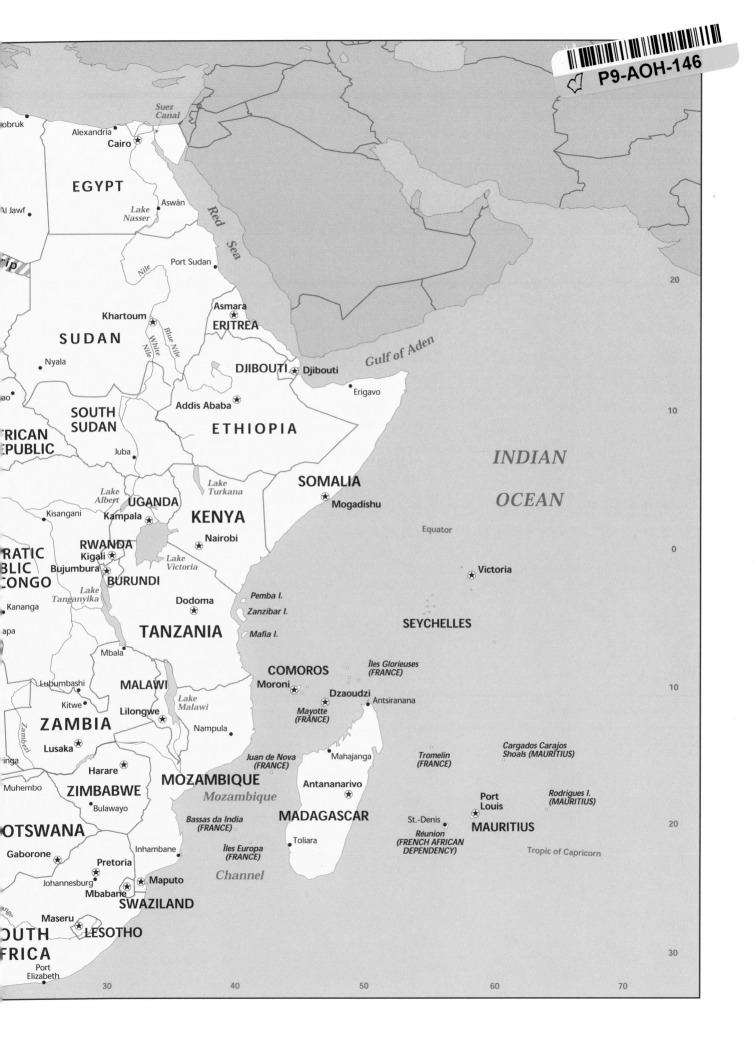

obruk

Alexandria
Cairo

EGYPT

Al Jawf

Lake Nasser

Aswān

Suez Canal

Red Sea

rip

Nile

Port Sudan

Khartoum

SUDAN

Nyala

Blue Nile

White Nile

Asmara
ERITREA

DJIBOUTI Djibouti

Gulf of Aden

ao

**SOUTH
SUDAN**

Addis Ababa

Erigavo

Juba

ETHIOPIA

RICAN
EPUBLIC

Lake Turkana

SOMALIA

Lake Albert

UGANDA

Kisangani
Kampala

KENYA

Mogadishu

**INDIAN

OCEAN**

Nairobi

Equator

RATIC
LIC
ONGO

RWANDA
Kigali
Bujumbura

BURUNDI

Kananga

Lake Victoria

Lake Tanganyika

Dodoma

Victoria

apa

Pemba I.

Zanzibar I.

SEYCHELLES

TANZANIA

Mafia I.

Mbala

Kanga

Lubumbashi

MALAWI

Kitwe

Lake Malawi

Lilongwe

Nampula

COMOROS
Moroni

Dzaoudzi
Antsiranana

*Îles Glorieuses
(FRANCE)*

*Cargados Carajos
Shoals (MAURITIUS)*

ZAMBIA

Lusaka

Zambezi

*Mayotte
(FRANCE)*

*Juan de Nova
(FRANCE)*

Mahajanga

*Tromelin
(FRANCE)*

inga

Harare

ZIMBABWE

MOZAMBIQUE

Antananarivo

Port
Louis

*Rodrigues I.
(MAURITIUS)*

Muhembo

Bulawayo

Mozambique

MADAGASCAR

St.-Denis

MAURITIUS

OTSWANA

Gaborone

Inhambane

*Bassas da India
(FRANCE)*

*Îles Europa
(FRANCE)*

Toliara

*Réunion
(FRENCH AFRICAN
DEPENDENCY)*

Tropic of Capricorn

Pretoria

Johannesburg

Maputo

Channel

Mbabane

SWAZILAND

Maseru

OUTH
FRICA

LESOTHO

Port
Elizabeth

Orange

20

10

0

10

20

30

30   40   50   60   70

WORLDMARK
ENCYCLOPEDIA OF THE NATIONS

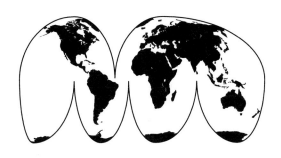

AFRICA

WORLDMARK
ENCYCLOPEDIA OF THE NATIONS,
THIRTEENTH EDITION

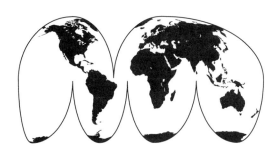

Volume 2
AFRICA

GALE
CENGAGE Learning

Detroit • New York • San Francisco • New Haven, Conn • Waterville, Maine • London

Worldmark Encyclopedia of the Nations, 13th Edition
Timothy L. Gall and Derek M. Gleason, Editors

Project Editors
Jason M. Everett and Kimberley A. McGrath

Contributing Editors
Kathleen J. Edgar and Elizabeth Manar

Managing Editor
Debra Kirby

Rights Acquisition and Management
Christine Myaskovsky

Imaging and Multimedia
John L. Watkins

Composition
Evi Abou-El-Seoud

Manufacturing
Rita Wimberley, Dorothy Maki

Product Manager
Douglas A. Dentino

Product Design
Kristine A. Julien

For product information and technology assistance, contact us at

Gale Customer Support, 1-800-877-4253.

For permission to use material from this text or product, submit all requests online at

www.cengage.com/permissions.

Further permissions questions can be emailed to

permissionrequest@cengage.com

While every effort has been made to ensure the reliability of the information presented in this publication, Gale, a part of Cengage Learning, does not guarantee the accuracy of the data contained herein. Gale accepts no payment for listing; and inclusion in the publication of any organization, agency, institution, publication, service, or individual does not imply endorsement of the editors or publisher. Errors brought to the attention of the publisher and verified to the satisfaction of the publisher will be corrected in future editions.

Library of Congress Cataloging-in-Publication Data

Worldmark encyclopedia of the nations / Timothy L. Gall and Derek M. Gleason, editors. -- 13th ed.
    p. cm.
  Includes bibliographical references and index.
  ISBN 978-1-4144-3390-5 (set) -- ISBN 978-1-4144-3391-2 (vol. 1) -- ISBN 978-1-4144-3392-9 (vol. 2) -- ISBN 978-1-4144-3393-6 (vol. 3) -- ISBN 978-1-4144-3394-3 (vol. 4) -- ISBN 978-1-4144-3395-0 (vol. 5) -- ISBN 978-1-4144-9090-8 (ebook)
  1. Geography--Encyclopedias. 2. History--Encyclopedias. 3. Economics--Encyclopedias. 4. Political science--Encyclopedias. 5. United Nations--Encyclopedias. I. Gall, Timothy L. II. Gleason, Derek M.
  G63.W67 2012
  910.3--dc23
                                2011049990

Gale
27500 Drake Rd.
Farmington Hills, MI 48331-3535

978-1-4144-3390-5 (set)   1-4144-3390-5 (set)
978-1-4144-3391-2 (vol. 1)   1-4144-3391-3 (vol. 1)
978-1-4144-3392-9 (vol. 2)   1-4144-3392-1 (vol. 2)
978-1-4144-3393-6 (vol. 3)   1-4144-3393-X (vol. 3)
978-1-4144-3394-3 (vol. 4)   1-4144-3394-8 (vol. 4)
978-1-4144-3395-0 (vol. 5)   1-4144-3395-6 (vol. 5)

This title is also available as an e-book
ISBN-13: 978-1-4144-9090-8   ISBN-10: 1-4144-9090-9

Contact your Gale, a part of Cengage Learning, sales representative for ordering information.

Printed in the United States
1 2 3 4 5 6 7 16 15 14 13 12

CONTENTS

For Conversion Tables, Abbreviations and Acronyms, Glossaries, World Tables, notes to previous editions, and other supplementary materials, see Volume 1.

READER'S GUIDE

GENERAL NOTE: The Thirteenth Edition of *Worldmark Encyclopedia of the Nations* (WEN) is comprised of five volumes. Volume 1 is dedicated to the United Nations and its related agencies. Volumes 2 through 5, "Africa," "Americas," "Asia and Oceania," and "Europe," contain entries on the countries of the world.

Reflecting the ever-changing status of the world geopolitical situation, the Thirteenth Edition includes entries for 196 countries and the Palestinian Territories, three more entries than the previous edition. This reflects the widely recognized independence of Kosovo and South Sudan that has occurred since the publication of the Twelfth Edition. It also recognizes the unique status of the Palestinian Territories, which, in the months leading up to the publication of this edition, were working to achieve membership in several peripheral United Nations agencies—a push toward formal recognition of statehood. Seven entries describe dependencies of the United Kingdom, United States, and the Netherlands. Previous editions have been cognizant of similar changes, including those in East Timor, Macau, and Hong Kong. Perhaps most dramatically, the Eighth Edition of this encyclopedia (1995) reported on the dissolution of the USSR, Czechoslovakia, and Yugoslavia; the unification of Germany; the unification of Yemen; and the independence of Eritrea. These changes resulted in 25 new country articles. Whereas the First Edition of the *Worldmark Encyclopedia of the Nations,* in one volume, contained 119 articles, the present Thirteenth Edition now contains 204.

Some notable foci for the Thirteenth Edition include coverage of the Arab Spring—the revolutionary fervor that carried across North Africa and the Middle East during 2011 and into 2012, deposing several long-standing dictators—and the global financial crisis, which, despite beginning in 2008, has led to economic recession or stagnation across much of the world that continued through 2011 and into 2012, especially among European countries and in other highly developed economies. Also for the Thirteenth Edition, each entry was submitted for review by subject-matter experts at universities across the United States and around the world, leading to greater continuity within each article and an authorial perspective conscious of region-wide context and historical relevance.

In compiling data for incorporation into the *Worldmark Encyclopedia of the Nations,* substantial efforts were made to utilize national government statistical resources, as well as all pertinent UN agencies, to compile the core information in each entry. Material received from official sources was reviewed and critically assessed by editors as part of the process of incorporation. In some cases, discrepancies between self-reported data and accepted international revisions, occasionally noted in figures such as unemployment and minority ethnic populations, highlight the political influences that weigh on national government statistic reporting. Materials and publications of the UN family and of intergovernmental and nongovernmental organizations throughout the world provided a major fund of geographic, demographic, economic, and social data.

In compiling historical, economic, and political data, primary materials generated by governments and international agencies were supplemented by data gathered from numerous other sources including newspapers (most notably *The European,* the *Financial Times,* the *New York Times,* and the *Wall Street Journal*); periodicals (most notably *Current History, Elections Today, The Economist,* the *Far Eastern Economic Review, Foreign Affairs,* and *World Press Review*); and thousands of World Wide Web sites hosted by government agencies and embassies. The base knowledge and access to a broad range of speciality academic publications enjoyed by subject-matter experts figures heavily in these sections as well.

The reader's attention is directed to the Glossary of Special Terms for explanations of key terms and concepts essential to a fuller understanding of the text.

COUNTRY NAMES: Country names are reported (as appropriate) in three forms: the short-form name (generally conformed to the US Central Intelligence Agency's *World Factbook 2011*), as commonly used in the text; the English version of the official name (generally conformed to the United Nations list of country names); and the official name in the national language(s). When necessary, textual usages of some short-form names have been rectified, usually through the substitution of an acronym for the official name, in order to strike a better balance between official usages and universal terminology. Thus the following short-form names have been adopted throughout (except in historical context to preserve accuracy): DROC (Democratic Republic of the Congo); ROC (Republic of the Congo); DPRK (Democratic People's Republic of Korea/North Korea); and ROK (Republic of Korea/South Korea).

MAPS: Spellings on the individual country maps reflect national usages and recognized transliteration practice. To clarify national boundaries and landforms, dark shading has been applied to waters, and lighter shading to lands not within that nation's jurisdiction. Cross-hatching has been used to designate certain disputed areas. Rivers that run dry during certain times of the year are indicated by dashed instead of solid lines.

FLAGS AND NATIONAL EMBLEMS: All depictions of flags, flag designations, and national emblems have been reviewed and, where necessary, corrected or changed to reflect their official usage as of 2012. In general, the term "national flag" denotes the civil flag of the nation.

CURRENCY: In most cases, currency conversion factors cited in the Thirteenth Edition are derived from figures available during the last quarter of 2011 or the first quarter of 2012. Differences between the official exchange rate and the actual exchange rate are noted as appropriate.

WEIGHTS AND MEASURES: The general world trend toward adoption of the metric system is acknowledged through the use of metric units and their nonmetric (customary or imperial) equivalents throughout the text. The two exceptions to this practice involve territorial sea limits, which are reported in nautical miles, and various production data, for which (unless otherwise stated) units of measure reflect the system in use by the country in question. All tons are metric tons (again, unless otherwise indicated), reflecting the practice of the UN in its statistical reporting.

HOLIDAYS: Except where noted, all holidays listed are official public holidays, on which government offices are closed that would normally be open. Transliterations of names of Muslim holidays have been standardized. For a fuller discussion on these points, and for a description of religious holidays and their origins and meanings, see the Glossary of Religious Holidays in this volume.

GEOGRAPHIC INFORMATION: To update the sections on Location, Size, and Extent; Topography, Climate, Flora and Fauna, and Environment, the World Bank's *World Development Indicators 2011* and CIA *World Factbook 2011* were two primary sources. Additional data was acquired from the Ramsar Convention on Wetlands (http://www.ramsar.org); UNESCO World Heritage Centre (http://www.whc.unesco.org); United Nations Environment Programme (http://www.unep.org); Weather Channel: Averages and Records (http://www.weather.com/common/home/climatology.html); and the International Union for Conservation of Nature (http://www.iucn.org).

POPULATION DATA: Data for the four rubrics describing population (Population, Migration, Ethnic Groups, Languages) were compiled from numerous publications of the US Department of State, the World Bank, the United Nations, and the Organization for Economic Co-Operation and Development (OECD), specifically its publication *Trends in International Migration*. Data on refugee populations generally comes from the United Nations. Population rankings are ordered based on data from the *World Factbook 2011* and include all full country entries in these volumes; this calculation excludes the Palestinian Territories and the seven dependency entries.

RELIGIONS: Data for this section were compiled in large part from the *2010 International Religious Freedom Report* released by the Bureau of Democracy, Human Rights, and Labor, US Department of State. This is an annual report to Congress compiled in compliance with Section 102(b) of the International Religious Freedom Act (IRFA) of 1998. The report includes the work of hundreds of State Department, Foreign Service, and other US government employees. The authors gathered information from a variety of sources, including government and religious officials, nongovernmental organizations, journalists, human rights monitors, religious groups, and academics.

TRANSPORTATION: Sources consulted for updated information on transportation include the *World Factbook 2011* and the World Bank's *World Development Indicators 2011*. Information on recent or ongoing transportation projects most often came from major news organizations such as the *BBC News International* and the *New York Times*.

HISTORY: In writing the History rubric, the entries relied heavily on the expertise of the academics reviewing and revising each country profile. Beyond the contributions of the subject-matter experts, the History rubrics have been maintained in previous editions and in between editions through the use of a variety of news and background information sources. Full country profiles—including information on the history, economy, political institutions, and foreign relations on most nations of the world—are provided by the US Library of Congress and by the US Department of State; similar formats are published by the *BBC News International*. In consulting news sources for up-to-date information on events, only reported facts (not editorials) were used. The *New York Times* and the *Washington Post* are more comprehensive than the *Wall Street Journal*, whose focus is placed on financial and business news. While the Web site of the United Nations was used extensively in compiling Volume 1 "United Nations," of the *Worldmark Encyclopedia of the Nations,* its coverage of such problems as politics in the Middle East and global terrorism pertained to and supported the updating of History rubrics of a number of countries. Other organizations that publish journals or studies on global current events, foreign policy, international relations, and human rights include Amnesty International; Human Rights Watch; *Foreign Affairs*, published by the Council on Foreign Relations; and *Great Decisions*, published by the Foreign Policy Association.

GOVERNMENT: The Government rubric is constructed by outlining the institutions of government as they were formed throughout a nation's modern history, up to those existing under the present constitution.

The US Library of Congress and the US Department of State chronicle constitutional changes and also provide information on the form of government. The online resource ElectionGuide (Electionguide.org) and the *World Factbook 2011* provide information on officeholders in place at the time of publication. The *BBC News International* "Country Profiles" cover current leaders and their political parties, and *The Economist* is comprehensive in its coverage of political structures and political forces in place and at work in the nations it profiles. The official government Web sites of individual nations were also consulted.

POLITICAL PARTIES: The *World Factbook 2011* was consulted for a list of political parties, and often, their leaders. *The Economist* also has sections in its country briefings labeled "political structure" and "political forces," which describe the political climate of each nation the magazine profiles. In addition, *The Economist* provides a brief history of the nation, which often includes the history of political parties. Editors also reviewed profiles of nations prepared by the US Department of State.

LOCAL GOVERNMENT: The *World Factbook 2011* lists the administrative subdivisions in each nation of the world. *The Economist* was consulted for a description of regional legislatures. ElectionGuide provides information on recent and upcoming subnational elections.

JUDICIAL SYSTEM: The US State Department *Background Notes* and the *World Factbook 2011* both provided basic information on each nation's judicial system. *The Economist* was consulted for a description of the legal systems of each nation it profiles. The US State Department's *Human Rights Reports* provide more in-depth details about the independence and fairness of the judiciary.

ARMED FORCES: Statistical data on armed forces was compiled from the *The Military Balance* (The International Institute for Strategic Studies), the *World Factbook 2011*, and other print and online sources including *Current World Nuclear Arsenals* maintained by the Center for Defense Information.

INTERNATIONAL COOPERATION: This section was updated using data provided by news agencies, the *World Factbook 2011*, and US State Department *Background Notes*.

ECONOMY: In addition to numerous official online sources, data on the economies of the world were compiled from the most recent editions of the following publications (and their publishers): *Country Commercial Guides* (US Department of State), *World Development Indicators 2011* (World Bank) and *Doing Business* reports (World Bank). *The Economist* was consulted for detailed information on economic structures and select indicators in its "Country Profiles" archive; it also included economic and political forecasts for the nations it profiled. *The Index of Economic Freedom* (Heritage Foundation) was also consulted for its measurement of independent variables into broad factors of economic freedom.

INCOME: Statistics on national income were obtained from sources published by the United Nations, the World Bank, and the US Central Intelligence Agency. CIA figures are for gross domestic product (GDP), defined as the value of all final goods and services produced within a nation in a given year. In most cases, CIA figures are given in purchasing power parity terms. Actual individual consumption, a statistic maintained by the World Bank, measures the percentage of a nation's GDP spent on various sectors of the consumer economy. Thus, public expenditures in sectors such as education, health, or military are not included in the calculation and account for the remaining percentage of GDP not included in actual individual consumption numbers.

LABOR: Labor statistics were compiled from the World Bank publication *World Development Indicators 2011* and the US State Department's *Human Rights Reports 2010*.

AGRICULTURE, FISHING, AND FORESTRY: In addition to government sources, statistical data for these sections was compiled from the following yearbooks published by the Food and Agriculture Organization of the United Nations: *Fishery Statistics; Production; Agriculture;* and *Forest Products.*

MINING: Data on mining and minerals production came from various online sources and from statistics compiled by the Minerals Information office of the US Geological Survey, US Department of the Interior, including the *Minerals Yearbook*. The *Minerals Yearbook* is published both electronically on the Internet and in various print formats available from the US Government Printing Office Superintendent of Documents. The *Yearbook* provides an annual review of mineral production and trade and of mineral-related government and industry developments in more than 175 countries.

ENERGY AND POWER: Key sources consulted include *Country Analysis Briefs* (US Energy Information Administration, US Department of Energy) and *World Development Indicators* (The World Bank). Special attention was given to renewable energy projects completed or underway in various countries; information for projects typically was found through major news agencies or on official government Web sites.

INDUSTRY: The primary source material for the Industry rubric was the *World Factbook 2011* and the US State Department's *Country Commercial Guides*, which provide a comprehensive look at countries' commercial environments, using economic, political, and market analysis. *Background Notes* were consulted for information on the industrial history and climate of each country profiled. *The Economist* and, to a lesser extent, *BBC News* were useful in providing background material for the Industry rubric.

SCIENCE AND TECHNOLOGY: Information in this section derived primarily from statistics of the UNESCO Institute for Statistics, the World Bank's *World Development Indicators,* and the World Intellectual Property Organization.

DOMESTIC TRADE: Source material for the Domestic Trade rubric came from the US State Department's *Country Commercial Guides* and *Background Notes.* Also used was *The Economist* and, to a lesser extent, the *BBC* for providing background material for the Domestic Trade rubric. The World Bank's *Doing Business* reports were consulted for information on conducting business in a nation, which included business hours and business regulations. Finally, most nations' government Web sites provided information on domestic trade.

FOREIGN TRADE: Sources consulted included the *Direction of Trade Statistics* (IMF Statistics Department, International Monetary Fund). The US State Department's *Country Commercial Guides* and *Background Notes* were also used. *The Economist* and the *World Factbook 2011* were consulted in listing import and export partners and key products traded. Various UN bodies—such as UNCTAD and UNESCO—provided up-to-date trade statistics. The principal trading partners table was constructed with information from the IMF's *Direction of Trade Statistics* publication.

BALANCE OF PAYMENTS: Balance of payments tables were computed from the International Monetary Fund's *Balance of Payments Statistics Yearbook.* In some cases, totals are provided even though not all components of those totals have been reported by the government of the country. Accordingly, in some instances numbers in the columns may not add to the total. Supplementing the IMF's *Balance of Payments Statistics Yearbook* were *The Economist's* "Country Briefings," the *World Factbook 2011,* and information taken from the US State Department, in particular, the *Country Commercial Guides.*

BANKING AND SECURITIES: Statistical data on securities listings and market activity was compiled from *International Banking Statistics* (www.bis.org/statistics) and the *World Factbook 2011,* which provides both the discount rate and prime lending rate for most nations. Various Web sites specific to the individual countries of the world were also consulted, especially for the most current information on active publicly traded companies and market capitalization for domestic exchanges.

INSURANCE: Primary sources for information on insurance included the online resources of the Insurance Information Institute, Rowbotham and Co. LLP., PricewaterhouseCoopers, the Swiss Reinsurance Company, and J. Zakhour & Co., as well as numerous national Web sites dealing with insurance.

PUBLIC FINANCE: In addition to official government Web sites, analytical reports from the US Department of Commerce, the *World Factbook 2011,* and the *Government Finance Statistics Yearbook* (International Monetary Fund) were consulted.

TAXATION: Information on Taxation was compiled from country data sheets published by international accounting firms (Deloitte and Ernst & Young). Addition informational was obtained from the US Commerce Department, *Doing Business* reports from the World Bank, and government Web sites of the countries of the world.

CUSTOMS AND DUTIES: Information on Customs and Duties was compiled from country data sheets published by the accounting firms of Deloitte and Ernst & Young. Additional information was obtained from the US Commerce Department, the World Trade Organization, and the government Web sites of the countries of the world.

FOREIGN INVESTMENT: Source material for the Foreign Investment rubric included the US State Department's *Country Commercial Guides,* which provided a comprehensive analysis of the foreign direct investment environments of the countries of the world. The International Monetary Fund's publications *International Financial Statistics Yearbook* and *Balance of Payments Statistics Yearbook,* and the US State Department's *Background Notes* were consulted for the information on foreign direct investment. Also used was information contained in the *World Factbook 2011. The Economist* was consulted in providing basic FDI figures and other relevant data.

ECONOMIC DEVELOPMENT: Source material for the Economic Development rubric included the US State Department's *Country Commercial Guides* and *Background Notes. The Economist* was consulted for economic and political forecasts for selected nations. The *Index of Economic Freedom* was also consulted for its broad description of economic freedom and development. Information on foreign aid was taken from the print publications and Web sites of the International Monetary Fund, World Bank, and the United States Agency for International Development (USAID). Information on long-term development plans was found most often on individual government Web sites.

SOCIAL DEVELOPMENT: Publications consulted in the preparation of this rubric include the US State Department's 2010 *Human Rights Reports,* the US Social Security Administration reports for each nation, and the World Bank's *World Development Indicators 2011.* Additional information was obtained from country-specific Web sites and general news publications.

HEALTH: Statistical sources consulted included the World Health Organization health profiles for each country as well as statistical information maintained by UNESCO. Numerous Web sites of individual nations of the world were also utilized. The World Bank's *World Development Indicators 2011* served as an additional resource.

HOUSING: The latest government population and housing census information available was used for each country through access of official government Web sites. Also of use was the World Bank publication *World Development Indicators 2011*. Web sites consulted included Habitat for Humanity (http://www.habitat.org), United Nations Human Settlements Programme (http://unhabitat.org) and the US Agency for International Development (http://www.usaid.gov).

EDUCATION: Data on Education was obtained from various UNESCO publications and statistics from the World Bank. The *World Factbook 2011* and the US State Department's *Background Notes* were also consulted.

LIBRARIES AND MUSEUMS: Some information concerning libraries and museums was accessed through official government Web sites of various countries when links were available to tourism, education, and/or cultural ministries or departments. In addition, the following Web sites were consulted: American Library Association (http://www.ala.org); International Federation of Library Associations and Institutions (http://www.ifla.org); Museums of the World (http://www.museum.com); and UNESCO (http://www.unesco.org).

MEDIA: Primary sources for this section include the annual *Editor & Publisher* publication *International Year Book*—which lists circulation figures for periodicals—online data provided by UNESCO, and media sections of the "Country Profiles" featured on the Web site of *BBC News International.* In addition, government and other Web sites related to the countries of the world were consulted. Additional sources consulted included the *World Development Indicators 2011, World Factbook 2011,* and US State Department's *2010 Human Rights Reports* (particularly with regard to freedom of the press).

ORGANIZATIONS: Lists of member countries were obtained through the official Web sites of a variety of prominent international organizations and associations, such as the International Federation of Red Cross and Red Crescent Societies, Amnesty International, Kiwanis International, the World Alliance of YMCAs, the World Organization of the Scout Movement, etc.

TOURISM, TRAVEL, AND RECREATION: Statistical sources consulted included the *Tourism Factbook,* published by the UN World Tourism Organization in 2011. Tourism Web sites of individual countries were also consulted. US Department of State per diem travel allowances are published online.

FAMOUS PERSONS: Entries are based on information available through March 2012. Where a person noted in one country is known to have been born in another, the country (or, in some cases, city) of birth follows the personal name in parentheses.

DEPENDENCIES: Source material for the Dependencies rubric was taken primarily from statistical Web sites maintained by the sovereign nation overseeing each dependency. Information also came from *Background Notes* and from the Web site of the United Nations. *The Economist* and the Web site of *BBC News* were also consulted.

BIBLIOGRAPHY: Bibliographical listings at the end of country articles are provided as a guide to further reading on the country in question and are not intended as a comprehensive listing of references used in research for the article. Effort was made to provide a broad sampling of works on major subjects and topics as covered by the article; the bibliographies provide, wherever possible, introductory and general works for use by students and general readers, as well as classical studies, recent contributions, and other works regarded as seminal by area specialists. The country article bibliographies were supplemented with information obtained from a search conducted in November 2011. An extensive bibliography listing key references related to the facts in this encyclopedia follows. However, it is not a complete listing since many fact sheets, brochures, World Wide Web sites, and other informational materials were not included due to space limitations.

PRINT PUBLICATIONS CONSULTED

Almanac of Famous People. 10th ed. Farmington Hills, MI: Cengage Gale, 2011.

Balance of Payments Statistics Yearbook. Washington, D.C.: International Monetary Fund, 2011.

Asian Development Bank, ed. *Asian Development Outlook 2011: South-South Economic Links.* Manila, Philippines: Asian Development Bank, 2011.

Central Intelligence Agency. *World Factbook 2011.* Washington, D.C.: US Government Printing Office, 2011.

Commonwealth Yearbook 2011. London: Commonwealth Secretariat, 2011.

Compendium of Tourism Statistics (2005–2009). 2011 ed. Madrid: World Tourism Organization, 2011.

Crystal, David. *The Cambridge Encyclopedia of Language.* 2nd ed. New York: Cambridge University Press, 1997.

Direction of Trade Statistics. Washington, D.C.: International Monetary Fund, quarterly.

Doernberg, Richard L. *Doernberg's International Taxation in a Nutshell.* 9th ed. Eagan, MN: Thomson Reuters Westlaw, 2012.

Dowie, Mark. *Conservation Refugees: The Hundred-Year Conflict between Global Conservation and Native Peoples.* Cambridge, MA: MIT Press, 2011.

Editor and Publisher International Yearbook 2010. New York: The Editor and Publisher Company, 2011.

Ellicott, Karen. *Countries of the World and Their Leaders Yearbook 2012.* Farmington Hills: Cengage Gale, 2011.

Emerging Stock Markets Factbook 2000. Washington, D.C.: International Finance Corporation, 2002.

Entering the 21st Century: World Development Report 1999/2000. New York: Oxford University Press, 2000.

Evandale's Directory of World Underwriters 2010. London: Evandale Publishing, 2011.

Food and Agriculture Organization of the United Nations. *FAO Statistical Yearbook.* New York: United Nations, 2010.

———. *FAO Yearbook: Fishery Statistics.* New York: United Nations, 2009.

———. *FAO Yearbook: Forest Products.* New York: United Nations, 2009.

Future Demographic-Global Population Forecasts to 2030. London: Euromonitor, 2012.

Global Development Finance. Washington, D.C.: The World Bank, 2011.

Global Education Digest. Montreal: UNESCO Publishing, 2011.

Government Finance Statistics Yearbook. Washington, D.C.: International Monetary Fund, 2011.

Health in the Americas. 2007 ed. Washington, D.C.: World Health Organization, 2007.

Health Information for International Travel 2005–2006. Philadelphia, PA: Mosby, 2005.

Historical Statistics 1960-1993. Paris: Organization for Economic Co-Operation and Development, 1995.

Insurance in the Arab World: Facts and Figures. Beirut: J. Zakhour & Co., undated.

International Civil Aviation Organization. *ICAO Statistical Yearbook, Civil Aviation Statistics of the World.* Montreal: International Civil Aviation Organization, annual.

International Committee of the Red Cross. *ICRC Annual Report 2010.* Geneva: ICRC Publications, 2011.

International Finance Corporation. *Doing Business 2012: Doing Business in a More Transparent World.* Washington, D.C.: International Finance Corporation, 2011.

International Financial Statistics Yearbook. Washington, D.C.: International Monetary Fund, 2008.

The International Insurance Fact Book. New York: Insurance Information Institute, 2012.

International Marketing Data and Statistics 2012. London: Euromonitor, 2012.

International Institute for Strategic Studies. *The Military Balance 2011.* London: Routledge, 2011.

International Save the Children Alliance Annual Report 2010, London: Cambridge House, 2011.

International Trade Statistics Yearbook. New York: United Nations, 2011.

Insurance in the Arab World: Facts and Figures. Beirut: J. Zakhour & Co., undated.

The International Insurance Fact Book, New York: Insurance Information Institute, 2011.

Key World Energy Statistics. Paris: International Energy Agency, 2011.

Little Data Book. Washington, D.C.: The World Bank, 2011.

Making Decisions on Public Health: A Review of Eight Countries. Geneva: World Health Organization, 2004.

McCoy, John F., ed. *Geo-Data: The World Geographical Encyclopedia, 3rd ed.* Farmington Hills, MI: Gale Group, 2003.

National Accounts for OECD Countries, Main Aggregates, Volume I, 2003–2010. Paris: Organization for Economic Cooperation and Development, 2011.

National Accounts Statistics: Main Aggregates and Detailed Tables. New York: United Nations, 2011.

Nordic Statistical Yearbook 2010. Stockholm: Nordic Council of Ministers, 2011.

Nuclear Power Reactors in the World. Vienna: International Atomic Energy Agency, 2006.

Organisation for Economic Co-operation and Development (OECD). *OECD Factbook 2011–2012.* Paris: OECD, 2011.

———. *Agricultural Policies in OECD Countries at a Glance 2011.* Paris: OECD, 2011.

———. *Education at a Glance 2011.* Paris: OECD, 2011.

———. *Health at a Glance 2011.* Paris: OECD, 2011.

———. *Government at a Glance 2011.* Paris: OECD, 2011.

Organization for Economic Co-operation and Development (OECD). *Revenue Statistics of OECD Member Countries 1965–1992.* Paris: OECD, 1993.

Population and Vital Statistics Report, January 2011. New York: United Nations, 2011.

Science & Engineering Indicators 2010. Washington, D.C.: National Science Foundation, 2010.

Sivard, Ruth Leger. *World Military and Social Expenditures.* Washington, D.C.: World Priorities, Inc., 1996.

Sources and Methods: Labour Statistics. Geneva: International Labour Office, 1996.

The State of the World's Children 2011. New York: Oxford University Press, 2011.

The State of the World's Refugees: Human Displacement in the New Millenium. New York: Penguin Books, 2006.

The State of the World's Refugees: Fifty Years of Humanitarian Action. New York: Oxford University Press, 2000.

Stockholm International Peace Research Institute. *SIPRI Yearbook 2011: Armaments, Disarmament and International Security.* London: Oxford University Press, 2011.

Tourism Market Trends: Africa, Madrid: World Tourism Organization, 2008.

Tourism Market Trends: Americas, Madrid: World Tourism Organization, 2008.

Tourism Market Trends: East Asia & the Pacific, Madrid: World Tourism Organization, 2008.

Tourism Market Trends: Europe, Madrid: World Tourism Organization, 2008.

Tourism Market Trends: Middle East, Madrid: World Tourism Organization, 2008.

Tourism Market Trends: South Asia, Madrid: World Tourism Organization, 2008.

Trends in International Migration 2004. Paris: Organization for Economic Co-Operation and Development, 2005.

United Nations Department of Economic and Social Affairs. *World Population Policies 2009.* New York: United Nations, 2010.

United Nations Development Program. *Human Development Report 2011.* New York: United Nations, 2011.

US Agency for International Development, Bureau for Management, Office of Budget. *US Overseas Loans and Grants and Assistance from International Organizations (The Greenbook).* Washington, D.C.: US Government Printing Office, 2011.

US Arms Control and Disarmament Agency. *World Military Expenditures and Arms Transfers 2005.* Washington, DC: U.S. Arms Control and Disarmament Agency, 2009.

US Department of the Interior, US Geological Survey. *Mineral Industries of Africa and the Middle East.* Washington, D.C.: US Government Printing Office, 2009.

——. *Mineral Industries of Asia and the Pacific.* Washington, D.C.: US Government Printing Office, 2009.

——. *Mineral Industries of Europe and Central Eurasia.* Washington, D.C.: US Government Printing Office, 2008.

——. *Mineral Industries of Latin America and Canada.* Washington, D.C.: US Government Printing Office, 2009.

Working Time Laws: A Global Perspective. Geneva: International Labour Office, 2005.

World Data on Education. Paris: International Bureau of Education, 2000.

World Development Indicators 2011. Washington D.C.: The World Bank, 2011.

World Development Report 1990: Poverty. New York: Oxford University Press, 1990.

World Development Report 1995: Workers in an Integrating World. New York: Oxford University Press, 1995.

World Development Report 1996: From Plan to Market. New York: Oxford University Press, 1996.

World Development Report 2003: Sustainable Development in a Dynamic World. Washington, D.C.: World Bank, 2003.

World Development Report 2006: Equity and Development. Washington, D.C.: World Bank, 2005.

World Development Report 2011. Washington, D.C.: World Bank, 2011.

The World Health Report: Make Every Mother and Child Count. Geneva: World Health Organization, 2005.

The World Health Report: Working Together for Health. Geneva: World Health Organization, 2006.

The World Health Report: A Safer Future: Global Public Health Security in the 21st Century. Geneva: World Health Organization, 2007.

The World Health Report: Primary Health Care (Now More Than Ever). Geneva: World Health Organization, 2008.

World Health Statistics 2011. Geneva: World Health Organization, 2011.

World Migration Report. New York: United Nations, 2011.

World Population Projections to 2150. New York: United Nations, 1998.

World Population Prospects: 2011. New York: United Nations, 2011.

World Resources Institute; United Nations Environment Programme; United Nations Development Programme; World Bank. *World Resources Report 2010–11.* New York: Oxford University Press, 2011.

World Urbanization Prospects. New York: United Nations, 2011.

Worldwide Corporate Tax Guide. New York: Ernst & Young, 2011.

Yearbook of Labour Statistics 2005. Geneva: International Labour Office, 2011.

WEB SITES CONSULTED

In the course of preparing this edition, hundreds of Web sites were consulted including the official Web site of each country of the world and those of various nongovernmental organizations worldwide. Of special significance are the Web sites listed below. These sites were accessed in 2011 and 2012 for information relevant to the rubrics listed above.

African Development Indicators 2011. http://data.worldbank.org/sites/default/files/adi_2011-web.pdf

American Library Association. http://www.ala.org

Amnesty International. http://www.amnesty.org

Asia Society. http://asiasociety.org/policy

BBC News. *Country Profiles.* http://news.bbc.co.uk/2/hi/country_profiles/default.stm

Central Intelligence Agency. *The World Factbook, 2011.* http://www.cia.gov/cia/publications/factbook/index.html

Council on Foreign Relations. http://www.foreignaffairs.org/

Country Forecasts. http://www.countrywatch.com

Country Overviews. http://www.developmentgateway.org

The Economist. http://www.economist.com/countries/index.cfm

ElectionGuide. http://www.electionguide.org

Energy Information Administration. *Country Analysis Briefs, 2011.* http://www.eia.doe.gov/emeu/cabs/

Foreign Policy Association. http://www.fpa.org/

Growth Competitiveness Index Rankings. http://www.weforum.org

Habitat for Humanity. http://www.habitat.org

Human Rights Watch. http://www.hrw.org/

Index of Economic Freedom. http://www.heritage.org

Insurance Information Institute. http://www.internationalinsurance.org/

International Banking Statistics. http://www.bis.org/statistics/index.htm

International Federation of Library Associations and Institutions. http://www.ifla.org

International Labour Organization, Department of Statistics. http://www.ilo.org/stat/lang--en/index.htm

International Monetary Fund. http://www.imf.org/

International Union for Conservation of Nature. http://www.iucn.org

Jurist World Law. http://jurist.law.pitt.edu/world/

L'Outre-Mer. http://www.outre-mer.gouv.fr/

Latin Business Chronicle. http://www.latinbusinesschronicle.com

Minerals Information Office, US Geological Survey, US Department of the Interior. http://minerals.usgs.gov/minerals/pubs/country/

Museums of the World. http://www.museum.com

National Science Foundation. Science & Engineering Indicators 2012. http://www.nsf.gov/statistics/seind12/

New York Times. http://www.nytimes.com/pages/world/index.html

OPEC Annual Report 2010. http://www.opec.org/opec_web/static_files_project/media/downloads/publications/Annual_Report_2010.pdf

Organization of American States Annual Report of the Inter American Commission on Human Rights. http://www.oas.org/en/iachr/docs/annual/2011/TOC.asp

Patent Applications by Country. http://www.wipo.int/ipstats/en/statistics/patents/

Political Resources on the Net. http://www.politicalresources.net

Population and Vital Statistics Report, January 2011. Series A, Vol. LXIII. http://unstats.un.org/unsd/demographic/products/vitstats/default.htm

Ramsar Convention on Wetlands. http://www.ramsar.org

TradePort. http://www.tradeport.org

United Nations. http://www.un.org/

United Nations Conference on Trade and Development (UNCTAD). http://www.unctad.org

United Nations Educational, Scientific, and Cultural Organization (UNESCO). http://www.unesco.org

———. *Education for All Global Monitoring Report 2011.* http://unesdoc.unesco.org/images/0019/001907/190743e.pdf

———. Statistics on Research and Development. http://www.uis.unesco.org

———. World Heritage Centre. http://www.whc.unesco.org

United Nations Food and Agricultural Organization. http://www.fao.org/

———. Production Statistics. http: http://faostat.fao.org/site/339/default.aspx

———. Trade Statistics. http: http://faostat.fao.org/site/342/default.aspx

———. Resource Statistics. http: http://faostat.fao.org/site/348/default.aspx

———. Forestry Statistics. http: http://faostat.fao.org/site/630/default.aspx

———. Fisheries Statistics. http: http://faostat.fao.org/site/629/default.aspx

United Nations Schedule of Mission Subsistence Allowance (MSA). http://www.un.org/depts/OHRM/salaries_allowances/allowances/msa.htm

United Nations Human Settlements Programme (UN-HABITAT). http://unhabitat.org

United Nations Statistics Division. http://unstats.un.org/unsd/default.htm

US Agency for International Development. http://www.usaid.gov.

US Department of State. *Background Notes.* http://www.state.gov/r/pa/ei/bgn

———. *Country Commercial Guides.* http://www.state.gov/e/eb/rls/rpts/ccg/

———. *International Religious Freedom Report 2010.* http://www.state.gov/g/drl/rls/irf/2010/index.htm

———. *Human Rights Reports, 2010.* http//www.state.gov/j/drl/rls/hrrpt/

US Library of Congress. http://lcweb2.loc.gov/frd/cs/profiles.html

The Wall Street Journal. http://online.wsj.com/public/us

The Washington Post. http://www.washpost.com/index.shtml

The Weather Channel. "Averages and Records." http://www.weather.com

The World Bank. http://worldbank.org

———. *Doing Business* database. http://www.doingbusiness.org

World Development Indicators, Country Overviews. http://www.developmentgateway.org

World Health Organization. Countries. http://www.who.int/countries/en/

World Intellectual Property Organization. http://www.wipo.int/portal/index.html.en

GUIDE TO COUNTRY ARTICLES

All information contained within a country article is uniformly keyed by means of small superior numerals to the left of the subject headings. A heading such as "Population," for example, carries the same key numeral (6) in every article. Thus, to find information about the population of Albania, consult the table of contents for the page number where the Albania article begins and look for section 6 thereunder. Introductory matter for each nation includes coat of arms, capital, flag (descriptions given from hoist to fly or from top to bottom), anthem, monetary unit, weights and measures, holidays, and time zone.

SECTION HEADINGS IN NUMERICAL ORDER

1	Location, size, and extent	27	Energy and power
2	Topography	28	Industry
3	Climate	29	Science and technology
4	Flora and fauna	30	Domestic trade
5	Environment	31	Foreign trade
6	Population	32	Balance of payments
7	Migration	33	Banking and securities
8	Ethnic groups	34	Insurance
9	Languages	35	Public finance
10	Religions	36	Taxation
11	Transportation	37	Customs and duties
12	History	38	Foreign investment
13	Government	39	Economic development
14	Political parties	40	Social development
15	Local government	41	Health
16	Judicial system	42	Housing
17	Armed forces	43	Education
18	International cooperation	44	Libraries and museums
19	Economy	45	Media
20	Income	46	Organizations
21	Labor	47	Tourism, travel, and recreation
22	Agriculture	48	Famous persons
23	Animal husbandry	49	Dependencies
24	Fishing	50	Bibliography
25	Forestry		
26	Mining		

SECTION HEADINGS IN ALPHABETICAL ORDER

Agriculture	22	Income	20
Animal husbandry	23	Industry	28
Armed forces	17	Insurance	34
Balance of payments	32	International cooperation	18
Banking and securities	33	Judical system	16
Bibliography	50	Labor	21
Climate	3	Languages	9
Customs and duties	37	Libraries and museums	44
Dependencies	49	Local government	15
Domestic trade	30	Location, size, and extent	1
Economic development	39	Media	45
Economy	19	Migration	7
Education	43	Mining	26
Energy and power	27	Organizations	46
Environment	5	Political parties	14
Ethnic groups	8	Population	6
Famous persons	48	Public finance	35
Fishing	24	Religions	10
Flora and fauna	4	Science and technology	29
Foreign investment	38	Social development	40
Foreign trade	31	Taxation	36
Forestry	25	Topography	2
Government	13	Tourism, travel, and recreation	47
Health	41	Transportation	11
History	12		
Housing	42		

FREQUENTLY USED ABBREVIATIONS AND ACRONYMS

AD—Anno Domini
a.m.—before noon
b.—born
BC—Before Christ
C—Celsius
c.—circa (about)
cm—centimeter(s)
Co.—company
Corp.—corporation
cu ft—cubic foot, feet
cu m—cubic meter(s)
d.—died
E—east
e.g.—exempli gratia (for example)
ed.—edition, editor
est.—estimated
et al.—et alii (and others)
etc.—et cetera (and so on)
EU—European Union
F—Fahrenheit

fl.—flourished
FRG—Federal Republic of Germany
ft—foot, feet
ft³—cubic foot, feet
GATT—General Agreement on Tariffs and Trade
GDP—gross domestic products
gm—gram
GMT—Greenwich Mean Time
GNP—gross national product
GRT—gross registered tons
ha—hectares
i.e.—id est (that is)
in—inch(es)
kg—kilogram(s)
km—kilometer(s)
kw—kilowatt(s)
kWh—kilowatt-hour(s)
lb—pound(s)
m—meter(s); morning

m³—cubic meter(s)
mi—mile(s)
Mt.—mount
MW—megawatt(s)
N—north
n.d.—no date
NA—not available
oz—ounce(s)
p.m.—after noon
r.—reigned

rev. ed.—revised edition
S—south
sq—square
St.—saint
UK—United Kingdom
UN—United Nations
US—United States
USSR—Union of Soviet Socialist Republics
W—west

A fiscal split year is indicated by a stroke (e.g. 2011/12).
For acronyms of UN agencies and their intergovernmental organizations, as well as other abbreviations used in text, see the United Nations volume.
A dollar sign ($) stands for US$ unless otherwise indicated.
Note that 1 billion = 1,000 million.

ALGERIA

Democratic and Popular Republic of Algeria
Al-Jumhuriyah al-Jaza'iriyah ad-Dimuqratiyah ash-Sha'biyah

CAPITAL: Algiers (Alger)

FLAG: The national flag consists of two equal vertical stripes, one green and one white, with a red crescent enclosing a five-pointed red star in the center. The crescent is more closed than those of other Muslim countries because the Algerians believe the long crescent horns bring happiness.

ANTHEM: *Kassaman (We Pledge).*

MONETARY UNIT: The Algerian dinar (DZD) is a paper currency of 100 centimes. There are coins of 1, 2, 5, 10, and 50 centimes and 1, 5 and 10 dinars, and notes of 10, 20, 50, 100, and 200 dinars. DZD1 = US$0.0133770 (or US$1 = DZD74.7550) as of December 2011.

WEIGHTS AND MEASURES: The metric system is the legal standard.

HOLIDAYS: New Year's Day, 1 January; Labor Day, 1 May; Overthrow of Ben Bella, 19 June; Independence Day, 5 July; Revolution Day, 1 November. Muslim religious holidays include Eid al-Fitr, Eid al-Adha, 1st of Muharram (Muslim New Year), and Milad an-Nabi. Christians observe their own religious holidays.

TIME: GMT.

¹LOCATION, SIZE, AND EXTENT

Situated in northwestern Africa along the Mediterranean Sea, Algeria is the largest country on the continent. Comparatively, it is slightly less than 3.5 times the size of Texas, with a total area of 2,381,740 sq km (919,595 sq mi). Extending about 2,400 km (1,500 mi) E–W and 2,100 km (1,300 mi) N–S, Algeria is bounded on the N by the Mediterranean Sea, on the E by Tunisia and Libya, on the SE by Niger, on the SW by Mali, on the W by Mauritania, and on the W and NW by the Western Sahara and Morocco; the total boundary length is 6,343 km (3,933 mi). Land boundary and claim disputes with Libya remained unresolved.

Algeria's capital city, Algiers, is located on the northern boundary of the country on the Mediterranean Sea.

²TOPOGRAPHY

The parallel mountain ranges of the Tell or Maritimes Atlas, comprising coastal massifs and northern inland ranges, and the Saharan Atlas divide Algeria into three basic longitudinal zones running generally east–west: the Mediterranean zone or Tell; the High Plateaus, including the regions of Great and Small Kabilia; and the Sahara Desert, accounting for at least 80% of Algeria's total land area. About half of Algeria is 900 m (3,000 ft) or more above sea level, and about 70% of the area is from 760 to 1,680 m (2,500 to 5,500 ft) in elevation. The highest point is Mount Tahat (3,003 m/9,852 ft) in the Ahaggar Range of the Sahara.

Only the main rivers of the Tell have water all year round, and even then the summer flow is small. None of the rivers are navigable. The mountainous areas of the High Plateaus are poorly watered; most of the rivers and streams (*oueds*) flow irregularly, since they depend upon an erratic rainfall for water. In the High Plateaus are many salt marshes and dry or shallow salt lakes (*seb-khas* or *shotts*). Farther south the land becomes increasingly arid, merging into the completely dry desert.

Algeria lies on the African Tectonic Plate, a seismically active area. Earthquakes on 10 October 1980 in a rural area southwest of Algiers left over 2,500 people dead and almost 100,000 homeless. An earthquake in May 2003 east of Algiers killed 2,200 people and left 51,000 homeless.

³CLIMATE

Northern Algeria lies within the temperate zone, and its climate is similar to that of other Mediterranean countries, although the diversity of the relief provides sharp contrasts in temperature. The coastal region has a pleasant climate, with winter temperatures averaging from 10° to 12°C (50° to 54°F) and average summer temperatures ranging from 24° to 26°C (75° to 79°F). Rainfall in this region is abundant—from 38 to 69 cm (15 to 27 in) per year and up to 100 cm (40 in) in the eastern part—except in the area around Oran (Ouahran), where mountains form a barrier against rain-carrying winds. When heavy rains fall (often more than 3.8 cm/1.5 in within 24 hours), they flood large areas and then evaporate so quickly that they are of little help in cultivation.

Farther inland, the climate changes; winters average from 4° to 6°C (39° to 43°F), with considerable frost and occasional snow on the massifs; and summers average from 26° to 28°C (79° to 82°F). In this region, prevailing winds are westerly and northerly in winter and easterly and northeasterly in summer, resulting in a general increase in precipitation from September to December and a decrease from January to August; there is little or no rainfall in the summer months.

In the Sahara Desert temperatures range from -10° to 34°C (14° to 93°F) with extreme highs of 49°C (120°F). There are daily temperature variations of more than 44°C (80° F). Winds are frequent and violent. Rainfall is irregular and unevenly distributed.

⁴FLORA AND FAUNA

The World Resource Institute estimates that there are 3,164 plant species in Algeria. In addition, Algeria was home to 100 mammal, 372 bird, 97 reptile, and 13 amphibian species. The calculation reflected the total number of distinct species residing in the country, not the number of endemic species.

Characteristic trees of northern Algeria are the olive and the cork oak. The mountain regions contain large forests of evergreens (Aleppo pine, juniper, and evergreen oak) and some deciduous trees. The forests are inhabited by boars and jackals, about all that remains of the many wild animals once common. Fig, eucalyptus, agave, and various palm trees grow in the warmer areas. Esparto grass, alfa, and drinn are common in the semiarid regions. On the coastal plain, the grape vine is indigenous.

Vegetation in the Sahara is sparse and widely scattered. Animal life is varied but scarce. Camels are used extensively. Other mammals are jackals, jerboas, and rabbits. The desert also abounds with poisonous and nonpoisonous snakes, scorpions, and numerous insects.

⁵ENVIRONMENT

The World Resource Institute reported that Algeria had designated 11.88 million hectares (29.35 million acres) of land for protection as of 2006. Water resources totaled 14.3 cu km (3.43 cu mi) while water usage was 6.07 cu km (1.46 cu mi) per year. Domestic water usage accounted for 22% of total usage, industrial for 13%, and agricultural for 65%. Per capita water usage totaled 185 cu m (6,533 cu ft) per year.

The United Nations (UN) reported in 2008 that carbon dioxide emissions in Algeria totaled 140,005 kilotons.

Algeria's principal environmental problem is encroachment of the desert onto the fertile northern section of the country. Soil erosion from overgrazing compounds the problem. To impede desertification, in 1975 the government began a project to erect a "green wall" of trees and vegetation 1,500 km (930 mi) long and 20 km (12 mi) wide along the northern fringes of the Sahara. The annual cost of this 20-year afforestation project was about $100 million.

Other significant environmental problems include water shortages and pollution. The small amount of water available in Algeria is imperiled by regular droughts. The threat is aggravated by lack of sewage control and pollutants from the oil industry, as well as other industrial effluents. The Mediterranean Sea is contaminated due to fertilizer runoff, waste from the oil industry, and soil erosion.

Algeria had 50 Ramsar Wetlands of International Importance. According to a 2011 report issued by the International Union for Conservation of Nature and Natural Resources (IUCN), the number of threatened species included 14 types of mammals, 9 species of birds, 8 types of reptiles, 3 species of amphibians, 36 species of fish, and 15 species of plants. Endangered species included the Barbary hyena, Barbary leopard, Barbary macaque, the Algerian nuthatch, the North African fire salamander, the African lion, the common otter, and the Mediterranean monk seal. The red gazelle and the Sahara oryx were listed as extinct as of 1994.

⁶POPULATION

The US Central Intelligence Agency (CIA) estimated the population of Algeria in 2011 to be approximately 34,994,937 which was 35th in population among the 196 nations of the world. In 2011 approximately 5.2% of the population was over 65 years of age with another 24.2% under 15 years of age. The median age in Algeria was 27.6 years. There were 1.01 males for every female in the country. The population's annual rate of change was 1.173%. The projected population for the year 2025 was 43,600,000. Population density in Algeria was calculated at 15 people per sq km (39 people per sq mi).

The UN estimated that 66% of the population lived in urban areas, and that urban populations had an annual rate of change of 2.3%. The largest urban areas, along with their respective populations, included Algiers, 2.7 million; and Oran, 770,000.

The population is concentrated in the cultivated areas of the northern Tell region near the Mediterranean coast. More than 90% of the populace lives in approximately one-eighth of the country. The plateau and desert regions are sparsely populated.

⁷MIGRATION

In 2011 the CIA estimated Algeria's net migration rate to be -0.27 migrants per 1,000 citizens. The total number of emigrants living abroad was 1.21 million, and the total number of immigrants living in Algeria was 242,300.

In 1962 some 180,000 Algerian refugees were repatriated from Tunisia and Morocco. After independence was declared in July 1962, about 650,000 French Algerians and more than 200,000 Harkis (Algerian Muslims who fought on the French side during the war of independence and chose to retain French citizenship) emigrated to France. The exodus reduced the French population in Algeria from about 10% of the total in 1961 to less than 1% in 1981. In the 1990s there were around 24,000 displaced people from Mali and Niger located in the southern Algerian regions of Tamanrasset, Adrar, and Illizi. In 1995 the UN High Commissioner for Refugees (UNHCR) began repatriating Tuareg refugees back to Mali and Niger. Repatriation was completed as of June 1998, benefiting some 6,302 Malians and 3,259 Nigeriens. By the end of 2011 the UNHCR reported that it was assisting some 91,000 refugees in the country including an estimated 4,000 Palestinians that were well integrated into Algerian society.

As a result of the war between the Polisario guerrillas and Morocco over the Western Sahara about 150,000 Sahrawi refugees fled to Algeria in the 1970s. In 2011 the government claimed this number had grown to 165,000, whereas the UNHCR estimated the number to be closer to 90,000. Charitable organizations alleged that the Sahrawi, a nomadic people, were being detained against their will and abused in Polisario camps located in Tindouf in southwestern Algeria. Over the past decade, Algerians have sought asylum in France, Spain, the United Kingdom, Switzerland, Belgium and Germany.

⁸ETHNIC GROUPS

The population consists almost entirely of mixed Arab-Berber ancestry. While most identify themselves by their Arab heritage, about 15% think of themselves as Berbers. The Berbers, who resemble the Mediterranean sub-race of Southern Europe, are de-

LOCATION: 18°57′ to 37°5′N; 8°44′W to 12°E. BOUNDARY LENGTHS: Mediterranean coastline, 1,104 kilometers (686 miles); Tunisia, 958 kilometers (595 miles); Libya, 982 kilometers (610 miles); Niger, 956 kilometers (594 miles); Mali, 1,376 kilometers (855 miles); Mauritania, 463 kilometers (288 miles); Morocco, 1,637 kilometers (1,017 miles). TERRITORIAL SEA LIMIT: 12 miles.

scendants of the original inhabitants of Algeria and are divided into many subgroups. The Kabyles (Kaba'il), mostly farmers, live in the compact mountainous section in the northern part of the country between Algiers and Constantine. The Chaouia (Shawiyyah) live in the Aurès Mountains of the northeast. The Mzab, or Mozabites, include sedentary date growers in the Ued Mzab oases. Desert dwellers are comprised of the Tuareg, Tuat, and Wargla (Ouargla). Europeans were of French, Corsican, Spanish, Italian,

and Maltese ancestry. Algeria's European population was estimated at less than 1% of the total population in 2011.

⁹LANGUAGES

The official and majority language is Arabic, with many variations and dialects. Many Algerians also speak French. "Arabization" has been encouraged by the government. About one-fifth of the population speaks a Berber dialect, particularly in Kabilia, in the Aurès and in smaller, relatively protected areas in the mountains and the Sahara. Berber is a distinct branch of the Hamitic language group; dialects vary from district to district. In antiquity, the Numidians wrote Berber in script form.

10 RELIGIONS

About 99% of the population practiced Islam, which, constitutionally, is the state religion. Except for a small minority of Kharijites (Ibadhis) in the Mzab region, most Muslims are adherents of the Maliki rite of the Sunni sect, with a few Hanafi adherents. Since the 1990s many non-Muslims have fled the country because of civil war and acts of terrorism by Islamic extremists. Estimates in 2010 placed the number of Christians and Jews between 12,000 and 50,000 with Seventh-Day Adventists accounting for the largest number of Christians. The Jewish community was estimated at less than 2,000 with no active congregations.

11 TRANSPORTATION

The CIA reports that Algeria has a total of 108,302 km (67,296 mi) of roads, of which 76,028 km (47,242 mi) are paved. There were 112 vehicles per 1,000 people in the country. Railroads extended for 4,723 km (2,935 mi). There were 143 airports, which transported 4.37 million passengers in 2009 according to the World Bank.

The railroad system consists principally of a main east–west line linked with the railways of Tunisia and Morocco and of lines serving the mining regions of Béchar (formerly Colomb Béchar); the esparto grass country on the High Plateaus; the date-producing areas of Biskra, Touggourt, and Tebessa; and the main port cities.

Roads are most adequate in the Tell zone, but in the mountainous and rural areas they are relatively poor. The French colonial administration built a good road system, partly for military purposes, which after independence deteriorated. However, new roads have been built linking the Sahara oil fields with the coast. Algeria's portion of the trans-Saharan highway—formally known as the Road of African Unity, stretching about 420 km (260 mi) from Hassi Marroket to the Niger border south of Tamanrasset—was completed in 1985.

Algiers is the principal seaport. Other significant ports are Arzew, Bejaïa (Bougie), Skikda (a large gas-exporting center also known as Philippeville), Oran, Annaba, Ghazaouet, and Mostaganem. Algeria's merchant fleet numbered 35 ships of 1,000 gross registered tons or over in 2010.

Fifty-seven airports have paved runways. There are also two heliports. The main international airport, H. Boumediene Airport, is about 20 km (12 mi) from Algiers. Constantine, Annaba, Tilimsen (Tlemcen), and Oran have smaller modern airports that could accommodate jet aircraft. Air Algérie, the national airline, provides international service.

12 HISTORY

Before the period of recorded history, the North African coastal area now known as Algeria was inhabited by Berber tribal groups, from whom many present-day Algerians are descended. Phoenician sailors established coastal settlements, and after the 8th century BC the territory was controlled by Carthage. Roman dominance dates from the fall of Carthage in 146 BC. Completely annexed in AD 40 the region, known as Numidia, became a center of Roman culture. Christianity flourished, as did agriculture and commerce; Numidian wheat and olives were shipped to Rome. By the mid-3rd century there were some 20 Numidian bishops. Despite the prosperity of the Roman cities and the cereal-growing countryside, there were frequent Berber revolts. The Roman influence gradually declined, especially after the Vandal invasion of 430–31. The Byzantine conquered eastern Numidia in the 6th century.

The Arab conquest began in 637 in the area known as Al-Maghrib al-Awsat or the Middle West and continued for a century. The Berbers accepted Islam but preserved their own traditional political and social institutions, in effect absorbing the invaders. Arabs from the east attacked in the 11th century. These newcomers, unlike their predecessors, were nomadic herders rather than farmers; they destroyed many of the towns and farms and reinforced a more pastoral type of economy. Almoravids from Morocco also took possession of part of the region in the 11th century, and they were succeeded by Almohads a century later. Although these and other dynasties and individuals united the territory and consolidated it with Morocco and Spain, local rulers retained considerable autonomy. Meanwhile, seafaring and piracy became important.

Spain conquered part of the coast in the early 16th century, and Algerians asked for aid from Aruj, known as Barbarossa, a Turkish pirate. He expelled the Spaniards from some of their coastal footholds, made himself sultan, and conquered additional territory. The area of Barbarossa's control was extended by his brother, Khayr ad-Din, also called Barbarossa, who placed his territory under the suzerainty of the Ottoman sultan in Constantinople. Until 1587 Algiers was governed by beylerbeys; from 1587 to 1659, by pashas, who were appointed for three-year terms; and after 1659, by aghas and finally by deys (28 deys in all, 14 of whom were assassinated). Other parts of what is now called Algeria were ruled either by Turkish officials or by local chieftains. Spain held a small area around Oran until 1708 and controlled it again from 1732 to 1791.

Algiers became increasingly independent of Constantinople and, joining with other states of the Barbary Coast, thrived on piracy. At this time it had diplomatic and trade relations with many European countries, including France. But with the defeat (though not suppression) of the Barbary pirates by US and European fleets during 1815–16 and with the growing European interest in acquiring overseas colonies, Algiers was seen as a possible addition to either the British or the French empire. In 1830 the French took over the principal ports; they gradually subjugated the Berbers, annexed the northern regions, and set up a system of fortified posts. Thereafter, sporadic revolts broke out, notably the guerrilla war from 1830 to 1847, led by the legendary hero Abd al-Qadir, and the Kabyle rebellion in 1871. Other sections, however, remained independent of France until the first decade of the 20th century.

Al-Jazair, as it was called in Arabic became, in French, Algérie a name that France applied to the territory for the first time in 1839. In 1848 northern Algeria was proclaimed an integral part of France and was organized into three provinces. Following the Franco-Prussian War of 1870–71, large numbers of Alsatians and other French colonizers settled the most fertile confiscated lands, as did other Europeans at the invitation of France. Muslims had no political rights except for limited participation in local financial delegations.

Following World War I France took the first steps toward making all of Algeria an integral part of France. In 1919 voting rights were given to a few Muslims, based on education and military service qualifications. French citizenship had previously been open to Muslims who renounced their Koranic status.

During World War II in exchange for loyalty to France, many Muslims hoped for political concessions, and moderates believed that France might be persuaded to grant Algeria a separate status while retaining close diplomatic, economic, and defense ties. In 1957 all Muslims became French subjects, but about nine million Muslims and 500,000 Europeans voted on separate electoral rolls for a joint assembly. Unsuccessful in obtaining further reforms and faring poorly in several apparently rigged elections, the moderate Muslim nationalist group led by Ferhat Abbas was greatly weakened.

War ensued in Algeria toppling several French governments before causing the demise of the Fourth Republic in May 1958. Younger nationalists had formed what would become known as the National Liberation Front (Front de Libération Nationale—FLN), and launched a guerrilla war on 1 November 1954. The FLN's National Liberation Army (Armée de Libération Nationale—ALN) perpetrated acts of terrorism and sabotage throughout Algeria and gained increasing mass support. Eventually, France was forced to maintain at least 450,000 troops in Algeria. During the hostilities the French army completely cleared many rural areas of their civilian populations and evacuated some two million Muslims to army-controlled *regroupment* centers or new large villages. Although the army gradually eliminated the power of the FLN to carry out large-scale attacks, the latter continued its terrorist acts against the French army, French settlers, and pro-French Muslims. Terrorist activities, mainly as a result of factional disputes, were also carried on by Algerian Muslims in France. During more than seven years of civil war, well over one million Muslim guerrillas and civilians and 10,000 French soldiers lost their lives.

French rightists and military groups in Algeria then brought Gen. Charles de Gaulle to power. To their surprise, however, he pursued a policy of preparing for Algerian independence. He offered self-determination to Algeria in September 1958. Referendums in France and Algeria on 8 April and 1 July 1962 approved a settlement, and independence was formally proclaimed on 3 July, despite a program of counterterrorism by the French Secret Army Organization in Algeria.

With independence achieved, a seven-man political bureau, established as the policy making body of the FLN, took over effective control of the country on 5 August 1962. Ahmed Ben Bella became the first premier, and Ferhat Abbas was chosen speaker of the assembly. The assembly adopted a constitution which was endorsed by referendum in September 1963.

Elected president in October, Ben Bella began to nationalize foreign-owned land and industry. Opposition to his authoritarian regime led to an outbreak of armed revolts in the Kabilia and Biskra areas in July 1964 and to open attacks on the regime by leading political figures. On 19 June 1965 the Ben Bella government was overthrown in a bloodless coup directed by Col. Houari Boumedienne, who was the first deputy premier and defense minister. The 1963 constitution was suspended, and a revolutionary council headed by Boumedienne took power. The new government shifted to a gradualist approach to national development, with deliberate economic planning and an emphasis on financial stability. During the 1970s the council nationalized the oil industry and initiated agrarian reforms. Boumedienne ruled by decree until June 1976, when a national referendum approved a Socialist constitution providing for a one-party state with a strong presidential system and an elected National Assembly. Boumedienne was elected president in December 1976 but died two years later.

The FLN Central Committee, with strong army backing, chose Col. Chadli Bendjedid as the party's leader, and his presidential candidacy was ratified by the electorate on 7 February 1979. He was reelected without opposition in January 1984 for a second five-year term. After a period of maintaining continuity with the previous regime, the Bendjedid government moved toward more moderate policies, expanding powers for the provinces and state enterprises and attempting to revitalize the FLN and government agencies. In foreign affairs, Algeria reduced its earlier support for liberation groups around the globe and for hard-line nonaligned positions. It patched up its dispute with Morocco over the Western Sahara and sharply reduced its aid to the Polisario. Algeria played a key role in helping the United States resolve the hostage crisis in 1981 and worked hard for the Arab Maghreb Union, a planned economic community (EC) for North Africa. Serious internal trouble developed in 1988 when young Algerians rioted over high prices, unemployment, and the dictatorship of an aging, inept, and corrupt revolutionary regime. Shocked by the 500 deaths in the streets, Bendjedid moved to liberalize his government. Political parties were allowed to form outside the FLN and the prime minister and cabinet were made responsible to the national assembly. He won a third term in 1989, supported by 81% of the electorate.

Burdened by heavy debts and low oil prices, Bendjedid was obliged to pursue austere economic policies and to abandon socialism for the free market-actions which further inflamed his opposition, now led by the Islamic Salvation Front (FIS). In 1989 the party won 55% of urban election seats while the FLN maintained power in the countryside. Elections to the national assembly, postponed six months, were held in December 1991 under relatively free conditions. FIS candidates won 188 out of 231 contested seats, needing only 28 more places in a second vote to control the 430-member Assembly. The FLN won only 16 seats.

The army intervened, arresting FIS leaders and indefinitely postponing the second-stage vote. Bendjedid resigned under pressure from the army and Mohammed Boudiaf, a hero of the revolution, returned from exile to lead the High State Council, which the army established. A harsh crackdown on Islamists began; the FIS was banned and its local councils were closed. As acts of terrorism continued by both sides in 1992 and 1993, the regime declared a state of emergency, set up special security courts, and arrested more than 5,000 people. Boudiaf was assassinated in June 1992 to be replaced by Ali Kafi with Redha Malek as prime minister in August 1993. In January 1994 Defense Minister Liamine Zeroual was named president and the five-man presidential council was abolished.

Zeroual released two top FIS leaders in September 1994 and began a dialogue with the FIS. After six weeks of apparently half-hearted talks, Zeroual ended the dialogue and called for new presidential elections. Opposition parties—including the FLN, the FIS, and other Islamist groups—met in late 1994 and early 1995 under the auspices of the Sant'Egidio Roman Catholic community in Italy to produce a national contract to end the violence through a transitional government that would include all parties. Zeroual rejected the meeting as foreign interference in Algeria's internal affairs and condemned the contract that it produced. He continued to attempt dialogue with the legalized opposition parties with no results.

While parties accounting for nearly 80% of the vote in the 1991 parliamentary elections were excluded from participating, Zeroual did have three opponents contesting the presidency in the November 1995 elections. The elections went ahead as scheduled. Despite widespread calls for boycotts and threats of violence, the government claimed 75% of registered voters participated in the election, which gave Zeroual the office of presidency with 61% of the votes. Opposition groups disputed the turnout figures.

Zeroual's first objective after election was to pass a new constitution that greatly expanded presidential powers. A national referendum passed with nearly 80% of the registered voters participating and 86% approving the new constitution. Although there were widespread irregularities and, despite opposition appeals to boycott backed by threats, the vote was generally viewed as reflecting Algeria's weariness with civil war. However, violence continued. From 1992 to 2003 fighting had claimed between 100,000–120,000 lives. Ramadan in 1997 (the traditional high point of terrorist activity) was the bloodiest ever, with daily reports of bombings and massacres.

Amidst ongoing violence, parliamentary elections were held in June 1997. Thirty-nine political parties registered for the elections with over 7,000 candidates contesting 280 seats in the National People's Assembly. The result was a victory for pro-government parties. Although the FIS and other religious parties were barred from participating, two moderate Islamist parties won more than 100 seats and received over 20% of the votes cast. Regional and municipal council elections were held in October 1997, with the RND (Rassemblement national pour la démocratie—National Democratic Rally) winning more than half of the seats.

In September 1998 President Zeroual gave a surprise address announcing that he would step down from power in February 1999, two years before his term was to expire. The decision was most likely due to infighting in the regime, which had become increasingly public. Forty-seven candidates presented themselves for election, but only seven made it to the final list with Abdelaziz Bouteflika emerging as the leading candidate. Alleging massive voter list fraud, four of the candidates withdrew from the contest two days before the 15 April election day. They were joined the following day by the other two candidates. The claims were rejected by the minister of the interior and the election went ahead with Bouteflika as the single candidate.

Following his victory, Bouteflika announced the "Civil Concord Plan," offering amnesty for Islamists who renounced violence. Voters overwhelmingly approved the plan in a national referendum. Some 5,500 rebels participated in the amnesty, and the AIS formally disbanded in 2000. Those guilty of murder, rape, or the placing of bombs were to be prosecuted; however, the death penalty would not be used, and no prison sentence would be longer

than 20 years. Although the plan was supported by the FIS, Berber protests over police brutality, ethnic discrimination, corruption, housing shortages, unemployment, and repression ensued. In May the mainly Berber party, the Rally for Culture and Democracy, withdrew from the government in protest against the government's handling of the unrest. In October Bouteflika agreed to a constitutional amendment granting national recognition to the Berber language, Tamazight. However, the language was not granted "official" status like Arabic.

In the aftermath of the 11 September 2001 terrorist attacks on the United States, the United States called upon all states to implement counterterrorism measures. Algeria pledged its support for the Bush administration's campaign against terrorism, and sent the United States a list of 350 Islamic extremists known to be living abroad who may have had contacts with Osama bin Laden's al-Qaeda network. Bouteflika made two official state visits to the US in 2001, the first such visits by an Algerian president in 15 years. In return for Algeria's aid, the Bush administration agreed to ease restrictions on arms sales to Algeria.

In parliamentary elections on 30 May 2002, the FLN won 199 of 389 seats in the national assembly; it was 1 of 23 parties participating. Four parties, including two Berber parties, boycotted the elections, which were marred by violence and low voter turnout (47%). In March 2003 French president Jacques Chirac visited Algiers, the first state visit by a French president since independence. His visit was primarily viewed as an act of reconciliation between France and Algeria, but Chirac also called on the government to end the 11-year old Islamic insurgency with dialog.

On 21 May 2003 an earthquake, which measured 6.7 on the Richter scale, struck along Algeria's northern coast. The worst hit areas were east of Algiers. More than 2,200 people were killed, over 9,000 were injured, and over 1,000 people went missing. 51,000 were made homeless in Algeria's most devastating quake in more than 20 years.

In a landslide victory Bouteflika was reelected to a second term in April 2004. Promising to devote himself to seeking "true national reconciliation," Bouteflika offered to invest more in the Berber Kabylia region and greater recognition of the Tamazight language. In January 2005 government arrested the head of the rebel Armed Islamic Group (GIA), Nourredine Boudiafi, and killed his deputy. It was declared that the group was virtually dismantled.

Resurgence in Islamic terrorist activity in North Africa took place at the end of 2006 and into 2007. The Salafist Group for Preaching and Combat (GSPC), an Algeria-based Sunni group that merged with al-Qaeda and was renamed al-Qaeda in the Islamic Maghreb (AQIM), claimed responsibility for roadside attacks and suicide bombings. One of the attacks killed 33 people, wounded hundreds more, and ripped off the façade of the prime minister's office. Parliamentary elections in May 2007 were marred by fighting between the military and armed groups; dozens were killed. In July a suicide bomber targeted a military barracks near Bouira, killing at least nine people. And in September 2007 at least 50 people were killed in a series of bombings.

In the face of widespread unemployment, utility outages, housing shortages, and militancy, Bouteflika managed an overwhelming victory at the polls in 2009 after the government amended the constitution in 2008 to remove presidential term limits. However, in December 2010 a sudden rise in the cost of living triggered riots across the country. Tax cuts and increases in food subsidies quelled the protests. In February 2011 government lifted the 19-year state of emergency restrictions. In March a reform commission began drafting new laws that, among other things, relaxed restrictions authorizing new political parties and permitted private ownership of broadcast media. Sporadic violent demonstrations by various groups continued, but were more narrowly focused or confined to specific regions.

Internationally, Algeria continues to experience border disputes with its neighbors. Since 1976 Algeria has supported the exiled Polisario Front (Polisario) from the Western Sahara, rebels who militarily oppose Moroccan administration of Western Sahara. In 2010 some 90,000–100,000 Sahrawi refugees lived in Polisario-run camps in Tindouf in southwest Algeria. The Sahrawi, a nomadic people comprising some 36 tribes, were being detained in the camps and according to international charities were being intimidated, repressed, punished, tortured, and denied basic human and civil rights by the Polisario. Algeria and Morocco accused each other of harboring militants and arms smuggling. Dormant disputes included Libyan claims of about 32,000 sq km (12,355 sq mi) still reflected on its maps of southeastern Algeria and Algeria's claim to Chirac Pastures in southeastern Morocco

13 GOVERNMENT

The government consists of executive, legislative and judicial branches, although the military has been the ultimate authority in Algeria since 1991. The president serves as chief of state and head of government. A 2008 amendment to the constitution abolished presidential term limits and separated the post of head of state from that of prime minister. The next presidential election was scheduled for 2014.

Algerian voters approved a new constitution in 1996 that further strengthened a dominant executive branch. Under the constitution, a second legislative body called the Council of the Nations (Senate) joined the existing National People's Assembly, or Al-Majlis Ech-Chaabi Al-Watani. The number of seats in the National People's Assembly was changed from 380 seats to 389 seats in the 2002 elections. Members are elected by popular vote to serve five-year terms. In the Council of Nations (Senate) with 144 seats; one-third of the members of the council are appointed by the president with the remaining two-thirds elected by indirect vote (local and regional government). Members serve six-year terms. The constitution requires half the council to be renewed every three years. The council was mandated to approve, by a three-fourths vote, legislation proceeding from the national assembly. Amendments to the constitution occurred in 2002 and 2008.

14 POLITICAL PARTIES

The first Algerian parties were born out of desire for liberation. One of the earliest active figures in the struggle for Algerian self-determination was Messali Hadj, who in 1925 formed the Star of North Africa (Étoile Nord Africaine) movement among Algerian workers and intellectuals in Paris. In 1937 they founded the Algerian People's Party (Parti Populaire Algérien—PPA). Banned in 1939 the PPA operated illegally and militantly under the Vichy regime, with strong support from students and workers.

In 1944 Ferhat Abbas formed the Friends of the Manifesto and of Liberty (Amis du Manifeste et de la Liberté—AML), a moderate reform group that was later transformed into the Democratic Union of the Algerian Manifesto (Union Démocratique du Manifeste Algérien—UDMA). In 1946 some AML members joined the PPA and, under Messali Hadj's leadership, formed a legal front organization, the Movement for the Triumph of Democratic Liberties (Mouvement pour le Triomphe des Libertés Démocratiques—MTLD). On a program favoring "the return of the Algerian people to national sovereignty," the MTLD won 5 of the 15 elected seats in the national assembly elections of 1 November 1946; in 1948, however, the MTLD lost all its seats and was reduced to semi-illegality. Two years later, it was suppressed by the police.

In 1951 an Algerian Front was formed by the MTLD, the UDMA, the Algerian Communist Party, and the Society of 'Ulema, a political-cultural organization. Policy differences in the following years resulted in the creation of three groups: supporters of Messali Hadj; centrists, who hoped to obtain constitutional advances by cooperating with the French administration; and a militant group who proposed violent action. By 1954 there was an open split. The centrist majority repudiated Messali Hadj's leadership. An activist group of nine members formerly associated with an MTLD splinter group calling for armed rebellion then established the Revolutionary Committee for Unity and Action (Comité Révolutionnaire d'Unité et d'Action—CRUA), with headquarters in Cairo, divided Algeria into six military zones and appointed commanders for each and launched a war with France on 1 November 1954.

Shortly thereafter, the CRUA changed its name to the FLN, and its forces became known as the National Liberation Army. The FLN was an amalgamation of various nationalist tendencies in Algeria. Its membership gradually incorporated most members of the former MTLD, most members of the UDMA, and members of the Society of 'Ulema, as well as former independents and young people with no previous political allegiance. Its goal was the complete independence of Algeria, and it appeared to have the support of the great majority of Muslims. After Messali Hadj broke with the FLN, he formed the National Algerian Movement (Mouvement National Algérien—MNA), supported mainly by Algerians in France. The MNA attacked both the FLN and the war through acts of terrorism in France, but lost influence following Hadj's imprisonment.

In August 1956 an FLN congress established an embryo parliament, the 34-member National Committee of the Algerian Revolution, enlarged in 1957 by 20 more members to a total of about 50 and a five-member executive body, the Executive and Coordinating Committee, enlarged in Cairo in 1957 by additional members. In September 1958 a provisional government was established with Ferhat Abbas as president and with headquarters in Cairo and Tunis. Benyoussef Ben Khedda succeeded Abbas as president in August 1961. President de Gaulle in effect recognized the FLN as the only political organization that had the authority to speak for the Muslims during peace negotiations with the French government. During this period, French expatriates in Algeria organized the Secret Army Organization, which violently opposed Algerian independence.

After independence, differences of opinion arose among the members of the Political Bureau, the FLN's policy-making body, regarding the organization of the FLN. While Ben Bella envisioned the creation of an elite party, Mohamed Khider (assassinated in Spain in January 1967) sought to create a broader mass party. The FLN mobilized popular political participation by forming mass organizations for peasants, youth, guerrilla veterans, and women. It organized itself into departmental federations, sections, and cells, staffed largely by former guerrillas (mujahedin). In April 1964 the first congress of the FLN adopted the Charter of Algiers, a guideline for government policy that provided for a wide range of agricultural, industrial, and social reforms. The FLN's National Charter of April 1976 outlined a plan for creating a Socialist system commensurate with Islamic principles. A new national charter adopted in January 1986 de-emphasized Socialism and placed greater stress on Islam. The chief organs of the FLN were the Central Committee, the highest policy-making body of both the FLN and the nation, the Political Bureau and the Secretariat. In the meantime, the Islamic Salvation Front (FSI), an umbrella organization comprising groups that supported government guided by Islamic law, established itself. In September 1989 the government approved a multiparty system, and by 31 December 1990, over 30 legal political parties existed, including the FSI, FLN, and the Socialist Forces Front (FFS).

With the annulment of elections several parties, notably the FSI, were outlawed. The main parties that participated in the June 1997 elections included the official government party, the RND; the Movement for a Peaceful Society (formerly Hamas); Ennahda (a moderate Islamic party); two ethnic-Berber parties, the FFS and the Rally for Culture and Democracy (RCD); and the FLN.

Twenty-three parties participated in the May 2002 parliamentary elections. Two Berber parties boycotted the elections, including the RCD and the FFS. The FLN took a majority of seats in the national assembly. Also winning seats were Islah, the RND, the Movement for a Peaceful Society (MSP), the Workers' Party (PT), the Algerian National Front (FNA), the Islamic Renaissance Movement, the Party of Algerian Renewal (PRA), and the Movement of National Understanding (MEN). Independents won 29 of 389 seats.

Elections for the national assembly on 17 May 2007 resulted in the FLN winning 23% of the vote (136 seats); RND 10.3% (61 seats); MSP 9.6% (52 seats); PT 5.1% (26 seats); RCD 3.4% (19 seats); FNA 4.2% (13 seats); others 34.6% (49 seats); and independents 9.8% (33 seats). In the 28 December 2009 elections for the Council of Nations the number of seats by party were as follows: FLN 29, RND 12, MSP 3, RCD 1, independents 3, presidential appointees (unknown affiliation) 24. In the 2009 presidential election the FLN standard bearer, Bouteflika, garnered more than 90% of the vote. Louisa Hanoune came in second with 4.2% of the vote. The next national assembly and Council of Nation elections were scheduled for 2012; the next presidential election for 2014.

15 LOCAL GOVERNMENT

In 1969 a governorate of 48 provinces (*wilayats*) system replaced the departments that had been established by the French. Each *wilaya* has its own elected people's assembly, executive council, and appointed governor (*wali*), who is responsible to the Ministry of the Interior. The 48 *wilayats* have subdivisions called *da'iraats* (districts), which are further subdivided into 1,552 communes.

The commune is the basic collective unit, governed by an assembly elected for four years.

In the 10 October 2007 elections the FLN won a majority of local council and assembly seats, taking control of 668 communes and 43 of the country's 48 cities. The RND lost its majority, retaining just 171 communes. The FFS won 65 communes and independents gained control over 77. Islamic parties declined in popularity overall.

In the 29 November 2007 elections the FLN won with only 43% of the population voting. Twenty-three parties and numerous independents contested the elections. Unlike the 2002 contest, no party called for a boycott. The RND, one of the FLN's two partners in the governing alliance loyal to President Bouteflika, came in second.

16 JUDICIAL SYSTEM

After independence, Algeria's judicial system was reorganized. Algerians replaced French magistrates and the judiciary was extended into regions of the country previously ignored. The judicial system comprises civilian and military courts. Civilian courts are divided into three levels. *Da'ira* courts hear disputes in civil and some criminal matters. *Wilaya* courts serve as the courts of first instance for remaining criminal cases and as courts of appeal for the *da'ira* courts. At the head of the system is the Supreme Court. The Special Court of State Security was abolished in 1995.

The constitution guarantees independence of the judiciary. However, executive branch decrees restricted some of the judiciary's authority. Judges are appointed by the executive branch without legislative approval, and the government can remove judges at will. A judge's term is 10 years.

Algeria's present legal codes, adopted in 1963, are based on the laws of Islam and of other Northern African and Socialist states, as well as on French laws. Efforts were made to harmonize the laws and legal procedures with those of the Maghreb nations. A first plan for judicial reorganization was approved in 1965; this was followed in 1966 with the beginning of large-scale structural reforms. A new civil code was promulgated in 1975 and a new penal code in 1982.

In civilian courts, Shariah (Islamic law) is applied to social issues. Defendants in civilian courts are afforded a wide range of procedural protections including a public trial, right to counsel, right to confront witnesses, and right of appeal.

Military courts have jurisdiction in cases involving military personnel and hear some cases in which civilians are charged with security-related and terrorism offenses.

The Constitutional Council reviews the constitutionality of treaties, laws, and regulations. The Constitutional Council was not part of the judiciary, but it had the authority to nullify unconstitutional laws. As the highest law of the land, the constitution prohibits torture and other cruel, inhuman or degrading treatment, as well as arbitrary arrest and detention. In criminal cases, the suspect has to be charged or released within 48 hours of incommunicado detention. However, the 1992 Antiterrorist Law provided up to 12 days of pre-arraignment detention.

In August 2002, President Bouteflika announced a major reorganization of the judiciary. He changed approximately 80% of the heads of the 187 lower courts and all but three of the presidents of the 37 higher-level courts. Women in Algeria have become a political force unheard of in the rest of the Arab world; as of 2007 women made up 70% of Algeria's lawyers and 60% of its judges.

17 ARMED FORCES

The International Institute for Strategic Studies (IISS) reported that armed forces in Algeria totaled 147,000 members in 2011. The force comprised 127,000 members from the army, 6,000 from the navy, and 14,000 from the air force. Armed forces represented 2.3% of the labor force in Algeria. Defense spending totaled $8.3 billion and accounted for 3.3% of gross domestic product (GDP).

Six months of military service was compulsory for males.

In April 2010 Algeria joined forces with its neighbors to form the Joint Military Staff Committee of Algeria, Mali, Mauritania, and Niger. Based in Tamanrasset, Algeria, the general purpose of the committee was to strengthen cooperation through shared intelligence and joint military operations in the fight against terrorism, drug trafficking, and illegal weapons trade. Specifically, the committee hoped to combine efforts to counter the threat from al-Qaeda. Regional and international leaders feared that al-Qaeda would establish bases in the Sahara, which could provide a safe haven for the terrorist organization if regional forces, such as the new committee, failed to take action.

18 INTERNATIONAL COOPERATION

Algeria was admitted to the UN on 8 October 1962 and was a member of ECA and all the non-regional specialized agencies, such as the ICAO, IFC, FAO, IAEA, ILO, IMF, UNESCO, UNHCR, UNIDO, World Health Organization (WHO), and the World Bank. Algeria was an observer in the World Trade Organization (WTO) and was a temporary member of the UN Security Council until December 2005. Algeria also participated in the African Development Bank, G-77, G-15, G-24, League of Arab States, African Union, the Organization of the Islamic Conference (OIC), the Arab Maghreb Union, the New Partnership for Africa's Development (NEPAD), OAPEC, and OPEC. The country was a partner in the OSCE. Algeria was a member of the Nonaligned Movement and the Organization for the Prohibition of Chemical Weapons. In cooperation on environmental issues, Algeria participated in the Basel Convention, Convention on Biological Diversity, Ramsar, CITES, the Kyoto Protocol, MARPOL, the Montréal Protocol, and the UN conventions of the Law of the Sea, Climate Change, and Desertification.

19 ECONOMY

The GDP rate of change in Algeria, as of 2011, was 3.3%. Inflation stood at 5%, and unemployment was reported at 9.9%. In 2010 GDP purchasing power parity (PPP) was estimated to be $251.1 billion, with GDP per capita estimated to be $7,300. Agriculture accounted for 8.3% of GDP, industry 61.6%, and services 30.1%. Oil and gas dominated the economy, representing 60% of budget revenues, 30% of GDP and 95% of export earnings.

Pre-independence, Europeans employed more than 90% of the workforce in industry and commerce. Following their departure in 1962, FLN governments nationalized the mining industry and created state farms and state-owned industries on abandoned farms and on expropriated French landholdings. Companies partnering with Algerian state enterprises were allowed to operate independently. In the 1980s the government decentralized companies, splitting over 90 state corporations into 300 specialized units. These enterprises adopted their own annual plans, determined the prices of their products, and invested their profits freely.

With the dawn of liberalization, a new money and credit law invited substantial international participation in the economy. In 1993 a revised investment code opened Algeria to foreign investment, and in 1995 investment promotion agencies were created to stimulate the economy, to liberalize foreign trade, and to encourage private sector competition. Into the new millennium the government committed to greater economic deregulation and diversification, but hydrocarbons remained the engine of growth. With average crude oil prices topping $100/bbl in 2011, Algeria recorded a sharp increase in export earnings and trade surplus.

20 INCOME

In 2010 GDP was estimated at $251.1 billion. GDP is defined as the value of all final goods and services produced within a nation in a given year and computed on the basis of PPP rather than value as measured on the basis of the rate of the exchange based on current dollars. The per capita GDP was estimated at $7,300. The annual growth rate of GDP was 3.3%. The average inflation rate was 5%. According to the World Bank, remittances from citizens living abroad totaled $2.1 billion or about $59 per capita and accounted for approximately 0.8% of GDP.

According to World Bank figures in 2009, household consumption in Algeria totaled $42.4 billion or about $1,211 per capita, measured in current US dollars rather than PPP. Household consumption included expenditures by individuals, households, and nongovernmental organizations on goods and services, excluding the purchases of dwellings. It was estimated that household consumption was growing at an average annual rate of 19.5%.

It was estimated that in 2006 about 23% of the population subsisted on an income below the poverty line established by Algeria's government.

21 LABOR

As of 2010 Algeria had a total labor force of 10.81 million people. Within that labor force, the CIA estimated in 2003 that 14% were employed in agriculture and 13.4% in industry. Unemployment was problematic with up to 50% of youth unemployed in 2005–06.

Algerian law permits collective bargaining by unions. While there are no legal restrictions on a worker's right to join a union, government approval is required by those workers seeking to form a union. Approximately two-thirds of Algerian workers were unionized as of 2005. Minimum wages are set by the government with the advice of the General Union of Algerian Workers (Union Générale des Travailleurs Algériens—UGTA). The standard workweek is 37.5 hours, and those employees who work past the standard workweek are allowed to receive "time-and-a-half" or "double-time," regardless of whether they worked during a holiday, a weekend, or on a normal work day. As of 2009 the minimum wage was around $203 per month. This amount was not considered a living wage. Health and safety regulations are also specified by law, but enforcement was irregular. The minimum age for employment is 16 years. However, child labor remained problematic in agriculture and in the informal economy, with 1.5 million working children and some 300,000 students dropping out of school each year to enter the labor force (2010).

²²AGRICULTURE

Roughly 17% of the total land is farmed. The country's major crops included wheat, barley, oats, grapes, olives, citrus, and fruits. Cereal production in 2009 amounted to 5.3 million tons, fruit production 3 million tons, and vegetable production 4.5 million tons. The soil was poor and subject to erosion, and the water supply was generally irregular and insufficient; about one-quarter of northern Algeria was completely unproductive.

Although agriculture accounted for about 8% of GDP, 14% of Algerians made their living in this sector. Prior to independence, European-owned agriculture accounted for about two-thirds of vegetable production and employed about 800,000 farm laborers, 700,000 of them Muslims. Most Muslim-owned farms were small—10 hectares (25 acres) or less—and were located mainly in marginal areas on the interior plains and on mountain slopes. The Muslim sector, comprising the bulk of the agricultural population, accounted for only one-third of vegetable production but nearly all the livestock.

Within six months of independence, at least half the European-owned land had been vacated. Algerian peasants soon began to work on these abandoned farms under a self-management system. During the 1960s the government established more than 2,300 state farms on expropriated French landholdings; by the end of the decade, these farms accounted for two-thirds of total agricultural production and employed about 500,000 workers.

In July 1971 President Boumedienne announced an agrarian program providing for the breakup of large Algerian-owned farms and their reorganization into cooperatives. The first stage of the plan, the registration of land ownership, began in March 1972. In the second stage, many absentee landlords were forced to hand over part of their land to the state. By July 1973, of a total of 5 million hectares (12.4 million acres) of public land, 1 million hectares (2.5 million acres) of cultivable land had been redistributed to 54,000 families of landless peasants (*fellahin*) and 1,348 cooperatives had been created.

By 1980 the number of cooperatives had increased to about 6,000; in the early 1980s, however, the government split large cooperatives into smaller units to improve efficiency. In 1982–83 about 450,000 hectares (1.1 million acres) of land previously nationalized were returned to private ownership, mostly in plots of 10 hectares (25 acres) or less. In 1987 the government further divided large state-owned farms into private cooperatives with long-term land leases. Farmers began to enjoy production and investment decision-making, as well as the right to keep profits.

With some 1.2 million members, the National Union of Algerian Peasants, established in March 1973, played a leading role in land reform. However, by 1995 most of the cooperatives had been dispersed because of internal disputes, and land was divided into individual plots. The government did not officially endorse this development, which compelled farmers to sell their produce on the black market. By 2008 the Ministry of Agriculture was considering land privatization to stimulate private investment, but fears of privatizing gains and socializing losses, tough going in the privatization of banking and other industries, as well as public and political opposition to privatization delayed reforms.

²³ANIMAL HUSBANDRY

The UN Food and Agriculture Organization (FAO) reported that Algeria had dedicated 32.9 million hectares (81.3 million acres) to permanent pasture or meadow in 2009. During that year, farmers tended 125 million chickens, 1.7 million head of cattle, and 5,700 pigs. The production from these animals amounted to 194,215 tons of beef and veal, 246 tons of pork, 266,214 tons of poultry, 166,934 tons of eggs, and 3.97 million tons of milk. Algeria also produced 13,000 tons of cattle hide and 25,739 tons of raw wool.

About half of the livestock was owned by only 5% of the herdsmen. In 2004 there were an estimated 18,700,000 sheep, 3,200,000 goats, 245,000 camels, 170,000 donkeys, 44,000 horses, and 43,000 mules. Algeria was self-sufficient in poultry, meat, and eggs, but had to import all inputs (chicks, hatching eggs, feed, veterinary products, and equipment). Algeria produced about one billion liters of milk annually, while consumption amounted to 3 billion liters.

²⁴FISHING

Algeria had 2,310 decked commercial fishing boats in 2008. According to the FAO, the annual capture totaled 138,833 tons. The export value of seafood totaled $10.92 million. Fishing is extensive along the coast but, compared with oil and gas, the industry is relatively undeveloped. Sardines, bogue, mackerel, anchovies, and shellfish are caught.

²⁵FORESTRY

Approximately 1% of Algeria was covered by forest. The FAO estimated the 2009 roundwood production at 102,600 cu m (3.62 million cu ft). The value of all forest products, including roundwood, totaled $14.4 million. Algeria's mountain ranges contain dense forests of evergreens (evergreen oak, Aleppo pine, and cedar) and deciduous trees. Warmer zones contain large numbers of fruit and palm trees. Algeria was an important producer of cork; other forestry products were firewood, charcoal, and wood for industrial use.

Reforestation projects included the planting of a "green wall" across Algeria from the Moroccan to the Tunisian frontier to halt the encroachment of the Sahara. During the first half of the 1980s reforestation proceeded at a rate of 52,000 hectares (128,000 acres) per year, but from 1984 to 1994 deforestation averaged about 45,000 hectares (111,200 acres) per year. In 2009 it was estimated that Algeria had 10% less forested land than in 1979.

²⁶MINING

In 2000 the government proposed allowing foreign investors to develop mineral deposits held by the national mining companies. The national geologic and mineral research office has identified many mineral deposits. However, they were located in remote areas that lacked infrastructure or government funding for development. With Algeria's proximity to Europe, its major minerals customer, the country's base and precious metals are of interest to foreign investors. Guerrilla activity, though, remains a significant deterrent.

Algeria's phosphate deposits at Djebel Onk, in the northeast, are among the largest in the world, covering about 2,072 sq km (800 sq mi). The deposits had an output of 1,017,000 metric tons in 2009, down from 1,805,000 tons in 2008. There are deposits of high-grade iron ore at Ouenza, near the Tunisian border. Production totaled 1,307,000 metric tons in 2009. Among other mineral production in 2009: bentonite, 32,000 metric tons in 2009, down from 53,000 metric in 2008; crude barite, 38,000 metric tons in 2009, down from 65,000 metric tons in 2006; salt (brine and sea salt), 269,000 metric tons in 2009, up from 197,000 metric tons in 2005; and hydraulic lime, estimated at 65,000 metric tons in 2009, up from an estimated 32,000 metric tons, in 2005. Marble, silver, kaolin, sulfur, fuller's earth, and strontium are also mined. The value of nonfuel mineral exports in 2009 was $770 million, down from $1.8 billion in 2008. Algeria has large deposits of celestite, diamond, manganese, quartz crystal, rare earth minerals, tungsten, and uranium, none of which have been mined.

27 ENERGY AND POWER

The World Bank reported in 2008 that Algeria produced 40.2 billion kWh of electricity and consumed 32.9 billion kWh, or 940 kWh per capita. All energy came from fossil fuels. Per capita oil consumption was 1,078 kg. Oil production totaled 2.078 million barrels of oil a day.

Oil and gas dominate the economy, accounting for about 30% of the GDP and 95% of all export earnings. Discovered in 1950, the country's proven natural gas reserves ranked tenth in the world, totaling an estimated 4.54 trillion cu m (160.4 trillion cu ft). In 2010 Algeria qualified as the sixth-largest gas exporter in the world producing about 85.14 billion cu m. A 500-km (310-mi) main pipeline connecting Hassi R'Mel to Arzew (between Oran and Mostaganem) opened in 1961, and branch lines to Oran and Algiers carried gas four years later. Since then, six more pipelines have come on stream including the first trans-Mediterranean gas pipeline (Transmed) to Europe via Sicily, built at a cost of $3 billion. The Transmed consists of three segments linking Algeria, 550 km (342 mi); Tunisia, 370 km (230 mi); and the Mediterranean to Sicily, 154 km (96 mi) underwater. In 2001 Algeria's total liquefied natural gas (LNG) export capacity amounted to over 6 billion cu m (212 billion cu ft) per year. The $2.3 billion Gazoduc Maghreb-Europe pipeline to Spain and Portugal via Morocco began operating in November 1996. Total dry exports of natural gas amounted to 55.28 billion cu ft in 2010.

Oil was discovered at Edjeleh and Hassi Messaoud in 1956 and at Al-Gassi in 1959; by 1969 the Franco-Algeria Cooperative Association (ASCOOP), a petroleum development company, had discovered eight major fields. Proven reserves of crude oil amounted to 12.2 billion bbl as of January 2011. There were four main pipelines linking the wellheads in the eastern Sahara with Algerian ports and a fifth with the Tunisian port of Sekhira; there were also several branch pipelines. In 2010 Algeria's total refinery capacity was more than 500,000 barrels per day. Algeria was the world's second-largest exporter of LNG; its exports, which went mainly to Western Europe, accounted for 19% of the world's total. There are four gas liquefaction plants, three at Arzew and one at Skikda, but they operate below capacity because of disrepair and lack of funds for spare parts.

The Société Nationale pour la Recherche, la Production, le Transport, la Transformation et la Commercialisation des Hydrocarbons (Sonatrach), founded in 1964 as the state-owned petroleum company, dominated production and transport of the oil and gas industry. On 24 February 1971 President Boumedienne announced the Algerian takeover of controlling interest in all French oil company subsidiaries and the nationalization of all pipelines and natural gas deposits. Holdings of all other foreign petroleum interests in Algeria were nationalized by the end of 1971. Subsequent agreements have generally treated foreign companies as minority partners in Algerian state enterprises. Contracts for sales of natural gas to Western Europe and the United States increased spectacularly in the 1970s, but decreased in the 1980s as world energy prices fell, pushing Algeria into severe debt.

By 1991 Sonatrach had reversed its monopolistic policy and formed joint ventures for new exploration contracts. In 2011 Anadarko, Eni, the British Gas Group (BG Group), British Petroleum (BP), Conoco-Phillips, Total, and others were actively engaged in various aspects of exploration and production in the industry, and Sonatrach reached out to foreign companies such as the Chinese giant Sinopec.

In 1996 Algeria signed a nuclear cooperative agreement with China, which built two nuclear research reactors in Algeria. In 2008 the government signed an agreement with China to cooperate on developing civilian nuclear power and to share research, training, and human resources. Algeria had significant uranium reserves and was developing plans to build its first nuclear power plant by 2020 as part of a larger scheme to diversify the energy sector. Algeria has no capacity for enriching uranium.

28 INDUSTRY

The industries of Algeria, which traditionally have been concentrated around Algiers and Oran, have included carpet mills, cement factories, chemical plants, automobile assembly plants, food-processing installations, oil refineries, soap factories, and textile plants. Other major industries have produced bricks and tiles, rolled steel, farm machinery, electrical supplies, machine tools, phosphates, sulfuric acid, paper and cartons, matches, and tobacco products.

Before independence, industry made significant gains. New enterprises were developed in food processing and packaging, textiles, leather, chemicals, metalworking, building materials, and farm machinery. A large steel plant was built at Annaba, a petroleum refinery at Algiers, a petrochemical complex at Arzew, and a phosphate production center at Djebel Onk, near the Tunisian border. Other industries were set up to produce automobiles, tractors, cement, rubber tires, and ammonia.

Between 1962 and 1974 the government nationalized industry. Foremost was the development of the hydrocarbons sector, including the building of refineries and natural gas liquefaction plants. To remain competitive, the oil and gas industry was restructured in the 1980s and 1990s, eventually opening to foreign investors. In 2011 Anadarko was the leading foreign producer generating more than 500,000 bbl of petroleum per day. Eni produced 84,000 bbl/day.

In the early 2000s the government spent $15 billion to restructure industry. By 2004 the estimated industrial production growth rate stood at 6%; however, this growth tapered and by 2010 the industry production growth rate registered a -3.6%. As of 2010 industry accounted for about 61.6% of the nation's GDP. The hydrocarbons sector (mostly petroleum and natural gas) alone accounted for 30% of GDP in 2010 and over 90% of export revenues.

Algerian industry has continued structural transformation toward a free-market economy. In August 2009 the government signed a memorandum of understanding with companies from the United Arab Emirates (Aabar) and Germany relating to the construction and operation of German automobile manufacturing plants in three Algerian sites. The plants, located in Taret, Ain Smara, and Oued Hamimine, were designed to produce the Sprinter and Unimog models of Daimler AG, as well as other all-wheel drive vehicles.

29 SCIENCE AND TECHNOLOGY

According to the World Bank, as of 2009 there were 84 patent applications in science and technology. Since independence, Algeria has made major technological advances, especially in steel and petrochemicals. However, by 2011 Algeria still had a severe shortage of skilled workers and was heavily dependent on foreign technologies.

Scientific training was conducted at several universities: Oran Es-Senia (founded in 1965); Constantine (founded in 1969); the Hovari Boumedienne University of Sciences and Technology (founded at Algiers in 1974); the Oran University of Sciences and Technology (founded in 1974); Tlemcen (founded in 1975); Annaba (founded in 1975); the Ferhat Abbas-Setif University of Setif (founded in 1978); Blida (founded in 1981); and Boumerdes (founded in 1981). From 1987–97 science and engineering students accounted for 58% of college and university enrollments. The government's National Bureau of Scientific Research operated 18 research centers in biology, anthropology, oceanography and fisheries, astronomy, astrophysics, geophysics, renewable energy, arid zones, technology transfer, and other fields.

In 2010 the Algerian parliament approved a plan to spend $1.4 billion on the development of scientific research programs over the next five years. The plan was specifically designed to reverse the brain drain that has resulted in large numbers of highly educated Algerian scientists leaving the country for better opportunities. At least 34 new research programs were slated to be implemented by government with the hope of increasing the number of scientific researchers in government programs from some 21,000 to 28,000.

30 DOMESTIC TRADE

European trading firms formerly played a major role in the economy; however, many Europeans, fearful of Muslim control, sold their holdings or gave them up in 1961–62. After independence, about one-half of the country's shops closed, and in 1963 state agencies began taking over nearly all wholesaling and marketing operations. Since 1996 the Algerian government has prioritized the privatization of state-owned enterprises.

The principal cities of the north are the largest trade centers. While most trade is done on a cash or credit basis, some bartering still occurs among the rural dwellers and in the Muslim quarters of cities. In the mountain regions local market days or special local fairs offer opportunities to exchange products depending on the season.

Normal business hours are from 8 a.m. to noon and 2 or 2:30 to 5:30 or 6 p.m., Saturday–Wednesday, and from 8 a.m. to noon on Thursday. Banks are generally open from 9 a.m. to 3 p.m., Monday–Thursday, but some banks close for lunch. Shopping is normally carried out from 8 a.m. to 12 p.m. and 2 to 6 p.m., Saturday–Thursday. Ramadan hours are shorter.

31 FOREIGN TRADE

Algeria imported $37.07 billion worth of goods and services in 2008, while exporting $52.66 billion worth of goods and services. Major import partners in 2009 were France, 15.1%; China, 11.6%; Italy, 9.1%; Spain, 7.3%; Germany, 6.8%; the United States, 4.9%; Tajikistan, 4.3%; and Turkey, 4.3%. Its major export partners were the United States, 22.9%; Italy, 12.6%; Spain, 11.9%; France, 9.8%; Netherlands, 7.2%; Canada, 5.4%; and Turkey, 4.4%.

Crude oil and natural gas accounted for nearly all of Algeria's export value; industrial equipment and semi-finished goods and foodstuffs, especially wheat, dominated the country's imports.

Principal Trading Partners – Algeria (2010)

(In millions of US dollars)

Country	Total	Exports	Imports	Balance
World	97,974.0	57,762.0	40,212.0	17,550.0
United States	15,947.0	13,830.0	2,117.0	11,713.0
Italy	12,835.0	8,780.0	4,055.0	4,725.0
France	9,879.0	3,777.0	6,102.0	-2,325.0
Spain	8,548.0	5,910.0	2,638.0	3,272.0
China	5,617.0	1,174.0	4,443.0	-3,269.0
Netherlands	4,644.0	4,164.0	480.0	3,684.0
Turkey	4,220.0	2,704.0	1,516.0	1,188.0
Canada	3,301.0	2,971.0	330.0	2,641.0
South Korea	3,134.0	1,158.0	1,976.0	-818.0
Belgium	2,697.0	1,921.0	776.0	1,145.0

(…) data not available or not significant.

(n.s.) not specified.

SOURCE: *2011 Direction of Trade Statistics Yearbook*, New York: United Nations, 2011.

Balance of Payments – Algeria (2009)

(In millions of US dollars)

Current Account		**160.0**
Balance on goods		7,784.0
Imports	-37,402.0	
Exports	45,186.0	
Balance on services		-8,695.0
Balance on income		-1,319.0
Current transfers		2,390.0
Capital Account		...
Financial Account		5,676.2
Direct investment abroad		-215.0
Direct investment in Algeria		2,760.0
Portfolio investment assets		...
Portfolio investment liabilities		...
Financial derivatives		...
Other investment assets		-7.0
Other investment liabilities		3,138.2
Net Errors and Omissions		**-2,319.6**
Reserves and Related Items		**-3,516.6**

(…) data not available or not significant.

SOURCE: *Balance of Payment Statistics Yearbook 2011*, Washington, DC: International Monetary Fund, 2011.

Surpluses accrued with the oil and gas price spikes in the mid-1970s. The 1986 collapse of oil prices forced the government to implement International Monetary Fund (IMF) stabilization programs. Algeria registered a trade surplus during most of the nineties, except during 1994, after a season of political turmoil. On 30 April 1998 the Algerian government chose not to re-subscribe to IMF structural programs. Coupled with low oil prices, this move brought about diminished export revenues, threatening a trade deficit. In the millennium sharply rising world oil prices created trade surpluses. In 2010 the country had a $19 billion trade surplus.

³²BALANCE OF PAYMENTS

Algeria has long had a current-accounts deficit, which pre-independence was covered by the French government. Although a more equitable balance of trade prevailed after independence (Europeans had been the chief consumers of foreign goods), a loss of capital and a decrease in French aid caused continued deterioration of Algeria's payments position. However, continued growth of the petroleum sector permitted substantial payments surpluses during the 1970s. In 1986 the fall of oil prices caused a large deficit and led to IMF restructuring of the economy. In 1991 government abolished many import restrictions with the exception of foreign exchange and external credit access. By 1996 Algeria had removed export restrictions and was encouraging foreign investment.

Debt rescheduling by the Paris Club and other lenders in the late1990s allowed the Bank of Algeria to increase its reserves of hard currency. Owing to high world oil prices, external debt fell from 8.1% of GDP in 2009 to 6.6% of GDP in 2010. In 2010 government expenditures amounted to an estimated $60.7 billion, approximately one billion more than revenues ($58.88 billion), equal to a deficit of -1.1% of GDP.

³³BANKING AND SECURITIES

The Bank of Algeria functioned as the central bank, headquartered in Algiers. It was government-owned, as were five other state-owned banks and one public development bank. Public sector banks controlled 90% of assets and deposits in the country. The 14 private banks were all subsidiaries of large international banking groups. In 2008 there were some 10 banking applications pending, but government had decided to freeze new authorizations. By 2011 efforts to privatize the sector were ongoing, but stiffly opposed by key forces in government and industry.

As of 31 December 2010 the central bank discount rate was 4%, and the commercial bank prime lending rate was 8%. There was no change in the rates from the previous year. Stocks of narrow money amounted to approximately $75 billion and stocks of broad money amounted to about $109 billion. Algeria had $162.9 billion in reserves of foreign exchange and gold, which was 15th best in the world.

Algeria has a history of state control over the banking sector. Following the separation of the French and Algerian treasuries in late 1962, the Directorate of Treasury and Credit was established as the government's fiscal agent. The state also established cooperative banks. Following the nationalization of banks in 1963, foreign banks ceased operations and were absorbed by three government-owned banks: the Foreign Bank of Algeria, the National Bank of Algeria, and the People's Credit of Algeria. There were

also four government banks for financing economic development and a savings institution that offered housing loans. These included the Algerian Development Bank, the Agricultural Bank for Rural Development, and the Maghreb Bank for Investment and Commerce. It was not until 1996 that private companies were permitted to set up money-changing shops following a directive issued by the Central Bank initiating open market operations. This change opened a field previously restricted to state-owned banks.

The Algiers stock exchange was opened in July 1999. With only three companies listed (a food processing company, a pharmaceutical company, and a hotel) the exchange was still in its early stages by 2008, and total market capitalization was less than $100 million by the end of 2007. Bonds issued in 1998 by Sonatrach, the national oil company, were rated in the Algiers stock exchange on 18 October 1999. As part of privatization, 11 state-owned companies were expected to trade on the stock exchange in the near future.

³⁴INSURANCE

In 1966 a state monopoly based on the Algerian Company of Insurance (ACI) and the Algerian Insurance of Reinsurance Fund (AIRF), replaced foreign insurance companies. However, liberalization and privatization brought changes to the industry and in 2008 7 of 16 companies operating in Algeria were private. The sector was highly concentrated with three companies holding 80% of market share. Algeria's generous social and pension systems obviated the need for health and life insurance; auto, property and casualty insurance accounted for 80% of premiums totaling some $811 million in 2008. Companies doing business in Algeria included: Compagnie Algérienne d'Assurances (CAA), the Compagnie Algérienne des Assurances Transports (CAAT), the Compagnie Centrale de Réassurance, the Agricultural Mutual Fund, the Algerian Fund Insurance for Workers in Education and Culture, the CAGEX Insurance Company, and Guarantee for Exports and the Société Nationale d'Assurances. In 1998 Trust-Algeria, the International Company of Insurance and Reinsurance, and Algerian Insurance were approved as Algerian Insurance Companies. The state insurer, Société Algérienne d'Assurance (SAA), was the top non-life and life insurer.

³⁵PUBLIC FINANCE

According to the CIA World Factbook, in 2010 Algeria recorded an estimated $58.88 billion in public revenue and $60.67 billion in public expenditures. The budget deficit amounted to 1.1% of GDP. Public debt was 6.6% of GDP, with $4.341 billion of the debt held by foreign entities. About 60% of government revenue came from petroleum and natural gas.

³⁶TAXATION

The most important sources of government revenue are oil and gas royalties. Algeria's tax system has been streamlined through the replacement of a number of different taxes by a value-added tax (VAT), a personal income tax, and a corporate profits tax. The corporation tax is 45% on distributed profits and 20% on reinvested earnings. Many fiscal advantages are accorded to developing and expanding industries and private investment. For established domestic industry and commerce there is a tax on production (a

Public Finance – Algeria (2009)

(In billions of dinars, budgetary central government figures)

Revenue and Grants	3,740.5	100.0%
Tax revenue	3,503.1	93.7%
Social contributions	...	...
Grants	...	...
Other revenue	237.5	6.3%
Expenditures	4,188.2	100.0%
General public services	804.5	19.2%
Defense	407.1	9.7%
Public order and safety	183	4.4%
Economic affairs	813.5	19.4%
Environmental protection	11.9	0.3%
Housing and community amenities	438.9	10.5%
Health	230.1	5.5%
Recreational, culture, and religion	85.8	2.0%
Education	600.7	14.3%
Social protection	612.8	14.6%

(...) data not available or not significant.

SOURCE: *Government Finance Statistics Yearbook 2010,* Washington, DC: International Monetary Fund, 2010.

single tax that is passed on to the consumer) and a tax on industrial and commercial activities.

Algeria's 1993 investment code offered foreign investment companies a three-year exemption from VAT, a property tax abatement, lower customs duties, and a two- to five-year exemption from corporate income taxes. However, by 2012 Algeria still had one of the most regressive taxation regimes among Middle Eastern and North African (MENA) countries and in the world. In 2012 the country was ranked 148th out of 183 economies on the World Bank's "Ease of Doing Business" index, down five rankings from 2011. On the tax indicator, Algeria ranked 164th out of 183 economies. Companies doing business in Algeria were required to make 29 payments per year including a 6.6% profit tax; 29.7% labor and other contributions tax; and 35.7% for other taxes amounting to 72% total tax rate. By contrast, MENA countries paid a total rate of 32.2% and Organisation for Economic Co-operation and Development (OECD) countries 42.7%.

37 CUSTOMS AND DUTIES

A customs union between Algeria and France allowed regulations applicable in the metropolis to apply also in Algeria, making Algeria a de facto adherent of the General Agreement on Trade and Tariffs (GATT). By a special agreement with the European Union (EU), Algerian industrial products were granted duty-free entry into the EU market. In addition, agricultural products received seasonal tariff reductions, while Algeria gave reciprocal treatment to EU imports. Algeria also concluded preferential customs agreements with Tunisia and Morocco and was a founding member of the Arab Maghreb Union (UMA), a trade union composed of Algeria, Libya, Mauritania, Morocco, and Tunisia that aimed to create a free trade zone.

For non-EU countries and nations not enjoying preferential trade status with Algeria, tariffs on imports ranged from 3–40% with additional duties (Taxe Spécifique Additionnelle) ranging from 20–110% on luxury goods. To join the WTO, Algeria lowered its rates to bring them within acceptable WTO levels. The government further abolished import licenses. The only imports subject to restriction were firearms, explosives, narcotics, and pork products.

In 2012 on the World Bank's "Ease of Doing Business" index, "Trade Across Borders," Algeria ranked 127th out of 183 economies, which was four rankings lower than 2011. The cost to import a container was $1,318 compared with $1,238 for MENA countries, and the cost to export a container was $1,248 compared with $1,057 for MENA countries.

38 FOREIGN INVESTMENT

Foreign direct investment (FDI) in Algeria recorded a net inflow of $2.85 billion according to World Bank figures published in 2009. FDI represented 2.02% of GDP.

Beginning in the 1990s Algeria gradually relaxed restrictions regarding foreign investment. Under investment codes issued in 1983 and 1986, Algeria's foreign investment regime was relatively restrictive. The government permitted foreign investment only in joint ventures with state-owned companies, although repatriation of profits was guaranteed. The economy's main hydrocarbon sector and many others were off limits.

A breakthrough occurred with the money and credit law of March 1990, which permitted majority foreign-owned joint ventures in almost all sectors except for hydrocarbons, electricity, railroads, telecommunications, and a few others. Nevertheless, the hydrocarbon law of November 1991 allowed foreign firms to exploit existing oil fields in partnership with the national petroleum company. The Investment Code of October 1993 no longer distinguished between investments made by foreigners or Algerians and granted new investors limited tax exemptions and reductions in duty on imported goods. In 1995 the government established the National Agency of Investment Development (Agence de Promotion, de Soutien, et de Suivi des Investissements—APSI) and regional investment promotion agencies to serve as a network of regional one-stop shops to reduce bureaucracy.

In August 2001 government reorganized public sector companies to facilitate investment. The 11 sectoral holding companies into which state economic enterprises (EPEs) had been organized in 1996 were replaced with 28 shareholding management companies and the National Privatization Council was renamed the State Shareholding Council. Nearly all sectors received some type of foreign investment, including the hydrocarbon sector where government auctioned exploratory contracts for particular blocks. Following a 2005 law that further liberalized hydrocarbons, and that forced Sonatrach to bid on domestic projects alongside foreign firms, as many as 30 foreign firms became engaged in petroleum exploration and production.

39 ECONOMIC DEVELOPMENT

Despite a dismal global economy in 2010, Algeria recorded a GDP growth rate of 3.3% most of which derived from petroleum and natural gas. By 2011 the country's key economic challenges were to diversify an economy dependent on hydrocarbons, to further relax state controls over the economy, and to increase employment opportunities for youth. On the 2011 Index of Economic Freedom, Algeria's economy was rated 132nd out of 179 in the world, falling within the "mostly unfree" category.

For much of the post-independence period, government favored socialist policies. Under the Charter of Algiers, workers managed enterprises while government owned them. Algeria's initial development phase from 1967–69 aimed to expand industry, improve agriculture, and train personnel. The second phase (1974–77) established a heavy industrial base and largely completed agricultural reforms. From 1978–79 government consolidated economic gains, limited oil and gas exports, and decentralized industry in order to develop the periphery. The five-year plan for 1980–84 shifted the emphasis from heavy to light industry and to neglected social areas, especially housing. The second five-year plan (1985–89) emphasized agriculture and water supply in order to reduce chronic food deficits, but industry (32%) and social infrastructure (27%) were allotted the largest shares of the proposed total investment.

In 1995 Algeria signed a three-year IMF program to reschedule a $13 billion debt with the Paris Club. Restructuring improved the balance of trade, reduced expenditures, and created surplus revenue. However, in 1998 government did not renew its IMF program, which resulted in an additional $31 million debt that year.

Trade surpluses in the early 2000s reduced foreign debt. By end of 2001 debt decreased to $22.5 billion, or 43% of GDP, and to $21.9 billion in 2004. In the early 1990s foreign debt had reached 72% of GDP. By 2010 thanks to implementation of a fiscal stimulus package, and high world prices for oil and gas, public debt fell to 6.6% of GDP.

In 2002 Algeria entered into an Association Agreement with the EU. Priorities were privatization, economic and trade liberalization, and employment. In 2005 the government increased spending on labor-intensive housing, as well as road and water projects. In September 2004 the government announced a $50 billion capital spending package covering the period 2005–09.

In 2010 Algeria launched a five-year $286 billion program to update infrastructure and to create jobs. The plan earmarked about $130 billion for the completion of large infrastructure projects including railways, roads, and water supply access, some of which were already underway. The remainder was allocated to create two million housing units; to invest in health, education, and sports; and to develop transportation, public works, and agriculture. To reduce the national debt (approximately $4 billion in 2010), the government pledged to complete the projects without foreign loans.

40 SOCIAL DEVELOPMENT

Algeria ranked below the world average in public expenditures in the social sector. In 2008 government spent 4.3% of GDP on education (89th worldwide), and in 2009 government spent 5.8% of GDP on health (114th worldwide). The UN Development Program (UNDP) Human Development Index (HDI), which measures prospects for a long and healthy life and quality education, ranked Algeria 96 out of 187 countries in the "medium" category of human development.

Employees and self-employed people receive insurance for old age, disability, sickness and death. The program is financed with contributions from employees and employers. Retirement is age 60 for men and age 55 for women and veterans, with early retirement available for those employed in heavy labor and for the disabled. Work injury benefits cover all employed individuals; however, only salaried workers are entitled to unemployment benefits.

The Family Code, based on Islamic principles, treats women as legal minors under the authority of the father, husband, or other male head of the family. The code permits polygamy and prohibits marriage between a Muslim woman and a non-Muslim man while allowing a Muslim man to marry outside the faith. In a court of law, a woman's testimony is not considered equal to a man's, and women do not have full legal guardianship of their children, requiring the father to sign all official documents.

Women constitute 19% of the work force. Traditional Islamic views prevent most women from seeking jobs outside the home. Labor laws prohibit sexual discrimination in the workplace, but these laws are not enforced. Spousal abuse is common, especially in rural areas. Spousal rape is not prohibited by law, and it accounted for an estimated 27% of domestic abuse. Many of the abused women were uneducated and illiterate.

Algeria's human rights record remains poor and includes extrajudicial killings, torture, and failure to control abuses by security personnel, including massacres of suspected Islamic militants. Ethnic tensions between Arabs and Berbers continue. The High Commission for Berber Affairs protects and promotes Berber language and culture.

41 HEALTH

According to the CIA, life expectancy in Algeria was 73 years in 2011. The country spent 5.8% of its GDP on healthcare, amounting to $268 per person. There were 12 physicians, 20 nurses and midwives, and 17 hospital beds per 10,000 inhabitants. The fertility rate was 2.3 while the infant mortality rate was 29 per 1,000 live births. In 2008 the maternal mortality rate, according to the World Bank, was 120 per 100,000 births. It was estimated that 88% of children were vaccinated against measles. The CIA calculated HIV/AIDS prevalence in Algeria to be about 0.1% in 2009.

Algeria's principal health challenges have been tuberculosis, malaria, trachoma, and malnutrition. In 2011 the average life expectancy was 74.5 years. The government has emphasized awareness of birth control, resulting in an estimated 64% of women aged 15 to 49 using some form of contraceptive. Approximately 95% of the population had access to adequate sanitation and 83% to improved water sources.

42 HOUSING

Severe housing shortages have plagued Algeria for decades. About half of all housing units are individual houses, with the remaining housing falling into three categories: traditional houses called *haouches*, flats or apartments, and shacks or other marginal arrangements. In 1964 the Ministry for Housing and Construction was created to aid in reconstruction and upgrading of damaged and substandard dwellings. The government's 1965 financial reform provided for regularization of ownership and collection of rents from some 500,000 nationalized or sequestered apartments and houses in the major cities.

Migration to the coastal cities during the 1960s and 1970s aggravated the housing problem, and in the 1974–77 development plan the government took steps to curb the flow. The 1980–84 development plan called for the construction of 450,000 new housing units; the building effort failed to meet the target because of shortages of construction materials. In 1982 the government committed more than $1.5 billion to prefabricated housing, some of it as part of a program to build "model villages" for workers on state farms or in state-owned enterprises. In 1998 the World Bank offered the nation a loan of $150 million for a 10-year program to improve and create low-income urban housing, thus eliminating urban slums.

Despite these efforts, 2003 reports indicated that the country still needed 1.5–2 million housing units. The average occupancy rate was at about 7.5 persons per household; with one report indicating that 52% of all households included 15–20 members. The Ministry of Housing and Urbanism announced plans to build one million new homes by the end of 2009, but street riots in May 2011, protesting government demolition of illegal housing, were evidence of the inadequacy of the plans and their implementation. In July 2011, a UN housing expert called on the government to democratize its housing policies, to make them more transparent, and to involve citizens directly in decision-making.

43 EDUCATION

In 2009 the World Bank estimated that 94% of age-eligible children in Algeria were enrolled in primary school. Secondary enrollment for age-eligible children stood at 67%. Tertiary enrollment was estimated at 31%. The pupil to teacher ratio for primary school was about 25:1 in 2005. The CIA estimated that Algeria had a literacy rate of 69.9%. In 2008 the government spent 4.3% of GDP on education.

Education in Algeria is patterned after the French system, but its scope has been greatly extended. Public primary and secondary schools were unified in 1976 and private schools were abolished. The government has given priority to teacher training, technical and scientific programs, as well as adult literacy classes.

Education is compulsory for 12 years, with most students beginning at age six. Basic education lasts nine years. Upon completion, students chose to continue in general secondary or to enroll in technical programs, each involving three more years of study. The academic year goes from September to June. The public schools are regulated jointly by the Ministry of Education and the Ministry of Religious Affairs and the study of Islam is a required part of the curriculum. Arabic is the official language of instruction, although French and Berber are also in widespread usage.

In 2011 there were some 80 universities and 658 technical and professional schools. The University of Algiers (founded in 1909), its affiliated institutes, and other universities enrolled 939,000 students; professional training schools enrolled 464,000 students in 2011. Universities provide diverse programs with an emphasis on development-related subjects. The National Conference of Universities was created in 2000 to serve as a coordinating body for higher education.

44 LIBRARIES AND MUSEUMS

The largest libraries in Algeria are those of the University of Algiers (over 800,000 volumes) and the National Library (founded in 1835, over 950,000 volumes). In 2005 the National Library (Bibliothèque nationale d'Algérie) had seven annex locations to supplement its main location in Algiers. Several sizeable university collections exist, including the University of Constantine (208,000 volumes), the University de Mentouri (240,000 volumes), and the University d'Oran Es-Senia (200,000 volumes). Other collections of size are the Municipal Library in Constantine (25,000 volumes) and the Aubert Library in Oran (26,000 volumes). The Pasteur Institute in Algiers has a special library of over 47,000 volumes, and the Institute of National Studies in Tiaret has a library of 25,000 volumes.

Museums of importance in Algiers include the Bardo National Museum of Prehistory and Ethnography (1928), the National Museum of Fine Arts of Algiers (1930), the National Museum of Antiquities and Islamic Art (1897), and the Museum of the Revolution (1968) with a collection of memorabilia celebrating Algeria's war of independence against France. Various regional museums are located at Constantine, El Biar (west of Algiers), Oran, Sétif, and Skikda. There was a fine antiquities museum in Cherchell, a decorative arts museum in Ghardaia Oasis, and a botanical garden in Beni-Abbes. The preservation of many of Algeria's cultural treasures has been under threat from anti-Western extremists.

45 MEDIA

In 2009 the CIA reported that there were 2.6 million telephone landlines in Algeria with a density of 100 phones per 100 people. Mobile phone subscriptions averaged 94 per 100 people. There were 25 FM radio stations, 1 AM radio station, and 8 shortwave radio stations. Internet subscriptions stood at 14 per 100 citizens. Broadband was initiated in 2003; in 2010 the country had about 572 Internet hosts. In 2009 there were some 4.7 million internet users. Satellite, cable, and radio telephone services linked Algeria with most other parts of the world.

Of the 45 daily publications in 2010, prominent newspapers included *Le Jeune Independant* and *Al-Moudjahid* with circulations of 392,000. Others included *El-Khabar* (circulation 530,000), *Quotidien d'Oran* (195,000), *Liberte* (120,000), *El-Watan* (70,000), *L'Expression* (29,000), *Djazair News* (20,000), and *Chorouk El-Youmi* (9,000). There are two state-owned French-speaking papers, *El-Moudjahid* and *Horizons* and two state-owned Arab speaking papers, *El-Chaab* and *El-Massa*.

Algeria had approximately 46 television stations. Satellite dish antennas are widespread and millions of citizens have access to European and Middle Eastern broadcast stations. The Algerian Press Service (APS) and the Algerian News Agency (ANA) are the primary news services.

Since 1993 President Bouteflika has maintained that media should ultimately be at the service of the state, therefore, radio and television remain primarily under government control. Radio-Télévision Algérienne operates the broadcast media and carries programming in Arabic, Berber dialects, and French. State-run radio operated several national networks and roughly 40 regional radio stations in 2007. Censorship is not a rule, but jail terms and fines are enforced against press coverage considered defamatory or insulting to the president, the army, and government officials.

In 2009 the Media Sustainability Index (MSI), which considers factors such as professionalism, management and business acumen, ranked Algeria as having an "unsustainable, mixed system."

On a scale of 0–4, with 4 being most sustainable, Algeria scored 1.51, compared to 1.63 for all Middle East and North African countries combined. According to Freedom House's "Freedom in the World" 2011 Index, which measures political rights and civil liberties including freedom of speech, Algeria was "not free."

⁴⁶ORGANIZATIONS

There are foreign and domestic chambers of commerce, industry, and agriculture in the major cities and the country has a national committee of the International Chamber of Commerce. The African Federation of Mines, Energy, Chemical and Allied Trade Unions is an organization of labor unions, seeking to advance the trade union movement by facilitating communication and cooperation among members and representing the interests of members before business organizations and government agencies. The leading trade union, Union Générale des Travailleurs Algériens (UGTA), sponsors many organizations in Algeria. The "professional trade sectors" affiliated with the UGTA include food, agriculture, construction, teachers, energy, finance, information sciences, light and heavy industry, health, social security, and telecommunications. There are some national associations for medical professionals, such as the Algerian Association of Medical Physicists.

The National Union of Algerian Youth (UNJA) was originally established by the FLN in 1969 as the youth wing of the FLN. Since then UNJA has broadened its youth representation and the Algerian National Youth Forum (FNJA) was established to represent other political tendencies. The National Union of Algerian Students (UNEA) and the National League of Algerian Students (LNEA) are active groups of university students. The Government's Ministry of Youth and Sports was established in 1998 and there are other national sports associations, some of which are linked to international associations as well. Other youth non-government organizations (NGOs) in Algeria include the Federation of Algerian Youth Hostels and the Union of Youth of Seguia El Hamra Río Oro. A scouting movement (Scouts Muslmans Algériens/Algerian Muslim Scouts) is also present.

Red Cross and Red Crescent societies, including one for youth, are active. There is a chapter of Amnesty International within the country. There are chapters of the Lions Club and Kiwanis International. The Society of St. Vincent De Paul also has members in Algeria.

Learned societies are active in such fields as anthropology, archaeology, geography, history, and various branches of medicine.

⁴⁷TOURISM, TRAVEL, AND RECREATION

The *Tourism Factbook*, published by the UN World Tourism Organization, reported 1.91 million incoming tourists to Algeria in 2009, who spent a total of $382 million. Of those incoming tourists, there were 284,000 from Europe and 258,000 from the Americas. There were 86,383 hotel beds available in Algeria. The estimated daily cost to visit Algiers, the capital, was $392.

Visitors need a valid passport and a visa. There are no required vaccinations, although inoculations against typhoid, tetanus, and rabies are recommended. Vaccination against yellow fever is required of those coming from an infected area.

Among popular tourist attractions are the Casbah and Court of the Great Mosque in Algiers, as well as excellent Mediterranean beaches, Atlas Mountains resorts, and tours of the Sahara Desert. The government has encouraged tourism as an increasingly important source of foreign exchange.

The most popular Algerian sport is football (soccer), which is played throughout the country by professionals and amateurs alike. Tennis is widely played as well.

⁴⁸FAMOUS PERSONS

The most famous Algerian of antiquity was St. Augustine (Aurelius Augustinus, b. 354–d. 430), a Church father and theologian who was born in eastern Numidia. An important 19th-century figure was Abd-el-Kader (Abd al-Kadir bin-Muhyi ad-Din al-Hasani, b. 1808–d. 1873), emir of Mascara, who led the resistance against the French invaders from 1830 to 1847. Two early figures in the drive for Algerian independence were Messali Hadj (b. 1898?–d. 1974), who organized several political movements and Ferhat Abbas (b. 1900–d. 1986), who led the first provisional government and was elected first speaker of the national assembly in 1962. Other important nationalist leaders include Ahmed Ben Bella (1916–2012), a founder of the FLN and the first premier of independent Algeria, who, after becoming president in 1963, was overthrown and imprisoned for 15 years until 1980; Belkacem Krim (b. 1922–d. 1970), a political leader in Kabilia; Benyoussef Ben Khedda (b. 1922–d. 1967), head of the provisional government in 1961–62; and Houari Boumedienne (Muhammad Boukharrouba (b. 1927–d. 1978), who overthrew Ben Bella in 1965 and became president in 1976. Boumedienne's successor as president and FLN leader was Col. Chadli Bendjedid (b. 1929).

Two renowned French Algerian writers are playwright Jules Roy (b. 1907–d. 2000) and novelist, playwright, and essayist Albert Camus (b. 1913–d. 1960), winner of the Nobel Prize for literature in 1957. Frantz Fanon (b. Martinique, 1925–d. 1961), a psychiatrist, writer, and revolutionary, was a leading analyst of colonialism.

⁴⁹DEPENDENCIES

Algeria has no territories or colonies.

⁵⁰BIBLIOGRAPHY

Algeria Investment and Business Guide: Strategic and Practical Information. Washington, DC: International Business Publications USA, 2012.

Benjamin, Roger. *Renoir and Algeria.* New Haven: Yale University Press, 2003.

Habeeb, William M, Rafael D. Frankel, and Mina Al-Oraibi. *The Middle East in Turmoil: Conflict, Revolution, and Change.* Santa Barbara, CA: Greenwood, 2012.

Hourani, Albert Habib. *A History of the Arab Peoples.* Cambridge, MA: Belknap Press of Harvard University Press, 2002.

Mathias, Grégor. *Galula in Algeria: Counterinsurgency Practice Versus Theory.* Santa Barbara, CA: Praeger Security International, 2011.

McDougall, James, ed. *Nation, Society and Culture in North Africa.* London: Frank Cass Publishers, 2003.

Naylor, Phillip C. *Historical Dictionary of Algeria.* 3rd ed. Lanham, Md: Scarecrow Press, 2006.

Roberts, Hugh. *Battlefield Algeria 1988–2002: Studies in a Broken Polity*. London: Verso, 2002.

Ruedy, John. *Modern Algeria: the Origins and Development of a Nation*. Bloomington: Indiana University Press, 2005.

Stora, Benjamin. *Algeria, 1830–2000: A Short History*. Ithaca: Cornell University Press, 2001.

Zeilig, Leo, and David Seddon. *A Political and Economic Dictionary of Africa*. Philadelphia: Routledge/Taylor and Francis, 2005.

ANGOLA

Republic of Angola

República de Angola

CAPITAL: Luanda

FLAG: The upper half is red, the lower half black; in the center, a five-pointed yellow star and half a yellow cogwheel are crossed by a yellow machete.

ANTHEM: *Angola Avanti (Forward Angola).*

MONETARY UNIT: The Angolan escudo was the national currency until 1977, when the kwanza (AOA) of 100 lwei replaced it. There are coins of 50 lwei and 1, 2, 5, 10, and 20 kwanza, and notes of 20, 50, 100, 500, and 1,000 kwanza. AOA1 = US$0.0105341 (or US$1 = AOA94.9300) as of January 2012.

WEIGHTS AND MEASURES: The metric system is used.

HOLIDAYS: New Year's Day, 1 January; Anniversary of Outbreak of Anti-Portuguese Struggle, 4 February; Victory Day, 27 March; Youth Day, 14 April; Workers' Day, 1 May; Armed Forces Day, 1 August; National Heroes' Day, 17 September; Independence Day, 11 November; Pioneers' Day, 1 December; Anniversary of the Foundation of the MPLA, 10 December; Family Day, 25 December.

TIME: 1 p.m. = noon GMT.

¹LOCATION, SIZE, AND EXTENT

Angola is located on the west coast of Africa, south of the equator. Angola is slightly less than twice the size of Texas, with a total area of 1,246,700 sq km (481,353 sq mi), including the exclave of Cabinda (7,270 sq km/2,810 sq mi), which is surrounded by the Democratic Republic of the Congo and the Republic of the Congo. Angola proper extends 1,758 km (1,092 mi) SE–NW and 1,491 km (926 mi) NE–SW; Cabinda extends 166 km (103 mi) NNE–SSW and 62 km (39 mi) ESE–WNW. Angola proper is bounded on the N and NE by the Democratic Republic of the Congo, on the SE by Zambia, on the S by Namibia, and on the W by the Atlantic Ocean. Its total boundary length, including Cabinda's, is 5,198 km (3,233 mi).

²TOPOGRAPHY

Topographically, Angola consists mainly of broad tablelands above 1,000 m (3,300 ft) in altitude; a high plateau (planalto) in the center and south ranges up to 2,400 m (7,900 ft). The highest point in Angola is Mt. Moco, at 2,620 m (8,596 ft), in the Huambo region; other major peaks are Mt. Mejo (2,583 m/8,474 ft), in the Benguela region, and Mt. Vavéle (2,479 m/8,133 ft), in Cuanza Sul.

Rivers are numerous, but few are navigable. There are three types of rivers in Angola: constantly fed rivers (such as the Congo River), seasonally fed rivers, and temporary rivers and streams. Only the Cuanza, in central Angola, and the Congo, in the north, are navigable by boats of significant size.

³CLIMATE

Angola's climate varies considerably from the coast to the central plateau and even between the north coast and the south coast. The north, from Cabinda to Ambriz, has a damp, tropical climate. The zone that begins a little to the north of Luanda and extends to Namibe, the Malanje region, and the eastern strip have moderate, tropical climates. Damp conditions prevail south of Namibe, dry conditions in the central plateau zone, and a desert climate in the southern strip between the plateau and the frontier with Namibia. There are two seasons: a dry, cool season from June to late September, and a rainy, hot season from October to April or May. The average temperature is 20°C (68°F); temperatures are warmer along the coast and cooler on the central plateau. The Benguela Current makes the coastal regions arid or semiarid. The annual rainfall is only 5 cm (2 in) at Namibe, 34 cm (13 in) at Luanda, and as high as 150 cm (59 in) in the northeast.

⁴FLORA AND FAUNA

The World Resources Institute estimates that there are 5,185 plant species in Angola. In addition, Angola is home to 296 mammal, 930 bird, 235 reptile, and 85 amphibian species. The calculation reflects the total number of distinct species residing in the country, not the number of endemic species.

Thick forests (especially in Cabinda and in the Uíge area in the north) cover the wet regions, and in the drier areas there is a thinner savanna vegetation. Fauna include the lion, impala, hyena, hippopotamus, rhinoceros, and elephant.

⁵ENVIRONMENT

The World Resources Institute reported that Angola had designated 12.55 million hectares (31.01 million acres) of land for protection as of 2006. Water resources totaled 184 cu km (44.14 cu mi) while water usage was 0.35 cu km (0.084 cu mi) per year. Domestic water usage accounted for 23% of total usage, industrial for

17%, and agricultural for 60%. Per capita water usage totaled 22 cu m (777 cu ft) per year.

The United Nations (UN) reported in 2008 that carbon dioxide emissions in Angola totaled 24,743 kilotons.

Long-standing environmental problems in Angola were aggravated by 30 years of war. The main problems included land abuse, desertification, loss of forests, and impure water. The productivity of the land was continually threatened by drought and soil erosion, which contributed to water pollution and silt deposits in rivers and dams.

The cutting of tropical rain forests for international timber sale and domestic use as fuel contributed to the destruction of the land.

Endangered species in Angola included the black-faced impala, three species of turtle (green, olive ridley, and leatherback), the giant sable antelope, the African slender-snouted (or long-snouted) crocodile, the African elephant, Vernay's climbing monkey, and the black rhinoceros. According to a 2011 report issued by the International Union for Conservation of Nature and Natural Resources (IUCN), the number of threatened species included 15 types of mammals, 23 species of birds, 4 types of reptiles, 39 species of fish, 6 types of mollusks, and 34 species of plants.

⁶POPULATION

The US Central Intelligence Agency (CIA) reported the population of Angola in 2011 to be approximately 13,338,541, which placed it at number 70 in population among the 196 nations of the world. In 2011, approximately 2.7% of the population was over 65 years of age, with another 43.2% under 15 years of age. The median age in Angola was 18.1 years. There were 1.02 males for every female in the country. The population's annual rate of change was 2.784%. The projected population for the year 2025 was 27,400,000. Population density in Angola was calculated at 11 people per sq km (28 people per sq mi).

The UN estimated that 59% of the population lived in urban areas, and that urban populations had an annual rate of change of 4%. The largest urban areas, along with their respective populations, included Luanda, 4.5 million; and Huambo, 979,000.

⁷MIGRATION

Estimates of Angola's net migration rate, as reported by the CIA in 2011, amounted to 0.82 migrants per 1,000 citizens. The total number of emigrants living abroad was 533,300, and the total number of immigrants living in Angola was 65,400. From the 1960s until the mid-1990s, Angola was ravaged by civil war, with terrible effects on the Angolan population and social structure. Although fighting stopped in 1994, it began again in 1996 and continued until 2002. There were still Angolan refugees living in 15 other countries as of 2011. Many Angolans also remained displaced within their country as a result of the civil war.

⁸ETHNIC GROUPS

The overwhelming majority of the population is Bantu, divided into a number of ethnolinguistic groupings. The main ones are the Ovimbundu, constituting some 37% of the population, the Kim-bundu, totaling 25% of the population, and the Bakongo accounting for 13%.

⁹LANGUAGES

Portuguese is the official language, although Bantu and other African languages (and their dialects) are used at the local level.

¹⁰RELIGION

Christianity is the primary religion, with Roman Catholicism being the largest denomination. As of 2010, the officials from Catholic Church reported a membership of about 55% of the population, though some government estimates placed the percentage as high as 70%.

Almost half the population (47%) follows some African traditional beliefs, usually in conjunction with other faiths. About 25% adhere to syncretic African Christian religions, the largest of which is the Kimbanguist Church, whose followers believe that the mid-20th century Congolese pastor Joseph Kimbangu was a prophet. Communities in rural areas of the country practice animism and other indigenous religions. There is also a small Islamic community. There are very few declared atheists in the country.

About 10% of all citizens are members of Protestant denominations, the largest of which include Methodists, Baptists, Seventh-Day Adventists, Congregationalists (United Church of Christ), and Assemblies of God. About 5% are members of Brazilian evangelical churches. The Muslim community has been estimated at between 80,000 and 90,000 members, with about half being immigrants from West Africa.

The constitution of 2010 defines the nation as secular, provides for the separation of church and state, and provides freedom of conscience, religion, and worship. The right to religious freedom is generally respected in practice.

¹¹TRANSPORTATION

Owing to war and neglect, Angola's road system has atrophied over the years. According to Portuguese estimates, there were 72,323 km (44,939 mi) of roads at the time of independence (1975), of which 8,371 km (5,201 mi) were paved. In the mid-1980s, these figures had increased to perhaps 80,000 km (50,000 mi), but by 2002 had fallen back to 76,626 km (47,615 mi), of which 19,156 km (11,904 mi) were paved. In 2011, according to CIA data, Angola had only 51,429 km (31,956 mi) of roads, of which 5,349 km (3,324 mi) were paved.

In addition to roads, there were 193 airports, which transported 274,869 passengers in 2009. Thirty-one airports had paved runways. Significant upgrades to the nation's airports were made in anticipation of hosting the 2010 Africa Cup of Nations football (soccer) tournament. About $130 million was spent on the construction of a new airport in Benguela and $99 million for a new airport in Lubango. International and domestic services were maintained by Transportes Aéreos de Angola (TAAG), Air France, Air Namibe, Sabena, South African Airways, TAP (Portugal), and several regional carriers. There were airstrips for domestic transport at Benguela, Cabinda, Huambo, Namibe, and Catumbela (near Lobito).

Angola also had approximately 1,300 km (808 mi) of navigable waterways, and three main railway lines: the Luando, Namibe, and Benguela railways, all of which experienced service disruptions as

LOCATION: Angola proper: 5°49′ to 18°3′S; 11°40′ to 24°5′ E. Cabinda: 4°21′ to 5°46′S; 12°2′ to 13°5′ E. BOUNDARY LENGTHS: Democratic Rep. of the Congo, 2,291 kilometers (1,423 miles); Zambia, 1,110 kilometers (690 miles); Namibia, 1,376 kilometers (855 miles); Atlantic coastline, 1,600 kilometers (995 miles). Cabinda: Democratic Rep. of the Congo, 220 kilometers (136 miles); Republic of the Congo, 201 kilometers (125 miles). TERRITORIAL SEA LIMIT: 20 miles.

a result of the civil war. The Luanda railway connected the national capital with the provincial capital of Malanje in the north. The Namibe railway ran from Angola's port of Namibe to the provincial capital of Menongue in the south.

The Benguela railway was formerly the main exit route for DROC and Zambian copper, extending through the country from the port of Lobito to the border with the DROC. Service resumed in 2001 between Lobito and Huambo. By mid-1992, normal passenger traffic resumed from Lobito to Ganda. East of Ganda, however, the route was still severely damaged, with at least 75 bridges in serious disrepair. In November 2001 a 99-year lease to operate the railway expired, and it was taken over by the Angolan government. Since 2006 restoration of the line, clearing of mines, and rebuilding of bridges have taken place largely by China International Fund, Ltd. (CIFL). The project was part of a national railway plan and was expected to be completed in 2011–12. When finished, the line should be able to carry some 4 million passengers and 20 million tons of freight annually.

12 HISTORY

Angola was inhabited first by people of the Khoisan group (Bushmen), and then by various Bantu peoples from farther north as well as east between 1300 and 1600. By the 15th century, several African kingdoms had developed in the area; the most notable included the kingdoms of the Kongo and Mbundu peoples. The Portuguese arrived on the coast in the late 15th century, and Luanda was founded as a trading settlement in 1575. The Portuguese developed trade with African nations, particularly with the Mbundu, whose ruler was called the *ngola* (from which the name of Angola comes). The slave trade assumed paramount importance during the 17th century, when slaves were carried to Portuguese plantations in Brazil. From the late 16th through the mid-19th century, Angola may have provided the New World with as many as two million slaves.

Slavery was formally abolished (with a 20-year grace period) in 1836, although under Portuguese rule forced labor was common until the early 1950s. Trade in other commodities was needed to replace the slave trade; hence, between 1870 and 1903 the Portuguese claimed control over more and more of the interior of the country. To strengthen their control, the Portuguese began building the Benguela railway in 1902. European domination continued until 1951, when Angola's status changed into an overseas province of Portugal. Increasing numbers of Portuguese settlers came to Angola, and by 1960 there were about 160,000 Europeans in the country.

Organized armed resistance to Portuguese rule began on 4 February 1961, when urban partisans of the Popular Movement for the Liberation of Angola (MPLA) attacked the São Paulo fortress and police headquarters in Luanda. Within six weeks, the war had been extended to the north by the rural guerrillas of another organization, the Union of Angolan Peoples, which later became the National Front for the Liberation of Angola (FNLA). The FNLA, headed by Holden Roberto, set up a revolutionary government-in-exile in Zaire on 3 April 1962. A third movement, the National Union for the Total Independence of Angola (UNITA), headed by Jonas Savimbi, came into being as the consequence of a split in the government-in-exile, of which Savimbi had been foreign minister. All three movements were divided by ideology, ethnic considerations, and personal rivalries; they were also active militarily in 1974 when the Portuguese decided to put an end to their African empire after the coup in Portugal on 25 April. After negotiations with FNLA, MPLA, and UNITA leaders, the Portuguese agreed on 15 January 1975 to grant complete independence to Angola on 11 November 1975. The agreement also established a coalition government headed by a three-man presidential council including MPLA leader António Agostinho Neto, Roberto, and

Savimbi. As independence day approached, however, the coalition government fell apart; mediation attempts by other African countries failed.

Thus, at the dawn of Angola's independence, each of three rival organizations had its own army and sphere of influence. The FNLA primarily represented the Kongo people; it was based in Zaire, and it received financial support mainly from China and the United States. Together UNITA and the FNLA established the Popular Democratic Republic of Angola (with its capital at Huambo) sustained with US funds, South African troops, and some white mercenaries (mostly former commandos in the Portuguese armed forces). UNITA had the support of the Ovimbundu, the largest ethnic group in Angola. The MPLA, a Marxist-oriented party, drew social support from mestiços in Luanda and other urban areas and from the Mbundu people. It received military as well as financial assistance from the USSR and from some 15,000 Cuban soldiers. The MPLA and Cuban forces soon seized the initiative, and by mid-February 1976 the FNLA and UNITA strongholds had fallen. On 11 February, the Organisation of African Unity (OAU) formally recognized the MPLA government in Luanda as the legitimate government of Angola. South African troops subsequently withdrew, but the Cuban forces remained to consolidate the MPLA's control over the country and provide technical assistance. By 1982 there were 18,000 Cuban troops in Angola, with the number reportedly rising to 25,000 during the first half of 1983 and to 30,000 in late 1986.

A coup attempt on 27 May 1977 by an MPLA faction opposed to the Cuban involvement was suppressed and followed by a massive purge of the party. Activist groups were reined in, and the organization became more centralized. Meanwhile, UNITA, which had never been rooted out of southern Angola, began to regroup. Despite the Cuban troops and Soviet-bloc military assistance, the MPLA government remained vulnerable to the UNITA insurgency, operating from the southern Angolan countryside and from Namibia. Implicated in this conflict was the government of South Africa, whose continual incursions into southern Angola in the late 1970s and early 1980s were aimed chiefly at the forces of the South West Africa People's Organization (SWAPO), who were using Angola as a base in their bid to force South Africa to give up Namibia. By 1983, South African soldiers were said to be permanently stationed in southern Angola; in December, South Africa launched a major offensive in the region. In addition to harassing SWAPO, South Africa continued to provide supplies to UNITA. The Angolan government resisted efforts by the United States to secure the withdrawal of Cuban troops in return for Namibian independence and a South African pullback.

Under an agreement brokered by the United States, South African troops withdrew from southern Angola in 1985 but continued to raid SWAPO bases there and to supply military aid to UNITA, including air support. In 1986, the United States sent about $15 million in military aid to UNITA, reportedly through Zaire.

Fighting escalated in 1987 and 1988 even as negotiations for a settlement progressed. An Angolan settlement became entangled with the resolution of civil war in and the independence of Namibia. A controversial battle at Cuito Cuanavale in 1988, at which South African and Angolan/Cuban forces were stalemated, led to a South African willingness to agree to end its involvement in Angola and eventually to withdraw from Namibia. Included in the settlement was the Cuban commitment to a phased withdrawal of its military forces from Angola by mid-1991.

Those two agreements, signed on 22 December 1988 in New York by Angola, South Africa, and Cuba, also included a pledge that the signatories would not permit their territories to be used "by any state, organization, or person in connection with any acts of war, aggression, or violence against the territorial integrity...of any state of southwestern Africa." This meant that South Africa would be prohibited from aiding UNITA, and Angola would remove the ANC's training bases.

All the major parties had been brought to the conclusion that a settlement was better than a prolongation of the fighting. The Soviet Union wanted to disentangle itself from Angola. The administration of US president Ronald Reagan wanted to take the lead in a successful resolution, and its Assistant Secretary of State for African Affairs, Chester A. Crocker, took the lead in the negotiations.

But as settlement in Namibia was moving forward, it proved much harder to bring the Angolan government and UNITA to terms. At a summit at Gbadolite involving 19 African leaders, MPLA Leader José Edvardo dos Santos and Savimbi shook hands publicly and endorsed the "Gbadolite Declaration" (cease-fire and reconciliation plan) on 22 June 1989. But from the start, the terms were disputed and swiftly unraveled. The parties returned to the battlefield.

Yet, the powers began to scale back their support. The relaxation of cold war tensions provided the basis for contacts between the warring parties. Progress moved in fits and starts, and in April 1991, Savimbi and dos Santos initialed an agreement that led to the establishment of a UN-supervised cease-fire and a process of national reconciliation.

Tension increased when UNITA took de facto control of several provinces, and its generals were withdrawn from the officially "merged" national army. Fighting broke out in Luanda in October, and more than 1,000 were killed in a week. UNITA gained control of 75% of the country. Its refusal to accept UN-brokered cease-fire terms agreed to by the government in May led to a Security Council resolution on 1 June 1993, condemning unanimously UNITA for endangering the peace process and to US recognition of the Angolan government on 19 May. In 1994, it was estimated that 1,000 were dying every day in the fighting.

On 20 November 1994, the Lusaka Protocol was signed, promising a new, if tenuous, era of peace in Angola. The third peace effort between the opposing groups, it was the first to guarantee a share of power to UNITA and the first to be supported by over 6,000 armed UN peacekeepers. Demobilizations of fighters were suspended and renewed as new offensives broke out and were halted. In 1995, the international community imposed sanctions against UNITA, though several governments violated them, including African countries serving as arms transshipment points. In September 1995, the United States pledged $190 million to support Angolan reconstruction and development at the Brussels Roundtable.

In 1997, the government and UNITA found themselves involved on opposite sides of the Zaire civil war (now the Democratic Republic of the Congo-DROC). UNITA supported its ally, President Mobutu Sese Seko, while the government backed Laurent Kabila. Following Kabila's victory in May 1997, and subsequent to the 1998 invasion of DROC by Rwanda and Uganda, dos Santos joined other SADC leaders in providing military support to the Kabila government. By July 1999, all sides at war had signed the Lusaka Accords leading to an eventual withdrawal of most foreign troops by 2003.

In Angola, full-scale war resumed as the government launched offensives in December 1998, and again in March 1999. In February 1999, the UN Security Council voted to end its peacekeeping operations after Secretary-General Kofi Annan declared there was no longer any hope of carrying out the 1994 Lusaka peace agreement. In August 1999, the Office for Coordination of Human Affairs estimated 2.6 million persons were internally displaced in Angola. The following month, Human Rights Watch released a 200-page report detailing how the UN deliberately overlooked evidence showing rearmament and retraining of soldiers by both sides in breach of the 1994 accords. In October 1999, UNITA's main headquarters at Bailundo and Andulo had fallen, and in February 2000, the Fowler report was issued on strengthening UN sanctions against UNITA.

In February 2002, prospects for peace changed dramatically when the army announced that it had killed Savimbi in an attack in southeastern Angola. In addition, the death from illness of Savimbi's second-in-command, General Antonio, further weakened UNITA's military capacity. In March 2002 UNITA commanders issued a joint communiqué with the Angolan army (FAA) confirming a cessation of hostilities and reiterating unequivocal support for a political settlement based on the 1994 Lusaka Peace Accord. A peace accord between the government and UNITA followed in April.

As disarmament, demobilization, and reintegration of the armed forces, the repatriation of refugees, and the arduous task of rebuilding the country got underway, dos Santos declared that he would not seek reelection in the elections scheduled for late 2003–early 2004. However, it was clear that his departure would depend on a successor who could be trusted not to prosecute him for human rights abuses and massive diversion of state funds.

In the meantime, beginning in 2004, tens of thousands of foreigners were expelled from the country in a crackdown on illegal mining and diamond trafficking. In December 2004, the government announced that 300,000 diamond dealers had been expelled. By September 2004, oil production in Angola had reached 1 million barrels per day. Angola joined the Organization of Petroleum Exporting Countries (OPEC) in 2007, bringing the number of countries in the organization to 12. Angola assumed the presidency of the cartel in 2009. By 2007, Angola was among the three fastest-growing oil exporters in the world, drawing attention from China, which provided billions of dollars in loans and development aid in return for favorable treatment of its oil interests. Indeed, in June 2005, Chinese Premier Wen Jiabao visited Angola, and promised to extend more than $2 billion in new loans, in addition to $3 billion in credit China had already given Angola. In 2006, Angola overtook Saudi Arabia as the largest petroleum supplier to China, and became the sixth largest oil exporter to the United States. In October 2007 Angola was pumping approximately 1.5 million barrels of oil a day, second to only Nigeria in Africa.

In August 2006, the government signed a peace agreement with a separatist group in the northern enclave of Cabinda. In October 2006, The UN refugee agency began final repatriation of Angolans who fled the civil war to the Democratic Republic of the Congo. In March 2007, the UN High Commissioner for Refugees, António Guterres, attended a ceremony hosted by Angola at which regional leaders officially marked the successful conclusion of the largest repatriation of refugees in Africa in that decade. Since the end of the 30-year civil war in Angola in 2002, when 457,000 Angolans were believed to be refugees in neighboring countries, nearly 410,000 had returned home by March 2007. The next priority for UNHCR was to find a solution for the Congolese refugees who had been in Angola for decades.

After successive postponements, dos Santos declared that parliamentary elections would be held in 2008 and presidential elections in 2009. The parliamentary contest went forward as scheduled, the first in 16 years. The MPLA won 82% of the vote, gaining 191 of 220 seats. Although international observers said the exercise fell short of meeting international standards for free and fair elections, the main opposition group, UNITA, accepted defeat. The presidential election was postponed yet again on the grounds that more time was required to revise the constitution. On 21 January 2010 parliament approved a new constitution that among other things abolished direct presidential elections. This change effectively guaranteed dos Santos the presidency for life as long as his party stayed in power and he maintained control over it.

In January 2010 separatist rebels in Cabinda staged an attack on a bus carrying the Togolese football (soccer) team on its way to compete in the Africa Nations' Cup beginning 10 January. A little-known offshoot of the Front for the Liberation of the Enclave of Cabinda (FLEC), a group promoting independence for the province of Cabinda, known as the Front for the Liberation of the Enclave of Cabinda-Military Position (FLEC-PM), claimed responsibility for the attack. A larger offshoot known as Armed Forces of Cabinda (FLEC-FAC) also claimed responsibility.

Three persons were killed—the bus driver, the team's assistant manager, and the media officer. Several players, two team doctors, and a journalist were injured. Secretary General of the FLEC-PM, Rodrigues Mingas, exiled in France, claimed the attack had been aimed at the Angolan forces at the head of the convoy. The Togo team returned home two days later, and having initially pulled out of the tournament, was disqualified from play. Angolan authorities condemned the shootings as an act of terrorism, and arrested two alleged operatives on 11 January as well as suspects believed connected with FLEC. Four suspects were tried—a priest, a lawyer, an economist, and a police officer. They were found guilty of crimes against state security, and sentenced from three to five years. Human rights groups including Human Rights Watch criticized the conviction for having targeted "activists" who they claimed were simply opposed to the government.

In February 2010, the Financial Action Task Force (FATF), a powerful, membership-based international organization that campaigns against money laundering and terrorist financing, placed tier-two, graduated sanctions on Angola for the nation's failure to commit to international standards on anti-money laundering and combating the financing of terrorism (AML/CFT). In the report, the FATF urged its members to "consider the risks arising from the deficiencies associated with [Angola]." Listed along with Angola in the tier-two bracket were North Korea, Ethiopia, and Ecuador. FATF is comprised of thirty-three of the most powerful nations and territories in the world, plus two regional organizations, including the Gulf Co-operation Council.

Angola was a member of the Southern Africa Development Community (SADC), and held the presidency of this body from September 2011 to September 2012.

[13] GOVERNMENT

The constitution of 1975 was amended in 1976 and again in 1980. Following a cessation of hostilities, a transitional government was established in December 1992 dominated by the MPLA. UNITA held six cabinet posts, and four other parties were also represented. In 1997, the MPLA and UNITA reached an agreement that allowed UNITA to participate in a Government of National Unity and Reconciliation. With the ruling party's approval, UNITA would nominate candidates for four ministerial positions: Trade, Geology and Mines, Health, and Hotels and Tourism. UNITA members would also occupy a number of deputy ministerial, governor, deputy governor, and ambassadorial posts. In early 1997, 70 elected UNITA deputies assumed their seats in the National Assembly, and Jonas Savimbi assumed the role of special advisor to President José Eduardo dos Santos.

The resumption of war in 1998 all but doomed this arrangement, and rendered the National Assembly nominally functional. In reality, it had little independence and did not have oversight over presidential appointments or the ability to initiate legislation. In 1999, dos Santos abolished the post of prime minister, vesting these powers in the director of his own office. He also created a parallel ministry of defense within the presidency.

The civil war officially ended in August 2002, after Jonas Savimbi died in a gun duel with government forces in February and UNITA signed a cease-fire agreement in April. In December 2002, Fernando da Piedade Dias dos Santos Nando was appointed prime minister, though the position had very little real power. Elections were originally slated for 2006, but they were constrained by the poor state of roads and railways. They were postponed by the president to 2008 (legislative) and 2009 (presidential), initially to allow more progress on the clearing of land mines, infrastructure development, and the return and resettlement of refugees.

Under the terms of a new constitution approved by parliament in January 2010, the President (José Eduardo dos Santos), who is both chief of state and head of government, was to be elected indirectly by members of the National Assembly for a 5-year term. This seat was now filled by the top-ranked candidate of the ruling party. Consequently, dos Santos was slated to stay in office until at least 2012 when the next parliamentary elections were due. There was also provision for a Vice President, who is Fernando da Piedade Dias dos Santos. In the unicameral 220 seat National Assembly, members are elected by direct popular vote in multi-member constituencies (130 from one national constituency and 90 from 18 provincial constituencies—5 per province) using the party-list proportional representation system; members serve 4-year terms. The president appoints and leads the Council of Ministers.

[14] POLITICAL PARTIES

In 2012, 78 political parties had legal status. Until 1974, the Portuguese suppressed movements and political parties that stood for self-determination and independence. The three leading political organizations at independence were the Popular Movement for the Liberation of Angola (Movimento Popular de Libertação de Angola—MPLA), founded in 1956; the National Front for the Liberation of Angola (Frente Nacional de Libertação de Angola—FNLA), founded in 1962; and the National Union for the Total Independence of Angola (União Nacional para a Independência Total de Angola—UNITA), founded in 1966. The victory of the MPLA and Cuban forces brought recognition to the MPLA government by the OAU and by most non-African countries. The MPLA-Workers' Party (MPLA—Partido de Trabalho, or MPLA-PT), a Marxist-Leninist vanguard party, was created in December 1977. UNITA remained in de facto control of part of the country, while the remnants of the FNLA continued low-level guerrilla activity in the northwest, as did the Front for the Liberation of the Cabinda Enclave.

Some 18 parties and 11 presidential candidates contested the 1992 elections. In the presidential contest, the MPLA's Dos Santos won 49.6% of the presidential vote and UNITA's Savimbi got 40.1%, requiring a runoff. Though international observers considered the elections reasonably free and fair, Savimbi repudiated the results and refused to participate in a second round. The contest was regarded as generally free and fair however; the MPLA won 54% of the votes and 129 seats, while UNITA took 34% of the votes and 70 seats. Also represented were the Angolan Democratic Forum (FDA), the Democratic Renewal Party (PRD), and the Angola Youth Worker, Peasant Alliance Party (PAJOCA). Separatist groups in Cabinda, such as the Frente Nacional de Libertação do Enclave de Cabinda (FLEC) and the National Union for the Liberation of Cabinda (UNLC) did not take part in the national elections. They continued to wage a low-level armed struggle for the independence of oil-rich Cabinda province.

Opposition parties were extremely weak and fractured. Thirteen of them contested the legislative elections in September 2008. The four that won seats had little apparent influence in the National Assembly. In that election the incumbent MPLA won 82% of the vote, gaining 191 of 220 seats. UNITA won 10.39% of the vote, garnering 16 seats. Three other parties—the Social Renewal Party (PRS), the New Democracy Electoral Union (ND), and the National Front for the Liberation of Angola (FNLA) shared the remaining 13 seats. At times opposition parties such as the UNITA Renovada, have formed working relationships with the MPLA, but these relationships have strengthened the ruling party's hands vis-a-vis splinter groups. According to a study conducted by the United States in 2010, the primary constraint to democratic development in Angola was the lack of effective political competition and political accountability. The next legislative elections were scheduled for 2012.

15 LOCAL GOVERNMENT

Angola consists of 18 provinces. Cabinda is geographically separated from the others. The provinces are divided into districts, municipalities and communes. The communes are led by commissioners who are appointed by the president on the recommendation of the MPLA-PT.

Provincial legislatures consisting of 55–85 members were created in 1980. In 1986, these legislatures were expanded up to 100 members each. In the 1992 elections, MPLA carried 14 of the provinces to UNITA's four. The civil war severely disrupted the performance of local government, and for many years, severed ties between Luanda and the outlying provinces.

In August 2007 the Council of Ministers passed a resolution to grant some municipalities control over their own budgets. This measure was extended to all municipalities in 2008. The central government has said that decentralization will be a gradual process and there is no timeline for fresh elections of sub national governments.

16 JUDICIAL SYSTEM

The legal system is based on Portuguese civil law system and customary law. Prior to independence, Portuguese civil and military law was applied by municipal courts, labor courts, ordinary courts, and administrative tribunals; final appeal was to the Metropolitan High Court in Lisbon. A 1978 law declared that people's courts with working class representatives would be courts of first instance. It also made provisions for criminal, police, and labor courts with lay judges whose voices would be equal to those of professional judges.

The judicial system is composed of municipal and provincial courts at the trial level and a Supreme Court at the appellate level. A constitutional court was established in May 2008. Municipal court judges are usually laymen. In theory, the Ministry of Justice administers provincial courts located in each of the 18 provincial capitals. The Supreme Court nominates provincial court judges. The judge of the provincial court, along with two laymen, acts as a jury.

In 1991, the constitution was amended to guarantee an independent judiciary. In practice, however, the president appoints the Supreme Court judges for life upon recommendation of an association of magistrates. Confirmation by the National Assembly is not required.

Several issues confront the legal system. The courts, which were crippled by the civil war, are perceived as ineffective and untrustworthy by the few who have access to them. The system lacks the resources and independence to play an effective role, and the legal framework is obsolete. Much of the criminal and commercial code dates to the colonial era with modifications from the Marxist era.

17 ARMED FORCES

The International Institute for Strategic Studies (IISS) reports that armed forces in Angola totaled 107,000 members in 2011. The force was comprised of 100,000 from the army, 1,000 from the navy, and 6,000 members of the air force. Armed forces represented 1.4% of the labor force in Angola. Defense spending totaled $3.9 billion and accounted for 3.6% of gross domestic product (GDP).

Defense responsibilities are vested in the Armed Popular Forces for the Liberation of Angola (Forças Amadas Populares de Libertação de Angola—FAPLA).

18 INTERNATIONAL COOPERATION

Angola, a UN member since 1 December 1976, participates in ECA and nonregional specialized agencies such as FAO, IAEA, IMF, ILO, UNESCO, UNIDO, WHO, and IFC; the nation is a member of the World Trade Organization (WTO; 1996) and the World Bank. Angola also participates in the African Development

Bank, G-77, the non-aligned movement, the ACP Group, Interpol, the New Partnership for Africa's Development (NEPAD), and the African Union. It is one of 14 countries in the SADC. Angola has observer status in the OAS and CEMA. It is also a participant of COMESA. As a result of offshore oil discoveries in the Gulf of Guinea, Angola strengthened cooperation with Equatorial Guinea and São Tomé and Principe. Angola also promotes the revival of the Community of Portuguese-Speaking Countries (CPLP). In environmental cooperation, Angola is part of the Convention on Biological Diversity, the Montréal Protocol, MARPOL, and the UN conventions on the Law of the Sea, Climate Change, and Desertification.

[19]ECONOMY

The GDP rate of change in Angola, as of 2011, was 3.7%. Inflation stood at 14.3%; unemployment data was unavailable. Angola had initially forecast a 9.7% GDP expansion in 2010; however in August of that year, the government sharply reduced its economic forecast in line with IMF predictions of 6.7%. The revised economic outlook came after the government admitted to owing $9 billion to foreign construction firms. Angola's total debt of $31.5 billion accounted for nearly 40% of GDP.

Angola was rich in natural resources, had a large petroleum industry, and had the potential to be a major agricultural producer. From 2002 to 2010, Angola experienced astounding economic growth. In 2004 the GDP grew by 12.2%, by 19% in 2005, and by over 20% in 2007. However, corruption and economic mismanagement have left most of the population impoverished. On Transparency International's Corruption Perception Index (CPI), the country ranked 168th in 2010 with a score of 1.9 on a scale of 1–10, where 1 was viewed as "highly corrupt" and 10 as "very clean." Angola was also ranked 146 out of 169 countries on the 2010 UN Development Program's (UNDP) Human Development Index (HDI). The HDI is a comparative measure of life expectancy, literacy, education, and standards of living for countries worldwide. It is a standard means of measuring well-being, especially child welfare.

Having both temperate and tropical zones, Angola had the potential for producing a wide variety of agricultural products, and once registered surpluses of coffee, sisal, cotton, and maize. The civil war created famine in many parts of the country, leaving most Angolans dependent on cassava as their staple crop. Farmers have been reluctant to return to their farms in part because land mines still litter the countryside. Over half of the country's food is imported.

Petroleum and diamonds have led Angola's growth. Economists estimated that Angola's alluvial reserves of diamonds totaled between 40 and 130 million carats. In addition, there were untapped diamond reserves in volcanic pipes known as kimberlites. Angola's six existing kimberlites, among the ten largest on earth, held an estimated 180 million carats worth several billion dollars. Diamond production (official and unofficial) was estimated to be about 8.5 million carats in 2010, worth some $995 million.

The offshore petroleum sector benefited from major investments during the war years. As of 2011, Angola was producing about 1.6 million barrels per day, which for technical reasons, was well under its estimated capacity of 1.9 million barrels. Angola was a member of OPEC, but OPEC was not enforcing quotas.

Crude oil accounts for 95% of exports, more than 72% of government revenues, and over 50% of the country's GDP.

In a move to diversify the economy, the Angolan parliament passed a biofuel law in March 2010 to establish regulations for the production of biofuels and for the participation of foreign companies in biofuel ventures. Although the biofuel law was hailed by some, opponents feared that the focus on agriculture for the production of biofuels would exacerbate the problem of food security. In other moves designed to link oil and gas with other sectors, the government required petroleum companies to source from local businesses and to employ more Angolans. A liquefied gas plant was scheduled to come on line in 2012, and there were plans underway to increase refining capacity at a plant in Luanda, and to build a second refinery in Lobito.

[20]INCOME

The CIA estimated that in 2011 the GDP of Angola was $115.9 billion. The CIA defines GDP as the value of all final goods and services produced within a nation in a given year and computed on the basis of purchasing power parity (PPP) rather than value as measured on the basis of the rate of the exchange based on current dollars. The per capita GDP was estimated at $5,900. The annual growth rate of GDP was 3.7%. The average inflation rate was 14.3%. It was estimated that agriculture accounted for 9.6% of GDP, industry 65.8%, and services 24.6%.

According to the World Bank, remittances from citizens living abroad totaled $82.1 million or about $6 per capita and accounted for approximately 0.1% of GDP in 2008.

As of 2011 the World Bank reported that actual individual consumption in Angola was 27.0% of GDP and accounted for 0.03% of world consumption. By comparison, the United States accounted for 25.44% of world individual consumption. The World Bank also estimated that 12.2% of Angola's GDP was spent on food and beverages, 3.9% on housing and household furnishings, 1.3% on clothes, 1.5% on health, 1.4% on transportation, 0.2% on communications, 0.6% on recreation, 0.8% on restaurants and hotels, and 3.6% on miscellaneous goods and services and purchases from abroad.

[21]LABOR

As of 2011, Angola had a total labor force of 8.24 million people. Within that labor force, the CIA estimated in 2003 that 85% were employed in agriculture, 7% in industry, and 8% in the service sector.

Near the end of the war in 2001, it was estimated that more than half of the population was unemployed or underemployed. Unemployment remained high in part because rural populations were reluctant to return home until land mines were cleared. Following the end of the civil war, unemployment decreased, but still remains high for a variety of reasons.

The constitution recognizes the right for Angolans to form unions, bargain collectively, and to strike. However, these rights are not respected in practice. While strikes are permitted by law, lockouts and the occupation of places of employment by workers were prohibited. Non-striking workers are also protected under the law. Armed forces personnel, firefighters, prison workers and police are prohibited from striking. Compulsory labor by children is also prohibited, although it is commonplace for children to work in the informal sector selling street wares or to work in the fields and to fetch water, gather wood fuel, process foods and prepare meals.

The government has established a 40-hour workweek, along with minimum health and safety standards, including 26 hours of rest per week. However, inadequate resources and weak capacity prevent the government from enforcing these standards. The minimum working age is 14, but the government is unable to enforce this standard. Although the legal minimum wage in 2010 was $106 per month, most wage earners hold second jobs, or reliy on the informal economy, subsistence agriculture, or income from abroad in order to survive.

22 AGRICULTURE

Roughly 3% of the total land is being farmed, and the country's major crops include bananas, sugarcane, coffee, sisal, corn, cotton, manioc (tapioca), tobacco, vegetables, and plantains. Cereal production in 2009 amounted to 1 million tons, fruit production 580,724 tons, and vegetable production 297,232 tons.

Agriculture was the backbone of the economy prior to the civil war. Diverse climatic conditions favor a wide variety of crops, and there is also considerable irrigation potential. Coffee production, primarily of the robust variety, at one time made Angola the world's fourth-largest producer. However, during the civil war almost all the plantations were abandoned, and crop disease set in. Moreover, widespread laying of landmines discouraged farmers from venturing into their fields.

Demining was largely responsible for increases in the production of tropical fruits by several-fold since 2005. Still, production of most crops remains far below 1974 levels. To stimulate agriculture, the government proposed land reform laws designed to reconcile overlapping traditional land use rights and colonial-era land claims. It also made land grants to facilitate commercial agricultural development. However, the lack of clear title to land tracts and the burdensome registration process in Angola continues to impede foreign investment in the agriculture sector.

As part of US president Barack Obama's Feed the Future initiative, US assistance in agriculture supported more than 8,600 Angolan farmers, cooperatives, and agribusinesses, particularly those working in coffee and bananas.

23 ANIMAL HUSBANDRY

The UN Food and Agriculture Organization (FAO) reported that Angola dedicated 54 million hectares (133.4 million acres) to permanent pasture or meadow in 2009. During that year, the country tended 7.1 million chickens, 5 million head of cattle, and 788,000 pigs. The production from these animals amounted to 111,096 tons of beef and veal, 79,555 tons of pork, 145,418 tons of poultry, 15,773 tons of eggs, and 221,223 tons of milk. Angola also produced 13,508 tons of cattle hide. The number of goats and sheep in 2004 was estimated to be 340,000.

Lack of a pastoral tradition among northern Angolans, abundance of the tsetse fly in many regions, and the poor quality of natural pastures were some of the factors most frequently cited to explain the lag in animal husbandry in Angola. What little there was of the livestock industry was virtually destroyed in the war years. In addition, widespread laying of mines significantly delayed development of the sector.

24 FISHING

Angola had 350 decked commercial fishing boats in 2008. The annual capture totaled 317,262 tons according to the UN FAO. The export value of seafood totaled $16.84 million.

Fresh fish, fishmeal, dried fish, and fish oil were produced for the domestic market and for export. During 1975–76, some of the processing plants were destroyed, and most of the modern fishing boats departed with refugees. In 2010 government was attempting to restore fisheries to greater economic prominence.

25 FORESTRY

Approximately 47% of Angola was covered by forest. The UN FAO estimated the 2009 roundwood production at 1.1 million cu m (38.7 million cu ft). The value of all forest products, including roundwood, totaled $43 million. Angola's large timber resources included the great Maiombe tropical rain forest in Cabinda. In addition, eucalyptus, pine, and cypress plantations covered 140,000 hectares (346,000 acres).

26 MINING

Diamonds are an important source of revenue to Angola, second only to petroleum. Petroleum accounted for more than 96% of exports by value ($11.5 billion), and diamonds accounted for $132 million or 1.1% of the value of exports in 2010. After the civil war ended in 2002, Angola began to restructure its diamond sector. The government in 2003 ended the four-year-old monopoly of the state-controlled diamond marketing company, Ascorp, which was controlled by the state diamond company Empressa Nacional de Diamantes de Angola (Endiama). Ascorp now competes with other private companies to buy diamonds from miners and small producers. The government also plans to build a new diamond cutting factory to create an industry of diamond cutting in Angola.

Official reported diamond production in 2010 was 13 million carats, up from 9.175 million carats in 2006 (90% gem quality, 10% industrial grade). However, that total does not include smuggled production. Sociedade Miniera de Catoca Ltd (SMC) is Angola's leading producer of diamonds, with an annual production of around 6.5 million carats from its Catoca kimberlite pipe. Reserves in the Catoca kimberlite were estimated to be 189.3 million carats. SMC is a joint venture of Endiama, the state-owned diamond mining company and the Joint Stock Company Almazy Rossii-Sakha (Russia), Odebrecht Mining Services Inc. (Brazil), and the Leviev Group (Israel).

Large iron ore deposits have been discovered in many areas. The deposits at Kassinga, with an estimated reserve of one billion tons of high-grade hematite iron ore, annually yielded millions of tons of ore exports before the civil war halted mining in 1975. Ferrangol, the state iron ore mining company, produced a slight quantity of ore in 1988; it has shown no output since. The mines in Lunda Norte and Lunda Sul provinces, previously controlled by UNITA rebel forces, were opened to foreign companies for exploration and development in 1996, and an Endiama-De Beers venture announced the discovery of 17 new kimberlites there in 2000. These areas contributed about $400 million to the annual $1.1 billion value of diamond production. SDM, an Endiama-Australian-Odebrecht venture formed in 1995 to mine alluvial diamonds in the Cuango River Valley, near Luzamba, produced 210,000 carats of high-quality diamonds in 2000; its annual capacity was estimated at 70,000 carats in 2010. Other such ventures saw their operations frequently suspended because of security problems. A feasibility study of the proposed Camafuca kimberlite estimated 23.24 million carats of diamonds valued at $109 per carat.

Salt production has remained steady at an estimated 35,000 metric tons annually from 2006 through 2010. Clay, granite, marble, and crushed stone were also reportedly mined throughout the country. The country is also rich in nickel, platinum-group metals, magnetite, copper, phosphates, gypsum, uranium, gold, asphalt, and feldspar.

27 ENERGY AND POWER

The World Bank reported in 2008 that Angola produced 3.99 billion kWh of electricity and consumed 3.41 billion kWh, or 256 kWh per capita. Per capita oil consumption was 609 kg. In 2011 oil production capacity was 1.94 million barrels of oil a day with actual production at about 1.6 million barrels per day.

Angola has extensive hydroelectric power resources that far exceeds needs. The Cambambe Dam, on the Cuanza River, provided Luanda's industries with cheap power. Two dams on the Catumbela River produced power for the Lobito and Benguela areas. Matala Dam in southern Cunene provided power to Lubango and Namibe. The Ruacana Falls Dam, near the Namibian border, was completed in the late 1970s, but the power station was in Namibia.

Boosting the nation's supply of energy had become a major focus for the government. In May 2010, the government announced a major partnership with neighboring Namibia to build another $1.1 billion hydropower station and storage dam along the Cunene River. The new project would require a 50% investment from each country, and was expected to be up and running by 2017. In September 2010, officials announced an $18 billion plan to overhaul Angola's hydroelectric dams and power grids through a soon-to-be-established oil fund. A major goal was to boost hydroelectric power generation capacity from 790 megawatts of electricity to 4,000 megawatts by 2016.

As of December 2010, Angola had become Africa's largest oil producer, a position traded by Angola and Nigeria over the preceding year. By mid-2011 Angola was producing at a level well below its peak capacity—about 1.6 million barrels per day (bpd), compared to an estimated capacity of 1.9 million bpd, due to technical problems. Oil production was expected to recover in the latter half of 2011, helped by the start-up of the 220,000 bpd Pazflor deepwater field. Estimates of Angola's proven oil reserves range from 9.5 billion to 13.5 billion barrels. Oil reserves are located along the Atlantic coast, mostly off the shore of Cabinda and in the northern border area between Quinzau and Soyo. In May 2011, the government resumed construction on the Angolan Sonaref oil refinery in Lobito. When completed, the facility was expected to have a capacity of 200,000 barrels of oil a day.

Gross natural gas production totaled 690 million cu meters in 2009. Total natural gas reserves were estimated at 309.8 billion cu m as of 2011. In 2002, Sonangol and Chevron Texaco joined forces in what evolved into a $5 billion project to develop liquefied natural gas from natural gas in Angola's offshore fields. Production was slated to begin in 2012.

The Angolan parliament passed a biofuel law in March 2010. The law set regulations for the production of biofuels and for the participation of foreign companies in biofuel ventures. Foreign enterprises were expected to build partnerships with local farmers and production companies as a means of boosting the local private sector. A number of biofuel projects had already been launched, including a 10,000-acre sugarcane plantation and bioenergy facility under construction near the Capanda hydroelectric dam and operated by Biocom, a partnership of Sonangol, Damer (Angola), and Odebrecht (Brazil). When completed in 2012, the Biocom bioenergy plant was expected to provide 160 GW of energy from ethanol produced from sugarcane.

28 INDUSTRY

Industry was dominated by oil and gas. In its pre-1975 prime, the Angolan industrial sector centered on petroleum refining and machinery, construction inputs, food processing, electrical products, chemicals, steel, and vehicle assembly. As a consequence of the civil war, Angola's industrial sector operated at a fraction of prewar levels. That production included food processing, textiles, soap, shoes, matches, paint, plastic bottles, and glues. In 1993, industrial production also included 9,000 tons of crude steel, 250,000 tons of cement, and 9 million barrels of refined petroleum products. Heavy industry for that year (cement, steel, oil refining, vehicle assembly, and tire production) accounted for about 15% of Angola's manufacturing output. Following the war Angola became an importer of machinery, vehicles, spare parts, and processed food.

In 2010, Angola surpassed Nigeria as the largest oil producer in sub-Saharan Africa. In that year the petroleum industry accounted for about half of the GDP and 95% of export revenues. Angola had one refinery located in Luanda operated by Sonangol, the state-owned oil company and regulator. Efforts had begun to increase capacity of the Luanda refinery from 40,000 bpd to 100,000 bpd, and work was underway to construct a second refinery in Lobito with projected production of 200,000 bpd. The US company Kellogg, Brown and Root had been retained to do most of the front-end engineering and design work for the Lobito operation. On the gas front, a consortium of Chevron, Sonangol, BP, Total, and Eni were developing a $5 billion liquefied natural gas plant at Soyo to take advantage of the country's estimated 25 trillion cubic feet of natural gas reserves. Construction by Bechtel began in February 2008 and the plant was scheduled to begin production in 2012.

Diamond mining figured importantly in Angola's economy. During the civil war many gemstones sold on the black market were considered "conflict diamonds" because they were traded to fund military operations. Since then Angola has taken measures to regulate the trade, and has become an active member in the Kimberley Process Certification Scheme (KPCS). KPCS was established in 2003 to prevent conflict diamonds from reaching world markets. In 2010 eight of 145 concessions were large-scale operations; diamond mining accounted for about 8.5 million carats worth nearly a billion dollars.

In 2009, SABMiller, one of the world's leading brewers, announced plans to build a new $125 million brewery in Angola to produce both beer and soft drinks. At least 500 new jobs from the venture were expected for residents in and around the plant site in Luanda. The company also planned to create incentives for local farmers to produce the corn, sugar, and barley needed for brewing, thus boosting the local economy while reducing the company's reliance on imports. SABMiller already has a successful brewing plant in the southern city of Lubango.

[29] SCIENCE AND TECHNOLOGY

The World Bank reported in 2009 that there were no patent applications in science and technology in Angola. Three decades of war and a severe shortage of skilled personnel have limited Angola's development of its extensive mineral reserves and abundant fertile land. Angola's research institutes included the Cotton Scientific Research Center in Catete, the Agronomic Research Institute in Huambo (founded in 1962), the Institute for Veterinary Research in Lubango (founded in 1965), the Angola Medical Research Institute in Luanda (founded in 1955), and the Angolan Directorate of Geological and Mining Services in Luanda (founded in 1914). The University Agostinho Neto (founded in 1963) had faculties of sciences, agriculture, medicine, and engineering, and the National Center of Scientific Investigation. The National Museum of Natural History and the National Anthropology Museum were located in Luanda.

[30] DOMESTIC TRADE

Practically all domestic trade was in Portuguese hands before independence, when state people's stores and consumer cooperatives were established in the cities. Over half of Angolan consumer goods were still imported from Portugal in 1998. For more than 40 years, after the war for independence began in 1961 and until the civil war ended in 2002, trade was stifled by fighting and population displacements. For many of those years barter was the norm as imports were strictly controlled due to a lack of foreign exchange. Although a privatization program was underway, few groups or individuals in the private sector had the financial and administrative capacity to purchase and effectively run large public corporations.

[31] FOREIGN TRADE

Angola imported $24.76 billion worth of goods and services in 2011, while exporting $65.63 billion worth of goods and services. Major import partners in 2010 were Portugal, 17.4%; China, 14%; the United States, 9%; Brazil, 6.6%; France, 5.8%; India, 5.3%; and South Africa, 6%. Its major export partners were China, 42.8%; the United States, 23%; India, 9.5%; and France, 4%.

Crude petroleum and petroleum products topped the commodities export list for Angola (95%), followed by diamonds and other precious and semiprecious stones. Seafood and shellfish exports were in third place. As of 2011, China and the United States purchased most of Angola's oil. Angola's imports included industrial goods and services such as machinery, automobiles, spare parts, oil field equipment, mining equipment, chemicals, aircraft and food stuffs.

[32] BALANCE OF PAYMENTS

In 2010 Angola had a foreign trade surplus of $32.25 billion. According to the CIA World Factbook, exports totaled $50.59 billion and imports totaled $18.34 billion. The current account balance was estimated at $7.202 billion. Reserves of foreign exchange and gold totaled $19.66 billion; external debt was $18.11 billion,

Principal Trading Partners – Angola (2010)				
(In millions of US dollars)				
Country	Total	Exports	Imports	Balance
World	...	46,437.0	...	...
China	22,940.0	20,736.0	2,204.0	18,532.0
United States	12,586.0	11,165.0	1,421.0	9,744.0
India	4,754.0	4,093.0	661.0	3,432.0
Portugal	3,431.0	680.0	2,751.0	-2,071.0
Taiwan	3,243.0	2,616.0	627.0	1,989.0
France	2,851.0	1,937.0	914.0	1,023.0
South Africa	2,723.0	1,783.0	940.0	843.0
Canada	1,782.0	1,574.0	208.0	1,366.0
Brazil	1,542.0	500.0	1,042.0	-542.0
Netherlands	1,048.0	700.0	348.0	352.0

(…) data not available or not significant.

(n.s.) not specified.

SOURCE: *2011 Direction of Trade Statistics Yearbook,* New York: United Nations, 2011.

Balance of Payments – Angola (2010)		
(In millions of US dollars)		
Current Account		**7,421.1**
Balance on goods		33,928.0
Imports	-16,666.9	
Exports	50,594.9	
Balance on services		-17,897.5
Balance on income		-8,171.8
Current transfers		-437.7
Capital Account		**0.9**
Financial Account		**-1,511.6**
Direct investment abroad		-1,340.4
Direct investment in Angola		-3,227.2
Portfolio investment assets		-273.5
Portfolio investment liabilities		3.0
Financial derivatives		...
Other investment assets		97.6
Other investment liabilities		3,228.9
Net Errors and Omissions		**-1,730.0**
Reserves and Related Items		**-4,180.3**

(…) data not available or not significant.

SOURCE: *Balance of Payment Statistics Yearbook 2011,* Washington, DC: International Monetary Fund, 2011.

and the stock of direct foreign investment at home was $88.4 billion and abroad was $5.096 billion. In early 2012, WTI and Brent Crude Oil were trading at over $100 a barrel, which was expected to sustain trade surpluses in the near term.

Opaque off-budget accounting in the oil sector and systemic corruption have made it difficult to calculate accurately the balance of payments. According to Global Witness, an $8.6 billion discrepancy existed in the 2008 oil accounts as reported by the Ministries of Finance and Petroleum and by Songangol, the state oil company. In 2002, the IMF reported that $900 million had disappeared from government finances in 2001. That amount was greater than the value of humanitarian assistance for Angola in 2002. Over $4 billion went unaccounted for from 1997 to 2005.

33 BANKING AND SECURITIES

In 2012, there were some 20 banks doing business in Angola including the Banco Nacional de Angola (BNA), which was the central bank, and which acted as the regulatory authority for the nation's other government-owned banks. Headquartered in Luanda, the bank's primary goal was to preserve the stability of the Angolan currency. It also acted in an advisory capacity to the government regarding monetary policy, as well as the primary executor of that policy. Prior to 1996, the BNA also held commercial accounts. However, in 1996 these were transferred to the Caixa de Credito Agro-Pecuaria e Pescas (CAP) to permit the BNA to concentrate on its regulatory functions. Concerns remained over the laxity of supervision of Angola's commercial banks. The Banco de Comercio e Industria (The Bank of Commercial and Industrial Commerce-BCI), formerly a Sonangol subsidiary, had been privatized. Some institutions made loans to small and medium-scale enterprises. Only about 6% of the population used banks.

In December 2010, the discount rate, the interest rate at which the central bank lends to financial institutions in the short term, was 25%. There were no securities exchanges in 2011, although in 2005 government announced its intentions to establish a stock market.

34 INSURANCE

At independence there were 26 insurance companies operating in Angola, 12 of which were foreign. Government nationalized the industry in 1978, creating the Empresa Nacional de Seguros (ENSA), a state-owned monopoly that inherited $53 million in annual premiums, of which 5% came from the oil industry. New legislation in February 2000 permitted local and foreign participation, and in 2001 AAA Seguros was created, 90% of which was owned by Sonangol, the state oil company. In 2008 Angola's insurance market consisted of seven insurance companies and 20 insurance brokers. In 2006 it was estimated that the industry generated some $100 million in business annually, 50% of which came from the oil industry.

35 PUBLIC FINANCE

In 2010 the budget of Angola comprised $40.41 billion in public revenue and $37.38 billion in public expenditures. The budget surplus amounted to 7.1% of GDP. Public debt was 20.3% of GDP, with $18.11 billion of the debt held by foreign entities. Debt was largely the result of previously large public sector deficits, high military expenditures, the fall of international oil prices in the late 1990s, and a centrally planned economy up to 1991. By 2011 oil and gas were still mainly controlled by the state oil company, Sonangol, and a parastatal was authorized to be the state's diamond distributor. A lack of transparency and weak oversight characterized the management of public accounts.

Money laundering and off–budget expenditures and oil revenue accounting were considered significant problems. In 2010, the National Assembly passed a new law to combat money laundering and terrorist financing. In 2011, the government established a Financial Intelligence Unit to implement provisions of the new law. A Financial Action Task Force on Money Laundering (FATF) report recognized that Angola had taken steps toward improving its AML/CFT (anti-money laundering and combating the financ-

ing of terrorism) regime. However, the Angolan commercial code, financial sector law, and telecommunications law all required substantial revision.

In November 2009, following Angolan efforts to make oil revenues more transparent, the IMF approved a 27-month Stand-by Arrangement (SBA) with Angola in the amount of approximately $1.4 billion to help the country cope with the effects of the global economic crisis. In June 2011, a visiting IMF team concluded its fifth review of the arrangement and gave positive marks to the government on implementation of the stabilization and reform agenda.

36 TAXATION

The 2003 investment laws and codes provided a number of tax incentives such as exemption from real estate taxes and corporate income tax up to specified levels of profit to encourage foreign investment in Angola. In 2012, the corporate tax rate was 35%, with the overall combined tax rate at 53.2%. This rate compared favorably to the sub Saharan average of 57.1%. It was somewhat higher than the OECD average of 42.7%. Angola ranked 149th among 181 countries surveyed on the Doing Business Index for 2012 in terms of tax friendliness.

Income tax for individuals ranged from 1 to 40% for employees, and from 3 to 60% for self-employed professionals. Also levied were inheritance and gift taxes, and a payroll tax for social security.

The main indirect tax was a manufacturer's sales tax with rates ranging from 5 to 50% on 100 listed products.

37 CUSTOMS AND DUTIES

Both specific and ad valorem duties were levied; but, as a member of the WTO, Angola was reviewing its tariffs and nontariff barriers. Specific duties were assessed by weight, and additional taxes were levied on luxury items. Preferential treatment was accorded to goods from Portugal, Mozambique, Guinea-Bissau, Cape Verde, and São Tomé and Princípe. All imports required a license and were handled by one of several state companies. Most exports were similarly handled by state agencies. Under the 2003 investment code, new investments received up to 15 years exemption from industrial taxes and smaller investments, $50,000 to $250,000, were exempted from all customs duties. Angola was eligible for tariff preferences under the US African Growth and Opportunity Act (AGOA). On the World Bank Doing Business Index for 2012, Angola ranked 163rd out of 181 countries surveyed for cost and ease of trading across borders.

38 FOREIGN INVESTMENT

Foreign direct investment (FDI) in Angola represented a net inflow of $2.21 billion according to World Bank figures published in 2009. FDI represented 2.92% of GDP. A new private investment law adopted in 2011 provided added benefits and incentives for investors. The threshold for such incentives was increased from investments of $100,000 under the old law to $1 million. The lack of clear title to land tracts and the burdensome registration process in Angola continues to be a significant impediment to foreign investment in the agriculture sector.

Petroleum is the engine of investment in Angola. In the 1990s some 15 foreign oil and gas companies, including Chevron, Texaco, ExxonMobil, Total, and Occidental invested more than $8 billion in Angola. From 1998 to 2001, driven by giant offshore discoveries, foreign direct investment (FDI) totaled about $5.6 billion. In 1999, investment was sustained by exploratory drilling in ultra-deep water, and between 2000 and 2004 annual FDI flows averaged $2.05 billion, peaking in 2003 at $3.5 billion. By 2005, ExxonMobil's Kizomba B deep water platform had come on stream, and Total was completing its Dalia platform. Other companies were constructing new platforms.

In 2010–2011, upgrades were being made to the Luanda refinery, and KBR was engineering a second refinery in Lobito. A consortium of Chevron, Sonangol, BP, Total, and Eni was developing a $5 billion liquefied natural gas plant at Soyo with production scheduled to begin in February 2012. In January 2011, Sonangol announced the results of a restricted tender for exploration of the pre-salt layer in 11 blocks off the central coast of Angola. Cobalt International Energy was awarded an operatorship in block 20 and a stake of 40%, and ConocoPhilips was awarded operatorship and stakes of 30% in blocks 36 and 37. Sonangol had an interest in all blocks.

The diamonds sector also received significant investment. In 2000, Angola set up ASCORP, a state-controlled company in partnership with Lev Leviev (Russian/Israeli diamond manufacturer), and established a monopoly on certified diamond buying. De Beers' plans to build a $30 million diamond processing facility in Luanda did not come to fruition, but in April 2003 the then newly established National Private Investment Agency (ANIP) announced it was seeking funding for a diamond cutting and polishing factory in Luanda. The next big phase of diamond sector investment was poised to commence in 2012 with exploitation of the kimberlite pipes.

Following the end of the civil war, the Angolan government endeavored to develop policies that were more investor-friendly. In 2003, the National Assembly passed laws that provided foreign corporations tax incentives and a legal framework for non-judicial dispute resolution; they also consolidated rules of incorporation. In addition, the government created the National Private Investment Agency (ANIP) to encourage and supervise FDI. Under the 2003 laws foreign companies continued to be guaranteed national treatment, the right to repatriate profits, and the right to indemnification for property nationalized or expropriated. The laws also made provisions for streamlining approvals. Approval requests for investments less than $5 million had to be processed in 15 days and requests for larger investments in 30 days.

Despite reforms, serious obstacles to FDI remain: poor infrastructure, a small market, favoritism in contracts for local firms, widespread corruption and registration costs that range from $20,000 to $60,000 for foreign corporations. The World Bank Doing Business in 2011 report identified Angola as one of the most time-consuming countries surveyed for establishing a business (171 out of 181 worldwide and 36 out of 46 for sub Saharan Africa). Launching a business typically required 68 days, compared with a regional average of 37 and an OECD average of 13 days. However, the government had established the "Guichet Único," or one-stop shop, under the Ministry of Justice, which brought together representatives of various ministries in one place to simplify and speed up registration. The Guichet Único succeeded in issuing 2,000 new business licenses in 2008.

[39] ECONOMIC DEVELOPMENT

On the Heritage Foundation's Index of Economic Freedom, Angola ranked 40th regionally, and 161st worldwide (2010), indicative that the country had far to go to transform its institutional environment to be more conducive to investment, jobs creation, and economic growth. Major constraints to economic development are the absence of linkages between the giant petroleum sector and other sectors, lack of diversification in the economy, upward pressure on the value of local currency, and the high costs of doing business. Government policies require foreign oil companies to increase local sourcing and to hire more Angolans, but there is a dearth of skilled labor, and Angola imports most of the physical resources required by the industry including processed foods.

Because of its oil wealth, Angola has not had to submit to multilateral supervision to the extent that other developing countries have. Nevertheless, in 2000, Angola entered into a Staff-Monitored Program (SMP) with the International Monetary Fund (IMF). Although the program lapsed in 2001, the IMF remained engaged in the country. The World Bank prepared a Transitional Support Strategy (TSS) as a short- to medium-term plan for involvement in Angola. These difficulties notwithstanding, the IMF in 2005 concluded that oil and diamonds would continue to form the backbone of Angola's economy. In 2007 an IMF team praised the government's macro-economic policies, but analysts were divided over the government's efforts to promote economic diversification and pragmatic development.

In 2012, the government's strategy appeared focused on large infrastructure and public works projects administered through the Gabinete de Reconstrução Nacional (GRN). However, analysts argued that the strategy was putting rehabilitation before development, and suggested that first Angola needed to train up its mid- and lower-level workforce to manage development so that it could implement large-scale projects and maintain sophisticated infrastructure. Only 16% of government employees have completed high school.

In a 2006 opinion poll administered by the International Republic Institute, 75% of respondents said unemployment was the most important issue facing the country. In this vein, some analysts believed that agriculture ought to be the focus of development. According to the World Bank, roughly two-thirds of the population earns its living from small-scale agriculture, but the government allocates less than 1% of its budget to the sector. Skeptics, however, point out that Angolan agriculture might not be competitive internationally given that oil has made the economy so expensive.

[40] SOCIAL DEVELOPMENT

Angola epitomizes the "resource curse." Despite immense oil and mineral wealth, poverty levels in countries like Angola and Nigeria are extremely high. In 2006 it was estimated that more than 40% of the Angolan population lived beneath the poverty threshold. In 2011 Angola's human resources were considered extremely undeveloped, and health and education services were poor. On the UN Human Development Index (HDI), Angola ranked 148th of 187 countries worldwide in 2010, falling within the "low development" category. The HDI is a comparative measure of life expectancy, literacy, education, and standards of living for countries worldwide. It is a standard means of measuring well-being, especially child welfare.

Social welfare is almost entirely dependent on affective networks. Individuals see themselves first as members of family, extended family, peer groups, clans, and ethnic groups. These relationships remain important in times of need and more generally for social advancement. The Roman Catholic Church also plays an integral part in the administration of welfare, health, and educational programs. A number of international nongovernmental organizations and international donors also provide humanitarian and development assistance, particularly in health and education.

Although women's rights are protected in the constitution, in practice there as discrimination in the workplace and in the home, and most women hold low-paid jobs. Spousal abuse against women is widespread. Credible evidence suggests that the majority of homicides against women are a result of domestic disputes. However, in 2011 about 38% of the elected legislators in the national government were female. Women and children are at high risk for mutilation from land mines, due to foraging in the fields for food and firewood. During the civil war, children were recruited to fight in both the government and UNITA forces. There were an estimated 1,500 children living on the street in Luanda in 2004, many of them engaging in prostitution.

Angola's government has a poor human rights record. Many Angolans have known little outside of war and violence. Security forces have reportedly been responsible for torture, beatings, rapes, and disappearances, and prison conditions were life-threatening.

41 HEALTH

According to the CIA, life expectancy in Angola was 54.59 years in 2011. The country spent 6.8% of its GDP on healthcare, amounting to $204 per person. There were 1 physician, 14 nurses and midwives, and 80 hospital beds per 10,000 inhabitants. The fertility rate was 5.6, while the infant mortality rate was 84 per 1,000 live births. In 2008 the maternal mortality rate, according to the World Bank, was 610 per 100,000 births. It was estimated that 77% of children were vaccinated against measles. Immunization rates for one-year-old children in 2007 were estimated at 47% for diphtheria, pertussis, and tetanus. Malnutrition affected an estimated 53% of children under five years of age. The CIA calculated HIV/AIDS prevalence in Angola to be about 2% in 2009.

Angola was in the yellow fever endemic zone. Cholera incidence was high. Risk of major infectious diseases including diarrheal diseases, hepatitis A, and typhoid fever was high. There was a resurgence of polio in 2007. Only a small fraction of the population received even rudimentary medical attention.

In 2011 the health sector continued to be a priority for US assistance to Angola. Funding for the President's Emergency Plan for AIDS Relief (PEPFAR) more than doubled from $7 million to $17.7 million in 2010. In addition, Angola was selected as one of the first three countries in the US President's Malaria Initiative, receiving $35 million in 2010. In 2010, USAID also received $4 million for family planning and reproductive health activities and provided $1,350,000 to combat polio in Angola.

42 HOUSING

Most people live in multi-family dwellings constructed in the 1960s, which have since deteriorated to the point that basic utilities are limited or unavailable. Housing shortages have led to urban slum developments. These are most prominent in Luanda, where about four million people live in a city designed for 700,000.

During the war for independence, a majority of the Portuguese residents abandoned homes that were then confiscated by the government. In fact, all urban land was considered to be property of the State. Management of dwellings was under the control of provincial governments, and leasing or other housing and property regulations were ambiguous or nonexistent. As a result, a UN report indicated that about 90% of urban residents lived in settlements without a clearly defined legal status. Over the years, the government has made some effort to expand housing, but projects have been insufficient to meet housing needs.

Access to clean water is a challenge for many rural households as the cost of installing sanitary systems is prohibitive. In July 2009, the government began a joint multi-year program with the UN and the non-governmental Institute of Medicine to provide safe, piped water to 100% of urban residents and 80% of rural residents by 2020. According to the CIA World Factbook, in 2008, 60% of urban dwellers had access to improved water supply and 86% of them had improved sanitary conditions. In the same year, 38% of rural dwellers had access to improved water supply, and 18% to improved sanitary facilities.

43 EDUCATION

In 2009 the World Bank estimated that 52% of age-eligible children in Angola were enrolled in primary school. Secondary enrollment for age-eligible children stood at 21%. Tertiary enrollment was estimated at 3%. Overall, the CIA estimated that Angola had a literacy rate of 67.4%, with far fewer females (54.2%) than males (82.9 percent) being literate. Public expenditure on education represented 4.4% of GDP in 2007.

Education was compulsory for children between the ages of six and ten. Primary education lasts six years, and secondary education consists of two cycles of three years each. There are also three-year vocational and four-year technical programs for secondary students. The pupil to teacher ratio for primary school was about 42:1 in 2003. The ratio for secondary school was about 18:1. In 2008 school life expectancy (primary to tertiary) was 11 years on average.

The language of instruction is Portuguese and vernacular languages. The academic year runs from October to July. The Ministry of Education oversees the national public programs.

The University Agostinho Neto (UAN) in Luanda was established in 1963 with faculties in science, engineering, law, medicine, economics, and agriculture. In 1998 the Catholic Church founded, also in Luanda, the Universidade Católica de Angola (UCAN). By 2011 the UAN had 40 faculties dispersed over most of the territory with autonomous public institutions in Benguela, Cabinda, Huambo, Lubango, Malanje, and Uige. Additionally, private universities sprung up with links to universities in Portugal, namely Universidade Lusíada, Universidade Lusófona and Universidade Jean Piaget—all located in Luanda. Others were local: Universidade Privada de Angola (Luanda and Lubango), Universidade Técnica de Angola (Luanda), Universidade Metodista (Luanda), Universidade Metropolitana (Luanda) and Instituto Superior de Ciências Sociais e Relações Internacionais (Luanda). Saudi

Arabia has announced the creation of an Islamic university in Luanda.

44 LIBRARIES AND MUSEUMS

The National Library of Angola was founded in Luanda in 1969. The library of the University of Luanda was founded in 1963. The Municipal Library in Luanda had more than 30,000 volumes. Additional libraries of note were the Geological and Mining Services Directorate Library (1914) in Luanda (40,000 volumes) and the National Historical Center Library (1982) with 12,000 volumes located in Luanda.

The Angola Museum (which contains Angola's historical archives), the Coffee Museum, Museum of Geology, National Museum of Natural History, National Museum of Archaeology, Central Museum of the Armed Forces, and National Museum of Anthropology are all located in Luanda. There are regional museums in Namibe, Huambo, Lobito, Lumbango, and Uíge. The Museum of Chitato, located in Dundo, houses a distinctive ethnographic collection featuring the art of the local Chokue people, recordings of local folk music, and a photographic collection dating to the 1880s. The Municipal Museum of New Lisbon houses a collection of traditional and modern African sculpture. Elinga Teatro is a modern urban art gallery and theater in Mutamba.

45 MEDIA

In 2010 the CIA reported that there were 303,200 telephone landlines in Angola. In addition to landlines, mobile phone subscriptions averaged 70 per 100 people with some 9 million cellular phones in use. There were 21 FM radio stations, 6 AM radio stations, and 7 shortwave radio stations. In 2011 the country had about 20,269 Internet hosts. In 2009 there were some 606,700 Internet users in Angola. Internet users numbered 3 per 100 citizens. International service is provided by 29 satellite earth stations, as well as by submarine fiber-optic cable links to Europe and Asia. The national newspaper is the government-owned *Jornal de Angola* (circulation in 2000 was 41,000); there are at least seven private weekly publications with circulations in the low thousands. Most people get their news and information by radio.

Most of the media is controlled by the state. Rádio Nacional de Angola broadcasts in Portuguese, English, French, Spanish, and major local languages; government-owned, it is the only station with the capacity to broadcast nationwide. Commercial radio stations include the Catholic Church's Radio Ecclesia and Radio Lac Luanda. The primary news agency is the Angola Press. The only television station is the government's Angola Public Television (Televisao Publica de Angola—TPA), which broadcasts in Luanda and in most provincial capitals.

The constitution provides for basic freedoms of speech and press, but in practice the government restricts these freedoms. Journalists are intimidated into self-censorship, and the government tightly restricts content of the main newspapers, television station, and radio broadcasts. Angola ranks 104th out of 178 countries in the 2010 Reporters without Borders world press freedom index; events since early September 2010 were likely to result in a lower ranking for 2011. In 2010 a journalist working for a radio station critical of the government was gunned down in his home, two journalists were physically attacked and injured, and a fourth was the target of intimidation. In 2008, a provincial radio reporter was suspended for 180 days for having covered protests. In 2007 a newspaper editor was jailed and in 2006 two journalists were murdered.

On Freedom House's "Freedom in the World 2011" index, Angola scored six on political rights and five on civil liberties, which placed the country in the category of "not free." The Freedom index rates countries on a scale of 1–7 with seven representing "least free." As of 2012 Angola had not yet participated in the Media Sustainability Index (MSI), which has surveyed media in 40 sub Saharan countries. The MSI ranks countries on criteria of free speech, professionalism, plurality of news sources, business acumen, and supporting institutions.

46 ORGANIZATIONS

Angola is rich in associational life despite decades of war. Organizations established by the MPLA include the Organization of Angolan Women, the Medical Assistance Service, and the Centers for Revolutionary Instruction. There are professional associations for a variety of fields.

The Angolan National Youth Council, founded in 1991, serves as a major nongovernmental organization representing the opinions and concerns of the nation's youth. The Association of Students of Higher Education (AEES: Associazao dos Estudiantes de Educacao Superior) and the National Union of Angolan Students (UNEA) represents major student movements. A scouting organization (Associação de Escuteros de Angola) is also present. There are branches of the YMCA and YWCA and several sports associations.

Angolan Action for Development (A.A.D.), the Angolan Women's Organization, and the League of Angolan Women (LIMA) are groups focusing on the political, social, and developmental issues and concerns of women. There are associations for professional women in the fields of journalism, law, and law enforcement. At the community level there are women's self-help and rotating credit associations.

Many NGOs provide aid to rural and poverty stricken populations. Among them are Africare-Angola and the ACM-YMCA of Kuanza Sul, which offers assistance to displaced persons. There are active chapters of the Red Cross, Caritas, UNICEF, and Publish What You Pay, an association of NGOs organized to promote transparency in oil and gas transactions.

47 TOURISM, TRAVEL, AND RECREATION

The *Tourism Factbook*, published by the UN World Tourism Organization, reported 366,000 incoming tourists to Angola in 2009, who spent a total of $554 million. Of those incoming tourists, there were 161,000 from Europe. There were 10,723 hotel beds available in Angola, which had an occupancy rate of 92%. The estimated daily cost to visit Luanda, the capital, was $501. Staying in rural areas could cost much less depending on type of accommodation.

Tourism was an important activity until 1972, when the guerrilla war and the subsequent civil war led to a precipitous drop in the number of tourists and hence tourist revenues. Beginning in the late 1990s, tourist numbers rebounded, but in 1996, only about 21,000 visitors came to the country. In 1997, the number jumped to 45,000 and increased to 52,000 the following year. In 2003, the number of visitors again jumped to 106,625. Tourism receipts totaled approximately $71 million.

In January 2010 Angola stepped onto the continental stage hosting the Africa Cup of Nations football (soccer) tournament. The nation invested $600 million for the construction of new stadiums in Cabinda, Huila, Benguela, and Camama.

⁴⁸FAMOUS PERSONS

António Agostinho Neto (1922–79), a poet and physician who served as the president of MPLA (1962–79) and president of Angola (1975–79), was Angola's dominant political figure. José Eduardo dos Santos (b. 1942) succeeded Neto in both these posts. Jonas Malheiro Savimbi (1934–2002), the son of a pastor, founded UNITA in 1966. Holden Roberto (1923–2007), headed the FNLA, and fought to liberate Angola from the Portuguese.

⁴⁹DEPENDENCIES

Angola has no territories or colonies.

⁵⁰BIBLIOGRAPHY

Anand, Sudhir, et al. *The Cost of Inaction: Case Studies from Rwanda and Angola.* Cambridge: Harvard University Press, 2012.

Hodges, Tony. *Angola: Anatomy of an Oil State.* Bloomington: Indiana University Press, 2004.

James, W. Martin. *Historical Dictionary of Angola.* Lanham, MD: Scarecrow Press, 2004.

Kreike, Emmanuel. *Re-creating Eden: Land Use, Environment, and Society in Southern Angola and Northern Namibia.* Portsmouth, NH: Heinemann, 2004.

McElrath, Karen, ed. *HIV and AIDS: A Global View.* Westport, CT: Greenwood Press, 2002.

Oyebade, Adebayo. *Culture and Customs of Angola.* Westport, CT: Greenwood Press, 2007.

Rotberg, Robert I. *Ending Autocracy, Enabling Democracy: The Tribulations of Southern Africa, 1960–2000.* Cambridge, MA: World Peace Foundation, 2002.

Zeilig, Leo, and David Seddon. *A Political and Economic Dictionary of Africa.* Philadelphia: Routledge/Taylor and Francis, 2005.

BENIN

Republic of Benin
République du Bénin

CAPITAL: Porto-Novo

FLAG: Two equal horizontal bands of yellow (top) and red with a vertical green band on the hoist side.

ANTHEM: *L'Aube Nouvelle (The New Dawn).*

MONETARY UNIT: The Communauté Financière Africaine franc (XOF), which was originally pegged to the French franc, has been pegged to the euro since January 1999 with a rate of 655.957 CFA francs to 1 euro. The CFA franc has coins of 1, 2, 5, 10, 25, 50, 100, and 500 CFA francs, and notes of 50, 100, 500, 1,000, 5,000, and 10,000 CFA francs. XOF1 = US$0.00207 (or US$1 = XOF481.263) as of 2011.

WEIGHTS AND MEASURES: The metric system is the legal standard.

HOLIDAYS: New Year's Day, 1 January; Anniversary of Mercenary Attack on Cotonou, 16 January; Labor Day, 1 May; Independence Day, 1 August; Armed Forces Day, 26 October; National Day, 30 November; Harvest Day, 31 December. Most religious holidays have been abolished, but Good Friday, Easter Monday, Christmas, Eid al-Fitr, and Eid al-Adha remain public holidays.

TIME: 1 p.m. = noon GMT.

¹LOCATION, SIZE, AND EXTENT

The People's Republic of Benin (formerly Dahomey) is situated in West Africa on the northern coast of the Gulf of Guinea, and has an area of 112,620 sq km (43,483 sq mi), extending 665 km (413 mi) N–S and 333 km (207 mi) E–W. For comparison's sake, Benin is slightly smaller than the state of Pennsylvania. Roughly wedge-shaped, Benin is bounded on the N by Niger, on the E by Nigeria, on the S by the Gulf of Guinea (Atlantic Ocean), on the W by Togo, and on the NW by Burkina Faso, with a total boundary length of 1,989 km (1,233 mi). The capital city of Benin, Porto-Novo, is located in the southeastern corner of the country.

²TOPOGRAPHY

Difficult to access because of sandbanks, the coast has no natural harbors, river mouths, or islands. Behind the coastline is a network of lagoons, from that of Grand Popo on the Togo border (navigable at all seasons) and joined to Lake Ahémé, to that of Porto-Novo on the east, into which flows Benin's longest river, the Ouémé, navigable for some 200 km (125 mi) of its total of 459 km (285 mi). Besides the Ouémé, the only other major river in the south is the Kouffo, which flows into Lake Ahémé, the largest lake in the country with an area of 100 sq km (39 sq mi). The Mono, serving from Parahoué to Grand Popo as the boundary with Togo, is navigable for 100 km (62 mi) but subject to torrential floods in the rainy season. Benin's northern rivers, the Mékrou, Alibori, and Sota, which are tributaries of the Niger, and the Pandjari, a tributary of the Volta, are torrential and broken by rocks.

North of the narrow belt of coastal sand is a region of lateritic clay, the main oil palm area, intersected by a marshy depression between Allada and Abomey that stretches east to the Nigerian frontier. North of the hills of Dassa, the height ranges from 60 to 150 m (200–500 ft), broken only by the Atakora Mountains (Chaine de L'Atakoria), stretching in a southwesterly direction into Togo.

³CLIMATE

South of Savalou, especially in the west, the climate is typically equatorial-hot and humid, with a long dry season from December to March, in which the dry harmattan blows in a northeasterly to southwesterly direction. Temperatures range between 22°C (72°F) and 35°C (95°F), with the average 27°C (81°F). The great rains fall from March to July; there is a short dry season from July to September and a short wet season from mid-September to mid-November. In the southwest, average rainfall is considerably lower and the dry season longer: at Grand Popo, for example, average rainfall is about 82 cm (32 in) as compared to about 127 cm (50 in) in Porto-Novo and Cotonou. Northern Benin has only one wet season (May to September, with most rain in August) and a hot dry season in which the harmattan blows for three or four months. Temperatures range from a maximum of 40°C (104°F) in January to a minimum of 13°C (56°F) in June.

Although rainfall, which is highest in central Benin (135 cm/53 in), decreases as one moves northward, it remains high (97 cm/38 in) in most of northern Benin. In the southwest region, average rainfall drops to 82 cm (32 in) per year. This region is sometimes referred to as the "Benin window." The uncharacteristically low level of precipitation is attributed to the destruction of native rain forest, which in turn caused a decrease in the evaporation of moisture into the air, resulting in fewer convection rains.

⁴FLORA AND FAUNA

The World Resources Institute estimates that there are 2,500 plant species in Benin. The coconut plantations of the coastal strip give way to oil palms and ronier palms growing as far north as

35

Abomey; these are in turn succeeded by savanna woodland, in which the vegetation of the Guinea forest and the vegetation of the southern Sudan are intermingled, and then by characteristic Sudanic savanna. Trees include coconut, oil palm, ronier palm, ebony, shea nut, kapok, fromager, and Senegal mahogany.

According to the World Resources Institute, Benin is home to 159 species of mammals, 485 species of birds, 99 species of reptiles, and 12 species of amphibians. These figures reflect total number of distinct species residing in the country, not the number of endemic species. Among the mammals in Benin are the elephant, lion, panther, monkey, and wild pig, as well as many kinds of antelope. Crocodiles and many species of snakes (including python, puff adder, and mamba) are widely distributed. Partridge, guinea fowl, and wild duck, as well as many kinds of tropical birds, are common. Insects include varieties of tsetse fly and other vectors of epidemic disease.

5 ENVIRONMENT

The main environmental issues facing the people of Benin are desertification, deforestation, wildlife endangerment, and water pollution. The spread of the desert into agricultural lands in the north is accelerated by regular droughts. Benin has also lost at least 59% of its forests from uncontrolled agricultural practices and fires. Between 1983 and 1993 alone, forest and woodland was reduced by 12%. For the period 1990-1995, deforestation occurred at an average rate of 1.25% per year.

The World Resources Institute reported that Benin had designated 2.61 million hectares (6.45 million acres) of land for protection as of 2006. Water resources totaled 25.8 cu km (6.19 cu mi) while water usage was 0.29 cu km (0.07 cu mi) per year. Domestic water usage accounted for 32% of total usage, industrial for 23%, and agricultural for 45%. Per capita water usage totaled 15 cu m (530 cu ft) per year. The UN reported in 2008 that carbon dioxide emissions in Benin totaled 3,873 kilotons.

Benin has two national parks and several game reserves. In addition, the government has set aside 5,900 hectares (14,580 acres) for nurseries to foster reforestation. Among the government organizations with responsibility for the environment are the National Commission for Combating Pollution and for the Protection and Improvement of the Environment, which is under the Ministry of Public Health, and the Ministry of Rural Development and Cooperative Action.

Factors that contribute to the endangerment of the wildlife in Benin are the same as those that threaten the forests. According to a 2011 report issued by the International Union for Conservation of Nature and Natural Resources (IUCN), the number of threatened species included 11 types of mammals, 6 species of birds, 4 types of reptile, 27 species of fish, and 14 species of plants. Threatened species include the cheetah, the sandbar shark, the green turtle, and the roan antelope.

6 POPULATION

In 2011, the US Central Intelligence Agency (CIA) estimated the population of Benin to be approximately 9,325,032, which placed it at number 89 in population among the 196 nations of the world. In 2011 approximately 2.7% of the population was over 65 years of age, with another 44.7% under 15 years of age. The median age

in Benin was 17.4 years. There was 1 male for every female in the country. The population's annual rate of change was 2.911%. The projected population for the year 2025 was 13,600,000. Population density in Benin was calculated at 83 people per sq km (214 people per sq mi).

The UN estimated that 42% of the population lived in urban areas, and that urban populations had an annual rate of change of 4.0%. The largest urban areas, along with their respective populations, included Cotonou, 815,000; and Porto-Novo, 276,000.

7 MIGRATION

Estimates of Benin's net migration rate, carried out by the CIA in 2011, amounted to zero. The total number of emigrants living abroad was 531,600, and the total number of immigrants living in Benin was 232,000. Seasonal labor migration to Nigeria and Ghana is both considerable and of long duration, but estimates of its extent are not available. In June 1998, Benin and Burkina Faso became the first African countries to take in refugees approved by United Nations High Commissioner for Refugees (UNHCR) for resettlement. At the end of 2010, the nation hosted 7,300 refugees, most of whom were from Togo. A repatriation program for Togolese refugees was established between Benin, Togo, and the UNHCR in 2007.

8 ETHNIC GROUPS

The population of Benin is 99% African. However, even though several of the larger groups in southern Benin are culturally and socially closely related, Benin is not ethnically or linguistically homogeneous, and there is a particularly marked division between the peoples of the south and those of the north. The largest ethnic group is that of the Fon and those of related ancestry, who make up about 39.2% of the population. The Adja and those of related ancestry make up about 15.2%. The Yoruba (about 12.3% of the population), essentially a farming people, came from Nigeria and are settled along the southeastern boundary of the country. The Bariba (about 9.2%) are the dominant people in northeast Benin. The Peul and those of related ancestry make up about 7% of the population, followed by the Ottamari at 6.1%, the Yoa-Lokpa at 4%, and the Dendi at 2.5%. The Aizo live in the south of the country and are predominantly farmers. The Goun, who are related to the Adja, are concentrated around Porto-Novo. In the northeast, the Somba subdivide into a number of distinct groups. The Fulani, traditionally nomadic herders, gradually are becoming sedentary. Other groups include the Holli, the Mina, and the Pilapila (or Yowa).

9 LANGUAGES

The official language is French. However, many African languages are spoken. Fon and Yoruba are the most important in southern Benin. In the north there are at least six major tribal languages, including Bariba (a subgroup of the Voltaic group in which the Mossi language is most important) and Fulani.

10 RELIGIONS

According to a 2002 census, about 27% of the population are nominally Roman Catholic, 24% are Muslim (primarily Sunni), 17% practice Voodoo (Vodun), and 5% are Celestial Christians. About

6% adhere to other traditional indigenous beliefs, and about 7% claim no religious affiliation. Even some who identify themselves as Christian or Muslim are likely to observe some traditional indigenous customs as well. The most common indigenous religion is Vodun, which spread to the Americas with slavery and later became a source for African-inspired religions such as Santeria (in the Spanish-speaking Caribbean), voodoo (in Haiti), and Candomble (in Brazil). The Vodun religion is based on a belief in one supreme being who rules over a number of lesser deities, spirits, and saints. Other religious groups include Methodists, The Church of Jesus Christ of Latter-Day Saints (Mormons), Jehovah's Witnesses, Rosicrucians, the Unification Church, Eckankar, Baha'is, Baptists, Assemblies of God, and Pentecostals. Freedom of religion is guaranteed by the constitution, and this right is generally respected in practice. There is no state-sponsored religion. Certain Christian and Muslim holidays are officially observed, along with one traditional indigenous holiday. An Ecumenical Day is celebrated in Ouidah each year on the first Wednesday of May.

11 TRANSPORTATION

As of 2010, the CIA reports that Benin has a total of 16,000 km (9,942 mi) of roads, of which 1,400 km (870 mi) are paved. Benin has 438 km (272 mi) of narrow-gauge railroad.

Benin is expected to benefit greatly from the World Bank funded reconstruction of the Abidjan-Lagos Corridor, also known as the West African Coastal Corridor. In 2010, the World Bank approved funding of $317.5 million to begin improvements on this important roadway, which stretches for 998.8 km (620 mi), linking the capital cities of Abidjan (Côte d'Ivoire), Accra (Ghana), Lomé (Togo), Cotonou (Benin) and Lagos (Nigeria). This corridor is one of the most highly traveled roadways on the continent. Developed in part by the Economic Community of West African Nations (ECOWAS), the corridor project implemented procedural reforms to promote a more efficient trade process, along with much-needed improvements to the physical infrastructure. The project was to be executed in two phases, with the first phase covering Ghana, Togo, and Benin, and the second phase covering Côte d'Ivoire and Nigeria.

Benin has approximately 150 km (93.2 mi) of navigable waterways, primarily along a portion of the River Niger, which forms the country's northern border. Regular transportation services from Parakou to Malanville and thence to Niamey (in Niger), either by road or, in the season when the Niger River is navigable, by river steamer, are important for the movement of produce to and from Niger via Cotonou, Benin's lone port. Until 1965, the port was serviced by a wharf built in 1891. In 1965, a new deep-water port, constructed with French and European Development Fund assistance and capable of handling one million tons annually, was opened. In the mid-1980s, the port was expanded to handle 3 million tons a year. Landlocked Niger has a free zone in the port area of Cotonou. Cotonou has served as a relief channel for goods destined for Nigeria. It also serves as the chief port for Niger. There is boat traffic on the lagoons between Porto-Novo and Lagos, Nigeria, as well as on the rivers. Benin has no merchant marine.

In 2010, Benin had five airports, but only one had a paved runway (Cadjehoun Airport). Located at Cotonou, Cadjehoun Airport has direct international jet service to Accra, Niamey,

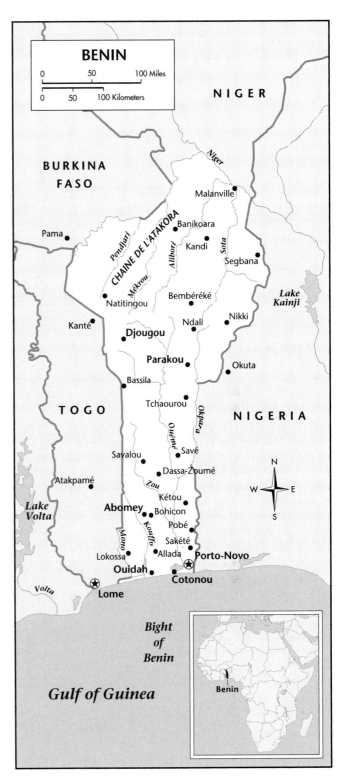

LOCATION: 0°47′0 to 3°47′E; 6°15′ to 12°25′ N. BOUNDARY LENGTHS: Niger, 190 kilometers (118 miles); Nigeria, 750 kilometers (466 miles); Atlantic coastline, 125 kilometers (78 miles); Togo, 620 kilometers (385 miles); Burkina Faso, 270 kilometers (168 miles). TERRITORIAL SEA LIMIT: 200 miles.

Monrovia, Lagos, Ouagadougou, Lomé, and Douala, as well as connections to other West African cities. There is a major airport at Parakou, and airfields of lesser importance at Natitingou, Kandi, and Abomey.

12 HISTORY

Benin (formerly Dahomey) has no geographical or historical unity and owes its frontiers to Anglo-French rivalry in the late-19th-century partition of Africa. This is especially marked in northern Benin, whose affinities are rather with the neighboring countries of West Africa than with the peoples of the south. Southern Benin has some historical unity, owing to the existence there of several kingdoms, all traditionally related and peopled by Fon and Adja (related to the Ewe of southern Togo and southeastern Ghana). Traditionally, the kingdoms of Allada, Abomey (or Dahomey), and Adjatché (later Porto-Novo) were founded when two brothers of the king of Allada created new states, respectively, north and southeast of Allada. Abomey conquered Allada in 1724, seized the port of Ouidah in 1727, and became a famous slave-trading kingdom. At this time, women soldiers ("Amazons") were recruited by Abomey for regular service.

The Portuguese–the first Europeans to establish trading posts on the West African coast–founded the trading post of Porto-Novo on what is now the Benin coast. They were followed by English, Dutch, Spanish, and French traders as the slave trade developed. The French established posts at Ouidah and Savé in the middle of the 17th century, and the English and Portuguese also built forts nearby in the early 18th century. The Portuguese fort at Ouidah, which remained Portuguese territory until 1961, was built in 1727. French, English, and Portuguese coastal trade continued, and as Yoruba power weakened, Abomey continually raided the Yoruba and expanded westward toward the Ashanti. Prisoners seized in these campaigns were sacrificed or exported as slaves until the latter half of the 19th century. European traders were closely controlled by the yevogan of Ouidah, the Abomey functionary stationed there, and subjected to substantial levies. It was not until the mid-19th century, with the gradual replacement of the slave trade by trade in palm oil, that European activity brought forth new developments. In 1857, the French established themselves in Grand Popo. In 1868, the French made a treaty with the king of Abomey by which they were permitted to establish a trading post at Cotonou. The British meanwhile established themselves in Lagos, which they annexed in 1861 in order to eliminate the slave trade. Anglo-French rivalry in Porto-Novo, in which successive local kings took different sides, eventually ended with a French protectorate there (1882) and British posts at various points farther west, which were abandoned by the Anglo-French agreements of 1888–89. However, Abomey remained outside French control, and its levies on European trade became increasingly irksome. War between Abomey and Porto-Novo broke out in 1889 over France's rights of sovereignty to Cotonou, and Béhanzin, who succeeded to the throne of Abomey in that year, attacked the French posts there. His forces included some 2,000 Amazons. Béhanzin next attacked Porto-Novo and Grand Popo in 1891. In 1893, a French expeditionary force commanded by Dodds took Abomey, and a French protectorate was declared. Renewed hostilities were followed by Béhanzin's surrender to the French in 1894. (He died in exile in Martinique in 1906). His successor, his brother Agoli Agbo, was exiled in 1899 for misadministration, and the kingdom of Abomey finally came to an end.

From 1892 to 1898, the territory took its modern shape with the exploration and extension of French control in the north. The construction of the railroad to the north was begun in 1900. Dahomey became a component colony of the federation of French West Africa in 1904. In 1946, under the new French constitution, it was given a deputy and two senators in the French parliament and an elected Territorial Assembly with substantial control of the budget. Under the reforms of 1956–57, the powers of the Territorial Assembly were extended, and a Council of Government elected by the Assembly was given executive control of most territorial matters. Universal adult suffrage and a single electorate were established at the same time. In September 1958, the territory accepted the French constitution proposed by General de Gaulle's government and opted for the status of an autonomous republic within the French Community, as provided by the new constitution.

On 4 December 1958, the Territorial Assembly became a national constituent assembly, and the Republic of Dahomey was proclaimed a member of the French Community. On 14 February 1959, a constitution was adopted; the first Legislative Assembly was elected on 3 April. Hubert Maga, chairman of the Dahomeyan Democratic Rally, was named prime minister on 18 May 1959. On 1 August 1960, Dahomey proclaimed its complete independence, and on 25 November a new constitution, calling for a strong unitary state, was adopted.

After independence, the country suffered from extreme political instability, with military coups in 1963, 1965 (twice), 1967, 1969, and 1972. The numerous and often ingenious efforts at constitutional government, including, from 1970–72, a three-man presidential council with a rotating chairman, failed for a number of reasons. The major ones were regionalism, especially the north-south differences, and the country's poor economy; unemployment was high for the relatively large number of educated Beninese and economic growth minimal.

The coup on 26 October 1972 established Maj. Mathieu Kérékou as the leader of a military regime. It represented a clear break with all earlier Dahomeyan administrations, introducing revolutionary changes in the political and economic life of the country. In late 1974, President Kérékou said that the national revolution would follow a Marxist-Leninist course, and the state sector was rapidly expanded by nationalization. As of 1 December 1975, the country's name was changed to the People's Republic of Benin by presidential proclamation.

In 1979, a National Revolutionary Assembly was elected from the single list of candidates offered by the Party of the People's Revolution of Benin, the only legal political organization. This body elected Kérékou to a new term as president in 1980.

In February 1990, after weeks of unrest and economic disorder, Kérékou convened a National Conference of Active Forces of the Nation to discuss Benin's future. The National Conference—the first of its kind in Africa—became a public critique of Kérékou's 17 years of rule. On 2 December 1990, a new constitution was adopted by popular referendum, and Kérékou was forced to turn over power to a transitional government to initiate the return to democracy. Presidential and parliamentary elections were held on 10 March 1991, and runoffs on 24 March resulted in a victory for then-prime-minister Nicephore Soglo. The conferees also changed the name of the country to the Republic of Benin. Referred to popularly as a "civilian coup," Benin's National Conference spawned several similar conferences throughout the continent.

Following a period of considerable tension between the executive branch and the legislature and in the wake of protests caused by the devaluation of the CFA currency, a second National Convention of Forces of Change was held, and calls were issued for new elections to be administered by a national electoral commission. After some delay, elections were held on 28 March 1995 and were considered to be generally free and fair, although the Constitutional Court heard complaints of irregularities in April and invalidated 13 seats. New elections for those seats were scheduled for May, amid opposition complaints that Soglo's dominance of the Benin Renaissance Party (PRB) would again lead to irregularities. After the squabbling, the PRB did in fact emerge with a plurality, holding 20 seats along with 13 held by parties aligned with Soglo and the PRB. In the presidential elections that followed in 1996, Soglo was defeated by his old rival Kérékou, who won the runoff by garnering 52.49% of the vote to Soglo's 47.51%. In sum, the 1990s proved quite remarkable for Benin with two transfers of presidential and legislative power freely and fairly at the ballot box, one of which marked the first successful transfer of power in Africa from a dictator to a democratically elected leader.

In presidential elections on 4 and 22 March 2001, Kérékou was easily reelected. In December 2002 the country launched its decentralization program, as three million people went to the polls to elect mayors and municipal councilors, who were previously appointed by the government. They were the first municipal and communal elections since the end of one-party rule in 1990. Soglo was elected mayor of Cotonou by its council in February 2003.

Having confirmed that he would step down after his term ended in 2006, President Kérékou put an end to the national debate over a constitutional review that would have removed the upper age limit of 70 and allowed him to run for a third consecutive term. The sharp divisions in the parliament and across the country triggered by this prospect—as well as the practical difficulties of budgeting for a national referendum—caused Kérékou, who was 72, to stand down. Former president, Nicephore Soglo, who also exceeded the age limit for candidates, was likewise ineligible to run.

Thomas Boni Yayi won the presidency in March 2006 with 74.5% of the vote. Yayi, a first-time politician, was formerly the head of the West African Development Bank. In 2007, his coalition won control of the general parliament, boosting his goal of passing anti-corruption reform measures. In the 2011 elections, Yayi was reelected in what observers described as a fair and transparent election.

13 GOVERNMENT

Under the 1990 constitution, the president is elected by popular vote to serve a five-year term as chief of state and head of government. The president is eligible for a second term. The president appoints a council of ministers to serve as his cabinet. The unicameral national assembly has 83 members elected by direct popular vote to serve four-year terms.

14 POLITICAL PARTIES

Following independence, the most important parties in the national assembly were the Dahomeyan Republican Party (Parti Républicain du Dahomey-PRD), the Dahomeyan Democratic Rally (Rassemblement Démocratique Dahoméen-RDD), and the Dahomey Democratic Union (Union Démocratique Dahoméenne-UDD). A coalition of these three parties took office, with Hubert Maga as prime minister, in 1959. In November 1960,

after losing a vote of confidence, the UDD ministers resigned, and the PRD and RDD united in the Dahomeyan Unity Party (Parti Dahoméen de l'Unité-PDU), again under Maga as prime minister. At the end of 1960, the PDU candidates overwhelmingly defeated the UDD and thereby gained complete control of the executive and the legislature. In 1961, the UDD was banned, and Dahomey became a one-party state.

After the fall of the Maga government in October 1963, the PDU was disbanded and replaced by the Dahomeyan Democratic Party (Parti Démocratique Dahoméen), which was in turn dissolved following the 1965 military coup. The Union for Dahomeyan Renewal (Union pour le Renouveau du Dahomey) was later formed, but it was dissolved after the military coup of December 1969.

The Kérékou regime, which took power in 1972, appeared at first to be unwilling to return to party government, but, following the adoption of a Marxist-Leninist policy in 1974, the government formed a political organization as the basis of a one-party state. This organization, which became known as the Party of the People's Revolution of Benin (Parti de la Révolution Populaire du Benin-PRPB), was the sole legal party until 1990.

Numerous parties have formed since then. The Democratic Renewal Party (PRD) came into the legislature in 1993. The Communist Party of Benin was registered in October 1993. In 1994, the Party for the Renaissance of Benin (PRB) was founded by Rosine Soglo, the wife of then-president Nicephore Soglo, who had previously aligned himself with no party but was quickly elected head of the PRB. The African Movement for Democracy and Progress (MADEP) has been a major party in elections since 1999.

The Key Force (FC), Alliance for Dynamic Democracy (ADD), and the Force Cowrie for an Emerging Benin (FCBE) emerged for the elections of 2007. That year, the FCBE gained 35 seats in the assembly, followed by the ADD with 20 seats, the PRD with 10 seats, and other parties and independents with 18 seats. In the 2011 elections, the FCBE won 41 seats, followed by an opposition coalition group known as the Union Fait la Nation with 30 seats and other parties with 12 seats.

In March 2006, Thomas Boni Yayi, an independent candidate, won the presidential election with 74.5% of the vote. Boni Yayi won a second term as president in the 2011 elections with 53% of the vote.

15 LOCAL GOVERNMENT

The country is divided into 12 departments for administrative purposes, and these, in turn, are divided into 77 communes. There are elected district, commune, town, and village councils.

Benin has been slow to decentralize. In December 2002, the country held its first municipal and communal elections since the end of one-party rule in 1990. However, central government has resisted devolution of budget authority to the communes, and several mayors were removed by municipal councils, allegedly for mismanagement.

16 JUDICIAL SYSTEM

The legal system in Benin is based on French civil law and local customary law. The 1990 constitution provided for establishment of a new constitutional court responsible for judicial review of the constitutionality of legislation and for deciding disputes between the president and the national assembly. This court began functioning in 1993. It consists of seven members, four of whom are appointed by the assembly and three by the president, all for a single five-year term. There is also a high court of justice responsible for hearing charges of crimes against the nation committed by the president or other government officials. This court consists of the members of the constitutional court and six additional members appointed by the assembly.

In the criminal justice system, convictions from lower criminal courts can be appealed to the court of appeals and the Supreme Court. The president of the Supreme Court is appointed by the president to serve a 5-year term. The members of the military may be tried in case of minor offenses at military disciplinary councils, but greater offenses are referred to civilian courts.

Human and civil rights are also enshrined in the constitution. Citizens have the right to a fair public trial, and criminal defendants enjoy the presumption of innocence, the right to counsel, and the rights to confront witnesses and have access to government-held evidence. While the judicial system is independent, it is not always impartial. A 2010 report from the US Department of State indicated that the judiciary was susceptible to corruption at all levels.

[17]ARMED FORCES

The International Institute for Strategic Studies reports that the Benin Armed Forces totaled 4,750 members in 2011. The force is comprised of 4,300 from the army, 200 from the navy, and 250 members of the air force. Armed forces represent .2% of the labor force in Benin. Defense spending totaled $139.9 million and accounted for 1% of GDP.

As of 2007, all Beninese between the ages of 18 and 35 are subject to military service "in the national interest." Under the law, all eligible youth must register for service within their commune. Those selected for training and service general serve a standard tour of duty of 18 months.

[18]INTERNATIONAL COOPERATION

Benin was admitted to UN membership on 20 September 1960, and is a member of ECA and several nonregional specialized agencies. The country joined the WTO on 22 February 1996. It is a member of the African Development Bank, the ACP Group, the West African Economic and Monetary Union, ECOWAS, the Organization of the Islamic Conference (OIC), the New Partnership for Africa's Development (NEPAD), G-77, and the African Union. The nation is part of the Franc Zone and the Community of Sahel and Saharan States (CENSAD). It is an observer in the OAS.

Benin has joined with Côte d'Ivoire, Niger, Burkina Faso, and Togo in the Conseil d'Entente, a loose grouping of like-minded states with a common loan-guarantee fund. Benin, as a member of the Niger Basin Authority, cooperates with other riparian states of the Niger River in planning the further use and development of the river for fishing, transportation, flood control, and hydroelectricity. The Organization Commune Bénin-Niger regulates common problems of transportation and communications. Benin became a member of the Association of African Petroleum Producers in 1987. The country is part of the Nonaligned Movement and the Organization for the Prohibition of Chemical Weapons.

In environmental cooperation, Benin is part of the Basel Convention, the Convention on Biological Diversity, Ramsar, CITES, the Kyoto Protocol, the Montréal Protocol, MARPOL, the Nuclear Test Ban Treaty, and the UN Conventions on the Law of the Sea, Climate Change, and Desertification.

[19]ECONOMY

Since the 1990 transition to a democratic government, Benin's economy has changed considerably as the government has privatized its state owned industries and has begun to attract external investment. Nevertheless, the economy remains underdeveloped, and poverty is widespread. Most citizens are dependent on subsistence agriculture, though cotton, palm oil, and cocoa are grown as cash crops. Regional trade in cotton and in consumer and processed goods produced by the industrial sector is import to the national economy. While mineral resources are limited, some limestone and marble are exploited commercially. There is also a small offshore oil exploration project that shows some potential.

The 2008–09 global financial crisis of had a significant impact on the nation's economy, especially noted by the drop in cotton exports. Real GDP growth in 2009 was reported at 2.7%, a decline from 5% in 2008. In 2010 the GDP growth rate was estimated at 2.5%. Inflation stood at 1.6%.

[20]INCOME

The CIA estimated that in 2010 the GDP of Benin was $13.99 billion. The CIA defines GDP as the value of all final goods and services produced within a nation in a given year and computed on the basis of purchasing power parity (PPP) rather than value as measured on the basis of the rate of the exchange based on current dollars. The per capita GDP was estimated at $1,500. The annual growth rate of GDP was 2.5%. The average inflation rate was 1.6%. It was estimated that agriculture accounted for 35.8% of GDP, industry 6.1%, and services 58.1%.

According to the World Bank, remittances from citizens living abroad totaled $242.5 million or about $26 per capita and accounted for approximately 1.7% of GDP.

As of 2011, the most recent study by the World Bank reported that actual individual consumption in Benin was 80.6% of GDP and accounted for 0.02% of world consumption. By comparison, the United States accounted for 25.44% of world individual consumption. The World Bank also estimated that 38.1% of Benin's GDP was spent on food and beverages, 11.2% on housing and household furnishings, 7.6% on clothes, 2.4% on health, 6.1% on transportation, 1.4% on communications, 1.8% on recreation, 6.5% on restaurants and hotels, and 1.7% on miscellaneous goods and services and purchases from abroad.

It was estimated that, in 2007, about 37.4% of the population subsisted on an income below the poverty line established by Benin's government.

[21]LABOR

In 2007, Benin had a total labor force of 3.662 million people. As of 2011, there was no reliable data on unemployment. Only about 5% of workers are employed in the formal wage sector. The labor market is highly dependent on informal employment, with small businesses hiring family members or apprentices than more highly skilled employees.

There are minimum wage scales for a number of occupations, with an average minimum wage at about $66 per month in 2010, which is not enough to provide a decent standard of living for a worker and family. Reports indicate that most of those in the formal wage sector make more than the minimum wage, but a significant number still must supplement their income through subsistence farming or work and trade in the informal sector. Laborers and domestics, generally part of the informal sector, tend to earn less than minimum wage. The law prohibits the employment or apprenticeship of children under the age of 14 in any enterprise, but allows children between the ages of 12 and 14 old to work as domestic servants or in temporary and seasonal light work, as long as it does not interfere with compulsory schooling. In practice, child labor is a serious problem, as much younger children are often sent to work in order to supplement the family income or in exchange for room, board, and education with a wealthier family.

The fundamental labor legislation provides for collective agreements between employers and workers, though the government is responsible for setting wages in the public sector. The National Consultation and Collective Bargaining Commission was established in 2009 to facilitate collective bargaining and enhance social dialogue. Labor laws relating to the formal wage sector also establish a 40- to 46-hour basic workweek, with a 24-hour rest period per week. Domestic and agricultural workers generally work more than 70 hours per week. The legislation also provides for paid annual leave and for family allowances for children. Although health and safety standards have been established, enforcement has been ineffective.

Trade union activity is concentrated in urban areas and particularly in the south, where most wage and salaried workers are employed. The constitution gives workers the right to organize, join unions, meet, and strike. However, the government does reserve the right to declare a strike illegal if it is thought to threaten social peace and order. As of 2010, around 75% of government workers were unionized, but the percentage is much smaller in the private sector.

22 AGRICULTURE

The local economy of Benin is based strongly on agriculture. About 90% of the total agricultural output is produced on family farms using low technology and focusing primarily on domestically consumed crops, such as cashews, corn, sorghum, millet, paddy rice, pineapples, cassava, yams, and beans. Cotton, palm oil, and peanuts are grown and exchanged for cash. However, the reliance on agriculture has kept much of Benin's population in poverty, as rapid increases in population tend to offset any economic gains. About 13% of the total land is arable. The agricultural sector is plagued by a lack of infrastructure, poor utilization of rural credit, and inefficient and insufficient use of fertilizer, insecticides, and seeds. The smuggling of crops for export or for sale on the domestic black market has resulted in understated crop figures. In 2009, cereal production amounted to 1.5 million tons, fruit production 386,024 tons, and vegetable production 397,701 tons.

Palm products were long Benin's principal export crop, but cotton has gained in importance, placing Benin as the third-largest

cotton producer in Africa in 2009. Despite improved production, however, cotton storage and ginning capacity are still insufficient. Many cotton farmers are adopting an organic farming program that preserves the health of local farmers and may offer valuable economic incentives. The new, organic crops have been christened "Peace Cotton" by local farmers because, with the help of European investors, these farmers are able to avoid the harsh chemical pesticides that have caused illness for many. In the 2007–08 planting season alone, over 320 farmers died from exposure to pesticides used in cotton production. In addition to the health benefits, many farmers see a growing market for an organic product and envision organic labels for their cotton that would attract higher prices. Benin was expected to produce 220 tons of organic cotton from October 2009 through 2012. Cotton exports account for more than one-third of overall export earnings.

In 2009, the United Nations Food and Agricultural Organization (FAO) offered an initial investment of $500,000 to the government to assist in increasing the nation's rice crop. Only about 8% of all arable land is used for growing rice, while thousands of hectares of low-lying flood plains are available for such a crop. Experts from the FAO believe that Benin can double the amount of rice produced each year, which would provide enough to satisfy local consumption and offer a surplus for export. With increased production, the potential earnings for rice cultivation in Benin have been estimated at over $55 million.

One measure under consideration to improve agricultural production is the use of solar-powered irrigation systems. In a 2010 study published by the Proceedings of the National Academy of Sciences, Stanford University researchers found solar-powered irrigation to be an effective, efficient, and environmentally friendly way to increase agricultural yield. Typically, crop irrigation in sub-Saharan countries such as Benin is the responsibility of village women, who tote buckets of water long distances to irrigate fruit and vegetable crops. During Benin's long dry season, this represents a particularly difficult task, and food security is never guaranteed. In an attempt to address this problem, Stanford researchers constructed large solar-powered water pumps in several villages and compared them against "control" villages, which used traditional means of irrigation. In the experimental villages, agricultural yield increased by three to five servings per person per day and allowed villagers to grow more finicky crops with higher market values. The excess food was brought to market for profit. According to researchers, the system costs $18,000 to set up and $5,750 per year to maintain. However, analysts have predicted that the system will pay for itself in two to three years, given higher crop yields.

23 ANIMAL HUSBANDRY

The UN Food and Agriculture Organization (FAO) reported that Benin dedicated 550,000 hectares (1.36 million acres) to permanent pasture or meadow in 2009. During that year, the country tended 16 million chickens, 2 million head of cattle, and 355,600 pigs. The production from these animals amounted to 23,538 tons of beef and veal, 5,317 tons of pork, 86,461 tons of poultry, 8,216 tons of eggs, and 73,171 tons of milk. Benin also produced 3,924 tons of cattle hide. In 2004, there were 700,000 sheep and 1,350,000 goats. Although the livestock population has increased,

Benin still imports substantial amounts of meat and poultry to meet local demand.

Most of Benin's cattle are in the north beyond the main trypanosomiasis (sleeping sickness) zone inhabited by the tsetse fly, but there is also a small hardy type in the lagoon area. Horses are rare, owing to the ravages of trypanosomiasis. Poultry are mainly confined to the south of the country.

24 FISHING

Ocean fishing, which had been carried on largely by Ghanaian fishermen, is gaining importance at Cotonou (where a fishing port was opened in 1971) and other coastal centers. Under an agreement with the Senegal government, Senegalese fishermen introduced deep-sea-fishing methods to the Beninese, and a national fishing company was established as a joint venture with Libya. Exports of fish commodities amounted to nearly $1.9 million in 2003. Lagoon and river fishing remain of primary importance. In 2003, fishery products accounted for 2.8% of agricultural exports. In 2008, the annual capture totaled 37,495 tons, according to the UN FAO.

25 FORESTRY

There are about 3.4 million hectares (nearly 8.4 million acres) classified as forest and woodland, about 31% of the total land area. Most forests are in northern Benin, and exploitation is subject to public control. Timber production is small. Firewood, charcoal, and building wood for local use are the most important forest products. The UN FAO estimated the 2009 roundwood production at 427,000 cu m (15.1 million cu ft). The value of all forest products, including roundwood, totaled $15.7 million. American Peace Corps volunteers have assisted with the development of the forestry sector, with special attention to the dilemma between ecological balance and fuelwood production.

26 MINING

With the exception of oil, Benin was relatively poor in mineral resources, all of which belonged to the government. Sedimentary phosphate deposits were located along the Mekrou River in the north. There was low-grade iron ore at Loumbou-Loumbou and Madekali, in the Borgou district, where surveys discovered resources of more than 500 million tons. Development of the hydroelectric power station was seen as a key factor in the future potential development of the iron ore and phosphate deposits. Limestone was quarried for use in cement plants. There was potential for small-scale gold mining in the Atacora gold zone in the northwest. Other mineral resources included chromium, rutile, and diamonds; small quantities of industrial diamonds were exported. In 2009 the country produced 1.5 million metric tons of hydraulic cement, 77,000 metric tons of clay, 20 kg (44 lbs) of gold, and 25,000 cu m (882,867 cu ft) of gravel.

27 ENERGY AND POWER

Production from the Sémé offshore oil field began in October 1982 by Saga Petroleum, a Norwegian firm working under a service contract. However, the field was closed in 1998 for economic reasons. From 1992 through 1998, the field produced about 22 million barrels of crude oil. While there have been some plans considered for redevelopment of the field, installations already in place have fallen into disrepair over the years, and it is expected that a very large financial investment would be needed to continue operations. In 2009, oil imports were estimated at 33,410 barrels per day, while oil exports were estimated at 10,840 barrels per day. Oil consumption in 2010 was estimated at 25,000 barrels per day.

In 2009, the government announced plans to begin a survey of the ultra-deep waters along the West African coast for potential oil reserves.

Electrical generating capacity in 2002 totaled 0.122 million kW. The World Bank reported in 2008 that Benin produced 136 million kWh of electricity and consumed 661 million kWh, or 71 kWh per capita. Roughly 37% of energy came from fossil fuels. Total electricity imports for 2000 were estimated at 651 million kWh.

An agreement was signed with Togo and Ghana in 1967 under which Benin receives low-cost electric power from the Akosombo Dam on the Volta River in Ghana. The Nangbeto hydroelectric dam on the Mono River was completed in 1987 as a joint project between Togo and Benin that feeds a power station supplying the southern regions of both countries.

28 INDUSTRY

Benin's industrial sector is underdeveloped, accounting for only about 6.1% of GDP in 2010. Industrial activity centers primarily on cotton ginning and cement production. The previously state-owned cotton-manufacturing corporation SONAPRA was fully privatized in 2008. There are also textile mills, food processing facilities, and some manufacturing of construction materials. Enterprises such as the Onigbolo cement factory and the Savé sugar refinery have characterized Benin's industrial sector. A textile factory at Parakout was revitalized with financing from the West African Development Bank. The industrial production growth rate was estimated at 3% in 2010.

29 SCIENCE AND TECHNOLOGY

The World Bank reported in 2009 that there were no patent applications in science and technology in Benin. Much of the scientific and technical research conducted in Benin is directed toward agriculture and is supported by France. As of 2011, the temporary headquarters of the Africa Rice Center (AfricaRice), a leading pan-African agricultural research organization, was located in Cotonou. Agricultural research focused on local production techniques is carried out as one of the activities of the Songhai Center, which has five sites in Benin offering advanced education and training in agriculture. The Entomological Research Center of Cotonou (CREC) is organized under the public health research unit of the ministry of health and conducts research in collaboration with local and international institutions. In 2011, the CREC was involved in research on malaria. The National University of Benin, which maintains ten branch locations, has faculties of scientific and technical studies, health sciences, and agriculture.

30 DOMESTIC TRADE

Except in Cotonou and Porto-Novo, retailers deal in a wide variety of goods rather than specializing in a few products. In the two larger towns, some shops specialize in such lines as dry goods, foodstuffs, and hardware. In the smaller towns, bazaars and individual merchants and peddlers deal in locally grown products

Principal Trading Partners – Benin (2010)

(In millions of US dollars)

Country	Total	Exports	Imports	Balance
World	3,600.0	1,250.0	2,350.0	-1,100.0
China	2,614.7	114.2	2,500.5	-2,386.3
France	575.5	3.8	571.7	-567.9
Malaysia	522.7	5.3	517.4	-512.0
United States	512.3	0.1	512.2	-512.1
India	416.2	126.8	289.4	-162.7
United Kingdom	341.9	0.0	341.8	-341.8
Netherlands	305.3	2.5	302.8	-300.3
Thailand	294.5	10.1	284.4	-274.3
Côte d'Ivoire	150.3	14.9	135.4	-120.5
Turkey	131.3	2.9	128.4	-125.4

(…) data not available or not significant.

(n.s.) not specified.

SOURCE: *2011 Direction of Trade Statistics Yearbook,* New York: United Nations, 2011.

Balance of Payments – Benin (2009)

(In millions of US dollars)

Current Account		**-755.8**
Balance on goods		-513.0
Imports	-1,737.8	
Exports	1,224.8	
Balance on services		-275.2
Balance on income		-33.0
Current transfers		65.3
Capital Account		**152.8**
Financial Account		**186.1**
Direct investment abroad		-31.2
Direct investment in Benin		134.3
Portfolio investment assets		-27.6
Portfolio investment liabilities		106.2
Financial derivatives		0.4
Other investment assets		-245.6
Other investment liabilities		249.8
Net Errors and Omissions		**-4.4**
Reserves and Related Items		**421.3**

(…) data not available or not significant.

SOURCE: *Balance of Payment Statistics Yearbook 2011,* Washington, DC: International Monetary Fund, 2011.

and a few imported items. Domestic trade is generally on a cash basis, but in the countryside barter is common. Advertising is not widely used.

Many small businesses are privately owned by Beninese residents, but a number of enterprises are held by foreigners, particularly French nationals.

Business hours are from 9:30 a.m. to 1 p.m. and from 4 to 7 p.m. Monday through Friday, from 3 to 7 p.m. on Saturday, and from 9 to 11 a.m. on Sunday. Banks are open on weekdays from 8 to 11 a.m. and 3 to 5 p.m. Monday through Friday.

31 FOREIGN TRADE

With few resources of its own, Benin consistently runs a trade deficit. Cotton is by far the leading product, accounting for more than one-third of all exports. Other export commodities include cashews, shea butter, textiles, palm products, and some seafood. Leading imports are foodstuffs, petroleum products, beverages, tobacco, capital goods, and other consumer products.

The port of Cotonou is a free-trade zone for products destined for Burkina Faso and Niger. In 2010, its port was home to the largest market of secondhand cars in West Africa.

According to the CIA, the total amount of merchandise exports was estimated at $1.25 billion in 2010, while merchandise imports were estimated at $1.78 billion. Major import partners in 2010 were China 35.2%; France, 8%; the United States, 7.2%; Malaysia, 5.9%; the United Kingdom, 4.8%; the Netherlands, 4.3%; India, 4.1%; and Thailand, 4%. Its major export partners were India, 26.4%; China, 21.4%; Niger, 6.5%; Nigeria, 5.6%; and Indonesia, 4.4%.

Benin is a member of the World Trade Organization, the Economic Community of West African States (ECOWAS), and the West African Economic and Monetary Union (WAEMU). The government has also established bilateral trade agreements with Germany, Tunisia, Switzerland, China, Portugal, Greece, France, and the United States.

32 BALANCE OF PAYMENTS

Large annual transfers from the French government and other sources are necessary for Benin to offset its chronic trade deficit. According to the CIA, merchandise exports had a trade deficit of $530 million in 2010. The current account balance, reflecting net trade in goods and services plus other net earnings and transfer payments, was estimated at -$485.1 million for that same year.

33 BANKING AND SECURITIES

In 1959, the Central Bank of the West African States (Banque Centrale des États de l'Afrique de l'Ouest-BCEAO) succeeded the Currency Board of French West Africa and Togo as the bank of issue for the member states of WAEMU, including Benin, Burkina Faso, Côte d'Ivoire, Guinea-Bissau, Mali, Niger, Senegal, and Togo. BCEAO notes, known as CFA francs (XOF), are unreservedly guaranteed by France. They are pegged to the euro at a fixed rate of XOF655.956 =€1.

Benin's banking sector was the fourth-largest in WAEMU in 2009 with 13 banks. Commercial banks include Ecobank-Benin, the Financial Bank, the Bank of Africa Benin, Diamond Bank, Societe Generale des Banques du Benin, Banque Atlantique du Benin, and Banque Régionale de Solidarite. Banque Sahelo-Sahélienne pour le Commerce et l'Investissement is a sub-regional Islamic bank that opened in 2004 and the African Investment Bank opened in 2006. The West African Development Bank is located in Cotonou.

The discount rate, the interest rate at which the central bank lends to financial institutions in the short term, was 4.25% in December 2009.

There is no securities market in Benin.

34 INSURANCE

As of 2009, there were eight insurance companies in the nation providing life and non-life insurance products. Insurance

Public Finance – Benin (2009)

(In billion of CFA francs, budgetary central government figures)

Revenue and Grants	631.83	100.0%
Tax revenue	506.2	80.1%
Social contributions	15	2.4%
Grants	77.4	12.3%
Other revenue	33.24	5.3%
Expenditures	772.36	100.0%
General public services	...	...
Defense	...	...
Public order and safety	...	...
Economic affairs	...	...
Environmental protection	...	...
Housing and community amenities	...	...
Health	...	...
Recreational, culture, and religion	...	...
Education	...	...
Social protection	...	...

(…) data not available or not significant.

SOURCE: *Government Finance Statistics Yearbook 2010*, Washington, DC: International Monetary Fund, 2010.

companies fall under the authority of the Direction du Contrôle des Assurances.

35 PUBLIC FINANCE

The government has struggled since the 1980s to get create a sustainable budget and shrink its massive external debt. By 1988, the external debt stood at $909 million. In 1989, the government rescheduled its arrears through the Paris Club. Then, in 1991, Benin began implementing a structural adjustment program supported by the World Bank. The program called for reduced fiscal expenditures, deregulation of trade, and the privatization of money-losing state-owned enterprises. In 2003, the World Bank and International Monetary Fund approved a comprehensive debt reduction package for Benin under the Heavily Indebted Poor Countries Initiative. Under this initiative, Benin received debt relief of about $460 million.

In 2010, the budget of Benin included $1.348 billion in public revenue and $1.73 billion in public expenditures. The budget deficit amounted to 3% of GDP. Public debt that year was 20.8% of GDP, with $2.8 billion of the debt held by foreign entities.

36 TAXATION

Personal income tax is levied on a four-tiered scale beginning at 10% on income ranging from XOF50,001 to XOF130,000 and progressing to 35% for income ranging from XOF530,000 and above. The corporate income tax for non-industrial companies is 30%, while industrial companies pay a rate of 25%. Oil companies involved in research, exploitation, production, and sale of hydrocarbons are taxed at rates between 35% and 45%. Property taxes in main towns for both individuals and corporations are levied at 5% for undeveloped property and 6% of the rental vale for developed property.

A value-added tax (VAT) with a standard rate of 18% was introduced in 1991. In 2003 an estimated three-fourths of VAT collected was collected on imports, despite the fact that most imports, including those pursuant to all government contracts and most investments, are exempt from VAT. There is also a 1% community solidarity levy.

37 CUSTOMS AND DUTIES

Benin and its fellow member states of WAEMU enacted a common external tariff (CET) in 2000. Customs duties are based on four categories of products: 0% on drugs, books, and condoms; 5% on essential goods, basic raw materials, capital goods, and specific inputs (semi-manufactured and manufactured goods used by local industries); 10% on inputs and intermediary products; and 20% on final consumption and all goods imported from outside of the WAEMU zone (such as frozen fish, used clothing, milk, oil, wheat flour, and cigarettes). The CET also includes a Community Solidarity Deduction (1%), a Statistical Duty (1%), an Import Cyclical Tax (10%), and a Regressive Protection Tax (10% and 20%). Imports are also subject to an 18% VAT at point of entry.

38 FOREIGN INVESTMENT

The government is eager to promote foreign investment and has taken several steps toward developing an investment-friendly business environment. Primary regulations are outlined by the 1990 investment code, revised in 2008. Under the revised guidelines and with the help of the Business Registration Center in Cotonou, many new businesses can be registered within two weeks. Benin has a bilateral investment agreement with France, Germany, and Great Britain.

The principal foreign investors are from Lebanon, India, Germany, France, and other Western countries. Rothmans-UK invested in the formerly state-run cigarette factory. An American private investor has entered the steel industry, manufacturing reinforcing bars and roofing materials. While current oil reserves are negligible, investments in further exploration possibilities offshore have been considerable.

Other arenas of interest to foreign investors are the potential for building apparel factors in Benin and investments in tourism. Tourism investment has been increasing, with plans to establish a tourism investment zone along the country's scenic coastline.

Foreign direct investment (FDI) in Benin has been steadily increasing since Benin's transition to a democratic government in the early 1990s. According to the UN Conference on Trade and Development, FDI averaged $39 million between 1985 and 1995. Since then, it has risen from $44 million in 2001 to $63 million in 2006. According to 2009 figures from the World Bank, FDI in Benin was a net inflow of $92.5 million. FDI represented 1.39% of GDP.

39 ECONOMIC DEVELOPMENT

Economic development is guided primarily within the context of IMF Poverty Reduction and Growth Facility (PRGF) and the Heavily Indebted Poor Countries (HIPC) Initiative with the IMF and the World Bank. Additional support strategies have been developed in cooperation with the African Development Bank and the Millennium Challenge Corporation of the United States.

In the 2000s, the government showed great progress in privatizing a majority of companies and displayed a willingness to shift its macroeconomic policies to comply with market-oriented reforms.

Nevertheless, a high incidence of poverty, a continued reliance on agriculture, and the ongoing struggle against government corruption have hindered economic growth. The government was expected to make improvements in physical and institutional infrastructures in order to build a stronger foundation for a sustainable economy. The government also planned to adopt programs and policies to improve the business climate through reforms to the land tenure system, the commercial justice system, and the financial sector. Investments to improve health and education were long-term priorities for national development strategies.

40 SOCIAL DEVELOPMENT

A social security program funded by employer and employee contributions was established in 1970 and updated in 2003. It provides pensions for old age, disability, and survivorship. Maternity benefits, worker's compensation, and a family allowance program, financed entirely by employers, are also offered. However, these benefits only apply to those within the formal wage economy. A majority of the population is self-employed or works in the informal job sector and falls outside the scope of these programs.

Although the law provides for equality for women, they are victims of discrimination in most areas of society. Domestic violence and spousal abuse are common, and the police generally hesitate to interfere. Although outlawed in 2003, female circumcision, also known as female genital mutilation (FGM), is still fairly common in some regions of Benin and among certain ethnic groups. As of 2010, an estimated 13% of all girls and women had been subjected to FGM, with a majority of cases occurring before the age of 13 and half of these occurring before the age of 5. Among the Bariba and the Peul, more than 70% of all girls and women had undergone the procedure. The practice is considered both physically and psychologically harmful to girls and women, and in some cases may cause death.

Child labor is widespread, as many children are sent to work to supplement the family income. Though the law sets the minimum work age at 14, children as young as seven have been employed on farms, in small business, at construction sites in urban areas, as street vendors, and as domestic servants. Some children from rural areas are indentured to agents who place the children in agricultural or domestic service jobs with the understanding that a portion of the child's wages would be sent back to his or her parents. In some cases, these children have been taken out of the country and placed in forced labor or prostitution rings. Under a traditional practice known as *vidomegon* ("placed child"), a child from a poor rural family will be placed with a wealthier family in exchange for room, board, and an education. If the child is set to work outside of their new home, their wages might be split between the host and biological families. Other times, the child simply works as a servant for the host family. In some cases, these children are subject to long, hard hours of work and receive inadequate care in return. A majority of children placed under *vidomegon* are girls.

Though the family code prohibits marriage under the age of 18 years, underage and forced marriages of girls and young women are also common, particularly in some rural areas. One traditional practice of forced marriage involves the abduction and rape of a girl by her intended groom. In some rural areas, a traditional practice of killing deformed and breech babies was still practiced. Prostitution of women and children is also a problem.

Corruption within the police force is widespread, with many reports of illegal detainments and physical abuse against prisoners. Living conditions at most prisons are considered to be extremely harsh, with frequent overcrowding, lack of proper sanitation facilities, inadequate medical care, and meager food rations.

41 HEALTH

Malaria, yellow fever, and meningitis were prevalent in some parts of the country as of 2007, and cholera had not been eradicated. The incidence of tuberculosis was 87 per 100,000 people in 2007. The HIV/AIDS adult prevalence rate was at 1.2% in 2009. An estimated 25% of children under five years of age were malnourished. Estimated average life expectancy in 2011 was 59.84 years.

As of 2011 there was one physician, eight nurses and midwives, and five hospital beds per 10,000 inhabitants. The country spent 4.1% of its GDP on healthcare, amounting to $32 per person.

According to the CIA, the infant mortality rate in 2011 was 61.56 per 1,000 live births. The total fertility rate was 5.31 in 2011. In 2008 the World Bank estimated the maternal mortality rate was 410 deaths per 100,000 births. It was estimated that 72% of children were vaccinated against measles. Approximately 16% of women used contraception in 2007.

42 HOUSING

Improvement in overall appearance and in sanitation facilities in towns and villages has been fostered by the government. Low-cost housing has been provided by a public corporation backed by French development funds.

Many residents have been looking to build more modern, Western-style homes; however, most of the construction materials for such structures need to be imported, making materials (and labor) too expensive for many residents. In the rural areas, the typical dwelling of northern Benin is a round building of beaten mud with a conical roof of thatch. In southern Benin, rectangular huts with sloping roofs of palm or straw thatch are more usual. Along the coastal lagoons, houses are often built on stilts.

At the 2002 census, there were approximately 1,210,463 households with an average household size of 5.59 people. About 47% of the population lived in multi-family dwellings, while 27% lived in separate single-family units, and 21.4% lived in smaller cabins or huts. 55% of all dwellings were made of earthen walls, while 32% had brick walls. Nearly 72% of all dwellings had sheet metal roofs, and 22% had thatch. Nearly 56% of dwellings had cement floors, and 40% had earth or sand.

43 EDUCATION

During the French colonial period, Benin produced the educational elite of French West Africa. The percentage of primary-school attendance was higher than that in any other French West African territory, largely because of intense missionary activity. The educational system is patterned on that of France, but changes have been introduced to modify the elitist system and adapt the curriculum to local needs and traditions. The most significant change has been the takeover of mission schools following legislation in 1975, by which the state made all education free, public, secular, and compulsory from ages 6 to 12.

Primary school covers a six-year course of study, followed by four years of lower secondary and three years of upper secondary classes. Secondary students have the option of attending one of the five vocational schools in the country. In 2009, the World Bank estimated that 95% of age-eligible children in Benin were enrolled in primary school. Secondary enrollment for age-eligible children stood at 20%. The student-to-teacher ratio for primary school was about 47:1 in 2005; the ratio for secondary school was about 24:1. In 2005, it was estimated that about 65% of all students completed their primary education.

The National University of Benin system, founded in 1970, has several campuses, with the largest (and main campus) being the University of Abomey-Calavi (in Cotonou). A variety of faculties are spread throughout the system to include studies in economics and management, law and politics, arts and social sciences, science and technology, health science, education, mathematics and physics, and agricultural science. There are several private institutions, as well. In 2011, there were 94 institutions of higher learning accredited by the Ministry of National Education. In 2009, tertiary enrollment was estimated at 6%. Overall, the CIA estimated that Benin had a literacy rate of 34.7%. Public expenditure on education represented 3.5% of GDP.

44 LIBRARIES AND MUSEUMS

The National Archives and National Library, which houses around 35,000 volumes, are in Porto-Novo. Also in the capital is the library of the National University of Benin (University of Abomey-Calavi in Cotonou) with 50,000 volumes. The library of the National University of Benin in Cotonou serves as a depository library of the United Nations. The French Cultural Center in Cotonou maintains a library of 30,000 volumes. In 2007, the International Federation of Library Associations and Institutions reported an estimated 70 public libraries, 45 school libraries, and 15 university libraries nationwide in Benin but noted that these figures, obtained from government sources, may have included a number of recently closed libraries. There are historical museums in Abomey and Ouidah, an ethnological museum in Porto-Novo, and Cotonou, and a museum of natural history and ethnography in Parakou. There are monuments and historical sites maintained by the government and three zoos and botanical gardens.

45 MEDIA

The nation's domestic telephone system is a mix of microwave radio relay, cellular, and open-wire systems. Overall quality can be described as fair. International communications are provided by seven satellite ground stations, while a fiber-optic submarine cable provides service to Asia and Europe. In 2009, the CIA reported that there were some 127,100 main phone lines and 5 million mobile cellular phones in use, with mobile phone subscriptions averaging 56 per 100 people.

While there are a number of independent media organizations, the government owns and operates the most influential sources and maintains this status by controlling broadcast range and infrastructure. As of 2010, there were an estimated 75 private, community, and commercial radio stations. Those operated by the government Office of Radio and Television and the French government-owned Radio France Internationale were the most prominent. There were five private stations and one government-owned television station. In 2003, there were an estimated 445 radios and 12 television sets for every 1,000 people. In 2010, the country had 1,286 Internet hosts. In 2009 there were about 2 Internet users for every 100 people.

In 2002 there was only one daily newspaper; *Ehuzu* (also known as *La Nation*), is the primary government publication, with a daily circulation of about 12,000. There are about 50 other newspapers and periodicals. Weeklies included *La Gazette du Golfe* (circulation 18,000) and *Le Forum de la Semaine*. Other publications included *L'Opinion* and *Tam-Tam Express* (8,000 every other week). All were published in Cotonou. There are also several general interest and a few special interest periodicals.

The Constitution of Benin ensures freedom of expression, including speech and the press, and the government is said to respect this freedom.

46 ORGANIZATIONS

The Chamber of Commerce and Industry of Benin is in Cotonou. There are professional organizations for teachers and doctors.

The Organization of Revolutionary Youth of Benin, founded in 1983, has about 150,000 members from all parts of Benin. The organization has direct relations with all youth-serving ministries of the Government and is affiliated with the Pan African Youth Movement and the World Federation of Democratic Youth. The Scoutisme Béninois is a scouting organization sponsoring both Boy Scouts and Girl Guides. There are also organizations of the Junior Chamber of Benin, YMCA/YWCA, and the Special Olympics.

Women's rights and support organizations include Women in Law and Development–Benin, the Female Jurists Association of Benin, and the Women's Justice and Empowerment Initiative (of Care International).

There are active chapters of the Red Cross, Amnesty International, Africare, Caritas, and Friends of the Earth.

47 TOURISM, TRAVEL, AND RECREATION

Benin has great potential for tourism, and the government is striving to develop this sector of the economy. The country has a rich cultural heritage, varied scenery, and impressive national parks. The tourist industry remains underdeveloped. For trips to the Pendjari game park, there is a small (21-room) hotel in Porga.

Tourist attractions include the lake village of Ganvie, two game parks in the north, the ancient royal city of Abomey, several museums, and beaches. Hunting lodges have been built to foster safaris in the two national parks, where efforts have also been made to preserve wild game. In the south are picturesque villages built on stilts over the waters of the coastal lagoons.

A visa is required for all visitors except those from Denmark, Germany, France, Sweden, and many of the African nations. Proof of vaccination against yellow fever is required in most of West Africa.

According to the *Tourism Factbook* published by the UN World Tourism Organization, there were 23,960 hotel beds available in Benin in 2009, which had an occupancy rate of 10%. The estimated daily cost to visit Porto-Novo (official capital), the capital, was $247. The cost of visiting other cities averaged $147. In 2005, Benin had more than 170,000 visitors.

⁴⁸FAMOUS PERSONS

Perhaps the most famous historical ruler in the area now known as Benin was Béhanzin (d. 1906), who was king of Abomey from 1889 until he was defeated by the French in 1894. The best-known modern Beninese are the political leaders Hubert Maga (1916–2000); Sourou-Migan Apithy (1913–1989); Justin T. Ahomadegbé (1917–2002); and Brig. Gen. Ahmed Mathieu Kérékou (b. 1933). Nicephore Soglo (b. 1934), a former World Bank economist, was elected president in 1991 in Benin's first multiparty presidential election. Djimon Diaw Hounsou (b. 1964, Cotonou) is an actor and model in the American film and television industry.

⁴⁹DEPENDENCIES

Benin has no territories or colonies.

⁵⁰BIBLIOGRAPHY

Benin Investment and Business Guide: Strategic and Practical Information. Washington, DC: International Business Publications USA, 2012.

Berzock, Kathleen Bickford. Benin: Royal Arts of a West African Kingdom. Chicago: Art Institute of Chicago; distributed by Yale University Press, 2009.

Caulfield, Annie. Show Me the Magic: Travels Round Benin by Taxi. London: Penguin, 2003.

Decalo, Samuel. Historical Dictionary of Benin. 3rd ed. Metuchen, NJ: Scarecrow Press, 1995.

Edgerton, Robert B. Women Warriors: The Amazons of Dahomey and the Nature of War. Boulder, CO: Westview Press, 2000.

Houngnikpo, Mathurin C. Determinants of Democratization in Africa: A Comparative Study of Benin and Togo. Lanham, Md.: University Press of America, 2001.

Kneib, Martha. Benin. Tarrytown, NY: Marshall Cavendish Benchmark, 2006.

Semley, Lorelle. Mother Is Gold, Father Is Glass: Gender and Colonialism in A Yoruba Town. Bloomington, IN: Indiana University Press, 2011.

Zeilig, Leo, and David Seddon. A Political and Economic Dictionary of Africa. Philadelphia: Routledge/Taylor and Francis, 2005.

BOTSWANA

Republic of Botswana

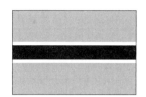

CAPITAL: Gaborone

FLAG: The flag of Botswana consists of five horizontal stripes. The top and bottom stripes are light blue and wider than the middle stripe, which is black. The blue stripes are separated from the black by thin white stripes.

ANTHEM: *Fatshe La Rona (Blessed Country).*

MONETARY UNIT: On 23 August 1976, the pula (BWP) of 100 thebe replaced the South African rand as Botswana's legal currency. There are coins of 1, 2, 5, 10, 25, 50 thebe and 1,2,5 pula, and notes of 10, 20, 50 ,100 and 200 pula. BWP1 = US$0.31524 (or US$1 = BWP7.16) as of 2011.

WEIGHTS AND MEASURES: The metric system is the legal standard.

HOLIDAYS: New Year's Day, 1 January; President's Days, 18–19 July; Botswana Day, 30 September; Christmas, 25 December; Boxing Day, 26 December. Movable holidays include Good Friday, Easter Monday, and Ascension.

TIME: 2 p.m. = noon GMT.

¹LOCATION, SIZE, AND EXTENT

A landlocked country in southern Africa, Botswana has a total area of 600,370 sq km (231,804 sq mi), extending 1,110 km (690 mi) NNE–SSW and 960 km (597 mi) EWE–WNW. Comparatively, the area occupied by Botswana is slightly smaller than the state of Texas. It meets Zambia at a point in the N and is bordered on the NE by Zimbabwe, on the SE and S by South Africa, and on the W and N by Namibia, with a total land boundary length of 4,013 km (2,493 mi).

²TOPOGRAPHY

The country is a broad tableland with a mean altitude of 1,000 m (3,300 ft). A vast plateau about 1,200 m (4,000 ft) in height, extending from near Kanye north to the Zimbabwean border, divides the country into two distinct topographical regions. The eastern region is hilly bush country and grassland (veld). The Tsodilo Hills in the northwest contain the highest point in the country at about 1,489 m (4,884 ft). To the west lie the Okavango Swamps and the Kalahari Desert. The only sources of year-round surface water are the Chobe River in the north, the Limpopo in the southeast, and the Okavango in the northwest. The Limpopo is the longest river in Botswana with a length of 1,600 km (1,000 mi). In seasons of heavy rainfall, floodwaters flow into the Makgadikgadi Salt Pans, Lake Ngami (the country's largest lake, 1,040 sq km/401 sq mi), and Lake Xau.

³CLIMATE

Most of the country has a subtropical climate, with cooler temperatures prevailing in the higher altitudes. Winter days are warm and nights are cool, with heavy frost common in the desert. Temperatures range from average maximums of 33°C (91°F) in January and 22°C (72°F) in July to average minimums of 18°C

(64°F) in January and 5°C (41°F) in July. Beginning in August, seasonal winds that blow from the west carry sand and dust across the country. Rainfall normally averages 45 cm (18 in) but ranges from 69 cm (27 in) in the north to less than 25 cm (10 in) in the Kalahari; drought conditions prevailed in the early and mid-1980s.

⁴FLORA AND FAUNA

Common trees in Botswana are the mopane, camel-thorn, motopi (shepherd's tree), and baobab. Botswana has natural game reserves for most animals found in southern Africa, including lions, leopards, cheetahs, elephants, giraffes, zebras, hippopotamuses, rhinoceroses, African buffalo, hyenas, and 22 species of antelope. The duiker (a small, horned antelope), wildebeest (gnu), and springbok (gazelle) are familiar. Furthermore, the World Resources Institute estimated that there are 2,151 plant species in Botswana, and it is home to 169 mammal, 570 bird, 133 reptile, and 28 amphibian species. The calculation reflected the total number of distinct species residing in the country, not the number of endemic species. According to a 2007 report issued by the International Union for Conservation of Nature and Natural Resources (IUCN), the number of threatened species included 8 types of mammals and 8 species of birds. Endangered species included the black rhinoceros, the African hunting dog, and the African savannah elephant. Burchell's zebra has become extinct.

⁵ENVIRONMENT

The World Resources Institute reported that Botswana had designated 17.44 million hectares (43.1 million acres) of land for protection as of 2006. Overgrazing due to the rapid expansion of the cattle population is a continuing threat to the vegetation and wildlife of Botswana. There are 5 game reserves, 3 game sanctuaries, and 40 controlled hunting areas. Natural hazards to the environment include seasonal winds from the west that blow sand and dust across the country. At the same time, the United Nations (UN) reported in 2008 that carbon dioxide emissions in Botswana totaled 4,994 kilotons.

Botswana has limited water supplies that are inadequate for its increasing population, and the nation's water shortage is exacerbated by periodic droughts. In 2006, water resources totaled 14.7 cu km (3.53 cu mi) while water usage was 0.19 cu km (0.046 cu mi). Domestic water usage accounted for 41% of total usage, industrial for 18%, and agricultural for 41%. Per capita water usage totaled 107 cu m (3,779 cu ft) per year. One major factor in Botswana's water supply problem is that 68% of the country is part of the Kalahari desert.

⁶POPULATION

The CIA estimates the population of Botswana in 2011 to be approximately 2,065,398, which placed it at number 142 in population among the 196 nations of the world. In 2011 approximately 3.9% of the population was over 65 years of age, with another 33.9% under 15 years of age. The median age in Botswana was 22.3 years. There were 1.01 males for every female in the country. The population's annual rate of change was 1.656%. The projected population for the year 2025 was 2,200,000. Population density in Botswana was calculated at 4 people per sq km (10 people per sq mi).

In 2010 the UN estimated that 61% of the population lived in urban areas, and that urban populations had an annual rate of change of 2.3%. The largest urban area was Gaborone, with a population of 196,000.

The prevalence of HIV/AIDS has had a significant impact on Botswana's the population. The AIDS epidemic causes higher death rates and lowers life expectancy.

⁷MIGRATION

Estimates of Botswana's net migration rate, carried out by the CIA in 2011, amounted to 4.82 migrants per 1,000 citizens. The total number of emigrants living abroad was 63,000, and the total number of immigrants living in Botswana was 114,800.

At least 50,000 Botswanans are working in South Africa at any particular time. In 1991 21,468 South African residents were listed as born in Botswana. In 1998, the United Nations High Commissioner for Refugees (UNHCR) had been planning to phase out its Botswana office by the end of the year. However, in October 1998 the influx of 2,500 asylum seekers from the Caprivi region of Namibia provided them with an urgent new caseload.

⁸ETHNIC GROUPS

The population, predominantly of Tswana stock (79%), is distributed among eight ethnic groups, Batswana being the largest. The others include Bamangwato, Bakwena, Bangwaketsi, Bakgatla, Barolong, Bamalete, and Batlokwa. The next largest single group of indigenous peoples is the Kalanga, which accounts for about 11% of the population. There are about 3% Basarwa (Bushmen). Kgalagadi and whites account for about 7%.

⁹LANGUAGES

Though English is the official language, it is only spoken by about 2.1% of the population (2001 census). Setswana is the most widely spoken language, spoken by about 78.2% of the population. About 7.9% of the population speak Kalanga and 2.8% speak Sekgalagadi. Other languages are used by about 8.6% of the population; 0.4% of the population did not specify their native language.

¹⁰RELIGIONS

The 2001 census estimated that 73% of the population are nominally Christian. Anglicans, Methodists, and the United Congregational Church of Southern Africa (formerly the London Missionary Society) are the largest groups. Other denominations include Lutherans, Roman Catholics, the Church of Jesus Christ of Latter-Day Saints (Mormons), Seventh-Day Adventists, Jehovah's Witnesses, Baptists, the Dutch Reformed Church, Mennonites, and other Christian denominations. Most people practice a blend of indigenous beliefs alongside of their Christianity. About 6% of the population claimed to be Badimo (African Traditional Religions), 0.4% Muslim, 0.3% Hindu, and 0.06% Baha'i. About 20.6% of the population claim no religious affiliation. Freedom of religion is provided for in the constitution and this right is generally respected. Religious groups, like all organizations within the country, must be registered with the state Registrar of Societies, a department of the Ministry of Labor and Home Affairs. Some Christian holidays are celebrated as public holidays.

¹¹TRANSPORTATION

The CIA reported that Botswana has a total of 25,798 km (16,030 mi) of roads, of which 8,410 km (5,226 mi) are paved. Bituminous roads were extended to the Zambian and Zimbabwean borders, thereby reducing Botswana's economic dependence on South Africa. Railroads in Botswana extend for 888 km (552 mi). The main railroad from Cape Town in South Africa to Bulawayo in Zimbabwe runs through Botswana for a distance of 641 km (398 mi), connecting Lobatse, Gaborone, and Francistown. Two branch lines totaling 71 km (44 mi) connect the coal field of Morupule and the copper-nickel complex at Selebi-Phikwe with the main line. These lines are owned by Botswana but operated by National Railways of Zimbabwe. In 1991, a new 165 km (103 mi) spur connecting Sua Pan to Francistown was completed, at a cost of $45 million.

There are 78 airports, which transported 233,515 passengers in 2009 according to the World Bank. Of these, 10 have paved runways. The government-owned Air Botswana operates scheduled flights to Francistown, Gaborone, Maun, and Selebi-Phikwe. There is international service to Johannesburg, South Africa; Mbabane, Swaziland; and Harare, Zimbabwe. A new international airport near Gaborone was opened in 1984.

¹²HISTORY

According to tradition, the founder of the Batswana ethnic group was a 14th-century chief named Mogale. His great-great-grandson Malope had three sons, Kwena, Ngwaketse, and Ngwato, who became the chiefs of the major groups that now inhabit Botswana.

The foundations of the modern state lie in between 1820–70, when the Batswana suffered many tribulations at the hands of the Matabele. In 1872 Khama III became chief of the Bamangwato. He was the son of Chief Sekgoma, the only Batswana chief who had succeeded in turning back the Matabele. Up to that time, the Batswana had no permanent contact with Europeans, except for

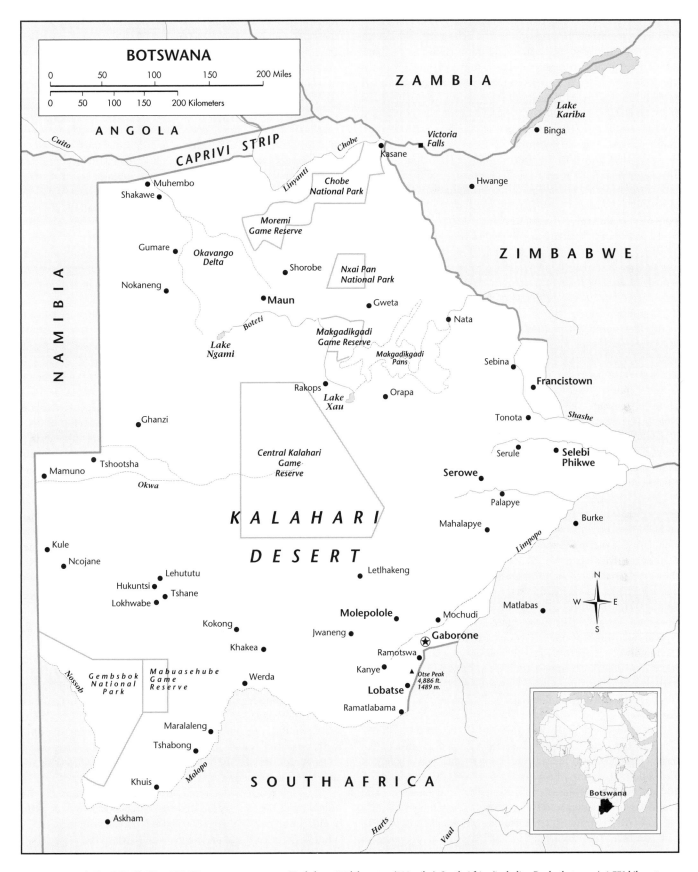

BOTSWANA

Scale: 0 – 50 – 100 – 150 – 200 Miles
0 – 50 – 100 – 150 – 200 Kilometers

ANGOLA

ZAMBIA

NAMIBIA

ZIMBABWE

SOUTH AFRICA

CAPRIVI STRIP

Cuito

Chobe

Linyanti

Victoria Falls

Lake Kariba

Binga

Kasane

Hwange

Muhembo

Shakawe

Chobe National Park

Moremi Game Reserve

Gumare

Okavango Delta

Nokaneng

Shorobe

Nxai Pan National Park

Maun

Gweta

Nata

Boteti

Lake Ngami

Makgadikgadi Game Reserve

Makgadikgadi Pans

Sebina

Francistown

Rakops

Lake Xau

Orapa

Tonota

Shashe

Ghanzi

Central Kalahari Game Reserve

Serule

Selebi Phikwe

Serowe

Tshootsha

Mamuno

Okwa

Palapye

Mahalapye

Burke

K A L A H A R I

D E S E R T

Limpopo

Kule

Ncojane

Lehututu

Hukuntsi

Tshane

Lokhwabe

Letlhakeng

Matlabas

Molepolole

Mochudi

Kokong

Jwaneng

Khakea

Gaborone

Ramotswa

Kanye

Otse Peak 4,886 ft. 1489 m.

Werda

Nossob

Gembsbok National Park

Mabuasehube Game Reserve

Lobatse

Ramatlabama

Maralaleng

Tshabong

Molopo

Khuis

Askham

Harts

Vaal

N W E S

Botswana

LOCATION: 17°47′ to 26°54′S; 20° to 29°21′E. BOUNDARY LENGTHS: Zimbabwe, 813 kilometers (505 miles); South Africa (including Bophuthatswana), 1,778 kilometers (1,105 miles); Namibia (South West Africa), 1,461 kilometers (908 miles). LOCATION: 17°47′ to 26°54′S; 20° to 29°21′E. BOUNDARY LENGTHS: Zimbabwe, 813 kilometers (505 miles); South Africa, 1,840 kilometers (1,141 miles); Namibia, 1,360 kilometers (843 miles).

the missionaries Robert and Mary Moffat and David Livingstone, who had established missions in the first half of the 19th century. But with increased exploration and the partition of southern Africa among the European powers, hostility developed between the Batswana and the Boer trekkers from the Transvaal. Khama III appealed to the United Kingdom for assistance, and in 1885 the whole of what was then known as Bechuanaland was proclaimed to be under the protection of Queen Victoria. The territory south of the Molopo River was constituted a crown colony called British Bechuanaland, and in 1895 it was incorporated into South Africa. The northern part of the territory, the Bechuanaland Protectorate, remained under the protection of the British crown, the powers of which, beginning in 1891, were exercised by the high commissioner in South Africa. The South African Act of Union of 1909, which created the Union (now Republic) of South Africa, provided for the eventual transfer to South Africa of Bechuanaland and the two other High Commission Territories, Basutoland and Swaziland, despite their requests to the contrary. The provision was dropped in 1961, after the withdrawal of South Africa from the Commonwealth.

The first significant political progress was made in 1921–22 with the creation of European and African advisory councils, added to which was a joint advisory council. In 1961, executive and legislative councils were created. A major step on the road to independence was taken in 1965 with the implementation of Bechuanaland's self-government constitution under Seretse Khama, the former chief-designate of the Bamangwato, who had become prime minister after Bechuanaland's first general elections. Final constitutional talks were held in London in February 1966, and on 30 September 1966, under the leadership of President Khama, the newly named Republic of Botswana came into being.

On 18 October 1969 the BDP, under the leadership of Sir Seretse Khama, was returned to power in the general elections, and he was sworn in for a second term as president on 22 October. Khama was reelected president after the BDP won 27 out of 32 regular elective seats in the National Assembly in national elections held on 26 October 1974. During this first decade of independence, Botswana refused to support the UN sanctions against South Africa because, although officially opposed to apartheid, Botswana recognized its own economic dependence on South Africa. Following the 1969 elections, President Khama banned the import of goods from the white minority regime in Rhodesia (now Zimbabwe). Tensions were high in the 1970s as Botswana harbored 20,000 refugees from Rhodesia, and Rhodesian forces several times crossed into Botswana on "hot pursuit" raids against guerrillas.

In elections held in October 1979, the BDP won 29 of the 32 elective seats, and Khama was elected to a fourth presidential term. He died in 1980 and was succeeded by Vice President Quett Ketumile Joni Masire, who was elected to a full five-year term on 10 September 1984. Masire was reelected on 7 October 1989 and the BDP won 31 and the BNF 3 of the elected assembly seats.

South Africa repeatedly, but fruitlessly, pressed Botswana to sign a mutual-security agreement, and it accused Botswana of harboring insurgents opposed to the Pretoria regime and allowing them to mount acts of terrorism and sabotage against South Africa, a charge Botswana denied. An attack by South African commandos on 14 June 1985, aimed at South African refugees,

killed at least 15 people in Gaborone. Further South African border violations and attacks on targets in Botswana took place during 1986, but such incursions had ended by 1988. In 1992 the two countries established formal diplomatic relations.

Before the 1994 legislative elections, the assembly was expanded to 44 seats, 40 of which would be elected, with the majority party given the right to appoint the remaining 4 seats. The opposition maneuvered before the election, attempting to form a broad coalition to unseat the BDP, which had so dominated the country since independence. Many opposition politicians insisted on electoral reforms, specifically the introduction of absentee balloting (20% of the population were migrant workers) and the lowering of the voting age from 21 to 18. On 15 October of that year, the elections were held and the BDP won a significant majority of seats in the assembly. The assembly named Masire president on 17 October. In November 1995, amidst worsening economic conditions and civil unrest, the government announced constitutional reforms, which limited the president to two terms, although a stipulation was added that the rule would not apply to the sitting president. The voting age was also lowered to 18, but no action was taken to introduce absentee balloting.

On 1 April 1998 Festus Mogae succeeded Quett Masire after the latter stepped down. Mogae was subsequently elected president in the 16 October 1999 polls with 54.3% of the National Assembly vote. He faced a number of issues such as environmental degradation, the need to diversify the economy, and political power struggles within the ruling party. In 2004 Mogae was reelected when the BDP won 51.7 % of popular votes and obtained 44 seats in the new parliament. In 2008 Mogae stepped down. After rejecting a proposal that the president be elected directly by the citizenry, parliament appointed Seretse Khama Ian Khama, the son of Sir Seretse Khama, the first president of Botswana, to succeed Mogae. He was inaugurated in April 2008. A total of 57 seats in the parliament were contested in the 2009 general election. The election was won by the BDP with 53.26 % of popular votes and obtained 45 seats in the new parliament. The largest opposition party, the BNF, won 21.94 % of the popular vote and 6 seats. The Botswana Congress Party (BCP) won 19.5% of the popular vote and 4 seats. Voter turnout in the 2009 general election was 76.71%. President Seretse Khama Ian Khama was elected president, extending his term by five years. The elections came as Botswana weathered a troubled economy, contracting at 10% in the midst of the global economic crisis, while citizens struggled with unemployment and decreased wages. In May-July 2010 seven BDP parliamentarians and the lone independent changed their membership to the newly created Botswana Movement for Democracy (BMD). In August 2010 two BMD members returned to the BDP, leaving the BMD with six seats. Regionally, the Botswana Democratic Party carries a reputation of effectively managing the country, the economy, and shrewdly attracting foreign investment.

Although much of Botswana's economy is based upon the diamond trade, the country has undertaken an effort to reduce its dependence on the industry; safari-based tourism is an increasingly important sector for Botswana in its quest for economic diversification. The government wants ethnic group members to move to villages, so that their ancestral lands may be developed for tourism. However, in December 2006, after a four-year trial, a group of bushmen won the right to keep their ancestral lands. During

Festus Mogae's decade-long tenure as president, Botswana's economy grew at a vibrant pace.

13 GOVERNMENT

Under the 1965 constitution, as subsequently modified, Botswana is a republic. It is Africa's longest continuous multiparty democracy. The president is the chief of state, chief executive, and commander-in-chief of the armed forces. He is elected by a simple majority of the National Assembly. The president appoints a cabinet from among the National Assembly members, including the vice president, who also serves as a cabinet minister. The president also has the power to declare war, and he can summon or dissolve the National Assembly at any time. He can veto any bill, but if it is passed again within six months, he must either sign it or dissolve the Assembly.

The bicameral parliament consists of a National Assembly and a House of Chiefs. Both the President and members of parliament are elected for five-year terms. The National Assembly comprises 63 seats—57 are directly elected members, 4 are appointed by the majority party and 2, the president and attorney general, serve as ex-officio members. After a no-confidence vote, the Assembly must be dissolved, or the president must resign. The House of Chiefs is largely advisory and consists of the chiefs of the eight principal ethnic groups, four chiefs elected from minority districts, and three others elected by the House. Any proposed bill relating to matters of tribal concern must be referred to the House of Chiefs before the Assembly can pass it. It was chaired by Chief Puso Gaborone beginning on 18 January 2009. Gaborone was still chief as of January 2012. All citizens of Botswana aged 18 and over are eligible to vote.

14 POLITICAL PARTIES

Botswana has had multiparty competition since independence, although the BDP, founded in late 1961 as the Bechuanaland Democratic Party by Seretse Khama, has won every election from 1966 to 2004. The BDP gained prominence by advocating a gradual approach to independence through democracy, nonracialism, and a multiparty state. While maintaining opposition to apartheid, the BDP acknowledged Botswana's economic dependence on apartheid South Africa and the need to maintain friendly relations. Other parties included the Botswana People's Party (BPP), founded in 1960; the Botswana Independence Party (BIP), founded in 1964 under the leadership of Motsamai Mpho; and the BNF, which put up its first candidates in 1969.

In the March 1965 elections, the BDP won 28 of the 31 contested seats, and the BPP took the other 3. Seretse Khama became prime minister and appointed Quett Masire as deputy prime minister.

In the elections on 26 October 1974, the ruling BDP raised its total of elective seats to 27, while the BNF won 2 seats, the BPP 2, and the BIP 1. In the elections of October 1979, the BDP won 29 seats, the BNF 2, and the BIP 1. In elections held in September 1984, the BDP won 29 seats, the BNF 4, and the BPP 1. The division in the October 1989 elections was BDP 31 and BNF 3. Since then, the opposing parties, largely concentrated in urban areas, formed a common front and threatened to boycott the 1994 elections unless electoral reforms were enacted. Principal among these demands were that the voting age be lowered from 21 to 18 and absentee balloting be allowed. 20% of the country's electorate were migrant workers. However, the coalition collapsed before the election and the BNF ran alone, winning 13 of the 40 contested seats, with the BDP taking the rest. The Assembly was enlarged to 44 seats prior to balloting with four seats appointed by the majority.

In the parliamentary elections held on 16 October 1999, the BDP won 33 out of the 40 parliamentary seats. The remaining seats went to the Botswana National Front (6 seats) and the Botswana Congress Party (1 seat). A number of minor parties formed a coalition, but did not capture any seats. These were the United Action Party, the Independence Freedom Party (IFP), and the Botswana Progressive Union (BPU).

In the parliamentary elections held on 30 October 2004, the BDP won 51.73% of the popular vote and 44 of the 57 seats contested. BNF won 26.06% of the popular vote and 12 seats; and BCP won 16.62% of the popular vote and only 1 seat. The other five, smaller, political parties that contested did not win any seat but in total won about 5% of the popular vote. These included the Botswana Alliance Movement (BAM—2.84% of the popular vote), Botswana People's Party (1.91% of the popular vote), the New Democratic Front (0.78% of the popular vote), and the Marx, Engels, Lenin, Stalin Movement of Botswana (MELS—0.03% of the vote).

In accordance with constitutional guidelines, Mogae stepped down in 2008 after ten years in office. He was succeeded by Vice President Seretse Khama Ian Khama, also of the BDP. In the October 2009 elections, the BDP continued its 43-year political reign, picking up 53.3% of the vote and 45 seats. Ian Khama was reelected, extending his term by five years. The BNF earned 21.9% of the vote and six seats, followed by the BCP with 19.1% and four seats. The BAM won one seat (2.2% of the vote) and one seat was earned by an independent. Between May-July 2010, seven BDP parliamentarians and an independent parliamentarian changed their membership to the newly created Botswana Movement for Democracy (BMD). However in August 2010, two BMD members returned to the BDP, leaving the BMD with six seats.

15 LOCAL GOVERNMENT

Local government is carried out by nine district councils and five town councils: Gaborone, Francistown, Lobatse, Jwaneng, and Selebi-Phikwe.

Executive authority in each district is vested in the district commissioner, who is appointed by the central government. The commissioner is assisted by the district council and the district development committee, which are partly appointed and partly elected. Botswana also has traditional village councils, called *kgotla*, which serve as public forums at which villagers can express opinions.

16 JUDICIAL SYSTEM

The 1965 constitution provides for a high court, a court of appeal, and lower courts (magistrate courts are located in each district). The chief justice, appointed by the president, is chairman of the Judicial Services Commission, which advises the president on the appointment of other judges and magistrates. The African Courts Proclamation of 1961 provides for courts with competence in matters of tribal law and custom, presided over by chiefs and headmen. A court of appeals for such cases was created in 1986. The customary courts handle marital and property disputes as well as minor offenses. The judiciary is independent of the executive and the legislative branches. The legal system is based on Roman-Dutch law and local customary law.

¹⁷ARMED FORCES

The International Institute for Strategic Studies reports that armed forces in Botswana totaled 9,000 members in 2011. The force is comprised of 8,500 from the army and 500 from the air force. Armed forces represent 1.1% of the labor force in Botswana. Defense spending totaled $941.9 million and accounted for 3.3% of the GDP.

¹⁸INTERNATIONAL COOPERATION

Botswana became a member of the UN on 17 October 1966 and is a member of the ECA and several nonregional specialized agencies. It is a member of the ACP, and the WTO (1995). It belongs to the Southern African Customs Union (with South Africa, Lesotho, Namibia, and Swaziland) and the Preferential Trade Area for East and Southern Africa. Botswana also participates in the African Development Bank, the Commonwealth of Nations, G-77, and the South African Development Community (SADC), which maintains a secretariat at Gaborone. In 2000 the United States and Botswana jointly established the International Law Enforcement Academy (ILEA) in Gaborone. Botswana is part of the Nonaligned Movement. In environmental cooperation, Botswana is part of the Basel Convention, the Convention on Biological Diversity, Ramsar, the Kyoto Protocol, the Montréal Protocol, the Nuclear Test Ban Treaty, and the UN Conventions on the Law of the Sea, Climate Change, and Desertification.

¹⁹ECONOMY

Most economists regard Botswana as one of Africa's major success stories. The GDP rate of change in Botswana, as of 2010, was 8.6%. Inflation stood at 7.1%, and unemployment was reported at 7.5%. The country's economy was dependent almost entirely on livestock production until the 1970s, when it became an important exporter of diamonds and other minerals. Then, the Botswana Development Corporation, adopting a conservative investment policy, actively sought foreign capital for investments in crop agriculture, tourism, and secondary industries. The rapid growth in diamond production helped Botswana achieve average high economic growth from independence through 2005. In 2005 it slowed somewhat to 3.3%, due to the Asian financial crisis and a cut in economic development spending. The impact of HIV/AIDS also continues to have an adverse effect on the economy. Despite its economic success, unofficial estimates place the unemployment rate at nearly 40%, with 30.3% of the population below the government established poverty line.

The diamond industry was developed in 1971 in cooperation with De Beers Consolidated Mines (Debswana). Botswana is the one of the world's largest producer of gem diamonds in value terms. It is also the one of the world's most diamond dependent economies. Diamond mining, which in 2006 stood at a record 34.3 million carats, accounts for more than one-third of Botswana's GDP and for 70–80% of export earnings. However, the industry took a hit in the midst of the global financial crisis as a result of lower demand. Botswana's diamond sales volume for 2009 was 37% lower than that of 2007. Demand has somewhat recovered, and Debswana planned to increase diamond production by 20% in 2011.

Botswana is the second largest mining producer by value in the world (South Africa is first). Botswana produces copper-nickel matte, and has significant coal deposits. Botswana also has exploitable deposits of platinum, gold, and silver. Exploration for petroleum and natural gas deposits has been underway in western Botswana. The country continues to encourage foreign direct investment in non-mining sectors of the economy, including light manufacturing, tourism, financial services, and pharmaceuticals.

In spite of the gains recorded by the mining sector, more than half of the population is dependent on subsistence agriculture and livestock farming. Farming, however, is hindered by inadequate rainfall and poor soil. Commercial farms played a critical role in agricultural and livestock production. Agriculture meets only a small portion of food needs and is a meager contributor to GDP, primarily through beef exports. Of Botswana's total output of sorghum, maize, millet, beans and pulses, 37% was produced by 100 of the 360 commercial farms. Ownership of the national herd of cattle was highly concentrated: 5% of households owned over 50%.

Although Botswana has an advanced infrastructure with good roads, communications, and dependable utilities, there is a general lack of technical and managerial skills among its workers.

In January 2010 the World Bank reported that Botswana's economy contracted by a sobering 8.3% in 2009. However, in the same report, the Global Monetary Organization offered a more encouraging forecast for 2010, predicting 4.8% growth for the year. The African Economic Outline reported that the economy was expected to grow 6.9% in 2011 and 7.0% in 2012.

²⁰INCOME

The CIA estimated that in 2010 the GDP of Botswana was $28.49 billion. The CIA defines GDP as the value of all final goods and services produced within a nation in a given year and computed on the basis of purchasing power parity (PPP) rather than value as measured on the basis of the rate of the exchange based on current dollars. The per capita GDP was estimated at $14,000. The annual growth rate of GDP was 8.6%. The average inflation rate was 7.1%. It was estimated that agriculture accounted for 2.3% of GDP, industry 45.8%, and services 51.9%.

According to the World Bank, remittances from citizens living abroad totaled $87.9 million or about $43 per capita and accounted for approximately 0.3% of GDP.

The World Bank reported that in 2009, household consumption in Botswana totaled $5.2 billion or about $2,498 per capita, measured in current US dollars rather than PPP. Household consumption includes expenditures of individuals, households, and nongovernmental organizations on goods and services, excluding the purchases of dwellings. It was estimated that household consumption was growing at an average annual rate of 7%.

The World Bank estimated that Botswana, with 0.03% of the world's population, accounted for 0.04% of the world's GDP. By comparison, the United States, with 4.85% of the world's population, accounted for 22.51% of world GDP.

As of 2011 the most recent study by the World Bank reported that actual individual consumption in Botswana was 32.2% of the GDP and accounted for 0.01% of world consumption. By comparison, the United States accounted for 25.44% of world individual consumption. The World Bank also estimated that 9.9% of Botswana's GDP was spent on food and beverages, 5.3% on housing and household furnishings, 2.0% on clothes, 2.1% on health, 4.2% on transportation, 0.9% on communications, 0.8% on recreation, 0.1% on restaurants and hotels, and 1.6% on miscellaneous goods and services and purchases from abroad.

21 LABOR

As of 2009 Botswana had a total labor force of 1.225 million people. Botswana's unions are concentrated mostly in the mining sector, and to a lesser extent in the country's railway and banking sectors. In 2010 only police, military, and prison personnel were prohibited from joining unions. An employment act controls employment contracts, work by women and children, wage guarantees, conditions of work, and paid holidays. The law severely restricts the right to strike. There was a government set minimum wage of $0.58 per hour in 2010 for most full-time workers in the private sector, which cannot provide a living wage to a worker and their family. However, most jobs in the formal sector of the economy paid in excess of the minimum wage. There is a maximum 48-hour workweek, although 40 hours per week can be found in most private sector jobs. Public sector employees had a 48 hour workweek. Although there are minimum safety and health standards, because of a lack of resources they are not regularly enforced.

22 AGRICULTURE

Crop production is hampered by traditional farming methods, recurrent drought, erosion, and disease. Roughly 1% of the total land is currently farmed, and most of the land under cultivation is in the eastern region. Major crops include sorghum, maize, millet, beans, sunflowers, and groundnuts. In 2009 cereal production amounted to 55,850 tons and grain was often imported from South Africa. Fruit production amounted to 6,000 tons, and vegetable production 25,821 tons.

Agricultural research has been devoted to soil conservation, grazing experiments, and developing and distributing improved strains of grain. The construction of dams and the drilling of boreholes to tap underground water are continuing government programs. In early 1990, the government changed its official agricultural policy to emphasize the production only of those foodstuffs that can be raised economically. The Arable Lands Development Program and the Tribal Grazing Land Policy are government programs designed to help farmers in communal areas.

In August 2009 the United States African Development Foundation (USADF) extended a grant of $100,000 to the Komku Development Trust, a community organization that will assist the herders of seven ethnic San communities in western Botswana in making the transition from subsistence cattle rearing to organized cattle ranching. The program will provide a link between ranchers and the Botswana Meat Commission, allowing for maximum commercial benefits to the ranchers. Projects such as these, beginning with the grassroots organizations, have the potential to create new jobs, increase income for farmers, and improve living conditions in some of the most impoverished communities.

23 ANIMAL HUSBANDRY

The UN Food and Agriculture Organization (FAO) reported that Botswana dedicated 25.6 million hectares (63.3 million acres) to permanent pasture or meadow in 2009. During that year, Botswana had 2.5 million head of cattle. Other livestock included goats, horses, and donkeys. Cattle are valued for wealth and prestige and are used in paying for a bride, but there is little of the cultural prohibition against selling cattle found in some other parts of Africa. Herds are grazed in the open veldt where water and grass are available; the borehole-drilling program is extending the available grazing land. A gradual upgrading of stock quality has been achieved through selective breeding, culling, and controlled grazing. A system of disease-control fences has been installed. A vaccine institute was opened in 1981 to deal with the threat of foot-and-mouth disease. In the mid-1980s, the Botswana Meat Commission's plant at Lobatse was the largest export abattoir in Africa. In 2010 meat production totaled 67,000 tons, with beef accounting for more than half of the total. Much of Botswana's annual beef production is exported to South Africa and Western Europe. Beef and beef products are Botswana's second-largest export earner (after minerals).

24 FISHING

Botswana is landlocked, but some fishing for local consumption is carried out by the inhabitants of the Limpopo River Valley and the Okavango region. In 2008, the annual capture totaled 86 tons according to the UN FAO.

25 FORESTRY

Approximately 20% of Botswana is covered by forest. The indigenous forests of northeast Ngamiland include the valuable mukwa, mukusi, and mopane woods. Some small-scale exploitation has taken place. The UN FAO estimated the 2009 roundwood production at cu m (3.71 million cu ft).

26 MINING

Botswana, home to the world's largest gem diamond mine, is a leading producer of diamonds by value. In 2009, Botswana was the third largest producer diamonds, after the Democratic Republic of Congo and Australia, with production of 17.7 million carats and sales of $1.7 billion that year. Nickel, cobalt, and soda ash production also play a significant role in the economy. The minerals industry employs over 13,000 workers, of whom about 50% are involved in mining and quarrying. The northeast contains copper, nickel, and precious metals; the northwest has copper and silver; and the south holds base and precious metals. Other valuable minerals produced included agate, clay, coal, cobalt, gold, salt, sand, silver, soda ash, and construction stone. Major mines are situated in regions with few job opportunities. Mineral rights (separate from surface rights) are vested in the state. For significant mineral operations, the government usually exercises its legal right to acquire mines for free an equity interest of 15–25%. Royalties are collected on the sales of certain minerals, such as 3% on base metals, 5% on gold, and 10% on diamonds. The 1999 Mines and Minerals Act, designed to promote foreign investment, diversify the economy, and reduce reliance on the diamond industry, continued to vest all mineral rights in the state, but introduced a new "retention license." The government retained an option to acquire up to a 15% interest in new ventures on commercial terms, thus abolishing its previous free equity participation. Favorable geologic environment and mineral investment climate, political stability, and low tax rates should make Botswana a target for foreign mineral investment.

The government maintained an equity position in most of the major mining companies, but the industry was operated, for the most part, on a privately owned free-market basis. In a 50–50 joint partnership with De Beers Centenary, the government owned Debswana Diamond, the country's largest mining company.

De Beers Botswana Mining (Debswana) and Botswana Concessions (BCL), both partly owned by the government, developed major mineral fields in the eastern and central regions in the 1970s. Starting in 1981 the Debswana diamond mine at Orapa had to stockpile diamonds to halt the decline in world prices. The world's largest gem diamond mine was opened at Jwaneng in 1982, and processing capacity was increased in 1996 by the addition of a fourth treatment line. Jwaneng, the richest diamond mine in Africa, treated 12 million tons of ore in 2009. Reserves and resources in Jwaneng's three main kimberlite pipes were reported to be 287.6 million tons at a grade of 143.6 carats per hundred tons. The Letlhakane Mine recovered 1 million carats in 2009. The Orapa Mine recovered 13 million carats in 2009. Total reserves and resources at Orapa were reported to be 652.9 million tons at a grade of 49 carats per hundred tons. Debswana completed an expansion at Orapa in 2000 that was designed to double production to 12 million carats per year and treat an additional 8.9 million tons per year of ore. It was expected to allow production from the open pit for 30 years, with the potential of extending the mine life by another 20 or 30 years by shifting to underground mining. The expanded facilities included a completely automated recovery plant (CARP), a 15-story building in which only X-ray technology is used to recover diamonds and no human picking or sorting is done. Botswana's diamond output for 2009 was 17.7 million carats, down from 34.3 million carats in 2006.

BCL developed a nickel-copper smelter at Selebi-Phikwe in the 1970s and owns the Phikwe, Selebi, and Selebi North mines. National output for mined copper in 2009 was estimated at 27,700 metric tons; for mined nickel was estimated at 32,740 metric tons; and for smelted cobalt, 330 metric tons. BCL's smelter produced 13,600 metric tons of copper and 24,000 metric tons of nickel. Reserves were reported at 27 million tons for BCL at a grade of 0.86% copper and 0.84% nickel, and for Tati Nickel's Phoenix Mine at 46 million tons at a grade of 0.32% copper and 0.56% nickel.

A brine mining and treatment facility at Sua Pan produced 264,000 metric tons of soda ash in 2009, and 170,000 metric tons of salt from natural soda ash, down from 243,945 metric tons in 2005. The country produced an estimated 30,000 kg of other precious gemstones, principally agate, in 2009. Gold output totaled 1,530 kg in 2009, down from 2,709 kg in 2005.

27 ENERGY AND POWER

Most electric power is generated thermally in installations run by the Botswana Power Corp., a public enterprise established in 1970. Electric generating capacity consists of the 132 MW Morupole coal-fired plant and the 60 MW coal-fired plant at Selebi-Phikwe.

The World Bank reported in 2008 that Botswana produced 631 million kWh of electricity and consumed 2.89 billion kWh, or 1,398 kWh per capita. Roughly 67% of energy came from fossil fuels. Coal production in 2007 consisted entirely of the bituminous type and totaled 1,000,000 tons. Coal is mined solely at Morupole by Anglo American, mostly for the generation of electricity. In 2008, per capita oil consumption was 1,102 kg.

In June 2010, the government secured a loan of $186 million from the African Development Bank for the construction of the Morupule B coal-fired power plant. The total cost of the 600 MW power station and accompanying distribution lines and substations is estimated at $1.7 billion. Earlier in 2010, the government secured a loan of $136 million from the World Bank and $825 million from a consortium that includes the Industrial and Commercial Bank of China. The project is expected to be up and running by 2012.

In April 2010 Botswana announced plans to open an ambitious biofuels processing plant in the country. The effort has been designed to provide green sector jobs and reduce the carbon footprint of a country heavily reliant on coal for energy. The plant will be funded by the National Petroleum Fund and was set to open in 2012. At first, meat tallow and used cooking oil will be used as the primary fuels. The plant will eventually shift to jatropha oil, which can be harvested at local plantations. Organizers said the plant will produce more than 13,000,000 gallons (50,000,000 liters) of biofuel each year.

28 INDUSTRY

Botswana has a small, but dynamic, manufacturing sector, which contributed approximately 7.9 % to the country's GDP in 2010. Average growth in this sector during the 1990s was 3.8% per year, and it was seen in the early 2000s as having the most growth potential in the country. The sector has diversified into textiles, beverages, chemicals, metals, plastics, and electrical products. The government parastatal, the Botswana Development Corp., has declined in significance relative to private initiatives, but still is a major promoter of industrial development with interests in brewing, sugar, furniture, clothing, tourism, milling, and concrete. Though promising, industrial development is limited by a small domestic market, weak infrastructure, import dependence, and small skilled labor force. Indeed this sector has seen slow growth since 2000, following the closure of the Hyundai vehicle-assembly plant and the emphasis on manufacturing as the main source of future growth has been questioned.

Local coal supplies the fuel required for Botswana's energy sector. Peak requirements are generally supplied by the South African grid. In 1991 Botswana also linked to the Zambian and Zimbabwean grids. Botswana has no hydroelectric power resources, but solar power has potential as an energy source.

The construction industry was the fastest growing sector of the economy in the 1980s, and rapid urbanization created a need for low-income housing. This sector has decreased in importance, however, as there has been a shortage of building material and supplies. On the other hand, the chemicals industry has expanded; soda ash (for use in steel, glass, paper, and detergent manufacturing industries) is an important commodity, and Botswana Ash is the leading soda ash company operating in the country. The production of copper and nickel has contributed to an increase in the local production of electrical components. The motor industry is growing, with vehicle assembly, tire manufacturing, leather finishing, paint manufacturing, batteries, and the manufacture of spare parts being government priorities and opportunities for foreign investment.

Diamond mining is the engine of growth in Botswana. Diamond mining has fueled much of the economic expansion and in 2011 accounted for more than one-third of GDP, as well as 80% of export earnings. Mining and livestock production remain the primary economic activities. Botswana has been referred to as the world's largest diamond producer in terms of the quality and grade of its diamonds. The country's growth is heavily dependent upon developments in the diamond industry, which in turn is affected by global economic conditions.

29 SCIENCE AND TECHNOLOGY

The University of Botswana (founded in 1976), the Botswana Agricultural College (founded in 1967), and Botswana Polytechnic, all located in Gaborone, offer training in science, agriculture, and engineering. In 1987–97, science and engineering students accounted for 37% of college and university enrollments. The Geological Survey of Botswana, founded in 1948, publishes mineral resource reports and bulletins. The World Bank reported in 2009 that there were no patent applications in science and technology in Botswana.

30 DOMESTIC TRADE

Small general stores usually carry a variety of items, but food, fuel, and clothing staples make up most of their stock. There are also a few wholesalers, and some traders act as local agents for larger firms. To augment their incomes, other traders operate postal or transport services, restaurants, butcheries, and bakeries. The traders play an important role as middlemen between the local livestock and crop producers and the slaughterhouses, factories, and exporters. There are also a number of South African and US franchises in Botswana, including fast food, supermarkets and department stores. Major US investors include Owens Corning, H.J. Heinz, Coca-Cola, IBM, Xerox, and Kentucky Fried Chicken. Such private sector foreign investments are encouraged by low corporate taxes and no prohibitions of foreign ownership. The government has eliminated all foreign exchange controls.

Business hours are 7:30 a.m. to 4:30 p.m., Monday through Friday with a 45-minute lunch break, and most retail businesses are also open Saturdays and Sundays until midday.

31 FOREIGN TRADE

Botswana imported $4.518 billion worth of goods and services in 2008, while exporting $4.419 billion worth of goods and services. Major import partners in 2009 were South Africa, the European Union (EU), and the United States. Its major export partners were the EU and South Africa. The government of Botswana has increased economic integration with the SADC, ratifying a Trade Protocol to ease trade barriers. With recurrent drought and only 5% arable land, Botswana imports much of its food and other basic needs, primarily through South Africa. Indirectly, the United

Balance of Payments – Botswana (2010)

(In millions of US dollars)

Current Account		**45.9**
Balance on goods		-208.5
Imports	-4,841.7	
Exports	4,633.3	
Balance on services		-482.1
Balance on income		-242.6
Current transfers		979.0
Capital Account		**19.0**
Financial Account		**-634.6**
Direct investment abroad		-0.3
Direct investment in Botswana		265.0
Portfolio investment assets		396.8
Portfolio investment liabilities		17.8
Financial derivatives		...
Other investment assets		-1,217.8
Other investment liabilities		-96.2
Net Errors and Omissions		**609.5**
Reserves and Related Items		**-39.8**

(…) data not available or not significant.

SOURCE: *Balance of Payment Statistics Yearbook 2011*, Washington, DC: International Monetary Fund, 2011.

States accounts for a sizeable portion of Botswana's imports (manufactured goods) and exports (diamonds).

Exports fell as a result of the 1997 East Asian financial recession, especially diamond exports, which dropped from $2.1 billion in 1997 to 1.7 billion in 1998. However, between 1999 and 2000 exports rebounded at a rate of 7.7%. By 2010 Botswana's exports were estimated to be $4.91 billion. Imports in 1997 and 1998 were $1.6 billion both years. These had risen to $4.767 billion by 2010. In 2003 diamonds accounted for 82.5% of exports and copper and nickel 4.9%, with the remainder being exports of beef, soda ash, and textiles. Leading imports included foodstuffs; vehicles and transport equipment; textiles; and petroleum products. Over the years Botswana has maintained a positive and healthy balance of payments.

32 BALANCE OF PAYMENTS

The CIA reported that in 2004 the purchasing power parity of Botswana's exports was $2.94 billion, while imports totaled $2.26 billion resulting in a trade surplus of $680 million. Because of the substantial diamond exports, Botswana always reports healthy trade surpluses. After falling slightly in 2001, diamond exports rose sharply in 2002 due to increased global demand. In 2004 international prices for diamond were raised three times which netted Botswana $2.8 billion in diamond exports, 95% of all export earnings. In 2010 Botswana had a foreign trade deficit of $952 million, amounting to 1.9% of GDP.

33 BANKING AND SECURITIES

Prior to 1976 Botswana belonged to the South African Monetary Area. Its currency, like those of Lesotho and Swaziland, was issued by the South African Reserve Bank. On 23 August 1976, however, the central Bank of Botswana was established, and Botswana began issuing its own currency. The Bank of Botswana has responsibility for administering exchange control delegated to it by the

Ministry of Finance and Development Planning. In 1999 the government launched a new loan guarantee scheme to support new, small businesses in non-diamond enterprises by providing partial security for loans.

In 2009 the discount rate, the interest rate at which the central bank lends to financial institutions in the short term, was 10%. The commercial bank prime lending rate, the rate at which banks lend to customers, was 11.46% in 2010.

In November 1996 the Bank of Botswana relaxed controls that prevented the dual listing of foreign companies on the Botswana Stock Exchange (BSE). Prior to this, any investment by a Botswanan-based entity in a foreign company was regarded as an external investment covered by the relevant rates and limits. There became free transferability of shares between the BSE and any other stock exchanges listing the shares. Nine companies had dual listed by the end of 1998, and the BSE had recorded a growth rate of 14%. As of November 2011 there were 35 market listings and 3 stock indexes.

In 1998 an investment bank was licensed; Investec Bank Botswana was set up to provide merchant banking and investment advisory services. The Botswana Development Corporation (BDC) and the National Development Bank (NDB) offer specialized development assistance.

[34] INSURANCE

The South African insurance giant, Metropolitan Life, established First Health Medical Administrator in Botswana in mid-September 1996. It launched Metropolitan Life of Botswana in 1997 in a joint venture with the Botswana Development Corporation (BDC), and had a 25% stake in the company. In a similar move several years ago, BDC established Botswana Insurance Holdings (BIHL) in conjunction with St. Paul (USA) and African Life. St. Paul Fire and Marine of Minnesota bought out Botswana General Insurance in November 1997.

[35] PUBLIC FINANCE

About half of the government's revenues in 1998 came from the diamond industry with another 20% from returns on foreign reserves. Tourism was becoming increasingly important, accounting for 12% of GDP in 2000. In 2010 the budget of Botswana included $4.165 billion in public revenue and $5.888 billion in public expenditures. The budget deficit amounted to 10.7% of GDP. Public debt was 22.6% of GDP, with $2.496 billion of the debt held by foreign entities.

The CIA estimated that in 2010 Botswana's central government took in revenues of approximately $4.656 billion and had expenditures of $5.638 billion. Public debt in 2010 amounted to 19.9 % of GDP.

[36] TAXATION

The basic corporate tax rate in 2010 was 15% (plus a 10% surcharge). For manufacturing companies, approved as such by the Minister of Finance, a reduced rate of 15% (5% company tax and 10% surcharge) applies. A withholding tax of 15% is assessed on the payment of all dividends and on the payment of interest on offshore loans. Taxes on such capital income may be reduced or eliminated in double taxation treaties. The capital gains rate is 25% and is assessed on 100% of the gains from real estate transactions

and on 50% of the gains from transactions in moveable property. Only 75% of the gain from the sale of shares in a company is subject to the tax. However, capital gains from the sale of shares of a company listed on the Botswana Stock Exchange are tax-exempt.

The income tax law establishes for individual incomes progressive rates ranging up to 25%, reduced from 30%. A local government tax is paid to the district or town council to finance social and sanitary services.

As of 7 January 2002 a value-added tax (VAT) with a standard rate of 10%, replaced Botswana's 10% sales tax which was imposed on fuel, liquor, cigarettes, motor vehicles, computers, domestic electrical appliances, and other consumer and luxury goods. The VAT had been raised to 12% by 2011.

[37] CUSTOMS AND DUTIES

Botswana belongs to a customs union called the Southern African Customs Union (SACU), with South Africa, Lesotho, Swaziland, and Namibia. South Africa levies and collects most of the customs, sales, and excise duties for the five member states, paying a share of the revenues to the other four. In addition, all customs duties are eliminated among the five countries. The SACU implements high protectionist tariffs on countries outside of the club, though, disheartening potential nonmember investors. In 1996 the SADC launched a free trade agreement for the elimination of tariff and nontariff trade barriers between its member countries (Angola, Democratic Republic of the Congo, Lesotho, Malawi, Mauritius, Mozambique, Namibia, Seychelles, South Africa, Swaziland, Tanzania, Zambia, and Zimbabwe).

South Africa has put in place a VAT for imports coming into the SACU from outside, but its implementation on Botswana's borders has so far been unsuccessful. Additionally, as a signatory of the General Agreement on Tariffs and Trades (GATT) and a member of the World Trade Organization, Botswana and the rest of the SACU were charged to reduce tariffs.

[38] FOREIGN INVESTMENT

Since independence in 1966, Botswana has been open to foreign investment. With the discovery of diamonds in 1967, this has also meant an economy dependent on diamond mining and, more importantly, the diamond monopoly strictly maintained by the De Beers Company. Highly developed auditing and security systems, developed to preserve the diamond monopoly, helped minimize corruption in Botswana and give its bonds the highest rating in Africa. Foreign direct investment (FDI) in Botswana was a net inflow of $251.6 million according to World Bank figures published in 2009. FDI represented 2.13% of GDP.

From 1966 to 1999, Botswana had the highest average growth rate in the world (9%). This did not translate into significant foreign investment outside of the mining sector, however, nor into a solution for chronic high unemployment (officially 21%, but generally thought to be closer to 40%). Moreover, recent controversy about "conflict diamonds" and the HIV/AIDS epidemic in Botswana have led to substantial divestment by traditional investors, De Beers of South Africa and Anglo American of the United Kingdom.

The government began actively encouraging foreign investment in the mid-1980s. Government policies offered attractive tax rates (10% on corporate income), including a five-year tax holiday, capital grants on new projects, and duty-free access to the large South African market (source of 80% of foreign direct investment). Botswana also enjoys duty-free access to the European Community for most of its products (source of 15% of foreign direct investment). Its liberal policies allow unrestricted repatriation of earnings and capital. Furthermore, it has a substantial financial assistance policy for foreign investors and has established an export-processing zone in Selebi-Phikwe. Investment law is scrupulously observed by the Botswana bureaucracy and courts. Investment incentives, including cash grants, have been offered to small and medium-scale investors for labor-intensive schemes, particularly outside urban areas. The complete liberalization of exchange controls occurred in February 1999.

In the late 1990s, with the exposure of the link between De Beers' purchases of uncontrolled raw diamonds to maintain its monopoly and socially corrosive brutality in diamond-producing countries, the diamond industry changed to a system of certified diamonds and a list of "Suppliers of Choice." Although Botswana's diamond mining company, Debswana, continued to be owned 50% by the Botswana government and 50% by De Beers Centenary, the latter, in 2002, became part of the private holding company De Beers SA, 45% owned by the London-based mining conglomerate Anglo-American, and 45% by the Oppenheimer Group. Botswana's two other major mining companies, Tati Nickel and BCL (copper, nickel, and cobalt), had become 85% owned and 50% owned respectively by LionOre Mining of Canada, to which Anglo-American had sold its shares.

The HIV/AIDS epidemic in Botswana, with over 24.8 % of the adult population estimated to be HIV positive in 2009, affects everything, including foreign investment. Anecdotal evidence suggests it has increased production and training costs for companies and reduced the pool of skilled labor available for foreign investors.

FDI is chiefly in mining. The largest investors have been the Anglo-American Corporation, which bought out De Beers, and LionOre of Canada, which then bought out Anglo-American interests.

Other areas of investment included specialty agricultural production; construction; and manufacturing of textile, health and beauty, agricultural and construction equipment products. The government seeks investments in infrastructure, telecommunications, tourism, and housing development.

Botswana's prudent financial and monetary policies have contributed to continued strong performance on Botswana's stock exchange.

[39] ECONOMIC DEVELOPMENT

Botswana has made job creation a top priority of government planning in the past few years. Although employment rates have grown, unemployment is formally estimated at 7%, but was closer to 40% in unofficial estimates in 2007.

The government has a long standing policy of promoting human capital development and health care. All education through the university level is free, but 18.8% of the population over 15 in 2009 was illiterate. Great importance is placed on the development of rural areas so as to reduce rural-urban migration.

In light of the limited resources, Botswana's government now follows "food security" agricultural policy of promoting only those foodstuffs that can be grown economically.

Botswana's long-term economic prospects are highly dependent on South Africa and its other southern African neighbors. The government has been a strong proponent of economic integration among the 15 members of the SADC. The organization's 2000 Trade Protocol called for the elimination of all tariff and nontariff barriers to trade by 2012 among the 11 countries signing the protocol.

Botswana has been rated the least-corrupt country in Africa, according to Transparency International. The country aims to diversify its economy away from minerals, and ecotourism is being promoted. Botswana has been a victim of the HIV/AIDS pandemic, and the government has taken steps to tackle the virus through prevention programs and the provision of advanced drug therapies to those infected. The Government of Botswana has put in place policies that enhance competitiveness, including a new Foreign Direct Investment Strategy, Competition Policy, Privatization Master Plan, and National Export Development Strategy.

[40] SOCIAL DEVELOPMENT

The first universal pension program was inaugurated in Botswana in 1996. It covers all residents aged 65 and older, and is funded completely by the government. It pays a flat-rate monthly pension, which is adjusted periodically according to the cost of living. Many social welfare needs are met through the provisions of tribal custom. Employed persons are covered by work injury laws, with the exclusion of casual workers and family labor. There are no statutory benefits for sickness and maternity. After 60 months of continuous employment, a severance unemployment benefit is available. Destitute residents are provided with a small monthly cash payment and food rations.

Traditional views of male dominance are pervasive in Botswana. Customary law allows men to physically punish their wives for wrongdoing and spousal abuse is common. Sexual harassment, rape, and other violence against women is widespread. Rape is especially serious considering the prevalence of HIV/AIDS. Women are accorded the same civil rights as men, but under traditional marriage laws, they require their husbands' consent to buy or sell property, obtain a loan, or sign a contract. There are legal provisions, however, that allow women to marry "out of common property" and thereby retain their legal rights. Polygamy is legal, but is not widely practiced.

While ethnic minorities are not subject to discrimination, some groups remain marginalized and underrepresented in government. Human rights are generally respected in Botswana. However, there are still reports of abusive police tactics, and prison conditions remain poor.

[41] HEALTH

The government stresses primary health care with emphasis on disease prevention and healthy living. According to the CIA, life expectancy in Botswana was 55 years in 2011. The country spent 16.6% of its GDP on healthcare, amounting to $612 per person. There were 3 physicians, 28 nurses and midwives, and 18 hospital beds per 10,000 inhabitants. The fertility rate was 2.8, while the infant mortality rate was 43 per 1,000 live births. In 2008, the maternal mortality rate, according to the World Bank, was 190 per 100,000 births. It was estimated that 94% of children were vaccinated against measles.

The major health problems are malnutrition and tuberculosis. As of 2007 malaria was prevalent. In 2007, there were 670 cases of tuberculosis per 100,000 people. Public health teams conduct tuberculosis and malaria control campaigns. It was estimated that 17% of children under five years of age were malnourished.

As if 2007 approximately 47.5% of married women were using contraception. Children one year of age were immunized as follows: diphtheria, pertussis, and tetanus, 97%; and measles, 90%.

The HIV/AIDS adult prevalence rate was 24.8% in 2009, the second highest in the world (after Swaziland). The rapid transmission of HIV in Botswana has been attributed to three main factors: the position of women in society, particularly their lack of power in negotiating sexual relationships; cultural attitudes to fertility; and social migration patterns. The government's goal was to have no new infections by 2016, and Botswana has been commended for being the first country in Africa to widely distribute antiretroviral drugs through its public health system.

42 HOUSING

There is no overcrowding in rural areas, but slums have developed in the larger towns. The Botswana Housing Corp., a public enterprise, concentrates its efforts on the main urban centers, where growth, therefore demand, is greatest. The 1999 National Policy on Housing has shifted some of the control of housing from government to private hands. Part of this policy includes the Poverty Alleviation and Housing Programme, a pilot program through which those who cannot afford to purchase a home might learn the skills necessary to build their own. This self-help policy is particularly helpful to rural residents.

Housing ranges from flats and bungalows to huts and all other structures intended for human use. Squatter-occupied "improvised" housing units account for about 2% of all housing. Of all housing units, about 30% were acquired through tribal authorities. Nearly 71% of the total land area in Botswana is under tribal control. Sanitation facilities included pit latrines and flush toilets; however, two-thirds of housing units had no facilities. The water supply is piped or drawn from wells, river beds, rivers, or other sources.

43 EDUCATION

In 2007, the World Bank estimated that 87% of age-eligible children in Botswana were enrolled in primary school. Secondary enrollment for age-eligible children stood at 60%. Tertiary enrollment was estimated at 8%. Overall, the CIA estimated that Botswana had a literacy rate of 81.2%. Public expenditure on education represented 8.9% of GDP.

The government aims to achieve universal education. Education is compulsory for students between the ages of 7 and 15. Education at the primary level lasts for seven years, though it is not compulsory. This is followed by three years of junior secondary school and two years of senior secondary school. Primary school enrollment in 2005 was estimated at about 84.5% of age-eligible students; 85% for boys and 84% for girls. In 2009 secondary school enrollment was about 55.9% of age-eligible students; 52.3% for boys and 59.5% for girls. It is estimated that about 93.3% of all students completed their primary education in 2005. The student-to-teacher ratio for primary school was at about 25:1 in 2005; the ratio for secondary school in 2009 was about 13.6. Schooling is conducted in Sestwana for the first four years and in English for the remaining years. The academic year runs from August to May.

Until 1961 primary schooling was completely financed by tribal treasuries, with some ethnic groups spending up to 70% of their budgets on education. Between 1985 and 1994, the government launched a major program of secondary school construction. As of 2009 public expenditure on education was 8.9% of GDP.

The University of Botswana, established on 1 July 1982 by an Act of Parliament, has a faculty of social sciences, education, sciences, agriculture, and humanities. In the 2005/06 academic year, it had 15,710 students.

44 LIBRARIES AND MUSEUMS

The Botswana National Library Service was founded in 1967 to provide nationwide public library service and act as the national library. There are 21 branches located throughout the country holding a total of 160,000 volumes; mobile library service is also provided. The main library is located in Gaborone has 65,000 volumes. The University of Botswana (1971) has over 250,000. The National Archives, with 20,000 items, are in Gaborone. The Botswana Libraries Consortium was established in 2003 as a cooperative organization of public, private, and academic libraries.

The renovated National Museum and Art Gallery in Gaborone houses a collection of the ethnography and natural history of Botswana, as well as sub-Saharan African art. There are also ethnographic museums in Kanye and Mochudi and a postal museum in Gaborone. In 1986 the Supa Ngwao Museum Centre in Francistown opened, holding ethnographic and historical installations.

45 MEDIA

In 2009 the CIA reported that there were 144,200 telephone landlines in Botswana. In addition to landlines, mobile phone subscriptions averaged 96 per 100 people. There were 8 FM radio stations, 13 AM radio stations, and 4 shortwave radio stations. Internet users numbered 6 per 100 citizens. In 2010, the country had 2,739 Internet hosts. In 2009 there were some 120,000 Internet users in Botswana. The government controls the content of nearly all radio and television broadcasts through the Botswana Press Agency (BOPA), which produces the free *Daily News* newspaper, Radio Botswana and Radio Botswana 2 (which broadcast nationally to most of the country), and Botswana Television (BTV). Radio Botswana broadcasts, in English and Setswana, a variety of news, educational, cultural, and entertainment programs. The privately-owned Gaborone Broadcasting Company (GBC) is the only other television station in the country; it broadcasts mostly foreign programming.

There is one daily newspaper in Botswana, the government published *Dikgang Tsa Gompieno* (or *Daily News*) in both English and Setswana. The government also publishes, in a bilingual edition, the monthly magazine *Kutlwaro*. Four independent newspapers were publishing on a weekly basis. *Mmegi Wa Digmang*, or *The Reporter*, is published in both Setswana and English. The major political parties publish monthly journals.

The constitution of Botswana ensures a free press and free speech, and the government is said to highly respect these rights.

⁴⁶ORGANIZATIONS

There is a chamber of commerce in Gaborone and there are some professional associations. The Botswana Council of Nongovernment Organizations (BOCONGO) serves as an umbrella group to encourage and support nongovernment organizations as recognized partners in national development. Member organizations (which numbered 84 as of 2012) include the Botswana Christian Council; the Cooperation for Research, Development, and Education; the Botswana Council of Women, and the Environmental Conservation Society.

Educational and cultural organizations include Botswana Society and the Botswana Technology Center. Youth organizations include Junior Achievement, Junior Chamber, Girl Guides, Boy Scouts, Botswana Christian Council Youth Unit, and the Young Women's Christian Association (YWCA). Most towns have women's clubs. The Emang Basadi Women's Association is a national organization promoting women's development and legal rights.

There are national chapters of the Red Cross Society, United Nations Children's Fund (UNICEF), and the Society of Saint Vincent de Paul. The Botswana Center for Human Rights was founded in 1996.

⁴⁷TOURISM, TRAVEL, AND RECREATION

The *Tourism Factbook*, published by the UN World Tourism Organization, reported 1.55 million incoming tourists to Botswana in 2009, who spent a total of $454 million. Of those incoming tourists, there were 1.3 million from Africa. There were 8,681 hotel beds available in Botswana, which had an occupancy rate of 36%. The estimated daily cost to visit Gaborone, the capital, was $210. The cost of visiting other cities averaged $147.

Botswana's well-stocked game reserves are its principal tourist attraction, with both hunting and photographic safaris available. Popular with tourists is the Okavango Delta region, which during the rainy season is a maze of waterways, islands, and lakes; it includes the Moremi Wildlife Refuge and nearby is Chobe National Park. In total, eight national parks and game reserves cover almost 20% of the land area of the country. The Kalahari Desert is another attraction, as are the country's tapestry weavers, potters, and rug makers. The Tsodilo Hills have cave paintings by the ancestors of the Basarwa (Bushmen), the earliest known inhabitants of Botswana. The government's "National Conservation Strategy and Tourism Policy" promotes tourism while protecting wildlife areas. All nationals except citizens of the United States, South Africa, Commonwealth countries, and most Western European countries, need visas for visits up to 90 days. Visitors are required to have a passport, ongoing/return ticket, and proof of sufficient funds for the stay. Proof of yellow fever and cholera vaccinations are required of travelers from infected areas. Antimalarial precautions are advisable.

⁴⁸FAMOUS PERSONS

Khama III (1837–1923), chief of the Bamangwato and a Christian convert, reigned for 48 years. His grandson, Sir Seretse Khama (1921–80), was Botswana's first president. Quett Ketumile Joni Masire (b. 1925) succeeded him in 1980. President Masire resigned in April 1998. In 2011 the president of Botswana was Lieutenant General Seretse Khama Ian Khama (b. 1953).

⁴⁹DEPENDENCIES

Botswana has no territories or colonies.

⁵⁰BIBLIOGRAPHY

Diamond, Larry and Marc F. Plattner. *Democratization in Africa.* Baltimore, MD: Johns Hopkins University Press, 2010.

Dibie, Robert A. *Non-Governmental Organizations (NGOs) and Sustainable Development in Sub-Saharan Africa.* Lanham, MD: Lexington Books, 2008.

FDI and Tourism: The Development Dimension: East and Southern Africa. New York: United Nations, 2008.

Good, Kenneth. *The Liberal Model and Africa: Elites against Democracy.* New York: Palgrave, 2002.

Kamoche, Ken M., ed. *Managing Human Resources in Africa.* New York: Routledge, 2004.

Lange, Matthew. *Lineages of Despotism and Development: British Colonialism and State Power.* Chicago: University of Chicago Press, 2009.

McKenna, Amy. *The History of Southern Africa.* New York: Britannica Educational Publishing, 2011.

Morton, Fred, Barry Morton, and Jeff Ramsay. *Historical Dictionary of Botswana.* Lanham, MD: Scarecrow Press, 1996.

Nolting, Mark. *Africa's Top Wildlife Countries: Botswana, Kenya, Namibia, Rwanda, South Africa, Tanzania, Uganda, Zambia & Zimbabwe, Also Including Burundi, Congo, Ethiopia, Lesotho, Malawi, Mozambique, Swaziland, Mauritius, and Seychelles Islands.* Ft. Lauderdale: Global Travel Publishers, Inc., 2008.

Rotberg, Robert I. *Ending Autocracy, Enabling Democracy: The Tribulations of Southern Africa, 1960–2000.* Cambridge, MA: World Peace Foundation, 2002.

BURKINA FASO

CAPITAL: Ouagadougou

FLAG: The flag consists of two equal horizontal stripes of red and green divided by a narrow gold band. A five-point gold star is at the center.

ANTHEM: *Le Ditanye (Anthem of Victory).*

MONETARY UNIT: The Communauté Financière Africaine franc (XOF) is a paper currency with one basic official rate based on the euro. It was originally pegged to the French franc. There are coins of 1, 2, 5, 10, 25, 50, 100, and 500 francs, and notes of 50, 100, 500, 1,000, 5,000, and 10,000 francs. XOF1 = US$0.00204 (or US$1 = XOF487.99) as of 2011.

WEIGHTS AND MEASURES: The metric system is the legal standard.

HOLIDAYS: New Year's Day, 1 January; Anniversary of the 1966 Revolution, 3 January; Labor Day, 1 May; Independence Day, 5 August; Assumption, 15 August; All Saints' Day, 1 November; Christmas, 25 December. Movable religious holidays include Eid al-Fitr, Eid al-Adha, Milad an-Nabi, Easter Monday, Ascension, and Pentecost Monday.

TIME: GMT.

¹LOCATION, SIZE, AND EXTENT

Burkina Faso (formerly Upper Volta), a landlocked country in West Africa, has an area of 274,200 sq km (105,869 sq mi), with a length of 873 km (542 mi) ENE–WSW and a width of 474 km (295 mi) SSE–NNW. Comparatively, the area occupied by Burkina Faso is slightly larger than the state of Colorado. Burkino Faso is bounded on the E by Niger, on the SE by Benin (formerly Dahomey), on the S by Togo, Ghana, and Côte d'Ivoire, and on the W and N by Mali. Burkina Faso has a total boundary length of 3,192 km (1,983 mi).

The capital city of Burkina Faso, Ouagadougou, is located in the center of the country.

²TOPOGRAPHY

Burkina Faso consists for the most part of a vast lateritic plateau in the West African savanna, approximately 198–305 m (650–1,000 ft) above sea level. The highest point (749 m/2,457 ft) of Téna Kourou is near the Mali border, southwest of Orodara. The land is slightly inclined toward the south and notched by valleys formed by the three principal rivers, the Black, White, and Red Voltas, and their main tributary, the Sourou. They are alternately dry or in flood and all are unnavigable. In general, the land is dry and poor.

³CLIMATE

The climate is characterized by high temperatures, especially at the end of the dry season. The humidity, which increases as one moves south, ranges from winter lows of 12–45% to rainy season highs of 68–96%. The harmattan, a dry east wind, brings with it spells of considerable heat from March to May, when maximum temperatures range from 40°C to 48°C (104° to 119°F). From May to October, the climate is hot and wet, and from November to March, comfortable and dry. January temperatures range from 7°C to 13° C (44° to 55°F). Average annual rainfall varies from 115 cm (45 in) in the southwest to less than 25 cm (10 in) in the extreme north and northeast. The rainy season lasts from four months in the northeast to six months in the southwest, from May through October. From 1969 to 1974, Burkina Faso suffered from drought, especially in the north, which is in the semiarid Sahel zone.

⁴FLORA AND FAUNA

The World Resources Institute estimated that there were 1,100 plant species in Burkina Faso. In addition, Burkina Faso was home to 129 species of mammals, 452 species of birds, 44 species of reptiles, and 11 species of amphibians. The calculation reflects the total number of distinct species residing in the country, not the number of endemic species.

Fauna, possibly the widest variety in West Africa, includes the elephant, hippopotamus, buffalo, monkey, crocodile, giraffe, various types of antelope, and a vast variety of bird and insect life.

⁵ENVIRONMENT

The World Resources Institute reported that Burkina Faso had designated 3.82 million hectares (9.45 million acres) of land for protection as of 2006. Water resources totaled 17.5 cu km (4.2 cu mi) while water usage was 1.7 cu km (0.408 cu mi) per year. Domestic water usage accounted for 13% of total usage, industrial for 1%, and agricultural for 86%. Per capita water usage totaled 60 cu m (2,119 cu ft) per year.

The UN reported in 2008 that carbon dioxide emissions in Burkina Faso totaled 1,693 kilotons.

The major environmental problems facing Burkina Faso are recurrent drought and the advance of the northern desert into the savanna. This trend toward desertification has been increased by overgrazing of pasture, slash-and-burn agriculture, and overcutting of wood for fuel. Almost all the trees within 40 km (25 mi) of the capital have been felled. The frequency of droughts in Burkina Faso and its location in the Sahara desert contribute to the nation's water supply problems. According to the World Health Organization (WHO), about 80% of all disease in Burkina Faso is caused by unsafe water. Pollution problems result from uncontrolled disposal of sewage and industrial wastes. Poor air quality caused by dust, smoke from cooking fires, and vehicular exhaust also poses a serious health hazard in urban centers.

The Ministry of Environment and Tourism is the principal government agency concerned with the environment. Burkina Faso has 12 national parks and wildlife reserves totaling 2.855 million hectares (7.05 million acres). The country has 15 Ramsar Wetlands of International Importance.

According to a 2011 report issued by the International Union for Conservation of Nature and Natural Resources (IUCN), the number of threatened species includes 9 species of mammals, 7 species of birds, 1 type of reptile, and 3 species of plants. Threatened species include the African hunting dog, the chimpanzee, and the African elephant. The Sahara oryx, or white oryx, has become extinct in the wild.

6 POPULATION

The US Central Intelligence Agency (CIA) reported the population of Burkina Faso in 2011 to be approximately 16,751,455, which placed it at number 61 in population among the 196 nations of the world. In 2011, approximately 2.5% of the population was over 65 years of age, with another 45.8% under 15 years of age. The median age in Burkina Faso was 16.9 years. There were 0.99 males for every female in the country. The population's annual rate of change was 3.073%. The projected population for the year 2025 was 25,400,000. Population density in Burkina Faso was calculated at 61 people per sq km (158 people per sq mi).

The UN estimates that 26% of the population lives in urban areas, and that urban populations has an annual rate of change of 6.2%. The largest urban area was Ouagadougou, one of West Africa's fastest growing cities, with an estimated population in 2011 of nearly 2 million.

The prevalence of HIV/AIDS has had a significant impact on the population of Burkina Faso. The AIDS epidemic causes higher death and infant mortality rates and lowers life expectancy. The rate was 1.2% in 2009.

7 MIGRATION

Burkina Faso's net migration rate, as reported by the CIA in 2011, was negligible. The total number of emigrants living abroad was 1.58 million, and the total number of immigrants living in Burkina Faso was 1.04 million. Seasonal labor migration in Burkina Faso, which began in the colonial period as a means of obtaining money for taxes, continued as a remedy for economic deficiencies. According to some estimates, as many as two million Burkinabé lived abroad at any one time, about half in Côte d'Ivoire and the rest throughout West Africa, where many were employed on coffee and cocoa plantations.

In January 2011, there were 531 refugees and 534 asylum seekers residing in Burkina Faso; and there were 1,145 Burkinabé refugees and 505 Burkinabé asylum seekers residing outside the country. As a result of a protracted political crisis in neighboring Cote d'Ivoire, more than 100,000 Burkinabé nationals returned to their home country in 2011. Subsequent to the 2011 rebellion in Libya, 566 Burkinabé returned from there to their home country.

8 ETHNIC GROUPS

There are more than 60 ethnic groups represented in the country. The principal ethnic group in Burkina Faso is the Mossi, who make up about 40% of the total population. They are mainly farmers and live in the central portions of the country. The Bobo, the second-largest ethnic group (about one million), are mostly farmers, artisans, and metalworkers living in the southwest around Bobo-Dioulasso. Other groups include the Gurunsi, Senufo, Lobi, Mande, and the nomadic Fulani, or Peul, who inhabit the areas near the country's northern borders. The number of nomads in the north has diminished since the Sahelian drought of the 1970s.

9 LANGUAGES

French is the official language of Burkina Faso. However, tribal languages belonging to the Sudanic family are spoken by 90% of the population. Moré, spoken by 55% of the population, is the most important indigenous language. The various ethnic groups speak their own languages.

10 RELIGIONS

About 61% of the population practice Islam, 19% practice Roman Catholicism, and approximately 4% are Protestant. A majority of the population also believes in aspects of traditional indigenous religion, and about 15% of the population practice traditional indigenous religions exclusively or principally.

Members of the Fulani and Dioula ethnic groups are predominantly Muslim. The majority of all the nation's Muslims are Sunnis, with minority groups belonging to the Shi'a, Tidjania, and Wahhabite sects. A large number of foreign missionary groups were active within the country, including the Assemblies of God, the Christian Missionary Alliance, the Campus Crusade for Christ, Baptists, Mennonites, Jehovah's Witnesses, Mormons, Seventh-Day Adventists, the World Evangelical Crusade, and the Pentecostal Church of Canada. Islamic missionary groups included the World Islamic League and Ahmadia.

Freedom of religion is guaranteed by the constitution, and this right is generally respected in practice. Since 2008 the country has participated in the US Trans-Sahara Counterterrorism Partnership program designed to combat religious extremism and terrorist groups such as Al Qaeda in the Islamic Maghreb (AQIM). However, there is no formal method of tracking terrorist flows at border checkpoints or at either of the country's two commercial airports. Religious groups have to register with the Ministry of Territorial Administration to obtain legal status. Certain Muslim and Christian holidays are observed as public holidays.

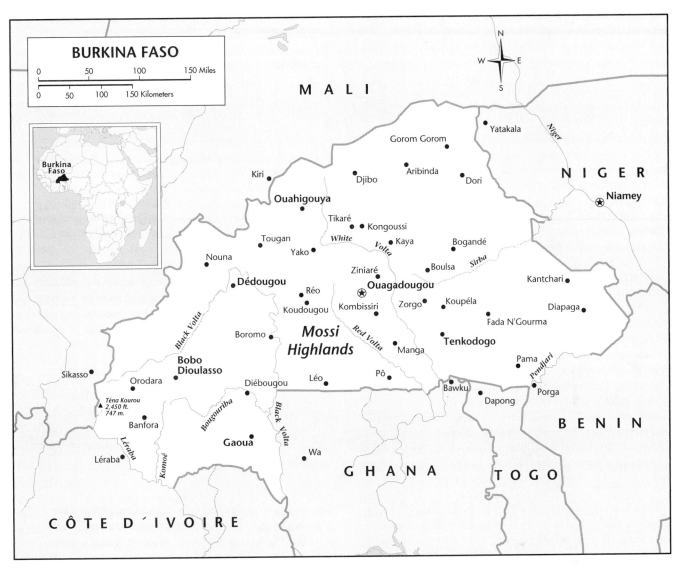

LOCATION: 9°30′ to 15°N; 2° to 5° W. BOUNDARY LENGTHS: Niger, 628 kilometers (390 miles); Benin, 306 kilometers (190 miles); Togo, 126 kilometers (78 miles); Ghana, 548 kilometers, (341 miles); Côte d'Ivoire, 584 kilometers (363 miles); Mali, 1,000 kilometers (621 miles).

11 TRANSPORTATION

The CIA reports that Burkina Faso had a total of 92,495 km (57,474 mi) of roads, of which 3,857 km (2,397 mi) were paved in 2004. There were 11 vehicles per 1,000 people in the country. Many of the secondary roads are not open year-round owing to flooding and poor maintenance. Railroads extend for 622 km (386 mi). There are 24 airports, which transported 79,345 passengers in 2009 according to the World Bank.

The 510-km (317-mi) Mossi Railroad in Burkina Faso is part of the line that begins at Abidjan, Côte d'Ivoire, and ends in Niger, some 1,145 km (710 mi) away. The line serves the towns of Banfora, Bobo-Dioulasso, Koudougou, and Ouagadougou; 25–40% of the railway traffic passes through Burkina Faso. A railroad from Ouagadougou to Tambao (353 km/219 mi) to exploit the mineral deposits was begun in October 1981 and completed by 1991.

There are international airports at Ouagadougou and Bobo-Dioulasso and numerous smaller airfields. In 2010, there were two airports with paved runways. Air Burkina, launched in 1967, is

government-run and has a monopoly on domestic service. It also flies to regional locations as far as Libreville in Gabon and to Paris, France.

12 HISTORY

Until the end of the 19th century, the story of Burkina Faso is the history of empire-building by the Mossi. Legend and tradition, as well as some ethnographic evidence, all suggest that the Mossi entered the region from the 11th to the 13th century as a warrior group from Central or East Africa and subjugated the weaker aboriginal Ninigi tribes.

They called their land Mogho ("country of the Mossi") and established five independent kingdoms—Tenkodogo, Yatenga, Gourma, Zandoma, and Ouagadougou. Each was ruled by a king, the *mogho* or *moro naba* ("ruler of the Mossi"), and Ouagadougou was the most powerful of the kingdoms.

Through the centuries, the Mossi population was augmented by groups of immigrants, such as the Hausa and the Fulani, who settled in Mossi territory but retained their ethnic identity. Contact and conflict with Islam came early. From the beginning of the 14th century, the Mossi had been engaged in recurrent wars with the neighboring empires of Mali and Songhai. They also occupied Timbuktu (now in Mali) at various times. After suffering defeat in the hands of Askia Daoud of Songhai in the 16th century, the Mossi ceased fighting with their powerful neighbors. Their warrior tradition and their internal unity continued, however.

By the 19th century, Mossi power seems to have declined. When the first known European incursions occurred late in the 19th century, internal dissension made the Mossi prey to the invaders. A French lieutenant, Voulet, was sent with an infantry column to subjugate the territory in 1896. Ouagadougou fell to Voulet in September of that year. The Mossi accepted French domination as a form of protection from their hostile neighbors.

In 1919, the French created a separate colony called Upper Volta (now Burkina Faso). But in 1932, Upper Volta's territory was divided among Niger, French Sudan (now Mali), and Côte d'Ivoire. Throughout the colonial period, the traditional political structure of the Mossi was retained; hence, the moro naba of Ouagadougou was regarded by the French as the emperor of the Mossi. When World War II (1939–45) broke out, the moro naba sent his two eldest sons to fight for France; more than 10,000 youths in the territory also followed suit. The restoration of Upper Volta as a territorial unit, long the aim of the traditional chiefs, became a reality in 1947. In 1958, voters in Upper Volta overwhelmingly approved the new constitution of the Fifth French Republic, and Upper Volta's territorial assembly voted to make the country an autonomous state within the French Community. By this time, the traditional chiefs had lost much of their influence, and political power was in the hands of the young, European-educated elite.

The republic achieved independent status on 5 August 1960. Maurice Yaméogo, leader of the Volta Democratic Union, became president. His government quickly took on an authoritarian cast and banned all opposition parties. In 1965, a single electoral list was offered to the people, and the opposition—joined by civil servants, trade unionists, and students—fomented riots. Yaméogo was replaced in January 1966 by Lt. Col. (later Gen.) Sangoulé Lamizana, a former army chief of staff, who suspended the 1960 constitution, dissolved the National Assembly, and formed a military-civilian cabinet.

During the 1970s and early 1980s, Upper Volta experienced severe political instability. A constitution that provided for an elected assembly was adopted in 1970, but factional struggle broke out and became so disruptive that in February 1974, President Lamizana announced that the military had again taken over the government. A new constitution was approved in 1977; under this constitution, Lamizana won election to the presidency in 1978. On 25 November 1980, however, Lamizana was deposed in a bloodless coup led by Col. Sayé Zerbo, who became president. Zerbo's government was overthrown on 7 November 1982 by yet another army coup, and Maj. Jean-Baptiste Ouédraogo was named president.

Under the moderate Ouédraogo regime, a military faction emerged that was suspected of having close ties to Libya. Prominent in this group was Capt. Thomas Sankara, who served as prime minister from January until May 1983, when he was purged by Ouédraogo. On 4 August 1983, Sankara seized power in what

was Upper Volta's third coup in as many years. As many as 20 persons may have died in the disturbances. After the coup, Sankara, who emerged at the head of the ruling National Revolutionary Council, sought to retain Upper Volta's traditional foreign aid ties with the West while establishing warm relations with such nations as Ghana, Libya, the USSR, and Cuba.

Sankara also sought to instill his nation with a spirit of revolutionary fervor. In August 1984, on the first anniversary of his rule, he renamed the nation Burkina Faso, meaning roughly "Land of Upright Men." He led a campaign against corruption and tax evasion; and he trimmed government spending by cutting the salaries of civil servants, an action that earned him the enmity of the nation's small but influential labor unions. A substantial number of politicians, soldiers, government officials, and labor leaders were jailed, and seven men were executed in 1984 for allegedly plotting to overthrow the government.

In December 1985, Burkina Faso took up arms against Mali. At issue was a strip of land 20- by 160-km (12- by 100-mi) that had triggered clashes first in 1974, and again in 1975. On 22 December 1986, the International Court of Justice ruled in favor of dividing the territory into roughly equal parts, a decision both nations accepted.

On 15 October 1987, faced by opposition among the trade unions and civil servants, the government was overthrown by an army unit. The putsch was led by Capt. Blaise Compaoré, the president's chief adviser who is also said to have been his inseparable companion. Sankara and 12 aides (including two of the coup plotters) were immediately shot, and Compaoré assumed the presidency. Executions of highly placed military men followed a coup attempt on 18 September 1989.

As the 1990s dawned, the authorities sought to legitimize their position at the ballot box. They championed the drafting of a new constitution that called for multiparty elections for president and a national legislature. In March of 1991, the ruling party abandoned its Marxist ideology and embraced free enterprise.

Elections were held for president in December 1991; a parliamentary election followed in 24 May 1992. Results from both were disputed, and they led to no changes in the government. Compaoré ran unopposed for president and his party, the Popular Democratic Organization-Worker's Movement (ODP-MT), carried the legislative elections. Only three opposition parties contested seats nationwide; 35 parties boycotted the poll, and only 35% of eligible voters voted. The ODP-MT won 78 of 107 seats, with 9 other parties splitting the remainder of the vote. The government convened on 15 June and Youssouf Ouédraogo was named prime minister. The introduction of multiparty competition was a major reform, but the lack of probity in the electoral process prompted critics to label the government and its reforms a "shamocracy."

Regionally, Compaoré conducted an active foreign policy in West Africa. He sent troops to Liberia and harbored dissidents from Gambia. This action alienated Compaoré from his fellow West African leaders and from western governments, including the United States, which recalled its ambassador in 1992. Burkina Faso continued its support for Liberian insurgent Charles Taylor and his NPFL despite a West-Africa-wide deployment of forces—ECOMOG—in Liberia to help resolve the lingering and bloody civil war there. Burkina Faso had refused to contribute forces to ECOMOG, despite international pressure, until 1995 when the

Compaoré regime announced it was satisfied with the cease-fire accord signed that year in Nigeria.

Compaoré played regional elder statesman in August 2006 by mediating the Inter-Togolese Dialog. He then successfully brokered a peace agreement between Laurent Gbagbo and Guillaume Soro of the Forces Nouvelles in Cote d'Ivoire in March 2007. He also engaged in diplomatic efforts in Guinea. In early 2011, Compaoré joined the ranks of international mediators who attempted, unsuccessfully, to resolve the political stalemate between Laurent Gbagbo and Alassane Ouattara in Cote d'Ivoire. He chaired the regional body, ECOWAS, in 2007. On the world stage, Burkina Faso was a non-permanent member of the UN Security Council in 2008–09.

Human rights violations have been commonplace under the Compaoré regime. The government has suppressed a vocal independent press, and the security forces have used excessive force against civil society demonstrations and government critics. In a case that was never resolved, Norbert Zongo, publisher and editor of the nationally-known *Indépendent* newspaper, was killed in an ambush about 100 kilometers south of Ouagadougou in December 1998. Zongo's newspaper had been investigating the death of Compaoré's brother's driver, who died as a result of torture in January 1998. In February 2000, the National Reconciliation Commission (NRC), established in November 1998, recommended that government arrange special trials of people implicated in economic crimes and political killings. Estimates placed the number of political killings since 1989 at 100 or more. In 2001, Compaoré established a fund of $7.75 million to compensate families of victims of political violence and rights abuses.

The May 2002 parliamentary elections marked the first time in Burkina Faso's history that three consecutive legislative elections were held without a military coup. It was also the first time that the single ballot was used in an election. Some 30 parties participated in the elections, but seats were shared between a few. The major winners were President Compaoré's Congress for Democracy and Progress (CDP) with 57 seats and the African Democratic Rally-Alliance for Democracy and Federation (ADF/RDA), which took 17 seats. The CDP maintained a majority in the 2007 elections with 73 seats. Tertius Zongo was named prime minister that year. On 21 November 2010, Compaoré was re-elected with more than 80% of the vote in elections deemed overall to be free, but not fair because of incumbent advantage. Four of seven presidential challengers alleged vote rigging in the exercise.

Owing to civil conflicts in neighboring Cote d'Ivoire, more than 150,000 Burkinabe immigrants and refugees returned home in 2002, and another 100,000 returned home from Cote d'Ivoire in early 2011 following Laurent Gbagbo's refusal to cede power after losing the December 2010 elections in that country.

In the first half of 2011 the country was rocked by a series of mutinies and looting by police and armed forces in the capital city and across the country. An attack from close range forced Compaoré to flee the presidential compound. After loyal forces succeeded in quelling the uprisings and restoring order, intense criticism and civil society pressure forced Compaoré to undertake extensive reforms. He dismissed 566 soldiers who had participated in the mutinies, replaced the Prime Minister, Defense Chief and security chiefs, dissolved the national election commission (CENI) and appointed new governors in all 13 regions.

13 GOVERNMENT

Under the constitution of 27 November 1960, Upper Volta was governed by a president, a council of ministers, and a National Assembly of 50 members. On 5 January 1966, President Lamizana suspended the constitution and dissolved the National Assembly, announcing that he would exercise legislative and executive power by ordinance and decree. A constitution approved in 1970 provided for eventual restitution of democratic institutions, although with a formal role in the government for the military. The 1970 constitution was suspended in February 1974, when the army again assumed full power.

A democratic constitution, adopted in 1977, provided for a president and a 57-member National Assembly. This document was abolished after the coup of 25 November 1980, and the Military Committee for Reform and National Progress (Comité Militaire de Redressement pour le Progrès National—CMRPN), led by Col. Sayé Zerbo, assumed power. The military coup of 7 November 1982 led to the abolition of the CMRPN and the formation of the People's Salvation Council (Conseil du Salut du Peuple—CSP) under Maj. Jean-Baptiste Ouédraogo. The CSP was itself dissolved by the military coup of 4 August 1983, which established the National Revolutionary Council (Conseil National de la Révolution—CNR), a body that included radical former CSP members. Under Capt. Thomas Sankara, its chairman and the head of state, the CNR was the supreme governmental authority and was assisted by a Council of Ministers. Following the October 1987 coup, this body was renamed the Popular Front, with Capt. Blaise Compaoré as its chief.

A new constitution, establishing the fourth republic, was adopted on 2 June 1991. Among other provisions, it called for an Assembly of People's Deputies with 107 seats (now 111). The president is chief of state, chairs a council of ministers, appoints a prime minister, who with the legislature's consent, serves as head of government. In April 2000, the constitution was amended, reducing the presidential term from seven to five years, enforceable as of 2005, and allowing the president to be reelected only once. Given insider pressure in 2010–11 to override this amendment (Article 37), it was unclear what the outcome would be in 2015. The legislative branch is a unicameral National Assembly (Assemblée Nationale) consisting of 111 seats. Members are elected by popular vote for five-year terms.

In April 2005, President Compaoré was re-elected for a third straight term. He won 80.3% of the vote, while Bénéwende Stanislas Sankara came a distant second with 4.9%. In the presidential election of November 2010, Compaoré won 80.15% of the vote followed by Hama Arba Diallo with 8.21% and Bénéwende Stanislas Sankara with 6.34%. Four other candidates shared the remainder of the votes. Luc Adolphe Tiao of CDP was named Prime Minister on 18 April 2011. The next presidential election was scheduled for 2015.

14 POLITICAL PARTIES

After the 1978 competitive presidential and legislative elections, the government recognized only the three largest parties in the National Assembly: the Voltaic Democratic Union-African Democratic Rally, the National Union for Democracy, and the Voltaic Progressive Union. The last subsequently merged with smaller groups to form the Voltaic Progressive Front.

Following the coup of 25 November 1980, all political parties were banned. To disseminate government views on a grass-roots level, the CNR, which took power in 1983, sponsored the formation of Committees for the Defense of the Revolution.

The Compaoré government legalized parties prior to holding elections on 24 May 1992. Compaoré's Popular Democratic Organization-Worker's Movement (ODP-MT) gained 78 seats. The National Convention of Progressive Patriots-Social Democratic Party (CNPP-PSD) won 12 seats, and the African Democratic Assembly (ADA) won 6. Eight other parties were represented in the Assembly of People's Deputies. Abstention of 65% of the voters diminished the significance of this election.

National Assembly elections were held 11 May 1997. Again, a boycott resulted in an approximate 50% voter turnout, with the CDP of President Compaoré winning 101 seats, the PDP 6 seats, the RDA 2 seats, and the ADF 2 seats.

In the municipal elections of September 2000, the CDP took 802 of 1,098 council seats based on a voter turnout of 68.4% in a field of 25 parties. The African Democratic Rally-Alliance for Democracy and Federation (ADF/RDA) took second place with 133 seats. Third place was taken by l'Union des Démocrates Libéraux (ULD), a pro-presidential group with 49 seats. The l'Union pour la Démocratie et la Fédération (UDF), an opposition group, took fourth place with 22 seats. The Party for African Independence (PAI) took fifth place with 20 seats. A number of younger parties including the Democratic Convention for Federation (CDF) took the remaining seats. Numerous complaints of fraud were brought forward to the Constitutional Court, but with little effect on the overall results.

The parliamentary elections of May 2002 saw the CDP retain its majority, but its control declined to 57 seats against 17 for ADF/RDA led by Hermann Yaméogo. The Party for Democracy and Progress (PDP/PS) of Joseph Ki-Zerbo won 10 seats; the CFD took 5; PAI, led by Philippe Ouedraogo, also took 5; while other parties won 17 seats. In the May 2007 elections the CDP gained strength by winning 73 seats. The ADF/RDA followed with 14 seats. The Union for the Republic, led by Toussaint Abel Coulibaly, came in with five seats, followed by the Union for Rebirth-Sankarist Movement (UNIR-MS) with four seats and the Coalition of Democratic Forces of Burkina (CFD-B) with three. The remaining seats went to eight other parties. Tertius Zongo was named prime minister that year. The next legislative elections were set for May 2012.

In the 21 November 2010 presidential election, Compaoré was reelected with 80.15% of the vote. He ran on the CDP ticket, but received support from the Presidential Movement Alliance (AMP) and from the ADF-RDA coalition. Four of the seven candidates challenged the vote, claiming that the electoral commission rigged it by allowing ineligible people to vote for Compaoré. The commission rejected the challenge without providing further details. Hama Arba Diallo of the Party for Democracy and Socialism came in second with 8.18% of the vote, followed by Bénéwende Stanislas Sankara of the UNIR-MS with 6.34%. The next presidential election was set for 2015.

15 LOCAL GOVERNMENT

In the 1995 municipal elections, President Compaoré's supporters won absolute majorities in 26 of 33 municipalities. Fewer than 10% of the eligible voters registered, and 25% of the registered voters abstained. The 24 September 2000 municipal elections were boycotted by a coalition of opposition parties known as the February the Fourteenth movement; as such, the ruling CDP party won in 40 of the 49 municipalities. In the April 2006 municipal elections, 46 parties won seats, but the CDP was the overwhelming victor claiming 12,854 of 17,786 total seats. The ADF-RDA came in second with 1,637 seats and the Union for the Republic (UPR) was third with 610. In 2011 Burkina Faso was divided into 13 regions, 45 provinces, 301 departments, 49 municipalities, and 7,285 villages.

16 JUDICIAL SYSTEM

The legal system is based on the French civil law system and customary law. At the apex of the judicial system is the Supreme Court and beneath it are courts of appeal at Ouagadougou and Bobo-Dioulasso. Courts of the first instance in Ouagadougou, Bobo-Dioulasso, Ouahigouya, and Fada N'Gourma deal with cases involving civil, criminal, and commercial law; a court at Ouagadougou specializes in common law. Following the 1983 coup, the CNR created tribunals to try former government officials for corruption and mismanagement. These "people's tribunals" infringed to some degree on the functions of courts of the first instance. In 1993, the "people's tribunals" were abolished.

In addition to the courts described above, traditional courts at the village level apply customary law in cases of divorce and inheritance. There is also a High Court of Justice to try the president and high government officials for treason or other serious crimes.

The June 1991 constitution provides a number of safeguards including a right to public trial, right to access to counsel and a right to appeal. In 1995, an Office of Ombudsman "Mediateur du Faso" was created for resolving disputes between the state and its citizens. Despite these safeguards, the judiciary is subject to interference by the executive. An example of this influence was the dropping of charges in 2006 against Marcel Kafando, the only person charged in the unresolved slaying of Norbert Zongo in December 1998.

17 ARMED FORCES

The International Institute for Strategic Studies (IISS) reported that armed forces in Burkina Faso totaled 11,200 members in 2011. The force was comprised of 6,400 from the army, 600 from the air force, and 4,200 members of the gendarmerie. Armed forces represented .2% of the labor force in Burkina Faso. Defense spending totaled $241.1 million and accounted for 1.2% of gross domestic product (GDP).

Burkina Faso has been a significant contributor of peacekeeping troops to troubled areas such as Darfur. In 2010 more than 1,000 Burkinabé troops were serving in four UN peacekeeping missions.

Military ties between the United States and Burkina Faso are strong. Burkina Faso is a partner in the Africa Contingency Operations Training and Assistance (ACOTA) program, and the United States has trained three 750-man battalions for peace support operations in Darfur. The US Embassy had established an English-language laboratory at a local military base. The government of Burkina Faso supports US efforts in the Sahel to combat extremism such as through the Trans-Sahara Counterterrorism Partnership (TSCTP). In May 2010, Burkina Faso hosted Flintlock, a multilateral military exercise.

18 INTERNATIONAL COOPERATION

Burkina Faso was admitted to UN membership on 20 September 1960. It is a member of ECA and several nonregional specialized agencies. It is also a member of the WTO (1995), the African Development Bank, the West African Economic and Monetary Union (WAEMU/UEMOA), the ACP Group, the Economic Community of West African States (ECOWAS/CEDEAO), the G-77, the Non-aligned Movement, the Organization of the Islamic Conference (OIC), and the African Union (AU). The nation is part of the Franc Zone and the Community of Sahel and Saharan States (CENSAD). Together with other countries of former French West Africa, it participates in the Council of the Entente. Burkina Faso also belongs to the Niger Basin Authority. In environmental cooperation, the nation is part of the Basel Convention, the Convention on Biological Diversity, Ramsar, CITES, the Montréal Protocol, and the UN Conventions on the Law of the Sea, Climate Change, and Desertification.

Burkina Faso served as a member of the UN Security Council from 2008–2009 and assumed the rotating, one-month presidency of the council in December 2009.

19 ECONOMY

The GDP rate of change in Burkina Faso, as of 2011, was 4.9%. Inflation stood at 3.6%, and unemployment was reported at 77%. While the nation experienced relatively strong growth in a global recession, Burkina Faso remained one of the poorest countries in the world. The country has a population growth rate of nearly 3.1% annually, is landlocked, has few natural resources under exploitation, depends on subsistence agriculture, and suffers from a weak industrial base. The main staples—millet, sorghum, maize, and rice—are grown for domestic consumption. Cotton, the principal export crop, is price sensitive. A significant portion of the labor force migrates to neighboring countries for work.

Environmental conditions for agriculture are precarious. Northern Burkina is Sahelian and subject to severe drought. Soils are lateritic and generally poor. However, efforts to expand agriculture to more fertile fields in river valleys have received support by the UN and donor countries, and projects to eradicate "river blindness" (onchocerciasis) have opened previously uninhabitable areas to cultivation and grazing.

Burkina's mineral sector holds potential, but is largely undeveloped. Long underestimated, the Poura gold reserves have proven to be capable of generating nearly 10% of export earnings annually. This potential has attracted foreign investors. In 2007 the country's only commercial gold mine was opened, and by 2010 gold had become the country's number one source of export revenue. In 2012, seven companies were engaged in 29 projects linked to gold mining in 13 mines around the country.

Zinc and silver deposits at Perkoa have been judged commercially viable. Significant limestone deposits basic to cement manufacturing are located near Tambao at Tin Hrassan. Other mineral resources are manganese, vanadium-bearing magnetite, bauxite, lead, nickel, and phosphates.

Manufacturing is limited to cotton and food processing (mainly in Bobo-Dioulasso) and import substitution heavily protected by tariffs. Some factories are privately owned, and others are scheduled to be privatized. Burkina Faso's revised investment code has helped to promote foreign investment.

20 INCOME

The CIA reported that in 2011 the GDP of Burkina Faso was $21.83 billion. The CIA defines GDP as the value of all final goods and services produced within a nation in a given year and computed on the basis of purchasing power parity (PPP) rather than value as measured on the basis of the rate of the exchange based on current dollars. The per capita GDP was estimated at $1,5 00. The annual growth rate of GDP was 4.9%. The average inflation rate was 3.6%. It was estimated that agriculture accounted for 34.1% of GDP, industry 23.2%, and services 42.8%.

According to the World Bank, remittances from citizens living abroad totaled $99.3 million or about $6 per capita and accounted for approximately .5% of GDP.

In 2007 the World Bank estimated that Burkina Faso, with 0.21% of the world's population, accounted for 0.03% of the world's GDP. By comparison, the United States, with 4.85% of the world's population, accounted for 22.51% of world GDP.

Recent data for household consumption in Burkina Faso was unavailable. Household consumption includes expenditures of individuals, households, and nongovernmental organizations on goods and services, excluding the purchases of dwellings. It was estimated that household consumption was growing at an average annual rate of 9.9%. In 2005, the World Bank reported that actual individual consumption in Burkina Faso was 75.1% of GDP and accounted for 0.03% of world consumption. By comparison, the United States accounted for 25.44% of world individual consumption. The World Bank also estimated that 38.4% of Burkina Faso's GDP was spent on food and beverages, 13.4% on housing and household furnishings, 2.5% on clothes, 2.1% on health, 5.9% on transportation, 0.8% on communications, 1.4% on recreation, 4.2% on restaurants and hotels, and 3.1% on miscellaneous goods and services and purchases from abroad.

21 LABOR

As of 2007, Burkina Faso had a total labor force of 6.668 million people. Within that labor force, CIA estimates in 2000 noted that 90% were employed in agriculture, 5% in industry, and 5% in the service sector. In 2010 the unemployment rate stood at 77% and was expected to rise still higher in 2011 owing to the return of economic migrants fleeing the political turmoil and violence in Cote d'Ivoire. High unemployment has historically forced a large part of the country's male labor force to migrate annually to neighboring countries in search of work.

Workers in the formal sector are permitted to join unions. About 60% of the country's public employees are union members, while around 25% of the workers in the private sector are unionized. Essential workers such as police officers are not allowed to unionize. Workers can strike to achieve their labor goals.

The minimum age for employment is 14 years. Because of subsistence agriculture and the large informal sector, child labor is common. Similarly, although a standard work week of 40 hours and a minimum monthly wage of $62 (2010) were guaranteed by law, minimum wage and other worker protections seldom applied to farmers, herders, and workers in the informal sector.

22 AGRICULTURE

Roughly 18% of the land is farmed by approximately 90% of the workforce, which is engaged in some form of subsistence agriculture. Crops for local consumption include peanuts, sesame, sorghum, millet, corn, and rice. Other subsistence crops are cassava, cowpeas, and sweet potatoes. Export and cash crops include cotton, shea nuts, tobacco, sugarcane, and peanuts. Cereal production in 2009 amounted to 3.6 million tons, fruit production 100,029 tons, and vegetable production 217,377 tons. Food production is constrained by rain-fed agriculture, generally poor soils, costly inputs, and farming techniques subject to flooding and drought. Burkina Faso is not self-sufficient in food.

The government has asserted that global climate change has had a dramatic effect on the nation's farms. Reportedly, the rainy seasons are beginning earlier and ending later than usual, with heavier and longer rains causing an increase in soil erosion and crops lost to flooding. In 2011 the World Bank was reviewing a project appraisal document that would provide $115 million to Burkina Faso to support development of agricultural production and food security support through 2015. The project design was deemed to be consistent with the Country Assistance Strategy (2010–2012) and with the African Union's Comprehensive African Agricultural Development Program's (CAADP) focus on markets and infrastructure.

For the benefit of small farmers, the government launched Operation 100,000 Ploughs in July 2011. The program provided significant subsidies that allowed farmers to purchase animal-drawn ploughs to replace the more common handheld hoes that are used for tilling the soil. The ploughs would allow workers to cover more ground in less time and provide a more efficient method of farming. The government expected to distribute 20,000 ploughs each year between 2011 and 2015, with at least half specifically provided for women, who are an important part of the agricultural workforce.

23 ANIMAL HUSBANDRY

The UN Food and Agriculture Organization (FAO) reported that Burkina Faso dedicated 6 million hectares (14.8 million acres) to permanent pasture or meadow in 2009. During that year, the country tended 37 million chickens, 9.5 million head of cattle, and 2 million pigs. The production from these animals amounted to 115,737 tons of beef and veal, 39,874 tons of pork, 33,029 tons of poultry, 34,664 tons of eggs, and 245,350 tons of milk. Burkina Faso also produced 18,930 tons of cattle hide. Further development depended on the availability of pasturage and water, as well as the import policies and tax levels of neighboring countries.

24 FISHING

Burkina Faso had 166 decked commercial fishing boats in 2008. The annual capture totaled 10,600 tons according to the UN FAO. The export value of fish totaled $157.2 million. The country had no access to the sea, and freshwater areas were limited. Fishing was mostly artisanal.

25 FORESTRY

Approximately 21% of Burkina Faso is covered by forest. The UN FAO estimated the 2009 roundwood production at 1.17 million cu m (41.4 million cu ft). The value of all forest products, including roundwood, totaled $275,000.

Almost all of Burkina Faso's primitive forest has been cut for fuel or cleared for farmland. Reforestation programs were launched in 1973. Deforestation proceeded at the rate of 0.2% per year during 1990–2000. In total, between 1990 and 2010, Burkina Faso lost 17.5% of its forest cover, amounting to around 1,198,000 hectares (2,960,322 acres).

26 MINING

Mining does not play a significant role in Burkina Faso's economy. However, government revenues are dominated by gold, the third-leading export commodity. Gold mining output for 2009 was 13,181 kg, and artisanal miners account for about 1,600 kg of annual production. In 2008, the Kalsaka, Mana, and Youga mines opened, and the Inata mine was commissioned in 2009. Investment and mining codes were revised in 2004, which has renewed interest by investors.

Exploitation of an estimated 15 million tons of high-grade manganese ore at Tambao awaited better commercial prospects and completion of a railway extension from Ouagadougou to Tambao. Bauxite deposits have been located in the regions of Kaya and Bobo-Dioulasso. Significant mineral deposits included copper at Gaoua and Wayen, graphite at Kaya, and phosphate at Kodjari. Four main deposits of limestone have also been discovered. For many years, iron has been worked at Ouahigouya and near Banfora to make farm and home implements. The Perkoa high-grade zinc ore deposit had resources of 7 million tons and planned to produce 60,000 tons per year with an estimated mine life of 15 years. Other deposits included cassiterite, cobalt, diamonds, granite, lead, marble, nickel, phosphate rock, pumice, salt, sand and gravel, uranium, and vanadium.

In recent years, Burkina Faso's government has made an effort to attract greater foreign investment and, as a result, has worked to foster growth in the gold mining industry. In his 2010 state-of-the-nation address, Prime Minister Zongo reported that gold production in Burkina Faso more than doubled from 2008 through 2009, with 5,000 kg reported in 2008 and 11,642 kg in 2009. About 1,350 new permanent jobs were created at four major mines as a result of increased production. Beginning in 2010, the government sought to initiate operations at gold mines in Essakane and Inata and at a manganese mine in Kier. Gold is the second largest export product, after cotton.

In October 2011, the board of the Extractive Industries Transparency Iniative (EITI), based in Oslo, Norway, determined that the country was making meaningful progress on governance criteria associated with extractives, and extended Burkina's "candidate status" within EITI for 18 months until April 2013. Publish What You Pay Burkina Faso received grants in 2010 and 2011 amounting to some $58,000 to strengthen civil society involvement in the implementation of EITI.

²⁷ENERGY AND POWER

The World Bank reported in 2008 that Burkina Faso produced 589 million kWh of electricity and consumed 653.3 million kWh, or 39 kWh per capita. The country consumed 9,000 barrels per day of oil in 2010. There were no known reserves of oil and gas. SONABEL (Société Nationale Burkinabé d'Electricité) was the state-owned utility supplying electricity to the country.

²⁸INDUSTRY

Industry accounted for about 23% of Burkina's GDP in 2011, yet employed only 2% of the population. The principal centers for economic activity are Bobo-Dioulasso, Ouagadougou, Banfora, and Koudougou, cities on the rail line to Abidjan, Côte d'Ivoire. Burkinabé industry reflects an interesting diversity, but is dominated by unprofitable state-controlled corporations. Important sectors are food processing, textiles, and leather, and small-scale operations including cigarettes, bricks, and light metal goods such as beds and agricultural implements.

Burkina Faso also has a brewery and moped and bicycle assembly plants. Cotton production, Burkina Faso's second-largest export, recorded about 700,000 480 lb. bales in 2011, about half the production level reached during the 2005–06 seasons. Gold surpassed cotton in 2010 to become the country's largest export revenue earner.

Since the turn of the millennium, efforts have been underway to diversify and to develop new industries such as the shea butter industry. Shea butter is a high quality skin moisturizer and a substitute for cocoa butter in the production of chocolate. The country has also made progress with privatization. In 2007, the government completed the privatization of Comptoir Burkinabé Precious Metals (CBMP), the National Centre for Information Processing (CENATRIN), the National Society of Film of Burkina (SONACIB), and that of ONATEL, by the transfer of 51% of the company's shares to Morocco TELECOM.

As for companies in the energy sector, namely the National Petroleum Company (SONABHY) and the National Society Burkina Faso electricity (SONABEL), privatization was ongoing. Similarly, privatization schemes for the Bureau of Mines and Geology of Burkina (BUMIGEB) and Control Centre of Motor Vehicles (CCVA) were continuing. Privatization of Ouagadougou and Bobo-Dioulasso airports was postponed pending construction of a new international airport at Donsin.

²⁹SCIENCE AND TECHNOLOGY

The World Bank reported in 2009 that there were no patent applications in science and technology in Burkina Faso. Public financing of science was 0.11% of GDP. Burkina Faso has a shortage of skilled scientists and technicians. Scientific and technical aid came chiefly from France. In 1997 there were 17 scientists and 16 technicians per million people, actively engaged in R and D. In 2008, agricultural research and development—the main focus of scientific research—amounted to $19.5 million.

Burkina Faso had four national institutes conducting research in agriculture, medicine, and natural sciences; and two French institutes conducting research in medicine, hydrology, and geology; and an international institute (founded in 1960) to combat endemic and transmitted diseases and malnutrition and to train medical workers in eight member African states. The University of Ouagadougou (founded in 1969) had institutes of mathematics and physics, chemistry, natural science, technology, and health sciences. A 14-nation school of engineering and rural equipment (founded in 1968) was located in Ouagadougou.

³⁰DOMESTIC TRADE

About 90% of the population is employed in subsistence farming, which results in small scale trade and barter centered on agriculture and basic necessities. Much of this trade occurs in the larger towns and cities during weekly markets. The country relies heavily on imports for capital goods and food products. Importers, mainly of Lebanese origin, wholesale and retail their own products, dealing in everything from matches to farm equipment. There are a limited number of privately-owned factories for cotton and textiles manufacturing and food processing. Insufficient economic activity leads many Burkinabé to migrate to surrounding countries in search of work. The main commercial centers are Ouagadougou and Bobo-Dioulasso.

³¹FOREIGN TRADE

Burkina Faso imported $2.25 billion worth of goods and services in 2011, while exporting $1.591 million worth of goods and services. Major import partners in 2010 were Cote d'Ivoire, 26.1%; France, 16%; and Togo, 5.3%, and Ghana, 4.7. Its major export partners were China, 17.3%; Belgium, 11.6%; Singapore, 9.3%; Indonesia, 7.6%; Turkey, 6.4%; Thailand, 4.8%; and Japan, 4.2%.

The leading imports are machinery and food products. Refined petroleum products also account for much of the nation's imports, along with cement, clinker, and fertilizers. Gold and cotton are Burkina Faso's largest export earners, with animal products coming in third. Vegetables, leather, oil seeds, and animal hides account for about 20% of exports.

Principal Trading Partners – Burkina Faso (2010)

(In millions of US dollars)

Country	Total	Exports	Imports	Balance
World	3,355.3	1,200.0	2,155.3	-955.3
Côte d'Ivoire	539.2	1.2	538.0	-536.8
France	337.0	7.0	330.0	-322.9
China	162.7	110.1	52.6	57.5
Belgium	142.0	73.7	68.3	5.4
Togo	86.7	1.4	85.3	-83.9
South Africa	76.7	...	76.7	-76.7
Canada	54.6	21.9	32.6	-10.7
Indonesia	54.1	48.4	5.6	42.8
Turkey	52.1	40.8	11.3	29.5
Belgium-Luxembourg n.s.	50.7	...	50.7	-50.7

(…) data not available or not significant.

(n.s.) not specified.

SOURCE: *2011 Direction of Trade Statistics Yearbook,* New York: United Nations, 2011.

Balance of Payments – Burkina Faso (2009)

(In millions of US dollars)

Current Account		-766.4
Balance on goods	-482.0	
Imports	-1,382.4	
Exports	900.4	
Balance on services	-406.8	
Balance on income	-5.5	
Current transfers	127.9	
Capital Account		281.5
Financial Account		172.1
Direct investment abroad	-34.1	
Direct investment in Burkina Faso	105.2	
Portfolio investment assets	-42.4	
Portfolio investment liabilities	...	
Financial derivatives	...	
Other investment assets	91.8	
Other investment liabilities	51.7	
Net Errors and Omissions		-48.4
Reserves and Related Items		361.3

(…) data not available or not significant.

SOURCE: *Balance of Payment Statistics Yearbook 2011*, Washington, DC: International Monetary Fund, 2011.

Public Finance – Burkina Faso (2009)

(In billions of CFA francs, budgetary central government figures)

Revenue and Grants	771.5	100.0%
Tax revenue	494.6	64.1%
Social contributions	...	
Grants	232.4	30.1%
Other revenue	44.5	5.8%
Expenditures	956.8	100.0%
General public services	...	...
Defense	...	...
Public order and safety	...	...
Economic affairs	...	...
Environmental protection	...	...
Housing and community amenities	...	...
Health	...	...
Recreational, culture, and religion	...	...
Education	...	...
Social protection	...	...

(…) data not available or not significant.

SOURCE: *Government Finance Statistics Yearbook 2010*, Washington, DC: International Monetary Fund, 2010.

32 BALANCE OF PAYMENTS

Burkina Faso's balance of payments has been chronically negative, as receipts from exports of goods and services traditionally do not cover the cost of imports. However, the balance of payments improved considerably over the 10-year period from 2000 to 2010. To offset trade imbalances, the country has had to rely on remittances from Burkinabé working abroad and on international credits and other forms of borrowing. Burkina Faso had a trade deficit of $57 million in 2008. Foreign exchange reserves including gold grew to $1.068 billion in 2010.

33 BANKING AND SECURITIES

In 1959, the Central Bank of West African States (Banque Centrale des États de l'Afrique de l'Ouest—BCEAO) succeeded the Currency Board of French West Africa and Togo as the bank of issue for the former French West African territories. In 1962, it was reorganized as the joint note-issue bank of Benin (then Dahomey), Côte d'Ivoire, Mauritania (which withdrew in 1973), Niger, Senegal, Togo, and Burkina Faso (then Upper Volta). BCEAO notes, known as CFA francs, are guaranteed by France without limitation. Foreign exchange receipts of Burkina Faso go into the BCEAO's exchange pool, which in turn covers its foreign exchange requirements.

As of 31 December 2010, the discount rate, the interest rate at which the central bank lends to financial institutions in the short term, was 4.25%.

In 2010 ten commercial banks including Ecobank operated within the country. Other banks included the International Bank for Commerce, Industry, and Agriculture of Burkina Faso, the National Development Bank (80% government-owned), the National Fund of Agricultural Credit of Burkina Faso (54% state-owned) and the state-owned National Fund of Deposits and Investment.

Microcredit initiatives, organized by cooperatives, NGOs and the public sector, have expanded to supply credit to small and medium enterprises, many of which are headed by women.

34 INSURANCE

Insurance companies had to be government-approved and were subject to government supervision. Automobile third-party liability insurance was compulsory. In 2010 nine insurance companies including Sonar (National Society for Insurance and Reinsurance, 51% state-owned), Foncias, UAB, and Colina operated in the country.

35 PUBLIC FINANCE

In 2010 the budget of Burkina Faso included $1.87 billion in public revenue and $2.343 billion in public expenditures. The budget deficit amounted to 5.9% of GDP. Public debt was 27.0% of GDP, with $2.032 billion of the debt held by foreign entities. Over 40% of government income was derived from customs duties; personnel expenses accounted for over 40% of outlays.

Burkina Faso began implementing IMF Structural Adjustment Programs (SAPs) in 1990 to rein in public spending and generate higher revenues. Through the privatization of state-owned enterprises and increased tax collection and caps on civil servant salaries, the SAPs improved tax collections and stabilized salaries with the result that budget surpluses were attained in 1991. A value-added tax took effect in 1993. An enhanced SAP negotiated in 1993 sought growth of 3–11% annually while curbing financial imbalances. In 2003, the IMF approved a three-year $34 million Poverty Reduction and Growth Facility (PRGF) Arrangement with Burkina Faso. In 2007 this program was extended to support economic reforms for the period 2007–10. Approximately 20% of the government budget was financed by foreign aid.

36 TAXATION

The contribution of direct taxation of all kinds to governmental revenue was relatively low. Individuals in the formal sector paid a single income tax, varying from 2 to 30% on salaries, tips, and other remuneration; business income tax rates varied between 10 and 45%.

Companies paid a combined tax rate of 43.6% on profits including a forfeit tax, and taxes on income from debt and investments. There were also a number of real estate taxes. Indirect taxes included customs duties and license fees. Burkina Faso also levied a value added tax (VAT) that varied from 15 to 20%. There was also a 1% statistical tax and a 1% community solidarity tax. Additional taxes were levied on industrial and agricultural products, livestock breeding, and fishing industry products. On the World Bank's Ease of Doing Business Index in 2011, Burkina Faso was ranked 30th out of 46 sub Saharan African countries in terms of being business tax-friendly.

In addition, there were consumption taxes on specified items, such as petroleum products and tobacco, and local taxes on motor vehicles.

37 CUSTOMS AND DUTIES

Burkina Faso made several trade reforms in the first decade of the 2000s. Most notably, almost all nontariff barriers to trade have been eliminated, and the maximum tariff has been lowered from 200 to 66%, except for petroleum, which still carries a 150% tariff. Burkina Faso is working with the World Trade Organization (WTO) to get its tariff rates within WTO parameters.

In 2011 it cost $2,412 to export and $4,030 to import a container of goods. These costs compared unfavorably to the average for sub Saharan Africa where the cost to export and import containers was $1,960 and $2,503 respectively. The World Bank ranked Burkina Faso 175th out of 191 economies overall on ease of trading across borders.

38 FOREIGN INVESTMENT

Foreign direct investment (FDI) in Burkina Faso represented a net inflow of $171.4 million according to World Bank figures published in 2009. FDI represented 2.11% of GDP. In the International Finance Corporation's (IFC) Doing Business 2010 report, Burkina Faso ranked 147th out of 183 countries, up from 155 in 2009 and 164 in 2008, reflecting efforts to encourage business growth. Reforms aimed at increasing foreign investment included the adoption of a labor code in May 2008, improving the process to transfer property, the elimination of commune authorization requirements, the creation of a one-stop shop to facilitate construction permits, a decrease of the corporate tax rate from 35% to 30%, and a decrease on dividend taxes from 15% to 12%. These reforms have accelerated mining development, and investors have opened four commercial gold mines and a manganese mine since 2007.

On Transparency International's Corruption Perception Index (CPI), Burkina scored 3 on a scale of 0 to 10, where "0" represents a perception that the country is very corrupt, and "10" that the country is corruption free. Its overall score placed it 100 out of 183 ranked countries.

39 ECONOMIC DEVELOPMENT

Burkina Faso's development plans have emphasized agriculture, infrastructure, and privatization. The 1991–95 plan allocated an estimated 75% of government investment to agriculture. The subsequent plan, developed with support by the International Monetary Fund (IMF), included a goal of 5% real annual growth in GDP, with inflation controlled to a maximum of 3% per year. The plan targeted privatization and encouraged foreign investment, particularly in industrial mining.

Beginning in the early 2000s, interest in mining accelerated, especially in gold. By 2010 gold had become the largest earner of foreign exchange, and by 2011 investors were engaged in nearly 30 projects connected with 13 separate gold mines throughout the country. A Poverty Reduction Strategy Paper (PRSP) for the country produced in July 2004 identified four pillars of development: broad-based economic growth, access to basic social services by the poor, increased employment opportunities and income generation for the poor, and good governance.

The country depended significantly on bilateral financial and technical assistance. France and the United States were the leading bilateral aid donors, with the US becoming the largest bilateral donor in 2011. In 2005, Burkina Faso and the US Millennium Challenge Corporation (MCC) signed a $12 million Threshold Country Program to build schools and increase girls' enrollment rates. In July 2008, Burkina Faso signed a 5-year compact for $480.9 million with MCC. The compact program aimed to combat poverty by building roads, improving rural land governance, and aiding farmers with agricultural development and irrigation projects. Bilateral US assistance in fiscal year 2011 was $22.25 million.

Economic development also has been guided multilaterally. In 1991, Burkina Faso began implementation of an IMF-backed Enhanced Structural Adjustment Facility (ESAF), and a Poverty Reduction and Growth Facility (PRGF). Burkina Faso reached its completion point for assistance under the IMF/World Bank Heavily Indebted Poor Countries (HIPC) initiative in 2000. The country completed a PRGF arrangement in 2002 that was fully disbursed. A three-year $34 million PRGF arrangement was approved in June 2003 to support the government's economic reform program for 2003–06. A follow-on PRGF arrangement was approved in April 2007 to support economic reform through 2010. In December 2009 the IMF conducted a fifth review of economic performance under the PRGF arrangement, approving access to $52.52 million, bringing total disbursements to $74.8 million.

In 2012, owing to world gold prices and increases in gold production, the economy was expected to continue modest expansion. However, high quality, long-term jobs in the mining sector are limited, and much more diversification in agriculture and industry is needed to stimulate sustained economic growth in the country.

40 SOCIAL DEVELOPMENT

Social security and social development are largely dependent upon affective networks, beginning with immediate family and extending to relatives, friends, members of clans and ethnic groups, and regional ties. Most Burkinabé link social improvement to education, but as subsistence farmers, most families need older children to help with cultivation and other tasks, and few can afford to send their children to school through high school or college.

Government social welfare programs exist, but subsistence farmers and the many Burkinabé employed in the informal sector fall outside the scope of these programs. A social insurance law provides employed persons with pensions for old age and disability, and widows of pensioners received survivor benefits equal to 50% of the insured person's pension. These programs are funded by equal contributions from employers and employees. Retirement age varies according to occupation. Medical coverage is limited to maternity benefits, consisting of 100% of regular earnings payable for 14 weeks. A worker's compensation program provides both temporary and permanent disability benefits and medical benefits. Employment-related family allowances are also paid to families with children under the age of 14. For those covered by such programs, benefits are often paid late or infrequently.

The constitution prohibits discrimination based on race, religion, or ethnic origin, but does not mention sexual discrimination. Women do not have equal opportunities to education and employment, and they did not have the same property rights as men. Spousal abuse is common and polygamy is legal. Female circumcision, also known as female genital mutilation (FGM), is widely practiced. Although government and NGOs are collaborating to curb the practice, it is estimated that up to 70% of the female population has undergone FGM. Child abuse remains a widespread problem.

Prison conditions are poor and facilities are overcrowded. Serious human rights violations continue and perpetrators of these abuses are rarely punished.

On the UN Human Development Index (HDI), Burkina Faso ranked 161st out of 169 countries worldwide in 2010, falling within the "low development" category. The HDI is a comparative measure of life expectancy, literacy, education, and standards of living for countries worldwide. It is a standard means of measuring well-being, especially child welfare.

41 HEALTH

According to the CIA, life expectancy in Burkina Faso was 54 years in 2011. The country spent 6.4% of its GDP on healthcare in 2009, amounting to $38 per person. There were 1 physician, 7 nurses and midwives, and 90 hospital beds per 10,000 inhabitants. The fertility rate was 6.07, while the infant mortality rate was 79.84 per 1,000 live births. In 2008 the maternal mortality rate, according to the World Bank, was 560 per 100,000 births. It was estimated that 75% of children were vaccinated against measles.

The CIA reported HIV/AIDS prevalence in Burkina Faso to be about 1.2% in 2009. This rate stabilized in 2005, was considered generalized for the population, and relatively low compared with all of sub Saharan Africa.

The major health problems were malnutrition, tuberculosis, and malaria. In 2007 there were 670 cases of tuberculosis per 100,000 people. Public health teams conducted tuberculosis and malaria control campaigns. It was estimated that 17% of children under five years of age were malnourished.

Approximately 47.5% of married women use contraception, though women, on average, have 6 children. As of 2007, 97% of children one year of age were immunized for diphtheria, pertussis, and tetanus.

42 HOUSING

Architecture in the metropolitan centers is essentially Western in appearance, exhibiting considerable French influence. African quarters typically consist of houses made of mud bricks or more costly cement concrete hollow blocks with galvanized iron roofs. Windows tend to be few and small so as to keep out the heat, shut out bright sunlight, and enhance privacy. In rural areas, the Mossi in particular live in round huts made of mud wattle with conical straw roofs or in rectangular mud brick or wattle huts with flat roofs.

Over the past decades, Burkina Faso has experienced housing shortages owing to population growth, urbanization, and poverty. According to the CIA World Factbook, in 2010 about 76% of the population had access to safe water, but only 11% had access to improved sanitation.

43 EDUCATION

In 2009 the World Bank estimated that 63% of age-eligible children in Burkina Faso were enrolled in primary school. This number was up considerably over 2005 when primary enrollment was about 45%. Secondary enrollment for age-eligible children stood at 15%; up 4% over 2005.

Tertiary enrollment was estimated at 3%. The average number of years of schooling was only six years. Of those enrolled in tertiary education, there were 100 male students for every 50 female students. Those who could afford it sent their children abroad for college and university studies.

A 10-year plan from 2000–2010 aimed to improve access to, quality, and management of basic education in the country. However, by 2012 the sector was far from achieving its Millennium Development Goal (MDG) targets for 2015. Much remained to achieve in areas of teacher training, equity in girls education, student retention, reducing overcrowding especially at the tertiary level, and improving the quality of education throughout the system.

In 2011, the UNDP estimated that Burkina Faso had an adult literacy rate of 28.7%, which was fifth lowest in the world. However, this figure represented nearly a 10% improvement over 2002. Public expenditure on education represented 4.6% of GDP.

All public education is free. Primary education is compulsory for six years (ages 6 to 12). Secondary students then have an option of continuing for seven years of general studies or seven to eight years of technical programs. The academic year runs from October to June. The language of instruction is French.

The Center for Higher Education was established in 1969, and in 1974 it became the University of Ouagadougou. The Université Polytechnique de Bobo-Dioulasso was organized in 1996. The primary administrative body is the Ministry of Secondary and Higher Education and Scientific Research.

44 LIBRARIES AND MUSEUMS

The largest library, now part of the University of Ouagadougou, was founded in 1969 and had 70,000 volumes as of 2002. Other libraries are attached to institutes such as the Center for Economic and Social Studies of West Africa and the Institute of Environmental and Agricultural Research. There is also a large library

(20,000 volumes) attached to the Grand Seminary of Koumi in Bobo-Dioulasso.

The French Cultural Center in Ouagadougou holds 30,000 volumes. The National Museum in Ouagadougou has a collection of the ethnography, costumes, and domestic artifacts of Burkina Faso. There is the Museum of Southwest Civilizations in Gaoua, a regional museum in Pobe, and, opened in 1990, a Provincial Museum of Music in Bobo-Dioulasso housing a number of traditional instruments.

In June 2009, the Ruins of Loropéni, located near the borders of Côte d'Ivoire, Ghana, and Togo, were inscribed as the nation's first UNESCO World Heritage Site. The site represented the best preserved of ten fortresses in the Lobi area, a major gold production region from the 14th through 17th centuries.

45 MEDIA

In 2010 the CIA reported that there were 144,000 telephone landlines in Burkina Faso. In addition to landlines, mobile phone subscriptions averaged 33 per 100 people with some 5.708 million mobile cellular phones in use. There were several privately-owned FM and AM radio stations, and three shortwave radio stations. Internet users numbered 1 per 100 citizens with some 1,877 Internet hosts (2010). Prominent newspapers in 2010, with circulation numbers listed parenthetically, included *L'Observatuer* (8,000), *Le Pays* (4,000), and *Sidwaya* (3,000). Some newspapers publish weekly or less frequently depending on human, financial, and material resources as well as content availability. The press agency Agence d'Information du Burkina is based in Ouagadougou.

Radio continues to be the dominant medium, but citizens are becoming increasingly enamored with the Internet and social media. In 2009 the country had 12 public, 19 commercial, 23 community, 19 religious, 4 international radio stations. Broadcasts were in French and 13 indigenous languages. Télévision Nationale du Burkina, the government-owned television station established in 1963, broadcasts in Ouagadougou and Bobo-Dioulasso with reach to other parts of the country. There are also three privately operated television stations.

The 1993 Information Code provides for freedom of speech and freedom of the press, but these freedoms are in large part circumscribed by the considerable power granted to government over the media sector, specifically through the Conseil Supérieur de Communication (CSC). The CSC is composed mostly of government-appointed members. Self-censorship is the norm, as the government is sensitive to criticism.

In 1998 Norbert Zongo, publisher and editor of *l'Indépendent*, was found burned to death in his car about 100 km (62 mi) south of the capital. His newspaper had been investigating the suspicious circumstances surrounding the death of the driver of the President's brother. The death was attributed to torture. In 2006 the only person charged in the Zongo affair was found not guilty, a verdict declared "scandalous" by Reporters Without Borders.

On the Media Sustainability Index (MSI), which ranks media according to free speech, professionalism, plurality of news sources, business acumen, and supporting institutions, the country scored 2.39 out of 4 possible points, a score that placed the country in the "near sustainability" category.

46 ORGANIZATIONS

The Chamber of Commerce, Industry, and Handicrafts of Burkina Faso is headquartered in Ouagadougou. There is also an Office for the Promotion of Burkinabé Enterprises. The National Farmers Union was created in 1987. Cooperative groups and unions are active, as are employers' and professional groups. Student movements have played an influential role in national politics. A national student union was founded in 1965 at the University of Ouagadougou. Other youth organizations include chapters of the Boy Scouts, Girl Guides, Junior Chamber, Youth For Christ, Catholic Youth Organization, and Red Cross Youth. There are several sports associations, including those representing the national sport, soccer, and pastimes such as tennis, handball, and tae kwon do. There is also a national organization for the Special Olympics.

At the community level, Burkina boasts a rich associational life with groups organized around work, faith, savings, mutual self help, age, gender, trades and civic interests. Towns and villages across the country feature famers and growers' associations, women's saving and investment groups, transporters, and dressmakers' and market sellers' associations. Home town and village associations, peer groups, and mutual self help societies are found in the country's regional capitals and abroad. There are national chapters of the Red Cross Society, Caritas, UNICEF, Amnesty International, Transparency International, Publish What You Pay, and the Extractive Industries Transparency Initiative (EITI).

47 TOURISM, TRAVEL, AND RECREATION

The *Tourism Factbook*, published by the UN World Tourism Organization, reported 269,000 incoming tourists to Burkina Faso in 2009, who spent a total of $82 million. Of those incoming tourists, there were 119,000 from Africa and 116,000 from Europe. There were 10,113 hotel beds available in Burkina Faso, which had an occupancy rate of 45%. The estimated daily cost to visit Ouagadougou, the capital, was $282. The cost of visiting other cities averaged $158.

Tourist attractions include the Nazinga, Arly, and "W" park game preserves. The National Museum and Museum of Music showcase the rich culture in Burkina. The market in the capital of Burkina, Ouagadougou, boasts crafts, art, and food, along with the Salon International de l'Artisanat de Ouagadougou (International Craft Show of Ouagadougou), the largest craft fair in Africa.

Every two years in the month of February Burkina Faso hosts FESPACO, the largest African film festival on the continent. FESPACO was held from 26February to 5 March 2011, with the next festival scheduled for 2013. The national football (soccer) team, "The Stallions" (Les Etalons), had qualified to play in the Africa Nations Cup in 2012. All visitors must have a passport, visa, and certificate of yellow fever vaccination.

48 FAMOUS PERSONS

The best-known persons are Maurice Yaméogo (1921–93), a former president of Upper Volta during 1960–66; Moro Naba Kougri (1930–82), the traditional sovereign of the Mossi; and Sangoulé Lamizana (1916–2005), a former army chief of staff, who was president of Upper Volta from 1966 to 1980. Capt. Thomas Sankara (1949?–87), who gained a following in the 1974 clashes with Mali and seized power in a 1983 coup; he was overthrown and executed in 1987. Capt. Blaise Compaoré (b. 1951) assumed the presidency after Sankara's execution.

⁴⁹DEPENDENCIES

Burkina Faso has no territories or colonies.

⁵⁰BIBLIOGRAPHY

Burkina Faso Investment and Business Guide: Strategic and Practical Information. Washington, DC: International Business Publications USA, 2012.

Engberg-Pedersen, Lars. *Endangering Development: Politics, Projects, and Environment in Burkina Faso.* Westport, CT: Praeger, 2003.

Manson, Katrina, and James Knight. *Burkina Faso.* Chalfont St. Peter: Bradt Travel Guides, 2006.

Zeilig, Leo, and David Seddon. *A Political and Economic Dictionary of Africa.* Philadelphia: Routledge/Taylor and Francis, 2005.

BURUNDI

Republic of Burundi

République du Burundi; Republika yu Burundi

CAPITAL: Bujumbura

FLAG: The national flag consists of a white circle in the center with arms extending to the four corners. The circle contains three red stars with green borders. Upper and lower fields formed by the circle and its arms are red; the fields on the sides are green.

ANTHEM: *Burundi Bwacu (Our Beloved Burundi).*

MONETARY UNIT: The Burundi franc (BIF) is a paper currency. There are coins of 1, 5, and 10 francs, and notes of 10, 20, 50, 100, 500, 1,000, 2,000, 5,000 and 10,000 francs. BIF1 = $0.00080 (or $1 = BIF1,219.53) as of 2011.

WEIGHTS AND MEASURES: The metric system is the legal standard.

HOLIDAYS: New Year's Day, 1 January; Unity Day, 5 February; Labor Day, 1 May; Independence Day, 1 July; Assumption Day, 15 August; Victory of UPRONA, 18 September; Rwagasore Day, 13 October; Ndadaye Day, 21 October; All Saints' Day, 1 November; Republic Day, 28 November; Christmas, 25 December. Movable religious holidays include Easter Monday, Ascension, Pentecost Monday, and Eid al-Fitr and Eid al-Adha.

TIME: 2 p.m. = noon GMT.

¹LOCATION, SIZE, AND EXTENT

Burundi is a landlocked country in east-central Africa with an area of 27,830 sq km (10,745 sq mi), of which about 7% consists of lakes. Comparatively, the area occupied by Burundi is slightly smaller than the state of Maryland. It extends 263 km (163 mi) NNE-SSW and 194 km (121 mi) ESE-WNW. Burundi is bounded on the N by Rwanda, on the E and S by Tanzania, and on the W by the Democratic Republic of the Congo, with a total boundary length of 974 km (605 mi).

Burundi's capital city, Bujumbura, is located in the western part of the country.

²TOPOGRAPHY

Burundi is a country mainly of mountains and plateaus, with a western range of mountains running north-south and continuing into Rwanda. The highest point is Mt. Heha at 2,670 m (8,760 ft). The only land below 914 m (3,000 ft) is a narrow strip of plain along the Ruzizi River (about 800 m/2,600 ft), which forms the western border north of Lake Tanganyika. From the mountains eastward, the land declines gradually, dropping to about 1,400 m (4,600 ft) toward the southeastern and southern border. The average elevation of the central plateau is about 1,525 to 2,000 m (5,000 to 6,500 ft). The major rivers form natural boundaries for most of the country. The Kanyaru and the Kagera separate Burundi from Rwanda along many sections of the common border. The Kagera and the Ruvubu are important as the southernmost sources of the Nile. Most of Burundi's southern border is formed by the Malagarasi River. The principal lakes are Tanganyika, Cohoha, and Rweru.

³CLIMATE

Burundi in general has a tropical highland climate, with a considerable daily temperature range in many areas. Temperature also varies considerably from one region to another, chiefly as a result of differences in altitude. The central plateau enjoys pleasantly cool weather, with an average temperature of 20°C (68°F). The area around Lake Tanganyika is warmer, averaging 23°C (73°F); the highest mountain areas are cooler, averaging 16°C (60°F). Bujumbura's average annual temperature is 23°C (73°F). Rain is irregular, falling most heavily in the northwest. Dry seasons vary in length, and there are sometimes long periods of drought. However, four seasons can be distinguished: the long dry season (June–August), the short wet season (September–November), the short dry season (December–January), and the long wet season (February–May). Most of Burundi receives between 130 and 160 cm (51–63 in) of rainfall a year. The Ruzizi Plain and the northeast receive between 75 and 100 cm (30–40 in).

⁴FLORA AND FAUNA

The World Resources Institute estimates that there are 2,500 plant species in Burundi. Of the remaining trees, the most common are eucalyptus, acacia, fig, and oil palms along the lakeshores. In addition, Burundi is home to 116 species of mammals, 597 species of birds, 80 species of reptiles, and 26 amphibian species. This calculation reflects the total number of distinct species residing in the country, not the number of endemic species.

Wildlife was abundant before the region became agricultural. Still found are the elephant, hippopotamus, crocodile, wild boar, lion, antelope, and flying lemur, as well as such game birds as guinea fowl, partridge, duck, geese, quail, and snipe. The crowned crane is prevalent. As the region becomes more densely populated, some species are dwindling or disappearing.

In Lake Tanganyika there is a great variety of fish, including the Nile perch, freshwater sardines, and rare tropical specimens. Most of the 133 fish species in Lake Tanganyika are found nowhere else in the world.

5ENVIRONMENT

Population pressure has placed high stress on the environment. Wildlife survives only in those areas of the country not heavily cultivated; rapid population growth is reducing the amount of uncultivated land. The cutting of forests for fuel is uncontrolled despite legislation requiring permits. Soil erosion due to deforestation, improper terracing, and overgrazing is also a serious problem. Burundi also has a problem with maintaining the purity of its water supply.

According to a 2008 report issued by the World Bank, the number of threatened species included 9 types of mammals, 8 species of birds, 18 species of fish, 6 species of amphibian, 1 type of mollusk, 4 types of other invertebrates, and 2 species of plants. Threatened species include the mountain gorilla, cheetahs, African elephants, and the whale-headed stork.

The World Resources Institute reported that Burundi had designated 154,800 hectares (382,519 acres) of land for protection as of 2006. Water resources totaled 3.6 cu km (0.864 cu mi) while water usage was 0.29 cu km (0.07 cu mi) per year. Domestic water usage accounted for 17% of total usage, industrial for 6%, and agricultural for 77%. Per capita water usage totaled 38 cu m (1,342 cu ft) per year.

The UN reported in 2008 that carbon dioxide emissions in Burundi totaled 180 kilotons.

6POPULATION

The US Central Intelligence Agency (CIA) estimated the population of Burundi in 2011 to be approximately 10,216,190, which placed it 81st in population among the 196 nations of the world. In 2011 approximately 2.4% of the population was over 65 years of age, with another 46% under 15 years of age. The median age in Burundi was 16.9 years. There were 0.98 males for every female in the country. The population's annual rate of change was 3.462%. The projected population for the year 2025 was 11,600,000. Population density in Burundi was calculated at 367 people per sq km (951 people per sq mi).

The UN estimated that 11% of the population lived in urban areas in 2010, and that urban populations had an annual rate of change of 4.9%. The largest urban area was Bujumbura, with a population of 455,000 (2009).

The prevalence of HIV/AIDS (3.3% in 2009) has had a significant impact on the population of Burundi. The AIDS epidemic causes higher death and infant mortality rates and lowers life expectancy.

7MIGRATION

Estimates of Burundi's net migration rate, reported by the CIA in 2011, amounted to 3.22 migrants per 1,000 citizens. The total number of emigrants living abroad was 356,000, and the total number of immigrants living in Burundi was 60,800. Burundi also accepted 9,849 refugees.

Since the early 1990s insecurity and instability have plagued the Great Lakes sub region, displacing large numbers of people. In 1994 with the outbreak of civil war and genocide in Rwanda, an estimated 270,000 Burundians living in Rwanda returned home. Additionally, several hundred thousand Rwandan refugees crossed the border into Burundi. By August 1996, compelled by insecurity within Burundi, most of these refugees returned to Rwanda, and by November 1996, facing insecurity in eastern DRC, some 120,000 Burundians returned home. As of 2007 nearly 100,000 Burundians were displaced internally and some 10,000 Congolese refugees resided in Burundi. Given chronic insecurity, efforts to repatriate refugees have been difficult.

A further source of conflict has resulted from the loss of lands when returnees come back home. Over 20,000 land disputes have been registered by the National Commission on Land and Other Properties. Although some land disputes have been resolved peacefully, many repatriated citizens found themselves homeless, fueling new violence.

8ETHNIC GROUPS

The population is made up mainly of Hutu, a Bantu people, traditionally farmers, who constitute about 85% of the inhabitants. A tall, formerly warrior Hamitic people, the Tutsi (Watutsi, Watusi, Batutsi), people, constitute about 14% of the population, but dominate the government and military. The earliest known inhabitants of the region were the Twa (Batwa), a Pygmy tribe of hunters, related to the Pygmies of the Democratic Republic of the Congo. They make up about 1% of the population. There are about 82,000 immigrant Africans. Europeans and Asians number about 5,000.

9LANGUAGES

The main language is Kirundi, a Bantu language. Both Kirundi and French are official languages. Swahili is used as a lingua franca along Lake Tanganyika and in the Bujumbura area.

10RELIGIONS

Estimates indicate that 62% of the population are Roman Catholic and 5% are Protestant. About 23% practice indigenous religions and about 10% are Muslim (primarily Sunni). Freedom of religion is guaranteed by the constitution and this right is generally respected in practice. Religious groups must register with the Ministry of Interior and maintain a headquarters within the country. The heads of major religions are given diplomatic status. Ascension Day, the Feast of the Assumption, Eid al-Fitr, Eid al-Adha, and Christmas are all observed as national holidays.

11TRANSPORTATION

A great hindrance to Burundi's economic development is lack of adequate transportation. The country is landlocked, and there are no railroads. Only about 7% of roads remain open in all weather; the rest are classified as local roads or tracks. The CIA reported that Burundi has a total of 12,322 km (7,657 mi) of roads, of which 1,286 km (799 mi) are paved. There are eight airports, but only one of them is paved.

Burundi is dependent on Tanzania, Uganda, Zambia, and the Democratic Republic of the Congo for its imports. Through

Bujumbura, Lake Tanganyika serves as the country's sole inland waterway, and as a link with Kigoma in Tanzania for rail shipment to Dar es Salaam.

Air service is maintained by Air Burundi, which operates domestic service and flies to Rwanda, Tanzania, and the Democratic Republic of the Congo. International service is also provided by Brussels Airlines and other airlines. As of 2009 the international airport in Bujumbura was the country's primary and only paved airport. There was one heliport.

12 HISTORY

The first known inhabitants of what is now Burundi were the Twa, a Pygmy tribe of hunters. Between the 7th and 10th centuries, the Hutu, a Bantu agricultural people, occupied the region, probably coming from the Congo Basin. In the 15th and 16th centuries, tall warriors, the Tutsi, believed to have come originally from Ethiopia, entered the area.

The Tutsi, a nomadic pastoral people, gradually subjugated the Hutu and other inhabitants of the region, although they adopted the Hutu language, as did the Twa, so that all three groups were Bantu-speaking. A feudal social system based on caste-the conquering Tutsi and the subjected Hutu-became the dominant feature of social hierarchy, and especially of economic and political relations. The Hutu did the farming and grew the food in return for cattle, but generally had no part in government. The Tutsi were the ruling caste and did no manual labor. To a certain extent, however, the castes were open to each other. Custom allowed a particularly worthy Twa or Hutu to rise to the rank of a Tutsi; conversely, an impoverished Tutsi who had fallen from his former estate could be assimilated into the Hutu.

The penetration of and eventual conquest by the Tutsi was reported as a slow and peaceful process that initiated a process of political integration. The ownership of land was gradually transferred from the Hutu tribes to the *mwami*, the semi-divine king of the Tutsi. The first mwami, Ntare I Rushatsi, is thought to have come to power in the 16th century. While the ruling mwami was in theory an absolute king, he was often regarded as *primus inter pares* among the *ganwa*, prince-like aristocrats of royal lineage. But the mwami had his court and his army, and he could not easily be removed from office.

The first European known to have reached the territory was John Hanning Speke, who traveled with Richard Burton to Lake Tanganyika in 1858. They paddled to the north end of the lake in their search for the headwaters of the Nile. In 1871, Stanley and Livingstone landed at Bujumbura and explored the Ruzizi River region. Subsequently, other explorers, principally German, visited Burundi. After the Berlin Conference of 1884–85, the German zone of influence in East Africa was extended to include Rwanda and Burundi. A German, Count von Götzen, discovered Lake Kivu in 1894. The first Roman Catholic missionaries came in 1898 and in 1899 the territories then known as Ruanda-Urundi officially came under the administration of German East Africa.

The German authorities made no changes in the indigenous organization, choosing only Tutsi for positions of colonial authority. They administered the territory through the traditional authorities in accordance with the laws and customs of the region. However, the history of Burundi under the German administration was marked by constant factional struggles and rivalry, in

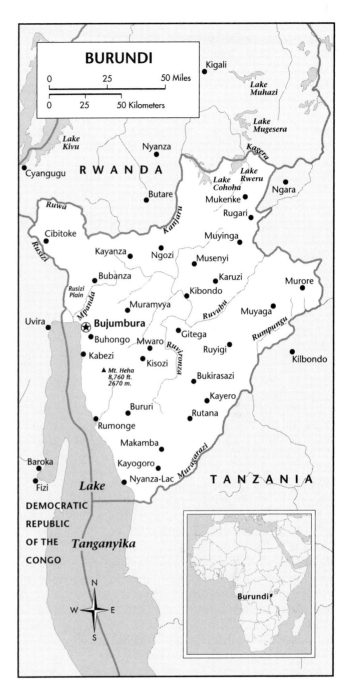

LOCATION: 2°20′ to 4°28′S; 29° to 30°50′E. BOUNDARY LENGTHS: Rwanda, 290 kilometers (180 miles); Tanzania, 451 kilometers (280 miles); Democratic Republic of the Congo, 233 kilometers (145 miles).

contrast to the peaceful state of affairs in Rwanda. When Belgian troops occupied the country in 1916, they found it in dissension and the three-year-old mwami, Mwambutsa IV, the center of court intrigue. In 1923 the League of Nations awarded Belgium a mandate to the region of Ruanda-Urundi. The Belgians adopted the same policy of indirect administration employed by the Germans, retaining the entire Tutsi-dominated hierarchy. In 1946 Ruanda-Urundi became a United Nations Trust Territory under Belgian administration.

On 18 September 1961 elections for the National Assembly were held in Urundi under the auspices of the UN. The result was a sweeping victory for UPRONA, the party headed by Prince Louis Rwagasore, eldest son of the mwami. On 13 October 1961, shortly after Prince Rwagasore had become premier, he was assassinated. Two leaders of the Christian Democratic Party were charged, convicted of responsibility for the murder, and executed.

The UN had strongly urged that Urundi and Ruanda come to independence united, since their relationship had long been close, their economies were integrated, and their people were ethnically one. However, the UN reluctantly decided that there was insufficient support for the union in both regions, and on 27 June 1962, the UN General Assembly passed a resolution that called for the creation of two independent nations, Burundi and Rwanda.

On 1 July 1962 Burundi became an independent, constitutional monarchy headed by King Mwambutsa IV. The king set up a government that comprised equal numbers of Hutu and Tutsi, with a Hutu as prime minister. In 1965 the assassination of the prime minister, and Mwambutsa's subsequent refusal to appoint a Hutu prime minister even though the Hutu won a parliamentary majority, began a destabilizing cycle of Hutu uprisings and government repression. Mwambutsa was deposed in July 1966 and was succeeded in September by his son, Charles, who then became known as Ntare V. On 29 November 1966 Ntare V was in turn overthrown by a military coup headed by the Tutsi prime minister, Col. Michel Micombero, who abolished the monarchy and declared Burundi a republic with himself as president.

In 1969 an alleged Hutu coup attempt ended in the arrest of 30 prominent businessmen and officials. Another Hutu-led coup attempt in April 1972 led to widespread civil war, in which mass killings of Hutu by Tutsi and of Tutsi by Hutu were reported. Ntare V was killed on 29 April 1972, reportedly by Hutu, which led to the massacre of 150,000 Burundian Hutu a month later. On 21 July 1973 the UN High Commissioner for Refugees reported that there were at least 85,000 Hutu refugees from Burundi, of whom an estimated 40,000 were in Tanzania, 35,000 in Zaire (now the Democratic Republic of the Congo), and 10,000 in Rwanda. President Micombero later conceded that more than 100,000 persons had been killed in the course of the 1972 insurgency, and perhaps hundreds of thousands of refugees had fled. Most of the deaths were among the Hutu, and educated Hutu were systematically massacred under Micombero's de facto military regime. By August 1972 nearly all educated Hutu had fled or been killed. During 1973 rebel bands conducted raids into Burundi from across the Rwandan and Tanzanian borders, and Burundi's relations with those two neighbors deteriorated. By the end of 1973, however, the government was fully in control.

On 1 November 1976 President Micombero was stripped of all powers in a bloodless military coup led by Lt. Col. Jean-Baptiste Bagaza, and the Supreme Revolutionary Committee (SRC) that subsequently took power named Bagaza president. The new regime, like the old, was dominated by Tutsi. At a party congress of UPRONA in 1979, a party central committee headed by President Bagaza was selected to replace the SRC, and civilian rule was formally restored. Although the military remained active in both the party and in the government, Bagaza encouraged land reform, electoral reform, and reconciliation. A new constitution was adopted in a national referendum in 1981, and a legislative assembly was elected in 1982. Bagaza was reelected unopposed to a new five-year term in 1984. However, after 1984 Bagaza's human rights

record worsened due to his suppression of religious freedom and political opposition. In September 1987, he was overthrown in a bloodless military coup while he attended a conference in Canada. Maj. Pierre Buyoya became president.

Buyoya withdrew recognition of opposition parties, suspended the 1981 constitution, and established his ruling Military Committee for National Salvation (CSMN). Ethnic violence erupted in 1988, and in response to rumors of the murder of Tutsi in the north, the army massacred between 5,000 and 25,000 Hutu. Over 100,000 were left homeless and 60,000 took refuge in Rwanda. Throughout 1988 an estimated 150,000 people were killed.

Major Buyoya agreed to the restoration of multiparty politics in 1991, and a new constitution was approved in March 1992. Competition between approved, ethnically balanced parties in the June 1993 election brought to office Burundi's first elected president, as well as its first Hutu president, Melchior Ndadaye. Ndadaye got 66% of the vote, while Buyoya received just 33%. Ndadaye began to talk of reform of the Tutsi-dominated armed forces, but on 21 October 1993 Ndadaye and several cabinet members were assassinated by a faction of Tutsi soldiers. Other cabinet officers, including Prime Minister Sylvie Kinigi, a Tutsi, took refuge in the French embassy. Ethnic violence continued, launching the country into civil war, with some 10,000 murdered and 800,000 fleeing the country. It has been estimated that as many as 100,000 were killed in this round of violence.

The military coup attempt failed, however, and Ndadaye's Burundi Democratic Front (FRODEBU) regained control, electing Cyprien Ntaryamira as president in January 1994. In February, Ndadaye's successor was inaugurated, but his coalition was unable to restore order. In an effort to negotiate peace, he went to Tanzania for consultations. On his flight home, the plane in which he was returning, along with Rwanda's President Habyarimana, was shot down near the Rwanda capital, Kigali, on 6 April 1994. Two other members of his cabinet also died in the attack. This crash marked the beginning of the Rwandan genocide.

The constitutionally provided line of succession left the post of president to Sylvestre Ntibantunganya. He served in a transitional capacity until October 1994 when the assembly elected him to serve a four-year term. In contrast to the genocide that erupted in Rwanda, Ntibantunganya managed to maintain relative stability in Burundi for a time. However, the influx of refugees from Rwanda and increased armament of Hutu and Tutsi groups fueled sporadic violence prompting the government to impose a curfew in Bujumbura in December.

The death toll attributable to ethnic strife and political problems continued to mount during the first half of 1995. In 1993 alone, an estimated 150,000 had died in ethnic violence between Hutu and Tutsi. The averting of a citywide strike in the capital of Bujumbura in early February 1995 helped ease the ethnic tension, but the relief was short-lived. On 11 March, Mines and Energy Minister Ernest Kabushemeye was shot to death as the violence flared anew. Later that month, fighting in the central market left four people dead. By 25 March, thousands of people were fleeing Bujumbura to escape the violence, and hundreds were feared dead in new fighting. The exodus grew to 50,000 refugees from a city with a total population of 300,000. Two suburbs where clashes had occurred were practically deserted.

The flare-up also affected refugees from neighboring Rwanda who had fled to seven northern Burundi camps to escape Hutu-Tutsi violence in their own country. An estimated 20,000 refugees undertook a two-day trek to Tanzania to escape the violence at one of the camps, which left 12 dead and 22 wounded. The seven camps, which once held more than 25,000 Rwandans, were closed by August 1996 as the last group of the refugees returned to its homeland.

Despite an Organization of African Unity (OAU) peace mission, the Hutu militias and Tutsi-dominated government army battled throughout the early days of June in Bujumbura's suburbs. The OAU mission was aimed at ending months of fighting between the majority Hutu and the Tutsi before the clashes could develop into an all-out war.

On 25 July 1996 Maj. Pierre Buyoya seized power in a coup backed by the Burundi military. The parliament continued to function, although during Buyoya's "Transition Period" its powers were severely curtailed. Soon thereafter, six East African nations cut trade ties to the country and imposed and economic embargo after demanding Maj. Buyoya restore parliament. The African leaders also demanded that Major Buyoya, president of Burundi from 1987 to 1993, begin peace talks with Hutu rebels. Yet ethnic violence escalated in the months following Major Buyoya's takeover. Each side blamed the other for the assassination in September of Archbishop Joachim Ruhuna, Burundi's senior Roman Catholic archbishop. In 1999 in his new role as facilitator of the Arusha Peace Process, Nelson Mandela asked all parties-the government, rebel forces, and international organizations-to sit down and discuss the issues. In the early months of 2000 several such meetings were held in Tanzania, leading up to the signing of the Arusha Peace and Reconciliation Agreement for Burundi on 28 August 2000. However, Mandela's efforts ran up against entrenched regional conflicts and ethnic animosities as several armed factions refused to accept the peace agreement.

Seeking to secure national borders, Burundian troops intervened in the conflict in the Democratic Republic of the Congo in 1998, but were redeployed to Burundi to engage rebels operating within the country and from across the Congolese border. In October 2002, Burundi's smaller rebel groups—the CNDD-FDD (National Council for the Defense of Democracy-Forces for the Defense of Democracy) of Jean Bosco Ndayikengurukiye and the Palipehutu-FNL (Forces for National Liberation) of Alain Mugabarabona—signed a cease-fire, followed by a similar agreement between the CNDD-FDD of Pierre Nkurunziza and the transitional government of Burundi. Only the Palipehutu-FNL of Agathon Rwasa had not signed a cease-fire with the transitional government by mid-June 2003.

Under the Arusha Accords, a three-year transitional government was inaugurated 1 November 2001 under the leadership of Pierre Buyoya. On 30 April 2003 Buyoya stepped down under the terms of the accord, making way for a Hutu vice president, Domitien Ndayizeye, to assume the presidency for the remaining 18 months. However, since the signing of the cease-fires, fighting between the army and CNDD-FDD rebels occurred daily. On 3 February 2003 the African Union authorized an African Mission in Burundi (AMIB), which fielded troops from South Africa, Ethiopia, and Mozambique to safeguard cantonment areas and to provide technical assistance to the disarmament and demobilization process. In late 2003 the Burundian government and the CNDD-FDD signed renewed cease-fire and power-sharing agreements. In March 2004 members of the CNDD-FDD assumed governmental and parliamentary offices. Many bilateral donors, as well as the World Bank, assisted in funding Burundi's disarmament, demobilization, and reintegration program for former rebel combatants. However, some conflict continued, and in August 2004 the extremist Palipehutu-FNL massacred more than 150 Congolese Tutsi refugees, and as of late 2005 continued to stage attacks.

Reaching a stable compromise on power sharing proved difficult. Although a post-transition constitution was approved in September 2004, the vote was boycotted by the Tutsi parties. In addition, the Arusha Peace Agreement mandated that local and national elections be held before the end of the transitional period on 31 October 2004, but transitional institutions were extended. On 28 February 2005, however, Burundians popularly approved a post-transitional constitution by national referendum, with elections scheduled for the summer of 2005. After local, parliamentary, and other elections in June and July, on 19 August 2005 the good governance minister, Pierre Nkurunziza, became the first post-transitional president.

In August 2006 former president Ndayizeye was accused of involvement in an alleged coup plot. However, he was acquitted by the Supreme Court in January 2007. In September 2006, the FNL and the government signed a cease-fire during talks in Tanzania. But by December 2006, international observers claimed the government had become increasingly authoritarian, and that it risked triggering unrest and eroding peace. Nonetheless, in February 2007 the UN concluded its peacekeeping mission and redirected its operations toward reconstruction.

A measure of stability was gained when Burundi became a member of the East African Community (EAC) in 2007 and entered the EAC Customs Union in July 2009. Membership in the union allows for free trade between the five member nations: Kenya, Tanzania, Uganda, Rwanda, and Burundi. In 2009 plans were advanced to adopt a single currency for the EAC. Member governments were also considering the formation of a political federation.

By end of 2011 the political scene remained highly unstable. In the run up to the presidential election in June 2010, all candidates opposing Nkurunziza pulled out of the race alleging electoral fraud, leaving Nkurunziza to be reelected by default. The opposition boycott of the election called into question the credibility of the process and the legitimacy of the results, and threatened to re-ignite conflict in the country.

¹³GOVERNMENT

Burundi has transitioned from a constitutional monarchy at independence to a modern republic with three branches of power. However, its government has never enjoyed a lengthy period of stability. Burundi's present constitution was ratified by referendum on 28 February 2005, replacing the 13 March 1992 instrument. The president serves as both the chief of state and head of government. The cabinet is a council of ministers appointed by the president.

The bicameral parliament consists of the Senate with 54 seats—34 members elected by indirect vote to serve five-year terms, with the remaining seats assigned to ethnic groups and former heads of state. The National Assembly had a minimum of 100 seats—60% Hutu and 40% Tutsi with at least 30% reserved for women—and additional seats appointed by a National Independent Electoral Commission to ensure ethnic representation. Members are elected to serve five-year terms with elections due in 2015.

14 POLITICAL PARTIES

Belgium first allowed political competition by parties after 1948. Two major forces emerged: the multi-ethnic Union for National Progress (Parti de l'Unité et du Progrès National—UPRONA), led by Tutsi Prince Louis Rwagasore, and the Belgium-supported Christian Democratic Party (Parti Démocrate Chrétien—PDC). Of the 23 registered political parties, only two retained political significance in the years following independence from Belgium: UPRONA, and the People's Party (Parti du Peuple–PP), an all-Hutu party. UPRONA, which initially controlled 58 seats in the assembly out of a total of 64, was soon torn by internecine leadership rivalries. Over time, these rivalries mirrored ethnic confrontation between Tutsi and Hutu. In the assembly, the PP merged with the Hutu wing of UPRONA to form the so-called Monrovia Group, while the Tutsi wing of UPRONA referred to itself as the Casablanca Group.

In the 2005 elections Burundi counted 30 registered political parties without representation in parliament and six parties with representation in one or both houses. The six major parties were the Front for the Defense of Democracy (CNDD-FDD) with 32 senate and 64 assembly seats; Burundi Democratic Front (FRODEBU) with 5 senate and 30 assembly seats; UPRONA with 2 senate and 15 assembly seats; and the National Council for the Defense of Democracy (CNDD), the breakaway party from the CNDD-FDD with 3 senate and 4 assembly seats.

In the June 2010 presidential election, 34 political parties registered initially, but by election day opposition candidates had pulled out of the race, claiming that the ballot was rigged in favor of Nkurunziza. Nkurunziza ran (and won) unopposed. In the July 2010 assembly elections, the CNDD-FDD won 81.2% of the vote and 81 seats, followed by UPRONA with 11.6% and 17 seats, and FRODEBU with 5.9% and 5 seats. Three seats went to other, small, parties. In the senate, the CNDD-FDD won 94.12% of the vote and 32 seats, followed by UPRONA with 5.88% and 2 seats.

15 LOCAL GOVERNMENT

Over time Burundi has transitioned from 8 to 17 provinces, including the capital city regions. Communal councils govern each of Burundi's 129 communes with 25 members per council. There were also local colline (hill) councils elections without party affiliation in 2005. Both of these local councils are directly elected.

16 JUDICIAL SYSTEM

The legal system of Burundi is based on German and French civil codes and customary law. It provides for 123 local tribunals and 17 tribunals of first instance in the provinces, and for courts of appeal, the Supreme Court of Burundi, and a constitutional court in Bujumbura. The task of the constitutional court was to review new laws for conformity to the constitution. The constitutional court also created a high court responsible for resolving charges of crimes by high-level government officials. A military court had jurisdiction over the armed forces. The president of the republic nominated members of the supreme and constitutional courts, with the Supreme Court of Burundi as the final court of appeal. At times, domination by Tutsis of the courts has abetted ethnic competition and rivalry in the country.

17 ARMED FORCES

According to the International Institute for Strategic Studies, armed forces in Burundi totaled 20,000 members in 2011, all of which were members of the army. Armed forces represented 1.1% of the labor force in Burundi. Defense spending totaled $200.6 million and accounted for 5.9% of gross domestic product (GDP).

18 INTERNATIONAL COOPERATION

Burundi belongs to several international organizations. It was admitted to UN membership on 18 September 1962 and is a member of ECA and several nonregional specialized agencies. It also belongs to the African Development Bank, G-77, the ACP Group, COMESA, the New Partnership for Africa's Development (NEPAD), and the African Union (AU). It became a member of the WTO on 23 July 1995. Burundi, Rwanda, and the Democratic Republic of the Congo form the Economic Community of the Great Lakes Countries (CEPGL), which is intended to foster development in the region of lakes Kivu and Tanganyika. Burundi also cooperates with Rwanda and Tanzania in the development of the Kagera River Basin. Burundi became a member of the East African Community (EAC) in 2007 and entered the EAC Customs Union in July 2009.

The UN Operation in Burundi (ONUB) established in May 2004, completed its mission early 2007. ONUB's mandate to reconcile and keep the peace among Tutsi, Hutu and other conflicted ethnic groups in the sub region was succeeded by the UN Integrated Office (BINUB) established by Security Council resolution 1719 of 26 October 2006.

Relations with neighbor Rwanda continued to be critical. In late October 2009, Burundi and Rwanda agreed upon an extradition treaty that would allow Rwanda to prosecute individuals in Burundi accused of participating in the 1994 genocide. 6,000 Burundians were suspected of participating in the genocide, lending special importance to the extradition treaty.

In environmental cooperation, Burundi is part of the Basel Convention, the Convention on Biological Diversity, CITES, the Kyoto Protocol, the Montréal Protocol, and the UN Conventions on Climate Change and Desertification.

19 ECONOMY

In 2010 the GDP was approximately $3.4 billion (purchasing power parity—PPP). At the official exchange rate GDP was $1.5 billion. The real growth rate was 3.9%. Per capita PPP was $300. Inflation stood at 9.8%. These figures placed Burundi near the bottom of global economic performance. For example, the country ranked 172nd worldwide in GDP PPP.

In 2011 Burundi was still largely a subsistence agriculture economy with agriculture accounting for 32% of the economy; industry 21% and services 47%. More than 90% of the population was engaged in cultivation of bananas, plantains, sweet potatoes and manioc—Burundi's staple crops. Nevertheless, 13% of all imports were foodstuffs, indicating a serious deficit in the efficiency of that sector. Much of the country's growth was based upon coffee and tea exports, which were vulnerable to world market price fluctuations, and subject to unpredictable weather conditions. Conflict, displaced persons, land disputes, soil erosion and poor governance were contributing factors to constrained economic performance, and by end of 2011 Burundi continued to rely heavily on aid from multi-national organizations.

Burundi's mineral sector was small, with a potential that remains undetermined. Gold, tungsten, columbo-tantalite, bastnaesite, and cassiterite each were mined in small quantities. Explorations have revealed petroleum under Lake Tanganyika and in the Ruzizi Valley, as well as large nickel deposits at Musongati. Copper, cobalt, and platinum are expected to be found in association with the nickel. Phosphate rock deposits have also been located.

The ongoing development of the EAC common market was one step to increase trade to, from, and within the sub region. The goal of the EAC was to establish a strong political federation by 2015. Towards that end, EAC members hoped to launch a new, single, shared currency by 2012.

[20]INCOME

The CIA estimated that in 2010 the GDP of Burundi was $3.397 billion. The CIA defines GDP as the value of all final goods and services produced within a nation in a given year and computed on the basis of purchasing power parity (PPP) rather than value as measured on the basis of the rate of the exchange based on current dollars. The per capita GDP was estimated at $300, meaning that most people were living at or below the poverty rate of $2 per day. According to the World Bank, remittances from citizens living abroad totaled $28.2 million or about $3 per capita and accounted for approximately 0.8% of GDP.

[21]LABOR

As of 2007 Burundi had a total labor force of 4.2 million people. Based on estimates from 2002 (the most recent available information as of January 2012), the CIA reported that 93.6% were employed in agriculture, 2.3% in industry, and 4.1% in the service sector. Most of the labor force was involved in subsistence farming. Although the country's labor code restricted child labor, some 640,000 minors were performing compulsory labor. In addition, children in rural areas under 16 years of age performed heavy manual labor.

Workers were legally permitted to form and join unions, although the army, gendarmie, and foreign workers were prohibited from unionizing. The labor code permitted strikes only after alternative remedies had been exhausted and six days notice given. Unions were permitted to be affiliated with international organizations. Civil servants made up the majority of union members. Approximately 50% of the country's public sector employees were union members; less than 10% of the formal workforce in the private sector were unionized. Burundi had a labor code mandating a 45-hour workweek, however, most people worked in the unregulated informal sector with little or no protection for rights.

[22]AGRICULTURE

In 2011 roughly 49% of the total land was farmed, with the average family plot size estimated at 0.8 hectares (2 acres). Major crops included coffee, cotton, tea, corn, sorghum, sweet potatoes, bananas, and manioc (tapioca). In 2009 cereal production amounted to 299,770 tons, fruit production 733,827 tons, and vegetable production 442,018 tons.

Coffee and tea exports comprised the majority of foreign earnings; coffee alone accounted for 39% of exports in 2004. Coffee is chiefly of the arabica variety. The government regulates the grading, pricing, and marketing of the coffee crop, and all coffee export contracts require approval.

The government has been encouraging cotton and tea production in order to diversify exports. Palm oil is obtained from trees in plantations along the shore of Lake Tanganyika. Tobacco and wheat cultivated in the highland areas also yield some cash income. However, much of the land has suffered a loss of fertility because of soil erosion from poor agricultural practices, irregularity of rainfall, lack of fertilizer, and shortened fallow periods.

[23]ANIMAL HUSBANDRY

The UN Food and Agriculture Organization (FAO) reported that Burundi dedicated 900,000 hectares (2.22 million acres) to permanent pasture or meadow in 2009. During that year, the country tended 5 million chickens, 553,538 head of cattle, and 202,926 pigs. The production from these animals amounted to 13,410 tons of beef and veal, 11,200 tons of pork, 6,862 tons of poultry, 2,057 tons of eggs, and 36,068 tons of milk. Burundi also produced 3,006 tons of cattle hide.

Social prestige has traditionally been derived from ownership of cattle. This cultural characteristic along with improved sanitary conditions, has resulted in the accumulation of large herds of poor-quality stock. For example, milk yields per cow average only 350 kg a year (17% of world average). Meat consumption was estimated at only 48 calories per person per day, only one-tenth of the world's average. Large herds also retarded economic development by reducing the amount of land available for crops, and they destroyed pastureland by overgrazing. Through various programs, the government was seeking to eliminate excess cattle, improve the remaining livestock, and introduce modern stock-raising methods.

[24]FISHING

There are three main methods of fishing in Lake Tanganyika: industrial, native, and traditional. Industrial fishing, which developed after 1946, is carried out by small trawlers accompanied by several rowboats. Native fishing occurs in catamarans equipped with lights, nets, and engines. Traditional fishing, which dates from time immemorial, is conducted in pirogues equipped with lights and landing nets. According to the UN FAO, in 2008 the annual capture totaled 17,766 tons.

[25]FORESTRY

Approximately 7% of Burundi (approximately 325,000 hectares) was covered by forest in 2011, an increase from 3.7% in 2000. The harvesting of wood has increased only slightly since the late 1970s, and the emphasis has now shifted to reforestation. The UN FAO estimated the 2009 roundwood production at 333,000 cu m (11.8

million cu ft). The value of all forest products, including round-wood, totaled $786,000.

26 MINING

Mining and energy accounted for about 1% of Burundi's GDP in 2004. The country has been known to produce columbium (niobium)-tantalum ore, gold, kaolin (china clay), tin, and tungsten ore, mostly for export, and limestone, peat, sand, and gravel for domestic consumption. Burundi has significant deposits of feldspar, kaolin, nickel, phosphate, platinum-group metals, quartzite, rare-earth metals, vanadium, and limestone for cement. There are gold deposits at Mabayi, Muyinga, Cankuzo, and Tora-Ruzibazi, where artisanal mining took place. After waning in the early 1990s, gold production rose to 1,000 kg in 1994 and 2,200 kg in 1996, and then dropped to 1,500 kg in 1997–2000. In 2009 gold mine production totaled an estimated 750 kg.

The government has tried to transfer technical skills to artisanal miners, to raise productivity and increase state revenues. The Burundi Mining Corp., a government-private venture, was exploring the possibility of producing gold on a commercial basis at Muyinga, where resources were estimated at 60 tons of gold. Deposits of cassiterite, columbite-tantalite, and wolframite associated with pegmatites have been found in Kayanza and Kirundo provinces. Nickel reserves, found in 1974, were estimated at 370 million tons (3%–5% of the world's total); high transportation costs, low world market prices, and political instability have delayed their exploitation.

Since 1993 foreign investment and development of Burundi's resources have been hindered by civil unrest, social strife, and economic sanctions imposed by regional states; the economy contracted by 23% in the period 1993–96. Although the sanctions were lifted in 1999, internal strife continued to hurt the economy. In 2000 Burundi joined with 19 other nations to form Africa's first free-trade area, and the World Bank and other international donors pledged to give $440 million in reconstruction aid to Burundi. In 2009 production of columbite-tantalite (gross weight) was 84,000 kg, and of peat, 9,800 metric tons. Tin mines produced an estimated 21 metric tons in 2009. Tungsten mine output totaled 194 metric tons in 2009.

27 ENERGY AND POWER

The World Bank reported in 2008 that Burundi produced 208 million kWh of electricity and consumed 163.5 million kWh, or 16 kWh per capita.

Two dams completed since 1984 have increased the amount of power production from hydroelectric installations, but Bujumbura and Gitega were the only two cities with municipal electricity service. Burundi imports its petroleum products from Kenya and Tanzania. Consumption of oil in 2009 was estimated at only 2,600 barrels per day. Given the high cost of petroleum, wood and peat accounted for 94% of energy consumption with peat offering an alternative to increasingly scarce firewood and charcoal. The government is promoting peat production and fostering the development of renewable energy resources such as solar electricity and biogas.

In 2008 oil was detected in the Ruzizi valley bordering the Democratic Republic of the Congo. The government awarded one of four blocks to the London-based Surestream Petroleum

company for exploration. Three blocks were still available for prospecting. In addition, a subsidiary of Amoco has held an oil exploratory concession in and around Lake Tanganyika.

28 INDUSTRY

In 2011 industrial activities were almost exclusively concentrated in Bujumbura and accounted for an estimated 21% of GDP in 2010. The industrial sector transforms to varying degrees agricultural and forestry products including cotton, coffee, tea, vegetable oil, and woods. There are also several small plants for soft drinks, blankets, footwear, soap, insecticides, building materials, furniture, and metal goods. The future of industrial development is largely dependent on security, political stability, improved electric power supply and transportation, as well as more efficient and cooperative commercial relations with neighboring countries. The Brarudi brewery, with a reputation in the sub region for producing quality beer, is the country's largest and most reliable source of tax revenue.

29 SCIENCE AND TECHNOLOGY

Burundi is on the receiving end of science and technology and is dependent upon many donors including the EEC, the World Bank, Belgium, France, the Federal Republic of Germany (FRG), the United States, Switzerland, and China for technical and other assistance. The National Center of Hydrometeorology, the Ministry of Geology and Mines, the Institute of Agronomical Sciences of Burundi (founded in 1960), and a medical laboratory devoted to nutritional studies are located in Bujumbura. The University of Burundi, in Bujumbura, has faculties of sciences, medicine, psychology and education, agriculture, and applied sciences. The Higher Institute of Agriculture is in Gitega.

From 1987–97 total expenditures for research and development totaled 0.3% of GDP with fewer than a thousand scientists and engineers actively engaged in research and development. The World Bank reported in 2009 that there were no patent applications in science and technology in Burundi.

30 DOMESTIC TRADE

The informal sector accounts for most of Burundi's domestic trade. Foodstuffs, beer, soft drinks, soap, insecticides, hardware, textiles, and cigarettes are traded wholesale and in small shops owned and run mainly by Greeks, Indians, and Arabs. Markets in towns and villages also provide centers for trade. All domestic trade is influenced by the coffee harvest, which from June–September, increases incomes and stimulates trading with an inflationary effect.

Business hours are usually 8 a.m. to noon and 2 to 5 p.m. on weekdays, and 8 a.m. to noon on Saturday. Banks are open 8 to 11:30 a.m. Monday-Friday.

31 FOREIGN TRADE

Burundi imported $336 million worth of goods and services in 2008, while exporting $71 million worth of goods and services. Major import partners in 2009 were Saudi Arabia, 15.4%; Belgium, 10.2%; China, 9.8%; Uganda, 7.9%; Kenya, 6.9%; France, 4.9%; and Germany, 4% . Its major export partners were Germany,

Principal Trading Partners – Burundi (2010)

(In millions of US dollars)

Country	Total	Exports	Imports	Balance
World	609.7	100.5	509.2	-408.7
Sa'udi Arabia	77.3	...	77.3	-77.3
Belgium	41.7	4.4	37.4	-33.0
Germany	40.4	21.1	19.3	1.8
Uganda	40.1	1.8	38.3	-36.5
China	39.8	3.1	36.7	-33.6
Kenya	35.3	1.7	33.6	-32.0
Zambia	31.1	...	31.1	-31.1
Asia n.s.	28.3	...	28.3	-28.3
France	22.5	1.9	20.6	-18.7
India	19.3	0.2	19.1	-18.9

(…) data not available or not significant.

(n.s.) not specified.

SOURCE: *2011 Direction of Trade Statistics Yearbook,* New York: United Nations, 2011.

Balance of Payments – Burundi (2010)

(In millions of US dollars)

Current Account		-323.1
Balance on goods	-337.2	
Imports	-438.4	
Exports	101.2	
Balance on services	-88.7	
Balance on income	-10.9	
Current transfers	113.6	
Capital Account		**75.7**
Financial Account		**63.4**
Direct investment abroad	...	
Direct investment in Burundi	0.8	
Portfolio investment assets	...	
Portfolio investment liabilities	...	
Financial derivatives	...	
Other investment assets	-43.6	
Other investment liabilities	106.2	
Net Errors and Omissions		**8.1**
Reserves and Related Items		**175.9**

(…) data not available or not significant.

SOURCE: *Balance of Payment Statistics Yearbook 2011,* Washington, DC: International Monetary Fund, 2011.

26%; Belgium, 11.2%; Sweden, 10.8%; Pakistan, 7.6%; and the United States, 4.6%.

Burundi became a member of the East African Community (EAC) in 2007 and entered the EAC Customs Union in July 2009. Membership in the union allows for free trade between the five member nations: Kenya, Tanzania, Uganda, Rwanda, and Burundi. Over the long-haul, the government anticipates that freer trade will lower prices on imports and generate higher export revenues.

32 BALANCE OF PAYMENTS

In 2010 Burundi had a foreign trade deficit of $403 million, amounting to 19.3% of GDP.

33 BANKING AND SECURITIES

The Bank of the Republic of Burundi is the nation's central bank and bank of issue. Established in 1967 as the Bank of the Kingdom of Burundi, the central bank acts in a supervisory capacity to the nation's banking industry, and is the bank of issue.

Some 12 commercial banks operate in Burundi including the Commercial Bank of Burundi, the Credit Bank of Bujumbura, the Belgian-African Bank of Burundi, and Ecobank. There are also a savings bank and a postal savings bank. Other financial institutions include the National Economic Development Bank and the Central Fund for Mobilization and Finance.

34 INSURANCE

Insurance companies operating in Burundi include the Commercial Union of Insurance and Reinsurance (Union Commerciale d'Assurances et de Réassurances—UCAR), the partly state-owned Insurance Co. of Burundi (Société d'Assurances du Burundi—SOCABU), and a branch of the General Insurance of France. Motor vehicle insurance is the only compulsory coverage.

35 PUBLIC FINANCE

In 2010 the budget of Burundi included $386.3 million in public revenue and $476.2 million in public expenditures. The budget

deficit amounted to 6.8% of GDP. Public debt was 31.1% of GDP, with $1.2 billion of the debt held by foreign entities. Total government expenditures, including consumption and transfer payments, dropped to 40 percent of GDP. Spending commitments made under the 2009 Finance Act and promised civil service salary increases were expected to increase the budget deficit.

Government outlays by function were as follows: general public services, 43.1%; defense, 27.7%; public order and safety, 2.8%; economic affairs, 5.2%; health, 2.6%; recreation, culture, and religion, 0.4%; education, 18%; and social protection, 0.2%.

36 TAXATION

Burundi has relatively high tax rates with the top income and corporate tax rates at 35 percent. A value-added tax (VAT) replaced the general sales tax on 1 July 2009. A significant portion of state revenues is generated by import and export duties and a tax on beer. In 2010 overall tax revenue as a percentage of GDP was 18 percent.

37 CUSTOMS AND DUTIES

Burundi's weighted average tariff rate was 5.6% in 2009. Since joining the East African Community, Burundi has lowered tariffs to bring them in line with other EAC member countries. The trade regime is relatively open, but the cost of trade reflects inadequate administrative capacity, poor infrastructure, and customs corruption. Non-tariff barriers also constrained trade.

Burundi is a member of the Common Market of Eastern and Southern Africa (COMESA) and, as a party to the Lomé Convention, receives preferential treatment by the European Union.

38 FOREIGN INVESTMENT

Foreign direct investment (FDI) in Burundi has fluctuated wildly depending on security and stability. In 2000 FDI reached $11.7

million, increasing to $48 million in 2002. However, according to World Bank figures, in 2009 the country recorded a net inflow of FDI of only $348,405. In 2009 FDI represented 0.03% of GDP. The expansion of mining and the potential oil and gas discoveries are expected to increase FDI substantially.

³⁹ECONOMIC DEVELOPMENT

In 2011 Burundi's economic freedom score was 49.6, ranking the country as one of the least free (148th overall) on the *2011 Index of Economic Freedom*. Its score improved by 2.1 points over 2010 owing to greater trade, monetary and investment freedom. Nonetheless, Burundi ranked 31st out of 46 countries in sub-Saharan Africa on the index. According to the index, the government appeared uninterested in restructuring the economy and reforming the regulatory environment. For example, obtaining licenses to attract foreign investment was subject to intrusive and inefficient regulations, and corruption was rife. Government revenues were too low to make meaningful public investments in economic and social development.

Consequently, Burundi remained dependent on foreign assistance for development programs and recurrent expenses. The African Development Bank, European Union, and Belgium were Burundi's principal providers of financial and technical support.

⁴⁰SOCIAL DEVELOPMENT

As in most of sub-Saharan Africa, the family remains the most important social welfare institution. To supplement affective networks, churches and charitable organizations run social centers for women and youth, and missions are needed to look after orphans and the aged. For the small percentage of wage earners, government social security insures against accidents and occupational diseases and provides old-age and disability pensions. Workers covered by the labor code are entitled to workers' compensation for temporary and permanent disabilities, but this safety net covers few persons.

The Transitional Constitution Act guarantees equal protection for all citizens, but it has not been effectively implemented. Women suffer job discrimination and sexual violence, which is rarely reported to the authorities. The stigma of rape is so pervasive that women are subject to ridicule by authorities, and often are required to provide food and other costs of incarcerating the rapist. Domestic violence is commonplace although no cases involving abuse of women have ever been heard in a Burundian court. Children are often used for forced labor, are subjected to violence, and have lost care givers to conflict and war.

Burundi's poor human rights record remains unchanged, with failure to control excesses by security forces, including reprisals against civilians following rebel attacks. Abductions are commonplace. Prison conditions are life threatening.

On the UN Development Program's (UNDP) human development index, which measures average achievements in three basic dimensions of human development: a long and healthy life, access to knowledge and a decent standard of living, Burundi scored 185th out of 187 ranked countries.

⁴¹HEALTH

According to the CIA, life expectancy in Burundi was 51 years in 2011. The country spent 13% of GDP on healthcare, amounting to $20 per person. There were 0 physicians, 2 nurses and midwives, and 7 hospital beds per 10,000 inhabitants. The fertility rate was 4.5 children per woman, while the infant mortality rate was 101 deaths per 1,000 live births. In 2008 the maternal mortality rate, according to the World Bank, was 970 deaths per 100,000 births. It was estimated that 91% of children were vaccinated against measles. The CIA reported the HIV/AIDS prevalence rate in Burundi to be about 3.3% in 2009. In 2011 Burundi received healthcare assistance from several donors, NGOs, and intergovernmental agencies, including the World Health Organization.

⁴²HOUSING

Most housing in rural areas is a beehive-shaped hut made of strips of wood woven around poles, and covered with tin (thatch has become scarce). The huts are generally not grouped into villages, but are organized in groups on a family basis. Government resettlement projects have favored mud brick and cement dwellings with roofs of corrugated iron sheets or ceramic tile. The average dwelling is a two- or three-room home, which generally houses about five people.

⁴³EDUCATION

Until 1954 all education was provided by religious missions; it was almost entirely limited to the primary grades. Education is now compulsory for children between the ages of 6 and 12. Primary education lasts for six years. General secondary education lasts for seven years. At the secondary level, students also have an option of technical studies (five years) or vocational schooling (seven years). The academic year runs from October to June. The languages of instruction in schools are Kisundi and French. The University of Burundi, in Bujumbura (founded in 1960), is the country's only institution of higher learning.

In 2009 the World Bank estimated that 99% of age–eligible children in Burundi were enrolled in primary school. Secondary enrollment for age–eligible children stood at 9%. Tertiary enrollment was estimated at 3%. Overall, as reported by the CIA, Burundi had an estimated literacy rate of 59.3%. Public expenditure on education administered by the Ministry of Education represented 8.3% of GDP.

⁴⁴LIBRARIES AND MUSEUMS

There are about 60 public libraries in Burundi, with the largest in and around the capital. Libraries in Bujumbura include the Public Library, which has 27,000 volumes; the library of the University of Burundi, with 192,000 volumes; and a specialized collection at the Department of Geology and Mines. The French Cultural Center in Bujumbura holds 33,000 volumes.

The National Museum in Gitega (founded in 1955) houses a collection of musical instruments, weapons, witchcraft implements, and a sizeable library. The Musée Vivant, established in 1977 in Bujumbura, contains exhibits reflecting all aspects of life in the country. It also includes a reptile house, aquarium, aviary, open-air theater, and botanical gardens.

⁴⁵MEDIA

In 2009 the CIA reported that there were 31,500 telephone landlines in Burundi. In addition to landlines, mobile phone subscriptions averaged 10 per 100 people. There were nearly a dozen private radio stations offering a balanced range of opinions and viewpoints, but they had limited transmission range. Listeners could also receive broadcasts from international shortwave transmitters including the BBC, France International and Voice of America (VOA). Internet users numbered 1 per 100 citizens, and only 2% of the population had access to the Internet in 2010.

Radio remained the most widely used medium for information dissemination. Privately owned radio stations included Radio Isanganiro, Bonesha FM, and African Public Radio (RPA). These stations broadcasted in French, Kirundi, and Kirundi Swahili. Some stations received funding from international donors. There were up to eight private newspapers, but they did not publish regularly, their readership was limited, and they were hampered by financial and infrastructural constraints.

In 2011 Freedom House rated the media as "not free," meaning that government dominated ownership of the media, cracked down on reporters perceived as unfavorable towards government, and forced journalists and editors to practice self-censorship. The government owned *Le Renouveau*, the only daily newspaper, as well as the public television and radio broadcasters with national coverage, National Radio and Television of Burundi.

Although there were no apparent government restrictions on Internet access, the National Communications Council barred websites from "posting documents or other statements by political organizations that disseminated hate or violence," and the government appeared to be intolerant of criticism that appeared online. For example, in July 2011 Jean-Claude Kavumbagu, editor of the online Net Press news agency, was detained on charges of treason. He had been previously imprisoned on various charges including criminal defamation. The July arrest was made following his criticism of the country's security forces.

46 ORGANIZATIONS

Various commercial, agricultural, cultural, social, and welfare organizations exist in Burundi. The Burundi Chamber of Commerce and Industry is located in Bujumbura. The UPRONA has affiliate labor, youth, and women's organizations.

The National Council of Churches of Burundi has a membership of 500,000 Protestant congregations. The group supports issues of social welfare, peace, reconciliation, human rights, and general educational as well as evangelical activities.

Youth organizations include the National Youth Council, the Young Catholics Movement, the Red Cross Youth, YMCA, Boy Scouts, and Girl Guides. There are sports associations representing such pastimes as tennis, handball, and track and field. There are a number of women's organizations, including the Burundi Women's Union, which serves to encourage participation in government and politics, and the multinational Women's International League for Peace and Freedom.

There are national chapters of the Red Cross Society, UNICEF, the Society of St. Vincent de Paul, and Caritas.

47 TOURISM, TRAVEL, AND RECREATION

Despite its many attractions, owing to insecurity, tourism in Burundi has declined since 1993. The *Tourism Factbook*, published by the UN World Tourism Organization in 2011, reported 201,000 incoming tourists to Burundi in 2009, who spent a total of $1.7 million. Of those incoming tourists, there were 141,000 from Africa. There were 1,420 hotel beds available in Burundi. The estimated daily cost to visit Bujumbura, the capital, was $187.

Burundi has many tourist attractions. Lake Tanganyika is internationally famous for its scenic beauty. Points of interest include Bujumbura, the capital, on Lake Tanganyika; Gitega, the former capital, with its museum and traditional handicraft center; and the Mosso area in the southeast, with its fairly abundant wildlife. The northeast has a great variety of tropical birds. Burundi is rich in folk art; the dances and drumming of the Tutsi are particularly well known.

All visitors require a valid passport and visa. A certificate of vaccination against yellow fever is recommended along with precautions for malaria.

48 FAMOUS PERSONS

Mwami Ntare I Rushatsi (c. 1500), a warrior and astute administrator, succeeded in unifying the country under Tutsi rule. Mwambutsa IV (1913–78), the last mwami under the Belgian administration, was deposed in July 1966. Prince Louis Rwagasore (1930–61), the son of Mwambutsa, was the founder of UPRONA. Michel Micombero (1940–83) was president from 1966 until 1976, when he was replaced by Jean-Baptiste Bagaza (b. 1946). Bagaza served until 1987, when he was succeeded by a military junta led by Pierre Buyoya (b. 1949).

49 DEPENDENCIES

Burundi has no territories or colonies.

50 BIBLIOGRAPHY

Burundi Investment and Business Guide: Strategic and Practical Information. Washington, DC: International Business Publications USA, 2012.

Eggers, Ellen. *Historical Dictionary of Burundi.* 3rd ed. Lanham, MD: Scarecrow, 2006.

Forster, Peter G. *Race and Ethnicity in East Africa.* New York: St. Martin's Press, 2000.

Janzen, John M. *Do I Still Have a Life?: Voices from the Aftermath of War in Rwanda and Burundi.* Lawrence: University of Kansas, 2000.

Jennings, Christian. *Across the Red River: Rwanda, Burundi, and the Heart of Darkness.* London: Phoenix, 2001.

McElrath, Karen, ed. *HIV and AIDS: A Global View.* Westport, Conn.: Greenwood Press, 2002.

Ould Abdallah, Ahmedou. *Burundi on the Brink, 1993–95: A UN Special Envoy Reflects on Preventive Diplomacy.* Washington, DC: United States Institute of Peace Press, 2000.

Scherrer, Christian P. *Genocide and Crisis in Central Africa: Conflict Roots, Mass Violence, and Regional War.* Westport, CT: Praeger, 2002.

Uvin, Peter. *Life After Violence: A People's Story of Burundi.* African Arguments. 2009.

Watt, Nigel. *Burundi: Biography of a Small African Country.* London: Hurst & Co, 2008.

Zeilig, Leo, and David Seddon. *A Political and Economic Dictionary of Africa.* Philadelphia: Routledge/Taylor and Francis, 2005.

CAMEROON

Republic of Cameroon
République du Cameroun

CAPITAL: Yaoundé

FLAG: The flag is a tricolor of green, red, and yellow vertical stripes with one gold star imprinted in the center of the red stripe.

ANTHEM: *O Cameroun, berceau de nos ancêtres (O Cameroon, cradle of our ancestors).*

MONETARY UNIT: The Communauté Financière Africaine franc (XOF), which was originally pegged to the French franc, has been pegged to the euro (€) since January 1999 with a rate of XOF655.957 = €1. The franc is issued in coins of 1, 2, 5, 10, 25, 50, 100, and 500 francs, and notes of 500, 1,000, 2,000, 5,000, and 10,000 francs. XOF1 = US$0.0020 (or US$1 = XOF495.33) as of 2011.

WEIGHTS AND MEASURES: The metric system is the legal standard.

HOLIDAYS: New Year's Day, 1 January; Youth Day, 11 February; Labor Day, 1 May; National Day, 20 May; Christmas, 25 December. Movable religious holidays include Ascension, Good Friday, Easter Monday, End of Ramadan (Djoulde Soumae), and Festival of the Lamb (Eid al-Adha or Djoulde Laihadji).

TIME: 1 p.m. = noon GMT.

¹LOCATION, SIZE, AND EXTENT

Situated in West Africa, Cameroon, shaped like an elongated triangle, contains an area of 475,440 sq km (183,568 sq mi), extending 1,206 km (749 mi) N–S and 717 km (446 mi) E–W. Comparatively, the area occupied by Cameroon is slightly larger than the state of California. It is bordered on the N and NE by Chad, on the E by the Central African Republic, on the E and S by the Republic of Congo, Gabon, and Equatorial Guinea, on the SW by the Gulf of Guinea (Atlantic Ocean), and on the W and NW by Nigeria, with a total boundary length of 4,993 km (3,103 mi). The coastline accounts for 402 km (249 mi) of this length.

Cameroon's capital city, Yaoundé, is located in the south central part of the country.

²TOPOGRAPHY

There are four geographical regions. The western lowlands (rising from sea level to 600 m/2,000 ft) extend along the Gulf of Guinea coast and average about 100 km (60 mi) in width. The northwestern highlands consist of forested volcanic mountains reaching over 2,440 m (8,000 ft) in height. Mt. Cameroon (4,095 m/13,435 ft), which stands isolated on the coast to the south, is the nation's only active volcano and the highest peak in West Africa. The central plateau region extends eastward from the western lowlands and northwest highlands to the border with the Central African Republic and northward to the Bénoué (Benue) River. It includes the Adamawa Plateau, at elevations of 900 to 1,500 m (2,950 to 4,920 ft). This is a transitional area where forest gives way to savanna. The northern region is essentially a vast savanna plain that

slopes down to the Chad Basin. Of the two main rivers, the Bénoué is navigable several months during the year, and the Sanaga is not navigable. Part of Lake Chad is in Cameroonian territory.

³CLIMATE

The southern and northern regions of the country are two distinct climatic areas. On the coast, the average annual rainfall ranges between 250 cm and 400 cm (100 in and 160 in); in the inland south, between 150 cm and 250 cm (60 in and 100 in). The western slopes of Mt. Cameroon receive 600 cm to 900 cm (240 in to 350 in) a year. The mean temperature ranges from 22° C to 29°C (72° F to 84°F) along the coast. In the south there are two dry seasons, November to March and June to August. The northern part of the country has a more comfortable climate. Total rainfall drops from 150 cm (60 in) a year in the central plateau to 60 cm (24 in) northward near Lake Chad, and the mean temperature ranges from 23° C to 26°C (73° F to 79°F), although it can reach 50°C (122°F) in the far north. The dry season in the north is from October to March.

⁴FLORA AND FAUNA

Cameroon possesses practically every variety of flora and fauna found in tropical Africa. The World Resources Institute estimates that there are 8,260 plant species in Cameroon. In addition, Cameroon is home to 322 species of mammals, 936 species of birds, 211 species of reptiles, and 192 species of amphibians. The calculation reflects the total number of distinct species residing in the country, not the number of endemic species. Major game animals include buffalo, elephant, hippopotamus, antelope, Derby eland, and kudu. Twenty-two primate species are known in the coastal forests along the Gabon border.

5 ENVIRONMENT

The World Resources Institute reported that Cameroon had designated 3.99 million hectares (9.87 million acres) of land for protection as of 2006. Water resources totaled 285.5 cu km (68.5 cu mi) while water usage was 0.99 cu km (0.238 cu mi) per year. Domestic water usage accounted for 18% of total usage, industrial for 8%, and agricultural for 74%. Per capita water usage totaled 61 cu m (2,154 cu ft) per year.

Cameroon has 20 national parks. Nevertheless, poaching is a major problem because of insufficient guards. Deforestation and wildlife preservation are major concerns in Cameroon. The Congo Basin has seen the fastest rate of deforestation in the world, in part due to lack of responsible ownership. To further the cause of wildlife preservation, the government of Cameroon opened two new national parks. Takamanda National Park (opened in November 2008) serves as a refuge for the Cross River gorilla, which is the most endangered species of gorilla in the world. Deng Deng National Park (opened in February 2009) protects a population of about 600 lowland gorillas, along with forest elephants, chimpanzees, buffalo, and bongo. Overgrazing is degrading the semiarid northern range lands. By the mid-1980s Cameroon had lost 40% of its mangrove swamps. The Dja Faunal reserve is a natural UNESCO World Heritage Site.

According to a 2011 report issued by the International Union for Conservation of Nature and Natural Resources (IUCN), the number of threatened species included 38 types of mammals, 20 species of birds, 4 types of reptile, 54 species of amphibians, 112 species of fish, 11 type of mollusk, 13 other species of invertebrates, and 378 species of plants. Threatened species include the cheetah, Allen's swamp monkey, the spotted eagle, and the Cameroon clawless otter.

Air pollution is a significant environmental problem in Cameroon. The main sources of pollution are industrial chemicals and vehicle emissions. The United Nations (UN) reported in 2008 that carbon dioxide emissions in Cameroon totaled 6,163 kilotons.

The country also has a problem with volcanic activity, flooding, and insect infestation. In August 1986 poisonous gases emanating from Lake Nyos in northwestern Cameroon killed 1,746 villagers, by official count. The lake lies within the crater of a dormant volcano, and scientists speculated that the toxic gases were released by molten rock that had seeped into the lake.

6 POPULATION

The US Central Intelligence Agency (CIA) estimated the population of Cameroon in 2011 to be approximately 19,711,291, which placed it at number 58 in population among the 196 nations of the world. In 2011 approximately 3.3% of the population was over 65 years of age, with another 40.5% under 15 years of age. The median age in Cameroon was 19.4 years. There were 1.01 males for every female in the country. The population's annual rate of change was 2.121%. The projected population for the year 2025 was 26,500,000. Population density in Cameroon was calculated at 41 people per sq km (106 people per sq mi).

The UN estimated that 58% of the population lived in urban areas in 2010, and that urban populations had an annual rate of change of 3.3%. The largest urban areas, along with their respective populations, included Douala, 2.1 million; and Yaounde, 1.7 million.

The prevalence of HIV/AIDS has had a significant impact on the population of Cameroon. The AIDS epidemic causes higher death and infant mortality rates, and lowers life expectancy.

7 MIGRATION

Estimates of Cameroon's net migration rate, carried out by the CIA in 2011, amounted to zero. The total number of emigrants living abroad was 279,200, and the total number of immigrants living in Cameroon was 196,600. Cameroon also accepted 25,000 refugees from Chad, 3,000 from Nigeria, and 24,000 from the Central African Republic.

In 1981 nearly 10,000 Cameroonians living in Gabon were repatriated following anti-Cameroonian demonstrations there. At the end of 1980 there were 110,000 refugees from Chad at a camp in Kousséri, but by the end of 1981, all but 25,000 had returned to Chad. The camp was closed in March 1982, with the remaining refugees transferred to the Poli region. In 1998 refugees arrived from Rwanda, Republic of Congo (ROC), and the Democratic Republic of the Congo (DROC).

8 ETHNIC GROUPS

Cameroon has an extremely heterogeneous population, consisting of approximately 250 ethnic groups. Cameroon Highlanders constitute the largest group at 31% of the total population. They include the Bamileke and the Bamoun. The Equatorial Bantu account for about 19% of the population, followed by the Kirdi at 11%, the Fulani at 10%, the Northwestern Bantu 8%, Eastern Nigritic 7%, and other African groups comprising 13%, Less than 1% are non-African.

9 LANGUAGES

French and English are the official languages. However, there are 24 major African language groups, with some 270 indigenous dialects spoken. Most belong to the Bantu and Semi-Bantu (or Sudanic) language groups.

10 RELIGIONS

About 69.2% of the population are at least nominally Christian, of whom approximately 38.4% are Roman Catholics and 26.3% are affiliated with Protestant denominations. Nearly 21% are nominally Muslim. About 5.6% are animists. Indigenous religions are practiced primarily in rural areas.

The Fulani people in the north are mainly Muslim, as are the Bamoun group of the western provinces and the Kirdi. The Christian missionaries (Protestants since 1845 and Roman Catholics since 1890) have been particularly active in other areas, with the English-speaking citizens of provinces of the western region being primarily Protestant and the French-speaking citizens in provinces of the southern and western regions being predominantly Catholic. Missionary groups include Baptists,

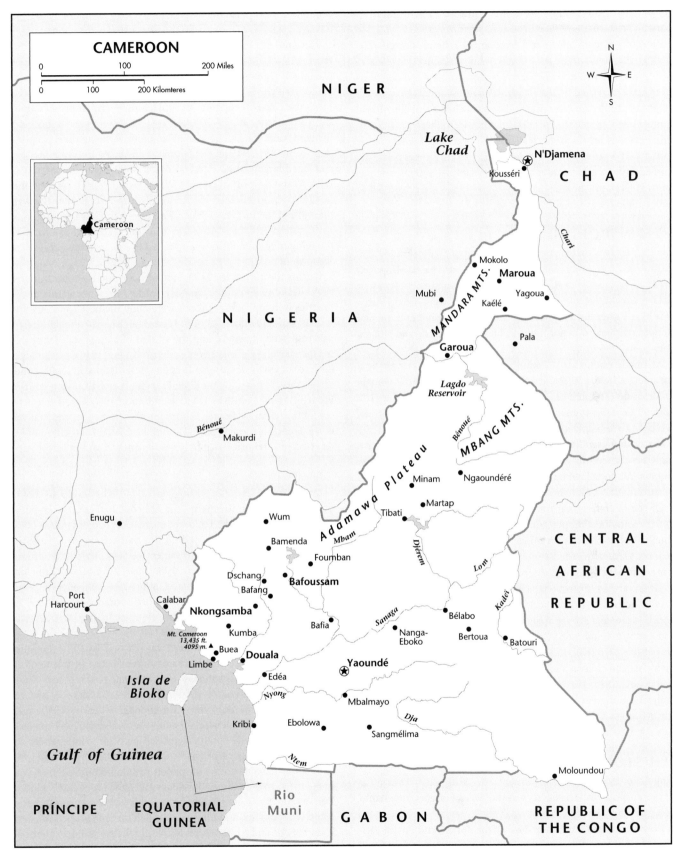

CAMEROON

0   100   200 Miles

0   100   200 Kilomteres

N I G E R

Lake Chad

N'Djamena

Kousséri

C H A D

Chari

Cameroon

Mokolo

Maroua

MANDARA MTS.

Mubi

Kaélé

Yagoua

Garoua

Pala

N I G E R I A

Lagdo Reservoir

Bénoué

MBANG MTS.

Makurdi

Adamawa Plateau

Minam

Ngaoundéré

Enugu

Wum

Tibati

Martap

Bamenda

Mbam

Foumban

Dschang

Bafoussam

Bafang

Nkongsamba

Bafia

Nanga-Eboko

Bélabo

Bertoua

Batouri

Kumba

Mt. Cameroon 13,435 ft. 4095 m. ▲

Buea

Douala

Yaoundé

Limbe

Edéa

Mbalmayo

Isla de Bioko

Nyong

Kribi

Ebolowa

Sangmélima

Dja

Moloundou

Gulf of Guinea

Ntem

Rio Muni

C E N T R A L

A F R I C A N

R E P U B L I C

Sanaga

Djérem

Lom

Kadéi

Bénoué

Calabar

Port Harcourt

PRÍNCIPE

EQUATORIAL GUINEA

G A B O N

REPUBLIC OF THE CONGO

LOCATION: 1°40′ to 13°5′N; 8°30′ to 16°11′ E. BOUNDARY LENGTHS: Chad, 1,047 kilometers (651 miles); Central African Republic, 822 kilometers (511 miles); Republic of the Congo, 520 kilometers (323 miles); Gabon, 302 kilometers (188 miles); Equatorial Guinea, 183 kilometers (114 miles); Gulf of Guinea coastline, 364 kilometers (226 miles); Nigeria, 1,921 kilometers (1,194 miles). TERRITORIAL SEA LIMIT: 50 miles.

Presbyterians, Methodists, Jehovah's Witnesses, the Unification Church, Seventh-Day Adventists, and Mormons.

Freedom of conscience and freedom of religion are guaranteed by the constitution and these rights are generally respected in practice. Relations between the government and religious groups are governed by the Law on Religious Congregations. All religious groups must register with the Ministry of Territorial Administration and Decentralization; however, there are no specific penalties for failure to register. The practice of witchcraft is considered a criminal offense, however, prosecution is generally applied only in conjunction with other criminal actions, such as murder. Certain Christian and Muslim holidays are celebrated as public holidays.

11 TRANSPORTATION

The CIA reports that Cameroon has a total of 50,000 km (31,069 mi) of roads, of which 5,000 km (3,107 mi) are paved. Unpaved roads are not usable in all seasons, and as a result the government has been rerouting and paving heavily used roads in order to provide all-weather links between agricultural areas and commercial shipping centers. A major highway between Yaoundé and Douala opened in 1985.

Railroads extend for 977 km (607 mi). The oldest railway line, constructed before 1927 and rebuilt in the mid-1980s, links Douala to Yaoundé (307 km/191 mi) and Douala to Nkongsamba (172 km/107 mi). On the Douala- Yaoundé line there is a spur from Ngoume to Mbalmayo (30 km/19 mi). Kumba is linked to the Douala-Nkongsamba line by another spur. The Trans-Cameroon Railway, Cameroon's most recently constructed line, extends the Douala-Yaoundé line northward 622 km (386 mi) to Ngaoundéré, a cattle-marketing city on the Adamawa Plateau.

Of the operating maritime ports in Cameroon, Douala is the busiest and most important. Lesser ports include Kribi, used chiefly for the export of wood, and Limbé, used only for palm-oil exports. Garoua, on the Bénoué River, is the main river port, but it is active only from July to September.

There are 34 airports, which transported 466,050 passengers in 2009 according to the World Bank. The main international airport is at Douala. Secondary international airports are at Yaoundé and Garoua. Cameroon Airlines, which went into operation one November 1971, flies to Paris, London, Frankfurt, Brussels, and many African cities; it also operates all scheduled domestic flights. Cameroon Airlines is jointly owned by the government and Air France. Among the other airlines serving Cameroon are Pan Am, Air Afrique, Alitalia, Swissair, Iberia, Air Zaire, Air Mali, and Nigeria Airways.

12 HISTORY

Linguistic evidence indicates that the area now known as Cameroon and eastern Nigeria was the place of origin of the Bantu peoples. After the 12th century AD, the organized Islamic states of the Sudanic belt, especially those of the Kanem and Fulani peoples, at times ruled the grasslands of northern Cameroon. Small chiefdoms dominated the western highlands and coastal area. Portuguese travelers established contact with the area in the 15th century, but no permanent settlements were maintained. Slaves, however, were purchased from the local peoples.

The modern history of Cameroon began in 1884, when the territory came under German rule after the explorer Gustav Nachtigal negotiated protectorate treaties with the local chiefs. Although British missionaries had been active in the area since 1845, the United Kingdom recognized the German protectorate, called Kamerun, which included areas that were later to become British Cameroons and French Cameroun. During their occupation from 1884 to 1914, the Germans advanced into the interior, cultivated large plantations, laid roads, and began constructing a railroad and the port of Douala. When World War I broke out, the territory was invaded by French and British forces. After the war one-fifth of the former German Kamerun, which was contiguous with eastern Nigeria, was assigned to the United Kingdom, and the remaining four-fifths was assigned to France under League of Nations mandates.

During the period 1919–39, France made notable contributions to the development of the territory. Agriculture was expanded; industries were introduced; roads were built; medical services were broadened; and more schools were established. Political liberty was restricted, however, and the system of compulsory labor introduced by the Germans continued. In August 1940 Col. Philippe Leclerc, an envoy of Gen. Charles de Gaulle, landed at Douala and seized the territory for the Free French. The birth of the Fourth French Republic and the UN trusteeship in 1946 signified a new era for the territory. French Cameroun was granted representation in the French National Assembly and the Council of the Republic. An elected territorial assembly was instituted and political parties were recognized, thus establishing a basis for Cameroonian nationalism.

Immediately after the setting up of the trusteeship in 1946, many parties began to emerge, but only one had effective organization and strength, the Union of Cameroon Peoples (Union des Populations du Cameroun—UPC). The party demanded immediate reunification of the British Cameroons and French Cameroun and eventual independence. In 1955 the UPC, accused of being under extreme left-wing influence, launched a campaign of sabotage, violence, and terror that continued sporadically until 1971, 11 years after independence. The death toll from this struggle was estimated at between 10,000 and 80,000.

A new stage in self-government was reached in 1957, when the French government created the autonomous state of Cameroun, and Cameroonian institutions were created along the lines of French parliamentary democracy. In 1958 the Legislative Assembly of Cameroun voted for independence by 1960, and France and the UN General Assembly assented. In 1959 the last step in the evolution of political institutions prior to independence took place when a government of Cameroun was formed and given full internal autonomy. Ahmadou Ahidjo became prime minister. Earlier in the year, on 1 January 1959, the Kamerun National Democratic Party had won the general elections in Southern British Cameroons, and John Foncha had become prime minister. Soon Foncha and Ahidjo were discussing the possibilities of unification upon the achievement of independence.

On 1 January 1960 Cameroun became an independent republic. Fierce UPC-led riots in the Dschang and Nkongsamba areas caused Ahidjo to summon French reinforcements to suppress the rebellion, but intermittent rioting continued. A draft constitution was approved in a referendum of 21 February, and on 10 April a new Cameroun National Assembly was elected. Ahidjo's Cameroun Union Party won a majority, and Ahidjo, who ran unopposed, was elected president in April 1960.

During 1960 consultations between Foncha and Ahidjo continued, and a proposed federation was tentatively outlined. On 11 February 1961 separate plebiscites were held in the Southern and Northern British Cameroons under the auspices of the UN. The voters in Southern Cameroons chose union with the Cameroun Republic, while those in Northern Cameroons opted for union with Nigeria, which was accomplished on 1 June 1961. During the months that followed, terrorist activity was renewed and the Cameroun Republic had to devote one-third of its national budget to the maintenance of public order.

A draft constitution for the federation was approved by the Cameroun National Assembly on 7 September 1961, and the new federation became a reality on 1 October. The Cameroun Republic became the state of East Cameroon, and Southern British Cameroons became the state of West Cameroon in the new Federal Republic of Cameroon, with Ahmadou Ahidjo as president and John Foncha as vice president. Both were reelected in 1965, but Foncha was later replaced as vice president and the office was abolished in 1972.

A proposal to replace the federation with a unified state was ratified by popular referendum on 20 May 1972; the vote was reportedly 99.97% in favor of unification. A new constitution went into effect on 2 June, under which the country was renamed the United Republic of Cameroon. Ahmadou Ahidjo remained president of the republic; running unopposed, he was reelected for a fourth five-year term on 5 April 1975. In June, by constitutional amendment, the office of prime minister was created, and Paul Biya was appointed to the post. Ahidjo, reelected unopposed, began his fifth five-year term as president in May 1980. In November 1982 he resigned and was succeeded by Biya; Ahidjo remained head of the ruling party, the Cameroon People's Democratic Movement (CPDM).

Biya proved more independent than Ahidjo had anticipated. Following allegations of a military coup plot allegedly masterminded by Ahidjo, the former president retired to France in August 1983 and Biya became party chairman. Ahidjo was sentenced to death (later commuted to life imprisonment) in absentia in February 1984. Biya's own presidential guard attempted to overthrow the government in April; the rebellion was stamped out by the army. Purges followed and 46 of the plotters were executed. A state of emergency was declared, which lasted several years. Late in 1984 the position of prime minister was abolished and the name of the country was changed to the Republic of Cameroon.

Despite democratic reform begun in 1990 with the legalization of political parties other than the CPDM, political power remains firmly in the hands of President Biya and a small circle of CPDM members from his own ethnic group. Biya was reelected on 11 October 1992 amid accusations of voting irregularities. Biya reportedly got 39% of the vote to 35% for John Fru Ndi. (Ndi briefly proclaimed himself president before the government released the polling figures.) In contrast, the 1 March 1992 legislative election was considered free and fair by international observers, although many parties boycotted the elections and the CPDM won several constituencies by default. But even though opposition parties were well-represented in the legislature (92 of 180 seats), there were, according to the 1992 constitution, few legislative or judicial checks on the president.

Following the elections, civil unrest erupted as the population expressed the widespread belief that Ndi had won the presidential elections. By late 1992 Ndi and his supporters were under house arrest and the international community had made clear its displeasure at the antidemocratic and increasingly violent turn the Biya regime was taking.

Biya agreed in May 1993 to hold a so-called Great National Constitutional Debate and in June he began preparing a draft of a new constitution to be adopted either by referendum or by the National Assembly of Cameroon. In 1994, 16 opposition parties formed a loose alliance, dominated by Ndi's Social Democrats, to work for constitutional and electoral reform. In October 1995, the CPDM reelected Biya as its leader. In December of that year the assembly adopted a number of amendments to address the power of the president. These reforms included a strengthening of the judiciary, the creation of a partially elected 100-member senate, the creation of regional councils, and the fixing of the presidential term to seven years, renewable once. Strikes and demonstrations became commonplace as Biya resisted implementation of reforms.

The May 1997 legislative elections were marred by mismanagement, vote-rigging, and fraud, resulting in the Supreme Court's cancellation of results in three constituencies (seven seats). Based on the misconduct of these elections, the opposition boycotted the October 1997 presidential elections, in which Biya claimed victory with 93% of the vote. To add further insult, Cameroon topped Transparency International's list of the most corrupt countries in the world in 1998, prompting the creation of an anticorruption body.

On 30 June 2002 the country held legislative and municipal elections that again were denounced by the opposition as fraudulent. The Supreme Court cancelled the results of nine constituencies, ordering new elections in these constituencies on 15 September. In the end, the CPDM won 149 of 180 seats.

The victory for the ruling party was cemented with the reelection of the 72-year old Paul Biya in October 2004, thus enhancing the chances of continued domination by the ruling party. By 2006, appeals were being heard in Biya's home province in favor of a constitutional amendment that would allow him to run for another term. Following the legislative elections in July 2007, in which Biya's party retained a sizable majority, the assembly amended the constitution to eliminate term limits in 2008. In October 2011 Biya was reelected president with 78% of the vote. His opponents rejected the result, alleging widespread fraud.

13 GOVERNMENT

Under the 1972 constitution, as amended in 1984 and 2008, Cameroon has nominally been a republic headed by a president elected by universal suffrage (from age 20) to serve five-year terms. Term limits for the president were abolished in 2008. The president appoints the ministers, vice-ministers, and regional functionaries; is the head of the armed forces; and promulgates the laws. The president can decree a state of national emergency and can be invested with special powers.

The legislative branch is composed of the unicameral National Assembly of Cameroon, with 180 members from 49 single and multi-seat constituencies. The assembly is directly elected to a five-year term by universal suffrage. Members meet three times a year in March, June, and November.

Government checks and balances remain extremely weak under a strong executive system.

14 POLITICAL PARTIES

The Cameroon National Union (Union Nationale Camerounaise—UNC) was Cameroon's sole legal political party until 1990. It was formed in 1966 through a merger of the Cameroon Union (Union Camerounaise) and the Kamerun National Democratic Party, the major political organizations, respectively, of the eastern and western regions, and four smaller parties. The UNC sponsors labor, youth, and women's organizations and provided the only list of candidates for the 1973, 1978, and 1983 legislative elections.

Ahmadou Ahidjo became the first head of the UNC in 1966 and continued in that capacity after his resignation as the nation's president in 1982. Following President Biya's assumption of emergency powers in August 1983, Ahidjo, then in France, resigned as party leader. Biya was subsequently elected party chief at a special party congress in September. In 1985, the UNC was renamed the Cameroon People's Democratic Movement (CPDM).

Opposition parties were legalized in 1990. In the elections to the assembly on 1 March 1992, the CPDM won 88 of the 180 seats; the National Union for Democracy and Progress (UNDP), 68 seats; the Union of Cameroonian Populations (UPC), 18 seats; and the Movement for the Defense of the Republic (MDR), 6 seats. The CPDM and the MDR formed a coalition.

In the presidential election of 11 October 1992 the voting was split by CPDM, 40%; Social Democratic Front (SDF), 36%; and UNDP 18%. The SDF accused Biya of stealing the election, but Biya was reelected to his post as head of the CPDM in October 1995.

In the May 1997 assembly elections the CPDM took 109 seats, the SDF 43, the UNDP 13, the UDC 5, others 3, and cancelled constituencies 7. The opposition, backed by international observers, declared the legislative elections highly flawed, and based on their perception of misconduct, the main opposition parties boycotted the presidential elections of October later that year.

The SDF and its allies in the Union for Change remained critical of Biya but are also critical of France, which they call an "accomplice of those in power." However, in 2000 the alliance reportedly was falling apart as the SDF sought to distance itself from the SCNC. The SCNC apparently was accusing the SDF of delaying independence for the northwest and southwest English-speaking provinces by refusing to force its English-speaking members of parliament to resign from the Francophone-dominated assembly. Moreover, some members of the opposition wanted their party leaders to join Biya's coalition government so they could share the spoils of office.

By 2000 Biya had shored up his government by forming a coalition with the northern-based UNDP, which had 13 assembly seats, and with the UPC, which had one seat. Together, the ruling coalition gave Biya a four-fifths majority in the assembly. The coalition government enjoyed support from seven of Cameroon's 10 provinces, and thus secured former President Ahidjo's north-south alliance, which he had created in 1958.

In the June and September 2002 assembly elections the CPDM took 149 seats, the SDF 22, the UDC 5, the UPC 3, and the UNDP 1. Voting irregularities in 9 constituencies (17 seats) in the June elections led to the subsequent by-elections in September for those seats. Nineteen of the SDF's seats came from the English-speaking northwest province. The biggest loser in the election was the UNDP: it had won 68 seats in 1992 and 13 seats in 1997. Observers attributed the party's poor showing to its participation in the CPDM-led government.

In the 11 October 2004 election President Paul Biya was re-elected with 70.9 % of the vote. His longtime opponent, John Fru Ndi scored 17.4%, Adamou Ndam Njoya took 4.5%, and Garga Haman Adji came in last with 3.7%. Biya's second seven-year term extended through October 2011; constitutionally he was not eligible to run for reelection.

In the July 2007 assembly elections, the Cameroon People's Democratic Movement remained the majority party. Voter turnout was low, and leaders of several opposition parties protested the results. By-elections were held on September 30 to determine 17 vacant seats after the Supreme Court nullified results in five districts. Following the by-elections, the allocation of seats in the assembly was as follows: CPDM 153 seats, SDF 16 seats, UNDP 6 seats, UDC 4 seats, Progressive Movement (MP) 1 seat.

Following the retention of a sizable majority by Biya's party in the 2007 legislative elections, the assembly amended the constitution to eliminate term limits in 2008. In October 2011 Biya was re-elected president with 78% of the vote. Despite claims of widespread fraud by opponents, Biya was sworn in for a sixth term on 3 November 2011.

The next legislative elections were scheduled to take place in mid-2012.

15 LOCAL GOVERNMENT

The Republic of Cameroon is divided into 10 administrative provinces, each placed under the jurisdiction of a governor appointed by the head of state. Each province is subdivided into departments, which are under the administrative control of divisional officers (préfets). In turn, departments are composed of arrondissements headed by assistant divisional officers (sous-préfets). Municipal officials are elected for five-year terms. Traditional institutions such as chiefdoms were in noticeable decline during the 1970s and 1980s, although traditional rulers were treated as administrative adjuncts and received a government salary.

In 1996 Biya's government organized relatively free and fair municipal elections where opposition candidates won in nearly every major city. However, three-fourths of the local councils are dominated by the ruling coalition. Municipal elections for 336 local councils were held on 30 June 2002, and were charged by church leaders and opposition politicians as being flawed; vote-buying, stuffing of ballot boxes, intimidation, and multiple voting were among the accusations brought by the opposition. In January 2003, Biya announced that the government would begin a major program of decentralization to complete the process of democratization begun by the June parliamentary and municipal elections. Beginning January 2012 the government embarked on the third generation of the effective transfer of powers and accompanying resources to local governments. Over 17 ministries are expected to be involved in the devolution of powers and resources for effective local and balanced development.

16 JUDICIAL SYSTEM

Cameroonian law has three main sources: local customary law, the French civil code, and British law. The Supreme Court of Cameroon, in addition to its other powers and duties granted by the constitution, gives final judgment on such appeals as may be granted by the law from the judgments of the provincial courts of appeal. The system also includes appeals courts in each of the 10 provinces, courts of first instance in each of the country's divisions, and a 15-member high court of justice, appointed by the assembly. Proposals for appointments and sanctions against magistrates throughout the republic are started by the Higher Judicial Council, of which the head of state is president. A court of impeachment has the right to try the president for high treason and cabinet ministers for conspiracy against the security of the state.

A state security court established in 1990 hears cases involving internal or external state security. Traditional courts that resolve domestic, probate, and minor property disputes remain an important element in the judicial system. These courts vary considerably according to region and ethnic group. Appeal is possible in most cases to traditional authorities of a higher rank.

Prior to the 1995 amendments (promulgated in 1996) to the 1972 constitution, the judiciary was supervised by the Ministry of Justice, part of the executive, and did not function as an independent branch of government. The December 1995 amendments called for a more independent judiciary. However, as of 2011 there continue to be reported abuses, including beatings of detainees, arbitrary arrests, and illegal searches. The judiciary has made efforts to enhance its independence and align itself with international standards.

17 ARMED FORCES

The International Institute for Strategic Studies reports that armed forces in Cameroon totaled 14,100 members in 2011. The force is comprised of 12,500 from the army, 1,300 from the navy, and 300 members of the air force. Armed forces represent 0.3% of the labor force in Cameroon. Defense spending totaled $580.3 million and accounted for 1.3% of gross domestic product (GDP).

18 INTERNATIONAL COOPERATION

Cameroon was admitted to UN membership on 20 September 1960 and is a member of ECA and several nonregional specialized agencies. Cameroon is also a member of the African Development Bank, G-77, the African Union, the Islamic Development Bank, the Monetary and Economic Community of Central Africa (CEMAC), the Organization of the Islamic Conference (OIC), the Central African States Development Bank, the New Partnership for Africa's Development (NEPAD), and the ACP Group. The nation is part of the Franc Zone. Cameroon was formally admitted to the Commonwealth of Nations in 1995. The nation is part of the Nonaligned Movement. In environmental cooperation, Cameroon is part of the Basel Convention, the Convention on Biological Diversity, CITES, International Tropical Timber Agreements, the Kyoto Protocol, the Montréal Protocol, and the UN Conventions on the Law of the Sea, Climate Change, and Desertification.

19 ECONOMY

Agriculture remains the mainstay of the economy, with 70% of the nation engaged in work on what are mostly coffee and cocoa farms. The business infrastructure is subpar. The government has made efforts in recent years to attract more foreign investment with the help of the International Monetary Fund (IMF) and the World Bank, however. The building of an oil pipeline through the country is expected to help business efforts. Despite these prospects, the unemployment rate remains high. The most recent estimates available as of January 2012 placed unemployed at 30% (2001). The economy is also hindered by corruption in government and economic mismanagement, which together create an unfavorable business climate. Although Cameroon is an economic leader in the region, its population lags behinds its neighbors in health and educational indicators.

Coffee and cocoa are Cameroon's principal agricultural exports, along with cork, wood, and cotton. Petroleum, basic manufactures, machinery, and transport equipment provide additional export revenues. The government is trying to stimulate more timber processing. Construction is a growth sector. In 2009 Cameroon began negotiations with the European Union to implement a Voluntary Partnership Agreement (VPA) designed to boost the timber industry. Cameroon has been working with the international Forest Stewardship Council in seeking certification for its forests, a process that involves an evaluation of acceptable forest management activities and the implementation of a tracking system for forest products.

International agencies like the IMF continue to press for increased budget transparency, privatization, and poverty reduction programs as a prerequisite to international economic assistance. In May 2009 the government signed a loan agreement with the International Fund for Agricultural Development (IFAD) for $13.7 million. The funds are earmarked for poverty reduction activities within rural communities. Although the United States is the leading investor (primarily in the energy sector) in Cameroon, its main trading partner is France.

In March 2010 Cameroon signed eight cooperation agreements with China, paving the way for a host of Chinese-sponsored projects in the agriculture, energy, road, postal, and information and communications technology industries. Among other projects, China agreed to open a $500 million bus manufacturing plant in Douala, the largest city in Cameroon, to supply busses to Cameroon and other central African nations.

The GDP rate of change in Cameroon, as of 2010, was 3%. Inflation stood at 1.9%.

20 INCOME

The CIA estimated that in 2010 the GDP of Cameroon was $44.33 billion. The CIA defines GDP as the value of all final goods and services produced within a nation in a given year and computed on the basis of purchasing power parity (PPP) rather than value as measured on the basis of the rate of the exchange based on current dollars. The per capita GDP was estimated at $2,300. The annual growth rate of GDP was 3%. The average inflation rate was 1.9%. It was estimated that agriculture accounted for 20% of GDP, industry 30.9%, and services 49.1%.

According to the World Bank, remittances from citizens living abroad totaled $147.6 million or about $7 per capita and accounted for approximately 0.3% of GDP.

The World Bank reports that in 2007 household consumption in Cameroon totaled $14.8 billion, measured in current US dollars rather than PPP. Household consumption includes expenditures of individuals, households, and nongovernmental organizations on goods and services, excluding the purchases of dwellings. It was estimated that household consumption was growing at an average annual rate of 9.8%.

In 2007 the World Bank estimated that Cameroon, with 0.29% of the world's population, accounted for 0.06% of the world's GDP. By comparison, the United States, with 4.85% of the world's population, accounted for 22.51% of world GDP.

As of 2011 the most recent study by the World Bank reported that actual individual consumption in Cameroon was 74.7% of GDP and accounted for 0.07% of world consumption. By comparison, the United States accounted for 25.44% of world individual consumption. The World Bank also estimated that 33.9% of Cameroon's GDP was spent on food and beverages, 14.2% on housing and household furnishings, 7.3% on clothes, 1.7% on health, 5.2% on transportation, 0.9% on communications, 1.2% on recreation, 4.5% on restaurants and hotels, and 2.7% on miscellaneous goods and services and purchases from abroad.

It was estimated that in 2000 about 48% of the population subsisted on an income below the poverty line established by Cameroon's government.

21 LABOR

As of 2010 Cameroon had a total labor force of 7.836 million people. Within that labor force, CIA estimates in 2001 noted that 70% were employed in agriculture, 13% in industry, and 17% in the service sector. Unemployment was estimated at about 30%.

Although workers are allowed to organize and join unions, there are numerous government-imposed restrictions. Private and public sector employees cannot belong to the same union, nor can a union include different or closely related sectors of the economy. In addition, under penalty of fines and/or prison for union members, a union must register with the government. In practice, unions have found it difficult to obtain registration. Those unions that are registered have been the subject of harassment and interference by the government. The law recognizes the right to strike, but only after mandatory arbitration. However, decisions arising from arbitration are not legally enforceable and can be overturned or even ignored by employers or the government. The right to strike is denied to national security personnel, civil servants and prison system employees.

There are minimum working age and safety and health regulations; however, a lack of resources has greatly compromised their enforcement. In 2008 the government increased the minimum wage in all sectors to XOF28,246 ($56) per month. However, the minimum wage did not provide for a decent standard of living for a worker and family. The workweek is set at 40 hours in public and private nonagricultural firms, and 48 hours in agricultural endeavors. The minimum age of employment is 14 years, although this is not enforced. Child labor remains a problem in Cameroon, as does forced and compulsory labor.

22 AGRICULTURE

Roughly 19% of the total land is farmed. The country's major crops include coffee, cocoa, cotton, rubber, bananas, oilseed, grains, and root starches. In 2009 cereal production amounted to 2 million tons, fruit production 2.8 million tons, and vegetable production 1.8 million tons.

Agriculture was the main source of growth and foreign exchange until 1978 when oil production replaced it as the cornerstone of growth for the formal economy. Agricultural development and productivity declined from neglect during the oil boom years of the early 1980s. Palm oil production has shown signs of strength, but the product is not marketed internationally. Cameroon bananas are sold internationally, and the sector was reorganized and privatized in 1987. Similarly, rubber output has grown in spite of Asian competition.

Cameroon is among the world's largest cocoa producers. Two types of coffee, robusta and arabica, are grown. Some cotton is exported, while the remainder is processed by local textile plants. Bananas are grown mainly in the southwest; rubber production occurs in the southwest as well. Small amounts of tobacco, tea, and pineapples are also grown.

23 ANIMAL HUSBANDRY

The UN Food and Agriculture Organization (FAO) reported that Cameroon dedicated 2 million hectares (4.94 million acres) to permanent pasture or meadow in 2009. During that year the country tended 33 million chickens, 6 million head of cattle, and 1.4 million pigs. The production from these animals amounted to 94,151 tons of beef and veal, 17,949 tons of pork, 33,086 tons of poultry, 9,874 tons of eggs, and 245,603 tons of milk. Cameroon also produced 13,000 tons of cattle hide.

Most stock breeding is carried out in the north. Ngaoundéré has one of the largest and best-equipped slaughterhouses in Africa. Meat production in 2009 was 78,00 tons. Meat products are exported to UDEAC countries. During 2002–04, livestock production was up 2.3% compared to 1999–2001. Attempts to improve livestock and hides and skins have been hindered by the social system, in which livestock constitutes a source of prestige, security, and wealth; by delays in the development of an effective transportation system; and by difficulty in controlling the tsetse fly.

24 FISHING

The fishing industry is not highly developed. Most fish are caught by artisan fishermen in rudimentary motorized pirogues. Cameroon had 59 decked commercial fishing boats in 2008. The annual capture totaled 138,000 tons according to the UN FAO. The export value of seafood totaled $102,000.

25 FORESTRY

The forested area of 23.9 million hectares (58.9 million acres) occupies about 42% of the land area. Forestry is mostly conducted in the Littoral, Center, South, and South West provinces. Of the 300 commercially valuable species, the principal types of trees felled are assié, azobe, dussil, eloorba, mahogany, sapele, sipo, illomba, ayus, iroko, dibetu, and silk cotton. Timber exports in 2003 were valued at $403.4 million. The UN FAO estimated the 2009 round-wood production at 2.62 million cu m (92.4 million cu ft). Wood sales make up the fourth-largest source of foreign revenue, but infrastructural problems and weak demand for lower-quality wood limits the development of the forestry sector. The value of all forest products, including roundwood, totaled $409.8 million.

The Congo Basin has seen the fastest rate of deforestation in the world, in part due to lack of responsible ownership.

In 2010 Cameroon signed an agreement with the European Union (EU) to ensure that all wood products exported from Cameroon to EU nations are derived from legally harvested timber from responsibly managed forests. Cameroon worked with the international Forest Stewardship Council to seek certification for its forests, a process that involves an evaluation of acceptable forest management activities and the implementation of a tracking system for forest products. Cameroon exports more timber products to Europe than any other African nation. About 80% of all Cameroon timber products go to member states of the European Union. Under the terms of the agreement, by 2012 all timber products shipped to Europe will carry licenses that show they have been legally harvested. Cameroon also pledged to certify all timber sent to non-European markets. Officials hope that this major initiative for responsible management will be a significant step in preserving the rainforests of the Congo Basin.

26 MINING

While Cameroon has steadily increased its oil production, the discovery and exploitation of other mineral resources have been slow. Bauxite deposits, in the Minam and Martap regions, have been estimated at 1 billion tons. Iron deposits containing an estimated 200 million tons have been discovered south of Kribi.

Other mineral deposits include diamonds, tin, gold, mica, marble, columbo-tantalite, silica sand, cassiterite, lignite, and rutile. Gold, the sole commercially exploited mineral, yielded an estimated 1,800 kg in 2009 and was produced by small-scale artisanal miners, mostly in the eastern part of the country. Limestone production was 100,000 metric tons, and production of pozzolana, ash for cement, was 600,000 metric tons in 2009. Diamond production in 2009 was estimated at 12,000 carats, and as with gold, was produced by small-scale artisanal miners.

27 ENERGY AND POWER

Cameroon began offshore oil production in 1977. Annual production has gradually fallen since 1985, and the decline is expected to continue as existing reserves are depleted. Cameroon's oil production totaled 77,230 barrels of oil a day in 2009, and its estimated reserves were 200 million barrels as of 1 January 2010, according to the Energy Information Administration (EIA). Per capita oil consumption was 372 kg in 2008. Field development and production began in the Kribi-Campo basin in the mid-1990s, and the Ebome field came online in 1996. As of 2002 the major operators were ExxonMobil, Shell, and TotalFina Elf. Work was under way on development of the Doba basin oil fields and the construction of a pipeline between Cameroon and Chad. With the aid of a $93

million loan from the World Bank, the Chad-Cameroon oil pipeline was completed in late 2003. In October 2002 Cameroon and Nigeria, both of whom claimed the potentially oil-rich Bakassi Peninsula, received a ruling on the dispute from the International Court of Justice, which granted the peninsula to Cameroon. Cameroon's petroleum consumption in 2009 was 77,230 barrels per day.

The country reportedly has large reserves of liquid petroleum gas, which are largely untapped. Natural gas production began in 2006. According to the EIA, Cameroon's natural gas reserves stood at 5 trillion cu ft as of 1 January 2010.

Hydroelectric resources remain the most readily exploitable form of energy in Cameroon, which, together with the Democratic Republic of Congo, is considered to have the greatest hydroelectric potential in Africa. Electrical energy is produced primarily by two hydroelectric stations on the Sananga River. Nearly 60% of the power from these stations goes to the aluminum smelter at Edéa. Cameroon's electrical capacity was 0.81 million kW in 2008, for which output for that year was 5.421 billion kWh, of which about 90% was from hydropower and the remainder from fossil fuels. Consumption amounted to 4.883 billion kWh in 2008. In 2008 roughly 24% of energy came from fossil fuels, while 5% came from alternative fuels.

In the 1980s hydroelectric capacity was expanded by an additional complex on the Sananga River (Song-Loulou) and a 72-MW generator (built with Chinese aid) on the Bénoué. However, despite Cameroon's impressive waterpower resources, the national electricity grid runs principally from Douala to Yaoundé and from Douala to Bafoussam. Most other areas are served by diesel-generated electricity or have no electricity at all. Cameroon's National Energy Plan attempts to prepare for a diminishing petroleum output. Hydro-Québec of Canada conducted a feasibility study of the Nachtigal Power Station, which could provide 280 MW of hydroelectric power on the Sananga River north of Yaoundé. In 1998, Hydro-Québec was awarded a contract to upgrade the Song-Loulou hydroelectric facility.

28 INDUSTRY

Industry accounted for 30.9% of GDP in 2010. Considerable advances in industrial development have been made in recent years, mostly in the south. Cameroon's first oil refinery opened at Limbé in May 1981. Since then, oil production has gained paramount importance for the country. Cameroon is sub-Saharan Africa's fifth-largest oil producer. The government, once a large shareholder in many industries, including aluminum, wood pulp, and oil refining, now advocates privatization. The government reported an annual growth of 8.2% in the manufacturing sector for 1998. Exports of logs and rubber were down 50% in 1998, partly because of tightening logging restrictions. There is a rubber factory in the Dizangué region, and about 20 large sawmills and 5 plywood factories and lumber mills.

The first industrial establishment not connected with agriculture processing and forestry was the Cameroonian Aluminum Refining Co. In 1957 the company opened at Edéa, importing ore from Guinea. Output was estimated at 74,800 metric tons in 1995. This was the only public sector monopoly not privatized by the year 2000. The most significant agricultural processing enterprises are the peanut and palm oil mills at Edéa, Douala, Bertoua, and Pitoa; soap factories at Douala and Pitoa; and tobacco factories at Yaoundé. Other concerns include a factory at Kaélé that produced cotton fiber and a cotton oil plant there that produces for export. There is a textile-weaving factory in Douala and a bleaching, dyeing, and printing factory in Garoua.

Cement plants are at Figuil and near Douala; in 1995, cement production was 620,000 tons, but demand for cement declined because of decreased public works. However, as of 2001, the construction sector has expanded, due in part to foreign financing of road construction. Residential and commercial construction is also underway. These construction projects boosted cement production. Several breweries supply both internal demand and surplus for export. Other manufactured products include beer and soft drinks, cigarettes, flour, chocolate, cocoa paste, construction materials, furniture, and shoes.

The $3.7-billion Chad-Cameroon oil pipeline, with estimated production at 225,000 barrels per day, was completed in late 2003. The project comprised approximately 300 oil wells, which are expected to extract approximately one billion barrels of oil over twenty-five years. Although Cameroon's oil production was expected to decline in 2011 (crude oil production was 77,230 barrels per day in 2009, down from 81,650 barrels per day in 2008) as older oil fields became exhausted and fewer new discoveries are made, the position of Kribi as the end point on the pipeline and Cameroon's refinery capacity could turn the nation into a major oil transport center. The government-controlled Sonara (Société Nationale de Raffinage) oil refinery in Limbe produces 45,000 barrels per day. In October 2002 the International Court of Justice ruled in Cameroon's favor in a border dispute with Nigeria over the Bakassi Peninsula. In August 2008 Nigeria officially handed over the region to Cameroon. The peninsula, which is located in the Gulf of Guinea, is believed to contain significant oil reserves, but no commercially viable deposits of oil had yet been discovered as of 2011.

29 SCIENCE AND TECHNOLOGY

The World Bank reported in 2009 that there were no patent applications in science and technology in Cameroon. The Ministry of Higher Education and Scientific Research is charged with formulating research policy and programs in Cameroon. It operates five university institutes and five research institutes concerned with soil science, hydrology, nutrition, psychosociology, demography, economics, geography, archaeology, botany and vegetal biology, and medical entomology. The French Institute of Scientific Research for Cooperative Development is located in Yaoundé. The universities of Buea, Yaoundé, and Douala (founded in 1977, 1962, and 1977, respectively) have Faculties of science. The University of Dschang (founded in 1977) offers training in agricultural sciences. In 1987–97, science and engineering students accounted for 45% of college and university enrollments. For the period 1990–01 there were only three researchers and four technicians actively engaged in research and development. High technology exports in 2006 totaled $2.94 million, accounting for only 2.71% of all manufactured exports.

30 DOMESTIC TRADE

Most imported consumer goods are distributed among the European population and the salaried and urban African workers. The internal markets are run by African entrepreneurs, while important import-export houses are controlled by Europeans, usually French. The main firms are found in Douala (the main port and industrial center) and Yaoundé (the capital city). The internal markets deal mainly with cattle, locally produced foodstuffs, and textiles, sewing machines, and radios. Trade in capital equipment and construction materials is practically restricted to the local industrialists and government contractors. Agricultural extension, modernization programs, cooperatives, and provident societies have all assisted in expanding markets. Credit, marketing of produce, transport of produce, and storage fall within their jurisdiction.

Usual office hours are from 7:30 a.m. to noon and from 1:00 to 3:30 p.m., Monday through Friday, and 8 a.m. to noon Saturday. Many businesses are open from 8 a.m. to 6 p.m. Banks are open 8 to 11:30 a.m. and 2:30 to 3:30 p.m.

31 FOREIGN TRADE

Cameroon imported $4.869 billion worth of goods and services in 2008, while exporting $4.371 billion worth of goods and services. Major import partners in 2009 were France, 21%; China, 11.7%; Nigeria, 10.8%; Belgium, 6.6%; and the United States, 4.3%. Its major export partners were Netherlands, 14.5%; Spain, 12.6%; Italy, 12.2%; China, 9.4%; the United States, 6.3%; France, 5.7%; Belgium, 4.5%; and the United Kingdom, 4.1%.

Imports included machinery, electrical equipment, transport equipment, fuel, pharmaceuticals, aluminum oxide, rubber, foodstuffs and grains, agricultural inputs, lubricants, and used clothing. Exports included crude oil, timber and finished wood products, cotton, cocoa, aluminum and aluminum products, coffee, rubber, bananas.

Principal Trading Partners – Cameroon (2010)			
(In millions of US dollars)			
Country	Total	Exports	Imports	Balance
---	---	---	---	---
World	8,750.0	3,900.0	4,850.0	-950.0
France	1,140.8	290.4	850.4	-559.9
China	1,015.0	419.8	595.3	-175.5
Spain	746.6	669.6	77.0	592.7
Netherlands	661.2	571.2	90.0	481.2
Nigeria	614.1	60.0	554.1	-494.2
Italy	534.3	412.5	121.8	290.7
United States	429.1	283.5	145.6	137.8
Belgium	378.7	131.3	247.4	-116.2
India	313.7	189.3	124.5	64.8
Germany	256.3	76.6	179.7	-103.1

(…) data not available or not significant.

(n.s.) not specified.

SOURCE: *2011 Direction of Trade Statistics Yearbook*, New York: United Nations, 2011.

32 BALANCE OF PAYMENTS

In 2010 Cameroon had a foreign trade deficit of $1.2 billion, amounting to 2.7% of GDP.

In the late 1970s, increased oil production compensated for the low world market prices of Cameroon's agricultural exports and helped the country achieve a favorable balance of payments. From 1994 to 1997 the volume and value of Cameroon's exports increased annually, in part due to the CFA currency devaluation. As of the early 2000s, cocoa and lumber exports have declined, due in part to lower world commodity prices. Petroleum remains Cameroon's chief export commodity. Cameroon has been attempting to attract further foreign investment into offshore and onshore concessions to raise export earnings. Cameroon imports primarily semiprocessed products and other industrial goods, machinery, and food products.

Exports of goods and services reached $5.64 billion in 2010. Imports grew to $6.41 billion in 2010, from $3.7 billion in 2004. The resource balance was consequently insignificant in both years, reaching $14 million in 2003, and $40 million in 2004. The current account balance was negative, improving from -$1.14 billion in 2009, to -$8.25 million in 2010. Foreign exchange reserves (including gold) grew to $3.665 billion in 2010.

33 BANKING AND SECURITIES

The bank of issue is the Bank of the Central African States (Banque des États de l'Afrique Central—BEAC), which replaced the Central Bank of the State of Equatorial Africa and Cameroon in November 1972. Its headquarters are in Yaoundé. In 1993, member states of the BEAC created a supranational supervisory authority, Commission Bancaire de l'Afrique Centrale (COBAC) in order to secure the region's banking system. The government's

Exchange Control Office controls all financial transactions effected between Cameroon and foreign territories.

Cameroon's banking system consisted of nine commercial banks with 60 branches in 1999. The major commercial banks, all with important foreign participation, were the Amity Bank, Banque Internationale du Cameroun pour l'Epargne et le Credit (the last bank to be privatized, in 1999), Caisse Commune d'Epargne et d'Investissement, Commercial Bank of Cameroon, Citibank, Societe General de Banque au Cameroun, Standard Chartered Bank, and the Societe Commerciale de Banque Credit Lyonnais-Cameroun. There was also a savings bank and a postal bank. Informal savings and loan systems known as tontines take the place of banks for many tribal members, with repayment enforced by social pressure.

In 2009 the discount rate, the interest rate at which the central bank lends to financial institutions in the short term, was 4.25%. At the end of 2010 the nation's gold bullion deposits totaled 0.90 tons.

In April 2003 the Douala Stock Exchange was declared open for business by Cameroon's prime minister Peter Mufany Musonge, although no exact date was given for the start of trading or the number of companies that will be listed. Cameroon has been criticized for a lack of transparency in its economic institutions and observers question whether the exchange will perform to international standards. The recently privatized electricity company, AES Sonel, is expected to be one of the first companies listed on the exchange when 5% of its shares are offered for sale to its employees; a sale required by an agreement between the company and the government.

34 INSURANCE

As of 2003 there were a number of foreign (predominately French) and domestic insurance companies doing business in Cameroon. However, foreign firms must have local partners. Cameroon was one of the 14 French-speaking African nations that adopted a common code with respect to the insurance sector. Enforcement of these new regulations led to the closure of some weak insurance companies and the restructuring of the sector.

35 PUBLIC FINANCE

In 2010 the budget of Cameroon included $3.779 billion in public revenue and $4.34 billion in public expenditures. The budget deficit amounted to 2.5% of GDP. Public debt was 9.6% of GDP, with $3.115 billion of the debt held by foreign entities.

Cameroon relies heavily on customs duties and direct taxes as sources of government revenue. Most of Cameroon's oil revenues do not appear in the national budget and are maintained in secret accounts abroad. The year 2000 budget was increased from $112 million to almost $2.2 billion in order to repay public debt, subsidize national education, public health, maintain infrastructure, and fund the police and armed forces. Also in 2000, the government of Cameroon was commended by the International Monetary Fund (IMF) for sound macroeconomic policies and thereby qualified for $2 billion in debt relief under the Heavily Indebted Poor Countries (HIPC) initiative. To reach the completion point, Cameroon met a number of triggers involving macroeconomic stability, commitment to a poverty reduction strategy, investment in social services as well as progress in privatization

---

Balance of Payments – Cameroon (2010)

(In millions of US dollars)

Current Account		-856.3
Balance on goods		-177.4
Imports	-4,662.6	
Exports	4,485.2	
Balance on services		-586.3
Balance on income		-238.6
Current transfers		146.0
Capital Account		147.0
Financial Account		527.4
Direct investment abroad		35.8
Direct investment in Cameroon		-0.6
Portfolio investment assets		-10.8
Portfolio investment liabilities		85.2
Financial derivatives		...
Other investment assets		550.6
Other investment liabilities		-132.8
Net Errors and Omissions		188.8
Reserves and Related Items		-6.8

(…) data not available or not significant.

SOURCE: *Balance of Payment Statistics Yearbook 2011*, Washington, DC: International Monetary Fund, 2011.

and reform of the forestry and transport sectors. In addition, Cameroon took steps to improve governance and fight official corruption. Following Cameroon's attainment of the Completion Point of the HIPC initiative in 2006, the IMF relieved Cameroon of the debts it and incurred before 1 January 2005, significantly lowering its debt burden and effectively freeing up resources to redeploy toward growth and poverty reduction.

The IMF reported that in 1999 government outlays by function were as follows: general public services, 43.6%; defense, 9.5%; public order and safety, 4.0%; economic affairs, 6.8%; housing and community amenities, 1.0%; health, 3.4%; recreation, culture, and religion, 0.7%; education, 12.0%; and social protection, 0.5%.

36 TAXATION

The tax on individual income ranged from 10–35% in 2010. Also levied were housing fund and employment taxes, a tax to finance Cameroon television, and social security taxes. The corporate tax rate was 38.5%. There is a 19.25% value-added tax (VAT) on goods and services sold in Cameroon, although some transactions are exempt. Other levies include taxes on business licenses, certain consumption goods, and stock dividend distributions.

37 CUSTOMS AND DUTIES

In accordance with the trusteeship agreement between France and the UN, all nations had equal tariff treatment in Cameroon when it was a trust territory. Many types of goods essential for economic, social, and educational development were exempt from duty. Export duties were moderate. Despite this situation, the direction of Cameroon's trade was to the franc currency zone and importers were required to secure import licenses for non-franc zone products. Following independence, the import licensing system was continued, but was lest strict for EU countries.

In 1994 Cameroon's new Regional Reform Program included reduced taxes on imports, from over 7% to 4%, and reduced the overall rate from a maximum 200% to a maximum 70% on luxury goods, and a minimum of 5% on necessities. Cameroon employs the common external tariff (TEC) using four categories: necessities, 5%; raw materials and equipment, 10%; semifinished goods, 20%; and finished products, 30%. There is also an excise tax and an indirect tax on consumer goods, of 25%.

The 2000 Financial Law was designed largely to attract foreign capital, providing exemptions from export duties on bananas, cocoa, coffee, cotton, rubber, sugar, palm oil, and medicinal plants. Legislation to establish free trade zones was enacted in 1990. Prohibited imports include certain sanitary products, chemicals, toxic waste, some cosmetics, and some food items.

38 FOREIGN INVESTMENT

Foreign direct investment (FDI) in Cameroon was a net inflow of $340.1 million according to World Bank figures published in 2009. FDI represented 1.53% of GDP.

Under the terms of a structural adjustment program, Cameroon has liberalized its investment code, eliminated most price controls, reduced import and export duties, and sought to privatize its parastatals. Foreign and domestic investors are provided with guarantees that substantially comply with international standards. Cameroon's investment code, enacted in 1990, eliminated

requirements for technology transfer and geographic location. Investments are not screened and foreign exchange privileges are not rationed. Investors can freely transfer dividends, return of capital, and interest and capital on foreign debt. The code requires at least 35% Cameroonian equity ownership in small- and medium-sized enterprises. In 1990, Cameroon also promulgated an industrial free zone (IFZ) regime which features a comprehensive package of incentives (a 10-year tax holiday and 15% corporate tax year beginning the 11th year) for enterprises which export at least 80% of their output, with licenses awarded by an independent regulatory agency, the National Office for Industrial Free Zones (NOIFZ). From 1996 to late 1999 the licensing process was suspended pending audits, but in 2002 the government declared all of Cameroon an IFZ, with benefits available to any enterprise meeting the export criterion. Cameroon has a special agreement with France only recently implemented which gives preferential treatment to France, including a special 15% tax and tax deductions for technical assistance.

Despite Cameroon's attractive investment code and IFZ regime, few foreign investors have come forward because of problems in its implementation. In 2011 Transparency International scored Cameroon at 52 on its International Corruption Perceptions Index, ranking 136th of 179 countries scored, making it the 27th among 46 African countries. In June 2003 the government got a soft official development assistance (ODA) loan from the World Bank for about $50 million to help it buy back $953.3 million of commercial debt and suppliers' credits at 14.5% face value. This loan was meant to increase Cameroon's attractiveness for foreign investment. While Cameroon's economy is one of the fastest growing in sub-Saharan Africa, red tape, high taxes, and corruption are the main obstacles for Cameroon's further expansion and foreign investment.

France has been the biggest source of foreign investment. The French company Pechiney has long owned the majority share of Alucam, the state aluminum complex, and in the privatization process begun in 1994, a French firm bought a state sugar mill in 1998; a French telecom firm was granted a mobile telephone license in 1999 and a French bank bought Cameroon's last state bank in 2000. South African firms acquired controlling shares in the privatized national railroad and the state-owned mobile telephone company. The Commonwealth Development Corporation had over £36 million ($58 million) invested in Cameroonian enterprises as of 1999, including CDC, HEVECAM, Printpak, SNEC, and SOCATRAL. In 2001 and 2002 the principal investors in the $2.2 billion Chad/Cameroon pipeline project were ExxonMobile with 40% (also the project operator), Petronas of Malaysia (35%), and ChevronTexaco (25%), with the US Export-Import Bank providing $158 million in loan guarantees for the project.

In June 2003, the government officially launched the Douala Stock Exchange (DSX), after more than three years of preparation and two missed launch dates, with the announced purpose of facilitating foreign investment in the Cameroon economy. its sole listing was (SEMC). Its first listing was Société des Eaux Minérales du Cameroun (SEMC). A second listing Société Africaine Forestière et Agricole du Cameroun (SAFACAM) was added in 2006.

In October 2005, a major investment plan for Alucam -the country's main aluminum smelter-was devised between the government and the Alcan Primary Metal Group. The investment plan was estimated to cost around $900 million and targeted an expansion and upgrade of the smelter and the construction of a new hydroelectric power station in Edea. A new cobalt mine was scheduled to open in Cameroon in 2010, but was delayed until 2012 due to the global financial crisis. The project could contribute more than $250 million a year to Cameroon's GDP and would make Cameroon the world's leading producer of cobalt.

39 ECONOMIC DEVELOPMENT

The government has initiated several efforts to further reduce its role in the economy and to promote private sector development during the 1990s and early 2000s, including reforms in taxation, tariffs, labor, and trade. Price controls were lifted in 1994 with the exception of pharmaceuticals, petroleum products, and goods and services produced by public monopolies. The government marketing board for coffee and cocoa was restructured and most restrictions on marketing and exporting were eliminated. During 1996 the government took bids from private companies for the privatization of the state-owned rubber company, shipping company, and railroad.

A prominent feature in Cameroon's economic development strategy was the development of an Industrial Free Zone (IFZ), which covers the entire country. Manufacturing and service industries authorized to operate under the program pay no duties on imported inputs, require no licenses, and are exempt from customs control. An IFZ firm must produce goods or services that are 80% export-bound and which are not environmentally destructive.

Multilateral aid from international financial institutions and UN organizations totaled $606 million in 1996. France agreed to loan $55 million in 1999 while the Paris Club agreed to reduce debt by 50% and reschedule payments through 2000. Total external debt in 2000 was $10.9 billion. Cameroon had a three-year $133.7 million Poverty Reduction and Growth Facility (PRGF) Arrangement with the International Monetary Fund (IMF) approved in December 2000 that was due to expire in December 2003. The country reached its decision point under the IMF/World Bank's Heavily Indebted Poor Countries (HIPC) initiative in October 2000, qualifying for some $2 billion in debt relief. The ongoing construction of the Chad-Cameroon oil pipeline in 2003 resulted in growth in the service sector. Economic development remained fragile, however, in part due to a decline in oil output. The government needs to focus on revenue collection, and target spending to key poverty-reduction policies such as health, education, and basic infrastructure.

Economic growth levels in 2010 were 3%. Projections for 2011 were 3.8% and 5.3% for 2012. While oil production is expected to pick up in the future (as a result of recently discovered oil fields), the overall effect on the economy will probably be offset by weak oil prices. Agriculture is expected to be an important growth sector, owing to high and steady returns on the production of cocoa, coffee, cotton, and timber.

40 SOCIAL DEVELOPMENT

Social services were introduced by the French in 1950. The law provides an employees' old age, disability, and survivors' pension plan, financed by employee and employer contributions. Benefits are also paid for occupational diseases and accidents. Old age (retirement) benefits are payable at age 60, or age 50 for early retirement. Maternity benefits are available for working women, but there are no general sickness benefits. There is a work injury insurance program covering all employed persons which provides cash benefits and medical care as well. Covered employees with children under the age of 14 receive a family allowance. Family assistance is a part of the traditional social system.

Although the constitution prohibits discrimination based on sex, under powerful customary laws, women do not have the same rights as men. Inheritance practices are dictated by tradition and custom, which favor male heirs. Custody of children after a divorce is determined by the husband's wishes, and spousal abuse is not accepted as grounds for divorce. Domestic violence is common and polygamy remains legal. Isolated cases of slavery were reported, largely Fulani enslavement of Kirdi. Many Fulani hired Kirdi at exploitive wage levels to perform tasks that the Fulani considered menial and beneath them. The law generally protects children from exploitation in the workplace and specifies penalties ranging from fines to imprisonment for infringement; however, child labor, particularly in informal sectors, remained a problem. The government specifically prohibits forced and compulsory labor by children, but there were reports that it occurred in practice.

There are over 200 different ethnic groups in Cameroon, and instances of ethnic favoritism are widespread. There are serious human rights abuses, including political and extrajudicial murders. Arbitrary detention and physical abuse of detainees is common. Although the press is independent and criticizes the government, the authorities seek to intimidate journalists. The government has also failed to cooperate with nongovernmental organizations monitoring human rights. Prison conditions are harsh and life threatening.

Cameroon signed the N'Djamena Declaration in 2010, which essentially calls for the end of the recruitment and use of children as soldiers. The recruitment and/or abduction of children to serve in armed conflicts in Africa has been a pressing issue for UNICEF and other international human rights organizations for many years. Along with a promise to halt recruitment efforts for child soldiers, the signatories of the N'Djamena Declaration have pledged to increase educational and employment opportunities for children once they have been released from military services.

41 HEALTH

According to the CIA, life expectancy in Cameroon was 54.39 years in 2011. The country spent 5.3% of its GDP on healthcare, amounting to $61 per person. There were 2 physicians, 16 nurses and midwives, and 15 hospital beds per 10,000 inhabitants. The fertility rate in 2011 was 4.7 children born per women, while the infant mortality rate was 60.91 per 1,000 live births. In 2008 the maternal mortality rate, according to the World Bank, was 600 deaths per 100,000 births. As of 2007 only an estimated 26% of the country's married women used any type of contraception. An estimated 29% of children under the age of five suffered from malnutrition. Approximately 62% of the population had access to safe drinking water and 92% had adequate sanitation. In 2007

Cameroon immunized children up to one year old for diphtheria, pertussis, and tetanus (80%); polio (79%); and measles (68%).

The Ministry of Public Health is responsible for the maintenance of all public health services. Many missionaries maintain health and leprosy centers. The government is pursuing a vigorous policy of public health improvement, with considerable success in reducing sleeping sickness, leprosy, and other endemic diseases. The demand for all types of health services and equipment is high and constant. The need for modern equipment is especially urgent, with many clinics using outdated equipment, some of which is imported illegally from Nigeria.

Malaria is prevalent in the Bénoué River valley, the basin of Lake Chad, the coastal region, and the forests of southern Cameroon. A large percentage of the adult population is affected. Other serious water-borne diseases are schistosomiasis and sleeping sickness, which is spread by the tsetse fly. Cameroon lies in the yellow fever endemic zone. The HIV/AIDS adult prevalence rate was 5.3% in 2009. The incidence of tuberculosis was 179 per 100,000 people in 2007.

⁴²HOUSING

Differences in climate, building materials, and patterns of living have resulted in a variety of traditional structures in rural areas. After 1946, the French government took measures to cope with growing urbanization, particularly in Douala and Yaoundé. There is still a housing shortage and many people still live in thatched hovels of mud and wood, with no running water or modern facilities. In 2000 only 62% of the population had access to improved water sources. The Cameroonian government has engaged in housing improvement and construction programs in urban and rural areas.

⁴³EDUCATION

In 2009 the World Bank estimated that 92% of age-eligible children in Cameroon, or 3,350,662 students, were enrolled in primary school. 1,268,655 students were enrolled in secondary schools. It is estimated that about 73% of all students complete their primary education. The student-to-teacher ratio for primary school was at about 46:1 in 2006; the ratio for secondary school was about 16:1 in 2009. Overall, the CIA estimated that Cameroon had a literacy rate of 67.9%. Public expenditure on education represented 3.7% of GDP.

Education is free in state schools and compulsory between ages 6 and 12. There are Francophone and Anglophone systems running side by side. The primary level of the Francophone system covers a six-year course of study. This is followed by four years of general secondary studies and three years of upper secondary studies. The primary schools of the Anglophone system cover a seven-year course, followed by five years of lower and two years of upper secondary studies. Both systems offer seven-year technical programs for secondary students as well. Working alongside the public schools are the missionary schools, which have been extremely important in the history of Cameroonian education. Government funds are available to mission and private schools. The school year runs from October to July.

There are two universities in the capital, in addition to those in Dschang, Nhaoundere, Duala and Buea. At Yaoundé University (founded in 1962), there are faculties of science, law and economics, and arts at Yaoundé, which maintains four regional campuses. Higher institutions attached to the university include the University Health Sciences Center, the Higher School of Sciences and Techniques of Information, the Institute of International Relations, the Advanced Teachers Training College, and the Polytechnic School. There is also a national school of public administration and an institute of business administration Tertiary enrollment was estimated at 9% in 2009. Of those enrolled in tertiary education, there were 100 male students for every 79 female students..

Officials from the African Union (AU) announced that the Cameroon-based hub of the proposed Pan-African University opened to students in September 2011, despite delays in the opening of two of the five other related hubs and continued concern over finances. The African Union announced plans to create the Pan-African University in 2008. Touted as a flagship institution of higher education, the university will consist of five regional schools, each specializing in a different discipline. Cameroon will host the Central Africa branch, specializing in social and human sciences and governance.

The University of Yaounde II is expected to serve as the host institute. Nigeria and Kenya were selected to represent West Africa and East Africa respectively, but political and financial issues emerged in choosing the South and North Africa branches. AU officials originally hoped to open all five branches in September 2010, but have since decided to go ahead with the first three branches in 2011, looking to 2012 as the opening date for the final two. Each of the branches requires a host institute of learning. Funding for each branch will come in three parts, with one third of the funds provided by the AU, one third from the host country, and one third from a lead partner. Sweden is expected to serve as Cameroon's lead partner.

⁴⁴LIBRARIES AND MUSEUMS

The National Archives is in Yaoundé and has an annex in Buea, where documents on colonial conditions and administration are stored. The National Archives also serves as the National Library of Cameroon and has a library of about 64,000 volumes in Yaoundé. The University of Yaoundé has about 90,000 volumes. There is a public library system with about 40 branches. The French Cultural Institute maintains a library in Douala with approximately 15,000 volumes. Douala also houses the Pan African Institute for Development Library, with about 13,000 volumes. The Cameroon Association of Librarians, Archivists, Documentalists and Museologists (ABADCAM) was established in 1974.

The Museum of Douala has prehistoric and natural history galleries devoted primarily to the main Cameroonian ethnic groups. The Museum of Bamounian Arts and Traditions at Foumban maintains objects of ancient art and a small library. The museums of Diamaré and Maroua at Maroua have ethnographic materials. Dschang has an ethnographic museum devoted to the Bamiléké and a fine-arts museum. Yaoundé has a museum of art and archaeology and a museum of Cameroonian art. There are also museums in Bamenda, Kousséri, and Mokolo.

45 MEDIA

The telecommunications network has been improving over the years. An automatic telephone exchange system links all important cities and towns. Cable, telegram, and telex services connect Cameroon to the outside world. In January 1974 a satellite telecommunications earth station was inaugurated, greatly improving the quality of Cameroon's international telephone service. However, service is still limited to mostly business and government use.

In 2009 Cameroon was selected as one of three countries to participate in the initial phase of the World Bank Group-sponsored Central African Backbone Program (CAB Program), which is designed to develop a high-speed telecommunications infrastructure in the region of Central Africa. The initial three-country project will serve as a model for expansion to eight additional countries, with a total estimated project cost of $215 million from 2009 to 2019.

In 2010 there were about 496,500 telephone landlines in Cameroon. In addition to landlines, there were 8.156 million mobile phones in use. In 2009 there were some 749,600 Internet users, about 4 per 100 citizens. Cameroon had 90 Internet hosts in 2010.

In 1987 Cameroon's radio and television networks were merged to form the Office de Radiodiffusion-Télévision Camerounaise (CRTV), which operates under the authority of the Ministry of Information and Culture. There are broadcasting stations at Yaoundé, Douala, Garoua, Buea, Bertoua, Bamenda, and Bafoussam, offering programs in French, English, and many African languages.

There were 2 FM radio stations, 9 AM radio stations, and 3 shortwave radio stations in 2009. In 2007, there were about 70 privately owned radio stations operating in the country; however, these were not officially licensed. The state-owned Cameroon Radio Television (CRTV) is the only officially recognized and fully licensed broadcaster in the country. In 2009, 33% of households had a television set. About 49% of households had a radio in 2007.

Most Cameroonian publications are issued irregularly and have small circulations. The majority are published in French, but some appear in Bulu, Duala, and other native languages of Cameroon. The major daily is the *Cameroon Tribune*, the official government newspaper, published in French in Yaoundé, with a weekly English-language edition; circulation was 66,000 in French and 20,000 in English as of 2002. There are 40 to 50 private newspapers, most of which are published sporadically.

The constitution guarantees freedom of the press, but in practice the threat of government censorship generally prevents opposition viewpoints from appearing in print, especially in the government-controlled press.

46 ORGANIZATIONS

The various economic interests of the country are represented in the Chamber of Commerce, Industry, and Mines in Douala and the Chamber of Agriculture, Pasturage, and Forests in Yaoundé. The Cameroonian Union of Professional Syndicates acts as a coordinating agency of the 20-odd syndicates of merchants and producers. There are also the Professional Banking Association and the Confederation of Small- and Medium-Sized Enterprises. The government has encouraged the formation of cooperatives. The National Produce Marketing Office, created in 1978, has a monopoly on marketing cocoa, cotton, coffee, peanuts, and palm kernels. It is responsible for the prices paid the producers, the quality of produce, and the development of production.

The Association to Fight Against Poverty and AIDS, founded in 1999, seeks to improve the lives of women through education, health, farming, economic development and women's rights. Cameroon Association for the Protection and Education of the Child was founded in 2002 to work on issues of children's welfare, particularly among disadvantaged and abused children of rural areas.

There are student unions based at the universities in Yaoundé and Douala. There are sports organizations in the country representing such pastimes as baseball, softball, badminton, and handball. There is also an organization of the Special Olympics. The Boy Scouts of Cameroon and Girl Guides are active in the country, as are chapters of the YMCA/YWCA.

Volunteer service organizations, such as the Lions Clubs International, are also present. There are national chapters of the Red Cross Society, Habitat for Humanity, UNICEF, the Society of St. Vincent de Paul, and Caritas.

47 TOURISM, TRAVEL, AND RECREATION

All visitors to Cameroon must have valid passports, visas, onward/return tickets, and certificates showing yellow fever immunization. The *Tourism Factbook*, published by the UN World Tourism Organization, reported 185,000 incoming tourists to Cameroon in 2006, who spent a total of $222 million. Of those incoming tourists, there were 97,000 from Africa and 63,000 from Europe.

There were 26,573 hotel beds available in Cameroon, which had an occupancy rate of 17%. The estimated daily cost to visit Yaounde, the capital, was $306. The cost of visiting other cities averaged $131.

Cameroon's chief tourist attractions are its forests, savanna, jungle, and wild game. The national parks and game reserves are equipped with camps for tourists. In October 2005, the government announced the creation of two new national parks, Boumba Bek and Nki. Together the parks house 283 bird species and 300 species of fish. The diverse ethnic groups, their cultures, and Cameroonian art have also proved of interest to visitors. There are several first-rate hotels in the major cities.

48 FAMOUS PERSONS

Ahmadou Ahidjo (1924–89) was president of Cameroon from 1960 until 1982. Paul Biya (b. 1933), after having served as prime minister since 1975, became president in 1982. William-Aurélien Eteki Mboumoua (b. 1933) was OAU secretary-general during 1974–78 and foreign minister of Cameroon during 1984–87. The best-known literary figures are the novelists Ferdinand Oyono (b. 1928) and Mongo Beti (1932–2001).

49 DEPENDENCIES

Cameroon has no territories or colonies.

50 BIBLIOGRAPHY

Austen, Ralph A. *Middlemen of the Cameroons Rivers: the Duala and Their Hinterland, c.1600-c.1960*. New York: Cambridge University Press, 1999.

Cameroon Investment and Business Guide: Strategic and Practical Information. Washington, DC: International Business Publications USA, 2012.

DeLancey, Mark W. and Mark Dike DeLancey. *Historical Dictionary of the Republic of Cameroon*. 3rd ed. Lanham, MD: Scarecrow Press, 2000.

Maynard, Kent. *Making Kedjom Medicine: A History of Public Health and Well-Being in Cameroon*. Westport, CT: Praeger, 2004.

Mbaku, John M. *Culture and Customs of Cameroon*. Westport, CT: Greenwood Press, 2005.

Zeilig, Leo, and David Seddon. *A Political and Economic Dictionary of Africa*. Philadelphia: Routledge/Taylor and Francis, 2005.

CAPE VERDE

Republic of Cape Verde
República de Cabo Verde

CAPITAL: Praia

FLAG: The flag consists of two white horizontal stripes above and below a red horizontal stripe in the lower half of a blue field. A circle of ten gold stars (representing major islands) is centered around the red stripe on the hoist side.

ANTHEM: *Cantico da Liberdade (Song of Freedom).*

MONETARY UNIT: The currency of Cape Verde is the escudo (CVE). There are coins of 1, 5, 10, 20, 50, 100, and 200 Cape Verde escudos, and notes of 200, 500, 1,000, 2,000, and 5,000 Cape Verde escudos. CVE1 = US$0.01166 (or US$1 = CVE84.085) as of 2011.

WEIGHTS AND MEASURES: The metric system is used.

HOLIDAYS: New Year's Day, 1 January; National Heroes' Day, 20 January; Women's Day, 8 March; Labor Day, 1 May; Children's Day, 1 June; Independence Day, 5 July; Assumption, 15 August; Day of the Nation, 12 September; All Saints' Day, 1 November; Immaculate Conception, 8 December; Christmas Day, 25 December.

TIME: 11 a.m. = noon GMT.

¹LOCATION, SIZE, AND EXTENT

Cape Verde, containing an area of 4,033 sq km (1,557 sq mi), is situated in the Atlantic Ocean about 595 km (370 mi) west of Dakar, Senegal. Comparatively, the area occupied by Cape Verde is slightly larger than the state of Rhode Island. Extending 332 km (206 mi) SE–NW and 299 km (186 mi) NE–SW, it consists of 10 islands and 5 islets, divided into a northern windward group (Barlavento)—Santo Antão, São Vicente, Santa Luzia [uninhabited], São Nicolau, Sal, Boa Vista, and two islets-and a southern leeward group (Sotavento)—Brava, Fogo, São Tiago, Maio, and three islets. The total coastline is 965 km (600 mi).

Cape Verde's capital city, Praia, is located on the southeastern coast of São Tiago Island.

²TOPOGRAPHY

The island chain is of volcanic origin. Fogo has the only active volcano, Pico do Cano (Mount Fogo), which reaches 2,829 m (9,281 ft) above sea level, the highest point in the nation. Peaks on Santo Antão and São Tiago reach 1,979 m (6,493 ft) and 1,392 m (4,567 ft), respectively. All but three of the islands are quite mountainous, with prominent cliffs and deep ravines. High ground and southwestern slopes support lush vegetation because of moisture condensation. Only four islands have year-round running streams. Mindelo on São Vicente is the principal port, but there are several other fine harbors.

³CLIMATE

A cold Atlantic current produces an arid atmosphere around the archipelago. There are two seasons: December–June is cool and dry, with temperatures at sea level averaging 21°C (70°F); July–November is warmer, with temperatures averaging 27°C (81°F). Although some rain comes during the latter season, rainfall is sparse overall. Accumulations are generally around 13 cm (5 in) annually in the northern islands and 30 cm (12 in) in the south. The archipelago is subject to cyclical droughts; a devastating drought began in 1968 and was broken only briefly in 1975, 1978, 1984, and 1986.

⁴FLORA AND FAUNA

The World Resources Institute estimates that there are 774 plant species in Cape Verde. In addition, Cape Verde is home to 26 species of mammals, 160 species of birds, and 20 species of reptiles. This calculation reflects the total number of distinct species residing in the country, not the number of endemic species.

There are trees typical of both temperate and tropical climates, depending on elevation. The only native mammal is the long-eared bat.

⁵ENVIRONMENT

The World Resources Institute reported that Cape Verde had designated 774,000 hectares (1.91 million acres) of land for protection as of 2006. Water resources totaled 0.3 cu km (0.072 cu mi) while water usage was 0.02 cu km (0.005 cu mi) per year. Domestic water usage accounted for 7% of total usage, industrial for 2%, and agricultural for 91%. Per capita water usage totaled 39 cu m (1,377 cu ft) per year.

The United Nations (UN) reported in 2008 that carbon dioxide emissions in Cape Verde totaled 308 kilotons.

Much of the land used for raising crops or livestock is too arid or steep for these purposes, resulting in soil erosion. Drought contributes to Cape Verde's land problems along with cyclones, volcanic activity, and insect infestation. The intense demand for wood as fuel has led to the virtual elimination of native vegetation. By 1978 nearly all indigenous plants in farmed areas and within a half-day's walk of small villages had been removed. The land and water supply is adversely affected by insecticides, pesticides, and fertilization. A resource still almost untapped is an estimated 80–90 million cu m of underground water, but the investment required to exploit it would be very large in relation to Cape Verde's resources.

In June 2009 Cidade Velha, located on Sao Tiago, was inscribed as the nation's first UNESCO World Heritage site. Cidade Velha, which dates back to the late fifteenth century, was the first colonial outpost in the tropics.

According to a 2011 report issued by the International Union for Conservation of Nature and Natural Resources (IUCN), the number of threatened species included 3 types of mammals, 4 species of birds, 24 species of fish, and 3 species of plants. Endangered species in Cape Verde included the Mediterranean monk seal, the northern bald ibis, the green sea turtle, and the hawksbill turtle.

6 POPULATION

The US Central Intelligence Agency (CIA) estimated the population of Cape Verde in 2011 to be approximately 516,100, which placed it at number 165 in population among the 196 nations of the world. In 2011 approximately 5.5% of the population was over 65 years of age, with another 32.6% under 15 years of age. The median age in Cape Verde was 22.7 years. There were 0.94 males for every female in the country. The population's annual rate of change was 1.446%. The projected population for the year 2025 was 680,000. Population density in Cape Verde was calculated at 128 people per sq km (332 people per sq mi).

The UN estimated that 61% of the population lived in urban areas in 2010, and that urban populations had an annual rate of change of 2.4%. The largest urban area was Praia, with a population of 125,000.

7 MIGRATION

Estimates of Cape Verde's net migration rate, carried out by the CIA in 2011, amounted to -0.66 migrants per 1,000 citizens. The total number of emigrants living abroad was 192,500, and the total number of immigrants living in Cape Verde was 12,100. Economic development has not kept pace with rapid population growth. This factor, in combination with the prolonged drought, has produced a sizable outflow of emigrants. By the early 1990s there were some 600,000 Cape Verdean emigrants in the United States, Europe, Latin America, and other African countries. Some 325,000 were in the United States alone—mostly in New England. Remittances to Cape Verde from emigrants enabled many of those who remained in the islands to survive the drought. In 1998 Cape Verde received some 2,000 refugees from Guinea-Bissau when violence erupted there.

8 ETHNIC GROUPS

About 71% of the inhabitants of Cape Verde are creole, descendants of Portuguese colonists and their African slaves, who came, most often, from what is today Guinea-Bissau. Another 28% of the inhabitants are entirely African. There is a small minority (1–2%) of Europeans on the islands.

9 LANGUAGES

Portuguese is the official language, but Crioulo, an archaic Portuguese dialect with a pronunciation that reveals African influences, is the spoken language of Cape Verde.

10 RELIGIONS

About 85% of the population of Cape Verde is nominally Roman Catholic. Protestant churches account for a small percentage, with the largest denomination being the Church of the Nazarene. Other denominations include the Seventh-Day Adventists, the Church of Jesus Christ of Latter-Day Saints, Assemblies of God, the Universal Church of the Kingdom of God, and various Pentecostal and evangelical groups. There are also small groups of Muslims and Baha'is. Several African traditional religions are practiced, especially on São Tiago, with some traditional elements infused in other religions.

Though there is no state religion, the Roman Catholic Church seems to enjoy a somewhat privileged status, including officially observed religious holidays. The constitutional right of freedom of religion is generally respected in practice. All associations, religious and secular, must register with the Ministry of Justice in accordance with the Law of Associations.

11 TRANSPORTATION

The CIA reports that Cape Verde has a total of 1,350 km (839 mi) of roads, of which 932 km (579 mi) are paved. There are 10 airports, which transported 776,469 passengers in 2009 according to the World Bank.

Commercial transportation is largely by coastal craft and domestic airlines. The ports of Mindelo on São Vicente and Porto Novo on Santo Antão are important as international fueling stops. The state-owned Companhia Nacional de Navigacao runs an inter-island ferry service. As of 2010 the merchant fleet of Cape Verde consisted of 13 ships of 1,000 GRT or over. Two deepwater berths at Praia Port were rehabilitated with international financing and provide modern cargo handling techniques.

In 1975 the international airport on Sal was renamed the Amilcar Cabral International Airport, in honor of the former nationalist leader of the African Party for the Independence of Guinea-Bissau and Cape Verde. It is an important refueling point on many African flights, with the second longest runway in Africa. Two new international airports were opened in the country in 2007 and 2009. The national airline is TACV Cabo Verde Airlines, which began service to Lisbon in 1985 and to Boston in 1987.

12 HISTORY

Parts of the Cape Verde Islands were probably discovered in about 1455 by António da Noli, a Genoese, who was in service to Prince Henry the Navigator of Portugal (Henrique o Navegador); the islands showed no signs of any previous human settlement, although new excavations in Sal Island might suggest earlier visitors. In 1462 São Tiago was the first island to receive permanent settlers. Plantation agriculture was established by the Portuguese community and worked by African slaves, who were brought in from the nearby Upper Guinea coast. There was a population of slaves and free Africans, and a population of creoles on the islands from this early period, and they retain strong, but complex cultural ties with the African mainland.

The islands produced trade goods; especially important were cattle, cotton cloths (*panos*) made by slave women, and rum (*grog*). These goods were used to purchase slaves and consumer items from slavers trading in the African interior and in the New World. The economy of the islands suffered from colonial restrictions on the production of potentially competitive export commodities, as well as from cyclical drought. Between 1747 and 1960 an estimated 250,000 Cape Verdeans died of famine.

The phase-out of the Atlantic slave trade and the abolition of slavery in the Portuguese Empire, coupled with an 1886 law providing for the settlement of former Cape Verde slaves on open lands, brought the end of Cape Verde's importance as a slave-trading center. The islands' historical role as a port of call (prior to the building of the Suez Canal) became important again in the mid-20th century, when they were used by Portuguese troops as a transit area for their African counter-insurgency campaigns. For five centuries the Portuguese were strong enough to keep the archipelago as a colony, until the African Party for the Independence of Guinea-Bissau and Cape Verde (Partido Africano da Independência da Guiné e Cabo Verde—PAIGC) took power on 5 July 1975. This Cape Verdean-led movement was engaged in 11 years of armed struggle in Guinea-Bissau (1963–74), until this precipitated a military coup in Portugal in April 1974. In turn this resulted in Portuguese decolonization in Africa, and an independence agreement was signed between Portuguese and PAIGC representatives on 30 December 1974, leading to the establishment of the two linked, but independent republics: the Republic of Guinea-Bissau on 24 September 1974 and the Republic of Cape Verde on 5 July 1975.

Cape Verde and Guinea-Bissau—where Luís de Almeida Cabral, a Cape Verdean, was president—were politically unified until a military coup in Guinea-Bissau toppled Cabral in November 1980. The Cape Verde wing of PAIGC subsequently broke its links with the mainland and temporarily abandoned the goal of unification and became known as the African Party for the Independence of Cape Verde (PAICV), dropping the G representing Guiné (the Portuguese designation for Guinea-Bissau). Diplomatic relations with Guinea-Bissau, severed at the time of the coup, were resumed in June 1982.

After 15 years of single-party rule by the PAICV, dissidents agitated to legalize an opposition party in 1990. A hastily assembled opposition coalition, the Movement for Democracy (MPD), won the 13 January 1991 legislative elections with 68% of the votes. In February an independent candidate, António Mascarenhas Monteiro, defeated the incumbent, Aristides Pereira, for the presidency with 72.6% of the vote. The governmental transition went smoothly and without violence.

In 1992 the new constitution came into force, and the government began to privatize state-run industries. I

On 11 and 25 February 2001, Pedro Pires (PAICV) was very narrowly elected president, and inaugurated on 22 March 2001. Pires won reelection in February 2006. In August 2011 Jorge Carlos Fonseca was elected president with 53.4% of the vote.

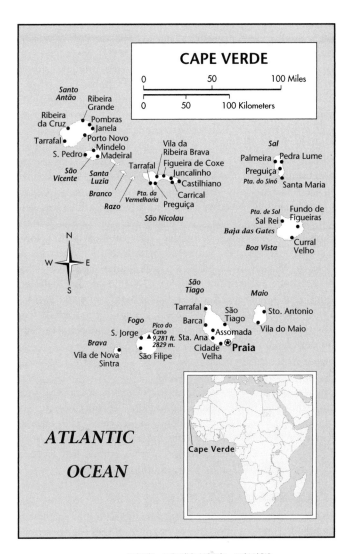

LOCATION: 14°48′ to 17°12′N; 22°40′ to 25°22′ W.
TERRITORIAL SEA LIMIT: 12 miles.

¹³GOVERNMENT

The prime minister, who heads the government, is nominated by the unicameral assembly and appointed by the president. A council of ministers is appointed by the president on the recommendation of the prime minister. As of 2011 the unicameral national assembly consisted of 72 seats, with members elected by popular vote to serve five-year terms.

The constitution was amended on 28 September 1990 to legalize opposition parties and revised again in 1992. It underwent a major revision on 23 November 1995, substantially increasing the powers of the president, and a further revision in 1999, to create the position of national ombudsman (*provedor de justiça*). It guarantees human rights and includes the principle of the separation of powers, a market-based economy, and individual rights and liberties. Multiparty democracy has peacefully prevailed ever since.

¹⁴POLITICAL PARTIES

The African Party for the Independence of Cape Verde (Partido Africano da Independência do Cabo Verde—PAICV) was the sole legal political party from 1975 until 1990. On 28 September 1990 the constitution was amended to legalize opposition parties. In the legislative elections held 13 January 1991, the PAICV was defeated by the Movement for Democracy (MPD), which garnered 68% of the vote. Through the 1990s and into the early 21st century, PAICV was the opposition in the national assembly.

In 1994 during an MPD party conference, two leading politicians split with the party and formed the Party for Democratic Convergence (PCD). Legislative elections were again held in 1995, with the MPD winning 50 of the 72 seats (the assembly had been shrunk since the 1991 balloting). The PAICV won 21 seats and the PCD won one seat. On 18 February 1996 Monteiro was reelected to the presidency, and Veiga retained his post as prime minister.

On 11 and 25 February 2001, Pedro Pires (PAICV) was very narrowly elected president, and inaugurated on 22 March 2001. Pires won reelection in February 2006. In August 2011 Jorge Carlos Fonseca was elected president with 53.4% of the vote; he defeated Manuel Inocencio Sousa. José Maria Pereira Neves has been prime minister since 1 February 2001. In January 2006 elections, PAICV won 52.3% and 41 seats to MPD's 44% and 29 seats. Legislative elections took place in February 2011; PAICV won 38 seats, MPD 32, and the Democratic and Independent Cape Verdean Union (UCID) 2.

[15] LOCAL GOVERNMENT

The islands are divided into 17 districts (conçelhos) and 31 freguesias, which are subdivisions of conçelhos. The conçelhos are: São Nicolau, Sal, Boa Vista, Maio, Brava, São Vicente, Praia, Tarrafal, Santa Cruz, Santa Catarina, Ribeira Grande, Porto Novo, Paúl, Calheta, Mosteiros, São Domingos, and São Filipe. There are local elections for the officials of these administrative units.

[16] JUDICIAL SYSTEM

In the colonial period, Cape Verde was subject to the Portuguese civil and criminal codes. Most provisions of these codes remain in effect. A Supreme Tribunal of Justice hears appeals from subregional and regional tribunals. Informal popular tribunals serve as courts of the first instance for minor disputes.

The 1992 constitution provides for a judiciary independent from the executive branch. The Supreme Tribunal of Justice has a minimum of five members, one appointed by the president, one appointed by the assembly, and three appointed by the Supreme Council of Magistrates. The Ministry of Justice and Labor appoints local judges.

Criminal defendants are presumed innocent and have the right to counsel, to public, nonjury trial, and to appeal.

[17] ARMED FORCES

The International Institute for Strategic Studies reports that armed forces in Cape Verde totaled 1,200 members in 2011. The force is comprised of 1,000 from the army, 100 from the coast guard, and 100 members of the air force. Armed forces represent 0.6% of the labor force in Cape Verde. Defense spending totaled $9.7 million and accounted for 0.5% of gross domestic product (GDP).

[18] INTERNATIONAL COOPERATION

On 16 September 1975 the Republic of Cape Verde was admitted to the UN. It belongs to the ECA and several nonregional specialized agencies. It is also a member of the African Development Bank, the ACP Group, ECOWAS, G-77, the African Union, the New Partnership for Africa's Development (NEPAD), and the Alliance of Small Island States (AOSIS). Cape Verde became a member of the WTO in 2008. In environmental cooperation, Cape Verde is part of the Basel Convention, the Convention on Biological Diversity, the London Convention, the Montréal Protocol, and the UN Conventions on the Law of the Sea, Climate Change, and Desertification.

[19] ECONOMY

Because Cape Verde suffers from a lack of natural resources, with the exception of a modest fishing industry, most revenue in the country is generated from the service sector. Tourism is one important developing industry.

Many Cape Verdeans work abroad and send money back to the islands, with an estimated 20% of GDP earned through remittances. While this has been a great boost to the economy, the government has begun to initiate campaigns that would bring these citizens, along with their skills and investment funds, back to the island. In May 2009 the government announced a program of reduced taxes and customs rates for emigrants who do business with Cape Verde. With recent investments in renewable energy sources and information technology, including connection to the West African Cable System, the government hopes that a business-friendly climate will bring its most successful expatriates home.

Tuna and lobster are the main fishing products. Bananas, maize, and beans are key crops, with cassava, sweet potatoes, coconuts, dates, and sugar cane also produced on small, low-technology farms for domestic consumption. Cape Verde is drought-prone, and less than 10% of its food requirements are met by local producers. Salt, pozzolana (a volcanic rock used in cement production), and limestone are mineral resources.

Cape Verde runs a high trade deficit as a result of high levels of foreign aid and remittances.

Perhaps Cape Verde's most important asset is its strategic economic location. It is an important refueling location for international air and ocean traffic. In 1997 a four-year World Bank-sponsored project designed to upgrade the port facilities at Porto Grande was completed. Two new ports were also built on the islands of Maio and Boa Vista.

In order to keep the tourist sector moving forward in the wake of the global financial crisis of 2008–09, the country managed to reduce prices, thereby attracting more visitors, and encourage foreign investment, thereby expanding the tourist industry through new construction projects.

The GDP rate of change in Cape Verde, as of 2010, was 5.4%. Inflation stood at 2.5%, and unemployment was reported at 21%.

[20] INCOME

The CIA estimated that in 2010 the GDP of Cape Verde was $1.908 billion. The CIA defines GDP as the value of all final goods and services produced within a nation in a given year and computed on the basis of purchasing power parity (PPP) rather than value as measured on the basis of the rate of the exchange based on current dollars. The per capita GDP was estimated at $3,800. The annual growth rate of GDP was 5.4%. The average inflation rate was 2.5%.

It was estimated that agriculture accounted for 9% of GDP, industry 16.2%, and services 74.8%.

The World Bank reports that in 2009 household consumption in Cape Verde totaled $1 billion or about $2,018 per capita, measured in current US dollars rather than PPP. Household consumption includes expenditures of individuals, households, and nongovernmental organizations on goods and services, excluding the purchases of dwellings. It was estimated that household consumption was growing at an average annual rate of 5.8%.

In 2007 the World Bank estimated that Cape Verde, with 0.01% of the world's population, accounted for less than 0.01% of the world's GDP. By comparison, the United States, with 4.85% of the world's population, accounted for 22.51% of world GDP.

As of 2011 the most recent study by the World Bank reported that actual individual consumption in Cape Verde was 87.2% of GDP and accounted for less than 0.01% of world consumption. By comparison, the United States accounted for 25.44% of world individual consumption. The World Bank also estimated that 26.6% of Cape Verde's GDP was spent on food and beverages, 27.7% on housing and household furnishings, 3.0% on clothes, 3.1% on health, 5.3% on transportation, 2.6% on communications, 2.7% on recreation, 2.4% on restaurants and hotels, and 3.6% on miscellaneous goods and services and purchases from abroad.

As of 2000 (the most recent year for which figures are available) an estimated 30% of the population lived below the poverty line.

21 LABOR

As of 2007 Cape Verde had a total labor force of 196,100 people. Unemployment was reported at 21% in 2010.

All workers are free to form and join unions of their choosing without interference from the government. About 22% of the country's workforce was unionized. The government generally respects the worker's right to strike, but this right has been limited at times by the government if an emergency situation or essential services might be affected.

In 2008 the legal minimum age for employment was lowered from 16 to 15. Children under 15 can work as apprentices under certain conditions. Minors under the minimum age cannot work at night, over seven hours per day, or in places that produce toxic products. However, enforcement by the government is rare.

Although there is no established minimum wage for the private sector, most private employers pay their workers what an entry-level government official would make, approximately $163 per month in 2010. However this is inadequate to support a family and most workers rely upon extended family help or second jobs. The legal workweek is limited to 44 hours for adults, with 12 consecutive hours per week for rest and premium rates of pay for overtime. Larger employers generally respect this restriction, but agricultural and domestic laborers work longer hours.

22 AGRICULTURE

Roughly 23% of the total land is farmed. The country's major crops include bananas, corn, beans, sweet potatoes, sugarcane, coffee, and peanuts. Cereal production in 2009 amounted to 7,380 tons, fruit production 21,218 tons, and vegetable production 17,422 tons.

The most widespread agricultural activity of the islands is gardening for domestic consumption. Frequent droughts often exacerbate an ongoing water shortage. Only the islands of São Tiago, São Vicente, São Nicolau, and Santo Antão have conditions suitable for raising cash crops. Bananas, the only agricultural export, are grown on irrigated land. Sugarcane, another cash crop, is used on the islands to produce rum.

Agriculture has been the focus of development aid programs since the 1960s, but progress has been frustrated by drought, locusts, overgrazing, and archaic cultivation methods.

The PAIGC has nationalized a few large-scale irrigated agricultural operations and began a program of land reform and cooperative agriculture; sharecropping was abolished. During 1976–80, 7,200 rainwater dikes were built. Torrential rains in 1984 destroyed much of this work, but by 1986, 17,000 dikes and 25,000 stone retaining walls had been completed. There has been little land redistribution, despite a 1982 law distributing farms over 5 hectares (12.5 acres)—1 hectare (2.5 acres) if irrigated—among the tenants if the land is not directly farmed by the owners.

In an effort to strengthen the agricultural sector, the government has begun promoting the commercialization of rural farms by bringing small farmers together into large agricultural companies. In 2010 the government met with farmers and landowners to encourage their participation in agricultural companies. The government explained the benefits, such as better access to modern equipment and a boost in production value as farmers organize for shared marketing ventures. The government has promised to provide training, organizational resources, and some microcredit financing options for farmers and landowners who are willing to partner together into agricultural companies under national development guidelines.

23 ANIMAL HUSBANDRY

The UN Food and Agriculture Organization (FAO) reported that Cape Verde dedicated 25,000 hectares (61,776 acres) to permanent pasture or meadow in 2009. During that year, the country tended 600,000 chickens, 45,000 head of cattle, and 231,640 pigs. The production from these animals amounted to 1,424 tons of beef and veal, 10,179 tons of pork, 7,520 tons of poultry, 1,948 tons of eggs, and 61,281 tons of milk. Cape Verde also produced 167 tons of cattle hide.

Periodic droughts have significantly lowered the capacity of the islands to pasture livestock.

24 FISHING

Cape Verde had 77 decked commercial fishing boats in 2008. The annual capture totaled 21,910 tons according to the UN FAO. The export value of seafood totaled $7.16 million.

The cold Canaries current, running adjacent to the islands, is an ideal environment for many kinds of marketable fish, and the fishing and fish-processing industries in the islands offer the best potential for expansion. Maritime resources are under-exploited.

25 FORESTRY

Approximately 21% of Cape Verde is covered by forest. The value of all forest products, including roundwood, totaled $891,000 in 2009.

Forests on the island have been cut down for fuel, and the drought damaged many wooded areas. Large-scale reforestation is under way as part of a program of water-resource development.

According to the World Bank, Cape Verde had about 850 sq km (328 sq mi) of forested land in 2010.

26 MINING

Mining's contribution to Cape Verde's economy is minimal, and the geological potential of the islands remains largely unexplored. Pozzolana (a volcanic rock used in pulverized form in the manufacture of hydraulic cement) from four mines on Santo Antão and salt are the only minerals exploited commercially, salt being a leading industry. In 2009 around 1,600 metric tons of salt were produced. Sal and Boa Vista have sea salt refineries and deposits of calcareous rocks, used in paving, building ornaments, and tile production. There are also deposits of kaolin, clay, gypsum, and basalt.

27 ENERGY AND POWER

The World Bank reported in 2008 that Cape Verde produced 257 million kWh of electricity and consumed 244.1 million kWh, or 473 kWh per capita. The country has no known oil or gas reserves. In 2009 oil consumption was estimated at 2,336 barrels per day.

The government has undertaken measures to expand domestic production of energy from renewable resources. Its goal is to generate 50% of the country's electricity needs from renewable sources by the year 2020; in 2010 that figure was only 3.2%.

28 INDUSTRY

The industrial sector in Cape Verde was born in the early 1990s, with garment and shoe production factories. Industry accounted for about 18% of GDP in 2000; a decade later, in 2010, that figure was 16.2%. Besides the salt refining, Cape Verdean products include frozen and canned fish, tobacco, bread and biscuits, and soft drinks. Rum is produced from locally grown sugarcane.

29 SCIENCE AND TECHNOLOGY

The World Bank reported in 2009 that there were no patent applications in science and technology in Cape Verde. The ECOWAS Center for Renewable Energy and Energy Efficiency (ECREEE), a specialized agency of the Economic Community of West African States (ECOWAS), was opened in the capital city of Praia in July 2010. The center is supported by the UN Industrial Development Organization (UNIDO) and the governments of Cape Verde, Austria, and Spain. It primarily serves as a regional center in support of research and development in renewable energy and energy efficiency technologies directed toward the West African Market. The ECREEE has worked to develop new energy programs for 18 countries in West Africa, all focusing on energy access and energy efficiency in key sectors of the economy. From its new offices in Cape Verde, the agency will serve as the primary implementing organization for those programs.

30 DOMESTIC TRADE

In 2010 nearly 75% of the economy was based on the service sector, with commerce, transportation, and public services as the strongest segments. Most consumer goods are imported and sold or distributed in the major centers of Praia and Mindelo by

Principal Trading Partners – Cape Verde (2010)

(In millions of US dollars)

Country	Total	Exports	Imports	Balance
World	786.9	44.5	742.4	-697.9
Portugal	349.6	11.7	337.8	-326.1
Netherlands	100.1	0.1	100.0	-99.9
Spain	82.9	32.2	50.7	-18.5
Brazil	33.1	0.7	32.4	-31.7
China	31.9	...	31.9	-31.9
Germany	18.0	...	18.0	-18.0
Japan	17.4	...	17.4	-17.4
United Kingdom	16.4	...	16.4	-16.4
Thailand	15.3	...	15.3	-15.3
France	14.8	0.3	14.5	-14.3

(…) data not available or not significant.

(n.s.) not specified.

SOURCE: *2011 Direction of Trade Statistics Yearbook,* New York: United Nations, 2011.

Balance of Payments – Cape Verde (2010)

(In millions of US dollars)

Current Account		**-184.3**
Balance on goods		-678.8
Imports	-814.2	
Exports	135.3	
Balance on services		222.2
Balance on income		-68.1
Current transfers		340.5
Capital Account		**39.9**
Financial Account		**243.9**
Direct investment abroad		0.2
Direct investment in Cape Verde		111.7
Portfolio investment assets		...
Portfolio investment liabilities		0.0
Financial derivatives		...
Other investment assets		-6.2
Other investment liabilities		138.2
Net Errors and Omissions		**-70.3**
Reserves and Related Items		**-29.1**

(…) data not available or not significant.

SOURCE: *Balance of Payment Statistics Yearbook 2011,* Washington, DC: International Monetary Fund, 2011.

EMPA, a state wholesale-retail company that controls the prices of many basic consumer goods.

Business hours for banking, government, and industry are 8 a.m. to 12 noon and 2 p.m. to 6 p.m. Commercial/retail hours are generally from 8 a.m. to 12:30 p.m. and 3 p.m. to 7 p.m. Some establishments are open on Saturdays from 9 a.m. to 1 p.m.

31 FOREIGN TRADE

Cape Verde imported $858 million worth of goods and services in 2008, while exporting $114 million worth of goods and services. Major import partners in 2009 were Portugal, 43.5%; Netherlands, 15.1%; Spain, 5.9%; China, 5%; Italy, 4.3%; and Brazil, 4.1%. Major export partners were Spain, 52.1%; Portugal, 21.5%; and Morocco, 6.9%.

Public Finance – Cape Verde (2009)

(In millions of Cape Verde escudos, central government figures)

Revenue and Grants	**43,377**	**100.0%**
Tax revenue	25,127	57.9%
Social contributions	4,360	10.1%
Grants	8,119	18.7%
Other revenue	5,771	13.3%
Expenditures	**48,054**	**100.0%**
General public services	13,930	29.0%
Defense	690	1.4%
Public order and safety	3,002	6.2%
Economic affairs	11,434	23.8%
Environmental protection	97	0.2%
Housing and community amenities	1,515	3.2%
Health	3,146	6.5%
Recreational, culture, and religion	547	1.1%
Education	8,017	16.7%
Social protection	5,676	11.8%

(…) data not available or not significant.

SOURCE: *Government Finance Statistics Yearbook 2010*, Washington, DC: International Monetary Fund, 2010.

Cape Verde has been increasingly dependent upon imports, especially foodstuffs and manufactured goods, a situation that has led to a severe trade imbalance. In 2010 approximately 82% of food was imported.

Major commodity export items were traditionally bananas and fish, and now also include re-exported fuel, garments, and shoes. In addition to food, major imports included industrial products, transport equipment, and petroleum.

32 BALANCE OF PAYMENTS

In 2010 Cape Verde had a foreign trade deficit of $449 million, amounting to 3.8% of GDP. Cape Verde's massive annual trade deficit is only partially offset by remittances from Cape Verdeans employed abroad. Annual payment deficits were substantial and could be met only through foreign assistance. The average import growth rate between 1990 and 1995 was 14%, compared to a GDP growth rate of 4%. Debt in 2000 reached $301 million. Due to foreign investment, largely in free-zone enterprises, exports rose during the 1990s and early 2000s.

33 BANKING AND SECURITIES

The Banco de Cabo Verde (BCV, Bank of Cape Verde) acts as the central bank to the country, although it has been privately held since 1999. Its primary mission is price stability. The bank's secondary function is to oversee the liquidity, operation, and solvency of the nation's financial system. Prior to 1993 the BCV also acted as a commercial and development bank, a function that was supplemented by the Caixa Economica de Cabo Verde (CECV), a savings bank. Since 1993 the bank's former commercial operations are now the responsibility of the Commercial Bank of the Atlantic (BCA), which is still majority state owned.

In March 1993 the financial market was opened for private and foreign banks, as long as at least 50% of the workers were Cape Verdean nationals.

In 1999 four Portuguese banks opened offices in Cape Verde: Totta and Acores, Caixa Geral de Depositos, Banco Nacional Ultramarino (BNU), and Banco Mello. The first totally private bank opened in 1999, the Banco Interatlantico.

In early October 1996 the Ministry of Economic Coordination held a conference in Praia to consider opening a stock exchange. With the help of GARSEE, a World Bank institution, the Capital Markets Implementation Committee was created (Comissão Instaladora do Mercado de Capitáis). The committee established the first stock exchange, the Bolsa de Valores de Cabo Verde, in March 1999 in Praia. The president of the Lisbon Stock Exchange, José Lemos, assisted GARSEE with the $500,000 project. The exchange became active in December 2005.

34 INSURANCE

There are several insurance companies in Cape Verde.

35 PUBLIC FINANCE

In 2010 the budget of Cape Verde included $520.7 million in public revenue and $680.8 million in public expenditures. The budget deficit amounted to 10.3% of GDP. Public debt was 65.0% of GDP, with $325 million of the debt held by foreign entities.

36 TAXATION

There are substantial tax incentives for foreign investors in Cape Verde. There is a consumption tax on nonpriority goods, ranging between 5% and 60% for hard liquor. In 2003 a 15% value-added tax (VAT) was introduced.

37 CUSTOMS AND DUTIES

Cape Verde is a member of the Economic Community of West African States (ECOWAS). In 1991 import tariffs were organized into a system of 10 ad valorem rates ranging between 5% and 50%. There is a customs tax of 7% and a consumption tax on luxury items ranging from 5–60%. There are no export controls. The import of narcotics is prohibited and pharmaceuticals can only be imported by the government.

38 FOREIGN INVESTMENT

Foreign direct investment (FDI) in Cape Verde was a net inflow of $119.8 million according to World Bank figures published in 2009. FDI represented 7.73% of GDP.

Prior to 5 July 1975 Portuguese corporations were the principal investors in the islands. On that date, foreign corporate landholdings were nationalized by the government. During the 1990s the shipbuilding and repair yard at Mindelo was jointly owned by the government and Portuguese investors; the fish-freezing plant was jointly owned by the government and Dutch investors; and the clothing factory by the government and 107 Cape Verdean nationals living abroad. Private enterprise is now encouraged by the government and has been a major objective of the on-going privatization effort. In 1993, to further encourage investment by Cape Verdean emigrants, the government created favorable tax conditions for such investors. A 100% tax exemption was granted to the first five years of a foreign exportation operation. After five years, a foreign-owned exportation company must pay a 10% tax, which after 10 years was capped at 15%. Foreign-owned industrial endeavors received an exemption for the first three years of operation, with progressively higher customs duties afterwards (25%, 50%, and 75%). The tourism and fishing industries were also granted tax breaks. By the mid-1990s most sectors of the economy were open to foreign investment, with highest priority given to light manufacturing, tourism, and fishing.

Most FDI has been in tourism (54%), with manufacturing accounting for 15.5% of FDI. The main sources have been Italy, Portugal, Spain (Canary Islands), and Hong Kong.

39 ECONOMIC DEVELOPMENT

The development plan adopted in 1991 sought to transform Cape Verde into an open-market style economy. The country's development priorities included the promotion of service-sector industries such as tourism, maritime services, and transshipping.

In 1994 the government announced a five-year plan to develop the fishing industry, focusing mostly on lobster and tuna. A free-trade port was projected, and offshore banking was planned. In 1997 the government adopted a four-year development plan that focused on debt management and sustainable development.

Cape Verde entered into an $11 million three-year Poverty Reduction and Growth Facility (PRGF) arrangement with the International Monetary Fund (IMF) in April 2002. Economic growth and international reserves increased in 2002, and inflation fell. The fiscal deficit was lower than expected, the balance of payments was stronger, and investment increased. The government that came into office in 2001 focused on implementing tight monetary policies and improving the social and economic infrastructure.

In November 2010 the International Monetary Fund announced that it had approved a 15-month Policy Support Instrument (PSI) for Cape Verde. According to the IMF, PSIs are intended for countries that may not need IMF monetary funding, but are able to benefit from IMF advice and endorsement of policy frameworks. Cape Verde's PSI is intended to consolidate macroeconomic stability and achieve sustained, broad-based growth.

As of 2011 economic reforms were aimed at developing the private sector and promoting foreign investment.

40 SOCIAL DEVELOPMENT

Old age, disability, and survivorship pensions are provided for employed persons with a special system for public employees. The system is funded with contributions from the insured person as well as the employer. Cash and medical benefits are provided for sickness, maternity, and work injury.

Company managers, shareholders, and owners are excluded from work injury coverage. Family allowances are payable to low income families with children under the age of 14.

The constitution bans sex discrimination, although social discrimination and violence against women persist. The penal code was amended to broaden the definition of sexual abuse and increase penalties.

Domestic violence against women is widespread and societal values discourage reporting these criminal offenses. Discrimination in the workplace continues in hiring, pay, and promotion. Women are often unaware of their rights and suffer unjust treatment in inheritance, family, and custody issues.

Child abuse and sexual violence against children are serious problems. Human rights are generally respected by the Cape Verde authorities although there have been reports of police abuse of detainees.

41 HEALTH

According to the CIA, life expectancy in Cape Verde was 71 years in 2011. The country spent 4.4% of its GDP on healthcare, amounting to $146 per person. There were 6 physicians, 13 nurses and midwives, and 21 hospital beds per 10,000 inhabitants. The fertility rate was 2.7 children per woman, while the infant mortality rate was 23 deaths per 1,000 live births. In 2008 the maternal mortality rate, according to the World Bank, was 94 deaths per 100,000 births. It was estimated that 96% of children were vaccinated against measles. The CIA calculated the HIV/AIDS prevalence rate in Cape Verde to be about 0.04% in 2001, the most recent year for which figures were available.

42 HOUSING

Housing on the islands varies greatly, from the elegant, Mediterranean-style homes of Europeans and middle-class Cape Verdeans to the simple timber and mud-block houses of peasants. At last estimate, approximately 95% of all housing units were one-floor dwellings. External walls are mostly of stone and clay, stone and cement, or all stone. Water supply is delivered by pipes, wells, tanks and cisterns, and other sources. As of 2008 about 84% of the population had access to safe drinking water. Only 54% of the population had access to improved sanitation systems.

43 EDUCATION

In the pre-independence period, education in the country followed the Portuguese system. Education under the independent government has been patterned after the program of popular education carried out in the liberated areas of Guinea-Bissau. The program stresses universal literacy and primary skills, with advanced education geared toward agricultural and technical skills for production.

Primary education is compulsory and lasts for six years. Secondary education consists of six more years divided into three cycles of two years each. At the second and third cycles, students may choose to switch to a technical or vocational school program.

In 2009 the World Bank estimated that 83% of age-eligible children in Cape Verde were enrolled in primary school. Secondary enrollment for age-eligible children stood at 63%. About 61% of age-eligible children were enrolled in some type of preschool program. The student-to-teacher ratio for primary school was 24:1 and the ratio for secondary school was about 18:1.

The most prominent institute of higher learning is the Universidade Jean Piaget de Cabo Verde. There are also a number of technical schools. In 2009 tertiary enrollment was estimated at 15%. Of those enrolled in tertiary education, there were 100 male students for every 124 female students. Overall, the CIA estimated that Cape Verde had a literacy rate of 76.6%.

The primary administrative body is the Ministry of Education and Human Resources. In 2009 public expenditure on education represented 5.9% of GDP.

⁴⁴LIBRARIES AND MUSEUMS

The Library of the National Assembly in Praia has about 5,000 volumes. The National Library of Cape Verde and the Cape Verde National Historical Archives can also both be found in Praia. The city also hosts a privately maintained technical and scientific library of 10,000 volumes. There is also a historical museum in the city.

⁴⁵MEDIA

In 2009 the CIA reported that there were 72,200 telephone landlines in Cape Verde. In addition to landlines, mobile phone subscriptions averaged 78 per 100 people; there were an estimated 277,700 mobile phones in use throughout the country.

In 2010 the country had 26 Internet hosts. Internet users numbered 30 per 100 citizens. There were approximately 150,000 Internet users in Cape Verde.

Newspapers in 2011 included the daily *Horizonte* and the weeklies *A Semana* and *Expresso das Ilhas*. The state-owned television station is Televisao Nacional De Cabo Verde. There were 22 AM radio stations.

The constitution of Cape Verde provides for free expression, and the government is said to uphold this right generally. Government authorization is not needed to establish newspapers, other printed publications, or electronic media.

⁴⁶ORGANIZATIONS

Cooperative organizations in agriculture, marketing, and labor have been formed. The Chamber of Commerce, Industry, and Services is located at Praia and the Chamber of Commerce, Industry, Agriculture, and Services of the Barlavento is located on São Vincente. The Council of Free Labor Unions serves as a network for unions, as does the National Union of Cape Verde Workers.

Mass organizations for youth and women are generally tightly controlled by the government. The Scout Association of Cape Verde is an active youth organization. There are national chapters of the Red Cross Society, Caritas, and UNICEF. Some volunteer service organizations, such as the Lions Clubs International, are also present.

⁴⁷TOURISM, TRAVEL, AND RECREATION

The *Tourism Factbook*, published by the UN World Tourism Organization, reported 287,000 incoming tourists to Cape Verde in 2009, spending a total of $355 million. Of those incoming tourists, there were 244,000 from Europe. There were 11,720 hotel beds available in Cape Verde, which had an occupancy rate of 45%. The estimated daily cost to visit Praia, the capital, was $254. The cost of visiting other cities averaged $137.

Tourism is an important source of revenue for the picturesque islands and has increased steadily since the mid-1980s. In 2002 there were 2,489 hotel rooms in the country; a decade later that number had risen almost five-fold.

The ruins at Cidade Velha on São Tiago and the beaches at Baia das Gates on Boa Vista hold considerable tourist interest. The three-day festival of Bais das Gatas, known for its music, has gained international fame. Hiking, fishing, and water sports are also popular.

⁴⁸FAMOUS PERSONS

Aristides Maria Pereira (1923–2011) was the cofounder, with Amilcar Cabral (1921–73), of the PAIGC. He became PAIGC secretary-general after Cabral's assassination. Pereira was the first president of the independent Republic of Cape Verde, a position he held until 1991. Luis de Almeida Cabral (1931–2009), a brother of Amilcar, became the first president of Guinea-Bissau; after being ousted, he went into exile in Cuba. Antonio Mascarenhas Monteiro was president (1991–2001). He was succeeded by Pedro Verona Rodrigues Pires (b. 1934). Cesaria Evora (1941–2011) gained an international reputation as a blues singer in the 1990s.

⁴⁹DEPENDENCIES

The Republic of Cape Verde has no territories or colonies.

⁵⁰BIBLIOGRAPHY

Broecke, Pieter van den. *Pieter van den Broecke's Journal of Voyages to Cape Verde, Guinea, and Angola, 1605–1612*. London: Hakluyt Society, 2000.

Cape Verde Investment and Business Guide: Strategic and Practical Information. Washington, DC: International Business Publications USA, 2012.

Lobban, Richard, and Marlene Lopes. *Historical Dictionary of the Republic of Cape Verde*. 4th ed. Metuchen, NJ: Scarecrow Press, 2007.

Schraeder, Peter J. *African Politics and Society: A Mosaic in Transformation*. Belmont, CA: Wadsworth, 2004.

Zeilig, Leo, and David Seddon. *A Political and Economic Dictionary of Africa*. Philadelphia: Routledge/Taylor and Francis, 2005.

CENTRAL AFRICAN REPUBLIC

République Centrafricaine

CAPITAL: Bangui

FLAG: The national flag consists of four horizontal stripes (blue, white, green, and yellow) divided at the center by a vertical red stripe. In the upper left corner is a yellow five-pointed star.

ANTHEM: *La Renaissance (Rebirth).*

MONETARY UNIT: The Communauté Financière Africaine franc (XAF), which was originally pegged to the French franc, has been pegged to the euro since January 1999 with a rate of XAF655.957 to 1 euro. The franc is issued in coins of 1, 2, 5, 10, 25, 50, 100, and 500 XAF francs, and notes of 50, 100, 500, 1,000, 5,000, and 10,000 XAF francs. XAF1 = US$0.0021 (or US$1 = XAF484.978) as of November 2011.

WEIGHTS AND MEASURES: The metric system is the legal standard.

HOLIDAYS: New Year's Day, 1 January; Anniversary of President Boganda's Death, 29 March; Labor Day, 1 May; National Day of Prayer, 30 June; Independence Day, 13 August; Assumption, 15 August; All Saints' Day, 1 November; Proclamation of the Republic, 28 November; National Day, 1 December; and Christmas, 25 December. Movable religious holidays include Easter Monday, Ascension, and Pentecost Monday.

TIME: 1 p.m. = noon GMT.

¹LOCATION, SIZE, AND EXTENT

Located entirely within the tropical zone of Central Africa, the Central African Republic (CAR) has an area of 622,984 sq km (240,535 sq mi), extending 1,437 km (893 mi) E–W and 772 km (480 mi) N–S. Comparatively, the area occupied by the Central African Republic is slightly smaller than the state of Texas. Entirely landlocked, it is bordered on the N by Chad, on the E by Sudan and South Sudan, on the S by the Democratic Republic of Congo and the Republic of the Congo, and on the W by Cameroon, with a total boundary length of 5,203 km (3,233 mi). The Ubangi and Mbomou rivers form much of the southern border; the eastern border coincides with the divide between the watersheds of the Nile and the Congo rivers. The CAR capital city, Bangui, is located in the southwestern part of the country.

²TOPOGRAPHY

The land consists of an undulating plateau varying in altitude from 610 to 762 m (2,000–2,500 ft). Two important escarpments are evident: in the northwest is a high granite plateau (rising to 1,420 m/4,659 ft), which is related to the Adamawa Plateau of Cameroon; in the northeast the Bongos Range rises to 1,368 m (4,488 ft) and extends into Sudan.

Soils are complex; sands and clays predominate, sometimes covered with a lateritic layer, over granite and quartz rocks. The land is well drained by two river systems: the Ubangi and its tributaries in the south, and the tributaries of the Chari and Logone rivers in the north.

³CLIMATE

The climate is tropical, with abundant rainfall of about 178 cm (70 in) annually in the south, decreasing to about 86 cm (30 in) in the extreme northeast. There is one rainy season (December–March) and one long, hot, dry season (April–November). Temperatures at Bangui have an average minimum and maximum range from 21°C (70°F) to 34°C (93°F).

Flooding is common during the rainy season. An unusually heavy rainfall beginning in August 2005 caused severe flood damage to homes in Bakala, Grimari, Kouango, and Bambari. Damage to local farmland, particularly in Ouaka, posed a threat of famine.

⁴FLORA AND FAUNA

The World Resources Institute estimated that there were 3,602 plant species in the Central African Republic. In addition, the Central African Republic was home to 187 mammal, 663 bird, 131 reptile, and 29 amphibian species. The calculation reflected the total number of distinct species residing in the country, not the number of endemic species.

The tropical rain forest in the southwest contains luxuriant plant growth, with some trees reaching a height of 46 m (150 ft). Almost every animal of the tropics is found, including the elephant, though its numbers have declined precipitously. The southwest boasts a colorful variety of butterflies.

According to a 2011 report issued by the International Union for Conservation of Nature and Natural Resources (IUCN), the number of threatened species included 8 types of mammals, 9 species of birds, 1 type of reptile, and 17 species of plants. Endangered species in the Central African Republic included the black rhinoceros and northern square-lipped rhinoceros.

Major losses have been reported in the elephant population. In 1979 it was disclosed that three-quarters of what had been the nation's elephant population at independence (40,000–80,000) had been killed so that the tusks could be sold for ivory. In the mid-1990s it was estimated that 90% of the nation's elephant population had been eliminated over the previous 30 years, 85% since

1982. A major massacre of some 500 elephants by poachers was recorded in 2007. Elephant hunting is now banned.

5 ENVIRONMENT

The World Resources Institute reported that the Central African Republic had designated 9.47 million hectares (23.39 million acres) of land for protection as of 2006. Water resources totaled 144.4 cu km (34.64 cu mi) while water usage was 0.03 cu km (0.007 cu mi) per year. Domestic water usage accounted for 80% of total usage, industrial for 16%, and agricultural for 4%. Per capita water usage totaled 7 cu m (247 cu ft) per year.

The United Nations (UN) reported in 2008 that carbon dioxide emissions in the Central African Republic totaled 253 kilotons.

The most significant environmental problems in the Central African Republic are desertification, water pollution, and the destruction of the nation's wildlife due to poaching and mismanagement. The encroachment of the desert on the country's agricultural and forest lands is due to deforestation and soil erosion. There are 13 national parks and wildlife reserves. The Dzanga-Sangha nature reserve in the southwest protects the nation's last rain forest. The Manovo-Gounda St. Floris National Park was a natural UNESCO World Heritage Site.

6 POPULATION

The US Central Intelligence Agency (CIA) estimated the population of the Central African Republic in 2011 to be approximately 4,950,027, which placed it at number 116 in population among the 196 nations of the world. In 2011 approximately 3.7% of the population was over 65 years of age, with another 41% under 15 years of age. The median age in the Central African Republic was 19.2 years. There were 1.03 males for every female in the country. The population's annual rate of change was 2.146%. The projected population for the year 2025 was 6,600,000. Population density in the Central African Republic was calculated at 7 people per sq km (18 people per sq mi).

The UN estimated that 39% of the population lived in urban areas and that urban populations had an annual rate of change of 2.5%. The largest urban area was Bangui, with a population of 702,000.

The prevalence of HIV/AIDS has had a significant impact on the population of Central African Republic. The AIDS epidemic causes higher death and infant mortality rates, and lowers life expectancy.

7 MIGRATION

As reported by the CIA, the Central African Republic's net migration rate in 2011 was negligible. The total number of emigrants living abroad was 129,300, and the total number of immigrants living in the Central African Republic was 80,500.

However, as of November 2011 nearly 8% of the Central African Republic's 4.5 million people were either internally displaced or living as refugees outside the country. In November 2011 the UN estimated the number of internally displaced persons (IDPs) at over 192,000 and the number of Central African refugees living in Cameroon and Chad at 162,000. At least 50% of these were children. According to 2010 figures from the UN Office for the Coordination of Humanitarian Affairs (OCHA), the Central African Republic hosted more than 31,000 refugees from the Democratic Republic of Congo and Sudan.

Since 2005 displacements have been caused by armed conflict pitting government forces against various armed groups in northern areas of the country. Owing to the signing of peace and reconciliation agreements, the number has fallen at times from a high of 200,000–108,000. However, the 2009 clashes between the army and splinter rebel groups, and attacks against civilians by the Lord's Resistance Army (LRA) caused new displacements.

A 2011 report by the Watchlist on Children and Armed Conflict and the Internal Displacement Monitoring Center (IDMC) asserted that the LRA was abducting children and using them as slaves and soldiers, forcing them to attack villages and kill others including children. These abuses counted among the six grave violations against children during times of conflict as identified by the UN Security Council. The report also documented attacks on schools and hospitals. In 2010 Human Rights Watch estimated that in the region the LRA had killed at least 2,000 persons and abducted 3,000 more since 2008.

8 ETHNIC GROUPS

The Central African Republic has more than 80 ethnic groups occupying specific regions of the country. The largest groups or groupings are the Baya to the west (33%), the Banda in the east (27%), and the Mandjia from the savanna (13%). They are followed by the Sara (10%) and the Mboum (7%). The Mbaka and the Yakoma account for 8% of the population. A small number of pygmies (Binga) are found in the forest region.

9 LANGUAGES

Many languages and dialects are spoken, including Arabic, Hunsa, and Swahili. Sangho, which originated along the Ubangi River, is the national language. French is the official language of government and is taught in the schools.

10 RELIGIONS

According to the 2003 census, 51% of the population were Protestants, 29% Roman Catholics, and 15% Muslims. Many of these followers incorporated traditional indigenous elements into their faith practices. Catholic and Protestant missions were scattered throughout the country; Islam was practiced primarily in the north. Missionaries included Lutherans, Catholics, Baptists, Grace Brethren, and Jehovah's Witnesses. Although the majority of them came from the US, France, Italy and Spain, missionaries from Nigeria and the Democratic Republic of Congo were also active in the country. All religious groups had to be registered with the Ministry of Interior.

The constitution provides for freedom of religion while prohibiting certain forms of religious fundamentalism. Prohibitions are mainly directed toward preventing extremism. Witchcraft and sorcery are illegal, although prosecutions are made generally in connection with other criminal activity such as murder. Under the 2009 penal code the death penalty for witchcraft was abolished.

11 TRANSPORTATION

The CIA reported that Central African Republic had 24,307 km (15,104 mi) of roads, of which 826 km (513 mi) were paved. There

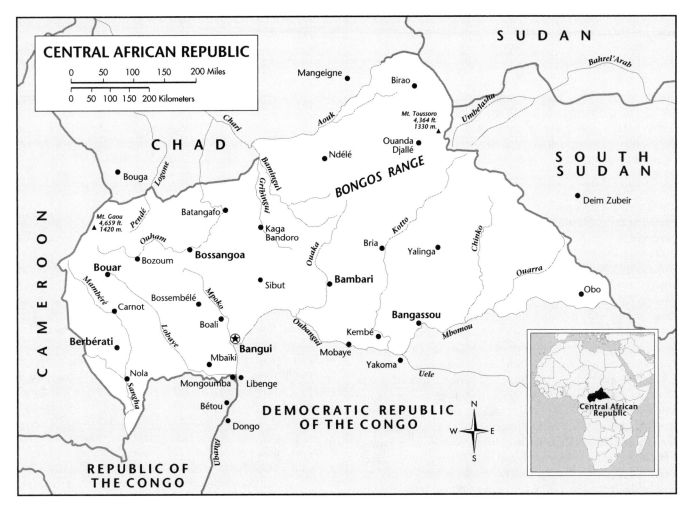

LOCATION: 2°13′ to 11°2′N; 14°25′ to 27°26′ E. BOUNDARY LENGTHS: Chad, 1,199 kilometers (745 miles); Sudan, 175 kilometers (109 miles); Democratic Republic of the Congo, 1,577 kilometers (980 miles); Republic of the Congo, 467 kilometers (290 miles); Cameroon, 822 kilometers (511 miles); South Sudan, 990 kilometers (615 miles).

were 37 airports. The Central African Republic had approximately 2,800 km (1,740 mi) of navigable waterways.

Most freight moves by river. The principal navigable rivers are the Ubangi, Sangha, Lobaye, and, subject to water level, tributaries of the Chari and Logone. Service on these latter is irregular during the dry season. Importantly, the Ubangi route connects the country to the Congo River port of Brazzaville, Republic of the Congo, where freight is transported by rail to the Atlantic port of Pointe-Noire. The port of Kilongo (at Bangui) is the largest in the country. Kilongo and the port of Nola were expanded to accommodate growth in maritime traffic.

There is an international airport at Bangui-Mpoko. In 2011 seven airlines provided international connections to Bangui including Air France, Ethiopian Airlines and Kenya Airways. Inter-RCA provided domestic service.

12 HISTORY

Before its colonial history, the area now known as the Central African Republic was settled by successive waves of peoples, mostly Bantu. Both European and Arab slave traders exploited the area in the 17th, 18th, and 19th centuries, and slave raids and intertribal wars were frequent until the French conquest. In the 19th

century the main population groups, the Baya and the Banda, arrived from the north and east, respectively, to flee the slave trade.

The French explored and conquered the country, chiefly from 1889, when an outpost was established at Bangui, to 1900, as part of a plan to link French colonies from the Atlantic to the Nile. The strongest and most sustained opposition to the French came from Sultan Senoussi, who was finally defeated in 1912. Isolated local revolts continued well into the 20th century, however. The strongest and bloodiest of these revolts, known as the War of Kongo-Wara, lasted from 1928 to 1931.

The territory of Ubangi-Shari was formally established in 1894 and its borders fixed by treaties between the European colonial powers. The western border with the German Cameroons was fixed by a convention with Germany in 1884. A convention of 1887 with Belgium's King Leopold II delineated the southern border with the Independent State of the Congo. The eastern border with the Sudan was fixed by an 1899 convention. These boundaries were drawn with little knowledge of the human geography of the area, so ethnic groups were sometimes separated into different territories. From 1906 to 1916, Ubangi-Shari and Chad were merged as a single territory. In 1910 Gabon, Middle Congo, and Ubangi-Shari (including Chad) were constituted administratively as separate colonies forming parts of a larger French Equatorial

Africa. Ubangi-Shari's resources were exploited by French companies, and abuses of the forced labor system were common.

In 1940 the colony quickly rallied to the Free French standard raised at Brazzaville, Congo. After World War II, the territory elected Barthélémy Boganda as its first representative to the French Parliament in Paris. In a referendum on 28 September 1958, Ubangi-Shari voted to become an autonomous republic within the French community. The Central African Republic was proclaimed with Boganda as president on 1 December 1958. On 30 April 1959, Minister of the Interior David Dacko was elected to succeed Boganda, who had died in a plane crash on 29 March. The country declared itself an independent republic on 13 August 1960, with Dacko as president. In 1961, the constitution was amended to establish a presidential government with a single-party system.

On 1 January 1966, a military coup d'etat led by Col. Jean-Bédel Bokassa overthrew Dacko (Bokassa's cousin), abolished the constitution, and dissolved the National Assembly. Bokassa, who became president in 1968 and president for life in 1972, proclaimed himself emperor of the newly formed Central African Empire on 4 December 1976. A year later, on that date, he crowned himself emperor in a lavish ceremony at an estimated cost of $25 million—a quarter of the nation's annual export earnings.

On 20 September 1979 Dacko, with French support, led a bloodless coup that overthrew Bokassa while he was out of the country. The republic was restored, and Bokassa, who took refuge in Côte d'Ivoire and France, was sentenced to death in absentia for various crimes, including cannibalism. Moreover, an African judicial commission reported that he had "almost certainly" taken part in the massacre of some 100 children for refusing to wear the compulsory school uniforms. In January 1981 six of his supporters, including two sons-in-law, were executed.

A new constitution allowing free political activity was approved by referendum in February 1981. A month later Dacko was elected, polling a bare majority against four rivals. Violence followed the election, which the losers claimed was fraudulent. Economic conditions failed to improve, and Dacko was overthrown on 1 September 1981 by a military coup led by army chief of staff Gen. André Kolingba. Kolingba became chairman of the ruling Military Committee for National Recovery, and the constitution and all political activities were suspended. The Kolingba regime survived an attempted coup in 1982 and an aborted return by Bokassa in 1983. On 21 November 1986 Kolingba was elected unopposed to a six-year term as president, and a new constitution was adopted establishing a one-party state. The new ruling party, the Central African Democratic Party (Rassemblement Démocratique Centrafricaine-RDC), nominated a list of 142 of its members, from which voters elected 52 to the new national assembly on 31 July 1987.

Bokassa made an unexpected return in October 1986 and was retried. On 12 June 1987 he was convicted of having ordered the murders of at least 20 prisoners and the arrest of the schoolchildren who were also killed. He was sentenced to death, but this was commuted to a life term in February 1988. He was released from prison on 1 September 1993, as a result of an amnesty. He died of a heart attack in Bangui on 3 November 1996 at age 75.

The 1990s proved to be a decade of unsteady democratization. In April 1991, under pressure from France, the IMF, and local critics, Kolingba agreed to legalize opposition parties, many of which had already formed a united front to press for further reforms. Elections were held on 25 October 1992, but widespread irregularities led to the Supreme Court dismissing the results for both the national assembly and the presidency. Elections were rescheduled, and on 19 September 1993 citizens elected Ange-Félix Patassé as head of the Movement for the Liberation of the Central African People (MLPC), president. A new national assembly of 85 members was elected. Patassé's party won only 33 seats, and Kolingba's RDC won 14 seats. Despite some irregularities, an international observer delegation certified the validity of the outcome.

Despite the 1994 national referendum and a new constitution instituting democratic reforms, nonpayment of salaries provoked three mutinies and widespread ethnic violence in 1996 and 1997. The French army quelled the mutinies, leaving over 100 people dead and hundreds more injured.

Mediation from four heads of neighboring states produced the Bangui Accord in January 1997. The accord included an 800-strong Inter-African Peace Force (MISAB) composed of six French-speaking countries, approved and supported by the UN and French government. In April 1998, the UN deployed a peacekeeping force of 1,498 military personnel called MINURCA. Its mandate was mainly to monitor implementation of the Bangui Accord. MINURCA succeeded in maintaining security, stability, and an environment conducive for peaceful elections.

On 22 November and 13 December 1998 parliamentary elections were held, overseen by MINURCA. The ruling MLPC won 47 of the 109 seats of the national assembly, but the opposition formed a parliamentary majority. Patassé won the presidential elections held on 19 September 1999, taking 51.6% of the vote. His runner-up, Kolingba, got 19.3%. Despite opposition allegations of rigging and irregularities, the UN and other international observers declared both elections generally free and fair.

The dawn of the millennium witnessed more civil unrest in the country. On 15 February 2000 a UN peace-building mission replaced MINURCA and UN troops were withdrawn. However, on 28 May 2001 Kolingba led an unsuccessful coup attempt against Patassé during which at least 59 people were killed and thousands fled Bangui during 10 days of violence. Chadian and Libyan troops, and rebel troops from the Congolese Liberation Movement (MLC) from the Democratic Republic of the Congo, aided Patassé in suppressing the coup attempt. Economic instability followed the aborted coup. Former army chief of staff, François Bozizé, was accused of being involved in the coup attempt and, in November, fighting broke out between government forces attempting to arrest Bozizé and Bozizé's supporters. Libya, Chad, and the UN intervened to attempt to resolve the conflict. Bozizé fled to Chad, but his supporters returned in October 2002, engaging the government in six days of heavy fighting. Libyan forces aided Patassé's troops in suppressing the rebellion.

On 15 March 2003 Bozizé staged a coup, captured Bangui, declared himself president, suspended the constitution, and dissolved parliament. Patassé, who had been in Niger for a meeting of African heads of state, fled to Cameroon. Bangui was ravaged by two days of looting and violence, in which at least 13 people were killed. Bozizé replaced the national assembly with a National Transitional Council (NTC) composed of the leading political factions, police and army personnel, and civil society representatives, including Nicolas Tiangaye, a prominent human rights advocate. His rule brought a measure of stability, but state sector arrears brought about strikes in February and March 2004, and his government squandered an opportunity to strengthen support in the countryside by failing to compensate people for their farms and businesses that were destroyed during the 2003 coup.

Despite these shortcomings, and his promise to step down at the end of the transition, Bozizé contested the 13 March 2005 presidential elections in which all of the leading opposition candidates were allowed to run except for Patassé. Bozizé won the run-off on 8 May 2005, defeating Martin Ziguélé, who ran on the former ruling party ticket of the MLPC. The National Elections Commission declared Bozizé the winner with 64.6% of the vote to 35.4% for Ziguélé. The election received a general declaration of fairness, although the absence of Patassé cast a shadow over the legitimacy of the process.

On 8 May 2005 Bozizé gained yet a further victory when his coalition, Convergence Nationale (Kwa Na Kwa—KNK), won 42 parliamentary seats in the legislative run-off vote. The MLPC came in second with 11 seats while the RDC managed only 8 seats. The remaining seats were won by independents or by smaller parties. In June, the African Union (AU) lifted sanctions against the country, which had been in effect since the 2003 usurpation of power.

The elections returned a sense of stability to the political scene. However, Patassé, who was living in exile in Togo, and whose supporters believed him to be the rightful head of state, could not be ruled out as leading a future uprising. Further, members of Kolingba's Yakoma tribe in the south, who dominated the army, posed a threat to Bozizé's government because of their widespread boycott of the second round of the legislative elections. In August 2006 Patassé was convicted in absentia of fraud and sentenced to 20 years' hard labor.

In October 2006 rebels seized Birao, a town in the northeast. In December French fighter jets fired on rebel positions in the northeast in support of government troops to regain control of the area. In February 2007 the rebel People's Democratic Front, led by Abdoulaye Miskine, signed a peace agreement with Bozizé in Libya and urged fighters to lay down their arms.

Following individual ceasefire agreements with the Popular Army for the Restoration of Democracy (APRD) and the Union of Democratic Forces for Unity (UFDR), the government and rebel groups signed the Libreville Comprehensive Peace Agreement in June 2008. Former president Ange-Felix Patassé returned from exile to the Central African Republic to participate in the talks. The accord resulted in the establishment of a new coalition government in January 2009, which included ministerial posts for APRD and UFDR leaders and two other opposition leaders.

Peace was short lived, however, when the Convention of Patriots for Justice and Peace (CPJP), a rebel splinter group, accused the government of failing to meet its commitments. Attacks by the CPJP, including seizure of the northern town of Ndélé, took place from June to October 2010, causing more population displacements. The attacks also disrupted the scheduling of the presidential election, which was postponed four times between April 2010 and January 2011.

Further destabilization resulted in 2008 from the LRA operating in the southeastern part of the country. Human Rights Watch reported that in the region the LRA had killed some 2,000 persons and abducted another 3,000—many of them children. In the meantime, per UN Security Council Resolution 1923 (May 2010), the joint UN mission to the Central African Republic and Chad—MINURCAT—withdrew from the country end of 2010. In October 2011 US President Barak Obama committed 100 battle-equipped military advisors to the Central African Republic to step up efforts to remove Joseph Kony, leader of the LRA, from the battlefield. The International Criminal Court had issued an arrest warrant against Kony for crimes against humanity in October 2005.

The 23 January 2011 presidential election occurred relatively peacefully. François Bozizé emerged the winner on the first round with 66% of the vote. Ange-Felix Patassé came in second with 20% and his former prime minister, Martin Ziguélé, with 6.5%. Reports from around the country generally confirmed the ballot as free and fair, although few independent observers were in place, and only 54% of voters turned out. The constitutional court dismissed opposition complaints of electoral commission bias. However, the court revised the results slightly to give Bozizé 64.37% and Patassé 21.41% of the vote.

Bozizé also emerged the clear winner in the legislative elections on 23 January and 27 March 2011. His party, the KNK, obtained 61 of the 100 assembly seats with the Presidential Majority party picking up another 11 seats. Independents won 26 seats.

In September 2011 some 15,000 people were displaced by an outbreak of fighting in the Bria diamond fields. The fighting was led by CPJP rebels, who had not agreed to the comprehensive peace accords. The Central African Republic government appealed to the UN for assistance, and by 2012 recommendations proposed by the UN Security Council Peacebuilding Commission were awaiting implementation.

Armed conflict between government forces and groups in northern parts of the country displaced 200,000 people between 2005 and 2008. The number of internally displaced residents declined to 108,000 after the signing of peace accords, but additional clashes have increased the number to more than 192,000 in 2010.

Civilians have suffered a range of human rights abuses, including killings, the looting and burning of villages, destruction of fields, loss of livelihoods, sexual violence, and the abduction and recruitment of children. The Central African Republic has signed the N'Djamena Declaration to end the recruitment of children into armed conflict. It also signed the Optional Protocol to the Convention on the Rights of the Child on the Involvement of Children in Armed Conflict (OPAC).

¹³GOVERNMENT

Government consists of three branches: the executive, legislative, and judiciary, with the executive by far the most powerful of the three. Presidential appointees and party loyalists dominate policy-making, law-making, and rulings in the other branches. The judiciary is not independent in matters of national import. On Freedom House's "Freedom in the World 2011" index, which measures political rights and civil liberties, the Central African Republic ranked as "partly free."

Since independence in 1960, the country has adopted, suspended, and amended the constitution several times. The 1959 constitution was suspended after the January 1966 coup, and the imperial constitution issued in December 1976 lapsed with Emperor Bokassa's fall in 1979. In early 1981 a new constitution was approved in a national referendum by 97.4% of the voters. This constitution provided for the election of a president and national assembly by universal adult suffrage. It also permitted competition by multiple parties. However, it was suspended following the military coup of 1 September 1981 in which executive and legislative power was subsumed by the ruling Military Committee for National Recovery (Comité Militaire pour le Redressement National), headed by Gen. André Kolingba. This committee was disbanded in 1985.

A new constitution adopted by plebiscite on 21 November 1986 established a one-party state and a 52-member national assembly; simultaneously, Kolingba was elected unopposed to a six-year term as president. The national assembly provided a forum for debate, but had little substantive impact on government policy.

In 1991, Kolingba was forced to legalize opposition parties. After the Supreme Court invalidated a 1992 election, new elections were conducted successfully in September 1993. For the 1993 elections the unicameral national assembly was enlarged to 85 members. Upon Kolingba's defeat, Ange-Félix Patassé, was installed and a transition to multiparty democracy took place. His coalition government was headed by the MLPC and included members of three other parties. Constitutional reforms passed by referendum in 1994 and instituted in 1995 and 1996 created a stronger prime minister, a constitutional court, and created regional assemblies. On 15 March 2003 former army chief François Bozizé dissolved parliament and suspended the constitution.

Prior to the March 2003 coup, the constitution provided for an independent judiciary, although it was subject to executive interference. The president could veto legislation, although the legislature could override his veto, and he could rule by decree under special conditions. Members of the national assembly served five-year terms. Suffrage was universal at age 21.

The national referendum on 5 December 2004 validated constitutional amendments proposed by the NTC including shortening the presidential term from six to five years, renewable only once; the strengthening of the office of the prime minister and the national assembly; and a reduction in fees required of political candidates.

14 POLITICAL PARTIES

The Central African Republic's independence party, the Movement for Social Evolution of Black Africa (Mouvement d'Évolution Sociale de l'Afrique Noire—MESAN), was founded by Barthélémy Boganda in September 1949. Boganda, himself a deputy in Paris for some years, had championed greater internal autonomy for the colony and an end to French administration.

Since independence, political parties have served the narrow interests of political leaders rather than aggregate citizen preferences and link citizens to their government. The five coups or attempted coups in the Central African Republic's history are symptomatic of this condition. Early antagonism to Boganda's

rule grew out of his personal monopoly of power and manipulation of electoral law, which made it difficult to contest seats within MESAN. In the 25 September 1960 election MESAN received 80% of the votes, while the newly founded Movement for the Democratic Evolution of Central Africa (Mouvement d'Évolution Démocratique de l'Afrique Centrale—MEDAC) received 20%. In February 1961, in a bid to consolidate power, the government dissolved MEDAC, and in December 1962 a constitutional amendment recognized MESAN as the sole party in the republic. That advantage was short-lived when in January 1966, a military coup d'état overthrew the government and all political activity was banned. MESAN would later be revived by Jean-Bédel Bokassa in 1972.

After Bokassa's fall, the single-party system was maintained and the ruling party changed its name to the Central African Democratic Union (Union Démocratique Centrafricaine—UDC). However, the February 1981 constitution opened the way for multiparty competition. Five parties competed in the presidential election of 15 March 1981. President David Dacko, the UDC candidate, received 50.2% of the vote. His chief opponent was Ange-Félix Patassé of the MLPC, who received 38.1%. Following the military coup of 1 September 1981, all political activity was again suspended. The MLPC was formally banned on 6 March 1982 after an unsuccessful coup that the government blamed on Patassé. Patassé subsequently fled to Togo.

The RDC, the sole legal political party adopted by the Kolingba regime, held its founding assembly in February 1987. The same year three opposition parties in exile in Paris, including the MLPC, established a coalition called the United Front.

In 1991 opposition parties were again legalized, and in October 1992 multiparty elections were held. The Supreme Court invalidated the results and on 19 September 1993, new elections led to Kolingba's defeat. His nemesis, Patassé, became president and the MLPC gained 33 of the 85 seats in the national assembly. The RDC won 14 seats.

Other parties in the government coalition included the Liberal Democratic Party, the Alliance for Democracy and Progress, and the David Dacko Movement (an informal grouping of supporters of the ex-president). In opposition, along with the RDC, were the Consultative Group of Democratic Forces (CFD), an alliance of 14 opposition groups; the Social Democratic Party; and the National Convention.

A record 849 candidates from 29 parties and 118 independents contested the parliamentary elections in November and December 1998. Patassé's MLPC won 47 of the 109 seats; Kolingba's RDC had 20; Dacko's MDD (Movement for Democracy and Development) got 8; and Abel Goumba's FPP (Patriotic Front for Progress) won 7 seats. Eleven of the 29 contesting parties won seats to the national assembly.

Patassé was reelected for a second presidential term with a narrow majority of 51.6% of the vote and sworn in as president on 22 October 1999. Kolingba came second (19.3%), Dacko third (11.1%), and Goumba fourth (6%) in the 10-candidate contest.

The national assembly was dissolved in March 2003 after François Bozizé seized power in a coup. Bozizé garnered 43% of the vote in the 13 March 2005 presidential elections and won the second run-off round on 8 May 2005 with 64.6% of the vote to 35.4% for Martin Ziguélé of the MLPC. André Kolingba of the RDC came in a distant third on the first round with 16.4% of the vote. Bozizé was supported on the second round with endorsements from Jean-Paul Ngoupandé of the Parti de L'unité Nationale, and the leader of the Forum Démocratique Pur la Modernité (Fodem), Charles Massi.

In the 8 May 2005 contest Bozizé's coalition, the KNK, won 42 parliamentary seats in the legislative run-off vote giving it the largest coalition in the 105-seat body. The MLPC came in second with 11 seats while the RDC managed only 8 seats. The remaining seats were won by independents or by smaller parties.

In the presidential election of January 2011, Bozizé won reelection with 64.4% of the vote, followed by Ange-Felix Patassé of the MLCP with 21.4%. Parliamentary elections were held on 23 January and 27 March 2011 with 61 of 100 seats conceded to Bozizé's KNK party and 11 more seats won by the Presidential Majority party. Independents took 26 seats with the remainder going to the MLPC and to the RDC parties.

15 LOCAL GOVERNMENT

The country is divided into 16 prefectures, 69 sub prefectures, and the autonomous commune of Bangui. In 1988 local elections created 176 municipal councils, each of which is headed by a mayor appointed by the president.

16 JUDICIAL SYSTEM

There are several civil courts, criminal courts, military courts, and a court of appeal situated in Bangui. At the apex is a Supreme Court, also located in Bangui, the members of which are appointed by the president.

There is also a High Court of Justice, a body of nine judges created to try political cases against the president, members of congress, and government ministers; this court has never convened. A constitutional court was created in 1996 to determine if laws passed by the national assembly conformed to the constitution. Three of its judges were appointed by the president, three by the president of the national assembly, and three by fellow judges.

The legal system is based on the French civil law system. Criminal defendants are presumed innocent with a right to counsel, to public trial, and to confront witnesses. Trials are public and frequently broadcast on national radio. Courts are undermined by inefficient management, shortage of trained personnel, salary arrears, and a lack of material resources. Significant case backlogs are not uncommon.

17 ARMED FORCES

In 2011 the International Institute for Strategic Studies (IISS) reported that armed forces in the Central African Republic totaled 2,150 members: 2,000 army regulars and 150 members of the air force. Armed forces represented 0.2% of the labor force in the country. Defense spending totaled $31.3 million and accounted for 0.9% of GDP.

Since 1986 the LRA, led by warlord Joseph Kony, has profited from weak territorial control and protection of civilians in the border regions of northern Uganda, Sudan, Central African Republic, and the Democratic Republic of the Congo. The LRA initially espoused a system of government based on the biblical Ten Commandments. Tactics have featured brutal abduction and exploitation of children as sex slaves, soldiers, and human battle

shields. Although the governments of the affected nations have worked to end the conflict through UN-assisted negotiations and military force, the LRA has consistently disregarded cease-fire agreements and has responded to military attacks by killing more civilians.

In October 2010 the affected governments met with leaders from the African Union to pool their resources to track down Kony. The ensuing plan proposed to utilize troops and cross-border intelligence from the four nations backed by military assistance from Nigeria and South Africa. In October 2011 US President Barak Obama committed 100 battle-equipped military advisors to the Central African Republic to strengthen efforts to remove Kony from the battlefield.

18 INTERNATIONAL COOPERATION

On 26 September 1960 the Central African Republic was admitted to the United Nations. The Central African Republic is a member of ECA and several nonregional specialized agencies. In 1959, together with Chad, the Congo, and Gabon, it formed the Equatorial Customs Union (Union Douanière Equatoriale—UDE) in which merchandise, property, and capital circulated freely. The Monetary and Economic Community of Central Africa (CEMAC) has superseded the UDE. The nation is part of the Franc Zone. The country is also a member of the African Development Bank, the Central African States Development Bank (BDEAC), the Community of Sahel-Saharan States (CENSAD), the New Partnership for Africa's Development (NEPAD), G-77, and the African Union, and is a signatory to the Lomé Convention. The Central African Republic is part of the Nonaligned Movement and is an observer in the Organization of the Islamic Conference (OIC). In environmental cooperation, the Central African Republic is part of the Convention on Biological Diversity, CITES, the International Tropical Timber Agreement (1994), the Montréal Protocol, the Nuclear Test Ban Treaty, and the UN Conventions on Climate Change and Desertification.

19 ECONOMY

In 2010 the GDP purchasing power parity was $3.446 billion, which came to an average of $700 per capita. In 2011 the economy was growing at a rate of 3.3% per year. Inflation stood at 0.9%, and unemployment was reported at 8%. Agriculture accounted for 53.8% of GDP followed by services at 31.7% and industry at 14.5%.

The economy, which is one of the world's least developed, is largely informal and handicapped by the Central African Republic's landlocked position, its poor transportation network, an unskilled workforce, corruption, misguided policies, and conflict. 85% of the workforce is engaged in subsistence agriculture growing manioc, corn, millet, bananas, and plantains for personal consumption. The economy qualified as "repressed," ranking 152nd out of 179 economies on the 2011 Index of Economic Freedom.

The extraction of rough diamonds and timber accounts for nearly 60% of exports. However, owing to smuggling and tax evasion, published figures on diamond production are unreliable. Coffee, tobacco, and cotton account for the remainder of exports. Livestock production increased in the early 1990s as the northern limit of the tsetse fly zone retreated south.

20 INCOME

In 2010 national revenues totaled $325.7 million and expenditures amounted to $335.2 million. The World Bank reported household consumption in 2009 to total $1.9 billion or about $380 per capita, measured in current US dollars rather than PPP. The Central African Republic had a relatively skewed income distribution with a gini coefficient of 0.42. The World Bank estimated that more than two-thirds of population lived below the national poverty threshold and that in order to climb out of poverty consumption would have to be increased by 50%.

In 2011 the World Bank reported that actual individual consumption in the Central African Republic was 91.8% of GDP and accounted for 0.01% of world consumption. By comparison, the United States accounted for 25.44% of world individual consumption. According to the World Bank 64.8% of GDP was spent on food and beverages, 9.9% on housing and household furnishings, 7.6% on clothes, 1.7% on health, 3.5% on transportation, 0.8% on communications, 1.7% on recreation, 1.9% on restaurants and hotels, and 3.6% on miscellaneous goods and services and purchases from abroad.

21 LABOR

As of 2007 the Central African Republic had a total labor force of 1.926 million people with the vast majority engaged in subsistence farming, herding, and fishing.

With the exception of military personnel, workers can join or form unions without prior authorization. Unions have the right to strike as long as certain procedures are followed. These include presenting demands to employers, receiving the latter's response, holding a conciliation meeting with the employer, and receiving a determination by an arbitration council that an agreement could not be reached. In addition, eight days advance notice of a planned strike is required.

A small portion of the labor force in the formal sector is affected by labor laws. The Central African Republic has a 40-hour workweek and a 48-hour rest period for government and most private sector employees. The government also sets minimum wage laws sector by sector. As of 2005 agricultural workers had the right to receive a minimum wage of $12 per month while office workers had the right to $28 per month. However, wage levels had not changed for more than two decades and the minimum wage was insufficient to support a worker and a family. There are general safety and health standards, but the Ministry of Labor and Civil Service does not define or enforce them. Although the labor code prohibits the employment of children under the age of 14, child labor is common and there were reported instances of forced labor.

22 AGRICULTURE

Agricultural output, dominated by subsistence farming, accounts for 53.8% of GDP. The Central African Republic is nearly self-sufficient in food production and has the potential to commercialize agriculture and to be an exporter of agricultural products.

Major crops include tree crops, cotton, coffee, tobacco, manioc (tapioca), yams, millet, corn, and bananas. Cereal production amounted to 250,667 tons, fruit production 256,762 tons, and vegetable production 99,206 tons.

23 ANIMAL HUSBANDRY

The UN Food and Agriculture Organization (FAO) reported that the Central African Republic dedicated 3.2 million hectares (7.91 million acres) to permanent pasture or meadow in 2009. During that year, the country tended 6.2 million chickens, 4 million head of cattle, and 800,000 pigs. The production from these animals amounted to 76,000 tons of beef and veal, 13,506 tons of pork, 4,396 tons of poultry, 1,324 tons of eggs, and 62,671 tons of milk. The Central African Republic also produced 11,000 tons of cattle hide. In 2004 there were an estimated 3,087,000 goats and 259,000 sheep. Honey production amounted to 13,000 tons in 2004.

24 FISHING

According to the FAO, in 2008 the annual capture totaled 15,000 tons. Fishing occurred along rivers with most of the catch sold or bartered on the Democratic Republic of Congo's side of the Ubangi. Pisciculture, launched in the 1950s, was also a major source of fish.

25 FORESTRY

Approximately 36% of the land is covered by forest, but only 3.4 million hectares (8.4 million acres) is dense forest, all in the south in areas bordering the Democratic Republic of Congo. Transportation bottlenecks on rivers and lack of rail connections seriously hinders commercial exploitation. Most timber ships out via the Ubangi and Congo rivers and then by rail to the Atlantic. More than a dozen types of trees are felled; 95% of the total is obeche, sapele, ebony, and sipo. The FAO estimated the 2009 roundwood production at 841,000 cu m (29.7 million cu ft). The value of all forest products, including roundwood, totaled $73.3 million.

26 MINING

Diamond mining was the country's leading industry and top export commodity in 2009. Mining accounted for about 4% of GDP and 40%-50% of export earnings. Diamonds were discovered in alluvial deposits in various parts of the country in 1935 and 1947. Production, which reached 609,360 carats in 1968, was put at 311,799 carats in 2009. However, sizable quantities are smuggled out of the country. About 60% of the nation's diamonds come from the upper Sangha region. Preliminary gold production in 2009 was put at 61 kg. Gold is still mined in alluvial deposits, by artisanal miners, primarily in the Bandas and the Bogoin-Boali greenstone belts.

Uranium was discovered in 1966 in the Bakouma region in the eastern part of the country, and there was further prospecting in the Berbérati and Bangassou areas; exploitation has not occurred, because of high start-up costs and poor transportation. Reserves are estimated at 5.7 metric tons at an average grade of 1.72% uranium. Iron deposits estimated at 3.5 million tons have been exploited, but production has ceased. The country also had deposits of nickel, graphite, ilmenite, lignite, monazite, rutile, manganese, cobalt, tin, copper, china clay, and limestone. The lack of adequate transportation and industrial infrastructure hindered the development of the nation's mineral industry. Little of the country's

Principal Trading Partners – Central African Republic (2010)

(In millions of US dollars)

Country	Total	Exports	Imports	Balance
World	480.0	140.0	340.0	-200.0
Netherlands	140.7	0.4	140.3	-140.0
South Korea	76.5	0.3	76.3	-76.0
France	68.1	7.9	60.2	-52.3
Belgium	44.0	33.4	10.5	22.9
Cameroon	41.9	0.0	41.9	-41.9
China	26.0	...	26.0	-26.0
United States	16.6	5.2	11.4	-6.3
Morocco	13.4	10.6	2.7	7.9
Brazil	11.1	0.2	10.9	-10.6
Congo, Dem. Rep of	11.1	10.6	0.5	10.1

(…) data not available or not significant.

(n.s.) not specified.

SOURCE: *2011 Direction of Trade Statistics Yearbook,* New York: United Nations, 2011.

400,000 sq km Precambrian terrain has been explored using modern investigation techniques.

27 ENERGY AND POWER

The World Bank reported in 2008 that the Central African Republic produced 160 million kWh of electricity and consumed 123.8 million kWh, or 25 kWh per capita. The capital city of Bangui was supplied by two hydroelectric generators and one thermal plant. A dam on the Mbali (a joint project with the Democratic Republic of Congo, opened in 1991, permitting year-round hydroelectric generation.

Exxon drilled an exploratory oil well in 1985, but further work was deemed economically infeasible. In 2009 daily oil imports were 2,418 bbl/day with a daily consumption of 2,000 bbl/day (2010). As of January 2011 the country had no known reserves of oil, natural gas or coal, although experts speculated that there could be oil deposits along the Central African Republic's northern border with Chad.

28 INDUSTRY

In 2010 industry contributed 14.5% of GDP, most of which consisted of artisanal diamond and gold mining. The Central African Republic was the world's 10th largest producer of diamonds. Textile and leather manufacturing were other leading industries. The largest single factory was a joint-venture textile complex (51% French owned) in Bangui, which handled spinning, weaving, dyeing, and the manufacture of blankets. All cotton produced in the country was ginned locally, with cotton-ginning plants scattered throughout the cotton-producing regions. Refined sugar and palm oil also were produced, as were soap, cigarettes, beer, bottled water, and soft drinks. Other light industries included paint, bricks and utensil manufacture, and motorcycle and bicycle assembly. Manufacturing primarily served local needs.

29 SCIENCE AND TECHNOLOGY

The World Bank reported in 2009 that there were no patent applications in science and technology in the Central African Republic. Among the research institutes were a study center on animal sleeping sickness in Bouar and an agricultural institute in M'Baiki. In addition, there was a National Institute of Textile Research and Food Crops located in Bambari, and the Pasteur Institute in Bangui that conducted research on various diseases. French institutes included the Institute of Scientific Research for Cooperative Development, at Bangui, and the experimental station of Maboké, in M'Baiki, under the direction of the National Museum of Natural History in Paris.

The University of Bangui has faculties of science and technology, health science, a polytechnic institute, and a research institute for mathematics teaching. The Central School of Agriculture is located in Boukoko, and the Territorial School of Agriculture is in Grimari. In the period 1990–2001, there were 27 technicians and 47 scientists and engineers per million people engaged in research and development. Also, in 1987–97, science and engineering students accounted for 30% of college and university enrollments.

30 DOMESTIC TRADE

Petty trade and barter define the majority of domestic economic transactions. Local produce, farming implements, cloth and imported clothing, and household necessities are sold at small shops and markets in towns and villages. No large-scale retail outlets are available. Lebanese and French businessmen control most of the wholesale and sizeable commercial operations. Whereas previously the government purchased and distributed agricultural products via a state trading company, company agents and middlemen buy cash commodities such as coffee, cotton and palm nuts and oil directly from producers for sale to large companies.

Artisanal diamond miners work under exploitative conditions, whereby in exchange for rice and implements, diggers are obliged to sell their product to crew bosses. Bosses sell the diamonds at considerable profit to middle-men, who sell them to exporters. Programs in support of the Kimberley Process aim to improve working conditions, secure fair payment for diggers, to increase transparency of transactions, and to strengthen the chain of custody "from earth to export" to prevent the trade of conflict (blood) diamonds.

A chamber of commerce in Bangui promotes trade and provides information to businesses. Local newspapers, company publications, handbills, billboards, and radio carry limited advertisements. Normal business hours are from 7 a.m. to noon and 2:30 to 6:30 p.m., Monday through Friday. Saturday hours are from 7 a.m. to noon.

31 FOREIGN TRADE

According to the CIA World Factbook, the Central African Republic imported $312.2 million worth of goods and services in 2010, while exporting $152.5 million worth of goods and services. Major import partners in 2009 were France, 14.7%; the United States, 9.6%; Cameroon, 9.1%; and Netherlands, 8.3%. Its major export partners were Belgium, 35.6%; China, 12%; Morocco, 11.2%; Democratic Republic of the Congo, 7.5%; and France, 6.3%.

Diamonds were the largest commodity export, sold either for jewelry (35%), or natural abrasives (35%). Officially, diamonds and timber accounted for approximately 60% of exports. However, the remoteness of alluvial sites, violent conflict over the control of diamond fields, and rampant corruption meant that a significant portion of the trade was illegal and accounted for. Leading agricultural exports included cotton (14%) and coffee (2.6%).

³²BALANCE OF PAYMENTS

The Central African Republic's deficits in trade and services are financed mainly through grants and low-cost loans. In the early 1980s, the country faced a severe balance-of-payments shortage caused by low world prices for exports and high fuel import costs. In an effort to balance payments, the government implemented an IMF structural adjustment program (SAP) from 1986 to 1990. The SAP aimed to reduce the size of the public sector and to increase private-sector investment. In 1998, the IMF approved a three-year SAP equivalent to $66 million. The IMF augmented and extended the program until it expired in 2002. The Central African Republic's first six-month emergency post-conflict assistance (EPCA) program expired in December 2004 and was not renewed because government failed to meet key macroeconomic targets. The Central African Republic has qualified as a Heavily Indebted Poor Country (HIPC) and successfully reached the completion point of the program in 2009.

³³BANKING AND SECURITIES

The central bank is the Bank of the Central African States (Banque des États de l'Afrique Central—BEAC), which also serves Cameroon, Chad, Republic of Congo, Equitorial Guinea, and Gabon—members of CEMAC. BEAC formulates and implements monetary policy for member states. It also preserves the stability of the common currency, the XAF franc, which is pegged to the Euro and whose convertibility is guaranteed by the French treasury. In 1972, BEAC replaced the Central Bank of the States of Equatorial Africa and Cameroon, which had been established in 1955 by French interests.

As of 2011 commercial banks operating within the Central African Republic included the Banque Intérnationale pour la Centrafrique (BICA), the Banque Populaire Maroco-Centrafricaine (BPMC), and the Commercial Bank Centrafrique. The BICA had the biggest share of deposits (40%) and was majority owned by Ecobank (72%). There was also the Postal Service's Caisse Nationale d'Epargne (savings bank) and the Bangui Cheques Postaux. Microfinance was conducted mostly by the Crédit Mutuel de Centrafrique (CMCA), which accounted for nearly all savings and credit transactions and 80% of the members in the microfinance sector.

There is no stock market, but two parallel, independent stock markets were under development in the CEMAC.

³⁴INSURANCE

In 1986 one state enterprise (SIRIRI) and eight foreign companies were represented in the Central African Republic, including La Mutuelle du Mans, Mutuelle Générale Française-Accidents, the Reliance Marine Insurance Company, Union Centrafricaine d'Assurances et de Réassurances, and l'Union des Assurances de Paris (IARD). By 2007 this number had decreased to only a few insurers. Motor vehicle insurance in the country is compulsory.

Because of weak property rights protection, many claims are settled informally between parties.

³⁵PUBLIC FINANCE

In 2010 the budget of Central African Republic tallied $334 million in public revenue and $362 million in public expenditures. The budget deficit amounted to 0.4% of GDP. The CIA reported that at the end of 2010 external debt totaled $402.8 million. $396 million of public debt was held by foreign entities.

The Central African Republic experienced a ballooning of debt in the 1970s owing to a rapidly expanding civil service, nationalization of enterprises, and expensive short-term borrowing coupled with falling commodity prices. Since the 1980s successive governments and the IMF have worked together to manage the economy. A 1980 austerity plan stabilized the budget and curbed foreign deficits by concentrating on agricultural production. A 1982 recovery plan, co-conducted with the IMF, preceded a formal SAP launched in 1987. A subsequent SAP agreed to in 1990, aimed to reduce the number of civil servants, reform pricing policies, and privatize the parastatal sector. In 1999 the IMF loaned the Central African Republic $11 million to fund unpaid government salaries. In 2008 the IMF and government jointly launched a HIPC initiative, which government completed in 2009.

³⁶TAXATION

The CIA estimated that in 2010 tax revenues accounted for 16.1% of GDP. In a study completed December 2010 the World Bank estimated that a medium-sized company doing business in the Central African Republic would pay a corporate tax rate of 30%; VAT 19%; social security contributions 19%; and property taxes 15%. The total tax rate as a percentage of profit amounted to 54.6%. In terms of "ease of doing business," the Central African Republic ranked second from last in sub Saharan Africa on the World Bank's June 2011 measure of business regulations.

³⁷CUSTOMS AND DUTIES

Customs and duties are governed by various rules and regulations depending on trade partner status with the Central African Republic. The Central African Republic along with five other states—Cameroon, Chad, Equatorial Guinea, Gabon, and Republic of Congo—established a customs union in 1983, the Central African Customs and Economic Union (Union Douanière et Economique de l'Afrique Centrale—UDEAC). UDEAC members have eliminated duties on most of the goods traded within their community. Trade within the XAF franc zone does not require a license.

UDEAC members levy a uniform customs tariff against third parties, but since the UDEAC countries are associated with the European common market, imports from EU countries receive a reduction in customs duties. Goods imported from countries outside UDEAC and outside the European common market are subject to duties, including a 5% duty on basic necessities, 10% on raw materials and capital goods, 20% on intermediate and miscellaneous goods, and 30% on consumer goods. Duty rate is applied on CIF (cost, insurance, freight). In addition, the Central African Republic applies excise taxes on luxuries such as beer, wine and spirits, tobacco, perfumes, and cosmetics. Customs evasion through the smuggling of goods to Democratic Republic of the Congo and Cameroon is common. Typically, these goods sell at 10–40% of retail price.

Gains derived from import duties in UDEAC member states go into the state budgets, but to offset the advantages gained by transit trade, especially to coastal countries, a share of import duties is deposited in a common fund.

38 FOREIGN INVESTMENT

Foreign direct investment (FDI) in the Central African Republic registered a net inflow of $42.3 million according to World Bank figures published in 2009. FDI represented 2.11% of GDP. The World Bank estimated that $1.5 billion in foreign resources over a three-year period (2008–10) would be needed to finance rehabilitation of infrastructure, agriculture, and social services.

Until the late 1980s the French government and French firms enjoyed a privileged relationship with the Central African Republic and dominated foreign investment in the country. However, private investment diminished with the decline of concessions. The nationalization of textiles, oil distribution, and river transport in 1974 also discouraged foreign investment.

In the early to mid-1980s the Kolingba government reaffirmed interest in foreign investment, encouraging public-private partnerships. The 1982 investment code provided incentives for the import of equipment and raw materials. Although this code was further liberalized in 2011, the Central African Republic remained dependent on foreign assistance from the World Bank, the European Union, the UN Development Program, the African Development Fund and bi-lateral donors. Given insecurity and uncertain government resolve to implement reforms, potential investors remained cautious.

39 ECONOMIC DEVELOPMENT

Independent economic development has been constrained by misguided policies, corruption, a limited tax base, an unskilled workforce, poor transportation networks, the Central African Republic's landlocked position, political uncertainty, instability and conflict.

The 1981–85 five-year plan called for XAF233,117 million in expenditures, including XAF83,363 million for rural transport and XAF54,935 million for agriculture and livestock raising. The 1986–90 plan called for XAF261.4 billion in spending (86% from foreign sources), with 53% for infrastructure and 35% for rural and regional development. Development expenditures were financed almost exclusively by donors and multilateral institutions. For example, the World Bank extended a $30-million loan in 1986.

Beginning in 1986 the government implemented a SAP to improve agricultural production, to encourage early retirement among government workers, and to privatize government enterprises. By the mid-1990s the goal of privatizing utilities and fuel distribution had not been met. Although the state-owned water company had been privatized, the electric utility and fuel distribution monopoly had yet to be reformed.

The 1994 devaluation of the XAF franc made products such as coffee, timber, cotton, and diamonds more attractive on the world market. On the other hand, prices for imports also rose, creating a period of high inflation in 1994. By 1995, the inflation rate had dropped to levels near the prevailing rate prior to devaluation. However, GDP growth was lackluster, and from 2001 to 2005 the country registered negative growth while inflation averaged 2.14% annually.

In this millennium, the IMF and World Bank have continued to partner with the Central African Republic to privatize state-owned businesses, fight corruption, streamline labor and investment codes, and reduce poverty through balanced economic growth. The Central African Republic's Poverty Reduction Strategy Paper (PRSP, 2008–2010) called for a doubling of per capita revenue by 2015 based on strong, sustainable economic growth. In 2009 the IMF recognized achievement of key goals by certifying the Central African Republic's attainment of the Heavily Indebted Poor Countries (HIPC) completion point. The government also adopted the CEMAC Charter of Investment, and was in the process of adopting a new labor code. Austerity measures have produced modest positive change as the economy grew by slightly more than 3% in 2010–11.

40 SOCIAL DEVELOPMENT

Government provides workers with a social safety welfare net, but in practice few workers are covered. Most of the labor force work in agriculture and informal sectors and receive no coverage or skills training. Civil servants and others working in the formal sector typically receive partial compensation owing to backlogs in processing and lack of funding. Benefits include old-age pensions at age 55 (men) or 50 (women); disability pensions at 30% of average monthly earnings; survivor benefits; prenatal and new-born allowances; and maternity leave. For social assistance, the vast majority of Central Africans depend on affective networks of extended family, friends, co-workers, pooled funds and mutual self-help groups.

Under the constitution all persons are equal, but in practice women, pygmies, orphans, the handicapped, physically deformed, and gay people face widespread discrimination. Single, widowed, and divorced women are not considered heads of households. Economic and educational opportunities for girls and women are limited. Polygamy remains legal and is widely practiced. Although banned by law, female genital mutilation is practiced in some rural areas. Spousal abuse and violence is a widespread problem. The government does not adequately fund programs for women and children.

The government's human rights record is poor. Freedom of speech and press are restricted. Arbitrary arrests and detention are common, police beat and torture detainees, and prison conditions are harsh. To end forced recruitment of child soldiers, representatives from the Central African Republic, Chad, Sudan, Nigeria, Niger, and Cameroon signed the N'Djamena Declaration on 10 June 2010. Signatories agreed to align policies with the Optional Protocol on the Involvement of Children in Armed Conflict, which is part of the Convention on the Rights of the Child, and championed by UNICEF and human rights organizations. The signatories also pledged to develop educational and employment opportunities for children released from military service, and to monitor the implementation of their commitments.

The main areas of social focus in the government's PRSP (2008–10) included education, health and HIV/AIDS, youth and sports, and employment. However, these priorities were severely underfunded. In 2010 the Central African Republic ranked 159th out of 169 countries on UNDP's Human Development Index. Six percent of the Central African Republic's population dies every year—a rate four times higher than in any African country. One in five children die before their fifth birthday, 60% of the population does not have access to potable water or basic sanitation, and 62% live on less than $1.25 a day (OCHA, 2010). In 2010 the UN Dispatch rated the humanitarian crisis in the Central African Republic as the world's fourth most under-funded and ignored.

41 HEALTH

According to the CIA, life expectancy in the Central African Republic was 47 years in 2011. The country spent 4.3% of its GDP on healthcare, amounting to $19 per person. Resources per 10,000 inhabitants amounted to 1 physician, 4 nurses and midwives, and 12 hospital beds. Thirty-seven percent of the population had to walk an average 6 miles (10 kilometers) to reach the closest health center. The fertility rate was 4.7, while the infant mortality rate was 112 per 1,000 live births. In 2008 the maternal mortality rate, according to the World Bank, was 850 per 100,000 births. It was estimated that 62% of children were vaccinated against measles. The CIA reported HIV/AIDS prevalence in the Central African Republic to be about 4.7% in 2009.

The most common diseases are bilharziasis, leprosy, malaria, tuberculosis, and yaws. Malaria, measles, and bacterial diarrhea are the main contributors to high death rates. The Central African Republic is a yellow fever endemic zone country. The Pasteur Institute at Bangui cooperates actively with vaccination campaigns. All medicine, antibiotics, and vaccine imports have to be authorized by the Ministry of Health.

Non-governmental organizations (NGOs) and government compensate for the lack of infrastructure and resources by dispensing healthcare from mobile clinics. Mobile crews around the country treat epidemic diseases, conduct vaccination and inoculation campaigns, and enforce local health regulations. They also research sleeping sickness, malaria, and other tropical diseases and devise prophylactic methods best suited to the rural population. In 2009–10 UNICEF financed the distribution of impregnated bed nets, a program designed to prevent malaria by placing at least one insecticide-treated mosquito net in each of 900,000 homes. Aid workers visited homes to demonstrate use of nets and to persuade families that sleeping under the nets could save their lives.

42 HOUSING

The Central African Republic struggles with overcrowding and inadequate shelter, particularly in rural areas where only 5% of the population live in permanent structures. The country's high poverty level contributes to a general inability to improve housing. According to UN-HABITAT, the number of households was projected to increase from 751,000 in 2000 to 1.1 million by 2015, thereby exerting tremendous pressure on housing stock and access to improved water sources and sanitation.

43 EDUCATION

Education is patterned after the French system. Although it is free, it is not particularly relevant to the needs of the country, and government schools are poorly staffed and under-resourced.

Faith-based schools typically guarantee students a higher level of learning and performance.

Education is compulsory the first six years of primary school (students between ages 6 and 12). A second stage of basic education covers a four-year course of study. Students can then choose to attend general secondary schools or technical schools, which offer three-year programs. The academic year runs from September to July. The primary language of instruction is French.

In 2009 the World Bank estimated that 67% of age-eligible children in the Central African Republic were enrolled in primary school. Secondary enrollment for age-eligible children stood at 10%. Tertiary enrollment was estimated at 2%. Of those enrolled in tertiary education, there were 100 male students for every 35 female students. The government's goal was to raise the primary school enrollment ratio to 73%, the completion rate to 74%, and to narrow the gap between boys and girls enrollment by 2010. As of 2009, public expenditure on education was estimated at 1.3% of GDP. The CIA estimated that the Central African Republic had a literacy rate of 55%.

Specialized institutions include two agricultural colleges, a national college of the performing and plastic arts, and the University of Bangui, founded in 1969.

44 LIBRARIES AND MUSEUMS

The French Institute of Scientific Research for Development and Cooperation maintains a research collection of 18,000 volumes in Bangui. The Agricultural Research Center in M'baïki has a library of 2,800 volumes. There is a municipal library in Bangui as well as a Roman Catholic mission library. The University of Bangui library has 26,000 volumes.

The Barthélémy Boganda Museum in Bangui (founded in 1964) includes collections on the ethnography, archaeology and natural history of the country. There are regional natural history and anthropology museums in Bouar and M'Baiki. The Labasso Museum in Bangassou (1975) features archaeological and anthropological exhibits from the Nzakara and Zandé areas.

45 MEDIA

The constitution provides for freedom of speech and of the press. However, in practice these freedoms are limited. In 2000, the president dissolved the High Broadcast Council, which had been created to regulate the media. In 2011 the government exercised close control over media operations and content.

In 2009 the CIA reported that there were 12,000 telephone landlines in the Central African Republic. Mobile phone subscriptions averaged 4 per 100 people, and internet users numbered 1 per 100 citizens. In 2010 the country had 20 Internet hosts. There were five FM radio stations, five AM radio stations, and one shortwave radio station. Most people got their news from radio.

Television broadcasting services are government-owned and operated by Radio-Télévision Centrafrique. Television transmissions are available only in Bangui, broadcasting in Sango and French. Satellite television is available. Radio Centrafrique is operated by the state; Radio Notre Dame by the Roman Catholic Church; Radio Ndeke Luka is backed by the UN; and RFI 1 Afrique, a satellite feed in French, rebroadcasts French news content and programming 24 hours a day. FM rebroadcasts of BBC

Africa Service in English are also available. In 2003, there were an estimated 80 radios and 6 television sets for every 1,000 people.

The nation's first daily newspaper, the government-controlled *E Le Songo*, began publication in 1986. Its circulation in 1995 was 2,000. *The Centrafrique Presse* was created by the government in 2001 to reflect the views of the ruling MLPC. Several private newspapers such as *Le Confident* publish sporadically, but few people read newspapers owing to low literacy and the relatively high cost of buying the papers. The official news agency is *Agence Centrafricaine de Presse* (ACAP). ACAP maintains a website with current news and information.

In 2009, a study showed that residents in Central Africa had the lowest quality and highest cost Internet and telephone services in all of Africa. Therefore, the Central African Republic along with two other countries was selected to participate in a World Bank Group sponsored initiative called the Central African Backbone (CAB). CAB aimed to develop high-speed telecommunications in Central Africa. The initial phase allocated $26.2 million for equipment and installation, and for strengthening the regulatory framework governing information and communications technologies (ICT). The CAB was co-sponsored by the African Development Bank and sought an additional $98 million from private investors to cover spending through 2019.

46 ORGANIZATIONS

Civil society in the Central African Republic is weak with most NGOs being only marginally sustainable. There are chambers for agriculture, livestock raising, water, forests, hunting, and tourism as well as for commerce, industry, mines, and handicrafts in Bangui. Rural cooperatives and community-based organizations are found throughout the country.

There are some professional and trade associations including the National Union of Teachers and School and University Administrators of the Central African Republic (NUTSUACAR). The National Olympic and Sport Committee (CNOS) coordinates national youth groups. Youth scouting organizations are active and there are Catholic youth organizations. There are national chapters of the Red Cross Society, Caritas, Habitat for Humanity, UNICEF, and the Society of St. Vincent de Paul. Community-based organizations such as women's rotating credit associations, market associations, transport and taxi drivers associations, and hairdressers and dressmakers associations are common.

47 TOURISM, TRAVEL, AND RECREATION

The *Tourism Factbook*, published by the UN World Tourism Organization, reported 52,400 incoming tourists to the Central African Republic in 2009, who spent a total of $6 million. Of those incoming tourists, there were 27,000 from Africa and 16,600 from Europe. There were 880 hotel beds available in the Central African Republic, which had an occupancy rate of 60%. The estimated daily cost to visit Bangui, the capital, was $171.

Development of the tourism industry in the Central African Republic is constrained owing to political unrest, insecurity, high costs, undeveloped infrastructure, and neglect. In 2007 bandits attacked a hunting party near Ndele town, killing a French national and injuring three others. The US issue periodic traveler advisories warning of bandits, poachers, and armed rebels. The main tourist attractions are hunting, fishing, game parks and waterfalls. Of special interest are the falls at Boali and Kembé, and the megaliths of Bouar. Ecotourism is popular in the southern Dzanga-Sangha National Park. The best time to visit the country is from November to April.

Visitors have to have a valid passport and a visa. A certificate indicating vaccination against yellow fever is also required.

48 FAMOUS PERSONS

Barthélémy Boganda (b. 1910–d. 1959), a dynamic leader of Central African nationalism, worked toward independence and attained virtually complete political power. The first president of the independent Central African Republic was David Dacko (b. 1930–d. 2003), who served from 1960 to 1966 and again from 1979 to 1981. Jean-Bédel Bokassa (b. 1921–d. 1996) overthrew Dacko in 1966, proclaimed himself emperor in 1976, and was himself ousted by Dacko in 1979. Gen. André Kolingba (b. 1936) seized power in 1981, and he served as president until he was defeated in the 1993 elections by Ange-Félix Patassé (b. 1937). Patassé served from 1993–2003, when he was deposed by rebel leader François Bozizé (b. 1946).

49 DEPENDENCIES

The Central African Republic has no territories or colonies.

50 BIBLIOGRAPHY

Central African Republic Investment and Business Guide: Strategic and Practical Information. Washington, DC: International Business Publications USA, 2012.

Kalck, Pierre and Xavier-Samuel Kalck. *Historical Dictionary of the Central African Republic.* 3rd ed. Lanham, MD: Scarecrow Press, 2005.

Woodfork, Jacqueline C. *Culture and Customs of the Central African Republic.* Westport, CT: Greenwood Press, 2006.

Zeilig, Leo, and David Seddon. *A Political and Economic Dictionary of Africa.* Philadelphia: Routledge/Taylor and Francis, 2005.

CHAD

Republic of Chad
République du Tchad

CAPITAL: N'Djamena (formerly Fort-Lamy)

FLAG: The flag is a tricolor of blue, yellow, and red vertical stripes.

ANTHEM: *La Tchadienne (The Chadian).*

MONETARY UNIT: The Communauté Financière en Afrique Centrale franc (XAF), which was originally pegged to the French franc, has been pegged to the euro since January 1999 with a rate of XAF655.957 to 1 euro. The franc is issued in coins of 1, 2, 5, 10, 25, 50, 100, and 500 francs and notes of 50, 100, 500, 1,000, 5,000, and 10,000 francs. XAF1 = US$0.00202 (or US$1 = XAF495.28) as of 2010.

WEIGHTS AND MEASURES: The metric system is the legal standard.

HOLIDAYS: New Year's Day, 1 January; National Holiday, 11 January; Labor Day, 1 May; African Independence Day, 25 May; Independence Day, 11 August; Assumption, 15 August; All Saints' Day, 1 November; Proclamation of the Republic, 28 November; Christmas, 25 December. Movable religious holidays include Eid al-Fitr, Eid al-Adha, Milad an-Nabi, Easter Monday, Ascension, and Pentecost Monday.

TIME: 1 pm = noon GMT.

¹LOCATION, SIZE, AND EXTENT

A landlocked country situated in northern central Africa, the Republic of Chad has an area of 1,284,000 sq km (495,755 sq mi), extending 1,765 km (1,097 mi) N–S and 1,030 km (640 mi) E–W. Comparatively, the area occupied by Chad is slightly more than three times the size of the state of California. It is bounded on the N by Libya, on the E by the Sudan, on the S by the Central African Republic, on the SW by Cameroon, and on the W by Nigeria and Niger, with a total boundary length of 5,968 km (3,708 mi).

The Aozou Strip of Chad, an area along the northern border of about 114,000 sq km (about 44,000 sq mi), was occupied and annexed by Libya in 1973. In February 1994 the International Court of Justice (ICJ) rejected Libya's claim to the territory. Armed clashes broke out with Nigeria in 1983 over several islands in Lake Chad that had emerged as the water level fell.

Chad's capital city, N'Djamena, is located in the southwestern part of the country.

²TOPOGRAPHY

The country's most marked feature is Lake Chad, which is situated at the foot of a gently sloping plain surrounded by vast marshes and fed chiefly by the Chari and Logone rivers. The surface area of the lake varies from about 9,842–25,641 sq km (3,800–9,900 sq mi). From this low point of 230 m (750 ft) above sea level, the land rises to a maximum of 3,415 m (11,204 ft) at Emi Koussi, an extinct volcanic peak in the Tibesti Mountains of northern Chad. The center of the country is primarily a shallow bowl known as the Bodélé Depression.

³CLIMATE

The three chief climatic zones are the Saharan, with a wide range of temperatures between day and night; the Sahelian, a semidesert; and the Sudanic, with relatively moderate temperatures. Extreme temperatures range from -12°–50°C (10°–122°F). At N'Djamena the average daily maximums and minimums are 42°C (108°F) and 28°C (73°F) in April and 33°C (91°F) and 14°C (57°C) in December. The rains last from April (in the south) or July (farther north) through October. Average annual rainfall is about 76 cm (30 in) at N'Djamena. In the far south it is as much as 122 cm (48 in), but at Faya-Largeau in the north it averages only 2.5 cm (1 in). A severe drought affected two-thirds of the country from 1967 through 1973 and again in the early 1980s, especially 1984. From 2008 to 2011 the entire Sahel region, Chad included, suffered from below-average rainfall and was revisited by drought. This drought was particularly devastating to the central regions of the country.

⁴FLORA AND FAUNA

Animal and plant life correspond to the three climatic zones. The World Resources Institute estimates there are 1,600 plant species. Furthermore, Chad is the natural habitat of 104 mammal, 531 bird, 53 reptile, and 10 amphibian species. This calculation reflects the total number of distinct species residing in the country, not the number of endemic species.

In the Saharan region the only flora is the date-palm groves of the oases. Palms and acacia trees grow in the Sahelian region. The southern or Sudanic zone consists of broad grasslands or prairies suitable for grazing. Elephants, lions, buffalo, hippopotamuses, rhinoceroses, giraffes, antelopes, leopards, cheetahs, hyenas, snakes, and a variety of birds are found in the savanna country.

5ENVIRONMENT

Chad has two national parks, five game reserves, and five Ramsar Wetlands of International Importance. The World Resources Institute reported that Chad had designated 11.49 million hectares (28.4 million acres) of land for protection as of 2006. Water resources totaled 43 cu km (10.32 cu mi) while water usage was 0.23 cu km (0.055 cu mi) per year. Domestic water usage accounted for 17% of total usage and agricultural for 83%. Per capita water usage totaled 24 cu m (843 cu ft.) per year. The United Nations (UN) reported in 2008 that carbon dioxide emissions in Chad totaled 385 kilotons.

The chief environmental problem is increasing desertification after a decade marked by below-normal rainfall and periodic droughts. Warring factions in Chad have damaged the environment and hampered the efforts of the government to address environmental problems for 25 years. Locust swarms periodically cause crop damage. The availability of fresh water is also a major problem.

According to a 2011 report issued by the International Union for Conservation of Nature and Natural Resources (IUCN), the number of threatened species included 13 types of mammals, 9 species of birds, 1 type of reptile, and 2 species of plants. Endangered species in Chad include the black rhinoceros, Dallon's gerbil, and African wild ass. The Sahara oryx, also called the scimitar-horned oryx, is extinct in the wild.

6POPULATION

The US Central Intelligence Agency (CIA) estimated the population of Chad in 2011 to be approximately 10,758,945, which placed it at number 77 in population among the 196 nations of the world. In 2011 approximately 3% of the population was over 65 years of age, with another 46% under 15 years of age. The median age in Chad was 16.8 years. There were 0.92 males for every female in the country. The population's annual rate of change was 2.009%. The projected population for the year 2025 was 16,900,000. Population density in Chad was calculated at 8 people per sq km (21 people per sq mi).

The UN estimated that 28% of the population lived in urban areas, and that urban populations had an annual rate of change of 4.6%. The largest urban area was N'Djamena, with a population of 808,000.

7MIGRATION

Estimates of Chad's net migration rate, carried out by the CIA in 2011, amounted to -3.84 migrants per 1,000 citizens. The total number of emigrants living abroad was 243,300, and the total number of immigrants living in Chad was 388,300. Chad also accepted 234,000 refugees from Sudan and 54,200 from the Central African Republic. At least 200,000 Chadians fled the country during the civil war in 1979–81, mostly to Cameroon and Nigeria. About 150,000 returned in 1982. In 1983 up to 200,000 of the estimated 700,000 Chadians in Nigeria were expelled as part of a general expulsion of foreigners. Beginning in 1983 tens of thousands of Chadians fled from Libyan-controlled northern Chad and other areas of the country. The government of Chad reported that more than 152,000 Chadians returned home between November 1985, when a general amnesty was proclaimed, and the end of June

1987. As of 1995 there were 42,900 Chadian refuges in Cameroon, 21,500 in the Central African Republic, 2,000 in Niger, and 1,300 in Nigeria. A total of some 10,500 Chadian refugees were repatriated from the Central African Republic between April 1995 and September 199, and from Niger between December 1997 and January 1999. The Chadian government, in agreement with the UN High Commissioner for Refugees (UNHCR), decided to facilitate the repatriation of another 55,000 Chadian refugees between 1999 and the end of 2000. According the United States Department of State, there are approximately 170,000 IDPs (Internally Displaced Persons) residing in 38 camps in the country, most of whom were displaced in 2005 as a result of interethnic fighting over scarce water and land resources during drought. As of September 2011 approximately 270,000 Sudanese refugees from Darfur remained in Chad. Most of these refugees are found in camps located along the eastern border with Sudan. Approximately 80,000 refugees from the Central African Republic live primarily in five camps in the south and approximately 5,000 refugees of various nationalities live in urban areas.

8ETHNIC GROUPS

The basic population of Chad derives from indigenous African groups whose composition has been altered over the course of years through successive invasions from the Arabic north. The present population is a mixture of at least 200 ethnic groups. The population can be broadly divided between those who follow the Islamic faith and the peoples of the south, by which is meant the five southernmost prefectures. The Arab invaders brought Islam perhaps as early as the 8th century, and today their descendants form a relatively homogeneous group localized in the regions of Chari Baguirmi and Ouaddai, but mostly seminomadic. Muslim indigenous groups include Arabs, Toubou, Hadjerai, Fulbe, Kotoko, Kanembou, Baguirmi, Boulala, Zaghawa, and Maba. Some indigenous groups such as the Salamat and the Taundjor, were largely Arabized by intermarriage over the years. Other Muslim peoples include the Fulani. Among the non-Muslim indigenous peoples, the most important (and the largest single group in Chad) are the Sara, about 30% of the population. They live in the valleys of the Chari and Logone rivers and are farmers of considerable skill. Others include the Ngambaye, Mbaye, Goulaye, Moundang, Moussei, and Massa. There are about 15,000 nonindigenous inhabitants, of whom about 1,000 are French.

9LANGUAGES

More than 120 languages and dialects are spoken by the different ethnic groups, but Arabic is commonly spoken in the north and Sara and Sango languages in the south. French and Arabic are the official languages.

10RELIGIONS

As of 2011 about 54% of the people were Muslims, 33% were Christians, and the remainder were followers of indigenous religions or no religion. Most of the people of northern Chad are Muslims. Islam in Chad has a long and rich history. As early as the 7th century Muslim traders from the Arabian peninsula entered the region. The religion received further impetus from traders and holy men both from Sudan and from northern Nigeria, who proselytized through the area around Lake Chad long before

CHAD

0 150 300 Miles

0 150 300 Kilometers

ALGERIA

LIBYA

Aouzou

Bardaï

Aozou Strip

TIBESTI

Zouar

SAHARA

DESERT

Grand Erg de Bilma

▲ *Emi Koussi*
11,204 ft.
3415 m.

Aozou Strip
The World Court, in
February of 1994, granted
administration of
the Aozou Strip to Chad.

BORKOU

Faya-Largeau

NIGER

Fada

ENNEDI

Bodélé

Depression

Howar

Berdoba

MASSIF DU KERKOUR NOURENE

Miski

Biltine

Abéché

S U D A N

Mao

Ati

Batha

Bol

Lake Chad

Farcha

⍟ **N'Djamena**

Mongo

N I G E R I A

Massenya

Abou Deïa

Azoum

Melfi

Am Timan

Chari

Bousso

Bongor

Logone

Léré

Pala

Laï

Doba

Salamat

Aouk

Sarh

Zakouma National Park

S O U T H
S U D A N

Moundou

Oulfam

Chad

CAMEROON

C E N T R A L   A F R I C A N   R E P U B L I C

W — E compass (N/S)

LOCATION: 7°26′ to 23°N; 13°28′ to 2°E. BOUNDARY LENGTHS: Libya, 1,054 kilometers (655 miles); Sudan, 1,360 kilometers (845 miles): Central African Republic, 1,199 kilometers (745 miles); Cameroon, 1,047 kilometers (651 miles); Nigeria, 88 kilometers (55 miles); Niger, 1,175 kilometers (730 miles).

the coming of Europeans. Protestant and Catholic missionaries have been in the territory only in this century. A majority of the nation's Muslims adhere to the mystical aspect of Islam known as Sufism. The Sufi order with the greatest number of adherents in Chad is the Tijaniyya. Most of the people of southern Chad are Christian, with a majority of Roman Catholics. Protestants tend to be affiliated with evangelical groups. Some people of the south, particularly those living in the valleys of the Chari and Logone rivers, follow African traditional religions. There are also small communities of Baha'is and Jehovah's Witnesses. The constitution provides for freedom of religion, but this right has been restricted by the government in some situations. For instance the Islamic group Faid al-Djariahas has been banned because of religious customs that are considered to be non-Islamic. The government also continues to closely monitor the activities of Islamist groups. All religious organizations must be registered with the Department of Religious and Traditional Affairs in the Ministry of the Interior. Though there is no state religion, a majority of the senior government officials are Muslim and some policies favor Muslims in practice. Certain Muslim and Christian holidays are officially observed.

11 TRANSPORTATION

Chad suffers from poor transportation both within the country and to outside markets; its economic development depends on the expansion of transport facilities. The CIA reports that Chad has a total of 33,400 km (20,754 mi) of roads, of which 267 km (166 mi) are paved. There are 56 airports. During the rainy season the roads become impassable and the economy slows down almost to a standstill.

The main export routes are to the Nigerian railhead of Maiduguri and the Cameroonian railhead of Ngaoundéré.

Most rivers flow but intermittently. On the Chari between N'Djamena and Lake Chad transportation is possible all year round. In September and October the Logone is navigable between N'Djamena and Moundou, and the Shari between N'Djamena and Sarh. Only 2,000 km (1,250 mi) of waterways are navigable all year.

Chad has 56 airports, eight of which had paved roads as of 2009. Air Tchad (60% state owned) provides internal service to 12 locations but suffers from lack of fuel and equipment. The international airport at N'Djamena was damaged in fighting in 1981, but is now served by several international carriers including Air Afrique, which is partly owned by Chad. Another major airport, developed as a military staging area, is located at Sarh.

12 HISTORY

Fine prehistoric rock engravings and paintings can be found in northern Chad dating from between 5000–2000 BC. In 2002 an international research team announced the discovery of the fossil remains of the earliest hominid on record. The six specimens, collected in Chad in 2001–2002, are the oldest hominid evidence and are dated between six and seven million years old.

As early as the 8th century BC Arabs and Berbers entered from the north and their records tell of the existence of great African empires—Kanem-Bornu, Baguirmi, and Ouaddai—between the 9th and 16th centuries. By the end of the 19th century many small states south of Lake Chad had become vassals of the northern sultanates, which conducted a flourishing slave trade.

Europeans began exploration of Chad in the 19th century. Chad was explored in part in 1822 by Dixon Denham and Hugh Clapperton, two British travelers. More detailed explorations were carried out by Heinrich Barth (1853) and Gustav Nachtigal (1870–71). In the decade after 1890 French expeditions gradually expanded French control of the lands to the south and east of Lake Chad. Complete conquest of the territory was achieved by 1913. The borders of Chad as they presently stand were secured by conventions between France and Germany (1894) and France and the United Kingdom (1898). In 1910 Gabon, Middle Congo, and Ubangi-Shari (which included Chad) were constituted administratively as colonies; together they formed French Equatorial Africa. Chad was separated in 1916 and became a colony in 1920.

On 26 August 1940 during World War II, French officials in Chad rallied to the Free French standard, making Chad the first colony to do so. N'Djamena, formerly Fort-Lamy, was an impor-

tant Allied air base on the route to the Middle East, and from there Col. Philippe Leclerc's troops departed to fight in the North African campaign. After 1945 Chad became one of the territories of French Equatorial Africa in the French Union, and in the referendum of 28 September 1958 the territory of Chad voted to become an autonomous republic within the French Community. On 26 November 1958 the territorial assembly became a constituent assembly and proclaimed the autonomous Republic of Chad. On 11 August 1960 Chad achieved full independence, with François (later Ngarta) Tombalbaye as head of state and prime minister. On 4 April 1962 a new constitution was proclaimed, and a new government formed with Tombalbaye as president.

By 1965 power had been consolidated and Chad was a one-party state. In 1965 there was full-scale rebellion in the Muslim north country, largely the result of Muslim resentment toward the Christian- and animist-oriented government in N'Djamena. Prominent in the rebellion was the National Liberation Front (Front de Libération Nationale–FROLINAT). In late 1968 President Tombalbaye requested and received the aid of French troops in combating the rebels. French troops were officially withdrawn from Chad in 1972 although technical advisers remained. In 1973 Libya, a major source of covert aid for the rebels, occupied and annexed the Aozou Strip in northern Chad.

On 13 April 1975 Tombalbaye's 15-year rule ended with an army coup and his assassination. Gen. Félix Malloum became the new president. Like his predecessor Malloum was a Southerner whose rule was opposed by the Muslim north. In 1976 however, a faction led by Hissène Habré split with FROLINAT and eventually formed the Armed Forces of the North (Forces Armées du Nord–FAN). Goukouni Oueddei, a powerful leader from the north with Libyan support, emerged as head of FROLINAT, but a FROLINAT advance south was stopped by additional French troops in 1978. In a government shuffle Malloum named Habré prime minister in 1978, but the two broke in early 1979 as antagonism between Muslims and Southerners intensified. After Habré's FAN party seized control of the capital, Malloum resigned as president on 23 March 1979 and fled the country. In April Habré became defense minister and Oueddei interior minister in a coalition government, which in August was reconstituted with Oueddei as president. In November it became the interim Government of National Unity, representing 11 armed factions, with Oueddei remaining as president and Habré as minister of defense.

Fighting between FAN and government forces broke out in March 1980, and Habré was dismissed from the cabinet in April. France withdrew its forces from Chad in May and the FAN-occupied Faya-Largeau in June, as well as holding part of N'Djamena. By October Libya had intervened on Oueddei's behalf and in December, an estimated 7,000 to 10,000 Libyan troops completed the conquest of Chad by occupying N'Djamena. Habré's forces fled to eastern Chad and Sudan.

Libya's action and proposed union with Chad angered other African leaders and France; Oueddei himself may have become alarmed at the growth of Libyan influence. At Oueddei's request Libyan troops withdrew in November 1981 and were replaced by a 3,600-man Organization of African Unity (OAU) peacekeeping force. These troops did nothing, however, to halt the FAN's subsequent advance from the east. On 7 June 1982 Habré's forces occupied the capital and Oueddei fled to Algeria. Habré declared himself president of Chad on 19 October 1982.

By early 1983 Habré's dictatorial regime had extended its control to southern Chad, but was meeting increasing difficulties in the north. Ousted president Oueddei formed a rival government and with a rebel army of about 3,000, captured the northern town of Faya-Largeau on 10 August 1983, with the support of Libyan aircraft and artillery. Although Habré's regime was characterized by widespread atrocities, France and the United States supported his quest for power, seeing him as a bulwark against Libya's Muammar el-Qaddafi. As of early 1984 Chad was effectively partitioned, with a chain of French military posts stretching across the center of the country. To the south the Habré regime was consolidating its position. France subsequently moved its defensive line 100 km (60 mi) to the north. Northern Chad, however, remained under the control of Libya and Oueddei's rebel forces, and there were growing fears that Libya was moving to annex the area.

A November 1984 agreement between France and Libya called for both countries to withdraw their forces from Chad, but although France complied, Libya reneged. French troops returned in 1985 to help repulse an enemy offensive. On 8 August Aozou and with it the entire disputed strip, fell to Chad, but a Libyan counteroffensive recaptured the settlement on 28 August. However, after a damaging Chadian raid on an air base within Libyan territory on 5 September, Libya agreed to a cease-fire effective 11 September. During 1987 fighting Chad captured US$500 million to US$1 billion worth of Libyan military equipment, most of it intact. US-supplied Stinger missiles allowed Habré's forces to neutralize Libya's air force. In 1987 Libya withdrew and Hissène Habré was officially recognized as president of the whole of Chad.

The struggle for Chad took another twist in November 1990. After a three-week campaign by guerrillas loyal to an ex-army commander, Idriss Déby, Habré's dictatorship fell. Déby was supported by Libya and Sudan, but he also was backed by the United States, France, and Nigeria. A French force of 1,200 assisted Déby against pro-Habré rebels, who were eventually put down in 1993.

In May 1992 Déby appointed a new prime minister, Joseph Yodoyman, who formed a new cabinet that included several opposition figures. A democratization process was agreed upon, parties were legalized and, by the end of 1992, 28 parties had registered. In April 1992 Yodoyman stepped down. He died in November.

A Sovereign National Conference that lasted from January to April 1993 brought together a diverse group of government, economic, military, and special interest representatives. It confirmed Déby as chief of state, established a new transitional government, elected 57 counselors to a Higher Transitional Council (a quasi-legislative body), and adopted the Transitional Charter, an interim constitution. This government was given a one-year mandate. Late in 1993 a technical commission of jurists was constituted, which began work on a new constitution, an electoral code, and a charter for political parties. In April 1994 Déby's mandate was extended by 12 months, and the work of the jurists was continued. Elections were scheduled for April 1995 but were postponed. The Transitional Council submitted a proposed constitution in 1994 calling for a directly elected president, a bicameral legislature, and a constitutional court.

Chad's long-standing territorial dispute with Libya over the Aozou Strip was taken up by the ICJ in June 1993. On 3 February 1994 the Court rejected Libya's claim to Chadian territory. Libyan withdrawal was slow, but was fully completed by May 1994. French forces remained in the area despite Libyan protests. In December 1994 the government announced an amnesty for exiled opposition politicians and for political prisoners, excluding Habré. Opposition activity expanded afterwards, but Déby was accused of sponsoring harassment despite the amnesty. Opposition forces coalesced early in 1995 to form the Political Parties Concentration (CPP) which, joining with Western nations—notably France—began calling for changes in the administration of the Transitional Council. In March ignoring such demands, the Transitional Council expanded its mandate to govern the country and removed the sitting prime minister. In August the chairman of the Transitional Council resigned amid allegations of fiscal mismanagement. Later that month the Council sponsored raids of opposition parties, and the government briefly detained a prominent opposition leader. Elections and the required constitutional referendum continued to be postponed.

In March 1996 the government signed a cease-fire agreement with 13 opposition parties for the constitutional referendum and elections to take place. The agreement was brokered by Gabon in Franceville with assistance from the Central African Republic and Niger. Though an election timetable was established and proceeded, numerous opposition groups, and particularly those who wished a federal governmental system rather than a unitary one, urged a boycott of the referendum polling. Despite these calls and opposition in the southern part of the country, 63.5% of the voters on 31 March 1996 agreed to adoption of the constitution.

The presidential elections could then proceed. The first round of voting took place on 2 June 1996 with Déby garnering 43.8% of the votes. The second round held on 3 July was contested between Déby and Wadal Abdelkader Kamagoué, representing the Union for Renewal and Democracy (Union pour le Renouveau et la Démocratie—URD, who had taken 12.4% of the voters in the first round. Déby was inaugurated as president on 8 August.

Legislative elections, though delayed again, took place in January and February 1997 with 658 candidates representing 49 political parties in polling for 125 national assembly seats.

Much of Déby's presidency since his 1996 inauguration has been engagement in negotiations or armed conflict with continuing dissident groups in the northern and southern regions of the country. Due to the desire to see the oil reserves from the Doba oil fields brought into production, his government has been particularly eager to bring a cessation to hostilities in the south, with mixed results. Outbreaks of violence continued to be reported in both the northern and southern regions and in 1998 Youssouf Togoimi left the government and his position as defense minister to form the Movement for Democracy and Justice in Chad (MDJT), and organized an armed rebellion against the government.

The Chadian security forces continue to be charged with human rights violations by various internal and international rights organizations. In October 1996 Amnesty International also accused France of participating in these violations in Chad. Despite various disagreements over the years, France continues to see maintenance of an armed force in Chad as essential to securing its strategic position as a border state of Libya and Sudan. Déby's government also continues to be accused of harassing the opposition, including detentions, prosecutions, and jail terms. Chadian forces took part in the UN peacekeeping mission in the Central African Republic in 1998 and in the Democratic Republic of the Congo from September of that year.

In January 1998 Déby's government stated its intention of requesting extradition of Hissène Habré from Senegal in order to prosecute him for human rights abuses and embezzlement of government funds. In a separate approach toward Habré, the Chadian Truth Commission, which spent 15 months studying charges against the former president, pressed for his criminal trial in Senegal, where he lived in exile after his ouster in 1990. They were joined by several international human rights organizations. In a 1992 report the Commission estimated that Habré's forces killed 40,000 Chadians, most of the deaths being attributed to his National Security Service. Habré was indicted in 2000 on charges of torture and crimes against humanity and placed under house arrest under the 1984 UN Convention Against Torture (CAT). However, in March 2001 Senegal ruled it did not have jurisdiction to try Habré in Senegal on torture charges during his tenure in power in Chad. On 18 August 2005 at the urging of Human Rights Watch, Prime Minister Pascal Yoadimnadji announced in a letter that all remaining Habré-era officials accused of human rights violations and still holding key government positions would be released from service of the Chadian government while awaiting trial.

On 20 May 2001 Déby won reelection as president with 63% of the vote in an election determined by credible sources to have been marked by fraud and vote-rigging. Six of the candidates opposing Déby were detained for questioning by the police, but were released within an hour. Although results from 25% of the polling stations were cancelled due to irregularities, Déby's reelection was confirmed and he was sworn in August for a second five-year term. During the campaign Déby promoted a US$3.5 billion development project from southern Chad to the coast of Cameroon. It was supported by an international consortium of companies with the ExxonMobil affiliate Esso Exploration and Production Chad, Inc. (EEPCI) serving as the primary operator. The Chad/Cameroon Development Project was the largest development project in the history of Chad; as many as 11,000 workers developed the Doba oil fields of southern Chad and built a 1,070 km (665 mi) pipeline to transport the oil from landlocked Chad to the coast of Cameroon. Of the total investment US$2 billion of this was invested in Chad. Planned for a 25-year production phase, Chad began to export oil extracted from the Doba Basin in late 2003, adding an estimated US$100 million to government revenues, an increase of approximately 40%. An estimated one billion barrels existed in oil reserves. The World Bank estimates that government income could increase annual government revenue from a minimum of US$80 million to US$100 million; Chad expects to receive between US$2.5 billion and US$5 billion in direct revenues from royalties, taxes, and dividends, depending on the price of oil over the Chadian oil field's production period. Despite the increase in oil revenue, 80% of the population relies on agriculture and subsistence farming, herding, and fishing. Although the government committed 80% of its future oil revenues on health, education, rural development, infrastructure, environment, and water, according to the World Bank, the government of Chad distributed US$67.7 million from oil revenues during 2004 for the priority poverty-reduction sectors, US$4.2 million for the oil production region, and US$12.7 million for the general budget.

In the first half of 2005 Chad netted US$102.5 million in net revenues. Chad estimated its direct oil revenues for the whole year would reach US$225 million. In July 2006 parliament approved the establishment of Chad's first state oil company, the Societe des Hydrocarbures du Tchad (SHT).

In November 2001 relations between Chad and the Central African Republic broke down when the Central African Republic army chief of staff, François Bozizé, fled to Chad after being accused of involvement in a failed coup attempt. Chad and the Central African Republic accused each other of supporting dissidents in cross-border attacks. Central African Republic President Ange-Félix Patassé claimed Chad was looking to annex part of the Central African Republic's oil-rich north as according to Patassé, 85% of the rebels occupying the north and center of the country were Chadians. In March 2003 rebels overthrew President Ange-Félix Patassé, and approximately 400 Chadian troops were sent to help stabilize the situation and back the self-declared president, Gen. Bozizé. The relations between the new Central African Republic government and Chad have significantly warmed.

In January 2002 the Chadian government and Togoimi's MDJT reached a peace agreement brokered by Libya. The accord provided for an immediate cease-fire, an amnesty for prisoners held by both sides, the integration of rebels into the national army, and government jobs for MDJT leaders. However, in May fighting between the two forces broke out in the far north of the country and 64 people were killed. As of 2003 skirmishing between government forces and the MDJT continued.

In January 2003 the government signed a peace agreement with the National Resistance Army (ANR), a rebel group operating in eastern Chad near the border with Sudan and the Central African Republic. The accord provided for an immediate cease-fire and an amnesty for prisoners. The following December a new peace agreement was signed with the northern rebels. Fighting between rebel groups, militias, and the government in the neighboring Darfur region of Sudan drove upwards of 180,000 refugees into eastern Chad, as well as sparking clashes between these militias and Chad's military. Tensions also remained high along the Central African Republic and Libyan borders, especially due to increased Central African Republic refugees amounting to 52,000, from clashes between central African rebels and the Central African Republic.

Much of the money initially earned on the pipeline was reportedly used to buy arms, and the influx of refugees as well as the nearby political instability has contributed to the unease. Although the Chadian government attempted to broker a peace accord between the Sudanese government and the Darfur rebels in April 2004, the Chadian army itself clashed with the Janjaweed militia, and the conciliatory attitude the Chadian government took with the Sudanese government was thought to be partly responsible for the 2004 uprising in the capital.

Drought, locusts, and a cholera epidemic in western Chad, in addition to the influx of primarily women and children refugees have also led to the general dissatisfaction of the 9.2 million people. Human rights criticism continued, fueled by such incidents as the imprisonment of a parliamentarian and the brief censure of media organizations.

By 2007 the situation in Sudan's Darfur region had worsened. Estimates placed the number of dead in Darfur as between 200,000 and 400,000. The border between Chad and Sudan had increasingly become the site of clashes and ethnic violence. After attacks by Janjaweed militia on Chadian villages on 31 March 2007, killing some 400 people, Libyan leader Col. Muammar Qaddafi took the lead in trying to broker a peace agreement between Chad and Sudan. Libyan and Eritrean military and security observers were sent to the border between Sudan and Chad in April 2007. Humanitarian aid organizations cared for 200,000 Sudanese refugees and 50,000 displaced Chadians in the eastern region of Chad. In early 2006 the UN warned that the violence in Chad was on its way to becoming a genocide, citing an increasing similarity to the situation in Sudan.

In May 2007 Sudan and Chad reached an agreement to attempt to stop fighting in Darfur from spilling over across the border between the two countries. However, heavy fighting flared up in eastern Chad in late 2007 after rebels seized government officers and vehicles. Hundreds were reported dead after a violent end to a month-long cease-fire in November. Rebel groups included the Union of Forces for Democracy and Development (UFDD) led by Mahamat Nouri, and the Rally of Forces for Change (RFC) led by the president's uncle. Rebel groups hoped to overturn the presidency of Idriss Déby. The fighting accompanied a November declaration of war by the UFDD against the French army, which maintains an army base in the country and comprises approximately half of a European Union (EU) peacekeeping force scheduled for deployment to Chad in December 2007.

In August 2007 both the government and opposition parties agreed to delay scheduled elections until 2009.

Tensions reignited between Chad and Sudan in May 2009, after Chad's government admitted to having conducted air raids against Chadian rebels in Sudanese territory. The announcement came just weeks after a reconciliation agreement between Chad and Sudan was signed, delivering a blow to the prospects of durable peace between the neighbors. Although Sudan denies supporting them, the Chadian rebels have ostensibly operated out of Sudan with impunity for years, using the country as a base out of which to run cross-border attacks. Following the raids the Chadian government signaled that it would continue to attack rebel positions in Sudan, while spokespeople for the Sudanese government argued that the attacks constituted an act of war against Sudan.

13 GOVERNMENT

According to the constitution of 1962, Chad was an indivisible, secular, democratic, and social republic with a president and national assembly. One-party rule was established and presidential elections were held on 15 June 1969, the first by universal suffrage. An official announcement on 16 June stated that President Tombalbaye, being the only candidate, had been reelected for a further seven years by 93% of the voters.

The National Assembly was dissolved after the coup of 13 April 1975 that ousted Tombalbaye. A provisional constitution, which came into force 16 August 1975, was abolished on 23 March 1979 when President Malloum fled. In October 1982 a National Consultative Council was formed with two representatives from each prefecture and two from N'Djamena. This body was to draft a new constitution by 1990, but it was replaced in the Déby coup on 1 December 1990.

The three-month long national conference in early 1993 established a new transitional government with a 57-member higher transitional council elected by the 254 conference delegates, and a transitional charter.

Work on a new draft constitution began near the end of 1993, and a provisional document was drafted and made public in 1994. The constitution, approved in a March 1996 referendum, mandates a directly elected president serving a five-year term, a bicameral legislature, and a constitutional court. The 1996 presidential election under this constitution returned Idriss Déby to the presidency, and 1997 legislative elections brought an absolute majority to Déby's Patriotic Salvation Movement (MPS) party, with three opposition parties sharing the remaining 62 seats. Déby was reelected in May 2001 and his MPS party won an overwhelming majority in the 21 April 2002 elections for the National Assembly. Although the 1996 constitution provides for a bicameral legislative branch, only the National Assembly functions, as the Senate has not yet been created. Senate members are to serve six-year terms, with one-third of representatives renewable every two years. Members of the National Assembly are elected for four-year terms in 25 single-member and 34 multi-member constituencies (155 seats total). In 2005 after an uprising in the capital that the president claimed was intended to overthrow him, the National Assembly approved a constitutional amendment that ended the two-term limit on the presidency, allowing Déby to run for a third term in 2006, which he won. Chad held presidential elections again in April 2011. President Deby won easily with approximately 88 percent of the vote, although turnout appeared low to international observers. Leading opposition figures boycotted the presidential elections due to concerns that deficiencies in the legislative elections had not been corrected. Municipal elections were scheduled for January 2012. Emmanuel Nadningar has been prime minister since 5 March 2010.

14 POLITICAL PARTIES

Prior to independence Chad was split politically. The Northerners, predominantly Muslim, were supporters of the Party of African Reunion (Parti de Regroupement Africain). The non-Muslim southern farmers were supporters of the Chad Progressive Party (Parti Progressiste Tchadien—PPT). In 1958 the Legislative Assembly of Chad was controlled by PPT members, who had a majority of 42 of the 65 seats. In the election of 31 May 1959, the PPT obtained 57 seats in the new Assembly and François (later Ngarta) Tombalbaye of the PPT became prime minister. In February 1960 four smaller parties joined forces to form the opposition African National Party (Parti National Africain—PNA). In 1962 the PNA was dissolved and Chad became a one-party state. In 1973 the name of the PPT was changed to the National Movement for Cultural and Social Revolution (Mouvement Nationale pour la Révolution Culturelle et Sociale—MNRCS). Following the 1975 coup the MNRCS was banned and the National Assembly was dissolved. As a consequence all formal political activity ceased.

In 1984 Habré established the National Union for Independence and Revolution (Union Nationale pour l'Indépendence et la Révolution—UNIR) with a 14-member Executive Bureau headed by himself and an 80-member Central Committee. After the Déby coup his MPS took over. Parties were legalized in 1992, and eventually 28 registered with the authorities. These parties have continued to evolve, unite, disband, and reform.

The 1996 constitution provides for many political parties with approximately 60 involved politically or culturally. In the 2002 elections seven major parties were represented in the National Assembly. The MPS had 110 assembly seats, the Rally for Democracy and Progress (RDP) 12, Federation Action for the Republic (FAR) 9, National Rally for Development and Progress 5, URD 5, and National Union for Democracy and Renewal (UNDR) 3. The remaining 11 seats were spread over a variety of other parties.

Emmanuel Nadingar of the MPS was named prime minister of Chad in March 2010 after Youssouf Saleh Abbas resigned from the post, following a series of government embezzlement scandals. Before assuming the premiership, Nadingar held the position of oil minister for the central African nation.

Parliamentary elections that were originally scheduled for November 2010 were rescheduled as the electoral commission claimed difficulties in procuring the appropriate resources in a timely manner. This included the equipment and staff members needed to compile voter registration data.

Leading up to the February 2011 elections, the MPS joined with the RDP to form the Alliance for the Renaissance of Chad (ART). In the elections the ART won 133 of the 188 seats in the assembly, followed by the National Union for Democracy and Renewal (UNDR) with 11. The remainder went to smaller parties.

15 LOCAL GOVERNMENT

Chad is divided into 18 regions, including the city of N'Djamena. Regions are subdivided into departments and communes. In many areas the traditional chief still retains power as the head of his people.

16 JUDICIAL SYSTEM

Since the 1990 coup the structure and functioning of the judicial system has been seriously disrupted. Because of the breakdown of law and order, as well as interference by the government and the military, the judiciary was unable to handle criminal cases. Many magistrates went on strike in 1993 to protest difficult working conditions and nonpayment of salaries.

Traditionally, the legal system was based on a combination of French civil law and Chadian customary law. The judicial system consisted of four criminal courts, four magistrate courts, four labor tribunals, 14 district courts in major cities, 36 justices of the peace in larger townships, and a court of appeal, the Appellate Court of N'Djamena. A supreme court was inaugurated in 1963 and abolished in 1975. A court of state security was established in 1976. Courts-martial, instituted early in the Déby regime to try security personnel, no longer operate and the remaining military magistrates sit as civilian judges on the N'Djamena Court of Appeals. In most rural areas where there is no access to these formal judicial institutions, sultans and chiefs preside over customary courts. Their decisions may be appealed to ordinary courts.

Under the transitional charter the Appellate Court of N'Djamena was charged with responsibility for constitutional review as well as review of decisions of lower courts and criminal convictions involving potential sentences of over 20 years.

The 1996 constitution guaranteed an independent judiciary. Though a supreme court was created and a functioning judicial system exists, it is clear that there continues to be significant interference in its independence, as the president names most judicial officials. The Supreme Court consists of one chief justice appointed by the president and 15 councilors chosen by both the president and National Assembly, all lifetime appointments. A Constitutional Council made up of nine judges elected to nine-year terms has the power to review legislation, treaties, and international agreements prior to their adoption. In local contexts customary and traditional law is recognized to the extent it does not interfere with national law or public order.

The Superior Council of Magistrates is to act as a guarantor of judicial independence.

17 ARMED FORCES

The International Institute for Strategic Studies reported that armed forces in Chad totaled 25,350 members in 2011. The force was comprised of an estimated 17,000 to 20,000 from the army, 350 from the air force, and 5,000 members of the republican guard. Armed forces represented 0.8% of the labor force in Chad. Defense spending totaled $296.7 million and accounted for 1.7% of gross domestic product (GDP).

The UN announced in May 2010 that it would withdraw all of its peacekeeping troops from Chad by the end of 2010. The UN mission in Chad, known as MINURCAT, had 4,375 military and civilian personnel deployed in Chad and the Central African Republic in May 2010. By the end of that year the UN peacekeepers had been withdrawn from Chad. This force was deployed in 2009 to protect hundreds of thousands of displaced refugees from Chad and the Darfur region of Sudan who faced threats from continuing violence along the border between the two countries. As of May 2011 according to the UN the withdrawal of the peacekeepers had not adversely affected security in the eastern part of the country.

18 INTERNATIONAL COOPERATION

Chad was admitted to UN membership on 20 September 1960 and is a member of the UN Economic Commission for Africa (ECA) and several nonregional specialized agencies. It is also a member of the African Development Bank; African, Caribbean and Pacific Group of States (ACP Group); the Central African States Development Bank (BDEAC), the Monetary and Economic Community of Central Africa (CEMAC), the Organization of the Islamic Conference (OIC), the Group of 77 (G-77), the New Partnership for Africa's Development (NEPAD), and the African Union. Chad joined the World Trade Organization (WTO) 19 October 1996. The nation is part of the Franc Zone and the Community of Sahel and Saharan States (CENSAD). Chad is part of the Non-Aligned Movement (NAM) and the Organization for the Prohibition of Chemical Weapons (OPCW). Chad, Cameroon, the Central African Republic, Niger, and Nigeria are members of the Lake Chad Basin Commission formed in 1964. Chad is also active in the Interstate Commission for the Fight against the Drought in the Sahel. In other environmental cooperation efforts, Chad is part of the Convention on Biological Diversity (CBD), the Ramsar Convention on Wetlands of International Importance, the Convention on International Trade in Endangered Species (CITES), the Montréal Protocol, the Nuclear Test Ban Treaty, the UN Convention on Climate Change, and the UN Convention to Combat Desertification (UNCCD).

¹⁹ECONOMY

The GDP rate of change in Chad as of 2010 was 5.1%. Inflation stood at 4%. The Chadian economy struggles with few natural resources and continual conflict. About 80% of the population is employed in subsistence agricultural, including farming, herding, and fishing. Agriculture accounts for about 21% of the GDP, with cotton, cattle, and gum Arabic as major exports. Oil exploration and production began in the early 2000s, but development of the sector has been hindered by the lack of foreign investment associated with ongoing civil conflicts. The country's history of instability, its position as a landlocked nation, and the high cost of energy are a few other factors contributing to Chad's financial difficulties. The nation continues to rely heavily upon foreign aid and investment.

The presence of oil in the southern Doba region enticed a US-based consortium led by ExxonMobil to invest in the country in the 2000s. The result was a $3.7 billion project (the country's GDP was $7 billion in 2007, based on the exchange rate) to export oil via a 1,000 km (621.37 mi) buried pipeline through Cameroon to the Gulf of Guinea. Chinese companies are also expanding exploration efforts and plan to build a refinery. The nation's total oil reserves have been estimated to be 1.5 billion barrels, although the oil industry considers the area underexplored. By comparison Iraq's oil reserves are estimated at 112 billion barrels. Oil exports began flowing in 2004.

The project suffered a setback in 2006 when the government of Chad amended its oil revenue management law. When rebels attacked the capital the president issued a state of emergency and placed the oil revenue funds under his direct command. Whether future oil revenues would be diverted to private uses became an issue. Then the government of Chad accused the oil companies of owing $500 million in taxes. The government instructed the consortium to cease operations and leave the country. The dispute was settled in 2007 after the oil companies agreed to pay the country more than $280 million in overdue taxes.

Livestock production is conducted following seasonal rain patterns and as a result of the extended drought is increasingly centered in the south. Industry is centered on cotton processing, but the sector suffered considerably from a variety of ills. Cotton, cattle, and gum arabic provide the bulk of Chad's non-oil export earnings.

²⁰INCOME

The CIA estimated that in 2010 the GDP of Chad was $17.36 billion. The CIA defines GDP as the value of all final goods and services produced within a nation in a given year and computed on the basis of purchasing power parity (PPP) rather than value as measured on the basis of the rate of the exchange based on current dollars. The per capita GDP was estimated at $1,600. The annual growth rate of GDP was 5.1%. The average inflation rate was 4%. It was estimated that agriculture accounted for 50.5% of GDP, industry 7%, and services 42.5%.

The World Bank reported that in 2009 household consumption in Chad totaled $5.4 billion or about $499 per capita, measured in current US dollars rather than PPP. Household consumption includes expenditures of individuals, households, and nongovernmental organizations on goods and services, excluding the purchases of dwellings. It was estimated that household consumption was growing at an average annual rate of 0.2%.

The World Bank estimates that Chad, with 0.14% of the world's population, accounted for 0.03% of the world's GDP. By comparison the United States with 4.85% of the world's population accounted for 22.51% of world GDP.

As of 2011 the most recent study by the World Bank reported that actual individual consumption in Chad was 59.8% of GDP and accounted for 0.02% of world consumption. By comparison the United States accounted for 25.44% of world individual consumption. The World Bank also estimated that 33.9% of Chad's GDP was spent on food and beverages, 5.7% on housing and household furnishings, 1.0% on clothes, 0.8% on health, 11.7% on transportation, 0.5% on communications, 2.8% on recreation, 0.3% on restaurants and hotels, and 2% on miscellaneous goods and services and purchases from abroad.

²¹LABOR

As of 2007 Chad had a total labor force of 4.293 million people. Within that labor force CIA estimates in 2006 noted that 80% were employed in agriculture, 10% in industry, and 10% in the service sector.

Although workers except those in the armed forces can form or join unions, authorization must be granted by the Ministry of the Interior. The right of collective bargaining is protected under the law, but the government can intervene under certain circumstances. The right to strike is also protected but in the public sector is limited by a decree that requires minimum services to be maintained. Over 90% of employees in the formal economy were unionized, excluding herders and subsistence cultivators.

Child labor in Chad is a problem. Although minors under the age of 18 are prohibited from working under circumstances that would impair the health, safety, or morals of a child, the means to enforce the law are lacking from the government. About one-fifth of all children between the ages of 6 and 18 work in the informal economy in urban areas. Children are also employed throughout the country in the agricultural and herding sectors, and as manual laborers, street vendors, and helpers in small shops in the country's urban centers.

Although there are occupational safety and health standards, these are rarely followed in the private sector and are nonexistent in the civil service.

²²AGRICULTURE

Roughly 3% of Chad's total land is currently cultivated. Cotton, sorghum, millet, peanuts, rice, potatoes and manioc comprise the country's major crops. Cereal production in 2009 amounted to 2.2 million tons, fruit production 117,857 tons, and vegetable production 104, 996 tons.

Prolonged periodic droughts and civil war and political instability have cut agricultural production and necessitated food relief. Because of drought annual cereal production can widely fluctuate. Chad's cereal yield during 2002–04 was 713 kg (1,571 lb) per person, up from 659 kg (1,453 lb) per person during 1992–94.

Since the 1960s cotton crops have accounted for a high percentage of Chad's export earnings. Cotton growing began about 1929 and spread gradually throughout southern Chad. Production was 84,500 tons in 2004, still far below the high of 174,062 tons in 1975–76. Production is dominated by the parastatal Coton Tchad, which regulates output, operates the ginneries and cottonseed oil works, and markets and exports both cotton and cottonseed. Chad's medium staple cotton is sold to 20 different countries; Germany, Portugal, and Japan are the principal customers. Although most cotton is exported, factories in Chad produce cottonseed oil for domestic consumption.

Production of peanuts has rapidly increased since the early 1990s, rising from an annual average of 164,000 tons during 1989–91 to an estimated 450,000 tons in 2004. Millet is the basic foodstuff, except in the Lake Chad area, where corn is the main cereal. Sugarcane is produced on a French-managed irrigated estate of about 3,000 hectares (7,400 acres) on the Shari River.

23 ANIMAL HUSBANDRY

The UN Food and Agriculture Organization (FAO) reported in 2009 that Chad had 45 million hectares (111.2 million acres) dedicated to permanent pasture or meadow. That same year the country tended 5.5 million chickens, 7.2 million head of cattle, and 29,240 pigs. The production from these animals amounted to 85,661 tons of beef and veal, 521 tons of pork, 5,133 tons of poultry, 3,064 tons of eggs, and 242,142 tons of milk. The country also produced 16,709 tons of cattle hide.

Live cattle, sheep, and goats are exported, with considerable smuggling, to Nigeria. Livestock is Chad's second most important export after cotton.

24 FISHING

Fish, either fresh or dried, forms an important element in the diet of the people living in the major valleys. Production is far below potential. In 2008 the annual capture of fish totaled 40,000 tons according to the FAO.

25 FORESTRY

Approximately 9% of Chad is covered by forest. The FAO estimated the 2009 roundwood production at 761,000 cu m (26.9 million cu ft). The value of all forest products including roundwood totals $6.73 million. The only exportable forest product is gum arabic, the yield of which averages 300 to 400 tons a year.

26 MINING

The mineral industry was poised to become a significant segment of Chad's economy as the Doba Basin petroleum project got under way. Exportation of crude oil began in 2004. Nonfuel mineral production in 2009 included: gold (100 kg); aggregate, sand and stone (350,000 metric tons); natron or soda ash (12,000 metric tons); and salt (10,000 metric tons) The country's undeveloped mineral resources included bauxite, columbium (niobium) and tantalum, diatomite, graphite, kaolin, quartz, soapstone, tin, thorium, tungsten, and uranium. There were also occurrences reported of chromite, copper, diamond, iron, lead, nickel, titanium, and zinc. The government actively encouraged foreign investment in the development of domestic hydrocarbons. Most trade was channeled through seaports in Cameroon and Nigeria. Petroleum produced

in the Doba Basin was exported by means of the Chad-Cameroon pipeline to a terminal in Kribi, Cameroon.

27 ENERGY AND POWER

Although Chad lacks coal, natural gas, and hydroelectric sources, the country does have crude oil reserves that totaled 126,170 barrels of oil a day in 2011.

Continental Oil Company in association with Shell Oil struck oil in the Kanem area north of Lake Chad in 1978, and wells briefly produced 1,500 barrels a day (about 80% of national consumption) before fighting disrupted the operation in 1980. An Exxon-led consortium drilled eight wells in the south during 1985–86. In 1988 interest in the region renewed and in November 1996 Exxon and the government of Chad signed an agreement outlining the development of oil reserves in the Doba Basin. In July 2003 the first oil began to be pumped following the completion of the Chad-Cameroon pipeline, which was built with the aid of a $93 million loan from the World Bank. A second project to develop oil fields in the Sedigi Basin with reserves put at 150 million barrels has been delayed. The problem arose after it was found that the pipeline to carry oil from the Sedigi Basin to a refinery and power plant in the capital of N'Djamena was of such poor quality that it could not be used.

The World Bank reported in 2008 that Chad produced 100 million kWh of electricity and consumed 96.8 million kWh, or 9kWh per capita. Only 2% of households in Chad are supplied with electricity.

28 INDUSTRY

Because it lacks power and adequate transportation, Chad is industrially one of the least developed countries in Africa. Cotton processing is the largest activity. Cottonseed oil is processed at Sarh and Moundou. Coton Tchad, the state-owned company that produces and exports cotton, is the country's main manufacturing concern.

Other enterprises include several modern slaughterhouses, a flour mill complex, a sugar refinery, and textile plants. There are also rice and peanut oil mills, a brewery, a soft drink plant, a soap factory, and a cigarette factory. Factories at N'Djamena also produce bicycles and mopeds, radios, and perfume.

29 SCIENCE AND TECHNOLOGY

N'Djamena has an institute for cotton research founded in 1939. The University of N'Djamena, founded in 1971, has faculties of sciences and of medicine and health. In 1987–97 science and engineering students accounted for 14% of college and university enrollments. There is a national telecommunications school in Sarh. Most research in Chad is dependent on foreign scientists and technicians; however, many foreign personnel were evacuated during the fighting of the early 1980s. Ostensibly, this is the reason the World Bank reported in 2009 there were no patent applications in science and technology in Chad.

30 DOMESTIC TRADE

More than 80% of the population is employed in agriculture either in subsistence farming, herding or fishing. Most local produce is sold directly to consumers or to intermediaries and barter is common. Company agents and intermediaries buy export crops

Principal Trading Partners – Chad (2010)

(In millions of US dollars)

Country	Total	Exports	Imports	Balance
World	5,900.0	3,400.0	2,500.0	900.0
United States	2,015.2	1,918.1	97.1	1,821.0
China	804.1	450.7	353.3	97.4
France	215.9	43.4	172.5	-129.2
Netherlands	152.9	123.8	29.1	94.6
Cameroon	146.7	0.2	146.5	-146.3
Germany	112.6	84.8	27.8	57.1
Belgium	42.7	0.0	42.7	-42.7
Sa'udi Arabia	38.0	0.0	38.0	-38.0
Italy	31.3	0.1	31.2	-31.2
Senegal	29.3	...	29.3	-29.3

(…) data not available or not significant.

(n.s.) not specified.

SOURCE: *2011 Direction of Trade Statistics Yearbook*, New York: United Nations, 2011.

at local markets or directly from the producers for sale to large companies. Distribution is largely unstructured, except for a few international and local companies. Most sell through retail points. A large portion of produce is transported by animals and carts, but trucks operate as well.

The country's domestic economy continues to rely heavily on foreign investment from the EU for both private and public sector concerns.

Business hours are 7:30 a.m. to 3:30 p.m. Monday through Thursday, and 7:30 a.m. to 1 p.m. on Friday. Commercial hours are generally from 7:30 a.m. to 12:30 p.m. and 4 to 8 p.m. Offices are closed Friday afternoons during Muslim prayer time and on Sundays.

31 FOREIGN TRADE

Chad imported $2.631 billion worth of goods in 2008 and exported $3.036 billion worth of goods and services. Major import partners are China 16.8%, France 16%, Cameroon 11.5%, the United States 6.9%, Italy 5.9%, and Ukraine 4.8%. Its major export partners are the United States and France, 89% and 4.7% respectively.

Cotton is Chad's primary export, making the economy's trade balance vulnerable to fluctuations in world cotton prices.

32 BALANCE OF PAYMENTS

Normally Chad has a deficit in trade and services that is offset or nearly offset by foreign assistance, largely from France. The country has a deficit of 11.6% of GDP.

33 BANKING AND SECURITIES

The Bank of the Central African States (Banque des États de l'Afrique Central—BEAC), is a joint bank that includes Cameroon, the Central African Republic, Congo, Equatorial Guinea, and Gabon. The adoption of the BEAC as its central bank was designed to strengthen the monetary solidarity and sovereignty of Chad and other member African nations, which would now control part of their foreign exchange and monetary policies. How-

ever, France continues to guarantee the convertibility of the Central African Franc (CFA franc). There are no securities exchanges in Chad.

34 INSURANCE

There are three local companies and about a dozen French companies providing insurance in Chad. The domestic insurance companies include Societe Mutuelle d'Assurances des Cadres (SMAC), Faugere and Jutheau (les Assureurs Conseils Tchadiens), and Star Nationale.

35 PUBLIC FINANCE

As of 2010 the budget of Chad included $1.972 billion in public revenue and $2.859 billion in public expenditures. Public debt was 26.5% of GDP with $1.743 billion of the debt held by foreign entities.

Customs duties are the principal revenue source. Privatization of government-owned enterprises continues under International Monetary Fund (IMF) restructuring plans.

36 TAXATION

A graduated income tax is imposed on civil servants and others who are paid fixed salaries or who have sufficient income. A head tax is imposed on all other persons, the amount varying according to regional levels of prosperity. There is also a domestic turnover tax and a corporate minimum tax. Further revenue is derived from business and professional licensing, from taxes on business transactions, real property, and profits, and from mining royalties.

37 CUSTOMS AND DUTIES

Customs duties, which are ad valorem, range from 5% on essential items to 30% for less essential products, in addition to an 18% value-added tax (VAT) applicable to all but the most basic goods. There is an extra tax on luxury products of 20% and automobiles have an excise tax of 51%. There are no quotas, and import licenses are no longer required. Prohibited imports include live animals, arms and munitions, pornography, narcotics, illicit drugs, and explosives.

38 FOREIGN INVESTMENT

Under the investment code issued in 1987, the government officially encouraged foreign private investment on two conditions: that the enterprise benefits the local population and that local materials are processed as far as possible. The code offers full foreign ownership to companies in Chad, except in national security or strategic industries. Benefits include preferential export duties and taxes, restrictions on the import of similar competitive products, preference in financial assistance from the Development Bank of Chad, and possible exemption from the sales tax and other fees and taxes for 15 years.

Foreign Direct Investment (FDI) in Chad had a net flow of $461.8 million according to World Bank figures published in 2009. FDI represents 6.75% of GDP. Political turmoil compounded by Chad's environmental difficulties has delayed significant foreign investments.

By far the most ambitious and innovative foreign investment project underway is the $3.7 billion Chad-Cameroon Petroleum Development and Pipeline Project, which entails drilling about

300 oil wells in Chad's Doha fields ($1.7 billion) and constructing a $2.2 billion 1,070 km (670 mi) pipeline to carry the oil across Cameroon and out into the Atlantic to a floating storage and loading facility for shipment to Europe and the United States.

The Chad-Cameroon pipeline is the largest energy infrastructure project in Africa and has taken decades to bring about. Though the first discovery well in the Doha field was drilled in 1974, it was not until 1994 that Houston-based ExxonMobil determined that at least one billion barrels of oil could be extracted, making investment profitable. Four years later a complex agreement had been reached between the oil companies—ExxonMobil (operator with 40% of private equity), ChevronTexaco (25% of private equity), and Petronas of Malaysia (35% of private equity), with Elf and Shell dropping out in 1999—the World Bank and other international financial institutions, and the Chad government.

The World Bank's contribution amounts to only 2.7% (including loans to Chad and Cameroon to finance their governments' share in the project), but the sign of its support was essential for the participation of the other investors. The pipeline project has World Bank backing on condition that there not be environmental damage and that the revenue be put into social welfare and development projects.

The government of Chad agreed to give up some of its sovereign control by having project management and expenditure overseen by an independent nine-member oversight committee, with four members from outside institutions and five representing Chad's religious, political, and community institutions. Revenues will go first to an escrow account in London, then to two commercial banks in Chad where the oversight committee is to see that 80% goes to priority areas (education, health, housing, and rural infrastructure) and 10% to a savings fund for the future, with the rest distributed according to a formula devised by the committee.

For their part the oil companies have been obliged to make over 60 changes in the proposed pipeline route to accommodate social and environmental concerns and to offer a "Sears catalogue" of items (bicycles, sewing machines, plows, community wells) as compensation to villagers along the route. The Clinton administration put an Export-Import Bank loan guarantee of $158.1 million behind the pipeline and the Bush administration approved Overseas Private Investment Corporation (OPIC) insurance up to $250 million for Houston-based Pride International, which is drilling oil wells for the project. The pipeline began operations in late 2004. Chad was expected to derive about $100 million a year in revenue from the sale of the oil from the three fields being developed, with a total of $2.5 billion over the estimated 28-year life of the project. Even before revenues began to flow, however, President Idriss Déby in early 2003 dismissed the head of the oversight committee because the official opposed the president's plans to use the revenue on such items as prisons and automobiles.

39 ECONOMIC DEVELOPMENT

Foremost among governmental objectives are the expansion and improvement of the transportation and telecommunications network, the expansion and diversification of agriculture, and the at-

tainment of food self-sufficiency. These goals have yet to be met. However, petroleum reserves promise future rewards.

40 SOCIAL DEVELOPMENT

Social services were introduced in Chad very slowly and have been largely disrupted by warfare. Salaried workers are entitled to old age, disability, and survivorship benefits. There are no statutory benefits for sickness, but there is a 50% maternity benefit for employed women. Employed persons are covered by a work injury law that is funded by employer contributions. Family allowances are available for working parents, and there is a birth grant awarded for the first three births of the first marriage.

The position of women in Chad is a subordinate one. While property and inheritance laws do not discriminate against women, tradition and local customs favor men. Women generally receive less education than men and do not have equal job opportunities. Rural women do most of the strenuous agricultural work in the fields, and girls are often married as young as 11 or 12. Female circumcision, also known as female genital mutilation, is widespread. Domestic violence and abuse are common, and women have limited recourse. Child labor continues to be a major problem.

The government's human rights record remains poor. A pattern of arbitrary violence continues, including arbitrary arrest and detention, torture, beatings, and other abuse. Prison conditions are life-threatening. The government continues to hold political prisoners and restricts freedom of speech and religion.

At the end of a three-day regional conference in Chad addressing issues concerning the rights and protection of children in areas of armed conflict, representatives from Chad, the Central African Republic, Sudan, Nigeria, Niger, and Cameroon signed the N'Djamena Declaration, which essentially calls for the end of the recruitment and use of children as soldiers. Signed on 10 June 2010 the binding document outlines the countries' commitments to align their policies with international standards, including those included in the Optional Protocol on the Involvement of Children in Armed Conflict, which is part of the Convention on the Rights of the Child. The meeting was hosted by the Chadian government and the UN Children's Fund (UNICEF). The recruitment and/or abduction of children to serve in armed conflicts in Africa has been a pressing issue for UNICEF and other international human rights organizations for many years. Along with a promise to halt recruitment efforts for child soldiers, the signatories of the N'Djamena Declaration have pledged to increase educational and employment opportunities for children once they have been released from military services. The signatories also agreed to establish a special committee charged with ensuring the implementation and monitoring of the agreed commitments. At the time of signing the declaration, the countries of Chad and Sudan had already signed and ratified the Optional Protocol.

41 HEALTH

As of 2011 according to the CIA life expectancy in Chad was 49 years. The total expenditure on healthcare in the country is 6.4% of its GDP, amounting to $42 per person. There are zero physicians, three nurses and midwives, and four hospital beds per 10,000 inhabitants. The fertility rate is 6.1 while the infant mortality rate is 124 per 1,000 live births. In 2008 the maternal mortality rate according to the World Bank was 1,200 per 100,000 births. It was estimated that 23% of children were vaccinated against measles. The CIA calculated HIV/AIDS prevalence to be about 3.4% in 2009.

All medicine, antibiotic, and vaccine imports must be authorized by the Ministry of Health. The most common diseases are schistosomiasis, leprosy, malaria, spinal meningitis, tuberculosis, and yaws, as well as malnutrition. An estimated 27% of the population have access to safe drinking water and 29% have adequate sanitation.

In Chad 60% of the women underwent female genital mutilation.

⁴²HOUSING

Forty thousand buildings and homes were destroyed during the civil war. According to the latest available figures, the total housing stock numbered 700,000 with 7.2 people per dwelling. In 2000 about 27% of the population had access to improved water systems and only 29% had access to improved sanitation systems.

⁴³EDUCATION

Sixty percent of age-eligible children in Chad were enrolled in primary school according to 2009 World Bank estimates. Secondary enrollment for age-eligible children stood at 9%. Tertiary enrollment was estimated at 2%. Of those enrolled in tertiary education, there were 100 male students for every 15 female students.

Overall, the CIA estimated that Chad had a literacy rate of 25.7%. Public expenditure on education represented 3.2% of GDP.

The educational system is patterned on France's and the primary language of instruction is French. Arabic is used in some schools. Private schools of an exclusively religious character (such as the catechism classes of Christian missions and the Muslim schools) receive no assistance from public funds, but the schools that conform to the officially-prescribed educational programs are aided by government grants. Education is theoretically compulsory between ages 6 and 12. Primary education lasts for six years followed by either general secondary education, which lasts for another seven years, or technical and vocational secondary education, which lasts for six. The academic year runs from October to June.

The University of N'Djamena is the only university in the country. The university has four faculties—exact and applied sciences; law, economics, and business administration; letters, languages, and human sciences; and medicine.

⁴⁴LIBRARIES AND MUSEUMS

Many of the libraries in Chad are the small private collections of research institutes in N'Djamena. The public library system includes a network of about 100 reading rooms. Among the largest is the Chadian National Institute for the Humane Sciences with 3,200 volumes, and the Educational Documentation Center with 3,300. Other notable libraries include the University of N'Djamena with about 12,000 volumes, the French Cultural Center in N'Djamena with 12,000 volumes, and the United States Information Agency, also in N'Djamena, with 3,000 volumes.

The National Museum in N'Djamena was founded in 1962 and has an excellent collection on the natural history, archaeology, and ethnography of Chad. The Museum of Abéché, which was founded in 1962 and formally opened in 1984, features an ethnographical collection. Fort-Lamy houses the country's premiere historical and public affairs museum with exhibits chronicling its fight for independence.

⁴⁵MEDIA

As of 2009 there were 13,000 landlines in Chad. In addition to the landlines, mobile phone subscriptions averaged 24 per 100 people. There were two FM radio stations, four AM radio stations, and five shortwave radio stations. Internet users numbered 2 per 100 citizens. Chad had five Internet hosts.

Postal and telephone service are under the direction of the Minister of Posts and Telecommunications. There are direct telephone connections between N'Djamena and Paris and several African capitals.

In 2009 Chad was selected as one of three countries to participate in the initial phase of the World Bank Group-sponsored Central African Backbone Program (CAB Program), which is designed to develop a high-speed telecommunications infrastructure in the region of central Africa. A 2009 study indicated that residents in central Africa had the lowest quality and highest cost Internet and telephone services in all of Africa. The initial phase investment of $26.2 million will be used for equipment and installation in restructuring the telecommunications infrastructure, and also to fund programs necessary to implement the laws and regulations that govern the information and communications technologies (ICT) sector. The initial three-country project will serve as a model for expansion to eight additional countries, with a total estimated project cost of $215 million from 2009 to 2019. The CAB Program, which is cosponsored by the African Development Bank, will also seek private sector investors for an additional $98 million in funds.

The Chad Press Agency publishes the daily news bulletin *Info-Tchad*. Other publications include the weekly *N'Djamena Hehdo* and the monthly *Tchad Et Culture*.

The Constitution and Transitional Charter ensure freedom of speech and the press, and the government is said to respect these rights. The Higher Council on Communications (mandated by the CNS) promotes free access to the media.

⁴⁶ORGANIZATIONS

The Chamber of Commerce, Agriculture, and Industry at N'Djamena has branches at Sarh, Moundou, Bol, and Abéché. In rural areas cooperatives promote the production and marketing of agricultural products. Fishermen and artisans also maintain cooperatives. Self-help tribal societies have grown rapidly, particularly in the larger towns, where members of ethnic groups act together to assist newcomers and to maintain links with those remaining in traditional areas. The Student Association of the University of Chad (AEUT) is one of the largest student organizations affiliated with the National Union of Chadian Students and Pupils (UGEST). Church youth organizations are active as are chapters of scouting and Girl Guide organizations. Sports organizations are active as well, including chapters of the Special Olympics.

The three primary human rights groups within the country are the Chadian Association for the Promotion of Human Rights, The Association for the Promotion of Fundamental Liberties in Chad, and the Chadian Human Rights League. There are national chapters of the Red Cross Society, Caritas, and UNICEF.

⁴⁷TOURISM, TRAVEL, AND RECREATION

Chad, a developing country, has gone through years of war and famine leaving its tourism industry very limited. Most visitors are attracted to the Zakouma National Park. The *Tourism Factbook*, published by the UN World Tourism Organization in 2011, reported 31,000 incoming tourists. Of these incoming tourists there were 16,000 from Europe. There were 1,434 hotel beds available in Chad. The estimated daily cost to visit N'Djamena, the capital, was $418. The cost of visiting other cities averaged $72.

Visitors must have valid passports and visas. Visitors must check in with the National Police within 72 hours of arrival and obtain a registration stamp. Vaccination for yellow fever is recommended.

⁴⁸FAMOUS PERSONS

Ngarta Tombalbaye (1918–75) was the first president of the independent Republic of Chad. Gen. Félix Malloum (b. 1932) became chief of state after the 1975 coup, but was ousted in 1979. Goukouni Oueddei (b. 1944) served (1979–82) as president and subsequently led a Libyan-backed rival government in northern Chad. Hissène Habré (b. 1942), a Muslim military leader, seized the capital in 1982 and became president. Idriss Déby (b. 1952) seized power in 1990 after a French-supported invasion from Sudan.

⁴⁹DEPENDENCIES

Chad has no territories or colonies.

⁵⁰BIBLIOGRAPHY

Azevedo, Mario Joaquim. *Roots of Violence: A History of War in Chad*. Australia: Gordon and Breach, 2004.

Chad Investment and Business Guide: Strategic and Practical Information. Washington, DC: International Business Publications USA, 2012.

Mays, Terry M. *Africa's First Peacekeeping Operation: The Oau in Chad, 1981-1982*. Westport, CT: Praeger, 2002.

Zeilig, Leo, and David Seddon. *A Political and Economic Dictionary of Africa*. Philadelphia: Routledge/Taylor and Francis, 2005.

COMOROS

Union of the Comoros
Udzima wa Komori;
Jumhuriyat al Qamar al Muttahidah

CAPITAL: Moroni

FLAG: Four equal horizontal bands of yellow (top), white, red, and blue with a green isosceles triangle based on the hoist; centered within the triangle is a white crescent with the convex side facing the hoist and four white, five-pointed stars placed vertically in a line between the points of the crescent.

ANTHEM: *Comoros Udzima wa ya Masiwa (The Union of the Great Islands).*

MONETARY UNIT: The Comorian franc (KMF) is the equivalent of the Communauté Financière Africaine franc (XOF), which has been pegged to the euro since January 1999 at a rate of 655.957 CFA francs to 1 euro. The Comorian franc is issued in notes of 500, 1,000, and 5,000 KMF 1 = US$0.00283 (or US$1 = KMF 346.413) as of 2011.

WEIGHTS AND MEASURES: The metric system is used.

HOLIDAYS: New Year's Day, 1 January; Second Coup d'état, 13 May; Independence Day, 6 July; Admission to UN, 12 November; Christmas Day, 25 December. The principal Muslim holidays are observed.

TIME: 3 p.m. = noon GMT.

¹LOCATION, SIZE, AND EXTENT

The Comoros are located at the northern entrance of the Mozambique Channel, between the eastern shore of the African continent and the island of Madagascar, which lies about 480 km (300 mi) to the SE. Comparatively, the area occupied by the Comoros Islands is slightly more than 12 times the size of Washington, DC. The islands have a combined area of 2,170 sq km (838 sq mi), of which Grand Comore (N'gazidja), the largest and northernmost island, comprises 1,148 sq km (443 sq mi); Mohéli (Mwali), lying to the S of Grand Comore, 290 sq km (112 sq mi); and Anjouan (Nzwani) to the E of Mohéli, 424 sq km (164 sq mi). There are also several small islands. The Comoros extend about 180 km (110 mi) ESE–WNW and 100 km (62 mi) NNE–SSW, with a total coastline of 340 km (211 mi). Mayotte, the fourth major island in the Comoros Archipelago, covering an area of 374 sq km (144 sq mi), is claimed by the Comoros, but remains under French territorial administration. The capital city Moroni, is located at the western edge of the island of Grand Comore.

²TOPOGRAPHY

The islands are volcanic in origin and their highest peak, Mt. Kartala at 2,360 m (7,743 ft), is an active volcano located near the southern tip of the island of Grand Comore. In the center of Grand Comore lies a desert lava field. To the north, a number of volcanic peaks rise from a plateau nearly 600 m (2,000 ft) in altitude. The island of Anjouan, to the southeast, has steep hills reaching heights of nearly 1,500 m (5,000 ft) in a central volcanic massif. Mohéli, to the west of Anjouan, has wide and fertile valleys, with a ridge in the center that reaches about 580 m (1,900 ft) above

sea level, and a thick forest cover. The lowest point is at sea level (Indian Ocean).

³CLIMATE

The climate in Comoros is humid and tropical, with coastal temperatures averaging about 28°C (82°F) in March and 23°C (73°F) in August. The monsoon season lasts from December to April. Rainfall in January averages 42 cm (16.5 in), while rainfall in October, the driest month, averages 8.5 cm (3.3 in). Cyclones and tidal waves are frequent in the summer.

⁴FLORA AND FAUNA

The World Resources Institute estimates that there are 721 plant species in Comoros. The rich volcanic soils on the islands foster profuse vegetation. Beyond the coastal zones, where mangroves predominate, there are coconut palms, mangoes, and bananas. Above them is a forest zone, with many varieties of tropical hardwoods. Broom, lichens, and heather grow on the highest peaks. The animal life is similar to that found on Madagascar. Comorian waters harbor the coelacanth, a rare primitive fish once thought to have been extinct for 70 million years. Fossil remains of the coelacanth dating back 400 million years have been found. Comoros is home to 15 species of mammals, 138 species of birds, and 28 reptile species. This calculation reflects the total number of distinct species residing in the country, not the number of endemic species.

⁵ENVIRONMENT

The World Resources Institute reported that Comoros had designated 721,000 hectares (1.78 million acres) of land for protection as of 2006. Water resources totaled 1.2 cu km (0.288 cu mi) while water usage was 0.01 cu km (0.002 cu mi) per year. Domestic water usage accounted for 48% of total usage, industrial for 5%, and agricultural for 47%. Per capita water usage totaled 13 cu m (459 cu ft) per year.

The UN reported in 2008 that carbon dioxide emissions in Comoros totaled 121 kilotons.

Although Mohéli has large tracts of fertile land not yet cultivated, parts of Anjouan are so densely populated that farmers have been forced to extend cultivation to the higher slopes, leading to deforestation and soil erosion, especially when crops are cultivated on slopes without adequate terracing. Population growth has also increased the demand for firewood, threatening the remaining forest areas. Soil erosion is aggravated by lack of terracing.

According to a 2011 report issued by the International Union for Conservation of Nature and Natural Resources (IUCN), the number of threatened species included 5 types of mammals, 9 species of birds, 3 types of reptiles, 6 species of fish, 63 species of other invertebrates, and 5 species of plants. Endangered species in the Comoros include the Anjouan sparrow hawk and Anjouan scops owl.

6 POPULATION

The US Central Intelligence Agency (CIA) estimated the population of Comoros in 2011 to be approximately 794,683, which placed it 158th in population among the 196 nations of the world. In 2011 approximately 3.1% of the population was over 65 years of age, with another 41.6% under 15 years of age. The median age in Comoros was 19 years. There were 0.98 males for every female in the country. The population's annual rate of change was 2.696%. The projected population for the year 2025 was 910,000. Population density in Comoros was calculated at 356 people per sq km (922 people per sq mi).

The UN estimated that 28% of the population lived in urban areas, and that urban populations had an annual rate of change of 2.8%. The largest urban area was Moroni, with a population of 49,000.

7 MIGRATION

Estimates of Comoros's net migration rate, carried out by the CIA in 2011, amounted to zero. The total number of emigrants living abroad was 38,600, and the total number of immigrants living in Comoros was 13,500. About 40,000 Comorians were living in France and 25,000 in Madagascar. About 16,000 were expelled from Madagascar in 1977–78, following a massacre there of Comorians in December 1976.

8 ETHNIC GROUPS

The islands' indigenous population consists almost entirely of persons of mixed African, Malagasy, Malay, and Arab descent. Ethnic groups include the Antalote, Cafre, Makoa, Oimatsaha, and Sakalava. Small numbers of Indians, Malagasy, and Europeans play an important part in the economy.

9 LANGUAGES

French and Arabic are the official languages. The main spoken language, Shaafi Islam (Shikomoro or Comoran), is akin to Swahili but has elements borrowed from Arabic. Other languages spoken include French, Malagasy, Swahili, Arabic, and Makua (an African language).

10 RELIGIONS

Islam is followed by about 99% of Comorians, almost all of whom are Sunni Muslims. Small groups of foreigners are Hindus or Christians. Following a 1999 military coup the May 2000 constitution did not allow for freedom of religion. The December 2001 constitution provides for freedom of religion, but a 2009 constitutional referendum made Islam the state religion. Proselytizing for any religion other than Islam is prohibited and converts from Islam may be prosecuted, though few cases have been enforced. The Grand Mufti, who is nominated by the president to serve in the Ministry of Islamic Affairs, serves as the government counsel on Islamic faith and law. The Birth of the Prophet Muhammad, Eid al-Fitr, Eid al-Kabir, and the Islamic New Year are observed as national holidays.

11 TRANSPORTATION

The CIA reports that Comoros has a total of 880 km (547 mi) of roads, of which 673 km (418 mi) are paved. There are four airports.

Each island has a ringed road, and there were some interior roads. There is an international airport at Hahaia, on Grand Comore; other islands have smaller airfields. All airports had paved runways. Air Comores (51% owned by Air France) provides regular inter-island flights. Air France and Air Madagascar provide service to Madagascar; Air Mauritius provides service to Mauritius; and South African Airways makes a weekly stop. There is a year-round port at Dzaoudzi, off the island of Mayotte. Expansion of the port of Mutsamudu to allow direct access to Anjouan was completed in 1985.

12 HISTORY

The Comoros are an archipelago of three small Indian Ocean islands that lie between East Africa and the northwestern coast of Madagascar. The three islands are called Grand Comore, Anjouan, and Mohéli. A fourth island, Mayotte, is claimed by Comoros but administered by France. In all likelihood they were visited in antiquity by Phoenician sailors. The first settlers were probably Melanesian and Polynesian peoples, who came to the Comoros by the 6th century AD; later immigrants arrived from East Africa, Arab lands, Indonesia, Persia, and Madagascar. The Portuguese discovered the islands in about 1503, and Frenchmen first landed in 1517. The Englishman James Lancaster visited the islands toward the end of the 16th century; at that time, and for many years afterward, Arab influence predominated over that of Europeans. Malagasy invasions also took place in the 16th century. In 1843 a Malagasy who ruled over Mayotte ceded the island to France, and in 1865 a Malagasy ruler of Mohéli signed a friendship treaty with France. A French protectorate was placed over Anjouan, Grand Comore, and Mohéli in 1886, and in 1908 the islands were joined administratively with French-ruled Madagascar. In World War II the islands were occupied by a British force and turned over to the Free French. The Comoros were granted administrative autonomy within the Republic of France on 9 May 1946, acquiring overseas territorial status, and on 22 December 1961 achieved internal autonomy under special statute. This status was amended on 3 January 1968 to give the territory greater internal autonomy.

On 11 December 1958, the territorial assembly voted to remain in the republic, but the cause of independence, championed by the Comoro National Liberation Movement based in Tanzania, was eventually embraced by the ruling coalition on the islands. An agreement for independence within five years was signed in Paris on 15 June 1973, and in a referendum held on 22 December 1974, a large majority on all islands except Mayotte voted in favor of independence. The vote was ratified by the French parliament, which decided that each island should vote separately on a new constitution. On 6 July 1975, nevertheless, the Comoros legislature unilaterally declared independence for all the islands, including Mayotte. The French government, rejecting the Comorian claim to Mayotte, ordered a separate referendum for the island. As preparations were made for the 1976 referendum, relations between France and the Comoros deteriorated. The Comorian government nationalized all French administrative property and expelled French officials. With strained French-Comorian relations as the backdrop, Mayotte voted on 7 February 1976 to remain part of France. The UN General Assembly, however, backed the Comorian claim to Mayotte in 1976 and 1979 resolutions.

Considerable domestic turmoil accompanied the birth of the new nation. The first Comorian government took power on 6 July 1975 and was led by Ahmed 'Abdallah. It unilaterally declared independence from France and was overthrown within a month on 3 August 1975 with the aid of foreign white mercenaries. A National Executive Council led by Prince Said Mohammed Jaffar was created. Jaffar was the leader of a group that favored a more conciliatory policy toward Mayotte and France. In January 1976 he was replaced by 'Ali Soilih who led a military coup that toppled Jaffar a year earlier. In 1977 Soilih's government changed the French names of the four islands (Grand Comore, Mohéli, Mayotte, and Anjouan) to N'gazidja, Mwali, Mahore, and Nzwani. Four unsuccessful coup attempts were launched during Soilih's rule. However, on 13 May 1978 Soilih was overthrown and killed by mercenaries led by Bob Denard, whose previous exploits in then Zaire (now the Democratic Republic of the Congo) and elsewhere made him infamous throughout Africa. Denard reinstalled the nation's first president, Ahmad 'Abdallah, who had been living in exile in Paris. Denard remained the true power behind 'Abdallah. Their government was close to right-wing elements in France and to South Africa, where the Comoros served as a conduit for supplies to the Renamo rebels in Mozambique. Soon after the coup, France agreed to restore economic and military aid, which had been suspended during the Soilih regime. Most African countries were, however, unhappy with the role of mercenaries in toppling the Soilih government and the Comoros were expelled from the Organization of African Unity (OAU).

In September 1978 Denard and his mercenaries were asked to leave the Comoros due to the international stigma their presence caused the island nation. This was a façade, as Denard remained the true power on the islands; however, the ruse did succeed in getting the Comoros back into the OAU. A new constitution was approved on 1 October 1978 by 99.31% of the voters. The new constitution created a federal Islamic republic in which each island was granted increased autonomy. On 22 October 'Abdallah, the only candidate, was elected president with a reported 99.94%

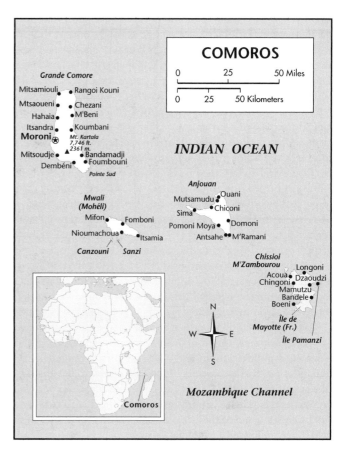

LOCATION: 43°1′ N to 44°32′ E; 11°21′ W to 12°25′ S.
TERRITORIAL SEA LIMIT: 12 miles.

of the valid votes. 'Abdallah was reelected unopposed with 99.4% of the vote in September 1984. There were coup attempts in 1985 and 1987. Elections to the national assembly were held in March 1987. By 1989, however, resentment for the overbearing influence of Denard and his men grew. Even 'Abdallah grew disenchanted and, with the backing of France and South Africa, he attempted to dislodge Denard's mercenaries. However, the move was thwarted when on 26 November 1989 a member of the presidential guard assassinated 'Abdallah. The presidential guard included European mercenaries and was under the command of Denard.

Said Mohamed Djohar, head of the Supreme Court, was appointed interim president pending a presidential election. With the help of Paris and Pretoria, on 15 December 1989 he forced Denard to relinquish power in exchange for safe passage to South Africa.

In January 1990 demonstrators protested the postponement of the presidential election that was scheduled for February. A French peacekeeping force enabled the government to lift political restrictions and conduct the presidential election as originally scheduled. The election was held on 18 February, but it was abandoned following allegations of fraud. On 4 March fresh elections were held in which no single candidate for the president received a majority of the votes. In a run-off election held one week later, Djohar won with 55% of the vote to the UNDC's (Union Nationale pour la Democratie aux Comores) Mohammed Taki Abdulkarim's 44%. In March Djohar appointed a government that included two of his opponents in the previous presidential election. Prince Said

Ali Kemal, a lawyer and grandson of the last Sultan of Comoros was one of the former presidential hopefuls who was made part of the coalition government. Djohar's coalition government survived three coup attempts and several ministerial defections. One coup attempt was launched on August 1990, by army rebels with help from European mercenaries. Another coup was attempted a year later and involved the president of the Supreme Court Ibrahim Ahmed Halidi, who announced that he was dismissing President Djohar and assuming the role of president. The bloodless coup received support from opposition parties who saw Djohar as corrupt and viewed the presidency itself as being vested with too much power. The coup was thwarted, however, and Djohar responded by ordering the arrest of several Supreme Court members, including Halidi, and imposing a month-long state of emergency. Djohar pledged to seek constitutional reforms and reshuffled his cabinet, bringing in disgruntled opposition members.

In January 1992, amid continued unrest, a new transitional government of national union was installed, as constitutional reforms were debated and prepared for referendum. A new constitution was voted on in June and was passed overwhelmingly. However, allegations of corruption against Djohar's son-in-law, Mohamed M'Changama, the minister of finance, plagued the regime. Amid heightened political unrest and a deteriorating economic situation, elections for the assembly produced a badly divided polity (the largest party had 7 of the 42 seats) and no consensus with the president on his choice of ministers could be reached. On 18 June 1992, Djohar dissolved the assembly, and legislative elections were held in December 1993 after long delays.

Supporters of Djohar won 24 of the 42 seats in the assembly, but members of the opposition rejected Djohar's appointment of Mohamed Abdou Madi as prime minister and the choice of Djohar's son-in-law as president of the assembly. Demonstrations against Djohar's authoritarian posture became frequent. A public sector strike began in April 1994 and grew quite acrimonious, and lasted until January 1995. Civil order continued to deteriorate as 1995 provincial elections were repeatedly postponed and as government after government collapsed. Djohar, however, remained in power, and his son and son-in-law held various ministerial posts.

By September 1995 conditions had deteriorated badly, and Bob Denard, from exile, staged a coup that resulted in the arrest of President Djohar. Denard appointed a close associate, Capt. Ayouba Combo, as the leader of a provisional government called the Transitional Military Committee. The Transitional Military Committee released political prisoners and in October transferred authority to two civilians, Mohammed Taki and Said Ali Kemal. Although France was no friend of Djohar, it was less enthusiastic about Denard's action and landed 1,000 troops to oust the coup leaders. In presidential elections held on 6 March 1996 and a runoff on 16 March, Mohammed Taki Abdulkarim won with 64% of the vote. Legislative elections on 1 and 8 December of that year resulted in an assembly situated as follows: National Rally for Democracy, 36 seats; National Front for Justice, 3 seats; independents, 4 seats.

In July 1997 security forces killed two people after separatists on Anjouan raised the French flag, blocked roads, and engaged in demonstrations demanding a return of French rule. Unrest quickly spread throughout Anjouan and Mohéli. On 3 August 1997 separatists on the island of Anjouan declared independence from the central government and were soon joined by the island of Mohéli. In early September 1997 President Taki dispatched the army in an unsuccessful attempt to reunify the islands. Hoping to find a peaceful solution to the situation, the OAU intervened in favor of a negotiated settlement. In October, despite the objections of the Taki's government, a referendum was held on Anjouan in which 99% of those voting supported independence. France, for its part, rejected demands by the islands to reestablish its sovereignty.

In November 1998 President Mohammed Taki died shortly after returning from a trip to Turkey and Spain. Interim president Ben Said Massounde took power in Grand Comore. A month later, a reported assassination attempt on Anjouan island leader Foundi Abdullah Ibrahim led to heavy fighting in the island. At least 60 people were reported killed. The assassination attempt and fighting was thought to have been instigated by Chamasse Said Omar, a political opponent of Ibrahim who was upset that the Anjouan leader wanted to negotiate a new relationship with the government of Grand Comore.

On 30 April 1999 interim president Massounde was toppled in a bloodless coup, and was replaced by Col. Azali Assoumani on 6 May 1999. The coup was triggered by unresolved issues in the negotiations with the separatist islands that would have given them greater autonomy within a political union of the three islands. The autonomy proposal, which caused widespread resentment on Grand Comore, erupted in rioting in which residents from the other islands were targeted and blamed for the harsh economic conditions on the main island. As the secession stalemate continued, the government announced on 21 March 2000 that it had foiled the country's 19th coup attempt since independence while Assoumani was in Saudi Arabia. Among the suspected plotters were two sons of the assassinated first president Ahmed 'Abdallah.

In 2001 a new constitution was adopted to accommodate a redefined system of government. Under the new system, each of the major islands elected its own president and parliament. A fourth union parliament and president was elected to consider national interests in foreign affairs and defense, while all other issues were handled by the individual island governments. The union presidency rotated between the three islands. Assoumani resigned his post on 16 January 2002 to run for president in the 14 April 2002 elections. In a poll boycotted by the other two candidates, he was elected with 75% of the vote and was sworn in 26 May 2002. In the interregnum, his prime minister, Jamada Madi Bolero, was appointed interim president and Djaffar Salim the interim deputy prime minister.

Following the election, the confederal arrangement went into effect, and the three islands of Mohéli, Anjouan, and Grand Comore assumed authority over most of their own affairs. President Assoumani's woes continued to mount in 2004 as the three island presidents and their supporters joined forces against the president's Convention pour le renouveau des Comores (CRC) party in the legislative elections. The results of this poll showed that the CRC had only a weak following, winning just 11 of 55 seats in the island parliaments, and 6 of the 18 seats up for reelection in the federal assembly. Col. Assoumani attempted to regain his posture by naming all members of his cabinet from the loyal ranks of his CRC party.

In the 2006 presidential elections, Assoumani was replaced by Ahmed Abdallah Sambi. Moving into 2008 government officials began to consider that the cost of sustaining four separate government administrations was causing a great strain on the nation's economy, consuming about 80% of the impoverished nation's GDP. In a May 2009 referendum Comorans voted for a new constitution advancing a streamlined government, with one rotating presidency, one unicameral assembly, and three governors (one for each island). While over 93% of the voters were in favor of the new structure, opponents claimed it was simply a ploy initiated by the incumbent union president, Sambi, to set himself up for greater power. The vote also allowed a one-year extension to Sambi's term as president, allowing time for the new system to be established.

This term extension was particularly unpopular among opposition leaders from Mohéli, the island next in line for the presidency under the 2001 agreement. As a result, Mohélian leaders began to consider secession, claiming that they would not accept Sambi as president after 26 May 2010, the date that his term was originally scheduled to end.

In elections held 7 November and 26 December 2010 (next to be held in 2014), Ikililou Dhoinine was elected president. Dhoinine obtained 61.1% of the vote compared to Mohamed Said Fazul with 32.7%. Abdou Djabir received 6.2% of the vote.

13 GOVERNMENT

Immediately prior to independence, the Comoros had partial autonomy and were governed by a 31-member Council of Ministers responsible to a Chamber of Deputies. The territory was represented in the French parliament by one senator and by two delegates to the French National Assembly. A high commissioner represented the French president. After independence was declared, the Chamber of Deputies was reconstituted as a national assembly. After the August 1975 coup, assembly was abolished; supreme power was subsequently vested in the National Council of the Institutions, headed by President 'Ali Soilih.

The constitution of 1978, the first for the Comoros, established a federal Islamic republic. Under this document, as amended in 1982, the president was elected to a six-year term, and there was an elected federal assembly of 42 members. Following the secession and subsequent breakup of the republic in 1997, the islands created a union consisting of semiautonomous islands led by their own presidents in addition to the president of the federal government, who retained control over defense, economic policy, and foreign affairs. The three island presidents were also vice presidents of the union. A new constitution was adopted in June 1992, and again in December 2001. It came into full operation following the election of the Assembly of the Union in 2004.

Under this constitution, the federal presidency rotated every four years among the elected presidents from the three main islands in the union. In the May 2009 referendum, Comorans voted for a new constitution that streamlined government allowing for one rotating presidency, one national parliament, and three governors (one for each island). Of the 33-member unicameral assembly, 15 assembly deputies were selected by the individual islands' local assemblies and 18 by universal suffrage. Deputies serve for five years.

14 POLITICAL PARTIES

In February 1982 the Comorian Union for Progress (Union Comorienne pour le Progrès—UCP) was established as the only legal party; in March; UCP members won 37 of 38 seats in the assembly in contested elections that also involved independents. In March 1987 UCP candidates won all 42 seats. Despite earlier assurances of a free ballot, few opposition candidates were allowed to run, and dissidents were subject to intimidation and imprisonment.

The UCP (known as Udzima) had been President Djohar's party until November 1991. But it had no seats in the assembly. On 10 September 1993, it merged with the Union for Democracy and Decentralization (UNDC), the largest party in the assembly with just seven seats. Before the dissolution of the assembly in June 1993, the Islands' Fraternity and Unity Party (CHUMA) had three seats, and the MDP/NGDC had five seats. No other party had more than two seats. Djohar hastily created his own party, the RDR, to contest the December 1993 elections. After 1993, the party distribution in the assembly was RDR and its coalition partners, 24 seats, and the UNDC and its allies, 18 seats.

A coup in September 1995 overthrew the Djohar government. A transitional government was set up after French military intervention removed the coup-plotters, and new elections were held in December 1996, resulting in an assembly situated as follows: National Rally for Development, 36 seats; National Front for Justice, 3 seats; independents, seats 4. In the April 2004 elections, the president's CRC party suffered a major defeat, winning only 6 of 18 seats up for election in the assembly, and just 11 of 55 seats in the island parliaments. There were some 20 parties on the scene including Forces pour l'Action Républicaine (FAR) led by Col. Abdourazak Abdulhamid, and the Forum pour la Redressement National (FRN), an alliance of 12 parties.

In the 2009 legislative elections, members of President Sambi's pro-union coalition won 19 seats in the assembly, followed by members of an autonomous coalition of parties with four seats and one seat going to an independent.

In the presidential elections of December 2010, ruling party candidate Ikililou Dhoinine won the presidency with 61% of the vote. Dhoinine served as vice president under Sambi. He will be the first Comoros president from Mohéli under the new constitution installed in May 2009.

15 LOCAL GOVERNMENT

Under the federal system, each of the main islands had its own president and elected legislature. The governors, formerly elected, were appointed by the president after the constitution was amended in 1982. As of 2011 there were governorships for each of the three islands and four municipalities: Domoni, Fomboni, Moroni, and Mutsamudu.

16 JUDICIAL SYSTEM

The legal system incorporates French and Islamic law in a new consolidated code. Most disputes are settled by village elders or by a court of first instance. The High Council as the Supreme Court (Cour Suprême) resolves constitutional questions, supervises presidential elections, and arbitrates any case in which the government is accused of malpractice. The High Council also reviews decisions of the lower courts, including the superior court of appeals at Moroni. The High Council consists of two members appointed by the president, two members elected by the assembly, and one elected by the council of each island; others are former presidents of the republic. Lower courts of the first instance are located in major towns. Religious courts on the islands apply Muslim law in matters relating to social and personal relationships.

The judiciary is largely independent of the executive and legislative branches. The constitution provides a number of safeguards including equality of all citizens before the law. However, it does not mention right to counsel.

The island of Mayotte has been administered by France since the Comoros unilaterally declared independence in July 1975. The Comoros claims Mayotte and officially represents it in international organizations, including the United Nations. The constitution of Mayotte states that the island is to be ruled by a prefect assisted by a secretary-general and a general council of 19 members.

17 ARMED FORCES

The International Institute for Strategic Studies reported in 2011 that armed forces in Comoros were constituted by small standing armies on each island. Defense spending totaled $22.4 million and accounted for 2.8% of gross domestic product (GDP).

18 INTERNATIONAL COOPERATION

On 12 November 1975 the Comoros became a member of the United Nations. The nation participates in the ECA, FAO, World Bank, IDA, IFAD, ILO, IMF, ITU, UNESCO, UNIDO, UPU, WHO, and WMO. It is also part of the African Development Bank, the ACP Group, G-77, the Arab League, the Organization of the Islamic Conference (OIC), and the Arab Monetary Fund. Comoros is a member of the Indian Ocean Commission, the Alliance of Small Island States (AOSIS), and COMESA. The nation is part of the Franc Zone. Comoros is part of the Nonaligned Movement. In environmental cooperation, Comoros is part of the Basel Convention, the Convention on Biological Diversity, Ramsar, CITES, the Montréal Protocol, MARPOL, and the UN Conventions on the Law of the Sea, Climate Change and Desertification.

19 ECONOMY

In 2010 GDP purchasing power parity (PPP) was $800 million. The GDP rate of change in Comoros was 2.1%. Inflation stood at 3% and unemployment was reported at 20%.

Comoros is an extremely poor nation, largely due to the country's dearth of natural resources and poor transportation system. Around 80% of the country's workforce is involved in agriculture, fishing, hunting, and forestry, all of which account for about 40% of the GDP. Still, Comoros relies heavily on supplemental food imports. Cassava, sweet potatoes, rice, and bananas are the staple crops along with yams, coconuts, and maize. Meat, rice, and vegetables are leading imports. Comoros is the world's second-largest producer of vanilla, with one third of exports going to France, and the world's leading producer of ylang-ylang, a perfume oil. Cloves and copra are also exported. Land access is a problem, as is overpopulation. The fishing industry has potential but is still largely undeveloped.

In 2010 services accounted for about 56% of the GDP and industry for about 4%. Tourism increased considerably in the 1990s

as a result of promotion by South African interests, but subsequent political upheaval discouraged potential visitors.

The unemployment rate in the country was around 20% and more than half of the population lived below the poverty line. To supplement incomes at home, about 150,000 Comorians living and working abroad sent money back to the islands. In cooperation with donors and international NGOs, Comoros was trying to foster better education for its workforce and was working to privatize many state-owned enterprises.

In April 2011 the International Monetary Fund predicted that Comoros's economic growth would rise by at least 2.5% by year-end, a 0.4 % increase from 2010. Additionally, growth was predicted to jump to 4% by 2013. Remittances and expansion in tourism and transport were expected to be the primary engines for growth, but fishing and agriculture sectors were also reported to be improving.

20 INCOME

The CIA estimated that in 2010 the GDP of Comoros was $800 million. The CIA defines GDP as the value of all final goods and services produced within a nation in a given year and computed on the basis of purchasing power parity (PPP) rather than value as measured on the basis of the rate of the exchange based on current dollars. The per capita GDP was estimated at $1,000. The annual growth rate of GDP was 2.1%. The average inflation rate was 3%. It was estimated that agriculture accounted for 40% of GDP, industry 4%, and services 56%.

According to the World Bank, remittances from citizens living abroad totaled $11.3 million or about $14 per capita and accounted for approximately 1.4% of GDP.

The World Bank reported that in 2009, household consumption in Comoros totaled $567 million or about $713 per capita, measured in current US dollars rather than PPP.

As of 2011 the World Bank reported that actual individual consumption in Comoros was 92.4% of GDP and accounted for less than 0.01% of world consumption. By comparison, the United States accounted for 25.44% of world individual consumption. The World Bank also estimated that 65.2% of Comoros's GDP was spent on food and beverages, 14% on housing and household furnishings, 5.1% on clothes, 1.4% on health, 0.8% on transportation, 1.0% on communications, 0.4% on recreation, and 0.5% on miscellaneous goods and services and purchases from abroad.

It was estimated that in 2002 about 60% of the population subsisted on an income below the poverty line established by Comoros's government.

21 LABOR

As of 2007 Comoros had a total labor force of 268,500 people. Within that labor force, CIA estimates from 1996 noted that 80% of the labor force was employed in agriculture, 10% in industry, and 10% in the service sector. Unemployment has been estimated at 20%.

The agriculture sector is largely subsistence. Fishing and local commerce are also small scale. To supplement incomes, many Comorians work abroad. In cooperation with international economic groups, Comoros is trying to educate its workforce and privatize state-owned enterprises.

The constitution provides the right for workers to create and join unions and strike. However, this provision affects only a small percentage of the population. The wage-earning labor force consists of fewer than 7,000 individuals, of which about 5,000 were government employees. The minimum age for employment is 15 years, but children generally work in subsistence farming and fishing, or as domestic servants. The government has few resources to enforce the minimum age restriction and there is no minimum wage. There are no occupational health and safety standards for the country's tiny manufacturing base. A 37.5-hour workweek is specified by law, with one day off every week and one month paid vacation annually.

22 AGRICULTURE

Roughly 59% of the total land was under cultivation. The country's major crops included vanilla, cloves, ylang-ylang (perfume essence), copra, coconuts, bananas, and cassava (tapioca). Other crops included sugarcane, sisal, peppers, spices, coffee, and various perfume plants such as abelmosk, lemon grass, jasmine, and citronella. The chief export crops were vanilla, cloves, ylang-ylang, and copra.

In 2009 cereal production amounted to 25,588 tons, fruit production 57,729 tons, and vegetable production 5,962 tons. Comoros is the world's largest producer of ylang-ylang, which is used in making perfumes and aromatherapy products. Comoros also is the second-largest producer of vanilla.

Comoros relies heavily on supplemental food imports, especially rice. Over half of all foodstuffs are imported, and about 50% of the government's annual budget is spent on importing food. Agricultural productivity is extremely low, and cultivation methods are rudimentary. Fertilizer is seldom used by smallholders. About 20% of the cultivated land belongs to company estates; 20% to indigenous landowners who live in towns and pay laborers to cultivate their holdings; and 60% to village reserves allotted according to customary law.

23 ANIMAL HUSBANDRY

The UN Food and Agriculture Organization (FAO) reported that Comoros dedicated 15,000 hectares (37,066 acres) to permanent pasture or meadow in 2009. Small amounts of livestock are raised. In 2004 there were an estimated 115,000 goats, 45,000 head of cattle, 21,000 sheep, and 5,000 asses. An estimated 1,100 tons of beef and 1,000 tons of other meat were produced in 2004, along with 4,550 tons of milk and 776 tons of eggs.

24 FISHING

In 2008 the annual capture totaled 16,000 tons according to the UN FAO.

25 FORESTRY

Approximately 2% of Comoros is covered by forest. The value of all forest products, including roundwood, is unknown. Forested areas amounted to about 8,000 hectares (20,000 acres) in 2000. Numerous fruit trees and tropical hardwoods are found. Some timber is produced, notably on the island of Grand Comore, which has about half of the country's remaining forests.

Roundwood production in 2003 amounted to 9,000 cu m (300,000 cu ft). Forest destruction is occurring at a rate of about 50 hectares per year. Much of the degradation is caused by population pressure and putting more land under cultivation.

26 MINING

As of 2011 there were no commercially exploitable mineral resources in the Comoros. Small quantities of clay, sand, gravel, and crushed stone were produced for domestic consumption, and the former French colony was dependent on imports to meet all its energy and cement needs.

Promotion of a new construction technique using lava and volcanic ash was expected to reduce cement imports and coral mining. In 2007 imports of cement totaled 41,508 tons, up from 29,985 tons in 2002. Political instability in recent years has continued to hurt the economy, and the outlook on minerals output was not expected to change significantly.

27 ENERGY AND POWER

The World Bank reported in 2008 that Comoros produced 52 million kWh of electricity and consumed 25.4 million kWh, or 32 kWh per capita.

In 2004 Comoros had no known reserves or production of petroleum, and imported whatever it consumed. Petroleum imports and consumption for that year stood at 1,000 barrels per day. With no proven coal reserves, there was no consumption or output of coal.

Electricity was the main source of power. As of January 2003 Comoros had an electrical generation capacity of 0.005 GW. In 2003 the consumption and generation of electricity each totaled 0.02 billion kWh. Of the power produced in 2002, 0.004 million kW was from thermal sources and 20% came from hydroelectric sources.

28 INDUSTRY

There are various small-scale industries, mostly for processing the islands' agricultural products. Aside from perfume distilleries (perfume is one of the country's main exports), the Comoros has sawmills, a soap factory, a printing plant, a small plastics factory, a soft-drink plant, and metalworking shops. Industry accounted for a mere 4% of GDP in 2010.

29 SCIENCE AND TECHNOLOGY

The World Bank reported in 2009 that there were no patent applications in science and technology in Comoros. There were no research institutes or institutions of higher learning in the Comoros.

30 DOMESTIC TRADE

Nearly 80% of the population was employed in agriculture, primarily subsistence farming. However, most of the farmland is owned by foreign investors and the majority of the nation's food products are imported. An underdeveloped transportation system limits domestic trade. A small industrial sector was focused on processing ylang-ylang and vanilla, which are produced primarily for export. The government was attempting to privatize commercial and industrial enterprises. Business hours were 7:30 a.m. to 2:30 p.m. Monday–Thursday, 7:30 to 11:30 a.m. Friday, and 7:30 a.m. to noon on Saturday.

31 FOREIGN TRADE

Comoros imported $143 million worth of goods and services in 2008, while exporting $32 million worth of goods and services. Major import partners in 2009 were France, 16.8%; Pakistan, 14.3%; United Arab Emirates, 8.5%; China, 6.8%; India, 5.6%; and Kenya, 4.9%. Major export partners were Turkey, 27.3%; France, 22.2%; Singapore, 18.9%; Italy, 6.6%; and Saudi Arabia, 5.4%.

Ylang-ylang essence, vanilla, cloves, copra, and other agricultural commodities made up the bulk of Comorian exports; of these, vanilla was by far the most important export earner. Imports included rice and other foodstuffs, petroleum products, and motor vehicles.

32 BALANCE OF PAYMENTS

In general, the chronic deficit on current accounts is counterbalanced by foreign aid, especially from France. By 2002 Comoros was in debt by $225 million. In 2004, the value of Comoros's exports was $34 million, and imports were valued at $115 million.

33 BANKING AND SECURITIES

The Central Bank of the Comoros was established in 1981. The Banque Pour l' Industrie et le Commerce, is the main commercial bank; the French Commercial Bank is also represented. The Banque de Développement des Comores is half state owned. The Banque Nationale de Paris Intercontinentale is the only international financial institution.

In 2005 the discount rate, the interest rate at which the central bank lends to financial institutions in the short term, was 3.59%.

There are no securities exchanges.

34 INSURANCE

Société Comorienne d'Assurances is based in Moroni. The Paris-based Préservatrice Foncière d'Assurances has an agent in Moroni.

35 PUBLIC FINANCE

In 2010 the budget of Comoros included $27.6 million in public revenue. The budget deficit amounted to 1.6% of GDP. Public debt was 39.5% of GDP, with $279.3 million of the debt held by foreign entities.

The Comoros government and the International Monetary Fund (IMF) agreed in 1990 to a structural adjustment program covering 1991 to 1993. The program provided $135 million and proposed a plan whereby the government diversified its exports, reduced public expenditures, and privatized its parastatal sector. Furthermore, the plan called for the abolishment of levies on export crops, privatization of the state-owned hotels, liquidation of the state-owned meat marketing company, initiation of a number of environmental projects, and the reduction of the number of civil servants. This last measure prompted civil disorder and economic disruptions. Concerned over the progress of reforms in 1993, the IMF and the government reassessed the program. Measures were adopted which persuaded the IMF to continue its support of the program. A military coup in 1999 halted most restructuring programs.

Principal Trading Partners – Comoros (2010)

(In millions of US dollars)

Country	Total	Exports	Imports	Balance
World	208.0	18.0	190.0	-172.0
France	39.1	5.7	33.4	-27.7
Pakistan	33.2	0.1	33.1	-33.0
United Arab Emirates	20.3	...	20.3	-20.3
India	17.9	7.6	10.3	-2.7
China	14.7	0.0	14.7	-14.7
Singapore	12.1	4.9	7.2	-2.3
Kenya	11.3	...	11.3	-11.3
Spain	9.6	0.0	9.6	-9.5
South Africa	8.5	...	8.5	-8.5
Belgium	7.0	0.1	6.9	-6.8

(…) data not available or not significant.

(n.s.) not specified.

SOURCE: *2011 Direction of Trade Statistics Yearbook*, New York: United Nations, 2011.

In 2010 the IMF and World Bank considered Comoros qualified for debt relief under the Heavily Indebted Poor Countries (HIPC) Initiative, but Comoros first needed to demonstrate satisfactory performance on the government's economic program by completing a series of reviews under the IMF's Extended Credit Facility (ECF). In 2011 the IMF deemed Comoros to be making progress on implementing reforms under the ECF, but still in need of bringing public wages under control, restructuring public utilities, and improving the provision of basic services to its population.

36 TAXATION

Tax collection, formerly the role of the island governors, became a federal responsibility following the 1982 constitutional revision.

37 CUSTOMS AND DUTIES

Import and export licenses are required, but often limited to a few firms. Since 1992 the government has reorganized and computerized the customs office, and introduced taxes on petroleum products and rice.

38 FOREIGN INVESTMENT

Foreign direct investment (FDI) in Comoros was a net inflow of $9.09 million according to World Bank figures published in 2009. FDI represented 1.7% of GDP. The economy was mainly supported by foreign aid and assistance, primarily from France, and to a lesser extent from Japan, Saudi Arabia, Kuwait, and the United Arab Emirates. A French company took over Comoros's electrical utility in 1997. A Swiss concern owns and operates the country's two main hotels. Officially, Comoros welcomes foreign investment and is prepared to offer incentive packages to potential investors.

39 ECONOMIC DEVELOPMENT

Development projects in the late 1980s and early 1990s focused on the agricultural sector, hydroelectric development, fishing, and start-up investment funds for small and intermediate enterprises. In addition, the European Development Funds provided resources for the redevelopment of the port at Moroni. International Monetary Fund (IMF) plans during the 1990s focused on agriculture diversification. In 1996 the country had an unemployment rate of 20% and one of the highest illiteracy rates in the world.

The government had several aims among which were to develop education and technical training, to improve health services, to reduce the high population growth rate, to privatize state-owned companies, to promote tourism, and to diversify exports. Remittances from abroad compensated somewhat for low economic performance and development.

In 2009 the World Bank injected $21.5 million into the economy through a three-year Poverty Reduction and Growth Facility (PRGF) to spur progress toward achieving the Millennium Development Goals (MDGs). Comoros was considered to have one of the least open economies in the world, and ranked near the bottom (167th) on the *2011 Index of Economic Freedom* published by the Heritage Foundation. In sub-Saharan Africa, Comoros ranked 42nd out of 46 countries.

40 SOCIAL DEVELOPMENT

On the United Nations Development Program's (UNDP) Human Development Index (HDI) for 2010, Comoros ranked 163rd, near the bottom of world. This ranking reflected the country's poor performance on key social indicators in education, health, and income.

Women occupied a subservient position in Comoros's highly traditional society, but this disadvantage was offset somewhat by Comoros's matrilineal social structure. Although women did not enjoy equal protection with men under the law, traditional custom granted women favorable inheritance and property rights. Isolated incidences of domestic violence against women were documented, but the government did not take action to protect women against it. Because of poverty, some families sent children as young as seven years old to live in other households where they worked as domestic servants. Priority in education was given to boys.

Prisons were overcrowded and lacked proper sanitation. Societal discrimination against Christians persisted. Isolated cases of human right abuses and political violence were reported.

41 HEALTH

According to the CIA, life expectancy in Comoros was 66 years in 2011. The country spent 8% of its GDP on healthcare, amounting to $28 per person. There were 2 physicians, 7 nurses and midwives, and 22 hospital beds per 10,000 inhabitants. The fertility rate was 3.9 births for every woman of childbearing age, while the infant mortality rate was 75 deaths per 1,000 live births. In 2008 the maternal mortality rate, according to the World Bank, was 340 deaths per 100,000 births. It was estimated that 79% of children were vaccinated against measles. The CIA calculated the adult HIV/AIDS prevalence rate in Comoros to be about 0.1% in 2009. In 2008, 95% of the population had access to improved water supply.

Lack of animal protein is a serious problem. In addition, a large percentage of the adult population suffers from malaria and there was a high incidence of tuberculosis and leprosy. The immunization rate in 2007 for diphtheria, pertussis, tetanus, and measles was estimated at 80% of children one year old.

42 HOUSING

In 2011 more than half of all housing units were straw huts with roofs of cocoa leaves. About 25% of the units were made of durable materials including stone, brick, or concrete. Of all housing units, nearly 90% were owned, 3% rented, and 3% occupied rent free. In 2008 about 36% of the population had access to improved sanitation systems.

43 EDUCATION

Education is compulsory for children between the ages of 7 and 16 years. Six years of primary education is required followed by seven years of secondary education—four years in the first stage followed by three years in the second stage.

In 2007 the World Bank estimated that 87% of age-eligible children in Comoros were enrolled in primary school. Secondary enrollment for age-eligible children stood at 15%. Tertiary enrollment was estimated at 5%. There are two technical schools and a teacher-training college near Moroni. In 2001 there were about 700 students enrolled in some form of higher education.

The CIA estimated that Comoros had a literacy rate of 56.5% in 2003. Public expenditure on education represented 7.6% of GDP in 2008.

44 LIBRARIES AND MUSEUMS

At independence there were two public libraries and three school libraries, with a total of 13,400 volumes. There is a National Center of Documentation and Scientific Research in Moroni as well as a National Museum of Comoros.

45 MEDIA

According to CIA estimates, in 2009 there were 25,400 telephone landlines in Comoros. In addition to landlines, mobile phone subscriptions averaged 15 per 100 people. There was one FM radio station, four AM radio stations, and one shortwave radio station. Radio-Comoros, a government agency, provided services on shortwave and FM in Comorian, French, English, Arabic, Malagasy, and Swahili. A national television station was launched in 2001 with assistance from China. Some Comorians were able to receive RFO Mayotte, run by French public radio and TV. There were also a number of local radio and television stations. Internet users numbered 4 per 100 citizens.

The primary weekly newspaper *Al Watwany* is published by the government; the weekly *L'Archipel* is published independently. There were several smaller private papers that published regularly, including *L'Archipel* (monthly). The government generally respected constitutional rights of speech and of the press, although varying levels of press freedoms were noted by Freedom House, with the greatest degree of freedom generally found on Grand Comore and Mohéli and the most repression experienced on Anjouan. In 2011 Freedom House ranked media freedom in the country as "partly free."

46 ORGANIZATIONS

There was a Chamber of Commerce, Industry, and Agriculture at Moroni. Youth organizations were developed in part through the national Union of Youth and Students of the Comoros (Union Jeunesse et des Etudiants des Comores—UJEC), founded in 1975.

Scouting organizations were also active for youth. There were some sports organizations. There were national chapters of the Red Crescent Society, Caritas, and UNICEF.

[47]TOURISM, TRAVEL, AND RECREATION

Since independence, chronic political instability and lack of attention have negatively impacted tourism. The *Tourism Factbook*, published by the UN World Tourism Organization, reported 14,600 incoming tourists to Comoros in 2007, who spent a total of $26.8 million. Of those tourists, there were 9,500 from Europe and 4,200 from Africa. There were 441 hotel beds available in Comoros. The estimated daily cost to visit Moroni, the capital, was $317. The cost of visiting other cities averaged $186.

Vaccination for yellow fever is recommended as well as anti-malarial precautions. A passport, visa, and return/onward ticket are required. Water sports are the primary recreational activities.

[48]FAMOUS PERSONS

Heads of state since independence include 'Ali Soilih (1937–78), who came to power as a result of the 1975 coup and who died after the 1978 takeover; and Ahmad 'Abdallah (1919–89), president briefly in 1975 and restored to power in 1978. Mercenary Bob Denard (France, 1929–2007) virtually ruled the country through figurehead presidents between 1978 and 1989, when France negotiated his departure after the assassination of 'Abdallah. Col. Assoumani Azali (b. 1959?) took power in a coup in 1999, assuming the titles of president, prime minister, and defense minister.

[49]DEPENDENCIES

The Comoros has no territories or dependencies.

[50]BIBLIOGRAPHY

Andrew, David, et al. *Madagascar and Comoros.* London, Eng.: Lonely Planet, 2008.

Comoros Investment and Business Guide: Strategic and Practical Information. Washington, DC: International Business Publications USA, 2012.

FDI and Tourism: The Development Dimension: East and Southern Africa. New York: United Nations, 2008.

Forster, Peter G. *Race and Ethnicity in East Africa.* New York: St. Martin's Press, 2000.

McElrath, Karen, ed. *HIV and AIDS: A Global View.* Westport, CT: Greenwood Press, 2002.

Ottenheimer, Martin and Harriet Ottenheimer. *Historical Dictionary of the Comoro Islands.* [computer file] Boulder, CO: netLibrary, Inc., 2000.

Penrith, James, and Deborah Penrith. *Madagascar & Comoros.* Oxford: Vacation Work, 2000.

Zeilig, Leo, and David Seddon. *A Political and Economic Dictionary of Africa.* Philadelphia: Routledge/Taylor and Francis, 2005.

CONGO, DEMOCRATIC REPUBLIC OF THE (DROC)

Democratic Republic of the Congo
République Democratique du Congo

CAPITAL: Kinshasa

FLAG: The flag is a sky blue field divided diagonally from the lower hoist corner to upper fly corner by a red stripe bordered by two narrow yellow stripes; a yellow, five-pointed star appears in the upper hoist corner.

ANTHEM: *Debout Congolaise (Arise Congolese).*

MONETARY UNIT: In 1997 the Congolese franc (CDF) replaced the zaire as the national currency. As of January 2012, the conversion rate was CDF1 = US$0.00110132 USD (US$1 = CDF908.000).

WEIGHTS AND MEASURES: The metric system is the legal standard.

HOLIDAYS: New Year's Day, 1 January; Commemoration of Martyrs of Independence, 4 January; Anniversary of the death of Laurent Désiré Kabila, 15 January; Anniversary of the death of Patrice Lumumba, 16 January; Labor Day, 1 May; Liberation Day (AFDL Anniversary), 17 May; Independence Day, 30 June; Parents' Day, 1 August; Christmas Day, 25 December.

TIME: In Kinshasa, 1 p.m. = noon GMT; in Lubumbashi, 2 p.m. = noon GMT.

¹LOCATION, SIZE, AND EXTENT

The Democratic Republic of the Congo is situated in central Africa and is crossed by the equator in its north-central region. It is the third-largest country on the continent, covering an area of 2,345,410 sq. km (905,568 sq. mi), with a length of 2,276 km (1,414 mi) SSE–NNW and a width of 2,236 km (1,389 mi) ENE–WSW. Comparatively, the area occupied by the country is slightly less than one-quarter the size of the United States, or about as large as the United States east of the Mississippi River. On the N it is bounded by the Central African Republic, on the NE by South Sudan, on the E by Uganda, Rwanda, Burundi, and Tanzania, on the SE and S by Zambia, on the southwest by Angola, and on the west by the Cabinda enclave of Angola and the Republic of the Congo (ROC), with a total boundary length of 10,744 km (6,661 mi). Its extreme western portion is a narrow wedge terminating in a strip of coastline along the Atlantic Ocean. The DROC and Zambia dispute the border to the east of Lake Mweru. Kinshasa, the capital, is located in the western part of the country.

²TOPOGRAPHY

The principal river is the Congo, which flows over 4,344 km (2,700 mi) from its headwaters to its estuary. The gigantic semicircular bend in the river, which is called the Lualaba in its upper course, delineates a central depression known as the cuvette, with an average altitude of about 400 m (1,312 ft). Around this densely forested section, which covers nearly half the area of the country, plateaus rise gradually to heights of 900–1,000 m (2,950–3,280 ft) to the north and south.

The highest altitudes are found along the eastern fringe of the country, on the edge of the Great Rift Valley, where dislocation of the strata has produced important volcanic and mountain masses, the most notable of which is Margherita Peak. Lying on the border

with Uganda, the peak rises to 5,109 m (16,762 ft), the third-highest point in Africa. Nyiragongo (11,365 ft/3,465 m), located south of Margherita Peak, is considered to be one of the most active volcanoes in Africa. On 10 January 1977, a lava lake poured out of the summit covering the countryside at speeds of 40 mph and killing about 2,000 people. It erupted again in 1982 and 1994. On 17 January 2002, lava flow from the volcano Nyiragongo forced the evacuation of Goma. Approximately 45 people died and 14 villages were damaged by the lava flow, leaving 12,000 people homeless. Mt. Nyamulagira, located about 15 km (9 mi) northwest of Nyiragongo, has erupted 34 times since 1882.

Savanna and park-forest vegetation predominate north and south of the equatorial forest belt; the southern savanna belt is far more extensive than the northern one. All major rivers are tributaries of the Congo; these include the Lomami, the Aruwimi or Ituri, the Ubangi, the Uélé, the Kasai, the Sankuru, the Lulua, the Kwango, and the Kwilu. The largest lakes include Tanganyika, Albert (L. Mobutu Sese Seko), Edward, Kivu, and Mweru, all of which form parts of the eastern border. Other large lakes are Mai-Ndombe and Tumba.

³CLIMATE

The climate is tropically hot and humid in the lower western and central regions, with frequent heavy rains from October or November through May south of the equator and from April to June and September to October in the north, while along the equator itself there is only one season. In the cuvette, temperatures average 24°C (75°F), with high humidity and almost no seasonal variation. Annual rainfall is between 130 cm and 200 cm (51 and 79 in). In the northern and southern plateaus there are wet and dry seasons, with temperatures slightly cooler in the latter and annual rainfall of 100–160 cm (39–63 in). The eastern highlands have temperatures averaging 18 to 24°C (64 to 75°F), depending on the season. Rainfall averages 120–180 cm (47–71 in).

⁴FLORA AND FAUNA

The World Resources Institute estimates that there are 11,007 plant species in the Democratic Republic of the Congo. In addition, the DROC is home to 430 mammal, 1,148 bird, 304 reptile, and 218 amphibian species. The calculation reflects the total number of distinct species residing in the country, not the number of endemic species.

The flora and fauna of the DROC include some 95% of all the varieties found in Africa. Among the many species of trees are the red cedar, mahogany, oak, walnut, the silk-cotton tree, and various palms. Orchids, lilies, lobelias, and gladioli are some of the flowers found, along with shrubs and plants of the euphorbia and landolphia families.

Larger species of mammals include the lion, elephant, buffalo, rhinoceros, zebra, leopard, cheetah, gorilla, chimpanzee, bonobo, wild boar, giraffe, okapi, and wild hog. The baboon and many kinds of monkeys are common, as are the jackal, hyena, civet, porcupine, squirrel, rabbit, and rat. Hippopotamuses and crocodiles are found in the rivers. Large snakes include the python, puff adder, and tree cobra. Lizards and chameleons are among the numerous small reptiles.

Birds species are similar to those common throughout Africa. They include the eagle, vulture, owl, goose, duck, parrot, whidah and other weaver birds, pigeon, sunbird, cuckoo, and swift, along with the crane, heron, stork, pelican, and cormorant. The rivers and lakes have many kinds of fish, among them catfish, tigerfish, and electric eels. Insects include various dragonflies, bees, wasps, beetles, mosquitoes, and the tsetse fly, as well as scorpions, spiders, centipedes, ants, and termites.

⁵ENVIRONMENT

The World Resources Institute reported that the Democratic Republic of the Congo had designated 19.61 million hectares (48.45 million acres) of land for protection as of 2006. Water resources totaled 1,283 cu km (307.8 cu mi) while water usage was 0.36 cu km (.086 cu mi) per year. Domestic water usage accounted for 52% of total usage, industrial for 17%, and agricultural for 31%. Per capita water usage totaled 6 cu m (212 cu ft.) per year.

Deforestation was caused by farming activity and the nation's dependency on wood for fuel. By 1985, 3,701 sq km (1,429 sq mi) of forestland had been lost. The DROC has nine national parks. There are five Natural World Heritage Sites, three biosphere reserves, and three Ramsar wetland sites.

In June 2010, the government reopened the Garamba National Park for tourism. Located along the border with Sudan, the park was listed as a UNESCO World Heritage Site in Danger in 1996, a distinction added because the park was home to 30 of the world's last remaining white rhinos. Militants from Uganda's Lord's Resistance Army took up residence in the park in 2005 after losing ground in southern Sudan. In a major campaign to save the park, the Congolese military welcomed Ugandan and UN troops to assist in driving the rebels out of the area. The Spanish government offered funding to rebuild areas of the park and to train park rangers and guides, to make the reserve an attractive and safe spot for tourists once again. Government officials hoped that renewed

tourism in the area would also renew interest and funding for the protection for the park's rare wildlife species.

The main environmental problem was poor water and sanitation systems, which resulted in the spread of insect- and rodent-borne diseases. The water was polluted by untreated sewage, industrial chemicals, and mining by-products. The UN reported in 2008 that carbon dioxide emissions in the DROC totaled 2,433 kilotons.

According to a 2011 report issued by the International Union for Conservation of Nature and Natural Resources (IUCN), the number of threatened species included 30 types of mammals, 35 species of birds, 4 types of reptile, 14 species of amphibians, 83 species of fish, 43 types of mollusks, 8 species of other invertebrates, and 83 species of plants. Endangered species in the DROC include the Marunga sunbird and the northern white and northern square-lipped rhinoceros.

In August 2009 the Congolese firm NOVACEL became the first in the nation to sign an Emissions Reduction Purchase Agreement (ERPA) with the World Bank. NOVACEL is the primary developer for the Ibi Bateke Carbon Sink Plantation Project, a reforestation effort encompassing 4,200 hectares (10,378 acres) of land on the Bateke Plateau, located about 92 mi (150 km) from Kinshasa. The World Bank agreed to purchase 500,000 carbon credits from the initiative, paid for through its BioCarbon Fund. In turn, the funds earned from the purchase will be used to implement programs that improve health, education, and agro-forestry activities. The plantation project is expected to trap an estimated 2.4 million tons of carbon dioxide between 2009 and 2039.

⁶POPULATION

The US Central Intelligence Agency (CIA) estimated the population of the Democratic Republic of the Congo in 2011 to be approximately 71,712,867, which placed it at number 19 in population among the 196 nations of the world. In 2011, approximately 2.6% of the population was over 65 years of age, with another 44.4% under 15 years of age. The median age in the DROC was 17.4 years. There were 1.03 males for every female in the country. The population's annual rate of change was 2.614%. The projected population for the year 2025 was 101,400,000. Population density in the DROC was calculated at 30 people per sq km (78 people per sq mi).

The UN estimated that 35% of the population lived in urban areas, and that urban populations had an annual rate of change of 4.5%. The largest urban areas, along with their respective populations, included Kinshasa, 8.4 million; Lubumbashi, 1.5 million; Mbuji-Mayi, 1.5 million; Kananga, 878,000; and Kisangani, 812,000.

The DROC's population in the east was significantly affected by warfare in the 1990s and early 2000s when an estimated four million people died, mostly from malnutrition and disease. This was the highest death rate connected to war since World War II. Many Congolese had been displaced or fled the country due to internal violence.

⁷MIGRATION

Estimates of Democratic Republic of the Congo's net migration rate, carried out by the CIA in 2011, amounted to -0.54 migrants per 1,000 citizens. The total number of emigrants living abroad

DEMOCRATIC REPUBLIC
OF THE CONGO

0   100   200   300 Miles

0   100   200   300 Kilometers

CENTRAL AFRICAN
REPUBLIC

SOUTH
SUDAN

CAMEROON

GABON

REPUBLIC
OF THE
CONGO

Congo Basin

ANGOLA

ZAMBIA

Democratic Republic
of the Congo

LOCATION: 5°28′ N to 13°27′ S; 12°12′ to 31°18′E. BOUNDARY LENGTHS: Central African Republic, 1,577 kilometers (980 miles); South Sudan, 628 kilometers (390 miles); Uganda, 765 kilometers (475 miles); Rwanda, 217 kilometers (135 miles); Burundi, 233 kilometers (145 miles); Zambia; 1,930 kilometers (1,206 miles); Angola, 2,511 kilometers (1,565 miles); Atlantic coastline, 37 kilometers (23 miles); Republic of the Congo, 2,410 kilometers (1,486 miles); Tanzania, 459 kilometers (285 miles). TERRITORIAL SEA LIMIT: 12 miles.

was 913,900, and the total number of immigrants living in Democratic Republic of the Congo was 444,700. The Democratic Republic of the Congo also accepted 132,295 refugees from Angola, 37,313 from Rwanda, 17,777 from Burundi, 13,904 from Uganda, 6,181 from Sudan, and 5,243 from the Republic of Congo. Political tensions and crises in neighboring African countries have resulted in large-scale migration to the DROC, and political turmoil in the DROC has resulted in out-migration as well. Many refugees were

resettled in the DROC through the aid of outside governments, private relief organizations, the UN, and UN-related agencies.

After a general amnesty for refugees and political exiles in 1978, some 200,000 (then) Zairians were repatriated from Angola, Zambia, Sudan, Tanzania, and Europe. There were 60,200 officially registered Zairians living in neighboring countries at the end of 1992, including 25,800 in Burundi, 16,000 in Tanzania, 15,600 in Uganda, and 2,300 in Sudan.

By early 1997, over 800,000 Rwandan Hutu refugees had returned to Rwanda from the DROC due to the armed rebellion in the country. There were still 250,000 Rwandan Hutus unaccounted for in the DROC at the beginning of 1997. The DROC harbored 400,000 Burundian refugees, 160,000 Angolans, 110,000 Sudanese, and 18,500 Ugandans as of May 1997. In 1998, more than 285,000 Angolans, Sudanese, Congolese, Ugandans, Rwandans, and Burundians remained in the DROC. Following the signature of an agreement between the DROC, Republic of Congo (ROC), and the UN High Commissioner for Refugees (UNHCR) in April 1999, some 36,000 Congolese were repatriated to Brazzaville, ROC. However, instability in Angola made similar repatriation for Angolans unlikely. Another repatriation effort was made in 2004, in which 11,166 Burundians and 2,011 Central Africans were repatriated. Also in 2004, more than 295,000 Congolese applied for asylum in Tanzania, Zambia, Rwanda, Uganda, South Africa, and the United Kingdom.

As a result of internal conflict that started in August 1998, more than 700,000 people were internally displaced. Some 95,000 sought asylum in Tanzania and 25,000 fled to Zambia. By 2011, approximately two million people were internally displaced due largely to widespread, continual sexual violence, particularly gender based against women and girls.

In 2011 the UN Refugee Agency appealed for $60 million to meet rudimentary needs of returning refugees. Refugee settlements were found up and down the Ubangui River; however, refugees have settled in the highest concentrations in North and South Kivu, Bas Congo, Katanga, Bandundu and Kasai. The humanitarian community believed the refugees along the Ubangui River would remain in the neighboring Republic of Congo (ROC) for the time being.

8 ETHNIC GROUPS

There are over 200 African ethnic groups, the majority of which are Bantu. Bantu-speaking peoples form about 80% of the population. Most of the rest are Sudanic-speaking groups in the north and northeast. Approximately 80,000–100,000 Pygmies are found in the cuvette. Among the Bantu-speaking peoples, the major groups are the Kongo, or Bakongo, in the southwest; the Luba, or Baluba, in East Kasai and Shaba; the Mongo and related groups in the cuvette area; the Lunda and Chokwe in Bandundu and West Kasai; the Bemba and Hemba in Shaba; and the Kwango and Kasai in Bandundu. The four largest groups—Mongo, Luba, Kongo (all Bantu), and the Mangbetu-Azande (Hamitic)—make up about 45% of the total population. Non-Africans include Belgians, Greeks, Lebanese, and Asian Indians.

Congo has experienced communal violence, the most violent of which in the 1990s and 2000s has been between the Lendu and Hema groups in Ituri District and between ethnic Hutu groups and Tutsis, including the Banyamulenge Tutsis, residing along the DROC-Rwanda and Burundi borders in the east.

9 LANGUAGES

As many as 700 languages and dialects are spoken in the DROC. Serving as regional lingua franca are four African languages: Lingala is used in the north from Kisangani to Kinshasa, as well as in the armed forces; Swahili, in the Kingwana dialect, is used in the east; Kikongo in the southwest; and Tshiluba in the south-central area. In addition, Lomongo is widely spoken in the cuvette. French is the official language and is widely used in government and commerce.

10 RELIGIONS

Until 1990, only three Christian churches were officially recognized denominations: the Roman Catholic Church; the Church of Christ in Congo (an umbrella group of Protestant churches); and the charismatic Kimbanguist Church, which claims to be the largest independent African church on the continent. As of 2010, Kimbanguists constituted about 10% of the population. About 50% of the population was Roman Catholic and about 20% Protestant--charismatic Protestant churches were growing rapidly in the 2000s. Another 10% of the population was Muslim. Others adhered to syncretic sects and traditional African beliefs. Protestant missionary groups included Lutherans, Baptists, Mormons, and Jehovah's Witnesses. There were small communities of Orthodox Christians and Jews.

Freedom of religion was provided for in article 26 of the transitional constitution, and this right was generally respected in practice. Religious groups were required to register with the government according to the Regulation of Nonprofit Associations and Public Utility Institutions statute; however, there were no penalties for failure to register. There was little sectarian violence in the country.

The Consortium of Traditional Religious Leaders provided a forum for the discussion of religious concerns between faiths and with the government. The Consortium was composed of leaders from the five major religious groups: Catholic, Muslim, Protestant, Orthodox, and Kimbanguist. The Catholic Church, which exercised considerable influence in political affairs, provided monitors throughout the country for the November 2011 elections. By the end of 2011, Cardinal Laurent Monsengwo, the leader of the Catholic Church in Congo, had declared the results of the presidential election to be seriously flawed, a position directly at odds with that of the President of the Republic.

11 TRANSPORTATION

The DROC had approximately 15,000 km (9,321 mi) of navigable waterways. Inland waterways-rivers and lakes-were the main channels of transportation. No single railroad ran the full length of the country, and paved highways were few and short. Lack of adequate transportation was a major problem affecting the development of the country. While the rivers, particularly the Congo and its tributaries, were mostly navigable, they were blocked at various points from through navigation by cataracts and waterfalls, making it necessary to move goods by rail or road between the navigable sections. Principal river ports were Kinshasa, Ilebo, Mbandaka, Kisangani, Kalemie, Ubundu, and Kindu. The chief seaport and only deepwater port was Matadi on the Congo River, 148 km (92 mi) from the Atlantic Ocean. Other seaports included Boma and Banana, also on the Congo below Matadi. The Congo Maritime Company was the national shipping line.

The CIA reports that Democratic Republic of the Congo has a total of 153,497 km (95,379 mi) of roads, of which 2,794 km (1,736 mi) are paved. Two major routes are from Kinshasa to Kikwit, and from Kinshasa to Boma. The road network is in a state of deterioration.

DROC railroads extended for 3,641 km (2,262 mi). Among the most important internal links were Lubumbashi-Ilebo, Kingala-Kindu, Ubundu-Kisangani, and Kinshasa-Matadi. In the early 1980s, the Kinshasa-Matadi line was extended by a Japanese company. A road and rail bridge across the Congo River at Matadi was completed in 1983. The southeastern network connected with the Angolan and Zambian railroad systems. In 1974, all railroads were consolidated under a single state-controlled corporation, SNCZ.

There were 198 airports in the DROC, 28 of which had paved runways. Air transport had become an important factor in the country's economy. The DROC had five international airports—N'Djili (Kinshasa), Luano (Lubumbashi), and airports at Bukavu, Goma, and Kisangani—which could accommodate long-distance jet aircraft. The former national airline, Air Zaïre, was organized in 1961 and flew to European and African cities, as well as within the country. It collapsed in the late 1990s because of insolvency. As of April 2012, the DROC had no national airline.

By the 2000s a number of private carriers served the DROC and regional destinations. However, the country had one of the worst air safety records in the world, due in part to its aging aircraft and poor maintenance. In April 2008 Hewa Bora Airways Flight 122 crashed on take-off in Goma killing some 44 people, most of which were on the ground. In 2010 a plane crashed in Bandundu killing 20 people. In April 2011 a UN commuter plane crashed at Kinshasa killing 32 people. On 8 July 2011 another Hewa Bora Airways flight crashed, this time while landing in Kisangani, killing 127 people. There were 51 survivors. Since 2008 the EU has banned all DROC registered airlines from flying to EU countries.

12 HISTORY

The earliest inhabitants of the area now called the DROC are believed to have been Pygmy tribes who lived by hunting and gathering food and using stone tools. Bantu-speaking peoples entered from the west by 150 AD, while non-Bantu-speakers penetrated the area from the north. These peoples brought with them agriculture and developed iron tools. In 1482, the Portuguese navigator Diogo Cão visited the mouth of the Congo River, marking the first known European contact with the region, but this did not lead to penetration of the interior. The Portuguese confined their relations to the Kongo kingdom, which ruled the area near the mouth of the Congo River as well as what is now the coast of northern Angola. A lucrative slave trade developed.

In the 16th century, the powerful Luba state developed in what is now Katanga Province; soon afterward, a Lunda state was established in what is now south-central DROC. In 1789, a Portuguese explorer, José Lacerdu e Almeida, explored in a cuvette and penetrated as far as Katanga, where he learned of the rich copper mines. A thriving Arab trade in slaves and ivory reached the Luba country from the east in the late 1850s or early 1860s.

The Scottish explorer David Livingstone reached the upper course of the Congo in 1871, when his whereabouts became unknown, and Welsh-American explorer Henry M. Stanley, commissioned by a US newspaper, located and rescued him (in modern Tanzania). In 1876–77, after the death of Livingstone, Stanley followed the river from the point that Livingstone had reached to its mouth. King Leopold II of Belgium commissioned Stanley to undertake further explorations and to make treaties with the tribal chiefs. In 1878, the monarch formed the International Association of the Congo, a development company, with himself as the chief stockholder. The Berlin Conference of 1884–85 recognized the Independent State of the Congo, set up by Leopold II under his personal rule, and its ultimate boundaries were established by treaties with other colonial powers.

International criticism and investigation of the treatment of the inhabitants, particularly on the rubber plantations, resulted in the end of personal rule in 1908. The territory was transferred to Belgium as a colony called the Belgian Congo, and in that year a law known as the Colonial Charter set up its basic structure of government.

The rise of nationalism in the various African territories following World War II seemed to have bypassed the colony, which remained without self-government (except for a few large cities) until 1959. The Congolese demanded independence and rioted, first in Léopoldville (now Kinshasa) and then in other parts of the colony. Following the first outbreaks, the Belgian government outlined a program for the gradual attainment of self-rule in the colony, but as the independence movement persisted and grew, Belgium agreed to grant the Congo its independence in mid-1960. It also promised to assist in the training of Congolese administrators, and to continue economic and other aid after independence.

Independence

The newly independent Republic of the Congo was inaugurated on 30 June 1960, with Joseph Kasavubu as its first head of state and Patrice Lumumba as its first premier. It was immediately confronted by massive economic, political, and social problems. A week after independence the armed forces mutinied, and separatist movements and intertribal conflict threatened to split the country. Following the mutiny and the ousting of its European officers, the Congolese National Army became an undisciplined and uncertain force, with groups of soldiers supporting various political and military leaders.

A major blow to the new republic was the secession of mineral-rich Katanga Province, announced on 11 July 1960 by Moïse Tshombe, head of the provincial government. The central government was hamstrung by the loss of revenues from its richest province and by the departure of Belgian civil servants, doctors, teachers, and technicians. After some assaults on Belgian nationals, Belgium sent paratroopers into the Congo, which appealed to the UN for help. Faced with the threatened collapse of a new nation, the UN responded with what grew into a program of massive assistance: financial, military, administrative, and technical. It established the UN Operation for the Congo (UNOC), sent in a UN military force (made up of contingents volunteered by nonmajor powers), and furnished considerable numbers of experts in administration, teachers, doctors, and other skilled personnel.

In September 1960, Kasavubu dismissed Lumumba as premier, and Lumumba announced that he had dismissed Kasavubu as head of state. The parliament subsequently rescinded both dismissals. Kasavubu then dismissed the parliament and with Col. Joseph-Désiré Mobutu, the army's newly appointed chief of staff, succeeded in taking Lumumba prisoner. UN troops did not interfere. As demands for Lumumba's release mounted, Lumumba was secretly handed over to the Katanga authorities, who had him put to death early in 1961. Shortly afterward, the UN Security Council for the first time authorized UN forces in the Congo to use force if necessary, as a "last resort" to prevent civil war from occurring.

In September 1961, after Katanga forces fired on UN troops seeking to secure the removal of foreign mercenaries, UN Secretary-General Dag Hammarskjöld flew to the Congo, where he boarded a plane for Northern Rhodesia (now Zambia) to meet with Tshombe. The plane crashed, killing him and all others on board. In December 1962, Katanga forces in Elisabethville (now Lubumbashi) opened sustained fire on UN troops. The UN troops then began broad-scale military operations to disarm the Katanga forces throughout the province. As they neared the completion of their task, Tshombe capitulated, and the secession of Katanga was ended on 14 January 1963.

Almost immediately, a new insurrection broke out, in the form of a series of rebellions. The rebels at one point exercised de facto control over more than half the country. As UN troops were withdrawn on 30 June 1964, the self-exiled Tshombe was recalled and offered the position of prime minister, largely at US and Belgian instigation. Tshombe promptly recruited several hundred white mercenaries to spearhead the demoralized national army. Rebel-held Stanleyville (now Kisangani) was recaptured in November 1964, when a US-airlifted contingent of Belgian paratroopers disarmed the insurgents. Widespread government reprisals against the population followed. By then, the rebellion had been contained.

Tshombe's attempt to establish a nationwide political base was successful in parliamentary elections held in early 1965, but on 13 October 1965 he was removed from office by Kasavubu, who attempted to replace him with Evariste Kimba, also from Katanga. When Kimba was not endorsed by the parliament, Gen. Joseph Desiré Mobutu, commander-in-chief of the Congolese National Army, seized power in a coup d'état on 24 November 1965 and assumed the presidency.

A new constitution adopted in June 1967 instituted a centralized presidential form of government, coupled with the creation of a new political movement, the Popular Movement of the Revolution (Mouvement Populaire de la Révolution—MPR). Tshombe's hopes for a comeback were dashed when he was kidnapped in June 1967 and imprisoned in Algeria, where he died two years later. His supporters, led by French and Belgian mercenaries, mutinied again in July 1967 but were finally defeated in November, in part because of logistical support of Mobutu extended by the US government. Other sources of opposition were summarily dealt with in 1968 with the disbanding of independent labor and student organizations.

Mobutu officially transformed the Congo into a one-party state in 1970, and in 1971, changed the name of the country, river, and currency to Zaire. (This name, an inaccurate rendition of the Kikongo word for "river," had been given by 16th-century Portuguese navigators to the river that later came to be known as the Congo.) This turned out to be the first step in a campaign of national "authenticity," which led not only to the Africanization of all European toponyms (a process that had already been applied to major cities in 1966) but also to the banning of Christian names (Mobutu himself changed his name to Mobutu Sese Seko).

Mobutu was elected without opposition to a new seven-year term as president in 1977, but he continued to face opposition, both external and internal. Former Katangan gendarmes, who had earlier fled to Angola, invaded (then) Shaba Province on 8 March 1977. Mobutu, charging that Cuba and the former USSR were behind the invasion, enlisted the aid of 1,500 Moroccan troops. The incursion was quelled by late May. In May 1978, however, the rebels again invaded Shaba and occupied Kolwezi, a key mining center. French paratroopers retook Kolwezi on 19 May and were later joined by Belgian troops, but several hundred foreigners and Zairians were killed during the eight-day rebel occupation. Troops from Morocco, Gabon, and Senegal replaced the French and Belgians in June; Zairian troops later reoccupied the region.

In 1981, Premier Nguza Karl-I-Bond resigned and became spokesman for an opposition group based in Belgium; however, he returned to Zaire in 1985 and was appointed ambassador to the United States in 1986. In June 1982, 13 former parliament members were jailed allegedly for trying to organize an opposition party. They were released in 1983, as part of an announced amnesty for political detainees and exiles, but six of the 13 were sent into internal exile in 1986.

In 1982, Mobutu resumed diplomatic ties with Israel, which had been broken in 1974; five Arab nations quickly cut ties with Zaire, and $350 million in promised Arab aid to Zaire was blocked. In 1983, Zaire sent 2,700 troops to Chad to aid the government against Libyan-backed rebels; they were withdrawn in 1984. Mobutu was reelected "unopposed" to a new seven-year presidential term in July 1984. In 1986 and 1987 there were reports that the United States was using an airbase in Zaire to supply weapons to the antigovernment guerrillas in neighboring Angola; Mobutu denied these charges and affirmed his support of the Angolan government.

For his support of western positions through the Cold War, Mobutu was handsomely rewarded. Western aid and investment and state seizures of private property made some individuals extraordinarily wealthy. Mobutu allegedly became the wealthiest person in Africa, with a fortune estimated at $7 billion, mostly in Swiss bank accounts. However, widely publicized human rights violations in the late 1980s put Mobutu on the defensive. He lobbied the US Congress vigorously, conducted public relations campaigns in Europe and North America and, until the collapse of his authority in the 1990s, managed to gain support from abroad. French and Belgian troops intervened in the Kinshasa unrest of 1990.

To stave off criticism, Mobutu promised to create a multiparty Third Republic. But, in fact, he raised the level of repression. He originally hoped to create two new parties, both of which would reflect his own political philosophy and join with his own MPR. Those opposed to Mobutu rejected this scheme, but the opposition was divided into a score of parties. With the army in disarray and disorder growing, Mobutu was forced to call a National Conference of approximately 2,800 delegates in September 1991 to draft a new constitution. Some 130 opposition parties joined together as the Sacred Union. Mobutu on several occasions suspended the Conference, but it continued to meet. It often failed to arrive at a consensus; when it did, Mobutu thwarted its decisions. Neither side was in a hurry to finish the Conference and get on with political reforms because the Conference allowed Mobutu to delay real political competition, while conferees received a handsome per diem for their attendance.

Mounting impatience for reforms unleashed widespread looting in Kinshasa in September 1991 and again the following year. Mobutu himself abandoned his presidential palace for the security of his yacht on the Congo River. On 16 February 1992, the Catholic Church organized a massive demonstration to reopen the National Conference. Thousands of marchers from all backgrounds converged on the stadium Tata Rafael. Police and soldiers opened fire on the marchers before they could reach their destination, killing hundreds of people.

In November 1991, Mobutu split the Sacred Union by naming Nguza Karl-I-Bond of the Union of Federalists and Independent Republicans (UFERI) as prime minister. Nguza closed the National Conference in February 1992. Pressure from inside and from western aid donors forced Mobutu to allow the Conference to resume in April. It sought to draft a new constitution and threatened to rename Zaire "Congo." On 14 August 1992, the Sacred Union got the Conference to elect Etienne Tshisekedi of the Union for Democracy and Social Progress (UDPS) as prime minister of a transitional government. Mobutu, who countered by forming a new government under his control and dismissing Tshisekedi in December 1992, controlled the army, the central bank, and the police. Continuing the struggle for control of the state, the Conference drafted a constitution and set a referendum date for April 1993, but it was never held. In March, Mobutu called a conclave of political leaders and named Faustin Birindwa as prime minister. The High Council of the Republic, the interim legislature, continued to recognize Tshisekedi, as did Zaire's principal economic partners abroad. Mobutu was able to incite ethnic violence through "ethnic cleansing policies," thereby dividing his opponents and then using his armed forces to quell the violence.

From that point, two parallel governments ruled Zaire. One controlled the country's wealth and the media; the other had a popular following and professed support from western governments. In September 1993, there was a minor breakthrough. Thanks to UN mediation, the rival powers agreed on a draft constitution for the Third Republic. The two legislatures were to combine into a single, 700-person assembly. New presidential and parliamentary elections were promised. However in January 1994, Mobutu dissolved both governments and a joint sitting of the two legislatures (the HCR-Parliament of Transition). It met on 19 January and appointed the Roman Catholic archbishop of Kisangani, Laurent Monsengwo, as its president. Tshisekedi organized a successful, one-day strike in Kinshasa.

In 1993, Mobutu's Bank of Zaire introduced new currency on three occasions, but it soon became worthless. Merchants would not accept it and riots broke out when soldiers could not spend their pay. French and Belgian troops were deployed in Kinshasa to help restore order as foreigners fled. Public employees also went on strike because of the economic conditions. Anarchy, corruption, uncontrolled violence, and poverty prevailed. Government authority dissolved, leaving the country to pillaging soldiers and roaming gangs. The situation led one journalist to call it "a stateless country." Shaba (Katanga) province declared its autonomy. AIDS was rife. The struggle of two rival claimants to power continued with neither able to mount much overt support.

Due, at least in part, to this chaotic domestic situation, a new outbreak of the Ebola virus was reported in May 1995. Ebola, a virulent disease for which there are no known treatments and which may kill as many as 90% of those infected by it, was responsible for approximately 250 deaths in this outbreak that occurred in Kitwit, a city of about 600,000, 402 km (250 mi) southeast of the capital. Hospitals lacked basic supplies, such as sterile dressings, gowns, and gloves. Many of those who died were medical professionals who had treated the first Ebola patients brought into medical facilities.

Meanwhile the nation was experiencing other problems on its eastern border. Civil war in neighboring Rwanda throughout 1994 and 1995 had forced over one million people to flee into North and South Kivu provinces where refugees settled into densely populated camps. These refugees, mostly Rwandan Hutus-many of whom had participated in the genocide against Rwandan Tutsis-quickly became a great strain on the region's scarce resources and in August 1995 the government stepped up efforts to repatriate them to Rwanda. Within a month, over 75,000 refugees had been expelled. However, the expulsion proved counterproductive. Many of the refugees were afraid of being imprisoned or killed by the Tutsi-led government of Rwanda. Some refugees fled into the countryside to avoid being deported while others returned across the border only hours after being expelled.

In October 1996, increasing insecurity, the high cost of living, and the destruction of the fauna and flora led the government of South Kivu province to initiate a series of repressive measures. These reprisals were directed against Rwandan Hutu refugees and against a group of ethnic Rwandans Tutsis, who claimed their ancestors had settled in Zaire more than a century before. This action prompted a rebellion by the Rwandans. By early November the provincial government had been overthrown; the major cities of the province had come under rebel control; and hundreds of thousands of Rwandan refugees were repatriated into Rwanda, attempting to flee the fighting.

At that point the rebellion took a strange turn as Laurent-Desiré Kabila took control. Kabila had originally fought with Lumumba for independence but had been living as a local warlord in the South Kivu province. Kabila's presence as the leader of the rebellion shifted its focus from protecting ethnic Rwandans to conducting a rebellion against the Mobutu government. Kabila obtained the backing of President Museveni of Uganda and Paul Kagame, the leader of the Rwandan Patriotic Front.

During the first few months of the rebellion, President Mobutu had been abroad to seek treatment for his prostate cancer. In mid-December, Mobutu returned, appointed a new defense minister, and reshuffled the army command. He also hired Serbian mercenaries and Rwandan Hutus to strengthen his army. In January 1997 the army launched a disastrous counteroffensive against the rebels. By February the rebels controlled nearly all of the Eastern provinces and were threatening to overtake the country. South African-brokered peace talks failed to bring about a cease-fire. The rebels soon took Kisangani, the nation's third-largest city without a fight in March. Any serious opposition to the rebels completely crumbled in the wake of their onslaught. In April, while the UN attempted to negotiate a meeting between Mobutu and Kabila (with Mobutu refusing), the rebels seized Lubumbashi, the second-largest city, and also took control of the diamond-rich province of Kasai.

As rebels closed in on the capital in May, Nelson Mandela hosted talks between Kabila and Mobutu aboard a South African ship.

Mobutu agreed to stand-down the army forces in Kinshasa but refused to agree on conditions for his departure. However, as rebel forces drew ever closer, Mobutu realized that his hopes of retaining any of his former power were misplaced, and he fled first to his hometown in the northern part of the country and then abroad. Kabila's forces entered the capital to a hero's welcome. Kabila announced that the country would return to using the name it had been known from 1960 to 1970, the Democratic Republic of the Congo.

While most citizens were glad to be rid of the brutal and corrupt government of Mobutu, and most Western nations were glad to be rid of an embarrassing remnant of the Cold War, Kabila soon proved to be an ambiguous hero. Most of Kabila's top associates were Tutsis in 1997 and were implicated in alleged massacres of Rwandan Hutu refugees in the Eastern Provinces, which they had controlled since November 1996.

By August 1998, a full-fledged war, which eventually involved nine African countries, erupted. It began with a disagreement between Kabila and his Rwandan and Ugandan allies over their future participation in the Congolese state, which soon led to Rwandan and Ugandan attacks on the eastern towns of Goma, Bukavu, and Uvira. With Southern African Development Community (SADC) members Angola, Namibia, and Zimbabwe supplying troops and materials to Congo, and Chad and Sudan also backing Kabila, US Assistant Secretary of State for Africa, Susan Rice, dubbed the conflict, "Africa's first world war."

Initially, a Congolese faction called the Rassemblement Congolais pour la Démocratie (RCD), which included former Mobutu supporters and Kabila dissidents, claimed popular support against the Kabila government to establish democracy in the DROC. This group never achieved wide popularity and some analysts believe it was principally a Rwandan creation to overthrow Kabila by proxy. In April through May of 1999, the RCD split into two factions with Ilunga claiming that Wamba dia Wamba no longer controlled significant forces. Shooting also broke out between sides of allied Ugandan and Rwandan forces in Kisangani leaving several dead. A third rebel group, the MLC of Jean-Pierre Bemba, controlled parts of Equateur Province and Province Orientale. The UN estimated that some 6,000 people died by the end of the first year of the Congo conflict, many of them civilians. The financial cost to Zimbabwe alone was estimated at $3 million per day.

In July 1999, all sides signed the Lusaka peace accords, and eventually the UN agreed to send some 5,000 peacekeepers under the MONUC mission to DROC to monitor the implementation of the accord. However, with more than half the national territory under rebel control, and with Kabila refusing to cooperate with the UN negotiator, a political and military stalemate ensued. The country fell further into economic chaos due to gross mismanagement of monetary and fiscal policy. On 16 January 2001, a presidential guard shot and killed Laurent Kabila. Kabila was succeeded by his adopted son, Joseph, who was confirmed unanimously by his father's appointed parliament to be the new head of state on 27 January 2001. In mid-January 2003 the assassination trial was concluded, and despite questionable evidence, 29 people were found guilty and condemned to death.

In August 2002, Joseph Kabila succeeded in concluding a peace deal with Rwanda, and with Uganda in September 2002 and March 2003. By April 2003 most foreign troops had withdrawn,

and Kabila had extracted commitments from his neighbors to respect pre-1997 Congolese borders.

Given his youth and inexperience, few observers thought Joseph Kabila could have orchestrated the power-sharing agreement signed in Pretoria on 17 December 2002 between his government, the Mouvement pour la Libération du Congo (MLC), the Rassemblement Congolais pour la Démocratie (RCD-Goma), the unarmed opposition, and civil society. The agreement permitted Kabila to remain president of the republic until elections were held, a condition on which he insisted throughout the Inter-Congolese Dialog (ICD) talks. However, despite the Pretoria agreement and the presence of several dozen French peacekeeping troops, fierce fighting continued in the northeast between the Hema and Lendu tribes over control of Bunia, a regional capital.

Fighting also continued in other parts of the country. In early 2003, the MLC rebel faction was accused of mass murder, cannibalism, rape, and other human rights abuses committed against Pygmies in Ituri located in the northeast. Fighting, raping, looting, and theft were also reported into June 2003 in towns and villages in the eastern Kivu provinces. Despite having signed a peace agreement in Sun City, South Africa in April 2003, the Rwandan-backed RCD-Goma captured the town of Lubero in June 2003.

In June 2003 concrete steps were taken to resolve the conflict and to implement the Pretoria Accord. A transitional power-sharing government with representation from all the main factions was charged with the responsibility of preparing the country for its transition to democratic elections in 2005. Implementation of the timetable, however, was slow with the government in no hurry to speed the transfer of power. Citizen protests over the delays culminated in a major demonstration organized by the Union for Democracy and Social Progress (UDPS) party in July 2005, and only under concerted pressure from donors did the parliament announce a new and presumably final elections deadline for March or April 2006. The enormous task of voter registration, which began in June 2005, proceeded apace throughout 2005, and the deadline for candidate registration was set for 17 January 2006.

Despite progress in moving the political transition forward, renewed clashes between armed factions operating in Ituri district and North Kivu province threatened to derail the process. Leaders of RCD-Goma were opposed to the transition, claiming that armed Hutu Interahamwe militias continued to conduct attacks on the Banyamulenge Congolese Tutsi population. It was also clear that RCD-Goma was interested in staying in power as long as possible, benefiting from the smuggling of cassiterite and other precious minerals from the DROC into Rwanda. Talks between Kabila and the Rwandan Hutu Democratic Forces for the Liberation of Rwanda (FDLR) aimed at disarming them and repatriating them to Rwanda broke down because the FDLR wanted to impose amnesty conditions that Rwanda refused.

The protracted fighting was responsible for an estimated 3.3 million war-related deaths in the Kivus between 1998 and 2002. This scale of human calamity had not been seen anywhere on the globe since World War II. In December 2005, the International Court of Justice ruled that Uganda would have to pay reparation to the DROC for looting during the 1998–2003 war. Meanwhile, the specter of a return of Rwandan armed forces to Congolese soil was very real.

In late 2005, the UN MONUC peace-keepers numbered over 16,500 strong and additional police were authorized to maintain order in the run-up to the elections. MONUC claimed to have successfully demobilized several thousand militia fighters in Ituri; however, some 2,000 militia members were thought to be operating with most of their weaponry in that area. While MONUC provided a deterrent to conflict, observers noted that the failure to restructure the armed forces, to disarm militias, and redirect the loyalty of soldiers to the central government presented a major obstacle to the success of the transition process. Congo's "gold curse" and the illegal exploitation of precious minerals from eastern Congo by rebel factions and foreign governments continued to fuel the fighting. In January 2006, eight MONUC soldiers were killed and several wounded allegedly in an attack by the Ugandan Lord's Resistance Army (LRA) rebels.

On 30 July 2006, presidential and multiparty parliamentary elections were finally held; they were the first free elections in 46 years. There was no clear winner in the presidential vote. Therefore, incumbent leader Joseph Kabila and opposition candidate Jean-Pierre Bemba faced off in a run-off election on 29 October 2006. In November, Kabila was declared the winner of the October run-off with 58% of the vote. The election had the approval of international monitors. However, in March 2007, government troops and forces loyal to Bemba clashed in Kinshasa. In April, Bemba exiled himself to Portugal, ending a three-week political stalemate in Kinshasa, during which he had sought refuge in the South African embassy.

In May 2007, the UN investigated allegations of gold and arms trafficking by UN peacekeepers in the Ituri region. War in the east was imminent in 2007. That August, international aid agencies prepared for a large increase in refugees fleeing instability in North Kivu. The total number of displaced people in North Kivu province alone swelled to more than 750,000 by October 2007. As of late 2007, the UN estimated that 1,000 lives were lost each day in the Congo, and also reported an epidemic of rape against women in eastern Congo. In November 2007, Congo reached an agreement with Rwanda to disarm Rwandan Hutu rebels, including former Rwandan soldiers and members of the militia known as the Interahamwe.

In January 2009, the Congolese and Rwandan armies conducted joint attacks against the FDLR and placed the leader of the group, General Laurent Nkunda, under house arrest in Rwanda. Following the operations, the FDLR elected a new leader and, through talks with the government, was officially recognized as a political party. In May 2009, the Congolese government passed an amnesty law that opened the door for the remaining rebel militia to disarm and join the national army. Officials hoped that these measures would pave the way to lasting peace. In the meantime, the joint Congolese-Rwandan force continued their offensive against the remaining rebels.

Starting in early 2004, the International Criminal Court opened investigations on war crimes and crimes against humanity in the Democratic Republic of Congo. From 2006 to 2011 five alleged war criminals either had charges drawn and subsequent warrants made or were brought to trial. The defendants in these trials were: Thomas Lubanga Dyilo, Germain Katanga, Mathieu Ngudolo Chui, Bosco Ntaganda, and Callixte Mbarushimana, brought up on charges such as: sexual slavery, rape, using children under fifteen to take active part in hostilities, mutilation, prosecution and murder.

On 28 November 2011, the DROC held a much anticipated, contested election, only the second since the constitution's inception, in which incumbent President Joseph Kabila was declared president amidst allegations of massive vote rigging. Against these allegations, Kabila's main opponent Etienne Tshisekedi declared himself president; however the Supreme Court upheld the results. By early December, SMS text capabilities were blocked by the government, followed shortly by the frequency blockage of RFI (Radio France International). Protests and violence followed in response to the election and the initial reports placed the death toll at eighteen people and 100 seriously injured.

By early 2012 a stalemate had ensued between the Kabila administration and the opposition, with the head of the Catholic Church, Cardinal Laurent Monsengwo, taking the position that the results of the election were invalid. The Catholic Church had trained and sponsored thousands of polling monitors to participate in the exercise, but the Church's observer mission had been stopped by the electoral commission from releasing its results, claiming that it was not a political entity. The EU, US, and UN stabilization force in the country, MONUSCO, also had expressed their deep concern with the results, and called for a peaceful resolution to the crisis.

13 GOVERNMENT

The DROC was a republic with a highly centralized government with executive power invested in the president. Since independence, the country has had numerous constitutions, constitutional amendments, and transitional constitutions. The latest iteration was approved in a national referendum in December 2005 by 84% of the voters, and promulgated in February 2006. The president nominates a vice president. He, along with the cabinet, is approved by the parliament. The legislative branch is bicameral and consists of a Senate of 108 seats, and a National Assembly composed of 500 members. Provincial assemblies elected the 108-member senate and provincial governors.

A basic law (loi fondamentale) was adopted in early 1960, before independence, pending the adoption of a permanent constitution by a constituent assembly. It provided for a division of executive powers between the head of state (president) and the head of government (premier). The premier and a cabinet known as the Council of Ministers were both responsible to the bicameral legislature on all matters of policy. This document was replaced by a constitution adopted in 1964 and modeled closely on the 1958 constitution of the French Fifth Republic. Under its terms, the president determined and directed the policy of the state and had the power to appoint and dismiss the prime minister. The powers of the parliament were sharply reduced. After his takeover in November 1965, Gen. Mobutu initially adhered to the 1964 constitution, but in October 1966 he combined the office of prime minister with the presidency. In June 1967 a new constitution was promulgated. It provided for a highly centralized form of presidential government and virtually eliminated the autonomy that provincial authorities had previously exercised.

The constitution was further amended on 23 December 1970 when the MPR was proclaimed the sole party of the republic. MPR primacy over all other national institutions, which resulted from the 1970 establishment of a single-party system, was affirmed in constitutions promulgated in 1974 and 1978. Instead of directly electing the president of the republic, voters confirmed the choice made by the MPR for its chairman, who automatically became the head of state and head of the government. The president's leading role in national affairs was further institutionalized by constitutional provisions that made him the formal head of the Political Bureau, of the Party Congress, and of the National Executive and National Legislative councils.

Organs of the MPR included the 80-member Central Committee, created in 1980 as the policy-making center for both party and government; the 16-member Political Bureau; the Party Congress, which was supposed to meet every five years; the National Executive Council (or cabinet); and the National Legislative Council, a unicameral body with 310 members. The Legislative Council was elected by universal suffrage from MPR-approved candidates. In practice, however, most government functions were directly controlled by President Mobutu through his personal entourage and through numerous aides and advisers. The constitution was amended in April 1990 to permit the formation of alternative parties.

In 1990, Mobutu was challenged by a rival government and he was unable to secure compliance with his decrees. In September 1993, the transitional Tshisekedi government elected by the National Conference in August 1992 and the Mobutu forces agreed on a draft constitution for the Third Republic and on an electoral process leading to a popular government in 1995. However, on 14 January 1994, Mobutu dismissed both governments and rival parliaments, a move that had little effect on the nation. Zaire had (as it had since 1992) two ineffectual governments, neither of which was capable of carrying out policy.

A rival legislature, the 435-member High Council of the Republic (HCR) was established by the National Conference in December 1992, and a government set up by the HCR and headed by Prime Minister Tshisekedi claimed to rule. Yet the army evicted his officers from government facilities. Mobutu repeatedly tried to remove Tshisekedi from office, but Tshisekedi refused to recognize Mobutu's authority to do so. Mobutu had de facto control of the administration but it was unable to act effectively. As a result of this stalemate, the government virtually collapsed.

With the overthrow of Mobutu in 1997, Zaire was renamed the Democratic Republic of the Congo, and the names of some provinces were changed. Bas-Zaire became Bas-Congo; Haut-Zaire became Province Orientale; Shaba assumed its former name, Katanga; and the two Kivus and Maniema were grouped together as one Kivu. In September 1997, Laurent Kabila had named several associates to the ministries, and others to governor posts. In November 1998 he approved a draft constitution, but it was not ratified by a national referendum; one outcome of the ongoing inter-Congolese dialogue was to be a new constitution. Laurent Kabila was assassinated in January 2001.

The December 2002 Pretoria agreement led to the establishment in June 2003 of a power-sharing transitional government led by President Joseph Kabila and co-led by four vice presidents who represented the five main armed factions, unarmed civilian opposition, civil society, and members of the previous Joseph Kabila government. The parliament was composed of a 500-member National Assembly and a 120-seat Senate with deputies appointed by the factions participating in the transition government. An electoral commission, a media-regulator, a truth and reconciliation commission, a national human rights watchdog, and an anticorruption commission rounded out the remaining temporary governmental bodies. The constitution was amended to change the age limit to 30 years old for presidential candidates, allowing Joseph Kabila (34 years old) to run.

In February 2006, a new constitution was formally adopted. The document was created to prepare the country for full democracy. Under the terms of the constitution, the president was to be elected and mandated to rule for two terms of five years. He also had to share power with an elected prime minister, chosen from the largest party elected to parliament. The parliament was to be elected and the judiciary (in theory) independent. In addition, the presidential age limit was reduced from 35 to 33. The number of provinces was increased from 10 to 26, but as of early 2012 that change had yet to take effect. The constitution was promulgated in front of the president of the African Union, Denis Sassou Nguesso, and South African President Thabo Mbeki, who had acted as a mediator in the Congo crisis. After the constitution was formed, a new national flag for Congo was adopted.

[14]POLITICAL PARTIES

In 2011 Congo had approximately 20–30 political parties plus coalitions of parties active on the national scene. Parties were identified foremost with leaders and by regional and ethnic identity; ideology and platform were of secondary importance.

Political activity was sharply restricted during the colonial period, but several dozen political parties had sprung into existence by early 1960, most of them small and based on local or ethnic organizations. Only the National Congolese Movement (Mouvement National Congolais—MNC) led by Patrice Lumumba entered the May 1960 elections and emerged with an effective national organization. Although the MNC captured only 30% of the popular vote, it formed alliances with two regional parties and controlled 64 of the 137 seats in the House of Representatives.

The national government subsequently organized in June 1960, however, won the backing of a much broader (although less cohesive) coalition which included Joseph Kasavubu's Bakongo Alliance (Alliance des Bakongo—ABAKO), the largest of the ethnic parties. Kasavubu became the country's head of state and in September 1960 ousted Lumumba. After Tshombe's accession to the post of prime minister in 1964, national and provincial elections were scheduled. In a rather belated effort to organize national support for his policies, Tshombe persuaded approximately 40 local formations to go to the polls under the hastily improvised label of the National Congolese Convention (Convention Nationale Congolaise—CONACO). The elections, held in March through April of 1965, gave CONACO 106 of the 166 seats in the lower house of the legislature. Kasavubu's subsequent dismissal of Tshombe in October 1965 and the failure of his handpicked successor, Evariste Kimba, to secure majority support in the CONACO-controlled lower house led to a complete stalemate, which was finally resolved only by Mobutu's seizure of power on 25 November 1965.

The new regime initially suspended all political parties, but in April 1967, Mobutu created the Popular Movement of the Revolution (Mouvement Populaire de la Révolution—MPR) in order to develop a political base for his regime. The constitution promulgated in June 1967 provided for the existence of "no more than two" political parties. However, all attempts to organize an opposition party to the MPR were summarily repressed, and the facade of bipartisanship was officially abandoned on 23 December 1970 when a constitutional amendment formally transformed the country into a single-party state. The chairman of the MPR held the office of head of state and head of the government after approval by the voters. Party and state were effectively one, and every citizen was automatically a member of the MPR. Of the four exiled opposition groups headquartered in Brussels, the Union for Democracy and Social Progress (Union pour la Démocratie et du Progrès Social—UDPS) appeared to be the most significant.

The constitution was amended to permit party activity in April 1990. By the time the National Conference was called in September 1991, more than 200 parties had emerged. Half of them belonged to the *mouvence présidentielle* but had no popular basis. The most important opposition parties formed a coalition known as the Sacred Union. These included the UDPS, the Union of Federalists and Independent Republicans (UFERI), the Unified Lumumbist Party (PALU) of Antoine Gizenga, and the Social Democratic Christian Party (PDSC). UFERI was later pried away from the Sacred Union by Mobutu's offer of the prime ministership to UFERI's Nguza Karl-I-Bond in November 1991.

In 1997, President Kabila outlawed all political parties and party activities until at least 1999 when elections were promised. However, party leaders such as Zahidi Ngoma (Les Forces du Future), and Olenghakoy (Forces for Renovation for Union and Solidarity-FONUS), who were previously jailed, did participate in the clergy-sponsored "Consultation Nationale" to discuss national issues. In April 2000, Tshisikedi of the UDPS traveled to the United States and Europe, signaling a thaw in the provisional ban on party activities.

In the run-up to the scheduled June 2006 elections, parties once again were legalized. The dominant players were Joseph Kabila's Party of the People for the Reconstruction of Democracy (Parti du Peuple pour la Reconstruction et la Démocratie—PPRD); the PDSC; FONUS; the National Congolese Lumumbist Movement (MNC); the MPR—divided into three factions; PALU; UDPS; and UFERI—divided into two factions.

In July 2006, presidential and parliamentary elections were held; they were the first free elections to be held in 46 years. There was no clear winner in the presidential vote. Therefore, incumbent leader Joseph Kabila and opposition candidate Jean-Pierre Bemba faced off in a run-off election on 29 October 2006. In November, Kabila was declared the winner of October's run-off election with 58% of the vote. The election had the approval of international monitors. In the July parliamentary elections, the PPRD came in first, with 22.2% of the vote and 111 seats; the Movement for the Liberation of Congo (MLC), headed by Bemba, came in second with 12.8% of the vote and 64 seats; followed by PALU with 6.8% of the vote and 34 seats; the Mouvement Social pour le Renouveau (MSR), 5.4% and 27 seats; and Forces du Renouveau, 5.2% and 26 seats. A number of other parties secured 3% or less of the vote. The Coalition of Congolese Democrats (CODECO), comprising 30 political parties, supported Pierre Pay-Pay wa Syakassighe in the 2006 Presidential Election.

In January 2011, parliament passed a proposal advanced by Kabila that permitted candidates to win an election on the first round with a simple majority, or less than 50% of the vote. This rule seriously disadvantaged opposition candidates and parties since they would be unable to join forces to defeat an incumbent on a second round. In December 2011, amidst allegations of vote-rigging and refusal by opposition parties to accept the results, the electoral commission declared Joseph Kabila the winner of the 28 November election with 49% of the vote. According to official tallies, Etienne Tshisekedi (UDPS) obtained 32% of the vote with other candidates sharing the remaining 19%. Tshisekedi countered by declaring himself president in December 2011, although his declaration affected no change in government. Some 18,864 candidates contested the 500 National Assembly seats. Senate elections were due on 13 June 2012.

15 LOCAL GOVERNMENT

Since independence, the number of provinces has varied from 6 to 21, with an autonomous capital district at Kinshasa (formerly Léopoldville). In 2011, there were ten provinces and the capital city of Kinshasa. According to the 2005 constitution, the provinces were to be sub divided into 26 provinces by 2009, but this change (le découpage) had not yet occurred. Certain provinces were better resourced than others, and a law requiring 40% of tax revenues to remain in the provinces favored provinces such as mineral-rich Katanga.

In 1966 the number of provinces was cut back to 12, later to 8, and then up to 10. At the same time, provincial autonomy, considerable in the republic's early years, was virtually eliminated following the adoption of a new constitution in 1967. The regions then were Bas-Zaire, Bandundu, Equateur, Haut-Zaire, Nord-Kivu, Shaba (formerly Katanga), Kasai-Oriental, Maniema and Sud-Kivu, and Kasai-Occidental. They were administered directly by regional commissioners. The regions were divided into 37 subregions (the former districts), of which 13 were major towns and their environs. These were further subdivided into 134 zones. Urban zones contained localities, while rural zones contained collectivities (chiefdoms), which in turn contained rural localities (groups of villages). Kinshasa, although autonomous, was organized like a region with subregions and zones.

Local administration was for years virtually coterminous with the local branch of the MPR. Regional, subregional, and zone commissioners were appointed by the central government. There were rural and urban councils. Urban councils were elected in 1977 and 1982; rural councils were elected in 1982. But the current breakdown of government left the operation of local government in doubt.

In April 1999, Laurent Kabila launched the CPP (Comité de pouvoir populaire), whose main purpose was to report to the authorities the needs of the population. CPP offices were located in each commune, and each neighborhood had its own representative. To some degree, their responsibilities overlapped with the existing local government. However, CPP more easily obtained funds to implement local projects, such as street lighting, sanitation, schools, and transportation. One example was the City Train, a tractor-trailer cab pulling a passenger wagon. In 2011, conventional local government administration was compromised by a weak tax base and inadequate funding.

¹⁶JUDICIAL SYSTEM

The judicial system was a civil legal system based on a Belgian version of French civil law. Tribal and customary law also applied in domestic affairs and in land tenure and property rights, especially in rural and remote areas of the country where there were no functioning courts.

The system comprised courts of first instance, appellate courts, a Supreme Court and the Court of State Security. Military courts handled cases involving the armed forces. Many disputes were adjudicated at the local level by administrative officials or traditional authorities. Although 1977 amendments to the constitution and subsequent revisions guaranteed an independent judiciary, in practice the president and the government influenced court decisions.

In theory, defendants had the right to counsel and a public trial. Appellate review was afforded in all cases except those involving national security and serious crimes adjudicated by the Court of State Security. Owing to the war in 1998, a provisional court (la Cour d'Ordre Militaire) was established.

The judicial system in Congo was broken in almost every way: from crumbling physical infrastructure to low salaries for judges, lawyers and clerks. Bribes and enticements compromised judgments and decisions at all levels, favoring the wealthy and influential.

¹⁷ARMED FORCES

The International Institute for Strategic Studies (IISS) reported that armed forces in the Democratic Republic of the Congo totaled an estimated 151,500 members in 2011. The force was comprised of 115,000 from the army, 7,000 from the republican guard, 6,703 from the navy, 2,548 from the air force, and 14,000 members of central staff. Armed forces represented 0.6% of the labor force in the DROC. Defense spending totaled $579.4 million and accounted for 2.5% of GDP.

The UN peacekeeping contingent in the DROC, which transformed itself into a stabilization mission (MONUSCO), was the largest UN mission in the world with over 20,000 personnel. The former mission, MONUC, had been set to expire in May 2010. Analysts advised that UN withdrawal would be catastrophic for stability and security because eastern border areas remained highly volatile and violent.

The LRA, led by warlord Joseph Kony, continued to operate in the four country border area of northeast Congo. LRA tactics have included child abduction, torture, slavery, and forced conscription. The UN estimated that nearly 2,000 people in the four-border region had been killed by the LRA between 2008 and 2011, with another 2,600 abducted.

In October 2010, leaders of Uganda, South Sudan, Central African Republic (CAR), and the DROC met with the African Union to forge an agreement to pool the resources of all four nations to defeat the LRA. The plan utilized troops and resources from all four nations, backed by military assistance from Nigeria and South Africa. It also included cross-border intelligence sharing and assistance from the African Union to track movements of LRA soldiers. In October 2011 US president Barack Obama committed 100 battle-equipped military advisors to neighboring CAR to strengthen efforts to remove Kony from the battlefield.

The International Criminal Court had an outstanding arrest warrant against Kony for crimes against humanity; he was still being pursued as of April 2012.

¹⁸INTERNATIONAL COOPERATION

The DROC was admitted to membership in the UN on 20 September 1960. It is a member of ECA and several non-regional specialized agencies and is a member of the WTO. The DROC is also a member of the African Development Bank, COMESA, the ACP Group, G-24, G-77, the SADC, the New Partnership for Africa's Development (NEPAD), and the African Union. The DROC is a member of the International Council of Copper Exporting Countries. The DROC, Rwanda, and Burundi form the Economic Community of the Great Lakes Countries (CEPGL). The DROC is part of the Nonaligned Movement.

The UN Stabilization Mission in the Democratic Republic of Congo (MONUSCO) was established (formerly the Observer Mission of the UN in the Congo [MONUC] in 1999) to assist in the disengagement of forces and the continuation of cease-fire agreements stemming from the 1998 civil war. In November 2009, the U.N. Security Council voted unanimously to expand and extend its arms embargo and related sanctions in the DROC for one year. The embargo, which has been in place since 2003, seeks to prevent illicit arms transfers to any armed groups other than the government's integrated army and police forces. The sanctions were extended through 29 November 2010. Since the initial authorization of MONUSCO, the mission's military strength has increased exponentially from 5,537 troops to 19,060 troops as of February 2012. In addition, the annual financial expenditure from the initial mission to 2011–12 has also increased significantly, from $55,271 to an estimated $1.49 billion.

The European Union has been conducting a Common Security and Defense Policy Mission to the Democratic Republic of Congo since 8 June 2005, following an official request from the government of the DROC. On 21 September 2010 the Council of the European Union voted to extend EU support in the DROC until 30 September 2012.

In environmental cooperation, the DROC is part of the Basel Convention, the Convention on Biological Diversity, Ramsar, CITES, the London Convention, International Tropical Timber Agreements, the Montréal Protocol, the Nuclear Test Ban Treaty, and the UN Conventions on the Law of the Sea, Climate Change and Desertification.

¹⁹ECONOMY

The GDP rate of change in Democratic Republic of the Congo, as of 2010, was 7.2%. Inflation stood at 26.2%, and unemployment was estimated to be 8.9% (as of 2008). Underemployment and unemployment in the conflict-prone eastern side of the country would likely make this figure much higher.

Mutinous military troops have periodically looted major urban centers bringing the economy to a virtual standstill. The economy has also been decimated by poor economic and monetary policies, systemic grand and petty corruption at all levels, protracted civil war, rapacious militias, crumbling infrastructure, bad transportation networks, weak rule of law, lack of sustained and regulated investment and low social development.

Intermittent war between 1996 and 2010 raised government debt, reduced revenue and economic output, increased corruption, caused a collapse of the banking system, and, because many industries and businesses could not operate, relegated much of the population to forms of barter. A UN report released in 2002 stated that over 85 multinational corporations, largely based in Europe, the United States, and South Africa, had taken advantage of the instability caused by war and violated ethical guidelines by dealing with criminal networks exploiting the DROC's natural resources, including gold, diamonds, coltan, cobalt, and copper. This activity must be seen against the backdrop of the plunder undertaken by the combatants themselves and other African nations involved in the fighting.

A large government deficit, primarily to pay salaries for the military and civil servants, was financed by printing currency. Hyperinflation, rapid devaluation, and abandonment of the formal economy ensued. As a result of the accompanying widespread uncertainty and civil disorder, most businesses that were unable to leave the country adopted a defensive stance, minimizing their exposure in the DROC and waiting for an upturn in the economy. After the civil war began in August 1998, the government depreciated the franc four times to keep up with inflation, which increased mistrust in the currency.

The government under Joseph Kabila in 2001 implemented stabilization measures designed to break the spiral of hyperinflation and currency depreciation caused by the war. The reform program reduced inflation from 500% in 200 to 7% in 2003. In that same year, a debt cancellation program under the Paris Club Heavily Indebted Poor Countries (HIPC) program came into effect, with 80% of the DROC's external debt being written off. By 2006, however, inflation had surged to 20% and the DROC lost its eligibility for interim debt relief because of fiscal overruns. International donors included the EU, World Bank, IMF, and African Development Bank; bilateral donors included Belgium, Canada, France, the US and China.

The government began to look toward Asia as a source of funding for development projects, particularly those involving reconstruction of the nation's war-damaged infrastructure. In late 2009, India offered funding of $25 million for the construction of water pumps throughout the country and $33.5 million that went toward the construction of a cement plant and the purchase of more than 340 Indian-made buses. In 2010, an additional loan of $42 million was offered by India for a new hydroelectric plant in Kakobola, of the western Bandundu province. This plant, which was expected to serve more than 1.9 million people, was under construction as of 2011. Another $168 million hydroelectric plant was planned for a location in central Congo, also with Indian financial support. Support for infrastructure development has also come from China. In July 2010, the World Bank and International Monetary Fund announced $12.3 billion of debt relief for the DROC to spur redevelopment.

In 2010 the World Bank predicted that the economy would grow steadily over the medium term at around 7% owing to investments and growth in extractives, and high world prices for raw materials. The Bank advised that continued restrictive monetary policy and fiscal discipline would be crucial to managing inflation. The World Bank also estimated that government's strategy to support large-scale infrastructure investments could significantly enhance growth, provided that high-return projects were prioritized. Investments combined with reforms to improve the business environment, especially trade facilitation measures were judged to be able to increase GDP growth.

20 INCOME

The CIA estimated that in 2010 the GDP of the DROC was $23.12 billion. The CIA defines GDP as the value of all final goods and services produced within a nation in a given year and computed on the basis of purchasing power parity (PPP) rather than value as measured on the basis of the rate of the exchange based on current dollars. The per capita GDP was estimated at $300. The annual growth rate of GDP was 7.2%. The average inflation rate was 26.2%. It was estimated that agriculture accounted for 37.4% of GDP, industry 26%, and services 36.6%.

The World Bank reported that in 2009, household consumption in the DROC totaled $5.9 billion or about $83 per capita, measured in current US dollars rather than PPP.

The World Bank estimated that the DROC, with 0.97% of the world's population, accounted for 0.03% of the world's GDP. By comparison, the United States, with 4.85% of the world's population, accounted for 22.51% of world GDP. It was estimated that in 2006 about 71% of the population subsisted on an income below the poverty line established by the Democratic Republic of Congo's government.

As of 2011 the most recent study by the World Bank reported that actual individual consumption in the Democratic Republic of the Congo was 69.0% of GDP and accounted for 0.02% of world consumption. By comparison, the United States accounted for 25.44% of world individual consumption. The World Bank also estimated that 44.3% of Congo's GDP was spent on food and beverages, 10.1% on housing and household furnishings, 3.5% on clothes, 2.8% on health, 2.4% on transportation, 0.6% on communications, 0.6% on recreation, 1.0% on restaurants and hotels, and 1.7% on miscellaneous goods and services and purchases from abroad.

21 LABOR

As of 2010 the DROC had a total labor force of 33.68 million people.

The law provides for the right to unionize with the exception of magistrates and military personnel. The right to strike is limited by restrictions (mandatory arbitration and appeal procedures), and the unions struggle to protect workers' rights due to the difficult economic situation and lax government enforcement.

The official workweek is 48 hours in six days, with one 24-hour rest period required every seven days. The legal minimum employment age is 18, although many children work to help feed their families. All wages and salaries were extremely low. Civil servants were paid irregularly, and supplemented their incomes through various types of rent-seeking and bribery.

22 AGRICULTURE

The country's major crops included coffee, sugar, palm oil, rubber, tea, cotton, cocoa, quinine, cassava (tapioca), manioc, bananas, plantains, peanuts, root crops, corn, and fruits. Cereal production in 2009 amounted to 1.6 million tons, fruit production 2.3 million tons, and vegetable production 542,645 tons.

The agricultural sector supported two-thirds of the population. Agricultural production has stagnated since independence and has become primarily subsistence focused on cassava, yams, plantains, rice, maize and sorghum. Plots averaged 1.6 hectares (four acres). The country was not drought-prone but was hindered by a poor internal transportation system, which impeded development of an effective national urban food-supply system. It was common to find small garden plots throughout Kinshasa and other cities. Domestic food production was insufficient to meet the country's needs, and many basic food products had to be imported.

The production of cash crops was severely disrupted by the wave of civil disorder that engulfed the country between 1960 and 1967, and production fell again after many small foreign-owned plantations were nationalized in 1973–74. By the mid-1990s, the production of the DROC's principal cash crops (coffee, rubber, palm oil, cocoa, tea) was mostly back in private hands. Commercial farmers numbered some 300,000, with holdings between 12 and 250 hectares (30 and 618 acres). Coffee was the DROC's third most important export (after copper and crude oil) and was the leading agricultural export. An estimated 80% of production came from the provinces of Orientale, Equateur, and Kivu. Only 10–15% of production was Arabica; coffee exports went mainly to Italy, France, Belgium, and Switzerland. The collapse of the International Coffee Agreement in 1989 quickly led to a doubling of exports by the former Zaire, whereupon the surplus entering the world market drove down prices rapidly.

Rubber was the second most important export cash crop. The plantation crop has been slowly recovering from nationalization. Some plantations were replanting for the first time in over 20 years. Oil palm production was concentrated in three large operations, two of them foreign-owned. Palm oil production remained profitable in the DROC due to a 100% tax on competing imported oil. The production of cotton engaged about 250,000 farmers, who annually produced about 8,000 tons. Domestic production, however, was not sufficient for the country's textile manufacturers.

23 ANIMAL HUSBANDRY

The UN Food and Agriculture Organization (FAO) reported that the DROC dedicated 15 million hectares (37.1 million acres) to permanent pasture or meadow in 2009. During that year, the country tended 19.8 million chickens, 755,000 head of cattle, and 965,000 pigs. The production from these animals amounted to 30,787 tons of beef and veal, 27,288 tons of pork, 61,339 tons of poultry, 5,266 tons of eggs, and 80,092 tons of milk. The DROC also produced 2,000 tons of cattle hide. A state agency managed large ranches, mainly in Katanga and West Kasai.

24 FISHING

The DROC had 25 decked commercial fishing boats in 2008. The annual capture totaled 236,000 tons according to the UN FAO. The export value of seafood totaled $419,000. Fish were the single most important source of animal protein in the DROC. Artisanal fish farming or pisciculture, provided families and small businessmen with a significant source of tilapia and income, especially in

Bandundu and Lower Congo provinces. PEMARZA, a state agency, carried on marine fishing.

25 FORESTRY

Approximately 68% of the Democratic Republic of the Congo was covered by forest. The UN FAO estimated the 2009 roundwood production at 4.45 million cu m (157.2 million cu ft). The value of all forest products, including roundwood, totaled $91.4 million.

The Congo basin possessed Africa's largest tropical evergreen forest; second largest in the world after the Amazon basin. Commercial development of the country's exploitable wooded area was underway, but difficult access to remote areas slowed exploitation. The Mayumbe area of Lower Congo was once the major center of timber exploitation, but forests in this area were nearly depleted. The more extensive forest regions of the central cuvette and of the Ubangi River valley have increasingly been tapped, utilizing the Ubangi and Congo River networks as access and transportation routes.

Foreign capital was necessary in order for forestry to expand, and the government recognized that changes in tax structure and export procedures would be needed to facilitate economic growth via the forestry sector.

26 MINING

Congo's minerals have been a source of conflict and chaos in the country. Foreign armies, warlords, militias, and Congolese generals have all been involved in illegal exploitation of gold, coltan and other minerals and precious stones in the Kivus and in Ituri District of Orientale Province. Typically, these operations carried high costs in environmental degradation and human exploitation. HIV/AIDS was highly prevalent in mining camps, and rapes of women were the highest in the world in these areas. In the 2000s, AngloGold Ashanti, subsidiaries and local partners were developing a major gold field in Mongbwalu in Ituri District, but in 2012 serious questions remained about the costs and benefits to human welfare, and the negative environmental impacts of that particular operation.

Mining was the country's leading industry in 2009, and diamonds, copper, and cobalt ranked first, second, and fourth, respectively, among export commodities. Mining has historically accounted for 25% of GDP and three-quarters of export revenues. In 2008 the mining sector's share of GDP was 13.4%. The outbreak of civil conflict in the DROC (then known as Zaire) in 1996 severely disrupted the economy, including metals mining, leaving diamond exports as the major source of revenue. Despite the collapse of much of the formal mining infrastructure, the DROC remained an important source of industrial diamond and cobalt.

The value of exports in 2008 was valued at $6.59 billion, of which cobalt accounted for 38%; copper, 35%; and diamonds, 1%. The public mining company La Générale des Carrières et des Mines (Gécamines) in 2002 reported total "global reserves" of 54 million tons of copper, 4.66 million tons of cobalt, and 6.4 million tons of zinc, expressed in contained metal. Gécamines, one of the country's most economically productive companies, produced all of its coal, cobalt, copper, and zinc. The Congo also produced, and was richly endowed with, cadmium, coal, columbium (niobium), and tantalum (locally referred to as "coltan"), germanium, gold, lime, manganese, petroleum, silver, crushed stone, sulfuric acid, tin, tungsten, uranium, and zinc. Uranium for the first US atomic bomb was mined in the former Zaire. Most foreign exploration activity and development-oriented feasibility work came to a halt in 1998, following the flare-up of a new full-scale civil war. Negotiations on a 1999 cease-fire agreement continued into 2001, and the decrease in military conflict permitted the government to address a proposal for new foreign investment and mining laws. Over half of the DROC's mineral exports took a circuitous route by air, riverboat, railway, and road from Shaba to the Matadi port (copper shipments could take 45 days to go from the plant to the dock), because the Benguela railway to Angola has effectively been closed since 1975; most of the rest went south by rail to South Africa, which was an important source of imports. Because of the size and wealth of its resources, the long-term potential of the Congo was more promising, and the country could return to world markets as an important supplier of cobalt, copper, diamond, and zinc, dependent on its ability to achieve political and economic stability and to put in place the legal and business framework needed to attract new foreign investment.

Until 1986, the former Zaire was the leading producer of industrial diamonds. The chief diamond-producing center was Mbuji Mayi, in East Kasai. The 80%-government-owned Société Minière de Bakwanga (MIBA) produced over 1.2 million carats of low-value, near-gem-quality stones in 2009. However, the majority of the diamonds produced by the DROC comes from artisanal mining in the Tshikapa, Kinsingani, and Mbujimayi regions. In 2009, artisanal production of diamonds totaled 17 million carats, compared with output in 2005 of 26.8 million carats.

Mine copper output in 2009 was 295,000 metric tons, up from 97,000 metric tons in 2005. Copper was produced exclusively in the Shaba Region (formerly Katanga), *shaba* meaning "copper" in Swahili. Gécamines holdings in the Copperbelt, in Shaba, contained one of the greatest concentrations of high-grade copper and coproduct cobalt resources in the world. First Quantum Minerals Ltd.'s small, high-grade Lonshi copper deposit began open pit mining in 2001; it contained a measured and indicated resource of 5.1 million tons grading 5.75% acid-soluble copper. In 2009, production of refined copper increased 247%.

The output of cobalt from mined ore was 29,000 metric tons in 2009, up from an estimated 24,500 metric tons in 2005. In 1994, Gécamines initiated a program to shift emphasis toward cobalt production, which jumped 57% that year, after falling 87% since 1987. Gécamines's strategy was to concentrate development and mining activities at cobalt-rich zones of several copper ore bodies, with plans to produce 10,000–15,000 tons of higher value cobalt by the end of 2002. Gécamines reported an increase of refined cobalt by 106% in 2009.

OM Group, Inc. (OMGI), of the United States, one of the world's largest consumers of refined cobalt, and l'Enterprise Générale Malta Forrest SPRL (EGMF) completed the first major foreign investment in Shaba in recent years; full operating capacity from their Luiswishi copper-cobalt mine was reached in 2000. As of early 2002, total resources remaining at the Luiswishi Mine-the only mine operating in Gécamines's Southern Group in 2001-were reported to be 7.5–8 million tons at a grade of 2.8% copper and 1.0% cobalt; the second phase of mining would develop 3.5 million tons of oxide reserves at a rate of 500,000 tons per year of ore. Anvil Mining NL of Australia and First Quantum announced

plans to develop the high-grade Dikulushi copper-silver deposit. Anvil also held a number of exploration licenses covering more than 43,000 sq km (16,600 sq mi), including gold and platinum prospects near Kalemie, copper and gold prospects near Kapulo, and copper prospects near Lungeshi. The Tenke Fungurume mine is the country's leading cobalt mine by capacity, and is a joint venture between Gécamines (17.5%) and Freeport McMoran Copper & Gold Inc. (US, 57.75%) and Lundin Mining Corp. (Canada, 27.75%). The Kolwezi copper-cobalt tailings project, operated by a 50–50 joint US-UK venture, was based on reprocessing of a resource of nearly 113 million tons grading 1.49% copper and 0.32% cobalt of oxide tailings from the Kingamyambo and Musonoi tailings dams; mining would be by high-pressure water monitor guns with the material pumped along a slurry pipeline to a new leach SX-EW plant.

Mined output of zinc (mineral content) fell from 172,000 tons in 1969 to zero in 1999 and 1,014 in 2001. Mined output of zinc totaled 17,000 metric tons in 2009. The Big Hill plant in Lumbumbashi has an annual capacity of 15,000 tons of zinc oxide.

Congo recorded no silver production in 2009, but did produce 76,242 kg in 2007 and 34,083 kg in 2008. Gold output was 3,500 kg in 2009, down from 10,300 kg in 2006. Cassiterite (tin ore) production totaled 10,000 metric tons in 2009, up from 4,400 tons in 2005.

According to the 1994 Constitution, the soil and subsoil belonged to the state. A new mining code was adopted in 2002, creating a framework of incentives conducive to private investment, including a change in the role of government from mining operator to mining regulator, creation of a single investment agreement framework, introduction of a special tax regime, and the option of issuing mining titles on a first-come-first-served basis, transparently managed. The government maintained at least partial ownership and generally majority ownership of all the productive and service sectors of the economy. In 2007, the government initiated a review of more than 60 mining contracts negotiated between 1998 and 2005. By the end of 2008, the government chose to terminate 23 of the contracts; most of the rest were determined acceptable or renegotiated.

²⁷ENERGY AND POWER

The World Bank reported in 2008 that the DROC produced 7.45 billion kWh of electricity and consumed 6.11 billion kWh, or 85 kWh per capita. Roughly 4% of energy came from fossil fuels, while 3% came from alternative fuels.

The Democratic Republic of the Congo (DROC) had reserves of petroleum, natural gas, coal, and a potential hydroelectric power generating capacity of around 100,000 MW. The DROC's Inga dams, alone on the Congo River, had the potential to generate 40,000 to 45,000 MW of electric power, sufficient to supply the electricity needs of the whole Southern Africa region. However, ongoing uncertainties in the political arena, and a resulting lack of interest from investors limited potential. The DROC was an exporter of electric power. During the 2000s electric power exports was transmitted to the Republic of Congo and its capital, Brazzaville, as well as to Zambia and South Africa.

The DROC had crude oil reserves second to, but far behind Angola's in southern Africa. As of 1 January 2011 the DROC's crude oil reserves came to 180 million barrels (Angola: 9.4 billion barrels as of 2010). In 2010, the DROC produced 21,100 barrels of petroleum per day. For that year, domestic consumption and net exports came to 13,000 barrels per day and 11,090 barrels per day, respectively. However, the DROC had limited refining capacity, and had to import refined petroleum products. In 2011 imports of refined petroleum products totaled 13,100 barrels per day. Oil product imports consisted of gasoline, jet fuel, kerosene, aviation gas, fuel oil, and liquefied petroleum gas.

As of 1 January 2011, the DROC had natural gas reserves of 991.1 million cu m (Angola: estimated 309.8 billion cu m as of 2011). As of 2011 there was no domestic production or consumption of natural gas.

28 INDUSTRY

Manufacturing in 2011 had yet to recover from war, instability, neglect and poor policies. Foreign exchange problems and a decline in local purchasing power due to hyperinflation (estimated at 357% in 2001 and 21.7% in 2005) also hindered industrial expansion. Much of the DROC's industry was limited to the processing of agricultural products (sugar, flour) and mineral-bearing ore (copper, zinc, cement). The production of consumer goods (beer, soft drinks, textiles) played a leading role in the sector, as did palm oil processing and cigarette making.

A five-year investment in the copper smelter in Katanga (then Shaba) was completed in 1990. However, the center was severely damaged by political unrest in 1992–93. The Maluju steel mill was unprofitable and closed in 1986. The Société Congo-Italienne de Raffinage (SOCIR) refinery operated at 50% of capacity and produced 2 million barrels of refined petroleum products in 1994. The country's domestic crude oil has been too heavy to be processed by the refinery although, as of 2000, the refinery resumed limited refining activity to process some imported crude oil.

Despite the war, reconstruction plans were underway during the 2003–05 period, including building, construction, construction for pipelines, communication and power lines, highways, roads, airfields, and railways. Construction for plants, mining and manufacturing, and buildings related to the oil and gas industry were also being undertaken. New policies implemented in 2010 to improve governance and rebuild infrastructure offered hope for a brighter future in industry.

29 SCIENCE AND TECHNOLOGY

The World Bank reported in 2009 that there were no patent applications in science and technology in the DROC. The General Commission on Atomic Energy, conducting research in peaceful application of atomic energy, was in Kinshasa, as were theInstitute of Tropical Medicine, the National Institute for the Study of Agronomical Research, the Institute of Nature Conservation, the Center for Geological and Mineral Research, and France's Bureau of Geological and Mineral Research. The University of Kinshasa (founded in 1954) had faculties of sciences, polytechnic, medicine, and pharmacy. The University of Kisangani (founded in 1963) had faculties of science and medicine. The University of Lubumbashi (founded in 1955) had faculties of sciences, polytechnic, veteri-

nary medicine, and medicine. Five university-level institutes offered training in information science, agronomy, and medicine.

30 DOMESTIC TRADE

Domestic trade was typically led by small- to medium-scale entrepreneurs, generally of Lebanese, Greek, Indian or Pakistani, and European extraction. Decades of corruption, poor economic policies, state control over enterprises and political unrest strangled trade. In the 1970s, Mobutu nationalized businesses in a program called "Zairianisation," handing over companies to cronies and clients who knew nothing about business. In short order firms and stores were run into the ground. By the mid-1990s, the government controlled 116 enterprises, of which 56 were fully publicly owned. Consequently, a large underground market operated within the country for decades.

In 2001, the government launched economic reforms, featuring the establishment of a commercial court and a new investment code that aimed to encourage foreign and domestic investment. These reforms achieved a measure of success, but were unable to overcome the damage wrought by decades of mutinies and looting by armed forces, widespread political turmoil and economic malaise.

The main distribution centers in the country were regional capitals including Kinshasa, Lubumbashi, Kisangani, Matadi, and Mbandaka. Other commercial centers included Likasi, Kolwezi, Kananga, and Mbuji-Mayi. High transportation costs and the lack of dependable road and rail systems in many areas hindered domestic trade. Much domestic trade was carried out in local weekly markets. One of the most colorful markets was the Congo River boats and barges that travelled between Kinshasa and Kisangani, carrying goods to be traded with villagers along the river.

Gratuities were a part of almost every commercial transaction conducted. Tips and gifts were routinely expected, particularly for licenses and permits. Soldiers and officials typically extorted money from businessmen and transporters along principal trade routes including the Kinshasa-Matadi highway.

Principal Trading Partners – Congo (DROC) (2010)

(In millions of US dollars)

Country	Total	Exports	Imports	Balance
World	9,900.0	5,400.0	4,500.0	900.0
China	2,763.3	2,242.1	521.1	1,721.0
Zambia	1,482.2	1,116.3	366.0	750.3
South Africa	813.5	10.1	803.4	-793.3
United States	599.5	496.6	102.9	393.8
Belgium	586.0	203.3	382.7	-179.4
Zimbabwe	333.8	46.7	287.1	-240.5
France	270.1	27.3	242.7	-215.4
Kenya	252.4	10.6	241.9	-231.3
Netherlands	193.4	49.9	143.5	-93.6
Uganda	154.3	1.5	152.8	-151.2

(…) data not available or not significant.

(n.s.) not specified.

SOURCE: *2011 Direction of Trade Statistics Yearbook*, New York: United Nations, 2011.

Usual business hours were from 8 a.m. to noon and from 2:30 to 5 p.m., Monday through Friday, and 7:30 a.m. to noon on Saturday. Most correspondence and advertising were in French. Because of high inflation and difficulty with banking, most transactions were conducted with cash; larger transactions were conducted with US dollars. Major credit cards and travelers' checks were not widely accepted.

³¹FOREIGN TRADE

Major import partners in 2009 were South Africa, 17.5%; Belgium, 9.8%; China, 9.8%; Zambia, 9.2%; France, 7%; Zimbabwe, 6.3%; and Kenya, 5.3%. DROC's major export partners were China, 41%; Zambia, 17.8%; the United States, 12.4%; Belgium, 8.6%; and India, 5.2%. Principal imports were consumer goods, foodstuffs, mining and other machinery, transport equipment, and fuels. The leading exports were diamonds, copper, cobalt, crude oil, coffee and timber. There was little value-added in Congo's exports, and little export revenue was re-invested in the domestic economy. During his administration, Mobutu routinely diverted much of the country's export revenues to special accounts held outside the country. The CIA reported that in 2011 exports totaled $10.93 billion and imports totaled $9.021 billion

³²BALANCE OF PAYMENTS

The CIA reported that DROC maintained a trade surplus from 2009 through 2011. However, substantial illegal exports, imports, and transfers of capital and profits abroad went unrecorded. Indeed, the central bank did not include adjustments for fraud of close to 100% for DROC's primary exports. In August 1991, the government permitted the zaire, then the national currency, to float because the central bank had exhausted its foreign exchange reserves. By statute, the government no longer controlled the import or export of capital or the foreign exchange markets. DROC had no external credit, almost no central bank reserves, and external financial operations were largely carried out by private entities. Large external payments arrears have not been cleared. In 2009, the external debt was estimated at $13.5 billion, up from $10.98 billion in 2005.

³³BANKING AND SECURITIES

The Central bank was the Bank of Congo (Banque Centrale du Congo). In 2011 some 25 commercial banks operated in the country, including the Bank of Kinshasa, Barclays Bank, Stanbic Bank, Citibank, and Ecobank. There were also a number of lending institutions aimed at providing loans to small- and medium-scale businesses in the informal sector. An indication of the deterioration of economic life was a strong disinclination by the public to keep money in banks.

In 2010 the central bank discount rate, the interest rate at which the central bank lends to financial institutions in the short term, was 22%, down from 70% in 2009. The commercial bank prime lending rate in the same year was 56.8%.

There were no securities exchanges in the DROC.

³⁴INSURANCE

In 2011, there were some 15 insurance firms doing business in DROC. In 1967, all private insurance companies had been abolished and replaced by the state-owned National Society of Insurance (La Société Nationale d'Assurances— SONAS). In 2011 SONAS still operated under the aegis of a government monopoly.

³⁵PUBLIC FINANCE

In 2010 the budget of Democratic Republic of the Congo included $700 million in public revenue and $2 billion in public expenditures. The budget deficit amounted to 9.9% of GDP. Public debt was 26.6% of GDP, with $13.5 billion of the debt held by foreign entities.

Public finance from the late 1970s to the 1990s was characterized by uncontrolled spending, poor tax collection, and large deficits, often covered by creating new money. Expenditures were almost entirely current. The state-owned copper mining company generated one-third of the government's revenue. Since coming to office, the Joseph Kabila administration, under the supervision of the IMF and the World Bank, has undertaken various economic reforms to improve governance and transparency in public finance. The program reduced inflation from over 500% in 2000 to about 10% by the end of 2001.

In June 2002, a three-year standby agreement was concluded with the IMF, but stabilization and welfare spending targets were missed because of the need for increased military spending. IMF-led programs to control public spending, manage currency fluctuation and inflation, and increase public revenues by stimulating economic growth continued into 2011 and beyond.

³⁶TAXATION

In the mid-1990s, personal income was taxed progressively, with a 50% ceiling on total payable tax. In 2012, the corporate tax rate was 40% of taxable profits. Profits of branches of foreign corporations were subject to the same rate of taxation. There was also a 221% sales tax on imports, exports, local manufactured goods, construction works, local services, and imported services. An employment tax of 33% was imposed on services by foreigners. Other taxes included an educational tax, property tax, and a transfer tax. Combined taxes totaled 339.7% compared with an average of 57.1% for sub Saharan Africa, and 42.7% for OECD countries. Congo ranked 165th out of 183 countries on the tax indicator of the World Bank's Doing Business Index for 2012.

³⁷CUSTOMS AND DUTIES

Congo adopted the Harmonized System in 1988. Most tariffs were ad valorem. The tariff rate system had four categories: 5% on basic necessities; 10% on raw materials and capital goods; 20% on intermediate and miscellaneous goods; and 30% on consumer goods. There was also an 18.7% value-added tax (VAT) based on CIF (cost, insurance, freight) plus the duty. The DROC was associated with the EU countries through the Lomé Convention, which provided for the reduction of tariff barriers between the signatories and EU members.

In order to improve business and investment opportunities in the DROC, the government under President Kabila adopted new custom codes and law to reflect the value added tax (VAT). Nonetheless, the DROC ranked 167th out of 183 countries on the "trade across borders" indicator of the World Bank's Doing Business Index for 2012. The cost of exporting a container of goods was $3,055 compared with $1,960 for sub Saharan countries and $1,032 for OECD countries. The cost of importing a container was $3,285 compared with $2,503 for sub Saharan countries, and $1,085 for OECD countries.

38 FOREIGN INVESTMENT

Foreign direct investment (FDI) in the Democratic Republic of the Congo was a net inflow of $951.4 million according to World Bank figures published in 2009. FDI represented 9% of GDP. FDI took a hit in 1973 when Asians and Europeans were barred from any commercial activity in five of the country's eight regions. Shortly thereafter, a policy of *Zairianisation* of the retail sector came into effect. Under these measures, expatriates were barred from a wide range of business activities, mostly in the retail and service sectors. Foreigners affected by this policy were compelled to sell their interests to Zairian nationals, many of whom turned out to be officials of the national party. Many of the new owners had no business experience, and quite a few of them simply liquidated the stock and never repaid the low-interest loans extended by the government for acquisition of the businesses. More frequently, *Zairianisation* involved some form of mixed ownership, with the government usually the major shareholder, but with management remaining in largely foreign hands.

Congo adopted a new investment code in 1979, which was updated to become more investor-friendly with World Bank guidance in 1986. However, the country's complex and arbitrary judicial system made implementation of this legal framework problematic at best.

The end of the Mobutu regime in May 1997 brought little respite as successive wars and off-budget, exploitation of mineral and timber resources followed. In 2001, timber investments by firms from Zimbabwe (about $300 million), Germany, Malaysia, and China were reported, but for the most part looting of the country's diamonds, gold, timber and tantalite deposits (used in mobile phones), by rival military groups replaced investment. With a semblance of peace in 2002 some foreign direct investment began to flow into the DROC again. In 2011 most FDI was directed at telecommunications, mining, and timber.

39 ECONOMIC DEVELOPMENT

From colonial times, economic development in the Congo has been almost exclusively extractive and exploitative. Under Belgian King Leopold II, who treated the Congo as his private fiefdom, rapacious agents pillaged the country for red rubber and ivory. The locals had their hands chopped off for not meeting quotas. During 50 years of Belgian state rule, forced labor and other abuses continued, but there were improvements to the country. The mining and export agriculture sectors developed and an extensive network of roads and railways was built. However, Congolese were not prepared to manage development, and at independence only a handful of college graduates existed.

The post-independence Mobutu regime oversaw turn-key construction projects, including the impressive Inga dams, but the vast transportation network, harbor facilities, iron and aluminum smelters, cement plants and mining companies were consistently under-capitalized, unmaintained and cannibalized. In most cases they lost so much value it was unprofitable for investors to take them over. In the 1970s and 1980s many development plans were hatched, including the occasional, vaguely conceived three-year plans, but they produced little economic growth.

From 1992 to 1997 any semblance of economic planning and development management evaporated. Intermittent wars and low-level conflict from 1997 to 2011, fueled by DROC's vast mineral wealth, further delayed economic development, particularly in the east. Government attempted to restore economic development through arrangements with multi-lateral institutions. In June 2002 the government negotiated a three-year $850 million Poverty Reduction and Growth Facility (PRGF) arrangement with the International Monetary Fund (IMF). In August 2005, the IMF completed the delayed fifth review of performance under the PRGF, triggering the release of a $39 million installment of the facility to the government despite the fact that several criteria had not been fulfilled. The IMF also extended the life of the PRGF from October 2005 to March 2006, to allow for completion of a sixth and final review. The IMF's Executive Board approved a new three-year program financed by an Extended Credit Facility (ECF) for the Government Economic Program (PEG 2) on 11 December 2009.

In 2007 the government adopted a Governance Contract laying out objectives in four areas (decentralization, public finance management, public administration, and transparency) and in three sectors (public enterprises, the mining sector, and the security sector, including the demobilization and reintegration of ex-combatants). The government put the Governance Contract measures in place in 2010 in an effort to improve governance and transparency in the forestry, mining, and oil sectors. These measures consolidated the HIPC Initiative reforms, enhanced investor confidence, and reassured development partners of government's commitment to grow the economy.

40 SOCIAL DEVELOPMENT

Social development in DROC was practically an oxymoron. Historical neglect of education and training in the country, policy failures, instability, and violence and discrimination against women retarded social development on a massive scale. On the UNDP's 2011 Human Development Index (HDI) Congo ranked last, 187th out of 187 countries.

A social insurance program theoretically protected employees in the formal sector by providing pensions for old age, disability, and survivorship. Contributions were made by employers and employees, with the government providing an annual subsidy. Retirement was at age 65 for men and age 60 for women, unless the person was "prematurely aged." Survivorship ceased when the widow or widower remarried. Workers were entitled to medical, dental, surgical, and hospital care, as well as medicine, appliances, and transportation. There was a family allowance for employed persons with one or more children. In reality, large segments of the population engaged in subsistence farming and were therefore excluded from coverage. Poor record-keeping, empty government coffers and rent-seeking meant that most Congolese had to change their "cradle to grave" mentality, and rely on family and affective networks for social welfare.

Discrimination and violence against women was widespread. A married woman had to obtain her husband's authorization before opening a bank account, accepting a job, obtaining a passport, or renting or selling real estate. Usually women were relegated to agricultural labor and household and child-rearing duties. The small percentage in the work force received less pay than men for comparable work and remained severely underrepresented in management positions. Domestic abuse was pervasive. Widows were generally deprived of all possessions including dependent children. Children were commonly forced into labor and military service.

In April 2010, the UN special representative on sexual violence in conflict declared DROC the "rape capital of the world." Amnesty International, an international human rights group, immediately echoed the warning, calling for increased focus on the issue. According to a Harvard Humanitarian Initiative report, roughly 60% of rapes in the DROC were perpetrated by gangs of armed men and more than half occurred inside the victims' homes. More troubling still were reports that an increasing proportion of rapes in the country were being carried out by civilians, indicating that a culture of impunity was rippling throughout the country.

Discrimination against ethnic Tutsi and indigenous Pygmies persisted. The human rights situation was extremely poor, especially in rebel-held areas. Abuses included large scale killing, disappearances, torture, rape, dismemberment, extortion, robbery, arbitrary arrest and detention, and harassment of human rights workers and journalists.

[41] HEALTH

According to the CIA, average life expectancy in the Democratic Republic of the Congo was 53.33 years in 2011. The country spent 7.3% of its GDP on healthcare, amounting to $16 per person. There was one physician, five nurses and midwives, and eight hospital beds per 10,000 inhabitants.

The departure of large numbers of European medical personnel in mid-1960 left the country's health services greatly weakened. Not a single African doctor had graduated at the time of independence. In 1960, 90 doctors of 28 nationalities recruited by the World Health Organization (WHO) were working in the country. The WHO's emphasis was on the training of national health workers, to prepare them to run their own health services. Most facilities were concentrated in the major cities.

Common diseases included malaria, trypanosomiasis, onchocerciasis, schistosomiasis, diarrheal diseases, tuberculosis, measles, leprosy, dysentery, typhoid, and hookworm. HIV/AIDS prevalence was 3.2 per 100 adults in 2007. The incidence of tuberculosis was 366 per 100,000 people in 2007.

Malnutrition was a serious health problem, especially among children; malnutrition was prevalent in an estimated 34% of all children under five years old. In 2007, 73% of children up to one year old were immunized against diphtheria, pertussis, and tetanus; polio (36%); and measles (70%), which was a huge increase over the previous decade. It was estimated that 76% of children were vaccinated against measles.

The fertility rate was 5.9, while the infant mortality rate was 126 per 1,000 live births. In 2008 the maternal mortality rate, according to the World Bank, was 670 per 100,000 births. In the same year, infant mortality was 78.43 per 1,000 live births.

An estimated 30% of married women were using contraception in 2007. Approximately 5% of the female population in the DROC has undergone female genital mutilation. The government had not published a policy opposing this procedure.

A 2010 UN survey indicated that some improvements had been made in health since 2000, but access to health care was still largely dependent on socio-economic factors; children from disadvantaged families were far less likely to have received standard vaccinations than were children from wealthier families. Millennium Development Goals included seven goals directly bearing on health. Reliable data on progress in meeting these goals by 2015 was difficult to obtain.

[42] HOUSING

The massive urban influx that began after independence led to a fourfold increase in the population of Kinshasa, creating a massive housing problem that was still far from solved. Tens of thousands of squatters were crowded into squalid shantytowns on the outskirts of the capital. Other, more prosperous migrants built themselves permanent dwellings. Unable to control the spread of unauthorized and generally substandard construction or to come up with adequate alternatives, the government tolerated what it could not prevent and began extending basic utilities to the new settlements. According to the CIA, about 80% of urban dwellers and 28% of the rural population had access to improved water sources in 2008, while only 23% of urban and rural people enjoyed improved sanitation facilities.

Housing fell under the responsibility of the Department of Public Health and Social Affairs. Public housing and home-building loans sponsored by the National Housing Office covered no more than a tiny fraction of the country's massive housing needs. Many housing units are traditional one-room adobe, straw, or mud structures, and less than half were modern houses of durable or semi-durable material containing one or more rooms.

[43] EDUCATION

School enrollment figures lagged. In 1998, there were about 4,022,000 students enrolled in primary school. In 1995, there were about 1,514,323 students enrolled in secondary school. It was estimated that about 38.9% of all students completed their primary education in 2005. The student-to-teacher ratio for primary school was about 34:1 in that same year; the ratio for secondary school was about 14.5:1. Tertiary enrollment was estimated at 6%. Of those enrolled in tertiary education, there were 100 male students for every 35 female students. The CIA reported that in 2001 the Democratic Republic of the Congo had a literacy rate of 67%.

The colonial system of education was notorious for training Africans to serve the colonial enterprise: elementary school attendance under the Belgians was one of the highest in Africa (56% in 1959), but was mostly limited to the first two grades; fewer than 10% of school-age children completed the six-year elementary cycle. One of the chief efforts of successive governments of the DROC was to graduate as many schoolchildren as possible beyond the elementary level.

University education was virtually nonexistent in the Belgian Congo prior to the mid-1950s. Up to that time, only a handful of Africans had been permitted to enroll in Belgian universities. Teacher-training institutions, religious seminaries, and advanced technical training in medicine, agronomy, and public administration were available, but did not lead to recognized university degrees. The Catholic University of Lovanium at Kinshasa (affiliated with the Catholic University of Louvain in Belgium) was organized in 1953. The State University of the Belgian Congo and Ruanda-Urundi at Lubumbashi was set up in 1955. A third university was established at Kisangani under Protestant auspices in

1962. A number of specialized institutes of higher learning were also created following independence.

In August 1971, the existing institutes and the three universities were amalgamated into a single national university system, the National University of Zaire (now the University of Kinshasa), organized into three separate campuses located in Kinshasa, Lubumbashi, and Kisangani. The three campuses were reorganized as separate universities in 1981. The DROC also had numerous university institutes, including ones specializing in agriculture, applied technology, business, teacher training, and the arts. In 1998, about 60,000 students were enrolled in some type of higher education program. Public universities were of low standard, and suffered frequent closures because of teacher and student strikes. Several private universities were founded in the 2000s, and though expensive by comparison with public schools, offered students a higher quality education.

In 2011, education was compulsory between ages 6 and 12. Primary school lasted for six years. General secondary school covered another six years; however, students could choose a six-year technical program or a five-year vocational program instead. The academic year ran from late September through May. The primary language of instruction was French.

⁴⁴LIBRARIES AND MUSEUMS

The National Library in Kinshasa holds an estimated 1.2 million volumes. The University of Kinshasa library has 300,000 volumes. Smaller academic libraries are attached to various specialized university institutes. The Kinshasa Public Library has 24,000 volumes, and is a part of a national system with nine branches.

There are several museums in the capital, including the Anthropology Museum, the Fine Arts Museum, the Private Museum of Zoology, and museums on the campus of the University of Kinshasa. There are regional museums at locations throughout the country, including Butemo, Kananga, Kisangani, Lubumbashi, Mbandaka, and Mushenge.

⁴⁵MEDIA

In 2009 the CIA reported that there were 40,000 telephone landlines in Democratic Republic of the Congo. In addition to landlines, mobile phone subscriptions averaged 15 per 100 people. There were over 200 private FM radio stations, 11 AM radio stations, 2 shortwave radio stations, and 4 television stations. Internet users numbered 1 per 100 citizens.

The postal, telephone, and telegraph services were owned and operated by the government, but were not reliable. In 2009, there were 40,000 main phone lines and 10.1 million mobile cellular phones in use nationwide.

State-controlled radio and television transmissions, operated under Radio-Television Nationale Congolaise (RTNC), were the prominent broadcasting stations, reaching the largest number of citizens. The RTNC radio broadcast of La Voix du Congo, was available in French, Swahili, Lingala, Tshiluba, and Kikongo. There was also Canal 5. There were an estimated 226 privately run radio broadcasting stations. In 2003, there were an estimated 385 radios and 2 television sets for every 1,000 people.

In 2010, the country had 3,005 Internet hosts. In 2008, there were some 290,000 Internet users in the Democratic Republic of the Congo. Internet cafés were popular in urban areas, but were considered expensive and out of reach for the average person. Rural and remote areas had unreliable cell phone and internet access.

In 2005 eight newspapers published daily with approximately 100 others publishing less frequently. Several of these newspapers were owned by politicians who used them to advance their political views. Circulations were limited in most cases to about 25,000. In 2011 several newspapers, including *le Phare* and *le Potentiel*, were published in Kinshasa and were available online.

While the constitution provided for freedom of speech and the press, the government restricted this right in practice, and reporters were forced to self-censor. In 2007 hundreds of media professionals took to the streets to protest government crackdowns and violence against reporters. In 2010 Human Rights Watch reported that violent crimes against journalists had worsened including murders, death threats, and physical attacks. In July 2009 the government cut Radio France Internationale's (RFI) signal, accusing the station of broadcasting reports contrary to government views, and of demoralizing troops fighting against Rwandan Hutu rebels. RFI was cut again in 2011 for its reporting on the elections. According to the Media Sustainability Index for 2010, Congo was judged to have an "unsustainable mixed system" whereby the country did not meet most of the criteria for free speech, plurality of news sources, professionalism, business management and institutional support. On the Freedom House Index of political rights and civil liberties, Congo was judged to be "not free."

⁴⁶ORGANIZATIONS

Associational life has undergone considerable change since independence. Under Mobutu it was highly politicized. Then robust boy- and girl-scout organizations were dismantled and replaced by MPR youth wings, which indoctrinated children in party patriotism. The Corps of Volunteers of the Republic (CVR), a quasi-political movement, including major student movements directly under the control of then president Mobutu, was created in February 1966. Its objectives were to promote "national reconstruction" and to "awaken national consciousness." The relative lack of enthusiasm generated by the CVR led to its being taken over in April 1967 by the MPR, and merged with the ruling party's Young Popular Movement of the Revolution.

Mobutu's conflict with the Roman Catholic Church provided the government with an excuse to ban all independent youth associations (most of which were church-related) and to replace them with party-controlled organizations. Student associations were similarly disbanded and superseded by an MPR-affiliated agency. Sports organizations were sponsored by the African Confederation of Sports for All.

In the 1990s democratic openings encouraged a blossoming of independent civil society. On many levels—media, women, youth, business, trades, arts, and human rights—associational life flourished. Congolese entrepreneurs have since founded thousands of NGOs to promote various causes ranging from improving the status of women to helping displaced persons.

Trade and professional organizations included the National Association of Private Enterprises of the Democratic Republic of the Congo (ANEZA), with nearly 1,000 members, and the chambers of commerce. The Coffee Board of the Democratic Republic of Congo promoted the coffee trade.

Human rights organizations operating within the country included the Committee of Human Rights Observers, The Christian Network of Human Rights and Civic Education Organizations, and the African Association for the Defense of Human Rights. There were also media associations. National chapters of the Red Cross Society, Caritas, the Society of St. Vincent de Paul, Habitat for Humanity and Publish What You Pay were active.

⁴⁷TOURISM, TRAVEL, AND RECREATION

The *Tourism Factbook*, published by the UN World Tourism Organization, reported 53,000 incoming tourists to the DROC in 2009. Of those incoming tourists, there were 31,000 from Africa. Hotel beds had an occupancy rate of 76%. The estimated daily cost to visit Kinshasa, the capital, was $398. The cost of visiting other cities averaged $139.

Congo's national parks were difficult to access, expensive, and some were dangerous to visit. Virunga National Park in the Virunga Mountains and high plains formerly was one of the best game preserves in Africa, known particularly for lions, elephants, and hippopotamuses. However, along with other parks, it was underfunded, understaffed and unprotected from poachers. Kahuzi-Biega Park, west of Lake Kivu, was one of the last refuges of the endangered mountain gorilla, but in the 2000s armed militias were hiding out in the area and conducting raids. Hippos in Lakes Albert and Edward were routinely massacred to provide meat for marauding rebels and bandits. The gargantuan Garamba National Park in the northeast, virtually inaccessible by road, was re-opened in 2010, but the Lord's Resistance Army continued to operate in that general area. Kinshasa formerly boasted two zoos and Mobutu's presidential garden; these had fallen victim to serious neglect by 2011.

One of the Congo's unique attractions was the presence of an orphanage for Bonobos located on the outskirts of Kinshasa at the Lukaya falls. In 2010 some 60 bonobos received protection in this sanctuary, which had the ultimate goal of eventually releasing the bonobos so they could readapt to life in the wild.

⁴⁸FAMOUS PERSONS

In the period of the transition to independence, two political leaders emerged as national figures: Joseph Kasavubu (1917–69), head of the ABAKO party, became the first chief of state; Patrice Emery Lumumba (1926–61) became the nation's first premier. Lumumba's subsequent murder made him a revolutionary martyr in Communist and many third-world countries. In 1960, Moïse Kapenda Tshombe (1919–69), who headed the government of Katanga Province, became prominent when he declared Katanga an independent state with himself as its president and maintained the secession until early 1963. Gen. Mobutu Sese Seko (Joseph-Désiré Mobutu, 1930–97), commander-in-chief of the Congolese National Army from 1961 to 1965, assumed the presidency after he deposed President Kasavubu on 25 November 1965. The MPR party congress promoted Mobutu to the rank of field marshal in December 1982. Laurent Désiré Kabila (1941–2001), seized power in May 1997 when he declared himself president and changed the name of the country back to the Democratic Republic of the Congo. After Kabila's assassination in 2001, Kabila's son Joseph Kabila (b. 1971) became president.

⁴⁹DEPENDENCIES

The DROC had no territories or colonies.

⁵⁰BIBLIOGRAPHY

Background Notes: Congo. Washington, D.C.: US Government Printing Office, 2000.

Clark, John Frank, Samuel Decalo, and Emizet F. Kisangani. *Historical Dictionary of Democratic Republic of the Congo (Zaire)*. Lanham, MD: Scarecrow Press, 2012.

Democratic Republic of the Congo Investment and Business Guide: Strategic and Practical Information. Washington, DC: International Business Publications USA, 2012.

Gondola, Ch Didier. *The History of Congo*. Westport, CT: Greenwood Press, 2002.

Jennings, Christian. *Across the Red River: Rwanda, Burundi, and the Heart of Darkness*. London: Phoenix, 2001.

Kisangani, Emizet F. *Civil Wars in the Democratic Republic of Congo, 1960–2010. Boulder*, CO: Lynne Rienner, 2012.

McElrath, Karen, ed. *HIV and AIDS: A Global View*. Westport, CT: Greenwood Press, 2002.

Mukenge, Tshilemalema. *Culture and Customs of the Congo*. Westport, CT: Greenwood Press, 2002.

Nzongola-Ntalaja, Georges. *The Congo from Leopold to Kabila: A People's History*. New York: Zed Books, 2002.

O'Ballance, Edgar. *The Congo-Zaire Experience, 1960–98*. New York: St. Martin's Press, 2000.

Vanthemsche, Guy. *Belgium and the Congo, 1885–1980*. New York: Cambridge University Press, 2012.

Zeilig, Leo, and David Seddon. *A Political and Economic Dictionary of Africa*. Philadelphia: Routledge/Taylor and Francis, 2005.

CONGO, REPUBLIC OF THE (ROC)

Republic of the Congo
République du Congo

CAPITAL: Brazzaville

FLAG: The flag consists of a green triangular section at the hoist and a red triangular section at the fly, separated by a diagonal gold bar.

ANTHEM: *La Congolaise (The Congolese).*

MONETARY UNIT: The Communauté Financière Africaine franc (XAF), which was originally pegged to the French franc, has been pegged to the euro since January 1999 with a rate of 655.957 francs to 1 euro. The franc is issued in coins of 1, 2, 5, 10, 25, 50, 100, and 500 francs and notes of 50, 100, 500, 1,000, 5,000, and 10,000 francs. XAF = US$0.0021 (or US$1 = XAF484.978) as of November 2011.

WEIGHTS AND MEASURES: The metric system is the legal standard.

HOLIDAYS: New Year's Day, 1 January; Labor Day, 1 May; Three Glorious Days, 13–15 August (including Independence Day, 15 August); Christmas Day, 25 December. Movable religious holidays include Good Friday and Easter Monday.

TIME: 1 p.m. = noon GMT.

¹LOCATION, SIZE, AND EXTENT

Lying astride the Equator, the Republic of the Congo contains an area of about 342,000 sq km (132,047 sq mi), extending approximately 1,287 km (798 mi) NNE–SSW and 402 km (249 mi) ESE–WNW. Comparatively, the area occupied by the Congo is slightly smaller than the state of Montana. It is bounded on the N by Cameroon and the Central African Republic, on the E and S by the Democratic Republic of Congo (DROC), on the SW by Cabinda (an enclave of Angola) and the Atlantic Ocean, and on the W by Gabon, with a total land boundary length of 5,504 km (3,413 mi) and a coastline of 169 km (105 mi).

The Congo's capital city, Brazzaville, is located in the southeastern part of the country.

²TOPOGRAPHY

The Congo is roughly divided into four topographical regions. The coastal region consists of a low, relatively treeless plain, with occasional high spurs jutting down from the Mayombé Escarpment. The escarpment region is made up of a series of parallel folds of moderate height (600–900 m/2,000–3,000 ft) that were once mostly forested. To the east and north of the escarpment, and forming the watershed between the Niari and Ogooué river systems, lies the plateau region, with savanna covering more than 129,000 sq km (50,000 sq mi) and separating the Congo and Ogooué basins. The northeastern region of the country is a swampy lowland covering some 155,000 sq km (60,000 sq mi); flooding is seasonal, with different tributaries of the Congo overflowing into one another. The country has two river systems: that of the coastal rivers, which flow into the Kouilou River, and that of the Congo River and its tributaries.

³CLIMATE

The Congo has a tropical climate characterized by high humidity and heat. There are two wet and two dry seasons. At Brazzaville, in the south, the average daily maximum temperature is 30°C (86°F) and the average minimum temperature 20° C (68°F). At Souanké, in the far north, the extremes are 29°C (84°F) and 18°C (64°F). Annual rainfall varies from 105 cm (41 in) at Pointe-Noire, in the southwest, to 185 cm (73 in) at Impfondo, in the northeast.

⁴FLORA AND FAUNA

The World Resources Institute estimates that there are 6,000 plant species in the Republic of the Congo. In addition, the Congo was home to 166 mammal, 597 bird, 149 reptile, and 58 amphibian species. The calculation reflected the total number of distinct species residing in the country, not the number of endemic species.

About half the land area was covered by okoumé, limba, and other trees of the heavy rain forest. On the plateaus, the forest gave way to savanna broken by patches of bushy undergrowth. The savanna supported jackals, hyenas, cheetahs, and several varieties of antelope; elephants, wild boar, giraffes, and monkeys dwelt in the forest.

⁵ENVIRONMENT

The World Resources Institute reported that the Republic of the Congo had designated 4.87 million hectares (12.04 million acres) of land for protection as of 2006. Water resources totaled 832 cu km (199.6 cu mi) while water usage was 35 cu km (8.4 cu mi) per year. Domestic water usage accounted for 59% of total usage, industrial for 29%, and agricultural for 12%. Per capita water usage totaled 8 cu m (283 cu ft) per year.

The United Nations (UN) reported in 2008 that carbon dioxide emissions in the Congo totaled 1,587 kilotons.

The most significant environmental problems in the Congo were deforestation, increases in urban population, and the protection of its wildlife. The Congo's forests are endangered by fires used to clear land for agriculture. Forests are also used as a source of fuel. The most accessible forest region, in the Kouilou-Mayombé Mountains, has been overexploited. From 1981–85, deforestation in the Congo proceeded at a rate of 22,000 hectares (54,400 acres) a year. From 1990–2000, deforestation occurred at a rate of about 0.1% per year. Deforestation accelerated during the 2000s, reaching an estimated rate of 0.17% from 2005 to 2010.

The Congo has nine protected areas. The two largest, the 7,800 sq km (3,000 sq mi) Léfini Reserve and the 2,600 sq km (1,000 sq mi) Odzala National Park, were established during the French colonial era. The country has one Wetland of International Importance at the Lake Télé Reserve.

According to a 2011 report issued by the International Union for Conservation of Nature and Natural Resources (IUCN), the number of threatened species included 11 types of mammals, 2 species of birds, 2 type of reptile, 46 species of fish, 5 types of mollusks, and 37 species of plants. Threatened species included the green turtle, the African sharp nose crocodile, the spotted hyena, and black crowned crane.

The Congo's urban centers are hampered by air pollution from vehicles and water pollution from sewage. Its water purity problem is most apparent in rural areas.

6 POPULATION

The US Central Intelligence Agency (CIA) World Factbook estimated the population of the Republic of the Congo in 2011 to be approximately 4,243,929, which placed it 126th in population among 196 nations worldwide. In 2011, approximately 2.7% of the population was over 65 years of age, with another 45.6% under 15 years of age. The median age in the Congo was 17 years. There were 1.03 males for every female in the country. The population's annual rate of change was 2.835%. The projected population for the year 2025 was 5,500,000. Population density in the Congo was calculated at 11 people per sq km (28 people per sq mi).

The UN estimated that 62% of the population lived in urban areas in 2009, and that urban populations had an annual rate of change of 3%. The largest urban area was Brazzaville, with a population of 1.3 million.

The prevalence of HIV/AIDS has had a significant impact on the population of Republic of the Congo. The AIDS epidemic causes higher death and infant mortality rates, and lowers life expectancy.

7 MIGRATION

Estimates of Republic of the Congo's net migration rate, reported by the CIA in 2011, amounted to -0.71 migrants per 1,000 citizens. The total number of emigrants living abroad was 208,600, and the total number of immigrants living in Republic of the Congo was 143,200. Within the country there was strong migration to urban centers from rural areas. Some French, Greek, and Lebanese immigrants have settled in the country.

In the 1990s the Republic of the Congo accepted tens of thousands of refugees from the Democratic Republic of the Congo (DROC) and Rwanda fleeing genocide, political turmoil and civil war. Citizens of the ROC also have fled to neighboring countries to escape internal political and ethnic violence. In 1999, fighting had displaced up to 1.8 million Congolese and forced another 300,000 to seek refuge in neighboring countries. In 2011, approximately 9,500 ROC citizens still resided in Gabon, although their refugee status expired that year.

In 2010 the UN High Commissioner for Refugees (UNHCR) appealed for $60 million to assist some 114,000 DROC refugees, 80% of whom were women and children, who had settled on the ROC side of the Ubangi River. Given insecurity in the DROC, the humanitarian community believed the refugees would remain in the ROC into 2012. According to UNHCR, as of December 2010, the country hosted 137,789 refugees and asylum seekers. Refugees and asylum seekers came from the DROC (128,334); Rwanda (7,586); Angola (863); and others (1,006).

8 ETHNIC GROUPS

The population belongs to four major ethnic groupings: the Kongo (48%), Sangha (20%), Teke (17%), and M'Bochi (12%). These groupings comprise more than 40 sub groups. Europeans and other groups make up 3% of the population. The Kongo occupy the area southwest of Brazzaville; the Teke, who live north of Brazzaville, are chiefly hunters and fishermen; the M'Bochi (or Boulangi) reside at the convergence of savanna and forest in the northwest. This group has furnished many migrants to urban centers, including the majority of Brazzaville's skilled workers and civil servants. There are about 12,000 Pygmies - possibly Congo's original inhabitants - in the high forest region. The largest number of Europeans living in the ROC are French nationals.

9 LANGUAGES

French is the official language. Several Bantu languages and dialects are spoken with Kikongo having the largest number of speakers. Monokutuba and Lingala are trade languages.

10 RELIGIONS

Almost 50% of the population is Christian, with about 90% of all Christians affiliated with the Roman Catholic Church. Protestant denominations include Methodists, Seventh-Day Adventists, the Church of Jesus Christ of Latter-Day Saints, and Jehovah's Witnesses. A small number of Christians practice Kimbanguism, a mixture of Christian and native customs and beliefs, which originated in the Democratic Republic of the Congo in the 1920s. About 48% of the population are animists. Nearly 2% are Muslims (Sunni and Chadian), most of whom are immigrants from North and West Africa who work or reside in urban centers.

The January 2002 constitution guarantees freedom of religion and freedom from discrimination on the basis of religious affiliation. All social, religious, and business organizations must register with the government. Certain Christian holidays are celebrated as national holidays. All organized religious groups have representation in the joint ecumenical council, which meets once a year.

REPUBLIC OF
THE CONGO

LOCATION: 3°42′ N to 5°1′ S; 11°7′ to 18°39′E. BOUNDARY LENGTHS: Cameroon, 520 kilometers (323 miles); Central African Republic, 467 kilometers (290 miles); Democratic Republic of the Congo, 1,625 kilometers (1,010 miles); Angola, 201 kilometers (125 miles); Atlantic coastline, 156 kilometers (97 miles); Gabon, 1,656 kilometers (1,020 miles). TERRITORIAL SEA LIMIT: 200 miles.

¹¹TRANSPORTATION

The CIA reports that Republic of the Congo has a total of 17,289 km (10,743 mi) of roads, of which 864 km (537 mi) are paved. There were 25 airports, six of which had paved runways. The Congo had approximately 1,120 km (696 mi) of navigable waterways.

The Congo-Ocean Railroad, completed in 1934, runs between Brazzaville on Pool Malebo and the ocean port of Pointe-Noire. Importantly, the 510-km (317-mi) line transports local freight,

and via connection to the Congo and Ubangi river systems, transports freight to and from landlocked Central African Republic. In the course of descending the Mayombé Escarpment, it crosses 172 bridges and travels through 12 tunnels. To relieve congestion on this stretch, a 91-km (57-mi) line was completed between Bilinga and Loubomo in 1985. The 285-km (177-mi) Comilog rail line was completed in 1962 to transport manganese ore extracted at Moanda, Gabon, from M'Binda on the Gabonese border to the Congo-Ocean line at Mont-Bélo.

Dense tropical forests, rugged terrain, swamps, and heavy rainfall made construction and maintenance of roads extremely costly. A Brazzaville-to-Duesso road was completed as far as Owando in the mid-1980s. Road travel in remote areas was difficult and unpredictable owing to flooding and poor maintenance.

River transportation was managed by the state-owned Trans-Congo Communications Agency. The river port of Brazzaville, which was the junction point of the Congo-Ocean Railroad and the Congo-Ubangi river system, was an important center for trade with the Central African Republic, Chad, and the DROC. A ferry connected Brazzaville with Kinshasa. Pointe-Noire was the Congo's only seaport and the terminus of the Congo-Ocean Railroad.

Brazzaville (Maya-Maya) and Pointe-Noire airports are the hubs of a network connecting the four equatorial republics. Lina-Congo, the former state-owned airlines was dissolved in 2002. In 2010, Trans Air Congo ran daily flights between Brazzaville and Pointe-Noir, Dolisie and Nkayi.

12 HISTORY

Although little is known of the early history of the Congo, it has been established that there was a Congo Empire that extended into present-day Angola and reached its height in the 16th century. The kingdom of Loango, which broke away from the Congo Empire, also prospered for a time. Another African state mentioned in the accounts of the first European explorers was the Anzico kingdom of the Teke. By the end of the 17th century, however, all these kingdoms had grown weak.

The coastal regions of the area became known to Europeans as early as the 15th century. The mouth of the Congo River was discovered by Portuguese sailor Diogo Cão in 1482. French trading companies, interested in slaves and ivory, appeared on the scene during the 17th century; by 1785, more than 100 French ships annually sailed up the coast. After the French Revolution, however, French interest in the area waned.

With the abolition of the slave trade, merchants began to seek new sources of commerce. The first forays into the interior began at this time, but extensive exploration came only toward the end of the 19th century, with Pierre Savorgnan de Bràzza and Henry Morton Stanley. In 1880, Bràzza signed a treaty with the powerful Teke tribal ruler Makoko, bringing the right bank of the Congo River under French control. The Congress of Berlin (1885) gave formal recognition to French claims to the region. The period after 1900 was marked by a slow but steady establishment of French administrative machinery. By 1910, Gabon, Middle Congo, and Ubangi-Shari (including Chad) were constituted administratively as colonies; together they constituted French Equatorial Africa, all under a governor general at Brazzaville. In 1940, French Equatorial Africa joined the Free French movement and the Allied war effort against the Axis powers. The first territorial assembly was elected in 1947. In a referendum held on 28 September 1958, the territory of Middle Congo voted to become an autonomous republic within the French Community.

The Territorial Assembly of the Middle Congo proclaimed the Republic of the Congo on 28 November 1958. On 8 December, Fulbert Youlou, mayor of Brazzaville and leader of the Democratic Union for the Defense of African Interests (UDDIA), was elected to head the provisional government. The adoption of a constitution on 20 February 1959 transformed the provisional government into the first official government of the republic. Legislative elections were held that June. The new National Assembly elected Fulbert Youlou prime minister on 27 June and president on 21 November.

The constitutional law of 4 June 1960, adopted by the French Parliament and by the Senate of the French Community, made it possible for a member state to become independent without leaving the community. The Republic of the Congo thus proclaimed its independence on 15 August 1960. President Youlou resigned on 15 August 1963, in the wake of anti-government rioting that threatened to turn into civil war. Alphonse Massamba-Debat became provisional president and was formally elected to the presidency on 19 December 1963; a new constitution was approved by national referendum that same month. In 1964, Massamba-Debat established relations with the USSR and China, and then announced the establishment of a "scientific Socialist state" with one-party control.

On 4 September 1968, Massamba-Debat resigned following a military coup that deprived him of most of his presidential powers. Capt. Marien Ngouabi then established a new revolutionary regime. Ngouabi was named president on 1 January 1969, and he proclaimed the People's Republic of the Congo the following December. Political stability proved difficult to achieve, however, and there were seven coup attempts during his seven years in office, which ended with his assassination on 18 March 1977. He was succeeded by Col. Joachim Yhombi-Opango, who abrogated the 24 June 1973 constitution. Yhombi-Opango resigned on 5 February 1979 and was succeeded in March by Col. Denis Sassou-Nguesso. A twenty-year treaty of friendship and cooperation with the USSR was signed in 1981. Sassou-Nguesso was reelected president in July 1984 and was chairman of the Organization of African Unity (OAU) during 1986–87.

The 1990s ushered in multiparty competition, but also was a tumultuous decade of armed uprisings and civil war. A four-month-long National Conference in 1991 led to the appointment of an interim government, headed by André Milongo. Pascal Lissouba won multiparty elections in 1992, but his unstable coalition, the Presidential Majority (la Tendence Présidentielle), was rocked by strikes and violent civil unrest. Legislative elections on 2 May 1993, gave way to armed conflict in June and July. To avoid civil war, the OAU and the president of Gabon brokered an accord that accepted first-round results and called for second-round elections on 6 October. The opposition alliance, the Union for Democratic Renewal-Congolese Workers' Party (URD-PCT), won seven of the 11 seats contested. Still, Lissouba's Pan-African Union for Social Democracy (UPADS) and its coalition partners won 69 of the 125 seats and Lissouba's shaky presidency continued. However, fighting broke out in the capital in November 1993, continuing into 1994 as armed forces loyal to Lissouba battled independent partisan militias.

On the one side was the northern M'bochi ethnic group, which had been aligned with the military government of Sassou-Nguesso. On the other side were two main southern groups, the Pool Lari and the coastal Vili. Transitional Prime Minister Milongo surrounded himself with Lari and Bakongo. Lissouba replaced them with his own people, the Nibolek, and "cleansed" the presidential guard. Although a mediation force was set up after a 30 January 1994 cease-fire, it was difficult to disarm the tribal factions.

In 1994, a government initiative to integrate military and security forces with members of tribal militias proved elusive. After the by-elections of 1995, the Lissouba regime took an authoritarian turn in the face of severe mismanagement and intractable street fighting, imposing restrictions on public demonstrations and eliminating press freedom.

In June 1997 Sassou-Nguesso's forces besieged the capital and shelled the parliament building. In October 1997, forces loyal to Sassou-Nguesso enlisted the help of Angolan troops and forced Lissouba into exile. Sassou-Nguesso once again assumed the reins of power and replaced the 1992 constitution with a Fundamental Act, conferring sweeping powers upon himself. He brought a degree of stability back to the country by forming a broad-based government that included former backers of Lissouba and Bernard Kolelas. The government convened a National Reconciliation Forum in January 1998, which elected a 75-member National Transition Council (NTC), replacing the National Assembly. Members of opposition parties and civil society were included in the NTC.

Civil conflict between the government and armed groups of southerners broke out again in mid-1998, intensifying in early 1999, before subsiding during the second half of the year. An estimated 10,000 people died and hundreds of thousands were displaced as rapes, looting, and destruction of many southern towns escalated.

The second half of 1999 saw the government regaining control over most of the south through military offensives, offers of amnesty, negotiations, and efforts to broaden the government's political base. The government signed a cease-fire and reconciliation accord with leaders of some rebel groups in November. In December 1999 Gabon's president, Omar Bongo, sponsored another accord, which involved the National Resistance Council (CNR), the only rebel group with military and political organization. With improved prospects for peace, Sassou-Nguesso declared a three-year transition period leading up to elections.

In presidential elections held 10 March 2002, Sassou-Nguesso was reelected president with 89.4% of the vote over Joseph Kignoumbi Kia Mboungou with 2.7%. In the legislative contest held 11 July 2002, the Democratic and Patriotic Forces (FDP) won 56 seats to 10 seats for other parties in the Senate, and 83 seats to 6 seats for the Union for Democratic Renewal (URD), 3 for the UPADS, and 45 seats for other parties. However, the most serious contenders--former president Lissouba and Prime Minister Kolelas--were banned from participation, and most parties boycotted the election.

In late March 2002 conflict erupted in the Pool region between government forces and "Ninja" rebels loyal to the Rev. Frederic Bitsangou (alias Pasteur Ntoumi) with the result that thousands of people were trapped or displaced with little or no relief. A peace agreement reached on 17 March 2003 between the government and Ntoumi guaranteed amnesty to combatants willing to disarm. However, disarmament proceeded slowly, and Ninja groups and government security units continued to skirmish in the Brazzaville suburbs in December 2003.

In January 2004, Pasteur Ntoumi announced that unless the government engaged in a national dialogue, allowed political exiles to return, and formed a new government of national unity, his forces would no longer disarm. An uneasy truce broken by sporadic security incidents, including rebel attacks on the country's main railway, ensued. In January 2005, Sassou-Nguesso formed a new government without opposition representation.

In June 2007, the Ninjas transitioned into "constructive opposition" committing to peaceful resolution of political and social issues within the Pool Department region. Government and the international community encouraged this move in 2008 by launching a National Program of Demobilization, Disarmament and Reintegration (NPDDR) to reintegrate ex-combatants into civilian society. Ntoumi was offered a government post in September 2007, but remained in hiding until December 2009, when he went to Brazzaville to take up the post. Bernard Kolélas, the founder of the Ninjas, died in Paris in 2009.

In the presidential elections of July 2009, the incumbent, Sassou-Nguesso, was reelected for another seven-year term, reportedly winning 78.6% of the vote. Members of the opposition boycotted the election, accusing the ruling party of electoral fraud—vote buying and failing to issue polling cards to opposition supporters. Despite claims by election observers of low voter turnout, the government reported a 66% participation rate. A corruption investigation against Sassou-Nguesso was undertaken by the French government in 2010 and continued into 2012.

In March 2010 the Congo received $2.4 billion in debt relief from the Paris Club.

13 GOVERNMENT

The government is comprised of an executive branch, a bicameral parliament with a National Assembly and Senate, and the judiciary. The current president, Dénis Sassou-Nguesso, is the chief of state and head of government. He abolished the post of prime minister in September 2009. A Council of Ministers serves by presidential appointment. Sassou-Nguesso is serving his second, and constitutionally last, seven year term and is due to step down in 2016.

Over the years, government structure in the ROC has changed depending on socialist and other influences. From 1979 to 1992, the ROC was governed under a constitution, approved by referendum on 8 July 1979 and amended in July 1984. The chairman of the 75-member Central Committee of the Congolese Labor Party (PCT) was the president of the republic and head of state. He was elected for an unspecified term as chairman (and therefore as president) by the party congress. Executive powers resided with the Council of Ministers, appointed by the prime minister and chaired by the president. The 153-member National Assembly, the sole legislative body, was elected by universal suffrage at age 18 from candidates named by the PCT.

On 15 March 1992, voters approved a new constitution, which provided for a mixed presidential-parliamentary form of government after the French model. Executive authority is vested in a directly elected president, who appoints the prime minister and cabinet. A National Assembly of 125 members was elected in two-round elections in June and July 1992. There was also a 60-member Senate. Pascal Lissouba was chosen president (61%) and his Pan-African Union for Social Democracy (UPADS) gained 39 seats. That legislature was dissolved in October and new legislative elections in May 1993 led to partisan fighting. A mediated settlement then confirmed a UPADS majority, yet fighting continued into 1994. In the view of many, the "democratic election" was the catalyst that unleashed tribal hatreds.

Soon after the defeat of Lissouba in the four-month 1997 civil war, Col. Denis Sassou-Nguesso formed a transitional government and replaced the 1992 constitution with a Fundamental Act. The Act gave additional powers to the executive making the president head of state and government, commander in chief of the armed forces with powers to appoint all members of the government, all senior military officers and government officials at subnational level. He was also mandated to direct the general policy of the government and to exercise regulatory powers.

In 1998, Sassou-Nguesso appointed a committee to draft a new constitution, which was approved by national referendum in January 2002. Under the constitution the bicameral parliament consists of the Senate with 72 seats and the National Assembly with 137 seats where members are elected to serve five-year terms. The president of the republic serves up to two seven-year terms. Legislative elections were held in 2007, Senate elections in 2008 and presidential elections in 2009. The next legislative elections were due in June 2012, Senate elections in 2013, and presidential elections in 2016.

14 POLITICAL PARTIES

In the past, political parties in the ROC mainly functioned to consolidate the individual power bases of politicians. Three political parties were active in the Middle Congo before the territory achieved its independence. Of these, the most important proved to be the Democratic Union for the Defense of African Interests (Union Démocratique de Défense des Intérêts Africain—UDDIA), founded by Abbé Fulbert Youlou. The UDDIA received 64% of the popular vote and won 51 of the 61 seats in the National Assembly elected in June 1959. Following the resignation of President Youlou and the dissolution of the Assembly in 1963, all political parties were banned. On 2 July 1964, the National Movement of the Revolution (Mouvement National de la Révolution—MNR), led by President Massamba-Debat, was officially established as the country's sole political party. A power struggle between the People's Militia and the army, tribal rivalries, and other conflicts led to Massamba-Debat's resignation in September 1968. The army commander in chief, Marien Ngouabi, then became head of state.

The Congolese Labor Party (Parti Congolais du Travail—PCT), created in December 1969 to succeed the MNR, had been based on the principles of Marxism-Leninism and democratic centralism. But, at its 1990 conference, the PCT abandoned this ideology. The 1979 constitution recognized the PCT as the sole party: all other political parties and any political activity outside the PCT were illegal. In the National Assembly elections of 8 July 1979, all candidates were PCT members.

After his assassination on 18 March 1977, Ngouabi was succeeded by Col. Joachim Yhombi-Opango, and in March 1979 by Col. Denis Sassou-Nguesso, who was reelected in July 1984. Elections due in July 1997 were delayed until the new constitution was adopted. The civil war and fighting between 1997 and 1999 restricted party activity. Sassou-Nguesso allowed some politicians from the former government to return and resume political activity in 1999, but he banned Lissouba and the former prime minister, Bernard Kolelas. They, along with former interior minister Col. Philippe Bikinkita, were sentenced to death in absentia on 5 May

2000 in the Brazzaville criminal court on charges of illegal detention, false imprisonment, and torture. The National Transitional Council (NTC), established in 1998, included representatives of opposition parties and members of civil society, but the NTC was criticized as being government-controlled and too narrow to represent Congo's 15 political parties.

In the absence of any serious competition, Sassou-Nguesso's coalition easily won the 2002 presidential and parliamentary elections. Opposition parties remained in disarray. President Sassou-Nguesso allowed Kolelas to return to Congo for his wife's funeral in October 2005 and subsequently asked that parliament grant Kolelas amnesty. Parliament complied with Sassou-Nguesso's request in December 2005.

Elections for the National Assembly were held in June and August 2007. The election results were as follows: PCT 46 seats, Congolese Movement for Democracy and Integral Development (MCDDI) 11 seats, Pan-African Union for Social Development (UPADS) 11 seats, Action Movement for Renewal (MAR) 5 seats, Movement for Solidarity and Development (MSD) 5 seats, independents 37 seats, others 22 seats.

In the 2008 Senate election, the Rally for the Presidential Majority (RMP) obtained 33 seats, the United Democratic Forces (FDU) 23 seats, and the UPADS 2 seats. Independents won 7 seats.

In the 2009 presidential contest, Denis Sassou-Nguesso was reelected with 78.6% of the vote; Joseph Kignoumbi Kia Mboungou obtained 7.5%, and Nicephore Fylla de Saint-Eudes obtained 7%, with others receiving the remaining votes.

15 LOCAL GOVERNMENT

There are 10 administrative regions and one federal district, each under the authority of a government commissioner. As of 2007, these were subdivided into 46 districts.

16 JUDICIAL SYSTEM

The legal system is based upon French civil law and customary law. The constitution provides for an independent judiciary, but in practice the judicial system is subject to interference by political leaders, and was nearly destroyed by the civil war.

The judicial system consists of traditional and local courts, courts of appeal, a Court of Accounts, the High Court of Justice, the Constitutional Court, and the Supreme Court. In rural areas, traditional courts continue to arbitrate local disputes, particularly property and inheritance cases, and domestic conflicts that can not be resolved within the family. The Court of Accounts' function is to hear cases related to mismanagement of government funds. The Constitutional Court's responsibility is to adjudicate the constitutionality of laws and judicial decisions. The High Court of Justice's function is to review judicial decisions or crimes involving the president and other high-ranking authorities in the conduct of their official duties. Local courts adjudicate criminal and civil complaints.

17 ARMED FORCES

The International Institute for Strategic Studies (IISS) reported that armed forces in the Republic of the Congo totaled 10,000 members in 2011. The force was comprised of 8,000 from the army, 800 from the navy, 1,200 members of the air force. Armed forces represented .8% of the labor force in the Congo. Defense spending totaled $155.5 million and accounted for 0.9% of GDP.

18 INTERNATIONAL COOPERATION

The Congo was admitted to the UN on 20 September 1960 and is a member of all of the specialized agencies except IAEA. It is also a member of the African Development Bank, the ACP Group, G-77, the Central African States Development Bank (BDEAC), the New Partnership for Africa's Development (NEPAD), and the African Union. The nation is part of the Franc Zone. Along with the Central African Republic, Gabon, and Cameroon, the country belongs to CEMAC, in which merchandise and capital circulate freely. Congo also is a signatory to the Lomé Convention and a member of the WTO. In addition to close ties with France and other Western European nations, the Congo has established friendly relations with China. Brazzaville is the African headquarters of WHO.

In 2011 Congo was elected to the UN Human Rights Council for a 3-year term. Congo held a seat on the UN Security Council during 2006–2007. Beginning in January 2006, President Sassou-Nguesso served a one-year term as Chairman of the African Union. He also served as a member of the ad hoc AU Heads of State High Committee on Libya and as an advisor during the 2011 leadership crisis in Cote d'Ivoire. In environmental cooperation, Congo is part of the Convention on Biological Diversity, Ramsar, CITES, International Tropical Timber Agreements, the Montréal Protocol, and the UN Conventions on Climate Change and Desertification.

19 ECONOMY

As of 2010, the gross domestic product (GDP) rate of change in Republic of the Congo was 9.1%. Inflation stood at 5.2%. Unemployment figures were unavailable, but under-employment and employment in the informal economy were high. Congo's economy qualified as "repressed," ranking 168th out of 179 economies on the 2011 Index of Economic Freedom.

Congo's economy is built on its petroleum resources, lumber, transport services, and agriculture. Congo's staple food crops are cassava, maize, plantains, yams, and sweet potatoes. The livestock industry is small and subject to health limitations imposed by the prevalence of the tsetse fly. Petroleum is Congo's most significant resource, contributing over 90% of exports. Production has increased as new fields were developed and improvements in recovery technology were implemented. The oil industry is concentrated in and around Pointe Noire.

After several prosperous years in the early 1980s, the price of oil declined and cast the Congolese economy into financial turmoil. The country experimented with state socialist approaches before embarking on market-style reforms in 1989. Early efforts at state-farm production of staple foods failed. The devaluation of Franc Zone currencies in 1994 resulted in inflation of 61%, but this subsided rather quickly. Reforms by the IMF and World Bank were in place when the civil war started in 1997. The economy worsened considerably in 1997, at -1.9% annual GDP growth, rebounding in 1998 to 2.5%, but fell again in 1999 due to renewed fighting. It grew at an average annual rate of 4.28% between 2001 and 2005 with a high of 8% in 2005 only to fall to -1.6% in 2007.

In 2006 the World Bank and the International Monetary Fund (IMF) instituted a debt relief program with the government to improve governance and financial transparency, especially relating to internal controls and the accounting system of the state-owned oil company (SNPC). They also called for an anti-corruption action plan. Funds freed up by debt relief were designated for poverty relief, although poverty reduction was slow and incremental. In 2010, Congo received some $1.9 billion in debt relief under the Heavily Indebted Poor Countries (HIPC) initiative.

20 INCOME

In 2010, the CIA estimated the GDP at $17.11 billion with an annual growth rate of 9.1%. GDP is the value of goods and services produced annually based on purchasing power parity (PPP). Per capita GDP was estimated at $4,100, which placed Congo in the lower ranks of medium income countries. The average inflation rate was 5.2%. It was estimated that agriculture accounted for 4.4% of GDP, industry 63.7%, and services 32%. According to the World Bank, remittances from citizens living abroad totaled $13.7 million in 2009, or about $3 per capita and accounted for approximately .1% of GDP.

As of 2011 the World Bank reported that individual consumption in the Republic of the Congo was 30.9% of GDP and accounted for 0.01% of world consumption. By comparison, the United States accounted for 25.44% of world individual consumption. The World Bank also estimated that 12.9% of Congo's GDP was spent on food and beverages, 5.2% on housing and household furnishings, 0.8% on clothes, 1.9% on health, 2.5% on transportation, 1.5% on communications, 0.7% on recreation, 2.4% on restaurants and hotels, and 0.7% on miscellaneous goods and services and purchases from abroad.

21 LABOR

As of 2007, the Congo had a total labor force of 1.514 million people mostly employed in the informal sector. Dating to the socialist era, formal sector wage earners - mainly civil servants – enjoyed a social welfare safety net. Formal sector employees were covered by old age, disability, maternity, funeral and survivorship benefits. Workers' compensation benefits were funded by employer contributions and included medical care. Employees were entitled to a family allowance for each child under 16 years of age, and there was a birth grant for the first three children.

In 2011 most individuals struggled to provide adequately for their families. The World Bank reported that dependence on the oil sector, lack of diversification in the economy and a small private sector had resulted in high levels of youth unemployment. It was estimated that 25% of people aged 15 to 29 in urban areas were unemployed. Youth also lacked appropriate market skills.

With the exception of the armed forces, workers are entitled to form and join unions. As of 2010, nearly all workers in the public sector and around 25% of those in the formal wage sector belonged to a union. However, this number represented only a small portion of workers since most were subsistence farmers or worked in the informal economy. The right to strike is guaranteed (except for those in the public sector). Workers have to file an intent to strike at least three days before the planned date of the strike and have to simultaneously participate in arbitration proceedings.

The standard workweek is seven hours per day, six days per week, with a one-hour lunch break per day. Overtime has to be paid for work over 40 hours. Compulsory overtime is not prohibited. As of 2010, the minimum wage was $109 per month in the formal economy. Due to high prices in urban areas and the demands of extended families, many workers, including health workers and teachers, have to accept additional employment, primarily in the informal economy. Though prohibited, child labor persists in the informal economy. Minimum occupational health and safety standards are only somewhat enforced.

22 AGRICULTURE

In 2011, agricultural activity was concentrated in the south, especially in the Niari Valley. The country's major crops include cassava (tapioca), sugar, rice, corn, peanuts, vegetables, coffee, and cocoa. Cereal production in 2009 amounted to 22,560 tons, fruit production 221,729 tons, and vegetable production 121,148 tons. Small amounts of tobacco were also grown.

In the 1990s, because of civil war and a steep drop in rural population, domestic production of cereals plummeted. By 1999, grain production was 80% less than it had been during 1989–91. However, crop production during 2002–04 was 4% higher than 1999–2001. Nonetheless, landholdings remained small, averaging less than 1.4 hectares (3.5 acres) per plot.

Export crops include coffee, cocoa, and palm oil. Since 1987, with the backing of the IMF and the World Bank, the government has encouraged agricultural development by abolishing state marketing boards and retail monopolies, freeing prices, removing tariffs on essential inputs, launching new agricultural credit institutions, and selling or closing state farms. Sugar output rebounded after a 1989 restructuring of the sugar industry, which has since been privatized.

23 ANIMAL HUSBANDRY

Animal husbandry is considered a potential growth area. The UN Food and Agriculture Organization (FAO) reported that the Congo dedicated 10 million hectares (24.7 million acres) to permanent pasture or meadow in 2009. During that year, the country tended 2.4 million chickens, 115,000 head of cattle, and 68,000 pigs. The production from these animals amounted to 5,417 tons of beef and veal, 11,025 tons of pork, 35,634 tons of poultry, 1,686 tons of eggs, and 39,267 tons of milk. The Congo also produced 308 tons of cattle hide.

24 FISHING

Most fishing is conducted for local consumption, although commercial fishing for export is growing. According to the FAO, the catch rose from 14,939 tons in 1970 to 45,577 tons in 1991, to 52,400 tons in 2003, and to 54,104 tons in 2008. Almost 50% of the annual catch was from saltwater fishing. The Congo had 1,970 decked commercial fishing boats in 2008. The export value of seafood totaled $95.38 million.

25 FORESTRY

Approximately 66% of the Republic of the Congo (some 22 million hectares – 54.3 million acres) is covered by forest. The FAO estimated the 2009 roundwood production at 2.43 million cu m (85.8 million cu ft). The value of all forest products, including

roundwood, totaled some $277.1 million, which was less than 4% of exports in 2010.

There are three main forest zones. Mayombé forest, covering about 1 million hectares (2.5 million acres), is the oldest forest under commercial exploitation and is almost exhausted. The Niari forest covers 3 million hectares (7.4 million acres) along the Chaillu River. The third zone, situated in the north, is the largest, with 15.5 million hectares (38.3 million acres). Because of constant flooding, however, it is the least exploited.

Okoumé, sapele, sipo, tiama, moaki, limba, and nioré are the main species of tree. Eucalyptus and pine are raised commercially in southern and coastal areas. Foreign private companies dominate commercial production. The Congolese Forestry Office was established in 1974 to implement reforestation, but development has been neglected owing to the oil boom. Isolated harvestable tracts, difficult weather conditions, and limited rail transport also inhibit expansion of the sector.

26 MINING

The Republic of the Congo's mineral sector, excluding oil, accounts for only a small part of the country's export earnings and its gross domestic product (GDP). In 2009, 93% of the country's export earnings came from oil, as did more than 50% of its GDP. Although potash was the primary mining product before the rapid growth of oil, production was not enough to make operations profitable and ceased after 1977. Gold, mined in the Mayombé area, reached 158 kg in 1967 but fell to an estimated 100 kg in 2009. Iron deposits estimated at 400 million tons have been found. AfriOre Ltd., of Canada, though inactive in the Congo, held exploration permits on the Boko Songo copper prospect, with 2 million tons of ore, and the Yanga Koubanza lead-zinc-copper prospect, with 5.5 million tons, both west of Brazzaville, and the company located high-grade copper mineralization at four other drilled prospects. Significant resources of magnesium, with by-products of salt, potash, and possibly chlorine, were being evaluated for development in the Makola and the Youbi magnesium salt evaporite deposits, in the Kouilou region.

In 2009 diamond production (artisanal) was estimated at 68,000 carats, up from 30,000 carats in 2003. Lime was also produced in 2009. Lime output that year was estimated at 400 metric tons. Hydraulic cement production totaled 105,000 metric tons in 2009.

27 ENERGY AND POWER

The Societe Nationale d'Electricite (SNE) manages the electric power sector. The World Bank reported in 2008 that the Congo produced 461 million kWh of electricity and consumed 543 million kWh, or 128 kWh per capita. Roughly 44% of energy came from fossil fuels, while 2% came from alternative fuels. Per capita oil consumption was 378 kg. Oil production totaled 302,200 barrels of oil a day.

There are two hydroelectric power facilities, the 15 MW Djoue and the 74 MW Bouenza (Moukoukoulou) plants. The ROC has been forced to import electric power from the Democratic Republic of the Congo to the make up the shortage in consumption. During the civil war, attacks on the Moukoukoulou facility cut the plant's capacity to around 55 MW, and destroyed large portions of the remaining power infrastructure.

Government planned to lower the nation's dependence on imported power by constructing new facilities and expanding those currently in use. In April 2010, the government signed a $700 million loan agreement with China to fund the construction of a hydroelectric dam in the north Sangha region; the Chinese-based Sinohydro Corporation was expected to be involved in construction of the dam during 2012. When complete, the hydroelectric project will provide almost enough power to supply the northern region of the country.

28 INDUSTRY

Industry is concentrated in the southern part of the country around Brazzaville and Pointe-Noire, and accounted for 64% of GDP in 2010. The largest industries are petroleum production, followed by food processing, including beverages and tobacco, chemicals, woodworking, metalworking and electrical industries, nonmetallic mineral products, paper and cardboard, and textiles. An oil refinery at Pointe-Noire, privatized in 1996, had a capacity of 21,000 barrels per day, but only 50% of the capacity was utilized. Other industries include sawmills, sugar refineries, and cement factories. In addition, artisans create distinctive jewelry, ceramics, and ebony and ivory sculptures.

29 SCIENCE AND TECHNOLOGY

The World Bank reported in 2009 that there were no patent applications in science and technology in the Congo. Science-related institutions include a Center of Research and Initiation of Technological Projects in Brazzaville, a Technical Center of Tropical Forestry in Pointe-Noire, and a Research Institute for Oils in Sibiti. Marien Ngouabi University in Brazzaville has a faculty of sciences and attached institutes of health sciences and rural development. Sibiti has an agricultural college, and Brazzaville contains a technical, commercial, and industrial college and a school for railway engineering. In addition, there is the Christian Polytechnic & Professional Institute of Arts, the Institute of Business & Economic Development, and the Mondongo Higher Institute of Agricultural Sciences.

30 DOMESTIC TRADE

Most domestic trade consists of agricultural products sold directly to consumers at town and village markets. Some products are sold to company agents and middlemen. Since colonial days, most of the country's domestic commerce is managed by West and North Africans and Lebanese. The country has developed a new investment code to attract foreign investment. However, high production costs, militant labor unions, and poor transportation systems have strangled investment and domestic productivity.

31 FOREIGN TRADE

The Congo imported $3.607 billion worth of goods and services in 2008, while exporting $9.2 billion worth of goods and services. Major import partners in 2009 were France, 20.9%; China, 12.1%; Italy, 9.7%; the United States, 9.1%; India, 6.5%; and Belgium, 4.6% . Its major export partners were the United States, 43.1%; China, 23.5%; France, 8.8%; and India, 6.2%.

Crude petroleum and products accounted for the vast majority of the Congo's commodity export revenues (90%). Diamonds and

Principal Trading Partners – Congo (ROC) (2010)

(In millions of US dollars)

Country	Total	Exports	Imports	Balance
World	11,187.0	8,200.0	2,987.0	5,213.0
United States	3,363.3	3,083.3	280.1	2,803.2
China	3,256.9	2,867.9	389.0	2,478.9
France	1,319.8	670.8	649.0	21.9
Taiwan	857.0	747.5	109.5	638.0
India	811.8	586.8	225.0	361.9
Spain	471.1	437.4	33.6	403.8
Netherlands	462.6	343.8	118.8	225.0
Italy	442.0	177.3	264.7	-87.5
Malaysia	212.6	171.6	41.1	130.5
Australia	211.3	196.0	15.3	180.8

(…) data not available or not significant.

(n.s.) not specified.

SOURCE: *2011 Direction of Trade Statistics Yearbook*, New York: United Nations, 2011.

Balance of Payments – Congo (ROC) (2007)

(In millions of US dollars)

Current Account		-2,181.0
Balance on goods	2,949.9	
Imports	-2,858.1	
Exports	5,808.0	
Balance on services	-3,208.3	
Balance on income	-1,884.7	
Current transfers	-38.0	
Capital Account		31.7
Financial Account		2,546.8
Direct investment abroad	…	
Direct investment in Congo, Republic of the	2,638.4	
Portfolio investment assets	-1.5	
Portfolio investment liabilities	…	
Financial derivatives	…	
Other investment assets	266.2	
Other investment liabilities	-356.4	
Net Errors and Omissions		-201.1
Reserves and Related Items		-196.4

(…) data not available or not significant.

SOURCE: *Balance of Payment Statistics Yearbook 2011*, Washington, DC: International Monetary Fund, 2011.

cement also supported the Congolese economy, as did wood exports, including lumber and plywood.

32 BALANCE OF PAYMENTS

Historically, the Congo has struggled with trade deficits and annual payments deficits. In March 2010, the Paris Club, an informal group of creditor nations, issued a $2.4 million debt cancellation for the ROC, easing what analysts described as an unsustainable debt burden. Brazil also joined the Paris Club in this initiative. With increased oil production and high world oil prices, the balance of payments has become manageable.

33 BANKING AND SECURITIES

Congo has one of the world's weakest banking sectors. In 2011, less than 5% of the population had bank accounts, and limited competition among banks resulted in high lending costs and limited access to capital by consumers and investors. In 2007 lending costs were approximately 15.5%.

The bank of issue is the Bank of the Central African States (BEAC), which serves all the members of the Central African Economic and Monetary Union (CEMAC). Commercial banks includes the Congolese Union of Banks, the International Bank of Congo, the Congolese Commercial Bank, and Ecobank. The National Development Bank of the Congo extends loans for economic development. The Congo has a 13% share in CEMAC's development bank, headquartered in Brazzaville. In 2007 some 86 microfinance institutions served the micro-finance sector.

At the end of 2009, the discount rate, the interest rate at which the central bank lends to financial institutions in the short term, was 4.25%. At the end of 2010, the nation's foreign exchange and gold reserves totaled $4.465 billion, 89th in the world. There is no securities market in the Congo. Normal banking hours are 6:30 to 11:30 a.m. Monday through Saturday.

34 INSURANCE

Like banking, the insurance sector is regulated and supervised by a regional body, the International Commission of Insurance Markets (Conférence Intérnationale des Marchés d'Assurances—CIMA). In March 1974, private insurance companies were nationalized and put under the Congo Insurance and Reinsurance Co. (ARC), which was 50% government owned. In 2007 two companies—the ARC and the Assurance Générale du Congo (AGC)—constituted the mainstay of the industry. Car insurance accounted for 54.4% of the market; fire hazard 15.5%, transport insurance 12.1% and other 17.3%.

35 PUBLIC FINANCE

In 2010 the budget of Republic of the Congo included $3.818 billion in public revenue and $2.599 billion in public expenditures. The budget surplus amounted to 7.7% of GDP. Public debt was 16.5% of GDP, with $5 billion of the debt held by foreign entities.

High dependence on oil revenues for public spending has imposed constraints on Congo. The collapse in oil prices in the mid-1980s dramatically decreased government revenues, which led to a surge in international borrowing. In 1985, Congo entered negotiation with the IMF for standby credits to satisfy domestic and foreign creditors. In 1986, Congo reluctantly submitted to an IMF structural adjustment program (SAP) for which the country received $40 million in funds and was able to reschedule its international payments. By 1988, Congo's external debt had risen to an unsustainable $4.1 billion. In 1989, a second structural adjustment program followed. In the late 1980s and early 1990s, weak oil prices and a massive public sector combined to drive up Congo's debt. Civil service salaries absorbed over half of the government's 1995 budget. The budget deficit rose from 5.5% of GDP in 1985 to 14% in 1991 and was estimated at 25% in 1998. In 1995, total external debt was approximately $5 billion with service on the debt amounting to 155% of revenues annually, one of the highest ratios in the world. Although the Paris Club agreed to reduce Congo's debt by 67%, debt reduction payments still reached $500 million in 1996. IMF and World Bank reform programs came to a halt when civil war erupted in 1997.

In March 2006, the World Bank and the International Monetary Fund (IMF) approved Heavily Indebted Poor Countries (HIPC) treatment for Congo, providing $1.9 billion in debt relief under the program, which Congo successfully completed in 2010. Total public external debt declined as a result from about $10 billion (or almost 200 percent of GDP) in 2004 to about $1.4 billion (or 12.5 percent of GDP) in 2010.

Strong oil prices in 2010–2011 meant that government would have significantly more resources at its command to invest in the public sector. The investment budget was estimated to reach approximately $2.2 billion in 2011, representing an increase of more than 50% compared to the investment budget of approximately $1.4 billion in 2010. The World Bank judged that government efforts to improve public finance management and procurement were positive.

Nonetheless, Congo's over-reliance on oil revenues meant that unless new oil discoveries were made, or unless the economy diversified, rising costs and unmet demands in the social sectors and infrastructure would place undue stress on the budget by 2015.

36 TAXATION

Compared with the OECD countries and with other countries in Africa, Congo has one of the most regressive tax structures. In the World Bank's "Doing Business" rankings, Congo scored 180th in the world in 2011. Companies paid a total tax rate of 65.9%, which included a profit tax of 18.1%, a labor tax and contributions of 32.5%, and other taxes amounting to 15.4%.

Individuals paid graduated income tax at rates of 1–50%, varying with an individual's marital status and number of dependents. Formal sector workers, of which there was a relatively small number, also paid social security taxes and regional income taxes.

37 CUSTOMS AND DUTIES

In 1983, CEMAC states - Cameroon, Central African Republic, Chad, Congo, Equatorial Guinea, and Gabon formed a Central African Customs Union (UDEAC). UDEAC provided low or no customs duties on most imported goods from member states. There were no free trade zones or free ports in the country.

On imports from non-UDEAC and non-EU common market countries, Congo imposed a 5% duty on basic necessities, 10% on raw materials and capital goods, 20% on intermediate and miscellaneous goods, and 30% on consumer goods. There was also an 18.7% value-added tax based on CIF (cost, insurance, freight) plus the duty. Significant nontariff trade barriers included import license requirements and a corrupt and inefficient customs system.

In 2011 the cost to import a container of goods to Congo was $7,709 compared to $2,503 on average for sub Saharan Africa and $1,085 for OECD countries. The cost to export a container from Congo was $3,818 compared with $1,960 on average for sub Saharan Africa and $1,032 for OECD countries.

38 FOREIGN INVESTMENT

Foreign direct investment (FDI) in the Republic of the Congo was a net inflow of $2.08 billion according to World Bank figures published in 2009. FDI represented 21.75% of GDP.

Virtually all foreign investment in the Republic of Congo has been in the oil and timber sectors, with the French company Total dominant in the oil sector. The second-largest oil investor has been ENI-Agip (Agip-Congo) of Italy. Chevron is the top US oil company engaged in the sector. Most of the oil industry is off-shore, employing foreign personnel. Investment in the wider economy has been hampered by numerous factors including political uncertainty, a poorly developed financial sector, inadequate and war-damaged infrastructure, the high cost of labor, difficulty in transporting raw materials, low productivity, and militant labor unions.

The 1973 investment code guaranteed the free transfer of capital, normally earned profits, and funds resulting from sales of foreign companies. Legislation adopted in 1982 reduced import duties and taxes on production equipment and profits on manufacturing and trading were tax exempt for the first five years. An updated investment code enacted in 1992 and amended in 1996 legislated equal treatment for domestic and foreign investors. This protection was reaffirmed by the Investment Charter, established by Law 6–2003 on January 18, 2003, which offered a range of guarantees to foreign investors including no discrimination or disqualification on all types of investment and equal justice under Congolese law.

In 1994, the regiment for participation by foreign oil companies was changed from the joint ventures that had prevailed since 1968 to production sharing agreements (PSAs), by which foreign oil companies operated under contracts with the national oil company, SNPC.

On-going privatization of state-owned enterprises in the oil distribution, oil refining, telecommunications, rail and water transportation, electricity, and water distribution sectors was designed to attract foreign investment.

Corruption remained a major deterrent to direct foreign investment. In 2010, on Transparency International's Corruption Perception Index (CPI), Congo was perceived as highly corrupt, ranking 154th out of 178 countries on the Index.

39 ECONOMIC DEVELOPMENT

Despite being resource-rich, Congo is a country with high poverty, a victim of the "resource curse." Development plans in the 1980s and 1990s called for the improvement of infrastructure (roads, electricity, water) and for the development of agriculture, forestry, and light industry; however, economic constraints caused those plans to be cut back sharply. In 1994, the Communauté Financière Africaine franc was devalued by half to boost economic activity. Although Congo derived export benefit from that policy, violent conflict and civil war in the 1990s to mid-2000s constrained economic development.

In the mid-1990s, Congo embarked on a path of economic reform, including reform of the tax, investment, labor, and hydrocarbon codes. Privatization of state-owned enterprises, particularly telecommunications and transportation, also occurred. The Paris Club agreed to a debt restructuring plan in 1996. But when war broke out in 1997, economic reform came to a halt. After re-election in 2002, President Sassou-Nguesso reestablished cooperation with international financial institutions, and launched an economic program, Nouvelle Espérance (New Hope), covering the period 2003–10.

In August 2005, the board of the IMF completed its first annual review of Congo's three-year poverty reduction and growth facility (PRGF) and gave a positive endorsement of progress in spite of opacity within the oil industry.

Congo's first full Poverty Reduction Strategy Paper (PRSP) was adopted in April 2008. The PRSP had five pillars: improving governance and consolidating peace and security; promoting growth and macroeconomic stability; enhancing access to basic social services; improving the social environment and integration of vulnerable groups; and combating HIV/AIDS. By 2011 a second generation PRSP was being prepared based on the government's objective of becoming an emerging economy by 2025. The second generation PRSP was to cover the period of 2011–2016.

In a 2011 report, the World Bank noted that the Republic of Congo had successfully completed its Heavily Indebted Poor Countries (HIPC) program. The Bank also reported that the economy grew significantly since 2008 through improvements in fiscal discipline and debt management. According to the 2010 IMF World Economic Outlook Report, the Republic of Congo was Africa's fastest growing economy in 2010.

Nonetheless, institutional constraints continued to hamper economic growth. In terms of economic openness, Congo ranked near the bottom in the world—169th out of 179 countries on the 2011 Economic Freedom Index.

40 SOCIAL DEVELOPMENT

In 2011 half the population lived below the poverty line and inequality remained high. Social indicators were far below those of countries with comparable levels of GNI per capita and meeting Millennium Development Goals (MDGs). Among others, MDGs to reduce maternal and child mortality were seriously off-track. On the 2011 UN' Human Development Index (HDI), which measures prospects for quality education and a long and healthy life, Congo ranked 137th among 169 countries.

The Fundamental Act prohibited discrimination based on race, gender, or religion, but many marriage and family laws discriminate against women. Polygamy is legal, while polyandry is not. Adultery is legal for men, but not for women. Women receive less education on average than men, and their salaries are generally lower. Women are not prominent at the highest levels of political or professional life. Domestic violence is widespread and rarely reported. Civil conflict increased the number of indigent children living on the streets of Brazzaville. The Union of Congolese Women promote the advancement of women through literacy and female education campaigns.

Pygmy minorities also face discrimination. They are often paid with food or goods for their labor, rather than with wages. Pygmies are underrepresented in government and are marginalized from government decision making.

Congo's human rights record has improved since the transition to democracy, but abuses continue. There are continuing reports of torture and extrajudicial killings, as well as disappearances, rapes, and arbitrary searches, arrests, and detention.

41 HEALTH

According to the CIA, life expectancy in the Republic of the Congo was 54 years in 2011. The country spent 2.7% of its GDP on healthcare, amounting to $70 per person. There was 1 physician, 8 nurses and midwives, and 16 hospital beds per 10,000 inhabitants. The fertility rate was 4.3, while the infant mortality rate was

81 per 1,000 live births. In 2008 the maternal mortality rate, according to the World Bank, was 580 per 100,000 births. It was estimated that 76% of children were vaccinated against measles. The CIA calculated HIV/AIDS prevalence in the Congo to be about 3.4% in 2009.

In 2010, approximately 50% of urban and 11% of rural inhabitants had access to safe water. In November 2010, there was an outbreak of polio that resulted in at least 201 cases of paralysis and 104 deaths. Government declared an emergency and announced plans to vaccinate the entire population using oral vaccine.

42 HOUSING

In 2008, more than 88% of all housing units were private houses. Owners occupied more than 60% of dwellings, tenants nearly 25%, and over 9% were occupied rent free. Close to one-third of all units had brick external walls, more than 25% had stone walls, nearly 16% had planks, and over 10% cob.

In 2008 about 71% of the population had access to improved water sources. However, only 30% of the population had access to improved sanitary facilities in 2008.

43 EDUCATION

The educational system is patterned after France with government-run schools, but changes are being introduced that adapt curriculum to local needs and traditions. Six years of primary school are compulsory. Secondary school covere a seven-year course of study; students can choose a general course of studies or a technical program for their secondary education. The academic year runs from October to June. The language of instruction is French.

Congo is making progress in school enrollment, but still has far to go in educating its population. In 2010 the World Bank estimated that 91% of age-eligible children in the Congo were enrolled in primary school. Tertiary enrollment was estimated at 6%.

The National University, which opened in Brazzaville in 1971, was later renamed Marien Ngouabi University. Overall, the CIA estimated that Republic of the Congo had a literacy rate of 83.8%. As of 2005, public expenditure on education was estimated at about 2.0% of GDP, or 8% of total government expenditures.

44 LIBRARIES AND MUSEUMS

Brazzaville is the center for libraries and museums. Marien Ngouabi University Library held some 20,000 volumes in 2002, and the National Popular Library held 15,000 volumes. The French Cultural Center housed a library of 33,000 volumes, and the World Health Organization held 40,000 volumes.

The National Museum of the Congo (1965), also in Brazzaville, contains ethnography displays and historical displays. There are regional museums in Pointe-Noire and Kinkala.

45 MEDIA

In 2009 the CIA reported that there were 24,300 telephone landlines in Republic of the Congo. Mobile phone subscriptions averaged 59 per 100 people. There were 18 radio and 10 TV stations, satellite TV service was available and rebroadcasts of international broadcasters were also available. Internet users numbered 7 per 100 citizens. In 2010 the country had 42 internet hosts. Generally, internet connectivity was poor even in Brazzaville, and was inaccessible in rural areas of the country.

Radio is the primary source of news and information. There are three government-owned radio stations and one government-owned television station, Tele Congo. Radio Brazzaville broadcast in French and local languages. Telecasts are in French, Kikongo, and Lingala. The news coverage and the editorial positions of the state-owned media reflect government priorities and views.

In 2009, there was one daily private newspaper being published in Brazzaville, *Dépeches de Brazzaville*; Some 50 other newspapers have been published irregularly. The information ministry runs the government news outlet, the Congolese News Agency. There are also a handful of periodicals and magazines, including *La Semaine Africaine*, a bi-weekly publication of the Catholic Church.

Although the constitution provides for free expression and a free press, reporters generally fear government retaliation for critical and unfavorable reports on government and ruling party performance; self-censorship was common. During the 2009 presidential elections, several international journalists reported physical attacks and intimidation. Few people can afford newspapers and salaries and working conditions for reporters are poor.

On the 2009 Media Sustainability Index (MSI), Congo scored 1.4 (scale 0–4), which relegated the country to the category of having an anti-free press. The MSI considered factors that contributed to the quality of journalism, effectiveness of management, and the legal environment supporting freedom of the press.

46 ORGANIZATIONS

There are Chambers of Commerce, Agriculture, and Industry in Brazzaville, Loubomo, Pointe-Noire, and Ouesso. In rural areas, cooperatives promote the production and marketing of agricultural products. Self-help societies are popular, especially in the larger towns. Some volunteer service organizations, such as the Lions Clubs International, are present.

Larger towns have vocational, faith-based, women's, and youth organizations. From the late 1960s to the early 1990s the Union of Socialist Youth of the Congo (UJSC), the youth wing of the Labor Party, was popular. Many government officials serving in 2011 once belonged to the UJSC. The Congolese Olympic Committee (COC) coordinate national youth sports organizations. There are scouting programs as well.

Many NGOs such as the Congolese Observatory for Human Rights, the national chapter of the Red Cross Society, and Caritas have offices in the capital city, Brazzaville.

47 TOURISM, TRAVEL, AND RECREATION

The *Tourism Factbook*, published by the UN World Tourism Organization, reported 85,000 incoming tourists to the Congo in 2009, who spent a total of $54 million. Of those incoming tourists, there were 40,000 from Europe and 30,000 from Africa. No data was available on the number of hotel beds available in the Congo. The US government estimated the daily cost of staying in Brazzaville in 2011 at $377, depending upon choice of accommodations and restaurants.

The main tourist attractions are the beaches near the Côte Sauvage region and water-skiing on the Kouillou and Congo rivers. All visitors need passports; visas need to be secured in advance. Vaccination for yellow fever is required and precautions for malaria are recommended.

⁴⁸FAMOUS PERSONS

The best-known figures from the ROC are Abbé Fulbert Youlou (1917–72), a former Roman Catholic priest who served as president from 1960 to 1963, as well as mayor of Brazzaville; Alphonse Massamba-Debat (1921–77), president from 1963 to 1968; and Marien Ngouabi (1938–77), who came to power in a 1968 coup and was president from 1968 to 1977. Denis Sassou-Nguesso (b. 1943?) became president in 1979; he served until 1992, and then again beginning in 1997. Prominent author and playwright Emmanuel Dongala-Boundzeki (b. 1941) is also a chemistry professor at Marien Ngouabi University in Brazzaville.

⁴⁹DEPENDENCIES

The Republic of the Congo has no territories or colonies.

⁵⁰BIBLIOGRAPHY

Attwater, Helen. *My Gorilla Journey*. Leicester, Eng.: Charnwood, 2000.

Congo Investment and Business Guide: Strategic and Practical Information. Washington, DC: International Business Publications USA, 2012.

Knight, Cassie. *Brazzaville Charms: Magic and Rebellion in the Republic of Congo*. London: Frances Lincoln, 2007.

Tayler, Jeffrey. *Facing the Congo: A Modern-day Journey into the Heart of Darkness*. New York: Three Rivers, 2000.

Zeilig, Leo, and David Seddon. *A Political and Economic Dictionary of Africa*. Philadelphia: Routledge/Taylor and Francis, 2005..

CÔTE D'IVOIRE

Republic of Côte d'Ivoire
République de Côte d'Ivoire

CAPITAL: Yamoussoukro

FLAG: The flag is a tricolor of orange, white, and green vertical stripes.

ANTHEM: *L'Abidjanaise (Song of Abidjan).*

MONETARY UNIT: The Communauté Financière Africaine franc (XOF), which was originally pegged to the French franc, has been pegged to the euro since January 1999 with a rate of 655.957 francs to 1 euro. It is issued in coins of 1, 5, 10, 25, 50, 100, 250, and 500 francs, and notes of 500, 1,000, 2,000, 5,000, and 10,000 francs. XOF1 = US$0.00215 (or US$1 = XOF465.2) as of 2011.

WEIGHTS AND MEASURES: The metric system is the legal standard.

HOLIDAYS: New Year's Day, 1 January; the Prophet's birthday, 5 February; Labor Day, 1 May; Independence Day, 7 August; Assumption, 15 August; All Saints' Day, 1 November; Christmas, 25 December. Movable religious holidays include Good Friday, Easter Monday, Ascension, Pentecost Monday, Eid al-Fitr, and Eid al-Adha.

TIME: GMT.

¹LOCATION, SIZE, AND EXTENT

The Republic of Côte d'Ivoire, on the south coast of the western bulge of Africa, has an area of 322,460 sq km (124,502 sq mi). Comparatively, the area occupied by Côte d'Ivoire is slightly larger than the state of New Mexico. Roughly rectangular in shape, it extends 808 km (502 mi) SE–NW and 780 km (485 mi) NE–SW. It is bordered on the N by Mali and Burkina Faso, on the E by Ghana, on the S by the Gulf of Guinea and the Atlantic Ocean, and on the W by Liberia and Guinea, with a total boundary length of 3,110 km (1,932 mi) and a coastline of 515 km (322 mi).

In 1983, Côte d'Ivoire's capital was moved to Yamoussoukro, about 225 km (140 mi) northwest of the former capital, Abidjan, in the south-central part of the country.

²TOPOGRAPHY

Except for the prolongation of the Guinea Highlands (in the northwest, from Man to Odienné), which has peaks of over 1,000 m (3,280 ft), the greater part of Côte d'Ivoire is a vast plateau, tilted gently toward the Atlantic. It is drained by four major rivers running roughly parallel from north to south—the Cavally (on the Liberian frontier), Sassandra, Bandama, and Komoé. They are not of much value for transportation, since they are sluggish in the dry season, broken by numerous falls and rapids, and subject to torrential flooding in the rainy season. Lake Kossou (Lac de Kossou), in the center of the country, has been formed by the impoundment of the Bandama. From Ghana to Fresco, the coast is almost a straight line, flat and sandy, with a series of deep lagoons behind it; from Fresco to the Liberian frontier, it is more broken, with small cliffs and rocky outcrops.

³CLIMATE

The greatest annual rainfall, about 200 cm (79 in), is along the coast and in the southwest. The coastal region has a long dry season from December to April, followed by heavy rains from May to September. Farther north, there is only one wet and one dry season, with rainfall heaviest in summer, culminating in September, and lightest in January. The country's lightest rainfall is in the northeast, averaging 109 cm (43 in) annually. Average temperatures along the coast range from 24° to 32°C (75° to 90°F) in January and from 22° to 28°C (72° to 82°F) in July. At Bouaké, in the center of the country, minimum and maximum temperatures in November, the hottest month, average 21° and 35°C (70° and 95°F); the range is from 20° to 29°C (68° to 84°F) in July, the coolest month. At Ferkéssédougou, in the far north, temperatures range from 21° to 36°C (70° to 97°F) in March and from 17° to 30°C (63° to 86°F) in November.

⁴FLORA AND FAUNA

The southern Côte d'Ivoire forest is a typical rain forest; it has a canopy at around 21–24 m (70–80 ft), with isolated trees pushing up above 37 m (120 ft). Farther north, the rain forest gives way to scattered stands of deciduous trees. Mahogany is widespread. Still farther north, oil palm, acacia, breadfruit, and baobab characterize the transition to true savanna, where shea nut and traveler's palm are common. The World Resources Institute estimates that there are 3,660 plant species in Côte d'Ivoire.

Côte d'Ivoire is home to 229 species of mammals, including jackals, hyenas, panthers, elephants, hippopotami, and numerous monkeys. Crocodiles and chameleons, as well as venomous serpents (horned vipers, mambas, and many others) and pythons, are numerous. A total of 702 bird species reside in Côte d'Ivoire. Not all are indigenous; among the indigenous birds are vultures, cranes, pigeons, turtle doves, parrots, and herons. Venomous spiders and scorpions abound.

The World Resources Institute estimates that the nation hosts 131 reptile species and 54 amphibian species. The species totals in this section reflect the total number of distinct species residing in the country, not the number of native species.

⁵ENVIRONMENT

Côte d'Ivoire faces environmental challenges related to deforestation and climate change, as well as agricultural and mining practices. Most of Côte d'Ivoire's forests, once the largest in West Africa, have been cut down by the timber industry, with only cursory attempts at reforestation. In 1960, there were 16 million hectares (39.5 million acres) of forest; by 2010, the Côte d'Ivoire's forested area measured less than 2 million hectares, according to the nation's environmental minister. Forestry guards have been unable to stop the illegal poaching in and clearing of the forests and have come under attack by poachers. Côte d'Ivoire's army in 2010 offered its assistance in protecting the remaining forests of the national parks and other protected areas. The environmental ministry was considering that offer as of 2011.

Côte d'Ivoire is also affected by desertification and climate changes, including decreased rainfall. Water pollution is a significant environmental problem due to chemical waste from industrial and mining sources and the heavy agricultural use of pesticides and fertilizers. The country's lack of sanitation facilities further contributes to the pollution problem.

The World Resources Institute reported that Côte d'Ivoire had designated 3.89 million hectares (9.61 million acres) of land for protection as of 2006. Water resources totaled 81 cu km (19.43 cu mi), while water usage was 0.93 cu km (0.223 cu mi) per year. Domestic water usage accounted for 24% of total usage, industrial for 12%, and agricultural for 64%. Per capita water usage totaled 51 cu m (1,801 cu ft) per year. The UN reported in 2008 that carbon dioxide emissions in Côte d'Ivoire totaled 6,379 kilotons.

There are three natural UNESCO World Heritage Sites and six Ramsar wetland sites in Côte d'Ivoire. According to the International Union for Conservation of Nature and Natural Resources (IUCN) Red List of Threatened Species, the number of threatened species in Côte d'Ivoire as of 2011 included 23 mammals, 15 birds, 6 reptiles, 14 amphibians, 45 fish, 3 mollusks, and 106 plants. Specific species included Pel's flying squirrel, the white-breasted guinea fowl, the thresher shark, and the red-capped monkey.

⁶POPULATION

The US Central Intelligence Agency (CIA) estimated the population of Côte d'Ivoire in 2011 to be approximately 21,504,162, which placed it at number 56 in population among the 196 nations of the world. In 2011, approximately 3% of the population was over 65 years of age, with another 39.8% under 15 years of age. The median age in Côte d'Ivoire was 19.6 years. There were 1.03 males for every female in the country. The population's annual rate of change was 2.078%. The projected population for the year 2025 was 30,800,000. Population density in Côte d'Ivoire was calculated at 67 people per sq km (174 people per sq mi).

The UN estimated that 51% of the population lived in urban areas, with an annual rate of change of 3.7%. The largest urban areas, along with their respective populations, included Abidjan, 4 million, and Yamoussoukro, 808,000.

The prevalence of HIV/AIDS has had a significant impact on the population of Côte d'Ivoire. The HIV/AIDS epidemic has led to higher death and infant mortality rates and lowered life expectancy.

⁷MIGRATION

Estimates of Côte d'Ivoire's net migration rate, calculated by the CIA in 2011, amounted to zero. The total number of emigrants living abroad was 1.17 million, and the total number of immigrants living in Côte d'Ivoire was 2.41 million. Côte d'Ivoire also accepted 25,615 refugees in that year. Flourishing economic activity in Côte d'Ivoire has attracted large numbers of workers from neighboring countries. From 1960 to the early 1990s, the country welcomed foreign workers, but in 1998, the government challenged the right of immigrants to own land and established rules to define "Ivoirians." A resident could not be a citizen without proving that both his or her parents had been born in an Ivoirian village. Migratory laborers from Burkina Faso, whose population was estimated at its peak as being more than one million, have worked chiefly on the cocoa and coffee plantations. After the violence of Côte d'Ivoire's 2002 civil war, 360,000 of these immigrants returned to their native Burkina Faso. In addition, Ghanaian, Guinean, Malian, Senegalese, and Mauritanian immigrants live in Côte d'Ivoire. In 2006, 38,000 Liberians lived in Côte d'Ivoire, but 30,000 of these immigrants returned to Liberia after peaceful elections were held there in 2005. Most of the non-African population consists of French and other Europeans, and Lebanese and Syrians.

⁸ETHNIC GROUPS

The ethnic composition of Côte d'Ivoire is complex, with more than 60 ethnic groups represented. The Akan group, which primarily occupies the eastern and central regions of the country, accounts for about 42.1% of the population. The Baoulé are the single largest subgroup of the Akan people, accounting for about 20% of the total population. The Voltaiques (Gur) account for about 17.6% of the population. The Northern Mandes from the northwest region of the country make up about 16.5% of the population. The Krou people in the southwest account for about 11%; the Bété are the largest subgroup. The Southern Mandes from the western regions account for about 10% of the population. Non-Africans include about 14,000 French and 130,000 Lebanese expatriates.

⁹LANGUAGES

The official language is French. Of the more than 60 African languages spoken by different ethnic groups, the most important are Agni and Baulé, spoken by the Akan group; the Kru languages; the Sénoufo languages; and the Mandé languages (especially Malinké-Bambura-Dioula).

¹⁰RELIGIONS

Estimates place the number of Muslims in Côte d'Ivoire at about 38.6% of the population and the number of Christians at 32.8%.

LOCATION: 2°30′ to 7°30′W; 4°20′ to 10°50′ N. BOUNDARY LENGTHS: Mali, 515 kilometers (320 miles); Burkina Faso, 531 kilometers (330 miles); Ghana, 668 kilometers (415 miles); Gulf of Guinea coastline, 507 kilometers (315 miles); Liberia, 716 kilometers (445 miles); Guinea, 605 kilometers (376 miles). TERRITORIAL SEA LIMIT: 12 miles.

About 17% of the population does not claim any religious affiliation or preference. About 11.9% of the population practices indigenous religions, either exclusively or in conjunction with other beliefs. A large variety of Christian denominations are represented in the country, including Roman Catholicism, Methodists, Southern Baptists, Seventh-Day Adventists, Assemblies of God, and the Church of Jesus Christ of Latter-Day Saints. A small percentage of people belong to the Harrist Church, a Protestant denomina-

tion founded in 1913 by the Liberian minister William Hade Harris. Syncretic religions, such as the Church of the Prophet Papa Nouveau and Eckankar, combine Christian tenets with African traditional customs and beliefs. There are also communities of Buddhists, Baha'is, and members of the International Society for Krishna Consciousness. Religious and political affiliation often follows ethnic and regional lines. Most Muslims live in the north and most Christians live in the south. Traditionalists are generally concentrated in rural areas in the north and across the center of the country. The Akan ethnic group traditionally practices a religion called Bossonism.

The constitution provides for freedom of religion; however, Christianity has historically enjoyed a privileged status in national life with particular advantage toward the Catholic Church. All religious groups must register through the Ministry of the Interior's Department of Faith-Based Organizations. Certain Muslim and Christian holidays are recognized as national holidays.

11 TRANSPORTATION

Côte d'Ivoire has one of the best-developed and best-maintained transportation systems in Africa. As of 2008, the nation's railway system consisted of a state-controlled section of a narrow gauge railroad that ran north from Abidjan through Bouaké and Ferkéssédougou to Ouagadougou, Burkina Faso, extending for 639 km (397 mi).

The CIA reports that Côte d'Ivoire has a total of 80,000 km (49,710 mi) of roads, of which 6,500 km (4,039 mi) are paved. The nation is expected to benefit greatly from the World-Bank-funded reconstruction of the Abidjan-Lagos Corridor, also known as the West African Coastal Corridor. In March 2010, the World Bank approved funding of $317.5 million to improve this important roadway, which stretches for 998.8 km (620 mi) and links the capital cities of Abidjan (Côte d'Ivoire), Accra (Ghana), Lomé (Togo), Cotonou (Benin), and Lagos (Nigeria). This corridor is one of the most highly traveled roadways on the continent. Developed in part by the Economic Community of West African States (ECOWAS), the corridor project was designed to implement procedural reforms that will support a more efficient trade process, along with much needed improvements to the physical infrastructure. The project was to be executed in two phases, with the first phase covering Ghana, Togo, and Benin, and the second phase covering Côte d'Ivoire and Nigeria. Construction in Ghana began in March 2012.

Côte d'Ivoire has approximately 980 km (609 mi) of navigable waterways. Harbor activity is concentrated at Abidjan (West Africa's largest container port), whose facilities include a fishing port and equipment for handling containers, and San Pedro, a deepwater port that began operations in 1971. There are also small ports at Sassandra and Tabou. Two nationalized shipping lines serve West Africa and Europe.

Air Ivoire, government-owned since 1976, operates domestic airline services and also flies to Ouagadougou, Burkina Faso, and Bamako, Mali. International flights to Paris, Dakar, and other African and European capitals are handled by Air Afrique, a joint venture owned by Côte d'Ivoire and other participating Yaoundé Treaty countries (72%) and by Air France and Union des Transports Aériens (28%). Côte d'Ivoire's principal airport, F.H. Boigny, is located in Abidjan. Secondary airports are located at Bérébi, Bouaké, Daloa, Man, Sassandra, Korhogo, Tabou, San Pedro, Guiglo, Bondoukou, Yamoussoukro, and Odienné. In 2009, 7 of the country's 27 airports had paved runways.

12 HISTORY

Little is known of the early history of the area now called Côte d'Ivoire. Most of its peoples entered the country from the northwest and the east in comparatively recent times, with the Kru-speaking peoples coming from west of the Cavally River (modern Liberia). European travelers described flourishing and well-organized states in the north and east, with strongly hierarchical social organization and elaborate gold weights and ornaments. These states, such as the Agni kingdom of Indénié and the Abron kingdom of Bondoukou, were closely related linguistically and socially to the neighboring Ashanti of modern Ghana and formed with them, along with the Fon of Dahomey (now Benin) and the Yoruba and Bini kingdoms in Nigeria, an almost continuous string of relatively rich and developed states of the Guinea forest zone. Nearer the coast, the scale of social organization was much smaller, and innumerable small units recognized no political superior.

Modern European acquaintance with the west coast of Africa began with the Portuguese discoveries of the 15th century, culminating in the discovery of the route to India around the Cape of Good Hope in 1488 and the establishment of trading posts along the Senegal coast and the Gulf of Guinea. The Portuguese and Spanish were soon followed by the Dutch and English. Gold, ivory, ostrich feathers, gum arabic, and pepper were succeeded by slaves as the major trading commodities. French activity in what is now Côte d'Ivoire began in 1687, when missionaries landed at Assinié. In 1843, Adm. Louis-Édouard Bouet-Willaumez established French posts at Assinié and Grand Bassam, where treaties with the local chiefs provided for the cession of land for forts in exchange for tribute to the chiefs (*coutumes*) at fixed rates and regular intervals.

After the Franco-Prussian War of 1870, the small garrisons of Assinié, Grand Bassam, and Dabou were withdrawn. French interests were confided to a resident trader named Verdier. He and a young assistant, Treich-Laplène, consolidated the French position along the coast. In 1887, Treich-Laplène signed treaties with Indénié, Bettié, Alangoa, and other chiefdoms of the interior, thus preventing British advances into eastern Côte d'Ivoire from Ashanti. Continuing northward to Kong, he joined forces with Col. Louis Binger, who had made his way from Bamako in French Sudan (Soudan Française, now Mali) to Kong and from there northeast to Ouagadougou in Upper Volta (now Burkina Faso) and back to Kong through Bondoukou. French claims to Upper Volta and northern Côte d'Ivoire, joining French Sudan and Niger in a continuous territory, were thus established. In 1893, the territory was renamed Côte d'Ivoire, and Col. Binger was appointed the first French governor. The new colony's frontier with Liberia was settled by a convention in 1892, and with the Gold Coast (modern Ghana) by the Anglo-French agreement of 1893. The northern border was not defined until 1947.

Despite these agreements, French control of Côte d'Ivoire was far from secured. Much of the region remained unexplored, and administrative control had yet to be effectively organized in those areas whose chiefs had concluded treaties with the French. More serious still, Samory Touré, a Malinké from Guinea who periodically fought the French, had moved southeast after the French capture of Sankoro in 1892 and was continuing his struggle against the invaders in the region of Kong. Not until 1898, after prolonged fighting, was he finally captured near Man. Systematic military operations in the densely forested area between the upper Cavally and the upper Sassandra were carried out from 1908 onward until French rule was finally established in Côte d'Ivoire on the eve of World War I. In other parts of the colony, intermittent revolts continued throughout this period, stimulated by the imposition of a poll tax and opposition of many of the chiefs to the substitution of a tax rebate for the coutumes promised in the treaties. Nevertheless, some 20,000 Ivoirian troops were raised in the colony during World War I, when the greater part of the French forces was withdrawn.

In the interwar years, Côte d'Ivoire became a considerable producer of cocoa, coffee, mahogany, and other tropical products. Although European planters produced about one-third of the cocoa and coffee and most of the bananas, the share of African planters rapidly increased throughout this period. The railroad, begun in 1904, did not reach the northern part of the colony until 1925. Until 1954, Grand Bassam (opened 1901) and Port Bouet (opened 1932) were the principal ports; that year, the deepwater port of Abidjan opened, following the cutting of the Ébrié Lagoon in 1950.

During World War II, Côte d'Ivoire, like the rest of French West Africa, remained under control of the Vichy government between 1940 and 1943. In 1941, the king of Bondoukou and thousands of his people made their way into the Gold Coast to join Gen. Charles de Gaulle's resistance forces. At the end of the war, Côte d'Ivoire was established as an overseas territory under the 1946 French constitution and given three deputies and three senators in the French parliament and an elected territorial assembly. By 1956, the territory produced 45% of all French West African exports, took in 30% of the imports, and seemed assured of continued economic advance.

In 1958, Côte d'Ivoire accepted the new French constitution in a referendum on 28 September and opted for the status of an autonomous state within the new French Community. On 4 December 1958, the Territorial Assembly, which had been elected by universal suffrage on 31 March 1957, formed itself into the Constituent Assembly and proclaimed the Republic of Côte d'Ivoire as a member state of the French Community. On 26 March 1959, the assembly adopted the first constitution of the new country. The legislature provided for in this constitution was chosen by a national election held on 17 April, and Félix Houphouët-Boigny was unanimously selected by the Assembly as prime minister on 27 April.

On 7 August 1960, the Republic of Côte d'Ivoire proclaimed its complete independence. On 31 October, a new constitution providing for a presidential system was adopted. In elections held on 27 November, Houphouët-Boigny was unanimously elected the country's first president. Although two plots to overthrow him, organized by government and party officials, were discovered in 1963, both failed, and in that year Houphouët-Boigny took over most key ministerial portfolios and consolidated his control over the Democratic Party of Côte d'Ivoire (PDCI).

Outbreaks of unrest plagued the Houphouët-Boigny government during the late 1960s and early 1970s. In 1969, some 1,500 unemployed youths were arrested in the course of widespread rioting. In 1970, disturbances broke out in Gagnoa, Bouaké, and Daloa. These incidents were followed in 1973 by an alleged conspiracy to overthrow the government. Following a brief trial, two army captains and five lieutenants were sentenced to death, while others were given jail sentences ranging from 15 to 20 years of hard labor. Before the sixth PDCI congress in 1975, President Houphouët-Boigny pardoned some 5,000 persons, among who were 145 political prisoners, some associated with the Gagnoa

disturbances. All death sentences were commuted to 20 years of hard labor. During this period, the government used a series of mass meetings called "dialogues" to win over new adherents. These public discussions were usually led by prominent members of the administration, and President Houphouët-Boigny often presided over them personally. During the second half of the 1970s, Houphouët-Boigny and the PDCI remained firmly in control, and Côte d'Ivoire became one of black Africa's most prosperous nations.

Houphouët-Boigny was reelected unopposed to his fifth five-year term as president in October 1980. The nation's first competitive National Assembly elections were held in the following month. The ruling PDCI allowed 649 candidates to compete for the 147 seats, with a runoff between the two best-placed candidates in each constituency where there was no majority choice. A total of 121 new members were elected, while 54 of the 80 deputies who ran for reelection were defeated. Relations with neighboring countries were generally favorable; in 1981, however, the death by suffocation of 46 Ghanaians who had been jailed near Abidjan on suspicion of drug smuggling led to friction with Ghana, which was resolved through Togolese mediation. Declining economic prospects in the early 1980s led to a series of strikes among professional workers, which Houphouët-Boigny accused a foreign power (presumed to be Libya) of fomenting.

Houphouët-Boigny won an unopposed sixth term as president in October 1985, reportedly receiving 100% of the vote in a turnout of over 99% of eligible voters. In the following month, fewer than 30% turned out for the National Assembly elections, in which 546 candidates—all members of the PDCI but not screened—competed for 175 seats. Only 64 deputies were returned to office. Côte d'Ivoire celebrated the 25th anniversary of its independence on 7 December 1985, and commemorated the occasion by releasing 9,500 convicted criminals from prison.

In 1990, Côte d'Ivoire entered a new political era as months of prodemocracy demonstrations and labor unrest led to the legalization of previously banned opposition parties. Even within the PDCI, a progressive wing called for further liberalization. The first multiparty presidential and legislative elections were held on 28 October 1990 and 25 November 1990, respectively. Houphouët-Boigny was reelected as president with 81% of the vote, and the PDCI carried 163 of the 175 seats. The remaining seats were won by other parties and independents, with the Ivoirian Popular Front (FPI) receiving 9; outside observers saw the elections as less than free and fair. That November, the National Assembly passed a constitutional amendment that allowed the Speaker to take over the presidency in the event of a vacancy (a provision eventually invoked on Houphouët-Boigny's death on 7 December 1993).

After the elections, popular disillusionment grew. Early in 1992, the president rejected the findings of his own investigative commission, which had found army chief of staff Gen. Robert Guei responsible for the shootings at Yopougon University in May 1991. Shortly thereafter, Houphouët-Boigny left for a four-month "private visit" to France. Rioting followed a mass demonstration in February 1992, and the government used this as a pretext to jail opposition leaders. In protest, the FPI withdrew from the National Assembly. Houphouët-Boigny continued to manage affairs from Paris until he returned in June to release the opposition leaders as part of an amnesty that also shielded accused soldiers.

After Houphouët-Boigny's death, power was transferred smoothly to Henri Konan Bédié, who became president until the 1995 elections. Born in 1934 in Dadiekro, Côte d'Ivoire, Henri Konan Bedié was of the Baoulé ethnic group. Bedié's ties to his idol Boigny began at a young age. During his initial schooling in Bokanda, Guiglo, and Dabopu, Côte d'Ivoire, he distributed newspapers of Boigny's political party, the Rassemblement Démocratique Africain. As he grew up, Bedié's aspirations became clearer. He traveled to France to study law at the University of Poitiers, after reconsidering a career in education, and worked his way through law school. He also obtained advanced degrees in economics and political science, as well as a doctorate in economics, and was appointed the first Ivoirian ambassador to the United States while still in his twenties. He opened the Ivoirian embassy in Washington, DC, during the last months of the Eisenhower administration and also established the Ivoirian mission to the UN when he was only 27. Bedié served as Minister of Finance and National Assembly President, as well as an advisor to the International Bank on Reconstruction and Development. Throughout his posts, Boigny was his most significant supporter.

Bédié proved to be a controversial leader. A split in the PDCI occurred on his watch, as departing Assembly members formed the Rally of the Republicans (RDR) and, later, the Republican Front. Bédié began cracking down on dissent, briefly imprisoning and exposing to beatings the editor of a prominent newspaper. In the year preceding the scheduled elections, Bédié instigated electoral reforms strictly limiting candidates who desired to run for president. Opposition parties decried the new electoral code and vowed to boycott the presidential elections.

Upholding their vow, the opposition parties boycotted the elections, held on 22 October 1995, in protest of Bédié's antidemocratic maneuvering since assuming office. Bédié was reported by government officials to have won 95% of the vote. Legislative elections were held in December. The opposition threatened to extend their boycott to these elections as well, but Bédié engaged the major parties in negotiations and agreed to allow representatives from the two largest parties to serve on the electoral commission overseeing the balloting. The elections were seen as relatively fair and resulted in a National Assembly with 146 seats held by the PDCI, 14 by the RDR, and 9 by the FPI. Presidential, legislative, and municipal elections were held, and Bédié was officially elected president.

Though Bédié's presidential win was seen as a significant accomplishment for the Baulé ethnic group, allegations of his corruption and discontent among Ivoirians continued to grow. After becoming president, Bédié maintained a low profile and granted few interviews to the press. Facing opposition from other politicians, Bédié invited members of some opposition parties to join his government. Only Bernard Zadi of the Union des Socieaux Démocrates party accepted, becoming minister of culture. Alassane Ouattara—a Mandé from the northern tribes—continued to be Bédié's most harsh enemy. Bédié had banned Ouattara's participation in the 1995 elections by claiming him a foreigner from neighboring Burkina Faso. Bédié subsequently stripped Ouattara of all outward signs of power and began a campaign against Ouattara's northern Dioulla-speaking tribes. Further, Bédié became very strict against any political opposition and went as far as to name a new director of the main television station to support his own agenda. Criticisms of corruption under his rule increased.

Many believed these actions could only lead to one outcome: a coup. Regardless, what occurred on 24 December 1999 shocked people around the world. On that day, Gen. Robert Gueï led a coup d'etat and overthrew Bédié. Familiar scenes ensued: gunfire, occupation of the public television station, and the president fleeing the country. However, never before had such an event occurred in the country that was often referred to as the "Ivoirian miracle." Bédié immediately sought refuge in the French ambassador's residence, who, along with the French government, denounced the coup. Bédié, who mistakenly assumed the loyalty of the military, was evacuated from Côte d'Ivoire soon after. While many people around the world, including numerous African leaders, condemned the coup, the streets of Abidjan filled with celebrations. The fact was that Bédié had become increasingly unpopular after the 1995 elections. Gueï rallied his supporters by pledging to honor all Ivoirians, no matter where they were born.

Many see Gueï's rise to power as a pro-Ouattara and pro-northern movement. Though he pledged to create conditions for democracy, fair elections, and a quick hand over of civilian rule, observers were skeptical. The party that had ruled for 39 years did not yet have time to recuperate from the shock.

Despite in-country support, Gueï and his office remained unstable. Many soldiers initially protested because of their lack of pay. Gueï's failure to address their concerns and offer payment resulted in increased corruption and bribery, with reported instances of soldiers and police officers stopping motorists at random and demanding payment through threats. All foreign debt repayment had been suspended. Gen. Gueï promised that as soon as political parties were formed, he would hold elections. They were tentatively set for October 2000, but the international community was concerned that Gueï had not ruled out his own presidential bid. Increasing military power and more defiance against Gueï's orders added to the tension in Côte d'Ivoire. Regional leaders, including US and French diplomats, warned Gueï against trying for the presidential bid, reasoning that his campaign would place international support for Côte d'Ivoire in jeopardy.

Presidential elections were held on 22 October. Fifteen of the nineteen candidates, including Ouattara and Bédié, were barred from running. Gueï proclaimed himself the winner, but it was widely believed that he had rigged the election, and the resulting violent popular uprising caused him to flee. Laurent Gbagbo of the FPI, who was believed to be the actual winner, was proclaimed president. The results were eventually determined to be 59.4% for Gbagbo and 32.7% for Gueï. The main opposition parties, Ouattara's RDR and Bédié's PDCI, boycotted the elections. Although they joined Gbagbo's supporters in demanding Gueï's departure, they also called for the election to be annulled. That same month, fighting erupted between the mainly southern Christian supporters of Gbagbo and the mainly northern Muslim supporters of Ouattara.

In March 2001, Gbagbo and Ouattara met for the first time since violence erupted between their supporters in October 2000, and both parties agreed to work toward national reconciliation. Also in March, Ouattara's RDR gained a majority in local elections, taking 64 communes while the PDCI won 58. The FPI secured 34 communes and 38 went to independent candidates. There were calls for new presidential and legislative elections. In the 7 July 2002 county elections, the FPI and the PDCI each won 18 of the 58 departments. In August 2002, the RDR was awarded four ministerial positions in the new government.

On 19 September 2002, as Gbagbo was out of the country, an attempted military coup took place, destabilizing Abidjan and Bouaké, among other cities. Assumed to be involved in plotting the coup, Guéï was killed, as were the Interior Minister and the former military commander of Bouaké. France increased its military presence in Côte d'Ivoire to protect its large French community, and ECOWAS planned to send a peacekeeping force. Approximately 200 US Special Forces were sent to assist the government in putting down the mutineers. The original mutiny spread quickly into a general uprising in the Muslim north against Gbagbo's southerner-dominated government. A cease-fire brokered by ministers from six African countries was signed by the government and rebels in Bouaké on 17 October, and direct negotiations between the Côte d'Ivoire Patriotic Movement (MPCI) and the government began on 30 October. The government agreed in principle to the idea of an amnesty and the reintegration of the mutineers into the army, but a political accord was not agreed upon. Further exacerbating the situation, two new rebel groups in the west emerged on 28 November—the Far Western Ivoirian People's Movement (MPIGO) and the Movement for Justice and Peace (MPJ). The MPCI continued to control the north while these two new groups controlled the southwest; the government continued to hold the majority of the south. France increased its troop presence, and by the end of December, close to 2,500 French troops were in Côte d'Ivoire.

Several resulting unification attempts and agreements were characterized by broken promises, missed deadlines, deadlock, incomplete implementation, and failure to achieve lasting peace. Following incidents between the MPIGO, MPJ, and French troops in January 2003, the two rebel groups agreed to participate in talks outside Paris on 15 January. Attending the talks were the three rebel movements, a government delegation, the political parties represented in the National Assembly, and the RDR. The talks resulted in a settlement to create a government of national unity and reconciliation in which the rebels would be represented. Gbagbo would remain as head of state but with diminished powers. Gbagbo signed the French-brokered Linas-Marcoussis Accord on 24 January, but tens of thousands of Ivoirians in Abidjan accused France of imposing the agreement and protested the deal on his return, attacking the French embassy and French-owned businesses. In a March meeting in Accra, Ghana, the parties involved in the power-sharing agreement finalized their plan for the creation of the government of national reconciliation: 10 cabinet posts were reserved for President Gbagbo's FPI; the PDCI, RDR, and MPCI each were granted 7 posts; and 7 posts were shared by the MJP and the MPIGO. Representatives of the rebel movements and those from the RDR failed to attend the inaugural cabinet meeting in Yamoussoukro on 13 March; only 21 of the newly appointed ministers attended. By mid-March, some 3,000 people had been killed in the fighting, and more than one million had been displaced. The first meeting of cabinet ministers in the new government was held on 17 April 2003.

The UN news network IRIN characterized the time after the Linas-Marcoussis Accord as a period of "no war, no peace." The peace accord faced major challenges. Political deadlock was punctuated with sporadic outbreaks of violence. The government lifted the curfew, French troops cracked down on lawlessness on the western side of the country, and a semblance of law and order was secured, albeit short-lived. Yet core problems of identity and citizenship, disarmament, and power sharing remained. Fresh fighting broke out soon after, followed by a trail of additional peace talks without resolution. A total cease-fire was agreed on 1 May 2003, and an "End of the War" declaration issued on 4 July. Both were broken, leading to another round of talks in Accra, Ghana, and the signing of the Accra III Agreement on 30 July 2004. However, September and October deadlines for legislative reform and rebel disarmament were not met by the parties. By 2004, a 10,000-strong UN peacekeeping force that included 4,000 French troops already in the country was deployed as part of the Linas-Marcoussis Accord to control the "zone of confidence" separating the rebel-held north and government-controlled south. Still, tensions continued to escalate, and violence at an opposition rally in March 2004, later reported to have been planned, killed 120 people.

Gbagbo tried to crush the rebellion but failed. Some experts on Côte d'Ivoire have interpreted some of Gbagbo's public statements to the effect that he never really accepted the Linas-Marcoussis agreement, but he was forced to accept it because he lacked the military capacity to crush the rebellion. On 4 November 2004, the Côte d'Ivoire Air Force launched a campaign against rebel positions, shattering terms of the cease-fire agreement of 2003. Two days later, a government aircraft bombed French barracks in Bouaké, killing nine French soldiers and one American civilian. The French brushed aside government claims that the attack was accidental and launched a retaliation attack that decimated the small Côte d'Ivoire force. This sparked several days of violent anti-French riots in Abidjan and elsewhere. On 15 November 2004, the UN Security Council placed Côte d'Ivoire under an immediate arms embargo and gave the government one month to get the peace process moving again. Ensuing talks sponsored by the African Union and mediated by South African president Thabo Mbeki culminated in the Pretoria Agreement, signed 6 April 2005, and a follow-up Pretoria II agreement in June 2005. The Pretoria agreements formally ended Côte d'Ivoire's state of war, tackling issues such as disarmament, demobilization, and reintegration (DDR); return of New Forces Ministers to government; legal issues surrounding national identity; and establishment of an independent electoral commission. The agreements also reaffirmed the legislative elections and the disarmament requirements of the Linas-Marcoussis Accord. The legal issues surrounding identity were reported to have been resolved, on paper at least, through constitutional amendments and presidential decrees following Pretoria II. The major challenge remained implementation.

Côte d'Ivoire's former colonial master, France, has enjoyed a complex love-hate, and often self-conflicting, relationship with the country. On the one hand, France provided military support for Gbagbo against the rebels. On the other hand, analysts saw French support within the 2003 accord for the rebel's uncompromising demand to change the Ivorian nationality legislation as legitimizing the rebellion. The change included removing the concept of the ethnic identity (Ivoirité) that denied electoral and land-ownership rights to a substantial minority, particularly those living in the north. In November 2004 and early 2005, anti-French riots swept through the government-run south. The French retaliated, attacking and destroying Gbagbo's air force.

The much-anticipated presidential elections scheduled for 30 October 2005, when President Laurent Gbagbo's mandate expired, were postponed in September. Disarmament initiatives agreed under the series of peace accords never materialized. On 14 October, the UN Security Council endorsed African Union proposals postponing the elections and allowed Gbagbo to remain in office for up to 12 more months. In return, President Laurent Gbagbo accepted UN resolution 1633, under which he would have to hand much of his power over to a new consensus prime minister charged with broad responsibilities for security and defense, and the task of organizing credible elections by the end of October 2006.

Six weeks behind schedule because of political disagreements among the rebels and opposition parties, and at the third such attempt in one month, a high-powered African Union delegation consisting of Olusegun Obasanjo, Thabo Mbeki, and Niger's president Mamadou Tandja, finally announced the appointment of Charles Konan Banny, governor of West Africa's central bank, as interim prime minister on 5 December 2005. The appointment of Banny, who was seen as independent-minded and potentially neutral, was broadly welcomed by parties to the conflict. Even the New Forces rebels, who had previously said that they would accept no one other than their own leader, Guillaume Soro, expressed support for Banny. This appointment finally gave some hope for the war-torn country after more than three years of conflict. Côte d'Ivoire won strong endorsements from parties to the conflict, raising a new glimmer of hope for peace. Banny was said to have international standing and good relations with Gbagbo and Ivoirian opposition leaders, assets that diplomats hoped would help him to turn his war-weary country around.

In February 2006, the main political rivals met on Ivorian soil for the first time since the 2002 rebellion. In June, however, militias loyal to Gbagbo did not meet their disarmament deadlines. In September, political and rebel leaders said they had failed to make any breakthrough on the main issues standing in the way of elections, particularly voter registration and disarmament. That month, the government resigned over a scandal involving the dumping of toxic waste in Abidjan.

In March 2007, government leaders and the New Forces rebels signed a power-sharing peace accord, mediated by Burkina Faso. Under the agreement, New Forces leader Guillaume Soro was named as prime minister. In May 2009, after nearly four years of delays, Prime Minister Soro announced that presidential elections would be held on 29 November 2009. Those elections were delayed, however, as the electoral commission worked to more clearly define the electoral roll by considering who was actually eligible to vote.

In January 2010, Gbagbo accused the commission of padding the voting registry with more than 400,000 ineligible voters. Opposition leaders claimed that the additional voters included members of northern ethnic groups who were not likely to support Gbagbo in the next election, and so they accused him of simply delaying the vote yet again. In response, Gbagbo dissolved both the government and the electoral commission in February 2010, claiming that a change was needed in order to ensure a government that served the people, not political parties. A number of demonstrations took place in the days following the dissolution, some of which turned violent and deadly; at least three people were killed as protesters clashed with security forces. A new unity government was formed two weeks later through negotiations mediated by President Blaise Compaore of Burkina Faso. While the new government included members from both of the main opposition parties, several key ministry positions were left empty as Gbagbo refused the nominations of opposition leaders. A new electoral commission was formed with a new president and four new vice presidents, with the rest of the previous members remaining at their posts. The new president of the electoral commission was from the same opposition party (Democratic Party of Ivory Coast) as the previous director.

The anticipated presidential election finally took place on 31 October 2010, with a preliminary result that gave Gbagbo 38% of the vote. Alassane Ouattara, a former economist for the International Monetary Fund and a popular figure in the Muslim north, won 32% of the vote. Because no candidate reached the 50% requirement, a runoff election was held 28 November 2010.

The runoff election set off a great outcry, as the electoral commission and the constitutional court each announced a different winner. The electoral commission posted results that placed Ouattara as the winner with 54% of the vote. This result was endorsed by UN observers, the European Union, France, and the United States, all of which called on Gbagbo to step down from office. A few days later, the constitutional court nullified the results from seven regions in the north heavily populated with Ouattara supporters, and declared Gbagbo the winner with 51% of the vote. The court claimed that there were serious irregularities in the vote for the disqualified regions, but other observers noted that, although some irregularities were apparent, they were not significant enough to overturn the initial count in favor of Ouattara.

Both Ouattara and Gbagbo stepped forward as victor, each choosing his own cabinet. Ouattara chose a New Forces rebel leader as his prime minister, leading many to fear a major conflict was brewing, since the government military forces sided with Gbagbo. Former South African president Thabo Mbeki was sent to mediate on behalf of the African Union, but he was unsuccessful. Meanwhile, fear of a renewed civil war led many companies and warehouses to shut down, resulting in widespread food and fuel shortages.

The crisis escalated through January as Gbagbo refused to step down. Ouattara and his chosen cabinet members were housed in a hotel heavily guarded by UN peacekeepers and New Forces rebels. Gbagbo ordered the UN peacekeepers to leave the country or risk being treated as part of the rebellion. The UN Security Council responded by extending the mandate of the mission for another six months. ECOWAS and the African Union suspended Côte d'Ivoire from their groups, stating that the country would be reinstated only when Gbagbo stepped down. The European Union, the United States, and some West African states imposed financial sanctions against the nation. These sanctions, along with the political crisis, caused a severe blow to the economy into 2011, especially in regard to the nation's primary export, cocoa. Both Ouattara and Gbagbo attempted to take control of cocoa purchases and exports in efforts to force the other out of power through financial means.

The African Union called for Gbagbo to step down by 24 March 2011. As that date passed without action, pro-Ouattara forces swept into the capital city of Yamoussoukro and then the city of Abidjan, where Gbagbo has been bunkered in his family's residence. On 4 April, UN and French forces intervened by initiating a series of airstrikes against the pro-Gbagbo military camps at the presidential palace and Gbagborsquo's home in an effort to stop the attacks against local civilians. The next day, the UN reported that three of Gbagbo's generals had stepped forward to negotiate with French officials concerning the terms for surrender, under which Gbagbo agreed to leave the country with a guarantee of safety for himself and the generals involved. Not long after news of these negotiations was made public, it was reported that pro-Ouattara forces had invaded the presidential residence. On 11 April 2011, the joint forces of the pro-Ouattara militia, the UN, and the French military succeeded in arresting Gbagbo. Alassane Ouattara was inaugurated 21 May 2011. In his speech, he called for Ivorian unity and peace as the nation moved forward to attempt reconciliation.

The political unrest took a heavy toll on the citizens of the nation. From November 2010 to April 2011, nearly 500 people were killed as a result of the crisis and nearly one million displaced. In January 2012, a UN Humanitarian Affairs officer called for continued humanitarian assistance for Côte d'Ivoire, especially in the west and southwest regions of the country. The UN Central Emergency Response Fund (CERF) allocated $8 million for life-saving projects in Côte d'Ivoire.

13 GOVERNMENT

Under the constitution of 23 July 2000, executive power is exercised by a president, elected for a five-year term by direct universal suffrage (from age 18). There is no term limit for the presidency. The president is head of state and commander in chief of the armed forces. The president has the right to negotiate and ratify treaties, and to propose and veto legislation; presidential vetoes may be overruled by a two-thirds vote of the legislature.

There is no vice president. The president appoints the prime minister, who is the head of the government. The prime minister in turn appoints the council of ministers (cabinet), who report to him. In the event a president is unable to serve out his term, the president of the national assembly assumes the role of president for 45–90 days and organizes a presidential election, the winner of which serves out the vacating president's term.

The unicameral National Assembly consists of 225 members, elected by direct universal suffrage for a five-year term in the same year as the president. The country had a de facto one-party system until May 1990, when opposition parties were allowed.

14 POLITICAL PARTIES

From 1959 to 1990, the only political party in Côte d'Ivoire was the Democratic Party of Côte d'Ivoire (Parti Démocratique de la Côte d'Ivoire—PDCI), headed by President Félix Houphouët-Boigny. The PDCI developed from the Côte d'Ivoire section of the African Democratic Rally (Rassemblement Démocratique Africain), formed in 1946. In the 1959 elections, Houphouët-Boigny

made it clear that parties that did not fully accept Côte d'Ivoire membership in the French Community would not be tolerated.

In May 1990, opposition parties were legalized and contested the 1990 elections. Among the two-dozen parties registered were the Ivoirian Popular Front (FPI), the Ivoirian Workers' Party (PIT), the Ivoirian Socialist Party (PSI), and the Ivoirian Human Rights League. In April 1994, some 19 parties formed a center-left opposition alliance, the Groupement pour la Solidarité (GPS). Also formed in 1994 was the Rally of the Republicans (RDR), a coalition of defectors from the PDCI. The 1995 legislative elections resulted in a National Assembly constituted as follows: PDCI, 146 seats; RDR, 14; and FPI, 9. The year 2000 marked the first time in almost 40 years that the PDCI was not in power. The 10 December 2000 and 14 January 2001 parliamentary elections were boycotted by the RDR. The FPI won 96 of 225 seats; the PDCI took 94; the RDR won 5, although it boycotted the elections; the PIT won 4; the Union of Democrats of Côte d'Ivoire (UDCI) took 1 seat; the Movement of Future Forces (MFA) won 1 seat; and independents secured 22 seats. Two seats were vacant.

Parties active in 2011 included the FPI, the PDCI, the RDR, and the Union for Democracy and Peace in Côte d'Ivoire (UDPCI), in addition to many others. Results from the December 2011 election awarded 127 seats to the RDR, 93 seats to the PDCI, and 5 seats to independents.

15 LOCAL GOVERNMENT

Côte d'Ivoire is divided into 19 regions, 90 departments, and 196 communes, each headed by an elected mayor, plus the city of Abidjan with 10 mayors. The central government chooses a prefect to head each region and department. The process of decentralization begun in 1977 has been regarded as the most thoroughgoing and effective in Francophone Africa.

16 JUDICIAL SYSTEM

The judicial system is based on the French civil law system and customary law. The Supreme Court heads the formal judicial system, which includes a Court of Appeals and lower courts. Military courts only try military personnel. Persons convicted by a military court may petition the Supreme Court. An independent Constitutional Council composed of seven members appointed by the president handles such issues as candidate eligibility in presidential and legislative elections, announcement of final election results, conduct of referendums, and constitutionality of legislation.

The judiciary is independent of the legislative and executive branches in ordinary criminal cases. Under the constitution and in practice, however, the judiciary accedes to the executive on political and national security issues.

17 ARMED FORCES

The International Institute for Strategic Studies reported that armed forces in Côte d'Ivoire totaled 17,050 members in 2011. The force was comprised of 6,500 from the army, 900 from the navy, 700 from the air force, 1,350 from the presidential guard, and 7,600 members of the gendarmerie. Armed forces represented

.2% of the labor force in 2011. Defense spending totaled $558.6 million and accounted for 1.5% of GDP in 2009.

18 INTERNATIONAL COOPERATION

Côte d'Ivoire was admitted UN membership on 20 September 1960 and is a member of the Economic Commission for Africa (ECA) and several non-regional specialized agencies, as well as the World Trade Organization (WTO) (1995). It belongs to the African Union and various other intergovernmental organizations, including the African Development Bank, the ACP Group, the Organization of the Islamic Conference (OIC), the New Partnership for Africa's Development (NEPAD), G-24, and G-77. Together with other countries of former French West Africa, Côte d'Ivoire participates in the West African Customs Union, and it was the organizer of the Conseil d'Entente, which unites Benin, Niger, Togo, and Burkina Faso in a customs union. In May 1975, Côte d'Ivoire was one of the signatories to a treaty that created ECOWAS, an economic organization that includes both French- and English-speaking West African countries. Côte d'Ivoire joined the Community of Sahel and Saharan States (CENSAD) in 2004. It is an associate member of the European Union. Abidjan is the headquarters for the African Development Bank and houses the secretariat of the Conseil d'Entente and the West African office of the World Bank.

Côte d'Ivoire is part of the Nonaligned Movement and the Organization for the Prohibition of Chemical Weapons. The UN Operation in Côte d'Ivoire (UNOCI) was established in 2004 to facilitate implementation of peace agreements designed to calm political unrest within the country; 41 nations are a part of the mission. In environmental cooperation, Côte d'Ivoire is part of the Basel Convention, the Convention on Biological Diversity, Ramsar, CITES, the London Convention, International Tropical Timber Agreements, the Montréal Protocol, MARPOL, the Nuclear Test Ban Treaty, and the UN Conventions on the Law of the Sea, Climate Change, and Desertification.

In March 2010, Ghana announced that it would set up a 13-member commission to address and formalize its maritime border with Côte d'Ivoire. The commission was to spearhead talks with Côte d'Ivoire in hopes of establishing a mutually acceptable border. Côte d'Ivoire had long attempted to clarify its maritime border with Ghana; however, after Ghana discovered massive offshore oil reserves in February 2009, Ivoirian authorities renewed their efforts to establish this border. Ministers from both countries attempted to underplay the possibility of a resource grab or oil dispute developing. The issue was still unresolved in January 2012.

19 ECONOMY

Côte d'Ivoire has an excellent network of paved roads and good telecommunications services, including internet access, two ports, and dependable air service, both of which support its economy. As the world's largest producer of cocoa beans and a top-ranked exporter of coffee and palm oil, Côte d'Ivoire depends on agricultural output for its financial success. This reliance upon cash crops has made the country highly susceptible to market fluctuations and weather conditions. Oil and gas revenues continue to increase, a promising sign for the country's prosperity, but Côte d'Ivoire's civil war and its aftereffects have resulted in slow economic growth and a loss of foreign investment.

For the first 15 years after independence, Côte d'Ivoire's economy expanded at a remarkable rate, reaching the double digits. During the 1980s and early 1990s, the nation experienced an economic slowdown due to falling export prices, rising import prices, and heavy debt-service costs. In January 1994, France devalued the CFA franc, which ultimately led to average growth rates of 7% per year between 1995 and 1998. The post devaluation boom waned in 1999, though, because of lower coffee, palm, rubber, and cocoa prices.

The attempted coup of 2002 dealt another blow to Côte d'Ivoire's economy, affecting everyone from business people to local artisans and farmers. The economy recovered slightly in 2004, with a GDP growth rate of 1.6% (as opposed to negative growth in 2002 and 2003). The situation deteriorated further when the president's troops attacked and killed nine members of the French peacekeeping force. A loss of foreign investment followed. GDP grew by 1.8% in 2006 and 1.7% in 2007, due in part to increased oil exports. The economy continued to grow in 2008 and 2009, at 2% and 4% respectively, but growth was challenged again in early 2010 by a turbine failure that led to power cuts.

The government has turned to international organizations for help in stabilizing its economy and controlling the national debt. In April 2009, the International Monetary Fund (IMF) agreed to write off $3 billion of the country's national debt. One month later, the Paris Club, a loose group of creditor governments from industrialized nations, agreed to ease and restructure the foreign debt of Côte d'Ivoire, reducing debt repayments from $4.6 billion to $391 million. The London Club agreed to similar debt restructuring in 2009, with the final agreement signed in 2010.

20 INCOME

The CIA estimated that in 2010 the gross domestic product (GDP) of Côte d'Ivoire was $37.02 billion. The CIA defines GDP as the value of all final goods and services produced within a nation in a given year, computed on the basis of purchasing power parity (PPP) rather than value as measured on the basis of the rate of the exchange based on current dollars. The per capita GDP was estimated at $1,800. The annual growth rate of GDP was 2.6%. The average inflation rate was 1.4%. It was estimated that agriculture accounted for 28.0% of GDP; industry, 21.3%; and services, 50.7%. According to the World Bank, remittances from citizens living abroad totaled $185.5 million, or about $9 per capita, and accounted for approximately .5% of GDP.

The World Bank reported that in 2010, household consumption in Côte d'Ivoire totaled $17 billion or about $791 per capita, measured in current US dollars rather than PPP. As of 2011, the most recent study by the World Bank reported that actual individual consumption in Côte d'Ivoire was 72.2% of GDP and accounted for 0.06% of world consumption. By comparison, the United States accounted for 25.44% of world individual consumption. The World Bank also estimated that 33.1% of Côte d'Ivoire's GDP was spent on food and beverages, 12.9% on housing and household furnishings, 2.5% on clothes, 3.0% on health, 7.9% on transportation, 2.1% on communications, 2.5% on recreation, 1.0% on restaurants and hotels, and 4.4% on miscellaneous goods and services and purchases from abroad.

World Bank figures show that in 2008 about 42.7% of the population subsisted on an income below the poverty line established by Côte d'Ivoire's government. The problem of poverty is more widespread in rural areas than in urban parts of the country, with 54.2% of rural dwellers living below the rural poverty line, and 29.4% of city dwellers living below the urban poverty line. The unemployment rate in 2010 was believed to have risen as high as 40–50% as a result of the civil war.

21LABOR

As of 2010, Côte d'Ivoire had a total labor force of 8.5 million people. Within that labor force, CIA estimates in 2007 noted that 68% were employed in agriculture.

With the exception of the police and the military services, all citizens can form or join a union. All unions must be registered, a process that takes three months and is routinely granted. Organized workers account for a very small segment of the workforce, because most are involved in the informal sector or agriculture. As of 2008, it was estimated that 15% of the workforce labored in the formal sector. Of those in the formal sector, approximately 60% were unionized. Collective bargaining is recognized, as is the right to strike. However, before a strike can be initiated, a six-day notification period must be given. The law does not prohibit anti-union discrimination.

The law provides a 40-hour workweek for all employees except agricultural workers, for whom longer working hours are permitted. The legal minimum work age is 14 years, but this is only enforced in large companies and in the civil service. Many children work on farms and do menial jobs in the informal sector in urban areas. A government-set minimum wage varies from sector to sector, with the lowest wage being around $78 per month in the industrial sector (as of 2008). Construction workers have a slightly higher minimum wage rate. Foreign workers are generally employed in the informal economy where labor laws do not apply.

22AGRICULTURE

Roughly 21% of Côte d'Ivoire's total land is under cultivation. Farming is intensive and efficiently organized, with most production in the hands of smallholders, though there are numerous European-owned plantations, far more than in neighboring West African countries. The country's major crops include coffee, cocoa beans, bananas, palm kernels, corn, rice, manioc (tapioca), sweet potatoes, sugar, and cotton.

Côte d'Ivoire is the world's leading producer of cocoa, accounting in 2011 for 36% of world production. Cocoa was in 2011 the nation's leading cash crop. Output rose from 379,000 tons in 1980 to 1,487,000 tons in 2011, in part because of the use of high-yield plants and improvement in planting methods and upkeep.

In 2011, Côte d'Ivoire was Africa's second-leading producer of coffee, topped only by Uganda. Côte d'Ivoire's coffee is grown in the southern and central parts of the country, almost entirely on smallholdings. Coffee production reached a peak of 367,000 tons in 1981 and then declined sharply because of drought and bush fires; since then, the nation's coffee production has varied greatly from year to year. In 2011, the total was 105,822 tons.

Other agricultural products include cereal (1.5 million tons produced in 2009), fruit (2.5 million tons), and vegetables (533,425 tons).

23ANIMAL HUSBANDRY

The UN Food and Agriculture Organization (FAO) reported that Côte d'Ivoire dedicated 13.2 million hectares (32.6 million acres) to permanent pasture or meadow in 2009. During that year, the country tended 33 million chickens, 1.5 million head of cattle, and 330,000 pigs. The production from these animals amounted to 41,518 tons of beef and veal, 14,468 tons of pork, 23,711 tons of poultry, 21,769 tons of eggs, and 103,439 tons of milk. Côte d'Ivoire also produced 5,454 tons of cattle hide. Sheep and goats are also raised, often as a secondary activity for many cattle herders.

Cattle are concentrated in the more northerly districts where tsetse flies are less prevalent. Nomadic production accounts for around half of cattle herds and is mainly undertaken by non-Ivoirian herders. Settled herders are concentrated in the dry north, mainly in Korhogo, Ferkessedougon, Bouna, Boundali, Odienne, and Dabakala. Milk production is small. In 2011, there were no processing facilities, but small-scale milk processing equipment was beginning to be available.

Pork production is periodically affected by African swine fever.

24FISHING

Africa's largest tuna fishing port is located in Abidjan; it handles roughly 100,000 tons of tuna each year. There are fish hatcheries in Bouaké, Bamoro, and Korhogo. Commercial fishing for tuna is carried on in the Gulf of Guinea, and sardines are also caught in quantity. Côte d'Ivoire had 62 decked commercial fishing boats in 2008. The annual capture totaled 58,000 tons according to the UN FAO. The export value of seafood totaled $103 million.

25FORESTRY

There are three types of forest in Côte d'Ivoire: rain forest, deciduous forest, and the secondary forest of the savanna region. The forested area is divided into two zones, the Permanent Domain (PD) and the Rural Domain (RD). The PD consists of classified forests, national parks, and forest areas. This includes major forested areas made up of 231 classified forest areas, 9 national parks and 3 forest reserves, 7 semi-classified forests, and 51 unclassified forests. The total area of the national parks and reserves is 1,959,203 hectares (4,841,191 acres). Forest exploitation activities are prohibited in the classified forest areas, which cover an estimated 4,196,000 hectares (10,368,000 acres); however, for maintenance purposes, limited logging is occasionally permitted.

Classified forests are spread throughout the country in three zones: 31.8% in the humid dense forest in the south, 30.5% in the semi-deciduous forests of central Côte d'Ivoire, and 33.7% in the savannah forests in the north. The RD, where logging is permitted, is extensive; however, the effective area for forestry production is estimated at 2.9 million hectares (7.2 million acres).

Côte d'Ivoire has what has been described as the world's fastest deforestation rate. In 2009, approximately 33% of Côte d'Ivoire was covered by forest. In 1983, the government acknowledged that the nation's forest area, which totaled approximately 16 million hectares (40 million acres) at independence in 1960, had dwindled to about 4 million hectares (10 million acres). Nevertheless, it still had the most extensive rain forest in Western Africa until 1993, when in response to the drop in cocoa and coffee prices, the country began to rely more heavily on wood exports. This increased focus on wood led to increased deforestation in the early 1990s.

At one time, mahogany was the only wood exploited, but now more than 25 different types of wood are utilized commercially. The major species planted are teak, frake, framire, pine, samba, cedar, gmelina, niangon, and bete. The increasing scarcity of forest resources has adversely impacted value-added industries, leaving lumber and veneer production in a steady state of decline.

The UN FAO estimated the 2009 roundwood production at 1.47 million cu m (51.9 million cu ft). The value of all forest products, including roundwood, totaled $337.2 million.

26MINING

In the early 21st century, minerals represented a minor component of the economy, of which petroleum was a leading industry. All mineral rights were vested in the state, the Ministère des Ressources Minières et Pétrolières was responsible for administering the sector, and oil prospecting and mining were subject to control of the state-owned Société d'Etat pour le Développment Minier de la Côte d'Ivoire (SODEMI). Mineral commodities were estimated to account for 10% of the country's exports, excluding the value of smuggled gold and diamonds; the government was planning to implement a diamond certification scheme to respond to worldwide concerns over conflict diamonds. Diamond output in 2004 was estimated at 230,000 carats, unchanged from 2003, but down from the 306,500 carats produced in 2002. Current production is unknown; Côte d'Ivoire's production of diamonds has been under United Nations sanctions since 2004. Although kimberlites were known to exist at Kanangone, Seguela, and Tortiya, diamonds were produced only from alluvial deposits at Tortiya and Seguela. Gold production in 2009 was 6,947 kg, compared to 1,243 kg in 2007. The Agbaou gold permit's resources were more than 26,000 kg. A number of foreign companies had gold interests in Côte d'Ivoire, among them a French consortium that in 1991 began to exploit a mine estimated to contain 500,000 tons of gold ore with a content of 7 grams of gold per ton. The country expects to boost its gold production by opening three new mines from 2010 to 2015. As of 2010, annual gold production was estimated at 7 tons. That figure is expected to increase to 20 tons per year by 2015. Tantalite production was estimated at 400 kg in 2008. Production of niobium (columbium) ore and tantalum ore were unknown in 2009. Also in 2009, Côte d'Ivoire produced cement, columbite, gravel and crushed rock, and sand. The production of building materials was a leading industry in the country.

The country's total iron ore resource has deposits at Monogaga, Mount Gao, Mount Klahoyo, Mount Nimba, Mount Segaye, Mount Tia, and Mount Tortro; poor infrastructure has hampered development of these resources..

27ENERGY AND POWER

Côte d'Ivoire has become in recent years an important supplier of energy to the sub-Saharan region as a result of its reserves of natural gas, excess electrical generating capacity, and recent offshore finds of oil and natural gas. In 2009, per capita oil consumption was 499 kg. Oil production totaled 43,833 barrels of oil a day.

Offshore oil was discovered in 1977, with production starting three years later. The bulk of the country's oil and gas wells (86%) are situated in shallow marine areas, with another 7% located in deep offshore wells. Only 7% of the country's oil and gas wells are onshore. Estimates by the *Oil and Gas Journal* have placed the country's proven petroleum reserves at 100 million barrels as of 1 January 2011. Production for 2010 was estimated at 44,880 barrels per day. Production at several offshore fields and blocks may push the nation's proven reserves and output totals higher. The Espoir field, which began producing in early 2002, is estimated to contain recoverable reserves of 93 million barrels of oil and 180 billion cubic feet of gas. Also, Block CI-40, which is jointly operated by Canadian Natural Resources, Svenska Petroleum, and the state oil corporation, Société Nationale d'Opérations Pétrolières de la Côte d'Ivoire (Petroci), and which lies 5 miles to the south of the Espoir field, is estimated to have recoverable oil reserves of 200 million barrels. Block CI-112, located off Côte d'Ivoire's western coast, is estimated by Vanco Energy Company to contain 2.7 billion barrels of oil in the block's San Pedro ridge and in other deposits.

As of 1 January 2011, the country was estimated to have of natural gas reserves of 1.00 trillion cu ft. In 2009, natural gas output and domestic consumption were each estimated at 56.5 billion cu ft.

Côte d'Ivoire's oil and gas industry is managed by Petroci. Founded in 1975, Petroci was restructured in 1998 into a holding company, Petroci Holding, with three subsidiaries: Petroci Exploration-Production, which handles upstream gas and oil activities; Petroci Gaz, which is responsible for the natural gas sector; and Petroci Industries-Services, which manages all other related services. Petroci Holding manages the three subsidiaries as well as the country's holdings in the gas and oil sectors.

The World Bank reported that Côte d'Ivoire produced 5.8 billion kWh of electricity in 2008. Fossil fuels provided 25% of that, while 2% came from alternative fuels. Côte d'Ivoire uses hydroelectric and thermal generating facilities to provide all of its electrical power. Although hydropower accounts for around two-thirds of its generating capacity, it accounts for less than half of the power generated. The use of natural gas–fueled power stations has turned Côte d'Ivoire into an exporter of electricity. Benin, Ghana, Burkina Faso, Mali, and Togo are among the countries connected to Côte d'Ivoire's power grid. Domestic consumption of electric power in 2008 was 3.84 billion kWh, or 178 kWh per capita. Compangnie Ivoirienne d'Electriciti (CIE) is the sole supplier of power, managing not only the government-owned generating plants but also the transmission and distribution of power. Although official estimates place the percentage of urban-dwellers with access to electricity at 77%, less than 15% of those living in rural areas have such access. In 2009, the World Bank reported that 47.3% of the overall population had access to electricity. Rural electrification is a government priority.

28INDUSTRY

Côte d'Ivoire's industrial activity is substantial by African standards. It accounted for 21.3% of GDP in 2010. The development of processing industries, especially in the Abidjan region, has been significant. Bouaké has become a large industrial center, and numerous thriving industries have been built up in the forest zone of the southern coastal region. These include palm oil mills, soap factories, a flour mill, fruit canning factories, a tuna canning factory, breweries, beer and soft drink plants, rubber processing plants, sugar mills, cotton ginning plants, and coffee- and cocoa-bean processing plants. The chemical and lubricant industries are also significant. In 2010, industrial production grew 4.5% with increased capacity utilization and plant expansion and renovation.

The lumber industry, producing largely for export, includes plywood factories and numerous sawmills. The construction materials industry is comprised of brick works, quarries, and cement plants. The Abidjan airport was completely renovated in 2001.

Recoverable oil reserves in the country amounted to 100 million barrels in 2011. According to the World Bank, petroleum products accounted for 3.58% of GDP in 2009, down from 6.22% in 2008. The oil refinery at Abidjan produces enough refined petroleum products for the country to be self-sufficient in them. Côte d'Ivoire is known more as an oil-refining country than an oil-producing one. Recoverable gas reserves amount to 1.1 trillion cubic feet, and the country is destined to become a gas exporter.

Cotton production is expanding in the north of the country, and a thriving textile industry has developed around it, including such activities as ginning, spinning, weaving, and printing.

Côte d'Ivoire continues to be one of the most industrialized sub-Saharan countries, but the precarious political situation prevents the country from exploiting this position fully.

29 SCIENCE AND TECHNOLOGY

The World Bank reported in 2009 that there were no patent applications in science and technology in Côte d'Ivoire. Scientific institutes in Côte d'Ivoire conduct research in such fields as tropical forestry, livestock and veterinary medicine, cotton and tropical textiles, coffee, cocoa, oils, rubber, savanna food crops, and citrus fruits. The French Institute of Scientific Research for Cooperative Development, founded in 1946, has a center in Abidjan and extensions in Bouaké and Man. The National University of Côte d'Ivoire in Abidjan includes faculties of sciences, medicine, and pharmacy, and an institute of renewable energy. A technical school in Bingerville offers training in electrical engineering, and a teachers' training college at Yamoussoukro includes schools of industrial technology and engineering. Science and engineering students account for roughly 31% of college and university enrollments.

In 2010, high technology exports were valued at $186.83 million; they accounted for 8% of the country's manufactured exports in 2009, up from 3% in 2002.

30 DOMESTIC TRADE

European firms play an important part in the economy, with the French and Lebanese populations having a strong influence in importing and marketing decisions. They buy and export lumber, coffee, cocoa, and palm oil products and import capital and consumer goods. Most European firms have their headquarters in Abidjan; many are also represented in Bouaké. Abidjan and Bouaké offer specialty shops in such lines as dry goods, foodstuffs, hardware, electrical appliances, and consumer electronics. In the smaller towns of the interior, bazaars and individual merchants and peddlers deal in locally grown products and a few imported items.

Domestic trade is generally on a cash basis, but in the countryside, bartering is common. Many shopkeepers extend credit to farmers until the end of the harvest season. Major credit cards are not generally used outside of Abidjan. Installment purchase

Principal Trading Partners – Côte d'Ivoire (2010)

(In millions of US dollars)

Country	Total	Exports	Imports	Balance
World	18,300.0	10,470.0	7,830.0	2,640.0
Nigeria	2,731.7	828.0	1,903.8	-1,075.8
Germany	1,734.4	667.7	1,066.7	-398.9
Netherlands	1,297.6	1,083.9	213.8	870.1
United States	1,283.5	1,104.6	178.9	925.8
Greece	822.8	672.9	149.9	522.9
Ghana	772.8	727.6	45.2	682.4
China	703.5	100.6	602.8	-502.2
Belgium	572.0	328.7	243.3	85.5
Italy	552.9	394.9	157.9	237.0
Burkina Faso	490.4	489.1	1.3	487.8

(…) data not available or not significant.

(n.s.) not specified.

SOURCE: *2011 Direction of Trade Statistics Yearbook,* New York: United Nations, 2011.

has been introduced for automobiles and major appliances. Prices and profit margins are regulated by the government for basic food products, many imported goods, and certain services.

Business hours are generally from 8 a.m. to noon and from 2:30 to 6:30 p.m., Monday through Friday, and from 8 a.m. to noon and from 3 to 6 p.m. on Saturday. Banks are normally open on weekdays from 9:30 a.m. to 1:30 p.m. and 2 to 5 p.m. Many businesses close during the month of August for vacation.

31 FOREIGN TRADE

Côte d'Ivoire has generally enjoyed a positive trade balance since independence. While cocoa and coffee were for a long time Côte d'Ivoire's major exports, they have been surpassed by oil. In 2008, Côte d'Ivoire's largest export commodities were petroleum oil, including crude oil, with 36% of total exports; cocoa, including cocoa beans, cocoa paste, and other cocoa products, 25%; rubber, 5%; wood products, 2%; prepared fish and caviar, 2%; and coffee, 1%.

Côte d'Ivoire imported $7.015 billion worth of goods and services in 2008, while exporting $10.25 billion worth of goods and services. Major import partners in 2009 were Nigeria, 20.7%; France, 14.2%; China, 7.2%; and Thailand, 5.1% . The country's major export partners were the Netherlands, 13.9%; France, 10.7%; the United States, 7.8%; Germany, 7.2%; Nigeria, 7%; and Ghana, 5.6%.

32 BALANCE OF PAYMENTS

In 2010, Côte d'Ivoire had a foreign trade surplus of $2.7 billion, amounting to 0.9% of GDP. Côte d'Ivoire's exports have diversified over the years, ranging from a reliance on cocoa, coffee, and other tropical agricultural products to new growth in light manufactured goods, petroleum products, and electricity. The success of these exports has led to a positive foreign trade balance; however, the country had external debt service arrears in the amount of $620 million and a total external debt in 2010 of $11.52 billion, or 31% of GDP.

Foreign exchange reserves, including gold, were $3.624 billion in 2010.

Balance of Payments – Côte d'Ivoire (2009)

(In millions of US dollars)

Current Account		**1,670.2**
Balance on goods		4,185.2
Imports	-6,318.1	
Exports	10,503.3	
Balance on services		-1,510.0
Balance on income		-890.1
Current transfers		-114.9
Capital Account		**103.8**
Financial Account		**-807.0**
Direct investment abroad		...
Direct investment in Côte d'Ivoire		380.9
Portfolio investment assets		-42.1
Portfolio investment liabilities		-8.8
Financial derivatives		...
Other investment assets		-1,432.0
Other investment liabilities		295.1
Net Errors and Omissions		**0.8**
Reserves and Related Items		**-967.8**

(…) data not available or not significant.

SOURCE: *Balance of Payment Statistics Yearbook 2011*, Washington, DC: International Monetary Fund, 2011.

Public Finance – Côte d'Ivoire (2009)

(In billions of francs, budgetary central government figures)

Revenue and Grants	**1,958.2**	**100.0%**
Tax revenue	1,772	90.5%
Social contributions	...	...
Grants	80.9	4.1%
Other revenue	105.3	5.4%
Expenditures	**1,878.4**	**100.0%**
General public services	...	...
Defense	...	...
Public order and safety	...	...
Economic affairs	...	...
Environmental protection	...	...
Housing and community amenities	...	...
Health	...	...
Recreational, culture, and religion	...	...
Education	...	...
Social protection	...	...

(…) data not available or not significant.

SOURCE: *Government Finance Statistics Yearbook 2010*, Washington, DC: International Monetary Fund, 2010.

33 BANKING AND SECURITIES

Côte d'Ivoire is a part of the Communaute Financiere Africaine, and in particular, the Union Economique et Monetaire de l'Afrique de l'Ouest (West African Economic and Monetary Union—UEMOA). The central bank for all UEMOA members is the Banque Centrale des Etats de l'Afrique de l'Ouest (BCEAO) in Dakar.

In 2010, the discount rate—the interest rate at which the central bank lends to financial institutions in the short term—was 4.25%. The commercial bank prime lending rate was 4.3%.

There are 15 commercial banks in Côte d'Ivoire. These include SGBCI, BIAO, BOCICI, SIB, Citibank, Paribas, BHCI, Ecobank, Bank of Africa, and HSBC Equator Bank. The African Development Bank is headquartered in Abidjan.

Public credit institutions provide credit to farmers and agricultural cooperatives, mortgages and personal loans, real estate financing, and loans to small industries. The Ivoirian Industrial Development Bank was inaugurated in 1965 to provide medium- and long-term credit for industrial projects. The National Agricultural Development Bank, created in 1968, extends loans to the agricultural community. The National Bank for Savings and Credit is the state savings institution.

Late in April 2011, banks reopened after being closed by the government for 10 weeks following the disputed elections in which ex-President Laurent Gbagbo attempted to stay in office.

As of 2011, a total of 38 companies were listed on the Regional Stock Exchange (BRVM). Total market capitalization as of that year was $6.04 billion. The BRVM office closed 11 February 2011, due to Côte d'Ivoire's political instability, relocating temporarily to Bamako, Mali. On 16 May 2011, the stock exchange resumed operation in Abidjan. At the end of the third quarter of 2011, the BRVM Composite Index was down 11.67% for the year.

34 INSURANCE

In 2009, there were 21 life insurance companies and 11 insurance companies offering non-life products in Côte d'Ivoire. Insurance companies are privately owned and very competitive, with foreign companies being the leading insurers. Insurance penetration was listed as 12.17%. Third-party motor liability insurance is compulsory. In 2009, all direct premiums written totaled $368 million, of which nonlife premiums accounted for $217 million.

35 PUBLIC FINANCE

In 2010, the budget of Côte d'Ivoire included $4.755 billion in public revenue and $5.158 billion in public expenditures. The budget deficit amounted to 2% of GDP. Public debt was 63.3% of GDP, down from 70.4% in 2005. In 2010, $11.52 billion of the public debt was held by foreign entities, as compared to $13.26 billion in 2010.

36 TAXATION

Côte d'Ivoire divides income into five categories according to its source: industrial and commercial profits, salaries and wages, marketable securities, land, and noncommercial profits. Each type is subject to its own specific tax. Individuals are taxed on their total income from all categories under the progressive Gen. Income Tax (IGR), which takes into account the number and type of persons in the taxpayer's household.

Income tax on individuals ranges from 2% to a maximum of 36%. Social security is withheld from employees at a rate of 3.2% of gross pay, with an additional 1%–2.5% withheld for the national tax for reconstruction. Real estate tax amounts to 11% of actual or potential income for landlords, plus a 4% tax on ownership.

Corporate income tax is set at 20% or 25%, based on the size of the company. Foreign-owned companies pay a tax of 20%. Companies pay a tax for Industrial and Commercial Benefits (BIC) at a rate of 35% of profits, with a 0.5% minimum rate on turnover. Water, oil, and electricity producers are subject to a minimum 0.1%

rate. Individually owned companies pay 25%. The tax on capital gains is included in the corporate tax. Subsidiaries of foreign corporations are subject to withholding tax of 12% (18% if the profit is exempt from corporate tax). The withholding tax on income from royalties is 20% and from interest, 18%. Dividends to non-residents are subject to 18% withholding, but this may be reduced to 10% or 12%. All withholding taxes may be reduced or eliminated by the terms of bilateral double-taxation prevention agreements. In June 2011, the UN reported that Côte d'Ivoire had double-tax treaties with 10 countries, the United States not included among them. Other than a tax on capital gains from securities, capital and capital gains are not taxed.

The main indirect tax is the value-added tax (VAT), which stood at 18% in 2011. Supplies to ships and aircraft are exempt from VAT. Also levied is a tax on service provided (TSP) of 10% on certain financial and other services, a business franchise tax, a petroleum products tax, and a tax on automobiles (50%–100%).

37 CUSTOMS AND DUTIES

A fiscal import duty, applied to all incoming goods regardless of origin, serves primarily as a source of revenue; in 2009, customs and duties made up 30.26% of the nation's tax revenues. Customs duties levied on goods vary to a maximum of 35%. An excise tax is levied on alcoholic beverages and tobacco; export duties and taxes are imposed on specified commodities. There is also the 18% VAT and a 2.6 % statistical tax that must be paid on all declarations. All imports valued at more than XOF1 million need licenses, which are issued on a quota basis. Bilateral customs agreements have been concluded with Burkina Faso, Niger, Benin, and some other countries. Tariff rates are determined by UEMOA, which sets uniform tariff rates (0%–20%) among its member countries.

38 FOREIGN INVESTMENT

Non-French foreign investment in Côte d'Ivoire was negligible until the issuance of the 1959 investment code, which eliminated all special privileges for French companies. A new investment code was adopted in 1984. To finance national investment, all businesses had to lend 10% of their profits to the government, but this loan was rebated if they reinvested twice that sum in government-approved industries. Investment incentives included tax holidays, export bonuses, duty-free imports of equipment and machinery, free repatriation of capital and profits, and tax stabilization clauses. The 1984 code was primarily intended to help small- and medium-sized enterprises, with greater incentives for firms locating outside the Abidjan area.

The New Investment Code of 1995 modified the code of 1984 to further encourage private sector investment for larger enterprises. Incentive packages were particularly aimed at attracting foreign investment in the petroleum, telecommunications, and mining sectors, which were being privatized.

As a venue for foreign direct investment, Côte d'Ivoire had in its favor an infrastructure that was well developed by third world standards (two ports with inland rail linkages, paved roads, advanced telecommunications facilities), a release from overwhelming external debt through the Paris Club and the HIPC (Highly Indebted Poor Countries) initiative of the IMF and World Bank, and, most famously at the time, a long record of political stability.

This record of political stability was broken with a coup in 1999, a popular uprising in 2000, and a troop mutiny in March 2002. The political turmoil created uncertainty in the private sector, which due to recent privatizations had delayed planned infrastructure improvements in the railroads, the petroleum sector, telecommunications, and electricity and water supply. Annual foreign direct investment (FDI) inflow fell over 43% between 1997 and 2001, from $450 million in 1997 to $256 million in 2001. Economic downturn in 2004 depleted the government's cash flow, reduced the tax base, and increased the country's debt. The political turmoil that followed seriously deteriorated the business climate, but by 2009, FDI showed some recovery; the World Bank reported that FDI net inflow was $380.9 million, representing 1.63% of GDP.

FDI has come primarily from France, which is the source of 55%–60% of accumulated FDI stock. The CIA reported in 2011 that FDI inflow accounted for 40%–45% of total capital in Ivorian firms, about 25% of which was French. Other important sources of FDI included the United States, United Kingdom, and Benelux countries (Belgium, the Netherlands, and Luxembourg).

39 ECONOMIC DEVELOPMENT

Since independence, Côte d'Ivoire has engaged in an economic program aimed at ending its reliance on outside assistance and at achieving self-sustained growth. Increased efforts to liberalize the economy by privatizing state-owned companies have helped to improve economic performance, as has increased capital investment. Côte d'Ivoire hopes to become classified as a "newly industrializing country" by the year 2025, but its development efforts have been undermined by the political instability of the September 2002 military coup attempt and the violence surrounding the November 2010 presidential election.

Côte d'Ivoire is one of countries with the highest potential in sub-Saharan Africa. It has one of the most developed economies on the African continent, rich natural resources, and a well-developed infrastructure, but it remains a country laboring under a fragile political situation and much social tension. The cocoa industry, although largely under government control, has suffered indirectly from this conflict. Both the tourism industry and trucking have suffered what may likely be permanent damage.

Under current conditions, the Côte d'Ivoire economy will remain highly vulnerable to commodity price variations and dependent upon outside assistance into the foreseeable future, a future mortgaged by its earlier levels of borrowing. In 2009–2010, Côte d'Ivoire negotiated and entered into agreements restructuring its Paris Club and London Club debts. The country's external debt at the end of 2010 was approximately $11.52 billion.

40 SOCIAL DEVELOPMENT

Contributions from employers and employees finance a social insurance system covering all employed persons; there is a special program for civil servants. Retirement age is set at 55 years. Employed women are entitled to a maternity benefit equal to 100% of salary for a total of 14 weeks. Work injury insurance is funded by employers at varying rates depending on the degree of risk in the job. A family allowance is available to all workers with children. In addition, there is also a birth grant and a maternity allowance.

Women play a subordinate role in society even though the constitution prohibits discrimination on the basis of gender. Domestic abuse occurs frequently but is generally not reported due to the shame it brings upon the family. Women are often forced into marriage, and inheritance practices favor men. Women's advocacy groups continue to address the indifference of authorities to female victims of violent crimes. Female circumcision, also known as female genital mutilation, was made illegal in 1998 but is still practiced, especially in the northern part of the country; as of 2007, approximately 40% of females had undergone female genital mutilation. The government has taken action against statutory rape of school girls by teachers, in part to combat low rates of enrollment due to teen pregnancies.

Security forces commit widespread abuses, including killings and arbitrary arrests and detentions. Journalists are regularly beaten and harassed, and the government restricts the freedom of press, assembly, speech, and movement.

41 HEALTH

According to the CIA, life expectancy in Côte d'Ivoire was 58 years in 2011. The country spent 4.6% of its GDP on healthcare, amounting to $55 per person. One physician, five nurses and midwives, and four hospital beds were available per every 10,000 inhabitants. The fertility rate was 3.9, while the infant mortality rate was 65 per 1,000 live births. In 2008 the maternal mortality rate, according to the World Bank, was 470 per 100,000 births. It was estimated that in 2010, 70% of children under the age of two were vaccinated against measles, and 85% against diphtheria, pertussis, and tetanus. The CIA calculated HIV/AIDS prevalence in Côte d'Ivoire to be about 3.4% in 2009.

Malaria, yellow fever, sleeping sickness, yaws, leprosy, trachoma, and meningitis are endemic. A broad program was set up in 1961 to control these and other diseases; compulsory vaccination against smallpox and yellow fever was instituted, efforts by mobile health units to track down cases and provide treatment were intensified, and general health measures were tightened both within the country and at the borders.

The HIV/AIDS adult prevalence rate was 3.4% in 2009. The high incidence of HIV/AIDS is attributed to a lack of HIV education programs. The incidence of tuberculosis was 139 per 100,000 people in 2010.

42 HOUSING

Housing remains an issue of major concern in Côte d'Ivoire, particularly in Abidjan, which has been the focus of continued migration from rural areas. Extensive slum clearance has been carried out in the former capital, but shantytowns still persist on the outskirts. About 70% of the housing in Abidjan is *habitats de cour*. These consist of a series of connected living units with shared outbuildings for kitchen and sanitation services. There is generally a shared courtyard, as well. It has been estimated that about 60% of the residents in Abidjan live in slum settlements. Police officers, soldiers, customs officials, top-level bureaucrats, and foreign salaried government employees receive free housing.

Habitat for Humanity estimates the housing deficit in Abidjan to be 12,000 houses per year. According to the latest available figures, the housing stock totaled nearly two million units, with about six people per dwelling. In 2008, according to the World Bank, only about 23% of the total population had access to improved sanitation systems; 80% had access to improved water systems.

43 EDUCATION

In 2009, the World Bank estimated that 57% of age-eligible children in Côte d'Ivoire were enrolled in primary school. Secondary enrollment for age-eligible children stood at 21%. Tertiary enrollment was estimated at 8%. Of the students who begin primary school, 59% of girls and 62% of boys complete their primary education. Overall, the CIA estimated that Côte d'Ivoire had a literacy rate of 48.7%. Public expenditure on education represented 4.6% of GDP.

Education is free at all levels. Schools are generally poorly equipped, with many lacking water and sanitary facilities. Primary education lasts for six years and secondary for seven years (four years of lower secondary followed by three years of upper secondary). Secondary students may choose a seven-year technical program instead of general studies.

In 2011, violence following the disputed elections of November 2010 interrupted schooling for an estimated one million students. UNICEF reported that 180 schools were looted, 20 hit by mortar shells, and 23 occupied by military forces. Many schools closed when a pro-Ouattara coalition called for civil disobedience, resulting in at least 800,000 children missing four to six months of school.

In 1996, the National University of Côte d'Ivoire split into three separate universities: the Université de Cocody, the Université d'Abobo-Adjamé, and the Université de Bouaké. Other universities and institutions also offer a variety of higher education programs.

44 LIBRARIES AND MUSEUMS

The National Library, in Abidjan, was created in 1968 from the former library of the French Institute of Black Africa and has a primarily scientific collection of over 75,000 volumes. The library of the African Development Bank at Abidjan, founded in 1970, has 40,000 volumes. A Public Information Center of the World Bank is also located in Abidjan. Abidjan has a municipal library with 50,000 volumes, the National University library with 95,000 volumes, and several small research libraries. The French Cultural Center holds 43,000 volumes.

The Museum of Côte d'Ivoire in Abidjan features ethnological, sociological, artistic, and scientific exhibits. The Native Costume Museum was founded in 1981 in Grand Bassam. Regional museums are located in Bondoukou, Bingerville, Abengourou, Bonova, Duekoue, and Vavova. A general interest museum was founded in 1992 in Korhogo.

45 MEDIA

In 2009, the CIA reported that there were 282,100 telephone landlines in Côte d'Ivoire. In addition to landlines, mobile phone subscriptions averaged 63 per 100 people. There were two FM radio stations, nine AM radio stations, and three shortwave radio stations. Internet users numbered 5 per 100 citizens. In 2010, the country had 9,865 Internet hosts. As of 2009, there were some 967,300 Internet users in Côte d'Ivoire. The major newspaper in

2010 was *Fraternite-Matin,* with a circulation of 80,000. Other papers included *Ivoir'Soir* (50,000), *Le Jour* (16,000), and *La Voie.*

Telephone and telegraph services were privatized in the late 1990s. All news media are owned or controlled by the government or the ruling PDCI. The government also controls radio and television broadcasting. Radio broadcasts are in French, English, and indigenous languages; television is in French only. Some international broadcasts are available, but transmission of some programming has been disrupted in the past by the government.

Though the constitution provides for free expression and a free press, the government imposes significant restrictions on print and electronic media; in 2011, military forces occupied *Notre Voie* to prevent its publishing articles favorable to Gbagbo.

⁴⁶ORGANIZATIONS

Chambers of commerce, industry, and agriculture have their headquarters in Abidjan, including the National Federation of Industry of Côte d'Ivoire. The International Labour Organization Regional Office for Africa is also in Abidjan. There are a number of employers' associations and agricultural producers' cooperatives. Some multinational trade and professional organizations are based in the country, including the Inter-African Coffee Organization and the African Union of Sports Medicine. A consumer cooperative also functions.

The African Music Rostrum, also based in Abidjan, is a multinational cultural organization that promotes African musical arts.

Côte d'Ivoire has many clubs devoted to various sports. There are at least three scouting organizations and several other youth organizations, many of which are related to religious organizations.

Amnesty International has chapters within the country. There are also national chapters of the Red Cross Society, Caritas, UNICEF, the Society of St. Vincent De Paul, and Habitat for Humanity.

⁴⁷TOURISM, TRAVEL, AND RECREATION

Côte d'Ivoire's attractions include fine beaches, specially built tourist villages, and photo safaris through the wildlife preserves; however, since 2002 the small tourism industry has declined due to political unrest. In June and December 2011, the US State Department issued travel warnings for US citizens, urging caution in the light of the potential for civil unrest.

The estimated daily cost to visit Yamoussoukro, the capital, was $253. The cost of visiting other cities averaged $103. Visas are required for all but citizens of the US and most West African countries. A vaccination certificate for yellow fever is needed from all foreign visitors.

Football (soccer) is a popular sport in Côte d'Ivoire, and the national team is one of the best in Africa. Several players, such as Didier Drogba and Gervinho, play for major European clubs and have achieved considerable success. The popularity of the sport even led to a ceasefire during domestic unrest in order to watch the national team participate in the 2006 World Cup. Côte d'Ivoire was the runner-up at the 2012 African Cup of Nations.

⁴⁸FAMOUS PERSONS

Queen Abla Pokou (b. 1720), the legendary heroine of the Baoulé people, led them to Côte d'Ivoire from the territory that is now Ghana. Félix Houphouët-Boigny (1905–1993) was the first African to be a French Cabinet minister (1956–69); he was elected as Côte d'Ivoire's first president in 1960 and was continually re-elected until his death. Henri Konan-Bédié (b. 1933) became president in 1993, a post he held until his ouster in a military coup in 2000 led by Robert Guéï. Laurent Koudou Gbagbo (b. 1945) defeated Guéï in presidential elections held later in 2000. The nation's outstanding literary figure, Bernard Binlin Dadié (b. 1916), is known abroad for several volumes of poetry and a novel; he has held many government posts, including minister of cultural affairs from 1977–86.

⁴⁹DEPENDENCIES

Côte d'Ivoire has no territories or colonies.

⁵⁰BIBLIOGRAPHY

Côte d'Ivoire Investment and Business Guide: Strategic and Practical Information. Washington, DC: International Business Publications USA, 2012.

Hamilton, Janice. *Ivory Coast in Pictures.* Minneapolis: Lerner Publications, 2004.

Kamoche, Ken M., ed. *Managing Human Resources in Africa.* New York: Routledge, 2004.

Sheehan, Patricia, and Jacqueline Ong. *Côte d'Ivoire.* New York: Marshall Cavendish Benchmark, 2000.

Zeilig, Leo, and David Seddon. *A Political and Economic Dictionary of Africa.* Philadelphia: Routledge/Taylor and Francis, 2005.

DJIBOUTI

Republic of Djibouti
République de Djibouti Jumhouriyya Djibouti

CAPITAL: Djibouti

FLAG: A white triangle, with a five-pointed red star within, extends from the hoist; the remaining area has a broad light blue band over a broad light green band.

ANTHEM: *Jabbuti (Djibouti).*

MONETARY UNIT: The Djiboutian franc (DJF) of 100 centimes is the national currency. There are coins of 1, 2, 5, 10, 20, 50, 100, and 500 Djibouti francs, and notes of 500, 1,000, 5,000, and 10,000 Djibouti francs. DJF1 = US$0.005662 (or US$1 = DJF180) as of April 2012.

WEIGHTS AND MEASURES: The metric system is in use.

HOLIDAYS: New Year's Day, 1 January; Labor Day, 1 May; Independence Day, 27 June; Christmas Day, 25 December. Movable religious holidays are Milad an-Nabi, Laylat al-Miraj, Eid al-Fitr, Eid al-Adha, and Muslim New Year (1st of Muharram).

TIME: 3 p.m. = noon GMT.

¹LOCATION, SIZE, AND EXTENT

Djibouti (formerly known as French Somaliland and then as the Territory of the Afars and the Issas) is situated on the east coast of Africa along the Bab al-Mandab, the strait that links the Red Sea with the Gulf of Aden. It is bordered by Eritrea to the N, Ethiopia to the N, W, and S, by Somalia on the SE, and by the Bab al-Mandab, Gulf of Tadjoura, and Gulf of Aden on the E. Djibouti encompasses approximately 23,200 sq km (8,958 sq mi) and has a total boundary length of 830 km (516 mi), which includes a coastline of 314 km (195 mi). Comparatively, the area occupied by Djibouti is slightly smaller than the state of Massachusetts.

Djibouti's capital city, Djibouti, is located in the eastern part of the country.

²TOPOGRAPHY

Originally formed by volcanic action that accompanied the uplifting and faulting of the East African shield and the Rift Valley system, Djibouti consists of a series of high, arid tablelands surrounding faults, within which are low plains. Many areas exhibit thick layers of lava flow. There are three principal regions: the coastal plain, fewer than 200 m (656 ft) above sea level; the mountains, averaging about 1,000 m (3,300 ft) above sea level; and the plateau behind the mountains, rising 300–1,500 m (984–4,921 ft). The highest point, Mt. Moussa Ali, rises to 2,028 m (6,654 ft) on the northern frontier. The saline Lake Assal, at 155 m (509 ft) below sea level, is the lowest point in Africa and the second-lowest in the world.

In general, the terrain is bare, dry, desolate, and marked by sharp cliffs, deep ravines, burning sands, and thorny shrubs. There is very little groundwater except in an area along the southern border with Somalia, and Djibouti is dependent on saline subterranean aquifers. Located above the meeting point of the Arabian and African tectonic plates, low magnitude earthquakes are common.

³CLIMATE

The climate is torrid, and rainfall is sparse and erratic. During the hot season, from May to September, daytime temperatures in the capital average 31°C (87°F), and the northeastern monsoon blows. During the warm season, from October to April, average daytime temperatures moderate to 37°C (99°F). Humidity is high all year, but annual rainfall averages less than 13 cm (5 in).

⁴FLORA AND FAUNA

The World Resources Institute estimates there are 826 plant species in Djibouti. On Mt. Goda, near Tadjoura, there are rare giant juniper trees, acacias, and wild olive trees. However, most of the vegetation is typical of the desert and semidesert, consisting of thorn scrubs and palm trees. The country is home to 106 mammal, 312 bird, 85 reptile, and 6 amphibian species. This number reflects the total number of distinct species in the country, not the number of endemic species. In its animal reserves, Djibouti has antelopes, gazelles, hyenas, and jackals.

⁵ENVIRONMENT

Djibouti's most significant environmental problems are deforestation, desertification, water pollution, and the protection of its wildlife. The World Resources Institute reported that Djibouti had designated 826,000 hectares (2.04 million acres) of land for protection as of 2006. Djibouti's forests are threatened by agriculture and the use of wood for fuel. The rare trees on Mt. Goda are protected within a national park. Water resources totaled 0.3 cu km (.072 cu mi) while water usage was 0.02 cu km (.0005 cu mi) per year. Domestic water usage accounted for 84% of total usage and agricultural for 16%. Per capita water usage totaled 25 cu m (883 cu ft.). The water supply is threatened by increasing salinity. Underwater nature reserves have been established in the Gulf of Tadjoura to prevent overfishing of tuna, barracuda, grouper, and other species. No hunting of wild animals is permitted, but abuses continue. Haramous-Loyada is a Ramsar Wetland Site. The UN reported in 2008 that carbon dioxide emissions in Djibouti totaled 487 kilotons.

According to a 2011 report issued by the International Union for Conservation of Nature and Natural Resources (IUCN), the number of threatened species included 8 types of mammals, 8 species of birds, 16 species of fish, and 2 species of plants. Threatened species include the spotted eagle, several species of sharks, the green turtle, the spotted hyena, and Grevy's zebra.

6 POPULATION

The US Central Intelligence Agency (CIA) estimates the population of Djibouti in 2012 to be approximately 774,389, which placed it at number 159 in population among the 196 nations of the world. In 2011, approximately 3.3% of the population was over 65 years of age, with another 35% under 15 years of age.

The median age in Djibouti was 21.8 years. There were 0.86 males for every female in the country. The population's annual rate of change was 2.237%. The projected population for the year 2025 was 1,100,000. Population density in Djibouti was calculated at 33 people per sq km (85 people per sq mi).

The UN estimated that 76% of the population lived in urban areas and that urban populations had an annual rate of change of 1.8%. The largest urban area was Djibouti, with a population of 567,000.

The prevalence of HIV/AIDS has had a significant impact on the population of Djibouti. The AIDS epidemic causes higher death and infant mortality rates, and lowers life expectancy.

7 MIGRATION

Estimates of Djibouti's net migration rate, carried out by the CIA in 2011, amounted to 5.33 migrants per 1,000 citizens. According to the World Bank, the number of emigrants as of 2010 is 13,500, which is about 1.5% of the population.

The number of immigrants is 114,100, which amounts to 13% of the population. The source countries for this immigration are Somalia, Ethiopia, and Yemen. The peoples of Djibouti, Somalia, and Eritrea are historically nomadic, migrating with flocks of camels and goats across borders that now separate their nations. Somalis from Djibouti have also historically sought work across the Gulf of Aden in Yemen and the Persian Gulf sheikdoms.

8 ETHNIC GROUPS

The Issa branch of the Somali people and related clans constitute 60% of all Djibouti's inhabitants; most live in southern Djibouti or in the capital. The Afars, a linguistically related people of north and west Djibouti, who also live in the Danakil depression of neighboring Ethiopia, number about 35%. The remaining 5% consists of French (about 3%), Arabs of Yemeni background, Ethiopians, and Italians.

9 LANGUAGES

Although French and Arabic are the official languages, the home languages of the vast majority of Djiboutians are Somali and Afar, both Cushitic languages of the Afro-Asiatic language family.

10 RELIGIONS

Over 94% of the population practices Sunni Islam, which is the state religion. However, the constitution provides for freedom of religion, and there is not widespread discrimination against other faiths. A small number of Djiboutians are Roman Catholic or Protestant (6%), or affiliated with the Baha'i Faith. A large foreign community also supports Greek and Ethiopian Orthodox churches. Proselytizing is not prohibited, but is discouraged. Islamic law (Shari'ah) may be applied to matters of family law and inheritance among Muslims; however, there are also civil courts available to handle similar cases involving non-Muslims. Religious groups must register with the Ministry of the Interior. The Ministry of Muslim Affairs oversees all Muslim activities. Milad an-Nabi, al Mi'raj, Eid al-Fitr, Eid al-Adha, and the Islamic New Year are observed as national holidays.

11 TRANSPORTATION

The CIA reports there are a total of 3,065 km (1,905 mi) of roads, of which 1,226 km (762 mi) are paved. Djibouti's lone railway links the capital with Addis Ababa.

A tarred road runs most of the distance from Djibouti city to Dikhil, Yoboki, and Galafi on the Ethiopian border, where it connects with the main Assab-Addis Ababa highway. Except for the 40-km (25-mi) road from Djibouti city to Arta, all other roads are rough. A secondary road connects Obock and Tadjoura, on the northern side of the Gulf of Tadjoura, with Randa and Dorra in the northern interior. A highway between Djibouti city and Tadjoura was completed in 1991.

Djibouti's improved natural harbor consists of a roadstead, outer harbor, and inner harbor. The roadstead is well protected by reefs and the configuration of the land. The inner harbor has five outer and six inner berths for large vessels. A quarter of Ethiopia's imports and half of its exports move through the port. Car ferries ply the Gulf of Tadjoura from Djibouti city to Tadjoura and Obock, ports of minor commercial importance.

There are 13 airports in the country. In 2009, three airports had paved runways. Ambouli Airport, about 6 km (4 mi) from the city of Djibouti, is the country's international air terminal. There are local airports at Tadjoura and Obock. Air Djibouti, partly government-owned and partly owned by Air France, provides domestic service to six centers and flies to a number of overseas destinations. In November 2009, the European Commission prohibited all flights from Djibouti from flying into European Union (EU) countries, citing security concerns as the driving factor in the decision. The move was directed against the aviation authorities in the country, which the European Commission labeled as negligent in their oversight. Along with Djibouti, the European Commission blacklisted Sao Tome and Principe and the Republic of the Congo in its November 2009 announcement.

¹²HISTORY

Somali (Issa) and Afar herders, who are nomadic, Muslim, and Cushitic-speaking, lived in and around Djibouti for hundreds of years before European explorers in the 19th century brought the region to the attention of the modern West. Obock and, later, Djibouti city were recognized as ports of great usefulness on the sea routes to India, Mauritius, and Madagascar. The Italians and British were active colonizers farther south along the Somali coast, and Britain gained control in areas that are now Yemen, the Sudan, and Egypt. France decided to establish its colonial foothold in 1862 along what is now the northeastern coast of Djibouti. This tentative venture became in 1884–85 the protectorates of Obock and Tadjoura, which were merged to form French Somaliland.

The administrative capital of French Somaliland was moved from Obock to Djibouti in 1896, a year before the boundaries of the colony were officially demarcated between France and Ethiopia. In 1898, a French consortium began building the narrow-gauge railway that finally reached Addis Ababa in 1917. During the Italian invasion and occupation of Ethiopia in the 1930s and during the early part of World War II (1939–45), there were constant border skirmishes between French and Italian forces. In December 1942, French Somaliland forces joined the Free French under Gen. Charles de Gaulle.

After World War II, French Somaliland gradually gained a measure of local autonomy. In 1957, it obtained a territorial assembly and a local executive council to advise the French-appointed governor-general. The following year, the voters of French Somaliland opted to join the French Community as an overseas territory, electing one deputy and one senator to the French National Assembly. In late 1958, the first elections to the local assembly were held under a system of proportional representation. In the second elections, held in 1963, plurality voting based on party lists in seven districts replaced proportional voting. The result was the election of an Afar leader as head of the executive council; the more numerous Issas felt they had been prevented by the new electoral procedures from gaining control of the council. In 1967, 60% of the voters in a special referendum opted to retain the colony's association with France, but the Issas again complained that the franchise lists had been unfairly restricted in a way that favored the Afars. After the referendum, French Somaliland became known as the Territory of the Afars and the Issas.

The country's independence movement had been led throughout the postwar period by the Issas, but their movement was opposed by Ethiopia, which wanted French control to continue, and by the Afars, who feared Issa domination. Finally, in 1975, the French began to accommodate increasingly strident demands for independence. The territory's citizenship law, which had favored the Afar minority, was revised to admit more Issas. In a referendum in May 1977, the now-enlarged Issa majority voted decisively for independence, which was officially established on 27 June 1977, as the country officially became the Republic of Djibouti. Hassan Gouled Aptidon, the territory's premier, had been elected the nation's first president by the territorial Chamber of Deputies three days earlier. Although Gouled, an Issa, appointed Afar premiers, and the cabinet was roughly balanced, the dominance of the Issas in administration led to political conflict, including cabinet crises. Gouled was reelected without opposition by universal suffrage in June 1981 and April 1987. A one-party Chamber of

LOCATION: 10°54′ to 12°43′N; 41°45′ and 43°27′ E. BOUNDARY LENGTHS: total coastline, 314 kilometers (196 miles); Somalia, 58 kilometers (36 miles); Ethiopia, 337 kilometers (210 miles); Eritrea, 113 kilometers (70 miles). TERRITORIAL SEA LIMIT: 12 miles.

Deputies list, elected without opposition in May 1982, consisted of 26 Issas, 23 Afars, and 16 Arabs. Only 12 seats were won by newcomers in the April 1987 election of a one-party list.

A new constitution was voted on in 1992, although opposition parties boycotted the vote. In December, legislative elections were held, which, according to the constitution, were to have been open to all parties. Due to administrative restrictions and opposition resolve not to participate, by election time, only two parties were officially allowed to contest seats: the ruling People's Rally for Progress Party (RPP) and the newly formed Democratic Renewal Party (PRD). Due to the antidemocratic nature of the electoral process, more than half the electorate refused to vote. The RPP was said to have won all 65 seats.

The human rights record of the authoritarian Gouled regime came increasingly under attack in the late-1980s and 1990s, with allegations of beatings; rapes; arbitrary, prolonged, and incommunicado detentions; and extra-judicial killings and disappearances of political/ethnic opponents of Gouled and union leaders. Journalists have also been harassed, intimidated, and detained. Dissatisfaction with Gouled contributed to an uprising by Afar guerrillas of the Front for the Restoration of Unity and Democracy (FRUD) in late 1991. FRUD gained control of some areas of the north and west. In February 1992, France deployed forces in Djibouti, and the Afars declared unilaterally a cease-fire. Presidential elections were held in March 1993. Five candidates contested the elections for president. The leader of the PDR, Mohamed Elabe, was Gouled's main opponent. But, again, fewer than half the electorate voted, and Gouled was reelected with officially 60% of the vote. Fighting continued with the Afar guerrillas, and a government counteroffensive checked the FRUD by July. Rebel bases in the north were occupied, and many opposition leaders were imprisoned, including Ali Aref Bourhan, for an alleged coup attempt. He was released in December 1993. By the end of 1993, about 35% of the central government's budgetary expenditures went toward maintaining "security"; that is, the military occupation of the north by troops of Somali origin.

In 1993, the FRUD suffered severe losses to a government offensive. In 1994, its leadership split over the issue of negotiations with the government. A more moderate wing then entered into negotiations and called a cease-fire. In March 1995, in compliance with the peace accords signed in December 1994, the majority of the FRUD disarmed, and the military integrated a segment of the insurgents into its ranks. Two FRUD leaders accepted ministerial posts.

Gouled became ill in December 1995 and spent several months in a hospital in France. During this period, there appeared a succession struggle between Ismael Omar Guelleh, Gouled's nephew, and Ismael Godi Hared. Both were close advisors of the president. In part to cut down on inter-party fighting, Gouled chose to remain at the helm after his convalescence. In February 1999, he announced his intention to retire and that he would not be a candidate for the scheduled April 1999 elections. At that point, the RPP named Guelleh, a key advisor and chief of staff to the former president for over 20 years, as its candidate. The FRUD, in alliance with the RPP, accepted Guelleh as its candidate, as well. An opposition coalition, which included the PRD (Democratic Renewal Party), the PND (National Democratic Party), and (unofficially) the FRUD-Renaissance, selected Moussa Ahmed Idriss as their candidate. An estimated 60% of the electorate participated, with Guelleh garnering 74% of the votes cast to 26% for Idriss. There was no official boycott of the elections, for the first time since Djibouti's independence from France in 1977.

In March 1996 the FRUD was given legal recognition as a political party. A radical wing of the FRUD, FRUD-Renaissance, which was led by Ahmed Dini, remained opposed to the cease-fire. Djibouti and Ethiopia jointly attacked the FRUD rebels in October 1997, and skirmishes continued in 1998. In February 2000, a reconciliation agreement was signed between Dini's faction and the government. In 2003, Dini was the first candidate on the candidate list of the opposition coalition; however, he did not win a seat in the parliament. That same year the moderate faction of FRUD became part of the political party known as the Union for the Presidential Majority (UMP).

In January 2003, Djibouti held a new round of parliamentary elections that the opposition claimed was highly fraudulent. By the official tally, the UAD opposition coalition was only 4,939 votes away from beating the presidential movement. Yet, because of Djibouti's winner-take-all system, the RPP won all 65 seats. For the first time in Djibouti's history, seven women won seats in the parliament.

In the presidential elections that followed on 8 April 2005, the opposition alleged irregularities and intimidation in the run-up to the contest and boycotted the polls on election day. With the absence of any opposition, President Guelleh was elected to another six-year term. In an effort to legitimize his victory, Guelleh claimed a 79% voter turnout. However, given a turnout of 48% in the parliamentary election just two years earlier, his claim was not credible. Following the election, Guelleh attempted to mend fences by announcing that he would step down after his second term and that he would not amend the constitution to seek a third term. However, the constitution was revised in 2010, and he won a landslide victory, securing 80% of the vote, in April 2011. He declared he would not seek a fourth term.

The electoral victories in 2005 cemented a nearly complete domination of government by the president's sub-clan, the Issa Mamassans, and severely restricted political space and economic opportunities for the Afar people. In 2005, reports began to surface of rebel insurrections allegedly led by disaffected elements of the FRUD. Among the leaders of the insurgency was Aramis Mohamed Aramis, an Afar and the son of a former FRUD commander, who was killed in 1991.

Djibouti is situated in one of the least stable regions of the world, and it occupies a highly strategic location facing the Saudi Arabian peninsula, straddling the choke point between the Red Sea and the Gulf of Aden. President Guelleh has maintained harmonious relations with neighbors and superpowers since his election in 1999. In 2004, the government signed a bilateral treaty with Eritrea promising economic, political, and social cooperation, and Djibouti continued to benefit from the significant transit of goods to and from land-locked Ethiopia via its well-developed seaport. Although a potential magnet for terrorists, the presence of French and American military bases in the country has served to dampen potential threats from Somalia's clan rivalries, which have destabilized greater Somalia and its self-declared autonomous states of Somaliland and Puntland. In November 2006, a UN report declared that several countries, including Djibouti, had openly defied a 1992 arms embargo on Somalia by supplying the rival Islamist administration in Mogadishu with arms. Djibouti denied the allegation.

In March and April 2007, a severe drought affected some inland areas. Area cattle farmers were particularly adversely affected. The UN World Food Program (WFP) declared that approximately 53,000 people would go without food unless further aid was found.

In 2007, Dubai World subsidiary DP World was in the process of building a new container terminal in a natural deepwater port at Doraleh as part of a $300 million public-private partnership with the government of Djibouti. It was hoped that the project, the first phase of which opened in December 2008, would boost Djibouti's status as a trading and transportation center. The shipping trade in the Red Sea was expected to double by 2015.

In 2008, the border conflict with Eritrea was renewed as Djibouti accused the Eritrean government of establishing troops in the territory of Ras Doumeira, a promontory on the Red Sea. Djibouti further accused its neighbor of having published maps that place the territory within Eritrea's own borders. In January 2009, the UN Security Council issued a resolution calling for the withdrawal of Eritrean troops from the disputed territory. In April 2009, the UN reported that Eritrea had not fulfilled this demand. The Eritrean government, however, insisted that there were no troops left on Djibouti soil.

Following the 11 September 2001 attacks, the United States decided to establish a military presence in the Horn of Africa in order to repel Islamist terrorism. Consequently, Camp Lemonnier, a former French Foreign Legion base, was renovated to accommodate US military personnel. In January 2007, Camp Lemonnier was expanded from 39 hectares (97 acres) to nearly 202 hectares (500 acres).

13 GOVERNMENT

Under the 1981 and 1992 constitutions, Djibouti is a parliamentary republic. The president, who according to the constitution must be an Issa, is elected by universal adult suffrage; the prime minister, who heads the cabinet, must be an Afar. The legislature consists of the unicameral Chamber of Deputies, whose 65 members are elected for five-year terms. Before 1992, candidates came from a single list submitted by the ruling party, the Popular Rally for Progress (RPP).

In January 1992, the Gouled government named a committee to draft a new constitution that would permit multiparty democracy, limit presidential powers, and establish an independent judiciary. On 4 September 1992, 75% of the voters approved the new constitution in a referendum. According to Djibouti's winner-takes-all electoral rules, the party obtaining a majority in a given district is awarded all the seats within that district, which explains how the FRUD won 36.9% of the vote in 2003 but took no seats in the parliament. In 2008, the UMP, the political party made up of the moderate faction of FRUD, won all seats in parliament.

In 2010, the parliament amended the constitution to allow the president to run for a third term. At the same time, the parliament modified the president's term from six years to five, and established a second legislative house (a senate).

14 POLITICAL PARTIES

Personalities and clan identities trump party labels, but the system is dominated by the ruling party and its coalition, the Union for the Presidential Majority (UMP), an alliance that includes the People's Rally for Progress (Rassemblement Populaire pour le Progrès—RPP), the Front for the Restoration of Unity and Democracy (FRUD), originally formed in 1991, PSD and PND. The opposition coalition, the Union for Democratic Changeover (UAD) is composed of the ARD, MRDD, UDJ, and formerly the PDD (expelled in December 2004).

Ruling party dominance harks back to October 1981, when a law was enacted that restricted political activity to the ruling RPP.

That year, the government temporarily detained the leaders of and banned the Djiboutian People's Party (Parti Populaire Djiboutien). Illegal Issa and Afar parties, including an Ethiopian-backed Afar party-in-exile and a Somali-backed Issa party-in-exile, waited in the wings. For the 1987 elections to the Chamber of Deputies, a single list of candidates was drawn up by the RPP, headed by President Gouled; about 90% of the nation's 100,985 voters cast ballots.

Despite the 1992 constitutional changes that legalized opposition parties, Djibouti remained tightly controlled by the RPP (People's Rally for Progress). On 18 December 1992, legislative elections were held, with the RPP gaining 74.6% of the vote and the Democratic Renewal Party (PRD) 25.4%. Other parties boycotted the elections on the grounds that Gouled did not consult the opposition in the "democratization" process. Most Afars did not vote. The RPP, therefore, won all 65 seats. Gouled was reelected, although not convincingly, on 7 May 1993. The four losing parties and FRUD, at the time a paramilitary organization in the north, accused the government of election fraud, a charge supported by international observers. Only 50% of the eligible voters were reported to have turned out.

In the December 1997 legislative elections, which generally were not considered credible, the RPP won 54 seats to the FRUD's 11, though their campaigns were supported by the RPP in alliance. The PRD and PND contested the elections and received 19.2% and 2.3% of the votes, respectively, but won no National Assembly seats. There were no female candidates in the election.

In February 1999, President Gouled designated his successor, his nephew and longtime advisor Ismael Omar Guelleh, who was then duly elected president on 9 April 1999 and installed on 8 May 1999. His cabinets reflected the proportional ethnic composition required by the constitution, with continued dominance of his Issa sub-clan. Barkat Gourad Hammado, the prime minister, was replaced by Mohamed Dileita Dileita on 4 March 2001.

Two groups, the Democratic Renewal Party (PRD) and the Democratic National Party (PND) have contested elections since 1992. FRUD-Renaissance, which separated from the FRUD in 1996, signed a peace accord in Paris on 7 February 2000 with the government, which also included a general release of prisoners held by both sides. The Movement for Unity and Democracy (MUD) allegedly is associated with the Somali National Movement operating out of northern Somalia. It is a coalition of Afar-oriented and Issa-oriented dissidents.

In the country's first full multiparty parliamentary elections, held 10 January 2003, the UMP, led by the RPP, garnered 62.2% of the vote to 36.9% for the FRUD, which won no assembly seats. In the capital, Djibouti-Ville, the opposition Union pour une Alternance Démocratique (UAD) took 44.9% of the votes, and the UMP 55%. President Ismail Omar Guelleh ran unopposed in the 8 April 2005 elections, guaranteeing him another six-year term in office. His appointed prime minister was Mohamed Dileita, who held the position as head of government since 4 March 2001.

In the 2008 legislative elections, the UMP again retained all 65 seats in the chamber of deputies. Mohamed Dileita of the People's Progress Assembly remained prime minister. Ismail Omar Guelleh of the People's Progress Assembly was reelected as president in 2011 with 80.6% of the vote.

15LOCAL GOVERNMENT

There are six *cercles*, or districts, with councils and appointed administrators: Ali Sabîh, Arta, Obock, Dikhil, Tadjoura, and Djibouti.

16JUDICIAL SYSTEM

The judicial system consists of courts of first instance, a High Court of Appeal, and a Supreme Court. Each of the six administrative districts also has a customary court. The legal system is a blend of French codified law, Shari'ah (Islamic law) and customary law of the native nomadic peoples.

The 1992 constitution is modeled on the 1958 French constitution. The judiciary is not completely independent of the executive branch. A state security court handles political trials and cases involving purported threats to national security. Political trials may be applied to the Supreme Court.

The Constitutional Council rules on the constitutionality of laws. The constitution states that the accused enjoys a presumption of innocence and has the right to counsel.

17ARMED FORCES

The International Institute for Strategic Studies reports that armed forces in Djibouti totaled 10,450 members in 2011. The force is comprised of 8,000 from the army, 200 from the navy, 250 from the air force, and 2,000 members of the gendarmerie. Armed forces represent 3.3% of the labor force in Djibouti. Defense spending totaled $80.1 million and accounted for 3.8% of GDP.

A total of 2,850 French troops were based near the city of Djibouti to deal with threats to French interests in the region as of 2010.

In January 2010, Djibouti approved the dispatch of 450 troops to Somalia to supplement the 2,500 soldiers that Burundi and Uganda each had operating in Mogadishu, Somalia's capital. The troops are necessary in fighting Somali insurgents, who from 2007 to 2012 have claimed the lives of 21,000 Somalis and driven over 1.5 million from their homes.

18INTERNATIONAL COOPERATION

Admitted to the UN on 20 September 1977, Djibouti belongs to ECA and all the nonregional specialized agencies except the IAEA. It is also a member of the WTO, the African Development Bank, G-77, the Arab League, the ACP Group, the Arab Monetary Fund, the Intergovernmental Authority on Development (IGAD), the Organization of the Islamic Conference (OIC), COMESA, the Community of Sahel and Saharan States (CENSAD), and the African Union. Djibouti is part of the Nonaligned Movement. In 1981, treaties of friendship and cooperation were signed with Ethiopia, Somalia, Kenya, and the Sudan. In environmental cooperation, Djibouti is part of the Convention on Biological Diversity, CITES, the Kyoto Protocol, the Montréal Protocol, MARPOL, and the UN Conventions on the Law of the Sea, Climate Change, and Desertification.

An ongoing border dispute between Eritrea and Djibouti nearly brought the nations to war in 1996 and 1999. In 2008, the conflict reappeared, with a UN resolution failing to resolve matters. Eritrean forces eventually retreated, and a buffer zone was created, though tensions remained. In 2010, a mediation deal was brokered through Qatar, and the conflict was still at a standstill as of early 2012.

19ECONOMY

Djibouti's economy depends largely on its proximity to the large Ethiopian market and a large foreign expatriate community. The country has a market-based, free-enterprise economy dependent on its strategic position at the narrow straits at the southern entrance to the Red Sea. Roughly 60% of all commercial ships in the world use Djibouti's waters from the Red Sea through the Bab al Mandeb strait into the Gulf of Aden to the Indian Ocean. The French military base in Djibouti is the country's largest single source of economic and commercial activity. The remainder of the money economy is service-oriented and centered on the free port of Djibouti, the railway terminus there, the airport, and government administration. The free port features a deepwater container terminal; France has committed substantial funds to its continuing modernization. There is also an active construction industry.

There is little arable farmland in Djibouti, and the country is subject to periods of severe drought. As a consequence, Djibouti produces only 3% of its food needs. Over half of the population derives its income from livestock: goats, sheep, and camels. A fishing industry has emerged, and the Islamic Development Bank helped finance a canning factory.

Since 1990, recession, civil war, and a high population growth rate combined to reduce per capita consumption by 35%. The border conflict between Ethiopia and Eritrea disturbed the normal commerce in which Djibouti allowed Ethiopia the use of its port and conducted regular trade relations. As a consequence, average annual growth of GDP between 1988 and 1998 was -3.1%, and the economy was at zero growth in 2001. The GDP rate of change in Djibouti, as of 2011, was 4.8%. Inflation stood at 7%, and unemployment was reported at 59% (though it was 83% in rural areas).

Because Djibouti has few exploitable natural resources and little industry, it is heavily dependent on foreign aid to finance development projects and support its balance of payments. The country has fallen behind on its debt payments and has had difficulty meeting the reform requirements set by foreign aid donors. Ethiopia has developed other trade routes, limiting Djibouti's port activity.

20INCOME

According to the World Bank, remittances from citizens living abroad totaled $32.5 million or about $43 per capita and accounted for approximately 1.5% of GDP. As of 2011 the most recent study by the World Bank reported that actual individual consumption in Djibouti was 65.7% of GDP and accounted for less than 0.01% of world consumption. By comparison, the United States accounted for 25.44% of world individual consumption. The World Bank also estimated that 30.9% of Djibouti's GDP was spent on food and beverages, 15.4% on housing and household furnishings, 1.7% on clothes, 2.8% on health, 5.2% on transportation, 0.3% on communications, 0.2% on recreation, 2.7% on restaurants and hotels, and 1.2% on miscellaneous goods and services and purchases from abroad. The World Bank estimates that Djibouti, with .01% of the world's population, accounted for less than 0.01% of the world's GDP. By comparison, the United States, with 4.85% of the world's population, accounted for 22.51% of world GDP. It was estimated that, in 2007, about 42% of the population subsisted on an income below the poverty line established by Djibouti's government.

21 LABOR

As of 2007, Djibouti had a total labor force of 351,700 people. Labor in the cash economy is concentrated in the city of Djibouti, particularly on the docks and in shipbuilding and building construction. The railway is a significant employer, as is the national government. However, there is no data available on occupational breakdown. Unemployment and underemployment are widespread; unemployment was estimated at 59% in 2007.

Workers were free to join unions and strike provided they complied with prescribed legal requirements. All unions must be legally sanctioned by the government, and 48 hours advance notice must be given to the Ministry of the Interior of a planned strike. Independent unions continue to be suppressed. In addition, those who participate in strikes may be arrested. Collective bargaining rarely occurs. A National Council on Work, Employment, and Professional Training was established by the government in 2008. It included members of unions, employers, and government officials. It was to serve in an advisory capacity.

The minimum wage for occupational categories was canceled in 2006. Wages were to be set by common agreement between employers and employees. Neither the previous minimum wage levels nor the new procedure was expected to create wages that would provide a worker or family a decent standard of living. By law, the standard workweek is 48 hours, spread over six days. A weekly rest period of 24 consecutive hours is also mandated by law, as is the provision of overtime pay. However, these regulations affect only the small fraction of the population that is involved in wage employment. The minimum age for child labor is 14 years old, although the lack of labor inspectors means that compliance is left largely to market forces. The government also lacks inspectors to enforce workplace safety standards; therefore, many workers face hazardous work conditions.

22 AGRICULTURE

Agriculture in Djibouti is very limited, due to acute water shortages in rural areas. Less than 1% of the total land is farmed, and the country's major crops include fruits and vegetables. Cereal production in 2009 amounted to 10 tons, fruit production 3,444 tons, and vegetable production 31,985 tons. Tomatoes are grown for domestic consumption. Date palms are cultivated along the coastal fringe. Famine and malnutrition in Djibouti have created a reliance on the distribution of food aid for millions of its people.

23 ANIMAL HUSBANDRY

The UN Food and Agriculture Organization (FAO) reported that Djibouti dedicated 1.7 million hectares (4.2 million acres) to permanent pasture or meadow in 2009. During that year, the country tended 297,000 head of cattle. The production from these and other animals amounted to 15,789 tons of beef and veal, 259 tons of pork, 5,786 tons of poultry, 353 tons of eggs, and 55,455 tons of milk.

Djibouti also produced 1,100 tons of cattle hide. Cattle, fat-tailed sheep, goats, and camels graze in the interior; hides and skins are exported.

24 FISHING

There is no local tradition of commercial fishing or seafaring, although the Gulf of Tadjoura, the Gulf of Aden, and the Red Sea are potentially rich sources of commercial and game fish. The UN FAO reported that, in 2008, the annual capture totaled 450 tons.

25 FORESTRY

Djibouti is virtually devoid of any forests. There are protected forests on mountain slopes, north of the Gulf of Tadjoura. The value of all forest products totaled $494,000.

26 MINING

Mining and manufacturing account for 3% of the GDP. Djibouti has been known to produce occasional small quantities of clays, granite, limestone, marble, salt, sand and gravel, and crushed and dimension stone for domestic construction projects. There was no cement production in the country; most imports came from Persian Gulf countries. Other mineral occurrences of potential economic interest included diatomite, geothermal fluids and mineral salts, gold, gypsum, perlite, petroleum, and pumice. Salt, extracted from evaporated pans by artisanal miners in the marshes of Tadjoura, was the only mineral produced in 2009. Salt production increased from the 53,099 metric tons produced in 2005 to an estimated 118,000 metric tons in 2009. Perlite mining started in 2009; gold exploration began in 2008. The outlook for the mineral industry was for little growth in the short run; constraints included small domestic markets, minimal known natural resources, and slow GDP growth.

27 ENERGY AND POWER

Djibouti has no proven reserves of oil or natural gas, nor any refining capacity. In addition, Djibouti has no known reserves of coal. The country's energy and power sector is dominated by electrical power generation. The World Bank reported in 2008 that Djibouti produced 280 million kWh of electricity and consumed 236.2 million kWh, or 312 kWh per capita. In 2008, imports of refined petroleum products totaled 7,987 barrels per day, with consumption placed at 12,000 barrels per day (2010). The port in Djibouti's capital city is an important oil shipment and storage site. The Dubai Ports Authority, which in 2000 was awarded a long-term contract to manage the port, hoped to increase its handling capacity to 300,000 metric tons per year over the next 20 years through modernization and expansion of port facilities.

In 2010, Djibouti received a $30 million loan from the Arab Fund for Development to jumpstart the construction of a 75-megawatt thermal electricity plant. The loan, repayable over 25 years at an interest rate of 2–5%, will cover only part of the $130 million facility. Other committed project contributors included the Kuwait Fund, the Saudi Fund, the Islamic Development Bank, and the Organization of the Petroleum Exporting Countries (OPEC). Together, those organizations pledged to commit more than $100 million to the construction of the plant.

28 INDUSTRY

Shipbuilding and urban construction traditionally have been industrial undertakings in Djibouti. Two main factories were a mineral-water bottling facility and a dairy, although small plants pro-

Principal Trading Partners – Djibouti (2010)

(In millions of US dollars)

Country	Total	Exports	Imports	Balance
World	520.0	100.0	420.0	-320.0
China	489.3	0.6	488.6	-488.0
Sa'udi Arabia	481.8	0.2	481.6	-481.4
Somalia	356.6	354.9	1.8	353.1
India	331.1	1.7	329.4	-327.7
Malaysia	198.2	0.0	198.2	-198.1
United States	139.6	2.7	136.8	-134.1
France	74.7	0.7	74.0	-73.3
Egypt	71.0	39.4	31.6	7.8
United Arab Emirates	65.7	17.7	48.0	-30.3
Brazil	60.5	...	60.5	-60.5

(…) data not available or not significant.

(n.s.) not specified.

SOURCE: *2011 Direction of Trade Statistics Yearbook,* New York: United Nations, 2011.

Balance of Payments – Djibouti (2010)

(In millions of US dollars)

Current Account		**50.5**
Balance on goods		-278.6
Imports	-363.8	
Exports	85.1	
Balance on services		216.6
Balance on income		17.4
Current transfers		95.2
Capital Account		**55.3**
Financial Account		**4.2**
Direct investment abroad		...
Direct investment in Djibouti		36.5
Portfolio investment assets		...
Portfolio investment liabilities		...
Financial derivatives		...
Other investment assets		-87.8
Other investment liabilities		55.5
Net Errors and Omissions		**-112.9**
Reserves and Related Items		**2.8**

(…) data not available or not significant.

SOURCE: *Balance of Payment Statistics Yearbook 2011,* Washington, DC: International Monetary Fund, 2011.

duce food, beverages, furniture, building materials, and bottled gas. With the help of France, Italy, the World Bank, OPEC, and the UN Development Program, Djibouti was promoting a project to develop geothermal energy resources. Interest was focused on the Goubet-Lac Assal region and, through this project, Djibouti hoped to become self-sufficient in energy.

29 SCIENCE AND TECHNOLOGY

Because Djibouti is an active volcanic zone, its two principal research organizations—the Higher Institute for Scientific and Technical Research and the Bureau of Geological and Mineral Research—concentrate on the earth sciences. The World Bank reported in 2009 that there were no patent applications in science and technology in the country.

30 DOMESTIC TRADE

The main commercial centers are around the Port of Djibouti, the international airport, and the railroad. Domestic trade is dominated by traffic in live sheep and camels, dates, and melons. The government maintains price controls on a number of essential commodities, including wheat flour, bread, sugar, and petroleum products. French citizens dominate the commerce of the city of Djibouti. Business hours normally are 7:30 a.m. to noon and 3:30 to 6 p.m., Sunday through Thursday. Banks are open Sunday–Thursday from 7 a.m. to 12 p.m. Banks and offices are closed on Fridays and Saturdays.

31 FOREIGN TRADE

In 2011, imports were $471.3 million, and exports were $80.4 million. Djibouti's major import partners in 2010 were China, 18%; Saudi Arabia, 17.7%; India, 12.9%; Malaysia, 7.5%; the United States, 5%; and Pakistan, 4.5%. Its major export partners as of 2010 are Somalia, 80.4%; Yemen, 4.1%; Egypt, 4.1; and the United Arab Emirates, 4%. About 75% of received US imports are consumed in Djibouti, while the remainder is forwarded to Ethiopia or northern Somalia. Exports include animal hides and skins, and coffee. Imports are vegetable products, foodstuffs, beverages, vinegar, tobacco, machinery and transportation equipment, and mineral products.

32 BALANCE OF PAYMENTS

Since independence, Djibouti has run large trade deficits, which have been offset by surpluses on services and by transfers attributable to the French base, port receipts, the national airline, the national airport, and grants from donors. In 2010, Djibouti had a foreign trade deficit of $179 million, amounting to 51.4% of GDP.

33 BANKING AND SECURITIES

The Djibouti Treasury was replaced in 1983 as the bank of issue and central bank by the new National Bank of Djibouti. Its duties include the licensing of new banks and their respective financial activities. The Central Bank officially recognizes eight money and exchange and transfer companies. However, many more are known to exist and operate on an informal basis. Known as "hawalas," these companies are widely used in Djibouti due to their better rates and simple operations.

The commercial bank prime lending rate was 10.3% in 2010.

There is no securities exchange.

34 INSURANCE

The State Insurance Co. of Somalia and about 10 European insurance companies provide most of the insurance coverage.

35 PUBLIC FINANCE

Increased military expenditures, declining tax receipts, and political unrest in bordering countries have exacerbated the deterioration of public finance in recent years. In 2010, the budget of Djibouti included $135 million in public revenue and $182 million in public expenditures. The budget deficit amounted .8% of GDP. Public debt was 58.1% of GDP, with $428 million of the debt held by foreign entities. France, a major provider of aid to Djibouti, has insisted that future aid packages be conditional on an overhaul of the country's muddled finances.

³⁶TAXATION

The individual income tax, payable by the employer, is collected by withholding from wages and salaries. In addition, the employee and the employer contribute to a medical and pension fund. There is a separate system for civil servants and soldiers. Private corporations and personal companies, as well as public companies and limited companies, pay a flat tax. Other taxes include property, stamp, and registration taxes.

³⁷CUSTOMS AND DUTIES

Formerly a "Free Zone," although the term only applied to the port, Djibouti now levies customs duties on most commodities, with most import taxes ranging from 5% to 40%. Luxury goods, such as cigarettes and alcoholic beverages, are taxed at higher rates, as much as 160%. Additionally, Djibouti requires import licenses for all those wishing to import or sell in the country.

³⁸FOREIGN INVESTMENT

Foreign investment is predominantly French, largely in connection with the military base and the port. Saudi Arabia, Pakistan, China, Korea, and Uganda have cooperation agreements. Foreign direct investment (FDI) in Djibouti was a net inflow of $96.9 million according to World Bank figures published in 2009. FDI represented 9.23% of GDP. Bilateral investment agreements (BITs) were concluded with Egypt and Malaysia in 1998 and with Switzerland in 2001. Tax relief is offered to some investors.

³⁹ECONOMIC DEVELOPMENT

In 1990, the Djiboutian government significantly expanded its public investment program. Projects in communications, agriculture, and fisheries, as well as in social and environmental areas, were planned. Execution of these plans was put on hold as a result of subsequent domestic disturbances. The Persian Gulf War of 1991 also disrupted investment programs sponsored by Iraq, Kuwait, and Saudi Arabia. Historically, French budgetary support of the Djibouti economy has been crucial to its stability, providing some 45% of foreign aid. However, the longstanding French financial commitment has weakened since 1989. Foreign aid has been partially supplemented by Djibouti's role as a major transit port for Ethiopian imports and exports, which continued to be central to the economy through 2011.

Per capita consumption dropped 35% during the late 1990s and 2000s, due to recession, civil war, and a high population growth rate (including immigrants and refugees). The government has fallen in arrears on long-term external debt and struggles to meet the demands of foreign aid donors. An ongoing dependence on food and energy imports has made Djibouti susceptible to changes in global food and energy prices.

⁴⁰SOCIAL DEVELOPMENT

Despite full legal protection, women generally play a subordinate role in the workplace and in the household. Customary law favors men in areas of inheritance and property rights. Domestic violence against women is treated as a family problem. As many as 98% of women have undergone female circumcision, also known as female genital mutilation (FGM), a painful and potentially life-threatening procedure. Although the procedure is illegal, no one has been prosecuted under those provisions. The government provides no funds to advance children's welfare.

Discrimination against minority ethnic clans in Djibouti is pervasive. The dominant clan, the Issa, control most government positions and are dominant in the military forces, as well. Djibouti's human rights record remains poor, despite the transition to a multiparty system. There are reports of police brutality, deplorable prison conditions, and illegal detentions.

⁴¹HEALTH

According to the CIA, life expectancy in Djibouti was 61.57 years in 2012. The country spent 6.4% of its GDP on healthcare, amounting to $84 per person. There were two physicians and eight nurses and midwives per 10,000 inhabitants. The fertility rate was 2.63, while the infant mortality rate was 53.31 per 1,000 live births. In 2008 the maternal mortality rate, according to the World Bank, was 300 per 100,000 live births. It was estimated that 73% of children were vaccinated against measles. The CIA calculated HIV/AIDS prevalence in Djibouti to be about 2.5% in 2009.

Malnutrition was severe and the incidence of tuberculosis high. Malaria was endemic. The incidence of tuberculosis was 734 per 100,000 people in 2007. There was a high risk of diarrheal diseases, hepatitis, and typhoid fever. Though most people (92 percent) have access to clean water, about 44 percent do not have access to adequate sanitation facilities, which exacerbates some health issues.

⁴²HOUSING

Djiboutian nomads generally live in branch-framed, transportable huts (*toukouls*), which are covered with woven mats or boiled bark pulled into fine strands and plaited; they are carried from place to place on camels. Good-quality urban housing is in short supply. Between 1960 and 2004, Djibouti City grew at an average annual rate of 4.5%, giving Djibouti one of the highest rates of urbanization in Africa. The pressures of urban growth have demanded an annual increase of at least 2,000 new dwellings. Unplanned urban shelters have made providing access to water, electricity, and sanitation facilities difficult. During the 2000s, the high cost of construction—a result of the need to import most construction materials—meant that most housing units were overcrowded, as the cost of building a basic residence was 2.5–7 times the average annual salary.

⁴³EDUCATION

The CIA estimates that Djibouti has a literacy rate of 67.9%. Public expenditure on education represented 8.4% of GDP. The World Bank estimated in 2009, that 44% of age-eligible children in Djibouti were enrolled in primary school. Secondary enrollment for age-eligible children stood at 24%. Tertiary enrollment was estimated at 3%.

Education is compulsory for six years at the primary level followed by seven years of secondary education. It is estimated that about 32% of all students complete their primary education. The student-to-teacher ratio for primary school was at about 34:1 in 2009. The University of Djibouti is the primary institute of higher education.

[44] LIBRARIES AND MUSEUMS

No information is currently available.

[45] MEDIA

From the city of Djibouti, telephone connections are available by satellite to Europe and the West and by landline to the main cities and towns of the interior. In 2010, the CIA reported there were 18,500 telephone landlines, and mobile phone subscriptions averaged 21 per 100 people.

All media are government-controlled. In 1983, Djibouti inaugurated a powerful state-owned AM radio transmitting station, built with French and FRG funds. A television service was first introduced in 1967. Both are state run and broadcast in French, Afar, Somali, and Arabic. In 2009, there was one FM radio station and two AM radio stations.

In 2010, the country had about 195 Internet hosts. In 2009, Internet users numbered 3 per 100 citizens.

Agence Djiboutienne d'Information is the official government press agency; it publishes in French. Each political party is allowed to publish a public journal. There are several opposition-run weeklies and monthlies that operate freely. The constitution provides for freedom of speech and the press, and the government is said to generally uphold these rights.

[46] ORGANIZATIONS

A chamber of commerce and industry, founded in 1912, has its headquarters in the capital. Youth organizations include the Association of Youth Homes in Djibouti, Djibouti Scout Association, and Red Crescent Youth of Djibouti (JCRD). There are some sports organizations in the country, as well. The Eglise Protestante (Protestant Church) offers educational and social welfare programs and religious evangelism. Volunteer service organizations, such as the Lions Clubs International, are also present. There are national chapters of the Red Crescent Society, Caritas, and UNICEF.

[47] TOURISM, TRAVEL, AND RECREATION

The *Tourism Factbook*, published by the UN World Tourism Organization, reported 52,800 incoming tourists to Djibouti in 2008; they spent a total of $16 million. There are 1,292 hotel beds available in Djibouti, which had an occupancy rate of 28%. The estimated daily cost to visit Djibouti, the capital, was $322. The cost of visiting other cities averaged $154. In addition to several seldom-visited sandy beaches along the Gulf of Tadjoura, tourist attractions include swimming and snorkeling off the islands in the Gulf of Tadjoura and the Bab al-Mandab. At Goubbet al-Kharab, at the western end of the Gulf of Tadjoura, there are steep cliffs and a bay turned dark green by black lava. Inland from this point is Lake Assal with a number of active volcanoes nearby. The Forest of the Day is a national park for rare trees on Mt. Goda. In the south, the alkaline Lake Abbé is visited by flocks of flamingos, ibis, and pelicans. Near Ali Sabîh are the famous red mountains and a national park full of various gazelles. Passports and visas are required; visas must be secured in advance. Antimalarial precautions are advisable, and yellow fever vaccinations are required if traveling from an infected area.

[48] FAMOUS PERSONS

Hassan Gouled Aptidon (1916–2006) was president from independence in 1977 until 1999, when he decided to step down; his nephew and handpicked successor, Ismael Omar Guelleh (b. 1947) was elected to the office in April 1999.

[49] DEPENDENCIES

Djibouti has no territories or colonies.

[50] BIBLIOGRAPHY

Alwan, Daoud A. *Historical Dictionary of Djibouti*. Lanham, MD: Scarecrow Press, 2000.

Djibouti Investment and Business Guide: Strategic and Practical Information. Washington, DC: International Business Publications USA, 2012.

Kalb, Jon, ed. *Bibliography of the Earth Sciences for the Horn of Africa: Ethiopia, Eritrea, Somalia, and Djibouti, 1620–1993*. Alexandria, VA: American Geological Institute, 2000.

Woodward, Peter. *The Horn of Africa: Politics and International Relations*. New York: I.B. Tauris, 2003.

Zeilig, Leo, and David Seddon. *A Political and Economic Dictionary of Africa*. Philadelphia: Routledge/Taylor and Francis, 2005.

EGYPT

Arab Republic of Egypt
Jumhuriat Misr al-'Arabiyah

CAPITAL: Cairo (al-Qāhira)

FLAG: Tricolor, sporting three horizontal stripes: red, white, and black. In the center white stripe stands the Egyptian coat of arms depicting the Eagle of ☒alā ad-Dīn Yūsuf ibn Ayyūb (Saladin), the great 12th-century AD Sultan of Egypt and Syria.

ANTHEM: *Bilady, Bilady, Bilady (My Country, My Country, My Country).*

MONETARY UNIT: The Egyptian pound (EGP) is a paper currency of 100 piasters or 1,000 milliemes. Legal currency are coins of 5, 10, 20, 25, and 50 piasters, notes of 25 and 50 piasters, and notes of 1, 5, 10, 20, 50, 100, and 200 pounds. EGP1 = US$0.1676 (or US$1 = EGP5.967) as of 2011.

WEIGHTS AND MEASURES: The metric system is the official standard, but various local units also are used: 1 feddan, consisting of 333.3 kassabah (or qasaba), equals 0.42 hectares (1.038 acres).

HOLIDAYS: Official government holidays include Old Calendarist Christmas, 7 January; Coptic Orthodox Epiphany, 19 January; National Police Day, 25 January; Sinai Liberation Day, 25 April; Labor Day, 1 May; Revolution Day, 23 July; Armed Forces Day, 6 October. Popular holidays include New Year's Day, 1 January; Evacuation Day, 18 June; Flooding of the Nile, 15 August; Popular Resistance Day, 24 October; Victory Day, 23 December. Movable holidays include Sham an-Nassim (Breath of Spring), the Monday following Orthodox Easter; several Muslim religious holidays, dated by the Hijri (Islamic) calendar, including the birthday of the Prophet Muhammad (Sunni account, 12 Rabi al-Awwal); Eid al-Fitr (1–3 Shawwal); Eid al-Adha (10–13 Dhu al-Hijjah); the 1st of Muharram (Muslim New Year).

TIME: 2 p.m. = noon GMT.

¹LOCATION, SIZE, AND EXTENT

Situated at the northeastern corner of Africa, the Arab Republic of Egypt has an area of 1,001,450 sq km (387,048 sq mi), extending 1,572 km (997 mi) SE–NW and 1,196 km (743 mi) NE–SW. However, the cultivated and settled area (Nile Valley, Delta, and oases) constitutes only about 3.5% of Egypt's land area; the Libyan and Western deserts occupy about 75% of the total. Comparatively, Egypt's area is slightly more than three times the size of the state of New Mexico. Beyond the Suez Canal in the east, the Sinai Peninsula overlaps into Asia; the Sinai was occupied by Israeli forces from 1967 to 1982.

Egypt is bounded on the N by the Mediterranean Sea, on the E by Israel and the Red Sea, on the S by Sudan, and on the W by Libya. The total land boundary length is 2,665 km (1,656 mi), and its total coastline is 2,450 km (1,522 mi). Egypt's capital city, Cairo, is located in the northeastern part of the country. In the SE corner is situated the Hala'ib Triangle, a territory that both Egypt and Sudan have claimed since 1956, and the adjoining Bir Tawil, *terra nullius*, which neither Egypt nor Sudan claims.

²TOPOGRAPHY

The altitude of Egypt ranges from 133 m (436 ft) below sea level in the Libyan Desert to 2,629 m (8,625 ft) above in the Sinai Peninsula. The Nile Delta is a broad, alluvial land, sloping to the sea for some 160 km (100 mi) with a 250-km (155-mi) maritime front between Alexandria (Al-Iskandariyah) and Port Said. South of Cairo, most of the country (known as Upper Egypt) is a tableland rising to some 460 m (1,500 ft). The narrow valley of the Nile is enclosed by cliffs as high as 550 m (1,800 ft) as the river flows about 900 km (560 mi) from Aswan to Cairo. The First Cataract—a series of cascades and rapids at Aswan (the other cataracts are in the Sudan)—forms a barrier to movement upstream.

The bulk of the country is covered by the Sahara, which north of Aswan is usually called the Libyan Desert. East of the Nile, the Arabian Desert extends to the Red Sea. The Western Desert consists of low-lying sand dunes and many depressions. Kharijah, Siwah, Farafirah, Bahariyah, and other large oases dot the landscape; another lowland, the Qattara Depression, is an inhospitable region of highly saline lakes and soils covering about 23,000 sq km (8,900 sq mi). The outstanding topographic feature is the Nile River, on which human existence depends because its annual floods provide the water necessary for agriculture. Before the completion of the Aswan High Dam in 1970, the floods, lasting generally from August to December, caused the river level to rise about 5 m (16 ft). Now, however, floodwaters can be stored, making it possible to provide year-round irrigation and to reclaim about 1 million feddans (about 1.04 million acres) of land. Damming the Nile resulted in the creation of Lake Nasser, a reservoir 292 km (181 mi) long and 9–18 km (6–11 mi) wide.

LOCATION: 21°35′ to 31°35′N; 25° to 36°E. BOUNDARY LENGTHS: Total coastline, 2,450 kilometers (1,520 miles); Israel, 255 kilometers (160 miles); Gaza strip 11 kilometers (7 miles); Sudan: 1,273 kilometers (790 miles); Libya, 1,150 kilometers (716 miles). TERRITORIAL SEA LIMIT: 12 miles.

³CLIMATE

Most of Egypt is a dry subtropical area, but the southern part of Upper Egypt is tropical. Northern winds temper the climate along the Mediterranean, but the interior areas are very hot. The temperature sinks quickly after sunset because of the high radiation rate under cloudless skies. Annual rainfall averages 2.5 cm (1 in) south of Cairo and 20 cm (8 in) on the Mediterranean coast, but sudden storms sometimes cause devastating flash floods. Hot, dry sandstorms, known as khamsins, come off the Western Desert in the spring. In Cairo, average temperatures range from 14°C (57°F) in January to 28°C (82°F) in July. Relative humidity varies from 68% in February to over 70% in August and 77% in December.

⁴FLORA AND FAUNA

The World Resources Institute estimates that there are 2,076 plant species in Egypt. In addition, Egypt is home to 118 species of mammals, 481 of birds, 107 of reptiles, and 11 of amphibians. The calculation reflects the total number of distinct species residing in the country, not the number of endemic species.

Plants are those common in dry subtropical and tropical lands, such as papyrus. Egypt has no forests but does have date palm and citrus groves; eucalyptus and cypress have been introduced. Sheep, goats, and donkeys are found throughout the country, and camels are found in all the deserts. Wild animals include the hyena, jackal, lynx, mongoose, and wild boar. The ibex may be found in the Sinai, and gazelles in the deserts. The Nile is adequately stocked with fish, but crocodiles have been reduced to a few along the shores of Lake Nasser. Reptiles include the horned viper and the hooded snake.

Centuries of human habitation in the Nile Valley have decimated Egypt's wildlife in that region. The hunting of any bird has been prohibited by law. The Wadi Al-Hitan (White Valley) became a natural UNESCO World Heritage Site in 2005.

5 ENVIRONMENT

The World Resources Institute reported that Egypt had designated 5.32 million hectares (13.15 million acres) of land for protection as of 2006. Water resources totaled 86.8 cu km (20.82 cu mi) while water usage was 68.3 cu km (16.39 cu mi) per year. Domestic water usage accounted for 8% of total usage, industrial for 6%, and agricultural for 86%. Per capita water usage totaled 923 cu m (32,595 cu ft) per year.

The UN reported in 2008 that carbon dioxide emissions in Egypt totaled 184,508 kilotons.

Egypt's environmental problems stem from its aridity, extremely uneven population distribution, shortage of arable land, and pollution. Soil fertility has declined because of overcultivation, and agricultural land has been lost to urbanization and desert winds. In addition, the nation's beaches, coral reefs, and wildlife habitats are threatened by oil pollution. Heavy use of pesticides, inadequate sewage disposal, and uncontrolled industrial effluents have created major water pollution problems. The expanded irrigation of desert areas after completion of the Aswan High Dam in 1970 has increased soil salinity and aided the spread of waterborne diseases.

According to a 2011 report issued by the International Union for Conservation of Nature and Natural Resources (IUCN), the number of threatened species included 17 types of mammals, 9 species of birds, 10 types of reptiles, 39 species of fish, and 2 species of plants. Endangered species include the Sinai leopard, northern bald ibis, and green sea turtle. The Sahara Oryx has been listed as extinct.

The National Committee for Environment, within the office of the prime minister, is the principal agency with environmental responsibilities.

6 POPULATION

The US Central Intelligence Agency (CIA) estimates the population of Egypt in 2011 to be approximately 82,079,636, which placed it at number 15 in population among the 196 nations of the world. In 2011, approximately 4.5% of the population was over 65 years of age, with another 32.7% under 15 years of age. The median age in Egypt was 24.3 years. There were 1.03 males for every female in the country. The population's annual rate of change was 1.96%. The projected population for the year 2025 is 103,600,000.

Population density in Egypt was calculated at 82 people per sq km (212 people per sq mi). The UN estimated that 43% of the population lived in urban areas in 2009, and that urban populations had an annual rate of change of 2.1%. The largest urban areas, along with their respective populations, include Cairo, 10.9 million; and Alexandria, 4.4 million.

7 MIGRATION

Estimates of Egypt's net migration rate, carried out by the CIA in 2011, amounted to -0.21 migrants per 1,000 citizens. The total number of emigrants living abroad was 3.74 million, and the total number of immigrants living in Egypt was 244,700. Egypt also accepted 70,000 refugees from Iraq, 70,198 from Palestinian Territories, and 12,157 from Sudan. In the early 1960s, most of the Greek population emigrated as the result of the government's nationalization measures; nearly all Jews, who formed less than 0.3% of the population in 1966, left the country after the 1967 war with Israel. With the completion of the Aswan High Dam in 1970, up to 100,000 Nubian tribesmen were moved from flooded parts of the upper Nile and resettled in the plain downstream. During the 1970s, there was significant internal migration from rural to urban areas. During the 1970s and first half of the 1980s, more than three million workers took jobs in other countries. In 1992, some 2,850,000 Egyptians were living abroad, including about one million in Libya and 850,000 in Saudi Arabia.

8 ETHNIC GROUPS

Ethnic groups of Eastern Hamitic stock make up about 99.6% of the population of Egypt; these include Egyptians, Bedouins, and Berbers. They are a product of the intermixture of ancient Egyptians with the invaders of many millennia from various parts of Asia and Africa. The remaining population is made up of minorities, including mainly Nubians, Armenians, Greeks, and other Europeans, primarily Italian and French.

9 LANGUAGES

The language of most of the population is Arabic, a Semitic tongue, which is Egypt's official language. Dialects vary from region to region and even from town to town. English and French are spoken by most educated Egyptians and by shopkeepers and others. The ancient language of Pharaonic Egypt, an Afroasiatic tongue, survives vestigially in the liturgy of the Copts, a sizable Christian sect dating back to the 4th century AD. The Nubians of Upper Egypt speak at least seven dialects of their own unwritten language. There are a small number of Berber-speaking villagers in the western oases.

10 RELIGIONS

The majority religion is Islam, of which the Sunnis are the largest sect, while many have adopted Sufi orders; Shi'a remain a tiny minority. According to official estimates, about 90% of the population are Muslim, and 8–10% are Christian, with the Coptic Orthodox Church the largest Christian denomination. Other denominations represented include Armenian Apostolic, Greek and Syrian Orthodox, Catholics (including Armenian, Chaldean, Greek, Melkite, Roman, and Syrian), and a variety of evangelical Protestant denominations. A Protestant community known as Ingili consists of 16 denominations, including Presbyterian, Anglican, Baptist, Brethren, Open Brethren, Revival of Holiness (Nahdat al-Qadaasa), and Church of God. There are small numbers of Seventh-Day Adventists, Jehovah's Witnesses, and The Church of Latter-day Saints (Mormons). The Jewish and Baha'i communities are extremely small. The 1971 constitution declares Islam the state religion. Though the constitution provides for religious freedom, the government has a long history of infringements upon this right. Government discrimination extends to both Muslim fundamentalists and Christians. The government only recognizes marriages of citizens who are adherents of Islam, Christianity, or Judaism, under which rubrics all citizens must be categorized on national identity cards. A card without a designation is generally considered to be invalid, and those without valid cards have difficulties registering for education, opening bank accounts, and/ or conducting other business transactions. However, in 2010, several members of the Baha'i faith successfully petitioned for cards marked with dashes in the religious identification field. Shari'ah (Islamic law) is the basis of family law for Muslims, but Christian and Jewish codes are also used in appropriate cases. While proselytizing is not officially prohibited, it is strongly discouraged, and conversions from Islam to another faith are rarely recognized by the government. Non-Muslim religious groups must register with the Ministry of Interior Religious Affairs Department to be officially recognized. While the law provides for the prosecution and punishment of those participating in the activities of unregistered religious groups, there have been no reports of such cases. Violent religious conflicts break out sporadically, often in response to religiously motivated attacks on individual Christians or Muslims.

11 TRANSPORTATION

The CIA reports that Egypt has a total of 65,050 km (40,420 mi) of roads, of which 47,500 km (29,515 mi) are paved. There are 43 vehicles per 1,000 people in the country. Railroads extend for 5,195 km (3,228 mi). In 1982, in an attempt to alleviate Cairo's notorious traffic congestion, work began on a city subway system. The first phase, five km (3 mi) long, was completed in 1987 at a cost of some $370 million. Cairo Metro, modeled after the Paris Metro, is the first subway to be built in Africa. Alexandria and Cairo are connected by both the Western Desert Highway, a high-speed toll road, and the busier Delta Road. Railroads are managed by the state-owned Egyptian Railways, founded in 1852.

Alexandria and Port Said are the nation's principal ports. Egypt's oceangoing merchant fleet consisted of 66 ships in 2010. Egypt has approximately 3,500 km (2,175 mi) of navigable waterways. Inland waterways include the Nile River, the Alexandria-Cairo Waterway, Lake Nasser, the 193.5 km (120 mi) Suez Canal, and many other smaller canals in the Nile River delta. However, the Nile River and the Suez Canal are the country's main inland waterways. Steamer service on the Nile is an important means of domestic transport. The modern Suez Canal was constructed between 1859 and 1869 under the supervision of the French engineer Ferdinand de Lesseps. In 1875, Great Britain became the canal's leading shareholder and the guarantor of its neutrality in 1888 under the Constantinople Convention. Management of the canal was entrusted to the privately owned Suez Canal Co. British rights over the canal were reaffirmed in the Anglo-Egyptian Treaty of 1936, then repudiated by Egypt in 1951. In 1956, Egypt nationalized the canal and placed it under the management of the

Suez Canal Authority, which had paid former stockholders $64 million by 1963. The canal was closed during the 1967 war with Israel and remained closed until 5 June 1975, when it resumed operations after having been cleared of mines and debris by teams of US, UK, and Egyptian engineers. During its first six months after resuming operations, the canal provided passage for a substantial number of dry-cargo ships but was used by only a comparatively small number of oil tankers, since the newer supertankers could not navigate the canal's 38-ft depth. The first phase of a project to widen and deepen the canal was completed in 1980, permitting ships of 53-ft draft (up to 150,000 tons) to pass through. The second phase includes increasing the navigable depth to 67 ft (up to 270,000 tons). Egypt also announced plans to build five tunnels under the canal and dig a second channel to permit the two-way passage of convoys; the first tunnel at the southern end of the canal was opened to traffic in 1980.

As of 2010, Egypt had 86 airports, of which 73 had paved runways; there were six heliports. These facilities transported 6.22 million passengers in 2009 according to the World Bank.

Cairo International Airport is used by numerous international airlines, including Egypt's own Egypt Air.

12 HISTORY

Egypt has one of the oldest recorded histories in Western civilization, dating back 5,000 years. The desert and the Nile cataracts provided protection against marauders, while the Nile River's annual flooding provided relatively stable irrigation and nutrient-rich silt for agriculture. The country was united into a centralized state about 3100 BC by Menes (or Narmer), king of Upper Egypt, who conquered Lower Egypt (essentially the Nile Delta) and established the first of some 30 dynasties, ruled over by a divine king, or pharaoh. Under Menes' dynastic successors, trade flourished, and the hieroglyphic form of writing was perfected. During the so-called Old Kingdom, the pharaohs of the fourth dynasty (c. 2613–2494 BC), of whom Cheops (Khufu) was the most notable, began to build the great pyramids as royal tombs. The twelfth dynasty of the Middle Kingdom (c. 1991–1786 BC) built vast irrigation schemes and developed a thriving civilization at Thebes; under their rule, the powerful scribal class developed a system of cursive writing called Hieratic. After a century of domination by Semitic peoples known as the Hyksos, who introduced the horse-drawn chariot, ancient Egypt attained its apex during the eighteenth dynasty (c. 1570–1320 BC) of the New Kingdom, under pharaoh Thutmose III, who extended the empire into Asia as far as the Euphrates. Amenhotep IV (also called Akhenaten/-on), with his queen, Nefertiti, attempted forcibly to replace Egyptian polytheism with monotheistic worship of the sun god Aten, or Aton. His son, the boy-king Tutankhamen, is most famous for his exquisite tomb and sarcophagus, which British archaeologist Howard Carter discovered in 1922.

In subsequent centuries, political instability weakened the kingdom, and Egypt was invaded by Assyria (673–663 BC), annexed by Persia (525 BC), and conquered by Alexander the Great (332 BC). Alexander established the Macedonian dynasty of the Ptolemies, which ruled Egypt from 323 to 30 BC. During this period, the city of Alexandria flourished as the intellectual center of the Hellenistic world. It sported two of the seven Wonders of the ancient world, the lighthouse at Pharos and the great library, in which were collected many of the literary works of the ancient world (it was damaged several times, and finally destroyed in the Muslim conquest of Egypt in AD 642). Religious scholars of the large Jewish community of ancient Alexandria, despite constant conflict with the Greek populace, produced the Septuagint (the Greek translation of the Hebrew Bible, or the Old Testament). The best-known ruler of the Ptolemies, Queen Cleopatra VII (sometimes designated as VI), was defeated, together with her lover Mark Antony, at the Battle of Actium in 31 BC by Gaius Octavius, later the Roman Emperor Augustus. After the official division of the Roman Empire following the death of Emperor Theodosius in AD 395, Egypt became part of the Eastern Roman (Byzantine) Empire.

Egypt played an integral role in the Muslim world after the Arab conquest by 'Amr ibn-al-'As in 639–42. Egypt's conquerors brought in settlers from Arabia and established firm control under the Abbasid caliphate (established in 749) and the Fatimids (909–1171), who founded Cairo as their capital in 969. The Fatimids were overthrown by Saladin (Salah ad-Din), founder of the Ayyubid dynasty, which gave way about 1250 to a local military caste, the Mamluks. The Mamluks continued to control the provinces after the conquest of Egypt by the Ottoman Turks in 1517.

Egypt remained a Turkish satrapy for four centuries. In 1805, an energetic Albanian soldier, Muhammad 'Ali, was appointed ruler (wali) of Egypt. He succeeded in establishing his own dynasty, which ruled the country, first under nominal Ottoman control and later as a British protectorate. Muhammad 'Ali destroyed Mamluk feudalism (already weakened by Napoleon's Egyptian campaign in 1798), stabilized the country, encouraged the planting of cotton, and opened the land to European penetration and development.

After the completion of numerous ambitious projects, including the Suez Canal (1869), Egypt became a world transportation hub, though one heavily burdened by debt. Ostensibly to protect its investments, England seized control of Egypt's government in 1882 and, at the time of the outbreak of World War I, made Egypt a protectorate (officially ending nominal Ottoman control). Eager to maintain its control of the Suez, the British tried to suppress independence efforts with violence and imprisonments, which only led to the 1919 Egyptian Revolution. Taking account of the gathering momentum of Egyptian nationalism, on 22 February 1922, the United Kingdom recognized Egypt as a nominally sovereign country under King Fuad but retained control over the conduct of foreign affairs, defense, security of communications, and the Anglo-Egyptian Sudan. Militant nationalism was represented by the Wafd Party, led by Sa'ad Zaghlul Pasha and, after his death, by Nahas Pasha. The conditions of association were revised in the 1936 Anglo-Egyptian Treaty, under which Britain maintained armed forces only in specified areas and especially along the Suez Canal. In that year, Farouk ascended the throne.

Egyptian nationalism gathered further momentum in World War II, during which Egypt was used as an Allied base of operations, and, in 1951, the government in Cairo abrogated the 1936 treaty. Royal extravagance, government corruption, the unsuccessful Palestine campaign against the newly-created state of Israel in 1948, and delays in long-expected social and political reforms motivated the 1952 Revolution, a successful military coup on 23 July 1952 by a group called the Society of the Free Officers. Initially, the Society aimed only to dethrone King Farouk I, whom they

replaced with his seven-month-old son Fuad. Within a year, however, the Society's aims had changed (as had its name). Reconstituted as "The Revolution Command Council," a republic was proclaimed on 18 June 1953, with Gen. Muhammad Naguib (Najib), the nominal leader of the officers, as its first president. The British-style parliament was dissolved and the monarchy abolished; the Muslim Brotherhood, which opposed the republic's overt secularism, was outlawed. Naguib, in turn, was forced out of power in 1954 by a younger man, Lt. Col. Gamal Abdel Nasser (Jamal 'Abd al-Nasir), the real architect of the revolution.

To increase the productive capacity of his country, Nasser entered into preliminary agreements with the United States, the United Kingdom, and the UN to finance in part a new high dam at Aswan. At the same time, he also negotiated economic aid and arms shipments from the Soviet Bloc when he was unable to obtain what Egypt needed from the West. Financial backing for the dam was subsequently withheld by the United States, whereupon, on 26 July 1956, President Nasser proclaimed the nationalization of the Suez Canal and announced that profits derived from its operations would be used for the building of the dam. (The last British occupation troops had been evacuated from their Suez Canal bases a month earlier.) The dam was completed with aid and technical assistance from the USSR.

Simultaneously, a crisis erupted between Egypt and Israel. Incidents involving Egyptian and Palestinian guerrillas (*fadayin*) and Israeli border patrols multiplied. On 29 October 1956, as part of a three-nation plot to bring down Nasser and reassert control over the Canal, Israeli armed forces swept into Egypt's Sinai Peninsula. The United Kingdom and France then issued an ultimatum to the belligerents to cease-fire. When Egypt rejected the ultimatum, Britain and France took military action in the Port Said area, at the northern end of the canal, landing troops and bombing Egyptian cities from the air. However, the intervention of the United States and the USSR, acting through the UN, led to the withdrawal of the British, French, and Israeli forces by March 1957.

On 1 February 1958, Egypt and Syria proclaimed their union in the United Arab Republic (UAR), under one head of state, one flag, a common legislature, and a unified army. The proclamation was approved by a plebiscite vote of 99.9% in Egypt and 99.98% in Syria. Nasser became president of the UAR, and a new cabinet was formed in March 1958, consisting of 2 Egyptian and 2 Syrian vice presidents, as well as 22 Egyptian and 12 Syrian ministers. Differing economic and political conditions prevented a complete fusion of the two regions, however. Nasser's economic measures were generally accepted, but his program of socialism and nationalization of banks and other commercial establishments were resented and opposed by Syrian businessmen. Syrian opposition to the union was crystallized when Nasser eliminated the separate regional cabinets and set up a unified cabinet in August 1961. On 28 September, the Syrian army revolted, and two days later it proclaimed Syrian independence. Even after the failure of the merger with Syria, Egypt, consistent with its Arab unity ideology, persisted in its attempts to form a union with other Arab states. Cooperation agreements were signed with Iraq, Yemen, Syria again, and Libya during the 1960s and early 1970s. None of these agreements produced a lasting, meaningful political union.

One reason for these political maneuverings was the continuing tension with Israel, which again erupted into open warfare on

5 June 1967, after the UN Emergency Force had on 19 May been withdrawn from the Egyptian-Israeli border at Egypt's demand; on 23 May, Egypt closed the Gulf of Aqaba to Israeli shipping. Israel quickly crippled the Egyptian air force and occupied the Gaza Strip and the Sinai to the Suez Canal, which was blocked and remained so until June 1975. A cease-fire was established on 8 June 1967. On 22 November 1967, the UN Security Council passed a resolution calling on Israel to withdraw from occupied Arab territories and for the recognition by the Arab states of Israel's right to independent existence within peaceful and secured frontiers. But neither side would agree to peace terms, and Israel continued to occupy the Gaza Strip and the Sinai. During the years after 1967, a "War of Attrition" was fought along the Canal with each side shelling the other and Israeli planes bombing Egyptian cities.

When Nasser died on 28 September 1970, his vice president, Anwar al-Sadat, became president. After a political crisis that resulted in the dismissal from office in May 1971 of 'Ali Sabri and other left-wing leaders who had been close to Nasser (they were subsequently convicted of treason), President Sadat firmly established his hold on the government and began to implement pragmatic economic and social policies. Beginning in July 1971 with the announcement of a 10-year development program, he quickly followed with the introduction in September of a permanent constitution and a series of financial measures designed to give more freedom to the banking system and to encourage investment of foreign and domestic capital. In a surprise move on 18 July 1972, Sadat ordered the expulsion of the 15,000 Soviet military advisers and 25,000 dependents who had come to Egypt after the 1967 war. After the ouster of the Russians, Egypt was able to improve relations with the United States, Europe, and the more conservative Arab states, which provided substantial financial assistance under the Khartoum Agreement to replace Suez Canal revenues (which had ceased when the Canal was closed by the 1967 war with Israel).

Frustrated in his ambition to recover the Sinai, President Sadat broke the 1967 cease-fire agreement on 6 October 1973 by attacking Israeli forces in the Sinai Peninsula in what is known as the Yom Kippur War (or October War); this assault was coordinated with a Syrian attack on Israeli forces occupying the Syrian Golan Heights. After initial successes, the Egyptian strike forces were defeated by the rapidly mobilized Israeli troops, who then crossed the Canal south of Isma'iliyah, destroyed Egypt's surface-to-air missile sites, and cut off the Egyptian 3rd Army. Syrian forces were repulsed; Egypt had lost its fourth war to Israel in 25 years. A ceasefire that came into effect on 24 October left Egyptian troops in the Sinai and Israeli troops on the west bank of the Canal. A series of disengagement agreements negotiated by US Secretary of State Henry Kissinger left Egypt in full control of the Canal and established a UN-supervised buffer zone in the Sinai between the Egyptian and Israeli forces. In November 1975, the Sinai oil fields at Abu Rudeis and Ra's Sudr were returned to Egypt.

President Sadat took a bold step toward establishing peace with Israel by going to Jerusalem in November 1977 and by receiving Israeli Prime Minister Menachem Begin at Isma'iliyah the following month. In September 1978, he entered into negotiations with Begin, mediated by US president Jimmy Carter, at Camp David, Maryland, where the two Middle East leaders agreed to a framework for a comprehensive settlement of the conflict. Following further negotiations, Sadat signed the Egyptian-Israeli Peace Treaty in Washington, DC, on 26 March 1979. The treaty provided for the staged withdrawal of Israeli forces from the Sinai, which was completed on schedule by 25 April 1982; set limits on forces and armaments for both sides; established a UN force to supervise the terms of the treaty; and called for full normalization of relations. However, the two nations were unable to agree on the question of autonomy for the Palestinians of the West Bank of the Jordan and in Gaza, as provided for in the Camp David framework. For their roles as peacemakers, Sadat and Begin were jointly awarded the 1978 Nobel Peace Prize. Other Arab leaders denounced the accords and sought to isolate Egypt within the Arab world.

Domestically, Sadat encouraged a shift from Nasser's socialism to greater free market conditions and some political liberalization, one result of which was an upsurge of activity by religious extremists. In early September 1981, Sadat ordered the arrest of 1,536 Muslims, Christian Copts, leftists, and other persons accused of fomenting violent acts. One month later, on 6 October, Sadat was assassinated in Cairo by four Muslim fundamentalists. The vice president, Muhammad Hosni (Husni) Mubarak, who had been Sadat's closest adviser, succeeded him as president and head of the National Democratic Party (NDP, which Sadat had founded in 1978), instituted a state of emergency, and immediately pledged to continue Sadat's policies, particularly the terms of the peace treaty with Israel. Relations with Israel cooled during 1982, however, especially after Israeli troops moved into Lebanon. In 1986, renewed efforts at normalization of diplomatic relations with Israel led to the resolution in Egypt's favor of a dispute over Taba, a tiny sliver of land, which had not been returned with the rest of the Sinai. The 30-year anniversary of Sadat's peace treaty with Israel was met in April 2009 with little celebration in Egypt. The 2009 conflict in Gaza between Israel and Hamas stained the treaty's legacy and reminded Egyptians that the comprehensive peace the treaty had originally promised remained elusive.

As a result of Arab fears of an Iranian victory over Iraq in their eight-year war (1980–88), Egypt, which had the largest army in the Arab world as well as an important arms industry, was welcomed back into the Arab fold following the 'Ammān Arab summit conference in November 1987. Egypt quickly renewed diplomatic relations with a number of Arab states and, in May 1989, ended its isolation by rejoining the Arab League, the headquarters of which returned to Cairo. Mubarak continued Sadat's policies of moderation and peacemaking abroad and gradual political liberalization and movement towards free market reforms at home. In July 1989, he became chairman of the Organization of African Unity for one year. In 1990, Egypt played a key role in the coalition to expel Iraq from Kuwait and in 1993 and 1994 was active in promoting the Israeli-Palestinian peace accord.

Mubarak was reelected president in 1987 and 1993. Parliamentary elections in 1987 were termed the fairest since 1952; 100 members of the opposition were elected to the 458-seat chamber. Opposition political forces, however, had become increasingly disenfranchised over the years. After Mubarak's third election, he conceded to their concerns and announced the government would hold a National Dialogue to hear the grievances of any legal political party. Representatives of the Muslim Brotherhood, an illegal but tolerated political grouping with massive appeal, were not invited. Just before the meeting, the Nasserists and the New

World Party announced they would not participate, essentially nullifying the work of the congress.

In 1995, legislative elections were again held, but, unlike the 1990 polling, the opposition parties announced they would not boycott these elections. The elections were held on 29 November and 6 December, and the ruling National Democratic Party (NDP) won 316 seats, losing several but retaining a vast majority. Although independents won more than 100 seats, nearly all of them were in reality firmly allied with the NDP. In January 1996, Mubarak replaced the sitting prime minister, Dr. Alif Sidqi, with Kamal Ahmed al-Ganzouri.

The most serious opposition to the Mubarak government came from outside the political system. Religious parties were banned and, as a consequence, Islamic militants resorted to violence against the regime, singling out Christian Copts and posing a threat to tourism, a major source of foreign exchange earnings. Starting in the mid-1990s, security forces cracked down violently on the militants, resorting to authoritarian measures, including arbitrary arrest, imprisonment, and torture to subdue the movement. However, it continued to gather strength, fueled by discontent with poor economic conditions, political autocracy, corruption, secularism, and Egypt's ties with the United States and Israel. In November 1997, militants murdered over 70 people at a popular tourist site in Luxor. It was alleged that Gamaa Islamiyya, one of Egypt's Islamic groups, was responsible for the attacks. However, in 1998 and 1999, the number of violent incidents decreased, and the government began releasing some of the jailed members of Islamist groups, said to number 20,000 by that time.

In September 1999, weeks after surviving an assassination attempt, Mubarak was elected to a fourth six-year term as president, running unopposed. Political opponents and Western observers criticized the ruling NDP's refusal to open the political system; greater political freedom, they said, would channel some of the political passion now given to outlawed Islamists into legal political parties, who could then use it to create a more open society and further marginalize the extremists. However, the government refused to implement electoral reforms. In February 2003, the state of emergency first declared in 1981 was renewed for another three years by President Mubarak.

Following the 11 September 2001 terrorist attacks on the United States, the United States called upon all states to adopt counterterrorism measures. Mubarak used the occasion to increase restrictions on the Islamic opposition, including members of the Muslim Brotherhood and Gamaa Islamiyya. After 11 September, Egyptian authorities referred increasing numbers of cases of Islamic militants to military courts. One of the leaders of the attacks on the World Trade Center and the Pentagon, Muhammad Atta, was Egyptian, as is Ayman al-Zawahiri, the leader of Egyptian Islamic Jihad and the head of al-Qaeda as of 16 June 2011 (following the 2 May 2011 killing of Osama bin Laden by US special forces). The high-profile positions of these Egyptians in the al-Qaeda organization caused some to place increased scrutiny on Egypt's ability to control Islamic extremism.

In 2005, Egypt changed its constitution to allow the opposition to contest presidential elections. Potential candidates had to meet strict criteria for participation, however, and religious parties remained banned, along with the Muslim Brotherhood (the only opposition organization with broad popular support). In the presidential election held on 7 September 2005, Mubarak gained a fifth consecutive term as president. The election was the first under the new system whereby multiple candidates might stand. In previous elections, Egyptians had voted yes or no for a single candidate chosen by parliament. In this election, all candidates were permitted to campaign freely and were given equal time on television. Mubarak faced nine opponents in the September election, although only two—Ayman Nour of the Tomorrow party, and Noaman Gomaa of the New Wafd party—had any real following. Without monitors in place in most of the nearly 10,000 polling stations, Mubarak supporters engaged in various acts of voter intimidation; other voting irregularities transpired, as well. The opposition to Mubarak came largely from a movement called "Kifaya" or "Enough." Kifaya supporters were permitted to protest without police intervention on the day of the election. Different groups affiliated with the Kifaya movement staged demonstrations for several months prior to the election.

In parliamentary elections held in November and December 2005, the Muslim Brotherhood won 34 seats, doubling the number of seats its members held in the last parliament, elected in 2000. The Muslim Brotherhood's candidates ran as independents, due to the outlaw status of the group. The Muslim Brotherhood solidified its position as the strongest opposition group in Egypt by winning an additional 42 seats in the second round of voting, and 12 in the third, to make a total of 88 seats in the new parliament. In total, the ruling NDP won 315 seats, noticeably fewer than the 388 it held in the outgoing parliament but nonetheless still above the two-thirds majority necessary to control legislation. Elections were marred by clashes between voters and security forces, leaving 12 dead.

In April 2006, parliament voted to extend the state of emergency, in place since 1981, until 2008. In late 2006, Mubarak pledged democratic and constitutional reforms in an address to parliament. In March 2007, the Egyptian public was asked to vote on 34 constitutional reforms, which dealt with three main issues. First, the government would be granted broad powers to monitor and detain people accused of terrorist activities. However, terrorism would not be specifically defined. Second, judges would have a limited role in monitoring elections, which were often called fraudulent. Third, religious political parties would be prohibited. The president would also have the power to dissolve parliament without a referendum. Human rights organizations criticized the proposed amendments, and when the results were officially announced, showing that 76% of voters had approved the changes in the referendum, they and Egyptian opposition groups said the poll was rigged. Indeed, Amnesty International called the constitutional changes the "greatest erosion of human rights in 26 years" in Egypt. Turnout was estimated at 27%.

In November 2006, Egypt became one of at least six Arab countries in the process of developing domestic nuclear programs to diversify energy sources. The potential proliferation of nuclear weapons by countries in the region, like Iran, makes Arab countries more interested in nuclear technology.

In 2009, rumors began to surface that Mubarak's son, Gamal, was being groomed to succeed his father in the next presidential elections. These rumors of political succession sparked an opposition campaign against the government in October 2009. Led by Ayman Nour, an opposition candidate in the 2005 election, the campaign focused on the election system, which organizers believed was so heavily stacked in favor of the Mubaraks that the next election would be simply a cover for a predetermined dynastic succession. Nour's campaign emphasized that the nation was meant to be a republic, not a kingdom; members of the Muslim Brotherhood supported this platform.

In late January 2011, as part of a wider wave of revolutions and protests in the Arab world known as "Arab Spring," and a few weeks after a major revolutionary uprising in Tunisia, thousands of Egyptians gathered in the streets of Cairo, Alexandria, and other cities, protesting against the rule of Mubarak, widespread unemployment, corruption, and poverty. Egypt's opposition leader, Mohamed El Baradei, a pro-democratic force who had served previously as Director General of the International Atomic Energy Agency, was prominent in the movement. Web networking sites like Facebook and Twitter facilitated rapid organization and assemblies of protesters; as a result, the Egyptian government temporarily shut down most Internet access in the nation. Crowds ignored a government-imposed curfew, which security forces refused to enforce. Though Mubarak offered some concessions, including sacking his cabinet, appointing a Vice President (the first in 30 years), and announcing that he would step down from office by September 2011, he balked at demands to resign; protestors called for a more immediate change in leadership. Following the announcement, violent clashes broke out between the pro and anti-Mubarak factions. After weeks of protest, Mubarak stepped down on 11 February, leaving all power to a military junta known as the Supreme Council of the Armed Forces (SCAF). After dissolving parliament and the Egyptian constitution, the Council issued a statement saying that they would supervise implementation of constitutional reforms, which Egyptian citizens overwhelmingly approved on 20 March 2011. One of the most important amendments limited the presidential term to two four-year periods. Some liberal members of Egyptian politics raised concerns over the timetable in which elections would occur, arguing that implementing elections too quickly might not leave the country enough time to form effective political groups.

13 GOVERNMENT

On 25 March 1964, President Nasser proclaimed an interim constitution, which remained in effect until a permanent constitution, drafted by the National Assembly, was approved by the electorate in a plebiscite on 11 September 1971; it, in turn, was dissolved by the Supreme Council of the Armed Forces in 2011. The 1971 constitution declared Egypt to be a democratic socialist state and an integral part of the Arab nation. Yet Egypt remained under state emergency law after the Sadat assassination in 1981, and, along with Mubarak's tough antiterrorism laws against Islamists, Egypt's government possessed sweeping powers of repression, even after Mubarak's removal. The state emergency law was partially lifted by the military government in January 2012.

Under the March 2011 referendum, the president of the republic is theoretically the head of state and supreme commander of the armed forces. The president is required to appoint a deputy and is limited to one term of two four-year periods. In addition, he appoints and retires civil, military, and diplomatic personnel in accordance with the law. However, the position was still vacant in October 2011, and the SCAF holds *de iure* control over executive

and military power, and even the interpretation of law. The prime minister, currently selected by the SCAF, heads the cabinet and oversees the daily operation of the government. The president's power to declare war and conclude treaties with foreign countries was subject to the approval of the People's Assembly, a unicameral legislative body that consisted of 444 elected and 10 appointed members serving five-year terms. A 264-member advisory body, the Shura Council, was formed in 1980. However, these bodies were dissolved by the SCAF in February 2011.

Until 2005, the People's Assembly nominated the president, who had to be confirmed by plebiscite for a six-year term. The constitution was amended by popular referendum in 1980 to permit Sadat to serve more than two terms. Vice President Mubarak, who became president upon Sadat's assassination, was confirmed in that office in national referendums in October 1981, 1987, 1993, and 1999.

An amendment passed by parliament in May 2005 and approved in a public referendum provided that the president was to be elected in direct, public elections to be contested by more than one candidate. In the presidential election held in September 2005, Mubarak was opposed by nine candidates. Official results had Mubarak winning 88.5% of the vote, with voter turnout at 23%. Ayman Nour of the Tomorrow party, who came in second place, took 7.3% of the vote, and Noaman Gomaa of the New Wafd party came in third with 2.8%. Elections to fill the presidency after Mubarak's resignation in February 2011 were expected to be held in 2012.

Suffrage is universal at age 18.

14 POLITICAL PARTIES

Since the founding of the republic in 1953, the president and his army colleagues dominated Egyptian politics. The Arab Socialist Union (ASU; founded by President Nasser as the Egyptian National Union in 1957) was the sole legal political party until 1976, when President Sadat allowed three minor parties to participate in parliamentary elections. In 1978, Sadat replaced the ASU with his own organization, the National Democratic Party (NDP), of which he became chairman. In elections held in June 1979, the NDP won 342 seats in the People's Assembly; the Socialist Labor Party (SLP), 29 seats; the Liberal Socialist Party, 3; and independents, 8. In 1980, however, Sadat denounced the SLP as the "agent of a foreign power," and 13 of the party's deputies defected either to join the NDP or to become independent members of the legislature, thus reducing the number of SLP seats to 16.

In January 1982, President Mubarak was elected without opposition as chairman of the NDP. In elections held in May 1984, the NDP won 390 seats in the National Assembly. The New Wafd (Delegation) Party, the middle-class successor of the dominant party of the pre-Nasser period allied with the Muslim Brotherhood, won 58. In the 1987 Assembly elections, the ruling NDP again won about 70% of the vote. Seventeen percent voted for an alliance of Socialist Labor, Liberal Socialist and, under their banner, the outlawed Muslim Brotherhood; 11% voted for the New Wafd. Elections in 1990 drew only some 25% of eligible voters when the opposition boycotted the poll, charging unfair and undemocratic procedures.

In 1995, the opposition contested the elections, but to little effect. Balloting was held on 29 November, and the NDP won a huge majority (317) of the body's 444 seats. Although independents won more than 100 seats, they were so closely allied with the NDP that nearly all of them joined the party after the elections. The New Wafd Party won 6 seats; the National Progressive Unionist Party won 5; the Socialists won 1; and the Nasserists won 1.

In elections for the National Assembly held in October and November 2000, the NDP took 353 of 444 elected seats. The New Wafd Party won 35; the New Delegation Party won 7; the National Progressive Unionist Party took 6; the Nasserists won 3; the Liberal Party took 1 seat; independents won 37 seats; and 2 seats remained vacant.

In November and December 2005, the Muslim Brotherhood won a total of 88 seats in the parliamentary elections; the NDP took 315 seats. Non-Muslim Brotherhood-affiliated parties took 14 seats, including the neo-liberal New Wafd Party, traditionally recognized as Egypt's largest opposition party. Independents won the rest of the seats.

In the parliamentary elections of 2010, Mubarak's own National Democratic Party (NDP) won 420 of the 508 elected seats in parliament. The vote was widely criticized by international observers, since there were reports of voter intimidation, interference, detentions, and ballot stuffing in favor of Mubarak. Protests escalated after the first round of voting (28 November) when preliminary results indicated that the Muslim Brotherhood had not won a single seat, despite the fact that they held 88 seats in the incumbent parliament. The Muslim Brotherhood and the New Wafd Party (another major opposition group) boycotted the runoff election of 5 December.

President Mubarak stepped down on 11 February 2011 as a result of weeks of anti-government protests. Control of the government was handed over to the SCAF, which appointed a new interim government cabinet in March 2011, with Essam Sharaf replacing Ahmed Shafiq as the new prime minister. Shafiq, whom Mubarak appointed before resigning, was considered to be too close to the old government to be acceptable to protestors.

15 LOCAL GOVERNMENT

Egypt traditionally has been divided into two regions: Lower Egypt (Wagh al-Bahari), north of Cairo, and Upper Egypt (As-Sa'id), south of the capital. Under the local government system established in 1960, Egypt is organized into 27 governorates, each headed by an appointed governor. The governorates are responsible for social, health, welfare, and educational services and for the social and economic development of their region. They are also required to supervise the city and village councils, which are constituted in a similar manner. Historically, real authority has resided in Cairo in a highly centralized regime, heavily burdened by bureaucracy. Since 1994, village mayors, who were previously elected, have been appointed by the Ministry of the Interior.

16 JUDICIAL SYSTEM

The judicial system is based on English common law, Islamic law, and especially the Napoleonic code; the Supreme Constitutional Court has the power of judicial review, as does the Council of State, which oversees the validity of administrative decisions. A tension exists between civil law derived from France and competition from promoters of Islamic law, who succeeded in amending the constitution to state that Shari'ah (Islamic) law is, in principle, the sole source of legislation. However, Shari'ah applies primarily to Muslims with regard to family, personal status, and inheritance matters, and non-Muslims have been allowed to maintain separate legislation in all matters except inheritance. Egypt accepts compulsory International Court of Justice (ICJ) jurisdiction, with reservations.

Simple police offenses, misdemeanors, and civil cases involving small amounts are subject to the jurisdiction of single-judge summary tribunals. The trial courts of the central tribunals, consisting of three justices each, sit in cases exceeding the jurisdiction of summary courts and also consider appeals. Traffic in narcotics and press offenses, considered serious crimes, are tried by the courts of appeals of the central tribunals in the first instance, sitting as assize courts. There are seven courts of appeals—at Cairo, Alexandria, Tantā, Al-Manṣurah, Asyut, Bani-Souef, and Ismailia—which sit in chambers of three judges. The highest tribunal is the Court of Cassation, composed of 30 justices, which sits in panels of at least 5 justices.

The 1971 constitution declared that the judiciary is independent of other state powers and that judges are independent and not subject to enforced retirement. The Supreme Constitutional Court is responsible for enforcing adherence to laws and regulations and for interpreting legislation and the constitution. The Office of the Socialist Public Prosecutor is responsible to the People's Assembly for the security of the people's rights, the integrity of the political system, and other matters.

The president appoints all civilian judges, from nominations by the Supreme Judicial Council, a body designed to assure the independence of the judiciary and composed of senior judges, lawyers, law professors, and the president of the Court of Cassation (the SCAF assumed these responsibilities after the resignation of Mubarak in February 2011). Judges are appointed for life, with mandatory retirement at age 64. The judiciary has demonstrated a good degree of independence from the executive branch.

The state of emergency in place since 1981 after the assassination of President Anwar Sadat led to detention without due process of many people. Emergency security courts try suspected terrorists whose only recourse upon conviction is an appeal for clemency to the president or prime minister.

17 ARMED FORCES

The International Institute for Strategic Studies reports that armed forces in Egypt totaled 468,500 members in 2011. The force is comprised of 340,000 from the Army, equipped with 3,855 main battle tanks, 412 reconnaissance vehicles, 520 armored infantry fighting vehicles, 4,750 armored personnel carriers, and 4,348 artillery pieces; 18,500 from the navy (including 2,000 coast guard personnel), equipped with four tactical submarines, one destroyer, 10 frigates, 48 patrol/coastal vessels and 15 mine warfare ships; 30,000 from the Air Force, equipped with 572 combat-capable aircraft, including 218 fighters, 223 fighter-ground attack aircraft, and 115 attack helicopters; and 80,000 members of the Air Defense command, equipped with both missile and gun-based air defense batteries. There were also 497,000 reservists divided among all services. Egypt's paramilitary forces were estimated at 330,000 active members, including a national guard of 60,000, a central security force of 325,000, and 12,000 border guards. Armed forces represent 3.2% of the labor force in Egypt. Defense spending totaled $17 billion and accounted for 3.4% of GDP.

18 INTERNATIONAL COOPERATION

Egypt joined the United Nations as a charter member on 24 October 1945 and participates in the Economic Commission for Africa (ECA), the Economic and Social Commission for Western Asia (ESCWA), and all the non-regional specialized agencies. The country is a member of the WTO. It belongs to the African Development Bank, the Arab Monetary Fund, COMESA (Common Market for Eastern and Southern Africa), G-15, G-24, G-77, the Organization of the Islamic Conference (OIC), the Council of Arab Economic Unity, the New Partnership for Africa's Development (NEPAD), the Community of Sahel and Saharan States (CENSAD), and the African Union (AU). It is also a member in OAPEC, a permanent observer at the Organization of American States (OAS), and a partner in the Organization for Security and Co-operation in Europe (OSCE).

Between 1958 and 1973, Egypt made several attempts to establish united or federated states with its Arab neighbors. Egypt and Syria formed the United Arab Republic from February 1958 to September 1961, when Syria broke away; the United Arab States, consisting of Egypt, Syria, and Yemen, survived formally from March 1958 through December 1961, although they never became a political reality; and a federation among Egypt, Syria, and Iraq was officially established in April 1963 but never implemented. On 1 January 1972, Egypt, Syria, and Libya established the Federation of Arab Republics to little practical effect. A formal merger attempt between Egypt and Libya, nominally consummated on 1 September 1973, dissolved in practice when relations between the two countries soured. Egypt became the first Arab state to normalize relations with Israel following the conclusion of the 1979 peace treaty. As a result of this act, however, Egypt's membership in the League of Arab States was suspended; Egypt did not rejoin the League until 1989. Arab League headquarters are in Cairo. Egypt plays a key role in the peace process between Israel and the Palestinian Authority. Egypt is part of the Nonaligned Movement and a member of the Permanent Court of Arbitration.

In environmental cooperation, Egypt is part of the Basel Convention, the Convention on Biological Diversity, Ramsar, CITES, the London Convention, International tropical Timber Agreements, the Kyoto Protocol, the Montréal Protocol, MARPOL, the Nuclear Test Ban Treaty, and the UN Conventions on the Law of the Sea, Climate Change, and Desertification.

19 ECONOMY

The Egyptian economy has been historically agricultural, with cotton as the mainstay. Land prices are extremely high because of the shortage of arable land, and food production is insufficient to meet the needs of its growing population. Although Egypt has expanded its private sector in recent years, industry remains centrally controlled and for the most part government-owned; since the 1950s, the government has developed the petroleum, services, and construction sectors, largely at the expense of agriculture.

Egypt's significant economic growth rate from 1975 to 1981, made possible in large measure through foreign aid and credits, had declined to about 5% by 1986. Revenues for 1985–86 from petroleum exports, Suez Canal traffic, tourism, and remittances

from Egyptians working abroad—all mainstays of the Egyptian economy—were eroded in the wake of sharp declines in international oil prices and developments in the Iran-Iraq war. Egypt's economic position was strengthened when the Gulf states and the United States rewarded the Egyptians for their role in forming the Arab anti-Iraq coalition, reducing external debt to about $40 billion in 1990. Egypt also has incentives to export to the United States through the Qualifying Industrial Zones program (administered by the Office of the United States Trade Representative), which permits duty-free Egyptian imports provided that 11.7% of the materials originate in Israel.

In the early 1990s, the collapse of world oil prices and an increasingly heavy debt burden led Egypt into negotiations with the International Monetary Fund (IMF) for balance-of-payments support. As a condition of the support, Egypt embarked on a comprehensive economic reform and structural adjustment program, under the aegis of the IMF and the World Bank. Egypt succeeded in stabilizing the macroeconomic fundamentals necessary for sustained economic growth in 1999. However, progress toward privatizing and streamlining the public sector and liberalizing trade policy was slow. Consequently, despite the improvements, the economy did not experience the economic growth necessary to reduce unemployment and generate the targeted 6–7% growth rates in the GDP.

Remittances from Egyptians working abroad bolstered the Egyptian economy somewhat. A more economically liberal cabinet was appointed in mid-2004, which announced far-reaching plans for economic reform. In September of that year, Egypt pushed through custom reforms, proposed income and corporate tax reforms, reduced energy subsidies, and privatized several enterprises. The tourism sector feared a downturn in tourist numbers when Islamic terrorists attacked resorts in the Sinai Peninsula in 2004 and 2005, but the industry performed better than expected. Despite the booms from 2005–2007, the standard of living failed to rise, and the government was still compelled to provide subsidies for basic necessities. Egypt strove to develop an export market for its natural gas resources, but improvement in the capital-intensive hydrocarbons sector did not ameliorate Egypt's chronic unemployment problem.

As a result of the 2008–09 global financial crisis, the annual economic growth rate declined from 7.2% in fiscal year 2007/08 to 4.7% in 2008/09.

In the first decade of the 21st century, Egypt initiated numerous development projects to increase the nation's information technology (IT) infrastructure in efforts to attract foreign investment in global IT partnerships and in the engineering services market. These efforts paid off, as major companies such as Microsoft, IBM, Oracle, and Alcatel took up residence in Egypt's Smart Village, the 600-acre technology park located in Cairo. In 2010, the government reaffirmed its continued commitment to increase the nation's investment potential in these areas and maintain its place as the global service delivery leader in the Europe, Middle East, Africa Region (EMEA). The government took steps to improve its industrial sector: in February 2010, the Industrial Development Authority announced plans to create three new industrial parks in Tenth of Ramadan City and Sadat City (both outside of Cairo) and

Borg el-Arab (outside of Alexandria). The gross domestic product (GDP) rate of change in Egypt, as of 2010, was 5.1%. Inflation stood at 12.8%, and unemployment was reported at 9.7%.

20 INCOME

The CIA estimated that, in 2010, the GDP of Egypt was $497.8 billion. The CIA defines GDP as the value of all final goods and services produced within a nation in a given year and computed on the basis of purchasing power parity (PPP) rather than value as measured on the basis of the rate of the exchange based on current dollars. The per capita GDP was estimated at $6,200. The annual growth rate of GDP was 5.1%. The average inflation rate was 12.8%. It was estimated that agriculture accounted for 13.5% of GDP, industry 37.9%, and services 48.6%.

According to the World Bank, remittances from citizens living abroad totaled $7.1 billion or about $87 per capita and accounted for approximately 1.4% of GDP.

The World Bank reports that, in 2009, household consumption in Egypt totaled $143.5 billion or about $1,749 per capita, measured in current US dollars rather than PPP. Household consumption includes expenditures of individuals, households, and nongovernmental organizations on goods and services, excluding the purchases of dwellings. It was estimated that household consumption was growing at an average annual rate of 5.3%.

As of 2011, the most recent study by the World Bank reported that actual individual consumption in Egypt was 76.9% of GDP and accounted for 0.71% of world consumption. By comparison, the United States accounted for 25.44% of world individual consumption. The World Bank also estimated that 34.8% of Egypt's GDP was spent on food and beverages, 13% on housing and household furnishings, 6.1% on clothes, 3.8% on health, 3.1% on transportation, 2.0% on communications, 2.0% on recreation, 2.4% on restaurants and hotels, and 3.7% on miscellaneous goods and services and purchases from abroad.

It was estimated that in 2005 about 20% of the population subsisted on an income below the poverty line established by Egypt's government.

21 LABOR

As of 2010, Egypt had a total labor force of 26.2 million people. Within the labor force, CIA estimates in 2001 noted that 32% were employed in agriculture, 17% in industry, and 51% in the service sector.

Egyptian workers obtained the legal right to organize trade unions in 1942. However, private-sector unions remain the exception, rather than the rule. In 2005, there were 23 trade unions, all of which were required to be members of the Egyptian Trade Union Federation (ETUF). The ETUF in 2005 had four million members. Approximately 25% of the Egyptian workforce were union members and were employed at state-owned companies. Collective bargaining is permitted, but is handled through a labor consultative council that includes employer, worker, and government representatives. Strikes are prohibited while these procedures are in effect. So-called "wildcat strikes" are prohibited. The government sets wages, benefits, and job classifications for government and other public-sector employees. In the private sector, employee compensation is set according to the country's laws on minimum wages.

For children in the nonagricultural sector, the law sets the minimum working age at 14 or at the age when basic schooling is completed (which is 15), whichever is higher. In addition, minors under the age of 18 are legally limited to the type of work and the conditions under which it is performed. However, child labor remains a problem. In 2005, an estimated two million children were working. The minimum wage for public-sector employees differed among sectors. The maximum number of hours that can be worked was 48 hours per week. Overtime rates of pay begin at 36 hours, with an extra differential rate for daytime and nighttime hours. A series of bonuses and other benefits generally triple minimum rate wages, thus offering a worker and a family a decent living standard. However, enforcement of health and safety regulations is sporadic.

22 AGRICULTURE

During the 1970s, despite substantial investment in land reclamation, agriculture lost its position as the dominant economic sector. Agricultural exports, which accounted for 87% of all merchandise export value in 1960, fell to 35% in 1974 and to 13% by 2004.

Traditionally, cotton has been the staple crop, but it is no longer important as an export. The country's major crops include cotton, rice, corn, wheat, beans, fruits, and vegetables. In 2009, cereal production amounted to 23.7 million tons, fruit production 10 million tons, and vegetable production 20.3 million tons. Substantial quantities of wheat are also imported despite increases in yield since 1970, and significant quantities of rice are exported. Citrus, dates, and grapes are the principal fruits by acreage. The government exercises a substantial degree of control over agriculture, not only to ensure the best use of irrigation water but also to limit the planting of cotton in favor of food grains. However, the government's ability to achieve this objective is limited by crop rotational constraints.

About one-quarter of the arable land is reclaimed from the desert, but these reclaimed lands only add 7% to the total value of agricultural production. The arable land (roughly 4% of Egypt's total area) is extremely productive and can be cropped two or even three times per year. Most land is cropped at least twice a year, but agricultural productivity is limited by salinity, which afflicts an estimated 35% of cultivated land, and drainage problems.

Irrigation plays a major role in a country the very livelihood of which depends upon a single river, the Nile; 99.9% of the arable land is irrigated. Most ambitious of all the irrigation projects is that of the Aswan High Dam, completed in 1971. A report published in March 1975 by the National Council for Production and Economic Affairs indicated that the dam was successful in controlling floodwaters and ensuring continuous water supplies but that water consumption had been excessive and would have to be controlled. Some valuable land was lost below the dam because the flow of Nile silt was stopped, and increased salinity remains a problem. Further, five years of drought in the Ethiopian highlands—the source of the Nile River's water—caused the water level of Lake Nasser, the Aswan High Dam's reservoir, to drop to the lowest level ever in 1987. In 1996, however, the level of water behind the High Dam and in Lake Nasser reached the highest level since the completion of the dam. Despite this unusual abundance of water supply, Egypt can only utilize 55.5 billion cu m (1.96 trillion cu ft) annually, according to the Nile Basin Agreement signed in 1959 between Egypt and Sudan. Another spectacular project designed to address the water scarcity problem is the New Valley (the "second Nile"), aimed at development of the large artesian water supplies underlying the oases of the Western Desert. Total investment in agriculture and land reclamation for the government's Third Plan (1993–1997) was EGP16,963 million.

The agrarian reform law of 1952 provided that no one might hold more than 190 feddans for farming and that each landholder must either farm the land himself or rent it under specified conditions. Up to 95 additional feddans might be held if the owner had children, and additional land had to be sold to the government. In 1961, the upper limit of landholding was reduced to 100 feddans, and no person was allowed to lease more than 50 feddans (1 feddan = 0.42 hectares). Compensation to the former owners was in bonds bearing a low rate of interest, redeemable within 40 years. A law enacted in 1969 reduced landholdings by one person to 50 feddans. By the mid-1980s, 90% of all land titles were for holdings of less than five feddans, and about 300,000 families, or 8% of the rural population, had received land under the agrarian reform program. According to a 1990 agricultural census, there were some three million small land holdings, almost 96% of which were under five feddans (2.1 hectares/5.2 acres). Since the late 1980s, many reforms attempting to deregulate agriculture by liberalizing input and output prices and by eliminating crop area controls have been initiated. As a result, the gap between world and domestic prices for Egyptian agricultural commodities has been closed.

The government plans massive irrigation and development projects to create new communities to alleviate population intensity in the valley, with the objective of increasing the percentage of populated areas from 5.3% to 25% of Egypt's total area. These projects are centralized in southern Egypt, by the Suez Canal, and Sinai. The government plans to create a new delta in the south of the Western Desert parallel to the Nile, adding 540,000 feddans (1,134,000 hectares/2,802,000 acres) to the cultivated area, to be irrigated by the Nile's water.

23 ANIMAL HUSBANDRY

Because of intensive cultivation of the soil, little land is available for animal husbandry, but efforts were made in the 1980s to increase the output of fodder per land unit and the productivity of livestock raising.

In 2009, the country tended 96 million chickens, 5 million head of cattle, 38,000 pigs; in 2005 Egypt tended 3,960,000 goats, 5,150,000 sheep, and 3,920,000 head of buffalo. The production from these animals amounted to 912,399 tons of beef and veal, 2,217 tons of pork, 662,014 tons of poultry, 194,761 tons of eggs, and 4.95 million tons of milk. Egypt also produced 34,307 tons of cattle hide and 7,932 tons of raw wool.

24 FISHING

Fishing is concentrated in the Nile Delta and River and in the Mediterranean and Red seas. Egypt had 3,140 decked commercial fishing boats in 2008. The annual capture totaled 373,815 tons according to the UN FAO. The export value of seafood totaled $4.3 million. Mullet and eels are caught in the Delta and sardines in the Mediterranean. There is a small-scale freezing and canning industry. Nevertheless, Egypt has been a net importer of fish. In the early 1980s, new fish-farming facilities were established at Maryut in the Delta.

25 FORESTRY

There is no significant forest cover in Egypt. Thus, the construction and furniture-making industries must rely on wood imports. The UN FAO estimated the 2009 roundwood production at 268,000 cu m (9.46 million cu ft). The value of all forest products, including roundwood, totaled $97.2 million. Furniture production engages about 40,000 people and is concentrated in the Damietta Governorate in the northern part of the Nile Delta. Softwood products come mostly from Russia, Sweden, and Finland; hardwood products from Romania, Croatia, and Bosnia.

26 MINING

In recent decades, crude oil, natural gas, and petroleum products have dominated Egypt's mineral industry. However Egypt is also a producer of ferroalloys, gold, iron ore, primary aluminum, steel, secondary copper, lead, and zinc and construction materials such as clay, gypsum, gemstones, dimension stone, and raw materials to make glass. Among non-fuel minerals, phosphate rock (around the Red Sea, along the Nile, and in the Western Desert) and iron ore are the most important in terms of value and ore grade. In 2009 Egypt also produced manganese ore, titanium, ilmenite, asbestos, barite, cement, bentonite, fire clay, kaolin, crude feldspar, fluorspar, gypsum and anhydrite, lime, nitrogen, salt, soda ash, sodium sulfate, basalt, dolomite, granite, dimension stone, gravel, limestone, marble blocks (including alabaster), glass sand, construction sand, talc, soapstone, pyrophyllite, and vermiculite, and there were occurrences of gold, ocher, sulfate of magnesia, and nitrate of soda. The government was engaged in efforts to partially privatize mining and metal assets. Although mineral resources have been exploited in Egypt since antiquity, including gemstones and zinc, some regions of the country remained geologically unexplored. Extraction of limestone, clay, and gypsum during World War II rose in response to the Allied armies' urgent demand.

In 2009 Egypt produced 6.2 million metric tons of phosphate rock, up from 972,000 metric tons in 2001. Egypt was the eleventh-largest cement producer in 2009, accounting for 1.5% of world production. Egypt also ranked seventh in direct-reduced iron in 2009, accounting for 4.5% of the world's production. Output of iron ore and concentrate was 2.5 million metric tons in 2003, unchanged since 2001. Development of an iron ore mine and steel plant near Aswan ceased in 2000 when the government charged the promoters with misappropriating public funds. Higher-quality deposits were being exploited in the Western Desert. Gold and copper deposits had not been of sufficient grade to justify profitable extraction, but, in 2009, the government designated gold production as a strategic project for the minerals sector.

27 ENERGY AND POWER

Egypt is an important non-Organization of Petroleum Exporting Countries (OPEC) energy producer, though it is a member of Organization of Arab Petroleum Exporting Countries (OAPEC). Commercial quantities of oil were first found in 1908, and more petroleum was found in the late 1930s along the Gulf of Suez. Later, large oil fields were discovered in the Sinai Peninsula, the Gulf of Suez, the Western Desert, and the Eastern Desert. The Abu

Rudeis and Ra's Sudr oil fields in the Sinai, captured by Israel in 1967, were returned to Egyptian control in November 1975, and the remaining Sinai oil fields reverted to Egyptian control by the end of April 1982. Egypt's proven crude oil reserves were estimated at 3.7 billion barrels as of 1 January 2005. Oil production in 2008 totaled 522,997 barrels of oil a day (down from 698,000 barrels per day in 2004 and 922,000 barrels per day in 1996). Approximately 50% of Egypt's oil production comes from the Gulf of Suez, with the Western Desert, Eastern Desert, and the Sinai Peninsula as the country's three other primary producing areas. Domestic per capita oil consumption was estimated at 867 kg in 2008. According to the CIA, oil exports for 2009 totaled approximately 163,000 barrels per day. The Suez Canal and the 322-km (200-mi) Sumed Pipeline from the Gulf of Suez to the Mediterranean Sea are two routes for oil from the Persian Gulf, which makes Egypt a strategic point of interest in world energy markets. Although the Suez Canal Authority (SCA) has deepened the canal so that it can accommodate the largest bulk freight carriers, the canal has undergone subsequent renovations during the 2000s to accommodate larger ships and make the area more attractive to tourism.

Major discoveries in the 1990s have given natural gas increasing importance as an energy source. According to data from Egypt's Ministry of Petroleum, the country's reserves of natural gas were estimated at 66 trillion cu ft, as of 1 January 2005, but probable reserves have been placed at or more than 120 trillion cu ft. Since the early 1990s, significant deposits of natural gas have been found in the Western Desert, in the Nile Delta, and off the Nile Delta shore near the city of Damietta (2002). Domestic consumption of natural gas has also risen as a result of thermal power plants converting from oil to natural gas. As of 2002, Egypt's production and consumption of natural gas are each estimated at 941 billion cu ft.

The Egyptian electric power system is almost entirely integrated, with thermal stations in Cairo and Alexandria and generators at Aswan. The World Bank reported in 2008 that Egypt produced 131 billion kWh of electricity and consumed 116.2 billion kWh, or 1,416 kWh per capita. Roughly 96% of energy came from fossil fuels, while 2% came from alternative fuels.

A $239 million electricity network link with Jordan was completed in 1998. In late 2002, Egypt announced that it would coordinate a regional energy distribution center to coordinate energy distribution among the nations of the region, including Egypt, Jordan, Syria, Lebanon, Iraq, Libya, Tunisia, Algeria, and Morocco.

In 2010, the government secured funding from the World Bank for construction of the 100-megawatt Kom Ombo Solar Power Plant in Southern Egypt and the 1,500-megawatt North Giza Power Plant on the outskirts of Cairo.

28 INDUSTRY

Egypt, at the time of the 1952 revolution, was much further advanced industrially than any other Arab country or indeed any country in Africa except South Africa. Under the socialist Nasser administration, the government coordinated industrial expansion and established an industrial base. As a result, bureaucracy and a dependence on political directives from the government became common to Egyptian industry. Since the early 1990s, the govern-ment promoted privatization as a way to eventually increase industrial output.

Industry accounted for 33% of GDP in 2004 and employed 17% of the labor force. The industrial production growth rate in 2004 was 2.5%. Major industrial products included textiles, chemicals (including fertilizers, polymers, and petrochemicals), pharmaceuticals, food processing, petroleum, construction, cement, metals, and light consumer goods. The clothing and textiles sector is the largest industrial employer.

Greater Cairo, Alexandria, and Helwan are Egypt's main industrial centers, producing iron and steel, textiles, refined petroleum products, plastics, building materials, electronics, paper, trucks and automobiles, and chemicals. The Helwan iron and steel plant, 29 km (18 mi) south of Cairo, using imported coke, processes iron ore mined near Aswan into sheets, bars, billets, plates, and blooms.

The petroleum industry accounts for approximately 40% of export earnings. Egypt is encouraging oil exploration, but natural gas is becoming the focus of the country's oil and gas industries. In 2005, the country's first liquefied gas export terminal began operations.

Egypt's industrial sector has undergone major reforms since World Bank adjustment programs went into effect during 1991, privatizing and restructuring state-owned enterprises. Some of the companies in important non-oil industries are technically in the private sector, but control still remains with the government.

29 SCIENCE AND TECHNOLOGY

Founded in 1971, the Academy of Scientific Research and Technology in Cairo is the national body responsible for science and technology. Egypt also has 12 specialized learned societies in agriculture, medicine, science, and technology. The National Research Center, also in Cairo, carries out research in pure and applied sciences. The Ministry of Agriculture has 20 attached research institutes in Cairo and Giza. Twenty other institutes conduct research in medicine, science, and technology.

In 2009, research and development (R&D) totaled 0.23% of GDP. In 2002, high-technology exports totaled $13 million, or 1% of manufactured exports. For the period 1990–01, there were 366 technicians and 493 researchers per million people actively engaged in R&D. Patent applications in science and technology as of 2009, according to the World Bank, totaled 490 in Egypt.

Located in Cairo are museums devoted to agriculture, geology, railways, and marine technology. In addition to polytechnic institutes in Cairo and Mansoura, Egypt in 1996 had 13 universities offering courses in basic and applied sciences. In 1987–97, science and engineering students accounted for 12% of college and university enrollments.

30 DOMESTIC TRADE

Cairo and Alexandria are the most important commercial centers. Virtually all importers, exporters, and wholesalers have offices in one or both of these cities. Egypt's retail trade is dominated by a large number of small, privately owned shops and vendors. Government cooperatives with hundreds of outlets also combine wholesale and retail activities. The principal retail centers have general and specialized stores as well as large bazaars. Smaller bazaars and open markets are found in the towns and villages. There are large wholesaling markets for meat and produce in Cairo, Al-

Principal Trading Partners – Egypt (2010)

(In millions of US dollars)

Country	Total	Exports	Imports	Balance
World	79,361.0	26,438.0	52,923.0	-26,485.0
United States	6,502.0	1,564.0	4,938.0	-3,374.0
China	5,314.0	430.0	4,884.0	-4,454.0
Italy	5,150.0	2,197.0	2,953.0	-756.0
Germany	4,585.0	572.0	4,013.0	-3,441.0
Sa'udi Arabia	3,706.0	1,591.0	2,115.0	-524.0
Turkey	2,877.0	999.0	1,878.0	-879.0
France	2,800.0	927.0	1,873.0	-946.0
India	2,779.0	1,228.0	1,551.0	-323.0
Spain	2,481.0	1,636.0	845.0	791.0
South Korea	2,328.0	534.0	1,794.0	-1,260.0

(…) data not available or not significant.

(n.s.) not specified.

SOURCE: *2011 Direction of Trade Statistics Yearbook*, New York: United Nations, 2011.

Balance of Payments – Egypt (2010)

(In millions of US dollars)

Current Account		**-4,504.0**
Balance on goods	-20,120.0	
Imports	-45,145.0	
Exports	25,024.0	
Balance on services	9,089.0	
Balance on income	-5,912.0	
Current transfers	12,439.0	
Capital Account		**-39.0**
Financial Account		**6,470.0**
Direct investment abroad	-1,176.0	
Direct investment in Egypt	6,386.0	
Portfolio investment assets	-445.0	
Portfolio investment liabilities	10,887.0	
Financial derivatives	…	
Other investment assets	-11,185.0	
Other investment liabilities	2,003.0	
Net Errors and Omissions		**-2,145.0**
Reserves and Related Items		**218.0**

(…) data not available or not significant.

SOURCE: *Balance of Payment Statistics Yearbook 2011*, Washington, DC: International Monetary Fund, 2011.

clude textiles (especially in cotton), food processing, and vehicle assembly. In 2001, about 51% of the work force was employed in the service sector, which also accounts for about 50% of GDP.

Government hours are 8 a.m. to 2 p.m., Saturday to Wednesday. Business hours vary widely. Typically, a business schedule in summer would be 8 a.m. to 2 p.m.; in the winter, from 9 a.m. to 1 p.m. and from 5 to 7 p.m., Saturday through Wednesday. Friday is the Muslim holy day, and most people do not work on Thursdays. While the official language is Arabic, commercial firms frequently employ English or French for business correspondence. Haggling (in Arabic, *momarsa*, auction), is a standard business process for determining a fair price for goods and services in Egypt. The Cairo International Trade Fair, held every spring, has been an important promotional event for a number of years.

[31]FOREIGN TRADE

Before 1973, when Egypt was linked to the then-Soviet Union, 55% of its exports went to Soviet bloc countries, which supplied 30% of its imports. In 2009, major import partners were the United States, 10.6%; China, 8.7%; Germany, 8%; Italy, 5.9%; Turkey, 5.2%; and Saudi Arabia, 4.5%. Its major export partners were Spain, 6.8%; Italy, 6.7%; the United States, 6.3%; India, 6.1%; Saudi Arabia, 5.8%; China, 4.3%; Libya, 4.3%; and Jordan, 4%. Trade with Libya and Saudi Arabia has increased in recent years.

Egypt imported $46.52 billion worth of goods and services in 2008, while exporting $25.34 billion worth of goods and services. In 2004, Egypt's major exports were finished products (38.4% of all exports); petroleum and petroleum products (38.3%); semifinished products (7.1%); and cotton, textiles, and garments (4.1%). Major imports were intermediate goods (29.5% of all imports); investment goods (22%); petroleum and petroleum products (14.1%); and consumer goods (durables and nondurables, 14%). Petroleum replaced cotton and cotton products as Egypt's principal export in 1976.

[32]BALANCE OF PAYMENTS

Egypt's total outstanding debt stood at $33.75 billion in 2004. However, Egypt's annual trade deficit increased steadily during the late 1990s and early 2000s. In 2010, Egypt had a foreign trade deficit of $9.2 billion, amounting to 6.6% of GDP. Merchandise exports, which continue to be dominated by oil, rose strongly to $12.3 billion in 2004, from $9 billion in 2003. However, imports soared by more than 40% to $21.6 billion. The wider trade deficit was offset by a considerable strengthening of services (fueled by tourism and Suez Canal revenues) and current transfers surpluses, leaving the current-account surplus little changed at 4.7% of GDP. The current-account surplus averaged 2.8% of GDP from 2001–05.

The government has attempted in recent years to improve its balance of payments through monetary and foreign-exchange policies that have kept interest rates high and made access to credit and foreign exchange for imports difficult. These policies, while improving the balance of payments situation, have had an overall negative impact on economic growth and the country's ability to encourage foreign investment.

exandria, and Mansoura. The franchising of fast food restaurants and retail chains continues to grow quickly, with both American- and Egyptian-based companies holding franchises.

Egypt's electronic commerce (e-commerce) sector is in its infancy. However, in 2004, the government passed a law to regulate the use of e-signatures and established the Information Technology Industry Development Agency (ITIDA), which was tasked with spreading e-government and e-business services. The Ministry of State for Administrative Development has launched a government portal that allows access to 23 services online, such as driving licenses and birth certificates. Telecom Egypt became the first public-owned entity to offer online billing to its customers. As of December 2005, there were 5 million Internet users in Egypt.

Though most farms are privately owned, manufacturing is largely controlled by the public sector. Domestic industries in-

33 BANKING AND SECURITIES

The Central Bank of Egypt (CBE) acts as the nation's central bank. It supervises all banks in Egypt except for Misr African International Bank, the Arab International Bank, and the Egypt Export Development Bank. Established in 1961, the CBE main duties are to ensure price stability, the soundness of the nation's banking system, to formulate and implement monetary policy, manage the nation's money supply, and act in a supervisory capacity over the various banks operating in Egypt. The CBE is managed by a Board of Directors, of which the Chairman is the CBE's Governor. There are also two Vice Chairmen/Deputy Governors, and 12 directors on the board.

In 2005, the discount rate, the interest rate at which the central bank lends to financial institutions in the short term, was 10%. At the end of 2005, the nation's gold bullion deposits totaled 2.43 million fine troy ounces. Since November 2002, a total of 11 banks have been licensed to perform electronic banking services. These include HSBC-Egypt, and Citibank.

In 1957, when foreign banks refused to finance Egypt's cotton crop after the Suez Canal was nationalized, the government took over all foreign banks and insurance companies. By the end of 1962, all banks had been nationalized. The number of registered banks dwindled to only four by 1971.

As of 1999, there were 69 banks operating in Egypt: 4 state-owned commercial banks; 29 commercial banks; 33 investment banks, and 7 specialized banks, including 20 foreign bank branches. The four state-owned commercial banks—the National Bank of Egypt, the Bank of Alexandria, the Banque du Caire, and the Banque Misr—dominate the sector due to their size in terms of assets, deposit base, and branches (an average of 200 branches each), accounting for 55% of the banking system's total assets. The national stronghold on the system becomes apparent when the public-sector banks' shares in joint-venture banks are taken into account, which reveals the big four to be holders of over 90% of the total assets of commercial banks. The dominance of the public sector is heightened if the National Investment Bank (NIB) is included. Holding the long-term resources mobilized by the social security system, the NIB possesses roughly 25% of total bank deposits. Private-sector ownership accounted for less than 30% of the banking sector in 2002, while the total assets of Egypt's banks in the same year amounted to $72 billion.

In 1975, the public sector was allowed to perform transactions freely with all banks, which became largely free to exercise all banking functions. The government's "open door" policy toward banking permitted international banks of good standing to establish branches in Egypt and exempted those banks from regulations governing the control of foreign exchange. In 1991, foreign exchange rates were liberalized. In 1992 and 1993, laws were passed allowing foreign bank branches to deal in Egyptian currency. In order to bring the Egyptian banking sector into line with international banking norms, banking law 155 of 1998 established a legal basis for the privatization of the four public-sector banks, but, by 2002, this process was just getting started.

Egyptians habitually have invested their funds in real estate, in foreign countries, or in gold. In June 1992, a comprehensive Capital Markets Law was passed, sparking a revival of the Cairo and Alexandria exchanges that had been dormant since 1961 nationalization. In 1994, Egypt had one of the world's best-performing stock markets, but the primary stock market remained thin. Most investors preferred to establish closed companies and to resort to bank loans. Stock trading in the secondary market was also limited. Nevertheless, Egypt's first corporate bond since 1951, issued by the German-Egyptian Hoechst Orient in May 1994, was almost three times oversubscribed. In 2004, the Egyptian stock market's capitalization totaled $38.516 billion. In that same year, a combined total of 792 companies where listed on the Cairo and Alexandria Stock Exchanges. Trading volume (by value) in 2004 totaled $5.608 billion, up from $3.278 billion in 2003.

34 INSURANCE

Until the 1950s, insurance companies operating in Egypt were mostly branches of foreign institutions. In July 1961, Egypt promulgated laws nationalizing all insurance companies. From 1996, the insurance market was dominated by four public-sector insurance companies (one of which was a re-insurance company), although three private-sector companies existed. Two joint ventures with foreign firms operated in the free zones. The domestic insurance market was closed to foreign companies, although they were able to operate as minority partners in Egypt's eight free zones.

As part of its IMF agreement, the government pushed a new, if still restrictive, insurance law through the People's Assembly in early May 1995. This allowed foreign access to the domestic market on the conditions that the foreign company owned no more than a 49% stake in the insurance company, that the manager of the company was Egyptian, and that the company met the capitalization requirement of $9 million. By 1998, the Egyptian parliament had passed a law allowing 100% ownership by foreign insurance companies, and complete privatization of public-sector insurance companies, but little progress has been made towards these goals. By 1999, there were 12 national insurance companies practicing in Egypt, and by 2003 there was $566 million in direct insurance premiums written, with non-life premiums accounting for $386 million.

Public Finance – Egypt (2009)		
(In millions of pounds, central government figures)		
Revenue and Grants	288,545	100.0%
Tax revenue	163,223	56.6%
Social contributions	…	…
Grants	7,984	2.8%
Other revenue	117,338	40.7%
Expenditures	356,944	100.0%
General public services	73,968	20.7%
Defense	22,531	6.3%
Public order and safety	16,170	4.5%
Economic affairs	23,002	6.4%
Environmental protection	1,259	0.4%
Housing and community amenities	18,200	5.1%
Health	15,783	4.4%
Recreational, culture, and religion	13,807	3.9%
Education	39,880	11.2%
Social protection	132,344	37.1%

(…) data not available or not significant.

SOURCE: *Government Finance Statistics Yearbook 2010*, Washington, DC: International Monetary Fund, 2010.

³⁵PUBLIC FINANCE

In 2010, the budget of Egypt included $46.82 billion in public revenue and $64.19 billion in public expenditures. The budget deficit amounted to 8% of GDP. Public debt was 80.5% of GDP, with $35.03 billion of the debt held by foreign entities.

The IMF reported that in 2002 government outlays by function were as follows: general public services, 35.7%; defense, 10.1%; public order and safety, 5.7%; economic affairs, 9.8%; housing and community amenities, 4.0%; health, 4.9%; recreation, culture, and religion, 9.6%; education, 19.2%; and social protection, 0.9%.

³⁶TAXATION

As of 2005, Egypt's standard corporate tax rate was 40%, although there was a reduced rate of 32% for industrial companies and profits made through export operations. Branches of foreign companies are treated the same as domestic companies. Oil production and prospecting companies are subject to a 40.55% tax on their profits.

Personal income tax is assessed according to a progressive schedule with a top rate of 40%.

The main indirect tax is the general sales tax (GST), set at 10% for most products, and 25% on a few others. Services are taxed at lower rates of 5% and 10%. There are also stamp duties that range from EGP100 to EGP600 ($17 to $100).

³⁷CUSTOMS AND DUTIES

Customs duties in Egypt serve not merely for protection but also for revenue. Under-invoicing is common, prompting customs officials to add 10–30% of invoice value to calculate the true value. In September 2004, Egypt's president issued a decree that reduced administrative fees and tariffs on imported goods. Generally, primary foodstuffs and raw materials were subject to a 2% ad valorem duty, followed by a 5% duty on capital goods, a 12% duty on intermediate goods, a 22% duty on nondurable consumer goods, a 32% duty on nondurable consumer goods, a 32% duty on semi-durable consumer goods, and a 40% duty on durable consumer goods. In addition, customs fees and tariffs on information technology machines, spare parts, and equipment have been reduced. However, items such as alcoholic beverages, tobacco and automobiles with engines larger than 2000 cc are subject to higher rates. Egypt assesses a 2% or 4% service fee on imports (depending on the customs duty assigned to the commodity) and a 5–25% sales tax is added to the final customs value of imports.

Free zones have been established in Alexandria, Cairo (Nasr City), Port Said, Ismailia, Damietta, Safaga, Sohag, and Suez; these are exempt from customs duties.

³⁸FOREIGN INVESTMENT

Egypt has declared that foreign private capital is both desired and welcome and that foreign capital investment has a place in the country's economic development. Investors in approved enterprises are assured of facilities for transfer of profits, withdrawal of capital, and employment of necessary foreign personnel. In 1974, Egypt sought specifically to encourage capital investments from multinational corporations in the West, so new projects financed with foreign capital were protected, capital was freed for re-export within five years of its investment in Egypt, and investment prof-

its earned within Egypt were allowed transfer abroad. In 1991, all foreign exchange transfer restrictions were lifted.

The main laws governing foreign investment are the Capital Market Law of 1992, as amended to increase stock market regulation in 1998; the Investment Incentives and Guarantees Law of 1997, establishing the regime for free trade zones (FTZs); and a series of laws in 1998 setting conditions for private (including foreign) participation in public banks, insurance, maritime transport, electricity distribution, and telecommunications.

Depending on their size, location, and other characteristics, new projects financed with foreign capital are exempt from taxation for five to ten years; in addition, payments of interest on foreign loans are not taxable, and investors are exempt from certain customs duties. To obtain approval, these projects must fall within the fields of industrialization, mining, energy, tourism, transportation, reclamation and cultivation of barren land, or animal husbandry. Applications must be made to the General Authority for Arab Investment and the Free Zones, which consists of the minister of state for Arab and foreign economic cooperation and seven other members. The bidding process for contracts has been made more transparent, but Egyptian bids are preferred up to 15% more than foreign bids. Since 1991, Egypt has liberalized its foreign trade by reducing the number of items on its list of banned imports. In 1990, the list covered 37% of all imports; in 1992, 11%; and in 1999, only apparel was banned. The use of other non-tariff barriers on imports and export restrictions has also been reduced. Bureaucratic barriers, however, still hamper investment. FTZs offer exemption from import duties, sales taxes, and taxes and fees on capital goods. A 1% tax is charged on warehoused goods and on exports from assembly plants. Investments are often located in the free zones of Alexandria, Cairo (Nasr City), Port Said, Ismailia, Damietta, Safaga, Sohag, and Suez. In 2003, to deal with the chronic shortage in foreign exchange, a law was passed requiring that 75% of foreign exchange earnings be converted into local currency.

Foreign direct investment (FDI) in Egypt was a net inflow of $6.71 billion according to World Bank figures published in 2009. FDI represented 3.56% of GDP. As of 2005, FDI stock totaled $15-$20 billion. In terms of portfolio investment, the Egyptian stock market declined nearly 60% in 2001, and did not recover by 2004.

The United Kingdom is Egypt's largest foreign investor, followed by the United States; both countries are very active in investing in the oil and gas sector. Other major investing countries are France, Italy, and Arab countries. A new Ministry of Investment was created in July 2004 to oversee investment policy, coordinating among the various ministries with investment-related areas of responsibility.

³⁹ECONOMIC DEVELOPMENT

At the time of the 1952 revolution, Egypt presented the familiar picture of a dual economy, having a small modern sector developed within a tradition-bound society. A rapidly expanding population was pressing hard on limited agricultural resources, while the nation as a whole faced severe problems of poverty, unemployment, unequal distribution of income and wealth, disease, political corruption, and illiteracy. Rapid industrialization was viewed as essential to economic improvement. The revolution was both a national revolution, Egyptianizing the economy by ridding it of foreign influence, and a social revolution, developing a "democratic, cooperative, socialist" society. The promised "socialism" was not at that time doctrinaire; it was pragmatically selective in its application. A major objective was the diversion of private investment from land into industry. In this earlier period, industrialization also was fostered through government creation and expansion of industrial firms.

In July 1961, in a major policy shift, socialist decrees brought virtually all economic activity under government ownership or control. The Charter for National Action, which elaborated the philosophy of Arab socialism, was approved by the National Congress of Popular Forces on 1 July 1962. It is clear that the Egyptian government had decided that industrialization and improvement of living standards could come only through central planning and direct government ownership and control of virtually the entire system of production and foreign trade.

Egypt inaugurated its first five-year development program in 1960. By the end of 1965, national income had increased in the five-year period by 39.6%; 171,000 new jobs had been created; and wages and salaries had increased by 54%. A second five-year development plan (1966–70) was canceled in 1967 because of the Arab-Israeli war, and annual plans were instituted. Shortly after the 1973 war, President Sadat introduced an "open door" economic development program that confirmed Egypt's socialist policy but decentralized decision making in the public sector, removed government constraints on the private sector, and attracted foreign private capital by liberalizing financial and trade regulations. As a result, most public-sector industries developed rapidly from 1973–79. A five-year development plan (1980–84) was replaced in 1982 by the new plan for 1982–87, of which the public sector was allocated 76.5% of the total funds. Of fixed investments in development projects, the industrial and mining sector was to receive 26%, transport and communications 16%, agriculture 12%, housing 11%, and electric power 8%. By 1987/88–1991/92 investment allocation for the public sector dropped to 62% and to 42% in the 1992/93–1996/97 plan. It aimed at the privatization of several sectors by encouraging the private sector to invest more capital. Egypt at the end of the 1990s was able to attract more foreign investment, cut the inflation rate, and decrease budget deficits.

As of the early 2000s, the state still controlled virtually all heavy industry, although agriculture was in private hands, and has been deregulated with the exception of the cotton and sugar sectors. This and other efforts at privatization have increased the growth of the economy. In 2010, public debt was 80.5% of GDP, and foreign debt amounted to $35.03 billion. A general sales tax was extended to the wholesale and retail levels of business in 2001. Increased spending on infrastructure projects in the early 2000s widened budget deficits once more. In 2003, after a series of currency devaluations, Egypt adopted a floating exchange rate mechanism—the Egyptian pound was no longer pegged to the dollar.

Although such events as the 1997 terrorist attacks at Luxor, the 11 September 2001 terrorist attacks on the United States, and the wars in Afghanistan and Iraq dampened the growth of tourism in Egypt, which experienced below-average growth rates in this sector, tourist arrivals were 10 times higher than global averages over the 2000–03 period and attracted some 25% of tourist arrivals to the Middle East. There were more than six million visitors to Egypt in 2003. This growth in arrivals generated $4.6 billion in tourism receipts, accounting for 22% of total exports of goods and services and 39% of services exports, making tourism the largest foreign currency earner in Egypt. In 2004, tourism was estimated to generate some $6.1 billion in revenue, although terrorist attacks in the Sinai Peninsula in 2004 and 2005 contributed to below-target tourist arrivals.

40 SOCIAL DEVELOPMENT

Employees pay 10–13% of their wages toward old age, disability, and survivor pensions. Retirement is set at age 60. A death grant and a funeral grant are also available. Employed persons aged 18 or older are covered by work injury insurance, except for casual workers, domestic workers, and the self-employed. Unemployment legislation has been in place since 1959 and covers all employed persons in the public and private sectors. It is funded by contributions from employers with deficits covered by the government.

Equality of the sexes is provided by law, but many aspects of law and traditional practice discriminate against women. Under Egyptian law, only males can transmit citizenship to their children or spouses. Women have won employment opportunities in a number of fields, but Egyptian feminists fear these gains will be halted by resurgent Islamic fundamentalism. Muslim female heirs receive half of the amount of a male heir, and Christian widows of Muslims retain no inheritance rights. The government continues its efforts to eradicate the widespread practice of female genital mutilation (FGM). Domestic abuse and violence is common. Because the concept of family integrity supersedes the well-being of the woman, few women seek redress from authorities.

Christian minorities in Egypt are often subject to discrimination and harassment. Extremists have attacked churches and have killed Christians, who also sometimes face discrimination in obtaining higher education and employment. Muslim converts to Christianity have been subject to harassment by police and have been charged under the Penal Code.

Human rights abuses of torture, extrajudicial killings, and prolonged pretrial detentions are on the decline. Arbitrary arrest and detention continue, and prison conditions remain poor. The government restricts freedom of press, assembly, religion, and expression. Islamic extremists also engaged in terrorist attacks, killing civilians. Human rights organizations do not have legal recognition, but they do operate openly.

41 HEALTH

Nearly all Egyptians have access to health care. Between 1982 and 1987 (during the first five-year plan), the government established 14 public and central hospitals, 115 rural health units, and 39 rural hospitals. In 2009 the country spent 4.8% of its GDP on healthcare, amounting to $113 per person. There were 28 physicians, 35 nurses and midwives, and 17 hospital beds per 10,000 inhabitants. An estimated 95% of the population had access to safe drinking water, and 94% had adequate sanitation.

Serious diseases in Egypt include schistosomiasis, malaria, hookworm, trachoma, tuberculosis, dysentery, beriberi, and typhus. Malaria and polio cases were small in number. The incidence of tuberculosis was 27 per 100,000 people in 2007. The CIA calculated HIV/AIDS prevalence in Egypt to be less than 0.1% in 2009. The HIV/AIDS adult prevalence rate was less than 0.1% in 2009. Life expectancy in 2011 was 70 years.

In 2011 the fertility rate was 2.8, while the infant mortality rate was 18 per 1,000 live births. In 2008, the maternal mortality rate, according to the World Bank, was 82 per 100,000 births. An estimated 60% of reproductive-age women practiced contraception in 2007. Abortion is legal only for medical reasons. The maternal mortality rate was 84 per 100,000 births in 2007. In 2007, Egypt vaccinated 98% of children up to one year old against tuberculosis; diphtheria, pertussis, and tetanus; in 2011, it was estimated that 95% of children were vaccinated against measles.

Although illegal since 1997, nearly of all Egyptian women undergo female genital mutilation. In 2007, there was a renewed effort to ban the practice.

42 HOUSING

Prior to 1952, most Egyptians lived in mud huts. Post-revolutionary governments, however, have actively concerned themselves with housing. In order to encourage rural housing activities on unfertile soil, "extension areas" have been allocated for villages. Efforts have been made to provide low-rent housing in towns; the units were constructed in cooperation with the Reconstruction and Popular Dwellings Co., in which the government held a share. Assisted by the state, which grants long-term and low-interest loans, cooperative societies also engage in housing construction. The state affords facilities for cooperatives to acquire land from the religious foundations.

According to the 1996 census, there were about 9.6 million apartments and 4.5 million rural homes throughout the country. About 2.6 million units were built from 1981–1999. There were nearly 400 slum/squatter areas housing over seven million people. In 1998, government subsidies helped build about 63,000 housing units. The new housing demand has been estimated at about 750,000 per year. In 2004, only about 260,000 units were available for sale. About 1.8 million housing units are vacant, partly because tenants cannot afford the cost of rent, but also because rent controls translate into low rents in some areas and landlords feel that the cost of maintenance would be higher than their return.

The government-sponsored National Housing Project, initiated to fulfill one of President Mubarak's campaign promises during the 2005 election, was expected to reach completion as expected by the end of 2011. The project called for the completion of 500,000 housing units. By August 2010, a total of 303,000 housing units had been completed, with an additional 215,000 under construction. Under the National Housing Project, the government sells land to private companies at a discount, under the stipulation that they will build low-income housing. Although the plan initially seemed to have been successful, it did not keep pace with the overall demand for housing, which some have noted to be as high as 360,000 units per year.

43 EDUCATION

The Education Act of 1953 provided free and compulsory education for all children between the ages of 6 and 15. The nine years of basic education are split into six years of primary education and three years of preparatory studies. Secondary schools cover three-year programs in either general or technical studies. Some students opt for five-year advanced technical studies programs in secondary school. The curriculum was updated in 1995 and includes a greater emphasis on vocational training, as well as on physics and foreign languages. The general secondary education certificate entitles the holder to enter a university.

In 2005, about 16% of age-eligible children were enrolled in some type of preschool program. In 2007, the World Bank estimated that 94% of age-eligible children in Egypt were enrolled in primary school. Secondary enrollment for age-eligible children stood at 71%. Tertiary enrollment was estimated at 28%. It is estimated that about 97.5% of all students complete their primary education. The student-to-teacher ratio for primary school was at about 26:1 in 2005; the ratio for secondary school was about 17:1.

A decree of 23 July 1962 provided free tuition at all Egyptian universities, which total 13 universities, and numerous institutes of higher learning. The traditional center for religious education in the Muslim world is Al-Azhar in Cairo, which in 1983 celebrated 1,000 years of teaching as the oldest continuously operating school in the world. Al-Azhar offers instruction in three faculties and 14 affiliated institutes and maintains its own primary and secondary schools.

There is also the American University in Cairo, which offers a wide range of undergraduate and graduate courses, as well as an American school in Cairo and one in Alexandria. The American Research Center in Cairo is supported by US universities and museums. It was established in 1948 to encourage the exchange of archaeologists and other researchers in almost all fields of interest.

Adult education, under the Ministry of Education, is increasingly important. Since 1993, the government has conducted a campaign against illiteracy. Business firms are required to combat illiteracy among their employees. Recent university graduates are being hired to lead literacy classes, and armed forces recruits are also expected to teach. In addition, the government has set up 3,000 one-class schools to teach a nontraditional study plan. These schools are aimed at girls who are unlikely to attend formal schooling, and as a result, are likely to remain illiterate. The schools provide vocational training and lessons on income generating businesses, in addition to the more traditional classes in Arabic, religion, sciences and arithmetic. In 2005, about 34% of the tertiary age population were enrolled in some type of higher education program. Overall, the CIA estimated in 2007 that Egypt had a literacy rate of 71.4%. Public expenditure on education represented 3.8% of GDP.

44 LIBRARIES AND MUSEUMS

In 2003, the Bibliotheca Alexandria was established on the site of the ancient library destroyed in a fire 2,000 years before. Bibliotheca Alexandria is the largest library in the Middle East and serves as a cultural center with exhibit areas, a planetarium, and a conference center. Egypt's other major libraries are the Egyptian National Library (2.5 million volumes), Alexandria University Library (with 15 collections, of which the largest, belonging to the Faculty of Arts, numbers 141,300 volumes), and the Cairo University Library (more than 1.4 million volumes). The National Library also functions as the main public library for the nation's capital and supervises 11 branch libraries located throughout the country. The Municipal Library in Alexandria contains one of the country's largest public library collections, with 23,390 Arabic and 35,400 European volumes.

One of the most important special libraries is the Scientific and Technical Documentation Division of the National Research Center at Cairo, which has the best collection of scientific and technical material in the Arab world. American University in Cairo sponsors a library system of nearly 400,000 volumes (primarily English language) and holds the Creswell Collection of Islamic art and architecture, comprising about 3,200 bound volumes. In all, Egyptian libraries affiliated with institutions of higher education hold over 35 million volumes. Assuit University sponsors 16 libraries with an approximate total of 177,274 Arabic volumes and 167,120 foreign books, as well as hundreds of periodicals.

The Egyptian National Museum, founded in 1902, contains unique exhibits from prehistoric times up to the 3rd century AD, and it also has a notable Department of Antiquities, established in 1835, which supervises excavations and administers archaeological museums. There are many specialized museums, including the Coptic Museum, devoted to the history of the old Christian Monophysites; the Museum of Islamic Art; the Greco-Roman Museum; the Agricultural Museum; the State Museum of Modern Art; the Islamic Archaeological Museum; the Railway Museum; and the Cotton Museum. There is a museum dedicated exclusively to the work of Mohmoud Mokhtar in Cairo. Several former royal palaces have been transformed into museums: the Al-Gawhara Palace in Cairo (a converted 19th century Ottoman palace), Ras at-Tin Palace in Alexandria, and Al-Montazah Palace in Montazah-Alexandria.

45 MEDIA

Telephone, telegraph, radio, and television services are operated by the state-owned Telecommunication Organization. Egypt operates a large and generally modern telecommunications system, which includes Internet and cellular services. Domestic service is provided through coaxial cable and microwave radio relay; international services are provided by five coaxial submarine cables, four satellite ground stations, tropospheric scatter radio, and microwave radio relay systems. In 2009, the CIA reported that there were 10.3 million telephone landlines in Egypt. In addition to landlines, mobile phone subscriptions averaged 67 per 100 people, with 55.3 million mobile cellular phones in use. There were 42 FM radio stations, 14 AM radio stations, and 3 shortwave radio stations. Internet users numbered 20 per 100 citizens. In 2010 the country had 187,197 Internet hosts.

As of 1999, 42 television stations operated in Egypt, broadcasting mostly in Arabic. In 2003, there were an estimated 339 radios and 229 television sets for every 1,000 people. Prominent newspapers in 2010, with circulation numbers listed parenthetically, included *Al Ahram* (900,000), *Al Akhbar* (780,000), *Al Goumhouriya* (900,000), and *Al Missa'* (405,000). There is also an English language newspaper, the *Egyptian Gazette* (40,000). *Arev* is a daily Armenian paper. There are two weekly Greek publications, *Phos* (20,000) and *Tachydromos-Egyptos* (2,000). *Le Journal D'Egypte* (weekly, 72,000) and *La Reforme* (daily) are the leading French publications.

On 23 May 1960, all Egyptian newspapers were nationalized and subjected to censorship. President Sadat ended formal press censorship in 1974, but the following year he set up a government council to supervise the newspapers. In 1981, President Mubarak revoked the ban on opposition newspapers, but the press remains sensitive to the wishes of the government. The Middle East News Agency is under the supervision of the information section of the Ministry of National Guidance. The constitution does provide for freedom of speech and press, though the government exercises control through media ownership, oversight, and a monopoly on resources such as newsprint.

In December 2009, the nation launched what is regarded as one of the largest digital archive projects in the world. The digital documentation of the National Archives of Egypt began in 2005 through the collaboration of the Ministry of Culture and the Ministry of Communications and Information Technology, with major technical support from IBM. The result is a digital archive of more than five million records representing more than 90 million documents, most of which is in the Arabic language. A major goal of the project was to increase the Arabic content of the Internet, while also providing a more efficient way to access the national archives. The project created 2,000 government jobs.

46 ORGANIZATIONS

Most organizations in Egypt serve occupational and professional (particularly agricultural) goals. The land reform law makes it compulsory for landholders who have obtained land under it to join cooperative societies (such as the Egyptian Seed Association) to help supply them with tested seeds, tools if available, and possibly markets. Several multinational organizations are based in Egypt, including the African Farmers Association and the Arab Labor Organization. The International Labour Organization has an office in Cairo. There are many chambers of commerce, representing various cities and various economic groups. The Federation of Egyptian Chambers of Commerce is in Cairo.

There are scholastic, archaeological, accounting, economic, historical, and other learned organizations. A national Academy of Scientific Research and Technology was established in 1971. The Egyptian Medical Association promotes research and education on health issues and works to establish common policies and standards in healthcare. There are also several associations dedicated to research and education for specific fields of medicine and particular diseases and conditions.

Egypt serves as a multinational center for many sports organizations, including Arab federations for boxing, fishing, basketball, judo, gymnastics, and fencing, to name a few. Many youth organizations are affiliated with religious institutions. Scouting programs are active, as are chapters of the YMCA/YWCA. The Egyptian Association of Women promotes higher education and professional training for women.

The multinational Arab Organization for Human Rights is based in Cairo. There are national chapters of the Red Crescent Society, CARE, the Society of Saint Vincent de Paul, UNICEF, and Caritas.

47 TOURISM, TRAVEL, AND RECREATION

Passports and visas are required of tourists. Visitors arriving from most African, American, and Caribbean countries need either a certificate of vaccinations against yellow fever or a location certificate from the Sudanese government stating that they have not been in southern Sudan within the previous six days.

Tourism has been a major foreign exchange earner, having grown steadily after the end of the Iran–Iraq war. The *Tourism Factbook*, published by the UN World Tourism Organization, reported 12.5 million incoming tourists to Egypt in 2009, who spent a total of $11.8 billion. Of those incoming tourists, 9.4 million came from Europe. 429,066 hotel beds were available in Egypt. The estimated daily cost to visit Cairo, the capital, was $267. The cost of visiting other cities averaged $133. Principal tourist attractions include the pyramids and Great Sphinx at Giza, the Abu Simbel temples south of Aswan, the Valley of the Kings at Luxor, and the Muhammad Ali Mosque in Cairo. Rides are available on *fellucas*, traditional sailing boats of the Nile.

Popular pastimes among Egyptians include card playing, movie-going, and sports such as football (soccer), swimming, tennis, and horse racing.

48 FAMOUS PERSONS

Egypt's first recorded ruler, or pharaoh, was Menes (or Narmer, fl. 3100? BC), who united the southern and northern kingdoms and founded the capital at Memphis. Notable successor pharaohs included Cheops (Khufu, fl. 26th cent. BC), who built the Great Pyramid at Giza; Thutmose III (r. 1504?–1450 BC), who greatly extended the empire through conquest; Amenhotep III (r. 1417–1379 BC), who ruled at the summit of ancient Egyptian civilization and built extensive monuments; his son Amenhotep IV (Akhenaten, r. 1379–1362 BC), who, with his queen, Nefertiti, instituted a brief period of monotheism; and Tutankhamen (r. 1361–1352 BC), whose tomb containing valuable treasures was found practically intact in 1922. Cleopatra VII (69–30 BC) was involved in the political conflicts of the Romans.

Philo Judaeus (13? BC–AD 50?) attempted to combine Greek philosophy with Judaism. Ptolemy (Claudius Ptolemaeus, fl. 2nd century AD) was the foremost astronomer of ancient times. Egyptian-born Plotinus (AD 205?–270) was a neoplatonic philosopher in Rome. Sts. Antony and Pachomius popularized Christian hermit and monasterial monasticism respectively in the 4th cent. AD. In the same century, Athanasius, patriarch of Alexandria, combated Arianism and established the biblical canon that the Protestant church would adopt.

The most notable of Egypt's rulers under the Muslim caliphate was Saladin (Salah ad-Din, 1138–1193), sultan of Egypt and Syria and founder of the Ayyubid dynasty. Muhammad 'Ali (1769–1849), of Albanian origin, is generally regarded as the founder of modern Egypt, having exercised effective control of the nation under nominal Ottoman authority; he established the dynasty that ended with the deposition of Faruk in 1952. 'Arabi Pasha (Ahmad 'Arabi, 1841?–1911) led a popular uprising against British intervention in 1882 but was defeated. Later, Sa'ad Zaghlul Pasha (1860?–1927), a founder of the Nationalist Party Wafd waged a fiery political fight against British rule.

No one had greater influence on Egypt during the 1950s and 1960s than Gamal Abdel Nasser (Jamal 'Abd al-Nasir, 1918–1970), the moving spirit of the army's revolt against the monarchy in 1952. As prime minister (1954–56) and president (1956–70), Nasser set Egypt on its socialist course and attempted to unify the Arab world through confederation. His successor as president,

Anwar al-Sadat (as-Sadat, 1918–1981), continued Nasser's policies but with important modifications, especially in relation to Israel and the United States; with Menachem Begin, he shared the Nobel Peace Prize in 1978 and negotiated the Egypt-Israel Peace Treaty of 1979. Upon Sadat's assassination in 1981, former air force chief of staff (1969–72) and vice-president (1975–81) Muhammad Hosni (Husni) Mubarak (b. 1928) became president of Egypt. Mohamed El Baradei (b. 1942) is the Director General of the International Atomic Energy Agency (IAEA). El Baradei and the IAEA were jointly awarded the Nobel Peace Prize in 2005.

The poet Sami al-Barudi (1839–1904) wrote popular and highly regarded verses about Islam's heroic early age. 'Abbas al-Aqqad (1889–1964) has been called the greatest contemporary Arab poet and the most original Arab writer. Involved in a political plot, he was jailed and composed an Arab "De Profundis" about his life in prison. Taha Husayn (1889–1973), the most widely known modern Egyptian intellectual leader, was minister of education from 1950 to 1952. The poet and essayist Malak Hifni Nasif (1886–1918) sought an improvement in the status of women. Ahmad Zaki Abu Shadi (1892–1955) was a renowned poet, essayist, and dramatist. Mahmud Taymur (1894–1973), a leading dramatist, wrote popular social satires and comedies. Um Kalthum (Fatma al-Zahraa Ibrahim, 1898?–1975) was the most famous singer of the Arab world. Mohammed Hassanein Heikal (b. 1923), journalist and author, was the outspoken editor of the influential newspaper *Al-Ahram* (1957–74) until he was forced by the government to resign. In 1988, Naguib Mahfouz (1912–2006) won the Nobel Prize for Literature. Ahmed Hassan Zewail (b. 1946) is an Egyptian-American chemist, and the winner of the 1999 Nobel Prize in chemistry for his work on femtochemistry.

49 DEPENDENCIES

Egypt has no territories or colonies.

50 BIBLIOGRAPHY

Asante, Molefi K. *Culture and Customs of Egypt*. Westport, CT: Greenwood Press, 2002.

Brier, Bob, and A. H. Hobbs. *Daily Life of the Ancient Egyptians*. 2nd ed. Westport, CT: Greenwood Press, 2008.

Bunson, Margaret. *Encyclopedia of Ancient Egypt*. New York: Facts on File, 2002.

Egypt Investment and Business Guide: Strategic and Practical Information. Washington, DC: International Business Publications USA, 2012.

Goldschmidt, Arthur. *Historical Dictionary of Egypt*. 3rd ed. Lanham, MD: Scarecrow, 2003.

McGregor, Andrew J. *A Military History of Modern Egypt: From the Ottoman Conquest to the Ramadan War*. Westport, CT: Praeger Security International, 2006.

Sullivan, Denis J, and Kimberly A. Jones. *Egypt: A Reference Handbook*. Westport, CT: Praeger Security International, 2008.

Supples, Kevin. *Egypt*. Washington, DC: National Geographic Society, 2002.

Zeilig, Leo, and David Seddon. *A Political and Economic Dictionary of Africa*. Philadelphia: Routledge/Taylor and Francis, 2005.

Zuehlke, Jeffrey. *Egypt in Pictures*. Minneapolis: Lerner, 2003.

EQUATORIAL GUINEA

Republic of Equatorial Guinea
República de Guinea Ecuatorial

CAPITAL: Malabo

FLAG: The flag is a tricolor of green, white, and red horizontal stripes; a blue triangle joins them at the hoist. The arms in the center of the white stripe hold a cotton tree (the national symbol), six stars—one for each physical division of the country—and the motto "Unidad, Justicia, Paz."

ANTHEM: *Caminemos pisando la senda (Let Us Tread the Path).*

MONETARY UNIT: Communauté Financière Africaine franc (XAF), which was originally pegged to the French franc, has been pegged to the euro since January 1999 with a rate of XAF655.957 to 1 euro. There are coins of 1, 2, 5, 10, 25, 50, 100, and 500 francs and notes of 50, 100, 500, 1,000, 5,000, and 10,000 francs. XAF1 = US$0.00196 (or US$1 = XAF491.559) as of April 2012.

WEIGHTS AND MEASURES: The metric system is the legal standard.

HOLIDAYS: New Year's Day, 1 January; Independence Day, 5 March; Labor Day, 1 May; Organisation of African Unity Day, 25 May; President's Birthday, 5 June; Armed Forces Day, 3 August; Human Rights Day, 10 December; Christmas, 25 December. Movable Christian holidays include Good Friday and Easter Monday.

TIME: 1 p.m. = noon GMT.

¹LOCATION, SIZE, AND EXTENT

Located on the west coast of Africa, Equatorial Guinea consists of a mainland enclave, Río Muni, and five inhabited islands: Bioko (between 1973 and 1979, Macías Nguema Biyogo, and before that Fernando Póo), Annobón (Pagalu during the 1970s), Corisco, Elobey Chico, and Elobey Grande. The total area is 28,051 sq km (10,831 sq mi), of which Río Muni, along with Corisco and the Elobeys, accounts for 26,017 sq km (10,045 sq mi) and Bioko, along with Annobón, 2,034 sq km (785 sq mi). Comparatively, Equatorial Guinea is slightly larger than the state of Maryland.

Río Muni is bounded on the N by Cameroon, on the E and S by Gabon, and on the W by the Gulf of Guinea (Atlantic Ocean), with a length of 248 km (154 mi) ENE–WSW and 167 km (104 mi) SSE–NNW. Bioko, situated 56 km (35 mi) W of Cameroon and about 259 km (161 mi) NW of Río Muni, extends 74 km (46 mi) NE–SW and 37 km (23 mi) SE–NW. Annobón is 686 km (426 mi) SW of Bioko; Corisco and the Elobeys are off the SW coast of Bioko, within sight of Gabon. The total boundary length of Equatorial Guinea is 835 km (519 mi), of which 296 km (183 mi) is coastline.

The capital city of Equatorial Guinea, Malabo, is located on the island of Bioko (Isla de Bioko).

²TOPOGRAPHY

Bioko and Annobón are volcanic islands that are part of the chain starting with the Cameroon Highlands and outcropping into the Atlantic as far as St. Helena. Río Muni is a fluvial mainland plateau, except for the sandy shore and the ridges of the Sierra Cristal range that separate the coast from the interior plateau. The Muni and Ntem rivers, on the south and north boundaries of Río Muni,

are estuaries navigable for about 20 km (12 mi); the Mbini River, midway between them, is typical of the cascading streams that drain all of Río Muni. Bioko has short cascading streams; Annobón has only storm arroyos. Most of the country, including the islands, is tropical rain forest. On Annobón, volcanic deposits restrict agriculture, and the Muni estuarial islands are sandy, but the rest of the country has tropical humus conducive to agriculture.

³CLIMATE

Equatorial Guinea has a tropical climate with distinct wet and dry seasons. From June to August, Río Muni is dry and Bioko wet; from December to February, the reverse exists. In between there is gradual transition. Rain or mist occurs daily on Annobón, where a cloudless day has never been registered. The temperature at Malabo, Bioko, ranges from 16°C to 33°C (61–91°F), though on the southern Moka Plateau normal high temperatures are only 21°C (70°F). In Río Muni, the average temperature is about 27°C (80°F). Annual rainfall varies from 193 cm (76 in) at Malabo to 1,092 cm (430 in) at Ureka, Bioko, but Río Muni is somewhat drier.

⁴FLORA AND FAUNA

The World Resources Institute estimates that there are 3,250 plant species in Equatorial Guinea. In addition, Equatorial Guinea is home to 153 mammal, 418 bird, 92 reptile, and 31 amphibian species. The calculation reflects the total number of distinct species residing in the country, not the number of endemic species.

The most common species of trees include palms and hardwoods. Yams and bananas were introduced by the early inhabitants and became staples. Monkeys, chimpanzees, elephants, and gray doves are common.

5 ENVIRONMENT

The World Resources Institute reported that Equatorial Guinea had designated 455,000 hectares (1.12 million acres) of land for protection as of 2006. Water resources totaled 26 cu km (6.24 cu mi) while water usage was 0.11 cu km (0.026 cu mi) per year. Domestic water usage accounted for 83% of total usage, industrial for 16%, and agricultural for 1%. Per capita water usage totaled 220 cu m (7,769 cu ft) per year.

The UN reported in 2008 that carbon dioxide emissions in Equatorial Guinea totaled 4,793 kilotons.

Equatorial Guinea's most significant environmental problems are deforestation, water pollution, desertification, and the preservation of wildlife. The forests are threatened by agricultural expansion, fires, and grazing. There are three Ramsar wetland sites in the country.

According to a 2011 report issued by the International Union for Conservation of Nature and Natural Resources (IUCN), the number of threatened species included 19 mammals, 5 birds, 5 reptiles, 4 amphibians, 29 fish, and 68 species of plants. Endangered species include the drill (Papio leucophaeus), seven species of monkeys, including Preuss's monkey, two species of bush babies, and the green sea turtle, hawksbill turtle, and olive ridley turtle.

6 POPULATION

The US Central Intelligence Agency (CIA) estimates the population of Equatorial Guinea in 2012 to be approximately 685,991, which placed it at number 166 in population among the 196 nations of the world. In 2011, approximately 4.1% of the population was over 65 years of age, with another 41.5% under 15 years of age. The median age in Equatorial Guinea was 19.1 years. There were 0.99 males for every female in the country. The population's annual rate of change was 2.607%. The projected population for the year 2025 was 970,000. Population density in Equatorial Guinea was calculated at 24 people per sq km (62 people per sq mi).

The UN estimated that 40% of the population lived in urban areas, and that urban populations had an annual rate of change of 3.1%. The largest urban area was Malabo, with a population of 128,000.

7 MIGRATION

Estimates of Equatorial Guinea's net migration rate, carried out by the CIA in 2011, amounted to zero. The total number of emigrants living abroad was 103,100, and the total number of immigrants living in Equatorial Guinea was 7,400. As many as 45,000 Nigerian laborers served in Equatorial Guinea in the early 1970s, mostly working on Bioko cocoa plantations. In 1975, Nigeria began evacuating those contract laborers, charging the Equatorial Guinean government with a long history of mistreating them.

Migration to Spain is a traditional and ongoing occurrence. Between 80–90% of Equatorial Guinean nationals who go to Spain do not return.

8 ETHNIC GROUPS

The largest single tribe is the Fang (Fon, or Pamúe), who entered Río Muni from the east largely between 1687 and 1926. The earlier Riomunians, who had probably arrived in the 14th century, were forced by the Fang to flee to the coast. The Bubi on Bioko are descendants of the indigenous African Bantu-speaking population that fled from the Cameroonian and Riomunian mainland in the 13th century; they are indigenous to Bioko island. Coastal tribes, sometimes referred to as Playeros, consist of Ndowes, Bujebas, Balengues, and Bengas. Fernandinos—descendants of mainland slaves liberated by the British navy in the 19th century—and Europeans, especially Spanish Asturians and Catalonians, have long dominated commerce and government. It is estimated that the 67 Fang clans represent more than 85% of the population. Europeans, mostly Spanish, number less than 1,000.

9 LANGUAGES

Spanish is the official language of the government, commerce, and schools. French is also an official language. The principal vernacular is Fang, which, like all the country's indigenous languages, is a Bantu tongue. Bubi and Ibo are also spoken. Annobón uses the fãd'Ambô, a pidgin form of Bantu speech with heavy 16th-century Portuguese inflection. Much petty commerce is conducted in pidgin English (Pichinglis).

10 RELIGIONS

Although African traditional religion has left its vestiges among the indigenous tribes, about 93% of the population is Christian. Within the Christian population, 87% are Roman Catholic and about 6% are Protestant, primarily Baptist and Episcopalian. About 5% of the population practice indigenous beliefs exclusively, but it has been reported that many Catholics include indigenous elements in their faith practice as well. There are small communities of Muslims, Baha'is, and other religious groups. Though there is no state religion, a 1992 law established an official preference for the Roman Catholic Church and the Reform Church of Equatorial Guinea, based on the traditional importance of these two denominations in popular culture. Other religious groups must register through the Ministry of Justice and Worship. Good Friday, Corpus Christi, Immaculate Conception, and Christmas Day are observed as national holidays.

11 TRANSPORTATION

The CIA reports that Equatorial Guinea has a total of 2,880 km (1,790 mi) of roads. There are seven airports.

The chief ports are Bata and Mbini in Río Muni and Malabo and Luba on Bioko. Bata, modernized in the 1970s, can accommodate up to four vessels of 20,000 tons each. There is regular service between Malabo and Bata. In 2010, the country had four merchant ships of 1,000 gross registered tons or more.

Bata's airport was the first major air transport facility. Malabo's airport was raised to jet standards in 1964 and became the focus of regional air services. A landing strip was built on Annobón in 1968. As of 2010 six of the seven airports had paved runways. Air transport between Bata, Malabo, and Douala, Cameroon, is provided by Equatorial Guinea Air Lines (Algesa). There is international air service to Gabon, Nigeria, Morocco, and Spain.

12 HISTORY

Although numerous archaeological discoveries indicate a very early Sangoan (modified Acheulean) culture throughout Equatorial Guinea, the earliest traceable inhabitants were Pygmies, remnants

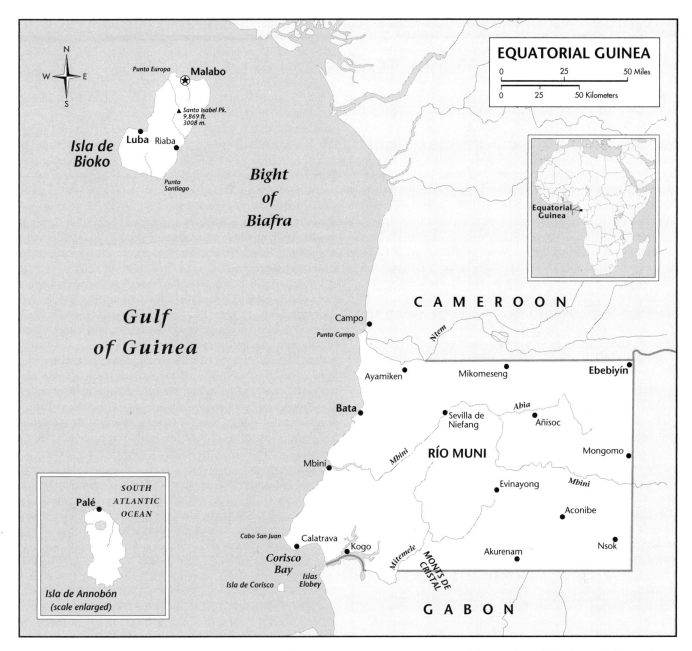

EQUATORIAL GUINEA

LOCATION: 1°1′ to 3°48′N; 8°26′ to 11°20′ E Annobón at 1°25′ S and 5°36′ E. BOUNDARY LENGTHS: Cameroon, 189 kilometers (118 miles); Gabon, 350 kilometers (218 miles); total coastline, 296 kilometers (183 miles). TERRITORIAL SEA LIMIT: 12 miles.

of whom remain in northeastern Río Muni. Bioko was apparently uninhabited when the Bubi came by sea from the mainland in the 13th century. Río Muni seems to have been occupied by the Bantu in a series of waves that superseded the Pygmies—first by the Bubi, before 1200; then by the Benga, Bujeba, and Combe, perhaps about 1300; and, finally, by the Fang from the Congo Basin, after 1687. Although Annobón was uninhabited in 1471 when the Portuguese discovered it, it was the only one of the territories later incorporated into Equatorial Guinea that they attempted to develop. The proprietorship of Annobón was ill administered, however, and it was virtually self-governing for 250 years. In 1778, Portugal transferred its nominal claims over Annobón, Fernando Póo, and the entire coast from the Niger Delta to Cape López (in modern Gabon) to Spain, in return for Spain's renunciation of pirate claims

in southern Brazil. Later that year, a Spanish expedition of occupation arrived from South America. The expedition withdrew in 1781 after disease and poor administration had cost the lives of 370 of the 547 Spaniards.

The primary Spanish mainland explorations were undertaken between 1875 and 1885. Catholic missionary efforts by the Claretians extended Spanish influence to Annobón (1884), completed the exploration of Fernando Póo (1883–1924), and began the penetration of Río Muni (1886–1925). The first effective efforts to penetrate the interior were undertaken in 1926–27 by Governor Ángel Barrera, who reportedly employed considerable force to subjugate the Fang. The administrative procedure for the colony was defined as the process of *reducción* (conquest), *repartimiento* (resettlement), and *encomienda* (placing in trust) of the indigenous people—the policy followed in Mexico and Peru 400 years earlier—but this time, the people were *encomendado* (entrusted) not to private masters but to the Claretians. After World War II (1935–45), the Franco government initiated a policy of heavy investment to turn Spanish Guinea into a model colony.

Spanish Guinea became a province of Spain in 1958. In 1964, two provinces (Fernando Póo and Río Muni) were created under an autonomous regional government. Political opposition and Protestant missions, both banned in Spain, were tolerated, and the regional regime of Bonifacio Ondó Edú was virtually self-governing internally. In 1966, independence was promised. Two years later, an opposition faction under Francisco Macías Nguema won the preindependence elections and organized a sovereign government on 12 October 1968, when the colony became the independent Republic of Equatorial Guinea. Within six months, hostility between Riomunians and Fernandinos had sharpened. The continued presence of Spanish civil servants, troops, and ships and the unchanged influence of Spanish plantation management provoked a crisis in 1969. Two coups failed, the Spanish were evacuated, medical services were suspended (until the World Health Organization restaffed them), and fiscal transactions ceased. However, within six weeks a new understanding was reached with Spain, under UN auspices, and Spanish subsidies were restored.

On 23 August 1972, Francisco Macías Nguema was proclaimed president for life; subsequently he assumed ministerial posts of defense, foreign affairs, and trade. In December 1974 an exile group, the Equatorial Guinean Liberation Front, and others charged that more than two-thirds of the National Assembly elected in 1968 had disappeared, and that many prominent persons, especially political opponents of the president, had been assassinated. It was estimated that a quarter of the country's population was in exile in Cameroon, Gabon, and Europe. On 3 August 1979, Macías Nguema was overthrown in a military coup led by his Spanish-trained nephew, Lt.-Col. Teodoro Obiang Nguema Mbasogo; the former president was tried shortly after the coup and executed on 29 September. International human rights organizations estimated that during his 11-year rule at least 50,000 people had been killed and 40,000 had been enslaved on state-owned plantations.

Under Obiang's leadership, the Supreme Military Council became the highest power in the country. The country continued to decay as corruption flourished and political opponents and others were imprisoned or put to death. Soviet influence was reduced, and economic and military cooperation with Spain was restored. A new constitution, approved in a referendum on 15 August 1982, provided that Obiang would remain head of state until 1989, when direct popular elections would take place. Parliamentary elections (based on a single list, with no political parties permitted) were held on 28 August 1983, and the PDGE won all 41 seats in the Chamber of People's Representatives in 10 July 1988 elections. Obiang was elected without opposition on 25 June 1989.

On 17 November 1991, a new constitution was adopted. Opposition parties began to be organized and sought official recognition in 1992. Eventually an election was held on 21 November 1993 and the PDGE won 68 of 80 seats. But the major opposition parties boycotted the election, and as many as 80% of the eligible voters refused to participate. The new cabinet was expanded from 34 to 42 members. On 25 February 1996, Obiang was reelected to the presidency for another seven-year term, receiving 98% of the vote. The poll was declared farcical by foreign observers. Despite a boycott of the elections by the three main opposition parties, voter turnout was 86%. Obiang's plan to form a government of national unity failed because the opposition's conditions for participation had not been met.

New wealth from substantial oil and gas reserves discovered off the coast in 1996 boosted the tiny country's impoverished economy, but the wealth did not reach the poor. Government corruption and mismanagement were rampant ,and some 80% of the wealth was amassed by less than 5% of the population, mostly Obiang's family clan. Growing discontent resulted in at least two coups d'état (the government attributed one in May 1997 to opposition Progress Party leader, Severo Moto) and a rebellion on Bioko island by members of the disenfranchised Bubi ethnic group in January 1998. A military court sentenced 15 of the 215 Bubi activists to death. In September Obiang suspended the sentence, under international pressure.

The ruling PDGE won 65 of the 80 seats in the second multiparty parliamentary elections held on 7 March 1999. In July 1999, the prime minister, Angel Serafin Seriche Dougan, and his government resigned, apparently to pave way for a government of national unity. The president offered to give a cabinet position to each of the opposition parties. Second multiparty legislative elections were held on 7 March 1999. Mainstream opposition parties participated in the elections, but along with the international community, denounced the elections for serious irregularities. The ruling PDGE won 75 of the 80 seats. (By 2004 the legislature had been increased to 100 seats.) The Convergence for a Social Democracy (CPDS) and the People's Union (UP) respectively got one and four seats.

In elections held 15 December 2002, Obiang officially was reelected with 97.1% to 2.2% of the vote for Celestino Bonifacio Bacale, but as in the past, the elections were marred by fraud, and held little credibility either domestically or abroad.

The judiciary, which often has come under international scrutiny, scheduled a national conference in January 2003. The purpose of the meeting was to improve human rights and strengthen the rule of law following criticism by rights groups, the opposition, and the Spanish government of the sentencing of 68 opposition activists for between six and 20 years in jail on charges of plotting to overthrow the president. Among those convicted were the leaders of three opposition parties. In August 2003, 31 of the condemned prisoners received amnesty. In elections held in April 2004, the PDGE and its allies won 98 of 100 seats and all but 7 of 244 municipal posts, but the results were judged not credible by international observers.

Political opponents twice attempted to overthrow the government in 2004. In March, Zimbabwean police impounded a plane originating from South Africa with 64 mercenaries on board destined for Equatorial Guinea. Simon Mann, the president of Executive Outcomes and the apparent ringleader, was sentenced to seven years in jail in Zimbabwe for trying to buy arms. In all, 22 people were convicted, including 9 tried in absentia. Allegedly backing the operation were Sir Mark Thatcher, son of Margaret Thatcher, Severo Moto, an Equatorial Guinean politician in exile in Spain, and the Spanish government. In October 2004, the military staged an abortive coup leading to the conviction of 23 soldiers.

Equatorial Guinea ranked 152 out of 159 countries on *Transparency International's Corruption Perceptions Index 2005*, with almost none of the economic benefits from the oil windfall trickling down to the average Equatorial Guinean. The judiciary was widely considered corrupt and dysfunctional. Further, Obiang's health appeared to be failing, and were he not to finish his third term, or not to seek a fourth term in 2009, his eldest son, commonly referred to as Theodorín, would be his heir apparent. Teodoro Nguema Obiang Mangue was also forestry minister, but was at odds with influential family members and factions within the elite.

In August 2006, the government resigned en masse. Obiang had accused the administration of corruption and poor leadership. A new prime minister, Ricardo Mangue, was named.

In February 2009, militants from the Niger delta region of Nigeria launched an unsuccessful coup attempt on the government of Equatorial Guinea in which fifteen attackers were arrested. While officials in Equatorial Guinea immediately accused the Movement of the Emancipation of the Niger Delta (MEND) as the responsible party, a spokesperson for the MEND denied the group's involvement in the attacks. MEND is just one of the insurgent groups fighting for a greater share of the country's oil wealth.

Though the next presidential elections were originally scheduled for 2010, in October 2009 Obiang announced that an early election would be held on 29 November of that year. The move was immediately condemned by some as being too soon for opposing candidates to initiate a campaign. As expected, Obiang was reelected with 95.8% of the vote.

In 2011 the government announced that it was creating a new capital city, named Djibloho. The proposed capital was to be located between Bata and Mongomo and was estimated to support 160,000 inhabitants.

13 GOVERNMENT

By referendum on 11 August 1968, Equatorial Guineans approved a constitution that became effective on Independence Day, 12 October 1968. The constitution required the country to join the UN and to coordinate Spanish financial, technical, and administrative assistance until total "Africanization" was achieved. Separatist activities on Bioko led to the suspension of the 1968 constitution in May 1971. The president assumed all powers and ruled by decree until a second constitution was approved by referendum in July 1973. Under this constitution, the only legal party, the United National Workers Party, designated deputies to the National Assembly and had the power to remove them. An article requiring election of the president by direct, secret, universal suffrage was suspended for President Francisco Macías Nguema, who had been proclaimed president for life on 23 August 1972. After the 1979 coup, a new constitution was drafted with UN assistance. Approved by 95% of the voters in a referendum on 15 August 1982, this document provided for elections every five years to a National Assembly, for the establishment of a Council of State, and for laws pertaining to human rights, which in practice are poorly defended under the law.

Since adopting the 17 November 1991 constitution, Equatorial Guinea has been a self-declared constitutional democracy with judicial integrity and multiparty elections. In reality, President Obiang Nguema runs the country with an iron fist, and his Democratic Party of Equatorial Guinea (PDGE) has no serious opposition. Lt.-Col. Obiang Nguema was inaugurated president on 12 October 1982, ran unopposed in 1989, and was reelected in 1996, 2002, and in 2009. Obiang appoints a prime minister, who nominally is head of government. A unicameral House of People's Representatives or Camara de Representants del Pueblo with 100 seats performs little or no check on the powerful executive. Members directly elected by popular vote serve five-year terms. The constitution was modified in 1995.

The legal system is a mix of customary law and civil law. Equatorial Guinea does not participate in any international law organizations.

14 POLITICAL PARTIES

Other than the ruling Partido Democrático de Guinea Ecuatorial (PDGE), there are 12 other registered parties. However, given the dominance of the PDGE, the system functions like a one-party state.

Following an abortive coup in March 1969, all existing political parties were merged into the United National Party (Partido Único Nacional) under the leadership of President Macías Nguema. Political activity outside this party was made illegal. The name of the party was later modified to United National Workers Party (Partido Único Nacional de los Trabajadores—PUNT). After the 1979 coup, all political parties were banned, and the ruling Democratic Party for Equatorial Guinea (PDGE) monopolized power and patronage. Among the opposition parties in exile in the mid-1980s were the National Alliance for the Restoration of Democracy and the Democratic Movement for the Liberation of Equatorial Guinea. A source of opposition is resentment by Biokans of mainland domination.

The 1991 constitution legalized political parties. and a January 1992 law on party formation initiated the process of party organization. However, it restricted party membership and activity to those who had lived continuously in Equatorial Guinea for 10 years. Since most opposition politicians had been in exile since independence, the effect was to prohibit serious opposition. Small parties—the Liberal Democrat Convention, the Popular Union, and the Progressive Democratic Alliance—were recognized in 1992. The Equatorial Guinea Progress Party (PPGE) was legalized after a long delay and, in 1993, the Socialist Party of Equatorial Guinea (PSGE) was approved. By mid-1993, 13 legal opposition parties stood prepared to contest elections, scheduled for 12 September. A number of opposition leaders were even granted amnesty. In 1995, the government reduced the residency requirement for politicians to five years leading up to an election. Political parties, however, continued to face harassment as of 2006.

In June 1997 the Progress Party, perhaps the only party that could constitute an alternative government, was banned by presidential decree. The government accused journalist Severo Moto, leader of the Progress Party, of plotting a coup against Obiang, by linking him to arms intercepted by Angolan authorities on a Russian boat destined for Equatorial Guinea in mid-May. Moto exiled himself to Spain.

The remaining opposition parties participated in the 7 March 1999 elections but rejected the results due to serious irregularities, challenging them in court. They also refused to take up their seats in the House. Once again, the ruling PDGE won an overwhelming majority with 75 of the 80 seats to 4 seats for the People's Union (UP), and 1 seat for the Convergence for a Social Democracy (CPDS). The international community also criticized the conduct of the elections. The opposition's presence in the National Assembly was further reduced when the UP dismissed two of its four parliamentary delegates in April, accusing them of endorsing Obiang's dictatorial government.

In the 25 April 2004 parliamentary elections—amid allegations of fraud—the PDGE and its affiliates took all but two seats in the expanded 100-seat parliament. They also won all but seven of the municipal posts around the country. In the 2008 elections, the PDGE took 89 seats, followed by the Electoral Coalition with 10 seats, and the CPDS with one seat. Ignacio Milam Tang of the PDGE was appointed as prime minister. The next legislative elections are set for 2012.

In the presidential elections of November 2009, Obiang Nguema was reelected with 95.8% of the vote. The primary opposition candidate, Placido Mico Abogo, received only 3.6% of the vote. The next presidential elections were set for 2016.

15 LOCAL GOVERNMENT

The country is divided into seven provinces, each headed by a governor appointed by the president. The provinces are divided into districts and 244 municipalities.

16 JUDICIAL SYSTEM

The court system, based on Spanish civil law and tribal custom, includes a Supreme Court, two appeals courts, lower provincial courts (first instance), military courts, and customary (traditional) courts. The courts apply a blend of traditional law, military law, and Franco-era Spanish law, which leads to some unpredictability in results. Appeals from courts of first instance are rare. A five-member Constitutional Council established in 1993 decides constitutional issues and releases election results. The customary courts composed of tribal elders adjudicate civil claims and minor criminal matters.

Under the 1991 constitution, the judiciary is not independent from the executive branch. In fact, all judges and clerks and other judicial personnel are appointed and dismissed at the will of the President. In addition, corruption is a problem because of low wages for judicial personnel.

Defendants have constitutional rights to an attorney and to appeal. However, in practice, these rights are not always afforded.

In January 1998, the treatment of Bubi ethnic group activists who were arrested after a rebellion and the conduct of the trial by a military court, which meted out 15 death sentences, were strongly criticized by Amnesty International and the European Parliament, respectively. Obiang suspended the death sentences in September 1998. Reports of serious and systematic human rights abuses in Equatorial Guinea continue.

17 ARMED FORCES

The International Institute for Strategic Studies reports that armed forces in Equatorial Guinea totaled 1,320 members in 2011. The force is comprised of 1,100 from the army, 120 from the navy, and 100 members of the air force. Armed forces represent .5% of the labor force in Equatorial Guinea. Defense spending totaled $26 million and accounted for 0.1% of GDP.

Military obligation in Equatorial Guinea is defined by selective compulsory military service, and a service obligation of two years; women hold only administrative positions in the Coast Guard (2011). The minimum age for service is 18 years.

18 INTERNATIONAL COOPERATION

Equatorial Guinea joined the UN on 12 November 1969; it participates in ECA and several nonregional specialized agencies. The nation is also a member of the African Development Bank, the ACP Group, the Central African States Development Bank (BDEAC), G-77, and the African Union. In December 1983, it joined the Central African Republic, the Congo, Chad, Cameroon, and Gabon in the Central African Customs and Economic Union (Union Douanière et Économique de l'Afrique Centrale—UDEAC); this organization is now known as the Monetary and Economic Community of Central Africa (CEMAC). The nation is part of the franc zone. Equatorial Guinea holds observer status in the WTO and the OAS. The country is part of the Nonaligned Movement. In environmental cooperation, Equatorial Guinea is part of the Convention on Biological Diversity, CITES, the Kyoto Protocol, MARPOL, and the UN Conventions on the Law of the Sea, Climate Change, and Desertification.

In February 2011, Obiang was elected as the president of the African Union. Human rights activists voiced their concern over the election, citing past allegations of embezzlement and election rigging against Obiang. There were additional concerns that Obiang would not be a suitable leader since the policies he has enacted in Equatorial Guinea do not always follow the same principles as the African Union. The president of the African Union serves a one-year term.

19 ECONOMY

Traditionally, Equatorial Guinea relied heavily upon its agricultural sector, with cocoa, coffee, and timber as the primary products. While much of the nation's population continues to rely upon farming for their survival, the national economy has been bolstered by the discovery and exploitation of oil reserves. The nation is the third-largest producer of crude oil in sub-Saharan Africa, following Nigeria and Angola. While the state maintains primary control of the industry, there are several strong foreign investors. The US-based companies of Exxon Mobil, Marathon Oil, and Amerada Hess, for instance, all have significant shares in the national companies. Other than oil, there are no other major industries, only small-scale factories producing goods for domestic use. Corruption remains a problem in Equatorial Guinea, with many of the political elite owning and controlling some of the country's most profitable businesses. As a result, while oil revenues have increased by more than 5,000% since 1995, the standard of living for most residents remains low. According to the International Monetary Fund (IMF), the government has maintained over $2 billion in foreign bank accounts, which have been used to finance the lavish lifestyles of the president and his family. Other natural resources that are undeveloped are titanium, iron ore, manganese, uranium, gold, and diamonds.

In 1985 Equatorial Guinea joined the CFA franc zone, improving the economic situation. In 1994, France devalued the CFA franc, causing its value to drop in half overnight, and raising the value of exports. Increased export revenue, together with newly exploited petroleum reserves, caused GDP to rise dramatically (over 50%) during 1996 and 1997. Between 2001 and 2005 GDP annual average growth rate was 27.78%, with a high of 65.6% in 2001 and a low of 6% in 2005. The growth rates in GDP were a result of discovery of new oil reserves and increases in the production of oil. Growth remained strong in 2008, when oil production peaked, but slowed in 2009–10, as the price of oil and the production level fell. The GDP rate of change in Equatorial Guinea in 2010 was –0.8%, but had risen to 7.1 percent in 2011. Inflation stood at 7% in 2011, and unemployment was reported at 22.3%.

²⁰INCOME

The World Bank reports that in 2009, household consumption in Equatorial Guinea totaled $2.5 billion or about $3,792 per capita, measured in current US dollars rather than PPP.

In 2007 the World Bank estimated that Equatorial Guinea, with 0.02% of the world's population, accounted for 0.02% of the world's GDP. By comparison, the United States, with 4.85% of the world's population, accounted for 22.51% of world GDP.

The CIA estimated that in 2011 the GDP of Equatorial Guinea was $26.11 billion. The CIA defines GDP as the value of all final goods and services produced within a nation in a given year and computed on the basis of purchasing power parity (PPP) rather than value as measured on the basis of the rate of the exchange based on current dollars. The per capita GDP was estimated at $19,300. The annual growth rate of GDP was -7.1%. The average inflation rate was 7%. It was estimated that agriculture accounted for 3.4% of GDP, industry 91.7%, and services 4.9%.

As of 2011, the most recent study by the World Bank reported that actual individual consumption in Equatorial Guinea was 30.2% of GDP and accounted for 0.01% of world consumption. By comparison, the United States accounted for 25.44% of world individual consumption. The World Bank also estimated that 12.6% of Equatorial Guinea's GDP was spent on food and beverages, 5.5% on housing and household furnishings, 1.6% on clothes, 2.2% on health, 2.5% on transportation, 1.2% on communications, 0.5% on recreation, 1.1% on restaurants and hotels, and 1.7% on miscellaneous goods and services and purchases from abroad.

²¹LABOR

As of 2009, Equatorial Guinea had a total labor force of 270,138 people.

As of 2011, workers had the right to form unions, but there was no legislation to prohibit antiunion discrimination in the workplace. In 2001 the Small Farmers Syndicate became the first legally recognized union. As of 2011, it was still the country's only legally recognized union, and there was no collective bargaining.

Wages are set by the government and employers, with little or no input by workers. There was a statutory monthly minimum wage of about $193 in 2011 for all workers. The legal minimum age for employment is 14, but the government does not enforce this. The standard legal workweek is set at 35 hours, with a 48-hour rest period.

²²AGRICULTURE

Roughly 11% of the total land is farmed, and the country's major crops include coffee, cocoa, rice, yams, cassava (tapioca), bananas, and palm oil nuts. Fruit production in 2009 amounted to 67,011 tons. In 2011 agriculture represented 3.4% of total GDP.

The island of Bioko has year-round rainfall, and the prevailing economic activity is cocoa cultivation. In Río Muni (on mainland Africa), where 80% of the population lives, food crops are the dominant economic activity, and cash crop cultivation is secondary. The main food crop is cassava; sweet potatoes are the second-largest food crop, followed by bananas.

Before independence, the main cash crops were cocoa, coffee, and palm kernels for palm oil. Guinean cocoa, of excellent quality, had an annual production of 38,000 tons in 1967. However, production experienced a sharp drop in the 1970s, falling to 4,512 tons in 1980. In 2010, production was estimated at 1,200 tons. Coffee of comparatively poor quality is grown in northern Río Muni, along the Cameroon border. The preindependence production of 8,959 tons in 1967 fell to 500 tons in 1978; the decline was mainly caused by forcible transfer of coffee farmers to the Bioko cocoa plantations. Coffee production was an estimated 3,300 tons in 2010. Actual cocoa and coffee production is higher, but official figures do not take into account quantities smuggled abroad rather than delivered to state marketing agencies.

²³ANIMAL HUSBANDRY

The UN Food and Agriculture Organization (FAO) reported that Equatorial Guinea dedicated 104,000 hectares (256,990 acres) to permanent pasture or meadow in 2009. During that year, the country tended 340,000 chickens, 5,100 head of cattle, and 6,300 pigs. Equatorial Guinea also produced eight tons of cattle hide.

Cattle and poultry production is rapidly reaching its preindependence levels of self-sufficiency with the financial help of the African Development Bank. However, production of domesticated animals is hindered by the presence of trypanosomiasis and other tropical deterrents.

²⁴FISHING

The fishing industry gained strength through the 1980s and is now almost entirely modernized; a tuna processing plant went into operation in 1990. Annobón subsists almost entirely on fishing and retains its traditional preeminence in offshore whaling and turtle gathering. Bioko is also a major fishing center, the chief catches being perch, tuna, mackerel, cod, pike, shark, and crayfish.

Equatorial Guinea had 66 decked commercial fishing boats in 2008. The annual capture totaled 5,400 tons according to the UN FAO. The export value of seafood totaled $30.74 million.

²⁵FORESTRY

Approximately 58% of Equatorial Guinea is covered by forest. Timber from Río Muni is Equatorial Guinea's leading export. Forests cover over 62% of the land area. The Río Muni area on the mainland produces okoumé and akoga from rain forests of considerable age. Even though the government has given permission to foreign firms, exploitation is difficult due to infrastructural problems. The government enacted a new forestry action plan in 1990 in an effort to strengthen the sector's development. The

UN FAO estimated the 2009 roundwood production at 419,000 cu m (14.8 million cu ft). The value of all forest products, including roundwood, totaled $16.4 million.

26 MINING

Petroleum, the country's leading industry and export commodity in 2009, was associated with Equatorial Guinea's rapid economic growth since 1996; natural gas was the country's fourth-leading industry. Geological surveys indicated occurrences of bauxite, alluvial gold, copper, diamond, titanium-bearing sands, ilmenite beach sands, lead, phosphates, zinc, iron, manganese, tantalum, and uranium in Río Muni; there has been no significant exploitation. A 1981 law stipulated that all mineral deposits were state property. Artisanal miners produced 200 kg of gold in 2009, and clay, gravel, and sand were also presumably produced.

27 ENERGY AND POWER

The World Bank reported in 2008 that Equatorial Guinea produced 92 million kWh of electricity and consumed 27.4 million kWh, or 41 kWh per capita. However, poor management and aging equipment has resulted in prolonged power blackouts. As a result, small gasoline and diesel-powered generators are used as backup power sources.

Since 1995, when significant offshore oil discoveries were made in the Gulf of Guinea, oil has become Equatorial Guinea's most important export. According to World Oil, Equatorial Guinea's proven oil reserves were put at 1.1 billion barrels, as of 1 January 2011. In 2010, oil production totaled 322,700 barrels of oil a day, of which crude oil accounted for over 90%. Domestic oil demand and net oil exports in 2010 were estimated at 2,000 barrels per day and 395,000 barrels per day, respectively.

Equatorial Guinea has proven natural gas reserves estimated, as of 1 January 2011, of 36.81 billion cu m, according to the CIA. The country's natural gas reserves are located off Bioko Island, which is the site of the nation's capital, Malabo, and mainly in the Zafiro and Alba oil and gas fields. Domestic consumption of natural gas is estimated for 2002 at 1.55 billion cu m.

28 INDUSTRY

Equatorial Guinea's manufacturing sector is very small. Sawmilling leads industrial production, followed by cement, bleach, and tuna canning plants. Small-scale soap manufacturing and food processing operations round out the industrial sector. The petroleum mining industry is growing rapidly, as large oil reserves have been discovered. Oil in 2006 accounted for over 87.1% of GDP and over 97% of exports. Proven oil reserves are estimated at 563.5 million barrels. Oil production increased from 17,000 barrels per day in 1996 to around 322,700 barrels per day in 2010. There is a methanol plant on Bioko Island that processes natural gas. Proven natural gas reserves are estimated at 36.81 billion cu m.

29 SCIENCE AND TECHNOLOGY

The World Bank reported in 2009 that there were no patent applications in science and technology in Equatorial Guinea. Spain,

Principal Trading Partners – Equatorial Guinea (2010)				
(In millions of US dollars)				
Country	Total	Exports	Imports	Balance
World	15,700.0	10,000.0	5,700.0	4,300.0
United States	2,382.3	2,083.3	299.0	1,784.3
Spain	1,191.1	867.5	323.6	543.9
China	1,045.8	544.2	501.6	42.6
Italy	1,003.4	880.6	122.7	757.9
South Korea	698.7	686.6	12.1	674.6
Canada	653.9	648.8	5.1	643.7
France	589.2	334.5	254.7	79.8
Netherlands	587.5	535.7	51.8	484.0
Brazil	561.2	510.0	51.2	458.8
Taiwan	413.7	413.6	0.1	413.5

(…) data not available or not significant.

(n.s.) not specified.

SOURCE: *2011 Direction of Trade Statistics Yearbook,* New York: United Nations, 2011.

China, and several other countries have provided Equatorial Guinea with technological assistance.

30 DOMESTIC TRADE

Most interior wholesale and retail trade has been maintained through *factorías* (small general agencies) managed by individual Spanish owners or the representatives of small firms. Most trade occurs in the major cities of Malabo and Bata.

Consumer price inflation has fluctuated quite a bit throughout the last decade. The inflation rate in 2010 was 8.2%, and it was 7% in 2011. Recent economic policies are designed to encourage foreign investment.

Normal business hours are 8 a.m. to 12 noon and 4 to 8:00 p.m., Monday through Friday, and 9 a.m. to 2 p.m. on Saturday. Spanish is the dominant business language, while French and English are also spoken.

31 FOREIGN TRADE

Equatorial Guinea imported $7.187 billion worth of goods and services in 2011, while exporting $13.65 billion worth of goods and services. Major import partners in 2010 were China, 21.4%; Spain, 13.8%; the United States, 12.7%; France, 10.9%; Cote d'Ivoire, 6.7%; the UK, 6.2; and Italy, 5.2%. Its major export partners were the United States, 24.3%; Italy, 10.3%; Spain, 10.1%; South Korea, 8.3%; Canada, 7.6%; China, 6.3%; Netherlands, 6.1%and Brazil, 5.9%.

The trade surplus was $6.483 billion in 2011. Leading exports for 2010 were petroleum, timber, and cocoa. Imports consisted primarily of machinery, building material, vehicles, food and beverages, and petroleum products.

32 BALANCE OF PAYMENTS

New oil and natural gas production improved Equatorial Guinea's balance of payments situation since the mid-1990s. Additional oil production that came online in 2001, combined with methanol gas exports from the new CMS-Nomeco plant, increased export earnings in the early 2000s. The country's debt service ratio fell from 20% of GDP in 1994 to less than 1% in 2005. Many of the aid programs Equatorial Guinea benefited from in the 1980s and 1990s had diminished or ceased altogether by 2000. Despite the continuance of a trade surplus, the current account balance was negative in both 2010 and 2011, at -$1.296 billion and -$941 million, respectively.

33 BANKING AND SECURITIES

The Bank of the Central African States (Banque des États de l'Afrique Centrale—BEAC) acts as the central bank for Equatorial Guinea. It is a joint central bank that includes Cameroon, the Central African Republic, Congo, and Gabon. The adoption of the BEAC as its central bank was designed to strengthen the monetary solidarity and sovereignty of Equatorial Guinea and other African nations. As a member of the CFA zone, Equatorial Guinea uses the CFA franc (XAF), whose convertibility is guaranteed by France.

In 2010 the discount rate, the interest rate at which the central bank lends to financial institutions in the short term, was 5.25%.

The story of commercial banking in Equatorial Guinea since independence has been a sorry one, and the lack of cheap and efficient commercial credit is blamed as a major obstacle to economic growth. Banking functions prior to independence were carried out mainly by the Banco Exterior de España (BEE), in association with two smaller Spanish institutions. Spanish banks almost stopped functioning after independence and withdrew altogether in 1972. As of 2010, there were only three banks operating in the country.

There are no securities exchanges.

34 INSURANCE

No information is available.

35 PUBLIC FINANCE

Equatorial Guinea made its first standby loan agreement with the IMF in 1985 and negotiated a structural adjustment agreement in 1988. Government problems with budget overruns and a continuing, structural imbalance of trade frustrated IMF technicians, who stopped payments in 1990. Nonetheless, the government reduced the 1990 budget and enacted key portions of the structural adjustment program: import price liberalization, economic diversification, utility rate increases, clarification of property rights, and private sector stimulus. With these steps taken and with petroleum revenues increasing, the IMF restarted the blocked structural adjustment program in December 1991. By 1994, however, repeated human rights violations and the failure to enact economic reform led to the suspension of most foreign economic assistance. In 1998, the government privatized distribution of petroleum products; petroleum revenues, along with sales taxes and duties, account for two-thirds of government revenues.

In 2010 the budget of Equatorial Guinea included $6.739 billion in public revenue and $6.984 billion in public expenditures. The budget deficit amounted to 1.7% of GDP. Public debt was 4.1% of GDP, with $794.3 million of the debt held by foreign entities.

36 TAXATION

Equatorial Guinea has a standard corporate tax rate of 35% in 2011, with a minimum 1% rate on turnover. There was a fuel tax

of XAF277 ($0.56) per liter. Property tax was assessed at a rate of 1%. A value-added tax of 15% was also in place.

37 CUSTOMS AND DUTIES

As a member of the six-nation Central African Economic Community (CEMAC), Equatorial Guinea shares customs systems and practices with its neighbors. The CEMAC makes trade with Central African countries much easier and more efficient. The tariff system is based on the CIF (cost, insurance, freight) value of imported goods, and is divided into four categories: basic necessities, raw materials and capital goods, intermediate and miscellaneous goods, and consumer goods.

38 FOREIGN INVESTMENT

Spain and France are the major aid donor countries working with the Equatorial Guinean government. Spain conditioned aid, however, on improvements in the human rights record and progress in the democratization effort. Other donors include China, Nigeria, and several other Western and Middle Eastern countries.

Foreign investment in the petroleum and lumber industries increased sharply during the late 1990s. Timber production increased by 70% in 1997, and petroleum production reached 85,000 barrels per day in the same year. Offshore drilling operations began production in 2000. In 2001, Equatorial Guinea had the world's fastest-growing economy, because oil production, with ExxonMobile as the main producer, reached 200,000 barrels per day. The inflow of foreign direct investment (FDI) jumped from an average of $22 million a year in 1997 and 1998 to an average of $120 million in 1999 and 2000. FDI inflow was $88 million in 2001. However, between 2002 and 2004 FDI inflow averaged $1.14 billion per year. According to figures from the UN Conference on Trade and Development (UNCTAD), Equatorial Guinea received the third-largest amount of foreign direct investment in sub-Saharan Africa in 2004. Foreign direct investment (FDI) in Equatorial

Public Finance – Equatorial Guinea (2009)		
(In billions CFA francs, budgetary central government figures)		
Revenue and Grants	**2,368.09**	**100.0%**
Tax revenue	905.66	38.2%
Social contributions	…	…
Grants	…	…
Other revenue	1,462.43	61.8%
Expenditures	**2,827.52**	**100.0%**
General public services	524.65	18.6%
Defense	175.62	6.2%
Public order and safety	17	0.6%
Economic affairs	1,608.9	56.9%
Environmental protection	113.3	4.0%
Housing and community amenities	171.52	6.1%
Health	45.32	1.6%
Recreational, culture, and religion	93.48	3.3%
Education	53.82	1.9%
Social protection	23.93	0.8%

(…) data not available or not significant.

SOURCE: *Government Finance Statistics Yearbook 2010,* Washington, DC: International Monetary Fund, 2010.

Guinea was a net inflow of $1.64 billion according to World Bank figures published in 2009. FDI represented 15.71% of GDP.

39 ECONOMIC DEVELOPMENT

During the 1990s, in conjunction with Spain, Equatorial Guinea focused on education, health, administrative reform, and economic infrastructures with little success. According to a 1996 International Monetary Fund (IMF) report, the production base of Equatorial Guinea was extremely small, the level of human capital very weak, and the country had no basic infrastructure. Mismanagement and corruption were widespread in public administration. US oil companies have invested in development of the country's infrastructure.

New oil and gas exploration and development of existing fields resulted in rapid growth in energy exports in the early 2000s. The government sold some state-owned enterprises, and attempted to establish a more favorable investment climate. However, in 2011 high oil revenues were cited as enabling poor management of public spending and, thus, were an impediment to economic growth.

As of 2011 there had been no formal agreements or arrangements with the IMF since 1996.

40 SOCIAL DEVELOPMENT

Old age, disability, sickness, and work injury laws cover employees, public officials, and military personnel. These programs are funded primarily from employers and the government, with a small contribution from the employee. Family allowances are also paid. Workers' medical benefits include free medical care, hospitalization, and medicine. However, subsistence farmers and agricultural workers are not covered by formal social security systems. The great majority of the population goes without potable water, electricity, basic education, or even minimal health care.

Women have the same legal rights as men, but in practice face discrimination. Male-dominated traditions and customs lead many parents to withdraw their daughters from school. Men are accorded favorable inheritance and property rights. Polygamy is common within the Fang ethnic group. Domestic violence against women is commonplace, and the government does not prosecute perpetrators. As of 2011, forced marriages were customary. In 2011, only about 10 percent of the elected legislators were female.

Human rights violations are commonplace. Human rights abuses include incommunicado detention, extrajudicial killings, torture, arbitrary arrest and detention, and searches without warrants.

41 HEALTH

According to the CIA, life expectancy in Equatorial Guinea was 62.75 years in 2012. The country spent 2.2% of its GDP on healthcare. There were 3 physicians, 5 nurses and midwives, and 19 hospital beds per 10,000 inhabitants. The fertility rate was 4.83, while the infant mortality rate was 75.18 per 1,000 live births. In 2008 the maternal mortality rate, according to the World Bank, was 280 per 100,000 births.

The national health system of Equatorial Guinea consists of four levels: health posts in each village of 600 people, dispensaries in health centers with a qualified nurse at the intermediate level, district level hospitals, and two referral hospitals at the most centralized level.

Health problems include malaria, parasitic disease, upper respiratory infections, gastroenteritis, and complications of pregnancy. In the continental zone, sickle cell anemia is common. Approximately 51% of the country's children were immunized against measles in 2007. In 2009 the HIV/AIDS adult prevalence rate was 5% in 2009. The incidence of tuberculosis was 135 per 100,000 people in 2011.

42 HOUSING

As part of the government's efforts at urban renewal, more than 1,000 families in Equatorial Guinea were displaced between 2003 and 2011 in order to clear land for development projects, which included high-end housing, hotels, and shopping centers. Relocation required families to purchase new dwellings that exceeded their financial capacity. Large-scale government constructions of "social housing" units have taken place, although many awaited the provision of utilities before residents could move into the units. The Chinese government has funded much of the construction effort.

43 EDUCATION

In 2000, the CIA estimated that Equatorial Guinea had a literacy rate of 87%, though the rate for women was much lower (80.5%) than that for men (93.4%). However, there was a slight increase in investment in education during the following 10 years, and, according to UNICEF estimates, the youth literacy rate (ages 15-24) for 2005-2010 was 98 percent for males and females.

Education is free and compulsory from 6 to 11 years of age. Primary education is for five years followed by four years of secondary in the first stage and three subsequent years of secondary education in the second stage.

In 2009, about 41% of age-eligible children were enrolled in some type of preschool program. Primary school enrollment that year was estimated at about 85% of age-eligible students. However, it is estimated that only about 54% of all students completed their primary education in 2009.

The Universidad Nacional de Guinea Ecuatorial is the primary institute of higher learning. As of 2009, public expenditure on education was estimated at 0.6% of GDP, or 4% of total government expenditures. Efforts were being made beginning in 2010 to continue improvements to the education system of Equatorial Guinea with some of the proceeds from oil sales.

44 LIBRARIES AND MUSEUMS

The Malabo Public Library, housed in three branches, contains some 17,000 volumes. The Claretian Mission at Malabo has about 4,000 volumes of Africana and Guineana and an archaeological-ethnographic museum. In Santa Isabel, the Mission Ethnological Museum houses a collection of the art of the Bubus people and stone sculptures of the Druids.

45 MEDIA

In 2010 the CIA reported that there were 13,500 telephone landlines in Equatorial Guinea. In addition to landlines, mobile phone subscriptions averaged 66 per 100 people. There were 3 AM radio stations, and 5 shortwave radio stations. Internet users numbered 2 per 100 citizens.

Equatorial Guinea has two government-owned radio stations broadcasting in Spanish, French, and local languages, including Fang, Bubi, and Combe. The only privately owned radio station is held by Teodoro Nguema Obiang Mangue, the president's son. There is one television station, also government-owned. Cable television is also available. *Poto Poto*, published in Spanish and Fang, may be the only daily national newspaper. There were several general-interest newspapers, including *La Gaceta*, a monthly publication with informal connections to the Government; *El Correo Guineo Ecuatoriano*, a bimonthly newspaper published by the Gaceta group; *La Opinion*, an opposition newspaper published every 2 to 3 weeks; *El Tiempo*, an opposition newspaper; and *Ebano*, a twice monthly publication of the Ministry of Information, Tourism, and Culture. *Egyptian Mail* is a national English-language publication.

Although the constitution of Equatorial Guinea provides for free speech and a free press, the government is said to severely restrict these freedoms in practice, censoring all criticism of the president and security forces. Access to foreign publications is limited.

46 ORGANIZATIONS

The government generally restricts the formation of nongovernmental organizations and associations. Apart from official and semiofficial organizations, most non government organizations are religious societies and sports clubs. In 2010, the only recognized labor union was the Small Farmers Syndicate. There is also an Equatorial Guinea Press Association. There is an International Lion's Club, and the Red Cross has an active chapter.

47 TOURISM, TRAVEL, AND RECREATION

Because Equatorial Guinea has undergone many years of international isolation, its tourism industry is very undeveloped, with limited hotel space available in Malabo and Bata. Attractions include the Spanish colonial architecture of Malabo, the beaches, and the tropical rain forests. A certificate of vaccination against yellow fever is required. A valid passport is needed; there are no visa requirements.

Equatorial Guinea and Gabon will co-host the biennial African Cup of Nations in 2012. The soccer tournament will be played in the Gabonese cities of Libreville and Franceville and in the Equatoguinean cities of Malobo and Bata.

There were hotel beds available in Equatorial Guinea. The estimated daily cost to visit Malabo, the capital, was $415.

48 FAMOUS PERSONS

Francisco Macías Nguema (1924–79) was president until his overthrow and execution in 1979. His successor, Lt.-Col. Teodoro Obiang Nguema Mbasogo (b. 1946), has ruled Equatorial Guinea since 1979.

49 DEPENDENCIES

Equatorial Guinea has no territories or colonies.

50 BIBLIOGRAPHY

Equatorial Guinea Investment and Business Guide: Strategic and Practical Information. Washington, DC: International Business Publications USA, 2012.

The History of Western Africa. New York: Britannica Educational, 2011.

Liniger-Goumaz, Max. *Historical Dictionary of Equatorial Guinea.* 3rd ed. Lanham, MD: Scarecrow Press, 2000.

Sundiata, I. K. *Equatorial Guinea: Colonialism, State Terror, and the Search for Stability.* Boulder, CO: Westview Press, 1990.

Zeilig, Leo, and David Seddon. *A Political and Economic Dictionary of Africa.* Philadelphia: Routledge/Taylor and Francis, 2005..

ERITREA

State of Eritrea
Hagere Ertra

CAPITAL: Asmara

FLAG: A red triangle divides the flag into two right triangles; the upper triangle is green, the lower one is blue. A gold wreath encircling a gold olive branch is centered on the hoist side of the red triangle.

ANTHEM: *Ertra, Ertra, Ertra (Eritrea, Eritrea, Eritrea).*

MONETARY UNIT: After becoming independent from Ethiopia, Eritrea used Ethiopian currency until November 1997. At this time the Nafka (ERN) was issued to replace the Ethiopian Birr at approximately the same rate. ERN1 = US$0.0653 (or US$1 = ERN15.32) as of November 2011.

WEIGHTS AND MEASURES: Eritrea uses the metric system.

HOLIDAYS: The following holidays are observed, New Year's Day, January 1; Independence Day, May 24; Martyrs' Day, June, 20; Anniversary of the Start of the Armed Struggle, September 1. Movable Islamic holidays include Eid al-Fitr, Eid al-Adha, and Milad an-Nabi. Movable Orthodox Christian holidays include Easter (Fasika) and Meskel.

TIME: 3 p.m. = noon GMT.

¹LOCATION, SIZE, AND EXTENT

Eritrea is located in eastern Africa. It occupies an area slightly larger than the state of Pennsylvania with a total area of 121,320 sq. km (46,842 sq. mi). Eritrea shares boundaries with the Red Sea on the N, Djibouti on the S, Ethiopia on the S, and Sudan on the W, and has a total land boundary of 1,626 km (1,010 mi) and a coastline of 2,234 km (1,388 mi). The capital city, Asmara, is located in the central portion of the country.

²TOPOGRAPHY

The topography of Eritrea is dominated by the extension of the Ethiopian north-south trending highlands, descending on the east to a coastal desert plain and on the northeast to hills and on the southwest to flat-to-rolling plains. Approximately 4% of the land is arable.

³CLIMATE

Eritrea is cooler and wetter in the central highlands. The western hills and lowlands are semiarid. Heavy rainfall occurs during June, July, and August, except in the coastal desert. The climate is temperate in the mountains and hot in the lowlands. Asmara, the capital, is about 2,300 meters (7,500 ft.) above sea level. Maximum temperature is 26°C (79°F). In the Danakil depression in Eritrea's southernmost province, highs of 60°C (140°F) are not uncommon. This is reportedly the hottest spot in the world. The weather is usually sunny and dry, with the short or *belg* rains occurring February–April and the big or *meher* rains beginning in late June and ending in mid-September.

⁴FLORA AND FAUNA

Eritrea is home to 70 species of mammals, 537 species of birds, 88 species of reptiles, and 9 species of amphibians. This calculation reflects the total number of distinct species residing in the country, not the number of endemic species. The giraffe and baboon are extinct in Eritrea. Populations of lion, leopard, zebra, and species of monkey, gazelle, antelope, and elephant continue to thrive, however. The coastal areas are home to many species of turtle, lobster, and shrimp. Plant life includes acacia, cactus, aloe vera, prickly pear, and olive trees.

⁵ENVIRONMENT

The World Resources Institute reported that Eritrea had designated 500,600 hectares (1.24 million acres) of land for protection as of 2006. Water resources totaled 6.3 cu km (1.51 cu mi) while water usage was 0.3 cu km (0.072 cu mi) per year. Domestic water usage accounted for 3% of total usage while agricultural for 97%. Per capita water usage totaled 68 cu m (2,401 cu ft.) per year. According to a United Nations (UN) report, in 2008 the carbon dioxide emissions in Eritrea totaled 579 kilotons. The most significant environmental problems in Eritrea are deforestation, desertification, soil erosion, overgrazing, famine, and damage to the infrastructure from warfare.

According to a 2011 report issued by the International Union for Conservation of Nature and Natural Resources (IUCN), the number of threatened species included 10 types of mammals, 12 species of birds, 6 types of reptiles, 18 species of fish, and 4 species of plants. Threatened species include the spotted eagle, the cheetah, the black crowned crane, the great white shark, the African wild ass, and the green turtle.

6 POPULATION

The US Central Intelligence Agency (CIA) estimated the population of Eritrea in 2011 to be approximately 5,939,484, which placed it at number 107 in population among the 196 nations of the world. In 2011 approximately 3.6% of the population was over 65 years of age, with another 42.1% under 15 years of age. The median age in Eritrea was 18.7 years. There were 0.98 males for every female in the country. The population's annual rate of change was 2.472%. The projected population for the year 2025 was 7,400,000. Population density in Eritrea was calculated at 51 people per sq. km (132 people per sq. mi). According to CIA, 22 % of the population lived in urban areas in 2010. The largest urban area was Asmara, with a population of 649,000.

7 MIGRATION

Estimates of Eritrea's net migration rate, carried out in 2011 by the CIA, amounted to zero. The total number of emigrants living abroad was 941,200, and the total number of immigrants living in Eritrea was 16,500. During Eritrea's struggle for independence, more than 750,000 fled the country, 500,000 of whom went to Sudan. Following Eritrea's liberation in 1991, many of these refugees returned voluntarily, although there were still some 315,000 in Sudan at the end of 1997. An Eritrean plan for repatriation from Sudan was implemented between 1994 and June 1995, with 25,000 refugees successfully repatriated. Another 80,000 returned on their own. Results of a data collection exercise conducted in Sudan in April 1998 suggested that 90% of Eritrean refugees (some 130,000) were willing to be repatriated. The Eritrean/Ethiopian border conflict had also displaced more than 300,000 people within Eritrea as of 1999. The UN High Commissioner for Refugees (UNHCR) began repatriating 150,000 Eritrean refugees from Sudan in 2001 due to renewed diplomatic relations between the two countries. In 2004 UNHCR assisted 9,893 voluntary returnees from Eritrea to Sudan.

8 ETHNIC GROUPS

Ethnologists classify Eritreans by nine prominent language groups. The Afar inhabit in the southeast, the Tigrinya in south central Eritrea, and the Tigre in the north. The Saho live in the south central/southeast. The Bilen live in central Eritrea, the Hadareb in the northwest, and the Kunama and Nara in the southwest. The ninth group, the Rashaida, inhabit the northwest. According to CIA data, in 2010 the Tigrinya represented (55% of the population), Tigre (30%), Saho (4%), Kunama (2%), Rashaida (2%), and Bilen (2%), and are believed to be the largest ethnic groups. The Afar, Beni Amir, and Nera together make up about 5% of the population.

9 LANGUAGES

The official languages of Eritrea are Arabic, Tigrinya, and English. Tigre is widely spoken in the western lowlands, on the northern coast, and in parts of the Sahel. Afar, Amharic, Kunama, and other minor ethnic group languages are also spoken.

10 RELIGIONS

According to a 2010 report, about 50% of all citizens are Sunni Muslims, while 30% are Eritrean Orthodox Christians and 13% Roman Catholics. Protestants, Seventh-Day Adventists, Jehovah's Witnesses, Buddhists, Hindus, and Baha'is are also represented in fairly small percentages. About 2% of the population practice indigenous religious beliefs. Geographically, Islam predominates in the eastern and western lowlands while Christianity is dominant in the highlands. Along ethnic lines, members of the Tigrinya group are primarily Orthodox Christian. Most of the Tigre, Nara, Afar, Saho, Beja, Rashaida, and Bilen are Muslim. The Kunama are generally Roman Catholic.

Though the constitution provides for freedom of religion, the government has not fully implemented the measures of the constitution since it was ratified in 1997, and there have been several reports of religious discrimination on behalf of the government. The government officially recognizes four main religions: the Eritrean Orthodox Church, Islam, Roman Catholicism, and the Evangelical (Lutheran) Church of Eritrea. All other religious groups are required to register with the government; however, the government has not approved any new registrations since 2002, despite the fact that several have fulfilled the necessary requirements. Religious groups must have approval from the government to conduct religious services and/or other activities and to publish and distribute religious materials. Religious organizations are prohibited from involvement in politics. Jehovah's Witnesses are particularly subject to discrimination both socially and from the government since their refusal to participate in national service is considered unpatriotic.

11 TRANSPORTATION

Eritrea's transport infrastructure suffered severe damage during the war for independence with Ethiopia. As of 2010 the CIA reports that Eritrea had a total of 4,010 km (2,492 mi) of roads, of which 874 km (543 mi) were paved. There were 13 airports. Massawa, the principal port, serves Eritrea and northern Ethiopia. The port, which has a 7-m (24-ft) channel and pier facilities capable of accommodating five or six large vessels, was damaged by bombing raids from February 1990 to May 1991. In early 1992 agreements were concluded between the Eritrean and Ethiopian governments to make Assab a free port for Ethiopia, making Ethiopia dependent on Eritrean ports for its foreign trade. Assab has an oil refinery and facilities capable of handling more than one million tons of goods annually.

A railway, which was almost completely destroyed during the war, once extended 317 km (197 mi) from Massawa on the Red Sea to Asmara, terminating near the Sudanese border. Reconstruction work on this railway, starting from Massawa, began in summer 1994. As of 2010 Eritrea had 306 km (190 mi) of rail line, all of it narrow gauge. In 2010, there were only four airports with paved runways. There was also one heliport. The airport at Asmara (Yohannes IV) handles international jet transportation. Repair of the railroad and highway network is necessary for the revival of agriculture and industry. The government of Eritrea has established a budget for transport rehabilitation, two-thirds of which is allocated for road repair to ensure that all parts of the country have access to modern roads.

12 HISTORY

Eritrea's strategic location on the Red Sea has made the history of this country one dominated by colonial rule. Turks, Egyptians,

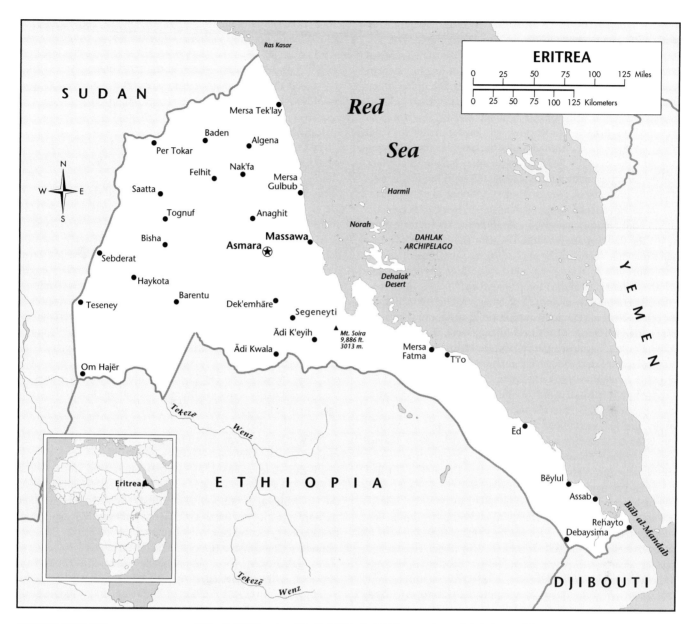

LOCATION: 15° N; 39°E. BOUNDARY LENGTHS: Djibouti, 113 kilometers (70 miles); Ethiopia, 912 kilometers (566 miles); Sudan, 605 kilometers (375 miles); coastline, 1,151 kilometers (717 miles). TERRITORIAL SEA LIMIT: 12 miles.

Italians, British, and Ethiopians have all colonized Eritrea over the years. During the modern European scramble for Africa, Eritrea fell under the colonial rule of Italy in 1890. Sustained resistance to Italian rule developed into a unified sense of Eritrean nationalism among the various ethnic groups in the country. For the first time, Eritrea was welded into a single political entity with unified political and social structures, which cut across the traditional divisions. It broadly followed the pattern of political development experienced in all other European colonies in Africa and which, in the vast majority of cases, formed the basis for eventual independence. Between 1936 and 1941 Eritrea, along with Italian Somaliland as part of the Italian East African Empire, was ruled together with Ethiopia for the first time. In 1941, after the Italians were defeated by Allied forces in the World War II, Eritrea and Somaliland were placed under the British Military

Administration, while Ethiopia regained its independence under Emperor Haile Selassie.

As a loser in World War II, Italy relinquished its legal right to its colonies in a 1947 treaty. The Four Power Commission (Britain, France, the Soviet Union, and the United States) was set up to decide on how to dispose of the former Italian colonies through negotiations. The agreement was to submit the matter to the UN General Assembly if negotiations were unsuccessful. The four countries could not agree on Eritrea's future. Britain proposed partition of Eritrea, with the western parts to go to the Sudan and the highlands and coastal strip to go to Ethiopia, while the United States suggested complete union with Ethiopia. France proposed a trust territory with Italian administration, while the Soviet Union argued for a trust territory under international administration. The problem was referred to the UN, which set up a commission of five countries (Burma, Guatemala, Norway, Pakistan, and South Africa) to study and propose a solution. The idea of partition was rejected outright. Guatemala and Pakistan proposed the standard formula of the UN Trusteeship leading to independence, but others favored close association with Ethiopia. For example, Norway wanted full union, while Burma and South Africa favored federation with some autonomy. Meanwhile, Ethiopian emperor Haile Selassie was working hard on the diplomatic front to acquire Eritrea. The United States backed Eritrea's federation with Ethiopia, and UN Resolution 390 was passed to that effect. This decision was made without giving due attention to the overwhelming presence of groups who were mobilizing the population for independence. From September 1951 Eritrea became an autonomous territory federated with Ethiopia. US strategic interests in the Red Sea and its close ties with the emperor played a major role in influencing the final decision. The United States put forth enormous pressure to have Ethiopia administer Eritrea, under "the Sovereignty of the Ethiopian Crown."

The federation lasted from September 1951 to 1962, but did not bring about harmonious integration of the entities. Ethiopia soon started to impose more direct rule at its will. The UN ignored Eritrea's protests against Ethiopia's intervention in their autonomous rule, and Ethiopia formally annexed Eritrea in 1962. A year earlier, in September 1961, the Eritrean Liberation Front (ELF) launched an armed struggle for independence. By 1970, when the Eritrean People's Liberation Front (EPLF) was created from within ELF, Eritrea had become the emperor's main preoccupation. After the emperor was overthrown in 1974, the self-styled Marxist military junta, called Dergue, stepped up its campaign against Eritreans. With the help of the Soviet Union, Korea, Cuba, and other countries in the Eastern Bloc, the Dergue sustained a very bitter war over Eritrea between 1978 and 1991. The war left Eritrea in complete ruins and created enormous land mine and population displacement problems. In terms of infrastructure, all basic services were virtually disrupted. Most towns were without services-such as electricity, water, and transportation-for much of the war years. Industrial sectors were wiped out and the ports were destroyed. Ethiopian forces bombed Massawa extensively during the last days of the war, killing many civilians, destroying most of the buildings, and depopulating the area. Towards the end of the war, Ethiopia had 500,000 troops under arms, half of them in Eritrea. At no time did the Eritrean forces number more than 100,000. It is estimated that the Dergue had spent $12 billion on military supplies for its war against Eritrea. In the 30 years of war, Eritrea lost more than 60,000 fighters and about 40,000 civilians. Hundreds of thousands were also forced into exile.

In May 1991 the EPLF captured the last Ethiopian outposts in Eritrea. Asmara, Eritrea's capital, was occupied on 24 May 24 1991. In the same year, the Tigrean People's Liberation Front (TPLF), which had also been fighting against the Dergue since 1975, took over the Ethiopian government forcing the president Mengistu Haile Mariam to flee Addis Ababa. The EPLF created a provisional government for Eritrea, until a referendum was carried out to determine the choice of the Eritrean people. The referendum was scheduled to take place in 1993. Although Eritrea had been absorbed into Ethiopia in 1962, Eritreans—unlike many Ethiopians—did not regard their struggle as one of secession. They never recognized Ethiopian legitimacy over their territory;

rather, they viewed their struggle as anticolonial, seeking to gain the independence they were denied by the UN in 1952. The referendum on 23–25 April 1993 proved that this was indeed the case. The great majority—98.5% of the 1,173,000 registered voters—voted for independence. The UN certified the results and on 24 May 1993 Eritrea became Africa's 52nd independent state. Four days later it was admitted to the UN and the Organization of African Unity (OAU).

The colonial boundary between Eritrea and Ethiopia, defined in a treaty between Italy and Ethiopia in July 1900, became the international boundary between the two sovereign states without modification, leaving Ethiopia a landlocked state once more. The decision was consistent with the cardinal article of an OAU charter adopted in 1963, stipulating that colonial boundaries were to be respected, and until May 1998 relations between the two countries were good. The Eritrean ports of Assab and Massawa remained open for Ethiopia free of charges. In May 1998 disagreement over the sovereignty of border villages erupted into all-out war. Between 2 and 6 May 1998 Eritrean soldiers invaded and occupied Badme, in northeastern Ethiopia. Other areas were subsequently occupied in Tigray State. Ethiopia later recaptured Badme, but fighting continued for two and a half years, interspersed with periods of inactivity. A US- and Rwanda-sponsored peace plan proposed in early June 1998 failed, as did arbitration efforts by the OAU with each side claiming to accept an OAU framework agreement while accusing the other of making impossible preconditions to its implementation.

The war, which according to the UN claimed the lives of an estimated 70,000 people on both sides, ended officially with a peace treaty, the Algiers Agreement, on 12 December 2000. Under the Algiers Agreement, some 4,200 UN soldiers commanded under the UN Mission in Ethiopia and Eritrea (UNMEE) remained on the border to monitor the so-called temporary security zone (TSZ) that separates the two countries. Experts from the Eritrea Ethiopia Boundary Commission (EEBC), established in April 2002, physically demarcated the internationally recognized boundary. However, Ethiopia rejected, as unjust and illegal, the ruling of the Permanent Court of Arbitration in The Hague following its decision on 13 April 2002. Legally, the ruling was binding and final. The Ethiopian government announced in November 2004 that it accepted the EEBC ruling and urged Eritrea to accept its full implementation, but Ethiopian prime minister Meles Zenawi later said he would accept border demarcation only in undisputed areas. In October 2005 the Eritrean government banned UN flights in the 25-km (15.5-mi) demilitarized TSZ, and by mid-November 2005 the UN Security Council expressed deep concern over rising tension in the shaky peace agreement over military movements by both parties towards the TSZ.

The UN Mission in Ethiopia and Eritrea ended in 2008 as the Eritrean government cut off fuel supplies and created restrictions that jeopardized the safety of UN personnel. Also in 2008, the border conflict between Eritrea and Djibouti was renewed as Eritrea was accused of establishing troops in the Djibouti territory of Ras Doumeira, a promontory on the Red Sea. Djibouti further accused its neighbor of having published maps that place the territory within Eritrea's own borders.

In January 2009 the UN Security Council issued a resolution calling for the withdrawal of Eritrean troops from the disputed territory. In April 2009 the UN reported that Eritrea had not fulfilled this demand. The Eritrean government, however, insisted that there were no troops left on Djibouti soil. The government of Eritrea has also been accused of supplying weapons and munitions to the militant Somali Islamist group al-Shabaab. Though the government has denied any involvement in the Somali Islamist struggle, the African Union urged the UN Security Council to impose sanctions against Eritrea in May 2009. This was the first time that the African Union had called for sanctions against one of its own members. Eritrea responded by suspending its own membership. This self-imposed exile from African Union ended in 2011. In August 2009 the Eritrea-Ethiopia Claims Commission (an international tribunal established in The Hague at the end of the border war) issued a ruling on the amount of compensation each country was to pay the other for damages caused during the border war. Eritrea was awarded $164 million, but was ordered to pay Ethiopia $174 million.

¹³ GOVERNMENT

After defeating the Ethiopian military government in May 1991, Eritrea functioned as a distinct political unit. Between the end of the war in May 1991 and the celebration of Independence Day on 24 May 1993, the EPLF formed a provisional government to run the country. The provisional government was comprised of a 28-member executive council. This provisional government organized elections at the village, district, and provincial level throughout the country to broaden popular participation. Following the referendum in May 1993 an interim administration was created to govern for four years. In this government, a national assembly was formed, consisting of the central committee of the EPLF and 60 other individuals. Ten out of the 60 seats were reserved for women. The assembly elected Isaias Afworki president. He also served as commander-in-chief of the armed forces and chaired the executive branch–the state council—whose members he nominated. The assembly ratified all of his nominations. This government was to serve until a constitutional commission prepared a constitution and the government organized elections.

In 1996 the 50-member constitutional commission submitted a draft document for public debate. It provided for multiparty democracy based upon Western standards featuring a full array of civil liberties. The resulting 1997 constitution provides for a 150-seat national assembly. When ratified, the constitution also called for national elections in May 1998, which were delayed by the war with Ethiopia, subsequently rescheduled for December 2001, and postponed indefinitely. By mid-2011, there were no elections in sight. Instead a 75-member transitional assembly remains as the legislative body.

The new constitution promulgated in 1997 provides for democratic freedoms, such as free speech, free assembly, and free association. However, the government clamped down the freedom of speech and the press, assembly, association, and religion, and in 2001 it closed all privately owned print media. According to international human rights agencies, including Human Rights Watch and Amnesty International, many journalists viewed as outspoken critics of the government have been arrested and held without trial. Eritrea also has a record of religious persecution over which the US State Department declared it a Country of Particular Concern in both 2004 and 2005. Human rights groups were not permitted

to operate in the country, except for the International Committee of the Red Cross (ICR).

¹⁴ POLITICAL PARTIES

The Eritrean Liberation Front (ELF) started the armed struggle for the independence of Eritrea in September 1961. In 1970 the Eritrean People's Liberation Front (EPLF) evolved from the ranks of the ELF with a new vision and program. Initially, both fronts intensified the war against Ethiopia. Both the ELF and the EPLF were mixed Muslim-Christian groups. However, they differed in the way they dealt with religious, ethnic, and regional differences inside their organizations. For example, the ELF organized itself into relatively autonomous separate units by regional, and therefore typically religious and ethnic, divisions. The EPLF on the other hand was comprised of units with mixed religion, ethnic, and regional backgrounds. By 1977 the two parties controlled most of the countryside. However, with their contradictions at the breaking point in 1978, the parties fought an all-out war against one another. By 1981 the EPLF had defeated and chased the ELF from Eritrea, leaving it the lone party operating in the country. Following its defeat in 1981, the ELF leadership divided into more than a dozen different factions. Some ELF members joined the EPLF while others fled to Sudan. After 1991 most of the former leadership returned to Eritrea to accept positions in the government or to form businesses. Others continued to discredit the government from outside the country. The Eritrean Islamic Jihad, a militant terrorist group, is a notable example.

One still unsettled issue is the nature and role of political parties. The EPLF government has opposed the creation of parties based on race, religion, region, or ethnicity. A split between Christian and Muslim-based parties would be disastrous because the Christian-Muslim divide in the country is about fifty-fifty. The EPLF itself is a good example of a party free of religious, ethnic, or regional basis. Since its inception in 1970, it represented a united front of people with very diverse political views who shared the common goal of obtaining the right of self-determination for Eritreans.

At its third congress on 10–17 February 1994, the EPLF adopted a new name, the People's Front for Democracy and Justice (PFDJ), and committed itself to widening its popular appeal to all sectors of the Eritrean society. The assembly, dominated by the PFDJ, declared a ban on opposition political activity until the implementation of the constitution, thereby giving the PFDJ a monopoly on power. Though a political party law was drafted by a committee of the assembly in January 2001, it had yet to be debated and approved by the assembly. Hence Eritrea remains a one-party state, with only the PFDJ allowed to operate legally.

¹⁵ LOCAL GOVERNMENT

Since independence in 1991, Eritreans have been participating in a process of electing governing councils for their villages, districts, and provinces. Between 1993 and 1997 both the central and local governments underwent a series of reorganizations. In 1996 Eritrea was restructured into six semiautonomous zones or regions, each consisting of several sub-zones. The change from 10 provinces to 6 zones was controversial, but gradually won public acceptance. Zones are administered by governors and have their own local assemblies. At the central level, the Ministry of Local

Governments oversees local affairs, and concerns itself with formulating national policy, regulations, and research and manpower development, leaving implementation responsibilities to regional and local governments.

¹⁶JUDICIAL SYSTEM

The legal system is a civil law system borrowed from Ethiopia's adaptation of the Napoleonic Code. The court system consists of courts of first instance, courts of appeals composed of five judges, and military courts, which handle crimes committed by members of the military. Traditional courts play a major role in rural areas, where village elders determine property and family disputes under customary law or in the case of Muslims, Shari'ah law. Although the judiciary appears to function independently of the executive branch, it suffers from lack of resources and training and there are signs of executive interference.

¹⁷ARMED FORCES

The International Institute for Strategic Studies reports that armed forces in Eritrea totaled 201,750 members in 2011. The force is comprised of an estimated 200,000 personnel from the army, whose equipment included 150 main battle tanks, 40 reconnaissance vehicles, 40 armored infantry fighting vehicles/armored personnel carriers, and more than 170 artillery pieces. The navy numbered 1,400 members. Primary naval units consisted of eight patrol/coastal vessels and three amphibious land craft. There were 350 members of the air force, which had 17 combat capable aircraft, including 13 fighters, in addition to 1 attack helicopter. Armed forces represent 9.4% of the labor force in Eritrea. Defense spending totaled $228.6 million and accounted for 6.3% of gross domestic product (GDP).

¹⁸INTERNATIONAL COOPERATION

Eritrea won its independence from Ethiopia on 24 May 1993 and joined the UN later that year. The country has since joined several specialized UN agencies, such as the FAO, ICAO, IAEA, IFC, UNESCO, UNIDO, the World Bank, and the WHO. Eritrea is a member of the African Union, the ACP Group, the African Development Bank, and the New Partnership for Africa's Development (NEPAD), and G-77. It also belongs to COMESA and the Community of Sahel and Saharan States (CENSAD). Eritrea is part of the Nonaligned Movement. In environmental cooperation, Eritrea is part of the Convention on Biological Diversity, CITES, and the UN Conventions on Climate Change and Desertification.

¹⁹ECONOMY

The Eritrean economy has yet to stabilize after years of armed struggle against Ethiopia. The economy was dealt a severe blow by the two-year war with Ethiopia (1998–2000). The war discouraged investment, destroyed crops, livestock, houses, and infrastructure, and displaced over one million people. The war greatly slowed economic growth (the economy contracted by 9% in 2000), largely due to a disruption in trade relations between the two countries. In addition, government purchases of military equipment used to fight the war drove the government deep into debt. Despite the end of the war, fears of a resurgence of hostilities, combined with poverty, illiteracy, and a weak transportation and communications infrastructure continue to hamper the investment climate. The military regime that ruled Ethiopia from 1974 to 1991 nationalized all housing and all large- and medium-sized businesses and services, including banks, in Eritrea. The post-independence government voiced a commitment to a market economy, although in practice the government and the ruling PFDJ party operate the economy under a command structure exercising tight controls on all economic activity. Successful companies that have been privatized are often reclaimed by the government.

Post war economic recovery was further hampered by four consecutive years of recurrent drought. The population, with 50% below the poverty line, is still largely dependent on food aid. Agriculture and livestock herding occupy over 80% of the population, taking place throughout the country, in both the highlands and lowlands. Long-term prospects for agricultural development appear to be strongest in the western lowlands. A small industrial sector shows signs of growth potential, but infrastructure and skilled labor is lacking.

The natural resource profile of Eritrea is not yet known with certainty. Known mineral resources include copper, zinc, lead, gold, silver, marble, granite, barite, feldspar, kaolin, talc asbestos, salt, gypsum, and potash. Petroleum resources are also suspected, located offshore. Eritrea's most significant economic assets may be its unspoiled coastline, which offers some of the best fishing and underwater diving in the world, and its two ports on the Red Sea. The government looks to mining as a source revenue and signed a contract with a Canadian firm to begin mineral extraction in 2010. Its lack of commitment to a true market economy, however, discourages most economic development.

²⁰INCOME

The CIA estimated that in 2010 the GDP of Eritrea was $3.625 billion. The CIA defines GDP as the value of all final goods and services produced within a nation in a given year and computed on the basis of purchasing power parity (PPP) rather than value as measured on the basis of the rate of the exchange based on current dollars. The per capita GDP was estimated at $600. The annual growth rate of GDP was 2.2%. The average inflation rate was 20%. It was estimated that agriculture accounted for 11.8% of GDP, industry 20.4%, and services 67.7%. The household consumption was estimated as growing at an average annual rate of 18.5%. As of 2011 the World Bank estimated that the poverty ratio was 69%.

²¹LABOR

As of 2007 Eritrea had a total labor force of 1.935 million people. Within that labor force, CIA estimates in 2004 noted that 80% were employed in agriculture, 10% in industry, and 10% in the service sector.

As of 2010 the right to form and join unions was limited by the government. All unions are run by the government and union leaders are usually government employees. Any union activity has to be sanctioned by the government. Workers can bargain collectively, but no collective bargaining agreements were known to exist as of 2010. Strikes are also allowed, but as of 2010, that right had not been exercised by workers.

The minimum working age is 18, but apprentices may be hired at age 14. However, enforcement of the nation's child labor laws has been ineffective. It is common for children in rural areas who were not in school to work on family farms, while in urban areas, some children work as street vendors. Most wage earners are employed by the public sector. Although there is no minimum wage in the private sector, a minimum wage does exist for the civil service sector. In 2010 it stood at $24 per month (though with a purchasing power of only $8) and is considered insufficient for supporting a worker and family with a decent standard of living. The workweek is set at 44.5 hours, with one rest day every week. Health and safety standards are not regularly enforced.

22 AGRICULTURE

Three-quarters of Eritrea's people are subsistence farmers who are dependent on unreliable rainfall to feed families that average seven children. Although these farmers have experienced relative peace and good harvests since May 1991, food production has not been able to keep pace with a rapidly expanding population. Harvests have been variable due to rainfall variations and pest infestations. The present government dissolved the former Ethiopian military regime's marketing board and reinstituted private markets for agricultural products. War, drought, deforestation, and erosion caused about 70–80% of the population to become dependent on food aid. Agricultural output, however, increased slightly during the 1990s, due to the ending of the war, favorable weather, and a newly developed seed and fertilizer distribution system. The army is involved in agricultural restoration, evidence of the government's commitment to agricultural reform. Roughly 5% of the total land is farmed. The country's major crops include sorghum, lentils, vegetables, corn, cotton, tobacco, and sisal. Cereal production in 2009 amounted to 226,899 tons, fruit production 4,944 tons, and vegetable production 47,489 tons. As of 2010 agriculture represented 11.8% of the national GDP.

23 ANIMAL HUSBANDRY

The UN Food and Agriculture Organization (FAO) reported that Eritrea dedicated 6.9 million hectares (17.1 million acres) to permanent pasture or meadow in 2009. During that year, the country tended 1.2 million chickens and 2 million head of cattle. The production from these animals amounted to 16,682 tons of beef and veal and 55,336 tons of milk. Eritrea also produced 4,834 tons of cattle hide and 625 tons of raw wool. Sheep, goats, cattle (especially zebu), and camels make up the majority of Eritrea's livestock. The government is emphasizing development of agriculture and animal husbandry in order to decrease the reliance on international relief, caused by war and drought.

24 FISHING

Independence from Ethiopia provided Eritrea access to about 1,011 km (628 mi) of Red Sea coastline. Because Eritrea now controls the coastline, long-term prospects for development of offshore fishing and oil are good. The Eritrean navy patrols the coastal waters to limit poaching by unauthorized non-nationals. The development of local fishing is expected to decrease the dependence on foreign food aid, even though fish has not been a major source of Eritreans' protein intake. In 2008 the annual capture totaled 1,665 tons according to the UN FAO.

25 FORESTRY

Approximately 15% of Eritrea is covered by forest. The UN FAO estimated the 2009 round wood production at 1,924 cu m (67,945 cu ft.). The value of all forest products, including round wood, totaled $974,000.

26 MINING

In 2009 mining and quarrying accounted for less than 1% of Eritrea's GDP. Eritrea produces basalt, cement, common clay, kaolin, coral, gold, granite, gravel, gypsum, laterite, lime, limestone (for other than cement), marble, pumice, quartz, salt, sand, and silica sand. The country also has known resources of chromium, copper, magnesium, zinc, lead, silver, barite, feldspar, talc, asbestos, iron ore, nickel-chromite, potash, and potassium. Marine salt is produced at Massawa and Assab. Quarries for limestone, clay or shale, and gypsum are located near Massawa. Artisanal gold production, extracted over a large area in the southwestern hills, was estimated at 50 kg in 2009, up from 25 kg in 2005, but down from 87 kg in 2007. Production totals for 2009 included: basalt, 45,000 metric tons, down from 211,053 metric tons in 2006; granite, 25,000 metric tons, down from 350,280 metric tons in 2005; marble blocks, 32,000 cu m, down from 1,860,146 cu m in 2006; and sand, 2,200,000 tons. The outlook for Eritrea's mineral industry is for gradual recovery from the war, with demand for gold, copper, basalt, granite, gravel, limestone, marble, and sand likely to increase.

27 ENERGY AND POWER

Oil and gas exploration in the Red Sea off Eritrea began in the 1960s, when Eritrea was part of Ethiopia. Following independence, the country began awarding production contracts in 1995. However, according to US Energy Information Administration, as of 2010 Eritrea had no proven reserves of crude oil or natural gas. It also has no known reserves of coal. As a result, the country as of 2010 has had no output of oil, natural gas or coal. In 2010 petroleum imports were estimated in 6,000 barrels a day. In 2009 consumption was estimated each at 3,864 barrels per day. In 2009 Eritrea's refinery had a capacity of 15, 000 barrels per day. The World Bank reported in 2008 that Eritrea produced 287 million kWh of electricity and consumed 285.1 million kWh, or 48 kWh per capita. Roughly 20% of energy came from fossil fuels. Per capita oil consumption was 138 kg.

28 INDUSTRY

Ethiopia nationalized Eritrea's 42 largest factories and systematically dismantled the Eritrean industrial sector during the protracted war of independence. By the end of the war, however, all production had stopped. Plants were generally inefficient, and most of these industries required significant investment to achieve productivity. According to the CIA, manufactured items in 2010 included food processing, beverages, clothing and textiles, light manufacturing, salt, and cement.

The government sought privatization of these industries, and issued incentives such as exemptions from income tax, preferential treatment in allocation of foreign exchange for imports, and provisions for remittance of foreign exchange abroad.

The oil industry has potential, as major oil deposits are believed to lie under the Red Sea. In 2001 the US firm CMS Energy entered into an exploration agreement with Eritrea for exploration in the Dismin Block in northeastern Eritrea. The construction industry is growing, as projects range from the construction and expansion of power plants; road, airport, and dam construction; upgrading sea ports; and the construction of schools and hospitals.

In 2010 industry had a 23.1 % share of the GDP.

[29]SCIENCE AND TECHNOLOGY

The World Bank reported in 2009 that there were no patent applications in science and technology in Eritrea. The University of Asmara, whose Italian and English sections were founded in 1958 and 1968, respectively, is the only facility of higher education in Eritrea offering courses in basic and applied sciences. It issues its *Seismic Bulletin* twice a year. The Eritrean Institute of Technology was opened in 2003 after the University of Asmara was ordered closed. The government however claims that reason for the opening of the college was to achieve equal distribution of higher learning in areas away from the capital city of Asmara. Similar colleges were opened in other prates of the country. College enrollment has dramatically increased in the country as a result of the opening of these institutions.

[30]DOMESTIC TRADE

Most of the population depends on subsistence farming, and so domestic commerce is not a significant part of the economy. There are, however, a number of thriving small businesses and factories within the Asmara area. These include restaurants, bars, Internet cafes, auto repair shops, crafts, a brewery, a cigarette factory, and a small glass and plastics producers. There are also several companies involved in making leather goods, and textile and sweater factories operating primarily for domestic consumption. Most local industries rely on outmoded technology and suffer from a lack of capital investment.

Business hours are 9:00 a.m. to 1:00 p.m., and 4:00 p.m. to 8:00 p.m., Monday through Saturday in Asmara; and 6:30 a.m. to 12:00 p.m. and 5:00 p.m. to 10:00 p.m. Monday through Saturday in Massawa and Assab. Banks are open from 8 a.m. to 12 p.m. and 2 p.m. to 4 p.m., Monday through Friday.

[31]FOREIGN TRADE

In 2010 exports were estimated at $19.1 million, while imports came to $695.9 million. Main exports were livestock, sorghum, and textiles. Imports were mainly processed goods, machinery, and petroleum. The major commercial partners included Saudi Arabia, 15.7%; Egypt, 11.9%; China, 11.1%; India, 8.9%; Germany, 7.2%; Italy, 7.2%; South Africa, 6.5%; Brazil, 5.9%; and South Korea, 4.3%.

[32]BALANCE OF PAYMENTS

In 2010 exports were estimated at $19.1 million, while imports came to $695.9 million, resulting in a trade deficit of $586.8 million. The trade gap is covered by external remittances from Eritrean expatriates, bank loans, and grants-in-aid; but mounting debt threatens the country. Eritrea's large trade gap results from a weak export base and the need to import large amounts of capital goods needed to rebuild the country's infrastructure and

industrial base. Economic growth slowed substantially due to the war with Ethiopia, largely due to the disruption of trade between the two nations, Ethiopia's boycott of the port of Assab, an increase in military spending, and the drafting of a large percentage of the work force into military service.

[33]BANKING AND SECURITIES

After the end of 1991, the Central Bank of Eritrea and the Commercial Bank of Eritrea were reestablished, having been nationalized by the Ethiopian military junta in 1984. The status of the National Bank of Eritrea (NBE) as central bank was clarified by a proclamation of April 1993. The Commercial Bank of Eritrea has a dozen branches across the country. It is the main retail bank and now has corresponding relations with both the Ethiopian and international banking systems. The Housing and Commerce Bank of Eritrea and the Agriculture and Industry Development Bank are also functioning, albeit at a very low capacity. In 1997 the government issued the Financial Institutions Proclamation, liberalizing the banking and insurance sectors to the private sector. In 2010 Eritrea had a stock of narrow money estimated at $1.342 billion, a stock of broad money estimated at $2.593 billion, and a stock of domestic credit estimated at $ 2.628 billion.

[34]INSURANCE

The National Insurance Corporation of Eritrea (NICE) was established in 1992. It engages in all classes of insurance and was the only insurance provider operating in Eritrea as of late 2011. Insurance coverage provided by NICE included life, motor, workers' compensation, and personal accident protection. It operates out of three locations: Asmara (headquarters), Massawa, and Assab.

[35]PUBLIC FINANCE

The state retains control over most of the land, mineral resources, and infrastructure of Eritrea. Most government revenues come from custom duties and taxes on income and sales. Massive infusions of foreign aid and investment are needed to restore the infrastructure and services and to develop private sector growth. Membership into the International Bank for Reconstruction and Development and the International Monetary Fund were approved in 1994. The government was set to invest heavily to upgrade and develop infrastructure and utilities. In 2010 the budget of Eritrea included $463.4 million in public revenue and $920.1 million in public expenditures. The budget deficit amounted to 20% of GDP. Public debt was 40.8% of GDP, with $1.048 billion of the debt held by foreign entities. The CIA estimated that in 2005 Eritrea's central government took in revenues of approximately $248.8 million and had expenditures of $409.4 million. Revenues minus expenditures totaled approximately -$160.6 million. Total external debt was $311 million.

[36]TAXATION

Customs duty and import and export taxes are 33.6% of government revenue; direct domestic tax (business and personal income taxes) are 27.8% of government revenue; domestic sales tax and taxes on services are 26.1% of government revenue. The main indirect taxes are municipal taxes, assessed at different local rates on goods and services.

³⁷CUSTOMS AND DUTIES

Eritrea applies the Common Market for Eastern and Southern Africa (COMESA) Common External Tariff of 0% for capital goods and raw materials, 10% for intermediate products, and 25% for finished products. Customs tariffs are based upon the item's CIF (cost, insurance, freight) value. There is a 2–10% rate on most goods. Luxury goods, such as electronic equipment and automobiles, are assessed at 25–35%. Capital goods, industrial inputs, books, livestock and seeds, school supplies, and pharmaceuticals are assessed at rates of 2–10%. Also, the Eritrean Customs Service levies sales taxes of 2%, 5%, and 15% on most goods.

³⁸FOREIGN INVESTMENT

Investment in Eritrea has come primarily from contributions of Eritrean exiles. International aid was restricted by the lack of international recognition of the Eritrean government's sovereignty, a problem resolved in the UN in April 1993. The government issued an investment code in December 1991 to encourage investment in the Eritrean economy. Incentives for investments in certain areas include exemption from customs and duties, exemptions from income tax, and special treatment regarding foreign currency exchange. While foreign direct investment (FDI) reached $61 million in 1997, it went down to $14 million in 1998.

By 1998 the Eritrean investment center had licensed 661 investment projects worth $562 million, of which $235 million was foreign. Annual FDI flows have remained remarkably steady, ranging from $31.7 million in 1998 to $38.7 million in 1997. In 2001 FDI inflow was $34.2 million. In 2010 FDI in Eritrea was a net inflow of $695,026,127, according to figures published by the World Bank. Major investors included the United States, South Korea, Italy, and China.

³⁹ECONOMIC DEVELOPMENT

The development priorities of the Eritrean government are food security, the development of a market-style economy, and the privatization of formerly nationalized enterprises. Encouraging the return of Eritrean exiles abroad is also a government goal in the reconstruction effort. The Emergency and Recovery Action Program was launched in late 1991 to focus on recovery of the transportation system (roads, railroads, and port and airport facilities), agriculture and fishing (including reliable water sources), and industry. Plans for 2000 were to invest $1 billion over the following decade to upgrade infrastructure and utilities. Regulatory requirements imposed by the government discouraged investment in the early 2000s, as had the 1998–2000 war with Ethiopia. The port in Massawa was rehabilitated, and an airport constructed there.

Other factors that negatively influence the economy include the small production and population base, limited supplies of hard currency, and the country's dependence on foreign donor aid. Food insecurity is one of the main problems that the country faces. In 2011, together with other nations of the Horn Africa, Eritrea faced a severe drought that threatened millions of people for starvation. The recurrence of droughts and reliance on external aid are the stumbling blocks for solid economic development policies in Eritrea.

⁴⁰SOCIAL DEVELOPMENT

During its struggle for independence, the EPLF created an elaborate system of social services. It launched a literacy program, a health care system (including hospitals), and a food distribution network. The provisional government mandated equal pay for equal work, and equal educational opportunities. However, in practice, traditional male privileges in education, employment, and the domestic sphere largely persist as a result of ingrained custom and uneven enforcement of the law. Domestic violence and abuse are pervasive and not addressed by the government. Officially the practice of female genital mutilation (FGM) is condemned, but it remains widespread. In 2004 it was estimated that 95% of women and girls had been subjected to FGM. But according to the 2011 Human Rights Watch report, the practice of FGM has been largely eliminated in urban areas through the efforts of government educational campaigns to discourage its practice. According to the same report, the human rights record remains poor. The government does not allow international human rights organizations to monitor prison conditions, and freedom of the press and speech is restricted.

⁴¹HEALTH

According to the CIA, life expectancy in Eritrea was 60 years in 2011. The country spent 3.0% of its GDP on healthcare, amounting to $10 per person. There were 1 physician, 6 nurses and midwives, and 12 hospital beds per 10,000 inhabitants. The fertility rate was 4.5 children per woman, while the infant mortality rate was 41.33 deaths per 1,000 live births. In 2008 the maternal mortality rate, according to the World Bank, was 280 deaths per 100,000 births. It was estimated that 95% of children were vaccinated against measles. The CIA calculated the HIV/AIDS prevalence rate in Eritrea to be about 0.8% in 2009. Approximately 61% of the population had access to safe drinking water and only 14% had adequate sanitation. Diarrheal disease, hepatitis, typhoid fever, and malaria remained significant health problems as of 2009.

⁴²HOUSING

After 30 years of war, thousands of returning refugees experienced a severe housing shortage, particularly in urban areas. In the 2000 border conflict, about 100,000 homes were destroyed and at least 450,000 Eritreans were displaced. Government and economic reform are needed before the housing situation can be fully addressed. Some international aid and foreign programs have helped ease the situation. In highland rural communities, most housing is built as a joint project of community members. These homes are generally made from wood, stone, and straw. Rural lowland homes are also made of wood and straw. Nomads build temporary shelters of wood and leaves. Concrete block and wood is generally used in urban housing.

⁴³EDUCATION

In 2009 the World Bank estimated that 36% of age-eligible children in Eritrea were enrolled in primary school. Secondary enrollment for age-eligible children stood at 27%. Tertiary enrollment was estimated at 2%.Overall, the World Bank estimated that Eritrea had a literacy rate of 67% as of 2011. Public expenditure on education represented 2.0% of GDP.

Education is compulsory for children between the ages of 7 and 14. Eritrea pursues as 2–5–3–4 education system: two tears in pre-primary, five years in elementary, three in middle school, and four in secondary. At tenth grade, students may choose to attend a three-year technical school. The academic year runs from September through June. The student-to-teacher ratio for primary school was about 38:1 in 2009; the ratio for secondary school was about 51:1.

44 LIBRARIES AND MUSEUMS

Asmara houses the library of the University of Asmara (60,000 volumes), the Asmara Public Library (28,000 volumes), and the library of the British Council (20,000 volumes). The National Museum in Asmara-located in a former palace-and the Archeological Museum, operated by the Department of Culture in Asmara, are the country's two principal museums.

45 MEDIA

In 2009 the CIA reported that there were 48,500 telephone landlines in Eritrea. In addition to landlines, mobile phone subscriptions averaged 3 per 100 people. There were two FM radio stations and two shortwave radio stations. Internet users numbered 5 per 100 citizens. In 2010 the country had 1,241 Internet hosts.

The government controls all nonreligious media, including one radio station, one television station, and three newspapers. The law prohibits private ownership of broadcast media. Religious media are prohibited from reporting on political news and events. Television broadcasts are Monday, Wednesday, and Saturday evenings in Tigrinya and Arabic languages. Dimtsi Hafash radio broadcasts daily in various local languages.

Private newspapers have been banned since 2001, as the government cited many journalists for endangering public security. The government-owned daily, *Asmara Herbet*, is published in Arabic and Tigrinya and had a 2002 circulation of 4,000. *Hadas Eritrea* is published three days a week. *Eritrea Profile* is a weekly English-language paper. *Tirigta* and *Geled* are weekly government youth papers. There are also electronic newspapers, namely *Capital Eritrea News, Shabait.com,* and *Shaebia,* all published in English.

46 ORGANIZATIONS

Professional organizations include the Teachers Union, Association of Eritreans in Agricultural Sciences, Eritrean Nurses Association, Eritrean Pharmacists Association, and the Eritrean Medical Association. There is an Association of War Disabled Veterans. Various trade unions formed the National Confederation of Eritrean Workers in September 1994. The Eritrean National Chamber of Commerce is in Asmara. There are also various religious humanitarian groups (Christian and Muslim), sports clubs, and art groups centered on music, theater, painting, and drawing. The National Union of Eritrean Youth Students has branches throughout the country and around the world. Planned Parenthood Association, the Red Cross Society, Caritas, and a Regional Center for Human Rights and Development all operate in Eritrea.

47 TOURISM, TRAVEL, AND RECREATION

Because Eritrea inherited the entire coastline of Ethiopia, there is long-term potential for development of tourism. Passports and visas are required. Proof of yellow fever vaccination may also be required if traveling from an infected area. The *Tourism Fact book*, published by the UN World Tourism Organization, reported 79,000 incoming tourists to Eritrea in 2009, spending a total of $26 million. Of those incoming tourists, there were 63,000 nationals living abroad. There were 13,509 hotel beds available in Eritrea, which had an occupancy rate of 30%. The estimated daily cost to visit Asmara, the capital, was $220. The cost of visiting other cities averaged $81.

48 FAMOUS PERSONS

Isaias Afworki (b. 1946) has been president of Eritrea since its independence from Ethiopia 24 May 1993.

49 DEPENDENCIES

Eritrea has no territories or colonies.

50 BIBLIOGRAPHY

Connell, Dan, and Tom Killion. *Historical Dictionary of Eritrea.* Lanham MD: The Scarecrow Press, 2011.

Denison, Edward. *Eritrea.* Chalfont St. Peter: Bradt, 2002.

Eritrea Investment and Business Guide: Strategic and Practical Information. Washington, DC: International Business Publications USA, 2012.

Negash, Tekeste. *Brothers at War: Making Sense of the Eritrean-Ethiopian War.* Athens: Ohio University Press, 2000.

Pool, David. *From Guerrillas to Government: The Eritrean People's Liberation Front.* Athens: Ohio University Press, 2001.

Prouty, Chris. *Historical Dictionary of Ethiopia and Eritrea.* 2nd ed. Metuchen, NJ: Scarecrow Press, 1994.

Tesfagiorgis, G. M. *Eritrea.* Santa Barbara, CA: ABC-CLIO, 2010.

Woodward, Peter. *The Horn of Africa: Politics and International Relations.* New York: I.B. Tauris, 2003.

Zeilig, Leo, and David Seddon. *A Political and Economic Dictionary of Africa.* Philadelphia: Routledge/Taylor and Francis, 2005.

ETHIOPIA

Federal Democratic Republic of Ethiopia

Yeltyop'iya Federalawi

CAPITAL: Addis Ababa

FLAG: The national flag is a tricolor of green, yellow, and red horizontal stripes with a blue disk and a yellow outlined star and rays in the center.

ANTHEM: *Whedefit Gesgeshi Woude Henate Ethiopia (March Forward, Dear Mother Ethiopia).*

MONETARY UNIT: The birr (ETB) is a paper currency of 100 cents. There are coins of 1, 5, 10, 25, and 50 cents, and notes of 1, 5, 10, 50, and 100 birr. ETB1 = US$0.05811 (or US$1 = ETB17.21) in 2011.

WEIGHTS AND MEASURES: The metric system is used, but some local weights and measures also are employed.

HOLIDAYS: Holidays generally follow the Coptic Church calendar. National holidays include Christmas, 7 January; Epiphany, 19 January; Victory of Adwa (1896), 2 March; Victory Day, 6 April; May Day, 1 May; New Year's Day, 11 September; Feast of the Holy Cross, 27 September. Movable Muslim holidays include Eid al-Fitr and Eid al-Adha. The Ethiopian Calendar consists of 12 months of 30 days each and a 13th month of five days (six days in a leap year). It is based on the Julian calendar, which is about seven years behind the Gregorian calendar used by most of the world.

TIME: 3 p.m. = noon GMT.

¹LOCATION, SIZE, AND EXTENT

Situated in eastern Africa, Ethiopia (formerly called Abyssinia) has an area of approximately 1,127,127 sq km (435,186 sq mi), with a length of 1,639 km (1,018 mi) E–W and a width of 1,577 km (980 mi) N–S. Comparatively, the area occupied by Ethiopia is slightly less than twice the size of the state of Texas. It is bounded on the N by Eritrea, on the NE by Djibouti, on the E and SE by Somalia, on the S by Kenya, and on the W by Sudan and South Sudan, with a total boundary length of 5,328 km (3,311 mi). The Ogaden region of eastern Ethiopia is claimed by Somalia and has been the subject of sporadic military conflict between the two nations since 1961; the southeastern boundary has never been demarcated. Ethiopia's capital city, Addis Ababa, is located near the center of the country.

²TOPOGRAPHY

Ethiopia contains a variety of distinct topographical zones. It is a country of geographical contrasts, varying from as much as 116 m (381 ft) below sea level in the Danakil depression to more than 4,600 m (15,000 ft) above in the mountainous regions. Ras Dashen, with an altitude of 4,620 m (15,158 ft), is the fourth-highest peak in Africa. The most distinctive feature is the northern part of the Great Rift Valley, which runs through the entire length of the country in a northeast-southwest direction at a general elevation of 1,500–3,000 m (4,900–9,800 ft). Immediately to the west is the High Plateau region; this rugged tableland is marked by mountain ranges.

East of the Great Rift Valley is the Somali Plateau—arid and rocky semidesert, extending to the Ogaden, which covers the entire southeastern section of the country. In the north, the Denakil Desert reaches to the Red Sea and the coastal foothills of Eritrea.

The western boundary of Ethiopia follows roughly the western escarpment of the High Plateau, although, in some regions, the Sudan plains extend into Ethiopian territory. Also, part of Ethiopia is the Dahlak Archipelago in the Red Sea.

Ethiopia's largest lake, Lake T'ana, is the source of the Blue Nile River. This river, which winds around in a great arc before merging with the White Nile in the Sudan, travels through canyons that reach depths of more than 1,200 m (4,000 ft). Several rivers in the southwest also make up a system of tributaries to the White Nile.

³CLIMATE

Ethiopian climate varies according to the different topographical regions. The central plateau has a moderate climate with minimal seasonal temperature variation. The mean minimum during the coldest season is 6°C (43°F), while the mean maximum rarely exceeds 26°C (79°F). Temperature variations in the lowlands are much greater, and the heat in the desert and Red Sea coastal areas is extreme, with occasional highs of 60°C (140°F). Heavy rainfall occurs in most of the country during June, July, and August. The High Plateau also experiences a second, though much milder, rainy season between December and February. Average annual precipitation on the central plateau is roughly 122 cm (48 in). The northern provinces receive less rainfall, and the average annual precipitation in the Ogaden is less than 10 cm (4 in). The westernmost region of Ethiopia receives an annual rainfall of nearly 200 cm (80 in). Severe droughts affected the country in 1982–84,1987–88, 1991, and 2002.

⁴FLORA AND FAUNA

The World Resources Institute estimates that there are 6,603 plant species in Ethiopia. In addition, Ethiopia is home to 288 mammal,

839 bird, 205 reptile, and 76 amphibian species. The calculation reflects the total number of distinct species residing in the country, not the number of endemic species.

In some areas, the mountains are covered with shrubs such as pyracantha, jasmine, poinsettia, and a varied assortment of evergreens. Caraway, carcade, cardamom, chat, coriander, incense, myrrh, and red pepper are common. The lakes in the Great Rift Valley region abound with numerous species of birds, and wild animals are found in every region. Among the latter are the lion, civet and serval cats, elephant, bush pig, gazelle, antelope, ibex, kudu, dik-dik, oribi, reed buck, wild ass, zebra, hyena, baboon, and numerous species of monkey.

5 ENVIRONMENT

Agencies responsible for environmental matters include the Ministry of Agriculture, the Forestry and Wildlife Development Authority, and the Ministry of National Water Resources. Simien National Park is a natural UNESCO World Heritage Site.

Ethiopia's forests are endangered. Each year, the nation loses 340 square miles of forest land. Its forests and woodland decreased by 3.4% between 1983 and 1993. From 1990–2000, the rate of deforestation was about 0.8% per year. Between 1990 and 2010, Ethiopia lost 18.6% of its forest cover or around 2,818,000 hectares. The government did not begin afforestation and soil conservation programs until the early 1970s.

Overgrazing, deforestation, and poor agricultural practices have contributed to soil erosion so severe, particularly in the Tigray and Eritrea regions, that substantial areas of farmland have been lost to cultivation. By 1994, an estimated 600,000 acres of arable land were washing away each year. The combined effects of severe drought and a 17-year civil war have also added to Ethiopia's environmental problems.

The World Resources Institute reported that Ethiopia had designated 18.62 million hectares (46.01 million acres) of land for protection as of 2006. Water resources totaled 110 cu km (26.39 cu mi), while water usage was 5.56 cu km (1.33 cu mi) per year. Domestic water usage accounted for 6% of total usage and agricultural for 94%. Per capita water usage totaled 72 cu m (2,543 cu ft) per year.

The UN reported in 2008 that carbon dioxide emissions in Ethiopia totaled 6,504 kilotons.

According to a 2011 report issued by the International Union for Conservation of Nature and Natural Resources (IUCN), the number of threatened species included 33 types of mammals, 24 species of birds, 1 type of reptile, 9 species of amphibians, 14 types of fish, 11 species of other invertebrates, and 24 species of plants. Endangered species in Ethiopia included the simian fox, African wild ass, Tora hartebeest, Swayne's hartebeest, Waliaibex (found only in Ethiopia), waldrapp, green sea turtle, and the hawksbill turtle.

6 POPULATION

The US Central Intelligence Agency (CIA) estimates the population of Ethiopia in 2011 to be approximately 90,873,739, which placed it at number 13 in population among the 196 nations of the world. In 2011, approximately 2.7% of the population was over 65 years of age, with another 46.3% under 15 years of age. The median age in Ethiopia was 16.8 years. There were 0.97 males

for every female in the country. The population's annual rate of change was 3.194%. The projected population for the year 2025 was 119,800,000. Population density in Ethiopia was calculated at 82 people per sq km (212 people per sq mi).

The UN estimated that 17% of the population lived in urban areas and that urban populations had an annual rate of change of 3.8%. The largest urban area was Addis Ababa, with a population of 2.9 million.

According to UNAIDS, Ethiopia has an adult HIV prevalence rate between 1.4% and 2.3%, an estimated total number of 1.3 million people living with HIV (PLHIV), and a total of 356,682 people requiring treatment. Ethiopia's HIV/AIDS epidemic pattern continues to be generalized and heterogeneous with marked regional variations. At the national level, the epidemiological trend over the past eight years has been stable, with HIV prevalence relatively low in rural areas and declining in urban areas. HIV prevalence among the adult population is lower than that of many other sub-Saharan African countries.

7 MIGRATION

Estimates of Ethiopia's net migration rate, carried out by the CIA in 2011, amounted to -0.01 migrants per 1,000 citizens. The total number of emigrants living abroad was 620,100, and the total number of immigrants living in Ethiopia was 548,000. Ethiopia also accepted 66,980 refugees from Sudan, 16,576 from Somalia, and 13,078 from Eritrea. Internal migration is from rural to urban areas. In the 1970s and early 1980s, up to 4.5 million people were displaced as a result of occasional drought, civil strife, and border fighting. In 1984–85, over 600,000 northern peasants were resettled, forcibly in some cases, to 77 sites in the more fertile west and south. Meanwhile, over 2.8 million rural inhabitants, mostly Oromo, were moved to collective villages. As the war for control of Ethiopia intensified between 1989 and 1991, more people were displaced.

After the change of government in 1991, 970,000 Ethiopian refugees returned home from neighboring countries. By November 1995, the United Nations High Commissioner for Refugees (UNHCR) had repatriated 31,617 Ethiopian refugees from Djibouti. Between 1993 and 1996, the UNHCR repatriated 62,000 from Sudan. In 1997, UNHCR had started planning the airlift of around 4,400 Ethiopian refugees remaining in Kenya.

According to the UNHCR, there were 65,461 Ethiopian refugees and 11,572 asylum seekers worldwide in 2005. There were 14,633 refugees in Sudan, 14,862 refugees and 1,992 asylum seekers in Kenya, and 22,976 refugees in the US, Canada, and Germany. As of 2005, Ethiopia was home to more than 204,940 refugees and 790 asylum-seekers settled in 19 camps and urban areas. Of the refugee population in Ethiopia, 59,090 were from Eritrea, 117,720 from Somalia, 24,980 from Sudan, and 3,150 from various other countries. The total refugee population is likely to rise due to new arrivals from Somalia and Eritrea. In July 2011, about 67% of the refugees within Ethiopia (160,000) were of Somali origin. In September 2011, some 20,000 people fled violence in Blue Nile State and sought protection in western Ethiopia. A total of 2,700 Kenyan refugees of Borena origin had been repatriated by the end of 2010.

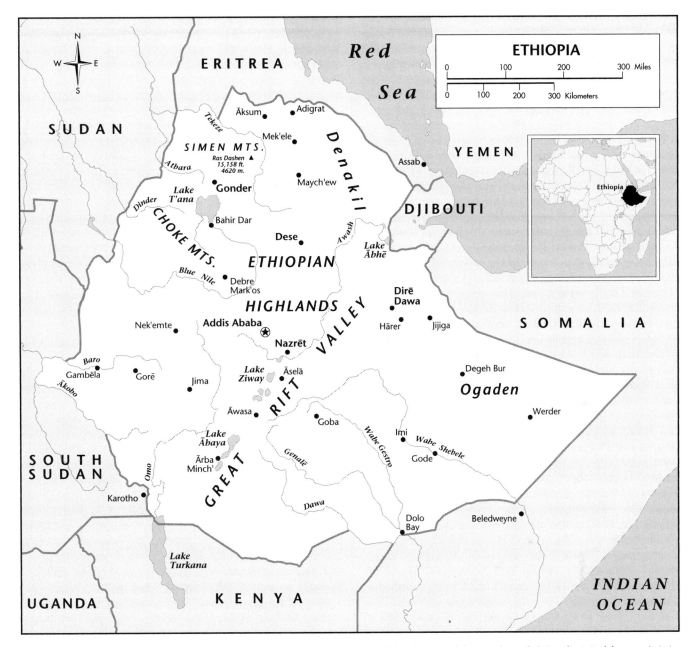

LOCATION: 3°30′ to 18°N; 33° to 48° E. BOUNDARY LENGTHS: Eritrea, 912 kilometers (566 miles); Djibouti, 337 kilometers (210 miles); Somalia, 1,626 kilometers (1,016 miles); Kenya, 830 kilometers (518 miles); Sudan, 769 kilometers (478 miles); South Sudan, 837 kilometers (520 miles).

8 ETHNIC GROUPS

Ethiopia is a composite of more than 77 ethnic groups. The Oromo represent approximately 34.5% of the population. The Amhara (26.9%) and Tigrean (Tigraway–6.1%) groups have traditionally been politically dominant. The Sidamo of the southern foothills and savanna regions account for 4%. The Somali (6.2%) and Afar (1.7%) inhabit the arid regions of the east and southeast. Nilotic peoples live in the west and southwest along the Sudan border. The Gurage account for 2.5% of the population, the Welaita for 2.3%, the Hadiya for 1.7%, the Gamo for 1.5%, and the Gedeo for 1.3%. The Shankella reside on the western frontier. The Beta Isreal live in the mountains of Simen. According to tradition, the name "Beta Israel" originated in the 4th century when the monarchs of Aksumite Empire embraced Christianity and the Beta

Israelites refused to follow suit. Some 14,000 were secretly flown to Israel via the Sudan during Operation Moses and Operation Jashua in 1984–85. Another 14,000 more were flown out of Addis Ababa in 1991 during Operation Solomon, and 4,500 are believed to remain. The Beja of the northernmost region, the Agau of the central plateaus, and the Sidamo of the southern foothills and savanna regions are the remnants of the earliest known groups to have occupied Ethiopia.

9 LANGUAGES

At least 77 different languages are spoken in Ethiopia. Most of these belong to the Semitic, Cushitic, and Omotic divisions of the Afro-Asiatic linguistic family. Amharic, the official language, is a Semitic tongue, the native language of perhaps 30%

of the people. Tigrinya and Tigray, also Semitic, are spoken in the north. Orominga, a Cushitic tongue, is widely spoken in the south. Somali and Afar, also Cushitic languages, are spoken in the east. Omotic tongues are spoken in the southwest. Nilo-Saharan language speakers live in the far southwest and along the western border. English is the principal second language taught in schools. Arabic is also spoken.

¹⁰ RELIGIONS

Christianity, Islam, and Judaism are indigenous to Ethiopia. The advent of Judaism in Ethiopia is unknown, but there is evidence that Judaism may have entered (modern-day) Ethiopia as early as the 8th century BC. The earliest reference to the Judaism in Ethiopia appears in the diary of Eldad Hadani, in the 9th century. Judaism was mainly concentrated in Northwest Ethiopia in the northern province of Gonder and west of Tigray province. Christianity in Ethiopia dates to the first century AD. King Ezana the Great of the Kingdom of Axum, declared Christianity a state religion in 330. The largest and oldest of the Christian denominations is the Ethiopian Orthodox Tewahedo Church, which was part of the Coptic Orthodox Church until 1959, when it was granted its own Patriarch by Coptic Orthodox Pope of Alexandria and Patriarch of All Africa Cyril VI. The Ethiopian Orthodox church has a membership of slightly more than 32 million people in Ethiopia, and is thus the largest of all Eastern Orthodox churches. Next in size are the various Protestant congregations, which include 13.7 million Ethiopians. Roman Catholicism has been present in Ethiopia since the 16th century and numbers 536,827 believers. Islam was introduced to Ethiopia when the followers of Prophet Mohammed, including his wife, fled persecution in Mecca and sought refuge in Aksum. They were received by the ruler of Ethiopia and settled in Negash in Northern Ethiopia. According to the 2007 national census, Islam is the second-most-widely practiced religion in Ethiopia, after Christianity, with over 25 million adherents. Ethiopia is believed to be the site of the oldest sultanate in the world, the Makhzumite Dynasty of Shewa founded in 896.

After the deposition of the emperor, the Ethiopian Orthodox Church lost most of its property (including an estimated 20% of all arable land) and political influence. In 2007, about 44% of Ethiopians were Ethiopian Orthodox Christians. Sunni Islam is practiced by about 34% of the population, most of whom inhabit the Somali, Afar, and Oromia regions of Ethiopia. About 19% of the population are Evangelical or Pentecostal Protestants, which is the fastest-growing religion in the country. Prominent Protestant churches include Mekane Yesus (5.3 million members, associated with the Lutheran church) and Kale Hiwot (6.7 million members, associated with Service in Mission), both of which are Evangelical. Other faiths represented in the country include Jehovah's Witnesses, Roman Catholics (Oriental and Latin Rite), Baptists, the Lutheran-Presbyterian Church of Ethiopia, Emnet Christos, Messeret Kristos (associated with the Mennonite mission), and Hiwot Berhan Church (associated with the Swedish Philadelphia Church. Animism and other traditional indigenous religions are represented by small groups. Although of Afro-Asiatic stock, the Beta Israel practice a form of Judaism that is of great antiquity and is traditionally attributed to ancient Arabian-Jewish or Egyptian-Jewish immigration. Few Falasha remain

after massive immigration and evacuation to Israel in 1984–85 and 1991. The Feles Mora consists of individuals who claim that their ancestors were Jews who were forced to convert to Ethiopian Orthodox. Many of these individuals are currently pursuing immigration to Israel. There are a large number of missionary groups working within the country.

Freedom of religion is guaranteed by the constitution, and this right is generally respected in practice. Though religious tolerance is generally widespread among established faiths, there have been instances of interfaith discrimination concerning newer religions. For instance, some tension has existed as both Orthodox Christians and Muslims have complained about the proselytizing of Jehovah's Witnesses and the Pentecostals. In some regions, there have also been incidents of violence between Orthodox Christians and Muslims. Religious groups and all other nongovernmental organizations, must register with the Ministry of Justice and renew their membership every three years. Epiphany, the Birth of the Prophet Muhammad, Good Friday, Easter, Meskel, Eid al-Adha, Eid al-Fitr, and Christmas are observed as national holidays. The government mandates a two-hour lunch break on Fridays to allow for the Muslim obligation of prayer.

¹¹ TRANSPORTATION

The CIA reports that Ethiopia has a total of 36,469 km (22,661 mi) of roads, of which 6,980 km (4,337 mi) are paved. There are 61 airports, which transported 2.91 million passengers in 2009, according to the World Bank.

It has been estimated that more than half of Ethiopia's produce is transported by pack animals, reflecting the country's rugged terrain and inadequate road network. About 75% of Ethiopian farms are more than a one-day walk from the nearest road. Bus services link provincial centers to the capital.

As of 2008, Ethiopia's merchant fleet consists of nine ships of 1,000 GRT or over. Neighboring Djibouti also serves as a depot for Ethiopian trade. Only one river, the Baro, is used for transport.

In 2010, the government confirmed its commitment to provide funding for a major railway network designed by the Ethiopian Railway Corporation. The project was expected to create 5,000 kilometers of new track through eight lines that will stem from the capital into other regions of the country. The Export and Import Bank of China will fund portions of the project. The first six lines were expected to be built before 2015, including five lines built by local contractors and one co-funded by the Chinese. The government set aside $336 million per year for the 2011–15 budgets as funding for the project. As of 2010, the nation had only one major railway, a 681-kilometer track that connects Addis Ababa with the port in Djibouti. Construction on the new railways is expected to create more than 300,000 jobs.

There were an estimated 17 airports with paved runways. The Addis Ababa airport handles international jet transportation. Before the civil war, the national carrier, Ethiopian Airlines, flew to numerous African, Asian, and European cities, and had sole rights to domestic air traffic.

¹² HISTORY

Humanlike fossils have been found in the Denakil depression dating back 3.5 million years; in 1981, the 4 million-year-old fossil bones of a direct ancestor of Homo sapiens were discovered in the Awash River Valley. Evidence of cereal agriculture dates back to about 5000 BC. Homer refers to the Ethiopians as a "blameless race," and Herodotus claims that they were known in his time as the "most just men"; to the Greeks, however, Ethiopia was a vague and semi-mythical area that did not exactly correspond to the modern country. Ethiopia first appears in written history as the Aksumite (or Axumite) Empire, which was probably established around the beginning of the Christian era, although national tradition attributes the foundation of the empire to Menelik I, the son of King Solomon and the Queen of Sheba. Christianity was introduced in the 4th century by Frumentius of Tyre, who was appointed bishop of the Ethiopian diocese by Patriarch Athanasius of Alexandria. The rise of Islam in the 7th century and the subsequent conquest of Egypt created a crisis for the Coptic Christian communities of northeast Africa. Ethiopia alone met the challenge, surviving until the 1970s as a Christian island in a Muslim sea.

The Aksumite dynasty suffered a slow decline. In 1137, the ruler of Lasta (now Lalibela), Tékla Haimanot, overthrew the Aksumite emperor, Del-Naad, and established the Zagwe dynasty. In 1270, the throne was again restored to the Solomonic dynasty, with the accession of Yekuno Amlak in the province of Shewa. Subsequently, Emperor Amda-Seyon 1 (r. 1314–44) reestablished the Ethiopian suzerainty over the Muslim principalities along the Horn of Africa. The Muslim penetration of the highland regions resumed in the early 16th century and, from 1527 to 1543, the Muslims threatened to overrun the entire empire. In 1541, Ethiopia enlisted the assistance of several hundred Portuguese musketmen against a jihad led by Imam Ahmad (known as Gragn, or "the left-handed"). Against these superior weapons, Ahmad was defeated and killed in battle in 1543.

The 18th and 19th centuries formed a period of political decentralization and incessant civil war; this period is called the Zamana Masafint ("Era of the Princes"). A young general named Lij Kassa Haylu established a powerful army, which defeated the forces of his rivals. He was crowned Emperor Tewodros (Theodore II) in 1855 and succeeded in reunifying the empire, but he was defeated and killed by a British expeditionary force under Gen. Robert Napier in 1868. Italy occupied the Eritrean ports of Aseb (1869) and Mits'iwa (1885) and annexed Eritrea in 1890. The Italian advance was stopped by the defeat and total rout of a large Italian army by the Emperor Menelik II at Adwa in 1896, an Ethiopian victory that is still commemorated as a national holiday. Italy, however, maintained control of Eritrea and also occupied the coastal region of Banadir (Italian Somaliland) in 1900. Meanwhile, France and the United Kingdom had obtained Somali coastal enclaves through purchase and a series of protectorate treaties concluded in the past with local tribal chieftains.

Menelik died in 1913. Three years later, his grandson and successor, Lij Yasu, was deposed in favor of his aunt, Empress Zauditu (Judith). Ras Tafari Mekonnen of Shewa was selected as heir apparent and head of government. On 2 November 1930, he was crowned Emperor Haile Selassie I. Italy invaded and conquered Ethiopia in 1935–36. Forced to flee the country, the emperor returned in 1941 with the aid of British forces. By a UN decision, Eritrea, which had been under British administration since 1941, was federated to Ethiopia in 1952 and was incorporated into the

empire 10 years later. By this time, an Eritrean secessionist movement was already stirring.

After an abortive coup in 1960, the emperor's political power began to lessen as political opposition increased. Guerrilla activity in Eritrea increased noticeably between 1970 and 1973; student and labor unrest also grew. After an official cover-up of catastrophic drought and famine conditions in Welo and Tigray provinces was uncovered in 1974, the armed forces overthrew the government. From 28 June to 12 September 1974, the emperor was systematically isolated and finally deposed. The monarchy was officially abolished in March 1975. Haile Selassie was killed while in the custody of security forces on 27 August 1975.

The new Provisional Military Administrative Council, also called the Dergue, came under the leadership of Maj. (later Lt. Col.) Mengistu Haile Mariam. The economy was extensively nationalized in 1975. Mengistu declared himself a Marxist-Leninist in 1976 and established close relations with Moscow. Perhaps 10,000 Ethiopians were killed in 1976–78 as the Dergue suppressed a revolt by civilian leftists that involved urban terrorism.

The war with Eritrean secessionists continued inconclusively until 1991. In mid 1977, Somalia invaded the Ogaden area to support the claims of ethnic Somalis there for self-determination. The assault was repulsed with the assistance of Soviet arms and Cuban soldiers in early 1978, when a 20-year treaty with the USSR was signed. Close links with Libya and the People's Democratic Republic of Yemen were established in 1981. In 1982, Ethiopian troops attempted without success to topple the Somali government by mounting an invasion of some 10,000 Ethiopian troops in support of the insurgent Somali Salvation Democratic Front. Hostilities with Somalia later eased, and diplomatic relations were reestablished in 1988. However, relations with the Sudan soured, as each country supported insurgent movements in the other.

A devastating drought and famine struck northern Ethiopia during 1982–84, taking an unknown toll in lives. Between November 1984 and October 1985, an international relief effort distributed 900,000 tons of food to nearly eight million people. Food aid continued on a reduced scale, while the government launched massive resettlement programs that critics said were really intended to hamper the operations of armed insurgents and to collectivize agriculture.

The Worker's Party of Ethiopia (WPE) was established as the sole legal political party in 1984. Two years later, a constitutional document was unveiled for discussion; after minor changes, it was approved by 81% of the voters in a referendum held on 1 February 1987. Later that year, another devastating drought struck northern Ethiopia, continuing into 1988.

Despite mobilizing one million troops and receiving massive Soviet bloc military aid, the government was not able to defeat the Eritrean and Tigrayan insurgencies. Led by the Eritrean People's Liberation Front (EPLF) and the Tigre People's Liberation Front (TPLF), which is part of a larger coalition, the Ethiopian People's Revolutionary Democratic Front (EPRDF) triumphed.

On 21 May 1991, Mengistu was forced to resign as president and fled to Zimbabwe. His vice president surrendered to EPRDF forces on May 27. The next day, Meles Zenawi, leader of the EPRDF, established an interim government. In July, delegates from the three victorious guerrilla groups agreed on a structure of an interim coalition government and to grant Eritrea the right to hold an internationally supervised referendum on independence.

In 1992, the multiparty government split sharply. The Oromo Liberation Front (OLF), the second-largest partner, withdrew from the coalition on 23 June. It claimed that the regional elections held on 21 June had been rigged by the EPRDF. The OLF and five other political groups had boycotted the elections. Some OLF forces took up arms against the government.

Amid the turbulence, the transitional government pledged to oversee the establishment of Ethiopia's first multiparty democracy. During 1993, a new constitution was drafted. For the transitional government, a 65-member Council of Representatives was created by the four constituent parties of the EPRDF, which was dominated by the TPLF, a Tigrayan ethnic party.

In June 1994, elections were held for the newly established Constituent Assembly. The EPRDF won 484 of 547 seats in a contest judged free and fair by observers. However, the majority of opposition candidates boycotted the elections under the banner of the Coalition of Alternative Forces for Peace and Democracy in Ethiopia (CAFPDE). The OLF also boycotted the election. The Assembly's first order of business was to draft a new constitution. When completed, the document called for the establishment of a bicameral legislature, a directly elected president, regional autonomy, the right to secession, and the division of the country into nine states. Elections were held in 1995 for the Federal Parliamentary Assembly, consisting of the directly elected Council of People's Representatives and the Council of the Federation. Opposition parties again boycotted the elections resulting in a commanding majority for the EPRDF—483 of 548 seats.

The political opposition's refusal to participate in elections has been a major problem for Ethiopia's fledgling democracy. Western governments and representatives of the OAU engaged the parties in talks prior to the 1995 balloting in the hopes of expanding participation, but opposition leaders insisted the government was impeding their efforts to fairly participate in the electoral process.

The Oromo Liberation Army (OLA), the armed wing of the OLF, has continued armed struggle against the Ethiopian government. Fighting intensified with a series of battles between May and August 1999. Both sides claimed victory, giving conflicting figures for the dead and injured. Over 2,000 OLA and government soldiers may have died in the fighting. Military forces also intensified operations against the Somali-based Al'Ittihad terrorist organization, rebel elements of the Ogaden National Liberation Front, and Tokuchuma (another terrorist group operating in eastern Ethiopia), both in the country and southern Somalia and in Northern Kenya. Ethiopia accused Eritrea and Somalia of financially supporting and training the OLF and Al'Ittihad.

Simmering tensions over border alignment with Eritrea came to a boil in 1998. Between 2 and 6 May 1998, Eritrean soldiers invaded and occupied Badme in northeastern Ethiopia. Other areas were subsequently occupied in Tigray State. Ethiopia later recaptured Badme, but fighting continued, interspersed with periods of inactivity. A US- and Rwanda-sponsored peace plan proposed in early June 1998 failed; so did arbitration efforts by the then-OAU. Each side claimed to accept an OAU framework agreement while accusing the other of making impossible preconditions to its implementation. The two-and-a-half-year war claimed the lives of an estimated 70,000 people on both sides, and cost both

countries—two of the world's poorest—an estimated $1 million a day, according to the United Nations. The bloody war formally ended on 12 December 2000 with a peace treaty, the Algiers Agreement.

Under the Algiers Agreement, some 4,200 UN soldiers commanded under the UN Mission in Ethiopia and Eritrea (UNMEE) remained on the border by July 2003. Their task was to monitor the so-called Temporary Security Zone (TSZ) that separates the two countries. Meanwhile, as part of the treaty, the Eritrea Ethiopia Boundary Commission (EEBC) demarcated the internationally recognized boundary. The EEBC, which was based in The Hague and comprised of five international lawyers chosen by both countries, was established to resolve boundary claims between the two neighboring countries. In its ruling of 13 April 2002, The Hague-based Permanent Court of Arbitration awarded the key town of Badme, where the war first flared up, to Eritrea. Ethiopia labeled the ruling "unjust and illegal," refused to accept it, and would not withdraw from Badme. Legally, the ruling is binding and final. Rejection of the ruling resulted in five years of no war and no peace between the neighbors since formal cessation of hostilities in 2000; this stalemate raised concerns over a possible relapse in fighting.

Since rejection of the border ruling of the Permanent Court of Arbitration by Ethiopia, Eritrea and Ethiopia have sent mixed messages and traded accusations as to which side is stalling implementation of the Algiers Agreement. For example, the Ethiopian government announced in November 2004 that it finally accepted the EEBC ruling and urged Eritrea to accept its full implementation, but Prime Minister Meles Zenawi later said he would accept border demarcation only in undisputed areas. Amidst rising tensions and international concerns over a military build-up on both sides of the border, the Eritrean government on 5 October 2005 banned UN flights in the 25-km demilitarized TSZ and UN night patrols by vehicle on its side of the TSZ. This action forced the UN mission in Eritrea (UNMEE) to vacate 18 of its 40 posts.

The UN Security Council passed a resolution in November 2005 imposing a one-month deadline for compliance and demanding that Eritrea rescind its flight and vehicle ban on the UN mission or face unspecified sanctions. Instead, Eritrea escalated the situation on 6 December 2005 by expelling 180 North America, Russian, and other international military observers, UN volunteers, and international civilian personnel. No reason was given for the action. Eritrea has repeatedly accused the international community, in particular the UN, of failing to enforce the EEBC boundary ruling. The same UN Security Council Resolution 1640 required both Ethiopia and Eritrea to withdraw their troops to the levels of 16 December 2004 and to both take immediate steps to start demarcation of their disputed boundary in accordance with the 2002 EEBC ruling by 23 December 2005.

On 22 December 2005, the EEBC ruled that Eritrea had caused the war with Ethiopia and violated international law when it invaded its neighbor in May 1998 and was "liable to compensate Ethiopia for damages caused by that violation of international law." However, both countries were likely to receive compensation from the other for breach of various international laws and for human rights abuses. This ruling did not change the separate EEBC ruling on boundaries between the two countries. The last meeting of the EEBC was held in September 2007, but no agreement was reached towards the emplacement of pillars on the ground.

As of December 2005, neither Eritrea nor Ethiopia had met its obligations under the UN resolution 1640 except for a partial withdrawal of troops from the border by Ethiopia. The military situation along the border remained tense and potentially volatile. In October 2006, then-UN Secretary General Kofi Annan urged Eritrea to pull back the troops it had moved into the buffer zone on the Ethiopian border. The UN stated the incursion was a major cease-fire violation. In November, Ethiopia and Eritrea rejected the EEBC proposal as a way of resolving the border dispute.

In 2008, the UN Mission in Ethiopia and Eritrea came to an end, as the Eritrean government cut off fuel supplies and created restrictions that jeopardized the safety of UN personnel. The UN Security Council voted unanimously to end the mandate. The stalemate over the border with Eritrea continued into 2009, with both countries arguing for control of the town of Badme.

Ethiopia's second multiparty elections took place on 14 May 2000 but were marred by irregularities and violence at a number of polling stations requiring the rescheduling of voting in certain constituencies. Voting was postponed in Somali regional states because of severe drought. The results gave parties the following number of seats: OPDO, 177; Amhara National Democratic Movement (ANDM), 134; TPLF, 38; Walayta, Gamo, Gofa, Dawro, and Konta People's Democratic Organization (WGGPDO), 27; EPRDF, 19; Somali People's Democratic Party (SPDO), 18; Gambela People's Democratic Movement (GNDM), 15; Kafa Shaka People's Democratic Organization (KSPDO), 10; ANDP, 8; Gedeyo People's Revolutionary Democratic Front (GPRDF), 7; South Omo People's Democratic Movement (SOPDM), 7; Benishangul Gumuz People's Democratic Unity Front (BGPDUF), 6; Bench Madji People's Democratic Organization (BMPDO), 5; Kembata, Alabaa, and Tembaro (KAT), 4; other regional political groupings, 22; and independents, 8. Forty-three seats were unconfirmed. On 8 October 2001, the Council of People's Representatives elected Woldegiorgis Girma president. Girma received 100% of the vote for a six-year term.

Ethiopia suffered yet another drought and food shortfalls in 2003–04. During the previous 30 years, rainfall levels gradually fell by as much as 23 mm a year, leaving some $12.6 million in need of food aid in 2003—or one in five of the population—at a cost of around $800 million. In 2004, the government began a program to move more than two million people away from the arid highlands of the east as a strategy to reduce vulnerability to drought and reduce food shortages.

Ethiopia held its third multiparty elections on 15 May 2005. The elections resulted in the EPRDF's disputed return to power. The EPRDF retained its control of the government with 327 of the 547 parliamentary seats, or 59% of the vote, while opposition parties shared 174 seats, or 32% of the vote. The opposition charged that the ruling EPRDF coalition had rigged the vote and engaged in acts of voter intimidation and violence, necessitating the rescheduling of voting in certain constituencies. On 8 June 2005, demonstrations, mounted by unarmed university students in Addis Ababa protesting the alleged electoral fraud and demanding investigations or a rerun, turned violent when police opened fire, killing some 42 people. At least one of the international observer groups, the European Union Election Observation Mission,

concluded that the election and electoral process had been below international standards. Both the Ethiopian government and electoral commission dismissed the report as biased, self-contradictory, and lacking credibility. With the controversy surrounding the elections, final official election results were not released until nearly four months later on 5 September. By the end of December 2005, the main opposition party, The Coalition for Unity and Democracy (CUD), was still boycotting the legislature.

Announcement of the final 2005 election results was followed by more violence starting November 1, when the opposition CUD led protests of the results, and at least 46 people were killed when security forces opened fire. More than 60,000 arrests are reported to have resulted, and Prime Minister Zenawi announced that 3,000 of them would face charges. On 28 December 2005, a Federal High Court judge remanded 129 opposition leaders, journalists, civil society members and a 15-year-old boy on charges related to violent demonstrations. The defendants claimed they were political prisoners, but the state charged the 129 with crimes ranging from treason to genocide and blamed opposition leaders for the deaths of 34 people and damages allegedly worth $110 million.

In 2006, Ethiopian troops crossed the border into Somalia to support the Somali transitional government headquartered in Baidoa. The Somali transitional government was locked in struggle with Islamists who had taken control of the capital city, Mogadishu, and much of Somalia. In October 2006, Prime Minister Meles Zenawi asserted that Ethiopia was technically at war with the Islamists because they had declared holy war on his country. In December 2006, amid fierce fighting, Ethiopian aircraft, tanks, and artillery were used to support the forces of the Somali transitional government. The Islamists were temporarily defeated, as their stronghold port of Kismayo was taken by government forces. The remaining factions, however, refused to consider peace talks unless Ethiopian forces withdrew from the fray. An agreement was reached, and the last Ethiopian troops left Mogadishu in January 2009.

In the May 2010 parliamentary elections, the ruling EPRDF and its allies steamrolled to victory, capturing 545 of the 547 seats in parliament. Although the electoral board hailed the vote as "peaceful, credible, fair, free, and democratic," election observers, including those from the European Union, said they found that the structure of the elections favored the ruling party.

For nearly two decades, the government has fought against rebel factions in the Ogaden region over that region's oil and gas reserves and the presence of foreign companies. The rebel Ogaden National Liberation Front (ONLF), which has been seeking independence for the region, has been responsible for several violent attacks against Ethiopian security forces and foreign oil companies. One of the worst attacks occurred in 2007 at an oil exploration field managed by the Chinese Sinopec Corp. Sixty-five Ethiopian soldiers and nine Chinese workers were killed as a result. While several attacks have occurred since then, a large faction of the ONLF began to seek a peace deal with the government. In October 2010, that faction, which represents about 80% of the rebels, signed a peace agreement with the government. However, representatives from the smaller Osman faction, named after former leader Admiral Mohamed Omar Osman, have called the deal irrelevant and threatened to continue attacks against any companies that do not gain their permission before setting up shop in Ogaden.

¹³GOVERNMENT

In name, Ethiopia was a constitutional monarchy between 1931 and 1974, but sovereignty was vested solely in the emperor, a hereditary monarch. The ruler appointed the prime minister, senators, judges, governors, and mayors. The emperor was assisted by the Council of Ministers and the Crown Council, the members of which he appointed.

After the military takeover in 1974, the parliament was dissolved and the provisional military government (PMG) established. The PMG assumed full control of the government and continued to rule through its provisional military administrative council, also called the Dergue, whose chairmanship Mengistu seized in February 1977. Government decisions were made by Mengistu on an ad hoc basis, sometimes in consultation with members of the Dergue's Standing Committee. Control over government ministries was maintained by assigning Dergue representatives to oversee their operations. The Commission for Organizing the Party of the Working People of Ethiopia acted as the Dergue's political arm.

The constitution approved by referendum on 1 February 1987 declared Ethiopia to be a people's democratic republic. A national assembly (Shengo), with 835 members chosen by proportional representation for the various nationalities, theoretically had supreme power. The president, who was elected to a five-year term by Shengo, acted as chief executive and commander-in-chief of the armed forces and nominated and presided over the cabinet and the state council, which had legislative power when the Shengo was not in session. The president also appointed top officials of the Workers' Party of Ethiopia (WPE), which was called the leading force in the state and society. The assembly held its first meeting on 9 September; the next day, it elected Mengistu president. It also redrew the political map, creating five "autonomous regions" in a doomed attempt to weaken the appeal of the independence movements. Despite the trappings of representative government, all power remained in Mengistu's hands. He was head of state and government, leader of the only party, and commander of the armed forces.

After Mengistu's defeat in May 1991, a transitional government was established, under the leadership of the Ethiopian People's Revolutionary Democratic Front, a coalition of parties opposed to the Dergue and led by President Meles Zenawi. Elections for a constituent assembly were held in June 1994. A new constitution was drafted, providing for a directly elected president, a bicameral legislature, regional autonomy with the right to secede, and a nine-state national structure. Elections to the newly established Federal Parliamentary Assembly were held in 1995; they resulted in a huge victory for the EPRDF owing to opposition boycotts. In the May 2000 elections, Zenawi's coalition gained 368 of the 548 seats in the Council of People's Representatives. The next presidential elections were scheduled for October 2007.

The Federal Parliamentary Assembly has two chambers. The Council of People's Representatives (Yehizbtewekayoch Mekir Bet), the lower chamber, has 547 members, who are elected for five-year terms in single-seat constituencies. The Council of the Federation (Yefedereshn Mekir Bet), or upper chamber, has 117 members chosen by state assemblies to serve five-year terms.

¹⁴POLITICAL PARTIES

In the past, there were no established political parties, although political factions existed on the basis of religion, ethnicity, regionalism, and common economic interests. In the 1970s, a number of illegal separatist groups became active militarily. They included the Eritrean People's Liberation Front (EPLF), Eritrean Liberation Front (ELF), the Oromo People's Democratic Organization (OPDO), Tigray People's Liberation Front (TPLF), Oromo Liberation Front (OLF), and Western Somali Liberation Front (WSLF). Eventually, EPLF defeated the ELF in Eritrea.

Two civilian left-wing parties, the Ethiopian People's Revolutionary Party and the All-Ethiopian Socialist Movement, were crushed by the Dergue in 1976 and 1977, respectively. In 1979, the Dergue established the Commission for Organizing the Party of the Working People of Ethiopia (COPWE) in order to lay the groundwork for a Marxist-Leninist party along Soviet lines. The Worker's Party of Ethiopia (WPE) was established in 1984 as the sole legal political party. Its 11-man politburo was headed by Mengistu.

The separatists successfully defeated Mengistu's forces, and, after Mengistu fled in May 1991, they established a transitional government under their coalition banner, the Ethiopian People's Revolutionary Democratic Front (EPRDF). The TPLF is the most prominent member of the EPRDF, which also includes the Ethiopian People's Democratic Movement (EPDM) and the Afar Democratic Union. The OLF is not part of the coalition. There are also numerous small, ethnic-based groups and several Islamic militant groups. Following 1994 elections to a transitional national assembly, 30 opposition groups—not including the OLF—formed the Coalition of Alternative Forces for Peace and Democracy in Ethiopia (CAFPDE) and began pressing for electoral reform. New elections were held in 1995 for a newly created Federal Parliamentary Assembly (consisting of two chambers). The elections, despite being overseen by international observers, were boycotted by the opposition and won by the EPRDF, which secured substantial majorities. Meles Zenawi of the EPRDF was chosen as prime minister.

The main parties contesting the 14 May 2000 elections were: Afar Democratic Association, Afar Democratic Union, Amhar National Democratic Movement, Ethiopia People's Revolutionary Democratic Front (EPRDF), Ethiopian Democratic Officers' Revolutionary Movement, Oromo People's Democratic Organization, and Tigre People's Liberation Front. There were approximately 58 national and regional parties, 29 of them belonging to the four-party coalition of the ruling EPRDF. Girma Woldegiorgis of the EPRDF was elected president by the house of representatives in 2001.

The EPRDF ruling coalition was returned to power in the contested elections of 15 May 2005 amidst opposition charges of widespread vote rigging and intimidation. A total of 10 parties and coalitions and one independent won the 547 parliamentary seats, which were split as follows: EPRDF, 327; CUD, 109; United Ethiopian Democratic Forces (UEDF) Alliance, 52; Oromo Federalist Democratic Movement, (OFDM) 11; ANDP, 8; GPDM, 3; Sheko and Mezenger People's Democratic Unity Organization

(SMPDUO), 1; Somali People's Democratic Party (SPDP), 24; Hareri National League (HNL), 1; Argoba Nationality Democratic Organization (ANDO), 1; and Independent, 1.

In the May 2010 parliamentary elections, the ruling Ethiopian Peoples' Revolutionary Democratic Front (EPRDF) won 499 seats, followed by the Somali Peoples Democratic Party (SPDP) with 24 seats, the Afar National Democratic Party with 8 seats, and the Benishangul Gumuz People's Democratic Party (BGPDP), which captured 9. Ethiopia's largest opposition group, the eight-party Ethiopia Federal Democratic Unity Forum (Medrek), won just one seat in the election. The Harari National League and the Argoba People Democratic Organization each took one seat, as well. A final seat went to an independent candidate.

15 LOCAL GOVERNMENT

According to a 2006 CIA report, Ethiopia has nine ethnically based states and two self-governing administrations—Addis Ababa and Dirē Dawa. Until 1987, Ethiopia was divided into 15 administrative regions, which in turn were subdivided into 103 sub-regions and 505 districts. In 1976, peasant associations were empowered to collect taxes and form women's associations, cooperatives, and militias. In the mid 1980s, an estimated 25,000 such peasant groups were in existence. Urban dwellers' associations were established for a variety of functions, including law and order.

In 1987, at its first sitting, the Shengo redrew the political map. It created five "autonomous regions" (Eritrea, Assab, Dirē Dawa, Ogaden, and Tigre). The remaining provinces were further subdivided into 24 administrative zones.

The establishment of regions was altered with the creation of the transitional government in 1991. In 1993, Eritrea gained its independence. The new regime called for 14 regional governments, but the June 1992 elections for 11 of the 14 regional assemblies were challenged, and widespread fraud was alleged. In the May 2000 elections, 3,300 regional and national seats were to be contested. Results of the third multiparty elections of 15 May 2005 were equally protested. The EPRDF alliance won half of the 10 state councils. According to the National Electoral Board of Ethiopia, a total of 1,920 Regional Council and City Administration seats were contested in 10 of the 11 regions.

16 JUDICIAL SYSTEM

The government of Ethiopia is now putting into place a decentralized federal system of courts consisting of regional and district courts consistent with the 1994 constitution. Each region has district (woreda), higher, and supreme courts. There are also local Shariah courts that hear religious and family cases involving Muslims. The Federal High Court and Federal Supreme Court have jurisdiction over cases involving federal laws, trans-regional issues, and issues of national import. The president and vice president of the Federal Supreme Court are recommended by the prime minister and appointed by the House of People's Representatives; for other federal judges, the prime minister submits to the House of People's Representatives for appointment candidates selected by the Federal Judicial Administrative Council.

The constitution provides for an independent judiciary; trials are public. Defendants have a right to legal counsel, and a public defender's office provides counsel to indigent defendants. The law, however, does not allow the defense access to prosecutorial evidence before the trial, and the current judiciary suffers from a lack of trained personnel and financial constraints. In 1995, the government began training new judges and prosecutors. However, it is estimated that the creation of a fully independent and skilled judicial system will take several decades.

In 1992, a special prosecutor's office was established. In 1994, this office began trying defendants charged with crimes against humanity during the Mengistu regime. As of 1997, approximately 1,300 detainees had been charged with war crimes. Up to 5,198 people had been charged with war crimes by the end of 1999.

The Council of People's Representatives in October 1999 passed enabling legislation to meet the constitutional requirement for the creation of a human rights commission and office of the ombudsman. The commission has full powers to receive and investigate all complaints of human rights violations made against any person. The commission was not made operational until 2005.

17 ARMED FORCES

The International Institute for Strategic Studies reports that armed forces in Ethiopia totaled 138,000 members in 2011. The force is comprised of 135,000 from the army and 3,000 members of the air force. Armed forces represent 0.3% of the labor force in Ethiopia. Defense spending totaled $1 billion and accounted for 1.2% of GDP.

18 INTERNATIONAL COOPERATION

Ethiopia is a charter member of the United Nations (UN), having joined on 13 November 1945; it belongs to the ECA and all the non-regional specialized agencies. A participant in the African Development Bank, G-24, and G-77. The former Ethiopian emperor Haile Selassie was a founder of the Organization of African Unity (OAU), which is now known as the African Union (AU). The AU secretariat and the UN Economic Commission for Africa are located in Addis Ababa. The nation has observer status in the WTO. It is part of COMESA, the ACP Group, the New Partnership for Africa's Development (NEPAD), and the Intergovernmental Authority on Development, a Horn of Africa regional grouping.

Ethiopian troops fought under UN command in the Korean conflict and served in the Congo (now the Democratic Republic of the Congo) in the early 1960s. The nation also supports the UN Operation in Burundi (est. 2004).

A border dispute with Eritrea resulted in war from 1998–2000. In 2000, the countries agreed to a United Nations-monitored cessation of hostilities and began the process of demarcating parts of the border. Although a basic border agreement was adopted in 2002, the two countries remain in dispute over the town of Badme. The UN peacekeeping mission ended in 2008 because the Eritrean government cut off fuel supplies and created restrictions that jeopardized the safety of UN personnel. In August 2009, the Eritrea-Ethiopia Claims Commission (an international tribunal established in The Hague at the end of the border war) issued a ruling on the amount of compensation each country was to pay the other for damages caused during the border war. Ethiopia was awarded $174 million but was ordered to pay Eritrea $164 million. Ethiopia's claim for $1 billion for environmental damages was dismissed. Though Ethiopia came out ahead in the ruling, the government argued that the amount did not reflect the extent of the damage suffered by the nation through the war.

Ethiopia is a member of the Nonaligned Movement and the Organization for the Prohibition of Chemical Weapons.

In environmental cooperation, Ethiopia is part of the Basel Convention, the Convention on Biological Diversity, CITES, the Montréal Protocol, and the UN Conventions on Climate Change and Desertification.

[19]ECONOMY

Ethiopia has experienced strong economic growth since 2002. With real GDP growth at or near double-digit levels since 2003, the country has consistently outperformed most other countries in Africa and expanded much faster than the continent-wide average, according to the African Development Bank. Real gross domestic product (GDP) has been 12.6% in 2004–05, 11.8% 2006–07, 11.2% 2007–08 and during the global financial crisis of 2008, Ethiopia had a growth rate of 10.8%. Growth is driven by the service sector (14.5%), followed by the industrial (10.2%) and agricultural (6%) sectors. Inflation stood at 8.5% in 2009 and 8.1% in 2010, and unemployment was reported at 20.9% in 2009.

Ethiopia's economy has undergone reforms since May 1991, when a market-oriented government came to power. Droughts, civil war, and cross-border conflicts have devastated the economy as much as socialist-style totalitarianism. The government continues to institute economic reforms designed to liberalize the economy and increase the role of private capital. Land, under Ethiopia's constitution, however, as of 2007 is owned by the government and leased to tenants. A large trade deficit hampers economic development.

Agriculture, hunting, forestry, and fishing engaged 85% of the Ethiopian population and account for almost half of GDP and 80% of exports. The agricultural sector is diverse, producing maize, sorghum, millet, other cereals (barley, wheat, and teff), tubers, and sugarcane. Coffee is the major export crop, generating 35% of Ethiopia's foreign exchange earnings. Livestock production is also important, responsible for around 20% of export earnings. Ethiopia's agriculture is plagued by periodic drought, soil degradation caused by inappropriate agricultural practices and overgrazing, deforestation, high population density, undeveloped water resources, and poor transport infrastructure, making it difficult and expensive to get goods to market. However, agriculture is the country's most promising resource. Potential exists for self-sufficiency in grains and for export development in livestock, flowers, grains, oilseeds, sugar, vegetables, and fruits.

The manufacturing sector, centered around Addis Ababa, produces construction materials, metal and chemical products, and basic consumer goods including food, beverages, leather, clothing, and textiles. Some large-scale industry is still state-owned, but a process of privation has been taking place since 1999.

Ethiopia produces gold and has additional undeveloped deposits of platinum, marble, tantalite, copper, potash, salt, soda ash, zinc, nickel, and iron. Natural gas is found in the Ogaden.

To break the cycle of famine, the government has promoted extension services and fertilizers in the hope that farmers could realize their potential and that poverty would be reduced. The progress in the country's economic fortunes that began in the 1990s was largely quashed by the 1998–2000 war and a sharp decline in international coffee prices. After the border war with Eritrea ended

in 2000, however, bumper crops were offset by farmers' inability to find markets for their goods.

Economic growth was modest in until 2004 when the economy recovered expanding by over 11% in 2005 and 2007 and over 10% in 2009 and 2010. The yoyo effect that has plagued the Ethiopian economy is largely due to the finicky weather patterns—droughts in late 2002 led to the economic recess of 2003, whereas normal weather patterns helped agricultural and GDP growth recover during 2004–07. More recently, issues with inflation and foreign exchange have become problems largely tied to the global economic crisis.

[20]INCOME

The CIA estimated that, in 2010, the GDP of Ethiopia was $86.12 billion. The CIA defines GDP as the value of all final goods and services produced within a nation in a given year and computed on the basis of purchasing power parity (PPP) rather than value as measured on the basis of the rate of the exchange based on current dollars. The per capita GDP was estimated at $1,000. Household income by percentage share of the lowest 10% was 4.1% and the highest 10%: 25.6% (2005). Investments made up 24.6 % of GDP in 2010.

According to the World Bank, remittances from citizens living abroad totaled $261.6 million or about $3 per capita and accounted for approximately 0.3% of GDP.

Consumption increased in 2010 by 7.8%. Private consumption is the main contributor to this growth in consumption, which grew from 75% of GDP in 2002 to 87.5% of GDP in 2009. Gross capital formation also increased by 11.5% in 2010 and is projected to grow by 13.3% in 2011. Both public and private capital formation contributed to this trend, but the public sector's contribution was nearly double that of the private sector. The World Bank reports that, in 2009, household consumption in Ethiopia totaled $24.3 billion or about $267 per capita, measured in current US dollars rather than PPP. Household consumption includes expenditures of individuals, households, and nongovernmental organizations on goods and services, excluding the purchases of dwellings. It was estimated that household consumption was growing at an average annual rate of 9.4%.

As of 2011 the most recent study by the World Bank reported that actual individual consumption in Ethiopia was 82.5% of GDP and accounted for 0.09% of world consumption. By comparison, the United States accounted for 25.44% of world individual consumption. The World Bank also estimated that 45.7% of Ethiopia's GDP was spent on food and beverages, 20.3% on housing and household furnishings, 5.1% on clothes, 1.8% on health, 1.8% on transportation, 0.2% on communications, 0.5% on recreation, 1.8% on restaurants and hotels, and 2.6% on miscellaneous goods and services and purchases from abroad.

[21]LABOR

The 1993 Labor Law provides workers with the right to form and join unions and engage in collective bargaining. This right, however, excludes many categories of employment, including teachers and civil servants. The right of workers to strike (and the employer's right to lockout) is also somewhat restricted. Both sides must seek conciliation efforts, provide 10 days' notice and give reasons for the strike or lockout. The government may refer labor disputes to arbitration, which is binding to the parties. As of 2005, about 300,000 workers were members of a union. Estimates by labor experts indicate that over 90% of union members were covered by collective bargaining agreements in that same year.

The legal minimum age for employment is 14, with special provisions for these workers up to age 18. However, child labor is widespread in both rural and urban areas. As of 2011, Ethiopia did not have a national minimum wage rate, although some public enterprises and government institutions had set their own minimum wage rates. For that same year, employees in the public sector had a minimum wage of $20 per month, while those in the insurance and banking sector had a rate of $21 per month. In neither case were these wage rates sufficient to provide a decent standard of living for a worker and family. The standard legal workweek was 48 hours with a 24 hour rest period. In addition, there was premium pay for overtime, while compulsory and/or excessive overtime was prohibited.

As of 2007, Ethiopia had a total labor force of 37.9 million people. Within that labor force, CIA estimates in 2009 that 85% were employed in agriculture, 5% in industry, and 10% in the service sector.

22 AGRICULTURE

Roughly 11% of the total land is currently farmed, and the country's major crops include cereals, pulses, coffee, oilseed, cotton, sugarcane, potatoes, qat, and cut flowers. Cereal production amounted to 15.5 million tons, fruit production 787,758 tons, and vegetable production 1.6 million tons.

Subsistence farming and livestock grazing, both inefficient, are the rule. Field crops account for 40% of gross agricultural output, cash crops for 20%, and livestock for the rest. In 2009, the government began implementing plans to increase commercial agriculture by allocating close to 3 million hectares for commercial agriculture. The amount allocated comprises 3% of Ethiopia's total land area, 4% of the total arable land in the country and close to 17% of the total land under cultivation. Since 2005, 1,100 foreign agricultural investors have registered, but only around 6% (64) are reported to be operational. There are 72 foreign investment projects above 5,000 hectares requesting a total land allocation of 2.9 million hectares and registering a total capital of B36.5 billion.

The coffee variety known as arabica may have originated in Ethiopia, and the word coffee is derived from Kaffa (Kefa), the region in the southwest that is still the largest coffee-producing area of the country. Coffee is the most valuable cash export crop. Coffee production was an estimated at 260,000 tons in 2004, the highest in Africa. Qat, the leaves from a shrub that are used to make tea and which have a mild narcotic effect, is another important cash export crop.

The most commonly produced cereal is teff (*Eragrostis abyssinica*), which is used to make the Ethiopian unleavened bread called *injera*. Corn and barley are the next most important grains, with an annual gross production of at least 1 million tons each. Sorghum, wheat, millet, peas, beans, lentils, and oilseeds are produced in substantial quantities; sugarcane and cotton are also grown.

The agricultural sector suffered severe damage from the civil war and its aftermath. Forced recruitment into the military led to a shortage of farm labor. Reforms aimed at introducing market-based incentives have been implemented, including freeing agricultural marketing and farm labor hiring practices. Emergency provisions of seeds, fertilizer, and other inputs have also been vital in rebuilding Ethiopia's agriculture. Since 1999, however, the border war with Eritrea and reduced harvests have caused Ethiopia to rely heavily on food donations from international organizations in order to ward off starvation.

23 ANIMAL HUSBANDRY

The UN Food and Agriculture Organization (FAO) reported that Ethiopia dedicated 20 million hectares (49.4 million acres) to permanent pasture or meadow in 2009. During that year, the country tended 38 million chickens, 50.9 million head of cattle, and 29,000 pigs. The production from these animals amounted to 363,095 tons of beef and veal, 1,751 tons of pork, 46,250 tons of poultry, 31,995 tons of eggs, and 1.48 million tons of milk. Ethiopia also produced 75,600 tons of cattle hide and 7,596 tons of raw wool.

Ethiopia has the largest livestock population in Africa, and this subsector accounts for 40% of gross agricultural output. In normal years, animal husbandry provides a living for 75% of the population. The country lacks facilities for fattening cattle brought in to slaughter, an adequate veterinary service, and breeding herds. The number of sheep and goats was estimated at 17 million and 9.6 million, respectively, but periodic drought may have made the actual number much lower. The number of horses was estimated at 1,500,000, mules at 325,000, donkeys at 3,800,000, and camels at 470,000. These were primarily pack animals.

Hides and skins constitute the country's second-largest export item and generally command high prices on the world market. In 2005, production of sheepskins was 10,800 tons and goatskins, 16,100 tons. In 2005, Ethiopia produced 39,000 tons of honey, more than any other nation in Africa.

24 FISHING

With the secession of Eritrea, Ethiopia lost access to an estimated 1,011 km (628 mi) of Red Sea coastline. In 1992, the Ethiopian and provisional Eritrean governments agreed to make Assab a free port for Ethiopia. Most Ethiopians do not eat seafood; hunting and fishing accounts for only a tiny fraction of the GDP. In 2008, the annual capture totaled 16,770 tons, according to the UN FAO.

25 FORESTRY

In the 1930s, more than 30% of Ethiopia consisted of forests, but that total has fallen to 13%. Boswellia and species of commiphora produce gums used as the basis for frankincense and myrrh, respectively. A species of acacia is a source of gum arabic. Eucalyptus stands, introduced in the 19th century, are a valuable source of firewood, furniture, and poles. Roundwood production was an estimated 94 million cu m (3.3 billion cu ft) in 2003; all but 2.5 million cu m (87 million cu ft) was for fuel. In 2009, approximately 12% of Ethiopia is covered by forest. The UN FAO estimated the 2009 roundwood production at 2.93 million cu m (103.4 million cu ft). The value of all forest products, including roundwood, totaled $3.2 million.

26 MINING

Ethiopia's main mineral export is gold, but the country has also been a producer of silver, tantalite, talc, soda ash, brick clay, feldspar, gemstones, diatomite, granite, anhydrite and gypsum, limestone, pumice, kaolin, salt, sand, and scoria. The country also has metal deposits of manganese, iron ore, platinum and nickel. Despite this, little of Ethiopia's expected mineral potential has been exploited, although foreign investment was increasing. Gold mine output in 2009 was estimated at 4,872 kg. Silver mine production in 2009 totaled 1,400 kg. Cement was the most important mineral industry in value and quantity. In 2009, hydraulic cement output totaled 2,300,000 metric tons, up from 1,568,624 metric tons in 2005. Substantial iron ore deposits were discovered in the Welega region in 1985. Other undeveloped resources included copper, semiprecious gemstones (agate, aquamarine, chalcedony, chrysoprase, emerald, garnet, jasper, obsidian, ruby, sapphire, spinel), molybdenum, mercury, palladium, rhodium, tungsten, zinc, apatite, bentonite, dolomite, potash, and quartz sand. Expected improvements in the general economic situation and the need to rebuild infrastructure were likely to increase demand for building materials and the viability of Eritrea's metals and industrial minerals deposits. The production of gold, silica sand, and silver is likely to increase in the near future; the outlook for niobium and tantalum depend on world market conditions.

27 ENERGY AND POWER

Ethiopia has a total generating capacity of 2,060 MW as of April 2011. The World Bank reported in 2008 that Ethiopia produced 3.78 billion kWh of electricity and consumed 3.42 billion kWh, or 38 kWh per capita. Hydroelectric power contributes 88% of the generation capacity in Ethiopia, and 11% comes from diesel with just 1% from geothermal. Per capita oil consumption was 393 kg. Since 2002, five hydroelectric power plants have been built and put into service with a total capacity of 1,437 MW. An additional five plants are on the drawing table, including the Grand Millennium Dam on the Nile River, which is expected to generate 5,250 MW.

A series of hydroelectric projects along the Omo River has been a source of controversy both within Ethiopia and in the eyes of some international environmental and human rights groups. The 300-megawatt Tekeze hydropower plant that was inaugurated in November 2009 was followed by the 420-megawatt Gilgel Gibe II project, which opened in January 2010. A third phase, the 1,100-megawatt Gilgel Gibe III, was under construction in 2011. The combined plants were expected to produce an energy surplus for the nation, once all three are running to full capacity. The projects would also regulate the annual flooding of the river, keeping the course navigable year round. However, the seasonal flooding of the river has become an important part of life for more than 500,000 residents of the Lower Omo Valley who practiced a form of flood retreat cultivation. Opponents of the project claimed that agricultural production in the valley will decline when the river is contained. The Ethiopian Power Corporation predicted that the Gibe III (south of Gibe I) dam would produce 6,500 gWh of energy a year, with potential revenues of $407 million per year in surplus energy exports to neighboring countries.

In 1997, due to high maintenance and operating costs, Eritrea and Ethiopia agreed to shut down their joint operations at the petroleum refinery at Assab and import refined petroleum products. Although Ethiopia has few proven hydrocarbon reserves, it is estimated to have considerable potential for oil and gas exploration.

28 INDUSTRY

While Ethiopia's industrial sector engages primarily in food processing, it also produces sugar, alcohol and soft drinks, cigarettes, cotton and textiles, footwear, soap, ethyl alcohol, and quicklime. Cement production is also significant. Industrial facilities are concentrated around Addis Ababa, depend heavily on agricultural inputs, and primarily serve the domestic market.

Industry made up 13% of GDP in 2009, and it employed only a fraction of the labor force; agriculture is by far the biggest employer and also the biggest contributor to the GDP (47%); services come in second with 45% participation in the GDP. Whereas agricultural growth rates were influenced by the weather, industry has managed to register stable growth rates—5.8% in 2001–02, 4.6% in 2002–03, 6.9% in 2003–04 and 9.5% in 2010.

Since 1991, privatization of Ethiopia's industry has been a major objective of the government. In 1995, the government established the Ethiopian Privatization Agency to help privatize companies. By 1999, about 180 government enterprises had been privatized, including Pepsi-Cola and Coca-Cola bottling plants, the St. George Brewery, and the Lega Dembi Gold Mine. Other companies for sale included the Kenticha Tantalum Mine, the Calub Gas Company, and the Wonji-Shoa Sugar Factory, hotels, tanneries, textile mills, and garment factories. By 2001, 123 enterprises had been privatized, and, since 2009, an additional 31 large-scale public enterprises have been put up for sale, and 12 additional enterprises are in the pipeline for sale.

Ethiopia has few proven oil and natural gas reserves, although the potential of these industries is seen as promising. Hydrocarbon exploration began in the Ogaden Basin in the 1920s, and, in 1994, the World Bank approved a $74 million loan to develop natural gas fields in the Ogaden Basin. As of 2002, there were plans to build an oil refinery.

One of the key components of Ethiopia's industrial success is its access to ports. Two thirds of Ethiopia's goods passed through the Eritrean port of Assab prior to the 1998–2000 border war. Ethiopia subsequently shifted its trade to Djibouti, but Port Sudan and Berbera in Somaliland were targeted as future outlets for trade.

29 SCIENCE AND TECHNOLOGY

Patent applications in science and technology as of 2009, according to the World Bank, totaled 12 in Ethiopia. Public financing of science was 0.17% of GDP. Scientific societies and research institutes in Addis Ababa include the Association for the Advancement of Agricultural Sciences in Africa, the Desert Locust Control Organization for Eastern Africa, the Ethiopian Mapping Authority, the Ethiopian Medical Association, the Ethiopian Institute of Geological Surveys, the Geophysical Observatory, the National Herbarium, the Institute of Agricultural Research, and the International Livestock Center for Africa. Another Institute of Agricultural Research is located in Sidamo. The University of Addis Ababa, founded in 1950, maintains faculties of science, technology, and medicine, a college of agriculture, and a school of pharmacy. The Alemaya University of Agriculture, founded in 1952, has faculties of agriculture and forestry and a division of natural and social sciences. Also in Ethiopia are the Jimma Junior College of Agriculture and the Polytechnic Institute at Bahir-Dar.

In 1987–97, science and engineering students accounted for 26% of college and university enrollments.

In October 2009, scientists announced the discovery of a fossilized partial skeleton in the Afar Rift (northeast of Addis Ababa) that may represent the oldest known ancestor of the human species. The 4.4 million-year-old bones represent a female of an animal species known officially as *Ardipithecus ramidus* and nicknamed Ardi. Ardi and the bones of about 36 other individuals were first discovered in Ethiopia in 1992, but researchers worked for 17 years to assess the bones in comparison to known species of apes (of similar age) and early human fossils, including the famous "Lucy" skeleton found in 1974 and dated at 4 million years old. Scientists believe that Ardi was about 1.2 meters (4 feet) tall and was adept at climbing trees and walking upright for short periods of time. Ardi shows similarities to both apes and humans, leading some scientists to believe that she may be one of the evolutionary links between the two.

³⁰DOMESTIC TRADE

Addis Ababa is the paramount commercial and distribution center. Most of the economy is monetary, but transactions are still conducted by barter in some of the more isolated rural sectors. Underdeveloped transportation systems prohibit domestic trade, particularly in agriculture. As of 2001, about 75% of all farms were more than half a day's walk from the nearest all-weather road. Even so, about 80% of the work force is employed in agriculture, which accounts for about 52% of the GDP. The 1999–2000 war with Eritrea and recurring droughts have severely effected the economy. Growth in the industrial sector has been further prohibited by the land tenure system, through which the government owns and leases all land.

In general, business hours are from 8:30 or 9 a.m. to 1 p.m. and from 2 p.m. to 5 or 6 p.m., Mondays through Fridays. Shops are open until 8 p.m. The national language, Amharic, is spoken along with English, the second official language. Credit cards are not widely accepted.

³¹FOREIGN TRADE

Agriculture accounts for 80% of Ethiopia's exports, and the major agricultural export crop is coffee, providing approximately 26% of Ethiopia's foreign exchange earnings, down from 65% a decade ago because of the slump in coffee prices since the mid 1990s and increases in other exports. Coffee exports generate more than half of Ethiopia's export returns, but the country's coffee production only accounts for 2.2% of the world's coffee exports. Other traditional major agricultural exports are leather, hides and skins, pulses, oilseeds, and the traditional "khat," a leafy narcotic that is chewed. Sugar and gold production has also become important in recent years. Leather, animal hides, and skins also bring in export revenues (9.9%). Other agricultural products, including vegetables, oilseeds, and cotton reflect the remainder of major exports (10%). Flowers and plant seeds are also a growing export commodity for Ethiopia and are expected to become the largest exporter if trends continue.

Ethiopia is heavily dependent on imported manufactures. Machinery, petroleum, and petroleum products represent the leading import items. In 2009, China was Ethiopia's largest import

Principal Trading Partners – Ethiopia (2010)				
(In millions of US dollars)				
Country	**Total**	**Exports**	**Imports**	**Balance**
World	11,246.2	2,580.1	8,666.1	-6,086.0
China	1,579.3	249.1	1,330.2	-1,081.1
United States	962.9	121.8	841.1	-719.2
Sa'udi Arabia	906.8	127.9	779.0	-651.1
Germany	389.5	188.0	201.5	-13.6
India	313.7	25.3	288.4	-263.1
Italy	269.0	54.6	214.4	-159.9
Sudan	236.5	83.2	153.3	-70.1
Turkey	229.5	37.2	192.3	-155.1
Belgium	206.7	135.0	71.7	63.4
Japan	136.2	41.9	94.3	-52.4

(…) data not available or not significant.

(n.s.) not specified.

SOURCE: *2011 Direction of Trade Statistics Yearbook*, New York: United Nations, 2011.

Balance of Payments – Ethiopia (2010)		
(In millions of US dollars)		
Current Account		**-425.4**
Balance on goods	-4,964.6	
Imports	-7,364.5	
Exports	2,400.0	
Balance on services	-302.0	
Balance on income	-63.6	
Current transfers	4,904.7	
Capital Account		**...**
Financial Account		**2,368.5**
Direct investment abroad	...	
Direct investment in Ethiopia	288.3	
Portfolio investment assets	...	
Portfolio investment liabilities	...	
Financial derivatives	...	
Other investment assets	1,084.6	
Other investment liabilities	995.6	
Net Errors and Omissions		**-2,929.9**
Reserves and Related Items		**986.8**

(…) data not available or not significant.

SOURCE: *Balance of Payment Statistics Yearbook 2011*, Washington, DC: International Monetary Fund, 2011.

partner, accounting for 16% of all imports followed by Saudi Arabia, India, Italy, and Japan.

in 2010, exports reached $1.716 billion, while imports grew to $6.992 billion. Ethiopia exported coffee, qat, gold, leather products, live animals, and oilseeds to China (13.9%), Germany (10.5%), Belgium (7.5%), Saudi Arabia (7.1%), the US (6.8%), and Sudan (4.6%). Imports included food and live animals, petroleum and petroleum products, chemicals, machinery, motor vehicles, cereals, and textiles and mainly came from China (15.1%), the (9.5%), and Saudi Arabia (8.8%).

³²BALANCE OF PAYMENTS

Ethiopia's balance of payments has been significantly affected by weather conditions, terms of trade, and emergency drought relief efforts provided by the international community. Under the Multilateral Debt Relief Initiative, the IMF Executive Board approved debt relief for Ethiopia, providing 100% debt relief on all debt incurred to the IMF before January 1, 2005, writing off approximately $161 million. The global economic downturn led to balance of payments pressures beginning in 2008 and has been partially alleviated by emergency funding from the IMF.

In 2008, the purchasing power parity of Ethiopia's exports, goods and services, was $3.514 billion, while imports totaled $9.616 billion, resulting in a trade deficit of $6.102 billion. In 2010, Ethiopia had a foreign trade deficit of $5.6 billion, amounting to 22.5% of GDP.

The International Monetary Fund (IMF) reported that, in 2001, Ethiopia had exports of goods totaling $433 million and imports totaling $1.63 billion. The services credit totaled $523 million and debit $526 million. According to UNCTAD, Foreign Direct Investment (FDI) flow to Ethiopia in 2010 was $148 million.

33 BANKING AND SECURITIES

The National Bank of Ethiopia (NBE), established in 1963, serves as the nation's central bank. Its primary functions include the regulation of the money supply and the availability of credit, management of the nation's foreign reserves, the licensing and supervision of banks, the regulation of interest rates, the issuance of paper currency and coins, and the fixing of exchange rates.

In January 1994, legislation was passed allowing for the establishment of private banks and insurance companies, but not the privatization of existing institutions, or the foreign ownership of such companies. The first private bank, Awash International, started operations at the end of 1994 and had eight branches by 1999. Seven other private banks have opened, including Dashen Bank, The Bank of Abyssinia, Wegagen Bank, NIB International, United Bank, Oromia CooperativeBank, and Lion International Bank. There are also two government-owned specialized banks: the Development Bank of Ethiopia (DBE); and the Construction and Business Bank (CBB). Between 2009 and 2010, all key areas of banking operations grew by an average of 20%, with deposits at 28.4%, loans at 21.1%, and foreign assets growing by 126.4%. Profits at most banks were up 45%, and shareholders received an average return of 27% percent on their investments.

A hallmark of the Ethiopian banking system has been the appearance of micro-lending institutions, which primarily are used by low-income micro-entrepreneurs in the nation's rural and urban areas. As of 2007, there were some 271 micro-lending institutions in the country.

There are no securities exchanges, and Ethiopians are legally barred from acquiring or dealing in foreign securities. A private-sector initiative plans to establish a market for buying and selling company shares by 2000. In 2008, Ethiopian Commodity exchange was created as a national agricultural exchange providing relevant and timely market information to farmers, wholesalers, etc. with a capital investment of B194 million.

34 INSURANCE

In January 1976, the 13 insurance companies operating in Ethiopia were nationalized and fused into an inclusive national insurance organization, the Ethiopian Insurance Corp. In 1994, the insurance industry was deregulated. Seven private insurance

companies opened between 1994 and 1997: United, Africa, Nile, Nyala, Awash, National, and Global. In 2009, Ethiopia had a total of ten insurance companies with a total of 175 branches nationally with over 52% of the branches in Addis Ababa. The insurance sector is largely geared towards corporate clients who insure their assets, business, and staff members. Private insurance makes up a negligible proportion of insurance premium deposits.

35 PUBLIC FINANCE

The Ethiopian fiscal year begins 8 July, in the Ethiopian month of Hamle. Ethiopia's public finances are under great budgetary pressure, as years of war and poverty have taken a heavy toll on the countryside, population, and infrastructure.

The US CIA estimated that, in 2010, the budget of Ethiopia included $4.36 billion in public revenue and $5.098 billion in public expenditures. The budget deficit amounted to 1.4% of GDP. Public debt was 39.3% of GDP, with $5.67 billion of the debt held by foreign entities. In 2005, under the Multilateral Debt Relief Initiative, Ethiopia's debt owed to the IMF was written off totaling approximately $161 million.

36 TAXATION

Ethiopia has a standard corporate tax rate of 30%. However, companies in the mining industry (excluding oil shale, petroleum, and natural gas) are taxed at rates of 35% for small-scale mining operations and 45% for large-scale mining operations. Income generated from petroleum, oil shale, and natural gas operations are subject to the 30% rate. Capital gains derived from the sale of buildings in municipal areas that are used for a business are subject to a 15% tax. Gains from the sale of company shares are taxed at 30%. A 5% tax is levied on royalties paid to residents and nonresidents, and a 2% ad valorem turnover tax on domestic sales. On 1 January 2003, Ethiopia replaced its sales tax with a value-added tax (VAT). As of 2011, the standard rate was 15%. Exempt from the VAT were food and pharmaceuticals.

37 CUSTOMS AND DUTIES

The primary purpose of the tariff system is to provide revenue rather than to protect Ethiopian industry or to prohibit the importation of certain commodities. However, there are restrictions on importing certain goods that compete with domestically produced goods. Excise tax brackets range from 10% for textiles to 100% for vehicles with engines larger than 1,800 cc. Taxes on imports are based on the cost, insurance and freight (CIF) value. Imports of certain agricultural and industrial tools and parts and many raw materials are duty-free.

38 FOREIGN INVESTMENT

Since May 1991, the climate for foreign investment has improved dramatically. Private investment policies are more liberal, commercial performance standards have been applied to public enterprises, taxes and tariffs have been reformed, and the currency has been devalued by 58%. The devaluation was the policy action required for the rescheduling of Ethiopia's foreign debt in 1992. Foreign exchange is now auctioned.

In 1996, a revised investment proclamation was approved that created additional incentives for foreign investors. Major provisions included duty-free entry of most capital goods and a cut in the capital gains tax from 40% to 10%. In addition, the government opened a number of previously closed sectors of the economy to foreign investment, although financial services, large-scale power production, telecommunications, and other public utilities remain off-limits. Official estimates are that, as of June 1996, 52 foreign investors had been given licenses. In 1998, amendments to the 1996 investment proclamation allowed Ethiopian expatriates and permanent residents the ability to invest in industries that had previously been reserved for nationals only.

The inflow of FDI peaked in 1997 at $288.5 million and has declined sharply since. In 2000, FDI inflow was $134 million and, in 2001, grew to $349 million. Subsequent years brought with them significant levels of capital inflow ($255 million in 2002, $465 million in 2003, and $545 million in 2004), but not enough for a country the size of Ethiopia. At the end of 2004, total FDI stocks amounted to only $2.5 billion. FDI in Ethiopia was a net inflow of $221.5 million according to World Bank figures published in 2009 and represented 0.78% of GDP.

39 ECONOMIC DEVELOPMENT

The policy of the Ethiopian government is to create the conditions necessary for sustained economic growth. Farmers have reacquired the economic freedom of price, production, and settlement. The government aspires to an agriculture-led industrialization and has focused its attention on food security, rural savings, and labor formation issues. The government holds all land and issues long-term leases to tenants. The 1996 economic reform plan promoted free markets and liberalized trade laws as essential to economic growth. Increased military expenditures during 1999 and 2000 largely due to the war with Eritrea threatened stability.

Ethiopia's per capita income, according to the CIA World Fact Book, is at about $1,000, up from $100 in 2001. In 2001, Ethiopia reached its decision point under the IMF/World Bank Heavily Indebted Poor Countries (HIPC) initiative and was to receive $1.9 billion in debt relief. Also in 2001, Ethiopia negotiated a three-year, $115 million Poverty Reduction and Growth Facility (PRGF) Arrangement with the IMF, which expired in March 2004. Although there was a bumper crop in 2000–01, the prices of coffee and cereals fell in 2001–02, and agricultural output was lower. Since July 2002, a severe drought affected Ethiopia; over 15 million people in Ethiopia and Eritrea alone were at risk of starvation in 2003.

The economy recovered well in 2004 and continued to grow substantially in 2005 due to a good performance in the agriculture sector. Since weather patterns were stable and favorable in 2005, analysts expected 2006 to be another good year for the Ethiopian economy. However, rising oil prices were expected to tone down the positive effect of the weather. The fact that the government owns all of the land in the country, which it leases to interested tenants, means that economic growth is seriously hindered because entrepreneurs cannot use that land as collateral for loans.

Through 2002–2005, Ethiopia instated the Sustainable Development and Poverty Reduction Program (SDPRP), Ethiopia's Poverty Reduction Strategy (PRS) and the primary vehicle for achieving the Millennium Development Goals (MDGs). The targeted development in SDPRP include infrastructure, human development, rural development, food security, and capacity building. In 2005, The PASDEP was introduced to carry forward strategic directions pursued under the SDPRP with particular emphasis on greater commercialization of agriculture and enhancing private sector development, industry, urban development, and a scaling-up of efforts to achieve the MDGs.

40 SOCIAL DEVELOPMENT

Other than modest government allocations for pensions, labor and social welfare for public employees, Ethiopia has no comprehensive public welfare or social security programs. Retirement is set at age 55 for public employees. Retired employees receive 30% of their average monthly salary during the last three years of employment. Most of the population depends on subsistence agriculture in deprived rural areas and therefore falls outside the scope of this limited retirement system.

Women have traditionally been restricted to subordinate roles in society. In rural areas, women are burdened with most of the strenuous agricultural and domestic work, while in urban areas, women are limited in their job opportunities. The civil code discriminates against women in family law and property issues. Domestic abuse is pervasive; societal norms inhibit most women from seeking intervention from the authorities. However, in 2004 a court was created to try cases of sexual abuse. Young women are still abducted for the purpose of marriage. The majority of girls are subject to female genital mutilation.

Human rights abuses persist, including arbitrary arrests, lengthy pretrial detention, and mistreatment of prisoners. However, the government encourages international human rights groups to send observers.

41 HEALTH

According to the CIA, life expectancy in Ethiopia was 56 years in 2011. The country spent 4.3% of its GDP on healthcare, amounting to $15 per person. There were 0 physicians, 2 nurses and midwives, and 2 hospital beds per 10,000 inhabitants. The fertility rate was 5.2, while the infant mortality rate was 67 per 1,000 live births. In 2008, the maternal mortality rate, according to the World Bank, was 470 per 100,000 births. It was estimated that 75% of children were vaccinated against measles.

42 HOUSING

Except in Addis Ababa, Hārer, Dirē Dawa, and a few other urban centers, most houses are built of mud or mortar and have thatched or tin roofs. In the rural areas the traditional thatched hut (*tukul*) is still the most common dwelling. A 2005 Habitat for Humanity report indicated that about 85% of all houses are made with mud, sticks, and thatch. Only about 8% of all housing units are built with stone walls. Housing shortages and overcrowding were still major concerns as of 2005. Only about 27% of the population had access to safe drinking water, and 10% had access to sanitation facilities. Homelessness is a pervasive problem in urban areas; it has been estimated that 80% of the residents in Addis Ababa are homeless or in substandard housing. The housing deficit for urban areas alone has been estimated at over 699,000 units, about 42% of the total housing stock in the nation.

Housing development and finance are the joint responsibility of the Ministry of Housing and Urban Development and the Housing and Savings Bank, which was established in November 1975. The government has developed the Ethiopian Housing Cooperative to encourage Ethiopia emigrants to return and build homes.

43 EDUCATION

In 2009, the World Bank estimated that 83% of age-eligible children in Ethiopia were enrolled in primary school. Secondary enrollment for age-eligible children stood at 26%. Tertiary enrollment was estimated at 4%. Of those enrolled in tertiary education, there were 100 male students for every 31 female students. Overall, the CIA estimated that Ethiopia had a literacy rate of 42.7%. Public expenditure on education represented 5.5% of GDP.

After the 1974 revolution, emphasis was placed on increasing literacy in rural areas. Practical subjects were stressed, as was the teaching of socialism. Public education is compulsory and free at the primary level, which covers eight years of study. The first cycle of secondary studies covers an additional two years. After this, students may choose another two years of preparatory studies or three-year technical or vocational studies. The academic year runs from September to July.

Primary school enrollment in 2005 was estimated at about 61.4% of age-eligible students; 64% for boys and 59% for girls. The same year, secondary school enrollment was about 27.7% of age-eligible students; 34% for boys and 22% for girls. It is estimated that about 55% of all students complete their primary education. The student-to-teacher ratio for primary school was at about 72:1 in 2005; the ratio for secondary school was about 54:1.

Addis Ababa University (formerly Haile Selassie I University) has extension centers in Alemaya, Gonder, Awasa, Bahir-Dar, and Debre Zeyit. The University of Asmara is a Roman Catholic institution. In 2005, about 3% of the tertiary age population was enrolled in some type of higher education program. The adult literacy rate for 2004 was estimated at about 41.5%, with 49.2% for men and 33.8% for women.

Ethiopia in 2005 began instituted a massive expansion to its higher education sector from 2 federal universities to 22 in just over a decade with another 10 to open in the next 10 years. The plan jointly managed by Ethiopian Ministry of Education and the current Ministry of Civil Services (formerly Ministry of Capacity Building) intends to provide access to higher education in remote areas with new campus sites proportionally located across the country. The huge expansion has increased number of students engaged in higher education at regional universities and has also resulted in a shortage of academic staff. It is estimated that 70% of faculty in the new universities are only qualified to bachelor degree level. Ethiopia has also facilitated and encouraged the establishment of private institutions of higher education, and there were as many as 60 such institutions in 2009. The Higher Education Relevance and Quality Agency in the Ministry of Education, responsible for quality audits and accreditations, has forced closure of over half of the private institutions for noncompliance and deficient instruction.

Ethiopia has been chosen as the site for a new African Institute for Mathematical Sciences (AIMS), a specialized institute of higher learning for those studying mathematics and science. The Ethiopia AIMS will be modeled after the current AIMS in South Africa, which opened in 2003 and has already trained more than 300 mathematicians. Primary funding for the new college will come from Canada, which is providing $19 million in funding for AIMS in Ghana and Senegal also. The Perimeter Institute for Theoretical Physics in Canada will serve as the primary consulting institution. Additional funding will be provided as part of a $2 million award from Google that was given to AIMS in 2010. The Ethiopia AIMS is expected to open by the end of 2013. Local officials hope that the new school will be a major step forward in providing high quality education for Ethiopian students who will be inspired to use their knowledge and experience within their homeland, rather than travel abroad for education and employment, as many currently do.

44 LIBRARIES AND MUSEUMS

The Addis Ababa University Library contains 550,000 volumes. The National Library, established in 1944, holds 164,000 volumes. The Alemaya University of Agriculture in Dirē Dawa holds 47,000 volumes. The first children's library in Ethiopia opened in 2003 in Addis Ababa. Addis Ababa is also the site of the Ethiopia Public Information Center, a depository library of the World Bank.

Addis Ababa is home to the National Museum, which houses a general collection of regional archaeology, history, and art; the Ethnographic Museum at the Institute of Ethiopian Studies, which includes collections of religious art, musical instruments, and ancient coins; the archaeological museum; the Natural History Museum; the Museum at the Holy Trinity Church; and the War Museum. There are regional museums in Harar, Makale, Wollamo Sodo, and Yirgalem. Many provincial monasteries and churches, as well as municipal authorities, maintain collections of documents, art, and antiquities.

45 MEDIA

In 2009, the CIA reported that there were 915,100 telephone landlines in Ethiopia. In addition to landlines, mobile phone subscriptions averaged 5 per 100 people. There were eight FM radio stations and one shortwave radio station. Internet users numbered 1 per 100 citizens.

All telephone and telegraph facilities are owned by the government and operated by the National Board of Telecommunications. The principal population centers are connected with Addis Ababa by telephone and radio circuits, and there is an earth-satellite station. In 2009, there were 915,100 main phone lines and 4 million mobile cellular telephones in use throughout the country.

Radio and television stations are run by the government. The Voice of Ethiopia radio service broadcasts mostly on AM in Amharic, but also in English, French, Arabic, and local languages. Ethiopian Television broadcasts about four hours daily. In 2001, there were eight radio stations and one television station. In 2003, there were an estimated 189 radios and 6 television sets for every 1,000 people.

In 2010, the country had 151 Internet hosts. As of 2009, there were some 447,300 Internet users in Ethiopia.

The two major daily newspapers (with estimated 2002 circulations and languages of publication) are *Addis Zeman* (40,000; Amharic) and the *Ethiopian Herald* (37,000; English), both published by the government at Addis Ababa. There are also several weeklies published by the government. There were about 28 private Amharic-language weeklies and 1 independent Tigrinya-language weekly. Most independently owned newspapers are printed at government-owned presses.

All newspapers are strictly censored by the Ministry of Information and National Guidance. A 1992 Press Law, along with the constitution of Ethiopia, provide for free speech and a free press. The government is reported to use legal mechanisms to repress press rights in practice.

46 ORGANIZATIONS

Since the 1974 revolution, peasants' and urban dwellers' associations, encouraged by the government, have been the chief voluntary societies. Ethiopia has a national chamber of commerce as well as regional and local ones. Trade unions are encouraged and supported through the Confederation of Ethiopian Trade Unions. The African Economic Community has an office in Addis Ababa.

The Institute of Ethiopian Studies promotes interest and research in the nation's history and culture. The Association for Higher Education and Development is a multinational organization formed in 1999 to promote education in the country. The Ethiopian Medical Association promotes research and education on health issues and works to establish common policies and standards in healthcare. There are also several associations dedicated to research and education for specific fields of medicine and particular diseases and conditions, such as the Ethiopian Diabetes Association.

The Ethiopian Youth League is a primary organization promoting education and job training. The National Union of Eritrean Youth and Students serves as an umbrella organization that develops local youth groups interested in promoting traditional culture and values. The Ethiopian Scouts Association is also active. There are several sports associations throughout the country. Branches of the YMCA/YWCA are also active. The African Center for Women is a multinational organization encouraging women's participation in development programs and providing various educational and training programs.

There are national chapters of the Red Cross Society, the Society of St. Vincent de Paul, UNICEF, and Habitat for Humanity.

47 TOURISM, TRAVEL, AND RECREATION

The *Tourism Factbook*, published by the UN World Tourism Organization, reported 330,000 incoming tourists to Ethiopia in 2008, who spent a total of $1.12 billion. Of those incoming tourists, there were 116,000 from Africa. There were 17,217 hotel beds available in Ethiopia. The estimated daily cost to visit Addis Ababa, the capital, was $378. The cost of visiting other cities averaged $87.

All visitors are required to have a valid passport and visa. Exit visas are required for visitors who stay more than 30 days. The chief tourist attractions are big-game hunting, early Christian monuments and monasteries, and the ancient capitals of Gonder and Aksum. There are seven national parks.

48 FAMOUS PERSONS

The most famous Ethiopian in national legend is Menelik I, the son of the Queen of Sheba and King Solomon, regarded as the founder of the Aksumite Empire. This tradition is contained in the *Kebra Negast*, or *Book of the Glory of Kings*. The most famous Christian saint of Ethiopia is Frumentius of Tyre (b. Phoenicia, d. c. 380), the founder of the Ethiopian Church. The 15th-century composer Yared established the Deggua, or liturgical music, of the Ethiopian Church. A 13th-century monarch, Lalibela, is renowned for the construction of the great monolithic churches of Lasta (now called Lalibela). Emperor Amda-Seyon I (r. 1313–44) reestablished suzerainty over the Muslim kingdoms of the coastal lowland regions. During the reign of King Zar' a-Ya'qob (1434–68), a ruler renowned for his excellent administration and deep religious faith, Ethiopian literature attained its greatest heights. Emperor Menelik II (1844–1913) is considered the founder of modern Ethiopia. Emperor Haile Selassie I (1891–1975) was noted for his statesmanship and his introduction of many political, economic, and social reforms. Lt. Col. Mengistu Haile Mariam (b. 1937) led the 1974 coup and was head of state from 1977 to 1991. Legesse ("Meles") Zenawi (b. 1955) became prime minister in 1995.

49 DEPENDENCIES

Ethiopia has no territories or colonies.

50 BIBLIOGRAPHY

Adejumobi, Saheed A. *The History of Ethiopia*. Westport, CT: Greenwood Press, 2007.

Clapp, Nicholas. *Sheba: Through the Desert in Search of the Legendary Queen*. Boston, MA: Houghton Mifflin, 2002.

Crummey, Donald. *Land and Society in the Christian Kingdom of Ethiopia: From the Thirteenth to the Twentieth Century*. Urbana: University of Illinois Press, 2000.

Ethiopia Investment and Business Guide: Strategic and Practical Information. Washington, DC: International Business Publications USA, 2012.

Grierson, Roderick. *Red Sea, Blue Nile: The Civilisation of Ancient and Medieval Ethiopia*. London, Eng.: Weidenfeld and Nicolson, 2002.

Henze, Paul B. *Layers of Time: A History of Ethiopia*. New York: Palgrave Macmillan, 2004.

Kamoche, Ken M., ed. *Managing Human Resources in Africa*. New York: Routledge, 2004.

Marcus, Harold G. *A History of Ethiopia*. Berkeley, CA: University of California Press, 1994.

McPherson, E. S. P. *Ethiopian Sovereignty and African Nationhood: Voice from the Ethio-Diaspora Call*. Brooklyn, NY: AandB Publishers, 2000.

Milkias, Paulos. *Ethiopia*. Santa Barbara, CA: ABC-CLIO, 2011.

Morell, Virginia. *Blue Nile: Ethiopia's River of Magic and Mystery*. Washington, DC: Adventure Press, 2001.

Shinn, David H., and Thomas P. Ofcansky. *Historical Dictionary of Ethiopia*. Lanham, MD: Scarecrow Press, 2004.

Woodward, Peter. *The Horn of Africa: Politics and International Relations*. New York: I.B. Tauris, 2003.

Zeilig, Leo, and David Seddon. *A Political and Economic Dictionary of Africa*. Philadelphia: Routledge/Taylor and Francis, 2005.

FRENCH AFRICAN DEPENDENCIES

MAYOTTE

Mayotte is the southernmost of the four main islands in the Comoros archipelago. It has an area of 374 sq km (144 sq mi). Mayotte lies in the Mozambique Channel about 480 km (300 mi) NW of Madagascar, at 12°49′ S and 45°17′ E.

Mayotte is surrounded by a coral reef, which encloses the islets of M'Zambourou (Grand Terre) and Pamanzi. Beyond the island's coastal plain, the Benara plateau reaches heights of 660 meters (2,165 feet). Mayotte's lowest elevation is sea level at the Indian Ocean. The average daily high temperature is 32°C (90°F); the average low is 17°C (63°F). Average annual precipitation is about 124 cm (49 in). Mayotte experiences periodic cyclones during the rainy season (November–May). The capital, Mamoudzou, is located on the northeast coast.

The population was estimated at 209,530 in 2011. Population density was 511 people per sq km (1,323 per sq mi). Some 46.4% of the population was 14 or younger, and 2.4% was 65 years of age or older. The population was growing at an annual rate of 1.533%. About half the population lived in urban areas in 2010, and urban areas had an annual rate of change of 2.5%. About 97% of the population is Muslim and 3% is Christian, mostly Roman Catholic. The official language is French, but only about one-third of the population uses it. A dialect of the African language, Swahili, is spoken throughout the island. The literacy rate is 86%. Illegal immigration, almost exclusively from Comoros, has been a problem. There were an estimated 13,329 illegal immigrants in 2008.

The infant mortality rate was 16.17 deaths per 1,000 live births in 2011, and life expectancy was 76.83 years. The fertility rate was 4 children born per woman as of 2011.

The gross domestic product (GDP) of Mayotte was $953.6 million in 2005 (most recent available information as of March 2012). The per capita GDP stood at $4,900. The labor force was estimated at 44,560 (2002), while the unemployment rate was 25.4% (2005). Vanilla, ylang-ylang (perfume essence), coffee, and copra are among the leading agricultural products. Agriculture covered 22,257 hectares (54,998 acres) in 2009, with bananas covering 4,600 hectares (11,367) and producing 17,000 tons (2003). Mayotte also has a lobster and shrimp industry, carried out across 74,000 sq km (28,572 sq mi) of its exclusive economic zone. Mayotte is France's largest aquacultural producer among its dependencies, producing 60 tons annually. Exports were valued at $6.7 million in 2009; imports totaled $502 million.

The island of Mayotte was originally ceded to France by its Malagasy ruler in 1843. Together with the other Comoros Islands, it was attached to the French overseas territory of Madagascar until 1946. At that time, the islands were given separate status within the French Republic.

Mayotte is the only island that, by popular vote, chose to retain its link with France instead of joining an independent Comoros.

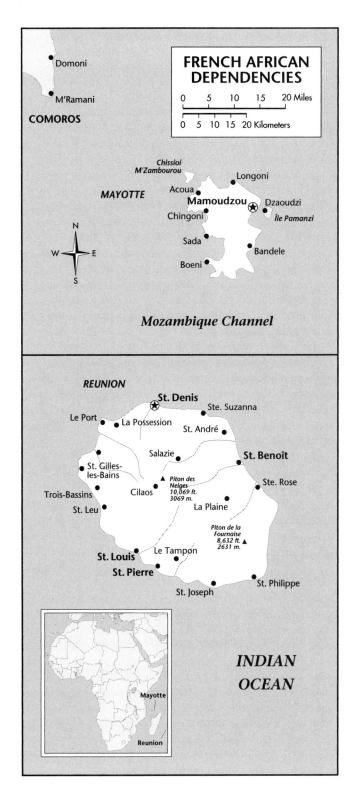

The Comoros referendum was held on 22 December 1974. Mayotte's decision to remain affiliated with France was confirmed in a separate referendum conducted on 8 February 1976. Some 99.4% of Mayotte voters favored remaining within France.

Mayotte's decision was opposed by the Comoros, which claimed the island as part of its territory. Comoros took the issue to the United Nations (UN). The UN Security Council passed a resolution on 7 February 1976, the day before Mayotte's referendum. The resolution declared Mayotte's referendum "aggression" against the sovereignty and territorial integrity of the Comoros. On 11 April another referendum was held in Mayotte. This time, 80% of the ballots were blank or were declared invalid. Of the valid ballots, 97.5% voted to remain affiliated with France.

The UN General Assembly called for incorporation of Mayotte within the Comoros on 21 October 1976. On 1 December 1976, France gave Mayotte a special status that would allow it to become either an overseas department of France or independent. A revision to Mayotte's legal standing made in 2007 paved the way for its conversion into an overseas department, and in January 2008 the government agreed to work toward this goal. A 2009 referendum in Mayotte resulted in a vote in favor of becoming an overseas department (95% in favor), and on 31 March 2011, the territory officially became the fifth overseas department of France. Status as an overseas department allows citizens to receive additional social benefits, although the transition process, which can take up to 25 years, also requires legal adjustments on the part of Mayotte, such as raising from 15 to 18 the legal age for women to marry and the outlawing of polygamy.

Attoumani Douchina served as president of the General Council, while Hubert Derache was appointed prefect on 22 July 2009. The General Council elects the president to a six-year term, and the next presidential election was scheduled for 2014. The General Council, with 19 members, last held elections in 2008. The Federation of Mahorans (UMP-RPR) won 8 seats, the Diverse Right won 4, independents won 4, and Citizens and Republic Movement, Democratic Movement, and Diverse Left each won 1 seat. Mayotte also elects two members to the French senate and one member to the French assembly.

As of 2009, there were 10,000 telephone landlines and 48,100 mobile cellular phones (2005). Television and radio is broadcast through the publicly owned French Overseas Network. There was one Internet host as of 2010.

RÉUNION

Réunion is the largest island in the chain of islands known as the Mascarene Archipelago. Réunion lies about 675 km (420 mi) E of Madagascar in the Indian Ocean. Réunion lies between 20°52′ and 21°22′ S and between 55°13′ and 55°50′ E. The island is 55 km (34 mi) long and 53 km (33 mi) wide, and has a coastline of 207 km (129 mi). It has an area of 2,510 sq km (969 sq mi).

Réunion is a volcanic island. It is mountainous, with 10 mountain peaks rising above 2,600 km (8,500 feet). One of the peaks, Piton de la Fournaise, is still an active volcano. The highest peak, Piton des Neiges, has an altitude of 3,069 meters (10,069 feet). Rosewood, ebony, ironwood, and other tropical hardwoods are represented in the forests near the coast. As of 2010, an estimated 35.2% of the total land area was covered by forest. Torrential riv-

ers are numerous. Carbon dioxide emissions totaled 2.8 kilotons in 2008.

The climate, generally tropical, varies with orientation and altitude. The mean annual temperature is 23°C (73°F) at sea level. The east coast receives almost daily precipitation. There, the total annual rainfall is 350 cm (140 in) annually. On the north coast, annual rainfall is only about half that. Cyclones threaten the island from December to April. The island has been devastated by powerful cyclones several times. The tropical cyclone monitoring center at Saint-Denis serves the entire Indian Ocean area. The waters surrounding Réunion are filled with rich and varied marine life.

The population was estimated to be 817,000 in January 2009. Population density was 312 people per sq km (808 per sq mi). The largest urban areas are Saint-Denis (population 140,733 in 2007) and Saint-Paul (101,023). About one-fourth of the islanders are of French origin, including those in the military. Réunion is the headquarters for French military forces in the Indian Ocean area. The vast majority of the population is Roman Catholic, with the remainder practicing Hinduism, Islam, or Buddhism.

There are about 2,724 km (1,703 mi) of roads. About half—1,300 km (810 mi)—are paved. Only the sugar plantations have functioning rail service. Pointe des Galets is the chief port, and Saint-Pierre is the main fishing port. Air France provides air service; steamer ships provide regular water transport.

Réunion was uninhabited when Portuguese explorer Pedro de Mascarenhas landed there on 9 February 1513. A few French colonists came in the 16th century to Bourbon Island, as it was then known. The French began using the island as a penal colony in the early 17th century.

In 1665, Réunion became an outpost of the French East India Company. Coffee and, after 1800, sugarcane, helped make the colony relatively prosperous. French immigration continued from the 17th to the 19th century. Others who settled on the island were Africans, Malays, Indochinese, and Chinese.

In 1793, the island received its present name, Réunion. With the mid-19th century came a decline in Réunion's prosperity. Slavery was abolished in 1848, and the Suez Canal opened in 1869, providing ships with a shorter route from Asia to Europe. Réunion lost its importance as a stopover on the East Indies route.

France has different categories for its overseas territories. Réunion became an overseas department of France in 1946. It was elevated to regional status in 1973. Réunion is represented in the French parliament by five deputies and three senators. Local administration is patterned on that of metropolitan France. There is a regional council of 45 elected members and a general council of 49 elected members.

Sugarcane, vanilla, tobacco, tropical fruit, vegetables, and corn are the primary agricultural products. Some 36,000 hectares (88,958 acres) of land were arable or under permanent crops in 2007. Sugarcane is an important crop, with 1.93 tons produced in 2010. In addition to sugar, rum and molasses, perfume essences, and lobster are among the exports. The fishing sector remained small, with only 307 small fishermen and 78 commercial fishermen in 2008 (down from 247 and 103, respectively, in 2007). Large-scale industrial fishing employed 169 people among 10 ships in 2008. Most of the industrial catch is exported. Fish imports amounted to 11,000 tons in 2008. Industrial growth came primarily through the construction and retail sectors.

The monetary unit is the euro. Manufactured goods, food, beverages, tobacco, machinery and transportation equipment, raw materials, and petroleum products are the main imports. The high cost of living in Réunion has been a continual cause of tension between native residents and the local government. In February 2012, a three-day series of riots was sparked by a protest rally in Saint Denis organized by truck drivers against the high cost of gasoline. The rally swelled into a riot as hundreds of residents, particularly youth, joined in to protest the high cost of utilities and food, and high rates of unemployment and poverty. As a result of the protests, officials promised to cut fuel prices, but residents continued to call for prices on food and utilities to be lowered to a rate more in line with that of mainland France. About 52% of the population lives below the poverty line and 30% are unemployed.

The unemployment rate for youth (ages 15–25 years old) is as high as 90% in some of the most disadvantaged neighborhoods. Unemployment for some 100,000 whites from metropolitan France is estimated at only 2.5%.

As of 2011, the school year included an austral summer holiday from December to February, as well as a holiday from early August to early September. There were an estimated 241,000 students from kindergarten through university levels as of 2010. Secondary students numbered 122,600 across 126 institutions. The University of La Réunion had 16,650 students.

Health services are comparable to that of mainland France. Municipalities have clinics with separate maternal wings. Tropical diseases are not reported, and no additional vaccinations are required for visitors.

GABON

Gabonese Republic
République Gabonaise

CAPITAL: Libreville

FLAG: The flag is a tricolor of green, golden yellow, and royal blue horizontal stripes.

ANTHEM: *La Concorde (Harmony).*

MONETARY UNIT: The Cooperation Financiere en Afrique Centrale franc (CFA), which was originally pegged to the French franc, has been pegged to the euro since January 1999 with a rate of CFA655.957 to 1 euro. It is issued in coins of 1, 2, 5, 10, 25, 50, 100, and 500 francs, and notes of 50, 100, 500, 1,000, 5,000, and 10,000 CFA francs. CFA1 = US$0.001997 (or US$1 = CFA502.33) as of 2011.

WEIGHTS AND MEASURES: The metric system is the legal standard.

HOLIDAYS: New Year's Day, 1 January; Day of Renewal, 12 March; Labor Day, 1 May; Africa Freedom Day, 25 May; Assumption, 15 August; Independence Day, 17 August; All Saints' Day, 1 November; Christmas, 25 December. Movable religious holidays include Easter Monday, Ascension, Pentecost Monday, Eid al-Fitr, and Eid al-Adha.

TIME: 1 p.m. = noon GMT.

¹LOCATION, SIZE, AND EXTENT

Situated on the west coast of Africa and straddling the equator, Gabon has an area of 267,667 sq km (103,347 sq mi), extending 717 km (446 mi) NNE–SSW and 644 km (400 mi) ESE–WNW. Comparatively, the area occupied by Gabon is slightly smaller than the state of Colorado. It is bordered on the N by Cameroon, on the E and S by the Republic of the Congo (ROC), on the W by the Atlantic Ocean, and on the NW by Equatorial Guinea, with a total boundary length of 3,436 km (2,135 mi), of which 885 km (550 mi) is coastline.

Gabon's capital city, Libreville, is located on the country's northwestern coast.

²TOPOGRAPHY

Rising from the coastal lowlands, which range in width from 30–200 km (20–125 mi), is a band more than 96 km (60 mi) wide forming a rocky escarpment, which ranges in height from 450–600 m (1,480–1,970 ft). This plateau covers the north and east and most of the south. Rivers descending from the interior have carved deep channels in the face of the escarpment, dividing it into distinct blocks, such as the Crystal Mountains (Monts de Cristal) and the Chaillu Massif. There are mountains in various parts of Gabon, the highest peak being Mt. Iboundji (1,575 m/5,167 ft). The northern coastline is deeply indented with bays, estuaries, and deltas as far south as the mouth of the Ogooué River, forming excellent natural shelters. Farther south, the coast becomes more precipitous, but there are also coastal areas bordered by lagoons and mangrove swamps. Virtually the entire territory is contained in the basin of the Ogooué River, which is about 1,100 km (690 mi) long and navigable for about 400 km (250 mi). Its two major tributaries are the Ivindo and the Ngounié, which are navigable for 80–160 km (50–100 mi) into the interior.

³CLIMATE

Gabon has the moist, hot climate typical of tropical regions. The hottest month is January, with an average high at Libreville of 31°C (88°F) and an average low of 23°C (73°F). Average July temperatures in the capital range between 20° and 28°C (68° and 82°F). From June to September there is virtually no rain but high humidity; there is occasional rain in December and January. During the remaining months, rainfall is heavy. The excessive rainfall is caused by the condensation of moist air resulting from the meeting, directly off the coast, of the cold Benguela Current from the south and the warm Guinea Current from the north. At Libreville, the average annual rainfall is more than 254 cm (100 in). Farther north on the coast, it is 381 cm (150 in).

⁴FLORA AND FAUNA

The dense green of the vegetation never changes, since plants flower and lose their leaves continuously throughout the year according to species. Tree growth is especially rapid; in the more sparsely forested areas, the trees tower as high as 60 m (200 ft), and the trunks are thickly entwined with vines. In the coastal regions, marine plants abound, and wide expanses are covered with tall papyrus grass.

Most tropical fauna species are found in Gabon. The World Resources Institute estimates that there are 6,651 plant species in Gabon. In addition, Gabon is home to 166 mammal, 632 bird, 130 reptile, and 41 amphibian species. Wildlife includes elephants, buffalo, antelope, situtungas, lions, panthers, crocodiles, and gorillas. The calculation reflects the total number of distinct species residing in the country, not the number of endemic species.

⁵ENVIRONMENT

Gabon's environmental problems include deforestation, pollution, and wildlife preservation. Forests are threatened by excessive logging activities. Gabon's coastal forests have been depleted, but there is a reforestation program, and most of the interior remains under dense forest cover.

Pollution of the land is a problem in Gabon's growing urban centers due to industrial and domestic contaminants. The United Nations (UN) reported in 2008 that carbon dioxide emissions in Gabon totaled 2,034 kilotons. The nation's water is affected by pollutants from the oil industry. The World Resources Institute reported that Gabon had designated 3.49 million hectares (8.62 million acres) of land for protection as of 2006. Water resources totaled 164 cu km (39.35 cu mi) while water usage was 0.12 cu km (0.029 cu mi) per year. Domestic water usage accounted for 50% of total usage, industrial for 8%, and agricultural for 42%. Per capita water usage totaled 87 cu m (3,072 cu ft) per year.

Wildlife poaching is a problem in some areas. In January 2011, five poachers were arrested when they were found with more than 30 chimpanzee heads and the head and hands of an endangered gorilla. According to a spokesman from the World Wildlife Fund, this was the biggest seizure of animal parts in Central Africa in the past ten years. The animal parts are generally sold in markets in Central and West Africa for spiritual use or traditional health remedies. As a result of population expansion accompanied by an increased demand for meat, poaching has become a significant threat to the nation's wildlife.

According to a 2011 report issued by the International Union for Conservation of Nature and Natural Resources (IUCN), the number of threatened species included 14 types of mammals, 4 species of birds, 3 types of reptiles, 3 species of amphibians, 61 species of fish, and 120 species of plants. Threatened species included Shelley's eagle owl, the thresher shark, the sun-tailed monkey, the clawless otter, and the black crowned crane. Gabon had the world's largest gorilla population. There are two national parks and four wildlife reserves in which hunting is banned. Gabon has nine Ramsar wetland sites.

⁶POPULATION

The US Central Intelligence Agency (CIA) estimated the population of Gabon in 2011 to be approximately 1,576,665, which placed it at number 152 in population among the 196 nations of the world. In 2011, approximately 3.9% of the population was over 65 years of age, with another 42.2% under 15 years of age. The median age in Gabon was 18.6 years. There were 0.99 males for every female in the country. The estimate for population growth rate in 2011 was 1.999%. The projected population for the year 2025 was 2,000,000. According to UN data for 2010, population density in Gabon was calculated at 6 people per sq km (16 people per sq mi).

The US Central Intelligence Agency (CIA) estimated that 86% of the population lived in urban areas in 2010, and that urban populations had an annual rate of change of 2.1%. The largest urban area was Libreville, with a population of 673,995.

⁷MIGRATION

The CIA's estimates of Gabon's net migration rate for 2011 amounted to -2.2 migrants per 1,000 citizens. The total number of emigrants living abroad was 25,200, and the total number of immigrants living in Gabon was 284,100. According to UN Migration Yearbook Gabon accepted 9,000 refugees. Because of its limited population and booming economy, Gabon has relied heavily on laborers from other African nations, including Benin, Cameroon, Equatorial Guinea, Mali, São Tomé and Príncipe, and Senegal. About 100,000–200,000 non-Gabonese Africans were believed to be in Gabon, many of them from Equatorial Guinea or Cameroon. Foreigners made up at least 20% of the population in Gabon. However, in September 1994 Gabon enacted laws requiring foreigners to pay residence fees or leave the country. By the deadline in February 1995 some 55,000 foreign nationals left the country, and 15,000 legalized their residency. According to UN Migration Yearbook, in 2010 foreigners made up about 19% of the population in Gabon.

⁸ETHNIC GROUPS

There are at least 40 distinct ethnic groups in Gabon. The Pygmies are said to be the original inhabitants. Only about 3,000 of them remain, scattered in small groups in the heart of the forest. The largest ethnic group, the Fang (about 30% of the population), came from the north in the 18th century and settled in northern Gabon. In the Woleu-Ntem part of Gabon, their direct descendants may be found almost unmixed with other Bantu ethnic strains. The Nzebi, Obamba, Eshira, Bapounou, and Batéké are other major groups. Smaller groups include the Omyènè, a linguistic group that includes the Mpongwe, Galoa, Nkomi, Orungu, and Enenga; these peoples live along the lower Ogooué, from Lambaréné to Port-Gentil. The Kota, or Bakota, are located mainly in the northeast, but several tribes have spread southward; they are well-known for their carved wooden figures. Other groups include Vili and the Séké. These other African groups and Europeans number about 154,000, including about 10,700 French and 11,000 people of dual nationality.

⁹LANGUAGES

French is the official language of the republic. The Fang language is spoken in northern Gabon, and other Bantu languages (Myene, Batéké, Bapounou/Eschira, Bandjabi) are spoken elsewhere in the country.

¹⁰RELIGIONS

Approximately 73% of the total population are Christian, with a majority of the people being Roman Catholic. Between 5% and 10% are Muslim; with a majority of these being foreigners. About 10% practice traditional indigenous religions (animism or voodoo) exclusively, but it is believed that a large number of Christians and Muslims also incorporate some elements of traditional religions within their practice. 5% of the population is not religious. Freedom of religion is guaranteed by the constitution and this right is generally respected in practice. While religious organizations are not required to register with the government, many do so in order to be assured of full protection of their constitutional rights. Easter Sunday and Monday, Ascension Day, Assumption

Day, Eid al-Fitr, Pentecost/Ascension, All Saints' Day, Eid al-Kebir (Eid al-Adha), and Christmas are observed as national holidays.

11 TRANSPORTATION

Until the 1970s, Gabon had no railroads. According to the CIA's 2004 estimates, Gabon had a total of 9,170 km (5,698 mi) of roads, of which 937 km (582 mi) were paved. Main roads connect virtually all major communities, but maintenance work is difficult because of heavy rainfall. A north–south road runs the length of the country, from Bitam to Ndendé. This main north-south link continues into Cameroon in the north and the Congo in the south. An east-west road connects Libreville and Mékambo. Farther south, another road runs from Mayumba to Lastoursville and Franceville.

Railroads extend for 810 km (503 mi). A 936-km (582-mi) railroad construction program, the Trans-Gabon Railway, began in October 1974. In its first stage, completed in 1983, the project linked the port of Owendo with the interior city of Booué (332 km/206 mi). The second stage, completed in December 1986, linked Booué with Franceville (357 km/222 mi) via Moanda, thus facilitating exports of manganese from the southeast and forestry exploitation in the same region. A proposed third stage would continue the line from Booué to Belinga in the northeast, where there are iron ore deposits.

The busiest ports are Port-Gentil, the center for exports of petroleum products and imports of mining equipment, and Owendo, a port that opened in 1974 on the Ogooué estuary, 10 km (6 mi) north of Libreville. Owendo's capacity, initially 300,000 tons, reached 1.5 million tons in 1979, when the port was enlarged to include timber-handling facilities. The smaller port at Mayumba also handles timber, and a deepwater port is planned for the city. In 1998, Gabon's merchant marine owned two vessels totaling 13,613 gross registered tons.

As of 2008, the merchant marine fleet consisted of two ships that were registered to foreign countries. In 2010, Gabon had approximately 1,600 km (994 mi) of navigable waterways, including 310 km (193 mi) on the Ogooué River.

As of 2010, Gabon had 44 airports, of which 13 with paved runways. According to the World Bank, 524,000 passengers were transported in 2009. There were three international airports: Libreville (Leon M'Ba), Port-Gentil, and Franceville. Air Gabon, a national airline, which had served European, West and Central African, and domestic destinations, was liquidated in 2006, and replaced by Gabon Airlines, which in turn ceased operating in early 2011. In October 2011, the Gabonese president Ali Bongo Ondimba announced that a new national airline would start operating in 2012. Numerous other airlines provide international flights. Air Affaires Gabon handled scheduled domestic service.

12 HISTORY

Bantu peoples began to migrate to what is now Gabon from Cameroon and eastern Nigeria at least 2,000 years ago. The Portuguese, who had sighted the coast as early as 1470, gave Gabon its name because the shape of the Río de Como estuary reminded them of a "gabao," a Portuguese hooded cloak. They also founded permanent outposts, notably at the mouth of the Ogooué River, and their missionaries followed shortly. After the Portuguese, the region was visited by the English, Dutch, and French. During the

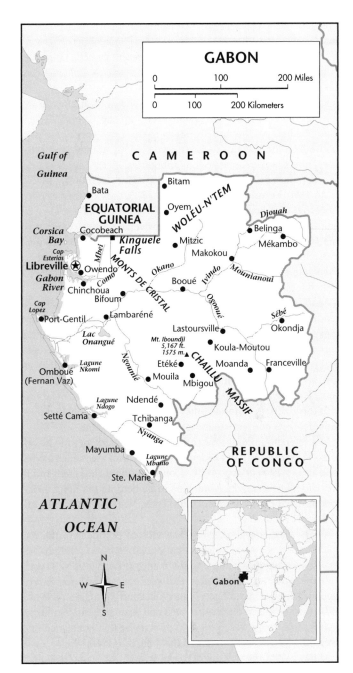

LOCATION: 2°19′ N to 3°55′ S; 9°18′ to 14°32′ E. BOUNDARY LENGTHS: Cameroon, 302 kilometers (188 miles); Republic of the Congo, 1,656 kilometers (1,029 miles); Atlantic coastline, 739 kilometers (459 miles); Equatorial Guinea, 386 kilometers (240 miles). TERRITORIAL SEA LIMIT: 12 miles.

17th century, the great French trading companies entered the slave trade. French Jesuit missionaries were active along the coast during this period, and their influence eventually extended to the powerful native kingdoms inland.

The abolition of the slave trade by France in 1815 ruined many merchants; but it did not end French interest in the Gabon coast. French vessels were entrusted to prevent the illegal slave trade; the search for new products for trade also led to French occupation of the coastal ports. In 1839, the French concluded a treaty with Denis, the African king whose authority had extended over the northern Gabon coast. The treaty ceded the kingdom to France in return for French protection. A similar treaty gave France much of the southern coast below the Ogooué, and gradually other coastal chiefs accepted French control. The present capital, Libreville ("place of freedom"), was founded in 1849 by slaves who had been freed from a contraband slave runner.

French explorers gradually penetrated the interior after 1847. During 1855–59, Paul du Chaillu went up the Ogooué River, where he became the first European to see a live gorilla. He was followed by the Marquis de Compiègne, Alfred Marche, and other explorers, who mapped out its tributaries. Pierre Savorgnan de Brazza explored almost the entire course of the river during 1876–78. In 1880, he founded Franceville. In 1885, the Congress of Berlin recognized French rights over the right bank of the Congo, an area that Brazza had explored extensively. In 1890, Gabon formally became a part of French Congo. It was separated into a district administrative region in 1903 and in 1910 was organized as a separate colony, part of French Equatorial Africa. In 1940, Free French forces ousted the Vichy government from Gabon.

Léon M'Ba and Jean-Hilaire Aubame had led the early independence movement in Gabon, but each had distinct political inclinations. M'Ba led the Gabon Democratic Bloc; Aubame led the Gabonese branch of the Party of African Reunion. The latter actively sought the formation of federal, supranational groupings in Africa, whereas the former was strongly opposed to such associations. Underlying the attitude of M'Ba was the belief that Gabon, with the greatest economic potential in the region, would end up supporting its poorer neighbors in any federal system.

In a referendum on 28 September 1958, the territory of Gabon voted to become an autonomous republic within the French Community. On 19 February 1959, a constitution was adopted, and a provisional government headed by M'Ba became the first official government of Gabon. Independence was formally proclaimed on 17 August 1960.

On 12 February 1961, M'Ba was elected president of the republic, heading a government of national unity in which Aubame served as foreign minister. Friction continued between M'Ba and Aubame, however, and after several years of political maneuvering, Aubame led a successful coup d'état on 18 February 1964. M'Ba was reinstated on the very next day through French military intervention, as provided for by a military agreement signed between the M'Ba government and the French in 1960.

M'Ba created the post of vice president in February 1967, and at his death on 28 November of that year, power was transferred peacefully to his vice president, Albert-Bernard Bongo. On 12 March 1968, Bongo announced the formal institution of a one-party system and the creation of the Gabon Democratic Party (PDG) as the country's sole legal political organization. He was reelected without opposition in 1973, 1979, and 1986. It was announced in 1973 that Bongo had taken the name of Omar and converted to Islam.

During the 1970s and early to mid-1980s, the exploitation of Gabon's huge natural resources progressed rapidly and, in 1975, the country became a full member of OPEC. In 1986, depressed oil prices caused a sharp decline in oil earnings, resulting in severe austerity measures in 1986 and 1987.

These austerities in the face of Bongo's ostentations led to internal pressures for reform in the late 1980s. In 1989, Bongo began talks with some elements of the underground Movement for National Recovery (MORENA). This divided MORENA, but it failed to stem the emergence of new movements calling for the establishment of multiparty democracy.

In March-April 1990, Gabon convened a national political conference to discuss changes to the political system. The PDG and 74 other organizations that attended essentially divided into two loose coalitions, the ruling PDG and its allies on one hand; and the United Front of Opposition Associations and Parties on the other. The conference approved sweeping reforms, including the creation of a national senate, decentralization of the budgetary process, and freedom of assembly and of the press. However, the killing of an opposition leader on 23 May 1990 led to riots in Port-Gentil and Libreville, which required France to send troops to protect its expatriates and corporate property.

Multiparty legislative elections were held in September-October 1990, but they were marred by violence and suspected fraud. Opposition parties had not yet been formally declared legal. In January 1991, the Assembly passed by unanimous vote a law legalizing opposition parties. Throughout 1991 and 1992, there was endemic unrest, government clamp-downs, and economic disruption. Still, the PDG reaffirmed its commitment to multiparty democracy. On 5 December 1993, multiparty presidential elections confirmed Bongo, who ran as an independent against Father Paul M'Ba Abessole, as president with 51% of the vote. Opposition parties protested the result and forced a postponement of the 26 December 1993 legislative elections. International observers complained of widespread procedural irregularities but found no evidence of deliberate fraud. Independent observers, however, reported the governmental policy of limitations on freedoms of speech, press, association and assembly, as well as the harassment of its critics.

Paul M'Ba Abessole, angry at the outcome, announced the formation of a rival government. Its core concerns included new presidential elections, the restoration of peace, and the maintenance of national unity. The rival administration was supported by a High Council of the Republic, later called the High Council of Resistance, composed mostly of defeated presidential candidates.

Bongo was harshly critical of the opposition government and appealed to its members to join his government in a show of unity. In January 1994, Gabon's Constitutional Court ruled that the elections had been fair. Civil unrest continued, however, as the country suffered from the devaluation of the CFA franc by 50%. Trade union demands for higher salaries led Bongo to impose a curfew, ostensibly to quell labor unrest but he also ordered security forces to destroy a radio transmitter operated by his political opponents and to attack a leading opposition figure's private house. The labor unrest lasted less than a week, but resulted in between 9 and 68 deaths, depending on whose figures are to be believed.

Negotiations on the creation of a unified government were held throughout 1994 to little effect. In September, the Organization of African Unity sponsored multilateral talks in Paris, which finally resulted in a tentative power-sharing agreement among Bongo's PDG and the main opposition parties. Legislative elections, which had been postponed in December 1993, were rescheduled for 1995 and Bongo agreed to bring opposition party members into a new government. The agreement essentially fell apart, however, when Bongo gave only 6 of 27 ministries to opposition members. At least two opposition members refused to participate in the government. By mid-1995, Bongo formed a functioning government with a modicum of opposition representation.

In July 1996, the Gabonese overwhelmingly approved a new constitution, calling for, among other things, a 91-member Senate. Legislative elections were held in December of that year, fully three years after they were scheduled. The PDG won a substantial majority (85 of 120 seats). When elections for the Senate were held in January and February 1997, the PDG again emerged as the dominant party, winning 54 of the 91 seats.

Opposition parties declared Paul M'Ba Abessole, head of the National Rally of Woodcutters (RNB), the real winner and they attempted to set up a rival government. In 1998 Omar Bongo was reelected president for a seven-year term with 66.6% of the votes. Pierre Mamboundou of the Union of the Gabonese People (UPG) party took a distant second with 16.5%, while Paul M'Ba Abessole (RNB) came third with 13.4%.

Bongo closed three newspapers after they reported allegations of corruption in his government. However, his appointment in January 2003 of Paul M'Ba Abessole to the post of third deputy prime minister suggested a clever move to co-opt the opposition. In November 2005, Bongo was reelected for a third seven-year term, thus reinforcing his status as the last of Africa's "Big Men."

In May 2009, President Bongo announced that he was temporarily suspending himself from official duties for health reasons and checked into a hospital in Spain for treatment. He died of a heart attack on 8 June. Bongo, who took office in 1967, was the longest-serving head of state in Africa. As a nation that has not experienced an organized, peaceful handover of power, government officials and citizens alike immediately feared the worst. Bongo's son, Defense Minister Ali Ben Bongo, closed the air, land, and sea borders of Gabon; defense forces were dispatched throughout the nation; and internet service was shut down. On 10 June, senate leader Rose Francine Rogombe was sworn in as the interim head of state.

In the August 2009 elections, the ruling party (Gabonese Democratic Party) supported Bongo's son, Ali-Ben Bongo, as a candidate for the presidency. Ali-Ben Bongo won the election with 42% of the vote. However, unprecedented violent mass protests began almost immediately after the announcement, primarily sparked by the opposition leaders, accusing the ruling party of fraud. Gendarmes and the military were deployed to Port-Gentil, the second-largest city and the opposition stronghold, and a curfew was imposed for more than 3 months. The Bongo family controlled several government offices throughout the 42-year term of Omar Bongo. During that time, the ruling family was accused of embezzling large sums of money from oil revenues to finance their lavish lifestyle. Opponents feared that Ali-Ben would continue that tradition. In late September 2009, after a review of eleven official complaints of election fraud, the constitutional court ordered an official recount. In October the court confirmed Bongo as the winner with 41.79% of the vote.

A partial legislative by-election was held in June 2010. PDG won three seats, while a newly created coalition National Union, composed largely of PDG defectors, won two. Both sides claimed victory.

In January 2011, André M'Ba Obame, the Secretary General of the UN coalition, declared himself president, claiming that he was the legitimate winner of the 2009 presidential election—according to official results he came third with 25.33% of the vote. He sought refuge at the UN Development Program headquarters in Libreville and formed a parallel government. In response, Ali-Ben dissolved the UN coalition for violating the constitutional provision for country's unity. In May 2011, Gabon's National Assembly declared M'Ba Obame's parliamentary mandate void. In June 2011, the Parliament adopted a law on the protection of personal data so that biometrics could be introduced in Gabon's future elections.

13 GOVERNMENT

Gabon is a parliamentary democracy with a presidential form of government. The president is elected by direct universal suffrage for a seven-year term; the 2003 constitutional amendment removed presidential term limits. The president, who is chief of state, appoints (and can dismiss) the prime minister, who in consultation with the president, selects and may dismiss members of the Council of Ministers. In 1967, the constitution was modified to provide for the election of a vice president, but in 1975, the office was abolished and replaced by that of a prime minister. The president has other powerful prerogatives: he appoints and can dismiss judges of the Supreme Court, has the authority to dissolve the National Assembly, declare a state of siege, delay legislation, and conduct referenda. In 1983, the constitution was amended officially to declare Gabon a one-party state. However, opposition parties were legalized in 1991.

The bicameral legislature consists of the Senate and the National Assembly. The Senate (created by constitutional re-write in 1990–1991 and finally put into being after 1997) is composed of 102 members who are elected by members of municipal councils and departmental assemblies and serve for six years. The National Assembly or Assemblée Nationale has 120 members who are elected by direct, popular vote to serve five-year terms. Legislation may be initiated by the president or by members of the assembly. The president may dissolve the assembly and call for new elections within 40 days and may also prorogue the body for up to 18 months. Legislation is subject to presidential veto and must then be passed by a two-thirds vote to become law. The voting age is 18.

14 POLITICAL PARTIES

When Gabon became independent in 1960, there were two major political parties. The Gabon Democratic Bloc (Bloc Démocratique Gabonais—BDG), led by Léon M'Ba, was an offshoot of the African Democratic Rally (Rassemblement Démocratique Africain—RDA), created by Félix Houphouet-Boigny of Côte d'Ivoire. The Gabon Democratic and Social Union (Union Démocratique et Sociale Gabonaise—UDSG), led by Jean-Hilaire Aubame, was affiliated with the Party of African Reunion (Parti de Regroupement Africain), an international movement created by Léopold-Sédar Senghor of Senegal. In the first elections after independence, neither party won a majority in the Assembly, and in the elections held in 1961, the leaders of the two parties agreed upon a single list of candidates; this joint list polled 99% of the votes. M'Ba became president and Aubame became minister of foreign affairs in a "government of national amity." This government lasted until February 1963, when the BDG element forced the UDSG members to choose between a merger of the parties and resignation from the government. The UDSG ministers all resigned, but Aubame was later appointed president of the newly created Supreme

Court. He resigned from this post in December 1963 and resumed his seat in the National Assembly.

In January 1964, M'Ba dissolved the Assembly and called for new elections on 23 February 1964. The UDSG was unable to present a list of candidates that would meet the electoral law, and when it seemed that the BDG list would be elected by default, the Gabonese military revolted and toppled the M'Ba government in a bloodless coup led by Aubame on 18 February 1964. French military forces intervened and reestablished the M'Ba government on 19 February. In the parliamentary elections held on 12 April 1964, the BDG list won 31 seats; the reorganized opposition gained 16 seats.

Another election was held in March 1967, in which M'Ba was reelected president and Albert-Bernard Bongo was elected vice president. M'Ba died on 28 November 1967, and Bongo became president on 2 December of that year. On 12 March 1968, the Democratic Party of Gabon (Parti Démocratique Gabonais—PDG), headed by Bongo, became the sole political party. On 25 February 1973, President Bongo was elected to his first full seven-year term. On 30 December 1979, Bongo was reelected with 99.85% of the more than 700,000 votes cast, a total that exceeded by far the number of registered voters. He was reelected again on 9 November 1986, reportedly receiving all but 260 of 904,039 votes cast. The single list of PDG National Assembly candidates was elected in February 1980, although independents were also allowed to run. In 1985, the list consisted of all PDG members, chosen by party activists from 268 nominated; only 35 incumbent deputies were retained. Thirteen women were elected. In 1983, three generals were elected to the central committee of the PDG, the first such admission of the military into high party ranks.

The Movement for National Reform (Mouvement de Redressement National—MORENA), an opposition group, emerged in 1981 and formed a government in exile in 1985. A number of persons were sentenced to long jail terms in 1982 for alleged participation in MORENA. All were released by mid-1986. In 1989, Bongo began talks with elements within MORENA, playing on division within their ranks. The resulting split ushered in the National Rally of Woodcutters (Rassemblement National des Bûcherons—RNB), and the MORENA-Original or Fundamental.

Emerging from the legalization of opposition party activity in March 1991 was the Association for Socialism in Gabon (APSG), the Gabonese Socialist Union (USG), the Circle for Renewal and Progress (CRP), and the Union for Democracy and Development (UDD).

Legislative elections were held in 1991, just prior to the legalization of political parties; the resulting National Assembly was constituted as follows: PDG, 64; Gabonese Party for Progress (PGP), 19; RNB, 17; MORENA-Originals, 7; Socialists, 9; others, 2. Presidential and legislative elections were scheduled for 1993, but only the presidential ballot was held, on 5 December. Protests over the fairness of the presidential election caused the government to postpone legislative elections.

Elections were delayed several times over the next three years, but were finally held on 15 and 29 December 1996, resulting in a National Assembly comprised as follows: PDG, 85; PGP, 10; RNB, 7; Circle of Liberal Reformers (CLR), 7; Socialists, 2. Elections for the newly created Senate were held on 19 January and 23 February 1997, resulting in a 91-seat chamber situated as follows:

PDG, 54; RNB, 19; PGP, 4; Republican and Democratic Alliance, 3; CLR, 1; Rally for Democratic Progress, 1; independents, 9; 2 seats undeclared.

National Assembly elections were held on 9 and 23 December 2001 with the resulting composition: PDG 86, RNB-RPG 8, PGP 3, Democratic and Republican Alliance (ADERE) 3, CLR 2, PUP 1, Social Democratic Party (PSD) 1, independents 13, others 3.

Elections into the Senate took place in January and February 2003. The results amounted to a repeat of the strength of parties after the 1997 poll. The PDG got 53 seats, RNB 20, PGP 4, ADERE 3, RDP 1, CLR 1, and Independents 9. The Senate elections were held in January 2009. PDG got 75 seats, RPG 6, Gabonese Union for Democracy and Development (UGDD) 3, CLR 2, Independent Centre Party of Gabon (PGCI) 2, PSD 2, UPG 2, ADERE 1, and independents 9. The next elections are to be held in January 2015.

In the December 2006 Assembly elections, the PDG retained its parliamentary majority, taking 82 of 120 seats (a decrease from the previous parliament). Thirteen more seats went to allies of the PDG, and the opposition party garnered 16 seats.

In the August 2009 presidential elections, the official results of the election placed Ali-Ben Bongo as the winner with 42% of the vote. However, mass protests began almost immediately after the announcement. Opposition leaders sparked several of these protests, accusing the ruling party of fraud and of initiating a coup rather than an election. In late September 2009, after a review of eleven official complaints of election fraud, the Constitutional Court ordered an official recount. As a result, in October the court announced Bongo as the winner with 41.79% of the vote. The primary opposition candidate, Pierre Mamboundou, came in second with 25.64%, followed by the former interior minister, Andre M'Ba Obame, with 25.33%.

The National Union, a coalition of several opposition parties, was given official recognition as a political party in April 2010. The party was founded one month earlier in an attempt to encourage a spirit of cooperation between several opposition parties that have often been at odds with one another. One of the new National Union leaders, Andre M'Ba Obame, campaigned as an independent candidate in the August 2009 presidential election, and came in third with 25.33% of the vote.

[15] LOCAL GOVERNMENT

Gabon is divided into nine provinces, administered by governors, which are subdivided into 36 prefectures, headed by prefects. There are also separate sub-prefectures, governed by sub-prefects. These officers are directly responsible to the government at Libreville and are appointed by the president. In some areas, the traditional chiefs still retain power, but their position has grown less secure.

[16] JUDICIAL SYSTEM

The civil court system consists of three tiers: the trial court, the appellate court, and the Supreme Court. The Supreme Court has three chambers: judicial, administrative, and accounts. The 1991 constitution, which established many basic freedoms and fundamental rights, also created a Constitutional Court, a body which considers only constitutional issues, and which has demonstrated a good degree of independence in decision-making. Some of its decisions on election freedoms were integrated into the electoral code of 1993, which formed the framework for the first multiparty presidential election held that year. In July 1995, the agreements to reform electoral procedures and to assure greater respect for human rights were approved by a national referendum.

The judiciary also consists of a military tribunal, which handles offenses under military law, a state security court (a civilian tribunal), and a special criminal court for cases of fraud and corruption involving government officials. There is no longer recognition of traditional or customary courts, although village chiefs continue to engage in informal dispute resolution.

The constitution provides for the right to a public trial and the right to counsel, but there is no right to a presumption of innocence. In addition, although the constitution ensures protection from arbitrary interference with privacy and correspondence, search warrants are easily obtained from judges, sometimes after the fact. A significant deterrent to political treason is the weak independence of the judiciary in state security trials where the influence of the executive may be of some import. The State Security Court is constituted by the government to consider state security matters; however, it had not met for years so its relevance is open to question.

17 ARMED FORCES

The International Institute for Strategic Studies reports that armed forces in Gabon totaled 4,700 members in 2011. The force is comprised of 3,200 from the army, 500 from the navy, and 1,000 members of the air force. Armed forces represent 0.9% of the labor force in Gabon. Defense spending totaled $204.3 million and accounted for 0.9% of gross domestic product (GDP).

France has its military base in Libreville with about 1,000 soldiers.

18 INTERNATIONAL COOPERATION

Gabon was admitted to the UN on 20 September 1960 and has become a member of some of its other specialized and related agencies, including ECA. Gabon is also a member of the African Union (AU), African Development Bank, World Bank, IMF, the ACP Group, G-24, G-77, the Central African States Development Bank (BDEAC), the Organization of the Islamic Conference (OIC), the New Partnership for Africa's Development (NEPAD), and the WTO. Gabon is one of six members of the Monetary and Economic Community of Central Africa (CEMAC). Libreville is the headquarters for the 13-member African Timber Organization of timber exporters and for the Economic Community of Central African States. Gabon left OPEC in 1995. The nation is part of the Franc Zone. Gabon belongs to the Nonaligned Movement. Gabon was elected to a non-permanent seat on the UN Security Council for January 2010 through December 2011 and assumed the rotating presidency in March 2010.

In environmental cooperation, Gabon is part of the Convention on Biological Diversity, Ramsar, CITES, the London Convention, International Tropical Timber Agreements, the Montréal Protocol, MARPOL, the Nuclear Test Ban Treaty, and the UN Conventions on the Law of the Sea, Climate Change, and Desertification.

19 ECONOMY

The GDP rate of change in Gabon, as of 2010, was 5.7%. Inflation stood at -1.3%, and unemployment was reported at 21%.

Thanks to oil revenues, Gabon's per capita income is over four times that of most sub-Saharan African countries. Over 40% of Gabon's GDP comes from petroleum and mining production. The petroleum industry generates 81% of export earnings and oil revenues account for roughly 46% of the government's budget. However, oil profits tend to benefit only the richest 20% of the population who receive 90% of the income. This income inequality has had unexpected consequences. In 2000, the government signed an agreement with the Paris Club to reschedule its official debt; however, because the country's per capita income is higher than the eligibility levels set by the World Bank/IMF Heavily Indebted Poor Countries Initiative, it failed to qualify for debt relief under that program. This is despite the fact that over 30% of the population lives in poverty.

Oil revenues are declining rapidly from its peak production in 1997 of 370,000 barrels per day. According to some estimates, Gabonese oil will be expended by 2025. Despite this, the planning for an after-oil era has started only recently. Moreover, oil revenues have not been spent efficiently. The lack of reinvestment in the economy, together with the government's mismanagement of its debt and failure to invest in new markets leaves the country vulnerable to market volatility. In 1986 Gabon saw its GDP drop by half after a dramatic fall in the world price for oil. Consequently, the government was forced to borrow money which substantially increased the country's debt problem with international lenders. The economy suffered a second dramatic shock in 1994 when France suddenly devalued the CFA franc, causing its value to drop in half overnight. Immediately, prices for almost all imported goods soared as the inflation rate shot up to 35%. In the face of dramatically escalating prices, uncertainty and anger led petroleum workers to strike for a doubling of their wages. The government reacted by imposing a national "state of alert." Lootings and burnings were reported as government troops tried to silence opposition parties. Unfortunately, because there is little value-added to Gabon's exports (oil and minerals), the devaluation has not helped Gabon's economy.

The economy was further hampered by inefficient parastatal enterprises that restrained private sector growth and by inefficient and over-sized administration. Under the pressure of the World Bank and IMF, the government embarked on a program of privatization of its state-owned companies and administration reform in the 1990s. However, the progress was slow. While the Bongo Ondimba administration reiterated its commitment to stated reforms, the goal is far from achieved.

Gabon imports the majority of its food; it is densely forested and only a fraction of the arable land is cultivated. Yet, in 2007, 60% of its population gained their livelihood in the agricultural sector, where the staple food crops are cassava, plantains, and yams.

Gabon's cash crops are palm oil, cocoa, coffee, and sugar. Palm oil is the most important of the four. The coffee sector was hard hit in the 1980s by low world prices and lower producer prices; coffee prices fluctuated in the 1990s and 2000s. Gabon is self-sufficient in sugar, which it exports to the United States and other countries. Rubber production has been promoted in recent years.

Content to remain dependent on oil and its other primary product exports, the government has not taken the steps necessary to diversify the economy. High labor costs, an unskilled workforce, and poor fiscal management continue to inhibit economic growth.

20 INCOME

The CIA estimated that in 2010 the GDP of Gabon was $22.48 billion. The CIA defines GDP as the value of all final goods and services produced within a nation in a given year and computed on the basis of purchasing power parity (PPP) rather than value as measured on the basis of the rate of the exchange based on current dollars. The per capita GDP was estimated at $14,500. In 2010, the World Bank estimated that Gabon, with 0.02% of the world's population, accounted for 0.3% of the world's GDP. By comparison, the United States, with 4.5% of the world's population, accounted for 19% of world GDP. CIA estimated that in 2010 agriculture accounted for 5,2% of GDP, industry 53.7%, and services 41.1%.

According to the World Bank, remittances from citizens living abroad totaled $11 million in 2005 (last available data), or about $7 per capita.

The World Bank reports that in 2010, household consumption in Gabon totaled $4.8 billion or about $2,900 per capita, measured in current US dollars rather than PPP. Household consumption includes expenditures of individuals, households, and nongovernmental organizations on goods and services, excluding the purchases of dwellings. It was estimated that household consumption was growing at an average annual rate of 5.5%.

As of 2011, according to the World Bank the actual individual consumption in Gabon was 36.3% of GDP and accounted for 0.01% of world consumption. By comparison, the United States accounted for 25.44% of world individual consumption. The World Bank also estimated that 13.3% of Gabon's GDP was spent on food and beverages, 6.2% on housing and household furnishings, 1.8% on clothes, 2.3% on health, 2.2% on transportation, 1.4% on communications, 0.9% on recreation, 1.0% on restaurants and hotels, and 3.5% on miscellaneous goods and services and purchases from abroad.

21 LABOR

As of 2010, Gabon had a total labor force of 714,500 people. Within that labor force, CIA estimated that 60% were employed in agriculture, 15% in industry, and 25% in the service sector.

In 1992, the former monopoly of the Gabonese Labor Confederation (COSYGA) was abolished and disassociated from the ruling Democratic Party of Gabon. As of 2010, the Ministry of Labor estimated that there were more than 136 unions, and about 40,000 union members in total: 10,000 in the public sector and 30,000 in the private sector. Almost all private sector workers were union members. Workers have the right to strike provided that attempts at arbitration have failed and eight days notice of the intent to strike is given. In the public sector, employees are allowed to strike provided that the strike does not jeopardize public safety. The government observes the resolution of labor disputes and takes an active interest in labor-management relations. Unions in each sector of the economy negotiate with employers over pay scales, working conditions, and benefits. Unions in Gabon are politically active and influential. Although discrimination on the basis of union membership is illegal, members of trade unions in both public and private sectors often faced discrimination.

As of 2010, the minimum wage was the equivalent of $166 per month. This wage did not provide a decent standard of living for a worker and family. The Labor Code provides many protections for workers, including a 40-hour workweek with a minimum rest period of 48 consecutive hours. However, the government did not always enforce the Labor Code provisions, especially in sectors where the majority of the labor force was foreign. Although the legal minimum working age was 16 and the government rigorously enforced this law in urban areas, child labor was a serious problem in rural areas and especially among noncitizen children working in informal sector.

22 AGRICULTURE

Roughly 2% of the total land is farmed, and the country's major crops include cocoa, coffee, sugar, and palm oil. The main food crops are cassava, plantain and maize. According to the World Bank and FAO, average annual cereal production amounts to approximately 33,000 tons. Given low production levels, in 2011, the country imported 177,000 tons of cereals. As of 2009, according to FAO, fresh fruit production was 9,058 tons, and vegetable production 38,217 tons.

Since independence, the dominant position of the petroleum sector has greatly reduced the role of agriculture. Gabon relies heavily on other African states and Europe for much of its food and other agricultural needs. According to the World Bank, as of 2009, food imports accounted for 17% of all merchandise imports. Until World War II (1939–45), agriculture was confined primarily to subsistence farming and the cultivation of such crops as manioc, bananas, corn, rice, taro, and yams. Despite some attempts to diversify and increase agricultural production - such as the set up of experimental stations and demonstration farms, and the establishment of cooperatives - agriculture received low priority until the 1976–81 development plan. The development of agriculture and small business has been hindered by a lack of international competition. Another problem is lack of transportation to markets.

Due to dwindling oil reserves, however, attempts to improve agricultural production increased. In 2010, the Gabonese government signed a joint venture agreement with OLAM, a Singapore-based company, for the development of 300,000 hectares of palm oil and rubber plantations between 2012 and 2016. OLAM will hold 70% of interest in this joint venture, the rest will be held by Gabon. Gabon wants to become the leading palm oil producer in Africa.

23 ANIMAL HUSBANDRY

The UN Food and Agriculture Organization (FAO) reported that Gabon dedicated 4.7 million hectares (11.5 million acres) to permanent pasture or meadow in 2009. During that year, the country tended 3.2 million chickens, 36,500 head of cattle, and 215,000 pigs. The production from these animals amounted to 5,751 tons of beef and veal, 10,376 tons of pork, 40,372 tons of poultry, 1,571 tons of eggs, and 53,137 tons of milk. Gabon also produced 212 tons of cattle hide.

Animal husbandry is limited by the presence of the tsetse fly, though tsetse-resistant cattle have recently been imported from Senegal to a cattle project. In 2009 there were an estimated 196,000 sheep and 92,000 goats. In an effort to reduce Gabon's reliance on meat imports, the government set aside 200,000 hectares (494,000 acres) in Gabon's unpopulated Savannah region for three ranches at Ngounie, Nyanga, and Lekabi. Currently, however, frozen imports are the most important source of beef, costing considerably less than locally produced beef. Poultry production satisfies about one-half of Gabon's consumption demand.

24 FISHING

While there have been recent improvements in the fishing industry, it is still relatively undeveloped. Gabon had 24 decked commercial fishing boats in 2008. The annual capture totaled 30,000 tons according to the UN FAO. The export value of seafood totaled $17.33 million. According to FAO, traditional fishing accounted in 2006 for half of total catch. The waters off the Gabonese coast contain large quantities of fish. Gabonese waters are estimated to be able to support an annual catch of 15,000 tons of tuna and 12,000 tons of sardines. The fishing fleet was formerly based chiefly in Libreville. A new fishing port, however, was built at Port-Gentil in 1979. Port-Gentil is now the center of operations for the industrial fleet. Plans for a cannery, fish-meal factory, and refrigerated storage facilities are underway. By international agreement and Gabonese law, an exclusive economic zone extends 322 km (200 mi) off the coast, which prohibits any foreign fishing company to fish in this zone without governmental authorization. However, since Gabon has no patrol boats, foreign trawlers (especially French and Spanish) often illegally capture tuna in Gabonese waters.

25 FORESTRY

Approximately 85% of Gabon is covered by forest. Gabon's forests have always supplied many of the necessities of life, especially fuel and shelter. The forests contain over 400 species of trees, with about 100 species suitable for industrial use. Commercial exploitation began as early as 1892, but only in 1913 was okoumé, Gabon's most valuable wood, introduced to the international market. Forestry was the primary source of economic activity in the country until 1968, when the industry was supplanted by crude oil as an earner of foreign exchange. Gabon is the largest exporter of raw wood in the region, and its sales represent 20% of Africa's raw wood exports. Forestry is second only to the petroleum sector in export earnings. Gabon's reserves of exploitable timber include okoumé, ozigo, ilomba, azobe, and padouk.

Gabon used to supply 90% of the world's okoumé, which makes excellent plywood, and also produces hardwoods, such as mahogany, kevazingo, and ebony. Other woods are dibetou (tigerwood or African walnut), movingui (Nigerian satinwood), and zingana (zebrano or zebrawood). The UN FAO estimated the 2009 roundwood production at 3.4 million cu m (120.1 million cu ft). The value of all forest products, including roundwood, totaled $948.7 million.

Exploitation had been hampered, to some extent, by the inadequacy of transportation infrastructure, a deficiency now alleviated by the Trans-Gabon Railway and Ndjole-Bitam highway. Reforestation has been continuously promoted, and selective thinning and clearing have prevented the okoumé from being forced out by other species. Over 50 firms are engaged in exploitation of Gabon's forests. Logging concessions covering about five million hectares (12.3 million acres) have been granted by the government, with the development of the least accessible areas largely carried out by foreign firms. Traditional demand in Europe for African lumber products has declined in recent years; during the 1980s, European demand for okoumé dropped by almost one-third. Markets in Asia (China, Japan), Morocco, and Israel, however, have become more receptive to African imports.

Since the adoption of the Forest Code in 2001, the official policy of Gabon has been to encourage downstream processing of timber. In November 2009, the government announced the ban on exports of unprocessed logs. However, the implementation of the new law was delayed through May 2010 and is seen to be detrimental to foreign investment and rural laborers in the short term.

26 MINING

Gabon was the richest of the former French Equatorial African colonies in known mineral deposits. In addition to oil, which accounted for 77% of the country's exports in 2009, Gabon was a world leader in manganese. Potash, uranium, columbium (niobium), iron ore, lead, zinc, diamonds, marble, and phosphate have also been discovered, and several deposits were being exploited commercially. Ownership of all mineral rights was vested in the government, which has increased its share of the profits accruing to foreign companies under development contracts.

The high-grade manganese deposits at Moanda, near Franceville, are among the world's richest. Reserves were estimated at 250 million tons with a metal content of 48%-52%. Production had been limited to a ceiling of 2.8 million tons a year, corresponding closely to the capacity of the cableway-at 76 km, Africa's longest overhead cable-used to transport the mineral to the Congo border, from where it was carried by rail to the port of Pointe Noire. The Trans-Gabon Railway provided an export outlet through the Gabonese port of Owendo. Use of the railroad has cut shipping costs by $20 million per year. Manganese was exploited by the Mining Co. of L'Ougoué (Comilog, an international consortium), which ranked among the world's lowest-cost producers. In 2009, an estimated 1.95 million metric tons of metallurgical-grade ore were extracted, down from 3.15 million metric tons in 20083. Annual production capacity at the Moanda Mine was 2.5 million tons, with reserves estimated to last 100 years.

Gabon also produced an estimated 190,000 metric tons each of clinker and hydraulic cement in 2008. In 2009, an estimated 500 carats of diamonds (gem and industrial) were produced, along with 300 kg of gold.

The Mékambo and Belinga iron fields in the northeastern corner of Gabon were ranked among the world's richest. Reserves were estimated as high as 1 billion tons of ore of 60%-65% iron content, and production could reach 20 million tons a year. Although iron was discovered there in 1895, it was not until 1955 that a full-scale commercial license was issued. Exploitation still awaited the establishment of a 225 km extension of the Trans-Gabon Railroad from Booué to Belinga; construction has been considered unprofitable, because of unfavorable market conditions.

The potential for new developments in columbium, gold, manganese, and possibly phosphate suggested a continued role for mining in the economy. The lack of adequate infrastructure inhibited new grassroots exploration and remained a major constraint on development of the well-defined iron ore deposit at Belinga.

27 ENERGY AND POWER

The World Bank reported in 2009 that Gabon produced 1.7 billion kWh of electricity and consumed 1.36 billion kWh, or 922.5 kWh per capita. Roughly 44% of energy came from fossil fuels, while 4% came from alternative fuels.

Gabon is the fifth-largest oil producer in sub-Saharan Africa, and has the region's third-largest oil reserves. Oil prospecting began in 1931. Deposits were found on the coast or offshore in the vicinity of Libreville and Port-Gentil, in the northwestern part of the country. Later, large deposits were found in the south. Oil from the northwest is channeled by pipeline to Cape Lopez, where there are loading facilities for export. Huge additional deposits were found on Mandji Island in 1962. The Rabi Kounga oil field is Gabon's largest oil field, while additional reserves were located in the offshore Tchatamba Marin and Etame fields.

Although Gabon's proven petroleum reserves rose from 1.3 billion barrels in 1996 to 2 billion barrels in 2009 according to US Energy Information Administration (EIA), the government is concerned about long-term depletion of resources. Total production of crude oil fell from a peak of 371,000 barrels per day to an estimated 227,900 barrels per day in 2010 (CIA). Per capita oil consumption was 1,214 kg as of 2009 (World Bank). Gabon's production goes primarily to the United States, France, China, Brazil, Argentina and, more recently, Taiwan. Oil exports in 2009 were estimated at 213,500 barrels per day (CIA).

As of 2010, reserves of natural gas reserves estimated at 1 trillion cu ft, by EIA. Production and consumption of natural gas in 2010 were estimated at 3 billion cu ft, each.

According to the World Bank, 53.2% of Gabon's electricity production derived from hydroelectric sources in 2009. As of 2011, hydroelectric stations were located at the Kinguélé and Tchimbélé dams on the Mbei River and at the Petite Poubara Dam on the Ogooué river. Grand Poubara was under construction. Production and distribution of electricity are maintained by the Energy and Water Company of Gabon (SEEG), which was formed in 1963. In 2011, Veoila Water India Africa, SEEG's majority shareholder (51%) since 1997, sold half of its shares to the French EDF (Eléctricité de France). The reminder was held by small and medium-sized Gabonese investors. Natural gas is the principal fuel for the thermal plants.

28 INDUSTRY

Gabon's industry is centered on petroleum, manganese mining, and timber processing. Most industrial establishments are located near Libreville and Port-Gentil. Virtually all industrial enterprises were established with government subsidies in the oil boom years of the 1970s. Timber-related concerns include five veneer plants and a large 50-year-old plywood factory in Port-Gentil, along with two other small plywood factories. Other industries include tex-tile plants, cement factories, chemical plants, breweries, shipyards, and cigarette factories. Gabonese manufacturing is highly dependent on foreign inputs, and import costs rose significantly in 1994 when the CFA franc was devalued. Increased costs and oversized capacity have made the manufacturing sector less competitive and it mainly supplies the domestic market. The government has taken steps to privatize parastatal enterprises.

Due to the fact that the Gabonese economy is dependent upon oil (crude oil accounts for over 80% of the country's exports, 43% of GDP, and 46% of state revenue), it is subject to worldwide price fluctuations. Gabon is sub-Saharan Africa's fifth-largest crude oil producer and exporter, although there are concerns that proven reserves are declining and production has declined as well. Thus the country has taken steps to diversify the economy, and to engage in further petroleum exploration. The Sogara oil refinery at Port-Gentil is the sole refinery in Gabon. The country produced 227,900 barrels per day in 2010, which was a decrease of 12% from the peak production levels.

29 SCIENCE AND TECHNOLOGY

The World Bank reported in 2009 that there were no patent applications in science and technology in Gabon. Gabon has a shortage of trained scientists and technicians and relies heavily on foreign-mostly French-technical assistance. In Libreville there are a French bureau of geological and mineral research, a technical center for tropical forestry, a research institute for agriculture and forestry, and a center for technical and scientific research. A laboratory of primatology and equatorial forest ecology is at Makokou, and an international center of medical research, concentrating on infectious diseases and fertility, is at Franceville. The University Omar Bongo, founded in 1970, has a faculty of sciences, schools of engineering and of forestry and hydraulics, and a health science center. The University of Sciences and Techniques of Masuke, at Franceville, founded in 1986, has a faculty of sciences. The Inter-provincial School of Health is located in Mouila. The African Institute of Information, at Libreville, trains computer programmers and analysts.

30 DOMESTIC TRADE

Most local produce is sold directly to consumers or to intermediaries at local markets in villages and towns, while imported goods are disposed of at the same time. Company agents and independent middlemen buy export crops at local markets or directly from the producers for sale to large companies. Both French and domestic companies carry on wholesale and retail trade in the larger cities. Nearly 70% of food products are imported. Large commercial companies generally sell hardware, food, clothing, tools, electrical goods, durable consumer goods, and cars. Medium-sized merchandise retail establishments are mostly operated by Syrian, Lebanese, or Asian expatriates. Small private companies are often owned by expatriates from elsewhere in West Africa and operate from market stalls. Gabonese have been trained in retailing in newly built stores. Those who qualify after training have been encouraged to buy the stores with government-sponsored loans. Advertising is carried by local newspapers, company publications, handbills, billboards, and radio and television stations.

Business hours are 8 a.m.-noon and 3–6 p.m., Monday through Friday, and 8 a.m.-1 p.m., Saturday. Banks are open 7:30–11:30

Principal Trading Partners – Gabon (2010)

(In millions of US dollars)

Country	Total	Exports	Imports	Balance
World	10,900.0	8,400.0	2,500.0	5,900.0
United States	2,336.6	2,069.6	267.1	1,802.5
China	1,114.0	865.8	248.2	617.6
France	1,046.7	254.4	792.3	-537.9
Malaysia	714.3	697.7	16.6	681.0
Australia	380.0	377.9	2.1	375.9
Spain	348.7	297.9	50.8	247.2
India	325.9	287.6	38.3	249.3
Trinidad and Tobago	302.9	299.3	3.6	295.8
Netherlands	265.9	153.7	112.2	41.5
Italy	227.3	135.8	91.5	44.2

(…) data not available or not significant.

(n.s.) not specified.

SOURCE: *2011 Direction of Trade Statistics Yearbook,* New York: United Nations, 2011.

Balance of Payments – Gabon (2005)

(In millions of US dollars)

Current Account		1,983.0
Balance on goods	4,105.0	
Imports	-1,358.8	
Exports	5,463.9	
Balance on services	-895.4	
Balance on income	-957.6	
Current transfers	-269.0	
Capital Account		...
Financial Account		-1,342.0
Direct investment abroad	-75.4	
Direct investment in Gabon	242.3	
Portfolio investment assets	7.6	
Portfolio investment liabilities	0.7	
Financial derivatives	...	
Other investment assets	-1,079.1	
Other investment liabilities	-438.1	
Net Errors and Omissions		-415.1
Reserves and Related Items		-225.9

(…) data not available or not significant.

SOURCE: *Balance of Payment Statistics Yearbook 2011,* Washington, DC: International Monetary Fund, 2011.

a.m. and 2:30–4:30 p.m., Monday through Friday. Mainly French is spoken.

31 FOREIGN TRADE

CIA estimated that Gabon imported $2.494 billion worth of goods and services in 2010, while exporting $9.371 billion worth of goods and services. Major import partners in 2010 were France, 29.4%; the United States, 9.9%; China, 9.2%; Belgium, 5.2%; Cameroon, 5.1%; and Netherlands, 4.2%. Its major export partners were the United States, 30.4%; China, 12.7%; Australia 5.5%, Malaysia, 5.3%; Trinidad and Tobago, 4.4%; and Spain, 4.4%.

Gabon has a record of trade surpluses. Until the late 1960s, timber was Gabon's main export. By 1969, however, crude petroleum had become the leader, accounting for 34% of total exports. Petroleum's share increased to 40.7% in 1972 and to 81.9% in 1974; it stood at 82.5% in 1985 and hovered around 80% during the 2000s (81% in 2010). Most of Gabon's oil goes to the United States.

Wood accounts for a substantial amount of export revenues—15% in 2011, according to the Association Interafricaine des Industries Forestières. Manganese is also important.

32 BALANCE OF PAYMENTS

Gabon's traditionally favorable trade balance does not always result in a favorable balance on current accounts, largely because of dividend payments and other remittances by foreign enterprises but also because of payments on large debts accumulated in the 1970s. Generally, however, an increasingly strong export performance and rising inflows of private and government capital have made Gabon's payments position one of the strongest of any African country.

The CIA reported that in 2010 Gabon's trade surplus was $6.877 billion.

33 BANKING AND SECURITIES

The bank of issue is the Bank of the Central African States (Banque des Etats de l'Afrique Centrale—BEAC), the central bank for Gabon. The adoption of the BEAC as its central bank was designed to strengthen the country's monetary solidarity and sovereignty with other African states belonging to BEAC. BEAC is Gabon's bank of issue, using the CFA franc, whose convertibility is guaranteed by France.

In 2010, the discount rate, the interest rate at which the central bank lends to financial institutions in the short term, was 3%. In 2010, the nation's gold bullion deposits totaled 0.013 million fine troy ounces.

Commercial banking in Gabon is largely controlled by French and other foreign interests. As of 2011, there was one development bank, and several commercial banks, including the Banque Internationale de Commerce et d'Industrie du Gabon (BICIG, a branch of BNP Paribas), the Union Gabonaise de Banque (UGB, a branch of Credit Agricole), and Citibank Gabon and Orabank Gabon.

The Gabonese Development Bank (BDG), 69.01% Gabonese-owned, is the nation's development bank. Other institutions concerned with development are the Credit Foncier du Gabon (CREFOGA, for housing), the Fund for Development and Expansion (FODEX, for small, to medium-sized firms), and the Banque Nationale de Credit Rural (BNCR, loans for agriculture).

A small regional stock exchange (BVMAC) headquartered in Gabon has been in operation since 2008. The securities market is poorly developed.

34 INSURANCE

In 1974, a national company known as SONAGAR was created, 36% owned by the government. In 1986, there were four French insurance companies represented in Gabon. In 1995, there were at least ten insurance companies doing business in Gabon. As of 2010, while the insurance penetration in Gabon was still low, it was significantly higher than the regional average.

35 PUBLIC FINANCE

The oil sector brings in around 50% of government revenues. Government finances are generally poorly managed. Large deficits have required borrowing from foreign creditors, although the government's failure to privatize state-owned enterprises and to fully account for oil revenues has soiled its reputation with international financial institutions. After the 1994 devaluation of the currency, Gabon was forced to reschedule its debt with the World Bank/IMF, the London Club of creditors, the African Development Bank, and the Paris Club. In 2007 Gabon issued a $1 billion sovereign bond to buy back a sizable portion of its Paris Club debt. In May 2010, a 3-year stand-by arrangement with the IMF expired, without Gabon fulfilling its responsibilities.

In 2010 the budget of Gabon included $3.557 billion in public revenue and $2.945 billion in public expenditures. The budget surplus amounted to 4.6% of GDP. Public debt was 25.8% of GDP, with $2.282 billion of the debt held by foreign entities.

36TAXATION

A progressive tax rate ranging from 0 to 35% is imposed on ordinary personal incomes (Deloitte). Additional taxes are levied on business transactions and on real property. In April 1995, a value-added tax (VAT) was introduced, replacing three turnover taxes. The standard VAT rate in 2011 was 18%. Other taxes include a 5% payroll tax, a property tax, and a financial transactions tax.

The standard corporate tax rate is 35% on net profits, with a minimum of 1% on turnover. There is a 20% withholding tax on dividends. Payments of interest, royalties, and for services are taxed at 10%. Government oil revenues are derived from royalty payments, a tax on petroleum company profits, a tax on exploration permits, and dividends paid by the petroleum companies.

37CUSTOMS AND DUTIES

Gabon is a member of Central African Economic and Monetary Community (CEMAC), which was created in 1994. Gabon's trade with other CEMAC members (Cameroon, the Central African Republic, Chad, Congo-Brazzaville and Equatorial Guinea) is subject to low or no customs duties. Gabon is a part of the franc zone, within which goods and capital flow without obstruction.

Import duties consist of a fiscal duty applied to all goods entering the CEMAC area, whatever their origin. Customs duties and taxes are based on the cost, insurance and freight (CIF) value. Basic products are taxed at 7.2%, raw materials at 29.8%, intermediate products and most food products at 53.4%, and luxury items 99.42%. In addition, there is an entry fee, a value-added tax (VAT) of 18% payable by all companies with a turnover of more than $400,000, a complementary import tax, and a special fee on postal and border imports. Imports from outside the franc zone and the European Union are subject to licensing fees and prior authorization is required. Export duties and taxes are levied on specific commodities.

38FOREIGN INVESTMENT

Foreign direct investment (FDI) in Gabon was a net inflow of $170.4 million according to World Bank figures published in 2010. FDI represented 1.3% of GDP.

Gabon has benefited from considerable private investment centered on the development of petroleum resources. French investments predominated and were concentrated in petroleum (Total) and manganese (COMILOG/ERAMET). France was Gabon's main supplier of goods. Since independence, however, Gabon

has sought additional sources of investment and US companies have invested in the lumber industry, oil exploration, and mining. French influence by sector is estimated at 63% in construction, 50% in petroleum, 30% in timber, 20% in chemicals, and 29% in transportation.

Gabon's investment code of 1998 conforms to regulations of the Central African Economic and Monetary Community (CEMAC), providing the same rights to foreign companies operating in Gabon as to domestic companies. There are no restrictions on foreign investment in Gabon. However, the government reserves the right to invest in the equity capital of ventures in certain sectors, such as mining and petroleum. In some sectors (i.e. pensions, hospitals, housing agencies) state-owned companies practically have a monopoly and foreign companies face unfair treatment. Moreover, Gabon's regulatory bodies are often subject to political influence, which also affects fair treatment and the sanctity of contracts. Certain sectors (i.e. mining, tourism, petroleum, forestry) have specific investment codes, which try to encourage investment through tax and customs incentives. Free transfer of capital is guaranteed and there are no restrictions on area of activity.

In January 1996, the government passed a new law on privatization that resulted in the sale of the electricity and water monopoly (SEEG) in 1997 to Veoila Water India Africa (51%), which in 2011 sold half of its shares to the French EDF (Eléctricité de France). Other companies to be privatized included Transgabonese Railway (OCTRA) and the International Telecommunications Office (OPT).

39ECONOMIC DEVELOPMENT

Economic liberalism tempered by planning is the basic policy of the Gabonese government, which seeks to make the most of the country's rich natural resources. Priority is being given to the agricultural sector, to reduce imports, and to diversify the economy. Limiting migration to the cities is also an important element in this strategy. Industrial development efforts are centered on resource processing industries. Building the infrastructure is also an identifiable priority.

The devaluation of the Communauté Financière Africaine franc in 1994 did not stimulate local production and discourage imports as expected. Realizing the need for structural adjustments to restore economic competitiveness, the government developed a new strategy in 1995 that encouraged private sector development, promoted privatization of state-owned enterprises, and increased the government's efforts in providing health and education services. A 1997 International Monetary Fund (IMF) report on Gabon criticized the government of overspending and failing to meet structural reform schedules. The government negotiated an 18-month stand-by arrangement with the IMF in 2000, which expired in 2002; Gabon met few of its targets.

Oil production fell in 2001, and non-oil activity rose by 4%. Oil prices were high in the early 2000s, and Gabon's current account balance improved from a deficit of 8.8% of GDP in 1999 to a surplus of 3.2% in 2000; it fell to a deficit of 1% of GDP in 2001, in part due to lower oil exports. In 2011, current account balance improved to a surplus of 15.6% (CIA). The IMF in 2003 encouraged Gabon's government to develop the non-oil sector as a way of replacing the oil and government sectors as the primary catalysts for economic growth and development. In May 2010, a 3-year standby arrangement with the IMF expired, without Gabon fulfilling its responsibilities.

40 SOCIAL DEVELOPMENT

Old age, disability, and survivor pensions are available to all employees and are funded by contributions from employees and employers. Special systems are in place for civil servants, military personnel, the self-employed, and state contract workers. Other benefits include maternity and medical coverage, and workers' compensation. A family allowance is available to all salaried workers with children under the age of 16. Agricultural workers and subsistence farmers are not covered by these programs.

Women have many legal protections and participate in business and politics, although they face discrimination in many areas. Polygamy is still common, and the property rights of women in polygamous marriages are limited. Women are required by law to obtain permission from their husband before leaving the country. Domestic abuse is prevalent, especially in rural areas. There is limited legal and medical assistance for rape victims.

Minority Pygmies maintain their indigenous community and decision-making structures. However, they suffer societal discrimination and severe poverty. Gabon's human rights record has improved in recent years, although there continue to be reports of the use of abuse by security forces. Prison conditions are harsh and life threatening.

41 HEALTH

Gabon's medical infrastructure is considered one of the best in West Africa. As of 2009, the World Bank estimated that 8.3% of GDP was spent on healthcare. This amounted to $266 per person. There were 3 physicians, 50 nurses and midwives, and 13 hospital beds per 10,000 inhabitants. Total expenditure on healthcare in Gabon in 2009 was an estimated 6% of GDP. Approximately 90% of the population had access to health care services. As of 2008, CIA estimated that 87% of the population had access to improved drinking water and 33% had adequate sanitation. The World Bank estimated that 55% of children were vaccinated against measles in 2010.

Most of the health services are public, but there are some private institutions, of which the best known is the hospital established in 1913 in Lambaréné by Albert Schweitzer. The hospital is now partially subsidized by the Gabonese government.

A comprehensive government health program treats such diseases as leprosy, sleeping sickness, malaria, filariasis, intestinal worms, and tuberculosis. In 2006 immunization rates for DPT and measles were 38% and 55% respectively. Gabon has a domestic supply of pharmaceuticals from a large, modern factory in Libreville.

According to CIA, the total fertility rate was 4.59 children per mother in 2011. In 2008, the maternal mortality rate was 260 per 100,000 live births, which, although extremely high, represented a significant drop from the previous decade. An estimated 10% of all births were low birth weight in 2007. In 2011, the infant mortality rate was 49.95 deaths per 1,000 live births and life expectancy was 52.49 years.

The HIV/AIDS adult prevalence rate was 5.2% in 2009, ranking among the top 20 in the world. The incidence of tuberculosis was 280 per 100,000 people in 2007.

42 HOUSING

Credit institutions make small loans for the repair of existing houses and larger loans (amounting to almost the total cost of the house) for the construction of new houses, but the cost of homeownership and maintenance has still been beyond the reach of most average citizens. Because of their higher credit rating, salaried civil servants and employees of trading companies receive most of the loans. The government has established a national habitation fund, and there have been a number of urban renewal projects. As of 2008, 95% of urban and 41% of rural dwellers had access to improved water sources (CIA). About 33% of urban and 30% of rural dwellers had access to improved sanitation systems. According to Population Reference Bureau, housing deficit was estimated to be between 133,000 and 200,000 dwellings in 2010.

43 EDUCATION

The educational system is patterned on that of France, but changes are being introduced gradually to adapt the curriculum to local needs and traditions. The government gives high priority to education, especially the construction of rural schools. Education is free and compulsory between the ages of 6 and 16. Primary school covers five years of study. Students then choose either general secondary courses or a technical school program, each of which cover seven years. The academic year runs from October to June. The primary language of instruction is French.

In 2009 the World Bank estimated that 81% of age-eligible children in Gabon were enrolled in primary school. Secondary enrollment for age-eligible children stood at 35%. Overall, the CIA estimated that Gabon had a literacy rate of 63.2%. It declined from 84% in 2004.

Omar Bongo University, at Libreville, includes faculties of law, sciences, and letters; teachers' training schools; and schools of law, engineering, forestry and hydraulics, administration, and management. In 1999, about 7% of the tertiary age population was enrolled in some type of higher education program.

In 2009 public expenditure on education was estimated at 3.8% of GDP.

44 LIBRARIES AND MUSEUMS

The National Library (founded in 1969), National Archives (1969), and Documentation Center (1980) together form a collection of 25,000 volumes. The Omar Bongo University in Libreville has 12,000 volumes. The Information Center Library in Libreville has 3,500 volumes. There are also American and French Cultural Centers in Libreville housing modest collections. The Museum of Arts and Traditions at Libreville is a general interest museum. The National Museum of Gabon is also in Libreville.

45 MEDIA

The Ministry of Information, Posts, and Telecommunications provides domestic services for Gabon and participates in international services. There are direct radiotelephone communications with Paris and other overseas points.

Radio-Diffusion Télévision Gabonaise (RTG), which is owned and operated by the government, broadcasts in French and indigenous languages. In 1981 a commercial radio station, Africa No. 1, began operations. The most powerful radio station on the continent, it has participation from the French and Gabonese governments and private European media. As of 2007, the government operated two TV stations and two radio broadcast stations. Transmissions of least 2 international broadcasters were accessible.

In 2010 the CIA reported that there were 30,400 main telephone lines and 1.61 million mobile cellular phones in use in Gabon. In addition to landlines, mobile phone subscriptions averaged 93 per 100 people. There were six FM radio stations, seven AM radio stations, and four shortwave radio stations. Internet users numbered 7 per 100 citizens. In 2010 the country had 90 Internet hosts. Prominent newspapers in 2010, with circulation numbers listed parenthetically, included *L'Union* (40,000).

The national press service is the Gabonese Press Agency. The government-controlled daily newspapers are *Gabon-Matin* and *L'Union*. The weekly *Gabon d'Aujourdhui*, is published by the Ministry of Communications. There are about nine privately owned periodicals which are either independent or affiliated with political parties. These publish in small numbers and are often delayed by financial constraints. Foreign newspapers are available.

The constitution of Gabon provides for free speech and a free press, and the government is said to support these rights. Several periodicals actively criticize the government.

46 ORGANIZATIONS

There is a chamber of commerce at Libreville. UNIGABON, a national organization was established in October 1959 and was renamed to Confédération Patronale Gabonaise (CPG) in 1978. CPG conducts liaison work among mining and timber companies, labor unions, public works societies, and transportation companies. There are some professional organizations, such as the Association of Editors of a Free and Independent Press and the Association of Sports Medicine.

Church organizations are active in the country and have a sizable following. They operate several mission schools and health centers. In rural areas, cooperatives promote the production and marketing of agricultural products. Among the tribes, self-help societies have grown rapidly, particularly in the larger towns, where tribal members act together as mutual-aid societies. There are youth and women's organizations affiliated with the PDG. The Alliance of YMCA's is also a major youth organization in the country, as are several scouting programs.

Volunteer service organizations, such as the Lions Clubs International and Rotary Clubs, are also present. There are national chapters of the Red Cross Society and Caritas.

47 TOURISM, TRAVEL, AND RECREATION

Gabon's tourist attractions include fine beaches, ocean and inland fishing facilities, and scenic sites, such as the falls on the Ogooué River and the Crystal Mountains. Many visitors come to see the hospital founded by Albert Schweitzer at Lambaréné. In addition, there are numerous national parks (covering about 10% of country's surface area) and wildlife reserves. Gabon is increasingly investing in ecotourism. President Ali Bongo Ondimba launched a project 'Green Gabon' aimed at valorizing and preserving Gabon's rich and diverse ecosystem.

Gabon and Equatorial Guinea co-hosted the biennial African Cup of Nations in 2012. The tournament was played in the Gabonese cities of Libreville and Franceville, and the Equatoguinean cities of Malobo and Bata.

The *Tourism Factbook*, published by the UN World Tourism Organization, reported 358,000 incoming tourists to Gabon in 2009, who spent a total of $13 million. The estimated daily cost to visit Libreville, the capital, was $484. The cost of visiting other cities averaged $317. Visitors must have a valid passport, visa, and evidence of yellow fever immunization.

48 FAMOUS PERSONS

The best-known Gabonese are Léon M'Ba (1902–67), the president of the republic from 1960 to 1967, and Omar Bongo (Albert-Bernard Bongo, 1935–2009), president from 1967 until his death. Born in Alsace (then part of Germany but now in France), Albert Schweitzer (1875–1965), a world-famous clergyman, physician, philosopher, and musicologist and the 1952 winner of the Nobel Prize for peace, administered a hospital that he established in Lambaréné in 1913.

49 DEPENDENCIES

Gabon has no territories or colonies.

50 BIBLIOGRAPHY

Dowie, Mark. *Conservation Refugees: The Hundred-Year Conflict between Global Conservation and Native Peoples.* Cambridge, MA: MIT Press, 2011.

Gabon Investment and Business Guide: Strategic and Practical Information. Washington, DC: International Business Publications USA, 2012.

Gardinier, David E. *Historical Dictionary of Gabon.* 3rd ed. Lanham, MD: Scarecrow Press, 2006.

Gray, Christopher J. *Colonial Rule and Crisis in Equatorial Africa: Southern Gabon, c. 1850–1940.* Rochester: University of Rochester Press, 2002.

McElrath, Karen, ed. *HIV and AIDS: A Global View.* Westport, CT: Greenwood Press, 2002.

Van Aarde, Rudi. *Congo Basin and Angola.* New York: Marshall Cavendish Reference, 2011.

Zeilig, Leo, and David Seddon. *A Political and Economic Dictionary of Africa.* Philadelphia: Routledge/Taylor and Francis, 2005.

THE GAMBIA

Republic of The Gambia

CAPITAL: Banjul (formerly Bathurst)

FLAG: The flag is a tricolor of red, blue, and green horizontal bands, separated by narrow white stripes.

ANTHEM: *For The Gambia, Our Homeland.*

MONETARY UNIT: In 1971 the dalasi (GMD), a paper currency of 100 butut, replaced The Gambian pound. There are coins of 1, 5, 10, 25, and 50 butut and 1 dalasi, and notes of 1, 5, 10, 25, and 50 dalasi. GMD1 = US$0.03367 (or US$1 = GMD29.7) as of November 2011.

WEIGHTS AND MEASURES: Both British and metric weights and measures are in use.

HOLIDAYS: New Year's Day, 1 January; Confederation Day, 1 February; Independence Day, 18 February; Labor Day, 1 May; Assumption, 15 August; Christmas, 25 December. Movable religious holidays include Good Friday, Easter Monday, Eid al-Fitr, Eid al-Adha, and Milad an-Nabi.

TIME: GMT.

¹LOCATION, SIZE, AND EXTENT

Located on the west coast of Africa, The Gambia has an area of 11,300 sq km (4,363 sq mi), extending 338 km (210 mi) E–W and 47 km (29 mi) N–S. Comparatively, The Gambia is slightly less than twice the size Delaware. Bounded on the N, E, and S by Senegal (with which it is joined in the Confederation of Senegambia) and on the W by the Atlantic Ocean, The Gambia has a total boundary length of 820 km (510 mi), of which 80 km (50 mi) is coastline. The Gambia's capital city, Banjul, is located on the Atlantic coast.

²TOPOGRAPHY

The Gambia River, the country's major waterway, starts in Guinea and follows a twisting path for about 1,600 km (1,000 mi) to the ocean. In its last 470 km (292 mi), the river flows through the Republic of The Gambia, narrowing to a width of 5 km (3 mi) at Banjul. During the dry season, tidal saltwater intrudes as far as 250 km (155 mi) upstream. Brown mangrove swamps line both sides of the river for the first 145 km (90 mi) from the ocean; the mangroves then give way to more open country and, in places, to red ironstone cliffs. The land on either side of the river is generally open savanna with wooded areas along the drainage channels. Elevation reaches a maximum of 73 m (240 ft).

³CLIMATE

The Gambia has a tropical climate with distinct cool and hot seasons. From November to mid-May there is uninterrupted dry weather, with temperatures as low as 16°C (61°F) in Banjul and surrounding areas. Hot, humid weather predominates the rest of the year, with a rainy season from June to October; during this period, temperatures may rise as high as 43°C (109°F) but are usually lower near the ocean. Along the coast, mean temperatures range

from 23°C (73°F) in January to 27°C (81°F) in June and range from 24° C (75°F) in January to 32°C (90°F) in May inland. Immediately before the rainy season begins is the hottest time of the year, with temperatures sometimes reaching 49°C (120°F) near Basse. The average annual rainfall ranges from 92 cm (36 in) inland to 145 cm (57 in) along the coast.

⁴FLORA AND FAUNA

The World Resources Institute estimates that there are 974 plant species in The Gambia. Forest types include tropical dry forest, wooded savanna, moist gallery forests along watercourses, and mangrove forests near the coast and main river stem. Fauna is diverse for such a small nation and includes 133 mammal, 535 bird, 58 reptile, and 14 amphibian species. Most large African mammals have been exterminated from the country, with the last elephant killed in 1913. A small population of hippos remains in River Gambia National Park. The calculation of total species reflects the total number of distinct species residing in the country, not the number of endemic species.

Birds and monkeys form the most commonly seen species of interest. It is not uncommon to see troupes of more than 100 baboons. The large number of different species of birds also attracts a number of tourists.

⁵ENVIRONMENT

The Gambia's environmental concerns include deforestation, desertification, and water pollution. The country lies in the eastern Sahel and is at risk of the Sahara gradually encroaching from the north. Deforestation is the most serious problem, with slash-and-burn agriculture, driven by the high population density, as the principal cause. The United Nations Educational, Scientific, and Cultural Organization (UNESCO) estimated the current deforestation rate at 6% annually in 2010. In the 1950s 34,000 hectares (84,000 acres) were set aside as forest parks, but by 1972, 11% of these reserves had been totally cleared. From 1981 to 1985 deforestation averaged 2,000 hectares (5,000 acres) per year. Reforestation programs have been set in place, and from 1990 to 2000 reforestation took place at a rate of about 1% per year. Bush fires set for clearing land for agriculture, careless fire use, and fires deliberately set by pastoralists to stimulate grass growth, represent some of the most important causes of deforestation.

A 30% decrease in rainfall over the last 30 years has increased the rate of desertification for The Gambia's agricultural lands. Water pollution is a significant problem due to lack of adequate sanitation facilities. Impure water is responsible for life-threatening diseases that contribute to high infant mortality rates.

The World Resources Institute reported that water resources totaled 8 cu km (1.92 cu mi) while water usage was 0.03 cu km (0.007 cu mi) per year. Domestic water usage accounted for 23% of total usage, industrial for 12%, and agricultural for 65%. Per capita water usage totaled 20 cu m (706 cu ft) per year.

Baobolon Wetland Reserve is a Ramsar wetland site. The Gambia's wildlife has been threatened by changes in habitat and poaching. According to a 2011 report issued by the International Union for Conservation of Nature and Natural Resources (IUCN), the number of threatened species included 10 types of mammals, 8 species of birds, 2 types of reptiles, 23 species of fish, and 4 species of plants. Threatened species include the African slender-snouted crocodile and the West African manatee.

Greenhouse gas emissions from The Gambia make only a very minor contribution to climate change. The United Nations (UN) reported in 2008 that carbon dioxide emissions in The Gambia totaled 396 kilotons. In 2011 The Gambia was a signatory to several international environmental treaties including the Kyoto Protocol, The Convention on Biological Diversity, and The Law of the Sea.

6 POPULATION

The US Central Intelligence Agency (CIA) estimated the population of The Gambia in 2011 to be approximately 1,797,860, which placed it at number 149 in population among the 196 nations of the world. In 2011 approximately 3.1% of the population was over 65 years of age, with another 40% under 15 years of age. The median age in The Gambia was 19.4 years. There were 1.03 males for every female in the country. The population's annual rate of change was 2.396%. The projected population for the year 2025 was 2,500,000. Population density in The Gambia was calculated at 175 people per sq km (453 people per sq mi).

The UN estimated that 58% of the population lived in urban areas and that urban populations had an annual rate of change of 3.7%. The largest urban area was Banjul, with a population of 436,000.

7 MIGRATION

Estimates of The Gambia's net migration rate, carried out by the CIA in 2011, amounted to -2.58 migrants per 1,000 citizens. The Gambia served as a staging point for Gambians and other West Africans to travel by boat to Morocco and Europe to seek economic opportunity as illegal immigrants. The total number of emigrants living abroad was 64,900, and the total number of im-

migrants living in The Gambia was 290,100. The Gambia also accepted 5,955 refugees. Each year, some 20,000–30,000 migrants from Senegal, Mali, and Guinea come to The Gambia to help harvest the groundnut crop. Gambians, in turn, move freely over national borders, which are poorly marked and difficult to police in West Africa. The Gambia also has an open-door policy for professionals, so it is used as a gateway to Europe and the Unites States.

8 ETHNIC GROUPS

Africans comprise 99% of the population in The Gambia. The Mandinka (Malinké), who make up an estimated 42% of the African population, came to The Gambia by the 13th century. The Fula account for about 18% of the population and live predominately in the eastern part of the country. Other major African groups include the Wolof (16%), Jola (10%), Serahule (9%), and others (4%). Wolofs live primarily in the northwest part of the country and urban areas, while Jolas reside in the southwest of the country and urban areas. The current president is of the Jola ethnic group. Only 1% of the population is non-African, including Syrians, Lebanese, and British. Non-Africans play a significant role in the economy.

9 LANGUAGES

English is the official language, but there are 21 distinct languages spoken. The principal vernaculars are Wolof, Fula, and Mandinka. Jola and Serahule are the next most commonly spoken languages. Most Gambians speak at least one language, and individual small villages may have as many as five languages spoken. Wolof serves as the major language of commerce, largely due to the economic importance of nearby Senegal, where Wolof is the primary spoken language.

10 RELIGIONS

About 90 % of Gambians follow Islam, which was introduced in the 12th century. Most Muslims are Malikite Sufis, but other branches include Tijaniyah, Qadiriyah, Muridiyah, and Ahmadiyah. The Lebanese population in the Banjul area represented a small Shi'a minority. About 9% of the population are Christians, mostly Roman Catholics; they live primarily in the Banjul area. Other Christian denominations include Anglicans, Methodists, Baptists, Seventh-Day Adventists, and Jehovah's Witnesses, along with other small evangelical groups. The Manjago and Jola are the ethnic groups with the largest amount of Christians. About 1% of Gambians, usually from the Jola ethnic group, practice traditional indigenous religions. In some areas, practices of animism are blended with Christianity or Islam. There is a small group of Baha'is. Freedom of religion is guaranteed by the constitution and this right is generally respected in practice. Religious groups are not required to register with the government, unless they wish to obtain the same benefits as other nongovernmental organizations. Both Biblical and Koranic studies are offered in public and private schools; participation is voluntary. Milad un-Nabi (the Birth of the Prophet Muhammad), Good Friday, Easter Monday, Assumption Day, Koriteh (Eid al-Fitr), Tobaski (Eid al-Adha), Yaomul

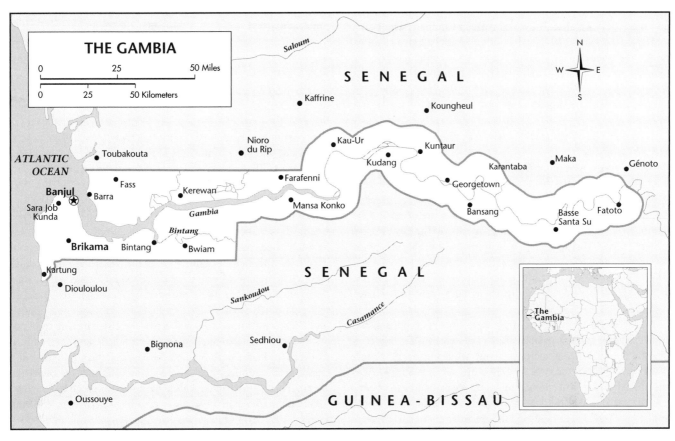

THE GAMBIA

SENEGAL

ATLANTIC OCEAN

Banjul

Brikama

SENEGAL

GUINEA-BISSAU

LOCATION: 13°10′ to 13°35′36″ N; 13°43′5″ to 16°49′31″ W. BOUNDARY LENGTHS: Senegal, 756 kilometers (470 miles); Atlantic coastline, 71 kilometers (44 miles). TERRITORIAL SEA LIMIT: 12 miles.

Ashura (the Islamic New Year), and Christmas are observed as national holidays.

11 TRANSPORTATION

The Gambia River not only provides important internal transport, but is also an international commercial link. Oceangoing vessels can travel 240 km (150 mi) upstream. Banjul, the principal port, receives about 300 ships annually. Ferries operate across the river and between Banjul and Barra. Other major ferry crossings exist near Farafeni, Janjanbureh, and Basse. The river and its tributaries provide 390 km (242 mi) of navigable waterways.

With the construction of major all-weather roads on both sides of The Gambia River, the waterway has become less significant for passenger traffic. In 2010 the main road on the south bank of the river was greatly deteriorated between the Kombo capital area and Janjanbureh. The CIA reported that The Gambia had a total of 3,742 km (2,325 mi) of roads, of which 723 km (449 mi) are paved.

In 2008 The Gambia's merchant marine totaled five vessels of 1,000 gross registered tons or more. There is an international airport (the country's only airport) at Yundum, 26 km (16 mi) from Banjul. The Gambia is one of only 25 nations in the world with only one airport. Air Gambia, 60% state owned, acts as an agent only. Foreign air carriers provide international service.

12 HISTORY

Archeological evidence in the form of stone axes and broken pottery, points to the existence of early habitation in The Gambia Riv-

er region around 2000 BC. In 470 BC Carthaginian sailors visited the river. Hannon the Carthaginian referred to The Gambia in his writings, making The Gambia known to the outside world. In AD 300 West African trading networks expanded as early empires established trading networks for people living in The Gambia River area. Later kingdoms of the Foni, Kombo, Sine-Salom, and Fulladou in The Gambia became trading partners of West Africa's great empires. Islam reached the Ghana Empire in the early 8th century, following the Arab conquest of North Africa.

Around AD 750, at Wassu, a large concentration of stone pillars was placed on the north bank of The Gambia River, the largest of which weighs about ten tons and stands about eight and a half feet above the ground. The stones likely mark the burial sites of kings and chiefs, similar to burial grounds of royalty in the Ghana Empire. In the 11th century Islamic leaders (Karamos) were buried like this, making some of the circles holy places.

Eastern Gambia was part of the great West African empires that flourished for a millennium, beginning with Ghana after AD 300. The relative political stability guaranteed by the empires permitted trade and movement of people throughout the region. Powerful kingdoms organized as families and clans of Wolof, Mandingo, and Fulbe (Fulani) formed larger social and political units. Small groups of Mandingos had settled in The Gambia by the 12th or 13th century, and a Mali-based Mandingo empire was dominant in the 13th and 14th centuries.

Portuguese sailors discovered The Gambia River in 1455; its navigability made it uniquely important for European traders seeking to penetrate the interior. In 1587 English merchants began to trade in the area. The Royal African Company acquired a charter in 1678 and established a fort on James Island, a small island in the river estuary. In 1765 the forts and settlements in The Gambia were placed under the control of the crown, and for the next 18 years The Gambia formed part of the British colony of Senegambia, with headquarters at Saint-Louis. In 1783 the greater part of Senegambia was handed back to France; The Gambia section ceased to be a British colony and was returned to the Royal African Company.

In 1816 Capt. Alexander Grant entered into a treaty with the chief of Kombo for the cession of Banjul Island. He renamed it St. Mary's Island and established a settlement on it that he called Bathurst (now Banjul). In 1821 the British settlements in The Gambia were placed under the administration of the government of Sierra Leone. This arrangement continued until 1888, except for the period 1843–66, when The Gambia had its own colonial administration. In 1888 The Gambia again became a separate colony. Its boundaries were defined following an agreement with France in 1889.

After 1888 The Gambia was administered by a governor assisted by an executive council and a legislative council. In 1902 St. Mary's Island was established as a crown colony, while the rest of the territory became a protectorate. In 1960 universal adult suffrage was introduced in the protectorate, and a 34-member house of representatives replaced the legislative council. The office of prime minister was created in 1962, and the executive council was reconstituted to include the governor as chairman, the prime minister, and eight other ministers. Dr. (later Sir) Dawda Kairaba Jawara, the leader of the Progressive People's Party (PPP), became the first prime minister. The Gambia attained full internal self-government on 4 October 1963, with Jawara as prime minister. An independence constitution, which was enforced starting in February 1965, established The Gambia as a constitutional monarchy within the Commonwealth.

On 23 April 1970, after a referendum, The Gambia became a republic with Jawara as the first president. He and the ruling PPP remained in power into the 1980s, weathering an attempted left-wing coup as well as a paramilitary rebellion in July 1981, which was quashed by Senegalese troops under a mutual defense pact signed in 1965. An estimated 500–800 people died in the uprising, and there was a large amount of property damage. In February 1982 the Confederation of Senegambia was formally constituted. Jawara was reelected to a new term as president that May, receiving 72.4% of the vote. He was reelected in March 1987, defeating two opponents with 59.2% of the vote and reelected again in April 1992. In that election, he received 59% of the vote to 22% for Sheriff Mustapha Dibba, who pulled in the most votes of his four rivals. Jawara's PPP was also returned to legislative power but with a reduced majority. The PPP fell from 31 to 25 of the elected seats in the 36-seat house of representatives.

In March 1992 Jawara accused Libya of arming a force led by Samba Samyang, the leader of the 1981 coup attempt. Libya denied involvement. He also made similar accusations against Libya and Burkina Faso in 1988. In May 1992 Jawara announced an amnesty for most members of the Movement for Justice in Africa (MOJA) which had been linked to the failed 1981 coup. In April

1993 two of MOJA's leaders returned from exile to organize as a political party.

Jawara was expected to retire midterm, but on 22 July 1994 he was overthrown in a bloodless military coup led by Lt. Yahya Jammeh, who had studied in the United States and held an honorary post in the Alabama National Guard. President Jawara took shelter on an American warship which, at the time, had been on a courtesy call. The junta of junior officers and a few civilians suspended the constitution, banned all political activity, detained its superior officers, and placed ministers of the former government under house arrest. The European Union (EU) and the United States suspended aid and pressed for a quick return to civilian rule. In 1995 Vice President Sana Sebally attempted another coup, ostensibly to return civilian rule, but it failed. Isolated from the west, Jammeh sought diplomatic ties with other marginalized nations. In 1994 he established relations with Libya. The next year, 1995, he established ties with Taiwan (incurring China's wrath and a break in relations). Economic accords were signed with Cuba as well as Iran.

On 26 September 1996 presidential elections were held in which Jammeh received 55.76% of the vote. Ousainou Darboe took 35.8% and Amath Bah earned 5.8%. Three former contenders, the PPP, The Gambia People's Party (GPP), and the National Convention Party, were blamed for The Gambia's problems and barred from competing. Two days later, Jammeh dissolved the Armed Forces Provisional Ruling Council, which he had formed upon taking power in 1994, and called for legislative elections in January 1997. The Alliance for Patriotic Reorientation and Construction won 32 of 45 contested seats (4 of the body's 49 are appointive). The elections were considered to have been relatively fair, although opposition candidates were harassed and there was almost no media exposure for any but the ruling party.

In 1998 tourism, the most important source of foreign currency, had risen to near pre-coup levels as Jammeh suppressed grumbling in the army, reestablished stability, and allowed some democratic reforms to move ahead. In February 1998 Jammeh made his first official visit to France. He signed a technical, cultural, and scientific accord in Paris designed to reinforce Franco-Gambian cooperation. In 1999 Jammeh raised The Gambia's international profile by mediating a dispute between Casamance rebels and the Senegalese government. The Asian Development Bank (ADB), the Organization of Petroleum Exporting Countries (OPEC), and the Islamic Bank approved a round of loans and credits for building and equipping schools and hospitals, and the International Monetary Fund (IMF) agreed to a second annual loan worth $11.8 million under the Enhanced Structural Adjustment Facility (ESAF).

However, in March 2000 the government was reeling from accusations of embezzlement of some $2-$3 million of Nigerian oil aid, the siphoning off of millions of dollars of a Taiwanese loan, and money laundering in connection with the privately held peanut processing and marketing company Gambian Groundnut Corporation (GGC). The government stepped up security measures and controls over the media, which it justified on the grounds of an alleged coup attempt on 15 January 2000. The coup may have been stage-managed as a pretext for increased security measures. In mid-April student protests ended with the deaths of 14 people. Local elections, scheduled for November 2000 were repeatedly postponed.

The 18 October 2001 presidential elections were conducted amidst charges of fraud, as thousands of Jola-members of Jammeh's ethnic group living across the border in Senegal reportedly helped reelect Jammeh who took 52.96% of the vote. Darboe of the United Democratic Party (UDP), who had formed a coalition with the PPP and the GPP of Hassan Musa Camara, came in second. Despite his allegations of voting and identity card fraud, Darboe conceded defeat. The EU, the Commonwealth, the United Kingdom, the UN, and Transparency International observers said they were relatively satisfied with the conduct of the election.

In 1999 the HIV/AIDS adult prevalence rate was estimated to be below 2%, one of the lowest rates in sub-Saharan Africa. The 2002 UN Human Development Report ranked The Gambia 160th out of 173 countries on the basis of real gross domestic product (GDP) per capita, adult literacy, and life expectancy. In February 2004 the government announced the discovery of large oil deposits, raising expectations of better economic times in The Gambia.

In December 2004 freedom of expression was severely strained when a new press law imposed jail terms for sedition and libel. A few days later, newspaper editor and outspoken critic of the law Deyda Hydara was shot and killed.

In August 2006 thousands of people fled into Gambia from Senegal's southern Casamance region; they were fleeing fighting between Senegalese troops and Casamance separatists.

Jammeh won a third term as president in elections held on 22 September 2006. He took 67.3% of the vote. Darboe won 26.6% and Halifa Sallah won 6% of the vote. On 25 January 2007 the ruling Alliance for Patriotic Reorientation and Construction (APRC) came in first in parliamentary elections (with 47 seats), retaining a tight hold on power in parliament.

In 2007 and 2008 President Jammeh received international attention for his claims that he could cure HIV/AIDS, asthma, and other illnesses using traditional medicine. The country's representative in the UN Development Programme was asked to leave The Gambia after publicly doubting Jammeh's claims, which included that patients who underwent his treatment could no longer infect others with HIV. Not long afterward, President Jammeh declared that homosexuals living in the country would be decapitated.

In April 2007 ten ex-army officers were sentenced to prison for planning a government takeover. A few years later in 2010, eight members of the military were sentenced to death after being accused of plotting a government coup and convicted of treason.

Other developments included the country's increasing importance as a conduit for drugs from Latin America to enter Europe. In May 2010 over two tons of cocaine, worth more than $1 billion, were seized in a single bust in The Gambia.

On November 24 2011 President Jammeh was reelected with 71.5% of the vote. The runner up candidate from the UDP received 17.4%, while the United Front candidate received 11.1%. A Commonwealth Observer Group presented a mixed review of the electoral process. The peacefulness of the election was lauded but observers noted that open military support for the president and the short campaign time did not allow for an even playing field. According to Freedom House, in the lead up to the 2011 elections President Jammeh threatened to stop government services to voters who did not support him.

13 GOVERNMENT

Under the republican constitution of 24 April 1970, as amended, the president, popularly elected for a five-year term was the head of state. Presidential powers included designating a vice president, who exercised the functions of a prime minister, and appointing cabinet members. The House of Representatives had 36 members elected by universal adult suffrage (at age 18), five chiefs elected by the Chiefs in Assembly, and eight appointed nonvoting members; the attorney general was also a member ex officio.

The military junta suspended the constitution on 22 July 1994, but following presidential elections two years later, a unicameral National Assembly was instituted, consisting of 49 members, 4 of whom were appointed by the president with the remainder standing for election. As of 2011 the assembly consisted of 53 members, 48 of which were popularly elected, and 5 of which were appointed by the president. They serve a five-year term.

14 POLITICAL PARTIES

The first Gambian political party, the Democratic Party, was formed in 1951 by Rev. John C. Faye. The Muslim Congress Party (CP) and the United Party (UP), led by Pierre S. N'Jie, were formed in 1952. The PPP, under the leadership of Sir Dawda Kairaba Jawara, was formed in 1958 and has governed the country since independence. The CP and the PPP merged in 1968. Two other parties were formed to compete in the 1977 elections, the National Liberation Party and the National Convention Party (NCP). In the elections of May 1982 the PPP won 27 seats (the same as in 1977), the NCP 3, and independents 5; in March 1987 the PPP won 31 seats and the NCP 5; and in April 1992 the PPP won 25 seats and the NCP 6. Other parties include or have included the GPP, the People's Democratic Organization for Independence and Socialism (PDOIS), The Gambian People's Democratic Party (PDP), and the MOJA.

After the 1994 coup, political parties were barred. The ban was lifted in August 1996, but three pre-coup parties, the PPP, The GPP, and the NCP remained proscribed. An independent electoral commission lifted the ban on these parties in August 2001. Elections for the House of Assembly were held on 2 January 1997 with members installed on 16 January 1997. Jammeh's APRC took 33 of 45 contested seats, the UDP took 7 seats, the National Reconciliation Party 2 seats, the PDOIS 1 seat, and independents 2 seats.

Members of opposition parties were harassed during Jammeh's annual tour in 1999 when he lashed out at them as a "gang of alcoholics." His own party weathered rough seas in early 2000 as its secretary-general, Phodey Makalo, disappeared with most of its funds. The July 22 Movement, which served Jammeh as a militia and political vehicle to launch his campaign, was reintegrated into the APRC.

Parliamentary elections were held on 17 January 2002 giving the APRC 45 of 53 seats. The PDOIS took three seats. Citing elections bias on the part of the Independent Electoral Commission (IEC), the main challenger to the APRC, the UDP boycotted the elections. APRC candidates ran unopposed in 33 of 48 constituencies. Former Head of State Jawara returned from exile in September 2002 upon condition that he resign from his party.

Prior to the presidential elections held in September 2006, new political alliances were in formation. In early 2006 Nigeria's President Olusegun Obasanjo, acting in his capacity as Chairman of the Commonwealth, visited Banjul in an effort to reconcile the government and opposition politicians. The result was a Memorandum of Understanding in which the ruling APRC and NADD, or National Alliance for Democracy and Development, pledged to forget the past and to work to create a level playing field for the 2006–07 elections. However, the APRC wound up dominating the elections. The presidential election was held on 22 September 2006. Jammeh was reelected president with 67.3% of the vote. He was challenged by Darboe (who won 26.6% of the vote) and Sallah (6.0%). Parliamentary elections were held on 25 January 2007. The APRC won 47 seats, retaining its hold on government. The UDP, led by Darboe, took 4 seats and the NADD, led by Sallah, won one seat. One seat was held by an independent candidate.

In the November 2011 elections the APRC, led by Jammeh, won reelection. Darboe, of the UDP came in second place, with Hamat Bah of the United Front coming in third place. Darboe rejected the results of the election and claimed the military vehicles on the streets represented intimidation to voters.

The next legislative elections were scheduled for 2012, and the next presidential elections for 2016.

¹⁵LOCAL GOVERNMENT

There are five administrative regions, each with a council, the majority of whose members are elected. The regions—Central River, Lower River, North Bank, Upper River, and Western—are subdivided into 35 districts administered by chiefs, called seyfos, with the help of village mayors and councilors. Banjul has a city council.

The power in village governments is vested in an alkalo, usually a member of the original family that founded the village, although they are occasionally elected.

¹⁶JUDICIAL SYSTEM

The judicial system is based on a composite of English common law, Koranic law, and customary law. It accepts compulsory International Court of Justice (ICJ) jurisdiction with reservations and includes subsidiary legislative instruments enacted locally. The constitution provides for an independent judiciary, and although the courts are not totally free from influence of the executive branch, they have demonstrated their independence on occasion.

The Supreme Court, presided over by a chief justice, has both civil and criminal jurisdiction. Formerly, appeals from any decision of the Supreme Court went before the court of appeals, whose judgments could be taken to the UK Privy Council. The January 1997 constitution provided for a reconfiguration of the courts with the Supreme Court replacing the Privy Council.

Muslim courts apply Shari'ah law in certain cases involving Muslim citizens, and in traditional matters chiefs rule on customary law and local affairs. District tribunals serve as appeals courts in cases of tribal law and custom. Cases of first instance in criminal and civil matters are handled by administrative officers who function as magistrates in courts located in each of the five administrative regions and Banjul.

¹⁷ARMED FORCES

The International Institute for Strategic Studies (IISS) reports that armed forces in The Gambia totaled 800 members in 2011, all of which are members of the army. Armed forces represent 1% of the labor force in The Gambia. Defense spending totaled $31.8 million and accounted for 0.9% of GDP. The branches of the military in 2011 included The Gambian National Army (GNA), Gambian Navy (GN), and the Republican National Guard (RNG).

The Gambia has provided observers to conflicts in other African nations, including Sudan from 2004 to 2011.

¹⁸INTERNATIONAL COOPERATION

The Gambia was admitted to the UN on 21 September 1965 and is a member of ECA and all the non-regional specialized agencies except IAEA. It also belongs to the World Trade Organization (WTO), the African Development Bank, the ACP Group, the Commonwealth of Nations, the Organization of the Islamic Conference (OIC), ECOWAS, G-77, the Community of Sahel and Saharan States (CENSAD), the New Partnership for Africa's Development (NEPAD), and the African Union. The government is participating in efforts to establish a West African Monetary Zone (WAMZ) that would include The Gambia, Ghana, Guinea, Liberia, Nigeria, and Sierra Leone. The union was scheduled to come on-stream in January 2003. It was later rescheduled for December 2009 and rescheduled again for 2015, at which point the six nations would have a unified currency. As of February 2011 Businessweek reported that Sierra Leone was the only country of the six on target for meeting the fiscal requirements necessary to establish the currency in 2015.

An agreement of confederation with Senegal, signed on 17 December 1981 and effective 1 February 1982, called for integration of the security services and armed forces of the two countries under the name Senegambia. The presidents of Senegal and The Gambia became president and vice president of Senegambia, respectively. The confederation was dissolved in 1989. The Gambia played an active role in ECOWAS efforts to resolve the civil wars in Liberia and Sierra Leone. The country contributed troops to cease-fire monitoring groups in 1990 (ECOMOG) and in 2003 (ECOMIL). The Gambia has also supported UN operations and missions in Ethiopia and Eritrea (est. 2000), Burundi (2004), and Côte d'Ivoire (2004), and Sudan (2004–2011). The Gambia is a part of the Nonaligned Movement and participates in the Organization for the Prohibition of Chemical Weapons.

In environmental cooperation, The Gambia is part of the Basel Convention, the Convention on Biological Diversity, Ramsar, CITES, the Kyoto Protocol, the Montréal Protocol, MARPOL, the Nuclear Test Ban Treaty, and the UN Conventions on the Law of the Sea, Climate Change, and Desertification.

¹⁹ECONOMY

The GDP rate of change in The Gambia was 5.7% in 2010, down from 6.7% in 2009. Inflation stood at 5.5% in 2010. In 2010 the IMF reported that real GDP growth in the country remained strong despite the global recession and a fall in tourism and remittances. Inflation was also low. GDP growth in 2010 was 0.7% better than the 0.5% predicted by the IMF.

The Gambia's light sandy soil is well suited to the cultivation of groundnuts, which are the country's principal agricultural export. About 75% of the population is engaged in crop production and raising livestock. However, groundnut production has fallen in recent years due to soil depletion and, in 1990, tourism overtook groundnut exports as the nation's number one export earner.

Significant export revenues are earned from fishing and re-export trade. Manufacturing is limited to food processing and the production of consumer goods like soap, soft drinks, and clothing.

The military's takeover of the country in 1994 resulted in a loss of $50 million in aid from the West, equal to about 10% of national income. In addition, tourism declined dramatically and Senegal, which surrounds The Gambia on three sides, closed the borders because of smuggling. When France devalued the Communauté Financière Africaine franc in 1994, The Gambia's goods were no longer competitive in the re-export trade. In 1998 the government appropriated a private peanut firm, thereby eliminating the largest purchaser of Gambian groundnuts.

Recent events indicate that The Gambian economy may be playing a large role in the smuggling of Latin American drugs to Europe.

20 INCOME

The CIA estimated that in 2010 the GDP of The Gambia was $3.494 billion. The CIA defines GDP as the value of all final goods and services produced within a nation in a given year and computed on the basis of purchasing power parity rather than value as measured on the basis of the rate of the exchange based on current dollars. The GDP based on actual exchange rate was $1.067 billion. The per capita GDP was estimated at $1,900 (purchasing power parity). The World Bank reported in 2003 that 58% of the population lived in poverty. The annual growth rate of GDP was 5.7%. The average inflation rate was 5.5%. It was estimated that agriculture accounted for 30.1% of GDP, industry 16.3%, and services 53.6%.

According to the World Bank, remittances from citizens living abroad totaled $79.8 million or about $44 per capita and accounted for approximately 2.3% of GDP. The World Bank reports that in 2009 household consumption in The Gambia totaled $589 million or about $328 per capita, measured in current US dollars rather than purchasing power parity.

In 2007 the World Bank estimated that The Gambia, with 0.02% of the world's population, accounted for less than 0.01% of the world's GDP. By comparison, the United States, with 4.85% of the world's population, accounted for 22.51% of world GDP. In terms of consumption The Gambia plays a similarly small role. As of 2011 the most recent study by the World Bank reported that actual individual consumption in The Gambia was 96.3% of GDP and accounted for less than 0.01% of world consumption. By comparison, the United States accounted for 25.44% of world individual consumption. The World Bank also estimated that 36.3% of The Gambia's GDP was spent on food and beverages, 7.6% on housing and household furnishings, 8.2% on clothes, 7.4% on health, 2.4% on transportation, 1.8% on communications, 5.8% on recreation, 0.4% on restaurants and hotels, and 3.9% on miscellaneous goods and services and purchases from abroad.

21 LABOR

As of 2007 The Gambia had a total labor force of 777,100 people. Within that labor force, CIA estimates in 1996 noted that 75% were employed in agriculture, 19% in industry, and 6% in the service sector.

The Labor Act of 1990 allows all workers (except civil servants, police, and military personnel) to form associations and trade unions. Approximately 10% of the workforce is unionized, which is about 30,000 workers. Strikes are permitted with 14 days' notice (21 days for essential services) to the commissioner of labor. Collective bargaining occurs even though unions are small and fragmented. Minimum wage and hours of employment are set by six joint industrial councils (commerce, artisans, transport, the port industry, agriculture, and fisheries), but only 20% of the labor force is covered by minimum wage legislation. The minimum wage was $.67 per day in 2011, although the US Department of State estimates most workers are paid above the minimum wage. Most Gambians pool their resources within extended families in order to meet their basic needs. Rural agricultural families typically receive a large share of their cash income from relatives in urban areas or abroad. The statutory working age is 18, but because of limited opportunities for secondary schooling, most children begin working at age 14.

22 AGRICULTURE

The country's major crops include rice, millet, sorghum, peanuts, corn, sesame, cassava (tapioca), and palm kernels. Cereal production in 2009 amounted to 310,964 tons, fruit production 8,939 tons, and vegetable production 9,331 tons.

The soil is mostly poor and sandy, except in the riverine swamps. High population density has reduced agricultural productivity as fields that were traditionally left to fallow for several years are now farmed almost every year. On upland soil the main food crops, besides groundnuts, are millet, sorghum, manioc, corn, and beans. Most landholdings range between five and nine hectares (12 and 22 acres). In 2008 the World Bank estimated only 4% of agricultural land to be irrigated, so irregular and inadequate rainfall has adversely affected crop production since the 1990's.

The principal cash crop is groundnuts, grown on some 111,000 hectares (275,000 acres). Mangos, bananas, oranges, papayas, and limes are grown mainly in the Western region where rainfall is highest. Oil palms provide oil for local consumption and kernels for export.

Much of the rice produced in The Gambia is farmed in tidal swamps along The Gambia River. If climate change reduces rainfall in the region as some models predict, the intrusion of saltwater further up the river could significantly reduce rice production.

23 ANIMAL HUSBANDRY

The UN Food and Agriculture Organization (FAO) reported that The Gambia dedicated 260,000 hectares (642,474 acres) to permanent pasture or meadow in 2009. During that year, the country tended 750,000 chickens, 432,000 head of cattle, and 27,000 pigs. The production from these animals amounted to 4,085 tons of beef and veal, 836 tons of pork, 7,439 tons of poultry, 3,203 tons of eggs, and 40,642 tons of milk. The Gambia also produced 483 tons of cattle hide. In 2005 the livestock population also included 270,000 goats and 148,000 sheep.

Animal husbandry practices change throughout the year. During the rainy season, livestock are constantly tended to protect agricultural crops. During the November–May dry season, livestock often roam freely. The Fula ethnic group is more commonly associated with animal husbandry and other ethnic groups often pay Fulas in cash or crops to husband their animals.

24 FISHING

In 2008 the annual capture totaled 42,645 tons according to the FAO. Fish is the most important source of animal protein for the majority of the population.

Bonga shad accounted for about 60% of the 2003 catch. Exports of fish products amounted to $1.1 million in 2002. A 1982 agreement with Senegal allows nationals of each country to operate fishing companies in the other's waters.

25 FORESTRY

Approximately 48% of The Gambia is covered by forest, although most of it is highly degraded. For instance, the FAO estimates closed canopy forest cover in 1946 at 60.1%. By 1999 this had decreased to only 0.7%. This is consistent with a broad trend of moist forest type environments being degraded, by fire and overharvesting, to more fire-prone savanna and woodland. The FAO estimated the 2009 roundwood production at 112,700 cu m (3.98 million cu ft). The value of all forest products, including roundwood, totaled $5.13 million.

Portions of The Gambia are covered by mangrove forest, open woodland, or savanna with woodland or bush. Wood resources are used for fuel (84%), poles, and rural housing construction. Roundwood removals were estimated at 750,000 cu m (26 million cu ft) in 2004.

26 MINING

The mineral industry was a minor component of The Gambia's economy. Clays for bricks, laterite, silica sand, cockleshell, and sand and gravel were exploited for domestic construction needs. Production of silica sand was estimated at 1,000,000 metric tons in 2009, down slightly from 1,065,000 metric tons in 2008. The Gambia has significant glass and quartz sand deposits, and resources of ilmenite, rutile, tin, and zircon. The government has encouraged exploration for gold. Large deposits of ilmenite were discovered along the coast in 1953 and were exploited by UK interests from 1956 to 1959. A new mineral and mining act was being developed.

27 ENERGY AND POWER

In February 2004 the government announced the discovery of large oil deposits. As of 2011 this has yet to be verified or developed. The country must import all of the fossil fuels it consumes. In 2002 consumption and imports of refined petroleum products each came to 1,980 barrels per day. There were no known imports or consumption of natural gas products or coal. All electric power is produced at thermal stations. In 2008 the World Bank reported that The Gambia produced 220 million kWh of electricity and consumed 165.4 million kWh, or 92 kWh per capita.

28 INDUSTRY

There is little industry in The Gambia. Industries include groundnut processing, fish processing, the processing of hides, building and repair of river craft, village handicrafts, and clothing manufacture. There are candle factories, oil mills, a soft drink factory, a distillery, a shoe factory, and a soap and detergent plant. Although the government provides incentives for industrial development, progress on that front has been slow. The Gambia produces industrial minerals for local consumption. Privatization has been slow,

Principal Trading Partners – The Gambia (2010)				
(In millions of US dollars)				
Country	Total	Exports	Imports	Balance
World	315.0	15.0	300.0	-285.0
China	218.5	12.8	205.7	-192.9
Brazil	89.5	0.3	89.2	-88.9
Senegal	74.1	0.2	73.9	-73.6
India	54.4	12.6	41.8	-29.1
Côte d'Ivoire	49.6	0.1	49.5	-49.4
Netherlands	40.1	1.4	38.7	-37.3
United States	36.1	3.7	32.3	-28.6
United Kingdom	31.5	5.4	26.1	-20.7
Indonesia	24.4	1.0	23.5	-22.5
Turkey	22.8	0.0	22.8	-22.8

(…) data not available or not significant.

(n.s.) not specified.

SOURCE: *2011 Direction of Trade Statistics Yearbook,* New York: United Nations, 2011.

except in the tourism and banking sectors. The largest industrial complex in the country, The Gambia Groundnut Company, formerly owned by the Alimenta group based in Switzerland, was taken over by the government in 1999. This led to a protracted legal battle and out-of-court settlement, after which the parties agreed to a compensation plan. The government subsequently reprivatized the company.

29 SCIENCE AND TECHNOLOGY

The World Bank reported in 2009 that there were no patent applications in science and technology in the country. The United Kingdom's Medical Research Council operates a field station (of its Dunn Nutrition Unit Laboratory in Cambridge) at Keneba, West Kiang, and a research laboratory on tropical diseases at Fajara, near Banjul. Gambia College, founded in 1978, has schools of agriculture, nursing and midwifery, and public health. The Gambia Ornithological Society, founded in 1974, is devoted to bird watching.

30 DOMESTIC TRADE

The marketing of the groundnut crop for export is handled by The Gambia Produce Marketing Board. About 75% of the population is employed in subsistence farming. Manufacturing is primarily based on agriculture and serves a domestic market. Cooperative banking and marketing unions finance the activities of a network of cooperatives in the groundnut-growing areas. Re-exportation of goods through the port of Banjul is a major contributing factor to the economy. Normal business hours are from 8 a.m. to 4 p.m. Monday–Thursday, and from 8 a.m. to 12:30 p.m. on Friday. Banking hours are from 8 a.m. to 1 p.m. Monday–Thursday, and from 8 a.m. to 11 a.m. on Friday. Shopping takes place between the hours of 9:30 a.m. and 12 p.m. and 2:30 to 6 p.m. Monday–Friday, and from 9 a.m. to noon on Saturday.

31 FOREIGN TRADE

The Gambia imported $306 million worth of goods and services in 2008, while exporting $107 million worth of goods and services. Major import partners in 2009 were China, 22.1%; Senegal,

Balance of Payments – The Gambia (2010)

(In millions of US dollars)

Current Account		**17.2**
Balance on goods		-68.9
Imports	-236.3	
Exports	167.4	
Balance on services		16.7
Balance on income		-8.1
Current transfers		77.5
Capital Account		...
Financial Account		**-15.7**
Direct investment abroad		...
Direct investment in The Gambia		37.4
Portfolio investment assets		...
Portfolio investment liabilities		...
Financial derivatives		...
Other investment assets		20.3
Other investment liabilities		-73.4
Net Errors and Omissions		**-94.7**
Reserves and Related Items		**93.3**

(…) data not available or not significant.

SOURCE: *Balance of Payment Statistics Yearbook 2011*, Washington, DC: International Monetary Fund, 2011.

9.3%; Brazil, 8.4%; Cote d'Ivoire, 4.7%; Netherlands, 4.6%; India, 4.5%; and the United States, 4.4%. Its major export partners were India, 47.5%; France, 12.6%; China, 10.9%; and UK, 7.4%.

Peanut products are by far The Gambia's leading export. However, peanut exports were depressed in the early 1980s, first by drought and then by low world prices. Other exports include fish, cotton lint, and palm kernels. The leading imports are food, manufactured goods, raw materials, fuel, machinery, and transport equipment.

Raw cashew nuts were an increasingly important export item in 2011. In 2010 The Gambian newspaper, *The Daily Observer*, reported a 300% increase in production from 2005–2010. The Cashew Alliance of The Gambia reported exports of 65,000 tons in 2011.

In 2004 The Gambia's primary export partners were India, 23.7%; the United Kingdom, 15.2%; France, 14.2%; Germany, 9.6%; Italy, 8.3%; Thailand, 5.9%; and Malaysia, 4.1%. The primary import partners in 2004 were China, 23.7%; Senegal, 11.6%; Brazil, 5.9%; the United Kingdom, 5.5%; the Netherlands, 4.5%; and the United States, 4.4%.

32 BALANCE OF PAYMENTS

In 2010 The Gambia had a foreign trade deficit of $64 million, amounting to 22.3% of GDP. In 2005 the value of The Gambia's exports was estimated at $140.3 million, and imports were valued at $197 million. The current account balance was estimated at -$20.54 million. In 2005 The Gambia had $81.55 million in reserves of foreign exchange and gold. The external debt burden was estimated at $628.8 million in 2003.

33 BANKING AND SECURITIES

The Central Bank of Gambia (CBG), the bank of issue, was established in 1971. The central bank discount rate in 2009 was 9% according to the CIA. The largest commercial bank is Stan-dard Chartered Bank Gambia, which is incorporated locally, with branches in Banjul, Bakau, Serrekunda, and Basse. The government no longer has an equity interest in the bank, in which the parent company holds 75% and Gambian shareholders 25%. The Gambia Commercial and Development Bank (GCDB) was wholly owned by the government but now has been sold to private interests, and the other commercial bank, the International Bank for Commerce and Industry (BICI), was, as of 1997, also privately owned.

The IMF reports that in 2001, currency and demand deposits—an aggregate commonly known as M1—were equal to $72.5 million. In that same year, M2—an aggregate equal to M1 plus savings deposits, small time deposits, and money market mutual funds—was $151.9 million.

34 INSURANCE

As of November 2011 the Central Bank of The Gambia listed 11 insurance companies operating in the country. The 1997 constitution granted regulation power over insurance companies to the CBG.

35 PUBLIC FINANCE

In 2010 the budget of The Gambia included $183.9 million in public revenue and $202.5 million in public expenditures. The budget deficit amounted to 2% of GDP. Public debt was 32.5% of GDP, with $525.7 million of the debt held by foreign entities.

The fiscal year extends from 1 July to 30 June. In the 1980s expansionary fiscal policies exacerbated a weakening economy; by 1985 the budget deficit reached 30% of GDP. An economic recovery program was initiated to reduce public expenditures, diversify the agricultural sector, and privatize the parastatal sector. This step preceded the 1988 agreement with the IMF for a SAP which helped the economy grow at an annual rate of 4% between 1990 and 1993.

36 TAXATION

As of 2010 the CIA estimated taxes and other government revenues represent 17.1% of GDP. Direct taxes provide only a small proportion of revenues, the greater proportion being derived from customs and excise duties and from foreign loans and grants-in-aid. Individuals are taxed on the basis of a graduated scale; companies are taxed at a flat rate on undistributed profits. The government revised the income tax system in March 1988 and enacted new sales taxes in April 1988 to broaden the tax base, improve tax collection, and rationalize the tax system.

37 CUSTOMS AND DUTIES

Customs duties are assessed by CIF (cost, insurance, and freight) value, as is the 10% national sales tax, from which some imports are exempt. Some commodities may be subject to excise taxes.

38 FOREIGN INVESTMENT

Foreign direct investment (FDI) in The Gambia was a net inflow of $39.4 million according to World Bank figures published in 2009. FDI represented 5.38% of GDP.

Joint ventures have been encouraged in The Gambia, but with the stipulation that a portion of the profits must be reinvested.

Under an ordinance passed in 1964, developing industries are exempt from profits tax for five years.

In 2002 the government embarked on a new effort to attract foreign investment, called the Gateway Project, financed by a World Bank loan. The Gambia Investment Promotion and Free Zone Agency (GIPZA) was established, with the first free zone planned for Banjui Airport. Gambia's foreign investment regime is open door and nondiscriminatory, with foreign companies treated the same as local companies. Incentives for setting up locations in the free zones include exemptions from taxes and customs duties, a ten-year tax holiday, and a reduced 10% corporate income tax rate for investments in the tourist sector. The government's priorities for foreign investment are agriculture, fisheries, tourism, light manufacture and assembly, energy, mineral exploration and exploitation, and telecommunications.

39 ECONOMIC DEVELOPMENT

Development goals have been focused on transportation and communications improvements, increases in rice and groundnut yields, and production diversity.

The historical importance of Great Britain to The Gambia has declined, as Gambia has turned increasingly to the International Development Association (IDA) and the European Development Fund, France, Germany, Switzerland, Japan, and Arab donors for aid. When Western aid ceased after the 1994 military takeover, The Gambia turned to Taiwan, Libya, Cuba, Nigeria, and Iran for economic support. Taiwan provided significant financial support for the paving of the North Bank road between Barra and Farafenni, completed in 2007.

In 2009 the World Bank reported that net official development aid accounted for 18.5% of Gross National Income (GNI). In 2010, in response to human rights abuses, the US Congress cancelled a disbursement of aid money aimed at combating drug smuggling in The Gambia and supporting military training. In 2000 The Gambia received $91 million in debt relief under the IMF/World Bank Heavily Indebted Poor Countries (HIPC) initiative, intended to reduce poverty and stimulate economic growth. The IMF began a three-year $27 million Poverty Reduction and Growth Facility (PRGF) Arrangement with The Gambia in 2002. As of January 2005 the World Bank had approved a total of 31 IDA credits for The Gambia for a total of approximately $272.7 million. The government has directed spending to social sectors in recent years, including agriculture, education, and health. A girls' scholarship program began in 2001 and was met with great success enrolling girls from poor households in school.

40 SOCIAL DEVELOPMENT

A national pension and disability system covers employed people in quasi-government institutions and in participating private companies. The retirement age is 55, with early retirement at 45. Worker's compensation laws have been in effect since 1940. Benefits include medical, surgical, hospital and nursing care, and medication. A special scheme exists for civil servants and the military. Agricultural workers and subsistence farmers are excluded from coverage.

As of 2011 the vice president was a female. Still, women play a small role in the political life of the country. In 2010 women held 7.6% of seats in parliament. Arranged marriages are common, and polygamy is practiced. Women face some discrimination in education and employment, although recent statistics indicate improvement. In 2010 girls and boys had equal enrollment numbers in primary and secondary education.

Inheritance rights, moreover, favor men. The painful and often life-threatening practice of female genital mutilation continues to be widespread and is opposed by organized women's rights groups. Domestic violence is widespread, and considered a family issue. Education for children is compulsory, in theory, but this provision is not enforced in practice. Child labor and trafficking children persists.

Human rights are improving but there are still significant problems in many areas. There were reports of arbitrary arrest, detention, and torture. The court system remains inefficient and corrupt. According to citizen reports, from January–March 2009, the president authorized an official witch hunt. Paramilitary troops and witch doctors were sent to several villages where residents were forcibly rounded up and transported to a secret location. According to victim reports, they were then forced to drink and bathe in a foul-smelling liquid that caused hallucinations, vomiting, stomach pains, and erratic behavior. Some deaths were also reported. According to reports from Amnesty International, up to 1,000 people were detained under accusations of witchcraft. In some villages, local leaders were simply told to sacrifice a red goat and a rooster to protect against the curse of sorcery. The Gambian inspector general of police claimed that all these reports were false. Other government officials could not be reached for comments. Belief in witchcraft is somewhat common in West Africa and an accusation of sorcery or witchcraft carries a stigma that may ruin the reputation of an individual and even an entire family or village.

The freedom of press has been severely restricted by the government. In August 2009 six journalists were each sentenced to two-years in jail for sedition after publishing statements that criticized the president. The statements specifically questioned the president's involvement in the 2004 unsolved murder of the prominent journalist, Hydara.

41 HEALTH

According to the CIA, life expectancy in The Gambia was 56 years in 2011. The country spent 5.5% of its GDP on healthcare, amounting to $26 per person. There were zero physicians, six nurses and midwives, and 11 hospital beds per 10,000 inhabitants. Dentists and pharmacists were also scarce, numbering less than 1 per 200,000 people. The fertility rate was 5.0, while the infant mortality rate was 78 per 1,000 live births. In 2008 the maternal mortality rate, according to the World Bank, was 400 per 100,000 births. It was estimated that 96% of children were vaccinated against measles.

Major health threats include malaria, HIV/AIDS, tuberculosis, and malnutrition. The CIA calculated HIV/AIDS prevalence in The Gambia to be about 2% in 2009. The incidence of tuberculosis was 233 per 100,000 people in 2007. Nearly half of all children die by age five, primarily because of malaria and diarrheal diseases. The most recent immunization rates available for children under one year old were as follows: tuberculosis, 98%; diphtheria, pertussis, and tetanus, 90%; polio, 29%; and measles, 87%.

The Gambia has hospitals in Banjul (Royal Victoria) and Bansang and a health clinic in Kombo, St. Mary. The country provided 62% of its people with safe water and 37% with adequate sanitation. Health conditions are poor.

Female genital mutilation is performed on nearly every woman in The Gambia. The government published a policy opposing female genital mutilation, but there had been no specific laws prohibiting it.

42 HOUSING

A Housing Finance Fund provides low-cost housing and related assistance. As of 2000 80% of urban and 52% of rural dwellers had access to improved water sources. The government has been looking into the use of alternative building materials to cut housing expenses. In 2001 about 75% of building materials were imported.

43 EDUCATION

The Gambia spent about 3.9% of GDP on education in 2010. In 2008 the World Bank estimated that 69% of age-eligible children in The Gambia were enrolled in primary school. Secondary enrollment for age-eligible children stood at 42%. Tertiary enrollment was estimated at 5%. The World Bank estimated the literacy rate at 46% in 2009.

Primary school is free and theoretically compulsory and lasts for nine years. Secondary schooling covers six years in two stages of three years each. Although it is compulsory, in reality not all students attend school. Even though it is free, the cost for school uniforms can be prohibitively expensive for some families. In 2010 the World Bank estimated that 71% of students complete primary school. The academic year runs September–July. The student-to-teacher ratio for primary school was at about 36:1 in 2010. Private schools provide education as well with 39% of all secondary students were enrolled in private schools in 2005.

The University of The Gambia was established in 1999 with four faculties and Gambia College, which in turn had nine schools in 2011 (Agriculture and Environmental Science; Arts and Sciences; Business and Public Administration; Education; Engineering and Architecture; Law; Medicine and Allied Health Services; Information Studies and Communications and a School of Graduate Studies and Research). Many university age students attempt to study overseas, often at community colleges in the US.

44 LIBRARIES AND MUSEUMS

The Gambia National Library in Banjul contains 115,000 volumes; it serves as both a national archive and a public library. School libraries are organized through the National Library. Gambia College in Brikama has a library of 23,000 volumes. The Yundum College Library at Banjul has 4,000 volumes, and the library of The Gambia Technical Training Institute has 3,880. Gambia Library and Information Services Association was formed in 1987. The Gambia National Museum, founded in 1982, is also in Banjul and features primarily archaeological and historical exhibits. The African Heritage Centre in Bakau serves as an art museum and gallery for local artists. The exhibits change as items are sold and new ones are offered. Tanje Village Museum offers exhibits on natural history as well as glimpses of village culture.

45 MEDIA

In 2009 the CIA reported that there were 49,000 telephone landlines in The Gambia. In addition to landlines, mobile phone subscriptions averaged 84 per 100 people. There were three FM radio stations and two AM radio stations, including one government operated and four private stations. Internet users numbered 8 per 100 citizens. The country had 1,453 Internet hosts.

In 2007 the government operated the single television station. In some parts of the country foreign cable and satellite service were available.

Prominent newspapers in 2010, with circulation numbers listed parenthetically, included the *Daily Observer* (2,000) and the *Point* (4,000). Though nominally independent, there have been allegations that the *Daily Observer's* editorial content was swayed toward promotion of the APRC.

The old and new constitutions provide for free expression, but the government is said to prohibit all dissenting political publication and broadcasting.

46 ORGANIZATIONS

The Gambia Chamber of Commerce and Industry represents many of the principal Gambian, British, and French firms. A network of cooperative societies functions within the groundnut-growing region. The Association of Farmers, Educators and Traders represents about 70,000 individuals. There are some professional associations, such as The Gambia Nurses Association, The Gambia Medical and Dental Association, and The Gambia Teachers Union. The Gambia Women's Finance Association helps promote business ownership among women. Youth organizations include The Gambia Scout Association, Girl Guides, and branches of YMCA/YWCA. There are several sports organizations in the country, including active branches of the Special Olympics. There are national chapters of the Red Cross Society, Caritas, and Amnesty International.

47 TOURISM, TRAVEL, AND RECREATION

All visitors need a valid passport. Visas are required for all nationalities except British, Canadian, and some EU passport holders. Vaccinations against yellow fever are required if traveling from an infected area. Tourism significantly increased during the 1990s and 2000s; however, outside of Banjul, facilities are limited and very basic. Main attractions are the 19th-century architecture in Banjul, beautiful beaches, and the ecotourism along The Gambia River. Popular sports are football (soccer) and wrestling.

The *Tourism Factbook*, published by the UN World Tourism Organization, reported 142,000 incoming tourists to The Gambia in 2009, who spent a total of $64 million. Of those incoming tourists, there were 115,000 from Europe. There were 6,743 hotel beds available in The Gambia. The estimated daily cost to visit Banjul, the capital, was $200. The cost of visiting other cities averaged $67.

48 FAMOUS PERSONS

The first prime minister of the independent Gambia and the first president of the republic until 1994 was Alhaji Sir Dawda Kairaba

Jawara (b. 1924). Col. Yahya A. J .J. Jammeh (b. 1965) seized power from Jawara in a bloodless coup in 1994.

⁴⁹DEPENDENCIES

The Gambia has no territories or colonies.

⁵⁰BIBLIOGRAPHY

Ebron, Paulla A. *Performing Africa*. Princeton, NJ: Princeton University Press, 2002.

Gambia Investment and Business Guide: Strategic and Practical Information. Washington, DC: International Business Publications USA, 2012.

Hughes, Arnold and Harry A. Gailey. *Historical Dictionary of The Gambia*. 4th. ed. Metuchen, NJ: Scarecrow Press, 2008.

Saine, Abjoulaye. *Culture and Customs of Gambia*. Westport, CT: Greenwood Press, 2012.

Van Aarde, Rudi. *West African Coast*. New York: Marshall Cavendish Reference, 2011.

Zeilig, Leo, and David Seddon. *A Political and Economic Dictionary of Africa*. Philadelphia: Routledge/Taylor and Francis, 2005.

GHANA

Republic of Ghana

CAPITAL: Accra

FLAG: The national flag is a tricolor of red, yellow, and green horizontal stripes, with a five-pointed black star in the center of the yellow stripe.

ANTHEM: *Hail the Name of Ghana.*

MONETARY UNIT: The Ghana cedi (GHC) is a currency of 100 pesewas. The Ghana cedi replaced the former cedi in 2007. There are coins of 1, 5, 10, 20, and 50 pesewas and 1 cedis, and notes of 1, 2, 5, 10, 20, and 50 cedis. GHC1 = US$0.61 (or US$1 = GHC1.64) as of 2011.

WEIGHTS AND MEASURES: The metric system is the legal standard.

HOLIDAYS: New Year's Day, 1 January; Anniversary of the Inauguration of the Fourth Republic, 7 January; Independence Day, 6 March; Labor Day, 1 May; Republic Day, 1 July; Christmas, 25 December; Boxing Day, 26 December. Movable religious holidays include Good Friday and Easter Monday.

TIME: GMT.

¹LOCATION, SIZE, AND EXTENT

Situated on the southern coast of the West African bulge, Ghana has an area of 238,540 square kilometers (92,100 square miles), extending 458 km (284 mi) NNE–SSW and 297 km (184 mi) ESE–WNW. Bordered on the E by Togo, on the S by the Atlantic Ocean (Gulf of Guinea), on the W by Côte d'Ivoire, and on the NW and N by Burkina Faso, Ghana has a total boundary length of 2,633 km (1,635 mi), of which 539 km (334 mi) is coastline. Comparatively, the area occupied by Ghana is slightly smaller than the state of Oregon. Ghana's capital city, Accra, is located on the Gulf of Guinea coast.

²TOPOGRAPHY

The coastline consists mostly of a low sandy shore behind which stretches the coastal plain, except in the west, where the forest comes down to the sea. The forest belt, which extends northward from the western coast about 320 km (200 mi) and eastward for a maximum of about 270 km (170 mi), is broken up into heavily wooded hills and steep ridges. North of the forest is undulating savanna drained by the Black Volta and White Volta rivers, which join and flow south to the sea through a narrow gap in the hills. Ghana's highest point is Mount Afadjato at 880 m (2,887 ft) in a range of hills on the eastern border.

Apart from the Volta, only the Pra and the Ankobra rivers permanently pierce the sand dunes, most of the other rivers terminating in brackish lagoons. There are no natural harbors. Lake Volta, formed by the impoundment of the Volta behind Akosombo Dam, is the world's largest manmade lake (8,485 square kilometers/3,276 square miles).

³CLIMATE

The climate is tropical but relatively mild for the latitude. Climatic differences between various parts of the country are affected by the sun's journey north or south of the equator and the corresponding position of the intertropical convergence zone, the boundary between the moist southwesterly winds and the dry northeasterly winds. Except in the north, there are two rainy seasons, from April through June and from September to November. Squalls occur in the north during March and April, followed by occasional rain until August and September, when the rainfall reaches its peak. Average temperatures range between 21 and 32°C (70 and 90°F), with relative humidity between 50% and 80%. Rainfall ranges from 83 to 220 cm (33 to 87 in) a year.

The harmattan, a dry desert wind, blows from the northeast from December to March, lowering the humidity and causing hot days and cool nights in the north; the effect of this wind is felt in the south during January. In most areas, temperatures are highest in March and lowest in August. Variation between day and night temperatures is relatively small, but greater in the north, especially in January, because of the harmattan. No temperature lower than 10°C (50°F) has ever been recorded in Ghana.

⁴FLORA AND FAUNA

The World Resources Institute estimates that there are 3,725 plant species in Ghana. In addition, Ghana is home to 249 mammal, 729 bird, 135 reptile, and 72 amphibian species. The calculation reflects the total number of distinct species residing in the country, not the number of endemic species.

Plants and animals are mainly those common to tropical regions, but because of human encroachment, Ghana has fewer large and wild mammals than in other parts of Africa.

[5] ENVIRONMENT

The World Resources Institute reported that Ghana had designated 3.63 million hectares (8.96 million acres) of land for protection as of 2006. Water resources totaled 53.2 cubic kilometers (12.76 cubic miles) while water usage was 0.98 cubic kilometers (.235 cubic miles) per year. Domestic water usage accounted for 24% of total usage, industrial for 10%, and agricultural for 66%. Per capita water usage totaled 44 cubic meters (1,554 cubic feet) per year.

The UN reported in 2008 that carbon dioxide emissions in Ghana totaled 9,801 kilotons.

Slash-and-burn agriculture and overcultivation of cleared land have resulted in widespread soil erosion and exhaustion. Overgrazing, heavy logging, overcutting of firewood, and mining have taken a toll on forests and woodland. About one-third of Ghana's land area is threatened by desertification. Industrial pollutants include arsenic from gold mining and noxious fumes from smelters. Water pollution results from a combination of industrial sources, agricultural chemicals, and inadequate waste treatment facilities.

Ghana has five national parks and four other protected areas; there are six Ramsar wetland sites. The ban on hunting in closed reserves is only sporadically enforced, and the nation's wildlife is threatened by poaching and habitat destruction. Songor, Ghana, was nominated for the UN Educational, Scientific, and Cultural Organization (UNESCO) Biosphere Reserve Program in 2011. The area is characterized by a unique combination of brackish/estuarine, freshwater, and marine ecosystems with mangroves, islands, and small patches of community protected forests. This site plays a significant role in the conservation of biological diversity as it serves as habitat for certain floral and faunal groups listed in the IUCN Red Data List of Endangered Species.

According to a 2011 report issued by the International Union for Conservation of Nature and Natural Resources (IUCN), the number of threatened species included 16 types of mammals, 13 species of birds, 5 types of reptiles, 12 species of amphibians, 44 species of fish, and 118 species of plants. Threatened species included the white-breasted guinea fowl, the hartebeest, Pel's flying squirrel, the black crowned crane, the red-capped monkey, and the great white shark.

[6] POPULATION

The US Central Intelligence Agency (CIA) estimates the population of Ghana in 2011 to be approximately 24,791,073, which placed it at number 47 in population among the 196 nations of the world. In 2011, approximately 3.5% of the population was over 65 years of age, with another 36.5% under 15 years of age. The median age in Ghana was 21.4 years. There were 1.00 males for every female in the country. The population's annual rate of change was 1.822%. The projected population for the year 2025 was 31,800,000. Population density in Ghana was calculated at 104 people per square kilometers (269 people per square miles).

The UN estimated that 51% of the population lived in urban areas, and that urban populations had an annual rate of change of 3.4%. The largest urban areas, along with their respective populations, included Accra, 2.3 million; and Kumasi, 1.8 million.

[7] MIGRATION

Estimates of Ghana's net migration rate, carried out by the CIA in 2011, amounted to -0.58 migrants per 1,000 citizens. The total number of emigrants living abroad was 824,900. Ghanaians primarily emigrate to the United States, Europe, and other parts of Africa, particularly Nigeria, Côte d'Ivoire, and Togo. The total number of immigrants living in Ghana was 1.85 million, or 8% of the population. Ghana also accepted refugees 35,653 from Liberia and 8,517 from Togo.

For generations, immigrants from Burkina Faso and Togo did much of the manual work, including mining, in Ghana; immigrant traders from Nigeria conducted much of the petty trade; and Lebanese and Syrians were important as intermediaries. In 1969, when many foreigners were expelled, Ghana's alien community was about 2,000,000 out of a population of about 8,400,000. In 1986, the government estimated that at least 500,000 foreigners were residing in Ghana, mostly engaged in trading.

Ghanaians also work abroad, some as fishermen in neighboring coastal countries. Many Ghanaians were welcomed in the 1970s by Nigeria, which was in the midst of an oil boom and in need of cheap labor. In early 1983, as the oil boom faded, up to 700,000 Ghanaians were expelled from Nigeria; soon after, however, many deportees were reportedly being invited back by Nigerian employers unable to fill the vacant posts with indigenous labor. But in May 1985, an estimated 100,000 Ghanaians again were expelled from Nigeria.

Ghana has a large scale of internal migration, estimated at 50% of the population. Expectations of higher wages and economic opportunities have encouraged urban migration. Annual urban population growth is 4%, while rural population growth is 1%.

The UN High Commissioner for Refugees (UNHCR) organized a plan for the voluntary repatriation of some 15,000 Liberian refugees; since June 1997, 3,342 have repatriated under the plan. Of those Liberian refugees remaining in Ghana, another 4,000 have expressed willingness to return to their homeland; however, the majority wish to stay in Ghana or be resettled in third countries. Repatriation efforts for both Liberian and Togolese refugees were ongoing in 1999. Also in 1999, both Liberian and Sierra Leonean refugees were still arriving in Ghana in sizable numbers. As of October 2011, there were approximately 18,000 Ivorian refugees who fled the country in 2010 and 2011 during the post-electoral crisis. The UNHCR has worked with the Ghana Refugee Board to ensure the safety of refugees and develop a national strategy for the local integration of long-staying refugees.

[8] ETHNIC GROUPS

It is fairly certain that Ghana has been occupied by Negroid peoples since prehistoric times. Members of the Akan family, who make up about 45.3% of the population, include the Twi, or Ashanti, inhabiting the Ashanti Region and central Ghana, and the Fanti, inhabiting the coastal areas. In the southwest, the Nzima, Ahanta, Evalue, and other tribes speak languages related to Twi and Fante. The Mole-Dagbon constitute about 15.2% of the population, the Ewe 11.7%, the Ga-Dangme 7.3%, the Gurma 3.6%, the Grusi 2.6%, and the Mande-Busanga 1%. Other tribes account for about 1.4% of the population. The Accra plains are inhabited by tribes speaking variants of Ga, while east of the Volta River are the Ewe

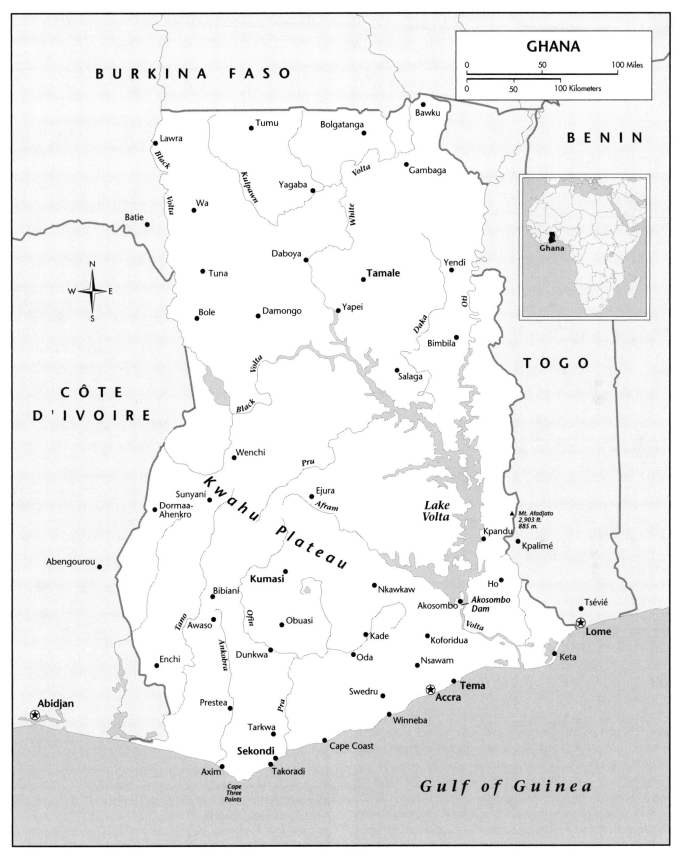

LOCATION: 4°45′ to 11°10′N; 1°12′E to 3°15′W. BOUNDARY LENGTHS: Togo, 877 kilometers (545 miles); Atlantic coastline, 539 kilometers (335 miles); Côte d'Ivoire, 668 kilometers (415 miles); Burkina Faso, 544 kilometers (338 miles). TERRITORIAL SEA LIMIT: 12 miles.

living in what used to be British-mandated Togoland. All these tribes are fairly recent arrivals in Ghana, the Akan having come between the 12th and 15th centuries, the Ga-Adangbe in the 16th century, and the Ewe in the 17th century. Most of the inhabitants of the Northern Region belong to the Mole-Dagbani group of Voltaic peoples or to the Gonja, who appear to bear some relation to the Akan. There are a small percentage of Europeans and other national groups.

9 LANGUAGES

Of the 56 indigenous languages and dialects spoken in Ghana, 31 are used mainly in the northern part of the country. The languages follow the tribal divisions, with Asante (14.8%) and Ewe (12.7%) being most prominent. Fante is spoken by about 9.9% of the population. Boron (Brong), Dagomba, Dangme, Dagarte (Dagaba), Akyem, Ga, and Akuapem are each spoken by less than 5% of the population. English is the official language and is the universal medium of instruction in schools. It is officially supplemented by five local languages.

10 RELIGIONS

An estimated 69% of the population belong to various Christian denominations, 15.6% are Muslims (though Muslim leaders claim the number is closer to 30%), and about 15.4% of the population follow traditional indigenous beliefs or other religions, including the Baha'i Faith, Buddhism, Judaism, Hinduism, Shintoism, Ninchiren Shoshu Soka Gakkai, Sri Sathya Sai Baba Sera, Sat Sang, Eckanker, the Divine Light Mission, Hare Krishna, and Rastafarianism. Christian denominations include Roman Catholics, three branches of Methodists, Anglicans, Mennonites, two branches of Presbyterians, Evangelical Lutherans, the Church of Jesus Christ of Latter-Day Saints, Seventh-Day Adventists, Pentecostals, Baptists, and Society of Friends (Quakers).

About 8.5% of the population practices indigenous religious beliefs and some Christians also include elements of indigenous religions in their own practices, particularly magic and divination. There are three primary branches of Islam within the country: Ahlussuna, Tijanis, and Ahmadis. A small number of Muslims are Shi'a. Zetahil, a religion that is unique to Ghana, combines elements of both Islam and Christianity. The indigenous religions generally involve a belief in a supreme being along with lesser gods. Veneration of ancestors is also common. The Afrikan Renaissance Mission, also known as Afrikania, is an organization which actively supports recognition and practice of these traditional religions. In many areas of the country, there is still a strong belief in witchcraft. Those suspected of being witches (usually older women) have been beaten or lynched and occasionally banished to "witch camps," which are small villages in the north primarily populated by suspected witches.

The law does provide protection for alleged witches. Freedom of religion is guaranteed by the constitution and this right is generally respected in practice. Although there is no state religion, religious education is part of the public school curriculum. Good Friday, Easter Monday, Eid al-Fitr, Eid al-Adha, and Christmas are observed as national holidays.

11 TRANSPORTATION

The government's development program has been largely devoted to improving internal communications; nevertheless, both road and rail systems deteriorated in the 1980s. Rehabilitation began in the late 1980s, with priority being given to the western route, which is the export route for Ghana's manganese and bauxite production and also serves the major gold-producing area. Rail lines are also the main means of transportation for such products as cocoa, logs, and sawn timber; they are also widely used for passenger service. There were 947 km (588 mi) of narrow-gauge railway in 2008, with the main line linking Sekondi-Takoradi with Accra and Kumasi.

The government transport department operates a cross-country bus service; municipal transport facilities are available in all main towns.

The Black Star Line, owned by the government, operates a cargo-passenger service to Canada, the United States, the United Kingdom, Italy, and West Africa. In 2008, Ghana had a merchant shipping fleet comprising four vessels of 1,000 gross registered tons or more. Lake transport service between Akosombo and Yapei is operated by Volta Lake Transport Co.

Ghana has no natural harbors. An artificial deepwater port was built at Sekondi-Takoradi in the 1920s and expanded after World War II. A second deepwater port, at Tema, was opened in 1962, and in 1963 further extensions were made. At a few smaller ports, freight is moved by surfboats and lighters. Ghana has approximately 1,293 km (803 mi) of navigable waterways. The major rivers and Lake Volta provide Ghana with its navigable waterways.

In 2010, there were 11 airports, of which seven had paved runways. Accra's international airport serves intercontinental as well as local West African traffic. Smaller airports are located at Sekondi-Takoradi, Kumasi, Tamale, and Sunyani. Ghana Airways, owned by the government, operates domestic air services and flights to other African countries and to the Federal Republic of Germany (FRG), London, and Rome.

The CIA reported that Ghana had a total of 62,221 km (38,662 mi) of roads as of 2006, of which 9,955 km (6,186 mi) were paved. Ghana is expected to benefit greatly from the World Bank funded reconstruction of the Abidjan-Lagos Corridor, also known as the West African Coastal Corridor. In March 2010, the World Bank approved funding of $317.5 million to improve this important roadway, which stretches for 998.8 km (620 mi), linking the capital cities of Abidjan (Cote d'Ivoire), Accra (Ghana), Lomé (Togo), Cotonou (Benin) and Lagos (Nigeria). This corridor is one of the most highly traveled roadways on the continent. Developed in part by the Economic Community of West African Nations (ECOWAS), the corridor project implemented procedural reforms designed to promote a more efficient trade process, along with much needed improvements to the physical infrastructure. The project was to be executed in two phases, with the first phase covering Ghana, Togo, and Benin, and the second phase covering Cote d'Ivoire and Nigeria.

12 HISTORY

Oral traditions indicate that the tribes presently occupying the country migrated southward roughly over the period 1200–1600. The origins of the peoples of Ghana are still conjectural, although the name "Ghana" was adopted on independence in the belief that Ghanaians are descendants of the inhabitants of the empire of Ghana, which flourished in western Sudan (present-day Mali), hundreds of miles to the northwest, more than a thousand years ago.

The recorded history of Ghana begins in 1471, when Portuguese traders landed on the coast in search of gold, ivory, and spices. Following the Portuguese came the Dutch, the Danes, the Swedes, the Prussians, and the British. Commerce in gold gave way to the slave trade until the latter was outlawed by Great Britain in 1807. The 19th century brought a gradual adjustment to legitimate trade, the withdrawal of all European powers except the British, and many wars involving the Ashanti, who had welded themselves into a powerful military confederacy; their position as the principal captors of slaves for European traders had brought them into conflict with the coastal tribes. British troops fought seven wars with the Ashanti from 1806 to 1901, when their kingdom was annexed by the British crown.

In 1874, the coastal area settlements had become a crown colony-the Gold Coast Colony-and in 1901 the Northern Territories were declared a British protectorate. In 1922, part of the former German colony of Togoland was placed under British mandate by the League of Nations, and it passed to British trusteeship under the UN after World War II. Throughout this period, Togoland was administered as part of the Gold Coast.

After a measure of local participation in government was first granted in 1946, the growing demand for self-government led in 1949 to the appointment of an all-African committee to inquire into constitutional reform. Under the new constitution introduced as a result of the findings of this committee, elections were held in 1951, and for the first time an African majority was granted a considerable measure of governmental responsibility. In 1954, further constitutional amendments were adopted under which the Gold Coast became, for practical purposes, self-governing. Two years later, the newly elected legislature passed a resolution calling for independence, and on 6 March 1957 the Gold Coast, including Ashanti, the Northern Territories Protectorate, and the Trust Territory of British Togoland, attained full independent membership in the Commonwealth of Nations under the name of Ghana. The Gold Coast thus became the first country in colonial Africa to gain independence. The nation became a republic on 1 July 1960.

During the period 1960–65, Ghana's first president, Kwame Nkrumah, steadily gained control over all aspects of Ghana's economic, political, cultural, and military affairs. His autocratic rule led to mounting but disorganized opposition. Following attempts on Nkrumah's life in August and September 1962, the political climate began to disintegrate, as government leaders accused of complicity in the assassination plots were executed or removed from office. A referendum in January 1964 established a one-party state and empowered the president to dismiss Supreme Court and High Court judges. Another attempt to assassinate Nkrumah occurred that month.

In February 1966, Nkrumah was overthrown. A military regime calling itself the National Liberation Council (NLC) established rule by decree, dismissing the civilian government and suspending the constitution. A three-year ban on political activities was lifted 1 May 1969, and after elections held in August, the Progressive Party, headed by Kofi A. Busia, formed a civilian government under a new constitution. During his two years in office, Busia lost much of his public following, and Ghana's worsening economic condition was the pretext in January 1972 for a military takeover led by Lt. Col. Ignatius Kutu Acheampong, who formed the National Redemption Council (NRC). Unlike the military rulers who came to power in 1966, however, the NRC made no plans for a rapid return to civilian rule. The NRC immediately repudiated part of the foreign debt remaining from the Nkrumah era and instituted an agricultural self-help program dubbed Operation Feed Yourself. By July 1973, the last 23 of some 2,000 persons arrested during the coup that brought the NRC to power had been released.

The NRC was restructured as the Supreme Military Council in 1976. A military coup on 5 July 1978 ousted Acheampong, who was replaced by Lt. Gen. Frederick Akuffo. Less than a year later, on 4 June 1979, a coup by enlisted men and junior officers brought the Armed Forces Revolutionary Council to power, led by a young flight lieutenant, Jerry Rawlings. Acheampong, Akuffo, and another former chief of state, A. A. Afrifa (who had engineered Nkrumah's overthrow in 1966), plus five others, were found guilty of corruption and executed in summary proceedings. Dozens of others were sentenced to long prison terms by secret courts. The new regime did, however, fulfill the pledge of the Akuffo government by handing over power to civilians on 24 September 1979, following nationwide elections. The Nkrumah-style People's National Party (PNP) won 71 of 140 parliamentary seats in the balloting, and PNP candidate Hilla Limann was elected president.

Ghana's economic condition continued to deteriorate, and on 31 December 1981 a new coup led by Rawlings overthrew the civilian regime. The constitution was suspended, all political parties were banned, and about 100 business leaders and government officials, including Limann, were arrested. Rawlings became chairman of the ruling Provisional National Defense Council. In the following 27 months there were at least five alleged coup attempts. Nine persons were executed in 1986 for attempting to overthrow the regime, and there remained concern over the activities of exile groups and military personnel.

A new constitution was approved by referendum on 28 April 1992 and Rawlings was elected with about 58% of the vote in a sharply contested multiparty election on 3 November 1993. The legislative elections in December, however, were boycotted by the opposition, and the ruling National Democratic Congress (NDC) was able to capture 190 of the 200 seats.

On 4 January 1993, the Fourth Republic was proclaimed and Rawlings was inaugurated as president. Opposition parties, assembled as the Inter-Party Coordinating Committee (ICC), issued a joint statement announcing their acceptance of the "present institutional arrangements" on 7 January, and further stated that they would continue to act as an elected opposition even though they had won no seats in the assembly.

Throughout the 1990s, Ghana's Northern Region has been the site of ethnic/tribal strife. The Kankomba, a landless, impoverished people, began to fight for economic rights against the dominant Nanumbia. In 1995, a curfew was imposed on the region amid massive strife.

Legislative elections were again held in 1996. By maintaining power throughout his elected term (1992–96), Rawlings became the head of the first Ghanaian government to serve a full term without being overthrown. In 1995, Rawlings set up an Electoral Commission charged with setting up and conducting free elections complete with international observers. The Commission enlisted the help of all registered opposition parties and conducted a massive drive to register voters. In the balloting, held 7 December 1996, 77% of the electorate turned out, a substantial improvement over the turnout in 1992. Most observers credited the increase with the Rawlings government's increased transparency.

In 1996, Rawlings was reelected to a second four-year term, having received about 58% of the vote to the Great Alliance Party candidate John Kufuor's 40%. The NDC took 133 seats in the 200-member assembly. The NPP emerged as the leading opposition, taking 60 of the remaining seats. The next presidential elections were held on 7 and 28 December 2000, with Rawlings barred by law from serving a third term. Kufuor won the election, taking 57.4% of the vote to NDC candidate and Rawlings' vice president John Atta Mills's 42.6% in the second round of voting (Kufuor won 48.4% of the vote in the first round, and Mills took 44.8%). Five other candidates contested the elections, and Rawlings relinquished power willingly. When Kufuor took office in January 2001, he began investigations into alleged corruption and human rights violations during the time Rawlings was in power, which caused consternation on Rawlings' part. Also on 7 December, parliamentary elections were held; the second round of voting was held on 3 January 2001, and the NPP took 100 of the 200 seats, to the NDC's 92. The elections were judged by international observers to be generally free and fair, although there were reports of government pressure on the media and voter intimidation.

Tension between Kufuor and Rawlings continued throughout 2001, and came to a head on 4 June when Rawlings, who was celebrating the anniversary of his 1979 takeover of power, gave a speech that implied Kufuor did not have the confidence of the military. This was seen as a threat of another coup, and thousands marched in protest of Rawlings' statement. One of Kufuor's first acts as president was to abolish the national holidays commemorating 4 June 1979 and the 31 December 1981 anniversary of the second coup that began the Rawlings era. Following Rawlings' speech, the military leadership stated its support of the Kufuor government.

One of the most well-known Ghanaians is Kofi Annan, the seventh secretary general of the UN. Born in Kumasi, Ghana, on April 8, 1938, Kofi Annan rose as a UN bureaucrat and was elected by the UN Security Council as Secretary General on 13 December 1996 and confirmed by the UN General Assembly four days later. Annan was the first black African to become Secretary General. Annan's tenure as Secretary General was renewed on 1 January 2002 for another five-year term. Annan and the UN jointly received the Nobel Peace Prize for "their work for a better organized and more peaceful world" on 10 December 2001.

In early 2003, Kufuor was host to talks between Côte d'Ivoire's new prime minister, Seydou Diarra, and representatives of the country's northern-based rebels in an attempt to reach an accord on a power-sharing agreement with President Laurent Gbagbo's government, after the civil war that broke out in the country in September 2002.

Ghana's leaders and citizens face unprecedented social threats. The National AIDS Control Programme (NACP) in Accra expected that by 2014 AIDS will account for 35% of all deaths. In 1994,

AIDS accounted for an estimated 3.5% of all deaths with some 200 people being infected daily. In February 2000, the estimated HIV prevalence was between 4% and 5% nationwide. HIV/AIDS affects the development of all sectors including health, education, the labor force, economy, transport and agriculture. To curb the pandemic, Ghana has launched a national crusade against it. In August 2005 Ghana started producing antiretroviral (ARV) drugs in the capital Accra as part of government plans to expand distribution of the life prolonging treatment for its HIV-positive citizens. This was achieved in a joint venture between Danpong Pharmaceuticals of Ghana and Adams Pharmaceuticals of China. The venture was expected to decrease the government bill for providing ARVs to some 2,600 patients by 45%, according to official sources.

Despite this setback to Ghana's development, in August 1999, representatives of Shell and Chevron signed a memorandum of understanding with representatives of Nigeria, Benin, Togo, and Ghana specifying that a gas pipeline traversing the four countries would be built. In February 2003, the heads of state of the four countries signed a treaty on establishing a legal and fiscal framework and a regulatory authority for the $500 million West African Gas Pipeline (WAGP). The pipeline will be designed to carry an initial volume of 195 million cubic feet of gas. In 2004 the US mining company Newmont entered Ghana's mining sector; it was projected they would invest up to $1 billion.

On 15 July 2004 the National Reconciliation Commission (NRC) formally wrapped up public hearings after 18 months and over 2,000 accounts of human rights violations. Modeled on South Africa's Truth and Reconciliation Commission, Kufuor's government set up the NRC on 3 September 2002 in order to foster national healing after human rights abuses and atrocities committed under Jerry Rawlings' and previous military regimes. Witnesses in the $5 million process included ordinary Ghanaians and high-profile individuals, such as former President Rawlings. Rawlings appeared before the commission in February to answer questions about his role in specific atrocities, including murder. The NRC submitted its final report and recommendations in October 2004. The government accepted many of the commission's recommendations through a White Paper that was produced in April 2005, including establishment of a Reparation and Rehabilitation Fund for victims of abuse, training and much-needed reform in operation of the security forces.

Kufuor won a mandate for a second term at the polls held on 7 December 2004. Kufuor defeated NDC's Atta Mills, winning 52.45% of the vote to Mills' 44.64%. Grand Coalition's Edward Mahama and the Convention People's Party (NPP) George Aggudey, polled 1.92 % and 1 %, respectively. Government claims of a coup attempt raised fears of unrest. One month before the elections the government arrested and questioned a group of people, including seven former soldiers, who were allegedly found with military helmets, body armor, a firearm and ammunition. However, the Electoral Commission reported a remarkable turnout of 85.1%, about 8.5 million Ghanaians, credited to an aggressive voter registration campaign mounted by the Electoral Commission. For the first time, registration included issue of picture identity cards and sought to eliminate fraud and build confidence in the electoral process. Both domestic and international observers pronounced the elections generally free, fair, and peaceful. There were a few incidents of intimidation and violence in which three people were reported killed. Eight political parties contested parliamentary elections that were run concurrently and four fielded presidential candidates. The 2004 election saw 30 new parliamentary constituencies added to the 2000 election, making a 230-member parliament. In the parliamentary elections, the ruling New Patriotic Party (NPP) won 128 seats, the National Democratic Congress (NDC), 94; the People's National Convention (PNC), 4; the Convention People's Party (CPP), 3; and an independent won 1 seat.

In June 2007, more than 600 million barrels of light oil reserves were discovered off Ghana's shore, offering the promise of relief from power shortages and an increased national prosperity. However, officials for Tullow Oil, which owns the property where the reserves were found, warned that it could be as many as seven years before the country began to see profits from the discovery. The discovery came just several months after Ghana celebrated the fiftieth anniversary of its independence, and was hailed as a turning point for the nation. President Kufuor declared that the oil reserves would help transform Ghana into an "African tiger."

Major floods devastated West Africa in September 2007, with Ghana bearing much of the natural disaster's brunt. An estimated 400,000 people were affected, with many homeless and at least 20 reported deaths. The flood was also linked to a contaminated water supply and an increased risk of disease outbreak, in addition to food shortages.

13 GOVERNMENT

Since independence, Ghana has experienced four military coups and ten changes of government. The military ruled Ghana by decree from 1972 to 1979, when an elected constituent assembly adopted a new constitution establishing a unicameral parliament and an executive branch headed by a president. On 31 December 1981, a military coup installed the Provisional National Defense Council (PNDC) as the supreme power; the constitution was suspended and the national assembly dissolved.

A consultative assembly, convened late in 1991 to draw up a new constitution, completed its work in March 1992. The government inserted a controversial amendment indemnifying officials of the PNDC from future prosecution for all acts of commission and omission during their term in office. In an April 1992 referendum, the constitution was approved by 92.5% of voters in a low turnout (58% of those eligible). It provided for a presidential system and a legislature (national assembly) of 200 members. Since the 1992 referendum, the government introduced multiparty competition.

The president is elected for a four-year term, and the constitution bars a third term.

14 POLITICAL PARTIES

The United Gold Coast Convention (UGCC) was established in 1947 with the declared aim of working for self-government at the earliest possible date. In 1949, as most of the UGCC leadership came to accept constitutional reform as an alternative to immediate self-government, the party secretary, Kwame Nkrumah, broke away and formed his own group, the Convention People's Party (CPP). In January 1950, Nkrumah announced a program of "positive action" for which he and the main leaders of the party were

prosecuted and sentenced for sedition. At the first elections held in 1951 under a new constitution, the CPP obtained 71 of the 104 seats, and Nkrumah and his colleagues were released from prison to enter the new government. In May 1952, Kofi A. Busia, of the University College, founded the Ghana Congress Party (GCP), which continued the UGCC position of trying to form alliances with traditional chiefs. The GCP's leadership was a mixture of dissatisfied former CPP members and the professional-oriented leadership of the UGCC. In 1953, Nkrumah was elected life chairman and leader of the CPP.

In 1954, the assembly and cabinet became all African. A new party, the Ashanti-based National Liberation Movement (NLM), was formed to fight the general centralizing tendencies of the CPP and also to maintain the position of the traditional rulers; the NLM leadership, except for Busia, consisted of former CPP members. In the elections held in 1956, however, the CPP retained its predominant position, winning 72 of 108 seats in the Legislative Assembly.

One of the first acts of independent Ghana under Nkrumah was the Avoidance of Discrimination Act (1957), prohibiting sectional parties based on racial, regional, or religious differences. This led the opposition parties to amalgamate into the new United Party (UP), opposing the government's centralization policies and the declining power of the traditional rulers. The effectiveness of the opposition was reduced following the 1960 election by the withdrawal of official recognition of the opposition as such and by the detention of several leading opposition members under the Preventive Detention Act (1958). In September 1962, the National Assembly passed by an overwhelming majority a resolution calling for the creation of a one-party state; this was approved by referendum in January 1964.

After the military takeover of February 1966, the National Liberation Council outlawed the CPP along with all other political organizations. The ban on political activities was lifted on 1 May 1969, and several parties participated in the August 1969 balloting. The two major parties contesting the election were the Progress Party (PP), led by Busia, which was perceived as an Akan-dominated party composed of former members of the opposition UP; and the National Alliance of Liberals (NAL), a Ewe- and CPP-dominated group under the leadership of the former CPP minister Komla Gbedemah. The PP won 105 seats in the 140-member National Assembly; 29 seats were captured by the NAL, and 6 by the five minor parties. In October 1970, the NAL merged with two of the smaller groups to form the Justice Party.

All political parties in Ghana were again disbanded following the January 1972 military coup led by Col. Acheampong. When political activities resumed in 1979, five parties contested the elections. The People's National Party (PNP), which won 71 of 140 seats at stake, claimed to represent the Nkrumah heritage; the Popular Front Party (PFP) and the United National Convention (UNC), which traced their lineage back to Busia's Progress Party, won 43 and 13, respectively. The Action Congress Party (ACP), drawing primary support from the Fante tribe, won 10 seats, while the leftist Social Democratic Front won 3. After the elections, the PNP formed an alliance with the UNC. In October 1980, however, the UNC left the governing coalition, and in June joined with three other parties to form the All People's Party. The coup of December 1981 brought yet another dissolution of Ghana's political party structure. Opposition to the Provisional National Defense Council (PNDC) was carried on by the Ghana Democratic Movement (organized in London in 1983) and a number of other groups.

With adoption of a new constitution in April 1992, the long-standing ban on political activity was lifted on 18 May 1992. Ghanaians prepared for the presidential and legislative elections to be held in November and December. The parties that emerged could be grouped into three clusters. The center-right group was the most cohesive and it consisted of followers of Kofi Busia. They formed the New Patriotic Party (NPP) and chose Adu Boaheu as their presidential candidate. The center-left group was Nkrumahists. Ideological and leadership differences kept them divided into five separate parties, of which the People's National Convention, a party led by ex-President Limann, was best organized. PNDC supporters comprised the third grouping. They favored continuity and, after forming the National Democratic Congress (NDC), were able to draft Rawlings as their candidate.

Rawlings eventually defeated Boaheu (58% to 30%) for the presidency. Opposition parties boycotted the December 1992 legislation elections, and the NDC carried 190 of the 200 seats. But the fear of one-party control prompted a split in the NDC. The official opposition in parliament was a faction of the ruling NDC.

Meanwhile, the NPP provided the most serious challenge to the NDC. It sees itself as defender of the new constitution. The NPP broke away from the opposition, the Inter-Party Coordinating Committee, by announcing in August 1993 its recognition of the 1992 election results, which the ICC had refused to accept.

On 7 December 1996, parliamentary elections were again held and while Rawlings's NDC maintained a majority, it fell from 190 seats in 1992 to 133 seats. The NPP, leading the opposition, won 60 seats. The People's Convention held 5 seats and the People's National Convention held 1. The elections were preceded by a massive voter registration drive and judged to be free and fair by international observers.

Leading up to the 2000 elections, the four main opposition parties formed the Joint Action Committee (JAC) to monitor the electoral register and campaign activities to ensure transparency. The elections for the National Assembly were held on 7 December 2000 and 3 January 2001. The NPP emerged the winner by a slim margin, taking 100 seats to the NDC's 92. The socialist People's National Convention took three seats, the socialist Convention People's Party took one seat, and independents won four seats. In the 7 and 28 December 2000 presidential elections, in addition to the NPP's candidate John Kufuor and the NDC's candidate John Atta Mills, the following five parties put presidential candidates forward: the People's National Convention, the Convention People's Party, the National Reform Party, the Great Consolidated Popular Party, and the United Ghana Movement.

On 7 December 2004, presidential and parliamentary elections were held simultaneously. Eight political parties competed in the parliamentary elections and four parties fielded candidates in the presidential elections. John Kufuor won a second four-year term as president in elections which had a turnout of 85.1% of registered voters, and was judged to be generally free, fair, and peaceful by both domestic and international observers. For a second time, Kufuor standing for the ruling NPP defeated his main challenger, NDC's Atta Mills. Kufuor won 52.45% of the vote to Mills' 44.64%.

Grand Coalition's Edward Mahama and the Convention People's Party (NPP) George Aggudey, won 1.92% and 1%, respectively.

In the parliamentary elections, only half of the eight parties contesting won seats in parliament. The ruling New Patriotic Party (NPP) won 128 seats, the National Democratic Congress (NDC), 94; the People's National Convention (PNC), 4; the Convention People's Party (CPP), 3; and independent, 1.

John Kufuor was constitutionally barred from running for a third term in the presidential elections of December 2008. With a runoff vote completed on 2 January 2009, John Evans Atta Mills of the National Democratic Congress narrowly defeated Nana Addo Dankawa Akufo-Addo of the incumbent New Patriotic Party (NPP), with 50.23% of the vote. While both parties alleged some voting irregularities, international observers called the elections fair and world leaders congratulated all parties on a peaceful resolution in a very close race. Mills took office on 7 January 2009 with John Dramani Mahama serving as vice-president. The next presidential and parliamentary elections were scheduled to take place in December 2012. John Atta Mills ran for his second term as president after defeating Nana Konadu Agyemang-Rawlings, wife of former President Jerry Rawlings, to become National Democratic Congress party's candidate. Nana Akufo-Addo ran as the primary opposition for the NPP.

All 230 seats in Parliament were up for re-election in 2008. The NDC won 114 seats and the NPP won 107. No other party won more than two seats. The next elections were scheduled for December 2012.

15 LOCAL GOVERNMENT

Ghana is divided into 10 regions: Eastern, Western, Ashanti, Northern, Volta, Central, Upper East, Upper West, Brong-Ahafo, and Greater Accra. In 1994, the 10 regions were further subdivided into 267 local administrative units. Local government in Ghana has traditionally been subject to the central government because responsibilities between the two were not well-defined. In late 1982, the government announced that town and village councils, which had been dissolved after the 1981 coup, would be run by people's and workers' defense committees. They were replaced by Committees for the Defense of the Revolution in 1984. The Local Government Law of 1988 and the Local Government Act of 1993 further empowered local governments, and set the stage for efforts to assist them with development planning, working with civil society, and less dependence on central government for resources.

Elections for 103 district assemblies, 4 municipal assemblies, and 3 metropolitan assemblies were conducted in March 1994. In April 2000, the World Bank approved a US$11-million credit for infrastructure development in Ghana's smaller cities. The Urban 5 Project is intended to support Ghana's decentralization program through capacity building, improvement of urban infrastructure, and delivery of services at the levels of the district assemblies. The project is part of an 11-year program. Local assembly elections were held in August 2002; 14,079 candidates competed in the elections, which were peaceful but marked by low voter turnout. District assembly elections were also held in 2006 and 2010. In 2010, 15,939 candidates contested the election. The next assembly elections were scheduled for 2014.

16JUDICIAL SYSTEM

The 1992 constitution established an independent judiciary and a number of autonomous institutions such as the Commission for Human Rights to investigate and take actions to remedy alleged violations of human rights. The new system is based largely on British legal procedures. The new court system consists of two levels: Superior Courts and lower courts. The superior courts include the Supreme Court, the appeals court, the high court, and regional tribunals. Parliament has the authority to create a system of lower courts. The old public tribunals are being phased out as they clear their dockets. The Courts Act of 2002 established the circuit courts, the magistrate courts, and special courts such as the juvenile courts.

The 1971 Chieftaincy Act gives the traditional courts powers to mediate local matters. Traditional courts in which village chiefs enforce customary tribal laws in resolving local divorce, child custody, and property disputes continue to operate alongside the new courts.

The constitution provides for an independent judiciary. However, in practice the judiciary is influenced on occasion by the executive branch, and is hampered by a lack of staff and financial resources. The government nominates any number beyond a minimum of nine members to the Supreme Court, subject to parliament's approval.

Defendants have the right to have a public trial, to be presumed innocent, to have an attorney, and to cross-examine witnesses. Under Kufuor's office there were improvements in human rights, freedom of expression, freedom of the press, and independence of the judiciary from the executive. Ghana's press is "one of the most unfettered" in Africa, according to the Commonwealth Press Union.

17ARMED FORCES

The International Institute for Strategic Studies reports that armed forces in Ghana totaled 15,500 members in 2011. The force is comprised of 11,500 from the army, 2,000 from the navy, and 2,000 members of the air force. Armed forces represented 0.1% of the labor force in Ghana. Defense spending totaled $1.1 billion and accounted for 1.7% of GDP.

The Ghanaian military provides support to UN and peacekeeping missions in eight countries or regions.

18INTERNATIONAL COOPERATION

On 8 March 1957, Ghana was admitted to the UN; the nation belongs to ECA and several nonregional specialized agencies. Ghana is also a member of the African Development Bank, the ACP Group, Commonwealth of Nations, G-24, G-77, the New Partnership for Africa's Development (NEPAD), and African Union. The nation is also a member of the WTO and holds observer status in the OAS. Ghana is also a member of the Commonwealth of Nations, and the African Union, the South Atlantic Peace and Cooperation Zone.

In November 1974, Ghana was admitted as a member of the International Bauxite Association and in June 1975 it ratified the treaty creating ECOWAS. From 2003–05, President John Agyekum Kufuor served as the chairperson of ECOWAS heads of state. In this capacity, he lead the country in taking on a strong role in the Côte d'Ivoire and Liberian peace process. The government is participating in efforts to establish a West African Monetary Zone (WAMZ) that would include The Gambia, Ghana, Guinea, Liberia, Nigeria, and Sierra Leone.

In 2003, Ghana sent troops to Côte d'Ivoire as part of the ECOWAS stabilization force. Ghana has also offered support to UN missions and operations in Kosovo (est. 1999), Lebanon (est. 1978), the Western Sahara (est. 1991), Ethiopia and Eritrea (est. 2000), Liberia (est. 2003), Sierra Leone (est. 1999), Burundi (est. 2004), Côte d'Ivoire (est. 2004), and the DROC (est. 1999). Ghana is part of the Nonaligned Movement.

In February 2010, IMF and government officials confirmed that Ghana will be the site for the IMF's second Regional Technical Assistance Center in West Africa (AFRITAC West 2). The mandate of the center is to offer assistance on issues such as tax and customs policies and administration, financial sector regulation and supervision, and financial management. AFRITAC West 2 will serve Ghana, Cape Verde, The Gambia, Nigeria, Liberia, and Sierra Leone, all of which face similar challenges in economic development.

In environmental cooperation, Ghana is part of the Convention on Biological Diversity, Ramsar, CITES, International Tropical Timber Agreements, the Kyoto Protocol, the Montréal Protocol, MARPOL, the Nuclear Test Ban Treaty, and the UN Conventions on the Law of the Sea, Climate Change, and Desertification.

19ECONOMY

The GDP rate of change in Ghana, as of 2010, was 5.7%. Inflation stood at 10.9%.

Ghana's economy is led by the agricultural sector, which employs about 56% of the labor force and accounts for approximately one-third of GDP. Its key crops are cassava, coco-yams (taro), plantains, and yams. Maize, millet, sorghum, rice, and groundnuts are also important staple crops. Agricultural crops which are sold for export include coffee, bananas, palm nuts, copra, limes, kola nuts, shea nuts, rubber, cotton, and kenaf. Cocoa, however, is the dominant export crop. Ghana produces meat, but not enough to satisfy local demand. The fishing industry, likewise, produces only about half of local demand.

Around 11% of the country's workforce remains unemployed and 29% of the nation's population lives below the poverty line. Ghana is still very dependent upon donations from international groups, such as the World Bank and the International Monetary Fund (IMF), and remittances from its citizens working abroad.

Ghana has significant deposits of gold, and important new investments were made in this sector in 1992. In that year, earnings from gold exports exceeded those of cocoa for the first time. Industrial diamonds are also produced. Ghana is a modest oil producer and refines petroleum products. Bauxite deposits are substantial but largely unexploited: the aluminum smelter at Tema uses bauxite imported from Jamaica. Significant manganese production occurs at Nsuta.

In addition, tourism and timber are growth areas. Timber reserves, however, are declining due to large-scale deforestation that is both legally approved and illegal. With respect to tourism, infrastructure and communications outside the main cities are poor, but tourism has become the country's third-largest source of foreign currency.

Prior to 1990, the economy was dominated by over 300 state-owned enterprises. Undisciplined spending by these parastatals together with large public sector wage increases, added substantially to the government's budget deficit and fueled inflation which peaked at 70% in 1995. In addition to the economic burden of public sector ownership the economy was also hampered by poor roads and an inadequate telecommunications sector. Economic reforms were instituted in the mid-1980s and by 1996 over 150 state owned enterprises had been privatized. After slowing somewhat, privatization got a boost in 2000 when the Kufuor administration focused on privatization and encouraging foreign investment. He declared his administration to usher in the "Golden Age of Business."

Kufuor's efforts were helped by a booming gold sector which boosted the GDP growth rate to 5.8% in 2004 and to 6.4% in 2007. Also, there was a higher demand for cocoa as a result of political turmoil in neighboring Côte d'Ivoire (the world's biggest cocoa producer prior to 2002).

Despite the economic progress, Ghana remains heavily reliant on international assistance from the World Bank, its largest donor. Most aid is tied to progress in the privatization program which is ongoing. In general, the government's sound macro-economic management has met with approval from the international community. Ghana was rewarded in 2006 with a $547 million US sponsored program designed to enhance agricultural and rural development in an effort to reduce poverty among small farmers by improving transportation and community services. It has also qualified for debt relief from the World Bank and the IMF.

The biggest boom to the economy is expected to come through the development of the nation's oil industry. The Ghanaian government announced the discovery of offshore oil reserves in 2007. The British company Tullow Oil is one of the primary investors, with approximately $750 million invested in the project. With over 600 million barrels of proven reserves, Ghana could see revenues of $20 billion by 2030. Largely due to the start of commercial oil production in 2010, economic growth has remained strong, with real GDP growth reaching an estimated 5.9% in 2010 compared to 4.7% in 2009. In 2011 Ghana was listed as *The World's Fastest Growing Economy in 2011* with an economic growth of about 20.146%. Real GDP growth of 11.0% was projected for 2012. Growth prospects have been aided by the country's increasingly democratic settlement and social stability, which have served to boost the confidence of investors and led to rising investment. Drawing on lessons learned from the oil-inspired conflicts in Nigeria, Ghana hopes to establish a strong oil industry for the benefit of its people.

20 INCOME

The CIA estimated that in 2010 the GDP of Ghana was $61.97 billion. The CIA defines GDP as the value of all final goods and services produced within a nation in a given year and computed on the basis of purchasing power parity (PPP) rather than value as measured on the basis of the rate of the exchange based on current dollars. The per capita GDP was estimated at $2,500. The annual growth rate of GDP was 5.7%. The average inflation rate was

10.9%. It was estimated that agriculture accounted for 33.7% of GDP, industry 24.7%, and services 41.6%.

In 2007 the World Bank estimates that Ghana, with 0.35% of the world's population, accounted for 0.05% of the world's GDP. By comparison, the United States, with 4.85% of the world's population, accounted for 22.51% of world GDP.

As of 2011 the most recent study by the World Bank reported that actual individual consumption in Ghana was 79.6% of GDP and accounted for 0.05% of world consumption. By comparison, the United States accounted for 25.44% of world individual consumption. The World Bank also estimated that 40.8% of Ghana's GDP was spent on food and beverages, 10.4% on housing and household furnishings, 7.3% on clothes, 4.5% on health, 4.7% on transportation, 0.2% on communications, 2.4% on recreation, 0.0% on restaurants and hotels, and 2.8% on miscellaneous goods and services and purchases from abroad. In 2009, household consumption in Ghana totaled $20.1 billion or about $812 per capita, measured in current US dollars rather than PPP.

According to the World Bank, remittances from citizens living abroad totaled $114.5 million or about $5 per capita and accounted for approximately 0.2% of GDP.

21 LABOR

As of 2010, Ghana had a total labor force of 10.56 million people. Within that labor force, CIA estimates in 2005 noted that 56% were employed in agriculture, 15% in industry, and 29% in the service sector.

Although freedom of association is provided by law, the government controls the right to unionize. Government has not, however, prevented the formation of unions. Less than 9% of workers in the formal economy are union members partially due to the weak economy. More workers, approximately 85%, are entering the informal sector which is not organized. The law protects the right to strike after mandatory arbitration, but this has not been utilized. Workers are also permitted to engage in collective bargaining.

The minimum working age is 15, but local custom and economic necessity encourage many children to work at much younger ages. The government, labor, and employers set a daily minimum wage of $2.49 which was in effect in 2011. The legal maximum workweek is set at 45 hours, but most collective bargaining agreements allow for a 40-hour week. Health and safety regulations are difficult to enforce due to lack of resources.

22 AGRICULTURE

Despite a wide range of natural resources, agriculture remains the lifeblood of the Ghanaian economy. Roughly 27% of the total land is farmed. In 2010 agriculture grew at 4.8%, lower than the 6.1% in 2009. Crop output and livestock production suffered that year from flooding in the northern regions of the country which caused the destruction of many farms.

Ghana is one of the world's top producers of cocoa. In 2009/10, cocoa output was nearly 640,000 tons; this followed a year of peak production (710,000 tons) in 2008/9. The government has continued to invest heavily to support cocoa farmers and the broader industry.

As a result of the 2008–09 global financial crisis, the Cocoa Board of Ghana (Cocobod) projected a financing gap of nearly $100 million in funds necessary to ensure production of the 2009–

10 crop. As part of a Trade Finance Facility, initiated to soften the impact of the economic crisis on Africa, the African Development Bank Group signed a pre-export finance deal in October 2009 for up to $1.2 billion. Officials believe that more than 100,000 metric tons have been illegally smuggled across the border to the Ivory Coast, where farmers often gain higher prices. The government estimates that the overall total production of cocoa, declared and undeclared, is more than 850,000 metric tons. With a goal to reach production of one million metric tons by 2012, the government hopes to tighten border surveillance and to consider measures that might discourage illicit trade by making prices more competitive.

In addition to cocoa, the country's major crops include rice, cassava (tapioca), peanuts, corn, shea nuts, and bananas. Cereal production in 2009 amounted to 2.6 million tons, fruit production 4.4 million tons, and vegetable production 518,811 tons.

Ghana continued to be a net food importer. Ghana's Ministry of Food and Agriculture estimated that Ghanaian agriculture may be operating at just 20% of its potential. Considerable potential exists for the development of agricultural exports including pineapples, tomatoes, soybeans, and cut flowers.

23 ANIMAL HUSBANDRY

The UN Food and Agriculture Organization (FAO) reported that Ghana dedicated 8.4 million hectares (20.6 million acres) to permanent pasture or meadow in 2009. Livestock can be raised only in the tsetse-free areas, mainly in the Northern Region and along the coastal plains from Accra to the eastern frontier. Ghana's indigenous West African shorthorn is one of the oldest cattle breeds in Africa. Ghanaian livestock farms which can be termed ranches are few; average livestock population for these outfits is about 400 animals. The elimination of deadly epizootic diseases by prophylactic inoculation of cattle (especially with the help of mobile immunization centers) resulted in a rise of the cattle. In 2009 the country tended 43.3 million chickens, 1.4 million head of cattle, and 521,000 pigs. The production from these animals amounted to 45,021 tons of beef and veal, 16,839 tons of pork, 116,200 tons of poultry, 19,800 tons of eggs, and 194,018 tons of milk. Ghana also produced 2,962 tons of cattle hide. Many live animals and much meat are imported (mainly from Nigeria) to satisfy local demand. A serious problem for the livestock industry continues to be the provision of adequate feed for animals during the dry season. Almost every household in Ghana rears a few animals for home consumption and as capital saving in case of crop failures.

24 FISHING

Ghana had 500 decked commercial fishing boats in 2008. The annual capture totaled 349,831 tons according to the UN FAO. The export value of seafood totaled $82.47 million. Round sardinella and European anchovies together accounted for 41% of the total catch. In 1973, an industrial fishing complex at Tema began production of canned pilchards and sardines. Lake Volta accounts for about half the freshwater catch. Considerable potential exists for the development of shrimp and fish exports.

25 FORESTRY

The forest area (primarily in the south) covers about 22% of the country. Since October 1972, the government has acquired a majority share in a number of foreign-owned timber companies. The Timber Marketing Board has a monopoly on the export of timber and timber products.

Among the roughly 300 timber-producing species are the warwa obech, mahogany, utile, baku, and kokrodua; species such as avodire, sapale, and makuri are considered the best in Africa. A ban on the export of 21 species was established in 1979 in order to encourage the production of sawn timber and timber products. The value of all forest products, including roundwood, totaled $160.8 million. The UN FAO estimated the 2009 roundwood production at 1.3 million cubic meters (45.9 million cubic feet), with 91% burned as fuel. Sawn wood exports in 2010 were $944 million. After cocoa and minerals, sawn timber and logs constitute the third-largest export item. The government is encouraging a shift to value-added timber exports in order to strengthen Ghana's position in the global market, create more employment, and bring in more foreign revenue.

26 MINING

Ghana's mining and quarrying sector in 2009, accounted for about 5.8% of the country's GDP. Employment in this sector is about 14,000 workers or under 1% of the country's labor force. Ghana was Africa's second-largest gold producer, behind South Africa, and was the continent's third-largest producer of aluminum metal and manganese ore. Extensive smuggling of gold, the top export of the Gold Coast, and of diamonds through the years has cut into government revenues, as well as high energy costs, which negated increased prices for gold and cocoa. In 2009, Ghana also produced hydraulic cement, salt, diamonds, silver, and bauxite.

Gold production in 2009, not including smuggled or undocumented production was 79,883 kg, down from 69,817 kg in 2006. Silver production increased from 3,142 kg in 2006 to 3,928 kg in 2009

Production of processed manganese ore, all from the Nsuta-Wassaw open-pit mine, was 1,007,000 metric tons in 2009, down from 1,659,000 metric tons in 2006. Only one relatively small bauxite deposit was worked, at Awaso. The site has been in production since 1941 by Ghana Bauxite Company (20% government owned); reserves have been estimated to last 30 years, and other ore reserves nearby were adequate to support mine life for a century. In 2009, production amounted to 440,000 metric tons, down from 727,000 metric tons in 2005. Akwatia, was the only formal operating diamond mine. However, over two-thirds of the diamonds produced were recovered by artisanal miners from alluvial and raised terrace gravel workings in the Birim Valley. Total production in 2009 (gem and industrial), and not including unreported artisanal production, amounted to 376,000 carats, down from 973,000 carats in 2006; total formal-sector production peaked in the 1970s at more than 2.5 million carats.

27 ENERGY AND POWER

The World Bank reported in 2008 that Ghana produced 8.36 billion kilowatt hours of electricity and consumed 6.25 billion kilowatt hours, or 252 kilowatt hours per capita. Roughly 28% of energy came from fossil fuels, while 6% came from alternative fuels. As of 2008 total installed capacity was 2.11 GW. The greatest single source of power is the Volta River Project, begun in 1962 and based on a hydroelectric installation at Akosombo, about 100 km (60 mi) northeast of Accra. Work on the Akosombo (or Volta

River) Dam was finished in 1965. The first stage of the electrification project was completed in mid-1967 and had a capacity of 512,000 kilowatts; by 1990, the plant's capacity had been expanded to 912 MW. Ghana's other major hydroelectric plant is at Kpong (160 MW). The Volta River Authority supplies 99% of the total national electricity consumption, 50–60% of which is absorbed by aluminum refining. Excess electricity is sold to Togo, Benin, and Côte d'Ivoire. A $150 million project to extend the main grid to northern Ghana was completed in 1991.

Beginning in the 1970s, oil exploration was conducted offshore and in the Volta River Basin. In 1979, an offshore field developed by Agri-Petco, a US company, began operations; it was later taken over by Primary Fuel, also a US company, but production ceased in 1986. Proved oil reserves were estimated at 660 million barrels, with refining capacity at 45,000 barrels per day, as of 2009. Per capita oil consumption was 405 kg. Oil production totaled 7,189 barrels of oil a day.

In December 2010, Ghana began pumping oil from the offshore Jubilee Field, thereby marking the beginning of Ghana's commercial oil mining operations. The Jubilee Field was discovered in 2007 and holds an estimated 1.5 billion barrels of oil. The site was developed and is operated by a consortium headed by UK-based Tullow Oil. The country expected to earn $400 million in oil profits in the first year of operations. Government officials forecast a 12% increase in the economic growth rate by the end of 2011. A second oil field discovered in September 2010 contains an estimated 1.4 billion barrels of oil.

28 INDUSTRY

Food, cocoa, and timber processing plants lead a list of industries that include an oil refinery, textiles, vehicles, cement, paper, chemicals, soap, beverages, and shoes. As part of its chemicals industry, Ghana produces rubber, aluminum, and pharmaceuticals. Much of Ghana's industrial base was nationalized over the years. Encouraged by the IMF, however, Ghana has largely ended its parastatal era. Between 1991 and 1999, more than two-thirds of the 300 public sector companies were divested, and the government decided to speed up privatization by contracting private consultants to manage the process.

In 2010, industry accounted for about 24.7% of GDP. Recent industrial activity has included a reopened glass factory, a new palm oil mill, a locally supplied cement plant, and facilities for milling rice, distilling citronella, and producing alcohol. Industry in Ghana is now oriented towards the fabrication of value-added semi-manufactured and finished products rather than just primary commodities for export-items such as furniture, jewelry, beer bottles, aluminum cooking utensils, fruit juice, and chocolate bars. The Tema industrial estate includes the Tema Food Complex, comprised of a fish cannery, flour and feed mills, a tin-can factory, and other facilities. The aluminum smelter at Tema is owned by Kaiser Aluminum and is one of Ghana's largest manufacturing enterprises.

The Tema Oil Refinery was in operation during 2011. Natural gas reserves, located primarily in the Tano fields, were estimated as of 1 January 2011 at 22.7 billion cu m. The 678 km (421 mi) West African Gas Pipeline began in August 2005 and was ready for commissioning in November 2007. The pipeline includes terminals in Tema and Takoradi and ,in December 2008, the first nat-

Principal Trading Partners – Ghana (2010)

(In millions of US dollars)

Country	Total	Exports	Imports	Balance
World	19,120.0	8,080.0	11,040.0	-2,960.0
China	2,237.9	112.0	2,126.0	-2,014.0
Nigeria	1,710.0	73.4	1,636.6	-1,563.2
United States	1,338.2	257.2	1,081.0	-823.8
Netherlands	1,005.3	532.3	473.0	59.3
United Kingdom	894.7	321.1	573.6	-252.5
Côte d'Ivoire	841.5	41.1	800.4	-759.3
France	792.1	260.9	531.2	-270.2
India	700.4	136.3	564.1	-427.7
Belgium	525.8	209.4	316.4	-107.0
South Africa	478.5	8.5	470.0	-461.5

(…) data not available or not significant.

(n.s.) not specified.

SOURCE: 2011 Direction of Trade Statistics Yearbook, New York: United Nations, 2011.

ural gas supply through the pipeline arrived in Ghana. The pipeline was to have an estimated capacity of nearly 14 million cubic meters (475 million cubic feet) a day.

29 SCIENCE AND TECHNOLOGY

The World Bank reported in 2009 that there were no patent applications in science and technology in Ghana. The Council for Scientific and Industrial Research founded in 1958 at Accra, advises the government on scientific matters, coordinates the national research effort, and disseminates research results. Attached to the council are 14 research institutes, many of which deal with land and water resources. Other learned societies and research institutions include the Ghana Institution of Engineers, the Pharmaceutical Society of Ghana, and the Geological Survey of Ghana, all at Accra; and the Ghana Science Association, the Ghana Meteorological Services Department, and the West African Science Association, all at Legon; and the Cocoa Research Institute at Tafo-Akimo. The Ghana Academy of Arts and Sciences was founded in 1959.

The University of Ghana, at Legon, has faculties of agriculture and science, a medical school, and institutes for medical research and for Volta River Basin studies. The University of Cape Coast has a faculty of science and a school of agriculture. The University of Science and Technology at Kumasim has faculties of agriculture, environmental and development studies, pharmacy and science, and schools of engineering and medical science. The country also has a computer science institute in Accra and eight technical institutes and polytechnics in various cities.

In 2008, high technology exports totaled almost $6 million, or 1% of manufactured exports. In 2010, high technology exports accounted for 2% of manufactured exports.

30 DOMESTIC TRADE

Subsistence farming is still the primary basis of the domestic economy. Although there are retail stores in all towns and main trading centers, most retail trade, particularly of food products, is still carried on in local markets, mainly by women. Larger wholesale and retail outlets (including supermarkets) are primarily located in

Balance of Payments – Ghana (2010)

(In millions of US dollars)

Current Account		-2,700.5
Balance on goods		-2,962.0
Imports	-10,922.1	
Exports	7,960.1	
Balance on services		-1,525.9
Balance on income		-535.0
Current transfers		2,322.4
Capital Account		337.5
Financial Account		3,970.5
Direct investment abroad		...
Direct investment in Ghana		2,527.4
Portfolio investment assets		723.0
Portfolio investment liabilities		-102.5
Financial derivatives		...
Other investment assets		...
Other investment liabilities		822.7
Net Errors and Omissions		-163.0
Reserves and Related Items		-1,444.6

(…) data not available or not significant.

SOURCE: *Balance of Payment Statistics Yearbook 2011*, Washington, DC: International Monetary Fund, 2011.

Public Finance – Ghana (2009)

(In billions of cedis, budgetary central government figures)

Revenue and Grants	6,803	100.0%
Tax revenue	4,616	67.9%
Social contributions	...	...
Grants	1,160	17.1%
Other revenue	1,027	15.1%
Expenditures	8,869	100.0%
General public services	...	...
Defense	...	...
Public order and safety	...	...
Economic affairs	...	...
Environmental protection	...	...
Housing and community amenities	...	...
Health	...	...
Recreational, culture, and religion	...	...
Education	...	...
Social protection	...	...

(…) data not available or not significant.

SOURCE: *Government Finance Statistics Yearbook 2010,* Washington, DC: International Monetary Fund, 2010.

Accra. The overseas marketing of primary agricultural products is effected through governmental marketing boards, which use trading companies and cooperatives as agents to purchase commodities from the producers. A value added tax of 12.5% applies to all consumer goods and services. An excise tax applies for certain products such as cigarettes and alcohol.

Normal business hours are from 8 a.m. to noon and 2 to 4:30 or 5 p.m., Monday through Friday; some companies also open on Saturday morning. Banks are open from 8:30 a.m. to 2 p.m., Monday through Thursday, and to 3 p.m. on Friday. English is widely spoken.

31 FOREIGN TRADE

Cocoa, gold, diamonds, base metals, aluminum, and wood were all substantial export products. In 2009, Ghana imported $10.18 billion worth of goods and services, while exporting $7.326 billion worth of goods and services. Major import partners were China (16.5%), Nigeria (12.2%), the United States (6.8%), Cote d'Ivoire (6.2%), France (5.2%), and the UK (4.3%) . Its major export partners were the Netherlands (13.2%), the UK (7.7%), France (5.8%), and Ukraine (5.7%).

32 BALANCE OF PAYMENTS

The CIA reported that in 2010 the purchasing power parity of the GDP was $61.97 billion.

In 2010 the current account balance was -2.324 billion. Ghana had a foreign trade deficit of $3 billion, amounting to 5.6% of GDP. Foreign exchange reserves (including gold) grew to $4.7 billion in 2010, increasing from $3.165 billion in 2009.

33 BANKING AND SECURITIES

The Bank of Ghana, established in 1957, is the central bank. Its primary mission is to supervise and regulate the nation's banking and non-banking financial sector. This includes licensing and

examination powers. The Bank of Ghana is governed by a Board of Directors, for which the bank's Governor is the Chairman. Below him are the First and Second Deputy Governors, and nine Directors.

In 2009, the discount rate, the interest rate at which the central bank lends to financial institutions in the short term, was 18%. At the end of 2008, the nation's gold deposits totaled 0.28 million ounces.

As of 2011, there were 30 licensed commercial banks operating in Ghana, including the Ghana Commercial Bank (GCB) and the Société Générale-Social Security Bank (SG-SSB). There are also 135 licensed rural and community banks, most of which are in the Ashanti (24) Central (21), Eastern (22) and Brong Ahafo (20) regions. Other banks include the Standard Chartered Bank of Ghana Africa Ltd. and The Trust Bank Limited. There were also 48 licensed non-bank financial institutions.

A stock exchange was opened in Accra in 1987. By 1994, the tiny exchange was up nearly 300%. International mutual fund managers and other foreign investors have shown increasing interest in Ghana, and in 1998, the Ghana Stock Exchange (GSE) was judged the best performing bourse in emerging markets. In 2011, the GSE had 36 listed companies. Market capitalization of companies in 2010 was $3.531 billion. At the end of 2011, the GSE composite index was 967.01.

34 INSURANCE

In 1962, the government set up the State Insurance Corp. (SIC) with the primary aims of tightening control over the activities of insurance companies (including their investment policies) and providing insurance coverage for the government and governmental bodies. In 1972, the SIC started a new subsidiary, the Ghana Reinsurance Organization, to curb the outflow of reinsurance premiums from the country. Insurance services were available as of 1997 through 16 companies, five of them classified as foreign (although a 1976 law required the latter to distribute 20%

of equity to the government and 40% to Ghanaian partners). As of 2010, Ghana had 23 non-life insurance companies, 17 life insurance companies, 2 reinsurance companies, 40 broking companies, 1 reinsurance broking company, and 1 loss adjusting company.

35 PUBLIC FINANCE

Ghana turned to the IMF as the economy approached bankruptcy in 1983. The IMF-sponsored stabilization program, known as the ERP (Economic Recovery Program), was pursued vigorously through its several phases, and borrowing from the IMF came to a temporary end in 1992. Many changes took place in the ten years of the program. The currency was devalued repeatedly; foreign exchange was auctioned. The cocoa sector was revamped, starting with higher producer prices, and privatized. Ghana's civil service was one of Africa's largest, therefore the number of civil service employees was reduced; and the state attempted to unburden itself of its parastatals. A systematic program removed government subsidies, and tax collection procedures were strengthened.

From 1995 to 1997, another IMF-backed structural adjustment program continued privatization, but public sector wage increases and defense spending countered austerity measures. Ghana's budgets have habitually been in deficit, financed mainly through the domestic banking system, with consequent rapid increases in the money supply and the rate of inflation. The third phase of the IMF program began in 1998, focusing on financial transparency and macroeconomic stability.

In 2002, Ghana received debt relief under the Heavily Indebted Poor Country (HIPC) program. It also benefited from the Multilateral Debt Relief Initiative in 2006. In 2009, Ghana signed a three-year Poverty Reduction and Growth Facility with the IMF to improve macroeconomic stability, private sector competitiveness, human resource development, and good governance and civic responsibility.

In 2010 the budget of Ghana included $5.518 billion in public revenue and $7.025 billion in public expenditures. Revenues minus expenditures totaled approximately -$1.5 billion. The budget deficit amounted to 7.6% of GDP. Public debt was 59.9% of GDP, with $6.759 billion of the debt held by foreign entities.

36 TAXATION

The basic corporate tax rate was 25% for companies in 2011, but there are different rates applicable to certain companies based on locational and sectorial incentives and carry over losses. Dividends are taxed at 8% and capital-gains are taxed at 15%. A personal income tax ranging from 0 to 25%. As of 30 December 1998, Ghana's sales tax of 15% was replaced by value-added tax (VAT) with a standard rate of 10%. In 2000, the standard VAT rate was increased to 12.5%, where it stood in 2011. Exempt from the VAT are vaccines, other specified drugs, and salt. A monthly salary tax of 5.5% on employees and 13% on employers finances the Social Security and National Insurance Trust pension program. There are also property and excise taxes, a 0–15% gift tax, and a 2.5% National Health Insurance levy on selected goods and services.

37 CUSTOMS AND DUTIES

Ghana uses the Harmonized Commodity Coding System (HS) to classify goods. The ad valorem tax is assessed with the Customs Valuation Code (CVC) formulated by the World Trade Organiza-

tion. In 2009, customs and other import duties represented 23% of tax revenue. Duty on most machinery and capital goods was 0%, the duty for raw materials and intermediate goods 10%, and the duty on most consumer goods 20%. The 12.5% VAT is also applied to imports on the basis of cost, insurance and freight (CIF) plus the duty. There are additional taxes on some products. There are import restrictions on cigarettes, narcotics, mercuric medicated soap, toxic waste, contaminated goods, foreign soil, and counterfeit notes and coins of any country. The import license system was abolished in 1989, but a permit is still required for the import of drugs, communications equipment, mercury, gambling machines, handcuffs, arms and ammunition, and live plants and animals. There are no controls on exports.

Ghana is a member of ECOWAS. The country also created free zones in May 1996, one located in the Greater Accra Region and two other sites at Mpintsin and Ashiem. The seaports and airport also qualify as free zones, as do companies that export more than 70% of products. These companies receive a ten-year corporate tax holiday and zero import tax.

38 FOREIGN INVESTMENT

Before the 1983 Economic Recovery Program, nationalized enterprise was the cornerstone of Ghanaian investment policy. Under the supervision of the IMF and World Bank, the government styled its policies on the model of a number of Asian countries where encouragement of the private sector and foreign direct investment (FDI) are considered essential to sustained economic growth. The principal law on FDI is the Ghana Investment Promotion Center (GIPC) Law of 1994, which governs investments in all sectors except minerals and mining (under the Minerals and Mining Act of 1986 as amended in 1994 and administered by the Minerals Commission), oil and gas (under the Petroleum Exploration and Production Law of 1984 administered by the Ghana National Petroleum Corporation-GNOC), and the free trade zones, established in 1996. The 1994 investment code guarantees the free transferability of dividends, loan repayments, licensing fees, and the repatriation of capital; provides guarantees against expropriation; and provides for dispute arbitration. Foreign investors are not subject to differential treatment on taxes, prices, or access to foreign exchange, imports, and credit.

The GIPC is responsible for promoting direct investment in Ghana. The only performance requirements are that a foreign investor must have at least $10,000 in capital for joint ventures, $50,000 for wholly foreign-owned ventures, and $300,000 for trading companies, and that the latter must employ at least 10 Ghanaians. The free trade zone consists of land near the seaports of Tema and Takoradi and the Kotoka Airport. To qualify for free zone incentives-a year corporate tax holiday and zero duty on imports-the business must export at least 70% of its output. Small enterprises-petty trading, taxi services with less than 10-car fleets, beauty and barber shops, small scale mining, pool betting businesses, and lotteries besides soccer-are reserved for Ghanaians.

Since 2000, the government has transformed its general foreign investment promotion strategy to specific firm target promotion directed at production centers of Europe and Asia. The objectives of the program are to attract firms that seek to local and sub-regional markets and which contribute to value-added production using raw materials available in Ghana.

Because a number of different agencies are involved in the promotion and monitoring of FDI in Ghana, published statistics tend to be unreliable and unreconciled. For the period 2000 to 2002, the GIPC reported it had licensed 510 projects representing a total investment of $351.2 million, $297.9 million of which was FDI and $53.3 million local funds. Of these, 342 were joint ventures and 169 wholly foreign-owned. From 1997 to 1999, FDI averaged $66.7 million a year (UNCTAD estimates), compared to the $100 million a year 2000 to 2002. In the first quarter of 2003, FDI was reported at a record-setting pace of $56.7 million, $49.7 million of which was for projects in the service sector. By the end of the year, capital inflows reached $88 million. In the first three quarters of 2004, FDI levels jumped to $85 million.

Ghana is the second largest recipient of FDI in Western Africa after Nigeria. Foreign direct investment (FDI) in Ghana was a net inflow of $1.68 billion according to World Bank figures published in 2009. FDI represented 6.44% of GDP. Inward stock in 2010 was $9 billion, and FDI outflow was $1.7 billion.

The major foreign investment projects in Ghana have been in mining and manufacturing. The United Kingdom has been the largest foreign investor, with investments exceeding $750 million, primarily through Lonmin Plc's 32% stake in the Ashanti Goldfields Corporation. The largest firm operating in Ghana is Valco, operated by the American company, Kaiser and Reynolds Aluminum, whose guaranteed use of electric power for aluminum refining made possible the building of the Volta Dam and its hydroelectric generating plant. In early 2003, a drought caused an energy crisis in Ghana and brought Valco's operations to a near standstill. Other American companies operating in Ghana include Teberebie Golfields Limited, CMS Generation (independent power producer), Affiliated Computer Services (since 2000, involved in developing offshore business process outsourcing projects), Regimanuel-Gray Limited (construction), Coca-Cola Company, Phyto-Riker (pharmaceuticals), Westel (ICT company formed by the partnership of Western Wireless International and Ghana National Petroleum Company), Pioneer Foods (Star-Kist Tuna), Union Carbide, Amoco, ChevronTexaco, and ExxonMobile.

39 ECONOMIC DEVELOPMENT

Recent economic policy has aimed at correcting basic problems in every phase of the economy: unemployment, low productivity, high production costs, the large foreign debt ($6.8 billion in 2010), low savings and investing, inflation (10.7% in 2010), and high private and government consumption. The country relies heavily on financial assistance from international lenders including the World Bank and the International Monetary Fund (IMF). Conditions of the loans include progress in privatizing state-owned enterprises and achieving macroeconomic performance targets.

The government's recently launched Vision 2020 plan aims at making Ghana a middle-income country through free-market reforms over the course of the next 25 years. Key elements of the plan include increased privatization of parastatals, a friendlier environment for foreign investment, renewed efforts to facilitate private-sector growth, and improvements in infrastructure and social welfare. Through mobilizing private sector management and capital, the government hopes to reduce its financial and managerial burden. By 2003, about two-thirds of 300 state-owned enterprises had been sold to private owners.

In 2002, Ghana reached decision point on the IMF/World Bank's Heavily Indebted Poor Countries (HIPC) initiative. In 2005, it became the 14th country to reach its completion point and received $3.5 billion in debt relief. The relief allowed Ghana to increase spending on education, health, programs to benefit rural areas, and improved governance. Ghana raised electricity, fuel, and municipal water rates, and raised taxes to stabilize its fiscal position, as part of the agreed-upon debt relief plan. In 2003, Ghana negotiated a three-year $258 million Poverty Reduction and Growth Facility (PRGF) Arrangement with the IMF, to support the government's economic reform program for 2003–05. In 2009, Ghana negotiated another three-year arrangement with the PRGF for $602.6 million to deal with macroeconomic instability. In 2006, Ghana signed a five-year, $547 million Millennium Challenge Corporation Compact, which aims to accelerate growth and reduce poverty by assisting in the transformation of Ghana's rural development and agricultural sector.

The economic growth during the 2000s was expected to continue in coming years. Agricultural production was expected to pick up, particularly in cocoa and food crops. The service sector was also anticipated to expand with improvements in the telecommunications, transport, and tourist sectors. The mining sector benefits from increased investments in gold production. The manufacturing sector, on the other hand, may likely continue to suffer because of the high inflation, increasing imports, and the strong exchange rate.

40 SOCIAL DEVELOPMENT

A social insurance system, initiated in 1965, covers all employed persons, with a special system for the military. There is voluntary coverage for the self-employed. Pensions are funded by 5% contributions from employees and 12.5% contributions from employers. The minimum pension is set at 37.5% of the average annual earnings in the three best years of earnings. There are no sickness or maternity benefits provided, however, employed persons receive worker's compensation. Agricultural workers and subsistence farmers are excluded from coverage in these programs.

Women play a prominent role in agriculture and domestic trade, and are represented at the highest levels of political life. Traditional courts, however, often deny women inheritance or property rights. Traditional customs also violate the human rights of children, including facial scarring and female genital mutilation. Violence against women is common and seldom reported. Among the Ewe ethnic group, a traditional practice called *trokosi* allows an individual or family to enslave a virgin daughter to a local priest or shrine for as long as three years as a means of assuring atonement for crimes committed by members of the family. Child labor and forced marriage continue.

Ethnic tensions and violence continue in the northern region. Some human right abuses continue, although significant improvements were made. Discrimination against persons with HIV/AIDS remains a problem, thus discouraging people from seeking testing.

41 HEALTH

Ghana spent 7.8% of its GDP on healthcare, amounting to $45 per person in 2009. Waterborne parasitic diseases are a widespread health hazard and the creation of Lake Volta and related irrigation systems has led to an increase in malaria, sleeping sickness, and schistosomiasis. The upper reaches of the Volta basin are seriously afflicted with onchocerciasis, a filarial worm disease transmitted by biting flies. Lymphatic filians in some remote villages of Ghana affect between 9.2 to 25.4% of the population. Control of filariasis in remote areas has been difficult. It was estimated that 93% of children were vaccinated against measles. A clinical trial to introduce the meningitis vaccine was instituted in 2007. Approximately 64% of the population had access to safe drinking water and 63% had adequate sanitation.

As of 2011, there was 1 physician, 11 nurses and midwives, and 9 hospital beds per 10,000 inhabitants. The total fertility rate in 2011 was estimated at 3.48 children born per woman. The infant mortality rate was 48.55 deaths per 1,000 live births. In 2008 the maternal mortality rate, according to the World Bank, was 350 per 100,000 births. According to the CIA, life expectancy in Ghana was 57 years in 2011.

It was estimated that 26% of children under five were malnourished. Goiter was present in 33% of school-age children. The HIV/AIDS adult prevalence rate was 1.8% in 2009. Two other common diseases were tuberculosis and measles.

Approximately 30% of women in Ghana have undergone female genital mutation, although Ghana's government has prohibited this under specific laws.

42 HOUSING

About 72% of all housing in Ghana are traditional compound houses, which consist of a large U-shaped structure with a shared central courtyard. There are usually seven or more rooms per structure. There are some flats and other types of housing in urban areas. In rural areas, wood, mud, or cement huts with sheet iron or mud roofs are more common. Overcrowding, defined as 2.5 persons or more per room, affects about 44.5% of all households. In rural areas, about 52% of the population use latrine sewage systems; 47% have no specific sewage systems. 18% of urban population and 7% of rural population have access to improved sanitation facilities. About 51% of rural dwellings are owner occupied. These are typically mud or mud brick huts. In urban areas, less than 20% of all housing units are owner occupied. As of 2008, about 90% of urban and 74% of rural households had access to improved drinking water sources.

Ghana's housing needs have been increasing as the main towns grow in population. In 1982, the government established the State Housing Construction Co. to help supply new low-cost dwelling units. The Bank for Housing and Construction finances private housing schemes on a mortgage basis. Under another housing ownership scheme, civil servants may acquire accommodations on purchase-lease terms. The Cocoa Marketing Board, the Social Security and National Insurance Trust, and other organizations have also invested in housing projects; nevertheless, most houses continue to be built without government assistance. Foreign mining companies provide housing for all their overseas employees and many of their African workers.

Recognizing that most private homes are too expensive for many citizens, the government has been working on programs addressing land and material costs and long-term financing for constructions. In December 2009 the government signed a deal with the South Korean firm STX to build 200,000 new homes in

10 cities by 2015. The total cost of the project was estimated at $10 billion. About 90,000 of the homes will be owned by the government, while the remainder will be sold to private owners.

43 EDUCATION

Most of the older schools, started by Christian missions, have received substantial financial help from the government, but the state is increasingly responsible for the construction and maintenance of new schools. Primary education has been free since 1952 and compulsory since 1961. Primary school lasts six years and is followed by six years of secondary schooling (at junior and senior levels). At the upper secondary level, students may choose to attend a three-year technical school. The academic year runs from September to June.

In 2009, about 70% of age-eligible children were enrolled in some type of preschool program. Primary school enrollment was estimated at about 76% of age-eligible students. The same year, secondary school enrollment was about 46% of age-eligible students. It is estimated that about 87% of all students complete their primary education. The student-to-teacher ratio for primary school was at about 33:1 in 2009; the ratio for secondary school was about 18:1. In 2009, private schools accounted for about 18% of primary school enrollment and 15% of secondary enrollment.

Ghana has three main universities: the University of Ghana, in Legon, outside Accra; the University of Science and Technology in Kumasi; and the University of Cape Coast. In 2009, about 9% of the tertiary age population was enrolled in some type of higher education program. In 2009, the World Bank estimated that Ghana had a literacy rate of 67%, 73% for males and 60% for females.

As of 2005, public expenditure on education was estimated at 5.4% of GDP.

44 LIBRARIES AND MUSEUMS

The Ghana Library Board maintains the Accra Central Library, 10 regional libraries, 53 district and branch libraries, mobile units, and children's libraries, with combined holdings of over five million volumes in 2008. The University of Ghana (Balme Library) in Legon has holdings of around 362,000 volumes and is the largest research library in Ghana. The University of Science and Technology Library has 310,000 volumes. The Research Library on African Affairs (formerly the George Padmore Memorial Library), which opened in Accra in 1961, maintains a collection of publications on various aspects of Africa.

The Ghana National Museum, in Accra, founded by the University College of Ghana and now operated by the Museum and Monuments Board, contains hundreds of exhibits illustrating the culture, history, and arts and crafts of Ghana and West Africa. The West African Historical Museum at Cape Coast, sponsored by the Museum and Monuments Board and the University of Cape Coast, opened in 1971. The Ghana National Museum of Science and Technology is at Accra. There are regional museums at Ho and Kumasi, which is also home to the Ghana Armed Forces Museum. The University of Ghana has several museums in Legon, maintained by the departments of geology and archaeology, and a teaching museum run by the Institute of African Studies.

45 MEDIA

In 2009 there were 267,400 main phone lines and 15.1 million mobile cellular phones in use. Mobile phone subscriptions averaged 63 per 100 people.

The National Communications Authority (NCA) is responsible for broadcast media licensing. The government-owned Ghana Broadcasting Corp. makes radio services available throughout the country in English and six other languages; an international radio service beams programs in English, French, and Hausa to all parts of Africa. A government-owned television service was established in 1965. There were 86 FM radio stations and 3 shortwave radio stations. There were three semiprivate television stations, one government station, and three cable networks. In 2010, the country had 41,082 Internet hosts. As of 2009, there were some 1.29 million Internet users in Ghana, and Internet users numbered 5 per 100 citizens.

According to the National Media Commission (NMC), Ghana has 106 newspapers (11 dailies, 67 weeklies, 23 bi-weeklies, and 5 tri-weeklies). The state-owned *Daily Graphic* is the oldest and most widely-read newspaper in Ghana. The other state-owned newspaper, the *Ghanaian Times,* had circulation numbers of 40,000 in 2010.

The government dominates all media, and though it is said to tolerate the small independent print media, it is reported to repress dissenting opinions during election times. The constitution does provide for free speech and press. President Kufuor was a supporter of press freedom and repealed a libel law though maintained that the media had to act responsibly. This policy helped decrease tensions between the private media and government.

46 ORGANIZATIONS

Cooperatives have played an important role in marketing agricultural produce, especially cocoa. The Cocoa Research Institute of Ghana promotes growth and development in the national cocoa industry and sponsors research in techniques for processing cocoa, coffee, shea, and kola. Their work is extended through the Ghana Cocoa Marketing Board. The National Chamber of Commerce, with headquarters in Accra, has 13 district chambers. The Ghana Employers' Association strives to promote better relations between workers and business owners. There are unions for a variety of occupations.

There are professional organizations for a number of careers and many of these are dedicated to research and education within their field, such as the Ghana Medical Association. National cultural associations—including associations of writers, musicians, artists, dancers, and dramatists—have been established. The Ghana Science Association was founded in 1958. The Ghana Academy of Arts and Science was founded in 1959.

National youth organizations include the Agricultural Youth Association, the Democratic Youth League of Ghana, the Ghana Scout Association, National Union of Ghanaian Students, Presbyterian Young People's Guild of Ghana, Student Christian Movement of Ghana, Green Earth Youth Organization, and groups of the YMCA/YWCA. There are several sports associations promoting amateur competition in such pastimes as tennis, squash, baseball and track and field.

Ghana Wildlife Society is active in matters of conservation and environmental protection. The Environmental Protection Association of Ghana supports conservation and resource management efforts, but also serves as an advocate for community health and rural development issues.

Volunteer service organizations, such as the Lions Clubs and Kiwanis International, are also present. Ghana has active chapters of the Red Cross, Habitat for Humanity, and Amnesty International.

47 TOURISM, TRAVEL, AND RECREATION

Tourism has become a major economic factor as well and is regarded as a primary growth industry. In particular, the government has begun to consider development in the sports industry as a way to boost the economy. The country sponsored the African Cup of Nations tournament in 2008. The sports minister has initiated a development plan that would increase private sector involvement in building local sports facilities and establishing sports programs for youth and adults.

Major tourist attractions include casinos, fine beaches, game reserves, and old British, Dutch, and Portuguese trading forts and castles. Indigenous dance forms and folk music thrive in rural areas, and there are many cultural festivals. The National Cultural Center is in Kumasi, the capital of the Ashanti region, an area rich in traditional Ghanaian crafts. There is an Arts Center in Accra, as well as the National Museum, the Alwri Botanical Gardens, and the burial place of W. E. B. Du Bois. Football (soccer) is the main sport of Ghana, although cricket, boxing, body building, golf, basketball, and track and field are also popular. Visas, proof of sufficient funds, and an onward/return ticket are required of all visitors, as well as proof of yellow fever vaccination. The *Tourism Factbook,* published by the UN World Tourism Organization, reported 803,000 incoming tourists to Ghana in 2009; they spent a total of $1.05 billion. Of those incoming tourists, there were 324,000 from Africa and 187,000 from Europe. There were 29,645 hotel beds available in Ghana, which had an occupancy rate of 75%.

The estimated daily cost to visit Accra, the capital, was $319 in 2011. The cost of visiting other cities averaged $143.

48 FAMOUS PERSONS

J. E. Casely Hayford (1867–1930), for 13 years a member of the Legislative Assembly, is remembered as a leading public-spirited citizen. Dr. J. E. K. Wegyir Aggrey (1875–1927), noted educational reformer, played a large part in the development of secondary education. Sir Henley Coussey (1891–1958) and Sir Emmanuel Quist (1882–1959) were distinguished jurists.

Persons from overseas who played a great part in the progress of Ghana were the Rev. Alexander Gordon Fraser (1873–1962), the first principal of Achimota School; Sir (Frederick) Gordon Guggisberg (1869–1930), who took the first steps toward Africanization of the public service and was instrumental in founding Achimota School; and Sir Charles Noble Arden-Clarke (1898–1962), who was governor of the Gold Coast during the preparatory years of independence (1948–57) and the first governor-general of Ghana. The writer, sociologist, and civil rights leader W(illiam) E(dward) B(urghardt) Du Bois (b. US, 1868–1963) settled in Ghana in 1961 and is buried in Accra.

Kwame Nkrumah (1909–72), the first president of the republic, served in that capacity until the military coup of February 1966; he died in exile in Guinea. J. B. Danquah (1895–1965), a lawyer, was named vice-president of the UGCC at the time of its founding in 1947. Detained along with Nkrumah after the Accra riots in 1948, he later helped to found the GCP. Arrested by Nkrumah in 1961, and again in 1964, he died in prison in 1965. Kofi Abrefa Busia (1913–78), a noted sociologist, was prime minister from October 1969 to January 1972. Flight-Lieut. Jerry (John) Rawlings (b. 1947), the son of a Scottish father and a Ghanaian mother, led successful military coups in 1979 and 1981. He was elected president in 1992, and reelected in 1996. John Kufuor (b. 1938) was president from 2001 to 2009. Kofi Annan (b. 1938) was secretary general of the UN from 1997 to 2006.

⁴⁹DEPENDENCIES

Ghana has no territories or colonies.

⁵⁰BIBLIOGRAPHY

Conrad, David C. *Empires of Medieval West Africa: Ghana, Mali, and Songhay*. Rev. ed. New York: Facts On File, 2010.

Ghana Investment and Business Guide: Strategic and Practical Information. Washington, DC: International Business Publications USA, 2012.

Gocking, Roger. *The History of Ghana*. Westport, CT: Greenwood Press, 2005.

Greene, Sandra E. *Sacred Sites and the Colonial Encounter: A History of Meaning and Memory in Ghana*. Bloomington: Indiana University Press, 2002.

Kamoche, Ken M., ed. *Managing Human Resources in Africa*. New York: Routledge, 2004.

Lentz, Carola, and Paul Nugent, eds. *Ethnicity in Ghana: The Limits of Invention*. New York: St. Martin's Press, 2000.

Nanang, David M. *Plantation Forestry in Ghana: Theory and Applications*. Happauge, NY: Nova Science Publishers, 2012.

Newell, Stephanie. *Literary Culture in Colonial Ghana*. Bloomington: Indiana University Press, 2002.

Osei, Akwasi P. *Ghana: Recurrence and Change in a Post-Independence African State*. New York: P. Lang, 1999.

Owusu-Ansah, David. *Historical Dictionary of Ghana*. 3rd ed. Lanham, MD: Scarecrow Press, 2005.

Salm, Steven J. *Culture and Customs of Ghana*. Westport, CT: Greenwood Press, 2002.

Zeilig, Leo, and David Seddon. *A Political and Economic Dictionary of Africa*. Philadelphia: Routledge/Taylor and Francis, 2005.

GUINEA

Republic of Guinea
République de Guinée

CAPITAL: Conakry

FLAG: The national flag is a tricolor of red, yellow, and green vertical stripes.

ANTHEM: *Liberté (Liberty).*

MONETARY UNIT: The syli, of 100 cauris, was introduced in October 1972, replacing the Guinea franc (GNF). In January 1986 the Guinea franc of 100 centimes was restored on a one-to-one basis with the syli. There are notes of 25, 50, 100, 500, 1,000, and 5,000 francs. GNF1 = US$0.00016 (or US$1 = GNF6,100) as of 2010.

WEIGHTS AND MEASURES: The metric system is the legal standard.

HOLIDAYS: New Year's Day, 1 January; Labor Day, 1 May; Anniversary of Women's Revolt, 27 August; Referendum Day, 28 September; Independence Day, 2 October; Armed Forces Day, 1 November; Day of 1970 Invasion, 22 November; Christmas, 25 December. Movable religious holidays include Eid al-Fitr, Eid al-Adha, and Easter Monday.

TIME: GMT.

¹LOCATION, SIZE, AND EXTENT

Guinea, on the west coast of Africa, has an area of 245,857 sq km (94,926 sq mi), extending 831 km (516 mi) SE–NW and 493 km (306 mi) NE–SW. Comparatively, the area occupied by Guinea is slightly smaller than the state of Oregon. Bordered on the N by Senegal, on the N and NE by Mali, on the E by Côte d'Ivoire, on the S by Liberia and Sierra Leone, on the W by the Atlantic Ocean, and on the NW by Guinea-Bissau, Guinea has a total boundary length of 3,719 km (2,311 mi), of which 320 km (199 mi) is coastline.

Guinea's capital city, Conakry, is located on the country's Atlantic coast.

²TOPOGRAPHY

Guinea owes its frontiers mainly to the accidents of the late 19th-century partition of Africa and has no geographic unity. The country can be divided into four regions: Lower Guinea (Guinée Maritime), the alluvial coastal plain; Middle Guinea, the plateau region of the Futa Jallon (Fouta Djalon), deeply cut in many places by narrow valleys; Upper Guinea (Haute Guinée), a gently undulating plain with an average elevation of about 300 m (1,000 ft), savanna country broken by occasional rocky outcrops; and the forested Guinea Highlands (Guinée Forestière), composed of granites, schists, and quartzites, including Mt. Nimba (1,752 m/5,747 ft), the highest peak in the country, at the juncture of Guinea, Liberia, and Côte d'Ivoire. The Niger River and its important tributary the Milo have their source in the Guinea Highlands; the Gambia River and Senegal River (whose upper course is called the Bafing in Guinea) rise in the Futa Jallon.

³CLIMATE

The coastal region and much of the inland area have a tropical climate with a long rainy season of six months, a relatively high and uniform annual temperature, and high humidity. Conakry's year-round average high is 29°C (84°F), and the low is 23°C (73°F); its average rainfall is 430 cm (169 in) per year. April is the hottest month; July and August are the wettest. Rainfall in the Futa Jallon is much less (about 150–200 cm/60–80 in) and more irregular, and temperatures are lower; moreover, the daily temperature range is much greater, especially during the dry season. In Upper Guinea, rainfall is lower than in the Futa Jallon. Rainfall in the highlands averages about 280 cm (110 in) annually; temperatures are relatively equable owing to the altitude.

⁴FLORA AND FAUNA

The World Resources Institute estimates that there are 3,000 plant species in Guinea. In addition, Guinea is home to 215 mammal, 640 bird, 95 reptile, and 48 amphibian species. The calculation reflects the total number of distinct species residing in the country, not the number of endemic species. There are a large number of endemic plant and animal species in the country. Conservation International has identified the forests of the region as one of 25 global Biodiversity Hotspot.

Dense mangrove forests grow along the river mouths. Farther inland, the typical vegetation of Lower Guinea is woodland dominated by parinari, with many woody climbers and bushes below. Gum copal is common near streams. The Futa Jallon has been subject to excessive burning, and the lower slopes are characterized by secondary woodland, much sedge (*catagyna pilosa*), and expanses of laterite; the higher plateaus and peaks have dense forest, and some plants found nowhere else in the world have been reported on them. Savanna woodland characterizes Upper Guinea, with only tall grass in large areas; trees include the shea nut, tamarind, and locust bean. There is moist rain forest along the border with Liberia.

The elephant, hippopotamus, buffalo, lion, leopard, and many kinds of antelope and monkey are to be found in Guinea, as well as crocodiles and several species of venomous snakes. Other notable wildlife includes a population of forest elephants in the Ziama Biosphere Reserve. Guinea's chimpanzee populations have attracted attention for impressive tool use and other abilities including teaching each other how to disable traps set by poachers.

⁵ENVIRONMENT

The United Nations (UN) reported in 2008 that carbon dioxide emissions in Guinea totaled 1,389 kilotons.

Centuries of slash-and-burn agriculture have caused forested areas to be replaced by savanna woodland, grassland, or brush. Mining, the expansion of hydroelectric facilities, and pollution contribute to the erosion of the country's soils and desertification. The World Resources Institute reported that Guinea had designated 1.5 million hectares (3.71 million acres) of land for protection as of 2006.

Guinea enjoys moderate water resources due to its geographic location. Water resources totaled 226 cu km (54.22 cu mi) while water usage was 1.51 cu km (0.362 cu mi) per year. Domestic water usage accounted for 8% of total usage, industrial for 2%, and agricultural for 90%. Per capita water usage totaled 161 cu m (5,686 cu ft) per year. Water pollution and improper waste disposal are also significant environmental problems in Guinea. Water-borne diseases contribute to the high infant mortality rate.

Guinea's wildlife has been seriously impacted by human encroachment and hunting, while aquatic resources are threatened by overfishing. A nature reserve has been established on Mt. Nimba, the highest peak in the country, as a UNESCO World Heritage Site. There are also 16 Ramsar wetland sites. According to a 2011 report issued by the International Union for Conservation of Nature and Natural Resources (IUCN), the number of threatened species included 22 types of mammals, 13 species of birds, 4 types of reptiles, 5 species of amphibians, 65 species of fish, 4 species of other invertebrates, and 22 species of plants. Threatened species included the African elephant, Diana monkey, and Nimba otter-shrew.

⁶POPULATION

The US Central Intelligence Agency (CIA) estimates the population of Guinea in 2011 to be approximately 10,601,009, which placed it at number 79 in population among the 196 nations of the world. In 2011, approximately 3.5% of the population was over 65 years of age, with another 42.5% under 15 years of age. The median age in Guinea was 18.6 years. There were 1.00 males for every female in the country. The population's annual rate of change was 2.645%. The projected population for the year 2025 was 15,900,000. Population density in Guinea was calculated at 43 people per sq km (111 people per sq mi).

The UN estimated that 35% of the population lived in urban areas, and that urban populations had an annual rate of change of 4.3%. The largest urban area was Conakry, with a population of 1.6 million.

⁷MIGRATION

Estimates of Guinea's net migration rate, carried out by the CIA in 2011, amounted to zero. The total number of emigrants living abroad was 532,700, and the total number of immigrants living in Guinea was 394,600. After independence from France in 1958, Guineans left the country in increasing numbers, mostly for Senegal and Côte d'Ivoire. In the early and mid-1980s, probably two million Guineans were living abroad, perhaps half of them in Senegal and Côte d'Ivoire. Many of them returned after the end of the Sékou Touré regime in 1984.

In 1997 there were around 420,000 Liberians and around 250,000 from Sierra Leone in Guinea. These refugees escaped from the fighting in their respective countries. The voluntary repatriation program begun for Liberians in March 1998 was suspended at the resumption of fighting. Out of the 120,000 who opted for repatriation, some 80,000 were returned before the Guinean-Liberian border was closed. The UN High Commissioner for Refugees (UNHCR) resumed repatriation of Liberian refugees in 2004, with 90,000 returning by 2007. As of 2010 there were 21,856 refugees from Liberia, 5,259 from Sierra Leone, and 3,900 from Cote d'Ivoire.

⁸ETHNIC GROUPS

Of Guinea's two dozen ethnic groups, three predominate: the Fulani, Malinké, and Soussou. The Fulani (sometimes called Peul), perhaps the largest single group (40% of the population), live mainly in the Futa Jallon. The Malinké, referred to in other parts of West Africa as Mandingo, and related peoples of the so-called Nuclear Mandé group (30%), live in eastern Guinea and are concentrated around Kankan, Beyla, and Kouroussa. The Soussou (20%), with related groups, are centered farther west and along the coast in the areas around Conakry, Forécariah, and Kindia. Related to them are the Dialonké, living farther east in Middle Guinea and western Upper Guinea. Smaller tribes make up the remaining 10% of the population. Toward the southeast, in the Guinea Highlands near the borders of Liberia and Côte d'Ivoire, are various Kru or peripheral Mandé groups; among them are the Kissi around Quéckédou, the Toma around Macenta, and the Koranko near Kissidougou. Notable among the 3,500 or so non-Africans are Lebanese and Syrians.

⁹LANGUAGES

French is the official language and the language of administration. In 1967, a cultural revolution was announced for the purpose of "de-Westernizing" Guinean education. A literacy program begun in 1968 sought eventually to teach all citizens to speak and write one of the eight principal local languages: Malinké (Maninkakan), Fulani (Pular), Soussou, Kpelle (Guerzé), Loma (Toma), Kissi, Coniagui, and Bassari, all of which belong to the Niger-Congo language group. After the fall of the Touré regime in 1984, French was again emphasized; however, the tribal languages are still spoken.

¹⁰RELIGIONS

About 85% of all Guineans, particularly the Fulani and Malinké, are Muslims; about 10% follow various Christian faiths; and most of the remaining 5% practice traditional African animist religions. Most Muslims belong to the Sunni sect, and practices, particularly public prayers and the prescribed fasts, are often combined with animist beliefs and ceremonies.

Christian missions were established in the 19th century, but converts have been few. Among Christian groups are Roman

GUINEA

LOCATION: 8° to 15° W; 7°35′ to 12°30′N. BOUNDARY LENGTHS: Senegal, 330 kilometers (205 miles); Mali, 932 kilometers (579 miles); Côte d'Ivoire, 605 kilometers (376 miles); Liberia, 563 kilometers (350 miles); Sierra Leone, 652 kilometers (405 miles); Atlantic coastline, 352 kilometers (219 miles); Guinea-Bissau, 386 kilometers (240 miles). TERRITORIAL SEA LIMIT: 12 miles.

Catholics, Anglicans, Baptists, Jehovah's Witnesses, Seventh-Day Adventists, and various other evangelical churches. There are a small number of Baha'is, Hindus, Buddhists, and observers of traditional Chinese religions. Freedom of religion is guaranteed by the constitution and this right is generally respected in practice. Though there is no state religion, some have claimed that Islam is generally favored by the government. The Birth of the Prophet Muhammad, Easter Monday, Assumption Day, Eid al-Fitr, Tabaski, and Christmas are observed as national holidays. The government has met with the Interreligious Council, a group of Anglican, Catholic, and Protestant leaders, to open a dialogue on electoral and governmental reform issues.

¹¹TRANSPORTATION

The CIA reported that Guinea has a total of 44,348 km (27,557 mi) of roads as of 2003 (the most recent estimates of 2011), of which 4,342 km (2,698 mi) were paved. Guinea has approximately 1,300 km (808 mi) of navigable waterways. Still, lack of an adequate and modern transportation network has hindered the country's development. For instance, one of the state owned railways running from Conakry to Kankan and was built between 1900 and 1914.

Conakry has a natural deepwater harbor that handles foreign cargo (mostly bauxite and alumina). Port modernization is scheduled with aid from the IDA, the African Development Bank, and the Federal Republic of Germany (FRG). A deepwater port at Kamsar, completed in 1973, handles the output of the Boké bauxite mine, as much as nine million tons a year. There are lesser ports at Kassa, Benty, and Kakande. Shallow inland waterways are navigable only by shallow-draft native crafts. A national shipping line is jointly owned with a Norwegian company.

In 2009 there were an estimated five airports with paved runways. Conakry's airport, Gbeesia, handles international jet traffic. Gbeesia, three smaller airfields at Labé, Kankan, and Faranah, and a number of airstrips are served by the national carrier, Air Guinée, which also flies to other West African cities.

12 HISTORY

Archaeological evidence indicates that at least some stone tools found in Guinea had been made by peoples who had moved there from the Sahara, pushed perhaps by the desiccation that had occurred in the Saharan region by 2000 BC. Agriculture had been practiced along the coast of Guinea by AD 1000, with rice the staple crop.

Most of Upper Guinea fell within the area influenced by the Ghana empire at the height of its power, but none of present-day Guinea was actually within the empire. The northern half of present-day Guinea was, however, within the later Mali and Songhai empires.

The Malinké did not begin arriving in Guinea until the 13th century; nor did the Fulani come in considerable numbers until the 17th century. In 1725, a holy war (jihad) was declared in Futa Jallon by Muslim Fulani. The onslaught was directed against the non-Muslim Malinké and Fulani; and it led ultimately to the independence of the Fulani of Futa Jallon. It also gave effect to their unity within a theocratic kingdom under Almamy Karamoka Alfa of Timbo.

Meanwhile, European exploration of the Guinea coast had begun by the middle of the 15th century; it was led by the Portuguese. By the 17th century, French, British, and Portuguese traders and slavers were competing with one another. When the slave trade was prohibited during the first half of the 19th century, Guinean creeks became hiding places for slavers harried by the ships of the British Royal Navy. French rights along the coast were expressly preserved by the Peace of Paris (1814), and French—as well as British and Portuguese—trading activities expanded in the middle years of the 19th century, when trade in peanuts, palm oil, hides, and rubber replaced that in slaves. The French established a protectorate over Boké in 1849 and consolidated their rule over the coastal areas in the 1860s. This inevitably led to attempts to secure a more satisfactory arrangement with the Fulani chiefs of Futa Jallon. A protectorate was established over the region in 1881, but effective sovereignty was not secured for another 15 years.

Resistance to the French advance up the Senegal and the Niger, toward Lake Chad, came from Samory Touré, a Malinké born in Upper Guinea. He had seized Kankan in 1879 and established his authority in the area southeast of Siguiri; but his attacks had spurred the inhabitants of the area to seek aid from French troops already established at Kita in the French Sudan (Soudan Français, now Mali) in 1882. Samory had signed treaties with the French first in 1886, and also in 1890. But on various pretexts both he and the French later renounced the treaties; so hostilities resumed. His capture in 1898 marked the end of concerted local resistance to the French occupation of Guinea, Ivory Coast (now Côte d'Ivoire), and southern Mali.

In 1891 Guinea was reconstituted as a French territory separate from Senegal, of which it had hitherto been a part. Four years later, the French territories in West Africa became a federation under a governor-general. The federation remained substantially unchanged until Guinea attained independence. In 1946, Africans in Guinea became French citizens, but the franchise was at first restricted to the Europeanized évoulés; it was not replaced by universal adult suffrage until 1957.

The End of Colonial Rule

In September 1958, Guinea participated in the referendum on the new French constitution. On acceptance of the new constitution, French overseas territories had the option of choosing to continue their existing status, to move toward full integration into metropolitan France, or to acquire the status of an autonomous republic in the new quasi-federal French Community. If, however, they rejected the new constitution, they would become independent forthwith. French president, Charles de Gaulle, had made it clear that a country pursuing the independent course would no longer receive French economic and financial aid or retain French technical and administrative officers. Anyway, the electorate of Guinea rejected the new constitution overwhelmingly. Guinea accordingly became an independent state on 2 October 1958, with Ahmed Sékou Touré, then the leader of Guinea's strongest labor union, as president.

During its first three decades of independence, Guinea evolved to become a slightly militant socialist state. The functions and membership of the ruling Parti Démocratique de Guinée (PDG) were merged with the various institutions of government, including the state bureaucracy. Thus, the unified party-state had nearly complete control over the country's economic and political life. Guinea expelled the US Peace Corps in 1966 because of alleged involvement in a plot to overthrow President Touré. Similar charges were directed against France, with which diplomatic relations were severed in 1965 and not resumed until 1975. An ongoing source of contention between Guinea and its French-speaking neighbors was the estimated half-million expatriates in Senegal and Côte d'Ivoire. Some of these were active dissidents who, in 1966, had formed the National Liberation Front of Guinea (Front de Libération Nationale de Guinée—FLNG).

International tension rose again in 1970 when some 350 men, including FLNG partisans and Africans in the Portuguese army, invaded Guinea under the leadership of white Portuguese officers from Portuguese Guinea (now Guinea-Bissau). The invasion was repulsed after one day, but this was followed by waves of arrests, detentions, and some executions. Between 1969 and 1976, according to Amnesty International, 4,000 persons were detained for political reasons, with the fate of 2,900 unknown. After an alleged Fulani plot to assassinate Touré was disclosed in May 1976, Diallo Telli, a cabinet minister and formerly the first secretary-general of the OAU, was arrested and sent to prison, where he died without trial in November.

In 1977, protests against the regime's economic policy, which dealt harshly with unauthorized trading, led to riots in which three regional governors were killed. Touré responded by relaxing restrictions, offering amnesty to exiles (thousands of whom returned), and releasing hundreds of political prisoners. Ties with the Soviet bloc were relaxed as Touré sought increased Western aid and private investment in Guinea's sagging economy.

Single-list elections for an expanded National Assembly were held in 1980. Touré was elected unopposed to a fourth seven-year term as president on 9 May 1982. According to the government radio, he received 100% of the vote. A new constitution was adopted that month, and during the summer Touré visited the United States as part of an economic policy reversal that saw Guinea seeking Western investment to develop its huge mineral reserves. New measures announced in 1983 brought further economic liberalization; private traders were even allowed to engage in produce marketing.

Touré died on 26 March 1984 while undergoing cardiac treatment at the Cleveland Clinic; he had been rushed to the United States after being stricken in Saudi Arabia the previous day. Prime Minister Louis Lansana Béavogui then became acting president, pending elections that were to be held within 45 days. On 3 April, however, just as the Political Bureau of the ruling Guinea Democratic Party (PDG) was about to name its choice as Touré's successor, the armed forces seized power, denouncing the last years of Touré's rule as a "bloody and ruthless dictatorship." The constitution was suspended, the National Assembly dissolved, and the PDG abolished. The leader of the coup, Col. Lansana Conté, assumed the presidency on 5 April, heading the Military Committee for National Recovery (Comité Militaire de Redressement National—CMRN). About 1,000 political prisoners were freed.

Conté suppressed an attempted military coup led by Col. Diarra Traoré on 4 July 1985. Almost two years later, it was announced that 58 persons, including both coup leaders and members of Touré's government, had been sentenced to death. However, it is believed that many of them, as well as Traoré, had actually been shot days after the coup attempt. All were identified with the Malinké, who were closely identified with the Touré regime. The military regime adopted free-market policies in an effort to revive the economy.

Multiparty Democracy Initiated

Under pressure locally and abroad, Guinea embarked on a transition to multiparty democracy, albeit with considerable reluctance from the military-dominated government. Government legalized parties in April 1992, but it did not really allow them to function freely. It postponed presidential elections for over a year (until 19 December 1993) and then annulled the results from two Malinké strongholds, claiming victory with 51.7% of the vote. The Supreme Court upheld the Ministry of the Interior's decision despite official protest from the opposition. Though international opinion on the elections was divided, it was generally conceded that the elections administration had been widely manipulated in favor of the PUP candidate, and in several instances the voting process was fraudulent.

The legislative elections were delayed until 11 June 1995. These elections were supposed to have preceded the presidential elections, but the regime switched the order in 1993. The opposition felt that scheduling the presidential election first gave the incumbent an unfair advantage in both elections. International observers found significant flaws in these elections as well, and afterwards, the opposition vowed to boycott the Assembly. Factionalism within the opposition alliance, CODEM, shattered this resolve, and by the time the Assembly was convened, 71 PUP representatives and 43 members representing 8 other parties assumed their seats.

The greatest threat to Conté's power came in February 1996, when mutineers commanded tanks, fired upon the presidential palace, and seized the president. The palace was all but destroyed, and some 30 to 50 people were killed, many of them civilians by stray bullets. Conté did strike a deal with the mutineers, agreeing to establish a multiparty grievance committee; but the committee was disbanded before it could issue its final report. No one received a death sentence, though 38 soldiers received sentences, 34 of them colonels, majors, captains, and lieutenants. Only six were Susu, and four of them received the lightest sentences. Conté gave in to the mutineers' demands by doubling soldiers' pay and taking over the defense department himself.

In December 1998, Guinea held its second round of multiparty elections. Though it was technically more acceptable than previous polling, the PUP marshaled the resources of the state and the public bureaucracy to conduct its campaign up-country. The opposition submitted a report detailing fraudulent and illegal election and campaign practices by the ruling party. Further, the Guinean Human Rights Organization and Amnesty International accused the government of routine torture-stripping, tying up, and beating opposition militants.

Before the international borders were reopened, the government seized Malinké RPG leader Alpha Condé for allegedly attempting to cross into Côte d'Ivoire. He and four RPG parliamentarians, and some 70 RPG militants were jailed. The Condé trial was repeatedly delayed, and the charges were changed to "recruitment of mercenaries with intent to overthrow the government." It was suspended shortly after it began in April 2000 when Condé's lawyers and the Court failed to agree on the legality of the arrest and the charges. Condé was being tried along with 48 others in the Cour de Sûreté de l'Etat (State Security Court).

The political climate in May 2000 was uneasy with fear that the Alpha Condé affair would drag on unresolved. Legislative and local elections were scheduled for later in the year, but the opposition renewed its calls to boycott them. Despite this adversity, municipal elections were held in June 2000 accompanied by violence in at least seven cities leading to several civilian deaths. Reports of arrests, beatings, rapes, and torture of protesters followed. The opposition indicated that it would boycott the legislative elections unless a neutral arbiter, such as an independent electoral commission, was established.

In mid-September 2000, the State Security Court convicted Condé of sedition and sentenced him to five years hard labor in prison, though later he was granted clemency. Seven of his 47 co-accused received lighter sentences, while the others were acquitted. The international community overwhelmingly Condémned the trial as a mockery of justice. Condé's five-year sentence would eliminate him from running in the presidential elections slated for 2003.

What amounted to a constitutional coup took place in November 2001. In one fell swoop, Conté and the PUP-dominated National Assembly amended the constitution to increase the length of a presidential term from five years to seven, and to remove term limits. The amendment also allowed the president to nominate local government officials. In June 2002 flawed parliamentary elections resulted in the ruling party's gain of a two-thirds majority in the Assembly.

Conté's declining health once fueled speculation that that he might not stand for reelection in 2003. Guinea, it was also argued, risked political chaos if Conté failed to run. The army, which is deeply divided by age, ethnicity and other factors, was thought likely to intervene. Conté did run in elections held on 21 December however; and official results indicated that he won a massive 95.3% of the vote. In turn, Mamadou Boye Barry of the UPR captured 4.6%. Since then the Conté administration continued on as it were. As of 2005, soldiers had yet to oust the elected régime. In April 2004, former Prime Minister Sidya Toure and Ba Mamadou of the Union of Democratic Forces (UFDG) were barred from traveling to neighboring Senegal. Both claimed they were on a private mission. In January 2005, Conté survived an apparent assassination attempt, when shots were fired on his motorcade in the capital.

Conté died in December 2008, sparking yet another immediate military coup. The junta leader, Captain Moussa Dadis Camara, suspended the constitution and organized a new ruling council of 32 members. Under international pressure to restore civilian rule, the junta originally agreed to organize new parliamentary and presidential elections by the end of 2009. The schedule for elections was soon changed with presidential polls set for 2010. Camara declared that no junta members would run for office in the elections, despite encouragement from supporters.

In September 2009, over 50,000 opposition members staged a public rally in protest of Camara's supposed plans for candidacy. Guinean troops opened fire on the protestors, killing at least 128 people and injuring numerous others. There were also several reports of troops beating and raping female protestors. Camara denied having any knowledge of the rapes. The UN Condémned the violence and issued a call for restraint on behalf of the Guinean government.

In December 2009, Camara was shot in the head by Aboubacar Chérif Diakité, a senior aide who feared that the government would make him a scapegoat in the ICC investigation. Camara was immediately taken for treatment in Morocco. In January 2010, he was transferred to a facility in Burkina Faso to recuperate. Amid such government turmoil, Camara agreed to stay abroad and his deputy, Jean Marie Dore, was appointed as interim prime minister. In March 2010, the interim government announced that presidential elections would be held on 27 June 2010.

By May 2010, at least 120 political parties had formed in anticipation of the election. Noting that such a large number of potential candidates would be unrealistic, the commission decided that each candidate must make a deposit of $80,000 in order to be approved for the ballot. The $80,000 figure was chosen as a compromise among suggestions from various party leaders, as some of the larger parties hoped to set the fee at more than $160,000. Even so, several opposition parties already protested against the fee, which was decidedly high in a struggling economy.

The June 2010 vote represented Guinea's first democratic ballot since gaining independence from France in 1958. Among the 24 candidates in the race, former prime minister Cellou Dalein Diallo, from the Union of Democratic Forces of Guinea (UFDG), took the lead with 39.72% of the vote, followed by Alpha Condé, of the Guinea People's Rally (RPG), with 20.67%. Although the

vote was deemed peaceful, leaders from the RPG challenged some of the poll results. A runoff election was held on 7 November. The runoff resulted in a relatively close victory for Condé, with provisional results giving him 52% of the vote over Diallo, who won 47.5%. The announcement of the results led to a few violent protests among Diallo's supporters. For his part, Diallo called for peace, but stated that he would challenge the election results in the nation's Supreme Court.

In December 2010, the Supreme Court rejected Diallo's suit and declared that there was insufficient evidence of voter intimidation. The court also rejected an earlier challenge made by the RPG, following the first round of voting. Upon this announcement, Diallo conceded defeat. Tensions between supporters of Condé and Diallo, which at times led to violence, continued through 2011.

13 GOVERNMENT

Guinea is a multiparty republic with a semi-authoritarian executive. Guinea's first constitution took effect on 12 November 1958 and was substantially amended in 1963 and 1974. Under the new constitution promulgated in May 1982 (but suspended in the military coup of April 1984), sovereignty was declared to rest with the people and to be exercised by their representatives in the Guinea Democratic Party (PDG), the only legal political party. Party and state were declared to be one and indivisible. The head of state was the president, elected for a seven-year term by universal adult suffrage (at age 18). A national assembly of 210 members was elected in 1980 from a single national list presented by the PDG; the announced term was five years, although the 1982 constitution and its precursors stipulated a term of seven (the assembly was dissolved after four years, in 1984). The constitution gave Assembly members control of the budget and, with the president, the responsibility to initiate and formulate laws.

Under the Touré regime there was no separation of functions or powers. The legislature, the cabinet, and the national administration were subordinate to the PDG in the direction and control of the nation. The assembly served mainly to ratify the decisions of the PDG's Political Bureau, headed by Touré, who was also president of the republic and secretary-general of the PDG. The assembly and the cabinet (appointed by Touré) implemented the decisions and orders of the party arrived at by the party congress, national conference, and the Political Bureau. Locally, PDG and government authority were synonymous.

The armed forces leaders who seized power after Touré's death ruled Guinea through the Military Committee for National Recovery (CMRN). Following the adoption by referendum of a new constitution on 21 December 1990, the CMRN was dissolved and a Transitional Committee of National Recovery (CTRN) was set up in February 1991 as the country's legislative body.

In 1993, the government created a 114-member national assembly. The assembly members are elected for a term of four years, 38 members in single-district constituencies, and 76 members by proportional representation. In July 1996, Lansana Conté created the post of prime minister.

The legislature was dissolved in 2008 by Camara. Elections tentatively scheduled for the end of 2011 had not yet occurred as of February 2012.

¹⁴POLITICAL PARTIES

From 1945, when political activity began in Guinea, until about 1953, the political scene was one of loose electoral alliances that relied more on the support of traditional chiefs and of the French administration than on political programs or organized memberships. After 1953, however, these alliances rapidly lost ground to the Guinea section of the African Democratic Rally (Rassemblement Démocratique Africain—RDA), an interterritorial organization founded in 1946. This section, known as the Guinea Democratic Party (Parti Démocratique de Guinée—PDG), was formed by Marxists determined to develop an organized mass political movement that cut across ethnic differences and had a strongly nationalist outlook. Their leader was Ahmed Sékou Touré, a prominent trade union leader in French West Africa. Regarded as the great-grandson of the warrior-chief Samory who had fought the French in the late 19th century, Touré had much support in areas where Samory had fought his last battles. But his strongest backers were the Susu in Lower Guinea. In 1957, the PDG won 57 of 60 seats in Territorial Assembly elections.

Convinced that the French Community proposed by De Gaulle would not result in real independence for the people of French West Africa, Touré called for a vote against joining the Community in the referendum of 28 September 1958. Some 95% of those voting in Guinea supported Touré in opting for Guinea's complete independence. In December 1958, the opposition parties fused with Touré's PDG, making it the only political party in the country. The precipitous withdrawal of the French bureaucracy in 1958 led, almost of necessity, to the PDG's inheritance of much of the structure of government.

During the 1960s, the PDG's party machinery was organized down to the grassroots level, with local committees replacing tribal authorities, and sectional, regional, and national conferences ensuring coordination and control. In 1968, a new local unit within the PDG, the Local Revolutionary Command (Pouvoir Révolutionnaire Local—PRL) was organized. By 1973, the PRL had assumed complete responsibility for local economic, social, and political affairs. There were 2,441 PRLs in 1981, each directed by a committee of seven members and headed by a mayor. Each of the 35 regions had a party decision-making body called a Federal Congress, headed by a secretary. A 13-member Federal Committee, headed by the regional governor, was the executive body. The 170 districts had similar bodies, called sections, congresses, and committees.

The Political Bureau, nominally responsible to a Central Committee, was the PDG's chief executive body. Until the military coup that abolished the PDG in April 1984, the Political Bureau was the focus of party and national power, and its members were the most important government ministers and officials, with Touré as chairman. The PDG and its mass organizations were outlawed after the 1984 coup.

Political parties were legalized in April 1992. Within a month, more than 30 parties had been formed, a number by government ministers who helped themselves to state funds and used the state agencies to promote their campaigns. The use of government vehicles for partisan activities and the disbursement of state monies to supporters were commonplace.

By July 1992, government had banned all political demonstrations. This hampered opposition parties preparing for National Assembly elections then scheduled for late 1992 and presidential elections scheduled for early 1993. Elections were delayed. By October 1993, 43 political parties were legally registered. At least a dozen were allied with the government Party for Unity and Progress (PUP) while nearly thirty belonged to a loose coalition, the Democratic Forum, whose objective was to present a common candidate to run against Conté. The Forum dissolved when two of its members admitted they had already made their campaign deposit, which legally entitled them to enter the race. At that point, the field of candidates widened pitting seven opposition leaders against Conté. In December 1993, despite official protests by the opposition, Lansana Conté officially won 51.7% of the vote. International observers noted isolated incidents of violence and destruction of ballot boxes, and further declared the campaigning and balloting unsatisfactory.

In 1993, the most significant national opposition parties were the Rally for the Guinean People (RPG), the Union for a New Republic (UNR), and the Party for Renewal and Progress (PRP). The PRP and the UNR later merged to form the UPR, which presented Mamadou Ba as its candidate in the December 1998 elections. In these elections, Ba took second place with 24.6% of the vote, Alpha Condé (RPG) received 16.9%, Jean-Marie Doré received 1.7% (UPG), and Charles Pascal Tolno (PPG) claimed 1.0%. Again, under protest from the opposition, Conté won on the first round with 54.1% officially. In the elections of December 2003, Conté's share rose to a massive 95%.

In the National Assembly, 38 seats are elected by single-member district, and 76 are assigned by proportional voting. In elections held in June 2002, all 114 members of the national assembly were elected directly for five-year terms. The PUP won 61.6% of the vote and controlled 85 seats; the UPR captured 26.6% of the votes and 20 seats; while other parties shared 11.8% of the vote and 9 seats between them.

The presidential election of June 2010 represented Guinea's first democratic ballot since gaining independence from France in 1958. With 24 candidates in the race, the top two were former prime minister Cellou Dalein Diallo from the Union of Democratic Forces of Guinea (UFDG), who captured 39.72% of the vote, and Alpha Condé of the Guinea People's Rally (RPG), who took 20.67%. While the vote was deemed peaceful, leaders from the RPG challenged some of the poll results. Since no candidate won the 50% required to win the election, a runoff was held on 7 November. The runoff resulted in a relatively close victory for Condé, with provisional results giving him 52% of the vote over Diallo, who won 47.5%. The announcement of the results led to a few violent protests among Diallo's supporters. For his part, Diallo called for peace, but stated that he would challenge the election results in the nation's supreme court.

The rivalry between Condé's RPG and Diallo's UFDG continued throughout 2011. Legislative elections scheduled for December 2011 had not occurred as of February 2012. Diallo claimed that prospects for a fair election were limited, with Condé having installed a personal friend as leader of CENI, the National Election Commission.

¹⁵LOCAL GOVERNMENT

Under the Touré regime, the local units of the PDG, the local revolutionary commands (PRLs), were responsible for the political and economic administration of rural areas. In principle, the PRLs regulated all commerce, farming, distribution of land, public works, and communications, as well as civil life and the people's courts in communities under their authority. Each PRL had a company of militia of 101 members, subdivided into 4 platoons and 12 groups.

In the early 1990s, Guinea embarked upon an ambitious decentralization program. Three hundred and three rural development communities (CRDs) were created each comprising several districts (groupings of villages). The 303 CRDs were divided proportionately among the existing 33 prefectures, and four natural regions. In 1994, the number of regions was increased to seven headed by governors appointed by the president. The prefectures are under the tutelage of appointed prefects, who in turn supervise sub-prefects. A sub-prefecture is the location for public services within a CRD.

CRDs and the districts within them represent the most decentralized political and financial public authority. Elections for CRD councils were last held in 1991, and little investment has made in them. However, through training and other investments, some CRDs have begun collecting hut, market, truck-stop, gravel pit, forestry, and other taxes. They have also begun to establish local development plans for schools, clinics, and mosques.

On 25 June 2000, the government organized municipal elections, which had been postponed from 29 June 1999 to December 1999, and then to June 2000 reportedly for budgetary reasons. The PUP ruling party claimed victory in 31 of Guinea's 38 communes, the Union for Progress and Renewal (UPR) won five local councils, the Assembly of Guinean People (RPG) one, and the Fight for Common Cause (LCC)—allied with the PUP—took one. Voter turnout was only 54%, or less than one-third of the adult population.

16 JUDICIAL SYSTEM

The judicial system is based on French civil law, customary law, and decree; legal codes are under revision, and Guinea has not accepted compulsory ICJ jurisdiction. In 1958 and 1965, the government introduced some customary law, but retained French law as the basic framework for the court system.

The system is composed of courts of first instance, two Courts of Appeal (in Kankan and in Conakry) and the Supreme Court. There is also a State Security Court (Cour de Sûreté de l'Etat), which tried the 1985 coup plotters, and conducted the Alpha Condé trial in 1999–2000. The legality of this court was debated in the February 1996 putsch. The Supreme Court ruled in favor of its validity since it predated the 1990 constitution, and the constitution failed to specifically address its existence. A military tribunal exists to handle criminal cases involving military personnel.

A traditional system of dispute resolution exists at the village and neighborhood level. Cases unresolved at this level may be referred to the courts for further consideration. The traditional system has been found to discriminate against women.

Although the 1990 constitution guarantees the independence of the judiciary, magistrates have no tenure and are susceptible to influence by the executive branch. The penal code provides for the presumption of innocence, the equality of citizens before the law, the right to counsel, and the right to appeal a judicial decision. This code is supported by the constitution, which provides

for the inviolability of the home; judicial search warrants are required by law. In reality, police and paramilitary personnel often ignore these legal protections.

In September 1996, the government announced the creation of a discipline council for dealing with civil servants who abuse their positions in the government. In June 1998, a special arbitration court was established to resolve business disputes.

17 ARMED FORCES

The International Institute for Strategic Studies reports that armed forces in Guinea totaled 12,300 members in 2011. The force is comprised of 8,500 from the army, 400 from the navy, 800 from the air force, 1,000 from the gendarmerie, and 1,600 members of the republican guard. Armed forces represented 0.4% of the labor force in Guinea. Defense spending totaled $119.9 million and accounted for 1.1% of GDP.

The CIA reported in 2009 that compulsory military service of 18 months existed for Guinean nationals between the ages of 18 and 25.

18 INTERNATIONAL COOPERATION

Guinea was admitted to the UN on 12 December 1958 and is a member of ECA and several nonregional specialized agencies. It is a member of the WTO. Guinea also belongs to the African Development Bank, the ACP Group, G-77, the New Partnership for Africa's Development (NEPAD), and the African Union. Guinea became a partner with Sierra Leone and Liberia in the Mano River Union in 1980, when it also joined Gambia and Senegal as a member of the Gambia River Development Organization. Guinea is also a member of the Economic Community of West African States (ECOWAS), although it was temporarily suspended prior to the Dec 2010 elections. The government is participating in efforts to establish a West African Monetary Zone (WAMZ) that would include The Gambia, Ghana, Guinea, Liberia, Nigeria, and Sierra Leone. In addition, Guinea belongs to the Niger Basin Authority and the Organization of the Islamic Conference (OIC). The International Bauxite Association was established in Conakry in 1974 with Guinea as a charter member. Guinea is part of the Non-aligned Movement.

In environmental cooperation, the country is part of the Basel Convention, Conventions on Biological Diversity and Whaling, Ramsar, CITES, the Kyoto Protocol, the Montréal Protocol, and the UN Conventions on the Law of the Sea, Climate Change, and Desertification.

19 ECONOMY

The GDP rate of change in Guinea, as of 2010, was 1.9%. This was an increase over the poor performance of 2009 (-0.3%). Inflation stood at 20% in 2010 according to the CIA.

Guinea remains one of the poorest countries in the world, despite its great development potential and wealth of natural resources. During its first years of independence, the Guinean government controlled the country's land and economy, and severely restricted the development of an industrial sector. Guinea has since worked to privatize many state-owned enterprises, though the country's weak infrastructure has hampered efforts at economic improvement. Around 76% of Guinea's work force is engaged in subsistence farming and approximately 47% of the country's population lives below the poverty line. The country has significant mineral resources and is working on developing its mining industry. It is believed that Guinea contains up to 50% of the world's reserves in bauxite. There are also significant reserves of iron ore, diamonds, and gold, and an undetermined amount of uranium. The mining sector accounts for about 70% of all exports.

For two decades after French withdrawal in 1958 the country was governed according to socialist-style economic management. Agriculture was collectivized and private commerce and industry repressed. In 1984, a major reform movement gained political power and reforms were instituted, aimed at developing a modern market economy. The collective farms were abolished, state-owned enterprises were liquidated, compulsory marketing through state agencies was abolished, food prices were decontrolled, and the government began actively to seek foreign investment for sectors other than mining and energy. Although the reforms were largely successful, the economy has been restrained by an underdeveloped infrastructure, including poor roads and communications systems, a lack of electricity, a weak judicial system, and unskilled workers. High levels of debt, unemployment, and underemployment also hamper economic progress.

To regain favor with the World Bank and IMF, the government instituted economic reforms in 2004. Price controls were loosened, government spending reduced, and tax collection improved. Unfortunately, inflation spiked after the reforms reaching 35% in 2005. This development was triggered by panic buying after the Liberian and Sierra Leonian conflicts. The result was a depreciated economy that left the population unable to afford food and fuel.

The country benefited slightly from the global demand for commodities in 2007, inching the growth rate up to about 2%. The 2008–09 global financial crisis slightly reduced demand for these commodities. Long term growth, however, is dependent on structural reforms that would improve the economic infrastructure.

The drug trade played an increasingly important role in Guinea's economy through 2011. In 2008 the UN Office on Drugs and Crime reported that greater quantities of Colombian drugs were being smuggled through Guinea en route to Europe. In November 2009 the son of the late President Lansana Conte was charged with drug trafficking.

20 INCOME

The CIA estimated that in 2010 the GDP of Guinea was $10.81 billion. The CIA defines GDP as the value of all final goods and services produced within a nation in a given year and computed on the basis of purchasing power parity (PPP) rather than value as measured on the basis of the rate of the exchange based on current dollars. The per capita GDP was estimated at $1,000. The annual growth rate of GDP was 1.9%. The average inflation rate was 20%. It was estimated that agriculture accounted for 25.8% of GDP, industry 45.7%, and services 28.5%.

According to the World Bank, remittances from citizens living abroad totaled $63.7 million or about $6 per capita and accounted for approximately 0.6% of GDP.

The World Bank reports that in 2009, household consumption in Guinea totaled $5.4 billion or about $508 per capita, measured in current US dollars rather than PPP. Household consumption includes expenditures of individuals, households, and nongovernmental organizations on goods and services, excluding the pur-

chases of dwellings. It was estimated that household consumption was growing at an average annual rate of 7.9%.

As of 2011 the most recent study by the World Bank reported that actual individual consumption in Guinea was 70.2% of GDP and accounted for 0.02% of world consumption. By comparison, the United States accounted for 25.44% of world individual consumption. The World Bank also estimated that 31.8% of Guinea's GDP was spent on food and beverages, 9% on housing and household furnishings, 4.7% on clothes, 8.3% on health, 5.4% on transportation, 0.2% on communications, 0.8% on recreation, 1.4% on restaurants and hotels, and 3.8% on miscellaneous goods and services and purchases from abroad.

21 LABOR

As of 2007, Guinea had a total labor force of 4.392 million people. Within that labor force, CIA estimates in 2006 noted that 76% were employed in agriculture, 12% in industry, and 12% in the service sector.

Most of the population relies on subsistence farming. Most of the wage and salary earners work in the public sector; mining is the other major source of salaried employment.

Guinea's Labor Code permits all workers (except military and paramilitary) to create and participate in labor organizations. The General Workers Union of Guinea (UGTG) and the Free Union of Teachers and Researchers of Guinea (SLECG) have emerged since the code ended the previously existing trade union monopoly system. However, the National Confederation of Guinean Workers (CNTG) remains the largest labor organization. Collective bargaining is protected by law. Salaried workers, including public sector civilian employees, have the right to strike, provided that they have given 10 days' notice of an intent to strike and that they are not engaged in an essential service. About 5% of the workforce is unionized.

The minimum working age is 16, and is enforced for large firms working in the formal economy. However, most children work, either in the informal economy or in agriculture. The work-week is technically 48 hours, but most people work longer hours. The labor code has provisions for a minimum wage but the government has yet to establish one, and most workers do not earn a living wage.

22 AGRICULTURE

Roughly 7% of the total land is farmed, and the country's major crops include rice, coffee, pineapples, palm kernels, cassava (tapioca), bananas, and sweet potatoes. In 2009 cereal production amounted to 2.7 million tons, fruit production 1.2 million tons, and vegetable production 409,433 tons.

The agricultural sector of the economy has stagnated since independence. The precipitate withdrawal of the French planters and removal of French tariff preference hurt Guinean agriculture, and drought conditions during the 1970s also hindered production.

Price controls have also had a dampening effect on output. In theory, until the reforms of the early 1980s, the state controlled the marketing of farm produce. However, even during the late 1970s, when all private trade in agricultural commodities was illegal, only a small amount of agricultural production actually passed through the state distribution system; some 500,000 private smallholders reportedly achieved yields twice as high as government collectives, despite having little or no access to government credit or research and extension facilities. During the 1970s and early 1980s, agricultural exports fell markedly, and food production decreased, necessitating rice imports of at least 70,000 tons a year. (In 1984, a drought year, 186,000 tons of cereal had to be imported.) However, some restrictions on marketing were removed in 1979 and 1981; more recently, prices were decontrolled and many state farms and plantations dissolved. These steps appeared to bring improvements.

23 ANIMAL HUSBANDRY

The UN Food and Agriculture Organization (FAO) reported that Guinea dedicated 10.7 million hectares (26.4 million acres) to permanent pasture or meadow in 2009. During that year, the country tended 20.1 million chickens, 4.7 million head of cattle, and 90,700 pigs. The production from these animals amounted to 47,960 tons of beef and veal, 1,957 tons of pork, 10,596 tons of poultry, 17,513 tons of eggs, and 140,282 tons of milk. Guinea also produced 9,523 tons of cattle hide.

The Fulani tend to dominate animal husbandry. Almost all the cattle are the small, humpless Ndama variety kept by the Fulani in Futa Jallon and Upper Guinea, where sheep and goats also are herded. The Ndama cattle are not susceptible to animal trypanosomiasis and, although very small, their yield in meat is good.

24 FISHING

Guinea's annual ocean fisheries potential exceeds 200,000 tons, according to World Bank estimates. Domestic artisanal fisherman only catch about 13% of the estimated annual yield. Guinea had 16 decked commercial fishing boats in 2008. The annual capture totaled 74,000 tons according to the UN FAO. The export value of seafood totaled $183,000. Tuna is the most important catch. Many species found in Guinean waters are among the richest in West Africa and command high value. A 1990 agreement with the European Union reflected a growing investment interest in the fishing sector. Since then, several small scale fishing ventures have been established, including a shrimp farming project financed by the African Development Bank, and development of private cold storage facilities in 14 different prefectures.

25 FORESTRY

Approximately 26% of Guinea is covered in forests. A further 24% of the country is covered in other wooded land such as savanna and partially deforested areas. The UN FAO estimated the 2009 roundwood production at 651,000 cu m (23 million cu ft). The value of all forest products, including roundwood, totaled $11.7 million.

The nation's forest resources have great economic potential, the major constraint on development being lack of adequate transportation. Important luxury woods like mahogany and rosewood grow in Guinean forests. Logging and sawmill facilities have been built in the Nzérékoré area.

26 MINING

Guinea's mineral production in 2009 consisted primarily of bauxite, cement, diamonds, gold, and salt. The country also had deposits of graphite, iron, limestone, uranium, nickel and manganese. However, these deposits remained undeveloped. In 2009, Guinea

was the world's fifth-leading bauxite producer. The mineral industry accounted for 67% of the $385.9 million in foreign direct investment in 2008.

The government has claimed that Guinea had 20 billion tons of bauxite reserves, with proven reserves of 18 billion tons. In 2009, Guinea's mine output of bauxite totaled an estimated 15.6 million metric tons wet-basis bauxite (metallurgical plus calcinable ore estimated to be 13% water), and 13.6 million metric tons dry-basis bauxite (wet-basis ore reduced to dry-basis, estimated to be 3% water). There was no recorded production from 2002 through 2009 of calcined bauxite.

In 2009, Guinea produced an estimated 18,091 kg of gold, including artisanal production, down from 19,945 kg in 2008. Artisanal production of gold was sold either directly to the Central Bank of Guinea or to collectors and ranges between 1,500 to 5,000 kg per year. Diamond production, including artisanal, in 2009 totaled 697,000 carats, of which 70–80% were of gem quality. Alumina production in 2009 was estimated at 530,000 metric tons. The country also produced cement, clays, salt, sand and gravel, and stone.

Iron ore was mined at Kaloum until 1967. Larger, richer deposits have been found in the Mount Nimba and Simandou mountain areas, along the Liberian border. In 1974, the Mifergui-Simandou and Mifergui-Nimba mining companies were formed to exploit the deposits, with the government retaining half interest in the firms. Reserves were estimated at 300–600 million tons. There was no iron ore production recorded during 2004–2009.

Several mining companies withdrew from mineral exploration projects in 2009. Prospecting and exploring are likely to slow down in the short run due to lack of a legislative framework that adequately defines the rights and obligations of investors and the government.

27 ENERGY AND POWER

The World Bank reported in 2008 that Guinea produced 920 million kWh of electricity and consumed 869.3 million kWh, or 82 kWh per capita. Guinea's electric power sector relies on hydropower and conventional thermal fuel to generate power.

In 2011 the CIA reported that Guinea has no known proven reserves of oil or natural gas. However, a Norwegian and Dutch company were exploring potential offshore reserves in 2010. Guinea also has no known coal reserves nor any oil refining capacity. The country must import whatever refined petroleum products or fossil fuels it consumes. In 2009, the CIA reported oil imports of 8,559 barrels per day. There were no imports or consumption of natural gas or coal in that year.

28 INDUSTRY

Industry accounted for 57% of GDP in 2010, 9% of which consisted of manufacturing. The manufacturing growth rate for 2010 was 3%. During the socialist years, a sizeable parastatal industrial sector emerged. Guinea had 234 state-run enterprises in 1985, but fewer than 60 remained in the government's portfolio a decade later. Manufacturing in Guinea consists of three elements: public enterprises with large staffs, producing below capacity; small private businesses, mostly engaged in producing beverages, bread, bricks,

Principal Trading Partners – Guinea (2010)

(In millions of US dollars)

Country	Total	Exports	Imports	Balance
World	2,550.0	1,450.0	1,100.0	350.0
China	513.5	50.0	463.5	-413.6
India	409.8	322.5	87.3	235.1
Chile	391.6	390.0	1.6	388.4
Netherlands	345.6	1.4	344.2	-342.8
France	215.5	47.4	168.2	-120.8
United States	197.0	103.3	93.7	9.6
Spain	187.2	157.8	29.3	128.5
Ireland	163.0	120.1	42.9	77.2
Russia	147.4	141.3	6.1	135.2
Belgium	136.1	62.3	73.8	-11.6

(…) data not available or not significant.

(n.s.) not specified.

SOURCE: *2011 Direction of Trade Statistics Yearbook*, New York: United Nations, 2011.

Balance of Payments – Guinea (2010)

(In millions of US dollars)

Current Account		**-329.2**
Balance on goods	66.3	
Imports	-1,404.9	
Exports	1,471.2	
Balance on services	-333.1	
Balance on income	-47.1	
Current transfers	14.7	
Capital Account		**16.9**
Financial Account		**313.4**
Direct investment abroad	…	
Direct investment in Guinea	101.4	
Portfolio investment assets	-0.1	
Portfolio investment liabilities	…	
Financial derivatives	…	
Other investment assets	-77.4	
Other investment liabilities	289.5	
Net Errors and Omissions		**38.7**
Reserves and Related Items		**-39.8**

(…) data not available or not significant.

SOURCE: *Balance of Payment Statistics Yearbook 2011*, Washington, DC: International Monetary Fund, 2011.

carpentry, and boilers/metalwork; and small nonindustrial units informally employing persons in a wide variety of occupations.

Among Guinea's other plants are agro-food processors, including a fruit cannery at Mamou, a fruit juice factory at Kankan, a tea factory at Macenta, a palm oil works at Kassa, a small tobacco factor at Beyla, two peanut oil works, at Dabola and at Agola, rice mills, a sugar complex consisting of two dams, a plantation, and a refinery. A textile complex at Sanoyah, a cement and plastics factories at Conakry, and a number of construction material plants are in operation. There is potential to develop a pharmaceuticals industry in Guinea.

Aluminum and bauxite are staples of the Guinean industrial economy. Global Alumina, a US based mining company is planning to open a $5.6 billion alumina refinery in Sangaredi. By 2008, the refinery was expected to reach full production but was delayed due to the 2008 political instability. As of April 2011 Global Alumina and its partner BHP were optimistic about resumption of construction.

In October 2009, Guinean authorities announced that the government had signed a major mining and oil investment deal with China, through which a Chinese development firm, the China International Fund, pledged to provide over $7 billion for infrastructure development in Guinea, including ports, railways, power plants, an administrative center, and low-cost housing in and around the capital of Conakry. The agreement was overturned in 2011 as part of a government effort to retain more control over industrial development and natural resources.

29 SCIENCE AND TECHNOLOGY

The World Bank reported in 2009 that there were no patent applications in science and technology in Guinea. The National Directorate for Scientific and Technical Research is in Conakry. The Center for Rice Research is in Kankan. The Pasteur Institute for Animalculture Research and the Institute for Fruit Research are in Kindia. Five colleges and universities, including the University Gamal Abdel Nasser in Conakry, offer degrees in basic and applied sciences.

30 DOMESTIC TRADE

Commerce was severely controlled through state trading enterprises until the end of the socialist era in 1984. Private Guinean traders can now import freely, the government having ended in 1992 its monopoly on imports of petroleum and pharmaceuticals. Prices for all goods other than imported rice and petroleum products were deregulated in 1986 and the private sector was permitted to engage in all levels of internal and external marketing. However, internal corruption and political conflicts have dissuaded foreign investment which is sorely needed to jump start commercial activity.

Business hours are 7:30 a.m. to 3 p.m., Monday through Thursday, 7:30 a.m. to 1 p.m. on Friday, and 7:30 a.m. to 1 p.m. on Saturday. Banks are normally open from 8 a.m. to 12:30 p.m., Monday through Saturday. French is the official language of businesses.

31 FOREIGN TRADE

Guinea imported $1.405 billion worth of goods and services in 2010, while exporting $1.468 billion worth of goods and services. Major import partners in 2010 were China, 11.5%; Netherlands, 6.3%; and France, 4.2%.. Its major export partners were India, 15.5%; Spain, 8%; Chile, 7.7%; Russia, 6.8%; Ireland, 6.1%; Ukraine, 5.7%; US, 5.2%; Denmark, 4.2%; Germany, 4.1%.

The mining industry accounted for about 70% of export earnings during the 2000s, including mostly bauxite and alumina, but also gold. In 2010 mining remained paramount, with bauxite, alumina, gold, and diamonds as the most important exports followed by coffee, fish, and agricultural products.

³²BALANCE OF PAYMENTS

In 2010 Guinea had a foreign trade deficit of $269 million, amounting to 3.3% of GDP. Ten years prior, Guinea had a trade surplus of $139.3 million.

³³BANKING AND SECURITIES

The Central Bank of Guinea acts as the nation's central bank. It was founded in 1960 after Guinea withdrew from the Central Bank of the West African States (Banque Centrale des États de l'Afrique de l'Ouest—BCEAO). In 2005, the discount rate, the interest rate at which the central bank lends to financial institutions in the short term, was 22.25%. More recent discount rate figures were unavailable as of early 2012. In 2010 the commercial bank prime lending rate, the rate at which banks lend to customers, was 24%.

There are six commercial banks in Guinea, including the Banque Internationale pour le commerce et l'industrie de la Guinée (BICIGUI); the Societe Generale des Banques en Guinee (SGBG); the Banque Islamique de Guinee (BIG); the Unione Internationale des Banques en Guinee (UIBG); and the International Commercial Bank de Guinée (ICBG), which was launched in Conakry in early November 1996. All involve French or US participation. However, there are no US banks operating in Guinea.

The commercial banking system in Guinea is marked by a high degree of fragility, a narrow financial base, and lending policies that are averse to risk, and are highly conservative. As a result, there is little money available to finance large investments. Instead, the banks focus on short-term lending with high interest rates, preferring to finance trade.

There are no securities exchanges in Guinea.

³⁴INSURANCE

There is a national insurance company, the National Society of Insurance and Reinsurance, and at least five other major companies based in Conakry.

³⁵PUBLIC FINANCE

In 2010 the CIA reported that the government of Guinea's budget was funded with $760.6 million in revenues but expenditures totaled $1.411 billion. The budget deficit was 14.3% of GDP. Taxes accumulated to 16.2% of GDP.

Guinea did not have a formal government budget until 1989. Since then, overly optimistic revenue projections, increasing civil service salaries and military expenditures, and diversion of public funds have resulted in deficits.

Total external debt was $2.843 billion in 2010.

³⁶TAXATION

Personal income and capital gains are taxed at 35%, which is also the corporate tax rate. Social security contributions totaled 18%. In 1996, the government introduced a value-added tax (VAT). In 2011 the standard rate was set at 18%. Exports, international transportation, and basic food items are exempted.

³⁷CUSTOMS AND DUTIES

Since 1994, import taxes have steadily increased. Import licenses are required for all imports regardless of country of origin and import duties are levied uniformly. Prohibited imports included arms, military equipment, and narcotics. There was also an 18% VAT on all imported products.

³⁸FOREIGN INVESTMENT

Foreign direct investment (FDI) in Guinea was a net inflow of $49.8 million according to World Bank figures published in 2009. FDI represented 1.21% of GDP. For comparison, the CIA reported in 2010 that investment was equivalent to 21.3% of GDP.

Guinea's national identity rests on its proud refusal to enter the French community in 1958 and its offers of economic assistance in exchange for political independence. Even though the country has gone through substantial political and economic liberalization since the passing of independence hero, Sékou Touré, in 1984, the legacy still inhibits the embrace of foreign investment. The only sectors of the economy in which private foreign investment were originally allowed after independence were mining and energy, but in the early 1980s agricultural investment was also being sought. During 1983–85, direct foreign investment amounted to $2.2 million.

An investment code following the 1984 coup indicated a new emphasis on private investment and incentives. It was replaced by the currently applicable investment code of 1987, as amended in 1995, which pledged national treatment, free repatriation of capital, special incentives for small and medium-size enterprises, nonmining exports, enterprises using over 70% local inputs, and those locating outside of Conakry. In 1989, under donor pressure, the government leased the operation of Conakry's water supply in a 10-year contract to a consortium led by the SARU and Vivendi companies of France operating as the management company SEEG (Société de Exploitation des Eaux de Guinée). After initial gains in efficiency, SEEG could not make further headway against nepotism and corruption and could not devise a way to get the government to pay its bills. Although the contract was renewed in June 2001, the private companies left in frustration. In 2003, under drought conditions, repeated riots in Conakry have protested the scarcity of water and electricity.

In 1992, investment policies were liberalized to permit private ventures in most sectors, including mining and telecommunications, and the Office of Private Investment Promotion (OPIP) was established as a one-stop shop to facilitate the process. By the revised mining code of 1995, foreigners could own up to 85% of mining ventures.

Diamond mining in Guinea has recently attracted explorations by De Beers (South Africa), Hymex and Trivalence Mining Corporations (Canadian), and Aredor Holding Company (Australia). Aredor has a reputation for nontransparent operations in gold mining in Guinea, leaving a few government officials wealthy and the local population with only a degraded and polluted environment. Gold mining in Guinea, like diamond mining, has until recently been mainly traditional and informal (illegal), but the Ghanaian company, Ashanti Goldfields, has operations in Guinea.

Some of the main concerns of foreign investors are the need for a stable judicial and economic framework, and increased stability along Guinea's southern borders.

³⁹ECONOMIC DEVELOPMENT

After independence, French-held financial, commercial, industrial, and distributive organizations were expropriated, and the national economy was divided into three sectors: a state sector, a mixed sector, and a sector for guaranteed private investment. By the mid-1970s, the private sector had become insignificant, and government policy increasingly leaned toward greater government control of the mixed enterprises and the state-sector companies. The 1987–91 recovery program called for $670 million in spending through 1989, with 42% for infrastructure and 24% for rural development. A major aim was to diversify the economy and reduce the heavy reliance on bauxite.

By 1990, the government had privatized the majority of its 180 public enterprises and closed over 300 state farms. From 1990 to 2000, the pace of structural reform slowed and debts increased as the economy failed to diversify. The Islamic Development Bank (IDB) granted two new loans to Guinea in 1997, and the Paris Club rescheduled a large portion of Guinea's bilateral debt, forgiving 50% of debt to France, and Russia forgave 70% of bilateral debt.

The government in recent years has taken steps to stimulate investment, encourage private-sector commercial activity, reduce the role of the state in the economy, and improve administrative and judicial frameworks. The government has also increased spending on education, health, infrastructure, banking, and justice sectors, and cut the government bureaucracy. Corruption and nepotism hamper economic development.

In 2000, Guinea was granted $800 million in debt relief under the International Monetary Fund (IMF)/World Bank Heavily Indebted Poor Countries (HIPC) initiative. In 2001, Guinea negotiated a three-year $81.3 million Poverty Reduction and Growth Facility (PRGF) Arrangement with the IMF, geared to support the country's efforts to stabilize the economy, promote growth, improve social services, and reduce poverty.

In 2003, the World Bank and the IMF cut off most of the financial assistance, and currently Guinea is not receiving any multilateral aid. The modest growth registered in 2005 was primarily caused by an increase in global demand and commodity prices on world markets. Although the inflation rate rose rapidly in 2004 and 2005 (to 35%), it since has reduced somewhat to 20% in 2010. Mining was expected to continue to be the prime growth engine, with most of the other sectors expected to stagnate in the short term. Government legislation in 2011 sought to increase government oversight of the mining industry in order to reduce corruption and protect the environment.

⁴⁰SOCIAL DEVELOPMENT

In the UN's 2011 Human Development Report, Guinea was ranked 178 in the world on the Human Development Index, an index including a mix of economic, health, educational, and quality of life factors.

There was a regression of social services during the Touré years. Although government sought to establish extensive social programs, they were badly organized and managed and, in the end, the treasury was empty. In 1994, social security legislation was updated, providing pensions at age 55 and cash sickness benefits for employed persons. Work injury laws, initiated in 1932, covers employed persons including agricultural salaried workers, domestic workers, apprentices, interns, and students at technical school. Officially, free medical treatment is available, as well as free care for pregnant women and for infants. In reality, health service is poor, and life expectancy is among the lowest in the world.

Women traditionally play a subordinate role in family and public life. The law prohibits discrimination based on gender, but is not effectively enforced. Violence against women is common, but the courts rarely intervene in domestic disputes. Inheritance customs favor male children over female children. Divorce laws favor men in awarding property and custody of children. Female genital mutilation (FGM), a practice that is both painful and often life-threatening, continues to be practiced in all parts of the country. A 2007 report by German Technical Cooperation (GIZ) found that 94% of surveyed respondents had subjected their daughters to FGM or intended to do so.

Human rights abuses include police abuse of prisoners, arbitrary detention, and torture. The government exercises its power to restrict unwanted political gatherings, sometimes with deadly force. In 2009, the military killed 157 citizens at an opposition rally in Conakry. A year after the massacre, no action had been taken against military officials.

⁴¹HEALTH

According to the CIA, life expectancy in Guinea was 58 years in 2011. The country spent 5.5% of its GDP on healthcare, amounting to $19 per person. There was one physician and three hospital beds per 10,000 inhabitants. The infant mortality rate was 61 per 1,000 live births. In 2008 the maternal mortality rate, according to the World Bank, was 6.8 per 1,000 births. It was estimated that 51% of children were vaccinated against measles. In 2008 20.8% of children under age five were underweight. The most common diseases for children under five years old were diarrhea, respiratory infections, helminthiasis, and malaria.

The Republic of Guinea lies along the "goiter belt" of the Atlantic coast from west to central Africa. Low iodine intake has led to goiter in predominantly rural areas. Yellow fever and smallpox had been brought under control, but schistosomiasis remained widespread.

The HIV/AIDS adult prevalence rate was 1.3% in 2009. Guinea has been revamping its health care system. Using the Bamako Initiative previously used by other sub-Saharan African nations, Guinea has set up several smaller health centers that offer immunization services, AIDS prevention and control, family planning, and tuberculosis control.

⁴²HOUSING

The most common rural dwelling is round, windowless, and made of wattle and daub or sun-dried mud bricks, with a floor of packed earth and a conical thatched roof. Urban dwellings are usually one-story rectangular frame or mud-brick buildings, generally without electricity or indoor plumbing. Conakry has a serious housing shortage.

⁴³EDUCATION

In 2009 the World Bank estimated that 73% of age-eligible children in Guinea were enrolled in primary school. Secondary enrollment for age-eligible children stood at 29%. Tertiary enrollment was estimated at 9%. Of those enrolled in tertiary education, there were 100 male students for every 34 female students. There were 74 female students for every 100 male students in primary and secondary education in 2009.

Overall, the CIA estimated that Guinea had a literacy rate of 29.5%. Public expenditure on education represented 2.4% of GDP. In 2010 there were 42 primary school students for each teacher.

Before Guinea became independent, its educational system was patterned on that of France and French was the primary language of instruction. All schools were nationalized in 1961. In 1968, a "cultural revolution," aimed at de-Westernizing Guinean life, was inaugurated; since then, eight vernaculars have been added to the school curriculum, and village-level programs have been set up to assist in the implementation of the plan. Although the French educational structure and its traditional degrees have been retained, African history and geography are now stressed. Education is free and compulsory between the ages of 7 and 13. Children go through six years of primary and seven years of secondary school. After this, students may choose to attend a three-year vocational school to complete their education. The academic year runs from October to June.

The Gamal Abdel Nasser Polytechnic Institute was established at Conakry in 1963. The Valéry Giscard d'Estaing Institute of Agro-Zootechnical Sciences was founded in 1978 at Faranah. The University of Conakry was founded in 1984.

44 LIBRARIES AND MUSEUMS

The chief book collection and main exhibition center are in the National Institute of Research and Documentation (67,000 volumes) at Conakry. The National Library (40,000 volumes) and the National Archives are also located in Conakry. There are also small university libraries in Kankan and Conakry.

The National Museum, at Conakry, has displays of the ethnography and prehistory of Guinea, as well as a collection of art, fetishes, and masks of the Sacred Forest. The capital also has two natural history museums, covering botany and geology. There are regional museums in Kissidougou, Nzérékoré, Youkounkoun, Beyla, and Boké.

45 MEDIA

Media access in Guinea is limited by lack of infrastructure and economic barriers. In 2009 the CIA reported that there were 22,000 telephone landlines in Guinea. In addition to landlines, mobile phone subscriptions averaged 56 per 100 people, or 5.6 million cellular phones in use. There were 5 AM radio stations, and 3 shortwave radio stations. Internet users numbered 1 per 100 citizens. In 2010 there were a total of 14 internet hosts.

Telephone, telegraph, and postal services are government-owned. Submarine cables connect Conakry with Dakar, Freetown, and Monrovia; telecommunication links by satellite are also available.

Radiodiffusion-Télévision Guinéenne broadcasts in French, English, Portuguese, Arabic, Creole, and local languages, as does TV-Nationale, the one television station in Guinea.

The government-owned *Horoya* is the only daily paper. There are also a number of private press weeklies, including *La Lance, L'Oeil, Le Democrat, L'Independant, La Nouvelle Tribune, L'Observateur,* and the satirical newspaper *Le Lynx*.

The constitution provides freedom of the press, though in practice the government imposes broad control and censorship. All media are owned or controlled by the government.

46 ORGANIZATIONS

Regional farm organizations are leagued in a national union of planters' cooperatives. Mass organizations associated with the RDA include the Youth of the Democratic African Revolution and the Revolutionary Union of Guinean Women. The Guinea Chamber of Commerce, Industry, and Agriculture has 70 affiliates.

National women's organizations include the Association Guinéenne des Femmes Diplômées des Universitiés and Commission Nationale des Femmes Travailleuses de Guinée. Scouting organizations are active for youth. Volunteer service organizations, such as the Lions Clubs International, are present. There is a national chapter of the Red Cross Society.

47 TOURISM, TRAVEL, AND RECREATION

The *Tourism Factbook*, published by the UN World Tourism Organization, reported 30,000 incoming tourists to Guinea in 2007, who spent a total of $4.9 million. Of those incoming tourists, there were 10,000 from the Americas and 9,000 from Europe. There were 5,394 hotel beds available in Guinea. The estimated daily cost to visit Conakry, the capital, was $266. The cost of visiting other cities averaged $105.

Visitors to Guinea must have a valid passport, visa, and international vaccination record (World Health Organization card). A certificate of vaccination against yellow fever is also required. Malaria precautions are recommended. An annual cultural festival that includes theatrical and dance groups is held in October.

48 FAMOUS PERSONS

A revered figure of the 19th century is Samory Touré (1830?–1900), a Malinké born in Upper Guinea, who conquered large areas and resisted French military forces until 1898. The founder of modern Guinea was his alleged great-grandson Ahmed Sékou Touré (1922–84), a prominent labor leader and political figure who became Guinea's first president in 1958. Guinea's best-known writer, Camara Laye (1928–80), wrote the novel *The Dark Child* (1953). Col. Lansana Conté (1934–2008) became president in 1984 and served until his death.

49 DEPENDENCIES

Guinea has no territories or colonies.

50 BIBLIOGRAPHY

Guinea Investment and Business Guide: Strategic and Practical Information. Washington, DC: International Business Publications USA, 2012.

O'Toole, Thomas. *Historical Dictionary of Guinea.* 5th ed. Lanham, MD: Scarecrow Press, 2005.

Schmidt, Elizabeth. *Cold War and Decolonization in Guinea, 1946–1958.* Athens: Ohio University Press, 2007.

Zeilig, Leo, and David Seddon. *A Political and Economic Dictionary of Africa.* Philadelphia: Routledge/Taylor and Francis, 2005.

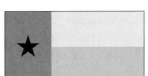

GUINEA-BISSAU

Republic of Guinea-Bissau
República da Guiné-Bissau

CAPITAL: Bissau

FLAG: The flag has equal horizontal stripes of yellow over green, with a red vertical stripe at the hoist bearing a black star.

ANTHEM: *Esta é a Nossa Pátria Bem Amada (This Is Our Well-Beloved Land).*

MONETARY UNIT: The Communauté Financière Africaine franc (XOF) replaced the Guinean peso as official currency in May 1997. Originally pegged to the French franc, it has been pegged to the euro since January 1999 with a rate of XOF655.957 to €1. The franc comes in coins of 1, 2, 5, 10, 25, 50, 100, and 500 francs, and notes of 50, 100, 500, 1,000, 5,000, and 10,000 francs. XOF1 = US$0.00204 (or US$1 = XOF487.99) as of December 2011.

WEIGHTS AND MEASURES: The metric system is used.

HOLIDAYS: New Year's Day, 1 January; Death of Amilcar Cabral, 20 January; Labor Day, 1 May; Anniversary of the Killing of Pidjiguiti, 3 August; National Day, 24 September; Anniversary of the Movement of Readjustment, 14 November; Christmas Day, 25 December. Movable religious holidays include Korité (end of Ramadan) and Tabaski (Feast of the Sacrifice).

TIME: 11 a.m. = noon GMT.

¹LOCATION, SIZE, AND EXTENT

Situated on the west coast of Africa, Guinea-Bissau, formerly Portuguese Guinea, has a total area of 36,120 sq km (13,946 sq mi), about 10% of which is periodically submerged by tidal waters. Comparatively, the area occupied by Guinea-Bissau is slightly less than three times the size of the state of Connecticut. Besides its mainland territory, it includes the Bijagós Archipelago and various coastal islands-Jeta, Pecixe, Bolama, and Melo, among others. Extending 336 km (209 mi) N–S and 203 km (126 mi) E–W, Guinea-Bissau is bordered on the N by Senegal, on the E and SE by Guinea, and on the SW and W by the Atlantic Ocean, with a total boundary length of 1,074 km (667 mi).

Guinea-Bissau's capital city, Bissau, is located on the country's Atlantic coast.

²TOPOGRAPHY

The country is swampy at the coast and low-lying inland, except in the northeast. At high tide, approximately 10% of the land in the coastal region is submerged. There are no significant mountains, but there is a central plateau rising to a couple hundred feet in elevation. Where the plateau stretches to the eastern frontier, it is called the Planalto de Gabú. This region has the nation's highest point, an unnamed point at 300 m (984 ft). The lowest point is at sea level (Atlantic Ocean). The most important rivers include the Cacheu, Mansoa, Geba, and Corubal.

³CLIMATE

Guinea-Bissau has a hot, humid, typically tropical climate, with a rainy season that lasts from mid-May to mid-November and a cooler dry season occupying the rest of the year. The average temperature in the rainy season ranges from 26–28°C (79–82°F).

Rainfall generally exceeds 198 cm (78 in), but droughts occurred in 1977, 1979, 1980, and 1983. The rainiest months are July and August. During the dry season, when the harmattan (dust-laden wind) blows from the Sahara, average temperatures do not exceed 24°C (75°F). The coldest months are December and January.

⁴FLORA AND FAUNA

Guinea-Bissau has a variety of vegetation, with thick jungle in the interior plains, rice and mangrove fields along the coastal plains and swamps, and savanna in the north. The World Resource Institute estimated that there were 1,000 plant species in Guinea-Bissau. Parts of Guinea-Bissau were rich in game, big and small. Several species of antelope, buffalo, monkeys, and snakes were found. In all, Guinea-Bissau was home to 101 mammal, 459 bird, 47 reptile, and 13 amphibian species. The calculation reflected the total number of distinct species residing in the country, not the number of endemic species.

⁵ENVIRONMENT

According to the World Resources Institute, Guinea-Bissau had designated 285,700 hectares (705,980 acres) of land for protection as of 2006. Water resources totaled 31 cu km (7.44 cu mi) while water usage was 0.18 cu km (.043 cu mi) per year. Domestic water usage accounted for 13% of total usage, industrial for 5%, and agricultural for 82%. Per capita water usage totaled 113 cu m (3,991 cu ft) per year.

The United Nations (UN) reported in 2008 that carbon dioxide emissions in Guinea-Bissau totaled 286 kilotons.

One of the most significant environmental problems in Guinea-Bissau was bush fire, which destroyed as many as 40,000 hectares (98,840 acres) of land per year and accelerated the loss of the nation's forests at a yearly rate of about 220 sq mi. In addition, owing to uncontrolled cutting, Guinea-Bissau had lost over 75% of its original mangrove areas by the mid-1980s, with the remaining swamps covering about 236,000 hectares (583,168 acres).

Another environmental issue was soil damage, caused by drought and erosion, as well as acidification and salinization. The Ministry of Natural Resources, created in January 1979, was responsible for making and enforcing environmental policy, but low state capacity and high levels of corruption meant that policies and regulations were weakly enforced.

Unexploded ordinances (UXOs) and embedded land mines dating to Guinea-Bissau's 1974 liberation war continued to litter the country in 2009. Guinea-Bissau signed the Ottawa Mine Ban treaty, pledging to eradicate all landmines and UXOs by 2011. Several non-government organizations (NGO) had also committed themselves to eradicating these dangerous devices; however, removal was expensive and procuring funds was difficult. In 2009 four deaths and ten injuries were attributed to UXOs. Otherwise fertile farmland sat idle as a result of land mines and UXOs.

According to a 2011 report issued by the International Union for Conservation of Nature and Natural Resources (IUCN), the number of threatened species included 12 mammals, 5 birds, 3 reptiles, 32 fish, and 4 plants. Threatened species included the Pygmy hippopotamus and the West African manatee.

⁶POPULATION

The US Central Intelligence Agency (CIA) reported the population of Guinea-Bissau in 2011 to be approximately 1,596,677, which placed it at number 147 in population among the 196 nations of the world. In 2011, approximately 3.2% of the population was over 65 years of age, with another 40.4% under 15 years of age. The median age in Guinea-Bissau was 19.5 years. There were 0.95 males for every female in the country. The population's annual rate of change was 1.988%. The projected population for the year 2025 was 2,300,000. Population density in Guinea-Bissau was calculated at 44 people per sq km (114 people per sq mi).

The UN estimated that 30% of the population lived in urban areas, and that urban populations had an annual rate of change of 3.0%. The largest urban area was Bissau, with a population of 302,000.

⁷MIGRATION

Estimates of Guinea-Bissau's net migration rate as reported by the CIA in 2011 were negligible. The total number of emigrants living abroad was 111,300, and the total number of immigrants living in Guinea-Bissau was 19,200. Guinea-Bissau also accepted 7,454 refugees.

In 1975, after the settlement of the guerrilla war against the Portuguese colonial administration, approximately 100,000 refugees returned from neighboring Senegal and Guinea. In 1998, a civil war erupted in Guinea-Bissau, prompting tens of thousands to flee the capital for the surrounding countryside and several thousands to cross into neighboring countries. Most refugees fled to Senegal and Guinea; others went as far as The Gambia and Cape Verde.

In 2011 the UN High Commissioner for Refugees (UNHCR) estimated that Guinea-Bissau hosted some 7,500 Senegalese refugees, mostly in rural areas. Given continuing insecurity in the Casamance region of Senegal, UNHCR indicated that repatriating

them would not be an option. Hence, UNHCR planned to support them with livelihoods programs and to help integrate them into national services and development programs.

⁸ETHNIC GROUPS

The largest ethnic groups were the Balanta (30%), the Fulani (20%), the Manjaca (14%), the Mandinga (13%) and the Pepel (7%). Of the nonindigenous people, the Cape Verdean mulatto community, which originated in the Cape Verde Islands, was the largest group, accounting for about 2% of the total population. There was also a small foreign community, consisting mainly of Portuguese, Lebanese and Syrian merchants.

In 2011 ethnic divisiveness was not a significant problem in Guinea-Bissau; however, some Balanta, who were the majority group in the army, viewed attempts to restructure the armed forces as akin to ethnic cleansing. Other groups harbored resentment toward the Balanta because of their dominance in the army. Low level conflicts were occurring between agriculturalists and pastoralists, and cattle theft between and among ethnic groups at times turned violent.

⁹LANGUAGES

Each ethnic group had its own language, subdivided into dialects. A Guinean "crioulo," or Africanized Portuguese patois, was the lingua franca. Portuguese was the official language. Given Guinea-Bissau's proximity to French-speaking neighbors, many educated Bissauans also spoke and read French.

¹⁰RELIGIONS

About 50% of the population, especially the Fulani and Mandinka, adhered to Islam. Some 40% of the population practiced traditional African religious beliefs or animism. Approximately 10% of the population was Christian, mostly Roman Catholic. Freedom of religion was provided for in the constitution and was generally respected. There were isolated cases of religious intolerance, extremism and sectarian violence in 2011.

¹¹TRANSPORTATION

The CIA reported that Guinea-Bissau had a total of 3,455 km (2,147 mi) of roads, of which 965 km (600 mi) were paved—generally trunk roads connecting the capital, Bissau with the provinces. There were 33 vehicles per 1,000 people in the country. There were nine airports.

Transportation facilities remain undeveloped, which hampered economic development, especially trade and the exploitation of minerals in the interior. Passenger service typically consisted of busses and trucks, bush taxis, and in Bissau, regular taxis. Secondary roads were laterite or dirt; many remote villages had no roads to accommodate regular passenger and commercial traffic.

Bissau was the main port. Expansion and modernization projects costing at least $48 million were undertaken in the early 1980s. Secondary ports and harbors included Buba, Cacheu, and Farim. As of 2008, the country's four largest rivers were navigable for some distance, with shallow water access possible to much of the interior via creeks and inlets. Bissau was also the site of a small international airport, while several aerodromes and landing strips served the interior. In 2009 there were two airports with paved runways. Linhas Aéreas da Guiné-Bissau (LIA), the national airline, provided service to Dakar, Senegal. Transportes Aéreos Portuguéses (TAP), Air Luxor, Air Guinée, Air Sénégal, and Cabo Verde Airlines (TACV) provided international service with much of the traffic routed through Dakar.

¹²HISTORY

The earliest inhabitants were hunters and fishermen who were replaced by the Baga and other peoples who came from the east. The Portuguese explorer Nuno Tristão arrived in the region in June 1446 and established the first trading posts. The slave trade developed during the 17th century; at its center was the port of Bissau, from which thousands of captive Africans were sent across the Atlantic to Latin America. Portugal retained at least nominal control of the area, and British claims to coastal regions were dismissed by arbitration in 1870. Nine years later, the area became a separate Portuguese dependency, administratively subordinate to the Cape Verde Islands. Portuguese Guinea's boundaries with neighboring French possessions were delimited in an 1886 treaty, and formal borders were demarcated by a joint commission in 1905. However, the interior was not effectively occupied until about 1920; nor did the Portuguese settle in the colony in large numbers. In 1951, together with other Portuguese holdings in Africa, Guinea was named a Portuguese overseas province.

In September 1956, a group of dissatisfied Cape Verdeans founded an underground movement to work for independence from Portugal. It was named the African Party for the Independence of Guinea and Cape Verde (Partido Africano de Independência da Guiné e Cabo Verde—PAIGC), and Amilcar Cabral became its secretary-general. On 19 September 1959, after more than 50 Africans had been killed during a dock strike that turned into a violent clash with police, Cabral called for an all-out struggle "by all possible means, including war." By 1963, large-scale guerrilla warfare had broken out in the territory.

During the ensuing years, PAIGC guerrillas, fighting a Portuguese force of about 30,000, increased their hold on the countryside. When Cabral was assassinated on 20 January 1973, reportedly by a PAIGC naval officer, Aristides Pereira took over the leadership of the movement, which on 24 September 1973 unilaterally proclaimed the independence of the Republic of Guinea-Bissau.

A PAIGC victory became near certain after 25 April 1974, when the Lisbon government was overthrown in a coup. The leader of the new regime, Gen. António de Spínola, was a former governor-general and military commander in Portuguese Guinea, and had become an advocate of peaceful settlement of the war. On 26 August 1974, the Portuguese government and the PAIGC signed an agreement in Algiers under which Guinea-Bissau was to attain independence from 10 September. The same agreement also provided for the removal of all Portuguese troops by 31 October as well as a referendum to determine the future status of the Cape Verde Islands.

The new government, under President Luis de Almeida Cabral, brother to Amilcar Cabral, had to deal with extensive economic dislocations brought about by the war. On 27 September 1974, the government announced its intention to control all foreign trade, and in May 1975, the legislature approved a program to nationalize all land and to confiscate property belonging to persons who had "collaborated with the enemy" during the war.

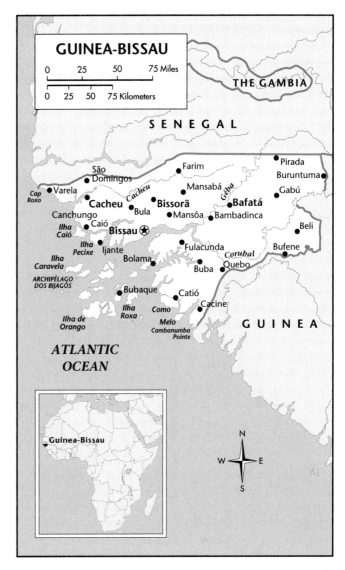

LOCATION: 10°52′ to 12°42′N; 13°38′ to 16°43′ W. BOUNDARY LENGTHS: Senegal, 338 kilometers (210 miles); Guinea, 386 kilometers (240 miles); Atlantic coastline, 398 kilometers (247 miles). TERRITORIAL SEA LIMIT: 12 miles.

In the first postindependence elections held in December 1976-January 1977, 80% of the population approved the PAIGC list of candidates for Regional Council membership. The 150-member National Assembly, selected by these representatives, convened on 13 March 1977. Luis Cabral was reelected president of Guinea-Bissau and of the 15-member Council of State, and Major João Bernardo Vieira was confirmed as the nation's vice president and as president of the National Assembly.

On 14 November 1980, President Cabral, a mestiço with close ties to Cape Verde, was overthrown by a group of Guinean blacks under Vieira's command. Severe food shortages and tensions in the alliance between Guinea-Bissau and Cape Verde had precipitated the bloody military coup, which led to the dissolution of the National Assembly and Executive Council, suspension of the constitution, arrest of the president, and temporary abandonment of the goal of unification with Cape Verde. A Revolutionary Council composed of nine military officers and four civilian advisers was named on 19 November, and a provisional government was appointed the following day. Diplomatic relations with Cape Verde, suspended at the time of the coup, were resumed in June 1982.

The National People's Assembly, reestablished in April 1984, adopted a new constitution in May. It also elected a 15-member Council of State to serve as the nation's executive body. As president of this council, Vieira served as both head of state and head of government. An abortive military coup took place in November 1985; in the aftermath, six persons were executed in July 1986 while another five died in detention. After ruling Guinea-Bissau as a one-party state for ten years, Vieira denounced single-party rule as elitist, inherently undemocratic, and repressive. In April 1991, Guinea-Bissau formally embraced multipartyism and adopted a new constitution. Four major opposition parties formed the Democratic Forum in January 1992 and sought to unseat PAIGC.

Elections scheduled for November 1992 were postponed until March 1993, giving the 11 opposition parties time to campaign and the multiparty electoral commission time to work out electoral procedures. They were again postponed until March 1994. On 17 March 1993, João da Costa, the leader of the Party for Renovation and Development (PRD), was implicated in an attempted coup. On 4 February 1994, the supreme military court acquitted him.

In July 1994, Guinea-Bissau held its first multiparty legislative and presidential elections. João Bernardo Vieira was elected president, narrowly defeating Koumba Yala with 52% to 48% of the vote. The PAIGC led decisively in the Assembly elections with 46% of the vote. In October, Vieira appointed Manuel Saturnino da Costa prime minister. In 1995, a coalition of opposition parties reformed the Democratic Forum, appointing da Costa as its leader.

The PAIGC reelected Vieira as party leader in May 1998, but he was nearly overthrown in June when army mutineers staged an unsuccessful coup. The coup attempt triggered a brief but devastating civil war. Upon Vieira's request, Senegal and Guinea sent 3,000 troops to restore order. Bombardments destroyed the main hospital, damaged schools and markets, and displaced thousands. The World Food Program and the Red Cross provided emergency services to an estimated 130,000 of these victims. Under a peace agreement signed in Abuja in November, presidential and legislative elections were to be held before March 1999.

In May 1999, following the dismissal of General Ansumane Mané, troops loyal to the general stormed the presidential palace. Some 70 people died in the assault. Vieira took refuge at the French Cultural Center, and later sought asylum at the Portuguese Embassy. He was allowed to leave for Lisbon after renouncing the presidency and promising to return for trial. Malam Bacai Sanha presided over the interim government, which ended the 11-month civil war.

In November 1999, National Assembly elections took place, and in January 2000, Sanha lost to Koumba Yala in presidential elections judged free and fair. On 24 January, President Yala appointed his close friend, Caetano N'tchama, prime minister. Despite the elections, the country had a parallel government in the form of the military junta. In November 2000, Mané revoked Yala's military appointments and fighting erupted between forces loyal to the government and supporters of the junta. After regaining control, loyalist forces announced on 30 November that Mané had been killed.

Yet another crisis ensued in January 2001 when the Guinea-Bissau Resistance (or RGB/MB) withdrew from the government, charging that it had not been consulted over a cabinet reshuffle and calling for N'tchama's dismissal. N'tchama was fired in March, leaving a number of issues for his successor including the detention of about 130 members of the military accused of supporting Mané, and the alleged involvement of Guinea-Bissau in the Casamance conflict in neighboring Senegal. Health, education, and other social sectors were seriously underfunded, and underpaid civil servants were demanding higher wages. In addition, thousands of weapons were in private hands, and newly graduated young people had few or no prospects of employment after leaving school. Yala announced in December 2001 that his government had foiled yet another coup attempt.

In November 2002, Yala dissolved the parliament and named Mario Pires prime minister. Yala arrested his defense minister on 30 April 2003 on charges of plotting a coup, and in June he held emergency talks with disgruntled military leaders and key ministers to prevent the collapse of his government. Under pressure from the UN Security Council to hold clean elections, Yala announced in June 2003 that parliamentary elections originally scheduled for 23 February and then pushed back to 20 April and then 6 July would be postponed yet again to August or September pending revision of the electoral roll. By July 2003, Yala's government owed six months in pay arrears to the army and civil service. In lieu of monetary remuneration, government workers were receiving payment in rice. In the words of then UN Secretary General Kofi Annan, the economy and government of Guinea-Bissau were on a precarious downward course.

In the meantime, relations with Senegal deteriorated over the Casamance conflict and the disputed Bissauan-Senegalese border, which had been demarcated by Portugal and France in 1960. In 1992 and 1995, Senegalese warplanes bombed suspected rebel bases in Guinea-Bissau alleged to be safe havens for Casamance rebels. In March 1996, the two governments reached an initial accord, and in 1999 through the mediation of President Jammeh of The Gambia, leaders of the two sides concluded an agreement. However, skirmishes continued into 2001 necessitating the intervention of the UN Secretary General. In March and April 2006, Guinea-Bissau soldiers fought on the side of Senegalese rebels along the southern border.

In September 2003, agreement was reached among the military and political parties to hold presidential and legislative elections. An interim civilian administration was also established, headed by President Henrique Rosa with Antonio Artur Rosa as prime minister. Elections followed in March 2004, which the PAIGC won. In October, the head of the armed forces was killed over problems that included outstanding wages. April 2005 saw the return from exile of ex-President Joao Vieira. The following month former president, Koumba Yala, declared he was still president, and he occupied the presidential residence, albeit briefly.

With international bodies overseeing the election processes, former military ruler Vieira won election for a five-year term, obtaining 52% of the vote to 47.6% for Malam Bacai Sanha. After a few weeks in office, Vieira dismissed the government of Prime Minister Carlos Gomes Junior. In March and April 2007, Prime Minister Aristides Gomes resigned after his government lost a no-confidence vote. Martinho Ndafa Kabi was appointed prime minister.

In June 2006, unions called for a three-day strike over the government's refusal to pay back wages for civil servants. Because government was incapable of meeting public sector payroll, the Economic Community of West African States (ECOWAS) promised to cover teachers' wages.

Further evidence of a failing state appeared in October 2006 when Guinea-Bissau was forced to request international aid to stop human traffickers from using its coastline to smuggle migrants, including Asians, to Europe. In June 2007, the UN and the International Monetary Fund warned international donors that they needed to rescue Guinea-Bissau from chaos and combat Latin American drug cartels.

In March 2009, President Vieira was assassinated by soldiers just hours after his longtime rival, the armed forces chief of staff General Batiste Tagme Na Waie, was killed by a bomb blast at his headquarters. Top military officers claimed that Vieira's death was not part of a coup attempt, but simply a random act of retaliation, as it was believed that Vieira was responsible for the blast that killed Na Waie. However, an armed group had made an attempt on the president's life in November 2008, attacking his residence and killing two of his guards. The speaker of parliament, Raimundo Pereira, was sworn in as interim president.

Elections to replace Vieira were held in June 2009. Malam Bacai Sanha, of the ruling African Party for the Independence of Guinea and Cape Verde (PAIGC), won the second round of balloting with 63% of the vote. Kumba Yala took second place. Carlos Gomes, Jr. was appointed prime minister. Observers viewed the electoral process as free, fair and transparent, but political instability continued.

On 1 April 2010, soldiers seized the prime minister and the army chief of staff in their offices in a mutiny. The prime minister was soon released, but General Jose Zamora Induta was ousted by the military and replaced by General Antonio Indjai. Indjai received appointment as Chief of Staff 30 June 2010. Induta was illegally detained until December 2010. The subsequent reappointment of Admiral Jose Americo Bubo Na Tchuto as Navy Chief of Staff, led to decisions by the United States to suspend its military assistance and by the European Union to terminate by September 30, 2010, its mission for the reform of Guinea-Bissau's security forces. Na Tchuto, along with Air Force Chief of Staff, Ibrahimia Papa Camera, were placed on the US Department of Treasury's Drug Kingpin list on 8 April 2010, freezing their assets and making it illegal for Americans to do business with them.

As a result of Indjai's appointment and Induta's unlawful detention, the European Union's Foreign Affairs Chief declared that the EU would reassess its aid to Guinea-Bissau in July 2010. The EU had allocated more than $150 million in aid to Guinea-Bissau for the 2008–13 period, reserving the right to withhold those funds if an acceptable solution was not reached.

On May 6, 2011, Lucinda Ahukarie, chief of one of the country's most credible law enforcement institutions, resigned over concern about the military's threats to her agency's fight against narcotrafficking. On 6 June, the National Assembly overwhelmingly adopted a law against female genital mutilation (FGM), which would allow penalties of up to 5 years in prison for perpetrators of FGM.

Several massive street demonstrations occurred in Bissau in 2011 to protest the government's failure to address the grievances of civil servants and retired armed forces personnel, especially the veterans of the liberation war, who demanded backpayments for salary and pensions. Protestors marched relatively peacefully, but were insistent that Prime Minister Gomes resign. In December 2011 President Sanha was flown to Dakar and then to Paris for emergency treatment. He was diabetic and had been dogged by health problems for some time.

¹³ GOVERNMENT

Nominally, the government of Guinea-Bissau consisted of three branches of power: the executive, the legislature (Assembly), and the judiciary. However, there was little separation of powers, and the armed forces Chief of Staff and high-ranking officers regularly meddled in government affairs.

The 1973 constitution was suspended following the 1980 coup. A constitution was ratified on 16 May 1984 by the reestablished National People's Assembly. In April 1991 a new constitution, providing for a multiparty system, was adopted and subsequently amended.

The 100-member Assembly is popularly elected for four-year terms. Before multiple parties were authorized in 1991, Assembly members had to belong to the ruling African Party for the Independence of Guinea and Cape Verde (PAIGC).

The president was titular head of government, popularly elected for a five-year, renewable, term. The president appointed a prime minister, who was the operational head of government. Malam Bacai Sanha was elected as president in July 2009, following the assassination of President Joao Bernardo Vieira. Carlos Gomes, Jr. was appointed prime minister.

¹⁴ POLITICAL PARTIES

Since the liberation era, the ruling African Party for the Independence of Guinea and Cape Verde (Partido Africano de Independência da Guiné e Cabo Verde-PAIGC) has been the dominant political party in the Republic of Guinea-Bissau country. Prior to 1991, it was the sole legal party in the country during a period of extreme intolerance. When Luis Cabral was president hundreds of political opponents were reportedly murdered and buried in mass graves.

The 1980 coup was condemned by Cape Verdean leaders of the PAIGC, and in January 1981 they broke with the Guinea-Bissau branch to form the African Party for the Independence of Cape Verde. The following November, Guinean party officials decided to retain the name PAIGC for their branch and to expel Cape Verdean founder-members from the party.

Opposition parties were legalized by a new constitution adopted in April 1991. A dozen parties were recognized. Among them were: the Party for Renewal and Development (PRD), which was composed of educated dissidents who quit the PAIGC because of its authoritarianism; the Social Democratic Front (FDS), led by one of the founders of the PAIGC, Raphael Barbosa; the Front for the Struggle for Guinea-Bissau's National Independence, which predates PAIGC and was led by Mindy Kankoila, an early independence leader who had been in exile for 40 years; the National Convention Party (mainly Muslims and FDS dissidents); and the League for the Protection of the Ecology (LPE). The most important opposition party was Bafata, the Guinea-Bissau Resistance-Bafata Movement. Many parties prior to the general elections of 1994 formed a coalition, including the PRD, the FDS, the LPE, the Movement for Unity and Democracy (MUD), and the Democratic Party for Progress (PDP).

Free and fair legislative elections on 3 July 1994 gave the PAIGC a majority of 62 seats. The Guinea-Bissau Resistance (RGB-MB) was second in balloting with 19 seats, 12 for the Social Renovation Party (PRS), 10 for the Front for the Liberation and Independence of Guinea-Bissau, and 6 for the Union for Change Coalition.

In the November 1999 Assembly elections, the Partido da Renovacao Social (PRS), won 38 seats, the Resistencia da Guine-Bissau-Movimento Ba-Fata (RGB-MB) 28 seats, and the PAIGC 24 seats. Five parties garnered the remaining 12 seats in this election, which were part of the second consecutive set of free and fair competitive elections in Guinea-Bissau. Despite Yala's promises to form a government of national unity, the PRS and its ally, RGB-MB dominated the cabinet.

In the Assembly elections held on 28 March 2004, the PAIGC captured 31.5% of the vote, followed by PRS with 24.8% and United Social Democratic Party with 16.1%. The Electoral Union won only 4.1% of the vote; APU got 1.3% and 13 other parties shared 22.2% between them. In terms of seats in the Assembly, PAIGC won 45, PRS got 35, and PUSD won 17. In turn, UE got 2 seats while APU won only 1 seat.

In the Assembly elections held 16 November 2008, the PAIGC increased its presence with 49.8% of the vote and 67 seats, followed by the PRS with 25.3% and 28 seats. Three newer parties gained seats in the Assembly, including the Republican Party for Independence and Development (PRID), with 7.5% of the vote and three seats; the New Democratic Party (PND) with 2.4% and one seat; and the Democratic Alliance with 1.4% of the vote and one seat.

The PAIGC also dominated the executive branch. In the June 2009 presidential election, Malam Bacai Sanha, the standard bearer for the ruling PAIGC, won 39% of the votes to 29% for Kumba Yala, a former president. Because no candidate obtained an absolute majority, a runoff election was held in July. Sanha defeated Yala in the runoff with 63% of the vote. Carlos Gomes, Jr. was appointed prime minister.

15 LOCAL GOVERNMENT

Guinea-Bissau consists of 8 regions, 37 sectors and a separate jurisdiction for the capital. Each region has a regional council, as does the capital, with membership consisting of elected representatives from the sectors. Local governments are underfunded, and real power and influence is exercised centrally from Bissau.

16 JUDICIAL SYSTEM

The judicial system was weak, corrupt, and law enforcement was unreliable. Remote areas of the country had no functioning courts and no policemen.

Civilian courts were patterned after the Portuguese colonial system. Nine Supreme Court judges were appointed by the president and served at his pleasure. The Supreme Court had jurisdiction over serious crimes and served as an appeals court for the regional military courts. There were nine regional courts, which were the first court of appeals for sectoral court decisions; the

regional courts heard felony cases and civil cases valued at over $1,000. There were also 24 sectoral courts, where judges were not necessarily trained lawyers; they heard civil cases under $1,000 and misdemeanor criminal cases.

State security cases were tried by civilian courts. Military courts tried only cases involving armed personnel under the code of military justice. In rural areas, persons were often tried outside the formal system either by traditional and customary law, or by informal settlements. Citizen and mob justice were also commonly practiced.

The 1991 constitution guaranteed civil rights and fundamental freedoms, including freedom of speech and freedom of religion. The constitution also provided for an independent judiciary, but rule of law was undercut by inadequate funding, low salaries, weak human capacity, poor training, crumbling infrastructure, and corruption. The president had authority to grant pardons and reduce sentences.

In 2011 the US Department of State, Bureau of International Narcotics and Law Enforcement (State/INL) implemented programs to increase the capacity of the justice sector and law enforcement to combat drug trafficking and other organized crime. INL funded two advisors and also contributed funds to support a rule of law program implemented by the UN Office on Drugs and Crime.

17 ARMED FORCES

The International Institute for Strategic Studies (IISS) reported that armed forces in Guinea-Bissau totaled an estimated 4,458 members in 2011. The force was comprised of 4,000 from the army, 350 from the navy, and 100 members of the air force. Armed forces represented 1% of the labor force in Guinea-Bissau. Defense spending totaled $55.4 million and accounted for 3.1% of gross domestic product (GDP). It was well-known that senior and high-ranking officers exercised political and economic power in the country.

18 INTERNATIONAL COOPERATION

Guinea-Bissau was admitted to the UN on 17 February 1974 and was a member of ECA and all the nonregional specialized agencies except IAEA. The nation was a member of the WTO and participated in the African Development Bank, the ACP Group, the African Union, ECOWAS, G-77, the non-aligned movement, the West African Economic and Monetary Union (WAEMU), the Community of Sahel and Saharan States (CENSAD), the Alliance of Small Island States (AOSIS), the New Partnership for Africa's Development (NEPAD), and the Organization of the Islamic Conference (OIC). It also belonged to OHADA, which harmonized business law among some 23 sub Saharan African states. In environmental cooperation, Guinea-Bissau was part of the Convention on Biological Diversity, Ramsar, CITES, and the UN Conventions on the Law of the Sea, Climate Change, and Desertification. The country was also part of an Interstate Committee for Drought Control in the Sahel (CILSS).

19 ECONOMY

Guinea-Bissau was one of poorest countries in the world with over 80% of the population relying on fishing and subsistence agriculture; most of the population lived below $2 a day. The industrial sector was small, and mining was undeveloped. Offshore oil reserves were unexploited, but offered potential for medium- to long-term growth. Guinea-Bissau's adoption of market-style economic policies had yet to overcome its initial embrace of socialist central planning.

As of 2011, the GDP rate of change in Guinea-Bissau was 3.5%. Inflation stood at 3.8%. In 2010, GDP was reported to be $1.78 billion. Agriculture accounted for 62% of GDP. Products included cashews, tropical fruits, rice, peanuts, cotton, and palm oil. Industry accounted for 12% of GDP, consisting mainly of cashew processing. Very little industrial capacity remained following the 1998 internal conflict. Trade and services accounted for the rest. In 2009 exports amounted to $114.8 million with cashews totaling $110.1 million, approximately 95% of exports. Other exports included fish, shrimp, peanuts, palm kernels, and sawn lumber.

In 2008 the major markets for these products were India (56.8%); Nigeria (35.6%); and Pakistan (1.2%). Imports totaled $146.4 million: food products ($58.1 million), and petroleum products ($35 million). Major suppliers were Portugal (24.5%), Senegal (17.2%), Pakistan (4.8%), and France (4.6%).

20 INCOME

The CIA estimated that in 2010 the GDP of Guinea-Bissau was $1.784 billion. The CIA defined GDP as the value of all final goods and services produced within a nation in a given year and computed on the basis of purchasing power parity (PPP) rather than value as measured on the basis of the rate of the exchange based on current dollars. The per capita GDP was estimated at $1,100. The annual growth rate of GDP was 3.5%. The average inflation rate was 3.8%. It was estimated that agriculture accounted for 62% of GDP, industry 12%, and services 26%.

According to the World Bank, remittances from citizens living abroad totaled $46.7 million or about $29 per capita and accounted for approximately 2.6% of GDP.

The World Bank estimated that Guinea-Bissau, with 0.02% of the world's population, accounted for less than 0.01% of the world's GDP. By comparison, the United States, with 4.85% of the world's population, accounted for 22.51% of world GDP.

As of 2011 the most recent study by the World Bank reported that actual individual consumption in Guinea-Bissau was 82.8% of GDP and accounted for less than 0.01% of world consumption. By comparison, the United States accounted for 25.44% of world individual consumption. The World Bank also estimated that 44.6% of Guinea-Bissau's GDP was spent on food and beverages, 17.2% on housing and household furnishings, 6.9% on clothes, 2.3% on health, 5.4% on transportation, 0.4% on communications, 3.2% on recreation, 0.4% on restaurants and hotels, and .4% on miscellaneous goods and services and purchases from abroad.

21 LABOR

As of 2007, Guinea-Bissau had a total labor force of 632,700 people. Within that universe, the CIA estimated that 82% were employed in agriculture, 9% in industry, and 9% in the service sector (2008).

The constitution granted workers the freedom to join and form trade unions; however, few people were employed in the formal sector, and unions were not strong. Few workers outside of the public sector were organized. There were 11 registered labor unions in 2002. Workers were allowed to strike provided that they gave notice of their intention to do so. Collective bargaining was permitted, but seldom occurred.

Minimum wages were established, but not enforced. The lowest legal monthly wage in 2002 was $20, which was not enough to support a family. The minimum age for employment was 14 years, but was not enforced outside of the small formal economy. Many children worked as street vendors or on family plots in rural communities. Health and safety standards set by the government were generally not enforced.

22 AGRICULTURE

Roughly 15% of the total land is arable or under permanent crops; the country's major crops included rice, corn, beans, cassava (tapioca), cashew nuts, peanuts, palm kernels, and cotton. Cereal production in 2009 amounted to 214,800 tons, fruit production 89,614 tons, and vegetable production 26,127 tons. In 2009, agriculture accounted for more than 60% of GDP, employed approximately 80% of the population, and comprised more than 90% of exports.

The country was divided into three major regions according to rainfall. The coast and river estuaries constituted the palm-tree (coconut) zone; intermediary and marshy areas comprised the rice-growing region; and the sandy areas of the savanna interior favored peanuts. In the 1950s, Guinea-Bissau exported about 40,000 tons of rice per year. However, recurrent droughts since 1962 have forced rice to be imported. Cashew nuts, palm kernels, and peanuts were the most important export crops. Tropical fruits such as mangoes held potential for greater cultivation.

The independence war reduced crop output by over one-third. Public investment, financed heavily by external borrowing, neglected agriculture in favor of the manufacturing sector. Agricultural recovery was hampered by inappropriate pricing policies, an overvalued exchange rate, and an inefficient marketing system. Price liberalization has improved trade, and important goods like rice are now traded informally with neighboring countries.

23 ANIMAL HUSBANDRY

The UN Food and Agriculture Organization (FAO) reported that Guinea-Bissau dedicated 1.1 million hectares (2.67 million acres) to permanent pasture or meadow in 2009. During that year, the country tended 1.8 million chickens, 620,000 head of cattle, and 410,000 pigs. The production from these animals amounted to 5,459 tons of beef and veal, 12,233 tons of pork, 2,326 tons of poultry, 1,029 tons of eggs, and 23,665 tons of milk. Guinea-Bissau also produced 1,397 tons of cattle hide.

Despite endemic tsetse fly, cattle raising occupied many Guineans, especially the Balanta in the interior. In 2005, there were an estimated 300,000 sheep and 335,000 goats.

24 FISHING

Guinea-Bissau had six decked commercial fishing boats in 2008. The annual capture totaled 6,750 tons according to the UN FAO. The export value of seafood totaled $4.57 million. Mullet accounted for about 44% of the annual catch. Agreements allowed the European Union countries to fish in national waters.

Fishing had the potential to become a viable industry. However, illegal and uncontrolled fishing was a significant problem, and constituted a major loss of revenue. Most fishing in Guinea-Bissau's waters was not done by Bissau-Guineans and no fish or seafood was processed in Guinea-Bissau for export.

25 FORESTRY

Approximately 72% of Guinea-Bissau was covered by forest. The UN FAO estimated the 2009 roundwood production at 170,000 cu m (6 million cu ft). The value of all forest products, including roundwood, totaled $1.88 million. Guinean forests and savanna woodland primarily supplied wood and timber for domestic consumption and fuel and construction material.

26 MINING

Mineral production (excluding natural gas and refined petroleum products) was not significant in 2009, and was limited to small-scale production of basalt, cement, clay, gold, limestone, salt, sand, silica sand, zircon, and laterites. Bauxite, diamonds, gold, and phosphate were economically promising minerals being explored; the Farim deposit had a phosphate resource of 166 million tons. Large deposits of bauxite, amounting to 200 million tons, were discovered in the Boé area in the late 1950s; lack of capital and transportation has hindered exploitation. The bauxite and phosphate resources were of low grade. The 1999 Mines and Minerals Act reformed mineral exploration and mine development and production, setting sizes and terms for exploration, mining, and prospecting leases.

27 ENERGY AND POWER

The World Bank reported in 2008 that Guinea-Bissau produced 70 million kWh of electricity and consumed 62.3 million kWh, or 39 kWh per capita. As of 2011 Guinea-Bissau had no proven reserves of petroleum or natural gas. There was no electricity production using renewable fuels.

28 INDUSTRY

Industry constituted a small part of Guinea-Bissau's economy, contributing approximately 12% a year to GDP. Industries included a sugar refinery and a rice and groundnut processing plant. Guinea-Bissau ranked sixth in the world in cashew production. Brewing and urban construction were also represented in the industrial sector.

In the late 1980s, Guinea-Bissau attempted to attract foreign interest in several enterprises, including a fish-processing plant, a plywood and furniture factory, and a plastics factory. Government plans to raise producer prices and to privatize parastatal trading companies in the 1990s were derailed by civil war in 1998.

Off-shore oil exploration began in the 1960s, but was slowed by border disputes with Senegal over exploratory blocks. Under a 1995 treaty, the two countries agreed to jointly manage the disputed area. Proceeds from the area were to be divided between Senegal and Guinea-Bissau on an 85:15 ratio, but Guinea-Bissau rejected those terms in order to negotiate a more balanced agreement.

On 8 June 2011, Houston-based Noble Energy announced it had joined a venture to explore for oil and gas 65 miles off the coast of Senegal and Guinea-Bissau beginning in summer 2011. The Kora prospect may hold up to 450 million barrels of oil.

29 SCIENCE AND TECHNOLOGY

The World Bank reported in 2009 that there were no patent applications in science and technology in Guinea-Bissau.

30 DOMESTIC TRADE

Domestic trade was mostly medium- and small-scale commercial transactions. Wholesaling and retailing in small shops was dominated by Lebanese merchants. Upcountry, most goods were traded in weekly open-air markets and daily in small shops located in and around the markets. Product distribution to inland areas was conducted by private carriers and by barge via the Geba River. Significant amounts of trade were barter.

Following Portuguese rule, the PAIGC introduced chains of all-purpose "people's stores," communally owned and managed; some of these were handed over to private traders beginning in 1985. The military conflict of 1998–1999 damaged infrastructure, which in turn severely disrupted agriculture. Normal business hours in the capital were 8 a.m. to 12 noon and 3 to 6 p.m., Monday-Friday.

31 FOREIGN TRADE

Guinea-Bissau imported $200 million worth of goods and services in 2008, while exporting $133 million worth of goods and services. Major import partners in 2009 were Portugal, 15.6%; Senegal, 15.3%; India, 11.6%; Netherlands, 8.4%; China, 7.8%; Thailand, 4.7%; and Brazil, 4.1% . Its major export partners were India, 69.7%; and Nigeria, 24.1%.

Cashew nuts accounted for more than 90% of exports with little to no value added to the product. Cashews were followed by fish, peanuts, palm kernels, and sawed lumber. The lumber trade shrunk in the late 1990s due to deforestation; properly managed, the fish sector was expected to grow. Imports included industrial and commercial supplies, fuels and lubricants, transport equipment and foodstuffs. Imported foods, beverages, and tobacco alone typically surpassed in value all of Guinea-Bissau's exports.

32 BALANCE OF PAYMENTS

Guinea-Bissau has had chronic balance-of-payments problems because of its annual trade deficit, which has persisted despite efforts to restructure trade by diversifying the range of commodities available for export and by establishing new trading partners and more favorable trade agreements. Foreign assistance is an essential element in meeting payments needs. Reserves of foreign exchange and gold were $168.6 million in 2009. The current account balance was -$82.6 million and -$100 million in 2010 and 2011, respectively.

33 BANKING AND SECURITIES

The Central Bank of the West African States (Banque central des états de l'Afrique de l'ouest—BCEAO) functioned as the central bank for Guinea-Bissau. It was the bank of issue for the CFA franc, which was the national currency, pegged to the Euro, and whose convertibility was guaranteed by the French treasury. The XAF franc was the currency of the West African Economic and Monetary Union (WAEMU or UEMOA), of which Guinea-Bissau was a member. The BCEAO generally supervised the financial sector of Guinea-Bissau. At the end of December 2009, the discount rate,

Principal Trading Partners – Guinea-Bissau (2010)

(In millions of US dollars)

Country	Total	Exports	Imports	Balance
World	330.0	120.0	210.0	-90.0
India	117.1	113.1	4.0	109.1
Portugal	60.1	0.4	59.7	-59.3
Senegal	46.2	0.0	46.2	-46.2
Nigeria	42.3	42.3	...	42.3
Colombia	16.2	...	16.2	-16.2
Spain	14.2	5.8	8.3	-2.5
China	13.9	3.5	10.4	-6.9
Togo	13.7	13.7	0.0	13.7
Cuba	11.9	...	11.9	-11.9
Côte d'Ivoire	9.3	0.0	9.3	-9.3

(…) data not available or not significant.

(n.s.) not specified.

SOURCE: *2011 Direction of Trade Statistics Yearbook,* New York: United Nations, 2011.

Balance of Payments – Guinea-Bissau (2009)

(In millions of US dollars)

Current Account		**-113.6**
Balance on goods		-80.7
Imports	-202.3	
Exports	121.6	
Balance on services		-53.8
Balance on income		-11.1
Current transfers		32.0
Capital Account		**65.8**
Financial Account		**-11.8**
Direct investment abroad		0.1
Direct investment in Guinea-Bissau		17.5
Portfolio investment assets		-19.1
Portfolio investment liabilities		-0.2
Financial derivatives		...
Other investment assets		3.7
Other investment liabilities		-13.7
Net Errors and Omissions		**-7.6**
Reserves and Related Items		**67.1**

(…) data not available or not significant.

SOURCE: *Balance of Payment Statistics Yearbook 2011,* Washington, DC: International Monetary Fund, 2011.

the interest rate at which the central bank lends to financial institutions in the short term, was 4.25%.

International banking and finance were problematic owing to a limited formal banking sector. ATMs were not available, credit cards were not accepted, currency exchange only existed at banks and hotels, wire transfer possibilities were extremely limited, and repatriation of funds was problematic. Purchases of goods and services were possible only in cash and in Franc CFA of the WAEMU. The US State Department recommended that travelers carry sufficient CFA with them when arriving in Guinea-Bissau.

The first investment bank in Guinea-Bissau, Banco Africano Ocidentale (BAO), was established in the first quarter of 1997 with joint Portuguese and Guinea-Bissau capital, and became the country's first commercial bank in 2001. In 2011 five commercial banks operated in the country.

Owing to small-scale commerce, microfinance held great potential. In 2009, a handful of micro-finance institutions served approximately 1,600 active borrowers, with about $600,000 in gross loan portfolios. On 7 June 2011 Ecobank and Bharti Airtel announced a joint venture to launch mobile banking in the country, and on 20 July 2011 the African Development Bank (AfDB) and Spain launched an initiative to scale up microfinance and support projects in the WAEMU countries through a Microfinance Capacity Building Fund.

There was no stock exchange in the country.

[34]INSURANCE

Since 1995, the insurance sector was regulated and supervised by the Inter-African Conference of Insurance Markets (CIMA), to which 13 African countries belonged, including neighboring Senegal. CIMA was regulated by the Regional Commission of Insurance Control (CRCA), which had a Council of Ministers as its highest body. Only one company was known to be operating in Guinea-Bissau—Alianca Seguradora.

[35]PUBLIC FINANCE

The budget deficit amounted to 2.4% of GDP. Public debt was 1.9% of GDP, with $941.5 million of the debt held by foreign entities.

Since independence, Guinea-Bissau has struggled to meet its balance of payments and service its debt sustainably. The government and the IMF initiated a structural adjustment program (SAP) in 1987 in order to reform public administration and the economy, control inflation and improve the debt service ratio. As part of this effort, government reduced petroleum subsidies, lowered customs duties and taxes on imports, and donors rescheduled the national debt. Following the 1998 war, foreign aid propped up the incumbent government. At the end of 2000, the country qualified for almost $800 million in debt relief under the Heavily Indebted Poor Countries (HIPC) initiative.

In December 2010, the country reached the completion point of the HIPC. Tax revenues exceeded predictions by 2% of GDP, reflecting a good cashew harvest. The government contained spending and kept domestic arrears on target. In May 2011, the Paris Club canceled $283 million of Guinea-Bissau's debt.

In 2010–11 the government appealed to bilateral donors to cover immediate operational expenditures such as payment of salaries. However, donors were reluctant to provide direct assistance of this type since the Court of Accounting was unable to act as an independent auditor of government accounts.

In May 2011, the Paris Club of creditors agreed to cancel $256 million of Guinea-Bissau's debt as a reward for progress in tackling poverty and boosting growth. An additional $27 million of bi-lateral debt was also cancelled. The World Bank projected that debt service reductions including the HIPC and the Multilateral Debt Relief Initiative (MDRI) would help the country complete its debt servicing by 2028.

[36]TAXATION

In 2010 the World Bank's *Doing Business* report estimated that a medium-sized business operating in Guinea-Bissau would, annually, make 46 tax payments, spend 208 hours in tax preparation, and pay a total tax rate of 45.9% of profit, slightly above the world average of 44.8%. Taxes comprised 15.8% social security contributions, 14.9% corporate income tax, 9% accident insurance, and 5.3% stamp duty on sales. The World Bank index ranked Guinea-Bissau's tax structure 26th of 46 sub Saharan African countries and 137th out of 183 countries worldwide.

37 CUSTOMS AND DUTIES

Import licenses were freely issued for most goods. Most imports were taxed, but luxury goods were more heavily taxed, while capital goods enjoyed special treatment. Duties were applied ad valorem; some common duties included rice (10%), gasoline (55%), diesel (15%), automobiles (40–95%), auto parts (36%), furniture (30%), and household appliances (25%). A 15–20% value-added tax (VAT) was also applied, as well as a 1% statistical tax and a 1% community solidarity tax. For WAEMU member countries, the average duties applied were 5% on raw materials and equipment, 10% on intermediate and selected goods, and 20% on other consumer goods.

In 2012, on the World Bank's "Ease of Doing Business" index, "Trade Across Borders," Guinea-Bissau ranked 117th out of 183 economies, which was one ranking lower than 2011. The duty to import a container amounted to $2,006 compared with $2,503 for sub Saharan African (SSA) countries, and the cost to export a container was $1,448 compared with $1,960 for SSA countries and $1,085 for OECD countries. Time required to export was estimated to be 23 days and required completion of six customs documents, whereas time to import required 22 days and six documents. In SSA countries on average the time required to export was 8 days and to import 37 days.

38 FOREIGN INVESTMENT

Foreign direct investment (FDI) in Guinea-Bissau amounted to a net inflow of $14 million according to World Bank figures published in 2009. FDI represented 1.67% of GDP. On the World Bank's "2011 Doing Business" survey, the country ranked 31st of 46 sub Saharan countries, and 176th out of 183 economies worldwide for starting a business. To improve the business climate, government established a Business Formation Center, and reduced the time it took to register a business from 216 days to 1 day. Corruption constituted a further constraint on investment.

Low investor confidence in the country was affected by perceptions of widespread corruption. In 2011, the country was considered "highly corrupt," scoring 2.2 on the Transparency International Corruption Perception Index (CPI) scale where 0 represented a "highly corrupt" political and economic climate and 10 a "highly clean" environment. The country ranked 154th on the world scale, and 35th in sub Saharan Africa.

39 ECONOMIC DEVELOPMENT

As of 2011 the GDP rate of change in Guinea-Bissau was 3.5%. Inflation stood at 3.8%. Historically, low levels of private investment have left the country dependent for growth on bi- and multi-lateral donor assistance. In May 2010, the IMF Executive Board approved a 3-year Extended Credit Facility (ECF) of $33.3 million to support Guinea-Bissau's medium-term economic program.

Since the 1980s economic development has been predicated on the development of agriculture and infrastructure. Foreign aid av-

eraged $64.3 million per year from 1982–85. Multilateral aid accounted for almost half this sum, chiefly from the IDA. The first development plan (1983–88) called for self-sufficiency in food supplies, with 25% of a $403.3 million investment going for construction and public works, 18% for rural development, and 14% for transport. The second development plan (1988–91) was totally financed by foreign aid. Numerous countries and intergovernmental organizations provided food aid, technical assistance, and balance-of-payments support. Following the 1998 war, donor commitments reached over $200 million.

The country implemented its first Poverty Reduction Strategy Paper (PRSP) in 2006–07. In mid-2011 government signed its second PRSP covering 2011–2015, which targeted economic stabilization, improved governance, rule of law, and achievement of the Millennium Development Goals (MDGs). As concerned the MDGs, it was largely conceded that the country would not meet its goals, but would continue nonetheless to strive for improvement in economic and social sectors.

In 2000, Guinea-Bissau qualified for almost $800 million in debt service relief under the International Monetary Fund (IMF)/ World Bank Heavily Indebted Poor Countries (HIPC) initiative, geared toward reducing poverty and stimulating economic growth. That year, it negotiated a three-year $18 million Poverty Reduction and Growth Facility (PRGF) Arrangement with the IMF to support the government's 2000–03 economic reform program. Following approval of the assistance, the IMF stated the country had lost budgetary control, with large unauthorized expenditures, particularly on defense. A drop in world cashew prices and a loss of foreign program financing in 2001 resulted in a decrease in economic activity.

Since 2006–2007, economic growth prospects have been relatively modest. Despite the global financial crisis, Guinea-Bissau achieved 3.5% growth in 2010. However, the dependence of the economy on a single export crop for its income and foreign reserves left the country vulnerable to climate, world prices and other external shocks. The economy was ranked 159th out of 179 economies worldwide on the 2011 Index of Economic Freedom, which measures the degree of openness or repressiveness of an economy.

40 SOCIAL DEVELOPMENT

Guinea-Bissau ranked far below the world average in public expenditures in the social sector. No reliable data was available on government expenditures on education as a percentage of GDP; in 2009, 8.6% of GDP was spent on healthcare. Two-thirds of the population lived under the $2/day poverty threshold; life expectancy was 47.5 years, and resilience was further weakened by the low availability of social services. The UNDP Human Development Index (HDI), which measures prospects for a long and healthy life and quality education, ranked Guinea-Bissau 176th out of 187 countries.

Provision of health services, including maternal and child care, nutrition programs, environmental sanitation, safe water distribution, and basic education, remained a social goal of the government, but low levels of funding, lack of technical and human resource capacity, and widespread corruption limited social progress. In lieu of a formal social welfare system, people relied on family, relatives and friends for support.

Although officially prohibited by law, discrimination against women persisted, especially in areas where Islamic law was dominant. Women had little access to education, and were responsible for most of the work on subsistence farms. The illiteracy rate for women was 82%. Domestic abuse against women was not only widespread, but also socially acceptable as a means of settling domestic disputes. Traditionally, female genital mutilation (FGM) has been commonly practiced, but in June 2011, the National Assembly overwhelmingly adopted a law against it, permitting penalties of up to 5 years in prison for perpetrators. However, enforcement of the law was expected to be problematic.

Some cases of arbitrary detention and the use of excessive force were reported, and members of the security forces were not held accountable for abuses of detainees' rights.

41HEALTH

According to the CIA, life expectancy in Guinea-Bissau was 47.5 years in 2011. The country spent 8.6% of its GDP on healthcare, amounting to $18 per person. There was 1 physician, 6 nurses and midwives, and 10 hospital beds per 10,000 inhabitants. The fertility rate was 5.7, while the infant mortality rate was 115 per 1,000 live births. In 2008 the maternal mortality rate, according to the World Bank, was 1,000 per 100,000 births. It was estimated that 76% of children were vaccinated against measles. The CIA calculated HIV/AIDS prevalence in Guinea-Bissau to be about 2.5% in 2009.

42HOUSING

Most traditional housing units were made of adobe, mud, and/or *quirinton*, a combination of woven branches and straw. Most of these units used petrol lamps for lighting; they did not have a sewage system or septic tank and water was usually available from wells or springs. Approximately 61% of the population had access to improved water sources, but only 21% to improved sanitation facilities in 2010. Though most of the population lived in rural areas, migration to urban areas has resulted in housing shortages. Civil war in 1998 destroyed about 5,000 homes.

43EDUCATION

Education was compulsory between the ages of 7 and 13. Primary school studies covered six years, followed by five years of secondary school. In 2009 the World Bank estimated that 52% of age-eligible children in Guinea-Bissau were enrolled in primary school. Secondary enrollment for age-eligible children stood at 11%. Tertiary enrollment was estimated at 3%. Private schools accounted for about 19% of primary school enrollment and 12.8% of secondary enrollment (2000). In 2011, the CIA reported that Guinea-Bissau had a literacy rate of 42.4%.

The 1998–99 civil war severely disrupted education, closing schools and keeping most of the country's children out of school for at least half a year. In 2000, UNICEF requested $5.22 million to rebuild and refurbish damaged primary schools, buy teaching materials and school supplies, train teachers, and provide other types of aid. In 2002 the government introduced the extended Public-Education-For-All (EFA) program whereby children in public schools no longer paid school fees or had to buy text books.

Amilcar Cabral University, the first public university in the nation, was established in 2003. The University of Colinas de Boe, a private university, also opened in 2003. There was no data available on the amount of public expenditure on education as a percentage of GDP.

44LIBRARIES AND MUSEUMS

The National Institute of Studies and Research (Instituto Nacional de Estudos e Pesquisa—INEP) in Bissau maintained a collection of 40,000 volumes, which included national archives and a museum. The Museum of Guinea-Bissau, also in Bissau, had a library of 14,000 volumes and maintained collections of interest in the fields of ethnography, history, natural science, and economics. There were municipal libraries in major cities. There were two museums in Bissau, the Museum of Portuguese Guinea and the National Ethnographic Museum.

45MEDIA

In 2009 the CIA reported that there were 4,800 telephone landlines in Guinea-Bissau. Mobile phone subscriptions averaged 35 per 100 people and constituted the preferred mode of communication. There was one FM radio station and four AM radio stations. Most people got their news and information from radio. Internet users numbered 2 per 100 citizens. In 2010 there were 82 internet hosts.

The main radio network was the government's Radiodifusão Nacional de Guiné-Bissau. Television consisted of the state national television station (RTGB) and the Portuguese-funded RTP Africa. Satellite television was also available via dish and subscription fees. The government news service was the Agencia Bissau Media e Publicacoes.

The government-owned daily, *Voz da Guine*, in Portuguese, had an estimated circulation of 6,000 in 2002. Privately owned newspapers (published once or a few times a week) include *Diario de Bissau, Banobero, Gazeta de Noticias, Fraskera*, and *No Pintcha*. These newspapers often delayed publication owing to financial constraints and dependence on the state-owned printing house, which frequently ran out of supplies.

The constitution provided for free speech and free press, but in practice state and private media professionals self-censored to avoid intimidation by government including detention, closures and other crackdowns. According to Freedom House's "Freedom in the World" 2011 Index, which measures the degree of political rights and civil liberties in countries, Guinea-Bissau was considered "partly free."

46ORGANIZATIONS

Guinea-Bissau has a rich tapestry of community-based organizations including faith-based, women's credit associations and youth cultural and sport groups. Trade associations included farmers and cashew growers, market-owners, shop-keepers, hair-dressers and barbers, dress-makers, mechanics and transport operators. A number of national-level NGOs with church and donor support included Caritas, Justice and Peace Commissions of the Catholic Church, human rights and legal assistance groups, and peacebuilding organizations such as the West Africa Network for Peacebuilding and Voz di Paz.

⁴⁷TOURISM, TRAVEL, AND RECREATION

The *Tourism Factbook*, published by the UN World Tourism Organization, reported 30,100 incoming tourists to Guinea-Bissau in 2007, who spent a total of $38.2 million. Of those incoming tourists, there were 13,400 from Africa and 10,300 from Europe. There were an unknown number of hotel beds available in Guinea-Bissau. The estimated daily cost to visit Bissau, the capital, was $278. The cost of visiting other cities averaged $88.

Tourism had great potential, but insecurity, poor infrastructure and the relatively high cost of visiting Guinea-Bissau discouraged growth in the sector. Game shooting had the potential to be a major attraction for many travelers as game was abundant in the open country as well as in the more inaccessible forest and jungle areas. 14% of the national territory was designated parkland, but services and related agencies were underfunded. Traditional cultural practices of various ethnic groups also were of interest. Bissau was run-down, but had an old town center adjacent to the port that featured colonial buildings, a liberation square and monument, a military fortress and former Portuguese quarter with narrow streets and houses. The island of Bubaque and the town of Bolama were cited for their charm and beauty.

In 2011 visitors were required to show a valid passport and an onward ticket. Visas could be secured upon arrival at the airport. Travelers from an infected area and from most of Africa and South America were required to have evidence of a yellow fever vaccination.

⁴⁸FAMOUS PERSONS

The best-known Guinean of recent years was Amilcar Cabral (1921–73), a founder of PAIGC, its first secretary-general, and a key figure in the war for independence until he was assassinated. Luis de Almeida Cabral (b. 1931), a cofounder of the liberation movement in September 1956 and the younger brother of Amilcar Cabral, subsequently became the first president of Guinea-Bissau; after release from detention by the Revolutionary Council in December 1981, he left the country. João Bernardo Vieira (1939–2009), leader of the Revolutionary Council, came to power in the 1980 coup. Vieira was deposed by rebels in 1999, made a political comeback in 2005, won election as president, but was assassinated in March 2009. Paulo Freire (1921–1997), a Brazilian educator and social theorist, put Guinea-Bissau on the world map through his involvement in an adult literacy campaign from May 1975–October 1976, which culminated in his 1978 widely-read book, *Pedagogy in Progress: Letters to Guinea-Bissau*.

⁴⁹DEPENDENCIES

Guinea-Bissau has no territories or colonies.

⁵⁰BIBLIOGRAPHY

Adebajo, Adekeye. Building Peace in West Africa: Liberia, Sierra Leone, and Guinea-Bissau. Boulder, CO: Lynne Rienner, 2002.

Guinea-Bissau Investment and Business Guide: Strategic and Practical Information. Washington, DC: International Business Publications USA, 2012.

Hawthorne, Walter. *Planting Rice and Harvesting Slaves: Transformations along the Guinea-Bissau Coast, 1400–1900.* Portsmouth, NH: Heinemann, 2003.

Paz, Voz di. *Roots of Conflicts in Guinea-Bissau: The Voice of the People.* Brussels, Belgium: Interpeace, 2010.

Schwab, Peter. *Designing West Africa: Prelude to 21st-Century Calamity.* New York: Palgrave, 2004.

Vigh, Henrik. *Navigating Terrains of War: Youth and Soldiering in Guinea-Bissau.* New York: Berghahn Books, 2006.

Zeilig, Leo, and David Seddon. *A Political and Economic Dictionary of Africa.* Philadelphia: Routledge/Taylor and Francis, 2005.

KENYA

Republic of Kenya
Jamhuri ya Kenya

CAPITAL: Nairobi

FLAG: The flag is a horizontal tricolor of black, red, and green stripes separated by narrow white bars. At the center is a red shield with black and white markings superimposed on two crossed white spears. Black symbolizes the majority population, red the blood shed in the struggle for freedom, green stands for natural wealth, and white for peace; the shield and crossed spears symbolize the defense of freedom.

ANTHEM: *Ee Mungu Nguvu Yetu (O God of All Creation).*

MONETARY UNIT: The Kenya shilling (KES) is a paper currency of 100 cents; the Kenya pound is a unit of account equivalent to 20 shillings. There are coins of 5, 10, and 50 cents, and 1, 5, 10, and 20 shillings; and notes of 50, 100, 200, 500 and 1000 shillings. KES1 = US$0.01158 (or US$1 = KES86.3568) as of 2012.

WEIGHTS AND MEASURES: The metric system is used.

HOLIDAYS: New Year's Day, 1 January; Labor Day, 1 May; Madaraka Day, 1 June; Kenyatta Day, 20 October; Uhuru (Independence) Day, 12 December; Christmas, 25 December; Boxing Day, 26 December. Movable holidays include Good Friday, Easter Monday, Eid al-Fitr, and Eid al-Adha.

TIME: 3 p.m. = noon GMT.

¹LOCATION, SIZE, AND EXTENT

Situated on the eastern coast of Africa, Kenya lies astride the equator. Its total area, including 11,230 sq km (4,336 sq mi) of water, is 582,650 sq km (224,962 sq mi), with a maximum length of 1,131 km (703 mi) SSE–NNW and a maximum width of 1,025 km (637 mi) ENE–WSW. Comparatively, the area occupied by Kenya is slightly more than twice the size of the state of Nevada. Kenya is bounded on the N by South Sudan and Ethiopia, on the E by Somalia, on the SE by the Indian Ocean, on the S by Tanzania, and on the W by Lake Victoria and Uganda. Kenya has a total land boundary length of 3,477 km (2,161 mi) and a coastline of 536 km (333 mi).

Kenya's capital city, Nairobi, is located in the south-central part of the country.

²TOPOGRAPHY

Kenya is notable for its topographical variety. The low-lying, fertile coastal region, fringed with coral reefs and islands, is backed by a gradually rising coastal plain, a dry region covered with savanna and thornbush. At an altitude of over 1,500 m (5,000 ft) and about 480 km (300 mi) inland, the plain gives way in the southwest to a high plateau, rising in parts to more than 3,050 m (10,000 ft), on which most of the population and the majority of economic activities are concentrated. The northern section of Kenya, forming three-fifths of the whole territory, is arid and of semidesert character, as is the bulk of the southeastern quarter.

In the high plateau area, known as the Kenya Highlands, lie Mt. Kenya (5,199 m/17,057 ft), Mt. Elgon (4,310 m/14,140 ft), and the Aberdare Range (rising above 3,962 m/13,000 ft). The plateau is bisected from north to south by the Great Rift Valley, part of the geological fracture that can be traced from Syria through the Red Sea and East Africa to Mozambique. In the north of Kenya the valley is broad and shallow, embracing Lake Rudolf (Lake Turkana), which is about 207 km (155 mi) long; farther south the valley narrows and deepens and is walled by escarpments 600–900 m (2,000–3,000 ft) high. West of the Great Rift Valley, the plateau descends to the plains that border Lake Victoria. The principal rivers are the Tana and the Athi, both flowing southeastward to the Indian Ocean, and the Ewaso Ngiro, which flows in a northeasterly direction to the swamps of the Lorian Plain.

³CLIMATE

The climate of Kenya is as varied as its topography. Climatic conditions range from the tropical humidity of the coast through the dry heat of the hinterland and northern plains to the coolness of the plateau and mountains; despite Kenya's equatorial position, Mt. Kenya is perpetually snowcapped. The coastal temperature averages 27°C (81°F), and the temperature decreases by slightly less than 2°C (3°F) with each 300 m (1,000 ft) increase in altitude. The capital, Nairobi, at 1,661 m (5,449 ft), has a mean annual temperature of 19°C (66°F); at 2,740 m (9,000 ft) the average is 13°C (55°F). The arid northern plains range from 21°-27°C (70–81°F).

Seasonal variations are distinguished by duration of rainfall rather than by changes of temperature. Most regions of the country have two rainy seasons, the long rains falling between April and June and the short rains between October and December. Average annual rainfall varies from 13 cm (5 in) a year in the most arid regions of the northern plains to 193 cm (76 in) near Lake Victoria. The coast and highland areas receive an annual average of 102 cm (40 in).

⁴FLORA AND FAUNA

The World Resources Institute estimates that there are 6,506 plant species in Kenya. The vegetation and animal life of Kenya reflect the variety of its topography and climate. Along the coastal region coconut trees flourish, with occasional mangrove swamps and rain forest. The vast plains of the hinterland and the northern regions are covered with grass, low bush, and scrub, giving way in the high-lying plains to typical savanna country of open grass dotted with thorn trees, and in the more arid regions to bare earth and stunted scrub. The highland areas are in parts densely forested with bamboo and valuable timber, the predominant trees being African camphor, African olive, podo, and pencil cedar.

Wildlife in Kenya abounds both in the sparsely populated areas and in the national parks and reserves that have been created for its protection. Kenya is home to 407 mammal, 1,103 bird, 261 reptile, and 76 amphibian species. The calculation reflects the total number of distinct species residing in the country, not the number of endemic species. Elephant, rhinoceros, lion, zebra, giraffe, buffalo, hippopotamus, wildebeest, and many kinds of buck are among the large mammals that abound on the plains and along the rivers. Kenya's diverse bird species include cranes, flamingos, ostriches, and vultures.

5 ENVIRONMENT

The World Resources Institute reported that Kenya had designated 6.91 million hectares (17.08 million acres) of land for protection as of 2006. Major problems of deforestation and soil erosion are attributed to growing population pressure. Furthermore, drought and desertification (to which 83% of Kenya's land area is vulnerable) threatened potential productive agricultural lands. Also of concern is the drop in water level at Lake Victoria. Water resources totaled 30.2 cu km (7.25 cu mi) while water usage was 1.58 cu km (.379 cu mi) per year. Domestic water usage accounted for 30% of total usage, industrial for 6%, and agricultural for 64%. Per capita water usage totaled 46 cu m (1,624 cu ft) per year. Water pollution from urban and industrial wastes posed a major environmental problem. The UN reported in 2008 that carbon dioxide emissions in Kenya totaled 11,227 kilotons.

Mount Kenya National Park is listed as a natural UNESCO World Heritage Site. Kenya has five Ramsar wetland sites. Game hunting and trade in ivory and skins have been banned, but poaching threatens leopards, cheetahs, lions, elephants, rhinoceroses, and other species. It is illegal to kill an animal even if it attacks. According to a 2011 report issued by the International Union for Conservation of Nature and Natural Resources (IUCN), the number of threatened species included 28 types of mammals, 31 species of birds, 6 types of reptiles, 7 species of amphibians, 68 species of fish, 17 types of mollusks, 55 species of other invertebrates, and 129 species of plants. Endangered species included the Sokoke scops owl, Taita blue-banded papilio, Tana River mangabey, Tana River red colobus, the green sea turtle, and the hawksbill turtle. There are 45 extinct species including the Kenyan rocky river frog and the Kenya oribi.

6 POPULATION

The US Central Intelligence Agency (CIA) estimated that the population of Kenya in 2011 was 41,070,934, which placed it at number 32 in population among the 196 nations of the world. In 2011, approximately 2.7% of the population was over 65 years of age, with another 42.2% under 15 years of age. The median age in Kenya was 18.9 years. There were 1.01 males for every female in the country. The population's annual rate of change was 2.462%. The projected population for the year 2025 was 51,300,000. Population density in Kenya was calculated at 71 people per sq km (184 people per sq mi).

The UN estimated that 22% of the population lived in urban areas, and that urban populations had an annual rate of change of 4.2%. The largest urban areas, along with their respective populations, included Nairobi, 3.4 million and Mombassa, 966,000.

The prevalence of HIV/AIDS has had a significant impact on the population of Kenya. The AIDS epidemic has caused higher death and infant mortality rates, and lowered life expectancy.

7 MIGRATION

Estimates of Kenya's net migration rate, carried out by the CIA in 2011, amounted to zero. The total number of emigrants living abroad was 457,100, and the total number of immigrants living in Kenya was 817,700. Kenya also accepted 173,702 refugees from Somalia, 73,004 from South Sudan, and 16,428 from Ethiopia. Throughout Kenya there is a slow but steady movement of the rural population to the cities in search of employment. Some Kenyans have emigrated to Uganda, and ethnic Somalis are present in significant numbers in Kenya's Northeastern Province. Kenya's refugee population included Somalis, Sudanese, Ethiopians, Ugandans, and a smaller group comprised of various other nationalities.

Far-reaching migratory changes took place in the years immediately preceding and following independence. By 1961, the post-1945 trend of net European immigration was reversed, and in the three years that followed, approximately 29,000 Europeans left Kenya. Permanent emigration in 1964 reached 9,860, while permanent immigration totaled 5,406. In the first year of independence, some 6,000 Britons renounced their citizenship and applied for Kenyan citizenship; during the same period, approximately 70,000 persons living in Kenya—the majority of them Asians—were granted British passports. After the United Kingdom limited immigration by Asians in 1967, a crisis situation developed in Kenya. Work permits, without which Asians could not stay in the country beyond a limited period, were not issued, and the United Kingdom denied entry to Asians from Kenya who wanted to work in the United Kingdom. In 1973, the Kenya government served 1,500 notices of termination to Asian employees (there were 300 in 1972) and announced that by the end of 1974 it aimed to completely Kenyanize the country's retail and wholesale trade. In 1975, the Ministry of Commerce and Industry ordered the closing of 436 businesses, most of which belonged to Asians.

8 ETHNIC GROUPS

African peoples indigenous to Kenya, who form 98% of the population, fall into three major cultural and linguistic groups: Bantu, Nilotic, and Cushitic. Although most of the land area is occupied by Cushitic and Nilotic peoples, over 70% of the population is Bantu. The Luo, a Nilotic people, live in an area adjacent to Lake Victoria. Other Nilotes-Turkana, Maasai, Pokot, Nandi, Kipsigis, and Tugen-occupy a broad area in the west from Lake Rudolf to the Tanzania border. Cushites such as the Galla and Somali live in the eastern and northeastern parts of the country. The Bantu reside mainly in the coastal areas and the southwestern uplands; the most significant Bantu peoples are the Kikuyu, Kamba, and

Luhya. The Kikuyu, who constitute the largest single ethnic group in Kenya, live for the most part north of Nairobi and have played a major role in the nation's political and social development. The estimated proportions of the major groups are Kikuyu 22%, Luhya 14%, Luo 13%, Kalenjin 12%, Kamba 11%, Kisii 6%, and Meru 6%. Other Africans constitute 15% of the total population. These smaller groups include the Bajuni, Kijikenda, Digo, and Nubians. Non-Africans (Arabs, Asians, and Europeans) account for no more than 1% of the population. The Arab community is centered on the Indian Ocean coast. The Swahili, a group of mixed Arab-Africans with a cultural affinity to the Arabs, also live in the coastal region. Most Asians in Kenya have origins traceable to the Indian subcontinent; living primarily in urban centers, they consist of at least 31 culturally separate groups but make up less than 0.4% of the nation's population. The European community, which has rebounded since the 1960s, is primarily of British origin. About 12% of the Europeans hold Kenyan citizenship. A 1984 law provides that people born in Kenya of non-Kenyan parents can no longer claim Kenyan citizenship.

9 LANGUAGES

Although there are linguistic groupings of very similar dialects, nearly all the African ethnic groups have their own distinct languages. Swahili (Kiswahili), however, increasingly has become an East African lingua franca, and in 1974 it became Kenya's official language, along with English. English remains in wide use in business and government, and parliamentary bills must be drafted and presented in that language. Both Gujarati and Punjabi are widely used among the Asian community.

10 RELIGIONS

Christians account for about 80% of the population, with Protestants accounting for 58% of all Christians and Roman Catholics accounting for 42%. About 10% are Muslim, with many living in the Northeastern Province, the Coast Province, and the northern region of the Eastern Province. Hindus, Sikhs, and Baha'is each account for less than 1% of the population. As in other African states with complex religious histories and some renewal of cultural self-consciousness, it is likely that a majority of ethnic Kenyans also hold traditional African beliefs. Foreign missionary groups include the African Inland Mission (Evangelical Protestant), the Pentecostal Assembly of Kenya, the Southern Baptist Church, and the Missionary Society of Britain (Anglican).The current constitution provides for freedom of religion and this right is generally respected in practice. Some of the latest amendments to the constitution included the implementation of government-funded Kadhi courts based on Shari'ah (Islamic) law for matters of family law pertaining to Muslims. A secular court still hears all criminal and civil proceedings and non-Muslims are directed to secular courts as well. However, some Christians regard the government sponsorship of these courts as preferentially treatment for Muslims. Religious organizations must register with the government Registrar of Societies; some small splinter groups have had their applications denied as the government did not consider them to be separate from their larger parent organization. The practice of witchcraft with the intent to cause harm is prohibited, but the offense is usually only prosecuted in cases that involve other crim-

inal charges, such as murder. Good Friday, Easter Monday, Eid al-Fitr, Christmas, and Diwali are observed as national holidays.

11 TRANSPORTATION

Half of Kenya's railway system was made up by the main line between the Ugandan border and Mombasa, the chief port.

A modern installation, the port at Mombasa serves Uganda, Tanzania, Rwanda, Burundi, the DROC, and the Sudan as well as Kenya. A national shipping line, 70% state owned, was created in 1987. There is steamer service on Lake Victoria. In 2008, the merchant marine had one ship of 1,000 gross registered tons (GRT) or over.

The CIA reported that Kenya had a total of 160,886 km (99,970 mi) of roads in 2008, of which 11,197 km (6,957 mi) are paved. The major road from Nairobi to Mombasa is well paved, and the government has undertaken a campaign to widen and resurface secondary roads. All-weather roads linking Kenya with the Sudan and Ethiopia have been completed. Over 80% of Kenya's total passenger and freight traffic use road transport.

Air travel transported 2.95 million passengers in 2009 according to the World Bank. There are major international airports at Nairobi (Jomo Kenyatta) and Mombasa (Moi International). The Nairobi air terminal, opened in 1958 and expanded in 1972 to receive jumbo jets, is a continental terminus for international services from Europe, Asia, and other parts of Africa. Air travel and air freight also are accommodated at Malindi, Kisumu, and numerous smaller airstrips. Kenya Airways flies to other nations of East Africa, the Middle East, Europe, and the Indian subcontinent.

12 HISTORY

Fossil remains show that humanlike creatures lived in the area of Lake Rudolf perhaps two million years ago. As early as the third millennium BC, cattle were being herded in what is now northern Kenya. Sometime in the first millennium BC, food-producing Cushitic-speaking peoples, possibly from the Ethiopian highlands, appeared in Kenya. During the Iron Age (c. AD 1000), the first Bantu speakers arrived, probably from points south and west, resulting in the retreat of Cushitic speakers. The Nilotic speakers entered at the end of the 16th century from the north or northwest, from South Sudan, and perhaps from the western Ethiopian borderland.

After their arrival, most groups settled into a pattern of slow and gradual movement highlighted by spurts of expansionist activity. For example, the Eastern Bantu (Kikuyu, Meru, Kamba, Pokomo, Teita, and Bajuni), possibly after settling in the area between Lamu and the Juba River, dispersed throughout southern and coastal Kenya. By 1400, the Kikuyu had reached the area near Mt. Kenya; they were joined there by the Meru in the 1750s. The Western Bantu (Luhya and Gusii) developed from an influx of Kalenjin (1598–1625) and Bantu (1598–1733) migrants. Other peoples, including the Luo, developed a strong ethnic identity and protected themselves from intruders. But as their population increased between 1750 and 1800, conflict arose, clans broke down, and another wave of migration ensued.

The Cushitic and Nilotic peoples (represented by Kalenjin ancestors of the Pokot, Nandi, Kipsigis, Kony, and Tugen) and others (such as the Turkana, Teso, and Galla) participated in independent movements beginning in the 16th century and lasting into the 18th. By 1800, the Kamba, acting as the chief carriers and go-betweens, dominated an extensive intergroup long-distance trade network that linked the interior to the East African coast. The last migrants into the country were the Somali, who did not enter northeastern Kenya in great numbers until the late 19th and early 20th centuries.

Meanwhile, another set of migrants settled on the Indian Ocean coast. As in the interior, the newcomers replaced the original hunter-gatherer inhabitants. In the period prior to the Common Era, Egyptians, Phoenicians, Persians, and possibly even Indonesians visited the coast. By the 10th century the Bantu had settled the coastal region in what the Arabs called the Land of the Zenj (blacks). As the area flourished, a mixed population of Arabs and Africans combined in creating the Swahili culture, a culture marked by its own language, a devotion to Islam, and the development of numerous coastal trade centers. Swahili cities such as Kilwa, Mombasa, and Pate remained independent of one another and of foreign control and, although they had little contact with the interior, grew wealthy from their mercantile contacts with India and Arabia.

Throughout the 16th century, following Vasco da Gama's landing at Malindi in 1498, the coastal cities struggled to remain independent of the external threats posed first by the Portuguese and then by the Omani Arabs. Although the Portuguese established posts and gained a monopoly of the trade along the Kenya coast, the Arabs eventually succeeded in driving out the Portuguese and reestablishing Arab authority in 1740. Independent Arab settlements persisted for a century until, during the rule (1806–56) of Sayyid Sa'id, a kind of unity was established. Arab control even in the 19th century continued to be confined to the coastal belt, however. In 1840, Sayyid Sa'id moved the capital of his sultanate to Zanzibar.

Europeans began to assert their influence in East Africa. After jostling with the Germans and the Italians for Zanzibari favors, the British emerged with a concession for the Kenya coast in 1887. European penetration of the interior had begun decades earlier with the explorations of two German missionaries, Johannes Rebmann and Johann Ludwig Krapf, in 1847–49, and by the English explorer John Hanning Speke at Lake Victoria in 1858. In 1886, the United Kingdom and Germany reached agreement on their respective spheres of influence in East Africa, and the Imperial British East African Company, a private concern, began establishing its authority in the interior two years later. In 1890, a definitive Anglo-German agreement was signed, and arrangements were made with the sultan of Zanzibar for protection to be extended to his mainland holdings. When the company failed in 1895, the United Kingdom assumed direct control over the "East African Protectorate." In December 1901, the railway linking Mombasa with Lake Victoria was completed, and in the following year the boundary between Kenya and Uganda was shifted some 320 km (200 mi) westward to its present position. European and Asian settlement followed the building of the railway, and by World War I the modern development of Kenya was clearly evident. In 1920 the protectorate, with the exception of the coastal strip (later ceded by Zanzibar), was declared a crown colony.

In the interwar years, the major challenge to European political power came from Asians who wanted equality with Europeans in governmental representative institutions. This challenge was successfully resisted, but in the postwar period a more dynamic threat came from African nationalism.

The Struggle for Independence

Africans made use of both legal and nonlegal methods in their struggle for independence from Europeans. The first efforts ended in the eruption of the Mau Mau movement, and a state of emergency was declared in October 1952. Supported primarily by the Kikuyu, Embu, and Meru tribes of Central Province, Mau Mau was a secretive insurrectionary movement that rejected the European domination over Kenya. The emergency lasted until late 1959, and cost over £55 million. At one time, more than 79,000 Africans were detained, and about 13,000 civilians (almost all African) were killed.

During the initial period of the emergency in 1954, the "Lyttelton" multiracial constitution was imposed on Kenyan political groups unable to agree among themselves. It provided both for African and Asian participation in a council of ministers with Europeans and a system of communal representation for each racial group, with a formula of equality of representation in legislative and executive institutions between Europeans and non-Europeans. The introduction of direct elections for Africans to the Legislative Council in 1957 was their first outstanding political gain. With the 1960 "Macleod" constitution came an African-elected majority in the Legislative Council; this represented a decisive shift in the direction of an African-controlled state of Kenya. Rapid advancement toward self-government and independence under African leadership was delayed, however, because of conflicts between the two major African political parties over the future constitutional structure of the country. A constitutional conference in London in early 1962 produced a "framework" constitution, which included formation of a national government representing both political parties. Following new national elections under this constitution in May 1963, Kenya became self-governing on 1 June. On 12 December 1963, Kenya became independent. Exactly one year later it became a republic within the Commonwealth of Nations, with Jomo Kenyatta as the country's first president. His political party, the Kenya African National Union (KANU), dominated the government, and leaders of a rival party, banned in 1969, were detained. On the other hand, some electoral choice was permitted: although all parliamentary candidates in 1969, 1974, and 1979 were KANU members, more than half the incumbents were unseated in the balloting.

An East African Community united Kenya, Tanzania, and Uganda in a common market and customs union until it was dissolved in 1977. Kenya has maintained remarkable political stability, despite territorial disputes with the Somali Democratic Republic, which resulted in sporadic fighting (1963–1968); and with Uganda (1970s). Tanzania closed its borders with Kenya between 1978 and 1983 because Kenya allegedly harbored Idi Amin's supporters after his fall.

Kenyatta died on 22 August 1978 and was succeeded by his vice president, Daniel Arap Moi, who was elected president without opposition a month later. In June 1982, the National Assembly voted unanimously to make Kenya formally a one-party state. On 1 August 1982, a group of junior air force officers, supported by university students and urban workers, attempted a military coup. Looting in Nairobi, particularly of Asian-owned stores, continued

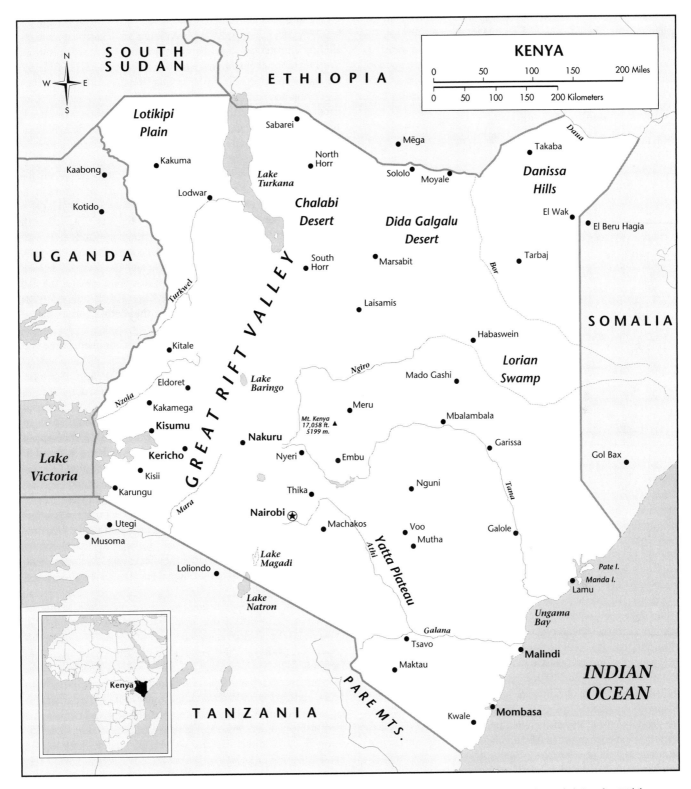

KENYA

0   50   100   150   200 Miles

0   50   100   150   200 Kilometers

LOCATION: 4°30′ N to 4°30′ S; 34° to 42°E. BOUNDARY LENGTHS: South Sudan, 232 kilometers (144 miles); Ethiopia, 861 kilometers (535 miles); Somalia, 682 kilometers (424 miles); Indian Ocean, 523 kilometers (325 miles); Tanzania, 769 kilometers (478 miles); Lake Victoria, 138 kilometers (86 miles); Uganda, 933 kilometers (580 miles). TERRITORIAL SEA LIMIT: 12 miles.

for days. This resulted in more than 500 people reported killed, dissolution of the entire 2,100-member air force, closing of Nairobi University, jailing of almost 1,000 persons, conviction and sentencing to death of 12 conspirators in the following months, and their reported execution in 1985. President Moi ran unopposed in the elections of September 1983; in the National Assembly voting during the same month, five cabinet ministers and 40% of all incumbents went down in defeat.

In 1986, Moi declared that KANU was above government, the parliament and the judiciary. Critics of Moi, even within KANU, were expelled from the party and government repression widened. Many opposition leaders were detained in July 1990 and in 1991 (including former vice president, Oginga Odinga), and clashes between pro-democracy demonstrators and police left five dead.

The Advent of Multiparty Democracy

As pressures mounted for political reform, the United States and 11 other donor nations pressed Moi to reduce government corruption, to improve its poor human rights record, and to institute economic reforms. In 1991, these donors withheld more than $350 million in aid. In December 1991, Moi and his party legalized multiparty politics, but opposition to Moi and civil unrest continued. Ethnic violence from 1991 to 1994 in the Rift Valley left over 3,000 Kikuyu and Luo dead, allegedly the work of "trained warriors" from Moi's ethnic group. In 1993, Africa Watch, a US-based human rights group, reported that as many as 1,500 Kenyans had been killed and over 300,000 displaced as a result of ethnic violence instigated by Moi's regime in the Rift Valley. In the lead-up to the 1997 general elections, ethnic fighting flared up in Mombassa, claiming over 42 lives. The death toll of these clashes pales in comparison to the Hutu-Tutsi genocide, but the social friction they caused provided Moi with what he termed "proof" that the country is too fractured along tribal lines to allow true multiparty democracy.

In Nairobi in January 1992, more than 100,000 attended the first legal antigovernment rally in 22 years. Through the years, the Forum for the Restoration of Democracy (FORD) had emerged as the main opposition. But a conflict between Kenneth Matiba and Odinga signaled ethnic divisions in the run-up to elections required by 21 March 1993. Moi, exploiting those weaknesses, delayed the elections until December. The opposition, divided into eight parties, saw its initial support fade away. Although the late December elections were generally peaceful, Matiba, Odinga, and Mwai Kibaki, of the Democratic Party of Kenya, refused to accept the results. Moi was reelected with 37% of the vote; Matiba had 26%, Kibaki 19%, and Odinga 17%. For the National Assembly, KANU won 100 of the 188 seats; FORD-Kenya, 31; FORD-Asili, 31; and DP, 23. However, many of Moi's cabinet ministers were defeated in their parliamentary contests.

Moi continued to demonstrate his authoritarianism in 1994 and 1995, as opposition groups struggled among themselves to present a united front. Moi's overtly heavy security apparatus stepped up internal oppression, leading the Kenyan Human Rights Commission to report that in the first nine months of 1995, security forces murdered 74 Kenyans in detention, 12 of whom were killed by torture. Violence conducted by unofficial Moi-supported gangs continued as well.

Despite this, opposition forces became vocal as the 1997 elections neared, demanding constitutional reform. Primary among the demands was a constitutional convention and at the very least parliamentary action limiting the powers of the president, and an electoral reform providing for a runoff election if no presidential candidate received more than 50% of the vote—a virtual certainty. Moi, elected with only 36% of the vote in 1992, publicly acknowledged the need for such reforms, but repeatedly postponed any action. This further inflamed opposition parties, and as protests

grew more violent, Moi's repression followed suit. By 9 September 1997, over 70 people had been killed in demonstrations, including 7 protestors killed by police in July in a massive Nairobi demonstration that saw police beating religious leaders inside the Kenya Presbyterian Church at midday. Images of bloodied clerics fleeing armed mobs in the international media outlets led to harsher criticism, further marginalization, escalating civil unrest, and violence. Moi refused to concede to opposition demands, insisting that democratic reforms would lead to the splintering of the country.

On 29 and 30 December 1997, Kenyans went to the polls without constitutional or electoral reform. Again, early hopes of a united opposition victory were dashed as divisions reemerged. Over nine parties split the opposition vote. Moi was reelected with 40% of the vote; Mwai Kibaki of the Democratic Party (DP) had 31%; National Democratic Party's (RDP) Raila Odinga had 11%; FORD-Kenya's M.K. Wamalwa had 8%; and Charity Kaluki Ngilu of the Social Democratic Party (SDP) had about 8%. Of the 210 seats of the National Assembly, KANU won 108; DP, 39; NDP, 21; FORD-Kenya, 17; SDP, 15; Safina and three other parties shared 7 seats.

Following the 1997 elections, civil unrest continued, crime and corruption increased, while the AIDS pandemic claimed at least 600 lives per day. In February 2000 the British Foreign Office minister in charge of Africa, Peter Hain, referred to corruption in Kenya as "the economic equivalent of AIDS." Still, Moi managed to survive a vote of no confidence moved by opposition MPs in October 1998. After 30 months of snubbing the IMF, the Kenyan government finally resumed formal relations with the IMF and in mid-January 2000, the IMF Board voted to resume aid to Kenya. The reestablishment of the East African Common Market was expected to increase trade among the three sister countries.

The opposition and civil society coalesced over the issue of constitutional reform. Bowing to mounting pressure and civil unrest, Moi finally consented to a Constitutional Review Commission Amendment Act, which became effective on 29 January 1999. However, squabbling over who should lead the review process delayed action into 2003.

Following much speculation, Moi went on record saying he would retire at the end of his term in 2002. Although it appeared in April 2002 that elections would be postponed for a year to allow for the drafting of the constitution, the polls were held on 27 December 2002. Mwai Kibaki's landslide victory with 62.2% of the vote over Moi's hand-picked candidate Uhuru Kenyatta with 31.3% ended 24 years of KANU rule under Moi. In the parliamentary vote, Kibaki's National Rainbow Coalition (NARC) won 125 directly elected and seven appointed seats for a total of 132 seats, compared to 64 directly elected and 4 appointed seats for KANU in a parliament of 224 seats. Overall the polls were judged peaceful, free, and fair. The next elections were scheduled to be held in 2007.

President Kibaki campaigned on a policy of generating economic growth, improving education, combating corruption, and implementing a new constitution. With international aid flowing back into Kenya, there have been some major achievements with reference to economic growth and improvements in the educational system. However, the constitutional process proceeded much slower due to disagreements between the partners in the coalition government. The Democratic Party (DP) led by Kibaki and National Alliance Party of Kenya (NAK) faction allied with Kibaki, favored a strong centralized presidential system, while the Liberal Democratic Party (LDP) faction—with fewer parliamentary seats in the coalition than the other two parties—preferred a federal parliamentary system with a strong prime minister while weakening the role of the president.

Raila Odinga, the leader of LDP, had hopes to become prime minister but the proposed new constitution was modified by the government during the Moi regime. The amendments retain a strong president, who controls a weaker prime minister. This resulted in a split between NAK and LDP, with the former campaigning for a "Yes" vote in the referendum on the constitution and the latter a "No." Uhuru Kenyatta's KANU party, which ruled Kenya for most of the postindependence era until its ouster in the 2002 elections was also vigorously campaigning for a "No" vote to the modified constitution. It was thought by some that the political wrangling and alignment over the referendum for the new constitution would imply a wider realignment before the 2007 elections. In addition to these disagreements, there was also a lack of progress in tackling the problem of corruption and the donor nations, particularly the British, strongly criticized the Kibaki government for lack of progress on this front.

In October 2004, Kenyan ecologist Wangari Maathai was announced as the winner of the Nobel Peace Prize. Professor Maathai, who was also Kenya's deputy environment minister, was the first African woman and the first environmentalist to win the prize. Maathai was honored for her campaign to save Africa's trees and for promoting social, economic, and cultural reforms that are ecologically viable. She is the founder of the Green Belt Movement, which has planted 20–30 million trees in Africa to counter deforestation and to slow desertification. The movement went on to campaign for education, nutrition, and other issues important to women.

Between December 2007 and April 2008, ethnic violence occurred in Kenya, the result of the 2007 presidential election, which reelected Kibaki amid allegations of fraud by his opponent Raila Amolo Odinga. Fraud allegations were corroborated by international observers. Nonviolent protests soon became violent and ethnically charged. More than 1,000 people were killed. Former UN secretary general Kofi Annan mediated negotiations between the two parties, forging a power-sharing agreement on 28 February 2008. The agreement established the office of prime minister and created a coalition government. Kibaki retained the presidency, while Odinga became prime minister.

In April 2010, Kenya's parliament approved a new and long awaited draft constitution, which outlined measures that could deeply curtail the powers of the presidency. The new constitution could revoke the president's power to appoint judges, and strike down the ability of cabinet members, who are tapped from parliament, to hold their seats in the legislature. The approval of parliament was only the first step in the process toward formal adoption. The draft must first be approved by the attorney general, who is allowed to make minor adjustments to the draft, and then by the voters, who must approve it in a national referendum. The draft constitution ran into a hurdle in May 2010 when the constitutional court ruled that the inclusion of Kadhi (Islamic) courts was illegal and discriminatory, as it favored one religion over the others. Kadhi courts, whose constitutionality has been challenged by many religious leaders, were introduced under British colonial rule as a way for Muslim families to settle personal matters, such as inheritance, divorce, personal status, and marriage. However, the court ruled that they are unconstitutional because they violate the principle of the separation of church and state. At the same time, the judges refused to remove clauses that condone the Kadhi courts, saying that such actions would violate the separation of powers.

The draft constitution was brought up for a national referendum in August 2010, gaining approval by more than 65% of the population in an election that was deemed fair and peaceful by international observers. Despite the court's initial ruling, the new constitution granted some legal recognition for Kadhi courts. It also included a bill of rights and substantial land reforms. A new senate and county governments were provided with some autonomy and a share of the national budget. The new constitution was officially signed by the president on 27 August 2010.

The Horn of Africa experienced a severe drought in 2010. By July 2011, more than 3.2 million Kenyans had been affected by what was considered the worst drought in 60 years. The loss of crops and livestock was coupled by soaring food prices. The government responded by dropping tariffs on imports of genetically modified maize in the hope of easing the burden, but this move was met by massive protests in the capital from those who believe that such a product is toxic.

13 GOVERNMENT

According to the constitution of 1963, as subsequently amended, the government of Kenya is led by a president who is chief of state, head of government, and commander-in-chief of the armed forces. The president is elected to serve a five-year term; he may, however, dissolve the National Assembly during his term, or the National Assembly may dissolve itself by a vote of no confidence, in which case a new presidential election must also be held. The president appoints the members of the cabinet (the vice president and the heads of the various ministries) from among members of the Assembly. The Assembly is barred by edict of the speaker from debating the conduct of the president. The cabinet is carefully balanced to maintain a multiethnic image, and the allocation of assistant ministerships is part of the communally arranged patronage system.

The unicameral National Assembly—established when the Senate and House of Representatives were merged by constitutional amendment in 1967—consisted of 224 members elected for a maximum term of five years, plus 12 national members nominated by the president and selected by parties in proportion to their parliamentary vote totals. In addition, the speaker of the Assembly and the attorney general are ex-officio members. Technically, MPs are allowed to introduce legislation, but in fact it is the attorney general who does so. Suffrage is universal at age 18.

The office of prime minister was created following a disputed election in 2007.

The constitution recognizes the principle of maximum allocation of governmental powers to local authorities, and provision is made for the establishment of provincial assemblies with local administrative powers. The central government may abridge or extend the powers of local government in the national interest.

14 POLITICAL PARTIES

Following a constitutional conference at Lancaster House in London in February 1960, two national African parties were formed, the Kenya African National Union (KANU) and the Kenya African Democratic Union (KADU). The fundamental difference between the two parties resided in the fact that KANU tended to represent those persons and tribes that were most closely associated with an urban-oriented nationalism and sought a highly centralized political system for Kenya, while KADU represented the more rural and pastoral tribes, who feared a concentration of power by any central government. The political conflicts between these two parties tended to become identified with tribalism, since each party had a core group of tribes committed to it. In the national elections of May 1963, KANU won a majority of seats in both houses of parliament, and its leader, Jomo Kenyatta, assumed power. KADU dissolved itself voluntarily in 1964 and joined KANU.

Since 1964, KANU has dominated Kenyan politics. In March 1966, 30 KANU members of the House announced that they had formed an opposition party, later named the Kenya People's Union (KPU), led by Oginga Odinga, a Luo, who had resigned his post as vice president. By-elections for the 30 seats, held in June 1966, resulted in the KPU's retention of only 9. In July 1969, Tom Mboya, the minister of economic planning, was assassinated. His death touched off old animosities between his tribe, the Luo, and the politically dominant Kikuyu, to which Kenyatta belonged. The government used the pretext of the assassination to ban the KPU and jail Odinga and other opposition leaders. In the 1969 elections, Kenyatta, who ran unopposed, and the KANU slate were returned to power. All parliamentary candidates also were KANU members in 1974 and 1979; however, there were many more candidates than constituencies, and in all three elections a majority of incumbents were unseated.

Following reports that Odinga, who had been freed in 1971, was planning to form a new, Socialist-oriented party, the National Assembly on 9 June 1982 declared Kenya a one-party state. In the wake of the attempted coup that August, Odinga was again detained, and treason charges were brought against his son, Raila Odinga, dean of the engineering school of the University of Nairobi. The treason charges were later dropped, but Oginga Odinga remained under house arrest from November 1982 to October 1983. By that time, presidential and parliamentary elections had been held, with some 900 KANU members vying for the 158 elective seats.

A clandestine dissident group known as Mwakenya was founded in 1981. In 1986, 44 persons were being held in connection with this group, 37 of whom were convicted of sedition. Other underground opposition groups emerged in the 1980s and in 1987 many joined to form the United Movement for Democracy (UMOJA, Swahili for unity).

In December 1991, the Moi government decided to end KANU's monopoly on legal political activity. A grand coalition known as the Forum for the Restoration of Democracy (FORD) was formed, but, before the December 1992 election, it fragmented into two factions—FORD-Kenya, headed by Oginga Odinga and FORD-Asili, led by Kenneth Matiba. The Democratic Party of Kenya (DP) was headed by Mwai Kibaki and the Kenya National Congress (KNC) by Chilube wa Tsuma. Three other parties were active, even in the face of persecution by Moi's police. In particular, government prevented opposition MPs, domestic and international human rights figures, and journalists from entering the security zones of the Rift Valley, where the government conducted a policy of ethnic cleansing against the area's non-Kalenjin population. In 1993 alone, the KANU-led government arrested 36 of the 85 opposition MPs.

In the run-up to the scheduled 1997 elections, opposition parties made a brief attempt at unity with the formation in 1995 of the united National Democratic Alliance. Factional bickering, however, rendered it stillborn. Also in 1995, the Safina Party was founded by Richard Leakey, the world-renowned paleoanthropologist and former head of the Kenya Wildlife Service, a post for which he was handpicked by President Moi. Leakey intended to organize an umbrella opposition party, but Moi promptly banned Safina. By 1996, however, several opposition parties had tentatively acknowledged their support of Safina. By March 1997 there were 26 registered political parties, but only 10 won parliamentary seats in the 1997 elections judged as fairly credible.

In the run-up to the 27 December 2002 elections, the opposition led by Mwai Kibaki organized a grand electoral alliance of four parties, the National Rainbow Coalition (NARC). The four parties in this coalition were Democratic Party led by Mwai Kibaki, Forum for the Restoration of Democracy-Kenya, Liberal Democratic Party, and National Party of Kenya. This coalition was victorious in the December 2002 elections, which elected Mwai Kibaki president, defeating Uhuru Kenyatta. The seats won by party were as follows: NARC 125, KANU 64, FORD-P 14, and other 7; ex-officio 2; seats appointed by the president: NARC 7, KANU 4, and FORD-P 1.

The 2007 presidential election reelected Kibaki, but there were allegations of fraud by his opponent Odinga. Violent protests followed, and a power-sharing agreement reached in early 2008 created the office of prime minister. Kibaki retained the presidency, while Odinga became prime minister.

The next elections were scheduled for December 2012.

15 LOCAL GOVERNMENT

Kenya is divided into seven provinces: Coast, Northeastern, Eastern, Central, Rift Valley, Nyanza, and Western. (The Nairobi area is separate and has special status.) These are subdivided into 63 districts, each headed by a presidentially appointed commissioner; provincial administration is closely supervised by the central government. There are two types of upper local authorities (municipalities and county councils) and four types of lower authorities (urban councils, township authorities, area councils, and local councils). The Nairobi area, administered by a city council, is the direct responsibility of the central government. Many of the councils raise their own revenues by taxes, construct and maintain roads, carry out public health schemes, construct and improve housing, support education, and provide agricultural and social welfare services.

16 JUDICIAL SYSTEM

The legal system is based on the 1963 constitution, the Judicature Act of 1967, and common law court precedent. Kenya accepts compulsory ICJ jurisdiction with reservations. Customary law, to the extent it does not conflict with statutory law, is used as a guide in civil matters concerning persons of the same ethnic group.

The judicial system consists of the Court of Appeal, which has final appellate jurisdiction, and subordinate courts. The High Court, sitting continuously at Nairobi, Mombasa, Nakuru, and Kisumu, and periodically at Eldoret, Kakamega, Nyeri, Kitale, Kisii, and Meru, consists of a chief justice and 24 associate judges, who are appointed by the president of the republic. The High Court has both civil and criminal jurisdiction, serving as an appellate tribunal in some cases and as a court of first instance in others. Lower courts are presided over by resident magistrates and district magistrates. Questions of Islamic law are determined by qadis' courts. Military courts handle court-martials of military personnel.

Although the constitution provides for an independent judiciary, the president has considerable influence over the judiciary. The president appoints the High Court Judges with the advice of the Judicial Service Commission. The president also has authority to dismiss judges, the attorney general, and other officials upon recommendation of a tribunal appointed by the president.

17 ARMED FORCES

The International Institute for Strategic Studies reports that armed forces in Kenya totaled 24,120 members in 2011. The force is comprised of 20,000 from the army, 1,620 from the navy, and 2,500 members of the air force. Armed forces represent 0.2% of the labor force in Kenya. Defense spending totaled $1.9 billion and accounted for 2.8% of GDP. Kenya contributed personnel to nine international peacekeeping missions, mainly in other African nations.

18 INTERNATIONAL COOPERATION

On 16 December 1963, Kenya became a member of the UN; the nation participates in ECA and several nonregional specialized agencies, such as UNESCO UNHCR, IAEA, FAO, IRC, IMO, the World Bank, and WHO. Kenya is also a member of the African Development Bank, the ACP Group, the Commonwealth of Nations, COMESA, G-15, G-77, the WTO, the New Partnership for Africa's Development (NEPAD), and the African Union. President Daniel Arap Moi was OAU chairman during 1981–82 and 1982–83. Nairobi has become increasingly important as a headquarters for international agencies (including the secretariat of the UN Environment Program) and as a convention center for world organizations.

On 26 June 1980, Kenya signed an agreement with the United States allowing the latter access to air and naval facilities at Mombasa. Since the US embassy bombings in August 1998, the World Trade Center attacks on 11 September 2001, and the November 2002 hotel bombing in Mombasa, the two nations have solidified their common front against international terrorism. The administration of US president George W. Bush designated Kenya a strategic regional pillar in the American national security strategy, and renewed airbase, port access, and overflight agreements with the Kenyan government.

The Kenyan government has played a key role in peace negotiations regarding the civil war in Sudan. On 9 January 2005, a Sudan North-South Comprehensive Peace Accord was signed in Nairobi.

Likewise, the government has participated in negotiations to reinstate a central government authority in Somalia.

In environmental cooperation, Kenya is part of the Basel Convention, the Convention on Biological Diversity, Ramsar, CITES, the London Convention, the Kyoto Protocol, the Montréal Protocol, MARPOL, the Nuclear Test Ban Treaty, and the UN Conventions on the Law of the Sea, Climate Change and Desertification.

Kenya is a member of the East African Community (EAC), a regional intergovernmental organization established by Kenya, Uganda, and Tanzania in 2000, and expanded to include Rwanda and Burundi in 2007. The EAC Common Market Protocol went into effect on 1 July 2010, under which the members agreed to implement legislation to remove barriers to the transport of goods, services, and workers across borders. The development of the common market is one step in the EAC's plan to increase trade to, from, and within the region and to establish a strong political federation by 2015.

19 ECONOMY

Kenya's is an agricultural economy supported by a manufacturing sector, much of which dates from the pre-independence period, and a tourism sector, which is an important foreign exchange earner. Kenya has few mineral resources. Kenya has a drought-prone agricultural sector in which maize is a principal staple crop, along with tubers-cassava, potatoes, and sweet potatoes. There is a shortage of arable land—only 12% is first-quality farm land—and little irrigation. Nonetheless, the country exports tea, coffee, cut flowers, and vegetables. Tea exports provide the largest share of foreign exchange earnings, followed by tourism. Coffee exports have suffered due to a decline in world coffee prices and a decline in production, which was caused in part by mismanagement.

Kenya had one of Africa's strongest economies in the 1980s, posting growth rates of 5% annually. Kenya's economic performance was below potential in the 1990s owing to a variety of problems, including intermittent drought, poor economic management, rampant corruption, a lack of investment, a deteriorating infrastructure, and on-off donor relations. GDP per capita fell and poverty climbed. In the early 1990s, political turmoil and poor harvests slowed growth. Disagreements over the direction of future investments led to a suspension of foreign aid in 1992 resulting in low growth and high inflation. Under a structural adjustment program supported by the World Bank and International Monetary Fund (IMF) in 1993, Kenya strengthened its free market by abolishing price controls, removing import licensing requirements, and floating the currency. The end of most financial controls occurred in 1995.

In 1997 a drought caused continuing power interruptions, slowed business and manufacturing, and cast doubts on the country's ability to sustain growth. Flooding during 1998 caused industry slowdowns. At the same time, government corruption was threatening $200 million in direct aid from the IMF and World Bank. The donor agencies' concern with official corruption was heightened in early 1996 when they learned that the government's request for a $50-million low interest loan coincided with its purchase of a $50-million private jet for the president. The purchase of the jet was a nonbudgeted expenditure hidden from the World Bank auditors. In August 1997, the IMF and World Bank, tired of Kenya's failure to clamp down on graft, ended talks on resuming aid, a move that resulted in cuts in bilateral aid programs. The government initiated its own Economic Recovery Strategy in September 1999 to improve public sector management.

Another drought in 1999–2000 caused water and energy to be rationed and reduced agricultural output. The IMF again provided loans to guide Kenya through the drought, but suspended them in 2001 when the government failed to implement anticorruption measures. Although ample rains returned in 2001, corruption—compounded with low investment and weak commodity prices—prevented any increase in economic growth. The new government installed after the elections of December 2002 committed itself to providing adequate education, a zero tolerance for corruption, and an economic environment conducive to domestic and foreign investment. However, the Kenyan economy continued to stagnate in 2002, real GDP growing by just 1.1%, compared with 1.2% in 2001. The sluggish performance was blamed on a number of factors, including election uncertainties, the continued suspension of donor assistance, low investor confidence, and the continuing deterioration in Kenya's infrastructure, which inflates business costs. The rise in oil prices in the second half of 2002 also did not help.

The 24-year reign of Daniel Arap and the MOI ended in December 2002 with the election of a new government. The new government inherited a host of problems and made some progress in rooting out corruption. Despite hopes of an economic revival under the reform-minded regime, economic growth continued to be sluggish in 2003, partly because of delays in securing a new agreement with the IMF. The economy began to gain ground and in 2005, posting a 5.2% growth in GDP. However, 2005 and 2006 brought allegations of government graft which led the World Bank and IMF to delay loans pending action by the government on corruption, which proved to be slow in materializing. Despite the inaction, the donors resumed lending. In 2007 the economy grew by 6% on a wave of horticultural exports which rose 65% to $1.12 billion to become the nation's largest foreign exchange earner.

The global financial crisis in 2008–09, combined with domestic political upheaval, dampened economic growth, which registered only 1.7% in 2008. Stronger growth returned in 2009 (2.6%). The GDP rate of change in Kenya, as of 2010, was 5%. Inflation stood at 4.2%, and unemployment was reported at 4%.

20 INCOME

The CIA estimated that in 2010 the GDP of Kenya was $66.03 billion. The CIA defines GDP as the value of all final goods and services produced within a nation in a given year and computed on the basis of purchasing power parity (PPP) rather than value as measured on the basis of the rate of the exchange based on current dollars. The per capita GDP was estimated at $1,600. The annual growth rate of GDP was 5%. The average inflation rate was 4.2%. It was estimated that agriculture accounted for 22% of GDP, industry 16%, and services 62%.

In 2011 the most recent study by the World Bank reported that actual individual consumption in Kenya was 85.9% of GDP and accounted for 0.11% of world consumption. By comparison, the United States accounted for 25.44% of world individual consumption. The World Bank also estimated that 32.9% of Kenya's GDP was spent on food and beverages, 10.7% on housing and household furnishings, 2.7% on clothes, 7.0% on health, 10.6% on transportation, 2.5% on communications, 5.3% on recreation, 4.1% on restaurants and hotels, and 0.6% on miscellaneous goods and services and purchases from abroad.

The World Bank reports that in 2009, household consumption in Kenya totaled $23.6 billion or about $574 per capita, measured in current US dollars rather than PPP. Household consumption includes expenditures of individuals, households, and nongovernmental organizations on goods and services, excluding the purchases of dwellings. It was estimated that household consumption was growing at an average annual rate of 3.8%. According to the World Bank, remittances from citizens living abroad totaled $1.7 billion or about $41 per capita and accounted for approximately 2.6% of GDP in 2009.

21 LABOR

The trade union movement is strong in Kenya and continues to pressure the government for better wages and improved living standards. However, union activity can result in dismissal or discrimination for employees. Complex rules severely limit the right to strike. The principal labor federation is the Central Organization of Trade Unions (COTU). Except for the 150,000–200,000 teachers believed to be members of Kenya National Union of Teachers and three other smaller unions, all unions are affiliated with the COTU. COTU, however, does little to pursue workers' rights.

As of 2010, Kenya had a total labor force of 17.9 million people. Within that labor force, CIA estimates in 2007 noted that 75% were employed in agriculture, 13% in industry, and 12% in the service sector. The minimum legal working age is 16, however this does not apply to the agricultural segment which accounts for 80% of the labor force. The number of child laborers was estimated at one million in 2010. The minimum wage ranged between $35 and $85 per month in 2010, depending on location, age, and skill level.

22 AGRICULTURE

Agriculture remains the most important economic activity in Kenya. Farming in Kenya is typically carried out by small producers who usually cultivate no more than two hectares (about five acres) using limited technology. Roughly 9% of the total land is farmed, and the country's major crops include tea, coffee, corn, wheat, sugarcane, fruit, and vegetables. Cereal production in 2009 amounted to 2.8 million tons, fruit production 2.9 million tons, and vegetable production 2.1 million tons.

From independence in 1963 to the oil crisis in 1973, the agricultural sector expanded by undergoing two basic changes: first, widespread acceptance of private ownership (replacing tribal ownership) and cash crop farming; second, the success of intensive nationwide efforts to expand and upgrade the production of African smallholders. Before World War II (1939–45) ended, agricultural development occurred almost exclusively in the "White Highlands," an area of some 31,000 sq km (12,000 sq mi) allocated to immigrant white settlers and plantation companies. Since independence, as part of a land consolidation and resettlement policy, the Kenya government, with financial aid from the United Kingdom, has gradually transferred large areas to African ownership. European-owned agriculture remains generally large-scale and almost entirely commercial.

After the 1973 oil crisis, agricultural growth slowed as less untapped land became available. Government involvement in marketing coupled with inefficient trade and exchange rate policies discouraged production during the 1970s. Coffee production booms in the late 1970s and in 1986 have in the past temporarily helped the economy in its struggle away from deficit spending and monetary expansion. Although the expansion of agricultural export crops has been the most important factor in stimulating economic development, much agricultural activity is also directed toward providing food for domestic consumption. Kenya's agriculture is sufficiently diversified to produce nearly all of the nation's basic foodstuffs. To some extent, Kenya also helps feed neighboring countries.

Kenya is one of Africa's leading tea producers. Black tea is Kenya's leading agricultural foreign exchange earner. The tea industry is divided between small farms and large estates. The small-scale sector, with more than 260,000 farmers, is controlled by the parastatal Kenya Tea Development Authority. Coffee is Kenya's third leading foreign exchange earner, after tourism and tea. Coffee is produced on many small farms and a few large estates. All coffee is marketed through the parastatal Coffee Board of Kenya. The suspension of the economic provisions of the International Coffee Agreement in July 1989 disrupted markets temporarily, driving coffee prices to historical lows.

Kenyan horticulture has become prominent and is now the third leading agricultural export, following tea and coffee. Fresh produce accounted for about 30% of horticultural exports. Flowers exported include roses, carnations, statice, astromeria, and lilies.

Kenya is the world's largest producer and exporter of pyrethrum, a flower that contains a substance used in pesticides. The pyrethrum extract, known as pyrethrin, is derived from the flower's petals. A drop in production during the mid-1990s was due to increasing production costs, disease damage, and slow payment by the parastatal Pyrethrum Board of Kenya. The growing demand for "organic" and "natural" pesticides has increased international demand for pyrethrin, despite the existence of synthetic chemical substitutes. Kenya also produces sisal, tobacco, and bixa annatto (a natural food coloring agent) for export.

To boost agricultural profits, in November 2010 the governments of Kenya and South Africa signed a memorandum of understanding to set a framework for greater cooperation in agricultural exports. South Africa had imposed strict health rules on the importation of livestock and livestock products and had banned avocados from Kenya due to fruit flies. Under this new level of cooperation, South African inspectors assisted Kenya in meeting the necessary standards to open up markets for the products. Kenya had also called upon South Africa to eliminate import tax on tea and white soda ash, thus expanding the market for those products. The agreement weighs heavily in favor of South Africa. The value of exports from Kenya to South Africa is estimated at about $43 million. The value of exports from South Africa to Kenya is $865 million.

23ANIMAL HUSBANDRY

The UN Food and Agriculture Organization (FAO) reported that Kenya dedicated 21.3 million hectares (52.6 million acres) to permanent pasture or meadow in 2009. During that year, the country tended 28.6 million chickens, 12.5 million head of cattle, and 334,689 pigs. The production from these animals amounted to 444,259 tons of beef and veal, 14,779 tons of pork, 23,940 tons of poultry, 57,057 tons of eggs, and 3.72 million tons of milk. Milk production is concentrated in the Rift Valley and Central Provinces. Together, these two provinces contain about 80% of Kenya's dairy cattle population. Dairy production accounts for about 12% of the total value of agricultural output. About 300,000 small dairy farmers produce 80% of the milk. Kenya also produced 55,440 tons of cattle hide and 1,633 tons of raw wool.

24FISHING

Commercial fishing takes place on the coast of the Indian Ocean and on the shores of lakes Baringo, Naivasha, Rudolf, and Victoria. In the Victoria region, commercial companies process and package filleted and frozen lake fish, which are sold throughout East Africa. Fish farms have been established in various parts of Kenya. Sportsmen who fish in the highland lakes and streams provide a small amount of government revenue in the form of licenses and fees. Kenya had eight decked commercial fishing boats in 2008. The annual capture totaled 133,286 tons according to the UN FAO. The export value of seafood totaled $49.68 million

25FORESTRY

Approximately 6% of Kenya is covered by forest. Both hardwoods and softwoods are produced in Kenya. The chief hardwoods are musheragi, muiri, mukeo, camphor, and musaise. The chief softwoods are podo, cedar, and cypress. The supply of softwoods is adequate for local needs, both for building and other purposes. Wattle, grown mainly on small African plantations, provides the base of an important industry. The UN FAO estimated the 2009 roundwood production at 1.25 million cu m (44 million cu ft). The value of all forest products, including roundwood, totaled $34.5 million.

26MINING

Kenya is chiefly known for its production of fluorspar, limestone, gemstones, salt, soapstone, and soda ash. Cement was a leading industry and export commodity in 2009. National output of crude salt was estimated at 24,125 metric tons in 2009. Fluorspar (acid-grade) production was reported at 15,667 metric tons in the same year, down from 98,248 tons in 2008 due to closure of Kenya's only fluorspar mine. Also in 2009, an estimated 1,500,000 tons of limestone were produced for cement. Kenya also produced secondary aluminum, anhydrite, barite, natural carbon dioxide gas, hydraulic cement, diatomite, feldspar, precious and semiprecious gemstones (amethyst, aquamarine, Iolite cordierite, green garnet, ruby, sapphire, and tourmaline), gold, gypsum, kaolin, refined secondary lead, lime, petroleum refinery products, crude steel, coral, granite, marble, industrial sand (glass), shale, sulfuric acid, and vermiculite. There are several gold deposits in the country.

27ENERGY AND POWER

Kenya has no known reserves of oil, natural gas, or coal. As a result, the country relies on imports to meet its fossil fuel needs. In 2010 Kenya's oil consumption was 78,000 barrels per day. Oil imports were 80,160 barrels per day in 2009. Petroleum products are refined at Mombasa both for export and for domestic use. Oil prospecting continues along the Indian Ocean coast and offshore, but prospects of a commercially viable strike seem remote after roughly 40 years of exploration.

There were no imports of natural gas in 2010 and no proved gas reserves by 2011.

The majority of Kenya's electric power generating capacity is based upon hydropower. Kenya's geothermal resources along the Great Rift Valley have been tapped by a plant near Lake Naivasha. The World Bank reported in 2008 that Kenya produced 7.06 billion kWh of electricity and consumed 6.02 billion kWh, or 147 kWh per capita. Roughly 16% of energy came from fossil fuels, while 7% came from alternative fuels. Per capita oil consumption was 465 kg.

28 INDUSTRY

According to the CIA Kenya's industrial production growth rate in 2010 was 4% . Although Kenya's manufacturing industries are small, they are the most sophisticated in East Africa. The manufacturing sector has been growing since the late 1990s and into the new century. The manufactures Kenya produces are relatively diverse. The transformation of agricultural raw materials, particularly of coffee and tea, remains the principal industrial activity. Meat and fruit canning, wheat flour and cornmeal milling, and sugar refining are also important. Electronics production, vehicle assembly, publishing, and soda ash processing are all significant parts of the sector. Assembly of computer components began in 1987. Kenya also manufactures chemicals, textiles, ceramics, shoes, beer and soft drinks, cigarettes, soap, machinery, metal products, batteries, plastics, cement, aluminum, steel, glass, rubber, wood, cork, furniture, and leather goods. It also produces a small number of trucks and automobiles. One quarter of Kenya's industrial sector is owned by UK investors; American investors are the next largest group.

Kenya has no known oil or natural gas reserves, although the government has conducted oil exploration. The oil refinery in Mombasa, built in 1959 and half-owned by the government, and major oil companies, typically operates at around 65% of its total capacity and is supposed to serve Kenya, Tanzania, Uganda, the DROC, Rwanda, Burundi, and offshore islands. Kenya deregulated its oil industry in 1994. Refinery products include gasoline, jet/turbo fuel, light diesel oil and fuel oil. The refinery's future is an important domestic issue in Kenya, and management is considering upgrading the facility rather than allowing the refinery to close.

29 SCIENCE AND TECHNOLOGY

Patent applications in science and technology as of 2009, according to the World Bank, totaled 38 in Kenya. Notable scientific institutions in Kenya include the UNESCO Regional Office for Science and Technology for Africa, in Nairobi; coffee and tea research foundations; grasslands and plant-breeding research stations; and numerous centers for medical, agricultural, and veterinary research. Medical research focuses on the study of leprosy and tuberculosis. The National Council for Science and Technology advises the government on scientific matters, and the Kenya National Academy of Sciences promotes advancement of learning and research. Both organizations were founded in Nairobi in 1977. The University of Nairobi, founded in 1956, has colleges of agriculture and veterinary sciences, health sciences, architecture

and engineering, and biological and physical sciences. Kenyatta University, founded in 1939 at Nairobi, has faculties of science and environmental education. Moi University, founded in 1984 in Eldoret, has faculties of forest resources and wildlife administration, science, technology, information sciences, environmental studies, health sciences, and agriculture. Edgerton University, founded in 1939 at Njoro, has faculties of agriculture and science. Other higher-education institutions include Jomo Kenyatta University College of Agriculture and Technology, Kenya Medical Training College, and Kenya Polytechnic, all in Nairobi, and five other institutes of science and technology elsewhere in the country.

The African Union announced plans to create the Pan-African University in 2008. Toted as a flagship institution of higher education, the university will consist of five regional schools, each specializing in a different discipline. Kenya was slated to host the East Africa branch, specializing in basic sciences, technology, and innovation. Nigeria and Cameroon were selected to represent West Africa and Central Africa respectively, but political and financial issues emerged in choosing the South and North Africa branches. AU officials originally hoped to open all five branches in September 2010, but have since delayed full operations until 2012. Each of the branches requires a host institute of learning. Funding for each branch was to come in three parts, with one third of the funds provided by the AU, one third from the host country, and one third from a lead partner. Japan was to serve as Kenya's lead partner.

30 DOMESTIC TRADE

Mombasa and Nairobi, the two principal distribution centers for imported goods, are linked by rail or highway to the towns in their immediate areas. The head offices of all the leading import and export firms, mining companies, and banks, not only for Kenya but also for East Africa as a whole, are in one or the other of these two cities. Warehousing facilities are extensive in both cities. Re-

Principal Trading Partners – Kenya (2010)

(In millions of US dollars)

Country	Total	Exports	Imports	Balance
World	17,241.0	5,151.0	12,090.0	-6,939.0
India	2,298.6	97.9	2,200.7	-2,102.8
China	2,000.4	35.6	1,964.8	-1,929.2
United Arab Emirates	1,490.5	83.9	1,406.6	-1,322.7
South Africa	1,261.9	39.3	1,222.6	-1,183.3
Sa'udi Arabia	1,001.7	16.4	985.3	-968.9
Netherlands	889.1	421.4	467.7	-46.3
United Kingdom	845.9	452.8	393.1	59.7
Japan	718.1	36.7	681.4	-644.7
Uganda	717.0	516.5	200.5	316.0
United States	694.6	295.5	399.1	-103.6

(…) data not available or not significant.

(n.s.) not specified.

SOURCE: 2011 Direction of Trade Statistics Yearbook, New York: United Nations, 2011.

Balance of Payments – Kenya (2010)

(In millions of US dollars)

Current Account		**-2,512.2**
Balance on goods		-6,303.0
Imports	-11,527.7	
Exports	5,224.7	
Balance on services		1,659.8
Balance on income		-155.4
Current transfers		2,286.4
Capital Account		**240.2**
Financial Account		**2,145.9**
Direct investment abroad		-1.6
Direct investment in Kenya		185.8
Portfolio investment assets		-51.2
Portfolio investment liabilities		33.5
Financial derivatives		...
Other investment assets		97.2
Other investment liabilities		1,882.1
Net Errors and Omissions		**267.7**
Reserves and Related Items		**-141.6**

(…) data not available or not significant.

SOURCE: *Balance of Payment Statistics Yearbook 2011,* Washington, DC: International Monetary Fund, 2011.

tail outlets are generally small and are often owned and operated by a wholesaler.

Office and shop hours are generally from 8 a.m. to 5 p.m., Monday-Friday, with lunchtime closing from 1 to 2 p.m. Normal banking hours are 9 a.m. to 3 p.m., Monday-Friday. The languages of business correspondence are English, Gujarati, and Swahili.

There are a number of advertising firms. Newspapers and trade magazines are the principal advertising media, but radio and cinema advertising are increasingly used. The annual, six-day Nairobi International Trade Fair is sponsored by the Agricultural Society of Kenya for the exhibition and promotion of products from all aspects of the agricultural, food processing, and construction industries.

31 FOREIGN TRADE

Kenya imported $10.4 billion worth of goods and services in 2008, while exporting $5.141 billion worth of goods and services. Major import partners in 2009 were India, 12.5%; China, 11.9%; UAE, 9.1%; South Africa, 8.1%; Saudi Arabia, 6.4%; the United States, 6.1%; and Japan, 5%. Its major export partners were UK, 11.4%; Netherlands, 9.9%; Uganda, 9.2%; Tanzania, 8.9%; the United States, 6%; and Egypt, 4.3%.

32 BALANCE OF PAYMENTS

In 2010 Kenya had a foreign trade deficit of $3.9 billion, amounting to 5.5% of GDP. The current account balance was -$2.636 billion in 2011, compared to the 2010 figure of -$2.328 billion.

33 BANKING AND SECURITIES

Kenya acquired its first separate currency on 14 September 1966, when the initial par value for the Kenya shilling was announced by the IMF. The new coin replaced, at par value, the East African shilling, previously issued for Kenya, Tanzania, and Uganda by the East African Currency Board, whose assets were divided by those nations following a June 1965 agreement.

The Central Bank of Kenya (CBK) was established in May 1966, taking over the administration of exchange control. Because the Kenya shilling soon became the strongest currency in East Africa, a black market for it developed. A complete ban on the export or import, or destruction of hard Kenyan currency was imposed in 1971 to discourage speculation.

The powers of the CBK were greatly reduced in the early 1990s with the liberalization of the financial sector. The commercial banks are free to set their own interest and exchange rates. The shilling has effectively been a convertible currency since the government signed Article VIII of the IMF Articles of Agreement in June 1994, and thereby pledged not to permit any restrictions on current international transactions. Foreign exchange is bought and sold in the interbank market in which the CBK is merely one player, although it intervened frequently with several large transaction in late 1994 and again in mid-1995, first to halt the appreciation of the shilling and then to stem its fall. The CBK retains responsibility for issuing treasury bills and bonds to cover the government deficit.

Of the 29 commercial banks operating in Kenya in 1985, several folded during a banking crisis in 1986. During the 2000s the financial sector was dominated by two multinational banks—the Standard Chartered Bank and Barclays Bank of Kenya; and the parastatal banks—Kenya Commercial Bank and National Bank of Kenya. They have branches in Nairobi and Mombasa and at least 25 other locales throughout the country. Other commercial banks include Citibank N.A., Euro Bank, and First American Bank.

Although they depend largely on the commercial sector for credit outlay, banks have started to turn to agriculture as an outlet. Land and agricultural banks provide financial assistance to farmers in the form of long-term loans for the discharge of onerous mortgages and the purchase of livestock, implements, fertilizer, and so forth. Short-term loans are granted for seasonal expenses.

The reputation of the banking sector has suffered from a series of scandals. The largest financial scandal in Kenyan history broke in 1993 when the CBK closed down Exchange Bank and a related company, Goldenberg International, a gold and jewelry firm. Exchange Bank was accused of failing to honor foreign exchange contracts and Goldenberg of securing privileged access to the now-scrapped export compensation scheme. The auditor-general has questioned billions of shillings of payments to Goldenberg under the scheme for gold exports that have not been proven.

The discount rate, the interest rate at which the central bank lends to financial institutions in the short term, was 7% in 2010. The commercial bank prime lending rate, the rate at which banks lend to customers, was 14.37%.

The Nairobi Stock Exchange (NSE) was founded in 1965 with six members. It was one of the largest stock markets in the sub-Saharan Africa (with South Africa, Nigeria, and Zimbabwe). The market received a small boost from the decision of the government to allow direct foreign investment in January 1995, but the limit on foreign ownership was 40%.

34 INSURANCE

Insurance companies must be registered and licensed. Categories of compulsory insurance include motor third-party liability

Public Finance – Kenya (2009)

(In millions of shillings, budgetary central government figures)

Revenue and Grants	**484,939**	**100.0%**
Tax revenue	445,167	91.8%
Social contributions	...	...
Grants	19,669	4.1%
Other revenue	20,103	4.1%
Expenditures	**619,826**	**100.0%**
General public services	137,893	22.2%
Defense	41,183	6.6%
Public order and safety	60,062	9.7%
Economic affairs	130,835	21.1%
Environmental protection	5,584	0.9%
Housing and community amenities	18,824	3.0%
Health	32,181	5.2%
Recreational, culture, and religion	5,095	0.8%
Education	144,439	23.3%
Social protection	43,730	7.1%

(…) data not available or not significant.

SOURCE: *Government Finance Statistics Yearbook 2010,* Washington, DC: International Monetary Fund, 2010.

for bodily injuries and cargo insurance for imports. The insurance regulatory body is the Ministry of Finance and Planning.

[35] PUBLIC FINANCE

The fiscal year extends from 1 July to 30 June. Due to mismanagement of public funds, government expenditures are closely watched. In 2010 the budget of Kenya included $7.017 billion in public revenue and $9.045 billion in public expenditures. The budget deficit amounted to 6.3% of GDP. Public debt was 50.9% of GDP, with $8.394 billion of the debt held by foreign entities.

[36] TAXATION

Corporate income tax was levied at 30% in 2011. The social security tax was 5%. A training or apprenticeship tax applied to each employee, as did an advance motor vehicle tax. Interest was taxed at 15%, and the land rate tax was 0.6%. Stamp duties were set at variable rates. The value-added tax (VAT) was 16% in 2011.

[37] CUSTOMS AND DUTIES

Most import license controls were dismantled in 1993. In 1997 an ad valorem import duty was imposed on rice, sugar, and milk. Priority items such as raw materials, spare parts, agricultural equipment, and medicines had a small import tariff. There were also excise-taxes on alcohol and tobacco. There were few export duties. In 1999 Kenya, Uganda, and Tanzania signed the East African Community (EAC) treaty that removed trade barriers by 2003.

Kenya operates six export processing zones, where manufacturers gain a 10-year corporate tax holiday (25% thereafter), a 10-year withholding tax holiday on dividend remittance, duty and VAT exemption on all imports except motor vehicles, and exemption from most other regulatory schemes. The Manufacturing Under Bond (MUB) program gives similar incentives to companies not located in the export processing zones.

[38] FOREIGN INVESTMENT

In 1964, in the wake of independence, foreign investment in Kenya went down considerably. In a move to reverse this trend, the government issued a white paper in 1965 welcoming foreign investment and encouraging joint ventures. Foreign investments in 1965 totaled $30 million, rising to $52 million in 1971. The pace of investment accelerated during the 1970s, and by 1984 it was estimated that US investment alone had a value of $350 million. In 1987, tax treaties with the United Kingdom, Germany, Zambia, Denmark, Norway, and Sweden were in force, but private foreign investment stagnated.

In the early 1990s, the government moved to encourage investment by liberalizing trade policies and removing impediments to the development of a free market. It was estimated in 1994 that foreign direct investment totaled more than $1 billion. The foreign direct investment stock in Kenya has remained at the $1 billion mark but increased slightly by 5% from $1 billion in 2001 to $1.1 billion in 2002; while outward stock remained insignificant. While in the 1990s flows of foreign direct investment (FDI) had stabilized at about $50 million, they drastically declined to $5 million in 2001 and $28 million in 2002, as confidence in the government of the president, Daniel Arap Moi, reached an all-time low. Investors were also deterred by widespread corruption, overregulation, and the government's on-off relations with donors. Foreign direct investment (FDI) in Kenya was a net inflow of $140.5 million according to World Bank figures published in 2009. FDI represented 0.48% of GDP.

The three largest affiliates of foreign transnational corporation investment in Kenya in the industrial sector were all from the United Kingdom and focused on tobacco, pharmaceutical, and food production. Other investments come from Germany and the United States. Regardless of the government's intentions to attract investment, power interruptions, poor roads, political turmoil, and rampant government corruption dissuaded most serious foreign investment.

[39] ECONOMIC DEVELOPMENT

Central to Kenyan government planning is a continuing expansion of the level of exports and diversification of products. Moreover, Kenya has sought the orderly introduction of large numbers of African farmers into former European agricultural areas. With the goal of full economic independence, the government continues to pursue Africanization of the private sector, particularly in commerce.

Kenya continues to assist private industry by tariff structures that permit the import of raw materials duty-free or at low rates; allow rebates or suspension of customs duties under certain conditions; and establish protective customs barriers. The 1979–83 development plan, Kenya's fourth, had as its main objective the alleviation of rural poverty. The 1984–88 development plan also emphasized the rural sector in calling for an annual real GDP growth of 4.9%.

Kenya has depended on external assistance for development financing, but the extent of that dependence has varied with domestic conditions. Whereas in the mid-1960s Kenya depended on external sources for 82% of its total development resources, by the early 1970s the proportion had fallen to only 45%. The late 1970s and 1980s brought renewed reliance on external loans, as the proportion of foreign financing needed to cover the annual government budget deficit rose from 28% in 1978–79 to 67% in 1981–82 and an estimated 89% in 1985–86.

Development in Kenya now depends on the private sector and on foreign and domestic investment as the parastatal sector is dismantled. Foreign exchange earnings were key to the sixth development plan (1989–93). Because of government mismanagement of funds during the period between 1996 and 1999, most development agencies (including the IMF and World Bank) refused to extend loans and gave up on structural reform programs. The government initiated its own Economic Recovery Strategy in 1999 to increase public sector management reliability, but there were doubts as to the effectiveness of the plan.

In 2000, the IMF renewed lending, in the amount of a three-year $193 million Poverty Reduction and Growth Facility (PRGF) Arrangement, which was further augmented due to the impact of severe drought conditions. An anticorruption authority set up by the government was declared unconstitutional in December 2000, and other Kenyan reforms stalled. The IMF and World Bank once again suspended their programs. In July 2003, the IMF indicated it would resume lending to Kenya, as the Fund was encouraged by the country's efforts to fight corruption and promote good governance.

The government turned to information and communications technology as a growth sector for the economy in 2010. The Kenya Information Communication Technology Board announced the launch of a major grant program to promote the development of businesses involved in providing software applications and local digital content. This followed an announcement by the Kuwait-based mobile phone operator Zain, which had plans to launch a third-generation (3G) network service across Kenya.

⁴⁰SOCIAL DEVELOPMENT

The National Social Security Fund operates a limited pension fund for employed persons. Retirees (age 55) are entitled to a lump sum equal to total contributions plus accrued interest. Disability and survivor benefits are also paid. Medical coverage for employees is available in government hospitals for certain illnesses including AIDS. Employers are also obligated to obtain private worker's injury insurance.

Facilities for social welfare have been largely in the hands of private and voluntary organizations. The government assists many of the voluntary organizations financially. The private and voluntary agencies are highly developed. There are societies that care for the blind, the deaf and mute, and the physically disabled, and voluntary organizations that care for the poor and destitute. Homes and hostels have been established throughout the country for the care of orphans, young offenders, and juvenile prostitutes.

In 2003 the government outlawed violence against women, although domestic violence is a widespread problem affecting over half of the women in Kenya. Rape is an increasing problem in the country. Women also lack the legal rights provided to men. Women must obtain written permission from their husbands or fathers in order to obtain a passport. In practice, permission is also required for women applying for credit. Although the Law of Succession stipulates that sons and daughters should receive equal inheritances, traditional custom continues to benefit male children.

Boys greatly outnumber girls in higher education. Female genital mutilation is widely practiced, especially among certain ethnic groups. Children are forced to marry against their will.

Ethnic tensions between Kenyan tribal groups are pronounced. Ethnic violence has occurred in the Rift Valley, as well as ethnically motivated fighting between Nubian and Luo populations, which erupted in Nairobi. Although most ethnic groups are represented in the government, Kikuyus sometimes face discrimination and harassment by government officials. Kenya's human rights record remains poor. There are many reports of extrajudicial killings, the use of excessive force, and arbitrary arrest. Prison conditions are poor, and there are lengthy pretrial detentions. Defendants do not have the right to appointed lawyers except for capital cases.

⁴¹HEALTH

The National Hospital Insurance Fund is the most important health insurance program in Kenya. Membership is compulsory for all civil servants. The government is attempting to improve and upgrade existing health facilities and opening new ones. Kenya produces cotton wadding domestically, but all other medical equipment and supplies are imported. High-quality private practitioners acquire sophisticated medical equipment, but the public sector acquires less expensive equipment. Kenya also has a well-developed pharmaceutical industry that can produce most medications recommended by the World Health Organization.

The government is attempting to reduce malnutrition and combat deficiency diseases. Among Kenya's major health problems are tuberculosis and protein deficiency, the latter especially among young children. Although the incidence of malaria has been reduced, it still is endemic in some parts of Kenya and is responsible for anemia in children.

Water supply, sanitation, bilharzia, and sleeping sickness also pose major problems. Schistosomiasis is endemic to some areas. Approximately 49% of the population have access to safe drinking water and 86% have adequate sanitation.

According to the CIA, life expectancy in Kenya was 55 years in 2011. The country spent 4.2% of its GDP on healthcare, amounting to $33 per person. The fertility rate was 4.9, while the infant mortality rate was 55 per 1,000 live births. In 2008 the maternal mortality rate, according to the World Bank, was 530 per 100,000 births. Malnutrition affected an estimated 33% of children under five. In 2011 it was estimated that 74% of children were vaccinated against measles.

In 2011 there was 1 physician, 12 nurses and midwives, and 14 hospital beds per 10,000 inhabitants. The government was encouraging the development of the private health care sector through tax incentives as well as other plans.

There has been a rapid spread of HIV/AIDS since the 1980s. The CIA calculated HIV/AIDS prevalence in Kenya to be about 6.3% in 2009.

The nation is vulnerable to droughts that wreak havoc on the health and well-being of the people and the strength of the economy. In January 2009, the government declared a national disaster for the southeastern and coastal areas of the country, as low rainfall during the planting season resulted in a severe shortage of food. Political unrest and high food prices were contributing factors to the crisis. The UN World Food Program (WFP) stepped up by expanding its existing Kenyan food distribution program from

1.2 million people to 2.5 million. The WFP operation in Kenya expected to spend $474 million to continue operations through March 2012.

42 HOUSING

Rapid urbanization has made it difficult for the government to keep pace in providing adequate housing for those in need. In Nairobi, the population density is 3,079 persons per sq km (almost 8,000 per sq mi). More than half of the city's residents live in temporary shelters, generally in one of over 100 slum communities throughout the city. One-room shanties in the slum areas of Nairobi, Mombasa, and Nakuru are typically about 3–5 sq m (32–54 sq ft)and house 5 to 6 people. The high level of poverty and the high cost of available land mean fewer urban dwellers are in a position to purchase property of their own.

Most housing in rural areas is privately built and owned by the residents. But many of these homes are built with traditional materials of mud and thatch and deteriorate in a relatively short time.

The central government is responsible for all housing projects and works closely with local authorities. Many new housing projects have been undertaken with financial aid from the National Housing Corp.

43 EDUCATION

In 2009 the World Bank estimated that 83% of age-eligible children in Kenya were enrolled in primary school. Secondary enrollment for age-eligible children stood at 50%. Tertiary enrollment was estimated at 4%. Overall, the CIA estimated that Kenya had a literacy rate of 85.1%. Public expenditure on education represented 7.0% of GDP. Primary education is free and compulsory for eight years. Children start school at the age of five or six and spend eight years at primary school; four years at secondary school and a further four years at the university. The academic year runs from October to July.

There are four main universities in Kenya. Kenyatta University was founded in 1972 and is located in Nairobi. The University of Nairobi was founded in 1956 as the Royal Technical College of East Africa. The Moi University was founded in 1984 at Eldoret. The Egerton University, located at Njoro, was founded in 1939. The language of instruction in all the universities is English.

44 LIBRARIES AND MUSEUMS

The Kenya National Library Service, founded in 1965 and located in Nairobi, maintains over 25 provincial and community branches. The largest public library is the McMillan Memorial Library, formerly a private institution, which was taken over by the Nairobi City Council in 1962; it includes a collection of Africana, and had two branches. In 1996, Kenya National Library Service launched the Camel Mobile Service to transport books to villages and settlements between 5 and 10 km (3 and 6 mi) away from the main regional libraries. The libraries of the University of Nairobi, with 500,000 volumes, are the best supported in Kenya. Kenyatta University in Nairobi has 166,000 volumes. The British Council maintains three branch libraries, and the National Archives in Nairobi holds 40,000 volumes.

The National Museum in Nairobi and the Ft. Jesus Museum in Mombasa are the largest in Kenya. There are numerous local museums, including the Kiriandusi Prehistoric Site in Gilgil, founded in 1928, the Gedi Ruins Museum south of Malindi, and museums in Kabarnet, Lamu, Meru, Narak, and Olergesailie. The Kapenguria Museum, opened in 1993, details Kenya's political development and struggle for independence.

45 MEDIA

Telecommunications services in Kenya's are unreliable and there has been little effort to modernize except for services directed at businesses. In 2009 the CIA reported that there were 664,100 telephone landlines in Kenya.

Kenya Broadcasting Corporation (KBC), the country's government-owned broadcaster, is the only station with a national network for television and radio programming. There were 24 FM radio stations, 18 AM radio stations, and 6 shortwave radio stations. Internet users numbered 10 per 100 citizens. In 2010, the country had 47,676 Internet hosts. As of 2009, there were some 3.9 million Internet users in Kenya.

Prominent newspapers in 2010, with circulation numbers listed parenthetically, included *Daily Nation* (170,000) and the *Standard* (200,000). The other dailies include: *Taifa Leo*, a Swahili newspaper, circulation 57,000; the *Kenya Times*, associated with KANU, 52,000; and the *Kenya Leo*, (in Swahili, 40,000 in 1995).

While there is no formal censorship, the press is sometimes subject to harassment from public officials who have been treated unfavorably.

46 ORGANIZATIONS

Voluntary societies are numerous. Some are affiliated with parent bodies in the United Kingdom; a few, such as the Rotary Club, the Round Table, Kiwanis, and the Lions Club, are affiliated internationally. The Red Cross, Habitat for Humanity, and Caritas are also active. African women's clubs, called Maendeleo ya Wanawake, have been organized throughout Kenya. Some are members of the umbrella organization of National Council of Women of Kenya. National youth organizations include the Kenya Scouts Association, YMCA/YWCA, Kenya UN Youth and Student Association, and 4-K Clubs (a branch of 4-H Clubs). There are several sports associations and clubs representing amateur athletes competing in such pastimes as cricket, lawn tennis, squash, tae kwon do, yachting, and badminton.

National organizations promoting arts and science include the Kenya National Academy of Sciences (est. 1983), the Kenya Medical Association, and the multinational African Academy of Sciences (est. 1985). Organizations dedicated to research and education include the African Medical and Research Foundation and the African Centre for Technology Studies.

The Kenya National Chamber of Commerce and Industry, founded in 1965, has its headquarters in Nairobi. The Central Organization of Trade Unions and the Federation of Kenya Employers are based in Nairobi. Organizations dedicated to promoting the concerns of industry, business, and labor include the Agricultural Society of Kenya, Tea Board of Kenya, Kenya Tea Growers Association, and Fresh Produce Exporters' Association of Kenya. The Kenya Consumer's Organization is also active.

The World Conservation Union has an office in Nairobi. Other nature conservancy organizations include the Wildlife Clubs of Kenya Association and Save the Elephants.

47 TOURISM, TRAVEL, AND RECREATION

Since Kenya attained independence in 1963, tourism has become the leading source of foreign exchange revenue. The *Tourism Factbook*, published by the UN World Tourism Organization, reported 1.82 million incoming tourists to Kenya in 2009; they spent a total of $1.1 billion. Of those incoming tourists, there were 1.2 million from Europe. There were 48,708 hotel beds available in Kenya, which had an occupancy rate of 92%.

Accommodations in the form of lodges and campsites are available in the more remote areas, as well as five-star hotels in the more popular regions. Safaris are the chief attraction, whether they are photographic, cultural, or even sport. Kenya also boasts over 30 national parks and game preserves. The largest game preserve is Tsavo National Park, home of over 500 bird species; covering an area of about 21,343 sq km (8,241 sq mi), it is one of the world's largest wildlife sanctuaries. Nairobi has a professional repertory theater and a National Theater; the capital hosts a Festival of African music in July. Other attractions include the mosques of Mombasa, the spectacular scenery of the Great Rift Valley, the coffee plantations at Thika, and the world-renowned Tree Hotels. Tourists also enjoy the dramatic view of Mt. Kilimanjaro, which rises in neighboring Tanzania. Scientists predicted that Kilimanjaro's ice cap, which had visibly shrunk during the 1990s, would completely disappear by 2015.

Travelers from infected countries must carry a certificate of vaccination against yellow fever. Precautions are also recommended against typhoid and malaria. A valid passport, visa, and onward/return ticket are required for entry into Kenya.

In 2011 the estimated daily cost to visit Nairobi, the capital, was $410. The cost of visiting other cities averaged $194.

48 FAMOUS PERSONS

The leading African figure in the modern history of Kenya was Jomo Kenyatta (1893?–1978). From the 1920s to the 1970s he was in the forefront of African nationalism. Imprisoned and restricted during the Mau Mau revolt for his alleged role in its organization, he was released in August 1961 and was president of independent Kenya from 1964 until his death. Another dominant African personality was Tom Mboya (1930–69), who commanded an international reputation as a political and labor leader. Oginga Odinga (1911–94), usually at odds with the ruling establishment, was vice-president from 1964 to 1966. Daniel Arap Moi (b. 1924), a son of poor farmers, was vice-president for 11 years before succeeding Kenyatta as president in 1978. He served until 2002, when he was succeeded by Mwai Kibaki (b. 1931).

Sir Michael Blundell (1907–93), a leader of the European community after World War II, came to be identified with those who sought to create a nonracial political society; he was a director of Barclays Bank of Kenya from 1968 to 1981. Richard Leakey (b. 1944) is a leading paleoanthropologist.

49 DEPENDENCIES

Kenya has no territories or colonies.

50 BIBLIOGRAPHY

Adoyo, James W., and Cole I. Wangai. *Kenya Political, Social, and Environmental Issues.* Hauppauge, NY: Nova Science Publishers, 2012.

Broch-Due, Vigdis, ed. *Violence and Belonging: The Quest for Identity in Post-Colonial Africa.* New York: Taylor and Francis, 2005.

Chau, Donovan C. *Global Security Watch—Kenya.* Santa Barbara, CA: Praeger, 2010.

Kamoche, Ken M., ed. *Managing Human Resources in Africa.* New York: Routledge, 2004.

Kenya Investment and Business Guide: Strategic and Practical Information. Washington, DC: International Business Publications USA, 2012.

Kilbride, Philip L, Collette A. Suda, and Enos H. N. Njeru. *Street Children in Kenya: Voices of Children in Search of a Childhood.* Westport, CT: Bergin and Garvey, 2001.

Maxon, Robert M., and Thomas P. Ofcansky. *Historical Dictionary of Kenya.* Lanham, MD: Scarecrow Press, 2000.

McElrath, Karen (ed.). *HIV and AIDS: A Global View.* Westport, Conn.: Greenwood Press, 2002.

Mwakikagile, Godfrey. *Ethnic Politics in Kenya and Nigeria.* Huntington, NY: Nova Science Publishers, 2001.

Sobania, N. W. *Culture and Customs of Kenya.* Westport, CT: Greenwood Press, 2003.

Watson, Mary Ann, ed. *Modern Kenya: Social Issues and Perspectives.* Lanham, MD: University Press of America, 2000.

Williams, Lizzie. *Nairobi and Rift Valley.* Bath: Footprint, 2012.

Zeilig, Leo, and David Seddon. *A Political and Economic Dictionary of Africa.* Philadelphia: Routledge/Taylor and Francis, 2005.

LESOTHO

Kingdom of Lesotho
Muso oa Lesotho

CAPITAL: Maseru

FLAG: The flag, adopted in October 2006, is a horizontal blue, white, and green tricolor with a black mokorotlo (the hat worn by indigenous Basotho people) in the center.

ANTHEM: *Lesotho Fatse la bo ntat'a rona (Lesotho, Land of Our Fathers)*.

MONETARY UNIT: Lesotho is part of the South African Common Monetary Area (CMA); the maloti (LSL) of 100 lisente, introduced in 1980, is on a par with the South African rand (ZAR), which also is legal tender. There are coins of 1, 2, 5, 10, 25, and 50 lisente, and notes of 10, 20, 50, 100 and 200. LSL1 = US$0.13 (or US$1 = LSL7.9) as of 2010.

WEIGHTS AND MEASURES: British and metric weights and measures are in general use.

HOLIDAYS: New Year's Day, 1 January; Moshoeshoe's Day, 12 March; Workers` Day, 1 May; Africa/Heroes` Day, 25 May; Family Day, 1st Monday in July; King's Birthday, 17 July; Independence Day, 4 October; National Sports Day, 6 October; Christmas, 25 December; Boxing Day, 26 December. Movable Christian holidays include Good Friday, Easter Monday, and Ascension.

TIME: 2 p.m. = noon GMT.

¹LOCATION, SIZE, AND EXTENT

Lesotho is an enclave within the Republic of South Africa, with an area of 30,355 sq km (11,720 sq mi), extending 248 km (154 mi) NNE–SSW and 181 km (112 mi) ESE–WNW. Comparatively, the area occupied by Lesotho is slightly smaller than the state of Maryland.

It is bordered on the E by the South African province of KwaZulu-Natal, on the S by the Western Cape Province, and on the W and N by the Free State, with a total boundary length of 909 km (565 mi). Lesotho claims that Basotho lands now part of South Africa were unjustly taken by force in the 19th century.

Lesotho's capital city, Maseru, is located on the country's northwest border.

²TOPOGRAPHY

Three distinct geographical regions, demarcated by ascending altitude, extend approximately north-south across Lesotho. The western quarter of the country is a plateau averaging 1,500–1,850 m (4,900–6,100 ft). The soil of this zone is derived from sandstone and, particularly in the westernmost region, is poor and badly eroded. The remainder of the country is highland. A zone of rolling foothills, ranging from 1,800–2,200 m (5,900–7,200 ft), forms the border between the lowlands and the mountains in the east.

The Drakensberg Range forms the entire eastern and southeastern border. A spur of this range, the Maluti Mountains, runs north and south. Where it joins the Drakensberg Range there is a high plateau ranging from 2,700–3,200 m (8,900–10,500 ft) in elevation. The highest point is Thabana Ntlenyana, 3,482 m (11,425 ft),

in the east. The rich volcanic soils of the foothills and mountains are some of the best in the country.

The sources of two of the principal rivers of South Africa, the Orange and the Tugela, are in these mountains. Tributaries of the Caledon River, which forms the country's western border, also rise here. The Orange and Caledon rivers, together with their tributaries, drain more than 90% of the country.

³CLIMATE

Temperatures vary widely from one geographical zone to another, and frequently within zones, depending on the altitude. In the lowlands, temperatures reach 32°C (90°F) or more in the summer and rarely fall below -7°C (19°F) in the winter. The range in the highlands is greater; temperatures sometimes fall below -18°C (0°F), and frost and hail are frequent hazards. Rainfall, which is mostly concentrated in the months from October to April, averages 71 cm (28 in) annually, varying from 191 cm (75 in) in parts of the mountains to as little as 60 cm (24 in) in the lowlands. Most of the rainwater is lost through runoff, and droughts are common.

⁴FLORA AND FAUNA

Grass is the natural vegetation in this virtually treeless country. The high plateau is covered with montane or subalpine grassland. Red oat grass forms a dry carpet in much of the Drakensberg foothill region. The country's small size, high elevation, and limited range of habitats restrict the variety of fauna. The World Resources Institute estimates that there are 1,591 plant species in Lesotho. In addition, Lesotho is home to 59 species of mammals, 311 species of birds, 40 species of reptiles, and 7 species of amphibians. The African lammergeier, a bird common in the mountains of Ethiopia but nowhere else in Africa, and the bald ibis, both of which are near extinction, are found in small numbers in the Drakensberg Range.

5 ENVIRONMENT

Much of the country has become denuded of its natural grass cover through uncontrolled grazing and rushing surface water. Related problems are severe soil erosion, soil exhaustion, and desertification. More than 3.5 million trees, mostly eucalyptus, have been planted as part of a gully control program, and for production of fuel and poles. The World Resource Institute reported that Lesotho had designated 6,800 hectares (16,803 acres) of land for protection as of 2006. Among the agencies with environmental responsibility is the National Environmental Secretariat of the prime minister's office. The UN reported in 2008 that carbon dioxide emissions in Lesotho totaled 240 kilotons.

In October 2009, the government signed a $25 million finance agreement with the World Bank in support of its long-term Metolong Dam and Water Supply Program, designed to increase the nation's supply of readily accessible, potable water. The overall program included projects aimed at both industrial and residential water needs. New projects were planned for the capital city of Maseru and at least four other urban areas. In 2006, domestic water usage accounted for 40% of total usage, industrial for 40%, and agricultural for 20%. Per capita water usage totaled 28 cu m (989 cu ft) per year. The government sought to increase the reliability and accessibility of treated water to 90% of the population in Maseru by 2013. Sanitation projects were also planned that would increase the level of adequate sanitation from 15% to 20% in Maseru during the same period of time.

Unlike neighboring South Africa, Lesotho is not rich in game and other wildlife. The famous Basuto pony, of almost pure Arabian stock, reached its peak of quality and quantity around the turn of the century. After suffering a decline because of ruinous trading practices, overstocking, overgrazing, disease, and drought, the pony has begun to make a comeback through a selective breeding program and improved feeding methods. Other vanishing species, including the wildebeest and blesbok, have been reintroduced in areas where they formerly were numerous. According to a 2011 report issued by the International Union for Conservation of Nature and Natural Resources (IUCN), the number of threatened species included 2 types of mammals, 7 species of birds, 1 species of fish, 2 species of invertebrates, and 4 species of plant. Threatened species included the blue crane, the brown hyena, the African lion and the lesser flamingo.

6 POPULATION

The US Central Intelligence Agency (CIA) estimates the population of Lesotho in 2011 to be approximately 1,924,886, which placed it at number 144 in population among the 196 nations of the world. In 2011, approximately 5.4% of the population was over 65 years of age, with another 33.5% under 15 years of age. The median age in Lesotho was 22.9 years. There were 0.97 males for every female in the country. The population's annual rate of change was 0.332%. The projected population for the year 2025 was 2,000,000. Population density in Lesotho was calculated at 63 people per sq km (163 people per sq mi).

The UN estimated that 27% of the population lived in urban areas, and that urban populations had an annual rate of change of 3.4%. The largest urban area was Maseru, with a population of 220,000.

7 MIGRATION

Estimates of Lesotho's net migration rate, carried out by the CIA in 2011, amounted to -8.42 migrants per 1,000 citizens. The total number of emigrants living abroad was 427,500, and the total number of immigrants living in Lesotho was 6,300. In 1996, around 60% of active male wage earners in Lesotho worked in South Africa.

8 ETHNIC GROUPS

Lesotho is ethnically homogeneous. At least 99.7% of the people are Sotho. Europeans, Asians, and other groups make up the remaining population.

9 LANGUAGES

The Sesotho (southern Sotho) language is spoken by virtually all the indigenous population. English shares with Sesotho the position of official language. Zulu and Xhosa are also spoken.

10 RELIGIONS

Christian missions have long been active in Lesotho. As a result, about 80% of the population are Christian. The primary Protestant denominations are the Lesotho Evangelical Church and the Anglican Church. Roman Catholics are also active in the country. An estimated 20% of the population practice indigenous religions. It is believed that many Christians incorporate some aspects of indigenous religions into their own faith practice as well. Christians are found throughout the country, while Muslims tend to be concentrated in the northeastern part of the country. Many of the Muslims are of Asian descent, while most of the Christians are indigenous Basotho. Freedom of religion is guaranteed by the constitution and this right is generally respected in practice. Good Friday, Easter Monday, Ascension Day, and Christmas are observed as national holidays.

11 TRANSPORTATION

The CIA reports that Lesotho has a total of 7,091 km (4,406 mi) of roads, of which 1,404 km (872 mi) are paved. A 2.6-km (1.6-mi) South African railway connects Maseru's industrial park to the Bloemfontein–Natal line, providing a valuable freight link to South Africa.

In 2010, Lesotho had 26 airports and only 3 had paved runways. Lesotho Airways and South African Airways maintain scheduled passenger service between Johannesburg and Moshoeshoe International, the new international airport 19 km (12 mi) outside of Maseru. Lesotho Airways also has regular service to Swaziland, Zimbabwe, and Mozambique, and to 28 domestic airstrips. Air taxis and chartered planes serve airstrips at Maseru and other centers.

12 HISTORY

What is now Lesotho was inhabited by San hunter-gatherers, pejoratively called the Bushmen by the whites, until about 1600, when refugees from local Bantu wars began to arrive. In 1818, Moshoeshoe, a minor chief of a northern tribe in what was to become Basutoland, brought together the survivors of the devastating Zulu and Ndebele raids and founded the Basotho nation. During the early days of its existence, the Basotho also had to contend with incursions by Boers from the Orange Free State. Moshoeshoe sought UK protection, but not before much land had been lost to white settlers. His urgent appeals for assistance went unheeded until 1868, when Basutoland became a crown protectorate. Moshoeshoe died in 1870. The following year, Basutoland was annexed to the Cape Colony, over the protests of both Basotho and Boer leaders. In 1880, the so-called Gun War broke out between the Basotho and the Boers over the attempt to disarm the Basotho in accordance with the provisions of the Cape Peace Preservation Act of 1878. A high point in Basotho history was the successful resistance waged against the Cape's forces.

In 1884, Basutoland was returned to UK administration under a policy of indirect rule. Local government was introduced in 1910 with the creation of the Basutoland Council, an advisory body composed of the British resident commissioner, the paramount chief, and 99 appointed Basotho members. In effect, the chiefs were allowed to govern for the next 50 years. Under a new constitution that became effective in 1960, an indirectly elected legislative body, the Basutoland National Council, was created.

A constitutional conference held in London in 1964 approved the recommendations for a pre-independence constitution that had been made by a constitutional commission. The new constitution went into effect on 30 April 1965, following the general election. The resident commissioner became the UK government representative, retaining powers for defense, external affairs, internal security, and the public service.

In April 1966, a conflict arose in parliament between the government and the opposition over Prime Minister Leabua Jonathan's motion requesting that the United Kingdom set a date for independence. To forestall passage of the motion, Paramount Chief Moshoeshoe II replaced 5 of his 11 senatorial appointees with 5 opponents of the government. The High Court subsequently invalidated that action, declaring that his right to appoint 11 senators did not entail the right of dismissal. The Senate and National Assembly eventually passed the independence motion, the latter by a vote of 32 to 28, but the dispute foreshadowed a constitutional crisis that was not conclusively resolved at independence. The final independence conference was held in June 1966. Charging that the United Kingdom was granting independence to a minority government, and demanding a more significant role for the paramount chief, delegates representing the opposition withdrew. Moshoeshoe II himself declined to sign the final accord.

Independence

The United Kingdom granted independence to the newly named Kingdom of Lesotho on 4 October 1966; Moshoeshoe II was proclaimed king on that date. The first general election following the attainment of independence was held in January 1970. When it appeared that the ruling party, the Basotho National Party (BNP), would be defeated, Prime Minister Jonathan, its leader, declared a state of emergency and suspended the constitution. The Basotho Congress Party (BCP), led by Ntsu Mokhehle, claimed that it had won 33 seats to the BNP's 23. Leabua Jonathan admitted he had

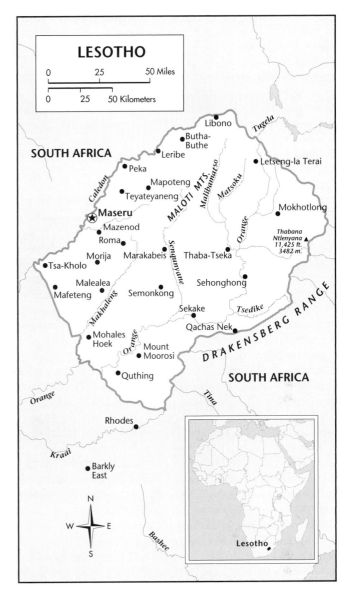

LOCATION: 28°35′ to 30°40′S; 27° to 29°30′E.

lost the election but nevertheless arrested the opposition leaders. The unrest, he said, was due to Communist influence, and since the majority of the people were behind him, he would suspend the constitution and hold new elections later. King Moshoeshoe II was placed under house arrest and in April 1970 the Netherlands gave him asylum. He was permitted to return in December.

Scattered attacks on police posts occurred in January 1974 in an alleged attempt by supporters of the BCP to overthrow the government of the ruling BNP. The abortive coup d'etat resulted in the arrest, killing, imprisonment, or exile of many people. In March 1975, 15 BCP followers were found guilty of high treason. The struggle against the Jonathan government continued through the late 1970s and early 1980s, with the Lesotho Liberation Army (LLA), the military arm of the BCP in exile, claiming responsibility for periodic bombings in Maseru, ambushes of government officials, and attacks on police stations. The Lesotho government charged that South Africa was allowing the LLA to use its territory as a base of operations.

Relations with South Africa deteriorated after that nation granted independence in 1976 to the Bantu homeland of Transkei, on Lesotho's southeastern border. When Lesotho, like all other nations except South Africa, declined to recognize Transkei, the Transkeian authorities closed the border with Lesotho, which also angered the apartheid South Africa government by harboring members of the banned African National Congress (ANC), an exiled South African insurgent group. On 9 December 1982, South African troops raided private residences of alleged ANC members in Maseru; 42 persons were killed, including at least 12 Basotho citizens. In the early 1980s, South Africa used economic pressures against Lesotho.

Parliamentary elections scheduled for August 1985 by the Jonathan government were called off because all five opposition parties refused to take part, charging that the voters' roll was fraudulent. Later that year, South Africa stepped up its destabilization activities, conducting a commando raid and aiding anti-government elements. On 1 January 1986, South Africa imposed a near-total blockade of Lesotho that resulted in severe shortages of food and essential supplies. On 20 January, a military coup led by Maj. Gen. Justin Metsing Lekhanya overthrew the government. All executive and legislative powers were vested in the king, acting on the advice of a six-man military council. On 25 January, a number of ANC members and sympathizers were flown from Lesotho to Zambia, whereupon South Africa ended its blockade of the country. All political activity was banned on 27 March.

There was widespread skepticism about the military government and its links to Pretoria, and agitation to return to civilian rule. In 1990, Lekhanya had Moshoeshoe II exiled (for a second time) after the king refused to agree to the dismissal of several senior officers. In November 1990, a new law was announced providing for a constitutional monarchy but barring Moshoeshoe from the throne. Later that month, Moshoeshoe's son (King Letsie III), was elected king by an assembly of chiefs.

In April 1991, rebel army officers staged a bloodless coup, forcing Lekhanya to resign. He was succeeded by Col. Elias Ramaema as leader of a military junta. In July 1992, the king was allowed to return to a hero's welcome.

Multiparty elections were scheduled for 28 November 1992, but they were postponed until 1993 because of delays in delimiting parliamentary constituencies. Finally, on 27 March 1993, in the first democratic elections in 23 years, the Basotho Congress Party, the major opposition party, won all 65 seats in the Assembly. The BCP formed a government under Prime Minister Dr. Ntsu Mokhehle. The BCP offered to nominate four BNP members but only one opposition politician accepted. Several cabinet members were appointed from opposition ranks.

On 25 January 1994, army troops mutinied in Maseru after the government refused their demands for a 100% pay increase. Prime Minister Mokhehle requested military assistance from South Africa, but that request was denied. After three weeks of sporadic fighting, the two factions within the military agreed to a Commonwealth-brokered deal for negotiations with the government.

In August 1994, Lesotho's first democratically elected government faced another challenge when King Letsie III suspended parliament and imposed a Ruling Council. The king had been angered by the Mokhehle government's creation of a board of inquiry to investigate the dethroning of his father. Although Letsie had the support of the security forces, his royal coup was condemned internally and internationally, and the United States cut off aid. On 14 September, the crisis was resolved when the king agreed to return the throne to his father. However, two years later King Moshoeshoe was killed in a car crash, and his son reclaimed the throne, much to the consternation of pro-democracy groups and Lesotho's neighbors.

Although the government increased military salaries in line with other government workers in 1995, an uprising three years later by a disgruntled faction of the Lesotho Defense Forces necessitated military intervention by Botswana and South Africa. Over 50 soldiers were taken into custody and charged with mutiny in September 1998 on the heels of rioting and looting that destroyed parts of the capital following the May elections in 1998. The violence cost Lesotho untold millions as it sent the economy into a tailspin.

The Lesotho Congress for Democracy (LCD) won the majority in parliament in the 23 May 1998 general elections, leaving the once-dominant Basotho National Party (BNP) and Basotholand Congress Party (BCP) far behind in total votes. Although international observers as well as a regional commission declared the elections to have reflected the will of the people, many members of the opposition accused the LCD of electoral fraud. The 1998 elections were the third multiparty elections in Lesotho's history. Nevertheless, after political riots following the disputed 1998 poll, an all-party forum called the Interim Political Authority was formed to level ground for the next poll. It proposed the restructuring of the Independent Electoral Commission, which happened, and the change of the model from winner-takes-all to mixed-member proportional representation. In the 25 May 2002 general elections, the ruling Lesotho Congress for Democracy was reelected by majority, winning all but one of the 80 constituency based seats.

In the February 2007 general elections, the LCD maintained its majority. These elections were held early, and some opposition members alleged that Prime Minister Mosisili called the polls early in order to stem defections from the LCD to the BCP and keep his ruling majority.

As of 2011, the Lesotho government remained a modified form of constitutional monarchy. The prime minister was head of government and had executive authority. The king serves a largely ceremonial function; he no longer possesses any executive authority and is proscribed from actively participating in political initiatives.

Lesotho remained among the poorest countries in Africa, with the majority of the population living below the poverty line on less than $1 per day. The percentage of the population living below the purchasing power parity (PPP) of $1.25 per day fell from 48 to 44% between 1995 and 2003. The United Nations (UN) classifies approximately 40% of Lesotho's population as "ultra-poor." Lesotho's economy was badly damaged by the shut-down of a textile industry quota system, resulting in the loss of jobs to cheaper Asian producers. The country remains dependent on neighboring South Africa as a buyer of its major natural resource, water, often referred to as "white gold" by the Basotho people. During 1995 and 1997, with intense construction activities involving the multi-million dollar Lesotho Highlands Water Project, Lesotho registered an impressive economic performance: the real gross domestic product (GDP) growth rate made Lesotho one of the top ten performers in Africa at this time. Completion of a major hydropower facility in January 1998 now permits the sale of water to South Africa, generating royalties that will be an important source of income for Lesotho.

Many of Lesotho's residents are employed in South Africa's mines, but in the early 21st century there was greatly reduced demand for these workers as mine deposits became increasingly exhausted. Local agriculture also experienced a decline in the early twenty-first century, thanks to droughts and the population ravages of AIDS. In 2007, the unemployment rate neared 50%.

In 2011, the World Bank estimated that Lesotho had the third highest adult HIV/AIDS prevalence in the world, at 23.2% of the adult population. Twenty-six percent of women and 19% of men in the 15 to 49 age bracket were infected. Each day, an estimated 62 people were newly infected and 50 people died due to HIV/AIDS. At the end of 2007, an estimated 270,000 people in the country were living with HIV/AIDS, 11,800 of them children. The number of AIDS orphans was estimated at 108,700 in 2007.

Poverty, lack of jobs, and food shortages in the subregion were driving rural to urban migration, and increasing the likelihood that young women and women heads of household would engage in commercial and risky sex to provide for their families.

13 GOVERNMENT

According to the 1993 constitution, the Kingdom of Lesotho is a monarchy with a bicameral parliament consisting of a National Assembly of 120 members: 80 elected by direct popular vote, and 40 by proportional vote, for five-year terms, and a Senate consisting of 33 members—22 chiefs and 11 others appointed by the ruling party.

Until 1993, the king was official chief of state (*motlotlehi*), and was designated by the College of Chiefs, according to Basotho custom. The prime minister (head of government) was appointed by the king and was a member of the majority party in the National Assembly. The cabinet was also appointed by the king, in accordance with advice of the prime minister, from among members of both houses of parliament.

Under the 1993 constitution, the monarch has become a figurehead, a "living symbol of national unity" with no executive or legislative powers. He is selected by traditional law and the College of Chiefs, which holds the power to determine who is next in the line of succession, and who shall serve as regent in the event that the successor is a minor. The College also may depose the monarch.

The leader of the majority party in the Assembly automatically becomes prime minister. Since 1998, the prime minister has been Pakalitha Mosisili, the leader of the Lesotho Congress for Democracy (LCD).

14 POLITICAL PARTIES

The Basotho National Party (BNP), formerly the Basutoland National Party, was founded in 1959 and was in the forefront of Lesotho's independence drive. The BNP long stood for maintaining diplomatic relations with South Africa and for a cautious approach to cooperation with other African states, in an attitude of "choose our friends but live with our neighbors." However, in the 1970s and early 1980s, the BNP played a more active role in opposing apartheid. By 1998, BNP had become the leading opposition party, as the Lesotho Congress for Democracy (LCD) took and consolidated its grip on power.

The Basotho Congress Party (BCP), founded in 1952 and formerly known as the Basutoland African Congress, is an outspoken Pan-Africanist party. The first party to demand independence, it subsequently opposed the "premature" granting of independence to a minority government. The third major party is the Marematlou Freedom Party (MFP). This party was formed in 1965 by the merger of two parties that had supported the chieftaincy.

In the general election held on 29 April 1965, the BNP won 31 seats, the BCP 25 seats, and the MFP 4 seats in the National Assembly. Chief Jonathan was defeated in the election, and Sekhonyana Maseribane was appointed prime minister. Chief Jonathan won a by-election on 1 June and assumed the office of prime minister. The two opposition parties, which together had polled 56.2% of the vote to 41.6% for the BNP (with 2.2% of the vote going to others), in an election in which only 62% of those eligible had voted, joined forces to protest the United Kingdom's granting of independence to a minority government. They also called for a more even distribution of executive power between the prime minister and the chief of state, and appealed to the UN, the Commonwealth, and the Organization of African Unity (OAU) in an unsuccessful bid to have the independence agreement rescinded.

The BCP claimed it had won 33 seats in the 60-seat National Assembly in the January 1970 general elections; the BNP won 23 seats, and the ballots for 4 seats had not been counted. Confusion over the outcome of the 1970 election, in which the United Democratic Party and the Communist Party participated but won no seats, resulted in suspension of the constitution by Prime Minister Jonathan, and political activities of opposition parties were subsequently restricted. Prime Minister Jonathan appointed two members of opposition parties to his cabinet in November 1975. The BCP then split into two factions: members of one accepted government posts, while leaders of the other organized an armed insurgency in exile.

The March 1993 election was contested by more than a dozen parties, but the chief vote getters were the BCP, still headed by Dr. Mokhehle, and the BNP, led by Evaristus Sekhonyana. Among the others were the MFP, the United Democratic Party (UDP), and the Communist Party of Lesotho (CPL). The BCP held all elected seats in the National Assembly, despite having won just over half the vote.

Since 1998, the dominant political party has been the ruling Lesotho Congress for Democracy (LCD) under the leadership of Dr. Pakalitha Mosisili. LCD won just over 60% of the votes in the May 1998 parliamentary elections. The major opposition parties included: the BNP, the BCP, led by Molapo Qhobela (24% of the 1998 vote); the Lesotho Labor Party/United Democratic Party Alliance (LLP/UDP), led by Charles Mofeli and Mamolefi Ranthimo; the Marematlou Freedom Party (MFP); the National Progressive Party (NPP); and the Sefate Democratic Union (SDU).

In the 25 May 2002 parliamentary election, the LCD garnered 54% of the vote, the BNP 21%, the Lesotho People's Congress or LPC 7%, and other parties took 18%. With the number of seats expanded from 80 to 120, the breakdown by party was: LCD 76, BNP 21, LPC 5, and other parties 18. Although opposition parties objected to the results, independent observers described the elections as free, fair, peaceful, lawful, and transparent—a model for Southern Africa.

In the February 2007 general elections, the LCD maintained its majority with 61 seats versus 17 for the All Basotho Convention (BSP), a splinter opposition party formed by former foreign minister Tom Thabane in October 2006. Pakalitha Mosisili of the LCD has been the prime minister since 1998. The next legislative elections are set for 2012.

15 LOCAL GOVERNMENT

There are 10 districts, each headed by a centrally appointed district administrator. District councils, established in 1944, were abolished in 1966. Each district is subdivided into wards, most of them presided over by hereditary chiefs allied to the royal family. During the period of military rule, each district was headed by a district secretary and a district military officer appointed by the central government and the defense force, respectively.

16 JUDICIAL SYSTEM

The legal system is based on English common law and Roman-Dutch law with judicial review of legislative acts in High Court and Court of Appeal. Lesotho accepts International Court of Justice (ICJ) jurisdiction with reservations.

The judicial system consists of the High Court, the Court of Appeal, subordinate courts, and the Judicial Service Commission (JSC). The members of the High Court are the chief justice, who is appointed by the chief of state, acting on the advice of the prime minister, and an unspecified number of puisne judges appointed by the chief of state, acting on the advice of the JSC. The Court of Appeal, which meets semiannually, is headed by a president, appointed by the chief of state, acting on the advice of the prime minister, and includes an unspecified number of justices of appeal, appointed by the chief of state, acting on the advice of the JSC. Parliament has the power of establishing subordinate courts and courts-martial. The High Court has unlimited original jurisdiction over civil and criminal matters, as well as appellate jurisdiction from subordinate courts.

Subordinate courts, comprising resident magistrate's courts, judicial commissioner's courts, and central and local courts, administer statute laws, while chiefs administer customary laws. There is no trial by jury. Military courts have jurisdiction only over military cases and their decisions are final.

17 ARMED FORCES

The International Institute for Strategic Studies reports that armed forces in Lesotho totaled 2000 members in 2011, all of which are members of the army. The service also had a 110-member air wing. Equipment included 22 reconnaissance vehicles and 12 artillery pieces. The air wing operated one patrol aircraft, three transport aircraft, and four utility helicopters. Armed forces represent 0.2% of the labor force in Lesotho. Defense spending totaled $86.1 million and accounted for 2.6% of GDP.

18 INTERNATIONAL COOPERATION

Lesotho became a member of the UN on 17 October 1966 and participates in ECA and several nonregional specialized agencies, such as the FAO, IFC, ULP, IMF, the World Bank, UNESCO, UNHCR, and the WHO. Lesotho is also a member of the Commonwealth of Nations, the ACP Group, the African Development Bank, the African Union, and G-77. The country's close relationship with South Africa is a major factor in its economic survival. Lesotho belongs to the Southern African Customs Union (SACU) and the Southern African Development Community (SADC). Lesotho is also part of the CMA that includes Namibia, Swaziland, and South Africa.

The country is part of the Non-Aligned Movement (NAM). In environmental cooperation, Lesotho is part of the Basel Convention, the Convention on Biological Diversity, the Kyoto Protocol, the Montréal Protocol, and the UN Conventions on Climate Change and Desertification.

19 ECONOMY

The GDP rate of change in Lesotho, as of 2010, was 2.4%. Inflation stood at 6.1%, and unemployment was reported at 45%. Lesotho is an agricultural country whose economy is based on subsistence agriculture, especially livestock. Land is controlled by the chiefs of the kingdom and cannot be privately owned. Textile-garment and agro-industrial enterprises dominate the industrial sector and tend to be state-owned, although privatization has increased. In 2007, Lesotho became the largest exporter of garments to the United States from sub-Saharan Africa with exports of $437 million. Manufacturing and construction businesses are mostly privately owned. It has a modest tourism sector. Other exports include diamonds, wool, and mohair. However, the global economic crisis of the late 2000s hit the Lesotho economy hard through loss of textile exports and jobs in that sector due largely to the economic slowdown in the United States, which was a major export destination, reduced diamond mining and exports, including weak prices for diamonds; drop in SACU revenues due to the economic slowdown in the South African economy, and reduction in worker remittances due to weakening of the South African economy and contraction of the mining sector and related job losses in South Africa. In 2009 GDP growth slowed to 0.9 percent, and an estimated 10,000 jobs were lost in the textile sector in late 2009.

Of prime economic importance is the water and electricity it sells to South Africa with whom its economic policy is closely tied. Many Basotho work in the South African mines and the South African rand is accepted as legal tender in Lesotho. Remittance from miners is an important source of income. As 35% of male wage earners are employed in South Africa, 54% of households in Lesotho are headed by women.

Lesotho has a large trade deficit, and is a recipient of aid from the World Bank and Western countries. Future economic growth is tied to the massive Lesotho Highlands Water Project (LHWP) completed in 1998. The project captures, stores, and transfers the headwaters of the Orange River system to industry clustered around Johannesburg, South Africa. Ancillary dams provide electricity. Following feasibility studies in 2005 and 2008, a second phase of the project, which began in 2011, was to increase electricity-generating capacity at the Muela hydropower station. Completion was anticipated in 2017, with water delivered to South Africa by 2018. In addition to its economic benefits, the project was slated to significantly lower Lesotho's carbon emissions.

²⁰INCOME

The CIA estimated that in 2010, the GDP of Lesotho was $3.303 billion. The CIA defines GDP as the value of all final goods and services produced within a nation in a given year, and computed on the basis of PPP, rather than value as measured on the basis of the rate of the exchange based on current dollars. The per capita GDP was estimated at $1,700. The annual growth rate of GDP was 2.4%. The average inflation rate was 6.1%. It was estimated that agriculture accounted for 7.1% of GDP, industry 34.6%, and services 58.2%.

According to the World Bank, remittances from citizens living abroad totaled $414.1 million or about $215 per capita and accounted for approximately 12.5% of GDP.

The World Bank reports that in 2009, household consumption in Lesotho totaled $1.2 billion or about $631 per capita, measured in current US dollars rather than PPP. Household consumption includes expenditures of individuals, households, and nongovernmental organizations on goods and services, excluding the purchases of dwellings. It was estimated that household consumption was growing at an average annual rate of 8.3%.

As of 2011 the World Bank reported that actual individual consumption in Lesotho was 106.1% of GDP and accounted for 0.01% of world consumption. By comparison, the United States accounted for 25.44% of world individual consumption. The World Bank also estimated that 41.3% of Lesotho's GDP was spent on food and beverages, 14.8% on housing and household furnishings, 13.3% on clothes, 7.7% on health, 6.1% on transportation, 1.9% on communications, 1.7% on recreation, 0.2% on restaurants and hotels, and 5.1% on miscellaneous goods and services and purchases from abroad.

²¹LABOR

With the exception of civil servants, workers have the right to unionize, but only about 10% of the workforce are union members. While strikes are technically legal, no legally sanctioned strikes have occurred since independence in 1966. The rights to bargain collectively and organize, while technically legal, are often restricted by the government. There are three small trade union federations: the Lesotho Trade Union Congress, the Lesotho Federation of Democratic Unions, and the Congress of Lesotho Trade Unions; these three organizations seldom cooperate with each other.

While there are restrictions on working hours and practices for children under 14, enforcement of these restrictions is ineffectual. Significant levels of child labor exist in Lesotho, and in 2011, the country was in the process of formulating an Action Program on the Elimination of Child Labor (APEC). The minimum wage is set by the government and varies from sector to sector. There is a sector-specific national minimum wage and a general minimum wage. The general minimum monthly wage varies from 878 to 958 maloti ($125 to $136). Examples of minimum monthly wages for other job categories include textile workers, 778 maloti ($111); construction workers, 1,040 maloti ($148); security guards, 1,181 maloti ($168); food service workers, 1,110 maloti ($158); and domestic workers, 339 maloti ($48). Minimum wages are updated every October 1 through the amended labor code minimum wage schedule. The national minimum wage does not provide a decent standard of living for a worker and family. Trade unions continue to engage the government on the matter. The Ministry of Labor is responsible for enforcing the minimum wage.

The law requires a maximum 45-hour workweek with 12 days of paid leave and paid holidays. Minimum occupational safety standards exist but the Ministry of Labor does not effectively enforce them. As of 2007, Lesotho had a total labor force of 854,600 people. Within that labor force, CIA estimates in 2002 noted that 86% were employed in agriculture, 7% in industry, and 7% in the service sector.

²²AGRICULTURE

Crop production in Lesotho is a high-risk, low-yield activity due to poor soil quality and a harsh climate. All land is held in trust for the Basotho nation by the king and may not be alienated. The local chiefs allocate farmland to individuals, and user rights are generally available to married males; nevertheless, one out of seven households is landless. A 1979 act increases security of tenure by recording rights of inheritance and allowing mortgaging and subletting of land. The average landholding per family head is 1.9 hectares (4.7 acres).

Most cultivated land is in the western lowlands. Roughly 11% of the total land is currently farmed, and the country's major crops include corn, wheat, pulses, sorghum, and barley. Cereal production amounted to 75,442 tons, fruit production 14,929 tons, and vegetable production 28,427 tons.

The country suffered from recurrent drought conditions in the 1980s and early 1990s. Lesotho is a large importer of grains and other foodstuffs.

Lesotho has one of the most advanced soil conservation programs in Africa. Terracing, grass stripping, and the construction of dams and irrigation canals are widely employed to cope with the severe erosion problems.

²³ANIMAL HUSBANDRY

The raising of livestock is the principal economic undertaking in Lesotho. The UN Food and Agriculture Organization (FAO) reported that Lesotho dedicated 2 million hectares (4.94 million acres) to permanent pasture or meadow in 2009. Grazing rights on all non-cultivated land are communal, and no limits are placed on the number of livestock permitted to graze an area. Lesotho's main exports are wool and mohair; in general, however, the quality of the livestock is poor and yields are low. In 2005 there were an estimated 850,000 sheep, 650,000 goats, 154,000 asses, 100,000 horses, 65,000 hogs, and 1,800,000 chickens. In 2009 Lesotho tended 616,496 head of cattle.

A number of livestock improvement centers were established, and Merino rams and Angora bucks were imported from South Africa for breeding purposes. Cattle, sheep, and goats are exported on the hoof. Hides and skins, usually from animals that have died of starvation or disease or have been slaughtered for human consumption, are also exported.

²⁴FISHING

Fishing has not yet been popularized, although the Malutsenyane River is one of the best natural trout fishing grounds in Africa. In 2008 the annual capture totaled 50 tons according to the UN FAO. There is virtually no commercial fishing.

25 FORESTRY

Lesotho is almost devoid of natural woodland, only a tiny 1% of the country is covered by forest. Trees have been planted in conjunction with soil conservation programs. Roundwood production in 2004 was estimated at 2.046 million cu m, all non-coniferous logs for fuel.

26 MINING

Lesotho has long been known as a source of diamonds, mostly from alluvial deposits, and was seeing a revival of its diamond mining industry. Geological surveys have revealed a limited variety of other exploitable mineral resources. In 2009 diamond production was estimated at 450,000 carats, up from 52,056 carats in 2005. Artisanal miners also produced small amounts of fire clay, gravel, dimension stone, and crushed rock for domestic consumption. Commercial interest in the mineral resources of Lesotho was limited to diamonds. The Lesotho Geological Survey has identified 39 kimberlite pipes and 343 dikes. The Letšeng Mine is the seventh largest kimberlite mine in the world and is known for producing large diamonds (greater than 108 carats), including the 603-carat Lesotho Promise.

In January 2010 the government granted a London-based joint venture the mining rights to the Kao kimberlite pipe, one of the largest kimberlite pipes in southern Africa. At the time of the announcement, Kao was estimated to hold 12.4 millions carets of diamonds.

The economy of landlocked Lesotho was based on subsistence agriculture, livestock, and remittances from migrant Basotho miners employed in South African gold mines. However, the number of migrant miners has fallen from an average of 110,000 in 1994, to 61,400 in 2003, and 35,000 in 2010. The revival of the diamond industry in Lesotho showed hope for some new opportunities for Basotho mineworkers and for replacing related lost government revenues. Exploration for iron, coal, and uranium continued.

27 ENERGY AND POWER

As of 2010 Lesotho had no proven reserves of oil, natural gas, or coal, and totally lacked any petroleum refining capacity. It was therefore, completely reliant upon imports to meet its refined oil, natural gas, and coal needs.

Lesotho's electric power is entirely hydroelectric, and is produced by the Muela hydroelectric facility. Muela is part of a jointly financed project with South Africa called the Lesotho Highlands Water Project. The project called for two 34-km (21-mi) tunnels to transport water from Lesotho's rivers to South Africa, with the first delivery in 1996 and maximum operation by 2020. Plans involved the construction of seven dams, as well as a hydroelectric plant that could meet almost all of Lesotho's power needs. The World Bank reported in 2008 that Lesotho produced 200 million kWh of electricity and consumed 488.9 million kWh, or 254 kWh per capita.

28 INDUSTRY

Lesotho has a wide variety of light industries, which include, among others, tire retreading, tapestry weaving, diamond processing, and production of textiles, shoes, electric lighting, candles, ceramics, explosives, furniture, and fertilizers. Manufacturing depends largely on agricultural inputs to support milling, canning, leather, and jute industries. In the 1980s, the Lesotho National Development Corporation promoted industrial development in the production of fruits and vegetables, tires, beer and soft drinks, parachutes, steel, and wire. In 1991, Lesotho inaugurated a television assembly plant. As the number of mineworkers has declined steadily over the past several years, a small manufacturing base has developed based on farm products and a rapidly growing apparel-assembly sector.

The garment industry has been a growth industry since the 1980s, making the country a major exporter of clothing and textiles, particularly denim. With the growth of the industry, however, there has also been increasing concern over environmental issues, specifically the so-called blue rivers carrying contaminants from illegal dumping of materials near the factory sites. In 2009, a number of allegations concerning illegal toxic dumping were brought to the attention of the government. In August 2009, two of the nation's biggest investors, Gap and Levi Strauss, announced they would launch their own investigations concerning the waste management practices of the industrial sites and pledged to implement stricter monitoring plans in order to protect the health of workers and nearby residents. The government has been blamed for much of the problem, for failing to designate an adequate number of well-managed industrial disposal sites.

In the early 2000s, there was growth in the manufacturing sector of the economy. Industry held a strong average annual growth of 10% between 1988 and 1998, and accounted for 38% of GDP in 2001. The major industrial contributor in 2000 was the Highlands Water Project, which began a second phase of construction in 2011. Lesotho has no known oil or natural gas reserves. Oil exploration took place in the 1970s, but those efforts were unsuccessful and exploration ceased. Textile exports to the United States accounted for $280 million in 2010, while also employing some 40,000 workers. Most textile facilities were owned by Taiwanese or Indian investors.

29 SCIENCE AND TECHNOLOGY

The World Bank reported in 2009 that there were no patent applications in science and technology in Lesotho. The Ministry of Agriculture, Cooperatives, and Marketing maintains a research station at Maseru, along with several experimental stations in the field. Lesotho's Geological Survey Department is headquartered in Maseru. The National University of Lesotho, founded in 1966 at Roma, has faculties of science and agriculture. Lesotho Agricultural College, founded in 1955, is located in Maseru.

30 DOMESTIC TRADE

Except for the northern regions, where Indians monopolized trading activities, domestic trade was handled by Europeans before independence. The Taiwanese also played a role. Nevertheless, more and more Basotho are currently taking out trading licenses. Traders play a central role in wool and mohair marketing, often acting as wool classers as well. The expertise of the traders varies widely. Some have regular suppliers and customers and maintain high quality, while others are prone to careless handling practices, lowering the market value of wool.

As of 2010 nearly 85% of the workforce was employed in some level of subsistence agriculture. About 35% of male wage earners had jobs in South Africa.

Normal business hours in urban areas are from 8 a.m. to 1 p.m. and from 2 to 4:30 p.m., Monday through Friday, and from 8 a.m. to 1 p.m. on Saturday. Banks are open from 8:30 a.m. to 1 p.m. Monday through Friday, and 9:30 to 11 a.m. on Saturday.

31 FOREIGN TRADE

Lesotho's chief exports are clothing, shoes, and road vehicles. Manufacturing accounted for 65% of exports in 1996. Other exports include wool and mohair, and food and live animals (7% each). The main imports are food, building materials, vehicles, machinery, medicines, and petroleum products. Lesotho imported $1.766 billion worth of goods and services in 2008, while exporting $985 million worth of goods and services. Major import partners in 2009 were South Africa, Asia, India, and the European Union. Its major export partners were South Africa Angola, the European Union, United States, Canada, China, and India.

Exports grew an average of 18.1% from 1993 through 1996, but declined slightly in 1998. Between 2001 and 2005, exports grew dramatically from $278.6 million to $749.9 million, an increase of 169% within a four-year period. Between 2001 and 2005, imports increased from $678.6 million to $1.4 billion, an increase of 103%. Increasingly, the United States has become a favorite destination for Lesotho's exports. Some 58.4% of exports went to the United States in 2010. Exports declined in 2009 due to weakened economic conditions worldwide—including South Africa's descent into recession—but recovered in 2010.

32 BALANCE OF PAYMENTS

Lesotho's chronic balance of payments deficit was partially offset by the flow of cash and material goods from Basotho workers in South Africa, but the end of this system in 1999 caused a higher total debt than usual. Revenues from the Highlands Water Project may offset losses. In 2010 Lesotho had a foreign trade deficit of $1 billion, amounting to 5.8% of GDP.

33 BANKING AND SECURITIES

Lesotho is a member of the Common Monetary Area. The 1974 agreement, which was revised in 1986, provided access to the South African capital market for the Lesotho banking system. Lesotho is responsible for its own monetary policy, and controls its own financial institutions, but management of the rand currency and the gold and foreign exchange reserves of the rand area remains the sole responsibility of South Africa. In 1980, the Lesotho Monetary Authority (now the Central Bank of Lesotho) began issuing loti as the national currency, but the South African rand remained legal tender and the loti was pegged at par with the rand.

Demand for credit in the private sector was strong during the 1990s in response to growth in the manufacturing, services, and construction sectors. In contrast, claims on central government were reduced as a result of the IMF-supported Structural Adjustment Program; in fact, the government was a net saver with

the domestic banking system in 1992. In the 1990s, interest rates remained positive in real terms and generally slightly higher than in South Africa due to higher margins.

The commercial bank sector is dominated by the government-owned Lesotho Bank and the South African-owned Stambic Bank, which acquired Barclays Bank's interest in Lesotho. Lesotho Bank was privatized in 1999. The Lesotho Building Finance Corporation merged with Lesotho Bank in April 1993 to facilitate an increase in the scale of domestic mortgage lending. The

---

Balance of Payments – Lesotho (2010)

(In millions of US dollars)

Current Account		**-421.4**
Balance on goods	-1,146.5	
Imports	-1,998.3	
Exports	851.8	
Balance on services	-468.2	
Balance on income	532.0	
Current transfers	661.2	
Capital Account		**123.3**
Financial Account		**-135.6**
Direct investment abroad	2.3	
Direct investment in Lesotho	117.0	
Portfolio investment assets	-0.2	
Portfolio investment liabilities	0.2	
Financial derivatives	...	
Other investment assets	-245.2	
Other investment liabilities	-9.6	
Net Errors and Omissions		**219.9**
Reserves and Related Items		**213.8**

(…) data not available or not significant.

SOURCE: *Balance of Payment Statistics Yearbook 2011,* Washington, DC: International Monetary Fund, 2011.

Public Finance – Lesotho (2008)

(In millions of maloti, budgetary central government figures)

Revenue and Grants	**8,879**	**100.0%**
Tax revenue	7,907	89.1%
Social contributions	...	...
Grants	122	1.4%
Other revenue	850	9.6%
Expenditures	**8,326**	**100.0%**
General public services	2,302	27.6%
Defense	335	4.0%
Public order and safety	568	6.8%
Economic affairs	2,568	30.8%
Environmental protection	10	0.1%
Housing and community amenities	143	1.7%
Health	806	9.7%
Recreational, culture, and religion	151	1.8%
Education	1,424	17.1%
Social protection	21	0.3%

(…) data not available or not significant.

SOURCE: *Government Finance Statistics Yearbook 2010,* Washington, DC: International Monetary Fund, 2010.

Lesotho Agricultural Development Bank (LADB) had served to mobilize rural savings and provide agricultural credit, but it was liquidated in 2000.

In 2010 the discount rate, the interest rate at which the central bank lends to financial institutions in the short term, was 10%. The commercial bank prime lending rate, the rate at which banks lend to customers, was 11.2%.

34 INSURANCE

In 2011 there were at least six insurance companies operating in Lesotho. During the 1998 destruction of commercial life, most firms were not covered by insurance, lengthening the rebuilding process.

35 PUBLIC FINANCE

Proceeds from membership in a common customs union with South Africa form the majority of government revenue. Lesotho receives aid from myriad sources, including the United States, World Bank, United Kingdom, the European Union, and Germany.

In 2010 the budget of Lesotho included $968.4 million in public revenue and $1.193 billion in public expenditures. The budget deficit amounted to 8.4% of GDP. Public debt was 46.5% of GDP, with $666.2 million of the debt held by foreign entities.

36 TAXATION

In 1960, a review of the tax structure was undertaken with a view toward ending the dual tax system, which made a distinction between Basotho and non-Basotho. It was decided that a basic tax, previously paid only by Basotho, would be paid by all male residents. A graded tax and a scaled income tax, both payable by all persons irrespective of race or sex, were subsequently imposed. The maximum tax rate for individuals is 35%, and in 2011 the statutory corporate tax rate fell from 15% to 10%. A 33.33% tax is paid on dividends. Lesotho has a value-added tax (VAT) system with a standard rate of 14%. Certain commodities are subject to variable VAT rates.

37 CUSTOMS AND DUTIES

Customs and duties constitute the predominant source of ordinary revenue. Lesotho, together with Swaziland, Botswana, and Namibia, is a member of a customs union with South Africa; consequently, no tariffs exist on most goods moving among them. South Africa levies and collects the bulk of the customs, sales, and excise duties for the five countries, paying a share determined by an established formula of total customs collections to the other four. Imports from outside the customs union, regardless of ultimate destination, are subject to the same tariff rates.

38 FOREIGN INVESTMENT

The government actively encourages foreign investment, particularly investment in manufacturing plants and agricultural projects. The Lesotho National Development Corporation (LNDC) promotes industrial estates, with such attractions as a 15-year discretionary tax holiday or accelerated depreciation allowances, plus LNDC capital participation of up to 25%.

Annual foreign direct investment (FDI) inflow into Lesotho was $269 million in 1997, but declined steadily for the rest of the decade, amounting to $119 million in 2000. For the period 1997 to 2000, net FDI equaled over one-fifth (21.8%) of its GDP, the highest such ratio in the world. According to the World Bank, FDI in Lesotho was a net inflow of $62.9 million in 2009. FDI represented 3.99% of GDP. Most FDI is concentrated in textiles, garments, and light manufacturing.

39 ECONOMIC DEVELOPMENT

The Lesotho government's development objectives are based on a food-security policy approach, built around small-scale irrigated agriculture projects and improved rural water supplies. Donors supported the fourth five-year plan (1988–91) with pledges of $390 million. Lesotho receives development assistance from the United States, United Kingdom, Germany, South Africa, Canada, Taiwan, the European Union, the World Bank, and various UN agencies.

In 2001, Lesotho negotiated a three-year, $35 million Poverty Reduction and Growth Facility (PRGF) arrangement with the IMF. Unemployment, poverty, and the HIV/AIDS pandemic are challenges for further economic development. The sale of the state telecommunications company in 2001 stood as evidence of Lesotho's continuing privatization program. The government in 2003 was committed to public sector reform and market-friendly policies, as illustrated by its support for the Lesotho Public Sector Improvement and Reform Project.

A review of Lesotho's economic performance in 2005 by the IMF welcomed the marked improvement seen across a range of macroeconomic indicators in recent years, noting in particular the lower fiscal deficits and improved balance of payments position. It also welcomed the government's commitment to increasing institutional capacity in order to better implement and monitor public spending programs, which will now be formulated in the context of a poverty reduction strategy. However, the IMF indicated that there was room for improvements in the economic policies in order for Lesotho to enhance labor skills, clear bottlenecks in infrastructure and public-sector delivery, and remove legal and administrative impediments to investment.

40 SOCIAL DEVELOPMENT

In the past, many social welfare programs were organized on the local level or by missions. But the need for concerted action to alleviate hardships brought about by severe droughts led to the creation in 1965 of a Social Welfare Department under the Ministry of Health (later the Ministry of Health and Social Welfare). Community development teams stimulate local initiative by conducting courses and forming voluntary community development committees. The Homemakers' Association, an organization long active in social welfare, has given family management courses in remote areas under a grant from the Oxford Committee for Famine Relief (Oxfam).

The roles of women are limited by law and by tradition. Married women are considered legal minors under customary law. They are unable to sign contracts and have no legal standing in a court of law. Domestic violence is a widespread problem, although it is considered unacceptable behavior. The government has pledged to improve the rights of women. Limited resources limit the ability of government to implement child welfare programs.

Some human rights violations were reported, including excessive use of force by police, long pretrial delays, and poor prison conditions. Crime is a serious problem in Lesotho.

41HEALTH

It was estimated that 85% of children have been vaccinated against measles. The CIA calculated HIV/AIDS prevalence in Lesotho to be about 23.6% in 2009.

According to the CIA, life expectancy in Lesotho was 45 years in 2011. The country spent 8.2% of its GDP on healthcare, amounting to $70 per person. There was 1 physician, 6 nurses and midwives, and 13 hospital beds per 10,000 inhabitants. The fertility rate was 3.3, while the infant mortality rate was 61 per 1,000 live births. In 2008, the maternal mortality rate, according to the World Bank, was 530 per 100,000 births. Lesotho's major health problems, such as pellagra and kwashiorkor, stem from poor nutrition and inadequate hygiene. It was estimated that 44% of children under five years of age were considered malnourished. Famines have resulted from periodic droughts. Approximately 91% of the population had access to safe drinking water and 92% had adequate sanitation.

Tuberculosis and sexually transmitted diseases (STDs) are also serious problems. The incidence of tuberculosis was 696 per 100,000 people in 2007. Children up to one year old were vaccinated at the following rates: diphtheria, pertussis, and tetanus, 83%; polio, 66%; and measles, 85%. About 43% of children suffered from goiter.

In April 2010, the head of the United Nations Children's Fund (UNICEF), Ann M. Veneman, visited Lesotho to stress the importance of education in reducing childhood illness in the country. Veneman used her visit to launch Facts for Life, a UN publication that delivers information to families and communities on how to prevent child and maternal deaths, diseases, injuries, and violence. The publication includes a chapter on how to manage childhood HIV/AIDS, placing a special emphasis on early detection. In Lesotho, one in ten children dies before reaching the age of five, mostly as a result of HIV/AIDS or preventable diseases, such as pneumonia and diarrhea.

The infant mortality rate per 1,000 live births was 56.42 in 2010. The total fertility rate was 3 children per woman in that year. Contraceptives were used by an estimated 23% of women. Estimated life expectancy in 2010 was 50.67. The government of Lesotho is making an effort to strengthen healthcare services.

The HIV/AIDS prevalence rate in Lesotho is one of the highest in the world, with nearly 23.2% of the population affected by the disease. With no sign that the infection rate is coming under control, the UN has projected that 36% of the adult population will be affected by 2023. At the end of 2006, only 31% of those infected by HIV/AIDS were receiving antiretroviral therapy. Young women between the ages of 15 and 24 have shown the highest rates of infection. An estimated 100,000 children have become AIDS orphans, as both parents have died from the disease. Several international agencies and foreign governments have offered aid for testing, treatment, and education programs designed to stop the spread of the disease.

42HOUSING

The Lesotho Housing and Land Development Corp. builds new housing for sale and rent, and a government-supported development program is building low-cost housing. The government has also begun to encourage private investment and ownership of housing through privatization of banking and legal reforms, the latter of which include the Law Reform Commission and the Land Policy Review Commission, which have been working on legislation to allow women equal rights in access to credit and land ownership.

43EDUCATION

The educational system in Lesotho reached a major milestone in May 2010, as the government passed the Education Act 2010, making free primary education compulsory for children ages 6 through 13. Free primary education was first introduced in 2000, as part of the nation's commitment to the global Education for All movement inspired by UNESCO. Since then, enrollment in primary education has jumped to 82% (80% boys and 84% girls). By making primary education compulsory, the government hopes to ensure that more children receive a basic education. In 2009 the World Bank estimated that 73% of age-eligible children in Lesotho were enrolled in primary school. Secondary enrollment for age-eligible children stood at 29%. Tertiary enrollment was estimated at 4%. Students may choose to attend craft schools after primary school instead of junior high. Those who complete junior high may opt for a two-year trade school instead of senior high. The languages of instruction are Sesotho and English.

In 2009, the CIA estimated that Lesotho had a literacy rate of 84.8%, one of the highest literacy rates in Africa, in part because Lesotho invests over 12% of its GDP in education. Contrary to most countries, in Lesotho female literacy (94.5%) is higher than male literacy. At the same time, Lesotho has achieved gender parity in primary education. Approximately 49% of primary school students are female and more than 50% of secondary school students are female. Most importantly, the probability of attending primary school is equal for children from the richest and the poorest households.

The government has pledged major investments in education, which it considers to be a driving force not only in economic development, but in improving the health and welfare of the nation's people.

Under the auspices of the Higher Education Subsector, a number of public institutions exist. These are the Lesotho College of Education (LCE), the National University of Lesotho (NUL) and Lerotholi Polytechnic (LP). LCE trains primary school teachers and junior secondary school teachers at both pre-service and in-service levels. It has slowly been turned into an autonomous institution to help improve its efficiency.

The NUL, the highest autonomous learning institution in the country, is committed to be a center of excellence in the country and the strengthening of its management operations is targeted in this regard.

The LP, traditionally classified under technical and vocational education and training, is also an autonomous institution. The LP has three schools that offer diverse fields at diploma and certificate levels. These are the School of Technology, the School of Built Environment, and the School of Commerce and Applied Studies. Its vision is to become a leading, self-sustaining and responsive university of science and technology.

44 LIBRARIES AND MUSEUMS

The Government Archive in Maseru has records dating from 1869. The Lesotho National Library, also in the capital, holds 88,000 volumes. The Thomas Mofolo Library at the National University of Lesotho is the largest library in the country with more than 170,000 books. The British Council maintains a library in Maseru, with 6,270 volumes and there is a library of 10,000 volumes at the Lesotho Agricultural College.

The National Teachers Training College in Maseru also has a notable library. The Lesotho National Library Service, founded in 1976, sponsors three public library branches: Leribe, Mafeteng, and Mokhotlong. The Lesotho Library Association was founded in 1978. The Lesotho National Museum in Maseruhas has collections on archaeology, ethnography, and geology. The Morija Museum has collections in the same fields.

45 MEDIA

The government operates postal and telephone services; the exchange at Maseru has been automatic since 1963. An earth satellite station was opened in 1986. In 2009, the CIA reported that there were 40,000 landline telephones in Lesotho. In addition to landlines, mobile phone subscriptions averaged 32 per 100 people.

Government-owned Radio Lesotho broadcasts in English and Sesotho; it is the only station with a national range. There were about seven privately owned radio stations. The government-owned Lesotho Television is the only television station in the country. In 2010, the country had 632 Internet hosts. Internet users numbered 4 per 100 citizens.

In 2011 Lesotho had approximately 18 newspapers and periodicals, most of which were weeklies. The major daily *Mphatlalatsane* was a daily Sesotho newspaper published in Maseru. The print media consisted of various newspapers in the Sesotho language and five English language weekly newspapers: *The Post*, *Lesotho Today*, *The Survivor*, *The Public Eye* and *The Mirror*, which are mostly free from editorial control by the government.

Moeletsi oa Basotho was published by the Roman Catholic Church with a circulation of 20,000; the Lesotho Evangelical Church`s publication, *Leselinyana le Lesotho* (*The Light of Lesotho*) had a circulation of 1500; and *Lentsoe la Basotho had a circulation 14,000.

The Constitution provides freedom of speech and the press, and the government is said to respect these rights in practice.

46 ORGANIZATIONS

Cooperative unions that are partly government-financed and government-sponsored, consumer cooperatives, artisan cooperatives, and the Progressive Farmers play an important part in economic and social development. There are also more than 100 active agricultural marketing and credit societies.

National youth organizations include the Association of Youth Cultural Clubs, Lesotho Scouts Association, Lesotho Work Camps Association, YMCA/YWCA, Lesotho Youth Federation, and the Student Representative Council of Lesotho. There are several sports organizations and clubs throughout the country, including branches of the Special Olympics. The Lesotho National Council of Women offers programs and activities to support and promote the development of women.

Volunteer service organizations, such as the Lions Clubs International, are present. The Red Cross, Caritas, the Society of St. Vincent de Paul, and Habitat for Humanity are active in the country.

47 TOURISM, TRAVEL, AND RECREATION

The Lesotho National Tourist Board promotes tourism, which is increasing but still underdeveloped. The *Tourism Factbook*, published by the UN World Tourism Organization, reported 344,000 incoming tourists to Lesotho in 2009, who spent a total of $40 million. Of those incoming tourists, there were 314,000 from Africa. There were 4,791 hotel beds available in Lesotho, which had an occupancy rate of 18%. The estimated daily cost to visit Maseru, the capital, was $266. The cost of visiting other cities averaged $90.

Permanent tourist camps are established in remote scenic areas for pony-trekking parties. The first such camp, consisting of bath and kitchen-equipped grass huts, was built at Marakabeis, near the end of the Mountain Road.

Although lacking in game, Lesotho has spectacular natural attractions in its mountains and in Malutsenyane Falls, as well as excellent trout fishing grounds. The rock paintings near Teyateyaneng are also a potentially important tourist site. The country's first national park, Sehlabathebe Mountain National Park, was established in 1970 in the Qacha's Nek District. There is a gambling casino in Maseru, along with mountain resorts and lodges.

Visas are not required for stays of up to 30 days, but a valid passport, proof of sufficient funds, and onward/return ticket are necessary. Vaccination against yellow fever is highly recommended and sometimes required.

48 FAMOUS PERSONS

Moshoeshoe (or Moshesh, 1786–1870), a chief of the Bakoena tribe in what was then northern Basutoland, is acclaimed as the founder of the Basotho nation. Moshoeshoe II (1938–96) served as king of Lesotho from October 1966 until January 1996, when he was killed in an automobile accident.

Crown Prince Letsie David Mohato (b. 1963), who had served as king during his father's 1989–94 exile, returned to the throne in February 1996 as King Letsie III. Chief Leabua Jonathan (1914–87), prime minister of Lesotho from its inception until 1986, was a leader in the drive for independence.

49 DEPENDENCIES

Lesotho has no territories or colonies.

50 BIBLIOGRAPHY

Dibie, Robert A. *Non-Governmental Organizations (NGOs) and Sustainable Development in Sub-Saharan Africa.* Lanham, MD: Lexington Books, 2008.

FDI and Tourism: The Development Dimension: East and Southern Africa. New York: United Nations, 2008.

Lundahl, Mats. *In the Shadow of South Africa: Lesotho's Economic Future.* Burlington, VT: Ashgate, 2003.

McElrath, Karen, ed. *HIV and AIDS: A Global View.* Westport, CT: Greenwood Press, 2002.

McKenna, Amy. *The History of Southern Africa.* New York: Britannica Educational Publishing, 2011.

Nolting, Mark. *Africa's Top Wildlife Countries.* Ft. Lauderdale: Global Travel Publishers, Inc., 2008.

Rosenberg, Scott, Richard F. Weisenfelder, and Michelle Frisbie-Fulton. *Historical Dictionary of Lesotho.* Lanham, MD: Scarecrow, 2003.

Zeilig, Leo, and David Seddon. *A Political and Economic Dictionary of Africa.* Philadelphia: Routledge/Taylor and Francis, 2005.

LIBERIA

Republic of Liberia

CAPITAL: Monrovia

FLAG: The national flag, dating from 1847, consists of 11 horizontal stripes, alternately red (6) and white (5), with a single five-pointed white star on a square blue field 5 stripes deep in the upper left corner.

ANTHEM: *All Hail, Liberia, Hail!*

MONETARY UNIT: The Liberian dollar (LRD) of 100 cents was linked to the US dollar until January 1998, when it switched to a rate determined by the floating market. The banknotes are in the denomination of 5, 10, 20, 50, and 100, while there are coins of 5, 10, 25, 50 cents, and 1 dollar. US notes and coins were also in circulation and were legal tender. LRD1 = US$0.0139860 (or US$1 = LRD71.5000) as of December 2011.

WEIGHTS AND MEASURES: US and UK weights and measures are used.

HOLIDAYS: New Year's Day, 1 January; Armed Forces Day, 11 February; Decoration Day, 2nd Wednesday in March; Birthday of J. J. Roberts (first president), 15 March; Fast and Prayer Day, 2nd Friday in April; National Redemption Day, 12 April; Unification Day, 14 May; Independence Day, 26 July; Flag Day, 24 August; Thanksgiving Day, 1st Thursday in November; Anniversary of 1985 Coup Attempt, 12 November; President Tubman's Birthday, 29 November; Christmas, 25 December. Good Friday and Easter Monday were movable religious holidays.

TIME: GMT.

¹LOCATION, SIZE, AND EXTENT

Located on the west coast of Africa, Liberia has an area of about 111,370 sq km (43,000 sq mi), with a length of 548 km (341 mi) ESE–WNW and a width of 274 km (170 mi) NNE–SSW. Comparatively, the area occupied by Liberia is slightly larger than the state of Tennessee. On the N it is bounded by Guinea, on the E by Côte d'Ivoire, on the S and SW by the Atlantic Ocean, and on the NW by Sierra Leone, with a total land boundary length of 1,585 km (985 mi) and a coastline of 579 km (360 mi).

Liberia's capital city, Monrovia, is located on the Atlantic coast.

²TOPOGRAPHY

There are three distinct belts lying parallel to the coast. The low coastal belt is about 40 km (25 mi) wide, with tidal creeks, shallow lagoons, and mangrove marshes. The land then rises to rolling hills, with elevations of 60–150 m (200–500 ft). The third belt, comprising the bulk of Liberia, is marked by abrupt changes of elevation in a series of low mountains and plateaus, less densely forested than the hilly region. The Nimba Mountains are near the Guinea frontier. The Wologizi Mountains reach a maximum of about 1,380 m (4,528 ft) with Mt. Wutuvi, the nation's highest point. Of the six principal rivers, all of which are at right angles to the coast and flow into the Atlantic Ocean, only the Farmington is of much commercial importance. Sandbars obstruct the mouths of all rivers, making entrance hazardous, and upstream there are rocky rapids.

³CLIMATE

The climate is tropical and humid, with little change in temperature throughout the year. The mean is 27°C (81°F), with temperatures rarely exceeding 36°C (97°F) or falling below 20°C (68°F). On the coast the heat is tempered by an almost constant breeze. Yearly rainfall is as high as 510 cm (200 in) on the coast, decreasing to about 200 cm (80 in) in areas farthest inland. There are distinct wet and dry seasons, most of the rainfall occurring between late April and mid-November. Average relative humidity in the coastal area is about 82% during the rainy season and 78% in the dry, but it may drop to 50% or lower between December and March, when the dust-laden harmattan blows from the Sahara.

⁴FLORA AND FAUNA

The World Resources Institute estimated that there were 2,200 plant species in Liberia. In addition, Liberia was home to 183 mammal, 576 bird, 80 reptile, and 42 amphibian species. The calculation reflected the total number of distinct species residing in the country, not the number of endemic species.

Liberia, together with neighbors Sierra Leone and Côte d'Ivoire, harbored most of West Africa's evergreen forests. There were about 235 species of trees with 90 of them present in potentially marketable quantities, including mahogany and ironwood. The bombex (cotton tree), the oil palm, and the kola tree were common. The wild rubber tree (Funtumia elastica) was indigenous, but the cultivated Hevea brasiliensis was the source of Liberia's commercial rubber. A variety of coffee peculiar to Liberia, Coffea Liberica, was formerly common but has given way to the preferred Coffea Robusta. Fruit trees included citrus varieties, the alligator apple, papaya, mango, and avocado. Pineapples grew wild.

Elephant and buffalo, once common in Liberia, had largely disappeared, but several species of antelope were found in the interior; two of these, the white-shouldered duiker and the zebra antelope, were particular to Liberia. A lemur called Bosman's potto and several species of monkey, including the long-haired and the Diana, were found in the forests. Wild pigs and porcupines existed in sparsely settled areas, and several members of the leopard group were also found. Most of the 15 species of snakes were venomous. Termite hills were found throughout the country. In some areas the tsetse fly was found, and driver ants and mosquitoes were common. Several varieties of snail acted as hosts in the propagation of enteric diseases. Among the birds were the hornbill, wild guinea fowl, cattle egret (cowbird), flamingo, woodpecker, and weaver.

5 ENVIRONMENT

The World Resources Institute reported that Liberia had designated 1.52 million hectares (3.76 million acres) of land for protection as of 2006. Water resources totaled 232 cu km (55.66 cu mi) while water usage was 0.11 cu km (.026 cu mi) per year. Domestic water usage accounted for 27% of total usage, industrial for 18%, and agricultural for 55%. Per capita water usage totaled 34 cu m (1,201 cu ft) per year.

The United Nations (UN) reported in 2008 that carbon dioxide emissions in Liberia totaled 674 kilotons.

At the beginning of the 1980s, Liberia was one of the last West African countries with significant primary forest reserves. By 2008 it possessed the core of the remaining West African forest belt, which extended from Guinea to Cameroon. However, deforestation has progressed rapidly owing to population pressure, commercial logging, firewood cutting, shifting agriculture, bushmeat demand, mining and weak protections against illegal and quasilegal activities. Massive cutting of Liberia's mangrove swamps has occurred in and around coastal cities like Monrovia. Hunting and loss of habitat have decimated wildlife along the coastal plain, and there were no longer any large herds of big game in the interior.

The water supply for many people was open sources such as streams, swamps, and shallow, uncovered wells. The Mano and St. John rivers were threatened by pollution from the dumping of iron ore tailings. Oil residue and untreated sewage and waste water found their way to coastal waters. The Environmental Protection and Management Law (EPML) of 2003 lacked implementing regulations and therefore was ineffective.

According to a 2011 report issued by the International Union for Conservation of Nature and Natural Resources (IUCN), the number of threatened species included 18 types of mammals, 11 species of birds, 5 types of reptiles, 4 species of amphibians, 53 species of fish, 1 type of mollusk, 8 other invertebrates, and 47 species of plants. The Jentink's duiker, the white-breasted guinea fowl, Pel's flying squirrel, the green turtle, and the Liberian mongoose are threatened species in Liberia.

In 2009 the president of Liberia declared a state of emergency as a plague of caterpillars swept through regions of the country. The species, identified as *Achaea catocaloides*, can emerge in sudden swarms, devouring crops and leaving behind contaminating feces. Over 400,000 residents from 100 villages were forced out of their homes by the infestation. The government immediately began a program to kill the insects by spraying pesticides, but much damage had already been done to valuable crops and water supplies in some areas.

6 POPULATION

The US Central Intelligence Agency (CIA) reported the population of Liberia in 2011 to be approximately 3,786,764, which placed it at number 128 in population among the 196 nations of the world. In 2011, approximately 3% of the population was over 65 years of age, with another 44.3% under 15 years of age. The median age in Liberia was 18.3 years. There were 1.00 males for every female in the country. The population's annual rate of change was 2.663%. The projected population for the year 2025 was 6,100,000. Population density in Liberia was calculated at 34 people per sq km (88 people per sq mi).

The UN estimated that 48% of the population lived in urban areas, and that urban populations had an annual rate of change of 3.4%. The largest urban area was Monrovia, with a population of nearly one million. Monrovia was built for a population of about 350,000 and along with other urban centers suffered from serious overcrowding.

The prevalence of HIV/AIDS has had a significant impact on the population of Liberia. The AIDS epidemic causes higher death and infant mortality rates, and lowers life expectancy.

7 MIGRATION

Liberia's net migration rate as reported by the CIA in 2011 was negligible. The total number of emigrants living abroad was 431,900, and the total number of immigrants living in Liberia was 96,300.

The Liberian civil war caused staggering displacements of the population in the 1990s and early 2000s when some 210,000 persons fled to Côte d'Ivoire, 420,000 to Guinea, 17,000 to Ghana, 14,000 to Sierra Leone, and 6,000 to Nigeria. By 2011 most of these refugees had returned home. However, in the violent aftermath of the political stalemate in Côte d'Ivoire in 2011, more than 163,000 Ivoirians crossed the border into Liberia seeking refuge. UNHCR appealed for $150 million to assist these refugees and the communities hosting them. By end of 2011 Côte d'Ivoire had stabilized sufficiently to allow Ivoirian refugees to begin returning home.

8 ETHNIC GROUPS

Liberia is peopled by some 28 ethnic groups and by descendants of freed slaves and captured peoples, who returned to the continent or who were brought to Liberia from intercepted ships. The indigenous peoples are believed to have migrated from the north and east between the 12th and 16th centuries AD, bringing with them elements of Egyptian and Arabian culture, such as the spinning and weaving of cotton and the smelting of iron. Linguistically, ethnic groups may be divided into three main groupings: the Mande people in the north and far west, the Kru tribes (including the Krahn) in the east and southeast, and the Mel in the northwest. The largest groups are the Kpellé (20.3% of the population),

Bassa (13.4%), Grebo (10%), Gio (8%), Mano (7.9%), Kru (6%), Lorma (5.1%), Kissi (4.8%), and Gola (4.4%).

About 2% of the population belonged to the historically dominant Americo-Liberian group, descendants of slaves from the United States. There were also two groups not strictly Liberian: the Mandingo, who were itinerant Muslim traders, and the Fanti fishermen, who came from Ghana and stayed for a few years at a time.

Because of intermarriage, ethnic divisions were becoming less distinct, especially in Monrovia. Nevertheless, there was a strong tendency among the indigenous people to preserve their identities, and ethnicity was at times a divisive dynamic in the country. In 2010, ethnic conflict erupted between indigenous groups and Mandigo peoples and ethnic conflict between the Krahn and Dan communities persisted in the north. In 2011, upon receiving the Nobel Peace Prize, President Johnson-Sirleaf announced that fellow Nobel recipient, Leymah Gbowee, a female Liberian human rights activist, would spearhead a national peace and reconciliation initiative to reunite the country. Lebanese and Syrian traders comprised the largest number of non-Africans.

9 LANGUAGES

English was the official language, but only about 20% of the people spoke or wrote it well; the remainder communicated mostly in one or more of 20 local languages including Vai, Bassa, and Loma. The international phonetic alphabet, introduced by missionaries, has facilitated the use of local languages for correspondence and publication of local newsletters.

10 RELIGIONS

The early settlers, freed American slaves, brought with them the culture and religion of the US deep South of the slavery era. Their descendants were generally adherents of Protestant denominations. Most Christians and a small Muslim minority retained elements of African belief systems, which consisted of practices such as ancestor veneration.

Liberians generally respected the constitutional principle of the separation of religion and state. However, conflict entrepreneurs exploited popular sentiments and politicized religion during the war to serve their personal interests. Because religious affiliation and ethnicity were closely linked, ethnic tensions persisted, most prominently between returning Mandingo, many of whom were Muslim, and Dan (Gio) and Mano in Nimba, as well as between Mandingo and Lorma in Lofa and Bong counties.

11 TRANSPORTATION

The CIA reported that Liberia had 10,600 km (6,587 mi) of roads, of which 657 km (408 mi) were paved. There were 29 airports. Transport infrastructure deteriorated significantly during the war years.

Private roads built by rubber and lumber companies were mostly laterite-surfaced. Paved trunk roads once connected Monrovia to the hinterlands as far as the Guinea, Sierra Leone, and Côte d'Ivoire borders. In 2011 reasonably paved roads carried travelers between Monrovia and border posts with Sierra Leone and Guinea at Bo Waterside and Ganta, respectively. However, owing to lack of maintenance since the war, many roads and bridges were nearly impassable during the rainy season; a trip from the capital to Maryland County in the east could take two or more days. Ex-

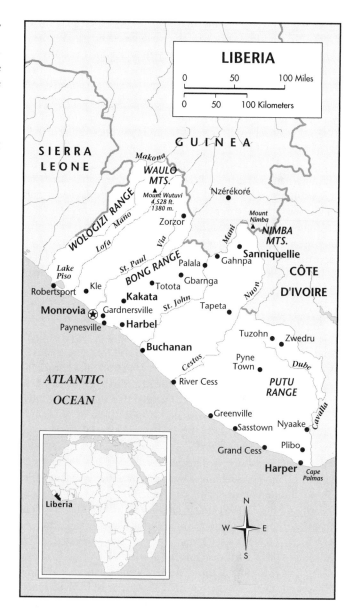

LOCATION: 4°20′ to 8°33′N; 7°22′ to 11°30′ W. BOUNDARY LENGTHS: Guinea, 563 kilometers (350 miles); Côte d'Ivoire, 716 kilometers (445 miles); Atlantic coastline, 538 kilometers (334 miles); Sierra Leone, 306 kilometers (190 miles). TERRITORIAL SEA LIMIT: 200 miles.

cept for short-line buses, virtually all of Liberia's common carriers were taxicabs.

Of Liberia's three railways, all were owned by foreign steel and financial interests under license by the Liberian Government and had been used to transport iron ore from mines to the ports of Buchanan and Monrovia. The Lamco Railroad closed in 1989 after iron ore production ceased. The other two were shut down by the civil war. Large sections of the rail lines have been dismantled, and an estimated 60 km (37 mi) exported for scrap.

The Free Port of Monrovia, opened in 1948, underwent substantial improvements during the late 1960s to accommodate ships with a draft up to 14 m (45 ft). A port used primarily for iron ore export was opened at Buchanan in 1963. These two deepwater ports handled over 98% of all cargo. Smaller ports, located at

Greenville and Harper, handled mainly timber exports. Owing to the war, Monrovia port closed for a period in 1999.

In 2011, 3,500 foreign-owned vessels transporting some 112 million gross tons registered under Liberia's flag of convenience. The Liberian registry, headquartered in Vienna, Virginia (USA), was the second largest in the world and represented approximately 11% of the world's ocean-going fleet. The registry provided the Liberian government with $15-$20 million in annual revenues in 2003.

Robertsfield, 58 km (36 mi) from Monrovia, was the site of the sole international airport. Prior to the war, medium-sized jets and small aircraft provided service from Spriggs Payne Airport on the outskirts of Monrovia to destinations upcountry. Air Liberia, founded in 1974, went defunct in 1990. In 2011 no domestic commercial airline was operating. In January 2011 Delta Airlines increased its flights between Atlanta and Monrovia to twice weekly. In 2011, seven major foreign airlines served Monrovia, five of them via stops in Accra.

12 HISTORY

It is believed that many of the peoples of Liberia migrated there from the north and east between the 12th and 16th centuries AD. Portuguese explorers first visited the coast in 1461, and Europeans traded with coastal tribes during the next three centuries. Modern Liberia was founded in 1822 by freed slaves from the United States. They were sent to Africa under the auspices of the American Colonization Society, a private organization whose purpose was "to promote and execute a plan for colonizing in Africa, with their own consent, the free people of color residing in the United States." The first settlement was on Providence Island near the present location of the capital city, Monrovia. Although the Society, with the help of the United States government under President James Monroe (after whom Monrovia is named), had arranged with local chiefs for a settlement, the colonists were attacked by indigenous peoples, disease, and barely maintained their foothold.

The first governors of the settlement were agents appointed by the Colonization Society, but in 1847 Americo-Liberians established the Republic of Liberia under a constitution modeled after that of the United States. The state seal shows a ship at anchor in a tropical harbor, and bears the inscription, "The Love of Liberty Brought Us Here." Thus began over a 130 years of Americo-Liberian domination over the 16 major indigenous ethnic groups within Liberia's borders.

Emigration to Liberia continued until the close of the U.S. Civil War, during which about 14,000 settlers went to Liberia under the auspices of the Society, and some 5,700 captives, liberated from slave ships on the high seas by the US Navy, were sent by the US government.

Although the United States refused to extend diplomatic recognition to independent Liberia until the civil war, several European governments did, including Britain and France. However, as the scramble for Africa reached its feverish pitch, Liberia's "century of survival" began. Neighboring British and French colonial powers, on one pretext or another, and by force of arms, encroached upon the infant republic. During the last quarter of the 19th century, Liberia lost considerable resource-rich territory to adjoining British

and French colonies. Pressure on Liberia's borders continued well into the 20th century.

Added to these dangers was Liberia's precarious economic position. In the 1870s, Liberia contracted for a $500,000 loan from European sources. Because of increasing world competition from Brazilian coffee, European sugar beets, and steamers, Liberia was unable to generate sufficient export revenue, and defaulted on this loan. Recession forced Liberia into a series of ever larger loans. Liberians were further compelled to allow collection of customs revenues by Europeans and Americans. Eventually, Liberia was able to secure a $5-million loan from a US firm, the Firestone Tire and Rubber Co., which set up rubber plantations in the country in 1926. The depression of the 1930s brought Liberia to the verge of bankruptcy, and government revenues fell in 1933 to a low of $321,000.

In the early 1930s, Liberia's political sovereignty was also seriously threatened. Accusations had begun to circulate internationally that Liberian laborers, with the complicity of government officials, were being recruited for transport to the Spanish island of Fernando Póo (now Bioko, in Equatorial Guinea) under conditions that resembled slave trading. A commission of inquiry, set up by the League of Nations at the request of Liberia's President Charles D. B. King, found some basis for the charges and implicated the vice president, who was forced to resign. President King also resigned.

Exportation of rubber from the new Firestone plantations began in 1934. The establishment of a U.S. air base in Liberia during World War II and the building of a port at Monrovia further stimulated development. William V. S. Tubman, elected president in 1944 and reelected for five additional terms, sought to unify the country by attempting to bridge the wide economic, political, and social gaps between the descendants of the original American ex-slaves and the tribal peoples of the interior. President Tubman, affectionately called "Uncle Shad," died at the age of 74, after 27 years in office. He was known as the "Maker of Modern Liberia" for his open door policy of unrestricted foreign investment and his Unification Policy.

Upon his death in 1971, Vice-President William R. Tolbert, Jr. assumed the reins of power. Tolbert was nominated by the True Whigs, Liberia's only legal political party, and, having been elected without opposition in October 1975, was inaugurated for an eight-year term in January 1976. Tolbert's term coincided with a deep economic depression, which sparked what would become a colonial revolution. The Progressive Alliance of Liberia (PAL) organized a protest against proposed increases in the price of rice. When violence and looting ensued, Tolbert was forced to subsidize rice to restore order, a sign that the True Whig government was coming to an end.

Doe Takes Power

On 12 April 1980 army-enlisted men staged a coup. Tolbert and at least 26 supporters were killed in the fighting. Thirteen officials were publicly executed 10 days later. The People's Redemption Council (PRC) led by Sgt. Samuel K. Doe, a Krahn tribesman, became head of state. Doe suspended the constitution, but a return to civilian rule was promised for 1985. Despite two coups attempts in 1981, the government declared an amnesty for all political prisoners and exiles. Forty political prisoners were released in September of that year, and another 20 were released in December. A draft constitution providing for a multiparty republic was issued in 1983 and approved by referendum in 1984.

In the elections of 15 October 1985, nine political parties sought to challenge Doe's National Democratic Party of Liberia (NDPL), but only three were allowed to take part. Doe was elected with 51% of the vote, and the NDPL won 21 of the 26 Senate seats and 51 of the 64 seats in the House of Representatives. Foreign observers declared the elections fraudulent, and most of the elected opposition candidates refused to take their seats.

In November 1985, military leader Thomas Quiwonkpa and an estimated 500 to 600 people died in an unsuccessful coup attempt-the seventh since Doe took power. Krahn troops retaliated, killing thousands of Gio, considered supporters of the coup leaders. In late December 1989, a small group of insurgents calling themselves the National Patriotic Front of Liberia (NPFL) led by Charles Taylor invaded Liberia. The rebel invasion soon pitted ethnic Krahn sympathetic to the regime against those victimized by it, Gio and Mano. Thousands of civilians were massacred on both sides. Hundreds of thousands fled their homes.

By June 1990, Taylor's forces laid siege to Monrovia. A third force led by Prince Yormie Johnson, split from the NPFL. Johnson quickly controlled parts of Monrovia prompting evacuation of foreign nationals and diplomats by the US Navy in August. To restore order, the Economic Community of West African States (ECOWAS) created the Economic Community Monitoring Group (ECOMOG) comprising some 4,000 troops from Nigeria, Ghana, Sierra Leone, The Gambia, and Guinea.

ECOWAS invited the principal Liberian players to meet in Banjul, Gambia to form a government of national unity. Exiled members of Liberia's leading political parties and associations elected Dr. Amos Sawyer, leader of the LPP to head an interim government of national unity (IGNU). Bishop Ronald Diggs of the Liberian Council of Churches became vice president. However, Taylor's NPFL refused to attend the conference, and the AFL, which formerly supported Doe, and the INPFL allied themselves against Taylor. Within days clashes erupted.

On 9 September 1990, Johnson's forces captured Doe at the port of Monrovia. His torture and execution were videotaped by his captors. ECOMOG was reinforced in order to protect the interim government headed by Dr. Sawyer. Sawyer was able to establish his authority over most of Monrovia, but the rest of Liberia was in the hands of various factions of the NPFL or of local gangs.

Repeated attempts to get Taylor and Johnson to cooperate with Sawyer proved fruitless. The war spilled into Sierra Leone, further complicating peacemaking and peacekeeping efforts. In April 1996, violence escalated in Monrovia. Roving gangs of heavily armed, leaderless teenagers recklessly sprayed the city with machine-gun fire and grenade launchers. More than 3,000 people were killed in the next two months and nearly every building in the capital suffered damage. Looters targeted international relief organizations, stealing radios, medicines, and cars.

On 8 May 1996, after more than 150,000 deaths and 13 peace accords, Liberia's four principal militias approved a peace plan that required an immediate halt to fighting, the removal of weapons and ammunition from the capital city of Monrovia, and the

return of about $20 million worth of vehicles and equipment stolen from international relief organizations. Additional troops from Ghana, Mali, Côte d'Ivoire, Niger, Burkina Faso, and Benin were brought in to enforce the peace accords, bringing the total number of foreign peacekeeping troops to 13,000. Meanwhile, it was apparent that disagreements over establishing an electoral commission and other difficulties in preparations would delay the proposed elections.

On 19 July 1997 some 500 international observers, including former US president Jimmy Carter, monitored the elections. They reported peaceful, mostly free and fair elections, although runners-up Johnson-Sirleaf and Kromah complained of irregularities. The official results gave Taylor the victory with 75.3% of the vote, while Johnson-Sirleaf obtained 9.6%. Taylor's National Patriotic Party (NPP) took 49 House seats and 21 seats in the Senate (out of 64 and 26 total seats respectively). On 2 August Taylor was inaugurated. He appointed a cabinet with some members of the transitional administration, and he established a nine-member national security council to maintain civil order.

Although insecurity prevailed in parts of Liberia, especially Lofa County, the last ECOMOG troops began leaving the country in October 1999. In July 1999, Taylor presided over the burning of a huge stockpile of weapons. By May 2000, much of Liberia was still in ruins, but international donors had made some progress in restoring agricultural production, reintegrating ex-combatants, and helping refugees and internally displaced persons resettle in their home areas.

Renewed fighting in 2000 led to a declaration of a state of emergency on 8 February 2002. Taylor lifted the emergency in September 2002, but by February-March 2003, the Liberians United for Reconciliation and Democracy (LURD) had made gains deep into territory previously held by government troops. Under ECOWAS supervision, the two sides met in Bamako in March 2003, the first such official encounter, and peace talks continued in Accra, Ghana. On 17 June, the two sides signed a cease-fire with commitments to a transition government without Taylor, but three days later Taylor declared that he would serve out his term to January 2004 with the possibility of seeking reelection.

On 11 August 2003, Taylor succumbed to international pressure, handed power over to his vice president, Moses Blah, and sought asylum in Nigeria where he remained in exile. A week later, under the auspices of ECOWAS and the international donor Contact Group (ICGL), the government, the LURD, and a new rebel group, the Movement for Democracy in Liberia (Model), signed a peace accord in Accra providing for an interim government, the National Transition Government of Liberia (NTGL) led by businessman, Gyudeh Bryant.

A National Transitional Legislative Assembly (NTLA), composed of warring factions, political parties, representatives of the counties, special interests, and civil society, replaced the House of Representatives and the Senate. A 15,000-strong peacekeeping force-the UN Mission in Liberia-(UNMIL) was established with a one-year mandate to enforce the peace. The mandate was later extended until March 2006. UNMIL began to demobilize and disarm combatants, but because donors underestimated the number of soldiers, funds were insufficient to implement rehabilitation and reintegration. Repatriation through the UN High Commissioner for Refugees (UNHCR) of the estimated 350,000 Liberian refugees was slow, but some 100,000 refugees returned on their own.

The political transition formally ended following the 11 October 2005 election between front-runners George Weah, an internationally renowned soccer (football) player, and Ellen Johnson-Sirleaf, a Harvard-educated international civil servant. Despite protests of fraud by Weah's youthful supporters of the Congress for Democratic Change (CDC), Johnson-Sirleaf was declared the winner on the 8 November second-round ballot with 59.6% of the vote to Weah's 40.4%. The new government was formed on 6 January 2006, making Johnson-Sirleaf Africa's first woman head of state.

Pressure for Taylor's extradition to face trial for alleged war crimes was mounting into 2006. His extradition was demanded by the UN Special Court of Sierra Leone, which charged him with 17 counts of war crimes. In addition, over 300 African and international human rights and activist groups and the UN High Commissioner for Human Rights demanded his extradition. However, Nigeria stated that it would not hand Taylor over without sufficient evidence of his crimes.

On 28 March 2006, the Nigerian government announced that Taylor had disappeared from his residence in Calabar, Nigeria. The next day, Taylor was arrested in Gamboru, along Nigeria's northeastern border with Cameroon. Nigerian authorities handed Taylor over to the UN in Sierra Leone. On 30 March, the UN Special Court of Sierra Leone requested permission to use the premises of the International Criminal Court in The Hague to carry out Taylor's trial, although the Special Court would conduct the proceedings of the trial. The trial, which started in The Hague in June 2007, lasted three and a half years, ending 11 March 2011. The hearings had been postponed four times in 2007. A verdict on 11 counts of war crimes, crimes against humanity and other serious violations of international for Taylor's alleged actions in Sierra Leone was expected in January 2012. Taylor maintained his innocence during the trial, dismissing the charges against him as lies and deceit.

In February 2006, it was announced that Johnson-Sirleaf had inaugurated a Truth and Reconciliation Commission (TRC) to investigate human rights abuses committed from 1979–2003, marking the end of civil war. The Commission released its findings in a report in June 2009, among which was a controversial recommendation that some 50 individuals, including Johnson-Sirleaf, not be permitted to participate in Liberian politics for 30 years. In Johnson-Sirleaf's case, the recommendation cited her role in financing Taylor's war-related activities in the early months of the first civil war, a role for which she later apologized and excused herself on the basis that once she knew the true extent of Taylor's character and intentions, she opposed him. In January 2011 the recommendation banning her and others from political participation was ruled unconstitutional. Although approximately a third of Liberians polled about the report thought it contributed to peace overall, members of the TRC had to go into hiding following the release of the report because of the controversy it generated.

In April 2007, the UN Security Council voted to lift its ban on Liberian diamond exports. The ban had been imposed in 2001 to stop the traffic in "blood diamonds," which had helped finance the civil war. President Johnson-Sirleaf had called for an end to the embargo as necessary to revive Liberia's economy. Britain's ambassador to the UN said the decision reflected confidence that the country had met the standards of the Kimberley Process Certification Scheme (KPCS), an industry initiative certifying the origins of diamonds entering international trade.

President Johnson-Sirleaf rolled out new measures in the fight against corruption in December 2009, offering financial compensation and job security to anyone who reported fruitful leads on acts of corruption. The measures were designed to protect and reward individuals who broke their silence about corruption. Under the program, 5% of any recovered funds would be given to the whistleblower, and if that person testified against their work superior, the government would arrange a job transfer for the employee. Analysts anticipated that it would take time before an accurate assessment of the effectiveness of the program could be made.

In a national referendum on 23 August 2011 to amend the constitution, all four proposals failed to receive the necessary two-thirds votes in order to pass. Changes concerned the retirement age for Supreme Court judges, residency requirements for presidential candidates, the date for holding elections, and plurality vs. absolute majority voting systems.

In December 2010 Johnson-Sirleaf announced that she would seek re-election in 2011, a reversal of her 2005 campaign promise. In the 11 October 2011 presidential election Johnson-Sirleaf garnered 43.9% of the vote against 32.7% for Winston Tubman, and 11.6% for Prince Yormie Johnson. Voter turnout was 71.8%. Despite general approval of the balloting by international observers, the opposition alleged fraud, and called for a boycott of the second round. On 8 November, only 38% of the voters went to the polls, electing Johnson-Sirleaf with 90.7% of the vote.

Four days prior to the first round of the election, it was announced that Johnson-Sirleaf had been awarded the Nobel Peace Prize. The timing of the announcement sparked outcries from the opposition. Johnson-Sirleaf and compatriot Leymah Gbowee, a female Liberian human rights activist, received their awards in Oslo on 10 December 2011 along with Tawakel Karman, a female Yemenese journalist and leader of protests in Yemen. The three women were recognized for their contributions to the non-violent struggle for the safety of women and for the rights of women to participate fully in peace-building processes. Shortly after the elections, Johnson-Sirleaf proposed that Gbowee lead a national peace and reconciliation initiative to restore dialog among the Liberian people.

As 2012 approached, Liberians faced many challenges. Many of the young ex-combatants had yet to be fully demobilized, disarmed and reintegrated into Liberian society. Unemployment was high. Local chiefs and residents complained that their lands were being confiscated and allocated to large companies for plantations. Low-level conflicts persisted between and among ethnic groups, and unresolved disputes existed over political jurisdictions.

13 GOVERNMENT

The Liberian republic was modeled after the United States. Its constitution, approved on 3 July 1984 and effective 6 January 1986, provided for a president and vice president elected jointly by universal suffrage (at age 18) for a six-year term with a limit of two consecutive terms. Candidacy was again allowed after the lapse of at least one term. The president was both the chief of state and head of government. He or she nominated judges from a list submitted by a commission, served as commander-in-chief of the armed forces, and had the right to veto legislation. Vetoes could be overridden by a two-thirds vote of both legislative houses. The legislature was divided into a Senate with 30 members elected by counties for nine years, and a House of Representatives with 64 members elected by equally apportioned constituencies for six years. In 2011, President Ellen Johnson-Sirleaf and her Vice President Joseph Boakai were serving Johnson-Sirleaf's second term.

The constitution proscribed the one-party state and guaranteed fundamental rights, such as free speech, press, and assembly. The president had the right to suspend certain rights by declaring a state of emergency in cases of war or serious civil unrest. A state of emergency, which must be confirmed by a two-thirds vote of both legislative houses, did not empower the president to suspend or abrogate the constitution, dissolve the legislature, suspend or dismiss the judiciary, or suspend the right of habeas corpus. The constitution guaranteed fundamental freedoms to all persons irrespective of ethnic background. Because of the country's unique history, the constitution stipulated that "only persons who are Negro or of Negro descent shall qualify by birth or by naturalization to be citizens of Liberia." Only citizens could own land.

14 POLITICAL PARTIES

Until recently, Liberian political history has been dominated by the True Whig Party (TWP). The TWP, organized in 1860, held power continuously for over a century (1878–1980). During that era presidents and members of the legislature, mainly Americo-Liberians, were de facto members of the party. A credible threat to True Whig domination arrived in 1979 when the Progressive People's Party (PPP) claimed to represent the interests of Liberia's indigenous peoples.

In March 1980, several PPP members were arrested, a move that along with the rice riots, triggered the April coup. Although all political activity was banned, many True Whig members retained their government posts.

Other parties, identified with individual politicians soon burst upon the scene. The National Democratic Party of Liberia (NDPL), established by former president Samuel K. Doe, was victorious in the 1985 elections. The newly formed Unity Party, Liberian Action Party, and Liberian Unification Party were allowed to participate in those elections. The United People's Party (UPP), probably the largest opposition grouping, was founded by Gabriel Baccus Matthews, formerly head of the PPP. The UPP was not allowed to field candidates in 1985, but was legalized in 1986. The National Patriotic Party (NPP) was led by Charles Taylor.

In May 2000, the opposition led by Dr. Togba-Nah Tipoteh, formed a loose coalition of eleven entities called the Collaborating Political Parties (CPP), which aimed to present a common candidate in 2003. In mid-2001, several key opposition leaders including Ellen Johnson-Sirleaf met in Abuja, Nigeria. They advanced a number of pre-conditions before going to elections. Among these were the restructuring the armed forces as stipulated by the Abuja Accords, holding elections for chiefs and mayors, conducting a census, dissolving NPP party cells in the civil service, stopping illegal funding of the NPP, guaranteeing opposition parties equal air time and reconstituting the elections commission (ECOM).

In June 2003, Charles Taylor's NPP, held 49 of 64 House seats, and 21 of 26 Senate seats. The Unity Party (UP) held 7 House seats and 3 Senate seats. The All Liberia Coalition Party held 3 House seats and 2 Senate seats. Three other parties held the 5 remaining House seats among themselves.

In the first round of the 2005 elections, George Weah emerged with 28% of the vote, Ellen Johnson-Sirleaf with 20%, and Charles Brumskine with 12%. Neither the Mandingo-backed LURD, nor the Krahn-dominated and Côte d'Ivoire-backed Model were able to transform themselves into political parties. In the run-off election, Johnson-Sirleaf obtained 59.4% to 40.6% for Weah. In the Senate election, the Coalition for the Transformation of Liberia (COTOL) won 7 seats followed by the NPP 4, the CDC, 3; the Liberian Party (LP) of Charles Brumskine, 3; the Unity Party (UP) of Charles Clarke, 3; and the Alliance for Peace and Democracy (APD) of Togba-na Tipoteh, 3. In the House of Representatives, the CDC secured 15 seats followed by the LP, 9; UP, 8; COTOL, 8; APD, 5; and NPP, 4.

In the presidential elections of 11 October 2011, Johnson-Sirleaf and her running mate, Joseph Boakai represented the Unity Party. With 16 parties contesting, Johnson-Sirleaf obtained 43.9% of the vote, Winston Tubman of the Congress for Democratic Change (CDC) 32.7%, and Prince Yormie Johnson of the National Union for Democratic Progress (NUDP) 11.6%. Despite allegations of fraud from the CDC and other opponents, international observers declared the contest reasonably free and fair. With no party having received an absolute majority on the first round, the second round occurred on 8 November. Amidst opposition calls to boycott, voter turn-out was low. Johnson-Sirleaf and Boakai won 90.7% of the vote.

In the 11 October 2011 House of Representatives elections the UP emerged victorious winning 24 seats. The CDC won 11 seats, the LP 7 seats, the NUDP 6 seats, and the NDC (National Democratic Coalition) 5 seats. The remaining 11 seats were won by six parties, with none gaining more than three seats. Half of the 30 Senate seats were also up for election. With 99 candidates contesting, the biggest winner was the NPP gaining 3 seats. The UP lost one seat, while the CDC and the NUDP each added one seat. Because of the large number of parties occupying seats in the legislature and their often irreconcilable differences, governance has been inefficient and cumbersome.

15 LOCAL GOVERNMENT

Liberia was divided into 15 counties and the federal district of Monrovia. The counties were Grand Cape Mount, Sinoe, Grand Bassa, Maryland, River Cess, Bomi, Grand Kru, Margibi, Lofa, Bong, Grand Gedah, Gbarpolu, River Gee, Nimba, and Montserrado.

The central government appointed county and territory superintendents. Counties were subdivided into districts headed by commissioners. There were also paramount, clan, and town chiefs. Cities elected their own mayors and councils.

16 JUDICIAL SYSTEM

The legal system was modeled on that of the United States. The 6 January 1986 constitution provided for the establishment of a Supreme Court consisting of a chief justice and four associate justices, to be appointed by the president from a panel recommended by a Judicial Service Commission. The consent of the Senate was required for these appointments and for the confirmation of lower court judges, to which a similar procedure applied. In theory, cases originated in magistrates' courts and could be taken for appeal to circuit courts or to the highest court. Serious cases originated in the circuit courts. Traditional courts were presided over by tribal chiefs. A labor court was created in 1986.

For many years, the judicial system suffered from corruption and domination by the executive. By mid-1990 the system had collapsed and justice administration was co-opted by the military commanders of various factions. In 1991, the Interim Government of National Unity (IGNV), revived the court system in the Monrovia area, and the National Patriotic Front of Liberia (NPFL) reopened courts in the areas under its control. After 1997, donors trained paralegals and human rights monitors to protect citizens up-country, and the US Department of Justice rebuilt magistrate courts, compiled 30 years of Supreme Court decisions, and published the Liberian Code so that judges and lawyers could have recourse to those decisions.

By 2011, the judiciary's ability to fulfill its function continued to be constrained by a lack of qualified personnel, insufficient funding, poor infrastructure, weak administration, and poor case-flow management and corruption. Rebuilding the courts was a major thrust of the Johnson-Sirleaf government.

17 ARMED FORCES

The International Institute for Strategic Studies (IISS) reported that armed forces in Liberia totaled 2,050 members in 2011. The force comprised 2,000 from the army and 50 members of the coast guard. Armed forces represented 0.1% of the labor force in Liberia. Defense spending totaled $22.1 million and accounted for 1.3% of gross domestic product (GDP).

18 INTERNATIONAL COOPERATION

Liberia was a charter member of the UN, having joined on 2 November 1945; it took part in ECA and several nonregional specialized agencies, such as UNESCO, FAO, ILO, the World Bank, UNIDO, IMF, and the WHO. Liberia belonged to the ACP Group, the African Development Bank, ECOWAS, G-77, the Nonaligned Movement, the Community of Sahel and Saharan States (CENSAD), the New Partnership for Africa's Development (NEPAD), and the African Union (AU). The government was participating in efforts to establish a West African Monetary Zone (WAMZ) that would include The Gambia, Ghana, Guinea, Liberia, Nigeria, and Sierra Leone.

Liberia and Sierra Leone formed the Mano River Union in 1973 to promote trade and economic cooperation between the two countries. Guinea joined in 1980, and Cote d'Ivoire in 2008. Leaders of Guinea, Liberia and Sierra Leone signed a nonaggression and antisubversion pact in 1986. In 2004 following the end of the civil war, the union was revitalized.

Technical assistance activities of the UN in Liberia have emphasized agricultural development, teaching, vocational training, and control of yaws and malaria. In 2003, the UN Mission in Liberia (UNMIL) was established for peacekeeping in support of the transitional government. At least 48 nations have offered support for UNMIL, whose mandate was extended by the UN Security Council to September 2012.

In environmental cooperation, Liberia is part of the Convention on Biological Diversity, International Tropical Timber Agreements, the Kyoto Protocol, the Montréal Protocol, MARPOL, the Nuclear Test Ban Treaty, and the UN Conventions on Climate Change and Desertification.

19 ECONOMY

The gross GDP in 2010 was estimated to be $1.691 billion growing at 5.1%. Inflation stood at 11.2%, and unemployment was reported at 85%. In 2002, the latest year for which data was available, it was estimated that agriculture accounted for 76.9% of GDP, industry 5.4%, and services 17.7%. Economic policies, regulations and structure were not conducive to growth. On the World Bank and Heritage Foundation's 2011 Index of Economic Freedom, Liberia's economy, considered "repressed," ranked 160 out of 179 worldwide.

The export agricultural sector consisted of cocoa, coffee, palm oil, rubber, and sugar cane. Financial mismanagement and the effects of civil war have created two economies, one centered around major urban centers and the other comprising the bulk of the country's rural hinterland. Although Liberia possessed significant reserves of gold, diamonds, iron ore and other minerals, major commercialization of mining had yet to occur.

The civil war left most of Liberia's economic infrastructure in shambles. Businessmen and capital fled to more productive markets as economic assets were plundered or destroyed by factional forces. President Johnson-Sirleaf, a Harvard-trained banker and administrator, had taken steps to reduce corruption and encourage private investment. Nonetheless, on Transparency International's Corruption Perception Index (CPI), Liberia ranked 91st worldwide, and scored 3.2 on a scale of 0–10 where 0 was "highly corrupt" and 10 "very clean."

In May 2010, the U.S. offered assistance toward reconstruction by approving a $15 million grant to Liberia through the Millennium Challenge Corporation (MCC). The three-year program included projects to improve land rights, trade policies and to educate girls and women.

In September 2010, the government passed legislation creating a new commercial code, a commercial court, and a framework for business law to bolster the development of the private sector and foreign investment. The country anticipated major investments in oil and iron ore from Chevron Corporation and ArcelorMittal. Timber and minerals were expected to contribute significantly to GDP in 2012.

20 INCOME

According to the CIA, in 2010 the GDP of Liberia totaled $1.691 billion. GDP was defined as the value of all final goods and services produced within a nation in a given year and computed on the basis of purchasing power parity (PPP) rather than value as measured on the basis of the rate of the exchange based on current dollars. The per capita GDP was estimated at $500. It was estimated that in 2000 about 80% of the population subsisted on an income below the poverty threshold.

According to the World Bank, remittances from citizens living abroad totaled $54.2 million or about $14 per capita and accounted for approximately 3.2% of GDP. The World Bank also estimated that Liberia, with 0.05% of the world's population, accounted for less than 0.01% of the world's GDP. By comparison, the United States, with 4.85% of the world's population, accounted for 22.51% of world GDP. As of 2011 the World Bank reported that actual individual consumption in Liberia was 60.2% of GDP and accounted for less than 0.01% of world consumption. By comparison, the United States accounted for 25.44% of world individual consumption. Some 17.9% of Liberia's GDP was spent on food and beverages, 13.9% on housing and household furnishings, 7.4% on clothes, 3.2% on health, 1.4% on transportation, 2.1% on communications, 1.0% on recreation, 0.4% on restaurants and hotels, and 4.2% on miscellaneous goods and services and purchases from abroad.

21 LABOR

As of 2007, Liberia had a total labor force of 1.372 million people. Within that labor force, the CIA reported in 2000 that 70% were employed in agriculture, 8% in industry, and 22% in the service sector. Although the bulk of the population was engaged in subsistence agriculture, an increasing number of Liberians were acquiring skills as machine operators, technicians and service employees.

Liberia's labor movement took root in 1951 with the formation of the Labor Congress of Liberia (LCL). However, following a major strike in 1955, the LCL leadership was arrested and the union dissolved. In 1958, it revived under the leadership of the Ministry for Social Affairs and functioned mainly as a government organ. To protest government interference in the LCL, the Congress of Industrial Organizations of Liberia (CIOL) organized in 1960. The Liberian Federation of Labor Unions formed in 1980 by a merger of the LCL and CIOL. After the war, Liberia counted 30 unions with a total of 60,000 members, most of whom were unemployed.

Formally, Liberia had minimum working ages, statutory minimum wages, and occupational safety and health standards, but none of these was effectively enforced. Child labor laws also were not enforced, especially in rural areas. Most people took available work regardless of wages or conditions.

22 AGRICULTURE

Liberians farmed roughly 5% of the total land area. Major crops included rubber, palm oil, coffee and cocoa, rice, cassava (tapioca), sugarcane, vegetables, bananas and other fruits. Cereal production in 2009 amounted to 292,983 tons, fruit production 233,128 tons, and vegetable production 82,801 tons.

With the exception of plantation farming, techniques were primitive. Farmers cleared up to two hectares (five acres) of wild forest or low bush each year, cultivated it with hand tools, and planted rice or cassava as the rainy season began. Because rice production was insufficient to meet local demand, government maintained a retail price ceiling on rice.

Liberian soils were prone to leaching in heavy rains, making them better adapted to tree-crop agriculture than to shifting field-crop production. Rubber was the leading cash crop. Before the war, six foreign-owned concessions produced over two-thirds of the rubber crop; Firestone's Harbel plantation was the largest in the world. Firestone ended its long association with Liberian rubber production with the sale of its interests to Japanese-owned Bridgestone in 1988.

23 ANIMAL HUSBANDRY

The UN Food and Agriculture Organization (FAO) reported that Liberia dedicated 2 million hectares (4.94 million acres) to permanent pasture or meadow in 2009. During that year, the country tended 6.5 million chickens, 39,000 head of cattle, and 230,060 pigs. The production from these animals amounted to 1,171 tons of beef and veal, 8,230 tons of pork, 15,949 tons of poultry, 5,322 tons of eggs, and 13,839 tons of milk. Liberia also produced 167 tons of cattle hide.

Poultry farming and marketing of eggs were on the increase. Experiments in crossing West African and Brahman cattle had not yet produced breeds resistant to the tsetse fly, but potential for developing resistant strains existed.

24 FISHING

In 2008, the annual capture totaled 7,890 tons according to the UN FAO. The fishing industry was dominated by the oceangoing trawlers of the Mesurado Fishing Co. The company also maintained a domestic distribution system that supplied a substantial amount of fish to the interior of the country. In 2008 the Bureau of National Fisheries (BNF) estimated that more than 250 unregulated "pirate boats" operated within 3 miles of shore, the zone reserved for artisanal fisheries. The BNF also estimated that some 8,000 unlicensed foreign artisanal boats using undersized nets and dynamite fished in Liberian waters. Approximately $10-$12 million was lost annually to illegal fishing. Sea turtles were hunted and their eggs illegally collected for local consumption. Liberia had no research facilities to study, monitor and report on threats to fish and aquatic life.

25 FORESTRY

In 2008 Liberia accounted for more than half of the Upper Guinean Forest, a fragmented band of tropical forest extending from Guinea to Cameroon—Africa's second largest forest block. Approximately 45% of Liberia was covered by forest, which totaled some 4.39 million hectares (ha) including 2.42 million ha classified as closed dense forest, 1.02 million ha of open dense forest, and .95 million ha of agriculture degraded forest. The UN FAO estimated the 2009 roundwood production at 420,000 cu m (14.8 million cu ft). The value of all forest products, including roundwood, totaled $5.47 million.

About 235 timber species grow in Liberia, of which 90 are potentially marketable, but natural stands of a single species were not common. Difficult access and poor transportation have restricted commercial logging, despite the existence of valuable African mahoganies and red ironwood. A number of foreign companies, mainly from the United States, have been granted concessions. Rubber and oil palm plantations cover a significant portion of forest area. In 2005, rubber alone employed 18,500 workers and accounted for 90% of total exports.

In 2009, government enlisted a European consortium to revitalize the timber industry. In May 2011, Liberia and the European Union signed an agreement to create a tracking system to prevent illegal timber exports to Europe. It was estimated that 20 to 40 percent of industrial wood derived from illegal sources.

26 MINING

In 2010, mineral production in Liberia was limited to diamonds, hydraulic cement, and gold. Mining accounted for 0.9% of GDP in 2010. Since December 1989, when mining revenues accounted for 22% of GDP, the mining sector has been severely damaged by years of civil war and political instability. Estimated production of gold in 2010 was 800 kg, up from 524 kg in 2008. Diamond production in 2010 was estimated at 25,000 carats, down from 28,368 carats in 2009, and from 47,007 carats in 2007. All of the country's diamond production comes from artisanal alluvial mining. In 2010, the country also produced 67,000 metric tons of hydraulic cement from a facility in Monrovia. Liberia's undeveloped resources included barite, chromium, kyanite, manganese, nickel, palladium, platinum, titaniferous sands, and uranium. Liberia's New Mining Law of 2000 gives the Ministry of Lands, Mines, and Energy the responsibility of issuing four types of mining license-exploration, Class A (for up to 25 years; are limited to 1,000 sq km; and are open to foreign investors), Class B (for 5 years; are renewable; allow mechanized production; and are open to foreign ownership), and Class C (covers artisanal mining; are good for one year intervals with expiration on December 31; and is open only to Liberians). Eastern Liberia was made up of rocks of Birimian age with significant potential for gold. Western Liberia was made up of rocks of Archean age that contained diamond, gold, iron ore, nickel, manganese, palladium, platinum, and uranium.

27 ENERGY AND POWER

The World Bank reported in 2008 that Liberia produced 335 million kWh of electricity and consumed 340.8 million kWh, or 90 kWh per capita. No electricity was produced from renewable resources. Active offshore oil exploration was anticipated in the Gulf of Guinea in 2012, although Liberia did not have any proven petroleum reserves as of 2011. No proven natural gas reserves had been discovered, either.

28 INDUSTRY

Before the civil war, Liberia's industrial sector was dominated by processing plants associated with its key agricultural outputs: rubber, palm oil, and lumber. The Liberian-owned Mesurado Group manufactured detergent, soap, industrial gas, and animal foods. Liberia also produced soft drinks, cement, plastics, shoes, recycled steel, and refined petroleum products. In addition, Liberia's industrial base produced rice and sugar, cookies and candy, candles, foam rubber, hand tools and aluminum parts, umbrellas, and batteries. The 1975 "Liberianization" law protected the production of rice, gasoline, and cement, and the operation of travel agencies, gas stations, and beer and soft drink distributors from foreign interference, despite free trade agreements.

The war significantly impacted industrial production. Between 1990 and 1996, rebel leaders and their business accomplices expropriated businesses using forced labor, stolen goods and stolen fuel. Forestry, mining, and rubber production techniques became environmentally unsound and unsustainable. Profits from these enterprises were squandered on arms and munitions. By 2004, industry accounted for only 9.8% of GDP, 5% of which was attributed to manufacturing. Government has since made minerals, timber, rubber and palm oil revitalization part of economic

Principal Trading Partners – Liberia (2010)				
(In millions of US dollars)				
Country	Total	Exports	Imports	Balance
World	18,279.7	847.4	17,432.3	-16,584.9
South Korea	5,942.2	0.4	5,941.8	-5,941.5
China	4,845.6	20.7	4,825.0	-4,804.3
Singapore	3,170.8	0.9	3,169.9	-3,169.0
Japan	2,115.8	0.4	2,115.3	-2,114.9
United States	376.8	167.7	209.1	-41.4
South Africa	262.3	249.4	13.0	236.4
Germany	184.7	33.1	151.7	-118.6
Spain	109.8	72.2	37.6	34.5
Italy	88.7	3.6	85.1	-81.5
Turkey	81.1	6.9	74.2	-67.3

(…) data not available or not significant.

(n.s.) not specified.

SOURCE: *2011 Direction of Trade Statistics Yearbook*, New York: United Nations, 2011.

recovery, but given the needs and scarce resources, progress was slow and gradual.

Since the war Liberia has regained its prominence as a flag of convenience, registering some 3,500 vessels with 112 million gross tons in 2011, approximately 11% of the world's shipping fleet. One-third of the oil imported to the US was transported by tankers registered under the Liberian flag.

The oil refinery at Monrovia was closed in 1984. By end of 2011, no viable oil or natural gas deposits had been discovered, although analysis of exploratory drilling indicated that the Liberian Basin held significant promise. In 2010 President Johnson-Sirleaf signed a three-year deal with Chevron to explore for off-shore oil. In late 2011, it was announced that Canadian Overseas Petroleum Limited had signed an Asset Acquisition Agreement with ExxonMobil Exploration and Production Liberia Limited with respect to the onward sale of certain of the interests in Block LB-13 offshore Liberia.

29 SCIENCE AND TECHNOLOGY

The World Bank reported in 2009 that there were no patent applications in science and technology in Liberia. Liberia had an agricultural experiment station in Suakoko; a geological, mining, and metallurgical society in Monrovia; and a research laboratory for the Mt. Nimba region, with headquarters in Robertsfield. The University of Liberia, founded in 1862, had colleges of agriculture and forestry, medicine, and science and technology. Cuttington University College, originally founded in 1889, has a science division, and the William V. S. Tubman College of Technology, founded in 1978, offered a three-year associate degree in engineering technology. All three institutions, as well as the Liberian Institute for Biomedical Research founded in 1952, were situated in Monrovia. Booker Washington Institute offered agricultural and industrial courses.

30 DOMESTIC TRADE

Before the civil war, internal trade was carried on mainly by large firms located in Monrovia with branches in other principal towns.

However, conflict destroyed nearly all businesses and production facilities and most foreign investors left the country. The infrastructure around major cities also suffered. As of 2011, domestic trade and manufacturing was limited, but on the rebound. A small business sector had resumed operations, primarily through Lebanese and Indian investors and businessmen. As of 2011, about 70% of the nation's work force was employed in subsistence agriculture. With some three-quarters of the population living on under $1/day, and 80% of the population unemployed, trade was often by barter.

³¹FOREIGN TRADE

Liberia imported $7.143 billion worth of goods and services in 2008, while exporting $1.197 billion worth of goods and services. Major import partners in 2009 were South Korea, 41.7%; China, 16%; Singapore, 14.1%; and Japan, 12.6% . Its major export partners were Germany, 29.3%; Poland, 18%; South Africa, 16.6%; Greece, 7.4%; the United States, 6.5%; and Norway, 5.5%.

In 2011, rubber continued to be the leading export, however, the lifting of sanctions on timber and diamonds had revitalized minerals and the timber trade. Imports were led by fuels, chemicals, machinery, transportation equipment, manufactured goods, and rice and other foodstuffs.

Several factors increased the cost of trade: import bans and restrictions, inadequate trade capacity and poor infrastructure, licensing, corruption and the minimal enforcement of intellectual property rights. According to the Heritage Foundation and World Bank, trade freedom in Liberia was comparatively low and the economy ranked 160th out of 179 worldwide on the 2011 Index of Economic Freedom, down three rankings from 2009.

³²BALANCE OF PAYMENTS

In 2010 Liberia had a foreign trade deficit of $1.3 billion. The balance of payments concerns transactions between an economy and the rest of the world in goods, services and income. Historically, Liberia has had a chronic payments deficit with large capital outflows and debt-service payments. During the war years, exports of foreign currency-earning raw materials such as iron, rubber, timber, diamonds, and gold plummeted. By 2011 exports of rubber, palm oil, timber and minerals were on the rebound.

³³BANKING AND SECURITIES

During the war most of the country's commercial banks had closed. By 2011, the banking system comprised the Central Bank of Liberia (CBL) and six mostly foreign-owned commercial banks. As part of Liberia's poverty reduction strategy, the CBL strengthened bank supervision. In 2008 it increased its net foreign reserves by $14.3 million, bringing the total level of reserves to $49.4 million. The positive trend in revitalizing the banking system was also evident in the CBL's increase of the minimum capital requirement of commercial banks operating in the country from $2 million to $6 million in 2008. In addition, the total capital of commercial banks nearly doubled in the period from 2006 to 2008, increasing from $21 million to $40.5 million.

By 2012 initiatives were underway to launch mobile banking with cell phones, reaching out to the country's 15 political subdivisions to make banking more accessible to the average Liberian living in the hinterlands. Less than 1% of the population had a bank

Balance of Payments – Liberia (2010)		
(In millions of US dollars)		
Current Account		-737.8
Balance on goods	-478.4	
Imports	-719.9	
Exports	241.5	
Balance on services	-921.7	
Balance on income	24.3	
Current transfers	638.1	
Capital Account		1,596.1
Financial Account		447.4
Direct investment abroad	...	
Direct investment in Liberia	452.9	
Portfolio investment assets	...	
Portfolio investment liabilities	...	
Financial derivatives	...	
Other investment assets	1.4	
Other investment liabilities	-6.8	
Net Errors and Omissions		847.1
Reserves and Related Items		-2,152.9

(…) data not available or not significant.

SOURCE: *Balance of Payment Statistics Yearbook 2011,* Washington, DC: International Monetary Fund, 2011.

account. In 2011 Access Bank Liberia (ABL) launched Liberia's first microfinance bank in an effort to serve the informal sector including low-income shop retailers, street vendors, craftsmen and farmers. ABL had five branches, 270 employees and more than 50,000 customers. Loans ranged from about $50 to $3,000.

In 2011 Liberia had no stock exchange, but plans were underway for its creation.

³⁴INSURANCE

Liberia had about a dozen insurance providers in 2011 offering health, automobile, property, and business insurance plans.

³⁵PUBLIC FINANCE

Since 2006 public finance has operated under the supervision of the World Bank and the IMF. The final 2010–2011 fiscal year budget of $369 million (ending June 30, 2011) was 6.3% higher than the initial budget submitted to the legislature, although 0.5% lower than the final budget the previous year. In FY 2010–2011, the Liberian Government committed to allocating 60% of its budget to poverty reduction strategy goals, and its expenditures for health and education increased by 10%. The budget deficit amounted to 0.7% of GDP. Public debt was 11.6% of GDP, with $3.2 billion of the debt held by foreign entities.

Government budgets were in balance up to the mid-1970s when oil price shocks and the collapse of agricultural export commodity prices caused high deficits. During the civil war, fiscal management collapsed. Recovery since 2004 has relied heavily on foreign aid, especially from the United States, Japan, the United Kingdom, France, Italy, Germany, China, and Romania. Taiwan and Libya were also significant bi-lateral donors.

The IMF launched Staff-Monitored Programs (SMP) in 2006 and 2007. These programs allowed the Johnson-Sirleaf administration to negotiate debt reduction with the World Bank and the

Public Finance – Liberia (2008)

(In thousands U.S. dollars, budgetary central government figures)

Revenue and Grants	**206,891.5**	**100.0%**
Tax revenue	169,865.3	82.1%
Social contributions	...	...
Grants	5,687.8	2.7%
Other revenue	31,338.4	15.1%
Expenditures	**201,258.8**	**100.0%**
General public services	109,271.6	54.3%
Defense	7,488.6	3.7%
Public order and safety	22,859	11.4%
Economic affairs	22,424.6	11.1%
Environmental protection	798.4	0.4%
Housing and community amenities	7,997	4.0%
Health	12,994.6	6.5%
Recreational, culture, and religion	2,658.2	1.3%
Education	13,642	6.8%
Social protection	1,174.7	0.6%

(...) data not available or not significant.

SOURCE: *Government Finance Statistics Yearbook 2010*, Washington, DC: International Monetary Fund, 2010.

IMF in 2008. Having reached its decision point in the HIPC debt relief initiative, the government implemented an IMF Poverty Reduction and Growth Facility (PRGF) from March 2008 to March 2011. The key objectives of the PRGF included managing public expenditures, fighting corruption, improving economic governance and bank supervision, establishing macroeconomic stability, and reducing external debt.

In September 2009, Liberia concluded the Governance Economic Management Assistance Program (GEMAP), which had permitted direct international involvement in revenue collection and economic governance. Further, the legislature passed the Public Finance Management Act of 2009, which governed all matters related to the management of public finances, and which specified the roles and responsibilities of the executive and legislative branches with regard to accountability in public finance. In June 2010, the IMF and World Bank determined that Liberia would be eligible for $4.6 billion in debt relief. In June 2011 the poverty reduction program ended, but the IMF approved a continuation of the Extended Credit Facility (ECF) through March 2012.

In a speech 12 July 2011, President Johnson-Sirleaf announced the launch of an Integrated Financial Management Information System (IFMIS) into the budget and expenditure management process. IFMIS was intended to address a number of budget management issues, efficiency, transparency and accountability. These were issues that she said "posed serious challenges in the mobilization and use of resources for reconstruction and development."

36 TAXATION

During the war years, Liberia's wealth was smuggled out of the country untaxed. In 1999, imports were improbably over three times the reported exports, a sign that many exports were going unreported. Of the $60 million in tax revenue collected in 1999, 22.4% came from income taxes on corporations and individuals,

16% from sales taxes, 30% from import duties, and 23% from Liberia's maritime registry.

Despite making progress, post-war Liberia remained a difficult country in which to conduct business. On Transparency International's Corruption Perception Index (CPI), Liberia ranked 91st out of 180 nations (11th in sub Saharan Africa), scoring 3.2 where 0 represented "highly corrupt," and 10 represented "very clean." On the World Bank's "Ease of Doing Business" index, which among other things measures the taxes and mandatory contributions that a medium-sized company must pay or withhold in a given year as well as the administrative burden in paying taxes, Liberia ranked 151st out of 183 countries.

In 2011 the World Bank estimated that a medium-sized company would make 33 tax payments annually totaling about 43.7% of gross profits. Statutory tax rates included a corporate income tax of 35% on profitable income, 7% on goods and services, and 10% on income received from money market accounts. Low-income taxpayers received a tax break in 2010, with their effective tax rate dropping from 25% to 20%. U.S. Treasury advisors were working with the Ministry of Finance to improve tax administration, strengthen internal controls, and increase revenue collection.

37 CUSTOMS AND DUTIES

Imports were subject to tariff duties, ranging from 2.5–25%, which constituted a major source of government income. Import duties were specific (based on weight) for some commodities, ad valorem (based on cost, insurance, and freight value) for others. Specific duties applied to foodstuffs, beverages, petroleum products, and certain rubber and textile products. All exports and some imports required licenses. Customs duties were 25% on luxury items such as alcoholic beverages, apparel, cosmetics, electronics, jewelry, and tobacco. The following goods could be imported into Liberia without incurring customs duty: 200 cigarettes or 25 cigars or 250 grams of tobacco products; 1 liter of alcoholic beverage; 100 grams (4 fl oz) of perfume; goods to the value of US$125.

Goods could be landed, stored, sorted, manufactured, repacked, reforwarded, or transshipped within the area of the Free Port of Monrovia without payment of customs duties. In December 2011, President Johnson-Sirleaf signed an executive order waving customs duties diesel fuel, pumps and spare parts for water treatment plants in the interests of national reconstruction and development.

38 FOREIGN INVESTMENT

Foreign direct investment (FDI) in Liberia recovered significantly since the war with a net inflow of $217.8 million according to World Bank figures published in 2009. FDI represented 24.85% of GDP. From 1999 to 2001, average FDI inflow was only $11.3 million, and was almost nonexistent in 2002 and 2003 at about $3 million and $1 million respectively. It increased modestly in 2004 to $20 million.

In 2008–09, government announced 39 business reforms, and the country attracted over $100 million in new investment in the first half of 2009. Liberia was the second country to obtain "compliant" status under the Extractive Industries Transparency Initiative (EITI). In 2010, the government enacted several pieces of legislation to modernize commercial transactions and expand commercial activities.

By 2011, foreign companies still faced several hurdles in Liberia. A restrictive regulatory environment meant that starting a business took an average of 35 days and corporate profits were taxed at a rate of about 44%. The Heritage Foundation and World Bank ranked Liberia 151st out of 183 countries worldwide for ease of doing business. President Johnson-Sirleaf had declared fighting corruption a top priority, but corruption was perceived as widespread.

Since 2008 the government had instituted restructuring and reform of key parastatals such as the Liberia Petroleum and Refinery Company (LPRC). Others, such the Agriculture and Industrial Training Bureau, the Bureau of State Enterprises and the National Food Assistance Agency were allocated minimal budgets in anticipation of their dissolution. By 2012 the government planned to dissolve or privatize dysfunctional and redundant state enterprises, thereby opening opportunities for FDI.

³⁹ECONOMIC DEVELOPMENT

Economic policy was guided by the IMF's Poverty Reduction and Growth Facility (PRGF), which was focused on four poverty reduction strategy pillars. In addition, the Governance and Economic Management Action Plan (GEMAP), created by the International Contact Group for Liberia and enacted by the legislature in 2005, improved the transparency of revenue collection and allocation.

Under IMF guidance, the government attempted to revive the economy through the reorganization of rubber production and other agricultural products. It imposed strict fiscal discipline and monetary reforms to enhance Liberia's investment climate. In addition to the lifting of timber sanctions in June 2006, the U.N. Security Council lifted sanctions on diamonds in April 2007 after determining that Liberia had instituted the necessary internal controls to comply with the Kimberley Process Certification Scheme (KPCS), the worldwide diamond-tracking mechanism established in 2003.

Government also was attempting to revitalize subsistence cultivation of rice, cassava, and greens, and to jumpstart cash crop production of cocoa, coffee and fruits. However, these initiatives were largely self-help backed by donors and foreign NGOs. By 2011 the private sector, NGOs and government were implementing more programs designed to assist Liberians engaged in petty trading and in other occupations in the informal sector.

⁴⁰SOCIAL DEVELOPMENT

Prior to the war, Liberia had provided social benefits for civil servants and workers in the formal sector, including medical benefits, leave and vacation and pensions. By 2004, the state had effectively collapsed, taking the economy and society with it. The war had claimed some 250,000 lives, half of them civilians. In 2011, some 500,000 internally displaced persons had yet to resettle, some 50,000 ex-combatants, many of them youth, were not fully disarmed and reintegrated, and more than 80% of the population remained unemployed. 75% of the population was subsisting on less than a dollar a day and depending on extended family, social networks and remittances to survive. In 2009, plans were under-

way to transfer the administration of pensions to the still defunct National Social Security and Welfare Corporation (NSWC).

Liberia ranked near the bottom of the world average in public expenditures in the social sector. GDP purchasing power parity, which was nearly last in the world (191st) was only $1.691 billion (2010 estimate). Social development was impeded by poor health, low literacy and low life expectancy. In 2003 only 42% of females could read and write, 20% of children were underweight (2007), 75% of the population did not have access to improved water sources, and life expectancy was 57 years at birth (194th in the world, 2011). The UNDP Human Development Index (HDI), which measures prospects for a long and healthy life and quality education, ranked Liberia 182nd out of 187 countries, in the "lowest" category of human development in 2011.

Rights for most women in the country were limited. Rural women remained largely subordinate in both public and private life. Women married under civil law had inheritance and property rights, but women married under tribal laws were considered property of their husbands. Domestic violence was widespread, and abused women had no recourse. Female genital mutilation was practiced by some ethnic groups. The awarding of the Nobel Peace Prize in 2011 to President Johnson-Sirleaf and to Leymah Gbowee, a human rights activist, for their contributions to promoting women's participation in peace, were expected to bring greater public attention to discrimination and marginalization of women in Liberia and the continent.

Ethnic discrimination was explicitly prohibited by law. Despite this provision, citizenship was legally available only to blacks. Only citizens could own land, and noncitizens were restricted from owning certain types of businesses. The government's human rights record was improving, and freedom of speech and association had greatly improved under the Johnson-Sirleaf administration.

⁴¹HEALTH

According to the CIA, life expectancy in Liberia was 57 years in 2011. The country spent 11.9% of its GDP on healthcare, amounting to $29 per person. There were 0 physicians, 3 nurses and midwives, and 7 hospital beds per 10,000 inhabitants. The fertility rate was 5.8, while the infant mortality rate was 80 per 1,000 live births. In 2008 the maternal mortality rate, according to the World Bank, was 990 per 100,000 births. It was estimated that 64% of children were vaccinated against measles. The CIA calculated HIV/AIDS prevalence in Liberia to be about 1.5% in 2009.

Aside from a small registration fee, rudimentary health care services were free of charge. In an effort to improve public health, a significant proportion of the fiscal budget was earmarked to restore public services such as health and education.

⁴²HOUSING

During the 1980s (the latest period for which housing data is available), the number of dwellings more than doubled, from 216,206 in 1981 to 500,000 as of 1988, with 4.8 people per dwelling. About 80% of the total housing stock was affected by the war. The 1998–2000 National Reconstruction Program prioritized housing, and the five-year plan (2001–05) also focused on reconstruction and new construction of adequate housing.

Many of the older corrugated-iron structures in Monrovia have been replaced with more modern dwellings, and houses of advanced design have been privately built to accommodate the growing urban population. The typical dwelling of the tribal people in the Liberian interior was the *rondavel*, a circular, one-room mud-and-wattle thatch-roofed hut, windowless and with a single low door. These rondavels were being replaced by large rectangular huts, also of mud and wattle, subdivided into two or more rooms and equipped with windows.

43 EDUCATION

In 2009 the World Bank estimated that 76% of age-eligible children in Liberia were enrolled in primary school. Secondary enrollment for age-eligible children stood at 20%. Overall, the CIA estimated that Liberia had a literacy rate of 57.5%. Public expenditure on education represented 2.8% of GDP, which was 144th in the world.

Education was compulsory from ages 6 to 16. Elementary school (primary) covered six years of study. This was followed by three years of junior high and three years of senior high school. The largest secondary school was the Booker Washington Institute, a vocational school located at Kakata, with about 1,500 students. The academic year ran from March to December.

There were three institutions of higher learning: the government-operated University of Liberia in Monrovia (established in 1862); Cuttington University College at Monrovia, an Episcopalian institution; and a three-year engineering school, the William V. S. Tubman College of Technology, founded at Monrovia in 1978. In 2001, there were about 44,000 students enrolled in tertiary education programs.

In the post-war years Liberia made significant gains in education. The Free and Compulsory Education Policy introduced in 2006, abolished tuition fees in public primary schools and reduced them for public secondary schools. This policy along with improved security has yielded substantial improvements in enrolment figures. Additionally, international NGOs, church organizations and private initiatives were helping reconstruct and re-equip schools and government had allocated a large portion of its budget to rehabilitate the education system.

Nonetheless, nearly 35% of the total population had no schooling at all, including 44% of females. The principal needs in the sector included rehabilitation of basic infrastructure, increased training and higher salaries for teachers, and increased family incomes or subsidization schemes so that more families could afford school supplies. Tertiary education also faced major challenges: the University of Liberia was understaffed and overcrowded.

44 LIBRARIES AND MUSEUMS

The government maintained a central public library in Monrovia, with 15,000 volumes. UNESCO also operated a library in Monrovia, and the Liberian Information Service had a research library in Monrovia. The University of Liberia and the Cuttington University College libraries have been slowly rebuilding their stock of books following looting during the 1990s.

The National Museum of Liberia was housed in the renovated Supreme Court building in Monrovia and the Tubman Center

of African Cultures was located in Robertsport. Other museums included the National Cultural Center in Cape Mount, the Africana Museum at Monrovia, the W. V. S. Tubman Library-Museum at Harper, and the Natural History Museum at the University of Liberia.

45 MEDIA

In 2009 the CIA reported that there were 2,000 telephone landlines in Liberia, and 842,000 mobile phones in use with subscriptions averaging 21 per 100 people. Mobile phone companies have introduced digital EDGE technology, making the Internet accessible in some rural areas.

There were 10 AM radio stations, 2 shortwave radio stations and several FM stations. Community radio was growing across the country. Internet functioned poorly, and users numbered 1 per 100 citizens. Prominent newspapers in 2010, with circulation numbers listed parenthetically, included the *Daily Observer* (30,000). Other newspapers included the *Analyst*, the *Heritage*, the *Inquirer*, and the *Vanguard* Newspaper, which published weekly. Since most Liberians could not afford to buy newspapers, circulation volumes were small. Online news sources also existed. Most people received their news and information by radio. Government has sought to transform the state broadcaster into a Public Service Broadcaster, and the government of China invested more than $1 million to help the Liberian Broadcast Service achieve a national footprint.

Freedom of speech and the press were guaranteed in the constitution, and the government generally respected these rights. In late 2010, the legislature passed a Freedom of Information (FOI) Act (2008), the first of its kind in West Africa. However, the sector struggled to overcome many constraints such as low pay and inadequate training for journalists.

In 2009, the Media Sustainability Index (MSI), which considers factors such as professionalism, management and business acumen, ranked Liberia as having an "unsustainable, mixed system." On a scale of 0–4, with 4 being most sustainable, Liberia scored 1.96. According to Freedom House's "Freedom in the World" 2011 Index, which measures political rights and civil liberties, Liberia was "partly free."

46 ORGANIZATIONS

Since 2003, civil society has been on the rebound, although many organizations remained dependent on support from abroad. Civic groups in Monrovia included the YMCA and YWCA, the Antoinette Tubman Children's Welfare Foundation, the Liberia Evangelistic Women Workers, the Red Cross, Boy Scouts, and Girl Guides. The Liberia Chamber of Commerce maintained headquarters in Monrovia. Numerous secret societies were found among various ethnic groups, although several of them suffered severe disruption during the war. Cultural groups included the Society of Liberian Authors, Liberian Arts and Crafts Association, and Liberian Research Association. There were sports associations promoting amateur competition in a variety of pastimes. The Boy Scouts of Liberia and Girl Guides had active troops. There were national chapters of the Red Cross Society, Caritas, the Society of St. Vincent de Paul, and Habitat for Humanity.

47 TOURISM, TRAVEL, AND RECREATION

The estimated daily cost to visit Monrovia, the capital, was $250. The cost of visiting other cities averaged $116. A few tourist-grade hotels operated in Monrovia, but these were mostly patronized by businessmen, diplomats and development workers. Certain missionary organizations offered accommodations upcountry. Football (soccer) was the national sport. Visitors had to obtain a visa and passport as well as provide proof of a yellow fever vaccination.

48 FAMOUS PERSONS

Joseph Jenkins Roberts (1809–76), who was governor under the Colonization Society at the time the republic was established, became its first and later its sixth president (1848–56, 1872–76) and gained the respect of the European colonial powers by his able exposition of Liberia's rights as a free and independent nation. The national heroine is Matilda Newport, who helped to repel an attack on the first struggling settlement. Among white Americans who went to Liberia to assist the early black settlers were Jehudi Ashmun (1794–1828) and Ralph Randolph Gurley (1797–1872), who together reorganized the colonists in 1824. William Vacanarat Shadrach Tubman (1895–1971) was president of Liberia from 1944 until 1971. Angie E. Brooks-Randolph (b. 1928) served as president of the 1969/70 UN General Assembly. William Richard Tolbert, Jr. (1913–80) succeeded Tubman as president. He was killed in the 1980 coup led by Samuel Kanyon Doe (1950–90), who subsequently assumed the titles of commander in chief of the armed forces and chairman of the PRC. Doe was in turn tortured and killed in 1990 by rebels loyal to Charles G. Taylor (b. 1948), the leader of the faction that gained control during the civil war. Taylor, who became president in 1997, fled in 2003, was captured and tried for war crimes in the Hague, and was awaiting the verdict of his trial. Ellen Johnson-Sirleaf (b. 1938) became the first elected female president of an African country in 2005. She and Leymah Gbowee, a female Liberian human rights activist, received the Nobel Peace Prize in 2011.

49 DEPENDENCIES

Liberia has no territories or colonies.

50 BIBLIOGRAPHY

Adebajo, Adekeye. *Building Peace in West Africa: Liberia, Sierra Leone, and Guinea-Bissau*. Boulder, CO: Lynne Rienner, 2002.

Beyan, Amos Jones. *African American Settlements in West Africa: John Brown Russwurm and the American Civilizing Efforts*. New York: Palgrave Macmillan, 2005.

Burin, Eric. *Slavery and the Peculiar Solution: A History of the American Colonization Society*. Gainesville: University Press of Florida, 2005.

Clapham, Christopher. *African Guerrillas*. Bloomington: Indiana University Press, 1998.

Dunn, D. Elwood. *Historical Dictionary of Liberia*. Lanham, MD: Scarecrow, 2001.

Higate, Paul. *Insecure Places: Peacekeeping, Power and Performance in Haiti, Kosovo, and Liberia*. New York: Palgrave Macmillan, 2009.

Liberia Investment and Business Guide: Strategic and Practical Information. Washington, DC: International Business Publications USA, 2012.

Liberian Women Peacemakers: Fighting for the Right to Be Seen, Heard, and Counted. Trenton, NJ: Africa World Press, 2004.

Olukoju, Ayodeji. *Culture and Customs of Liberia*. Westport, CT: Greenwood Press, 2006.

Zeilig, Leo, and David Seddon. *A Political and Economic Dictionary of Africa*. Philadelphia: Routledge/Taylor and Francis, 2005.

LIBYA

CAPITAL: Tripoli (Tarabulus)

FLAG: The 2011 revolution replaced the Gaddafi regime's solid green national flag with the Libyan Independence flag, flown from 1951 to 1969. The national flag is tricolor, composed of horizontal red, black, and green stripes, with a white crescent and moon formation inhabiting the central black stripe.

ANTHEM: As of January 2012, the Transitional National Council (TNC) had yet to replace officially the previous regime's national anthem, *Almighty God.* However, it was expected that *Ya Biladi (Oh My Country)*, the independence anthem from 1951–1969, would officially replace the previous anthem.

MONETARY UNIT: The Libyan dinar (LYD) of 1,000 dirhams is a paper currency. There are coins of 1, 5, 10, 20, 50, and 100 dirhams, and notes of ¼, ½, 1, 5, and 10 dinars. LYD1 = US$0.76923 (or US$1 = LYD1.2648) as of 2011.

WEIGHTS AND MEASURES: The metric system is the legal standard, but some local weights and measures are used.

HOLIDAYS: During Qadhafi's rule of Libya, official holidays included: UK Evacuation Day, 28 March; US Evacuation Day, 11 June; Anniversary of the revolution, 1 September; and Constitution Day, 7 October. The TNC decided to wait for national elections before officially declaring new holidays. These were expected to include Anniversary of the revolution, February 17, and Liberation Day, October 23. Anniversary of the revolution, 1 September, and Constitution Day, 7 October, were not likely to be included among the new national Holidays. Muslim religious holidays include Eid al-Fitr, Eid al-Adha, the 1st of Muharram, and Milad an-Nabi.

TIME: 2 p.m. = noon GMT.

¹LOCATION, SIZE, AND EXTENT

Situated on the coast of North Africa, Libya is the fourth-largest country on the continent, with an area of 1,759,540 sq km (679,362 sq mi), extending 1,989 km (1,236 mi) SE–NW and 1,502 km (933 mi) NE–SW. Comparatively, the area occupied by Libya is slightly larger than the state of Alaska. It is bounded on the N by the Mediterranean Sea, on the E by Egypt, on the SE by the Sudan, on the S by Chad and Niger, on the W by Algeria, and on the NW by Tunisia, with a total land boundary length of 4,348 km (2,702 mi) and a coastline of 1,770 km (1,100 mi).

The Aouzou Strip (114,000 sq km/44,000 sq mi) in northern Chad was claimed and had been occupied by Libya since 1973; in a judgment on 3 February 1994, the UN International Court of Justice returned the Aouzou strip to Chad. Monitored by an observer force deployed by the UN Security Council, Libyan forces withdrew on 31 May 1994. However, Chadian rebels from the Aouzou still reside in Libya. Libya also claims about 19,400 sq km (7,490 sq mi) of Nigerian territory.

Libya's capital city, Tripoli, is located on the Mediterranean coast.

²TOPOGRAPHY

Libya forms part of the North African plateau extending from the Atlantic Ocean to the Red Sea. The highest point is Bikku Bitti, or Bette Peak, a 2,267-m (7,438-ft) peak in the extreme south. The chief geographical areas are Tripolitania, Cyrenaica, the Sirte Desert, and Fezzan. Tripolitania, in the northwest, consists of a series of terraces rising slowly from sea level along the coastal plain of Al-Jifara to a sharp escarpment. At the top of this escarpment is an upland plateau of sand, scrub, and scattered masses of stone, with elevations of up to 1,000 m (3,300 ft). Farther south are depressions extending from east to west. Here are found many oases and artesian wells.

The Sirte Desert is a barren area along the Gulf of Sidra separating Tripolitania and Cyrenaica. An upland plateau rising to about 600 m (2,000 ft) gives a rugged coastline to Cyrenaica. This plateau, the Jabal Akhdar, contains three of Libya's leading cities—Benghazi, Al Baydā, and Darnah. Farther south the desert is studded with oases such as Jālū and Al Jaghbūb. The Fezzan, in the southwest, is largely a series of depressions with occasional oases. There are no perennial rivers in the country.

³CLIMATE

The climate has marked seasonal variations influenced by both the Mediterranean Sea and the desert. Along the Tripolitanian coast, summer temperatures reach between 40 and 46°C (104 and 115°F); farther south, temperatures are even higher. Summers in the north of Cyrenaica range from 27 to 32°C (81 to 90°F). In Tobruk, the average January temperature is 13°C (55°F); July, 26°C (79°F). The ghibli, a hot, dry desert wind, can change temperatures by 17–22°C (30–40°F) in both summer and winter.

Rainfall varies from region to region. Rain falls generally in a short winter period and frequently causes floods. Evaporation is high, and severe droughts are common. The Jabal Akhdar region of Cyrenaica receives a yearly average of 40–60 cm (16–24 in). Other regions have less than 20 cm (8 in), and the Sahara has less than 5 cm (2 in) a year.

⁴FLORA AND FAUNA

The World Resources Institute estimates that there are 1,825 plant species in Libya. The primary plant is the deadly carrot (Thapsia garganica). Other flora are various cultivated fruit trees, olive trees, date palms, junipers, and mastic trees. In addition, Libya is home to 87 mammal, 326 bird, 68 reptile, and 5 amphibian species. The calculation reflects the total number of distinct species residing in the country, not the number of endemic species. Goats and cattle are found in the extreme north. In the south, sheep and camels are numerous.

⁵ENVIRONMENT

The World Resources Institute reported that Libya had designated 122,900 hectares (303,693 acres) of land for protection as of 2006. The UN reported in 2008 that carbon dioxide emissions in Libya totaled 57,287 kilotons.

A major environmental concern is the depletion of underground water as a result of overuse in agricultural developments, causing salinity and seawater penetration into the coastal aquifers. Water resources total 0.6 cu km (0.144 cu mi), while water usage is 4.27 cu km (1.02 cu mi) per year. Per capita water usage totaled 730 cu m (25,780 cu ft) per year. Domestic water usage accounts for 14% of total usage, industrial for 3%, and agricultural for 83%. The Great Manmade River Project, developed to transport water from large aquifers under the Sahara Desert to coastal cities, is the world's most extensive water supply project. Another significant environmental problem in Libya is water pollution. The combined impact of sewage, oil by-products, and industrial waste threatens the nation's coast and the Mediterranean Sea generally. The desertification of existing fertile areas is being combated by the planting of trees as windbreaks.

According to a 2011 report issued by Human Rights Watch, landmines remain a persistent threat to civilian and animal life throughout the country. These include mines left during the Libyan war with Chad, desert battles of World War II, and the 2011 uprising.

According to a 2011 report issued by the International Union for Conservation of Nature and Natural Resources (IUCN), the number of threatened species included 12 types of mammals, 3 species of birds, 5 types of reptiles, 24 species of fish, and 2 species of plant. Endangered species in Libya included the Mediterranean monk seal, the leopard, and the slender-horned gazelle. The Bubal hartebeest and Sahara oryx are extinct.

⁶POPULATION

The US Central Intelligence Agency (CIA) estimated the population of Libya in 2011 to be approximately 6,597,960, which placed it at number 102 in population among the 196 nations of the world. This figure includes approximately 166,510 non-nationals. In 2011, approximately 4.6% of the population was over 65 years of age, with another 32.8% under 15 years of age. The median age in Libya was 24.5 years. There were 1.05 males for every female in the country. The population's annual rate of change was 2.064%. The projected population for the year 2025 was 8,100,000. Population density in Libya was calculated at 4 people per sq km (10 people per sq mi).

In 2011, the CIA estimated that 78% of the population lived in urban areas, and that urban populations had an annual rate of change of 2.1%. The largest urban area was Tripoli, with a population of 1.1 million.

⁷MIGRATION

Estimates of Libya's net migration rate, carried out by the CIA in 2011, amounted to zero. The total number of emigrants living abroad was 110,100, and the total number of immigrants living in Libya was 682,500. Libya also accepted 8,000 refugees. The number of Italians was as high as 70,000 during the period of colonial rule. In 1964 Italians numbered 30,000, but most left after their land and property were nationalized in 1970. There were 30,000 Jews in Libya in 1948, but because of the Arab-Israeli conflict the community had virtually disappeared by 1973. The demographic statistics on Libyan Jews were expected to change, however, as several Jewish leaders expressed a desire to return in the wake of the 2011 uprising that deposed former dictator Mu'ammar al-Qadhafi.

About 100,000 Libyans were in exile in the mid-1980s; with the fall of Qadhafi, this number was expected to decline, as many members of the exiled opposition began returning to Libya in 2011 (including members of the TNC). The CIA reported that, as of 2007, approximately 8,000 inhabitants of the Palestinian Territories sought refuge in Libya.

The nomadic inhabitants of Libya follow regular patterns of migration; nomadic tribes in the south normally ignore international frontiers. Since the discovery of oil, there has been significant internal migration from rural to urban regions. The 2011 uprising has led to an additionally exodus of the Libyan population.

⁸ETHNIC GROUPS

For thousands of years the inhabitants of Libya were Berbers. Arabs started arriving in the 7th century AD, displacing or assimilating their Berber predecessors. The latest estimates indicate that 97% of the total population is comprised of Berbers and Arabs. The remaining 3% are made up of Greeks, Maltese, Italians, Egyptians, Pakistanis, Turks, Indians, and Tunisians.

⁹LANGUAGES

Arabic is the official language; since 1969, its use in daily life, even by foreigners, was encouraged by government decree during the Qadhafi regime. The TNC had yet to institute an official linguistic policy as of January 2012. English, which is also used in some government publications, has replaced Italian as the second language; however, Italian is still widely understood. Berber is spoken by small communities, especially in Tripolitania. Native speakers constitute about 5% of the population. In 2011 there were demonstrations by native Berber speakers seeking official inclusion in the new constitution.

¹⁰RELIGIONS

Islam is Libya's official religion, and the government publicly supports a preference for a moderate practice of Islam. About 97% of the people are Sunni Muslim. There are small Christian communities in the country, including Roman Catholics, Greek Orthodox, Coptic Christians, and members of nondenominational evangelical Unity churches. The Great Green Charter on Human Rights of the Jamahiriya Era provided, in theory, for some degree of religious freedom, and this right is generally respected in practice. The TNC issued statements affirming continued support for religious freedom in 2011. During the Qadhafi era, the practice of Islam was strictly monitored by the government, with a particularly aim to oppose any extremist or militant sects that could be viewed as a threat to the government. Though minority religions were generally tolerated, the government placed a number of restrictions, which essentially limited the practice of non-Muslim faiths. Proselytizing of other faiths was prohibited. The government limited the number of public places of worship allowed to Christians and, as of 2010, there were no known places of worship for Hindus, Baha'is, or Buddhists. Religious groups, under Qadhafi, were allowed to hold worship services in private homes.

¹¹TRANSPORTATION

The CIA reported that Libya has a total of 100,024 km (62,152 mi) of roads, of which 57,214 km (35,551 mi) are paved. Transportation varies from dirt tracks suitable for camels and donkeys to a coastal highway extending for 1,822 km (1,132 mi) between the Tunisian and Egyptian borders. At the end of 1968, this highway was connected with a north–south road to Sabhā. Further extensions to Murzūq and Ghat were later completed, as well as a spur to Birāk. Roads also connect the Cyrenaica coastal centers with the interior.

The main ports are Tripoli, Benghazi, Qasr Ahmad (the port for Misrata), and Tobruk. Crude oil export terminals include Port Brega (Marsá al-Burayqah) and Ras Lanuf. As of 2010, Libya's merchant fleet had 27 vessels of 1,000 gross registered tons (GRT) or more.

There are 137 airports (59 with paved runways), which transported 1.15 million passengers in 2009 according to the World Bank. There are also two heliports. Libya's two international airports are Tripoli Airport (34 km/21 mi south of Tripoli) and Benina Airport (19 km/12 mi from Benghazi). Libyan Arab Airlines, established in 1965, operates to neighboring Arab countries, central and southern Africa, and Europe. Many major world airlines serve Libya. Due to the shifting political climate following the 2011 uprising, however, international flights were subject to periodic interruptions, cancellations and suspension of service. There is also regular domestic service, with airports at Tobruk, Port Brega, Ghat, Ghadamis, Misrata, and Al Baydā.

¹²HISTORY

Archaeological evidence indicates that a Neolithic culture, skilled in the domestication of cattle and the cultivation of crops, existed as far back as 6000 BC along the Libyan coast. To the south, in what is now the Sahara, hunters and herdsmen roamed what was then a well-watered savanna. Increasing desiccation and the coming of the Berbers about 2000 BC, presumably from southwestern Asia, ended this period. The pharaohs of the so-called Libyan dynasties who ruled Egypt (c. 950–720 BC) are thought to have been Berbers. Phoenician seafarers, who arrived early in the first millennium BC, founded settlements along the coast, including one that became Tripoli.

Around the 7th century BC, Greek colonists settled in Cyrenaica. In succeeding centuries, the western settlements fell under the sway of Carthage; the eastern settlements fell to the Egyptian dynasty of the Ptolemies in the 4th century BC. When the Romans defeated Carthage in the Punic Wars of the 3rd and 2nd centuries BC, they occupied the regions around Tripoli. In 96 BC, they forced Egypt to surrender Cyrenaica, and Roman influence later extended as far south as the Fezzan. Libya became very prosperous under Roman rule; with the decline of Rome, western Libya fell in the 5th century AD to Germanic Vandal invaders, who ruled from Carthage. In the 6th century, the Byzantines conquered the Vandals and ruled the coastal regions of Libya until the Arab conquest of the 7th century. The Arabs intermixed with the Berbers, who were gradually absorbed into the Muslim Arab culture.

Western Libya was administered by the Aghlabids of Tunisia in the 9th century, and by the Fatimids of Tunisia and then Egypt in the 10th. During the 11th century, invasions by two nomadic Arab peoples, the Banu Hilal and Banu Sulaym, destroyed many of the urban and agricultural areas. Normans from Sicily occupied Tripoli and surrounding regions in 1145 but were soon displaced by the Almohads of Morocco; during the 13th century, the Hafsids of Tunisia ruled western Libya. The eastern regions remained subject to Egyptian dynasties. In the 16th century, Spanish invaders seized parts of the coast, turning over control of Tripoli to the crusading Knights of the Order of St. John of Jerusalem. The Ottoman Turks occupied the coastal regions in 1551, ruling the country until 1711, when Ahmad Qaramanli, of Turkish origin, wrested semiautonomous status from Istanbul. Pirate captains, operating out of Tripoli, raided the Mediterranean and the Italian coasts. The Qaramanlis ruled until 1835, when the Ottomans again assumed control.

In September 1911, the Italians invaded Libya, meeting fierce resistance from both Turks and indigenous Libyans. A peace treaty of 17 October 1912 between Turkey and Italy placed Libya formally under Italian rule, but the Libyans continued their resistance. Led by a Muslim religious brotherhood, the Sanusi Sufi Order, the Libyans (with some Turkish help) fought the Italians to a standstill during World War I. Following the war, and particularly after the accession of Benito Mussolini to power in Italy, the Italians continued their often-brutal efforts to conquer Libya. Alleged concentration camps in Eastern Libya and forced migration still loom large in Libyan memory of Italian occupation. In 1931, 'Umar al-Mukhtar, a leader of the Sanusi, was captured and executed, and in 1932 the Italian conquest was completed. The legacy of Mukhtar (nicknamed "Lion of the Desert") created a national symbolism for self determination. Libyan rebels would renew

LOCATION: 19°30′ to 33°N; 9°30′ to 25°E. BOUNDARY LENGTHS: Mediterranean coastline, 1,770 kilometers (1,100 miles); Egypt, 1,115 kilometers (693 miles); Sudan, 383 kilometers (238 miles); Chad, 1,054 kilometers (655 miles); Niger, 354 kilometers (220 miles); Algeria, 982 kilometers (610 miles); Tunisia, 459 kilometers (285 miles). TERRITORIAL SEA LIMIT: 12 miles, but all of the Gulf of Sidra south of 32°30′ is claimed.

Mukhtar's anti-imperialist slogan, "We Win or We Die" as a rallying cry for the 2011 uprising against Qadhafi. In World War II, Libya became a main battleground for Allied and Axis forces, until it was occupied by victorious British and Free French troops.

The Treaty of 1947 between Italy and the Allies ended Italian rule in Libya and, when the Allies could not decide upon the country's future, Libya's fate was left to the UN. On 21 November 1949, the UN General Assembly voted that Libya should become an independent state. On 24 December 1951, Libya gained independence, with Muhammad Idris al-Mahdi as-Sanusi as king. Following the 1959 discovery of oil, the monarchy rapidly began developing production infrastructure.

On 1 September 1969, a secret army organization, the Free Unionist Officers, deposed the king and proclaimed a republican regime. On 8 September, the revolutionary Command Council (RCC) announced the formation of a civilian government. This government resigned on 16 January 1970, and a new cabinet was formed under Col. Qadhafi, chairman of the RCC. Later that year, the United Kingdom and the United States closed their military installations. On 15 April 1973, Qadhafi called for a "cultural revolution" based on Islamic principles. In subsequent months, hundreds of "people's committees" were established to oversee all sectors of the nation's political, cultural, and economic life. In April 1974, Qadhafi withdrew from the supervision of daily administrative functions (these were assumed by Maj. Abdul Salam Jallud), but he remained the effective head of state of Libya.

Qadhafi sought to make Libya the axis of a unified Arab nation. Union was achieved with Egypt, Tunisia, Morocco, Syria, and Sudan at various times, but only on paper. Subsequent relations with the many Arab nations, including Egypt and Tunisia, were often tense. Libya itself, despite rhetorical support for radical Palestinians, remained on the sidelines in Arab-Israeli conflicts.

Qadhafi was equally active in Africa. In 1973, he annexed from Chad the disputed Aouzou Strip, an area that may contain rich deposits of uranium. In 1979, his armed forces tried unsuccessfully to prop up the failing regime of Idi Amin in Uganda. Libya sent over 10,000 troops into Chad in 1980 in support of the regime of Goukouni Oueddei, and a union of the two nations was proposed. Intense international pressure, however, led to a Libyan withdrawal in November 1981. After the fall of Oueddei's regime in June 1982, Qadhafi provided military support for Oueddei's efforts to topple the new French-backed government in Chad. Libya's and Oueddei's forces were in control of much of northern Chad until 1987, when Chadian forces ousted them, capturing or destroying $1 billion in Libyan military equipment, and attacking bases inside Libya itself. In 1989, after acknowledging his error in moving into Chad, Qadhafi agreed to a cease-fire and the submission of the dispute over the Aouzou Strip to the Court of International Justice. The Court settled the dispute in Chad's favor in 1994.

Qadhafi was also accused of supporting subversive plots in such countries as Morocco, Niger, Sudan, Egypt, Tunisia, Ghana, Burkina Faso, Nigeria, The Gambia, Somalia, Senegal, and Mali, and of providing material support for a variety of insurgents, including the Irish Republican Army, Muslim rebels in the Philippines, and Japanese and German terrorists. Qadhafi did find some support in small, poor black African countries, eager for Libyan aid. In 1982, however, he suffered a setback when the annual Organization of African Unity (OAU, now the African Union) summit scheduled for Tripoli failed to convene because of disputes over Libya's policies in Chad and its support of Polisario guerrillas in Western Sahara. As a result, Qadhafi was denied his term as OAU chairman. In contrast, in February 1997 in a deliberate jab at the UN Security Council's sanctions against Libya over the Lockerbie bombing affair, the OAU Ministerial Council met in Tripoli, the first time this meeting had been convened outside of its headquarters in Addis Ababa, Ethiopia.

In 1981, two Libyan jets were shot down by US fighters over the Gulf of Sidra, an arm of the Mediterranean claimed by Qadhafi as Libya's territorial waters. In 1982, the United States, charging Qadhafi with supporting international terrorism, banned oil imports from Libya and the export of US technology to Libya. In January 1986, the United States, citing "irrefutable evidence" of Libyan involvement in Palestinian attacks on airports in Rome and Vienna the previous month, ordered all Americans to leave Libya and cut off all economic ties as of mid-1986. In March, a US naval task force struck four Libyan vessels after US planes entering airspace over the Libyan-claimed Gulf of Sidra were fired upon. On 15 April, following a West Berlin bomb attack in which US servicemen were victims, US warplanes bombed targets in Tripoli and Benghazi. Libya said that Qadhafi's adopted daughter was killed and two of his sons were wounded in the attack. Qadhafi survived several reported assassination and coup attempts in the 1980s and 1990s and the opposition of Islamist groups, which prompted him to crack down on militants in 1993.

Prior to the 2011 uprising, Qadhafi's most serious challenge in the recent past was from abroad, in the form of tough sanctions imposed since 1992 and 1993 on Libya by the UN Security Council after he refused to surrender two men suspected in the terrorist bombing of a Pan American passenger jet over Lockerbie, Scotland, in 1988. The UN resolutions (nos. 731 and 883) prohibited sales of equipment and air travel to Libya and froze its overseas bank deposits but, significantly, did not ban sales of petroleum products. Throughout the period of sanctions, the United States repeatedly attempted to persuade the UN to impose an oil embargo against Libya, but it was not successful. After numerous pleas to the UN by Arab and African countries and organizations to the UN Security Council to lift the sanctions, and numerous rounds of negotiations, in August 1998 Qadhafi eventually agreed to hand over the two Libyan suspects in the Lockerbie bombing for trial in the Netherlands before Scottish judges. The suspects were transferred to the Netherlands in April 1999. This decision led to an easing of tensions, with a suspension of the UN sanctions (although they were not lifted at the time) and Britain resuming full diplomatic relations in July 1999. The United States, however, remained committed to the branding of Libya as a supporter of international terrorism and therefore a pariah state. In January 2001, the Scottish court in the Netherlands found one of the two Libyan defendants guilty of involvement in the Lockerbie bombing, and sentenced him to life imprisonment. The other Libyan was acquitted. US President George W. Bush stated sanctions would remain in place not only until Libya compensated for the bombing of the aircraft, but also until Libya admitted guilt and expressed remorse for the act. In mid-2002, Libya stated that it was ready, in principle, to pay families of the victims of the bombing compensation in the amount of US$2.7 billion ($10 million for each of the 270 victims). In August 2003, Libya accepted responsibility for the actions of its officials and payment of the compensation to the victims' families. UN sanctions were lifted in September 2003, and US International Emergency Economic Powers Act (IEEPA) sanctions were lifted in September 2004.

In early September 1995, Libya began deporting thousands of Arab workers, primarily Palestinian, Sudanese, and Egyptian. In a speech on 1 September 1995, Qadhafi stated that foreigners (including some 30,000 Palestinians) were being expelled in order to create jobs for Libyans, although the move was widely interpreted as punishment of the PLO for holding peace talks with Israel. Qadhafi stated that many of those being deported were Islamic militant "infiltrators" posing as migrant workers. On 6–7 September, at least 30 people were killed in Benghazi when armed Islamic militants battled Libyan security forces during a roundup of workers for deportation. By 11 September, 7,000 Egyptians had been expelled, and thousands of Palestinians were stranded either at sea or at the border with Egypt. The deportations continued into October, when 650 Palestinians were stranded aboard a ferry off the coast of Cyprus, and 850 were still camped on the Egyptian border.

In the 1980s and 1990s, Qadhafi saw his regime challenged by democracy advocates, discontented military personnel and Islamist groups. Several assassination attempts were reported, both within the military and from armed Islamist groups. In the mid 1980s, the Qadhafi regime instituted an initiative known as the "Stray Dogs Policy" in which extra-judicial assassination and kidnappings of dissidents were undertaken throughout the world. In March 1997 the General People's Committee (GPC) adopted the Charter of Honor, imposing collective punishment on Libyans convicted of crimes of disorder, such as sabotage, drug and arms trafficking, and "terrorists, criminals, saboteurs and heretics." The charter was clearly aimed at opponents of the regime. Loose definitions included in the Libyan Penal Code at the time (such as "disseminating information that may harm the reputation of the nation") also criminalized criticism of the Qadhafi regime.

In March 1996, as many as 400 prisoners—many of them government opponents and Islamic militants—broke out of a prison near Benghazi. The ensuing clash with Libyan troops was viewed by many observers as an indication of significant antigovernment feeling in eastern Libya. In June of the same year, the Qadhafi regime perpetrated what has been called its worst human rights violation. Prisoners, many of them jailed for political violations, held at the Abu Salim facility outside of Tripoli undertook a general strike to protest living conditions. Allegedly under the support of Abdallah al-Senussi, prison officials executed 1,200 of the demonstrators in under three hours. The regime did not begin to inform families of the victims until 2001. Although Saif Qadhafi promised an official inquiry into the prison massacre in 2006, this never occurred under his father's regime.

In May 2001, Libya sent troops into the Central African Republic to aid President Ange-Félix Patassé and his supporters, to regain power after a failed coup attempt. It withdrew its troops in December 2002; Qadhafi stated the mission of restoring peace and stability to the country had been achieved. That month, Libya denied allegations put forward by the Democratic Republic of the Congo (DROC) that it was sending troops and equipment into Congolese territory along the border with the Central African Republic. On 13 December, the DROC government wrote the UN Security Council to condemn Libya's actions and demand an immediate withdrawal of Libyan troops from its territory. The DROC accused Libya of aiding the Movement for the Liberation of the Congo (MLC), a rebel group.

In January 2003, Libya was elected by secret ballot to head the UN Commission on Human Rights. The votes were 33 in favor, 3 opposed, and 17 abstentions. This caused international controversy, and led to calls for reform of the UN. In 2006, a new Human Rights Council was created to replace the UN Commission on Human Rights. The Human Rights Council is meant to be a standing body meeting year-round to promote and protect human rights with a membership that excludes the worst human rights violators. The United States, the Marshall Islands, Palau, and Israel voted against the Council's creation. They claimed the Council would have too little power, and that human rights-abusing nations might still take control of the body.

In December 2003, Libya publicly announced its intention to rid itself of weapons of mass destruction (WMD) and Missile Technology Control Regime (MTCR)-class missile programs. It cooperated with the United States, the United Kingdom, the IAEA, and the Organization for the Prohibition of Chemical Weapons toward these objectives. Libya also signed the IAEA Additional Protocol, and became a state party to the Chemical Weapons Convention. In May 2006, the United States announced it was restoring full diplomatic relations with Libya. The country was elected by the UN General Assembly to one of the 10 two-year seats on the UN Security Council. Libya's term on the UN Security Council, which began 1 January 2008, expired at the end of 2009.

In the wake of civilian protests in Tunisia and Egypt, a series of anti-government demonstrations began in Libya in mid-February 2011. Although Libyan activists scheduled a "Day of Rage" on 17 February, protests began ahead of schedule. This came as a response to the arrest of human rights lawyer Fathi Terbil, an attorney representing families of the 1996 Abu Salim prison massacre. The protests rapidly took a violent turn when warplanes and militia began to fire on the crowds. Fighting between pro- and anti-government forces continued as the protestors neared the capital of Tripoli, putting pressure on Qadhafi to step down. Government forces led a bloody crackdown on protestors near the capital; all government buildings were reported to have been burned to the ground. Within what seemed a matter of days, the anti-government forces were organized under the leadership of former justice minister Mustafa Abdel Jalil as the TNC. The rebels established a 30-member leadership council that they declared as the country's sole official representative and quickly began to seize control of several areas of eastern Libya, centered on the city of Benghazi. Qadhafi issued statements that blamed drugs and al-Qaeda for the uprising.

The 2011 outbreak of demonstrations led to renewed foreign relations troubles for Qadhafi. The Arab League officially suspended Libya's membership on 22 February, following reports of attacks against unarmed demonstrators. A host of Western nations, including the United States, Italy, the United Kingdom and France, quickly moved to condemn the attacks. By 10 March, France officially severed diplomatic ties with the Qadhafi regime, and declared formal recognition of the TNC as the legitimate representatives of the Libyan people. The pro-Qadhafi military retaliated against the rebels with heavy air strikes to maintain control of the western areas around Tripoli. By 8 March 2011, the UN reported that more than 1,000 people had been killed in the uprising and that nearly 200,000 had fled the country. As the battle continued, the NATO defense ministers began to consider the implementation of an international no-fly zone over Libya. This essentially banned military flights by Libyan government forces through Libyan airspace. However, some feared that any foreign intervention could trigger even greater violence. On 19 March 2011, military operations began following the 17 March declaration of UN resolution 1973, which was passed under the mandate to protect civilians. A power coalition including the United States, United Kingdom, Qatar, and France began enforcement of a no-fly zone over Libya, in addition to naval blockades. This was followed by the 23 March Operation Unified Protector, at which point enforcement of civilian protection was transferred to NATO. The UN issued sanctions against Qadhafi and his government, and the International Criminal Court stated that it would investigate Qadhafi and his sons for crimes against humanity.

After the UN voted to ban flights over Libyan airspace, Qadhafi's government said that it would call a ceasefire and stop military operations against anti-Qadhafi rebels. When this statement proved to be a false promise, American and European troops began strikes by air and sea against Qadhafi's forces. The allied forces said that they would stop the attacks once they saw a true ceasefire from Qadhafi. The Arab League called an emergency meeting to discuss the turn of events in Libya and elsewhere in the Arab world. Qadhafi showed no signs of stepping down and threatened to shut off the flow of Libyan oil to the United States, France, and the United Kingdom. The Libyan leader also threatened to unleash terrorist attacks in Europe as retaliation against NATO operations in the country. By 23 March 2011, British forces reported that Libya's air force was no longer able to fight. The allied forces then moved to increase pressure on Qadhafi's ground forces.

In April 2011, African Union (AU) members offered a peace proposal to rebel leaders in Benghazi in an attempt to end the two-month-long conflict in Libya. The African Union had already met with Qadhafi to discuss the proposal. The rebels agreed to look over the proposal but refused to hold a truce without Qadhafi stepping down. In May 2011, Libyan rebels gained ground in the city of Misrata, driving Qadhafi's forces from the third largest city in the country. The International Criminal Court was attempting to produce arrest warrants for Qadhafi for crimes against humanity and deliberately targeting civilians; on 27 June 2011, judges in The Hague, Netherlands, issued indictments for Qadhafi, his son Saif (considered the most likely successor to his father), and Abdulla Senussi, the former Libyan intelligence chief accused of masterminding the 1996 Abu Salim Prison massacre. Warrants were also issued for members of the Qadhafi family, who sought refuge in Algeria and Niger.

The so-called "Battle of Sirte" led to the capture of Qadhafi on 20 October 2011. Sirte, Qadhafi's hometown, had previously been the site of fierce struggles between loyalist and opposition fighters and was considered the last holdout for the Qadhafi regime's power. The Libyan leader was captured by rebel forces later that day and died soon after; the exact circumstances surrounding his death remain disputed. The TNC issued statements promising a full investigation into the capture and killing of the former leader. On 23 October 2011, representatives of the TNC officially declared the liberation of Libya and announced a formal end of the conflict.

13 GOVERNMENT

Under Qadhafi, the Libyan Arab Republic was established on 1 September 1969, and a new constitution was announced by the revolutionary Command Council (RCC) on 11 December 1969. The constitution, which was effectively superseded by the principles of Qadhafi's "Green Book," proclaimed Libya to be "an Arab, democratic, and free Republic, which constitutes part of the Arab nation and whose objective is comprehensive Arab unity." Supreme authority rested with the 12-member RCC, which appointed both the prime minister and cabinet. Qadhafi, as chairman of the RCC, was the effective head of state and commander in chief of the armed forces. In March 1977, the nation's name was changed to the Socialist People's Libyan Arab Jamahiriya, and the "authority of the people" was proclaimed by a newly convened GPC. The people theoretically exercised their authority through a system of some 600 people's congresses and committees. At the top of this system was the GPC, which replaced the RCC as the supreme instrument of government. The 760 GPC members were chosen out of about 2,700 representatives of the basic people's congresses. All executive and legislative authority was vested in the GPC, but it met for only two weeks a year and delegated most of its authority to its own Secretariat and to the GPC, in effect the cabinet, which was appointed by the Secretariat. GPC members served three-year terms. Voting for local people's congresses, whose elected members selected members of the GPC, was mandatory for those over 18. In 1979, Qadhafi gave up his official post as secretary-general of the GPC to become a "private citizen." As "Leader of the revolution," however, he remained the de facto head of state. He also remained the commander of the armed forces and virtually all power was concentrated in him and his close advisers. In 1988, public discontent with shortages led Qadhafi to limit the authority of revolutionary committees, release many political prisoners, and remove restrictions on foreign travel and private enterprise.

The formation of the TNC was officially announced on 27 February, shortly following the outbreak of the 2011 uprising. In the TNC's foundational declaration, the Council defined itself as a provisional ruling authority, to be dissolved following a popular constitutional referendum and free elections. The Council has issued statements maintaining a commitment to democratic rule, widespread human rights reforms, protection of minority rights, and the formation of civil society. National elections were slated to take place by June 2012.

14 POLITICAL PARTIES

Prior to the 2011 uprising, political parties did not play an important role in Libya's history. All political parties were banned in 1947 by British administrators, but many groups soon emerged to debate their country's future. By 1949, the Tripolitanian National Congress Party, led by Bashir Sadawi, was the leading party. However, it was dissolved in 1952, following local disorders, after Libya's first election campaign. Formation of and membership in political parties continued to be a criminal offense under the Qadhafi regime's penal code. In December 2011, the formation of the first political party, the Libya Motherland Party, was announced. Leader Abdullah Benun stated that the party would look to the moderate Islamist Justice and Development Party of Turkey as a potential model.

In 1971, the RCC founded the Libyan Arab Socialist Union as an alternative to political parties. It was viewed as an organization to promote national unity but functioned little since 1977. Seven exiled opposition groups agreed in Cairo in January 1987 to form a joint working group, but their work had no discernible impact on political conditions in Libya until the outbreak of the 2011 uprising, in which the dissident Libyan Diaspora played a fundamental role. The following groups have been in opposition to the government: Fighting Islamic Group, Islamic Martyrs' Movement, Libyan Ba'athist Party, Libyan Conservatives' Party, Libyan Democratic Movement, Libyan Democratic Authority, Libyan Democratic Conference, Libyan Movement for Change and Reform, Libyan National Alliance, Movement of Patriotic Libyans, National Front for the Salvation of Libya, Libya Islamic Group, and Supporters of God.

Mustafa Abdul Jalil served as the chairman of the TNC. Beginning on 23 October 2011, Abd al-Rahim al-Keeb took office as the TNC prime minister.

15 LOCAL GOVERNMENT

Jamahiriya, a Qadhafi-era neologism, meant "state of the masses." Politically implementing this system theoretically involved a process of total decentralization of power, whereby all decisions would be left to the citizens via direct democracy. One source claimed that in 1998 the GPC divided Libya into 26 governorates (Sha'biyah), each to be headed by the secretary of a people's committee. However, other sources differed on the structure of the local government. According to some sources, Libya was divided into 3 provinces, 10 governorates, and 1,500 administrative communes. One source listed a subdivision of 34 governorates. There were municipal people's congresses, as well as vocational, production, professional, and craft people's congresses. Although in theory Qadhafi planned to decentralize power to the 600 popular congresses, most decision-making power was tightly controlled by the central government. The municipal people's congresses appointed people's committees to execute policy. This was expected to change with the June 2012 elections announced by the TNC.

16 JUDICIAL SYSTEM

Qadhafi's Proclamation of People's Authority designated the Holy Koran as the law of society. Prior to the 2011 uprising, the Libyan legal system largely followed Egyptian codes and precedents. All cases relating to personal status were dealt with according to Muslim law. Cases of the first instance were heard by courts of first instance, followed by appeals courts. A separate body called the Shari'ah Court of Appeals heard cases appealed from the lower courts involving Islamic law. There was also a Supreme Court, consisting of a president and judges appointed by the GPC. It dealt with constitutional and legislative questions referred to it and heard administrative cases. Special revolutionary courts tried political offenses. Upon coming to power in 2011, the TNC maintained that judicial reforms formed a broad goal of its vision for the future.

17 ARMED FORCES

Prior to the 2011 uprising, the International Institute for Strategic Studies reports that armed forces in Libya totaled 76,000 members. The force was comprised of 50,000 from the army, 8,000 from the navy, and 18,000 members of the air force. Armed forces

represented 3.2% of the labor force in Libya. Defense spending totaled $3.5 billion and accounted for 3.9% of GDP.

18 INTERNATIONAL COOPERATION

Libya joined the UN on 14 December 1955 and is a member of ECA and several nonregional specialized agencies, such as the FAO, UNESCO, IAEA, IFC, ILO, the World Bank, and the WHO. The country joined the Arab League in 1953, the OAU in 1963, and OPEC in 1962. In January 1968, it was a founding member of OAPEC, along with Saudi Arabia and Kuwait. Libya also belongs to the African Development Bank, the Arab Bank for Economic Development in Africa, the Arab Fund for Economic and Social Development, the Council of Arab Economic Unity, the Community of Sahel and Saharan States (CENSAD), the Arab Maghreb Union, the New Partnership for Africa's Development (NEPAD), and G-77. Under Qadhafi, the country was an observer in the WTO.

In September 2009, Qadhafi and Venezuelan leader Hugo Chavez took the lead in talks at the second South America-Africa (ASA) summit, urging leaders from both continents to consider the establishment of a "NATO of the south." While the primary topics of the summit meeting included energy, food security, and the global economic crisis, Qadhafi promoted the adoption of a military-style defense pact between African and South American nations as a counter measure toward US and European powers. Chavez agreed that such an alliance could create a "balanced world." Thirty world leaders attended the summit, including those from Argentina, Zimbabwe, and the Democratic Republic of the Congo. The third ASA summit was scheduled to be held in Libya in 2011, but was indefinitely delayed as a result of the uprising.

Under Qadhafi, Libya was listed as a State Sponsor of Terrorism by the United States, even though the government offered strong commitments to the UN to renounce and fight against terrorism. Libya was part of the Nonaligned Movement. In environmental cooperation, Libya is part of the Basel Convention, the Convention on Biological Diversity, the London Convention, the Montréal Protocol, and the UN Conventions on Climate Change and Desertification.

19 ECONOMY

Until the late 1950s, Libya was one of the poorest countries in the world with about 80% of the population engaged in agriculture and animal husbandry. In 1950, per capita annual income was about $40, while Libya's most valuable source of foreign earnings was the revenue received for leasing bases to the United Kingdom and United States. (The bases were vacated in 1970.) But with the discovery of the Zaltan oil field in 1959, the economic horizons of the country were dramatically enlarged. The first oil pipeline, from B'ir Zaltan to the coast, was opened in 1961. More oil fields were subsequently discovered; in 1970 oil output of 159.9 million tons was achieved.

However, in the early 1990s the UN-imposed an air embargo on the country because of its efforts to build weapons of mass destruction. Libya's resulting isolation slowed the pace of oil exploration through the absence of major foreign oil companies. Lack of outlets limited the development of refineries, petrochemicals, and gas facilities. In 2002, in an effort to integrate its economy back into the international system, the government embarked on economic reforms. The government devalued the official exchange rate of the dinar by 51% to increase the competitiveness of its firms and to attract foreign investment. At the same time it cut its customs duty rate by 50% on most imports to offset the effects of the currency devaluation. Despite the reforms, the government continued to manage the economy along socialist lines maintaining controls on credit, trade, and foreign exchange.

When the government announced in 2003 that it would abandon efforts to obtain weapons of mass destruction, the embargo was lifted, and foreign investment began to return. Before the lifting of the embargo, Libya had 12 oil fields with reserves of 1 billion barrels or more each, and two others with reserves of 500 million–1 billion barrels. Oil companies were eager to exploit Libya's resources further, and Libya began to court actively foreign companies to help develop its production capacity from 1.5 million barrels per day to 2 million barrels per day over a five-year period and to 3 million barrels per day by 2015. As of 2010, approximately 1.8 billion barrels per day were produced; oil production was significantly disrupted by the 2011 uprising.

Petroleum products and natural gas account for almost all the value of exports and for one-quarter of GDP. Oil revenues have lifted the country's per capita GDP significantly, although much of the income has been lost to waste and corruption. Wealth is unevenly distributed, failing to reach the poorer segments of the society. The GDP rate of change in Libya, as of 2010, was 4.2%, and inflation stood at 3%. About 30% of the labor force was unemployed, a number that increased following the 2011 uprising. The TNC maintained that reintegration and employment opportunities for rebel fighters was of fundamental concern.

Economic prospects outside of the petroleum sector are limited. Poor soil and climatic conditions constrain agricultural output, although the manufacturing sector has expanded to include the processing of petrochemicals, iron, steel, and aluminum.

20 INCOME

The CIA estimated that in 2010 the GDP of Libya was $90.57 billion. The CIA defines GDP as the value of all final goods and services produced within a nation in a given year and computed on the basis of purchasing power parity (PPP) rather than value as measured on the basis of the rate of the exchange based on current dollars. The per capita GDP was estimated at $14,000. The annual growth rate of GDP was 4.2%. The average inflation rate was 3%. It was estimated that agriculture accounted for 2.6% of GDP, industry 63.8%, and services 33.6%. According to the World Bank, remittances from citizens living abroad totaled $14.4 million or about $2 per capita. It was estimated that about 33% of the population subsisted on an income below the poverty line established by Libya's government.

21 LABOR

As of 2010, Libya had a total labor force of 1.729 million people. Within that labor force, CIA estimates in 2004 noted that 17% were employed in agriculture, 23% in industry, and 59% in the service sector. Under Qadhafi, foreign workers, who did much of the blue-collar and technical work, were not treated with equality under Libyan labor law, and could stay in the country solely for the duration of their employment contracts. At the time of the 2011 uprising, the largest employer was the government, which operated public utilities, public works, several banks, the port and harbor organizations, and other enterprises.

Under Qadhafi, the National Trade Unions' Federation was the official trade organization, and any independent union or association was prohibited. All Libyan workers were required to join a trade union. Foreign workers could not join unions and enjoyed little protection. There was no collective bargaining; the government controlled all employment matters. Strikes were not permitted.

There is no information about the prevalence of child labor, although the minimum age for employment is legally set at 18 years old. The maximum legal workweek is 48 hours. The average family wage was estimated at $208 a month in 2010, but employees are irregularly paid, especially in the public sector.

22 AGRICULTURE

Roughly 1% of the total land is dedicated to agriculture, and the country's major crops include wheat, barley, olives, dates, citrus, vegetables, peanuts, and soybeans. Cereal production in 2009 amounted to 207,177 tons, fruit production 376,287 tons, and vegetable production 892,697 tons. Until 2011, agriculture was the only economic sector in which private ownership was still important. Cereals are grown in Tripolitania and Cyrenaica; agriculture in the Fezzan is concentrated in the oases. Virtually all crops are grown for domestic consumption. Nevertheless, most agricultural products must be imported.

Libya has invested a significant share of national revenue in agriculture in the hope of someday becoming agriculturally self-sufficient; cultivation has been changing from subsistence farming to highly mechanized operations. Areas singled out for development included the Al-Jifara Plain in Tripolitania; the Jabal Akhdar, east of Benghazi; part of the Fezzan; and the oases of Kufrah and Sarir. In the Kufrah oasis, large, untapped water reserves are being utilized to help provide fodder for sheep. Under Qadhafi, a government agency marketed farm produce and had authority to operate cooperatives and farms. The Agricultural Bank was provided with sufficient capital to make short- and long-term loans easily available.

23 ANIMAL HUSBANDRY

The UN Food and Agriculture Organization (FAO) reported that Libya dedicated 13.5 million hectares (33.4 million acres) to permanent pasture or meadow in 2009. During that year, the country tended 27 million chickens and 185,000 head of cattle. The production from these animals amounted to 30,786 tons of beef and veal, 100,010 tons of poultry, 55,641 tons of eggs, and 462,860 tons of milk. Libya also produced 973 tons of cattle hide and 9,394 tons of raw wool.

Before the transformation of the economy by the discovery of oil, livestock was an important sector, providing transport, clothing, food, and skins for tents. South of the Jabal areas, a wide belt of drought-resistant vegetation extending across most of the country is still used by nomadic and seminomadic herdsmen for grazing. In the Fezzan, the nomads move about between oases or other places where vegetation is suitable for their animals. Libya's livestock are vulnerable to disease and drought, and annual losses have reached as high as 60%.

24 FISHING

Libya had 99 decked commercial fishing boats in 2008. The annual capture totaled 47,645 tons according to the UN FAO. The export value of seafood totaled $14.48 million. Fishing is of minor importance, although Libya has excellent fishing grounds laden with tuna, sardines, and other fish.

25 FORESTRY

There are no significant forested areas in Libya. The only important forest areas in Libya are shrubby juniper growths in the Jabal Akhdar areas of Cyrenaica. A few conifers are found in more isolated districts. Tripolitania has some forest remnants in inaccessible regions. Encroaching sand dunes in the north create a need for afforestation, and many acacia, Aleppo pine, carob, cypress, eucalyptus, olive, and palm trees have been planted. Dune fixation, both for reforestation and to preserve agricultural land, has been an important part of the forestry program. The UN FAO estimated the 2009 roundwood production at 116,000 cu m (4.1 million cu ft). The value of all forest products, including roundwood, totaled $1.87 million.

26 MINING

The nonfuel sector of the Libyan mining industry was negligible. Petroleum was Libya's leading industry in 2009, although oil production has fallen to under 50% of output in 1970. Libya was the fourth-largest crude oil producer in Africa, after Nigeria, Algeria, and Angola. Nonhydrocarbon mineral production in 2009 consisted of lime, gypsum, hydraulic cement, salt, and sulfur (as a by-product of petroleum and natural gas). Estimated production in 2009 included: 260,000 metric tons of lime; 300,000 tons of gypsum; 130,000 metric tons of sulfur (by-product of petroleum and natural gas); 6.5 million metric tons of hydraulic cement; and 40,000 metric tons of salt. Libya had large reserves of iron ore in the Fezzan. The Wadi ash-Shatti iron ore deposit was estimated to contain 1.6 billion tons of oolitic hematite, limonite, chamosite, and siderite with a grade range of 30–48% iron. There were also deposits of magnesium salts (7.5 million tons) and potassium salts (1.6 million tons) in Maradah, south of the Port Brega oil terminal; potash in the Sirte Desert; and magnetite, phosphate rock, and sulfur. In 2009, mining and quarrying employed 44,190 workers, or 2.8% of Libya's work force.

27 ENERGY AND POWER

The World Bank reported in 2008 that Libya produced 28.7 billion kWh of electricity and consumed 24.6 billion kWh, or 3,728 kWh per capita. Demand for electric power in Libya is growing rapidly at a rate of about 6–8% per year. Demand was anticipated to reach between 5.8 and 8GW by 2020. Roughly 99% of energy came from fossil fuels.

Libya is a major exporter of oil, mainly to Italy, Germany, France, and Spain. The country is also a member of the Organization of Petroleum Exporting Countries (OPEC). Because Libya is a member of OPEC, its crude oil production is subject to a quota. In 2010, Libya's oil output averaged an estimated 1.79 million barrels per day. Domestic oil demand in 2010 was estimated at an average of 289,000 barrels per day. Net exports that year were estimated at 1.39 million barrels per day. Libya's domestic refining sector is made up of five refineries—Ras Lanuf, Az Zawiya, Tobruk, Brega, and Sarir.

In addition to oil, Libya has large proven reserves of natural gas, which as of 2010 were estimated by the Oil and Gas Journal to contain 55 trillion cu ft. However, these reserves are thought to be larger because they are largely unexplored and unexploited. Potential reserves have been placed by Libyan experts at 70–100 trillion cu ft. Libya is looking to expand its output of natural gas, in part as a replacement for oil in electric power generation, thus freeing up more oil for export, and for natural gas exports to Europe.

28 INDUSTRY

Libyan manufacturing industries developed significantly during the 1960s and 1970s, but fell far behind the petroleum sector of the economy in the 1980s. The refining sector was adversely affected by the UN embargo; several projects for expanding domestic refining were delayed. When UN sanctions were suspended in 1999, foreign oil companies showed a keen interest in investing in the exploration and production of oil in Libya. The 2011 ousting of the Qadhafi regime similarly resulted in renewed interest in investment in Libyan oil production sectors.

The petrochemicals industry is centered at the Marsá al-Burayqah plant, which produces methanol, ammonia, and urea. Although it operates well below capacity, the plant produces quantities of urea and ammonia that far exceed domestic demand. The Abu Kammash petrochemical complex produces ethylene dichloride (EDC), polyvinyl chloride (PVC), and vinyl chloride monomer (VCM). The iron and steel complex at Misrata began operations in 1990.

Libya's other manufacturing industries are small, lightly capitalized, and devoted primarily to the processing of local agricultural products (tanning, canning fruits and vegetables, milling flour, and processing olive oil), and to textiles, building materials, and basic consumer items. Handicraft products include carpets and rugs, silver jewelry, textiles, glassware, and leather goods. The industrial production growth rate was 2.7% in 2010.

29 SCIENCE AND TECHNOLOGY

The World Bank reported in 2009 that there were no patent applications in science and technology in Libya. There is a predominance of foreign labor in scientific and technical positions. Al-Fatah University at Tripoli (founded in 1973) has faculties of science, engineering, agriculture, medicine, pharmacy, veterinary medicine, nuclear engineering, and petroleum and mining engineering. The University of Garyounis at Benghazi (founded in 1955) has faculties of science and engineering. Bright Star University of Technology at Marsá al-Burayqah (founded in 1981) has faculties of basic engineering science, electrical and electronic engineering, mechanical and production engineering, chemical engineering, and petroleum engineering. Al-Arab Medical University at Benghazi was founded in 1984. Sabhā University has faculties of science, agriculture, medicine, and engineering. A posts and telecommunications institute is at Tripoli.

30 DOMESTIC TRADE

Tripoli, the leading port and transportation center, is the focus of trading activities. In 1978, Qadhafi announced that individuals should cease engaging in trade or marketing, and in 1979 the

Principal Trading Partners – Libya (2010)

(In millions of US dollars)

Country	Total	Exports	Imports	Balance
World	56,550.0	46,050.0	10,500.0	35,550.0
Italy	17,600.0	14,029.0	3,571.0	10,458.0
France	7,258.0	5,767.0	1,491.0	4,276.0
China	6,364.0	4,096.0	2,268.0	1,828.0
Germany	5,128.0	3,728.0	1,400.0	2,328.0
Spain	4,397.0	4,030.0	367.0	3,663.0
United States	2,720.0	1,988.0	732.0	1,256.0
Turkey	2,513.0	387.0	2,126.0	-1,739.0
United Kingdom	2,294.0	1,749.0	545.0	1,204.0
South Korea	1,707.0	155.0	1,552.0	-1,397.0
Tunisia	1,705.0	655.0	1,050.0	-395.0

(…) data not available or not significant.

(n.s.) not specified.

SOURCE: *2011 Direction of Trade Statistics Yearbook,* New York: United Nations, 2011.

Balance of Payments – Libya (2010)

(In millions of US dollars)

Current Account		**16,801.0**
Balance on goods	24,376.0	
Imports	-24,559.0	
Exports	48,935.0	
Balance on services	-5,717.0	
Balance on income	-30.0	
Current transfers	-1,828.0	
Capital Account		...
Financial Account		**-10,339.0**
Direct investment abroad	-2,722.0	
Direct investment in Libya	1,784.0	
Portfolio investment assets	-4,396.0	
Portfolio investment liabilities	...	
Financial derivatives	...	
Other investment assets	-4,889.0	
Other investment liabilities	-116.0	
Net Errors and Omissions		**-2,292.0**
Reserves and Related Items		**-4,170.0**

(…) data not available or not significant.

SOURCE: *Balance of Payment Statistics Yearbook 2011,* Washington, DC: International Monetary Fund, 2011.

31 FOREIGN TRADE

Libya imported $24.73 billion worth of goods and services in 2010, while exporting $41.8 billion worth of goods and services. Major import partners in 2010 were Italy, 16.3%; China, 10.3 %; Turkey, 9.7%; France, 6.8%; Germany, 6.4%; South Korea, 6.2%; Egypt, 5.7% and Tunisia, 4.8%. As of 2010, its major export partners were Italy, 31.6%; France, 13%; China, 9.2%; Spain, 9.1%; Germany 8.4% and the United States, 4.5%. Libya has long enjoyed a favorable trade balance because of exports of crude oil. Crude petroleum and petroleum products make up the majority of Libya's export commodity market. Other exports include natural and manufactured gas, hydrocarbons, and chemicals.

32 BALANCE OF PAYMENTS

In 2010 Libya had a foreign trade surplus of $17.1 billion, amounting to 18.9% of GDP. Due to Libya's dependence on oil exports, the balance of trade and current accounts balance fluctuate widely based on international oil prices. The current account balance was a surplus equal to 15% of GDP in 2009, but it was less than half that of the 2008 surplus (38.3%), as the 2008–09 global financial crisis sent many European countries into recession and weakened world demand in Libya's primary export market.

33 BANKING AND SECURITIES

The Central Bank of Libya, established in 1956, supervises the national banking system, regulates credit and interest, and issues bank notes. It also regulates the volume of currency in circulation, acts as a banker to the government, provides clearinghouse facilities for the country's commercial banks, and administers exchange control. In 2010, the discount rate, the interest rate at which the central bank lends to financial institutions in the short term, was 9.52%. Libya formerly had branches of many Arab, Italian, and British commercial banks; they were nationalized in 1969. The government ruled that 51% of the capital of each should be taken over by the government, which paid the value of this share. Thus, the Banco di Roma became Umma Bank, Barclays Bank eventually became Jamahiriya Bank, and the Banco di Sicilia became the Sahara Bank. The commercial department of the Central Bank was merged with two small banks to form the National Commercial Bank. In 1972, a reorganization of the commercial banks left the Jamahiriya and Umma banks owned by the Central Bank of Libya; two other institutions, the Sahara Bank and the Wahda Bank, were jointly owned by the Central Bank and private interests.

The National Agricultural Bank, established in 1957, provides advice and guidance on agricultural problems, advances loans to farm cooperatives, and generally assists the agricultural community. The Industrial and Real Estate Bank, founded in 1965, made loans for building, food-processing, chemical, and traditional industries; later it was divided into the Savings and Real Estate Bank and the Development Bank. A decree in 1966 abolished interest on loans made by the government development banks. In 1972/73, the government created the Libyan Arab Foreign Bank, later renamed Jamahiriya Foreign Bank, owned by the Central Bank of Libya, to invest in foreign countries. In 1981, its role in foreign investment was taken over by the Libyan Arab Foreign Investment Co.

private import-export trade was banned. In 1981, all shops were closed and replaced by huge supermarkets with stocks purchased by the state. Until 2011, about a dozen basic commodities were price-subsidized; a rationing system had been established in 1984. Because of an acute shortage of consumer goods, including food staples, some private stores were allowed to reopen by 1987. Under Qadhafi, the nation depended heavily on imports for basic food products. The sale of alcohol is prohibited; this was not expected to change in the post-Qadhafi era.

An annual international trade fair is held in Tripoli each March. Normal business hours are 7 a.m. to 2 or 2:30 p.m., Saturday through Thursday. Banks are open Saturday through Thursday from 8:30 a.m. to 12:30 p.m. in winter and from 8 a.m. to 12 p.m. in summer. Summer banking hours also include 4 to 5 p.m., Saturday through Wednesday.

On 15 March 2012, the Libyan stock exchange reopened for the first time since the fall of Qadhafi in 2011. The reopening of the exchange, which included 10 companies and an estimated capitalization of $3 billion, was extolled by the TNC as a sign of the country's return to political and economic stability. Publicly traded firms in Libya were comprised almost entirely of banks and insurers, with the lone exception of a cement company. Oil, telecommunications, and real estate firms were expected to join the exchange later in 2012. Foreign investors were permitted to hold up to a 10% stake in Libyan enterprises.

34 INSURANCE

During the Qadhafi era, all classes of insurance were available through the Libya Insurance Co. and Al-Mukhtar Insurance Co., both state enterprises. All licensed vehicles require third-party liability insurance, and all imported goods must be insured.

35 PUBLIC FINANCE

In 2010 the budget of Libya included $42.31 billion in public revenue and $38.92 billion in public expenditures. Public debt was 3.3% of GDP, with $6.386 billion of the debt held by foreign entities. Under Qadhafi, there were two budgets, one for ordinary expenses, the other (and larger one) for development. By law, 15% of total oil revenue was put aside yearly into the country's reserves, while 70% of the remainder went to development expenditures. All non-oil revenues were assigned to cover ordinary expenditures, and any shortfall was made up by transferring some of the petroleum revenues from the development budget. If funds from petroleum revenues were not sufficient to cover development expenses, planned projects were postponed. Although the Qadhafi government used part of its oil revenue to finance internal development (new schools, hospitals, roads), much was wasted.

36 TAXATION

Prior to the 2011 revolution, individual income taxes were levied at different rates for income from real estate, agriculture, commerce, industry, crafts, independent professions, and wages and salaries. Corporate taxes ranged from 20 to 60%. Also levied were a 16.7% royalty on petroleum production, a general income tax of up to 90%, and a Jihad tax. Indirect taxes were mainly sales taxes applied at various rates.

37 CUSTOMS AND DUTIES

Qadhafi's government maintained extremely tight import controls, even by regional standards, making Libya a difficult place to do trade. Libya utilized a single-column tariff schedule. Goods from all countries were subject to the same duties. Also levied were customs surcharges totaling 15% of the application customs duties. Almost all customs duties were ad valorem.

38 FOREIGN INVESTMENT

Foreign direct investment (FDI) in Libya was a net inflow of $1.71 billion according to World Bank figures published in 2009. FDI represented 2.74% of GDP. Outside of the oil industry, foreign investment in Libya has been limited. Prior to 2011, no foreign investment was allowed in certain areas, including banking, insurance, domestic commerce, and foreign aid. A minimum of 51% of the capital of joint stock companies had to be held by Libyans, and the chairman of the board of directors was required to be a Libyan national. With the massive increase in oil revenues in the 1970s, Libya became a major exporter of capital. Economic cooperation agreements were signed with many African countries, and in 1976 Libya purchased 10% of the shares of the Italian auto company Fiat; it sold its Fiat holdings in 1986 for about $3 billion.

39 ECONOMIC DEVELOPMENT

Under Libya's first five-year development plan (1963–68), several long-run measures were taken to raise industrial production and to expand and improve the quality of agriculture. Development plans through 1980 continued to prioritize agricultural development. The 1981–85 development plan called for investment primarily in industry (23%), followed by agriculture (18%). A drop in oil income caused a contraction in planned projects, however.

Libya increased its deposits in foreign banks in 1986, while at the same time reducing its outstanding debt. Deposits rose and fell based on oil prices, which were particularly high during the 1990–91 Persian Gulf Crisis. The economy was weakened by a US asset freeze that totaled $1 billion in 1994. The 1999 lifting of sanctions saw increased foreign investment.

In 2003, the government planned to diversify the economy away from its total dependence on oil. Tourism was one sector targeted for development. The Tourism Development Bank, with 80% of its shares held by the private sector, was one example of this initiative. During the 2000s Qadhafi also urged Libyans to undertake investment projects such as road and port construction, as well as communication and industrial production projects. Qadhafi reiterated the need to establish people's socialism as the foundational economic structure of society, whereby companies would not be owned by the state, but by the people who run them, assisted by foreign investors if necessary. In July 2004, Libya applied for membership in the WTO; as of late 2012 Libya had the status of a WTO observer. The goal of increasing oil production to 3 million barrels per day by 2012 was unlikely to be met.

40 SOCIAL DEVELOPMENT

Under Qadhafi's legal system, all employees were entitled to sickness, invalid, disability, death, and maternity benefits and unemployment payments. The cost of these programs was shared by employers, employees, and the government. Survivor benefits were paid to widows, siblings, or sons. Rehabilitation programs were provided for sick and disabled employees to provide them with new employment opportunities. Lump sum grants were provided for maternity, births, and funerals. There were no statutory benefits for unemployment, and there were limited family benefits under Social Care Fund legislation.

Despite a constitutional proclamation providing equality for women, customary Islamic restrictions still applied in 2011. Women were granted full legal rights, but few women worked outside of the home, and those who did remained in low-paid positions. There is evidence to suggest that younger, urban women are gradually becoming more emancipated. Younger women in urban areas have largely discarded the veil, although in rural areas it is still widely used. Women must obtain their husband's permission in order to leave the country. Violence against women remains a serious problem and is not discussed publicly.

There have been many reports of continuing human rights violations, including torture. Under Libyan law, persons could be detained incommunicado for unlimited periods, and the government defended its practice of imprisoning political dissenters. Under Qadhafi, citizens did not have the right to legal counsel or to fair public trials. The government discriminated against ethnic and tribal minorities, and restricted freedom of speech, press, movement, assembly, religion, and association. The TNC has faced allegations of human rights violations, although as of late 2011, no charges against the rebels had been filed.

41 HEALTH

According to the CIA, life expectancy in Libya was 75 years in 2011. The country spent 3.0% of its GDP on healthcare, amounting to $417 per person. There were 19 physicians, 68 nurses and midwives, and 37 hospital beds per 10,000 inhabitants. The fertility rate was 2.6, while the infant mortality rate was 17 per 1,000 live births. In 2008 the maternal mortality rate, according to the World Bank, was 64 per 100,000 births. It was estimated that 98% of children were vaccinated against measles. The CIA calculated HIV/AIDS prevalence in Libya to be about 0.3% in 2009.

Widespread diseases include typhoid, venereal diseases, and infectious hepatitis. With the assistance of the World Health Organization, Libya has eradicated malaria, once a major problem. Tuberculosis is still prevalent.

42 HOUSING

Increasing urbanization has created slum conditions in the major cities. There have been slum clearance and building projects since 1954. Postponement of housing projects occasionally led to public protests and illegal occupation of partially completed units, which occurred in January 2011, shortly before the broader uprising against Qadhafi. Low-income families have been allowed to buy ready-made houses from the state at 10% of cost or to build their own homes with interest-free loans. Real estate was the main area of private investment until 1978, when most tenants were made owners of their residences. The state paid full compensation to landlords for confiscated property and resold it to tenants at subsidized prices. As of 2008, an estimated 97% of urban dwellers had access to improved sanitation facilities.

43 EDUCATION

Overall, the CIA estimated that Libya had a literacy rate of 82.6% in 2003 (most recent information available as of March 2012). When Libya attained independence, about 90% of its population was illiterate, and there were few university graduates. Since then, the government has invested heavily in education, which is free at all levels. In 1985, the number of years of compulsory schooling was increased from six to nine years. Many students are enrolled in kindergarten programs of one or two years. Basic (primary) education covers nine years of study. This is followed by four years of specialized secondary education or four years of vocational school. The academic year runs from September to June. In 2009 gross primary school enrollment, which compares the total number of students enrolled to the number of children that are age-eligible, was 107%. Gross secondary school enrollment was 68%.

About 90% of male students completed primary school, and 87% of female students completed primary school.

The two main universities are Al-Fatah University and University of Garyounis. The Bright Star University of Technology at Marsá al-Burayqah was founded in 1981. There are also two higher institutes of technology and one of mechanical and electrical engineering.

As of 2003, public expenditure on education was estimated at 2.7% of GDP.

44 LIBRARIES AND MUSEUMS

The National Library in Benghazi holds 150,000 volumes, including the official documents of the Arab League. The public library in Benghazi has 14,000 volumes. Libya's largest library, with 295,000 volumes, is at the University of Garyounis; the Government Library in Tripoli has 37,000 volumes. The National Archives, which have an extensive collection of documents relating to the history of Tripolitania under Ottoman rule, are in Tripoli. In addition, France and Italy maintain cultural centers with libraries in the national capital. The Libyan Studies Center in Tripoli holds 100,000 volumes.

The museums exhibit mainly antiquities excavated from various Greek, Roman, Byzantine, and Arabic sites. The Department of Antiquities is responsible for all museums and archaeological sites in the country. Tripoli houses the Archaeological Museum, Epigraphy Museum, Ethnographic Museum, Natural History Museum, Prehistory Museum, and Islamic Museum. There are other museums, mainly archaeological, at Cyrene, Homs, Gaigab, Germa, Leptis Magna, Tokrah, Zanzur, Marsa Susah, and Sabrata.

45 MEDIA

In 2010, the CIA reported that there were 1.228 million telephone landlines in Libya. In addition to landlines, there were 5 million mobile cell phones in use in 2009. Mobile phone subscriptions averaged one per person. There were 16 FM radio stations, 3 AM radio stations, and 3 shortwave radio stations. Under Qadhafi, postal, telephone, and wireless services were owned and operated by the government. The Socialist People's Libyan Arab Jamahiriya Broadcasting Corp. broadcasted on radio in Arabic and English, and on television in Arabic, English, Italian, and French. In 2010, Libya had 12,432 Internet hosts. As of 2009, there were some 353,900 Internet users in Libya.

Prior to 2011, there were three major daily newspapers. *Al-Fair Al-Jadeed* (*New Dawn*) was published in Tripoli. The other dailies included *Al-Jihad* and *Libyan Press Review*. All print media was owned by the government. Qadhafi's government restricted all expression and opinion on matters deemed crucial to the regime. All political activities, including publication and broadcasting, which were not officially approved were banned. Vague laws existed by which any speech or expression could be interpreted as illegal.

46 ORGANIZATIONS

There are chambers of commerce in Tripoli and Benghazi. Until 2011, Libya had few nongovernment organizations. Membership in an illegal organization was made a capital offense in 1975. Youth organizations included the General Union of Great Jamahiriya Students, which had a membership consisting of all Libyan students registered at both secondary and tertiary educational institutions throughout the country. Prior to 2011, there was also a Libyan Public Scout and Girl Guide movement. Several sports associations and clubs were active throughout the country. The Gaddafi Charity Foundation encouraged volunteer efforts in social welfare and human rights programs. The Red Crescent Society and Caritas had active national chapters.

47 TOURISM, TRAVEL, AND RECREATION

The *Tourism Factbook*, published by the UN World Tourism Organization, reported 34,000 incoming tourists to Libya in 2007; they spent a total of $190 million. There were 27,334 hotel beds available in Libya. The estimated daily cost to visit Tripoli (Tarabulus), the capital, was $448. The cost of visiting other cities averaged $160. Tourists are attracted to Libya's climate, extensive beaches, and magnificent Greek and Roman ruins. However, the disruption of the 2011 uprising has hindered Libyan tourism. Under Qadhafi, visitors were required to register at the nearest police station within three days of arrival to avoid problems either during their stay or when departing.

48 FAMOUS PERSONS

As Roman emperor, Septimius Severus (r. 193–211) was responsible for initiating an extensive building program at his native Leptis Magna. Muhammad bin 'Ali as-Sanusi (1780?–1859), the founder of the Sanusi order, established its headquarters in Cyrenaica in the 1840s. Muhammad Idris al-Mahdi as-Sanusi (1890–1983), his descendant, was Libya's first king, ruling the country from its independence until he was deposed in 1969. Col. Mu'ammar Muhammad al-Qadhafi (1942–2011) became the actual ruler of the country at that time and led Libya until his death. Omar al-Muntasser (1939–2001) became secretary-general of the GPC in 1987.

49 DEPENDENCIES

Libya has no territories or colonies.

50 BIBLIOGRAPHY

Cirincione, Joseph, Jon B. Wolfsthal, and Miriam Rajkumar. *Deadly Arsenals: Nuclear, Biological, and Chemical Threats.* 2nd ed. Washington, DC: Carnegie Endowment for International Peace, 2005.

Libya Investment and Business Guide: Strategic and Practical Information. Washington, DC: International Business Publications USA, 2012.

Matar, Khalil I. and Robert W. Thabit. *Lockerbie and Libya: A Study in International Relations.* Jefferson, NC: McFarland, 2004.

The Middle East. Washington, DC: CQ Press, 2005.

Morgan, Jason, and Toyin Falola. *Culture and Customs of Libya.* Westport, CT: Greenwood Publishing Group, 2010.

O'Sullivan, Meghan L. *Shrewd Sanctions: Statecraft and State Sponsors of Terrorism.* Washington, DC: Brookings Institution Press, 2003.

St. John, Ronald Bruce. *Historical Dictionary of Libya.* 4th ed. Lanham, MD: Scarecrow Press, 2006.

St. John, Ronald Bruce. *Libya and the United States: Two Centuries of Strife.* Philadelphia: University of Pennsylvania Press, 2002.

Vandewalle, Dirk J. *History of Modern Libya.* 2nd ed. New York: Cambridge University Press, 2012.

Zeilig, Leo, and David Seddon. *A Political and Economic Dictionary of Africa.* Philadelphia: Routledge/Taylor and Francis, 2005.

MADAGASCAR

Republic of Madagascar
République de Madagascar;
Repoblika n'i Madagaskar

CAPITAL: Antananarivo

FLAG: The flag consists of a white vertical stripe at the hoist flanked at the right by two horizontal stripes, the upper in red, the lower in green.

ANTHEM: *Ry Tanindrazanay Malala O (Our Beloved Fatherland).*

MONETARY UNIT: The Malagasy ariary (MGA) is the official currency of Madagascar. The ariary is only one of two circulating currencies in the world with division units not based on a power of ten, but instead each ariary consists of five iraimbilanja. On 1 January 2005 the ariary replaced the Malagasy franc. One Malagasy franc was valued at 0.2 ariarys (one iraimbilanja). There are coins of 1, and 2 iraimbilanja, MGA1, 2, 4, 5, 10, 20, 50, and notes of MGA100, 200, 500, 1000, 2000, 5000, 10000. MGA1 = US$0.0004485 (or US$1=MGA2229.67) as of January 2012.

WEIGHTS AND MEASURES: The metric system is generally used.

HOLIDAYS: New Year's Day, 1 January; Commemoration of 1947 Rebellion(Martyrs' Day), 29 March; Labor Day, 1 May; Independence and National Day, 26 June; All Saints' Day, 1 November; Christmas, 25 December; Anniversary of the Democratic Republic of Madagascar, 30 December. Movable religious holidays include Good Friday, Easter Monday, Ascension, and Pentecost Monday.

TIME: 3 p.m. = noon GMT.

¹LOCATION, SIZE, AND EXTENT

Situated off the southeast coast of Africa, Madagascar is the fourth-largest island in the world, with an area of 587,040 sq km (226,657 sq mi), extending 1,601 km (995 mi) NNE–SSW and 579 km (360 mi) ESE–WNW. Comparatively, the area occupied by Madagascar is slightly less than twice the size of Arizona. It is separated from the coast of Africa by the Mozambique Channel, the least distance between the island and the coast being about 430 km (267 mi). The coastline of Madagascar is 4,828 km (3,000 mi). Madagascar claims a number of small islands in the Mozambique Channel—the Îles Glorieuses, Bassas da India, Juan de Nova, and Europa—covering about 28 sq km (11 sq mi), which are administered by France.

Madagascar's capital city, Antananarivo, is located near the center of the island.

²TOPOGRAPHY

Madagascar consists mainly of a block of crystalline rocks. It is generally described as a plateau, rising sharply from the narrow plain of the east coast and descending in a series of steps to the strip of sedimentary rocks along the west coast. The high plateau is much indented and, on the eastern edge, cut by deep gorges and waterfalls.

There are numerous volcanic outcrops that produce heights over 1,800 m (6,000 ft); the highest point is Mount Maromokotro (2,876 m/9,436 ft) in the Tsaratanana Massif. The eastern coast is almost straight and has very few anchorages. Behind its coral beaches there is an almost continuous line of lagoons from Foulpointe to Farafangana. These are linked by manmade channels to

form an inland waterway called the Pangalanes Canal. The island's major rivers flow westward and are navigable for about 160 km (100 mi) inland.

³CLIMATE

The climate of the eastern and northwestern coasts is dominated by the almost constant blowing of the southeasterly trade winds, which carry heavy rains during the austral winter (May to September). The central plateau and the western coast are sheltered from these winds but receive rain from the monsoon winds, which blow during the austral summer (October–April). Neither the trade winds nor the monsoons reach the southern part of the island, which consequently receives little rain and is, in places, a semidesert. The central plateau enjoys a tropical mountain climate with well-differentiated seasons. Generally speaking, the climate throughout the island is moderated by altitude, with the coast being hotter (average temperatures 21–27°C/ 70–80°F) and wetter than the plateau (average temperatures 13–19°C/ 55–67°F). Toamasina (Tamatave), on the east coast, has 284 cm (112 in) of rainfall annually, while Antananarivo, inland, has about 140 cm (55 in). Occasional cyclones have been devastating.

⁴FLORA AND FAUNA

The flora and fauna of Madagascar have developed in isolation from those of Africa, and the flora is highly specialized. Scientists maintain that Madagascar was originally covered with evergreen forests in the wetter areas of the east and north, which gave place to savanna on the plateau and semiarid vegetation in the south. Much of the original vegetation was destroyed by burning, so that the evergreen forest is now found only in a narrow strip along the steep eastern edge of the plateau, from north to south. Where the forest was destroyed, it was replaced by bush known as savoka, especially in the narrow east coast plain. There are a few small patches of deciduous forest in the northwest and west and mangrove swamps are general along the northwest and west coasts. The greater part of the plateau has a covering of laterite and fertility is low. The extreme south is free of laterite, but lack of rainfall prevents the greater fertility from being of much practical use. The World Resources Institute estimates that there are 9,505 plant species in Madagascar.

The fauna is remarkable chiefly because of the presence of 28 species of lemur, a lower primate largely confined to Madagascar. The island has 32 species of chameleon. Among the species of birds, 105 are found nowhere else in the world. The same is true for about 80% of the island's flowering plants and more than 95% of its reptiles. Madagascar is also unusual in its lack of poisonous snakes and, except for recent introductions, useful mammals.

Madagascar is home to 165 mammal, 262 bird, 383 reptile, and 226 amphibian species. The calculation reflects the total number of distinct species residing in the country, not the number of endemic species. In 2011 a new bird species was discovered in Madagascar. The forest dwelling bird discovered in the Beanka rainforest was named *Mentocrex beankaensis* and can be distinguished from similar birds by its plumage and size. The bird is largely nocturnal and was therefore difficult to locate for study even after the first sightings.

5ENVIRONMENT

Erosion, caused by deforestation and overgrazing, is a serious problem in Madagascar. Many farmers burn off their old crops at the end of winter and damage surrounding forests. By 1994, 75% of Madagascar's forests had been eliminated. The World Resources Institute reported that Madagascar had designated 1.52 million hectares (3.76 million acres) of land for protection as of 2006. Water resources totaled 337 cu km (80.85 cu mi) while water usage was 14.96 cu km (3.59 cu mi) per year. Domestic water usage accounted for 3% of total usage, industrial for 2%, and agricultural for 95%. Per capita water usage totaled 804 cu m (28,393 cu ft) per year. Water pollution, caused mainly by sewage, is also a significant environmental problem in Madagascar. The Ministry of Animal Husbandry, Water, and Forests is the chief government agency with environmental responsibilities. The UN reported in 2008 that carbon dioxide emissions in Madagascar totaled 2,250 kilotons

According to a 2011 report issued by the International Union for Conservation of Nature and Natural Resources (IUCN), the number of threatened species included 65 types of mammals, 35 species of birds, 134 types of reptiles, 67 species of amphibians, 85 species of fish, 24 types of mollusks, 76 species of other invertebrates, and 280 species of plants. Endangered species in Madagascar include the Alaotra grebe, Madagascar pochard, Madagascar fish eagle, and seven species of lemur. There are nine extinct species, including Delalande's coua and the Malagasy hippo. Worldwide trade in endangered and extinct species has created a market for Madagascar's exotic snakes and tortoises. The looting and smuggling of these species has decimated animal habitats and caused severe ecological harm.

6POPULATION

The US Central Intelligence Agency (CIA) estimates the population of Madagascar in July 2011 to be approximately 21,926,221, which placed it at number 53 in population among the 196 nations of the world. In 2011, approximately 3.1% of the population was over 65 years of age, with another 43.1% under 15 years of age. The median age in Madagascar was 18.2 years. There were 0.99 males for every female in the country. The population's annual rate of change was 2.973%. The projected population for the year 2025 was 28,600,000. Population density in Madagascar was calculated at 37 people per sq km (96 people per sq mi).

The UN estimated that 30% of the population lived in urban areas, and that urban populations had an annual rate of change of 3.9%. The largest urban area was Antananarivo, with a population of 1.8 million.

7MIGRATION

Estimates of Madagascar's net migration rate, carried out by the CIA in 2011, amounted to zero. The total number of emigrants living abroad was 79,800, and the total number of immigrants living in Madagascar was 37,800. Since independence, government policy has been uniformly opposed to immigration in any form. The advent of independence led to some emigration of foreign nationals, but it was not until the early 1970s, when the government undertook policies of national control and nationalization of foreign businesses, that foreign residents began leaving in any appreciable numbers.

8ETHNIC GROUPS

The Malagasy people are the result of the intermingling of immigrants. The original immigrants are believed to have been members of an Afro-Malagasy race that lived on the East African littoral. Later arrivals were Africans, Arabs, and, much more recently, immigrants from Europe, China, and India. The general population can be divided into 18 tribes, with no single group holding a majority. Major ethnic groupings include the Malayo-Indonesian (including the Merina and related Betsileo) and the Cotiers (mixed African, Malayo-Indonesian, and Arab ancestry-the Betsimisaraka, Tsimihety, Antaisaka, and Sakalava). The Merina and Betsileo live in the central highlands and show evidence of Asian origin, while the coastal peoples, such as the Betsimisaraka, Tsimihety, and Sakalava, are of predominantly African origin. The Merina have been the ascendant group since the late 18th century. The course that colonialism took in Madagascar strengthened their domination of the political and intellectual life of the island. Resentment of the Merina and their dominant position by the other ethnic groups is still a source of social unrest. The Indo-Pakistani community is commonly referred to as the Karana. There were about 20,000 Karana in the country in 2004. There are also significant numbers of French, Creole, and Comoran peoples.

9LANGUAGES

The principal and official languages are French and Malagasy. Malagasy is a Malayo-Polynesian language which has different but mutually intelligible dialects and is spoken throughout Madagascar. The Merina dialect has come to be considered the standard literary form of the language. Instruction in French is preferred by the coastal peoples, as it avoids connotations of Merina cultural dominance.

10 RELIGIONS

Christianity was introduced to the Malagasy in the early 19th century. About 50% of the Malagasy are Christians, though most are believed to practice some type of indigenous religious beliefs in conjunction with Christianity. The most prominent denominations are Roman Catholicism, the Reformed Protestant Church of Jesus Christ in Madagascar (FJKM), Lutheranism, and Anglicanism. Other groups include Seventh-Day Adventists, Jehovah's Witnesses, and the Church of Jesus Christ of Latter-Day Saints.

A number of citizens practice indigenous beliefs exclusively. Although there are many variations in detail, nearly all of these traditional Malagasy share certain basic religious ideas, the central one being belief in the soul and its immortality. Besides the almighty (Andrianahary or Zanahary), secondary divinities are recognized, especially the earliest inhabitants of the island (Vazimba), legendary kings and queens, and other great ancestors. The burial places and other places of special significance in the lives of these secondary deities are objects of veneration and pilgrimages, during which special rites are performed.

Muslims, concentrated mostly in the north and northwest, account for between 10% and 15% of the population. There is also a small number of Hindus among the Indian population.

The constitution allows for freedom of religion and this right is generally respected in practice, but the government restricted the activities of some religious groups following the 2009 coup. All religious groups must register with the Ministry of Interior for legal status. The Council of Christian Churches in Madagascar (FFKM) is an organization of Roman Catholic, Reformed, Lutheran, and Anglican officials that have participated in a number of national programs addressing a wide variety of political and social issues. However, the group stepped back somewhat from public action following the 2009 coup, since there were some members that did not support new regime. Some religious leaders have been harassed, detained, arrested, assaulted, and even killed by police and state security forces following the 2009 coup, primarily in relation to their political stand against the government.

11 TRANSPORTATION

Madagascar's railway system largely consisted of four main railroads, all publicly operated. These run from Toamasina to Antananarivo, with a branch from Moramanga to Lake Alaotra; from Antananarivo to Antsirabe; and from Fianarantsoa to Manakara on the east coast.

The CIA reports that Madagascar has a total of 65,663 km (40,801 mi) of roads as of 2003, of which 7,617 km (4,733 mi) are paved .The main roads radiate from Antananarivo to Mahajanga and Antsiranana, to Toamasina, to Fianarantsoa, and to Ihosy, from which one branch goes to Toliara (Tuléar) and another to Tolänaro (Fort Dauphin). The road from Antananarivo to Fianarantsoa is tarred, as are portions of the other main routes. There are 27 vehicles per 1,000 people in the country.

The three major ports are Toamasina, Nosy Be, and Mahajanga; Toliara and Antsiranana are also important. There are at least 13 other ports, engaged mainly in coastal trade. Madagascar has approximately 600 km (373 mi) of navigable waterways.

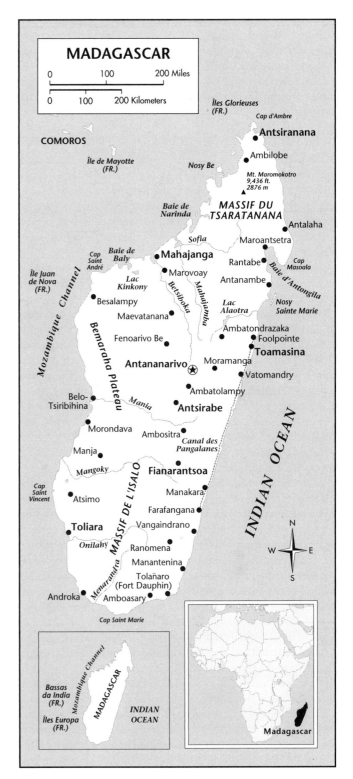

LOCATION: 43°12′ to 50°17′E; 11°57′ to 25°38′ S. TERRITORIAL SEA LIMIT: 12 miles.

There was considerable freight traffic along the Pangalanes Canal, which runs parallel to the east coast from Toamasina to Farafangana for a distance of 700 km (435 mi). As of 2009, the merchant fleet consisted of eight vessels of 1,000 gross registered tons (GRT) or more.

In 2011 there were 84 airports, which transported 499,526 passengers in 2009 according to the World Bank. The principal international airport is in Ivato, near Antananarivo. Air Madagascar (the national airline), Air France, Alitalia, Aeroflot, Air Mauritius, and Air Tanzania also provide international service. Air Madagascar, which is owned partly by Air France, also services internal locations.

12 HISTORY

Madagascar had no human inhabitants until about 2,500 years ago, when immigrants came, probably from Indonesia via the East African coast. This wave of immigration continued for at least 1,000 years, and there was also an influx of African peoples. Additional immigrants from Africa, Arabia, and the Persian Gulf and, much later, from Europe, India, and China did little more than supplement a fully settled population.

The earliest written histories of the Malagasy are the *sorabe*, in the Malagasy language using Arabic script. A Portuguese ship sighted the island and sailed along the coast in 1500. In 1502, the island was named Madagascar by the Portuguese, after the island of the same name originally reported by Marco Polo. During the 16th and 17th centuries, attempts were made by the Portuguese, British, Dutch, and French to establish settlements. All these efforts failed, and Madagascar became the lair of pirates who lived on Nosy Sainte Marie and intermarried with the Malagasy.

Among the Malagasy themselves, three main kingdoms appeared to be that of the Merina in the central plateau, the Sakalava in the west, and the Betsimisaraka in the east. Under King Andrianampoinimerina (r. 1787–1810), the foundations were laid for the primacy of the Merina kingdom.

Andrianampoinimerina was succeeded in 1810 by Radama I, his son, under whose guidance the Merina kingdom extended its rule over the major portions of the island (especially over the Betsimisaraka kingdom and the south). Radama welcomed Europeans to assist in the modernization of the kingdom and to further his conquests. On Radama's death in 1828, he was succeeded by his wife, Ranavalona I, whose hostility to the innovations in her husband's reign led to a persecution of the Malagasy Christians and eventually to the expulsion of the Europeans after an Anglo-French bombardment of Toamasina in 1845.

Radama II, who succeeded his mother in 1861, was sympathetic to the French but was murdered in 1863. Shortly after this, Rainilaiarivony, who was to become prime minister and consort to three successive queens, took control of the government. The last three decades of Malagasy independence during the 19th century were marked by continued attempts of those opposed to innovation to undermine the prime minister's authority. He therefore slowed modernization and tried to retain independence by seeking British friendship against the French. The latter claimed a protectorate over parts of the Sakalava kingdom by virtue of treaties made in 1840, and disputes over this claim and over French properties on the island resulted in a war in 1883 which ended in 1885 with a treaty giving the French control over Merina foreign policy.

The British recognized the French position under the terms of the Anglo-French Agreement of 1890, in exchange for French recognition of a British protectorate over Zanzibar. This exchange cleared the way for the French annexation of Madagascar in 1896. Malagasy resistance, especially in the south, was not finally overcome until 1904, however. Gen. Joseph Gallieni, governor-general from 1896 to 1905, opened the first government schools (hitherto all schools had been in the hands of the missions), established a free medical service for Malagasy, encouraged the study of Malagasy language and customs by the creation of the Malagasy Academy (Académie Malgache), and introduced new tropical crops in order to promote economic development. The impress of his policies remained substantial until the end of World War II. His successors, career colonial officials, struggled to promote economic growth. However, their efforts were impeded by a combination of World War I, subsequent economic difficulties in France, and the prolonged depression of the 1930s, together with the absence of easily exploitable resources, the distance of Madagascar from its main markets, and the shortage of labor.

During World War II, the Vichy French retained control of Madagascar until it was occupied in 1942 by British troops to prevent its naval facilities from being used by the Japanese. In 1943, French administration was restored under Gen. de Gaulle's Free French government. Madagascar became a French overseas territory in 1946. All Malagasy thus became French citizens, but only a limited number were accorded the franchise (mainly those with some education or experience of European ways in the French civil services or armed forces). A Territorial Assembly was established, with some control of the budget. It was composed entirely of members indirectly elected by provincial assemblies. The latter were wholly elected bodies, but there were separate electorates (and separate seats) for the French citizens of metropolitan status (including Europeans, Réunionnais, and some Malagasy given such status) and for Malagasy citizens of local status. Although the latter had a majority of the seats in both provincial and territorial assemblies, the number of seats assigned to the metropolitan electorate was most disproportionate to its numerical strength. This system was denounced by the nationalists, who had secured a majority of the Malagasy seats in the Territorial Assembly as well as the three Malagasy seats in the French National Assembly.

In March 1947, a rebellion broke out, and for a time the French lost control of the east coast. Europeans and loyal Malagasy were murdered and roads cut. The suppression of the rebellion required substantial forces and took more than a year. Loss of life was estimated at 11,000. The nationalist movement was disrupted by the rebellion and subsequent repressions, but was not destroyed. A period of reform beginning in 1956 resulted in abolition of the dual electorate system, placed Malagasy in important government positions, and led to the rebirth of serious political activity.

The End of French Rule

In the referendum of 28 September 1958, Madagascar overwhelmingly voted for the new French constitution and became an autonomous republic in the new French Community. As the Malagasy Republic, it became a sovereign independent nation on 26 June 1960 and on 20 September 1960 was elected to UN membership.

The constitution that was adopted in October 1958 and amended in June 1960 provided Madagascar with a strong presidential form of government. The president, Philibert Tsiranana, remained in power until May 1972, when there were riots throughout Madagascar. The protests were led by a nationalist, leftist coalition of students, teachers, laborers, and urban unemployed. The repression that followed these demonstrations led to the fall of the Tsiranana government on 18 May. Gen. Gabriel Ramanantsoa was immediately asked to form a nonpolitical "government of national unity," which was composed of 11 ministers (5 military and 6 civilian). Ramanantsoa effectively destroyed the coalition by raising the minimum wages, providing strike pay, annulling the head and cattle taxes, prosecuting corrupt officials, and introducing price and currency controls. The new government also broke diplomatic ties with South Africa, established relations with the Communist bloc, withdrew from the franc zone, and arranged for the withdrawal of French military forces under new cooperation agreements with France.

On 5 February 1975, following a period of social and ethnic unrest, Ramanantsoa was replaced as head of state by Col. Richard Ratsimandrava, who was assassinated in an attempted coup six days later. A military Directorate composed of 18 officers was immediately formed and assumed all governmental authority. The Directorate was superseded on 13 June by the all-military Supreme Council of the Revolution, headed by Didier Ratsiraka, who had been minister of foreign affairs in the Ramanantsoa government.

In December 1975, a draft constitution was approved in a referendum by 95% of the voters and the Second Malagasy Republic, to be called the Democratic Republic of Madagascar, was proclaimed. Ratsiraka was installed as president on 4 January 1976, thus remaining head of state.

The new regime accelerated growing state control of the economy, and Madagascar turned to the former USSR and the Democratic People's Republic of Korea for military aid. By 1979, however, growing economic difficulties forced Ratsiraka to develop closer ties with the West. Unemployment, inflation, and scarcities of basic foodstuffs caused serious rioting and social unrest in the early 1980s. Ratsiraka was elected to a new term as president on 7 November 1982. During 1986–87, the government was shaken by student protests against educational reforms, rioting in the port of Toamasina, attacks on Indo-Pakistani enterprises in four major urban centers, and famine in the south because of food-supply problems. By early 1987, the governing coalition appeared to be unraveling. On May Day, four of the parties called for the resignation of the government and early elections.

Democratization Unleashed

In July 1992, after seven weeks of pro-democracy protests, Ratsiraka finally agreed to dissolve the cabinet and begin talks with the opposition. He also offered to hold a referendum on a new constitution by the end of 1992. Although he rejected demonstrators' demands that he resign, Ratsiraka released Albert Zafy, a popular opponent, and offered to form a coalition government with opposition leaders. Protests continued, and government troops fired on demonstrators in Antananarivo, killing as many as 50 people. In August, Ratsiraka asked his prime minister, Guy Willy Razanamasy, to form a new government and to "install democracy." By November, Ratsiraka agreed to share power with a transitional government headed by Zafy, his main rival. Ratsiraka's Revolutionary Supreme Council stepped down from power.

The democratization process survived an attempted coup on 29 July 1992, led by a faction of the Active Forces known as the Lifeblood Committee. On 19 August 1992, a new constitution was approved by national referendum. Ratsiraka's supporters interfered with the voting, seeking greater provincial autonomy. However

the interior peoples, especially the Merina, strongly supported the new constitution. This was followed on 25 November by a presidential election, which a team of foreign observers deemed free and fair. Zafy defeated Ratsiraka, but without an absolute majority. In a runoff election on 10 February 1993, Zafy got 67% of the vote to Ratsiraka's 33%. The president was installed in March, amid violent confrontations between Ratsiraka's supporters and government forces.

Parliamentary elections were held in June 1993 for the new National Assembly. Twenty-five parties won representation with Zafy's Forces Vives (FV) taking the largest block of seats-48. Eight parties had more than five seats. The National Assembly elected Francisque Ravony prime minister—55 votes to 45 for Roger Ralison (FV), and 35 for former Maoist leader, Manandagy Rakotonirina.

Communal (territorial) elections, the first step in creation of the Senate, were held in November 1995, but President Zafy's day in the sun was short-lived. He was impeached in September 1995, and then defeated by Ratsiraka in competitive elections in December 1996. On February 10, 1997, Ratsiraka became the second African head of state, after Mathieu Kérékou of Benin, to have lost and then reclaimed the presidency via competitive elections.

An extensive revision of the 1992 constitution was approved narrowly in a March 1998 constitutional referendum. International observers found the conduct of the referendum generally free and fair, but problems involving the compilation of voter lists, distribution of electoral cards, and other issues led to charges of fraud and manipulation. The revised constitution reduced checks and balances and strengthened the presidency at the expense of the National Assembly. Parliamentary elections held in May 1998 generally were free and fair, but there were credible complaints of electoral fraud. In November 1999, municipal elections were held for 1,392 mayoral posts and 20,000 council seats.

After 29 years of dormancy, the Senate reconvened in May 2001. However, a national crisis ensued following the 16 December 2001 presidential election when challenger Marc Ravalomanana claimed to have won the election outright over incumbent Didier Ratsiraka, thereby eliminating the need for a run-off. The official results gave Ravalomanana 46.2%, forcing him into a runoff with Ratsiraka (40.9%). Albert Zafy (Rasalama) claimed 5.4%, Herizo Razafimahaleo 4.2%, D. Rajakoba 1.8%, and P. Rajaonary 1.6%. With Ratsiraka refusing to step down, Ravalomanana and his supporters mounted strikes and protests culminating in Ravalomanana's seizure of the presidency in February 2002. Operating from his provincial fiefdom, Toamasina, Ratsiraka commanded his armed forces to lay siege to the capital, blowing up key bridges and cutting off foodstuffs and other critical supplies. The violence resulted in more than 70 deaths. US recognition of Ravalomanana in June 2002 was followed by international approval, forcing Ratsiraka in July 2002 to seek exile in France ending seven months of political and economic chaos in the country.

Ravalomanana's first 18 months in power were marked by his consolidation of power, which was countered by a reorganization of opposition parties. None of the opposition parties, however, presented a serious challenge to Ravalomanana's power. Indeed, the president's first moves were to punish supporters of the old government including the last prime minister, Andrianarivo, who was detained and put on trial. However, under pressure from

Zafy's forces, Ravalomanana pardoned those serving sentences of less than three years and invited others to apply for amnesty. The influential Madagascar Council of Churches led the movement for reconciliation resulting in broad support for compromise.

In December 2002, the president's party, Tiako-I-Madagasikara (TIM), dominated national assembly elections. However, in the November 2003 municipal polls, TIM's opponents gained 18 of 45 of the most important mayoral posts up for election. The results speak to the importance of local power bases in Madagascar.

Internationally, Ravalomanana was able to restore donor confidence in the economy, largely through the leadership of his prime minister, Jacques Sylla. Gradually, the administration established productive relations with African states that were expected to lead to Madagascar's admission to the Southern Africa Development Community (SADC). Moreover, Madagascar qualified as one of the first African states to be eligible for funding under the US Millennium Challenge Account (MCA). The MCA agreement was signed in early 2005. France and the United Kingdom have also been supportive of the Ravalomanana government.

Ravalomanana won a second term in 2006 but faced ongoing criticism from opposition leaders. Leading into the presidential elections, he resisted European calls for a new electoral law and a more independent elections commission. In January 2009, following ongoing anti-government protests, the mayor of Antananarivo and opposition leader, Andry Rajoelina, stepped forward, calling for President Ravalomanana's resignation. Ravalomanana responded by having Rajoelina ousted from his mayoral post and setting security forces against pro-Rajoelina demonstrators in the capital. A faction of the military mutinied in support of Rajoelina and seized the president's office in March 2009. President Ravalomanana offered his resignation, ceding power to the military, which immediately installed Rajoelina as president. Shortly thereafter, an arrest warrant was issued against Ravalomanana, who fled to Swaziland. Thousands of citizens took to the streets as supporters of both Rajoelina and Ravalomanana clashed in protests that lasted through several weeks. In April 2009, Ravalomanana supporters, including several members of the military, proclaimed their own government and the expected return of Ravalomanana as their leader.

The international community condemned the actions of the pro-Rajoelina military takeover and no country officially recognized the Rajoelina government. The African Union and the Southern African Development Community (SADC) both suspended the membership of Madagascar, citing an unconstitutional change of government. In August, leaders from Madagascar's four major political parties met to consider the formation of an interim government until the next presidential elections.

An agreement was finally reached in October 2009, when three cabinet posts were approved. Rajoelina was accepted as president, but only with the stipulation that he would not run in the next presidential election. Emmanuel Rakotovahiny was selected as vice president and Eugene Mangalaza was named prime minister. However, after failing to agree on who should fill several key positions in the new government, Rajoelina formally rejected the power-sharing agreement in December 2009. He issued a presidential degree to dismiss the prime minister chosen in the agreement and replaced him with Colonel Albert Camille Vital, an officer in the army. President Rajoelina also declared that parliamentary elections would be held in March 2010. However, Rajoelina made no mention of a presidential ballot. Instead, Rajoelina said voters would get to choose a new prime minister and vote to approve Madagascar's new constitution. Under the provisions of the country's existing constitution, Rajoelina is five years too young to hold his office. The approval of a new constitution would be necessary for the legitimacy of his candidacy in presidential elections. When the March 2010 deadline passed with no elections, the African Union issued sanctions against Rajoelina and several of his key officials. These sanctions included travel restrictions and the freezing of foreign assets.

The referendum for constitutional reform finally came to a vote in November 2010. The electoral commission reported that the referendum had passed with 74% of the vote; voter turnout was estimated at more than 50%. New presidential and legislative elections, after several delays, were scheduled for March 2012. Omer Beriziky served as prime minister of Madagascar in 2011.

¹³GOVERNMENT

The constitution of 21 December 1975, like that of the First Republic, provided for a strong presidential system of government. The president was elected for a seven-year term and was both chief executive and head of state. The president was assisted by the Supreme Council of the Revolution (Conseil Supreme de la Révolution—CSR), which was to be "the guardian of the Malagasy Socialist Revolution." The president, as chairman of the CSR, named two-thirds of its members outright and chose the other third from a list submitted by the National People's Assembly. The premier, the designated head of government, was appointed by the president and assisted by a cabinet.

The 19 August 1992 constitution of the Third Republic provides for a head of state, the president, who is elected by universal suffrage to serve a five-year term. The president chooses a prime minister from a list of candidates nominated by the national assembly. The prime minister appoints the Council of Ministers.

The constitution provides for a two-chamber legislature—a 127-member national assembly (reduced from 160 members by a 2007 referendum) and a senate. Members of the national assembly are elected by universal suffrage to serve four-year terms. Regional assemblies elected by direct suffrage select two-thirds of the members of the 90-seat senate, with the remaining one-third appointed by the president for a four-year term. Suffrage is universal at age 18.

¹⁴POLITICAL PARTIES

Following World War II, the Democratic Movement for Malagasy Renewal (Mouvement Démocratique de la Rénouvation Malgache—MDRM), founded by several prominent nationalists, demanded that Madagascar be declared a free state within the French Union. The French, however, organized the island as an overseas territory, granting the vote to few Malagasy. In the wake of the 1947 rebellion, the leaders of the MDRM, whom the French accused of planning and leading the revolt, were convicted of treason and sentenced to death (later commuted to life imprisonment). Charges of French brutality in the suppression of the revolt, however, gained considerable sympathy for the nationalist cause.

After independence, the Social Democratic Party of Madagascar and the Comoros (Parti Social Démocrate de Madagascar et des Comores—PSD) became the dominant political organization in the Malagasy Republic. It was organized in 1957 under the leadership of Philibert Tsiranana, the son of a Tsimihety peasant, and advocated a gradual approach to independence. In the Assembly elections of September 1960, the PSD won 75 seats out of 107. In the 1965 and 1970 elections, it increased its representation to 104 seats. The PSD was supported principally by peasants and other conservative elements, and favored strong ties with France. Tsiranana, who became president in 1960, was reelected in 1965 and again in 1972, just prior to his overthrow. The only real alternative during this period was the pro-Soviet Party of the Congress of Independence (Ankoton'ny Kongresi'ny Fahaleorantenan Madagaskara—AKFM), founded in 1958.

Other parties represented regions, provinces, tribes, or religious groups, but displayed little national strength. The most significant of the regional parties was the Movement for the Independence of Madagascar (Mouvement National pour l'Indépendance de Madagascar—MONIMA) which was led by Monja Jaona from Toliara. It represented the more radical intellectuals and landless peasants of the south. As a result of its armed opposition to the central government in April 1971, which was quickly and harshly suppressed, MONIMA became a truly left-wing opposition movement with support among students and urban radicals. Though MONIMA was banned, these elements led the series of demonstrations against the Tsiranana regime that resulted in its fall in May 1972. The ban on MONIMA was lifted in June.

After the assassination of the new head of state, Richard Ratsimandrava, in February 1975, all political parties were banned. The new constitution institutionalized the ban by providing for the creation of a sole party, to be called the National Front for the Defense of the Révolution (Front National pour la Defense de la Révolution—FNDR).

In effect, however, the FNDR became an umbrella group under which parties survived as "revolutionary associations." MONIMA withdrew from the FNDR in 1977 but returned in 1981, bringing the number of parties in the FNDR to seven. The chief party was Ratsiraka's Vanguard of the Malagasy Revolution (Avant-garde de la Révolution Malgache—AREMA). On 29 May 1977, it won control of almost all provincial and local bodies, and on 30 June 1977, in an election in which voters were presented with a single FNDR list, AREMA won 112 Assembly seats to 16 for the PCI and 9 for two other parties.

In the presidential election of 7 November 1982, President Ratsiraka won reelection with 80.17% of the vote. His sole opponent, Monja Jaona, leader of MONIMA, was removed from the CSR and temporarily placed under house arrest after he called for a general strike to protest the election results. In elections in August 1983, AREMA again won a commanding majority in the Assembly. MONIMA left the FNDR in 1987.

Since the democratic changes of 1992 and 1993, numerous political organizations have operated in Madagascar. In 1991, Albert Zafy founded the National Union for Development and Democracy (UNDD). Zafy was supported in the 1993 elections by Forces Vive (FV), an informal alliance that included the UNDD and the AKFM-Fanavaozana, a breakaway group from the MFM (Mouvement pour le pouvoir prolétarien).

Following his defeat in the presidential elections of February 1993, Didier Ratsiraka created a new party, the Vanguard for Economic and Social Recovery (ARES—Avant Gardes pour le Redressement Économique et Social). Ratsiraka turned on his former policies by proposing a federalist arrangement that would give more autonomy to the provinces. In the elections of 17 May 1998, which were credibly free and fair, Ratsiraka was leading AREMA, now named the Association for the Rebirth of Madagascar, which took 62 seats, LEADER/Fanilo 15, AVI 14, RPSD 11, AFFA 6, MFM 3, AKFM/Fanavaozana 3, GRAD/Iloafo 1, Fihaonana 1, and independents 34 seats.

In the municipal elections on 14 November 1999, AREMA captured three of the six regional capitals, having previously held just one. The biggest losers were established opposition party candidates such as former president Albert Zafy, who was beaten in his own political stronghold of Antsiranana. Marc Ravalomanana, a 50-year-old businessman and a principal donor of funds to the AVI centrist party, won the mayorship of Antananarivo, the capital city. Although the vote was marred by poor organization, almost all the 1,392 mayorships and 20,000 council seats were contested by at least two candidates. Many of these were independents, which seemed to signal that local elections were no longer being run from national party headquarters in the capital.

In the 15 December 2002 parliamentary elections, Ravalomanana's I Love Madagascar (TIM) party captured a combined total of 125 out of 160 seats in parliament. The election results (minus presidential appointments) were as follows: TIM 103, FP 22, AREMA 3, LEADER/Fanilo 2, RPSD 5, TTS 2, HBM 1, and independents 22 seats. The opposition criticized the poll as manipulated by the president's party.

In the 2007 legislative elections, TIM won 106 seats in the national assembly; LEADER/Fanilo won only one seat and Independent candidates won 20 seats. Under the terms of a 2009 power-sharing agreement, new general elections were scheduled for 2011 but postponed until May 2012. A compromise deal left Rajoelina as interim president until the next elections, while also allowing the return from exile of ousted president Ravalomanana.

15 LOCAL GOVERNMENT

Prior to the Ravalomanana regime, Madagascar was divided into six provinces, subdivided into 28 regions comprising 148 departments, and further divided into nearly 1,400 communes. At the local level were some 11,393 fokontany (village or urban neighborhood organizations) with an elected president and council. All levels of the Malagasy state were organized in hierarchical fashion within the jurisdiction of the Ministry of the Interior.

During the 1996 campaign, former president Didier Ratsiraka promised to draft laws that would make provinces autonomous. He subsequently sponsored workshops to gather input and share ideas with regional leaders. This controversial plan transferred power from the central government to the provinces and municipalities, and to administrative subdivisions for tax collection, service provision, and development planning. However, it was widely feared that provincial autonomy would threaten Madagascar's political unity.

Ravalomanana introduced a new structure that makes 22 new regions the main administrative units. Consequently, the power of the six autonomous provinces was greatly reduced, which was reflected in their shrinking budgets. While the regional leaders are centrally appointed, the municipal mayors, who exercise considerable power, are elected by direct popular vote.

16 JUDICIAL SYSTEM

The Malagasy judicial system is based on the French tradition. During the 1960s and 1970s the nation began a move from a bifurcated judicial system (customary courts for most Malagasy and local courts for foreign residents and urbanized Malagasy) to a single judicial system. At the top of the judicial system is the Supreme Court in Antananarivo. Other courts include the Court of Appeal, also in Antananarivo; courts of first instance for civil and criminal cases; ordinary and special criminal courts; and military courts. There are also a High Court of Justice to try high officials and a High Constitutional Court. Military courts presided over by civilian magistrates hear cases involving national security.

The traditional courts (dina) continue to handle some civil disputes and recently have been used in criminal cases because of inconvenience and inadequacy of the formal court system. Decisions by dina are not subject to the formal procedural protections of the formal court system. In some cases, however, they may be challenged at the appeals court level. Dina's authority depends upon the mutual respect and consensus of the parties to abide by the ruling. Dina punishments are sometimes severe and include capital punishment.

The 1992 constitution guarantees an independent judiciary, and in practice the judiciary appears to be independent from the executive.

17 ARMED FORCES

The International Institute for Strategic Studies reports that armed forces in Madagascar totaled 13,500 members in 2011. The force is comprised of 12,500 from the army, 500 from the navy, and 500 members of the air force. Armed forces represent 0.2% of the labor force in Madagascar. . The paramilitary Gendarmerie National is the main force for the maintenance of public order and internal security. In 2011 defense spending totaled $194.1 million and accounted for 1% of GDP.

18 INTERNATIONAL COOPERATION

Madagascar was admitted to the UN on 20 September 1960 and is a member of ECA and several nonregional specialized agencies, such as the FAO, IAEA, the World Bank, UNESCO, UNHCR, UNIDO, and WHO. It is also a member of the WTO, the African Development Bank, the ACP Group, the Arab Bank for Economic Development in Africa, G-77, the African Union, Indian Ocean Commission, and COMESA. Madagascar is a member of the Nonaligned Movement. In environmental cooperation, the country is part of the Basel Convention, the Convention on Biological Diversity, Ramsar, CITES, the Kyoto Protocol, the Montréal Pro-

tocol, the Nuclear Test Ban Treaty, and the UN Conventions on the Law of the Sea, Climate Change, and Desertification.

19 ECONOMY

Madagascar is a poor country, with over 50% of the population falling below the poverty level. Its agriculture-based economy supports a majority of the labor force. There are substantial mineral deposits. Industry is centered on food processing. Though Madagascar has a considerable diversity of minerals, their remote locations have discouraged extraction. Chromite, graphite, and mica are exported along with gems such as topaz, garnets, and amethysts. Private mining interests have been invited to develop Madagascar's gold deposits, as well as ilmenite, zircon, rutile, nickel, platinum, and bauxite. There has also been renewed interest in Madagascar's oil potential. Madagascar is rich in biodiversity, and many plants and animals found there exist nowhere else in the world. Hence, ecotourism is a sector of the economy with great potential for development.

The agricultural sector, which accounted for 29.3% of GDP in 2010, is prone to cyclone damage and drought. Rice is the staple crop although Madagascar has sought to diversify crop production by promoting maize and potatoes. Cassava, bananas, and sweet potatoes are also important. Export crops are coffee, vanilla, and cloves, with coffee as the most important. The sugar sector has been revived with the help of French investments.

Madagascar sponsored an Export Processing Zone in 1991 and important investments have been made in tourism. Government efforts to strengthen the market economy have been erratic, while corruption and political instability have constrained growth. The country's infrastructure remains poor, with inadequate roads preventing the transportation of agricultural products from farm to market. Railroads and the port system are also undeveloped, although the telecommunications system is being revamped.

20 INCOME

The CIA estimated that in 2010 the GDP of Madagascar was $19.41 billion. The CIA defines GDP as the value of all final goods and services produced within a nation in a given year and computed on the basis of purchasing power parity (PPP) rather than value as measured on the basis of the rate of the exchange based on current dollars. The per capita GDP was estimated at $900. The annual growth rate of GDP was -2%. The average inflation rate was 8.1%. It was estimated that agriculture accounted for 26.5% of GDP, industry 16.7%, and services 56.8%. According to the World Bank, remittances from citizens living abroad totaled $10.3 million or about $0 per capita and accounted for approximately 0.1% of GDP.

The World Bank estimates that Madagascar, with 0.28% of the world's population, accounted for 0.03% of the world's GDP. By comparison, the United States, with 4.85% of the world's population, accounted for 22.51% of world GDP.

As of 2011 the most recent study by the World Bank reported that actual individual consumption in Madagascar was 75.6% of GDP and accounted for 0.04% of world consumption. By comparison, the United States accounted for 25.44% of world individual consumption. The World Bank also estimated that 46.5% of Madagascar's GDP was spent on food and beverages, 14.6% on housing and household furnishings, 3.1% on clothes, 3.4% on health, 2.4% on transportation, 0.3% on communications, 0.5% on recreation, 1.0% on restaurants and hotels, and -0.8% on miscellaneous goods and services and purchases from abroad.

The World Bank reports that in 2009, household consumption in Madagascar totaled $7 billion or about $318 per capita, measured in current US dollars rather than PPP. Household consumption includes expenditures of individuals, households, and nongovernmental organizations on goods and services, excluding the purchases of dwellings. It was estimated that household consumption was growing at an average annual rate of 0.8%.

21 LABOR

As of 2007, Madagascar had a total labor force of 9.504 million people. Both public and private sector workers have the right to establish and join labor unions of their choice. However, only 10% of the total force was unionized in 2010. Unions are required to register with the government, but authorization is customarily given. The law provides for collective agreements between employers and trade unions. Strikes are legally permitted.

Working conditions are regulated by the constitution and the labor code. The law sets the minimum working age at 14 (18 where the work is hazardous) but this minimum is enforced only in the small formal sector of the economy. In the large agricultural sector, many children work with their parents on family farms. The minimum wage was $35 per month in 2010, but this is not regularly enforced due to harsh economic realities. The standard legal workweek is 40 hours in industry and 42.5 hours in agriculture.

22 AGRICULTURE

Roughly 6% of the total land is arable or under permanent crops, and the country's major crops include coffee, vanilla, sugarcane, cloves, cocoa, rice, cassava (tapioca), beans, bananas, and peanuts. Although Madagascar's economy is essentially agricultural, much of the land is unsuitable for cultivation because of its mountainous terrain, extensive laterization, and inadequate or irregular rainfall. Only about 5% of the land area is cultivated at any one time. Large-scale plantations dominate the production of sisal, sugarcane, tobacco, bananas, and cotton, but, overall, Malagasy agriculture is dependent mainly on small-scale subsistence farmers cultivating less than one hectare (2.47 acres) of land.

A wide variety of food crops is grown. Rice is the staple of the Malagasy diet, though the yield is insufficient to meet the country's needs. Cereal production in 2009 amounted to 4.4 million tons, fruit production 996,768 tons, and vegetable production 357,612 tons.

23 ANIMAL HUSBANDRY

More than half the land is used for raising livestock. Cattle occupy an important place in the Malagasy economy. They are, however, more important as evidence of wealth than as sources of meat and dairy products. Only since the end of World War I has the consumption of meat become widespread among Malagasy, and now beef consumption is relatively high compared with other African countries. Cattle are employed to trample the rice fields and to draw plows and small carts. Most cattle are of the humped zebu type. Madagascar has vast natural pastures (60% of total land area) and is free of cattle diseases; there is, therefore, considerable potential for increasing production.

The UN Food and Agriculture Organization (FAO) reported that Madagascar dedicated 37.3 million hectares (92.2 million acres) to permanent pasture or meadow in 2009. During that year, the country tended 26 million chickens, 9.8 million head of cattle, and 1.4 million pigs. The production from these animals amounted to 134,676 tons of beef and veal, 64,424 tons of pork, 68,613 tons of poultry, 14,369 tons of eggs, and 525,522 tons of milk. Madagascar also produced 21,240 tons of cattle hide.

24 FISHING

Despite the island's long coastline, fishing is relatively undeveloped as an industry in Madagascar. On the east coast, with its stormy seas and absence of harbors, fishing is restricted mainly to the coastal lagoons and has been aptly characterized as virtually an extension of inland freshwater fishing. In the northwest, sardine and tuna are caught, and dried fish find a ready market. Dried fish also are prepared in the southwest. Lobsters, prawns, and shrimps are exported. Commercial maritime fishing is carried out by four joint-venture companies that operate along the northwest coast and account for most exports. Vessels from European Union nations are allowed to take up to 11,000 tons of tuna and prawns a year. French investment has helped establish a tuna cannery. Madagascar had 73 decked commercial fishing boats in 2008. The annual capture totaled 120,464 tons according to the UN FAO. The export value of seafood totaled $121.7 million.

25 FORESTRY

Approximately 22% of Madagascar is covered by forest. The main objectives of forestry policy have been to arrest further destruction of the woodlands; to pursue a systematic reforestation program in the interests of soil conservation and the domestic demand for construction timber; and to continue to meet the domestic need for firewood, of great importance in view of the absence of petroleum or exploited coal deposits. Eucalyptus, introduced at the end of the 19th century, acacias (especially mimosa), and various kinds of pine have been extensively used in reforestation. Raffia is the only forest product exported in any quantity. The UN FAO estimated the 2009 roundwood production at 277,330 cu m (9.79 million cu ft). The value of all forest products, including roundwood, totaled $36.2 million.

An illegal timber market has developed as so-called timber barons have begun to plunder the poorly protected national forests for valuable lumber that is then smuggled into China. Logs from rare rosewood trees are particularly valuable, in part because it is both scarce and protected. Unfortunately, the government has been unable, or some would say unwilling, to enforce laws that protect the environment and regulate the lumber trade. In 2009, the illegal operations amounted to an estimated $167 million. While the government has made some arrests and continues to consider new policies and actions to stop the enterprise, political instability has moved the focus of government to other pressing matters. Local environmental groups have also claimed that the government is getting a cut of the revenues from the operations, making it unlikely that the illegal trade will stop anytime soon. The desperate state of the economy contributes to the problem, as hundreds of poor citizens are more than willing to work for the timber barons, who pay as little as $2.50 per day for cutting and logging trees.

26 MINING

Madagascar's mining sector is primarily known for its production of chromite (chemical- and metallurgical-grade), as well as for the production and export of phlogopite mica and high-quality crystalline flake graphite. Madagascar is also a significant producer of ilmenite.

In 2009, output of chromite (marketable lumpy ore and gross weight concentrate) was 43,000 metric tons, down from 73,000 metric tons in 2008, and down significantly from the 105,000 metric tons produced in 2005, as a result of competition from South Africa. Graphite shipments (all grades) in 2009 totaled 5,000 metric tons. Output of mica (phlogopiute) in 2009 totaled 358 metric tons.

Deposits of gems (amazonite, amethyst, beryl, citrine, cordierite, garnet, sapphire, and tourmaline) have been exploited, as have those of ornamental stones (agate, apatite, and aragonite-69% of total ornamental stone production-calcite, jasper, and labradorite) and stones for electrical geodes (quartz-industrial, rose, and smoky-and celestine). In 2009, amethyst, emerald, ruby, and sapphire production totaled 20,000 kg, 55 kg, 30 kg, and 2,100 kg, respectively. Emerald is produced near Manamjary; ruby at Andilamena and Vatomandry; and sapphire at Ilakaka, Manombe, Marosely, and Sakara.

In 2009, Madagascar also produced mine gold (almost all was produced by artisanal miners and smuggled out of the country), natural abrasives, feldspar, kaolin, marble, marine salt, and dimension stone. Industrial calcite, clays, sand and gravel, and stone were presumably produced as well. Bastnaesite and monazite were not produced after 1996, although large deposits occurred of both, as well as of pyrochlore, and contained fergusonite, xenotine, euxenite, and uranium.

Extensive prospecting has led to the discovery of recoverable deposits of iron ore (910 million tons of resources; the 360-million-ton deposit near Soalala was the most valuable), bauxite (330–335 million tons in resources, found in the southeastern part of the country), nickel (168 million tons; the largest resources were in the Ambatovy lateritic deposit), coal, copper, lead, manganese, platinum, tin, titanium, zinc, and zirconium. Madagascar's considerable mineral potential has remained relatively unexploited; the main factors for this were the need for major infrastructure repairs; the country's poor power distribution systems; inadequate health and education facilities; and the inability to reform the economy and deal with chronic malnutrition, deforestation, land erosion, and population growth. After the government was overthrown in 2009 by a military coup, issuance of permits was suspended to consider revising mining contracts. Most of Madagascar's mining and mineral processing operations are privately owned, including gemstone, graphite, salt mines, and cement plants.

27 ENERGY AND POWER

Madagascar had no known reserves of oil, or natural gas as of 1 January 2012. Nor does the country have any recoverable coal reserves. As a result, Madagascar must rely upon imports to meet its fossil fuel needs, although the country does have a small refining capacity.

Madagascar's demand and imports of petroleum products in 2009 averaged 16,390 barrels per day. In 2012, Madagascar had no imports or consumption of natural gas. Madagascar's only oil refinery was established at Toamasina in 1966.

The World Bank reported in 2008 that Madagascar produced 1.11 billion kWh of electricity and consumed 1.14 billion kWh, or 52 kWh per capita.

28 INDUSTRY

Industry consists largely of processing agricultural products and textile manufacturing. The industrial centers are in the high plateau and near the Toamasina port. Industrialization has been severely hampered by inadequate internal transportation and a restricted local market. Industry accounted for 16.2% of GDP in 2010. Most plants operated at less than one-third of full capacity.

The majority of industrial enterprises process agricultural products: rice, sugar, flour, tobacco, tapioca, and sisal. In addition, there are some meat-packing plants. Urea- and ammonia-based fertilizers are produced in a plant that opened in 1985. Madagascar produces pulp for paper and cement. Other industrial enterprises include cotton spinning and weaving mills and three automobile assembly plants.

The government-owned petroleum refinery at Toamasina has a capacity of 15,000 barrels per day, but it has been operating at reduced capacity since it was hit by a hurricane in 1994. The petroleum sector was liberalized in 1996, and the state oil company SOLIMA was privatized in 2000. Oil and gas exploration holds great potential for the country.

Other industries include meat processing, soap, breweries, tanneries, sugar, textiles, glassware, cement, automobile assembly plant, paper, petroleum, and tourism.

29 SCIENCE AND TECHNOLOGY

Patent applications in science and technology as of 2009, according to the World Bank, totaled 1 in Madagascar. Public financing of science was 0.14% of GDP. France is the leading supplier of scientific and technical aid to Madagascar, and there are French research institutes in the country to study geology, hydrology, tropical forestry, and veterinary medicine.

The National Center of Applied Research in Rural Development, founded in 1974 at Antananarivo, conducts research into agriculture, forestry, fisheries, zoology, and veterinary studies. Also in the capital is a government department of agronomical research, the National Institute of Geodesy and Cartography, and the Pasteur Institute, which is devoted to biological research. The University of Antananarivo, founded in 1961, has departments of sciences, agriculture, polytechnics, and health sciences, and an Institute and Geophysical Observatory. The University of Fianarantsoa, founded in 1988, has departments of mathematics, physics-chemistry, engineering, and computer science. The University of Mahajanga, founded in 1977, has faculties of natural sciences, medicine, and dentistry and stomatology.

30 DOMESTIC TRADE

Antananarivo, the capital and largest city, is the principal distribution center for the island. Toamasina, Mahajanga, Antsiranana, Toliara, and Tolänaro are the commercial centers for the provinces in which they are located. Distribution and packaging are being gradually modernized. Most general merchants in the small eastern communities are Chinese; most on the west coast are Indian. Domestic trade is small due to low-incomes of most residents and relatively high prices. Business is conducted in French and Malagasy. Advertising and marketing are not common.

Business hours vary, but are generally from about 8 a.m. to noon and 2 to 5:30 p.m. on weekdays and from 8 a.m. to noon on Saturdays. Banks are open 8 to 11 a.m. and 2 to 4 p.m. Monday through Friday.

31 FOREIGN TRADE

Madagascar consistently runs a trade deficit. Exports consist mainly of unprocessed agricultural products and some extracted minerals. Textiles are Madagascar's major export commodity, followed by spices, coffee, and gemstones. Other exports include preserved fruit and shellfish.

Refined petroleum products were formerly imported in large quantities, but development of domestic refinery capacity altered this pattern. Madagascar now exports a small amount of petroleum products to East Africa and to other Indian Ocean islands. Crude petroleum still must be imported.

Madagascar imported $1.958 billion worth of goods and services in 2008, while exporting $1.412 billion worth of goods and services. Major import partners in 2009 were Thailand, 18.6%; China, 15.3%; France, 5.8%; South Africa, 4.8%; the United States, 4.6%; and India, 4.4%. Its major export partners were France, 32.1%; the United States, 16.1%; Germany, 6.4%; and China, 5%.

32 BALANCE OF PAYMENTS

Madagascar's payments balance is chronically negative. Since private investment has been limited, the deficits have been covered by foreign aid grants, official loans, and the use of central bank reserves from good years. In 1981, Madagascar was refused credit by its suppliers because of worsening deficits. The IMF provided a standby loan in 1982, conditional on devaluation of the currency, increased agricultural sector investments, producer price increases for rice and cotton, and the imposition of a ceiling on the minimum wage. These measures had a positive effect, although export production continued to decline. Consequently, further standby credits were negotiated and, in the late 1980s, Madagascar's debt was periodically rescheduled, conditional on further trade liberalization, tighter government spending controls, privatization of the state's banks, improvement of credit access, and the opening up of financial markets to foreigners. France and Germany canceled significant portions of Madagascar's debt at that time.

In 2010, the CIA estimated that Madagascar had $1.172 billion reserves of foreign exchange and gold reserves. Furthermore, in 2010 Madagascar had a current balance of -$2.106 billion.

33 BANKING AND SECURITIES

Upon leaving the franc zone in June 1973, the government established the Central Bank of the Malagasy Republic (Banque Centrale de la République Magache). Also organized at that time were the Malagasy National Development Bank, an agricultural credit institution, and the National Investment Co., an industrial investment bank. In June 1975, the Ratsiraka government nationalized all private financial institutions. In December 1976, Bankin'ny Tantsaha Mpamokatra (BTM) was established as the national rural development bank, Bankin'ny Indostria (BNI) as the national industrial development bank, and Banky Fampandrosoana ny Varotra (BFV) as the national bank for commerce. There was also a savings bank and a postal checking account system.

Economic reforms in 1988 allowed private foreign investment in the banking sector for the first time since the banks were nationalized. In 1989, the Banque Nationale de Paris was the first

---

Principal Trading Partners – Madagascar (2010)

(In millions of US dollars)

Country	Total	Exports	Imports	Balance
World	3,580.0	1,080.0	2,500.0	-1,420.0
France	634.5	294.6	339.9	-45.3
China	531.6	95.6	436.0	-340.4
United States	230.5	102.9	127.6	-24.7
South Africa	211.8	19.9	191.9	-172.0
Singapore	139.0	17.1	121.9	-104.7
Mauritius	138.3	15.8	122.5	-106.7
Bahrain	136.4	0.0	136.4	-136.4
Germany	117.8	63.0	54.8	8.2
Kuwait	112.6	0.1	112.5	-112.5
Canada	95.9	5.0	90.9	-85.9

(…) data not available or not significant.

(n.s.) not specified.

SOURCE: *2011 Direction of Trade Statistics Yearbook*, New York: United Nations, 2011.

Balance of Payments – Madagascar (2005)

(In millions of US dollars)

Current Account		-262.0
Balance on goods	-592.0	
Imports	-1,427.0	
Exports	834.0	
Balance on services	-117.0	
Balance on income	-80.0	
Current transfers	163.0	
Capital Account		192.0
Financial Account		-6.0
Direct investment abroad	…	
Direct investment in Madagascar	85.0	
Portfolio investment assets	…	
Portfolio investment liabilities	…	
Financial derivatives	…	
Other investment assets	11.0	
Other investment liabilities	-102.0	
Net Errors and Omissions		91.0
Reserves and Related Items		349.0

(…) data not available or not significant.

SOURCE: *Balance of Payment Statistics Yearbook 2011*, Washington, DC: International Monetary Fund, 2011.

French bank to open a private bank, the BMOI, since 1975. Financial sector liberalization has been a key condition of adjustment support.

The discount rate, the rate at which the central bank lends to commercial banks in the short term, was 5% in 2010. The commercial bank prime lending rate, the rate at which banks lend to customers, was 46% in 2010.

There are no securities exchanges in Madagascar.

34INSURANCE

In June 1975, as part of the government's Malagasization program, all insurance companies were nationalized. Most of these had previously been French. Foreign companies now operate only as coinsurers. Some of the insurance companies doing business in Madagascar included, in 1998: Avotra Mutuelle Générale d'Assurances Malagasy, Caledonian Insurance Co., Compagnie Malgache d'Assurances et de Reassurances, and Mutuelle d'Assurances Malagasy.

35PUBLIC FINANCE

In 2000, Madagascar started the preparation of a Poverty Reduction Strategy Paper (PRSP) under the Heavily Indebted Poor Countries (HIPC) initiative. By the end of the year, the IMF and the World Bank agreed that Madagascar had filled the requirements of the HIPC and together they reached a decision point for debt relief. As a result, various organizations, including the IMF, the Paris Club, and the African Development Bank awarded Madagascar grants or debt cancellations worth a total of $355 million dollars in 2001.

In 2010 the budget of Madagascar included $896.9 million in public revenue and $1.547 billion in public expenditures. The budget deficit amounted to 2% of GDP. Public debt was 29.3% of GDP, with $2.43 billion of the debt held by foreign entities.

36TAXATION

Indirect taxes produce much more revenue than direct taxes. The most important indirect taxes are import duties, a value-added tax (20% as of 2011), customs fees, and consumption taxes. Import licenses are not necessary, and exports have been liberalized. Direct taxation consists of a graduated personal income tax. A corporate profits tax is levied at 23% or 0.5% of annual gross revenue beyond $100,000. There is a 10% property tax, a 23% tax on interest, and a 5% tax for health insurance contributions.

37CUSTOMS AND DUTIES

Between 1960 and 1972, most Malagasy production went to France, where it was sold at subsidized prices. In return, preferential treatment was given to French imports. This reciprocal arrangement guaranteed the Malagasy a reliable return for their exports and enabled the French to pay low import duties and virtually monopolize the Malagasy market. Similar trade agreements were arranged with some European Community countries.

Beginning in 1972, however, the government restricted imports as much as possible and began the progressive cancellation of preferential arrangements to ensure greater diversity in supply sources. Import constraints were tightened during the early 1980s because of a severe shortage of foreign exchange but were liberalized in 1986. In 1988, Madagascar began a three-stage compre-

Public Finance – Madagascar (2008)		
(In billions of ariary, central government figures)		
Revenue and Grants	**3,257.7**	**100.0%**
Tax revenue	2,087.2	64.1%
Social contributions	137.1	4.2%
Grants	980.4	30.1%
Other revenue	53	1.6%
Expenditures	**3,567.7**	**100.0%**
General public services	1,616.2	45.3%
Defense	166.1	4.7%
Public order and safety	134.2	3.8%
Economic affairs	819.3	23.0%
Environmental protection	48.7	1.4%
Housing and community amenities	...	...
Health	197.6	5.5%
Recreational, culture, and religion	12.1	0.3%
Education	525.4	14.7%
Social protection	48.3	1.4%

(…) data not available or not significant.

SOURCE: *Government Finance Statistics Yearbook 2010*, Washington, DC: International Monetary Fund, 2010.

hensive tariff reform to simplify and reduce rates. Imported goods were divided into five categories and taxed at rates of 10–50%.

Customs duties continue to be an important source of revenue for Madagascar, as they are for many developing countries. The current tariff system consists of four kinds of duties: an import tax for crude materials, spare parts and inputs; capital goods; consumer goods; custom fees; a consumption tax; and a value-added tax of 20%.

38FOREIGN INVESTMENT

Prior to independence, nearly all private investment was French. The investment code of 1973 required that the Malagasy government own at least 51% of most new foreign projects, especially those involving strategic sectors of the economy. Import duties on equipment, excise on products, and taxes on profits were reduced or waived. Priority was given to enterprises in the allocation of foreign exchange and in the sale of goods and services to the state and its enterprises. In 1974, the government embarked on a socialist course, nationalizing large foreign enterprises without compensation and imposing strict controls on imports, prices and foreign exchange. There was little private foreign investment under these restrictive policies. The economy contracted and productivity declined. In 1994, under the pressure and guidance of the IMF, the World Bank, and donor states, a new liberalized policy framework was instituted. In 1997, the government announced that 45 state enterprises were set for privatization by the end of 1998, but only two companies had been privatized by mid-1999. Nonetheless, public foreign investment is encouraged.

A new code that became operational in 1986 allowed some exporters tax holidays of up to eight years, and there were special incentives for small enterprises. Foreign investors had the right to transfer dividends freely. The investment code of 1990 provided further incentives to foreign private investors and was opposed by local businesses for that reason. Rules covering foreign exchange and the number of foreign employees were relaxed. Small- and medium-size companies were provided tax exemptions through the first ten years of operation.

A number of export processing zones were set up in Madagascar. These have attracted investors from Europe, Mauritania, and Asia. Foreign direct investment (FDI) in Madagascar was a net inflow of $543.5 million according to World Bank figures published in 2009. FDI represented 6.33% of GDP.

39 ECONOMIC DEVELOPMENT

The 1982–1984 development plan, more modest than the previous one owing to limited resources, called for a shift from social investments (especially education and health) to agriculture, industry, and infrastructure. The following 1984–87 plan called for spending centered mainly on transport improvements and agricultural development. The 1986–90 plan, which superseded the 1984–87 plan, had 30% of the budget coming from private sources and 40% from foreign sources. The plan called for investments of 47% in agriculture in the ongoing effort to achieve food self-sufficiency and crop diversification.

Antigovernment strikes, corruption, and a lack of commitment have limited progress on the reforms since the early 1990s. In March 1997, a World Bank structural adjustment credit of $70 million was approved; in July 1999, a $100 million credit, and $40 million from the International Monetary Fund (IMF). The GDP growth rate increased steadily since these credits were allocated to Madagascar. However, external debt remained at $4 billion throughout the decade. One good sign during this period was a decrease in inflation, from 45% in 1993 to 6.2% in 1998.

In 2000, Madagascar was approved for $1.5 billion in debt service relief under the IMF/World Bank Heavily Indebted Poor Countries (HIPC) initiative. In 2001, it negotiated a $111.3 million three-year Poverty Reduction and Growth Facility (PRGF) Arrangement with the IMF. The PRGF was due to expire in November 2004. Also in 2001, the Paris Club approved a debt cancellation of $161 million, and the African Development Bank (AfDB) approved a debt cancellation of $71.46 million and granted an additional credit of $20 million to fight HIV/AIDS and poverty. Foreign direct investment in Madagascar's export processing zone strengthened the country's balance of payments position from 1997–2001, real GDP growth rate averaged 4.75%, and inflation was limited. The government embarked on an agenda of regulatory reform and public enterprise in 2002. Poverty, however, remained a constraint on growth and development.

Madagascar's ongoing political crisis continued to negatively impact key economic indicators and the business sector in 2011. Madagascar did not meet eligibility requirements for the African Growth and Opportunity Act (AGOA); this resulted in the loss of thousands of jobs.

40 SOCIAL DEVELOPMENT

Old age, disability and survivor's pensions are funded by 1% contributions by employees and 3.5% by employers. There is a National Social Security Fund that provides family allowances and workers' compensation for wage earners. Employed women receive 14 weeks of maternity leave at 50% of pay. An employment-related system for family allowances is available to residents of Madagascar or France.

Women enjoy a highly visible and influential position in society, occupying some important posts in business and in the public sector. Domestic abuse is not widespread and women have recourse when reporting abuse to authorities. A 2003 amendment to the penal code specifically prohibits domestic violence. Child labor persists.

Human rights are generally respected. Excessive pretrial detention is a problem in Madagascar, sometimes extending for periods that surpass the maximum sentence for the alleged offense.

41 HEALTH

All medical services in Madagascar are free. Each province has a central hospital and local clinics, dispensaries, and maternity-care centers are supplemented by mobile health units. The main hospitals are the Hospital Befelatnana and Fort Dauphin Hospital. The country spent 4.1% of its GDP on healthcare, amounting to $18 per person. There were 2 physicians, 3 nurses and midwives, and 3 hospital beds per 10,000 inhabitants. The fertility rate was 4.6, while the infant mortality rate was 41 per 1,000 live births. In 2008 the maternal mortality rate, according to the World Bank, was 440 per 100,000 births. It was estimated that 64% of children were vaccinated against measles. According to the CIA, life expectancy in Madagascar was 61 years in 2011.

Malaria remains one of the major health problems. The strategies of the fight against malaria consist of early care of malaria cases, drug interaction for pregnant women, and eradication of adult insects in the central highlands where malaria is common. In a February 2010 survey conducted by the United States and the World Health Organization (WHO), up to 40% of the malaria drugs found in Madagascar failed quality tests. The majority of the problematic medicine either contained impurities or lacked sufficient doses of the active ingredient that serves to combat the virus. According to the WHO, while much of the deficient medicine maintained some effectiveness, the failed drugs could not reliably stave off the deadly disease.

International sanctions against the government of Madagascar caused a severe food shortage in July 2011. According to a UN, almost 70% of the people living in the south of the island were suffering from food insecurity. Even before the sanctions, the country had been reported as having one of the highest malnutrition rates in the world. The UN urged nations to reconsider sanctions.

42 HOUSING

Malagasy houses, although constructed of varying materials in different parts of the island (brick and wood in the plateau, thatch and leaves in the west, and often on stilts in the east), are always rectangular, sited north–south, with the doorway opening to the west. In the central plateau, they are often two stories high and have outside terraces. The rapid growth of towns after World War II created grave problems of housing and sanitation, especially in Antananarivo, whose situation on a rocky promontory aggravates the difficulties of overcrowding.

43 EDUCATION

In 2007 the World Bank estimated that 98% of age-eligible children in Madagascar were enrolled in primary school. Secondary enrollment for age-eligible children stood at 24%. Tertiary enrollment was estimated at 4%. Of those enrolled in tertiary education, there were 100 male students for every 89 female students. Overall, the CIA estimated that Madagascar had a literacy rate of 68.9%. Public expenditure on education represented 3.0% of GDP.

Education is free and compulsory for five years. This is followed by four years of lower secondary education. Students may then attend a three-year program in either general upper secondary studies or technical school studies. The academic year runs from October to July.

The University of Madagascar in Antananarivo, established in 1961, also has campuses at Antsiranana, Fianarantsoa, Mahajanga, Toamasina, and Toliara. Also in Antananarivo are the Rural College of Ambatobe and the National Institute of Telecommunications and Posts.

44 LIBRARIES AND MUSEUMS

The principal libraries are the National Library in Antananarivo, with 236,000 volumes, and the university library, with 195,000 volumes. Other important libraries include the National Archives (30,000 volumes), the Antananarivo municipal library (23,000), and the Albert Camus Cultural Center Library (35,000).

The palace of the queen in Antananarivo contains important art, archaeological, and historical exhibits, especially concerning the Merina kingdom. Other museums in the city are the Gallery of Fine Arts; the University of Madagascar's Museum of Art and Archaeology; the Folklore, Archaeology, Paleontology, and Animal Museum; the Historical Museum, and a natural history museum. There is also an oceanographic research museum in Nosy Be, a regional museum in Toamasina, and university museums in Fianarantsoa and Tuléar.

45 MEDIA

In 2009 there were 181,200 main phone lines and 5.9 million mobile cell phones in use, an average of 31 per 100 people. Internet users numbered 2 per 100 citizens. In 2010, the country had 27,606 Internet hosts.

The government-owned Radio-Télévision Malagasy broadcasts in French, Malagasy, and English, and telecasts in French and Malagasy; Radio Madgasi Kara, also state-owned, broadcasts in French and Malagasy. There are a few privately operated stations for both radio and television.

Prominent newspapers in 2010, with circulation numbers listed parenthetically, included *Madagascar Tribune* (12,000) and *Midi-Madagasikara* (25,500), *Atrika* (circulation 13,000), *Imongo Vaovao* and *Maresaka* (5,000). All are published in Antananarivo. Despite prior censorship of all print media, the press is independent and quite outspoken.

In August 2009, Madagascar, along with Kenya, South Africa, Uganda, Tanzania, and Mozambique, became the direct beneficiaries of a $600 million undersea broadband investment project. The project was commissioned by SEACOM, an umbrella organization that included local African governments and telecommunication companies, and involved 9,300 miles of advanced, undersea, fiber-optic cables running through the Indian Ocean from South Africa to Kenya, via Madagascar. Before the cable went live in the final week of July 2009, the Indian Ocean seabed along the

eastern coast of Africa remained the last major region in the world not to be connected by high-speed, underwater cables. The SEACOM cable provided the East Africa region with direct access to the network of undersea Internet cables that run to Europe and South Asia. Internet access existed in East Africa for years before SEACOM but, previous to the 2009 cable, businesses, schools, and individuals in the region could access the Internet only through slow dial-up providers, or through prohibitively expensive satellite connections.

46 ORGANIZATIONS

There are hundreds of cooperatives, and the Ratsiraka government has been encouraging *fokonolona*, or village organizations, to stimulate planned agricultural undertakings. Chambers of commerce, originally established in 1902, are located in a dozen towns. The national branch is the Chamber of Commerce, Industry, Art and Agriculture of Antananarivo, which serves as a multipurpose group for tourism and trade. There are also seven major employers' organizations.

Tanora Tonga Saina is the government-sponsored youth movement. There are also scouting programs and a number of religiously and/or politically affiliated groups for youth. There are branches of Junior Chamber and YMCA/YWCA. A variety of sports associations are also active.

There are national chapters of the Red Cross Society, UNICEF, and Habitat for Humanity.

47 TOURISM, TRAVEL, AND RECREATION

Tourism has been encouraged by the government as a source of foreign exchange since the mid-1980s, with an exception for the years 1991 and 2002, when the industry suffered due to civil unrest. The *Tourism Factbook*, published by the UN World Tourism Organization, reported 163,000 incoming tourists to Madagascar in 2009; tourists spent a total of $518 million. Of those incoming tourists, there were 111,000 from Europe. Tourists are attracted to the city of Antananarivo, home to the largest open air market in the world. The hot springs town and resort of Antsirabe is also popular to visitors who enjoy boating and swimming.

Valid passports and visas are required to enter Madagascar. Certificates of vaccination against cholera and yellow fever are necessary of persons arriving from an infected area. Precautions against malaria are strongly advised.

In 2010 the estimated daily cost to visit Antananarivo, the capital, was $237. The cost of visiting other cities averaged $167.

48 FAMOUS PERSONS

The poet Jean-Joseph Rabéarivelo (1901–37) published several volumes of poetry (*Volumes, Presques Songes, Sylves*). Jacques Rabémananjara (b. 1913), a founder of the MDRM, is well known for his verse play, *Les Dieux Malgaches*. Philibert Tsiranana (1910–78), a Tsimihety teacher, founded the PSD, and became Madagascar's first president in May 1959. Gen. Gabriel Ramanantsoa (1906–79) was head of state from May 1972 to February 1975. Adm. Didier Ratsiraka (b. 1936) became head of state in June 1975 and president of the republic in January 1976. He served in that position until 1993, when he lost an election to Albert Zafy (b. 1927), who was president until 1996. Ratskiraka was elected president once again in 1997, and served until 2002. That year, he and Marc Ravalomanana (b. 1949) both claimed the presidency during an election controversy; Ratsiraka fled the country and Ravalomanana became president.

⁴⁹DEPENDENCIES

Two offshore islands, Nosy Boraha and Nosy Be, are considered to be integral parts of the country.

⁵⁰BIBLIOGRAPHY

Allen, Philip M. and Covell, Maureen. *Historical Dictionary of Madagascar*. Lanham, MD: Scarecrow Press, 2005.

Business in Madagascar for Everyone Practical Information and Contacts for Success. Washington, DC: International Business Publications USA, 2012.

Campbell, Gwyn. *An Economic History of Imperial Madagascar 1750–1895: The Rise and Fall of an Island Empire*. New York: Cambridge University Press, 2005.

Harmon, Daniel E. *Southeast Africa: 1880 to the Present: Reclaiming a Region of Natural Wealth*. Philadelphia, PA: Chelsea House Publishers, 2002.

Larson, Pier M. *History and Memory in the Age of Enslavement: Becoming Merina in Highland Madagascar, 1770-1822*. Oxford: J. Currey, 2000.

Madagascar Investment and Business Guide: Strategic and Practical Information. Washington, DC: International Business Publications USA, 2012.

Randrianja, Solofo, and Stephen Ellis. *Madagascar: A Short History*. Chicago: University of Chicago Press, 2009.

Roberts, Jonathan. *Mythic Woods: The World's Most Remarkable Forests*. London: Weidenfeld and Nicolson, 2004.

Stevens, Rita. *Madagascar*. Philadelphia, PA: Chelsea House, 1999.

Zeilig, Leo, and David Seddon. *A Political and Economic Dictionary of Africa*. Philadelphia: Routledge/Taylor and Francis, 2005.

MALAWI

Republic of Malawi

CAPITAL: Lilongwe

FLAG: Three equal horizontal bands of red (top), black, and green; a white sun disc is centered on the black band, its surrounding 45 white rays extend partially into the red and green bands; black represents the native peoples, red the bloodshed in their struggle for freedom, and green the color of nature; the sun represents Malawi's economic progress since attaining independence.

ANTHEM: *Mulungu dalitsa Malawi (Oh God Bless Our Land of Malawi).*

MONETARY UNIT: The kwacha (MWK) of 100 tambala is the national currency; it replaced the Malawi pound on 28 August 1970 and was linked with the pound sterling until November 1973. There are coins of 1, 2, 5, 10,50 tambala and 1, 5, 10 kwacha and notes of 50 tambala and notes of 10, 20, 50,100, 200 and 500 kwacha. MWK1 = US$0.0061 (or US$1 = MWK163.82) as of 2011.

WEIGHTS AND MEASURES: The metric system is the legal standard.

HOLIDAYS: New Year's Day, 1 January; John Chilembwe Day, 15 January; Martyrs' Day, 3 March; Labor Day, May 1; Kamuzu Day, 14 May; Republic or National Day, 6 July; Mothers' Day, 17 October; National Tree Planting Day, 21 December; Christmas, 25 December; Boxing Day, 26 December. Movable holidays include Good Friday and Easter Monday.

TIME: 2 p.m. = noon GMT.

1 LOCATION, SIZE, AND EXTENT

A landlocked country in southeastern Africa, Malawi (formerly Nyasaland) has an area of 118,480 sq km (45,745 sq mi), of which 24,400 sq km (9,420 sq mi) consists of water, chiefly Lake Malawi (also known as Lake Niassa). Comparatively, the area occupied by Malawi is slightly smaller than the state of Pennsylvania. Malawi extends 853 km (530 mi) N–S and 257 km (160 mi) E–W. It is bounded on the N and E by Tanzania, on the E, S, and SW by Mozambique, and on the W by Zambia, with a total boundary length of 2,881 km (1,790 mi).

Malawi's capital city, Lilongwe, is located in the central part of the country.

2 TOPOGRAPHY

Topographically, Malawi lies within the Great Rift Valley system. Lake Malawi, a body of water some 580 km (360 mi) long and about 460 m (1,500 ft) above sea level, is the country's most prominent physical feature. About 75% of the land surface is plateau between 750 m and 1,350 m (2,460 and 4,430 ft) above sea level. Highland elevations rise to over 2,440 m (8,000 ft) in the Nyika Plateau in the north and at Mt. Sapitwa (3,000 m/9,843 ft). The lowest point is on the southern border, where the Shire River approaches its confluence with the Zambezi at 37 m (121 ft) above sea level.

3 CLIMATE

Variations in altitude in Malawi lead to wide differences in climate. The vast water surface of Lake Malawi has a cooling effect, but because of the low elevation, the margins of the lake have long hot seasons and high humidity, with a mean annual temperature of 24°C (75°F). Precipitation is heaviest along the northern coast of Lake Malawi, where the average is more than 163 cm (64 in) per year; about 70% of the country averages about 75–100 cm (30–40 in) annually.

In general, the seasons may be divided into the cool (May to mid-August); the hot (mid-August to November); the rainy (November to April), with rains continuing longer in the northern and eastern mountains; and the post-rainy (April to May), with temperatures falling in May. Lilongwe, in central Malawi at an elevation of 1,041 m (3,415 ft), has a moderately warm climate with adequate rainfall. The average daily minimum and maximum temperatures in November, the hottest month, are 17°C (63°F) and 29°C (84°F), respectively; those in July, the coolest month, are 7°C (45°F) and 23°C (73°F).

4 FLORA AND FAUNA

Grassland, thicket, and scrub are found throughout the country. There are indigenous softwoods in the better-watered areas, with bamboo and cedars on Mt. Sapitwa; evergreen conifers also grow in the highlands. Mopane, baobab, acacia, and mahogany trees are found at lower elevations. The World Resource Institute estimated that there are 3,765 plant species in Malawi in 2011.

There are many varieties of animal life. The elephant, giraffe, and buffalo are found in certain areas; hippopotamuses dwell on the shores of Lake Malawi. The kudu, duiker, bushbuck, tsessebe, wildebeest, and hartebeest are among the antelopes to be found. Other mammals in Malawi are the baboon, monkey, hyena, wolf, zebra, lion, nocturnal cat, badger, warthog, and porcupine. Malawi is home to 207 species of mammals, 658 species of birds, 108 species of reptiles, and 56 species of amphibians. The calculation reflects the total number of distinct species residing in the country, not the number of endemic species.

Reptiles are plentiful and include freshwater turtle, crocodile, tortoise, marsh terrapin, chameleon, lizard, and many varieties of snakes; the Egyptian cobra has been found in the Shire Valley. Fish abound in the lakes and rivers; species include bream, bass, catfish, mudfish, perch, carp, and trout. The mbuna is a tropical fish protected within the waters of the Lake Malawi National Park. Malawi is rich in insect life and has species in common with tropical West Africa and Tanzania.

5 ENVIRONMENT

The World Resources Institute reported that Malawi had designated 1.84 million hectares (4.54 million acres) of land for protection as of 2006. Almost all fertile land is already under cultivation, and continued population pressure raises the threat of soil erosion and exhaustion, as well as infringement on forest resources for agricultural purposes. The demand for firewood has significantly depleted the timber stock. Water resources totaled 17.3 cu km (4.15 cu mi) while water usage was 1.01 cu km (.242 cu mi) per year. Domestic water usage accounted for 15% of total usage, industrial for 5%, and agricultural for 80%. Per capita water usage totaled 78 cu m (2,755 cu ft) per year.

The preservation of Malawi's wildlife is a significant environmental issue. Protected areas include Lake Malawi National Park, which is a natural UNESCO World Heritage Site, and Lake Chilwa, which is a Ramsar wetland site. Some of the nation's fish population is threatened with extinction due to pollution from sewage, industrial waste, and agricultural chemicals and siltation of spawning grounds. According to a 2011 report issued by the International Union for Conservation of Nature and Natural Resources (IUCN), the number of threatened species included 7 types of mammals, 15 species of birds, 1 reptile, 5 species of amphibians, 101 fish, 7 types of mollusks, 9 species of other invertebrates, and 14 species of plants. Threatened species included the African elephant, cheetah, and African wild dog.

The United Nations (UN) reported in 2008 that carbon dioxide emissions in Malawi totaled 1,055 kilotons.

6 POPULATION

The US Central Intelligence Agency (CIA) estimated the population of Malawi in 2011 to be approximately 15,879,252, which placed it at number 63 in population among the 196 nations of the world. In 2011 approximately 2.7% of the population was over 65 years of age, with another 45.1% under 15 years of age. The median age in Malawi was 17.2 years. There were 0.99 males for every female in the country. The population's annual rate of change was 2.763%. The projected population for the year 2025 was 22,900,000. Population density in Malawi was calculated at 134 people per sq km (347 people per sq mi).

The UN estimated that 20% of the population lived in urban areas in 2010, and that urban populations had an annual rate of change of 5.3%. The largest urban areas, along with their respective populations, included Blantyre, 856,000; and Lilongwe, 821,000.

The prevalence of HIV/AIDS has had a significant impact on the population of Malawi. The AIDS epidemic causes higher death and infant mortality rates, and lowers life expectancy. The CIA estimated that in 2009, there were 51,000 AIDS related deaths.

7 MIGRATION

Estimates of Malawi's net migration rate, carried out by the CIA in 2011, amounted to zero. The total number of emigrants living abroad was 212,600, and the total number of immigrants living in Malawi was 275,900. Accelerating migration from rural to urban areas contributed to an annual urban growth rate of about 6% in the early 1990s. Between October 1992 and mid-1996, 1.3 million Mozambican refugees repatriated from Malawi; the return of refugees to Mozambique was complete.

8 ETHNIC GROUPS

The people of Malawi belong mainly to various Central Bantu groups. The Chewa (32.6% of the population in 2008) are primarily located in the central regions of the country. The Nyanja (5.8%) live primarily in the south and the Lomwe (Alomwe, 17.6%) live south of Lake Chilwa. Other indigenous Malawians include the Tumbuko (8.8%), Sena (3.6%), Tonga (2.1%), and Ngonde (1%). The Ngoni (an offshoot of the Zulus from South Africa, 11.5%) and Yao (13.5%) arrived in the 19th century. There are a few thousand Europeans, mainly of British origin, including descendants of Scottish missionaries. There are also small numbers of Portuguese, Asians (mainly Indians), and persons of mixed ancestry.

9 LANGUAGES

Numerous Bantu languages and dialects are spoken. Chichewa, the language of the Chewa and Nyanja, is spoken by more than half the population, but the Lomwe, Yao, and Tumbuko have their own widely spoken languages, respectively known as Chilomwe, Chiyao, and Chitumbuka. English and Chichewa are the official languages.

10 RELIGIONS

According to a 2010 report, Christians account for 80% of the population, with the largest groups being affiliated with the Roman Catholic and Presbyterian (Church of Central Africa Presbyterian—CCAP) churches. There are smaller numbers of Anglicans, Baptists, Evangelicals, and Seventh-Day Adventists. Muslims account for approximately 13% of the population, with most belonging to the Sunni sect. Tribal religionists account for a small percentage of the population. There are also small numbers of Hindus, Baha'is, Rastafarians, and Jews.

11 TRANSPORTATION

The CIA reports that Malawi has a total of 15,451 km (9,601 mi) of roads, of which 6,956 km (4,322 mi) are paved. Malawi has approximately 700 km (435 mi) of navigable waterways. In terms of railroads, the main line consists of a single-tracked, narrow gauge rail line that runs from Salima to Nsanje, a distance of 439 km (273 mi), and is operated by Malawi Railways. The line was extended from Salima to Lilongwe in 1977 and was later extended to Mchinji, on the border with Zambia. At Chipoka, 32 km (20 mi) south of Salima, the railway connects with the Lake Malawi steamer service, also operated by Malawi Railways. The railway line extends, in the south, from Nsanje to the port of Beira in Mozambique. The Central African Railway Co., a subsidiary of Malawi Railways, operates the 26 km (16 mi) span from Nsanje to the Mozambique border. Malawi Railways was privatized in 1999.

Until 1982 about 95% of Malawi's foreign trade passed through Mozambican ports, mainly by rail connections, but by 1987, because of insurgent activity in Mozambique, over 95% of Malawi's exports were moving through South Africa's port of Durban. The use of this longer route, with only road transport through Malawi, was costing $50 million a year in extra transport expenses. Since 1990, when Mozambican rebels closed down the route, goods have been shipped through Zambia. As of 1999 major Malawi ports and harbors include Chipoka, Monkey Bay, Nkhata Bay, and Nkhotakota. Malawi has navigable waterways on Lake Malawi and on the Shire River.

There are 32 airports, which transported 157,007 passengers in 2009, according to the World Bank. Malawi's principal airports include Kamuzu International Airport, at Lilongwe and Chileka at Blantyre. Air Malawi, the national airline established in 1967, provides international and domestic air service. National carriers to some other countries in the region operate complementary services to Malawi. There are no direct services to Asia and the Pacific or the Americas.

12 HISTORY

Malawi has been inhabited for at least 12,000 years; its earliest peoples were nomadic hunter-gatherers. By the 13th century, Bantu-speaking migrants had entered the region. The Chewa peoples had become dominant by the early 16th century; their clans were consolidated under the leadership of a hereditary ruler called the *karonga*. Before the coming of the Europeans in the second half of the 19th century, Malawi was an important area of operations for Arab slave traders. The incursion of slaving took a heavy toll on the inhabitants, although the Chewa state never came under direct Arab rule. One of the major stated objectives of British intervention in the territory was to stamp out the slave trade.

The first European to explore the area extensively was David Livingstone, whose reports in the 1850s and 1860s were instrumental in the establishment of a series of mission stations in Nyasaland (as Malawi was then known) during the 1870s. In 1878 the African Lakes Company was formed by Scottish businessmen to supply the missions and provide a legitimate alternative to the slave trade. As the company extended its operations, it came into conflict with Yao tribesmen and Arab outposts toward the northern end of Lake Malawi. Fighting ensued in 1887–89, and pacification was completed only some years after the British government had annexed the whole of the territory in 1891. To Sir Harry Johnston, the first commissioner of the protectorate, fell the task of wiping out the remaining autonomous slave-trading groups. These antislavery operations were assisted by gunboats of the Royal Navy.

Nyasaland attracted a small group of European planters in the first decades of the 20th century. This group settled mainly in the Shire Highlands, and its numbers were never large. The territory was viewed by the imperial government as a tropical dependency, rather than as an area fit for widespread white settlement; much of the friction that marred race relations in the Rhodesias was therefore minimized in Nyasaland. Missionaries and colonial

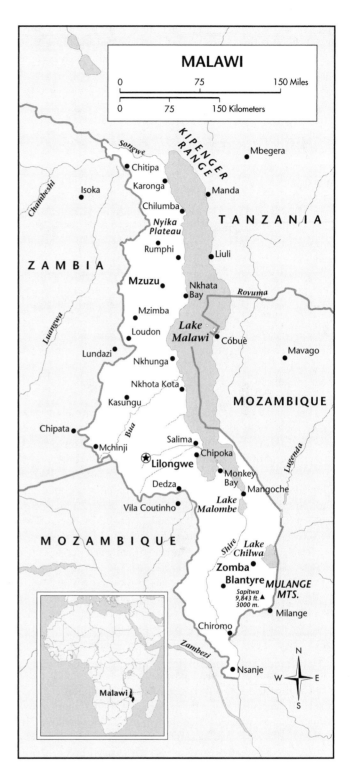

LOCATION: 9°27′ to 17°10′S; 32°20′ to 36°E. BOUNDARY LENGTHS: Tanzania, 451 kilometers (280 miles); Mozambique, 1,497 kilometers (930 miles); Zambia, 820 kilometers (510 miles).

civil servants consistently outnumbered planters in the European community, and lands occupied by European estates accounted for only a small part of the total land area.

Between World Wars I and II, the policy of the imperial government was built around the concept of indirect rule—that is, increasing the political responsibility of the African peoples by building on the foundations of their indigenous political institutions. Although this policy was not implemented at a rapid pace, it was generally assumed that Nyasaland would ultimately become an independent African-led state. In 1953, however, Nyasaland was joined with the two Rhodesias—Northern Rhodesia (now Zambia) and Southern Rhodesia (now Zimbabwe)—in the Central African Federation. The Africans' reaction to this political arrangement was hostile. Disturbances sparked by opposition to the federation in 1959 led to the declaration of a state of emergency, and some Africans, including Dr. Hastings Kamuzu Banda, were detained.

The African political leaders imprisoned in Southern Rhodesia were released in April 1960, and they gathered African support for the Malawi Congress Party (MCP). The MCP increased the campaign against federation rule and in the August 1961 elections polled more than 90% of the vote, winning all of the 20 lower-roll seats and two of eight upper-roll places. An era of "responsible" government then began, with the MCP obtaining five, and eventually seven, of the 10 available executive council positions. At a constitutional conference held in London in November 1962, it was agreed that Nyasaland should become fully self-governing early in 1963, and that Banda, who headed the MCP, should become prime minister. On 19 December 1962 the British government announced acceptance in principle of the right of Nyasaland to secede from the federation.

In February 1963, as scheduled, Nyasaland became a self-governing republic. In July, at a conference held at Victoria Falls, it was decided that the Central African Federation would break up by the end of the year. In October Banda visited the United Kingdom and successfully negotiated full independence, effective in mid-1964 after a general election based on universal adult suffrage. Accordingly, on 6 July 1964 Nyasaland became a fully independent Commonwealth country and adopted the name Malawi. On 6 July 1966 Malawi became a republic, and Banda assumed the presidency. After the constitution was amended in November 1970, Banda became president for life.

During the first decade of Banda's presidency, Malawi's relations with its black-ruled neighbors were sometimes stormy. At the opening session of the MCP convention in September 1968, President Banda made a claim to extensive territories outside the present boundaries of Malawi. The claim covered the whole of Lake Malawi and parts of Tanzania, Mozambique, and Zambia.

The Tanzanian government asserted that President Banda could make territorial claims only because he had the support of South Africa, Rhodesia (which at that time had a white minority government), and Portugal (which then still ruled Mozambique). In fact, in 1967 Malawi had become the first black African country to establish diplomatic relations with white-ruled South Africa; in August 1971, moreover, Banda became the first black African head of state to be officially received in South Africa, which supplied arms and development funds to Malawi.

The Banda government also faced some internal opposition. In October 1967 the Malawi government announced that a group of rebels, numbering about 25, wearing police uniforms, and posing as insurgents from Mozambique, had entered Malawi with the intention of killing President Banda and his ministers. Eventually, eight of the rebels were convicted of treason and sentenced to death; five others, including Ledson Chidenge, a member of the national assembly, were sentenced to death for the murder of a former official of the MCP.

Banda continued to rule Malawi with an iron hand through the 1970s and into the late 1980s. Several thousand people were imprisoned for political offenses at one time or another during his rule. One of these was former justice minister Orton Chirwa, leader of an opposition group in exile, who in May 1983 was sentenced to death after having reportedly been abducted from a town across the Zambian border in late 1981. Chirwa's sentence was commuted to life imprisonment in 1984. He died in prison in October 1992. Three government ministers and a member of the assembly—two of them key leaders of the MCP, with one of them, party secretary-general Dick Matenje, regarded as a possible successor to Banda—died in the middle of May 1983 in a mysterious car accident. Another staunch critic of the Banda regime, the journalist Mkwapatira Mhango, was killed together with nine members of his family in a bomb attack in Lusaka, Zambia, in 1989.

A serious problem in the 1980s concerned the activities of the Mozambique National Resistance (MNR), which, in its efforts (backed by South Africa) to bring down the government in Maputo, seriously disrupted Malawi's railway links with Mozambique ports. As a result, an increasing share of Malawi's trade had to be routed by road through Zambia and South Africa at great expense. In 1987 Malawi allowed Mozambican troops to patrol areas along their common border and sent several hundred troops into northeast Mozambique to help guard the railway leading to the port of Nacala. Other critical problems for Malawi, particularly during the late 1980s and the early 1990s were the nation's growing debt burden, severe drought, and the nearly one million refugees from Mozambique, most of whom have now returned to Mozambique.

In 1992 Banda's grip began to weaken. In March Malawi's eight Roman Catholic bishops issued a pastoral letter protesting detention without trial and harsh treatment of political prisoners. University students demonstrated. Wildcat strikes and rioting in Blantyre and Lilongwe followed the arrest of opposition trade unionist Chakufwa Chihana in May. Nearly 40 were killed by police gunfire in the first significant antigovernment demonstrations since 1964. Chihana was released on bail in September and he formed a new group, the Alliance for Democracy (AFORD), which campaigned for multiparty elections. In December, Chihana was sentenced to two years for sedition.

Pressure mounted (including threats by aid donors abroad to suspend assistance), and in October Banda agreed to hold a referendum early in 1993 on whether Malawi should remain a one-party state. In the referendum, on 14 June 1993, 63% of those voting favored adopting multiparty democracy. In July and November 1993, the assembly passed bills eliminating from the constitution single-party clauses (such as Hastings Kamuzu Banda's life presidency), appending a bill of rights, establishing a multiparty electoral law, and repealing detention without trial provisions of the Public Security Act. Dialogue among various major parties resulted in the establishment of a National Consultative Council and a National Executive Committee, with representatives from all registered parties, to oversee changes in the constitution, laws, and election rules and procedures. In December 1993 security forces disarmed Banda's paramilitary MCP Young Pioneers.

On 16 May 1994 the assembly adopted a provisional constitution, and the country held its first multiparty elections the following day. Bakili Muluzi of the UDF, a former cabinet minister, defeated Banda (MCP), Chihana (AFORD), and Kamlepo Kalua (Malawi Democratic Party). Of the 177 assembly seats contested, the UDF took 84, the MCP took 55, and AFORD 36. Muluzi immediately ordered the release of political prisoners and closed the most notorious jails. The new constitution took effect on 18 May 1995.

Malawi's second multiparty elections were held on 15 June 1999. The balloting showed a distinct regional cast to party constituency. Leading the UDF, Muluzi emerged the winner with 51.4% of votes in the presidential elections, followed by the MCP candidate, Gwanda Chakuamba, with 44.3%. Muluzi's UDF won 94 of 193 parliamentary seats, four short of a simple majority. Chakuamba's MCP took 63 seats, and its electoral ally, the AFORD, won 31; four seats went to independents. The results confirmed the regional voting trend set in 1994, with the UDF winning the densely populated south, the MCP strong in the central region and all of AFORD's seats coming from the rugged north.

Although international observers declared the contest free and fair, opponents alleged that the UDF had rigged the elections, and refused to recognize the outcome. Attempts to seek legal redress were rebuffed, leading to riots and the razing of 10 mosques in the north. At least two people were killed. Muluzi was inaugurated in Blantyre on 21 June 1999.

Severe food shortages in 2002 affected some 3.2 million people. The shortages exacerbated living conditions for more than 65% of the population considered "poor," and for some 15% of the adult population infected with HIV/AIDS. Widows of AIDS victims were increasingly subjected to property grabbing by relatives.

In July 2002 the assembly rejected proposals to amend the constitution to allow Muluzi to run for a third term in 2004. The third presidential elections were held on 20 May 2004. Bingu wa Mutharika, the UDF candidate who had been hand-picked by outgoing President Muluzi, was declared the victor.

Immediately after being elected president in 2004, Mutharika fell out of favor with his predecessor and supporter, Muluzi, because of Mutharika's zero tolerance policy toward corruption. Once out of the presidency, Muluzi refused to retire as head of UDF and remained its chair. Muluzi's staunch supporters accused Mutharika of persecuting and harassing them through his campaign to end corruption. There was talk of firing Mutharika from the UDF. On 5 February 2005 Mutharika announced his resignation from the UDF and formed his own political party, the Democratic Progressive Party (DPP).

Mutharika's formation of his own party effectively relegated the UDF to an opposition rather than a ruling party. Thus, on paper, the opposition parties formed the largest bloc in the assembly, while Mutharika's party, the DPP, did not have any seats. Muluzi aggressively sought the cooperation of the other opposition parties (which included John Tembo's MCP and Gwanda Chakuamba's Republican Party) to oust Mutharika through impeachment proceedings. He promised that once Mutharika was removed, a national governing council composed of the leaders of the three major political parties would rule the country. Such a promise contradicted the constitution, which notes that in the event of a vacancy in the presidency, the vice president automatically takes over.

In October 2005, there were a number of demonstrations both for and against Mutharika's impeachment. UDF supporters marched in the commercial capital of Blantyre, demanding the immediate impeachment and removal of Mutharika from office. The demonstrations turned violent with marchers vandalizing cars of opposition MPs. On 24 October 2005, as an impeachment motion was tabled in the assembly by UDF.

In the May 2009 presidential elections Mutharika won a second term in office with 65.9% of the votes. International observers reported concerns over voting irregularities and the role of state-owned media in securing the election for the incumbent. Members of the opposition Malawi Congress Party claimed that they were denied access to official vote-counting centers, but reluctantly accepted Mutharika as the winner.

¹³GOVERNMENT

Malawi officially became a republic on 6 July 1966, and its first constitution was adopted that year. The current constitution took effect on 18 May 1995 reaffirming the president as the head of state and supreme executive authority. Legislative power is vested in a unicameral assembly of 193 seats, with members elected by popular vote to serve five-year terms.

¹⁴POLITICAL PARTIES

Malawi was officially a one-party state from October 1973 until July 1993. The Malawi Congress Party (MCP) was the national party and Hastings Kamuzu Banda was its president for life. All candidates for the assembly had to be members of the MCP.

For years the opposition groups in exile achieved little success in their efforts to unseat the Banda government. The Socialist League of Malawi (LESOMA), with headquarters in Harare, was directed by Attati Mpakati until his assassination in March 1983. A second group, the Malawi Freedom Movement (MAFREMO), based in Tanzania, was led by Orton Chirwa, who was seized by Malawi authorities in late 1981 and imprisoned for life until his death in 1992. The Congress for the Second Republic, also based in Tanzania, was led by former External Affairs Minister Kanyama Chiume. The Save Malawi Committee (SAMACO) was formed in Lusaka, Zambia, in 1983.

In September 1992, trade unionist Chakufwa Chihana formed the Alliance for Democracy (AFORD) before being convicted of sedition. AFORD and others pushed successfully for a referendum on adopting a multiparty system, and the United Democratic Front (UDF) combined with a coalition in exile (the United Front for Multiparty Democracy) late in 1992.

From the introduction of multiparty competition in May 1994 to the elections in 2004, the UDF and its leader, Bakili Muluzi, dominated the political arena. In the 1994 presidential contest, Muluzi garnered 47.3% of the vote, and his party 84 of the 177 elective seats in the assembly. Muluzi obtained 51.4% of the vote in the 1999 presidential poll, and the UDF won 94 of 193 assembly seats. However, a shake-up in UDF hierarchy in 2003 revealed vulnerabilities in the party's leadership and organization. This led to Muluzi handpicking his successor, Bingu wa Mutharika, who narrowly won 36% of the vote in the controversial May 2004 elections. Furthermore, UDF won only 49 out of the 193 seats in parliament, showing that the dominance the UDF had during Muluzi's tenure had considerably waned. Bingu wa Mutharika then abandoned the UDF and moved on to form his own political party, the Democratic Progressive Party (DPP), a move which infuriated Muluzi ,who attempted to lure other opposition parties to join him in impeaching Mutharika.

Since the 2003 shake-up in the UDF hierarchy, dissenters from this shake-up have formed their own political parties. The splinter group parties from the UDF include the National Democratic Alliance (NDA) founded by Brown Mpinganjira, who fell out of favor with Bakili Muluzi. At the general elections of May 2004 this party won 8 out of 193 seats. Brown Mpinganjira later deregistered his party and rejoined the UDF. Other former UDF and non-UDF leaders of smaller parties formed a loose electoral alliance called the Mgwirizano Coalition. This coalition includes seven smaller parties: Malawi Democratic Party, Malawi Forum for Unity and Development, Movement for Genuine Democratic Change, National Unity Party, People's Progressive Movement, People's Transformation Party, and Republican Party. Gwanda Chakuamba, founder and leader of the Republican Party, was the presidential candidate for the Mgwirizano Coalition in the May 2004 elections. He won 26% of the vote and the Mgwirizano Coalition won 27 out of 193 seats.

In the May 2009 legislative elections, the DPP gained control of the assembly by winning 114 seats. The MCP came in next with 26 seats, followed by the UDF with only 17 seats. Thirty-two seats were gained by independent candidates and four were won by candidates from other parties. The next legislative elections are set for May 2014. In the May 2009 presidential election, Bingu wa Mutharika was reelected with 66% of the vote. John Tembo of the MCP was the next leading candidate with 30.7% of the vote. The next presidential election is set for 2014.

15 LOCAL GOVERNMENT

Malawi is divided into 28 districts. District councils provide markets, postal agencies, roads, and rural water supplies and exercise control over business premises and the brewing and sale of beer. More important, however, are the councils' responsibilities for primary education. Some of the councils run public health clinics. Council expenditures are mainly financed from direct government education grants, calculated to meet the salaries of teachers in most of the district schools. Other sources of revenue include annual taxes on all males over the age of 17 years who are residents in the district and charges for services rendered.

Town councils have powers similar to those of the district councils, but with greater emphasis on the problems that arise in urban areas. Their main functions are sewerage, removal of refuse, the abatement of nuisances, construction and maintenance of roads, and, in some cases, the provision of fire-fighting services. Revenue for town councils comes mainly from direct taxes on property.

16 JUDICIAL SYSTEM

Since 1969 Malawi has operated under two parallel court systems. The first is based on the United Kingdom legal system with local courts and a local appeals court in each district. Formerly, these courts heard all cases of customary law and had wide statutory, criminal, and civil jurisdiction. The upper layers consist of the Supreme Court of Appeal, the high court, and magistrates' courts.

A chief justice and four puisne judges appointed by the president staff the high court. There is a chain of appeals from the local courts up to the Supreme Court of Appeal.

A second system was established in November 1969, when the assembly empowered the president to authorize traditional African courts to try all types of criminal cases and to impose the death penalty; the president was also permitted to deny the right of appeal to the high court against sentences passed by the traditional courts, a right formerly guaranteed by the constitution. Traditional court justices are all appointed by the president. Appeals from traditional courts go to the district traditional appeals courts and then to the national traditional appeal court. Appeals from regional traditional courts, which are criminal courts of the first instance, go directly to the national traditional appeal court.

In 1993 the attorney general suspended the operation of regional and national level traditional courts in response to a report by the National Consultative Council on problems in the workings of the traditional court system. Since then the trend is toward moving serious criminal and political cases from traditional to modern courts. Education and training seminars have led to some improvements in the functioning of the local traditional courts.

The constitution provides for an independent judiciary, which is respected in practice. Defendants have the right to public trial, to have an attorney, to challenge evidence and witnesses, and to appeal. The constitution superseded many old repressive laws. The high court may overturn old laws that conflict with the constitution.

17 ARMED FORCES

The International Institute for Strategic Studies reports that armed forces in Malawi totaled 5,300 members in 2011, all of which are members of the army. Armed forces (including an air wing and a naval detachment) represent 0.1% of the labor force in Malawi. Defense spending totaled $169.5 million and accounted for 1.3% of gross domestic product (GDP).

18 INTERNATIONAL COOPERATION

Malawi became a member of the UN on 1 December 1964; the nation participates in ECA and several nonregional specialized agencies, such as the FAO, World Bank, ILO, IFC, UNESCO, UNIDO, and the WHO. Malawi also belongs to the WTO, the African Development Bank, the ACP Group, the Commonwealth of Nations, COMESA, G-77, the African Union, and the Southern Africa Development Community (SADC). The country is a member of the Nonaligned Movement and the Organization for the Prohibition of Chemical Weapons. The government has offered support to UN missions and operations in Kosovo (est. 1999), Liberia (est. 2003), the DRC (est. 1999), and Burundi (est. 2004).

In environmental cooperation, Malawi is part of the Basel Convention, the Convention on Biological Diversity, Ramsar, CITES, the Kyoto Protocol, the Montréal Protocol, MARPOL, the Nuclear Test Ban Treaty, and the UN Conventions on Climate Change and Desertification.

19 ECONOMY

Landlocked Malawi is a poor country where wealth is concentrated in the hands of a small elite. Most of the population (over

90%) is engaged in subsistence agriculture producing a variety of crops, including maize (corn), beans, rice, cassava, tobacco, and groundnuts (peanuts). Production does not always meet domestic demand although traditionally Malawi has been self-sufficient in the production of maize. Agriculture accounts for over one-third of gross domestic product (GDP) with about 90% of export revenues coming from the sale of tobacco, tea, and sugar. The sector experienced severe droughts in 1979–81, 1992, 1994, and 2001–02 which caused the GDP to decline by as much as 8%.

Periodic flooding also plagues Malawi. Manufacturing is small-scale, directed mainly to the processing of export crops. The fledgling mining sector in Malawi is slowly growing with the support of international financing.

Poor roads, lack of skilled labor, substandard electricity, water, and telecommunications infrastructure has had a negative impact on the economy. The government is inefficient, corrupt, and heavily in debt, which further constrains economic growth. Environmental challenges include deforestation and erosion.

These structural inefficiencies have left the country heavily dependent on international economic assistance from the International Monetary Fund (IMF), the World Bank, and individual donor nations. The donors, concerned about human rights abuses in Malawi, have tied support to human rights reforms. The donors have also pressed for improved educational facilities and increased attention to the problems of HIV/AIDS and the environment. Continued improvement in building a market economy and increased fiscal discipline in government spending are also required. In response, the government instituted an anticorruption campaign in 2005 and continued its efforts to privatize state owned businesses. By 2005 about 50% of the more than 90 state-owned enterprises had been sold to private hands, 22% were actively being offered for privatization, and an additional 13% had been earmarked for future transfer to the private sector.

In 2006 the country was approved for in debt service relief under the IMF/World Bank Heavily Indebted Poor Countries Initiative. In 2007 the US granted Malawi eligibility status to receive financial support within the Millennium Challenge Corporation (MCC) initiative.

The GDP rate of change in Malawi, as of 2010, was 6.6%. Inflation stood at 8%.

²⁰INCOME

The CIA estimated that in 2010 the GDP of Malawi was $12.98 billion. The CIA defines GDP as the value of all final goods and services produced within a nation in a given year and computed on the basis of purchasing power parity (PPP) rather than value as measured on the basis of the rate of the exchange based on current dollars. The per capita GDP was estimated at $800. The annual growth rate of GDP was 6.6%. The average inflation rate was 8%. It was estimated that agriculture accounted for 33.4% of GDP, industry 21.7%, and services 44.9%.

According to the World Bank, remittances from citizens living abroad totaled $900,000. The World Bank reports that in 2009, household consumption in Malawi totaled $2.9 billion or about $184 per capita, measured in current US dollars rather than PPP.

As of 2011 the most recent study by the World Bank reported that actual individual consumption in Malawi was 89.3% of GDP and accounted for 0.02% of world consumption. By comparison,

the United States accounted for 25.44% of world individual consumption. The World Bank also estimated that 22.1% of Malawi's GDP was spent on food and beverages, 14.3% on housing and household furnishings, 2.1% on clothes, 11.9% on health, 12.6% on transportation, 1.6% on communications, 7.1% on recreation, 1.7% on restaurants and hotels, and 9.5% on miscellaneous goods and services and purchases from abroad.

According to World Food Program poverty is both widespread and severe with 40% of the population living on less than $1 per day in 2010.

²¹LABOR

As of 2007 Malawi had a total labor force of 5.747 million people. Within that labor force, CIA estimates in 2003 noted that 90% were employed in agriculture, 5% in industry, and 5% in the service sector. Union membership is quite low due to the small number of workers in the formal sector of the economy. Between 12% and 18% of the workforce was unionized in 2010. The only labor federation was the Malawi Congress of Trade Unions, to which all unions belonged. In theory, unions have the right to organize, bargain collectively, and strike, but in practice labor relations are still in development.

The minimum working age is 14, but many children work due to cultural norms, agricultural predominance, and severe economic hardship. In 2010 the urban minimum wage amounted to approximately $0.94 per day; in all other areas, it was approximately $0.70. Minimum wage rates did not provide a decent standard of living for a worker and family. The legal maximum workweek is 48 hours but this regulation is not generally enforced.

²²AGRICULTURE

The agricultural sector is drought-prone and experienced severe droughts in 1979–81, 1992, and 1994. About 77% of the total land area of Malawi is under customary tenure—that is, subject to land allocation by village headmen based on traditional rights of succession by descent. Roughly 22% of the total land is farmed. The country's major crops include tobacco, sugarcane, cotton, tea, corn, potatoes, cassava (tapioca), sorghum, pulses, groundnuts, and Macadamia nuts. Cereal production in 2009 amounted to 4 million tons, fruit production 989,427 tons, and vegetable production 320,037 tons. Malawi is self-sufficient in food production (except during droughts).

Tobacco was first grown in 1889 near Blantyre in southern Malawi. Most production continues to come from the central region (around Lilongwe). Tobacco production was estimated at a record 160,014 tons in 1996 but fell to 69,500 tons in 2004. Malawi exports more than 95% of the tobacco it produces, which generates some 70% of all foreign earnings. As of 2010 Malawi was the top producer of burley leaf tobacco.

Tea, a major export crop, is produced mostly on estates; about 16,000 hectares (40,000 acres) are in tea plantations, mainly in the Mulanje and Thyolo districts. Although subsistence farmers participate in the production of export crops more extensively now than in the pre-independence period, much customary agriculture is still devoted to cereal production. Pressure of population on the land is mounting and, in a few areas, expansion of acreage under export crops has been discouraged in favor of food production. Maize (corn) is the staple food crop. Late rains, floods, and an increasing Mozambican refugee population kept maize production from meeting domestic demand during the mid-1990s.

23 ANIMAL HUSBANDRY

Animal husbandry plays a minor role in the economy. Pressure on the land for cultivation is sufficiently intense in many areas to rule out stock-keeping on any scale. The UN Food and Agriculture Organization (FAO) reported that Malawi dedicated 1.9 million hectares (4.57 million acres) to permanent pasture or meadow in 2009. During that year, the country tended 15.7 million chickens, 1 million head of cattle, and 1.6 million pigs. The production from these animals amounted to 26,629 tons of beef and veal, 25,132 tons of pork, 15,306 tons of poultry, 16,376 tons of eggs, and 50,863 tons of milk. Malawi also produced 2,927 tons of cattle hide.

In October 2009 the Shire Highlands Milk Producers Association (SHMPA) announced the beginning of a multiyear program cosponsored with the Netherlands-based Intervet/Schering-Plough Animal Health. The program is designed to support local small-scale dairy farmers in efforts to improve the health of dairy cows and the quality of milk produced. Intervet/Schering-Plough will provide funds to build and equip a new veterinary laboratory and will also offer training and education programs on animal nutrition and breeding practices. The SHMPA (established in 1985) has noted that one of the greatest difficulties faced by many small-scale milk farmers has been access to artificial insemination and veterinary services. Training in milk collection logistics and farm management may also be offered through the program, as needed. The Shire Highlands are located on the southern plateau region of Malawi.

24 FISHING

The growing commercial fishing industry is concentrated mainly in Lake Malawi, with small-scale activity in Lake Malombe, Lake Chilwa, and the Shire River. Fish farming is carried on in the south. Large employers of labor in the southern region are the major buyers, and much of the catch is sold directly to them. Fish from Lake Malawi contribute about 70% of animal protein consumption. In 2008 Malawi had 47 decked commercial fishing boats and the annual capture totaled 70,019 tons according to the UN FAO. The export value of seafood totaled $357,000.

25 FORESTRY

Approximately 34% of Malawi is covered by forest. Natural forests are extensive, and in the high-altitude regions, the Forestry Department is engaged in a softwood afforestation program. However, Malawi's annual rate of deforestation was 2.4% during 1990–2000. Sizable plantations of pine, cypress, and cedar have been established. The UN FAO estimated the 2009 roundwood production at 520,000 cu m (18.4 million cu ft). The value of all forest products, including roundwood, totaled $11.3 million.

26 MINING

Paladin Energy opened Malawi's first uranium mine at Kayelekera in the northern part of the country in 2009, and in 2010 production increased to 790 metric tons from 115 ton in 2009. Production was constrained by power outages. Uranium accounted for nearly 10% of Malawi's exports by value in 2010. Most of the mining

and mineral processing operations in Malawi are privately owned, including the cement plants, the Kayelekera uranium mine, the Mchenga coal mine, and the Nyala ruby and sapphire mine. Small-scale and artisanal miners produce aggregates, brick clay, gemstones, and lime. From 2009 to 2010 employment in the mineral industry increased to 21,022 workers from 11,565. In 2010 uranium production increased by 587%, sulfuric acid by an estimated 493%, ornamental stone by 80%, coal, by 34%, lime, by 23%, and limestone for use in the cement industry by 22%. Bentonite production decreased by 87% in 2010, and gemstones by 33%. From 2009 to 2010 the share of the mining sector in the GDP increased to 2% from 1%; most of the increase was attributable to increased uranium production.

27 ENERGY AND POWER

Malawi as of 2011 had no known petroleum or natural gas reserves. Nor did it have any oil refining capacity. However, the country does have small recoverable reserves of coal. Malawi's coal production increased to 79,186 metric tons in 2010 from 59,201 in 2009 because of increased demand from the brewery, cement, and tobacco industries. About 140,000 tons per year was consumed by the brewery, cement, ethanol, sugar, tea, textile, and tobacco industries.

In 2007 demand for petroleum products averaged 7,188 barrels per day, all of which was imported. There was no recorded demand for imports of natural gas in that year. Low-grade bituminous coal reserves were known about for many years, but mining did not begin until the last decades of the 20th century.

Both the consumption and the production of electric power are small, even by African standards. The World Bank reported in 2008 that Malawi produced 1.68 billion kWh of electricity and consumed 1.73 billion kWh, or 109 kWh per capita.

28 INDUSTRY

After a decade of rapid expansion—11% average growth per year in the 1970s—the pace of manufacturing growth slowed to 3.6% during 1980–90, and during 1990–2000, to 1.7%. In 2010 industry accounted for 21.7% of GDP.

Although Malawi's manufacturing sector is small, it is diverse. The processing of tea, tobacco, sugar, coffee, cement, and cotton accounts for most of its output. Factories manufacture soap, detergents, cigarettes, furniture, cookies, bread, blankets and rugs, clothing, and mineral waters. Other installations include a gin distillery, a cotton mill, and two textile plants. Brick making is well established. Roofing tiles are also produced, and radios are assembled. Other products made in Malawi include agricultural implements, bicycle frames, polishes, edible oils and fats, cattle foodstuffs, flour, matches, fishing nets, rope, twine and yarns, toiletries, and footwear. Two plants in Malawi retread tires, and its industries make a wide range of metal products.

29 SCIENCE AND TECHNOLOGY

The World Bank reported in 2009 that there were no patent applications in science and technology in Malawi. Research stations for tea, tobacco, and other aspects of agriculture conducted their activities under the auspices of the Ministry of Agriculture. The Ministry of Forestry and Natural Resources maintains forestry and fisheries research units.

The University of Malawi includes Bunda College of Agriculture and Kamuzu College of Nursing, both at Lilongwe; Malawi Polytechnic and the College of Medicine at Blantyre; and Chancellor College at Zomba, which has a faculty of science. The Geological Survey of Malawi, founded in 1921, is headquartered in Zomba. The Medical Association of Malawi, founded in 1967, is headquartered in Blantyre.

30 DOMESTIC TRADE

Domestic trade is concentrated in the larger towns, since transportation of goods to most rural areas is difficult and most rural residents have extremely low incomes. Local markets and stands for produce and baked goods prevail.

A small manufacturing sector is located near Blantyre, which is the country's major commercial center. There are a few larger supermarkets and grocery stores in Lilongwe, but with limited inventories. Karonga and Nsanje are the main trading ports. Zomba is a regional commercial center for agriculture. Licenses are required for all persons engaged in trading; fees vary with the nature of the business.

Business hours are 7:30 or 8 a.m. to noon and 1 or 1:30 p.m. to 4:30 or 5 p.m., Monday through Friday, and 7:30 or 8 a.m. to noon or 12:30 p.m. on Saturday. Banks are open weekdays from 8 to 12:30 p.m. (to 11:30 a.m. on Wednesday and 10:30 a.m. on Saturday).

31 FOREIGN TRADE

Malawi mostly exports tobacco. Other commodity exports include tea , sugar , coffee (4.0%), and woven cotton fabrics . In 2008 Malawi exported $1.189 billion worth of goods and services. Its major export partners were Germany, 11.5%; India, 8.5%; South Africa, 7.2%; Russia, 7.1%; Zimbabwe, 7.1%; the United States, 7%; and Netherlands, 6.3%. Malawi imported $1.675 billion worth of goods and services in 2008. Major import partners in 2009 were South Africa, 38.2%; India, 7.7%; Zambia, 6.5%; China, 5.8%; France, 4.8%; and Tanzania, 4.6%.

32 BALANCE OF PAYMENTS

Malawi runs an annual deficit on current accounts, which is generally mitigated but not annulled by capital inflows, mostly in the form of development loans. The current account balance in 2010 was estimated at -$502 million.

33 BANKING AND SECURITIES

The Reserve Bank of Malawi was established in Blantyre in 1964. It took over, by stages, the functions in Malawi of the former Bank of Rhodesia and Nyasaland, until that bank wound up its affairs in June 1965. The main duties of the reserve bank are to maintain currency stability and to act as banker to the government and to the commercial banks. The reserve bank administers exchange control and acts as registrar for local registered stock. The reserve bank also handles the issue of treasury bills on behalf of the government.

Malawi's financial services are unsophisticated and basic. Aside from the central bank, there are five licensed commercial banks, which are dominated by the two government-owned banks, the National Bank of Malawi (NBM) and the Commercial Bank of Malawi (CBM). In 1999 the NBM was 48% owned by

Principal Trading Partners – Malawi (2010)

(In millions of US dollars)

Country	Total	Exports	Imports	Balance
World	3,030.0	1,130.0	1,900.0	-770.0
South Africa	686.4	83.2	603.2	-520.0
India	131.7	30.6	101.0	-70.4
Germany	130.0	106.9	23.1	83.8
Zambia	125.1	12.2	112.9	-100.7
China	116.7	28.6	88.1	-59.5
United States	109.9	69.1	40.8	28.3
Zimbabwe	105.1	81.8	23.3	58.5
Tanzania	77.1	4.9	72.2	-67.4
Canada	74.9	71.1	3.9	67.2
Russia	73.9	73.9	0.0	73.9

(…) data not available or not significant.

(n.s.) not specified.

SOURCE: *2011 Direction of Trade Statistics Yearbook,* New York: United Nations, 2011.

Balance of Payments – Malawi (2009)

(In millions of US dollars)

Current Account		**-562.6**
Balance on goods		-726.9
Imports	-1,995.3	
Exports	1,268.4	
Balance on services		21.2
Balance on income		-109.6
Current transfers		252.7
Capital Account		**398.8**
Financial Account		**275.7**
Direct investment abroad		19.2
Direct investment in Malawi		75.8
Portfolio investment assets		-0.1
Portfolio investment liabilities		…
Financial derivatives		…
Other investment assets		6.8
Other investment liabilities		174.0
Net Errors and Omissions		**-233.8**
Reserves and Related Items		**121.9**

(…) data not available or not significant.

SOURCE: *Balance of Payment Statistics Yearbook 2011,* Washington, DC: International Monetary Fund, 2011.

Press Corporation Limited (PCL), and 39% by the Agriculture Development and Marketing Corporation (ADMARC); CBM was 23% owned by PCL, 22% by the Malawi government in direct shareholding, and 17% by the Malawi Development Corporation (MDC). The Malawi government owns MDC and ADMARC, and is PCL's largest shareholder (49%). As of 31 March 1999 total assets of the five banks reached about $300 million. The other three commercial banks are the First Merchant Bank Limited, the Finance Bank of Malawi, and Indefinance.

The Investment and Development Bank of Malawi (Indebank), formed in 1972 with foreign and local participation, provides medium- and long-term credit. Although the country's financial market has been liberalized, the sole mortgage finance institution, the New Building Society (NBS), which came into operation at independence in March 1964, faces no competition. The NBS's assets stood at $244.5 million in 1995.

A subsidiary of Indebank, the Investment and Development Fund (Indefund), finances small and medium-sized enterprises. The Malawi Development Corporation (MDC), which services the needs of large-scale industry, is state-owned. The Post Office Savings Bank (POSB) was restructured in 1994 and licensed as a commercial bank, the Malawi Savings Bank (MSB). Other major financial institutions include Loita Investment Bank, the Leasing and Financing Co. of Malawi (LFC), the Malawi Rural Finance Company (MRFC), and the Finance Corporation of Malawi (FINCOM).

The IMF reports that in 2001, currency and demand deposits—an aggregate commonly known as M1—were equal to $136.1 million. In that same year, M2—an aggregate equal to M1 plus savings deposits, small time deposits, and money market mutual funds—was $268.3 million.

In 2009 the discount rate, the interest rate at which the central bank lends to financial institutions in the short term, was 15%. At the end of 2005 the nation's gold bullion deposits totaled 0.01 million fine troy ounces.

The Malawi Stock Exchange (MSE) was established in December 1994 along with Stockbrokers Malawi to deal with listed company shares and to act as a broker in government and other securities approved by the Reserve Bank of Malawi (RBM). The stock exchange had no listings until November 1996, when shares in NICO were put up for sale. Since November 1994 the RBM has marketed treasury bills of varying maturities (30, 61, 91, and 182 days) in an attempt to encourage greater participation by the private sector. As of 2010 MSE had 15 listed companies.

34 INSURANCE

Most insurance firms operating in Malawi are owned or sponsored by parent companies in the United Kingdom. However, the leading company, the National Insurance Co. (NICO), is owned by Malawi interests. Motor vehicle insurance is compulsory.

35 PUBLIC FINANCE

Government revenues derive from import duties, income taxes on companies and individuals, income from government enterprises, excise duties, licenses, and value-added taxes. The fiscal year runs from 1 April to 31 March. Government consumption, which had an average annual growth rate of 7.0% during the 1980s, declined by 4.0% annually during the 1990s, and by 9.5% in 1998. Education, health, and agriculture were the three biggest items on the budget for 2000. In 2010 the budget of Malawi included $1.735 billion in public revenue and $1.769 billion in public expenditures. The budget deficit amounted to 0.7% of GDP.

The CIA estimated that in 2005 Malawi's central government took in revenues of approximately $844.6 million and had expenditures of $913.9 million. Revenues minus expenditures totaled approximately -$69.3 million. Public debt in 2010 was 40.4% of GDP, with $1.234 billion of the debt held by foreign entities.

36 TAXATION

Individuals pay taxes on all income from Malawi, whether they are residents or nonresidents. Most operating businesses are required to prepay estimated tax on a quarterly basis. The corporate income tax in 2011 was 30%. Branches of foreign companies were taxed at 35%, but reduced rates applied to insurance businesses (21%), and to ecclesiastical, charitable or educational institutions or trusts (25%). Companies operating in export processing zones (EPZs) are exempt from corporate tax, and companies operating in priority areas can qualify for a ten-year exemption, followed by a reduced 15% tax rate, when the exemption expires. Other tax allowances are offered—for mining companies, for manufacturers, for exports, for training, among others—as investment incentives. Royalties, rents, fees and commissions are subject to a 20% withholding tax. Interest from banks is also subject to a 20% withholding rate if the interest is over MWK10,000 ($61.91).

The income of individuals and partnerships is taxed according to a graduated scale with rates from 0–30%. For 2004 the government introduced a new top rate of 40%, and raised the threshold for taxable income from MWK30,000 to MWK \36,000 (about $187 to $223). Municipal taxes are based on property valuations.

Malawi's main indirect tax is a 16.5% value-added tax (VAT) which applies to goods and selected services, including luxury goods and electronics, as well as imports.

37 CUSTOMS AND DUTIES

Trade licenses are required for the import and export of certain goods, including military uniforms, wild animals, some food, and military equipment. Malawi is a member of the Southern African Development Community (SADC) and the Common Market for Eastern and Southern Africa (COMESA), granting trade preferences to member states. The country also has bilateral trade agreements with Zimbabwe and South Africa, granting the duty-free exchange of goods.

In 1998 the government eliminated export taxes on tobacco, sugar, tea, and coffee. Machinery, basic foodstuffs, and raw materials are admitted with a 10–5% tax. In July 1999 the maximum tariff rate was reduced from 30% of value to 25%. Tariffs on intermediate goods and raw materials were reduced from 10% to 5% and from 5% to 0%, respectively.

Luxury goods are assessed at higher rates than ordinary consumer items. Excise duties are levied for revenue purposes on spirits, beer, cigarettes and tobacco, petroleum products, and certain other items.

38 FOREIGN INVESTMENT

The government actively encourages foreign investment, particularly in agriculture and in import-substitution and labor-intensive industries. Foreign direct investment (FDI) in Malawi was a net inflow of $60.4 million according to World Bank figures published in 2009, and FDI represented 1.28% of GDP. Incentives such as exclusive licensing rights, tariff protection, and liberal depreciation allowances are offered. These incentives also include a tax allowance of 40% for new buildings and machinery, 20% for used buildings and machinery, and a 100% deduction for a manufacturing company's operating expenses for the first two years. Other incentives are: no import duty on heavy goods vehicles, raw materials for manufacturing, a maximum import tariff rate of 25%, no withholding tax on dividends, and tax holidays. Exporters do not have to pay the normal taxes or import duties. Repatriation of dividends and profits are freely permitted.

Encouraged by the formation of the Malawi Development Corp. and the implementation of a development plan, foreign investment increased in the mid-1960s. A sugar scheme on the lower Shire River was financed to a great extent by foreign investment, as were a distillery and a brewery. The large plantation enterprises were originally established with capital largely from the United Kingdom. Exploration for oil under Lake Malawi began in 1999, but has not yielded any positive results so far.

39 ECONOMIC DEVELOPMENT

During the first decades of independence, agricultural development was emphasized. The government sought to implement this policy by providing the family farmer with basic agricultural support facilities, such as extension services, training, irrigation, and research, and by increasing the output of fertile areas through farm credit, marketing, and processing facilities. During this period, four major agricultural developments were sponsored: the Shire Valley Agricultural Development Project in the south; the Lilongwe Land Development Program and the Central Region Lakeshore Development Project, both in the Central Region; and the Karonga Rural Development Project in the north.

In 2000 Malawi was approved for $1 billion in debt service relief under the IMF/World Bank's Heavily Indebted Poor Countries (HIPC) initiative, to support poverty reduction efforts through expenditures on health, education, and rural development, among other areas. Also in 2000 Malawi negotiated a three-year $58 million Poverty Reduction and Growth Facility (PRGF) Arrangement with the IMF, which expired in December 2003. In September 2002 the IMF approved $23 million in emergency relief to support large imports of food due to shortages that year, and to fight malnutrition and starvation, particularly among those affected with HIV/AIDS. A new three-year PRGF was signed with the IMF, worth $56 million, which commenced in July 2005. The main aim of the new PRGF was to restore fiscal discipline, with the priority on reducing domestic debt. Other government initiatives in the early 2000s targeted improvements in roads, and with participation from the private sector, improvements in railroads and telecommunications.

The United Kingdom has traditionally been Malawi's principal aid donor. South Africa has been a significant source of aid as well, especially in financing construction in the capital at Lilongwe and the railway extension from Lilongwe to Mchinji. Other significant aid donors have included the European Union, France, Canada, Germany, Japan, the United States, Denmark, the African Development Bank, and the World Bank/IDA.

40 SOCIAL DEVELOPMENT

Pension systems exist for public employees only. Government hospitals and clinics provide some medical services free to residents. Employers are required to obtain private worker's injury insurance. Worker's compensation is provided for disability and survivor benefits.

The constitution specifies equal rights for women and minorities, but women face widespread discrimination in the home and in employment opportunities. Spousal abuse is common, and the authorities rarely intervene. Inheritance practices often leave widows without their share of the family's assets. Women are much more likely to be illiterate than their male counterparts. Polygamy is practiced among some Muslims.

Socially, homosexual relationships are looked down upon in Malawi, and gay sex is criminalized.

Some human rights abuses continued to occur under the democratic government. The use of excessive force and the mistreatment of prisoners are reported. Human rights organizations are free to operate openly and without restrictions.

41 HEALTH

Health services, which rank among the poorest in Africa, are under the jurisdiction and supervision of the Ministry of Health and are provided to Africans free of charge. In 2011 the country spent 9.1% of its GDP on healthcare, amounting to $19 per person. Approximately 80% of the population had access to health care services. As of 2011 it was estimated that there were fewer than 2 physicians 100,000 people, 3 nurses and midwives, and 11 hospital beds per 10,000 inhabitants. Approximately 57% of the population had access to safe drinking water and 77% had adequate sanitation. Access to safe water and sanitation at times has been severely impeded by war.

The major health threats are malnutrition, malaria, tuberculosis, measles, dysentery, and bilharzia. Hookworm and schistosomiasis are widespread. The incidence of tuberculosis was 413 per 100,000 people in 2007. Malawi also has one of the highest HIV/AIDS prevalence rates, with nearly 12% of the adult population infected with the disease. The nation has shown some progress in providing education and treatment options for those who live with HIV/AIDS. A June 2009 report indicated that nearly 250,000 of the estimated 1 million people who are HIV positive have obtained free anti-retroviral drugs through government sponsored programs. The report further indicated that 77% of those receiving treatment were able to lead normal lives.

The fertility rate was 5.5 children born per woman, while the infant mortality rate was 69 per 1,000 live births. In 2008 the maternal mortality rate, according to the World Bank, was 510 deaths per 100,000 births. It was estimated that 92% of children were vaccinated against measles. About 32% of married women were using contraceptives. The major cause of infant death in Malawi is diarrheal disease. According to the CIA, life expectancy in Malawi was 54 years in 2011.

42 HOUSING

About 90% of the population live in rural areas. The traditional dwelling, used by anywhere from 45–65% of the total population, is a single-family home made of mud brick walls and a thatched roof. There are some more permanent structures, which are made with concrete, stone, or burnt brick walls and iron sheet, concrete, or asbestos roofs. Most dwellings have two or three rooms and the average household size is about 4.3 people. In 1998, at least 86% of dwellings were owner occupied. Only about 2.5% of residences had access to indoor piped water. Most drinking water was taken from boreholes, unprotected wells, and/or rivers and streams. About 74% of the population (both urban and rural) used pit latrines. About 22% had no toilets at all. Only 4.9% of the population had access to electricity. Wood is typically used for cooking fuel and paraffin is used for lighting.

Government-built houses are either rented or sold. The Malawi Housing Corp. has also developed housing plots in order to relocate urban squatters.

43 EDUCATION

Control of education, including mission schools, is in the hands of the Ministry of Education. Attendance is compulsory for eight years at the primary level. Secondary education lasts for four years. The academic year runs from September to July.

In 2009 the World Bank estimated that 91% of age-eligible children in Malawi were enrolled in primary school. Secondary enrollment for age-eligible children stood at 25%. It is estimated that about 57% of all students complete their primary education. The student-to-teacher ratio for primary school was at about 70:1 in 2003; the ratio for secondary school was about 46:1 in 2005.

The University of Malawi has four constituent colleges at Zomba, Lilongwe, and Blantyre. A new medical school was established in Blantyre. In August 2009 the nation marked the opening of the Amalika Teacher Training College, the first of six such colleges that will be established by 2014 through the partnership of Development Aid from People to People (DAPP) in Malawi, Planet Aid-USDA, and the government of Finland. When completed, the six colleges are expected to graduate a total 1,000 primary school teachers each year. In 2009 tertiary enrollment was estimated less than 1 %. Overall, the CIA estimated that Malawi had a literacy rate of 62.7%.

44 LIBRARIES AND MUSEUMS

The Malawi National Library Service, founded in 1968, has more than 804,000 volumes and maintains a nationwide interloan system with headquarters in Lilongwe, regional branches in Blantyre, Mulanje, Luchenza, Mzuzu, and Karonga, and a number of smaller rural libraries and library centers. The largest library is that of the University of Malawi (375,000 volumes). The US Information Agency maintains a small library in Lilongwe, and the British Council has libraries in Blantyre and in the capital. The National Archives are in Zomba and contain 40,000 volumes.

The Museum of Malawi (1959), in Blantyre, has a collection displaying the nation's archaeology, history, and ethnography. The Cultural and Museum Center Karonga serves as a museum of natural history, including dinosaur fossils and other prehistoric remains. Other museums include the Lake Malawi Museum in Mangochi and a regional museum in Mzuzu. There is also a postal museum in Namaka housed in a traditional postal carrier's rest hut.

45 MEDIA

In 2009 the CIA reported that there were 175,000 telephone landlines in Malawi. In addition to landlines, mobile phone subscriptions averaged 16 per 100 people.

Radio broadcasting services were provided in English and Chichewa by the state-owned Malawi Broadcasting Corp. over two stations in 2004. In 2009 there were 9 FM radio stations, 5 AM radio stations, and 2 shortwave radio stations. State-owned Television Malawi was the only national television broadcaster. In 2003 there were an estimated 499 radios and 4 television sets for every 1,000 people. In 2010 the country had 870 Internet hosts and Internet users numbered 5 per 100 citizens.

The Daily Times, published in English in Blantyre, appears Monday through Friday and had a circulation of 22,000 in 2002. The other major daily publications were *Computer Monitor, Michiru Sun, The Enquirer*, and *U.D.F. News* (United Democratic Front). *The Malawi News*, a weekly, had a circulation of 30,000. Other weeklies include *The Independent, The Nation*, and *The New Express*.

Though previously strictly controlled by the government, the media enjoy new constitutional provisions suspending censorship powers. The government is said to respect these new provisions.

46 ORGANIZATIONS

The Malawi Chamber of Commerce and Industry has its headquarters at Blantyre. A branch of the British Medical Association has been organized in Zomba. In the larger towns, musical societies and theater clubs have been established.

The League of Malawi Women and the League of Malawi Youth are active. Other national youth organizations include the Catholic Students Community of Malawi, Malawi Young Pioneers, Student Alliance for Rural Development, and the Student Christian Organization of Malawi. A variety of sports associations are also active.

Service clubs include the Rotary, Lions Clubs, and the British Empire Service League. Some social welfare and economic development groups have organized under the umbrella of the Council for Nongovernmental Organizations in Malawi, established in 1985. International organizations with active chapters include the Salvation Army, Habitat for Humanity, UNICEF, and the Red Cross.

47 TOURISM, TRAVEL, AND RECREATION

Tourist facilities are improving with the development of Malawi. The major cities and resorts are not as limited as the smaller, rural areas. The main tourist attraction in Malawi is Lake Malawi; the visitor is well served there by hotels and recreational facilities. There are also eight-day excursions around the lake available. Game parks, Mt. Mulanje, and Mt. Zomba also attract the tourist trade.

The *Tourism Factbook*, published by the UN World Tourism Organization, reported 755,000 incoming tourists to Malawi in 2009, spending a total of $48 million. Of those incoming tourists, there were 574,000 from Africa. A passport, proof of sufficient funds, and onward/return ticket are required for entry into Malawi. Upon entry, a 30-day visa is issued. Proof of vaccination against yellow fever is required for travelers from infected areas. In 2011 hotel beds available in Malawi had an occupancy rate of 58%. The estimated daily cost to visit Lilongwe, the capital, was $243. The cost of visiting other cities averaged $154.

48 FAMOUS PERSONS

The dominant historic political figure is Dr. Hastings Kamuzu Banda (1906–97). After a long period of medical practice in England, and a brief one in Ghana, he returned to Nyasaland in 1958 to lead the Malawi Congress Party. Following the declaration of a state of emergency, Banda was detained from March 1959 to April 1960. He became Malawi's first prime minister in 1963, and in 1966 he became Malawi's first president; he was named president for life in 1971 and ruled without interruption until ousted in a 1994 election mandated by constitutional reform. Bakili Muluzi (b. 1943) was president from 1994–2004. Bingu wa Mutharika (b. 1934) was reelected as president in 2009.

⁴⁹DEPENDENCIES

Malawi has no territories or colonies.

⁵⁰BIBLIOGRAPHY

Harmon, Daniel E. *Southeast Africa: 1880 to the Present: Reclaiming a Region of Natural Wealth.* Philadelphia, PA: Chelsea House Publishers, 2002.

Kalinga, Owen J. M., and Cynthia A. Crosby. *Historical Dictionary of Malawi.* 4th ed. Lanham, MD: Scarecrow Press, 2012.

Malawi Investment and Business Guide: Strategic and Practical Information. Washington, DC: International Business Publications USA, 2012.

Mandala, Elias C. *The End of Chidyerano: A History of Food and Everyday Life in Malawi, 1860–2004.* Portsmouth, NH: Heinemann, 2005.

McElrath, Karen, ed. *HIV and AIDS: A Global View.* Westport, CT: Greenwood Press, 2002.

Zeilig, Leo, and David Seddon. *A Political and Economic Dictionary of Africa.* Philadelphia: Routledge/Taylor and Francis, 2005.

MALI

Republic of Mali
République du Mali

CAPITAL: Bamako

FLAG: The flag is a tricolor of green, yellow, and red vertical stripes.

ANTHEM: *Le Mali (Mali).*

MONETARY UNIT: The Malian franc, a paper currency that had been floating with the French franc, was replaced in June 1984 by the French Community Franc (XOF). There are coins of 1, 2, 5, 10, 25, 50, and 100 francs and notes of 50, 100, 500, 1,000, 5,000, and 10,000 francs. XOF1 = US$0.0019 (or US$1 = XOF525.2) as of 2012.

WEIGHTS AND MEASURES: The metric system is the legal standard.

HOLIDAYS: New Year's Day, 1 January; Armed Forces Day, 20 January; Democracy Day, 26 March; Labor Day, 1 May; Africa Day, 25 May; Independence Day, 22 September; Christmas, 25 December. Movable religious holidays include Eid al-Fitr, Eid al-Adha, Milad an-Nabi, and Easter Monday.

TIME: GMT.

¹LOCATION, SIZE, AND EXTENT

A landlocked country in West Africa, Mali has an area of about 1,240,000 sq km (478,767 sq mi), extending 1,852 km (1,151 mi) ENE–WSW and 1,258 km (782 mi) NNW–SSE. Comparatively, Mali is slightly less than twice the size of Texas. Bounded on the N and NE by Algeria, on the E and S by Niger, on the S by Burkina Faso and Côte d'Ivoire, on the SW by Guinea, on the W by Senegal, and on the W and NW by Mauritania, Mali has a total boundary length of 7,243 km (4,661 mi). Mali's capital city, Bamako, is located in the southwestern part of the country.

²TOPOGRAPHY

There are few prominent surface features in Mali, which is crossed by two river systems-the Niger and the Senegal. In the southwest there are low mountains deeply notched by valleys formed by the coursing of water. A second upland, in the circle formed by the Niger River, is virtually a plateau and contains Hombori Tondo-the highest point in Mali at 1,155 m (3,789 ft). In the northeast is Adrar des Iforas, an extension of Algeria's Ahaggar Mountains. The republic is divided into three natural zones. The Sudanese zone is an area of cultivation covering some 200,000 sq km (77,200 sq mi) in the south and in the inland delta (a pre-Tertiary lake bed into which the upper Niger once flowed). The Sahel stretches east to west through the center of the country and the Sahara stretches across the northern region. A number of seasonal lakes can be found in the central Sahel region.

³CLIMATE

Southern and western Mali have a Sudanese climate with a short rainy season from June to September. Rainfall averages 140 cm (55 in) at Sikasso in the far south. To the north is the Sahelian zone, a semiarid region along the southern border of the Sahara. At Gao,

in Mali's northeast Sahel, rainfall is about 23 cm (9 in) a year. Actual year-to-year rainfall, however, is extremely erratic. In the Sahelian zone there are considerable variations of temperature, especially in April, May, and June, the period of maximum heat, and in December, when the hot, dry harmattan blows. Continuing north, one gradually enters into a Saharan climate, marked by the virtual absence of rain and an extremely dry atmosphere. Over 40% of the country is desert and unsuitable for agriculture.

The year is divided into three main seasons varying in length according to latitude: October-January, a cool and dry season; February-May, a hot and dry season; and June-September, a season of rains characterized by lower temperatures and an increase in humidity. Between 1968 and 1974, Mali, with neighboring Sahel states, experienced the worst drought in 60 years. Drought returned during 1982–85, and there is continuing concern over the southward advance of the desert.

⁴FLORA AND FAUNA

The World Resources Institute estimates that there are 1,741 plant species in Mali. In addition, Mali is home to 134 mammal, 624 bird, 107 reptile, and 32 amphibian species. The calculation reflects the total number of distinct species residing in the country, not the number of endemic species. According to the World Conservation Monitoring Centre, 0.7% of Mali's animals are endemic and 0.6% of its vascular plant species are.

The Saharan zone of Mali, an area of fixed dunes and false steppes, contains vegetation made up of thick-leaved and thorny plants (mimosas and gum trees). The vegetation of the Sahelian zone resembles that of the steppes, with thorny plants and shrubby savannas. The Sudanese zone is an area of herbaceous vegetation; its trees are West African mahogany, rosewood, kapok, baobab, and shea.

In the Saharan, or desert zone, animal life includes dorcas and maned wild sheep, the latter being in the mountains. Notable wildlife includes the threatened Saharan cheetah, with less than 250 individuals left through North Africa; it may no longer be present in Mali. In the Sahelian region are found oryx, gazelle, giraffe, wart hog, ostrich, bustard, red monkey, and cheetah, as well as lion, jackal, fox, hyena, and cynhyena. In the Sudanese zone there are large and small antelope, buffalo, elephant, lion, and monkey, plus such small game as hare, bustard, guinea fowl, quail, pigeon, and such water birds as duck, teal, sandpiper, peetweet, godwit, and woodcock. Other birds include pelican, marabou, ibis, egret, heron, eagle, and vulture.

⁵ENVIRONMENT

Mali's natural resources and wildlife are stressed by drought, deforestation, and erosion. All of these factors may be exacerbated in the future as some climate change models predict significant reduction of rainfall in West Africa.

The World Resources Institute reported that Mali had designated 2.6 million hectares (6.43 million acres) of land for protection as of 2006. The nation's wildlife is threatened by drought, poaching, and the destruction of the environment. Mali has a national park and four animal reserves that cover a total of 808,600 hectares (1,998,100 acres), as well as six forest reserves covering 229,400 hectares (566,900 acres). In addition, the Sahel has an elephant reserve of 1,200,000 hectares (2,965,000 acres) and a giraffe reserve of 1,750,000 hectares (4,324,000 acres). However, the authorities lack the means to prevent poaching of protected animals or cutting down of trees for firewood. According to a 2011 report issued by the International Union for Conservation of Nature and Natural Resources (IUCN), the number of threatened species included 12 types of mammals, 9 species of birds, 1 type of reptile, 3 species of fish, and 7 species of plants. Threatened species include the addax, cheetah, and barbary sheep. The Sahara oryx has become extinct in the wild.

Water resources total 100 cu km (23.99 cu mi) while water usage is 6.55 cu km (1.57 cu mi) per year. Domestic water usage accounts for 9% of total usage, industrial for 1%, and agricultural for 90%. Per capita water usage totals 484 cu m (17,092 cu ft) per year. The United Nations (UN) reported in 2008 that carbon dioxide emissions in Mali totaled 579 kilotons.

⁶POPULATION

The US Central Intelligence Agency (CIA) estimates the population of Mali in 2011 to be approximately 14,159,904, which placed it at number 67 in population among the 196 nations of the world. In 2011, approximately 3% of the population was over 65 years of age and 47.3% under 15 years of age. The median age in Mali was 16.3 years. There were 0.98 males for every female in the country. The population's annual rate of change was 2.61%. The projected population for the year 2025 was 22,300,000. Population density in Mali was calculated at 11 people per sq km (28 people per sq mi).

The UN estimated that 36% of the population lived in urban areas, and that urban populations had an annual rate of change of 4.4%. The largest urban area was Bamako, with a population of 1.6 million.

⁷MIGRATION

Estimates of Mali's net migration rate, carried out by the CIA in 2011, amounted to -5.23 migrants per 1,000 citizens. The total number of emigrants living abroad was 1.01 million, and the total number of immigrants living in Mali was 162,700. Mali also accepted 6,300 refugees. The Fulani, Tuareg, and other nomadic groups of northern Mali move freely across desert borders to and from neighboring countries. As many as two million Malians migrate seasonally to Côte d'Ivoire, Senegal, and Libya. In addition, 150,000 Malians fled to Algeria, Burkina Faso, and Mauritania in the early 1990s to escape government repression. Between June 1995 and 1999, some 131,780 Malian refugees returned home from Algeria, Burkina Faso, Mauritania, Niger, and Senegal. Malian refugees of Tuareg and Moor ethnic origin continue to return. There is also increasing migration from rural to urban areas.

⁸ETHNIC GROUPS

The main ethnic groups of Mali are the Mande, including the Bambara, Malinke, and Sarakole, accounting for about 50% of the total population. Other groups include the Peul (or Fulani), accounting for 17%; the Voltaic, making up 12%; the Songhai, constituting 6%; the Tuareg and Moors 10%; and other groups 5%. The Bambara, mostly farmers, occupy all of central Mali bounded by the Côte d'Ivoire frontier in the south and Nara and Nioro in the north. Malinke live chiefly in the regions of Bafoulabé, Kita, and Bamako. The Peul (or Fulani), semisedentary herdsmen, are to be found throughout the republic, but mainly in the region of Mopti. The Songhai—farmers, fishermen, and merchants—live along the banks and islands of the Niger River, east of the inland delta. The nomadic Tuareg, of Berber origin, are mainly in the north, in the Adrar des Iforas. The Minianka, largely farmers, populate the region of Koutiala, and the Senufo, also farmers, are found principally in the region of Sikasso. The Dogon, often considered to be the first occupants of Mali, are believed to have survived because of inaccessibility of their villages in the Hombori cliffs. The Dogon have won international esteem for their unique ceremonial artifacts. The majority of the peoples in Mali are Negroid; the Tuareg are classified as Caucasoid; and the Puel (Fulani) are of mixed origin.

⁹LANGUAGES

French, the official language, is the language of administration and of the schools and is the main unifying tongue for the country's diverse population elements. There are virtually as many languages as there are ethnic groups. However, Bambara—widely spoken in western, central, and southern Mali—is understood by about 80% of the population. The Semitic-speaking Arabs and Hamitic-speaking Tuareg are the only groups with a traditional written language, although in recent years other languages, most of which belong to the Niger-Congo group of African languages, have come to be written. Fulani is spoken in the Niger delta, and Songhai in the east and northeast.

¹⁰RELIGIONS

It is estimated that about 90% of the people are Muslims, the vast majority being Sunnis. Among them the Islamic fundamentalist sect of Dawa al Tabligh has grown in Kidal, Mopti, and Bamako.

LOCATION: 10°10′ to 25°N; 4°15′ E to 12°15′ W. BOUNDARY LENGTHS: Algeria, 1,376 kilometers (855 miles); Niger, 821 kilometers (510 miles); Burkina Faso, 1,202 kilometers (747 miles); Côte d'Ivoire, 515 kilometers (320 miles); Guinea, 932 kilometers (579 miles); Senegal, 418 kilometers (260 miles); Mauritania, 2,237 kilometers (1,390 miles).

The Wahabi movement is important in Tombouctou. About 1% of the population are Christian, with a split of about two-thirds Catholics and one-third Protestant. Most of the remainder practice indigenous religions. Freedom of religion is guaranteed by the constitution and this right is generally respected in practice. The constitution also defines the country as a secular state. Mawloud, the Prophet's Baptism, Easter Monday, Eid al-Fitr (Ramadan), Tabaski (Eid al-Adha), and Christmas are observed as national holidays.

11TRANSPORTATION

The CIA reported in 2010 that Mali had a total of 18,709 km (11,625 mi) of roads as of 2005, of which 3,368 km (2,093 mi) were paved. There were 20 airports. Mali had approximately 1,800 km (1,118 mi) of navigable waterways. Foremost in importance among these waterways is the great Niger River.

Transportation is controlled by the government's Malian Transport Authority. Mali has some 593 km (368 mi) of railroad, all of it narrow gauge, and served by diesel electric locomotives. The main line, from Dakar in Senegal to Bamako, runs a twice-weekly passenger service. There is more frequent service between Bamako and Koulikoro, the last stop on the line, and between Bamako and Kayes. The World Bank has helped finance the modernization of the Malian rail system.

A major project, completed in 1986, was the construction of a 558-km (347-mi) road between Gao and Sévare, near Mopti, to be part of a trans-Sahara highway linking Algeria and Nigeria.

Mali is landlocked but it is served by the port of Dakar in Senegal. The Niger River, which in Mali is 1,782 km (1,107 mi) long, is navigable except for a 59-km (37-mi) stretch between Bamako and Koulikoro (the main river port), where it is cut by rapids. The Bani River, a tributary of the Niger, is navigable for 224 km (139 mi) between San and Mopti. Regular service on the Niger is generally maintained from July through January. The Senegal is navigable between Kayes and Saint-Louis, Senegal. Mali, Senegal, and Mauritania make up the Senegal River Development Organization.

There were over twenty airports as of 2010, 12 of which were served by commercial airliners. An international airport is at Senou, 14 km (9 mi) from Bamako. Air Mali, the state-owned airline, flies to Gao, Mopti, Kayes, Nioro, Tombouctou, Nara, Yelimané, and Goundam. There are also airports at Ségou, Tessalit, Bourem, and Kidal. In 1992, Mali joined the ten other signatories of the Yaoundé Treaty and became a partner in Air Afrique.

12 HISTORY

The recorded history of the area now called Mali begins with the empire of Ghana. This means it dates from about the 4th century AD. At its height in the 10th century, the Ghana Empire occupied eastern Senegal, southwest Mali, and southern Mauritania and carried on a steady trade across the Sahara with Arab states. It disintegrated by the 13th century and was succeeded by the Mali Empire, from which the independent republic takes its name.

The Mali Empire reached its peak in the 14th century under Mansa Musa (r. 1312–37), who captured Tombouctou and made Mali a center of Muslim scholarship. Tombouctou and Djenné became key centers for trans-Sahara trade. By the 17th century, however, the empire had ceased to exist, and the Tuareg took much of the northern area.

Meanwhile, to the east, the Songhai Empire was founded around AD 700 in the middle region of the Niger River. Later centered at Gao, the empire was at its zenith after the capture of Tombouctou in 1468. The chief rulers in this period were Sonni Ali Ber (r. 1464–92) and Askia Muhammad I (r. 1492–1528). In 1591, the Songhai fell to an invading Moroccan army, which established secure bases at Gao, Tombouctou, and Djenné. Under Moroccan rule, a military caste known as the Arma developed, which controlled the countryside, but by 1780, the area had become fragmented into petty states.

In the 19th century, al-Hajj Umar, a member of the Tukulor tribe, waged a Muslim holy war against the pagans of the area. In 1862, he conquered Ségou and Macina, and the next year he plundered Tombouctou. He was killed in 1864 while trying to put down a rebellion. Around 1880, the French began their advance into what was to become the Republic of Mali. They were opposed from 1882 to 1898 by Samory Touré, a Malinke leader who was ultimately captured and exiled. The capture of Sikasso in 1898 completed the French conquest.

Under French administration, the area became known as French Sudan (Soudan Français) and was a part of French West Africa. Achievements of French rule included the building of the Dakar-Bamako railway and a Niger Delta development scheme. In 1946, the Sudanese became French citizens, with representation in the French parliament. Under the constitution of 1946, the franchise was enlarged and a territorial assembly was established. Universal suffrage was established in 1957, when enlarged powers were conferred on the territorial assembly, which was also given the right to elect a council of ministers responsible for the administration of internal affairs. In 1958, under the constitution of the Fifth French Republic, French Sudan became an autonomous republic, called the Sudanese Republic, within the French Community.

Independence

In January 1959, in Dakar, representatives of the Sudanese Republic, Senegal, Dahomey (now Benin), and Upper Volta (now Burkina Faso) drafted a constitution of the Federation of Mali (named after the medieval African empire), but only the assemblies of the Sudanese Republic and Senegal ratified it and became members of the federation. Later that year the new Mali Federation asked the French Community to grant it complete sovereignty while permitting it to remain a member of the Community. The Mali Federation became a sovereign state in June 1960.

Discord soon arose over external and internal policy, and on 20 August 1960, the federation was dissolved. On 22 September 1960, the Sudan declared itself independent as the Republic of Mali. Modibo Keita, a cofounder of the African Democratic Assembly and political secretary of the Mali Federation's African Federation Party, took control of the government. The break with Senegal was followed by the decision to leave the French Community. All ties between Senegal and Mali were severed, and Mali embargoed trade with or through Senegal until 1963, when an accord was reached.

The one-party dictatorship led by President Keita evolved into a socialist regime modeled on that of the People's Republic of China. However, by 1968, economic problems and discontent became severe. On 19 November, Keita was overthrown in a bloodless coup led by Lt. (later Gen.) Moussa Traoré. The 1960 constitution was abolished, and a 14-member Military Committee for National Liberation took command. The junta brought Mali back into the franc zone in 1968 and opened its doors to investment from nonsocialist as well as socialist countries.

Lt. Traoré became president in 1969, following an interim period of Yoro Diakité's presidency. (Diakité was expelled from the Military Committee in 1972 and died in the prison salt mines of Taoudenni in 1973.)

The military regime's efforts to improve the economic situation in Mali were frustrated by the prolonged period of drought that began in 1968 and peaked in 1972–73. It was estimated that during that time one-third of the population was rendered destitute. Severe drought conditions also prevailed in 1982–85.

In 1978, 29 army and police officers were convicted of plotting against the regime, and political unrest continued in later years. Traoré was elected president in 1979 under a new constitution, which also confirmed Mali as a one-party state. He was reelected in 1985. Fighting broke out between Mali and Burkina Faso on 25 December 1985 over possession of the Agacher Strip, an arid tract of land along their common border. About 65–70 men were killed before a cease-fire on 30 December. On 22 December 1986 the International Court of Justice, to which the dispute had been submitted in 1983, divided 2,952 sq km (1,140 sq mi) between the two countries in roughly equal parts.

Democratization

On 26 March 1991, Lt. Col. Amadou Toumani Touré engineered a coup that toppled the Traoré government. Following bloody confrontations between youth groups and the army in 1990 and 1991 in which more than 200 were killed, Touré immediately set up a National Reconciliation Council which appointed a broad-based Transitional Committee for Popular Salvation to oversee the transition to civilian democracy. In May 1991, a public trial broadcast over Malian radio eventually resulted in the February 1993 conviction of former President Traoré and three associates, who received death sentences for the March 1991 massacres.

A crisis was averted with a national conference, which included 48 political parties and some 700 civic associations. The participants met from 29 July to 14 August 1991, drafting new electoral rules, party statutes, and a new constitution, which was adopted by referendum in January 1992, and established an agenda for the transition. There were elections for municipal councilors and National Assembly deputies and, finally, presidential elections on 12 and 26 April 1992. Dr. Alpha Oumar Konaré, the leader of the Alliance for Democracy in Mali (ADEMA) became Mali's first democratically elected president with 69% of the vote. The Third Republic was launched. ADEMA also won 76 of the 116 National Assembly seats.

One of the last acts of the Touré transitional government was to negotiate (with Algerian mediation) a peace treaty in April 1992 with rebel Tuaregs in the north. The government acknowledged the Northerners' special status, and the Tuaregs renounced their claims to independence. Algeria agreed to guarantee the truce, which ended two years of fighting. In 1992 and 1993, between 60,000 and 100,000 Tuareg refugees returned from abroad. In February 1993, the government and the rebel group, the Unified Movements and Fronts of Azawad (MFUA), agreed to integrate MFUA guerrillas into the national army and, in May 1994, arrived at a further agreement to implement the 1992 National Pact. In May 1995, President Konaré personally visited refugee camps in bordering states in an effort to assure Tuareg refugees that it was safe to return home. In March 1996, after 3,000 Tuareg rebels had been integrated into the military, there was a massive ceremonial burning of their surrendered weapons in downtown Tombouctou. In January 2000, some 1,000 Tuaregs returned home to northern Mali from Niger.

A culmination of pressures led to a new government in April 1993. Abdoulaye Sekou Sow replaced Younoussi Touré as prime minister, and the National Congress of Democratic Initiative (CNIT) took a portion of the ministerial portfolios. However, this government was short-lived. Student disgruntlement with the economy, high unemployment, the negative effects of structural adjustment, and the devaluation of the XOF franc contributed to much popular dissatisfaction and to the fall of the Sow government in February 1994. In the subsequent government, ADEMA took 11 of the 16 ministries. Several ADEMA members left the party following Ibrahim Boubacar Keita's election as secretary of ADEMA and his appointment as prime minister. The detractors formed the Movement for Independence, Renaissance, and African Integration (MIRIA). The Patriotic Movement for Renovation (MPR) was also formed at this time, along with a splinter from the CNID, the Party for National Liberation (PARENA). Upset with the pace of reforms, students continued their violent unrest, re-

sulting in the January 1996 arrest of several student leaders. The crackdown was widely criticized, and in late January 1996, the CNID introduced a motion of no confidence in parliament, which the government was able to survive.

Malians took a step toward national healing in January 1999 when President Alpha Oumar Konaré commuted death sentences imposed on Traoré and his wife after they were convicted of embezzlement. The successful rural community elections of May-June 1999 strengthened Mali's quest for decentralized democracy. In spite of the low voter turnout caused by the boycott of the radical left, opposition groups won nearly 40% of the 10,000 council seats, though none of the parties won more than 10% of the seats. Given this new avenue for political participation, observers felt that the radical left, grouped under the Collectif des Partis Politiques de l'Opposition (COPPO), marginalized by its boycott, would want to contest future elections.

In February 2000, President Alpha Konaré announced a new national government spearheaded by Prime Minister Mande Sidibe, whose main task was to relaunch the economy. Konaré's cabinet included seven women and seven colonels. Six former ministers remained in government, including Foreign Minister Modibo Sidibe. Despite criticisms of corruption and failed economic policies, under Konaré, government became more representative and responsive to citizens. Society also became more open to debate. More than 40 newspapers, including 4 of 5 daily papers, were privately owned. Although the state controlled television, some 15 private radio stations operated in Bamako, and more than 40 stations broadcast freely up-country. Having served as chairman of ECOWAS, and being one a few African heads of state to stand down after completing his constitutional term of office, Alpha Konaré enhanced Mali's reputation internationally.

On 28 April 2002, Amadou Toumani Touré, nicknamed "ATT," emerged as the leader of the first-round presidential election with 29% of the vote, defeating former prime minister and rival, Ibrahim Boubacar Keita. In the run-off election on 12 May, Touré obtained 64% of the vote, defeating Soumaila Cissé to become the second democratically elected president of the Republic of Mali. Cissé won 35.6% of the vote. Eleven francophone African leaders witnessed the transfer of power from one constitutionally elected president to another—the first in Mali's history. Touré was reelected for a second term in 2007.

In 2006, the rebel Tuareg cause was renewed as militants stepped forward with accusations against the government of marginalization due to poor representation in government and the military. A May 2006 Tuareg raid in the town of Kidal resulted in a speedy peace deal signed in June. However, not all Tuareg groups were in agreement with the deal and sporadic violence continued through 2008. In December 2008, the North Mali Tuareg Alliance for Change (ATNMC) launched a raid against a military base in northern Mali, killing over 20 people. The military responded in January 2009 with a successful offensive against rebel bases in the northeast. The next month, nearly 700 Tuareg militants surrendered their arms in a ceremony that welcomed them into the regular army and marked the beginning of a new peace process. The government pledged to invest more resources into the economic development of the Tuareg homelands, but called upon the Tuareg to give up their demand for regional autonomy. Though the leader of the ATNMC was still at large, the government seemed confident that a permanent peace could be achieved.

In April 2010, the president announced a series of proposed constitutional reforms designed to reassess the balance of power within the government and thereby strengthen the nation's democratic structure. The amendments included the creation of a national senate, a state audit, and an independent regulatory authority for broadcasting. While the powers of the president would remain strong, the reforms would increase the powers of the constitutional court and the participation of political parties. In the spirit of increased democracy, the president did not propose a change to the two-term limit of the presidency. Despite public opposition in late 2011, the referendum was scheduled to coincide with presidential elections in April 2012.

13 GOVERNMENT

After independence, Mali was governed by the 1960 constitution, which provided for a national assembly. This body was abolished by the Keita regime in January 1968. Following the military coup of November 1968, the constitution itself was abolished and a provisional regime, the Military Committee for National Liberation, was established.

A long-awaited constitution was drawn up by the Military Committee in 1974 and endorsed in a public referendum on 2 June 1974. In this first national ballot since 1964, 99% of the electorate voted for acceptance. The constitution, which took full effect in 1979 and was amended in 1981, provided for a president with a six-year term, an 82-member national assembly, and a one-party system. The assembly was elected for a three-year term. There was universal suffrage at age 21. The 1979 constitution was replaced by a new constitution adopted by referendum in January 1992.

As of March 2012, the national assembly had 147 seats, with popularly elected members serving five-year terms. The president, elected by popular vote, chooses the prime minister who selects a cabinet.

14 POLITICAL PARTIES

The first political party in Mali, the Sudan Progressive Party (Parti Soudanais Progressiste—PSP) was an affiliate of the French Socialist Party. It dominated political activity in French Sudan for 10 years. It was followed by the Sudanese Union, a revolutionary, anticolonial party, which had its main strength in the towns. In the two elections of autumn 1946, the Sudanese Union won 32% and 38% of the total votes.

The PSP continued to maintain its majority in the Territorial Assembly until the end of 1955, when a split in its ranks enabled the Union to capture a majority. By March 1957, the Sudanese Union won 60 of the 70 seats in the new Territorial Assembly, and in the Legislative Assembly election of March 1959 it obtained 76.3% of the votes and all the seats. After the break with Senegal, it emerged as the only party in the Republic of Mali, one with control that extended even to the smallest Muslim villages through its national political bureau. In the parliamentary elections of April 1964, the single list of 80 deputies presented by the Sudanese Union was elected by 99.5% of the voters. The party was disbanded at the time of the 1968 coup d'état.

The Democratic Union of Malian People (Union Démocratique de Peuple Malien—UDPM) was created as the sole legal political party in 1979. It chose the presidential candidate and the single list of candidates for the National Assembly. In National Assembly elections in 1979, UDPM candidates received 99.89% of the votes cast; in 1982, 99.82%; and in 1985, 99.47%.

Shortly after the military coup in March 1991, some 48 parties were functioning, of which 23 contested the 1992 elections and 10 elected deputies to the National Assembly. The Alliance for Democracy in Mali (ADEMA) was the majority party, but with the change in prime minister and government on 12 April 1993, opposition parties were brought into cabinet; the National Committee for a Democratic Initiative (CNID) gained three cabinet posts.

In 1997, ADEMA held 76 seats in parliament and CNID held 9. Other parties represented in the National Assembly included the Sudanese Union/African Democratic Rally (US/RAD) with eight seats; the Popular Movement for the Development of the Republic of West Africa with six seats; Rally for Democracy and Progress (RDP) and the Union for Democracy and Development (UDD) with four seats each; and four other parties with the remaining seats. The UDPM, the former ruling party, attempted to relaunch itself in mid-1993, but the Supreme Court rejected its application for official recognition. It applied again in 1995 and was again rejected. Splits in ADEMA and CNID in 1995 resulted in the formation of the Movement for Independence, Renaissance, and African Integration (MIRIA)—headed by former vice president Traoré, the Patriotic Movement for Renovation (MPR), and the party for National Renovation (PARENA). In anticipation of the 1997 elections, PARENA announced it would form an alliance with ADEMA. However, flaws in the electoral process led to cancellation of the results by the Constitutional Court. The repeat elections, though ruled free and fair by international observers, were boycotted by 18 opposition parties.

In 2000, ADEMA had not lost its grip on the National Assembly, holding 130 of 147 seats, with 12 more held by allied parties, and only 5 by the opposition. Despite the tradition of male domination in Mali, 18 seats were held by women, and women held 6 cabinet posts in the government.

Elections to the Assembly were held 14 July and 28 July 2002, giving Amadou Toumani Touré's government a substantial show of popular support with the following breakdown of seats: L'Espoir (Hope) 2002 coalition 66, ADEMA 51, other parties 30. Despite Touré's attempt to ensure balance in the cabinet, the two main coalitions, Espoir 2002 and Alliance pour la République et la démocratie (ARD), criticized the new cabinet as being unrepresentative. L'Espoir 2002 objected to having received only two positions more than the ARD, even though they had backed the president in the second round of the elections. Nevertheless, Espoir did take most of the nonministerial parliamentary positions.

On 1 June 2003, in the presence of over 5,000 people gathered from around the country and abroad, Soumaila Cissé, vice president of ADEMA, who lost against Touré in the presidential election, announced the creation of a new party, Rally for Republic and Democracy (URD). The URD was expected to welcome an outflow of ADEMA supporters, perhaps as many as 25 deputies. ADEMA was working hard to stem the flow and estimated that no more than 10 of its deputies would defect to the URD.

The Alliance for Democracy and Progress, a coalition between ADEMA, URD, and other parties supporting the presidency of Touré, formed in December 2006. This was followed by the formation of the Front for Democracy and the Republic (FDR), a coalition of political parties including RPM and PARENA established to oppose Touré.

In the legislative elections of 2007, the Alliance for Democracy and Progress (ADP) won 113 of the 147 seats in the assembly, followed by the Front for Democracy and the Republic (FDR) with 15 seats. The African Solidarity for Democracy and Independence (SADI) took with four seats. Fifteen seats were gained by independent candidates. In the presidential elections of 2007, Amadou Toumani Touré was reelected with 71.2% of the vote, followed by Ibrahim Boubacar Keita of the Rally for Mali with 19.2%. The next elections were scheduled for 2012.

15 LOCAL GOVERNMENT

In recent years, Mali has undertaken an ambitious decentralization program, which involves the capital district of Bamako and eight regions: Gao, Kayes, Kidal, Koulikoro, Mopti, Segou, Sikasso, and Tombouctou. The state retains an advisory role in administrative and fiscal matters, and it provides technical support, coordination, and legal recourse to these levels. Opportunities for direct political participation and increased local responsibility for development have been improved.

In August-September 1998, elections were held for urban council members, who subsequently elected their mayors. In May–June 1999, citizens elected their communal council members for the first time. Female voter turnout was about 70% of the total, and observers considered the process open and transparent. With mayors, councils, and boards in place at the local level, newly elected officials, civil society organizations, decentralized technical services, private sector interests, and donor groups began partnering to further development.

16 JUDICIAL SYSTEM

Mali's legal system derives from French civil law and customary law, and provides for judicial review of legislative acts in a Constitutional Court (which was formally established on 9 March 1994). Mali has not accepted compulsory ICJ jurisdiction.

A Supreme Court was established in Bamako in 1969. It is made up of 19 members, nominated for five years. The judicial section has three civil chambers and one criminal chamber. The Supreme Court has both judicial and administrative powers. The administrative section deals with appeals and fundamental rulings.

The Court of Appeal is also in Bamako. There are two magistrate courts of first instance, a labor court, and a special court of state security. Customary courts have been abolished. The 1992 constitution established a separate constitutional court and a High Court of Justice charged with responsibility for trying senior government officials accused of treason.

The 1992 constitution guarantees independence of the judiciary. Constitutional provisions for freedom of speech, press, assembly, association, and religion are generally respected. Nonetheless, the executive has considerable influence over the judiciary. The president heads the Superior Judicial, the body that supervises judicial activity, and the Ministry of Justice appoints judges and oversees law enforcement. Trials are public, defendants have the right to an attorney of their choice, and court-appointed attorneys are available to indigent defendants in criminal cases. However, the judicial system has a large case backlog resulting in long periods of pretrial detention.

17 ARMED FORCES

The International Institute for Strategic Studies reports that armed forces in Mali totaled 7,350 members in 2011, all of which are members of the army. Armed forces represented 0.3% of the labor force in Mali. Defense spending totaled $319.6 million and accounted for 1.9% of gross domestic product (GDP), as reported by the CIA in 2006.

In April 2010 Mali joined forces with its neighbors to form the Joint Military Staff Committee of Algeria, Mali, Mauritania, and Niger. Based in Tamanrassett, Algeria, the general purpose of the committee is to strengthen cooperation through shared intelligence and joint military operations in the fight against terrorism, drug trafficking, and illegal weapons trade. Specifically, the committee hopes to combine efforts against the increasing regional threat from al-Qaeda. Regional and international leaders fear that al-Qaeda intends to establish bases in the Sahara, which could provide a safe haven for the terrorist organization if regional forces, such as the new committee, fail to take action.

18 INTERNATIONAL COOPERATION

Mali was admitted to the UN on 28 September 1960, and is a member of several nonregional specialized agencies, such as the FAO, UNSECO, UNIDO, the World Bank, IFC, IAEA, ILO, and the WHO. It also belongs to the African Development Bank, the ACP Group, G-77, ECOWAS, the Organization of the Islamic Conference (OIC), the New Partnership for Africa's Development (NEPAD), the Community of Sahel and Saharan States (CENSAD), the African Union, the West African Development Bank, the West African Economic and Monetary Union, and the WTO.

With Senegal and Mauritania, Mali comprises the Senegal River Development Organization. It is also a partner in the Liptako-Gourma regional development scheme with Burkina Faso and Niger. Mali is a member of the International Committee for the Control of the Drought in the Sahel (CILSS)

As a member of ECOWAS, Mali is participating in the six-nation group mediating the conflict in neighboring Côte d'Ivoire. In 2003, Mali contributed 200–300 troops for peacekeeping operations in the war-torn country. Mali has also offered support to UN missions and operations in Liberia (est. 2003), Sierra Leone (est. 1999), Burundi (est. 2004), and the Democratic Republic of the Congo (est. 1999). Mali is a member of the Nonaligned Movement.

In environmental cooperation, Mali is part of the Basel Convention, the Convention on Biological Diversity, Ramsar, CITES, the Kyoto Protocol, the Montréal Protocol, and the UN Conventions on the Law of the Sea, Climate Change and Desertification.

The government has maintained close ties with Algeria, particularly as allies in the struggle against Islamist terrorist groups of North Africa. Al-Qaeda in the Islamic Maghreb is believed to have its primary bases of operation in the Sahara regions of Algeria, Mali, and Niger. In June 2009, Mali forces successfully captured an al-Qaeda base near the Algerian border. In October 2009, the United States agreed to supply the Malian army with $5 million worth of equipment to aid in the fight against al-Qaeda. The equipment included vehicles, communication devices, and clothing, among other supplies. Sporadic action against Al-Qaeda continued through 2011. In October 2011 the Mauritania Army conducted an air raid with Malian assistance on an alleged al-Qaeda camp near the border. Mali is a member of the Trans-Sahara Counter Terrorism Partnership (TSCTP), which provides US government resources for security collaboration in the region.

19 ECONOMY

In 2010 Mali's economy grew at a moderate pace. The GDP rate of change in Mali, as of 2010, was 4.5%. Inflation stood at 2.5%, and unemployment was reported at 3%. It was estimated that agriculture accounted for 45% of GDP, industry 17%, and services 38%.

Economic activity in Mali centers on domestic agricultural and livestock production. Vast stretches of Sahara desert limit Mali's agricultural potential and subject the country to severe, prolonged, recurrent drought. In the 1980s a severe drought reportedly wiped out upwards of 80% of Malian herds. In periods of adequate rainfall, Mali approaches food self-sufficiency. The GDP growth rates are affected by the rainfall as well.

About 80% of the population was engaged in agriculture as of 2009. Irrigated lands along the Niger River have been the focus of infrastructure development loans designed to increase the production of rice. Historically, livestock production was a mainstay of the Malian economy. About 10% of the population is nomadic. The dry savannah plains are free of the tsetse fly and production has been oriented to serve the growing market in Côte d'Ivoire to the south.

Key sectors of economic growth in recent years have been in cotton production and gold: Mali was a leading producer and exporter of cotton in sub-Saharan Africa, and one of the largest producers of gold in West Africa.

Mali is rich in cultural and natural heritage and holds significant tourist potential. In 2010 the US Department of State recorded tourism as Mali's 3rd largest export, contributing 2.4% to GDP. Cultural attractions include ancient mosques such as the one in Djenne, the world's largest structure made of mud and a World Heritage Site, as well as the Dogon culture's cave dwellings. Although wildlife struggles in the country, notable animals such as elephants and giraffe hold potential for wildlife viewing.

State-centered policies pursued in the years following independence were largely unsuccessful and led to a reintegration of the Malian economy into the XOF franc zone. Subsequent economic plans imposed on Mali, first by the French and then by the IMF, sought to dismantle the parastatals, privatize industry, and disengage the government from manipulative agriculture policies and price controls. These measures were hindered by the influential Malian civil service, the drought in the early 1980s and, in 1986, the fall in cotton prices, which led the government to suspend its debt-servicing obligations and to a suspension of IMF and World Bank credits. However, deficits fell sharply in 1990 and 1991 as a result of higher taxes and reduced civil service and parastatal demands. Unfortunately, the political repercussions of the government's austerity measures led to its downfall in 1991. The new government, however, continued the structural adjustment process, and the effort to reduce the budget deficits was intensified.

In January 1994 France devalued the XOF franc, cutting its value in half. The devaluation was designed to encourage new investment, particularly in the export sectors of the economy, and discourage the use of hard currency reserves to buy products that could be grown domestically. Unlike exporting countries, however, Mali imported most of its food, had little to export, and therefore, benefited little from the devaluation. A period of inflation, where the rate approached 35%, followed devaluation in 1994. However, the reforms ultimately helped the economy grow at 5% annually between 1996 and 2007 with inflation down to a manageable 2.5% in 2007.

Despite the economic improvement, Mali remains heavily dependent on international aid from multilateral organizations (most significantly the World Bank, the African Development Bank, and Arab Funds) and bilateral programs funded by the European Union, France, United States ($117.87 million in 2010), Canada, Netherlands, and Germany. As of 2009, unemployment has been estimated at about 30%.

20 INCOME

The CIA estimated that in 2010 the GDP of Mali was $16.77 billion. The CIA defines GDP as the value of all final goods and services produced within a nation in a given year and computed on the basis of purchasing power parity (PPP) rather than value as measured on the basis of the rate of the exchange based on current dollars. The per capita GDP was estimated at $1,200. The annual growth rate of GDP was 4.5%. Per capita GDP, not adjusted for purchasing power parity, was $691, making Mali among the ten poorest nations on earth. In 2010, the average inflation rate was 2.5%.

Remittances play a major role in Malian income. According to the World Bank, remittances from citizens living abroad totaled $404.7 million in 2008, or about $29 per capita and accounted for approximately 2.4% of GDP.

As of 2011 it was estimated that household consumption was growing at an average annual rate of 2.4%. As of 2011 the most recent study by the World Bank reported that actual individual consumption in Mali was 74.5% of GDP and accounted for 0.02% of world consumption. By comparison, the United States accounted for 25.44% of world individual consumption. The World Bank also estimated that 36% of Mali's GDP was spent on food and beverages, 13% on housing and household furnishings, 3.6% on clothes, 3.3% on health, 7.4% on transportation, 0.7% on communications, 2.3% on recreation, 1.4% on restaurants and hotels, and 2.2% on miscellaneous goods and services and purchases from abroad.

21 LABOR

As of 2007, Mali had a total labor force of 3.241 million people. Within that labor force, the CIA estimates in 2005 noted that 80% were employed in agriculture, 10% in industry, and 10% in the service sector.

With the breakup of the Mali Federation in 1960, all the unions in the country joined together to form the National Union of Malian Workers (Union National des Travailleurs du Mali—UNTM). The UNTM was disbanded at the time of the 1968 coup, but was reestablished in 1970. Most workers organized in Mali belong to a union that is a member of the UNTM federation. A second federation, the Syndicated Confederation of Malian Workers, was formed following a split in the UNTM in 1997. The two groups divide the nation's 12 unions between them. In 2002, essentially all wage earners were union members. The constitution provides for the right to strike within certain limitations in some sectors. For instance, civil servants and state-employed workers must engage in mediation and give two weeks' notice of intent to strike.

Workers in the formal industrial sector may start to work as young as 12, with parental permission. However, this provision does not apply to the millions of children working in rural areas or in the urban informal economy. Wage workers are given extensive protection under the labor laws, including a maximum workweek, a minimum wage, and a specified number of days of paid annual leave. In 2008, the minimum wage was increased to XOF28,465, or $52 per month. The legal maximum workweek was set at 40 hours in industry, and 45 hours for agricultural laborers. Foreign, even illegal, workers are provided with the same protections.

22 AGRICULTURE

Roughly 4% of the total land is farmed, and the country's major crops include cotton, millet, rice, corn, vegetables, and peanuts. Cereal production in 2009 amounted to 6.3 million tons, fruit production 295,685 tons, and vegetable production 897,651 tons. The CIA reported cotton as Mali's number one export in 2010.

Millet and sorghum are cultivated mainly in the areas around Ségou, Bandiagara, and Nioro. Paddy rice is cultivated on irrigated farms in the area around Mopti, Ségou, and Niafounké. Cereals are produced for subsistence by 90% of farmers. Peanuts are grown in the Sudanese zone, as are cotton, fruits, vegetables, and henna. The shea tree nut, which grows wild, is exploited by Malians for its oil. Output fluctuates widely as a result of the amount and distribution of rainfall. Cotton is Mali's major foreign exchange earner. Buoyant world prices have increased foreign exchange earnings from cotton.

The Niger Office, now a state-controlled agency, was set up in 1932 to aid in improving cotton and rice production. It developed the irrigation and modern cultivation of some 81,000 hectares (200,000 acres) in the dry inland delta of the Niger. The infrastructure includes a dam (2.6 km wide/1.6 mi), irrigation canals, ditches and dikes, and such installations as housing stores, warehouses, rice and oil mills, cotton-ginning factories, sugar refineries, soap factories, research stations, schools, and dispensaries. Growing cotton in irrigated fields did not succeed and was abandoned in 1970. All cotton is now grown in nonirrigated fields in the regions of Bamako, Ségou, and Sikasso.

In April 2010, the Red Cross launched a massive relief operation to help hundreds of thousands of people in northern Mali and Niger who were suffering from the aftermath of a failed harvest. According to the Red Cross, some 250,000 people in those countries were short of food in April 2010, while millions more were suffering the effects of food insecurity. Rainfall in Northern Mali and Niger was 70% below the annual average in 2009, severely affecting the harvest and straining the abilities of herders to maintain their livestock. Because there were far more cows than the land could support, the Red Cross agreed to purchase 20,000 head of cattle from local herders. The meat harvest from those animals was used to feed the hungry. The whole operation cost the Red Cross tens of millions of dollars, almost triple the amount the agency had budgeted for Mali and Niger in 2010.

23 ANIMAL HUSBANDRY

The UN Food and Agriculture Organization (FAO) reported that Mali dedicated 34.7 million hectares (85.6 million acres) to permanent pasture or meadow in 2009. During that year, the country tended 35 million chickens, 8.7 million head of cattle, and 79,100 pigs. The production from these animals amounted to 110,566 tons of beef and veal, 2,309 tons of pork, 38,382 tons of poultry, 5,099 tons of eggs, and 763,197 tons of milk. Mali also produced 20,970 tons of cattle hide and 341 tons of raw wool.

Virtually all cattle are owned by nomads, who make up 10% of the population. Principal nomadic ethnic groups include the Tuareg and the Fulani (Peul). Cattle herding is centered in the Sahel (Nioro-Nara), the central Niger Delta (Ségou-Mopti-Bandiagara-Niafounké-Goundam), and the curve of the Niger (Tombouctou-Gao). A significant portion of trade in live animals is clandestine, because of higher prices in neighboring countries. Principal clients for cattle are Côte d'Ivoire and Ghana, and for sheep and goats are Côte d'Ivoire and Algeria. Meat and cattle are also exported to other African neighbors, such as Guinea, Senegal, Niger, and Benin.

There are two modern slaughterhouses, in Bamako and Gao. Livestock exports are the third-largest source of foreign exchange after cotton and gold.

24 FISHING

The Niger and its tributaries are extensively fished, and the Mopti region, where the Niger and Bani rivers flood the delta during the rainy season, accounts for 90% of the catch. The Senegal River accounts for most of the rest. Fishermen use nets, harpoons, and snares. In 2008 the annual total national capture equaled 100,000 tons according to the UN FAO. About 90% of the fishing catch is dried or smoked for domestic consumption and export; Nile tilapia and North African catfish are the main species. River fishing was severely affected by the 1968–74 and 1982–85 droughts.

25 FORESTRY

Approximately 10% of Mali is covered by forest. The UN FAO estimated 2009 roundwood production at 412,900 cu m (14.6 million cu ft). The value of all forest products, including roundwood, totaled $439,000.

Forests and woodlands are estimated to cover some 13.1 million hectares (35.6 million acres), or about 10.8% of the total land area. A total of six forest reserves cover 229,400 hectares (566,900 acres). Mali's Water and Forests Service works to preserve and increase the amount and quality of general and classified forest domain and to assure reasonable exploitation. Mali's total forest area includes 530,000 hectares (1,346,200 acres) of plantation forest.

Wood is Mali's primary energy source, and overcutting for fuel is a serious problem. The UN FAO estimates that Mali lost 11.8% of its forest between 1990 and 2010. Many climate change models depict a continuation of the reduction in rainfall that has occurred in West Africa in the preceding decades. Given this, forests under pressure from bush fires and fuel cutting may not regenerate into the same species of diverse forests that now exist in the south of Mali.

26MINING

Mali's mineral sector is dominated by gold mining. The country is Africa's third-largest gold producer, behind South Africa and Ghana, with gold accounting for 80% of Mali's total exports in 2009. Gold mining employs about 8,000 workers, with wages of $163 million. Total gold mine output (metal content) was 42,364 kg (93,397 lbs) in 2009, up from 41,160 kg (90,742 lbs) in 2008. The Morilla gold mine, opened in 2001, produced 10,637 kg (23,451 lbs) in 2009, from a resource of 140,000 kg (308,647 lbs). The Loulo mine produced 10,936 kg (24,110 lbs) of gold in 2009. The Kalana underground mine produced 519 kg (1,144 lbs) that year. Gold production increased in 2009 due to the start of operations at the Syama mine and the reopening of the Tabakoto mine.

In 2011, political instability and war in much of Africa helped increase the nation's gold mining industry as investors brought their business to Mali instead of competitors such as Guinea, Cote d'Ivoire, and Ghana. While the euro and other currencies were fluctuating with the global economic crisis, investors sought after gold because it would not drop in value. The German Pearl Gold company holds a 25 percent stake in Mali's gold mines, which are believed to hold 1.75 million ounces of recoverable gold.

Mali, in 2009, also produced gypsum and salt. Salt output in that year totaled 6,000 metric tons. Gypsum production in 2009 totaled an estimated 8,700 metric tons. Artisanal gold miners have also found diamonds in the Kenieba area.

Mali's mining sector remains underdeveloped due to a lack of infrastructure needed to support mining. Bauxite, iron, calcium, kaolin, copper, manganese, phosphate, tin, zinc, lead, marble, and lithium deposits have been located. Manganese reserves were 7.5 billion tons, of 30–40% grade ore. Western Mali had numerous bauxite deposits, ranging from 10 to 580 million tons, at 2–48% aluminum content. Phosphate reserves were estimated at 10 million tons, with anhydrous phosphate content of 31%. There was a marble quarry at Sélinkégni, a limestone quarry at Diamou, and a phosphate complex at Bourem. Mineral exploration interest was focused on diamond, gold, and oil.

All mines were owned by the state; some quarries were privately owned. At the request of mining companies, the government set up a regional mining office in Kayes to eliminate the 500 km journey between Bamako and the primary mining region in western Mali for routine administrative operations. The government eliminated the tax on insurance for vehicles used on mining sites, and reduced taxes on sales by mining companies (from 6–3%) and on proceeds from the transfer of shares in mining companies (from 20–10%). The government also lengthened the tenure for medium-scale mining permits, and introduced a four-year permit for small-scale mining. To address Mali's underdeveloped transportation network, the Africa Development Fund approved a loan to finance the multinational Kankan-Kouremale-Bamako road project in Guinea and Mali.

27ENERGY AND POWER

The World Bank reported in 2008 that Mali produced 490 million kWh of electricity and consumed 552.2 million kWh, or 39 kWh per capita. This energy is largely sourced outside of the country. Mali, as of 2012 had no known reserves of crude oil, natural gas, or refining capacity. There was no demand for imports of natural gas in that same year. In 2010 it was estimated that electricity provided only 1% of total energy usage in the country (the rest coming from wood, charcoal, or other sources).

In October 2010, the government inaugurated a new Chinese-built thermal power plant that added 55 MW to the nation's electricity generation capacity, moving total capacity to 180 megawatts operated by the state power company EDM (Energie du Mali). The new plant will be operated by the Burkina Faso-based company Sopam for five years, after which time operation will be transferred to EDM.

28INDUSTRY

Mali has a small industrial sector, mostly enterprises producing textiles and consumer goods. Groundnut-oil, rice-polishing, fruit-preserving, sugar-distilling, tea, and cottonseed-oil and cottonseed-cake plants are in operation, as are slaughterhouses. Industrial facilities include a vinegar factory, a cigarette factory, a soft-drink plant, a flour mill, a shoe factory, a tannery, and two textile plants. Other plants make tiles, furniture, farm implements, batteries, paint, and cosmetics and assemble radios, bicycles, and motorcycles. There are a few construction related facilities, including a brick factory, a ceramics factory, and a cement plant.

29SCIENCE AND TECHNOLOGY

The World Bank reported in 2009 that there were no patent applications in science and technology in Mali. Mali has a shortage of trained scientists and technicians and relies heavily on foreign, chiefly French, assistance. A French tropical agronomy research center is located in Bamako. The National Directorship for Meteorology, also in Bamako, publishes bulletins on agrometeorology and climatology. National centers for fruit and zootechnical research are located in Bamako. A national association for mineral research and mining is located in Kati. The National Center of Scientific and Technological Research in Bamako coordinates all research activity in Mali. National schools of engineering and of medicine and pharmacology are also in Bamako. The Rural Polytechnic Institute of Katibougou provides instruction and conducts research in agronomy, agricultural economics, stockbreeding, forestry, veterinary science, and rural technology. In 1987–97, science and engineering students accounted for 12% of college and university enrollments.

In 2010 the Malaria Research and Training Center at the University of Bamako opened a new biosafety laboratory designated for the production of genetically modified mosquitoes that are resistant to malaria. The lab is part of an ongoing joint research program between the University of Bamako and Keele University in the United Kingdom. The program was designed to research the potential for producing genetically modified mosquitoes that are resistant to malaria and that will be able to pass those resistant genes on to its offspring. Researchers hoped to begin outdoor field tests, in specially designed cages, by 2014. The ultimate goal is to have the ability to release a large number of the malaria-resistant insects in areas throughout the world, with the hope that the modified insects will steadily outnumber the rest, leading to a major decrease in the spread of disease.

Principal Trading Partners – Mali (2010)

(In millions of US dollars)

Country	Total	Exports	Imports	Balance
World	5,100.0	2,250.0	2,850.0	-600.0
Senegal	540.1	0.3	539.8	-539.5
France	415.7	6.3	409.4	-403.2
Côte d'Ivoire	374.1	1.0	373.1	-372.1
China	316.5	63.9	252.6	-188.7
South Africa	108.8	0.2	108.7	-108.5
Germany	92.8	3.0	89.8	-86.8
South Korea	89.3	84.0	5.2	78.8
Belgium	85.3	6.0	79.2	-73.2
Italy	69.7	8.7	61.0	-52.3
India	57.2	2.7	54.5	-51.8

(…) data not available or not significant.

(n.s.) not specified.

SOURCE: *2011 Direction of Trade Statistics Yearbook,* New York: United Nations, 2011.

Balance of Payments – Mali (2009)

(In millions of US dollars)

Current Account		**-654.9**
Balance on goods		-212.6
Imports	-1,986.3	
Exports	1,773.7	
Balance on services		-471.2
Balance on income		-457.4
Current transfers		486.3
Capital Account		**384.1**
Financial Account		**892.3**
Direct investment abroad		30.9
Direct investment in Mali		718.5
Portfolio investment assets		-60.3
Portfolio investment liabilities		21.3
Financial derivatives		-1.6
Other investment assets		-370.7
Other investment liabilities		554.3
Net Errors and Omissions		**-175.2**
Reserves and Related Items		**-446.3**

(…) data not available or not significant.

SOURCE: *Balance of Payment Statistics Yearbook 2011,* Washington, DC: International Monetary Fund, 2011.

³⁰DOMESTIC TRADE

Following independence, the government initiated an extensive program for the organization of rural cooperatives in the villages, with central purchasing organizations in the chief towns of the administrative districts. However, Mali's postindependence socialism has recently given way to emphasis on free trade and private enterprise. Agriculture is the basis of the economy. Significant small scale local trade of agricultural commodities including rice, vegetables, and meat exists in markets throughout Mali. Historically, during the Mali Empire, the economy centered on trading salt from the north with gold from mines in the south.

Since 1988, the government has been working on economic reforms that include a large scale privatization process and legal changes to encourage domestic commerce. For instance, business

applications can generally be processed through a single ministry, in a program called *guichet unique* or "one window." This reform allows businesses to open sooner and with far less red tape than before. The government has also eliminated price controls on consumer goods and developed both a commerce code and commercial courts to encourage fair business development.

Normal business hours are from 8 a.m. to noon and from 3 to 5 p.m., Monday-Saturday. On Fridays, most businesses close at noon. Banks are open from 8 a.m. to 2:30 p.m., Monday-Thursday, and from 8 a.m. to 12:30 p.m., Friday and Saturday.

³¹FOREIGN TRADE

Mali imported $2.358 billion worth of goods and services in 2008, while exporting $294 million worth of goods and services. Major import partners in 2009 were Senegal, 12.8%; France, 10.9%; Cote d'Ivoire, 9.4%; China, 5.9%; and South Korea, 4.8%. Its major export partners were China, 20.9%; Thailand, 7.4%; Morocco, 5.8%; South Korea, 5.7%; Indonesia, 4.9%; Burkina Faso, 4.2%; and France, 4.1%.

Cotton, gold, and livestock are Mali's leading exports. Increased cotton production and rising world prices have increased foreign exchange receipts, as has increased gold production. The 50% devaluation of the XOF franc in 1994 helped boost cotton, livestock, and other exports but doubled the cost of imports. Comparing 1994 to the index year of 1987, export activity decreased by 5% while import activity rose by 10%. Machinery and equipment, construction materials, petroleum, foodstuffs, and textiles are imported.

Since 1999 gold has emerged as Mali's primary export commodity, providing modest forest exchange reserves. In 2011 Mali was Africa's third-largest producer of gold.

³²BALANCE OF PAYMENTS

Mali's chronic deficit in trade and other goods and services is largely offset by aid from other governments and international organizations. The balance of payments is sharply influenced by the volume in cotton exports and the world price of cotton, the price of gold, the volume of official livestock exports, and the value of government-purchased imports. Mali's minimal industrial base and its dependence on imported machinery and petroleum negatively impact its balance of payments. Major imports to Mali include petroleum, machinery and equipment, construction materials, foodstuff, and textiles.

The CIA estimated that Mali's current account balance was -$723.9 million in 2010. In 2011 the figure had worsened to -$789.6 million.

³³BANKING AND SECURITIES

In 1959, the Central Bank of the West African States (Banque Centrale des États de l'Afrique de l'Ouest—BCEAO) succeeded the Currency Board of French West Africa and Togo as the bank of issue for the former French West African territories, known now as the franc zone: Benin, Burkina Faso, Côte d'Ivoire, Mali, Niger, Senegal, and Togo. Foreign exchange receipts of the member states went into the franc zone's exchange pool, which in turn covered their foreign exchange requirements. In July 1962, however, Mali withdrew from the BCEAO and West African Monetary

Union and established a bank of its own, the Bank of the Republic of Mali, which issued a new currency, the Malian franc.

In 1967, Mali returned to the franc zone, with its franc set at half the value of the XOF franc. In March 1968, the banking system was reorganized, and the Central Bank of Mali was established as the central issuing bank. In December 1982, Mali's application to rejoin the West African Monetary Union was rejected, as Upper Volta (now Burkina Faso), which had a border dispute with Mali, continued to oppose Mali's readmission until 1983. In 1984 it rejoined the BCEAO and the monetary union.

In addition to the Central Bank, commercial banks in 1997 included: the Bank of Africa, Banque Commerciale de Sahel, Banque Malienne de Crédit et du Depots, and the Financial Bank Mali. Development banks in Mali include the Banque de Développment du Mali and the Banque Nationale de Développment Agricole. Domestic savings have increased since 1994. Along with other members of the Union économique at minétaire ouest-africaine (UEMOA), Mali now faces the problem of diversifying credit instruments in favor of small and medium-sized enterprises, which have historically relied upon informal sources of investment.

The discount rate, the interest rate at which the central bank lends to financial institutions in the short term, was 16% as of 2010, a drastic increase from 4.25% the previous year.

34 INSURANCE

There were at least six insurance companies in Mali as of 2012, the largest being the National Fund of Insurance and Reinsurance, a state company. Third-party motor insurance is compulsory.

35 PUBLIC FINANCE

In 2010 the budget of Mali included $1.5 billion in public revenue and $1.8 billion in public expenditures. The budget deficit

---

Public Finance – Mali (2009)

(In billions of francs, budgetary central government figures)

Revenue and Grants	909.5	100.0%
Tax revenue	624.3	68.6%
Social contributions	…	
Grants	184.6	20.3%
Other revenue	100.7	11.1%
Expenditures	996.9	100.0%
General public services	…	…
Defense	…	…
Public order and safety	…	…
Economic affairs	…	…
Environmental protection	…	…
Housing and community amenities	…	…
Health	…	…
Recreational, culture, and religion	…	…
Education	…	…
Social protection	…	…

(…) data not available or not significant.

SOURCE: *Government Finance Statistics Yearbook 2010*, Washington, DC: International Monetary Fund, 2010.

---

amounted to 2.8% of GDP. Public debt was 43.1% of GDP, with $3.024 billion of the debt held by foreign entities.

Mali participated in various IMF programs in the late 1990s and early 2000s. In order to fulfill its IMF responsibilities, the country has been privatizing companies for the past several years. Privatization efforts in the cotton industry occurred during 2005–12, and the main telecommunications company was privatized in 2009. Mali was judged eligible for the Heavily Indebted Poor Countries (HIPC) initiative and has been benefiting from it since 2000 as a budgetary support.

36 TAXATION

Elements of a progressive taxation system were introduced in 1992. There is a tax on business profits and a general income tax with a graduated rate. The statutory rate tax rate on corporate profits was 35% in 2011. There is also a value-added tax (VAT) with a standard rate of 18% as of 2011 for most goods and services, as well as an excise tax on alcoholic beverages, fuels and lubricants, cartridges and bullets, tobacco, and other goods. In addition, there are taxes on property, livestock, motor vehicles, and firearms and a head tax, among others. There are also registration and stamp fees (XOF1,500 as of 2011).

37 CUSTOMS AND DUTIES

Customs duties constitute the leading source of government income and are imposed on both imports and exports. Import policies have been liberalized and import licensing eliminated since 1988. Duties on most goods range from 5 to 30% for imports from countries that do not belong to the West African Economic Community (CEAO), except for taxes on luxury goods, including cars and videocassette recorders, which vary from 80 to 100%. Duties for imports from CEAO members are approximately half the rate charged to nonmembers.

38 FOREIGN INVESTMENT

Foreign investment in Mali is relatively small and is mainly in retail trade or light industry. With independence and Mali's announcement of an economic policy aimed at "planned socialism," private foreign investment came to a standstill in 1961. By 1968, after seven years of almost no private foreign investment, the trend was reversed and Mali specifically requested private foreign investment to aid its development. The parastatal sector was to be dismantled, although it has remained a significant part of the economy.

The 1991 investment code offers certain incentives, mostly in the form of tax holidays of 5–10 years to companies prepared to invest in certain areas. In the three free zones, companies are granted permanent exemption from all fees and taxes, but must sell 20% of their production on the national market. Foreign and national investors are treated equally by law.

In 1998, annual foreign direct investment (FDI) inflows to Mali fell to $35.8 million, down from $74.3 million in 1997. FDI inflow increased to $51.3 million in 1999, and for 2000 and 2001 averaged $104.6 million. In 2002 FDI peaked at $244 million but fell to $132 million in 2003 and $180 million in 2004. FDI in Mali was a net inflow of $109.1 million according to World Bank figures published in 2009. FDI represented 1.21% of GDP.

39 ECONOMIC DEVELOPMENT

The 1994 devaluation of the XOF franc resulted in increased exports of cotton, livestock, gold, and other products, but raised the price of imports. Strong prices for cotton worldwide, combined with record production in Mali in 1995, were both positive factors for the Mali economy. Sporadic droughts and the instability in Cote d'Ivoire in the late 1990s have been setbacks to economic development.

The government has taken steps to liberalize the regulatory climate in order to encourage foreign investment. Price controls on consumer goods (including on petroleum products), import quotas, and export taxes have all been eliminated. Privatization of state-owned enterprises continued throughout the 1990s and into the 21st century. In 1999, Mali negotiated a $64 million four-year Poverty Reduction and Growth Facility (PRGF) arrangement with the International Monetary Fund (IMF). In 2003, Mali was granted $675 million in debt service relief under the IMF/World Bank Heavily Indebted Poor Countries (HIPC) initiative to improve governance, strengthen social services, and develop infrastructure and key productive sectors.

Mali received $117.87 million in bilateral aid from the US Department of State and USAID. The country also has received $461 million through a Millennium Challenge Corporation contract to provide irrigation to 5,200 hectares of agricultural land and to make capital improvements to the international airport. In 2009 Official Development Aid (ODA) accounted for 11.1% of GNI, as reported by the World Bank. This represented a meaningful reduction since 2006, when it accounted from 15% of GNI.

Economic development in Mali is limited by lack of infrastructure, the large dispersed nature of population centers in a geographically large country, corruption, and the nascent state of industry and value added production. In 2012 the World Bank's "Doing Business" report ranked Mali at 146 out of 183 economies in ease of conducting business operations.

40 SOCIAL DEVELOPMENT

Social welfare services are available mainly in urban areas, basically as an extension of labor benefits and medical aid under the labor code, which includes provisions for medical care, workers' compensation, and retirement benefits. Pensions were paid for by employee contributions of 3.6% and employer contributions in the amount of 5.4%. A system of family allowances, implemented in 2004 for wage earners, provides maternity and children's allowances, along with classes in prenatal and infant care. Employers are required to provide free sick leave to their employers, as well as maternity benefits equal to 100% of earnings for 14 weeks. Under tribal organization, the individual's basic welfare needs are traditionally cared for by the group. This system, however, is breaking down as the country develops.

The government has made a special effort to improve the status of women, and a few women have entered government employment. Yet, social and cultural factors still sharply limit educational and economic opportunities for most women. Despite legal protections, most women face active discrimination in the areas of divorce, inheritance, and child custody. Domestic abuse and violence against women is a common and tolerated problem. Women have little access to legal services. Female genital mutilation, a painful and often life-threatening procedure, is also commonly performed on young girls. It was estimated by German Development Agency (GTZ) that in 2007 92% of women between 15 and 49 had undergone this procedure. The government is actively seeking to eliminate this practice. Child labor persists. Human rights are generally respected, although prison conditions remain poor.

In August 2009, the Malian parliament passed a controversial new family law designed to strengthen and protect the rights of women. The passage was immediately met with protests throughout the country as demonstrators called the law a violation of Islamic faith. One of the most contentious points of the law was the right of inheritance for women and for children born out of wedlock. The words "paternal power" in regards to family law were changed to "parental power," thus implying a greater role for women in family matters, and part of the legislation implied that women are not required to obey their husbands. The law also raised the legal age for marriage to eighteen. The leader of Mali's High Islamic Council urged the president not to sign the law as leading imams and Muslim scholars claimed that the lawmakers were traitors to Allah. The leader of the National Union of Muslim Women's Association stated that most women in the nation do not support the law, claiming that only the "intellectual" minority is in favor of it. As a result, the president refused to sign the law.

41 HEALTH

According to the CIA, life expectancy in Mali was 49 years in 2011. The country spent 11.1% of its GDP on healthcare, amounting to $38 per person. There were 1 physician, 3 nurses and midwives, and 6 hospital beds per 10,000 inhabitants. The fertility rate was 6.5, while the infant mortality rate was 101 per 1,000 live births. In 2008 the maternal mortality rate, according to the World Bank, was 830 per 100,000 births. It was estimated that 71% of children were vaccinated against measles. The CIA calculated HIV/AIDS prevalence in Mali to be about 1% in 2009.

Most health care is provided by the public medical services. At Bamako are the Institute of Tropical Ophthalmology and the Marchoux Institute for Leprosy, which, in addition to treating patients, carry out research. The number of private doctors and well-equipped medical institutions is small. Pharmaceutical policies have resulted in the destruction of the public network of drug distribution. Despite the high level of healthcare investment, lack of organization and misappropriation of money has impaired the effectiveness of the healthcare system.

The principal diseases are malaria, leprosy, tuberculosis, enteritis and other intestinal diseases, cholera, pneumonia, and infectious and parasite-related diseases such as schistosomiasis, onchocerciasis, guinea worm, and trypanosomiasis. Anemia, malnutrition, and tetanus are also widespread.

42 HOUSING

Providing housing in the wake of rapid urbanization has been an ongoing challenge for the government of Mali. An estimated 45% of all residents in Bamako were living in substandard settlement housing, often in neighborhoods defined as slum or squatter settlements. Less than 2% of the district population had connections to sewage facilities. Only about 17% had in-home water connections. The government has tried to set new programs in place to stop the spread of the informal slum and squatter settlements and to upgrade such housing to higher standards.

Formal housing structures in Bamako are like those of a European city. Elsewhere, housing ranges from similar urban structures to the tents of Tuareg nomads, the circular mud huts with thatched roofs characteristic of the indigenous African villages, and traditional Sudanese architecture. The latter employs a common building material called *banco*, a mixture of wet mud and straw that dries into a hard, almost cement-like consistency. This is applied over wooden frames and can be used for buildings of several stories. The buildings resemble those in North Africa and the Middle East. The UNESCO World Heritage-listed Great Mosque in Djenne, Mali, is the world's largest structure made of mud and uses this building material.

Government activity is largely concentrated on improvement of urban housing and sanitation. The Real Estate Trust, a public corporation established in 1949, provides housing loans to persons wishing to build on their own land.

43 EDUCATION

In 2009 the World Bank estimated that 73% of age-eligible children in Mali were enrolled in primary school. Of these students only 55% are expected to complete primary school. Secondary enrollment for age-eligible children stood at 28% in 2010. Tertiary enrollment was estimated at 6%. Of those enrolled in tertiary education, there were 100 male students for every 45 female students. Overall, the CIA estimated that Mali had a literacy rate of 46.4%. Public expenditure on education represented 4.4% of GDP.

The Malian school system begins with an initial primary cycle of six years, followed by a six-year cycle of secondary schooling (divided into two three-year stages). At the upper secondary level, students may opt to attend technical schools (two to three years) or vocational schools (four years). The academic year runs from October to June.

In 2010, about 3% of age-eligible children were enrolled in some type of preschool program. The student-to-teacher ratio for primary school was about 50:1 in 2010, a slight improvement from 54:1 in 2005.

The University of Mali has four faculties: medicine, pharmacy and dentistry; technical sciences; juridical and economic sciences; and languages, arts, and humanities. The university also has schools for business administration, engineering, and teacher training. The Rural Polytechnic Institute of Katibougou is in Koulikoro.

44 LIBRARIES AND MUSEUMS

The National Library and Archives (20,000 volumes), a municipal library, and the library of the Islamic Center, both located in Bamako, opened in 1987. In addition, the French Cultural Center, with 27,000 volumes, serves as a public library, and there is a US Information Service library as well as several other privately run libraries. The Public Reading Franco-Malian Operation, founded in 1977, sponsors about 52 public-reading libraries in the district of Bamako. Tombouctou has a center of historic research with libraries and museums containing valuable Arabic manuscripts. The National Museum, which also has a library, is in Bamako, as is the Sudanese Museum, detailing the country's history as the for-

mer French Sudan. Regional museums are located in Gao and Sikasso, and there is a historical museum in Tombouctou.

45 MEDIA

The constitution of Mali provides for free speech and a free press, and the government is said to respect these rights in practice.

In 2009 the CIA reported that there were 81,000 telephone landlines in Mali. In addition to landlines, mobile phone subscriptions averaged 29 per 100 people with a total of 3.7 million mobile cell phones in use. There was 1 FM radio station, 230 AM radio stations, and 1 shortwave radio station.

In 2011, the state-owned broadcaster Office de Radiodiffusion Television du Mali (ORTM), operated the nation's only television station, launched in 1993. In 2010, the country had 524 Internet hosts. In 2009, there were some 249,800 Internet users in Mali. Internet users numbered 2 per 100 citizens.

Prominent newspapers in 2010 included *Bulletin Quotidien* and *Les Echos* (circulation 25,000). Several newspapers have been forced to shut down for lack of adequate funding. Those papers still in business are often published sporadically. On average, there may be 10 or 12 papers available for purchase on any given day.

46 ORGANIZATIONS

There is a Chamber of Commerce and Industry in Bamako and a Chamber of Commerce in Kayes. There are youth and women's affiliates of the UDPM. The government is hoping to increase food production through the formation of village cooperatives. The Committee for the Coordination of NGOs in Mali works with organizations involved with emergency relief, environmental improvement and preservation, and community development.

A Junior Chamber program is available for youth. There are a number of sports associations throughout the country and volunteer service organizations, such as the Lions Clubs International, are also present. A few health organizations are active. There are national chapters of the Red Cross Society, Caritas, and Amnesty International.

47 TOURISM, TRAVEL, AND RECREATION

The *Tourism Factbook*, published by the UN World Tourism Organization, reported 160,000 incoming tourists to Mali in 2009, who spent a total of $286 million. Of those incoming tourists, there were 73,000 from Europe, 45,000 from Africa, and 27,000 from the Americas. There were 10,498 hotel beds available in Mali. The estimated daily cost to visit Bamako, the capital, was $250. The cost of visiting other cities averaged $141.

Mali is world renowned for its traditional music, which is believed to be the progenitor to American blues music, brought to the US through the slave trade. Musical influences come from many local ethnic groups as well as historical influence from Moorish (ancient Moroccan) music. Ali Farka Touré was the most famous Malian musician and died in 2006.

A government tourist organization was created in April 1974 to develop hunting, fishing, and sightseeing in Mali, particularly in the areas around Mopti, Tombouctou, and Gao. There are modern motels in Bamako and in Tombouctou, the ancient capital of Muslim learning and culture, previously forbidden to foreigners. Other attractions are Mali's national parks and game reserves. Football (soccer) is a popular sport.

A visa must be obtained for entry into Mali for citizens of all but a few neighboring countries. A vaccination certificate for yellow fever is also needed if traveling from an infected area. Typhoid, tetanus, meningitis, and hepatitis immunizations are recommended.

⁴⁸FAMOUS PERSONS

Early figures associated with the area of present-day Mali include Mansa Musa (r. 1312–37), ruler of the Mali Empire, and Sonni 'Ali Ber (r. 1464–92) and Askia Muhammad I (r. 1492–1528), rulers of the Songhai Empire. Later figures include al-Hajj 'Umar (1797–1864), who plunged the entire area into a bloody holy war before he was killed while trying to put down a rebellion, and Samory Touré, (1835–1900), who fought the French at the head of a Malinke army for 16 years (1882–98). Modibo Keita (1915–77) was, until November 1968, a leading figure in the political life of the country. He became the first president of the Republic of Mali in 1960. Moussa Traoré (b. 1936) was president of Mali from 1969 to 1991. Alpha Oumar Konaré (b. 1946) was elected president in 1992; he served until 2002. Brigadier Gen. Amadou Toumani Touré (b. 1948) is considered the founder of Mali's democratic movement; he won the presidential elections in 2002.

⁴⁹DEPENDENCIES

Mali has no territories or colonies.

⁵⁰BIBLIOGRAPHY

Conrad, David C. *Empires of Medieval West Africa: Ghana, Mali, and Songhay.* New York: Chelsea House, 2010.

Imperato, Pascal J., ed. *Historical Dictionary of Mali.* Lanham, MD: Scarecrow Press, 2008.

Le Quellec, Jean-Loíc. *Rock Art in Africa: Mythology and Legend.* New York: Rizzoli International, 2004.

Mali Investment and Business Guide: Strategic and Practical Information. Washington, DC: International Business Publications USA, 2012.

Perinbam, B. Marie. *Family Identity and the State in the Bamako Kafu, c.1800–c.1900.* Boulder, CO: Westview, 1997.

Schulz, Dorothea E. *Culture and Customs of Mali.* Santa Barbara, CA: Greenwood, 2012.

Soares, Benjamin F. *Islam and the Prayer Economy: History and Authority in a Malian Town.* Ann Arbor: University of Michigan Press, 2005.

Zeilig, Leo, and David Seddon. *A Political and Economic Dictionary of Africa.* Philadelphia: Routledge/Taylor and Francis, 2005..

MAURITANIA

Mauritanian Islamic Republic
[French] *République Islamique de Mauritanie;*
[Arabic] *Al-Jumhuriyah; al-Islamiyah al-Muritaniyah*

CAPITAL: Nouakchott

FLAG: The flag consists of a gold star and crescent on a light green field.

ANTHEM: *Hymne National de la Republique Islamique de Mauritanie (National Anthem of the Islamic Republic of Mauritania).*

MONETARY UNIT: The ouguiya (MRO), a paper currency of 5 khoums, issued by the Central Bank of Mauritania, replaced the Communauté Financière Africaine franc on 29 June 1973. There are coins of 1 khoum and 1, 5, 10, and 20 ouguiyas, and notes of 100, 200, 500, and 1,000 ouguiyas. MRO1 = US$0.003431 (or US$1 = MRO289) as of April 2012.

WEIGHTS AND MEASURES: The metric system is the legal standard.

HOLIDAYS: New Year's Day, 1 January; Labor Day, 1 May; African Liberation Day, 25 May; Anniversary of the Proclamation of the Republic, 28 November. Movable religious holidays include Laylat al-Miraj, Eid al-Fitr, Eid al-Adha, 1st of Muharram (Muslim New Year), and Milad an-Nabi.

TIME: GMT.

¹LOCATION, SIZE, AND EXTENT

Situated in West Africa, Mauritania has an area of 1,030,700 sq km (397,955 sq mi). Mauritania extends 1,515 km (941 mi) NE–SW and 1,314 km (816 mi) SE–NW. Comparatively, Mauritania is slightly larger than three times the size of the state of New Mexico. It is bordered on the NE by Algeria, on the E and S by Mali, on the SW by Senegal, on the W by the Atlantic Ocean, and on the NW and N by the Western Sahara, with a total estimated boundary length of 5,828 km (3,621 mi), of which 754 km (469 mi) is coastline.

Mauritania's capital city, Nouakchott, is located on the Atlantic Coast.

²TOPOGRAPHY

There are three distinct geographic regions in Mauritania: a narrow belt along the Senegal River valley in the south, where soil and climatic conditions permit settled agriculture; north of this valley, a broad east-west band characterized by vast sand plains and fixed dunes held in place by sparse grass and scrub trees; and a large northern arid region shading into the Sahara, advancing south several kilometers each year, and characterized by shifting sand dunes, rock outcroppings, and rugged mountainous plateaus that in a few places reach elevations of more than 500 m (1,640 ft). The high point, Mount Ijill at about 915 m (3,002 ft), is near Fdérik. The country is generally flat.

³CLIMATE

Although conditions are generally desertlike, three climatic regions can be distinguished. Southern Mauritania has a Sahelian climate; there is one rainy season from July to October. Annual rainfall averages 66 cm (26 in) in the far south; at Nouakchott the annual average is 14 cm (5.5 in).

Trade winds moderate the temperature in the coastal region, which is arid. The average maximum temperature at Nouadhibou for January is 26°C (79°F), and for October 32°C (90°F); average minimums are 13°C (55°F) for January and 19°C (66°F) for July.

Most of Mauritania north of Atar—about two thirds of the country—has a Saharan climate. Daytime temperatures exceed 38°C (100°F) in most areas for over 6 months of the year, but the nights are cool. Average annual rainfall at Atar is 10 cm (4 in).

⁴FLORA AND FAUNA

The World Resources Institute estimates there are 1,100 plant species in Mauritania. The country is the natural habitat of 94 mammal, 521 bird, 74 reptile, and 3 amphibian species. These figures reflect the total number of distinct species in the country, not the number of endemic species. In the desert, there are some cacti and related species; oases support relatively luxuriant growth, notably date palms. In the south are grasses and trees common to the savanna regions, particularly the baobab tree but also palms and acacias. The far south, in the Senegal River valley, has willows, jujube, and acacias. Lions, panthers, jackals, crocodiles, hippopotami, hyenas, cheetahs, otters, and monkeys survive in the south; in the north there are antelope, wild sheep, ostrich and other large birds, and ducks.

⁵ENVIRONMENT

World Resources Institute estimates that Mauritania, as of 2006, had designated 1.1 million hectares (2.72 million acres) of land for protection. Water resources total 114 cu km (2.74 cu mi), while water usage was 1.7 cu km (.408 cu mi) per year. Domestic water usage accounts for 9% of total usage, industrial for 3%, and agriculture for 88%. Per capita water usage totals 554 cu m (19,564 cu ft) per year. The nation also has a problem with water pollution, resulting from the leakage of petroleum and industrial waste along with sewage into the nation's ports and rivers. A government-built dam on the Senegal River is expected to alleviate the country's water problems and stimulate agriculture. According to the UN, carbon dioxide emissions totaled 1,949 kilotons, as of 2008.

Deforestation is a severe problem because of the population's growing need for firewood and construction materials. Slash-and-burn agriculture has contributed to soil erosion, which is aggravated by drought. The expansion of the desert into agricultural lands is accelerated by limited rainfall, deforestation, the consumption of vegetation by livestock, and wind erosion. The expansion of domestic herds onto grazing land formerly restricted to wildlife has also taken a serious toll on the environment, both in erosion and in encroachment on wildlife species.

According to a 2011 report issued by the International Union for Conservation of Nature and Natural Resources (IUCN), the number of threatened species included 15 types of mammals, 11 species of birds, 3 types of reptiles, 32 species of fish, and 1 species of invertebrate. Threatened species include the African gerbil, African slender-snouted crocodile, and barbary sheep. The Sahara oryx has become extinct in the wild.

6 POPULATION

The US Central Intelligence Agency (CIA) estimates the population of Mauritania in 2012 to be approximately 3,359,185, which placed it at number 133 in population among the 196 nations of the world. In 2011, approximately 3.4% of the population was over 65 years of age, with another 40.4% under 15 years of age. The median age in Mauritania was 19.5 years. There were 0.93 males for every female in the country. The population's annual rate of change was 2.323% in 2012. The projected population for the year 2025 was 4,400,000. Population density in Mauritania was calculated at 3 people per sq km (8 people per sq mi).

The UN estimated that 41% of the population lives in urban areas and that urban populations have an annual rate of change of 2.9%. The largest urban area is Nouakchott, with a population of around 709,000.

7 MIGRATION

Estimates of Mauritania's net migration rate, carried out by the CIA in 2011, amounted to -0.91 migrants per 1,000 citizens. The total number of emigrants living abroad was 118,000, and the total number of immigrants living in Mauritania was 99,200. In seasonal grazing migrations, cattle are moved every year and are led to neighboring Senegal for sale. The droughts of the 1970s and early 1980s led to mass migrations to the towns. The population was only 5% nomadic in 2000, compared to 12% nomadic in 1988 and 83% in 1963. Some tribesmen of the Senegal River valley go to Dakar in Senegal for seasonal work or to engage in petty trade. A few thousand Mauritanians live in France.

8 ETHNIC GROUPS

Moors (Maures), the main ethnic group, are a Caucasoid people of Berber and Arab stock, with some black admixture. The Moors are further divided into ethno-linguistic tribal and clan groups. Other groups, all black, are the Tukulor, Sarakolé, Fulani (Fulbe), Wolof, and Bambara. The black population is found largely in southern Mauritania and in the cities. About 40% of the total population is a Moor/black admixture; 30% are Moors; and 30% are black. There are also small numbers of Europeans, mainly French and Spanish (the latter from the Canary Islands), and a small colony of Lebanese traders. Freed slaves or the descendants of freed slaves are known as haratin or Black Moors. There have been many reports of official government discrimination against ethnic minorities, particularly relating to procedures in the issuance of national identification cards, which must be obtained in order to vote. Racial and cultural tensions exist between the Moors and the Afro-Mauritanians (which include groups such as the Wolof and Soninke). There is also tension between the White Moors, who are the most dominant in politics, and the Black Moors, who may be looked down on due to their slave ancestry. The distinction between White Moors and Black Moors is not one of color, since intermarriages with a variety of ethnic groups have resulted in many dark-skinned White Moors and lighter-skinned Black Moors.

9 LANGUAGES

Arabic is the official language. The Arabic spoken in Mauritania is called Hasaniya. Wolof, Peular, and Soninke are spoken in southern Mauritania and recognized as national languages. French is widely used, particularly in business, but its status as an official language was eliminated in the 1991 constitution.

10 RELIGIONS

The constitution declares Islam to be the religion of both the state and its people. As such, over 99% of the population is Muslim, most of whom are Sunnis. The Qadiriya and the Tijaniya are influential Islamic brotherhoods. The few thousand Christians and a very small number of Jews are mostly foreigners.

11 TRANSPORTATION

Modern forms of transport are still undeveloped. The CIA reports there are a total of 11,066 km (6,876 mi) of roads in Mauritania. 2,966 kilometers (1,843 mi.) are paved. Railroads extend for 728 km (452 mi). There are 28 airports, which transported 142,355 passengers in 2009, according to the World Bank. Nine airports have paved runways, and two of the airports can accommodate international travel. In addition, there are two deepwater ports.

12 HISTORY

Tens of thousands of years ago, the Sahara was both lush and filled with game. Desiccation eventually forced the inhabitants southward, a process that in the 3rd and 4th centuries BC was speeded by the Berbers, who had domesticated the camel. As the Berbers pressed down from the north toward the Senegal River valley, black Africans who lived in the path of the invaders moved further to the south. From the 9th century, a Berber tribe, the Lamtuna, and two other Berber groups cooperated in the control of a thriving caravan trade in gold, slaves, and ivory from the south. They took desert salt and North African goods in exchange.

The Almoravids, a group of fervent Muslim Mauritanian Berbers, conquered northwest Africa and much of Spain in the 11th century. They had, in turns, hostile and peaceful trade relations

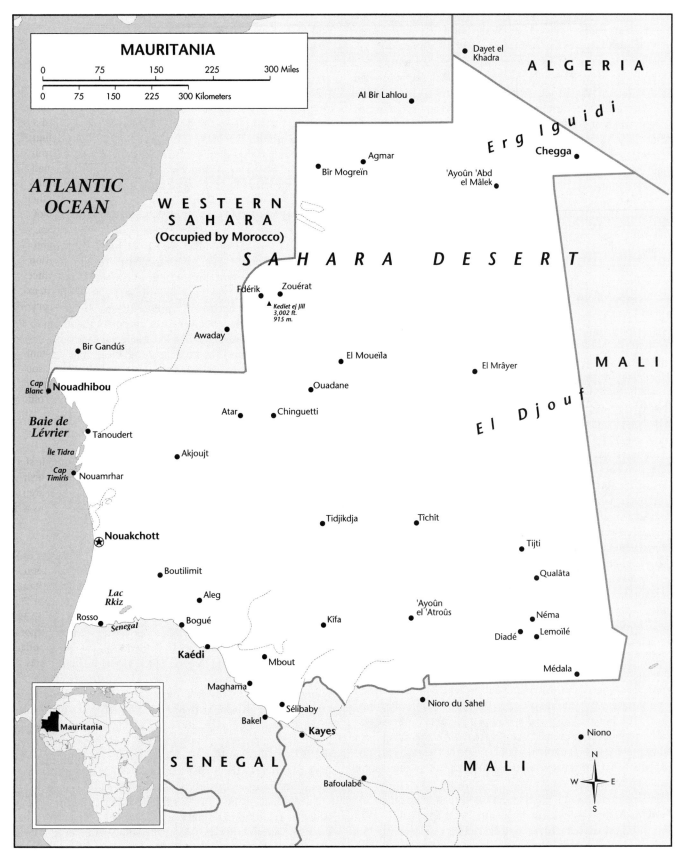

MAURITANIA

ATLANTIC OCEAN

WESTERN SAHARA (Occupied by Morocco)

ALGERIA

Erg Iguidi

SAHARA DESERT

MALI

El Djouf

Dayet el Khadra

Al Bir Lahlou

Agmar

Bîr Mogreïn

'Ayoûn 'Abd el Mâlek

Chegga

Fdérik

Zouérat

Kediet ej Jill 3,002 ft. 915 m.

Awaday

Bir Gandús

El Moueïla

El Mrâyer

Ouadane

Cap Blanc

Nouadhibou

Atar

Chinguetti

Baie de Lévrier

Tanoudert

Île Tidra

Akjoujt

Cap Timiris

Nouamrhar

Tidjikdja

Tîchît

Tijti

Nouakchott

Qualâta

Boutilimit

Lac Rkiz

Aleg

'Ayoûn el 'Atroûs

Néma

Rosso

Bogué

Senegal

Kifa

Diadé

Lemoïlé

Kaédi

Mbout

Médala

Maghama

Sélibaby

Nioro du Sahel

Bakel

Kayes

Niono

SENEGAL

MALI

Bafoulabé

N W E S

Mauritania

LOCATION: 14°42′ to 27°N; 4°30′ to 17°7′W. BOUNDARY LENGTHS: Algeria, 463 kilometers (288 miles); Mali, 2,237 kilometers (1,390 miles); Senegal, 813 kilometers (505 miles); Atlantic coastline, 754 kilometers (468 miles); Western Sahara, 1,561 kilometers (970 miles). TERRITORIAL SEA LIMIT: 12 miles.

with the black African empire of Ghana. Their authority in the Mauritanian region had declined by the late 11th century. After the Almoravid empire was destroyed in the 12th century, the Mali kingdom, successor to Ghana, extended over southeastern Mauritania and dominated trade in the area. Later, Mali was succeeded by the Songhai of Gao, whose empire fell to Moroccan invaders in 1591. Meanwhile, during the 14th and 15th centuries, nomadic Arab tribes of Yemeni extraction, the Banu Maqil, moved into Mauritania. By the 17th century, they had established complete dominance over the Berbers. They called themselves the Awlad-Banu Hassan. The Arabs and Berbers in Mauritania have since thoroughly intermingled with an Arabized Mauritania.

The Portuguese were the first Europeans to arrive, attracted in the 15th century by the trade in gold and slaves; later, the gum arabic trade became important. Competition for control was keen among Portuguese, French, Dutch, and English traders. The issue was resolved in 1815 when Senegal was awarded to France in the post-Napoleonic war settlement. During the 19th century, the French explored the inland regions and signed treaties with Moorish chieftains. Penetration of the desert zone was accelerated around the turn of the century in attempts to thwart Moorish raids on the Senegal River tribes. A Frenchman, Xavier Coppolani, was responsible for the signing of many treaties and played a key role in the extension of French influence in the area. By 1903, he was in control of Trarza, the Moors' main base for raids on the river tribes. Coppolani was killed in 1905, but his work was completed by Gen. Henri Gouraud, who gained effective control of the Adrar region by 1909. Mauritania was established as a colony in 1920, but its capital was located at Saint-Louis in Senegal. Mauritania thus became one of the eight territories that constituted the French West Africa federation.

In 1946, a Mauritanian Territorial Assembly was established, with some control over internal affairs. During the next 12 years, political power increasingly passed to local political leaders. Mauritania voted for the constitution of the Fifth French Republic at the referendum of 28 September 1958; it thus became a self-governing member of the French Community. The Islamic Republic of Mauritania was proclaimed in November 1958, while complete independence was attained on 28 November 1960.

Since independence, Mauritania has experienced three successful coups in up to 10 attempts. The grounds for these lay in part in the human and civil rights abuses committed by the various governments in power. The black minority, located largely in the south, has staged anti-discrimination protests and campaigned against slavery in Mauritania. Officially, slavery has been banned since 1981, but a law that makes slavery a punishable offense was not implemented until 2007. As of March 2012, there had been only one prosecution under the law, despite the fact that the United Nations states that between 10 and 20 percent of the population remains enslaved.

In foreign affairs, the government has turned increasingly toward the Arab world. Mauritania joined the Arab League in 1973 and withdrew from the franc zone during the same year; but ties with Europe, especially France, and the United States remain strong. The disastrous drought that struck Mauritania and the rest of the Sahel region during 1968–74 elicited substantial aid from the EC, the United States, Spain, France, and the Arab countries.

On 14 November 1975, the governments of Spain, Morocco, and Mauritania reached an agreement whereby Spain agreed to abandon control of the Spanish Sahara by 28 February 1976 and to share administration of the territory until then with Morocco and Mauritania. On 14 April 1976, Morocco and Mauritania announced a border delimitation agreement under which Morocco received more than two-thirds of the region (including the areas with the richest phosphate deposits). Morocco in effect annexed Western Sahara.

Morocco's action drew condemnation from across the world. The Popular Front for the Liberation of Saguia al-Hamra and Río de Oro (generally known as Polisario) even proclaimed Western Sahara as the Saharan Arab Democratic Republic. When Polisario forces, supported by Algeria, launched a war in the region, the guerrilla raids on the Mauritanian railway, iron mines, and coastal settlements, including Nouakchott, forced Mauritania to call French and Moroccan troops to its defense. The effects of the war weakened the government both economically and politically, and in July 1978, Moktar Ould Daddah, Mauritania's president since 1961, was overthrown by a military coup. On 5 August 1979, Mauritania formally relinquished its portion of the disputed territory, except for the military base of LaGuera, near Nouadhibou. Morocco also occupied and then annexed Mauritania's portion of that territory. Mauritania thereafter pursued a policy of strict neutrality in the Morocco-Polisario conflict, a policy that strained relations with Morocco.

In the wake of the 1978 coup, the constitution was suspended, and the National Assembly and the ruling Mauritanian People's Party (PPM) were dissolved. After a period of political uncertainty, Lt. Col. Khouna Ould Haydalla became chief of state and chairman of the ruling Military Committee for National Salvation as of 4 January 1980. There were unsuccessful attempts to overthrow his government in 1981 and 1982. Amnesty International claimed in 1983 that more than 100 political prisoners, including a former president and former prime minister, were being held in total darkness in underground cells in the desert. These prisoners were freed shortly after a military coup on 12 December 1984 brought Col. Moaouia Ould Sidi Mohamed Taya to power as chief of state.

However, as the economy faltered, racial, ethnic, and class tensions increased; the society became increasingly polarized. The lines were drawn between the Maurs or Moors—aristocrats who have dominated government—and black African slaves or descendants of slaves, who have adopted Moorish culture, but remain second-class citizens on the other. Although the government refuses to release census data, it is estimated that Moors account for 30–60% of the population. (The CIA estimates that Moors make up 30% of the population; blacks, 30%; and mixed Moor/black, 40%.) The black population, which is concentrated along the Senegal River border, has organized an underground Front for the Liberation of Africans in Mauritania (FLAM); grievances were linked with an unsuccessful coup attempt in 1987.

Interethnic hostilities in 1989 exploded when a border dispute with Senegal led to race riots that left several hundred Senegalese dead in Nouackchott. The Moorish trading community in Senegal was targeted for retaliation. Thousands of refugees streamed across the border in both directions. Mass deportation of "Mauritanians of Senegalese origin" fueled charges that Mauritania was trying to eliminate its non-Moorish population. Africa Watch estimated that at least 100,000 black slaves were being held in Mauritania.

Against this backdrop, the military conducted a bloody purge from September 1990 through March 1991 during which some 500 mostly black soldiers were murdered. Taya legalized opposition parties in July 1991, but he also stepped up Arabization policies. Parliament granted the perpetrators of the purge legal immunity in May 1993.

On 26 January 1992, Taya was elected in Mauritania's first multiparty presidential election with 63% of the vote. Ahmed Ould Daddah, the strongest of the four rivals and half-brother of Mauritania's first president, gained 33% of the vote. However, the election was marked by fraud. The legislative elections that followed in March were boycotted by 6 of the 14 opposition parties. Taya's Democratic and Social Republican Party (PRDS) easily won 67 of 79 Assembly seats.

Multiparty municipal elections were held in 1994, and the PRDS won control of 172 of the nation's 208 administrative districts. Presidential elections were held on 12 December 1997. Main opposition parties claimed that campaign conditions favored the reelection of Taya to a second six-year term and called for a boycott of the elections. Kane Amadou Moctar, the first black African ever to run for the presidency, presented himself as a non-aligned candidate with a platform promising to fight slavery, assist the return of Mauritanian refugees from Senegal, and reform the fisheries policy. The elections took place without incident, and Taya was declared the winner, taking 90% of the votes. Turnout was estimated at 70%, despite the opposition boycott. Moctar received less than 1% of the vote. Opposition leaders described the poll as a "masquerade," citing reports of widespread irregularities that included children casting ballots and polls remaining open as late as 11 p.m.

Despite multiparty elections, Mauritania was far from a free society. Opposition politicians were harassed and arrested. In 1994 and again in 1998, Cheikh Sadibou Camara of the Union for Democracy and Progress (UDP) was arrested for suggesting that the slave trade was continuing—publicly stating the suggestion was considered a crime in the country. Anti-Slavery International, based in London, presented an annual antislavery award to Camara in November 1998. The government also harassed journalists and suspended publication of newspapers and magazines on numerous occasions.

In June 2003, the government was dealing with a coup attempt that nearly overthrew Taya. As many as 40 people were injured and six killed in two days of heavy fighting in the capital on 8–9 June. Sala Ould Henena, who was fired from the army because of his opposition to the government's ties with Israel, was accused of leading former and mid-ranking army officers in the putsch. In response to the coup, the United States sent a 34-member military assessment team to Nouakchott to analyze US Embassy security needs. Analysts suspected that the cabal may have been provoked by a government crackdown earlier in the month against 32 Islamic leaders for their alleged ties to a foreign network of Islamic extremists and to former Iraqi leader Saddam Hussein.

On 7 November 2003, Mauritania's third presidential election since adopting the democratic process in 1992 took place. Incumbent President Taya was reelected. Several opposition groups alleged that the government had used fraudulent means to win the elections but did not elect to pursue their grievances via available legal channels. The elections incorporated safeguards first adopted in 2001 municipal elections: published voter lists and hard-to-falsify voter identification cards.

There was little doubt though that Taya had been attracting opposition from among key segments of the population. In 1999, Mauritania became only the third Arab League state to establish full diplomatic relations with Israel. Taya's links to Israel and his pro-Western, pro-US foreign policy had come under increasing criticism in the largely Muslim country. In June 2005, an attack on an army base in the Sahara left 15 soldiers dead; it was blamed on insurgents from Algeria. All this seems to lend credence to allegations that Taya had been insensitive to the desires of Mauritanians or that he had become too arrogant and too powerful to be bothered by what people thought about his government.

On 3 August 2005, President Taya was deposed in a bloodless coup. Military commanders, led by Colonel Ely Ould Mohammed Vall, seized power while President Taya was attending the funeral of Saudi Arabia's King Fahd. There was no public protest in his support, and dancing was reported on the streets of Nouakchott. Colonel Vall established the ruling Military Council for Justice and Democracy to run the country. The council dissolved the parliament and appointed a transitional government.

In June 2006, voters in a referendum approved constitutional changes to limit the president to two five-year terms in office. Mauritania held a number of elections that began in November 2006 with a parliamentary vote and culminated on 25 March 2007 with the second round of the presidential election. A new democratically elected government under President Sidi Mohamed Ould Cheikh Abdallahi was inaugurated on 19 April 2007.

In April 2007, Mauritania was readmitted to the African Union after the first democratically elected president, Sidi Ould Cheikh Abdallahi, took office; the country had been suspended from the organization after the 2005 coup. Another coup propelled General Mohamed Ould Abdelaziz to power in August 2008, as he deposed Abdallahi. The African Union imposed sanctions on Mauritania in February 2009, and the European Union cut its cooperation with the country soon after. Both organizations demanded that the democratically elected president be allowed to return to power.

Fresh elections were scheduled for July 2009, but many analysts questioned early on the degree to which they would be free and fair. In the run-up to the elections, General Abdelaziz stepped down from power and retired from the military in April 2009 in an attempt to legitimize his candidacy. However, this move provoked an outcry from several leaders in Mauritania, who viewed Abdelaziz's moves with suspicion, believing that the election's fate was predetermined by the military junta. Abdelaziz won the election and became president. According to the US Department of State, the elections of 2009 brought the country back to constitutional rule; under Mauritania's constitution, the president elected by popular vote is elected for a five-year term. The next election will be held in 2014.

¹³GOVERNMENT

The constitution of 20 May 1961 declared Mauritania to be an Islamic republic. This constitution, which placed effective power in the hands of a president who was also head of the only legal political organization, the Mauritanian People's Party, was suspended in 1978 by the new military regime. Subsequently, executive and legislative powers were vested in the Military Committee for National Salvation. A draft constitution was published in 1980 but later abandoned; like the 1961 document, it called for a popularly elected president and National Assembly.

The July 1991 constitution delegates most powers to the executive. The president is to be elected by universal suffrage for a five-year term. The prime minister is appointed by the president and designated head of government. Parliament is composed of a bicameral legislature. The Senate, or Majlis al-Shuyukh, has 56 seats with 17 up for election every two years. Its members are elected by municipal leaders to serve six-year terms. The National Assembly, or Majlis al-Watani, has 95 seats with members elected by popular vote to serve five-year terms. These institutions pose no serious challenge and, moreover, are controlled by the president's party, although competing political parties were legalized in July 1991.

14 POLITICAL PARTIES

As elsewhere in French West Africa, formal political movements developed in Mauritania only after World War II (1939–45). Horma Ould Babana, the leader of the first party to be established, the Mauritanian Entente, was elected to the French National Assembly in 1946. His party was considered too radical by the traditional chiefs, who organized a more conservative party, the Mauritanian Progressive Union (UPM). The UPM won 22 of 24 seats in the 1952 elections for the Territorial Assembly. In the 1957 elections, the first under universal adult suffrage, 33 of 34 persons elected to the Territorial Assembly were UPM members. In 1958, the UPM absorbed the weakened Entente into its organization, forming a single party, the Mauritanian Regroupment Party (PRM).

After independence, Prime Minister Moktar Ould Daddah in May 1961 set up a presidential system of government, and, in the subsequent presidential election, he was the only candidate. In December 1961, a new single party was formed, the Hizb Shab, or Mauritanian People's Party (Parti du Peuple Mauritanien—PPM). The PPM included minority parties as well as the PRM. By 1965, the single-party system had been established by law. President Ould Daddah was reelected in 1966, 1971, and 1976, but the PPM was dissolved after his ouster in 1978. No political parties functioned openly from 1978 until the 1991 military coup.

The Front for the Liberation of Africans in Mauritania (FLAM) was instrumental in stirring the 1989 unrest that ultimately led to multiparty elections. During this period of partisan organization, Taya formed the Democratic and Social Republican Party (Parti Republicain et Democratique Social—PRDS).

Chief among some 14 opposition parties has been the Union of Democratic Forces (UFD), which supported the runner-up in the January 1992 presidential election and boycotted the March parliamentary election. In May 1992, the UFD changed its name to UFD-New Era. In March 1993, it was weakened by the departure of eight centrist leaders to form a new political grouping. Also active are the Rally for Democratic and National Unity (RDU), the Union for Progress and Democracy (UPD), the Mauritanian Renewal Party (PMR), the People's Progressive Party (PPP), the Socialist and Democratic People's Union (SDPU), the Democratic Center Party (DCP), the Popular Front (FP), and El Har, a 1994 splintering of the UFD-New Era. The technically illegal Islamist party, Ummah, is very popular. The Action for Change (AC) party, which held four seats in the National Assembly following the October 2001 elections, was banned in January 2002.

After Taya won reelection in 2003, the Assembly was overwhelmingly dominated by his party, the PRDS. After Col. Vall took power in 2005, opposition politicians appeared to have become more involved, at least indirectly, in public decision making. For many years following 1998, Cheikh El Avia Ould Mohamed Khouna served as prime minister. On 8 August 2005 Sidi Mohamed Ould Boukakar became prime minister.

The Party of Democratic Convergence was banned in October 2005 because it was regarded as having breached Mauritanian law.

In the 2006 elections for the national assembly, the Coalition of Majority Parties (CPM), which includes the Union for the Republic; Union of Democratic Center; Republican Party for Democracy and Renewal; and Mauritanian Party for Unity and Change, and Democratic Renewal, won 63 seats. The Coordination of Democratic Opposition, representing a coalition of the Popular Progressive Alliance; Rally of Democratic Forces; Union of the Forces for Progress; National Pact for Democracy and Development; and the Alternative or El-Badil party, won 27 seats. The National Rally for Reform and Development took four seats and the Popular Front took one.

A presidential election was held on 11 March 2007. Since no candidate received a majority of the votes, a second round was held on 25 March between the top two candidates, Sidi Ould Cheikh Abdallahi and Ahmed Ould Daddah. Abdallahi won the second round with nearly 53% of the vote and took office in April.

In the senate elections of 2009, CPM won 45 seats, followed by COD with 7 seats and the National Rally for Reform and Development with 4 seats. The next legislative elections were expected in 2011 but were postponed until March 2012.

Mohamed Ould Abdel Aziz of the Union for the Republic deposed former president Sidi Ould Cheikh Abdellahi in a 2008 coup. He was victorious in the 2009 election, winning the presidency with 52.6% of the vote. The next presidential election was expected to take place in 2014. Moulaye Ould Mohamed Laghdaf, an independent, was appointed as prime minister following the 2008 coup.

15 LOCAL GOVERNMENT

Mauritania is divided into the city of Nouakchott and 12 regions, each with a governor and a commission. The regions are subdivided into 49 departments. Elections to municipal councils were held in December 1986 and again in 1992. The January-February 1994 municipal elections led to PRDS control of around 170 of the 208 municipalities, a majority retained by the PRDS in 1999.

Local elections were held in 2001, but the polls were marred as much by opposition boycott as by charges of massive fraud. All results for Nouakchott were annulled and a rerun ordered, although the reasons for such action remained unclear, given the boycott by opposition.

16 JUDICIAL SYSTEM

The 1991 constitution completely revised the judicial system, which had previously consisted of a lower court in Nouakchott, labor and military courts, a security court, and a Supreme Court in addition to *qadi* courts, which handled family law cases.

The revised judicial system includes lower-, middle-, and upper-level courts, each with specialized jurisdiction. The security court was abolished, and 43 department-level tribunals now bridge the traditional qadi and modern court systems. These courts are staffed by qadis or traditional magistrates trained in Koranic law. General civil cases are handled by 10 regional courts of first instance. Three regional courts of appeal hear challenges to decisions at the department level. A Supreme Court, headed by a magistrate named by the president to a five-year term, reviews appeals taken from decisions of the regional courts of appeal.

The 1991 constitution also established a six-member constitutional court, three members of which are named by the president, two by the national assembly president, and one by the senate president.

While the judiciary is nominally independent, it is subject to pressure and influence by the executive, which controls the appointment and dismissal of judges. The system is strongly influenced by rulings and settlements of tribal elders based on Shari'ah and tribal regulations.

The Codes of Civil and Criminal Procedure were revised in 1993 to bring them into line with the guarantees of the 1991 constitution, which provides for due process of law.

[17]ARMED FORCES

The International Institute for Strategic Studies reports that armed forces in Mauritania totaled 15,870 members in 2011. The force is comprised of 15,000 from the army, 620 from the navy and 250 members of the air force. Armed forces represent 1.5% of the labor force in Mauritania. Defense spending totaled $366.4 million and accounted for 5.5% of GDP. In April 2010, Mauritania joined forces with its neighbors to form the Joint Military Staff Committee of Algeria, Mali, Mauritania, and Niger. Based in Tamanrassett, Algeria, the general purpose of the committee is to strengthen cooperation through shared intelligence and joint military operations in the fight against terrorism, drug trafficking, and illegal weapons trade. Specifically, the committee hopes to combine efforts against the increasing regional threat from al-Qaeda. Regional and international leaders fear that al-Qaeda intends to establish bases in the Sahara, which could provide a safe haven for the terrorist organization if regional forces, such as the new committee, fail to take action.

[18]INTERNATIONAL COOPERATION

Admitted to the UN on 27 October 1961, Mauritania is a member of ECA and several nonregional specialized agencies, such as the FAO, IFC, IMF, the World Bank, UNESCO, UNIDO, and the WHO. It is also a member of the ACP Group, the Arab Bank for Economic Development in Africa, African Development Bank, the Council of Arab Economic Unity, the Arab Fund for Economic and Social Development, the Organization of the Islamic Conference (OIC), G-77, the Arab League, the African Union, the New Partnership for Africa's Development (NEPAD), the Arab Maghreb Union, and the WTO. Mauritania has joined with Senegal and Mali to form the Organization for the Development of the Senegal River (Organisation pour la Mise en Valeur du Fleu-

ve Sénégal-OMVS). Mauritania is a member of the Nonaligned Movement.

In environmental cooperation, Mauritania is part of the Basel Convention, the Convention on Biological Diversity, Ramsar, CITES, the Montréal Protocol, MARPOL, the Nuclear Test Ban Treaty, and the UN Conventions on the Law of the Sea, Climate Change, and Desertification.

The country is also a member with neighboring states of the Interstate Committee to Combat Drought in the Sahel (CILSS).

[19]ECONOMY

The GDP rate of change in Mauritania, as of 2011, was 5.1%. Inflation stood at 7.242% and unemployment was reported at 3%. While Mauritania is an agricultural country, historically largely dependent on livestock production, its significant iron ore deposits have been the backbone of the export economy in recent years. The droughts of the 1970s and 1980s transformed much of Mauritania, as the herds died off and the population shifted to urban areas. In 1960, 85% of the population lived as nomadic herders. By 2000, that percentage had fallen to 5%, and nearly one-third of the population lives in the district of Nouakchott. Offshore oil reserves have been identified and are estimated at one billion barrels. Substantial oil production and exports were projected to average 75,000 barrels per day. While initially promising, those projects have failed to materialize. Gold and diamond prospecting hold potential as growth areas.

Most of Mauritania is desert or semiarid. Less than 1% of Mauritania receives sufficient rain for crop production, and that 1% is drought-prone. Leading staple crops are millet, sorghum, rice, corn, sweet potatoes and yams, pulses, and dates. The country is not agriculturally self-sufficient, and this situation has been aggravated by increasing urbanization. As of 2011, mismanagement of food stocks had lessened the benefits of an otherwise strong harvest.

The droughts have led to a buildup of foreign debt leaving the country dependent on financial aid flows from international donors. Mauritania became eligible for debt relief under the IMF/World Bank's Heavily Indebted Poor Countries (HIPC) initiative in 2000, and debt service relief reached $1.1 billion by 2002, which almost halved Mauritania's debt burden. Foreign assistance accounted for 90% of investment from 1998–2001. In 2007, the GDP growth rate was estimated at less than one percent.

With Mauritania focusing on growth in agriculture, mining, and the building and public works sector, the economy made significant strides out of the 2008–09 global financial crisis. In 2009, the economy declined by 1.2%. Non-oil GDP growth for 2011 through 2014 is estimated to average between 5.3% and 5.8% annually. The International Monetary Fund estimated due to economic reforms, the country's economy grew by 5% in 2011. In 2010, there was a resumption of IMF financial assistance to Mauritania after a 19-month hiatus.

[20]INCOME

According to CIA estimates, the GDP of Mauritania as of 2011 was $7.242 billion. The CIA defines GDP as the value of all final goods and services produced within a nation in a given year and computed on the basis of purchasing power parity (PPP) rather than on value as measured on the basis of the rate of the exchange based on current dollars. The per capita GDP was estimated at $2,200. The annual growth rate of GDP was 5.1%. The average inflation rate was 6.5%. It was estimated by the CIA that in 2011 agriculture accounted for 19.2% of GDP, industry 36.6%, and services 44.1%. According to the World Bank, remittances from citizens living abroad totaled $1.9 million or about $1 per capita.

[21]LABOR

Trade unions are grouped into three federations, of which the oldest is the Union of Mauritanian Workers (Union des Travailleurs de Mauritanie), which is affiliated with the ICFTU. The newer ones are the General Confederation of Mauritanian Workers, formed in 1994, and the Free Confederation of Mauritanian Workers. Approximately 90% of the formal segment of the economy is unionized. The right to strike is guaranteed by law. Collective bargaining is also permitted. As of 2007, Mauritania's labor force totaled 1.318 million people. The CIA estimates of 2001 (the most recent figures available as of January 2012) noted that 50% of the population is employed in agriculture, 10% in industry, and 40% in the service sector.

Children under the age of 14 are prohibited by law from engaging in nonagricultural work. In practice, this regulation is not enforced. The guaranteed minimum workweek for most nonagricultural laborers is 40 hours with guaranteed overtime pay. However, domestic employees may work for up to 56 hours per week.

[22]AGRICULTURE

Less than 1% of the total land is currently farmed. Settled agriculture is restricted to the strip of land along the Senegal River and oases in the north. The country's major crops include dates, millet, sorghum, rice and corn. Cereal production in 2009 amounted to 212,709 tons, fruit production 23,191 tons, and vegetable production 3,737 tons. In general, landholdings are small. Overall agricultural development has been hampered not only by unfavorable physical conditions but also by a complicated land-tenure system (modified in 1984) that traditionally rested on slavery, inadequate transportation, and the low priority placed on agriculture by most government developmental plans. The country's traditional dependence on food imports has been heightened by drought.

The Mauritanian government has encouraged agricultural development of the Senegal River valley. In June 2008, a World Bank mission visited the country with the aim of energizing the agriculture and livestock sectors, two sectors that will be called upon to provide impetus in view of Mauritania's declining oil production.

[23]ANIMAL HUSBANDRY

The UN Food and Agriculture Organization (FAO) reported that Mauritania dedicated 39.3 million hectares (97 million acres) to permanent pasture or meadow in 2009. During that year, the country tended 4.3 million chickens and 1.7 million head of cattle. The production from these animals amounted to 25,801 tons of beef and veal, 132 tons of pork, 10,677 tons of poultry, 5,576 tons of eggs, and 424,714 tons of milk. Mauritania also produced 3,870 tons of cattle hide. The Moors tend to regard their cattle as symbols of wealth and prestige; this attitude discourages the herders from selling or slaughtering the animals. Total meat production in 2005 was estimated at 89,349 tons, with mutton accounting for

28% and beef for 26%. Reported figures are incomplete, however, since animal smuggling is common and much trade unrecorded.

[24]FISHING

Traditional fishing is carried out along the Senegal River and traditional sea fishing at Nouakchott and Nouadhibou. With a potential catch of 600,000 tons, fishing employs 1.2% of the labor force and contributes about 5% to GDP. It is estimated that more than $1 billion worth of fish is netted each year within the 320-km (200-mi) exclusive economic zone, but little of this sum benefits the treasury because the government lacks means of control and enforcement. The country had 166 decked commercial fishing boats in 2008. The annual capture totaled 195,328 tons according to the UN FAO. The export value of seafood totaled $157.2 million.

Since 1980, any foreigners wishing to fish in Mauritanian waters have been required by law to form a joint venture in which Mauritanian citizens or the government holds at least 51% of the capital. All of the catch must be landed in Mauritania for process and export, and each joint venture must establish an onshore processing facility. By 1987, over a dozen fishing companies had been established in Nouadhibou, including public and private interests from Algeria, France, Iraq, the Republic of Korea, Kuwait, Libya, Nigeria, Romania, Spain, and the former USSR.

[25]FORESTRY

Less than 1% of Mauritania is covered by forest. The UN FAO estimates of 2009 noted the roundwood production at 3,000 cu m (105,944 cu ft.). The value of all forest products, including roundwood, totaled $218,000. Sizable tree stands found in the southern regions are not fully exploited. The principal forest product is gum arabic, which is extracted from wild acacia trees that grow in the south. Until 1972, private traders collected and exported the gum; since 1972, it has officially been a monopoly of the state trading company, Société Nationale d'Importation et d'Exportation (SONIMEX). Nevertheless, much gum continues to be smuggled across the borders, particularly to Senegal.

[26]MINING

Iron ore mining and processing accounted for more than 38% of Mauritania's export earnings in 2009, which totaled $522 million. Iron ore output (metal content) was estimated at 6.7 million metric tons in 2009. Iron ore production by gross weight that same year totaled 10.3 million metric tons.

Gypsum output, from some of the greatest reserves in the world, was estimated at 36,928 metric tons in 2009. In 2009, Mauritania also produced cement, salt, crude steel, sand and gravel, and stone. Mauritania was rich in copper; in the 1980s, the mine at Akjoujt was estimated to contain 100 million tons of ore averaging 2.25% copper, with trace amounts of gold. In 1996, gold recovery from tailings at the mine was discontinued because the stockpile was depleted. The nearby Guelb Moghrein Project, which contained resources of 23.7 million tons (144 grams per ton of cobalt, 1.88% copper, and 1.41 grams per ton of gold), is an open pit mine wholly owned and operated by Mauritian Copper Mines. The mine employed 1,051 workers in 2009 and had a remaining lifespan of 7.5 years. Phosphate deposits, and reserves of platinum, palladium, and nickel, have been identified, and prospecting continued for petroleum, tungsten, and uranium. Mineral exploration efforts were focused on diamond (on the Archean Reguibat craton), gold (in the Inchiri region), oil (offshore), and continued evaluation of copper-gold, kaolin, and peat deposits.

27 ENERGY AND POWER

The World Bank reported in 2008 that Mauritania produced 547 million kWh of electricity and consumed 403.6 million kWh, or 123 kWh per capita. The CIA 2010 oil production estimates were 11,640 barrels of oil a day. Oil consumption during that same year was 20,000 barrels a day.

28 INDUSTRY

Fish processing, the principal industrial activity, is carried out in Nouadhibou. By far the largest fish processor is Mauritanian Fish Industries (IMAPEC), a Spanish company in which the Mauritanian government acquired a 51% share in 1980. IMAPEC has facilities for salting, drying, canning, and freezing fish and for producing fish flour; virtually all of its output is exported. Overfishing is a problem, however, as is mismanagement of the fishing sector and the lack of an effective governmental fisheries policy. The government is modernizing the fisheries sector through port extension and the development of warehouses. Other small industries include chemical and plastic plants, food and beverages, metal products, building materials, and cookie factories.

The first desalination plant in Africa was completed at Nouakchott in January 1969, with a capacity of 3,000 cu m (106,000 cu ft) a day. A rolling mill at Nouadhibou, built in 1977, produced small quantities of iron rods and steel. A petroleum refinery in Nouadhibou, with an annual capacity of 1 million tons, opened in 1982, shut down in 1983, and resumed operation in 1987 with help from Algeria. Algeria also helped revitalize a sugar refining plant. Similarly, Kuwaiti and Jordanian interests reopened the steel mill after a shutdown. Each of these operations represents a drain on state revenues, and the government has shifted policy toward the promotion of less ambitious industrial development.

The government has signed exploration contracts with the Canadian Rex Diamond Mining Corporation, the American BHP Minerals and Bab-Co, the French La Source, and the Australian Ashton West Africa Property Limited in order to find gold, oil, phosphate, aluminum, and copper in Mauritania. Mauritania, as of 2006, had an estimated one billion barrels of proven oil reserves.

29 SCIENCE AND TECHNOLOGY

A research institute for mining and geology, founded in 1968, is at Nouakchott. The Economic Community of West Africa has an institute in Nouadhibou-Cansado conducting research in the fisheries industry. The World Bank reported in 2009 that there were no patent applications in science and technology in Mauritania.

The Higher Scientific Institute, founded in 1986 at Nouakchott, has departments of mathematics, physics, chemistry, biology, geology, computer studies, natural resources, and ecology.

30 DOMESTIC TRADE

Most trade is done at or near the "Friendship Port" of Nouakchott. The seaport of Nouadhibou is a main center for fishing operations. Most consumer goods are sold through small shops or boutiques, although some medium-sized supermarkets are becoming more common. Arabic is the official language, but French is the business language. Normal business and banking hours are from 7:30 a.m. to 3 p.m. Sunday through Thursday, though it is somewhat common for businesses to open a little later in the morning than scheduled.

31 FOREIGN TRADE

Mauritania imported $2.633 billion worth of goods and services in 2011, while exporting $2.745 billion worth of goods and services. Iron ore and fish products are the primary exports. Major import partners in 2010 were China, 12.3%; France, 11.4%; Netherlands, 10.8%; Belgium, 5.7%; Brazil, 4.6%; and Spain 4.5%. Its major export partners were China, 41.5%; France, 9%; Cote d'Ivoire, 6.3%; Italy, 6.2%; Japan, 6%; Spain, 5.6%; and Netherlands, 4%.

32 BALANCE OF PAYMENTS

Mauritania had an external debt of $2.344 billion in 2010. According to the CIA, that same year exports were valued at $2.04 billion and imports $2.029 billion.

33 BANKING AND SECURITIES

At independence, Mauritania became a member of the West African Monetary Union (Union Monétaire Ouest Africaine-UMOA), but withdrew in 1973 to demonstrate its independent economic identity. When it withdrew, the government also relinquished membership in the African Financial Community (Communauté Financière Africaine-CFA), the currency of which—the CFA franc—was freely convertible to French francs. Mauritania then created its own currency, the ouguiya, and a national bank, the Central Bank of Mauritania (Banque Centrale de Mauritanie), which was established in 1973.

After privatization in 1989, banks in Mauritania included Banque Arbe Libyene-Mauritanienne pour le Commerce Extérieur et le Développement (BALM). BALM, founded in 1990, was 51% owned by Libyans and 49% owned by the state. Other banks included Banque Al-Baraka Mauritanie Islamique (BAMIS), Banque Mauritanie pour le Commerce Internationale (BMCI),

Principal Trading Partners – Mauritania (2010)

(In millions of US dollars)

Country	Total	Exports	Imports	Balance
World	3,640.0	1,890.0	1,750.0	140.0
China	1,193.8	880.4	313.4	567.0
France	500.7	210.3	290.4	-80.0
Netherlands	391.5	85.4	306.1	-220.8
Spain	233.3	118.7	114.6	4.1
Belgium	199.3	55.7	143.6	-87.9
Italy	173.4	145.3	28.1	117.3
Japan	163.2	128.2	35.0	93.1
Côte d'Ivoire	147.7	134.4	13.3	121.1
United States	141.7	49.8	91.9	-42.0
Brazil	116.4	...	116.4	-116.4

(…) data not available or not significant.

(n.s.) not specified.

SOURCE: 2011 Direction of Trade Statistics Yearbook, New York: United Nations, 2011.

and Banque Nationale de Mauritania (BNM). BAMIS, established in 1990, was 50% Saudi-owned and 10% BCM-owned. BMCI, founded in 1990, was 10% BCM-owned, and 90% of the bank was held by private interests. BNM, established in 1988, was 50% state-owned.

A significant drawback for the Mauritanian economy, partly due to the small number and low income of the population, was a dearth of domestic capital. The poor reputation of the domestic banking system, notwithstanding its overhaul, discouraged local savings.

In 2009 the central bank discount rate was 9%. The commercial bank prime lending rate was 17% in 2010.

34 INSURANCE

Insurance was handled by 13 foreign companies until July 1974, when the Mauritanian government assumed full control of insurance and reinsurance. All insurance business was controlled by the Mauritanian Insurance and Reinsurance Co.

35 PUBLIC FINANCE

Mauritania's budget is habitually in deficit. In 2010, the budget of Mauritania included $770 million in public expenditures. The budget deficit amounted to 3.8% of GDP. Public debt was 54% of GDP, with $2.391 billion of the debt held by foreign entities.

36 TAXATION

Mauritania had a corporate income tax rate of 25% in 2011, with a 2.5% minimum rate on turnover. According to the CIA, Mauritania's tax rate comprises 26.4% of the country's GDP. Capital gains are taxed at the corporate rate. However, the tax may be deferred if the gains are used to acquire new fixed assets in the country in the following three fiscal years. Dividends are subject to a 10% withholding tax, which can be deducted if the recipient of the dividends is subject to corporate income tax. The major indirect taxes are import duties, a turnover tax on exports and mining companies, a value-added tax (VAT) of 14% (2011), excise levies on petroleum, tobacco, a service tax, and a tax on vehicles.

37 CUSTOMS AND DUTIES

Along with other members of the West African Economic Community (CEAO), Mauritania imposes a revenue duty (*droit fiscal*) and a customs duty (*droit de douane d'entrée*) on most imported goods. Customs duties range from a minimum of 9% to a maximum of 27% for essential goods or non-luxury goods. Imports are also subject to the 14% VAT. Exports are not restricted, although both imports and exports require a license.

Since 1970, Mauritania has had a trade agreement with Senegal, allowing primary products to be traded between the two countries duty-free. Mauritania is also a member of ECOWAS.

38 FOREIGN INVESTMENT

With the nationalization of the mining sector in 1974, private foreign investment dropped drastically. Extension of government control over imports and domestic trade further curtailed the activity of foreign capital, as did ethnic clashes in 1989–91. In 1993, the government started to privatize parastatals, and by 1999, only 17% of GDP was accounted for by state-owned companies; 20% of Mauritanian companies were state-owned, including the telephone and postal services, utilities, transportation, radio and television, and mining production. According to the World Bank, foreign direct investment (FDI) in Mauritania was a net outflow of $38.3 million according to World Bank figures published in 2009. FDI represented 1.27% of GDP.

An investment code, approved in 1979, provided for tax holidays of up to 12 years on exports, imports of raw materials, and reinvested profits. The 1989 Investment Code guaranteed equal and free movement of capital in and out of Mauritania, in all sectors. It also provided incentives to new enterprises like a temporary tax reduction. Amendments have been made to the code to require hiring of Mauritanians. Tax preferences are offered for using local materials and investing in priority sectors, like agriculture, minerals, and fish processing.

Foreign investment has been small since the ethnic violence of 1989 to 1991. However, in 1999, the government introduced new initiatives to attract foreign investment. From 1997 to 1999, the average annual inflow of foreign direct investment (FDI) was negligible, ranging from $100,000 to $900,000. In 2000, inflows increased to $9.2 million and then, in 2001, to $30 million. Foreign private investors include Mobil Oil of the United States, NAFTAL of Algeria, and Elf Aquitaine of France in the petroleum sector; MINPROC and IFC of Australia in the gold sector; and CNF of China, the Al-Baraka Group of Saudi Arabia, and IFAFOOD of France in the fishing sector.

39 ECONOMIC DEVELOPMENT

Until the export earning capacity of Mauritania improves, its economy will remain fragile. External deficit management dominates the public investment horizon. Mauritania obtained assistance from the World Bank and loans from the IMF throughout the late 1990s and 2000s. The country withdrew its membership in the Economic Community of West African States (ECOWAS) in 2000 and increased commercial ties with Morocco and Tunisia (members of the Arab Maghreb Union), particularly in telecommunications. The IMF has stressed the need for banking and exchange rate reform and improved governance. Nearly all of Mauritania's external debt was forgiven following its qualification under the Heavily Indebted Poor Countries (HIPC) program in 2000. From 2006 to 2009, Mauritania participated in an IMF-backed Poverty Reduction and Growth Facility arrangement. Support from the IMF and World Bank halted due to the 2008 coup but was restored one year later after presidential elections. In 2011, the government continued to emphasize the reduction of poverty, improvement of health and education, and privatization of the economy as policy priorities.

40 SOCIAL DEVELOPMENT

The National Social Security Fund administers family allowances, industrial accident benefits, insurance against occupational diseases, and old age pensions. Pensions are paid for by 1% contributions from employees and 2% contributions from employers. Employed women are entitled to a cash maternity benefit and payable up to 14 weeks. Workers and their families who are covered under the labor code are entitled to medical benefits. There is also a family allowance and a birth grant.

Opportunities for Mauritanian women are severely limited by social and cultural factors. Although they have the right to vote, women face considerable legal discrimination. According to Shari'ah law, the testimony in court of two women equals that of one man. The law mandates equal pay for equal work and, in the public sector, this law is respected and applied. Education is not compulsory, and dire financial circumstances force many children to work. In addition, many young workers are displaced or orphaned children who were forced into labor by their guardians, particularly in agricultural fields. Laws prohibiting child labor are rarely enforced.

In January 2010, 34 Mauritanian Islamic scholars signed a religious decree, or fatwa, that condemned and banned the practice of female genital mutilation (FGM) in the country. More than 70% of Mauritanian girls undergo the procedure, which removes part or all of a woman's external genitalia. Analysts said that, because people often correlate the practice with Islam, the strong Islamic condemnation of the practice will serve to stigmatize the act and reduce its practice.

Slavery was abolished many times in Mauritania, the most recent law outlawing the practice having been passed in 2007. Despite this, there are still slaves in the rural areas, where a barter economy thrives. The UN estimates that at least 10% of all Mauritanians are enslaved. Weak laws for the protection of domestic workers have also contributed to a work climate akin to slavery among those so employed.

Some human rights abuses are reported including the use of excessive force to disperse demonstrators and inadequate prison conditions. Reliance on foreign investment from China seems to perpetuate negligence to human rights causes, which are less commonly recognized in China than in the US or Western Europe.

41 HEALTH

Mauritania's public health system consists of administrative units and health facilities organized in pyramid style. There were approximately 300 basic health units at the village level, about 130 health posts, and some 50 health centers. The health system is mostly public, but liberalization of private practice in the past several years has led to marked increase in the number of practitioners in the private sector. According to the CIA, life expectancy in Mauritania was 61.53 years in 2012. The country spent 5.7% of its GDP on healthcare in 2009. There were 1 physician, 7 nurses and midwives, and 4 hospital beds per 10,000 inhabitants. The fertility rate was 4.22, while the infant mortality rate was 58.93 per 1,000 live births in 2012. In 2008, the maternal mortality rate, according to the World Bank, was 550 per 100,000 births. It was estimated that 59% of children were vaccinated against measles. The CIA calculated HIV/AIDS prevalence in Mauritania to be about 0.7% in 2009.

The main health problems include malaria, tuberculosis, measles, dysentery, and influenza. Guinea worm remains a major problem. Pregnancy complications are common due to unhygienic conditions and lack of medical care. In non-drought years, the staple diet of milk and millet is nutritionally adequate, if somewhat deficient in vitamin C. Immunization rates for children up to one year old were: tuberculosis, 93%; diphtheria, pertussis, and tetanus, 50%; polio, 50%; and measles, 53%.

42 HOUSING

Construction accounts for a small fraction of GDP. The chief construction company, the Building Society of Mauritania, is hampered by inadequate manpower and capitalization. To encourage housing development, the government introduced new regulations in 1975 to encourage builders and to compel civil servants to purchase their own property and thus relieve the demand for public housing. The phenomenal growth of Nouakchott and the effects of rural migration, impelled by drought, have strained housing resources.

43 EDUCATION

Overall, the CIA estimated that Mauritania had a literacy rate of 51.2%, with far fewer women (43.4%) than men (59.5%) being literate. Public expenditure on education represented 2.9% of GDP. In 2009, the World Bank estimated that 76% of age-eligible children in Mauritania were enrolled in primary school. Secondary enrollment for age-eligible children stood at 16%. Tertiary enrollment was estimated at 4%. Of those enrolled in tertiary education, there were 100 male students for every 42 female students.

Six years of basic education are compulsory. A three-year lower secondary (college) program offers general education. Following this stage, students may choose to attend a three-year senior secondary school (lycee) or a technical school program of three or five years. The lycee programs offer specializations in arts and literature; natural sciences; mathematics, physics, and chemistry; or Koran (Koran) and Arabic studies. The academic year runs from October to June.

The National Institute of Higher Islamic Studies was established in Boutilimit in 1961, and the National School of Administration was founded in 1966 at Nouakchott. The University of Nouakchott, founded in 1981, has a faculty of letters and human sciences and a faculty of law and economics.

44 LIBRARIES AND MUSEUMS

The National Library at Nouakchott (10,000 volumes) and the National Archives (3,000) were both founded in 1955. The National Library is the depository for all the country's publications. There is a small library at the University of Nouakchott in the capital, as well as a French cultural center. The National Museum is also located in Nouakchott and has archaeology and ethnography collections. There are several Arab libraries in the major towns.

45 MEDIA

Many of Mauritania's post offices have telephone or telegraph services. There are direct telephone communications from Nouakchott to Paris. Administrative contact within the country is maintained by radiotelephone. Two earth-satellite stations came into service in 1985–86. In 2010, the CIA reported there were 71,600 telephone landlines in Mauritania. In addition to landlines, mobile phone subscriptions averaged 85 per 100 people. There was

1 FM radio station, 14 AM radio stations, and 1 shortwave radio station. Internet users numbered 2 per 100 citizens.

The government operates all national radio and television networks, broadcasting in French, Arabic, and several African languages. Residents with satellite receivers and dish antennas receive television broadcasts from France and other Arab countries. Telecasts are in French and Arabic.

The constitution provides for freedom of speech and the press; however, the law requires that copies of every newspaper be submitted to the Ministries of Interior and Justice for approval before distribution.

46 ORGANIZATIONS

The Chamber of Commerce, Industry, Agriculture, and Ranching is in Nouakchott. Youth organizations include the National Union of Students and Pupils of Mauritania and the Association of Scouts and Guides of Mauritania. Several sports associations are active within the country. The Lion's Club has active programs. The International Association of French-Speaking Women has a base in the country. The World Conservation Union has an office within the country. The Red Crescent Society and Caritas are active as well.

47 TOURISM, TRAVEL, AND RECREATION

Tourists are attracted to Atar, the ancient capital of the Almoravid kingdom, and Chinguetti, with houses and mosques dating back to the 13th century. Popular sports are rugby, surf fishing, tennis, football (soccer), basketball, and swimming. The US Department of State estimates the daily cost of staying in Nouakchott, the capital, is $200. The cost of visiting other cities averages $111.

There are few facilities for tourists, except in the capital, and travel is difficult outside of Nouakchott. Most visitors need a valid passport and visa; the visa requirement is waived for French and Italian nationals. A certificate of vaccination against yellow fever may be required if traveling from an infected area. Precautions against typhoid are recommended.

48 FAMOUS PERSONS

Abu Bakr ibn Omar (Boubakar), paramount chief of the Lemtouna, defeated Ghana in 1076. His lieutenant and cousin, Yusuf ibn Tashfin, conquered Morocco in 1082 and most of Spain in 1091. The best-known contemporary Mauritanian is Moktar Ould Daddah (1924–2003), president from 1961 until 1978; after being ousted, he was eventually allowed to go to France. Lt. Col. Khouna Ould Haydalla (b. Spanish Sahara, 1940) became prime minister and chief of staff of the armed forces in 1978 and assumed the presidency in 1980. Col. Maaouya Ould Sid Ahmed Taya (b. 1941), who had been prime minister (1981–84), was president from 1984 to 2005. Col. Ely Ould Mohamed Vall (b. 1953) became the new military leader of Mauritania in 2005.

49 DEPENDENCIES

Since relinquishing its claim to Western Sahara, Mauritania has no territories or colonies.

50 BIBLIOGRAPHY

Bales, Kevin. *Disposable People: New Slavery in the Global Economy*. Rev. ed. Berkeley: University of California Press, 2007.

Calderini, Simonetta. *Mauritania*. Santa Barbara, CA: Clio Press, 1992.

Mauritania Investment and Business Guide: Strategic and Practical Information. Washington, DC: International Business Publications USA, 2012.

Pazzanita, Anthony G. *Historical Dictionary of Mauritania*. 3rd ed. Lanham, MD: Scarecrow Press, 2008.

Robinson, David. *Paths of Accommodation: Muslim Societies and French Colonial Authorities in Senegal and Mauritania, 1880–1920*. Athens, Ohio: Ohio University Press, 2000.

Zeilig, Leo, and David Seddon. *A Political and Economic Dictionary of Africa*. Philadelphia: Routledge/Taylor and Francis, 2005.

MAURITIUS

Republic of Mauritius

CAPITAL: Port Louis

FLAG: The national flag consists of four horizontal stripes of red, blue, yellow, and green.

ANTHEM: *Glory to Thee, Motherland, O Motherland of Mine.*

MONETARY UNIT: The Mauritius rupee (MUR) is a currency of 100 cents. There are coins of 5, 10, 20 and 50 cents and 1, 5, 10 and 20 rupees, and notes of 5, 25, 50, 100, 200, 500, 1,000 and 2,000 rupees. MUR1 = US$0.03326 (or US$1 = MUR30.06) as of 2011.

WEIGHTS AND MEASURES: The metric system is in general use; traditional weights and measures also are employed.

HOLIDAYS: New Year, 1–2 January; Abolition of slavery, 1 February; National Day, 12 March; Labor Day, 1 May; Arrival of Indentured Labourers, 2 November. Christian, Hindu, Muslim and Chinese holidays also are observed.

TIME: 4 p.m. = noon GMT.

¹LOCATION, SIZE, AND EXTENT

Mauritius is situated in the Indian Ocean about 900 km (559 mi) E of Madagascar and 2,000 km (1,250 mi) off the nearest point of the African coast. The island of Rodrigues, an integral part of Mauritius, is located about 560 km (350 mi) off its northeastern coast. The two islands of Agalega lie 1,122 km (697 mi) to the N of Mauritius; also to the N is the St. Brandon Group (Cargados Carajos Shoals). Mauritius has a total area of about 2,040 sq km (788 sq mi), of which the island of Mauritius occupies 1,860 sq km (720 sq mi); the island of Rodrigues, 110 sq km (42.5 sq mi); and the other offshore islands, 71 sq km (27 sq mi). Comparatively, the area occupied by Mauritius is slightly less than 10.5 times the size of Washington, DC. Mauritius extends 61 km (38 mi) N–S and 47 km (29 mi) E–W, and has a coastline of 177 km (110 mi).

The nation also claims the Chagos Archipelago, which includes Diego Garcia, a British dependency about 1,900 km (1,200 mi) NE, and co-manages with France Tromelin Island, about 555 km (345 mi) NW. The Organization of African Unity (OAU) has supported Mauritius's claim to Diego Garcia.

The capital city of Mauritius, Port Louis, is located on the island's northwest coast.

²TOPOGRAPHY

Mauritius is mostly of volcanic formation and is almost entirely surrounded by coral reefs. A coastal plain rises sharply to a plateau 275 to 580 m (900 to 1,900 ft) high. Piton de la Rivière Noire, the highest peak, reaches 828 m (2,717 ft). The longest river is the Grand River South East, which stretches from the center of the country to the central eastern border with a distance of 40 km (29 mi).

³CLIMATE

The subtropical maritime climate is humid, with prevailing southeast winds. The temperature ranges from 18° to 30°C (64° to 86°F) at sea level, and from 13° to 26°C (55 to 79°F) at an elevation of 460 m (1,500 ft); the warmest season lasts from October to April, the coolest from June to September. From October to March southeast trade winds bring heavy rains to the central plateau and windward slopes, which have a yearly average rainfall of over 500 cm (200 in). On the coast rainfall averages about 100 cm (40 in) annually. Daily showers occur from April to September, and occasional tropical cyclones between December and April.

⁴FLORA AND FAUNA

Mauritius originally was covered by dense rain forest, which included heath and mossy forest at higher elevations and coastal palm savanna. As of 2011 there was a total of 711 indigenous plant species, including 246 that were endemic. Mauritius was home to 14 mammal, 137 bird, 35 reptile, and 2 amphibian species. This calculation reflects the total number of distinct species residing in the country, not the number of endemic species. Mauritius was home to two indigenous snakes, the Boleyria multicarinata and Casarea dussumieri; also indigenous to Mauritius was the now extinct dodo bird, one of many exotic animal species that thrived in isolation from predators including man. European settlers introduced dogs, cats, rats, monkeys, wild pigs, sambur deer, and mongoose and most species of present vegetation.

⁵ENVIRONMENT

The main environmental problems facing Mauritius are water pollution, soil erosion, and preservation of its wildlife. The sources of water pollution are sewage, agricultural and other chemicals.

The erosion of the soil occurs through deforestation. Mauritius had designated 6,800 hectares (16,803 acres) of land for protection as of 2006. Water resources totaled 2.2 cu km (0.528 cu mi) while water usage was 0.61 cu km (.146 cu mi) per year. Domestic water usage accounted for 25% of total usage, industrial for 15%, and agricultural for 60%. Per capita water usage totaled 488 cu m (17,234 cu ft) per year.

In 2008 carbon dioxide emissions in Mauritius totaled 3,884 kilotons.

According to a 2011 report issued by the International Union for Conservation of Nature and Natural Resources (IUCN), the number of threatened species included 6 types of mammals, 11 species of birds, 7 types of reptiles, 13 species of fish, 26 types of mollusks, 71 species of other invertebrates, and 88 species of plants. Endangered species on the island of Mauritius include the pink pigeon, Round Island boa and keel-scaled boa, green sea turtle, and Mauritius varieties of kestrel, parakeet, and fody. Endangered species on Rodrigues include distinctive varieties of brush warbler, fody, flying fox, and day gecko. Extinct species include the Mauritian duck, the Mauritius blue pigeon, the red rail, Rodrigues little owl, and the giant day gecko.

[6] POPULATION

Population censuses are conducted every ten years and the latest was conducted in 2011. As at 31 December 2010 the population for Mauritius stood at 1,245,289, and 1,283,415 for the whole of the republic which includes Rodrigues and other dependencies. The US Central Intelligence Agency (CIA) estimated the population of Mauritius in 2011 to be approximately 1,303,717, which placed it at number 150 in population among the 196 nations of the world. In 2011 approximately 7.5% of the population was over 65 years of age, with another 21.8% under 15 years of age. The median age in Mauritius was 32.7 years. There were 0.97 males for every female in the country. The population's annual rate of change was 0.729%. The projected population for the year 2025 was 1,400,000. Population density in Mauritius was calculated at 639 people per sq km (1,655 people per sq mi).

The United Nations (UN) estimated that 42% of the population lived in urban areas, and that urban populations had an annual rate of change of 0.8%. The largest urban area was Port Louis, with a population of 149,000.

[7] MIGRATION

Estimates of Mauritius's net migration rate carried out by the CIA in 2011 amounted to zero. The total number of emigrants living abroad was 140,700, and the total number of immigrants living in Mauritius was 42,900. A small number of Mauritians emigrate each year, principally to Australia, Europe, and Canada.

[8] ETHNIC GROUPS

The largest group on Mauritius, about 68% of the population, is Indo-Mauritian, consisting of immigrants from India and their descendants. About 27% of the islanders are Creole (mixed European and African), 3% Sino-Mauritian, and 2% Franco-Mauritian.

[9] LANGUAGES

Although English and French are both official languages, French is widely used and is more popular than English; however, Creole, derived from French, is the most widely spoken by 80.5% of the population. A number of Asian languages are used in some groups, including Bhojpuri (spoken by about 12.1% of the population), Hindi, Urdu, Tamil, and Hakka. On Rodrigues virtually the entire population speaks Creole.

[10] RELIGIONS

According to a 2000 census (the latest for which data is available), Hindus constituted about 48% of the total population. Roman Catholics accounted for about 24% of the population, while other Christian denominations accounted for about 9%. Other Christian denominations included Seventh-day Adventist, Assemblies of God, Christian Tamil, Church of England, Pentecostal, Presbyterian, Evangelical, Jehovah's Witnesses, and the Church of Jesus Christ of Latter-day Saints (Mormons). About 17% of the population were Muslims, with a majority being Sunni. There were small numbers of Buddhists and animists. Throughout the country there is a strong correlation between religious affiliation and ethnicity. Those of Indian descent are primarily Hindu or Muslim. Those of Chinese descent are often nominally Buddhist but practice as Catholics, since they often admit their children to Catholic schools. Creoles and Europeans are primarily Catholic. Freedom of religion is guaranteed by the constitution and this right is generally respected in practice. Though there is no state religion, a parliamentary decree allows that certain religions represented before independence (Roman Catholicism, the Church of England, Presbyterianism, Seventh-day Adventist, Hinduism, and Islam) are entitled to annual subsidies from the government. Other religions are registered by the Registrar of Associations in order to attain legal, tax-exempt status. Though there has been some social and political tension between the Hindu majority and the Christian, Muslim, and Creole minorities, there are few reports of violence or blatant discrimination. Thaipoosam Cavadee, Chinese Spring Festival, Maha Shivaratree, Ougadi, Ganesh Chathurthi, Eid al-Fitr, Divali, Assumption of Mary, All Saints' Day, and Christmas are observed as national holidays.

The island of Rodrigues is predominantly Catholic.

[11] TRANSPORTATION

According to 2010 World Bank development indicators, Mauritius had 2,028 km (1,260 mi) of roads of which 98 percent were paved. There were 159 vehicles per 1,000 people in the country. In 2008 the country had three merchant ships in service of 1,000 gross registered tonnage (GRT) or more. In 1999 the Port Louis harbor completed a major expansion and modernization. In 2011 there were two airports, which transported 1.257 million passengers in 2010 according to the World Bank. Air Mauritius provides about four flights weekly to Rodrigues from the main airport at Plaisance, as well as over 40 weekly international flights. In early 2001 Air Mauritius concluded an alliance with Delta Airlines. Other major airlines serving Mauritius are Air France, British Airways, Air India, Air Zimbabwe, Lufthansa (Condor), Singapore Airlines, South African Airways and Emirates.

[12] HISTORY

Long uninhabited Mauritius was probably visited by Arab and Malay seamen and later by Portuguese and other European voyagers. However, significant contact did not take place until the

Dutch, under Admiral Wybrandt van Warwijck, arrived in 1598. They named the island after their stadtholder, Prince Maurice of Nassau. Settlers arrived in 1638; their settlements were abandoned in 1710, however, and the French took possession in 1715, sending settlers from Réunion in 1721. The island was governed by the French East India Company until 1767, and by the French government for the next 43 years, except for a brief period of independence during the French Revolution. During the Napoleonic wars French-held Mauritius became a major threat to British shipping in the Indian Ocean, and Britain occupied it in 1810.

The French settlers established Mauritius as a sugar plantation economy, which then gained ascendancy under British rule. Major control of the cane fields and sugar refineries remained within the French community; lacking any appreciable British settlement, the island stayed French in culture. Abolition of slavery in the British Empire caused an acute labor problem as the former slaves, African and Malagasy in origin, left the sugar fields to go into other occupations. To offset this loss, the United Kingdom (UK), from 1835, allowed the planters to import indentured laborers from India. The system continued until 1923, with 450,000 Indians migrating to Mauritius.

The constitution of 1831 provided for a Council of Government in which representation was largely by Europeans, although a few Creoles won nomination. The constitution of 1886 provided for a council of 27 members, including 10 elected members. The electorate was limited by property qualifications, which denied the population of Indian descent elective representation until 1926. The constitution of 1947 abolished property qualifications and extended the franchise to both sexes. Since 1948 the Indian population has dominated the elective seats. As a result of a constitutional conference held in London in September 1965, Mauritius was granted full internal self-government.

Mauritius became independent on 12 March 1968 and one month later became a member of the UN. Disturbances at the time of independence between Muslims and Creoles forced declaration of a state of emergency, at which time UK troops from Singapore aided in restoring order. Sir Seewoosagur Ramgoolam, chief minister in the colonial government, became the first prime minister after independence. Ramgoolam's Mauritius Labor Party (MLP) held power alone or in coalition with others until June 1982 when an alliance of the Mauritian Militant Movement (MMM) and the Mauritian Socialist Party (PSM) captured all 60 directly elected seats on the island of Mauritius. This coalition, known as the MMM/PSM coalition, formed a government and the MMM leader, Aneerood Jugnauth, became prime minister. In March 1983 however, 11 of the 19 ministers, all MMM members, resigned and new elections were called. Aneerood Jugnauth created a new political party, the Mouvement Socialiste Militant (MSM). The MSM partnered with the MLP and the MSM/MLP won a clear mandate and once again won the 1987 Legislative Assembly Elections.

Jugnauth's coalition, this time partnering with the MMM, received a landslide victory in the September 1991 general elections, winning 59 of 62 directly-elected seats. As promised the Alliance MSM/MMM amended the constitution, making Mauritius a republic within the Commonwealth. Since 12 March 1992 Queen Elizabeth II has been replaced by a president of the Republic of Mauritius.

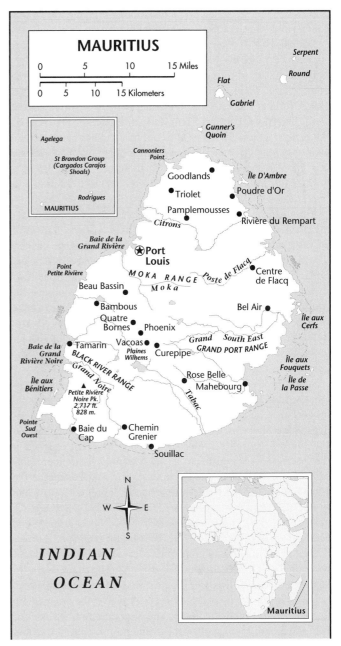

LOCATION: 19°50′ to 20°5′S; 57°18′ to 57°48′ E. TERRITORIAL SEA LIMIT: 12 miles.

In 1993 there was trouble in the coalition when a prominent minister in the MMM met officials of the MLP. The minister was fired by Jugnauth. The MMM underwent a split with some of them following the fired minister while the rest formed a new political party, the Renouveau Mouvement Militant (RMM). General elections were held in 1996 and the MMM/MLP won a landslide victory winning all the 62 elected seats. Dr. Navinchandra Ramgoolam became prime minister. Cassam Uteem and Angidi Veeriah Chettiar were later nominated as president and vice president.

Trouble in the MMM/MLP coalition resurfaced in June 1997 when Ramgoolam fired MMM's leader, Paul Bérenger, who was vice premier and minister of Foreign Affairs. Seven cabinet ministers belonging to MMM resigned in protest and, together with other elected MMM candidates, joined the parliamentary opposition group. This precipitated a second cabinet reshuffle since Ramgoolam took power in 1995. This left the labor party in power with only small parties aligned with it. Bérenger's place was now occupied by the vice president of the Labor Party, Kailash Purryag.

This unbalanced configuration provoked fears of a repeat of the ethnic clashes that had rocked Mauritius in 1968; however, ethnic violence did not materialize. in February 1999 after three days of rioting in the capital Port Louis and other parts of the country, the country gradually returned to normal. Clashes between Rastafarians and police were triggered by the death in police custody of a popular reggae singer, Kaya. Three protesters were killed, a policeman died of heart failure, and over 100 were wounded in the clashes.

Although the country had suffered corruption scandals under the previous administration of Prime Minister Navin Ramgoolam, Mauritius has largely avoided the corruption scourge characterizing much of Africa. After winning the September 2000 elections, the coalition government under Jugnauth and Bérenger stated that its priorities were to boost local and foreign investor confidence and to relaunch the economy. A notable feature of the 2000 general election was the agreement between Jugnauth and Bérenger to split the prime minister post between them. This allowed for the first time in postindependence Mauritius that the post of prime minister be occupied by a non-Hindu.

Mauritius is one of a few sub-Saharan African countries to attain the rank of middle-income status and rule by constitutional process; the country has had only four prime ministers since independence. In February 2002 Cassam Uteem and Angidi Veeriah Chettair, respectively the president and vice president, resigned in the space of a week refusing to sign anti-terror legislation prompted by the 11 September attacks on the World Trade Center in the United States (US). An interim president, Supreme Court Chief Justice Arianga Pillay, signed the bill into law, which was twice passed by the parliament owing to strong support from Prime Minister Aneerood Jugnauth. The constitution requires the president either to sign the bill into law or leave office. Karl Offmann was nominated president and Raouf Bundhun vice president. In September 2003 the five-time premier, Sir Aneerood Jugnauth, kept his coalition and campaign promise to hand over the premiership in midterm to the MMM leader and stepped down; his deputy, Paul Raymond Bérenger, became prime minister. On 7 October 2003 Sir Aneerood Jugnauth was sworn in as president of the republic after Karl Offmann stepped down a year and a half after assuming power. Raouf Bundhun remained vice president. In 2007 Aneerood Jugnauth was renominated as president. Parliamentary elections held in 2005 returned Navin Chandra Ramgoolam to office as prime minister.

An important turning point for Mauritius occurred in 2005 as both of its primary exports, sugar and textiles, were affected by changes brought to the preferential status it had negotiated with European and US markets since the 1970s. In the case of sugar, proposals by the European Union (EU) reduced sugar prices by 37.5% during the period of 2005–2007. Under the Sugar Protocol Mauritius enjoyed an annual fixed quota of over 500,000 metric tons at prices just under two-thirds of the world market price. Mauritian textiles were guaranteed duty-free entry into European markets under the Lomé Convention with the EU, and a series of Multi Fiber Arrangements (MFA) renewed in 1977 and three

subsequent times allowed Mauritian textiles to benefit from trade quotas into the US market. The MFA came to an end in 2005. The removal of special trade status exposed Mauritius to stiff competition from low-cost textile producers, notably China, and has also been the source of the loss in tens of thousands of jobs since 2005 in the Export Processing Zone (EPZ). With the comparative advantage evaporated, many investors have relocated to other low-cost countries. As one of the measures to revive the economy, Pravind Jugnauth, deputy prime minister and minister of finance and economic development, announced in April 2005 that Mauritius would become a duty-free island within four years, in order to attract tourists and trade and give Mauritians easier access to quality products at affordable prices.

Analysts believe growing unemployment and a worsening economy helped to narrowly squeeze the opposition MLP-led Alliance Sociale into power in parliamentary elections that were held 3 July 2005. This alliance included five other parties: the Mauritian Party of Xavier-Luc Duval (Parti Mauricien Xavier-Luc Duval—PMXD), Mauritian Social Democratic Party (Parti Mauricien Social-Démocratique—PMSD), The Greens (Les Verts), the Republican Movement (Mouvement Républicain—MR) and the Mauritian Militant Socialist Movement (Mouvement Militant Socialiste Mauricien—MMSM). It beat the outgoing coalition composed of MSM and MMM. The Alliance Sociale coalition won 48.8% of the vote and 38 of the 62 elected seats compared to 42.6% of the vote and 22 seats won by the MSM/MMM/PMSD coalition. The turnout was 81.5%. Navinchandra Ramgoolam, the MLP leader, replaced Bérenger as the prime minister and formed a new government.

¹³GOVERNMENT

The Mauritian government is parliamentary with executive power vested under the constitution in a ceremonial president and an executive prime minister, who is leader of the majority party in parliament. The president and vice president are elected by the National Assembly to serve five-year terms. The prime minister heads a Council of Ministers, which is responsible to a unicameral Legislative Assembly. Of its maximum 70 members, 62 are nominated by universal suffrage (age 18), and as many as 8 "best losers" are chosen from runners-up by the Electoral Supervisory Commission by a formula designed to give at least minimal representation to all ethnic groups and underrepresented parties.

¹⁴POLITICAL PARTIES

The MLP, headed by Prime Minister Sir Seewoosagur Ramgoolam, received support during 35 continuous years in office (1947–82) from the Hindu and Creole communities and some Muslims; often sharing power in those years was the Muslim Committee of Action (MCA). The PMSD has long represented the Franco-Mauritian and Creole landowning class.

A new political party, the MMM, was formed in the late 1960s. Its leaders were imprisoned in 1971 after the MMM called for a general strike to protest legislation banning strikes in industries controlled by MMM affiliates. The party leadership was later freed, and in the 1976 elections the MMM won more seats than the MLP. The MLP brokered a post electoral coalition with the PMSD and formed government. In the 1982 elections the MMM captured 42 seats in parliament and joined the PSM in a ruling coalition under

Aneerood Jugnauth; unlike the MMM, which had strong Creole representation, the PSM was primarily Hindu.

Jugnauth's government fell apart in the early months of 1983 in the course of a power struggle within the MMM that led to the prime minister's expulsion from his own party. Jugnauth then formed the MSM which, in alliance with the MLP, captured 37 of 62 directly elected seats in the August balloting. The MMM won 19 seats, the PMSD 4, and a Rodrigues-based party, the Organisation du Peuple Rodriguais (OPR) won 2. In August 1987 elections the MSM, in alliance with the MLP and PMSD, won 39 of 62 directly elected seats; a three-party coalition including the MMM won 21 seats, and the OPR won 2 seats.

The legislative elections of 15 September 1991 resulted in the MSM/MMM alliance getting 59 seats (53% of the vote) and the MLP/PMSD alliance 3 seats (38%). By October 1993 however, the MMM had divided into two factions; one remained in the government and the other, headed by former Foreign Minister Paul Bérenger, took opposition seats in parliament.

Legislative elections held in December 1995 saw a newly solidified MMM/MLP coalition win 60 seats (35 for MLP and 25 for MMM) of the 62 elected seats. The Rodrigues Movement had two seats, two seats were given to the OPR, one to the Gaetan Duval Party, and one to Hizbullah. The MMM/MLP coalition fell apart in June 1997 with the firing of Bérenger from the vice premiership, leaving the MLP in power with small parties aligned with it.

Following the reconfiguration of an opposition alliance comprising Aneerood Jugnauth's MSM and Paul Bérenger's MMM, the coalition successfully swept the 11 September 2000 elections, winning 52.3% of the vote and holding the MLP/PMSD to 36.9%, and the OPR to 10.8%. The breakdown of seats was 54 for the MSM/MMM, 6 for the MLP/PMSD, and 2 for the OPR. Sir Aneerood Jugnauth stepped down as he had promised and handed the premiership over to Paul Bérenger on 30 September 2003. Bérenger was to lose it in the 2005 elections.

In parliamentary elections held on 3 July 2005, the opposition Alliance Sociale led by the MLP, and also incorporating the PMXD, PMSD, The Greens, MR and MMSM, narrowly won the elections garnering 48.8% of the vote and winning 38 of the 62 contested seats. The Alliance Sociale ousted the MSM/MMM alliance, which won 42.6% of the vote and 22 parliamentary seats. The two remaining seats for Rodrigues were won by OPR, which took only 0.8% of the vote. According to the constitution President Aneerood Jugnauth allocated an additional eight seats to ethnic groups, bringing total representation to 42 Alliance Sociale, 24 MSM/MMM, and 4 OPR.

In the May 2010 legislative elections, the Alliance of the Future (AF), led by Prime Minister Navinchandra Ramgoolam, won 41 seats in the unicameral assembly. The alliance represented a coalition government that included Ramgoolam's MLP, the MSM, the PMXD, and supporters from other parties. The MMM won 18 seats, followed by the Rodrigues Movement with 2, and the Mauritian Solidarity Front with 1. Aneerood Jugnauth was renominated as president in November 2010 by a unanimous vote of the assembly.

15 LOCAL GOVERNMENT

There are nine administrative districts and three dependencies. Of the nine administrative districts, five are found in urban areas and are called municipalities, and four in rural areas and are called district councils. The lowest level of local government is the village council, of which there are 124, composed of elected as well as nominated members; above the village councils are four district councils. Mayors govern the major towns through the setting up of different commissions.

The three dependencies are Rodrigues, Agalega Islands and Carajos Shoals. In 2002 the Rodrigues Regional Assembly (RRA) was created with the aim of devolving power to Rodriguans.

Municipal council elections were held on 2 October 2005 followed by village council elections on 11 December 2005. According to the prevailing electoral law, elections at municipal and village level should be held every five years. At the last municipal election, the Alliance Sociale won all the wards in all the five municipalities, except in one of the four wards of the town of Beau Bassin-Rose Hill where the MSM/MMM alliance won three of the seven council positions. As for the village council elections, they were mostly won by pro Alliance Sociale supporters. In 2011, a new Local Governance Act was voted in the Mauritian parliament.

16 JUDICIAL SYSTEM

The statutes are based mainly on old French codes and on more recent laws with British precedents. The Supreme Court has a chief justice and eleven other judges who also serve on the Court of Criminal Appeal, the Court of Civil Appeal, the Intermediate Court and the Industrial Court. There is also the Subordinate Court which is made up of forty magistrates. Final appeal can be made to the UK Privy Council.

The president nominates the chief justice in consultation with the prime minister; then with the advice of the chief justice also appoints the associate judges. The president nominates other judges on the advice of the Judicial and Legal Service Commissions.

The legal system provides fair public trials for criminal defendants. Defendants have the right to counsel, including court-appointed counsel in case of indigence.

Mauritius has had a good record of freedom of the press and rule of law, except for isolated incidents. These include a rough economic period and unrest in the 1970s when the government attempted to impose some restrictions, particularly on newspapers opposed to its policies; arbitrary arrests became more frequent, but fierce opposition led to the abolition of the laws. There were also local and international concerns over government plans to put in place sanctions against private radio stations which had angered the government over coverage of an explosion in the northern city of Grand-Baie in August 2004.

From 2007 onwards there have been a number of ferocious attacks of a certain section of the written press and this has been reflected in the Mauritius losing 40 places on the Reporters Without Borders Index from 25th position in 2007 to 65th position in 2010.

17 ARMED FORCES

All defense and security duties were carried out in 2011 by a 2,000-personnel paramilitary police force. The forces within this structure were an estimated 500-member Coast Guard and an estimated 1,500-member Special Mobile Force. Armed forces represent 0.4% of the labor force in Mauritius. Defense spending totaled $55.3 million and accounted for 0.3% of gross domestic product (GDP).

18 INTERNATIONAL COOPERATION

Mauritius joined the UN on 24 April 1968 and belongs to the Economic Commission for Africa (ECA) as well as several nonregional specialized agencies, such as the UN Food and Agriculture Organization (FAO), the International Atomic Energy Agency (IAEA), the World Bank; the UN Educational, Scientific and Cultural Organization (UNESCO); the UN Industrial Development Organization (UNIDO), and the World Health Organization (WHO). The nation participates in the World Trade Organization (WTO), the African Development Bank, the Common Market for Eastern and Southern Africa (COMESA), the Commonwealth of Nations, the Group of 77 (G-77); the African, Caribbean and Pacific *Group* of States (ACP Group); Alliance of Small Island States (AOSIS), Small Island Developing States (SIDS) and the African Union. In 1984 Mauritius joined Madagascar and Seychelles in establishing the Indian Ocean Commission; Comoros and France (as the representative of Réunion) joined in 1985. Mauritius also is a member of the Southern African Development Community (SADC). The country is part of the Non-Aligned Movement (NAM).

In environmental cooperation Mauritius is part of the Basel Convention, the Convention on Biological Diversity (CDB), the Ramsar Convention on Wetlands of International Importance, the Convention on International Trade in Endangered Species (CITES), the Kyoto Protocol, the Montréal Protocol, International Convention for the Prevention of Pollution from Ships (MARPOL), the Nuclear Test Ban Treaty, the UN Convention on Climate Change, and the UN Convention to Combat Desertification (UNCCD).

19 ECONOMY

Mauritius has a diverse economy based on export-oriented manufacturing (mainly clothing), sugar, and tourism. Most of production is done by private enterprise, but the State Trading Corporation controls imports of products such as rice, flour, petroleum, and cement. Sugarcane covers approximately 45% of the island's land area and 90% of cultivated land; it accounts for 25% of export earnings. The financial and information and communications technology (ICT) services sector of the economy is expanding, as is the tourism sector. As of 2011 Mauritius had concluded 36 tax treaties under the Double Tax Agreement (DTA) upon which rests the offshore sector. The business climate for foreign investors is excellent as Mauritius ranked 17th globally on the World Bank's Ease of Doing Business Index.

Important to Mauritius's industrial development is the EPZ founded in the early 1970s in which imported goods and raw materials are processed for export. EPZ products include textiles and clothing, electrical components, and diamonds. Legislation gives investors in EPZ enterprises tax relief, duty exemption on most imports, unlimited repatriation of capital and profits, and cut-rate electricity. However, some of the country's larger manufacturing industries were moving their labor-intensive production to Madagascar and other African countries.

The economy grew at an impressive average rate of 6% in the early 1980s. However, economic growth started to decline in 1988 as the economy experienced some of the problems associated with success, including labor shortages, rising inflation, and capacity constraints. In the early 1990s the economy showed signs of a modest recovery with solid real growth and low unemployment. Adverse weather conditions reduced the importance of sugarcane to the Mauritian economy in the late 1990s, but exports of cane brought in almost 8% of the GDP. To further enhance its competitive advantage, in 1992 the government passed legislation for the creation of a commercial free port in Port Louis. The free port provides warehousing as well as facilities for processing foods and materials for reexport to destinations around the world. Between 1988 and 1998 the economy grew at an annual rate of approximately 5.3%, which is approximately where it stood in 2001.

In 2006 faced with rising oil prices and sugar and textile trade preference erosion, the government began a multi-year plan to diversify and balance the economy on a microeconomic level. This involved expanding the seafood industry, tourism, the knowledge hub, and business processing outsourcing (BPO). Real growth in 2007 was the highest since 2000.

In 2009 the World Bank ranked the nation as first in Africa for ease of doing business. The government's goal was to expand upon this recognition and become one of the top ten business-friendly locations in the world. Toward that goal the government announced in April 2009 a new national strategic plan to promote the ICT sector. The announcement was made at the opening of the ICT Business Pre-Incubator Cell at the Mauritian University of Technology, a program designed to encourage local and national entrepreneurship. Also in April the government met with US trade representatives to review the US-Mauritius Trade and Investment Framework Agreement (TIFA), which promotes cooperation between nations for ease of trade. The value of two-way trade between the two nations was at $227 million in 2008. Leading exports to the United States include textiles and apparel, cut diamonds and jewelry, live animals, prepared fish, optical and medical equipment, and perfume.

The tourist industry took a hit during the global financial crisis of 2008–09, leading to a rise in unemployment to about 8% in June 2009. The government responded with an allocation of about $47 million from the state budget for social programs assisting those affected by the crisis. Additionally, the government continues to support a special poverty eradication program designed to empower the 8% of the population that remains below the poverty line, although there is no official poverty line in Mauritius. This effort is coordinated through the National Empowerment Foundation (NEF), which promotes programs in literacy and life skills training. The 2009 budget included $17.5 million for NEF programs.

The projected growth rate for Mauritius in January 2010 was estimated to reach 4.1%, representing a substantial economic acceleration from the crawling 1.5% growth rate Mauritius had in 2009. With its sights set on becoming a high growth economy, Mauritius forged an agreement with the EU for a 2010–2012 budget support program worth 100.74 million euros (US$130.25682). The funding was meant to offer budgetary stability as the government continued its programs of economic reforms. The first disbursement of 30.2 million euros (US$39.0486) was granted by the EU in August 2010. That same month the government of Mauritius approved a major stimulus package aimed at boosting the tourism and export sectors. In 2011 the government of Mauritius attempted, in its budget entitled Rebalancing Growth—Consolidating Social Justice, to weather the storms caused by the prolonged world economic worries. As of 2010 the GDP rate of change in Mauritius was 4%, while inflation stood at 5.8 % and unemployment was reported at 7.3%.

[20]INCOME

The CIA estimated that in 2010 the GDP of Mauritius was $18.06 billion. The CIA defines GDP as the value of all final goods and services produced within a nation in a given year and computed on the basis of purchasing power parity (PPP) rather than value as measured on the basis of the rate of the exchange based on current dollars. The per capita GDP was estimated at $13,500. The annual growth rate of GDP was 3.6%. The average inflation rate was 2.9%. It was estimated that agriculture accounted for 4.8% of GDP, industry 24.6%, and services 70.5%.

According to the World Bank remittances from citizens living abroad totaled $215 million or about $162 per capita and accounted for approximately 1.2% of GDP.

The World Bank reports that in 2009 household consumption in Mauritius totaled $6.4 billion or about $4,915 per capita, measured in current US dollars rather than PPP. Household consumption includes expenditures of individuals, households, and nongovernmental organizations on goods and services, excluding the purchases of dwellings. It was estimated that household consumption was growing at an average annual rate of 2.1%.

As of 2011 the most recent study by the World Bank reported that actual individual consumption in Mauritius was 74.7% of GDP and accounted for 0.03% of world consumption. By comparison the United States accounted for 25.44% of world individual consumption. The World Bank also estimated that 23.5% of Mauritius's GDP was spent on food and beverages, 20.4% on housing and household furnishings, 3.7% on clothes, 4.1% on health, 8.5% on transportation, 1.9% on communications, 4.1% on recreation, 2.2% on restaurants and hotels, and 0.5% on miscellaneous goods and services and purchases from abroad.

Mauritius does not have a poverty line. However, on the basis of available census and survey data, the Central Statistics Office has come up with poverty-related indicators which indicate that around 8% of the population can be classified as poor.

[21]LABOR

As of 2011 Mauritius had a total labor force of 537,300 people. Within that labor force CIA estimates in 2007 noted that 9% were employed in agriculture, 30% in industry, and 31% in the service sector. Mauritius also had some 33,000 foreign workers employed mainly in the textile and construction industry who came from China, Bangladesh, Sri Lanka and India.

Unions have the legal right to organize, strike, and bargain collectively, and the trade union movement is active. There were over 335 labor unions in 2001 with 111,231 members, representing about 22% of the workforce. Workers are granted the right to strike, but this is severely curtailed by a mandatory cooling-off period and compulsory binding arbitration. Antiunion discrimination is prohibited and an arbitration tribunal handles complaints of such discrimination. Although the law protects collective bar-

gaining, there are not enough safeguards in place to protect employees from discriminatory actions by employers.

The minimum working age is 15 with restrictions for those under age 18. However, child labor and exploitation is still practiced and penalties for infractions are minimal. Minimum wages are set by the government, and cost-of-living allowances are mandatory. The minimum wage ranged from $3.53 to $12.30 per week in 2002, but due to a labor shortage and contract negotiations, actual wages are about double this figure. The standard legal workweek is 45 hours.

[22]AGRICULTURE

Roughly 48% of the total land is currently farmed and the country's major crops include sugarcane, tea, corn, potatoes, bananas, and vegetables. Cereal production in 2009 amounted to 839 tons, fruit production 24,317 tons, and vegetable production 71,732 tons.

Sugarcane is the major crop. In 2010 sugarcane occupied 40% of Mauritius's total land area. It is an estate economy with 9 large estates. Small operations account for 40% of the land cultivated and are grouped into cooperatives. Sugar's importance has diminished in recent years as manufacturing, tourism, financial and ICT services, and resort schemes have grown.

Tea production in Mauritius has been on the decline, disadvantaged by production cost increases, labor shortages, and low world prices. The area under tea cultivation declined from 2,905 hectares (7,178 acres) in 1990 to 760 hectares (1,878 acres) in 2006. Tobacco production provides the raw material for most locally produced cigarettes. In recent years horticultural products have been successfully grown for export, including flowers (mainly anthuriums), tropical fruits, and vegetables.

Almost any crop can be grown on Mauritius, but sugar as a monocrop means almost all cereals must be imported, including rice, the staple food. Potatoes and other vegetables are grown in the sugar fields between rows of cane.

Two of the largest sugar producers in Mauritius merged operations in November 2009 in an effort to better allocate land and resources between them and to increase efficiency through economies of scale. The decision to merge was driven by the EU ending its Sugar Protocol, a series of bilateral agreements between the EU and certain African, Caribbean, and Pacific countries, including Mauritius. The Sugar Protocol, which took effect in 1975, gave affected countries preferential access to European sugar markets at high, fixed prices. In Europe raw sugar prices were expected to fall by 36% as a result of the EU ending this program, which was to be phased out in stages from 1 October 2009 through 2015. Sugar exports in 2008 accounted for roughly 2 % of Mauritius's GDP and 14% of the value of exports.

[23]ANIMAL HUSBANDRY

Mauritius dedicated 7,000 hectares (17,297 acres) to permanent pasture or meadow in 2009. During that year the country tended 13.7 million chickens, 7,237 head of cattle, and 14,108 pigs. The production from these animals amounted to 7,893 tons of beef and veal, 3,568 tons of pork, 40,238 tons of poultry, 8,921 tons of eggs, and 142,584 tons of milk. Mauritius also produced 233 tons of cattle hide.

24 FISHING

With the decline of the sugar industry, Mauritius decided to develop other sectors of the economy, including the seafood sector. Mauritius had 20 decked commercial fishing boats in 2008. The annual capture totaled 6,152 tons according to the FAO. The export value of seafood totaled $109.4 million.

25 FORESTRY

Approximately 17% of Mauritius is covered by forest. In 2009 roundwood production was estimated at 8,500 cu m (300,175 cu ft). The value of all forest products, including roundwood, totaled $5.43 million.

26 MINING

There were few mineral resources in Mauritius. In 2009 Mauritius produced 57,160 metric tons of fertilizers, an estimated 2,301 metric tons of marine salt, and 56,000 metric tons of semi-manufactured steel. Historically, mineral output consisted of the local production and use of basalt construction stone, coral sand, lime from coral, and solar-evaporated sea salt. Concerns have been raised about the impact of coral sand mining on coastal lagoons. Polymetallic nodules occurred on the ocean floor northeast of Tromelin Island containing iron, manganese, and cobalt. However, these minerals were abundant on land. The near-term outlook for the exploitation of minerals other than construction materials was negligible.

27 ENERGY AND POWER

Mauritius as of 1 January 2011 had no proven reserves of crude oil, natural gas, coal, or petroleum refining capacity. As a result it is totally dependent upon imports to meet its fossil fuel needs.

In 2009 electric power production in Mauritius totaled 2.27 billion kWh and consumption 2 billion kWh. As of 1 January 2010, 79% of electricity was produced using imported fossil fuel. In line with the Maurice Ile Durable project launched in 2008, 21% of the electricity generation was from renewable sources. A significant portion of all primary energy consumed came from bagasse, or sugarcane waste. Hydroelectricity and wind energy accounted for the rest. In recent years a massive operation of sale of compact fluorescent lamps at a highly discounted price to residential customers was carried out.

28 INDUSTRY

Since 1986 EPZ export earnings have led those of the sugar sector. Investors were primarily from Mauritius itself and Hong Kong. The textile industry was the leading sector in the EPZ, with more than 90% of the EPZ's goods being produced for the United States and Europe; with the change in Mauritius's trade status taking effect in 2005, export earnings were under severe pressure. Other important products include chemicals, electronics, nonelectrical machinery, transportation equipment, precision engineering, skilled crafts, toys, nails, razor blades, and tires. Industry accounted for 29.9% of GDP in 2005. Mauritius is also emerging as a major business and financial center.

Manufacturing centers on the processing of agricultural products, sugarcane in particular. Of the nine large sugar-producing estates, two have their own factories. Normal production varies between 600,000 to 700,000 metric tons, but adverse weather during the late 1990s reduced these figures. Molasses and rum are among the sugar by-products produced in Mauritius. Local tobacco is made into cigarettes, and factories are maintained to process tea. Other small industries produce goods for local consumption, such as beer and soft drinks, shoes, metal products, and paints.

29 SCIENCE AND TECHNOLOGY

Patent applications in science and technology as of 2009 totaled two in Mauritius. In 1997, the latest year for which data is available, there were 201 scientists and engineers and 126 technicians per million people that were engaged in research and development (R and D); R and D expenditures that year totaled $27.659 million or 0.29% of GDP. Of that amount government sources accounted for 94.7%, with foreign sources accounting for the remaining 5.3%. High technology exports in 2002 totaled $29 million, or 2% of the country's manufactured exports.

The Mauritius Institute in Port Louis, founded in 1880, is a research center for the study of local fauna and flora. The Mauritius Sugar Industry Research Institute, founded in 1953, is located at Réduit. The University of Mauritius, founded in 1965 at Réduit, has schools of agriculture, engineering, and science. The University of Technology, founded in 2000, has a school of innovative technologies and engineering. In 2010 science and engineering students accounted for 39% of university enrollments. The Albion Fisheries Research Centre was founded in 1981. The Agricultural Research and Extension Unit was established within the Ministry of Agriculture in 1994. The Mauritius Oceanography Institute was created in 2000. The Regional Sugarcane Training Center for Africa, located in Réduit, is sponsored by the UN Development Program. The Port Louis Museum maintains collections of fauna, flora and geology of Mauritius and other islands of the Mascarene region.

30 DOMESTIC TRADE

Port Louis is the commercial center and the chief port. A wide variety of goods are distributed through the standard channels of importers, wholesalers, retailers, and supermarkets. Franchising, mainly in restaurants, has become quite popular. The first Kentucky Fried Chicken opened in Mauritius in 1983 and as of 2011 had a fleet of twenty restaurants. The first McDonald's opened in 2001.

The government maintains price and markup controls on a number of consumer goods, including rice, onions, iron and steel bars, edible oils, certain appliances, pharmaceuticals, sporting goods, timber, and many others. A 1998 Consumer Protection Act extended government pricing controls to several other basic commodities, such as cheese, butter, canned and frozen meats, and sugar. A 15% value-added tax (VAT) tax is applied.

The Mauritius Freeport, a customs duty-free zone in the port and airport, turned the country into a major regional distribution, transshipment, and marketing center. This zone provides facilities for warehousing, transshipment operations and minor processing, simple assembly, and repackaging.

Business hours are from 9 a.m. to 4 p.m., Monday through Friday, and 9 a.m. to 12 p.m. on Saturday. Banks are open from 9:30 a.m. to 3 p.m., Monday through Thursday, and 9 a.m. to 4 p.m. on Friday. Shops operate from 10 a.m. to 5 p.m., Monday through

Principal Trading Partners – Mauritius (2010)

(In millions of US dollars)

Country	Total	Exports	Imports	Balance
World	6,641.0	2,239.1	4,401.9	-2,162.8
India	951.6	16.9	934.6	-917.7
France	773.8	397.4	376.4	21.0
China	572.9	7.1	565.9	-558.8
United Kingdom	521.6	427.4	94.2	333.2
South Africa	472.2	114.1	358.1	-244.0
United States	299.9	197.8	102.1	95.6
Spain	242.9	127.4	115.4	12.0
Italy	237.3	143.7	93.6	50.2
Japan	162.6	19.9	142.7	-122.9
Australia	140.4	7.1	133.4	-126.3

(…) data not available or not significant.

(n.s.) not specified.

SOURCE: *2011 Direction of Trade Statistics Yearbook,* New York: United Nations, 2011.

Friday, and from 10 a.m. to 12 p.m. on Saturday in Port Louis and from 10 a.m. to 5 p.m. in the rest of the country. Most shops open from 10 a.m. to 12 p.m. on Sunday. Most business is conducted in English and French.

31 FOREIGN TRADE

Mauritius imported $5.1 billion worth of goods and services in 2011, while exporting $2.5 billion worth of goods and services. Major import partners in 2009 were India 18.7%, China 12.6%, France 11.8%, and South Africa 8.7%. Its major export partners were the United Kingdom 27%, France 21.2%, the United States 8.3%, Madagascar 6.4%, Italy 5.5%, South Africa 4.6%, and Spain 4.6%.

Mauritius imports more than it exports, but the difference is taken care of by revenues from tourism and other services. Mauritius had $2.601 billion in foreign exchange reserves and gold in 2010. The country held an external debt burden of $4.7 billion.

32 BALANCE OF PAYMENTS

In 2010 Mauritius had a foreign trade deficit of $925 million, amounting to .6% of GDP.

33 BANKING AND SECURITIES

The Bank of Mauritius is the central bank. There were 19 commercial banks operating in the country in 2011. Six were locally owned, including The Mauritius Commercial Bank Limited and the State Bank of Mauritius Limited, both of which dominated the market. The government-controlled Development Bank of Mauritius was established in March 1964 to provide loans for agricultural and industrial enterprises. The other 16 banks are offshore, offering attractive tax rates, especially to US investment in India. Foreign exchange reserves at the Bank of Mauritius stood at $ 2.5 billion in 2011. In 2010 total commercial bank assets were estimated at $26 billion.

The government made it clear early in the first quarter of 1997 that the Bank of Mauritius would intervene in the foreign exchange market in order to stabilize the value of the rupee. Interventions by the central bank helped the rupee to rebound after its decline against most foreign currencies during the first nine months of 1996. In 1997 the Mauritian rupee was freely convertible.

A market for securities or shares was not new to Mauritius when the Stock Exchange of Mauritius (SEMDEX) opened in 1989. Shares of companies had been traded in Mauritius in a market environment since the 19th century. The main difference between the market organized by Chambre de Courtiers de l'île Maurice and the market in its present form is the legal framework within which dealings in shares must now take place, and the regular meetings for share dealing. The stock market was opened to foreigners in 1994. In 2011 the market had 52 listed companies, and a capitalization that grew from $55 million in 1989 to $5.6 billion in 2011.

In October 2010 Mauritius launched its first commodities and currency exchange, known as the Global Board of Trade (GBOT). GBOT initially offered trading in gold and silver and currency pairings with the US dollar/Mauritius rupee (USD/MUR), the South African rand/US dollar (ZAR/USD), euro/US dollar (EUR/USD), the British pound/US dollar (GBP/USD), and the Japanese yen/US dollar (JPY/USD). Officials hope to add a wider array of commodities in the not too distant future.

34 INSURANCE

There are at least 20 insurance companies operating in Mauritius. In 2010 the value of all direct insurance premiums written totaled $491.7 million. As of that same year one of the top insurers was Swan, with gross written premiums of $97.3 million. The country's leading life insurer in 2010 was British American Insurance (BAI), which had gross written life insurance premiums of $203.7 million.

35 PUBLIC FINANCE

From the mid-1970s to 1981 the ratio of fiscal deficit to GDP increased from under 10% to 14% due to deficit public spending. During the 1980s an export-oriented economy caused the fiscal

Balance of Payments – Mauritius (2010)

(In millions of US dollars)

Current Account		**-799.6**
Balance on goods		-1,895.8
Imports	-4,157.3	
Exports	2,261.5	
Balance on services		711.3
Balance on income		201.7
Current transfers		183.3
Capital Account		**-4.8**
Financial Account		**840.5**
Direct investment abroad		-129.4
Direct investment in Mauritius		431.0
Portfolio investment assets		-138.6
Portfolio investment liabilities		-45.4
Financial derivatives		…
Other investment assets		-3,851.4
Other investment liabilities		4,574.2
Net Errors and Omissions		**172.9**
Reserves and Related Items		**-209.0**

(…) data not available or not significant.

SOURCE: *Balance of Payment Statistics Yearbook 2011,* Washington, DC: International Monetary Fund, 2011.

Public Finance – Mauritius (2009)

(In millions of rupees, central government figures)

Revenue and Grants	**67,195**	**100.0%**
Tax revenue	52,729	78.5%
Social contributions	2,769	4.1%
Grants	2,783	4.1%
Other revenue	8,914	13.3%
Expenditures	**65,572**	**100.0%**
General public services	17,765	27.1%
Defense	...	...
Public order and safety	5,599	8.5%
Economic affairs	6,731	10.3%
Environmental protection	2,093	3.2%
Housing and community amenities	1,127	1.7%
Health	5,840	8.9%
Recreational, culture, and religion	698	1.1%
Education	10,314	15.7%
Social protection	15,405	23.5%

(…) data not available or not significant.

SOURCE: *Government Finance Statistics Yearbook 2010,* Washington, DC: International Monetary Fund, 2010.

deficit to decline to 3% of GDP by 1989 and to 2% by 1991. The deficit reached 4.6% in 1997 and 6.3% in 2002. In 2010 the deficit stood at 4.5%.

In 2010 the budget of Mauritius included $2.114 billion in public revenue and $2.583 billion in public expenditures. The budget deficit amounted to 4.6% of GDP. Public debt was 60.5% of GDP with $4.695 billion of the debt held by foreign entities. As of 2011 the total external debt had reached 11.7% of GDP.

The International Monetary Fund (IMF) reported that GDP per capita had increased from $1,295 in 1980 to $7,303 in 2010. Macroeconomic and political stability, robust institutions, an efficient administration, a favorable regulatory environment, and a well-developed financial system explained this performance.

[36] TAXATION

As of 2011 Mauritius had a corporate income tax rate of 15%. However, companies were required to set up a Corporate Social Responsibility Fund (CSR) equivalent to 2% of their preceding year's profits to implement programs for the needy or to finance an approved nongovernmental organization (NGO). Mauritius has double-taxation prevention treaties with 36 countries.

The progressive scale for individual income tax, ranging from 5–30%, was replaced in 2007 by a flat schedule of 15% rate on taxable income.

A general sales tax (GST) averaging 5% was imposed in 1983. As of 7 September 1998 the GST was replaced by a VAT with a standard rate of 10%. On 1 July 2001 the standard rate was raised to 12% and then as of 7 January 2002 to 15%, where it remained as of 2011. The VAT applies to all goods and services except those specifically exempted. The exempt list includes basic foodstuffs, basic services (medical, hospital and dental), basic utilities (water and electricity), and all exported goods and services.

[37] CUSTOMS AND DUTIES

Mauritius maintains a list of preferred trading partners to which it gives preferential tariff rates. Taxes on imports from the preferred list are levied at 0–80%. Imports of goods from other countries at the 55% rate or higher are subject to an additional 10% duty. A VAT of 15% is levied on all imports. Vehicles, petroleum, alcohol, cigarettes, and furniture are subject to special excise duties of up to 360%.

Most imports require a license and state enterprises control the import of rice, wheat, flour, petroleum, cement, tea, tobacco, and sugar. There are few export controls except the need for licenses to export sugar, tea, vegetables, fruits, meat, fish, textiles, pharmaceuticals, gold, live animals, coral, and shells.

Mauritius is a member of the SADC, which launched a free trade area in 2008. The country is also a member of COMESA, which gives preferential rates of duty between member states.

[38] FOREIGN INVESTMENT

The government offers a variety of investment incentives including, for industries in the EPZ, a corporate tax exemption of at least 10 years followed by a low corporate tax rate of 15 percent, an exemption from import duties on capital goods and most raw materials; free repatriation of profits, dividends, and invested capital; a waiver of income taxes on dividends for 10 years, and reduced tariffs for electricity and water. All foreign investment must obtain approval from the prime minister's office, except in the offshore business center and the stock exchange. Businesses in Freeport receive exemption from company tax and tax on dividends, preferential rates for storage, halved port handling charges, and exemption from import duty and sales tax on finished goods and machinery. Foremost among foreign investors are those from Hong Kong, followed by French, South African, German, Indian and more recently, Chinese interests. In 2002 the government set up the Integrated Resorts Scheme (IRS) to attract high net worth non-citizens desiring to acquire an immovable property of not less than $500,000 in Mauritius for personal residence. The investor and his/her spouse and dependents are granted resident permits to live in Mauritius.

Foreign ownership of services such as accounting, law, medicine, computer services, international marketing, and management consulting was limited to 30% in 1997. However, with the further opening up of the Mauritian economy, 100% foreign ownership is allowed on the island. In December 2000 the Investment Promotion Act was passed, designed to streamline the investment process, and in 2006 the Business Facilitation Act allowed for the setting up of business within three working days. The Board of Investment (BOI) acts as the facilitator for all forms of investment in Mauritius and guides investors through the necessary processes for doing business in the country.

Total foreign direct investment (FDI) was $33 million in 1996. However, because foreign investors have not been registering with the Central Bank since the abolition of exchange controls in 1994, it is generally cautioned that official statistics underestimate the amount of foreign investment in the country. Not included is the increasingly important offshore financial sector. In 1997 FDI inflow rose to $56 million, mainly due to investments from South Africa in the banking sector. FDI inflow fell to $12.7

million in 1998, but increased to $55 million in 1999, most investments coming from South Africa. In 2000 FDI inflow reached almost $260 million, mostly due to France Telecom's purchase of a 40% share of Mauritius Telecom as part of their strategic alliance. Over the years FDI has significantly increased and in 2011 stood at $ 430 million. This upsurge is mainly due to the development of new types of investment such as ICT, seafood, biomedical and knowledge.

39 ECONOMIC DEVELOPMENT

France has backed training for labor, a stock exchange (which opened under the Stock Exchange Act of 1988), and irrigation projects. The EU is supporting efforts at diversifying agriculture. The Mauritius plan to become an international financial center advanced as liberalized currency rules were put into effect in 1986. As at 2011 some 34,000 global business companies are currently registered, with investments predominantly directed to India, China, the Far East and Africa. Mauritius is the leading financial center through which funds are invested in India. In 1995 Mauritius became the 12th member of the SADC; since then the SADC has been an important trading partner with imports increasing at a yearly average of about 1.88%, while exports increased by around 10.38%.

Massive investment from the government in infrastructure has been earmarked for the next ten years and that to the tune of $1 billion. This is in line with making Mauritius a hub for trading and investment in the Indian Ocean. Through the Chinese EXIM Bank, China has provided a number of preferential loans for the extension of the existing airport as well as the building of new roads. Mauritius's privileged relationship with India has also allowed for a line of credit worth $100 million in 2001 for the development of information technology on the island.

The government is putting effort into information and communications technologies, in an effort to diversify the economy away from its reliance upon sugar, textiles and apparel, and tourism. The government developed a five-year Sugar Sector Strategic Plan for 2001–05 to restructure the sugar industry, including reducing the labor force and the number of sugar mills in operation. Mauritius's EPZ firms have sizable investments in Madagascar's EPZ, and have been affected by political upheavals there. Nonetheless, growth in Mauritius was strong in the mid-2000s and social conditions were improving. A rising unemployment rate was a concern, however; the unemployment rate was estimated at 10.5% in 2005. The government has passed anti-money laundering and anti-terrorism legislation. Promoting a more open and liberalized economy, the island was able to attract a number of key investors. With GDP growth rates averaging 5–6% in the mid-2000s, Mauritius's economic success was reflected in more equitable income distribution, reduced infant mortality rates, increased life expectancy, and greatly-improved infrastructure.

40 SOCIAL DEVELOPMENT

Mauritius has a comprehensive welfare system that offers free education, free healthcare, and a universal system of pensions that supplements an earnings-related pension system. The universal pension covers all residents and is financed entirely from government sources. The universal pension pays a fixed sum according to the age of the pensioner. Employee pension benefits are determined by the number of years worked. A program of family allowances assists needy families with more than three children. Employment-related sickness and maternity benefits are provided as well as workers' compensation and unemployment benefits, rent assistance, and a funeral grant.

In 2011 the Equal Opportunity Act was enacted. The constitution prohibits discrimination based on gender. Although women do not face significant legal discrimination, most remain limited to traditional subordinate roles in the household and in the workplace. Domestic violence is pervasive and is often related to drug and alcohol abuse. In 1997 the Protection from Domestic Violence Act was passed and provides protection to victims of domestic violence. The government is committed to promoting the rights of children and in 2003 an Ombudsperson for Children was created.

41 HEALTH

As of 2011 there were an estimated 11 physicians, 37 nurses and midwives, and 33 hospital beds per 10,000 inhabitants. In the same year the country spent 5.5% of its GDP on healthcare, amounting to $383 per person. The entire population of Mauritius had access to safe water and adequate sanitation.

The average life expectancy in Mauritius in 2011 was 74.48 years and the infant mortality rate was 13.3 deaths per 1,000 live births. The maternal mortality rate was 36 per 100,000 live births in 2011. The total fertility rate in 2011 was estimated at 1.79 children born per woman. It was estimated that 75% of women were using contraception in 2011.

According to World Health Organization reports, 5.3% of children 3–6 years of age were anemic. Immunization rates for children up to one year old were: tuberculosis, diphtheria, pertussis, tetanus, poliomyelitis and hepatitis B 89%, and measles 99%. The island of Mauritius has a high prevalence of non-insulin dependent diabetes. Physical inactivity and glucose intolerance through obesity are suggested culprits. In order to fight this situation, a national action plan on physical activity had been set up for 2011–2014.

The high rates of coronary heart disease seen in Asian Indians, African-origin Creoles, and Chinese in this rapidly developing country may point to future problems in this region. Most deaths are cardiovascular disease-related. Nearly 40% of Mauritius's male population were smokers in 2009. In 2008 the government legislated against smoking.

The HIV/AIDS adult prevalence rate was 2.4% in 2011. The incidence of tuberculosis was 66 per 100,000 people in 2009.

42 HOUSING

In 2011 there were two basic types of houses—92% of houses were made of concrete, and 4.5% were galvanized iron/tin structures. In the same year there were 356,900 housing units nationwide. Of these about 77.6% were detached houses, 16.6% were semi-detached homes or blocks of flats. About 99% of all dwellings were privately owned. The average household size was 3.6 persons. About 94.2% of all dwellings had indoor piped water, 99.4% had electricity, 95.5% had an indoor kitchen, 95.5% had an indoor bathroom and 96.4% had flush toilet. However, only 50% of Rodriguan households had these basic amenities.

43 EDUCATION

Education is free up to college level and is compulsory for six years. The educational system is based largely on the British school system. Primary school covers six years of study. This is followed by seven years of secondary studies (five years lower and two years upper). The academic year runs from January to October at primary and secondary levels and from August to May at tertiary level.

In 2009 about 95% of age-eligible children were enrolled in some type of preschool program. Primary school enrollment in the same year was estimated at about 94% of age-eligible children. Secondary school enrollment was about 82% of age-eligible students. It is estimated that nearly all students complete their primary education. The student-to-teacher ratio for primary school was at about 22:1 in 2009; the ratio for secondary school was about 17:1. In 2009 private schools accounted for about 25% of primary school enrollment and 73% of secondary enrollment.

Postsecondary institutions include the University of Mauritius; the University of Technology, Mauritius; the Mauritius College of the Air; the Mauritius Institute of Education; and the Mahatma Gandhi Institute. There are several polytechnic schools and about 30 private organizations that offer tertiary-level programs of study. Many university students study in Europe, India, Australia, and the United States. As of 2010 46.9% of the tertiary age population was enrolled in some type of higher education program. Of those enrolled in tertiary education, there were 100 male students for every 125 female students. The adult literacy rate for 2009 was estimated at about 84.4%, with 88.2% for men and 80.5% for women.

As of 2009 public expenditure on education was estimated at 3.2% of GDP, or 14.3% of total government expenditures.

44 LIBRARIES AND MUSEUMS

Libraries include the Mauritius Institute Public Library (75,000 volumes), the Mauritius Archives (36,000), and the University of Mauritius Library (100,000). The National Library located at Port Louis and opened in 2000 had a collection of 317,000 items as of 2011. The Sugar Industry Research Institute Library maintains a unique collection of 29,870 volumes on all aspects of sugarcane cultivation and manufacture. The Mahatma Gandhi Institute in Moka operates a library with a collection of 87,000 books in various languages. Most municipalities and/or local councils are equipped with public libraries. Of these the Port Louis municipal library, known as the City Library, has a collection of 50,000 items and the Curepipe Municipal Library (the Carnegie Library), has a collection of over 100,000 items.

The Mauritius Museums Council operates the Natural History Museums in Port Louis (1880) and in Mahébourg (1950). Port Louis is also home to a stamp museum, the Blue Penny (2001). The Sugar Museum (2003) is to be found in Pamplemousses. The Folk Museum of Indian Immigration (1991) is in Moka at the Mahatma Gandhi Institute.

45 MEDIA

In 2010 the CIA reported that there were 379,100 telephone landlines in Mauritius. In addition to landlines mobile phone subscriptions averaged 83.38 per 100 people. There were four FM radio stations and nine AM radio stations. Internet users numbered 22 per 100 citizens.

There were over a dozen privately-owned newspapers across the country. Leading daily newspapers (with 2002 circulations) included *L'Express* (35,000), *Le Mauricien* (35,000), *The New Nation* (15,000), and *The Sun* (unavailable), each published in Port Louis in both French and English. There were three major Chinese language newspapers.

All parts of the island were linked by telegraph, telephone, and postal services.

The state-owned Mauritius Broadcasting Corporation (MBC) provides radio and television service in French, English, Hindi, Urdu, Tamil, Telegu, Creole and Mandarin. In 2001 the government established the Independent Broadcast Authority, which is intended to issue licenses and formulate regulations for private broadcast licenses. The members of the group are primarily representatives of government ministries as well as from civil society, and the chair is appointed by the prime minister. In 2011 there were three independent privately-owned radio stations in operation. Private television stations have yet to come to the island. In 2010 there were an estimated 420 radios and 350 television sets for every 1,000 people. In 2010 the country had 36,653 Internet hosts. As of 2009 there were some 290,000 Internet users in Mauritius.

Free speech and press are constitutionally provided and said to be respected by the government.

46 ORGANIZATIONS

There are various commercial and scholarly organizations of the western type, including the Mauritius Chamber of Commerce and Industry, the Indian Traders' Association, the Mauritius Employers' Federation, The Mauritius Cooperative Agricultural Federation, and the Mauritius Cooperative Union.

National youth organizations include the Young Socialists, the Mauritius Scout Association, the Mauritius Student Association for the UN, the Mauritius Union of Students Councils, the Mauritius World Federalist Youth, the Mauritius Young Communist League, Junior Chamber International, the National Federation of Young Farmers Clubs, and YMCA/YWCA. Several sports associations are active, including those representing such sports as football, basketball, badminton, karate, tae kwon do, squash, tennis, table tennis, boxing, yachting, and golf. The International Council of Hindu Youth also has a base in Mauritius.

The Institute for Consumer Protection, founded in 1983, serves as both a consumer protection agency and as an agency for the promotion of maternal and infant health. The Mauritius Family Planning Association (1957) is very active in the field of sexual and reproductive health including family planning. The Mauritius Wildlife Foundation is concerned about the conservation and preservation of the endangered local plant and animal species. Civil society is equally well represented in Mauritius and as at 2011 there were 350 NGOs and civil society organizations (CSOs) registered under the umbrella of the Mauritius Council of Social

Services. International organizations with active chapters in the country include the Red Cross, Amnesty International, Caritas, Transparency and Soroptimist. The multinational Indian Ocean Commission, founded in 1982, is based in Mauritius.

47TOURISM, TRAVEL, AND RECREATION

Tourism is one of the major pillars of the economy and has contributed significantly to the overall development of the country. The government has made efforts to promote upscale tourism and attract visitors from more countries. In addition to the nation's beaches, lagoons, and other scenic sites, tourist attractions include the colonial architecture of Port Louis, an extinct volcano in Curepipe, the fishing port and naval museum at Mahebourg, and the Botanical Gardens at Pamplemousses. Football (soccer) is the national sport. Badminton, volleyball, basketball, tennis, and water sports are also popular. Many of the hotels also have golf facilities. In 2011 about 871,000 tourists visited Mauritius, who spent a total of $1.39 billion. Of those incoming tourists there were 580,000 from Europe, primarily from France. There were 23,235 hotel beds available in Mauritius, which had an occupancy rate of 54%.

In 2010 tourist arrivals from January through September increased by 6.2% in comparison to figures from the previous year. Officials stated that the boost represented a significant increase in arrivals from emerging markets such as China and India. Luxury tourism has been a primary subsector.

Visitors must have a valid passport, onward/return ticket, hotel confirmation, and sufficient funds for the stay. All travelers are required to carry a visa except nationals from the United States and most European countries. In 2011 the estimated daily cost to visit Port Louis, the capital, was $241.

48FAMOUS PERSONS

Sir Seewoosagur Ramgoolam (1900–85), the first leader of independent Mauritius, was prime minister from 1968 to 1982, when Anerood Jugnauth (b. 1930) succeeded him. Jugnauth served as prime minister from 1982 to 1995, and then again from 2000 to 2003, when he was named president. Navinchandra Ramgoolam (b. 1947), was prime minister from 1995 to 2000, 2005 to 2010, and is currently serving his third mandate.

49DEPENDENCIES

Dependencies are Rodrigues, the Agalega Islands and the Cargados Carajos Shoals.

50BIBLIOGRAPHY

Kamoche, Ken M., ed. *Managing Human Resources in Africa.* New York: Routledge, 2004.

Mauritius Investment and Business Guide: Strategic and Practical Information. Washington, DC: International Business Publications USA, 2012.

NgCheong-Lum, Roseline. *Culture Shock! Mauritius. A Guide to Customs and Etiquette.* 4th ed. Tarrytown, NY: Marshall Cavendish Editions, 2009.

Vaughan, Megan. *Creating the Creole Island: Slavery in Eighteenth-Century Mauritius.* Durham, NC: Duke University Press, 2005.

Younger, Paul. *New Homelands: Hindu Communities in Mauritius, Guyana, Trinidad, South Africa, Fiji, and East Africa.* New York: Oxford University Press, 2010.

Zeilig, Leo, and David Seddon. *A Political and Economic Dictionary of Africa.* Philadelphia: Routledge/Taylor and Francis, 2005..

MOROCCO

Kingdom of Morocco
Al-Mamlakah al-Maghribiyah

CAPITAL: Rabat

FLAG: The national flag consists of a green five-point star at the center of a red field.

ANTHEM: *Hymne Chérifien (Hymn of the Sharif).*

MONETARY UNIT: The dirham (MAD) is a paper currency of 100 Moroccan centimes. There are coins of 1, 5, 10, and 20 Moroccan centimes and ½, 1, and 5 dirhams, and notes of 5, 10, 50, 100, and 200 dirhams. MAD1 = US$0.11959 (or US$1 = MAD8.3619) as of 2010.

WEIGHTS AND MEASURES: The metric system is the legal standard.

HOLIDAYS: New Year's Day, 1 January; Anniversary of the King's Accession, 3 March; Labor Day, 1 May; National Day, 14 August; Anniversary of the Green March, 6 November; Independence Day, 18 November. Movable religious holidays include Eid al-Fitr, Eid al-Adha, 1st of Muharram (Muslim New Year), and Milad an-Nabi.

TIME: GMT.

¹LOCATION, SIZE, AND EXTENT

Situated at the northwestern corner of Africa, with its northernmost point only 29 km (18 mi) south of Gibraltar, Morocco claims a total area of 446,550 sq km (172,414 sq mi), of which the Western Sahara comprises 252,120 sq km (97,344 sq mi). The Western Sahara is claimed and administered by Morocco, but as of 2011, sovereignty remained unresolved. Comparatively, Morocco is slightly larger than the state of California. Morocco extends 1,809 km (1,124 mi) NE–SW and 525 km (326 mi) SE–NW. Morocco proper is bordered on the N by the Mediterranean Sea and the two Spanish enclaves of Ceuta and Melilla, on the E and SE by Algeria, on the S by Western Sahara, and on the W by the Atlantic Ocean, with a total land boundary length of 2,018 km (1,254 mi) and a coastline of 1,835 km (1,140 mi).

Morocco's capital city, Rabat, is located on the Atlantic coast.

²TOPOGRAPHY

Morocco proper is divided into three natural regions: (1) the fertile northern coastal plain along the Mediterranean, which also contains Er Rif, mountains varying in elevation up to about 2,400 m (8,000 ft); (2) the rich plateaus and lowlands lying between the three parallel ranges of the rugged Atlas Mountains, which extend from the Atlantic coast in the southwest to Algeria and the Mediterranean in the northeast; and (3) the semiarid area in southern and eastern Morocco, which merges into the Sahara Desert. The Atlas Mountains, with an average elevation of 3,350 m (11,000 ft), contain some of the highest peaks of North Africa, including Mt. Toubkal (4,165 m/13,665 ft), the highest of all. South of the Atlas are the Anti-Atlas Mountains, with volcanic Mt. Siroua (3,300 m/10,800 ft). The Western Sahara is rocky, sandy, and sparsely populated, unsuited for agriculture but rich in phosphate deposits.

Morocco has the most extensive river system in North Africa. Moroccan rivers generally flow south or westward to the Atlantic or southeastward toward the Sahara; the Moulouya (Muluya), an exception, flows 560 km (348 mi) northeast from the Atlas to the Mediterranean. Principal rivers with outlets in the Atlantic are the Oumer, Rebia, Sebou (Sebu), Bou Regreg, Tensift, Draa, and Sous (Sus). The Ziz (Zis) and Rheris are the main rivers flowing southward into the Sahara.

³CLIMATE

The rugged mountain ranges and the Atlantic Ocean moderate the tropical heat of Morocco. Temperatures in Casablanca range from an average minimum of 7°C (45°F) to a maximum of 17°C (63°F) in January and from a minimum of 18°C (64°F) to a maximum of 26°C (79°F) in July. Temperature variations are relatively small along the Atlantic coast, while the interior is characterized by extreme variations. The eastern slopes of the Atlas Mountains, which divert the moisture-laden Atlantic winds, have a rigorous pre-Saharan climate, while the western slopes are relatively cool and well watered. The rainy seasons are from October to November and from April to May. Maximum annual rainfall (75–100 cm/30–40 in) occurs in the northwest. Other parts of the country receive much less; half of all arable land receives no more than 35 cm (14 in) a year.

⁴FLORA AND FAUNA

The World Resources Institute estimates that there are 3,675 plant species in Morocco. In addition, Morocco is home to 129 mammal, 430 bird, 102 reptile, and 14 amphibian species. The calculation reflects the total number of distinct species residing in the country, not the number of endemic species.

Extensive stands of cork oak exist in the Atlantic coastal region, while rich evergreen oak, cedar, and pine forests are found on the slopes of the Atlas. In the steppe region, shrubs, jujube trees, and the mastic abound, and along the wadis there are poplars, willows, and tamarisks. The olive tree is widely distributed, but the oil-yielding argan tree, unique to Morocco, grows only in the Sous Valley. The desert is void of vegetation except for occasional oases. Although the lion has disappeared, panthers, jackals, foxes, and gazelles are numerous. The surrounding waters abound in sardines, anchovies, and tuna.

⁵ENVIRONMENT

The World Resources Institute reported that Morocco had designated 470,100 hectares (1.16 million acres) of land for protection as of 2006. Water resources totaled 29 cu km (6.96 cu mi) while water usage was 12.6 cu km (3.02 cu mi) per year. Domestic water usage accounted for 10% of total usage, industrial for 3%, and agricultural for 87%. Per capita water usage totaled 400 cu m (14,126 cu ft) per year.

The UN reported in 2008 that carbon dioxide emissions in Morocco totaled 46,368 kilotons.

Livestock overgrazing, clearing of forests for fuel, and poor soil conservation practices have led to soil erosion and desertification. Pollution of Morocco's water and land resources is due to the dumping of industrial wastes into the ocean, the country's inland water sources, and the soil. Water supplies have also been contaminated by the dumping of raw sewage and coastal waters have been polluted by oil. The nation's environment is further challenged by pesticides, insect infestation, and accidental oil spills. The Ministry of Housing Development and Environment considers environmental impact as an integral part of its development strategy.

Destruction of wildlife has occurred on a large scale, despite strict laws regulating hunting and fishing. Moreover, the drainage of coastal marshlands to irrigate cultivated land has significantly reduced the numbers of crested coots, purple herons, and marbled and white-headed ducks. According to a 2011 report issued by the International Union for Conservation of Nature and Natural Resources (IUCN), the number of threatened species included 18 types of mammals, 10 species of birds, 11 types of reptiles, 2 species of amphibians, 47 species of fish, 7 species of invertebrates, and 32 species of plants. Endangered species in Morocco include the Barbary hyena, Barbary leopard, waldrapp, Spanish imperial eagle, Mediterranean monk seal, and Cuvier's gazelle. The Bubal hartebeest is extinct. The Sahara oryx is extinct in the wild.

⁶POPULATION

The US Central Intelligence Agency (CIA) estimated the population of Morocco in 2011 to be approximately 31,968,361, which placed it at number 38 in population among the 196 nations of the world. In 2011, approximately 6.1% of the population was over 65 years of age, with another 27.8% under 15 years of age. The median age in Morocco was 26.9 years. There were 0.97 males for every female in the country. The population's annual rate of change was 1.067%. The projected population for the year 2025 was 36,600,000. Population density in Morocco was calculated at 72 people per sq km (186 people per sq mi).

The UN estimated that 58% of the population lived in urban areas, and that urban populations had an annual rate of change of 2.1%. The largest urban areas, along with their respective populations, included Casablanca, 3.2 million; Rabat, 1.8 million; Fes, 1 million; Marrakech, 909,000; and Tangier, 768,000.

⁷MIGRATION

Estimates of Morocco's net migration rate, carried out by the CIA in 2011, amounted to -3.77 migrants per 1,000 citizens. The total number of emigrants living abroad was 3.02 million—nearly 10% of Morocco's population—and the total number of immigrants living in Morocco was 49,100. The Moroccan government encourages emigration because of the benefit to the balance of payments of remittances from Moroccans living and working abroad. There is some seasonal migration within Morocco as workers move into cities and towns after planting and harvesting are finished. Over 200,000 people migrate permanently to the cities each year; the urban share of the total population increased from 29% to 58% between 1960 and 2010.

Spain has two enclaves on the Moroccan coast, Melilla and Ceuta, which are ringed by fences to keep Moroccans and other Africans out. In August 2004, several hundred Africans attempting to migrate to Europe broke through the fence at Melilla.

The war in Western Sahara has been a cause of significant migration, both of settlers from Morocco proper and of refugees to Algeria. The UN High Commissioner for Refugees (UNHCR) established a presence in the Western Sahara Territory beginning in 1997.

⁸ETHNIC GROUPS

Arab-Berbers constitute 99.1% of the total population. Berbers (sometimes referred to as Amazigh), who compose an estimated 60% of the population, are concentrated largely in the northern regions of the Rif, the middle plains of the Atlas, and the Sous Valley. Arabs are distributed principally along the Atlantic coastal plain and in the cities. The Berbers and Arabs are closely intermingled and bilingualism is common. Formerly the Jewish community played a significant role in the economic life of the country, but its numbers decreased from about 227,000 in 1948 to an estimated 10,000 in 1989. Jews make up only about 0.2% of the population. Other groups made up the remaining 0.7%, including French, Spanish, Italian, and Algerian nationals living in Morocco.

⁹LANGUAGES

Although classical Arabic is the written and official language, Darija, an Arabic dialect peculiar to Morocco, is widely spoken; it can hardly be understood by Arabs of the Middle East. The Amazigh dialects, principally Rifi, Tamazight, and Tashilhit, are spoken in more remote mountainous areas by about one-third of the populace. However, in an effort to preserve their cultural and linguistic heritage, the Amazigh have successfully campaigned for government support of Amazigh language education. French is often used as the language of business, government, and diplomacy. Spanish is also spoken.

¹⁰RELIGIONS

More than 98.7% of Moroccans are Sunni Muslims. The activity of other sects (chiefly Sufi) has diminished since independence. The Shi'a Muslims present in the nation are primarily foreign residents. Most of the country's practicing Christians are part of the foreign community, with a majority of them affiliated with the Roman Catholic Church. Rabat and Casablanca have small Protestant communities. There are between 3,000 and 4,000 Jews in the country, also mostly in the Casablanca and Rabat urban areas. There are small numbers of Baha'is and Hindus. Islam was officially declared the state religion in 1961, but full religious freedom is theoretically accorded to Christians and Jews. However, the government does place several restrictions on religious activities and participation. It is illegal to attempt to convert any Muslim to another faith or to distribute non-Muslim Arabic-language literature, such as Bibles, and traditional Islamic law requires punishment for Muslims who convert. The legal system consists of Shari'ah (Islamic law) courts and Rabbinical (Jewish) courts. Religious-based political parties are prohibited, except for those that are Islamic oriented. The Birth of the Prophet Muhammad, Eid al-Fitr, Eid al-Adha, and Islamic New Year are observed as national holidays.

11 TRANSPORTATION

The CIA reports that Morocco has a total of 57,625 km (35,807 mi) of roads, of which 35,664 km (22,161 mi) are paved. Railroads extend for 2,110 km (1,311 mi). The railroad system is administered by the National Railroad Office, and about 1,003 km (623 mi) of rail are electrified. Diesel-operated trains are used on the remainder. The main lines run from Marrakech to Casablanca, Rabat, and Sidi Kacem and then branch north to Tangier and east to Meknès, Fès, and Oujda (on the Algerian border).

Casablanca is by far the most important port; the second largest in Africa, it accounted for 40% of goods loaded and unloaded. Tangier is the principal passenger and tourist port. Mohammedia handles most oil imports and can accommodate 100,000-ton tankers. There are also regional ports at Safi, Agadir, and Nador, and 10 minor ports. The Moroccan Navigation Co. (Compagnie Marocaine de Navigation—COMANAV), the largest shipping company, is 96% government owned. The country's merchant marine consisted of 30 vessels of 1,000 gross registered tons (GRT) or more as of 2010.

There are 58 airports, which transported 4.93 million passengers in 2009 according to the World Bank. Morocco has eight international airports, at Casablanca, Rabat, Tangier, Marrakech, Agadir, Fès, Oujda, and Al-Hoceima. The government-controlled Royal Air Maroc was founded in 1953; the airline also provides domestic service through a subsidiary, Royal Air Inter.

12 HISTORY

The Amazigh, the earliest known inhabitants of Morocco, suffered successive waves of invaders in ancient times: the Phoenicians, Carthaginians, Romans (1st century BC), Vandals (5th century AD), and finally the Byzantines (6th century). In 682, when the Arabs swept through North Africa, Okba (Uqba ibn-Nefi) conquered Morocco. Under successive Moorish dynasties, beginning with Idris I (Idris bin Abdallah) in 788, the Amazigh groups were united and the Islamic faith and Arabic language adopted. The Idrisid dynasty, an offshoot of the Umayyad dynasty, with its capital at Fès (founded in 800), lasted until 974, when it was overthrown by the Amazigh. Rising in the Sahara in the early 11th century, the powerful Muslim sect of the Almoravids extended its conquests over North Africa and ultimately into Spain. Abdallah bin Yasin, its chief, was proclaimed ruler over Morocco in 1055. In 1147, the Almohad sect (Al-Muwahhidun), led by Abd al-Mumin bin Ali,

conquered the Almoravids and ruled Morocco until 1269, when the Marinid (Beni Marin) dynasty came to power.

In the 16th century, the Saudi dynasty, the new monarchical line, began. Ahmad al-Mansur (called Ad-Dahabi, "the Golden"), the greatest of the Saudi kings, ruled from 1578 to 1603 and inaugurated the golden age of Moroccan history. He protected Morocco from Turkish invasion, strengthened the country's defenses, reorganized the army, and adorned his magnificent capital at Marrakech with the vast booty captured in Timbuktu (1591). The decadence of the last Saudi kings brought Morocco under the control of the Filali dynasty, of mixed Arab and Amazigh descent, which continued to modern times.

Trade with France and other European countries became increasingly important in the 18th and 19th centuries, and when the French in 1844 defeated the combined Moroccan and Algerian forces at Isly, France became the ascendant power. Spain, under an agreement with France, invaded and occupied northern Morocco in 1860. There followed some 45 years of trade rivalry among the European nations in Morocco. The Act of Algeciras, signed on 7 April 1906 by representatives of the United States, Germany, the United Kingdom, France, and Spain (among others), established the principle of commercial equality in Morocco and provided for a joint Spanish-French police force in Moroccan ports.

On 30 March 1912, after France had ceded some 260,000 sq km (100,000 sq mi) of the French Congo to Germany, the French imposed a protectorate in Morocco under Marshal Louis Lyautey. The Moroccans, led by Abd al-Karim, a guerrilla leader, fought for independence in the Rif War (1921–26) but were defeated by the combined French and Spanish forces, although sporadic fighting continued in Morocco until 1934.

A nationalist movement first took shape around the Plan of Reforms (1934) submitted to the French government by a group of young Moroccans. In 1934, the National Action Bloc was formed, and Alal al-Fasi became the uncontested nationalist leader. In December 1943, the Bloc was revived as the Istiqlal (Independence) Party, which during and after World War II pressed for independence and reforms. It received support from the Sultan, Sidi Mohammed bin Yusuf, later King Mohammed V, who became the symbol of the independence struggle. He was exiled in late 1953, and two years of terrorism ensued. After lengthy negotiations, the Franco-Moroccan agreement of 2 March 1956 granted independence, and Mohammed V became king of Morocco. Incorporated into the new nation was Tangier, once British territory, which had come under the rule of a consortium of powers in 1906 and since 1923 had been the center of an international zone.

After the death of Mohammed V on 26 February 1961, his son was crowned King Hassan II and became head of government. Hassan II increased his political power throughout the 1960s. In 1962, a constitutional monarchy was established, with the king retaining extensive powers. In June 1965, after student riots and other disorders, Hassan II declared a state of emergency and assumed all legislative and executive powers. A revised constitution promulgated in 1970 and approved by popular referendum gave the king broad personal power but reestablished parliament and ended the state of emergency. An attempted coup d'état by right-wing army officers in July 1971 forced the king to accept, at least in principle, the need for a more broadly based government. A third constitution, approved by referendum on 1 March 1972,

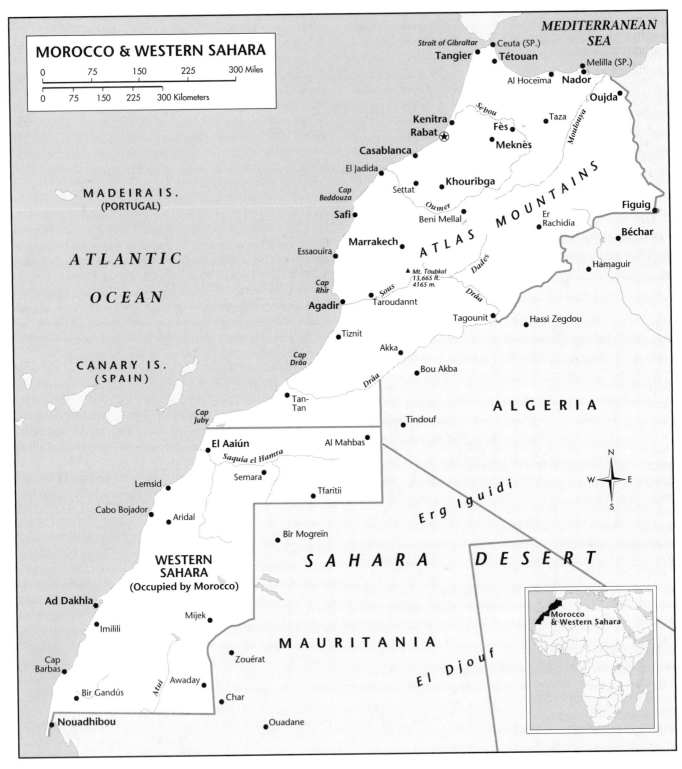

MOROCCO & WESTERN SAHARA

0　75　150　225　300 Miles

0　75　150　225　300 Kilometers

MADEIRA IS.
(PORTUGAL)

ATLANTIC

OCEAN

CANARY IS.
(SPAIN)

MEDITERRANEAN
SEA

Strait of Gibraltar　Ceuta (SP.)
Tangier　Tétouan
Melilla (SP.)
Al Hoceïma　Nador
Oujda
Kenitra　Taza
Rabat ⊛　Fès
Meknès
Casablanca
El Jadida
Khouribga
Settat　Er
Rachidia
Safi　Beni Mellal
Figuig
Marrakech
Essaouira　Béchar
Mt. Toubkal
13,665 ft.　Hamaguir
4165 m.
Cap
Rhir　Sous
Agadir　Taroudannt
Tagounit　Hassi Zegdou
Tiznit
Akka
Cap
Dràa　Bou Akba
Drâa
Tan-
Tan　Tindouf

ATLAS MOUNTAINS
Sebou
Oumer
Dadès
Drâa

ALGERIA

Cap
Juby

El Aaiún　Al Mahbas
Saquia el Hamra
Lemsid　Semara
Tfaritii
Cabo Bojador
Aridal

Erg Iguidi

WESTERN
SAHARA
(Occupied by Morocco)

Bîr Mogreïn

SAHARA　DESERT

Ad Dakhla
Mijek
Imilili

Cap
Barbas　Zouérat
Bir Gandús
Atui　Awaday
Char
Nouadhibou　Ouadane

MAURITANIA

El Djouf

Morocco
& Western Sahara

LOCATION: 27°40′ to 35°56′N (23° to 35°56′N including Western Sahara); 0°58′ to 13° W (0°58′ to 16°21′W including Western Sahara). BOUNDARY LENGTHS: (excluding Western Sahara): total coastline, 1,835 kilometers (1,140 miles); Algeria, 1,559 kilometers (974 miles); Western Sahara, 443 kilometers (275 miles). TERRITORIAL SEA LIMIT: 12 miles.

transferred many of the king's executive and legislative powers to a parliament which was to have two-thirds of its members directly elected. However, a second coup attempt in August 1972 caused the king to renew the emergency decrees.

In 1975, after Spain announced its intention of withdrawing from sparsely populated but phosphate-rich Spanish Sahara (now the Western Sahara), the king pressed Morocco's claim to most of the territory. Following the government's well-organized "Green

March" of about 350,000 Moroccans into the territory in November, Spain ceded the northern two-thirds of the region to Morocco and the southern third to Mauritania. However, Algeria refused to recognize the annexation and supported the claim to the territory by guerrillas of the Popular Front for the Liberation of Saguia al-Hamra and Río de Oro, better known as Polisario. The movement, based in the Algerian border town of Tindouf, proclaimed Western Sahara as the Saharan Arab Democratic Republic (SADR). In 1979, Mauritania renounced its claim to the southern part of the territory, which Morocco then occupied and annexed. By the early 1980s, Morocco had moved up to 100,000 soldiers into Western Sahara in a costly effort to put down the Polisario revolt. The army built a wall of earth and sand around the productive northwestern coastal region, containing about 20% of the total area, the towns of El Aaiún and Samara, and phosphate mines; later, three-quarters of the Western Sahara was enclosed. In the meantime, Polisario received not only military support, mainly from Algeria and Libya, but also diplomatic support from some 50 countries and from the OAU, which in 1982 seated a delegation from the SADR, provoking a walkout by Morocco and more than a dozen other members. In 1984, Morocco resigned from the OAU when it seated the SADR at its annual summit meeting. Earlier, in 1981, the king's agreement under African pressure for a referendum in the territory provoked strong criticism from Morocco's Socialist Party.

In 1988, UN Secretary General Perez de Cuellar persuaded Moroccan and Polisario representatives to accept a peace plan that included a cease-fire (effective in September 1991) and a referendum for the territory on independence or integration with Morocco. The vote was scheduled for 1992 but has been blocked by disagreement by the two sides on details, especially over voter eligibility. The UN force sent to mediate the struggle, MINURSO (UN Mission for the referendum in Western Sahara) has been struggling to hold the referendum. In 1997, UN Secretary General Kofi Annan sent former US Secretary of State James Baker to the region in hopes of ending the intransigence. Throughout the stalemate, the Moroccan government has repeatedly been accused of human rights violations in the Western Sahara.

Serious street riots, protesting against an imminent price hike for basic foodstuffs (subsequently canceled), ensued in June 1984 as the IMF demanded austerity measures in return for new credits. Between 1984 and 1994 King Hassan's government maintained close relations regionally and with Saudi Arabia and the other Gulf states and was the first Arab nation to condemn the Iraqi invasion of Kuwait. A 1984 treaty with Libya calling for a federation of the two countries was abrogated following the Libyan denunciation of the king for officially receiving Israeli Prime Minister Shimon Peres in July 1986. Israeli Prime Minister Rabin made a public visit in 1993 as the king continued to play a moderate role in the search for an Arab-Israel settlement, mediating the 1994 Israeli treaty with Jordan. In 1989, after a border agreement restored relations with Algeria, Morocco promoted the formation of the Arab Maghreb Union of the states of North Africa.

In 1993, after pro-government parties won most local elections the previous year, parliamentary elections were held. The two largest opposition parties, the Istiqlal and USFP, won over 40% of the vote, but center-right parties of the ruling coalition gained a slim majority in the vote's second stage amid charges of election fraud. When the opposition refused to join in a new coalition, a cabinet of technocrats and independents was approved by the king under Prime Minister Mohamed Karim Lamrani, who promised to accelerate the privatization of state-owned enterprises.

Meanwhile, the country's political opposition grew quite vocal in their discontent, prompting government reprisals. The country's most famous Islamist politician, Abdelsalam Yassine, was imprisoned, and Istiqlal joined forces with an Islamist organization to form a substantial opposition party. In response, King Hassan proposed in 1996 to make all of parliament directly elected. Previously, one-third of the deputies were appointed, giving the king power to undermine any opposition majority. The king also proposed the creation of a second chamber of advisers—a move seen by opposition parties as simply replacing one rubber stamp chamber with another. Still, the proposals were put to a vote on 13 September and approved by, officially, 99% of the population.

Elections for the new chambers were scheduled for 1997. In the months leading up to the elections, opposition skepticism waned as the government made repeated assurances that voting would be fair and the results would be respected. In June 1997 elections for 24,523 municipal council and commune seats were held and judged to be fair. The Bloc democratique won 31.7% of the seats, but control remained for the Entente nationale with 30.3% and the RNI, 26.4%.

Following the local elections, legislation in 1997 set up the new bicameral parliament approved in the 1996 constitutional referendum. The Chamber of Representatives would consist of 325 members directly elected for five-year terms. The Chamber of Advisors would be made up of 270 members selected by indirect election: 162 would represent local authorities, 81 trade chambers, and 27 employees' associations. In the same 1996 referendum 16 new regional councils, with members chosen for six-year terms by indirect election through an electoral college representing professions and local governments, had been established, and elections for these took place in October 1997.

The Chamber of Representatives elections took place on 14 November 1997. Some 48% of the voters participated. The Bloc democratique won 34.3% of the vote, the Entente nationale 24.8%, and the center-right parties 27.3%. In a direct appeal to young voters on the part of most of the parties, 43% of the new chamber was made up of members less than 45 years of age. Indirect elections for the Chamber of Advisors were held on 5 December 1997. The right and center-right parties predominated, as was expected, winning 166 of the 270 seats. The new two-house parliament met for the first time in January 1998.

On 4 February 1998 King Hassan appointed Abd ar-Rahman el-Youssoufi, leader of the USFP, as prime minister. This was a groundbreaking event, as it was the first time an opposition member had been appointed prime minister. The Youssoufi government attempted to tackle corruption and promote transparency of government. Though results were, on the whole, disappointing, King Hassan praised the government in March 1999.

On 23 July 1999 King Hassan died of a heart attack. He was succeeded by his eldest son, as Mohammed VI. One of his first important moves was to dismiss King Hassan's longtime interior minister and advisor, Driss Basri. Basri had been considered the real power behind King Hassan, so this move gave a clear indication that Mohammed VI planned to reign in control of his government. Upon assuming the throne, he pledged his commitment to constitutional monarchy, political pluralism and economic liberalism. Mohammed VI claimed he would address problems of poverty, corruption, and Morocco's human rights record, and would engage in job creation.

Like most Islamic countries of the world, Morocco's government feels under threat from an internal Islamist movement, which itself is divided. The various groups have moved to fill the perceived void in social services: blood banks and medical clinics, food pantries, homeless shelters, and schools. Parliamentary elections were held on 27 September 2002, and the Islamist Justice and Development Party (PJD) trebled its seats, coming in third with 42 of 325 parliamentary seats; however, it was denied any ministerial posts in the governing coalition formed by the Socialist Union of Forces for Progress (which took 50 seats) and the nationalist Istiqlal Party (which won 48 seats). The PJD would like to see Islamic law applied nationwide, including a ban on alcohol and a provision to have women wear veils. Morocco's largest and most vocal Islamist organization, Justice and Charity, works outside of the electoral process. Justice and Charity formally rejects the king and the Moroccan constitution, and thus is prevented from participating in organized politics as a party. Justice and Charity's leader instructed his followers to boycott the elections entirely. The group is gaining in popularity; estimates place its membership from between 50,000 and 500,000, and it is especially popular among those under age 30.

Moroccan authorities began a crackdown against Islamist groups, including the Salafist Combatants. Mosques and bookshops were closed, and detentions and arrests of Islamists increased. Critics of the government's actions stated that the crackdown failed to address problems such as poverty and ignorance, which cause radicalism. In June 2002, three Saudis and seven Moroccan nationals, including three women, were arrested and accused of being part of an al-Qaeda plot to plan terrorist acts in Morocco and against Western ships crossing the Strait of Gibraltar.

On 11 July 2002, Moroccan frontier guards planted the national flag on the uninhabited island of Perejil (Leila in Arabic), claimed by Spain. Spain landed troops to "recapture" the island, which Morocco claimed was equivalent to an act of war. The eviction of the Moroccan soldiers took place without any casualties. The United States helped to negotiate a deal to remove all forces from the island. The incident was one of a series of disputes between Spain and Morocco over a number of issues, including fishing rights, illegal immigration by Moroccans to Spain, the Spanish occupation of Ceuta and Melilla on the northern coast of Morocco, and the status of Western Sahara. Full diplomatic ties were reestablished between Spain and Morocco in January 2003. In 2005, King Juan Carlos of Spain made a state visit to Morocco.

In May 2003, Morocco's largest city, Casablanca, experienced a suicide terrorist attack which left 45 people dead and more than 100 people injured. The bombings were a simultaneous attack on a hotel, two Jewish owned restaurants, and a Jewish cemetery. By August of that same year four men were sentenced to death, two were suicide bombers who survived, and 83 others were imprisoned as fear increased that Islamic extremism was spreading. An organization alleged to have ties to al-Qaeda, the Moroccan Islamic Combat Group, was suspected of the Casablanca terrorist attack. This group was also suspected in the 11 March 2004 Madrid train bombing, leading to the pursuit and arrest of Moroccan suspects in Spain and throughout Europe.

In 2003, King Mohammed VI announced an initiative aimed at modernizing Moroccan society by granting new rights to women. He also celebrated the birth of his first son and heir, named Hassan after his grandfather, by ordering the release of over 9,000 convicts and reducing the jail sentences of more than 38,000 inmates. By 2004 parliament passed legislation on women's rights. The king also continued to maintain close ties with other Arab nations, as did his father. In 2003, Saudi Crown Prince Abdullah visited Morocco for talks about Iraq and the Palestinian territories. Mohammed VI further pursued his human rights agenda in 2004 by pardoning 33 prisoners, establishing a "truth commission," the Equity and Reconciliation Commission, headed by a former political prisoner. In hearings, about 200 people gave public testimony about past human rights abuses in Morocco.

After US designation of Morocco as a major non-NATO ally in 2004, Morocco's parliament approved a free trade agreement with the United States in 2005. However, in mid-2005 a protectionist movement sprang up in Morocco as 22 civil society groups formed a national coalition fighting against the free trade agreement with the United States. In August 2005, an 18-year-old Moroccan was arrested for the creation of the Zotob computer worm. Across the United States, the Zotob worm affected the computer operations of more than 100 companies, exploiting a flaw in the Windows 2000 operating system.

Regarding Western Sahara, efforts were undertaken in the late 1990s to register voters eligible for a referendum to be held in the region. Morocco stated that approximately 200,000 people were eligible as voters, while Polisario stated only 70,000 people were natives of the territory. In November 2001, King Mohammed VI declared the UN's plan to hold the referendum on Western Sahara "null." Negotiations between the two parties had taken place in 2000 and 2001 under the guidance of former US Secretary of State and UN envoy to Western Sahara James Baker and a "Framework Agreement" was drawn up to make Western Sahara an autonomous part of Morocco for a five-year period, after which a referendum would be held to determine if the region would become independent. Another option would allow for the division of the territory, with one part going to Morocco and the rest becoming an independent Western Saharan state. In January 2003, Polisario rejected a new proposal for the territory put forward by Baker, which did not guarantee enough autonomy for the group to relinquish its demand for a referendum on independence. However, by July they accepted a peace plan that Morocco still opposed. In September of that year the rebels released 243 Moroccan prisoners. In 2004, when South Africa formally recognized Polisario, Morocco responded by recalling its ambassador from Pretoria. In a continuing effort to clear the way for a peace settlement in Western Sahara, Polisario released their last (404) Moroccan prisoners in August 2005. At the end of April 2007, Morocco and the Polisario Front agreed to hold direct talks for the first time under the terms of a unanimously passed UN Security Council resolution.

In January 2010, the US-based advocacy group Human Rights Watch reported that, throughout 2009, Morocco reversed much of the progress it had made on reducing the heavy-handedness of government policy. When King Mohammed took the throne in 1999, he made concerted efforts to move away from the repression that defined his father's rule. As a result, Western nations established closer ties with Morocco than it did other Middle Eastern and North African nations. Each year, thousands of tourists from the United States and Europe flock to the country. But in 2009, the king appeared to break with his liberalizing traditions. A crackdown on peaceful dissent was reported in Morocco that year, especially against those who criticized the monarchy, Islam, or the government's approach to the disputed territory known as Western Sahara.

Following the January 2011 anti-government protests in Tunisia and Egypt, Moroccan protestors took to the streets, calling for a series of reforms that would transfer more power out of the hands of King Mohammad VI and into the authority of parliament. Nationwide protests that took place on 20 February were generally peaceful, but some rioting occurred in the north, and at least five people were killed in a fire set at a local bank. On 21 February, the king responded by announcing the creation of a new Social and Economic Council with a mandate to indentify and implement reforms that would promote "total synergy" between the people and the government. Activists then took their cause to the Internet, using social-networking sites to plan a second major demonstration scheduled for 20 March, at which they expected to raise support for the establishment of a constitutional monarchy. On 1 July 2011, a referendum was held to approve a new constitution, which was ratified with 98.5% vote. The new constitution, while retaining the king's overriding authority, provided additional powers to parliament and the prime minister. On 25 November 2011 parliamentary elections were held throughout the country; the moderate Islamist Justice and Development Party (PJD) won a majority.

13 GOVERNMENT

The Moroccan crown is hereditary and is passed on to the oldest male descendant in direct line or to the closest collateral male relative. The king, claiming descent from the Prophet Mohammad, is commander of the faithful and the symbol of national unity. He makes all civil and military appointments and signs and ratifies treaties. He can dismiss the parliament (if in session) and bypass elected institutions by submitting a referendum to the people on any major issue or whenever parliament rejects a bill he favors. He presides over the cabinet, and if the integrity of the national territory is threatened or events liable to jeopardize the functioning of Morocco's national institutions occur, he may declare a state of emergency.

The constitution of 1992 was amended by referendum in 1996. The national legislature became bicameral with the lower house elected directly and the upper house consisting of two-thirds of its members elected and one-third appointed by the king. The Chamber of Representatives consists of 395 members directly elected for five-year terms. The Chamber of Advisors consists of 270 members selected by indirect election: 162 represent local authorities, 81 trade chambers, and 27 employees' associations. In an effort to include the opinions of young people, the voting age was lowered from 20 to 18 in 2002. Suffrage is universal. In July 2011, a referendum was held for a new constitution, which was ratified by 98% of the votes. The new constitution enhanced parliamentary powers.

14 POLITICAL PARTIES

Morocco has a well-developed multiparty system with varying numbers of officially recognized parties and remarkably stable and long-lived leadership.

The largest traditional party is the Istiqlal (Independence) Party, whose leader after its formation in 1943 was Alal al-Fasi. The Istiqlal, once a firm supporter of the throne, now follows a reformist program and backs the king on specific measures only; it had no representation in the government from 1963 to 1977.

The National Union of Popular Forces (Union Nationale des Forces Populaires—UNFP) was formed in September 1959, following a split in the ranks of the Istiqlal in January of that year. At that time, the UNFP was a coalition of left-wing ex-Istiqlalis, trade unionists, resistance fighters, and dissident members of minor political parties and drew support from the modern cities (Casablanca) and the Sous River Valley. Among its leaders were Mehdi bin Barka; Muhammad al-Basri, a leader of the Liberation Army in 1953–55; Abderrahim Bouabid; and Mahjub bin Sadiq, head of the Moroccan Labor Union (Union Marocaine du Travail—UMT). The party fell victim to factionalism and was further weakened by the political neutrality of the UMT after 1963, by the kidnapping and disappearance of Bin Barka in France in 1965, and by other apparent instances of government repression, including the imprisonment of Bin Sadiq in 1967.

In 1970, the UNFP and Istiqlal, having lost some popular support, formed the National Front to boycott the elections. The Front was dissolved in 1972, by which time the split between the political and trade union wings of the UNFP had become open, and in 1973 many UNFP leaders were arrested and tried for sedition in connection with civil disorders and guerrilla activities. The UNFP formally split into two parties in 1974, the more radical trade union wing calling itself the UNFP and the political wing forming the Socialist Union of Popular Forces (Union Socialiste des Forces Populaires—USFP).

The program of the Moroccan Communist Party has often been close to that of the UNFP. From 1969 to 1974, the Communist Party was banned, but since then it has appeared under various names. Two communist parties contested the 1997 elections, the Party of Renewal and Progress (PRP) and the Organization of Action for Democracy and the People (OADP), with the PRP obtaining nine seats in the lower house and seven in the upper house, while the OADP obtained four in the lower house and none in the upper house. The USFP, Istiqlal, PRP, and OADP formed the Democratic Block.

The National Entente block was made up of three parties: the conservative Popular Movement (MP), the conservative National Democratic Party (PND), and the centrist Constitutional Union.

The Center block was made up of the National Rally of Independents (RNI), the Democratic and Social Movement (MDS), and the National Popular Movement (MNP).

In addition, there are various other parties of liberal, socialist, or Islamist orientation, the latter represented by the moderate Constitutional and Democratic Popular Movement (MPCD), which changed its name at the end of 1998 to the Party of Justice and Development (PJD).

King Hassan II sometimes worked through the party system and sometimes ignored it. In 1963, royalist forces united into the

Front for the Defense of Constitutional Institutions. A leading party in the Front was the Popular Movement (Mouvement Populaire—MP), the party of Amazigh mountaineers. Governments formed by Hassan II have consisted of MP members, followers of royalist front parties, and independents and technocrats loyal to the king. Following 1993 elections, which saw Istiqlal and the USFP winning a majority of the elected seats, the king used his power to appoint friendly deputies to the seats he controlled. Opposition parties protested by refusing to participate in the government. In 1996, the king submitted for referendum revisions to the constitution allowing for direct election for all members of parliament, a move greeted with initial suspicion but ultimately heralded as democratic as the 1997 elections for the newly comprised body approached. The various parties formed into Blocks, as listed above, though maintaining separate candidate lists. The results showed 15 parties gaining seats in the lower house and 13 obtaining seats in the upper house.

Twenty-six political parties participated in the 27 September 2002 elections for the Chamber of Representatives. The USFP took 50 seats; Istiqlal won 48; the Justice and Development Party (PJD) won 42; the National Rally of Independents won 41 seats; the Popular Movement took 27; the National Popular Movement took 18; the Constitutional Union won 16; and 15 other parties were represented. Women were guaranteed 10% of the seats. Two new political parties were recognized by the government for the 2002 elections—the Moroccan Liberal Party (PLM) and the Alliance of Liberties (ADL), which aimed to involve the youth and women in political action. The ADL won four seats in the Chamber of Representatives. The Islamist Justice and Development Party trebled the number of its seats in parliament, coming in third behind the USFP and Istiqlal. Justice and Charity, said to be the largest Islamist group, remains banned.

In the 2002 elections, parties were organized in the following blocks: the left-wing block, comprised of the USFP; the Party for Progress and Socialism (PPS), formerly the Communist Party; the Leftist Unified Socialist Party (PGSU), formerly the OADP; and the Socialist Democratic Party. The center-right block is comprised of the Istiqlal Party and the PJD. The Berberist block includes the Popular Movement (MP); the National Popular Movement (MNP); and the Social Democratic Movement (MDS). The conservative block consisted of the National Rally of Independents (RNI) and the Constitutional Union (UC). Driss Jettou was named prime minister. In the 2003 local and district elections, more than 30% of the 23,000 seats were won by the conservative Istiqlal Party and the left-wing USFP. The mainstream Islamist PJD party won less than 3% of the vote.

In the 2007 elections for the chamber of representatives, the Independence Party took 52 seats, followed by the PJD with 46, the MP with 41, the RNI with 39, USFP with 38, UC with 27, PPS with 17, the Democratic Forces Front (FFD) with 9, MDS with 9, and the Al Ahd Party with 8. The remaining 39 seats were won by other parties. Abbas El Fassi of the Independence Party was appointed as prime minister. The next legislative elections were set for 2012 but were moved up to November 2011 following the July 2011 Constitutional Referendum. The PJD won a parliamentary majority and was charged with forming the new government.

15 LOCAL GOVERNMENT

Local administration still follows many French and Spanish procedural patterns, but final authority rests with the king through the Ministry of the Interior. Morocco is divided into 16 regions and subdivided into 62 prefectures, 37 provinces, and 2 *wilayas* (urban administrative divisions). Each province and prefecture has a governor appointed by the king. The provinces and prefectures select councils or assemblies, which hold public sessions in the spring and fall. The assemblies are largely restricted to social and economic questions.

The provinces are divided into administrative areas, called *cercles*, each headed by a superqaid (*caidat*). Each cercle is subdivided into rural and urban communes, each headed by a qaid or a pasha, respectively, and assisted by a council. Councilors are elected for six-year terms, and each council is comprised of 9 to 51 members, depending on the size of the commune. The council president, chosen by secret ballot, presents the budget and applies the decisions of the council. Real power, however, is exercised by the qaid or pasha. The communes are supervised by the Ministry of the Interior, which retains final decision-making authority. In communes with less than 25,000 inhabitants, councilors are elected based on a one-round relative majority; in communes exceeding 25,000 inhabitants, proportional representation was used.

16 JUDICIAL SYSTEM

Morocco has a dual legal system consisting of secular courts based on French legal tradition, and courts based on Jewish and Islamic traditions.

The secular system includes communal and district courts, courts of first instance, appellate courts, and a Supreme Court. The Supreme Court is divided into five chambers: criminal, correctional (civil) appeals, social, administrative, and constitutional. The Special Court of Justice may try officials on charges raised by a two-thirds majority of the full Majlis. There is also a military court for cases involving military personnel and occasionally matters pertaining to state security. The Supreme Council of the Judiciary regulates the judiciary and is presided over by the king. Judges are appointed on the advice of the council. Judges in the secular system are university-trained lawyers. Since 1965 only Moroccans may be appointed as judges, and Arabic is the official language of the courts.

There are 27 Sadad courts, which are courts of first instance for Muslim and Jewish personal law. Criminal and civil cases are heard, and cases with penalties exceeding a certain monetary amount may be appealed to regional courts. The Sadad courts are divided into four sections: Shari'ah; rabbinical; civil, commercial, and administrative sections; and criminal.

17 ARMED FORCES

The International Institute for Strategic Studies reports that armed forces in Morocco totaled 195,800 members in 2011. The force was comprised of 175,000 from the army, 7,800 from the navy, and 13,000 members of the air force. Armed forces represented 2.1%

of the labor force in Morocco. Defense spending totaled $7.6 billion and accounted for 5% of GDP.

The Polisario Front opposition forces were estimated between 3,000 and 6,000. Moroccan troops were stationed in five countries on peacekeeping missions.

18 INTERNATIONAL COOPERATION

Morocco became a member of the UN on 12 November 1956 and participates in ECA and several nonregional specialized agencies, such as the FAO, ILO, IAEA, the World Bank, IMO, UNSECO, UNHCR, UNIDO, and the WHO. The nation is a member of the African Development Bank, the Arab Bank for Economic Development in Africa, the Arab Fund for Economic and Social Development, the Arab Maghreb Union, the European Bank for Reconstruction and Development, the Organization of the Islamic Conference (OIC), G-77, the Community of Sahel and Saharan States (CENSAD), and the Arab League. Morocco is an observer in the OAS and a partner in the OSCE.

In recent decades, Morocco has pursued a policy of nonalignment and has sought and received aid from the United States, Western Europe, and the former USSR. Relations with Algeria and Libya have been tense, especially since Morocco's takeover of the Western Sahara. In 1988, UN Secretary General Perez de Cuellar negotiated with Morocco and Polisario (a group seeking sovereignty for the Western Sahara as the Saharan Arab Democratic Republic) to accept a cease-fire and to hold a referendum for the territory to determine whether it will be independent or integrate with Morocco. Although the vote was scheduled for 1992, it has been blocked by disagreements over voter eligibility, and sovereignty was unresolved as of April 2012. The UN Mission for the Referendum in Western Sahara (MINURSO, est. 1991) was supported by 29 countries in 2011. In 1989, Morocco restored relations with Algeria; it maintains relations with Saudi Arabia and the other Gulf states and condemned the Iraqi invasion of Kuwait.

In environmental cooperation, Morocco is part of the Basel Convention, Conventions on Biological Diversity and Whaling, Ramsar, CITES, the London Convention, the Kyoto Protocol, the Montréal Protocol, MARPOL, the Nuclear Test Ban Treaty, and the UN Conventions on Climate Change and Desertification.

19 ECONOMY

The GDP rate of change in Morocco, as of 2010, was 3.2%. Inflation stood at 2.5%, and unemployment was reported at 9.8%.

The major resources of the Moroccan economy are agriculture, phosphates, and tourism. Sales of fish and seafood are important as well. Industry and mining contribute over one-third of the annual GDP. Morocco is one of the world's largest producers of phosphates and the price fluctuations of phosphates on the international market greatly influence Morocco's economy. Tourism and workers' remittances have played a critical role since independence. Morocco has a free trade agreement with the EU. Morocco suffers from poverty, urban overcrowding, inadequate housing infrastructure, and illiteracy, which reaches 83% for women in rural areas.

The high cost of imports, especially of petroleum imports, is a major problem. Another chronic problem is unreliable rainfall, which produces drought or sudden floods. Reduced incomes due to drought have caused GDP to fall periodically, while good

rainfall can provide a significant boost to GDP. Morocco and the United States negotiated a free trade agreement in 2004 that immediately eliminated tariffs on 95% of bilateral trade, with the remaining tariffs to be eliminated by 2013. That agreement went into effect in January of 2006.

While many nations entered recessions in 2009, the Moroccan government announced economic growth of 5.3% in 2009 and 2.4% in 2010. The increases came primarily through internal economic demand, with small increases in foreign trade. The tourist industry is expected to remain stable, in part through a government allotment of $37.3 million in June 2009 to reduce the impact of global recession on the industry.

20 INCOME

The CIA estimated that in 2010 the GDP of Morocco was $151.4 billion. The CIA defines GDP as the value of all final goods and services produced within a nation in a given year and computed on the basis of purchasing power parity (PPP) rather than value as measured on the basis of the rate of the exchange based on current dollars. The per capita GDP was estimated at $4,800. The annual growth rate of GDP was 3.2%. The average inflation rate was 2.5%. It was estimated that agriculture accounted for 17.1% of GDP, industry 31.6%, and services 51.4%.

According to the World Bank, remittances from citizens living abroad totaled $6.3 billion or about $196 per capita and accounted for approximately 4.1% of GDP.

The World Bank reports that in 2009, household consumption in Morocco totaled $52.1 billion or about $1,628 per capita, measured in current US dollars rather than PPP. Household consumption included expenditures of individuals, households, and nongovernmental organizations on goods and services, excluding the purchases of dwellings. It was estimated that household consumption was growing at an average annual rate of 4%.

As of 2011 the most recent study by the World Bank reported that actual individual consumption in Morocco was 64.6% of GDP and accounted for 0.18% of world consumption. By comparison, the United States accounted for 25.44% of world individual consumption. The World Bank also estimated that 24.3% of Morocco's GDP was spent on food and beverages, 12.4% on housing and household furnishings, 3.6% on clothes, 3.8% on health, 6.3% on transportation, 3.6% on communications, 2.3% on recreation, 4.1% on restaurants and hotels, and -3.3% on miscellaneous goods and services and purchases from abroad.

21 LABOR

As of 2010, Morocco had a total labor force of 11.63 million people. Within that labor force, CIA estimates in 2006 noted that 44.6% were employed in agriculture, 19.8% in industry, and 35.5% in the service sector.

Although the law provides for the right to form unions, the government interferes with the labor movement. Morocco's 17 trade unions are organized within three federations, and represent about half a million of the country's estimated nine million workers. Employees have the right to strike after engaging in arbitration. Work stoppages do occur, but security forces sometimes break up striking workers. Collective bargaining is utilized on a limited basis.

The 48-hour workweek is established by law, and overtime pay rates apply to all work in excess of 48 hours. At least one day of rest must be granted per week. In 2010, the minimum wage was $1.20 per hour for industrial work and $6.30 per day for agricultural workers. The minimum wage is not effectively enforced in the informal sector. There is also legislation covering health, sanitation, and safety standards for a small number of workers.

22 AGRICULTURE

Roughly 21% of the total land is arable or under permanent crops, and the country's major crops include barley, wheat, citrus fruits, grapes, vegetables, and olives. Cereal production in 2009 amounted to 10.4 million tons, fruit production 3.4 million tons, and vegetable production 5.3 million tons.

The bulk of the indigenous population carries out traditional subsistence farming on plots of less than five hectares (12 acres). A temperate climate and sufficient precipitation are especially conducive to agricultural development in the northwest.

Morocco is essentially self-sufficient in food production. Grain plantings are typically triggered by autumn rainfall and last through mid-January. Irregularity in rainfall necessitates the importation of grains during drought years. Principal export crops are citrus fruits and vegetables.

The government distributed some 500,000 hectares (1,235,500 acres) of farmland formerly owned by European settlers to Moroccan farmers in the late 1960s and the 1970s. To encourage Moroccans to modernize the traditional sector, the Agricultural Investment Code of 1969 required farmers in irrigated areas to meet the minimum standards of efficiency outlined by the government or lose their land. These standards applied to all farms of five hectares (12 acres) or more.

Dams and irrigation projects were begun under French rule and have continued since independence. In traditional areas, irrigation is by springs and wells, diversion of streams, and tunnels from the hills, as well as by modern dams and reservoirs. There are dams and irrigation projects on most of the country's major rivers, including the Sebou River in the northwest, which, along with its tributaries, accounts for some 45% of Morocco's water resources.

23 ANIMAL HUSBANDRY

The UN Food and Agriculture Organization (FAO) reported that Morocco dedicated 21 million hectares (51.9 million acres) to permanent pasture or meadow in 2009. During that year, the country tended 165 million chickens, 2.9 million head of cattle, and 8,000 pigs. The production from these animals amounted to 177,974 tons of beef and veal, 760 tons of pork, 422,426 tons of poultry, 203,327 tons of eggs, and 1.39 million tons of milk. Morocco also produced 21,125 tons of cattle hide and 55,029 tons of raw wool.

Livestock raising contributes about one-third of agricultural income. Livestock fares poorly on the overgrazed pasture, and periods of drought reduce growth on permanent pastureland as well as the output of fodder crops. Even though most of the import licensing system has been abolished, licenses are still required for imported livestock and animal genetic materials, in an effort to protect local production.

24 FISHING

Morocco had 2,978 decked commercial fishing boats in 2008. The annual capture totaled 995,773 tons according to the UN FAO. The export value of seafood totaled $1.06 billion. Fishing has been a major industry since the 1930s. The industry is centered in Agadir, Safi, and Tan-Tan. In some years, Morocco is the world's largest producer of the European sardine (Sardina pilchardus).

The waters off Western Sahara are particularly rich in seafood. Coastal fishing supplies the Moroccan fish processing industry, which is concentrated in the southern cities of Layoun, Tan Tan, Tarfaya, and Agadir. The canning industry processes mostly sardines and to a lesser extent mackerels and anchovies. Many of the plants use obsolete equipment, and government support to develop and introduce new technology to the industry has lagged.

Aquacultural production consists mainly of seabass, sea bream, oysters, tuna, and eel, which are produced for export to Europe. The principal aquaculture farms are located in Nador and Hoceima on the Mediterranean Sea, Oulidida on the Atlantic Ocean, and Azrou on an inland lake.

Much of the fish catch is processed into fish meal, fertilizer, and animal fodder.

25 FORESTRY

Approximately 12% of Morocco is covered by forest. The UN FAO estimated the 2009 roundwood production at 495,000 cu m (17.5 million cu ft). The value of all forest products, including roundwood, totaled $80.9 million.

Forests provide subsistence for families engaged in cork gathering, wood cutting, and other forestry occupations. Cork, the principal forest product, is grown in state-owned cork oak forests. Other commercial trees are evergreen oak, thuja, argan, and cedar. Esparto grass and vegetable fiber are other important forest products.

26 MINING

Morocco was the third-largest producer of phosphate rock (behind the United States and China), had 88.5 billion tons in proved reserves, and was the largest phosphate exporter. The 2009 output of phosphate rock, including by Western Sahara, was 25 million tons (gross weight). All phosphate was produced by the state-owned Office Chérifien des Phosphates, founded in 1920, which was responsible for managing and controlling all aspects of phosphate mining. The combined capacity of the main facilities-at Youssoufia, Benguerir, BouCraa, Sidi Chenan, and Khouribga-was 25 million tons per year.

Morocco also had significant deposits of copper ore and produced 18,000 metric tons in 2009 (gross weight concentrates), down from 18,500 metric tons in 2008. Iron ore production (gross weight) in 2009 was 10,000 metric tons, down from 9,000 metric tons in 2008. Other minerals produced in 2009 included: lead (gross weight concentrate, 36,000 metric tons); barite (700,000 metric tons); rock salt (estimated at 240,000 metric tons); and acid-grade fluorspar (60,000 metric tons, down from 56,724 metric tons in 2008). In addition, Morocco produced antimony, cobalt, gold, mercury, silver, arsenic trioxide, bentonite, hydraulic cement, feldspar, fuller's earth (smectite), gypsum, mica, montmorillonite (ghassoul), phosphoric acid, marine salt, talc and pyrophyllite, and a variety of crude construction materials. Morocco also had the capacity to produce zircon, and had the only anthracite mine in the Mediterranean area-Jerada, in the Oujda region.

Plans called for increased domestic processing of phosphate into phosphoric acid for export. The government owned the subsoil mineral rights for all minerals. Exploration and new discoveries of oil and gas would yield sulfur and ammonia, which were needed for phosphate fertilizers. The government is pursuing additional joint ventures with international mining companies, and is also considering privatization of selected state-owned mining assets. Lead, silver, and zinc outputs are expected to decrease.

27 ENERGY AND POWER

The World Bank reported in 2008 that Morocco produced 20.8 billion kWh of electricity and consumed 23.2 billion kWh, or 727 kWh per capita. Roughly 94% of energy came from fossil fuels, while 1% came from alternative fuels. Per capita oil consumption was 474 kg. Oil production totaled 500 barrels of oil a day. Morocco has only small deposits of oil and natural gas. However, since many of its sedimentary basins have yet to be explored, those figures could rise.

28 INDUSTRY

In 2010 industry accounted for 31.6% of GDP, down from 35.7% in 2001. The industrial production growth rate was 4.4% in 2010. Leading industrial sectors were phosphate mining, manufacturing and handicrafts, construction and public works, and energy. Morocco holds some of the world's largest phosphate reserves and is a leading producer, trailing the United States and China.

The manufacturing sector produces light consumer goods, especially foodstuffs, beverages, textiles, matches, and metal and leather products. Heavy industry is largely limited to petroleum refining, chemical fertilizers, automobile and tractor assembly, foundry work, asphalt, and cement. Many of the processed agricultural products and consumer goods are primarily for local consumption, but Morocco exports canned fish and fruit, wine, leather goods, and textiles, as well as such traditional Moroccan handicrafts as carpets and brass, copper, silver, and wood implements.

There are two oil refineries, one at Mohammedia and one at Sidi Kacem. There are also several petrochemical plants, a polyvinyl chloride factory, and many phosphate-processing plants. The Mahgreb-EU pipeline has been operating since 1996. There are several plants assembling cars and small utility vehicles. A number of cement factories are also in operation. The Safi industrial complex, opened in 1965, processes phosphates from Youssoufia, pyrrhotites from Kettara, and ammonia.

Ownership in the manufacturing sector is largely private, but the government owns the phosphate-chemical fertilizer industry and much of the sugar-milling capacity, through either partnership or joint financing. It is also a major participant in the car and truck assembly industry and in tire manufacturing.

29 SCIENCE AND TECHNOLOGY

Patent applications in science and technology as of 2009, according to the World Bank, totaled 177 in Morocco. Public financing of science was 0.64% of GDP. Research institutions included the Scientific Institute (founded in 1920) in Rabat, which does fundamental research in the natural sciences, and the Scientific Institute of Maritime Fishing (founded in 1947) in Casablanca, which studies oceanography, marine biology, and topics related to development of the fishing industry.

30 DOMESTIC TRADE

Consumer-ready products are freely traded by the private sector through companies that distribute them to wholesalers, distributors, or directly to retailers. The government intervenes directly in domestic trade through price subsidies at the retail level for staples such as flour, vegetable oil, and sugar. The government has planned to phase out these subsidies over an extended period in order to avoid social unrest. Support prices, once a major incentive to promoting government-supported crops, have been eliminated.

Casablanca, the chief port, is the commercial center of Morocco. Other principal distribution centers include Safi, Agadir, and Tangier. Wet markets are open-air produce markets common in rural and urban areas. Central markets are found in major cities and contain many small shops selling mainly domestic products. Numerous family-operated grocery outlets are scattered throughout the country and are where food products are typically sold in Morocco. There are also a growing number of supermarkets in major metropolitan areas; over half of them are in Casablanca and Rabat. Retail establishments include department stores in the main cities and shops and specialty stores. Bazaars cater especially to the tourist trade.

The first franchise, Pizza Hut, was established in 1992. Franchises covered such goods and services as fast food, clothing, office supplies, furniture, cosmetics, auto repair and office cleaning services. In addition to Pizza Hut, US-based franchisers in Morocco included McDonald's, Pepsi-Cola, New Balance, and Midas.

Business hours are generally from 8 or 8:30 a.m. to 6:30 p.m., with a two-hour lunch break, but some shops stay open later. Large stores are open from 9 a.m. to 1 p.m. and from 3 to 7 p.m. Souks (the commercial quarter of a city) are open Monday to Sunday from 8:30 a.m. to 1 p.m. and from 2:30 to 6 p.m.

Principal Trading Partners – Morocco (2010)

(In millions of US dollars)

Country	Total	Exports	Imports	Balance
World	53,081.0	17,559.0	35,522.0	-17,963.0
France	9,010.0	3,592.0	5,418.0	-1,826.0
Spain	6,978.0	2,838.0	4,140.0	-1,302.0
United States	3,103.0	602.0	2,501.0	-1,899.0
China	3,042.0	238.0	2,804.0	-2,566.0
Italy	2,824.0	744.0	2,080.0	-1,336.0
Germany	2,133.0	524.0	1,609.0	-1,085.0
Sa'udi Arabia	2,097.0	23.0	2,074.0	-2,051.0
India	1,541.0	972.0	569.0	403.0
Moldova	1,414.0	170.0	1,244.0	-1,074.0
United Kingdom	1,204.0	459.0	745.0	-286.0

(…) data not available or not significant.

(n.s.) not specified.

SOURCE: *2011 Direction of Trade Statistics Yearbook,* New York: United Nations, 2011.

```
┌─────────────────────────────────────────────────────┐
│ Balance of Payments – Morocco (2010)                 │
│                                                       │
│ (In millions of US dollars)                          │
│                                                       │
│ Current Account                            -4,209.0  │
│   Balance on goods              -15,062.0            │
│     Imports          -32,646.0                       │
│     Exports           17,584.0                       │
│   Balance on services             5,109.0            │
│   Balance on income              -1,242.0            │
│   Current transfers               6,986.0            │
│ Capital Account                         ...          │
│ Financial Account                        1,364.0     │
│   Direct investment abroad         -580.0            │
│   Direct investment in Morocco    1,241.0            │
│   Portfolio investment assets       -22.0            │
│   Portfolio investment liabilities  132.0            │
│   Financial derivatives               ...            │
│   Other investment assets           880.0            │
│   Other investment liabilities     -287.0            │
│ Net Errors and Omissions             -167.0          │
│ Reserves and Related Items          3,012.0          │
│                                                       │
│ (…) data not available or not significant.           │
│                                                       │
│ SOURCE: Balance of Payment Statistics Yearbook 2011, │
│ Washington, DC: International Monetary Fund, 2011.   │
└─────────────────────────────────────────────────────┘
```

```
┌─────────────────────────────────────────────────────┐
│ Public Finance – Morocco (2009)                      │
│                                                       │
│ (In millions of Dirhams, central government figures) │
│                                                       │
│ Revenue and Grants       246,648        100.0%       │
│   Tax revenue            175,566         71.2%       │
│   Social contributions    29,768         12.1%       │
│   Grants                   2,800          1.1%       │
│   Other revenue           38,513         15.6%       │
│                                                       │
│ Expenditures             238,975        100.0%       │
│   General public services   ...           ...        │
│   Defense                   ...           ...        │
│   Public order and safety   ...           ...        │
│   Economic affairs          ...           ...        │
│   Environmental protection  ...           ...        │
│   Housing and community amenities ...     ...        │
│   Health                    ...           ...        │
│   Recreational, culture, and religion ... ...        │
│   Education                 ...           ...        │
│   Social protection         ...           ...        │
│                                                       │
│ (…) data not available or not significant.           │
│                                                       │
│ SOURCE: Government Finance Statistics Yearbook 2010, │
│ Washington, DC: International Monetary Fund, 2010.   │
└─────────────────────────────────────────────────────┘
```

31 FOREIGN TRADE

Morocco imported $34.19 billion worth of goods and services in 2008, while exporting $14.49 billion worth of goods and services. Major import partners in 2009 were France, 17%; Spain, 14.9%; China, 7.5%; Italy, 6.8%; Germany, 6.4%; the United States, 5.7%; and Saudi Arabia, 5.1% . Its major export partners were Spain, 22.1%; France, 20.1%; and India, 4.9%.

As part of the government's trade liberalization process, a widespread antismuggling campaign has sharply reduced the amount of goods illegally entering Morocco. A large amount of hashish illegally exits the country.

In 2010, Moroccan exports were clothing and textiles, electric components, inorganic chemicals, transistors, crude minerals, fertilizers (including phosphates), petroleum products, citrus fruits, vegetables, and fish. Imports to Morocco included crude petroleum, textile fabric, telecommunications equipment, wheat, gas and electricity, transistors, and plastics.

32 BALANCE OF PAYMENTS

In 2010 Morocco had a foreign trade deficit of $11 billion, amounting to 1% of GDP. Remittances from Moroccans working abroad, foreign aid, and a growing tourist industry have helped to offset chronic trade deficits. The current-account balance for 2010 was estimated at -4.63 billion.

33 BANKING AND SECURITIES

The Bank of Morocco (Bank al-Maghrib), the central bank, has the sole privilege of note issue. It is required to maintain a gold or convertible-currency reserve equal to one-ninth of its note issue. The Ministry of Finance is responsible for the organization of banking and the money market. In February 1996 the central bank gave clearance for banks and finance houses to issue corporate bonds.

Public sector financial organizations specializing in development finance include the National Bank for Economic Development, Moroccan Bank for Foreign Trade, National Agricultural Credit Bank, and Deposit and Investment Fund. Also instrumental in development finance is the Bureau of Mineral Exploration and Participation, which has participatory interests in the production of all coal, petroleum, lead, and manganese. The National Bank for Economic Development, established in 1959, has been particularly active in financing manufacturing. The Agricultural Credit Bank makes loans to credit organizations, public institutions, and cooperatives. Private individuals borrow from local agricultural credit banks or from the agricultural credit and provident societies.

In 2010 the discount rate, the interest rate at which the central bank lends to financial institutions in the short term, was 6.5%.

The stock exchange (Bourse des Valeurs) at Casablanca, established in 1929, handles mostly European and a few North African issues. The Casablanca stock market underwent a program of reform in 1993. The government approved legislation to turn the bourse into a private company with stock held by brokers, to create new stock-trading bodies and to channel the funds of small savers into share issues and unit trusts.

34 INSURANCE

In 1995, the government stepped in to rescue the ailing insurance industry after studies uncovered financial difficulties in a number of firms. The authorities stepped in to prevent collapses which could affect related financial services such as savings and investment, as well as the interlinked banking sector. However, in September 1995, the government abandoned its attempts to restructure five state insurance companies and put them into liquidation. The companies, then already in temporary receivership, were Compagnie Atlantique d'assurances et de réassurances, Arabia Insurance Co., Assurances la victoire, Assurances la renaissance, and Réunion marocaine d'assurances et de réassurances (Rémar). Their combined losses are estimated at up to $550 million, mostly accumulated through pay-outs on car insurance, where the high accident rate had not been adequately reflected in premiums. Outstanding policies were transferred to the state finance company, Caisse de dépôt et de gestion (CDG). A new code has since been drawn up for insurance companies, establishing reserve requirements similar to those applying to the banking sector. In 2000, the insurance companies AXA-Al Amane and CAA announced a merger that created insurance giant AXA Assurance Maroc, which was still operating in Morocco as of 2011.

³⁵PUBLIC FINANCE

In 2010 the budget of Morocco included $23.42 billion in public revenue and $27.08 billion in public expenditures. The budget deficit amounted to 4.1% of GDP. Public debt was 58.2% of GDP, with $27.06 billion of the debt held by foreign entities. Some privatization has taken place since 2000 in order to reduce government deficits.

³⁶TAXATION

As of 2011 the corporate income tax rate was 30%. Social security contributions were 20.1%. A vehicle tax of MAD4,500 ($538) also applied. Local service tax on urban land was levied at 10.5%. The main indirect tax is Morocco's value-added tax (VAT) with a standard rate of 20% in 2011, but with various reduced rates from 7% to 14% for more basic goods and services.

All wage earners are liable to a progressive tax on salaries, remunerations, and allowances under the General Income Tax (IGR). There are several types of deductions that can be applied in calculating an individual's taxable base income. There are also social security taxes and supplementary taxes on professional and rental income.

³⁷CUSTOMS AND DUTIES

The policy of import liberalization that began in 1967, has continued and new commodities have been added to the list of items not subject to quotas. In the 1970 general import program, items not subject to quotas accounted for 75% of the imports. Most goods do not require import licenses. In 2011 ad valorem tariffs on textiles, apparel, footwear, and travel goods ranged from 2.5 to 30%.

Agreements between Morocco and the European Community (now the European Union) have provided for mutual tariff concessions. Citrus tariffs were cut 80% by the European Community by the mid-1970s; tariffs on canned fruit and vegetables were reduced more than 50%; and fish products, wine, olive oil, and cereals were given special concessions. In return, Morocco reduced its minimum tariffs by 30% and adjusted quotas on imports to Morocco.

The import tariff does not apply within the free zone of the Port of Tangier.

³⁸FOREIGN INVESTMENT

Foreign direct investment (FDI) in Morocco was a net inflow of $1.97 billion according to World Bank figures published in 2009. FDI represented 2.16% of GDP.

Foreign investment declined somewhat during the 1960s and 1970s because of political uncertainty and the government's Moroccanization policy requiring majority Moroccan ownership of foreign banks, trading companies, insurance firms, and small manufacturing plants. Many foreign firms either sold out or closed down before 30 September 1974, the first deadline for compliance with Moroccanization policies. In an effort to attract foreign capital, the government passed a new investment code in August 1973 that offered substantial tax concessions to private investors. To encourage badly needed foreign investment, a revised code introduced in 1982 permitted foreign investors 100% ownership of local companies in certain sectors and unrestricted transfer of capital. The effective repent in 1990 of the Moroccanization law and regulatory changes, including tax breaks and streamlined approval procedures, led to a more than threefold increase in foreign investment inflows in the four years following its enactment.

A new investment code was passed in 1995 that provided income tax breaks for investments in certain regions, crafts and export industries; and import duty reductions; especially during the first five years of operation. It also contained foreign exchange provisions that favored foreign investors.

The US-Morocco Free Trade Agreement (FTA), negotiated in 2004 and implemented in 2006, encouraged more US investors to take advantage of duty-free access to both US and European markets. In addition to tariff elimination, the FTA with Morocco includes investment provisions and commitments to increase access to the Moroccan services sector for American firms.

³⁹ECONOMIC DEVELOPMENT

Government policy stresses expansion and development of the economy, essentially through foreign investment. Morocco decided to abide by the International Monetary Fund's (IMF's) Article VIII, thus beginning the privatization of 112 public entities—mainly manufacturing enterprises, hotels, and financial institutions—slated for divestiture under the 1989 privatization law. Keeping major industries under government control, Morocco proceeded to open up investment only partially, keeping the majority of revenues from the phosphates and mining, banking and securities industries. Between 1993 and 2005, 66 Moroccan state-owned industries were fully or partially privatized, including the tobacco distribution company Régie des Tabacs, Banque Centrale Populaire, and 35% of Maroc Telecom to Vivendi (an additional 16% was sold in 2005).

Morocco instituted a series of development plans to modernize the economy and increase production during the 1960s. Net investment under the five-year plan for 1960–64 was about $1.3 billion. The plan called for a growth rate of 6.2%, but by 1964 the growth rate had only reached only 3%. A new three-year plan (1965–67) targeted an annual growth rate of 3.7%. The main emphasis of the plan was on the development and modernization of the agricultural sector. The five-year development plan for 1968–72 called for increased agriculture and irrigation. The development of the tourist industry also figured prominently in the plan. The objective was to attain an annual 5% growth rate in GDP; the real growth rate actually exceeded 6%.

Investment during the 1970s included industry and tourism development. The five-year plan for 1973–77 envisaged a real economic growth of 7.5% annually. Industries singled out for development included chemicals (especially phosphoric acid), phosphate production, paper products, and metal fabrication. Tourist development was also stressed. In 1975, King Hassan II announced a 50% increase in investment targets to allow for the effects of inflation. The 1978–80 plan was one of stabilization and retrenchment, designed to improve Morocco's balance-of-payments position, but the 4% annual growth rate achieved was disappointing.

The ambitious five-year plan for 1981–85, estimated to cost more than $18 billion, aimed at achieving a growth rate of 6.5% annually. The plan's principal priority was to create some 900,000 new jobs and to train managers and workers in modern agricultural and industrial techniques. Other major goals were to increase production in agriculture and fisheries to make the country self-sufficient in food, and to develop energy (by building more hydroelectric installations and by finding more petroleum and other fossil fuels), industry, and tourism to enable Morocco to lessen its dependence on foreign loans. The plan called for significant expansion of irrigated land, for increased public works projects such as hospitals and schools, and for economic decentralization and regional development through the construction of 25 new industrial parks outside the crowded Casablanca-Kénitra coastal area. Proposed infrastructural improvements included the $2-billion rail line from Marrakech to El Aaiún; a new fishing port at Ad-Dakhla, near Argoub in the Western Sahara; and a bridge-tunnel complex across the Strait of Gibraltar to link Morocco directly with Spain. Large industrial projects included phosphoric acid plants, sugar refineries, mines to exploit cobalt, coal, silver, lead, and copper deposits, and oil-shale development.

Outstanding foreign debt service and commitments remain a significant obstacle to economic development. The 1992 financing requirements were mostly covered, largely because of grants and bilateral credit. Despite the cancellation by Saudi Arabia of $2.8 billion of debt, the total still exceeded $23 billion. Despite rescheduling through both the Paris Club of official creditors and the London Club of commercial creditors, servicing the debt accounted for 30% of exports of goods and services. The economic plan of 1999–2004 included the creation of jobs, promotion of exports and tourism, resumption of privatization, and infrastructure construction.

In 2011 the Moroccan economy benefitted from several free trade agreements, but it was also exposed to the economic faltering of its main export market, the European Union. The Moroccan government sought to mitigate its liabilities in the export market—primarily textiles and clothing—by expanding the banking and financial sectors, which enjoyed international credibility and encouraged international investment. Modest growth of 5% was projected for 2012.

40 SOCIAL DEVELOPMENT

The social security system covers employees and apprentices in industrial and commercial fields and the professions, as well as agriculture and forestry. There is also voluntary coverage for persons leaving covered employment, and voluntary complementary insurance is available. Benefits include maternity allowances, disability pensions, old age pensions, death allowances, and allowances for illness. Employees contributed 3.96% of earnings, and employers contributed 7.93% of payroll. Workers with children under 12 years of age are also entitled to a family allowance.

Women comprise about 35% of the work force and are employed mostly in the industrial, service, and teaching sectors. They have the right to vote and run for office, although they are much more likely to be illiterate than men. Women do not have equal status under Islamic family and estate laws. Under these codes, a woman can only marry with the permission of her legal guardian, which is usually her father. Husbands may initiate and obtain a divorce more easily than women, and women inherit less than male heirs. Child labor is common, particularly in the rug making and textile industries. Young girls often work as domestic servants. Employment of children under the age of 12 is prohibited by law. Domestic violence remains a widespread problem. Prison conditions remain poor.

41 HEALTH

According to the CIA, life expectancy in Morocco was 72 years in 2011. The country spent 5.3% of its GDP on healthcare, amounting to $156 per person. There were 6 physicians, 9 nurses and midwives, and 11 hospital beds per 10,000 inhabitants. The fertility rate was 2.3, while the infant mortality rate was 33 per 1,000 live births. In 2008 the maternal mortality rate, according to the World Bank, was 110 per 100,000 births. It was estimated that 98% of children were vaccinated against measles. The CIA calculated HIV/AIDS prevalence in Morocco to be about 0.1% in 2009.

Health conditions are relatively poor, but programs of mass education in child and parent hygiene, as well as government-supervised health services in schools and colleges, have helped to raise standards. Campaigns have been conducted against malaria, tuberculosis, venereal diseases, and cancer. However, gastrointestinal infections, malaria, typhoid, trachoma, and tuberculosis remain widespread. The World Health Organizations and UNICEF have cooperated in the government's campaigns against eye disorders and venereal diseases. The health system is comprised of three sectors: a public sector consisting of both the Ministry of Public Health and the Health Services of the Royal Armed Forces, a semi public sector, and a private sector. These together have been responsible for the dramatic reduction in mortality rates.

42 HOUSING

Since the 1950s, several million Moroccans have moved from the countryside to the urban centers to escape rural unemployment. Housing and sanitation, consequently, have become urban problems. The government is engaged in a low-cost housing program to reduce the slum areas, called *bidonvilles*, that have formed around the large urban centers, especially Casablanca and Rabat.

In 2010, the UN recognized the government of Morocco for major improvements in human settlements by bestowing the award known as the Scroll of Honor. Specifically, the recognition was given to the Moroccan Ministry of Housing and Urban Development and its associated agency, the Al Omrane Group, for the success of the Cities without Slums project. Beginning in 2004, the project's goal was to improve living conditions and responsibly clear the slum areas in 85 cities by 2012. By October 2010, Al Omrane had successfully improved or eliminated 45.8% of the nation's slums, affecting the lives of 1.6 million residents.

43 EDUCATION

In 2009 the World Bank estimated that 90% of age-eligible children in Morocco were enrolled in primary school. Secondary enrollment for age-eligible children stood at 35%. Tertiary enrollment was estimated at 13%. Of those enrolled in tertiary education, there were 100 male students for every 89 female students. Overall, the CIA estimated that Morocco had a literacy rate of 52.3%. Public expenditure on education represented 5.6% of GDP.

The general school system includes modern secular public institutions, traditional religious schools, and private schools. Nine years of education are compulsory, but many girls leave school at a younger age than boys, and girls are a minority in secondary as well as primary schools. Primary school covers six years of study, followed by three years of continued basic studies (college). Students may then attend a general secondary school (lycée) for three years or a technical school for two or three years. At about seventh or eighth grade, some students may opt for vocational school programs. The language of instruction in primary schools is Arabic during the first two years, and both Arabic and French are used for the next three years. French is partly the language of instruction in secondary schools. The traditional religious schools are attended by only a small fraction of students. The government is committed to a unified public school system but has permitted private schools to continue because of the lack of alternative resources.

Morocco has six universities. Al-Qarawiyin University at Fès, founded in 859, is reputed to be the oldest university in the world; it was reorganized in 1962–63 as an Islamic university, supervised by the Ministry of Education. The first modern Moroccan university, the University of Rabat (now the Muhammad V University), was opened in 1957. Other universities are Muhammad bin Abdallah (founded 1974), in Fès; Hassan II (1975), Casablanca; Cadi Ayyad (1978), Marrakech; and Muhammad I (1978), Oujda. There are about two dozen colleges and conservatories.

44 LIBRARIES AND MUSEUMS

The General Library and Archives (1920) in Rabat is the national library, with holdings of 600,000 volumes. Its notable collection of medieval books and manuscripts, of particular interest to Muslim scholars, contains 1,600 ancient manuscripts of famous Islamic writers, including an important treatise by Averroës and classical treatises on medicine and pharmacy. The Muhammad VI Library of the Al Akhawayn University has a collection of over 65,000 books as well over 450 national and international academic journals, magazines and newspapers. The University Sidi-Mohomed Ben Abdelleh, in Fès, holds 225,000 volumes. There are various European and Colonial institutes through the country holding small collections. Of the 18 public libraries in Morocco, the largest is in Casablanca, with almost 360,000 volumes.

The Division of Museums, Sites, Archaeology, and Historic Monuments of the Ministry of Cultural Affairs administers 11 museums in major cities and at the ancient Roman site of Volubilis, northwest of Meknès. In some cities, such as Fès and Marrakech, small houses of historic and artistic interest have been preserved as museums. The Museum of Moroccan Arts and the Museum of Antiquities are in Tangiers. Also in Tangiers is the Forbes Museum, which holds a collection of lead soldiers that belonged to the American Malcolm Forbes. There are archeological museums in Tétouan, Rabat, and Larache. The National Science Museum and the Postal Museum are in Rabat. There are Ethnographic Museums in Chefchaouen and Tétouan.

45 MEDIA

In 2009 the CIA reported that there were 3.5 million telephone landlines in Morocco. In addition to landlines, mobile phone subscriptions averaged 79 per 100 people. There were 27 FM radio stations, 25 AM radio stations, and 6 shortwave radio stations. Internet users numbered 32 per 100 citizens. Prominent newspapers in 2010, with circulation numbers listed parenthetically, included *Al Ittihad al Ichtiraki* (110,000), *Al Alam* (100,000), *Le Matin du Sahara et du Maghreb* (100,000), as well as three other major newspapers.

Radiodiffusion Television Marocaine presents programs in Arabic, in Berber dialects, and in English, French, and Spanish. The television service, with studios in Casablanca and Rabat, presents daily programs in Arabic and French. A private television station, 2M International, began broadcasting in French and Arabic in 1989.

Press freedom is guaranteed by the constitution, and censorship of domestic publications was lifted in 1977, but criticism of Islam, the king, the monarchical system, or Morocco's claim to the Western Sahara is not permitted.

46 ORGANIZATIONS

The Moroccan Trade, Industry, and Handicrafts Association encourages economic development. Chambers of commerce, industry, and agriculture function in most Moroccan cities. British, French, Spanish, and international chambers of commerce are active in Tangier.

Morocco has several drama societies, music organizations (notably the Association for Andalusian Music), and artists' associations. The multinational Islamic Educational, Scientific, and Cultural Organization is based in Rabat. Professional organizations include societies of doctors, pharmacists, lawyers, and engineers. There are several other associations dedicated to research and education for specific fields of medicine and particular diseases and conditions. Societies have been formed to encourage the study of economics, geography, prehistory, sociology, and statistics. There are associations of primary- and secondary-school teachers, parents, older students, and alumni. The National Center for Planning and Coordination of Scientific and Technical Research was established in 1981.

There are at least two major student political groups: the National Union of Moroccan Students and the General Union of Moroccan Students. There are youth movements affiliated with political parties and religious institutions. Scouting programs are also active in the country. There are sports associations representing a wide variety of pastimes, such as tennis, tae kwon do, squash, yachting, and badminton.

The National Mutual Aid Society, a welfare organization with many subdivisions, is headed by Princess Lalla Aïcha, the king's sister. Volunteer service organizations, such as the Lions Clubs International, are also present. The Red Crescent Society and Caritas are also active.

47 TOURISM, TRAVEL, AND RECREATION

The *Tourism Factbook*, published by the UN World Tourism Organization, reported 8.66 million incoming tourists to Morocco in 2009; they spent a total of $7.98 billion. Of those incoming tourists, there were 4 million from nationals residing abroad and 3.6 million from Europe. There were 164,612 hotel beds available in Morocco, which had an occupancy rate of 33%. The estimated daily cost to visit Rabat, the capital, was $288. The cost of visiting other cities averaged $250.

Morocco's scenic variety and beauty, fascinating medieval cities, and favorable climate contribute to a steadily increasing flow of tourists. Tourism is one of the fastest-growing areas of the Moroccan economy and a valuable foreign exchange earner. Casablanca and Marrakech are favorite tourist destinations. Coastal beach resorts offer excellent swimming and boating facilities. Sports associations are widespread, particularly for football (soccer), swimming, boxing, basketball, and tennis.

In late 2010 the government unveiled a 10-year development plan designed to double the amount of tourist receipts and make tourism the second largest sector of the economy after agriculture. The main banks of the nation signed agreements with the government to fund a number of tourism-based projects, such as hotels and resort facilities. Foreign investors were also welcomed.

⁴⁸FAMOUS PERSONS

Important leaders and rulers include Idris I (Idris bin 'Abdallah, r. 788–91), of the Umayyad dynasty, who came to Morocco and was able to consolidate much of the area. His son Idris II (r. 791–804) founded Fès, the early capital. Yusuf bin Tashfin (r. 1061–1106), a religious reformer, conquered much of Spain and northern Africa. Muhammad bin Tumart (1078?–1130) founded the Almohad sect and developed a democratic form of government. The founder of the Almohad dynasty, 'Abd al-Mumin bin 'Ali (1094?-1163), conquered Morocco and parts of Spain. Yakub al-Mansur (r. 1184–99), who controlled all of North Africa west of Egypt, encouraged architecture and scholarship. Ahmad al-Mansur (r. 1578–1603) drove all foreign forces out of Morocco, conquered the western Sudan, and established commercial and other contacts with England and Europe. Mawlay Isma'il (r. 1672–1727) reunited Morocco and organized a harsh but effective centralized government. A capable and strong ruler famous for his justice was Muhammad bin 'Abdallah (r. 1757–90).

Morocco has attracted many great minds, and it has been said that none of the great names in western Arabic philosophy is unconnected with Morocco. Avicenna (Ibn Sina, or Abu 'Ali al-Husayn, 980?–1037), a great Persian physician and philosopher and an author of long-used textbooks on medicine, who was born near Bukhoro (Bukhara), lived for a number of years in Morocco. So did Avenzoar (Ibn Zuhr, or Abu Marwan 'Abd al-Malik bin Abu-'l-'Ala' Zuhr, c. 1090?–1162), physician and scholar, born in Sevilla, Spain, and author of important medical treatises. Averroës (Ibn Rushd, or Abu al-Walid Muhammad ibn Ahmad ibn Rushd, 1126–98), greatest Arab philosopher of Spain, was born in Córdoba and lived in Morocco for many years. The doctor and philosopher Abubacer (Abu Bakr Muhammad bin 'Abd al-Malik bin Tufayl, d. 1118) was likewise brought to the Moroccan court from Spain.

Among distinguished native-born Moroccans was Ahmad bin 'Ali al-Badawi (c. 1200?–76), a Muslim saint who was active principally in Egypt. The great traveler Ibn Battutah (Abu 'Abdallah Muhammad bin Battutah, 1304–68?) visited and wrote about many countries of Africa, Asia, and Europe. The poetry of Muhammad bin Ibrahim (d. 1955) is read throughout the Islamic world.

A famous fighter for Moroccan independence was 'Abd al-Karim (Muhammad 'Abd al-Karim al-Khattabi, 1882?-1963), who led a long campaign in the 1920s against French and Spanish forces. King Mohammed V (1909–61) gave up his throne as a gesture for independence, was arrested and exiled by the French, and returned in 1955 to become the first ruler of newly independent Morocco. He was succeeded by his son Hassan II (1929–1999), who continued his father's modernization program and expanded Morocco's territory and mineral resources by annexing Western Sahara. Mohammed VI (b. 1963) became king following his father's death in 1999.

⁴⁹DEPENDENCIES

Morocco has no territories or colonies.

⁵⁰BIBLIOGRAPHY

Bowles, Paul. *The Stories of Paul Bowles.* New York: Harper Perennial, 2006.

Hourani, Albert Habib. *A History of the Arab Peoples.* Cambridge, MA: Belknap Press of Harvard University Press, 2002.

McDougall, James, ed. *Nation, Society and Culture in North Africa.* London: Frank Cass Publishers, 2003.

Morocco Investment and Business Guide: Strategic and Practical Information. Washington, DC: International Business Publications USA, 2012.

Njoku, Raphael C. *Culture and Customs of Morocco.* Westport, CT: Greenwood Press, 2006.

Park, Thomas K., and Aomar Boum. *Historical Dictionary of Morocco.* Lanham, MD: Scarecrow Press, 2006.

Pazzanita, Anthony G. *Historical Dictionary of Western Sahara.* Lanham, MD: Scarecrow Press, 2006.

Pennell, C. R. *Morocco Since 1830: A History.* New York: New York University Press, 2000.

Wilde, Tatiana. *Insight Guide Morocco.* London: Insight Guides, 2012.

Zeilig, Leo, and David Seddon. *A Political and Economic Dictionary of Africa.* Philadelphia: Routledge/Taylor and Francis, 2005.

MOZAMBIQUE

Republic of Mozambique
República de Moçambique

CAPITAL: Maputo (formerly Lourenço Marques)

FLAG: The flag consists of broad stripes of green, black, and yellow, separated by narrow bands of white. Extending from the hoist is a red triangle; centered on the triangle is a yellow five-pointed star upon which is a white book over which are crossed the black silhouettes of a hoe and an AK47 rifle.

ANTHEM: *Patria Amada (Lovely Fatherland).*

MONETARY UNIT: The Mozambique escudo, linked until 1977 with the Portuguese escudo, was in June 1980 renamed the metical (MZM); it is a paper currency of 100 centavos. There are coins of 1, 5, 10, and 50 centavos and 1, 2, 5, and 10 meticais, and notes of 50, 100, 500, and 1,000 meticais. MZM1 = US$0.0376648 (or US$1 = MZM26,550) as of 2011.

WEIGHTS AND MEASURES: The metric system is in use.

HOLIDAYS: New Year's Day, 1 January; Heroes' Day, 3 February; Women's Day, 7 April; Workers' Day, 1 May; Independence Day, 25 June; Victory Day, 7 September; Day of Revolution, 25 September; Christmas, 25 December.

TIME: 2 p.m. = noon GMT.

¹LOCATION, SIZE, AND EXTENT

Located on the southeastern coast of Africa opposite the island of Madagascar, Mozambique (Moçambique), formerly known as Portuguese East Africa, has an area of 799,380 sq km (308,642 sq mi), of which land constitutes 786,380 sq km (303,623 sq mi) and inland water 13,000 sq km (5,019 sq mi). Comparatively, the area occupied by Mozambique is slightly less than twice the size of the state of California. The country extends 2,016 km (1,253 mi) NNE-SSW and 772 km (480 mi) ESE-WNW. It is bordered by Tanzania on the N, the Indian Ocean (Mozambique Channel) on the E, the Republic of South Africa on the S, Swaziland, South Africa, and Zimbabwe on the W, and Zambia and Malawi on the NW, with a total boundary length of 7,041 km (4,375 mi), of which 2,470 km (1,535 mi) is coastline.

²TOPOGRAPHY

Mozambique is 44% coastal lowlands, rising toward the west to a plateau 150 to 610 m (500–2,000 ft) above sea level and on the western border to a higher plateau, 550 to 910 m (1,800–3,000 ft), with mountains reaching a height of nearly 2,440 m (8,000 ft). The highest mountains are Namuli (2,419 m/7,936 ft) in Zambézia Province and Binga (2,436 m/7,992 ft) in Manica Province on the Zimbabwean border. The most important rivers are the Zambezi (flowing southeast across the center of Mozambique into the Indian Ocean), the Limpopo in the south, the Save (Sabi) in the center, and the Lugenda in the north. The most important lake is the navigable Lake Malawi (Lake Niassa); Lake Cahora Bassa was formed by the impoundment of the Cahora Bassa Dam. In the river valleys and deltas, the soil is rich and fertile, but southern and central Mozambique has poor and sandy soil, and parts of the interior are dry.

³CLIMATE

Two main seasons, one wet and one dry, divide the climatic year. The wet season, from November through March, has monthly temperature averages of 27–29°C (81–84°F), with cooler temperatures in the interior uplands. The dry season lasts from April to October and has June and July temperatures averaging 18–20°C (64–68°F). The average annual rainfall is greatest, about 142 cm (56 in) over the western hills and the central areas, and lowest, 30 cm (12 in) in the southwest.

Droughts are common in Mozambique, with severe droughts generally occurring every three to four years. A severe drought began to affect the central region of the country in 2001, and others hit in 2003, 2007, and 2009. Cyclones, tropical storms, and flooding are also common. There was widespread flooding in the Zambezi River Basin in Tete, Manica, Sofala, and Zambezia provinces in late 2006 and early 2007, and localized flooding in some areas occurs annually. Cyclone Jokwe, in March 2008, left at least 16 dead and affected almost 200,000. Cyclones Dando and Funso, which hit in January 2012, killed more than two dozen and displaced thousands. Due to such conditions, in 2012, the UN estimated that 146,500 people, mostly in Zambézia and Tete provinces, needed humanitarian assistance in the first half of 2012.

⁴FLORA AND FAUNA

The World Resources Institute estimates that there are 5,692 plant species in Mozambique. Thick forest covers the wet regions where there are fertile soils, but the drier interior, which has sandy or rocky soils, supports only thin savanna vegetation. Extensive stands of hardwood such as ebony, flourish throughout the country. Mozambique has elephants, buffalo, wildebeests, zebras, palapalas, hippopotami, lions, crocodiles, nyalas, and other southern

African game species. The World Resource Institute estimates that Mozambique is home to 228 mammal, 685 bird, 195 reptile, and 59 amphibian species. The calculation reflects the total number of distinct species residing in the country, not the number of endemic species. According to a 2011 report issued by the International Union for Conservation of Nature and Natural Resources (IUCN), the number of threatened species included 12 types of mammals, 24 species of birds, 8 types of reptiles, 3 species of amphibians, 55 species of fish, 3 types of mollusks, 55 species of other invertebrates, and 51 species of plants. Endangered species in Mozambique include the green sea, hawksbill, olive ridley, and leatherback turtles.

5 ENVIRONMENT

The World Resources Institute reported that Mozambique had designated 4.53 million hectares (11.19 million acres) of land for protection as of 2006. Other significant environmental problems included the loss of 70% of the nation's forests. The nation lost 7.7% of its forest and woodland between 1983 and 1993 alone. Mozambique has since launched reforestation projects, mostly involving the planting of conifers and eucalyptus. From the 1990s to the early 2000s, the rate of deforestation changed dramatically; it was -3.7% from 1990 to 2005. In 2000–05, the annual rate of deforestation was -0.3%; the rate was 0.58% in 2007.

Water resources total 216 cu km (51.82 cu mi) while water usage is 0.63 cu km (0.151 cu mi) per year. Domestic water usage accounted for 11% of total usage, industrial for 2%, and agricultural for 87%. Per capita water usage totaled 32 cu m (1,130 cu ft) per year. The purity of the nation's water supply is also a significant issue. Surface and coastal waters have been affected by pollution. The UN reported in 2008 that carbon dioxide emissions in Mozambique totaled 2,598 kilotons.

6 POPULATION

The US Central Intelligence Agency (CIA) estimated the population of Mozambique in 2012 to be approximately 23,515,934, which placed it at number 50 in population among the 196 nations of the world. In 2011 approximately 3% of the population was over 65 years of age, with another 45.9% under 15 years of age. The median age in Mozambique was 16.8 years. There were 0.98 males for every female in the country. The population's annual rate of change was 2.442%. The projected population for the year 2025 was 31,200,000. Population density in Mozambique was 29 people per sq km (75 people per sq mi).

The UN estimated that 38% of the population lived in urban areas, and that urban populations had an annual rate of change of 4.0%. The largest urban areas, along with their respective populations, included Maputo 1.6 million and Matola 761,000.

The prevalence of HIV/AIDS (a rate of 11.5%, the 8th highest in the world) has had a significant impact on the population of Mozambique. The AIDS epidemic causes higher death and infant mortality rates and lowers life expectancy.

7 MIGRATION

Estimates of Mozambique's net migration rate, carried out by the CIA in 2011, amounted to -2.18 migrants per 1,000 citizens. The total number of emigrants living abroad was 1.18 million, and the total number of immigrants living in Mozambique was 450,000.

Between April 1974 and the end of 1976, an estimated 235,000 of the 250,000 Portuguese in Mozambique fled the country. Famine and war produced another exodus in the 1980s, but this time of blacks. An October 1992 peace agreement left 4.5 million internally displaced and 1.5 million refugees abroad. Of the latter at the end of 1992, some 1,058,500 were in Malawi; about 200,000 in South Africa, 136,600 in Zimbabwe, 75,200 in Tanzania, 48,100 in Swaziland, and 26,300 in Zambia. By May 1993 about 750,000 people in both categories had returned home. Mozambique traditionally supplies seasonal farm workers to South Africa farmers.

In October 1992, the 16-year civil war ended with a peace treaty. Between 1992 and 1996 the Office of the UN High Commissioner for Refugees (UNHCR) completed the largest repatriation project it has ever conducted in Africa. Over 1.3 million refugees returned to Mozambique from Malawi, 241,000 returned from Zimbabwe, 23,000 returned from South Africa, and 32,000 returned from Tanzania.

8 ETHNIC GROUPS

Nearly the total population (99.66%) is made up of indigenous tribal groups, including the Shangaan, Chokwe, Manyika, Sena, and Makua. Overall, there are 10 major ethnic clusters. The largest, residing north of the Zambezi, is the Makua-Lomwé group, representing about 37% of the total population. The Yao (Ajawa) live in Niassa Province. The Makonde live mainly along the Rovuma River. Other northern groups are the Nguni, who also live in the far south, and the Maravi. South of the Zambezi the main group is the Tsonga (about 23%), who have figured prominently as Mozambican mine laborers in South Africa. The Chopi are coastal people of Inhambane Province. The Shona (about 9%) dwell in the central region. Also living in Mozambique are Euro-Africans, accounting for about 0.2% of the population; Europeans make up 0.06%, and Indians constitute 0.08%.

9 LANGUAGES

Portuguese remains the official language, though it is spoken as a first language by only about 10.7% of the population; about 27% speak Portuguese as a second language. Different African ethnic groups speak their respective languages. The most prominent of these are Emakhuwa, spoken by about 25.3% of the population, Xichangana by 10.3%, Elomwe by 7%, Cisena by 7.5%, and Echuwabo by 5.1%.

10 RELIGIONS

According to the 2007 census, of the eight million or so Mozambicans who claim religious affiliation, about 28.4% are Roman Catholic; 27.7% are Protestant; and 18% are Muslim, though some Muslim leaders claim a much larger percentage of adherents. Reports from the National Institute of Statistics stated the remainder of the population does not claim adherence to any religion or creed. However, local scholars claim that most of the population follows traditional indigenous customs and beliefs either exclusively or in conjunction with other religious traditions. Veneration of ancestors plays an important role in traditional customs as do *curandeiros*, the traditional healers or spiritualists who are consulted for healing, luck, and solutions to problems. The strongest Muslim communities are located in the northern provinces and along the coastal strip. Central provinces are predominantly Cath-

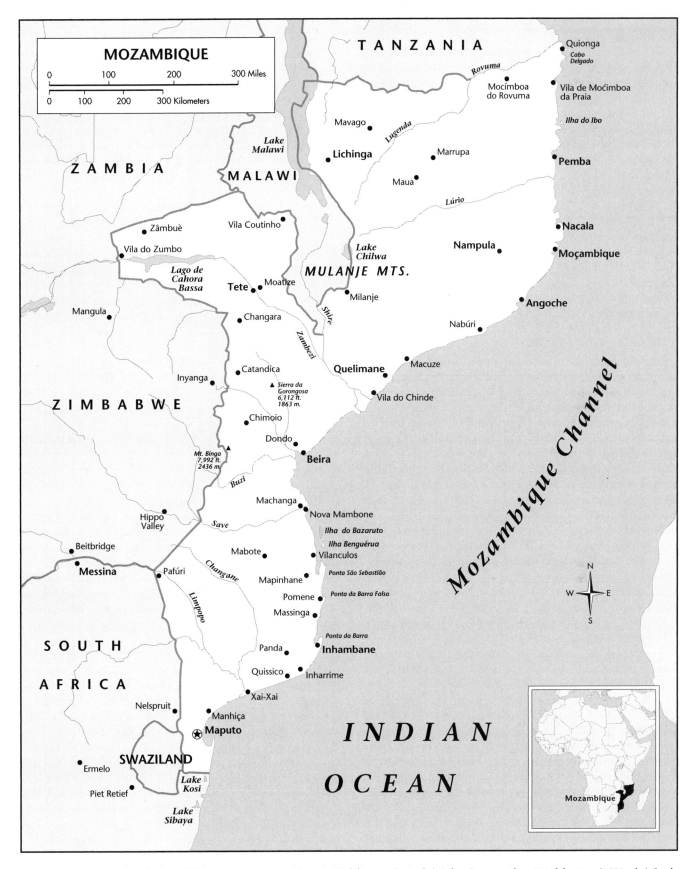

olic and the southern regions have the most Protestants. There are also small groups of Jews, Hindus, and Baha'is across the country.

The Republic of Mozambique is a secular state, and freedom of religion is provided for in the constitution. As of 2010 there were at least 749 denominations registered with the Department of Religious Affairs of the Ministry of Justice. Registration is required by law, and an organization must have at least 500 members in good standing to be registered. However, unregistered groups have been allowed to worship without restrictions. The largest of the African Independent Churches in the country is the Zion Christian Church. Other Christian denominations include Anglican, Greek Orthodox, Presbyterian, Methodist, Baptist, Seventh-day Adventist, Congregational, Church of Jesus Christ of Latter-day Saints, Nazarene, Jehovah's Witnesses and other Pentecostal, evangelical, and apostolic organizations. The evangelical Christians are reported as the fastest growing religious groups in the country. Among Muslims, only Sunni and Ismaili communities are registered. No religious holidays are officially observed, though individuals are generally allowed days off for their own religious observances. National Family Day is observed on December 25.

11 TRANSPORTATION

Transport networks are of major importance to the economy. Mozambique's landlocked neighbors—Malawi, Zambia, Zimbabwe, and Swaziland—along with South Africa are the main users of the Mozambican transport system.

The railways are the best-developed sector, with three good rail links between major Mozambican ports and neighboring countries. By independence in 1975 almost the entire railway system was owned by the state and passed into the hands of the newly independent government. The route system is all narrow gauge, with the single largest user being South Africa. There are six routes that make up the majority of the country's railroads: the Nacala Corridor, connecting Nacala to Malawi (300 km, 186 mi); the Sena Corridor, linking Beira via Dondo to the coalfields at Moatize (513 km, 319 mi) and to Malawi (370 km, 230 mi); the Beira Corridor, connecting Beira to Zimbabwe (315 km, 196 mi); the Limpopo Corridor, linking Maputo with Zimbabwe (534 km, 332 mi); the Resano Garcia line, connecting Maputo to South Africa (88 km, 55 mi); and the Goba line, linking Maputo to Swaziland (68 km, 42 mi). All in all railroads extend for 3,116 km (1,936 mi).

Construction on a new railway connecting the northern coal mining area of Moatize with the port of Nacala began in late 2009. The $500 million project, funded in part by the European Union (EU), the Netherlands, and Denmark, will include reconstruction of parts of the Sena line, which once linked Moatize to the port of Beira, and the Nacala-Malawi railway, which linked the ports by those names. All of these rail links were damaged by war. While the primary purpose of the project was to rebuild the transportation routes for the coal industry, the government also hoped the effort would place Mozambique as a regional transshipment route.

In July 2010 Mozambique announced plans to build a $132 million bridge across the Zambezi River to connect mainland Mozambique with an inland province of Tete. Bridge planners billed the project as a huge economic infrastructure investment that would not only benefit Tete and Mozambique, but also landlocked African states in the region, such as Malawi and Zimbabwe. Tete is known to hold some of the largest coal reserves in the world.

Analysts say the bridge will provide miners with much improved market access for the coal.

The CIA reported that Mozambique has a total of 30,331 km (18,847 mi) of roads, of which 6,303 km (3,917 mi) are paved. There are 13 vehicles per 1,000 people in the country. Few roads were suitable for trucks and passenger cars. In April 2010 the US Agency for International Development (USAID) offered $300 million to rebuild roads and to improve the water and sanitation infrastructure in parts of Mozambique. The funds were part of a five-year $507 million project of the US Millennium Challenge Account. The project allowed for upgrades on about 500 km (310 mi) of roadways.

Maputo, by far the leading port, has an excellent multipurpose harbor, with exceptional loading, unloading, and storage facilities. It is a major outlet for South Africa, Swaziland, Zimbabwe, Zambia, Malawi, and the eastern Democratic Republic of Congo (DROC). Other ports include Beira, Nacala, and Inhambane. The Mozambican merchant fleet consisted of two cargo ships of 1,000 GRT or more in 2010. Mozambique has approximately 460 km (286 mi) of navigable waterways. Mozambique's navigable waterways consisted of the Zambezi River to Tete and along Cahora Lake.

In 2010 there were 23 airports with paved runways. There are a total of 106 airports, which transported 490,019 passengers in 2009 according to the World Bank. Mozambique Air Lines (Linhas Aéreas de Moçambique—LAM), the state airline, operates both international and domestic services. The National Enterprise of Transport and Aerial Labor (Empresa Nacional de Transporte e Trabalho Aéreo—TTA) also provides domestic service. Maputo and Beira have international airports.

12 HISTORY

Mozambique's earliest inhabitants were hunter-gatherers often referred to as Bushmen. The land was occupied by Bantu peoples by about AD 1000. In the following centuries, trade developed with Arabs who came across the Indian Ocean to Sofala. The first Europeans in the area were the Portuguese, who began to settle and trade on the coast early in the 16th century. During the 17th century the Portuguese competed with Arabs for the trade in slaves, gold, and ivory, and set up agricultural plantations and estates. The owners of these estates, the *prazeiros*, were Portuguese or of mixed African and Portuguese blood (mestiços); many had their own private armies. Mozambique was ruled as part of Goa until 1752, when it was given its own administration.

Until the late 1800s Portuguese penetration was restricted to the coast and the Zambezi Valley. The African peoples strongly resisted further expansion, but they were ultimately subdued. By the end of the 19th century, the Portuguese had made boundary agreements with their colonial rivals, the United Kingdom and Germany, and had suppressed much of the African resistance. Authority was given to trading companies such as Mozambique Company, which forced local people to pay taxes and work on the plantations. After the Portuguese revolution of 1926, the government of Portugal took a more direct interest in Mozambique. The trading companies' influence declined, and Mozambique in 1951 became an overseas province of Portugal.

As in other Portuguese territories, African resistance to Portuguese rule grew stronger as the British and French colonies in

Africa began to win their independence. Gradually, various liberation movements were formed. On 25 June 1962 these groups united to form the Mozambique Liberation Front (Frente de Libertação de Moçambique—FRELIMO) and elected Eduardo C. Mondlane as its first president. The armed struggle began on 25 September 1964, when FRELIMO guerrillas trained in Algeria went into action for the first time in Cabo Delgado. By 1965 fighting had spread to Niassa and by 1968 FRELIMO was able to open fronts in the Tete region. By that time it claimed to control one-fifth of the country. In response, the Portuguese committed more and more troops, military supplies, and military aid funds to the territory. On 3 February 1969 Mondlane was assassinated in Dar es Salaam, Tanzania; the acting leader of FRELIMO, Samora Machel, became president of the organization in December 1970.

The turning point in the struggle for independence came with the Portuguese revolution of 25 April 1974. Negotiations between Portuguese and FRELIMO representatives led to an independence agreement in Zambia in September. Mozambique became officially independent at midnight on 24–25 June 1975, and the People's Republic of Mozambique was proclaimed in ceremonies on 25 June. Machel, who had returned to Mozambique on 24 May after 13 years in exile, became the nation's first president. He quickly affirmed Mozambique's support of the liberation movement in Rhodesia, and guerrilla activity along the Rhodesian border increased. On 3 March 1976 Mozambique closed its border with Rhodesia, severed rail and communications links, and nationalized Rhodesian-owned property. Because the transit fees paid by Rhodesia had been a major source of foreign exchange revenue, the action aggravated Mozambique's economic ills. During this period Rhodesian forces conducted land and air raids into Mozambique to punish Black Nationalist guerrillas based there. These raids ended and the border was reopened in 1980, following the agreement that transformed Rhodesia into Zimbabwe. However, South African airmen bombed Maputo in 1981 and 1983 in retaliation for Mozambique's granting refuge to members of the African National Congress (ANC), a South African Black Nationalist group.

The Mozambique National Resistance (RENAMO), created in 1976, allegedly by Portuguese settler and business interests with white Rhodesian (Central Intelligence Organization) backing, conducted extensive guerrilla operations in Mozambique during the 1980s. With an armed strength estimated as high as 12,000, RENAMO blew up bridges and cut rail and road links and pipelines. After the loss of its Rhodesian support, RENAMO received substantial aid from South Africa and also had bases in Malawi. Voluntary support for RENAMO within Mozambique was difficult to ascertain, but there was known to be considerable disaffection with the government because of food shortages and resistance by peasants to being resettled onto communal farms. In addition to these political problems, Mozambique experienced widespread floods in 1977–78 and recurrent drought periodically from 1979, especially in 1992.

On 16 March 1984 Mozambique and South Africa signed a nonaggression pact at Nkomati whereby Mozambique agreed to keep the ANC from using Mozambican territory for guerrilla attacks on South Africa, while South Africa agreed to stop supporting RENAMO. Nevertheless, South Africa continued to aid RENAMO and as a result, in 1985 Mozambique pulled out of the commission that monitored the nonaggression pact. On 19 Octo-

ber 1986 President Machel and 33 others were killed when their Soviet-built jetliner crashed inside South Africa while returning to Maputo. Mozambican officials accused South Africa of employing a radio beacon to lure the craft off course to its destruction, but an international commission found that the crash was caused by negligence on the part of the Soviet crew. On 3 November 1986 FRELIMO's Central Committee elected Foreign Minister Joaquim A. Chissano president. In 1987 despite the jetliner crash and Mozambican claims that RENAMO and South Africa were responsible for the massacre of 386 people in a village near Inhambane, Mozambique and South Africa revived their nonaggression pact. However, fighting intensified and hundreds of thousands of Mozambicans fled to Malawi and Zimbabwe.

In 1990 there was movement toward resolving the civil war. There were serious signs in the late 1980s that FRELIMO was moderating its views. At its 1989 Congress FRELIMO formally abandoned its commitment to the primacy of Marxism-Leninism. The first peace talks in 13 years were scheduled for Blantyre, Malawi, but they broke down just before they were to open. In August, government and rebel leaders concluded three days of talks in Rome. That same month Chissano announced that FRELIMO had agreed to allow opposition parties to compete openly and legally. Finally in November government and RENAMO agreed to appoint the Italian government and the Catholic Church as mediators in peace talks.

It took until 4 October 1992 to sign a peace treaty ending the war, but sporadic fighting and new RENAMO demands slowed down the implementation process. Chissano and Afonso Dhlakama, RENAMO's leader, signed an agreement that called for the withdrawal of Zimbabwean and Malawian troops that had assisted government forces guarding transport routes and the regrouping of both government and RENAMO soldiers at assembly points. It called for the formation of a new national army composed of half government and half RENAMO troops. A joint commission of government and RENAMO, along with a small UN monitoring force and other joint commissioners, the police, and intelligence services were to oversee the agreement's implementation. In addition, multiparty elections were to be held within a year.

Delays troubled the process practically from the start. RENAMO was slow to appoint its representatives to the joint commissions. The UN Operation in Mozambique (UNOMOZ) was formally approved in December 1992, but no troops arrived until March 1993, and it was midyear before 6,000 troops were deployed. RENAMO failed to implement the provision for demobilization and all of the provisions regarding freedom of movement and political organization in areas it controlled. New RENAMO demands were put forward almost monthly, and despite direct meetings between Dhlakama and Chissano and an October 1993 visit by UN Sec. Gen. Boutros Boutros-Ghali, the delays continued.

Political party activity picked up as efforts to resolve the civil war continued. By the end of 1996, 22 parties were active. In March 1993 government presented a draft electoral law to opposition parties, but not until late July was a meeting convened to discuss it. The opposition parties demanded a two-thirds majority on the National Electoral Commission. After Boutros-Ghali's visit a compromise (10 out of 21 for the opposition parties) was agreed to. Delays also marked the effort to confine armed forces in designated areas.

Elections first scheduled for 1993 were conducted on 27–29 October 1994. On the presidential ballot Chissano won 53.3% of the vote to Dhlakama's 33.7%. The remainder was split among 10 other contenders. On the legislative ballot FRELIMO took 44% of the popular vote to RENAMO's 37.7%. FRELIMO had 129 seats and RENAMO 112. The Democratic Union took nine seats. Dhlakama disputed the fairness of the vote, and UN observers agreed that it had been less than ideal, but insisted that the announced results were sufficiently accurate. More than 2,000 international observers agreed. Chissano formed the new government on 23 December with the entire cabinet made up of FRELIMO MPs. Early in 1996 the Chissano government announced that it would postpone municipal elections slated for later that year until 1997. In presidential and parliamentary elections held in December 1999, Chissano defeated Dhlakama 52.29% to 47.71%, while his party took 133 seats against 117 for RENAMO in the parliamentary contest.

The next elections were held on 1 December 2004. In these elections Armando Guebuza, the new FRELIMO candidate, won 63.7% of the votes and the RENAMO candidate, Afonso Dhlakama, got 31.7%. In the parliamentary elections FRELIMO won 62% (1.8 million) of the votes, RENAMO 29.7% (905,000 votes) and 18 minor parties shared the remaining 8%. Under the proportional system FRELIMO won 160 of the parliamentary seats and RENAMO won 90. The election results were contested by RENAMO and were widely criticized by international observes such as the EU Election Observation Mission to Mozambique. Nevertheless, although the elections had shortcomings it was agreed that the shortcomings did not affect the final result in the presidential election, which was decisively in favor of FRELIMO. The new FRELIMO president, Armando Guebuza, was sworn in as president of the republic on 2 February 2005 without the blessing of Dhlakama and RENAMO. Dhlakama was absent at the inauguration. In spite of the protests over the elections, RENAMO agreed to participate in the parliament and the Council of State. In the 2009 presidential and assembly of the republic elections, Guebuza won the election with 75% of the vote. Dhlakama and Daviz Simango trailed with 16.5% and 8.6% respectively. In the parliamentary election FRELIMO won 191 seats, followed by RENAMO with 51 seats and 8 for the Democratic Movement of Mozambique (MDM). Elections were held again in 2009, with Guebuza winning over 76% of the vote.

In October 2005 work began on a Unity Bridge over the Ruvuma River, intended to link Mozambique with its neighbor Tanzania. The bridge was inaugurated on 12 May 2010 by the presidents of Mozambique and Tanzania.

With the return of normalcy to the war-torn country in the mid-1990s, Mozambique attempted to address the huge problem of the repatriation of the millions of refugees. By 1996 1.6 million had returned. In 1997 Mozambique had become relatively stable, but remained mired in poverty. International investment, following structural adjustment programs initiated by the World Bank, poured in as the country engaged in a wholesale privatization of formerly state-owned enterprises on a scale unmatched anywhere in the world. In mid-2003 Mozambique was set to benefit from an $11.8 million disbursement from the International Monetary Fund (IMF), following a positive review of its economic performance under the IMF's Poverty Reduction and Growth Facility (PRGF). In 2005 it was reported that Mozambique's economy had

been growing at 8% a year since 1996. In 2006 the World Bank cancelled most of Mozambique's debt as part of a program sponsored by the Group of Eight (G-8) nations, and the following year Chinese President Hu Jintao pledged to provide interest-free loans for agriculture, health, and education.

Despite these measures and a dramatic increase in overall prosperity, more than half of the population reportedly still lives in poverty, and in 2009 an estimated 11.5% of the population was infected with HIV/AIDS. Food insecurity also remains an issue for some 600,000 people affected by cyclical droughts and flooding. The country was hit by particularly damaging floods in February 2007. In March of that same year nearly 100 people were killed in an accidental explosion at a weapons arsenal in the capital, with hundreds more injured.

Former president Joaquim Chissano was chosen for the inaugural Mo Ibrahim Prize in October 2007, which honors a retired African head of state for excellence in leadership. Chissano was chosen for his role in bringing peace to Mozambique.

¹³GOVERNMENT

The constitution of the People's Republic of Mozambique became effective at midnight on 24–25 June 1975. Under the constitution and its revision enacted during 1977–78, Mozambique was a republic in which FRELIMO was the sole legal party. The president was the chief of state; the president of FRELIMO had to be the president of the republic. He acted on the advice of the Council of State Ministers, which he appointed and over which he presided. He also appointed provincial governors. The position of prime minister was created in a 1986 constitutional revision. The National People's Assembly, with 226 members, was the supreme organ of the state. Elections to the Assembly were held in 1977 and 1986, with the candidates chosen from a single FRELIMO slate.

A revised constitution with a multiparty system of government came into force on 30 November 1990. The name of the country was changed from the People's Republic to the Republic of Mozambique. Governmental institutions remain otherwise unchanged. According to the 1990 constitution the president is to be elected by universal adult suffrage for a five-year term and may be reelected only once. The Assembly of the Republic replaced the People's Assembly. Its 250 deputies are to be elected for five-year terms.

¹⁴POLITICAL PARTIES

FRELIMO, the sole legal political party until 1991, was founded in 1962 by the merger of three existing nationalist parties. Formation of FRELIMO did not mean complete political unity. Splinter groups or organizations began to appear in Cairo, Nairobi, and elsewhere, but none of these splinter organizations ever received the support of the Organization of African Unity (OAU), which gave official recognition only to FRELIMO.

In August 1973 five anti-FRELIMO groups formed the National Coalition Party (Partido de Coligação Nacional—PCN). The PCN program called for a referendum on the country's future and the restoration of peace and multiracialism. The organized opposition from the Portuguese community took the form of the Independent Front for the Continuation of Western Rule (Frente Independente de Continuidade Ocidental—FICO, or "I stay"). FICO called for Portugal to continue the war against FRELIMO. In fact, however, the Portuguese government chose to recognize FRELIMO. After the formation of a provisional FRELIMO government in September 1974, the PCN was dissolved and its leaders detained.

Two years after independence, in 1977, FRELIMO was transformed from a liberation movement into a Marxist-Leninist vanguard party dedicated to the creation of a Socialist state. FRELIMO formally downgraded its ideological commitment at its July 1989 congress. Proposals to broaden party membership and decision making were also adopted. The new constitution in force in November 1990 legalized a multiparty system. Since then activity has been vigorous. FRELIMO and RENAMO (created in 1976 as a dissident armed force) have been most popular, the latter especially in the central regions. Parties included the Mozambican National Union (UNAMO), a splinter from RENAMO, and several smaller parties, including the Democratic Party of Mozambique (PADEMO) and the Mozambique National Movement (MONAMO). They geared up for multiparty presidential and legislative elections in October 1994.

The elections were held on 27 October 1994, and FRELIMO took 129 seats, RENAMO 112, and the Democratic Union 9. FRELIMO head Chissano won the presidential election with 53% of the vote to RENAMO's candidate Dhlakama's 33%, with the rest split among 10 candidates.

By 1996 Mozambique had nearly two dozen political parties officially registered with the state. In addition to FRELIMO and RENAMO, the Democratic Union, a coalition of three smaller parties, was founded in 1994. UNAMO ran a strong presidential race, and the Liberal Democrats won almost 2% of the votes in the legislative elections.

In the presidential elections held in December 1999, Dhlakama lost again to Chissano, but gained 14 points over 1994. In the legislative polls, RENAMO's 38.81% was only a slight improvement over 37.7% in 1994. This translated to 133 parliamentary seats against 117 for RENAMO in the 250-seat assembly. In September 2000 Renamo-UE member Raul Domingos was expelled from the party, but he continued to hold his parliamentary seat as an independent. In mid-2002 FRELIMO announced that Armando Guebuza would be its candidate in the 2004 elections following Chissano's announcement earlier that he would not stand for a third term.

Chissano and Dhlakama met a number of times over 2001–2002 to discuss RENAMO's claim that the 1999 elections were rigged. RENAMO threatened to form a separate government in its stronghold, the six central and northern provinces. Barring this radical move, RENAMO leaders demanded that Chissano name the governors of these provinces from among RENAMO's ranks. But Chissano refused to take such action on constitutional grounds. RENAMO's electoral alliance with 10 small parties, the RENAMO-Electoral Union, said that its own parallel count gave Dhlakama 52% in the presidential race and the coalition 50% in the 1999 legislative polls.

Mozambique is dominated by FRELIMO and RENAMO, so much so that it is extremely difficult for anybody to achieve electoral success under the banner of any other party. However, there is a plethora of smaller parties. In the elections held in December 2004, 18 smaller parties, alongside FRELIMO and RENAMO, contested in the elections. However, as expected, FRELIMO and RENAMO shared 92% of the vote while the other 18 parties got

only 8% of the vote. In these elections, FRELIMO got 160 parliamentary seats while RENAMO received 90 seats. The presidential candidate for RENAMO, Armando Guebuza, won 63.7% of the votes, while RENAMO's candidate, Afonso Dhlakama, received 31.7% of the votes in 2004. In the 2009 elections, Guebuza won with just over 76% of the vote; Dhlakama and Simango trailed with 14.9% and 8.8% respectively. In the parliamentary election, FRELIMO won 191 seats, followed by RENAMO with 51 seats and 8 for the MDM. Aires Bonifacio Ali became prime minister in January 2010.

15 LOCAL GOVERNMENT

All of Mozambique outside the capital is organized into 10 provinces subdivided into 128 districts. Districts are further divided into municipalities and localities. The capital city of Maputo is considered an 11th province. Each provincial government is presided over by a governor, who is the representative of the president of the republic and is responsible to FRELIMO and the national government for his activities. Each province also has a provincial assembly which legislates on matters exclusively bearing on that province. District, municipal, and local assemblies were established in 1977; local elections were held in that year and in 1986. Some 20,230 deputies for 894 local assemblies were elected by adult suffrage at age 18 from candidates chosen by local units of FRELIMO or, in their absence, by other local groups. Deputies of the provincial, district, and municipal assemblies were elected by the local bodies.

Elections were held in 1998 and were scheduled again for October 2003. RENAMO boycotted the first local polling in 1998, accusing the government of fraud. That resulted in a turnout of just 14.4% and a landslide victory for FRELIMO. In the November 2003 local assembly elections turnout was generally low, about 30% of the voters, but far better than the turnout in the 1998 elections. The ruling FRELIMO party won in the greater majority of the 33 municipalities. Among the reasons cited for the low turnout in the 2003 local elections and the apathy of voters were an overall lack of trust in political parties and the perception among voters that their votes would not bring about any changes in the government. Nevertheless, EU observers declared the local polling free and fair, but warned that a low voter turnout was a matter of concern for future elections.

16 JUDICIAL SYSTEM

The legal system is based on Portuguese civil law and customary law. The formal justice system is bifurcated into a civil/criminal system under auspices of the Ministry of Justice and a military justice system under joint supervision of the Ministries of Defense and Justice. At the apex is the Supreme Court, which hears appeals from both systems. The provincial and district courts are below the Supreme Court. There are also special courts such as administrative courts, customs courts, fiscal courts, maritime, and labor courts. Local customary courts, part of the civil/criminal system, handle estate, divorce, and other social and family issues. Although the constitution provides for a separate Constitutional Court, one has never been established; in its absence the Supreme Court reviews constitutional cases.

Since abolition of the Revolutionary Military Tribunal and establishment of the Supreme Court in 1988, those accused of crimes against the state are tried in civilian courts under standard criminal procedural rules.

The 1990 constitution declares the establishment of an independent judiciary with judges nominated by other jurists instead of designated by administrative appointment. It is the president, however, who continues to appoint the justices of the Supreme Court.

In nonmilitary courts all criminal defendants enjoy presumptions of innocence, have the right to legal counsel, and the right of appeal; however, the judicial system suffers from lack of qualified judicial personnel and financial resources.

[17] ARMED FORCES

The International Institute for Strategic Studies reports that armed forces in Mozambique totaled 11,200 members in 2011. The force is comprised of 10,000 from the army, 200 from the navy, and 1,000 members of the air force. Armed forces represent 0.1% of the labor force in Mozambique. Defense spending totaled $175.8 million and accounted for 0.8% of gross domestic product (GDP) in 2006.

Mozambique had observers in three UN missions in the region.

[18] INTERNATIONAL COOPERATION

Mozambique was admitted to the UN on 16 September 1975 and takes part in UN Economic Commission for Africa (ECA) and several nonregional specialized agencies, such as the Food and Agriculture Organization (FAO), International Labour Organization (ILO), IMF, the World Bank, UN Educational, Scientific, and Cultural Organization (UNESCO), UNHCR, UN Industrial Development Organization (UNIDO), and the World Health Organization (WHO). The country also belongs to the World Trade Organization (WTO); African, Caribbean and Pacific Group of States (ACP Group), the Commonwealth of Nations, the Organization of the Islamic Conference (OIC), the African Development Bank, G-77, and the African Union. Mozambique plays a leading role in the Southern African Development Community (SADC). Mozambique is a member of the Nonaligned Movement. The country has supported UN operations and missions in East Timor (est. 2002), Burundi (est. 2004), and the Democratic Republic of Congo (DROC; est. 1999). In environmental cooperation, Mozambique is part of the Basel Convention, the Convention on Biological Diversity, the Convention on International Trade in Endangered Species (CITES), the Kyoto Protocol, the Montréal Protocol, the UN Convention on Climate Change, and the UN Convention to Combat Desertification (UNCCD).

[19] ECONOMY

Mozambique, with its agricultural economy and considerable mineral reserves, is a poverty-stricken country. Civil war, ineffective socialist economic policies, and severe droughts plague Mozambique's economy, leaving it heavily dependent on foreign aid. In 2008, it was estimated that more than half of the population lived below the poverty line. As of 2010 unemployment was reported at 21%. Approximately 81% of the population is employed in agriculture, mostly on a small-scale subsistence level. The sector suffers from inadequate infrastructure, commercial networks,

and investment. However, a majority of Mozambique's arable land is still uncultivated, leaving room for considerable growth.

After the country achieved its independence in 1975, the leaders of FRELIMO's military campaign rapidly established a one-party state allied to the Soviet bloc and instituted a socialist style economy. Under this system the economy suffered from the use of outdated data collection systems, geared to a state-managed economy that failed to measure the vitality of the private sector. A brutal civil war from 1977 to 1992 only furthered the country's economic woes.

In the late 1980s the country began a program of economic reform including a privatization program that has been one of the most successful in Africa. Since then more than 1,200 smaller state-owned enterprises have been privatized. Despite the improvements Mozambique remains dependent on foreign aid for a large portion of its annual budget. However, much of its once substantial foreign debt has been reduced to a manageable level through forgiveness and rescheduling under the Heavily Indebted Poor Countries (HIPC) and Enhanced HIPC initiatives run by the World Bank and the IMF.

The 1992 peace accords, which halted the 16-year civil war, brought much needed relief from military activities. The return of rain in 1992 after one of the worst droughts on record and continuing peace meant that many Mozambicans were able to farm their lands again, making them less dependent on food aid. However, the country's economic problems were compounded in 2000 when some of the worst flooding in the history of the country killed and displaced many citizens.

In the decade from 1997 to 2007, Mozambique's GDP grew at an average 9 percent per year. The global economic crisis slowed this growth from 2008–2009. In 2010, the growth rate was 8.3%, but the cost of energy and food rose and there were riots. Growth had slowed to 7.2% in 2011.

Tourism has been targeted as a growth industry for the nation. The development of the tourist sector has been made possible by foreign investment, particularly through companies from South Africa, China, Kuwait, and the United Arab Emirates. In 2010 the government approved deals for 400 new hotels and resorts to be built throughout the country and expected the total investment in the tourism sector to reach about $2 billion within the next decade.

[20] INCOME

Mozambique's gross domestic product (GDP) rate of change as of 2011 was 7.2% and inflation stood at 11.7%. The CIA estimated that in 2011 the GDP of Mozambique was $23.87 billion. The CIA defines GDP as the value of all final goods and services produced within a nation in a given year and computed on the basis of purchasing power parity (PPP) rather than value as measured on the basis of the rate of the exchange based on current dollars. The per capita GDP was estimated at $1,100. It was estimated that agriculture accounted for 28.4% of GDP, industry 26.9%, and services 44.7% in 2011.

According to the World Bank, remittances from citizens living abroad totaled $111.1 million or about $5 per capita and accounted for approximately 0.5% of GDP.

In 2007 the World Bank estimated that Mozambique, with 0.32% of the world's population, accounted for 0.03% of the world's GDP. By comparison the United States, with 4.85% of the world's population, accounted for 22.51% of world GDP.

The World Bank reported that in 2009, household consumption in Mozambique totaled $8.3 billion or about $360 per capita measured in current US dollars rather than PPP. Household consumption includes expenditures of individuals, households, and nongovernmental organizations on goods and services, excluding the purchases of dwellings. It was estimated that household consumption was growing at an average annual rate of 0.4%. In 2011, the World Bank reported that actual individual consumption in Mozambique was 72.7% of GDP and accounted for 0.03% of world consumption. By comparison, the United States accounted for 25.44% of world individual consumption. The World Bank also estimated that 45.6% of Mozambique's GDP was spent on food and beverages, 6.8% on housing and household furnishings, 4.3% on clothes, 3.4% on health, 2.9% on transportation, 0.1% on communications, 1.5% on recreation, 0.3% on restaurants and hotels, and 2.2% on miscellaneous goods and services and purchases from abroad.

It was estimated that in 2001 about 70% of the population subsisted on an income below the poverty line established by Mozambique's government.

21 LABOR

As of 2011 Mozambique had a total labor force of 9.973 million people. Within that labor force CIA estimated that 81% were employed in agriculture, 6% in industry, and 13% in the service sector (figures from 1997). The law provides for workers to organize and join unions, although less than 1% of the workforce are union members. The vast majority of those unionized are in larger urban areas where industries are located. There is a constitutional right to strike with the exception of government employees, police, military personnel, and employees of other essential services. There are two labor federations. The law protects the right of workers to engage in collective bargaining and prohibits anti-union discrimination.

The minimum working age is 15, but many children work on family farms or in the informal urban economy. On 27 April 2011 the government announced new minimum wages. There were 13 different minimum wages, ranging from $54 per month for farm workers to $105 for electricity and gas workers, and $173 in the financial sector. Civil service minimum wages were frozen at $77. None of these minimums provides a living wage, and most workers earn more or engage in additional labor or family farming to supplement their earnings. The legal workweek is 44 hours. The government has enacted health and environmental laws to protect workers, but these provisions are ineffectually enforced.

22 AGRICULTURE

Roughly 6% of the total land is currently farmed, and the country's major crops include cotton, cashew nuts, sugarcane, tea, cassava (tapioca), corn, coconuts, sisal, citrus and tropical fruits, potatoes, and sunflowers. Cereal production in 2009 amounted to 1.8 million tons, fruit production 360,899 tons, and vegetable production 207,129 tons. The majority of Mozambique's workforce is employed in subsistence agriculture, which has been greatly affected by periodic drought and flooding. Agricultural pursuits supported over 81% of the population and provided about 28.4% of the

GDP in 2011. Since independence there has been a serious decline in agricultural production, attributed to the collapse of rural transport and marketing systems when Portuguese farmers and traders left the country. In the 1980s state farms received the bulk of agricultural investment, but the yields were poor.

In April 2010 the government reported the largest cashew nut crop since 1997, with production at more than 95,000 tons. Cashew nut production is expected to reach 120,000 tons a year by 2015. Mozambique is a net importer of food; in 2004 the trade deficit in agricultural products was $218.6 million.

In 2009 USAID launched a four-year $20 million agro-business program in Mozambique designed to improve the competitiveness of private sector agriculture. The program targeted eight crops, known as value chains, as being most profitable based on demand and production potential. These value chains include maize, soybeans, bananas, and cashew nuts. Forestry was also included in the program.

23 ANIMAL HUSBANDRY

The FAO reported that Mozambique dedicated 44 million hectares (108.7 million acres) to permanent pasture or meadow in 2009. Animal husbandry, however, is an underdeveloped sector in the Mozambican economy. A lack of credit, deadly epizootic diseases, and other diseases carried by the tsetse fly make a commercially viable animal husbandry industry impractical for many African traditional farmers, who predominate in this sector. In 2009 the country tended 18 million chickens, 1.2 million head of cattle, and 1.3 million pigs. The production from these animals amounted to 29,333 tons of beef and veal, 98,033 tons of pork, 32,513 tons of poultry, 11,634 tons of eggs, and 89,991 tons of milk. Mozambique also produced 2,500 tons of cattle hide.

24 FISHING

The potential catch is estimated at 500,000 tons of fish and 14,000 tons of prawns. In 2008 Mozambique had 328 decked commercial fishing boats. The annual capture totaled 119,645 tons according to the FAO. The export value of seafood totaled $96.4 million. South African trawlers are allowed to fish in Mozambican waters in return for providing a portion of their catch to Mozambique. The EU and Japan have each entered into agreements designed to help develop the fishing industry.

25 FORESTRY

Approximately 50% of Mozambique is covered by forest, which constitute an estimated 30.6 million hectares (75.6 million acres). Wood production is from natural forests and is almost entirely consumed by the local rural populations for fuel and construction. The timber industry is centered along the Beira Railroad and in Zambézia Province where sawn and construction timber are produced for the nearby South African market. The FAO estimated the 2009 roundwood production at 1.3 million cu m (46.1 million cu ft). The value of all forest products, including roundwood, totaled $81.1 million.

26 MINING

Mozambique's rich mineral deposits remain largely undeveloped. After the end of the civil war, efforts began to revive the economy, with the minerals sector playing an important role. In 2011 mining accounted for 3% of GDP. In 2009 Mozambique produced bauxite, beryl, marine salt, cement, gravel and crushed rock, marble (block and slab), limestone, sands and tantalite. Zambézia, Nampula, and Tete provinces had large deposits of columbite, tantalite, beryl, semiprecious stones, feldspar, kaolin, and coal. Manica Province produced copper and bauxite. Also known to occur were deposits of diatomite, fluorspar, guano, gypsum, iron ore, limestone, manganese, mica, nepheline syenite, perlite, phosphate rock (resources of 274 million tons), rare earths, silica sand, precious and ornamental stones (agate, amethyst, aquamarine, emerald, garnet, jasper, morganite, rose quartz, tigereye, and tourmaline), and titanium. Resources of heavy-mineral sands totaled 14 billion tons containing 300 million tons of ilmenite, as well as zircon and rutile.

Production of bauxite totaled 3,612 metric tons in 2009, down from 5,443 metric tons in 2008. Gold was also produced in 2009 by artisanal miners. Official production of gold in 2009 totaled 511 kg, up from 298 kg in 2008. Limestone, gravel and crushed rock, marine salt, sands and granite were also produced in 2003. Mozambique's only graphite mine closed in 1999 because of a tax dispute. Most of Mozambique's mining and mineral processing operations were privately owned, including the cement plants, the Marropino tantalum mine, the Moma mineral sands mine, and the Mozal aluminum smelter.

27 ENERGY AND POWER

In August 2010 Anadarko Petroleum Corporation, the second-largest natural gas producer in the United States, discovered oil in the Rovuma Basin of the northern province of Cabo Delgado. Anadarko was granted exploration rights in 2006. Although the discovery sparked a great deal of optimism, the company must still conduct further investigations to determine the commercial viability of the find. Oil companies from Malaysia, Norway, and Italy are also currently conducting exploration projects in Mozambique. Also in August 2010 the government announced its approval for a $2 billion hydroelectric project to be built on the Zambezi River downstream from the existing Cahora Bassa project. The state-owned electric company Electricidade de Moçambique (EDM) will maintain 20% ownership of the project, with the remainder owned by the fifty-fifty joint venture of Energia Capital (Mozambique) and Camargo Correia (Brazil). The new Mphanda Nkuwa facility is expected to generate 1,500 megawatts of electricity when completed.

As of 1 January 2008 Mozambique had natural gas reserves of 127.4 billion cu m. Recoverable coal reserves have been placed at 234 million short tons, but additional reserves in the country's Moatize mines in the northwestern part of the country have been estimated at 2.4 billion short tons.

Mozambique is totally reliant upon imports of refined petroleum products.

Mozambique's electric power sector is heavily based upon hydroelectric generation. The World Bank reported in 2008 that Mozambique produced 15.1 billion kWh of electricity and consumed 10.3 billion kWh, or 450 kWh per capita. Roughly 7% of energy came from fossil fuels while 14% came from alternative fuels.

A proposed hydroelectric dam project along the Zambezi has received strong criticism from international and local environmentalists who believe that the construction of dams for hydroelectricity may limit the supply of water to the greater region. As of 2009 only 20% of the population of Mozambique had access to electricity. The new dam project would provide power primarily for neighboring South Africa. Non-government groups such as the Maputo-based Justica Ambiental (JA) are encouraging the government to continue considering green options such as biofuels, solar, and wind for the nation's power needs rather than the large-scale dams that produce large quantities of cheap electricity at the expense of the environment.

In March 2009 the Brazilian-owned mining company Vale announced plans for a $1.3 billion coal mining project that is expected to produce 11 million tons of coal per year. The mine will produce both metallurgical coal, used in the production of steel, and thermal coal, used in the generation of electricity. Most of the product will be exported. In 2009 the state-owned fuel company Petromoc announced that its biofuel project was producing nearly 80,000 liters (21,100 gallons) of biofuel per day. The fuel is produced primarily from copra (dried coconut meat). Petromac announced plans to expand production by also increasing harvests of copra and jathropa. The seeds of the jathropa shrub are used to produce biofuel oil.

In February 2010 Anadarko announced that it had discovered a deepwater natural gas well about thirty miles off the coast of Mozambique. The discovery was significant in that it represents the first major natural gas find off the coast of east Africa, a huge geographic area where exploration had been intensifying.

In May 2010 the state-owned energy company CMH secured a $100 million loan from the Development Bank of Southern Africa and the French Development Agency (AFD) for the expansion of natural gas production operations in the country. CMH will use the funds to realize its financing obligations with the South African company Sasol, which operates a facility in the southern province of Inhambane, Mozambique.

28 INDUSTRY

Manufacturing is centered mostly in food processing and beverages. Food, beverages, and tobacco processing account for 62% of all manufacturing. Industry is concentrated around the larger cities of Maputo, Matola, Beira, and Nampula. Mozambique's industrial sector is primarily centered on the processing of locally produced raw materials, such as sugar, cashews, tea, and wheat. Brewing and textile production emerged in the 1980s along with cement, fertilizer, and agricultural implement manufacturing. Other industries make glass, soaps, oils, ceramics, paper, tires, railway equipment, radios, bicycles, and matches. Major investments in aluminum processing, steel production, mineral extraction, fertilizer, and sugar production have been planned. According to the CIA, Mozambique had an industrial production growth rate of 8% in 2010.

Economic reforms of the early 1990s promoted private ownership of industry and brought about a significant decline in the number of parastatals; from 1990 to 2000 over 1,200 smaller businesses had been divested and 37 large enterprises had been privatized. Only 11 large state-owned companies remained including the national airline, telephone, electricity, insurance, oil and gas exploration, port and rail, airports, water supply, and fuel distri-

Principal Trading Partners – Mozambique (2010)

(In millions of US dollars)

Country	Total	Exports	Imports	Balance
World	7,750.0	3,200.0	4,550.0	-1,350.0
Netherlands	1,824.9	1,182.0	642.9	539.0
South Africa	1,693.1	466.3	1,226.8	-760.5
Portugal	262.5	108.3	154.2	-45.8
India	232.1	30.4	201.7	-171.3
China	209.6	79.6	130.0	-50.5
Japan	130.1	3.9	126.3	-122.4
Germany	99.9	20.4	79.5	-59.1
United States	90.7	16.4	74.3	-57.8
Togo	64.8	3.0	61.7	-58.7
United Kingdom	58.8	1.4	57.4	-56.1

(…) data not available or not significant.

(n.s.) not specified.

SOURCE: *2011 Direction of Trade Statistics Yearbook,* New York: United Nations, 2011.

Balance of Payments – Mozambique (2010)

(In millions of US dollars)

Current Account		**-1,113.3**
Balance on goods		-1,179.2
Imports	-3,512.4	
Exports	2,333.3	
Balance on services		-506.3
Balance on income		-84.6
Current transfers		656.8
Capital Account		**345.5**
Financial Account		**768.9**
Direct investment abroad		0.8
Direct investment in Mozambique		789.0
Portfolio investment assets		0.3
Portfolio investment liabilities		1.1
Financial derivatives		…
Other investment assets		-179.5
Other investment liabilities		157.2
Net Errors and Omissions		**66.5**
Reserves and Related Items		**-67.7**

(…) data not available or not significant.

SOURCE: *Balance of Payment Statistics Yearbook 2011,* Washington, DC: International Monetary Fund, 2011.

29 SCIENCE AND TECHNOLOGY

According to the World Bank, patent applications in science and technology as of 2009 totaled 18 in Mozambique. Public financing of science was 0.53% of GDP. Eduardo Mondlane University in Maputo, founded in 1962, has faculties of agricultural sciences, biology, engineering, mathematics, medicine, veterinary science, and sciences. Maputo also has the National Directorate of Geology, the Cotton Research Institute, the National Institute of Health, and the Meteorological Service. In 2008 Mozambique's high technology exports were 3.6 % of its manufactured exports.

30 DOMESTIC TRADE

The cities of Maputo, Beira, and Nampula are the main centers of commercial life, where it is estimated that 50% of all imported products are consumed. Maputo and Beira are trading centers and ports of entry. There is not a well-established distribution system for local or imported goods. Many local manufacturers sell or distribute their products on their own. Larger retailers import high volumes of goods and sell the excess to other smaller retailers. National distribution of regional products has been hindered by a poor transportation system. Credit cards are not widely accepted.

Business hours are 8:30 a.m. to noon and 2 to 5 p.m. Mondays through Fridays, and 8 a.m. to 12 noon on Saturdays.

31 FOREIGN TRADE

Mozambique imported $3.846 billion worth of goods and services in 2011, while exporting $2.646 billion worth of goods and services. Major import partners in 2010 were South Africa 28.6%, China 10.3%, Australia 7.2%, India 5.8%, US 4.7%, and Portugal 4.1%.. There is a considerable amount of unofficial trade along the borders as well as unreported fish exports to Asia.

Traditionally, shrimp accounted for the largest portion of Mozambique's export revenues (26%). Other exports included electric current (23%), fruits and nuts (15%), cotton (7.3%), and sugar (2.1%). In 2011 Mozambique's exports were worth $2.3 billion. Commodities exported included aluminum, cashew nuts, prawns, cotton, sugar, citrus, timber, bulk electricity, and natural gas. Main markets were Belgium, South Africa, and Zimbabwe.

32 BALANCE OF PAYMENTS

Mozambique has traditionally had a balance of payments deficit and relies heavily on imported consumer and capital goods. In 2010 Mozambique had a foreign trade deficit of $1.8 billion amounting to 10.3% of GDP. The current account deficit was -$1.385 billion in 2011, compared to the 2010 figure of -$999 million.

Mozambique is taking steps to improve its trade balance, however, by increasing the production of locally manufactured and agricultural goods. By the early 2000s exports had risen over 40% since 1996. A faster rise in export earnings has been hampered in part by bankruptcies in the cashew processing industry and poor prices for the sale of electricity generated by the Cahora Bassa hydroelectric dam.

In 1999 Mozambique qualified for $3.7 billion in debt service relief under the HIPC initiative. This amount was subsequently augmented to $4.3 billion. This debt relief improved the country's

bution companies. Government policy now supports the development of private enterprise fully.

The construction sector showed strong growth in the early 2000s, as projects to rebuild roads, bridges, schools, clinics, and other basic infrastructure were underway. There are considerable natural gas reserves, both onshore and offshore, but they have yet to be fully developed. As of 2011 Mozambique was still seeking investors in the oil refinery sector as the two oil refinery projects the government approved were put on hold by investors following the financial crisis that hit most developed economies. In addition, the Moma titanium mine has been a benefit for the economy as it produced about 7% of world supply titanium minerals.

balance of payments. Prior to HIPC approval Mozambique owed $8.3 billion in foreign debt. HIPC reduced the eligible debts held by participating creditors by 90% or close to $3 billion.

³³BANKING AND SECURITIES

The Mozambican branch of the defunct Portuguese National Overseas Bank was nationalized without compensation. By a decree of 23 May 1975 it was reconstituted as the Bank of Mozambique (Banco de Moçambique—BM). Functioning as a central bank, it served as the government's banker and financial adviser and as controller of monetary and credit policies. It was also an issuing bank, a commercial bank, and the state treasury; the bank managed Mozambique's external assets and acted as an intermediary in all international monetary transactions.

In 1978 the government nationalized four of the five remaining commercial banks; the Banco Standard Totta de Moçambique remained private. In that year a second state bank, the People's Investment Bank, was created and given responsibility for supervising a building society, the Mozambique Credit Institute (the industrial bank), and the National Development Bank.

After 1992 the government's economic reform program began to tackle the financial sector. Foreign banks were allowed to invest in Mozambican financial institutions, in 1994 interest rates were deregulated, and in 1995 the commercial activities of the central bank were assumed by a newly created institution, the Banco Comercial de Moçambique (BCM). By 1997 the government had privatized the BCM and the Banco Popular de Desenvolvimento (BPD).

In 2011 the commercial bank prime lending rate, the rate which banks lend to customers, was 16%. The discount rate in 2010, the interest rate at which the central bank lends to financial institutions in the short term, was 3.25%.

³⁴INSURANCE

In 1977 all insurance companies were nationalized and Empresa Moçambicana de Seguros was established as the sole state insurance enterprise. This company continued functioning during 2012, although the government had plans to sell minority holdings in the company.

³⁵PUBLIC FINANCE

The government's role in the economy has diminished during the past decade as the country has recovered from civil war. Preparations for privatization of many state-run industries and utilities began in 2002, and the tax code was revised.

The CIA estimated that Mozambique's central government took in revenues of approximately $3.342 billion and had expenditures of $3.986 billion in 2011. Revenues minus expenditures totaled approximately -$644 million. Total external debt was $5.437 billion. In 2010 the budget of Mozambique included $2.346 billion in public revenue and $2.898 billion in public expenditures. The budget deficit amounted to 5.3% of GDP in 2011. Public debt was 43% of GDP, with $5.437 billion of the debt held by foreign entities.

³⁶TAXATION

Under Portuguese rule, taxation and tax collection were full of inequities and corruption at all levels of government. In 1978, after independence, much higher and more progressive taxes were introduced. These included an income tax on wages, salaries, and other benefits. As of 2005 Mozambique had a standard corporate tax rate of 32%. However, income derived from the breeding and agricultural sectors was subject to a 10% rate for the period 2003 through 2010. Capital gains and branch offices are taxed at the corporate rate. Dividends, interest, and royalties are subject to a 20% withholding tax. A VAT with a standard rate of 17% (as of 2005) is charged on most goods and services. Exemptions from VAT include basic foodstuffs, medicines and pharmaceuticals, books and journals, bicycles, agricultural inputs and fishing implements, waste disposal, and burial and cremation services.

³⁷CUSTOMS AND DUTIES

Both import and export licenses are required for all goods. The average nominal customs tariff rate was reduced from 18% to around 10% in 1996, although duties on imported goods ranged from 0–30%, depending upon whether it is a primary, intermediate, or consumer good. In 2008 the Mozambican parliament reduced duties per agreements with the SADC. Certain products, such as potatoes, beans, and most fruits from South Africa, retained a 15% duty through 2010 in an effort to protect domestic agricultural industries. The country chaired the SADC from 1990 to 2000 and houses its Communications Commission (SATCC) in Maputo.

³⁸FOREIGN INVESTMENT

The liberalizing of Mozambique's economy began with the initiation of its economic recovery plan (ERP) in January 1987. Included in the program were measures to stimulate the private sector, an effort reinforced in 1990 by further legislation. In June 1993 the investment code was reformed to put foreign and local investors on an equal footing with respect to fiscal and customs regulations. The parastatal sector has been progressively privatized..

Certain tax incentives are available to encourage foreign direct investment (FDI), including a 50–80% reduction in taxes. The flow of capital is liberal. Regulations issued in 1999 established an Industrial Free Zone Council, which approved the first free zone enterprise in Maputo—Mozal, an aluminum smelter. Companies in the free zone must engage in nontraditional industry and export at least 85% of production.

In 1998 FDI inflow to Mozambique totaled about $235 million, up 365% from 1997. FDI inflows peaked at $382 million in 1999 then fell to $139 billion in 2000. In the period 1998 to 2000 Mozambique's share of world FDI inflows was almost twice its share of world GDP, a considerable improvement on its performance 1988 to 1990, when its share of FDI flows was only 30% of its share of world GDP. In 2009 FDI in Mozambique was a net inflow of $881.2 million, according to World Bank figures published in 2009, which represented 9% of GDP.

The leading sectors for foreign investment in Mozambique have been industry, agribusiness and fishing, finance, and tourism. The driving force behind the country's FDI inflows has been mining and some processing industries. Put together they had drawn global transnational corporations (TNCs) into the economy. In recent years these TNCs have not invested in any major projects. Many projects in the pipeline have not become operational.

³⁹ECONOMIC DEVELOPMENT

The government of Mozambique has abandoned its postindependence preference for a socialist organization of society, which it had tried to effect through the creation of cooperatives, state farms, and industries. In cooperation with the IMF, Mozambique is reforming its economy and preparing for a post-civil war period of economic growth. Progress has been slow, however. Growth sectors include agriculture and related processing industries, transportation, and mining.

In 1999 Mozambique's eligible debts were reduced by 90% by the IMF, World Bank, the Paris Club, and other multilateral lending agencies under the HIPC initiative. The country also hoped for 100% debt relief from the United States and gained complete debt cancellation from the United Kingdom. Debt stood at $8.3 billion before 1999 and $5.7 billion after reforms. A variety of infrastructure development projects have been carried out, including a road and railway from Maputo to Johannesburg.

The Economist Intelligence Unit forecasts that the economic expansion Mozambique experienced between 2000–2005 will continue for the next few years, boosted by overall macroeconomic stability, policy reforms and continuing strong donor support against a background of broad-based expansion across most sectors of the economy, including agriculture, transportation, and tourism sectors. Over 1,200 state-owned enterprises were privatized, most of them small. In 2003 Mozambique was operating under a three-year $76 million PRGF Arrangement with the IMF. Floods in 2000 and food shortages in 2002 curtailed economic development. Riverine flooding damaged some 32,000 hectares (79,073 acres) of crops and rendered unusable 22,610 hectares (55,871 acres) of cropland in 2011. This loss had a local impact, although it represented less than 1 percent of national cropland.

⁴⁰SOCIAL DEVELOPMENT

Foreign aid is used in assisting Mozambican Labor and Social Welfare Ministries with building infrastructure to benefit the most disadvantaged groups in the country including disabled and abandoned children. The country is upgrading employment and professional training centers.

Despite government rhetoric and constitutional provisions mandating equal rights for both sexes, legal and social discrimination against women is pervasive. Women may not work outside of the home without the husband's permission. Inheritance rights, furthermore, strongly favor men over women. Tradition and custom lead many families to withdraw their daughters from school at an early age. Sexual harassment in the workplace is prevalent. Domestic violence against women, including beating and spousal rape, is widespread. Women believe that their husbands have the right to beat them. However, in 2011 almost 40 percent of the People's Assembly was made up of women. Child prostitution persists, and there is continuing abuse and exploitation of street children in urban areas.

Human rights abuses have been in decline, but there is evidence of systemic police brutality. Prison conditions are poor and, in some cases, life threatening.

⁴¹HEALTH

Almost all health care services are provided by the government's National Health Service. The army maintains its own health posts and two hospitals. Traditional healers continue to play a significant role. All medical products must be registered with the Ministry of Health and, due to currency constraints, Mozambique is entirely dependent on bilateral and multilateral donors for its drug needs. Only 39% of the population has access to health care services. In 2011 the country spent 4.7% of its GDP on healthcare, amounting to $25 per person.

According to the CIA, life expectancy in Mozambique was 52 years in 2012. There were 0.027 physicians, 3 nurses and midwives, and 8 hospital beds per 10,000 inhabitants. The shortage of medical supplies and trained personnel has remained severe throughout Mozambique. In 2007 immunization rates were as follows: tuberculosis 84%; diphtheria, pertussis, and tetanus 72%; polio 71%; and measles 77%.

In 2012 the fertility rate was 5.4, while the infant mortality rate was 76.85 per 1,000 live births. Only 6% of women of the ages 15 to 49 used contraception as of 2007. An estimated 20% of all births were underweight. The maternal mortality rate in 1989–95 skyrocketed to 1,500 per 100,000 live births, but in 2008 the maternal mortality rate, according to the World Bank, was 550 per 100,000 births.

The prevalence of HIV/AIDS has severely impacted the people of Mozambique, with some 12.5% of adults affected by the epidemic, representing one of the highest prevalence rates in the world. In 2010 the United States agreed to finance a $1 billion program aimed at reducing the trend of new HIV infections and providing greater access to treatment for those suffering with HIV/AIDS. The program was expected to run from 2010 through 2015 and represented the latest of continuing partnerships with the United States in the fight against the disease. In 2004 the United States offered $37.5 million in funds for HIV/AIDS related programs. Funding for 2009 was boosted to $250 million. The CIA calculated HIV/AIDS prevalence in Mozambique to be about 11.5% (for those of all ages) in 2009.

⁴²HOUSING

At last estimate more than 60% of housing units were constructed of woven straw, about 15% of cane and wood sticks, and nearly 10% of bricks and concrete. In 2008, less than half of Mozambicans had access to clean water. Approximately 65% of all households use well water, nearly 20% river and spring water, almost 10% piped outdoor water, and less than 5% piped indoor water. Nearly 96% were without electricity and 83 percent did not have access to adequate sanitation facilities.

⁴³EDUCATION

The education system in Mozambique has slowly been rebuilt after the civil war, which destroyed at least 50% of primary schools. In 1990 private schooling was reintroduced. Education is compulsory for seven years, but in practice, most students do not study for the full compulsory period. Primary school covers the first seven years. This is followed by five years of general secondary education or five years of technical school. The academic year runs from August to June.

In 2009 the World Bank estimated that 91% of age-eligible children in Mozambique were enrolled in primary school. Secondary enrollment for age-eligible children stood at 15%. Overall, the CIA estimated that Mozambique had a literacy rate of 47.8%. The adult literacy rate for 2004 was estimated at about 47%, with 62.3% for men and 31.4% for women. Public expenditure on education represented 5.0% of GDP. The student-to-teacher ratio for primary school was at about 66:1 in 2005; the ratio for secondary school was about 32:1.

Eduardo Mondlane University is established in Maputo. The objective of the government is to promote the spread of education at all levels through democratization guided by the state. In 2005 about 1% of the tertiary age population was enrolled in some type of higher education program.

44 LIBRARIES AND MUSEUMS

The National Library of Mozambique, founded in 1961, contains 110,000 volumes. There is a small public library system. The principal museums in Maputo are the Museum of Natural History, founded in 1911, specializing in natural history and ethnography; the Freire de Andrade Museum, specializing in minerals; and the Military History Museum. Beira and Nampula have general museums, Manica has a natural history museum, and Isla da Inhaca, near Maputo, has a museum of marine biology. The National Museum of Ethnology is in Nampula.

45 MEDIA

Postal and telecommunications services are government-operated. In the larger cities telephones are automatic. In 2010 there were 88,100 landlines and 7.224 million mobile cell phones in use, an average of 35 per 100 people.

Radio Moçambique, the official radio service, broadcasts in Portuguese, English, Afrikaans, and local languages. TV Mozambique is the government-owned television service. Several private stations are operational, including about 40 community radio and television stations that are partially subsidized by the government and UNESCO.

In 2009 Mozambique became the direct beneficiary of a $600 million undersea broadband investment project that promised to revolutionize commerce and education in one of the least-connected areas of the world. The project was commissioned by SEACOM, an umbrella organization that included local African governments and telecommunication companies and involved 9,300 miles of undersea fiber optic cables running through the Indian Ocean from South Africa to Kenya. The SEACOM cable carried the promise of affordable, fast Internet for millions in the East African region. In 2011 the country had 82,804 Internet hosts. In 2009 Internet users numbered 3 per 100 citizens.

Major daily newspapers included *Notícias* and *Diario do Moçambique*. Both papers are representative of the ruling party, as is the weekly publication *Domingo*. There are a number of smaller independent publications.

The constitution, the 1991 Press Law, and the 1992 Rome Peace Accords provide for free expression including free speech and a free press; however, though some improvements were reported, the government has restricted some press freedoms.

46 ORGANIZATIONS

The Mozambique Chamber of Commerce, founded in 1980, is located in Maputo. Only a small percentage of the nation's workers belong to unions. There is a national teachers' union.

FRELIMO has emphasized mass organizations, such as the Organization of Mozambican Women and the Organization of Mozambican Youth. Scouting programs and active chapters of the YMCA/YWCA are available for youth. There are also several sports associations promoting competitions for amateur athletes.

There are national chapters of the Red Cross Society, Habitat for Humanity, the Society of St. Vincent de Paul, the UN Children's Fund (UNICEF), and Caritas.

47 TOURISM, TRAVEL, AND RECREATION

Tourism is regarded as a major growth industry for the nation, which has reported an increase in the number of tourists from 250,000 in 2000 to 3.1 million in 2009. The *Tourism Factbook*, published by the UN World Tourism Organization, reported 3.11 million incoming tourists to Mozambique in 2009, who spent a total of $217 million. Of those incoming tourists, there were 2.6 million from Africa. There were 18,412 hotel beds available in Mozambique, which had an occupancy rate of 27%. The estimated daily cost to visit Maputo, the capital, was $238. The cost of visiting other cities averaged $220. In 2010 tourism accounted for 2.5% of the GDP. The government would like to see that rise to 7% by 2025.

The coastal town of Pemba offers the third-largest natural bay in the world with white sand beaches and coral reefs that can be easily reached by most swimmers. Diving and water sports are popular in this town. The northern half of Mozambique Island, which has a number of old churches and mosques, has been declared a UNESCO World Heritage Site.

All foreign nationals need visas, which must be obtained prior to traveling. Yellow fever immunizations are required if traveling from an infected country.

48 FAMOUS PERSONS

Eduardo C. Mondlane (1920–69) was the first president of FRELIMO. His successor and later the first president of independent Mozambique, was Samora Moïsés Machel (1933–86). Joaquim Alberto Chissano (b. 1939), foreign minister since independence, succeeded Machel as president in 1986; he served until 2005 and was succeeded by Armando Guebuza (b. 1943). Chissano won the Mo Ibrahim Prize in 2007.

49 DEPENDENCIES

Mozambique has no territories or colonies.

50 BIBLIOGRAPHY

Azevedo, Mario, Emmanuel Nnadozie, and Tome Mbuia Joao. *Historical Dictionary of Mozambique.* 2nd ed. Lanham, MD: Scarecrow Press, 2003.

Fitzpatrick, Mary. *Mozambique.* 3rd ed. Hawthorne, Victoria, Australia: Lonely Planet, 2010.

Harmon, Daniel E. *Southeast Africa: 1880 to the Present: Reclaiming a Region of Natural Wealth.* Philadelphia: Chelsea House Publishers, 2002.

Manning, Carrie L. *The Politics of Peace in Mozambique: Post-conflict Democratization, 1992–2000*. Westport: CT: Praeger, 2002.

McElrath, Karen, ed. *HIV and AIDS: A Global View*. Westport, CT: Greenwood Press, 2002.

Mozambique Investment and Business Guide: Strategic and Practical Information. Washington, DC: International Business Publications USA, 2012.

Ndege, George O. *Culture and Customs of Mozambique*. Westport, CT: Greenwood Press, 2007.

Rotberg, Robert I. *Ending Autocracy, Enabling Democracy: The Tribulations of Southern Africa, 1960–2000*. Cambridge, MA: World Peace Foundation, 2002.

Zeilig, Leo, and David Seddon. *A Political and Economic Dictionary of Africa*. Philadelphia: Routledge/Taylor and Francis, 2005.

NAMIBIA

Republic of Namibia

CAPITAL: Windhoek

FLAG: A wide red stripe edged by narrow white stripes divides the flag diagonally from lower hoist corner to upper fly corner; the upper hoist-side triangle is blue and charged with a yellow, 12-rayed sunburst; the lower fly-side triangle is green.

ANTHEM: *Namibia, Land of the Brave.*

MONETARY UNIT: The Namibian dollar (NAD) of 100 cents is in use; NAD1 = US$0.12051 (or US$1 = NAD8.29) as of 2011.

WEIGHTS AND MEASURES: The metric system is in use.

HOLIDAYS: New Year's Day, 1 January; Independence Day, 21 March; Workers' Day, 1 May; Casinga Day, 4 May; Africa Day, 25 May; Ascension Day, June 2; Heroes' Day, 26 August; Human Rights Day, 10 December; Christmas, 25–26 December. Movable religious holidays include Easter and Easter Monday.

TIME: 2 p.m. = noon GMT.

¹LOCATION, SIZE, AND EXTENT

A vast land of desert and semidesert along the southwestern coast of Africa, Namibia covers 825,418 sq km (318,696 sq mi). Comparatively, the area occupied by Namibia is slightly more than half the size of the state of Alaska. It extends 1,498 km (931 mi) SSE–NNW and 880 km (547 mi) ENE–WSW (excluding the Caprivi Strip). Namibia is bordered by Angola and Zambia in the N, by Botswana in the E, by South Africa to the SE and S, and by the Atlantic Ocean to the W, with a total land boundary length of 3,936 km (2,446 mi) and a coastline of 1,572 km (977 mi).

The enclave of Walvis Bay (1,124 sq km/434 sq mi) was administered from 1977 to 1994 as part of South Africa's Cape Province, as were 13 offshore islands. Walvis Bay was reincorporated into Namibia on 1 March 1994. Namibia's capital city, Windhoek, is in the center of the country.

²TOPOGRAPHY

Namibia is largely an elevated, waterless plateau partly suitable for arid grazing. The average altitude is 1,080 m (3,543 ft) above sea level; the high point, near the coast, is Konigstein, at 2,606 m (8,550 ft). Along almost the entire range of the coast there are sandy wastes and high, reddish sand dunes. The coastal strip comprises the Namib Desert, and the eastern region is part of the Kalahari Desert. All four permanent rivers form borders: the Kunene and Okavango in the north, the Zambezi in the northeast, and the Orange (Oranje) in the south.

³CLIMATE

Namibia's climate is the driest in Africa, with sunny, warm days and cooler nights, especially during the winter months. The average temperature along the coast is the summer is 23°C (73°F); in winter, the average temperature is 13°C (55°F). The fertile

northern strip is always warmer, having a climate similar to that of southern Angola.

Much of Namibia is a land of perennial drought. The annual rainfall, which is concentrated in the November-March period, generally averages more than 70 cm (28 in) in the far north, 2.5–15 cm (1–6 in) in the south, and 35 cm (14 in) in the central plateau. But the rains often fail: some regions have gone nearly a century without a drop of rain.

⁴FLORA AND FAUNA

The World Resources Institute estimates that there are 3,174 plant species in Namibia. In addition, Namibia is home to 192 species of mammals, 619 species of birds, 215 species of reptiles, and 40 species of amphibians. This calculation reflects the total number of distinct species residing in the country, not the number of endemic species. The Namibian Wildlife Trust, organized in 1982, works closely with the Department of Nature Conservation to maintain the habitat and to prevent poaching of threatened fauna and avifauna. Twelve nature conservation areas cover 99,616 sq km (38,462 sq mi). Among these are the 22,270 sq km (8,603 sq mi) Etosha National Park, one of Africa's best-run and least-visited animal preserves; a smaller game park near Windhoek; and the Namib Desert Park (23,401 sq km/9,035 sq mi), east of Swakopmund. There is a seal reserve at Cape Cross, north of Swakopmund.

In the game parks and the neighboring grazing areas, there are the tallest elephants in the world, along with rhinoceroses; an abundance of lions, cheetahs, and leopards; ostriches; and a profusion of ungulates, including the giraffe, zebra, kudu, eland, black-faced impala, hartebeest, springbok, gemsbok, and wildebeest. Namibia is one of two countries in the world (with Mali) where there are elephants living in desert conditions. Desert elephants tend to have smaller bodies and larger feet than other elephants. Birds of prey are numerous, as are the Kori bustard and the Karroo korhaan. Among the unique flora are the desert welwitschia and many varieties of aloe. According to a 2011 report issued by the International Union for Conservation of Nature and Natural Resources (IUCN), the number of threatened species included 12 types of mammals, 25 species of birds, 4 types of reptiles, 1 species of amphibian, 27 species of fish, and 26 species of plants. Threatened species include the black rhino, cave catfish, and the wild dog. Burchell's zebra has become extinct.

⁵ENVIRONMENT

Namibia's environmental concerns include water pollution and insufficient water for its population. Nearly all of the urban population has safe water. The United Nations (UN) reported in 2008 that carbon dioxide emissions in Namibia totaled 3,034 kilotons. Deforestation and soil erosion also threaten the nation's land. Agricultural chemicals, such as dichlorodiphenyltrichloroethane (DDT), pose a threat to the environment due to excessive usage. The World Resources Institute reported that Namibia had designated 4.28 million hectares (10.58 million acres) of land for protection as of 2006. Water resources totaled 45.5 cu km (10.92 cu mi) while water usage was 0.3 cu km (0.072 cu mi) per year. Domestic water usage accounted for 24% of total usage, industrial for 5%, and agricultural for 71%. Per capita water usage totaled 148 cu m (5,227 cu ft) per year.

⁶POPULATION

The US Central Intelligence Agency (CIA) estimated the population of Namibia in 2011 to be approximately 2,147,585, which placed it at number 140 in population among the 196 nations of the world. In 2011 approximately 4.1% of the population was over 65 years of age, with another 34.2% under 15 years of age. The median age in Namibia was 21.7 years. There were 1.01 males for every female in the country. The population's annual rate of change was 0.873%. The projected population for the year 2025 was 2,800,000. Population density in Namibia was calculated at 3 people per sq km (8 people per sq mi).

The UN estimated that 38% of the population lived in urban areas in 2010, and that urban populations had an annual rate of change of 3.3%. The largest urban area was Windhoek, with a population of 342,000 in 2009.

The prevalence of HIV/AIDS has had a significant impact on the population of Namibia. The AIDS epidemic causes higher death and infant mortality rates, and lowers life expectancy.

⁷MIGRATION

Estimates of Namibia's net migration rate, carried out by the CIA in 2011, amounted to 0.20 migrants per 1,000 citizens. The total number of emigrants living abroad was 16,500, and the total number of immigrants living in Namibia was 138,900. Namibia also accepted 4,700 refugees. Namibia's migrant labor force exceeds 100,000. Ovambo from northern Namibia have moved south since the 1920s to work in the diamond mines near the mouth of the Orange River, in the port of Walvis Bay, and in the cities and towns of the interior. Ovambo formerly migrated by the thousands to work in the gold mines of South Africa, but that traffic has diminished. Some Ovambo have gravitated from neighboring

Angola into northern Namibia. The resurgence of war in Angola in mid-1998 drove thousands of refugees into Namibia.

⁸ETHNIC GROUPS

About 87.5% of the population is black; 6% is white; and 6.5% is mixed. Approximately 50% of total population belong to the Ovambo tribe, the largest group, who live mainly in the well-watered north. The second-largest group, constituting 9% of the population, is the Kavango, who reside along the Okavango River. The Damara, accounting for 7% of the populace, live east of the arid coast and to the south of the Ovambo, and the Herero, a herding people who live north of Windhoek, account for another 7%. The Nama, herders in the deep south, make up 5% of the population; the Caprivians, living in the easternmost portion of the strip, total 4%; the San (Bushmen) 3%; the Basters of Rehoboth, a farming community of mixed origin, 2%; and the Tswana 0.5%. The white population lives predominantly in central and southern Namibia. The Coloureds (peoples of mixed descent) live largely in Windhoek and other cities. Historically, the San have been marginalized, with limited access to educational and employment opportunities.

⁹LANGUAGES

The official language of Namibia is English; however, it is only used by about 7% of the population. Afrikaans is the common language used by most people, including about 60% of the white population. Approximately 32% speak German. Ovambo, in any of several dialects, is widely used throughout the country, and Herero is widely spoken in Windhoek. Other indigenous languages are also used by the various tribes.

¹⁰RELIGIONS

The first missionaries to proselytize in Namibia were British Congregationalists and Methodists; German and Finnish Lutherans; and German-speaking Roman Catholics. As a result, more than 90% of Namibians identify themselves as Christians, with the largest denominations being Lutheranism, Roman Catholicism, and Anglicanism. Other groups include Baptists, Methodists, Pentecostals, evangelicals (charismatics), and Mormons (The Church of Jesus Christ of Latter-day Saints). There are also a number of Independent African churches (Zionist churches) that blend traditional African beliefs with Christianity. A number of members from the Afrikaner ethnic group belong to the Reformed Church of Namibia. Nearly 10% of the population practices indigenous religions. One notable custom is the ritual fire, which some tribes keep burning continuously to ensure life, fertility, prosperity, and the happiness of ancestors. There are small numbers of Jews, Muslims (Sunni), Buddhists, and Baha'is in the country.

The constitution provides for religious freedom and this right is generally respected in practice. Religious groups must register with the Ministry of Trade and Industry to obtain tax-exempt status. Good Friday, Easter Monday, Ascension Day, and Christmas are observed as national holidays.

¹¹TRANSPORTATION

The CIA reports that Namibia has a total of 64,189 km (39,885 mi) of roads, of which 5,477 km (3,403 mi) are paved. The

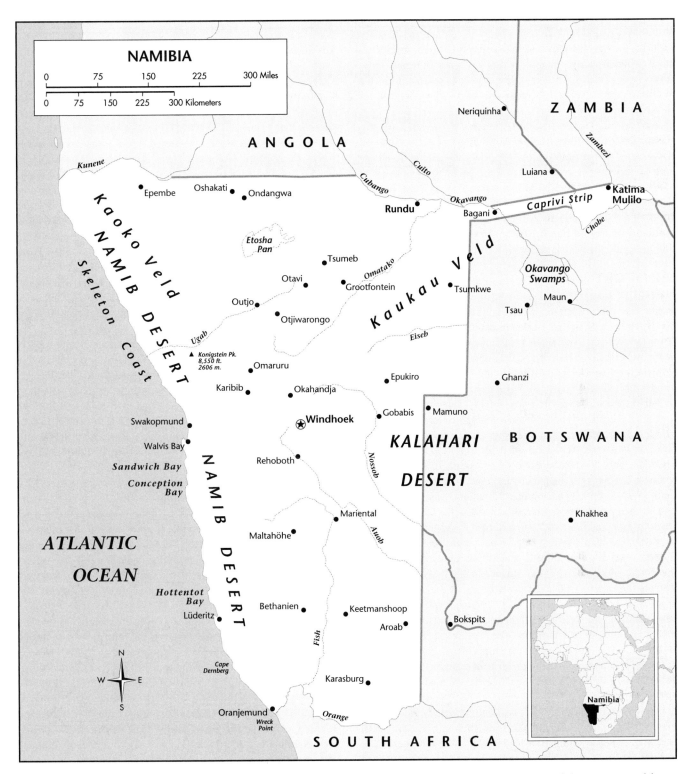

NAMIBIA

0　75　150　225　300 Miles

0　75　150　225　300 Kilometers

LOCATION: 11°44′ to 25°16′E; 16°58′ to 28°58′ S. BOUNDARY LENGTHS: Angola, 1,376 kilometers (855 miles); Zambia, 233 kilometers (144 miles); Botswana, 1,360 kilometers (850 miles); South Africa, 966 kilometers (600 miles); Atlantic Ocean, including Walvis Bay, 1,489 kilometers (921 miles). TERRITORIAL SEA LIMIT: 12 miles.

Trans-Kalahari Highway links Namibia and Gauteng Province in South Africa. The Trans-Caprivi Highway links Namibia to Zambia, Zimbabwe, and northern Botswana. Namibia's rail system consists of a main line from South Africa connecting east of Karasburg and continuing to Keetmanshoop (with a side branch to Lüderitz), Mariental, and Windhoek before heading eastward to the ranching area of Gobabis and north to the copper-mining area of Tsumeb. Westward from Windhoek and also southwestward from Tsumeb, the main rail lines link the interior with Swakopmund and Walvis Bay.

Walvis Bay, a South African enclave from 1977 to 1994, has been the main handler of Namibia's imports and exports and the home of the territory's once-vital fishing fleet since the 1920s. About 95% of all Namibian seaborne trade is transshipped there. Lüderitz, the site of the first German entry in 1883, has lost its status as a port because of harbor silting and poor transport links. However, it remains a center of the territory's crayfish industry. In 2010 Namibia had one merchant vessel, a cargo ship, of 1,000 GRT or more.

There are 129 airports, which transported 454,855 passengers in 2009, according to the World Bank. An estimated 21 airports had paved runways in 2010. Namibia's international airport (Windhoek International) is near Windhoek, with other modern facilities at Rundu, Grootfontein, Walvis Bay, Lüderitz, Keetmanshoop, and Oranjemund. Other towns have dirt airstrips, and many white Namibians fly their own aircraft from their farms to the urban centers. South African Airways links Windhoek to Europe and to the principal cities in South Africa.

12 HISTORY

Paintings of animal figures on rock slabs in Namibia testify to at least 25,000 years of human habitation there. The San (Bushmen) may have been Namibia's earliest inhabitants. The Damara also claim to be the true indigenous Namibians, who were compelled to welcome waves of Herero and Ovambo from the north. By the 19th century, the Damara, Ovambo, and Herero were the largest indigenous ethnic groups. The Kavango and the Caprivians were settled in the areas where they now reside. There was competition for land, mostly between the Ovambo and the Herero. But then the invaders arrived. First came the Hottentots (now called Nama), brown-skinned peoples of mixed parentage from South Africa. They had guns, and conquered a large swath of southern and central Namibia from the Herero and the Damara. The Germans came in 1883, initially as commercial colonizers and missionaries and then as soldiers. With military might, the Germans in the 1890s moved inland across the desert from Walvis Bay (which had been annexed by the British in 1878 and incorporated into Cape Colony in 1884) to Windhoek, establishing forts and subjugating the Herero and Damara. The Germans forcibly took land and cattle from the Herero, whose revolt was suppressed by the Germans at a cost of about 65,000 Herero lives. A Nama revolt met a similar fate in 1904. In 1985 the UN Whitaker Report classified the aftermath as an attempt to exterminate the Herero and Nama peoples, and, therefore, one of the earliest attempts of genocide in the 20th century. In 2004 the German government recognized and apologized for the events but ruled out a financial compensation for the victims' descendants.

When World War I broke out, the South Africans invaded Süd-West Afrika, as the German colony was then known. The South Africans wished to annex the territory, but the new League of Nations granted South Africa a mandate instead. From 1920 to 1946 South Africa administered the mandatory territory as if it were an integral part of its union, but neglected social services and the Ovambo-Kavango sphere in the north.

After World War II, South Africa refused to acknowledge the jurisdiction of the UN over Namibia as a successor organization to the League of Nations. Instead, it progressively integrated Namibia into its union. In the 1950s senators from German South West Africa sat in the South African parliament. The UN took South Africa before the International Court of Justice, which gave ambiguous verdicts in 1962 and 1966, but in 1971 it decisively declared South Africa's occupation of Namibia illegal. In 1978 the UN Security Council rejected South Africa's annexation of Walvis Bay.

Meanwhile, in 1960 representatives of the indigenous majority had formed the South West Africa People's Organization (SWAPO) to seek independence and black majority rule. Beginning in 1966, but especially after 1977, SWAPO used guerrilla tactics with varying success. South Africa countered by building up its armed forces along Namibia's borders with Zambia and Angola, where SWAPO had established bases and from where it launched raids.

In 1978 South Africa ostensibly accepted a Western-sponsored plan for an independent Namibia, but at the same time sponsored elections for a constituent assembly (opposed by the UN) that resulted in the victory of a white-dominated multiethnic party, the Democratic Turnhalle Alliance. Representatives of the United States, the United Kingdom, the Federal Republic of Germany, France, and Canada then attempted to devise a formula acceptable to South Africa that would permit Namibia to proceed to independence in accordance with UN Security Council Resolution 435 of 1978.

A "transitional government of national unity," composed of South African-appointed members of six parties, was installed in 1985. The South African administrator-general retained the right to veto legislation, and South Africa continued to exercise authority over foreign affairs and defense. On 13 December 1988, seven months of US-mediated (with observers from the Soviet Union) negotiations resulted in the signing of the Protocol of Brazzaville, by which South Africa agreed to implement the UN Plan for Namibia.

The process to implement UN Resolution 435 on 1 April 1989 started off shakily. In contravention of SWAPO president Sam Nujoma's assurances to the UN to abide by a cease-fire and repatriate only unarmed insurgents, around 2,000 armed members of the People's Liberation Army (PLAN), SWAPO's military wing, crossed into northern Namibia from Angola. South African forces were authorized to oppose them and 375 PLAN fighters were killed. This misunderstanding was overcome by negotiations and peace was restored.

Elections, held 7–11 November 1989, were certified as free and fair. This transitional period involved the return of some 42,000 refugees and the return of SWAPO politicians and PLAN fighters in exile. SWAPO took 57% of the vote, just short of the two-thirds necessary to allow it a free hand in drafting a constitution. The main opposition Democratic Turnhalle Alliance (DTA) received 29%. By 9 February 1990 the constituent assembly had drafted and adopted a constitution based on the 1982 constitutional principles. Namibia became independent on 21 March 1990. Nujoma was sworn in as president by UN Sec. Gen. Javier Pérez de Cuéllar.

On 1 March 1994, the reincorporating of Walvis Bay into Namibia was completed through an agreement with South Africa.

By the late 1990s secessionist sentiments were growing among the 92,000 Lozi of the Caprivi Strip in northeastern Namibia. They formed the Caprivi Liberation Front, led by Mishake Muyongo, former SWAPO executive secretary. On 2 August 1998 Caprivi Liberation Army (CLA) rebels attacked military, police, and other government installations around Katima Mulilo in Caprivi. Namibia declared a state of emergency that lasted three weeks. Six soldiers and police officers, and several civilians died in the attack. Many rebels were captured or killed by security forces. By December 1998 about 2,250 Namibians from the Caprivi region had crossed into Botswana, allegedly fleeing persecution by the Namibian Defense Force, and 2,232 of them were given asylum in Botswana. In 2005 over 130 Caprivians were being held for trial on charges of treason, of which 13 were lodging complaints under one of the several international and regional human rights treaties applicable in the country.

In November 1998 SWAPO used its two-thirds majority in the legislature to change the constitution to allow Nujoma a third term of office. This move attracted widespread national and international criticism in what some observers called a "torpedoing of democracy" to suit certain individuals. Nujoma went on to win the (substantially free and fair) elections held on 30 November and 1 December 1999.

Namibia maintained neutrality in its foreign policy until the late 1990s, when 2,000 Namibian solders were sent to help President Laurent Kabila of the Democratic Republic of the Congo fight rebels. By August 2001 all but 150 of these troops had returned home. In December 1999 Namibia allowed Angolan troops to use its territory to pursue rebels from the National Union for the Total Independence of Angola (UNITA). Between December 1999 and January 2000, scores of civilians were wounded or killed. The death of UNITA leader Jonas Savimbi in February 2002 and the subsequent peace accord between UNITA and the Angolan government ended bouts of "hot pursuit" across the Namibian-Angolan border in connection with the quarter-century-long civil war in Angola. In 2003 the Namibian and Botswanan governments accepted the demarcation of their joint border along the Kwando, Linyanti, and Chobe rivers.

In June 2003 Namibia was included in free trade talks with the United States as part of the Africa Growth and Opportunity Act (AGOA). It also received more than $37 million over five years in assistance from the Global Fund to fight HIV/AIDS and is one of 14 countries that benefitted from a US$15 billion, five-year emergency plan for HIV/AIDS that was coordinated by the US government.

In 2007 Nujoma stepped down as president of SWAPO, passing leadership of the organization to Hifikepunye Pohamba, who had been elected as president of Namibia in 2005.

13 GOVERNMENT

The Namibia constitution adopted on 21 March 1990 is considered a model of democratic government. Universal suffrage and a strong emphasis on human rights and political freedom are prominent. An independent judiciary and legal obligations to improve the disadvantaged sectors of the population are written into the government. Namibia has a bicameral legislature. It consists of a national assembly of 72 deputies elected for a five-year term, and up to six members appointed by the president, and a national council comprised of two members from each of 13 regions elected for a six-year term. The national council functions purely in an advisory capacity. The president is elected by direct, popular vote and serves as head of state and government and commander in chief of the defense force for no more than two five-year terms. The constitution was amended in November 1999 specifically to allow Nujoma (alone) a third term, a move that attracted criticism

both from within the country and the international community. There is also an independent ombudsman to investigate complaints and take action in defense of the interests of individuals and organization in their dealings with the state.

14 POLITICAL PARTIES

The South West Africa People's Organization (SWAPO) is the largest political party, and during the struggle for independence, it was recognized by the OAU and the UN General Assembly as the sole legitimate representative of the Namibian people. SWAPO had a military wing—the People's Liberation Army (PLAN)—that was engaged in war with South Africa during the struggle. SWAPO's support comes chiefly from the Ovambo people of the north and from urban areas. The Democratic Turnhalle Alliance (DTA), a white-led amalgam of constituent ethnic parties, was the main opposition party in Namibia's first two elections. It narrowly lost the main opposition role (partly due to early alleged financial links with white South Africa) to the new (formed in March 1999) Congress of Democrats (CoD) in the 1999 elections. Three other parties—the United Democratic Front (UDF), the Monitor Action Group (MAG), and the Democratic Coalition of Namibia—won at least a seat in the 1994 and 1999 elections. There are also several small ethnic parties, most of which were represented in the bodies appointed in 1985.

In the 1989 elections to the constituent assembly, SWAPO gained 41 seats (57.3%); the DTA 21 seats (28.6%); the United Democratic Front, four seats (5.6%); and the Action Christian National, three seats (3.5%). The other parties collectively gained three seats on 5% of the vote. In the 1994 elections SWAPO maintained its commanding majority in the assembly, taking 73.9% of the vote, which translated to 53 seats. DTA held 15 seats; United Democratic Front, 2 seats; and one each by the Democratic Coalition of Namibia and the Monitor Action group. In the November/December 1998 elections for the national council, SWAPO took 21 seats, DTA 4, UDF 1 seat. In the November/December 1999 presidential elections, Nujoma performed even better that in previous elections, winning 76.8% of the vote. Ben Ulenga of the CoD had 10.5%; Katuurike Kaura of DTA, 9.6%; and Chief Justice Garoëb of the UDF, 3%. SWAPO swept 55 of the 72 assembly seats; CoD and DTA, got 7 each; UDF, 2; MAG, 1.

The results of the 15–16 November 2004 assembly elections gave again a vast majority to SWAPO, with 76.3% of the vote going to Hifikepunye Pohamba, followed by CoD (7.3%), DTA (5.2%), the National Unity Democratic Organization (NUDO, 4.2%), UDF (3.8%), the Republican Party (RP, 1.9%), and MAG (1.1%). Hifikepunye Pohamba was elected as president.

In the general elections of November 2009 Hifikepunye Pohamba was reelected for a second term as president, winning 76% of the vote. SWAPO maintained its majority in the assembly by winning 75% of the vote (54 seats). The Rally for Democracy and Progress (RDP) won 11.3% of the vote (8 seats), followed by the DTA with 3.2% (2 seats), NUDO with 3% (2 seats), and UDF with 2.4% (2 seats). All People's Party (APP), CoD, the Republican Party, and the South West Africa National Union (SWANU) each gained one seat. While opposition leaders contested the results through allegations of fraud, international observers called the election free and fair.

¹⁵LOCAL GOVERNMENT

There are 13 regions in Namibia. The most populous is Omusati, followed by Ohangwena, Khomas, Kavango, Oshana, Oshikoto, Otjozondjupa, Erongo, Caprivi, Kunene, Karas, Hardap, and Omaheke. They are governed by elected councils. Local governments (municipalities, towns, and villages) have elected councils.

¹⁶JUDICIAL SYSTEM

The court system retains Roman-Dutch elements inherited from South Africa, along with elements of the traditional court system. The formal court system is arranged in three tiers: 30 magistrates' courts, the high court, and the Supreme Court. The Supreme Court serves as the highest court of appeals and also exercises constitutional review of legislation.

The traditional courts handle minor criminal offenses such as petty theft and violations of local customs. In 1991 a presidential commission recommended that the traditional courts be maintained, provided they act consistently with the constitution and laws. Legislation enacted in 1993 intended to bridge the gap between traditional and magistrates' courts by creation of a system of community courts.

The constitution calls for an independent judiciary, as well as an extensive bill of rights protecting freedom of speech, press, assembly, association, and religion, and a guarantee of redress for those whose fundamental rights have been violated. It provides for an ombudsman to deliver free legal advice upon request.

Because of a shortage of trained magistrates and lack of legal counsel, courts typically face a significant backlog of cases awaiting trial. The government appointed the first public defender in 1993, and renewed funding for representation for indigent defendants.

Although the constitution specifically prohibits discrimination on the grounds of sex, race, color, ethnic origin, religion, creed, or social or economic status, some customary and apartheid-based laws dating from before independence have not yet been repealed.

¹⁷ARMED FORCES

The International Institute for Strategic Studies reports that armed forces in Namibia totaled 9,200 members in 2011. The force is comprised of 9,000 from the army and 200 members of the navy. Armed forces represent 1.9% of the labor force in Namibia. Defense spending totaled US$541.1 million and accounted for 3.7% of gross domestic product (GDP). Namibia participated in five UN peacekeeping efforts in Africa.

¹⁸INTERNATIONAL COOPERATION

Namibia became a member of the UN on 23 April 1990; it belongs to ECA and several nonregional specialized agencies, such as the FAO, IAEA, ILO, ITU, UNESCO, UNHCR, the World Bank, and the WHO. It also serves as a member of the African Development Bank, the ACP Group, the Commonwealth of Nations, G-77, the African Union, and the WTO. In the subregion, Namibia belongs to the South Africa Customs Union (SACU) and to the Southern Africa Development Community (SADC). Namibia is also part of the Common Monetary Area (CMA) that includes Lesotho, Swaziland, and South Africa. Namibia is a member of the Nonaligned Movement.

In environmental cooperation, Namibia is part of the Basel Convention, the Convention on Biological Diversity, Ramsar, CITES, the Kyoto Protocol, the Montréal Protocol, and the UN Conventions on the Law of the Sea, Climate Change, and Desertification.

¹⁹ECONOMY

Namibia's economy is dependent on a few primary commodity exports, including minerals (mainly diamonds, uranium, zinc, lead, copper, tin, lithium, and cadmium), livestock (both meat and hides), and fishing. The CIA reported that in 2010 mining contributed 8% of GDP, but provided more than 50% of foreign exchange earnings. Diamonds alone contribute approximately 10% of the national GDP. Tourism is also a growing Namibian industry. The economy is highly linked to that of South Africa, in spite of gaining independence from that country in 1990. Eighty percent of Namibia's imports originate there, and transport and communications infrastructure are strongly linked with South Africa. The Namibian dollar continues to be linked at parity to the South African rand.

Although one of the most prosperous African countries, the country's high per capita income level (approximately US$5,200) is unevenly distributed and obscures one of the most unequal income distributions on the African continent. The HIV/AIDS pandemic is also having a devastating effect on the economy as about 180, 000 people were infected with the virus by 2009. Nonetheless, a democratically elected government is following economic and social policies aimed at the development of previously neglected regions of the country and that respond to the major challenges faced by the population.

The economy has a superior transport and communications infrastructure, an extensive natural resource base, a small population, and a stable government committed to competitiveness in attracting investment. Large oil and gas reserves were discovered in 2000. For these reasons analysts believe that Namibia's economy holds enormous potential for long-term economic growth.

Although tourism accounted for less than 3% of GDP in 2002, it grew faster than any other sector of the economy. Ecotourism is an important segment of the tourism industry, as Namibia has a wide variety of wildlife and striking scenery.

The global economic crisis of 2008–09 caused a decline in economic growth and an increase in unemployment. By February 2010, however, the Namibian economy had recovered and was again strong. The GDP rate of change in Namibia in 2010 was 4.4%. Inflation stood at 4.6%, and unemployment was reported at 51.2%.

²⁰INCOME

The CIA estimated that in 2010 the GDP of Namibia was US$14.6 billion. The CIA defines GDP as the value of all final goods and services produced within a nation in a given year and computed on the basis of purchasing power parity (PPP) rather than value as measured on the basis of the rate of the exchange based on current dollars. The per capita GDP was estimated at US$6,900. The annual growth rate of GDP was 4.4%. The average inflation rate was 4.6%. It was estimated that agriculture accounted for 7.3% of GDP, industry 34.4%, and services 58.4%.

In 2007 the World Bank estimated that Namibia, with 0.03% of the world's population, accounted for 0.02% of the world's GDP. By comparison, the United States, with 4.85% of the world's population, accounted for 22.51% of world GDP. According to the World Bank, remittances from citizens living abroad totaled US$13.6 million or about US$6 per capita and accounted for approximately .1% of GDP.

As of 2012 the most recent UN report stated that about 38% of the population lived below the poverty level established by Namibia's government. Some 25% of the population lived on US$1 per day.

The World Bank reported that in 2009 household consumption in Namibia totaled US$6.1 billion or about US$2,843 per capita, measured in current US dollars rather than PPP. Household consumption included expenditures of individuals, households, and nongovernmental organizations on goods and services, excluded the purchases of dwellings. It was estimated that household consumption was growing at an average annual rate of 11.1%. As of 2011 the World Bank reported that actual individual consumption in Namibia was 62.3% of GDP and accounted for 0.01% of world consumption. By comparison, the United States accounted for 25.44% of world individual consumption. The World Bank also estimated that 19.1% of Namibia's GDP was spent on food and beverages, 11.5% on housing and household furnishings, 3.4% on clothes, 5.6% on health, 6.4% on transportation, 0.5% on communications, 1.8% on recreation, 2.9% on restaurants and hotels, and 1.6% on miscellaneous goods and services and purchases from abroad.

21 LABOR

In 2010 the Namibian labor force was estimated at 789,100 people. Unemployment was reported at 51.2%. Approximately 16.3% of the labor force was employed in agriculture, 22.4% was employed in industry, and 61.3% was employed in services.

The constitution provides freedom of association, including the right to form and join trade unions, which was extended to public servants, farm workers, and domestic employees under the Labor Act of March 1992. The principal trade union organizations are the National Union of Namibian Workers (NUNW), a SWAPO-aligned federation, and the Namibia Federation of Trade Unions (NFTU). The main public service and construction unions are affiliates of the Namibia People's Social Movement (NPSM), formerly known as the Namibian Christian Social Trade Unions. Workers generally have the right to strike. Collective bargaining is permitted but is virtually only practiced in the mining and construction industries.

The minimum legal working age is 14; however, child labor remains prevalent, especially in rural areas. There is no legal minimum wage, and many workers have difficulty maintaining a decent standard of living. The legal workweek is set at 45 hours, with a mandatory 24-hour rest period per week. The government implements health and safety standards.

22 AGRICULTURE

Roughly 1% of the total land is farmed. The country's major crops include millet, sorghum, peanuts, and grapes. Cereal production in 2009 amounted to 111,738 tons, fruit production 38,384 tons, and vegetable production 55,734 tons. Agriculture consists of two sectors: a commercial sector with some 50,000 workers (producing 80% of annual yields), and a subsistence sector situated largely in communal areas. Colonialism left Namibia with a three-tier agricultural production system: 4,000 commercial ranches; 20,000 stock-raising households; and 120,000 mixed-farming operations. The ranches displaced local farmers on 66% of the viable farmland and left only 5% of the land to the 120,000 mixed-farming operations.

Corn (maize) is grown primarily in the area known as the Grootfontein-Otavi-Tsumeb triangle, where farms are much smaller than in other parts of the country. Corn production in 2004 amounted only to 33,000 tons (down from 50,000 tons in 1991). Recent droughts have created a dependency on grain imports. Namibia is dependent on South Africa for corn, sugar, fruit, and vegetables.

Caprivi and Kavango in the northeast have potential for extensive crop development. Communal farms there are estimated to produce 60% of their staple food, such as mahango (which is also used to brew beer). Cotton, rice, and vegetable production have begun on an experimental basis in Kavango. An irrigation project at Hardap Dam near Mariental produces corn, alfalfa, feed corn, and grapes.

23 ANIMAL HUSBANDRY

The UN Food and Agriculture Organization (FAO) reported that Namibia dedicated 38 million hectares (93.9 million acres) to permanent pasture or meadow in 2009. Livestock production is the major agricultural activity, making up more than 90% of that sector's output. In 2009 the country 2.5 million head of cattle. In 2005 there were an estimated 2,900,000 sheep and 2,100,000 goats. In 2005 meat production totaled 107,600 tons, including 77,300 tons of beef, 14,000 tons of mutton, and 5,000 tons of goat meat. Karakul pelts have been a leading export, but the world market is currently depressed. Namibia has ideal conditions for commercial breeding of ostriches, and of other African game animals for meat, hide, trophy, and tourism purposes.

24 FISHING

The fish stocks of the rich Benguela current system were seriously depleted in the late 1970s and throughout the 1980s. Most species, however, recovered somewhat by the late 1990s as a result of conservation programs. Fishing and fish processing are among the nation's best prospects for employment and economic growth. In early 1992 a new fisheries code was presented to the legislature, which stressed employment and training opportunities for Namibian citizens, profit reinvestment, and revenue gain for the nation. After independence in 1990, the volume of the nominal catch skyrocketed nearly tenfold. Namibia had 218 decked commercial fishing boats in 2008. The annual capture totaled 372,822 tons according to the UN FAO. The export value of seafood totaled US$375.6 million.

25 FORESTRY

Approximately 9% of Namibia is covered of forests and woodland, including woodland savanna, all in the north and northeast. Most of the timber is used locally.

26MINING

Namibia is among the world's premier producers of gem diamonds. The mineral industry accounts for 20% of GDP and about two-thirds of the country's exports by value. More than 6,000 workers are employed by the minerals industry. The most valuable minerals are diamonds, uranium, copper, silver, lead, zinc, gold, pyrite, and salt. Diamonds are mainly recovered from a 96 km (59.6 mi) stretch along the coastline north of the Orange River; which produced 1,192,000 carats in 2009. Also produced in 2009 were white arsenic, lead, manganese, fluorspar, semiprecious stones (agate, amethyst, garnet, pietersite, rose quartz, sodalite, and tourmaline), dolomite, granite, marble, sulfur (pyrite concentrate), and wollastonite.

In 2008 mine copper output was estimated at 37,956 metric tons (copper content); mine lead, 20,000 metric tons (metal content); zinc concentrate, 47,000 metric tons (metal content); and salt, 781,800 metric tons. Rössing Uranium, owned by Río Tinto-Zinc, of the United Kingdom, produced uranium oxide at the world's sixth-largest producing uranium mine, at Swakopmund. Namibia was the fourth-largest producer of uranium in 2009, accounting for 9% of world production. Coal has been discovered in southeastern Namibia.

27ENERGY AND POWER

The World Bank reported in 2008 that Namibia produced 2.1 billion kWh of electricity and consumed 3.83 billion kWh, or 1,782 kWh per capita. Roughly 72% of energy came from fossil fuels, while 7% came from alternative sources. Per capita oil consumption was 823 kg.

In May 2010 the government announced a major partnership with neighboring Angola to build a US$1.1 billion hydropower station and storage dam along the Kunene River. The new project will involve a 50% investment from each country. If all goes well, the plant is expected to be up and running by 2017. Both governments look to hydropower as a way to improve the generally unreliable electrical supply in their nations.

The Caprivi Link Interconnector line, linking Namibia to power networks in Zambia, Zimbabwe, and other African neighbors, came online in November 2010. The link allows the region of Caprivi, which was once dependent on electricity supplied from South Africa, to receive power from a greater variety of sources. The Ruacana hydroelectric power station is being expanded to increase output from 240 megawatts to 320 megawatts by mid-2012. A feasibility study for a proposed Orange River plant is expected to be completed in 2013.

28INDUSTRY

Namibia's small industrial sector has centered on meat packing and fish processing, with some production of basic consumer goods. There are furniture and clothing factories, metal and engineering works, assembly plants for imported components, and a cement plant (which, however, closed in 1999 due to pollution risks to the lives of workers and residents in the area).

In 2010 the industrial sector contributed 34.3% of the national GDP. The government has committed to a mixed-market economy and aims to diversify the economy away from its traditional reliance upon the mining sector, encouraging private-sector investment and export-oriented manufacturing industries. The African Economic Unit reported that construction contracted in 2010 driven mainly by the decline in residential building construction, which was caused by the tightening of credit and a high level of household indebtedness.

Namibia remains underexplored with regard to oil and natural gas, but its greatest potential in the hydrocarbon sector remains with natural gas. The main significant discovery as of 2002 was the Kudu gas field off Luderitz. Originally involving big multinationals such as Shell and ChevronTexaco, these companies withdrew leaving the state-owned National Petroleum Corporation of Namibia (Namcor) in charge. Serica Energy signed an agreement with the Namibian government in early 2012 for oil exploration. The agreement was worth US$3 million; US$2 million came in the form of shares in Serica Energy. Plans were to construct a moderate-size electric power generation plant in Orangemund, a pipeline to the Western Cape in South Africa, and potentially two electric power plants there. The primary partners in the Kudu gas field project are Namcor, NamPower, Energy Africa, and South Africa's Electricity Supply Commission (ESKOM).

29SCIENCE AND TECHNOLOGY

The Namibia Department of Agriculture and Rural Development, founded in 1979 at Windhoek, supports extensive research on natural resources and ecology. The Desert Ecological Research Unit of Namibia, founded in 1963 at Swakopmund, carries out exploration and research in the Namib Desert and semiarid Namibia. The University of Namibia has a faculty of science. The Namibia Scientific Society, at Windhoek, is concerned with ornithology, speleology, botany, archaeology, herpetology, astronomy, and ethnology. Natural science exhibits are displayed at the Lüderitz Museum, the Museum Swakopmund, and the National Museum at Windhoek. In 1987–97, science and engineering students accounted for 4% of college and university enrollments. In 2002 Namibia's high technology exports totaled US$6 million, or 1% of its' manufactured exports. The World Bank reported in 2009 that there were no patent applications in science and technology in Namibia.

30DOMESTIC TRADE

Windhoek is the country's major commercial center. A good road network, increasingly paved, facilitates trade and communications around the country. The marketing and distribution systems are mainly controlled by foreign investors and managers from South Africa and Germany. Domestic trade is heavily dependent on South African imports for most consumer goods; there is also significant South African presence in domestic investment, mainly in the form of pension funds, life insurance, and transactions between commercial banks. Business hours are from 7:30 a.m. to 4:30 or 5 p.m., Monday through Friday. Many businesses are closed from mid-December to mid-January for a summer holiday.

31FOREIGN TRADE

Namibia imported US$5.152 billion worth of goods and services in 2008, while exporting US$4.277 billion worth of goods and services. Major import partners in 2009 were South Africa, Angola, the European Union, the United States, Canada, China, and India. Main exports in 2011 were diamonds, processed fish, other minerals, animals and derived products, and beverages and other foods.. The Walvis Bay enclave is an export-processing zone, with the potential of becoming a center for re-exports toward Angola, South Africa, Zimbabwe, and Botswana.

Leading imports are vehicles and transport equipment, petroleum products and fuel, chemicals, foodstuffs, and machinery and electrical equipment. South Africa (80%), the United States (4%), Germany (2%), and Japan are the leading suppliers for Namibia's imports.

³²BALANCE OF PAYMENTS

Traditionally, Namibia has maintained a trade surplus resulting from its valuable mineral exports. However, over 95% of Namibia's consumption and investment goods are imported, resulting in wide fluctuations in the merchandise trade surplus due to the constant changes in world mineral prices. In 2010 Namibia had a foreign trade deficit of US$1.1 billion, amounting to 2% of GDP.

Namibia joined the International Monetary Fund in September 1990, when it began opening more to foreign trade. Since then, the current account has grown to maintain a surplus, due to surpluses in net current transfers, particularly in Southern African Customs Union (SACU) receipts and foreign development assistance not linked to capital assets. Germany, the United States, and Scandinavian countries are the principal bilateral donors. Although revenues from the SACU are expected to decline for Namibia as a result of the 2002 new arrangements, they still represent an important financial source for the government.

³³BANKING AND SECURITIES

Banking activities have recorded strong growth since independence in 1990 as the range of financial institutions operating in Namibia has expanded. Total assets of the four main commercial banks more than doubled in 1991–95, and during 1995 bank lending to the private sector rose by 34%, that represented 92% of total domestic credit, of which 41% comprised loans to individuals. There have been no banking failures since independence, but the regulatory regime inherited from South Africa is being brought more into line with international norms under a new banking institutions act that was due to come into effect in 1997.

First National Bank Namibia and Standard Bank Namibia have the largest branch networks and remain wholly owned subsidiaries of their South African parent banks. Other commercial banks included the Commercial Bank of Namibia (CBN, a subsidiary of the Geneva-based Société financière pour les pays d'outre mer, or SFOM), South Africa's Nedcor Bank, FirstRand Limited, and Bank Windhoek (in which South Africa's ABSA Bank is the main shareholder). In mid-1996, Bank Windhoek completed a merger with the Namibia Building Society. The City Savings and Investment Bank (CSIB) was launched in 1994 as Namibia's first indigenously owned financial institution. At that time it had a single branch in Windhoek, but has since grown.

In 2010 the discount rate, the interest rate at which the central bank lends to financial institutions in the short term, was 10%.

Within four years, the Namibian Stock Exchange (NSE), which started operations in October 1992, grew to become sub-Saharan Africa's second-largest in terms of market capitalization, next to the Johannesburg Stock Exchange (JSE). The NSE is increasingly being used by local firms to raise capital for business expansions,

Balance of Payments – Namibia (2010)		
(In millions of US dollars)		
Current Account		-314.2
Balance on goods	-785.7	
Imports	-4,914.7	
Exports	4,129.0	
Balance on services	148.2	
Balance on income	-563.9	
Current transfers	887.3	
Capital Account		112.5
Financial Account		-470.4
Direct investment abroad	-4.4	
Direct investment in Namibia	795.9	
Portfolio investment assets	-695.1	
Portfolio investment liabilities	4.4	
Financial derivatives	...	
Other investment assets	-470.2	
Other investment liabilities	-101.0	
Net Errors and Omissions		-378.9
Reserves and Related Items		1,051.0

(…) data not available or not significant.

SOURCE: *Balance of Payment Statistics Yearbook 2011*, Washington, DC: International Monetary Fund, 2011.

while foreign investors are buying into Namibian equities through new listings and rights offers, which have been mainly oversubscribed. Some 95% of the NSE's overall market capitalization comprises dual-listings of South African parent groups of Namibian subsidiaries. Thirteen different companies were listed in 2001, when local market capitalization was US$151 million. As of 2011 a total of 42 companies were listed on the NSE.

³⁴INSURANCE

The government embarked on a considerable shake-up of the insurance and pensions sector during the 1990s, over which the South African mutual societies had the biggest influence. Premium income continued to be invested mainly in South African assets following independence, overriding Namibian insurance funds like the Government Institutions Pension Fund (GIPF).

Legislative amendments of 1995 required that 35% of Namibian-generated funds under management be reinvested in specified local assets. A long-term insurance bill tabled at the end of 1996 made it compulsory for South African mutuals to establish Namibian-registered public companies and match net liabilities with local assets. As part of their asset localization measures, Sanlam and Old Mutual launched the first Namibian unit trusts in 1995. Other major insurance companies include Metropolitan Life and Mutual and Federal Insurance Company.

³⁵PUBLIC FINANCE

Although per capita GDP is one of the highest in Africa, the majority of Namibia's people live in poverty. The economy is one of the most advanced in the region, but income distribution is very skewed. In order to combat this problem, the government continues to concentrate its spending on social services. A large portion of the budget is also allocated to development projects, including boosting the construction industry and expanding the infrastructure. The CIA estimated that in 2010 Namibia's central government took in revenues of approximately US$3.103 billion and had expenditures of US$3.847 billion. Revenues minus expenditures totaled approximately -US$77 million. Public debt in 2010 amounted to 20.1% of GDP.

The IMF reported that in 2002, the most recent year for which it had data, government outlays by function were as follows: general public services, 26.4%; defense, 9.0%; public order and safety, 9.8%; economic affairs, 10.4%; housing and community amenities, 9.0%; health, 10.6%; recreation, culture, and religion, 2.2%; education, 22.4%; and social protection, 7.3%.

36 TAXATION

There is a progressive personal income tax with a top rate of 35%. The basic tax on corporate profits is 35%. Nonresident shareholders are taxed 10% on dividends, and there is a tax on undistributed profits. Mining companies, and oil and gas extraction companies are taxed at special rates. As of 27 November 2001, a value-added tax (VAT) replaced the 8% general sales tax (GST), with a standard rate of 15%. Exempted from VAT are education, medical services, hotel accommodations, and public transportation. There are also excise taxes on luxury goods.

37 CUSTOMS AND DUTIES

Namibia is part of the Southern African Customs Union (SACU), Preferential Trade Area for Eastern and Southern Africa (PTA), the Common Market for Eastern and Southern Africa (COMESA), and the SADC Free Trade Protocol. No tariffs exist on most goods moving between members, but there is a 15% duty on non-imports from nonmember nations, plus a 15% sales duty. It also has signed bilateral trade agreements with over 20 major trading nations around the world. Imports from outside the union are subject to a common tariff rate based on the Harmonized System of Import Classification; most imports need licenses. South Africa levies and collects most of the customs and excise duties for the other members and then pays each a share, based on an established formula. Namibia has double taxation agreements with South Africa, the United Kingdom, Sweden, and Germany, and is a member of the UN, the World Bank, the International Monetary Fund, and the World Trade Organization.

38 FOREIGN INVESTMENT

International investment, mostly South African, has historically played an important role in Namibia. In addition, there is significant UK and US investment in mining. Several international oil and gas distribution as well as fishing companies operate in Namibia. In December 1990 foreign investment legislation was liberalized. In April 1993 Namibia announced a program of private-sector investment incentives that included lower taxes, grants, and development loans. In 1994 the government created an export processing zone at Walvis Bay. Foreign direct investment (FDI) in Namibia was a net inflow of US$490.2 million according to World Bank figures published in 2009. FDI represented 5.29% of GDP. Namibia's goal is to create an infrastructure that will serve as a reexport center for southern Africa, including Angola, South Africa, Zimbabwe, and Botswana.

Public Finance – Namibia (2007)		
(In millions of Namibian dollars, budgetary central government figures)		
Revenue and Grants	**18,356**	**100.0%**
Tax revenue	16,969	92.4%
Social contributions	81	0.4%
Grants	205	1.1%
Other revenue	1,100	6.0%
Expenditures	**17,139**	**100.0%**
General public services	3,704	21.6%
Defense	1,683	9.8%
Public order and safety	1,565	9.1%
Economic affairs	1,947	11.4%
Environmental protection	...	...
Housing and community amenities	1,151	6.7%
Health	1,669	9.7%
Recreational, culture, and religion	360	2.1%
Education	3,418	19.9%
Social protection	1,642	9.6%

(…) data not available or not significant.

SOURCE: *Government Finance Statistics Yearbook 2010,* Washington, DC: International Monetary Fund, 2010.

39 ECONOMIC DEVELOPMENT

Namibia's government will continue to build and diversify its economy around its mineral reserves. Priorities include expanding the manufacturing sector, land reform, agricultural development in the populous north, and improved education and health opportunities. Transfer of Walvis Bay and 12 offshore islands to Namibia in 1994 returned to Namibia its deepwater port and 20% of its offshore rights. In 2011 the fishing industry employed over 10, 000 workers.

The five-year development program started in 1994 set an annual growth rate target of 5%, highlighting government budget cuts and foreign investment and trade. As of 2002 GDP growth since the mid-1990s had averaged 3.5% a year. Unemployment remained high, at around 30% of the labor force, and economic growth was not substantial enough to significantly reduce poverty. The 2004–05 budget aimed to limit the fiscal deficit to 1.6% of GDP. The Namibian Stock Exchange (NSX) continues to expand, gaining weight particularly in sub-Saharan Africa.

40 SOCIAL DEVELOPMENT

By many economic and social indicators, including population per physician, per hospital bed, and per telephone, Namibia is statistically better off than many other sub-Saharan African countries. However, such comparisons also mask the huge disparities between rural and urban Namibia, and between its black and white populations.

The government is obliged by the constitution to promote actively the welfare of the people, including gender, racial and regional equality. Considerable discrimination against women exists in both formal and customary law. Community property laws, for example, define women as legal minors, unable to enter into any kind of contract without the husband's signature. In the absence of this permission, women may not open a bank account or purchase property. Some measures were taken to address these inequities through the Married Person's Equality Bill, which outlaws discrimination against women in civil marriages. However, the law does not affect practices in customary, or traditional, marriages. Domestic abuse and violence are widespread, and cultural views of women exacerbate the problem.

Human rights are generally respected. However, there are excesses by security forces, and prison conditions remain harsh. Indigenous San peoples have historically faced discrimination from Namibia's other ethnic groups. The government has attempted to redress the marginalization of the San by increasing their participation in decision-making on issues that affect them. These efforts have been applied unevenly, and the San remain relatively isolated and largely excluded from national decision making.

[41]HEALTH

In 2011 average life expectancy was 52.19 years and infant mortality was 45.59 per 1,000 live births. The total fertility rate in 2011 was estimated at 2.49 children born per woman. The country spent 12.1% of its GDP on healthcare, amounting to US$258 per person. There were 4 physicians, 28 nurses and midwives, and 27 hospital beds per 10,000 inhabitants. It was estimated that 76% of children were vaccinated against measles. The maternal mortality rate was estimated at 180 deaths per 100,000 live births in 2008.

The Namibian government is considering fortifying foods with vitamin A and/or iron. Vitamin A deficiencies were seen in 20.4% of children under age five and goiter is a common problem.

The HIV/AIDS adult prevalence was 13.1% in 2009, the seventh highest rate in the world. The epidemic was worst in the northeastern part of the country, where rates of infection were as high as 29% of the population. In March 2011 the HIV prevalence rate for pregnant women was reported at 19%. This poses a particular concern as the country has set a goal to raise an HIV-free generation by 2015. Several programs have been implemented to help reach the goal, including the Prevention of Mother to Child Transmission program (PMTCT). This program works to keep the newest generation of Namibians HIV-free.

HIV/AIDS is the leading cause of mortality, followed by pneumonia, tuberculosis, and malaria. The prevalence of both measles and polio was low.

[42]HOUSING

There is a sharp contrast in housing standards between white and black Namibians, primarily because the economic imbalance between these groups has not evened out since the end of apartheid. A majority of the population is rural, where most dwellings are self-constructed from local materials. A 2007 housing deficit of 80,000 was believed to have increased between 2007 and 2011. The figure was a substantial increase over the 1990s, when the housing backlog was estimated at 45,000 units. In 2011 the government prioritized housing access for low-income residents, although housing prices were often too steep even for middle-income citizens. Microfinance was suggested as a way to create a more inclusive housing environment.

[43]EDUCATION

Education is compulsory for 10 years between the ages of 6 and 16. Primary education is for seven years, and secondary lasts for five years. The academic year runs from February to November. In 2009 the World Bank estimated that 89% of age-eligible children in Namibia were enrolled in primary school. Secondary enrollment for age-eligible children stood at 54%.

Higher education is provided primarily by the University of Namibia, the Polytechnic of Namibia, and the Colleges of Education (at Windhoek, Ongwediva, Rundu, and Caprivi). There is an Academy for Tertiary Education for adult students. Tertiary enrollment was estimated at 9%. Of those enrolled in tertiary education, there were 100 male students for every 132 female students. Overall, the CIA estimated that Namibia had a literacy rate of 85%. Public expenditure on education represented 6.4% of GDP.

[44]LIBRARIES AND MUSEUMS

Public libraries serve most cities and towns in an extensive network. The National Archives and a public library (78,000 volumes) are both located in Windhoek, as is the National Library, which contains about 90,000 volumes. The library of the University of Namibia at Windhoek holds 86,800 volumes.

There is a National Museum of Namibia in Windhoek, with an emphasis on the natural and human sciences, and local museums in Lüderitz, Swakopmund, Gobabis, Omaruri, Outjo, Tsumeb, and other towns. The State Museum in Windhoek features objects from the cultures of the Nama, Bushman, Herero, Ovambo, and other Southern African peoples. The Lüderitz Museum features displays of diamond mining.

[45]MEDIA

Namibia has good quality telephone service, with at least 18 automatic telephone exchanges that can put callers in touch with 63 countries. In 2009 the CIA reported that there were 142,100 telephone landlines in Namibia, while mobile phone subscriptions averaged 56 per 100 people. Communication with rural areas is provided by about 65 fixed radio stations and 500 mobile stations. Fax machines and telex services are readily available.

The government-owned Namibian Broadcasting Corp. transmits radio programs in English, German, Afrikaans, and African languages. Television relays from South Africa began in the Windhoek and Oshakati areas in 1981. In 2009 there were 2 FM radio stations, 39 AM radio stations, and 4 shortwave radio stations. In 2010 the country had 76,020 Internet hosts. Internet users numbered 6 per 100 citizens.

Four major daily newspapers are published in Windhoek, including *Namib Times* (7,000) and the *Namibian* (27,000). *Tempo* is a Sunday paper with a circulation of above 11,000. The government owns and operates the Namibia Press Agency. The government also owns one biweekly newspaper, *New Era*, and two magazines, *Namibia Today* and *Namibia Review*.

The constitution provides for free speech and a free press, and the government is said to generally respect those rights. However, the government-owned Namibian Broadcasting Corporation operated most radio and television services, and though it provides significant coverage of opposition opinions, there have been many complaints of bias in the reporting of sensitive issues.

[46]ORGANIZATIONS

There are two chambers of commerce in Windhoek. Professional and trade associations exist for teachers, miners, journalists, architects, jewelers, and members of the tourist industry. The National Scientific Society promotes research and education in the fields of national history, ethnology, archaeology, zoology, botany, and geology.

National youth organizations include the Namibian National Students Organization, the National Youth Council of Namibia, the SWAPO Youth League of Namibia, Junior Chamber, and Boy Scouts of Namibia. A number of sports associations are active within the country, representing such pastimes as sailing, badminton, baseball, and tennis. Women's organizations include the Sister Namibia Collective and the Namibia National Women's Organization. The YWCA has chapters in Namibia.

Volunteer service organizations, such as the Lions Clubs International, are also present. The Red Cross and the Society of St. Vincent de Paul are also active in the country.

47 TOURISM, TRAVEL, AND RECREATION

Namibia's prime tourist attractions are game viewing, trophy hunting, and the scenic beauty of its deserts. In the west, Swakopmund is a Hanseatic-style resort town populated by Namibians of German descent. It is the center for tours of the nearby Namib dunes, and for visits to the wild Skeleton Coast to the north. In the south, the Fish River Canyon, 85 km (53 mi) long and 700 m (2,300 ft) deep, ranks second in size to the Grand Canyon.

The *Tourism Factbook*, published by the UN World Tourism Organization, reported 931,000 incoming tourists to Namibia in 2008, who spent a total of US$469 million in 2009. Of those incoming tourists, there were 676,000 from Africa. There were 8,239 hotel beds available in Namibia, which had an occupancy rate of 60%. The estimated daily cost to visit Windhoek, the capital, was US$270. The cost of visiting other cities averaged US$195. Vaccinations are required if traveling from an infected area. All nationals except those of Japan, Germany, the United States, and 42 other countries are required to carry a visa for stays of up to 90 days.

48 FAMOUS PERSONS

Herman Toivo ja Toivo (b. 1915), the founder of SWAPO and the leader of Namibian nationalism, languished in a South African prison from 1966, when he was convicted of treason, until his release in March 1984. Sam Nujoma (b. 1929) was the leader of SWAPO from 1960 to 2007, and served as first president of Namibia, from 1990 to 2005.

49 DEPENDENCIES

Namibia has no territories or colonies.

50 BIBLIOGRAPHY

Ejikeme, Anene. *Culture and Customs of Namibia*. Santa Barbara, CA: Greenwood, 2011.

Gordon, Robert J. *The Bushman Myth: The Making of a Namibian Underclass*. 2nd ed. Boulder, CO: Westview Press, 2000.

Kreike, Emmanuel. *Re-creating Eden: Land Use, Environment, and Society in Southern Angola and Northern Namibia*. Portsmouth, NH: Heinemann, 2004.

Leys, Colin. *Namibia's Liberation Struggle: The Two-Edged Sword*. London: J. Curry, 1995.

McElrath, Karen, ed. *HIV and AIDS: A Global View*. Westport, CT: Greenwood Press, 2002.

McKenna, Amy. *The History of Southern Africa*. New York: Britannica Educational Publishing, 2011.

Minahan, James. *Miniature Empires: A Historical Dictionary of the Newly Independent States*. Westport, CT: Greenwood Press, 1998.

Namibia Investment and Business Guide: Strategic and Practical Information. Washington, DC: International Business Publications USA, 2012.

Nolting, Mark. *Africa's Top Wildlife Countries*. Ft. Lauderdale: Global Travel Publishers, Inc., 2008.

Orizio, Riccardo. *Lost White Tribes: The End of Privilege and the Last Colonials in Sri Lanka, Jamaica, Brazil, Haiti, Namibia, and Guadeloupe*. New York: Free Press, 2001.

Rotberg, Robert I. *Ending Autocracy, Enabling Democracy: The Tribulations of Southern Africa, 1960–2000*. Cambridge, MA: World Peace Foundation, 2002.

Sparks, Donald L. *Namibia: The Nation After Independence*. Boulder, CO: Westview Press, 1992.

Zeilig, Leo, and David Seddon. *A Political and Economic Dictionary of Africa*. Philadelphia: Routledge/Taylor and Francis, 2005.

NIGER

Republic of Niger
République du Niger

CAPITAL: Niamey

FLAG: The flag is a tricolor of orange, white, and green horizontal stripes, with an orange circle at the center of the white stripe.

ANTHEM: *La Nigérienne.*

MONETARY UNIT: The Communauté Financière Africaine franc (XOF), which was originally pegged to the French franc, has been pegged to the euro (€) since January 1999 with a rate of XOF655.957 = €1. The franc comes in coins of 1, 5, 10, 25, 50, 100, 200, 250, and 500 francs, and notes of 1,000, 2,000, 5,000, and 10,000 francs. XOF1 = US$0.0020 (or US$1 = XOF495.33) as of 2011.

WEIGHTS AND MEASURES: The metric system is the legal standard.

HOLIDAYS: New Year's Day, 1 January; Anniversary of 1974 military takeover, 15 April; Labor Day, 1 May; Independence Day, 3 August; Proclamation of the Republic, 18 December; Christmas, 25 December. Movable religious holidays include Eid al-Fitr, Eid al-Adha, and Milad an-Nabi.

TIME: 1 p.m. = noon GMT.

¹LOCATION, SIZE, AND EXTENT

A landlocked country, the Republic of Niger is the largest state in West Africa, with an area of 1,267,000 sq km (489,191 sq mi), extending 1,845 km (1,146 mi) ENE–WSW and 1,025 km (637 mi) NNW–SSE. Comparatively, the area occupied by Niger is slightly less than twice the size of the state of Texas. Bordered on the N by Libya, on the E by Chad, on the S by Nigeria, on the SW by Benin and Burkina Faso, on the W by Mali, and on the NW by Algeria, Niger has a total boundary length of 5,697 km (3,540 mi). Niger's capital city, Niamey, is located in the southwestern part of the country.

²TOPOGRAPHY

Niger is four-fifths desert, and most of the northeast is uninhabitable. The southern fifth of the country is savanna, suitable mainly for livestock raising and limited agriculture. In the north-central region is the volcanic Aïr Massif, reaching a height of 1,944 m (6,376 ft) on Mount Gréboun, the nation's highest point. Massifs along the Libyan border average about 800 m (2,600 ft). The southern plateau is at an elevation of 300–500 m (1,000–1,650 ft). The Niger River flows for about 563 km (350 mi) through southwestern Niger. To the north of the Niger are many ancient stream channels that flow periodically during wet weather. A portion of Lake Chad is situated in the southeastern corner of the country.

³CLIMATE

Niger, one of the hottest countries in the world, has three basic climatic zones: the Saharan desert in the north, the Sahel to the south of the desert, and the Sudan in the southwest corner. The intense heat of the Saharan zone often causes the scant rainfall to evaporate before it hits the ground; at Bilma, in the east, annual rainfall is only 2 cm (0.79 in). On the average, rainfall in the Aïr Massif is limited to a maximum of 25 cm (10 in) annually, and most of it comes during a single two-month period. At Agadez, in the northern Sahel, annual rainfall averages 16.5 cm (6.5 in), but yearly totals often vary greatly. In the south, rainfall is higher. It averages 56 cm (22 in) at Niamey, in the southern Sahel, and 87 cm (34 in) at Gaya, in the Sudanese zone. The rainy season is from May through October, with most rain in July and August. At Niamey, the average maximum daily temperature fluctuates from 31°C (88°F) in August to 41°C (106°F) in April. Nights are cool—below 20°C (68°F) from November to February.

⁴FLORA AND FAUNA

The World Resources Institute estimates that there are 1,460 plant species in Niger. The northern desert has vegetation only after rare rainfalls. The savanna includes a vast variety of herbaceous vegetation, with such trees as bastard mahogany, kapok, baobab, and the shea tree (karité). In addition, Niger is home to 123 mammal, 493 bird, 60 reptile, and 8 amphibian species. The calculation reflects the total number of distinct species residing in the country, not the number of endemic species. There are antelope, lion, waterbuck, leopard, hyena, monkey, wart hog, and countless varieties of bird and insect life. In the Niger River are crocodiles, hippopotamuses, and sometimes manatee. Turtles, lizards, pythons, horned vipers, and other varieties of snakes abound.

⁵ENVIRONMENT

The United Nations (UN) reported in 2008 that carbon dioxide emissions in Niger totaled 909 kilotons.

In Niger serious depletion of vegetation has been caused by the burning of brush and grass to prepare for the planting of crops, often on marginal land; by overgrazing of range lands; and by tree cutting for fuel and construction. Soil erosion and increasing desertification have also occurred.

The World Resources Institute reported that Niger had designated 8.41 million hectares (20.79 million acres) of land for protection as of 2006. Water resources totaled 33.7 cu km (8.09 cu mi) while water usage was 2.18 cu km (0.523 cu mi) per year. Domestic water usage accounted for 5% of total usage and agricultural for 95%. Per capita water usage totaled 156 cu m (5,509 cu ft) per year.

With Benin and Burkina Faso, Niger administers "W" National Park, of which 334,375 hectares (826,254 acres) are in Niger. There are also several game reserves, but resources for safeguarding protected fauna are insufficient. The nation's wildlife is endangered by unlawful hunting and poaching. Protected areas included 2 natural UN Educational, Scientific, and Cultural Organization (UNESCO) World Heritage sites and 12 Ramsar wetland sites. According to a 2011 report issued by the International Union for Conservation of Nature and Natural Resources (IUCN), the number of threatened species included 12 types of mammals, 7 species of birds, 1 species of invertebrate, and 4 species of plants. Threatened species include the addax, cheetah, and dama gazelle. The Sahara oryx has become extinct in the wild.

6 POPULATION

The US Central Intelligence Agency (CIA) estimated the population of Niger in 2011 to be approximately 16,468,886, which placed it at number 62 in population among the 196 nations of the world. In 2011 approximately 2.4% of the population was over 65 years of age, with another 49.6% under 15 years of age. The median age in Niger was 15.2 years. There was one male for every female in the country. The population's annual rate of change was 3.643%. The projected population for the year 2025 was 27,400,000. Population density in Niger was calculated at 13 people per sq km (34 people per sq mi).

The UN estimated that 17% of the population lived in urban areas, and that urban populations had an annual rate of change of 4.7%. The largest urban area was Niamey, with a population of 1 million.

7 MIGRATION

Estimates of Niger's net migration rate, carried out by the CIA in 2011, amounted to zero. The total number of emigrants living abroad was 386,900, and the total number of immigrants living in Niger was 202,200. Most of the northern area of Niger was inhabited by migratory peoples who followed their flocks and herds through the mountainous countryside. During the 1968–75 Sahelian drought, however, these people were forced to leave the north. Many nomads migrated to urban areas in order to keep from starving, but some later returned. As many as 500,000 people may have moved to Nigeria since the drought. About 100,000 returned in early 1983, when many foreigners were expelled from Nigeria. Thousands more Nigeriens were expelled from Nigeria in 1985 and in 1986; Algeria expelled about 2,000 of the 50,000 Nigerien nomads in southern Algeria. The migration from rural to urban areas has continued.

A five-year civil war (1990–95) between rival factions of Tuareg rebels drove many Tuaregs into big towns or neighboring countries such as Burkina Faso and Algeria. With the signing of a peace agreement in April 1995 came the implementation of a repatria-

tion program. Repatriation of Nigerien refugees from Algeria and Mali was completed by 1998. In 1999 some 3,589 Malian refugees were repatriated; however, some Malians remained on refugee sites, refusing to return to their homeland.

8 ETHNIC GROUPS

The Hausa are the largest ethnic group, forming 55.4% of the total population. The Djerma-Songhai, the second-largest group, constitutes 21% of the population. They, like the Hausa, are sedentary farmers living on the arable southern tier. The Djerma-Songhai are concentrated in the southwest; the Hausa, in south-central and southeast Niger. Many of Niger's inhabitants are nomadic or semi-nomadic livestock-raising peoples, including the Fulani, or Peul (8.5%), the Tuareg (9.3%), and the Beri Beri or Kanouri (4.7%). Arab, Toubou, and Gourmantche peoples make up the remaining 1.2% of the populace, along with some 1,200 French expatriates.

9 LANGUAGES

French is the national and official language, but it is spoken by only a small minority of the people. The various ethnic groups use their own local languages. Hausa is spoken all over the country as the language of trade. Djerma is also used extensively.

10 RELIGIONS

More than 98% of the population are Muslim, with about 95% Sunni and the remainder Shia. Christians, including both Catholics and Protestants, constitute less than 2% of the population; they tend to be concentrated in Maradi, Niamey, and other urban centers with expatriate populations. There are a small number of Baha'is, located primarily in Niamey and in communities on the west side of the Niger River, bordering Burkina Faso. Traditional indigenous religions are also practiced by a small percentage of the population. Though relations between religious communities are generally amicable, there have been reports of tension between certain fundamental Muslims and various Christian organizations. The constitution provides for freedom of religion and no particular religion is designated as a state religion. However, the government retains the right to monitor religious expression that might be considered detrimental to public safety and national unity. The constitution prohibits the formation of political parties based on religious doctrines. Religious organizations are registered with the Interior Ministry. Milad un-Nabi (the Prophet Muhammad's birthday), Easter Monday, Eid al-Fitr, Laylat al-Qadr, Eid al-Adha, Muharram, and Christmas are observed as national holidays.

11 TRANSPORTATION

Landlocked Niger relies heavily on road and air transportation. The CIA reports that Niger has a total of 18,949 km (11,774 mi) of roads, of which 3,912 km (2,431 mi) are paved. The principal road runs from west to east, beginning at Ayorou, going through Niamey, Dosso, Maradi, and Zinder, and ending at Nguigmi. A 902 km (560 mi) all-weather stretch between Niamey and Zinder was opened in 1980. Extending from the main route are roads from Niamey to Burkina Faso (not paved), from Zinder to Algeria through Agadez (with tough desert driving on dirt tracks), from Dosso to Benin, and from Birni Nkonni and Maradi to Nigeria. A 602 km (385 mi) highway between Tahoua and the uranium

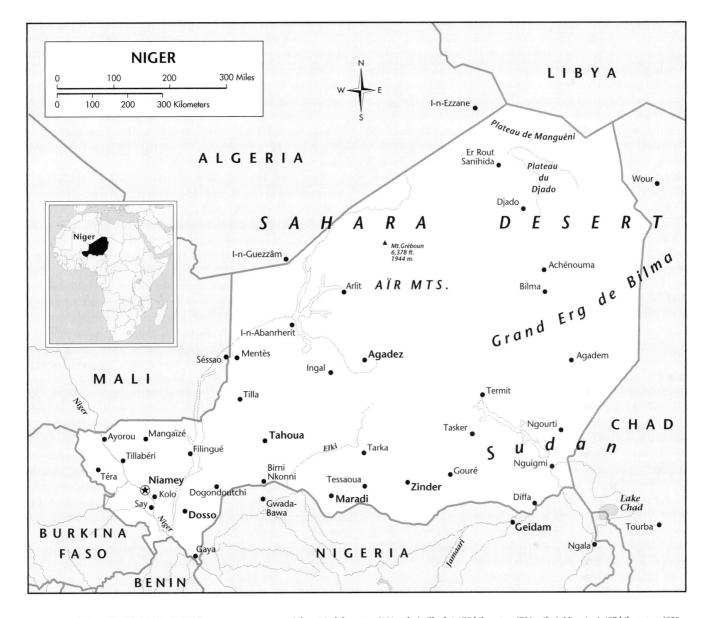

LOCATION: 12° to 23°30′N; 0°30′ to 15°30′ E. BOUNDARY LENGTHS: Libya, 354 kilometers (220 miles); Chad, 1,175 kilometers (730 miles); Nigeria, 1,497 kilometers (930 miles); Benin, 190 kilometers (118 miles); Burkina Faso, 628 kilometers (390 miles); Mali, 821 kilometers (510 miles); Algeria, 956 kilometers (594 miles). Broken lines indicate rivers and lakes that are dry for most of the year, only filling with water during infrequent rainy periods.

mines at Arlit was completed in 1981. SNTN National Transport Company, a government joint venture with a private French company, is the most important road hauler and has a monopoly over certain routes.

Niger's most important international transport route is by road to the rail terminus at Parakou, Benin. From there, Organisation Commune Benin-Niger (OCBN), a joint Benin-Niger railway, operates service to the Benin port of Cotonou. Niger has approximately 300 km (186 mi) of navigable waterways. The Niger River composes most of these navigable waterways, extending from Niamey to Gaya on the Benin frontier from September through March.

There are 27 airports. There were 10 airports with paved runways in 2010. The international airport is at Niamey. There are domestic airports at Agadez, Maradi, Zinder, Arlit, and Tahoua.

Niger is a participant in the transnational Air Afrique, which provides international service along with several other airlines.

12 HISTORY

Through extensive archaeological research, much evidence has been uncovered indicating that man has been present in northern Niger for over 600,000 years. By at least 4000 BC, a mixed population of Libyan, Berber, and Negroid peoples had evolved an agricultural and cattle-herding economy in the Sahara. Written history begins only with Arab chronicles of the 10th century AD. By the 14th century, the Hausa had founded several city-states along the southern border of what is today the Republic of Niger. About 1515 an army of the Songhai Empire of Gao (now in Mali), led by Askia Muhammad I, subjugated the Hausa states and captured the Berber city of Agadez, whose sultanate had existed for many generations. The city had been important largely because of its position on the caravan trade routes from Tripoli and Egypt into the Lake Chad area. The fall of the Songhai Empire to Moroccan invaders in 1591 led to expansion of the Bornu Empire, which was centered in northeast Nigeria, into the eastern and central sections of the region. The Hausa states and the Tuareg also remained important. It was probably during the 17th century that the Djerma settled in the southwest. Between 1804 and 1810 a devout Fulani Muslim named Usman dan Fodio waged a holy war against the Hausa states, which he subjugated along with a part of the Bornu Empire west of Lake Chad. About that time, European explorers began to enter the area, starting with a Scot, Mungo Park, in 1805–06.

Bornu, Hausa, and Fulani entities vied for power during the 19th century, a period during which political control was fragmented. The first French military expeditions into the Niger area at the close of the 19th century were stiffly resisted. Despite this opposition French forces pushed steadily eastward and by 1900 had succeeded in encircling Lake Chad with military outposts. In 1901 the military district of Niger was created as part of a larger unit known as Haut-Sénégal et Niger. Rebellions plagued the French forces on a minor scale until World War I, when a major uprising took place. Some 1,000 Tuareg warriors attacked Zinder in a move promoted by pro-German elements intent on creating unrest in French and British African holdings. British troops were dispatched from Nigeria to assist the French in putting down the disturbance. Although this combined operation broke the Tuareg resistance, not until 1922 was peace fully restored. In that year, the French made Niger a colony.

Niger's colonial history is similar to that of other former French West African territories. It had a governor but was administered from Paris through the governor-general in Dakar, Senegal. From 1932 to 1947, Niger was administered jointly with Upper Volta (now Burkina Faso) for budgetary reasons. World War II barely touched Niger, since the country was too isolated and undeveloped to offer anything of use to the Free French forces.

In 1946 the French constitution conferred French citizenship on the inhabitants of all the French territories and provided for a gradual decentralization of power and limited participation in indigenous political life. On 28 September 1958 voters in Niger approved the constitution of the Fifth French Republic, and on 19 December 1958 Niger's Territorial Assembly voted to become an autonomous state, the Republic of Niger, within the French Community. A ministerial government was formed by Hamani Diori, a deputy to the French National Assembly and secretary-general to the Niger branch of the African Democratic Rally (Rassemblement Démocratique Africain—RDA). On 11 July 1960 agreements on national sovereignty were signed by Niger and France, and on 3 August 1960 the Republic of Niger proclaimed its independence. Diori, who had been able to consolidate his political dominance with the help of the French colonial administration, became Niger's first president. His principal opponent was Djibo Bakary, whose party, known as the Sawaba, had been banned in 1959 for advocating a no vote in the 1958 French constitutional referendum. The Sawaba was allegedly responsible for a number of unsuccessful attempts to assassinate Diori after 1959.

Diori was able to stay in power throughout the 1960s and early 1970s. His amicable relations with the French enabled him to ob-

tain considerable technical, military, and financial aid from the French government. In 1968 following a dispute between the ruling Niger Progressive Party (Parti Progressiste Nigérien—PPN) and the civil service over alleged corruption of civil service personnel, the PPN was given a larger role in the national administration. Over the years Diori developed a reputation as an African statesman and was able to settle several disputes between other African nations. However, unrest developed at home as Niger, together with its Sahel neighbors, suffered widespread devastation from the drought of the early 1970s.

On 15 April 1974 the Diori government was overthrown by a military coup led by Lt. Col. Seyni Kountché, the former chief of staff who subsequently assumed the presidency. Madame Diori was killed in the rebellion, as were approximately 100 others, and the former president was detained from 1974–80 under house arrest. Soon after the coup French troops stationed in Niger left at Kountché's request.

The economy grew markedly in the late 1970s, chiefly because of a uranium boom that ended in 1980. The Kountché regime, which was generally pro-Western, broke diplomatic relations with Libya in January 1981 in alarm and anger over Libya's military intervention in Chad. Relations with Libya slowly improved, and diplomatic ties resumed in 1982. Nevertheless Niger continued to fear Libyan efforts at subversion, particularly among the Tuareg of northern Niger. In October 1983, an attempted coup in Niamey was suppressed by forces loyal to President Kountché. Kountché died of a brain tumor in November 1987, and then Col. Ali Saibou, the army chief of staff, was appointed president.

In 1989 Saibou created what he intended to be a national single party, The National Movement for a Developmental Society (Le Mouvement National pour la Société de Développement—MNSD). However, the winds of democratic change ushered in multiparty competition. At the forefront for political reform was the labor confederation, which organized a widely observed two day long general strike. Following the example of Benin, a national conference was held from July to October 1991 to prepare a new constitution. The conferees appointed an interim government led by Amadou Cheiffou to work alongside the Saibou government to organize multiparty elections. Widespread fighting in the north and military mutinies in February 1992 and July 1993 postponed the elections, but a new constitution was adopted in a December 1992 referendum.

Niger's first multiparty elections took place on 27 February 1993. Mamadou Tandja, who succeeded Saibou as MNSD leader, came in first with 34%. However, with Mohamadou Issoufou's support, Mahamane Ousmane defeated him in the March runoff with 54% of the vote. In the legislative elections, the MNSD won the largest number of the seats (29), but a coalition of nine opposition parties, the Alliance of the Forces of Change (AFC) dominated the National Assembly with 50 of the 83 seats. Prime Minister Issoufou led the AFC.

The new government found itself threatened by an insurgency in the north. In March it reached a three-month truce with the major Tuareg group, the Liberation Front of Air and Azaouak (FLAA), and was able to extend it for three more months. By September, however, the Tuaregs had split into three factions and only one, the Front for the Liberation of Tamoust (FLT), agreed to renew the truce for three more months. Some Tuaregs, chiefly under the Liberation Army of Northern Niger (Armée Revolutionnaire de Libération du Nord Niger—ARLNN) continued the rebellion, prompting more government reprisals.

The Tuareg raids created tension with Libya, suspected of inciting the insurgencies, and divided Nigerians over issues of favoritism. The government appeared biased in favor of members of the Djerma-Songhai (or Zarma-Songhai), one of Niger's five major ethnolinguistic groups. In April 1995 a tentative peace was reached via the joint mediation of Algeria, Burkina Faso, and France. However, ethnic disturbances continued in the south of the country.

In late 1994 disagreements between the president and the leadership of the National Assembly resulted in a political stalemate lasting throughout 1995. In the legislative elections of 12 January 1995, the AFC succumbed to factionalism allowing the MNSD to win a slight majority (29 seats). The MNSD formed a ruling coalition with its allies in the Democratic and Social Convention (24 seats). However, the two sides fought over the appointment of a prime minister, and then-prime minister, Hama Amadou, and President Ousmane fought over International Monetary Fund (IMF) austerity measures. In January 1996 Col. Ibrahim Baré Maïnassara (known as Baré) toppled Ousmane and dissolved the Assembly. The military regime suspended political parties and civil liberties, and placed the president, prime minister, and president of the Assembly under house arrest. Despite Baré's pledge to restore democracy, donors cut assistance to Niger.

In May 1996 voters approved a new constitution that strengthened the powers of the executive. However, only 40% of the electorate voted. Baré lifted the ban on political parties and in the July elections, despite evidence of massive fraud, declared himself the winner with 52% of the vote. Ousmane received 19%, Tandja Mamadou 16%, Mahamadou Issoufou 8%, and Moumouni Amadou Djermakoye 5%. Baré's Union of Independents for Democratic Renewal (UNIRD) took 52 of 83 Assembly seats in the November 1996 legislative elections.

On 9 April 1999 while boarding his helicopter, President Baré died in a hail of assassin's bullets. Political gridlock gripped the country, eroded public confidence in government, and allowed the military to intervene. The day prior to the assassination, opposition leaders had called on Baré to step down. Maj. Daouda Mallam Wanké said the presidential guard had opened fire in self-defense, and his junta later described the murder as an unfortunate accident. Few people believed it was, and the coup was roundly condemned by the international community. Baré's widow, Clemen Aicha Baré, filed claims against Wanké as the prime perpetrator and against the former prime minister Ibrahim Assane Mayaki for his alleged role in the assassination.

In October 1999 Wanké made good on his promise to return the country to civilian rule. Despite allegations of vote rigging, seven candidates contested the presidential elections. In the first round, Mamadou Tandja (MNSD) took 32.3% of the vote to Mahamadou Issoufou's Nigerien Party for Democracy and Socialism (PNDS) 22.8%. In the 24 November runoff, Tandja was elected with 59.9% to Issoufou's 40.1%. Observers declared the second round free and fair. In the 24 November Assembly elections, five of seven parties won seats. The MNSD took 38 of 83 seats, the Democratic and Social Convention (CDS) 17, the PNDS 16, the

Rally for Democracy and Progress (RDP) 8, and the Nigerien Alliance for Democracy and Progress (ANDP) 4.

The new National Assembly passed an amnesty for perpetrators of the January 1996 and April 1999 coups to avoid "the spirit of revenge or any form of resentment." Eight members of Maïnassara Baré's party dissented. Tandja said his top priority would be to work for political, social, and institutional stability, essential for national recovery.

In May 2002 Niger and Benin submitted a boundary dispute between them to the International Court of Justice (ICJ) in the Hague. At issue were sectors of the Niger and Mékrou rivers and islands in them, in particular Lété Island. This dispute was resolved in Niger's favor by the court in 2005.

On 30 July 2002 soldiers from three garrisons in the southeastern Diffa Region mutinied, protesting low and overdue salaries and improper working conditions. The mutiny threatened Niamey, but troops loyal to the government put down the 10-day rebellion on 9 August. In December at least 80 of the mutineers who were arrested in August escaped from prison.

In early 2004 the government established an all-party dialogue and conflict resolution forum, the National Council for Political Dialogue (Conseil National de Dialogue Politique—CNDP). In May 2004 rumors of a new Tuareg rebellion surfaced following the desertion of former Tuareg rebels from the army, which coincided with armed attacks and banditry in the north. However, in July and December 2004 the country held successful local, presidential, and parliamentary elections. Tandja was reelected in the presidential poll, a first for a Nigerien president.

Despite its convincing victory in the December 2004 polls, the ruling MNSD party faced serious social and economic challenges heading into 2006. A major food crisis in the second half of 2005 was portrayed as a famine in the international media and by UN agencies, and was strongly criticized by donor governments as the result of poor governance. Following the introduction of taxes on basic foodstuffs, the government became the target of major social protests, and ultimately had to withdraw the measures. Ultimately, an estimated 3 million of Niger's 12 million people were facing hunger, and some 32,000 children were thought to be severely malnourished. While President Tandja blamed food shortages on climatic factors and locust invasions, the main opposition party, the PNDS, accused the government of diverting aid, and criticized it for its slow reaction and mismanagement of the crisis.

In May 2009 Tandja announced a plan for a national referendum that would amend the constitution by removing the two-term limit on the presidency. When opposition leaders and labor unions protested against the plan, Tandja dissolved parliament and assumed greater executive powers. In June 2009 the constitutional court ruled that the referendum was unlawful, leading Tandja to dissolve that body too, claiming emergency powers to rule by decree. Despite continued protests from within the nation and criticism from the international community, the referendum proceeded as planned on 4 August 2009. Though opposition groups called for a boycott, the measure was approved by 92.5% of the vote. Tandja claimed that his motive in seeking additional terms in office was based on a need for more time to complete a series of economic development projects. Critics saw the move as a major step away from democratic rule and expressed concern that the completion of Tandja's economic projects would profit the government more than the general population.

On 18 February 2010 a military coup ensued as armored vehicles descended on Niger's capital in a surprise assault on the presidential palace. President Tandja was removed from the palace and taken to another house on the grounds. Given the growing discontent over Tandja's term extension and the resulting international sanctions, the coup came as little surprise to local analysts. The military junta responsible for the coup identified themselves as the Supreme Council for the Restoration of Democracy; their appointed leader was Col. Salou Djibo. The group immediately announced the suspension of the constitution and the dissolution of all state institutions. A few days after seizing the president, a spokesman for the group reported that the new government intended to draft a new constitution and hold democratic elections. The civilian council presented its draft constitution in August 2010. The charter reduced the powers of the president and reinstated the position of prime minister as the head of government. It established a limit of two five-year terms for the president and called for parliamentary elections to be held every five years. The draft also called for changes that would create greater transparency in business and industry. The constitutional referendum was held on 31 October 2010. With 52% turnout the new constitution was approved by more than 90% of voters. A first round of presidential elections and parliamentary elections were held on 31 January 2011. Mahamadou Issoufou of the PNDS and Seini Oumarou of the MNSD competed in the second-round presidential elections on March 12. Issoufou won the presidency with about 58% of the vote and took office on 7 April 2011 with Brigi Rafini named as prime minister.

13 GOVERNMENT

The constitution of 8 November 1960 established the president of the republic, elected for a five-year term by direct universal suffrage, as chief of state and head of the executive branch. Legislative power was invested in a 50-member unicameral National Assembly. This constitution was suspended following the military coup of 15 April 1974, when the National Assembly was also dissolved. All executive and legislative power was taken over by the Supreme Military Council, composed of army officers. The president of the Supreme Military Council was president of the council of ministers (cabinet) and head of state. Seyni Kountché held this office from 1974 to 1987. Most cabinet officers were civilians in 1987.

In 1987 a national development council was established to serve as a constituent assembly on a nonparty basis. It drafted the constitution of the Second Republic that came into force on 24 September 1989.

A national conference from July to October 1991 drafted a multiparty democratic constitution that was approved by national referendum on 26 December 1992. It established the Third Republic with a National Assembly of 83 deputies chosen by popular and competitive elections, a president likewise elected, and a prime minister elected by the Assembly. The new government with Mahamane Ousmane as its head was sworn in on 23 April 1993.

Political gridlock led to a relatively bloodless coup led by then Col. Ibrahim Baré Maïnassara in January 1996. Within six months the regime had drafted and submitted for national referendum a new constitution with a significantly strengthened executive.

The document was approved on 12 May 1996 ushering in the short-lived Fourth Republic. In flawed elections Baré Maïnassara declared himself winner over four other candidates on the first round, and his UNIRD party won a majority of seats in the Assembly.

Baré Maïnassara was assassinated on 9 April 1999 by his presidential guard. Maj. Daouda Wanké reappointed Ibrahim Assane Maiyaki as prime minister for the transition government. He then appointed a transitional cabinet consisting of 20 members, most of whom were civilian. Wanké also replaced seven of Niger's regional military leaders. He announced that he would not run for the presidency and disqualified all military and security personnel, as well as all members of the transitional government from standing for election. Wanké named a 60-member independent national election commission to oversee the establishment of the election roles and the polling. The CRN renounced any form of remuneration during the transition period and moved to reduce by half the salaries of future members of government.

The constitution of the Fifth Republic, adopted 18 July 1999, provides for a semi-presidential government. The president, who may stand for two five-year terms, is head of state, and appoints the prime minister (head of government) from a list of three candidates proposed by the parliamentary majority. The president names all 23 cabinet ministers and other high-ranking civilian and military officials. Presidential actions must be countersigned by the prime minister. The National Assembly can unseat the prime minister through a no-confidence vote. The president can dissolve the 113-member National Assembly (expanded from 83), assume emergency powers, and convene the Council of the Republic in the event of a constitutional crisis. The National Assembly has the power to pass a motion of no confidence in the government.

This Fifth Republic constitution created four new bodies: the Constitutional Court, the Superior National Defense Council, the Council of the Republic (a conflict resolution body), and the Economic, Social, and Cultural Council. The Council of the Republic was created to end the political impasse that brought down the Third Republic through the military coup in 1996. Amnesties for those involved in both the 1996 and 1999 coups were part of the constitutional draft.

14 POLITICAL PARTIES

Parties emerged only after World War II. In 1946 the RDA became dominant with the help of several labor unions. By 1948 its popularity waned, and the PPN, the local branch of the RDA, was unable to reelect its candidate to the French National Assembly. Meanwhile, other parties, based on regional interests, gained strength.

In 1957 Djibo Bakary, leader of a dissident RDA group, helped form a socialist party that became known as the Party of the African Regrouping (Parti du Regroupement Africain—PRA). Branches were quickly established in most of the other French-African territories.

Shortly before the voting on the French constitution in September 1958, the PPN joined with chiefs and dissident PRA members to form a coalition, the Union for the Franco-African Community (Union pour la Communauté Franco-Africaine), led by Hamani Diori, leader of the PPN. On 14 December 1958 the Sawaba, led by Djibo Bakary, was defeated by the new coalition, which won 54 of the 60 seats in the Assembly. Following full independence Diori became president of the republic. Diori consolidated the position of the PPN by allying himself with Niger's powerful Muslim traditional chiefs, exiling Bakary, and banning the Sawaba in 1959. In 1964 and 1965 Bakary organized attacks from abroad on Diori's life.

The PPN became the only legal party under the Diori regime. In the October 1970 elections, Diori won 99.98% of the votes cast, and the PPN won 97.09% of the votes cast for the National Assembly. After the coup of 15 April 1974, the military government suppressed all political organizations in the country. Both Diori and Bakary, who returned from exile, were imprisoned until 1980.

In 1989 Saibou created the MNSD, which was intended to be the sole legal party, but the constitutional referendum of December 1992 authorized a multiple party system. In the legislative elections on 12 January 1995 some 774 candidates ran for 83 Assembly seats. The MNSD won a slight majority (29 seats) and formed a coalition with the CDS (24 seats). The coalition was factious, and in January 1996, leaders of a military coup dissolved the Assembly, overthrew the president, and banned political parties. Following the approval of a new constitution in May, political parties once again were allowed to exist.

In flawed presidential elections in July 1996, Baré Maïnassara took 52.22%, Mahamane Ousmane 19.75%, Mamadou Tandja 15.65%, and two other candidates took the remaining 12% of the vote. Legislative elections were held again in November 1996 for the reinstated 83-seat National Assembly. The pro-Maïnassara UNIRD won 52 seats, the Nigerian Alliance for Democracy and Progress-Zaman (ANDPS-Zaman Lahiya) 8, Union of Patriots, Democrats, and Progressives (Union des Patriotes Démocratiques et Progressistes—UPDP-Shamuwa) 4, Union for Democracy and Social Progress (Union pour la Démocratie et le Progrès Social—UDPS-Amana) 3, coalition of independents 3, with the remaining 6 seats divided among three other parties.

In the October–November 1999 presidential elections, Mamadou Tandja won convincingly with 32.3% on the first round and 59.9% on the second. Mahamadou Issoufou (PNDS) came in second with 22.8% and 40.1%. The others were Mahamane Ousmane (CDS) with 22.5%, Hamid Algabid (RDP) with 10.9%, Mumouni Djermakoye Amadou (ANDP) with 7.7%, Andre Salifou (UDPD) with 2.1% and Amadou Ali Djibo (Union of Independent Nigerians, Union des Nigériens Indépendants—UNI) with 1.7% of the vote.

A new political landscape emerged after the elections. The CDS of former president Ousmane rallied behind MNSD to catapult Tandja and MNSD to victory in the 24 November second round. Formerly CDS was pitted against MNSD as part of the Alliance du Changement (AC) in the multiparty elections of 1991. Ousmane and Tandja were sworn enemies until General Baré's coup ousted Ousmane in 1996. The coup threw CDS and MNSD into the opposition, and made them both members of the umbrella alliance, the Front pour la Restauration et Défense de la Démocratie (FRDD) to compete in the elections in November 1996. FRDD had comprised eight parties including MNSD, CDS, and Issoufou's party, PNDS.

In the National Assembly elected on 24 November 1999, 5 of 19 contending parties won seats. MNSD took 38 of 83 seats, CDS 17, PNDS 16, RDP 8, and ANDP 4. Thus, the MNSD-CDS coalition had 55 of 83 seats. With its 16 seats Issoufou's PNDS took leadership of the opposition coalition. The main allies of the opposition were the RDP and the ANDP bringing the coalition to 30 seats.

The November–December 2004 general elections saw the re-election of Mamadou Tandja and reinforced the dominance of the ruling coalition, the Alliance des Forces Démocratiques (AFD), comprising five parties led by MNSD. Tandja won with 65.5% of the vote to 34.5% for Mahamadou Issoufou. In the legislative contest, MNSD took 47 seats, followed by CDS with 22, PNDS (the main opposition party) with 17, the Social and Democratic Rally with 7, RDP with 6, ANDP with 5, and the Party for Socialism and Democracy in Niger with 1; others took a total of 8 seats. In all the ruling coalition secured 88 of 113 seats.

In the October 2009 legislative elections, MNSD won 76 seats, followed by the Social Democratic Rally (RSD) with 15 seats, and the RDP with 7 seats. The Nigerien Self-Management Party, the Rally of Nigerien Patriots, the Workers' Movement Party, and the Union of Independent Nigeriens each gained one seat. Eleven seats were won by independent candidates.

In the January 2011 legislative elections following the 2010 coup, the PNDS-Tarrayya won 39 seats, followed by the National Movement for a Developing Society-Nassara (MNSD-Nassara) with 26 seats, the Nigerien Democratic Movement for an African Federation (MODEN/FA) with 23, the ANDP with 8, the RDP with 7, Union for Democracy and the Republic-Tabbat with 6, the CDS with 3 and the Union of Independent Nigeriens with 1.

A first round of presidential elections was held 31 January 2011. These marked the first elections since the February 2010 military coup. Of the ten candidates three were leading: Mahamadou Issoufou of the Social Democratic Party and two former prime ministers—Seini Oumarou of MNSD and Hama Amadou of MNSD-Nassara. In the March 2011 runoff Issoufou came out ahead with 58% of the vote; Oumarou received 42% of the vote. The elections were reportedly peaceful and fair. Issoufou was inaugurated on 7 April 2011 and named Brigi Rafini as Prime Minister.

15 LOCAL GOVERNMENT

Niger consists of 8 regions (departments), subdivided into 36 districts (arrondissements) and a capital district. Democratization and demands for better governance have led to decentralization and popular participation in local government. However, devolving authority from the national level required adequate electoral safeguards. In 1999 the Supreme Court ordered rerun elections in five regions. Opponents objected on the grounds that their candidates had held a clear lead over those of the president's party. The ensuing deadlock contributed to the crisis of government and to the 9 April coup.

16 JUDICIAL SYSTEM

The legal system, which is seriously under-resourced and subject to executive pressures and corruption, mirrors French civil law with important customary-law modifications. The High Court of Justice, which is appointed by the National Assembly from among its own membership, is empowered to try the president and members of the government for crimes or offenses committed in performance of their official duties. Defendants and prosecutors may appeal verdicts from lower courts, first to the Court of Appeals and then to the Supreme Court, which sits as the highest court of appeal. The seven-member Constitutional Court has jurisdiction over electoral and constitutional matters, including ruling on the constitutionality of laws and ordinances, as well as compliance with international treaties and agreements. A Court of State Security tries crimes against the state.

Notably, the Constitutional Court has overruled several presidential decrees, rejected more than one third of the candidates in the local elections in April 2004, and forced the government to change the electoral code and reschedule the local elections.

Traditional and customary courts hear cases involving divorce or inheritance. There are no religious courts. Customary courts, located in larger towns and cities, are presided over by a legal practitioner with basic legal training who is advised about local tradition by a local assessor. The actions of chiefs in traditional courts and of the presiding practitioner in customary courts are not regulated by the code provisions. Appeals can be taken from both customary and traditional courts to the formal court system.

[17] ARMED FORCES

The International Institute for Strategic Studies reports that armed forces in Niger totaled 5,300 members in 2011. The force is comprised of 5,200 from the army and 100 members of the air force. Armed forces represent .2% of the labor force in Niger. Defense spending totaled $144.3 million and accounted for 1.3% of GDP.

Niger's primary military missions include guaranteeing national sovereignty by protecting its national interests against aggression, participating with and reinforcing police in civil defense matters, countering the proliferation of small arms, contributing to regional security, and supporting international peacekeeping operations.

Niger participated in four UN peacekeeping missions in Africa. While Nigerien forces have expressed a desire to actively combat terrorism and secure their borders, resources are stretched thin protecting mining and petroleum investments, participating in international peacekeeping operations, and dealing with residual banditry. Primary partners for security cooperation include France, China, Algeria, and Morocco.

In April 2010 Niger joined forces with its neighbors to form the Joint Military Staff Committee of Algeria, Mali, Mauritania, and Niger. Based in Tamanrassett, Algeria, the general purpose of the committee is to strengthen cooperation through shared intelligence and joint military operations in the fight against terrorism, drug trafficking, and illegal weapons trade. Specifically, the committee hopes to combine efforts against the increasing regional threat from al-Qaeda. Regional and international leaders fear that al-Qaeda intends to establish bases in the Sahara, which could provide a safe haven for the terrorist organization if regional forces, such as the new committee, fail to take action.

[18] INTERNATIONAL COOPERATION

Niger was admitted to the UN on 20 September 1960, and is a member of UN Economic Commission for Africa (ECA) and several other nonregional specialized agencies, such as the Food and Agriculture Organization (FAO), International Labour Organization (ILO), the World Bank, International Atomic Energy Agency (IAEA), UNESCO, UN Industrial Development Organization (UNIDO), and the World Health Organization (WHO). Niger is also a member of the World Trade Organization (WTO), the Af-

rican Development Bank, the West African Development Bank; African, Caribbean and Pacific Group of States (ACP Group), the Economic Community of West African States (ECOWAS), the Commonwealth of Nations, Group of 77 (G-77); the Community of Sahel and Saharan States (CENSAD), the Organization of the Islamic Conference (OIC), the New Partnership for Africa's Development (NEPAD), the West African Economic and Monetary Union, the Niger River and Lake Chad Basin Commissions, and the African Union. It has joined with Benin, Côte d'Ivoire, Burkina Faso and Togo in the Council of the Entente, a customs union with a common solidarity fund. The nation is part of the Franc Zone.

Niger is a member of the Nonaligned Movement. The government has offered support to UN missions and operations in Liberia (est. 2003), Burundi (est. 2004), Côte d'Ivoire (est. 2004), and the Democratic Republic of the Congo (DROC, est.1999). In environmental cooperation, Niger is part of the Basel Convention, the Convention on Biological Diversity, the Ramsar Convention on Wetlands, the Convention on International Trade in Endangered Species (CITES), the Kyoto Protocol, the Montréal Protocol, the Nuclear Test Ban Treaty, the UN Convention on Climate Change, and the UN Convention to Combat Desertification (UNCCD).

[19] ECONOMY

The gross domestic product (GDP) rate of change in Niger as of 2010 was 7.5%. Inflation stood at 0.1%.

Niger is an arid, landlocked country with much of its territory forming a portion of the Sahara. It is one of the poorest countries in the world with its population ranking last on the UN Human Development Index (HDI). Most of its people live in a marginally productive and highly drought-prone band of arable land along Niger's southern border with Nigeria. The economy is based on subsistence farming even though less than 3% of the land is under cultivation. A drought and locust infestation in 2005 led to food shortages for as many as 2.5 million Nigerians. Agriculture and livestock production employed an estimated 90% of the labor force in 2007. The formal economy generates few jobs.

Niger has some of the world's largest uranium deposits and uranium mining is a mainstay of Niger's export economy. Exports of uranium helped the country enjoy rapid economic growth during the 1960s and 1970s. However, revenues dropped by almost 50% in the late 1980s due to a decline in world demand. When prices rebounded in 2006, exports surged to contribute over 55% of foreign exchange earnings. In addition to uranium there are exploitable deposits of gold and oil potential, as well as deposits of coal, phosphates, iron, limestone, and gypsum.

Before 2000 a history of military rule and a bad debt repayment record kept foreign aid and investment from entering the country. The government also maintained inefficient monopolies in water, power, and telecommunications. The economy received a shock in January 1994 when France devalued the Central African Franc (CFA franc), causing its value to drop in half overnight. The devaluation of the CFA franc improved Niger's trade relationship with Nigeria and boosted revenue from the export of such products as livestock, peas, onions, and cotton. Still the country's economy was in need of reform. In 1998 encouraged by the World Bank, the government began a privatization program that successfully privatized its telecommunications monopoly, while leaving the electric utility and oil distribution company in government hands.

Democratic rule was restored in 2000, but the new government was faced with serious economic problems. The treasury was empty and government workers went unpaid. The International Monetary Fund (IMF) and the World Bank encouraged economic reforms and made the county eligible for debt relief under their Heavily Indebted Poor Countries (HIPC) initiative, in the amount of $115 million. Freed of its debt service obligation, Niger was able to direct funds to basic health care, primary education, HIV/AIDS prevention, rural infrastructure, and other programs geared at poverty reduction. In 2005 the IMF canceled all Niger's debt to it (approximately $111 million) incurred before January 2005. In 2006 the African Development Fund (ADF) canceled $193 million in debt for Niger. The World Bank announced that approximately $745 million in debt relief for Niger would be phased in over the next 37 years.

In early 2010 political instability caused many international organizations to withhold aid funds from the nation. In May 2010 the World Bank reestablished aid funding to Niger by promising $40 million in budgetary aid, primarily to provide relief for severe food shortages which plagued the nation. According to the UN at least 60% of the population was expected to face the threat of severe food shortages by the end of 2010. The announcement of funding came a few days after the military junta began its own major food drive and distribution program, with hopes of providing free food for at least 1 million people of the estimated 10 million people in need. Since inauguration of the elected government in April 2011, most donor countries, including the United States and European Union, started to reengage in several key sectors. Foreign aid represents 8.3% of Niger's GDP and over 40% of government revenues.

²⁰INCOME

The CIA estimated that in 2010 the GDP of Niger was $11.05 billion. The CIA defines GDP as the value of all final goods and services produced within a nation in a given year and computed on the basis of purchasing power parity (PPP) rather than value as measured on the basis of the rate of the exchange based on current dollars. The per capita GDP was estimated at $700. The annual growth rate of GDP was 7.5%. The average inflation rate was 0.1%. It was estimated that agriculture accounted for 39% of GDP, industry 17%, and services 44%.

As of 2011 the most recent study by the World Bank reported that actual individual consumption in Niger was 76.9% of GDP and accounted for 0.02% of world consumption. By comparison, the United States accounted for 25.44% of world individual consumption. The World Bank also estimated that 37.6% of Niger's GDP was spent on food and beverages, 10.2% on housing and household furnishings, 5.5% on clothes, 3.5% on health, 6.1% on transportation, 0.6% on communications, 4.0% on recreation, 4.0% on restaurants and hotels, and 2.7% on miscellaneous goods and services and purchases from abroad. According to the World Bank remittances from citizens living abroad totaled $89.1 million or about $5 per capita and accounted for approximately 0.8% of GDP.

It was estimated that in 1993 about 63% of the population subsisted on an income below the poverty line established by Niger's government.

²¹LABOR

As of 2007 Niger had a total labor force of 4.688 million people. Within that labor force CIA estimates in 1995 noted that 90% were employed in agriculture, 6% in industry, and 4% in the service sector.

The minimum wage varies for each class and category of salaried employees. The lowest minimum wage was approximately $57 per month in 2010, which does not provide a family with a decent standard of living. The legal workweek is 40 hours for most occupations, with some legal workweeks extending to 72 hours. The minimum age for employment is 14 years old. This is observed in the formal sector of the economy, but child labor persists in the informal economy and in agriculture.

The Union of Workers' Syndicates of Niger (Union des Syndicats des Travailleurs du Niger—USTN) is the only trade union federation. It was founded in Niamey in 1960 and is affiliated with the African Trade Union Confederation. USTN has 38 member unions. Its head is appointed by the government. Unions represent a very small segment of the population; most members are government workers. Except for police and security forces, employees are permitted to engage in strikes.

²²AGRICULTURE

Roughly 11% of the total land is farmed, and the country's major crops include cowpeas, cotton, peanuts, millet, sorghum, cassava (tapioca), and rice. Cereal production in 2009 amounted to 3.5 million tons, fruit production 262,236 tons, and vegetable production 749,961 tons.

Although only 2.8% of Niger's area is cultivated, farmers increased their production following the 1968–75 drought, and in 1980 the country became self-sufficient in food crops. The most plentiful rains in 30 years fell during the 1992–1993 season, pushing agricultural production up by 64%. Irrigation and off-season farming projects are of keen interest to the government and foreign donors. During 1990–2000, agricultural production grew by an annual average of 3.2%. Almost 90% of the active population is engaged in crop cultivation or animal husbandry.

Agricultural techniques are still rudimentary; there are a few tractors in use, and most farmers do not keep draft animals. Very little fertilizer is used. Over 95% of agriculture is on farms of less than five hectares (12 acres), with the average about three hectares (7.5 acres). Cowpeas are only competitive as an export in neighboring Nigeria's market due to transportation costs. The government of Niger is encouraging crop diversification and the raising of export crops like onions, garlic, peppers, and potatoes, in addition to cowpeas.

Peanuts, formerly the main source of agricultural export revenue, are planted mainly in the Zinder area. Production increased from 8,980 tons in 1945 to a high of 298,000 tons in 1967. Because of a lack of producer incentives, production declined to only 87,000 tons in 1982, and only a fraction of that total was delivered to the government marketing agency, SOMARA, which had a monopoly on pricing and marketing peanut products until 1986.

Cotton, introduced in 1956 to reduce Niger's dependence on peanuts, has also suffered from lack of grower incentives. Production of seed cotton rose from 218 tons in 1956 to 6,682 tons in 1967 but was only around 5,000 tons in 2009.

In April 2010 the Red Cross launched a massive relief operation to help hundreds of thousands of people in northern Mali and Niger who were suffering from the aftermath of a failed harvest. According to the Red Cross, some 250,000 people in those countries were short of food in April 2010, while millions more were suffering the effects of food insecurity. Rainfall in Northern Mali and Niger was 70% below the annual average in 2009, severely affecting the harvest and straining the abilities of herders to maintain their livestock. Because there were far more cows than the land could support, the Red Cross agreed to purchase 20,000 head of cattle from local herders. The meat harvest from those animals was used to feed the hungry. The whole operation cost the Red Cross tens of millions of dollars, almost triple the amount the agency had budgeted for Mali and Niger in 2010.

23 ANIMAL HUSBANDRY

The FAO reported that Niger dedicated 28.8 million hectares (71.1 million acres) to permanent pasture or meadow in 2009. Almost half the land area of Niger is classified as pasture but, like agriculture, animal husbandry has suffered greatly from insufficient rainfall. About 12% of Niger's GDP comes from livestock production, which engages 29% of the population. Official statistics of Niger seriously underrepresent total exports—most animals are herded across borders without documentation.

Meat production, which had dropped to 38,000 tons in 1973, was an estimated 106,000 tons in 2011. In 2009 the country tended 11 million chickens, 9.3 million head of cattle, and 40,000 pigs. The production from these animals amounted to 192,006 tons of beef and veal, 1,467 tons of pork, 10,688 tons of poultry, 4,719 tons of eggs, and 707,104 tons of milk. Niger also produced 35,000 tons of cattle hide. There is a tannery at Maradi. Sandals, briefcases, and fine ladies handbags of high quality are produced in small numbers but seldom exported.

Meat exports are inspected and controlled by the customs service before leaving the country. Only inspected, tuberculin-tested cattle are used in export meat production. The Niger River Valley south of Say is infested by the tsetse fly, and trypanosomiasis is, therefore, a major cattle disease.

24 FISHING

In 2011 the annual capture totaled 30,000 tons according to the FAO.

There is no commercial fishing on a wide scale, but fishing is an appreciable source of revenue for the Sorko on the Niger River and the Boudouma on Lake Chad. The fishermen on Lake Chad consume most of their catch. Most of the total annual catch was from the Niger River and its tributaries; a small amount is from the Lake Chad region.

25 FORESTRY

The forest domain is only about 1% of Niger's surface. The FAO estimated 2009 roundwood production at 411,000 cu m (14.5 million cu ft). The value of all forest products, including roundwood, totaled $648,000. Small amounts of gum arabic are extracted from acacia trees. Some tree planting has been undertaken, mainly with acacia species, but deforestation remains a serious problem. About 1,328 hectares (3,281 acres) were reforested annually during 1990–2000, and hundreds of thousands of trees have been planted, but these are highly vulnerable to drought.

26 MINING

Uranium dominated Niger's mining sector, ranking it fifth in the world in terms of production. Uranium mining was the country's leading industry in 2009, as well as its leading export commodity, accounting for around 75–90% of exports. In 2009 Niger produced 3,243 metric tons of uranium. A uranium boom occurred in the late 1970s, but with the reduction in world demand in the 1980s, prices fell, although the government was partly protected by contracts negotiated earlier. Niger exports the uranium that generates 80% of France's electricity. Cement, brick, and chemical production were other leading industries, and Niger also produced clays, bituminous coal, gold, gypsum, limestone, molybdenum (in connection with uranium ore), phosphate rock, salt, sand and gravel, stone, cassiterite tin, and tungsten (and, at times, columbite, in connection with cassiterite).

Although uranium was the only mineral to be significantly developed, Niger was rich in a number of other minerals. The country's first gold mine, the Samira Hill open pit, was opened in 2000 by Niger's prime minister, and intended to produce 10,000 tons per day of ore. The combined reserves of Samira Hill and the nearby Libiri deposit were 10.1 million tons (2.2 grams per ton of gold). Gold output in 2009 was officially estimated at 1,852 kilograms. In addition, there were some natron and sodium sulfate deposits, an estimated 650 million tons of iron ore deposits at Say, near Niamey, and 400 million tons of phosphate deposits in "W" National Park in the Niger River Valley. There were also unexploited deposits of manganese, lithium, copper, zinc, lead, silver, cobalt, kaolin, feldspar, gypsum, limestone, marble, and clay.

In 2009 the government announced construction on the Imouraren mine, which will become the world's second-largest uranium mine. The project is a result of an agreement between the government of Niger and the French nuclear energy company Areva, which holds a majority share. The open-pit mine in northern Niger is expected to be operational in 2012.

27 ENERGY AND POWER

Even though Niger has proven crude oil reserves, the country previously had no refining capacity and imported all the refined oil it consumed. A $5 billion deal with China National Petroleum Corporation in 2008 led to the building of a refinery in Zindar. Commercial oil production was scheduled to begin at the end of 2011 with the projected refining rate of 20,000 barrels per day. In 2009 imports and demand for refined petroleum products each averaged 4,000 barrels per day.

Niger produced only a small amount of coal in 2009. Output and demand for coal in that year each came to 198,000 short tons. There were no recorded imports, production, or consumption of natural gas in 2009 by Niger.

Niger's electric power generating sector is completely reliant upon fossil fuels. Of the nation's 0.105 million kWh of generating capacity, all was fossil fuel dedicated. The World Bank reported in

2008 that Niger produced 200 million kWh of electricity and consumed 691.7 million kWh, or 42 kWh per capita.

28 INDUSTRY

Niger's manufacturing sector is small and consists mainly of the processing of domestic agricultural commodities. Agricultural products are processed at a groundnut oil plant, rice mills, flour mills, cotton gins, and tanneries. A textile mill and a cement plant operate, and light industries produce beer and soft drinks, processed meats, noodle products, baked goods, soaps and detergents, perfume, plastic and metal goods, farm equipment, canned vegetables, pasta, and construction materials. The 1994 devaluation of the CFA franc made light manufacturing more competitive by decreasing the cost of local inputs by 50%, but also raised the price of imports dramatically. There is potential for development of fertilizer, seed, and equipment production in the agribusiness sector. There is a small cotton industry.

29 SCIENCE AND TECHNOLOGY

The World Bank reported in 2009 that there were no patent applications in science and technology in Niger. Niger relies heavily on foreign sources for technical expertise, and French agencies are especially active; the Bureau of Geological and Mineral Research, the French Company for the Development of Textile Fibers, the Institute of Fruit and Citrus Fruit Research, and the French Institute of Scientific Research for Development and Cooperation all have offices in Niamey.

The National Institute of Agronomical Research of Niger in Niamey maintains two soil-science stations, at Tarka and Kolo. There is also a national office of solar energy and a veterinary laboratory in Niamey. The Livestock Service of Niger has a Sahelian experimental station at Filingué for breeding zebu cattle and a center for goat breeding and poultry raising at Maradi. The University of Niamey, founded in 1971, includes faculties of science, agronomy, and health services, and institutes of radioisotopes and of research on the teaching of mathematics. The National Museum of Niger, founded in 1959 in Niamey, has a zoo, a geological and mineral exhibition, and paleontology and prehistory museums.

30 DOMESTIC TRADE

The main domestic commercial center in Niger is in the capital city of Niamay. Merchants and peddlers in the small villages sell such items as beverages, cigarettes, soap, cloth, perfume, and batteries. About 90% of the workforce is employed in subsistence farming and only 6% are involved in industry and commerce. Large foreign concerns, usually French-owned, import products to be sold in stores in Niamey and in the secondary cities. In 1997 and 2000 the government made revisions to its investment code in an effort to encourage much needed foreign investment.

The work day is typically from 7:30 a.m. to 12:30 p.m. and 3:30 p.m. to 6:30 p.m. in government offices, Monday through Friday. Private businesses generally are open during those hours also.

31 FOREIGN TRADE

Niger imported $1.62 billion worth of goods and services in 2010, while exporting $484 million worth of goods and services. Major import partners in 2010 were China 44.9%, France 11.6%, the United States 6.2%, United Kingdom 4.7%, Nigeria 3.9%, Japan

Principal Trading Partners – Niger (2010)

(In millions of US dollars)

Country	Total	Exports	Imports	Balance
World	1,120.0	900.0	220.0	680.0
China	301.7	0.2	301.5	-301.3
France	281.1	1.3	279.8	-278.5
Nigeria	251.5	138.3	113.2	25.2
French Polynesia	122.3	...	122.3	-122.3
Côte d'Ivoire	83.5	0.5	83.0	-82.5
United States	79.8	24.6	55.1	-30.5
Belgium	66.7	0.0	66.7	-66.7
Netherlands	56.7	0.4	56.3	-55.9
India	56.6	9.5	47.1	-37.7
South Africa	52.3	0.3	52.0	-51.7

(…) data not available or not significant.

(n.s.) not specified.

SOURCE: *2011 Direction of Trade Statistics Yearbook,* New York: United Nations, 2011.

Balance of Payments – Niger (2009)

(In millions of US dollars)

Current Account		-1,320.1
Balance on goods	-797.3	
Imports	-1,794.2	
Exports	996.9	
Balance on services	-634.8	
Balance on income	-38.8	
Current transfers	150.9	
Capital Account		247.1
Financial Account		886.8
Direct investment abroad	-89.4	
Direct investment in Niger	815.3	
Portfolio investment assets	-29.7	
Portfolio investment liabilities	10.2	
Financial derivatives	...	
Other investment assets	112.4	
Other investment liabilities	68.0	
Net Errors and Omissions		2.9
Reserves and Related Items		183.3

(…) data not available or not significant.

SOURCE: *Balance of Payment Statistics Yearbook 2011,* Washington, DC: International Monetary Fund, 2011.

3.5%, and the Netherlands 3.4%. Imports were led by consumer goods, petroleum, foodstuffs, transportation vehicles, machinery, bridge equipment, and industrial products. Niger's major export partners were France 41.9%, Japan 14.3%, the United States 13.2%, and Nigeria 7.8%. Primary exports included uranium, livestock, gold, cowpeas, and onions. Trade figures show that uranium accounted for about 54% of exports by value. The demand for uranium has steadily decreased since the 1980s.

32 BALANCE OF PAYMENTS

Niger's balance of payments deficit is usually offset by large amounts of bilateral and multilateral aid. The CIA reported that in 2010 the purchasing power parity of Niger's exports was $1.04

Public Finance – Niger (2007)

(In billions of CFA francs, budgetary central government figures)

Revenue and Grants	**396.1**	**100.0%**
Tax revenue	233.2	58.9%
Social contributions	...	...
Grants	118.5	29.9%
Other revenue	44.3	11.2%
Expenditures	**415**	**100.0%**
General public services	...	...
Defense	...	...
Public order and safety	...	...
Economic affairs	...	...
Environmental protection	...	...
Housing and community amenities	...	...
Health	...	...
Recreational, culture, and religion	...	...
Education	...	...
Social protection	...	...

(...) data not available or not significant.

SOURCE: *Government Finance Statistics Yearbook 2010,* Washington, DC: International Monetary Fund, 2010.

billion while imports totaled $1.794 billion, resulting in a trade deficit of $754 million.

33 BANKING AND SECURITIES

The Central Bank of the West African States (Banque Centrale des États de l'Afrique de l'Ouest—BCEAO) is the bank of issue for Niger and other West African states. Niger has a monetary committee that reports to the BCEAO and works under BCEAO general rules but possesses autonomy in internal credit matters.

Two development banks remained following the collapse of the Banque de Développement de la Républica du Niger (BDRN) in 1990: Crédit du Niger (CN), and the Caisse Nationale du Crédit Agricole (CNCA). Three commercial banks collapsed in Niger between 1988 and early 1992: the Banque Internationale pour le Commerce et L'industrie-Niger (BICI-N); the Banque de Cédit et de Commerce (BCC), which the African Development Bank's Nigeria Trust Fund agreed to take over following the collapse of the parent bank; and the Bank of Credit and Commerce International (BCCI). Banque Meridien-BIAO du Niger was taken over in September 1995 in a combined purchase by Banque Belgolaise of Belgium, which took 35%, and Cofipa, a European investment group (15%); the remaining 50% of the equity was sold to private Nigerian interests. The bank changed its name to BIA-Niger. The Banque Arabe Libyenne et Nigérienne pour le Commerce Extérieur (Balinex) was rescued in March 1992 by Libya.

In 2009 the money market rate, the rate at which financial institutions lend to one another in the short term, was 5.3%. The discount rate, the interest rate at which the central bank lends to financial institutions in the short term, was 4.25%.

34 INSURANCE

As of 1986 third-party automobile liability was compulsory, and no life insurance was being written. In 1987 automobile insurance accounted for 45% of all premium revenues. In 1997 there were at least five major insurance companies operating in Niger, among them La Société Nigérienne d'Assurances et de Réassurances (SNAR LEYMA). Transport, accident, fire, retirement, and all-risk insurance products were being offered.

35 PUBLIC FINANCE

In 2010 the budget of Niger included $320 million in public revenue and $320 million in public expenditures. The budget deficit amounted to 8.9% of GDP. Public debt was 17.2% of GDP, with $2.1 billion of the debt held by foreign entities. The CIA estimated that in 2010 Niger's central government took in revenues of approximately $800.4 million, including $134 million from foreign sources, and had expenditures of $1.3 billion. Estimated total external debt in 2009 was $990.9 million.

Budgets are nominally balanced but only through the infusion of foreign loan funds and grants. Expenditures have been severely constrained because of the fall in receipts from the sale of uranium ore due to decline in world demand. The end of the uranium boom in the late 1980s left the public sector poorly equipped to adapt, as public expenditures had focused on infrastructure and construction projects at the expense of agricultural development. Uranium exports earnings more than halved from 1987 to 1998. Niger never completely recovered from the CFA franc devaluation. Consequently, heavy foreign debts were incurred.

In December 2000 Niger qualified for enhanced debt relief under HIPC and concluded an agreement with the Fund on a Poverty Reduction and Growth Facility (PRGF). Debt relief provided under the enhanced HIPC initiative significantly reduced Niger's annual debt service obligations. In December 2005 Niger received 100% multilateral debt relief from the IMF, which translates into the forgiveness of approximately $86 million in debts to the IMF, excluding the remaining assistance under HIPC.

In 2010 the Niger economy was recovering from the effects of 2009 and was also hurt when the international community cut off non-humanitarian aid in response to Tandja's moves to extend his term as president. Nearly half of the government's budget is derived from foreign donor resources. Future growth may be sustained by exploitation of oil, gold, coal, and other mineral resources. Privatization is underway in Niger, but more for budgetary and financial rather than structural purposes.

36 TAXATION

Although both a proportional and a general income tax of 60% are levied, few citizens of Niger are more than marginally taxed since their incomes are too low. The most important sources of revenue are the taxes on industrial and commercial profits and the turnover tax on domestic goods and imports. Niger has value-added tax (VAT) with a standard rate set at 19% in 2010. Other significant sources of revenue from taxes are social security contributions, the registration tax, and excises on petroleum products, alcohol, and cigarettes. The corporate tax rate is 30%.

37 CUSTOMS AND DUTIES

In general two main taxes make up the tariff system. A fiscal import duty of 5–66% is applied to almost all incoming goods, regardless of origin, and serves as a source of revenue. A common external tariff (CET) of maximum 22% is levied on all goods from non-WAEMU (West African Economic and Monetary Union) countries. There are also a VAT of 15–20%, a statistical tax of 1%, and a community solidarity tax of 1%. Goods imported from countries that have trade agreements with Niger pay a minimum customs duty, while those from other countries are subject to a higher general tariff. Goods from EU countries other than France are dutiable at less than the minimum.

38 FOREIGN INVESTMENT

Except for uranium mining, foreign private capital has not been easy to attract to Niger. Prospective investors are discouraged by Niger's periods of military rule, small markets, inadequate infrastructure, bureaucratic delays, shortage of local capital, lack of skilled labor, and exorbitant transportation costs.

Niger's investment codes are liberal, with tax relief and tariff protection depending on the level of investment. Further advantages accrue to those investing in small-scale enterprise. The government seeks foreign investment in most sectors, and private-sector investment in parastatal enterprise is welcome.

In the period 1998 to 2000, Niger's share of world foreign direct investment (FDI) inflows was only one-tenth of its share of world production of goods and services. In 1997 FDI inflow peaked at $25.5 million, and then fell to $9 million in 1998. In 1999 the year President Baré was assassinated, FDI inflow dwindled to $300,000. In 2000 FDI inflow recovered to $19.3 million, but fell to $2 million in 2002 and then recovered to $11 million in 2003. FDI in Niger was a net inflow of $738.9 million according to World Bank figures in 2009, representing 13.73% of GDP.

39 ECONOMIC DEVELOPMENT

Government development programs have had three basic aims: first, to diversify production of foodstuffs; second, to develop underground water resources; and third, to develop and improve the country's infrastructure. France is the leading bilateral aid donor.

In 2000 the IMF approved a three-year $76 million Poverty Reduction and Growth Facility (PRGF) arrangement for Niger, to support the government's economic reform and poverty reduction program. The World Bank, Paris Club creditors, and the African Development Bank have provided assistance to the country under the HIPC initiative. Niger has enacted revisions to the investment, petroleum, and mining codes, with attractive terms for investors. The country depends upon FDI for economic development. As of 2002 five of twelve state-owned enterprises scheduled for privatization had been sold to private hands.

In August of 2005 an IMF mission visited Niamey, the capital of Niger, to evaluate Niger's performance under its PRGF arrangement. It was determined that as a result of the food crisis, budget implementation was weaker than targeted, but more importantly the first review of the PRGF has not yet been concluded. Niger was ranked bottom of the HDI for 2005.

Potential extraction of resources such as gold and oil provided a pathway toward greater economic growth for Niger. In 2011 the China National Petroleum Company invested in oil exploration in the Agadem block as well as a refinery north of Zinder. Niger's mineral resources attracted significant foreign interest; however, that interest has been tempered by poor infrastructure and political instability.

40 SOCIAL DEVELOPMENT

The National Social Security Fund provides pensions, family allowances, maternity benefits, and workers' compensation for employed persons, technical students and apprentices. These programs are financed by a 1.6% contribution from employees, and 2.4% contribution of payroll from employers. There is a special system for civil servants. Retirement is set at ages 58–60. These programs apply only to the minority of citizens who are formally employed, and subsistence farmers are excluded.

In 2004 a separate Ministry of Women's Promotion and Child Protection was established to promote and protect women and children. Women face both legal and social discrimination, particularly in rural areas. Men are recognized as the legal head of household, and in cases of divorce, the husband receives custody of all children under eight years of age. According to Islamic family code men have preferential inheritance and property rights. Domestic abuse is common and women do not seek redress due to ignorance of the legal system and social stigmatization. Marriages at an early age are common, and young girls may be sent to live with her husband's family from the age of ten. Female genital mutilation, a practice that is both painful and potentially life threatening, is practiced by some ethnic groups.

Prison conditions are poor and facilities are overcrowded. International human rights organizations are permitted to visit facilities. Human rights in Niger are improving.

At the end of a three-day regional conference in Chad addressing issues concerning the rights and protection of children in areas of armed conflict, representatives from Chad, the Central African Republic, Sudan, Nigeria, Niger, and Cameroon signed the N'Djamena Declaration, which essentially calls for the end of the recruitment and use of children as soldiers. Signed on 10 June 2010 the binding document outlines the countries' commitments to align their policies with international standards, including those included in the Optional Protocol on the Involvement of Children in Armed Conflict, which is part of the Convention on the Rights of the Child. The meeting was hosted by the Chadian government and UNICEF. The recruitment and/or abduction of children to serve in armed conflicts in Africa has been a pressing issue for UNICEF and other international human rights organizations for many years. Along with a promise to halt recruitment efforts for child soldiers, the signatories of the N'Djamena Declaration have pledged to increase educational and employment opportunities for children once they have been released from military services. The signatories also agreed to establish a special committee charged with ensuring the implementation and monitoring of the agreed commitments.

According to the UN at least 60% of the population was expected to face the threat of severe food shortages by the end of 2010. By July 2010 drought conditions throughout the nation had worsened the crisis, leading the UN World Food Program to expand existing operations to a total of about $213 million for an estimated 7.9 million people.

41 HEALTH

According to the CIA life expectancy in Niger was 53.4 years in 2011. The country spent 5.9% of its GDP on healthcare, amounting to $21 per person. There were no physicians, one nurse and midwife, and three hospital beds per 10,000 inhabitants. The total fertility rate in 2011 was estimated at 7.6 children born per woman, which was the highest rate in the world. The infant mortality rate was 112.2 per 1,000 live births. Only an estimated 14% of women used contraception. In 2011 the maternal mortality rate was 1,600 per 100,000 live births.

Common diseases reported in Niger were measles, guinea worm, leprosy, and deaths from diarrheal diseases. The incidence of tuberculosis was 157 per 100,000 people in 2007. The HIV/AIDS adult prevalence rate was 0.8% in 2009. In Niger an estimated 20% of women suffer from female genital mutilation. Approximately 59% of the population had access to safe drinking water and only 20% had adequate sanitation in 2007.

Immunization rates for children up to one year old included: diphtheria, pertussis, and tetanus 89%, and measles 83%. About 40% of children under five years old were considered malnourished. The goiter rate was 35.8 per 100 school-age children.

42 HOUSING

The government has been working on projects to increase housing, particularly for low-income families through the Federal Housing Authority created in 1976. The Crédit du Niger offers housing loans. Most government buildings and many houses in the metropolitan centers are essentially French in style. The Tuareg nomads live in covered tents, while the Fulani live in small collapsible huts made of straw mats. The villagers in the east live in round straw huts. In the center of the country villagers construct houses of banco, a mixture of mud and straw that has, when dried, a hard cement-like consistency.

43 EDUCATION

The adult literacy rate in 2009 for men was 42.9% and 15.1% for women, for an overall literacy rate of 28.7%. Public expenditure on education represented 4.5% of GDP in 2009.

The educational system is patterned on that of France, but changes are gradually being introduced to adapt the curriculum to local needs and traditions. Schooling is compulsory for six years for children ages 6 to 12. While primary schooling lasts for six years, secondary lasts for seven years in two cycles of four and three years. The academic year runs from October to June. In 2009 about 3% of age-eligible children were enrolled in some type of preschool program. Primary school enrollment in 2010 was estimated at about 59% of age-eligible students—65% for boys and 52% for girls, while secondary school enrollment was about 13% of age-eligible students—16% for boys and 11% for girls. It was estimated that about 41% of all students completed their primary education. The student-to-teacher ratio for primary school was at about 39:1 in 2010; the ratio for secondary school was about 28:1. Additional education occurs through thousands of Koranic schools.

In 1963 the National School of Administration was founded in Niamey. Tertiary enrollment was estimated at 1%. Of those enrolled in tertiary education, there were 100 male students for every 34 female students. The Université Abdou Moumouni in Niamey is the primary institution of higher learning. The Islamic University of West Africa at Say, mostly financed by the OIC, was inaugurated in 1987.

44 LIBRARIES AND MUSEUMS

There are state-run libraries in the large municipalities and libraries maintained by religious orders, the military, and professional and other groups. The Regional Center of Research and Documentation for the Oral Tradition in Niamey was founded in cooperation with UNESCO in 1968; it preserves the oral history of West Africa and has a library of 5,000 volumes. Abdou Moumouni University in Niamey holds 25,000 volumes. The French Cultural Center in Niamey also holds 25,000 volumes.

The National Museum of Niger, which has ethnographic and paleontological exhibits, is also in Niamey, as are a zoo, botanical gardens, craft workshops, and youth training centers. There are regional museums throughout the country, including the National Museum of Colonial History in Aba, the Archeology Museum in Nsukka, and the National War Museum of Umauhia, and a regional museum in Zinder.

45 MEDIA

In 2010 the CIA reported that there were 83,600 telephone landlines in Niger. In addition to landlines, mobile phone subscriptions were 3.81 million.

There were five FM radio stations, six AM radio stations, and four shortwave radio stations in 2009. The Voice of the Sahel and Télé-Sahel, the government's radio and television broadcasting units, respectively, broadcast in French, Djerma, Hausa, Tamachek, Kanuri, Fulfuldé, Toubou, Gourmantché, and Arabic. There are several private stations. In 2010 there were three television stations. In 2008, 10% of households had a television set and 43% had a radio set. In 2010 the country had 172 Internet hosts. Internet users numbered 1 per 100 citizens.

Prominent newspapers in 2010 with circulation numbers listed parenthetically, included *Le Sahel* (5,000) and the weekly *Le Sahel Dimanche* (3,000); a monthly, the *Journal Officiel de la République du Niger*, is also published. All are government publications. There are about 12 private publications, usually published weekly or monthly. These include *Le Republicain* (3,000) and *La Tribune du Peuple* (3,000).

The 1996 constitution provides for freedom of speech and the press, though the current government is said to limit press freedom and stifle political discussion through intimidation, harassment, and detention.

46 ORGANIZATIONS

The Chamber of Commerce, Agriculture, Industry, and Handicrafts of Niger has headquarters at Niamey. There are also chambers of commerce in Agadez, Maradi, Tahoua, and Zinder. National youth organizations include the National Samariya Youth Movement, the Nigerien Student Union of the University on Niamey, Junior Chamber, and the Scout Association of Niger. There are several active sports associations within the country. There are several women's organizations promoting equal rights and government participation for women. The World Conservation

Union has an office in Niamey. There are national chapters of the Red Cross Society and Caritas.

47 TOURISM, TRAVEL, AND RECREATION

The government has promoted both domestic and international tourism since 1984. The "W" National Park along the Niger River offers views of a variety of fauna, including lions, baboons, elephants, 350 species of birds, and 500 plant species. Other tourist attractions include Agadez's 16th-century mosque, one of the oldest in West Africa; villages built on piles in Lake Chad; the annual six-week gathering of nomads near Ingal; the Great Market and Great Mosque in Niamey, and the Sahara desert. Nigeriens engage in game hunting, fishing, swimming, and a variety of team sports. Visas are required for most travelers, as is a vaccination certificate for yellow fever and possibly cholera.

The *Tourism Factbook*, published by the UN World Tourism Organization, reported 66,000 incoming tourists to Niger in 2009; they spent a total of $86 million. Of those incoming tourists, there were 42,000 from Africa. There were 3,320 hotel beds available in Niger, which had an occupancy rate of 49%. The estimated daily cost to visit Niamey, the capital, was $221. The cost of visiting other cities averaged $156.

48 FAMOUS PERSONS

Hamani Diori (1916–89), a former schoolteacher, became leader of the local section of the PPN in 1946, became president of the General Council of the Republic of Niger in 1958, and was president of the Republic of Niger until April 1974, when he was deposed by a military coup. Seyni Kountché (1931–87) became head of state after the coup of 1974 and ruled the country until his death. Col. Ibrahim Bare Maïnassara (1950–99), who led a coup in January 1996 that ousted the democratically elected government, was assassinated in May 1999. He was succeeded by Daouda Malam Wanké, head of the presidential guard, who held the post until December 1999.

49 DEPENDENCIES

Niger has no territories or colonies.

50 BIBLIOGRAPHY

Alidou, Ousseina. *Engaging Modernity: Muslim Women and the Politics of Agency in Postcolonial Niger.* Madison: University of Wisconsin Press, 2005.

Behnke, Alison. *Niger in Pictures.* Minneapolis, MN: Twenty-First Century Books, 2008.

Connah, Graham. *Forgotten Africa: An Introduction to Its Archaeology.* New York: Routledge, 2004.

McKenna, Amy. *The History of Western Africa.* New York: Britannica Educational Publishing, 2011.

Niger Investment and Business Guide: Strategic and Practical Information. Washington, DC: International Business Publications USA, 2012.

Zeilig, Leo, and David Seddon. *A Political and Economic Dictionary of Africa.* Philadelphia: Routledge/Taylor and Francis, 2005..

NIGERIA

Federal Republic of Nigeria

CAPITAL: Abuja

FLAG: The national flag consists of three vertical stripes. The green outer stripes represent Nigerian agriculture. The white center stripe represents unity and peace.

ANTHEM: *Arise, All Compatriots.*

MONETARY UNIT: On 1 January 1973, the Nigerian pound was replaced by the naira (NGN) of 100 kobo. There are coins of 50 kobo and 1 and 2 naira, and notes of 5, 10, 20, 50, 100, 200, 500, and 1000 naira. NGN1 = US$0.0062 (or US$1 = NGN162.30) as of 2011.

WEIGHTS AND MEASURES: As of May 1975, the metric system is the official standard, replacing the imperial measures.

HOLIDAYS: New Year's Day, 1 January; National Day, 1 October; Christmas, 25 December; Boxing Day, 26 December. Movable Christian religious holidays include Good Friday and Easter Monday; movable Muslim religious holidays include Eid al-Fitr, Eid al-Adha, and Milad an-Nabi.

TIME: 1 p.m. = noon GMT.

¹LOCATION, SIZE, AND EXTENT

Located at the extreme inner corner of the Gulf of Guinea on the west coast of Africa, Nigeria occupies an area of 923,768 sq. km (356,669 sq mi), extending 1,127 km (700 mi) E– W and 1,046 km (650 mi) N – S. Comparatively, the area occupied by Nigeria is slightly more than twice the size of the state of California. It is bordered by Chad on the N E, by Cameroon on the E, by the Atlantic Ocean (Gulf of Guinea) on the S, by Benin (formerly Dahomey) on the W, and by Niger on the N W and N, with a total boundary length of 4,900 km (3,045 mi), of which 853 km (530 mi) is coastline. The borders between Nigeria and Chad and Nigeria and Cameroon are disputed, and there have been occasional border clashes.

Nigeria's capital city, Abuja, is located in the center of the country.

²TOPOGRAPHY

Along the entire coastline of Nigeria lies a belt of mangrove swamp forest from 16 to 96 km (10 to 60 mi) in width, which is intersected by branches of the Niger and innumerable other smaller rivers and creeks. Beyond the swamp forest is a zone, from 80 to 160 km (50 to 100 mi) wide, of undulating tropical rain forest. The country then rises to a plateau at a general elevation of about 600 m (2,000 ft) but reaches a maximum of 2,042 m (6,700 ft) on the eastern border in the Shebshi Mountains, and the vegetation changes from woodland to savanna, with thick forest in the mountains. In the extreme north, the country approaches the southern part of the Sahara.

The Niger, the third-largest river of Africa, enters Nigeria from the northwest and runs in a southeasterly direction, meeting its principal tributary, the Benue, at Lokoja, about 550 km (340 mi) from the sea. It then flows south to the delta, through which it empties into the Gulf of Guinea via numerous channels. Other main tributaries of the Niger are the Sokoto and Kaduna rivers. The second great drainage system of Nigeria flows north and east from the central plateau and empties into Lake Chad. Kainji Lake, in the northwest, was created by construction of a dam on the Niger above Jebba.

³CLIMATE

Although Nigeria lies wholly within the tropical zone, there are wide climatic variations in different regions of the country. Near the coast, the seasons are not sharply defined. Temperatures rarely exceed 32°C (90°F), but humidity is very high and nights are hot. Inland, there are two distinct seasons: a wet season from April to October, with generally lower temperatures, and a dry season from November to March, with midday temperatures that surpass 38°C (100°F) but relatively cool nights, dropping as low as 12°C (54°F). On the Jos Plateau, temperatures are more moderate.

Average rainfall along the coast varies from about 180 cm (70 in) in the west to about 430 cm (170 in) in certain parts of the east. Inland, it decreases to around 130 cm (50 in) over most of central Nigeria and only 50 cm (20 in) in the extreme north.

Two principal wind currents affect Nigeria. The harmattan, from the northeast, is hot and dry and carries a reddish dust from the desert; it causes high temperatures during the day and cool nights. The southwest wind brings cloudy and rainy weather.

⁴FLORA AND FAUNA

The World Resources Institute estimates that there are 4,715 plant species in Nigeria. The natural vegetation is divisible into two main sections directly related to the chief climatic regions of the country: (1) high forest, including both swamp and rain forests,

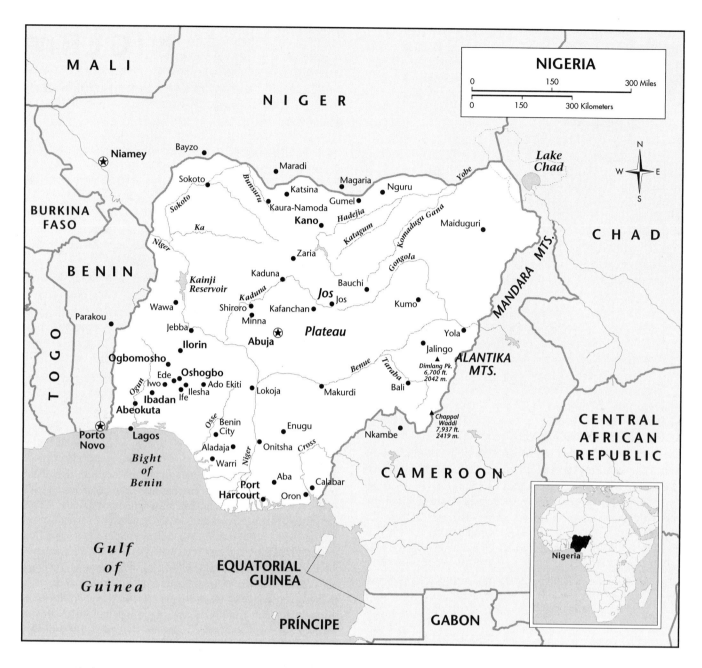

NIGERIA

LOCATION: 2°30′ to 14°30′E; 4°30′ to 14°17′ N. BOUNDARY LENGTHS: Chad, 87 kilometers (55 miles); Cameroon, 1,690 kilometers (1,050 miles); Atlantic coastline, 853 kilometers (530 miles); Benin, 773 kilometers (480 miles); Niger, 1,497 kilometers (930 miles). Broken lines indicate rivers and lakes that are dry for most of the year, only filling with water during infrequent rainy periods. TERRITORIAL SEA LIMIT: 30 miles.

and (2) savanna. Along the coastal area, the mangrove tree predominates, while immediately inland is freshwater swamp forest, which is somewhat more diversified and includes varieties of palms, the abura, and mahogany. North of the swamp forest lies near the rain forest, which forms a belt with an average width of some 130 km (80 mi). Here, trees reach as much as 60 m (200 ft) in height. Principal trees include the African mahogany, iroko, African walnut, and the most popular export wood, the obeche. Farther inland, the rain forest becomes displaced by tall grass and deciduous trees of small stature, characteristic of the savanna.

Animal species include 290 mammals, 899 birds, 155 reptiles, and 73 amphibians. Few large animals are found in the rain forest; gorillas and chimpanzees in decreasing numbers are present, as well as baboons and monkeys. Reptiles abound, including crocodiles, lizards, and snakes of many species. Although many kinds of mammals can be found inland from the rain forest, these are not nearly so plentiful as in East or South Africa. Nigeria possesses two dozen species of antelope, but large concentrations of animals, even the common antelope, are rarely observed. The hippopotamus, elephant, giraffe, leopard, and lion now remain only in scattered localities and in diminishing number. Wildcats, however, are more common and widely distributed. Wildlife in the savanna includes antelope, lions, leopards, gazelles, and desert hyenas.

⁵ENVIRONMENT

The World Resources Institute reported that Nigeria had designated 5.65 million hectares (13.97 million acres) of land for protection as of 2006. Water resources totaled 286.2 cu km (68.66 cu mi) while water usage was 8.01 cu km (1.92 cu mi) per year. Domestic water usage accounted for 21% of total usage, industrial for 10%, and agricultural for 69%. Per capita water usage totaled 61 cu m (2,154 cu ft) per year.

Many of Nigeria's environmental problems are those typical of developing states. Excessive cultivation has resulted in loss of soil fertility. Increased cutting of timber has made inroads into forest resources, exceeding replantings. Between 1983 and 1993 alone, Nigeria lost 20% of its forest and woodland areas.

Oil spills, the burning of toxic wastes, and urban air pollution are problems in more developed areas. In the early 1990s, Nigeria was among the 50 nations with the world's highest levels of carbon dioxide emissions, which totaled 96,500 kilotons, a per capita level of 0.84 metric tons. The UN reported in 2008 that carbon dioxide emissions in Nigeria totaled 95,194 kilotons.

Water pollution is also a problem due to improper handling of sewage. The principal environmental agencies are the Environmental Planning and Protection Division of the Federal Ministry of Works and Housing, and the analogous division within the federal Ministry of Industry.

According to a 2011 report issued by the International Union for Conservation of Nature and Natural Resources (IUCN), the number of threatened species included 26 types of mammals, 14 species of birds, 4 types of reptiles, 13 species of amphibians, 59 species of fish, 11 species of invertebrate, and 172 species of plants. Threatened species include the drill, Presuu's red colobus, and the Ibadan malimbe. The Sahara oryx has become extinct in the wild.

⁶POPULATION

The US Central Intelligence Agency (CIA) estimates the population of Nigeria in 2011 to be approximately 155,215,573, which placed it at number 8 in population among the 196 nations of the world. In 2011, approximately 3.2% of the population was over 65 years of age, with another 40.9% under 15 years of age. The median age in Nigeria was 19.2 years. There were 1.04 males for every female in the country. The population's annual rate of change was 1.935%. The projected population for the year 2025 is 217,400,000. Population density in Nigeria was calculated at 168 people per sq km (435 people per sq mi).

The UN estimated that 50% of the population lived in urban areas, and that urban populations had an annual rate of change of 3.5%. The largest urban areas, along with their respective populations, included Lagos, 10.2 million; Kano, 3.3 million; Ibadan, 2.8 million; Abuja, 1.9 million; and Kaduna, 1.5 million.

Lagos has the highest population density of any major African urban conglomeration. The prevalence of HIV/AIDS has had a significant impact on the population of Nigeria. The AIDS epidemic causes higher death and infant mortality rates, and lowers life expectancy.

⁷MIGRATION

Estimates of Nigeria's net migration rate, carried out by the CIA in 2011, amounted to -0.10 migrants per 1,000 citizens. The total number of emigrants living abroad was 1 million. The total number of immigrants living in Nigeria was 1.13 million, or 1% of the total population. Nigeria also hosted 5,778 refugees in 2011. Nigeria is an important destination country for migrants in the West Africa region. Immigrants are drawn from neighboring nations by economic opportunity. Most Nigerians abroad live in Sudan, the United States, or the United Kingdom. There has been a marked increase in the number of Nigerians emigrating for educational purposes. Within Nigeria, expectations of economic opportunities have increased urban migration.

On 17 January 1983, Nigeria, suffering from an economic crisis brought about by decreased earnings from oil, ordered all resident aliens to leave the country. Some 700,000 Ghanaians departed during the following weeks, as did smaller numbers from Benin, Cameroon, Chad, Mali, Niger, Togo, and Burkina Faso. In 1985 about 200,000 to 250,000 aliens were expelled, including about 100,000 from Ghana and 50,000 from Niger.

⁸ETHNIC GROUPS

There are more than 250 different ethnic groups within the country, none of which holds a majority. The four largest ethnic groups are the Hausa and Fulani, which together account for about 29% of the population; the Yoruba, accounting for 21% of the population; and the Ibos with 18% of the population. The Ijaw of the South Delta make up 10% of the people, followed by Kanuri (4%), the Ibibio (3.5%), and the Tiv (2.5%).Yoruba predominate in Ogun, Ondo, Oyo, and Osun states. The Ibo (Igbo) predominate in Anambra, Imo, Abia, and Enugu states. The Hausa and Fulani constitute the largest single groups in Sokoto, Kaduna, Jigawa, Katsina, and Kano states. Other important groups include the Kanuri in Borno and Yobe states; the Edo (Bini) in Edo State; the Ibibio in Akwa Ibam State; the Ijaw (Ijo) in Rivers State; the Tiv in Benue and Plateau states; and the Nupe in Niger State.

⁹LANGUAGES

The official language is English, although there are over 500 distinct indigenous tongues. Hausa is the mother tongue of more than 40% of the inhabitants of the northern states. Yoruba is commonly used in southwestern urban centers, including Lagos. Ibo and Fulani are also widely spoken. Ethnic divisions roughly reflect the distribution of other vernaculars.

¹⁰RELIGIONS

Religious affiliation in Nigeria is strongly related to ethnicity, with rather distinct regional divisions between ethnic groups. The northern states, dominated by the Hausa and Fulani groups, are predominantly Muslim while the southern ethnic groups have a large number of Christians. In the southwest, there is no predominant religion. The Yoruba, the majority ethnic group in the southwest, practice Christianity, Muslim, and/or the traditional Yoruba religion, which centers on the belief in one supreme god and several lesser deities. The Ibo of the east are primarily Catholic or Methodist, with some traditional practices included. Overall statistics indicate that about 50% of the population are Muslim, with a majority practicing the Sunni branch of the faith. About 40% are Christian and about 10% practice traditional African religions or no religion at all. Many people include elements of traditional beliefs in their own practice of Christianity or Islam. The Christian community is composed of Roman Catholics (the largest denomination), Methodists, Anglicans, Baptists, Presbyterians, and members of Evangelical and Pentecostal groups. Though the constitution prohibits state and local governments from declaring an official religion, a number of states have recently adopted various forms of the Islamic criminal and civil law known as Shari'ah, a move which many Christians believe to be an adoption of Islam as the de facto religion. The constitution also provides for freedom of religion, however, some states have restricted religious demonstrations, processions, or gatherings as a matter of public security. Business owners and public officials have been known to discriminate against individuals of a faith different than their own in matters of providing services and hiring practices. The same type of discrimination exists between members of different ethnic groups.

11 TRANSPORTATION

The CIA reported that Nigeria has a total of 193,200 km (120,049 mi) of roads as of 2004, of which 28,980 km (18,007 mi) were paved. Nigeria is expected to benefit greatly from the World Bank funded reconstruction of the Abidjan-Lagos Corridor, also known as the West African Coastal Corridor. In March 2010, the World Bank approved funding of $317.5 million to improve this important roadway, which stretches for 998.8 km (620 mi), linking the capital cities of Abidjan (Côte d'Ivoire), Accra (Ghana), Lomé (Togo), Cotonou (Benin) and Lagos (Nigeria). This corridor is one of the most highly traveled roadways on the continent. Developed in part by the Economic Community of West African Nations (ECOWAS), the corridor project included procedural reforms to promote a more efficient trade process, along with much needed improvements to the physical infrastructure. The project was to be executed in two phases, with the first phase covering Ghana, Togo, and Benin, and the second phase covering Côte d'Ivoire and Nigeria.

The main waterways are the Niger and Benue rivers and a system of navigable creeks and lagoons in the southern part of the country. The Niger is navigable to Onitsha by large riverboat and to Lokoja by barge throughout the year. Ports farther upstream on the Niger and Benue can be reached in the high-water season. Inland waterways total about 8,575 km (5,328 mi). Lagos remains Nigeria's principal port, handling more than 75% of the country's general cargo. Other ports are Port Harcourt, Calabar, and the delta port complex of Warri, Sapele, Koko, Burutu, Bonny, and Alesa Eleme. The merchant marine operated a fleet of 98 ships of 1,000 gross registered tons or more in 2010.

Most of the railway system is single tracked and consists of two generally north–south lines, originating in Lagos and Port Harcourt. The westerly situated route runs northeast from Lagos through Ibadan, Ilorin, and Kaduna to Kano. An easterly situated line runs from Port Harcourt through Enugu and Makurdi, and joins the western line at Kaduna. Extensions carry the former north to Nguru and the latter north to Kaura-Namoda. Three branch lines connect other industrial and commercial centers to the main system. A 645-km (400-mi) extension of the Port Harcourt line from Kafanchan to Maiduguri, linking the main system with the northeastern corner of the country, was completed in 1964. However, years of neglect have seriously reduced the capacity and utility of the railway system.

There are 54 airports, which transported 1.37 million passengers in 2009 according to the World Bank. Air traffic has been growing steadily. International service is provided from Lagos (Murtala Muhammed), Port Harcourt, and Kano airports by more than two dozen international airlines; a cargo-oriented international airport is located in Abuja. Air Nigeria is the national air carrier. It was founded in 2004 and began operations in 2005.

12 HISTORY

The history of Nigeria prior to the beginnings of British administration is not well documented. There is archaeological evidence, however, that an Iron Age culture had been present sometime between 500 BC and AD 200, and agriculture and livestock raising long before then. About the 11th century AD, Yoruba city-states developed in western Nigeria, and some, such as Benin, became powerful kingdoms in later centuries. During medieval times, northern Nigeria had contact with the large kingdoms of the western Sudan (Ghana, Mali, and Songhai) and with countries of the Mediterranean across the Sahara. Islamic influence was firmly established by the end of the 15th century, and Kano was famous not only as a center of Islamic studies but also as a great commercial entrepôt of the western Sudan. Until the arrival of the British, northern Nigeria was economically oriented toward the north and east, and woven cloth and leatherwork were exported as far as the North African ports of the Mediterranean. At the beginning of the 19th century, a jihad, or holy war, led by a Fulani sheikh, Uthman dan Fodio, established Fulani rule over the surviving Hausa kingdoms, until the British conquest at the end of the century.

In the south, the Portuguese were the first Europeans to establish close relations with the coastal people. In the late 15th century, they established a depot to handle trade goods and slaves from Benin. The Portuguese monopoly was broken after a century, and other European nations participated in the burgeoning slave trade. The British abolished slave trading in 1807, and thereafter British policy was directed at enforcing that ban on other nations. Interest in legitimate commerce developed slowly, but the discovery of the mouth of the Niger in 1830 provided an important impetus. The extension of British influence over Nigeria was gradual and, initially at least, unplanned. In 1861, the British annexed the island of Lagos, an important center of palm oil trade; thereafter, they gradually extended their influence over the adjacent mainland of Yorubaland.

In 1887, British influence over the eastern coast, which had been promoted since 1849 by consular agents, was regularized by the establishment of the Oil Rivers Protectorate. This too was gradually extended inland and became the Niger Coast Protectorate in 1894. The acquisition of the interior of Nigeria, however, was accomplished largely by Sir George Goldie, founder of the Royal Niger Company, who by 1885 had eliminated commercial competition on the Niger and, by claiming treaties with responsible African authorities, had secured recognition of British influence over the Niger Basin by the European powers at the Berlin Conference. This influence was far more fancied than real; but it provided the basis for British rule over northern Nigeria, which was consolidated by a series of punitive expeditions culminating in the establishment of the Protectorate of Northern Nigeria in 1900.

The three separate administrative units were finally amalgamated in 1914 into the Colony and Protectorate of Nigeria, with

Sir Frederick Lugard as governor-general. Despite the ostensible unification, the administrative individuality of the three separate regions—North, East, and West—was maintained. The chief characteristic of British rule in Nigeria was its system of local administration, known as indirect rule. In real terms though, indirect rule depended on a system of centralized political units with local (or native) chiefs at the lowest rungs of the hierarchy. It functioned well in the North, with variable success in the West, and poorly in the East.

After World War II, increasing pressures for self-government resulted in a succession of short-lived constitutions. The constitution of 1954 established a federal form of government, greatly extending the functions of the regional governments. A constitutional conference of May and June 1957 decided upon immediate self-government for the Eastern and Western regions, the Northern to follow in 1959. The step from self-government to independence was quickly taken. On 1 October 1960, Nigeria became a fully independent member of the British Commonwealth, and on 1 October 1963 it became a republic. Nnamdi Azikiwe was elected the first president of the Federal Republic of Nigeria.

Internal unrest began almost as soon as Nigeria raised its own flag; but its roots lay in the complex ethnic composition of the regions. It boiled over to resentment over the domination of the federal government by Northern elements, and culminated in a military coup on 15 January 1966. Organized by a group of Eastern junior army officers, the coup led to the deaths of the federal prime minister, Sir Abubakar Tafawa Balewa; the premier of the Northern Region, Sir Ahmadu Bello; and the premier of the Western Region, Chief S. L. Akintola. By 17 January, Maj. Gen. Johnson Aguiyi-Ironsi, commander-in-chief of the army, had suppressed the revolt and assumed supreme power. He suspended the constitution and dissolved the legislature, established a military government, and appointed military governors to replace the popularly elected civilian governors in the regions. On 29 July 1966, mutinous elements in the army, largely Northern army officers, staged a countercoup, killed Gen. Ironsi, and replaced him with Lt. Col. Yakubu Gowon as head of the military government. The July coup led to the massacre of thousands of Easterners residing in the Northern Region and to the exodus of more than one million persons (mostly Ibos) to the Eastern Region.

On 28 May 1967, Col. Gowon assumed emergency powers as head of the Federal Military Government and announced the division of the country into 12 states. The Northern Region was split into 6 states; the Mid-West, Western, and Lagos areas each became separate states; and 3 states were formed from the Eastern Region. Rejecting the realignment, Eastern Region leaders announced on 30 May the independent Republic of Biafra, with Lt. Col. Odumegwu Ojukwu as head of state. On 6 July, the federal government declared war on the fledgling republic. By the time the war ended on 12 January 1970, Biafra had been reduced to about one-tenth of its original 78,000-sq-km (30,000-sq-mi) area; a million or more persons had perished, many from disease and starvation; many more had become refugees at home or abroad. Following the surrender, many Ibos returned to their former positions in Lagos, and Gowon's military regime sought to rehabilitate the three Eastern states as quickly as possible.

In October 1970, with the civil war behind him, Gowon set 1976 as the target date for Nigeria's return to civilian rule. Political change came slowly, however, and in October 1974, Gowon announced an indefinite postponement of plans for the transfer of power. The regime's recalcitrance in this and other areas, including its failure to check the power of the state governors and to reduce the general level of corruption, led to Gowon's overthrow on 29 July 1975. His successor, Brig. Murtala Ramat Muhammad, moved quickly in dismissing large numbers of officials, many of them corrupt and inefficient; and in establishing an ombudsman commission. One of his plans was to establish a new capital territory in the center of the country, at Abuja. On 13 February 1976, Muhammad was assassinated in the course of an abortive coup. He was replaced as head of the government by the former chief of staff of the armed forces, Lt. Gen. Olusegun Obasanjo, who pledged to carry on his predecessor's program. In March 1976, a decree established a 19-state federation. Political party activity was again permitted in late 1978, and a new constitution took effect on 1 October 1979, the day Alhaji Shehu Shagari took office as president. Leader of the conservative National Party of Nigeria, he also had the support of the Nigerian People's Party (NPP), led by former president Azikiwe. The NPP withdrew its support in 1981, leaving Shagari at the head of a minority government. In August 1983, Shagari won reelection to a second term as president; in late December, however, he was ousted in a military coup.

The new military regime, led by Maj. Gen. Muhammadu Buhari, provoked growing public dissatisfaction because of its increasingly authoritarian character, and a military coup on 27 August 1985 brought Maj. Gen. Ibrahim Badamasi Babangida to power. Assuming the title of president, Babangida promised greater respect for human and civil liberties; yet he banned Second Republic party officials from participation in politics for 10 years. A return to full civilian rule was pledged by 1992, with local elections on a nonparty basis, the creation of a constituent assembly, the establishment of no more than two political parties, state elections, a national census, and finally presidential elections. The first step in the process—local elections on 12 December 1987—were marred by irregularities. To deal with Nigeria's economic troubles, stemming from the fall of world oil prices in the 1980s, Babangida inaugurated a "homegrown" Structural Adjustment Program (SAP) prompted by the IMF but not directed by them. It involved cuts in public spending, decreased state control over the economy, stimulation of exports, devaluation of the currency, and rescheduling of debt.

A mostly elected Constituent Assembly met in 1988 and approved modifications in the 1979 constitution. The process of party formation proved awkward in a society as heterogeneous as Nigeria's. None of the 13 potential parties gained Babangida's approval. Instead, he decided to create two new parties, one "a little to the right" of center, another "a little to the left." Neither challenged government effectively.

Babangida's guided program of transition from military rule to a democratic civilian Third Republic was due for completion in 1992. But it was marked by crisis after crisis. Clashes between Muslims and Christians in 1991 and 1992 spread through northern cities. Hundreds were killed in the rioting itself and then by the army seeking to contain the riots. Pro-democracy groups also emerged across society, in part from frustration with the excesses of military rule; and because of suspicion that the military might renege on plans to turn over power to elected civilians.

In elections for state governors and assemblies, the National Republican Convention (NRC) won 13 of 30 assemblies and 16 governorships. The Social Democratic Party (SDP) carried 17 and 14, respectively. But voter indifference and fear of intimidation was high. When state governments took office, intraparty wrangling and political violence marred their performance.

Nonetheless, by January 1992, Nigerians geared up for the national presidential and legislative elections scheduled for later in the year. Nigeria's first successful census since independence (results announced in March 1992) indicated a population of 88.5 million, some 20 million fewer than estimated. The election register had to be revised downward, from 70 million to 39 million voters. On 20 May 1992, the government banned all political, religious, and ethnic organizations other than the two approved political parties.

In legislative elections held on 4 July, the left-of-center SDP won 47 of the 91 Senate seats and 310 of the 593 seats in the House of Representatives. The right-of-center NRC won 37 and 267 seats, respectively. The ruling military council pushed back the transition date until January 1993; it also postponed the inauguration of the National Assembly to coincide with the formal take-off of the Third Republic.

In August and September, the country began the process of narrowing the field of presidential candidates from 20 to 2 in preparation for the December elections. But on 17 November 1992, Babangida announced a third delay in the transfer of power from 2 January until 27 August 1993. Political violence and charges of electoral fraud disrupted the first round of presidential primaries that year. The second round, held in September, was flawed, too. Faced with a virtual breakdown of the electoral machinery, the military council suspended the primary results in October. All 23 of the presidential aspirants were banned from future political competition. These disruptions were compounded by high levels of student and labor unrest, detentions of dissidents, and ethnic and religious violence. Nonetheless, the military council promised to give way to an elected civilian administration in 1993.

A new round of presidential nominations took place in March 1993. Chief M.K.O. Abiola (SDP) and Alhaji Bashir Tofa (NRC), both Muslim businessmen with ties to Babangida, won nomination. The presidential election of 12 June took place amid a flurry of legal efforts to halt it and great voter confusion. Abiola apparently defeated Tofa handily, 58.4% to 41.6% according to unofficial results.

But the National Electoral Commission set aside the results on 16 June. A week later, Babangida annulled the election citing irregularities, poor turnout, and legal complications. Abiola, backed largely by the Yoruba people, demanded to be certified as president-elect. Civil unrest followed, especially in Lagos.

After weeks of uncertainty and tension, Babangida resigned the presidency and his military commission on 26 August 1993. He handpicked a transitional council headed by Chief Ernest Shonekan. By mid-November, Gen. Sani Abacha forced Shonekan to resign and he installed himself as head of state. On 18 November 1993, he abolished all state and local governments and the national legislature. He replaced many civilian officials with military commanders. He banned political parties and all political activity and ordered strikers to return to work. The following week, he named an 11-member Provisional Ruling Council composed mainly of generals and police officials. He also created a 32-member Federal Executive Council to head government ministries. It included prominent civilians and some prodemocracy and human rights activists.

On 11 June 1994, Abiola proclaimed himself president and then went into hiding. He was arrested later that month, an action that portended much that was to come for Nigeria. Massive protests followed Abiola's arrest, but Abacha's military repressed the demonstrators violently. On 6 July Abiola pleaded not guilty to three counts of treason; the following day laborers went on strike to protest the Abacha regime. In the following months millions of Nigerian workers walked out in support of Abiola and refused to attend scheduled government talks. Abiola remained in prison through June 1996, when his outspoken wife Kudirat Abiola was assassinated. Strikes and protests continued in support of the sanctity of the vote, and of Abiola's mandate.

In August, General Abacha fired his army and navy commanders. Two weeks later he banned several newspapers, declaring that his government had absolute power and would not give in to prodemocracy demonstrators. Late in September, claiming that it was part of his plan to "rejuvenate the machinery of government," Abacha removed all civilians from his ruling council. Three months later he suspended habeas corpus and continued to round up and jail opponents. At the same time he rejected a court order demanding the release of Abiola from prison for medical treatment. In March 1995 Abacha ordered the arrest of former Nigerian leader Olusegun Obasanjo on suspicion of treason. Later in the month he dissolved labor unions and jailed their leaders. On 25 April Abacha canceled a 1 January 1996 deadline for the return of civilian rule and refused to discuss the matter. Though he lifted a ban on political parties in June 1995, Abacha placed tight restrictions on their operations. The July convictions in secret trials of 40 suspected traitors brought international condemnation and demands of leniency from critics of the Nigerian government. Ultimately Abacha relented on 1 October, commuting the death sentences of his convicted opponents and declaring that he would relinquish power to an elected government in 1998.

Despite these promises, many outside observers remained skeptical, largely due to fallout from the case of Ken Saro-Wiwa, leader of the Movement for the Survival of Ogoni People. Sentenced to death in October 1995 for a quadruple murder, many believed that Saro-Wiwa had been convicted on trumped-up charges stemming from his opposition to a proposed drilling agreement in Nigeria's main oil-producing region. The executions in early November of Saro-Wiwa and eight others brought a torrent of criticism from the international community and resulted in Nigeria's suspension from the British Commonwealth and an embargo from the European Union on arms and aid to Nigeria. Bowing to this pressure, the Abacha government amended in May 1996 the law under which Saro-Wiwa and the others had been convicted and offered to hold talks on the matter with the United Kingdom.

Abacha announced efforts in November 1996 to spur economic change and raise living standards in the country, a pronouncement met with skepticism by an increasingly angry opposition. By December, opponents of the government detonated two bombs aimed at Col. Mohammed Marwa, head of the Nigerian military. Col. Marwa escaped both attacks.

In April 1998, four of Nigeria's five major political parties nominated Abacha as their presidential candidate. Amid opposition accusations that the transition plan was designed to prolong Abacha's rule, legislative elections held on 25 April were heavily boycotted. Nigeria's political fortunes changed suddenly on 8 June when Abacha died of an apparent heart attack. General Abdoulsalami Abubakar took charge and promised to continue Abacha's transition. On 7 July, Abiola died of a suspected heart failure while still in custody.

On 20 July General Abubakar announced a new plan for return to civilian rule culminating in a transfer of power in May 1999. On 5 December local council elections took place with three parties qualifying to move on to state and national elections by winning at least 5% of the vote in 24 of 36 states. On 11 January 1999 elections for state governorships and legislatures were held.

Elections for president and the national legislature were held on 27 February 1999. Former Nigerian leader Olusegun Obasanjo (PDP) won the presidential elections with 62% of the vote, while Olu Falae, the candidate for the Alliance for Democracy (AD) and the All Peoples Party (APP), received 38%. Despite Falae's charges of election rigging, international observers from the Carter Center and the National Democratic Institute reported that available evidence of electoral abuse and other irregularities were unlikely to have affected the overall results. In April Olu Falae closed his case against Obasanjo after a federal appeals court in Abuja rejected two pleas. Power was handed over officially to the new government in May. Twenty heads of state attended Obasanjo's inauguration on 4 June, some two decades after he left office as a military ruler.

Obasanjo promised to restore law and order, fight corruption, and unify Nigeria's ethnically and religiously diverse peoples. The federal government increased the oil-producing states' share of revenue from 3% to 13%. However, these states were demanding a 50% share, so the increase did not resolve disputes over local ownership, control of resources, and embezzlement. In 1999, Nigeria was second on Transparency International's list of most corrupt countries (Cameroon was first). In 2011, Nigeria ranked 37 on the list of most corrupt countries.

In 1999, fighting in the Delta region killed several hundred people while outbreaks of fighting between Yorubas and Hausa in the area of Lagos resulted in hundreds more deaths. The Igbo demanded reparations of $87 billion for the 1967–70 civil war. In February 2000, days of violent clashes between Muslims and Christians killed as many as 750 persons (mostly Igbo Christians, other southeasterners, and some Yorubas) in Kaduna, and destroyed several churches and mosques following announcements that a fuller application of Islamic law, Shari'ah, would be introduced in Zamfara and at least five other northern states. In principle, Shari'ah only affects Muslims, but its implementation has caused great consternation among non-Muslims.

In June and July 2001, between 100 and 200 people were killed in Nasarawa state in fighting between the Tiv and other ethnic groups. In October, more than 200 villagers were killed by the army in the east-central state of Benue in retaliation for the murder of 19 soldiers amid fighting between the Tiv and Junkun. From 7–13 September 2001 in the central city of Jos, about 915 lives were lost in inter-communal violence between Muslims and Christians, although the nongovernmental organization Human Rights Watch described the conflict as more political and economic than religious.

On 27 January 2002, more than 1,000 people died as a result of a series of explosions at an army munitions dump in Lagos. Many of the victims had fallen into a canal and drowned as they tried to leave the northern neighborhood of Ikeja. In February, some 100 people were killed in Lagos in ethnic clashes between Yorubas and Hausa. Thousands fled their homes. In November, more than 200 people were killed in riots between Muslims and Christians in Kaduna, following the publication of a newspaper article suggesting that the prophet Muhammad would have wished to marry one of the Miss World contestants competing in that beauty pageant to be held in Abuja on 7 December. The pageant was subsequently moved to London. Also in November, the Nigerian government intervened to save the life of Amina Lawal, a 30-year old woman sentenced to death by stoning after she was found guilty in a Shari'ah court of having had extra-marital sex. Her case provoked large-scale protests from the international community.

In October 2002, the International Court of Justice (ICJ) ruled in favor of Cameroon in its territorial dispute with Nigeria over the oil-rich Bakassi peninsula. Fighting between the two countries over the region broke out in 1994, at which point Cameroon requested a world court ruling on the border dispute. The decision was not subject to appeal. On 12 June 2006 Nigerian President Obasanjo and Cameroonian President Paul Biya signed an agreement in New York on implementing the ICJ decision. Within two months, Nigeria withdrew its troops. On 14 August 2008, Nigeria formally ceded Bakassi to Cameroon.

Nigerians, once dominated by the military, have become disappointed in the civilian rule initiated in 1999. But Nigerians have had to contend with increasing poverty, ethnic strife, religious intolerance, declining standards in health and education, and a stagnant economy. In 2000, an estimated 60% of the population lived below the poverty line. From 1999 until the end of 2002, approximately 10,000 people had been killed in political and sectarian fighting. In December 2001, Chief Ajibola Ige, the sitting attorney general and minister of justice of the federal government, was murdered in the bedroom of his home at Ibadan. Chief Ige's murder has remained unsolved, as have those of several other high-ranking politicians from the ruling PDP. These murders, a rising wave of crime in the country, as well as the militarization of the Niger Delta, cast doubts on the efficacy of the security agencies. It also served as a spur to calls for a decentralized police force, or one structured by region and/or state.

For many, the general elections of 2003 were critical to finding solutions to these and other questions, and could move the country forward. In 2002, 24 new political parties had joined the fray after the Supreme Court declared as invalid some of the conditions that the Independent National Electoral Commission (INEC) had imposed on associations seeking a license to operate as political parties. The presidential race attracted more candidates, but public debates on issues were no clearer or deeper. The larger political parties did not face much challenge either.

The 2003 elections left the PDP in greater control of government. In the presidential poll, Obasanjo won 61.9% of the votes; former military head of state and candidate of the All Nigeria People's Party (ANPP), Muhammadu Buhari, took 31.2%. The AD, with a large Yoruba following, did not field a candidate in apparent support of Obasanjo's candidacy. The PDP also won 73 seats in the Senate and 213 in the House of Representatives; ANPP won 28 and 95 seats, while the AD took 6 and 31 seats respectively. The PDP won control of government in 28 states, ANPP got 7, and ADP won only in Lagos State. The results were contested at all levels. Buhari filed a suit against Obasanjo's victory that went all the way to the Supreme Court; it drew a dissenting opinion in favor of the appellant.

In July 2003, an attempt was made with support from a detachment of the police to forcibly remove from power Chris Ngige, governor of the PDP-controlled Anambra State in the east. Subsequent efforts involved the burning down of major government symbols and the withdrawal of security details from Ngige. A senior police officer, a judge, and several minor actors in the saga were dismissed. In early 2004, Obasanjo declared a state of emergency in central Plateau State, also controlled by the PDP. In September 2005, yet another PDP governor, this time of oil-rich Bayelsa State, was arrested in London on suspicion of money laundering. He returned to Nigeria but was removed from office and prosecuted for various economic offences. At the federal level, Obasanjo had been locked in battle with several segments of the PDP. He also openly accused his deputy, Vice President Atiku Abubakar of disloyalty after an apparent disagreement over succession in 2007.

Obasanjo's economic policy was controversial. Continued increases in the price of petroleum products put his administration at odds with organized labor and civil society. The PDP enacted a law that made it more difficult to form and maintain a single labor federation in Nigeria. Obasanjo negotiated a debt-forgiveness deal with Nigeria's creditors and consistently affirmed a commitment to antipoverty programs. Not many jobs were being created and federal government units were downsized. In 2006 Obasanjo served notice that thousands of jobs were to be erased in the public sector. However, in April of that year, with the help of record-high oil prices, Nigeria became the first African nation to pay off its debt to the Paris Club of rich lenders.

Beginning in January 2006, militants in the Niger Delta attacked pipelines and other oil facilities and kidnapped foreign oil workers. The rebels demanded more control over the region's oil wealth. Companies confined employees to heavily fortified compounds, allowing them to travel only by armored car or helicopter.

In May 2006, the Senate rejected proposed changes to the constitution, which would have allowed President Obasanjo to stand for a third term in 2007. Governorship and state assembly elections were held on 14 April 2007, while the presidential and national assembly elections were held on 21 April. Umaru Yar'Adua of the ruling People's Democratic Party was proclaimed winner of the presidential election. However, his chief rivals rejected the results, and international monitors held that the voting, which took place amid chaos, fraud, and violence, was not credible. The election in one sense marked an important milestone for democracy, as Nigeria—Africa's most populous nation, largest oil producer, and second largest economy—handed power for the first time from one elected civilian government to another. However, because the elections were considered to be seriously flawed, worse even, than the marred elections in 1999 and 2003, it could be seen that Nigeria's democracy had taken a step backward. Yar'Adua, a 56-year-old governor of the remote northern state of Katsina, won

24,638,063 votes. His nearest rival, Muhammadu Buhari, a former military dictator, had less than one-fourth as many votes, with 6,605,299 votes. The unwritten sectarian rules in Nigeria, aimed at keeping the peace in the ethnically and religiously divided nation, held that the president in 2007 should be a Muslim from the north because Obasanjo is a Christian from the southwest.

Three weeks after Yar'Adua took office as president, in June 2007, a general strike was called. Unions desired a reversal on tax and fuel-price increases and on the sale of two state-owned oil refineries. These actions had been pushed through in Obasanjo's final days in office. The government agreed to withdraw a five-point increase in the value-added-tax rate, to halve the rise in fuel prices, and to review privatization policies, but those moves failed to avert the strike.

The Yar'Adua administration began to distance itself from its predecessor, in part by showing unprecedented restraint in allowing the legislative and judicial branches to operate free from influence. In October 2007 Patricia Etteh, the speaker of the federal House of Representatives, resigned over allegations of corruption, after intense legislative and public pressure. As of mid-February 2008, electoral tribunals and the courts had nullified at least 6 gubernatorial, 9 Senate, 11 House, and 14 state-level House of Assembly elections from April 2007. On 26 February 2008 a tribunal upheld the results of the April 2007 presidential election.

In August 2008, Nigeria officially ceded land from the oil-rich Bakassi peninsula to Cameroon, ending a long-standing dispute between the two countries. Part of the land had traded hands in 2006, following the 2002 international court ruling in favor of Cameroon.

In mid-2008, an oil crisis developed within the nation as falling oil prices and declining production levels posed a serious threat to the economy. By year-end, oil production was cut by nearly 20% due to the continued violence between the government and militant groups in the oil-rich delta region. In January 2009, the value of the naira had dropped by 20% within only a few weeks time, due to the loss of oil revenues. The president assembled a team of advisors to address the impending financial crisis and plans were made toward deregulation of the oil sector by dropping government subsidies and privatizing some refineries. In May 2009, the Nigerian Labor Congress launched a massive protest against the deregulation plans, claiming they would only result in local fuel shortages and higher fuels prices for residents. Violence continued as the Movement for the Emancipation of the Niger Delta (MEND) claimed responsibility for the destruction of two major oil pipelines. The Ijaw National Congress, representing the largest ethnic group in the region, accused the national military of killing over 1,000 civilians during the course of the conflict and called upon the UN to intervene.

The progress of negotiations, along with other government business, came to a halt in November 2009 when President Umaru Yar'Adua was admitted to a hospital in Saudi Arabia with what was later diagnosed as pericarditis. The president was still hospitalized one month later, leading members of the national assembly to call for an official transfer of power to the vice president, Goodluck Jonathan. Jonathan stepped in as acting president on 10 February 2010. In April 2010, Jonathan swore in a new cabinet. Yar'Adua died on 5 May 2010 and Jonathan was sworn in as president and commander-in-chief of the armed forces not long afterwards. Former Kaduna state governor Namadi Sambo was approved as the vice president on 17 May. The next presidential elections took place on 16 April 2011. After some controversy, Jonathan was named the candidate by his People's Democratic Party (PDP). The PDP guidelines establish a rotating system for nominations, alternating between candidates from the Muslim north and Christian south. Because Jonathan is a southerner, the PDP stated that its 2011 candidate would be a northerner. However, Jonathan announced his intention to run for the presidency on 18 September 2010.

In an effort to clear up some of the uncertainty surrounding procedures for the 2011 elections, Jonathan signed the 2010 Electoral Act in August 2010. The act stipulated the order in which elections must be held by placing legislative elections first, followed by presidential elections, and then gubernatorial elections. In the past, the schedule of elections was entirely at the discretion of the Independent National Electoral Commission (INEC). The act also stated that the INEC must publish the date of the election no less than 90 days in advance, and political parties may have until 60 days before polling to submit their candidates. Additionally, the INEC was permitted to revise the voter registration rolls until 60 days before election day; in the 2006 Electoral Act, the INEC had to submit the final voter registrations at 120 days before the polls. While the 2011 election was originally scheduled for January, it was postponed to April to allow INEC to conduct the election more swiftly and give parties more time for primaries. Some 21 out of 63 registered political parties fielded candidates. Jonathan won the election with 58.89% of the vote, with Muhammadu Buhari of the Congress for Progressive Change coming in second.

In 2009, the Boko Haram Islamist movement killed hundreds in northeastern Nigeria as part of a violent campaign to impose Shari'ah law on the entire country. In July, security forces killed the movement's leader. Clashes between Muslims and Christians in Jos killed around 300 people in January and March 2010. In October 2010, Nigeria marked 50 years of independence, but celebrations in Abuja were marred by deadly bomb blasts. The Islamist group Boko Haram, loosely modeled on the Taliban movement, claimed responsibility for numerous attacks. On Christmas Eve, Boko Haram carried out bomb attacks near Jos, killing at least 80 people and sparking clashes between Christians and Muslims that resulted in 200 deaths. Despite attempts by the government to start negotiating with Boko Haram in 2011, the Islamist group carried out further attacks, including a suicide bomb attack on UN headquarters in Abuja that killed 23 people in August 2011. In December, nearly 70 people were killed in fighting between security forces and Boko Haram militants in the northeastern states of Yobe and Borno. On Christmas day, 40 people were killed by bomb attacks by Boko Haram.

13 GOVERNMENT

The 1979 constitution, promulgated by the outgoing military government, established a federal system resembling that of the United States, with a directly elected president and vice president (whose names appear on the same ballot) and separate executive, legislative, and judicial branches.

The military government that took command after the December 1983 coup suspended the 1979 constitution. The president held executive and legislative authority, in consultation with the 28-member Armed Forces Ruling Council, and appointed the cabinet.

After the Abacha seizure of power on 17 November 1993, the 1979 constitution remained suspended. A military-dominated Provisional Ruling Council (PRC) ruled by decree. A 32-member Federal Executive Council managed government departments, and the PRC dissolved the elected national and state legislatures and the local councils, replacing elected civilian governors with military administrators. The PRC also announced that it would hold a constitutional conference to plan for the future and to establish a timetable for a return to democracy. On 21 November 1993, Abacha signed a decree restoring the 1979 constitution (Second Republic). Nonetheless, legal experts disagreed which documents should form the basis for Nigerian government and law.

The new constitution, which became law in May 1999, restored constitutional rule under the Fourth Republic. Nigeria became a federal republic comprising 36 states and a Federal Capital Territory at Abuja. The national legislature is bicameral with 109 Senate seats and 360 House seats. Members of both houses are elected by universal suffrage (age 18) to a four-year term. The president is elected to no more than two four-year terms. The president chairs a Federal Executive Council, which he appoints.

14 POLITICAL PARTIES

Ethnic, religious, and regional differences have hindered the formation of a truly national Nigerian political party in Nigeria. Before 1966, the major parties were the Northern People's Congress (NPC), overwhelmingly dominant in the Northern Region and possessing a plurality in the federal House of Representatives; the National Council of Nigerian Citizens (NCNC), dominant in the Eastern Region and junior partner in coalition with the NPC in the federal House of Representatives; and the Action Group, majority party in the Western Region and the leading opposition group in the federal legislature. Policies and platforms of the major parties were similar, generally supporting welfare and development programs. Following the 1959 elections, the NCNC joined in a coalition with the NPC in the federal government.

The first national elections in independent Nigeria, held on 30 December 1964, were contested by two political alliances: the Nigerian National Alliance (NNA), led by Sir Ahmadu Bello, premier of the Northern Region, and the United Progressive Grand Alliance (UPGA), led by Michael Okpara, premier of the Eastern Region. The NNA comprised the NPC, the Western-based Nigerian National Democratic Party, and opposition parties representing ethnic minorities in the Eastern and Mid-Western regions. The UPGA included the NCNC, the Action Group, the Northern Elements Progressive Union (the main opposition party in the Northern Region), and the United Middle Belt Congress (a non-Muslim party strongly opposed to the NPC). Northerners feared Ibo domination of the federal government and sought support from the Yoruba, while the UPGA accused the Muslim Northerners of anti-Southern, antidemocratic, and anti-Christian attitudes. The election results, announced on 6 January 1965, gave a large majority to the NNA (198 of 267 constituencies). Before the balloting began, the UPGA charged that unconstitutional practices were taking place and announced that it would boycott the elections, in which only 4 million of the 15 million eligible voters actually cast ballots. On 4 January 1965, President Azikiwe called on

Prime Minister Balewa to form a new government. In the supplementary elections held on 18 March 1965, the UPGA won all 51 seats in the Eastern Region and 3 seats in Lagos. This was followed by announcement of an enlarged and reorganized cabinet on 31 March. Ten months later the Balewa government was overthrown, the military assumed power, and on 24 May 1966 all political parties were banned.

When legal political activity resumed in 1978, five parties emerged: the National Party of Nigeria (NPN), representing chiefly the North and an educated, wealthy elite; the Nigerian People's Party (NPP), strong among the Ibos and slightly to the left of the NPN; the Unity Party of Nigeria (UPN), Yoruba-led and welfare-oriented; the People's Redemption Party, advocating radical social change; and the Great Nigeria People's Party, espousing welfare capitalism. Shagari, the NPN presidential candidate, received the most votes (33.9%) in the 11 August 1979 presidential election, with Obafemi Awolowo of the UPN a close second (29.2%). In National Assembly elections held on 7 and 14 July 1979, the NPN won 36 of the 95 Senate seats and 168 of 440 House of Representatives seats. The UPN was second with 28 and 111, respectively; the NPP third with 16 and 78. Each of the five parties won control of at least two state governments in elections held 21 and 28 July 1979. In the presidential election of August 1983, incumbent President Shagari of the NPN won reelection to a second four-year term, polling 12,047,638 votes (47%). Obafemi Awolowo of the UPN placed second with 7,885,434 votes (31%). That same month, Shagari's NPN posted victories in Senate and House elections. However, there were widespread charges of irregularities in the balloting. All existing political parties were dissolved after the December 1983 coup.

During the 1990s two parties, the right-of-center National Republican Convention (NRC) and a left-of-center Social Democratic Party (SDP) were permitted limited activity during the transition from military rule. The two-chamber National Assembly to which they were elected never was granted genuine power. On 12 June 1993, Nigerians apparently elected Moshood Abiola, a wealthy businessman, president, but General Ibrahim Babangida annulled the vote over alleged corruption. Ernest Shonekan replaced him for the interim, and on 17 November General Sani Abacha took power, suspending all partisan and political activity. The May 1994 legislative elections were widely boycotted by foes of Abacha's military regime. On 1 October 1995, Abacha announced a three-year program for return to civilian rule.

Political parties, suppressed by the military government, were allowed to form in July 1998. Three parties were registered by the Provisional Ruling Council for participation in local, state and national elections: the All People's Party (APP) led by Mahmud Waziri; the People's Democratic Party (PDP) led by Soloman Lar; and the Alliance for Democracy (AD), led by Ayo Adebanjo.

In the February 1999 election Obasanjo (PDP) won 62.8% of the vote; Olu Falae (AD/APP), received 37.2%. In the Senate, the PDP claimed 66 seats, the APP 23, the AD 19, with 1 other seat. In the House of Representatives, the PDP took 215 seats, the APP 70, the AD 66, and others 9. International observers reported some flaws, but generally approved the results.

The three registered parties suffered from leadership squabbles. Two factions claimed leadership of the AD, which is dominant only in the Yoruba southwest. The APP elected a new chairman in December 1999, after its former chairman, Mahmud Waziri, defected to the PDP. In December 2002, 24 new political parties registered for the 2003 elections.

The 2003 elections were held as scheduled. They confirmed the PDP as Nigeria's largest political party. The All Nigeria's People's Party (ANPP) was the second-largest party. Muhammadu Buhari, ANPP candidate for president in 2003, and its chair, Don Etiebet, each had their positions challenged.

In September 2006, the Alliance for Democracy, the Justice Party, the Advance Congress of Democrats, and several other minor political parties merged to form the Action Congress (AC).

In the 2007 presidential election, Umaru Yar'Adua of the PDP won 24,638,063 votes. In second place was Muhammadu Buhari of the ANPP (6,605,299 votes). Obasanjo's vice president, Atiku Abubakar, of the Action Congress (AC), won 2,637,848 votes. There were 15 other candidates running. In the 21 April 2007 legislative elections, the PDP prevailed. In the Senate, the PDP won 87 seats, the ANPP won 14, and AC won 6. In the House of Representative, the PDP won 263 seats, the ANPP won 63, and the AC won 30.

The next presidential election was scheduled for 2 April 2011. The election was cancelled on the same day it was meant to take place as the National Electoral Commission discovered that many polling stations did not have the necessary materials. The vote was rescheduled for 16 April, but many Nigerians suspected an overall plan of electoral fraud. Many citizens spent hours, and large sums of money, to travel to the villages where they were registered to vote, only to find the polls closed. Many of those who returned to their homes were not expected to make the costly journeys again, meaning that far fewer people were likely to participate in the election. The election took place on 16 April, but was followed almost immediately by riots and dissent when Goodluck Jonathan was declared the winner with 57% of the vote. His primary rival was Muhammadu Buhari, a northern Muslim from the Congress for Progressive Change (CPC). Buhari accused election officials of fraud, claiming that there were a number of irregularities in some regions of the country. A series of violent demonstrations occurred in the north as the result of the vote, leaving more than 500 people dead. The next presidential elections were scheduled for 2015.

In the 2011 senate elections, the PDP won 45 seats, the AC won 13 seats, the ANPP 7, the CPC 5, and others 4. In the house, the PDP won 123 seats, the AC 47, the CPC 30, the ANPP 25, and others 9. The next legislative elections were also scheduled for 2015.

15 LOCAL GOVERNMENT

In March 1976, a reorganization of Nigeria's major administrative divisions was undertaken. The 12 preexisting states were reconstituted into 19 states as follows: Ogun, Ondo, and Oyo states were created out of the former Western State; Imo and Anambra states from East-Central State; Niger and Sokoto states from North-Western State; Benue and Plateau states from Benue-Plateau State; and Bauchi, Borno, and Gongola from North-Eastern State. Seven other states remained basically unchanged except for minor boundary adjustments and some name changes; these are (with original names where applicable, in parentheses) Lagos, Kaduna (North-Central), Kano, Bendel (Mid-West), Cross River (South-Eastern), Rivers, and Kwara. The Federal Capital Territory of Abuja comprises 7,315 sq km (2,824 sq mi) and was carved from the central part of the country between Kaduna, Plateau, and Niger states. By law, a fixed proportion of federally collected revenue is allotted monthly to the states and localities.

Under the military regime established in 1983, all state governors were appointed by the ruling council; in 1987, all but one governor was a military officer. The governor of each state served as chairman of an appointed state executive council. By the end of the Babangida regime in August 1993, there were 30 states (as of 2006, there were 36) governed by elected state legislatures and governors. On 18 November 1993, these governments were abolished and the civilian governors were replaced by military commanders.

The transition to civilian rule announced 20 July 1998 led to local council elections on 5 December 1998. The PDP, APP, and AD qualified to present candidates to state and national elections by winning 5% of the vote in 24 states. The state governorships and legislatures were contested on 11 January 1999. In 2002, the PDP controlled 21 state governments.

After the 2003 election, PDP controlled 28 state governments. Nearly all local government councils in these states, and many in states controlled by other parties, were also run by the PDP. However, the commitment of its leadership to a system of autonomous local government was questionable. Many PDP governors (and non-PDP governors) reportedly diverted funds meant for local government; a law, the Monitoring and Allocation and Local Government Act, has made such action illegal. Shortly after May 2003, the federal government postponed local government elections to enable a panel appointed by it to examine the workings of the system. The reasoning for postponement was questionable, as the panel's report was not published. In July 2006, the Supreme Court ruled that the Federal Government lacked constitutional powers to monitor the 36 states of the Federation and consequently struck down all aspects of the Act.

The next local election took place on 14 April 2007, which gave the PDP control over 28 of the 36 states. In the 2011 elections, the opposition Action Congress of Nigeria captured additional governorships for a total of 6 out of the 36 state governors. The ruling PDP continued to possess the majority of governorships, with 23 state governors as of 2011. The next election was scheduled for 2015.

16JUDICIAL SYSTEM

Both the suspended 1979 constitution and the never-implemented 1989 constitutions, as well as the new constitution promulgated on 29 May 1999, provide for an independent judiciary. In practice, the judiciary is subject to executive and legislative branch pressure, influence by political leaders at both the state and federal levels, and suffers from corruption and inefficiency.

Under the 1999 constitution, the regular court system comprises federal and state trial courts, state appeals courts, the Federal Court of Appeal, the Federal Supreme Court, and Shari'ah (Islamic) and customary (traditional) courts of appeal for each state and for the federal capital territory of Abuja. Courts of the first instance include magistrate or district courts, customary or traditional courts, Shari'ah courts, and for some specified cases, the state high courts. In principle, customary and Shari'ah courts have jurisdiction only if both plaintiff and defendant agree, but fear of legal costs, delays, and distance to alternative venues encourage many litigants to choose these courts.

Trials in the regular court system are public and generally respect constitutionally protected individual rights, including a presumption of innocence, the right to be present, to confront witnesses, to present evidence, and to be represented by legal counsel. However, low compensation for judges, understaffing, poor equipment, bribery, special settlements, and a host of developmental factors decrease the reliability and impartiality of the courts.

Under the Abubakar government, military tribunals continued to operate outside the constitutional court system, but they were used less and less frequently as military rule waned; the tribunals officially were disbanded by the implementation of the new constitution and the return to civilian rule. The tribunals had in the past been used to try both military personnel and civilians accused of various crimes, but groups asserted that these tribunals failed to meet internationally accepted standards for fair trial.

In October 1999, the governor of Zamfara signed into law two bills passed by the state legislature aimed at instituting Shari'ah law in the state. As a result, school children were being segregated by sex in Zamfara schools, some public transportation, and some health facilities. There were fears among non-Muslims that despite legal provisions, women and other groups would be subjected to discrimination in Shari'ah courts. As of early 2003, 11 other northern states had adopted various forms or adaptations of Shari'ah law, including: Sokoto, Kebbi, Niger, Kano, Katsina, Kaduna, Jigawa, Yobe, Bauchi, Borno, and Gombe. Some of these states have issued sentences of public caning for consumption of alcohol, amputations for stealing, and death by stoning for committing adultery. Some sentences have been carried out, but no life has been taken in the pursuit of a decision by a Shari'ah court. Those found guilty for adultery have had the verdicts reversed on appeal.

According to the federal government, religious police in Kano State (also called *Hisba*) have assumed police functions with no official authorization to do so, as have ethnic militias, such as the Odu'a People's Congress.

The judiciary has faced testing moments since the 2003 polls. Obasanjo himself accused the judiciary of corruption; some legal practitioners also traded accusations against judges in open court. Election petitions at all levels brought with them allegations of bribery and witness tampering. Acting through the National Judicial Council, a body chaired by Nigeria's Chief Justice, the judiciary moved to cleanse its own house. Several judicial officers were dismissed, disciplined in other ways, or exonerated after due hearing. The stated offenses ranged from receiving undue gratification to passing judgments that were patently illegal or procedurally wrong, or that brought the judiciary to ridicule.

17ARMED FORCES

The International Institute for Strategic Studies reports that armed forces in Nigeria totaled 80,000 members in 2011. The force is comprised of 62,000 from the army, 8,000 from the navy, and 10,000 members of the air force. Armed forces represented 0.3% of the labor force in Nigeria. Defense spending totaled $5.7 billion and accounted for 1.5% of GDP. Nigeria has observers and peacekeeping forces stationed in Burundi, Côte d'Ivoire, the DROC,

Eritrea/Ethiopia, Liberia, Sierra Leone, South Sudan, Sudan, and Western Sahara.

18 INTERNATIONAL COOPERATION

Nigeria was admitted to the UN on 7 October 1960, and since that time has become affiliated with ECA and several nonregional specialized agencies, such as the FAO, ILO, IAEA, the World Bank, UNESCO, UNHCR, UNIDO, and the WHO. The nation is also a member of the Commonwealth of Nations, the WTO, the ACP Group, the African Development Bank, G-15, G-24, G-77, the Organization of the Islamic Conference (OIC), the New Partnership for Africa's Development (NEPAD), the Community of Sahel and Saharan States (CENSAD), and the African Union. Nigeria joined OPEC in June 1971. In May 1975, Nigeria became a founding member of ECOWAS. Among other regional organizations of which Nigeria is a member are the Niger Basin Authority and the Lake Chad Basin Commission. The government is participating in efforts to establish a West African Monetary Zone (WAMZ) that would establish a common currency among its member nations—The Gambia, Ghana, Guinea, Liberia, Nigeria, and Sierra Leone.

Nigeria is a member of the Nonaligned Movement. The government has supported UN missions and operations in Kosovo (est. 1999), Western Sahara (est. 1991), Ethiopia and Eritrea (est. 2000), Liberia (est. 2003), Sierra Leone (est. 1999), Burundi (est. 2004), Côte d'Ivoire (est. 2004), South Sudan (est. 2011), Sudan (est. 2005), and the DROC (est. 2000).

In environmental cooperation, Nigeria is part of the Basel Convention, the Convention on Biological Diversity, CITES, the London Convention, the Kyoto Protocol, the Montréal Protocol, the Nuclear Test Ban Treaty, and the UN Conventions on the Law of the Sea, Climate Change and Desertification.

19 ECONOMY

The Nigerian economy, with an enterprising population and a wealth of natural resources, offers tremendous potential for economic growth. However, poor economic policy, political instability, and an over reliance on oil exports have created severe structural problems in the economy. Agriculture remains the basic economic activity for the majority of Nigerians, employing a majority of the labor force. Crop yields have not kept pace with the average population growth, and Nigeria must import most of its food.

When the oil boom of the 1970s came to an end in the early 1980s, Nigeria's failure to bring domestic and foreign expenditures in line with its lower income led to a rapid buildup of internal and external deficits. Nigeria deferred payments on its large foreign debt, adopted austerity measures, scaled back ambitious development plans, and introduced a foreign exchange auction system that devalued the naira. These policies had a positive effect and from 1986 to 1990 real GDP grew at a 5.4% average annual rate.

However, in 1992 real GDP grew at only 4.1%, while the large government deficits, 10% of GDP in 1992, continued to expand. A crippling blow to the economy came in mid-1994 when oil workers in the southeast, unhappy with the way the central government collected oil revenue without giving any back, went on strike. With daily output down 25% because of the strike, the government's lack of revenue forced it to stop servicing most of its $28 billion external debt. In the meantime the budget deficit reached $1 billion, over 12% of GDP.

In 1996, the World Bank reported that an estimated $2 billion in oil revenues from the early 1990s was diverted in a secret government bank account. There were also reports that significant amounts of oil revenue were being lost due to fraudulent practices at the country's oil terminals. In response, the Nigerian government appointed two inspection firms to oversee the loading of crude oil tankers.

By 2004 external debt stood at $31 billion. The next year, Nigeria carved out a deal to have some 60% of the debt the country owed to the Paris Club forgiven; Nigeria pledged to repay about $12 billion. High unemployment and declining productivity hampered growth. As of 2006, the pace of privatizing state-owned enterprises and balancing the budget was slow, but liberalization of the telecommunications sector was underway. The government also committed itself to privatizing the country's four state-owned oil refineries, and to developing several small, independently owned refineries.

The government's 2008 budget stressed improvements in infrastructure, which is the main impediment to growth. While other economies continued to suffer from the global economic downturn, Nigeria posted a robust growth rate of 7.07% for the third quarter of 2009, up nearly a full percentage point from the same period a year before. Although the growth rate dropped slightly from the second quarter, analysts thought the overall economic forecast was strong, driven largely by gains in the oil sector.

Crude oil accounted for over 95% of government revenue in 2008. That year, however, an oil crisis developed due to continued violence between the government and militant groups in the oil-rich delta region. The conflict centers on the distribution of wealth. Local groups within the delta region want to see a greater amount of oil revenues funneled back into their own communities, rather than settling only in the pockets of the government. Oil production was cut by nearly 20% by year-end 2008. In January 2009, the value of the naira had dropped by 20% within only a few weeks, due to the loss of oil revenue. The president assembled a special team of economic advisors to address the impending financial crisis and plans were made toward deregulation of the oil sector by dropping government subsidies and privatizing some refineries. In May 2009, the Nigerian Labor Congress launched a massive protest against the deregulation plans, claiming they would only result in local fuel shortages and higher fuel prices for residents. Government fuel subsidies in 2008 kept the price of a liter of gas to an average of 44 cents. Those subsidies cost the government a total of $4.3 billion dollars.

The GDP rate of change in Nigeria, as of 2010, was 8.4%. Inflation stood at 13.9%, and unemployment was reported at 4.9%. Nigeria anticipated a boom in manufacturing through the development of the Lekki Free Trade Zone (LFTZ) in Lagos. With significant funding from Chinese investors, this free trade zone was expected to welcome a number of Chinese manufacturers, particularly those producing goods such as furniture, electronics, heavy machinery, and pharmaceuticals. Since Nigeria currently imports a vast majority of its goods, the foreign investment offered not only a source of new jobs and revenue, but also a variety of products for the local market. Sixty percent of the LFTZ is held by Chinese investors, with the remaining 40% in the hands of the

Lagos state government. In 2010 the project began its first phase of construction, which involved basic infrastructure improvements such as roads and power and water connections. Some 135 local and foreign companies indicated interest in the project. Planners projected that the LFTZ would become operational in 2012, generating $647 million annually and creating one million new jobs.

20 INCOME

The CIA estimated that in 2010 the GDP of Nigeria was $377.9 billion. The CIA defines GDP as the value of all final goods and services produced within a nation in a given year and computed on the basis of purchasing power parity (PPP) rather than value as measured on the basis of the rate of the exchange based on current dollars. The per capita GDP was estimated at $2,500. The annual growth rate of GDP was 8.4%. The average inflation rate was 13.9%. It was estimated that agriculture accounted for 31.9% of GDP, industry 32.9%, and services 35.2%.

According to the World Bank, remittances from citizens living abroad totaled $9.6 billion or about $62 per capita and accounted for approximately 2.5% of GDP.

The World Bank estimates that Nigeria, with 2.13% of the world's population, accounted for 0.45% of the world's GDP. By comparison, the United States, with 4.85% of the world's population, accounted for 22.51% of world GDP.

As of 2011 the most recent study by the World Bank reported that actual individual consumption in Nigeria was 71.6% of GDP and accounted for 0.44% of world consumption. By comparison, the United States accounted for 25.44% of world individual consumption. The World Bank also estimated that 41.3% of Nigeria's GDP was spent on food and beverages, 13.1% on housing and household furnishings, 4.2% on clothes, 2.2% on health, 3.4% on transportation, 0.2% on communications, 0.9% on recreation, 0.5% on restaurants and hotels, and 2.6% on miscellaneous goods and services and purchases from abroad.

21 LABOR

As of 2010, Nigeria had a total labor force of 50.48 million people. Within that labor force, CIA estimates in 1999 (most recent figures available as of February 2012) noted that 70% were employed in agriculture, 10% in industry, and 20% in the service sector.

The four labor federations were merged in 1978 into the Nigerian Labour Congress (NLC), which was strengthened by legislation establishing a compulsory dues checkoff system. Unions were strengthened by government decrees and a new constitution in 1999. Freedom of association and the right to strike were restored. The NLC is the only legal trade union organization (outside the petroleum industry).

In March 2011, President Jonathan signed a new minimum wage act after threats of strikes and prolonged negotiations. The new law states that once an employer in the public or private sector has a workforce of 50 people, he or she must pay the minimum wage of NGN18,000 ($118.00) per month. The act more than doubled the previous minimum wage of approximately NGN7,500 ($50) per month. Despite the passage of the act, concerns remained over the implementation and enforcement of the minimum wage and the fact that many organizations, especially in the agricultural sector, employ less than 50 workers.

The workweek is set at 40 hours, but there is no law prohibiting excessive compulsory overtime. Children as young as 13 may work with special restrictions. In reality, as a result of crumbling public schools and dire economic conditions for many citizens, children of all ages work. The law stipulates minimum occupational health and safety standards, but such standards are not effectively enforced.

22 AGRICULTURE

Agriculture is an important sector of Nigeria's economy, engaging about 70% of the labor force. Agricultural holdings are generally small and scattered; farming is often of the subsistence variety, characterized by simple tools and shifting cultivation. These small farms produce about 90% of the total food. Nigeria's diverse climate, from the tropical areas of the coast to the arid zone of the north, make it possible to produce virtually all agricultural products that can be grown in the tropical and semitropical areas of the world. The economic benefits of large-scale agriculture are recognized, and the government favors the formation of cooperative societies and settlements to encourage industrial agriculture. Large-scale agriculture, however, is not common. Despite an abundant water supply, a favorable climate, and wide areas of arable land, productivity is restricted, owing to low soil fertility in many areas and inefficient methods of cultivation.

The agricultural products of Nigeria can be divided into two main groups: food crops, produced for home consumption, and export products. Prior to the civil war, the country was self-sufficient in food, but imports of food increased substantially after 1973. Bread, made primarily from US wheat, replaced domestic crops as the cheapest staple food for much of the urban population. The most important food crops are yams and manioc (cassava) in the south and sorghum (Guinea corn) and millet in the north. Roughly 36% of the total land is farmed, and the country's major crops include cocoa, peanuts, cotton, palm oil, corn, rice, sorghum, millet, cassava (tapioca), yams. Cereal production in 2009 amounted to 21 million tons, fruit production 10.3 million tons, and vegetable production 8.8 million tons. Production of cassava was 36.8 million tons in 2009 (highest in the world); yams was 29.1 million tons (highest in the world); citrus fruit, 3.8 million tons (second highest in the world); cocoyams (taro), 2.98 million tons (highest in the world); and groundnuts, 2.97 million tons (third highest in the world).

Although cocoa is the leading non-oil foreign exchange earner, growth in the sector has been slow since the abolition of the Nigerian Cocoa Board. The dominance of smallholders in the cocoa sector and the lack of farm labor due to urbanization holds back production. Nigeria produced 363,610 tons of cocoa in 2009, fourth in the world. While cocoa was significant in the country's economic development, its role has declined in part due to aging farmers and trees. In 2010–11, Nigeria produced 280,000 tons of cocoa. Favorable weather and rising prices are expected to encourage greater growth in 2012.

After cocoa, rubber is the second-largest non-oil foreign exchange earner. Despite favorable prices, production has fallen from 155,000 tons in 1991 to 89,000 tons in 2010. Low yield, aging trees, and lack of proper equipment have inhibited production.

²³ANIMAL HUSBANDRY

The UN Food and Agriculture Organization (FAO) reported that Nigeria dedicated 38 million hectares (93.9 million acres) to permanent pasture or meadow in 2009. During that year, the country tended 184.5 million chickens, 16.4 million head of cattle, and 7.2 million pigs. The production from these animals amounted to 287,842 tons of beef and veal, 209,495 tons of pork, 243,453 tons of poultry, 510,583 tons of eggs, and 1.2 million tons of milk. Nigeria also produced 45,900 tons of cattle hide. Over 90% of the nation's cattle are found in the north, owned mostly by nomadic Fulani. The prevalence of the tsetse fly in other areas restricts the majority of cattle to the fly-free dry savanna areas. The cattle owned by the Fulani and Hausa consist mainly of zebu breeds; cattle in the south are mainly Shorthorns. There were also an estimated 57 million goats and 36 million sheep in 2010.

Improvements in stock, slaughterhouse, cold storage, and transport facilities have made parts of Nigeria almost self-sufficient in meat production, but many Nigerians outside the north suffer protein deficiency in their diet. The Livestock and Meat Authority controls operations in transport and slaughtering in the north.

²⁴FISHING

Nigeria had 224 decked commercial fishing boats in 2008. The annual capture totaled 541,368 tons according to the UN FAO. The export value of seafood totaled $56.83 million. Fish is an important dietary element and one of the few sources of animal protein available to many Nigerians. Fishing is carried on in Nigeria's many rivers, creeks, and lagoons, and in Lake Chad; trawlers operate along the coast.

Both federal and state governments are encouraging the development of local fisheries, inland and at sea, by sponsoring research, stocking reservoirs, and offering training in improved fish culture and fishing gear. Fish ponds have been established in the southern part of the country.

²⁵FORESTRY

Approximately 10% of Nigeria is covered by forest. High forest reserves occur mostly in Ogun, Ondo, and Oyo states; savanna forest reserves, chiefly in the northern states, are limited in value, yielding only firewood and local building materials. The UN FAO estimated the 2009 roundwood production at 9.42 million cu m (332.6 million cu ft). The value of all forest products, including roundwood, totaled $45.7 million. Exports of timber and finished wood products were banned in 1976 in order to preserve domestic supplies. The ban was subsequently lifted and the forestry sector recorded gains. However, the country suffers from desertification, anemic reforestation efforts, and high levels of domestic wood consumption. Nigeria has one of the highest deforestation rates of natural forest in the world. In 2010 forestry imports totaled $539 million.

²⁶MINING

The oil sector is the cornerstone of the Nigerian economy. Other leading industries include cement and other construction materials, chemicals, fertilizer, ceramics, and steel.

Nigeria produced 230 metric tons (gross weight) of cassiterite tin concentrate in 2009, down from 1,818 metric tons in 2006. A smelter at Jos produces refined tin for export. In 2009, production of columbium and tantalum concentrates (gross weight) totaled 180 metric tons. Nigeria has plentiful supplies of limestone, and production totaled 3.9 million tons in 2009. In addition, Nigeria produces barite, clays, feldspar, gold, granite, kaolin, lead, marble, shale, and topaz. Gypsum output declined from 579,000 metric tons in 2007 to 300,000 metric tons in 2009. Nitrogen production was halted in 1999. Iron ore production only amounted to 99,000 metric tons in 2009, even though extensive iron deposits includes reserves of 2,500 million tons with an average content of 37%.

To attract local and foreign investment in the development of the nonfuel minerals sector and to broaden the country's industrial base, the Mining and Minerals Decree No. 34, enacted in 1999, provided for three-year tax holidays, exemption from customs duties for mining equipment, convertibility of foreign currency, and free transferability of funds. It also reaffirmed that all mineral rights were to be held by the federal government, although the national legislature was debating reallocation of mineral rights to the states. However, the country's reputation for civil strife, corruption, environmental degradation, fraud, poor infrastructure, and political uncertainty continued to temper international investors' interest in most projects. The adoption of Islamic Shari'ah law in many of the northern states added uncertainty to internal mineral projects in northern Nigeria. Militants claiming to fight for redistribution of oil revenue have regularly blown up pipelines, although such incidents have decreased since 2009. Shell claims that 70% of oil spilled in the Niger delta during 2006–2010 was caused by sabotage and theft.

²⁷ENERGY AND POWER

Nigeria is one of the largest producers of oil in the world and the largest oil producer in Africa. It is a major oil supplier to the United States and Western Europe. Nigeria is also a member of the Organization of Petroleum Exporting Countries (OPEC).

In 2011, the country produced an estimated 2.46 million barrels of oil per day, of which crude oil accounted for 2.3 million barrels per day. In 2010, net exports and domestic consumption of oil were estimated at 2.1 million barrels per day and 279,000 barrels per day, respectively. Crude oil refining capacity in 2009 was estimated at 505,000 barrels per day. As a member of OPEC, Nigeria is subject to a crude oil production quota. As of August 2011, that quota was set at 1.96 million barrels per day.

Nigeria's proven reserves of natural gas makes the country one of the world's top 10 countries so endowed, and the largest in Africa. Nigeria's natural gas reserves were 185 trillion cu ft in 2010. Nigeria produced an estimated 1.02 trillion cu ft of natural gas, with domestic demand for that year at 176 billion cu ft and exports estimated at 848 billion cu ft.

In May 2010, Nigeria's state-run oil company, the Nigerian National Petroleum Company, signed a $23 billion deal with China to build three new refineries and a fuel complex in Nigeria. Under the agreement, China would supply the funds in order to benefit from Nigeria's massive oil and gas exports. At the time of the agreement, Nigeria was the twelfth-largest oil producer in the world but imported some 85% of its fuel needs from other countries. This paradox could be explained by the fact that Nigeria's four state-run refineries were in a state of disrepair. With the huge infusion of Chinese capital, Nigeria hoped to reverse this trend.

Nigeria also has coal deposits. In 2010, Nigeria had coal reserves estimated at 2 billion tons and proven reserves of 650 million tons, with domestic consumption and production each estimated at 0.09 million short tons.

The World Bank reported in 2008 that Nigeria produced 21.1 billion kWh of electricity and consumed 19.1 billion kWh, or 123 kWh per capita. Approximately 73% of energy came from conventional thermal sources, while hydropower accounted for the remainder. Nigeria's electric generating capacity is heavily dedicated to conventional thermal sources. In 2010 the government announced the sell of the state-owned Power Holding Company of Nigeria, which had held a monopoly over electricity generation for many years. The entire nation struggles from a lack of power and frequent blackouts. In 2008, reports indicated that the government would need to commit to an investment of $85 billion to create the necessary infrastructure to produce electricity nationwide, 24 hours a day. The government hoped privatization of the sector would translate into a better supply at a quicker pace.

28 INDUSTRY

Industry accounted for 32% of GDP in 2010, mostly in the oil sector. Due to the high costs of production that result from inadequate infrastructure, Nigeria's manufacturing capacity utilization remains low. An estimated 10% of the labor force is employed in the industrial sector.

The oil sector supplies 95% of foreign exchange earnings and some 90% of total exports. Nigeria's crude oil refining capacity was estimated at 505,000 barrels per day in 2009. There are four state-owned refineries in Nigeria, and hydrocarbon production is centered around Eleme, Warri, and Kaduna. Sabotage, fires, extended maintenance, and management problems plague the oil industry, however. There has been political unrest over the issue of the equitable sharing of Nigeria's oil profits with the population.

The textile industry is still in early stages of development. Between 60% and 70% of all raw materials used in textile production come from local sources. Foreign investment in the textile industry is led by Chinese and Indian investors. Other areas of expansion include cement production, tire production, and furniture assembly. Other important industries include sawmills, cigarette factories, breweries, sugar refining, rubber, paper, soap and detergent factories, footwear factories, pharmaceutical plants, tire factories, paint factories, and assembly plants for consumer electronics. Nigeria has five state-owned motor-vehicle assembly plants for Volkswagen, Peugeot, and Mercedes products, which were privatized by 2007.

29 SCIENCE AND TECHNOLOGY

The World Bank reported in 2009 that there were no patent applications in science and technology in Nigeria. Learned societies include ones for ecology, engineering, entomology, fisheries, forestry, genetics, geography, medicine, microbiology, nutrition, and veterinary medicine. The Federal Ministry of Science and Technology has 25 attached research institutes that focus on cereals, cocoa, lake ecology, horticulture, forestry, livestock, root crops, veterinary medicine, oceanography and marine sciences, oil palms, rubber, and tropical agriculture, among other areas. The Geological Survey of Nigeria, founded in 1919, is concerned with geological mapping, mineral exploration, geophysical and geochemical surveys, and consultation on geological problems.

The National Museum branch in Jos, founded in 1989, has zoological and botanical gardens and a transport museum. Obafemi Awolowo University in Ile-Ife has a natural history museum founded in 1948. Nigeria has 60 universities and colleges offering courses in basic and applied science. Science and engineering students account for about 40% of college and university enrollments.

The Nigerian Academy of Science, founded in 1977, promotes and coordinates scientific and technological activities, trains scientists, advises the government on scientific matters, and organizes symposia and lectures.

The African Union announced plans to create the Pan-African University in 2008. Touted as a flagship institution of higher education, the university consisted of five regional schools, each specializing in a different discipline. The University of Lagos was to host the West African node designated for earth and life sciences. Kenya and Cameroon were selected to represent East Africa and Central Africa respectively, but political and financial issues emerged in choosing the South and North Africa branches. AU officials originally hoped to open all five branches in September 2010, but all branches were not expected to open until 2012.

30 DOMESTIC TRADE

The distribution of consumer goods is effected largely through a complex network of intermediary traders, who extend the area of distribution and often break down products into very small units for delivery to the ultimate consumer. A few trading companies, especially those with European equity and management, carry full product lines. Village markets are universal but tend to be more highly organized in the densely populated areas of the south. The great market centers such as Ibadan and Kano are attended by many thousands daily. Domestic commerce is limited by poor infrastructure, widespread fraud and corruption, and shortages of fuel that are exacerbated by illegal smuggling of gasoline across Nigeria's borders. The economy is still primarily cash based. Advertising has increased markedly since independence. Newspapers, magazines, radio, television, billboards, and movies are all utilized.

Businesses and government offices are generally open from 8 a.m. to 4 p.m., Monday through Friday. In the Muslim north, establishments close at 1 p.m. on Friday so that Muslim workers can attend Jumat services. Supermarkets and stores are open from 8:30 a.m. to 5 p.m., Monday through Friday, and from 7:30 a.m. to 1 p.m. on Saturdays. A large number of smaller shops and restaurants are often open from sunrise to near midnight.

31 FOREIGN TRADE

Nigeria's exports have been on a dramatic upswing. Between 1998 and 1999, they grew more than three-fold, and by 2000 nearly doubled again. Exports were dominated by fuels and mining products (about 95%). Agricultural products composed about 2% of Nigeria's exports. Cocoa is the largest agricultural export. Leading imports are machinery, chemicals, transportation equipment, manufactured goods, and food.

Nigeria imported $34.18 billion worth of goods and services in 2008, while exporting $76.33 billion worth of goods and services. In 2008, Nigeria's leading markets were: the United States (34% of

Principal Trading Partners – Nigeria (2010)

(In millions of US dollars)

Country	Total	Exports	Imports	Balance
World	116,000.0	79,000.0	37,000.0	42,000.0
United States	32,951.0	28,507.0	4,444.0	24,063.0
India	11,482.0	9,361.0	2,121.0	7,240.0
China	8,335.0	971.0	7,364.0	-6,393.0
Netherlands	7,430.0	2,881.0	4,549.0	-1,668.0
Brazil	6,868.0	5,919.0	949.0	4,970.0
Spain	5,607.0	5,247.0	360.0	4,887.0
France	5,324.0	3,048.0	2,276.0	772.0
Germany	3,780.0	2,295.0	1,485.0	810.0
South Africa	3,380.0	2,527.0	853.0	1,674.0
United Kingdom	3,098.0	1,102.0	1,996.0	-894.0

(…) data not available or not significant.

(n.s.) not specified.

SOURCE: *2011 Direction of Trade Statistics Yearbook,* New York: United Nations, 2011.

all exports); India (9.8%); Brazil (9%); Spain (6.8%); and France (4.5%). Leading suppliers were China (13.9% of all imports); the United States (9.3%); the Netherlands (8.6%); the United Kingdom (4.9%); and France (4.4%).

³²BALANCE OF PAYMENTS

Exports are dominated by oil, and with oil prices forecast to remain relatively high against a background of rising production from 2005–10, substantial trade surpluses were predicted. The trade surplus was estimated at $14 billion in 2010, amounting to 1.7% of GDP. In 2010, the current-account surplus was $21.85 billion.

³³BANKING AND SECURITIES

In 1892, Nigeria's first bank, the African Banking Corp., was established, patterned along British lines. Before World War II, two large British banks, the Bank of British West Africa and Barclays Bank, virtually monopolized Nigerian banking. After 1945, a number of African-owned banks entered the field; between 1946 and 1952, however, more than 20 such banks failed. The bank of issue became the Central Bank of Nigeria (CBN) in 1958. It regulated most commercial banking operations in Nigeria, but the federal Ministry of Finance retained control of most international activities of the financial sector. The Nigerian Industrial Development Bank (NIDB) was established in 1964 to provide long- and medium-term financing to concerns in the industrial nonpetroleum, mining, and tourist sectors.

The 1969 Banking Decree required that all banking institutions be incorporated in Nigeria, and a 1976 law gave the government 60% ownership of all foreign banks. The Banking Decree also established minimum capital requirements for licensed banks, based on the total deposits. Important additional sources of credit were provided by thrift and loan societies and by the branches of the National Development Corporation. The National Bank for Commerce and Industry helped finance smaller enterprises. Merchant banking expanded rapidly from 1973 onward, when the Union Dominican Trust Company began operations.

With the adoption of the Structural Adjustment Program (SAP) in 1986, the licensing of new banks was liberalized. In July 1990

the state banks were privatized. Beginning in 1990 the country allowed the establishment of foreign banks, but 60% of the foreign banks that were established in Nigeria had to be held by Nigerian interests. In the same year the government began a program to establish 500 community banks. From 1985 to 1993, the number of banks rose from 40 to 120, but declined to 89 in 1998. There were over 100 banks in Nigeria in 2011; the main banks included the Guaranty Trust Bank, Access Bank, First City Monument Bank, Skye Bank, MainStreet Bank Limited (formerly Afribank), Fidelity Bank, Diamond Bank Limited, United Bank for Africa (with Banque Nationale de Paris and Bankers Trust shareholdings), Union Bank of Nigeria, and First Bank of Nigeria (partly owned by Standard Chartered.

Nigerian banks felt the 2009 credit crunch just as strongly as those in other nations. As the banks faltered, the government provided a $4 billion bailout package for nine key lenders. In 2010, Nigeria launched the Asset Management Company of Nigeria to cover non-performing loans and to recapitalize these lenders. In December of the same year, the government launched a $500 million loan facility for small and medium-sized businesses, which was funded and operated by the Nigerian Bank of Industry.

In 2011, currency and demand deposits—an aggregate commonly known as M1—were equal to $36 billion. In that same year, M2—an aggregate equal to M1 plus savings deposits, small time deposits, and money market mutual funds—was $76 billion. In 2011, the money market rate, the rate at which financial institutions lend to one another in the short term, was 15%. In 2009, Nigeria's central bank gold reserves totaled 0.63 million fine troy ounces.

The Nigerian (formerly Lagos) Stock Exchange (NSE) began operations on 1 July 1961, following passage of the Lagos Stock Exchange Act; the government promulgated regulations for the exchange and provided that all dealings in stock be carried out only by members of the exchange. The Securities and Exchange

Balance of Payments – Nigeria (2010)

(In millions of US dollars)

Current Account		**2,476.0**
Balance on goods		20,237.0
Imports	-53,461.0	
Exports	73,698.0	
Balance on services		-19,231.0
Balance on income		-18,623.0
Current transfers		20,092.0
Capital Account		**...**
Financial Account		**-6,999.0**
Direct investment abroad		-915.0
Direct investment in Nigeria		6,049.0
Portfolio investment assets		-1,121.0
Portfolio investment liabilities		3,717.0
Financial derivatives		...
Other investment assets		-14,524.0
Other investment liabilities		-204.0
Net Errors and Omissions		**-5,207.0**
Reserves and Related Items		**9,730.0**

(…) data not available or not significant.

SOURCE: *Balance of Payment Statistics Yearbook 2011,* Washington, DC: International Monetary Fund, 2011.

Public Finance – Nigeria (2008)

(In billions of naira, budgetary central government figures)

Revenue and Grants	2,386.9	100.0%
Tax revenue	68.5	2.9%
Social contributions	...	...
Grants	...	...
Other revenue	2,318.4	97.1%
Expenditures	2,793.7	100.0%
General public services	...	...
Defense	...	...
Public order and safety	...	...
Economic affairs	...	...
Environmental protection	...	...
Housing and community amenities	...	...
Health	...	...
Recreational, culture, and religion	...	...
Education	...	...
Social protection	...	...

(...) data not available or not significant.

SOURCE: *Government Finance Statistics Yearbook 2010*, Washington, DC: International Monetary Fund, 2010.

Commission (SEC) fixed prices of all new securities, and regulated the prices of those already being traded. Transactions of 50,000 shares or more were subject to SEC approval. The government encouraged public issues of shares by Nigerian companies in an effort to mobilize local capital for the country's development. The exchange, in Lagos, with branches in Kaduna and Port Harcourt, dealt in government stocks and in shares of public companies registered in Nigeria. After the provision of new investment incentives under the Nigerian Enterprises Promotion Decree of April 1974, activity on the stock exchange increased.

In a bid to encourage foreign interest in the NSE, a computerized central securities clearing system (CSCS) was installed on 14 April 1997, although it got off to a quiet start. The custodian bank for the system was Nigeria International Bank/Citibank. The benefit of the system was that trades would be settled within one week and eventually within two days, compared with the long delays hitherto experienced in effecting share transfers after purchases and sales. On 21 April 1997, a CBN directive lifted the restrictions on equity ownership of individual and corporate investors in Nigerian banks. Under this legislation, it was possible for an individual or another corporation to own up to a 100% share in a bank. Prior to the directive, the maximum shareholding for an individual was just 10%, while for companies it was 30%.

Market capitalization of the Nigerian Stock Exchange (NSE) was $40 billion in 2011, with 207 companies listed. The NSE All Share Index was down 18.5% in 2011 to 20,730.63.

34 INSURANCE

The Nigerian Reinsurance Corp. requires foreign insurance companies to reinsure 20% through the corporation. In 1976, the government took a 60% interest in foreign-owned insurance companies. The only compulsory insurance is that for motor vehicles. Laws of 1976 and 1977 regulate insurance firms, particularly those in the life insurance field, and provide for their registration, inves-

tigation, and minimum capitalization. The regulatory body is the Director of Insurance, under the Federal Ministry of Trade (Insurance Division). In 2011, Nigeria had 17 life insurance companies, 32 non-life insurance companies, 10 composite companies, and 2 re-insurance companies. The total net insurance premiums was $609 million. It contributed 0.72% to the economy. In 2011, Nigeria's leading life was Aiico, which grew 67.35% from 2009 to 2010 and had gross written life insurance premiums of $51 million in 2011.

35 PUBLIC FINANCE

The federal government is responsible for collecting taxes on income, profits, and property, as well as import and export taxes and excise duties. It also runs the national transportation system. The petroleum sector provides over 83% of budgetary revenues. A large share of these revenues is redistributed to state governments. The budget is consistently in deficit. In 2010 the budget deficit amounted to 6.7% of GDP. Some $9.462 billion of public debt was held by foreign entities.

Public investment flourished during the oil boom years of the 1970s. When the oil market prices collapsed in the 1980s however, the Nigerian government maintained its high level of spending, thus acquiring substantial foreign debt. Although privatization efforts began in 1986, increased government spending outside the official budget since 1990 has damaged public finance reform. Through privatization, the government sold state-owned banks, fuel distribution companies, and cement plants. Nigeria sought to sell the troubled Nigerian Airways before it ceased operations in 2006. Also in 2006, Nigeria became the first African nation to pay off its multi-billion dollar Paris Club debt. Nigeria agreed to pay the Paris Club $12.4 billion in exchange for the remainder of its $30 billion official debts being written off. This agreement facilitated a sharp reduction in its external debt, which declined from 36% of GDP in 2004 to less than 4% of GDP in 2007. It had risen to 13.4% of GDP by 2010.

36 TAXATION

With the restoration of democracy, most state and local governments have found it necessary to introduce their own local levies in the face of dwindling revenues from the Federation Account to the State and Local Governments.

Nigeria had a standard corporate tax rate of 30%, as of 2011, plus a 2% education tax. A reduced rate is available for companies engaged in manufacturing, agricultural production or mining solid minerals, and for wholly export-oriented enterprises. There was also a capital gains tax of 10% on the disposal of assets inside or outside of Nigeria, although there were some exemptions. There is a withholding tax of 10% on dividends, interest income, rental income and royalties. There is also a tax on companies engaged in upstream (exploration and production) activities in the petroleum sector.

Under the Personal Income Tax Act, both Nigerian and foreign residents in Nigeria are subject to a progressive tax on their worldwide income, with a top rate of 25%. Property taxes are assessed by state governments.

In 1993, the Value-added Tax Decree (VAT Act) abolished the Sales Tax Decree of 1986, establishing a VAT with a standard rate of 5% (as of 2011) chargeable on most goods and services. Exempted goods include medical and pharmaceutical products, basic foodstuffs, books and educational materials, baby products, locally manufactured fertilizers, all exports, plants and machinery used in export processing zones (EPZs). States are also authorized to impose a tax on goods and services rendered in the state. Excise duties on beer, tobacco, textiles, and other goods are also levied.

³⁷CUSTOMS AND DUTIES

The federal government levies customs duties on most imports, but these duties were substantially reduced in 1986 and in 1995. The import duty varies from 5–60%, averaging 12%. All imports are also subject to a 7% port surcharge and a 5% VAT. The paperwork necessary for exporting and importing is lengthy. The taxation system has been widely avoided and valuations are arbitrary.

Prohibited exports include raw hides and skins, timber and building materials, raw palm kernels, and unprocessed rubber (to protect building and processing industries). Most goods produced in Nigeria may be freely exported. Prohibited imports include live chicks, flour, vegetable oils, gypsum, mosquito repellent coils, plastic domestic articles, used tires, and weapons.

³⁸FOREIGN INVESTMENT

Nigeria is West Africa's most populous country, and one of the most developed. Investment in the petroleum industry was carried out on a very large scale in the 1970s, including funds devoted to production, refining, and petrochemicals. The petroleum industry was largely nationalized during that period. Upstream operations are dominated by the Shell Petroleum Development Company of Nigeria. The company has been involved in conflict with local groups, particularly the Movement for the Survival of the Ogoni People (MOPOS), which accused Shell of causing life-threatening environmental damage, while the company contends that the damage was caused by interference with its operations. Downstream, two consortiums with foreign participation have controlled about 30% of the market: TotalFinaElf Nigeria Plc and Unipetrol/Agip. However, in 2005, Majestic Oil (Sierra Leone) acquired Unipetrol's 24.22% share in the West Africa Oil Refinery when the company failed to invest in the rehabilitation of the facility.

In December 1989, a new Nigerian Enterprises Decree permitted 100% foreign ownership in any new venture except those in banking, oil, insurance, and mining. The government uses an open tender system for awarding government contracts. However, a patronage system exerts powerful influence over the awarding of such contracts. Government scandals, political instability, and endemic corruption (Nigeria is regularly ranked among the most corrupt countries in the world, often at the top of the list) have inhibited foreign investment. Corporate profits, except for those of oil companies, are taxed at 30%.

In 1992 the Nigerian Free Zone Act was passed establishing the Nigerian Export Processing Zone Authority (NEPZA). Free trade zones (FTZ), so renamed in 2001, are expanses of land with improved ports and/or transportation, warehousing facilities, uninterrupted electricity and water supplies, advanced telecommunications services and other amenities to accommodate business operations. Under the free trade zone system, as long as end products are exported (although 25% can be sold in the domestic market), enterprises are exempt from customs duties, local taxes, and foreign exchange restrictions, and qualify for incentives-tax holidays, rent-free land, no strikes or lockouts, no quotas in EU and US markets, and, under the 2000 African Growth and Opportunity Act (AGOA), preferential tariffs in the US market until 2012. When fully developed, free zones are to encompass industrial production, offshore banking, insurance and reinsurance, international stock, commodities, and mercantile exchanges, agro-allied industry, mineral processing, and international tourist facilities.

In 1995 the military government decreed the establishment of the Nigerian Investment Promotion Commission (NIPC) and the liberalization of the foreign exchange market. These, with amendments, remain the bases of Nigeria's policy of encouraging foreign investment. Foreign direct investment (FDI) inflow was reported at $1.5 billion in 1997, and about $1 billion in both 1998 and 1999. In late 2002, the Nigerian government announced that since the return to an elected government in May 1999, around $57 million in FDI had flowed into the country, from a total of 170 foreign companies.

Nigeria receives the largest amount of FDI in Africa and is the 19th largest recipient in the world. In 2009, FDI reached $11 billion, representing nearly 30% of the GDP. The stock of US FDI in Nigeria in 2009 was $5.4 billion, up from $3.4 billion in 2008. US FDI in Nigeria is concentrated largely in the petroleum/mining and wholesale trade sectors. ExxonMobil and Chevron are the two largest US corporate players in offshore oil and gas production.

³⁹ECONOMIC DEVELOPMENT

The agriculture sector was the focus of intense development interest during the 1990s, with food self-sufficiency the goal. In 1990, agriculture was the subject of a separate three-year development plan involving public and private spending targets concentrating on the family farmer. The program included price stabilization plans and schemes to revitalize the palm oil, cocoa, and rubber subsectors. The Agricultural Development Projects continued through the decade, but implementation of goals was difficult. The country still imports most of its wheat from the United States.

An integrated petrochemical industry was also a priority. Using the output of the nation's refineries, Nigeria produced benzene, carbon black, and polypropylene. The development of liquid natural gas facilities was expected to lead to the production of methanol, fertilizer, and domestic gas. Nigeria's refineries operated at less than optimal rates throughout the 1990s and into the first decade of the twenty-first century.

The Obasanjo administration in the early 2000s was supporting private-sector-led, market-oriented economic growth, and had begun economic reform programs. Privatization of state-owned enterprises continued. A Stand-By Arrangement with the International Monetary Fund (IMF) approved in 2000 lapsed in 2001 as the government's economic reform program went off track. By 2005, Nigeria had negotiated a deal for forgiveness of 60% of its debt with the Paris Club. Nigeria settled its debt with the Paris Club in 2006.

With offshore oil production increasing, the need to renegotiate Nigeria's OPEC quota was a priority in 2011. However, OPEC refused to raise the production quota for Nigeria and other oil-producing countries. The Nigeria sought to maintain good relations with Western powers and to promote Nigeria as a leading international and regional power.

40 SOCIAL DEVELOPMENT

A 2004 law established a unified system of mandatory individual accounts for public employees. The system is not fully implemented in the private sector. The National Social Insurance Trust Fund holds contributions previously made and will transfer the funds into a private pension. Old age pensions are available after age 50, and are not payable abroad. Medical benefits are provided to insured employees of firms with 10 or more workers. Employers fund work injury insurance. There is limited social assistance and health care benefits provided to families.

Although sex discrimination is banned under the constitution, traditional practices still deprive women of many rights and the adoption of Shari'ah law by many northern states has more severely limited the rights and freedom of women. A woman may not obtain a passport without her husband's permission. It is customary for all assets to be turned over to the parents after the death of a male, leaving the widow economically destitute. Segregation by gender occurs in some schools, health facilities, and, in some states, on public transportation. Purdah, the Islamic practice of completely segregating a woman from men other than those within her family, is practiced in some families, primarily in the north. In Shari'ah courts, women's testimony is given less weight than that of men. Female genital mutilation (FGM) is widespread throughout the country despite government opposition. Domestic violence is widespread, and wife beating is permissible under the penal code.

As of 2011, Nigeria's human rights situation had improved, but serious abuses remained. Arbitrary arrest and detention were still used to silence the government's critics. Reports of torture and extrajudicial killings persisted, and prison conditions were considered to be life threatening. Overcrowding and poor sanitary conditions were compounded by limited food, water, and medicine for inmates. Sentences of stoning and amputation were still imposed.

In 2010 at the end of a three-day regional conference in Chad addressing issues concerning the rights and protection of children in areas of armed conflict, representatives from Chad, the Central African Republic, Sudan, Nigeria, Niger, and Cameroon signed the N'Djamena Declaration, which called for the end of the recruitment and use of children as soldiers. The signatories also agreed to establish a special committee charged with ensuring the implementation and monitoring of the agreed commitments.

41 HEALTH

Nigeria's health care delivery system consists of a network of primary, secondary, and tertiary facilities. As of 2011, there were 4 physicians, 16 nurses and midwives, and 5 hospital beds per 10,000 inhabitants. The target areas for mass procurement of medical equipment are the teaching hospitals. The lack of proper facilities and inadequate remuneration of public sector health care workers have also spurred the development of a limited number of privately-owned hospitals which cater to those who can afford them. The country is in need of medical supplies and equipment. Some pharmaceuticals are manufactured in Nigeria. Approxi-

mately 57% of the population had access to safe drinking water and 63% had adequate sanitation. The country spent 6.4% of its GDP on healthcare, amounting to $69 per person.

Despite the receding influence of such endemic diseases as yellow fever, health problems in Nigeria remain acute. Malaria and tuberculosis are the diseases of most frequent incidence, but serious outbreaks of cerebrospinal meningitis still occur in the north. Just under half of all deaths are thought to be among children, who are especially vulnerable to malaria and account for 75% of registered malaria deaths. The prevalence of child malnutrition for children under age five was 46%. Goiter was present in 20% of all school-age children. Nigeria had the highest number of measles cases reported of all African nations and diarrheal diseases remain prevalent. It was estimated that 41% of children were vaccinated against measles in 2008.

Schistosomiasis, guinea worm, trachoma, river blindness, and yaws are other diseases of high frequency. Progress has been made in the treatment of sleeping sickness (trypanosomiasis) and leprosy. The former has been nearly eliminated by the introduction of new drugs, while the introduction of sulfone therapy has nearly halted the incidence of new cases of leprosy in the eastern states. A program for the eradication of river blindness and malaria has been undertaken in cooperation with the World Health Organization.

The total fertility rate in 2011 was 4.73 children per woman surviving her childbearing years. Only 12.5% of married women used contraceptives. The life expectancy was 47.56 years in 2011. In that year the infant mortality rate was 91.54 per 1,000 live births. The maternal mortality rate was 840 per 100,000 live births in 2008.

The government was also working on the control of sexually transmitted diseases, including HIV/AIDS, through public education and behavior change. HIV/AIDS reached epidemic levels in Nigeria. The HIV/AIDS adult prevalence was 3.6% in 2009.

In March 2011, the National Emergency Management Agency (NEMA) reported that more than 400 children had died in the northern state of Zamfara as a result of lead poisoning associated with illegal gold mining operations in the region. The NEMA report included deaths from November 2010 to March 2011. The UN had earlier reported about 400 deaths between the months of March and October 2010.

42 HOUSING

Housing generally has not ranked high on the scale of priorities for social spending, and state governments have tended to rely upon local authorities to meet the problem. Efforts at providing low-cost rural housing have been minimal, despite the creation of the Federal Mortgage Bank of Nigeria in 1977, and shantytowns and slums are common in urban areas. Overcrowding in urban housing is a serious problem. It has been estimated that about 85% of the urban population live in single rooms, often with eight to twelve persons per room. Living conditions are poor.

43 EDUCATION

In 2007 the World Bank estimated that 61% of age-eligible children in Nigeria were enrolled in primary school. Secondary enrollment for age-eligible children stood at 26%. About 74% of all students complete their primary education in 2010. The student-to-teacher ratio for primary school was at about 36:1 in 2010; the ratio for secondary school was about 28:1. In 2010, private schools accounted for about 8% of primary school enrollment and 22% of secondary enrollment.

The 1979 constitution made primary education the responsibility of the states and local councils. State and federal authorities have concurrent powers over postprimary education. The first six years of primary education were made compulsory in 1976. These are followed by six years of general secondary studies or technical school studies. Primary education begins in the local language but introduces English in the third year. The academic year runs from October to July.

The advancement in education in the southern states, compared with the relative lag in the northern states, reflects the contribution of Christian missions to the Nigerian educational system. Teacher-training colleges are operated by missions or voluntary societies; their schools, however, are regulated and largely supported by the government. There are 13 federal polytechnic colleges and 14 state-owned polytechnic colleges. A major obstacle to the further advancement of education in Nigeria is the shortage of qualified teachers; large numbers of foreigners are employed, particularly by the universities. The adult literacy rate for 2010 was estimated at about 71.6%, with 79.3% for men and 63.7% for women. Public expenditure on education was estimated at less than 1% of GDP.

44 LIBRARIES AND MUSEUMS

The National Library of Nigeria was founded in Lagos in 1962 and has over one million volumes, including some 35,000 UN documents and the National Information and Documentation Center. In 2011 there were 22 state branches of the National Library. The National Archives are in Enugu State. State governments have libraries in their respective capitals and in all the local government headquarters. Almost all of the 20 universities have libraries. The largest public library in Kano holds over 300,000 volumes. The chief university library is that of the University of Ibadan, which contains 450,000 volumes. Other sizable university collections are at the University of Lagos (375,000 volumes), the University of Ife (401,000), and the University of Nigeria at Nsukka and Enugu (717,000). The High Court of Lagos State holds a collection of 600,000 volumes. There are dozens of other privately maintained collections throughout the country.

The National Museum in Lagos contains many specimens of Nigerian art, mostly pieces of statuary and carvings, remarkable for their variety and quality. It also has archaeological and ethnographic exhibits. Other museums represent more specialized interests: the museum at Ife opened in 1955 in response to halt the looting of national art treasures, and contains world-renowned bronze and terra cotta heads; the decorative arts museum at Benin City has a collection of bronzes; and that at Oron has a valuable collection of ancestor carvings. The museum at Jos, opened in 1952 originally as the National Museum, is a center of research into the prehistoric culture of Nigeria. The Esie Museum, at Ilorin in Kwara State, has stone antiquities, and the National Museum at Kaduna has archaeological and ethnographic exhibits, including a "craft village." The Owo Museum, in Ondo State, displays arts, crafts, and ethnographic relics. There are also museums in Kano, Argungu, and Oshogbo. Lagos also houses the Centre for Black and African Art and Civilization.

45 MEDIA

Nigeria's efforts to expand and modernize its fixed-line telephone network have been hampered by its faltering efforts to privatize its former national telephone monopoly NITEL. Domestically, wireless telephony has grown rapidly, spurred in part by the slow pace of fixed-line modernization and expansion efforts. There are four wireless operators in Nigeria, all of which operate nationally. International service to Europe and Asia is provided by fiber-optic submarine cable. Three Intelsat satellite ground stations also offer international service. In 2009, there were some 1.4 million main phone lines and about 73 million mobile cellular phones in use. Mobile phone subscriptions averaged 47 per 100 people.

Telephone and telegraph communications are the responsibility of the Federal Ministry of Communications through its parastatal NITEL. Trunk lines and UHF links connect all the major towns, and all of these have exchange units, including automatic exchanges at Lagos, Ibadan, Kaduna, Kano, Jos, and Port Harcourt. Postal services are provided by another parastatal-NIPOST. There are post offices at local-government headquarters and other major towns.

Radio broadcasting is the joint responsibility of the federal and state governments, operating under the Federal Radio Corp. of Nigeria, created in 1978; state radio stations broadcast in English and local languages. In 2009 there were 36 AM, 83 FM radio stations, and 11 shortwave radio stations. Television, introduced in 1959, now operates throughout the country under the direction of the Nigerian Television Authority, with stations in all state capitals and channels set aside for the state governments. Several states also run their own stations. In 2007, there were nearly 70 national and regional television stations controlled by the federal government as well as several private TV stations and cable and satellite services. In 2010, the country had 1,378 Internet hosts. As of 2009, there were some 43.9 million Internet users in Nigeria. Internet users numbered 28 per 100 citizens.

In 2011 there were 25 major daily newspapers in Nigeria, some of them published by the federal or state governments. Leading daily newspapers, with daily circulation numbers in 2009 listed parenthetically, included *Punch* (34,264), *Sun* newspapers (25,632), *Vanguard* (25,241), *Guardian* (25,222), *Thisday* (21,703), and *Tribune* (8,314). *Compass, Daily Independent, Leadership, National Life, New Nigeria,* and *Mirror* had daily circulation numbers around 1,600.

The constitution provides for freedom of speech and of the press and the government generally respected these rights; however, there were problems in some areas, particularly in restrictions on antigovernment reports.

46 ORGANIZATIONS

Cooperatives are very important in Nigerian economic life. Many different societies are included in this category—consumers' societies, thrift and credit societies, and others—but the most important are the marketing societies, which play a significant role in handling export produce, and sometimes in the production of both food and cash crops. Examples include the African Groundnut Council and the Cocoa Producers' Alliance. However, the Structural Adjustment Program is gradually replacing cooperatives with farmers' societies and export societies. There are chambers of commerce in all 19 state capitals and Abuja, and a National Association of Chambers of Commerce, Industry, Mines, and Agriculture in Lagos and Abuja.

The Girl Guides, the Boy Scouts, YWCA organizations, Muslim societies, Jamat Aid groups, and other community, social, and service groups are active in all towns and villages. There are sports clubs in Lagos and all the state capitals and national chapters of sports associations. Other national youth organizations include the National Association of Nigerian Students, the Ahmadyya Youth Association of Nigeria, 4-H, and the Catholic Youth Organization of Nigeria. National women's organizations include the Nigeria Association of University Women and the National Center for Women in Development.

Literary and art associations meet regularly in Lagos, Kaduna, Enugu, and other major cities. Nigerian Academy of Sciences promotes public interest and education in the sciences. The Nigerian Medical Association promotes research and education on health issues and works to establish common policies and standards in healthcare. There are several other associations dedicated to research and education for specific fields of medicine and particular diseases and conditions.

The Constitutional Rights Project, founded in 1990, is a social action group. Volunteer service organizations, such as the Lions Clubs and Kiwanis International, are also present. International organizations with national chapters include Amnesty International, the Society of St. Vincent de Paul, Habitat for Humanity, Caritas, and the Red Cross.

47 TOURISM, TRAVEL, AND RECREATION

There are five-star hotels in Lagos, Abuja, and Kaduna, and first-class hotels in all the state capitals. All of the cities have museums, which attract visitors to their historical artifacts. Many of the beaches are underdeveloped and lack accommodations and tourist facilities. Sports and social clubs offer facilities for swimming, sailing, tennis, squash, golf, and polo.

A passport valid for at least six months from visa purchase, return/onward ticket, and proof of sufficient funds are required for entry into Nigeria. Citizens of 106 countries including the United States and Canada also need visas. Travelers from infected areas are required to show a certificate of yellow fever vaccination. Precautions are recommended against malaria, meningitis, and typhoid.

The *Tourism Factbook*, published by the UN World Tourism Organization, reported 6.05 million incoming tourists to Nigeria in 2009; they spent a total of $791 million. Of those incoming tourists, there were 4.2 million from Africa. There were 43,875 hotel beds available in Nigeria, which had an occupancy rate of 87%.

The estimated daily cost to visit Abuja, the capital, was $508. The cost of visiting other cities averaged $186.

48 FAMOUS PERSONS

Famous Nigerians of the 19th century include 'Uthman dan Fodio (d. 1817), who founded the Fulani empire at the beginning of the century, and Samuel Ajayi Crowther (1809–92), a Yoruba missionary of the Church of England who was consecrated first bishop of the Niger Territories in 1864.

The Palm Wine Drinkard and other stories by Amos Tutuola (1920–1997) exploit the rich resources of traditional Nigerian folk tales. Benedict Chuka Enwonwu (1921–1994), Nigeria's leading painter and sculptor, gained international fame, as has Wole Soyinka (b. 1934), a prominent playwright who was awarded the 1986 Nobel Prize for Literature, the first African so honored. Novelists of note include Chinua Achebe (b. 1930) and Cyprian Ekwensi (1921–2007). Sports figures include Dick Tiger (1929–71), twice world middleweight champion and once light-heavyweight champion.

Herbert Macaulay (1864–1946) is regarded as the father of Nigerian nationalism. Among contemporary political figures, Dr. (Benjamin) Nnamdi Azikiwe (1904–96), long one of the leading West African nationalists and formerly premier of the Eastern Region, was a founder of the NCNC and first governor-general and president of independent Nigeria. Former chief rival of Azikiwe and founder of the Action Group, Chief Obafemi Awolowo (1909–87) resigned as premier of the Western Region to lead the opposition in the federal House of Assembly. The hereditary leader of the Hausa-Fulani ruling class in northern Nigeria and leader of the NPC until his assassination in January 1966 was Alhaji Sir Ahmadu Bello, sardauna of Sokoto (1909–66), who became prime minister of the Northern Region in 1954. The first prime minister was Alhaji Sir Abubakar Tafawa Balewa (1912–66), who also was assassinated in the 1966 coup. Chief Simeon Olaosebikan Adebo (1913–94), a leading Nigerian diplomat, has held several UN posts. Maj. Gen. Yakubu Gowon (b. 1934) headed the Federal Military Government from July 1966 to July 1975, when he was deposed in a bloodless coup during his absence from Nigeria at an OAU meeting. Gowon is credited with formulating the postcivil war policy of reconciliation with the Ibos that resulted in the country's rapid recovery. Alhaji Shehu Shagari (b. 1925) served in several high government posts before being elected president in 1979. Reelected in 1983, he was subsequently deposed in a military coup from which Maj. Gen. Muhammadu Buhari (b. 1942) emerged as leader of the Supreme Military Council and head of state. Basketball player Hakeem Alajuwon (b. 1963) was named one of the 50 Greatest Players in NBA History by the National Basketball Association in 1996–97.

49 DEPENDENCIES

Nigeria has no territories or colonies.

50 BIBLIOGRAPHY

Falola, Toyin. *Culture and Customs of Nigeria*. Westport, CT: Greenwood Press, 2001.

Gordon, April A. *Nigeria's Diverse Peoples: A Reference Sourcebook*. Santa Barbara, CA: ABC-CLIO, 2003.

Nigeria Investment and Business Guide: Strategic and Practical Information. Washington, DC: International Business Publications USA, 2012.

Okafor, Victor O. *Nigeria's Stumbling Democracy and Its Implications for: Africa's Democratic Movement*. Westport, CT: Praeger Security International, 2008.

Oyewole, Anthony, and John Lucas. *Historical Dictionary of Nigeria*. 2nd ed. Lanham, MD: Scarecrow Press, 2000.

Zeilig, Leo, and David Seddon. *A Political and Economic Dictionary of Africa*. Philadelphia: Routledge/Taylor and Francis, 2005..

RWANDA

Republic of Rwanda
Republika y'u Rwanda

CAPITAL: Kigali

FLAG: The national flag has three horizontal bands of sky blue (top, double width), yellow, and green, with a golden sun with 24 rays near the fly end of the blue band.

ANTHEM: *Rwanda nziza (Rwanda, Our Beautiful Country).*

MONETARY UNIT: The Rwanda franc (RFW) is a paper currency. There are coins of 1, 5, 10, 20, and 50 francs and notes of 100, 500, 1000, 2000, and 5000 francs. RFW1 = US$0.00171 (or US$1 = RFW586.25) as of 2010.

WEIGHTS AND MEASURES: The metric system is the legal standard.

HOLIDAYS: New Year's Day, 1 January; National Heroes Day, 1 February; Genocide Memorial Day, 7 April; Labor Day (May Day), 1 May; Independence Day, 1 July; National Liberation Day, 4 July; Assumption, 15 August; Patriotism Day, 1 October; All Saints' Day, 1 November; Christmas, 25 December; Boxing Day, 26 December. Movable religious holidays include Good Friday and Easter.

TIME: 2 p.m. = noon GMT.

¹LOCATION, SIZE, AND EXTENT

Rwanda, a landlocked country in east-central Africa, has an area of 26,338 sq km (10,170 sq mi), extending 248 km (154 mi) NE–SW and 166 km (103 mi) SE–NW. Comparatively, the area occupied by Rwanda is slightly smaller than the state of Maryland. It is bordered on the N by Uganda, on the E by Tanzania, on the S by Burundi, and on the W and NW by the Democratic Republic of the Congo (DROC), with a total boundary length of 893 km (555 mi).

Rwanda's capital city, Kigali, is located near the center of the country.

²TOPOGRAPHY

Rwanda lies on the great East African plateau, with the divide between the water systems of the Nile and Congo rivers passing in a north–south direction through the western part of the country. To the west of the divide, the land drops sharply to Lake Kivu in the Great Rift Valley; to the east, the land falls gradually across the central plateau to the swamps and lakes on the country's eastern border. Almost all of Rwanda is at least 1,000 m (3,300 ft) above sea level; the central plateau is between 1,500 and 2,000 m (4,950 and 6,600 ft) high. Its grassy highlands are the core areas of settlement of Rwanda's peoples. In the northwest on the border with the DROC are the volcanic Virunga Mountains; the highest peak, Mt. Karisimbi (4,519 m/14,826 ft), is snowcapped. Lake Kivu, 1,460 m (4,790 ft) above sea level, drains into Lake Tanganyika through the sharply descending Ruzizi River. The Kagera River, which forms much of Rwanda's eastern border, flows into Lake Victoria.

³CLIMATE

The high altitude of Rwanda provides the country with a pleasant tropical highland climate, with a mean daily temperature range of less than 2°C (4°F). Temperatures vary considerably from region to region because of the variations in altitude. At Kigali, on the central plateau, the average temperature is 21°C (70°F). Rainfall is heaviest in the southwest and lightest in the east. A long rainy season lasts from February to May and a short one from November through December. At Gisovu, in the west, near Kibuye, annual rainfall averages 160 cm (63 in); at Gabiro, in the northeast, 78 cm (31 in); and at Butare, in the south, 115 cm (45 in).

⁴FLORA AND FAUNA

Wildlife was abundant before the region became agricultural. There are still elephants, hippopotamuses, buffalo, cheetahs, lions, zebras, leopards, monkeys, gorillas, jackals, hyena, wild boar, antelope, flying lemurs, crocodiles, guinea hens, partridges, ducks, geese, quail, and snipe. Because the region is densely populated, these are becoming fewer, and some species are disappearing.

Though largely deforested, remaining woodlands include small areas of tropical forests along the western border, north and south of Lake Kivu. The most common trees are eucalyptus imported from the south in the 1890s, acacias, and oil palms.

The World Resources Institute estimates that there are 2,288 plant species in Rwanda. In addition, Rwanda is home to 206 mammal, 665 bird, 97 reptile, and 31 amphibian species. The calculation reflects the total number of distinct species residing in the country, not the number of endemic species.

⁵ENVIRONMENT

The World Resources Institute reported that Rwanda had designated 200,800 hectares (496,188 acres) of land for protection as of 2006. Water resources total 5.2 cu km (1.25 cu mi) while water usage is 0.15 cu km (0.036 cu mi) per year. Domestic water usage accounts for 24% of total usage, industrial for 8%, and agricultural for 68%. Per capita water usage totals 17 cu m (600 cu ft) per year. The UN reported in 2008 that carbon dioxide emissions in Rwanda totaled 715 kilotons.

The ability of the nation's agricultural sector to meet the demands of its large population is complicated by the overuse and infertility of the soil. Soil erosion and overgrazing also pose serious problems.

Rwanda's remaining forested area is under intense pressure from uncontrolled cutting for fuel. During 1981–85, deforestation averaged 3,000 hectares (7,400 acres) per year. Between 1990 and 2000, the average rate of deforestation was 3.9% per year. Malaria and sleeping sickness have spread because forest clearing and irrigation have increased the breeding areas for disease-carrying insects. In 2011, the government announced plans to implement a new environmental management program aimed at radically reducing the deforestation rate and starting the reforestation process. The project aims to reduce total deforestation to 15% and increase reforestation to 20% by 2016. The majority of funding (91.7%) for this work is through a $1.4 million grant through the African Development Fund (ADF), with the balance to be paid by the Rwandan government.

In northeastern Rwanda the beautiful Kagera National Park is a game reserve sheltering many types of wildlife. Volcano National Park, which surrounds Mt. Karisimbi and was Africa's first wildlife park, is one of the last existing homes of the mountain gorilla. Historically, the national parks have suffered from uncontrolled poaching and unauthorized cultivation, although rates declined during the 2000s. According to a 2011 report issued by the International Union for Conservation of Nature and Natural Resources (IUCN), the number of threatened species included 20 mammals, 12 birds, 8 amphibians, 9 fish, 2 invertebrates, and 4 plants. Threatened animal species included the chimpanzee, African elephant, and black rhinoceros. Sixteen species of fish have become extinct.

6 POPULATION

Rwanda is the most densely populated country in Africa. The US Central Intelligence Agency (CIA) estimated the population of Rwanda in 2011 to be approximately 11,370,425, which placed it at number 73 in population among the 196 nations of the world. In 2011, approximately 2.4% of the population was over 65 years of age, with another 42.9% under 15 years of age. The median age in Rwanda was 18.7 years. There were 0.99 males for every female in the country. The population's annual rate of change was 2.792%. The projected population for the year 2025 was 15,800,000. Population density in Rwanda was calculated at 432 people per sq km (1,118 people per sq mi). The UN estimated that 19% of the population lived in urban areas, and that urban populations had an annual rate of change of 4.4%. The largest urban area was Kigali, with a 2009 population of 909,000.

7 MIGRATION

Estimates of Rwanda's net migration rate, carried out by the CIA in 2011, amounted to 1.06 migrants per 1,000 citizens. In 2010 net migration—immigrants in Rwanda minus the emigrants from Rwanda—was 15,109 persons. Over the years, Rwanda has accepted thousands of refugees from the DROC and Burundi. Before independence, many Rwandans, compelled by famine and under-employment, migrated to the DROC, Uganda, and Tanzania. Political discord between the Hutu and Tutsi caused thousands of Tutsi to flee their homeland even before the 1994 genocide, many of them going to Burundi and Uganda.

With renewed violence in 1994, one half of Rwanda's population (then 7.5 million) was forced to flee their homes. Of these displaced persons, 2.4 million refugees fled to neighboring countries; in the years since the fighting ceased, many have returned. In 1996, violence in Burundi forced 100,000 Rwandans to repatriate. After the civil war in the DROC in October of 1996, 720,000 of the 1.1 million Rwandan refugees there were forced to repatriate. In 1996 and early 1997, Tanzania returned 480,000 Rwandan refugees from its western regions. Another 10,000 returned from Uganda. In addition, one million refugees who left Rwanda in the 1950s and 1960s have also returned since 1994. By the end of 1997, fewer than 100,000 Rwandan refugees remained outside the country.

As of 31 December 2011, under a cessation clause declaration of the UN High Commission for Refugees (UN HCR), Rwandans living abroad lost their HCR refugee status, leaving them with three options: to return to Rwanda, to seek asylum, or to stay where they were and adhere to that nation's immigration laws. Estimates of the total number of those Rwandans who fled the country as a result of the genocide and were still living abroad varied from 60,000 to 65,000 in 2009 to as many as 73,000 in 2011. Not all those who fled were willing to return. In 2008 the International Organization for Migration (IOM) began working in Rwanda to facilitate the movement of refugees, assisting those who wanted to migrate to a third country.

8 ETHNIC GROUPS

The population of Rwanda is about 84% Hutu, a Bantu people who are traditionally farmers. The Tutsi, a pastoral people, constitute about 15% of the total population, but many have fled into neighboring territories for refuge, especially since civil strife began in 1959. The Tutsi migrated to Rwanda sometime before the 15th century. An enormous amount of tension exists between the Hutu and the Tutsi, which has frequently led to violence, most notably in the 1994 genocide. There are also some Batwa (Twa), hunters related to the Pygmies of the DROC. The earliest known inhabitants of the region, the Batwa constitute about 1% of the population of Rwanda. There are also small numbers of Asians and Europeans.

9 LANGUAGES

The main language is Kinyarwanda, a member of the Bantu language family. The official languages are Kinyarwanda, French, and English. Kiswahili, a form of Swahili, is used in commercial centers.

10 RELIGIONS

European missionaries, notably the White Fathers, introduced Christianity to Rwanda in the late 19th century. A 2002 census showed the population to be 57% Catholic and 26% mainline Protestant. Seventh-Day Adventists accounted for about 11% of the population and Muslims accounted for about 5%. A small number of people practice indigenous religions exclusively, but it is believed that many adherents of other faiths incorporate traditional elements into their own practice. These elements include belief in a supreme being, Imaana, and a number of lesser deities, who can be communicated with through the spirits of ancestors. There are small groups of Baha'is, Hindus, and others. There are several foreign missionary groups. The constitution allows for freedom of religion; however, some minority groups have reported restrictions and discrimination from local government authorities. Good Friday, Easter, Assumption, and Christmas are observed as national holidays.

11 TRANSPORTATION

The CIA reports that Rwanda has a total of 14,008 km (8,704 mi) of roads, of which 2,662 km (1,654 mi) are paved. Five principal roads connect Kigali to other Rwandan cities, and an asphalt road connects Butare and Cyangugu. Most roads become impassable during the rainy season, and there are few bridges. Bus service connects Kigali to the 10 prefectures. The most important roads for landlocked Rwanda's external trade run from Kigali to Kibungo and from Kigali to Kakitumba, connecting the capital city by road and rail with Indian Ocean ports in Tanzania and Kenya. About 90% of foreign trade is via the Kakitumba route, which leads to the Kenyan ports via Uganda. Rwanda has no railroads. There is traffic on Lake Kivu to the DROC from Gisenyi, Kibuye, and Cyangugu, using native craft and shallow-draft barges.

There are nine airports, four of which have paved runways. International airports are at Kigali-Kanombe and at Kamembe, served by several international carriers. Direct flights to and from Europe are available through Brussels, Paris, and Athens. Internal air traffic is provided by RwandAir.

12 HISTORY

Stone Age habitation reaching back as far as 35,000 years has been reported in the region now called Rwanda. The first known inhabitants of the area were the Batwa, a pygmoid group following hunting and gathering subsistence patterns. Later, between the 7th and 10th centuries AD, the Hutu people arrived, probably from the region of the Congo River basin. They spoke Bantu and followed a settled, agricultural way of life. Between the 14th and 15th centuries, the Tutsi, a pastoral people of Nilotic origin, arrived from the north and formed numbers of small and independent chieftaincies. At the end of the 15th century, a few of these chieftaincies merged to form a state, near Kigali, under the leadership of Ruganzu I Bwimba. In the 16th century, the Tutsi dynasty began a process of expansion that continued into the late 19th century under the prominent Tutsi leader Kigeri IV Rwabugiri (d. 1895).

The Tutsi conquest initiated a process of political integration. The ownership of land was gradually transferred from the Hutu to the *mwami*, the king of the Tutsi, who became the supreme head and, in theory, absolute master of the country. He was the incarnation of the state and enjoyed an almost divine prestige. A feudal social system based on caste was the dominant feature of social relations between the conquering Tutsi and the subject Hutu, especially in terms of economic and political relations. The ownership of cattle, a vital element in the social system, was controlled by the Tutsi, who in turn parceled out their use to the Hutu. The Hutu did the farming and grew the food, but had no part in government, while the Tutsi did no manual labor. The separation of the castes was not complete; intermarriage, especially between Tutsi

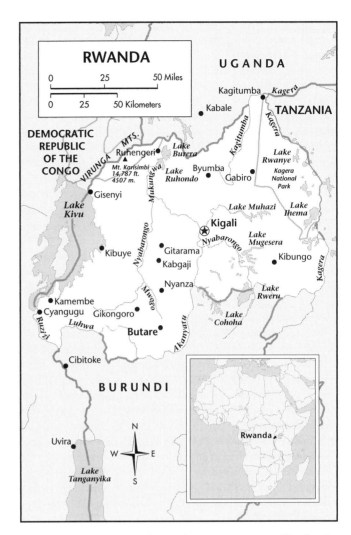

LOCATION: 1°4′ to 2°50′S; 28°51′ to 30°55′ E. BOUNDARY LENGTHS: Uganda, 169 kilometers (105 miles); Tanzania, 217 kilometers (135 miles); Burundi, 290 kilometers (180 miles); Democratic Republic of the Congo (DROC), 217 kilometers (135 miles).

men and Hutu women, was common. The northwest remained Hutu-controlled and the Hutu language, Kinyarwanda, was eventually adopted by the Tutsi.

The first European known to have explored the region was John Hanning Speke, who traveled with Richard Burton to Lake Tanganyika in 1858, where he turned north in his search for the headwaters of the Nile. In 1871, Stanley and Livingstone landed at Bujumbura (now the capital of neighboring Burundi) and explored the Ruzizi River region. After the Berlin Conference of 1884–85, the German zone of influence in East Africa was extended to include Rwanda and Burundi, and in 1894, a German lieutenant, Count von Götzen, arrived at Lake Kivu. Roman Catholic missionaries soon followed. After the mwami submitted to German rule without resistance in 1899, the Germans administered the territory through the traditional authorities in accordance with the laws and customs of the region. Belgium occupied the territory in 1916 during World War I, and was awarded a mandate known as Ruanda-Urundi (present-day Rwanda and Burundi) by the League of Nations in 1923. In 1925, an administrative union was formed between the Ruanda-Urundi mandate and the Belgian Congo (now the DROC). A key policy of Belgian rule was the strengthening of the effective control of the Tutsi dynasty—under Belgian supervision—throughout Ruanda.

In 1946, Ruanda-Urundi became a UN trust territory under Belgian administration. Events in Africa after World War II aroused Hutu political consciousness and led the Hutu to demand the abolition of social and political inequalities. In November 1959, a Hutu revolution began, continuing sporadically for the next few years. Many Tutsi either were killed or fled to neighboring territories during the nationwide anti-Tutsi campaign named the "wind of destruction." The Belgian authorities, along with the Roman Catholic missionaries, provided crucial support to the Hutu during this troubled period. A provisional government, republican in tendency and composed predominantly of members of the Parmehutu Party, was set up in Ruanda in October 1960. In the following January, the leaders of the Parmehutu proclaimed the deposition of the mwami and the creation of a republican regime. The new regime was recognized de facto by the administering authority, but the UN declared it to have been established by irregular and unlawful means.

On 25 September 1961, legislative elections and a referendum on retaining the institution and person of the mwami were held in Ruanda at the insistence of the UN General Assembly and under the supervision of the UN Commission for Ruanda-Urundi. The elections gave the Parmehutu, led by Grégoire Kayibanda, an overwhelming majority. Approximately 95% of the electorate took part in the referendum, voting four-to-one to abolish the monarchy. The UN strongly urged both Ruanda and Urundi to come to independence united as one nation, but reluctantly agreed that neither country wished to do so. On 27 June 1962, the UN General Assembly passed a resolution providing for the independent states of Rwanda and Burundi, and on 1 July, Rwanda became an independent country.

In December 1963, following an abortive invasion by Tutsi refugees from Burundi, a massive retaliation was launched against the remaining resident Tutsi population, causing the death of an estimated 12,000 Tutsi. The massacre was the signal for a renewed exodus of Tutsi elements into the neighboring territories of Uganda, Tanzania, the DROC, and Burundi. In all, approximately 150,000 Tutsi fled between 1959 and 1964.

In January 1964, the monetary and economic union that had existed between Burundi and Rwanda was terminated. Despite severe economic difficulties, Kayibanda was reelected to a third four-year term as president in 1969. However, continuing internal unrest led the Rwandan army to overthrow the Kayibanda government in July 1973, and Maj. Gen. Juvénal Habyarimana assumed the presidency. His regime, dominated by officers from the north, took a more moderate stand on the issue of Hutu-Tutsi relationships than had the previous administration.

In 1975, he institutionalized his military regime, creating a one-party state under his National Revolutionary Movement for Development (MRND). A system of ethnic quotas was introduced that formally limited the Tutsi minority to 14% of the positions in the workplace and schools.

Under Habyarimana's corrupt and authoritarian regime, popular discontent grew through the 1980s. In November 1990 Habyarimana announced that political parties would be permitted in 1991, and that ethnic affiliations would be abolished from national identity cards. Several new parties emerged in 1990 and 1991. The greatest threat to the regime came in October 1990, when over 1,000 Tutsi refugees invaded Rwanda from Uganda. This group, called the Rwanda Patriotic Front (RPF) had considerable success, considering that around 1,000 French, Belgian, and Zairian paratroopers helped defend the government in Kigali. Government forces retaliated by massacring Tutsi. A cease-fire was worked out later in October, and Uganda, Burundi, and Zaire (now DROC) agreed to send in peacekeeping forces to supervise it, but fighting broke out again in January 1991. Further cease-fires were negotiated between government and Tutsi rebels in Brussels, Belgium, in March 1991 and in Arusha, Tanzania, in July 1992, but fighting continued.

In April 1992 Habyarimana appointed an opposition politician, Dismos Nsengiyaremye, as prime minister. The new cabinet included 9 members of the MRND and 10 opposition party members. Their supporters fought in the streets. Hardliners around Habyarimana were accused of trying to sidetrack the democratization process. By June the government had officially recognized 15 opposition parties. Talks with Tutsi leaders regarding power sharing continued, but the Hutu-Tutsi division appeared to be beyond reconciliation. A power sharing agreement was signed in Tanzania in January 1993, but failed to end the fighting. Another peace agreement was signed on 4 August 1993. On 5 October 1993, the UN Security Council authorized a peacekeeping force to assist in implementing the agreement. Unrest continued and no transitional government, which the agreement called for, was established.

In 1994 a total breakdown occurred. In February the minister of public works was assassinated. His supporters, in turn, murdered an opposition politician. In April, a rocket downed an airplane carrying the presidents of Rwanda and Burundi back to Kigali from regional peace talks in Tanzania. All aboard were killed. From that point on, Rwanda became a killing field, as members of the Rwandan army and bands of armed Hutu massacred Tutsis and many moderate Hutus, including Prime Minister Agathe Uwilingiyimana. The extremist Coalition for the Defense of the Republic (CDR) encouraged and directed the killing. In response, the RPF stepped up its liberation efforts.

By July 1994 several hundred thousand persons had been killed and several hundred thousand more had fled their homes and the country to Burundi, Tanzania, and Zaire. The RPF occupied over half the country, seizing Kigali and restoring some semblance of order. While the international community was aware of the genocide occurring in Rwanda, little was done until the RPF had occupied a large part of the country. The UN approved a large expansion of the limited peacekeeping force in the area as the RPF consolidated its control and established a government of national unity, headed by a Hutu president, Pasteur Bizimungu. Major General Paul Kagame, a leader of the RPF, became minister of defense and vice president. The government announced that Hutu refugees, numbering in the millions, were safe to return to Rwanda, but few believed them, and conditions at the refugee camps, primarily in Zaire, began to deteriorate as disease and starvation became rampant. A 70-member Transitional National Assembly was formed in late 1994 in the hopes of returning order to the country. In February 1995, the UN Security Council created the International Criminal Tribunal for Rwanda.

Meanwhile, the government of Zaire's policy of forcible repatriation proved catastrophic, as thousands of refugees died or disappeared. From April 1994 to 1997, some 100,000 Hutu refugees lost their lives when Interahamwe ("those who attack together"), guerillas suspected of having perpetrated the genocide in Rwanda, were allowed free reign in the camps. In Rwanda, almost 90,000 suspected killers were arrested and detained in miserable conditions in whatever facilities the government could find, including soccer stadiums. The slow pace of the trials was a cause of considerable concern, but UN and Rwandan authorities defended the thoroughness, offering it as evidence that the government was not interested in wholesale revenge. Of the nearly 90,000 prisoners, only 1,946 had been indicted by 1997. A process of *gacaca*, or trial by local communities, began in June 2002 to speed up the trials of some 119,000 detainees.

When it became clear to Rwanda that the refugee camps in Zaire had become little more than training camps for Hutu paramilitaries, Rwandan and Ugandan troops enlisted Zairian rebel leader Laurent Kabila to oust longtime dictator Mobutu Sese-Seko. In less than eight months, Mobutu was overthrown; Kabila was made president of the Democratic Republic of the Congo, as Zaire had been renamed, in May 1997. A year later, irreconcilable differences between Kabila and Kagame and Yoweri Museveni of Uganda, led to "Africa's first world war," eventually involving nine African countries. Peace talks in South Africa in 2002 resulted in a formal cease-fire, troop withdrawals, and a plan for a transitional government in the DROC, to which Rwanda's proxy, the RCD-Goma, was a signatory. By June 2003, with the backing of UN (MONUC) troops, implementation of the transition plan had commenced, but fighting between Congolese soldiers, rebel groups, and Rwandan regulars continued.

In addition to conducting the gacaca trials, Rwanda faced several challenges to national healing and rebuilding. In April 2002, Bizimungu was jailed for possessing documents the government said advocated civil disobedience and ethnic division. (He was held until 2004, when he was sentenced to 15 years in prison, but released in April 2007 after receiving a presidential pardon.) In May 2002, the DROC filed a case with the International Court of Justice in The Hague that accused Rwanda of genocide against 3.5 million people in DROC. By late 2002, some 19,000 Rwandan refugees had been repatriated home from Tanzania, as well as another 5,000 from Zambia. In June 2003, Kagame signed a new constitution approved by national referendum into law, but international human and civil rights groups feared the constitution would limit multiparty pluralism and freedom of expression.

In July 2003, the government announced that presidential elections would be held on 25 August and parliamentary elections on 29 September, ending nine years of transitional rule. In the first post-genocide presidential election, and the first multiparty election since independence in 1962, Paul Kagame won a landslide victory. He ran on a platform of increased justice, economic growth, national unity, and good governance.

In March 2005, the main Hutu rebel group, the Democratic Liberation Forces of Rwanda (FDLR), one of several groups accused of creating instability in the DROC, announced it was ending its armed struggle. Many of the FDLR's members were accused of taking part in the 1994 genocide. Rather than disarming, some of the FDLR militants fled across the border to the DROC to escape government forces. Rwanda invaded the DROC twice in attempts to defeat the remaining Hutu militias. In January 2009, the Congolese and Rwandan armies joined forces in an attack against them and succeeded in arresting the group's leader, General Laurent Nkunda. As of March 2012, Nkunda was believed to be under house arrest in Rwanda.

Kagame was reelected in the August 2010 presidential elections in a landslide victory, winning 93.1% of the vote. Although the vote was deemed to be fair, some called the election a charade due the absence of prominent competition; the three primary rivals were also from the RPF. Opposition groups, such as the unregistered Democratic Green Party, were not permitted to field candidates. The government also has been criticized widely for its control over the press and intolerance for dissent, leading many to believe that a second term in office for Kagame was assured long before the election took place.

13 GOVERNMENT

The constitution of December 1978 provided for a unitary republic with executive, legislative, and judicial branches. The executive was headed by a president elected for a five-year term who presided over the council of ministers and was commander in chief of the armed forces. The secretary-general of the National Revolutionary Movement for Development, the sole legal political party, was empowered to act in the president's stead in the case of incapacity. The president shared legislative power with the country's unicameral legislature, the National Development Council, which consisted of 70 members.

A new constitution legalizing independent parties was adopted on 18 June 1991. The redefined executive branch consisted of an elected president, a prime minister, and a Council of Ministers chosen from the legislature. The unicameral legislature retained the original name of National Development Council.

The 4 August 1993 Peace Accord signed with the RPF called for a 22-month transition period leading to multiparty elections and the establishment of several new institutions. By 1994, the RPF had established control of the country, instituting a government of national unity, headed by President Bizimungu, himself a Hutu.

In May 1995, the 70-seat transitional national assembly (TNA) created a new constitution. In early 2000 Bizimungu resigned, accusing the Tutsi-controlled parliament of unfairly investigating his allies on corruption charges. The vice president, Paul Kagame was inaugurated 22 April 2000, the country's first Tutsi president since independence from Belgium in 1962. In 2001 four additional seats—two for women and two for youth—were added to the TNA.

The 2003 constitution did not drastically change the composition of government. The executive arm of the government is comprised of the chief of state, the president, and the prime minister, who is head of the government. A Council of Ministers is appointed by the president.

The parliament is comprised of two bodies: an 80-seat Chamber of Deputies and a 26-seat Senate. The Chamber of Deputies consists of 53 members elected by popular vote, 24 women elected by local bodies, and 3 members selected by disabled and youth organizations. In the Senate, twelve members are elected by local communities, while eight are appointed by the president, four are appointed by the Political Organizations Forum, and two are representatives of institutions of higher learning.

14 POLITICAL PARTIES

In the last years of Belgian administration, many political organizations were formed. In March 1957, Kayibanda and other young Hutu leaders issued the *Hutu Manifesto* demanding a continuation of Belgian rule until the Hutu were better prepared to assume a role in political affairs. In June 1957, they formed the Hutu Social Movement, which, in 1959, became the Party of the Hutu Emancipation Movement (Parti du Mouvement de l'Emancipation Hutu—Parmehutu). Parmehutu thereupon set a policy of ending Tutsi rule, drawing political definitions along ethnic lines, and abolishing the feudal system.

The Rwanda National Union Party (Union Nationale Rwandaise—UNAR), founded in September 1959 by Prosper Bwanakweli and backed by the mwami, was the leading monarchist party, calling for immediate self-government and independence under a hereditary (Tutsi) constitutional monarchy.

In the 1961 elections, Parmehutu received 77.7% of the votes cast; UNAR won 16.8%, and other minority parties 5.5%. Under a system of proportional representation, 35 of the 44 seats in the National Assembly went to Parmehutu. Parmehutu extended its control in the 1969 elections, and thereafter became the only political party in Rwanda until its disbanding by the military in 1973.

In 1975, President Habyarimana founded and became party president of the MRND, which became the nation's only legal party. Party membership was automatic at birth. The president of the MRND was the sole candidate in national presidential elections and appointed the party's secretary-general and central committee. In December 1981, the 64 deputies to the National Development Council were elected from 128 candidates chosen by the MRND. In the elections of December 1983, 140 MRND candidates vied for 70 seats in an enlarged council; 17 former deputies were defeated.

In November 1990, the president announced that opposition political parties would be permitted to organize in 1991. Several new parties emerged, including the Democratic Republican Movement (MDR), the Liberal Party (LP), the Democratic and Socialist Party (PSD), and the Coalition for the Defense of the Republic (CDR). The latter, headed by Martin Bucyana, was charged with provoking the 1994 massacres. Cracks within the RPF and TNA widened following corruption probes and political and ethnic infighting.

Following President Bizimungu's resignation, Kagame was elected president on 17 April 2000 during a special joint session of parliament. Under the Arusha peace accord, the number of seats by party in the transitional government was predetermined and shared by eight parties: FPR 13, Democratic Republican Movement (MDR), 13; Democratic and Socialist Party (PSD), 13; Liberal Party (PL), 13; Christian Democrats (PDC), 6; RPA, 6; Rwandan Socialist Party (PSR), 2; Islamic Democrats (PDI), 2; and others, 2.

Legislative elections on 29 September 2003 saw 8 parties and 17 independents compete for representation. On 1 October the RPF won a clear victory with 40 seats. The PSD earned 7 seats, and the PL, 6. Legislative elections in 2008 awarded 42 seats to the RPF,

7 to the PSD, and 4 to the PL. The next legislative elections were scheduled for 2013.

In the August 2010 presidential elections, Kagame was reelected to another seven year term in a landslide victory with 93.1% of the vote. The next presidential elections were scheduled for 2017. Pierre Damien Hamumuremyi became prime minister on 7 October 2011.

15 LOCAL GOVERNMENT

Rwanda in 2000 adopted a policy of decentralization in which the country is divided into 4 provinces plus the city of Kigali. It is further administratively subdivided into 30 districts, 416 sectors, and 2,148 cells. Decentralization has given local governments powers and authorities previously reserved for the central government. Local elections took place in 2011, with RPF candidates winning the majority of races.

16 JUDICIAL SYSTEM

The Rwandan legal system is based on Belgian and German civil codes and customary local laws. The main courts in Rwanda are the Supreme Court of six justices, the High Courts of the Republic, provincial courts, district courts, and mediation committees.

Although the constitution provides for an independent judiciary, certain provisions also give the executive branch and the president authority to appoint and dismiss judges. When the president has the opportunity to nominate Supreme Court judges, two nominations are required for each open seat. In practice, the courts are susceptible to government influence and manipulation.

The constitution guarantees defendants the right to counsel, but not a publicly-funded defense. A shortage of attorneys leaves many criminal defendants unrepresented. Presumption of innocence and the right to present evidence in one's own defense are not guaranteed. The government has sought help from the international community to rebuild the judiciary and appoint lower court officials.

17 ARMED FORCES

The International Institute for Strategic Studies reported that armed forces in Rwanda totaled 33,000 members in 2011. The force was comprised of 32,000 from the army and 1,000 members of the air force. Armed forces represented 0.7% of the labor force in Rwanda. Defense spending totaled $353.4 million and accounted for 2.9% of GDP.

In 2009, Rwanda withdrew its troops from the DROC and began the process of restructuring the military and demobilizing thousands of troops, with the end goal of a military consisting of 20,000 soldiers and more than 100,000 reserves.

18 INTERNATIONAL COOPERATION

Rwanda was admitted to the UN on 18 September 1962, and is a member of most nonregional specialized agencies, including the FAO, the World Bank, UNESCO, UNIDO, and the WHO. It is also a member of the WTO, the African Development Bank, the ACP Group, COMESA, G-77, New Partnership for Africa's Development (NEPAD), and the African Union. In 1976, Rwanda joined Burundi and Zaire (now the DROC) in the Economic Community of the Great Lakes Countries, formed to develop the economic potential of the basin of Lakes Kivu and Tanganyika; its headquarters are in Gisenyi. In 1977, Rwanda joined Burundi and Tanzania in forming an economic community for the management and development of the Kagera River Basin. Uganda became a part of the community in 1980. Its headquarters are in Kigali. Rwanda is part of the Nonaligned Movement. Rwanda became a member of the East African Community (EAC) in 2007.

In 2009 Burundi and Rwanda agreed to an extradition treaty that allowed Rwanda to prosecute individuals in Burundi accused of participating in the 1994 genocide against the ethnic Tutsi. In 2008, the National Public Prosecution Authority compiled a list of 6,000 Burundians suspected of participating in the 1994 genocide.

In environmental cooperation, Rwanda is part of the Convention on Biological Diversity, CITES, the Kyoto Protocol, the Montréal Protocol, the Nuclear Test Ban Treaty, and the UN Conventions on climate Change and Desertification.

19 ECONOMY

Rwanda has an agricultural economy with relatively few mineral resources. The country's high population density puts pressure on the land and the economy. Soil erosion has limited growth in the agricultural sector. The manufacturing base is limited to a few basic products. The limited number of export products produced—primarily tea, coffee, and pyrethrum, which is used in insect repellents—leaves the country vulnerable to market fluctuations.

While the five years of civil war that culminated in the ethnic massacres of 1994 decimated Rwanda's economic base and impoverished the population, Rwanda's economy has improved steadily since 1996. In the post-war period the government began an ongoing program of privatization that led to the transfer of a number of government-owned companies to private enterprise, including several tea estates, a mobile phone provider, and the complete banking sector. Trade policies were liberalized, tax collection was improved, and the banking system was reformed. Agricultural reforms included improved farming methods and increased use of fertilizers.

The economy of Rwanda was likely to benefit from its membership in the East African Community (EAC), a regional intergovernmental organization established by Kenya, Uganda, and Tanzania in 2000, and expanded to include Rwanda and Burundi in 2007. The EAC Common Market Protocol went into effect on 1 July 2010. Under this protocol, members agreed to implement legislation that would remove barriers to the transport of goods, services, and workers across borders. The development of the common market is one step in the EAC's plan to increase trade to, from, and within the region and to establish a strong political federation by 2015.

Rwanda's economy showed an average growth rate between 2006 and 2010 of 7.3%, with the service sector the largest contributor to GDP since 2006. Rwanda's exports of goods and services rose 31.7% in 2011, due to growth in coffee, tea, and mining; however, the nation remained highly dependent on grants from its development partners. Rwanda was expected to realize economic growth of 7.6% in 2012.

20 INCOME

The CIA estimated that in 2010 the GDP of Rwanda was $12.16 billion. The CIA defines GDP as the value of all final goods and services produced within a nation in a given year and computed on the basis of purchasing power parity (PPP) rather than value as measured on the basis of the rate of the exchange based on current dollars. The per capita GDP was estimated at $1,100. The annual growth rate of GDP was 6.5%. The average inflation rate was 6.4%. It was estimated that agriculture accounted for 42.1% of GDP, industry 14.3%, and services 43.6%.

The World Bank reported that in 2009, household consumption in Rwanda totaled $4.2 billion or about $372 per capita, measured in current US dollars rather than PPP. As of 2011, the most recent study by the World Bank reported that actual individual consumption in Rwanda was 80.1% of GDP and accounted for 0.01% of world consumption. By comparison, the United States accounted for 25.44% of world individual consumption. The World Bank also estimated that 44.9% of Rwanda's GDP was spent on food and beverages, 15.5% on housing and household furnishings, 2.7% on clothes, 2.8% on health, 4.1% on transportation, 0.4% on communications, 1.0% on recreation, 1.4% on restaurants and hotels, and 1.8% on miscellaneous goods and services and purchases from abroad.

According to the World Bank, remittances from citizens living abroad totaled $92.6 million in 2008, or about $8 per capita and accounted for approximately 0.8% of GDP.

21 LABOR

As of 2007, Rwanda had a total labor force of 4.446 million people. Within that labor force, CIA estimates in 2000 (most recent information available as of March 2012) noted that 90% were employed in agriculture, 5% in industry, and 5% in the service sector.

A new labor code guaranteeing freedom of association was adopted in May 2009; however, it did not secure the same rights for public employees. Under the code, labor disputes are required to go to arbitration if agreement is not reached. Strikes are forbidden unless all procedures have been followed. In 2011 there were two reports of the government attempting to break up unions, in one case by a mass dismissal of employees, and in another by not renewing the contracts of union activists.

The Central Union of Rwandan Workers (CESTRAR) is Rwanda's largest and formerly sole authorized trade union organization. Other unions include the Union Association of Health Personnel in Rwanda; the Interprofessional Union of Workers of Rwanda; the Union of Secondary School Teachers; and the Association of Christian Unions, which represents public and private sector workers, small businessmen, and subsistence farmers.

The minimum legal age for regular employment is 18 (14 for apprenticeships or light work). The minimum age does not apply to subsistence agriculture. Minimum wages vary with position and sector. The legal standard workweek was raised from 40 hours to 45 hours in May 2009. The daily minimum wage for workers in the tea industry ranged from RWF500–750 ($0.85–1.28) and from RFW1000–1500 ($1.60–2.55) for construction workers.

22 AGRICULTURE

Roughly 56% of Rwanda's total land is arable or under permanent crops. Except for heavily eroded regions, the soil has good humus content and is fertile, especially in the alluvial valleys and in the volcanic soils of the northwest. Subsistence agriculture predominates, with the small family farm of about 1 hectare (2.5 acres) the basic agricultural unit.

The country's major crops include pineapple, cotton, groundnuts, sorghum, millet, wheat, cotton, sweet potatoes, mangoes, pawpaw, sugarcane, cassava, and sesame. The plantain crop is used principally for making beer and wine. Coffee, grown by some 600,000 smallholders, is the chief cash crop. Coffee and tea together generally contribute 80% to export earnings. Rwanda also exports quinine and pyrethrum. Cereal production in 2009 amounted to 650,627 tons, fruit production 3.2 million tons, and vegetable production 421,352 tons.

Rwanda has endured devastating periods of famine. In 1928–29, more than 400,000 Rwandans died or were forced to migrate; in 1943–44, the figure was 300,000. Government planning has aimed at mitigating such catastrophes by striving for annual increases of food-crop production. Included in the government effort has been the introduction of rice cultivation by agronomists from Taiwan and China. Export diversification has been encouraged by the government, including production of alternatives such as sunflowers, and fruits and vegetables for the European winter market.

23 ANIMAL HUSBANDRY

The UN Food and Agriculture Organization (FAO) reported that Rwanda dedicated 450,000 hectares (1.11 million acres) to permanent pasture or meadow in 2009. During that year, the country tended 2 million chickens, 1.5 million head of cattle, and 310,833 pigs. The production from these animals amounted to 23,400 tons of beef and veal, 6,519 tons of pork, 2,460 tons of poultry, 2,321 tons of eggs, and 146,395 tons of milk. Rwanda also produced 5,325 tons of cattle hide.

The number of cattle owned by an individual has traditionally been a key indicator of status in Rwanda's social system. This factor has resulted in the accumulation of large herds of poor-quality stock. The government is striving to introduce modern stock-raising methods and improve the quality of the nation's cattle as part of its Vision 2020 program for alleviating poverty.

24 FISHING

Fishing in the lakes and rivers is principally for local consumption. In 2008, the annual capture totaled 9,050 tons according to the UN FAO.

25 FORESTRY

Approximately 18% of Rwanda is covered by forest. Erosion and cutting (due to farming and stock raising) have almost entirely eliminated Rwanda's original forests. Remaining growths are concentrated along the top of the Nile-Congo divide and on the volcanic mountains of the northwest. There are scattered savanna woodlands in the eastern prefectures.

There are few commercially exploitable woodlands; most existing growths are too inaccessible for easy development, although they are used locally for fuel and building. The UN FAO estimated the 2009 roundwood production at 1.21 million cu m (42.8 million cu ft). The value of all forest products, including roundwood, totaled $2.37 million.

In 2010, the National Forestry Authority (NAFA) drafted a three-year plan for management of Rwanda's forest resources, with an eye to developing agro-forestry and raising public awareness of the importance of Rwanda's forests.

26 MINING

Before the massacres of 1994, mineral commodities typically provided 10% of export earnings, mainly from concentrates of tin, tungsten, and colombium-tantalum ores, and gold bullion. By the mid-2000s, Rwanda had recovered most of the mineral output lost in 1994, although many obstacles continued blocking full utilization of existing resources. Among them were the absence of high-grade ores, the lack of sufficient capital, massive population displacements, a 65% poverty rate, a shortage of skilled labor, the country's landlocked status, high transportation costs, high oil prices, and civil unrest. In 2009, mining and quarrying accounted for less than 1% of Rwanda's gross domestic product (GDP). That year, Rwanda produced 9% of the world's tantalum and 1% of its tungsten.

In 2009 estimated mineral production included: 1,300 metric tons of tin ore (metal content), compared to 215 metric tons in 2005; tungsten ore, 1,500 metric tons, compared to 557 metric tons in 2005; cement, 100,000 metric tons; and columbite-tantalite ore and concentrate (gross weight), 430,000 kg, up from 276,000 kg in 2005. Recorded mined gold output in 2009 was 20 kg. Some lava beds of the west and northwest contained potassium compounds useful for fertilizers. Exploitation of the country's peat deposits could become necessary to meet the subsistence farming sector's energy needs.

The Rwandan mineral industry consisted mostly of a number of small cooperatives and individual artisanal miners who produced ores and concentrates from scattered locations generally in a 30-km-wide (18-mi-wide) zone that extended east–west through Kigali. In 2000, the government privatized Régie d'Exloitation et de Développement des Mines, the state mining exploration company.

27 ENERGY AND POWER

All of Rwanda's refined petroleum products are imported. In 2010, demand and imports of refined petroleum products each totaled 6,000 barrels per day. Rwanda has no proven reserves of coal, crude oil, or oil refining capacity; however, a Canadian firm began exploring the northwest corner of Rwanda for oil in 2007, and in 2010 moved its focus to seismic surveys and environmental impact assessments of Lake Kivu, which is known to contain methane. In 2011 the Finnish firm Wärtsilä was building a 25 MW power plant to be fueled by methane drawn off the lake. The plant was to be operational late in 2012, after which an additional 75 MW capacity would be added. Proven natural gas reserves were estimated at 56.630 trillion cubic meters in 2010.

The World Bank reported in 2008 that Rwanda produced 160 million kWh of electricity and consumed 272.9 million kWh, or 24 kWh per capita. Most of the country's electric power came from four hydroelectric stations. Additional power is imported from the DROC.

28 INDUSTRY

The industrial sector as a whole contributed 14.3% to GDP in 2010; the industrial production growth rate in 2010 was 7.5%.

Most industrial activity centers on food processing. Manufacturing and processing establishments are at the artisan level, turning out items such as pottery, wicker baskets, bricks, shoes, tile, and insecticide. Rwanda has light industry which produces sugar, coffee, tea, flour, cigars, beer, wine, soft drinks, metal products, and assembled radios. Rwanda also has textile mills, soap factories, auto repair shops, a match factory, a pyrethrum refinery, and plants for producing paint, cement, pharmaceuticals, and furniture.

29 SCIENCE AND TECHNOLOGY

The World Bank reported in 2009 that there were no patent applications in science and technology in Rwanda. The Institute of Agronomical Sciences of Rwanda, attached to the Ministry of Agriculture, and the Institute of Scientific and Technological Research have their headquarters in Butare, and the Directorate of Geological and Mineralogical Research within the Ministry of Industry is in Kigali. The National University of Rwanda, in Butare, has faculties of sciences, medicine, agriculture, and applied sciences. Science and engineering students account for about 30% of college and university enrollments.

30 DOMESTIC TRADE

Kigali is the main commercial center in Rwanda. There are a few small supermarkets in Kigali offering imported items at rather high prices. However, smaller outdoor marketplaces selling locally produced foods and goods predominate in most areas. Nearly 90% of the work force is employed in agriculture, primarily at a subsistence level.

Business hours are from 8 a.m. to noon and from 2 to 5 p.m., Monday through Friday, and from 8:30 a.m. to 12:30 p.m. on Saturday. Banks are open from 8:30 a.m. to noon and from 2 to 6 p.m., Monday through Friday, and from 8 a.m. to 1 p.m. on Saturday.

31 FOREIGN TRADE

Rwanda imported $1.047 billion worth of goods and services in 2008, while exporting $226 million worth of goods and services. Major import partners in 2009 were Kenya, 16.6%; Uganda, 15%; United Arab Emirates, 6.9%; China, 6.6%; Belgium, 5.6%; Germany, 4.9%; Tanzania, 4.8%; and Sweden, 4%. Major export partners were Kenya, 33.4%; DROC, 13.4%; China, 7%; Thailand, 6.1%; the United States, 5.4%; Swaziland, 5.4%; Belgium, 5.1%; and Pakistan, 4.2%.

Rwanda's main commodity exports are coffee (56%) and tea (27%). It has been difficult for Rwanda to attract foreign investment. One notable investor in the coffee industry is Starbucks, which opened an office in Kigali in 2009. With an investment of over $3.7 million in loans to coffee farmers, the company has taken great efforts to work with local farmers to improve the quality and value of their crops. Other exports include gold (17%) and animal hides and skins (0.9%).

Rwanda entered the EAC Customs Union in July 2009. Membership in the union allows for free trade between the five member nations: Kenya, Tanzania, Uganda, Rwanda, and Burundi. The government expects lower prices on imports and greater revenues from exports as a result.

Principal Trading Partners – Rwanda (2010)

(In millions of US dollars)

Country	Total	Exports	Imports	Balance
World	1,655.0	255.0	1,400.0	-1,145.0
Kenya	345.0	140.9	204.1	-63.2
Uganda	191.9	7.8	184.2	-176.4
China	90.6	35.2	55.4	-20.3
United Arab Emirates	89.5	1.6	87.8	-86.2
Congo	68.9	56.4	12.5	43.9
Tanzania	60.6	1.2	59.4	-58.2
United States	54.0	20.3	33.8	-13.5
Belgium	51.0	12.3	38.6	-26.3
Germany	46.9	14.4	32.5	-18.1
South Africa	34.2	0.2	34.0	-33.8

(…) data not available or not significant.

(n.s.) not specified.

SOURCE: *2011 Direction of Trade Statistics Yearbook*, New York: United Nations, 2011.

Balance of Payments – Rwanda (2010)

(In millions of US dollars)

Current Account		**-421.0**
Balance on goods		-787.0
Imports	-1,084.0	
Exports	297.0	
Balance on services		867.0
Balance on income		-46.0
Current transfers		658.0
Capital Account		**286.0**
Financial Account		**152.0**
Direct investment abroad		…
Direct investment in Rwanda		42.0
Portfolio investment assets		…
Portfolio investment liabilities		21.0
Financial derivatives		…
Other investment assets		-28.0
Other investment liabilities		117.0
Net Errors and Omissions		**-6.0**
Reserves and Related Items		**-10.0**

(…) data not available or not significant.

SOURCE: *Balance of Payment Statistics Yearbook 2011*, Washington, DC: International Monetary Fund, 2011.

32 BALANCE OF PAYMENTS

In 2010 Rwanda had a foreign trade deficit of $946 million, amounting to 18.6% of GDP. UN figures show that since 2006, Rwanda's imports have increased an average of 31.6% per year, while in comparison, exports between 2006 and 2009 increased only by an average of 14% per year, leading to an increasingly large trade deficit. On 31 December 2010, foreign exchange reserves including gold were estimated to be $812.8 million, up from the previous year-end figure of $742.7 million.

33 BANKING AND SECURITIES

From 1922 until the independence of the Zaire (now DROC) in 1960, the monetary and banking systems of Rwanda and Burundi were integrated with those of the Congo. In July 1962, upon becoming independent, Rwanda and Burundi formed a joint monetary union administered by a common central bank. This bank was dissolved, and its functions as a central banking institution transferred, in April 1964, to the National Bank of the Republic of Rwanda. The Banque Nationale du Rwanda (BNR) was looted in July 1994 but reopened later in the year and has since reopened its branches in Butare and Ruhengeri. The bank imposes foreign exchange controls and administers the import licensing system.

In 2011 fourteen banks were licensed to operate in Rwanda. The International Monetary Fund reports that at the end of 2010, the stock of broad and narrow money was $1.243 billion. In 2010, the discount rate, the interest rate at which the central bank lends to financial institutions in the short term, was 7.75%. The commercial bank lending rate was 16%.

The Rwanda Stock Exchange (RSE) began operations on 31 January 2011, offering shares of brewer Brasseries et Limonaderies du Rwanda (BRALIRWA). The RSE replaced the Rwanda-Over-The-Counter (OTC) market that opened 31 January 2008.

34 INSURANCE

A number of companies offer automobile and other insurance in Rwanda. In 2011, 92% of the population had national health coverage, which cost $2.00 per year.

35 PUBLIC FINANCE

In 2010 the budget of Rwanda included $1.169 billion in public revenue and $1.366 billion in public expenditures. The budget deficit amounted to 0.4% of GDP. Public debt was 20.2% of GDP, with external debt making up less than 5% of GDP.

36 TAXATION

Direct taxation includes a tax on industrial and commercial profits, levied at 30% in 2010. Taxes on dividends and a turnover (sales) tax are also levied. Indirect taxation, forming the bulk of government tax revenue, is derived largely from import and export duties.

Individual taxes are levied in accordance with a progressive, five-bracket schedule, with a top rate of 30%. Additional deductions in calculating taxable income including pension payments, disability benefits, medical expenses, travel expenses, and on-the-job meal and training expenses. Diplomats and diplomatic staff, high ranking executives of international organizations, as well as persons and companies under special agreements ratified by law are given special tax exemptions. Privileged persons include those dealing in exports as well as with donor-funded projects under an agreement with the government of Rwanda and the donor.

A contribution of 8% of salary is made to Rwanda's Social Security, with the employer contributing 5% and the employee, 3%.

Rwanda has legislated a value-added tax (VAT) with a standard rate of 18% on all taxable goods and services.

37 CUSTOMS AND DUTIES

Import duties have been the most important source of tax revenues since independence. There are two kinds of duties, both levied ad valorem: customs duties, averaging 15–30%, and revenue duties, averaging 5–15% (up to 60% for some goods). A 1% handling fee is also levied. Most imports require a license. Rwanda is a member of Common Market of Eastern and Southern Africa (COMESA).

Rwanda's joining the EAC in 2007 resulted in the removal of trade tariffs between Rwanda and other member nations, and the adoption of a common external tariff schedule applied by all member nations to non-member nations. While tariffs for some items were reduced, the loss of revenue was to be mitigated by increased sales.

38 FOREIGN INVESTMENT

While Rwanda has attempted to attract foreign investment through modifications of its investment code, foreign investment in Rwanda has been hampered by a weak judicial system unable to settle technical business issues, a weak domestic market, and low return on investment. Also cited as hindrances to foreign investment are the nation's dependence on raw materials, finished products, and skilled technical workers from abroad. Rwanda's infrastructure also is perceived as weak, and the cost of transport high. Despite these perceived roadblocks, the World Bank stated in 2010 that great improvements in ease of doing business had been noted over the 2008 evaluation. Foreign direct investment (FDI) in Rwanda was a net inflow of $118.7 million according to World Bank figures published in 2009. FDI represented 2.28% of GDP. In 2010 foreign aid represented approximately 50% of the government's budget.

39 ECONOMIC DEVELOPMENT

Rwanda's attempt to establish food self-sufficiency has delayed many of its development plans in other sectors. Rwanda typically receives foreign aid from various European donors and the EU. Rwanda's economic development goals were defined in its Vision 2020 program, the aim of which is to transform Rwanda from a poor, subsistence agriculture-based economy to a knowledge-based, service-oriented economy. The means of accomplishing this focused on reforms in the business environment, investment in infrastructure, improvement in agricultural productivity, and the development of skills needed for economic modernization.

Rwanda's Economic Development and Poverty Reduction Strategy (EDPRS) contains three key economic growth strategies—an economy-wide increase in agricultural and manufacturing production; the creation of economic opportunities for the poorest Rwandans through public works, credit, and direct support; and the strengthening of political and economic governance.

In 2010 the government announced a seven-year plan focused on economic growth through the development of infrastructure and industrial production. The plan set a target to increase electricity access by 30% and energy production from a capacity of 70 MW to 1,000 MW. By 2017, the government also hoped to increase access to clean water to 100% of the population, and to promote industrial production by about 12% annually.

40 SOCIAL DEVELOPMENT

Social security programs aimed at meeting the individual's basic welfare needs have been established in law since independence. Old age pensions for workers, sickness and maternity benefits, and payments for those injured on the job are provided for all salaried workers. The system is funded by contributions from employees and employers. While most of the population live in poverty and engage in subsistence agriculture, the majority (92%) are covered by government health insurance. Old age pensions are available beginning at age 55, unless the person is deemed prematurely aged.

Although sex discrimination is outlawed by the constitution, and the 1999 Inheritance and Marital Property Law gave women the right to inherit property from their husbands and fathers, the right to inherit only applies in the case of a legal marriage contract. Only 60% of marriages in Rwanda are bound by a legal contract, leaving 40% of wives with no inheritance rights. However, women are guaranteed representation in the legislature, with 24 seats reserved for women. As a result of the 2008 elections, Rwanda became the first nation in the world to have a female majority in its legislature. Prior to the elections, women held 48% of the seats, already the most gender-equal legislature in the world.

Domestic violence and wife beating are prevalent. Child labor and human trafficking are widespread.

Elections in 2010–11 were peaceful, but the time leading up to them was marred by two high-profile political murders and a series of grenade attacks. Opposition parties faced roadblocks in registration as well. The government's human rights record remains poor. Arbitrary arrest and detention continue, as well as life-threatening prison conditions. Freedom of speech and of the press is severely restricted.

41 HEALTH

According to the CIA, life expectancy in Rwanda was 58 years in 2011. The country spent 9.4% of its GDP on healthcare, amounting to $48 per person. There was less than one physician, 5 nurses and midwives, and 16 hospital beds per 10,000 inhabitants. The fertility rate was 4.9, while the infant mortality rate was 64 per 1,000 live births. In 2008 the maternal mortality rate, according to the World Bank, was 540 per 100,000 births. It was estimated that 92% of children were vaccinated against measles. The CIA calculated HIV/AIDS prevalence in Rwanda to be about 2.9% in 2009, with approximately 170,000 living with HIV/AIDS.

Major disease risks for Rwanda include bacterial diarrhea, tuberculosis, dengue fever, yellow fever, hepatitis A, typhoid fever, malaria, and rabies. Poor sanitation measures and water pollution also cause serious health problems; it was estimated that in 2008, 65% of the population had access to safe drinking water and only 54% access to improved sanitation facilities. The incidence of tuberculosis was 106 per 100,000 people in 2010.

The WHO, the UN FAO, and UNICEF provide aid in public health services. Since the late 1960s, the UN, Belgium, France, and the United States have been assisting Rwanda in specific health-related projects.

42 HOUSING

The traditional rural Rwandan house is beehive-shaped, made of mud bricks and poles, and covered with thatch. Prior to the genocide, these residences were scattered throughout the farmlands and accounted for 89% of Rwanda's housing units; however, the government National Habitat Program aimed at improving rural housing conditions and providing new housing for a large number of returning genocide survivors, brought villagization. Villagization is meant to construct rural village communities where better public services and utilities might be provided. This project

has been met with controversy because it is believed that some rural residents might be forcibly relocated to the new villages and consolidated into specific settlement areas. Part of the program includes a directive to zone particular areas for housing and prohibit residence in nondesignated areas. Government policies also have been criticized for focusing on returning refugees instead of addressing the existing housing shortage.

Rapid urbanization of Rwanda has led to the spread of unplanned urban settlements with inadequate access to utility services. One of the aims of Vision 2020 is that 30% of the population lives in planned cities rather than these unplanned settlements. To meet the demand for housing, it was estimated in 2007 that 8,500 to 10,000 new housing units would be needed each year. In the remaining urban areas, an additional 15,000 would be needed annually.

About 94% of all households live in a single-family structure. In 2008, 54% of all households had access to improved sanitation. Sixty-five percent had access to an improved water source. About 86% of all housing is owner occupied.

43 EDUCATION

As of 2010, about 10% of age-eligible children were enrolled in some type of preschool program. In 2008 the World Bank estimated that 96% of age-eligible children in Rwanda were enrolled in primary school. The student-to-teacher ratio for primary school was about 64:1 in 2010; the ratio for secondary school was 29:1. Tertiary enrollment was estimated at 5%. Overall, the CIA estimated that Rwanda had a literacy rate of 70.4%, and that public expenditure on education represented 4.1% of GDP.

There were no public schools in Rwanda until the 1950s, and secondary education was then attainable only at a school founded in 1929 at Butare by Roman Catholic missionaries. With independence, Rwanda began a major expansion of its educational programs; in 1989, education accounted for 25.4% of total government expenditure. However, the Catholic Church continues to play a leading role in education.

Education is free and compulsory for six years, generally for children ages 7 to 13. Primary school is for six years; however, not all students who enroll in primary school complete the six years, and those who do may take additional years to do so. Primary school is followed by three years of junior and three years of senior secondary education. Technical school programs are available for students at the secondary level. Most primary and secondary schools are under the direction of religious missions, but many receive state subsidies. The academic year runs from September to June.

The National University of Rwanda at Butare was founded in 1963 by the government and a Canadian Roman Catholic order. Other known institutions are the African and Mauritian Institute of Statistics and Applied Economics in Kigali.

44 LIBRARIES AND MUSEUMS

The largest library collection is at the National University, which has approximately 199,000 volumes. There is a government library in Kigali, with about 15,000 volumes, and smaller collections are found in the administrative centers of the other prefectures. A National Library was founded in 1989 and has a collection of about 6,000 volumes. A library of 30,000 volumes is maintained at the

Dominican Monastery in Kigali and the French Cultural Institute also maintains a collection in the capital. The Kigali Public Library, Rwanda's first public library, was still under construction as of January 2012.

The National Museum in Butare contains an important collection for the study of the cultural evolution of the country and is housed in a building inaugurated in January 1989. An ethnological museum is maintained in Kabgayi and a geological museum in Ruhengeri. Kigali is home to the Geological Museum of Rwanda.

45 MEDIA

In 2009 the CIA reported that there were 33,500 telephone landlines in Rwanda. In addition to landlines, mobile phone subscriptions averaged 24 per 100 people. Mobile telephone penetration in Rwanda started slowly in comparison to other nations in the region because the market was closed to competition until 2006. In December 2009, MTN International, the leading mobile phone network company in Africa, announced plans for an additional $18 million upgrade and expansion of its mobile network in Rwanda, bringing the company's total year-end investment in the Rwandan network to about $100 million. In 2009–11, Rwanda was the fastest growing mobile market in Africa.

In 2009 there were eight AM radio stations and one shortwave radio station. Broadcasts occur in French, Swahili, and Kinyarwanda. In 2010 the country had about 815 Internet hosts. As of 2009, there were some 450,000 Internet users in Rwanda. Internet users numbered 5 per 100 citizens.

In 2010, more than ten newspapers, including weeklies, biweeklies and dallies, were available in Rwanda; however, readership remains low. The three with highest readership were *Umuseso, Imvaho Nshya,* and *New Times.* Others include *Kinyamateka, Jeune Afrique,* and *Rwanda Champion.*

The Fundamental Law provides for freedom of the press. However, it is said that the government harasses and intimidates the media at any reporting of views contrary to its goals. In 2002, Asuman Bisiika, a Ugandan citizen and editor of the Rwanda Herald, was deported to Uganda after publishing articles critical of the Rwandan government.

46 ORGANIZATIONS

Many of the commercial, agricultural, and welfare organizations founded under the Belgian administration have continued in operation since independence. There is a chamber of commerce and industry in Kigali; the Rwanda Private Sector Federation assists in business and trade. The government has also supported the growth of agricultural cooperatives.

Scouting and YMCA/YWCA programs are available for youth. Sports associations promote amateur competitions for athletes of all ages. Organizations dedicated to promoting the rights of women include the Federation of African Women Peace Networks, Pro-Femmes, and the Rwandan Women's Network. There are national chapters of the Red Cross Society, CARE International, UNICEF, the Society of St. Vincent de Paul, and Caritas.

47 TOURISM, TRAVEL, AND RECREATION

While tourism declined in the 1990s due to war and economic factors, the country is again attracting visitors with its mountain gorillas, wild game preserve, and the hiking opportunities in the Volcano National Park and the Akagera National Park.

A valid passport is required of all tourists, and a visa is required for many others. Malaria, meningitis, hepatitis, and typhoid are health risks.

The *Tourism Factbook,* published by the UN World Tourism Organization, reported 699,000 incoming tourists to Rwanda in 2009; they spent a total of $218 million. Of those incoming tourists, there were 591,000 from Africa. The estimated daily cost to visit Kigali, the capital, was $275. The cost of visiting other cities averaged $169.

48 FAMOUS PERSONS

Kigeri IV Rwabugiri (d. 1895) was one of the most famous rulers of the pre-colonial Rwanda kingdom. Grégoire Kayibanda (1924–76), the first president of independent Rwanda, studied for the priesthood and became a teacher. He founded Parmehutu, the party that led the move to independence. Juvénal Habyarimana (1937–94) became president in July 1973 and remained in office until 1994, when a new government was established with Pasteur Bizimungu (b. 1951) as president. Paul Kagame (b. 1957), the founder of the RPF and president of the country, is most well known for his role on the Rwandan genocide in 1994, and his destabilizing role in the Second Congo War.

49 DEPENDENCIES

The Republic of Rwanda has no territories or colonies.

50 BIBLIOGRAPHY

Adekunle, Julius. *Culture and Customs of Rwanda.* Westport, CT: Greenwood Press, 2007.

Adelman, Howard and Astri Suhrke, eds. *The Path of a Genocide: the Rwanda Crisis from Uganda to Zaire.* New Brunswick, NJ: Transaction Publishers, 2000.

Carr, Rosamond Halsey. *Land of a Thousand Hills: My Life in Rwanda.* New York: Viking, 1999.

Chrétien, Jean-Pierre. *The Great Lakes of Africa: Two Thousand Years of History.* New York: Zone Books, 2003.

Education in Rwanda: Rebalancing Resources to Accelerate Post-Conflict Development and Poverty Reduction. Washington, DC: World Bank, 2004

Jennings, Christian. *Across the Red River: Rwanda, Burundi, and the Heart of Darkness.* London, Eng.: Phoenix, 2001.

Rwanda Investment and Business Guide: Strategic and Practical Information. Washington, DC: International Business Publications USA, 2012.

Scherrer, Christian P. *Genocide and Crisis in Central Africa: Conflict Roots, Mass Violence, and Regional War.* Westport, CT: Praeger, 2002.

Turner, Pamela S. *Gorilla Doctors: Saving Endangered Great Apes.* Boston: Houghton Mifflin, 2005.

Twagilimana, Aimable, and Learthen Dorsey. *Historical Dictionary of Rwanda.* Lanham, MD: Scarecrow Press, 2007.

Zeilig, Leo, and David Seddon. *A Political and Economic Dictionary of Africa.* Philadelphia: Routledge/Taylor and Francis, 2005..

SÃO TOMÉ AND PRÍNCIPE

CAPITAL: São Tomé

FLAG: The flag consists of three unequal horizontal stripes of green, yellow, and green; there is a red triangle at the hoist, and two black stars on the yellow stripe.

ANTHEM: *Independéncia Total (Total Independence).*

MONETARY UNIT: The dobra (STD) is equal to 100 centimos. There are coins of 50 centimos and 1, 2, 5, 10, and 20 dobras, and notes of 50, 100, 500, and 1,000 dobras. STD1 = US$0.0000509 (or US$1 = STD19,641) as of 2010.

WEIGHTS AND MEASURES: The metric system is used.

HOLIDAYS: New Year's Day, 1 January; Martyrs' Day, 4 February; Labor Day, 1 May; Independence Day, 12 July; Armed Forces Day, first week in September; Farmers' Day, 30 September. The principal Christian holidays also are observed.

TIME: GMT.

¹LOCATION, SIZE, AND EXTENT

São Tomé and Príncipe, the smallest country in Africa, lies in the Gulf of Guinea, about 360 km (225 mi) off the west coast of Gabon. The nation has an area of 1,001 sq km (386 sq mi). Comparatively, the area occupied by São Tomé and Príncipe is slightly less than 5.5 times the size of Washington, DC. São Tomé extends about 49 km (30 mi) NNE–SSW and 29 km (18 mi) ESE–WNW. Príncipe has a length of approximately 21 km (13 mi) SSE–NNW and a width of 15 km (9 mi) ENE–WSW.

São Tomé and Príncipe's capital city, São Tomé, is located on the northeast coast of the island of São Tomé.

²TOPOGRAPHY

The islands form part of a chain of extinct volcanoes and are both quite mountainous. Pico de São Tomé, the highest peak on São Tomé, is 2,024 m (6,640 ft) above sea level. Most other peaks rise to only a little more than half that height. Príncipe's plateau area, extending along the northwestern coast, is larger than that of São Tomé. Pico de Príncipe is Príncipe's tallest mountain, reaching 948 m (3,109 ft) above sea level.

³CLIMATE

The islands are tropical, but temperature varies a good deal with altitude. Coastal temperatures average around 27˚C (81˚F), but the mountain regions average only 20˚C (68˚F). Seasons are distinguished more by a change in precipitation than by a change in temperature. From October to May, the northern regions of São Tomé and Príncipe receive between 100 and 150 cm (40 to 60 in) of rain. The southern portions receive about 380 to 510 cm (150 to 200 in).

⁴FLORA AND FAUNA

The World Resource Institute estimates that there are 895 plant species in Sao Tome and Principe. In addition, Sao Tome and Principe is home to 14 mammal, 112 bird, 15 reptile, and 9 amphibian species. The calculation reflects the total number of distinct species residing in the country, not the number of endemic species.

Except for the coastal flatlands where cocoa and coffee plantations predominate, São Tomé and Príncipe are dominated by forestland. Above 1,370 m (4,500 ft), the tropical rain forest changes to cloud-mountain forest. There is little livestock, but domestic fowl are abundant.

⁵ENVIRONMENT

Water and land pollution are the most significant problems in São Tomé and Príncipe. The purity of the nation's water supply is questionable due to the lack of adequate water treatment systems. The nation's forests are also threatened due to overuse and there is no regulatory policy to regulate their preservation. The nation's cities are threatened by inadequate sewage treatment. Soil erosion and soil exhaustion are other major environmental problems. The UN reported in 2008 that carbon dioxide emissions in Sao Tome and Principe totaled 128 kilotons.

According to a 2011 report issued by the International Union for Conservation of Nature and Natural Resources (IUCN), the number of threatened species included 5 types of mammals, 12 species of birds, 4 types of reptiles, 3 species of amphibians, 12 species of fish, 1 type of mollusk, 1 species of other invertebrate, and 35 species of plants. Threatened species include the São Tomé short-tail, São Tomé sunbird, the West African seahorse, and at least six species of sharks.

⁶POPULATION

The US Central Intelligence Agency (CIA) estimates the population of Sao Tome and Principe in 2011 to be approximately 179,506, which placed it at number 177 in population among the 196 nations of the world. In 2011, approximately 3.1% of the population was over 65 years of age, with another 44.7% under 15 years of age. The median age in Sao Tome and Principe was 17.5 years. There were 1.00 males for every female in the country. The population's annual rate of change was 2.052%. The projected population for the year 2025 was 230,000. Population density in Sao Tome and Principe was calculated at 186 people per sq km (72 people per sq mi).

The UN estimated that 62% of the population lived in urban areas, and that urban populations had an annual rate of change of 2.8%. The largest urban area was Sao Tome, with a population of 60,000.

⁷MIGRATION

Estimates of São Tomé and Príncipe's net migration rate, carried out by the CIA in 2011, amounted to -9.33 migrants per 1,000 citizens. The total number of emigrants living abroad was 36,200, and the total number of immigrants living in São Tomé and Príncipe was 5,300. Historically, São Tomé and Príncipe received a substantial flow of what was allegedly temporary immigration in the form of contract labor. The *serviçais*, as they were called, came largely from Angola and Mozambique to work on the cocoa plantations; many were never repatriated. More recently, plantation labor has come from drought-stricken Cape Verde. Before 1974, Cape Verdeans were subsidized by the Portuguese government to settle on São Tomé and Príncipe in an effort to boost the islands' plantation economy. After the April 1974 revolution in Portugal and the coming of independence to the Portuguese territories, almost all the 3,000–4,000 European settlers left, while several hundred Angolans fled to São Tomé. Subsequently, more than 10,000 São Toméan exiles returned from Angola, and most Cape Verdeans left São Tomé.

⁸ETHNIC GROUPS

Most of the island's permanent residents are Fôrros, descendants of the Portuguese colonists and their freed African slaves, who came from Gabon and the Guinea coast. Along the southeast coast of São Tomé lives a group called the Angolares, the descendants of Angolan slaves, shipwrecked in the 16th century, who established independent fishing communities. Others include the mestico, servicais (contract laborers from Angola, Mozambique, and Cape Verde), tongas (children of servicais born on the islands), and Europeans, primarily Portuguese.

⁹LANGUAGES

Portuguese, the official language, is spoken in a Creole dialect that reveals the heavy influence of African Bantu languages.

¹⁰RELIGIONS

Christianity is the dominant religion, with Roman Catholics constituting about 85% of the total population and Protestants constituting about 12%. The primary Protestant groups are Evangelicals, New Apostolic, and Seventh-Day Adventists. Approximately 2% of the population is Muslim. Some residents include traditional faith practices in their observance of Christianity or Islam. The constitution provides for religious freedom. Religious groups must register with the government, but there have been no reports of restrictions placed on unregistered groups. Ash Wednesday, Good Friday, All Souls' Day, and Christmas are observed as national holidays.

¹¹TRANSPORTATION

Transportation networks on São Tomé and Príncipe reflect the plantation economy. Schooners are the main means of transportation for people living far from town. The CIA reports that São Tomé and Príncipe has a total of 320 km (199 mi) of roads, of which 218 km (135 mi) are paved, although often in disrepair and about a third are impassable after a heavy rainfall. Roads outside of the capital lack streetlights and many require a 4-wheel drive vehicle. There are no railroads. The Merchant Marine reported three ships of 1,000 GRT or more in 2010.

There are 3 airports, one of which is international, which transported 50,716 passengers in 2009 according to the World Bank. In 2010, all of the airports had paved runways. The international airport at São Tomé is served by the Trans Air Portugal (TAP), which has a weekly flight to Lisbon. A national airline (STP Airways) was launched in 2007 as a joint venture with Angola's national airline Transportes Aéreos de Angola (TAAG). It was banned from flying to the EU because of security concerns, but was reorganized and now has flights to Lisbon three times a week. Aeroflot makes occasional stops and weekly fights are available to a number of African locations.

São Tomé and Santo António are the main ports; large freighters must be unloaded from their anchorage by barge because the ports are not deep enough to accommodate them. As of 2011, a deepwater port designed to accommodate containers was scheduled to be constructed at Fernao Dias, 10 miles north of São Tomé city. The government is working to make the new port a regional hub for container shipping in West Africa.

¹²HISTORY

São Tomé and Príncipe were probably uninhabited volcanic islands when the Portuguese landed there in 1471. In 1485, São Tomé was made a donatário (concession) of João de Paiva; the donatário provided for de Paiva to administer and profit by his administration of São Tomé according to Portuguese law. Subsequently, São Tomé served as a slave station.

The islands were settled by a group of Europeans and their African slaves. In 1493, 2,000 Jewish children were taken to São Tomé in an effort to populate the islands and raise the children as Christians, but by 1532 only 50 or 60 were left. It was Portuguese policy to deport its criminals, *degradados*, and orphans to remote colonial areas, and many of São Tomé's earliest male settlers came in this fashion. Female settlers were more often African slave women, and from the ensuing marriages a large mestiço population developed. A third group, separate from the European and mestiço populations, consisted of Angolares, descendants of shipwrecked Angolan slaves.

By the mid-16th century, the islands were Africa's leading exporter of sugar. São Tomé and Príncipe were taken over by the Portuguese crown in 1522 and 1573, respectively. Eventually, sugar lost its commercial importance, but in the early 19th century, two new cash crops, coffee and cocoa, were introduced, and by 1908 São Tomé had become the world's largest producer of cocoa. Plantation slavery or slave-like contract labor remained the basis of island labor for hundreds of years, and even when slavery formally ended in 1869, the plantations employed laborers "recruited" on "contract" from other areas of Portuguese-speaking Africa. In 1906, Henry Nevinson published his book, *A Modern Slavery*, which exposed the use of involuntary recruits, unacceptably high labor mortality, and poor work conditions on the islands. The outcry resulted in a boycott of São Tomé cocoa. The scandal occasioned some reforms, but oppressive conditions continued. As late as 1953, the governor of São Tomé ordered Portuguese troops to open fire on striking plantation workers, leaving nearly 1,000 people dead, an action that aroused nationalist feeling.

Independence

A liberation group formed in the islands in 1960, but Portuguese control made it impossible to wage an effective guerrilla war. The organization, the Committee for the Liberation of São Tomé and Príncipe (later renamed the Movement for the Liberation of São Tomé and Príncipe—MLSTP), remained in exile in Gabon until it was recognized by Portugal in 1974 as the sole legitimate representative of the people of São Tomé and Príncipe.

An independence agreement was concluded between Portuguese and MLSTP negotiators on 26 November 1974, and a transitional government was installed on 21 December. On 12 July 1975, São Tomé and Príncipe achieved full independence. On the same day, Manuel Pinto da Costa, the secretary-general of the MLSTP, was inaugurated as the country's first president.

Following an alleged plot to overthrow the government, about 1,500 troops from Angola and Guinea-Bissau were stationed on the islands in 1978 at Pinto da Costa's request. Soviet, East European, and Cuban personnel were also reportedly on the islands. In 1979, Prime Minister Miguel dos Anjos da Cunha Lisboa Trouvoada was arrested and charged with attempting to seize power. His post was assumed by Pinto da Costa, and the MLSTP was reported to be seriously split. In the early 1980s there was unrest on Príncipe, apparently provoked by separatists. By 1985, São Tomé and Príncipe had begun to establish closer ties with the West.

Multiparty Democracy Launched

In 1990, a new policy of *abertura*, or political and economic "opening," was adopted. It led to the legalization of opposition parties and direct elections with secret balloting. The secret police were purged and freedom of association and press were encouraged. A number of groups, many led by politicians in exile, united as the Party of Democratic Convergence-Group of Reflection (PDC-GR) and were led by Miguel Trovoada. An independent labor movement was launched and strikes were legalized. Abertura was also reflected in the evolution of a market economy and the privatization of state farms and enterprises.

On 20 January 1991, the nation held its first multiparty legislative elections. The former ruling party (MLSTP) was defeated by the PDC-GR. PDC-GR got 54.4% (33 seats) of the vote, the MLSTP 30.5% (21 seats), and the Democratic Opposition Coalition (CODO) 5.2% (1 seat). In the presidential election on 3 March 1991, Trovoada was elected unopposed. In 1992, the government imposed a strict structural adjustment program at the behest of

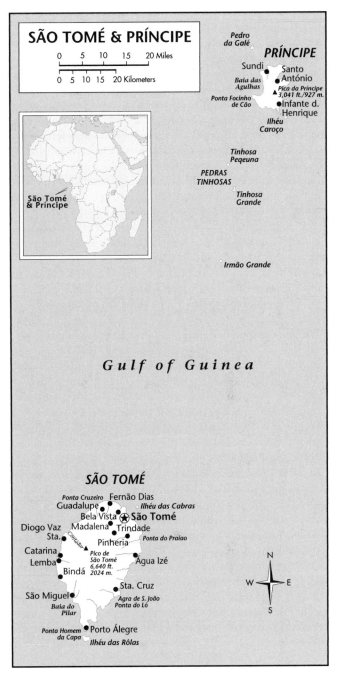

LOCATION: São Tomé: 0°13′N and 6°37′E. Príncipe: 1°37′N and 7°24′E.
TERRITORIAL SEA LIMIT: 12 miles.

the IMF and the World Bank, which increased the price of gasoline and depreciated the value of the currency by 40%. The measures prompted massive demonstrations and calls for the dissolution of the government headed by Prime Minister Daniel Lima dos Santos Daio. The parliament then appointed Norberto Alegre prime minister, who then formed a new government.

In 1993, the PDC-GR continued to dominate the central government, but partisan activity accelerated. The president and the prime minister, both PDC-GR, also became involved in a dispute over interpretation of the constitution on the separation of powers. In November, a joint communique by four opposition parties accused government of "leading the country towards a social ex-

plosion" and denounced its "authoritarian and repressive attitude."
By 1994, Trovoada was forced to again dissolve the government
amid continued protests. The PDC-GR was increasingly seen as
corrupt and complacent, but Trovoada was viewed with equal
skepticism. After firing Alegre, Trovoada appointed a new prime
minister from the PDC-GR, but the PDC-GR refused to acknowledge the president's right to do so, expelled the prime minister
from the party, and refused to participate further with the government. In response, Trovoada announced new elections for 2 October 1994. The MLSTP won 27 seats; the PCD-GR, 14; and the Independent Democratic Action Party, 14. Carlos Alberto Monteiro
Dias da Graça was appointed prime minister. Regional elections
were held on Príncipe in March 1995, resulting in a commanding
majority for the MLSTP.

A bloodless coup in August 1995 led by five Army officers
temporarily disbanded the government, but international pressure reversed the coup and by year's end, a new government of
national unity was created, headed by Prime Minister Armindo
Vaz d'Almeida. In June 1996, Trovoada won presidential elections,
taking 52% of the vote to (MLSTP) Manuel Pinto Costa's 48% in a
rerun. The election was deemed generally free and fair by international observers, despite allegations of an unconstitutional modification of the voter lists between the first and second rounds. In
September, the prime minister resigned and was replaced, after
much infighting, by Raul Vagner de Conceição Bragança Neto. In
March 1998 the civil service went on strike, the first since independence, demanding payment of six months of wage arrears, but
government coffers were then said to be empty. Demobilized soldiers threatened to destabilize the country, demanding financial
benefits provided for by a pact that ended the 1995 coup.

In the 8 November 1998 election, the MLSTP took 31 of the 55
parliamentary seats. The ADI won 16 and the PCD-GR, 8 seats.
After Trovoada's veto of the first cabinet, Prime Minister Guil-
herme Posser da Costa formed a government in January 1999, announcing an austerity program to relaunch the economy and end
corruption.

On 3 September 2001, a relatively unknown wealthy businessman, Fradique Melo Bandeira de Menezes, became São Tomé and
Príncipe's third president as the result of free and fair elections
held in July. Barred from seeking a third term, President Trovoada needed a successor who would protect his political and financial interests. It was widely speculated that Trovoada and his son
Patrice believed they could control de Menezes from behind the
scenes. De Menezes adopted a widely popular platform, ran a successful campaign, and gained enough votes on the first round to
defeat Manuel Pinto da Costa, the candidate of the Movimento
de Libertacao de São Tomé e Príncipe-Partido Social Democrata
(MLSTP-PSD).

Despite de Menezes' efforts to clean up government and to
eradicate poverty, instability and corruption continued to undermine social and economic progress in the period 2002–2006.
Much of the instability could be attributed to the islands' inherently unstable governance structure—there were seven prime ministers since 2001—and to the intense political competition related to
the discovery of oil, auctioning of oil blocks, and desire to control
revenues.

In March 2002, legislative elections were held eight months
ahead of schedule resulting in a divided parliament with no par-

ty winning a majority. The unity government formed afterwards,
which had been agreed to prior to the election, proved fractious
and weak. Efforts to strip the president of his powers including his
right to renegotiate an oil agreement with Nigeria, were rebuffed.
A decision to call for fresh legislative elections was reneged upon,
and in April 2003, riots broke out resulting in one death and much
damage to public property.

A military coup on 16 July 2003 led to the deposing of de Menezes, who was in Nigeria at the time, and the arrests of the senior
members of government. However, the president and cabinet were
reinstalled following international pressure and an agreement that
a new government be formed with oversight over governmental
affairs by an international committee. In October, the first oil licensing round was held, but only one block was awarded to a consortium of American and Norwegian companies.

In September 2004, de Menezes dismissed the government of
Maria das Neves over a corruption scandal. The successor government became embroiled in a similar scandal involving embezzlement at the government's aid agency, Gabinete de Gestao da
Ajuda. Five more oil blocks were awarded in April 2005, but the
process was marred by allegations of corruption in the adjudica-
tion process. A public sector strike in June 2005 led to the resignation of Vaz de Almeida; central bank governor Maria do Carmo
Silveira was appointed the new prime minister. In July, President
de Menezes called for a referendum on the country's constitutional form of government. The referendum sparked controversy,
but had been agreed to as a condition in a memorandum of understanding signed by the president and party representatives in
2003. Nevertheless, on 24 November the National Assembly rejected the motion for a referendum by 45 votes to 5. General elections were held in March 2006, with the coalition of MDFM-PCD
winning 37% of the vote and 23 seats in the National Assembly;
Tome Vera Cruz became the prime minister on 21 April 2006.
MDFM is the Force for Change Democratic Movement (MDFM)
and PCD is the Party for Democratic Covergence.

Presidential elections were held on 30 July 2006. De Menezes
was the victor, winning 60.6% of the vote. In November 2007, de
Menezes dismissed and replaced several ministers in his government in the midst of public criticism over the nation's management of the economy. In February 2008, de Menezes appointed
Patrice Trovoada as prime minister. On 20 May 2008, the government collapsed after losing a parliamentary vote of confidence.
The opposition leaders claimed that Trovoada had failed to establish the reforms promised when he was first appointed. He was
replaced by Joaqim Rafael Branco in June 2008. In March 2010,
de Menezes issued an executive decree that scheduled new elections for 2010. In those elections, Trovoada's ADI party fells two
seats shy of gaining a majority in the National Assembly. A new
government was formed in August and Trovoada was appointed
Prime Minister.

13 GOVERNMENT

On 12 July 1975, São Tomé and Príncipe, formerly considered
overseas territories of Portugal, became an independent democratic republic. The constitution, drafted by a constituent assembly, took effect on 12 December 1975. The president was chief of
state, elected by the 40-member National Assembly for a term of
four years. The prime minister, who was elected to a five-year term

by the National Assembly on the recommendation of the MLSTP, appointed and headed the cabinet.

A new constitution announced by da Costa in 1989, was adopted by the National Assembly in April 1990, approved in an August referendum, and went into force in September 1990. Under the 1990 constitution, the president is elected for a maximum of two five-year terms, and is nominally in charge of foreign affairs and defense. The prime minister is chosen by the National Assembly and approved by the president. Members of the 55-member National Assembly serve a four-year term. Suffrage is universal at age 18.

The power-sharing configuration of government presents a pattern for political conflict that appears to be well-established. Under the country's semi-presidential system, the president must form a government with the opposition. Both presidents Trovoada and de Menezes were embroiled in conflicts with parliament largely stemming from the vague constitutional separation of powers.

14 POLITICAL PARTIES

On 15 October 1974, the government of Portugal recognized the Movement for the Liberation of São Tomé and Príncipe (Movimento de Libertação de São Tomé e Príncipe—MLSTP) as the sole legitimate representative for the islands. The party, formed in exile in 1960, at a Pan-African conference in Ghana, originally called itself the Committee for the Liberation of São Tomé and Príncipe (Comité de Libertação de São Tomé e Príncipe—CLSTP). In 1965, CLSTP publicly demanded independence and economic reforms for the islands. At a conference in Guinea in 1972, the CLSTP changed its name to the MLSTP and moved its headquarters to Gabon. Until the declaration of 15 October 1974, the MLSTP remained partially underground and in exile, expressing itself through a legal party, the Pro-Liberation Movement Association, led by the poet Alda de Espírito Santo. After independence, the MLSTP became the only political party. Until 1991, Manuel Pinto da Costa was secretary-general of MLSTP and president of the republic.

With the legalization of opposition party activity, several politicians returned from exile to organize their followers. Miguel Trovoada, an MLSTP founder who had been exiled after challenging da Costa's leadership, formed the Democratic Convergence Party-Group of Reflection (PCD-GR) and, in the 1991 elections, it captured control of the National Assembly and the presidency. The Democratic Opposition Coalition (CODO) and the Christian Democratic Front (FDC), and other parties together captured 15% of the vote for the legislature.

In December 1992, the MLSTP came back to score a series of landslide victories in municipal and regional elections. It took control of six of the eight regional governing bodies. In the 1994 elections, the MLSTP solidified its control, taking 27 of the 55 seats. The PDC-GR took 14, as did the Independent Democratic Action Party. Only 42% of registered voters turned up. There was a bloodless and short-lived coup amid massive popular unrest due to wage stagnation in 1995. The military leaders held power only briefly before returning the civilian government to power. In 1996, a government of national unity headed by Prime Minister Armindo Vaz d'Almeida was inaugurated.

Nine parties contested the 8 November 1998 parliamentary elections. The MLSTP further solidified it parliamentary grip to 31 seats. The Independent Democratic Action Party (ADI) increased its seats to 14, whereas the PCD-GR) got only 8 seats. São Tomé and Príncipe was one of 15 countries whose politicians formed the Union of African Parties for Democracy and Development (UAPDD) in Namibia in October 1998, aimed at promoting the interests of the continent.

In the July 2001 presidential elections, de Menezes benefited from the support of the Independent Democratic Action Party (ADI), the country's largest, but comparatively weak opposition, and five other political forces including the PCD, UNDP, Codo, PRD, and the PPP. Under the country's semi-presidential formula, the dominant parties in the parliament wield considerable powers. Therefore, although this coalition reflected the self-interests of the leaders of these political entities, it assured de Menezes of a constituency sufficient to score 56.3 % to 39 % of the vote over Pinto da Costa. Three other opposition figures took 5% of the vote.

On 3 March 2002, São Toméans went to the polls to elect a new parliament. The results ended in a deadlock for the MLSTP-PSD, which gained 39.6% of the vote, and Force for Change Democratic Movement (MDFM-PCD), which took 39.4% of the ballots. Ue-Kedadji coalition received 16.2%. The number of seats by party was: MLSTP-PSD 24, MDFM-PCD 23, Ue-Kedadji coalition 8.

In the run-up to the March 2006 elections, the two main opposition parties—the Force for Change Democratic Movement (MDFM) and the Party for Democratic Convergence (Partido de Convergencia Democrática—PCD) announced a renewal of their alliance. It remained to be seen whether smaller parties would join them. The Ue-Kedadji coalition (comprised of the ADI, PRD, Uniao Nacional para Democracia e Progresso—UNDP, Codo, and Partido Popular do Progresso—PPP remained split over the announcement by the ADI in October 2005 that it intended to contest the elections on its own. An outright victory by the MLSTP-PSD, which had been predicted, and which would have ensured a more stable governance arrangement, was not realized in the March 2006 elections. Instead, the MDFM-PCD won 37% of the vote and 23 seats to MLSTP's 28.9% and 19 seats. ADI won 20% and 12 seats.

Presidential elections were held on 30 July 2006. De Menezes was the victor, winning 60.6% of the vote. In second place was Patrice Trovoada, son of Miguel Trovoada, who took 38.8% of the vote. A third candidate, Nilo Guimarães, won 0.6% of the vote. Voter turnout was estimated at 64.9%.

In the August 2010 legislative elections, the Independent Democratic Action Party (ADI) took 26 of the 55 seats in the national assembly. The alliance of the Movement for the Liberation of São Tomé and Príncipe —Social Democratic Party (MLSTP-PSD) took 21 seats, followed by the Democratic Convergence Party—Reflection Group with 7 seats, and the alliance of the Force for Change Democratic Movement—Democratic Convergence Party (MDFM-PCD) with 1 seat. Although the ADI obtained the most seats, it fell two seats short of the overall majority. Patrice Trovoada of the ADI was elected as prime minister, but he added three ministers from other parties to his government.

15 LOCAL GOVERNMENT

São Tomé and Príncipe is divided into two provinces, corresponding to the two islands, and seven counties, of which six are on São Tomé, each governed by its own assembly. Príncipe was granted political and administrative autonomy, which it has exercised since 29 April 1995.

16 JUDICIAL SYSTEM

The accord signed on 26 November 1974 between the Portuguese government and the MLSTP served as the legal code in the islands until 12 December 1975, when a new constitution was formally implemented.

The present legal system, based on Portuguese law and customary law, provides for an independent judiciary and affords litigants in civil cases the right to a fair public trial and a right to appeal. It affords criminal defendants a public trial before a judge as well as legal representation. A shortage of trained lawyers, however, makes implementing this right difficult. The highest court is the Supreme Court, which is appointed by and accountable to the National Assembly.

17 ARMED FORCES

The force is comprised of army, coast guard, and presidential guard. Defense spending totaled $2.5 million and accounted for 0.8% of GDP.

A small citizen's army was formed by the Movement for the Liberation of São Tomé and Príncipe (MLSTP) government after Portuguese troops were withdrawn. There are also several hundred Angolan troops. Portugal announced in October 2009 that it would send police instructors to São Tomé and Príncipe to train about 70 new officers there, illustrating the long-lasting cooperation between the countries. São Tomé and Príncipe began to seriously pursue police reform when an elite group of Angola-trained security forces stormed the capital police headquarters to protest working conditions and pay. The Portuguese training program was designed to bring São Tomé and Príncipe's police forces up to 200 officers.

18 INTERNATIONAL COOPERATION

São Tomé and Príncipe, admitted to the United Nations on 16 September 1975, takes part in ECA and several nonregional specialized agencies, such as the FAO, the World Bank, the ILO, UNESCO, UNIDO, and the WHO. The nation is also a member of the ACP Group, the African Development Bank, G-77, the Alliance of Small Island States (AOSIS), the New Partnership for Africa's Development (NEPAD), and the African Union. The country has observer status in the WTO. São Tomé and Príncipe is part of the Nonaligned Movement. In environmental cooperation, the nation is part of the Convention on Biological Diversity, CITES, the Montréal Protocol, MARPOL, and the UN Conventions on the Law of the Sea, Climate Change, and Desertification.

19 ECONOMY

The gross domestic product (GDP) rate of change in São Tomé and Príncipe, as of 2010, was 4.5%. The annual rate of Inflation, which peaked at 37% in 2008, had declined to just under 12% in 2010. The government credited the improvement to an upturn in food and fuel prices, a shortened rainy season, and election related spending by political parties. In 2011, however, it was on the

rise again, hovering around 15%. Unemployment was reported at 16.65%.

São Tomé and Príncipe is one of the poorest countries in the world with an estimated 50% of the population living in poverty. It has to import over 90% of its resources and is not self-sufficient in food. The economy is based largely on cocoa production, which represents about 95% of the nation's exports. This sector is particularly vulnerable to drought and the inadequacy of the nation's infrastructure. The industrial sector is undeveloped. By some estimates, the informal sector, fueled by urban migration in search of economic opportunity, constitutes more than 60% of the economy.

The country is heavily dependent on foreign assistance, which has left it indebted to foreign creditors. Its development partners are pressing for reforms that would open the economy to increased foreign investment, which should lead to improved exports, and the enhanced foreign exchange needed to pay its debts.

When the country achieved independence from Portugal in 1975, it adopted a socialist model and the state took control over most of the economic resources, including the large cocoa plantations run by the Portuguese. In the 1980s, however, the state began the transition to a market economy and a multiparty democracy. The large estates were subdivided into small parcels and placed in the hands of the workers. The scale of the holdings, however, permitted little more than subsistence agriculture, which still engages most of the nation's workforce.

International organizations have been working with the government to take the economy beyond its subsistence state. An island paradise, rich in exotic wildlife and unspoiled beaches, the country has potential as a tourist destination. However, the government has been slow to invest in this sector. Rich volcanic soil and abundant rainfall could also sustain increased agricultural production of fruits and vegetables for export to European markets.

São Tomé and Príncipe may have an untapped supply of petroleum in its territorial waters in the Gulf of Guinea, a known oil zone that is being explored through the help of foreign investors. The economy rose an estimated 6% by 2007 because of increases in public expenditures and oil-related capital investment. A major oil find could substantially improve the country's economic prospects, although managing increased oil revenues could pose significant political challenges.

The Financial Action Task Force (FATF), a Paris-based international organization dedicated to combating money laundering and terrorist financing, implicated São Tomé and Príncipe in its February 2010 report for not addressing strategic deficiencies related to the financing of terrorism and money laundering. In its report, the group urged the government of São Tomé and Príncipe to address the related issues and warned that the FATF will take action against the country—such as a recommendation for economic sanctions—if meaningful progress is not made.

20 INCOME

The CIA estimated that in 2010 the GDP of Sao Tome and Principe was $311 million. The CIA defines GDP as the value of all final goods and services produced within a nation in a given year and computed on the basis of purchasing power parity (PPP) rather than value as measured on the basis of the rate of the exchange based on current dollars. The per capita GDP was estimated at

$1,800. The annual growth rate of GDP was 4.5%. The average inflation rate was 13%. It was estimated that agriculture accounted for 14.7% of GDP, industry 22.9%, and services 62.4%.

According to the World Bank, remittances from citizens living abroad totaled $2 million or about $11 per capita and accounted for approximately 0.6% of GDP.

The World Bank estimates that São Tomé and Príncipe, with less than 0.01% of the world's population, accounted for less than 0.01% of the world's GDP. By comparison, the United States, with 4.85% of the world's population, accounted for 22.51% of world GDP.

As of 2011, the most recent study by the World Bank reported that actual individual consumption in São Tomé and Príncipe was 96.0% of GDP and accounted for less than 0.01% of world consumption. By comparison, the United States accounted for 25.44% of world individual consumption. The World Bank also estimated that 55.4% of São Tomé and Príncipe's individual consumption was spent on food and beverages, 11.8% on housing and household furnishings, 3.7% on clothes, 5.2% on health, 9.2% on transportation, 1.2% on communications, 1.4% on recreation, 1.2% on restaurants and hotels, and 2.5% on miscellaneous goods, services, and purchases from abroad.

It was estimated that in 2004 about 54% of the population subsisted on an income below the poverty line established by São Tomé and Príncipe's government.

21LABOR

As of 2007, Sao Tome and Principe had a total labor force of 52,490 people.

Agriculture and fishing support most of the population. Laborers for the plantation sector come from mainland Africa and Cape Verde on a contract basis; Angola, Mozambique, and Nigeria are the major sources of contract labor. Plantation laborers gained a 400% wage increase on the eve of independence. Soon after, labor disruptions and the reorganization of production reduced the output of plantation crops. In 2007, the workforce consisted of about 52,490 people.

Unemployment can reach up to 50% of the workforce, largely because of the unpopularity of plantation work among the Fôrros. Unrelated to the former sole union (an affiliate of the MLSTP), or any political party, the Independent Union Federation (IUF) was formed in 1992 to take advantage of freedom of association provisions now in the constitution. Workers may organize and bargain collectively. However, the IUF has had little luck in organizing the workers on the large state-owned plantations. The government remains the primary mediator for labor, even though privatization has reduced the relative role of the government as an employer.

While the minimum age for employment is legally set at 18, children occasionally do work, especially on state-run plantations. Conditions on the largest state-owned plantations—the nation's largest job sector—have been described as "medieval." The free housing and medical care, which the workers are promised, are inadequate. Food and clothing, supposed to be provided at low cost in "company stores," are typically more expensive than on the open market. Safety and health regulations are ineffectually enforced. The minimum wage is legally set at $14 per month. The workweek is set at 40 hours, but this is only practiced in the modern economic sector.

22AGRICULTURE

Out of 96,000 hectares (237,221 acres) of land in São Tomé and Príncipe, 10,000 hectares (24,711 acres) are arable. Roughly 57% of the total land is currently farmed, and the country's major crops include cocoa, coconuts, palm kernels, copra, cinnamon, pepper, coffee, bananas, papayas, and beans. Cereal production amounted to 4,182 tons, fruit production 33,379 tons, and vegetable production 9,268 tons.

Plantation agriculture has long dominated the economy of the islands. Before nationalization in 1975, private companies owned more than 80% of the arable land. Their plantations were managed by São Tomé mestiços, Cape Verdeans, and São Tomé Europeans. About 11,000 small proprietors owned the rest of the arable land. The nationalization law limited the private holdings to 100 hectares (247 acres) and reorganized 29 plantations into 15 state companies. In 1985, however, the government began legally recognizing the right of individual families to cultivate land within the state plantations. The two largest plantations were leased to European management in 1986.

A variety of microclimates enables the cultivation of diverse tropical crops, but soils are especially suited for cocoa (introduced from Brazil in the late 19th century), which is the major export crop. About half of all cultivated land is used for cocoa production. Labor disruptions, a reduced workweek, inadequate investment in repair and maintenance, and the use of work time to conduct management and cooperative training programs combined to lower the cocoa output from 10,000 tons in 1975 to 3,900 tons in 1987. Cocoa exports accounted for about 90% of export earnings. Coconuts are the second most important crop.

Since 1990, a World Bank and IMF-sponsored structural adjustment program aimed at diminishing the dependence on cocoa exports and food imports have driven economic policy. The program called for fundamental land reform and accompanying measures to stimulate cultivation of food crops for local consumption.

23ANIMAL HUSBANDRY

The UN Food and Agriculture Organization (FAO) reported that Sao Tome and Principe dedicated 1,000 hectares (2,471 acres) to permanent pasture or meadow in 2009. During that year, the country tended 420,000 chickens, 4,800 head of cattle, and 2,620 pigs. The production from these animals amounted to 225 tons of beef and veal, 606 tons of pork, 1,316 tons of poultry, 467 tons of eggs, and 7,121 tons of milk. Sao Tome and Principe also produced 21 tons of cattle hide.

African swine fever plagued the livestock sector, largely pigs, once in 1979 and again in 1992, necessitating the destruction of the entire herd of some 30,000 animals. Disease severely affected chicken and egg production in 1993. There is no tsetse-borne disease in São Tomé, but production is limited by tuberculosis. In 2009 there were an estimated 3,000 sheep and 5,200 goats.

24FISHING

Sao Tome and Principe had 25 decked commercial fishing boats in 2008. The annual capture totaled 4,250 tons according to the UN FAO. The export value of seafood totaled $94,000.

Sao Tome and Principe's fishing waters, which span 130,000 sq. km., are rich in marine resources, containing a potential fisheries biomass of 12,000 tons annually. Nevertheless, fishing contributes less than 3% to the nation's GDP. Most fish are caught for local consumption, although European Union (EU) vessels catch tuna in island waters under license and there are fishing agreements with Angola and Portugal. Foreign assistance has focused more recently on artisanal fishing. The IMF has highlighted the sector as a potential area for economic development, although past investments by the government have not significantly contributed to GDP; rather, it has exacerbated the country's debt service burden.

25 FORESTRY

About 27% of São Tomé and Príncipe are covered with primary, though inaccessible, forest. Wood is used on the plantations for fuel to dry cocoa beans and elsewhere as a building material. Unrestricted cutting has been the rule in spite of the legal sanctions against it. In 1993, new forest regulations were issued and guards were trained to enforce them. Reforestation and scientific foresting have been enforced to avoid further loss. The UN FAO estimated the 2009 roundwood production at 9,000 cu m (317,832 cu ft). The value of all forest products, including roundwood, totaled $1.18 million.

26 MINING

The mineral industry was not significant in the islands, and mineral wealth remained largely unexplored. Lime deposits were exploited for the local market, and small clay and stone open-pit operations supplied the construction industry.

27 ENERGY AND POWER

The World Bank reported in 2008 that Sao Tome and Principe produced 41 million kWh of electricity and consumed 20.1 million kWh, or 112 kWh per capita.

Hydroelectric facilities are on the Contador River on São Tomé. About 60% of São Tomé's 0.14 million kWh of electric power in 2002 were produced by hydroelectricity; the rest was thermal. Total installed capacity in the islands was 10,000 kW in 2002. Demand for electric power in 2002 totaled 0.013 million kWh. Most of São Tomé is electrified, but only a quarter of the nation's households have electricity.

São Tomé has no proven reserves of oil, natural gas, or coal, nor any refining capacity. All fossil fuel needs are met by imports of refined oil products. In 2002, imports and demand each averaged 630 barrels per day. Distillates and gasoline comprised the bulk of these imports, at 430 barrels per day and 140 barrels per day, respectively.

In May 2011, the government awarded a Nigerian oil company rights to exploration in a block of the country's exclusive zone. The block covers 4,288 square kilometers (1,632 miles). São Tomé has six other blocks that may be awarded to additional oil companies in the next few years.

28 INDUSTRY

São Tomé has very little industry; the industrial sector constituted about 23% of the GDP in 2010. Light construction items—textiles, soap, beer, fish, bread, and palm oil—are produced on the islands. The development of oil resources in its territorial waters promises a new addition to the industrial sector. In January 2006, Chevron Corp. began exploration drilling in the Gulf of Guinea on a block jointly owned by São Tomé and Nigeria.

29 SCIENCE AND TECHNOLOGY

The World Bank reported in 2009 that there were no patent applications in science and technology in Sao Tome and Principe. The Ministry of Agriculture maintains a library in São Tomé. The Center of Technical and Scientific Documentation, also in São Tomé, has an extensive library of specialized documents on agriculture and fisheries.

30 DOMESTIC TRADE

The landholding population of São Tomé and Príncipe grows some produce for the local market, but not on a large scale. Similarly, the Angolare population of São Tomé supplies fish to the local market. However, domestic agriculture and industry are not sufficient to fully supply local consumption, causing the country to rely heavily on imports for most goods. The port towns of São Tomé and Santo António are the principal commercial and distribution centers.

Business hours are Monday through Friday, 7:30 a.m. to 4:30 p.m.

31 FOREIGN TRADE

Sao Tome and Principe imported $99 million worth of goods and services in 2008, while exporting $13 million worth of goods and services. Major import partners in 2009 were Portugal, 56.2%; Brazil, 6.5%; Malaysia, 6%; the United States, 4.5%; and Japan, 4.3% . Its major export partners were UK, 32.9%; Netherlands, 26.8%; Belgium, 21%; and Portugal, 4.3%.

São Tomé and Príncipe's trade balance depends on price levels for cocoa, which accounts for about 90% of export earnings. Copra is also exported. The value of imports was four times that of exports in 2006. The leading imports are machinery and electrical equipment, food, and petroleum products.

32 BALANCE OF PAYMENTS

In 2010, São Tomé and Príncipe had a foreign trade deficit of $83 million, amounting to 41.2% of GDP. Since the country cannot supply enough food and clothing for its own people, imports remain high, while export revenues vary according to world agricultural prices. There is also an outflow of remittances for workers employed under contract from abroad.

33 BANKING AND SECURITIES

The Banco Nacional de São Tomé e Príncipe is the central bank and also handles commercial banking. In 1999, several senior central bank officials were dismissed in connection with the embezzlement of $1 million. The bank governor himself was dismissed on suspicion of corruption, and a government investigation of the bank led to the resignation of a finance minister.

Until the mid 2000s, the country's oldest bank, Banco Internacional de Sao Tome e Principe, a joint venture between Portugal's Caixa Geral de Depositos and Sao Tome, was the only bank on the islands. Since then government liberalization of the financial sector has led to the creation of eight more. Still, the market for banking services is small, underdeveloped, and concentrated in urban areas. Interest rates on loans tend to be double the rates in neighboring countries, making credit hard to acquire by small and medium sized firms. The percent of nonperforming loans exceeds 15%. There is no stock exchange.

³⁴INSURANCE

SAT Assurance, headquartered in Cameroon, is the only insurance company serving the islands. There is also an insurance fund for civil servants.

³⁵PUBLIC FINANCE

In 2010, the budget of São Tomé and Príncipe included $35.56 million in public revenue and $38.64 million in public expenditures. The budget deficit amounted to 3.6% of GDP. Public debt was 67.8% of GDP, with $318 million of the debt held by foreign entities.

In 1987, the government instituted an IMF structural adjustment program to encourage private sector growth. This goal has been the focus of economic reform since the early 1990s. São Tomé and Príncipe has traditionally received foreign aid from the UN Development Program, the World Bank, the EU, Portugal, Taiwan, and the African Development Bank. In late 2000, the country qualified for enhanced debt relief through the IMF's Heavily Indebted Poor Countries (HIPC) Initiative.

³⁶TAXATION

Sao Tome and Principe is dependent on import taxes and excise duties, particularly on imported petroleum products. The tax system, generally viewed as outdated and complex, is plagued by weak enforcement, which has led to significant arrears. International organizations, including the Millennium Challenge Corporation, an aid arm of the U.S. Government, are working with the country to improve implementation of the tax code.

Tax reforms enacted in 2009 changed the personal income tax from a flat rate of 13% to a progressive schedule ranging from 10 to 20%. Excise taxes ranging from 5 to 250% are imposed on petroleum products, motor vehicles, alcoholic drinks, tobacco, and services. The social security contribution is 6% of gross salaries and the property tax is 15% on registered value, although exemptions and deductions are available for buildings used as dwellings by owners and their families. There is a 5% sales tax. Corporate income is now taxed at a flat rate of 25%, down from the previous range of 25 to 45%.

In 2008, excise taxes on petroleum and petroleum products accounted for 18% of all tax revenue. Tax revenues were 17.4% of GDP in 2010, up from 13.2% in 2001. The IMF reported that tax revenue collections for the first half of 2011 had exceeded projected levels.

³⁷CUSTOMS AND DUTIES

As of 2011, all imports require a license. Duties are levied on basic goods at 5%, on luxury goods at 20%, and on other goods at 10%. Investment goods are taxed at between 10% and 20%. The duty on imports of raw materials is 5%. Free trade zones were established

Principal Trading Partners – São Tomé and Príncipe (2010)

(In millions of US dollars)

Country	Total	Exports	Imports	Balance
World	136.0	11.0	125.0	-114.0
Portugal	61.1	0.4	60.8	-60.4
Malaysia	20.3	0.0	20.3	-20.3
Netherlands	10.1	4.8	5.3	-0.5
South Korea	5.8	0.1	5.6	-5.5
Belgium	5.4	1.8	3.7	-1.9
Gabon	4.6	0.0	4.6	-4.6
Japan	2.3	0.0	2.2	-2.2
China	2.3	0.0	2.3	-2.3
Egypt	2.0	2.0	...	2.0
France	1.9	0.6	1.3	-0.7

(…) data not available or not significant.

(n.s.) not specified.

SOURCE: *2011 Direction of Trade Statistics Yearbook*, New York: United Nations, 2011.

Balance of Payments – São Tomé and Príncipe (2010)

(In millions of US dollars)

Current Account		**-107.4**
Balance on goods		-87.4
Imports	-99.4	
Exports	12.1	
Balance on services		-22.3
Balance on income		-0.4
Current transfers		2.6
Capital Account		**40.3**
Financial Account		**61.0**
Direct investment abroad		-11.0
Direct investment in São Tomé and Príncipe		24.6
Portfolio investment assets		...
Portfolio investment liabilities		...
Financial derivatives		...
Other investment assets		18.8
Other investment liabilities		17.6
Net Errors and Omissions		**2.3**
Reserves and Related Items		**3.8**

(…) data not available or not significant.

SOURCE: *Balance of Payment Statistics Yearbook 2011*, Washington, DC: International Monetary Fund, 2011.

in 1998, allowing foreign companies to import materials duty free for the manufacture of products for re-export.

Travelers to Sao Tome and Principe are allowed to bring with them reasonable quantities of tobacco, perfume, and gifts duty free. There are no restrictions on cameras, although alcoholic beverages are prohibited and currency must be declared on arrival.

³⁸FOREIGN INVESTMENT

Foreign direct investment (FDI) in Sao Tome and Principe was a net inflow of $7.5 million according to World Bank figures published in 2009. FDI represented 3.94% of GDP.

Since independence, investments have been minimal. An investment code adopted in 1986 allows free transfer of profits, dividends, and liquidated assets, and also exemption from export duties. Some investors may qualify for tax and import-duty exemptions.

In 1999, the government granted Island Oil Exploration Limited the right to develop an offshore logistics center and port to support future oil and gas operations. The combination of foreign investment related to oil exploration and spending on the construction of a new deep-water port has helped the economy expand in 2011. However, the long-term outlook is dependent on the discovery of recoverable oil reserves. The government also hopes for increased investment in the tourism sector.

Important bilateral partners include China, India, and Brazil as well as the neighboring African nations like Nigeria and Angola.

39 ECONOMIC DEVELOPMENT

Since 1987, a World Bank and IMF-sponsored structural adjustment program with the objective of weaning the economy of its dependence on cocoa exports and foodstuff imports drove economic policy. Since 1991, the government has imposed fiscal and economic austerity measures, continued to devalue the currency, reformed the banking sector, raised electricity and fuel prices, and continued to privatize the nonagricultural sector. In 2000, the country became eligible for $200 million in debt relief under the IMF/World Bank Heavily Indebted Poor Countries (HIPC) initiative, and international donors pledged additional aid in 2001. In 2005, the government signed on to a new three-year IMF Poverty Reduction and Growth Facility (PRGF) program worth $4.3 million. In August 2009, the government forged a loan agreement with Portugal designed to peg the nation's currency (the dobra) to the euro, a move that officials hope will ensure financial stability and attract foreign investment.

With the help of the United Nations Development Programme, the government hopes to stabilize cocoa production through long-lease arrangements with private-sector management companies. A shift to black pepper and arabica coffee could revitalize the coffee sector. Food self-sufficiency depends on the success of the government's policy of turning fringe cocoa land over to mixed-agriculture family farmers. Projects to export plantains, cocoyam, and citrus fruits to Gabon are under study. The pork herds are to be reestablished. The fishing, forestry, and tourist industries are being revitalized. The government plans to promote the development of additional food processing and construction material industries, as well as to improve the paved road network.

Other initiatives still in development as of 2011 include tax reform, a new customs code, and revised regulations aimed at reducing the time required to start a business from over 140 day to 4 days.

40 SOCIAL DEVELOPMENT

A national social security system was initially set up in 1979, and was amended in 1990. Old age, disability, and survivorship benefits are paid to all employed persons, including civil service and the military. There are also sickness and maternity benefits, worker's compensation, and a voluntary program for the self-employed. Retirement is set at age 62 for men and age 57 for women.

Women enjoy constitutional equality with men, and some have been government ministers, but in general, they are limited to a subordinate role by the traditional culture. Female literacy is much lower than that of men, and women are underrepresented in the professions. Traditional views inhibit women from seeking redress for domestic abuse and violence. Economic opportunities are further limited to women due to a very high teenage pregnancy rate.

Human rights were generally well respected, although the country suffers from an inefficient judicial system and harsh prison conditions.

41 HEALTH

According to the CIA, life expectancy in Sao Tome and Principe was 66 years in 2011. The government spent 8.7% of its GDP on healthcare, amounting to $91 per person. There were 5 physicians, 19 nurses and midwives, and 32 hospital beds per 10,000 inhabitants.

The fertility rate was 3.7, while the infant mortality rate was 52 per 1,000 live births. The government hopes that crop diversification will help alleviate malnutrition, which continues to plague the country. Tuberculosis is present in the country and presents an increasingly serious health concern. The incidence of tuberculosis was 107 per 100,000 people in 2007. It was estimated that 90% of children were vaccinated against measles.

Access to medical care is limited, the level of care is low, and some medicines are not available. There is one hospital and several foreign-run clinics on the island of Sao Tome. Persons with a serious illness travel out of the country for care.

42 HOUSING

Housing on the islands varies greatly, from the estate houses of the plantation headquarters to the thatch huts of the plantation laborers. Some town buildings are wooden; others are mud block with timber, as are plantation-labor dormitories. At the 2001 census, there were about 33,887 occupied dwellings. Of these, about 35% were built in 1975 or earlier. Wood, cement, and zinc are the most common building materials for walls, floors, and roofs. The 2001 housing census, still the most recent government census as of January 2012, was used by the government to structure its poverty reduction program during the 2000s, which focused on improving rural housing.

43 EDUCATION

The school system before independence was the same as that of Portugal. Schooling is free and compulsory through the 6th grade. However, teachers are poorly trained and teaching materials inadequate. Primary education is for four years and secondary has two stages: the first five years are followed by two more years. In 2009, the World Bank estimated that 97% of age-eligible children in Sao Tome and Principe were enrolled in primary school. The student-to-teacher ratio for primary school was at about 31:1 in 2005.

Secondary enrollment for age-eligible children stood at 32%. There is only one high school, which is overcrowded and underfunded with between 60 and 70 students per classroom. The high school is on the island of Sao Tome and students from Principe wishing to attend must find accommodations to continue their studies.

Tertiary enrollment was estimated at 4%. The Polytechnic Institute of São Tomé and Príncipe is a public institution, established in 1997 primarily as a teacher's college. Its first class graduated in 2001. A private institution, Instituto Universitario de Contabilidade, Administracao e Informatica, was established in 1993. Many students seeking a college education go overseas and a few receive scholarships to study in Portugal. Once there, they tend not to return after graduation.

The government allocates about 20% of the national budget to health and education. Overall, the CIA estimated that São Tomé and Príncipe had a literacy rate of 84.9%.

44 LIBRARIES AND MUSEUMS

São Tomé maintains libraries at the Center for Technical and Scientific Documentation (45,000 volumes) and the national assembly (1,000 volumes). A general National Museum was founded in 1976 and located in the Fortress of Saint Sebastian, constructed in 1585. Its exhibits are mainly of African and religious art.

45 MEDIA

In 2009, the CIA reported that there were 7,800 telephone landlines in São Tomé and Príncipe. In addition to landlines, mobile phone subscriptions averaged 39 per 100 people with an estimated 64,000 cellular phones in use. However, making an international call into the country can be more difficult than calling out. Before 2007, a company half-owned by the government controlled a monopoly over the telecommunication sector. Since then, the market has been opened to competition and the country has benefited from enhanced service that now exceeds that available in most African countries. Internet subscriptions stood at 16 per 100 citizens, although internet cafes are popular with young people. In 2010, the country had 1,514 Internet hosts serving some 26,700 users. There are no government restrictions on access to the Internet or reports that the government monitors email or Internet chat rooms.

The national government operates radio and television broadcasts in Portuguese. The radio station broadcasts 17 hours a day and a television broadcasts five to six hours a day. A regional radio station on Principe started broadcasting in 1999. About 45% of households have a television set. There were no independent radio or television stations, but there is no law forbidding them. The Voice of America, Radio International Portugal, and Radio France International all rebroadcast locally. In 2010, there was 1 FM radio station, 5 AM radio stations, and 1 shortwave radio station.

The constitution provides for the freedoms of speech and of the press and the government generally respects these rights in practice.

46 ORGANIZATIONS

Cooperative movements sponsored by the MLSTP function as part of the government's economic development program. The Youth Movement for the Liberation of São Tomé and Príncipe is a major youth organization for youth ages 15 to 24. There are some sports associations, such as the São Tomé and Príncipe Athletic Federation (track and field) and the São Tomé and Príncipe Football Federation. There are YMCA/YWCA branches in the country. The Red Cross and Caritas also have national chapters.

47 TOURISM, TRAVEL, AND RECREATION

The *Tourism Factbook*, published by the UN World Tourism Organization in 2011, reported 15,200 incoming tourists to Sao Tome and Principe who spent a total of $8.3 million. Of those incoming tourists, there were 6,400 from Europe and 5,200 from nationals residing abroad. There were 609 hotel beds available in Sao Tome and Principe. The estimated daily cost to visit Sao Tome, the capital, was $271. The cost of visiting other cities averaged $305.

São Tomé and Príncipe's scenic beauty, wildlife, and unique historic architecture have the potential to attract tourists, but even though the islands have been a port of call for voyagers for centuries. Tourist facilities are minimal and restricted largely to the port towns and their environs. The first tourist hotel opened in 1986 and the government has encouraged greater private investment in the tourist sector. Two sports facilities opened in 1992. São Tomé has beautiful white sand beaches and a number of coffee and cocoa plantations to explore. All visitors must have visas. A yellow fever vaccination certificate is required if traveling from an infected area.

48 FAMOUS PERSONS

Rei Amador (d. 1596), who rebelled against the Portuguese and almost overran the island in 1595, is a national hero. Alda de Espírito Santo (b.1926) is a poet and nationalist leader. Manuel Pinto da Costa (b.1937), the secretary-general of the MLSTP, became the country's first president on 12 July 1975, a post he held until his party was defeated in the elections of 1991. Miguel Trovoada (b.1936) succeeded Manuel Pinto da Costa as president; he served until 2001. Fradique de Menezes (b.1942) began his presidency in 2001.

49 DEPENDENCIES

São Tomé and Príncipe has no territories or colonies.

50 BIBLIOGRAPHY

Gillespie, Rosemary G., and David A. Clague, eds. *Encyclopedia of Islands.* Berkeley: University of California Press, 2009.

Millennium Challenge Corporation. *São Tomé and Príncipe: Millennium Challenge Corporation Working with São Tomé and Príncipe to Develop and Implement Sound Fiscal Policies.* Washington, DC: Millennium Challenge Corporation, 2007.

Zeilig, Leo, and David Seddon. *A Political and Economic Dictionary of Africa.* Philadelphia: Routledge/Taylor and Francis, 2005.

SENEGAL

Republic of Senegal
République du Sénégal

CAPITAL: Dakar

FLAG: The flag is a tricolor of green, yellow, and red vertical stripes; at the center of the yellow stripe is a green star.

ANTHEM: *Pincez, Tous, vos Koras, Frappez les Balafons (Pluck your koras, strike the balafons).*

MONETARY UNIT: The Communauté Financière Africaine franc (XOF) is the national currency. There are coins of 1, 2, 5, 10, 25, 50, 100, and 500 francs, and notes of 50, 100, 500, 1,000, 5,000, and 10,000 francs. XOF1 = US$0.00202 (or US$1 = XOF495.28) as of 2010.

WEIGHTS AND MEASURES: The metric system is the legal standard.

HOLIDAYS: New Year's Day, 1 January; Independence Day, 4 April; Labor Day, 1 May; Day of Association, 14 July; Assumption, 15 August; All Saints' Day, 1 November; Christmas, 25 December. Movable religious holidays include Eid al-Fitr, Eid al-Adha, Milad an-Nabi, Good Friday, Easter Monday, Ascension, and Pentecost Monday.

TIME: GMT.

¹LOCATION, SIZE, AND EXTENT

Situated on the western bulge of Africa, Senegal has a land area of 196,722 sq. km (75,954 sq mi), extending 690 km (429 mi) SE–NW and 406 km (252 mi) NE–SW. Comparatively, the area occupied by Senegal is slightly smaller than the state of South Dakota. It is bordered on the N and NE by Mauritania, on the E by Mali, on the S by Guinea and Guinea-Bissau, and on the W by the Atlantic Ocean. It is the westernmost point of the African mainland. On the NE the boundary is set by the Senegal River, and on the E by the Falémé River. Senegal surrounds the long, narrow Republic of The Gambia on three sides. The total boundary length of Senegal is 2,640 km (1,640 mi), of which 531 km (330 mi) is coastline.

Senegal's capital city, Dakar, is located on the Atlantic coast. Dakar boasts a population of 2.777 million, representing 22% of total Senegal's population.

²TOPOGRAPHY

The northern part of the Senegal coast has dunes from Cap Vert to Saint-Louis, but to the south are muddy estuaries. Behind the coast is a sandy plain, which extends north to the floodplain of the Senegal River. The Casamance region in the south, isolated from the rest of Senegal by the Republic of The Gambia, is low but more varied in relief, while to the southeast lie the Tamgué foothills, which rise to a maximum altitude of 581 m (1,906 ft.). Much of the northwest of Senegal (known as the Ferlo) is semidesert, but the center and most of the south, except for the forest of Casamance, are open savanna country. The major rivers include the Senegal, Saloum, Gambie, and Casamance. These generally flow from east to west toward the Atlantic.

³CLIMATE

Temperatures are lowest along the coast and highest inland; rainfall is highest in the south and lowest in the north. The wet season, which lasts from June to October, is shorter in the north and longer in the south, especially near the southwest coast. The average annual rainfall ranges from 34 cm (13 in) at Podor in the extreme north to 155 cm (61 in) at Ziguinchor, in the southwest. At Dakar, the average is 57 cm (22 in); at Tambacounda, in the interior, it is 94 cm (37 in). Temperatures vary according to the season, with the highest temperatures registered in the northeast. At Dakar, during the cool season (December–April), the average daily maximum is 26°C (79°F) and the average minimum 17°C (63°F); during the hot season (May–November), the averages are 30°C (86°F) and 20°C (68°F).

An unusually heavy season of rain beginning in August 2005 caused severe flooding in Dakar and the surrounding region. At least 50,000 people had to abandon their homes for makeshift shelters. Unsanitary conditions brought about by flood damage sparked a cholera epidemic that affected over 27,000 nationwide; at least 400 people died from the disease. During 2010, Dakar and the surrounding region experienced increased severe flooding.

⁴FLORA AND FAUNA

The World Resources Institute estimates that there are 2,086 plant species in Senegal. Vegetation varies in different areas of Senegal, depending on the average rainfall. The most tropical part of southern Casamance has mangrove swamps and remnants of high forest, including oil palms, bamboo, African teak, and the silk-cotton tree. The dry thornland of the northeast has spiny shrubs, especially acacia, including the gum-bearing species. Trees, which are widely spaced in this region, include the African locust bean, tallow tree, and gingerbread plum, along with cassias and acacias.

In addition, Senegal is home to 191 mammal, 612 bird, 92 reptile, and 32 amphibian species. The calculation reflects the total number of distinct species residing in the country, not the number of endemic species. The lion and leopard are occasionally found in the northeast, as are chimpanzees, elephants, hippopotamuses, and buffalo. The wild pig, hare, guinea fowl, quail, and bustard are widely distributed. Insects and birds are abundant, and there are numerous lizards, snakes, and other reptiles.

Wildlife populations are threatened by poaching, deforestation, overgrazing, soil erosion, desertification, and overfishing

5 ENVIRONMENT

The World Resources Institute reported that Senegal had designated 2.16 million hectares (5.33 million acres) of land for protection as of 2006. Senegal has at least six national parks. Game in forest reserves is classified by law as partially or completely protected, but poaching remains a problem. Protected areas included four Ramsar wetlands and two natural UNESCO World Heritage Sites. According to a 2011 report issued by the International Union for Conservation of Nature and Natural Resources (IUCN), the number of threatened species included 16 types of mammals, 10 species of birds, 6 types of reptiles, 45 species of fish, and 9 species of plants. Threatened species include the western giant eland and four species of turtle (green sea, olive ridley, hawksbill, and leatherback). The Sahara oryx has become extinct in the wild.

Much of the land is threatened with desertification because of overgrazing, inadequately controlled cutting of forests for fuel, and soil erosion from overcultivation. Dakar suffers from such typical urban problems as improper sanitation (especially during the rainy season, when sewers overflow) and air pollution from motor vehicles. Senegal's cities have produced about 0.6 million tons of solid waste per year. Important environmental agencies include the Ministry of Scientific and Technical Research, which is responsible for coordinating all research and development in Senegal.

Niokolo-Koba National Park, a UNESCO World Heritage Site, is located in an upper stretch of the Gambia River. The park is 9,130 sq. km. Its altitude ranges from 16 m (52 ft) to 311 m (1,020 ft). Niokolo-Koba National Park is world-renowned for its wildlife and the only place in Senegal where there are populations of giraffe, elephant, and lion.

Water resources totaled 39.4 cu km (9.45 cu mi) while water usage was 2.22 cu km (0.533 cu mi) per year. Domestic water usage accounted for 4% of total usage, industrial for 3%, and agricultural for 93%. Per capita water usage totaled 190 cu m (6,710 cu ft.) per year.

The UN reported in 2008 that carbon dioxide emissions in Senegal totaled 5,474 kilotons.

6 POPULATION

The US Central Intelligence Agency (CIA) estimates the population of Senegal in 2011 to be approximately 12,643,799, which placed it at number 71 in population among the 196 nations of the world. In 2011, approximately 2.8% of the population was more than 65 years of age, with another 43.3% less than 15 years of age. The median age in Senegal was 18 years. There were 0.99 males

for every female in the country. The population's annual rate of change was 2.557%. The projected population for the year 2025 was 17,400,000. Population density in Senegal was calculated at 64 people per sq km (166 people per sq mi).

The UN estimated that 43% of the population lived in urban areas, and that urban populations had an annual rate of change of 3.3%. The largest urban area was Dakar, with a population of 2.8 million.

7 MIGRATION

Estimates of Senegal's net migration rate, carried out by the CIA in 2011, amounted to -1.90 migrants per 1,000 citizens. The total number of emigrants living abroad was 636,200, and the total number of immigrants living in Senegal was 210,100. Senegal also accepted 19,630 refugees. There is considerable seasonal migration between The Gambia and Senegal in connection with cultivation and harvesting of peanuts.

Many Senegalese migrate to Europe for work. Many are permitted by visa and some enter illegally. Trans-Saharan travel routes and boats abet African workers migrating to Europe. Popular destinations are France, Spain, and Italy.

8 ETHNIC GROUPS

The largest ethnic group is the Wolof, who makes up about 43.3% of the total population; they live mainly in the northwest. The Pular rank as the second-largest group, constituting 23.8% of the population. Closely related to the Wolof are the Serer (14.7%), in west-central Senegal, who are skilled peanut cultivators, and the Lebu, mostly fishermen and farmers, concentrated in the Dakar area. Other important groups are the Diola of Casamance (Jola), making up 3.7% of the populace; the Mandinka, in the southeast and in Casamance, accounting for 3%; the Soninke constituting 1.1%; the Tukulor, who live predominantly in the northeast; and the Fulani (Peul) and Bambara, scattered throughout the country. Europeans and Lebanese make up about 1% of the total population; other various groups constitute the remaining 9.4%.

9 LANGUAGES

French, the official language, is the language of administration and of the schools. Indigenous languages are also widely spoken, the major ones being Wolof, Pular, Diola, and Mandingo.

10 RELIGIONS

Government reports indicate that about 94% of the people are Muslim, with members of the Tijaniya and Muridiya brotherhoods having great social, political, and economic influence. About 4% of Senegalese are Christians, including Roman Catholics and a number of Protestant denominations. The remaining 2% practice exclusively traditional indigenous religions or no religion at all. The constitution provides for the freedom of religion and defines the country as a secular state. However, the government does offer grant money to religious organizations through an application process that is open to all. Registration is not required, but most organizations do so in order to obtain full legal status to conduct business. The government encourages and supports Muslim pilgrimages to the Mecca and Catholic pilgrimages to the Vatican. Tabaski (Abraham's sacrifice), Tamkharit, the Birth of the Prophet Muhammad, Korite (end of Ramadan), Easter Monday,

Ascension, Pentecost, Feast of the Assumption, All Saints' Day, and Christmas are observed as national holidays.

11 TRANSPORTATION

The CIA reports that Senegal has a total of 14,008 km (8,704 mi) of roads as of 2006, of which 4,099 km (2,547 mi) are paved. There are 23 vehicles per 1,000 people in the country. As of 2008, Senegal had 906 km (562 mi) of railroad, all narrow gauge and all owned by the government. The main lines run from Dakar to Thiès and thence to Kidira on the Mali border, and from Thiès to Saint-Louis. There are also branch lines from Guinguineo to Kaolack, from Louga to Linguère, and from Diourbel to Touba, serving the peanut-growing areas. There are modern roads from Dakar to Thiès, Saint-Louis, and Matam, and from Dakar to Kaolack and on through The Gambia to Ziguinchor in Casamance.

Favorably located at the westernmost point of the continent and possessing up-to-date equipment, Dakar is one of the largest deep-water seaports on the West African coast, a major import-export center and a port of call for freight and passenger ships. The port can accommodate ships of up to 100,000 tons. The Senegalese Maritime Navigation Co. (Compagnie Sénégalaise de Navigation Maritime—COSENAM), a river and ocean freight transport line in which the government has an 84% share, was founded in 1979. Senegal has approximately 1,000 km (621 mi) of navigable waterways. The Senegal River, which has a sandbar across its mouth, is navigable by shallow-draft vessels all year round from Saint-Louis to Podor (225 km/140 mi) and between August and October as far as Kayes in Mali (924 km/574 mi). It is closed to foreign ships. The Saloum is navigable by oceangoing vessels to the important peanut port of Kaolack, 114 km (71 mi) upriver. The Casamance River is navigable to Ziguinchor, although not without difficulty.

In 2009 there were 10 airports with paved runways. Dakar's Yoff International Airport, a West African air center, is served by many foreign airlines. Air France, Air Senegal, and Air Afrique maintain routes connecting Saint-Louis, Thiès, Ziguinchor, Kédougou, Tambacounda, and 10 other towns with secondary air fields. Air Senegal is 50% owned by the government and 40% by Air Afrique, in which Senegal also holds a 7% share.

12 HISTORY

Very little is known about the history of Senegal before the 16th century. The major feature seems to have been the gradual movement into Senegal of the Wolof and Sérer peoples from the northeast, who reached their present positions between the 10th and 15th centuries AD. At various times parts of Senegal were included in the empires of Tekrur, Ghana, and Mali. At the height of its power at the beginning of the 14th century, Mali controlled the Falémé and Upper Senegal. That century saw the emergence of the Jolof Empire, controlling the six Wolof states of Jolof, Kayor, Baol, Walo, Sine, and Salum. In the middle of the 16th century, Kayor revolted and conquered Baol, but the other Wolof states continued to admit a shadowy suzerainty of Jolof. As the power of Kayor and Baol increased toward the end of the 17th century, however, Jolof's power declined, probably because it was cut off by those states from access to the sea and European trading. The 18th and early 19th centuries were marked by struggles among the northernmost Wolof states and by sporadic Mauritanian attacks on them.

European activities in Senegal began with the arrival of the Portuguese at the Cap Vert Peninsula and the mouth of the Senegal River in 1445. The Portuguese enjoyed a monopoly on trade in slaves and gold until the 17th century, when they were succeeded by the Dutch, who virtually dominated all trade by 1650. The later 17th century brought the beginnings of the Anglo-French rivalry, which dominated the 18th century in Senegal as elsewhere. Throughout the 17th and 18th centuries, the main trading activities were the export of slaves and of gum arabic. Peanut cultivation by African peasants, the foundation of Senegal's modern economy, began in the mid-19th century.

French rule was confined to the old trading posts of Saint-Louis (founded in 1659), Gorée, and Rufisque until its expansion under the Second Empire, during the governorship of Gen. Louis Faidherbe (1854–65). The French occupation of Senegal was consolidated and extended under the Third Republic during the last three decades of the 19th century. In 1871, Senegal was again allowed to send a deputy to the French parliament, a right that had been abolished under the Second Empire. In the following decade, municipalities on the French model were established in Saint-Louis, Gorée, Dakar, and Rufisque, and only the inhabitants of these towns took part in the elections of the deputy.

Between 1895 and 1904, a series of decrees consolidated eight territories into a French West Africa federation, of which Dakar became the capital. In 1920, a Colonial Council, partly elected by the citizens of the old towns and partly consisting of chiefs from the rest of Senegal, replaced the elected General Council previously established for the four towns. All the elected bodies were suppressed in 1940 but restored at the end of the war, and in 1946 Senegal was given two deputies in the French parliament. Under the constitution of 1946, the franchise was extended and a Territorial Assembly was established in Senegal. Universal suffrage was established in 1957. In 1958, Senegal accepted the new French constitution and became an autonomous republic within the French community.

On 17 January 1959, in Dakar, representatives of French Sudan (now Mali), Senegal, Dahomey (now Benin), and Upper Volta (now Burkina Faso) drafted a constitution for a Federation of Mali, but only the assemblies of French Sudan and Senegal ratified it and became members of the federation. The Mali Federation became a sovereign state on 20 June 1960, but conflicting views soon led to its breakup. On 20 August, the Legislative Assembly of Senegal proclaimed Senegal's national independence and announced its withdrawal from the federation. A new republican constitution was adopted on 25 August, and on 5 September, Léopold-Sédar Senghor was elected president and Mamadou Dia became prime minister, in effect retaining a position he had held since 1957.

After an attempt by Dia to avoid a vote of no-confidence in the National Assembly by calling out the national police, the legislature met in a special session on 17 December 1962 and overthrew Dia's government by a motion of censure. Dia was arrested, and Senghor was elected by unanimous vote of the deputies as head of government. Less than three months later, the electorate approved a new constitution that abolished the post of prime minister and made the president both chief of state and head of the executive branch. A constitutional amendment in 1970 reestablished the office of prime minister, and Abdou Diouf, former minister of planning and industry was appointed to the post on 26 February 1970. Dia, in detention since 1962, was released in March 1974 as part of an independence celebration.

Having been reelected president in 1968, 1973, and 1978, Senghor resigned as president at the end of 1980 and was succeeded by Diouf. In the summer of 1981, 2,000 Senegalese troops were sent to The Gambia to put down an attempted military coup there. The Confederation of Senegambia was constituted in February 1982 with Diouf as president. Under the terms of confederation, the two countries pledged to integrate their armed and security forces, form an economic and monetary union, and coordinate foreign policy, communications, and possibly other endeavors. The Senegambia agreement was dissolved on 30 September 1989. Diouf was elected to a full term as president on 27 February 1983, receiving 83.5% of the vote in a five-candidate contest. All parties were guaranteed equal access to the media, but the secret ballot was optional, and independent observers reported widespread electoral irregularities. The office of prime minister constitutionally regarded as the president's successor was once again abolished in April 1983.

The ruling Parti Socialiste Sénégalais (PS) was victorious in municipal and rural elections held in November 1984, although 12 of the 15 registered parties boycotted the polls. Diouf liberalized the political process and restructured his administration, making it less corrupt and more efficient. Government advocated modulated reform in the face of reactionary elements in the PS.

In the 1988 national elections, Diouf carried 77% of the vote and the PS took 103 of the 120 seats in the National Assembly. Despite a generally fair election, opposition protests escalated into rioting in Dakar. The city was placed under a three-month state of emergency. Diouf's principal opponent, Maitre Abdoulaye Wade of the Democratic Party, was among those arrested and tried for incitement. Afterwards, Diouf met with Wade and tensions eased.

In April 1989, a nationwide state of emergency was declared and a curfew imposed in Dakar after rioters killed dozens of Mauritanians. Protesters had been enraged by reports of the killing of hundreds of Senegalese in Mauritania. Relations with Mauritania were broken and armed clashes along the border and internal rioting led to the expulsion of most Mauritanians residing in Senegal. Diplomatic relations were reestablished in April 1992 and the northern border along the Senegal River was reopened.

In April 1991, Wade accepted the post of Minister of State in Diouf's cabinet. Diouf appointed Habib Thiam as prime minister on 7 April 1991, who then appointed the Council of Ministers in consultation with President Diouf.

Diouf and PS again won reelection in February 1993. His margin of victory, however, shrank to 58% versus 32% for Wade. The PS took only 84 seats in the May legislative elections and the PDS increased its representation from 17 to 27 seats. The Jappoo Leggeeyal Senegalese Party and the Democratic League won three seats each. Two other parties took the other three seats. Wade and other opponents denounced the elections as fraudulent, though international observers declared them generally free and fair. When the vice president of the Constitutional Court was murdered after the elections were officially certified, Wade and other PDS members were charged in the slaying. He and MPs with parliamentary immunity were later released. Political discontent followed these events and an opposition party demonstration in 1994 left six police officers dead and many civilians injured.

In November 1996, the government initiated a decentralization policy that devolved considerable political and administrative authority to the provinces. In July 1998, it undertook a major reshuffling of ministers and ministerial posts, and in November, it signed a peace accord with Guinea-Bissau that was intended to establish a buffer zone along the southern border. In keeping with the accord, the Senegalese army withdrew its 2,500 troops supporting then president, Joao Bernardo Vieira. Togolese, Gambian and Nigerian soldiers under ECOMOG replaced the Senegalese troops.

Since December 1983, the Movement of Democratic Forces of the Casamance (MFDC) has waged a low-level separatist war against the Senegalese government. The Movement splintered in 1991 and signed peace accords with the Senegalese government in 1991, 1993 and in December 1999 in Banjul. In 1992 and 1995, Senegalese warplanes bombed rebel bases in Guinea-Bissau suspected of providing safe havens and resupply points for the rebels. In March 1996, the two governments reached an accord. President Jammeh of The Gambia, who belongs to the same dominant Diola ethnic group of the Casamance, and officials in Guinea-Bissau have mediated the conflict. Despite Abdoulaye Wade's campaign promises to end the insurgency through negotiations and military means, by June 2003 the fighting continued unabated. A deal reached in December 2004 has held up reasonably; but it could be undermined by in-fighting in the ruling PDS or between groups in the Casamance region.

In January 1999, the PS won highly controversial Senate elections by a landslide, taking all 45 elected seats. However, a boycott by the two largest opposition parties undermined the Senate's credibility. The bill to create the Senate had been pushed through by the PS-dominated National Assembly in February 1998, thereby increasing the ruling party's representation. The voting rules also ensured a majority of PS politicians in the electoral college.

In April 2000, Abdoulaye Wade was inaugurated as Senegal's third president. The February elections were the first in Senegal's history to result in a change of government. Although Diouf won 41.3% of the vote on the first round, PS defectors Moustapha Niasse (AFP) and Djibo Leyti Ka (URD) threw their support behind Wade to give him 58.5% on the 19 March second round. His victory not only ended 40 years of rule by the Parti Socialiste, but it also ended speculation that Senegal's quasi-democracy was moribund. Using their cell phones, Senegalese youth called in results, which were broadcast by electronic media to prevent fraud.

Wade's record over his first three years in office was mixed. In December 2001, he became head of the Economic Community of West African States (ECOWAS), and the Union Economique et Monétaire Ouest-Africaine (UEMOA). In April 2002, Senegal hosted an international conference on the New Partnership for Africa's Development (NEPAD). As promised, he began building primary schools around the country. However, strikes by postal workers, bank employees, and teachers indicated considerable social unrest owing to unmet wage and benefits demands. The government's delay of local elections in the fall of 2001 and the replacement of elected officials with appointees (délégations spéciales) were widely criticized as antidemocratic.

Wade also fell out with some of the young bright stars with whom he rode to power in 2000. One example is Idrissa Seck. As prime minister, Seck claimed to know Wade's vision intimately; so he needed no prodding to work seamlessly with the president. Yet Seck's dismissal in April 2004 seemed questionable. In July 2005, he was arrested for inflating public contracts; when this spurred protests, he was jailed and then charged for undermining state security. Seck's supporters believed however that his travails were all political, that he had become influential in the PDS and announced his candidature for the 2007 presidential elections. All this, they argued, made him a threat to Wade's political ambition. In February 2006, Seck was released from jail after charges against him were dropped.

The Wade government released a poverty reduction strategy paper (PRSP) within the specified timeframe. It reduced the budget deficit, and improved relations with the IMF.

In August 2006, the army launched an offensive against rebels from a faction of the MFDC in Casamance. That month, Senegal and Spain agreed to jointly patrol the Senegalese coast to stop the flight of illegal migrants to Europe. Many migrants set off for Europe from Senegal in unseaworthy boats. Later that year, Spain and Senegal agreed to a series of measures to stem the flow of illegal migration to the Canary Islands. Spain agreed to grant 4,000 Senegalese temporary work permits until 2008.

In February 2007, Wade was reelected president with some 56% of the vote, which was enough to avoid a second-round ballot. After being elected, Wade warned that corruption cases involving his opponents would be reopened. The Socialist Party, in opposition, declared it would challenge the results. That June, legislative elections were held, and Wade's ruling coalition increased its majority in parliament. The elections were boycotted by the opposition. In June 2009, the parliament voted to create the new post of vice president, to be appointed by the president. Political opposition leaders speculate that the new post has been designed specifically as a means for Wade to position his son, Karim, as the next president. Karim Wade was appointed to a senior ministry point in May. Despite a constitutional two-term limit, the Constitutional Court announced in January 2012 that Wade could stand for a third term.

In 2008, Senegal finished in tenth position on the Ibrahim Index of African Governance based solely on the government's good record of successful dealings with its people. Senegal has a long history of international peacekeeping and regional mediation. On 22 February 2011, Senegal severed diplomatic ties with Iran, saying Tehran supplied Cassamance rebels with sophisticated weapons that were used by rebels and caused the deaths of Senegalese soldiers.

13 GOVERNMENT

Under the 2001 constitution, the president of the republic is head of state. The prime minister is head of the government, and appoints the Council of Ministers in consultation with the president.

Legislative power is exercised by the 150-member National Assembly, elected to serve five-year terms, and a 100-seat Senate. The Senate was abolished as a result of the 2001 constitutional referendum, but reestablished in 2007. Of the 100 members of the Senate, 35 are indirectly elected and the remaining 65 members appointed by the president.

14 POLITICAL PARTIES

The Senegal branch of the French Socialist Party (SFIO) won the first postwar elections largely because its leaders constituted the only organized party that had contacts in all parts of the colony. It sought to establish political and juridical equality between French and Senegalese citizens. In 1948, however, its leaders, Ahmadou Lamine-Guèye and Léopold-Sédar Senghor, quarreled. Senghor left the SFIO and founded a new party, the Senegalese Democratic Bloc (Bloc Démocratique Sénégalais—BDS), which was based more in the rural areas than in the old communes, from which Lamine-Guèye derived his political support. The new party emphasized social and economic rather than juridical issues and geared its program closely to peasant interests and grievances. In 1951, it won both Senegalese seats in the French National Assembly and, in 1952, 43 of the 50 seats in Senegal's Territorial Assembly.

In the French National Assembly, Senghor had meanwhile taken a leading part in creating a new parliamentary group, the Overseas Independents (Indépendants d'Outre—MerIOM), emphasizing African and colonial problems. It was, however, confronted by another African party, the African Democratic Rally (Rassemblement Démocratique Africain—RDA), founded in October 1946 by African deputies hostile to the provisions of the constitution of 1946 regarding the overseas territories. Although the RDA substantially reduced the number of seats held by the IOM in the French parliament, in Senegal it made no inroads on the two established parties, the BDS and the SFIO.

Senghor and his associate Mamadou Dia secured overwhelming majorities at the parliamentary elections in 1956 and launched a campaign to unite all Senegalese parties. They faced the opposition of Lamine-Guèye, who sponsored a first attempt to create an African Socialist movement loosely associated with the SFIO, and of the RDA leadership, which aimed at bringing about the unity of all parties within the RDA.

In 1956, Senghor's party, the BDS, was reorganized to become the Popular Senegalese Bloc (Bloc Popular Sénégalais), which took a strongly nationalistic stance. In the Territorial Assembly elections in 1957, the first held under complete universal suffrage, it won 47 seats, while the SFIO won only 12. Lamine-Guèye and Senghor were reconciled in 1958 and their respective parties fused in April 1958 to form the Senegalese Progressive Union (Union Progressiste Sénégalaise—UPS). The UPS supported the new French constitution in the referendum of September 1958, and in the elections to the Senegal legislature in 1959 it won all 80 seats. After independence in 1960, the UPS remained the dominant political party. President Senghor was its secretary-general, and the party's National Council was responsible for major national policy decisions. In 1976, the UPS changed its name to the Senegalese Socialist Party (Parti Socialiste Sénégalais—PS), after joining the Socialist International.

There was no legal opposition party from 1966 until 1974, when Abdoulaye Wade obtained permission from Senghor to create the Senegalese Democratic Party (Parti Démocratique Sénégalais—PDS). The PDS won 17 Assembly seats in 1978, compared with 83 for the PS.

In 1981, the constitution, which had restricted the number of political parties to four, was amended to end all restrictions. In 1982, the government amended the electoral law for the legislature so that half the deputies would be elected on a basis of proportional representation, while the remaining members were chosen by direct suffrage. This helped the regime win the 1983 presidential and legislative elections in which Diouf received 83.5% of the votes cast. Presidential and legislative elections held in 1988 were marred by rioting in cities and minor conflicts in rural areas, but Diouf officially received 73.2% of the votes cast.

Seven parties contested the National Assembly elections of 9 May 1993. The PS won 84 seats; the PDS won 27; the Jappoo Leggeeyal ("Let Us Unite") Party and the Democratic League won three seats each; the Independence and Labor Party (PIT) won two seats; and the Senegalese Democratic Union/Renewal party got one.

Although many people have lamented Senegal's "stalled" democratic transition, democrats may be encouraged by the growth of party competition. From 1983 to 1993, the PDS increased its share of representation in the Assembly from 8 to 27 seats, while the number of PS seats declined from 111 to 84. In presidential elections over the same period of time, Abdoulaye Wade's percentage of the vote climbed from 15% to 32%, while Diouf's dropped from 83% to 58%. The number of officially recognized parties in Senegal has gone from one in 1973 to 26 in 1997. From 1978 to 1996, the number of parties contesting legislative elections went from 4 to 14.

In the February/March 2000 presidential elections, eight parties presented candidates. Diouf's PS enjoyed the support of several tiny parties, and a coalition of four parties known as the Convergence Patriotique (CP). The CP comprised the Bloc des Centristes Gainde (BCG) led by Jean-Paul Dais, the Parti Liberal Senegalais (PLS), led by Ousmane Ngom, Serigne Diop's Parti Démocratique Sénégalais-Renovation (PDS-R), and the Parti Africain de l'Indépendence (PAI) of Majmouth Diop. The PAI was once Marxist, while the three others emerged from splits in the PDS. On the other hand, Wade's PDS claimed the backing of the Pole de Gauche, a left-wing coalition of the And-jeff/Parti Africain pour la Démocratie et le Socialisme (AJ/PADS), and the Ligue Démocratique-Mouvement Travail (PIT).

However, the real difference in the outcome of the 19 March second round was the support of Moustapha Niasse (AFP) and to a lesser extent, Djibo Ka (URD), both defectors from the PS who formed their own parties. Wade's subsequent appointment of Niasse as his prime minister all but confirmed the belief among Niasse's supporters that they were voting for a Wade-Niasse ticket. On the first round, Diouf obtained 41%, Wade 30%, Niasse 17%, Ka 7%, with four other candidates picking up the remaining 4% of the vote. Wade's second round alliance gave him an easy victory over Diouf with 58.5% of the vote.

The parliamentary elections held on 29 April 2001 gave Abdoulaye Wade's SOPI coalition an overwhelming victory with 89 seats to 11 for the AFP, 10 for the PS, and 10 for other parties. In the municipal and local elections of 12 May 2002, Wade's coalition, the Convergence des actions autour du Président en perspective du 21ème siècle (CAP 21) captured a majority of the 433 posts. The opposition joined forces under the Cadre Permanent de Concertation (CPC), which included the Parti de l'indépendence et Travail (PIT), the Parti Socialiste (PS), the Union pour le Renouveau Démocratique (URD), and Alliance des Forces de Progrès (AFP). They attacked the government for failing to privatize the electric utility, for bungling groundnut sector reforms, and for mishandling relations with unions and multilateral lending institutions.

In the presidential election of February 2007, Abdoulaye Wade of the PDS was reelected with 55.9% of the vote. The next elections for the assembly were held in June 2007. The election was boycotted by 12 opposition parties, including the former ruling Socialist Party, which resulted in a record-low, 35% voter turnout. The SOPI coalition, led by President Wade's PDS, won 131 seats; others won 19 seats. In the August 2007 Senate elections, 34 seats were won by the PDS, the AJ/PADS party won 1 seat, and 65 other seats were to be appointed by the president.

The next presidential election was scheduled for 26 February 2012.

15 LOCAL GOVERNMENT

Senegal's local administrative organization consists of eleven regions; Fatick, Kaolack, Kolda, Ziguinchor, Tambacounda, Saint-Louis, Thiès, Diourbel, Louga, Matam, and Dakareach headed by an appointed governor and an elected local assembly. The regions are divided into 34 departments, each headed by a prefect, who is assisted by two special secretaries. The departments in turn are divided into 103 districts (*arrondissements*), each headed by a subprefect. In rural areas the basic administrative unit is the ru-

ral community, usually made up of a group of villages with a total population of about 10,000.

In 1996 the assembly passed a comprehensive decentralization law that devolves significant authorities to lower levels of government for taxation, service delivery, and local management of resources, although implementation has been slow and uneven.

16 JUDICIAL SYSTEM

The legal system is based on French civil law. In 1992 the Supreme Court was replaced by the Council of State for Administrative Questions, the Constitutional Council, and a Court of Appeals (*Cour de Cassation*). Judicial review of legislative acts takes place in the Constitutional Court; the Council of State audits the government's accounting office. Senegal accepts compulsory ICJ (International Court of Justice) jurisdiction with reservations.

The constitution declares the independence of the judiciary, from the executive, the legislature, and the armed forces. Judges are appointed by the president after nomination by the minister of justice. In practice, low pay and political ties make magistrates vulnerable to outside pressures.

Criminal defendants are presumed innocent until proven guilty and are afforded public trials, and the right to legal counsel, among other procedural rights. Muslims have the right to choose customary law or civil law for cases involving family inheritance.

17 ARMED FORCES

The International Institute for Strategic Studies reports that armed forces in Senegal totaled 13,620 members in 2011. The force is comprised of 11,900 from the army, 950 from the navy, and 770 members of the air force. Armed forces represent .3% of the labor force in Senegal. Defense spending totaled $335.5 million and accounted for 1.4% of GDP.

Senegal has supplied troops for service in several UN peacekeeping efforts. France maintains an estimated 1,100 military personnel in Senegal.

In 2010 rebels from the Movement of Democratic Forces of Casamance, a separatist group in Senegal, launched attacks that caused hundreds of residents to flee into The Gambia. The rebels, known by the French acronym MFDC, have been fighting a low-level insurgency for independence in the Casamance region of Senegal since the early 1980s. The government and the MFDC signed a peace accord in 2004, but sporadic violence continues to plague the region and displace civilians.

18 INTERNATIONAL COOPERATION

Senegal was admitted to the UN on 28 September 1960 and is a member of ECA and several nonregional specialized agencies, such as the FAO, IAEA, the World Bank, ILO, UNESCO, UNIDO, and the WHO. Senegal was a member of the UN Security Council in 1988–89. Senegal is a member of the ACP Group, the African Development Bank, ECOWAS, the Organization of the Islamic Conference (OIC), G-15, G-77, the WTO, the West African Economic and Monetary Union (WAEMU), the Community of Sahel and Saharan States (CENSAD), and the African Union. The nation is also a part of the Organization for the Development of the Senegal River (founded in 1975) and the Organization for the Development of the Gambia River (founded in 1978). Senegal remains in the Franc Zone. It was one of the founding governments of the New Partnership for Africa's Development (NEPAD).

Senegal has sent troops to Côte d'Ivoire as part of an ECOWAS peacekeeping force. The country has also offered support to UN missions and operations in Kosovo (est. 1999), Liberia (est. 2003), Burundi (est. 2004), and the DROC (est. 1999). Senegal is part of the Nonaligned Movement.

In environmental cooperation, Senegal is part of the Basel Convention, Conventions on Biological Diversity and Whaling, Ramsar, CITES, the Kyoto Protocol, the Montréal Protocol, MARPOL, the Nuclear Test Ban Treaty, and the UN Conventions on the Law of the Sea, Climate Change and Desertification.

[19]ECONOMY

The GDP rate of change in Senegal, as of 2010, was 4.2%. Inflation stood at 1.2%, and unemployment was reported at 48%. Although tourism and services provide a majority of GDP, most of the workforce is employed in agriculture, with peanuts as a primary export commodity. Fishing and phosphate mining are also important exchange industries.

In 1979 Senegal began a long-term structural adjustment program under the direction of the World Bank, the IMF, and bilateral donors. The program was aimed at reducing government deficits, the rate of inflation, and the negative trade balance. The government carried out a major program of privatization of the parastatal enterprises, reducing or eliminating its holdings in 30 of the approximately 40 institutions targeted. Some success was realized and from 1991 to 1992 the economy grew. However, due to depressed economic conditions, low world prices for its exports, and its lack of international competitiveness, Senegal failed to meet most of its 1992 structural adjustment targets. Consequently, the country sank deeper into debt and low or no growth was predicted for 1993.

In January 1994, France devalued the CFA franc, causing its value to drop in half. Immediately, prices for almost all imported goods soared as the inflation rate hit 32%. In the face of rising prices, thousands demonstrated against the government. The government responded by imposing temporary price controls in an effort to prevent price-gouging by local merchants and halt the sharp rise in inflation.

After the initial shock, the devaluation began to pay dividends. Senegal was also helped by debt rescheduling and more than $1.5 billion in financial aid from the World Bank and other international donors. Into 2007, Senegal continued to depend heavily on foreign assistance, which represented about 23% of overall government spending.

As of 2007, more than 80% of GDP represented private activity and significant parastatal companies had been privatized, including water, telecommunications, mining, and aviation. However, the government still remained the country's largest single employer.

Tourism declined as a result of the 2008–09 global financial crisis, prompting industry leaders to call upon the government for support. In particular, agencies have asked the government to reduce its tax on flights into the country, which accounts for more than 50% of the cost of airfare. The global crisis has also been responsible for a serious decline in the amount of remittances sent to Senegal from citizens overseas. An estimated $2 billion in remittances are sent each year, with more than 70% of all Senegalese who live and work overseas sending money to family members who remain in Senegal. For some rural residents, these remittances are their sole source of income.

The economy of Senegal depends heavily on foreign aid. In 2009, Senegal received an aid package of $3.7 million from the US Agency for International Development (USAID) to further improve agricultural production and reduce rates of malnutrition. The same year, the United States approved $13.9 million in funding from the Millennium Challenge Corporation that will be used toward improvements in water supply and roads throughout the country. In January 2009, China pledged $11.5 million for public projects that will include a new children's hospital and a national theater in Dakar. The IMF approved a policy support instrument for Senegal in 2010; it was scheduled to run through 2013 to assist with economic reforms.

[20]INCOME

The CIA estimated that in 2010 the GDP of Senegal was $23.88 billion. The CIA defines GDP as the value of all final goods and services produced within a nation in a given year and computed on the basis of purchasing power parity (PPP) rather than value as measured on the basis of the rate of the exchange based on current dollars. The per capita GDP was estimated at $1,900. The annual growth rate of GDP was 4.2%. The average inflation rate was 1.2%. It was estimated that agriculture accounted for 14.9% of GDP, industry 21.4%, and services 63.6%.

According to the World Bank, remittances from citizens living abroad totaled $1.4 billion or about $108 per capita and accounted for approximately 5.7% of GDP.

The World Bank reported that in 2009, household consumption in Senegal totaled $10.7 billion or about $845 per capita, measured in current US dollars rather than PPP. Household consumption includes expenditures of individuals, households, and nongovernmental organizations on goods and services, excluding the purchases of dwellings. It was estimated that household consumption was growing at an average annual rate of 5.3%.

The World Bank estimated that Senegal, with 0.18% of the world's population, accounted for 0.03% of the world's GDP. By comparison, the United States, with 4.85% of the world's population, accounted for 22.51% of world GDP.

As of 2011 the most recent study by the World Bank reported that actual individual consumption in Senegal was 80.5% of GDP and accounted for 0.04% of world consumption. By comparison, the United States accounted for 25.44% of world individual consumption. The World Bank also estimated that 42.9% of Senegal's GDP was spent on food and beverages, 13.3% on housing and household furnishings, 4.3% on clothes, 4.3% on health, 3.2% on transportation, 4.4% on communications, 1.9% on recreation, 0.8% on restaurants and hotels, and 1.1% on miscellaneous goods and services and purchases from abroad.

It was estimated that in 2001 about 54% of the population subsisted on an income below the poverty line established by Senegal's government.

[21]LABOR

As of 2010, Senegal had a total labor force of 5.532 million people. Within that labor force, CIA estimates in 2007 noted that 77.5%

were employed in agriculture, 11.5% in industry, and 11% in the service sector.

Senegal's fundamental labor legislation is based on the French overseas labor code of 1952, which provides for collective agreements between employers and trade unions, for the fixing of basic minimum wages by the government on recommendation of advisory committees. The code also provides for paid annual leave and for child allowances. The right to strike is recognized by law, and there are special labor courts. The largest trade union organization is the National Confederation of Senegalese Workers, which since 1970 has been the official union affiliated with the ruling PS. Its major rival is the National Union of Autonomous Labor Unions of Senegal. The industrial workforce is almost totally unionized. Although the relative number of union members is small, they have considerable political power due to their control of vital segments of the economy.

The minimum working age is 16, when minors may work in apprenticeships. The prohibition of child labor is strictly enforced in the formal sector, but somewhat less so in the informal and traditional economies. The labor law provides for a workweek of 40 to 48 hours and minimum occupational and safety and health regulations. However, these labor regulations are not effectively enforced outside of the formal economy. The minimum wage was $0.42 per hour in 2010.

22 AGRICULTURE

Most of Senegal lies within the drought-prone Sahel region, with irregular rainfall and generally poor soils. With only about 5% of the land irrigated, the heavy reliance on rain-fed cultivation results in large fluctuations in production. Most Senegalese farms are small (1.4 hectares/3.9 acres), and about 60% are in the so-called Peanut Basin, east of Dakar. Much of the agricultural land is still communally owned.

Roughly 13% of the total land is farmed, and the country's major crops include peanuts, millet, corn, sorghum, rice, cotton, tomatoes, and green vegetables. Cereal production in 2009 amounted to 1.9 million tons, fruit production 223,228 tons, and vegetable production 577,870 tons.

Since independence, the Senegalese government has developed a system of generally small cooperatives to rationalize agricultural production and marketing and to free the farmers from chronic indebtedness to private traders; these were replaced in 1984 by a network of "village sections" with financial autonomy. Parastatal agencies guarantee minimum prices of major agricultural crops, including peanuts, millet, sorghum, rice, and cotton.

In theory, all peanuts are processed locally, and prices of processed peanut oil and other peanut products are set by parastatal agencies. Production of unshelled peanuts varies widely because of periodic drought, and production is frequently underreported because of unauthorized sales to processors in neighboring countries. Cotton, Senegal's other major export crop, is produced and marketed under the direction of the Society for the Development of Textile Fibers (Société de Développement des Fibres Textiles—SODEFITEX).

In the mid-2000s, the government began to intensify its promotion of agricultural programs targeted at domestic food production, particularly rice. Projects along the Senegal River have shown such significant progress that the government projected potential self-sufficiency in rice by 2012. In a country where food security is a major issue and the cost of imported food is high, this would be a major achievement. Additional aid for agriculture was offered in August 2009, as the European Union (EU) allocated more than $15.6 million (€10.9 million) in grant funds to benefit small farmers in Senegal. As part of the EU Food Facility program, funds will be used to support projects of crop diversification and collective farming that will improve the efficiency of small farms and boost local production. In association with the UN World Food Program, additional projects will provide food in exchange for work on irrigation and flood prevention projects. All of these projects are designed to address the challenge of food security in the nation as well as boost the local economy.

23 ANIMAL HUSBANDRY

The UN Food and Agriculture Organization (FAO) reported that Senegal dedicated 5.6 million hectares (13.8 million acres) to permanent pasture or meadow in 2009. During that year, the country tended 44 million chickens, 3.3 million head of cattle, and 332,260 pigs. The production from these animals amounted to 62,224 tons of beef and veal, 11,565 tons of pork, 37,203 tons of poultry, 22,339 tons of eggs, and 313,407 tons of milk. Senegal also produced 9,325 tons of cattle hide. Hides are exported or used in local shoe production and handicrafts.

Raising livestock is a primary activity in the northern section of Senegal and a secondary one for farmers in the southern and central regions. Cattle are raised mainly by the Sérer and by nomadic Fulani. Sheep and goats are important in parts of the southwest. Cattle imported from Mauritania meet part of the nation's meat requirements, but livestock are also exported to neighboring countries. Substantial quantities of cheese, butter, and canned and powdered milk are imported.

The poultry sector consists of a few commercial producers and an important informal sector that also raises the chicks produced by the commercial sector. In 1996, an outbreak of Newcastle disease disrupted local egg production, and producers began vaccinating chicks at the breeding farms. Due to the large size of the traditional poultry sector, there is always disease present.

24 FISHING

Senegal has a flourishing fishing industry, and Dakar is one of the most important Atlantic tuna ports. Senegal had 176 decked commercial fishing boats in 2008. The annual capture totaled 447,754 tons according to the UN FAO. The export value of seafood totaled $251.7 million.

25 FORESTRY

Approximately 44% of Senegal is covered by forest. Bushfires are common in Senegal. The high frequency of fire combined with overgrazing contributes to the desertification of woodlands in Senegal. Timber production is small, with firewood and charcoal being the most important forest products. Senegal is highly vulnerable to declining rainfall and desertification. The UN FAO estimated the 2009 roundwood production at 794,000 cu m (28 million cu ft.), a 76% decline compared with 2004. In 2009, the value of all forest products, including roundwood, totaled $6.2 million.

²⁶MINING

Phosphate rock, fertilizer, petroleum refining, and the production of construction materials were among the minerals produced by Senegal in 2009. Mining has taken on added importance for Senegal's economy in the postindependence era, with phosphate rock, phosphoric acid, fertilizer production, artisanal gold, and petroleum exploration playing key roles in the country's economy. In 2009, production of aluminum phosphate was estimated at 4,000 metric tons. Calcium phosphate production that same year was estimated at 948,000 metric tons, up from 645,000 metric tons in 2008. Calcium phosphate-based fertilizer production was 1,451,000 metric tons in 2009. In addition to the Taiba phosphate rock mine already exploited northeast of Dakar, the government has identified deposits at Matam, whose 40.5 million tons of reserves would likely remain unexploited under existing phosphate market conditions.

Salt output was estimated at 222,000 metric tons in 2009. Senegal accounted for 6% of global fuller's earth (attapulgite) production in 2009. Also produced were hydraulic cement, fuller's earth (attapulgite) and other clays, natural gas, crude oil, limestone, and sand. The government's estimate of unreported gold production in 2009 was placed at 5,354 kg. Many foreign companies had active exploration permits in Sabodala and Kanoumering, where Precambrian (Birimian) metamorphic rocks were exposed and significant reserves of gold have been reported. Iron ore reserves of 600 million tons have been identified in the Faleme, Farangalia, and Goto deposits, with a forecast capacity of 12 million tons per year; their development, though, could not justify the cost of creating the extensive port shipping and rail infrastructure needed to exploit the deposits. Eastern Senegal also had 350,000 tons of marble, as well as deposits of peat, uranium, titanium, serpentine, and other minerals.

In 2000, a newly elected government included among its top priorities the development of the country's inadequate infrastructure by improving the highway system, modernizing railroads, and constructing a new airport. In 2001, the African Development Bank Group approved an $18.7 million loan to help finance the 148-km Diamniadio-Mbour-Kaolack road project. The Ministère des Mines, de l'Energie at de l'Hydraulique was responsible for the administration over natural resources, and the Direction des Mines et de la Géologie was responsible for the mining sector.

²⁷ENERGY AND POWER

The World Bank reported in 2008 that Senegal produced 2.4 billion kWh of electricity and consumed 1.93 billion kWh, or 153 kWh per capita. Roughly 57% of energy came from fossil fuels, while 1% came from alternative fuels. Per capita oil consumption was 234 kg. Senegal, as of 2010, imported 36,290 barrels of oil per day. Senegal had no proven reserves of natural gas as of 2011. There are extensive reserves of peat along the coast between Dakar and Saint-Louis.

²⁸INDUSTRY

Senegal's manufacturing sector registered annual growth increases consistently during the 1980s, 1990s, and into the 2000s. Agro-industry (oil mills, sugar refineries, fish canneries, flour mills, bakeries, beverage and dairy processing, and tobacco manufacturing) plays a key role. Especially important are groundnut-processing mills. The textile industry includes four cotton-ginning mills, factories for weaving, dyeing, and printing cloth, and plants that produce mattresses, thread, and hats. Cement, refined petroleum products, fertilizers, and phosphoric acid are produced. Other industrial products include plywood, boats, bicycles, soap, leather goods, paints, acetylene, sulfuric acid, and cigarettes. The industrial production growth rate was 4.9% in 2011.

Senegal's oil potential has yet to be completely ascertained. There is a refinery at Dakar, with production capacity of 27,000 barrels per day. Petrosen, the state-owned oil company, is encouraging exploration.

²⁹SCIENCE AND TECHNOLOGY

The World Bank reported in 2009 that there were no patent applications in science and technology in Senegal. The African Regional Center for Technology, with 30 member states, has its headquarters in Dakar. Most research facilities in Senegal deal with agricultural subjects. Dakar has centers for mining and medical research and a research institute on African food and nutrition problems. An institute of research for oils and oilseeds is at Bambey. The Senegalese Institute of Agricultural Research, with headquarters at Dakar, operates a national center of agronomical research at Bambey, a national laboratory of livestock and veterinary research at Dakar, an oceanographic center at Dakar, and numerous other technical facilities throughout the country.

The University Cheikh Anta Diop de Dakar, founded in 1949, has faculties of medicine and pharmacy and of sciences, and research institutes in psychopathology, leprosy, pediatrics, renewable energy, applied tropical medicine, applied mathematics, health and development, environmental science, adontology and stomatology, applied nuclear technology, and the teaching of mathematics, physics, and technology. The University of Saint Louis has an applied mathematics unit. Other facilities for scientific training include a polytechnic school at Thiès; an international school of sciences and veterinary medicine, representing 13 French-speaking countries, at Dakar; and an institute of nutritional technology at Dakar.

³⁰DOMESTIC TRADE

Dakar is not only the capital and largest city of Senegal but also the nation's largest consumer market and a major commercial and industrial center of West Africa. Many large trading firms have headquarters in France. Lebanese residents also play an important role in trade, however, many of their businesses are gradually being replaced by Senegalese merchants. A small number of supermarkets and larger retail stores deal primarily in imported goods. A few foreign franchise firms have made their way into the country.

Smuggling of goods from The Gambia is a serious problem, since such illicit imports undercut Senegalese products in price. A large informal domestic trade takes place in the Dakar marketplace known as Sandaga. Here, street vendors sell a wide variety of goods from cosmetics and shoes to stereo equipment.

Principal Trading Partners – Senegal (2010)

(In millions of US dollars)

Country	Total	Exports	Imports	Balance
World	6,501.4	2,059.3	4,442.1	-2,382.8
France	973.8	95.0	878.8	-783.8
Mali	491.1	490.8	0.3	490.4
Nigeria	455.5	4.8	450.7	-445.9
China	413.3	15.3	398.0	-382.6
India	327.8	205.8	122.0	83.8
Spain	224.0	57.3	166.7	-109.5
Switzerland	212.6	163.1	49.5	113.6
Netherlands	202.4	21.8	180.5	-158.7
Thailand	161.9	2.6	159.2	-156.6
Italy	144.3	45.8	98.5	-52.7

(…) data not available or not significant.

(n.s.) not specified.

SOURCE: *2011 Direction of Trade Statistics Yearbook,* New York: United Nations, 2011.

Since Senegal ratified the WTO agreement in 1995, the government's role in domestic trade has been reduced. Subsidies for rice, sugar, wheat, and flour have been eliminated.

Normal business hours are from 8 or 9 a.m. to noon and 3 to 6 p.m., Monday-Friday, and 8 or 9 a.m. to noon on Saturday. Banks are usually open 7:45 a.m. to 12:15 p.m. and 1:30 to 3:45 p.m., Monday-Friday.

31 FOREIGN TRADE

Senegal imported $4.474 billion worth of goods and services in 2008, while exporting $2.112 billion worth of goods and services. Major import partners in 2009 were France, 20%; Nigeria, 9.2%; China, 9%; Thailand, 5.5%; and Spain, 4.3% . Its major export partners were Mali, 19.3%; Switzerland, 8.3%; India, 8.2%; France, 5.8%; and UK, 4.2%. The most important commodity exports for

Balance of Payments – Senegal (2009)

(In millions of US dollars)

Current Account		**-864.8**
Balance on goods		-2,028.2
Imports	-4,125.0	
Exports	2,096.8	
Balance on services		-129.0
Balance on income		-180.8
Current transfers		1,473.2
Capital Account		**305.1**
Financial Account		**484.2**
Direct investment abroad		-77.1
Direct investment in Senegal		331.1
Portfolio investment assets		-91.3
Portfolio investment liabilities		-1.6
Financial derivatives		…
Other investment assets		-128.2
Other investment liabilities		451.4
Net Errors and Omissions		**-171.3**
Reserves and Related Items		**246.8**

(…) data not available or not significant.

SOURCE: *Balance of Payment Statistics Yearbook 2011,* Washington, DC: International Monetary Fund, 2011.

Senegal are shellfish, fish, refined petroleum products, peanut oil, inorganic chemicals, and fertilizers.

32 BALANCE OF PAYMENTS

Since independence, as in colonial times, Senegal's balance of payments has generally run a deficit on current accounts, mainly covered by foreign aid from France (and, more recently, from other EU members). Remittances from Senegalese working in France, together with small inflows of private capital, have also helped cover the shortfalls. The Economist Intelligence Unit reported that in 2010 Senegal had a trade deficit of $2.042 billion. The current account balance was -$1.167 billion that same year.

33 BANKING AND SECURITIES

In 1959, the Central Bank of the West African States succeeded the Currency Board of French West Africa and Togo as the bank of issue for the former French West African territories. In 1962, it was reorganized as the joint note-issue bank of Benin, Côte d'Ivoire, Mauritania (which left in 1973), Niger, Senegal, Togo, and Upper Volta (now Burkina Faso), members of the West African Economic and Monetary Union (UEMOA). BCEAO notes, known as CFA francs, are guaranteed by France without limitation, formerly to the French franc and now to the euro. Foreign exchange receipts of the member states go into the franc area's exchange pool, which in turn covers their foreign exchange requirements. In 1973, the member states of the BCEAO signed new statutes that, among other things, provided for increased Africanization of bank personnel, transfer of headquarters from Paris to Dakar, and greater participation of the bank in the development activities of member states.

Commercial banks operating in Senegal include the International Bank for Occidental Africa (French-owned), Banque Internationale pour le Commerce et l'Industrie du Senegal, Credit Lyonnais, Banque Senegalo Tunisienne, Ecobank, Societe Generale, Citibank, and Banque Islamique du Senegal. The most significant development bank is the government-controlled National Development Bank of Senegal, which participates in development projects and provides credit for government organizations, mixed societies, and cooperatives. Another development financing institution is the Housing Bank of Senegal. A new credit institution, the National Fund for Agricultural Credit, was created in 1984.

The discount rate, the interest rate at which the central bank lends to financial institutions in the short term, was 0.25% in 2010, a significant decrease compared to the 2009 figure of 4.25%.

There are no securities exchanges in Senegal.

34 INSURANCE

As of 2011, at least 20 companies provided insurance in Senegal. Third-party motor insurance is compulsory.

35 PUBLIC FINANCE

Although Senegal's finances are recorded as being in balance each year, in fact the country has run persistent deficits since 1976, generally covered by foreign aid. Senegal qualified for debt relief under the Heavily Indebted Poor Countries (HIPC) Initiative. Progress on the structural reforms required for the program is on track, but slow. From 1987 to 1998, Senegal's fiscal deficit fell from 12% of GDP to 7% of GDP. Donor mandated economic reforms have helped the government to restrain spending while the closing of tax loopholes has increased revenues helping Senegal to reduce the deficit.

In 2010 the budget of Senegal included $2.726 billion in public revenue and $3.315 billion in public expenditures. The budget deficit amounted to 5.2% of GDP. Public debt was 32.1% of GDP, with $3.858 billion of the debt held by foreign entities.

36 TAXATION

In 2011 the World Bank estimated the total tax rate on commercial profits at 46%. Generally, capital gains are taxed at the corporate rate. However if the gains are used to acquire new fixed assets in Senegal within three years, or arise from a merger or other acquisition, the tax can be deferred. Dividends and royalties are subject to withholding taxes. Interest income is subject to a 15% tax.

Individual taxes include a salary tax on the employee and a general income tax with rates ranging up to 50%. Indirect taxes have long been the mainstay of Senegal's tax system, with import duties by far the most important. Other indirect taxes include the business license tax, export taxes, a real estate tax, and registration and stamp taxes. The value-added tax (VAT) has a standard rate of 18% (2011).

37 CUSTOMS AND DUTIES

In January 2000, Senegal put into effect a new tariff scheme that conforms to the common external tariff (CET) scheme agreed on by member nations of the West African Economic and Monetary Union (WAEMU). Under this new tariff structure, Senegal has four simple tariff rate categories: 0% on cultural and scientific goods, agricultural inputs, and capital goods and computer equipment not available from local production; 5% on raw materials, crude oil, and cereals for industry; 10% on semifinished products, intermediate goods, diesel and fuel oil; and 20% on consumer goods, capital goods and computer equipment available from local production, and vehicles. However, there also exists an array of other import tariffs, with a maximum combined rate of 52% and a value-added tax (VAT) of 18% applied to all imports.

In 1982 Senegal abolished its import licensing system, opening the market to all countries on an equal basis; previously, only products from the franc zone and the European Union (EU) could be imported without a license. Certain import restrictions exist on agricultural and industrial products that support the Senegalese economy.

38 FOREIGN INVESTMENT

Following independence, Senegal's economic policy shifted from a largely laissez-faire, noninterventionist stance to a policy of increasing government participation in economic affairs. By 1975, the government had effectively nationalized groundnut trade and processing, assumed majority control of the two main phosphate companies, and nationalized water distribution and electricity production. Half a generation later, in 1991, a slow privatization of the parastatal sector was under way.

In spite of its parastatal tradition, Senegal encourages private investment, which remains substantial. The investment code, enacted in 1962 and significantly revised in 1972, 1978, and 1981, encourages both domestic and foreign private investment in industrial, agricultural, mineral, transport, tourist, and other enterprises that conform to the goals of the national development program. Incentives include tax advantages and exemptions from customs and duties.

An industrial free trade zone located outside Dakar offers preferential access to West African Economic Community, ECOWAS, and European Economic Community countries. Aside from exchange-control regulations, there are no restrictions on the repatriation of capital and earnings for amounts up to XOF200,000; above this amount, prior government approval is required. By the beginning of 1992, 15 firms had begun operations in the zone. In December 1983, Senegal signed a bilateral investment treaty with the United States, becoming the first sub-Saharan African nation to do so.

Foreign investment rose steadily from 13.8% of GDP in 1993 to 16.5% in 1997. In 1997, annual foreign direct investment (FDI) inflows peaked at $176 million; following this there was some decline in the early 2000s. World Bank figures reported FDI reaching a high of $398 million in 2008, and declining to $237 million in 2010. Most private investment in Senegal has come from France, and the telecommunications sector has attracted the most foreign investment.

39 ECONOMIC DEVELOPMENT

Senegal's development program addresses the basic problems encountered by Senegal's economy: lack of diversified output, the inefficiency of investments, the role of state in economic activity, and the excessive expansion of domestic consumer demand. These problems have been partly addressed by programs focusing on food self-sufficiency, fishing, and tourism, and by strengthening high-return activities. Projects such as the Manantali irrigation project, the phosphate-to-fertilizer recovery project, and the trawler modernization program are examples of what Senegal is doing within this policy framework. In the area of manufacturing, capacity utilization improvement, equipment modernization, and low-capital production are emphasized. Since 1994, the government has made progress in privatizing state-owned enterprises, reducing labor costs to improve competitiveness in the manufacturing sector, and liberalizing trade by eliminating export subsidies and removing restrictions on certain strategic imports. Private economic revenues accounted for roughly more than 80% of GDP in 2005, but trade liberalization had not progressed as much as planned.

In 2000, Senegal became eligible for around $800 million in debt service relief under the International Monetary Fund (IMF)/World Bank Heavily Indebted Poor Countries (HIPC) initiative. In 2003, the IMF approved a $33 million three-year Poverty Reduction and Growth Facility (PRGF) Arrangement for Senegal, to support the government's economic reform program. In September of 2005, the World Bank and the IMF backed a deal to cancel about $55 billion of debts owed by 18 of the world's poorest countries, 14 of which are in sub-Saharan Africa including Senegal. The government is committed to continue the donor-supported economic reform program as outlined in the IMF's three-year poverty reduction and growth facility (PRGF). Senegal's Agency for the Promotion of Investment (APIX) aims to promote foreign investment. In 2007 Senegal and the IMF agreed to a new, nondisbursing, Policy Support Initiative program which was completed in 2010. Senegal received its first disbursement from the $540 million Millennium Challenge Account compact it signed in September 2009 for infrastructure and agriculture development. An additional agreement with the IMF, signed in 2010, was expected to expedite economic reforms through 2013. Government investment in the power sector was a priority for 2012 following widespread protests against power shortages in 2010.

40 SOCIAL DEVELOPMENT

Since 1955, a system of family allowances for wage earners has provided modest maternity and child benefits. The system is financed by employer contributions at the rate of 7% of gross salary; an additional 15% contribution finances a fund for occupational health and accident coverage. Shared equally by employer and employee is a 6% contribution to a fund for general medical and hospital expenses. In addition, employees contribute 4.8% of gross salary to a retirement fund and employers contribute 7.2%. The retirement age is 55. This program covers employed persons, including domestic, seasonal, and day workers.

According to the UN only 20% of women participate in the work force. Discrimination against women is widespread in both education and employment. Although prohibited by law, female genital mutilation (FGM) is practiced by ethnic groups in rural areas. A 2010 report in Global Times cited a government study showing FGM prevalence at 28% of women nationally, with the highest incidence in the rural parts of the southeast. Women in urban areas, however, were making progress in the workplace. The government adopted legislation mandating fines and prison terms of up to three years for sexual harassment. Although minority religions are protected under law and are free to practice their religions, non-Muslims may face discrimination in civil, political, or economic matters.

Despite the vigorous multiparty political activity, there have been charges of human rights violations and electoral irregularities, as well as restrictions on freedom of press and association. Security forces commit abuses including arbitrary arrest and detention, beatings, and torture.

41 HEALTH

According to the CIA, life expectancy in Senegal was 56 years in 2011. The country spent 5.7% of its GDP on healthcare, amounting to $59 per person. There were 1 physician, 4 nurses and midwives, and 3 hospital beds per 10,000 inhabitants. Major health problems include measles and meningitis along with such water-related diseases as malaria, trypanosomiasis, onchocerciasis, and schistosomiasis. The CIA calculated HIV/AIDS prevalence in Senegal to be about 0.9% in 2009.

Infant mortality was 51 deaths per 1,000 live births in 2011. In 2008 the maternal mortality rate, according to the World Bank, was 410 per 100,000 births. It was estimated that 79% of children were vaccinated against measles.

A 2010 survey conducted by the United States and the World Health Organization (WHO), found that up to 40% of the malaria drugs in Senegal failed quality tests. The majority of the problematic medicine either contained impurities or lacked sufficient doses of the active ingredient that serves to combat the virus. According to the WHO, while much of the deficient medicine maintained some effectiveness, the failed drugs could not reliably stave off the deadly disease.

42 HOUSING

Most housing in Dakar is like that of a European city. Elsewhere, housing ranges from European-type structures to the circular mud huts with thatched roofs common in villages. Since World War II, the growth of Dakar and other towns has been rapid, with government activity largely concentrated on improvement of urban housing and sanitation.

43 EDUCATION

In 2009 the World Bank estimated that 73% of age-eligible children in Senegal were enrolled in primary school. Secondary enrollment for age-eligible children stood at 21%. Tertiary enrollment was estimated at 8%. Of those enrolled in tertiary education, there were 100 male students for every 54 female students. Overall, the CIA estimated that Senegal had a literacy rate of 39.3%. Public expenditure on education represented 5.8% of GDP.

Education is compulsory for six years of primary school, for students between ages 6 and 12. For those attending secondary school, there are options for a seven-year general education (in two cycles of four years and three years) or a five-year technical or vocational program (in two cycles of three years and two years). The academic year runs from October to July.

The University of Dakar has two graduate schools and numerous research centers. For more than 30 years, the University of Dakar offered free tuition and generous subsidies to students. However, in 1994 it began implementing new austerity measures aimed at scaling back enrollment, raising academic standards and getting students to pay for more of the cost of their education. A polytechnic college opened at Thiès in 1973. Other colleges include a national school of administration at Dakar and a school of sciences and veterinary medicine for French-speaking Africa.

In 2010 the government of Senegal announced the commitment of $1.3 million for the establishment of a new African Institute for Mathematical Sciences (AIMS) to be built near Mbour. Primary funding for the new college came from Canada, which provided $19 million in funding for AIMS in Ghana and Ethiopia, in addition to Senegal. The Perimeter Institute for Theoretical Physics in Canada served as the primary consulting institution. Additional funding was provided as part of a $2 million award from Google. The Senegal AIMS was modeled after the AIMS in South Africa, which opened in 2003 and has already trained more than 300 mathematicians. AIMS Senegal opened in September 2011 and partnered with universities in France to train local faculty members and provide for visiting faculty and lecturers.

44 LIBRARIES AND MUSEUMS

There are four major libraries in Senegal, all located in Dakar. The oldest is the Archives of Senegal, founded in 1913, which has a collection of more than 26,000 volumes. The largest is the Central Library of the University of Dakar, founded in 1952, which has more than 306,000 volumes. The Basic Institute of Black Africa (Institut Fondamental d'Afrique Noire—IFAN) and the Alliance Française maintain libraries of more than 70,000 and 7,000 volumes, respectively. In addition to these major facilities, there are specialized libraries attached to various research institutes. The Museum of African Art in Dakar and the History Museum and the Museum of the Sea on Gorée Island are operated by IFAN.

There are natural history museums in Dakar and Saint-Louis and a local museum in Saint-Louis.

45 MEDIA

In 2009 the CIA reported that there were 278,800 telephone landlines in Senegal. In addition to landlines, mobile phone subscriptions averaged 55 per 100 people, or 8.34 million cell phones in use. Telephone and telegraph services, publicly owned and operated, are good by African standards, particularly in the coastal area and in the main centers of peanut production. French submarine cables connect Dakar with Paris, Casablanca, Conakry (Guinea), and Recife (Brazil), and radiotelephone facilities are also in operation. The postal system provides international telephone facilities.

The government-operated radio and television service has transmitters throughout the country. The two national radio networks based in Dakar broadcast mostly in French, while the regional stations in Rufisque, Saint-Louis, Tambacounda, Kaolack, and Ziguinchor, which originate their own programs, broadcast primarily in six local languages. In 2009, there were more than 25 privately owned radio stations. There were 8 FM radio stations, 20 AM radio stations, and 1 shortwave radio station. There are no privately owned television stations in the country, but French and South African satellite services are available. In 2010, the country had 241 Internet hosts. Internet users numbered 7 per 100 citizens.

The constitution guarantees freedom of opinion, which the press is generally free to exercise. The main newspapers in circulation in 2010 were: *Le Soleil du Sénégal*, the PS party newspaper, with an estimated circulation of 45,000, and *Sud Quotidien* (30,000). There are also several weekly newspapers and magazines.

46 ORGANIZATIONS

There are chambers of commerce, industry, and agriculture in the principal cities. Professional and trade associations also exist. The Consumers International Subregional Office for West and Central Africa is located in Dakar. The Alliance Française sponsors lectures and concerts. Of the many sport and social associations in the towns, those for soccer are especially popular, but racing clubs, aero clubs, and automobile clubs are also active. National youth organizations include the Democratic Youth Movement, the Socialist Youth Movement, Young Workers Movement, YMCA, and the Senegalese Scout Confederation. The John F. Kennedy Center Dakar encourages youth participation in volunteer efforts.

Volunteer service organizations, such as the Lions Clubs International, are also present. The Daniel Boitier Center in Dakar is a Roman Catholic organization for the study of social and economic problems. Panos Institute networks with community groups and organizations to encourage community development projects. The African Council of AIDS Service Organizations is based in Dakar. Other social action groups include the Femmes Developpement Entreprise en Afrique, Goree Institute, and Hope Unlimited. International organizations with national chapters include Amnesty International, Defence for Children International, Caritas, Habitat for Humanity, UNICEF, and the Red Cross.

47 TOURISM, TRAVEL, AND RECREATION

The *Tourism Factbook*, published by the UN World Tourism Organization, reported 875,000 incoming tourists to Senegal in 2007; they spent a total of $637 million. Of those incoming tourists, there were 438,000 from Africa and 324,000 from Europe. There were 31,229 hotel beds available in Senegal, which had an occupancy rate of 35%. The estimated daily cost to visit Dakar, the capital, was $325. The cost of visiting other cities averaged $195.

The comfortable climate, variety of cultural attractions, attractive physical features such as the coastal beaches and the 5,996-sq-km (2,315-sq-mi) Niokolo-Koba National Park, and the relative proximity to Europe have all combined to make Senegal an increasingly popular vacation area and international conference center. Gorée Island, near Dakar, has many former slave houses, where perhaps 20 million slaves were kept before being shipped to America between 1536 and 1848. Wrestling and fishing are popular, and hunting is allowed from December to May on an 80,000-hectare (198,000-acre) reserve.

48 FAMOUS PERSONS

Blaise Diagne (1872–1934) was the first African to be elected to the French parliament and to hold office in the French government as an undersecretary of state. Léopold-Sédar Senghor (1906–2001), president of Senegal from 1960 until his retirement in 1980, was a French-language poet of distinction; in 1984, he became a life member of the French Academy, the first black African to receive that honor. Abdou Diouf (b. 1935) was president of Senegal (1981–2000), after serving as prime minister (1970–80). Abdoulaye Wade (b. 1926) became president in 2000. Among Senegalese writers are Birago Diop (1906–89), author of short stories, and David Diop (1927–60), an internationally known poet. Ousmane Sembene (1923–2007) was a film director and writer of international repute. Cheikh Anta Diop (1923–86), RND leader, wrote many works of distinction on African history.

49 DEPENDENCIES

Senegal has no territories or colonies.

50 BIBLIOGRAPHY

Berg, Elizabeth L. *Senegal*. 2nd ed. New York: Marshall Cavendish Benchmark, 2010.

Getz, Trevor R. *Slavery and Reform in West Africa: Toward Emancipation in Nineteenth-century Senegal and the Gold Coast*. Athens: Ohio University Press, 2004.

Lambert, Michael C. *Longing for Exile: Migration and the Making of a Translocal Community in Senegal, West Africa*. Portmouth, NH: Heinemann, 2002.

Robinson, David. *Paths of Accommodation: Muslim Societies and French Colonial Authorities in Senegal and Mauritania, 1880–1920*. Athens: Ohio University Press, 2000.

Ross, Eric. *Culture and Customs of Senegal*. Westport, CT: Greenwood Press, 2008.

Senegal Arabia Investment and Business Guide: Strategic and Practical Information. Washington, DC: International Business Publications USA, 2012.

Zeilig, Leo, and David Seddon. *A Political and Economic Dictionary of Africa*. Philadelphia: Routledge/Taylor and Francis, 2005.

SEYCHELLES

Republic of Seychelles

CAPITAL: Victoria

FLAG: The flag is made up of five oblique bands of (left to right) blue, yellow, red, white, and green.

ANTHEM: *Koste Seselwa* (Seychellois Unite).

MONETARY UNIT: The Seychelles rupee (SCR) is a paper currency of 100 cents. There are coins of 5, 10, and 25 cents and 1, 5, 10, 20, 25, 50, 100, 1,000, and 1,500 rupees and notes of 10, 25, 50, and 100 rupees. SCR1 = US$0.08183 (or US$1 = SCR12.221) as of 2010.

WEIGHTS AND MEASURES: The metric system is the legal standard.

HOLIDAYS: New Year's, 1–2 January; Labor Day, 1 May; National Day, 5 June; Independence Day, 29 June; Assumption, 15 August; All Saints' Day, 1 November; Immaculate Conception, 8 December; Christmas, 25 December. Movable religious holidays include Good Friday, Easter Monday, Corpus Christi, and Ascension.

TIME: 4 p.m. = noon GMT.

¹LOCATION, SIZE, AND EXTENT

Seychelles, an archipelago in the Indian Ocean, consists of an estimated 115 islands, most of which are not permanently inhabited. The second-smallest country in Africa, Seychelles has an area of 455 sq km (176 sq mi), of which Mahé, the principal island, comprises 144 sq km (56 sq mi). Comparatively, the area occupied by Seychelles is slightly more than 2.5 times the size of Washington, DC. There are two main clusters: one is a granitic group, centering around Mahé; the other, to the SW, includes the coralline Aldabra Islands and the Farquhar group. Situated about 1,600 km (1,000 mi) off the east coast of Africa, Mahé extends 27 km (17 mi) N–S and 11 km (7 mi) E–W.

The capital city of Seychelles, Victoria, is located on the island of Mahé.

²TOPOGRAPHY

The Seychelles Islands are the highest points of the Mascarene Ridge, an Indian Ocean ridge running in a generally N–S direction. The granitic islands rise above the sea surface to form a peak or ridge which, in the case of Mahé, attains an elevation of 912 m (2,992 ft) at Morne Seychellois, the highest point. Rugged crests, towering cliffs, boulders, and domes contribute to the islands' great natural beauty. Here and there, in the hollows in the rock relief, are pockets of lateritic soil, often very thin and easily eroded. Mahé; possesses white, sandy beaches behind which are flats of coral and shell known locally as plateaus. Small streams descending the mountain slopes deposit alluvial material, creating the most fertile soils on the island. The coralline Seychelles are, in contrast, low lying, rising only a few feet above the surface of the sea. Many have the typical Indian Ocean lagoon. Soils tend to be thin, with poor moisture retention. These islands are suited only to the coconut palm and a few other species.

³CLIMATE

Although the Seychelles Islands lie close to the equator, their maritime situation results in coastal temperatures that are fairly constant at about 27°C (81°F) throughout the year. At higher altitudes, temperatures are lower, especially at night. Mean annual rainfall at sea level on Mahé is 236 cm (93 in); in the mountains there may be as much as 356 cm (140 in) a year. On the southwestern coral islands, rainfall is much lower, averaging about 50 cm (20 in) a year on Aldabra. May to October is the relatively dry sunny season; in this period, the southeast monsoon winds bring brief showers every two or three days. The northwest monsoon arrives in December and continues until March, bringing frequent and heavy rain. Humidity is high, especially in the coastal areas.

⁴FLORA AND FAUNA

The World Resource Institute estimates that there are 250 plant species in Seychelles. In addition, Seychelles is home to 25 mammal, 238 bird, 38 reptile, and 12 amphibian species. The calculation reflects the total number of distinct species residing in the country, not the number of endemic species.

Primary forest is found only on Praslin and Curieuse islands, northeast of Mahé. On Praslin, native forests of coco-de-mer have been protected in small reserves; its fruit, a huge coconut weighing up to 18 kg (40 lb), is the largest seed in the world and this is the only place where the palm is found growing wild. Virtually all the broadleaf evergreen rain forest has been cut down. In its place are the coconut plantations, with occasional patches of vanilla. Other existing trees are native to the islands and have adapted to the local conditions. Underplanting is quite usual and includes avocado, breadfruit, banana, cinnamon, mango, papaya, patchouli, and pineapple.

Sharks abound in the surrounding oceans, but on land there are no reptiles or mammals that present a threat to human life. The most noteworthy animal is the giant tortoise; once very plentiful, the species is now sorely depleted. Bird life includes dozens of the world's rarest species, but there are very few insects.

5 ENVIRONMENT

The World Resource Institute reported that Seychelles had designated 3,800 hectares (9,390 acres) of land for protection as of 2006. The UN reported in 2008 that carbon dioxide emissions in Seychelles totaled 623 kilotons.

Seychelles does not have the resources to maintain a comprehensive program of environmental regulation. The monitoring of the environment is complicated by the fact that the nation consists of 15 islands distributed over a 1.3 million sq km area. Seychelles has no natural fresh water resources. In addition, the nation has a water pollution problem due to industrial by-products and sewage. Fires, landslides, and oil leakage also affect the environment in Seychelles.

The government Environmental Management Plan of Seychelles 1990–2000 proposed 12 areas of environmental regulation. The Aldabra atoll is a native preserve on the UNESCO World Heritage list, as is the Vallée de Mai Nature Reserve. The Port Launay Coastal Wetlands are listed as a Ramsar site. The Ministry of Planning and External Relations and the Ministry of National Development hold principal environmental responsibility.

According to a 2011 report issued by the International Union for Conservation of Nature and Natural Resources (IUCN), the number of threatened species included 5 types of mammals, 10 species of birds, 10 types of reptiles, 6 species of amphibians, 17 species of fish, 36 types of mollusks, 64 species of other invertebrates, and 61 species of plants. The olive ridley, hawksbill, and green sea turtles and the Seychelles black parrot, Seychelles magpie robin, and Seychelles warbler are threatened species. The Aldabra brush warbler and the Seychelles parakeet (or parrot) have become extinct.

In 2011 Seychelles signed the Nagoya Protocol, a supplementary agreement to the Convention on Biological Diversity. It provided for benefit sharing among genetic researchers working to maintain biodiversity.

6 POPULATION

The US Central Intelligence Agency (CIA) estimates the population of Seychelles in 2011 to be approximately 89,188, which placed it at number 184 in population among the 196 nations of the world. In 2011, approximately 7.1% of the population was over 65 years of age, with another 21.9% under 15 years of age. The median age in Seychelles was 32.5 years. There were 1.03 males for every female in the country. The population's annual rate of change was 0.945%. The projected population for the year 2025 was 100,000. Population density in Seychelles was calculated at 196 people per sq km (76 people per sq mi), making it one of the most densely populated countries in Africa.

The UN estimated that 55% of the population lived in urban areas, and that urban populations had an annual rate of change of 1.3%. The largest urban area was Victoria, with a population of 26,000.

7 MIGRATION

Estimates of Seychelles's net migration rate, carried out by the CIA in 2011, amounted to 1.03 migrants per 1,000 citizens. The total number of emigrants living abroad was 12,300, and the total number of immigrants living in Seychelles was 10,800. Entry for the purpose of employment is strictly controlled. Since the 1950s, some retirees from the United Kingdom have settled in Seychelles. Applying to citizenship required fees totaling SCR25,500 ($2,087) in 2011.

8 ETHNIC GROUPS

There are no distinct ethnic divisions, apart from small Indian and Chinese groups constituting about 1% of the total population. The bulk of the population is Seychellois, a mixture of African, French-European, and Asian strains.

9 LANGUAGES

Creole, a simplified form of French with borrowings from African languages, has been the first language since 1981 and is the initial language in public schools; it is spoken by about 91.8% of the population. English and French are also widely spoken as second languages. English is the first language of about 4.9% of the population. English, Creole, and French are all considered to be official languages; English is the official language of the National Assembly.

10 RELIGIONS

According to the most recent estimates, Roman Catholics constituted about 82% of the Christian community; Anglicans totaled another 6%. Other Christian groups include Baptists, Seventh-Day Adventists, the Assemblies of God, the Pentecostal Church, Nazarites, and Jehovah's Witnesses. Hindus, Muslims, and Baha'is are also present. The constitution provides for freedom of religion and there is no state religion; however, the government does offer sometimes substantial financial assistance to churches from the state budget, primarily in the form of grants, through an application process that is open to all. Good Friday, Easter, Corpus Christi, Assumption of Mary, All Saints' Day, Immaculate Conception Day, and Christmas are observed as national holidays.

11 TRANSPORTATION

The CIA reports that Seychelles has a total of 458 km (285 mi) of roads, of which 440 km (273 mi) are paved. One road encircles the island and another runs across the island by way of the central mountain ridge.

Until the opening of the international airport on Mahé in 1971, the Seychelles Islands were entirely dependent on the sea for their links with the rest of the world. Until 1970 passenger and cargo service by ship was irregular. In the early 1970s, however, new deepwater facilities were dredged at Victoria Harbor. Private ferries connect Mahé to Praslin and La Digue. As of 2010 there were nine merchant ships of 1,000 GRT or more.

There are 14 airports, which transported 564,580 passengers in 2009 according to the World Bank. Eight airports had paved runways. Seychelles International Airport is at Pointe Larue on Mahé. Flights to London, Zürich, Frankfurt, and Rome are in service via Air Seychelles, the national carrier. Air France's scheduled flights connect Seychelles with Europe. Ligne Aérienne Seychelles (LAS), a private line, ran charter flights to Australia, Singapore, Botswana, and Malawi.

12 HISTORY

The Portuguese explorer Vasco da Gama discovered the Seychelles Islands (then uninhabited) in 1502, and an English expedition visited the islands in 1609. The name Seychelles derives from the Vicomte des Séchelles, Louis XV's finance minister. The French first claimed the islands in 1756, but colonization did not begin until 1768, when a party of 22 Frenchmen arrived, bringing with them a number of slaves. As competition grew among European nations for the lucrative trade with India and Asia, more and more seamen called at the islands to provision their vessels and to pick up commodities useful for trade.

The French and British battled for control of the islands between 1793 and 1813. French bases were blockaded in 1794 and again in 1804; on each occasion, the French capitulated. Under the Treaty of Paris (1814), the islands, together with Mauritius, were ceded to Britain. Both before and after the cession, the islands were administered from Mauritius as dependent territories. When the British made clear that they would enforce the ban on slavery throughout the Empire, many of the French landowners who had continued to import African slaves, largely from Mauritius and Réunion, departed for Africa and elsewhere, taking their slaves with them. However, with slavery ended, thousands of liberated slaves and others came into the islands. Indian labor was introduced to work on the plantations and some Chinese immigrants became shopkeepers.

In 1872, a Board of Civil Governors was created, increasing the degree of political autonomy; a Legislative Council and an Executive Council were established in 1888. On 31 August 1903, the islands became a crown colony, no longer subordinate to Mauritius. By this date, the cosmopolitan character of Seychelles had been established. Intermarriage between the descendants of the French, African, and Asian populations produced the Seychellois of today.

In 1948, the first elections were held, filling four seats on the Legislative Council. A new constitution was written in 1966 and promulgated in 1967. It vested authority in a governor and a Governing Council. General elections, the first based on the principle of universal adult suffrage, were held in December 1967 for the new Legislative Assembly. Further amendments to the constitution in March 1970 gave the Seychellois greater autonomy over affairs of internal government.

Seychelles achieved independence at 12:05 AM on 29 June 1976. Upon independence, the UK government recommended the transfer from the British Indian Ocean Territory to Seychelles of the island groups of Aldabra and Farquhar and the island of Desroches. These islands, which had been detached from Seychelles in 1965, were duly returned to the new republic.

James Richard Marie Mancham, then leader of the conservative Seychelles Democratic Party, became president on independence, heading a coalition government that included Seychelles People's United Party (SPUP) leader France Albert René as prime minister. Mancham was overthrown by a coup on 5 June 1977 and went

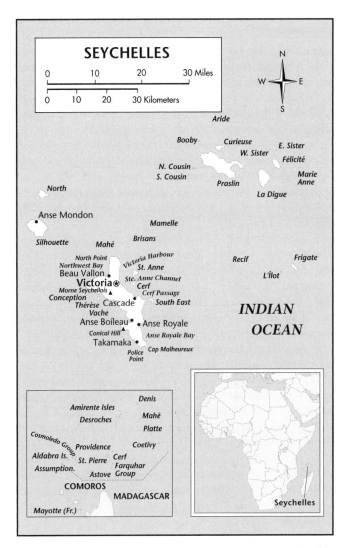

LOCATION: 3°41′ to 10°13′S; 46°12′ to 56°17′ E. TERRITORIAL SEA LIMIT: 12 miles.

into exile; René became president. He suspended the constitution, dismissed the legislature, and ruled by decree.

In 1978, a new political party, the Seychelles People's Progressive Front (SPPF), absorbed the SPUP. The constitution of March 1979, adopted by referendum, established a one-party state as the country drifted toward a Marxist political system. In November 1981, about 50 mercenaries recruited in South Africa landed in Mahé, briefly seized the airport, and apparently planned to return Mancham to power; however, Seychellois troops forced them to flee. Tanzanian troops, airlifted to Seychelles following this incident, also played a part in restoring order after an abortive army mutiny of 17–18 August 1982 took at least nine lives. All Tanzanian troops had left the country by the end of 1984. A number of other plots have been alleged since then.

René was reelected president without opposition in June 1984. Since then, the Seychelles made progress economically and socially. Under rising pressure to democratize, in December 1991, René agreed to reform the electoral system. Multiparty elections were held in July 1992 (the first since 1974), and the prospect of reconciliation between René and Mancham supporters was raised.

Many dissidents, including Mancham, returned from exile. In June 1993, 73% of the voters approved a new constitution providing for multiparty government.

Since the introduction of multiparty competition, the SPPF has remained dominant, but has gradually seen its popularity weaken. Presidential and National Assembly elections were held 23 July 1993, with René winning the presidency and the SPPF capturing all but one of the directly elected legislative seats. In the 1998 contest, René obtained 66.7% of the presidential vote and his party captured 30 of 34 seats. In August 2001 elections, René again defeated his opponents, but this time by only 54.19%, and in National Assembly elections in December 2002—the first to be held separately from presidential elections—the SPPF captured 23 seats to 11 for the SNP.

In April 2004, after 27 years in power, René—barred constitutionally from running for a third term—handed over power to his vice president James Michel. The move gave Michel time to establish himself, and as SPPF party chair, René continued to exercise power behind the scenes. One sign of this power was the expansion of the central committee from 20 to 25 members composed of former ministers and key civil servants. In the annual SPPF congress in May 2005, Vice President Joseph Belmont was named to be Michel's running mate.

After winning elections in 2006, there was a six month boycott by the opposition party, and Michel responded by dissolving the assembly in 2007, with elections to fill vacancies taking place that year. Independent organizations certified the election as free and fair.

The country suffered an economic crisis in 2008 after defaulting on loan payments. It received assistance from the IMF and World Bank as it drastically reformed its fiscal policy in 2009 and 2010.

13 GOVERNMENT

The 1976 constitution provided for a multiparty system, but was replaced in 1979 with a document authorizing a one-party state. The June 1993 constitution reestablished multiparty elections for president and for a National Assembly consisting of 33 members, 22 directly elected and 11 allocated on a proportional basis. The president is both head of state and head of government and appoints a cabinet of ministers from outside the National Assembly. Typically, the president also holds key ministerial posts. While the 1993 constitution guarantees extensive political and civil liberties, it also allows the curtailment of freedom of expression in order to protect "the reputation, rights, and freedoms of private lives of persons." This is a thinly veiled limitation on the freedom of the press. The independent media was the target of restrictions under the René administration.

In 1996 the SPPF successfully introduced constitutional changes, including the enlargement of the National Assembly to 35 (with 10 members to be chosen by proportional representation) and creation of the post for a vice president. In 1998 the United Opposition (UO) boycotted the National Assembly meetings protesting the SPPF's heavy-handed behavior. In 2011 the National Assembly was comprised of 34 seats, 25 elected by popular vote and 9 allocated on a proportional basis to parties winning at least 10% of the vote.

Parliamentary elections may be concurrent with presidential elections. The president and members of the National Assembly serve five-year terms.

14 POLITICAL PARTIES

Before 1978 there were two political parties, the Seychelles Democratic Party (SDP) and the Seychelles People's United Party (SPUP), both founded in 1964. In the last legislative elections prior to independence, on 25 April 1974, the SDP won 13 of 15 elective seats and the SPUP 2. Appointments in June 1975 brought total party strength to 18 for the SDP and 7 for the SPUP. The successor to the SPUP, the Seychelles People's Progressive Front (SPPF), was established in 1979 as the sole legal party, with the avowed objective of creating a Socialist state; the SDP was declared to have "disappeared." There were at least three opposition groups in exile. In the 1979 parliamentary elections, 55 candidates sanctioned by the SPPF competed for 23 elective seats in the People's Assembly. In the 1983 parliamentary elections, 17 of the 23 elected candidates ran unopposed; and in the December 1987 elections, 36 candidates, all of them members of the SPPF, competed for the 23 seats in the People's Assembly.

After René's announcement of a return to multiparty democracy, parties began to organize in preparation for an election to a constituent assembly in July 1992. Many dissidents returned from exile and the Democratic Party (DP) was reestablished. Also established were the Seychelles Party (PS), the Seychelles Democratic Movement (MSPD), and the Seychelles Liberal Party (SLP).

After the 23 July 1993 elections, eight opposition members obtained seats in the 33-seat National Assembly. René won the presidential election with 59.5% of the vote. The Parti Seselwa, the Seychellois National Movement, and the National Alliance Party opposed the adoption of the new constitution in 1993 and contested the July 1993 elections as the United Opposition (UO) coalition. Its presidential candidate, former president Mancham, received 36.6% of the vote. The SPPF won 21 legislative seats to the DP's 1. The SPPF was also given 6 of the 11 seats apportioned according to the percentage of the votes won; the DP, 4 seats; and the UO, 1 seat.

In the 1998 elections, the SPPF captured 30 seats; the UO three; and the DP only one seat. The Reverend Wavel Ramkalawan replaced James Mancham as leader of the opposition, and in late 1998, the UO changed its name to the Seychelles National Party (SNP). In National Assembly elections held in December 2002, the SPPF captured 23 seats to 11 for the SNP. The SPPF retained a strong grassroots structure throughout the islands.

In the July 2006 presidential election, James Michel of the SPPF was elected to the post with 53.7% of the vote. Wavel Ramkalawan of the SNP won 45.7% of the vote, followed by Philippe Boulle of the United Opposition (a three-party coalition) with 0.6%.

In the May 2007 legislative elections, both the SPPF and the SNP retained exactly the same number of seats, at 23 and 11 respectively. In the May 2011 presidential election, incumbent James Michel was reelected to his second five-year term in office, winning 55.4% of the vote; his main opponent, Wavel Ramkalawan of the SNP, won 41.4%.

Presidential elections in 2011 reelected Michel. The next scheduled elections were set for 2016.

¹⁵LOCAL GOVERNMENT

There are 23 administrative districts that were formerly SPPF district branch committees. In 2003, SPPF delegates to a special party congress agreed that members of district committees would be appointed rather than elected. Each district is headed by a principal secretary, and governance is divided among the Departments of Community Development, Administration and Finance, Projects, District Administration, and an Audit Unit.

¹⁶JUDICIAL SYSTEM

Magistrates' courts are normally the courts of the first instance. The Supreme Court hears appeals and takes original jurisdiction of some cases. An independent Appeal Court was established in 2005. The president of Seychelles appoints the chief justice—a naturalized citizen—and also appoints all other judges from other Commonwealth countries on seven-year contracts.

Civil law is based on the French Napoleonic Code, while criminal law follows the British model. Members of the armed forces accused of serious offenses are tried by court-martial unless the president decrees otherwise. Executive and ruling party dominance in the judicial system has been challenged unsuccessfully.

The Constitutional Court convenes weekly, or as needed, to consider constitutional and civil liberties issues. The Court of Appeal convenes twice a year and considers appeals from the Supreme Court and Constitutional Court only. In addition, an industrial court and a rent tribunal exist.

In May 2010, the government of Seychelles and the United Nations Office of Drugs and Crime (UNDOC) announced plans to establish a regional judicial center in the island nation for the prosecution of pirates. Piracy was becoming a major problem for Seychelles, particularly as Somali pirates have moved into the southern waters surrounding the country to elude international patrols. Pirates captured in the waters of East Africa and the Arabian Peninsula have generally been transported to a regional UN-backed center in Kenya for prosecution, which was the only approved center for such prosecutions.

However, by March 2010 that system was overburdened, leading Kenya to refuse to accept new suspects. The government of Seychelles began prosecuting piracy in that same month, when 11 pirates were captured off its coast through the efforts of the Seychelles Coast Guard and the European Union Naval Force Somalia Operation (EU NAVFOR). The local courts were enabled for such prosecution through previous amendments to the Seychellois criminal code that allow the courts to prosecute suspected pirates under universal jurisdiction. The EU and UNDOC previously established a counter-piracy training program in Seychelles to train and equip the Coast Guard, police, and prison officials in the appropriate manner to receive and detain suspects.

Although the new regional center eased some of the immediate burden on the Kenyan system, Seychelles, with a prison that houses only 100 inmates, is too small to offer major support. Although suspects can now be tried in national court, those convicted will be returned to Somalia to serve out their sentences. The new regional center was funded by the UN, EU, Australia, Canada, and Germany.

¹⁷ARMED FORCES

The International Institute for Strategic Studies reports that armed forces in Seychelles totaled 200 members in 2011, all of which were members of the army. Defense spending totaled $41.1 million and accounted for 2% of GDP.

¹⁸INTERNATIONAL COOPERATION

Admitted to the United Nations on 21 September 1976, Seychelles participates in ECA and several nonregional specialized agencies, such as the IAEA, FAO, the World Bank, UNCTAD, UNESCO, UNIDO, and the WHO. The nation belongs to the ACP Group, the African Development Bank, COMESA, SADC, the Cross-border Initiative in Eastern and Southern Africa (CBI), the Alliance of Small Island States (AOSIS), and the Indian Ocean Commission. It also belongs to the Commonwealth of Nations, G-77, and the African Union. The country has observer status in the WTO. It is part of the Nonaligned Movement. IN environmental cooperation, Seychelles is part of the Basel Convention, the Convention on Biological Diversity, CITES, the London Convention, the Kyoto Protocol, the Montréal Protocol, MARPOL, the Nuclear Test Ban Treaty, and the UN Conventions on the Law of the Sea, Climate Change, and Desertification. It signed the Nagoya Protocol in 2011.

¹⁹ECONOMY

The gross domestic product (GDP) rate of change in Seychelles, as of 2010, was 6.2%. Deflation stood at 2.2%, and unemployment was reported at 2%. Seychelles highly productive economy is based primarily on tourism and fishing, particularly tuna fishing. Tourism employs about 30% of all Seychellois and provides over 70% of hard currency earnings.

The manufacturing sector has also contributed to economic growth. Crop production is limited by mountainous terrain and low soil fertility, leaving the Seychelles dependent on imports for beef, rice, potatoes, and some fresh produce.

Seychelles became a major tourist destination after the opening of its international airport in 1971. Stiff international competition for tourist dollars caused the government to take steps to broaden the economic base by promoting the development of fishing and light manufacturing. The tourism industry was adversely affected by the 11 September 2001 terrorist attacks in the United States and the subsequent decline in air travel.

Since 1990, a program to privatize the economy has resulted in progress in several sectors. In 1995 the American food company Heinz and Co. purchased 60% of the previously state-owned Seychelles Tuna Canning Factory. In addition most state-owned agricultural land has been turned over to private control. In 2005 and 2006 the government took more steps to liberalize trade by removing import licenses. The Seychelles rupee had been overvalued for years, and in 2006 it was allowed to depreciate, falling by 10% in the first few months of 2007.

In 2007 there was a significant upturn in tourism, and real GDP grew by 5.8%. The global financial crisis of 2008–09 dealt a major blow to the economy, as tourism fell by 15% in the first quarter of 2009, leading to an overall 8% decline in the economy for that year. By the end of that year, the World Bank reported that the national debt of Seychelles had reached 123% of GDP. After defaulting on a Eurobond interest payment, the government turned to the International Monetary Fund (IMF) for assistance, receiving $26 million in emergency support in November 2008 and $31 million in December 2009 to support economic reforms. Through diligent management, the government met all of the targets set by the IMF for getting the economy back on track, and economic growth recovered by 2010. The recovery was attributed largely to a rebound in tourism.

An additional round of relief came in the form of cancelled debt as the Paris Club of creditors cancelled about $70 million of the nation's debt through two major agreements, the second of which went into effect in July 2010. The figure amounted to about 45% of the debt owed to Paris Club members. The remainder of the debt was restructured for repayment over 18 years, with a five-year grace period. Continued government efforts to liberalize the economy provided the opportunity to bring the national debt under control more quickly than expected.

20INCOME

The CIA estimated that in 2010 the GDP of Seychelles was $2.053 billion. The CIA defines GDP as the value of all final goods and services produced within a nation in a given year and computed on the basis of purchasing power parity (PPP) rather than value as measured on the basis of the rate of the exchange based on current dollars. The per capita GDP was estimated at $23,200. The annual growth rate of GDP was 6.2%. The average inflation rate was -2.2%. It was estimated that agriculture accounted for 2.9% of GDP, industry 30.8%, and services 66.2%.

According to the World Bank, remittances from citizens living abroad totaled $12.5 million or about $140 per capita and accounted for approximately .6% of GDP.

The World Bank reports that in 2009, household consumption in Seychelles totaled $549 million or about $6,159 per capita, measured in current US dollars rather than PPP. Household consumption includes expenditures of individuals, households, and nongovernmental organizations on goods and services, excluding the purchases of dwellings. It was estimated that household consumption was growing at an average annual rate of 15.8%.

21LABOR

As of 2006 Seychelles had a total labor force of 39,560 people. Within that labor force, CIA estimates in 2006 noted that 3% were employed in agriculture, 23% in industry, and 74% in the service sector.

The Seychelles Federation of Workers' Union was the country's largest union. The Seychelles National Trade Union ceased operations in 2007; the Seychelles National Union began operations in 2009. Historically, trade unions have been associated with political parties. Employees have the right to organize and bargain collectively, but in practice most wages were set by the government—the country's largest employer. The government has the right to review and approve labor contracts between individuals and large firms. Approximately 15–20% of the workforce was unionized in 2011.

The minimum age for employment is 15, but children are encouraged to attend school until the 9th or 10th grade. Apprenticeships and vocational programs are available to those who leave school early. The minimum wage applied only to public sector jobs, and it stood at $186 per month in 2011; the private sector was encouraged, not mandated, to grant the minimum public sector wage. Most workers also receive a variety of free public services. Nonetheless, the minimum wage did not provide for a decent living, and the private sector generally paid higher wages in an effort to attract workers. The legal maximum workweek is 45 to 55 hours, but most government workers work less than that. Some private sector employees worked as many as 60 hours per week.

The government has issued comprehensive occupational health and safety regulations but they are not effectively enforced due to a lack of resources. Employees are allowed to leave dangerous job sites, report employers, and seek compensation.

22AGRICULTURE

Out of 46,000 hectares (113,668 acres) of land in Seychelles, only 1,000 hectares (2,471 acres) are arable. The country's major crops include coconuts, cinnamon, vanilla, sweet potatoes, cassava (tapioca), copra, and bananas. Fruit production amounted to 2,310 tons and vegetable production to 2,594 tons.

Tea planting began in the early 1960s. Sweet potatoes, yams, breadfruit, and cassava are grown in small quantities but are not sufficient to satisfy the local demand. Oranges, lemons, grapefruit, bananas, and mangoes meet the local requirement only in season.

23ANIMAL HUSBANDRY

In 2009, the country tended 370,000 chickens, 350 head of cattle, and 5,175 pigs. The production from these animals amounted to 863 tons of beef and veal, 471 tons of pork, 1,193 tons of poultry, 769 tons of eggs, and 6,576 tons of milk. Seychelles has continued to seek self-sufficiency in the production of animal products as a means to lower its trade deficit.

24FISHING

In 2008, the annual capture totaled 69,172 tons according to the UN FAO. Per capita fish consumption in the Seychelles is very high, yet the development of industrial fishing is at its early stages. The development of port services for foreign tuna fishing fleets since the early 1980s has raised incomes and living standards, while diminishing the role of artisanal fishing.

Foreign vessels fishing in Seychellois waters must be licensed to operate within the 322-km (200-mi) economic zone, which encompassed one of the world's richest tuna-fishing grounds. French investments have focused on tuna fishing and canning. The European Community, Korea, and Japan hold the key licenses to Seychelles coastal fishing.

25FORESTRY

Although approximately 89% of Seychelles is covered by forest, little virgin forest remains. The UN FAO estimated the 2009 value of all forest products at $99,000. Coconut plantations are the main source of timber, aside from imports. Imports of forest products rose to 4.2 million in 2010, up substantially from 1.4 million in 2006.

26MINING

Seychelles' mineral production in 2004 consisted granite dimension stone, gravel and crushed rock, and sand. Although

Principal Trading Partners – Seychelles (2010)

(In millions of US dollars)

Country	Total	Exports	Imports	Balance
World	1,050.1	400.1	650.0	-249.9
Sa'udi Arabia	212.3	...	212.3	-212.3
France	127.5	59.3	68.2	-8.9
United Kingdom	92.9	63.8	29.1	34.7
South Africa	86.7	2.5	84.2	-81.7
Italy	85.0	37.3	47.7	-10.4
Spain	77.5	10.9	66.6	-55.7
Singapore	61.4	1.3	60.1	-58.8
Japan	44.5	36.1	8.4	27.7
India	40.3	7.7	32.6	-24.9
Mauritius	37.9	13.6	24.3	-10.7

(…) data not available or not significant.

(n.s.) not specified.

SOURCE: *2011 Direction of Trade Statistics Yearbook*, New York: United Nations, 2011.

production of guano (a phosphate fertilizer comprising bird droppings, extracted from Assumption) ceased in the mid-1980s, a plant with a capacity of 5,000 tons per year remained; modest production was unofficially reported in the mid-1990s. Output of granite dimension stone in 2004 was estimated at 93,000 metric tons, up from 92,120 metric tons in 2002. Gravel and crushed rock output in 2004 was estimated at 213,000 metric tons, up from 212,926 metric tons in the previous year. Sand production in 2004 was estimated at 2,200 metric tons, up from 2,165 metric tons in 2002. Polymetallic nodules were known to occur on the ocean bottom near the Admirante Islands. The Seychelles comprised 40 granitic and at least 50 coralline islands.

27 ENERGY AND POWER

The World Bank reported in 2008 that Seychelles produced 260 million kWh of electricity and consumed 248.7 million kWh, or 2,788 kWh per capita. All fossil fuel and refined petroleum product consumption was met by imports. In 2010 imports averaged 8,000 barrels per day, twice that of 2004 levels.

A government announcement in 2010 stated that two foreign companies would begin drilling for oil in the archipelago by the end of 2012. It was to be the first major oil exploration in Seychellois territory.

28 INDUSTRY

In 2011 manufacturing contributed 15% to 20% of GDP, varying based on output of the Indian Ocean Tuna cannery. The tuna cannery opened in 1987 and was privatized in 1995 with a 60% purchase by U.S.-based Heinz Inc. The tuna business has grown rapidly, and the joint venture between Heinz and the government is one of the largest employers in Seychelles.

Other factories are smaller and process local agricultural products. A tea factory handles locally grown tea. Others process copra and vanilla pods and extract coconut oil. There is a plastics factory, a brewery and soft drink bottler, and a cinnamon distiller. Salt, cigarettes, boats, furniture, steel products, publications, animal feeds, processed meats, dairy products, paints, and assembled televisions are also produced. Oil exploration is underway, and

geophysical and geochemical analyses indicate potential for commercial production.

29 SCIENCE AND TECHNOLOGY

The World Bank reported in 2009 that there were no patent applications in science and technology in Seychelles. The University of Seychelles American Institute of Medicine paralleled the curriculum of US medical schools. The University of Seychelles offered degrees in computing and information technology and tropical, coastal, and marine sciences.

30 DOMESTIC TRADE

The small Chinese merchant class plays an important part in the retail trade. The variety of domestic goods for sale is very limited. There are price controls on most foodstuffs. The capital of Victoria is the major commercial center of the island. Shops range from supermarkets to a traditional open-air market. A small handicrafts and pottery industry creates products primarily for tourists.

Normal business hours are 8 a.m. to noon and 1:30 to 4 p.m., Monday–Friday; 8 a.m. to noon on Saturday. Most business is conducted in English, but French is widely spoken.

31 FOREIGN TRADE

Seychelles imported $831 million worth of goods and services in 2008, while exporting $464 million worth of goods and services. Major import partners in 2009 were Saudi Arabia, 17.4%; Spain, 7.9%; South Africa, 7.1%; France, 6.7%; Brazil, 6.4%; Singapore, 5.4%; Germany, 4.1%; and the United States, 4%. Its major export partners were UK, 28.1%; France, 21%; Italy, 10.7%; Japan, 7.9%; and Spain, 5.4%.

Seychelles' major exports were canned tuna, frozen fish, cinnamon, copra, and reexported petroleum. As with many small island nations, Seychelles imports most manufactured goods and a number of foodstuffs.

Balance of Payments – Seychelles (2010)

(In millions of US dollars)

Current Account		-225.1
Balance on goods		-336.5
Imports	-736.8	
Exports	400.2	
Balance on services		150.7
Balance on income		-64.6
Current transfers		25.4
Capital Account		275.3
Financial Account		239.1
Direct investment abroad		-6.2
Direct investment in Seychelles		167.3
Portfolio investment assets		27.2
Portfolio investment liabilities		-2.5
Financial derivatives		...
Other investment assets		8.5
Other investment liabilities		44.8
Net Errors and Omissions		13.2
Reserves and Related Items		-302.5

(…) data not available or not significant.

SOURCE: *Balance of Payment Statistics Yearbook 2011*, Washington, DC: International Monetary Fund, 2011.

³²BALANCE OF PAYMENTS

In 2010 Seychelles had a foreign trade deficit of $231 million, amounting to 4.3% of GDP. Development aid, income from tourism, and earnings from reexports have generally been sufficient to offset Seychelles' persistent visible trade deficit.

The rise of exports consistently outpaced the growth of imports in Seychelles during the 2000s. Reflecting this trend, the current account balance ballooned from -$284.2 million in 2009 to -420.1 million in 2010.

³³BANKING AND SECURITIES

The Seychelles Monetary Authority, established in 1978 as the bank of issue, became the Central Bank of Seychelles in 1983. The central bank discount rate, the rate at which the government lends money to banks, was 5.13% in 2007. The commercial bank prime lending rate, the rate at which banks lend to customers, was 12.703% in 2010.

Commercial banks included the Barclays, Nouvobanq, Banque Française Commerciale Océan Indien, Bank of Baroda, and Habib Bank. Development of an offshore banking center began in 1999.

The Seychelles Stock Exchange was set to open in 2011. It was expected to list a number of Seychellois companies and large hotels on its exchange.

³⁴INSURANCE

All private insurance companies were nationalized in 1983 and their business transferred to the State Assurance Corp. Insurance Acts in 1995 and 2008 liberalized the insurance industry and led to the development of an offshore insurance industry. H Savy Insurance Company and the State Assurance Company are still the two main providers of insurance.

³⁵PUBLIC FINANCE

In 2010 the budget of Seychelles included $316.5 million in public revenue and $310.3 million in public expenditures. The budget surplus amounted to 4.4% of GDP. Public debt was 58.8% of GDP, with $1.549 billion of the debt held by foreign entities.

Annual budgets of increasing deficits were common in the 1980s. The public sector is responsible for two-thirds of Seychelles' employment. Public investment focuses on social and physical infrastructure, tourism, and export activities. Some privatization has occurred in recent years, including the privatization of the Seychelles Tuna Canning Factory, 60% of which was purchased by Heinz in 1995.

A public finance crisis in 2009 led to a default on Eurobond interest payments, but it also allowed for a more sustainable restructuring of public spending, culminating in the forgiveness of $70 million of debt and a delayed repayment schedule.

³⁶TAXATION

The Seychellois tax code was greatly reformed in 2010, largely as a result of its 2009 fiscal crisis. Personal income tax was set at 15%, down from its previous level of 18.75%. This standardized of the personal income tax rate and demonstrated the government's broader commitment to a simpler, more regular tax code. A preferential goods and services tax, previously levied at 10%, was to

be replaced by a value-added tax levied at 15% in 2012. The maximum business tax rate was reduced from 40% to 33%, and tax free status was revoked for companies and lowered for sole traders and

Seychelles has also signed tax information exchange agreements with foreign countries as an effort to add transparency to its offshore banking sector. It did so with the Netherlands in 2010.

³⁷CUSTOMS AND DUTIES

The Seychellois government places quotas on certain imports (such as motor vehicles) and other types of restrictions on other items. Prohibited goods include arms and ammunition, dangerous drugs, pornographic materials, and spearguns. Import tariffs a variable trade tax from 0% to 50%, and a 15% GST (to become at VAT in 2012).

The Seychelles International Trade Zone offers tax benefits and other advantages to exporters.

³⁸FOREIGN INVESTMENT

Foreign direct investment (FDI) in Seychelles was a net inflow of $248.6 million according to World Bank figures published in 2009. FDI represented 32.52% of GDP. Tourism was a major target of foreign investors in 2011; other sectors promoted by the Seychelles Investment Bureau, a government entity, included fisheries, agriculture, industry, and offshore banking.

³⁹ECONOMIC DEVELOPMENT

The 1985–89 plan sought to create jobs and emphasized developing cash crops, tourism, and the fishing industry. The 1990–94 plan emphasized the need to attract foreign investment. Of considerable interest to donors in the 1990s was the 10-year plan to improve the Seychelles environment.

Dependence on tourism revenues depressed the economy during a 2008 global recession. Tourism continued to drive the

Public Finance – Seychelles (2009)

(In millions of rupees, central government figures)

Revenue and Grants	**4,174.3**	**100.0%**
Tax revenue	2,911.1	69.7%
Social contributions	375.2	9.0%
Grants	365.3	8.8%
Other revenue	522.6	12.5%
Expenditures	**3,729.5**	**100.0%**
General public services	2,058.2	55.2%
Defense	148.6	4.0%
Public order and safety	...	...
Economic affairs	...	...
Environmental protection	...	...
Housing and community amenities	...	...
Health	359.4	9.6%
Recreational, culture, and religion	...	...
Education	...	...
Social protection	...	...

(…) data not available or not significant.

SOURCE: *Government Finance Statistics Yearbook 2010,* Washington, DC: International Monetary Fund, 2010.

economy in 2011, facilitating development in construction as well as public spending to upgrade infrastructure. Efforts to diversify the Seychellois economy focused on the growth of an offshore banking center, which the country regarded as a new pillar of its economy. Industrial prospects remained limited primarily to light manufacturing, and agriculture and fisheries accounted for a small portion of the GDP. Tapping oil reserves remained a lucrative, though unproven, prospect.

40 SOCIAL DEVELOPMENT

All citizens residing in Seychelles territory and resident foreign employees are entitled to participate in the social security fund. Benefits are provided for old age, disability, survivorship, sickness, and maternity. Employees and employers are required to make monthly contributions. Retirement is set at age 63 with at least five years of residency. There is also a workers' compensation scheme. Health services are provided under the National Health Plan.

Traditional Seychelles culture is matriarchal and women are accorded considerable respect within society. However, violence against women, particularly domestic violence, remains a problem and has been linked to alcohol abuse. Women are fairly well represented in both the public and private sectors. Inheritance laws do not discriminate against women.

Human rights are generally respected although prison conditions were poor and pretrial delays prolonged as much as three years due to judicial inefficiencies.

41 HEALTH

According to the CIA, life expectancy in Seychelles was 74 years in 2011. The country spent 4.2% of its GDP on healthcare, amounting to $366 per person. There were 15 physicians, 79 nurses and midwives, and 39 hospital beds per 10,000 inhabitants. The fertility rate was 2.3, while the infant mortality rate was 11 per 1,000 live births.

It was estimated that 97% of children were vaccinated against measles. Seychelles has also reached the goal of attaining at least 90% immunization DPT (diphtheria, pertussis, and tetanus). No cases of polio, measles, or neonatal tetanus were reported, however leprosy was still present. In 2007 there were reports of Chikungunya, a form of viral fever spread by mosquito bites.

42 HOUSING

Most homes were made of stone block with corrugated iron roofs; others are constructed of wood frames and walls. Some rural houses were thatched. Special housing was available for citizens who lost their homes due to natural disasters.

43 EDUCATION

In 2009 the World Bank estimated that 94% of age-eligible children in Seychelles were enrolled in primary school. Secondary enrollment for age-eligible children stood at 97%.Overall, the CIA estimated that Seychelles had a literacy rate of 91.8%. Public expenditure on education represented 5.0% of GDP.

Since 1980, public education has been free and compulsory for 10 years for children between the ages of 6 and 16. Six years of primary education are followed by five years of secondary education. Vocational courses are offered for secondary students.

The University of Seychelles, the first independent, non-profit university in the nation, was opened in 2009. Located at Anse Royale, the university offered undergraduate and pre-graduate courses in business administration and computing and information systems in collaboration with the University of London. A foundation studies program was offered at the university to assist potential students without the necessary qualifications for enrollment. There was also a teacher-training college and a polytechnic institute. Only members of the National Youth Service were eligible to apply to the teacher-training college. Many students continued to study abroad, mainly in the United Kingdom.

44 LIBRARIES AND MUSEUMS

The National Archives and a National Library (80,000 volumes) are both located in Victoria (Mahé Island). Seychelles Polytechnic University has 12,000 volumes. The Seychelles National Museum of History is located in the same building as the National Library. There is also a Seychelles Natural History Museum in Victoria.

45 MEDIA

In 2009 the CIA reported that there were 22,100 telephone landlines in Seychelles. In addition to landlines, mobile phone subscriptions averaged 105 per 100 people. There was 1 FM radio station, 1 AM radio station, and 2 shortwave radio stations. Internet subscriptions stood at 39 per 100 citizens. In 2010 the most prominent newspaper, with its circulation listed parenthetically, was the *Seychelles Nation* (3,500).

Radio-Television Seychelles, which is government owned, broadcasts in English, French, and Creole. Television service, controlled by the government, began in 1983. License fees for privately owned radio and television stations are so high that an independent media has not been able to develop.

The press was not entirely free, and most journalists practiced self-censorship. There were legal reprisals for those who those highly critical of the government.

46 ORGANIZATIONS

Trade groups include the Seychelles Chamber of Commerce and Industry and the Seychelles Farmers' Association. The Women's Association and the Youth Organization are arms of the SPPF. Other youth organizations include the National Youth League of the Seychelles and the Scout and Guide Movement of the Seychelles. There are several sports associations representing such pastimes as tennis, squash, yachting, and track and field. There are national chapters of the Red Cross and Caritas.

47 TOURISM, TRAVEL, AND RECREATION

The *Tourism Factbook*, published by the UN World Tourism Organization, reported 158,000 incoming tourists to Seychelles in 2009; they spent a total of $302 million. Of those incoming tourists, there were 122,000 from Europe. There were 5,080 hotel beds available in Seychelles, which had an occupancy rate of 54%. The estimated daily cost to visit Victoria, the capital, was $447.

The prosperity of Seychelles depends on tourism. Visitors can enjoy coral beaches, water sports including scuba diving, waterskiing, and windsurfing, and boat or yacht tours of the islands.

The archipelago's wildlife is also a popular tourist attraction. Valid passports are required, but visas are not.

A decline in tourism revenues in 2008, stemming from a global recession, triggered a financial crisis for the Seychellois government. Tourism also directed large amounts of foreign investment and spending on public infrastructure.

48 FAMOUS PERSONS

Sir James Richard Marie Mancham (b. 1939), leader of the SDP, became Seychelles' first president in 1976. He was deposed in 1977 by France Albert René (b. 1935), who served until 2004.

49 DEPENDENCIES

Seychelles has no territories or colonies.

50 BIBLIOGRAPHY

Carpin, Sarah. *Seychelles*. 6th ed. Hong Kong: Odyssey, 2005.

Gillespie, Rosemary G., and David A. Clague, eds. *Encyclopedia of Islands*. Berkeley: University of California Press, 2009.

Skerrett, Adrian. *Birds of the Seychelles*. Princeton, NJ: Princeton University Press, 2001.

Vine, Peter. *Seychelles*. 2nd ed. London, Eng.: Immel Publishing, 1992.

Zeilig, Leo, and David Seddon. *A Political and Economic Dictionary of Africa*. Philadelphia: Routledge/Taylor and Francis, 2005.

SIERRA LEONE

Republic of Sierra Leone

CAPITAL: Freetown

FLAG: The national flag is a tricolor of green, white, and blue horizontal stripes.

ANTHEM: Begins "High we exalt thee, realm of the free, Great is the love we have for thee."

MONETARY UNIT: The leone (SLL) is a paper currency of 100 cents. There are coins of 10, 50, 100 and 500 cents, and notes of 1000, 2000, 5000 and 10000 leones. SLL1 = US$0.000233 (or US$1 = SLL4,300.00) as of February 2012.

WEIGHTS AND MEASURES: The metric system is employed.

HOLIDAYS: New Year's Day, 1 January; Independence Day, 27 April; Bank Holiday, August; Christmas, 24–25 December; Boxing Day, 26 December. Movable religious holidays include Good Friday, Easter Monday, Whitmonday, Eid al-Fitr, Eid al-Adha, and Milad an-Nabi.

TIME: GMT.

¹LOCATION, SIZE, AND EXTENT

Situated on the west coast of Africa, Sierra Leone has an area of 71,740 sq km (27,699 sq mi), extending 338 km (210 mi) N–S and 304 km (189 mi) E–W. Comparatively, the area occupied by Sierra Leone is slightly smaller than the state of South Carolina. It is bounded on the N and E by Guinea, on the SE by Liberia, and on the S and W by the Atlantic Ocean, with a total boundary length of 1,360 km (845 mi), of which 402 km (250 mi) is coastline. In addition to the mainland proper, Sierra Leone also includes the offshore Banana and Turtle islands and Sherbro Island, as well as other small islets.

Sierra Leone's capital city, Freetown, is located on the Atlantic Coast.

²TOPOGRAPHY

The Sierra Leone Peninsula in the extreme west is mostly mountainous, rising to about 884 m (2,900 ft). The western part of the country, excluding the Peninsula, consists of coastal mangrove swamps. Farther east, a coastal plain extends inland for about 100–160 km (60–100 mi); many rivers in this area are navigable for short distances. Stretches of wooded hill country lead east and northeast to a plateau region generally ranging in elevation from 300 to 610 m (1,000 to 2,000 ft). There are peaks of over 1,830 m (6,000 ft), reaching a maximum of 1,948 m (6,390 ft) at Loma Mansa (Bintimani) in the Loma Mountains.

³CLIMATE

Temperatures and humidity are high, and rainfall is heavy. The mean temperature is about 27°C (81°F) on the coast and almost as high on the eastern plateau. There are two distinct seasons: the dry season, from November to April, and the wet season, over the rest of the year, with the heaviest precipitation in July, August, and September. Rainfall is greatest along the coast, especially in the mountains, where there is more than 580 cm (230 in) annually, but it averages more than 315 cm (125 in) a year in most of the country, with 366 cm (144 in) at Freetown. The relative humidity ranges from an average of 80% during the wet season to about 50% during the dry season.

⁴FLORA AND FAUNA

About 25–35% of the land area, mostly in the north, consists of savanna or grasslands; 20–25%, mostly in the south-center, is low bush; another 20–25%, in the southeast, is secondary forest or high bush; 10–20% is swampland; and 3–5% is primary rain forest. The World Resources Institute estimates that there are 2,090 plant species in Sierra Leone.

Animal species include 197 mammal, 626 bird, 69 reptile, and 46 amphibian species. The calculation reflects the total number of distinct species residing in the country, not the number of endemic species. The emerald cuckoo, which has been described as the most beautiful bird in Africa, is found in Sierra Leone, although it has disappeared from the rest of West Africa. Other species include the Senegal firefinch, common bulbul, little African swift, Didric cuckoo, bronze manakin, cattle egret (or "tickbird"), and many birds that breed in Europe but winter in Sierra Leone. Crocodiles and hippopotamuses are indigenous to the river regions of the coastal plain.

⁵ENVIRONMENT

The World Resources Institute reported that Sierra Leone had designated 292,300 hectares (722,289 acres) of land for protection as of 2006. Water resources totaled 160 cu km (38.39 cu mi) while water usage was 0.38 cu km (0.091 cu mi) per year. Domestic water usage accounted for 5% of total usage, industrial for 3%, and agricultural for 92%. Per capita water usage totaled 69 cu m (2,437 cu ft) per year. Water pollution is a significant problem in Sierra Leone due to mining by-products and sewage. The nation's cities produce an average of about 0.3 million tons of solid waste per year.

Population pressure, leading to an intensification of agriculture, has resulted in soil depletion, while lumbering, cattle grazing, and slash-and-burn farming have decimated the primary forest. Agricultural lands are gradually replacing forestlands due to the need for food by a population that increased by 80% during the period between 1963 and 1990. The forests of the Sierra Leone Peninsula are protected. The Sierra Leone River Estuary is a Ramsar Wetland Site. Government agencies with environmental responsibilities include the Ministry of Agriculture, Natural Resources, and Forestry, Ministry of Mines, Ministry of Lands and Human Development, Ministry of Energy and Power, and Ministry of Economic Planning and National Development. The UN reported in 2008 that carbon dioxide emissions in Sierra Leone totaled 1,312 kilotons.

Hunting for food has reduced the stock of wild mammals, and Cutamba Killimi National Park, which has some wildlife species found only in this part of West Africa, is exploited by poachers. According to a 2011 report issued by the International Union for Conservation of Nature and Natural Resources (IUCN), the number of threatened species included 17 mammals, 10 birds, 3 reptiles, 2 amphibians, 47 fish, 3 other invertebrates, and 48 plants. Threatened species in Sierra Leone include the white-breasted Guinea fowl, Diana monkey, the African sharp-nosed crocodile, and several species of shark.

6 POPULATION

The US Central Intelligence Agency (CIA) estimates the population of Sierra Leone in 2011 to be approximately 5,363,669, which placed it at number 112 in population among the 196 nations of the world. In 2011, approximately 3.7% of the population was over 65 years of age, with another 41.8% under 15 years of age. The median age in Sierra Leone was 19.1 years. There were 0.94 males for every female in the country. The population's annual rate of change was 2.249%. The projected population for the year 2025 was 8,100,000. Population density in Sierra Leone was calculated at 75 people per sq km (194 people per sq mi).

The UN estimated that 38% of the population lived in urban areas, and that urban populations had an annual rate of change of 3.3%. The largest urban area was Freetown, with a population of 875,000.

The prevalence of HIV/AIDS has had a significant impact on the population of Sierra Leone. The AIDS epidemic causes higher death and infant mortality rates, and lowers life expectancy.

7 MIGRATION

Estimates of Sierra Leone's net migration rate, carried out by the CIA in 2011, amounted to -4.25 migrants per 1,000 citizens. The total number of emigrants living abroad was 267,000, and the total number of immigrants living in Sierra Leone was 106,800. Sierra Leone also accepted 27,311 refugees.

Historically, there has been considerable movement over the borders to and from Guinea and Liberia. In the mid-1980s, the number of non-native Africans was estimated at 30,000. Since the civil war in 1991, hundreds of thousands of refugees have left Sierra Leone. The UN High Commissioner for Refugees (UNHCR) began repatriating refugees in 1997.

8 ETHNIC GROUPS

The African population is composed of some 20 native ethnic groups, constituting nearly 85% of the total population. The two largest are the Mende (about 31% of the population) and Temne (about 35%). Other peoples, making up the remaining 30% of the African populace, include the Limba (8%), Kono (5%), Mandingo (2%), Loko (2%), Bullom, Fulani, Gola, Kissi, Koranko, Krim, Kru, Loko, Malinke, Sherbro, Susu, Vai, and Yalunka. Creoles (also Kriole or Krio), the descendants of freed Jamaican slaves who settled in the Freetown area in the late 18th century, account for the remaining 2% of the total population. Refugees from Liberia's recent civil war also live in Sierra Leone, along with small numbers of Europeans, Lebanese, Pakistanis, and Indians.

9 LANGUAGES

English is the official language; however, it is used regularly only by the literate minority. The Mende and Temne languages are widely spoken in the south and north, respectively. Krio, the mother tongue of the Creoles, derived largely from English, with words added from various West African languages, is the lingua franca and a first language for about 10% of the population, but is understood by 95%.

10 RELIGIONS

A 2010 report estimates that the population is 77% Muslim, 21% Christian, and 2% practitioners of traditional indigenous religions. Muslims were traditionally concentrated in the northern part of the country, and Christians in the south. However, the civil war that ended in 2002 prompted relocation by large masses of the population. Reportedly, many syncretic practices exist, with up to 20% of the populace practicing a mixture of either Muslim or Christianity with traditional indigenous religions. There are small communities of Hindus, Jews, and Baha'is. Freedom of religion is guaranteed by the constitution and this right is usually respected in practice. Religious groups are not required to register with the government. The Birth of the Prophet Muhammad, Good Friday, Easter Monday, Eid al-Fitr, Eid al-Adha, and Christmas are observed as national holidays. The Inter-Religious Council serves an important role in civil society and works to promote the peace process within the country.

11 TRANSPORTATION

The CIA reported that Sierra Leone had a total of 11,300 km (7,021 mi) of roads in 2002, of which 904 km (562 mi) were paved. In 1970 there were more than 580 km (360 mi) of railway, but by the end of 1975, following an IBRD recommendation, Sierra Leone had dismantled most of its rail system and replaced it with new roadways; since the mid-1980s, only 84 km (52 mi) of narrow-gauge railway has remained, connecting the closed iron mines at Marampa with the port of Pepel, on the Sierra Leone River. The line remains operable but is in limited use. There are nine airports, which transported 21,784 passengers in 2009 according to the World Bank.

Freetown has one of the finest natural harbors in the world, with an excellent deepwater quay, built in 1953. In 1970, work was completed on an extension that provides the port with berth facilities for six to eight ships and about 24 hectares (60 acres) of storage area. Pepel specializes in the export of iron ore, and Point Sam, the Sherbro River terminal, handles bauxite and rutile. Bonthe and Sulima are other ports. Sierra Leone has many rivers; however, some are navigable only over short distances for about three months of the year, during the rainy season. About 600 km (373 mi) of Sierra Leone's waterways are navigable year round.

12 HISTORY

Archaeological research indicates that by AD 800 the use of iron had been introduced into what is now Sierra Leone and that by AD 1000 the coastal peoples were practicing agriculture. Beginning perhaps in the 13th century, migrants arrived from the more advanced savanna lands to the north and east.

European contact began in 1462 with the Portuguese explorer Pedro da Cintra, who gave the mountainous Peninsula the name Sierra Leone ("Lion Mountains"). From the 16th to the early 19th century, the region was raided for slaves for the Atlantic trade, and later in the 19th century, it was ravaged by African war leaders and slavers.

The colony of Sierra Leone was founded by British philanthropists to relieve the horrors of this slave trade. Granville Sharp, a leader in the movement to abolish slavery, planned it as a home for African slaves freed in England. In 1787, he sent out the first settlers to what he called "The Province of Freedom." In the following year, one of the Temne kings and his subordinate chiefs sold and ceded a strip of land on the north shore of the Sierra Leone Peninsula to Capt. John Taylor on behalf of the "free community of settlers, their heirs and successors, lately arrived from England, and under the protection of the British Government." A few years later, they were joined by settlers of African origin from England, Nova Scotia (freed slaves who, as loyalists, had fled the American Revolution), and Jamaica.

The Sierra Leone Company, of which Sharp was a director, was formed in 1791 to administer the settlement. The land did not prove as fertile as described, and the settlement was the victim of attacks by neighboring tribes and by a French squadron. The burden of defense and settlement proved too heavy for the company, and Sierra Leone was transferred to the crown in 1808. The colony received additions of land up to 1861 through various treaties of friendship and cession from the local chiefs.

After 1807, when the British Parliament passed an act making the slave trade illegal, the new colony was used as a base from which the act could be enforced. Beginning in 1808, hundreds, and sometimes thousands, of slaves were freed each year, most of them remaining in Sierra Leone. In 1896, a British protectorate was declared over the hinterland of Sierra Leone, which was separate from the colony. Revolts in 1898 were provoked mainly by attempts to extend British colonial jurisdiction into the protectorate.

During Sierra Leone's colonial history, indigenous people waged several unsuccessful revolts against British rule. In the Hut Tax War of 1898, a Northern front, led by Bai Bureh, and Southern front both took up arms against the British. Hundred were killed

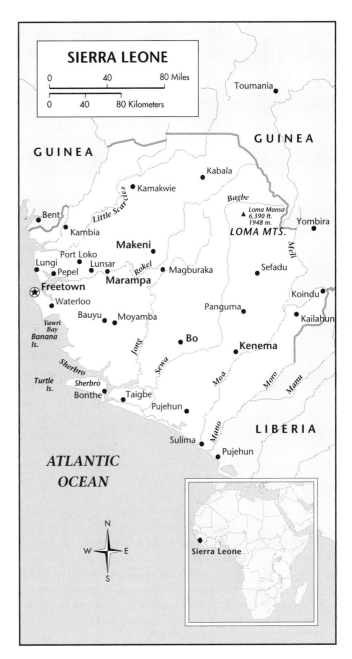

LOCATION: 6°55′ to 10°N; 10°16′ to 13°18′W. BOUNDARY LENGTHS: Guinea, 652 kilometers (405 miles); Liberia, 306 kilometers (190 miles); Atlantic coastline, 406 kilometers (252 miles). TERRITORIAL SEA LIMIT: 12 miles.

on both sides over the course of several months. Bai Bureh was captured on 11 November 1898. He was sent into exile in the Gold Coast (now Ghana). Nearly 100 of his supporters were hanged by the British. Although riots and other labor disturbances continued to occur throughout colonial rule, no other major uprisings occurred.

A 1924 constitution provided for the election of three members to a Legislative Council on a restricted franchise, and the constitution of 1951 provided for an elected majority, resulting in African rule. In 1957, the Legislative Council was replaced by a House of Representatives, most members of which were elected, and the literacy requirement for voters was dropped. In 1958, Milton Margai became Sierra Leone's first prime minister; in 1960, he led a delegation to London to establish conditions for full independence.

Independence

Sierra Leone became an independent country within the Commonwealth of Nations on 27 April 1961. Milton Margai continued as prime minister until his death in 1964, when he was succeeded by his half-brother, Albert Margai, who held office until the national elections in March 1967. The outcome of the elections was disputed, but the All-People's Congress (APC) claimed a plurality of the seats in the House of Representatives. Before Siaka Stevens, chairman of the APC, could take office as prime minister, he was ousted in a bloodless coup led by the army chief, Brig. David Lansana. Martial law was declared, and a National Reformation Council remained in control for 13 months, until 18 April 1968, when it was overthrown by the Anti-Corruption Revolutionary Movement, a military group that formed the National Interim Council. On 26 April 1968, Stevens was installed as prime minister of a civilian government. Continuing political unrest prompted the declaration of a state of emergency in 1970 and a ban on the newly created United Democratic Party, an opposition group whose leaders were arrested.

In 1971, after an abortive military coup which was suppressed with aid from Guinea, a new constitution was adopted. The country was declared a republic on 19 April 1971. Two days later, Siaka Stevens, then prime minister, became the nation's first president. National elections were held in May 1973, and the APC won a nearly unanimous victory following the decision of the opposition Sierra Leone People's Party to withdraw its candidates because of alleged electoral irregularities. An alleged plot to overthrow Stevens failed in 1974, and in March 1976, he was elected without opposition for a second five-year term as president. In 1978, a new constitution was adopted, making the country a one-party state.

An economic slowdown, coupled with revelations of government corruption, led to a general strike in September 1981, called by the Sierra Leone Labour Congress; some labor leaders and other government critics were temporarily detained under emergency regulations, but the government met a key demand of the strikers by moving to reduce the prices of basic commodities. Violence and irregularities marked the parliamentary elections held in 1982, which were limited to the APC.

Stevens did not run for reelection as president in 1985, yielding power to his handpicked successor, Maj. Gen. Joseph Saidu Momoh, the armed forces commander, whose nomination by the APC was ratified in his unopposed election in October 1985. Parliamentary elections were held in May 1986. Following an alleged attempt to assassinate Momoh in March 1987, over 60 persons were arrested, including First Vice President Francis Minah, who was removed from office. An extensive reshuffling of the cabinet followed. Further reports of alleged coup attempts followed.

In April 1991, Sierra Leone was invaded from Liberia by forces commanded by Liberian rebel Charles Taylor. Domestic support within Sierra Leone mounted and by 29 April 1992, Momoh was overthrown in a military coup. Momoh fled to Guinea. A National Provisional Ruling Council (NPRC) was created but, shortly afterward, on 2 May, the head of the five-member junta Lt. Col. Yahya was arrested by his colleagues and replaced by 29-year-old Capt. Valentine Strasser, who was formally designated head of state.

The Strasser government soon began ruling by a series of decrees and public notices limiting political freedoms. The NPRC dissolved parliament and political parties. Strasser talked of returning Sierra Leone to multiparty democracy, but his main goal was to end the fighting in the southeast where the forces of the National Patriot Front of Liberia (NPFL) and Sierra Leone dissidents were engaging a weakly-committed Sierra Leone armed force. Forces from the ECOWAS Monitoring Group sought to create a buffer along the boundary between the two countries. A rebellion led by Foday Sankoh of the Revolutionary United Front (RUF) simmered throughout 1993, although it seemed to falter as the Liberian rebels across the border lost ground. Facing a military stalemate, in November 1993 Strasser announced a unilateral cease-fire, an amnesty for rebels, and issued a timetable for a transition to democracy.

Through 1992 and 1993, Strasser used the security situation to consolidate his power. In December 1992, the government executed 26 alleged coup plotters from the Momoh government. In mid-1993, Strasser arrested his vice president, Capt. Solomon Musa. Policy was formulated and implemented by the NPRC, which established a Supreme Council of State comprising NPRC members, military officers and one civilian.

In 1996, Deputy Brig. Gen. Julius Maada Brio ousted Strasser and provided him safe conduct out of the country. Presidential and parliamentary elections took place in February 1996, but were opposed violently by rebel forces resulting in 27 deaths. Neither candidate, Ahmad Tejan Kabbah (United Peoples Party) or Dr. John Karefa-Smart, received a majority of the vote and a runoff election was held on 15 March 1996. Kabbah won the election with 59.4% of the vote.

In May 1997, Maj. Johnny Paul Koromah of the Armed Forces Revolutionary Council (AFRC) overthrew Kabbah. Clashes between the rebels and Nigerian troops followed, forcing 12,000 Freetown residents to flee the capital. With ECOMOG's support, President Kabbah returned from exile on 10 March 1998. However, rebel forces remained firmly in control of the north, the Kono diamond field, and areas along the Liberian border.

A violent rebel offensive in January 1999 led by the AFRC and Revolutionary United Front (RUF) forced the evacuation of diplomatic and foreign aid personnel from Freetown. As many as 5,000 residents were killed, 150,000 dislocated, and 20% of Freetown was destroyed. Rebels amputated the hands and feet of thousands of civilians "to send a message" to the government. Human rights reports documented unspeakable abuses on all sides. The attack was repelled, but rebels gained control of two-thirds of the country.

In March 1999, President Kabbah was forced to grant temporary amnesty to Corporal Foday Sankoh of the RUF. Sankoh received four ministerial positions and three deputies, bringing the rebel presence in government to seven. Peace talks resumed, and a cease-fire was signed in May. In July, Jesse Jackson and ECOWAS chairman, Gnassingbe Eyadema, were present at the signing of the Lomé Peace Accord. In December 1999, ECOMOG forces began their withdrawal to be replaced by 11,000 UN observer troops (UNAMSIL), which eventually reached troop strength of 17,000.

Disgruntled over the distribution of ministries in the unity government, the RUF resumed war in early May 2000, captured 500 UN personnel, and advanced to within 25 miles of the capital. However, on 17 May, Foday Sankoh was captured and eventually died in government custody in July 1993. Liberian President Charles Taylor, a supporter of the RUF, helped obtain the release of some of the peacekeepers, but insisted that Sankoh be part of the solution to the war. By June 2000, the rebels offered to trade their remaining captives for Sankoh's release, but the trade never materialized. Instead UNAMSIL routed the RUF and other armed groups, and concluded a peace agreement, which became fully effective January 2002. President Kabbah and his party won overwhelming victories at the presidential and parliamentary polls that followed on 14 May 2002.

Kabbah proceeded with restructuring and downsizing the army and security forces, and began to prosecute war criminals under a UN Special Court. In October 2002, Kabbah established a Truth and Reconciliation Commission (TRC) to accelerate emotional healing. The TRC's mandate expired in April 2004. By February 2003, some 1,400 people had provided testimony containing information about 3,000 victims who had suffered more than 4,000 violations, including 1,000 deaths and 200 cases of rape and sexual abuse. Militarily, nearly 50,000 combatants were demobilized and disarmed of some 15,000 weapons. Koroma, who escaped from the police in a failed coup attempt in 2003, had not been heard from and was presumed dead. In May 2003, authorities in Liberia produced the corpse of Col. Mosquito, the RUF bush commander.

UNAMSIL completed the first phase of its downsizing in late 2002 and in early May 2005, UN Secretary-General Kofi Annan said that the remaining troops except for a small rapid reaction force would be phased out by end of 2005. In local elections on 22 May 2004—the first such elections in over 30 years—the strong showing of the main opposition party APC sent a general message of discontent to the SLPP.

In June 2004, the first UN Special Court of Sierra Leone began its first trial of leaders of the pro-government militias, the Civil Defense Force (the Kamajors), and the RUF. In March 2005, trials for the AFRC defendants began. By early 2006, 13 people had been indicted (three posthumously-Foday Sankoh, Sam 'Mosquito' Bockarie, and Johnny Paul Koroma). Liberian President, Charles Taylor, who also faced 17 counts of war crimes charges under the Court, was exiled in Nigeria. In March 2006, Nigerian authorities handed Taylor over to the UN in Sierra Leone. The UN Special Court requested permission to use the premises of the International Criminal Court in The Hague to carry out Taylor's trial, although the Special Court would still conduct the proceedings of the trial. Taylor's war crimes trial started in The Hague in June 2007. However, hearings were postponed four times in 2007. The trial was reconvened in January 2008. Taylor's trial continued into July 2009, when the former Liberian president took the stand in his own defense in The Hague. In his defense statements, Taylor adamantly maintained his innocence, denying any involvement in the atrocities. Although a verdict was expected in 2011, none came, and lawyers for Taylor were seeking to reopen the case in early 2012.

Presidential and parliamentary elections were held in August 2007. Ernest Bai Koroma was elected president and his All People's Congress, formerly in opposition, won a majority in parliament. Koroma was sworn in as president on 17 September 2007. He won 54.6% of the vote in a run-off with the incumbent vice-president Solomon Berewa. Koroma is an insurance broker; he said he wanted to govern Sierra Leone as a businessman would. Koroma promised to fight corruption in his inaugural speech, and said he would combat the mismanagement of state resources.

Poverty, particularly as it affected war orphans and internally displaced people, continued to be a major challenge for the government into 2008. Approximately US$300 million dollars of international aid was poured into the country each year, beginning in 2000, in efforts to support post-conflict reconstruction. Most of the money, however, went toward rebuilding the government. In 2008 there were seven resettlement camps, inhabited by the internally displaced, that had been recognized as new townships by the government. The camps were meant to serve as temporary shelters. However, the residents there have not been able to obtain the financial resources to return to their previous homes. In 2007, the UN Development Programme ranked Sierra Leone as the least developed of the 177 countries that it analyzed.

13 GOVERNMENT

A new constitution came into force on 1 October 1991, replacing the June 1978 constitution and subsequent modifications. However, it was suspended by the military junta after the 29 April 1992 coup. Shortly thereafter, the parliament and political parties were dissolved and the NPRC ruled by decree through a Supreme Council of State (SCS) and a Council of State Secretaries (CSS-Cabinet). In November 1993 they announced a timetable leading to multiparty democracy and general elections in 1996. The constitution was suspended after the military coup in May 1997, but came into force again following the reinstatement of the Kabbah government in March 1998. A short-lived government of national unity was formed in October 1999 as part of the Lomé Peace Accords.

In February 2002, a district block (proportional) representation system for the election of MPs came into force, replacing the first-past-the-post constituency system, which was reinstated for the 2007 elections. As of 2011, the unicameral parliament had 124 seats—112 elected by popular vote and 12 filled by paramount chiefs elected in separate polls; members serve five-year terms.

14 POLITICAL PARTIES

Party politics in Sierra Leone have a long and lively history. The Sierra Leone People's Party (SLPP), formed in 1951, dominated politics from its inception until 1967, when the All People's Congress (APC) claimed to have won a plurality of the seats in a disputed parliamentary election. The SLPP combined the Sierra Leone Organization Society, founded in the protectorate in 1946, and the Freetown People's Party, founded in the colony by the Rev. Etheldred Jones, also known as Lamina Sankoh. Although the SLPP won only two of the seven seats open to election in 1951, it was given recognition when the indirectly elected protectorate members and eight paramount chiefs joined with it. In 1953, Milton Margai became chief minister, and in 1957, the SLPP won 26 of the 39 seats being contested.

During the pre-APC period, the National Council of Sierra Leone (NCSL), founded in 1951, was the principal opposition group. It was influential only in the colony and favored a federal constitution with separate assemblies for the colony and the protectorate. When universal adult suffrage was introduced in 1957, the NCSL lost all its seats in the legislature. The United People's Party

(UPP) was founded in 1956 by Cyril Rogers-Wright and Wallace Johnson to unite the interests of the colony and the protectorate. In the 1957 general elections, it won one seat in the legislature and gained three more after election petitions to the courts, so that it then constituted the principal legislative opposition.

In September 1958, Siaka Stevens and Milton Margai's half-brother, Albert Margai, withdrew from the SLPP and formed the People's National Party (PNP) to pursue a more militant policy. In 1960, the PNP and UPP joined the United National Front of all parties for the April constitutional talks in London. A national coalition government was formed, and Albert Margai became a cabinet minister.

Stevens left the United Front to form a new opposition group, the Elections Before Independence Movement (EBIM). Expelled from the PNP, he transformed the EBIM into the APC and, with support from younger radicals and much of the trade union movement, campaigned for a neutralist foreign policy and the need for a general election before independence. In March 1961, Stevens and some of his supporters were charged with sedition, libel, and incitement and were jailed just before independence under emergency regulations. They were later released and acquitted of the charges.

In the election of 25 May 1962, the SLPP won 28 of 62 seats for ordinary members of the House of Representatives, the APC 16, the Sierra Leone Progressive Movement 4, and independents 14. After the election returns were announced, 12 of the independents declared themselves members of the SLPP, and Milton Margai was able to form a new government. Upon his death on 28 April 1964, Albert Margai became prime minister. Thirteen months of military rule followed the disputed 1967 elections, after which Siaka Stevens, leader of the APC, became prime minister.

Siaka Stevens, president from 1971 to 1985, created the APC in 1960. The APC dominated from 1967 until April 1992. In September 1970, another opposition group, the United Democratic Party, was formed. Shortly afterward, a state of emergency was declared, and on 8 October, the party was banned. The SLPP won 15 seats in the 1977 elections, the last in which an opposition party was allowed to participate. In the 1983 balloting, 173 candidates competed for 66 seats, and the remaining 19 elective seats (mostly held by members of the outgoing government) were uncontested. In 1978, a new constitution made the APC the sole legal party, and the SLPP was formally dissolved. Members of parliament were required to declare themselves members of the APC on penalty of losing their seats.

In the 1986 balloting, 335 candidates competed for the 105 popularly elected seats. Over half the sitting members, including three cabinet ministers, were defeated and over 60% of those elected were newcomers to the House. After the April 1992 military coup, all political parties were banned and parliament was dissolved. In 1993 a timetable was prepared for a return to civilian rule and a multiparty democracy. Captain Valentine Strasser assumed leadership during the 1992 coup, but was overthrown in 1996.

In February 1996, Ahmad Tejan Kabbah, candidate of the National People's Party, was elected president with 59.4% of the vote. Fifteen parties registered for the 1996 elections. In the parliamentary competition for 80 seats (68 elected members; 12 paramount chiefs), the SLPP took 27 seats, the UNPP 17, the PDP 12, the APC 5, the NUP 4, and the DCP 3. These were the first elections since the former House of Representatives had been shut down by the military coup of April 1992. In November 1999, the RUF changed its name to the Revolutionary United Front Party (RUFP) and Foday Sankoh gave addresses around the country as though he were running for president.

With a cease-fire in place, presidential elections were held in May 2002. In a landslide victory, Ahmed Tejan Kabbah, candidate of the SLPP obtained 70.06% of the vote to defeat Ernest Koroma of the APC. Koroma received 22.4% of the vote, while the Peace and Liberation Party (PLP) gained 3%, and others took 4.59%. The Revolutionary United Front Party (RUFP) and its chairman Foday Sankoh were thoroughly discredited. In the parliamentary contest for 112 elected seats, the SLPP captured 83 seats, the All People's Congress (APC) 27 seats, and the PLP 2 seats.

In May 2004, the APC won local elections in Freetown, but also fared well elsewhere winning 22% of the vote, 4 councils, and 116 councilors. The SLPP, which continued to dominate overall, won 70% of the vote, 15 councils, and 330 councilors. Independents elected 10 councilors, but won no councils. Both the SLPP and APC alleged that the other side was guilty of vote-rigging, coercion, and multiple- and under-aged voting.

At the SLPP convention in September 2005, Solomon Berewa, the country's vice president, assumed leadership of the party and was designated the party's candidate for the 2007 presidential elections. Berewa defeated Charles Margai—son of the late prime minister Albert Margai—and a number of other aspirants. At its convention the main opposition party, the APC, chose Ernest Koroma, a Muslim, who also was confirmed as party chairman. A number of independents formed a new party, the Republican Movement, and several small parties met in June 2005 to strategize on the creation of a "third force." In addition, Charles Margai left the SLPP to form his own party, the People's Movement for Democratic Change (PMDC).

Presidential and parliamentary elections were held in August 2007. Koroma was elected president and his All People's Congress, formerly in opposition, won a majority in parliament. Koroma was sworn in as president on 17 September 2007. He won 54.6% of the vote in a run-off with Solomon Berewa. As a result of the August parliamentary elections, the APC took 59 seats, the SLPP 43 seats, and the PMDC 10 seats.

The next elections were scheduled for 2012.

15 LOCAL GOVERNMENT

Sierra Leone is divided into the Western Area (the former colony) and the Northern, Eastern, and Southern provinces (formerly the protectorate). The three provinces are divided into a total of 12 districts with some 150 chiefdoms. Local government in the Western Area is administered by municipalities. Rural areas are governed by village committees, which send members to district councils, which in turn are represented in a rural area council.

Each province has a resident minister as administrative head. Local units within the provinces are, in ascending order of importance, villages, extended villages or sections, chiefdoms, and district councils. The district councils, which contain elected members as well as paramount chiefs, are responsible for primary education, health centers, agricultural extension work, social welfare, community development, and transportation services (roads, bridges, and ferries). The war incapacitated local government by severely disrupting social institutions, and uprooting some two million refugees and internally displaced persons.

16 JUDICIAL SYSTEM

Local courts apply traditional law and customs in the chiefdoms. Elected indigenous leaders preside over the local courts. Magistrates hold court in the various districts and in Freetown, administering the English-based code of law. Appeals from magistrates' courts are heard by the High Court, which also has unlimited original civil and criminal jurisdiction. Appeals from High Court decisions may be made to the Court of Appeal and finally to the Supreme Court, consisting of a chief justice and not fewer than three other justices. The attorney general is a cabinet minister and head of the state law office, which is administered by the solicitor-general. Many of the justices, magistrates, and other lawyers are Sierra Leoneans trained in British universities or at Inns of Court in London. Judges serve until the age of 65.

The judiciary is not independent in practice and remains subject to manipulation. A UN Special Court for Sierra Leone, established at the end of the war, continued to hear cases of alleged war criminals in 2011.

17 ARMED FORCES

The International Institute for Strategic Studies reports that armed forces in Sierra Leone totaled 10,500 members in 2011, all of which were members of joint forces. Armed forces represented 0.5% of the labor force in Sierra Leone. Defense spending totaled $108.8 million and accounted for 2.3% of GDP.

18 INTERNATIONAL COOPERATION

Admitted as the 100th member of the UN on 27 September 1961, Sierra Leone participates in ECA and several nonregional specialized agencies, such as the FAO, IAEA, ILO, UNCTAD, UNESCO, UNIDO, and the WHO. The country belongs to the WTO, the ACP Group, the African Development Bank, Commonwealth of Nations, ECOWAS, G-77, Organization of the Islamic Conference (OIC), the Islamic Development Bank, the New Partnership for Africa's Development (NEPAD), the Non-Aligned Movement, and the African Union. In 1980–81, then president Siaka Stevens served as chairman of the Organization of African Union (OAU) and Freetown hosted the organization's summit conference in July 1980. Sierra Leone is also a member of the International Criminal Court with a Bilateral Immunity Agreement of protection for the US military (as covered under Article 98).

In October 1973, Sierra Leone and Liberia concluded the Mano River Union agreement, aimed at establishing an economic union of the two countries; Guinea joined the union in 1980. Trade restrictions among the three nations were abolished in 1981 and a common external tariff was established for most items of trade. The government is participating in efforts to establish a West African Monetary Zone (WAMZ) that would include The Gambia, Ghana, Guinea, Liberia, Nigeria, and Sierra Leone.

Sierra Leone signed a defense pact with Guinea in 1971 allowing for the exchange of some army personnel. The UN Mission in Sierra Leone (UNAMSIL) was established in 1999 to cooperate with government officials by monitoring the implementation of peace agreements and the disarmament of civil and revolutionary forces. UNAMSIL is supported by 31 countries. Sierra Leone is part of the Nonaligned Movement.

In environmental cooperation, Sierra Leone is part of the Convention on Biological Diversity, Ramsar, CITES, the Montréal Protocol, MARPOL, the Nuclear Test Ban Treaty, and the UN Conventions on the Law of the Sea, Climate Change, and Desertification.

19 ECONOMY

The GDP rate of change in Sierra Leone, as of 2010, was 5%. Inflation stood at 11.7%. Although Sierra Leone is a potentially rich country with diverse resources, which include diamonds, gold, rutile, bauxite, and a variety of agricultural products, the economy has been severely depressed over the past two decades. About two-thirds of the population engages in subsistence agriculture, which accounts for 52.5% of national income. The country has a chronic balance-of-payments deficit aggravated by a rebellion in the export-producing diamond regions of the country. The economy suffers from low production, poor export performance, large budget deficits, shortage of essential goods, deterioration of infrastructure, inability to service external debts, a pervasive parallel market, an influx of refugees from the civil war in Liberia, and inflation.

The government adhered to a structural adjustment program established in 1991–92 that called for a reduction in the number of civil service employees, increased privatization of the economy, increased taxation, and fiscal discipline. The program produced some improvements in the stability of the exchange rate and reduced inflation. Consequently, although some donors suspended aid, Sierra Leone gained the support of the World Bank, IMF, and other international agencies.

Civil unrest in 1997 and the Army's takeover of the democratically elected government cast doubt on whether support would last. Less than a third of $230 million dollars pledged in 1996 for the first stage of a five-year recovery program was given and it was likely that the donors would renege on the remainder if the political situation worsened. In 1997, GDP weakened by 20%, and remained at this depressed rate; in 1998, GDP gained by only 0.7%. Peace talks in 1998 broke down during the same year, and fighting continued until the cessation of hostilities in January 2002.

Since then, massive infusions of outside assistance have helped Sierra Leone begin to recover. Sierra Leone qualified for $950 million in debt relief under the IMF/World Bank Heavily Indebted Poor Countries (HIPC) initiative. The smuggling of diamonds out of the country remains a catalyst for instability and undermines the legitimate economy. Bauxite and rutile mines that were closed during the war reopened in 2005.

In May 2011, Sierra Leone's government cut their fuel subsidy, causing prices to jump by 30 percent. The cut was made so that money could be allocated toward meeting debt obligations under International Monetary Fund programs. Analysts worried that the cut and public reactions to it would affect the 2012 presidential elections.

20 INCOME

The CIA estimated that in 2010 the GDP of Sierra Leone was $4.72 billion. The CIA defines GDP as the value of all final goods and services produced within a nation in a given year and computed on the basis of purchasing power parity (PPP) rather than value as measured on the basis of the rate of the exchange based on current dollars. The per capita GDP was estimated at $900. The annual growth rate of GDP was 5%. The average inflation rate was 11.7%. It was estimated that agriculture accounted for 48% of GDP, industry 31%, and services 21%.

According to the World Bank, remittances from citizens living abroad totaled $46.7 million or about $9 per capita and accounted for approximately 1% of GDP.

The World Bank reports that in 2009, household consumption in Sierra Leone totaled $1.6 billion or about $304 per capita, measured in current US dollars rather than PPP.

As of 2011 the most recent study by the World Bank reported that actual individual consumption in Sierra Leone was 99.2% of GDP and accounted for 0.01% of world consumption. By comparison, the United States accounted for 25.44% of world individual consumption. The World Bank also estimated that 4.9% of Sierra Leone's GDP was spent on food and beverages, 9% on housing and household furnishings, 7.2% on clothes, 14.2% on health, 2.7% on transportation, 2.5% on communications, 3.1% on recreation, 1.1% on restaurants and hotels, and 4.7% on miscellaneous goods and services and purchases from abroad.

21 LABOR

As of 2007, Sierra Leone had a total labor force of 2.207 million people. Subsistence agriculture was the occupation of a vast majority of the population.

The 1991 constitution provides for the right of association, and all workers (including civil servants) have the right to join trade unions of their choice. The trade union movement in Sierra Leone, one of the oldest in West Africa, dates back to 1913, when Wallace Johnson organized the Customs Employees Union. Under his influence, other unions developed, and in 1943, the first Sierra Leone Trade Union Council (TUC) was formed. The Sierra Leone Council of Labor, which replaced the TUC in 1946, merged in May 1966 with the Sierra Leone Federation of Labor to form the Sierra Leone Labor Congress (SLLC). All unions are members of the SLLC, although membership is voluntary. In the mid-1980s, the SLLC had over a dozen constituent unions totaling about 40,000 members. With the decline of manufacturing, union membership has declined since then, although exact figures are unavailable. In 2010, about 40% of workers in the formal economy were unionized.

The minimum working age is 18, but this is not enforced and children routinely work as vendors and petty traders in urban areas and work seasonally on family subsistence farms in rural areas. The standard workweek is 38 hours but most workweeks exceed that amount. Health and safety regulations set by law are not enforced. The minimum wage was $6.35 per month in 2010.

In 2010 youth unemployment was extremely high in Sierra Leone—60%—severely limiting the economic prospects for many young people in the country. In an effort to address this type of embedded problem, the UN Development Program in Sierra Leone launched in 2007 the Youth Enterprise Development program, which aimed to develop entrepreneurial skills in young people in the country. While well funded and considered to be quite successful by many analysts, the three-year program was scheduled to end in 2012.

22 AGRICULTURE

Most Sierra Leoneans live on small, scattered farms, following a scheme of bush-fallow rotation, slash-and-burn field preparation, and limited use of fertilizer. Roughly 9% of the total land is farmed, and the country's major crops include rice, coffee, cocoa, palm kernels, palm oil, and peanuts. Cereal production in 2009 amounted to 867,516 tons, fruit production 249,707 tons, and vegetable production 248,957 tons.

Rice, grown by 80% of farmers, is the most important subsistence crop and, along with millet in the northeast, is a food staple. The Rice Research Institute, which is located in the Northern Province, breeds high-yielding varieties for seed. Other domestic food crops include cassava, yams, peanuts, corn, pineapples, coconuts, tomatoes, and pepper.

Coffee is grown in the eastern and southern provinces. Cocoa is grown in the Kenema and Kailahun districts of the Eastern Province and in the Pujehun District of the Southern Province, mainly on smallholdings of about 0.4–1.2 hectares (1–3 acres). Palm produce is derived from stands of wild palms, mainly in the northeast and southeast. Although there is substantial local consumption of palm kernels, they are a major agricultural export. Piassava, a raffia palm fiber used for broom and brush bristles, is grown in the swampy areas of the extreme south. Small amounts of kola nuts are also exported, and modest crops of bananas, pineapples, and sugarcane are grown.

23 ANIMAL HUSBANDRY

The UN Food and Agriculture Organization (FAO) reported that Sierra Leone dedicated 2.2 million hectares (5.44 million acres) to permanent pasture or meadow in 2009. During that year, the country tended 7.8 million chickens, 350,000 head of cattle, and 52,000 pigs. The production from these animals amounted to 7,850 tons of beef and veal, 3,112 tons of pork, 16,913 tons of poultry, 7,732 tons of eggs, and 30,526 tons of milk. Sierra Leone also produced 1,827 tons of cattle hide. Large numbers of Ndama cattle were kept, mainly by nomads in the savanna area of the northeast.

24 FISHING

Fresh fish is not a staple for the country as a whole but is much prized in Freetown and other parts of the Peninsula. The fishing industry, which once was confined to inshore waters, has spread into the middle waters and includes canoe, industrial, freshwater, and shellfish fisheries. Shrimp is the main export. The government has a joint venture agreement with Maritime Protection Services Sierra Leone Ltd., the purpose of which is to prevent poaching, protect artisanal fishing, increase revenue, and conserve maritime resources. In 2008, the annual capture totaled 203,582 tons according to the UN FAO. The export value of seafood totaled $13.01 million.

25 FORESTRY

Approximately 38% of Sierra Leone is covered by forest. Much of Sierra Leone's rain forests have been cleared, with only remnant areas in the south and east; intensive farming gradually eliminated most of the forest area. Most prime forestland is in the government estate in the mountainous eastern half of the country and in the Western Area hills. The UN FAO estimated the 2009 roundwood production at 123,600 cu m (4.36 million cu ft). The value of all forest products, including roundwood, totaled $6.34 million. Forests comprise both evergreen and semi-deciduous rain forests, swamp forests, mangrove forests, and significant areas of secondary and regenerating forests. The Gola Forest in the southeast is the largest remaining tract of rain forest.

26 MINING

The mining of diamonds was Sierra Leone's leading industry in 2010. In addition to diamonds, the country is also a producer of cement, gypsum, and salt. Civil strife adversely affected investment in natural resource development in the 1990s. Sierra Leone adopted a new Mines and Minerals Act in 2009 that vests the state with all rights of ownership and control of minerals.

Diamond output in 2009 was reported at 437,516 carats, down from 400,843 carats in 2008. However, these figures do not reflect smuggled artisanal output. Alluvial diamonds, first discovered in Kono District in 1930, were widely scattered over a large area, but particularly along the upper Sewa River. The main diamond deposits were the Koidu and Tongo fields. In 2010, the government and Koidu Holdings S.A. signed an agreement for the Kouidu kimberlite project located in the Kono district. Gold production in 2009 totaled 270 kg.

Cement production in 2010 totaled 300,980 metric tons, up from 236,240 metric tons in 2009. Rutile and ilmenite are also mined. Sierra Leone is known to have reserves of bauxite and other minerals including antimony, cassiterite, columbite, corundum, fluorspar, lead, lignite, magnetite, molybdenum, monazite, platinum, silver, tantalite, tin, titanium, tungsten, and zinc.

A 1999 amendment to the 1994 Mines and Minerals Act introduced procedures for sale and export of precious minerals by license holders, and penalties for unlawful possession or smuggling of precious minerals. In 2001, Sierra Leone and Angola introduced a diamond certification scheme in response to UN sanctions aimed at prohibiting importation of diamonds from rebel-controlled areas in the countries. The Kimberley Process Certification Scheme (KPCS) was established in 2003 to authenticate the origin of rough-cut diamonds so that sales do not fund civil conflicts.

In July 2010, the Chinese firm Shangdong Iron and Steel struck a deal with African Minerals Tonkolili for a 25% share in the latter's iron ore mining project in Sierra Leone. The $1.5 billion investment will be used to finance the construction of the mine, which is expected to result in about 5,000 new jobs for Sierra Leoneans throughout the construction and operational phases. As part of the deal, Shandong guaranteed that it will purchase iron ore from the mine at reasonable rates, thus providing much needed revenue for Sierra Leone. The first shipment of ore was expected to be available by the end of 2011. By the end of 2012, the mine was expected to have a production capacity of 25 million tons per year.

27 ENERGY AND POWER

The World Bank reported in 2008 that Sierra Leone produced 58 million kWh of electricity and consumed 75.1 million kWh, or 14 kWh per capita. In 2009 and 2010, US-based Anadarko Petroleum Corp discovered two oil fields off the coast of Sierra Leone, boosting the hopes of the government that the addition of oil wealth may be possible within a few years. Upon announcing the second discovery in November 2010, officials from Anadarko said they would be working closely with the government to accelerate appraisals of the fields and further exploration in the area throughout 2011.

28 INDUSTRY

Industry accounted for 31% of GDP in 2010, and is oriented toward the processing of raw materials and of light manufactured goods for domestic consumption. The sector has suffered from a lack of foreign exchange, high import costs, unreliable local services, and political instability. The Wellington Industrial Estate, covering 46 hectares just east of Freetown, was developed in the 1960s by the government to encourage investments. Its factories produce a variety of products, including cement, nails, shoes, oxygen, cigarettes, beer and soft drinks, paint, and knitted goods. Timber for prefabricated buildings is milled, and another factory produces modern furniture. Small factories in the Freetown area process tuna and palm oil. Oyster farming and shrimp production dominate the fishing industry. Village craft products include a popular cloth, rope, sail canvas, boats, wood carvings, baskets, and leather goods.

29 SCIENCE AND TECHNOLOGY

The World Bank reported in 2009 that there were no patent applications in science and technology in Sierra Leone. The Institute of Marine Biology and Oceanography, founded in 1966, is affiliated with Fourah Bay College of the University of Sierra Leone at Freetown. The college itself, founded in 1827 by the Church Missionary Society, has faculties of engineering and pure and applied sciences. Also part of the university is Njala University College (founded in 1964), which has faculties of agriculture and environmental sciences, and the College of Medicine and Allied Health Sciences (founded in 1987). A paramedical school in Bo operates with funds from the government and the European Community. The Ministry of Mines has a geological survey division to locate mineral deposits and advise on all matters relating to the earth. The Sierra Leone Medical and Dental Association, founded in 1961, is headquartered in Freetown.

30 DOMESTIC TRADE

Freetown is the principal commercial and distribution center. Internal trade is normally carried on by trading firms that deal in a variety of merchandise. Bo is the commercial center for the central region of the country, with most significant trading activity in ginger, rice, coffee, cocoa, and palm oil and kernels. Makeni, in central Sierra Leone, is a trading center for the Temne people, who mainly produce rice.

Normal business hours are from 8 a.m. to 12 p.m. and 2 to 4:45 p.m., Monday through Friday, with a half day on Saturday. Banks are open from 8 a.m. to 1:30 p.m., Monday through Thursday, and 8 to 2 p.m. on Friday.

31 FOREIGN TRADE

Sierra Leone imported $560 million worth of goods and services in 2008, while exporting $216 million worth of goods and services. Principal imports are foodstuffs, machinery and transportation equipment, fuels, and lubricants. Civil war inhibited foreign trade between 1995 and 1999. Sierra Leone's most important ex-

Principal Trading Partners – Sierra Leone (2010)

(In millions of US dollars)

Country	Total	Exports	Imports	Balance
World	1,358.2	350.0	1,008.2	-658.2
South Africa	149.0	0.5	148.5	-148.1
China	117.4	9.3	108.1	-98.8
Belgium	116.2	87.7	28.5	59.2
United States	94.1	27.0	67.1	-40.1
United Kingdom	77.2	12.2	65.0	-52.9
Côte d'Ivoire	74.5	17.1	57.4	-40.4
Malaysia	63.4	2.2	61.2	-59.0
Netherlands	55.0	21.9	33.1	-11.2
India	54.6	6.3	48.3	-42.0
Romania	53.4	46.0	7.4	38.7

(…) data not available or not significant.

(n.s.) not specified.

SOURCE: *2011 Direction of Trade Statistics Yearbook*, New York: United Nations, 2011.

Balance of Payments – Sierra Leone (2010)

(In millions of US dollars)

Current Account		**-482.9**
Balance on goods		-373.0
Imports	-735.9	
Exports	362.9	
Balance on services		-83.6
Balance on income		-48.5
Current transfers		22.3
Capital Account		**22.7**
Financial Account		**101.4**
Direct investment abroad		…
Direct investment in Sierra Leone		86.6
Portfolio investment assets		-22.1
Portfolio investment liabilities		3.0
Financial derivatives		…
Other investment assets		-11.8
Other investment liabilities		45.7
Net Errors and Omissions		**37.4**
Reserves and Related Items		**321.4**

(…) data not available or not significant.

SOURCE: *Balance of Payment Statistics Yearbook 2011*, Washington, DC: International Monetary Fund, 2011.

ports are diamonds and rutile. Other exports include vegetable oil, fresh fish, shellfish, coffee, and cocoa. Major import partners in 2009 were South Africa, 14.6%; China, 7.6%; Malaysia, 6.7%; the United States, 5.9%; Cote d'Ivoire, 5.6%; France, 5.1%; India, 4.7%; UK, 4.5%; and Netherlands, 4.1%. Its major export partners were Belgium, 27%; the United States, 12%; Netherlands, 8%; UK, 7.5%; Cote d'Ivoire, 6.2%; China, 4.4%; and Greece, 4.1%.

Sierra Leone's exports to Belgium are mainly in the form of diamond exports to Antwerp. An immense black market for diamonds exists, probably accounting for the majority of exports from Sierra Leone.

³²BALANCE OF PAYMENTS

In 2010 Sierra Leone had a foreign trade deficit of $305 million, amounting to 3.1% of GDP. Sierra Leone's frequently negative balance of trade and habitual deficit in current accounts are somewhat counterbalanced by capital inflows, generally from foreign governments.

³³BANKING AND SECURITIES

The Bank of Sierra Leone, established in 1963, is the central bank and bank of issue. The Banking Act of 1964 provides for the regulation of commercial banks by the central bank, including the control of money supply. Poor revenue collection, failure to control expenditures, and heavy debt servicing requirements as a result of past borrowing characterized government finances in the 1980s and early 1990s.

In 2012 there were twelve commercial banks operating in the country. Standard Chartered Bank Sierra Leone and Barclays Bank of Sierra Leone are both foreign banks that are locally incorporated, with Sierra Leonean staff. The International Bank of Trade and Industry opened in 1982, with funds from Lebanese and Sierra Leonean investors.

The National Development Bank was established in 1968 to finance agricultural and industrial projects. The National Cooperative Development Bank, established in 1971, serves as a central bank for all cooperatives and makes modest loans to individual farmers and cooperatives for agricultural improvements. Sierra Leone also has a Post Office Savings Bank. Most banks closed during the rebel attacks of the late 1990s.

There is no securities exchange in Sierra Leone.

³⁴INSURANCE

The National Insurance Co. is government owned. All insurance companies in Sierra Leone are supervised by the Ministry of Finance.

³⁵PUBLIC FINANCE

In 2010 the budget of Sierra Leone included $96 million in public revenue and $351 million in public expenditures. The budget deficit amounted to 6.9% of GDP. Public debt was 29.3% of GDP, with $1.61 billion of the debt held by foreign entities. The government of Sierra Leone has been prevented from having any significant economic influence in the country thanks to a shortage of foreign exchange, deep-seated corruption, and uncertainty surrounding the civil wars that periodically take place.

³⁶TAXATION

Corporate income tax was taxed at a statutory rate of 30% in 2010. Social security contributions were assessed at 10%, and a tax on interest was levied at 15%. Municipal license fees and a vehicle tax were applied as well. The goods and services tax was 15%. Income tax rates were progressive, ranging from 25 to 40% as of 2011.

³⁷CUSTOMS AND DUTIES

A common external tariff was adopted in 2005 by the Economic Community of West African States. It provided for four bands of tariff assessment: 0, 5, 10, and 20%. A diamond export tax of

Public Finance – Sierra Leone (2009)

(In billions of leones, budgetary central government figures)

Revenue and Grants	**1,250.45**	**100.0%**
Tax revenue	698.87	55.9%
Social contributions	...	
Grants	500.34	40.0%
Other revenue	51.24	4.1%
Expenditures	...	...
General public services	...	...
Defense	...	...
Public order and safety	...	...
Economic affairs	...	...
Environmental protection	...	...
Housing and community amenities	...	...
Health	...	...
Recreational, culture, and religion	...	...
Education	...	...
Social protection	...	...

(...) data not available or not significant.

SOURCE: *Government Finance Statistics Yearbook 2010,* Washington, DC: International Monetary Fund, 2010.

5% applied as of 2010. Import duties ranged from 0 to 30%. Textbooks, medical equipment, agricultural inputs, and machinery could arrive duty free.

38 FOREIGN INVESTMENT

The government encourages the development of plantations and the investment of foreign private capital in agriculture and worthwhile new enterprises. Safeguards are provided against nationalization, and repatriation of capital, profits, and interest is permitted. Legislation in 1983 offered tax relief for up to five years, preferential access to import licenses, exemption from customs and duties on capital equipment and new materials, and special bonuses for companies setting up outside Freetown.

Sierra Leone attracted few foreign investors in the early 1990s. Progress in reforming the economy was expected to reverse that trend, but renewed civil disturbances in 1997 threatened those prospects. Rex Mining, the first company to invest in Sierra Leone after the civil war, suspended work at its diamond mine after the military coup in May of 1997. Production in the rutile and bauxite plants resumed in 2000, but continuance was unsure because of political unrest.

Foreign Direct Investment (FDI) was $521 million in 2010. This consisted of $36 million in inward FDI flows and $495 million (21.8% of GDP) in inward FDI stocks. Most of this investment was in the mining sector.

39 ECONOMIC DEVELOPMENT

The Sierra Leone government, in addition to stabilizing its balance-of-payment and budgetary deficits and meeting its debt obligations, seeks investors in its mining sector. A parallel economy, lawless conditions, and a crumbling infrastructure continue to constrain economic growth. The government encourages foreign investment.

In 2001, the International Monetary Fund (IMF) approved a $169 million three-year Poverty Reduction and Growth Facility (PRGF) Arrangement for Sierra Leone, to support the government's economic reform program. In 2002, Sierra Leone became eligible for nearly $950 million in debt service relief under the IMF/World Bank Heavily Indebted Poor Countries (HIPC) initiative. The IMF continued working with Sierra Leone through 2011, approving a new three-year program in 2010 worth $45 million.

Relative political stability benefitted mining industries, as did government tax incentives. The discovery of offshore oil reserves in 2009 and 2010, though several years from profitability, offered potential for future economic growth.

40 SOCIAL DEVELOPMENT

All employees in the public and private sectors are covered under the social insurance plan initiated in 2001. There is voluntary coverage for the self-employed. The program is funded by employee and employer contributions, with the government providing funding for government employees only. Old age, disability, and survivorship benefits are available. Employers provide medical care for employees and their families through collective agreements.

Women are guaranteed equal rights under the constitution, and a number of women have held prominent posts. Even so, discrimination and violence against women are frequent. Women carry out most of the strenuous agricultural work, and are responsible for child rearing. Girls were denied an education more often than boys, and traditional beliefs kept women confined to the household. They do not have equal access to economic opportunities, health care, or social freedoms. Female genital mutilation, a practice which is painful and sometimes life threatening, is an entrenched cultural practice. It is estimated that as many as 80–90% of girls and women may have been affected. There is considerable local opposition to advocates campaigning to have the practice banned. Domestic abuse and violence is a widespread social problem.

The government's human rights record has improved, although there are continued reports of the mistreatment of detainees and illegal detention.

41 HEALTH

According to the CIA, life expectancy in Sierra Leone was 48 years in 2011. The country spent 13.3% of its GDP on healthcare, amounting to $44 per person. There were 0 physicians, 2 nurses and midwives, and 4 hospital beds per 10,000 inhabitants. The fertility rate was 5.2, while the infant mortality rate was 123 per 1,000 live births. In 2008 the maternal mortality rate, according to the World Bank, was 970 per 100,000 births. It was estimated that 71% of children were vaccinated against measles. The CIA calculated HIV/AIDS prevalence in Sierra Leone to be about 1.6% in 2009. Sierra Leone had an estimated 4 hospital beds per 10,000 people in 2007.

With WHO and UNICEF technical assistance, an endemic diseases control unit reduced the incidence of sleeping sickness and yaws, and began a leprosy control campaign. Malaria, tuberculosis, and schistosomiasis remain serious health hazards, as does malnutrition.

Sierra Leone has posted some of the highest infant and maternal mortality rates in the world, due in part to widespread malnutrition and lack of investment in targeted health programs. However, in May 2010, the government launched a new program of free medical care for all pregnant women, nursing mothers, and children under the age of five in government-sponsored hospitals. The $90 million program included an increase in the number of care providers.

42 HOUSING

As of the 2004 census, there were an estimated 967,300 households counted representing about 4,836,500 people. Village houses in the provinces are traditionally made of sticks with mud walls and thatch or grass roofs; they may be circular or rectangular in shape. In some villages, wattle-and-daub construction has been replaced by sun-dried mud blocks, and roofs of grass, palm thatch, or palm tiles are giving way to corrugated iron sheeting. In Freetown, older two-story wooden houses have been being replaced by structures built largely of concrete blocks, with corrugated iron or cement-asbestos roofs.

The government has made reconstruction a priority and has initiated a National Housing Policy to work on programs of reform, resettlement, and reconstruction.

43 EDUCATION

The CIA estimated in 2009 that Sierra Leone had a literacy rate of 35.1%. Public expenditure on education represented 4.3% of GDP. Primary education is neither wholly free nor compulsory, but the ultimate goal of the government is to provide free primary school facilities for every child. Primary school lasts for three years, followed by three years of junior secondary school and three years of senior secondary school.

Fourah Bay College, the oldest institution of higher learning in West Africa, was founded in 1827 by the Church Missionary Society, primarily to provide theological training. It was affiliated with the University of Durham in England in 1876 and received a royal charter in 1959 as the University College of Sierra Leone. In 1967, the University of Sierra Leone was chartered with two constituent colleges, Fourah Bay (in Freetown) and Njala University College (in Moyamba District).

44 LIBRARIES AND MUSEUMS

The library of Fourah Bay College, University of Sierra Leone, founded in 1827, has 200,000 volumes. Public collections are maintained by the Sierra Leone Library Board. The central public library collection is at Freetown, which holds 80,000 volumes. There are at least 10 branch locations. The American Cultural Center and the British Council both maintain small collections. The Sierra Leone National Museum contains documents concerning Sierra Leone and its history and various works of sculpture, especially Nomolis stone fetishes representing seated figures of unknown origin that have been found in the Mende areas. The Sierra Leone Railway Museum opened in 2005.

45 MEDIA

In 2009 the CIA reported that there were 32,800 telephone landlines in Sierra Leone. In addition to landlines, mobile phone subscriptions averaged 20 per 100 people. The Sierra Leone Broadcasting Service manages radio and television transmissions. Radio Sierra Leone, the oldest broadcasting service in English-speaking West Africa, broadcasts mainly in English, with regular news and discussion programs in several indigenous languages and a weekly program in French. The Sierra Leone Television Service was inaugurated in 1963. Private stations do exist, but license fees are high, prohibiting some sources from operating on a regular basis. As of 2009 Sierra Leone had one AM radio station, nine FM radio stations, and two television stations. In 2010, the country had about 281 Internet hosts. As of 2009, there were some 14,900 Internet users in Sierra Leone.

The only major daily newspaper is the government-owned *Daily Mail*, but there were several privately owned weekly newspapers. The 1991 constitution provides for free speech and a free press. However, this right has been restricted at times. In 2010 journalists often practiced self-censorship.

46 ORGANIZATIONS

There is a chamber of commerce in Freetown. The cooperative movement has grown rapidly since the 1960s. National youth organizations include the National Union of Sierra Leone Students, Sierra Leone Association of Students in Economics and Commerce, Sierra Leone Scouts Association, YMCA/YWCA, and the Sierra Leone National Youth League. There are several sports associations in the country with programs for amateur athletes of all ages.

Several voluntary associations exist, mostly in the Freetown area; most of these are women's religious, cultural, political, or economic groups. Coordinating bodies include the Federation of Sierra Leone Women's Organizations, and the United Church Women. The Sierra Leone Association of Non-Governmental Organizations serves as another coordinating group. International organizations with national chapters include Amnesty International, Caritas, and the Red Cross.

47 TOURISM, TRAVEL, AND RECREATION

Sierra Leone has magnificent beaches, including Lumley Beach on the outskirts of Freetown, perhaps the finest in West Africa. Natural scenic wonders include Bintimani and the Loma Mountains, Lake Sonfon, and the Bumbuna Falls. There are several modern hotels in Freetown, as well as a luxury hotel and casino at Lumley Beach. There has been a slow response from the international community to change the image of the country to that of a tourist destination. A certificate of vaccination against yellow fever is required if traveling from an infected area. The *Tourism Factbook*, published by the UN World Tourism Organization, reported 37,000 incoming tourists to Sierra Leone in 2009; tourists spent a total of $25 million. Of those incoming tourists, there were 13,000 from Africa and 11,000 from Europe. There were 2,997 hotel beds available in Sierra Leone, which had an occupancy rate of 36%. According to 2011 UN World Tourism Organization estimates, the average cost of staying in Freetown was $195 per day. The cost of visiting other cities averaged $95.

⁴⁸FAMOUS PERSONS

Sir Samuel Lewis (1843–1903) was a member of the Legislative Council for more than 20 years and the first mayor of Freetown. Sir Milton Augustus Strieby Margai (1895–1964), the grandson of a Mende warrior chief, was the founder of the SLPP and the first prime minister of Sierra Leone, a post he held until his death. Sir Albert Michael Margai (1910–80) succeeded his half-brother as prime minister from 1964 to 1967. Siaka Probyn Stevens (1905–88), the founder of the APC, was prime minister from 1968 to 1971 and became the republic's first president from 1971 to 1985. John Musselman Karefa-Smart (1915–2010) served as minister of lands, mines, and labor, in which capacity he organized Sierra Leone's diamond industry, and also served as assistant director-general of WHO from 1965 to 1970. Davidson Nicol (1924–94) was his country's permanent representative to the UN from 1969 to 1971, served as president of the Security Council in 1970, and became executive director of UNITAR in 1972. Foday Sankoh (1937–2003) was the leader of the Revolutionary United Front, a guerrilla group that terrorized villages in the early 1990s. In 2010 Olufemi Terry won the Caine Prize for African Writing, regarded as Africa's leading literary award. The prize recognized Terry's short story "Stickfighting Days," which details the life of a boy who lives in a slum and uses sticks to fight other boys.

⁴⁹DEPENDENCIES

Sierra Leone has no territories or colonies.

⁵⁰BIBLIOGRAPHY

Adebajo, Adekeye. *Building Peace in West Africa: Liberia, Sierra Leone, and Guinea-Bissau.* Boulder, CO: Lynne Rienner, 2002.

Cubitt, Christine. *Local and Global Dynamics of Peacebuilding: Postconflict Reconstruction in Sierra Leone.* New York: Routledge, 2012.

Day, Lynda Rose. *Gender and Power in Sierra Leone: Women Chiefs of the Last Two Centuries.* New York: Palgrave Macmillan, 2012.

Fyle, C. Magbaily. *Historical Dictionary of Sierra Leone.* Lanham, MD: Scarecrow, 2006.

Greene, Graham. *The Heart of the Matter.* New York: Viking, 1948.

Larémont, Ricardo René. *Borders, Nationalism, and the African State.* Boulder, CO: Lynne Rienner, 2005.

Sierra Leone Investment and Business Guide: Strategic and Practical Information. Washington, DC: International Business Publications USA, 2012.

Zeilig, Leo, and David Seddon. *A Political and Economic Dictionary of Africa.* Philadelphia: Routledge/Taylor and Francis, 2005..

SOMALIA

CAPITAL: Mogadishu (Muqdisho)

FLAG: The national flag is light blue with a five-pointed white star in the center.

ANTHEM: *Somalia Hanolato (Long Live Somalia).*

MONETARY UNIT: The Somali shilling (SOS) of 100 cents is a paper currency. There are coins of 1, 5, 10, and 50 cents and 1 shilling, and notes of 5, 10, 20, 100, 500, and 1,000 shillings. SOS1 = US$0.00069527 (or US$1 = SOS1,438.3 as of 2006). Official rates were unavailable between 2007 and 2010. The black market rate was SOS23,000 per US dollar in 2007.

WEIGHTS AND MEASURES: The metric system is the legal standard.

HOLIDAYS: New Year's Day, 1 January; Labor Day, 1 May; National Independence Day, 26 June; Foundation of the Republic, 1 July. Muslim religious holidays include Eid al-Fitr, Eid al-Adha, Ashura, and Milad an-Nabi.

TIME: 3 p.m. = noon GMT.

¹LOCATION, SIZE, AND EXTENT

Situated on the horn of East Africa, Somalia has an area of 637,657 sq km (246,201 sq mi), extending 1,847 km (1,148 mi) NNE–SSW and 835 km (519 mi) ESE–WNW. Comparatively, the area occupied by Somalia is slightly smaller than the state of Texas. It is bounded on the N by the Gulf of Aden, on the E and S by the Indian Ocean, on the SW by Kenya, on the W and NW by Ethiopia, and on the NW by Djibouti, with a total land boundary of 2,340 km (1,454 mi) and a coastline of 3,025 km (1,880 miles). The boundary with Djibouti has been fixed by international agreement, but the western border with Ethiopia remains in dispute.

Somalia's capital city, Mogadishu, is located on the Indian Ocean coast.

²TOPOGRAPHY

The northern region is somewhat mountainous, containing two main ranges, the Migiurtina and the Ogo, with plateaus reaching between 900 and 2,100 m (3,000–7,000 ft). To the northeast there is an extremely dry dissected plateau that reaches a maximum elevation of nearly 2,450 m (8,000 ft). South and west of this area, extending to the Shabeelle River, there is a plateau region called the Mudug Plain whose maximum elevation is 685 m (2,250 ft). The region between the Juba and Shabeelle rivers is low agricultural land, and the area that extends southwest of the Jubba River to Kenya is low pastureland.

The Jubba and Shabeelle rivers originate in Ethiopia and flow toward the Indian Ocean. They provide water for irrigation but are not navigable by commercial vessels. The Shabeelle dries up before reaching the ocean. Despite its lengthy shoreline, Somalia has only one natural harbor, Berbera.

³CLIMATE

Somalia has a tropical but not torrid climate, and there is little seasonal change in temperature. In the low areas the mean temperature ranges from about 24°C to 31°C (75°F to 88°F). The plateau region is cooler, the southwest warmer. The periodic winds, the southwest monsoon (June-September), and the northeast monsoon (December-March) influence temperature and rainfall. Rain falls in two seasons of the year, heavy rains from March to May and light rains from September to December. Average annual rainfall is estimated at less than 28 cm (11 in). Droughts are not infrequent.

⁴FLORA AND FAUNA

The World Resources Institute estimates there are 3,028 plant species in Somalia. In addition, Somalia is home to 182 types of mammals, 642 species of birds, 222 types of reptiles, and 32 species of amphibians. The calculation reflects the total number of distinct species in the country, not the number of endemic species. Along with its large livestock herd, Somalia has one of the most abundant and varied stocks of wildlife in Africa. Animal life includes the elephant, lion, wildcat, giraffe, zebra, hyena, hippopotamus, waterbuck, gazelle, dik-dik, lizard, crocodile, turtle, porcupine, baboon, and boar. There are a large variety of snakes, the best known being the puff adder, the spitting cobra, and the krait. Domestic animals are camels, sheep, goats, and cattle. The most common birds are the ostrich, duck, guinea fowl, bustard, partridge, green pigeon, sand grouse, and heron.

Acacia thorn trees, aloes, baobab, and candelabra trees are native to the semiarid regions. Trees that provide frankincense and myrrh are native to the region as well. Southern forests include eucalyptus and mahogany. Mangrove, kapok, and papaya grow along the rivers. Coconut, dune palm, pine, juniper, cactus, and flowering trees such as the flamboyant were imported and have become widespread in the populated areas.

⁵ENVIRONMENT

The World Resources Institute reported that Somalia had designated 190,400 hectares (470,489 acres) of land for protection as of 2006. Water resources totaled 15.7 cu km (3.77 cu mi) while water usage was 3.29 cu km (0.789 cu mi) per year. Domestic agricultural water usage accounted for nearly 100% of total usage. Per capita water usage totaled 400 cu m (14,126 cu ft) per year. The increasing aridity of the Somali climate, coupled with excessive timber cutting and overgrazing, have led to deforestation and desertification. In nearly every five-year period, Somalis can anticipate two years of drought. Overgrazing between Mogadishu and Chisimayu has resulted in the gradual movement of coastal sand dunes inland, posing a serious threat to agricultural areas and human habitation. The United Nations (UN) reported in 2008 that carbon dioxide emissions in Somalia totaled 601 kilotons.

The hunting and trapping of antelopes and gazelles for their skins was banned in 1969. However, many species continue to be adversely affected by growing numbers of livestock, exclusion from watering spots by human settlement, and the cutting of bush vegetation and tree cover. According to a 2011 report issued by the International Union for Conservation of Nature and Natural Resources (IUCN), the number of threatened species included 15 types of mammals, 12 species of birds, 4 types of reptiles, 27 species of fish, 1 type of mollusk, and 21 species of plants. Threatened species in Somalia include the black rhinoceros, cheetah, Pelzeln's dorcas gazelle, Swayne's hartebeest, several species of shark, and the green sea, hawksbill, and leatherback turtles.

⁶POPULATION

The US Central Intelligence Agency (CIA) estimated the population of Somalia in 2011 to be approximately 9,925,640, which placed it at number 86 in population among the 196 nations of the world. In 2011 approximately 2.4% of the population was over 65 years of age, with another 44.7% under 15 years of age. The median age in Somalia was 17.8 years. There were 1.00 males for every female in the country. The population's annual rate of change was 1.603%. The projected population for the year 2025 was 13,900,000. Population density in Somalia was calculated at 16 people per sq km (41 people per sq mi).

The UN estimated that 37% of the population lived in urban areas and that urban populations had an annual rate of change of 4.1%. The largest urban area was Mogadishu, with a population of 1.4 million.

⁷MIGRATION

Estimates of Somalia's net migration rate, reported by the CIA in 2011, amounted to -11.81 migrants per 1,000 citizens. The total number of emigrants living abroad was 812,700, and the total number of immigrants living in Somalia was 22,800. Since about half of all Somalis are nomadic or semi-nomadic, there are substantial movements back and forth across the frontiers in the normal range of grazing activities. Within the country there has been

a gradual migration toward the south and southwest, especially since the north was drought-stricken in the 1970s and early 1980s. A campaign of political terror began in 1986; the effects were so severe that an estimated three-quarters of the population was internally displaced between 1988 and 1993.

The conflict with Ethiopia led to the influx of many refugees from the Ogaden, most of them ethnic Somalis. In 1990 an estimated 586,000 refugees were being assisted by the UN High Commissioner for Refugees in refugee camps. The government claimed the total number of people in refugee camps exceeded 1.3 million. Yet the political violence in Somalia was so extreme that about 600,000 people fled the country between 1988 and 1991.

After Siyad Barre's regime fell in January 1991, fighting began between 16 different rival factions in Somalia. These clan wars and the long drought led to over 900,000 Somalis fleeing to neighboring nations.

⁸ETHNIC GROUPS

The majority of Somalis speak a Cushitic language—such as Somali—and are closely related to other Cushitic speakerssuch as the Oromo of Ethiopia and northwest Kenya. It is believed that the Somalis descend from people who migrated from the equatorial lakes of Africa to settle in the area of Somalia's two rivers to intermix with pastoral groups from the north and migrants from the Arabian Peninsula, the Persian Gulf, and perhaps Southeast Asia. Ethnic Somalis, who make up about 85% of the population, are divided into two main clan families: the Samaal, which includes the Darod, Isaaq, Hawiye, and Dir clan groups, and the Saab, which includes the Rahanweyn and Digil clans and other smaller clan groups. The Samaal are principally nomadic or semi-nomadic pastoralists; the Digil and Rahanweyn are primarily farmers and sedentary herders. There are also small Bantu-groups who are living along the Shabeelle and Jubba rivers. Other smaller minority groups include the Benadiri, the Rer Hamar, Brawanese, Swahili, Tumal, Yibir, Yaxar, Madhiban, Hawrasmae, Muse Dheryo, and Faqayaqub. The non-indigenous population consists primarily of Arabs, Italians, Pakistanis, and Indians. The Italians are mainly engaged in teaching, business, and banana production; the Arabs, Pakistanis, and Indians are primarily shopkeepers.

⁹LANGUAGES

Somali, classified as a lowland Eastern Cushitic language, is spoken by all Somalis, with dialectal differences that follow clan family divisions. Loanwords from Arabic, English, and Italian have been thoroughly assimilated by Somali phonetic rules. Until 1972 the official languages of Somalia were oral Somali, Arabic, English, and Italian. In 1973 a written form of Somali, with a script based on the Latin alphabet, was adopted as the nation's chief official language. This official script largely replaced the use of English and Italian in newspapers and public documents. The official script is used in all schools. However, Arabic, English, and Italian are all still widely spoken and understood.

¹⁰RELIGIONS

The Somalis are primarily Sunni Muslims adhering to the Shafi'i legal school. According to tradition, their original ancestors were

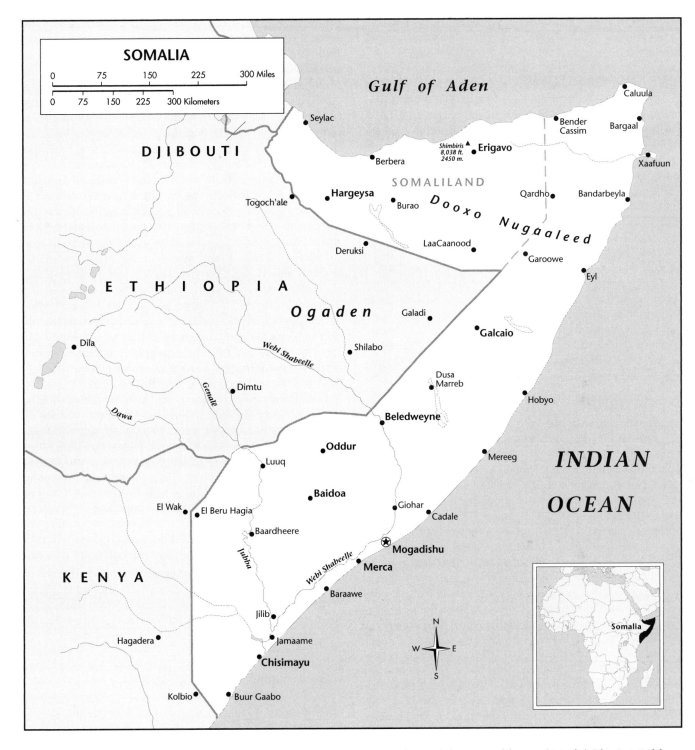

LOCATION: 12° N to 1°39′ S; 41°30′ to 51°E. BOUNDARY LENGTHS: Total coastline, 3,025 kilometers (1,874 miles); Kenya, 682 kilometers (424 miles); Ethiopia, 1,626 kilometers (1,016 miles); Djibouti, 58 kilometers (36 miles). TERRITORIAL SEA LIMIT: 200 miles.

of the Qurayshitic lineage of the Prophet Muhammad. Except for a small number of urbanites influenced by higher education, all Somalis belong to one of the following Sufi (Islamic mysticism) orders: Qadiriyyah, Salihiyyah, Ahmadiyyah, and Rifaiyyah. As Muslims, they adhere to the law of the Shari'ah (Islamic law) whenever it does not conflict with local customary law. A small,

extremely low-profile Christian community does exist. The nation's Transitional Charter provides for freedom of religion, but there are restrictions on non-Muslim religious practices. Proselytizing of any religion but Islam is illegal. In 2009 the transitional government ratified legislation to implement Shari'ah across the entire nation, but in practice local judicial systems combine

Shari'ah with other traditional laws. Eid al-Fitr, Eid al-Adha, Muharam (Islamic New Year), and Mi'raaj are observed as national holidays.

11 TRANSPORTATION

The CIA reports that Somalia has a total of 22,100 km (13,732 mi) of roads, of which 2,608 km (1,621 mi) are paved. A 1,054-km (655-mi) road constructed with Chinese financing and work crews, completed in 1978, tied together the northern and southern parts of the country for the first time. There are no railways and no commercial water transport facilities.

The ports of Mogadishu, Chisimayu, and Berbera are served by vessels from many parts of the world, as well as by Somali and Arab dhows. Mogadishu in recent years handled more than 70% of Somalia's export and import traffic. In 2008 the United Arab Emirates (UAE) operated one merchant marine cargo ship out of Somalia.

The CIA reports there are 59 airports. However, there are only seven airports with paved runways. The major airfields are in Mogadishu and Berbera. International air service has been provided by the state-owned Somali Airlines (among other carriers), which also has regular flights connecting Mogadishu with regional centers and with Kenya, Djibouti, Saudi Arabia, the Comoros, Yemen, the Persian Gulf states, Frankfurt, Cairo, and Rome.

12 HISTORY

Somalia was known as the Land of Punt by ancient Egyptians, who came to Somalia's northern shores for incense and aromatic herbs. In the 9th or 10th century AD Somalis began pushing south from the Gulf of Aden coast. About this time, Arabs and Persians established settlements along the Indian Ocean coast. During the 15th and 16th centuries Portuguese explorers attempted without success to establish Portuguese sovereignty over the Somali coast. Meanwhile, the main coastal centers continued to be controlled by Arab merchant families under the nominal suzerainty of the sultanate of Oman, which transferred its seat to Zanzibar in the early 19th century.

After the British armed forces occupied Aden in 1839, they developed an interest in the northern Somali coast. By 1874 Egyptians occupied several points on the shore, but their occupation was short-lived. From 1884 to 1886 the British signed a number of "protectorate" treaties with Somali chiefs of the northern area. The protectorate was first administered by the resident in Aden and later (1907) by the colonial office. From 1899 to 1920 British rule was constantly disrupted by the "holy war" waged by Muhammad 'Abdallah Hasan (generally known in English literature as the "Mad Mullah").

Italian expansion in Somalia began in 1885, when Antonio Cecchi, an explorer, led an Italian expedition into the lower Juba region and concluded a commercial treaty with the sultan of Zanzibar. In 1889 Italy established protectorates over the eastern territories then under the nominal rule of the sultans of Obbia and of Alula, and in 1892 the sultan of Zanzibar leased concessions along the Indian Ocean coast to Italy. Direct administrative control of the territory known as Italian Somaliland was not established until 1905. The Fascist government increased Italian authority through its extensive military operations. In 1925 the British government, in line with secret agreements with Italy during World War I, transferred the Jubaland (an area south of the Jubba River) to Italian control. During the Italo-Ethiopian conflict (1934–36), Somalia was a staging area for Italy's invasion and conquest of Ethiopia. From 1936 to 1941 Somalia and the Somali-inhabited portion of Ethiopia, the Ogaden, were combined in an enlarged province of Italian East Africa.

In 1940–41 Italian troops briefly occupied British Somaliland but were soon defeated by the British, who conquered Italian Somaliland and reestablished their authority over British Somaliland. Although the Ogaden was returned to Ethiopia in 1948, British administration over the rest of Italian Somaliland continued until 1950, when Italy became the UN trusteeship authority. A significant impetus to the Somali nationalist movement was provided by the UN in 1949 when the UN General Assembly resolved that Italian Somaliland would receive its independence in 1960. By the end of 1956 Somalis were in almost complete charge of domestic affairs. Meanwhile, Somalis in British Somaliland were demanding self-government. As Italy agreed to grant independence on 1 July 1960 to its trust territory, the United Kingdom gave its protectorate independence on 26 June 1960, thus enabling the two Somali territories to join in a united Somali Republic on 1 July 1960. On 20 July 1961 the Somali people ratified a new constitution, drafted in 1960, and one month later confirmed 'Aden 'Abdullah Osman Daar as the nation's first president.

From the inception of independence, the Somali government supported the concept of self-determination for the people of the Somali-inhabited areas of Ethiopia (the Ogaden section), Kenya (most of the northeastern region), and French Somaliland (now the Republic of Djibouti), including the right to be united within a greater Somalia. Numerous border clashes occurred between Somalia and Ethiopia and between Somalia and Kenya. Soviet influence in Somalia grew after Moscow agreed in 1962 to provide substantial military aid.

Abdirashid 'Ali Shermarke, who was elected president in 1967, was assassinated on 15 October 1969. Six days later, army commanders seized power with the support of the police. The military leaders dissolved parliament, suspended the constitution, arrested members of the cabinet, and changed the name of the country to the Somali Democratic Republic. Maj. Gen. Jalle Mohamed Siad Barre, commander of the army, was named chairman of a 25-member Supreme Revolutionary Council (SRC) that assumed the powers of the president, the Supreme Court, and the National Assembly. Siad Barre was later named president.

In 1970 President Siad Barre proclaimed "scientific socialism" as the republic's guiding ideology. This Marxist ideology stressed hard work and public service and was regarded by the SRC as fully compatible with Islam. A number of industries and large firms, especially foreign banks and oil companies, were nationalized. Self-help projects were instituted to clean up the towns and villages, construct roads and sidewalks, dig and maintain wells and irrigation canals, build infirmaries and schools, and stabilize sand dunes. In 1972 the SRC proclaimed the adoption of a Latin script for Somali; in 1973 it inaugurated widespread literacy campaigns. The drought that affected large areas of Africa from 1968 to 1973 became severe in Somalia in late 1974, and in November of that year the SRC declared a state of emergency, set up relief camps, and initiated food rationing.

Controversy arose in 1975 over US charges that the Soviet Union was developing a military installation at the port of Berbera. Somalia denied the charges and invited inspection by journalists and US congressmen, who reported that they had found evidence of Soviet missile-handling facilities there. Somali officials did acknowledge receipt of Soviet military and technical advisers. Meanwhile, Ethiopia claimed that a Soviet-equipped Somalia represented a threat to its security. That same year, Siad Barre extended formal recognition to the Western Somali Liberation Front in the Ogaden. Somali forces took part in the fighting but were defeated in 1977, soon after the Soviet Union had swung its support to Ethiopia. Late in the year, Siad Barre expelled the Soviets. Relations with the United States warmed and in 1980, in return for military and economic aid (about $80 million in 1982), Siad Barre agreed to allow the United States use of air and naval facilities at the northern port of Berbera and at Mogadishu, facilities that had been built by the Soviets.

A new constitution was ratified in 1979. On 30 December 1979 an unopposed list of 171 candidates was elected to the People's Assembly which, the following month, elected Siad Barre unanimously to a new term of office (unopposed elections were again held on 31 December 1984). In October 1980 Siad Barre declared a state of emergency and reestablished the SRC, responding to the activities of an Ethiopian-backed opposition movement, the Somali Salvation Democratic Front (SSDF). The state of emergency was lifted in March 1982, but at midyear the insurgents, supported by a reported 10,000 Ethiopian troops, invaded Somalia. By December, however, only a small area was in insurgent or Ethiopian hands.

In January 1986 Siad Barre met with Lt. Col. Mengistu Haile Mariam, Ethiopia's head of state, in Djibouti in an effort to improve relations between the two countries. Two other meetings of Somali and Ethiopian officials were held in May and August, but no agreement was reached. After Barre's unopposed reelection on 23 December 1986—the first direct presidential election in Somalia—Barre appointed a prime minister for the first time, Lt. Gen. Mohamed 'Ali Samater—the first vice president and minister of defense. The SSDF had virtually crumbled by the end of 1986, but in 1987 another insurgent group, the Somali National Movement, was conducting operations in the north (the former British Somaliland). In February 1987 relations between Somalia and Ethiopia deteriorated following an Ethiopian attack on six settlements. Growing out of the Soviet shift to the Ethiopian side, American-Somali relations became closer during the administration of US president Ronald Reagan. This included a 10-year agreement providing US forces access to naval and air facilities at Berbera and increasing US military aid to Somalia.

In 1988 both the Ethiopian and Somali governments, faced by growing internal resistance, pledged to respect their border, but by 1990 the Somali regime was losing control. Armed resistance from the SSDF, the Somali Democratic Alliance (SDA), the Somali Democratic Movement (SDM), the Somali National Movement (SNM), the Somali Patriot Movement (SPM), and the United Somali Congress (USC) were turning Somali territory into a death trap. Government forces were no less ruthless. Each was led by a clan leader or local warlord. Donor nations threatened to cut off aid unless the atrocities ended.

In March 1990 Barre called for dialogue and, possibly, an end to single-party rule, but he was eventually ousted and, in January 1991, he fled Mogadishu. The USC seized the capital, but fighting continued. The SNM controlled much of the north and declared its territory the independent state of Somaliland. By December, the USC had split in two. One faction was led by Ali Mahdi Muhammad, the interim president, the other by Gen. Muhammad Farrah Aideed. They were from different sub-clans of the Hawiye clan. The fighting continued and the warring factions prevented people from planting and harvesting crops. Several hundred thousand people died. Far more were threatened by starvation. Over a half-million fled to Kenya. Contagious disease spread through refugee camps inside the country. The starvation and total breakdown of public services was publicized in the western media. Calls for the UN to intervene mounted. Yet, the food relief that was sent was stolen by soldiers and armed looters. Private relief efforts were frustrated and subject to extortion. Late on 3 December 1992 the UN Security Council passed a resolution to deploy a massive US-led international military intervention (UNITAF—United Task Force) to safeguard relief operations. By the end of December, Aideed and Ali Mahdi had pledged to stop fighting. The UNITAF spread throughout the country. Violence decreased dramatically, but later gunmen began to appear again.

US forces shifted their mandate toward the UN-Boutros-Ghali position of trying to confiscate arms and "technicals" (vehicles with mounted heavy weapons). Although the problem of relief distribution had largely been solved, there was no central government and few public institutions. Local warlords and their forces became increasingly emboldened.

By early 1993 over 34,000 troops from 24 UN members—75% from the United States—were deployed. Starvation virtually ended, a modicum of order was restored, and hope had returned. Yet, little was done to achieve a political solution or to disarm the factions. From January 1993 until 27 March, 15 armed factions haggled in Addis Ababa, Ethiopia, and finally reached agreement to end hostilities and to form a transitional national council for a two-year period to serve as the political authority in Somalia.

On 4 May 1993 the relief effort, Operation Restore Hope, was declared successful and the number of US forces was sharply reduced. Command of relief, disarmament, and reconstruction work was assumed by the UN. This effort, United Nations Operation in Somalia II (UNOSOM II), featured Pakistani, US, Belgian, Italian, Moroccan, and French troops, commanded by a Turkish general. However, on 23 June 1993, 23 Pakistani soldiers were killed in an ambush, and the UN Security Council ordered the arrest of those responsible. Gen. Aideed's forces were blamed and a $25,000 bounty was placed on Aideed's head.

Mogadishu subsequently became a war zone. In early October 1993, 18 US Army Rangers were killed and 75 were wounded in a firefight, known as the Battle of Mogadishu or the Black Hawk Down incident. American public opinion turned against the effort, forcing President Bill Clinton to withdraw US troops. Despite diplomatic overtures by his special envoy Charles Oakley and an inclusive UN—and then Ethiopian—sponsored set of talks, mediation failed. Kenya's President Daniel Arap Moi also mediated. After the US pullout, some 19,000 UN troops remained. Security Council Resolution (897) redefined the UNOSOM II mandate, emphasizing peacemaking and reconstruction, but it was a recognition that the assertive, coercive strategy of the UN had failed and that a more neutral role was necessary.

The United States completed its withdrawal of troops in March 1995, after which Mogadishu again disintegrated into chaos. The last of three major battles was engaged after peace talks between the factions collapsed in November 1996. Some 300 people, many civilians and aid workers, were killed in a month of fighting.

The hope for restored order was rekindled with the death of Gen. Aideed on 1 August 1996. Aideed's rivals declared a cease-fire, although his son and successor, Hussein Muhammad Aideed, vowed revenge and renewed the fight.

Because the factional splits were not based on ideological, religious, or issue differences, but instead were quests for power and riches, there was little hope for the restoration of a central government, and by the year 2000 the country was split into four pieces: Somaliland to the far north, Puntland to the northeast, South Mogadishu controlled by Hussein Muhammad Aideed, and North Mogadishu dominated by Ali Mahdi. Islamic courts took on the task of establishing law and order.

Despite overtures by Libya to influence the political configuration, clan elders met in neighboring Djibouti, and at the Arta Peace Conference on 26 August 2000 established a three-year Transitional National Government (TNG) with Abdiqassim Salad Hassan as president. The purpose of the TNG was to restore stability. However, the TNG controlled only pockets of the capital and country, and by August 2003 the TNG was due to expire.

Meanwhile, on 14 April 2003 citizens in the self-declared republic of Somaliland went to the polls to elect a president in Somaliland's first multiparty election. After disputing the results, the Kulmiye party's presidential candidate, Ahmad Muhammad Silanyo, said that the intervention of elders and others had persuaded him to accept the outcome, perhaps with promises for a power-sharing deal. Incumbent president Dahir Riyale Kahin of the Unity of Democrats Party (UDUB) was declared the winner by the Somaliland Election Commission (SEC), a decision that later was confirmed by the constitutional court.

By July 2003 more than 350 delegates had gathered for a national conference held in Kenya—Somalia's 14th peace talks in ten years—to vote on a parliament that would elect an interim president, who would then appoint a prime minister. Delegates, who were to elect a president from among more than 30 candidates, broke through a serious impasse by selecting a federal system of government and nominating a 351-member parliament to serve a four-year term. However, Hassan threatened to withdraw from the talks unless various grievances were resolved, including complaints that the parliament was too large, that elders alone should elect the president, and that Arabic must not be considered a second language. Further, the proposal to federate the country according to existing jurisdictions was rejected by Hassan because in his opinion it would dismember Somalia into a collection of small states and deepen existing divisions in the country. Indeed, some counterterrorism experts feared that a federal system would encourage warlordism and provide safe havens for international terrorists. Finally, in late 2004 a new federal transitional parliament (FTP) was formed.

Moving the FTP to Somalia proved a dangerous proposition. The prime minister's first visit to Mogadishu was marred by an explosion at a rally, and in November 2005 six people were killed and 20 injured in an attack on his convoy. That same month, the son of an FTP official was shot and killed, and some 12 people were killed and 21 wounded as the result of fighting triggered by Islamist militias bent on closing cinemas and video stores. In early 2006 clan militias killed some 30 people and wounded 70 more in fighting in the southern port city of Chisimayu and in towns in Mudug and Galguduud.

In December 2005 the peace process was jeopardized further when the Mogadishu faction of the FTP elected a regional council to govern Banaadir (greater Mogadishu). Many of those elected belonged to the Hawiye clan, which surrounded Mogadishu. Some observers viewed this development as a direct affront to the authority of, as well as a formal break with, the Jowhar interim government.

The following month, thanks to mediation by Yemen, President Yusuf and Parliament Speaker Sharif Hassan Sheikh Aden (the leader of the Mogadishu faction) declared that they would cooperate with each other, and in February the FTP met on Somali soil for the first time at a food warehouse in the central town of Baidoa. Some 205 of the 275 members of parliament attended. Surrounded by heavy security, President Yusuf made strong appeals for peace, unity, and national security. Those not attending the meeting were mostly Mogadishu warlords, who were determined to move the government from Jowar (56 miles north of Mogadishu) back to Mogadishu. They also disagreed over the perceived need for foreign peacekeepers in the country.

According to a report by the International Crisis Group (ICG), international donors were most likely to succeed in promoting peace in Somalia by not backing one faction over another in the divided TFG (Transitional Federal Government) and instead supporting the transitional federal charter, reviving the parliament, and establishing a government of national unity. This approach, according to ICG, stood the best chance of preventing Somalia from becoming a haven for terrorists.

From March to May 2006 scores of people were killed and hundreds injured during fierce fighting between rival militias in Mogadishu. It was the worst violence in almost a decade. In June and July militias loyal to the Union of Islamic Courts took control of Mogadishu and other parts of the south after defeating clan warlords. Ethiopian troops crossed the border into Somalia to support the Somali transitional government headquartered in Baidoa. In September the transitional government and the Union of Islamic Courts began peace talks in the Sudanese capital, Khartoum. That month Somalia's first known suicide bombing took place. President Yusuf was targeted outside parliament in Baidoa. In October 2006 Ethiopian Prime Minister Meles Zenawi asserted that Ethiopia was technically at war with the Islamists because they had declared holy war on his country. In December 2006, amid fierce fighting, Ethiopian aircraft, tanks, and artillery were used to support the forces of the Somali transitional government. The Islamists were temporarily defeated. In January 2007 the Islamists abandoned their last stronghold, the port town of Kismayo. President Yusuf entered Mogadishu for the first time since taking office in 2004. That month the United States carried out air strikes in southern Somalia; the United States said it was targeting al-Qaeda personnel being sheltered there. President Yusuf defended the US attack. The interim government imposed a three-month state of emergency. In February 2007 the UN Security Council authorized a six-month African Union (AU) peacekeeping mission for Somalia. In March AU peacekeepers landed at Mogadishu amid fierce fighting between insurgents and government forces backed by Ethiopian troops. The Red Cross said it was the worst fighting in 15 years. By April 2007 the UN stated more than 320,000 Somalis had fled fighting in Mogadishu since February.

In June 2007 a US warship shelled suspected al-Qaeda targets in Puntland. That month, Prime Minister Ghedi escaped a suicide car bomb attack on his compound. Ethiopian Prime Minister Zenawi visited Mogadishu and said he would withdraw his troops once peace was established. That July a national reconciliation conference opened in Mogadishu and came under mortar attack. Islamist leaders did not attend the talks. In August the nongovernmental organization (NGO) Human Rights Watch accused Ethiopian, Somali, and insurgent forces of war crimes, and the UN Security Council of indifference regarding the conflict. Ethiopian forces fired in Mogadishu in October on demonstrators who were protesting at the presence of what they called foreign invaders. The heaviest fighting in Mogadishu was taking place since April and Ghedi resigned. In November Nur Hassan Hussein, also known as Nur Adde, was sworn in as new prime minister. Top UN officials stated in November 2007 that the country had higher malnutrition rates, more current bloodshed, and fewer aid workers than Darfur. Indeed, at that time Somalia shared with Darfur and the Democratic Republic of the Congo the designation of being the worst humanitarian disasters on the planet.

In January 2009 Sheik Sharif Sheik Ahmed was elected president by the Somali parliament.

Despite some progress, Somalia remains a very unstable nation. Piracy in the waters of the Gulf of Aden and the Indian Ocean has caused international concern. In mid-December 2008 the UN Security Council approved a resolution allowing countries to pursue Somali pirates on land as well as at sea. While piracy is dangerous, desperate young men feel that the risk is worthwhile, since they have typically earned over $100 million per year in ransom for captured ships.

In August 2010 the long-awaited Consultation Draft Constitution was introduced to the nation by the Independent Federal Consultation Commission (IFCC). The 29-member IFCC received the mandate to prepare a draft constitution in 2004, but efforts were hindered by more pressing issues of national security. In September 2010, just a few weeks after the unveiling of the consultation draft, Prime Minister Omar Abdirashid Ali Sharmarke resigned from his post. Sharmarke and President Ahmed disagreed over issues concerning the draft constitution, but details of the exact nature of the disagreement are not known. Claiming that he was unable to work with the president, Sharmarke told reporters that his resignation sprung from national interests rather than personal reasons, since the lack of unity within the government created political instability that the insurgents used to their advantage. Mohamed Abdullahi Mohamed was nominated as the new prime minister and approved by a parliamentary vote of 297 to 95. Mohamed was educated in the United States and served as an official at the Somali embassy in Washington DC. He was sworn in as prime minister on 31 October 2010.

As of 2011 Al-Shabaab, a splinter group of the Islamic Courts Union, controlled large sections of the southern parts of Somalia where it is said to have imposed its own strict form of Shari'ah law.

Al-Shabaab describes itself as waging jihad against "enemies of Islam," and was engaged in combat against the TFG and the African Union Mission to Somalia (AMISOM).

13 GOVERNMENT

Somalia is perhaps the world's best-known example of a failed state. Its governments have been as fractured as they have been ineffective and since independence have only nominally ruled the territory within its borders. Since 1991 there has been no recognized permanent central government, and both Somaliland and Puntland—formally part of Somalia—have declared their autonomy. Puntland, which has exercised self-rule since 1998, has not declared its intention to become independent, while Somaliland seeks international recognition as an independent state.

From July 1961 to October 1969 Somalia was a parliamentary democracy based on the principle of separation of powers. After the army's seizure of power in October 1969, Maj. Gen. Siad Barre was named chairman of the 25-member SRC, which then elected him president. A constitution, approved in January 1979 by the ruling Somali Revolutionary Socialist Party (SRSP) and ratified by popular referendum on 25 August, vested legislative authority in the People's Assembly of 177 members serving five-year terms. This assembly could be dissolved by a two-thirds vote of its members or by the president. The People's Assembly was given the right to elect the president to a six-year, renewable term. (This was changed in 1984 to a direct popular election for a seven-year term.) The president was authorized to appoint members of the cabinet and to act as its chairman. He was declared commander in chief of the armed forces, with the power to declare war and to appoint the president of the Supreme Court. An article of the document allowed him to invoke emergency rule. On 24 October 1980 Siad Barre issued a decree suspending those constitutional provisions that were incompatible with the state of emergency triggered by the conflict with Ethiopia.

Large-scale fighting among clan factions from 1989 to January 1991 brought about the collapse of the Barre regime and his flight from Mogadishu. An interim administration (based on the 1969 constitution) was created by the United Somali Congress, but it collapsed in November 1991 and its two warring factions plunged Somalia into total civil war. The northern province declared its independence on 18 May 1991 as the sovereign state of Somaliland, the name it bore under British colonial rule. That independence, so far, has brought relatively orderly rule. On 5 May 1993 Mohammed Ibrahim Egal was elected president by members of the central committee.

Barre's overthrow in June 1991 marked the end of viable central government. Some 15 armed factions have been fighting continuously, except for the relatively peaceful early months of UN-US administration from December 1992 until around June 1993. UNOSOM II was technically in control until March 1995, when the UN withdrew the last of its troops from the country. With the UN's departure, the country split into zones controlled by the various factions. Gen. Aideed's death on 1 August 1996 renewed prospects for political stability as rival warlords Osman Ali Atto and Ali Mahdi Muhammad declared a cease-fire. It was also hoped that the moderate Osman Atto, Aideed's clansman and a former advisor, would assume control of Aideed's forces. But Aideed's immediate successor, his son Hussein Muhammad Aideed, renewed the fight against his father's rivals.

Sheikh Sharif Sheikh Ahmed was elected president in January 31, 2009. A transitional governing entity with a five-year mandate, known as the Transitional Federal Institutions (TFIs), was established in October 2004; the TFIs relocated to Somalia in June 2004. In 2009 the TFIs were given a two-year extension to October 2011. In June 2011 Abdiweli Muhammad Ali was named prime minister of Somalia.

Although not yet recognized as an independent nation, Somaliland maintains an army, a police force, a currency, and a judicial system, and it levies taxes. It has not been free of the factional fighting that pervades the south, but it enjoys far more stability and less lawlessness. It successfully held parliamentary elections in September 2005, although the opening of the 82-member body was marred by protests outside the building and a brawl inside. Nonetheless, because of concern with extremists and instability in the Horn of Africa, the United States, United Kingdom, and the European Union (EU) were reported to be leaning toward recognition of Somaliland as an independent state.

14 POLITICAL PARTIES

Political parties in Somalia may be thought of more accurately as collections of clans and sub-clans vying with each other for political power. Prior to October 1969 Somalia had a nominal multi-party system of government where opposition in parliament came from within the majority party as well as from opposition parties. The Somali Youth League (SYL), the largest party, was formed in 1943 as the Somali Youth Club. Its program included the unification of all Somalis (including those in Kenya, Ethiopia, and French Somaliland); social, political, and economic development; and nonalignment in international affairs. It represented almost all government personnel, entrepreneurs, and skilled and quasi-skilled workers of the southern area (formerly Italian Somaliland). In the first national elections after independence, held on 30 March 1964, the SYL won an absolute majority of 69 of the 123 parliamentary seats. The remaining seats were divided among 11 parties. In general elections held in March 1969, the ruling SYL, led by Mohammed Ibrahim Egal, was returned to power. A total of 64 political parties contested the elections. In October 1969 the SRC prohibited all political parties and announced that elections would be held in due course. In 1976, the SRC was abolished and its functions transferred to the leadership of the newly formed SRSP, which was led by the former SRC members. Siad Barre was general secretary of the SRSP, which remained the sole legal party until his overthrow in January 1991. Subsequently, the SNM seized control of the north and established the independent state of Somaliland. Since then, armed factions largely identified with clans and sub-clans divided up the territory as they fought and negotiated to expand their influence.

Many of the factions bear the titles of political parties: e.g., the Somali Democratic Movement, the Somali National Union, the Somali Patriotic Movement, and the USC. In fact, their bases are not national. The USC controlled Mogadishu and much of central Somalia until late in 1991 when it split into two major factions. Aideed's Somali National Alliance (SNA) identified with the Habar Gadir sub-clan of the Hawiye clan and Ali Mahdi's Somali Salvation Alliance (Abgal sub-clan of the Hawiyes). Currently the latter exists as the "Group of Twelve" coalition and these are the two dominant claimants to national power.

Aideed was killed on 1 August 1996 and was succeeded by his son, Hussein Muhammad Aideed. Some observers believe he could be displaced by Osman Ali Atto, an elder clansman and former Aideed advisor who was a rival of the general's at the time of the latter's death. Osman Atto is considered more moderate than Aideed, and more receptive to a political solution for Somalia.

The main political factions comprising the FTP are the National Salvation Council (NSC); the Somali Restoration and Reconciliation Council (SRRC); and various civil society and traditional leaders. The 90-member cabinet is split between proponents of locating the government at Jowhar and those who want to move it back to Mogadishu. Somaliland's main parties are the Democratic United National Party (UDUB), led by the president; Kulmiye ("unifier"); and the Justice Party (UCID).

In January 2009 the Somali parliament elected Sheik Sharif Sheik Ahmed as Somalia's new president. Sheikh Sharif of the Alliance for the Reliberation of Somalia (ARS) defeated more than a dozen other candidates, including the current prime minister, Nur Hassan Hussein. Sheikh Sharif is an Islamist cleric whose moderate views and emphasis on peaceful accord are considered by many to be a welcome relief from the reign of the transitional president, Abdullahi Yusuf Ahmed, who resigned his position in December 2008. His support is strong in Mogadishu and southern Somalia.

Under the terms of a 2009 UN deal, the Somali government and parliament were expected to enact a new constitution and hold new elections before 20 August 2011. However, in April 2011 the government announced that elections would be postponed until sometime in 2012, in order to have more time to complete the constitution and ensure adequate security measures. President Sheikh Sharif Sheikh Ahmed was expected to run for re-election.

15 LOCAL GOVERNMENT

Somalia is divided into 18 regions (*gobolka*): Awdal, Bakool, Banaadir, Bari, Bay, Galguduud, Gedo, Hiiraan, Jubbada Dhexe, Jubbada Hoose, Mudug, Nugaal, Sanaag, Shabeellaha Dhexe, Shabeellaha Hoose, Sool, Togdheer, and Woqooyi Galbeed.

Until 1973 the country was divided into eight regions, each headed by an official chosen by the central government. The regions were subdivided into 48 districts, headed by district commissioners also appointed by the government. There were 83 municipalities and sub-municipalities. The powers of the municipal councils included local taxation, town planning, registry and census, public services, and approval of the local budget. The major educational, economic, and social services were financed and maintained by the central government, which also exerted supervisory control over the municipal councils through its power to remove mayors and to dissolve the councils.

16 JUDICIAL SYSTEM

Owing to the collapse of national government, no national judicial system exists. However, much of the country has reverted to Shari'ah with the possibility for appeals; secular courts exist in some localities. The UN operation in Somalia oversaw administration of the Somalia penal code in those areas under UN supervision. Islamic law and traditional mediation continue to be applied to settle disputes over property and criminal offenses. The fear of renewed anarchy interferes with impartial administration of justice, and prosecution of war crimes is difficult.

In 1993 plans were released for a three-tier judicial system with courts of appeals, regional courts, and district courts. In the self-declared Republic of Somaliland, adoption of a new constitution is pending and the pre-1991 penal code is in effect. In North Mogadishu and part of South Mogadishu, the middle Shabelle, Gedo, and Hi'ran regions, court decisions are based only on Shari'ah law.

Historically, under the 1961 constitution the Supreme Court was the highest juridical organ of the republic, having ultimate jurisdiction over all civil, penal, and administrative matters and over all rights established by the constitution and by the laws of the state. Other judicial organs were qadi courts (Muslim courts), district courts, provincial courts, and courts of assize. Judicial organs of second instance were a tribunal of qadis, a court of appeals, and an appeals court of assize. Somali citizens participated as jurors in the courts of assize and the appeals court of assize. The Ministry of Justice administered the prison system and the offices and employees of the judicial organs. It prepared projects and regulations dealing with judicial matters and it supervised notaries, the bar, and the Office of State Attorney.

When the SRC assumed all judicial as well as executive and legislative powers in October 1969, it suspended the Supreme Court. However, the court was reopened in December 1969, and the rest of the court system was left much as before. A new national security court was empowered to rule on cases involving persons accused of attempting to undermine the independence, unity, and security of the state. The 1979 constitution established the Constitutional Court (composed of the Supreme Court and delegates to the People's Assembly) to decide on the constitutionality of laws. It also empowered the Higher Judicial Council, chaired by the president and composed of high-ranking SRC members, to be responsible for the selection, promotion, and discipline of members of the judiciary.

17 ARMED FORCES

The International Institute for Strategic Studies (IISS) reports that armed forces in Somalia totaled 2,000 members in 2011, all of whom are members of an army allied to the transitional government. Armed forces represent 0.1% of the labor force in Somalia. Defense spending totaled $53.4 million and accounted for 0.9% of GDP.

The regular armed forces disintegrated in the revolution of 1991, leaving the nation awash with Russian, Chinese, and European weapons. Clan gangs armed with these weapons terrorized relief workers during their humanitarian efforts sponsored by international and private organizations and battled a UN and US expeditionary force to a standstill. Between December 1992 and March 1994 over 100,000 US military personnel served in Somalia. The national armed forces did not reform during the 2000s, and the country remained torn between the Republic of Somaliland declared by the SNM in the north and insurgent groups in the south. There was no data on military expenditures for 2005 or on the exact number of armed Somalis.

Djibouti announced in late January 2010 that it would send 450 troops to Somalia to supplement the AU contingent already present in the country. The 450 Djiboutian troops would supplement the 2,500 soldiers that Burundi and Uganda each had operating in Mogadishu.

In June 2010 the government called for an emergency summit of East Africa's Intergovernmental Authority on Development (IGAD) to plead for much needed assistance in the war against al-Qaeda. As a result, the group agreed to send 2,000 additional troops as soon as possible to serve within AMISOM. The members of IGAD have also determined to work with the UN Security Council to secure up to 20,000 additional troops for deployment throughout the country.

On 27 July 2010 AU leaders agreed to send more troops to Somalia. AU leaders decided to remove AMISOM's official cap of 8,100 troops, giving AU countries more flexibility to bolster the peacekeeping force in the country. At the time of the meeting, 6,200 AMISOM troops were stationed in Somalia. Jean Ping, the AU's commission chairman, said AU leaders were committed to adding at least 4,000 more to this force.

In December 2010, there were unofficial reports that al-Shabab and Hizbul Islam (a second major Islamist group) were planning to join forces in their fight against the government. Together, these two groups control much of south and central Somalia.

18 INTERNATIONAL COOPERATION

Somalia, which joined the UN on 30 September 1960, participates in ECA and several non-regional specialized agencies, such as the UN Food and Agricultural Organization (FAO), the World Bank, ILO, UNESCO, UNHCR, UNIDO, and the World Health Organization (WHO). It is also a member of the ACP Group, the African Development Bank, the Arab Fund for Economic and Social Development, the Council of Arab Economic Unity, the Islamic Development Bank, the Organization of the Islamic Conference (OIC), the New Partnership for Africa's Development (NEPAD), the Community of Sahel and Saharan States (CENSAD), G-77, the Arab League, and AU.

Since 1960 the Somali government has sponsored a policy known as Pan-Somalism that strives for the unification of all Somali populations within the region into a Greater Somalia. This issue has a major impact on relations with Ethiopia, Kenya, and Djibouti and tensions between Somalia and these countries has escalated to violence in the past. Somalia is part of the Nonaligned Movement. In environmental cooperation, Somalia is part of CITES, the Montréal Protocol, and the UN Conventions on the Law of the Sea and Climate Change.

In April 2011 Prime Minister Mohamed Abdullahi Mohamed, who was sworn in by the interim government on 31 October 2010, issued an order calling for all UN agency officials associated with the UN mission to Somalia to become residents in Mogadishu by the end of June 2011. Only about half of the 1,500 mission members have been based within the country, with the remainder taking offices in neighboring Kenya for security reasons. Mohamed claimed that the UN agencies should be present within the country in order to best understand the problems affecting the country.

19 ECONOMY

Somalia's economy, one of the poorest in the world, is an agricultural one based primarily on livestock and, to a lesser extent, on farming. The GDP rate of change in Somalia, as of 2010, was 2.6%.

Livestock accounts for about 40% of GDP and a large percentage of export earnings, mainly from Saudi Arabia. Bananas are the main cash crop and account for nearly 50% of export earnings. Other crops produced for domestic consumption are cotton, maize, and sorghum.

There are plans to develop the fishing industry. Northern Somalia is the world's largest source of incense and myrrh. There has been little exploitation of mineral resources, which include petroleum, uranium, and natural gas.

Since 1990 the economy has been a shambles, the consequence of drought and of protracted civil strife which has left the country without central authority. By early 1992 virtually all trade, industrial, and agricultural activities had stopped, large numbers of people were forced from their homes, and more than six million people were at risk of starvation.

In 1993 donors pledged $130 million toward Somalia's reconstruction. The aid, together with good rains and increased stability, helped ease the food situation and few communities were at risk of widespread famine in 1997; however, the lack of rains in spring 2001 caused major food shortages in the south of the country. Continued hostilities and the lack of a central authority in 2007 prevented significant improvements in economic conditions.

The UN through its various relief agencies is the country's largest employer. Although Somalia was largely still in a state of anarchy in 2011, the telecommunications sector was functioning, with most major cities having wireless telephone services. Money exchange services have filled the void created by the absence of a formal banking sector. Hotels, guarded by private militias, operate in Mogadishu and consumer goods can be found in the city's markets.

Profiteering from counterfeiting has rapidly debased Somalia's currency, and the country's arrears to the International Monetary Fund (IMF) have continued to grow.

20 INCOME

The CIA estimated that in 2010 the GDP of Somalia was $5.896 billion. The CIA defines GDP as the value of all final goods and services produced within a nation in a given year and computed on the basis of purchasing power parity (PPP) rather than value as measured on the basis of the rate of the exchange based on current dollars. The per capita GDP was estimated at $600. The annual growth rate of GDP was 2.6%. It was estimated that agriculture accounted for 65% of GDP, industry 10%, and services 25%.

21 LABOR

As of 2007, Somalia had a total labor force of 3.447 million people. Within that labor force, CIA estimates in 1975 noted that 71% were employed in agriculture, 15% in industry, and 14% in the service sector.

Since the overwhelming majority of the population was engaged in stock herding or agriculture, the number of unemployed was not large, but there was considerable unemployment in the urban centers.

Labor codes were enacted in the early 1960s for minimum wages, hours of work, employment of women and children, vacations, and collective bargaining. After the 1969 revolution the SRC dissolved the existing unions and took action to organize the General Federation of Somali Trade Unions along lines more in keeping with its plans for a Socialist state, but it was believed to have ceased functioning with the collapse of the government in 1992. The constitution of Somaliland provided the right to unionize. As of 2010 the Somaliland Trade Union Organization (2004), which claimed to have 26,000 members, was an umbrella organization cover 21 unions. However, it undertook no activities in 2010. There are no systems in place to implement acceptable work conditions, child labor regulations, workweek standards or wage minimums.

22 AGRICULTURE

The country's major crops include bananas, sorghum, corn, coconuts, rice, sugarcane, mangoes, sesame seeds, and beans. Cereal production in 2009 amounted to 215,368 tons, fruit production 214,768 tons, and vegetable production 101,020 tons.

There are two main types of agriculture, one indigenous and the other introduced by European settlers. The Somalis have traditionally engaged in rain-fed dry-land farming or in dry-land farming complemented by irrigation from the waters of the Shabeelle and Jubba rivers or from collected rainwater. The rainy season lasts from April to June and these rains typically bring about 75% of Somalia's annual cereal production. Corn, sorghum, beans, rice, vegetables, cotton, and sesame are grown by both methods. Bananas and sugarcane have been the main commercial crops, grown on irrigated land along the two rivers. Sugarcane is cultivated at Giohar and Jilib. Somalia is the world's leading producer of frankincense.

Between 1975 and 1991 all land was nationalized. Existing customary rights were generally honored, but the state took over large areas of irrigable land in the river valleys. Plantations had to register to obtain a concession grant, with the value of the land itself excluded from the selling price. In 1993 privatization and assistance from Italy (the main market for banana exports) began to help revitalize the agricultural sector.

23 ANIMAL HUSBANDRY

The majority of Somalis raise livestock; in some areas, particularly in the north, this is the only means of subsistence. During the civil war, herds were looted and killed. The UN FAO reported that Somalia dedicated 43 million hectares (106.3 million acres) to permanent pasture or meadow in 2009. During that year, the country tended 3.4 million chickens, 5.4 million head of cattle, and 4,200 pigs. Somalia also produced 12,000 tons of cattle hide.

Having no official central government, the traditional Somali system of customary law and politics has been instrumental in maintaining economic stability. Somalia's animal herding sector is stronger than that of either of its neighbors, Kenya or Ethiopia. By Somali custom, the cross-border livestock trade is facilitated by brokers who certify that traded livestock are not stolen and thus act as insurance agents for cross-border trading. Fees are lower on the Somali side of the cross-border trade than on the Kenyan side, indicating that rustling may be a more severe problem in Kenya than in Somalia.

24 FISHING

Approximately 1% of the population is engaged full-time in fishing. Somalia had nine decked commercial fishing boats in 2008.

The annual capture totaled 30,000 tons according to the UN FAO. The export value of seafood totaled $4.59 million.

Fish-processing plants produced fish flour, inedible oil, and semi-refined edible oil. One of the government's aims has been to establish fishing cooperatives; in 1975 thousands of nomads from the drought-affected area were resettled in fishing villages.

25 FORESTRY

Approximately 11% of Somalia is covered by forest. The UN FAO estimated the 2009 roundwood production at 110,000 cu m (3.88 million cu ft). The value of all forest products, including roundwood, totaled $15.8 million. Somalia is one of the few areas in the world where frankincense is produced; incense trees of the genus Boswellia are found in the northeast. Gum arabic is also produced in small quantities. In the scant forests along the rivers of the Jubba region, Euphorbia ruspoli is milled and used for the production of banana crates.

26 MINING

The Somali minerals sector, which was not a significant economic force before the 1991 overthrow of the government, failed to expand in the ensuing years of political and economic instability. In 2003 small quantities of gypsum, marine salt, and sepiolite (meerschaum) were exploited, and the country also presumably produced clays, sand and gravel, crushed and dimension stone, and limestone (for lime manufacture and/or agriculture). Officially reported mineral and trade data have been unavailable owing to lack of a central government since 1991 and the secession of Somaliland and Puntland. The civil war forced the closure of Somalia's cement plant and oil refinery (a leading industry) and halted exploration for natural gas and other resources. There were unexploited deposits of anhydrite, bauxite, columbite, feldspar, natural gas, iron ore, kaolin, quartz, silica sand, tantalum, thorium, tin, and uranium, and recent discoveries of amethyst, aquamarine, emerald, garnet, opal, ruby, and sapphire.

In 2006 dimension stone production of granite, marble, and sandstone began in Somaliland, and in 2008 niobium and tantalum mining started as well. Somaliland had more than 1,600 workers employed in artisanal mining in 2006. Mining of gemstones in Somaliland has been limited by a lack of modern equipment, civil strife, and damage to the infrastructure; an EU-funded NGO was working with Somaliland's government to exploit gemstone resources. Tin was mined by the British before World War II, and charcoal was once the fifth-leading export commodity.

27 ENERGY AND POWER

Somalia has no reserves of oil, or coal, nor any refining capacity, but does have modest reserves of natural gas. The World Bank reported in 2008 that Somalia produced 315 million kWh of electricity and consumed 297.8 million kWh, or 30 kWh per capita. Oil production totaled an estimated 110 barrels per day in 2010.

Somalia relies on imported petroleum products for the production of its electric energy. The CIA estimates of 2009 noted that the country consumed 3,827 barrels of oil a day.

28 INDUSTRY

Before the start of civil war in the early 1990s, the manufacturing sector was beginning to develop. However, all industries suffered major losses during the civil war. Industries mainly serve the domestic market and, to a lesser extent, provide some of the needs of Somalia's agricultural exports, such as the manufacture of crates for packing bananas. Most industries have been looted, however, and many sold for scrap metal.

The most important industries were the state-owned sugar plants at Jowhar and Jilib, an oilseed-crushing mill, and a soap factory. Other industries manufactured corrugated iron, paint, cigarettes and matches, aluminum utensils, cardboard boxes and polyethylene bags, and textiles.

The fish and meat canning export industries operate below capacity. Textiles are produced at the SOMALTEX plant, which supplies virtually the entire domestic market. Most major enterprises are government-owned, but private plants produce food, beverages, chemicals, clothing, and footwear. There are also plants for milk processing, vegetable and fruit canning, and wheat flour and pasta manufacturing, as well as several grain mills. Local craft industries produce sandals and other leather products, cotton cloth, pottery, baskets, and clay or meerschaum vessels.

There is one natural gas field, but exploration and exploitation of oil and natural gas has been suspended since political conflict began.

29 SCIENCE AND TECHNOLOGY

In 1993 the Somali National University in Mogadishu had departments of medicine, agriculture, veterinary medicine, engineering, geology, and industrial chemistry. Also located in Mogadishu were the Institute for the Preparation of Serums and Vaccines, the Laboratory of Hygiene and Prophylaxy, and the Society of Medicine and Tropical Hygiene. In Mogadishu there is the school of public health, a veterinary college, the Geological Survey Department of the Ministry of Water Development and Mineral Resources, and the Survey and Mapping Department of the Ministry of Public Works. A technical college is located in Burao. The World Bank reported in 2009 that there were no patent applications in science and technology in Somalia.

30 DOMESTIC TRADE

Despite the lack of a central government, domestic commerce in Somalia is still active, although on a small scale. Some merchants, using satellite telephones or radios, coordinate distribution networks that transport food and other goods between various rival territories. Small shops barter or sell a limited number of such imported and domestic items as tea and coffee, kerosene, sugar, cotton goods, spices, cereals, skins, hides, and ghee. Outside the urban centers, the barter system is often employed. In the urban centers, small traders deal essentially in a cash economy.

Mogadishu is a primary business and commercial center and hosts a large number of shops and markets offering a variety of goods. In the south, at the mouth of the Juba River, Kismayu serves as an important port, particularly for banana exports. Hargeisa serves as a watering and trading center for many of the nation's nomadic herders.

Usual business hours are from 8 a.m. to 12:30 p.m. and from 4:30 p.m. to 7 p.m., Saturday–Thursday.

31 FOREIGN TRADE

Somalia imported $798 million worth of goods and services in 2008, while exporting $300 million worth of goods and services. Major import partners in 2009 were Djibouti, 29.9%; Kenya, 7.8%; China, 7.3%; Pakistan, 7%; Brazil, 6.4%; Yemen, 4.8%; Oman, 4.6%; and UAE, 4.5% . Its major export partners were UAE, 53%; Yemen, 18.5%; and Oman, 13.4%.

Exports consist largely of livestock (camels, sheep, and goats), bananas, hides, and fish. Principal imports are manufactures, petroleum products, food, and petroleum. Imports also include guns, medicine, and khat (a stimulant leaf chewed by Somalis). Foreign trade is handled by local traders who coordinate transactions despite factional fighting and the lack of a central government. Many traders in the north have relocated from Berbera to Bosaso in order to avoid foreign exchange regulations imposed by the self-proclaimed Somaliland government in the northwest. Livestock is normally driven from northeast Ethiopia to ports and then shipped to Saudi Arabia.

32 BALANCE OF PAYMENTS

Since independence, Somalia has consistently had an unfavorable balance of payments on current accounts, caused by deficits of trade and invisible transactions. In the 1980s Somalia depended on direct transfers and capital assistance from other governments and became even more dependent after civil war and ensuing anarchy broke out in 1991.

33 BANKING AND SECURITIES

The Central Bank of Somalia, a government institution with branches in every region, controls the issue of currency and performs the central banking functions of the state. All banks were nationalized in 1970. The Central Bank was set up in 1960. The Commercial and Savings Bank, formed in 1975 from a merger of the National Commercial Bank and the Somali Savings and Credit Bank, was closed in June 1990. The Somali Development Bank was created in 1983, and the Commercial Bank of Somalia was opened in July 1990. The formal banking system no longer functions.

34 INSURANCE

A small number of European agencies which had acted as agents for foreign insurance companies were replaced by a state-owned insurance company, the National Insurance Co. of Somalia, in 1972.

35 PUBLIC FINANCE

The Somali budget has been in deficit since the early 1970s. Some $3 billion of debt was held by foreign entities. Disintegration of the national economy since 1991 has led to relief and military intervention by the UN. No central government authority existed as of 2006, so there was no functioning system of civil administration to collect and disburse public finances.

36 TAXATION

Direct taxes are imposed on income and profits, when officials can collect them. In 1986 tax rates on wages and salaries ranged from 0%–18.9%. Income from trade and the professions was taxed at rates of up to 35%. Indirect taxes are imposed on imports, exports,

Principal Trading Partners – Somalia (2010)

(In millions of US dollars)

Country	Total	Exports	Imports	Balance
World	1,778.3	515.7	1,262.6	-746.9
Djibouti	388.7	1.6	387.1	-385.4
United Arab Emirates	322.2	262.5	59.6	202.9
Yemen	163.5	101.1	62.4	38.7
Oman	127.4	66.3	61.2	5.1
Kenya	103.5	2.3	101.2	-98.9
Pakistan	97.0	5.6	91.4	-85.8
India	87.1	8.3	78.7	-70.4
China	80.9	1.5	79.4	-77.8
Brazil	69.9	...	69.9	-69.9
Sa'udi Arabia	36.9	17.0	19.9	-2.8

(…) data not available or not significant.

(n.s.) not specified.

SOURCE: *2011 Direction of Trade Statistics Yearbook,* New York: United Nations, 2011.

mortgages, vehicle registration, sugar, alcohol, and a number of other goods and services.

37 CUSTOMS AND DUTIES

Customs and duties are levied primarily to provide income for the state and to offer protection to local industries. Most duties are ad valorem and range from 0% to 100%. Unspecified goods are dutiable at 25% ad valorem. A general sales tax of 10% for imported goods is also levied.

38 FOREIGN INVESTMENT

Foreign direct investment (FDI) in Somalia was a net inflow of $108 million according to World Bank figures published in 2009. Civil strife and the lack of a central government have discouraged foreign investment. Although the UN and associated foreign governments spent $4 billion dollars to restore order to the country, no productive assets remained after their departure in 1995. The only economic spin-off appears to have been contracts issued to local companies to dispose of military debris and trash. Foreign investment in the late 1990s centered on the communications structure in mobile phone technology and energy creation, but continuation of political conflicts well into 2002 drove away investment.

39 ECONOMIC DEVELOPMENT

Successive Somali governments have sought to stimulate production in all sectors of agriculture, commerce, and industry. However, drought, inflation, civil strife, and the rise of oil prices have severely hampered these programs. Government priorities prior to the civil war included the expansion of the fishing fleet, food self-sufficiency based on the development of the Baardheere dam project, livestock breeding, meat export programs, and transport and telecommunication improvements.

Clan warfare has left Somalia without a central government since 1991. Economic development at the beginning of the new millennium was expected to be devoted in large part to the rebuilding of the Somali civil administration. The ongoing civil disturbances and clan rivalries have interfered with any broad-based economic development and international aid arrangements. The return of peace and security to the whole country was considered essential for viable economic growth.

⁴⁰SOCIAL DEVELOPMENT

Since 1989 internal fighting and widespread drought conditions have severely disrupted government and its ability to provide social services. Private humanitarian agencies tried to fill the need but fighting, extortion, and the activities of armed factions and looters chased many of them away. The UN has also tried to help, but it too finds operations difficult. Somalia in effect has no national government, and current data for social services is unavailable.

Although the constitution prohibits discrimination based on sex or ethnicity, societal discrimination and violence against women and children are prevalent. Women play a subordinate role in Somalia's culture and politics. Polygamy is practiced and female genital mutilation is nearly universal. The punishment for murdering a woman is half as severe as that for killing a man. Rape is a common occurrence.

Serious human rights violations included suppression of civil and political rights, disappearances, arbitrary detention, and harsh prison conditions. Many civilians continue to be killed in factional fighting.

⁴¹HEALTH

According to the CIA, life expectancy in Somalia was 50 years in 2011. The country spent 2.6% of its GDP on healthcare. There was less than one physician and one nurse or midwife per 10,000 inhabitants. The fertility rate was 6.4, while the infant mortality rate was 109 per 1,000 live births. In 2008 the maternal mortality rate, according to the World Bank, was 1,200 per 100,000 births. It was estimated that 24% of children were vaccinated against measles. The CIA calculated HIV/AIDS prevalence in Somalia to be about 0.7% in 2009.

In 1972 all health facilities and the services of all private medical personnel were placed under state control. Government policy was eventually to provide free medical treatment for all. One of the self-help projects instituted by the SRC was the construction of local clinics.

Somalia had a high incidence of tuberculosis, schistosomiasis, and pulmonary disturbances. Malaria and intestinal parasites were endemic. Serious dietary deficiencies were found, particularly in the north. Only about a third of the population had access to pure drinking water, which was rarely available outside the larger cities. Water outside these centers needs to be filtered, boiled, or chemically treated. Somalis, however, take few of these precautions.

Though Somalia was declared to be polio free in 2007, the only way for the nation to maintain that status is through intervention from the WHO and the UN Children's Fund. Two rounds of polio vaccinations in 2011 intended to reach 800,000 children.

⁴²HOUSING

Years of civil war and a 2004 tsunami took a toll on the nation's housing stock. The war caused internal migration and displacement to the extent that some areas are highly overpopulated while other neighborhoods have been abandoned. A vast majority of the population lives in slums or partially destroyed housing.

Development schemes aided by UN and foreign assistance programs have helped alleviate some housing shortages. Town planning and housing are under the jurisdiction of municipalities, and assistance is given by the central government only when it has approved a project submitted by the municipality. The typical Somali house is either a cylindrical hut with a conical thatched roof or a rectangular hut with an angular roof of thatch or metal.

⁴³EDUCATION

Overall, the CIA estimated that Somalia had a literacy rate of 37.8% in 2001 (the most recent available figure as of January 2012). Private schools were closed or nationalized in 1972 and all education was put under the jurisdiction of the central government. In 1975 primary education was made compulsory. A minimum of eight years of schooling at the primary level is mandatory; however, many prospective students, particularly among the nomadic population, cannot be accommodated. Secondary education lasts for four years.

Primary school enrollment in 1995 was estimated at less than 10% of age-eligible students. The same year, secondary school enrollment was at less than 6% of age-eligible students.

Mogadishu University is the primary source for higher education. All institutions at the higher level had 817 teachers and 15,672 students in 1986.

⁴⁴LIBRARIES AND MUSEUMS

The National Museum of Somalia in Mogadishu maintains a highly specialized library (3,000 volumes) dealing primarily with African and Somali culture, government, and history. The National Library, under the supervision of the Ministry of Higher Education and Culture, has 9,000 volumes, and the Somali Institute of Public Administration also has a book collection; both are in Mogadishu. The Amoud University Library has about 65,000 volumes. The National Museum in Mogadishu is a restored residence of the Viceroy of the Sultan of Zanzibar. Besides its comprehensive collection of Somali ethnographic material, the museum has local art objects, fossils, and old coins.

⁴⁵MEDIA

The CIA reports there are 100,000 telephone landlines in Somalia. In addition to landlines, mobile phone subscriptions averaged 7 per 100 people. There are 11 AM radio stations and 1 shortwave radio station. Internet users number 1 per 100 citizens. In 2010 the country had only three Internet hosts.

The transitional government operates Radio Mogadishu. There are several privately owned radio and television stations, many of which are local or regional in range. Most of the country can receive transmissions from British Broadcasting.

There are two daily newspapers, one government and one independent. There is also an English-language weekly newspaper and several other small weekly papers. Freedom of speech and the press are severely limited, according to reports. Factional infighting creates an atmosphere of mistrust, and media representatives such as comedians, actors, and journalists have been arrested, detained, or otherwise harassed. Most news comes from foreign broadcasts.

46 ORGANIZATIONS

Private organizations that existed in the 1960s have largely been replaced by government-sponsored groups. Among party-controlled groups are the Union of Somali Cooperatives Movement, the Somali Women's Democratic Organization, and the Somali Revolutionary Youth Organization.

There are active sports associations promoting amateur competitions among athletes of all ages in pastimes such as squash, tennis, badminton, dance sport, and weightlifting; some of these, such as the Somalia Football Federation, are affiliated with international organizations as well.

Volunteer service organizations, such as the Lions Clubs International, are also present. There is a national chapter of the Red Crescent Society.

47 TOURISM, TRAVEL, AND RECREATION

The estimated daily cost to visit Mogadishu, the capital, was $208. The cost of visiting other cities averaged $169. Somalia's modest tourist industry has declined since the civil war began in 1991. Every person entering Somalia is required to have a valid passport and a proper visa. An official certificate showing immunization against yellow fever is necessary if traveling from an infected area.

Before the war, Somalia offered lovely beaches, excellent diving, and numerous species of East African wildlife.

48 FAMOUS PERSONS

The most important historical figure in Somali history is Muhammad 'Abdallah bin Hasan (known popularly in English literature as the "Mad Mullah"). He was born about 1860 and during his youth devoted himself to religious studies. In August 1899, with his followers of the Salihiyyah confraternity, he declared a holy war against the British, Italians, and Ethiopians. His resistance to the British lasted until his death in November 1920. Muhammad, also known as one of Somalia's greatest poets, was the first to call for Somali unity. Other important historical figures include Sharif Abu Bakr bin 'Abdallah al-'Aydarus (d. 1503), who founded the Qadiriyyah confraternity in the Somali region; Sheikh 'Ali Maye Durogba of Marka (d. 1917), who founded the Ahmadiyyah sect in Somalia; and Sheikh Muhammad Guled (d. 1918), who started the Salihiyyah sect in Somalia.

'Abdullahi 'Issa Mohamed (b. 1921) was prime minister during the Italian trusteeship administration (1956–1960) and was Somalia's first foreign minister. Aden 'Abdullah Osman Daar (b. 1908) is regarded as the Somali most responsible for bringing about the transition of the Somali territory from dependence to independence; he was the nation's first president. Abdirashid 'Ali Shermarke (b. 1919–d. 1969) was Somalia's first prime minister after independence and the nation's second president. He was assassinated on 15 October 1969 by a member of his bodyguards. Maj. Gen. Jalle Mohamed Siad Barre (b. 1921–d. 95) was the leader of the bloodless coup that took over the government six days later and established the SRC. He subsequently became president of the Somali Democratic Republic. Mohamed 'Ali Samatar (b. 1931), first vice-president and minister of defense, became prime minister in 1986. Mohammed Farah Aidid (b. 1934–d. 96) was the clan leader that gained control over much of Somalia during the civil war. His son, Hussein Aidid (b. 1962), a former US marine, took over after his death. Abdiqasim Salad Hassan (b. 1941) was recognized as president in exile in Djibouti in 2000, serving until 2004. In October of that year, Abdullahi Yusuf Ahmed (b. 1934) was named the transitional president of Somalia. Osman Hasan Ali (b. 1950) became famous as the wealthy financier of clan militias during the civil war.

49 DEPENDENCIES

Somalia has no territories or colonies.

50 BIBLIOGRAPHY

Abdullahi, Mohamed Diriye. *Culture and Customs of Somalia.* Westport, CT: Greenwood Press, 2001.

Besteman, Catherine and Lee V. Cassanelli, eds. *The Struggle for Land in Southern Somalia: The War behind the War.* Boulder, CO: Westview Press, 2003.

Mohamoud, Abdullah A. *State Collapse and Post-Conflict Development in Africa: The Case of Somalia (1960–2001).* West Lafayette, IN: Purdue University Press, 2006.

Mukhtar, Mohamed Haji. *Historical Dictionary of Somalia.* Lanham, MD: Scarecrow, 2003.

Somalia Investment and Business Guide: Strategic and Practical Information. Washington, DC: International Business Publications USA, 2012.

Woodward, Peter. *The Horn of Africa: Politics and International Relations.* New York: I.B. Tauris, 2003.

Zeilig, Leo, and David Seddon. *A Political and Economic Dictionary of Africa.* Philadelphia: Routledge/Taylor and Francis, 2005.

SOUTH AFRICA

Republic of South Africa

Republiek van Suid-Afrika

CAPITAL: Pretoria (administrative); Cape Town (legislative); Bloemfontein (judicial)

FLAG: Two equal width horizontal bands of red and blue separated by a central green band that splits into a horizontal Y, the arms of which end at the corners of the hoist side; the Y embraces a black isosceles triangle from which the arms are separated by narrow yellow bands; the red and blue bands are separated from the green band and its arms by narrow white stripes.

ANTHEM: *National Anthem of South Africa.*

MONETARY UNIT: The South African rand (ZAR) is a paper currency of 100 cents. It is used throughout the South African monetary area. There are coins of 1, 2, 5, 10, 20, and 50 cents and 1, 2, and 5 rand, as well as notes of 10, 20, 50, 100, and 200 rand. ZAR1 = US$0.125998 (or US$1 = ZAR7.93662) as of 2012.

WEIGHTS AND MEASURES: The metric system is in use.

HOLIDAYS: New Year's Day, 1 January; Human Rights Day, 21 March; Freedom Day, 27 April; Workers' Day, 1 May; Youth Day, 16 June; Women's Day, 9 August, Heritage Day, 24 September; Day of Reconciliation, 16 December; Christmas, 25 December; Goodwill Day, 26 December. Movable religious holidays include Good Friday and Ascension; Family Day is a movable secular holiday.

TIME: 2 p.m. = noon GMT.

¹LOCATION, SIZE, AND EXTENT

The area of South Africa is 1,219,912 sq km (471,011 sq mi). Comparatively, the area occupied by South Africa is slightly less than twice the size of the state of Texas. Considered as a whole, South Africa extends 1,821 km (1,132 mi) NE–SW and 1,066 km (662 mi) SE–NW. It is bounded on the N by Botswana and Zimbabwe (formerly Rhodesia), on the NE by Mozambique and Swaziland, on the E by the Indian Ocean, on the S by the confluence of the Indian and Atlantic oceans, on the W by the Atlantic Ocean, and on the NW by Namibia. South Africa also controls two small islands, Prince Edward and Marion, which lie some 1,920 km (1,200 mi) southeast of Cape Town. South Africa's capital city, Pretoria, is located in the northeastern part of the country.

²TOPOGRAPHY

South Africa has a mean altitude of about 1,200 m (3,900 ft), and at least 40% of the surface is at a higher elevation. Parts of Johannesburg are more than 1,800 m (6,000 ft) above sea level. There are three major zones: the marginal regions, which range in width from 80 to 240 km (550 mi) in the east to 60 km (30 mi) in the west and include the eastern plateau slopes, Cape folded belt, and western plateau slopes; a vast saucer-shaped interior plateau, separated from the marginal zone by the Great Escarpment; and the Kalahari Basin, only the southern part of which projects into north-central South Africa. The land rises steadily from west to east to the Drakensberg Mountains (part of the Great Escarp-

ment), the tallest of which is Mt. Injasuti (3,408 m/11,181 ft), on the border with Lesotho.

The coastal belt of the west and south ranges between 150 and 180 m (500 and 600 ft) above sea level and is very fertile, producing citrus fruits and grapes, particularly in the Western Cape. North of the coastal belt stretch the Little and the Great Karoo highlands, which are bounded by mountains, are semiarid to arid, and merge into sandy wastes that ultimately join the arid Kalahari Desert. The high grass prairie, or veld, of the Free State and Gautengis is famous for its deposits of gold and silver. From the Drakensberg, the land falls toward the Indian Ocean in the rolling hills and valleys of KwaZulu-Natal, which are covered with rich vegetation and, near the coast, subtropical plants, including sugarcane.

The two most important rivers draining the interior plateau are the Orange (with its tributary the Vaal), which flows into the Atlantic Ocean, and the Limpopo, which empties into the Indian Ocean through Mozambique. Of the fast-flowing rivers, with steeply graded courses that produce spectacular waterfalls, the largest is the Tugela, which rises in the Mont-aux-Sources and flows swiftly to the Indian Ocean.

³CLIMATE

South Africa lies almost wholly within the southern temperate zone, and its climate is more equable than that of corresponding northern latitudes because of its surrounding waters. Temperature differentials between east and west coasts stem from the influences, respectively, of the warm Mozambique (Agulhas) Current and the cold Benguela Current. The average daily minimum temperature at Durban, on the east coast, ranges from 11°C (52°F) in July to 21°C (70°F) in February; on the west coast, at Port Nolloth, the range is from 7°C (45°F) to 12°C (54°F) during the corresponding months. Temperatures are cooler in the highlands: at Johannesburg, the average daily minimum is 4°C (39°F) in June and July and 14°C (57°F) in January. On the high veld, there are sharp differences of temperature between day and night, but there is less daily fluctuation nearer the coast.

Rainfall is unpredictable in large parts of the country, and prolonged droughts are a serious restriction on farming in such areas. While the mean annual rainfall is 46 cm (18 in), 21% of the country receives less than 20 cm (8 in) and 31% gets more than 60 cm (24 in). Much of South Africa gets its rain in the summer months, but the western coastal belt is a winter rain area. Along the south coast of the Cape, rain falls during both seasons. In December 2010 and continuing into January 2011, South Africa was hit with a series of floods that killed at least 39 people. The flooding was most prominent in the eastern part of the country, with the worst of the floods hitting the Eastern Cape Province and the KwaZulu-Natal Province.

⁴FLORA AND FAUNA

The variety of South Africa's climate and altitude accounts for its diversified flora and fauna. Major vegetation zones include the forest and palm belt of the east, south, and southwest coasts; the temperate grasslands (veld) of the eastern portion of the interior plateau; the desert and semidesert (Karoo) vegetation of the western interior; and the bushveld (savanna) of the Kalahari and the northeast. Of the 200 natural orders of plants in the world, over 140 are represented; South Africa also has a floral kingdom found nowhere else. There are 200 species of euphorbia, about 350 different kinds of heath in the Cape Province alone, and more than 500 species of grass. Wild flowers (including the protea, South Africa's national flower) grow in great profusion throughout the Cape region.

Aardvarks, jackals, lions, elephants, wild buffalo, hippopotami, and various kinds of antelope are still found in some parts of the country. In the great game parks, animals may be seen living in their natural surroundings. The variety of both smaller mammals and plants is so extensive that they have not yet all been identified. The World Resources Institute estimates that there are 23,420 plant species in South Africa. In addition, South Africa is home to 320 mammal, 829 bird, 364 reptile, and 119 amphibian species. The calculation reflects the total number of distinct species residing in the country, not the number of endemic (native) species.

⁵ENVIRONMENT

Recent industrialization and urbanization have taken their toll on the South African environment, as have such agricultural practices as veld fires, overgrazing of livestock, and intensive use of pesticides. Soil erosion and desertification are two more significant environmental issues in South Africa. Three hundred to four hundred million tons of soil are lost per year. The country's limited water resources have been impaired by mineralization, eutrophication, and acidic mine drainage. The country's cities produce about 4.2 million tons of solid waste per year. Air pollution in urban areas stems primarily from coal burning and motor vehicle

exhausts. The UN reported in 2008 that carbon dioxide emissions in South Africa totaled 433,173 kilotons.

The principal environmental bodies of South Africa are the Department of Water Affairs, the Department of Environmental Affairs, and the Department of National Health and Population Activities. The World Resources Institute reported that South Africa had designated 7.37 million hectares (18.22 million acres) of land for protection as of 2006. Water resources totaled 50 cu km (12 cu mi), while water usage was 12.5 cu km (3 cu mi) per year. Domestic water usage accounted for 31% of total usage, industrial for 6%, and agricultural for 63%. Per capita water usage totaled 264 cu m (9,323 cu ft) per year.

South Africa has taken a more prominent role in the arena of climate change through the opening of the Nansen-Tutu Center for Marine Environmental Research in 2010. The center was launched through the joint efforts of the University of Cape Town Marine Research Institute and the Nansen Environmental and Remote Sensing Center in Norway. The goal of the project is to maintain a long-term, systematic program of data collection from the three oceans surrounding southern Africa—the South Atlantic Ocean, the Indian Ocean, and the Southern Ocean. Marine environments and ecosystems will be closely monitored, and researchers will document the current effects of climate change and develop modeling strategies to predict its future impact on the African continent and beyond. The initial annual budget, supplied by both Norwegian and African partners, was about $500,000 per year. Funding was expected to average about $1.5 million per year between 2010 and 2016.

According to the International Union for Conservation of Nature and Natural Resources (IUCN) Red List of Threatened Species, the number of threatened species in South Africa as of 2011 included 24 types of mammals, 40 species of birds, 21 types of reptiles, 20 species of amphibians, 87 species of fish, 21 types of mollusks, 134 species of other invertebrates, and 97 species of plants. Specific species included the riverine rabbit, Cape Mountain zebra, Treur River barb, and several species of butterfly. Twelve species have become extinct, including the cape warthog, bluebuck, Burchell's zebra, and quagga.

There are numerous nature and game reserves and national parks. Some 120 rare Addo elephants are protected in Addo Elephant National Park, 56 km (35 mi) north of Port Elizabeth; Bontebok National Park (near Swellendam, Cape Province) is a habitat for the last surviving herd of bontebok antelope; Mountain Zebra National Park (near Cradock, in Cape Province) is a refuge for several hundred rare mountain zebras and springbok; and Kruger National Park, in northeastern Transvaal, has almost every species of South African wildlife in its natural habitat.

⁶POPULATION

The US Central Intelligence Agency (CIA) estimated the population of South Africa in 2011 to be approximately 49,004,031, which placed it at number 25 in population among the 196 nations of the world. Approximately 5.7% of the population was over 65 years of age, with 28.5% under 15 years of age. The median age in South Africa was 25 years. There were 0.99 males for every female in the country. The population's annual rate of change was -0.38%. The projected population for the year 2025 was 54,400,000. Popu-

LOCATION: 16°28′ to 32°54′E; 22°8′ to 34°50′ S. BOUNDARY LENGTHS: Botswana, 1,778 kilometers (1,105 miles); Zimbabwe, 225 kilometers (140 miles); Mozambique, 491 kilometers (305 miles); Swaziland, 449 kilometers (279 miles); total coastline, 2,954 kilometers (1,836 miles); Namibia, 1,078 kilometers (670 miles); Lesotho, 909 kilometers (565 miles). TERRITORIAL SEA LIMIT: 12 miles.

lation density in South Africa was calculated at 40 people per sq km (104 people per sq mi).

The UN estimated that 62% of the population lived in urban areas in 2009 and that urban populations had an annual rate of change of 1.2%. The largest urban areas, along with their respective populations, included Johannesburg, 3.6 million; Cape Town, 3.4 million; Ekurhuleni (East Rand), 3.1 million; Durban, 2.8 million; and Pretoria, 1.4 million.

The prevalence of HIV/AIDS has had a significant impact on the population of South Africa. The AIDS epidemic causes higher death and infant mortality rates and lowers life expectancy.

⁷MIGRATION

Estimates of South Africa's net migration rate, carried out by the CIA in 2011, amounted to -6.19 migrants per 1,000 citizens. The total number of emigrants living abroad was 878,100, and the total number of immigrants living in South Africa was 1.86 million. South Africa also accepted 10,772 refugees from the Democratic Republic of Congo, 7,818 from Somalia, and 5,759 refugees from Angola. Preference was given in the past to immigrants of those countries from which South Africa's present white population is derived. Between 1963 and 1984, the number of immigrants averaged about 37,000 annually, and the number of emigrants about 12,000. After 1984, immigration fell, and, perhaps as a consequence, the white population actually declined.

8 ETHNIC GROUPS

Legal separation of the racial communities was a cornerstone of government policy through most of the 20th century. This racial policy, often called apartheid but referred to in South African government circles as "separate development," created and maintained one of the most rigidly segregated societies in the world. During the 1970s and 1980s, enforcement of separatist policies eased, but the division of the population into four racial communities—Africans (blacks), whites, Coloureds, and Asians—remained. The rules of apartheid were formally abolished in 1991, but most citizens still describe themselves as one of the four traditional categories.

At the 2001 census, about 79% of the population were black Africans. Whites accounted for about 9.6% of the total population. About 60% of the whites were descendants of Dutch, French Huguenot, and German settlers, and about 40% were of British descent; South Africans of European, especially Dutch, descent are called Afrikaners. The so-called Coloureds, accounting for about 8.6% of the total population, are a long-established racial amalgam of white, Hottentot, and African, Indian, and Malay lineage. Asians made up about 2.5% of the population; they included descendants of Indian, East Indian, and Chinese indentured laborers who were not repatriated after their brief period of service as miners. There were a few thousand Khoikhoi within the country, an indigenous nomadic people who are primarily sheep and cattle herders.

9 LANGUAGES

The interim constitution adopted in 1993 recognized 11 languages as official at the national level: Afrikaans, English, Ndebele, Sepedi, Sesotho, Swazi, Tsonga, Tswana, Venda, Xhosa, and Zulu. All were still recognized officially in 2012.

Afrikaans is a variant of the Dutch spoken by the 17th-century colonists, and it includes lexical items, phrases, and syntactic structures from Malay, Portuguese, the Bantu group, Hottentot, and other African languages, as well as from English, French, and German. Afrikaans has borrowed from English words such as *gelling* (gallon), *jaart* (yard), *sjieling* (shilling), and *trippens* (three pence), while English has taken *kraal, veld,* and other Afrikaans words. More than 70% of South African whites are bilingual. Afrikaans is the primary language of about 13.3% and English of 8.2%. The most widely spoken primary language is Zulu, spoken by about 23.8% of the population. Xhosa follows with about 17.6% of the population as primary speakers. Sepedi is spoken by 9.4% of the population, Setswana by 8.2%, Sesotho by 7.9%, and Tsonga by 4.4%. The remaining 7.2% included speakers of German, Portuguese, and other languages.

10 RELIGIONS

According to the 2001 census, approximately 80% of the population claimed to be Christian, with the largest group of Christian churches linked to the African Independent Churches. These included the Zion Christian Church (accounting for about 11% of the population) and the Apostolic Church (about 10% of the pop-

ulation), as well as some Pentecostal offshoots that were founded as breakaways from various missionary churches, or the so-called Ethiopian churches.

The Dutch Reformed churches made up about 6.7% of the population and included the Nederduits Gereformeerde, Nederduitsch Hervormde, and the Gereformeerde Churches. The next-largest denomination was the Roman Catholic Church at 7.1% of the population, followed by the Methodists at 6.8%, Anglicans at 3.8%, Lutherans at 2.5%, Presbyterians at 1.9%, Baptists at 1.5%, and Congregationalists at 1.1%. There were a number of Pentecostal and charismatic churches as well as congregations of Greek Orthodox and Seventh-Day Adventists. About 87% of all whites were Christian, as were about 80% of all Blacks and 87% of all Coloureds. About 1.2% of the population was Hindu and another 1.5% was Muslim, with most adherents being of Indian descent.

There were very small numbers of Jews, Buddhists, Confucians, and Rastafarians. About 16% of the population claimed no formal religious affiliation, but many of these individuals practiced traditional indigenous customs, including the veneration of deceased ancestors and the use of herbs and therapeutic techniques. Some combine traditional practices with Christianity.

Freedom of religion is guaranteed by the constitution and there is no state religion. Religious groups are not required to register with the government, but may apply as public benefit organizations to obtain certain tax benefits. Relations between most religious groups are amicable. Good Friday and Christmas are observed as national holidays.

11 TRANSPORTATION

South Africa's transportation network is among the most modern and extensive on the continent. The CIA reported that South Africa had a total of 362,099 km (224,998 mi) of roads in 2002, of which 73,506 km (45,675 mi) were paved.

The South African Transport Service, a government department, operates the railways, principal harbors, South African Airways, and some road transportation services. South Africa's railroad network consists entirely of narrow gauge rail. The railroads extend for 22,051 km (13,702 mi); of that total, 10,436 km (6,491 mi) were electrified.

South Africa's seven ports, owned and operated by the government, include the deepwater ports of Durban, Port Elizabeth, and Table Bay (at Cape Town); other ports with good facilities are Richards Bay, Saldanha Bay, East London, and Mosselbaai (or Mossel Bay). There are 578 airports, which transported 12.5 million passengers in 2009 according to the World Bank.

The government-owned South African Airways operates both international and domestic flights. O.R. Tambo International Airport (ORTIA), near Johannesburg, is the major international airport; other international airports are located at Cape Town and Durban.

In 2010, the Standard Bank Group of South Africa announced the signing of a memorandum of understanding with China Railway group for the construction of a $30 billion high-speed railway network to link some of the major cities in the nation. The project sought to expand investment and development in manufacturing and trade.

12 HISTORY

Fossil skulls suggest that South Africa may have been one of the earliest sites of human evolution. Little is known of the original settlers, but when Europeans first arrived, there were two distinct groups of peoples—the San nomadic hunters of the western desert upland country, and the Hottentots, a pastoral people who occupied the southern and eastern coastal areas. Before 100 AD, Bantu-speaking peoples entered the Transvaal from the north, settling territories in the north and east.

In 1488, the Portuguese sailor Bartholomeu Dias arrived at the Cape of Good Hope, and on Christmas Day of 1497, Vasco da Gama reached KwaZulu-Natal. The first European settlement at the Cape was made in 1652 under Jan van Riebeeck on behalf of the Dutch East India Co., which needed a refreshment station on the route to the East. Because there was a shortage of farm labor, the Dutch imported slaves from West Africa, Madagascar, and the East Indies, and because of the scarcity of European women, mixed marriages took place, eventually producing the Cape Coloured people. Huguenot settlers joined the small Dutch settlement in 1688. Continued demands for meat and relatively poor agricultural production encouraged the development of cattle farming, which in turn led to the need for more grazing land. Settlements were established on the coastal plain, along the valleys, and on the Great Karoo. The European population multiplied, but the San and Hottentots declined in numbers. The first contacts with Bantu-speaking Africans were made along the Great Fish River, which, in 1778, the Cape authorities proclaimed the boundary between the colonists and the Africans. The first serious clash came in 1779, when invading Xhosa were driven back across the river border. Three more frontier wars were fought by 1812.

In 1795, Britain occupied the Cape, and in 1814, the area was ceded to the United Kingdom by the Treaty of Vienna. The free Coloured inhabitants of the Cape were given the same legal and political status as whites, and in 1834, slavery was abolished. Because of severe droughts and in reaction to British policy and administration, about 6,000 Boers (Dutch farmers) undertook the Great Trek in 1836, migrating northward into the present Orange Free State and the Transvaal. Some crossed the Drakensberg Mountains into Natal. The British annexed Natal in 1843 and extended their rule over Kaffraria in 1847, Griqualand West in 1871, and Zululand and Tongaland in 1887. The Transvaal was annexed in 1877 but returned to independence after a revolt in 1881, culminating in a British defeat by the Boers at Majuba Hill. In 1881, Swaziland was also declared independent. After a war between the Boers and Basutos, the British proclaimed Basutoland (now Lesotho) a British territory, and in 1884 it became a British protectorate. The British granted local self-government to the Cape in 1872 and to Natal in 1897.

Meanwhile, the spread of European settlements into areas occupied by Africans led to the setting aside of large native reserves and to the development of separate white and black communities. In 1860, indentured Indians were brought into Natal to work on the sugarcane plantations; by 1911, when India halted the emigration because of what it called "poor working conditions," more than 150,000 Indians had come to South Africa as contract laborers. It was in South Africa, while pursuing the Indians' claims of injustice, that Mohandas (Mahatma) Gandhi, then a young lawyer, developed his philosophy of nonviolent resistance.

The discovery around 1870 of diamonds along the Orange and Vaal rivers and in the Kimberley district led to an influx of foreigners and brought prosperity to the Cape and the Orange Free State. Railways were built and trade increased. The discovery of gold on the Witwatersrand in 1886 brought in thousands of additional newcomers and made Transvaal potentially the wealthiest state. Tension between the Boers and the outsiders attracted to Transvaal was accentuated by an unsuccessful attempt to capture Johannesburg in 1896, led by Leander Starr Jameson (Jameson Raid), and culminated in the South African (or Boer) War (1899–1902). After a desperate struggle against the larger British forces, the Boer republics of Transvaal and the Orange Free State gave up their independence by the Treaty of Vereeniging on 31 May 1902, but shortly thereafter they were granted self-government by the British. In a convention during 1908–9, the leaders of the Afrikaners, together with those from the Cape and Natal, drafted a constitution for a united South Africa that passed the British Parliament as the South Africa Act in 1909, becoming effective on 31 May 1910. The constitution provided for a union of the four territories or provinces, to be known as the Union of South Africa. In 1913, the Union Parliament passed the Bantu Land Act, setting aside 8.9 million hectares (22 million acres) of land as black areas; an additional 6.3 million hectares (15.6 million acres) were added to the black homelands by another parliamentary act in 1936. The Act created a system of land tenure that deprived the majority of South Africa's inhabitants of the right to own land, which had major socioeconomic repercussions.

The Union of South Africa fought with the Allies in World War I, signed the Treaty of Versailles, and became a member of the League of Nations. In 1920, the League gave South Africa a mandate over the former German colony Namibia, which lasted until 1946 when South Africa refused to recognize UN authority over the area and regarded it as an integral part of the country. In 1926, a British declaration granted South Africa national autonomy and equal legal status with the United Kingdom. Mining and industrialization advanced in the period between the two wars. More intensive exploitation of the wealth of the country led to better living standards. South Africa sent troops to fight the Nazis in World War II, although many Afrikaners favored neutrality. In 1948, the National Party (NP) took power, influencing the general character of life in South Africa and, in particular, enforcing its policies of apartheid, or racial separation (officially called "separate development" after 1960) of whites and nonwhites.

South Africa's white electorate approved a republican form of government in a 1960 referendum, and South Africa became a republic on 31 May 1961. The republican constitution did not deviate substantially from the former one, the only major change being the substitution of a president for the monarch as the head of state. As a result of objections from nonwhite members of the Commonwealth of Nations to South Africa's presence, South Africa withdrew its application for continued Commonwealth membership in 1961.

The immediate period surrounding the creation of the republic was one of mounting pressures applied to the government because of its apartheid policies. In 1960, black unrest swelled to the point where a state of emergency was declared. On 21 March 1960, a black demonstration was staged against the "pass laws," laws requiring blacks to carry "reference books," or internal passports, thus enabling the government to restrict their movement into urban areas. The demonstration resulted in the killing at Sharpeville of 69 black protesters by government troops and provided the touchstone for local black protests and for widespread expressions of outrage in international forums. During 1964, the government acted to stiffen its control over blacks living in white areas. After 1 May 1963, the General Law Amendment Act allowed the government to hold people for consecutive 90-day periods without trial (the length was decreased to 15 days in 1966). In 1965, the Suppression of Communism Amendment Bill renewed the government's authority to detain for security reasons persons who had completed prison sentences.

During the mid-1970s, the Portuguese colonial empire disbanded and blacks came to the fore in Mozambique and Angola, two former Portuguese territories. South African troops joined the Angolan civil conflict in an attempt to prevent a Soviet-backed faction from coming to power. Unsuccessful, the troops withdrew in March 1976. South Africa subsequently launched sporadic attacks on Angola (which supported insurgents seeking to end South African rule over Namibia) and Mozambique and aided insurgencies in both countries; these operations (and other raids into Botswana, Lesotho, and Zimbabwe) were apparently in response to the aid and political support given by South Africa's neighbors to the African National Congress (ANC), a black nationalist group.

Beginning in June 1976, the worst domestic confrontation since Sharpeville took place in Soweto, on the outskirts of Johannesburg, where blacks violently protested the compulsory use of Afrikaans in schools; suppression of the riots by South African police left at least 174 blacks dead and 1,139 injured. The Afrikaans requirement was subsequently modified. During the late 1970s, new protest groups and leaders emerged among the young blacks. After one of these leaders, 30-year-old Steven Biko, died on 12 September 1977 while in police custody, there were renewed protests. As a result, on 4 November, the UN Security Council approved a mandatory arms embargo against South Africa, the first ever imposed on a member nation.

By 1981, the government had designated four of the ten black homelands as "sovereign" states: Bophuthatswana, Ciskei, Transkei, and Venda. All members of the ethnic groups associated with these homelands automatically lost their South African citizenship; the government's stated intent to grant independence to the remaining six homelands meant that the vast majority of South Africa's blacks would eventually lose their South African citizenship. In an effort to conciliate nonwhites and international opinion, the government scrapped many aspects of apartheid in the mid-1980s, including the "pass laws" and the laws barring interracial sexual relations and marriage. A new constitution established legislative houses for Coloureds and Indians in 1984, although only 31% and 20% of the respective eligible voters went to the polls.

These measures failed to meet black aspirations, and in July 1985, as political violence mounted, the government imposed a state of emergency in 36 magisterial districts that lasted over seven months. The districts comprised nearly all of the urban black population, and during this time 7,996 persons were detained and 757 people died due to political violence, by government count. A new, nationwide state of emergency was imposed in June 1986, with police and the military exercising extraordinary powers of arrest and detention. At least 4,000 and possibly as many as 10,000 people were detained in 1986, including over 1,400 aged 18 or under.

In 1984, South Africa and Mozambique signed the Nkomati Accord, by which each country pledged not to aid the antigovernment forces in the other country. Also in 1984, South Africa signed an agreement to withdraw the forces it had sent into southern Angola to forestall aid to guerrillas in Namibia. However, the government continued to hold its neighbors responsible for ANC violence, and South African raids into Botswana, Zambia, and Zimbabwe were conducted during 1986. In 1987, the government announced that it was withdrawing the troops it had sent into Angola to aid rebels fighting against the Angolan government, which was supported by Cuban and Soviet troops.

In July 1987, the government cracked down on the United Democratic Front (UDF), an umbrella organization of over 600 civic, sports, church, trade union, women's, professional, youth and student bodies opposed to apartheid. Some 22 of its leaders were charged with treason, and many more were forced to go underground. The government banned 17 antiapartheid organizations, including the UDF and the largest trade union, on 24 February 1988. Repression increased throughout 1987 and 1988, as did protests against state policies. Some alternative newspapers, including *New Nation* and *Weekly Mail*, were prohibited briefly from publishing. Various antiapartheid leaders were assassinated by secret hit squads using police and military intelligence. Others were detained and otherwise restricted, while still others were served with banning orders. Protest strikes and demonstrations mounted in retaliation, as did organization efforts among antiapartheid activists.

In 1989, President P.W. Botha resigned as head of the NP after a mild stroke in January. He was replaced by F. W. de Klerk who, on 15 August, was also named acting state president. After the general election, held 6 September, de Klerk was elected to a five-year term as president.

De Klerk launched a series of reforms in September 1989 that led to the release of ANC leader Nelson Mandela and others on 10 February 1990. The ANC and other resistance militants, including the Communist Party, were legalized. Mandela had been in prison 27 years and had become a revered symbol of resistance to apartheid.

At that point, the ANC began to organize within South Africa, and government began "talks about talks" with the ANC. In August 1990, the ANC suspended its armed struggle, and most leaders of the ANC returned from exile. Still, fighting continued, largely between ANC activists and supporters of the Zulu-dominated Inkatha Freedom Party, strongest in Natal province. More than 6,000 people were killed in political violence in 1990 and 1991; many were victims of fighting provoked by a "third force" of operatives employed by hardliners within the Defense Force and the police.

In 1991, de Klerk introduced and parliament passed measures to repeal laws that had institutionalized apartheid policies (the Land Act [1913 and 1936], the Group Areas Act [1950], and the Population Registration Act [1950]). A number of repressive security acts were repealed as well.

In July, the ANC convened its first full conference in South Africa in 30 years. They elected Mandela president and Cyril Ramaphosa as secretary general. Oliver Tambo moved from president to the new post of national chairman.

Meanwhile, negotiations continued over constitutional changes and plans for nonracial elections and the transition to majority rule. Numerous parties engaged in the first Convention for a Democratic South Africa (CODESA) starting in December 1991. On 14 September 1991, the government, the ANC, and Inkatha signed a pact to end factional fighting. Other groups signed on, but the agreement hardly stemmed the high levels of violence. The militant right wing refused to cooperate with any negotiations and agreements. In order to strengthen his negotiating hand, de Klerk called a whites-only referendum for 17 March 1992. Of the 85% turnout, 68.7% supported de Klerk's efforts to negotiate a settlement. By May, however, CODESA talks had slowed, and the ANC mounted a series of mass protests. After 42 residents were murdered at Boipatong Township by Zulu hostel dwellers allegedly assisted by police, the ANC withdrew from CODESA. On 7 September, 24 ANC supporters were killed by the Ciskei army troops as they marched in protest on the homeland's capital.

Later that month, negotiations began again between the government and the ANC. A summit held on 26 September between Mandela and de Klerk produced a Record of Understanding that met several key ANC demands. This angered KwaZulu Chief Mangosuthu G. Buthelezi, who withdrew from the talks. In February 1993, government and the ANC reached agreement on plans for a transition to democracy. Multiparty negotiations followed in April. An interim parliament was to be elected for a five-year period after a general election in April 1994. All parties gaining over 5% of the vote would be represented in the new cabinet. The new parliament would also serve as a constituent assembly to iron out details of a new constitution. The broad guidelines were agreed upon by the government, the ANC, and other parties in late December 1993. A transitional Executive Council was established to oversee some aspects of government, including security. Inkatha, led by Buthelezi, and the right-wing Conservative Party refused to participate and boycotted the talks on multiparty government. Just a few days before the scheduled elections, however, Inkatha agreed to participate. White conservatives tried to hold out for an Afrikaner homeland, but the white right was divided on whether to participate in preelection talks, participate in the election itself, or take up arms as a last resort. There were inefficiencies and some claims of electoral fraud and intimidation, especially by the ANC against Inkatha in Natal province. Despite these concerns, the elections proceeded relatively peacefully and with great enthusiasm. They were pronounced "free and fair" by international observers and the independent Electoral Commission.

The results left the ANC as the major winner with 62.5%. The NP gained 20.4%; the Inkatha Freedom Party, 10.5%; the Freedom Front, 2.2%; the Democratic Party, 1.7%; and the Pan-Africanist Congress, 1.2%. ANC, was awarded 252 of the 400 seats in parliament. It was the governing party in all but two of the nine regions. The IFP carried KwaZulu/Natal and the NP held the Western Cape. Mandela became president and Thabo Mbeki (ANC) and de Klerk (NP) were named deputy presidents. Even Buthelezi was persuaded to take a ministerial post in the cabinet.

In May 1994, the Constitutional Assembly convened to lay the groundwork for the new constitution. All parties were included in the initial sessions, but Inkatha boycotted the Assembly's draft-ing of an interim constitution when its demand for international mediation on regional autonomy was not met. At the same time, violent clashes between Inkatha and ANC supporters flared anew in the Natal Province.

South Africa held local elections on 1 November 1995, although last-minute changes to the interim constitution allowed for seven provinces—including KwaZulu Natal—to delay elections until 1996. The ANC also swept the provincial elections, with the NP winning the largest minority share of the vote.

Bishop Desmond Tutu convened a Truth and Reconciliation Commission in early 1996 to expose apartheid atrocities committed in the years of white rule. Although those who refused to cooperate with the commission could be subject to criminal penalties, the commission granted immunity and amnesty to those who admitted their roles in apartheid crimes. Testimony in a 1995 court case also linked death squads to the highest levels of government, including the prime minister's office.

In 1997, the Constitutional Court ratified the new constitution after rejecting a draft submitted in 1996. The new constitution was inaugurated in February 1997. It granted a strong central government with some limited powers vested in the provinces. Inkatha, which boycotted the drafting sessions to the end, accepted the Constitutional Court's decree.

The NP withdrew from the government of national unity immediately after ratification of the constitution to take its place as the official opposition party. De Klerk, who would leave politics in August 1997, also resigned his post to head the opposition party.

By 1997, the exuberance of the new constitutional era and two years of economic expansion had given way to uncertainty in the months following ratification. South Africa was struggling with the new political structure, a flagging economy, revolutions of the Truth and Reconciliation, and a crime wave seemingly out of control. The latter was deemed by citizens as the number one problem facing the new government. The murder rate had grown to ten times higher than the murder rate in the United States. Robbery, assault, and carjackings had left downtown Johannesburg in ruins, and vigilante groups were prevalent throughout the nation. The high crime rate had deterred foreign investment and affected the tourist industry, as well.

Early in 1999, Nelson Mandela, president of South Africa since 1994, delivered his final "state of the nation" address. The vote in June 1999 passed without a single political killing and was quickly embraced by all political parties. Despite the increase in crime in the nation, the second parliamentary elections held in June 1999 were peaceful and generally fair. In the 3 June elections, the ruling African National Congress (ANC) won 266 of 400 parliamentary seats (63%), just one seat shy of the two-thirds majority required to change the constitution. Thabo Mbeki was sworn in as South Africa's second democratically elected president at a glittering inauguration ceremony, which saw Nelson Mandela step down after steering the country away from apartheid rule and oppression. However, the one-sided vote in favor of ANC was itself troubling. Critiques noted that the dominance of the ANC had the coloring of a de facto one-party state.

The first four years of Mbeki in office were marked by an active foreign policy and controversy over his AIDS policy. Along with Botswana, South Africa sent peacekeeping forces to Lesotho in 1999 to quell rioting and civil unrest following the 1998 elections there. Subsequently, the government played host to the belligerents of Africa's "first world war" in the Great Lakes region, helping them reach power sharing and peace agreements in December 2002 and April 2003. In addition to sending peacekeeping troops to the DROC, South Africa also took the lead in providing peacekeepers for Burundi in early 2003 following peace negotiations by Nelson Mandela in that country. Mbeki was one of four African heads of state who championed the New Partnership for Africa's Development (NEPAD), a continent-wide initiative that promised accountable governance in exchange for donor resources and technical assistance. South Africa hosted the World Summit on Sustainable Development in Johannesburg in August 2002.

However strong Mbeki's record, it was tarnished by his response to the flawed March 2002 elections in Zimbabwe, and by his de-linking of HIV—the virus that the world scientific community says causes AIDS—from the disease itself. His government's reluctance to introduce antiretroviral therapy damaged his credibility at home and abroad.

The dominance of the ANC was clearly illustrated in the 14 April 2004 elections. Mbeki won reelection and the ANC obtained 69.7% of votes cast on the national ballot, winning 279 seats. This majority theoretically allowed the ANC to change the constitution, though the party pledged not to do so. Only about 56% of eligible voters took part in the election. The main opposition party, the Democratic Alliance, also obtained an increased percentage on the national ballot—12.4% or 50 seats in the national assembly.

Same-sex marriage became legal in South Africa on 30 November 2006, when the Civil Unions Bill was enacted. South Africa became the fifth country, and the first in Africa, to legalize same-sex marriage. As of early 2012, 10 countries had legalized same-sex marriages.

In the 2009 elections, Jacob Zuma of the ANC won with nearly 66% of the vote. The ANC won 264 seats in the legislature, with their nearest challenge, the Democratic Alliance, winning 67 seats.

Although South Africa's economy is highly developed, the exclusionary nature of apartheid and distortions caused in part by the country's international isolation until the 1990s left major weaknesses. As of 2011, the economy was in a process of transition as the government sought to address the inequities of apartheid, stimulate growth, and create jobs. South Africa has become increasingly integrated into the international system, and foreign investment has increased dramatically. Still, the economic disparities between population groups are expected to persist for many years, remaining an area of priority for the government.

South Africa was awarded a nonpermanent seat on the UN Security Council for 2011–12.

13 GOVERNMENT

The terms of the new constitution adopted in February 1997 were hammered out prior to the 29 April 1994 election. There is a 400-seat National Assembly chosen by proportional representation (200 nationally and 200 from regional lists). Following the implementation of the new constitution on 3 February 1997, the former senate was disbanded and replaced by the National Council of Provinces, with essentially no change in membership and party affiliations—although the responsibilities were somewhat changed. Of 90 total members, 10 come from each province or region and are selected by each provincial assembly. The members serve as

both a legislature and a constituent assembly. They also elect the president and deputy presidents.

Although the degree of autonomy and the level of power given to the regions remain contentious with the IFP's longstanding grievance about the way power is devalued to the regions, the nine provinces have assemblies based on the total number of votes cast in the general election. Thus, the number of members each provincial legislature has depends on the number of votes cast divided by 50,000. The executive branch of the provincial governments is, like the legislatures, allocated proportionally.

14 POLITICAL PARTIES

The early division in the South African party system was between those who promoted Afrikaner nationalism and those Afrikaans-speaking and English-speaking persons who worked together toward goals on which both sides could agree. When General Louis Botha formed the first cabinet in 1910, he combined the moderate Afrikaners and English into the South African National Party, which confronted an English-speaking opposition. Soon afterward, however, General J.B.M. Hertzog formed the National Party (NP), dedicated to placing the interests of South Africa above those of the British Empire and to developing the Afrikaner group until it was as powerful as the English South Africans.

Hard-pressed by Hertzog's NP in 1920, General Jan Christiaan Smuts, who succeeded Botha, fused the South African National Party with the English-speaking Unionists, establishing the alignment of the English-speaking, except those in the Labour Party (LP), with moderate Afrikaners. The LP allied itself with Hertzog, who achieved office in 1924. Together they carried through the so-called civilized labor policy, designed to safeguard a wide area in the economy for white labor.

Economic crisis during the Depression forced a new alignment of parties that brought Hertzog and Smuts into coalition in 1933 and fusion in the United Party (UP) in 1934. Daniel F. Malan broke with Hertzog in 1934 to form the "purified" NP, dedicated to a more exclusive and radical Afrikaner nationalism than Hertzog had ever preached.

When World War II broke out, Hertzog wished to remain neutral. Smuts swung the House of Assembly in support of the Allies and became prime minister with the support of all English-speaking South Africans and a substantial group of moderate Afrikaners in the UP. Malan won the 1948 election, the first whose campaign was waged chiefly on the racial issue. The sharpest division between the two parties arose from NP efforts to remove the Coloureds from the common voting roll.

The basic division in the party system was between the NP, which favored the policy of apartheid, or totally separate development of the different races, and the UP, which favored social and residential segregation but economic integration. The members of the NP were mainly Afrikaans-speaking while those of the UP were English-speaking, but each party had a considerable number of members of the other language group. Beginning in 1950, the Nationalists implemented their program of apartheid. Between 1953 and 1987, the NP won nine successive parliamentary elections under four party leaders: Malan (in 1953); Hendrik Frensch Verwoerd (1958, 1961, 1966); Balthazar Johannes Vorster (1970, 1974, 1977); and Pieter W. Botha (1987). Vorster, who succeeded Verwoerd as prime minister after the assassination of Verwoerd in 1966, left the office in 1978 to become president. In the following year, however, he was forced to resign because of a political scandal involving the misappropriation of government funds to finance clandestine political and propaganda activities in the United States, Norway, and other Western countries. The Nationalists' program met with little effective opposition from the UP, which formally disbanded in 1977. In that year, leaders of the UP and its splinter group, the Democratic Party, which had formed in 1973, established the New Republic Party (NRP), with support from English-speaking voters in Natal and the Eastern Cape. The NRP endorsed continuing white rule, but with a softening of apartheid. In the same year, another merger produced the Progressive Federal Party (PFP), which drew its main backing from English-speaking voters in urban areas and stood for universal suffrage within a federal system, with guarantees of minority rights. In the 1987 elections, the NP increased its representation from 116 (in 1981) to 123 seats. The PFP fell from 26 to 19 seats; the NRP lost 4 of its 5 seats. In 1989, the last national race-based parliamentary elections, the NP suffered a setback, winning just 48% of the vote and 93 seats. The PFP dissolved itself in favor of the Democratic Party, which took 33 seats.

The Conservative Party (CP) opposed any form of power sharing with nonwhites. It was led by a former cabinet minister, Andries Treurnicht. The CP became the official opposition party after winning 23 seats in the 1987 elections and 39 in 1989.

Several Coloured and Indian parties participated in the August 1984 elections for the houses of Parliament created for their respective ethnic groups. The Labour Party, a Coloured party headed by the Rev. Allan Hendrickse, won 76 of the 80 directly elected seats; it opposed the new constitution, advocated repeal of all discriminatory measures, and said that it was campaigning on behalf of all nonwhites but was vague on the question of whether it would accept a unitary state governed on the principle of one-person, one-vote. All five Indian parties participating in the elections favored protection of minority rights and rejected government in a unitary state on the basis of one-person, one-vote. The National People's Party won 18 and Solidarity 17 of the 40 directly elected seats; the two parties formed a governing alliance in January 1986.

In 1985, the government repealed a law that had prohibited people of different racial groups from belonging to the same political party.

Several extraparliamentary organizations of Africans and Asians have formed on a national basis. The African National Congress (ANC) and the South African Indian Congress have cooperated with each other and have sought to cooperate with white liberal organizations. Banned in 1960, the ANC turned from its earlier tradition of nonviolence toward sabotage and other terrorist acts. In 1987, the government offered to legalize the group if it renounced violence. From 1987 onward, talks were held outside the country between the ANC and diverse groups of white South Africans.

Notable among the more militant African groups was the Pan-Africanist Congress (PAC), which broke away from the ANC in 1959 and was banned in 1960. The ANC and PAC had been recognized by the UN General Assembly as "the authentic representatives" of the people of South Africa. During the 1970s, a loose coalition of African student groups known as the Black Consciousness Movement developed under the leadership of Steven Biko. The United Democratic Front (UDF) was founded in 1983, claiming at its peak to be a multiracial alliance of nearly seven hundred groups representing nearly two million people. It dissolved itself in August 1991, after having continued resistance to apartheid while the ANC was in exile. Considerable ferment occurred among political parties in the run-up to the 1994 elections. The Inkatha Freedom Party (IFP), headed by Zulu Chief Mangosuthu Buthelezi, at first had a cozy relationship with the NP, but that dissolved once the NP began negotiating in earnest with the ANC. Not until just days before the elections in 1994 did the IFP agree to run candidates. It captured over 10% of the national vote and managed to win the election for the provincial government in Natal. The Freedom Front (FF) became the electoral vehicle for Gen. Constand Viljoen, former head of the Defense Force. He contested the results (2.2% of the vote, nine seats) despite resistance from the CP and other right-wing bodies. The FF sought to work within the system to achieve the creation of an autonomous Afrikaner state.

In February 1993 the ANC allowed minority parties to participate in the government for five years after the end of apartheid. Also in February 1993 the first nonwhites entered the cabinet, thus broadening the base of the NP.

The 1994 elections resulted in an overwhelming victory for the ANC, headed by Nelson Mandela, as did the 1995 local elections. The new government included six ministers from the NP and the IFP.

Any political party that wins 20% or more of the National Assembly votes in a general election is entitled to name a deputy executive president; any party that wins 20 or more seats in the National Assembly is entitled to become a member of the governing coalition. As of 1997 the ANC, the IFP, and the NP constituted a Government of National Unity.

In the second post-apartheid parliamentary elections in 1999, the ANC won handsomely, taking 266 of 400 parliamentary seats (66%), just one seat shy of the two-thirds majority required to change the constitution. The remaining seats went to 12 other parties as follows: Democratic Party (DP) 38; Inkatha Freedom Party (IFP) 34; New National Party (NNP) 28; United Democratic Movement (UDM) 14; African Christian Democratic Party (ACDP) 6; Pan Africanist Congress (PAC) 3; United Christian Democratic Party (UCDP) 3; Vryheidsfront/Freedom Front (VF/FF) 3; Federal Alliance (FA) 2; Minority Front (MF) 1; Afrikaner Eenheids Beweging (AEB) 1; and Azanian People's Organization (Azapo) 1.

In the third post-apartheid parliamentary elections in 2004, the ANC won decisively, taking 279 of 400 parliamentary seats (69.7%), more than the two-thirds majority required to change the constitution. The remaining seats went to 11 other parties as follows: Democratic Alliance (DA) 50; Inkatha Freedom Party (IFP) 28; United Democratic Movement (UDM) 9; Independent Democrats (ID) 7; New National Party (NNP) 7; African Christian Democratic Party (ACDP) 6; Pan Africanist Congress (PAC) 3; United Christian Democratic Party (UCDP) 3; Vryheidsfront/Freedom Front (VF/FF) 4; Minority Front (MF) 2; Azanian People's Organization (Azapo) 2.

In 2009, presidential election results were as follows, Jacob Zuma, African National Congress , 65.90% of the total votes; Helen Zille, Democratic Alliance, 16.66%; Congress of the People,

Mosiuoa Lekota, 7.42 %; Inkatha Freedom Party, Mangosuthu Buthelezi ,4.55%.

In the 2009 legislative elections, the ANC won 264 seats, the DA 67 seats, the Congress of the People (COPE) 30 seats, IFP 18 seats, and other parties 21 seats. The next legislative and presidential elections were set for 2014.

15 LOCAL GOVERNMENT

Historically, the four provinces—Cape, Natal, Transvaal, and Orange Free State—dealt chiefly with local matters, such as hospitals, roads, municipal government, and educational matters that can be classified as general affairs (applying to all population groups). The provinces receive annual subsidies from the national government. Elected provincial councils were abolished in 1986 and replaced by regional services councils, with representation by local authorities. Executive power in each province is exercised by an administrator and executive committee appointed by the state president and responsible to the national government.

Under the 1984 constitution, local government was to be assigned to the three parliamentary houses, as applicable, or, in regard to general affairs, to the Department of Constitutional Development and Planning. However, residents in each (segregated) residential area, including blacks, elected primary local authorities, who rendered certain services as well as represented their constituents at the provincial level. As far as local government and administration for whites were concerned, elected municipal councils were retained. The local affairs of blacks living in the six black homelands within the Republic of South Africa were administered by the respective homeland governments.

Under the post-1994 election arrangements, nine provincial governments were established (Northern Province, Gauteng, Mpumalanga, Free State, Kwazulu-Natal, Eastern Cape, Western Cape, Northern Cape, and North-West). Their legislatures were determined (in size and party representation) by proportional representation.

16 JUDICIAL SYSTEM

The Constitutional Court in Johannesburg is the highest court for constitutional matters. It has the final say on the constitutionality of governmental laws and powers. The Supreme Court of Appeals, with its seat in Bloemfontein, is the highest court for all nonconstitutional matters. In 2012, there were 384 regional magistrates' offices vested with certain judicial as well as administrative powers.

The common law of the Republic of South Africa is Roman-Dutch law, which has evolved from the uncodified law of the Netherlands as it existed when the Cape of Good Hope was ceded to Great Britain. It has been influenced by English common law in procedures more than in substantive matters. Trial by jury was abolished in 1969.

Black tribal chiefs and headmen have limited jurisdiction to hear cases in traditional courts. There are appeals courts, divorce courts, and children's courts for blacks. In self-governing black homelands, lower courts have been established by the legislative assemblies. Following the passage of the Traditional Courts Bill in 2008, in 2010 the traditional courts were aligned with the standards and regulations set forth in the South African constitution.

The judiciary has moved in the direction of more independence from the other branches with instances of alleged political interference with courts on the decline.

17 ARMED FORCES

The International Institute for Strategic Studies reports that armed forces in South Africa totaled 62,082 members in 2011. The force was comprised of 37,141 from the army, 6,244 from the navy, 10,653 from the air force, and 8,044 members of the South African Military Health Service. Armed forces represented 0.4% of the labor force in South Africa. Defense spending totaled $8.9 billion and accounted for 1.7% of GDP.

18 INTERNATIONAL COOPERATION

South Africa became a charter member of the UN on 7 November 1945 and has technically remained a member continuously, despite past disputes and international sanctions over apartheid and the country's unwillingness to place its League of Nations mandate, Namibia, under UN international trusteeship. Namibia gained independence in 1990. South Africa is part of ECA and several nonregional specialized UN agencies, such as the FAO, the World Bank, IAEA, UNHCR, UNESCO, UNIDO, ILO, and the WHO. The nation is also a member of the ACP Group, WTO, the African Development Bank, the New Partnership for African Development (NEPAD), the Commonwealth of Nations, G-24. G-77, the Southern African Custom Union, and the Southern African Development Community. South Africa served as the African Union's first president from July 2003 to July 2004.

The nation was diplomatically isolated from other states on the African continent after Angola and Mozambique gained independence in 1975 and Zimbabwe in 1980. This left South Africa as the continent's only white-minority regime. South African teams were excluded from international competition, such as the Olympic Games (from 1960). Following changes in South Africa's political situation, the country was reinstated to international competition by the International Olympic Committee.

South Africa has supported peace negotiations in a variety of African nation conflicts, including UN missions and operations in Ethiopia and Eritrea (est. 2000), Liberia (est. 2003), Burundi (est. 2004), and the DROC (est. 1999). The nation is part of the Nonaligned Movement and a member of the Zangger Committee and the Nuclear Suppliers Group (London Group).

In environmental cooperation, South Africa is part of the Antarctic Treaty, the Basel Convention, Conventions on Biological Diversity and Whaling, Ramsar, CITES, the London Convention, the Kyoto Protocol, the Montréal Protocol, MARPOL, the Nuclear Test Ban Treaty, and the UN Conventions on the Law of the Sea, Climate Change, and Desertification.

In 2010, South Africa was elected for a two-year term on the UN Security Council. The term began on 1 January 2011.

In April 2011, reports revealed that South Africa had been exporting weapons to some of the top non-democratic, repressive countries. The National Conventional Arms Control committee reported arms deals between 10 of the 25 worst-performing countries of the 2010 Global Peace Index including Libya, Saudi Arabia, Syria, Guinea Bissau, and Equatorial Guinea.

¹⁹ECONOMY

The opening of the political process to all South Africans and the election of a new multiracial government in 1994 marked a turning point in South Africa's economic history. With a modest agriculture sector (though known for excellent fruits and wine), fabulous mineral wealth (gold accounts for over one-third of exports), a diverse manufacturing sector (centered in metals and engineering, and especially steel-related products), and growing financial services and tourism sectors, South Africa's influence extends well beyond its borders.

The GDP rate of change in South Africa, as of 2010, was 2.8%. Inflation stood at 4.5%, and unemployment was reported at 23.3%. Although the white minority enjoys living standards equal to those in the rest of the industrialized world, most of the remaining 85% of the population have subpar living standards common to the developing world. The high prevalence of HIV/AIDS (over 20% of the adult population) remains the major obstacle to achieving economic growth. High unemployment, rigid labor laws, low skill levels, crime, and corruption hamper economic progress. Emigration has also emerged as one of South Africa's challenges, as South Africans who are highly skilled find better markets for their skills abroad, especially in Australia, New Zealand, the United Kingdom, Canada, and the United States.

South Africa has a mixed economy, with substantial government intervention. A number of state-owned enterprises exist jointly with a strong private sector. The government maintains a budget surplus and pursues conservative economic policies aimed at controlling inflation. State-owned enterprises are managed to promote social goals like job creation and services for low-income households. Nevertheless, the government maintains a commitment to privatization and open markets. A chief characteristic of the private sector is the high concentration of ownership by a small group of integrated conglomerate structures.

South Africa's transportation infrastructure includes modern airports and well-developed roads, although there is a shortage of public transportation. There is an efficient telecommunication system that supports cellular and internet services. The power system, however, is hampered by aging plants.

The 2008–09 global financial crisis left South Africa, like much of the world, reeling. During its height, the country's economy slipped into recession, marked by a sharp decline in its manufacturing and mining sectors. The overall economy declined by 6.4% in the first quarter of 2009, which was the largest decline since 1984. At the same time, however, the construction sector enjoyed a much-needed boost as the nation prepared to sponsor the FIFA (Fédération Internationale de Football Association) World Cup in 2010.

In 2010, efforts to create new jobs were hindered, in part, by union-negotiated wage increases that were intended to provide a better standard of living for many workers, particularly those within the garment manufacturing industry. Many garment factories closed down as they found it difficult to accommodate the higher labor costs at a time when product demand and sales were down. A large number of companies that remained in business did so by illegally refusing to pay the new minimum wages. Since so many citizens were seeking employment, these jobs were readily filled. The government began to push companies to comply with minimum wage laws or face forced closure. However, the resulting closures left an even greater dilemma concerning unemployment. In Newcastle, the government initiated a moratorium on factory shutdowns and began working more closely with the national bargaining council for union and employer representatives to urge factory owners to create business plans that would accommodate the legal minimum wage without major layoffs.

²⁰INCOME

The CIA estimated that in 2010 the GDP of South Africa was $524 billion. The CIA defines GDP as the value of all final goods and services produced within a nation in a given year, computed on the basis of purchasing power parity (PPP) rather than value as measured on the basis of the rate of the exchange based on current dollars. The per capita GDP was estimated at $10,700. The annual growth rate of GDP was 2.8%. The average inflation rate was 4.5%. It was estimated that agriculture accounted for 3% of GDP, industry 31.2%, and services 65.8%. According to the World Bank, remittances from citizens living abroad totaled $902.3 million, or about $18 per capita, and accounted for approximately .2% of GDP.

The World Bank reported that in 2009, household consumption in South Africa totaled $174.6 billion or about $3,564 per capita, measured in current US dollars rather than PPP. Household consumption includes expenditures of individuals, households, and nongovernmental organizations on goods and services, excluding the purchases of dwellings. It was estimated that household consumption was growing at an average annual rate of 3.1%.

As of 2011, the most recent study by the World Bank reported that actual individual consumption in South Africa was 71.7% of GDP and accounted for 0.74% of world consumption. By comparison, the United States accounted for 25.44% of world individual consumption. The World Bank also estimated that 16.6% of South Africa's GDP was spent on food and beverages, 13.1% on housing and household furnishings, 3.7% on clothes, 8.0% on health, 11.0% on transportation, 1.5% on communications, 3.0% on recreation, 1.7% on restaurants and hotels, and 5.9% on miscellaneous goods and services and purchases from abroad.

²¹LABOR

As of 2010, South Africa had a total labor force of 17.39 million people. Within that labor force, CIA estimates in 2007 noted that 9% were employed in agriculture, 26% in industry, and 65% in the service sector. The constitution provides for the rights to unionize and strike, both of which are reinforced by the Labor Relations Act of 1995. The Labor Relations Act provides protection to workers. The government does not interfere with collective bargaining. In industries and trades where employers and employees are not organized, the Minister of Labor, acting on the advice of the government-appointed wage board, may prescribe compulsory wages and conditions of employment.

The standard workweek is 45 hours. In addition, the law also authorizes four months of maternity leave for women and time-and-a-half pay for overtime. Some collective agreements provide for three weeks' annual leave, and many industries work a five-day week. Employers must provide satisfactory working conditions and accident-prevention measures. Enforcement of safe working conditions is irregular, although the government is making attempts to improve the means of enforcement. The National

Economic Forum, a tripartite structure representing labor, business, and government, is involved in nurturing job creation and job training.

There is no legally mandated national minimum wage; rather, negotiations between labor and management set minimum wage standards industry by industry. In addition, the Minister of Labor can set wages by sector. As of 2010, the rate for farm workers was about $0.88 per hour. The minimum wage for domestic workers (working at least 27 hours per week) was between $0.67 and $0.98 per hour. Compliance with minimum wage rates averaged between 65% and 90%, depending on region. Employment of minors under 15 is illegal. Child labor laws are enforced in the formal economy, but in the agricultural and informal sectors, child labor is widespread. The Ministry of Welfare does allow exceptions to the child labor laws in some sectors of the economy, such as in the performing arts.

Public sector union workers began a series of strikes over the issue of wage increases and housing allowances on 18 August 2010; strikes lasted until 6 September 2010. The strikes, which included an estimated 1.2 million public servants, led to temporary closures of several schools and hospitals. The unions demanded a pay increase of 8.6% and a housing allowance of ZAR1,000 ($141). After a series of negotiations, the unions accepted a deal that included a 7.5% wage increase and a ZAR800 ($115) housing allowance.

22 AGRICULTURE

Many areas suffer from erratic rainfall and soil erosion. The worst drought of the 20th century in southern Africa resulted in near to total crop failure in 1992. Many farmers subsequently abandoned the countryside for urban areas. Except for rice, tea, coffee, and cocoa, the country is typically self-sufficient in essential food production.

Roughly 13% of the total land is farmed, and the country's major crops include corn, wheat, sugarcane, fruits, and vegetables. Cereal production in 2009 amounted to 14.6 million tons, fruit production to 5.9 million tons, and vegetable production to 2.3 million tons.

Sugarcane, indigenous to the Natal coastal belt, was grown before World War II in quantities sufficient to export. Increasing domestic demand after the war absorbed the total output, but with a rise in production and an expansion of the capacity of sugar mills, South Africa became a large sugar exporter. Deciduous and citrus fruits, some of them exported, are also profitable. Vegetables, peanuts, sunflower seeds, groundnuts, soy beans, coffee, ginger, tobacco, cotton, and various types of fodder plants are used domestically. Wine is an important product.

To boost trade in agriculture, in November 2010 the governments of Kenya and South Africa signed a memorandum of understanding that set a framework for greater cooperation in agricultural exports. South Africa had imposed strict health rules on the importation of livestock and livestock products and banned avocados from Kenya due to fruit flies. Under this new level of cooperation, South African inspectors assisted Kenya in meeting the necessary standards to open up markets for the products. Kenya has also called upon South Africa to eliminate import tax on tea and white soda ash, thus expanding the market for those products. The value of exports from Kenya to South Africa is estimated at

about $43 million. The value of exports from South Africa to Kenya is $865 million.

23 ANIMAL HUSBANDRY

Until the end of the 19th century, cattle were kept mainly for draft purposes and bred for strength and endurance; meat and fat needs were provided by sheep. The cattle gave little milk and yielded poor-quality meat, while the sheep gave only fat mutton and no wool. The introduction of foreign breeds and crossbreeding gradually improved the stock, providing excellent meat, wool of fairly good quality, and good milk yields. The country's sheep breeds consist mainly of Merino for wool and Dorpes for mutton. Cattle breeds include the introduced Hereford and Aberdeen Angus as well as the indigenous Afrikaner. Dairy cows are mostly Fresian, forming a well-developed dairy industry.

The UN Food and Agriculture Organization (FAO) reported that South Africa dedicated 83.9 million hectares (207.4 million acres) to permanent pasture or meadow in 2009. During that year, the country tended 125 million chickens, 13.8 million head of cattle, and 1.6 million pigs. The production from these animals amounted to 804,453 tons of beef and veal, 173,963 tons of pork, 1.23 million tons of poultry, 345,165 tons of eggs, and 2.85 million tons of milk. South Africa also produced 89,670 tons of cattle hide and 35,414 tons of raw wool.

24 FISHING

After Morocco, South Africa is Africa's most important fishing nation. The Fisheries Development Corp., established in 1944, has helped modernize equipment, secure better conditions of life for fishermen, and stimulate the catching and canning of fish. The commercial fishing fleet is operated mainly from Cape Town harbor. South Africa had 973 decked commercial fishing boats in 2008. The annual capture totaled 643,686 tons according to the UN FAO. The export value of seafood totaled $441.9 million.

More than 90% of the catch is taken from the productive cold waters off the west coast. Shoal fishing by purse-seine accounts for most of the volume. Hake accounts for 70% of all deep-sea landings. Anchovy, pilchard, mackerel, round herring, snoek, abalone, kingklip, rock lobster, oysters, and mussels are other important species. One-third of the hake catch and nearly all of the abalone are exported. Anchovy, pilchard, and round herring are processed into fishmeal, fish oil, and canned fish.

Rock lobster is caught mainly along the western and southern Cape coasts, with much of it processed into frozen lobster tails for export. About 75% of the lobster catch is exported. South Africa ceased whaling in 1976 and is a member of the International Whaling Commission.

Oyster farming at Knysna began decades ago. Interest in mariculture has grown in recent years and permits have been granted for farming abalone, prawns, red-bait, and mud crab.

Besides commercial fishing, there are thousands of anglers who fish for recreation from the shore and small craft. There are size restrictions and limits for sport fishing. A total ban has been placed on the catching of four species: the great white shark, Natal bass, and the potato and brindle bass.

25FORESTRY

Approximately 5% of South Africa is covered by forest. Cutting in indigenous forests is strictly controlled. Commercial forestry covers 1.2 million hectares (31 million acres), with pine and commercial softwoods, eucalyptus, and wattle the principal timbers produced. South Africa is an important producer of wattle and wattle extract, used in the tanning of leather. Domestic timber production satisfies 90% of domestic needs. Wood is imported for furniture manufacture, railroad ties, and high-quality paper. The UN FAO estimated the 2009 roundwood production at 18.9 million cu m (667 million cu ft). The value of all forest products, including roundwood, totaled $1.46 billion.

26MINING

Since the late 19th century, South Africa's economy has been based on the production and export of minerals, which, in turn, have contributed significantly to the country's industrial development. One of the largest and most diverse mineral producers, in 2009, South Africa was the largest producer and exporter of chromium, as well as the leading producer of aluminosilicates (andalusite), gold, vanadium, gem diamonds, ferrochromium, platinum (89% of world reserve base of platinum-group metals, or PGMs), and manganese (24% of world reserve base of ore). South Africa was also the second-largest producer of zirconium and titanium minerals, as well as a major producer of cobalt, copper, iron ore, lead, nickel, silver, uranium, zinc, aggregate and sand, asbestos, dimension stone, fluorspar, lime, limestone, phosphate rock, sulfur, and vermiculite. South Africa was self-sufficient in the vast majority of its mineral needs, the bulk of which were produced in the northern half of the country. South Africa was among the top five countries in terms of reserves, ranking first in reserves of andalusite, chromite, gold, manganese, PGMs, and vanadium. De Beers, the South African mining giant, accounted for 94% of the country's diamond production and controlled 80% of the world's uncut diamond trade.

In 2009, the mining industry accounted for 8.8% of South Africa's GDP. The leading export earners in 2009 were (in descending order): PGMs, gold, coal, iron ore, manganese, nickel, chromite, and copper. The production of iron, steel, chemicals, and fertilizers ranked among the country's top industries.

The 2009 output of PGMs (platinum, palladium, rhodium, ruthenium, iridium) was 271,393 kg. Production came almost exclusively from mines in the Bushveld Complex, north of Pretoria. Anglo American Platinum Corp. Ltd. (Anglo Platinum) was the world's largest PGM producer in 2009, accounting for 54% of South Africa's production.

Primary gold output in 2009 was 197,628 kg, down from 212,571 in 2008. South Africa's gold output in 2009 accounted for about 8% of world production, compared to 13% from China and around 9% of world output by Australia and the United States.

Iron ore and concentrate output (by metal content) in 2009 was 55.3 million tons (preliminary). Kumba Resources Ltd. expanded the Sishen iron ore mine's capacity in 2009 so that ore production totaled 39.4 metric tons, up from 34 metric tons in 2008. The Sishen Mine was previously owned by Iscor, South Africa's largest crude steel producer.

Chromium output in 2009 (gross weight) was 6,865,000 tons (preliminary), compared to 9,682,000 tons in 2008. Mined copper output in 2009 was 105,000 metric tons (preliminary), down from 109,000 metric tons in 2008. The country's total copper reserve base (metal content) was 13 million tons. Antimony production in 2009 (by gross weight) was put at 2,400 metric tons (preliminary). Proven and probable reserves of antimony amounted to 1.5 million tons, and mineral resources exclusive of reserves totaled 8.6 million tons. The country's total antimony reserve base was 200,000 tons. South Africa is the world's fourth-largest antimony producer after China, Russia, and Bolivia.

Output of manganese ore and concentrate (primarily metallurgical-grade, but also chemical) was 4,576,000 tons (gross weight) in 2009, up from 6,806,000 tons in 2008. Total proven reserves were 12.8 million tons (44.61% manganese, 7.30% iron), and measured, indicated, and inferred resources were 237 million tons (41.24% manganese, 7.98% iron). The country's total manganese reserve base was four billion tons.

Production outputs for the other principal metals in 2009 were: vanadium, 14,353 metric tons (with a reserve base of 12 million tons); titanium (ilmenite and rutile concentrates), 2,220,000 tons (with a reserve base of 244 million tons); zirconium concentrate (baddeleyite and zircon), 387,000 tons (a reserve base of 14 million tons); and mined nickel (metal content), 34,605 metric tons (a reserve base of 12 million tons). South Africa also produced cobalt, lead, silver, uranium, and zinc.

Preliminary output of natural gem and industrial diamonds in 2009 were put at 2.5 million carats and 3.6 million carats, respectively. Approximately 80% of South Africa's diamond production in 2009 came from mines owned by De Beers Consolidated Mines Ltd. The country's total diamond reserve base was 1,127 million carats. Alluvial diamonds were discovered along the Orange River in 1867, and surface diamonds, at Kimberley, in 1870.

Preliminary output of other industrial minerals in 2009 included: vermiculite, 193,334 metric tons; feldspar, 101,394 metric tons; and limestone and dolomite, 22,789,000 metric tons. South Africa also produced aluminosilicates (andalusite, with a reserve base of 51 million tons), barite, calcite, hydraulic cement, clays (attapulgite, bentonite, fire clay, raw and calcined flint clay, and kaolin), fluorspar (acid-grade and metallurgical-grade, with a total reserve base of 80 million tons), tiger's eye (semiprecious gem), gypsum, industrial or glass sand (silica), lime, crude magnesite, mica, nitrogen, perlite, phosphate rock (a reserve base of 2.5 billion tons), natural mineral pigments (ochers and oxides), salt, natural sodium sulfate, dimension stone (granite, norite, and slate), crushed and broken stone (quartzite and shale), aggregate and sand, sulfur, talc and pyrophyllite (wonderstone), and brick clay.

The South African minerals industry operated on a free-enterprise, market-driven basis. Government involvement was primarily confined to ownership of the national electric power supply and the national oil and gas exploration company. Mineral land holdings and production have historically been controlled either by the government or by private entities. However, under the new Minerals and Petroleum Resources Act, existing mineral rights will revert to the South African government, unless companies act within a five-year period to convert "old order" exploration and mining rights into "new" rights under terms specified in the new legislation. Since 1994, the minerals industry has undergone a major corporate restructuring, or "unbundling," aimed at simplifying a complex system of interlocking ownership, at establishing separate core commodity-focused profit centers, and at diversifying and rationalizing nonperforming assets. In 2009, the government amended the Diamond Export Levy Act of 2007 and the Mineral and Petroleum Resources Royalty Administration Act of 2008. The government's Black Economic Empowerment Program required that black ownership of the mining industry reach 15% by 2009 and 26% by 2014.

South Africa's well-developed railway and port infrastructure was built mainly to transport mineral products, and minerals continue to constitute a major part of the nation's freight. However, the impact of HIV/AIDS on the able-bodied skilled and semi-skilled work force in the country is of concern to investors.

27 ENERGY AND POWER

South Africa is the second-largest energy producer on the African continent, surpassed only by Algeria, and the continent's largest consumer of energy. Growth and development of the nation's power sources, particularly electricity, are a primary concern for the government. The state-owned Eskom, the largest power utility in Africa, generates nearly 90% of its electricity from coal. The World Bank reported in 2008 that South Africa produced 255.5 billion kWh of electricity and consumed 232.2 billion kWh, or 4,739 kWh per capita. Roughly 87% of energy came from fossil fuels, while 3% came from alternative fuels. With frequent shortages and only about 80% of the population having access to electricity, the company has built additional coal-fired power stations and diesel-fueled gas turbines, which are cheaper to produce but pose a serious concern for the environment.

Coal is the primary energy source produced and consumed in South Africa. South Africa has only small proven reserves of oil. Per capita oil consumption was 2,756 kg. Oil production totaled 13,000 barrels of oil a day in 2008.

In 2009, natural gas production was 1.9 billion cu m and consumption was 5.4 billion cu m. South Africa imported 3.5 billion cu m in 2009.

South Africa's synthetic fuels industry is highly developed and is backed by offshore condensate and natural gas production in Mossel Bay and a plentiful supply of coal. The South African Coal, Oil, and Gas Corporation (SASOL) is the world's leader in oil-from-coal technology. SASOL operates two coal gasification plants in Secunda and one in Sasalburg. SASOL has the capacity to produce 150,000 barrels per day, mostly to the gasoline market. South Africa's other leading synthetic fuel producer is the Petroleum Oil and Gas Corporation of South Africa (PetroSA) with capacity of 50,000 barrels per day.

In 2010, the South African government signed a memorandum of understanding with the Chinese solar panel firm Suntech Power Holdings to develop solar plants in South Africa. Though the memorandum had no specific financial terms, an initial investment of between $350 million and $400 million was expected to build a 100-MW solar power plant. Officials from Suntech noted that the photovoltaic market in South Africa could be worth more than $1 billion.

28 INDUSTRY

The manufacturing sector has evolved over the past 70 years, beginning with light consumer industry in the 1920s and expanding into heavy industry with the creation of ISCOR (Iron and Steel Corporation of South Africa) in 1928. Industry is localized in Gauteng, Western Cape, the Durban-Pinetown area of KwaZulu-Natal, and the Port Elizabeth-Uitenhage area of Eastern Cape.

The largest industrial sector is the metal products and engineering sector dominated by ISCOR, now privatized. South Africa is the world's largest gold, platinum, manganese, chromium, vanadium, aluminosilicates, and titanium producer; the second-largest of vermiculite and zirconium; third for fluorspar; fourth for antimony; and fifth for zinc, coal, lead, and uranium. Companies like Columbus Stainless Steel and Billiton's Hillside Aluminum Smelter produce processed industrial minerals, instead of just primary commodities. A dip in gold prices during the late 1990s threatened the gold mines, but only temporarily. South Africa is a major pulp and paper producer. The chemical sector centers on sizeable fertilizer production and the Modderfontein explosives factory. In 2011 the industrial production growth rate was 4%.

29 SCIENCE AND TECHNOLOGY

The World Bank reported in 2009 that there were no patent applications in science and technology in South Africa. Public financing of science was 0.93% of GDP. Among South Africa's earliest research ventures was the Royal Observatory at the Cape of Good Hope, established by the British Admiralty in 1820. Societies of leading engineers, architects, chemists, metallurgists, and geologists were organized in the 1890s, and the South African Association for the Advancement of Science was established in 1902. The Council for Scientific and Industrial Research (founded in 1945) has 13 research divisions. The Atomic Energy Corporation established an experimental nuclear reactor in 1965 and has since directed the government's nuclear program. In 1970, it was announced that its researchers had devised a new uranium-enrichment process, subsequently developed by the national Uranium Enrichment Corp. The Scientific Advisory Council to the Minister of National Education (established in 1962) promotes the application of scientific knowledge and recommends national science policies and programs.

On 17 September 2009, the South African government successfully launched its first satellite. The SumbandilaSat is designed to collect information on weather patterns and climate change as it affects Africa. The $3.5 billion satellite was funded by the government of South Africa and developed by the South African commercial firm, Sunspace, but sent into orbit on a Russian rocket launched from Kazakhstan.

In December 2010, the government launched the South Africa Space Agency (SANSA) and introduced the National Space Strategy developed through the Ministry of Science and Technology. SANSA is responsible for implementing the new space program, which is designed to promote research in the areas of astronomy, earth observation, communications, navigation, and space physics. International cooperation in space-related activities is another major goal of the space strategy.

The Hartebeestheek Radio Astronomy Observatory's 26-meter-diameter antenna was originally constructed to serve as a tracking station for NASA's Deep Space Network. In May 2010, South Africa was chosen to host the prestigious International Astronomical Union (IAU) Office for Astronomy Development (OAD). The country was 1 of 20 that had placed bids for the honor. The office was to be established in Cape Town at the South Africa Astronomical Observatory (SAAO) Headquarters, which houses the Southern African Large Telescope. Researchers and educators from both the SAAO and the IAU were planning to work together on educational and outreach programs that may lead to further developments in the science of astronomy.

The city of Johannesburg is home to a geological museum, the Adler Museum of the History of Medicine, and the James Hall Museum of Transport. Botanical and zoological gardens are located, respectively, in Durban and Pretoria. South Africa has 30 universities and colleges offering courses in basic and applied sciences.

³⁰DOMESTIC TRADE

South Africa has largely dismantled its old economic system that involved extensive government involvement in the domestic economy through state-owned enterprises. Approximately 90% of the population and consumer market surrounds the cities of Johannesburg, Cape Town, Durban, Pretoria, and Port Elizabeth.

Retail establishments are extremely diverse, ranging from local convenience stores and specialty shops to department stores, supermarkets, and chain stores. There are some wholesale outlet stores as well, and hypermarkets are beginning to find a place in some suburban areas. In rural areas, merchants sponsor cooperative stores. Nearly 90% of consumer goods are domestically sourced.

The number of franchises continues to grow. However, there have been significant increases in cellular communications, real estate, office building and home services, and consumer goods retailing. There are also many advertising agencies.

Business hours for most offices and shops are from 8 a.m. to 1 p.m. and 2 p.m. to 4:30 p.m., Monday through Friday, and from 8:30 a.m. until 1 p.m. on Saturday. Banks are usually open from 9 a.m. to 3:30 p.m. weekdays and from 8:30 to 11 a.m. on Saturdays.

³¹FOREIGN TRADE

Gold, diamonds and other metals and minerals are the most valuable export commodities. Exports of gold, platinum, coal, and iron account for approximately 17% of commodity exports. The share of gold as a percentage of total merchandise exports fell from 51.4% in 1980 to 13% in 2000. In 1995, processed primary product exports exceeded those of gold for the first time. South Africa imported $77.04 billion worth of goods and services in 2008, while exporting $76.86 billion worth of goods and services. Major import partners in 2009 were China, 17.2%; Germany, 11.2%; the United States, 7.4%; Saudi Arabia, 4.9%; and Japan, 4.7%. Its major export partners were China, 10.3%; the United States, 9.2%; Japan, 7.6%; Germany, 7%; UK, 5.5%; and Switzerland, 4.7%.

In 2011, South Africa announced plans to push for a free trade agreement between the South African Development Community (SADC), the East African Community (EAC), and the Common Market for East African States (COMESA). Such an agreement could offer substantial benefits to a market that includes 27 countries with a combined GDP of nearly $1 trillion. Talks began in December 2011.

³²BALANCE OF PAYMENTS

Gold invariably represents the great majority of the country's international reserves. In 2010 South Africa had a foreign trade deficit of $2.3 billion, amounting to 4.9% of GDP. The current account balance in 2010 was -$9.987 billion, an improvement over the 2009 figure of -$11.33 billion.

³³BANKING AND SECURITIES

The South African Reserve Bank (SARB), the central bank of issue, began operations in 1921 and in 1924 assumed liability for the outstanding notes of the commercial banks. It is the fourth-oldest central bank to have been established outside Europe. It purchases

---

Principal Trading Partners – South Africa (2010)

(In millions of US dollars)

Country	Total	Exports	Imports	Balance
World	161,962.0	81,821.0	80,141.0	1,680.0
China	21,192.0	10,385.0	10,807.0	-422.0
Germany	14,537.0	5,505.0	9,032.0	-3,527.0
United States	13,258.0	7,631.0	5,627.0	2,004.0
Japan	10,448.0	6,614.0	3,834.0	2,780.0
India	9,413.0	5,656.0	3,757.0	1,899.0
United Kingdom	8,802.0	5,366.0	3,436.0	1,930.0
Netherlands	4,810.0	2,507.0	2,303.0	204.0
Sa'udi Arabia	4,625.0	347.0	4,278.0	-3,931.0
Italy	4,106.0	2,328.0	1,778.0	550.0
Iran	3,546.0	73.0	3,473.0	-3,400.0

(…) data not available or not significant.

(n.s.) not specified.

SOURCE: *2011 Direction of Trade Statistics Yearbook*, New York: United Nations, 2011.

Balance of Payments – South Africa (2010)

(In millions of US dollars)

Current Account		**-10,117.0**
Balance on goods		3,838.0
Imports	-81,862.0	
Exports	85,700.0	
Balance on services		-4,453.0
Balance on income		-7,225.0
Current transfers		-2,278.0
Capital Account		**31.0**
Financial Account		**10,376.0**
Direct investment abroad		-382.0
Direct investment in South Africa		1,565.0
Portfolio investment assets		-3,916.0
Portfolio investment liabilities		14,386.0
Financial derivatives		…
Other investment assets		-2,590.0
Other investment liabilities		1,311.0
Net Errors and Omissions		**3,507.0**
Reserves and Related Items		**-3,796.0**

(…) data not available or not significant.

SOURCE: *Balance of Payment Statistics Yearbook 2011*, Washington, DC: International Monetary Fund, 2011.

and disposes of the entire gold output. In September 1985, because of a net outflow of capital arising from South Africa's declaration of a state of emergency, a two-tier foreign-exchange system was adopted by the bank, involving a commercial rand for current transactions and a financial rand for investments or disinvestments by nonresidents. At the same time, certain debt payments, mainly to foreign banks, were frozen. Limited payments were resumed in April 1986, and the two-tier foreign-exchange system was discarded.

Each bank is required to maintain a reserve balance with the South African Reserve Bank equal to 8% of its short-term liabilities. Since the commercial banks have restricted themselves to traditional functions, many other institutions have been established to make loans or investments to stimulate economic growth and development. The government has sponsored financial institutions such as the Development Bank of South Africa, the Corporation for Public Deposits, the Industrial Development Corp. (IDC), the Fisheries Development Corp., and the Corporation for Economic Development.

In 2009 the discount rate, the interest rate at which the central bank lends to financial institutions in the short term, was 7%. The commercial bank prime lending rate, the rate at which banks lend to customers, was 11.708%.

South Africa is home to the Johannesburg Stock Exchange (JSE). The JSE dwarfs all sub-Saharan Africa's other active stock exchanges put together. On 8 November 1995, the JSE underwent its "Big Bang" when the Stock Exchange Control Act came into effect, changing the system under which the market had operated for years. New capital adequacy requirements placed major financial obligations on broking firms, and the easy fixed-commission system for brokers disappeared. Most visibly, the traditional trading floor—the open outcry market—became a thing of the past as firms carried out all their trading by computer. The restructuring of the stock exchange also allowed banks to enter the securities markets as stockbrokers for the first time. However, market capitalization during the 2000s was significantly less than peak levels in 1995.

34 INSURANCE

Automobile third-party liability, unemployment insurance, and workers' compensation insurance are all compulsory, the last of which is a virtual government monopoly. At the beginning of 1994, a consortium of black investors negotiated a deal to buy 51% of African Life, a life insurance company serving over two million customers, from majority share holders. Other insurance companies include Old Mutual and Sanlam.

Life insurance companies and pension funds are controlled by the Registrar of Financial Institutions. The main long-term capital institutions are the pension funds and life assurance companies, which invest mainly on the JSE secondary market.

35 PUBLIC FINANCE

The fiscal year runs from 1 April to 31 March. The minister of finance presents the budget to parliament in March for authorization of expenditures and imposition of the necessary taxes. In 1994, the ANC inherited a government that owned about half of all capital assets, one-quarter of them parastatal corporations. Since then, privatization has moved slowly, but steadily.

The US Central Intelligence Agency (CIA) estimated that in 2010 the budget of South Africa included $103.1 billion in public revenue and $126.2 billion in public expenditures. The budget deficit amounted to 5.5% of GDP. Public debt was 33.2% of GDP, with $80.52 billion of the debt held by foreign entities.

36 TAXATION

In 2001, South Africa's territorial system of taxation (or source-based system) was replaced with one based on worldwide incomes for resident companies, including resident branches of foreign companies. In order to preserve some of South Africa's appeal as an offshore location for international headquarters, a separate regime for nonresident International Holding Companies (IHCs) is maintained, which allows for income from foreign subsidiaries to not be counted in the IHC's tax liability (under Controlled Foreign Entity provisions in the tax law).

As of 2011 the standard corporate tax rate in South Africa was 28%. The dividend tax was 10%, and property tax was levied at 0.1%. An occupational injuries insurance contribution was set at 1.6%; unemployment insurance contributions were 1.0%, as were skill development contributions. A fuel tax was assessed at 22%.

Individual income tax is assessed according to a progressive scale. Above an exempted limit, gifts are taxed at 20%, but there is no inheritance tax. The transfer of property is taxed on a progressive scale depending on the value of the property. Royalties paid to nonresidents are subject to a withholding tax of 12%. Capital gains were taxed at 28% as of 2011.

The main indirect tax is South Africa's value-added tax (VAT), with a standard rate of 14% (2011). However, certain fuels, exports, some farming goods and basic foodstuffs, and international transport are zero-rated. Residential rents, educational services, some financial services and domestic passenger transport are exempt from the VAT. Other taxes include provincial and city taxes.

Public Finance – South Africa (2009)

(In millions of rand, central government figures)

Revenue and Grants	**682,814**	**100.0%**
Tax revenue	611,829	89.6%
Social contributions	15,290	2.2%
Grants	2,958	0.4%
Other revenue	52,737	7.7%
Expenditures	**801,199**	**100.0%**
General public services	...	...
Defense	...	...
Public order and safety	...	...
Economic affairs	...	...
Environmental protection	...	...
Housing and community amenities	...	...
Health	...	...
Recreational, culture, and religion	...	...
Education	...	...
Social protection	...	...

(...) data not available or not significant.

SOURCE: *Government Finance Statistics Yearbook 2010,* Washington, DC: International Monetary Fund, 2010.

37 CUSTOMS AND DUTIES

Although South Africa has signed the General Agreement on Tariffs and Trade (GATT) and has been liberalizing import controls with the intention of eventually removing them completely, some classes of imports are still subject to licenses and control regulations. Many goods enter South Africa duty-free. Goods that are subject to a duty pay an average rate of 12%. High tariffs were being reduced for protected industries such as textiles and automobiles.

South Africa maintains a common customs area with Botswana, Lesotho, Namibia, Swaziland, and the black homelands of Bophuthatswana, Ciskei, Transkei, and Venda through the South African Customs Union. Common customs, excise, and a value-added tax (VAT) of 14% are levied. Specific excise duties are levied on beverages, tobacco, petroleum products, and motor vehicles. Ad valorem excise duties are levied on office machinery, film, and luxury consumer goods. Export licenses are required for a number of products.

38 FOREIGN INVESTMENT

Despite a considerable increase in recent years in domestic savings available for investment, foreign capital investment plays a significant role in South African economic development, and a number of manufacturing and industrial concerns have been established by the United Kingdom, the United States, and continental European companies since World War II. UK capital has been invested primarily in manufacturing, heavy engineering, and in the development of new gold fields in Transvaal and the Orange Free State. US investments are mainly in mining and manufacturing, and in wholesale and retail trade.

The establishment of a multiracial government in 1994 and the lifting of sanctions led to an increase in foreign investment in South Africa. The number of multinational corporations with direct investments or employees in South Africa increased by over 20%. By 1997, total foreign direct investment (FDI) exceeded $18 billion. The inflow of FDI in 1997 was over $3.8 billion but fell to $561 million in 1998. Inward FDI flows increased to $1.5 billion in 1999 and to $888 million in 2000. Contrary to worldwide trends in the economic slowdown of 2001, FDI inflow in South Africa reached a record $6.79 billion. However, the flows declined to $757 million in 2002 to $720 million in 2003 and $585 million in 2004. In 2005 FDI inflows were boosted by the Goldfields-Norilsk and Metcash-Metzo deals and the takeover of Amalgamated Banks of South Africa (ABSA)—one of the country's "big four" banks—by Barclays of the United Kingdom, and the purchase by Vodafone of a further 15% stake in the mobile-phone operator, Vodacom.

Barclays' purchase was the largest single FDI inflow into South Africa since the transition to multiparty rule in 1994. The inflows from both Barclays and Vodafone have stimulated foreign interest in South Africa and signal a vote of confidence for the country's political and economic prospects for the medium and long term. The United Kingdom has been the largest investor with almost half of the total, followed by the United States, Germany, the Netherlands, Malaysia, and Switzerland. Manufacturing and business services gained the lion's share of FDI, led by telecommunications; major investors included Petronas, SDC Communications, Dow Chemicals, Telecom Malaysia, Coca-Cola, and Lafarge. Foreign direct investment (FDI) in South Africa was a net inflow of $5.35 billion according to World Bank figures published in 2009. FDI represented 1.88% of GDP.

39 ECONOMIC DEVELOPMENT

The recession of 1989 to 1993 was provoked by a drop in investment from 24% to 15%. With the inauguration of multiracial government in 1994, this investment was restored from about $13 billion in 1994 to about $18 billion in 1998, creating new jobs and generating growth. Tremendous changes in the structure of the economy were required to relieve the pressures of poverty and inequality that resulted from apartheid. A realistic strategy that attended to popular expectations and aspirations as well as to sound economic principles was needed, with the goals of reducing tariffs and other restrictive practices, linking wages and output, ending exchange controls, reforming taxes, and optimizing welfare allocations. The government implemented a Growth, Employment, and Redistribution (GEAR) plan to cover the years 1996–2000. The plan was successful in bringing macroeconomic stability to the country, but formal employment continued to decline, and wealth remained unequally distributed along racial lines.

South Africa has what may be called a dual economy—one comparable to industrialized nations and another comparable to developing countries. Trade liberalization increased from the early 1990s to the 2000s. The government continued to be committed to responsible fiscal management while increasing spending on infrastructure, social services, and socio-economic "upliftment" programs. The government adopted plans to encourage development in specific regions and in small and medium enterprise development, in part to promote growth and the creation of jobs.

In 2009, President Zuma announced a three-year $98 billion spending program to provide funding for schools, transportation, housing, and sanitation projects. Pledging to make the fight against poverty a priority of his administration, he also promised to create 4 million jobs by 2014. A plan to reach this goal was revealed in February 2012. It focused primarily on infrastructure development, prioritizing the building of additional higher education facilities and road construction. Addressing other issues of economic and social development, the president promised to find ways to cut violent crime by 10%.

40 SOCIAL DEVELOPMENT

South Africa has a comprehensive system of social legislation, which includes unemployment insurance, workers' compensation, old age pensions, disability pensions, war veterans' pensions, pensions for the blind, maternity grants, and family allowances. The first statutory benefits were initiated in 1928, and the system was updated in 2004. The cost of most of these benefits is borne by the national government, but the cost of industrial accident insurance is borne by employers, while contributions to the unemployment insurance fund are made by employers, employees, and the government. The retirement age is 65 for men and 60 for women. Sickness and maternity benefits both pay 45% of weekly earnings; maternity benefits are payable up to a total of 26 weeks. The government funds assistance to families of limited means.

The ANC government of national unity sought to provide more social services for its black constituents within the constraints of a weakened economy. Its top priorities are housing, health, education, and the creation of more jobs in the formal economic sector.

Despite legal protection, sex discrimination is still widespread, especially in connection with economic issues including wage disparity, credit access and property rights. Domestic abuse is widespread, and victims who seek redress are not treated adequately by law enforcement, medical personnel, or the judicial system. The incidence of rape is extremely high due to general lack of security and the prevailing attitude condoning violence against women. There are many governmental and nongovernmental organizations monitoring and promoting human rights for women.

Although South Africa's human rights record has improved, there are continued reports of detainees dying in custody. Criminal activity is widespread, and vigilante and mob justice is increasing. Prison conditions are harsh.

Widespread poverty is noted as the primary cause for the high crime rate in South Africa. Economic policies directed toward bridging the economic and educational gaps between the nation's whites and blacks may help relieve some of these difficulties.

41 HEALTH

The South African government increased its spending in the public and private sectors of health care. South Africa's governmental policy has been directed toward a more streamlined and equitable public health service to bridge the country's social and ideological divisions. Emphasis on better health care resulted in numerous projects to expand and modernize existing hospitals and clinics, as well as build new ones. There was also emphasis on preventive health care, as well as a greater demand for laboratory analysis and therapeutic equipment and disposables. Most electronic and high-tech equipment is imported. Provincial administrations maintain most major hospitals and receive subsidies from the national government. Hospital care is free for those unable to bear the costs, but medical treatment is generally conducted on a private basis.

About 80% of doctors take care of urban citizens. Large sectors of the population live in conditions nearer to those of a developing country. There are about 700 hospitals, with Baragwanath Hospital near Johannesburg the largest in southern Africa.

There are medical schools at the universities of Cape Town, Stellenbosch, Witwatersrand, Pretoria, Natal, and the Orange Free State. Between 1959 and 1994, most black medical students attended the medical school at the University of Natal. In addition, the Medical University of Southern Africa (near Pretoria) was opened for black students in 1978. Following the introduction of democracy in 1994, the government sought to reverse the discrimination against blacks by building many new community clinics. However, the money to fund these clinics came from the medical school budgets funded publicly. The South African Institute for Medical Research in Johannesburg is well known for its studies of silicosis and other diseases to which mine workers are subject.

According to the CIA, life expectancy in South Africa was 52 years in 2011. The country spent 10.4% of its GDP on health care, amounting to $485 per person. The prevalence of HIV/AIDS has had a harsh impact in South Africa, with about 17.8% of the adult population infected with the virus in 2009. This represents the fourth-highest adult prevalence rate in the world. The estimated total number of people living with HIV/AIDS is 5.6 million, the

second highest in the world. Beginning in 2003, the government approved a major drug distribution program to treat those with HIV, offering free medications for many of the poorest citizens. In 2009, the government initiated more programs to provide antiretroviral drugs for 80% of those infected with HIV. A major program to distribute antiretrovirals to infants and pregnant women who have tested positive for HIV began in 2009. These programs represented a major reversal in the South African government's previous policies toward HIV/AIDS. The former president, Thabo Mbeki, denied the connection between HIV and AIDS and planted fears that antiretrovirals were poisonous. Each year, about 59,000 babies are born with HIV.

Other prevalent infectious diseases reported in South Africa included tuberculosis, measles, typhoid, malaria, and viral hepatitis. Leprosy has been reduced to less than 1 per 100,000, but malaria and tuberculosis still cause serious problems. Smoking remains a significant health risk.

There were 8 physicians, 41 nurses and midwives, and 28 hospital beds per 10,000 inhabitants in 2011. The total fertility rate was estimated at 2.3 children born per woman. Infant mortality in that year was 43.2 deaths per 1,000 live births. In 2008 the maternal mortality rate, according to the World Bank, was 410 per 100,000 births. It was estimated that 62% of children were vaccinated against measles.

42 HOUSING

In the late 1990s, there was an explosive growth of shacks and shantytowns surrounding South Africa's major urban areas. In 1994, the housing backlog was estimated to be 1.2 million homes for the black population, while there was a surplus of white housing units of 83,000. This backlog and demand translated into the need to build 250,000 dwelling units a year in the last years of the 20th century, or roughly 1,000 units per working day; however, only about one-tenth of that number—25,000 dwelling units—were built each year, leaving the country with a serious housing shortage. Most of the black townships and squatter settlements lack the basic infrastructure and services of water, sewage, and electricity. Efforts to solve South Africa's housing problem must focus not only on construction but also on servicing current and prospective sites by building roads and providing electricity, sanitation, and water.

At the 2001 census, there were about 11,205,705 households counted, which translates into about the same number of dwelling units. About 55.6% of all households were living in what was described as a house on a separate stand; 16% of all households were living in shacks. Some 32.3% of all households had access to piped water inside their dwelling. Another 29% had piped water in their yard. Nearly 52% of all dwellings had some type of flush toilet. Another 27% used pit latrines.

In 2010, the UN recognized the Johannesburg Social Housing Company (Joshco) for major improvements in human settlements by bestowing the award known as the Scroll of Honor. Established in 2004, this government-supported group has provided affordable housing with improved living conditions and basic services for tens of thousands of poor families through community development projects. These projects generally involved the conversion of abandoned buildings or derelict buildings in slum districts into livable housing units.

⁴³EDUCATION

In 2009, the World Bank estimated that 85% of age-eligible children in South Africa were enrolled in primary school. Secondary enrollment for age-eligible children stood at 72%. Overall, the CIA estimated that South Africa had a literacy rate of 86.4%. Public expenditure on education represented 5.4% of GDP.

The challenge facing the post-apartheid government has been to create an educational system that provides quality education to all citizens of South Africa. The educational legacy left by the apartheid government has not been easy to dismantle. Literacy rates among blacks remain low, and educational facilities in the townships and rural areas need to be upgraded. During the apartheid government, education for whites was free and compulsory between the ages of 7 and 16, but attendance was not generally compulsory for blacks. Adult literacy was close to 100% for whites and about 50% for blacks in the mid-1980s.

After the Soweto riots of 1976, the national government increased expenditures for black education, and black student enrollment rose sharply. The government reported by the early 1990s that primary and secondary schools enrolled about one million white students; 5.8 million blacks; 900,000 Coloured; and 300,000 Asians.

The Government of National Unity established a National Ministry of Education in 1994 and an educational system comprised of nine provincial subsystems was developed. National policies set clear educational guidelines, and the Provincial Legislatures were accorded significant authority in setting specific priorities and policies for each province.

In 1995, President Mandela launched the Presidential Lead Project on Developing the Culture of Learning and Teaching. The program revised school governance structures, increasing school attendance and renovating hundreds of schools around the country.

Education is now compulsory for nine years, which is covered by six years of primary school and three years of junior secondary school. Students may then enter either a two-year technical school program or a three-year general senior secondary program.

South Africa has 21 universities and 15 technikons (technology institutes) that provide tertiary level vocational training. The government of South Africa has shown a strong commitment to the development of higher education and has begun to attract substantial investment from foreign agencies and organizations for education development. The African Institute for Mathematical Sciences (AIMS) was established in 2003 to promote higher education in math and science for all African students. From 2003 through 2010, the center graduated 305 students, 95% of whom continued on for education at the master's and doctorate levels. A majority of those students have remained in Africa to pursue their careers. The government of South Africa provides $1.3 million per year for teaching and research programs at AIMS. In September 2010, the African Institute for Mathematical Sciences was awarded $2 million from Google for its Next Einstein Initiative, a plan to launch three new AIMS centers in Senegal, Ghana, and Ethiopia by 2013.

In 2010, Stellenbosch University in South Africa launched its new journalism center, Mediafrica. The center strengthened the reputation of the university's journalism department, which was already considered to be one of the top 12 journalism schools in Africa, according to the UN Educational, Scientific, and Cultural Organization (UNESCO). The mission of the center is to train journalists and other media workers in investigative reporting, with an emphasis on ethical reporting. Mediafrica offers programs in print, video, and other media.

⁴⁴LIBRARIES AND MUSEUMS

The National Library of South Africa is made up of two branches, one in Pretoria (formerly known as the State Library, 787,000 volumes) and one in Cape Town (formerly known as the South African Library, 750,000 volumes). The University of Witwatersrand's main collection holds over one million volumes. Major public libraries are located in Johannesburg (850,000 volumes) and Cape Town (1.4 million volumes).

The Kaffrarian Museum in King William's Town has imposing collections of indigenous animals. The National Museum in Bloemfontein contains an ictidosaur skeleton and the Florisbad human fossil skull. The East London Museum houses the first coelacanth to be caught (the entire family had previously been thought to be extinct). The South African National Gallery is in Cape Town. Founded in 1871, it houses an extensive European collection as well as one of Africa's finest collections of contemporary African art. The South African Cultural History Museum is also in Cape Town, as is the Castle Military Museum, which opened in 1995. Robben Island, 12 km (7.5 mi) from Cape Town, is a former prison and is now a museum. Johannesburg has several archaeological museums as well as the University Art Galleries of the University of Witwatersrand. Pretoria houses the Kruger Museum, chronicling the life of Paul Kruger; the Natural Cultural History Museum; and the Museum of Anthropology and Archaeology.

⁴⁵MEDIA

South Africa has the best and most modern telecommunications system in Africa. Domestic services are provided by a mix of open-wire lines, microwave radio relay links, fiber-optic and coaxial cable, radiotelephone stations, and wireless local loops. International services are provided by a pair of submarine cables and three Intelsat satellite ground stations. In 2009, there were some 4.3 million main phone lines and mobile phone subscriptions averaged 94 per 100 people.

The South African Broadcasting Corp. (SABC), a semigovernmental organization, offers transmissions in English, Afrikaans, and nine Bantu languages. It derives its income from listeners' licenses and from its commercial services. External broadcasting services are operated by the Voice of South Africa. The country's first television service was begun in January 1976 under government auspices. In 1981, a separate channel began broadcasting in native languages. There are several privately held television and radio stations. In 2009, there were 14 FM radio stations, 347 AM radio stations, and 1 shortwave radio station. Internet users numbered 9 per 100 citizens.

The English and Afrikaans populations have their own newspapers, distinguished not only by language but also by the variety and slant of news. Nearly all newspapers in South Africa are published by members of the Newspaper Press Union (NPU). Its main function is to hear and decide complaints against the press in cases where the complaints do not fall under the jurisdiction of the courts. The Media Council, established by the NPU, seeks to maintain editorial standards and to deal with infringements of the NPU press code. Prominent newspapers in 2010, with circulation numbers listed parenthetically, included *Die Burger* (105,841), the *Sowetan* (225,000), and *Beeld* (111,958), as well as 13 other major newspapers.

The constitution provides for free speech and a free press, and the government now is said to respect these rights. News coverage and editorial opinion is vigorous and unfettered.

46 ORGANIZATIONS

The cooperative movement began before the consummation of the Union, concentrating then as now on marketing agricultural produce. The movement's rapid advance, however, dates from 1922, when the first Cooperative Societies Act was passed. Every branch of farming has its own associations, to which about 75% of all farmers belong; these groups are affiliated with provincial organizations, which, in turn, are members of the South African Agricultural Union. The Agricultural Research Council is an important group for the advancement of the farming industry. Other similar groups include the Sugar Milling Research Institute, the South African Sugarcane Research Institute, and the ARC-Institute for Tropical and Subtropical Crops.

The South African Federated Chamber of Industries is the chief employers' organization. The Association of Chambers of Commerce (ASSOCOM) was formed in 1892 to promote commerce and industry in South Africa. In 1990, the South African Chamber of Business (SACOB) was formed by the merger of the Association of Commerce and Industry and the South African Federated Chamber of Industries. One hundred and two chambers of commerce and industry are members of SACOB.

To provide special aid to Afrikaans-speaking businesspeople, the Afrikaanse Handelsinstituut was established in Pretoria in 1942. It now assists all Afrikaner businesses involved in commerce, finance, and mining. Membership is offered if at least half the capital of a firm is owned by Afrikaners.

The Royal Society of South Africa, founded in 1877, is the leading scholarly organization. The South African Academy of Science and Arts was founded in 1909 and is based in Arcadia. The Geological Society of South Africa (founded in 1895) has published important research in its transactions, and its influence extends beyond South Africa. The African Music Society, an international organization that specializes in the recording of music of all parts of Africa, has its headquarters near Johannesburg. Shakespeare Society of Southern Africa is based in Grahamstown. Other organizations have been established for studies in Afrikaans, archaeology, economics, medicine, technology, and other fields. Groups for hobbyists and other amateur actives are also available, such as the All Breeds Cat Club, the Cape Lancia Club (a car club), and the Federation of Rose Societies of South Africa (R.O.S.A).

Organizations dedicated to health and welfare include the Association of Societies for Occupational Safety and Health, Health Systems Trust–South Africa, the South African Medical Research Council, the Democratic Nursing Organization of South Africa, and the Colleges of Medicine of South Africa. The South African Medical Association promotes research and education on health issues and works to establish common policies and standards in healthcare. There are several other associations dedicated to research and education for specific fields of medicine and particular diseases and conditions, such as the Cancer Association of South Africa and Diabetes South Africa.

There are a number of sports associations throughout the country. National youth organizations include the ANC Youth League, Girl Guides Association of South Africa, Junior Chamber, National Catholic Federation of Students, YMCA/YWCA, South African Scout Association, South African Student Congress, South African Young Christian Workers, and Youth for Christ. Sports associations promote amateur competition among athletes of all ages for a variety of pastimes.

Women's organizations include the ANC Women's League, the African Gender Institute, National Council of Women of South Africa, the Nisaa Institute for Women's Development, and programs through the Office on the Status of Women. Black Sash Trust is an organization, primarily of women, dedicated to promoting human rights and civil liberties through the principles of democracy.

There are several national environmental associations in the country, including Birdlife South Africa, Endangered Wildlife Trust, the Grassland Society of Southern Africa, Wildlife and Environment Society of South Africa, African Conservation Trust, and the Environmental Monitoring Group.

National organizations promoting causes of social justice include the Friedrich Naumann Foundation–Africa Regional Office and the Legal Resources Centre. There are national chapters of the Red Cross Society, Caritas, Habitat for Humanity, the Society of St. Vincent de Paul, UNICEF, and Amnesty International.

47 TOURISM, TRAVEL, AND RECREATION

The tourism industry is based on private enterprise, but the government oversees tourist facilities through the South African Tourist Corporation, which also promotes tourism abroad. In addition to the principal cities and many ocean beaches, popular attractions include the Kruger National Park, situated in the northeast on the Mozambique and Zimbabwe borders, and several game reserves; the Castle of Good Hope fortress at Cape Town (built during 1662); and the Kimberley Mine Museum at the site of the famous Big Hole diamond mine. Entertainment facilities include symphony halls, theaters, movies, nightclubs, and discos. Among popular pastimes are golf, tennis, bowls (lawn bowling), hunting, horse racing, rugby, football (soccer), cricket, and water sports. The *Tourism Factbook*, published by the UN World Tourism Organization, reported 9.93 million incoming tourists to South Africa in 2009; they spent a total of $8.68 billion. Of those incoming tourists, there were 7.8 million from Africa. In 2011 the estimated daily cost to visit Pretoria/Tswane was $341. The cost of visiting other cities averaged $317.

48 FAMOUS PERSONS

Among the most famous tribal leaders in what is now South Africa were Shaka (1773–1828), who built the Zulu into a powerful nation, and Cetewayo (d. 1884), who led the Zulu in an unsuccessful war against the British in 1879. Other outstanding figures of 19th-century South Africa were Stephanus Johannus Paulus (Oom Paul) Kruger (1825–1904), president of the Transvaal and leader of the Boers, and British-born Cecil John Rhodes (1853–1902), entrepreneur and empire builder, after whom the Rhodesias (now Zambia and Zimbabwe) were named. Jan Christiaan Smuts (1870–1950), statesman and military leader, was one of the great men of the first half of the 20th century. He and two other prime ministers of Boer descent—Louis Botha (1862–1919) and James Barry Munnik Hertzog (1866–1942) —attempted to merge the two white nationality groups in a common loyalty to the British Commonwealth. Daniel François Malan (1874–1959), an Afrikaner Nationalist leader, led his party to victory in 1948 and served as prime minister (1948–54) when South Africa's racial separation policies were codified. Hendrik Frensch Verwoerd (1901–66), Nationalist prime minister from 1958 until his assassination, vigorously enforced separate development of the races and created the black homelands. His successor, Balthazar Johannes Vorster (1915–83), served as prime minister from 1966 until his elevation to the presidency in 1978; he resigned in the following year because of a political scandal. Pieter Willem Botha (b. 1916) became prime minister in 1978 and president in 1984. Frederik Willem de Klerk (b. 1936) was the last state president of apartheid South Africa, serving from 1989 to 1994.

Among the best-known South African writers in the English language was Olive (Emily Albertina) Schreiner (1855–1920), whose *Story of an African Farm* has become a classic. A collection of short stories about Afrikaner farmers, *The Little Karoo*, by Pauline Smith (1882–1957), is regarded as a masterpiece. South African authors of novels and short stories such as Sarah Gertrude Millin (Liebson, b. Russia, 1889–1968), Alan Stewart Paton (1903–88), Sir Laurens Van der Post (1906–96), Peter Abrahams (b. 1919), Ezekiel Mphahlele (b. 1919), Nadine Gordimer (b. 1923), Dan Jacobson (b. 1929), and John M. Coetzee (b. 1940) have won considerable attention in the United Kingdom and the United States. Ignatius Roy Dunnachie Campbell (1901–57) was an eminent South African poet, and his friend William Charles Franklyn Plomer (1903–73) was a highly regarded novelist, poet, essayist, and critic. Athol Fugard (b. 1932) has written internationally acclaimed plays about South African race relations.

Well-known authors and poets in the Afrikaans language are Cornelis Jacob Langenhoven (1873–1932), author of the national anthem; Christian Frederick Louis Leipoldt (1880–1947); N.P. van Wyk Louw (1906–70); the poet, playwright, and critic Uys Krige (1910–87), who also wrote in English; and André Brink (b. 1935). Eugène Nielsen Marais (1871–1936), a journalist, lawyer, poet, and natural historian, was an outstanding student of animal and insect behavior. Breyten Breytenbach (b. 1939) has earned international recognition as an important Afrikaans poet; he served seven years in prison (1975–82) after pleading guilty to a passport violation and to illegal contacts with an African political group.

V. (J.E.A.) Volschenck (1853–1935) is sometimes called the "father of South African art," and Anton Van Wouw (b. Netherlands, 1862–1945) is called the "doyen" of South African sculpture. Other artists include the painters Robert Gwelo Goodman (b. England, 1871–1939), Jacob Hendrik Pierneef (1886–1957), and Walter W. Battiss (b. England, 1906–82), also an authority on Bushman art; and sculptor Coert Laurens Steynberg (1905–82).

Other noted South Africans include historian George McCall Theal (b. Canada, 1837–1919); the physical anthropologist Raymond Arthur Dart (b. Australia, 1893–1988); Clement Martyn Doke (b. England, 1893–1983), an authority on Bantu philology; the social anthropologist Isaac Schapera (1905–86); Louis Franklin Freed (b. Lithuania, 1903–81), a specialist on tropical diseases; and pioneer open-heart surgeon Christiaan Neething Barnard (1922–2001). Lord Henry de Villiers of Wynberg (1842–1914) was chief justice of Cape Colony and of the Union of South Africa.

South Africa's first Nobel Prize winner (for peace in 1961) was Chief Albert John Luthuli (1898–1967), a former president of the ANC, who maintained a policy of nonviolence and of cooperation between whites and blacks. Desmond Mpilo Tutu (b. 1931), the secretary general of the South African Council of Churches during 1979–84 and an outspoken foe of apartheid, received the 1984 Nobel Prize for peace. As archbishop of Cape Town, he became the Anglican primate for southern Africa in 1986. Nelson R. Mandela (b. 1918), a prominent leader of the ANC, was sentenced to life imprisonment in 1964; his release was a principal demand of antigovernment activists. He became South Africa's first president elected in fully representative democratic elections. Oliver Tambo (1919–93), the president of the ANC since 1977, directed the group from exile. Another outspoken critic of the government was the Rev. Allan Boesak (b. 1945), a UDC founder and the former president of the World Alliance of Reformed Churches. More conciliatory toward the regime was Gatsha Buthelezi (b. 1928), the chief of the Zulu people, who heads the Inkatha movement.

49 DEPENDENCIES

South Africa has no territories or colonies. South Africa once maintained a civil administration and a military presence in Namibia. Namibia, a sovereign state, is discussed under its own heading elsewhere in this volume.

50 BIBLIOGRAPHY

Afolayan, Funso S. *Culture and Customs of South Africa.* Westport, CT: Greenwood Press, 2004.

Foster, Douglas. *After Mandela: The Struggle for Freedom in Post-Apartheid South Africa.* New York: W. W. Norton, 2012.

Guest, Emma. *Children of AIDS: Africa's Orphan Crisis.* Sterling, VA: Pluto Press, 2001.

Kamoche, Ken M., ed. *Managing Human Resources in Africa.* New York: Routledge, 2004.

Lawson, George. *Negotiated Revolutions: The Czech Republic, South Africa and Chile.* Burlington, VT: Ashgate, 2005.

Mandela, Nelson. *The Struggle is My Life.* Rev. ed. New York: Pathfinders, 1986.

McElrath, Karen, ed. *HIV and AIDS: A Global View.* Westport, CT: Greenwood Press, 2002.

Rotberg, Robert I. *Ending Autocracy, Enabling Democracy: The Tribulations of Southern Africa, 1960-2000.* Cambridge, MA: World Peace Foundation, 2002.

Saunders, Christopher and Nicholas Southey. *Historical Dictionary of South Africa.* 2nd ed. Lanham, MD: Scarecrow, 2000.

South Africa Investment and Business Guide. Washington, DC: International Business Publications USA, 2012.

Stapleton, Timothy J. *A Military History of South Africa: From the Dutch-Khoi Wars to the End of Apartheid.* Westport, CT: Praeger Security International, 2010.

Stengel, Richard. *Nelson Mandela: Portrait of an Extraordinary Man.* London: Virgin, 2012.

Younger, Paul. *New Homelands: Hindu Communities in Mauritius, Guyana, Trinidad, South Africa, Fiji, and East Africa.* New York: Oxford University Press, 2010.

Zeilig, Leo, and David Seddon. *A Political and Economic Dictionary of Africa.* Philadelphia: Routledge/Taylor and Francis, 2005.

SOUTH SUDAN

Republic of South Sudan

CAPITAL: Juba

FLAG: The national flag features three equal horizontal bands of black (top), red, and green; the red band is edged in white; a blue isosceles triangle based on the hoist side contains a gold, five-pointed star.

ANTHEM: *South Sudan Oyee (Hurray).*

MONETARY UNIT: The South Sudanese Pound (SSDG). There are notes of 10, 25, 50, and 100 South Sudanese Pounds. SSDG1 = US$0.374 (or US$1 = SSDG2.6765) as of 2011.

WEIGHTS AND MEASURES: The metric system is the legal standard.

HOLIDAYS: Independence Day, 9 July.

TIME: 3 p.m. = noon GMT.

¹LOCATION, SIZE, AND EXTENT

South Sudan covers an area of just over 664,329 sq km (256,499 sq mi). The country, located in east-central Africa, has a 5,413-km (3,383-mi) border and shares boundaries with the Central African Republic to the west, Kenya and Uganda to the southeast, Ethiopia to the east, and Sudan to the north. The nation is slightly smaller than Texas.

²TOPOGRAPHY

South Sudan is made up of a vast plain through which the White Nile flows northward. The White Nile joins with the Blue Nile north of the border in Khartoum, Sudan, to form the great Nile River. South Sudan's plains are broken up by scattered hills covered in thick vegetation. The Sudd, one of the world's largest wetlands, covers over 30,000 sq km or about 15% of South Sudan's total area. The highest elevation is at Mount Kinyeti (3187 m/10,456 ft) along the southern border with Uganda. Other peaks along the range, all of which exceed 3000 m (9843 ft), include Imatong, Didinga, and Dongotona.

³CLIMATE

Average temperatures range from 23°C (73°F) in the winter to 31°C (88°F) in the summer. Rainfall averages around 120 cm (47 in) and is heaviest in the south and decreases toward the north. Rainfall is dictated by the annual shift of the Inter-Tropical Convergence Zone.

⁴ENVIRONMENT

Although agriculture is a staple of the economy, agricultural land is threatened by the advancing of the desert and rising temperatures. Due to uncontrolled hunting, the nation's wildlife is threatened. Endangered species include the waldrapp, northern white rhinoceros, slender-horned gazelle, and hawksbill turtle. The Sahara oryx has become extinct in the wild.

⁵FLORA AND FAUNA

In the western part of the country, there is a broad-leafed tropical woodland and forest region; grass covers much of the east. Date palms line the banks of the Nile. Wildlife includes most of the mammals, birds, and reptiles common to central Africa.

⁶POPULATION

In 2011 the Central Intelligence Agency (CIA) reported that the population of South Sudan was 8,260,490. The number was the result of a disputed census, and some population estimates range as high as 9.28 million. The population density was calculated at 13 people per sq km, and 22% of the population lived in urban areas. Only 2.6% of the population was over the age of 65, and 44.4% of the population was under 15 years of age. Juba, the capital, is the largest city with an estimated population of 250,000.

⁷MIGRATION

Before the country achieved independence, many people from South Sudan had migrated to Khartoum, the capital of Sudan. South Sudanese living in Khartoum at the time of independence in July 2011 were permitted to choose South Sudanese citizenship and, according to an agreement between the two nations, permitted to return to South Sudan. Years of civil war have displaced an estimated 80,000 people throughout the former Sudan. Furthermore, the CIA reported that approximately 21,000 refugees from the Democratic Republic of Congo and Ethiopia resided in South Sudan in 2011.

⁸ETHNIC GROUPS

Dinka, the predominant ethnic group, accounts for nearly half of the population. Other groups include Nuer, the second largest ethnic group, as well as the Shilluk, Azande, and Bari.

⁹LANGUAGES

Both English and Arabic are widely spoken and understood, although English is the official language of South Sudan. The provisional constitution recognizes the right of indigenous groups to speak their own languages. In all, around 400 diverse dialects of Nilotic, Nilo-Hamitic, and Sudanic languages are spoken.

¹⁰RELIGIONS

Most South Sudanese are either Christian or hold animist beliefs. A smaller percent of the population is Sunni Muslim. The largest Christian denominations are the Roman Catholic Church of Sudan and the Episcopal Churches of Sudan. Other Protestant groups represented in the nation include the African Inland Church, the Sudan Interior Church, the Church of Christ, Presbyterians, Seventh-day Adventists, Methodists, and Jehovah's Witnesses.

¹¹TRANSPORTATION

A lack of basic infrastructure posed a major challenge for South Sudan. In 2011 the nation still lacked comprehensive road system which, despite measuring approximately 7000 km (4,375 mi), had only 60 km (38 mi) of paved roads. Likewise, South Sudan had 24 airports, most of which had unpaved runways. There were 236 km of railroad as of 2011.

¹²HISTORY

South Sudan was politically fragmented before the arrival of European colonizers and consisted of ethnic groups similar in relative size and geographic location to contemporary demographics. South Sudan's resources, primarily slave labor, gold, ivory, and timber, drew significant interest from European powers. An Egyptian invasion in the 1870s created the province of Equatoria, which included the former Sudan and parts of northern Uganda. Present-day South Sudan remained largely ungoverned, and its lack of central authority made it susceptible to slave raiders.

In 1885, an Islamic crusade led by Muhammad ibn Abdalla toppled foreign authority in Khartoum and created the Mahdist regime. Official Mahdist rule, however, ended in 1898 with the resurgence of British authority. Britain's Lord Kitchener defeated the Mahdists at the Battle of Omdurman and organized the region under the Anglo-Egyptian Condominium. Despite the joint title, the Anglo-Egyptian Condominium was, in operation, purely British. Nonetheless, British rule in the area that makes up modern-day South Sudan was far from comprehensive. Much of the British influence arrived via English-language education provided by Christian missionaries.

South Sudan gained independence from the Anglo-Egyptian alliance on 1 January 1956 after a nearly three year transitional process as a province of Sudan. During the creation of the new state, neither the secular or Islamic nature of the government nor its federal or unitary structure was addressed. The Khartoum government backed away from previous promises to form a secular, federal government, and southern army officers promptly revolted, initiating the first of two civil wars.

During the war, an initially hard line approach by the Khartoum government, led by General Ibrahim Abboud from 1958 until 1964, gave way to more conciliatory civilian governance.

Meanwhile, southern leaders were divided, with some arguing for a federal reunification and others advocating for secession. The prolonged civil war, in addition to its military casualties, displaced thousands of Sudanese citizens who fled to neighboring countries. It also stalled the development of the Sudanese economy.

After a series of ineffectual governments failed to negotiate a peace, a leftist coalition of military leaders, led by Colonel Gaafar Muhammad Nimeiri, took control of the Sudanese government in Khartoum. Nimeiri's government replaced his predecessors' Islamist ideology with a Communist ideology, winning the support of the Soviet Union in the process. However, after an assassination attempt by Communist insiders, Nimeiri purged the Communist Party and resultantly lost the support of the Soviet Union. Nimeiri exhausted his only other political option, which was to negotiate with neighboring Ethiopia and Uganda to end the three nations' mutual support of neighboring rebel groups. Afterward, he began negotiations with southern rebels, reaching a peace agreement in 1972 that allowed for limited autonomy in the south.

The accord signed in 1972 lasted only 11 years. Nimeiri realigned with Islamist elements in Khartoum who, after Chevron's discovery of oil in the south in 1979, pushed hard to dissolve the 1972 agreement. In 1983, Nimeiri made Arabic the official language, rescinded southern autonomy, and placed southern military forces under the authority of Khartoum. Southern Sudanese military officers mutinied once again, initiating a second civil war that did not officially end until 2005. Movements within the Khartoum government to soften the government's stance toward the south were consistently defeated by Islamists. The Islamist influence was cemented by a coup orchestrated by General Umar al-Bashir and supported by elements in the military. Al-Bashir's government became known as the National Islamic Front (NIF) and vigorously continued the war against the Sudan People's Liberation Movement (SPLM) in the south. It also supported radical Islamist groups within its borders, prompting UN sanctions in 1996. NIF policies garnered support for the SPLM both within and outside Sudan. The SPLM united under Colonel John Garang and were bolstered by the efforts of Ethiopia, Eritrea, Uganda, and Kenya to broker an end to the conflict.

In 1997, after the Khartoum government suffered significant military defeats against the SPLM, they signed several agreements that ended fighting among major groups of government and rebel fighters. These accords included the Khartoum, Nuba Mountains, and Fashoda Agreements. SPLM leaders who signed the agreements then worked with the Khartoum government against remaining SPLM forces. Following these initial agreements, major talks sponsored by the Intergovernmental Authority for Development were held in Kenya in 2002 and 2003. Negotiations brokered by retired Kenyan General Lazaro Sumbeiywo resulted in the Machakos Protocol. The following year, on 19 November 2004, the two sides agreed to a final peace deal rendered by the United Nations Security Council (UNSC) in Nairobi. It marked only the fifth time the UNSC had ever met outside of New York. The UNSC adopted Resolution 1574 and created a timeline that marked 31 December 2004 as the date for the Government of Sudan and the SPLM to sign a final agreement. After fulfilling that obligation, both sides formally signed the Comprehensive Peace

SOUTH SUDAN

LOCATION: 10°13′ to 3°48′ N; 25°29′ to 34°37′ E. BOUNDARY LENGTHS: Central African Republic, 989 kilometers (615 miles); Democratic Republic of the Congo, 639 kilometers (397 miles); Ethiopia, 934 kilometers (580 miles); Kenya, 232 kilometers (144 miles); Sudan, 2,184 kilometers (1,357 miles); Uganda, 435 kilometers (270 miles).

Agreement on 9 January 2005. An estimated 2.5 million people died from starvation or drought during the two civil wars.

The Comprehensive Peace Agreement signed in January 2005 provided for six years of southern Sudanese autonomy followed by a referendum on independence. It also established the Government of National Unity (dominated by the National Congress Party or NCL) and the interim Government of Southern Sudan (dominated by the SPLM) and outlined steps toward the sharing of wealth, power, and security between the two parties. A major point in the agreement called for a 2011 referendum for independence in the south. In the 9 January 2011 referendum, more than 99% of Southern Sudanese voted for independence from Sudan. On 9 July 2011, the country became Africa's 54th independent nation.

13 GOVERNMENT

The Government of South Sudan (GOSS) and the Assembly of South Sudan are based in Juba, Central Equatoria State. The governments of the country's ten states and their parliaments are located in the capitals of each respective state, as they were before independence. South Sudan is a democracy with a president and a bicameral legislature. The bicameral legislature consists of 332 members of a National Legislative Assembly as well as 50 members of the Council of States. All legislative members serve four year terms.

As a result of the terms set forth in the Comprehensive Peace Agreement (CPA), the April 2010 ballot included twelve separate elections in Southern Sudan for regional, local, and national representatives. Southern Sudanese voters overwhelmingly elected SPLA leader Salva Kiir as president of Southern Sudan in those elections (giving him 93% of the vote over his rival and former SPLA ally Lam Akol). At the time of his election as president of the autonomous Southern Sudan, Kiir served, in effect, as vice president to Sudan's president Omar Hassan Ahmad al-Bashir. Although tasked to run a unity government with al-Bashir, Kiir was noted for making increasingly secessionist remarks in the run up to his inauguration. On 21 May 2010, Kiir was sworn in as the first democratically elected president of Southern Sudan. He continued in the post as president of South Sudan after voters opted for independence in the January referendum.

14 POLITICAL PARTIES

South Sudanese politics are largely controlled by the National Congress Party (NCL) and the Sudan People's Liberation Movement (SPLM). Other, smaller political parties include Sudan People's Liberation Movement–Democratic Change (SPLM–DC), Sudan African National Union (SANU), United Democratic Front (UDF), Union of Sudan African Parties (USAP 1), Union of Sudan African Parties (USAP 2), South Sudan Democratic Front (SSDF), and United Democratic Salvation Front (UDSF).

15 LOCAL GOVERNMENT

South Sudan is divided into 10 states: Central Equatoria, Eastern Equatoria, Jonglei, Lakes, Northern Bahr el Ghazal, Unity, Upper Nile, Warrap, Western Bahr el Ghazal, and Western Equatoria.

16 JUDICIAL SYSTEM

As of August 2011, the judicial system in place before independence remained in place. It included a supreme court, a court of appeals, high courts, and county courts. The supreme court consists of seven justices, one who serves as president, one who serves as deputy president, and five other justices who do not have other titles. While most cases are presented before a panel of three justices, cases involving changes to the constitution are heard before the entire panel. Before full independence, John Wol Makec was president of the Supreme Court of Southern Sudan, and Chan Reec Madut was deputy president.

17 ARMED FORCES

The South Sudan National Army, the primary component of the South Sudan Armed Forces, transitioned into a formal, national military from its previous role as a rebel militia fighting on behalf of the SPLM. In 2011 following national formation, the government focused its efforts on removing underage fighters from its ranks as well as preventing military-age males from joining other armed groups. The government has occasionally missed payments to soldiers, inciting rioting among those unpaid.

Following border clashes with Sudan, the UN committed to the deployment of 7,000 peacekeeping troops in South Sudan in 2011.

18 INTERNATIONAL COOPERATION

South Sudan hosts ambassadors from a number of countries as well as representatives from the European Union Office, Arab League of Nations, African Union, Japan International Cooperation Agency, World Bank, and Swiss Cooperation Office. The nation has missions abroad in several African countries as well as in Australia, Norway, Belgium, the United Kingdom, Canada, and the United States.

19 ECONOMY

For most South Sudanese, economic survival depends on subsistence farming and cattle rearing. The White Nile valley offers prime agricultural land. According to the CIA, the government generates 98% of its revenue through oil exports but depends on cooperation with Sudan to utilize a pipeline to the Red Sea. A previous 50-50 revenue sharing agreement between South Sudan and Sudan expired in 2011. The government targeted a 6% economic growth rate for 2011, and a 7.2% growth rate for 2012.

Foreign aid receipts have totaled more than $4 billion since 2005, with most of the financing coming from the UK, United States, Norway, and the Netherlands.

20 INCOME

The Government of South Sudan estimated its gross domestic product (GDP) to be $13 billion in 2011. The per capita GDP stood at $1,546. Poverty is widespread in South Sudan, and much of the population has no reliable source of income. Household consumption totaled $4 billion, or $525 per capita.

21 LABOR

In 2008, 53% of those working in South Sudan were unpaid family workers. Some 12% were paid employees.

22 AGRICULTURE

Agriculture plays an important role in daily life in South Sudan. Seventy-eight percent of households depend on crop farming or animal husbandry as their primary source of livelihood. South Sudanese crops include sorghum, maize, rice, millet, wheat, pineapple, cotton, groundnuts, sweet potatoes, mangoes, pawpaw, sugarcane, cassava, sesame, and gum. The government of South Sudan estimated that roughly half of its 82 million hectares were arable.

23 ANIMAL HUSBANDRY

There are an estimated 10–20 million head of cattle in the White Nile River valley, reflecting the importance of animal husbandry to South Sudanese. Cattle rustling is a major source of conflict, often stoking ethnic tensions and leading to retributive violence. Chicken, goats, pigs, horses, donkeys, sheep, and other animals are also tended by South Sudanese.

24 FISHING

In the southern provinces and towns, fish is a diet staple. The Nile River yields about 110 varieties of fish, including Nile perch, tilapia, catfish, mudfish, lungfish, moon fish (opah), and electric fish. The commercial fishing sector remains undeveloped.

25 FORESTRY

Roughly 29% of South Sudan is covered by forest. The country supplies a large amount of the world's gum arabic, a substance extracted from the acacia tree and used in the production of medicines, candies, inks, and adhesives. Commercial logging harvests both teak and mahogany.

26 MINING

South Sudan has regions believed to be rich in gold and uranium. It has additional resources in iron ore, silver, copper, aluminum, coal, chromium ore, zinc, mica, diamond, quartz, and tungsten. Commercial mining operations, in their infancy before the start of the civil war, vacated during the conflict, leaving most of the mineral assets untouched.

27 ENERGY AND POWER

South Sudan is one of the poorest countries in the world despite the large quantities of oil contained in the country. Much of the economy depends on this oil, though most people rely on agriculture and farming for their livelihoods. Petroleum discoveries in the south-central region of the former Sudan led to exports of crude oil in 1999. Since then, increases in oil production together with high oil prices in world markets have attracted foreign investment into the area. These developments gave a boost to the economy and serve as a point of tension between Sudan and South Sudan. South Sudan contains a vast majority of the oil wealth, but the pipeline runs through Sudan.

Most South Sudanese still relied on diesel generators for electricity as of 2011. The government has promoted hydroelectric projects to potential investors.

28 INDUSTRY

South Sudan lost many of its industries during the civil war. These industries included sugar, textile, cement, fruit, vegetable, and timber processing plants. As of 2011, the largest manufacturing plant was the Southern Sudan Beverages Ltd, which produces both beer and soft drinks. The Ministry of Commerce, charged with expanding South Sudan's manufacturing industry, sought growth in agro-based industrialization.

29 SCIENCE AND TECHNOLOGY

There was no available data on the status of science and technology in South Sudan in 2011.

30 DOMESTIC TRADE

Most basic goods arrive from Sudan, making South Sudan largely dependent on its northern neighbor.

31 FOREIGN TRADE

In 2011, South Sudanese exports totaled $9.51 billion while imports were $5.33 billion. The resulting balance of trade was a surplus of $4.18 billion. The most important export is oil. Other important exports include oil seeds, especially sesame (22%), cotton (17%), sheep (12%), gold (7.6%), vegetable oil (6.4%), crude vegetable materials (5.3%), and sugar (3.7%). The main imports are a broad range of industrial goods, petroleum products, and foodstuffs, most of which are imported from Sudan.

32 BALANCE OF PAYMENTS

As of 2011 South Sudan did not carry major external debt.

33 BANKING AND SECURITIES

The Bank of Sudan regulates 30 commercial investment and agricultural banks. Commercial banks include Ivory Bank, Nile Commercial Bank, Buffalo Commercial Bank, Bank of Ethiopia, KCB Bank Group, and Equity Bank. There are several microfinance and microcredit institutions in the country, yet only about 1% of households in South Sudan have a bank account.

34 INSURANCE

In 2009, only a handful of foreign-based commercial insurance companies, licensed by the Southern Sudanese government, operated in South Sudan. Insurance products included fire, accident, life, pension, and private and commercial motor vehicle protection.

35 PUBLIC FINANCE

Government estimates in 2009 pegged total government expenditures at US3.04 billion, or roughly 23% of GDP.

36 TAXATION

Government documents published in 2007 advocated an income tax that exempted those making no more than 300 Sudanese pounds per month. For all others, income tax rates were fixed at 10%. Dividends and capital gains were included as income, and a number of standard exemptions were also included.

37 CUSTOMS AND DUTIES

There were no reported customs and duties being levied by the government as of 2011.

38 FOREIGN INVESTMENT

Foreign investment in South Sudan derives predominantly from oil companies. In 2009 the government created the Southern Sudan Investment Authority, which sought to encourage and regulate foreign investment. As a part of its investment policy, the government pledged not to nationalize any businesses.

39 ECONOMIC DEVELOPMENT

Economic development was a primary goal of South Sudan's first government in 2011. Industries such as fruit canning and cotton spinning, in operation prior to the civil war, were in need of restoration, and other planned developments, including paper making and palm oil production, awaited financial and logistical support.

Beginning in 2009, the government sought investors to develop hydroelectric power along rapids south of Juba to stabilize the power supply to the capital. Additional hydroelectric projects were identified in other regions.

Since the signing of the CPA in 2005, major roads were cleared of mines and internal air transport was restored. Few conference or business facilities exist outside of Juba.

40 SOCIAL DEVELOPMENT

The Child Act passed by the Southern Sudanese government in 2008 enunciated protections for children against abuse, early marriage, negative or harmful social customs, and child labor. The protections were reaffirmed in the 2011 Transitional Constitution of the Republic of South Sudan. The document also protected indigenous languages, separation of church and state, and ethnic and gender equality. Freedom of expression and the media, as well as the right to access basic services, were also enshrined.

41 HEALTH

Lack of access to clean water has caused serious health problems in South Sudan, as several diseases are carried through the water supply. Additionally, widespread starvation and malnutrition has resulted from chronic instability and warfare. Malaria, schistosomiasis, sleeping sickness, tuberculosis, and various forms of dysentery all persist throughout the country.

In 2006 the CIA reported that the infant mortality rate was 102 deaths per 1000 live births. The HIV/AIDS infection rate, as of 2009, was 3.1%.

42 HOUSING

Tukuls, cone-shaped dwellings made of mud, serve as homes for 83% of the population.

43 EDUCATION

Out of the population over the age of 14, only 27% are literate. There is a wide disparity between male and female literacy rates: 40% for males compared to 16% for females. Only 37% of the population above the age of six have ever attended school. UNESCO reported that in 2011 the student–teacher ratio was 100:1 and nearly double that in other states. Furthermore, only 12% of teachers were female. In 2010, 262,300 male students were enrolled in primary school compared to 164,000 female students. That number dwindled to 15,700 male students and 6,700 female students by the end of primary school. In the last grade of secondary school, enrollment numbered 1,300 for male students and 400 for female students.

The few South Sudanese who obtain higher education typically do so in other countries. In an effort to encourage their return, the government announced a program in August 2011 to repay the student loans of nationals willing to return to South Sudan and work in the public or non-profit sector.

44 LIBRARIES AND MUSEUMS

There were no libraries or museums of note in South Sudan as of 2011.

45 MEDIA

Only 15% of households in the country own a phone. Some 59% of those living in urban areas have a phone, compared to 8% in rural areas. There are three mobile phone service providers in the country.

46 ORGANIZATIONS

The World Health Organization, the YWCA, and several microfinance organizations have offices in South Sudan. Numerous organizations were present before South Sudanese independence, and most were expected maintain offices in the country.

47 TOURISM, TRAVEL, AND RECREATION

Civil war and conservative Islamic rule discouraged tourism in Sudan after colonial independence. Previously, big-game hunting in the South Sudanese rain forest and boat excursions on the Nile attracted foreign tourists. As of 2011, the government had identified seven national parks and twelve game reserves. These reserves, inaccessible during the civil war, are home to large populations of animals. In 2011 the Ministry of Wildlife and Tourism was tasked to work on both the preservation and commercialization of these regions. At least 75 commercial hotels and lodges operated in South Sudan in 2011, with roughly half of them based in Juba.

Wrestling matches between two young men, organized as a celebration of the harvest season, were a traditional event in South Sudanese culture. The competition attracted numerous spectators and was accompanied by singing and drumming. Basketball is popular and several South Sudanese players have been drafted by teams in the US National Basketball Association (NBA). Soccer is also an important sport in many villages and is a favorite South Sudanese pastime.

48 FAMOUS PERSONS

The recording artist Yaba Angelosi is from South Sudan. Current NBA player Luol Deng plays for the Chicago Bulls, and former player Manute Bol (d. 2010) was also born within South Sudan's borders. Bol, at 7 ft 7 in (2.31 meters), has the distinction of being one of the tallest players to ever play in the NBA.

49 DEPENDENCIES

South Sudan has no territories or colonies.

50 BIBLIOGRAPHY

Beswick, Stephanie. *Sudan's Blood Memory: The Legacy of War, Ethnicity, and Slavery in Early South Sudan*. Rochester, NY: University of Rochester Press, 2004.

Natsios, Andrew S. *Sudan, South Sudan, and Darfur: What Everyone Needs to Know*. New York: Oxford University Press, 2012.

SUDAN

Republic of the Sudan
Jumhuriyat as-Sudan

CAPITAL: Khartoum

FLAG: The national flag consists of a tricolor of red, white, and black horizontal stripes, with a green triangle at the hoist.

ANTHEM: *Nahnu Djundulla Djundulwatan (We Are the Army of God and of Our Land).*

MONETARY UNIT: The Sudanese dinar (SDG) is a paper currency of 100 piasters (qurush) or 1,000 milliemes. SDG1 = US$0.373622 (or US$1 = SDG2.67650) as of 2012.

WEIGHTS AND MEASURES: The metric system is the legal standard, but a highly diverse system based on Egyptian and British standards is in local use.

HOLIDAYS: Independence Day, 1 January; Unity Day, 3 March; Uprising Day, 6 April; Decentralization Day, 1 July; Christmas, 25 December. Movable Muslim religious holidays include the 1st of Muharram (Muslim New Year), Eid al-Fitr, Eid al-Adha, and Milad an-Nabi.

TIME: 2 p.m. = noon GMT.

¹LOCATION, SIZE, AND EXTENT

Situated in northeast Africa, Sudan covers an area of 1,861,484 sq km (718,723 sq mi). It is bounded on the N by Egypt, on the NE by the Red Sea, on the E by Eritrea and Ethiopia, on the S by South Sudan, on the W by Chad, on the SW by the Central African Republic, and on the NW by Libya.

The Anglo-Egyptian Agreement of 19 January 1899 established the parallel of 22°N as the international boundary between Egypt and Sudan. In 1902, however, a special administrative boundary was delineated between the Nile and the Red Sea, in order to facilitate the administration of nomadic tribes and to maintain the continuity of certain tribal areas in the border region. In 2001, the countries agreed to discuss the creation of an "area of integration" for this overlapping territory and both governments agreed to withdraw military forces from the region. The Egypt-Sudan boundary west of the Nile runs 892 km (554 mi); east of the Nile, the international boundary is 383 km (238 mi), and the administrative boundary is 357 km (222 mi). Including this administrative line, Sudan's total boundary length is 6,751 km (4,195 mi). South Sudan seceded from Sudan by national referendum, which became official 9 July 2011.

Sudan's capital city, Khartoum, is located in the northeast central part of the country.

²TOPOGRAPHY

The greatest part of Sudan is a vast plain traversed by the northward-flowing Nile River and its tributaries. Widely separated mountain chains and many hilly areas often reach altitudes of more than 2,000 m (6,500 ft). The northern area is mainly desert, including the Nubian Desert, with rock at or near the surface covered by thin soils of low fertility. The western undulating sandy wastes merge into the Red Sea Hills to the east.

The dominating geographic feature is the Nile River, formed near Khartoum by the confluence of the Blue Nile and White Nile rivers. There are natural harbors at Port Sudan (Bur Sudan) and Suakin on the Red Sea.

³CLIMATE

In the northern plains and desert region, average temperatures range from 32°C (90°F) in winter (November to February) to 42°C (108°F) in summer (March to June); the hottest months are May and June. In the central and southern regions, average temperatures are 27° to 29°C (80° to 85°F). Rainfall decreases from south to north, the annual average varying from 120 cm (47 in) in the south to less than 10 cm (4 in) in the north; the rainy season is from July to September. Climatic hazards-sandstorms in the northern deserts and flooding rains in the central belt-often interfere with railroad traffic. The most temperate climate occurs in the Red Sea Hills.

⁴FLORA AND FAUNA

The World Resources Institute estimates that there are 3,137 plant species in Sudan. In addition, Sudan is home to 302 mammal, 952 bird, 162 reptile, and 15 amphibian species. The calculation reflects the total number of distinct species residing in the country, not the number of endemic species.

The acacia desert shrub and acacia short-grass shrub grow in the northern desert and the grasslands of the west. The broadleafed tropical woodland and forest region is for the most part in the southwest, where areas of luxuriant growth and closed forests are found; grass covers much of the steppe area of the southeast. Date palms line the banks of the Nile. Wildlife includes most of the mammals, birds, and reptiles common to central Africa. Many varieties of fish are found in the rivers and in the coastal waters of the Red Sea.

5 ENVIRONMENT

A shortage of potable water inhibited agriculture, animal husbandry, and human settlement in much of Sudan. Water resources totaled 4.6 cu km (1.1 cu mi) while water usage was 37.32 cu km (8.95 cu mi) per year. Domestic water usage accounted for 3% of total usage, industrial for 1%, and agricultural for 96%. Per capita water usage totaled 261 cu m (9,217 cu ft) per year. The water on the nation's coasts was also polluted by industrial by-products, oil, and sewage. Sudan's cities produced about 1.1 million tons of solid waste per year.

The nation's agricultural land was threatened by the advance of the desert. Government agencies vested with environmental responsibilities included the National Committee for Environment (within the National Council for Research) and the ministries of agriculture, natural resources, irrigation, energy, and health. The World Resources Institute reported that Sudan had designated 11.41 million hectares (28.19 million acres) of land for protection as of 2006. The UN reported in 2008 that carbon dioxide emissions in Sudan totaled 11,512 kilotons.

Due to uncontrolled hunting, the nation's wildlife was threatened. Protected areas included Dinder National Park, an ecologically sensitive area between the sahel and highlands, which was listed as a Ramsar wetland site and under threat from encroachment by cattle herding. According to a 2011 report issued by the International Union for Conservation of Nature and Natural Resources (IUCN), the number of threatened species included 15 types of mammals, 15 species of birds, 3 types of reptiles, 19 species of fish, 45 species of invertebrates, and 16 species of plants. Threatened species included the waldrapp, northern white rhinoceros, Tora hartebeest, slender-horned gazelle, painted hunting dog and hawksbill turtle. The Sahara oryx has become extinct in the wild.

6 POPULATION

The US Central Intelligence Agency (CIA) reported the population of Sudan in 2011 to be approximately 36,787,012, which placed it at number 34 in population among the 196 nations of the world. In 2011, approximately 2.7% of the population was over 65 years of age, with another 42.1% under 15 years of age. The median age in Sudan was 18.5 years. There were 1.03 males for every female in the country. The population's annual rate of change was 2.484%. The projected population for the year 2025 was 56,700,000. Population density in Sudan was calculated at 20 people per sq km (52 people per sq mi).

The UN estimated that 40% of the population lived in urban areas, and that urban populations had an annual rate of change of 3.7%. The largest urban area was Khartoum, with a population of 5 million.

7 MIGRATION

Estimates of Sudan's net migration rate, as reported by the CIA in 2011, amounted to -0.29 migrants per 1,000 citizens. The total number of emigrants living abroad was 967,500, and the total number of immigrants living in Sudan was 753,400. As a result of

the war between the Sudanese government and the Sudan People's Liberation Army in the south and ongoing instability, UNHCR reported a population of concern nearly 2 million people in early 2011. This population was composed of 387,288 refugees originating from Sudan, 23,713 asylum seekers and 7,070 returnees. Within Sudan there were 178,308 refugees, 6,046 asylum seekers and 1,624,100 internally displaced persons (IDPs).

Since the 1970s, the Sudanese government has welcomed refugees as a result of war or famine. As a result of the UN High Commissioner for Refugees (UNHCR) repatriation programs, 25,000 Eritreans and 62,000 Ethiopians were sent home in 1994 and 1995. In 2004 Sudan experienced a political and humanitarian crisis; a severe drought coupled with genocide in Darfur as the government supported Arab militias against Black Sudanese. Over 50,000 people died and 1.6 million Black Sudanese were displaced. The UN labeled Sudan the "world's worst humanitarian crisis" in 2004. At the end of 2004, there were also 662,302 internally displaced persons who were at a camp in West Darfur, and another 37,416 former Eritrean refugees in Sudan.

8 ETHNIC GROUPS

Prior to the partitioning of the country, Sudanese Arabs accounted for an estimated 70% of the population. In all, there were nearly 600 ethnic groups, with the Fur, Beja, Nuba, and Fallata being among the most prominent. Foreigners constituted 2% of the total populace.

9 LANGUAGES

Arabic, the official language, was the mother tongue of about half the population. Besides standard Arabic, Nubian and Ta Bedawie were also commonly spoken. English (also an official language) was used widely, in many cases serving as a lingua franca among the southern tribes. In all, more than 400 diverse dialects of Nilotic, Nilo-Hamitic, and Sudanic languages were spoken.

10 RELIGIONS

The state religion was Islam, primarily Sunni. As an important transit station for Mecca-bound African pilgrims, Sudan remained intimately linked with the Islamic world. Among the Muslims, religious brotherhoods (tarigat) played an important role in sectarian and communal life. The two most popular brotherhoods were the Ansar, which was closely associated with the Umma Party, and the Khatimia, which was associated with the Democratic Unionist Party. The dominant National Congress Party was also primarily Muslim.

11 TRANSPORTATION

The CIA reported that prior to division, Sudan had a total of 19,232 km (11,950 mi) of roads as of 2000, of which 12,655 km (7,863 mi) were paved. Railroads extended for 4,508 km (2,801 mi). There were 32 airports, which transported 606,558 passengers in 2009 according to the World Bank. Sudan had approximately 4,068 km (2,528 mi) of navigable waterways.

With the exception of a few interurban bus lines and taxi systems, all land, sea, river, and air transportation facilities were owned by the state. The country's railroad linked most of the main towns of Sudan. The principal terminals were: Khartoum and Port Sudan in the east; Wadi Halfa' in the north (on the Egyptian bor-

LOCATION: 23° to 9°N; 22° to 38° E. BOUNDARY LENGTHS: Egypt 1,273 kilometers (789 miles); Red Sea coastline, 853 kilometers (529 miles); Eritrea, 605 kilometers (376 miles); Ethiopia, 769 kilometers (478 miles); Central African Republic, 175 kilometers (109 miles); Chad, 1,360 kilometers (845 miles); Libya, 383 kilometers (238 miles); South Sudan, 2,184 kilometers (1,357 miles). TERRITORIAL SEA LIMIT: 12 miles.

der); Al Ubayyid in the center of the country; and Nyala in the west. 'Aṭbarah on the Nile River (north of Khartoum) was an important junction and seat of the central administration, repair shops, and equipment-manufacturing plants of the Sudan Railways Corp.

In 1966, a bridge linking Khartoum North and Omdurman, and the enlargement of the bridge on the White Nile between Khartoum and Omdurman were completed, facilitating the circulation of traffic around these three towns. A major road (1,197 km/744 mi) linking Port Sudan with Khartoum was completed in 1980.

Sudan, as of 2008 and prior to being divided, had 4,068 km (2,530 mi) of navigable inland waterways, of which 1,723 km (1,072 mi) on the Blue and While Nile rivers were open year round. River transport services linked many communities. The White Nile route between Kusti and Juba (1,436 km/892 mi) was of crucial importance. Port Sudan, on the Red Sea, was primarily a cargo port, handling all of Sudan's cotton exports as well as most food imports. Passenger traffic was insignificant except for Mecca-bound pilgrims. A small Sudanese merchant marine was founded with assistance from the former Yugoslavia.

Prior to partition, there were 19 airports with paved runways. There were also four heliports. The international airport was at Khartoum. The state-owned Sudan Airways Corp., founded in 1947, linked the main cities and provided extensive international service. Flights to the south were suspended in the mid-1980s because of the civil war.

12 HISTORY

The salient events in recorded Sudanese history occurred in the northern half of the country. The kingdom of Kush (or Cush), rich in gold and iron and sustained by irrigation from the Nile flood-waters, broke away from Egyptian rule about 1000 BC. It became a separate kingdom, with its capital at Napatan, and developed under the pervasive influence of Egyptian culture. It conquered Egypt for a time (736–657 BC), moved its capital to Meroe (now Merowe) in 538 BC, and was destroyed about AD 350 by the Ak-sumite (or Axumite) Empire in Ethiopia.

Following the fall of Kush, two successor kingdoms arose: Maqurra, in northern Sudan, with its capital at Old Dongola and Alwa, in central Sudan, with its capital at Soba. Maqurra fell in the 15th century to an alliance of Arabs and Mamlukes from Egypt. Around the beginning of the 17th century, Alwa was conquered by an alliance of Arabs and a loose confederation of tribes ruled by the "Black Sultans" of the Funj dynasty, with their capital at Sennar. The inhabitants of the south, until the 20th century, lived in primitive tribal isolation, interrupted only by explorers and pe-rennial slave raiding.

In the 1820s, the autonomous Ottoman viceroy of Egypt, Mu-hammad 'Ali, defeated the Funj sultan and brought Sudan under Turco-Egyptian rule, which lasted until 1885. By then, most of the Sudanese tribes had revolted against the harshness and corruption of the regime and rallied under the leadership of a northern ship-wright, Muhammad Ahmad bin 'Abdallah. He proclaimed him-self the Mahdi (Rightly Guided One), whose coming to achieve the complete victory of Islam had been prophesied in Muslim tra-dition. After decisively defeating a series of punitive expeditions, the Mahdi took possession of Khartoum in 1885, whereupon his troops captured and beheaded the governor, Gen. Charles Gor-don, one of the British officers in the employ of Egypt. The Mah-di installed himself as head of a theocratic state, which survived until 1898, when an Anglo-Egyptian invasion force under Gen. Horatio Herbert Kitchener defeated the Mahdi's successor, the Khalifa ('Abdallah bin Muhammad), in the battle of Omdurman. British rule was set up under a nominal Anglo-Egyptian "condo-minium" following a French attempt to seize parts of Sudan, an effort thwarted by Kitchener at Fashoda (now Kodok) in an inci-dent that almost provoked a war between France and Great Brit-ain. British administration did much to restore law and order, re-press slave trading, and bring modern government and economic stability to Anglo-Egyptian Sudan, as it was then called.

Sudanese nationalism erupted after World War I with Egyptian support and received its decisive impetus during World War II, when British-led Sudanese troops distinguished themselves in re-pelling a vastly superior Italian force. An Egyptian scheme to join Egypt and Sudan in a dual monarchy under King Faruk miscar-ried, as did other proposals for the "unity of the Nile Valley." Pro-longed Anglo-Egyptian negotiations for agreement on a mutual-ly acceptable form of Sudanese independence reached fruition in 1953, after Faruk was deposed.

The Republic of the Sudan, under a parliamentary government, was proclaimed on 1 January 1956. On 17 November 1958, a mili-tary dictatorship was installed, headed by Lt. Gen. Ibrahim Ab-boud, commander-in-chief of the armed forces, after a bloodless coup that had the support of some party leaders. President Ab-boud's military regime was overthrown on 26 October 1964, and civilian politicians ruled for the next five years.

A revolutionary council led by Col. Gaafar Mohammed Nimei-ri (Ja'far Muhammad Numayri) overthrew the government in a bloodless coup on 25 May 1969 and established the Democratic Republic of the Sudan. The new government suspended the con-stitution, the Supreme Council of State, the National Assembly, and all political parties. The ex-president and former ministers were arrested. Nimeiri became prime minister in October 1969. On 25 May 1971, he proclaimed that Sudan would become a one-party state, with the Sudanese Socialist Union the sole political organization. A provisional constitution was promulgated on 13 August 1971, and Nimeiri, running unopposed, was elected presi-dent in September, receiving 98.6% of the votes cast. One of Ni-meiri's most significant acts was to bring an end to the sporadic civil war that had plagued Sudan since independence. A settle-ment with autonomist forces in the south was reached in Febru-ary 1972, when negotiators for the Sudanese government and the South Sudan Liberation Front, the Anyanya rebels, agreed on a cease-fire and on autonomy for the southern provinces.

Nimeiri was reelected without opposition in 1977 and 1983, but his regime had to weather considerable turmoil both domestically and in relations with neighboring countries, especially Libya. An abortive left-wing coup attempt in July 1971 led to the execution of leading Sudanese Communists; the banning of the Trade Union Federation, the Public Servants Union, and the Teachers Union (all formerly Communist-dominated); and the expulsion of East German security advisers. Another alleged coup was foiled in Jan-uary 1973, and an abortive, Libyan-inspired attempt on Nimeiri's life was disclosed by the Sudanese government in April 1974. Stu-dent riots and disclosure of yet another abortive coup came in Oc-tober 1974, and during the following year the Nimeiri government faced and successfully suppressed at least two military rebellions.

In July 1976, an attempted coup by the Ansar brotherhood, al-legedly with Libyan support, was crushed. In subsequent years, Nimeiri charged repeatedly that Libya was aiding Muslim dissi-dents in Sudan. On 16 March 1984, Omdurman was bombed by what Sudan, Egypt, and the United States claimed (but Libya de-nied) was a Libyan air force TU-22. Nimeiri declared a state of emergency in April 1984 to cope with protests over rising prices and a new government Islamization program (in July of that year, the National People's Assembly rejected his attempt to make Su-dan an official Islamic state). The state of emergency ended in Sep-tember 1984, but by then a new rebellion was under way in the south, which had become alienated by Nimeiri's efforts to restrict its autonomy and apply Shari'ah (Muslim law). Many Sudanese were shocked by the execution of Mahmoud Mohammed Taha, a popular Muslim political and religious leader, for heresy (in criticizing the application of Shari'ah) in January 1985. Riots broke out in the spring of 1985, when, in order to gain new loans from international creditors, Nimeiri removed subsidies on basic commodities, causing prices to rise. On 7 April 1985, Nimeiri was replaced by a military council headed by Gen. Abdel-Rahman Swar ad-Dhahab. The country was renamed the Republic of Sudan, the ruling Sudanese Socialist Union was abolished, political and press freedom was restored, and food prices were lowered. Sudan reverted to a policy of nonalignment in foreign policy, backing away from its close ties with Egypt and the United States.

Unrest in the South

General elections held in April 1986 resulted in a moderate civilian coalition government headed by Prime Minister Sadiq al-Mahdi. The government's chief problem was the continuing rebellion by the Sudan People's Liberation Movement (SPLM), which controlled much of the south and prevented voting there. The SPLM halted air traffic (including food relief) to the south and opposed two major projects vital to the economy—oil exploration and a canal that would provide water to the parched north. The coalition government was headed by the northern-based Ummah Party. It began searching for a formula to unite the country with the SPLM which, unlike the earlier Anyanya, was also committed to unity. Divisions with government over meeting key SPLM demands, most especially the repeal of Islamic law, prolonged the civil war. In March 1989, a new government composed of Ummah Party and Democratic Unionist Party (DUP) ministers agreed to accommodate the SPLM.

However, on 30 June 1989, a group of army officers led by Brig. Omar Hasan al-Bashir overthrew the civilian government. Mahdi was arrested and fighting in the south escalated. The coup makers created a National Salvation Revolutionary Command Council (RCC), a junta composed of 15 military officers assisted by a civilian cabinet, suspending the 1985 transitional constitution, abrogating press freedoms, and dissolving all parties and trade unions. In September 1989 the government sponsored a "National Dialogue Conference on the Political System" which produced a proposal for a new federal system of government. On 23 April 1990, Umar Hassan Ahmad al-Bashir declared a state of emergency and dissolved parliament. An alleged coup attempt prompted that move. The following day, 28 officers were court martialed and executed.

Despite these measures and the efforts by third parties to further peace, including former US President Jimmy Carter and Nigeria, few positive results were obtained. With the fall of Ethiopia's Marxist government in 1991, the SPLM rebel faction lost its chief patron. A 1992 government offensive, coupled with a major political split in the SPLM, reduced rebel-held territory while increasing casualties and displaced persons with the latter numbering, at times, over 2 million.

Civilian rule returned nominally to Sudan in 1993, when the RCC was formally dissolved and al-Bashir was declared president. However, he retained control over the military, and the government was dominated by the fundamentalist National Islamic Front (NIF), under the leadership of Hassan al-Turabi. Al-Bashir was elected president with a reported 75% of the vote in the 1996 national elections, which were boycotted by major opposition

groups. Following the elections, al-Turabi was elected speaker of parliament.

Because of its militant Islamic policies, Sudan became increasingly isolated. Sudan further distanced itself from the West by giving sanctuary to Muslim rebels from Tunisia and Algeria, to the Hezbollah (Party of God), to Palestinian rebels, and to the Lord's Resistance Army in Uganda. Sudan also accepted military assistance from Iran. The regime further radicalized Islamic practice by purging the civil service, the armed forces, the judiciary, and the educational system of non-Muslims, and by promulgating a penal code based on Islamic law. The UN General Assembly condemned Sudan's human rights violations in 1993. The United States designated Sudan as a terrorist country that year; tensions with Egypt developed as well.

Under international pressure, Sudan adopted a new constitution in 1998 providing for a multiparty government; registration of new parties began in 1999. In the same year, fighting in the oil-rich southern part of the country escalated into wholesale destruction. Human rights abuses multiplied as factional rivalries intensified between rebels loyal to SPLM leader John Garang and militants of the Nasir faction of the SPLM. The latter rejected all cooperation with the Islamic north. Famine relief efforts in the region had to be suspended owing to rebel attacks. In March 2000, a number of nongovernmental organizations (NGOs) left the country after refusing to comply with restrictions imposed by rebel authorities.

In the meantime, a power struggle between President Bashir and Hassan Turabi, who was a party leader, parliamentary speaker, and architect of the nation's Islamist policies, ended with Turabi's forced removal and the dismissal of the National Assembly in a military raid ordered by Bashir in December 1999. In widely boycotted and discredited elections held in December 2000, Bashir was reelected and the NCP gained 355 seats to 5 for nonpartisans in the National Assembly. The struggle between Bashir and Turabi continued; Bashir had Turabi imprisoned from March 2004 to June 2005.

On 26 May 2004, the Khartoum government and the Sudan People's Liberation Army (SPLA) signed a power-sharing agreement in Naivasha, Kenya. On 19 November the two sides signed a pledge to end the 21-year civil war in front of the 15 UN Security Council members meeting in Nairobi; it was only the fourth time the Security Council had met outside its New York headquarters. On 9 January 2005, a comprehensive peace agreement was signed, ending more than two years of intense negotiations. In July 2005, John Garang of the SPLM was sworn in as vice president of Sudan (Bashir remained president). Just three weeks later Garang was killed in a helicopter crash. Rioting broke out in Khartoum and other cities upon news of his death.

In September 2005, a power-sharing government was formed in Khartoum. That October, an autonomous government was formed in the south, according to the January 2005 peace agreement. Former rebels dominated the administration.

Darfur

Beginning in 2003 in Darfur—the western region of Sudan, which is slightly larger than France—Arab nomads, supported by the Khartoum military and government-backed Janjaweed militia groups began to attack the Fur people, subsistence farmers who make up the major ethnic group in the region. The Fur were supported by the rebel Sudan Liberation Movement/Army (SLM/A) and the Justice and Equality Movement (JEM) faction of the SLM/A. The SLM/A in early 2003 began to attack government and military outposts, with the intent of gaining influence in the affairs of the region after having been systematically marginalized socioeconomically.

The government armed the nomads and sent the Janjaweed, which translated means "men with guns on the backs of beasts," to raid black villages on horseback, on camels, and in trucks, with guns and machetes. The Janjaweed rampages resulted in what has been called one of the world's worst humanitarian crises with countless rapes, the murders of more than 70,000 people, and the displacement of nearly 2 million people.

The rebels claimed the depopulation of villages and consequent changes in land ownership were part of a government strategy to change the entire demography of Darfur. The government denied all humanitarian agencies access to the region; refugees were housed in camps on the border of Chad. In April 2004, the two sides agreed to a temporary cease-fire to allow for humanitarian agencies to reach those in need of help, but the Janjaweed continued their attacks. In May 2004, the UN condemned the attacks on civilians and called on the Khartoum government to prevent the Janjaweed from carrying out strikes against the black African population. In July 2004, the US Congress declared the mass killings of civilians in Darfur to be genocide. By 2007, the number of dead—many from hunger and disease in addition to violence—was estimated at between 200,000 and 400,000.

In May 2006, the Khartoum government and the SLM/A in Darfur signed a peace agreement. Two smaller rebel groups rejected the accord. That August, Sudan rejected a UN resolution calling for a UN peacekeeping force in Darfur. President Bashir said the force would compromise Sudan's sovereignty. However, an African Union (AU) peacekeeping force was deployed in the country beginning in 2004, and by May 2007 its strength was 7,000 troops. In April 2007, Sudan announced it would accept a partial UN troop deployment to reinforce AU peacekeepers in Darfur, but not the 20,000-member force called for originally. That May, the International Criminal Court (ICC) issued arrest warrants for a minister and a Janjaweed militia leader suspected of war crimes in Darfur.

On 29 May 2007, US President George Bush announced he was imposing new unilateral economic sanctions against Sudan for failing to allow the deployment of UN forces and end its support for the Janjaweed. In July, the UN Security Council authorized a peacekeeping force of 26,000 troops for Darfur. Sudan said it would cooperate with the UN-AU Mission in Darfur (UNAMID). At the end of September 2007, hundreds of Darfurian rebels overran an AU peacekeeping base in Darfur, killing at least 10 soldiers, possibly kidnapping dozens more, and seizing heavy weapons and other supplies. The UN took over command of the Darfur peacekeeping operation from the AU on 31 December 2007.

By that time, the situation in Darfur had become more complex and dangerous. The Terjem and the Mahria, heavily armed Arab tribes that raped and pillaged together as Janjaweed militias, faced off in South Darfur, raiding each other's villages and causing Arab tribesmen to flee into displacement camps. The new Arab-versus-Arab dimension complicated the already dire crisis. The crisis was further compounded by the location of most of the country's oil in the south and by most of the infrastructure in the north. Leaders were confronted with reforming an extremely militarized government and with equitably dividing Sudan's large and growing oil profits. By December 2007, leaders from the government and the south announced that they had resolved most of their differences and that the SPLM would rejoin the national unity government. However, to make matters worse, refugees from Ethiopia and Chad were crossing into Sudan, where they found conditions as bad as or worse than those they left.

In March 2009, the International Criminal Court issued an arrest warrant for Sudanese president Omar al-Bashir on charges of war crimes and crimes against humanity. Thousands of citizens took to the streets in central Khartoum to show their support for their president, who scoffed at the warrant. In an address to those assembled, al-Bashir asserted that the true criminals were the leaders of the United States and Europe.

Relations between Sudan and the United States appeared to warm later in the year as on 20 October 2009 the United States unveiled a controversial new approach to Sudan that advocated engagement over isolation for the government of Khartoum. While the new plan included both incentives and sanctions—depending on the government's behavior and the progress achieved with human rights in the Darfur region—analysts described the policy as more conciliatory than the previous Bush-era policy to Sudan. Sudan appeared to welcome many aspects of the new proposal. Many human rights groups criticized the proposal as too lenient, citing the moral ambiguity of engaging with a government run by an internationally wanted war criminal. At the time of the announcement, the details of the sanctions and incentives were kept classified by the Obama administration. A referendum on the future status of Darfur was expected in 2012.

North-South Partition

The nation's first multi-party elections in 24 years were held from 11 to 13 April 2010, with voters called to the polls to elect a president, 450 members for the national assembly, and local government officials for 25 states. Incumbent Omar al-Bashir, representing the National Congress Party, was the favored candidate because his leading opponents, Sadiq al-Mahdi of the Ummah party and Yassir Arman of the Sudan People's Liberation Movement, cited electoral rigging and withdrew from the race. Many opposition parties boycotted the election. Several difficulties were reported from polling stations in the south, including a lack of printed ballots and confusion over voter registration lists. One week following the vote, counters were still waiting for the delivery of several ballot boxes, leading the National Elections Commission to announce an official delay in the results.

When the official results for the presidency were released 26 April, al-Bashir was declared the winner with 68% of the vote. Despite having withdrawn from the race, Arman received 22%. Salva Kiir of the Sudan People's Liberation Movement (SPLM) was declared the leader of the semi-autonomous south with 93% of the vote.

The 2005 Comprehensive Peace Agreement (CPA), which had ended the north-south war, had given Southern Sudan considerably more autonomy from the north, and, most importantly, the opportunity to vote for independence five years later. After numerous debates and delays, the referendum for independence in the south took place on 9 January 2011. Voting was orderly, and the Southern Sudan Referendum Commission reported that the measure had passed with some 3,792,518 (98.83%) votes in favor of separation. As a result, South Sudan became an independent country on 9 July 2011.

Although the referendum was peaceful, rebel activity continued on the border between the Sudan and South Sudan, particularly in the Abyei region, which was dubbed "Sudan's Jerusalem" since it was claimed by both northern and southern Sudan and was in dispute for years. In April 2011, fighting between South Sudan's army and rebel groups broke out in two states in the region, resulting in an estimated 180 deaths. Two separate incidents of fighting occurred in Unity and in the Upper Nile states, both parts of South Sudan. In both cases, clashes occurred between rebel groups and the South Sudanese army, although the first involved the Sudan People's Liberation Army, based in South Sudan, and the second was led by a former northern army commander. South Sudan was eventually able to restore order, but observers worried that the new state army would not be able to hold South Sudan together after independence.

In June 2011, Sudan's government and representatives from South Sudan signed an agreement to co-govern controversial border states. UN troops from Ethiopia were dispatched into Abyei to diffuse tensions and prevent the deal from unraveling. Although no actual ceasefire was reached, each side made compromises to ensure the administration of Blue Nile and Southern Kordofan states. On 9 July 2011 the South's secession became official, and Africa's newest state was greeted with much fanfare in the south marked by ceremonies, speeches, parades and visiting heads of state. Nonetheless, periodic and deadly clashes between Sudanese and South Sudanese forces continued along the border regions throughout 2011.

13 GOVERNMENT

Historically, the government experienced several coups and reconfigurations. A constitution took effect on 8 May 1973—Sudan's first permanent governing document since independence in 1956. It established a presidential system and a one-party state, with the Sudanese Socialist Union (SSU) as the only political party. Nominated by the SSU for a six-year renewable term, the president (after confirmation by national plebiscite) appointed vice presidents, a prime minister, and cabinet ministers, who were answerable to him. The president was also supreme commander of the armed forces.

That constitution was suspended on 6 April 1985. A temporary constitution was established on 10 October 1985, pending a permanent one to be drawn up by the National Assembly elected in 1986. A six-member civilian Supreme Council, including a president, was established as the nation's executive body in 1986, replacing the military council that had seized power in 1985.

After a 1989 military coup, the 1985 transitional constitution was suspended. In January 1991, the RCC imposed Islamic law in the six northern provinces. Executive and legislative authority was vested in a 15-member Revolutionary Command Council (RCC). Its chairman, acting as prime minister, appointed a 300-member transitional National Assembly. In mid-October 1993, Bashir dissolved the RCC and officially declared himself president. On 30 October 1993, President Bashir announced a new, predominantly civilian cabinet that consisted of 20 federal ministers, most of whom retained their previous cabinet positions. On 9 February 1995, Bashir abolished three ministries and divided their portfolios to create several new ministries. These changes had the effect of increasing the National Islamic Front's presence at the ministerial level and consolidating its control over the Ministry of Foreign Affairs. Bashir was elected to a five-year term in March 1996. In 1998, a new constitution was promulgated that nominally provided for a multiparty political system. Registration of new parties took place in 1999.

Under the comprehensive peace agreement of 2005, a bicameral national legislature was established, consisting of a Council of States (50 seats; members indirectly elected by state legislatures to serve six-year terms) and a National Assembly (450 seats; members presently appointed, but in the future 75% of members to be directly elected and 25% elected in special or indirect elections; to serve six-year terms). The 2005 agreement led to the eventual independence of South Sudan in 2011.

14 POLITICAL PARTIES

Prior to the partition in July 2011, Sudan had some 15 political parties dominating national politics. As was true during Sudan's struggle for independence, political parties were personality- and regionally-based first, followed by ideology or party platforms. The most powerful force before 1958 was the Ansar sect and the Ansar-sponsored Ummah Party. Other parties were closely affiliated with the Khatmiyah sect, led by Sayyid 'Ali al-Mirghani; the leftist-dominated labor unions; the Graduates Congress, an organization of college graduates; and leaders of the black tribes of the south. For the first three years of the country's independence, these parties were strongly divided on such issues as union with Egypt (opposed by the Ummah Party); alignment with the West in economic and foreign affairs (opposed by the Khatmiyah, the labor unions, and the Graduates); Communism (courted by elements in most parties and labor unions); political secularization (sought by leaders not aligned with the religious sects); federalism (demanded by southern spokesmen); and fear of the royal aspirations of the Mahdi family. These divisions helped bring about the downfall of several coalition cabinets and finally weakened the parliamentary system to the point where the army could successfully carry out a coup without encountering resistance. Political activity was banned in 1958 and was not resumed until the overthrow of the Abboud government in October 1964.

During the mid-1960s, two regional parties—the Southern Front, formed in 1964 by Southerners living in the north, and the Sudan African National Union (SANU), formed in 1966 by Sudanese exiles in Uganda—advocated self-determination and independence for the south.

In 1966, the Ummah Party split into two groups, one conservativeand one progressive. The following year, the Democratic Unionist Party (DUP) was formed from the amalgamation of the National Unionist Party and the People's Democratic Party. In the May 1968 elections, the DUP won 101 of 218 parliamentary seats, while no other party captured more than 36.

After the 1969 military takeover, existing political parties were banned and a special attempt was made, beginning in 1971, to suppress the powerful Communist Party. The 1973 constitution provided for a one-party state, with the Sudanese Socialist Union (SSU), established by Nimeiri in 1971, as the sole legal political organization. In elections for the National People's Assembly, only candidates approved by the SSU were allowed to run.

In April 1986, in the first free elections held since 1968, the Ummah Party won 99 of 301 parliamentary seats, the DUP won 63, and the fundamentalist National Islamic Front (NIF) won 51. The remaining seats went mainly to regional parties, but 37 seats from the south were unfilled because of the civil war and the boycott of the elections by the Sudanese People's Liberation Front. The Ummah Party, the DUP, and four southern parties formed a coalition government, with the NIF in opposition. In August 1987, the coalition fell apart when the DUP broke away from the Ummah Party after an election in which it lost one of its two seats on the Supreme Council to an Ummah candidate, reportedly because the DUP candidate had been a close aide of Nimeiri. Prime Minister Sadiq al-Mahdi, aligned with the Ummah Party, retained his position until his overthrow in June 1989.

The Revolutionary Command Council (RCC) banned all parties in 1989 except for the NIF, whose members and supporters held most key positions. After the dissolution of the RCC in October 1993, the NIF further tightened its grip on the state. The RCC's executive and legislative powers were transferred to the president and the Transitional National Assembly (TNA), Sudan's appointed legislative body, which was replaced by the National Assembly elected in March 1996.

The main opposition to the central government became the Sudan People's Liberation Movement (SPLM), which joined forces in 1997 with a new alliance of northern rebels known as the National Democratic Alliance. This opposition was sponsored by Ethiopia and Eritrea and encouraged by the United States, which held the government of Sudan responsible for sponsoring international terrorism and for committing atrocities against its Christian population in the south.

The 1998 constitution (revised in 2000) recognized political parties other than the NIF for the first time since 1989. However, parties had to accept the constitution and refrain from advocating or using violence against the regime. Approved parties included the ruling National Congress Party (NCP) led by Ibrahim Ahmed Umar, the Popular National Congress (PNC) led by Hassan al-Turabi, and over 20 minor pro-government parties. In the fall of 1998, the National Islamic Front (NIF) changed its name to the National Congress Party.

In presidential elections held in December 2000, al-Bashir was reelected president with 86.5% of the vote, followed by Ja'afar Muhammed Numayri with 9.6%. Three other candidates received less than a combined 4% of the vote. In the boycotted parliamentary elections of 13–22 December 2000, the NCP took 355 of 400 seats.

In 2005, under the terms of a Comprehensive Peace Agreement (CPA), a Government of National Unity (GNU) was formed by the National Congress Party (NCP) and Sudan People's Liberation Movement (SPLM). The NCP, which came to power by military coup in 1989, is the majority partner.

In the 2010 elections, President al-Bashir was reelected to his post with 68.2% of the vote. In the elections for the national assembly, the NCP won 323 seats, followed by the SPLM with 99 seats, the Popular Congress Party with 4 seats, the Democratic Unionist Party with 4 seats, the Umma Federal Party with 3 seats, the Umma Renewal and Reform Party with 2 seats, the Democratic Unionist Party-Original with 2 seats, and the Sudan People's Liberation Movement-Democratic Change with 2 seats. Seven seats were won by members of other parties and/or independents. Four seats were left vacant.

15 LOCAL GOVERNMENT

Local government experienced reorganizations in 1983, 1989, 1994, 1998 and 2003. The constitutional decree of 2 February 1994 created 26 states, each subdivided into provinces and districts. President Bashir stated his intention to devolve executive and legislative powers "never experienced in remote areas" to state governments. In theory, states were to be led by elected governors, deputy governors, and a cabinet of ministers. The Sudanese National Assembly passed the Sudan Constitution of 1998, and a Local Government Act was adopted that year. The 2003 Local Government Act separated the local executive and legislative organs, established an elected local council, defined its competencies, and specified financial resources. Southern Sudan created its own Local Government Act in 2009.

16 JUDICIAL SYSTEM

Historically, the judicial system was largely subservient to the president and his administration. The court system included regular courts (both criminal and civil), special security courts, military courts, and tribal courts. The chief justice of the Supreme Court, as the senior judge, presided over the judiciary and according to the 1973 constitution, was directly responsible to the president through a council headed by the president. Civil justice was administered by the Supreme Court, courts of appeal, and lower courts, while criminal justice was administered by major courts, magistrates' courts, and local people's courts. There was also a Constitutional Court of nine justices. Since 2005, the National Judicial Service Commission was tasked with overall administration of the court system.

As of 20 January 1991, the now defunct Revolutionary Command Council imposed Islamic law in the northern states. For Muslims, justice in personal matters such as domestic relations and probate, was administered by Muslim law courts, which formed the Shari'ah Division of the Sudan judiciary. The Shari'ah Division included a court of appeal, high courts, and qadis' courts. The president of the Shari'ah judiciary was the grand qadi.

17 ARMED FORCES

The International Institute for Strategic Studies (IISS) reported that armed forces in Sudan totaled 109,300 members in 2011. The force was comprised of 105,000 from the army, 1,300 from the navy, and 3,000 members of the air force. Armed forces represented .9% of the labor force in Sudan. Defense spending totaled $1.4 billion and accounted for 1.4% of GDP.

During years of civil war, the Sudanese armed forces, largely Muslim, faced an estimated 25,000 rebels of the Sudanese People's Liberation Army and another 3,000 in other opposition groups. South Sudan, by virtue of its geography, replaced Sudan in the latter half of 2011 as one of the four, border countries waging war on the Lord's Resistance Army (LRA), led by warlord Joseph Kony. Kony's outlaw group had since the late 1980s terrorized civilians in the border regions of northern Uganda, Sudan, Central African

Republic, and the Democratic Republic of the Congo. LRA tactics included abduction, torture, and murder of thousands of civilians. Governments of all four border nations were committing troops and sharing intelligence in order to defeat the LRA. The International Criminal Court had an outstanding arrest warrant against Kony for crimes against humanity, and the US was committing 100 battle-equipped soldiers to assist in the hunt for Kony.

18 INTERNATIONAL COOPERATION

Sudan joined the UN on 12 November 1956; it participated in ECA and several nonregional specialized agencies, such as the FAO, UNESCO, UNHCR, the World Bank, IAEA, and the WHO. The nation belonged to the African Development Bank, the Arab Bank for Economic Development in Africa, the Arab Fund for Economic and Social Development, the Islamic Development Bank, the ACP Group, the Council of Arab Economic Unity, the Organization of the Islamic Conference (OIC), G-77, the Arab League, the Community of Sahel and Saharan States (CENSAD), COMESA, the New Partnership for Africa's Development (NEPAD), and the African Union. Sudan held observer status in the WTO.

Although the government had shown cooperation in international counterterrorism talks, Sudan remained on the US list of State Sponsors of Terrorism for its alleged support of such groups as the Egyptian Islamic Jihad, the Palestinian Islamic Jihad, Hamas, and (formerly) the Lord's Resistance Army. Sudan was part of the Nonaligned Movement. In environmental cooperation, Sudan was part of the Convention on Biological Diversity, CITES, the Kyoto Protocol, the Montréal Protocol, the Nuclear Test Ban Treaty, and the UN Conventions on the Law of the Sea, Climate Change, and Desertification.

19 ECONOMY

Sudan had an agricultural economy. Cotton and gum arabic accounted for almost a quarter each of export earnings. Domestic crops included grain sorghum, millet, wheat, sesame seeds, and peanuts. The livestock sector was sizable as well, particularly camels and sheep, which were exported to Arab countries. Agriculture was threatened by droughts, which have led to famines. The industrial sector was limited to light industries and agricultural processing. Mineral exploration was limited although asbestos, chromium and mica were mined. Economic development was hindered by a poor transportation system that increased the cost of transporting goods over long distances. Prior to partition, Sudan was Africa's largest country.

The economy since the early 1970s has been on the verge of collapse owing to recurring civil war. The wars have resulted in an estimated 2 million deaths, and 5 million displaced persons. Despite the 2005 peace accords, ethnic and tribal fighting continued in the three states region. The Darfur region experienced some of the worst human rights abuses imaginable, including systematic and widespread murder, rape, abduction and forced displacement. The UN took command of the Darfur peacekeeping operation in 2007, but hostilities and instability continued into 2011 seriously disrupting the economy.

In 1997 Sudan began working with the IMF to implement economic reforms designed to transition from a socialist to a market-based economy. Petroleum discoveries in south-central Sudan turned things around when Sudan began exporting crude oil in the last quarter of 1999. In 2000 the IMF restored Sudan's voting rights. Increased oil production, enhanced light industry, and an expansion of export processing zones helped the economy grow at an annual rate of over 6% between 2001 and 2005. However, arrears to the IMF exceeded $1 billion and, by 2007, total foreign debt was approaching 100% of GDP, which stood at about $81 billion.

Increases in oil production together with high oil prices in the world markets attracted foreign investment into the country which gave a boost to the economy sending the GDP growth rate above 10% in 2007.

The GDP rate of change in Sudan, as of 2010, was 3.7%. Inflation stood at 4.5%, and unemployment was reported at 18.7%. The economy continued to depend on the oil sector, but services and utilities played an increasingly important role. Nonetheless, as much as 40% of the population lived below the poverty line and relied on subsistence agriculture for their livelihoods.

20 INCOME

The CIA estimated that in 2010 the GDP of Sudan was $100 billion. The CIA defines GDP as the value of all final goods and services produced within a nation in a given year and computed on the basis of purchasing power parity (PPP) rather than value as measured on the basis of the rate of the exchange based on current dollars. The per capita GDP was estimated at $9,400. The annual growth rate of GDP was 3.7%. The average inflation rate was 4.5%. It was estimated that agriculture accounted for 10.6% of GDP, industry 34.6%, and services 54.8%.

According to the World Bank, remittances from citizens living abroad totaled $2 billion or about $81 per capita and accounted for approximately 3% of GDP.

The World Bank reported that in 2009 household consumption in Sudan totaled $38.3 billion or about $1,042 per capita, measured in current US dollars rather than PPP. Household consumption included expenditures of individuals, households, and nongovernmental organizations on goods and services, excluding the purchases of dwellings. It was estimated that household consumption was growing at an average annual rate of 0.6%.

As of 2011 the World Bank reported that actual individual consumption in Sudan was 79.8% of GDP and accounted for 0.18% of world consumption. By comparison, the United States accounted for 25.44% of world individual consumption. The World Bank also estimated that 45.3% of Sudan's GDP was spent on food and beverages, 15.9% on housing and household furnishings, 3.7% on clothes, 1.6% on health, 6.5% on transportation, 0.1% on communications, 2.3% on recreation, 0.1% on restaurants and hotels, and 2.9% on miscellaneous goods and services and purchases from abroad.

21 LABOR

As of 2007, Sudan had a total labor force of 11.92 million people. Within that labor force, CIA estimates in 1998 noted that 80% were employed in agriculture, 7% in industry, and 13% in the service sector. It was estimated that in 2002 about 18.7% of the population was unemployed.

The trade union movement was reconstituted after the 1971 coup attempt. Strikes, banned by the government in May 1969, were legalized in 1985. The 1989 coup, however, brought a swift end to the strong labor movement which had been growing under the Sadiq al-Mahdi administration. The National Salvation Revolution Command Council (RCC) abolished labor unions and prohibited strikes by decree on 30 June 1989. The right to organize and join a union has since been restored, but the government dominated the leadership of all unions and tightly controlled their activities. The largest union was the Sudan Workers Trade Union Federation with some 800,000 members in 2002.

Slavery and forced labor continued to persist in Sudan. Prior to separation, slaves were generally taken in one of the southern war zones and then sent north to work as domestic servants, agricultural workers, or to be sent abroad. The minimum wage was about $11 per month and was insufficient to support the average family. Although the minimum age for employment was 18 years, it was not enforced and children as young as 11 years old worked full-time in all areas including industry. The legal workweek was six eight-hour days, with Fridays designated as rest days.

22 AGRICULTURE

Prior to partition of the country, roughly 58% of the total land was used for agriculture, with irrigated farming dominant in the north along the banks of the Nile and other rivers. The country's major crops included cotton, groundnuts (peanuts), sorghum, millet, wheat, gum arabic, sugarcane, cassava (tapioca), mangos, papaya, bananas, sweet potatoes, and sesame. Cereal production in 2009 amounted to 5.6 million tons, fruit production 1.3 million tons, and vegetable production 1.9 million tons.

Government regional development schemes played a decisive role in the economy since the 1920s. The Gezirah Scheme, located between the Blue and White Niles near their confluence at Khartoum, was the world's largest under single management and provided a substantial portion of foreign exchange and government revenue. The 354-km (220-mi) Jonglei Canal started in 1978 but never finished was meant to drain the Sudd swamp and channel water from the White Nile to the arid northern Sudan and to Egypt. Built by a French consortium at a projected cost of $260 million, the unfinished canal would help irrigate up to 243,000 hectares (600,000 acres). The project was halted by SPLA attacks in 1984. In 2008, Egypt and Sudan said they would restart work on the canal, but it did not appear to be a priority for the government of Sudan.

Over the years the public and private agricultural sectors have invested heavily in land preparations, pesticides, and related inputs. Agricultural funding for such projects came from the World Bank, the African Development Bank, and the International Fund for Agricultural Development. However, these projects increased debt significantly and led to debt-repayment problems.

Officials anticipated that investments in agriculture, particularly those aimed at increasing wheat production, would lead to food self-sufficiency by 2015. Increased production in rice and sorghum, which were hot weather crops, was also expected as a result of government investment.

23 ANIMAL HUSBANDRY

The UN Food and Agriculture Organization (FAO) reported that in 2009 Sudan dedicated 117.2 million hectares (289.6 million acres) to permanent pasture or meadow. During that year, the country tended 42.4 million chickens and 41.6 million head of cattle. The production from these animals amounted to 339,664 tons of beef and veal and 7.31 million tons of milk. Sudan also produced 58,800 tons of cattle hide and 54,668 tons of raw wool.

Cattle in the southern rainfall area were mainly shorthorn zebu of Asian origin and the longhorn sanga. Nomadic or seminomadic pastoral tribes owned the bulk of the cattle. Sudanese sheep had hairy coats and were grown for meat rather than wool. They were owned almost exclusively by nomadic or seminomadic tribes. Widespread smuggling reduced income available to the government from livestock exports.

24 FISHING

In 2008, prior to national partition, the annual capture totaled 65,500 tons according to the UN FAO. The Nile River yielded some 110 varieties of fish including the popular Tilapia; the Red Sea was another valuable fishing ground.

25 FORESTRY

Approximately 29% of Sudan (prior to partition) was covered by forest, which amounted to 61.6 million hectares (152.2 million acres). The UN FAO estimated the 2009 roundwood production at 2.17 million cu m (76.7 million cu ft). The value of all forest products, including roundwood, totaled $6.19 million. Timber production, apart from cutting for local village needs, was confined to forests lying within reach of navigable rivers or areas served by roads and railways. Sudan supplied over 80% of the world's needs of gum arabic, extracted from the acacia. The Ministry of Agriculture and Natural Resources maintained forests, administered public preserves, and operated sawmills.

26 MINING

Sudan was not rich in mineral resources and the mineral sector has traditionally made a negligible contribution to the economy, although rising production of gold and crude petroleum in recent years has substantially increased the sector's influence. In 2008, nonfuel mining accounted for 0.6% of Sudan's gross national product (GNP).

Estimated mineral production in 2009 included salt, 35,793 metric tons; mine chromite (gross weight), 14,087 metric tons (reported); gold, from the Red Sea Hills, 1,922 kg, down from 2,276 kg in 2008 (excluding artisanal output); gypsum, 30,000 metric tons; and hydraulic cement, 1,000,000 metric tons, up from 370,000 metric tons in 2008. Sudan presumably also produced clay and/or shale for cement, limestone for cement, lime, construction aggregate and fill, other construction materials (clays, sand and gravel, and stone), and marble for export. In 2009 Sudan produced an estimated 413 kg of silver. Sudan was also known to have deposits of barite, copper, iron ore (large reserves near Port Sudan), kyanite, lead, nickel, silver, tungsten, wollastonite, and zinc; however, little exploitation of these deposits was expected, because of civil unrest.

27 ENERGY AND POWER

The World Bank reported in 2008 that Sudan produced 4.52 billion kWh of electricity and consumed 3.99 billion kWh, or 108 kWh per capita. Roughly 31% of energy came from fossil fuels, while 1% came from alternative fuels and the rest from hydro–

power. Per capita oil consumption was 372 kg. Oil production totaled 511,329 barrels of oil a day.

Sudan has seen its proven reserves of crude oil increase dramatically since 2001. Sudan's proven oil reserves, as of 1 January 2011, were 5 billion bbl. In 2010, oil production was 514,300 barrels per day and oil consumption was 98,000 barrels per day. Oil exports totaled 383,900 barrels per day in 2009, while oil imports totaled 11,820 barrels per day. Sudan also had proven natural gas reserves totaling some 84.95 billion cu m (3 trillion cu ft). As of 1 January 2005, according to the Oil and Gas Journal, the country's crude oil refining capacity was estimated at 121,700 barrels per day at three refineries: Port Sudan at 21,700 barrels per day; El Gily at 50,000 barrels per day; and at Khartoum at 50,000 barrels per day.

In a move to boost the economy through the development of sustainable, clean energy, Sudan signed a deal with the French-owned Solar Euromed for the construction of three solar power plants, one in each of the three Darfur states. The plants were expected to be operational by the end of 2014. The government anticipated that the project would be one of many leading toward a more sustainable and reliable energy source for the nation.

In August 2010, the government of Sudan announced plans to build a new four-reactor nuclear power plant by 2030. As the first step, the country will build a smaller research reactor with assistance from the International Atomic Energy Agency (IAEA). The research reactor will facilitate training of future staff and will be used to produce radioisotopes for medical use. The larger power plant project was expected to cost anywhere between $3 billion and $6 billion. It was considered necessary as a means to help the nation boost and maintain an adequate supply of electricity to accommodate projected increases in industry and population. As of 2010, only about 20% of the country had electricity. The government hoped to raise that figure to 80% by the end of 2020. Developments in hydroelectric plants and alternative energy sources such as solar and wind power were also being considered to meet these goals.

Principal Trading Partners – Sudan (2010)

(In millions of US dollars)

Country	Total	Exports	Imports	Balance
World	20,460.0	10,500.0	9,960.0	540.0
China	8,200.1	6,049.2	2,150.9	3,898.4
Japan	1,218.0	1,116.4	101.6	1,014.7
India	1,123.0	585.7	537.3	48.4
Sa'udi Arabia	877.7	114.4	763.3	-649.0
United Arab Emirates	822.5	262.3	560.1	-297.8
Egypt	680.7	37.8	642.9	-605.0
Germany	353.3	17.5	335.9	-318.4
Uganda	300.8	0.3	300.5	-300.2
Turkey	255.3	4.7	250.5	-245.8
Ethiopia	230.8	139.4	91.4	47.9

(…) data not available or not significant.

(n.s.) not specified.

SOURCE: *2011 Direction of Trade Statistics Yearbook,* New York: United Nations, 2011.

28 INDUSTRY

In 2010 industry accounted for 34.6% of Sudan's GDP. Production included oil, cotton ginning, textiles, cement, edible oils, sugar, soap distilling, shoes, petroleum refining, pharmaceuticals, armaments, and automobile/light truck assembly. In the 1980s industrial output fell to a low of 5% of capacity because of scarce foreign exchange, suspension of import licenses and letters of credit. There were shortages of raw materials, skilled labor, and energy. Prior to this difficult period, Sudan's import-substitution strategy supplied many items that had formerly been imported. Textiles, the largest industry, were part of a decade-long (1985–95) rehabilitation project. There were a number of cotton ginning plants, including the large Gezira plant. Other factories processed cotton seed and groundnuts into oil and cake. The Kenana sugar complex, commissioned in 1980, was one of the largest sugar plantation and refining installations in the world, jointly owned by the Sudanese government, the governments of Kuwait and Saudi Arabia, and other private interests.

29 SCIENCE AND TECHNOLOGY

Patent applications in science and technology as of 2009, according to the World Bank, totaled 3 in Sudan. The National Council for Research, founded in 1970 at Khartoum, was responsible for planning and directing national research programs in agriculture, medicine, energy, and other fields. The Agriculture Research Corporation of the Ministry of Agriculture, founded in 1904, had its headquarters in Wad Medani, and a Forestry Research Center and the Geological Research Authority operated in Khartoum. The universities of Gezirah, Juba, Khartoum, and Nilayn all had faculties or colleges in scientific and technical fields, and the Sudan University of Science and Technology, founded in 1950 at Khartoum, had colleges of agriculture, engineering, and sciences.

30 DOMESTIC TRADE

Omdurman was Sudan's commercial center for livestock and handicrafts. The cities of El Fasher, El Gedaref, and Kassala served as regional trade and market centers, primarily for agricultural goods. The few modern shops featured imported products. Most retail trade was conducted in open-air markets or in stalls in buildings near market centers. Because of the low literacy rate, newspaper advertising was of limited significance. Window and sidewalk displays and outdoor advertising were the principal marketing aids. An international trade fair was held annually at Khartoum.

Markets usually were open from 7 a.m. to 2 p.m., in order to escape the afternoon heat. Business hours were from 8 a.m. to 2 p.m. and 6 p.m. to 8 p.m., Saturday through Thursday, with Friday as the day of rest. Normal banking hours were 8:30 a.m. to noon, Saturday through Thursday. Government hours were 8 a.m. to 2:30 p.m.

31 FOREIGN TRADE

Prior to the split in 2011, Sudan imported $20.02 billion worth of goods and services in 2008, while exporting $16.11 billion worth of goods and services. Major import partners in 2009 were France, 23.3%; Italy, 19.1%; Germany, 9.2%; and Spain, 4.9%. Its major ex-

Balance of Payments – Sudan (2010)

(In millions of US dollars)

Current Account		**156.8**
Balance on goods		2,564.9
Imports	-8,839.4	
Exports	11,404.3	
Balance on services		-2,067.6
Balance on income		-2,471.6
Current transfers		2,131.2
Capital Account		...
Financial Account		**650.1**
Direct investment abroad		...
Direct investment in Sudan		2,063.7
Portfolio investment assets		-14.3
Portfolio investment liabilities		21.4
Financial derivatives		...
Other investment assets		-2,785.7
Other investment liabilities		1,365.1
Net Errors and Omissions		**-859.9**
Reserves and Related Items		**52.9**

(…) data not available or not significant.

SOURCE: *Balance of Payment Statistics Yearbook 2011*, Washington, DC: International Monetary Fund, 2011.

port partners were China, 60.3%; Japan, 14%; Indonesia, 8.6%; and India, 4.9%.

Sudan's main exports included oil and petroleum products, cotton, sesame, livestock, groundnuts, gum arabic, and sugar. Other exports included gold, vegetable oil, and crude vegetable materials. Principal imports included foodstuffs, manufactured goods, refinery and transport equipment, medicines and chemicals, textiles, and wheat.

32 BALANCE OF PAYMENTS

In 2009 the current accounts deficit stood at 11.5% of GDP due to the global crisis. In 2010 Sudan had a foreign trade deficit of $3 billion, amounting to 3.3% of GDP. The country's external debt stood at $37.7 billion in 2010, approximately $12 billion higher than in 2005. The country had a habitual payments deficit, most of the debt servicing was in arrears, and international credit was generally not available to Sudan. Remittances from Sudanese working abroad were discouraged by inequitable exchange rate policies. Sudan began implementing IMF macroeconomic reforms in 1997, and began exporting crude oil in 1999, which improved the balance of payments.

33 BANKING AND SECURITIES

The central bank was the Bank of Sudan with some 14 branches throughout the country. In 2011, 32 commercial banks were doing business in the country. In the run up to the referendum on southern secession, Sudan saw its currency depreciate considerably on the black market with the Central Bank's official rate also losing value as the Sudanese people started to hoard foreign currency. The Central Bank intervened heavily in the currency market to defend the value of the pound and the Sudanese government introduced a number of measures to restrain excess local demand

for hard currency, but uncertainty about the secession increased the demand for foreign exchange.

In July 2011, the government of Sudan introduced newly designed currency notes in a move that generated serious complaints from newly independent South Sudan. Although South Sudan unveiled its own currency earlier in the month, many South Sudanese still possessed the former, no longer valid Sudanese, currency. The government of Sudan estimated that nearly $2 billion in Sudanese pounds were in circulation in South Sudan at the time. The central bank claimed that the issuance of new currency was a precautionary measure designed to protect the economy from destabilization. According to South Sudanese estimates, the decision could cost the government of South Sudan $700 million and violated a previous agreement with Sudan to wait six months before introducing a new currency. Sudanese representatives claimed that the move was gradual, allowing for about three months for the full exchange of currency.

Sudan's traditional banking system was inherited from the Anglo-Egyptian condominium (1899–1955). When the National Bank of Egypt opened in Khartoum in 1901, it obtained a privileged position as banker to and for the government, allowing it to operate as a semiofficial central bank. Other banks followed, but the National Bank of Egypt and Barclays Bank dominated and stabilized banking in Sudan until after World War II. Post-World War II prosperity created a demand for an increasing number of commercial banks.

Before Sudanese independence, there had been no restrictions on the movement of funds between Egypt and Sudan, and the value of the currency used in Sudan was tied to that of Egypt. This situation was unsatisfactory to an independent Sudan, which established the Sudan Currency Board to replace Egyptian and British money. It was not a central bank because it did not accept deposits, lend money, or provide commercial banks with cash and liquidity. In 1959, the Bank of Sudan was established to succeed the Sudan Currency Board and to take over the Sudanese assets of the National Bank of Egypt. In February 1960, the Bank of Sudan began acting as the central bank of Sudan, issuing currency, assisting the development of banks, providing loans, maintaining financial equilibrium, and advising the government.

Banks were nationalized in 1970 but in 1974 foreign banks were allowed to open branches in Sudan. In December 1990 the government decided to adopt Islamic banking principles. Seven banks in Sudan were based on the principles of Islamic banking that had been introduced in September 1984, namely Faisal Islamic Bank of Sudan (FIBS), Islamic Cooperative Development Bank, Tadamun Islamic Bank of Sudan, Sudanese Islamic Bank, Al-Baraka Bank, Islamic Bank of Western Sudan, and Bank of Northern Sudan.

No stock exchange existed in the Sudan.

34 INSURANCE

All foreign insurance companies were nationalized in 1970, a condition that later was relaxed. There were at least 20 Sudanese insurance companies in 1997 and a National Reinsurance Co. In 2003 Sudan adopted an Insurance Act that gave powers to an Insurance Commission established to regulate the industry, including licensing and enforcement of rules. In 2011 some 12 major insurance companies were doing business in Sudan.

35 PUBLIC FINANCE

In 2010 the budget of Sudan included $11.06 billion in public revenue and $13.15 billion in public expenditures. The budget deficit amounted to 3% of GDP. Public debt was 94.2% of GDP, with $37.73 billion of the debt held by foreign entities.

Sudan's budgets were in deficit from the 1960s through the 1990s. The budget deficit soared to 22% of GDP in 1991/92, which aggravated inflation. As of 2000, neither the budget deficit nor inflation showed signs of shrinking because of civil war. The IMF reported that the Staff Monitored Program (SMP) for 2009–10 missed its key targets because of larger than envisaged fiscal deficits. The deficits were caused by weak external inflows and foreign exchange. The IMF also reported that the Heavily Indebted Poor Countries (HIPC) program should be continued.

The International Monetary Fund (IMF) reported that in 1999 budgetary outlays by function were as follows: general public services, 54.7%; defense, 27.5%; public order and safety, 7.8%; economic affairs, 1.1%; housing and community amenities, 0.1%; health, 1.0%; recreation, culture, and religion, 0.1%; and education, 7.6%.

36 TAXATION

Sudan, as of 2012, had a standard corporate tax rate of 15%, considerably reduced over the rate of 35% in 2005. The combined tax rate was 36.1%, which compared to 57.1% for sub Saharan Africa and with 42.7% for OECD countries. Worldwide, Sudan ranked 103rd among nations on the taxation criteria of the World Bank's "Doing Business 2012" report.

Capital gains derived from the sale of land and buildings were subject to a tax rate of 5%. Capital gains from the sale of automobiles were taxed at 2.5%. Other capital gains and dividends were not taxed.

Other taxes included an income tax on salaries, various consumption and production taxes, stamp duties, miscellaneous fees and charges, including a development tax, and the Zakat, an annual religious tax of 2.5% on entities operating in Sudan. The personal income tax was first imposed in July 1964, and an income tax on Sudanese working abroad was added later. Income from property, hitherto exempt from any tax, became subject to the business profits tax on 1 January 1964. There was also a value-added tax (VAT) of 15%.

37 CUSTOMS AND DUTIES

Sudan had a liberal trade policy, although it restricts imports of some goods considered competitive with those produced locally. The customs tariff applied to goods from all countries except Egypt and Jordan, which received preferential treatment. On the World Bank's "Doing Business in 2012" report, Sudan ranked 151st worldwide for ease of doing business. It cost $2,050 to export a container of goods compared to $1,960 for sub Saharan Africa and $1,032 for OECD countries. Importing a container cost $2,900 compared to $2,503 for sub Saharan Africa and $1,085 for OECD countries. The time to import goods was estimated at 46 days compared to 37 on average in sub Saharan Africa, and to 11 in OECD countries.

Most tariff rates were ad valorem and ranged from zero to 1,100%. Export duty was 10% on cotton and gum arabic and 5% for all other items. Specific rates were applied mostly to alcoholic beverages and tobacco. Commodities not included in the tariff schedule were dutiable at 40% ad valorem. Also levied were royalties, a consumption tax of 10%, and a 10% defense tax. An additional tax of 5–150% was imposed on a list of 122 items. The average tariff rate in 1999, as determined by the IMF, was 19.3%. The customs service was known to be extremely corrupt. In 1997, the United States implemented a trade embargo on Sudan because of terrorist activities.

38 FOREIGN INVESTMENT

Foreign direct investment (FDI) in Sudan was a net inflow of $2.68 billion according to World Bank figures published in 2009. FDI represented 4.91% of GDP.

Until the millennium, Sudan was unfavorable to investors. In 1971, Sudan nationalized the holdings of foreign investors, mostly British. A privatization effort and a move toward a mixed economy began slowly in the early 1980s and picked up momentum via negotiations with the IMF in 1985. The 1980 Encouragement of Investment Act provided for repatriation of profits, tax incentives, customs relief, industrial rates for transport and electricity. However, the introduction of Shari'ah law in 1983 (unenforced since 1985), along with foreign exchange shortages, discouraged investors through 1986. In 1990, the government invited foreign investors to purchase companies in the parastatal sector. Key properties in the agricultural, tourist, transportation and communications sectors were identified as candidates for privatization under the National Economic Salvation Program. In 1992, the creation of four free-trade zones was announced in an attempt to encourage additional foreign investment.

In 1999, a new investment act guaranteed the equal status of foreign and national projects and encouraged investment in the sectors of agriculture, industry, and tourism, amongst others. It gave total tax exemptions for business profits and customs duties for 10 years on capital projects and 5 years for nonstrategic industries. Change in investor confidence proved dramatic. Foreign investment in 2001 increased to $574 million and, between 2002 and 2004, FDI averaged $1.2 billion reaching $1.51 billion in 2004. Encouraged by the oil industry, by 2009 it had jumped to $2.68 billion.

39 ECONOMIC DEVELOPMENT

For decades Sudan accumulated foreign debt and by the early 1990s it had become the largest debtor to the World Bank and IMF. However, in 1993 its failure to service its international debt, together with a poor human rights record, drove the World Bank to suspend financing for 15 development projects, and led to a suspension in voting rights in the IMF.

Economic development has been driven by two key factors: the government's commitment to food self-sufficiency, which has led to a reallocation of investment in agriculture and other productive sectors, and increased oil exploitation since 2000. Privatizing the parastatal sector also encouraged growth. However, in the 1990s the country's foreign debt regularly exceeded its annual GDP, which was unsustainable. Nonetheless, increases in oil production were expected to protect real GDP growth at around 8.0% despite world recession.

Sudan was not ranked on the Heritage Foundation's 2011 Index of Economic Freedom because of lack of data owing to political instability. According to the Foundation, the last time the Sudan was fully graded was in 2000, when it received a score of 47.2. In 2011 the world average was 59.7 on a scale of 1–100, where 100 points represented the freest economy.

40 SOCIAL DEVELOPMENT

The social insurance system provided benefits for employed persons and the self-employed. Domestic workers, home workers, and family laborers and subsistence farmers, who made up a significant percentage of the labor force, were excluded. A separate program served the armed forces and public employees. The social insurance system was funded by employee contributions of 8% of wages, with employer contributions of 15% of payroll. Self-employed individuals contributed 25% of their monthly income. The program included old-age and disability pensions, workers' compensation, and survivor benefits. Retirement was set at age 60, but reduced for those in arduous labor.

The fundamentalist Islamic government has redefined the place of women in society. Formerly, the state guaranteed basic rights and freedoms to women of any religion. They were afforded opportunities in trades, the professions, and higher education. However, with the advance of extremism, these freedoms no longer exist. Women were excluded from the civil service and received limited educational opportunities. They were no longer free to travel abroad without the permission of a male family member. Women who walked in public with an uncovered head or who were wearing slacks were often stopped and taken to police stations. Female university students in Khartoum were sentenced to be flogged, reportedly for wearing pants. Female circumcision (also referred to as female genital mutilation), although illegal, was prevalent, especially in the most drastic form. The city of Khartoum ordered the separation of the sexes in public to conform with strict Muslim law. This separation required barriers between men and women at social events and banned them from sitting facing each other; the law dictated that the barriers be observed at weddings, parties, and picnics and prohibited certain other practices perceived as inappropriate in an Islamic society. The government did not stop violence against women. Women in Darfur were especially vulnerable, where rape and assaults were commonplace.

Sudan's human rights situation remained dismal. Government and SPLA continued to regularly commit abuses, including massacres, kidnapping, enslavement, forced conscription, and rape. According to human rights groups, the practice of slavery has grown as a result of the civil war that has intermittently raged in the Sudan since its independence in 1956. Freedom of speech, press, assembly, association, and political choice were repressed throughout the Sudan.

In June 2010 Sudan joined representatives from Chad, the Central African Republic, Sudan, Nigeria, Niger, and Cameroon in signing the N'Djamena Declaration, which essentially called for the end of the recruitment and use of children as soldiers, a policy aligned with international standards, including the Optional Protocol on the Involvement of Children in Armed Conflict, which was part of the Convention on the Rights of the Child. The signatories agreed to establish a special committee charged with ensuring the implementation and monitoring of the agreed commitments. Sudan had a head start in the process, since it had already signed and ratified the Optional Protocol.

41 HEALTH

According to the CIA, life expectancy in Sudan was 58 years in 2011. The country spent 6.9% of its GDP on healthcare, amounting to $95 per person. There were 3 physicians, 8 nurses and midwives, and 7 hospital beds per 10,000 inhabitants. The fertility rate was 4.1, while the infant mortality rate was 69 per 1,000 live births. In 2008 the maternal mortality rate, according to the World Bank, was 750 per 100,000 births. About 10% of women were using contraception in 2007, and an estimated 89% of Sudanese women underwent female genital mutilation. It was estimated that 82% of children were vaccinated against measles. The CIA calculated HIV/AIDS prevalence in Sudan to be about 1.1% in 2009.

The central government operated most research laboratories and dispensaries. Hospital facilities and medical and public health services were free. In 2008, 57% of the population had access to improved sources for drinking water and 34% had access to adequate sanitation.

42 HOUSING

Most Sudanese lived in simple houses of their own; others living and working on the schemes rented from agricultural-scheme authorities. Over half of all housing units were *gottias*—single rooms with round mud walls and a conical straw roof; about one-third were *menzils*-multi-room houses with toilet facilities. Of all dwellings, over 80% were owner-occupied. Almost every house, even in the cities, had a walled courtyard or garden. In the big cities, bungalows were provided for important government officials and high-level foreign employees. A national housing authority provided low-cost housing to government employees, rural schoolteachers, and persons in low-income groups. A town-planning ordinance provided for slum clearance and replanning of towns. Khartoum had a number of modern apartment buildings.

43 EDUCATION

In 2009 the World Bank estimated that 40% of age-eligible children in Sudan were enrolled in primary school. Overall, the CIA estimated that Sudan had a literacy rate of 61.1%.

Schooling was compulsory for eight years of basic education. This was followed by three years of general secondary school. At the secondary level, vocational programs for industrial, commercial, and agricultural studies were available for boys. Home economic programs were available for girls. The academic year ran from July to March.

The University of Khartoum was established in 1956. A branch of Cairo University was opened at Khartoum in 1955. Other institutions included the Islamic University of Omdurman and the universities of El-Gezirah (at Wad Madanī) and Juba. In 1999 (the latest year for which data was available), it was estimated that about 7% of the tertiary age population was enrolled in some form of higher education.

⁴⁴LIBRARIES AND MUSEUMS

The University of Khartoum Library, in eight branches, was the principal library network with 350,000 volumes. The Library of the Ahfad University for Women had a collection of about 80,000 books. The library at the Institute of Education in Bakhter Ruda had 28,000 volumes; the Khartoum Polytechnic collection had 30,000 volumes; and the Educational Documentation Center, also in Khartoum, had 20,000 volumes. Minor library facilities were maintained by secondary schools, houses of worship, government agencies, and foreign community centers. The National Records Office, in Khartoum, served as the national archives and contained over 20 million documents, including 13,000 bound volumes covering Sudanese history since 1870.

There were antiquities museums in Khartoum and Merowe, which was also the site of excavations of buildings from the kingdom of Kush. The Khalifa's tomb in Omdurman contained relics of Mahdist and other recent history. The National Botanic Garden in Khartoum contained rare specimens of Sudanese flora. Khartoum also had an ethnographic museum, a natural history museum, and the Sudan National Museum. There were also museums at Al Ubayyid, Port Sudan, Wadi Halfa', Wad Madanī, Merowe, Omdurman, and other locations.

⁴⁵MEDIA

In 2009 the CIA reported that there were 370,400 telephone landlines in Sudan. In addition to landlines, mobile phone subscriptions averaged 36 per 100 people. There were 12 FM radio stations, 1 AM radio station, and 1 shortwave radio station. Internet users numbered 10 per 100 citizens.

The Sudan Broadcasting Service, the government-controlled radio network, transmitted daily in Arabic, English, French, Amharic, Somali, and other languages. Television service was inaugurated in 1963; an earth satellite station was completed in November 1974. The government controlled all radio and television broadcasts, with particular attention to ensuring that content was consistent with government policies. The only privately owned radio station was strictly limited to music.

Much of the press was privately owned, but the state still had great influence over public and private publications. Prominent newspapers in 2010 included *Al Khartoum* (circulation 25,000).

The constitution provided for freedom of thought, expression, and press as regulated by law. In practice, the government was said to severely limit free speech and the press through intimidation, surveillance, and economic control. Sudan television had a permanent military censor to ensure that all broadcasts reflected government views. In 2009 it was reported that government frequently harassed, tortured, censored and denied journalists their civil liberties.

In 2009 the Media Sustainability Index, which ranks the media of some 40 African countries on criteria of freedom of speech, professionalism, plurality of news sources, business management, and supporting institutions, ranked Sudan 1.60 on a scale of 1–4, in which 4 represented a fully sustainable system. Sudan's system was judged to be an "unsustainable mixed system" where the media minimally met objectives and elements of the government and legal system were opposed to a free media system.

⁴⁶ORGANIZATIONS

Sudan had a rich panoply of associational life of cooperatives, trades, professions, gender, youth, sports, religion, culture and tribal groups. The cooperative movement, which began in the 1930s, had achieved prominence, especially in the irrigation schemes. In the Gezirah Scheme, tenant farmers formed many cultural, educational, and recreational groupings.

The Sudan Chamber of Commerce (Khartoum), comprising both local and foreign business interests, performed various functions for the government. There were several smaller chambers, most of them organized by resident European and Egyptian traders. More than 30 clubs served foreign and minority groups and business firms. Such clubs served as principal centers of social activity in Sudanese towns.

The National Center for Research, established in 1991, promoted study and research in various branches of science. The multinational African Laser, Atomic and Molecular Sciences Network was based in Khartoum.

National youth organizations included the General Sudanese Students Union, Girl Guides Association of The Sudan, YMCA/YWCA, Sudan Boy Scouts Association, and Sudan International Youth and Student Movement for the UN. Other youth programs and organizations were sponsored through the Supreme Council of Youth and Sports.

The Babiker Badri Scientific Association for Women's Studies served as a social action group for the rights and education of women. There were national chapters of the Red Cross Society, UNICEF, the Society of St. Vincent de Paul, and Caritas.

⁴⁷TOURISM, TRAVEL, AND RECREATION

The *Tourism Factbook*, published by the UN World Tourism Organization prior to partition, reported 420,000 incoming tourists to Sudan in 2009, who spent a total of $299 million. Of those incoming tourists, there were 161,000 from East Asia and the Pacific, 100,000 from Africa, and 100,000 from Europe. There were 11,225 hotel beds available in Sudan. The estimated daily cost to visit Khartoum, the capital, was $408.

The main tourist attractions were big-game hunting in the forests of the south, boat excursions down the Nile through the forest and desert, deep-sea fishing, the Red Sea Hills, the underwater gardens at Port Sudan, and archaeological sites in the north. Horse racing was popular in the Sudan since its introduction in 1929. However, during the civil war and the advent of Islamic rule, tourism in the Sudan dropped significantly. In 2001 there were only 50,000 tourists. Visitors to Sudan required a passport and a visa. A vaccination certificate against yellow fever was also required if traveling from an infected area. Precautions against typhoid, meningitis, and malaria were recommended.

⁴⁸FAMOUS PERSONS

The one Sudanese to achieve world renown in modern history was the Mahdi (Muhammad Ahmad bin 'Abdallah, 1843–85), who set out on a self-appointed mission to purify Islam, a mission he hoped would carry him ultimately to Istanbul and to the apex of the Muslim world. Under his banner, the people of Sudan rose against their Egyptian overlords and for over a decade kept most of their country free from foreign rule. The Mahdi died shortly after the seizure of Khartoum. His able but harsh successor, the Khalifa ('Abdallah bin Muhammad at-Ta'a'ishi, d. 1899), organized an independent government, which lasted until 1898, when an Anglo-Egyptian expeditionary corps reconquered Sudan.

The Mahdist wars provided the background for the exploits of famous British soldiers and administrators, among them generals Charles George Gordon (1833–85), Horatio Herbert Kitchener (1850–1916), and Sir Francis Reginald Wingate (1861–1953), the first governor-general of the condominium, as well as other foreign officers and explorers in the service of Egypt, such as the Italian Romolo Gessi (1831–81), the German Emin Pasha (Eduard Carl Oscar Theodor Schnitzer, 1840–92), the American Charles Chaillé-Long (1842–1917), and the Austrian Sir Rudolf Carl von Slatin (1857–1932).

Osman Digna ('Uthnab Abu Bakr Digna, c. 1840–1926), an organizer and leader of the Mahdist armies, and Sayyid 'Abd ar-Rahman al-Mahdi (1885–1959), posthumous son of the Mahdi, are revered by Sudanese. The most influential figure in recent years was Gaafar Mohammed Nimeiri (Ja'far Muhammad Numayri, (1930–2009), leader of Sudan from the 1969 coup until 1985. Sadiq al-Mahdi (b. 1936) was prime minister during 1966–67 and 1986–89. He was overthrown in a coup led by Field Marshal Omar Hasan Ahmad al-Bashir (b. 1944) who subsequently became a dictatorial president.

⁴⁹DEPENDENCIES

Sudan had no territories or colonies.

⁵⁰BIBLIOGRAPHY

Essien, Kwame, and Toyin Falola. *Culture and Customs of Sudan.* Westport, CT: Greenwood Press, 2009.

Lobban, Richard A., Jr., Robert S. Cramer, and Carolyn Fluehr-Lobban. *Historical Dictionary of the Sudan.* Lanham, MD: Scarecrow Press, 2002.

O'Sullivan, Meghan L. *Shrewd Sanctions: Statecraft and State Sponsors of Terrorism.* Washington, DC: Brookings Institution Press, 2003.

Patterson, Donald. *Inside Sudan: Political Islam, Conflict, and Catastrophe.* Boulder, CO: Westview Press, 2003.

Sudan Investment and Business Guide: Strategic and Practical Information. Washington, DC: International Business Publications USA, 2012.

Totten, Samuel. *Oral and Documentary History of the Darfur Genocide.* Santa Barbara, CA: Praeger, 2011.

Woodward, Peter. *The Horn of Africa: Politics and International Relations.* New York: I.B. Tauris, 2003.

Zeilig, Leo, and David Seddon. *A Political and Economic Dictionary of Africa.* Philadelphia: Routledge/Taylor and Francis, 2005.

SWAZILAND

Kingdom of Swaziland

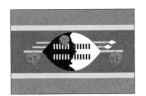

CAPITAL: Mbabane (administrative and judicial); Lobamba (royal and parliamentary)

FLAG: Blue, yellow, crimson, yellow, and blue stripes with the shield and spears of the Emasotsha regiment are superimposed on the crimson stripe.

ANTHEM: *Nkulunkulu Mnikati wetibusiso tema Swati (O God, bestower of the blessings of the Swazi).*

MONETARY UNIT: The lilangeni (pl. emalangeni; SWL) of 100 cents is a paper currency equal in value to the South African rand, which also is legal tender. It was introduced in 1974. There are coins of 1, 2, 5, 10, 20, and 50 cents, 1 lilangeni, 2 emalangeni, 5 emalangeni, and notes of 2, 5, 10, 20, and 50 emalangeni. SWL1 = US$0.16129 (or US$1 = SWL6.2) as of 2011.

WEIGHTS AND MEASURES: The metric system replaced imperial weights and measures in September 1969.

HOLIDAYS: New Year's Day, 1 January; Commonwealth Day, 2nd Monday in March; National Flag Day, 25 April; Birthday of King Sobhuza II, 22 July; Umhlanga (Reed Dance) Day, last Monday in August; Somhlolo (Independence) Day, 6 September; United Nations (UN) Day, 24 October; Christmas Day, 25 December; Boxing Day, 26 December. Movable religious holidays include Good Friday, Holy Saturday, Easter Monday, Ascension, and the Incwala Ceremony.

TIME: 2 p.m. = noon GMT.

¹LOCATION, SIZE, AND EXTENT

A landlocked country in southern Africa, Swaziland has an area of 17,363 sq km (6,704 sq mi), extending 176 km (109 mi) N–S and 135 km (84 mi) E–W. Comparatively, the area occupied by Swaziland is slightly smaller than the state of New Jersey. It is bounded by Mozambique on the NE and by the Republic of South Africa on the SE, S, W, and N, with a total boundary length of 535 km (332 mi).

Swaziland's capital city, Mbabane, is located in the northwest part of the country.

²TOPOGRAPHY

The country is divided west-to-east into four well-defined regions, the first three being of roughly equal breadth. The four regions extend north and south and are known as the high, middle, and low veld, and the Lebombo plain and escarpment. The high veld on the west has an average altitude of 1,050 to 1,200 m (3,445 to 3,937 ft). The middle veld averages about 450 to 600 m (1,476 to 1,969 ft), and the low or bush veld less than 300 m (984 ft). The Lebombo plain, at an average height of 610 m (2,000 ft), extends to the Lebombo escarpment, which is part of the Lebombo Mountains in the east. The entire country is traversed by rivers or streams, making it one of the best watered areas in southern Africa. The longest river is the Great Usutu, which stretches roughly from west to east across the center of the country for a total distance of 217 km (135 mi).

³CLIMATE

The high veld has a humid near-temperate climate with about 140 cm (55 in) of mean annual rainfall. The middle veld is subtropical and somewhat drier, with about 85 cm (33 in) of annual rainfall; the low veld, almost tropical, is sub humid, receiving about 60 cm (24 in) of rain in an average year. Rainfall tends to be concentrated in a few violent storms in the summer (October–March). Temperatures range from as low as -3°C (27°F) in winter in the highlands to as high as 42°C (108°F) in summer in the lowlands. At Mbabane, temperatures average 20°C (68°F) in January and 12°C (54°F) in July.

⁴FLORA AND FAUNA

Grassland, savanna, mixed bush, and scrub cover most of Swaziland. There is some forest in the highlands. Flora includes aloes, orchids, and begonias. Large indigenous mammals include the blue wildebeest, kudu, impala, zebra, waterbuck, and hippopotamus; however, wildlife has become very scarce outside the protected areas. Crocodiles live in the lowland rivers. Bird life includes the European stork, sacred ibis, and gray heron. The World Resource Institute estimates that there are 2,715 plant species in Swaziland. In addition, Swaziland is home to 124 mammal, 490 bird, 111 reptile, and 41 amphibian species. The calculation reflects the total number of distinct species residing in the country, not the number of endemic species.

⁵ENVIRONMENT

The chief environmental problem is soil erosion and degradation, particularly because of overgrazing. Population growth and the increased demand for fuel have threatened the country's forests, and the resulting deforestation has contributed to the loss of valuable soil. Swaziland has at least four protected areas for wildlife—two wildlife sanctuaries and two nature reserves—totaling 40,045 hectares (98,953 acres), all in the northern half of the country. The World Resources Institute reported that Swaziland had designated 53,900 hectares (133,190 acres) of land for protection as of 2006. Water resources totaled 4.5 cu km (1.08 cu mi), while water usage was 1.04 cu km (.25 cu mi) per year. Domestic water usage accounted for 2% of total usage, industrial for 1%, and agricultural for 97%. Per capita water usage totaled 1,010 cu m (35,668 cu ft) per year.

Another significant environmental problem in Swaziland is air pollution from transportation vehicles and emissions from other countries in the area. The United Nations (UN) reported in 2008 that carbon dioxide emissions in Swaziland totaled 1,063 kilotons.

Water pollution from industrial and agricultural sources is also a problem, as well as contamination by untreated sewage, which contributes to the spread of life-threatening diseases.

According to a 2011 report issued by the International Union for Conservation of Nature and Natural Resources (IUCN), the number of threatened species included 5 mammals, 11 birds, and 11 plants. Burchell's zebra has become extinct. Threatened marine species include the Baltic sturgeon, Danube salmon, and marsh snail. The cheetah and the cape vulture are listed among the vulnerable species.

6 POPULATION

The US Central Intelligence Agency (CIA) estimated the population of Swaziland in 2011 at approximately 1,370,424, which placed it at number 149 in population among the 196 nations of the world. In 2011 approximately 3.6% of the population were over 65 years of age, with another 37.8% under 15 years of age. The median age in Swaziland was 20.3 years. There were 0.99 males for every female in the country. The population's annual rate of change was 1.204%. The projected population for the year 2025 was 1,500,000. Population density in Swaziland was calculated at 79 people per sq km (205 people per sq mi).

The UN estimated that 21% of the population lived in urban areas, and that urban populations had an annual rate of change of 1.5%. The largest urban area was Mbabane, with a population of 74,000.

The population doubled since the nation gained its independence from Great Britain in 1968. The relatively rapid increase in population raised concerns over food security and land divisions. Most of the population (80%) lived in rural areas in traditional, family-based, farm communities. According to custom every son was given a portion of the family farm as his own once he married. This portion was where he built his own home and supported his own family through farming and cattle raising. As the population increased, there were fewer and smaller portions of land available and smaller plots were not large enough to support herds of cattle and/or harvests large enough to support larger families.

The prevalence of HIV/AIDS has had a significant impact on the population of Swaziland, with the number of AIDS orphans growing. The HIV/AIDS epidemic caused higher death and infant mortality rates and lowered life expectancy. As of 2006 Swaziland acknowledged that it was grappling with a humanitarian crisis caused by the devastating HIV/AIDS pandemic. According to UNAIDS, the Joint United Nations Programme on HIV/AIDS, Swaziland had the highest prevalence rates of HIV/AIDs in the world, ahead of neighboring Botswana, which made some strides against the disease. Combined with several years of equally devastating drought and famine, HIV/AIDS significantly undermined the economy, which was already dependent on the regional giant South Africa. As of 2009 the HIV/AIDS adult prevalence rate was 25.9%.

In the midst of such daunting challenges, King Mswati III often came under heavy local and international criticism for lavish living, including luxury cars and mansions for his thirteen wives.

7 MIGRATION

Estimates of Swaziland's net migration rate, carried out by the CIA in 2011, amounted to zero. The total number of emigrants living abroad was 160,300, and the total number of immigrants living in Swaziland was 40,400. Over the years, there has been a noticeable drift of educated Africans, many of whom have acquired citizenship in the United Kingdom, from South Africa to Swaziland. Conversely, many itinerant asylum seekers were making a practice of using Swaziland as a stepping stone to gain access to South Africa in the 2000s.

8 ETHNIC GROUPS

The indigenous African population in Swaziland constituted 97% of the total populace and comprised more than 70 clans, of which the Nkosi Dlamini, the royal clan, was dominant. Europeans made up the remaining 3%.

9 LANGUAGES

English and SiSwati, spoken by almost all Swazi, were the official languages. Government business was conducted in English.

10 RELIGIONS

Most of the population was Christian, with about 40% affiliated with the Zionist Church, professing a blend of Christianity and indigenous ancestral worship. About 20% of the population were Roman Catholic. Other Christian denominations included Anglicans, Methodists, and Mormons (the Church of Jesus Christ of Latter-day Saints). About 10% of the population were Muslims and there were small groups of Jews and Baha'is. Muslims and Baha'is were generally located in urban areas. The constitution provided for religious freedom; however, local chiefs had significant power in determining what practices were consistent with local traditions and customs. Religious groups were required to consult with local chiefs before establishing new places of worship, and government permission was required for building new churches in urban areas. Non-Christian religious groups have been denied broadcasting privileges on government-owned radio and television networks. There is some tension between Christian groups, primarily over matters of politics. Good Friday, Easter Monday, Ascension Day, and Christmas are observed as national holidays.

11 TRANSPORTATION

The CIA reported that Swaziland had a total of 3,594 km (2,233 mi) of roads, of which 1,078 km (670 mi) were paved. A highway runs between the southern boundary with South Africa and the eastern boundary with Mozambique. Railroads extended for 300 km (186 mi). All railways were narrow gauge and link iron mines at Ngwenya with the Mozambique Railway and the port of

Maputo in Mozambique. In the 1970s a 94 km (58 mi) southern spur was constructed to the South African border. A 115 km (71 mi) northern spur to the South African border was completed in 1986. In 2009 out of a total of 15 airports there was only one with a paved runway. Matsapa Airport, near Manzini, provided service via Royal Swazi National Airways to South Africa, Mozambique, Zambia, Malawi, Zimbabwe, Botswana, Kenya, and Tanzania.

12 HISTORY

Like other parts of southern Africa, Swaziland was originally occupied by hunting and gathering peoples known as Bushmen. In the 16th century, according to tradition, Bantu-speaking peoples advanced southwest to what is now Mozambique. During the migration, these groups disintegrated to form the various ethnic groups of southern Africa. In fact, however, the Swazi did not appear to have broken away from the main body of the Bantu until the middle of the 18th century. The Swazi emerged as a distinct ethnic group at the beginning of the 19th century and were in constant conflict with the Zulu; they moved gradually northward and made their first formal contact with the British in the 1840s, when their ruler, Mswati II, applied to the United Kingdom for help against the Zulu. The United Kingdom succeeded in improving relations between the two ethnic groups.

About this time the first Europeans came to Swaziland to settle. The independence of Swaziland was guaranteed by the United Kingdom and Transvaal governments in 1881 and 1884, but owing to the excessive number of concessions, including land, grazing, and mineral rights granted to European entrepreneurs by King Mbandzeni during the 1880s, the United Kingdom decided some form of control was necessary. In 1890 a provisional government was established, representing Swaziland, the United Kingdom, and the Transvaal. From 1894 to 1899, the Transvaal government undertook the protection and administration of Swaziland. After the South African (Boer) War of 1899–1902, the administration of Swaziland was transferred to the British governor of the Transvaal. An order in council established the relationship between the Swazi and the United Kingdom in 1903, providing the basic authority under which British administration was conducted for 60 years.

Independence

Responsibility for Swaziland was transferred in 1907 to the high commissioner for South Africa. An elected European Advisory Council was constituted in 1921. By the provisions of the Native Administration Proclamation of 1941, the position of the ngwenyama (paramount chief) as native authority was recognized. In 1963 constitutional discussions looking toward independence were opened in London. The following year elections for a legislative council were held under the country's first constitution. After further constitutional talks in London in 1965, Swaziland became an independent nation within the Commonwealth on 6 September 1968.

On 12 April 1973 King Sobhuza II, who had been head of the Swazi nation since 1921, announced that the constitution had been repealed and that he had assumed supreme executive, legislative, and judicial powers. In 1979 a new parliament was chosen, partly through indirect elections and partly through royal appointment.

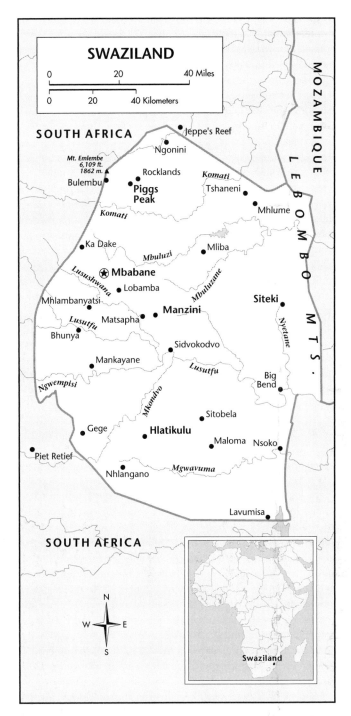

LOCATION: 25°43′ to 27°20′S; 30°48′ to 32°8′ E BOUNDARY LENGTHS: Mozambique, 108 kilometers (67 miles); South Africa, 446 kilometers (277 miles).

After Sobhuza died in 1982, a prolonged power struggle took place. At first his senior wife, Queen Mother Dzeliwe, became head of state and regent. Members of the Liqoqo, the king's advisory council, seized effective power and appointed a new "Queen Regent" in August 1983—Ntombi, one of Sobhuza's other wives. At that time it was announced that Makhosetive, the 15-year-old son of Ntombi and one of Sobhuza's 67 sons, would ascend the throne upon reaching adulthood. He was crowned King Mswati III on 25 April 1986. The intrigues continued until the new king approved the demotion of the Liqoqo back to its advisory status.

By tradition, the king reigns along with his mother or a ritual substitute, the ndlovikati (*lit.* she-elephant). The former was viewed as an administrative head of state and the latter as a spiritual and national head of state, with real power counterbalancing that of the king. During the long reign of Sobhuza II, the reign of the ndlovukati became more symbolic. As of 2011 the king ruled through his prime minister and cabinet.

In 1982 South Africa and Swaziland secretly signed a security agreement. Under pressure from South Africa, Swaziland arrested and deported members of the African National Congress (ANC), the leading Black Nationalist group in South Africa. On three different occasions in late 1985 and 1986, South African commando squads conducted raids in Swaziland, killing a number of ANC members and supporters. In November 1987 a new parliament was elected and a new cabinet appointed. Obed Dlamini was the prime minister from 1989 until 1993. In September and October 1993, popular elections were held for parliament, and a new prime minister, Prince Mbilini, took office, replacing Dlamini, who was defeated in the second round of voting. Barnabas Sibusiso Dlamini became Prime Minister in October 2008.

The Swaziland Federation of Trade Unions (SFTU) and the National Association of Civil Servants (NACS) organized strikes as a means to pressure the government for greater democratic control by the people of Swaziland. The strikes led the government to ban trade unions in 1995. The ban was later lifted, but the country was again disrupted in 1996 by a general strike supported by the SFTU. Three leaders were detained, and a Constitutional Review Commission was formed, charged with the task of soliciting views from the Swazi nation as to the type of constitution preferred. The commission met with all the country's constituencies and submitted a report to government officials.

The history of Swaziland during the early 2000s was dominated by controversy over drafting of the new constitution. In July 2005 after release of several drafts—in May 2003 and November 2004—and missed deadlines, parliament passed the Swaziland constitution. The king signed it 26 July 2005, and the new constitution entered into force January 2006. However, the constitution did not open up the political space to political parties, as civil society and human rights organizations in Swaziland and elsewhere had expected. Rather, the new constitution encoded the king's absolute governing powers into the land's grand law, reinforcing the ban on political parties and allowing human rights clauses to be suspended by the king if he finds them in conflict with some undefined "public interest."

Political, civil society, and human rights organizations, and the international community were unanimous in their criticism of the process that resulted in the new document, calling it palace controlled, nontransparent, not consultative enough, and undemocratic. The constitution was written by two commissions led by the king's brothers, Prince Mangaliso Dlamini and Prince David Dlamini, who was also the justice minister. Critics charged that widely publicized "consultation" meetings with traditional leaders, called by King Nswati III, were window dressing. They further alleged that the king's last-minute decision to channel approval of the constitution through a parliament he controlled, reversing his earlier decision to decree the constitution into law, was designed to mask a faulty process and to gain back door legitimacy for the document. However, several attempts to challenge the process

legally failed. For their part, royalists contended that democracy was a dividing force in the country, whereas the monarch was a strong unifying force. The king repeatedly asserted that the constitution enjoyed the full support of the Swazi people.

¹³GOVERNMENT

Swaziland was a constitutional monarchy until King Sobhuza II repealed the constitution in 1973 and assumed absolute power through a state of emergency decree, which was still in force as of 2006. The king then ruled the country as king-in-council, on the advice of his former cabinet and two traditional Swazi councils, one consisting of all the chiefs and other notables; the other of the king, the queen mother, and (in theory) all adult males.

A constitution was promulgated in 1978. In 1979 a new parliament was created with a House of Assembly consisting of 50 members, 40 of whom were chosen by indirect election and 10 appointed by the crown; the 20-member Senate had 10 members chosen by indirect election and 10 appointed by the crown. To become law, legislation passed by parliament had to be approved by the crown. The cabinet was presided over by a prime minister appointed by the crown from among the members of parliament.

In response to popular moves calling for reform, King Mswati III appointed several commissions to review the tinkhundla (local government) system. In July 1992 the second Tinkhundla Review Commission (popularly called Vusela II) reported to the king. Government accepted its main recommendations—increase tinkhundla centers, allow direct representation in parliament, and institute a secret ballot. Opposition parties complained that Vusela II did not consult a broad range of Swazis and that the reforms did not address the issue of the legality of political parties. The king followed the Vusela II recommendations, rejected the creation of a multiparty system and, on 21 August 1993, the electoral process got started with nomination of candidates. On 25 September primary elections selected three candidates for each district. In October runoff elections, voters chose 55 members for the House of Assembly. The king appointed 10 more. A 30-member Senate was chosen, with 10 members elected by the House of Assembly and 20 appointed by the king.

Mswati was reluctant to share power. He ruled by decree, even though the Court of Appeal ruled against the legality of such decrees. He was often criticized for silencing his opponents in a heavy-handed manner. The king's disregard for the rule of law triggered what the Integrated Regional Information Networks (IRIN) News Network called a rule-of-law crisis. In November 2002 in protest of government's refusal to abide by Swaziland's Court of Appeal's decisions on two important rulings, the six members of the court resigned *en masse* and refused to hear cases for a period of two years. In a stinging report released in July 2004, Amnesty International, the international human rights organization, challenged Swaziland to "back up its recent commitments to international human rights standards by re-establishing the rule of law and confronting the systematic violation of civil, political, economic and social rights." Facing considerable international pressure for democratization and adherence to the rule of law, Prime Minister Absolom Dlamini made overtures to the court, which resumed hearing cases in November 2004.

The state heavily controlled the media, and strictly restricted freedom of expression. For instance, the palace instituted a press ban on photographs of King Mswati's cars, following embarrassing exposure of his lavish tastes and purchase of the world's most expensive automobile, reported to have cost $500,000. Some local pro-democracy groups were forced to hold political demonstrations in neighboring countries after a government ban on political meetings and the brutal force with which demonstrators had been handled.

14 POLITICAL PARTIES

All parties were banned under the 1978 constitution, but this ban was defied by the People's United Democratic Movement (PUDEMO), the Swaziland Liberation Front, the Swaziland Youth Congress (SWAYOCO), the Swaziland Communist Party, the Imbokodvo National Movement (INM), the Ngwane National Liberatory Congress (NNLC), the Swaziland National Front, and the Convention for Full Democracy in Swaziland, which operated openly. PUDEMO went so far as to declare itself legal in February 1992, and to demand a national convention of all political factions and a referendum on the constitution.

After many postponements, new elections were held in 1998. Amidst tight military and police security, Swazis went to the polls on 24 October 1998 in parliamentary elections. Over 85,000 people voted, which was an estimated 40% of the voting population. During the voting, harassment by the authorities of anti-electoral groups like PUDEMO and SWAYOCO, which were encouraging a boycott because they believed the elections would be rigged, was widespread. In addition to the 53 elected members of parliament, the king selected 10 more for the House of Assembly, 20 senators, and 10 cabinet ministers. The king also reappointed Prime Minister Sibusiso Dlamini to head the new government following the 1998 general elections.

In March 2005 Swaziland's High Court upheld a ban on legal recognition of opposition political parties, dealing a serious blow to Swaziland's two largest political organizations, PUDEMO and NNLC, which together with labor unions sought to challenge and forestall the new draft constitution. The pro-democracy groups argued that the constitutional process was illegal as it had gone against a 2002 decision by the Court of Appeal that ruled King Mswati III had no legal basis to decree laws. In their judgment the five justices invoked another decree, a 1973 state of emergency pronounced by Mswati's father, King Sobhuza, which gave absolute power to the monarchy and banned organized political opposition to royal rule. The 2005 constitution approved by the king and parliament maintained the ban on political parties. However, some local groups believed the government's recently-published policy guidelines for the creation, registration and running of nongovernmental organizations provided small openings for political activity.

Pro-democracy groups vowed to continue testing provisions of the constitution in court. In October 2005 there were firebombing incidences in several locations of Mbabane which the government blamed on the opposition party PUDEMO and other antiroyalist political groups. PUDEMO denied the claims.

Elections for the House of Assembly were held in September 2008. On 16 October 2008 Mswati III appointed Barnabas Sibusiso Dlamini to be prime minister. The House of Assembly had 65 seats by the 2003 election; 10 were appointed by the king and 55 elected by popular vote. The 66th member was the Speaker of the House who could be elected from outside the House as sanctioned by Section 102 of the constitution. The Senate had 30 members. Ten Senators, half of whom had to be female, were elected by members of the House of Assembly so as to represent a cross section of Swazi society. The next elections were scheduled to take place in 2013.

15 LOCAL GOVERNMENT

Swaziland is divided into four districts: Hhohho, Manzini, Shiselweni, and the largest, Lubombo. District commissioners are appointed by the central government. Mbabane, Manzini, and two other towns have municipal governments. Paralleling statutory government structure is a traditional system consisting of the king and his traditional advisors, traditional courts, and 55 tinkhundla sub regional districts in which traditional chiefs are grouped.

16 JUDICIAL SYSTEM

The dual judicial system consists of a set of courts based on a western model and western law and a set of national courts which follows Swazi law and custom. The former consists of a Court of Appeal and a High Court, plus magistrate's courts in each of the four districts. The traditional courts deal with minor offenses and violations of traditional Swazi law and custom. Sentences in traditional courts are subject to appeal and review to the Court of Appeals and High Court. The king has authority to appoint a special tribunal with its own procedural rules in treason and sedition cases.

The judges of the courts of appeal are expatriates, usually from South Africa, and serve on a two-year renewable contract basis. Local judges serve indefinitely on good behavior.

Although the courts were supposed to be independent of executive and military control or influence, there have been poor relations between the judiciary and the government. Matters came to a head in November 2002. The government refused to follow rulings of the Supreme Court of Appeal on two major cases, one declaring the king`s frequent decrees as illegal, and another ordering the return to their homes of Chief Mliba Fakudze and 200 of his followers forcibly evicted and exiled from their homes in Macetjeni by the government in 2000, after defying an apparent palace order installing King Mswati's brother, Prince Maguga Dlamini, as their new chief. Government defiance sparked public protests, international condemnation, and resulted in the resignation of the entire bench in November 2002. Relations began to turn around in November 2004 when the Court of Appeal resumed hearing cases after promises by the new Prime Minister Absolom Dlamini that the government would respect court decisions. However, tensions reappeared in 2011, when 80 lawyers boycotted national courts following the suspension of a judge accused of criticizing King Mswati.

17 ARMED FORCES

The force was comprised of the Umbutfo Swaziland Defense Force, a ground force with an air wing. The force had fewer than 3,000 personnel and functioned as a border patrol and an internal security force. A royal guard battalion was formed in 1982. Defense spending totaled $285.5 million and accounted for 4.7% of gross domestic product (GDP) in 2006.

¹⁸INTERNATIONAL COOPERATION

Swaziland joined the UN on 24 September 1968 and participated in the UN Economic Commission for Africa (ECA) and several nonregional specialized agencies, such as the Food and Agriculture Organization (FAO), UN Educational, Scientific, and Cultural Organization (UNESCO), UN Industrial Development Organization (UNIDO), the World Bank, and the World Health Organization (WHO). Swaziland also belonged to the African, Caribbean and Pacific Group of States (ACP Group), the African Development Bank, the Commonwealth of Nations, Group of 77 (G-77), World Trade Organization (WTO), the Southern African Customs Union (SACU), The Common Market for Eastern and Southern Africa (COMESA), the Southern African Development Community (SADC), and African Union. The country was also a part of the Non-Aligned Movement (NAM). In environmental cooperation, Swaziland was part of the Convention on Biological Diversity, Convention on International Trade in Endangered Species (CITES), the Montréal Protocol, the Nuclear Test Ban Treaty, the UN Convention on Climate Change, and the UN Convention to Combat Desertification (UNCCD).

¹⁹ECONOMY

Swaziland's economy was based on free market principles, although nearly 60% of Swazi territory was held by the Crown in trust for the Swazi nation. The benefits of a modern economy were primarily enjoyed by the growing urban population. The majority supported itself through subsistence agriculture on rural homesteads. Agriculture was hampered by overgrazing, soil depletion, droughts, and floods. It was estimated that in 2009 nearly 69% of the population lived in poverty, with about 40% of the labor force unemployed. The GDP rate of change in Swaziland, as of 2010, was 2%. Inflation stood at 5%, and unemployment was reported at 4%. A combination of declining revenues and increased spending led to budget deficits after 2000.

A relatively diversified industrial sector accounted for the largest component of the formal economy at 46% of GDP in 2008. The industrial sector produced garments, textiles, and light manufactured products. Because of its small size, Swaziland relied heavily on the export sector, composed primarily of large firms with predominantly foreign ownership. Sugar and wood pulp were the main foreign exchange earners. There was little mining in Swaziland with only coal, diamonds, and quarry stone mines active. However, money sent home from Swazi miners working in South Africa accounted for a sizable percentage of national income.

Surrounded almost entirely by South Africa, Swaziland's economy was heavily influenced by its dominant neighbor from whom it received over 90% of its imports and sent about 70% of its exports. The economy benefited considerably from investments that might otherwise have gone to South Africa during the period when there were international sanctions imposed on that country. On the other hand, the Swazi economy would likely continue to suffer as a reformed South Africa attracted investment that had been going to Swaziland. This overwhelming presence led some analysts to view the Swazi economy as a small, developing part of the much larger South African economy.

Swaziland's membership in the SACU with South Africa, Botswana, Lesotho, and Namibia, allowed for the virtually unimpeded exchange of goods between the countries, subject to South Africa's import control requirements.

The fiscal deficit in Swaziland grew to 13% of GDP by February 2011. At that time the government announced plans to cut spending and raise taxes to help regain strength in the economy. The budget cuts were expected to cut the deficit to 7.5% of GDP by March 2012.

Facing financial insolvency, Swaziland appealed to neighboring South Africa for a loan of $355 million in August of 2011. Though South African officials viewed the loan as necessary to preserve regional stability, many people were skeptical of how the money would be used, suggesting that it would merely preserve the opulent lifestyle of King Mswati.

²⁰INCOME

The CIA estimated that in 2010 the GDP of Swaziland was $6.067 billion. The CIA defines GDP as the value of all final goods and services produced within a nation in a given year and computed on the basis of purchasing power parity (PPP) rather than value as measured on the basis of the rate of the exchange based on current dollars. The per capita GDP was estimated at $4,500. The annual growth rate of GDP was 2%. The average inflation rate was 5%. It was estimated that agriculture accounted for 8.6% of GDP, industry 42%, and services 49.4%. In 2007 the World Bank estimated that Swaziland, with 0.02% of the world's population, accounted for 0.01% of the world's GDP. By comparison the United States, with 4.85% of the world's population, accounted for 22.51% of world GDP.

According to the World Bank, remittances from citizens living abroad totaled $93.5 million or about $68 per capita and accounted for approximately 1.5% of GDP.

The World Bank reported that in 2009, household consumption in Swaziland totaled $2.2 billion or about $1,593 per capita, measured in current US dollars rather than PPP. Household consumption includes expenditures of individuals, households, and nongovernmental organizations on goods and services, excluding the purchase of dwellings. It was estimated that household consumption was growing at an average annual rate of 3.8%.

As of 2011 the most recent study by the World Bank reported that actual individual consumption in Swaziland was 69.9% of GDP and accounted for 0.01% of world consumption. By comparison the United States accounted for 25.44% of world individual consumption. The World Bank also estimated that 29.9% of Swaziland's GDP was spent on food and beverages, 14.4% on housing and household furnishings, 4.3% on clothes, 5.1% on health, 4.8% on transportation, 0.9% on communications, 2.3% on recreation, 0.4% on restaurants and hotels, and 1.9% on miscellaneous goods and services and purchases from abroad.

It was estimated that in 2006 about 69% of the population subsisted on an income below the poverty line established by Swaziland's government.

²¹LABOR

As of 2007 Swaziland had a total labor force of 457,900 people. About 80% of the formal private sector was organized. The Swaziland Federation of Trade Unions was the major labor organization. There was also an employers' federation, as well as a second, breakaway labor group, the Swaziland Federation of Labor Officially. The right to strike was severely limited, but unions still engaged in strikes.

The minimum age of employment was 15, and children were rarely employed in the formal economy. Child labor was more common in the agricultural and informal economies, particularly in the eastern cotton growing region. Swaziland had a legally-mandated sliding scale of minimum wages depending on the type of work. The minimum monthly wage for a domestic servant was approximately $45 (SWL300) in 2011. For an unskilled worker it was $63 (SWL420) and for a skilled worker, $90 (SWL600). These minimum wages generally did not provide a decent standard of living for a worker and family. Wage arrears, particularly in the garment industry, were common. The government protects workers with health and safety regulations. The maximum workweek was set at 48 hours, with one day of rest.

In a November 2009 report of the International Trade Union Confederation (ITUC) on labor standards in the SACU, Swaziland was listed as the worst offender of workers' rights. There were several legal restrictions and limitations on collective bargaining and the right to organize and the law did not allow worker strikes. Child labor was considered to be a problem as well.

The issue of workers' rights inspired government opposition from a somewhat surprising source, the Congress of South African Trade Unions (COSATU) in South Africa. COSATU was affiliated with the South African ruling ANC and served as the nation's largest, most powerful trade union. The group initiated several campaigns against the regime of King Mswati III, primarily through the coordination of pro-democracy rallies inside and outside of Swaziland and by offering assistance to underground Swazi unionists. As a result of their public actions, COSATU and the Pro-Democracy Movement for Swaziland gained support in much of the southern region of South Africa. Such support may lead the government of South Africa to take action against the Swazi regime.

²²AGRICULTURE

Swazi Nation Land (SNL), which comprised over 60% of the total land area, was held in trust by the crown for the Swazi people and supported about 70% of the population. Nearly half of the remaining land, which was freehold title, was owned by Europeans; the rest was owned by government or parastatal bodies. Under the traditional land tenure system, farmers tilled small plots, averaging less than 3 hectares (7.4 acres), but had no title or right to sell this land. The average freehold title farm, by contrast, was about 800 hectares (2,000 acres), and over 60% of freehold title cropland was irrigated. In this modern sector, agriculture expanded considerably in the early 1970s, mainly because of improved irrigation, better strains, and widespread introduction and use of fertilizers. Roughly 11% of the total land was farmed in 2009, and the country's major crops included sugarcane, cotton, corn, tobacco, rice, citrus, pineapples, sorghum, and peanuts. In 2009 cereal production amounted to 61,470 tons, fruit production 102,875 tons, and vegetable production 11,311 tons. Sugar was the most important cash crop, and corn was the staple crop. Most of the sugar produced was exported to Western Europe and North America. Much of the sugar was exported to the European Union (EU), in

accordance with the Sugar Protocol of the Lomé Convention; increasing amounts, however, were sold and refined domestically.

Between 1970 and 1982, 17 Rural Development Areas were established to assist traditional farmers; the program was planned to extend eventually to all Swazi Nation Land. The 1991–92 drought caused corn and cotton production to seriously decline; as a result the government sought emergency food assistance. By 1999 crop production was 90% of what it had been during 1989–91.

²³ANIMAL HUSBANDRY

Livestock raising, like agriculture, was divided into two sectors: a traditional system of grazing on communal lands for subsistence needs and modern commercial ranches on freehold title land. The UN FAO reported that Swaziland dedicated 1 million hectares (2.55 million acres) to permanent pasture or meadow in 2009. During that year the country tended 3.2 million chickens, 585,000 head of cattle, and 30,000 pigs. The production from these animals amounted to 21,846 tons of beef and veal, 1,535 tons of pork, 6,083 tons of poultry, 2,946 tons of eggs, and 56,883 tons of milk. Swaziland also produced 1,700 tons of cattle hide.

²⁴FISHING

In 2008 the annual capture totaled 70 tons according to the UN FAO. Several commercial fish farms have been established, and some Rural Development Areas had fish ponds.

²⁵FORESTRY

Swaziland's forests—pine and eucalyptus—were among the world's largest planted forests, covering 161,000 hectares (398,000 acres), or about 9% of the land area. The total forest area in 2000 was 522,000 hectares (1,290,000 acres), or 30% of the land area. Of Swaziland's planted forests, half supplied the Usutu Pulp Mill, a large export earner producing unbleached wood pulp. About 3% of Swaziland's forests were in protected nature reserves and game sanctuaries. The UN FAO estimated the 2009 roundwood production at 330,000 cu m (11.7 million cu ft). The value of all forest products, including roundwood, totaled $68.1 million. The value of all forest products, including roundwood, totaled $68.1 million in 2009.

²⁶MINING

The historic mineral sector of Swaziland has essentially collapsed. The kingdom contained the world's oldest known mine site, the Lion Cavern at the Ngwenya Iron Mine on Bomvu Ridge, northwest of Mbabane. Carbon-14 dating estimated that mining of hematite (libomvu) and specularite ochres for cosmetic and ritual uses took place at the site from 43,000–41,000 BC until at least 23,000 BC; the mine was closed in 1977. Mining's role in Swaziland's economy was declining in recent years, and as of 2004 accounted for only a minor factor in its overall economy. Asbestos mining ceased in 2000, diamond mining ceased in 1996, and mining of the once-major export of iron ore stopped in the late 1970s (it reached 2.24 million tons in 1975).

In 2009 Swaziland produced an estimated 240,000 cu m of quarry stone products, and also produced brick clay, anthracite coal, pyrophyllite, and sand and gravel. Small-scale unreported gold mining took place. The mining of chrysolite fiber asbestos, once the dominant source of mining revenue, employed 1,000 workers at Bulumbe, one of the world's largest asbestos mines, but ceased because of declining reserves, environmental concerns, and weak markets. In 2000 the last year of asbestos production, 12,690 metric tons was produced. An estimated 500 metric tons of ferrovanadium was produced in 2009. Although fewer than 1,000 Swazis were directly employed in the mining sector, 1,000 people processed timber from the country's extensive pine populations for mines in South Africa, and 10,000-15,000 Swazis were employed in South African mines.

27 ENERGY AND POWER

The World Bank reported in 2008 that Swaziland produced 470 million kWh of electricity and consumed 1.51 billion kWh, or 1,102 kWh per capita. However, Swaziland's primary fossil fuel resource is coal. The country has no proven reserves of oil or natural gas, and thus must rely on imports to meet its petroleum and natural gas needs.

As of 2011 Swaziland had no proven reserves of crude oil or natural gas, nor any petroleum refining capacity.

Coal was Swaziland's only fossil fuel resource. As of 2008 these reserves came to 159 million short tons. Production for coal in 2010 came to 351,000 short tons, while consumption was 251,000 short tons. There were no known oil or natural gas reserves in Swaziland.

28 INDUSTRY

Manufacturing consisted primarily of the following export-oriented industries: wood pulp production, drink processing, fruit canning (Swazican), and sugar processing. Manufacturing growth in the mid-1990s was mostly attributable to increased production of drink processing at Bromor Foods and the sugar-based production activities of the Royal Swaziland Sugar Corporation and Cadbury Confectioneries. Swaziland's three sugar mills have an annual production capacity of 500,000 tons. Usutu Pulp Mill, Swaziland's largest employer, was the leading wood pulp processing company, with an annual capacity to produce 220,000 tons of bleached kraft pulp. Sappi, a London-based company, managed the Usutu Pulp Mill. Cement, agricultural machinery, electronic equipment, and refrigerator production were also important parts of Swaziland's manufacturing sector. Textiles, footwear, gloves, office equipment, confectionery, furniture, glass, and bricks were also manufactured. Industry accounted for over 40% of GDP.

Sanctions against South Africa in the late 1980s and internal unrest inspired interest in the relocation of South African-based industry, such as Coca-Cola, in Swaziland. Reexports of South Africa manufactures with "Made in Swaziland" labels also appeared at that time. The industrial sector growth of the 1980s slowed in the early 1990s as stability returned to South Africa and sanctions were eliminated. Textile manufacturing, which flourished when South African tariffs were high, began to wither when they were equalized.

Creation of the SADC further marginalized previous industry benefits to operating in Swaziland. The privatization of state-owned industry in 2000 increased foreign interest in Swaziland's industrial sector.

29 SCIENCE AND TECHNOLOGY

The University of Swaziland, founded originally as part of the University of Botswana, Lesotho, and Swaziland in 1964, had faculties of agriculture and science. The Swaziland College of Technology, founded originally in 1946 as a trade school, offered courses in various fields of engineering. The Geological Survey and Mines Department, founded in 1946 at Mbabane, conducted mining research, and three other institutes conduct agricultural research. In 2002 high technology exports were valued at $3 million, or 1% of the country's manufactured exports. The World Bank reported in 2009 that there were no patent applications in science and technology in Swaziland.

30 DOMESTIC TRADE

South Africa's substantial presence in Swaziland's domestic economy essentially meant that South African business was the driving force in Swaziland's domestic commerce. South African employers and investors dominated certain sectors of local trade. However, the government worked on programs to encourage local ownership and operation of small- to medium-sized establishments. A few franchises were established. Bargaining was an accepted practice in many Swazi business deals. The most developed distribution routes were those connecting to South Africa. Mbabane and Manzini were the principal commercial centers. Manufactured articles were generally available in all urban centers and were marketed mostly by South Africans.

Business hours are from 8:15 or 8:30 a.m. to 1 p.m. and from 2 to 5 p.m., Monday-Friday, and from 8:15 or 8:30 a.m. to 1 p.m., Saturday. Banks are open weekdays from 8:30 a.m. to 1 p.m. and Saturdays from 8:30 to 11 a.m.

31 FOREIGN TRADE

Swaziland's exports have traditionally equaled a significant portion of GDP. As a result the country's entire economy tended to mirror world commodity prices, and especially the state of the South African economy.

The value of exports rose steadily during the 1990s, while the value of imports rose until 1997, when purchases suddenly dropped by 27%. This was probably due to the creation of the South African free trade area. Principal exports in 2003 included sugar, soft drink concentrates (a large US investment), wood pulp and lumber, cotton yarn, and fruit. Principal imports were motor vehicles, machinery, transport equipment, food, petroleum products, and chemicals. Swaziland imported $1.643 billion worth of goods and services in 2008, while exporting $1.417 billion worth of goods and services. Its major export partners were South Africa, 80%; the EU, 10%; and Mozambique, 10%.

Almost 96% of imports either originated in or traveled through South Africa, and direct sales to and transshipments through South Africa accounted for about 72% of Swaziland's exports. About 12% of exports went to the EU.

32 BALANCE OF PAYMENTS

A decline in long-term capital inflows, increasing government deficits, and a drop in donor assistance plagued Swaziland with a current account deficit for much of the 1990s. The goods and services account had been negative since the 1980s. Payments made

Balance of Payments – Swaziland (2010)

(In millions of US dollars)

Current Account		**-388.6**
Balance on goods		-149.9
Imports	-1,955.2	
Exports	1,805.4	
Balance on services		-412.1
Balance on income		-226.1
Current transfers		399.5
Capital Account		**14.4**
Financial Account		**87.8**
Direct investment abroad		-3.9
Direct investment in Swaziland		135.7
Portfolio investment assets		49.7
Portfolio investment liabilities		4.7
Financial derivatives		...
Other investment assets		-161.6
Other investment liabilities		63.3
Net Errors and Omissions		**55.5**
Reserves and Related Items		**230.9**

(…) data not available or not significant.

SOURCE: *Balance of Payment Statistics Yearbook 2011*, Washington, DC: International Monetary Fund, 2011.

by SACU to Swaziland, along with donor assistance, offset this deficit, but these sources of revenue were threatened. Increased government deficits also weakened the position of the current account. Revenue from SACU, which made up 60% of the fiscal revenue base and 25% of the GDP in 2008 and 2009 collapsed by more than 60% for 2010 and 2011, while expenditure levels gradually increased to 45% of GDP in 2009 and 2010. By 2010 Swaziland had a foreign trade deficit of $484 million, amounting to 4.1% of GDP.

The Economist Intelligence Unit reported that in 2005 the PPP of Swaziland's exports was $2.007 billion while imports totaled $2.096 billion, resulting in a trade deficit of $89 million.

33 BANKING AND SECURITIES

The Central Bank of Swaziland was the nation's central bank. Swaziland has experienced excess liquidity for some time. The nation's commercial banks were Standard Bank, First National and the Nedbank as of 1998. The government reconstructed the Swaziland Development and Savings Bank in that year after a 1995 bankruptcy. The Swaziland Building Society provided mortgages for housing.

The International Monetary Fund (IMF) reported that in 2001 currency and demand deposits, an aggregate commonly known as M1, were equal to $62.2 million. In that same year M2, an aggregate equal to M1 plus savings deposits, small time deposits, and money market mutual funds, was $189.7 million.

In 2005, the money market rate, the rate at which financial institutions lend to one another in the short term, was 3.47%. The discount rate, the interest rate at which the central bank lends to financial institutions in the short term, was 7%.

The Swaziland Stock Market was established in July 1990. In 2011 there were a handful of listed public companies, as some listed government stock options, listed debentures, government guaranteed stock and non-trading mutual funds.

34 INSURANCE

The Swaziland Royal Insurance Corporation, 41% state owned, began operating in 1974. It was majority-owned by South African insurance and reinsurance companies. The Swaziland National Provident Fund was a mandatory savings institution for employees.

35 PUBLIC FINANCE

In the past the government maintained a prudent fiscal policy by avoiding large deficits and restricting public sector growth. From 1987 to 1991 large budgetary surpluses were registered, and the government began making repayments on the external debt as a net creditor to the bank. Budgetary deficits during the 1990s–2000s reflected extravagant government spending on the monarch and his family. The civil service was overstaffed as well, prompting a reduction of 5,000 employees in 2000. In 2010 the budget of Swaziland included $961.7 million in public revenue and $1.379 billion in public expenditures. The budget deficit amounted to 11.9% of GDP. Public debt was 14.6% of GDP, with $468.4 million of the debt held by foreign entities.

Government outlays by function were as follows: general public services, 30.6%; defense, 7.6%; public order and safety, 8.1%; economic affairs, 21.1%; housing and community amenities, 3.6%; health, 8.0%; recreation, culture, and religion, 0.6%; education, 19.8%; and social protection, 0.4%.

36 TAXATION

Swaziland had a progressive personal income tax system with rates ranging from 0–30%. There were no local taxes. As of the year ending December 2010 the corporate income tax was levied at a rate of 30%. There was no capital gains tax, tax on dividends from companies paid to residents, or estate taxes. Swaziland had double taxation treaties with several countries including South Africa. The standard rate for the sales tax was increased from 14% in 2010, with higher rates for items like liquor (25%) and tobacco. Exempted from sales tax were fresh foodstuffs, drugs, medicines, furniture and building supplies.

37 CUSTOMS AND DUTIES

Swaziland belonged to the SACU with South Africa, Lesotho, Botswana, and Namibia. South Africa levied and collected most of the customs, sales, and excise duties for the five member states, paying a share of the revenues to the other four. Local import duties were applied to wines, spirits, and beer. Swaziland also signed a double taxation agreement with the United States in 2000.

38 FOREIGN INVESTMENT

Foreign direct investment (FDI) in Swaziland was a net inflow of $65.7 million according to World Bank figures published in 2009. FDI represented 2.19% of GDP.

Cognizant of its subordinate relationship to South Africa, Swaziland fostered an investment climate agreeable to foreign businesses. More than half of all enterprises were foreign-owned or joint ventures. South African investment consistently accounted for around 45% of FDI. It is surmised that UK entities injected the largest portion of the remaining 55%, followed by Taiwan. The United States, Denmark, the Netherlands, and Germany were also present. Foreign investors paid a reduced 10% corporate tax and were exempted from withholding tax on dividends for the first 10 years.

In 1997 Swaziland experienced divestment of FDI amounting to -$15.1 million, but in 1998 annual FDI inflow rose to $151 million. Inflow was $100 million in 1999, but there was a reverse flow of -$18.5 million in 2000. FDI inflow was $68 million in 2001, $48.7 million in 2002, and $60.8 million in 2003. FDI grew by 10.4% in 2003 and much of this growth was through reinvested earnings. FDI in Swaziland was a net inflow of $65.7 million, according to World Bank figures published in 2009. FDI represented 2.19% of GDP. There was no policy of encouraging Swazis or Swazi business to invest abroad generally, but a handful of Swazi businesses invested abroad, primarily in South Africa.

[39]ECONOMIC DEVELOPMENT

The growth that was experienced in past years left unaffected the 60% of Swazis who lived on small family farms. While manufacturing employment rose, about half of Swazis were unemployed and actively seeking work. Economic activity weakened in the early 2000s, however, in part due to drought and closures by foreign firms. Food shortages and the spread of HIV/AIDS exacerbated the dire conditions of high unemployment, income inequality, and poverty. A National Emergency Response Committee (NERCHA) was established in 2001 to combat HIV/AIDS.

Consistent commodity prices for sugar and wood pulp during 2011 were expected to sustain modest economic growth. The continuing rise in the value of the rand against the US dollar threatened to make export-oriented industries less profitable. A decrease in government salaries, combined with the implementation of a value-added tax (VAT), was the basis for economic growth between 2011 and 2014. The measures were also the conditions under which the government could secure much-needed financing from the IMF.

[40]SOCIAL DEVELOPMENT

Social services developed slowly. A system of pensions existed for formerly-employed persons. Old age, disability, and survivorship were covered. The program was funded by 5% contribution by both employees and employers. Retirement was allowed between ages 45 and 50 and pensions could be paid as a one-time lump sum or divided into installments. Private work injury insurance was mandatory for all employers.

On paper Swaziland, Africa's last absolute monarchy, seemed willing to respect and uphold women's rights. The country was a signatory to the Convention on the Elimination of All Forms of Discrimination against Women, and its 2005 constitution clearly embraced equality for all before the law. In practice, however, things were different. Women did not have full legal equality with men, and a married woman was virtually a legal minor. A woman could not open a bank account, buy land, or leave the country without her husband's permission. In addition, women did not automatically transmit citizenship to their children, and could not transfer property to them. Domestic violence was commonplace, and rape was viewed as a minor offense by most men. Women were inhibited from reporting violence, and the court system was

unsympathetic. Child abuse was also a widespread social problem despite legislation protecting the rights of children.

There were continued reports of the use of excessive force by police and torture during interrogation. The law did not provide for freedom of speech and of the press, and the government restricted these activities. However, human rights organizations were permitted to operate.

[41]HEALTH

According to the CIA, life expectancy in Swaziland was 46 years in 2011. The country spent 5.8% of its GDP on healthcare, amounting to $156 per person. There were 2 physicians, 63 nurses and midwives, and 21 hospital beds per 10,000 inhabitants. The fertility rate was 3.5, while the infant mortality rate was 52 per 1,000 live births. In 2008 the maternal mortality rate, according to the World Bank, was 420 per 100,000 births. It was estimated that 95% of children were vaccinated against measles. Major health problems include bilharzia, typhoid, tapeworm, gastroenteritis, malaria, kwashiorkor, and pellagra. Traditional healers were still consulted by a majority of the population. Approximately 43% of the population had access to safe water, and 36% had adequate sanitation. About 56% of the population had access to health care services.

Swaziland, like many African nations, was significantly impacted by the prevalence of HIV/AIDS and, in fact, had the highest prevalence rate in the world, with an estimated 25.9% of adults living with the disease in 2011. In 2009 international aid groups were alarmed by the increasing number of combined HIV/AIDS and tuberculosis (TB) cases. That year about 80% of the people with HIV/AIDS also suffered from TB. An average of 14,000 new TB cases have been diagnosed every year. Moreover, by November 2009, many of the TB cases proved to be drug resistant.

About 42.6% of pregnant women tested positive for HIV. One charity, Swaziland for Positive Living, promoted a campaign to encourage male circumcision as a way to lower the risk of contracting HIV. Trials in Kenya, Uganda, and South Africa showed that the operation seemed to reduce the risk of contracting the disease by 60% for males. However, the monarch and his top aides consistently renounced HIV awareness and prevention campaigns as merely scare tactics and claimed that the HIV/AIDS epidemic was greatly exaggerated by pharmaceutical firms seeking business. Assistance in prevention and treatment of HIV/AIDS came primarily through international aid organizations and foreign nations.

In 2011 the infant mortality rate was estimated at 63.09 deaths per 1,000 live births. Maternal mortality in 2007 was estimated at 589 deaths per 100,000 live births. The total fertility rate in 2011 was estimated at 3.11 children born per woman. In 2009 the government of Japan offered a grant of $2.57 million to Swaziland for a three-year campaign to improve maternal and child health and welfare programs in the nation. A major goal of the programs was to encourage male involvement in the care of wives and infant children in the first few months after birth. Such a goal was difficult to achieve in a society in which traditional gender roles were clearly defined and maintained, and in which native customs prevailed over modern medical knowledge and practice. Traditional Swazi customs prohibited men from maintaining physical contact with their wives and newborn children for at least six months after a birth. Although women were encouraged to breast-feed their infants for at least six months, traditional care included the use of traditional medicines and foods that may be detrimental to the health of the child.

In 2011 total life expectancy was estimated at 48.66 years.

The immunization rates for children under one year of age were as follows: diphtheria and pertussis, tetanus, 71%; and measles, 60%.

⁴²HOUSING

The search for jobs in urban settings caused a housing shortage in these areas. Several squatter settlements developed, accounting for as much as half of annual shelter production in cities. It was estimated that about 60% of the urban population resided in temporary shelters, and that number grew as more and more households were unable to afford the high cost of home ownership. In response, the government has worked with international programs, such as the World Bank, to create and improve urban housing. In 2001 the Swaziland National Housing Board provided over 1,000 rental units and 500 units for ownership to low- and middle-income families.

⁴³EDUCATION

In 2009 the World Bank estimated that 83% of age-eligible children in Swaziland were enrolled in primary school. Secondary enrollment for age-eligible children stood at 29%. Tertiary enrollment was estimated at 4%. Overall, the CIA estimated that Swaziland had a literacy rate of 81.6%. Public expenditure on education represented 7.8% of GDP.

The majority of primary and secondary schools were run by missions with grants from the government. Children went through seven years of primary and five years of secondary schooling in three- and two-year cycles. Schooling was not compulsory and nominal fees were charged to parents. The academic year ran from August to May.

Higher education was provided by the University of Swaziland and the Swaziland College of Technology.

⁴⁴LIBRARIES AND MUSEUMS

The Swaziland National Library Service was founded in 1971; with 250,000 volumes, it had 12 branches throughout the country and operated school libraries at secondary levels. There was also a mobile library service. The University of Swaziland in Kwaluseni had 180,000 volumes. The Swaziland Library Association was founded in 1984. The Swaziland National Museum in Lobamba, founded in 1972, contained collections primarily of ethnographic material and cultural objects of South Africa Bantu groups.

⁴⁵MEDIA

In 2009 the CIA reported that there were 44,000 telephone landlines in Swaziland. In addition to landlines, mobile phone subscriptions averaged 55 per 100 people. There were three FM radio stations, two AM radio stations, and three shortwave radio stations. Internet users numbered 8 per 100 citizens.

The government-operated Swaziland Broadcasting Service broadcasted radio programs in English and SiSwati and television programs in English. In 2010 the country had 2,335 Internet hosts. In 2009 there were some 90,100 Internet users in Swaziland.

There were two major daily English language newspapers, the *Times of Swaziland* and the *Swaziland Observer*, with circulations in 2010 of 25,000 and 18,000, respectively. Freedom of speech and of the press were said to be limited, especially on political matters.

⁴⁶ORGANIZATIONS

There were more than 123 cooperative societies, including the Swaziland Central Cooperatives Union. The National Chamber of Commerce and Industry is in Mbabane. The Swaziland National Consumers' Association was established in 1994. There were active professional associations, such as the Swaziland Nurses Association and Swaziland National Association of Teachers.

Educational organizations included the Swaziland Educational Research Association and Fundza, which works to establish school libraries throughout the country.

National youth organizations included the Swaziland Boy Scouts Association, Swaziland Workcamp Association, and the Swaziland Youth Forum. There were several sports associations in the country promoting amateur competition for athletes of all ages in a variety of pastimes; many of these groups were affiliated with international counterparts, as well as with the Swaziland Olympic and Commonwealth Games Association.

Volunteer service organizations, such as Lions Clubs International and Rotary Club, were also present. Social action and development groups included the Human Rights Association of Swaziland and Emanti Esive (Water for Community Development), a health and wellness organization. There were national chapters of the Red Cross Society; UN Children's Fund, formerly United Nations International Children's Emergency Fund (UNICEF); and Caritas.

⁴⁷TOURISM, TRAVEL, AND RECREATION

Swaziland offers the tourist a magnificent variety of scenery and casinos at Mbabane, Nhlangano, and Piggs Peak. The tea estates near the Mdzimba Mountains are also an attraction. Popular sports are tennis, squash, hiking, fishing, white-water rafting, lawn bowls (bowling on a green), and golf. If traveling from an infected area, vaccination against yellow fever is required. Precautions against cholera, typhoid, polio, and malaria are recommended. Passports and travel documents are required of all visitors as well as visas from more than 145 countries including China and Russia.

The *Tourism Factbook*, published by the UN World Tourism Organization, reported 1.34 million incoming tourists to Swaziland in 2009, who spent a total of $40 million. Of those incoming tourists, there were 1.2 million from Africa. There were 2,947 hotel beds available in Swaziland, which had an occupancy rate of 53%. The estimated daily cost to visit Mbabane, the capital, was $342. The cost of visiting other cities averaged $138.

According to 2005 US Department of State estimates, the daily cost of staying in Mbabane was $247.

⁴⁸FAMOUS PERSONS

Sobhuza II (1899–1982) was king, or ngwenyama, of the Swazi nation from 1921 until his death. Mswati III (b. 1968) became king in 1986.

[49] DEPENDENCIES

Swaziland has no territories or colonies.

[50] BIBLIOGRAPHY

Booth, Alan R. *Historical Dictionary of Swaziland.* Lanham, MD: Scarecrow Press, 2000.

Fitzpatrick, Mary, et al. *South Africa, Lesotho and Swaziland.* Hawthorn, Victoria: Lonely Planet Publications, 2004.

McElrath, Karen, ed. *HIV and AIDS: A Global View.* Westport, CT: Greenwood Press, 2002.

Penn, Helen. *Unequal Childhoods: Children's Lives in Developing Countries.* New York: RoutledgeFalmer, 2005.

Swaziland Investment and Business Guide: Strategic and Practical Information. Washington, DC: International Business Publications USA, 2012.

Zeilig, Leo, and David Seddon. *A Political and Economic Dictionary of Africa.* Philadelphia: Routledge/Taylor and Francis, 2005.

TANZANIA

United Republic of Tanzania
Jamhuri Ya Muungano Wa Tanzania

CAPITAL: Dodoma

FLAG: The flag consists of a black diagonal stripe running from the lower left corner to the upper right corner, flanked by yellow stripes. The diagonal stripes separate two triangular areas: green at the upper left and blue at the lower right.

ANTHEM: *Mungu ibariki Afrika (God Bless Africa).*

MONETARY UNIT: The Tanzanian shilling (TZS) of 100 cents is a paper currency. There are coins of 50, 100, and 200 cents and notes of 500, 1,000, 2,000, 5 000, and 10,000 shillings. TZS1 = US$0.0063 (or US$1 = TZS159.504) as of 2011.

WEIGHTS AND MEASURES: The metric system is used.

HOLIDAYS: New Year`s Day, 1 January; Zanzibar Revolution Day, 12 January; Chama Cha Mapinduzi Day, 5 February; Union Day, 26 April; International Workers' Day, 1 May; Farmers' Day, 7 July; Nyerere Day, 14 October; Independence Day, 9 December; Christmas, 25 December. Movable religious holidays include Eid al-Fitr, Eid al-Adha, Milad an-Nabi, Good Friday, and Easter Monday.

TIME: 3 p.m. = noon GMT.

¹LOCATION, SIZE, AND EXTENT

Situated in East Africa just south of the equator, mainland Tanzania lies between the area of the great lakes—Victoria, Tanganyika, and Malawi (Niassa)—and the Indian Ocean. It contains a total area of 945,087 sq km (364,900 sq mi), including 59,050 sq km (22,799 sq mi) of inland water. Comparatively, the area occupied by Tanzania is slightly larger than twice the size of the state of California. It is bounded on the N by Uganda and Kenya, on the E by the Indian Ocean, on the S by Mozambique and Malawi, on the SW by Zambia, and on the W by Zaire, Burundi, and Rwanda, with a total boundary length of 4,826 km (2,999 mi), of which 1,424 km (885 mi) is coastline. Tanzania claims part of Lake Malawi, although its internationally recognized boundary is the eastern shore.

The section of the United Republic known as Zanzibar comprises the islands of Zanzibar and Pemba and all islets within 19 km (12 mi) of their coasts, as well as uninhabited Latham Island, 58 km (36 mi) south of Zanzibar Island. Zanzibar Island lies 35 km (22 mi) off the coast, and Pemba Island is about 40 km (25 mi) to the Ne. The former has an area of 1,657 sq km (640 sq mi), and the latter 984 sq km (380 sq mi).

Tanzania's capital city, Dodoma, is located in the center of the country, the town is 486 kilometers west of the former capital of Dar es Salaam.

²TOPOGRAPHY

Except for the islands and a coastal strip varying in width from 16 to 64 km (10–40 mi), Tanzania lies at an altitude of over 200 m (660 ft). A plateau averaging 900–1,800 m (3,000–6,000 ft) in height makes up the greater part of the country. Mountains are grouped in various sections. The Pare range is in the northeast, and the Kipengere Range is in the southwest. Kilimanjaro (5,895 m/19,340 ft), in the north, is the highest mountain in Africa.

On the borders are three large lakes: Victoria, the second-largest freshwater lake in the world, exceeded only by Lake Superior; Tanganyika, second only to Lake Baykal as the deepest in the world; and Lake Malawi. Lakes within Tanzania include Natron, Eyasi, Manyara, and Rukwa.

Tanzania has few permanent rivers. During half the year, the central plateau has no running water, but in the rainy season, flooding presents a problem.

Two-thirds of Zanzibar Island, to the center and the east, consists of low-lying coral country covered by bush and grass plains and is largely uninhabited except for fishing settlements on the east coast. The western side of the island is fertile and has several ridges rising above 60 m (200 ft). Masingini Ridge, at 119 m (390 ft), is the highest point on the island. The west and center of Pemba Island consists of a flat-topped ridge about 9.5 km (6 mi) wide, deeply bisected by streams. Pemba is hilly, but its highest point is only 95 m (311 ft). Apart from the narrow belt of coral country in the east, the island is fertile and densely populated.

³CLIMATE

There are four main climatic zones: (1) the coastal area and immediate hinterland, where conditions are tropical, with temperatures averaging about 27°C (81°F), rainfall varying from 100 to 193 cm (40 to 76 in), and high humidity; (2) the central plateau, which is hot and dry, with rainfall from 50–76 cm (20–30 in), although with considerable daily and seasonal temperature variations; (3) the semitemperate highland areas, where the climate is healthy and bracing; and (4) the high, moist lake regions. There is little seasonal variation in the Lake Victoria area, but the eastern sections average only 75–100 cm (30–40 in) of rain, while the western parts receive 200–230 cm (80–90 in). A small area north of Lake Niassa receives 250 cm (100 in) of rain. There are two rainy seasons in the north, from November to December and from March through May. In the south there is one rainy season, from November to March.

The climate on the islands is tropical, but the heat is tempered by sea breezes that are constant throughout the year, except during the rainy seasons. The seasons are well defined. From December to March, when the northeast monsoon blows, it is hot and comparatively dry. The heavy rains fall in April and May, and the lesser in November and December. It is coldest and driest from June to October, during the southwest monsoon.

⁴FLORA AND FAUNA

The World Resources Institute estimates that there are 10,008 plant species in Tanzania. Common savanna species cover most of the drier inland areas—amounting to about one-third of the country—between altitudes of 300 and 1,200 m (1,000 and 4,000 ft). Two main types of closed-forest trees-low-level hardwoods and mountain softwoods-are found in high-rainfall areas on the main mountain masses and in parts of the Lake Victoria Basin. Wooded grasslands are widely scattered throughout the country. The drier central areas include bushlands and thickets. Grasslands and heath are common in the highlands, while the coast has mangrove forest. There are over 10,000 species of plants throughout the country.

In addition, Tanzania is home to 375 mammal, 1,056 bird, 335 reptile, and 132 amphibian species. The calculation reflects the total number of distinct species residing in the country, not the number of endemic species. The population of wild mammals is roughly 4 million and includes species of antelope, zebra, elephant, hippopotamus, rhinoceros, giraffe, and lion. Various types of monkeys are plentiful. Insect life, consisting of more than 60,000 species, includes injurious species and disease carriers. There are 25 poisonous varieties among the 100 species of snakes. Fish are plentiful.

The flora and fauna of Zanzibar and Pemba are varied. Mammals common to both are galagos, fruit-eating and insectivorous bats, genets, mongooses, small shrews, rats, and mice. Zanzibar has the leopard, Syke's monkey, civet, and giant rat. Unique species of tree coney are found on Pemba and Tumbatu Islands. There are also five unique mammals-Kirk's colobus (monkey), two elephant shrews, duiker antelope, and squirrel.

⁵ENVIRONMENT

The Ministry of Natural Resources and Tourism, the Tanzania National Parks Department, and the Ministry of Lands, Housing, and Urban Development are the government agencies entrusted with environmental responsibilities in Tanzania. One of the nation's major concerns is soil degradation as a result of recent droughts. Also of concern is the drop in water level at Lake Victoria. In 2006 water resources totaled 91 cu km (21.83 cu mi) while water usage was 5.18 cu km (1.24 cu mi) per year. Domestic water usage accounted for 11% of total usage and agricultural usage for 89%. Per capita water usage totaled 135 cu m (4,767 cu ft) per year. The nation's land is also affected by the related problem of desertification.

The World Resources Institute reported that Tanzania had designated 34.27 million hectares (84.68 million acres) of land for protection as of 2006. The Greater Mahale Ecosystem along the shores of Lake Tanganyika in northwestern Tanzania is considered by some to be the gem of the nation's natural resources. About 75% of the ecosystem is comprised of woodland and forest that is minimally accessible to human development and travel. The area is home to one of the largest chimpanzee populations on earth and supports a diversity of other plant and animal species. In 2009 a new research center was opened at Mahale State Park (located within the greater ecosystem) to serve as a hub for international researchers. The center is funded primarily by the European Commission, with additional support from the Frankfurt Zoological Society and the Tanzanian National Parks Service.

According to a 2011 report issued by the International Union for Conservation of Nature and Natural Resources (IUCN), the number of threatened species included 35 types of mammals, 42 species of birds, 16 types of reptiles, 51 species of amphibians, 174 species of fish, 15 types of mollusks, 65 species of other invertebrates, and 297 species of plants. The nation's marine habitats are threatened by damage to its coral reefs caused by the fishing industry's use of dynamite. Threatened species included the Uluguru bush-shrike, green sea turtle, hawksbill turtle, olive ridley turtle, and Zanzibar suni. At least 16 species of fish have become extinct.

⁶POPULATION

The US Central Intelligence Agency (CIA) estimates the population of Tanzania in 2011 to be approximately 42,746,620, which placed it at number 30 in population among the 196 nations of the world. In 2011, approximately 2.9% of the population was over 65 years of age, with another 42% under 15 years of age. The median age in Tanzania was 18.5 years. There were 0.98 males for every female in the country. The population's annual rate of change was 2.002%. The projected population for the year 2025 was 67,400,000. Population density in Tanzania was calculated at 45 people per sq km (117 people per sq mi).

The UN estimated that 26% of the population lived in urban areas, and that urban populations had an annual rate of change of 4.7%. The largest urban area was Dar es Salaam, with a population of 3.2 million.

The most densely populated regions are the well-watered or elevated areas, particularly in the fertile Usambara Mountains around Kilimanjaro and Meru, on the shores of Lake Victoria, in the Southern Highlands, and in the coastal areas around Tanga and Dar es Salaam

The prevalence of HIV/AIDS has had a significant impact on the population of Tanzania. The AIDS epidemic causes higher death and infant mortality rates, and lowers life expectancy which was 52.85 years in 2011.

⁷MIGRATION

Estimates of Tanzania's net migration rate, carried out by the CIA in 2011, amounted to -0.53 migrants per 1,000 citizens. The total number of emigrants living abroad was 316,900, and the total

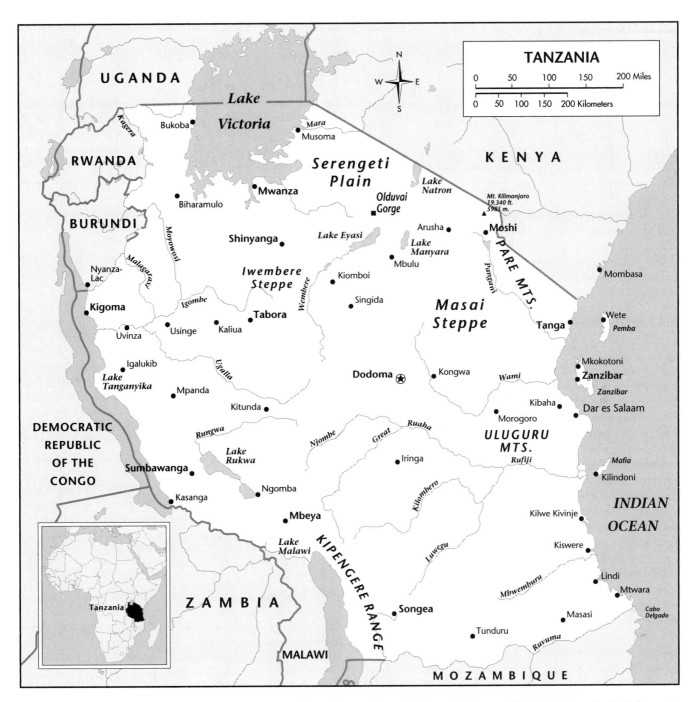

LOCATION: 1° to 11°45′ S; 29°21′ to 40°25′E. BOUNDARY LENGTHS: Uganda, 418 kilometers (260 miles); Kenya, 769 kilometers (478 miles); total coastline (including coasts of Zanzibar and Pemba islands), 1,271 kilometers (790 miles); Mozambique, 756 kilometers (470 miles); Malawi, 451 kilometers (280 miles); Zambia, 322 kilometers (200 miles); Democratic Republic of the Congo, 459 kilometers (285 miles); Burundi, 451 kilometers (280 miles); Rwanda, 217 kilometers (135 miles). TERRITORIAL SEA LIMIT: 50 miles.

number of immigrants living in Tanzania was 659,200. Tanzania also hosted more than half a million refugees, more than any other African country. 352,640 of the refugees came from Burundi and 127,973 where from the Democratic Republic of the Congo.

Out of an estimated Asian population of 100,000 in 1967, almost half, most of them with British passports, had left the country by 1980. Arabs, who were the dominant group on Zanzibar before the 1964 revolution, despite forming less than 20% of the population, fled after the event to the mainland or the Middle East. There is some emigration of laborers seeking work in neighboring countries, but Tanzanians who leave the country without authorization are subject to prosecution on return. During the clove harvest, labor moves from the towns to the clove plantations, from Zanzibar to Pemba, and from the mainland territories to Pemba. Urban authorities are empowered to return the unemployed to their villages.

⁸ETHNIC GROUPS

Mainland-native Africans constitute 99% of the total population. About 130 small people groups have been categorized into 5 ethnic groups distinguishable by their physical characteristics and languages. Approximately 95% of Tanzanians may be roughly classified as Bantu, a comparatively recent blend mainly of Hamitic and Negroid stocks. Tribes range in membership from only a few thousand to the Sukuma tribe, which numbers more than two million. Other major tribes include the Nyamwezi, Makonde, Haya, and Chagga. The Luo, east of Lake Victoria, are the only people of Nilotic origin; the Masai of the northern highlands are Nilo-Hamites. A very small number of Bushmen-like people are scattered throughout northern Tanzania, where small tribes of Cushitic origin also live. The inhabitants of Zanzibar and Pemba are chiefly descendants of mainland Africans or are of mixed African and Arab extraction. The remaining 1% of the population is made up of non-Africans, including Arabs, Asians, and Europeans.

⁹LANGUAGES

Most Tanzanians speak variations of Bantu languages and dialects. Various languages also have Hamitic or Nilotic origins. Swahili (or Kiswahili) is the official language, as well as the lingua franca, and is understood in most parts of the country, although its usefulness declines toward the west. English, also an official language, is the primary language of commerce, administration, and higher education. Generally, Swahili is seen as the unifying language of the country between different ethnic groups, who each have their own languages. English serves the purpose of providing Tanzanians with the ability to participate in the global economy and culture. Kiunguja, a form of Swahili, and Arabic are widely spoken in Zanzibar. The first language typically learned by a Tanzanian is that of his or her ethnic group, with Swahili and English learned thereafter.

¹⁰RELIGIONS

Since religious affiliation has been removed from government censuses as of 1967, reliable statistics on religious association are difficult to obtain. However, a 2010 report indicates that about 62% of the total population is Christian and 35% is Muslim. The Christian churches represented include Roman Catholic, Pentecostal, Protestant, Seventh-day Adventist, the Church of Jesus Christ of Latter-day Saints, and Jehovah's Witnesses. A majority of the Muslims are Sunni, while others belong to one of several Shi'a groups. On the island of Zanzibar, about 98% of the inhabitants are Muslim. There are small communities of Buddhists, Hindus, Sikhs, and Baha'is. Religious freedom is guaranteed by the constitution. The law forbids religious discrimination, but some Muslims believe that they are disadvantaged with less representation in civil service, government, and other public institutions. A 2001 Mufti Law allows the president of Zanzibar to appoint a mufti (Islamic leader) as a Zanzibar government official who settles religious disputes involving Muslims and generally monitors Muslim activities on the island. On the mainland, the National Muslim Council of Tanzania (BAKWATA) is a nongovernmental organization that has elected their own mufti. All religious groups must register with the Registrar of Societies of the Ministry of Home Affairs (mainland) or the Chief Government Registrar (Zanzibar). Good Friday, Easter Monday, Eid al-Fitr, Eid al-Hajj, and Christmas are observed as national holidays.

¹¹TRANSPORTATION

The CIA reported that Tanzania had a total of 91,049 km (56,575 mi) of roads as of 2010, of which 6,578 km (4,087 mi) are paved. The Central Line of railway extends 1,255 km (780 mi) from Dar es Salaam to Kigoma; its main branch lines are Tabora to Mwanza (381 km/237 mi) and Kaliua to Mpanda (211 km/131 mi). The Northern Line, extending from Dar es Salaam and Tanga to Moshi and Arusha, is linked to the railway systems of Kenya and Uganda. The 1,857-km (1,154-mi) Tazara railway, operated by the Tanzania-Zambia Railway Authority, links Dar es Salaam in Tanzania with Kpiri Mposhi in Zambia; 962 km (598 mi) of the line are in Tanzania. The Tazara railway is used mainly to transport goods for Zambia and Malawi.

Tanzania has a small national merchant shipping line of three freighters and one tanker. The principal ports on the mainland are Dar es Salaam, Mtwara, Tanga, and Lindi, all of which are managed by the Tanzanian Harbours Authority. Tanzanian ports handle cargo for landlocked Zambia, Zaire, Uganda, Rwanda, and Burundi. Freight and passenger vessels serve Mwanza and other Lake Victoria ports, among them Bukoba and Musoma. A joint Burundian-Tanzanian shipping company operates on Lake Tanganyika, and the Tanzanian Railways Corporation operates vessels on lakes Tanganyika, Victoria, and Niassa. Tanzania's rivers are not navigable.

Tanzania has 124 airports, which transported 683,541 passengers in 2009 according to the World Bank. Most internal air services are operated by Air Tanzania, which also flies internationally. Charter companies operate flights to government-maintained airports, landing fields, and privately owned airstrips. Foreign airlines provide service from international airports at Dar es Salaam and in the vicinity of Mt. Kilimanjaro (opened in 1971). There is also an international airport on Zanzibar.

¹²HISTORY

Paleontologists Louis and Mary Leakey, working at Olduvai Gorge and elsewhere in northern Tanzania, uncovered fossil evidence that humanlike creatures inhabited the area at least as early as 3.7 million years ago. Excavations of Stone Age sites have revealed that the hunter-gatherers of the late Stone Age, known as Bushmen, were gradually displaced by successive waves of Cushitic, Bantu, and Nilotic peoples. By the 1st millennium AD, the Iron Age Urewe culture had developed along the western shore of Lake Victoria.

Arabs from the Persian Gulf area were engaged in trade along the Indian Ocean coast by the 9th century AD and by the 12th century had established trading posts on the mainland and the offshore islands. Intermarriage between the Arabs and coastal Bantu-speaking peoples resulted in the emergence of the Swahili people, culture, and language. (Swahili literally means "of the coast.")

The first contacts of European nations with the East African coast were incidental to their quest for acquiring spices. In 1498, Vasco da Gama rounded the Cape of Good Hope, and thereafter the Portuguese established trading and supply posts on the East

African coast for their ships on the way to India. Eventually, the Portuguese lost control of the sea routes, and in 1698, the Ya'aruba imam of the Ibahdi Arabs of Oman, Sa'if bin Sultan, expelled the Portuguese from every position that they held north of Mozambique. The Ibahdis of Oman long remained in at least nominal control of East Africa, and there was a lucrative trade in slaves and ivory.

Sayyid Sa'id bin Sultan (the ruler of Oman during 1806–56), above all others, must be regarded as the founder of modern Zanzibar. Sa'id first visited Zanzibar in 1828, and in 1840, he made the island his capital. A believer in free trade, he encouraged foreign merchants, including Indians, broke up Arab monopolies, and made commercial treaties with the United States and the United Kingdom. Zanzibar is indebted to him most for his establishment of the clove tree. By the time he died in 1856, he had established a large, loosely held empire that included Oman, Zanzibar, and the East African coast inland to the Great Lakes and the Congo. Zanzibar produced three-quarters of the world's clove supply on plantations worked by slaves from the mainland. British pressure triggered the cessation of the slave trade in 1876, although slavery itself was not abolished until 1897.

The rise of Zanzibar as a commercial center was largely due to its trading links to the interior. Many of the caravan routes that stretched across East Africa were pioneered by African mainland societies. For example, the Yao living around Lake Malawi supplied the southern Tanzania trading town of Kilwa with slaves and ivory. African societies that gained control over the trade routes enhanced their power and wealth. In northeast Tanzania, a powerful trading and military state emerged in the 1860s in Urambo. Its leader, Mirambo was an excellent military and commercial strategist. He challenged the position of coastal traders in the area as well as the leading states that were closely aligned to Zanzibar.

The first Europeans to explore the interior were the British Sir Richard Francis Burton and John Hanning Speke, who crossed the country in 1857 to search for the source of the Nile, which Speke identified in 1858. In 1866, Sultan Majid of Zanzibar began building the coastal town of Dar es Salaam ("Haven of Peace"). In 1871, Scottish missionary and explorer David Livingstone had reached Ujiji when his whereabouts became unknown to the outside world; the Anglo-American explorer Henry Morton Stanley, commissioned by a US newspaper, located him there later in that year. Tanganyika (the name for the mainland prior to the 1964 union with Zanzibar) came under German influence in 1884–85, when Karl Peters concluded treaties with chiefs of the interior in order to secure a charter for his German East Africa Company.

In 1890, two treaties between Germany and Great Britain were signed: the first partitioned the territories on the mainland hitherto controlled by the sultan of Zanzibar; the second officially recognized Anglo-German spheres of influence, excluded Germany from the Upper Nile, and established a British protectorate over Zanzibar and Pemba. Tanganyika and Ruanda-Urundi (now Rwanda and Burundi) became recognized as German East Africa in 1891. As they occupied the interior, the German-led troops put down African opposition and uprisings. Intense military opposition to the European imperialism was led by Mirambo of the Nyamwezi in northwest Tanzania, by Mkwawa of the Hehe in southern highlands and by Meli of the Chagga around Kilimanjaro. However, the most bloody and intense opposition to German rule was the Maji-Maji war from 1905–1907. This war was inspired by Kinjekitile, a charismatic spiritual leader from southern Tanzania, succeeded in uniting a large number of African societies to fight the Germans. People who took Kinjekitile's medicine were told that the "white man's' bullets" could not harm them. After initial battlefield successes, the Germans initiated a scorched earth policy that eventually starved southern Tanzania into submission. During World War I, a small German force led by Gen. Paul von Lettow-Vorbeck fought a long defensive guerrilla war against British armies, and much of Tanganyika was laid waste.

Moving Toward Independence

Following the defeat of Germany during the First World War , the United Kingdom administered Tanganyika as a mandate of the League of Nations starting from 1920. It instituted a system of indirect rule whereby European bureaucrats administered African affairs through local or native chiefs. The United Kingdom promoted the economic integration of its East African territories by establishing a regional customs union of Tanganyika, Kenya and Uganda. It also tried to boost economic growth in the region by encouraging the cultivation of export crops.

The United Kingdom created an all white Legislative Council for Tanganyika in 1926. Africans became part of the Legislative Council much later starting from 1945. In 1946, Tanganyika became a UN trust territory. After 1954, the Tanganyika African National Union (TANU) petitioned the UN Trusteeship Council to put pressure on the UK administration to establish a timetable for independence. TANU-supported candidates won the elections of 1958–60 for the Legislative Council, and Julius Nyerere became chief minister in September 1960. On 9 December 1961, Tanganyika became an independent nation. On 9 December 1962, it was established as a republic, headed by Nyerere as president.

In Zanzibar, a Legislative Council with an elected element had been established in 1957. On 24 June 1963, a deeply divided Zanzibar attained internal self-government; it became completely independent on 10 December 1963 under the (ZNP) Zanzibar Nationalist Party. On 12 January 1964, however, the ZNP government was overthrown by African nationalists allowing ZNP's bitter rivals the ASP (Afro-Shirazi Party) to take power. The sultan, who had fled, was deposed, and Abeid Karume was installed as president. On 26 April 1964, Tanganyika merged with Zanzibar and became the United Republic of Tanganyika and Zanzibar, with Nyerere as president; in October, the name was changed to Tanzania. Karume, still president of Zanzibar and a vice president of Tanzania, was assassinated on 7 April 1972; his successor as head of the Zanzibar Revolutionary Council was Aboud Jumbe.

Under Nyerere, Tanzania became steadily more socialist. In international affairs, Tanzania`s Pan-Africanist government became one of the strongest supporters of majority rule in southern Africa, backing liberation movements in Mozambique, Southern Rhodesia (now Zimbabwe) and South Africa. Growing ideological differences between the East African Community's three members (Kenya, Tanzania, and Uganda) led to the breakup in 1977 of the 10-year-old organization. Tanzania's border with Kenya remained closed until 1983. On 30 October 1978, Ugandan forces invaded Tanzania; Nyerere retaliated by sending 20,000 Tanzanian troops into Uganda. Ugandan President Idi Amin's forces were routed in April 1979, and former president Milton Obote, who had been living in exile in Tanzania, was returned to power. In 1982, Tanzanian troops helped put down an army mutiny in the Seychelles.

In 1980, Nyerere was reelected without opposition to his fifth and last term as president. During the early 1980s, Tanzania was plagued by poor economic performance, and there was a small, unsuccessful army mutiny against Nyerere in January 1983. There was also rising dissatisfaction in Zanzibar over the islands' political ties to the mainland; an attempt to overthrow Jumbe in June 1980 failed. In 1984, Jumbe and his colleagues, including his Chief Minister Seif Shariff Hamad, attempted to push for more autonomy for Zanzibar. As a result, Aboud Jumbe was pressured by the union government to resign his posts as vice president of Tanzania and president of Zanzibar in January 1984. His Chief Minister, Seif Shariff Hamad was detained. Ali Hassan Mwinyi, Jumbe's successor, was elected president of Zanzibar in April 1984. He was succeeded by Idris Abdul Wakil in October 1985. Mwinyi succeeded Nyerere as president of Tanzania in November 1985, following presidential and parliamentary elections, and was reelected in 1990. Mwinyi identified with reformists in the ruling party, Chama Cha Mapinduzi (CCM), seeking greater political and economic liberalization, and in 1990 Nyerere resigned as chairman of the CCM. On 14 October 1999 Julius Nyerere died of leukemia. Idris Wakil, died shortly after on 15 March 2000.

Liberalization was not easy to attain. Except for religion, the CCM controlled almost all areas of social affairs. Party cells at work and in the community shadowed Tanzanians constantly. In February 1992, at an extraordinary national conference of CCM, delegates voted unanimously to introduce a multiparty system. On 17 June 1992, Mwinyi signed into law constitutional amendments that allowed new parties (with certain exceptions) to participate in elections. The first multiparty elections since the reinstitution of multiparty politics were local government elections held in 1994. In the elections the ruling party CCM soundly defeated the opposition parties. Despite strong government and CCM support for liberalization, the state is at least rhetorically committed to socialism as the concept of "socialism and self-reliance" is retained in article nine of the union constitution.

Rifts between the mainland (Tanganyika) and Zanzibar grew in the 1990s, often linked to the ongoing Christian-Muslim division. In December 1992, in violation of the constitution, the government in heavily Muslim Zanzibar covertly joined the Organization of Islamic Countries (OIC). In August 1993, parliament debated a motion calling for constitutional revisions to create a separate government for Tanganyika, to parallel the Zanzibar government. At that point, Zanzibar agreed to withdraw from the OIC and to allow Tanzanians from the mainland to visit without passports.

In April 1993, fundamentalist Muslims were arrested for attacking owners of pork butcheries in Dar es Salaam. Demonstrations at their trials led to more arrests and a government ban on the Council for the Propagation of the Koran. Around the same time the government also arrested an evangelist pastor named Christopher Mtikila who had formed a political party not recognized by the government. Mtikila, a populist preacher, accused the government of selling the country off to Arabs and Zanzibaris and his actions helped to heighten Christian-Muslim tensions. Mwinyi shuffled his cabinet several times in 1993 to balance Christian and Muslim interests. Later under the Mkapa regime, religious tensions became apparent again when Muslims protested over the arrest of a religious leader from the Mwembechai Mosque in Dar es Salaam on the grounds that he was threatening peace and stability through his provocative sermons. In a demonstration that followed the arrest, two people were shot dead by the police and 135 demonstrators were arrested.

The constitutional amendment of 1992 resulted in the elections of October 1995, the first multiparty elections in Tanzania since the 1960s. However, the CCM commitment to a fair and open election was questioned. CCM candidate Benjamin Mkapa was elected union president in a vote that opposition parties and international observers considered flawed. On Zanzibar, international observers and the opposition Civic United Front (CUF) believed that CCM intimidation and vote rigging influenced the election results for the islands' government to favor CCM. The CUF claimed victory, only to have the CCM reject the results. The CCM-dominated electoral commission then declared CCM candidate Salmin Amour the winner of the presidential race and gave the CCM the majority of seats in Zanzibar's House of Representatives. CUF boycotted sessions of the Zanzibar House and refused to recognize the Amour government until a 1999 Commonwealth-brokered agreement was reached between the two rival parties. Despite the agreement, political tensions on the islands were high as the October 2000 elections approached.

Among the major problems inherited by President Benjamin Mkapa was the social and economic burden of catering for the welfare of 700,000 refugees living in camps near the northern and western borders. Tanzania had taken in some 500,000 Rwandan refugees who fled the violence in their country since 1980. In one day at the height of the 1994 genocide in Rwanda, 200,000 refugees crossed over the border. Additionally, the government took in 200,000 refugees from Burundi. The strain on the country's resources, coupled with incursions into Tanzania by Tutsi dominated Burundi government forces chasing Hutu rebels, led the government to close its borders in 1995. In February 1997, Tanzania implemented its much-criticized plan to repatriate or expel its refugee population. In 1998 Tanzania severed its relations with Burundi and refused to recognize the military government of Maj. Pierre Buyoya. In response, Burundi closed its embassy in Dar es Salaam. Repatriation of Rwandan refugees was nearly completed by end of 2002.

On 7 August 1998, simultaneous bombings of the US embassies in Nairobi and Dar es Salaam-claiming 11 Tanzanian lives in Dar es Salaam-were attributed to Osama bin Laden's al-Qaeda organization. Combined investigations and close cooperation between the Tanzanian and US governments facilitated the capture of a number of the terrorists. However, in early 2003 Western governments issued warnings to their citizens of possible terrorist threats on Zanzibar, which had a devastating impact on the economy with some hotel bookings down by 50%.

In October 2000, Tanzanians went to the polls reelecting Benjamin Mkapa and giving the ruling CCM party 244 of 272 seats in the parliament. The CUF disputed the results in Zanzibar, and in January 2001 after the government declared a protest march illegal, security forces shot and killed approximately 30 persons, seriously injured 300, and displaced some 2,000 more. On 26 February 2001, in what appeared to be a revenge murder, the CCM secretary general for Pemba was found killed with machete slashes to his skull and body. Following year-long talks between the CCM and CUF, a constitutional amendment act was passed by the Zanzibari parliament on Pemba island towards the implementation of a reconciliation agreement signed by the two parties in October 2001. The passage of the act meant a review of the judiciary and Zanzibar Electoral Commission (ZEC), as well as the introduction of a director of public prosecution.

Presidential and parliamentary elections were held on 14 December 2005. Originally scheduled for 30 October, the elections were postponed due to the death of a vice presidential candidate. These polls were the third since the country returned to multiparty rule in 1992. They were also significant in that the incumbent President Benjamin Mkapa, who served two consecutive terms, stepped down in accordance with the constitution. Jakaya Kikwete was elected president winning 80.3% of the votes. Kikwete was subsequently re-elected for his second and final term on 31 October 2010. The next presidential election was scheduled for 2015.

Elections for the presidency of Zanzibar and its House of Representatives took place on 30 October 2005, as scheduled. Amani Abeid Karume of CCM won 53.18% of the votes and Seif Sharif Hamad of CUF won 46.07% of the votes in the presidential election. Voter turnout was high at 90.8% of registered voters. Immediately after the results were announced, riots broke out and a number of people were beaten and shot by the police. CUF protested the results claiming that Karume had won the presidency in Zanzibar through vote rigging. In the Zanzibar House of Representatives, CCM won 30 of the 50 seats and CUF took 19, with one seat being invalidated. Unlike most of the preceding elections, the 2010 elections proceeded peacefully. After years of intense debates between Civic United Front (CUF) and CCM, the two political parties finally reached a power-sharing agreement. On 29 January 2010, the unicameral Zanzibar House of Representatives adopted as law a bill that outlined the parameters of a government of national unity and called for a popular referendum on the plan. On 31 July 2010, Zanzibari voters gave their approval in the first-ever referendum to amend the constitution to allow for a unity government in Zanzibar. Ali Mohamed Shein, the immediate past union vice president, was elected president of Zanzibar on 31 October 2010.

China has increasingly been looking for new sources of oil to feed its burgeoning economy. It is looking to Africa as a supplier of its energy needs. In June 2006, Chinese prime minister Wen Jiabao visited Tanzania, on a seven-nation African tour to secure energy agreements and strengthen economic ties. Premier Wen signed agreements to help Tanzania's health, transportation, and communications sectors.

In August 2006, the African Development Bank (AfDB) announced the cancellation of more than $640 million in debt owed by Tanzania. The AfDB said it was impressed with Tanzania's economic record and the level of accountability of its public finances.

Tanzania faced a number of issues and challenges. According to the UNDP human development report for 2011, Tanzania ranked 152nd out of 187 countries, making it one of the world's poorest nations. The HIV adult prevalence rate was 11% with over 2 million people infected with the virus. The US State Department reported in 2010 that while Tanzania had improved its respect for human rights, the government's overall record remained poor. Despite improvements, members of the police and security forces committed unlawful killings and mistreated suspected criminals.

The most serious violations of human rights resulted from election-related violence in Zanzibar in 2001 and in October 2005.

¹³GOVERNMENT

A new constitution, replacing the 1965 interim document, went into effect in April 1977 and was substantially amended in October 1984 and in 1992. It has been amended numerous times since then.

The president, who is both chief of state and head of government, can be elected for no more than two five-year terms by universal adult suffrage. Before the constitutional amendments in 1992, the sole legal party Chama cha Mapinduzi (CCM) nominated the president. Two vice presidents, whom he appointed, assisted him: one was the prime minister and the other was the president of Zanzibar. The president is assisted by a vice president and cabinet. If the president of Tanzania is from Zanzibar, the vice president must be from the mainland and vice-versa.

Presidential and legislative elections are held concurrently, and in each legislative constituency. All candidates in competing in elections must belong to political parties. If the president withholds his assent from a bill passed by the assembly, it does not become a law unless the assembly passes it again by a two-thirds majority. The president may dissolve the assembly and call for new presidential and legislative elections if he refuses to assent to a law passed by such a majority within 32 days of its passage. The unicameral National Assembly elected in 2010 had 343 members. These included the Attorney General, five members elected from the Zanzibar House of Representatives to participate in the Parliament, the special women's seats which are made up of 30% of the seats that a given party has in the House, 181 constituent seats of members of Parliament from the mainland, and 50 seats from Zanzibar. Also in the list were 48 appointed for women and the seats for the 10 nominated members of Parliament. Laws passed by the National Assembly are valid for Zanzibar only in specifically designated union matters.

The Revolutionary Council of Zanzibar, which held power on the islands since 1964, adopted a separate constitution in October 1979, which it replaced in January 1984. The new constitution provides for a popularly elected president and a 75-member Council of Representatives, 50 of whom are popularly elected and 25 appointed. The government of Zanzibar has exclusive jurisdiction over internal matters, including immigration, finances, and economic policy. Since the 1990s, a trend toward greater autonomy for Zanzibar has been the basis of political tension with the mainland.

The Articles of Union and Acts of Union of 1964 provided for two governments: the union government, which also handled mainland issues, and the Zanzibar government, which dealt with nonunion matters pertaining to Zanzibar. The Tanganyikan constitution of 1962 was amended to accommodate the two government arrangement, which has remained in place ever since. However, the two-government system has been criticized as favoring Zanzibar because there is no separate government for the mainland. Moreover, Zanzibar's representation in parliament is considered to be disproportionate to its small population. In August 1993, following Zanzibar's attempt to join the OIC in violation of the constitution, the National Assembly adopted a resolution that provided for the possibility of setting up a mainland or Tanganyikan government to parallel that of Zanzibar. The issue of a federated system with three governments has remained a bone of contention between CCM and the opposition parties.

Renegotiation of the Union pact was the key issue of the 1995 elections, the first contested elections on Tanzania in 20 years. Although the former ruling party emerged from those elections with the Zanzibar presidency and a majority in the House of Representatives, the secessionist movement remained strong on the islands. The Zanzibar government established its own department of revenue and foreign affairs.

14 POLITICAL PARTIES

At independence in 1961, Tanganyika (Tanzania Mainland) had a multiparty political system. The Tanganyika African National Union (TANU), established in 1954, was the overwhelmingly dominant political party in preindependence Tanganyika. Other political parties of this era included the United Tanganyika Party, the African National Congress, and the All Muslim National Unity of Tanganyika. In Zanzibar, there were three important political parties prior to independence. These were the ZNP (Zanzibar Nationalist Party, ASP (Afro-Shirazi Party), and ZPPP (Zanzibar and Pemba People's Party). On 5 February 1977, ASP the ruling party of Zanzibar and TANU merged into the Chama Cha Mapinduzi (CCM) or Revolutionary Party. It became the sole legal political party in Tanzania. All candidates had to be approved by the CCM and were permitted to campaign only on the CCM platform. Elections within the single party framework were competitive, however. In the balloting on 13 and 27 October 1985, 328 candidates competed for 169 elective seats in the National Assembly. In 1987, former president Julius K. Nyerere was reelected chairman of the CCM. He stepped down in 1990, to be succeeded by Ali Hassam Mwinyi.

The CCM used to favor nonracism and African socialism. The basic aims, laid down in Nyerere's Arusha Declaration of 1967, were social equality, self-reliance, economic cooperation with other African states, *ujamaa* (familyhood), and the development of forms of economic activity, particularly in rural areas, based on collective efforts. However, since the late 1980s, CCM slowly transformed itself into a pro-market, pro-business party. The CCM conceives of economic modernization and free market policies as ways to raise the living standards of the citizens of Tanzania, one of the poorest countries in the world. CCM hopes to continue to privatize and modernize the economy through the acquisition of new and modern technology. The CCM is divided into locally organized branches, which are grouped into districts, which in turn are grouped into regions. The 172-member National Executive Committee is the principal policymaking and directing body of the CCM. A central committee of 18 members is elected at periodic party congresses.

Although Tanzania amended its constitution in 1992 to become a multiparty state, the CCM still controls government. Other parties have tried to organize, and have complained of harassment by government and CCM activists. Before taking part in elections, new parties undergo a six-month probation during which they can recruit and organize. Parties representing regional, racial, ethnic, or religious groups are explicitly prohibited.

Multiparty elections were held in Zanzibar on 25 October 1995 and union-wide on 29 October 1995. International observers and opposition parties accused the CCM of voter fraud and intimidation of opposition candidates in Zanzibar. While Civic United Front (CUF) claimed victory, on 26 October, the election commission declared CCM presidential candidate Salmin Amour the winner by 1,565 votes over the CUF's Seif Shariff Hamad. The CCM also won 26 of the 50 seats in the House of Representatives. Citing fraud in the election, the CUF boycotted the House and refused to recognize the Amour government. CCM-CUF tension in Zanzibar increased dramatically after the government arrested eighteen CUF members and charged them with treason, an offense punishable by death. Four of those charged with treason were CUF members of the Zanzibar House of Representatives. The Commonwealth Secretary General, Chief Emeka Anyaoku, tried to reconcile the two parties. An agreement was reached between the two parties in 1999 but tensions on the island remained high as CUF charged CCM with not living up to the agreement. As the 2000 elections approached, the treason suspects were still behind bars and clamoring to run for office from prison.

The Union election held on 29 October 1995 was so disorganized that it was cancelled in Dar es Salaam and held again on 19 November. In the presidential election, CCM candidate Benjamin Mkapa won with 61.8% of the vote. Former Deputy Prime Minister Augustino Mrema of the National Convention for Constitutional Reform received 27.7%; Ibrahim Lipumba of the Civic United Front won 6.4%, and John Cheyo of the United Democratic Party captured 3.97%. Parliamentary election results saw the CCM win 59.2% of the vote and 186 seats; NCCR, 21.83% and 16 seats; CUF, 5% and 24 seats; Chadema, 6.2% and 3 seats, and UDP, 3.3% and 3 seats.

As of the October 2000 elections there were 12 permanently registered opposition parties: Civic United Front/Chama Cha Wananchi (CUF), the National Convention for Constitutional Reform (NCCR-Mageuzi), the Union for Multiparty Democracy (UMD), Chama cha Demokrasia na Maendeleo (CHADEMA), the National League for Democracy (NLD), the Tanzania Peoples Party (TPP), the Tanzania Democratic Alliance (TADEA), the National Redemption Alliance (NRA), the Popular National Party (PONA), the United Peoples Democratic Party (UPDP), the United Democratic Party (UDP), and the Tanzania Labor Party (TLP).

In the presidential elections on 29 October 2000, CCM candidate Benjamin William Mkapa was reelected president with 71.7% of the vote, defeating CUF candidate Ibrahim Haruna Lipumba who garnered 16.3%. TLP candidate Augustine Lyatonga Mreme managed to obtain 7.8%, and John Momose Cheyo of the UDP 4.2%. In the National Assembly, the CCM won 244 of 272 seats to 16 for the CUF, 4 for CHADEMA, 3 for TLP, and 2 for UDP. In the Zanzibar House of Representatives the CCM won 34 seats to 16 for CUF. However, on Zanzibar the elections and postelections period were marred by violent civil unrest.

The results of the 2005 National Assembly election were as follows: CMM, 206 seats; CUF, 19 seats; CHADEMA, 5 seats; other, 2 seats; 37 women were appointed by the president, and Zanzibar representatives, 5 seats. The results of the 2005 Zanzibar House of Representatives election were as follows: CCM, 30 seats; CUF, 19 seats; and 1 seat was nullified with a rerun scheduled.

In the December 2005 Union elections , ten political parties fielded candidates for the presidency of Tanzania. Benjamin Mkapa of CCM stepped down as mandated by the constitution. CCM fielded Jakaya Kikwete who won the presidency with 80.3% of the votes, while Sauti ya Umma (SAU) was represented by Henry Kyara and CUF supported Ihrahim Lipumba who won 11.7% of the votes. Other presidential candidates included Emmanuel Makaidi of National League for Democracy (NLD); Freeman Mbowe of Chama cha Demokrasia na Maendeleo (CHADEMA) (won 5.9% of the votes); Augustine Mrema of Tanzania Labour Party (TLP); Christopher Mtikila of Democratic Party (DP); Sengondo Mvungi of National Convention for Construction and Reform-Mageuzi (NCCR-Mageuzi) also supported by the Forum for the Restoration of Democracy (FORD), National Reconstruction Alliance (NRA), Union for Multiparty Democracy (UMD), and United People's Democratic Party (UPDP); Anna Senkoro of Progressive Party of Tanzania-Maendeleo (PPT-Maendeleo); and Leonard Shayo of Demokrasia Makini (MAKINI). Jakaya Kikwete was re-elected with 62.8% of the vote for his second and final term on 31 October 2010. The ruling CCM party won 186 out of the 239 directly elected seats. The next presidential and national assembly elections were scheduled for 2015.

On 31 July 2010, the citizens of Zanzibar voted to change the political landscape through a referendum that amended the constitution to allow for a power sharing agreement between parties. The referendum was approved by a 66.4% of the votes. Under the new guidelines, a unity government will consist of a president chosen from the winning party in general elections, a first vice president from the second-place party, and a second vice president from the winning party. Government ministers will be allocated on a proportional basis.

15 LOCAL GOVERNMENT

Mainland Tanzania is divided into 26 administrative regions, which are subdivided into districts. Zanzibar and Pemba are divided into five regions. Regional commissioners are appointed by the central government, as are district commissioners and development directors for the districts.

The units of local government are district development councils. Each district development council includes elected members, but these bodies are only advisory. In Zanzibar, revolutionary committees are responsible for regional administration.

16 JUDICIAL SYSTEM

Mainland Tanzanian law is a combination of British, African customary law, and Islamic law. Local courts are presided over by appointed magistrates. They have limited jurisdiction, and there is a right of appeal to district courts, headed by either resident or district magistrates. Appeal can be made to the High Court, which consists of a chief justice and 29 judges appointed by the president. It has both civil and criminal jurisdiction over all persons and all matters. Appeals from the High Court can be made to the five-member Court of Appeal. Judges are appointed to the Court of Appeal and the High Court by the president on the advice of the chief justice and to courts at lower levels by the chief justice.

In 1985, the Zanzibari courts were made parallel to those of the mainland. Islamic courts handle some civil matters. Cases concerning the Zanzibari constitution are heard only in Zanzibari courts. All other cases may be appealed to the Court of Appeal of the Republic.

Although declared independent by the constitution, the judiciary is subject to executive branch influence and is criticized as inefficient and corrupt. Questions have been raised as to the availability of a fair trial in politically charged cases.

17 ARMED FORCES

The International Institute for Strategic Studies reports that armed forces in Tanzania totaled 27,000 active members and reservists numbering 80,000 in 2011. The navy had an estimated 1,000 personnel. The Air Defense Command numbered an estimated 3,000. Police field forces, which included naval and air units, numbered 1,400. Armed forces represented 0.1% of the labor force in Tanzania. Defense spending totaled $119.8 million and accounted for 0.2% of GDP.

18 INTERNATIONAL COOPERATION

Tanganyika was admitted to UN membership on 14 December 1961, and Zanzibar on 16 December 1963; following their union into what was eventually called Tanzania, the two regions retained a single membership. Tanzania is a member of ECA and several nonregional specialized agencies, such as the FAO, ILO, the World Bank, UNESCO, UNHCR, UNCTAD, and the WHO. It is also a member of the African Development Bank, the East African Development Bank, the Commonwealth of Nations, the ACP Group, G-6, G-77, the WTO, the Southern African Development Community (SADC), and the African Union. Along with Rwanda, Burundi, and Uganda, it belongs to the Kagera Basin Organization. Julius Nyerere, Tanzania's first president, was one of the founding members of the Nonaligned Movement. Tanzania, Uganda, and Kenya signed an East African Cooperation Treaty in September 1999. A second treaty establishing a Customs Union was signed in March 2004.

In environmental cooperation, Tanzania is part of the Basel Convention, the Convention on Biological Diversity, CITES, the Kyoto Protocol, the Montréal Protocol, and the UN Conventions on the Law of the Sea, Climate Change, and Desertification.

19 ECONOMY

Tanzania has an agricultural economy whose chief commercial crops are sisal, coffee, cotton, tea, tobacco, pyrethrum, spices, and cashew nuts. The GDP rate of change in Tanzania, as of 2010, was 6.5%. Inflation stood at 7.2%, and unemployment was reported at 4.34%. As of 2008, agriculture accounted for 27% of GDP, provided over 80% of exports, and employed 80% of the workforce. Tanzania's industrial sector is one of the smallest in Africa. Plagued by water and power shortages, the sector is limited to food processing services and light manufacturing of textiles and apparel for the domestic market. There is limited exports of manufactured goods. The most important minerals are gold and diamonds.

After 25 years of socialist experimentation Tanzania achieved important advances in education and health. However, poor economic performance led the government, in 1986, to adopt market-style reforms in conjunction with the IMF structural adjustment program. Reform measures included a revaluation of the exchange rate, removal of price controls, a restructuring of the financial sector, and a liberalized trade regime.

Since then, significant progress has been made in revitalizing the economy and donors have pledged additional funds to rehabilitate Tanzania's economic infrastructure and relieve its debt burden. In 2006, Tanzania received $3.8 billion in debt relief under the Multilateral Debt Relief Initiative (MRDI).

By 2007, the economy was improving, with the mining, tourism, agriculture, construction, telecommunications, and utilities sectors all showing potential for growth. The government had sold off state-owned enterprises, was welcoming foreign investment, and had implemented strict fiscal and monetary policies. Nevertheless, Tanzania's macroeconomic progress had not translated into better lives for its rural poor and the country remains one of the poorest in the world. In 2009, 36% of the population was living below the poverty line and the public debt was estimated at 22% of GDP.

In July 2010, the government announced plans to invest in the development of the nation's fiber optics network and methane gas production as a means of reaching a new goal to become a middle-income economy by 2020. The government hoped to boost the mining industry through improvements in power supply, sponsored in part by the World Bank and the United States. In 2010, Tanzania was the third largest producer of gold in the world, with substantial reserves of uranium, nickel, and coal. In June 2011, the World Bank approved a $2.8 billion loan for Tanzania, to be released over four years, in an effort to decrease poverty, increase economic growth, and secure political stability. An additional $28.8 million was being considered to help Tanzania's energy sector.

20 INCOME

In 2007 the World Bank estimated that Tanzania, with 0.58% of the world's population, accounted for 0.07% of the world's GDP. By comparison, the United States, with 4.85% of the world's population, accounted for 22.51% of world GDP. The CIA estimated that in 2010 the GDP of Tanzania was $58.44 billion. The CIA defines GDP as the value of all final goods and services produced within a nation in a given year and computed on the basis of purchasing power parity (PPP) rather than value as measured on the basis of the rate of the exchange based on current dollars. The per capita GDP was estimated at $1,400. The annual growth rate of GDP was 6.5%. The average inflation rate was 7.2%. It was estimated that agriculture accounted for 42% of GDP, industry 18%, and services 40%.

According to the World Bank, remittances from citizens living abroad totaled $23.3 million or about $1 per capita.

The World Bank reports that in 2009, household consumption in Tanzania totaled $13.3 billion or about $312 per capita, measured in current US dollars rather than PPP. Household consumption includes expenditures of individuals, households, and nongovernmental organizations on goods and services, excluding the purchases of dwellings. It was estimated that household consumption was growing at an average annual rate of 3.4%.

As of 2011 the most recent study by the World Bank reported that actual individual consumption in Tanzania was 81.5% of GDP and accounted for 0.08% of world consumption. By comparison, the United States accounted for 25.44% of world individual consumption. The World Bank also estimated that 58.7% of Tanzania's GDP was spent on food and beverages, 9.5% on housing and household furnishings, 5.6% on clothes, 0.9% on health, 3.2% on transportation, 0.1% on communications, 0.8% on recreation,

0.0% on restaurants and hotels, and 1.6% on miscellaneous goods and services and purchases from abroad.

21 LABOR

As of 2010, Tanzania had a total labor force of 23.39 million people. Within that labor force, CIA estimates in 2002 noted that 80% were employed in agriculture, 10% in industry, and 10% in the service sector. In 1964, by legislation of the National Assembly, the existing 13 trade unions were dissolved and amalgamated into a single national institution, the National Union of Tanzanian Workers. This was reorganized in 1978 to take in Zanzibar trade union activity as the Organization of Tanzania Trade Unions (OTTU), which still is the only labor union organization. The OTTU was renamed the Tanzania Federation of Trade Unions (TFTU) in 1995. Strikes are permitted after a lengthy and complicated arbitration procedure which delays a resolution for months. Collective bargaining does not regularly occur, and public sector employee wages and benefits are set by the government.

With the permission of a parent, a child as young as 12 years old may work on a day-to-day basis. Employment of a long-term contractual nature cannot begin until a minor is at least 15. Enforcement of these provisions is inadequate and has actually declined in recent years with increased privatization. The standard workweek is 40 hours for government workers, while most private employers retain a 44 to 48-hour workweek. Tanzania has a government-mandated minimum wage, and no worker in Tanzania can be paid less than this mandatory minimum rate of pay. Employers in Tanzania who fail to pay the Minimum Wage may be subject to punishment by Tanzania's government. As of 2011 the minimum wage fixed by law varied from one sector to another. For example, as of 2011, it was TZS65,000 ($40) per month for hotel workers and TZS350,000 ($218) per month for workers in the minerals sector.

22 AGRICULTURE

The economy of Tanzania depends heavily on agriculture. The country's major crops include coffee, sisal, tea, cotton, pyrethrum (insecticide made from chrysanthemums), cashew nuts, tobacco, cloves, corn, wheat, cassava (tapioca), bananas, fruits, and vegetables. Fruit production amounted to 4.5 million tons and vegetable production to 1.8 million tons in 2009.

Growth and development of the agricultural sector is often supported by foreign aid and investment. In 2009, the government received $30 million from the World Bank as part of the East African Agricultural Productivity Program. The program benefits the countries of Kenya, Ethiopia, and Tanzania by supporting regional cooperation in new technology, training, and dissemination programs for the major commodities of dairy, cassava, rice, and wheat. The same year, the United States African Development Foundation (USADF) provided grants to promote agricultural research and education through grassroots cooperative organizations such as the Association of Mango Growers ($98,000), the Mbingu Organic Cocoa Outgrowers Association ($91,000), and Uncle Milo's General Traders Limited ($241,000), the latter of which supports small-scale sunflower oilseed growers.

Roughly 5% of the total land is farmed , with about two-thirds belonging to farmers owning or operating farms of five hectares (12.4 acres) or less. A massive collectivization and cooperative agricultural program was begun in 1967; by the end of 1980, 8,167 self-help villages, involving more than 14 million people, had been established. The program was coupled with the takeover of large estates.

Tanzania is one of Africa's leading producers of sisal. Tanzania is the third leading producer of cloves, which are grown mostly on Pemba. Tanzania is also an important producer of coconuts, mostly from the island of Zanzibar. In March 2011, Tanzania's average coffee prices reached an all-time high, averaging about $7 per kg ($3.18 per lb).

23 ANIMAL HUSBANDRY

Although large areas are unsuitable for livestock because of the tsetse fly, considerable numbers of cattle, sheep, and goats are kept, and livestock raising makes a substantial contribution to the economy. The UN Food and Agriculture Organization (FAO) reported that Tanzania dedicated 24 million hectares (59.3 million acres) to permanent pasture or meadow in 2009. During that year, the country tended 30 million chickens, 19.1 million head of cattle, and 455,000 pigs. The production from these animals amounted to 247,187 tons of beef and veal, 13,159 tons of pork, 47,043 tons of poultry, 32,533 tons of eggs, and 953,034 tons of milk. Tanzania also produced 48,300 tons of cattle hide and 5,792 tons of raw wool.

24 FISHING

With over 6% of Tanzania's area consisting of open lake waters, inland fishing, especially on Lake Tanganyika, occupies an important place in the economy. There is also fishing in the Indian Ocean. Nile perch, dagaas, and tilapias are the main species caught. Tanzania had 17 decked commercial fishing boats in 2008. The annual capture totaled 325,476 tons according to the UN FAO. The export value of seafood totaled $145.2 million.

25 FORESTRY

Approximately 38% of Tanzania is covered by forest. There are about 13,000,000 hectares (32,000,000 acres) of permanent forest reserves. Small plantations for fast-growing trees have been established in these reserves. On the islands, remains of former forests are found only in two reserves. The UN FAO estimated the 2009 roundwood production at 2.31 million cu m (81.7 million cu ft). The value of all forest products, including roundwood, totaled $39.8 million.

26 MINING

With the rebirth of the gold industry, in 1999, gold has dominated the mineral industry in Tanzania; in 2009 the country accounted for 2% of the world's gold mine production. Because of significant exploration successes and government investment incentives, Tanzania's mining sector has been playing an increasingly important role in the economy. Mining and quarrying accounted for 2.8% of GDP in 2008. Gold was the top export commodity in 2009, valued at $1.08 billion and accounting for 41% of total exports. Diamond exports accounted for 1% of exports, and all other minerals, 1%.

Output of refined gold in 2009 totaled 39,112 kg, up from 36,434 kg in 2008. With the opening of three new mines, gold production is expected to increase in the short term but is likely to decrease after 2012 due to the shutdown of the Golden Pride Mine near Isanga.

Diamond output in 2009 was 181,874 carats, down from 237,676 carats in 2008. Diamonds, 85% of which were gem-quality or semigem-quality, were mined at the Williamson field, in Mwadui. The deposits were jointly-owned by the government and Petra Diamonds Ltd. (UK). Diamond production has declined since the 1967 peak (988,000 carats), because of depletion of higher-grade ores and equipment failure. Production hit a low in 1994, of 17,177 carats. Diamond resources were 114 million tons containing 6.5 million carats. The output of other gemstones (including amethyst, aquamarine, chrysoprase, emerald, garnet, kyanite, opal, peridot, lolite, ruby, sapphire, tanzanite, and tourmaline) was 1,068,481 kg in 2009, compared to 2,498,637 in 2006. African Gem Resources, the new owner of block C of the Merlani mining area, estimated that block C, with resources of 2.24 million tons of ore, grading 22 carats per ton, contained two-thirds of the world's known deposits of tanzanite. Tanzania is the world's only producer of tanzanite.

In 2009 Tanzania produced 8,105 metric tons (preliminary) of crude gypsum and anhydrite, as well as calcite, hydraulic cement, crushed limestone, salt, and presumably stone, and sand and gravel. Resources of limestone totaled 1,370,852 tons; marble resources for lime production totaled 2,679 tons; and calcitic marble resources amounted to 121 million tons. No iron ore or graphite was produced in 2009. Resources and proven reserves of iron ore, in Itewe, Liganga, and the Uluguru Mountains, totaled 103 million tons. Deposits of cobalt, copper, lead, mica, nickel, phosphates, tin, titanium, tungsten, and uranium were also known to occur, and companies were exploring for cobalt and nickel and planning to produce copper concentrate from a gold mine.

In April 2010, Tanzania's parliament passed the Mining Act 2010 to address public concerns that foreign mining companies were unfairly profiting from Tanzania's minerals. The Mining Act 2010 increases the mining royalties paid to the government from 3% to 4% on precious and base metals and from 5% to 6% on gemstones and diamonds. Additionally, the law mandates that the government must own a stake in all future mining projects. Analysts say the new mining law will bring Tanzania's royalty rates more in line with other African nations.

27 ENERGY AND POWER

Tanzania has proven reserves of natural gas and coal but must rely on imports for all its crude oil. Coal is Tanzania's most abundant resource. Recoverable coal reserves totaled of 220 million short tons as of 2008. In 2010, coal output totaled 105,000 short tons.

The World Bank reported in 2008 that Tanzania produced 4.41 billion kWh of electricity and consumed 3.56 billion kWh, or 83 kWh per capita. Roughly 11% of energy came from fossil fuels, while 1% came from alternative fuels. Per capita oil consumption was 446 kg.

Development in the northern mining areas of the country has been delayed due to chronic power shortages. But industry is not the only sector that struggles with the lack of power. In 2010 the World Bank announced a loan agreement of $150 million for a new power transmission project in the north. The same month, the government signed a $45 million financing agreement with the United States for a project to include construction and rehabilitation of 24 power stations on the mainland and Zanzibar. The project also included the installation of a 100-MW submarine power cable between the mainland and Zanzibar. US funding comes as part of a larger $698 million grant under the US Millennium Challenge program, with funds designated for water, energy, and infrastructure improvements.

28 INDUSTRY

Along with the results of parastatal inefficiencies; fuel and import costs, lack of foreign exchange, power shortages, lack of spare parts, and unreliable local services have tested the manufacturing sector severely. Over 80% of state-owned companies have been privatized, including tobacco and cashew farms, mines, the brewery, and a cigarette factory. Tanzanian industry is centered on the processing of local agricultural goods. Some products are exported to neighboring countries: textiles and clothes, shoes, tires, batteries, transformers and switchgear, electric stoves, bottles, cement, and paper. Other industries include oil refining, fertilizers, rolling and casting mills, metal working, beer and soft drinks, vehicle assembly, bicycles, canning, industrial machine goods, glass and ceramics, agricultural implements, electrical goods, wood products, bricks and tiles, oxygen and carbon dioxide, and pharmaceutical products. In the early 2000s, the industrial sector was relatively weak, but made small gains in the production of cement, soft drinks, corrugated iron sheeting, food processing, chemicals, leather products, and textiles. The construction industry was growing at a slow pace. In 2010 the industrial production growth rate was 7%.

29 SCIENCE AND TECHNOLOGY

The World Bank reported in 2009 that there were no patent applications in science and technology in Tanzania. The Tanzania Commission for Science and Technology, founded in 1958 at Dar es Salaam, advises the government on science and technology policy. Much of the scientific and technical research in Tanzania is directed toward agriculture. Facilities include the Livestock Production Research Institute at Dodoma (founded in 1905), the National Institute for Medical Research at Amani and Mwanza (founded in 1949), the Silviculture Research Institute at Lushoto (founded in 1951), the Agricultural Research Institute of the Ministry of Agriculture at Mlingano (founded in 1934), and the Tropical Pesticides Research Institute at Arusha (founded in 1962). The University of Dar es Salaam (founded in 1961) has faculties of science, medicine, and engineering and an institute of marine sciences; Sokoine University of Agriculture at Morogoro (founded in 1984) has faculties of agriculture, forestry, and veterinary medicine. The Open University of Tanzania (founded in 1992 at Dar es Salaam) has faculties of science, technology, and environmental studies.

30 DOMESTIC TRADE

Dar es Salaam is Tanzania's main distribution center. Mombasa, in Kenya, and inland Tanzanian towns also serve as trade centers. Previously, Tanzania used nontariff trade barriers to protect local industries and domestic commerce. With trade liberalization, tar-

iff barriers have been adjusted for this purpose. Most retail shops are small, privately owned establishments.

Normal business hours are 7:30 am to 2:30 p.m., Monday through Friday; firms that take a lunch break at noon may stay open to 4 or 4:30 p.m. Banks are open from 8:30 am to noon, Monday through Friday, and 8:30 to 11 a.m. on Saturday.

31 FOREIGN TRADE

The chief imports are transport equipment and intermediate and industrial goods machinery. The big traditional export commodities for Tanzania are coffee, fish and shellfish, and fruits and nuts. Other exports include unfinished tobacco and cotton. The start of large-scale gold mining has resulted in dramatic increases in export earnings for this nontraditional sector. Tanzania imported $6.334 billion worth of goods and services in 2008, while exporting $3.809 billion worth of goods and services. Major import partners in 2009 were China, 15.5%; India, 15%; South Africa, 7.6%; Kenya, 6.7%; UAE, 4.5%; and Japan, 4.2%. Its major export partners were India, 12.1%; China, 9.4%; Japan, 6.7%; Netherlands, 5.9%; UAE, 5.4%; and Germany, 4.9%.

Tanzania is a member of the East African Community (EAC), a regional intergovernmental organization established by Kenya, Uganda, and Tanzania in 2000, and expanded to include Rwanda and Burundi in 2007. The EAC Common Market Protocol went into effect on 1 July 2010, under which the members have agreed to implement legislation that will remove barriers to the transport of goods, services, and workers across borders. The development of the common market is one step in the EAC's plan to increase trade to, from, and within the region and to establish a strong political federation by 2015. EAC members hoped to launch a new, single, shared currency in 2012.

32 BALANCE OF PAYMENTS

In 2010 Tanzania had a foreign trade deficit of $2.3 billion, amounting to 13.2% of GDP. Tanzania typically runs a current account deficit, although long term capital investment from abroad resulted in surpluses for several years during the 1970s. The cur-

Principal Trading Partners – Tanzania (2010)

(In millions of US dollars)

Country	Total	Exports	Imports	Balance
World	11,217.1	3,515.2	7,701.9	-4,186.7
China	1,741.0	365.1	1,375.9	-1,010.8
India	1,470.3	232.6	1,237.7	-1,005.1
South Africa	661.9	35.1	626.9	-591.8
Kenya	604.8	51.3	553.5	-502.2
United Arab Emirates	502.3	117.0	385.3	-268.3
Japan	473.0	141.7	331.4	-189.7
Singapore	324.6	7.1	317.6	-310.5
Bahrain	260.0	...	260.0	-260.0
Germany	254.6	94.4	160.2	-65.9
Netherlands	220.6	93.2	127.4	-34.2

(...) data not available or not significant.

(n.s.) not specified.

SOURCE: *2011 Direction of Trade Statistics Yearbook*, New York: United Nations, 2011.

Balance of Payments – Tanzania (2010)

(In millions of US dollars)

Current Account		**-1,978.2**
Balance on goods	-2,828.3	
Imports	-7,125.1	
Exports	4,296.8	
Balance on services	241.9	
Balance on income	-215.7	
Current transfers	823.9	
Capital Account		**606.5**
Financial Account		**1,588.1**
Direct investment abroad	...	
Direct investment in Tanzania	433.4	
Portfolio investment assets	...	
Portfolio investment liabilities	3.2	
Financial derivatives	...	
Other investment assets	-75.2	
Other investment liabilities	1,226.7	
Net Errors and Omissions		**132.5**
Reserves and Related Items		**-348.9**

(…) data not available or not significant.

SOURCE: *Balance of Payment Statistics Yearbook 2011,* Washington, DC: International Monetary Fund, 2011.

rent account deficit was $1.978 billion in 2010. Agricultural marketing reforms and flexible exchange policies are expected to provide export growth in upcoming years, as exports move from the underground to the official market.

33BANKING AND SECURITIES

On 5 February 1967, Tanzania nationalized all banks after the adoption of the Arusha Declaration. From then until 1991, banking was a state monopoly led by the central Bank of Tanzania (BoT) and the National Bank of Commerce (NBC). In 1991, the financial services sector was opened to private and foreign capital. In 1993, the first private banks opened their doors. These were Meridien BIAO and Standard Chartered, the latter being among the UK-owned banks that were nationalized in 1967. Meridien's Zambian-based African network collapsed in 1995, and Stanbic of South Africa took over the Tanzanian subsidiary after its seizure by the BoT. The Kenyan-owned Trust Bank opened in March 1995, to be followed by Eurafrican Bank (a Belgian-led venture). Also in early 1995, the only private bank to be majority-owned by indigenous Tanzanians, First Adili Bank, began business.

The BoT was the central bank and bank of issue, providing advice to the NBC. The NBC, which used to account for over 75% of the country's transactions, was split in 1997 into NBC 1997 and the National Microfinance Bank (NMB). Other Tanzanian banks include the People's Bank of Zanzibar, the Tanzania Investment Bank, the Tanzania Housing Bank, the Rural Cooperative and Development Bank (CRDB), and the Tanganyika Post Office Savings Bank. Foreign banks include Citibank, Stanbic Bank, Standard Charter, Bank of Great Britain, Akiba Commercial Bank, and Exim Bank.

In 2010 the discount rate, the interest rate at which the central bank lends to financial institutions in the short term, was 8.25%.

The Dar es Salaam Stock Exchange (DSE) was incorporated in 1996 as a company limited by guarantee without a share capital. It became operational in April, 1998. The DSE is a non-profit making body created to facilitate the Government implementation of the reforms and in the future to encourage wider share ownership of privatized and all the companies in Tanzania. In 2011 the securities being traded were ordinary shares of 14 listed companies, 5 corporate bonds and 8 Government of Tanzania bonds. Major companies trading on the DSE are Tanzania Breweries Limited, Tanzania Tea Packers Limited, TOL Limited (producer of industrial gases), CRBD Bank Public Limited Company, National Microfinance Bank Plc, and Tanzania Cigarette Company Limited.

In 2009 the government opened a new bank in Dar es Salaam specifically for the economic empowerment of women. Women may open accounts at the Tanzanian Women's Bank with only an ID card or passport and with a minimum deposit of 3,000 Tanzanian shillings (about $2). Most other banks in the country require documented proof of wealth, such as title deeds, and a much larger minimum deposit. Financial advice and services focused on drawing women into the business world, but men were also permitted to hold accounts at the bank.

34INSURANCE

All insurance companies were nationalized in 1967. After the adoption of free market policies, several insurance emerged to complement the National Insurance Corporation of Tanzania, that covers life, fire, automobile, marine, and general accident insurance. The other major insurance companies include Heritage Insurance Company, Reliance Insurance Company and Jubilee Insurance Company.

35PUBLIC FINANCE

In 2010 the budget of Tanzania included $4.263 billion in public revenue and $5.644 billion in public expenditures. The budget deficit amounted to 6.1% of GDP. Public debt was 23.3% of GDP, with $8.226 billion of the debt held by foreign entities. The Tanzanian budget covers cash expenditures and receipts for the mainland only, and does not include Zanzibar government revenues and expenditures. Total expenditures include a development budget and revenues include profits from privatization sales. The fiscal year ends on 30 June. Since 1986, the government has improved its fiscal and monetary policies, with mixed results. Tanzania qualified for debt relief under the Heavily Indebted Poor Countries (HIPC) Initiative.

36TAXATION

The corporate income tax rate in 2011 was 30% of taxable profits. Withholding taxes include: a 10% general rate for dividends (5% for companies listed on the Dar es Salaam Stock Exchange); 10% for interest; 15% on royalties; and a 10% rate on rents for residents (15% rate for nonresidents). Capital gains are treated as ordinary business income and subject to the corporate rate.

Income taxes are also levied on wages and salaries. There is a Housing Levy and a Vocational Education Training Levy on gross payroll. There is a value-added tax (VAT) with a standard rate of 18%, as of 2011. Exemptions from VAT include computers, tour operations, hospital equipment, and investments in educational equipment. Other taxes include a stamp duty on sales, a transport withholding tax, local government development levies, an entertainment tax (for non-VAT-registered taxpayers), and airport and seaport departure charges.

37 CUSTOMS AND DUTIES

Tanzania has a single column tariff with many items dutiable ad valorem. Customs duties range from 0–25%, not including the VAT. In 1992, the government abolished duties and taxes on raw materials for industry as part of an economic reform program. In 1995, a uniform 5% tax was levied on imported capital goods. Import duties and sales tax apply according to the value of goods. There are no export controls, except for protected wild animals, and there are no prohibited imports, except for narcotics and other internationally prohibited drugs. Import and export licenses are not needed.

38 FOREIGN INVESTMENT

From independence in 1961, Tanzania followed state-centered socialist policies. With the initiation of economic reforms in 1986, investment interest in Tanzania has grown considerably in all sectors. Under the Tanzania Investment Promotion Policy of 1990 the Investment Promotion Center was established and by 1997, it had approved about 1,025 projects worth $3.1 billion. The operations of foreign banks were authorized in 1991, and the banking industry was substantially reformed to make it more competitive. The Tanzania Investment Act of 1997 was strengthened by the Land Act of 1999 and the Village Land Act of 1999, which provide the right to acquire land in urban and rural areas, respectively.

As a further impetus for reform, the Tanzanian government has taken steps to qualify under the US Africa Growth and Opportunity Act (AGOA) that mandates tariff-free and quota-free access to the US market for countries making market-based reforms. Foreign direct investment (FDI) in Tanzania was a net inflow of $414.5 million according to World Bank figures published in 2009. FDI represented 1.94% of GDP. The 10 leading countries that have invested in Tanzania are the United Kingdom, the United States, Kenya, Canada, South Africa, China, Germany, Italy, the Netherlands, and India. Foreign investment has mainly gone into mining, manufactures, agriculture, and tourism.

39 ECONOMIC DEVELOPMENT

The fourth five-year development plan (1981–86) was not fully carried out because of Tanzania's economic crisis. Among the projects implemented were an industrial complex, a pulp and paper project, a machine-tool plant, a phosphate plant, and the development of natural gas deposits. The Economic and Social Action Plan of 1990 scaled back the government's ambitions and sought to continue moderate growth in the economy, improve foreign trade, and alleviate some of the social costs of economic reform. Development planning is now conducted on an annual basis, with recent development priorities set in the areas of transport infrastructure, health, and education.

In 2000, the International Monetary Fund (IMF) approved a three-year $181.5 million Poverty Reduction and Growth Facility (PRGF) Arrangement for Tanzania (it expired in June 2003). With the inception of this program, GDP growth averaged more than 5%, while inflation declined to below 5%. The servicing of Tan-

zania's over $8 billion external debt absorbs around 40% of total government expenditures. In 2001, Tanzania became eligible for $3 billion in debt service relief under the IMF/World Bank Heavily Indebted Poor Countries (HIPC) initiative.

The government has taken steps to attract foreign investment, including revamping tax codes, floating the exchange rate, licensing foreign banks, and creating an investment promotion center to trim bureaucratic red tape. Poverty remains pervasive, however, and is the main target for economic development. In 2010 the government announced plans to develop the nation's fiber optics network and methane gas production in order to become a middle-income economy by 2020. In 2011 the World Bank approved a $2.8 billion loan for Tanzania, to be released over four years and targeted at basic development and infrastructure.

40 SOCIAL DEVELOPMENT

A social insurance system was implemented in 1998. It covers employees in the private sector, and some public workers and self-employed persons. Domestic workers are excluded, although voluntary coverage is available. Employers contribute 10% of payroll and employees contribute 10% of their wages. Coverage includes old age, disability, and survivorship payments, as well as medical care and maternity benefits. The labor code requires employers to provide severance pay to employees with continuous service of at least three months.

The government advocates equal rights and employment opportunities for women. However, discrimination and violence against women are widespread. The law does not specifically address spousal abuse and victims are hesitant to seek assistance. Female genital mutilation is prevalent. Rape is a significant problem, and the police are ill equipped to deal with the few cases that are actually reported. In Zanzibar, unmarried women who become pregnant and are under the age of 21 are subject to two years' imprisonment. Inheritance laws favor men.

Sexual abuse among children has become a major concern for the nation. In 2011 a UNICEF survey indicated that more than 30% of girls and more than 13% of boys experienced some type of sexual abuse before the age of 18. The survey also found that among those youth who reported having sexual intercourse before the age of 18, 29% of girls and 17.5% of boys said the encounter was forced. Earlier in the year, reports indicated a high occurrence of rape among young girls living alone or in groups in ghettos that provide barely adequate and easily invaded temporary housing for those attending senior schools miles away from their family homes. Living without parental or other adult protection, these schoolgirls are particularly vulnerable to sexual assaults. As a result, some schools report dropout rates of up to 20% for girls between the ages of 13 and 17, primarily due to pregnancy. The incidence of sexual abuse among children may be higher, as it is believed that many cases are not reported. The education minister pledged to make the issue a priority and urged teachers to take the imitative in protecting the most vulnerable children.

Tanzania's human rights record remains poor. Police abuse of prisoners and detainees is widespread. Prison conditions are poor, and dysentery, malaria, and cholera are common. There are reports that the government has blocked the registration of local human rights organizations.

⁴¹HEALTH

According to the CIA, life expectancy in Tanzania was 56 years in 2011. The country spent 18% of its GDP on healthcare, amounting to $25 per person. There was less than one physician, 2 nurses and midwives, and 11 hospital beds per 10,000 inhabitants. The fertility rate was 5.5, while the infant mortality rate was 68 per 1,000 live births. In 2008 the maternal mortality rate, according to the World Bank, was 790 per 100,000 births. It was estimated that 91% of children were vaccinated against measles.

In 1975, the government began to nationalize all hospitals, including those run by Christian missions; private medical practice was ended in 1980. Medical treatment is free or highly subsidized in company clinics as well as hospitals. The pyramid structure of Tanzania's national health care system, stressing primary care at an affordable cost, makes it a pioneer in sub-Saharan Africa. Approximately, 54% of the population had access to safe drinking water and 90% had adequate sanitation. An estimated 80% of the population had access to healthcare services. Life expectancy was 52.85 years in 2011.

There were close to 3,000 rural health facilities, 17 regional hospitals, and 3 national medical centers. Medical staff morale was low due to declining wages and management and operational difficulties in the central medical stores and domestic pharmaceuticals industries. Imports of drugs were overseen by the Pharmaceutical Board; there were four local manufacturers.

Special programs of disease control have been carried out with the assistance of the World Health Organization and UNICEF for most major diseases, including malaria, tuberculosis, sleeping sickness, schistosomiasis, poliomyelitis, and yaws. An estimated 44% of children under five were malnourished.

The prevalence of female genital mutilation was lower than most African nations. Although prohibited by law, the government has not effectively stopped the procedure.

The HIV/AIDS adult prevalence rate was 5.6% in 2009, one of the highest in the world. The Tanzanian government is working to stop the spread of AIDS by improving the treatment of sexually transmitted diseases. Intervention on some STDs has shown a reduction in HIV prevalence.

⁴²HOUSING

Tanzania has developed a serious urban housing shortage as a result of the influx of people to the towns. There have been government initiatives to develop housing sector since independence. Such attempts include establishment of National Housing Corporation in 1962. This was responsible for combating housing shortages in urban centers. The defunct Tanzania Housing Bank was established in 1972 to provide loans for housing construction and rehabilitation of the houses in upgraded squatter settlements. In recent years Government has being playing a facilitation role by creating an enabling environment for private sector, individuals and other institutions to take part in housing development. Housing development is guided by the Settlement Development Policy of 2000. In the implementation of the Policy, the government approved a National Mortgage facility. The department is also responsible for overseeing quality housing development in the country in collaboration with the UN-HABITAT. The govern-

ment plans to provide soft housing loans to enable low income earners to build quality houses.

A significant number of dwellings are constructed from mud and poles or from mud bricks and blocks. A smaller percentage of dwellings are made of concrete and stone, or of baked and burned bricks. Piped indoor water is available to about one-fourth of households and over half have private toilets. The housing deficit in urban areas was estimated at 1.2 million units.

⁴³EDUCATION

Education is compulsory for seven years, generally for children between the ages of 7 and 14. This is covered by a two-stage primary school program (four-years plus three-years). Students may then attend four years of lower secondary and two years of upper secondary school. In the upper secondary level, students choose three courses of study from the following topics: languages, arts, social sciences, mathematics, sciences, commercial subjects, military science, and technology. All senior secondary students take a course in political education. The academic year runs from September to July.

In 2009 the World Bank estimated that 96% of age-eligible children in Tanzania were enrolled in primary school. In 2000 (the latest year for which data was available), secondary school enrollment was about 4.6% of age-eligible students. It is estimated that about 54.2% of all students completed their primary education in 2005. The student-to-teacher ratio for primary school was at about 56:1 in 2005.

The University College in Dar es Salaam opened in 1961 and achieved university status in 1970. The Sokoine University of Agriculture, at Morogoro, was founded in 1984. Other educational facilities in Tanzania include trade schools, the Dar es Salaam Technical College, University College of Lands, Architecture, and Survey (Formerly Ardhi Institute of Dar es Salaam), the Institute of Finance Management and a political science college (both in Dar es Salaam), the College of African Wildlife Management at Mweka, the Institute of Development Management at Morogoro, and the College of National Education in Korogwe. The School of Art at Bagamoyo, devoted to preserving traditional cultures, is one of the few national art schools in sub-Saharan Africa. In 1995, an Open University was established to offer distance learning programs to students in remote areas. The first university to be established on Zanzibar, the University of Zanzibar, opened in 1998.

Overall, the CIA estimated that Tanzania had a literacy rate of 69.4%. Public expenditure on education represented 6.8% of GDP.

⁴⁴LIBRARIES AND MUSEUMS

The Tanzania Library Service was established in 1964. It maintains the National Central Library in Dar es Salaam (656,000 volumes), 20 regional public libraries, a school library service, and a rural extension service. The British Council Library and the American Center Library are also in Dar es Salaam. The other major library is the University of Dar es Salaam Library (750,000 volumes). The library at Dar es Salaam Technical College circulates books by mail to all parts of the country. Also in the capital is the library of the East African Literature Bureau. Zanzibar's National Archives has a collection of Arabic manuscripts. The Tanzanian Library Association was founded in 1973.

The National Museums of Tanzania, with branches in Dar es Salaam and Arusha, have ethnographical, archaeological, historical, geological, and natural history sections; the discoveries from Olduvai Gorge are located there. The Department of Geological Survey maintains a geological museum in Dodoma. There are also museums in Arusha, Bagamoyo, Mikumi, Mwanza, and Tabora.

In Zanzibar, the Government Museum has extensive exhibits illustrating the history, ethnography, industries, and natural history of Zanzibar and Pemba. Tabora has the Livingstone and Stanley Memorial site. There is a fine arts museum in Marangu.

45 MEDIA

In 2009 the CIA reported that there were 173,552 telephone landlines in Tanzania. In addition to landlines, mobile phone subscriptions averaged 40 per 100 people. In 2010, there were 173,552 main phone lines and 17.6 million mobile cell phones in use nationwide.

Radio Tanzania, a government corporation, broadcasts internally in Swahili and English and abroad in English, Afrikaans, and several indigenous African languages. Radio Tanzania Zanzibar broadcasts in Swahili. Private radio and television stations broadcast from Dar es Salaam. There were 12 FM radio stations, 11 AM radio stations, and 2 shortwave radio stations. Internet users numbered 2 per 100 citizens.

In 2010 there were about 110 newspapers published in English and Kiswahili, including 19 dailies and 53 weeklies. Many of the papers were privately owned. The largest dailies, both published in Dar es Salaam, are the government-owned *Daily News* (in English), with a circulation of about 50,000 in 2002, and the CCM-owned *Uhuru* (in Swahili), with a circulation of 100,000. *Kipanga* (in Swahili) is published on Zanzibar by the government. The constitution provides for freedom of speech and the press; however, the government is said to pressure journalists into self-censorship.

46 ORGANIZATIONS

In most of the larger centers, chambers of commerce represent commercial, agricultural, and industrial interests. Rural cooperatives, dissolved in 1976, were reintroduced in 1982 to take over from state bodies the functions of crop purchasing and distribution of agricultural products. There are professional associations and unions for a number of fields, such as the Tanzania Teachers' Union and the Tanzania Sports Medicine Association. The Tanzania Consumers Protection Association is active.

The CCM has five principal affiliates: the Umoja Wa Wawawake Wa Tanzania, a women's organization; the Youth League; the Workers' Organization; the Union of Cooperative Societies; and the Tanzania Parents' Association. Cultural organizations include the National Kiswahili Council, which promotes the use of the Swahili language.

The Tanzanian Scout Association, Girl Guides, and YMCA/YWCA programs are available for youth. There are also several sports associations offering youth programs for athletes interested in a variety of pastimes, such as badminton, cricket, lawn tennis, squash, and track and field.

Social action groups include the Rotary Club, the Catholic Women Organization of Tanzania, the Center for Human Rights Promotion, National Peace Council of Tanzania, and the Tanzania Gender Networking Program. The multinational African Medical and Research Foundation-Tanzania is based in Dar es Salaam. The Center for Women and Children's Rights, established in 1998, and the Huruma Rehabilitation Programme, established in 1994, are dedicated to promoting and supporting the rights and social welfare of women. Volunteer service organizations, such as the Lions Clubs International, are also present. International organizations with national chapters include Amnesty International, Habitat for Humanity, Africare, Caritas, and the Red Cross.

47 TOURISM, TRAVEL, AND RECREATION

The *Tourism Factbook*, published by the UN World Tourism Organization, reported 714,000 incoming tourists to Tanzania in 2009, who spent a total of $1.19 billion. Of those incoming tourists, there were 349,000 from Africa and 233,000 from Europe. There were 56,562 hotel beds available in Tanzania, which had an occupancy rate of 48%. Tanzania has great natural resources along its Indian Ocean coastline, 29 game reserves and 13 national parks, especially the 14,763 sq km (5,700 sq mi) Serengeti National Park, famed for its profusion of wildlife. Tourists also enjoy the dramatic view of Mt. Kilimanjaro. As of 2006, scientists were predicting that Kilimanjaro's ice cap, which had visibly shrunk during the 1990s, would completely disappear by 2015. Other attractions are the national dancing troupe and the ebony wood sculptures of the Makonde tribe. Visas are required and are valid for Zanzibar as well. In 2011 the estimated daily cost to visit Dar es Salaam, the capital, was $273. The cost of visiting other cities averaged $187.

48 FAMOUS PERSONS

The most famous 19th-century Zanzibari was Sayyid Sa'id bin Ahmad al-Albusa'idi (b. Oman, 1791–1856), who founded the Sultanate. Mkwawa, chief of the Hehe, carried on guerrilla warfare against the Germans for three years until he was betrayed for a reward in 1898. The Germans cut off his head and sent it to the anthropological museum in Bremen; in 1961, Mkwawa's skull was returned to the Hehe. The foremost present-day figure is Julius Kambarage Nyerere (1922–99), the founder and first president of independent Tanganyika (and later of Tanzania) from 1962 to 1985, when he stepped down. He was succeeded by 'Ali Hassan Mwinyi (b. 1925), who had been president of Zanzibar during 1984–85. Abeid Karume (1905–72), a sailor of Congolese origin, was the first president of Zanzibar and first vice president of Tanzania until his assassination. He was succeeded by Aboud Jumbe (b. 1920), who resigned both posts in 1984. Since 1985, the president of Zanzibar has been Idris Abdul Wakil (b. 1925–2000). Edward Moringe Sokoine (1938–84), a prime minister during 1977–80 and 1983–84, was regarded as Nyerere's most likely successor until he died in a car crash. Salim Ahmed Salim (b. 1942) was a president of the UN General Assembly during 1979–80, a foreign minister during 1980–84, and a prime minister during 1984–85. An internationally known Tanzanian runner is Filbert Bayi (b. 1953), a former world record holder at 1,500 m. Benjamin William Mkapa (b. 1938) was the third Presided of the United Republic of Tanzania (1995–2005) and former Chairman for the Revolutionary State Party (Chama Chama Mapinduzi, CCM). Jakaya Mrisho Kikwete (b. 1950) is the 4th and current President of Tanzania. He assumed the presidency in August 2005 after serving for several years as a government minister. Kikwete was also Chairperson of the African Union from 31 January 2008 to 2 February 2009.

⁴⁹DEPENDENCIES

Tanzania has no territories or colonies.

⁵⁰BIBLIOGRAPHY

Kamoche, Ken M., ed. *Managing Human Resources in Africa.* New York: Routledge, 2004.

McElrath, Karen, ed. *HIV and AIDS: A Global View.* Westport, CT: Greenwood Press, 2002.

Ofcansky, Thomas P. *Historical Dictionary of Tanzania.* 2nd ed. Lanham, MD: Scarecrow Press, 1997.

Plummer, Mary Louisa, and Daniel Wright. *Young People's Lives and Sexual Relationships in Rural Africa: Findings from a Large Qualitative Study in Tanzania.* Lanham, MD: Lexington Books, 2011.

Tanzania Business Law Handbook: Strategic Information and Laws. Washington, DC: International Business Publications USA, 2012.

Tanzania Investment and Business Guide. Washington, DC: International Business Publications USA, 2012.

Zeilig, Leo, and David Seddon. *A Political and Economic Dictionary of Africa.* Philadelphia: Routledge/Taylor and Francis, 2005.

TOGO

Republic of Togo
République Togolaise

CAPITAL: Lomé

FLAG: The national flag consists of five alternating horizontal stripes of green and yellow. A five-pointed white star is at the center of a red square that spans the height of the top three stripes.

ANTHEM: *Terre de nos aïeux (Land of Our Fathers).*

MONETARY UNIT: The Communauté Financière Africaine franc (XOF) is a paper currency of 100 centimes. There are coins of 1, 2, 5, 10, 25, 50, 100, and 500 francs and notes of 50, 100, 500, 1,000, 5,000, and 10,000 francs. XOF1 = US$0.00204 (or US$1 = XOF487.99) as of December 2011.

WEIGHTS AND MEASURES: The metric system is the legal standard.

HOLIDAYS: New Year's Day, 1 January; National Liberation Day, 13 January; Economic Liberation Day, 24 January; Victory Day, 24 April; Independence Day, 27 April; Labor Day, 1 May; Martyrs' Day, 21 June; Assumption, 15 August; All Saints' Day, 1 November; Anniversary of the failed attack on Lomé, 24 September; Christmas, 25 December. Movable religious holidays include Easter Monday, Ascension, Whitmonday, Eid al-Fitr, and Eid al-Adha.

TIME: GMT.

¹LOCATION, SIZE, AND EXTENT

Situated on the west coast of Africa, Togo has an area of 56,785 sq km (21,925 sq mi), extending 510 km (317 mi) N–S and 140 km (87 mi) E–W. Comparatively, the area occupied by Togo is slightly smaller than the state of West Virginia. Togo is bounded on the N by Burkina Faso, on the E by Benin, on the S by the Gulf of Guinea, and on the W by Ghana, with a total boundary length of 1,703 km (1,058 mi), of which 56 km (35 mi) is coastline.

Togo's capital city, Lomé, is located on the Gulf of Guinea coast.

²TOPOGRAPHY

Togo is traversed in the center by a chain of hills, the Togo Mountains, extending roughly southwest into Ghana and northeastward into Benin and averaging about 700 m (2,300 ft) in height. The highest elevation is Mt. Agou (986 m/3,235 ft). To the north and west of these hills, the Oti River drains in a southwesterly direction into the Volta River, which constitutes a part of the upper boundary with Ghana. To the north of the Oti River Valley lies gently undulating savanna country. From the southern spurs of the central hills, a plateau stretches gradually southward to a coastal plain. The coastline consists of a flat sandy beach thickly planted with coconut trees and partially separated from the mainland by lagoons and lakes that are the former estuaries of several rivers.

³CLIMATE

Togo has a humid, tropical climate, but receives less rainfall than most of the other countries along the Gulf of Guinea. In the south there are two rainy seasons, from March to early July and in September and October. The heaviest rainfall occurs in the hills of the west, southwest, and center, where the precipitation averages about 150 cm (60 in) a year. North of the Togo Mountains there is one rainy season, lasting from April to August. Rainfall in this region averages 100 cm (40 in) a year. The coast gets the least rainfall, about 78 cm (31 in) annually. The average maximum and minimum temperatures are 30°C (86°F) and 23°C (73°F) at Lomé, on the southern coast, and 35°C (95°F) and 15°C (59°F) at Mango, in the north.

⁴FLORA AND FAUNA

The World Resources Institute estimates that there are 3,085 plant species in Togo. In addition, Togo is home to 175 mammal, 565 bird, 108 reptile, and 19 amphibian species. The calculation reflects the total number of distinct species residing in the country, not the number of endemic species.

Natural vegetation was chiefly of the savanna type, luxuriant in the rainy season, brittle grass and shrub during the dry season. Dense belts of reeds were found along the coastal lagoons. Much of the largest wildlife has been exterminated in the southern area, but in the north, elephants and lions still can be found. Hippopotamuses and crocodiles live in and along the rivers, and monkeys are fairly common. The coastal swamps abound in snakes.

⁵ENVIRONMENT

As of 2006, the World Resources Institute reported that Togo had designated 603,200 hectares (1.49 million acres) of land for protection. Water resources totaled 14.7 cu km (3.53 cu mi), while water usage was 0.17 cu km (0.041 cu mi) per year. Domestic water usage accounted for 53% of total usage, industrial for 2%, and agricultural for 45%. Per capita water usage totaled 28 cu m (989 cu ft) per year.

The UN reported in 2008 that carbon dioxide emissions in Togo totaled 1,315 kilotons.

The dense tropical rain forests that once covered much of the country are now found only along the river valleys and in isolated pockets of the Atakora Mountains. Slash-and-burn agriculture and the cutting of wood for fuel are the major causes of forest depletion. Between 1990 and 2010, Togo lost an average of almost 3% of its forest and woodland each year, resulting in a loss of almost 58 percent of its forests in a 20-year period. Soils are generally of poor quality, requiring intensive fertilization and cultivation to be productive. The soil and water supply are threatened by pesticides and fertilizers. The nation's land is also threatened by desertification.

Water pollution is a significant problem in Togo. Contamination of the water supply contributes to the spread of disease.

Responsibility in environmental matters is vested in the Ministry of Rural Development and the Ministry of Environment and Tourism. The government of Togo has tried to protect the nation's environment through a comprehensive legislative package, the Environmental Code of 1988.

The nation's wildlife population was at risk due to poaching and the clearing of land for agricultural purposes. According to a 2011 report issued by the International Union for Conservation of Nature and Natural Resources (IUCN), the number of threatened species included 11 types of mammals, 5 species of birds, 3 types of reptiles, 2 species of amphibians, 24 species of fish, and 10 species of plants. Threatened species included the African elephant, Diana monkey, and West African manatee.

6 POPULATION

The US Central Intelligence Agency (CIA) estimated the population of Togo in 2012 to be approximately 6,961,049, which placed it at number 101 in population among the 196 nations of the world. In 2011, approximately 3.1% of the population was over 65 years of age, with another 40.9% under 15 years of age. The median age in Togo was 19.3 years. There were 0.97 males for every female in the country. The population's annual rate of change was 2.762%. The projected population for the year 2025 was 9,300,000. Population density in Togo was calculated at 119 people per sq km (308 people per sq mi).

The UN estimated that 43% of the population lived in urban areas, and that urban populations had an annual rate of change of 3.9%. The largest urban area was Lomé, with a population of 1.6 million.

The prevalence of HIV/AIDS has had a significant impact on the population of Togo. The AIDS epidemic causes high death and infant mortality rates, and lowers life expectancy.

7 MIGRATION

Togo's net migration rate, estimated by the CIA in 2011, was negligible. The total number of emigrants living abroad was 368,700, and the total number of immigrants living in Togo was 185,400. Togo also accepted 5,000 refugees. There was a steady migration of laborers from rural to urban areas. Members of the Ewe group migrated to and from Ghana, with as many as 100,000 people seeking work in Ghana annually. There was also much movement of Ouatchi, Adja, Kabré, and Losso peoples to and from Benin. Some

of the illegal immigrants expelled from Nigeria in 1983 were Togolese; moreover, Togo suffered the disruptive effect of the hundreds of thousands of Ghanaians who returned home from Nigeria via the Togolese coastal roads during that time. About 7% of the population consisted of noncitizens.

As of January 2011 there were 14,051 refugees and 151 asylum seekers residing in Togo, and 18,330 refugees and 1,032 Togolese asylum seekers residing outside the country.

8 ETHNIC GROUPS

Native Africans constitute 99% of Togo's total population. About 37 tribal groups comprise a mosaic of peoples of distinct languages and histories. The main ethnic group consists of the Ewe and related peoples such as the Ouatchi, Fon, and Adja; they live in the south and constitute about 20–25% of the population. Next in size are the Kabye, accounting for about 10–15% of the population. As elsewhere in Africa, political and ethnic boundaries did not coincide. Thus, the Ewe are divided by the Togo-Ghana boundary, and large numbers of Ouatchi, Adja, Kabye, and Losso live in adjacent Benin. Other significant groups are the Mina (5% of the population), Cotocoli (10–15%), Moba (10–15%), Gourma, Akposso, Ana, Lamba, Ehoué, and Bassari.

Within Togo's complex ethnic, linguistic, and racial makeup, a major distinction can be made between the tribes of Sudanic origin that inhabit the northern region and those of the Bantu type found in the south. There was some residual confrontation between these groups owing to religious and cultural differences and the political, economic, and development competition that evolved between southerners and northerners in colonial times. The remaining 1% of Togo's population is non-African, mostly European and Syrian-Lebanese.

9 LANGUAGES

French is the official language. Most newspapers are printed in French, and trade and commerce passing through Anécho and Lomé usually are conducted in that language; however, the public schools combine French with Ewe and Mina in the south, and Kabiye and Dagomba in the north. In northern Togo, Hausa was also widely spoken. Pidgin English and French were used widely in the principal trading towns. In all, more than 44 different languages and dialects were spoken in Togo.

10 RELIGIONS

The most recent statistics indicate that about 29% of the population was Christian. About 20% of the population was Sunni Muslim. Nearly 51% of Togolese practice a variety of traditional indigenous religions or other faiths, including Vodoun (Voodoo), which was believed to have originated in the region that is now Togo. Most of the Muslims live in the central and northern parts of the country, while Christians are found primarily in the south. Freedom of religion is guaranteed by the constitution, and this right is generally respected in practice. Faiths are tolerant of each other, and religious extremism and sectarian violence are rare. The government recognizes three faiths as state religions: Roman Catholicism, Protestantism, and Islam. Religious groups fitting into other categories must register as an association with the government to obtain the same rights as the state religions. Easter Monday, Ascension, Pentecost Monday, Assumption, Eid al-Fitr,

All Saints' Day, Tabaski, and Christmas are observed as national holidays.

11TRANSPORTATION

The CIA reported that Togo had a total of 7,520 km (4,673 mi) of roads in 2007, of which 2,376 km (1,476 mi) were paved. There were eight airports, of which two had paved runways. Togo had approximately 50 km (31.1 mi) of navigable waterways.

The country has two main trunk lines. The first, completely paved since 1980, ran north from Lomé to the border with Burkina Faso; the second was a coastal road running from Lomé to Aného and onward to the Benin border. Because of extreme variations in weather, the roads that were not paved required constant attention. During the dry season, they were very dusty, and during the rainy season they became extremely muddy and were frequently washed out.

Togo is expected to benefit greatly from the World Bank-funded reconstruction of the Abidjan-Lagos Corridor, also known as the West African Coastal Corridor. In March 2010, the World Bank approved funding of $317.5 million to improve this important roadway, which stretches for 998.8 km (620 mi), linking the capital cities of Abidjan (Côte d'Ivoire), Accra (Ghana), Lomé (Togo), Cotonou (Benin), and Lagos (Nigeria). This corridor was one of the most highly traveled roadways on the continent. Developed in part by the Economic Community of West African Nations (ECOWAS), the corridor project implemented procedural reforms to promote a more efficient trade process, along with much needed improvements to the physical infrastructure. The project was to be executed in two phases, with the first phase covering Ghana, Togo, and Benin, and the second phase covering Côte d'Ivoire and Nigeria.

As of 2008, Togo had 532 km (331 mi) of meter gauge (narrow gauge) railroad, including three major lines from Lomé: to Kpalimé (116 km/72 mi), to Aného (44 km/27 mi), and to Atakpamé and Blitta (276 km/171 mi). An 80-km (50-mi) spur went to Tabligbo. The rail system was operated by Chemin de Fer Togolais.

Togo lacks a natural harbor, but in 1968 a major deepwater port east of central Lomé was completed with a loan from the Federal Republic of Germany (FRG). An autonomous free port at Lomé serves landlocked Burkina Faso, Niger, and Mali. There is also a phosphate-handling port at Kpémé. A small merchant-shipping fleet was created in 1974 as a joint venture with the FRG. In 2008, there were 10 ships of 1,000 gross registered tons or over. As of 2008, Togo's navigable inland waterways consisted of a 50 km (31 mi) stretch of the Mono River, in which navigation was seasonal and dependent upon rainfall.

There were only two airports with paved runways. The international airport at Lomé linked Togo with other countries of West and Central Africa and with Europe; a second international airport, at Niamtougou, was completed in the early 1980s. Among the international airlines serving Togo are Air France, Brussels Airlines, and Ethiopian Airlines. Air Togo operates domestic service, flying to airstrips at Atakpamé, Sokodé, Sansanné-Mango, Lama-Kara, Niamtougou, and Dapaong.

12HISTORY

Between the 12th and the 18th centuries, the Ewe, Adja, and related peoples, who now constitute a majority of the population of southern Togo and adjoining Ghana, came to this area from the

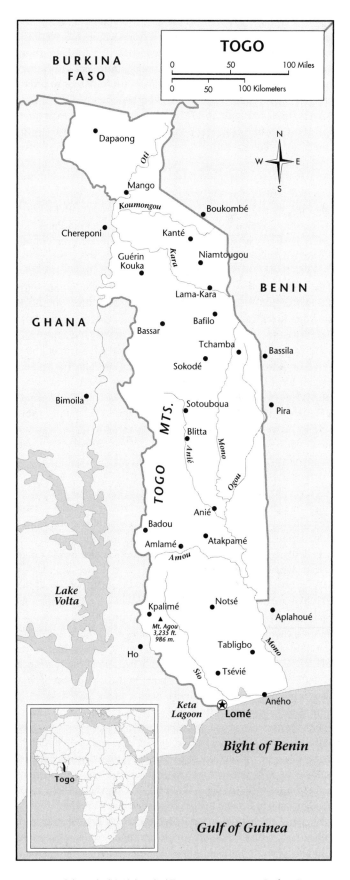

LOCATION: 6°5′ to 11°11′N; 0°5′ to 1°45′ E. BOUNDARY LENGTHS: Burkina Faso, 126 kilometers (78 miles); Benin, 644 kilometers (400 miles); Gulf of Guinea coastline, 56 kilometers (35 miles); Ghana, 877 kilometers (545 miles). TERRITORIAL SEA LIMIT: 30 miles.

Niger River Valley as a result of pressure from the east. Portuguese sailors visited the coast in the 15th and 16th centuries. Slave shipments began from Grand Popo (now in Benin), Petit Popo (now Anécho), and other coastal villages; traders introduced the growing of cassava, coconuts, corn, and other crops in order to provision their slave ships. The French established trading posts at Petit Popo in 1626 and again in 1767, but abandoned them each time. The French were again active there and at Porto-Séguro, east of Lomé, from 1865 to 1883.

German traders came to Grand Popo as early as 1856, but did not arrive in significant numbers until 1880. Germany finally established control over the area, its first African acquisition, on 5 July 1884, when Dr. Gustav Nachtigal made a treaty with the chief of Togo, a village on the north side of a lagoon behind Porto-Séguro. The treaty established a German protectorate over a small coastal enclave, and the village name eventually was given to the entire territory. The Germans established a capital first at Baguida, then at Zebe, and in 1897 at Lomé. Boundary delimitations with the British and French were made in 1897 and 1899. Although the Volta River formed a natural boundary between Togo and the Gold Coast (now Ghana), as a result of the negotiations, the frontier diverged from the river about 320 km (200 mi) north of Lomé and descended diagonally, so that the so-called Volta Triangle on the left bank became part of the Gold Coast. The boundary arrangements resulted in splitting the Ewe, Adja, Ouatchi, Fon, and other peoples between the Gold Coast, Togo, and Dahomey (now Benin). As the Germans extended their control to the north, they built roads and railroads and established administrative, legal, economic, educational, and other institutions.

Soon after the outbreak of World War I (1914–18) in August 1914, neighboring French and British units gained control of Togo. In a provisional arrangement, the British took the coastal area and the railways, and the French assumed control of the interior. League of Nations mandates were established in 1922.

Following World War II, both the United Kingdom and France placed their spheres of Togoland under UN trusteeship. Beginning in 1947, leaders of the Ewe people repeatedly petitioned the UN, first for Ewe unification and subsequently for Togoland unification. At the time, the Ewe were under three different administrations: the Gold Coast, British Togoland, and French Togoland. For nine years thereafter, the Togoland question was before the UN. Its resolution was difficult not only because of the resistance of the British and French governments to the Ewe demands, but also because both the Ewe and non-Ewe of the two Togolands were deeply divided on the form self-determination should take. The problem was partially resolved by a plebiscite (a vote by an entire country or people) held in British Togoland on 9 May 1956 under UN supervision. A majority of the registered voters decided in favor of integration of British Togoland with an independent Gold Coast. Consequently, when the Gold Coast became the independent state of Ghana, British Togoland ceased to exist.

On 28 October 1956, in a referendum held in French Togoland, 72% of the registered voters chose to terminate French trusteeship and to accept the status of internal autonomy and continued association with France that had been proffered them by the French government. This unilateral effort to terminate French trusteeship was not accepted by the UN.

In April 1958, new elections were held under UN supervision. The Committee for Togolese Union, pledged to secure complete independence, won control of the Togo Assembly, and its leader, Sylvanus Olympio, subsequently became prime minister. On 13 October 1958, the French government announced that full independence would be granted, and on 27 April 1960, the Republic of Togo became a sovereign nation, with Olympio as president.

President Olympio was assassinated on 13 January 1963 by military insurgents. At the insurgents' behest, Nicolas Grunitzky, the exiled leader of the Togolese Party for Progress, returned to Togo and formed a provisional government. He abrogated the constitution, dissolved the National Assembly, and called new elections. In the May 1963 balloting, Grunitzky was elected president, a new 56-member National Assembly was chosen, and a new constitution was approved by national referendum.

Grunitzky held office through 1966. The final months of his presidency were marked by antigovernment demonstrations involving many of Olympio's former supporters and sympathizers. On 13 January 1967, the Grunitzky government was overthrown by a military coup led by Col. Kléber Dadjo, who was succeeded in April 1967 by Lt. Col. Étienne Éyadéma. The constitution was again suspended, the Assembly dissolved, and Éyadéma declared himself president.

In 1969, Éyadéma proposed the establishment of a national party of unification, the Togolese People's Rally (Rassemblement du Peuple Togolais-RPT). At its first party congress in November 1971, the RPT representatives opposed the idea of constitutional government and asked for a national referendum in support of the Éyadéma regime. This took place in January 1972, with 99% of the population voting for Éyadéma. Survivors of a 1970 plot to overthrow the regime were pardoned after the referendum, and several former members of Olympio's government joined the RPT. Others of Olympio's supporters went into exile or into business, and there was no coherent opposition to the government.

In 1974, Éyadéma began to advocate a "cultural authenticity" policy, stimulated at least in part by the crash of his private plane in January 1974, from which he escaped uninjured. The crash (the cause of which he believed suspicious) followed his nationalization of the phosphate industry and appeared to spur his drive for further Africanization in Togo. At this time, Éyadéma dropped his first name, Étienne, using instead his African second name, Gnassingbé.

Éyadéma was reelected as president without opposition on 30 December 1979, when the voters also approved a draft constitution for what was called the Third Republic (succeeding the republics headed by Olympio and Grunitzky). A 67-member National Assembly was elected at the same time. Éyadéma remained firmly in control in the early 1980s, despite the disruptions caused by Nigeria's expulsion of illegal immigrants and the economic decline attributable to falling phosphate prices. An alleged plot to assassinate Éyadéma on 13 January 1983, while French president François Mitterrand was visiting Togo, apparently misfired. Éyadéma reportedly blamed Gilchrist Olympio, the son of the former president, for the coup attempt.

On 23–24 September 1986, about 60 insurgents, mostly Togolese in exile, attempted to seize control of Lomé but were repulsed. About 150 French and 350 Zairian troops were flown in to help restore order. The official death toll was 26. The coup attempt was reportedly financed by Gilchrist Olympio, who was sentenced to death in absentia. Another 12 men were given death sentences, and 14 were sentenced to life imprisonment. Éyadéma accused Ghana and Burkina Faso of aiding the insurgents. In National Assembly elections on 24 March 1985, 216 candidates, all approved by the RPT, contested 77 seats; only 20 deputies were reelected. Éyadéma was elected unopposed to a new seven-year term as president on 21 December 1986.

Opposition to Éyadéma's rule came to a head in March 1991 when, after police clashes with thousands of antigovernment demonstrators, the government agreed to institute a multiparty system and to grant amnesty to dissidents. On 28 August 1991, Éyadéma ended 24 years of military rule by surrendering authority to Joseph Kokou Koffigoh, an interim prime minister selected by a National Conference. The RPT was to be disbanded and Éyadéma barred from running for the presidency.

In October and November 1991, armed forces loyal to Éyadéma failed several times to overthrow Koffigoh. On 3 December 1991, however, they attacked the government palace and seized him. The French refused to help Koffigoh; instead, he was forced to compromise; he then formed a coalition government with Éyadéma and legalized the RPT.

On 5 May 1992, opposition leader Gilchrist Olympio was severely wounded in an ambush, and in July another opposition figure was assassinated. The transitional government several times rescheduled the referendum on a new constitution. Finally, on 27 September 1992, it was approved. The legislative and presidential elections were postponed again and again until August 1993.

The Army, composed largely of Kabyé (Éyadéma's group) never accepted Éyadéma's ouster, the National Conference, or Koffigoh. Eventually, Koffigoh's interim government was dissolved in 1992, and Éyadéma consolidated his powers. However, in January 1993 he reappointed Koffigoh prime minister of a government which cooperated closely with Éyadéma, now president. On 25 August 1993, Éyadéma easily won reelection as president (97% of the vote). The electoral process, however, was marred by a low turnout (all major opposition candidates refused to participate) and serious irregularities.

Following delays, legislative elections were held in two rounds in February 1994. With the exception of Olympio's Union of the Forces of Change (UFC), the main opposition parties participated. The RPT reportedly took 33 of the 81 seats in the first round. The Action Committee for Renewal (CAR) won 19. Koffigoh's New Force Coordination failed to take a single seat. Nonetheless, the armed forces continued to attack opposition politicians. The second round voting was marred by violence, with armed gangs attacking voting stations and opposition supporters. Still, international observers declared the election satisfactory.

On 24 February 1994 the National Electoral Commission released results for 76 seats as follows: opposition, 38 seats; RPT, 37 seats; Koffigoh, 1 seat. The Supreme Court ordered new elections for 3 seats of the Action Committee for Renewal and the Togolese Union for Democracy, lowering their totals to 34 and 6 seats, respectively. Defections from the CAR to the RPT and the merging of the Union of Justice and Democracy (UJD) with the RPT gave the RPT a narrow majority with 42 seats.

In June 1998 Éyadéma officially won the presidential elections with 52%, but the opposition rejected the election as rigged. Éya-

déma's dubious victory precipitated a national crisis, and led the opposition to boycott the legislative elections delayed and then scheduled for March 1999. In July, the RPT and opposition parties signed the Lomé Framework Agreement, which included a pledge by Éyadéma to respect the constitution and not to seek another term. The Agreement ensured among other things political rights for opposition leaders, the safe return for refugees, and compensation for victims of political violence. Éyadéma also agreed to dissolve the National Assembly in March 2000 and hold new legislative elections, to be supervised by an independent national election commission (CENI). The March deadline passed, as did deadlines in October 2001 and March 2002. The elections were finally held on 27 October 2002, but under a boycott from the Union of the Forces for Change (UFC) and the Action Committee for Renewal (CAR), grouped as the Coalition of Democratic Forces (CFD). The RPT took 72 of the 81 seats.

In December 2002, parliament amended the constitution to allow Éyadéma to seek a third term, and to bar Gilchrist Olympio, leader of the UFC, from running by instituting residence requirements. In February 2003, a new nine-member CENI was formed, including four representatives each of the RPT and the opposition umbrella group CFD. The ninth member was the president of the Lomé Court of Appeal. However, the UFC withdrew from the CFD because it regarded CENI's mandate as curtailed by the government, and because it regarded the CFD's actions and strategies as incoherent. In June, Éyadéma won the election with 57.8% of the vote, but no international observers were present, and the opposition refused to accept the outcome as a free and fair expression of the will of the people.

Facing a new political stalemate, the government initiated talks in late 2003 and into 2004 with the opposition via the Cotonou Convention platform (2000) sponsored by the EU. Despite the regime's new promises to implement reforms, the opposition mostly boycotted the talks. In December 2004, the boycott seemed to be having an effect as Éyadéma dissolved the parliament and announced new elections for 2005. However, in February 2005, he died unexpectedly. The problem of succession followed; Éyadéma's son, Faure Gnassingbé, took his place. Although Gnassingbé had the support of the army, strong pressure from ECOWAS forced him to step down and to organize fresh elections. On 24 April, Gnassingbé won the election, but again the opposition dismissed the exercise as fraudulent, and neither the EU nor the United States recognized the outcome as legitimate. In rioting that followed, some 500 people were killed, and thousands fled the country in the face of government crackdowns. Gnassingbé also appointed his brother Kpatcha Gnassingbé to be defense minister.

In the months that followed, Nigerian President Obasanjo insisted on a government of national unity with an opposition prime minister. Bowing to concerted pressure, Gnassingbé finally appointed an opposition leader, Edem Kodjo—a former head of the OAU—to be the new prime minister. However, this appointment was refused by the UFC. Talks held in Rome between Gnassingbé and Gilchrist Olympio sponsored by the Italian Catholic community of Sant Egidio, revealed a number of sticking points including a mutually acceptable electoral framework and constitutional rules. Specifically, the opposition demanded a return to the 1992 constitution while the RPT refused to reverse the amendments made in 2002 that disqualified Olympio's candidacy, but allowed

Gnassingbé to hold office. In the meantime, Lomé became a dangerous city beset by violent organized crime. Owing to government crackdowns, poor military accountability, and harassment by pro-government militias, the number of Togolese seeking refuge in neighboring Benin and Ghana grew to about 45,000 by 2006.

In April 2006, reconciliation talks between the government and the opposition resumed. That August, the government and the opposition signed an agreement providing for the participation of opposition parties in a transitional government. In September, Yawovi Agboyibo, long-time leader of the opposition Committee of Action for Renewal, was named prime minister and given the task of forming a unity government and organizing elections. In February 2007, Olympio returned from exile briefly. In April 2009, a coup attempt over Faure, allegedly led by his half-brother, Kpatcha Gnassingbe, was unveiled, leading to the arrests of Kpatcha, 18 soldiers, and 10 civilians, all of whom were accused of some level of involvement. In May 2009, the nation's constitutional court announced a plan for democratic reform, including presidential elections to be held in February and March of 2010.

In January 2010 separatist rebels in Cabinda, Angola, staged an attack on a bus carrying the Togolese national football (soccer) team from the Republic of Congo to the Africa Nations' Cup tournament in Cabinda. A little-known offshoot of the Front for the Liberation of the Enclave of Cabinda (FLEC), a group promoting independence for the province of Cabinda, known as the Front for the Liberation of the Enclave of Cabinda-Military Position (FLEC-PM), claimed responsibility for the attack. A larger off-shoot known as Armed Forces of Cabinda (FLEC-FAC) also claimed responsibility.

Three persons were killed—the bus driver, the team's assistant manager, and the media officer. Several players, two team doctors, and a journalist were injured. Secretary General of the FLEC-PM Rodrigues Mingas, exiled in France, claimed the attack had been aimed at the Angolan forces at the head of the convoy. The Togo team returned home two days later, and having initially pulled out of the tournament, was disqualified from play. The other members of Togo's group, including Ghana, decided to continue play. Prime Minister Gilbert Houngbo called for three days of national mourning for the victims beginning 11 January. The following day, the Togo captain, Emmanuel Adebayor, announced his retirement from international football, stating that he was "haunted by the events" of that terrible afternoon.

On 4 March 2010, Faure Gnassingbe of the Togolese People's Rally was reelected as president with 60.9% of the vote. Jean-Pierre Fabre, a candidate from the UFC, came in second with 33.9% of the vote. Fabre declared the election fraudulent, leading hundreds of supporters of the opposition to stage a series of riots, most of which were quickly dispersed by tear gas. With this new election, the Gnassingbe family began its 44th year in power. After several weeks of negotiations, it was announced in May that a power-sharing agreement had been reached between the two leading parties through which the UFC, under the new leadership of Gilchrist Olympio, son of Sylvanus Olympio, would receive eight ministerial posts in a coalition government. However, shortly after the agreement, the UFC rejected the deal and suspended Olympio. The majority of the party had been against the deal.

In 2011 the opposition continued to stage weekly protest marches in Lomé. In addition, the Truth and Reconciliation Commission (TRC), established in 2006 following the police-led killings, continued its investigations, which covered the period 1958 through 2005. Initially scheduled to last only three months, the TRC was scheduled to conclude and to present its findings in 2012.

¹³GOVERNMENT

Before the reign of Éyadéma, Togo was considered a republic in transition to democratic rule. However, under Éyadéma and his son Fauré Gnassingbe, Togo was ruled like an autocratic dynasty. According to the constitution, the president was elected by popular vote for a five-year term. In December 2002, the National Assembly amended the constitution, revoking the two-term limit on the presidential office (allowing Éyadéma to run again), instituting a single rather than two-round system of voting (to prevent the opposition from forcing a run-off against their best-placed candidate), insisting that presidential candidates be residents of Togo for at least 12 months prior to the election (to prevent Gilchrist Olympio from running), and to lower the minimum age for presidential candidates to 35, (enabling Fauré Gnassingbé to run). The 81-seat National Assembly was selected in national, multiparty elections, but performed minimal checks on the executive. In 2011, Freedom House ranked Togo as "partly free," with a political rights score of 5 and a civil liberties score of 4 on a scale of 1–7 where 7 represented "least free" and 1 "most free."

Formerly, the constitution of 30 December 1979 provided for a president nominated by the RPT and elected for a seven-year term by universal adult suffrage at age 18. The president would nominate and preside over the cabinet and could rule by decree after declaring a state of emergency. Members of the National Assembly were to be nominated by the RPT and directly elected for five years. The legislature, which may be dissolved by the president, met twice a year.

A new constitution mandating multiparty elections was approved in a referendum on 27 September 1992. Although opposition parties were permitted, they were subject to intimidation and coercion. Chief of state, President Gen. Gnassingbé Éyadéma, held power between April 1967 and February 2005, which made him sub-Saharan Africa's longest ruling leader at the time. The cabinet was a Council of Ministers appointed by the president and the prime minister. Given the weakness of the legislature, and the RPT's majority, public decision-making authority resided with the executive.

¹⁴POLITICAL PARTIES

As of 2011, three political parties dominated the landscape—the incumbent Togolese People's Rally (RPT), the Union of Forces for Change (UFC), and the Action Committee for Renewal (CAR). There were also a number of smaller parties with representation in the National Assembly. Parties typically identified with the personality and ethnic group of their leader, rather than with ideology or platform.

In the first Territorial Assembly elections in 1946, there were two parties, the Committee of Togolese Unity (Comité de l'Unité Togolaise—CUT) and the Togolese Party for Progress (Parti Togolais du Progrès—PTP). The CUT was overwhelmingly successful, and Sylvanus Olympio, the CUT leader and Assembly president, campaigned for Ewe reunification. The CUT controlled all Assembly seats from 1946 to 1952. In the 1952 elections, however, the CUT was defeated, and it refused to participate in further elections because it claimed that the PTP was receiving French support. In the territorial elections of 1955, the PTP won all 30 Assembly seats, and when Togo was given autonomy in 1956, Nicolas Grunitzky, PTP leader, became prime minister.

In the UN-supervised elections of April 1958, the CUT regained power with a demand for independence from France, while the PTP and the Union of Chiefs and Peoples of the North (Union des Chefs et des Populations du Nord-UCPN) advocated that Togo remain an autonomous republic within the French Union. The two defeated parties merged in October 1959 to form the Togolese People's Democratic Union (Union Démocratique des Populations Togolaises—UDPT), under Grunitzky's leadership.

In the post-independence period, parties struggled against one-party rule and incumbent party domination. From 1969 till the legalization of opposition parties in 1991, Togo was a one-party state. In March 1961, the National Assembly enacted legislation that based elections to the Assembly on a party-list system, with a single ballot in which a majority would be decisive. In the April 1961 elections, which were held on this single-list system, candidates from the alliance of the UDPT and the Togolese Youth Movement (Mouvement de la Jeunesse Togolaise—Juvento) were prevented from registering and were not permitted on the ballot. Consequently, the new Assembly consisted entirely of CUT members.

After Olympio (who had become president in 1960) was assassinated by military insurgents, Grunitzky, who was living in exile in Benin (then Dahomey), was invited back to Togo to form a provisional government. Grunitzky announced that free elections would be held, but in fact the delegates of the four leading parties—UDPT, Juvento, the Togolese Unity Movement (Unité Togolaise, formed from the CUT after Olympio's assassination), and the Togolese Popular Movement (Mouvement Populaire Togolais)—as well as the insurgents' Committee of Vigilance, agreed on a single national union list of candidates. In the elections of 5 May 1963, Grunitzky became president and Antoine Meatchi vice-president; a new 56-member Assembly was elected; and a new constitution was approved by national referendum. In early 1967, however, Grunitzky was deposed, and a military regime took power, with no constitution and no legislature.

Organized political activity was suspended until 1969, when the Togolese People's Rally (Rassemblement du Peuple Togolais-RPT) was founded as the nation's sole legal political party. The President heads the RPT, which has a Central Committee and a Political Bureau. In the 1979 and 1985 legislative elections, all candidates were nominated by the RPT. In the 1994 legislative elections, however, other parties participated.

Political opposition to Éyadéma became bolder after 1990. For years, an anti-Éyadéma group, the Togolese Movement for Democracy (Mouvement Togolais pour la Démocratie), functioned in exile from Paris. After opposition parties were legalized on 12 April 1991, and especially after the National Conference engineered a governmental change in August 1991, other parties began to function, albeit in an atmosphere of threat from the armed forces and pro-Éyadéma gangs. Among the country's parties as

of 1996 were the Coordination des Forces Nouvelles (CFN), Rally of the Togolese People (RPT), Togolese Union for Democracy (UTD), Action Committee for Renewal (CAR), Union for Democracy and Solidarity (UDS), Pan-African Sociodemocrats Group (GSP, an alliance of three radical parties: CDPA, Democratic Convention of African Peoples; PDR, Party for Democracy and Renewal; and PSP, Pan-African Social Party), Union of Forces for Change (UFC), and Union of Justice and Democracy (UJD).

All major opposition parties boycotted the 1993 elections, delaying elections until February 1994. The winners distributed the seats as follows: CAR 36, RPT 35, UTD 7, UJD 2, CFN 1. However, as a result of defections from the CAR to the RPT and the merging of the UJD with the RPT, representation in the National Assembly in August 1997 was RPT 42, CAR 32, UTD 5, CFN 1, independent 1, giving Eyadema's party a narrow majority.

Disagreements between the divided opposition and the RPT thwarted efforts to achieve a national consensus on how the 1998 elections were to be conducted. The opposition boycotted the elections in March 1999 to protest the alleged cheating by Éyadéma and his supporters in the June 1998 presidential election. But progress was made in defining the role of the national electoral commission (CENI), and by April 2000, the two sides agreed to return to the table to discuss endorsement of an electoral bill and related issues pertaining to national reconciliation. Legislative elections were delayed throughout 2000, 2001, and early 2002; they were finally held on 27 October 2002. The elections were judged to be democratic and transparent by international election observers, but the two main opposition parties—the UFC and the CAR—grouped as the Coalition of Democratic Forces (CFD), boycotted the elections, and the RPT emerged with 72 of the 81 seats. Also winning seats were the Rally for Democracy and Development (Rassemblement pour le soutien de la démocratie et du développement—RSDD), 3; the Union for Democracy and Social Progress (Union pour la démocratie et le progrès social—UDPS), 2; Juvento, 2; the Believers' Movement for Equality and Peace (Mouvement des croyants pour l'égalité et la paix—MOCEP), 1; and an independent won 1 seat.

In early 2003, the UFC pulled out of the CFD umbrella opposition organization, due to disagreements with its strategies and its agreement to sit on the newly reformed electoral commission, CENI, which the UFC judged to be manipulated by the government. In the June 2003 presidential contest, Éyadéma scored 57.8% of the vote to 33.7% for the UFC candidate, Emmanual Bob-Akitani, Gilchrist Olympio's replacement. In the April 2005 presidential contest, Bob-Akitani ran against Éyadéma's son, Faure Gnassingbé, and was defeated 60.1% to 38.3%. The main opposition declared both polls fraudulent, and refused to accept the results. The UFC and the CAR remained outside the government of national unity.

In the 2007 legislative elections, the Rally for the Togolese People won 39.4% of the vote and 50 seats in the assembly. The UFC won 37% of the vote and 27 seats, followed by CAR with 8.2% and 4 seats. In 2010, Fauré Gnassingbé was reelected as president with 60.9% of the vote. The prime minister is Gilbert Houngbo (since 2008). The next presidential election was scheduled for 2015, and the next parliamentary election was scheduled for 2012.

15 LOCAL GOVERNMENT

Togo is divided into five administrative regions—Maritime, Plateaux, Centrale, Kara, and Savanes—each supervised by an inspector. The regions are subdivided into 30 prefectures and four sub-prefectures. Inspectors and prefects are appointed by the president. The prefectures and sub-prefectures are subdivided into cantons.

Democratic decentralization was ongoing at the local community level. The country is composed of 30 communes, 9 of them "fully independent" with an elected mayor, and 21 "semi-independent" with the prefect acting as mayor. Communes have popularly elected municipal councils.

16 JUDICIAL SYSTEM

The legal system is based on French and customary law, blending elements of African traditional law and the Napoleonic Code. In practice, the judiciary is subject to the influence and control of the executive branch.

Supervision of the judiciary is the responsibility of the Superior Council of Magistrates, established in 1964. Members include the president of the republic as chairman, the minister of justice, the president and vice president of the Supreme Court, and others. A Constitutional Court is the highest court of jurisdiction in constitutional matters. The Supreme Court sits in Lomé; there are also a sessions court (Court of Assizes) and an Appeals Courts. Tribunals of first instance are divided into civil, commercial, and correctional chambers; labor and children's tribunals; and the Court of State Security, which was set up in September 1970 to judge crimes involving foreign or domestic subversion. A Tribunal for Recovery of Public Funds handles cases involving misuse of public funds.

Defendants in criminal cases are presumed innocent and are afforded the right to counsel. Village chiefs or a Council of Elders can try minor criminal cases in rural areas. Appeals from such rulings can be taken to the regular court system.

Trials are open and judicial procedures are generally respected. However, the judicial system suffers from a lack of personnel and remains overburdened.

17 ARMED FORCES

The International Institute for Strategic Studies (IISS) reports that armed forces in Togo totaled 8,550 members in 2011. The force was comprised of 8,100 from the army, 200 from the navy, and 250 members of the air force. Armed forces represented 0.3% of the labor force in Togo that year. Defense spending totaled $95.9 million and accounted for 1.6% of GDP.

Equipment included two main battle tanks and nine light tanks. The air force had 16 combat capable aircraft that included four fighter ground attack aircraft. The country's navy had two coastal patrol vessels. Paramilitary forces numbered 750 members.

18 INTERNATIONAL COOPERATION

Togo was admitted to the UN on 29 September 1960. It was a member of ECA and several nonregional specialized agencies, such as the World Bank, UNESCO, UNIDO, the ILO, FAO, and the WHO. Togo also belonged to the African Development Bank, the ACP Group, the Arab Bank for Economic Development in Africa, ECOWAS, G-77, the WTO, the Organization of the Islamic Conference (OIC), the West African Economic and Monetary Union, the New Partnership for Africa's Development (NEPAD), the Community of Sahel and Saharan States (CENSAD), and the African Union. Togo has been an active member of the Conseil d'Entente, which includes Côte d'Ivoire, Niger, Burkina Faso, and Benin. Togo hosted the signing ceremony for the Lomé Convention (providing for preferential treatment by the European Community for developing countries) in February 1975.

In environmental cooperation, Togo is part of the Convention on Biological Diversity, Ramsar, CITES, International Tropical Timber Agreements, the Kyoto Protocol, the Montréal Protocol, MARPOL, the Nuclear Test Ban Treaty, and the UN Conventions on the Law of the Sea, Climate Change, and Desertification.

19 ECONOMY

The GDP in Togo was $6.324 billion in 2011. The rate of change in Togo, as of 2011, was 3.8%. Inflation stood at an estimated 4.5%. Owing to state intervention in and control over the economy, the Heritage Foundation ranked Togo's economy 153rd out of 179 economies in the world in 2011, which was considered "repressed" on the Index of Economic Freedom.

Togo's economy is largely agricultural, with 46 percent of the GDP coming from agriculture and over 65% of the population engaged in subsistence and commercial agriculture. Togo is drought-prone, but has the potential to be food self-sufficient in years of ample rainfall. Coffee, cocoa, and cotton are the major cash crops; food crops include corn, sorghum, millet, cassava, and yams. The nation also has an active commercial sector and significant phosphate deposits upon which it draws for foreign exchange.

Uncertainty in the political climate has discouraged foreign investment, donor contributions, and the stability needed for economic progress. By 2006, Togo was $105 million in arrears to the World Bank and owed $15 million to the African Development Bank (ADB). In an effort to regain the confidence of the donor community, Togo resumed talks to restart development assistance. Successful legislative elections in 2007 led to a grant of €26 million from the EU. In 2011 Togo reached an agreement with the IMF that led to the forgiveness of 95% of its debt.

20 INCOME

The CIA estimates that in 2011 the GDP of Togo was $6.324 billion. The CIA defined GDP as the value of all final goods and services produced within a nation in a given year and computed on the basis of purchasing power parity (PPP) rather than value as measured on the basis of the rate of the exchange based on current dollars. The per capita GDP was estimated at $900. The annual growth rate of GDP was 3.8%. The average inflation rate was 4.5%. It was estimated that agriculture accounted for 46% of GDP, industry 23%, and services 31%.

According to the World Bank, remittances from citizens living abroad totaled $306.8 million in 2009, or about $45 per capita and accounted for approximately 5.1% of GDP.

In 2007 the World Bank estimated that Togo, with 0.09% of the world's population, accounted for 0.01% of the world's GDP. By comparison, the United States, with 4.85% of the world's population, accounted for 22.51% of world GDP.

As of 2011 the most recent study by the World Bank reported that actual individual consumption in Togo was 100.8% of GDP and accounted for 0.01% of world consumption. By comparison, the United States accounted for 25.44% of world individual consumption. The World Bank also estimated that 53.8% of Togo's GDP was spent on food and beverages, 9.4% on housing and household furnishings, 5.3% on clothes, 3.8% on health, 16.3% on transportation, 2.1% on communications, 2.0% on recreation, 2.4% on restaurants and hotels, and 1.7% on miscellaneous goods and services and purchases from abroad.

It was estimated by the World Bank that in 2006 about 62% of the population subsisted on an income below the poverty line established by Togo's government.

21 LABOR

As of 2007, Togo had a total labor force of 2.595 million people. Within that labor force, the CIA reported that in 1998, 65% were employed in agriculture, 5% in industry, and 30% in the service sector. The majority of families engage in subsistence farming.

Trade unions once were the base for left-wing opposition to the military regime and were subsequently incorporated into the one-party system. The Central Committee of the RPT dissolved the central bodies of all Togolese trade unions in December 1972, and the National Workers Confederation of Togo (Confédération Nationale des Travailleurs du Togo—CNTT) was established in 1973 as the sole national union. In 1991, the National Conference suspended the automatic withholding of CNTT dues for all workers, and it froze CNTT's assets. Several trade unions left the CNTT, some of which then affiliated with two new federations: the Labor Federation of Togolese Workers and the National Union of Independent Syndicates. After 1991 Togo's labor federations took a more active role in independent collective bargaining. As of 2010, about 60–70% of the workforce in the formal, wage economy was unionized.

The minimum working age is 14 (18 for certain industrial employment), but it is not enforced, and many children work in the informal sector and on family plots. The minimum wage was raised to $58 in 2008, but it does not provide a living wage for a family. The workweek is limited to 72 hours, with one mandatory rest period of 24 hours.

About 9,000 people, 60% of them women, work in Togo's export processing zone (EPZ) in Lomé where some 60 foreign companies operate. In theory, workers have the same rights as workers elsewhere in Togo, but in practice are subject to various abuses and have been denied the right to organize into unions. In 2011, the first union of export processing zone workers organized to defend workers' rights in the EPZ.

22 AGRICULTURE

Roughly 46% of the total land is farmed. The country's major crops include coffee, cocoa, cotton, yams, cassava (tapioca), corn, beans, rice, millet, and sorghum. Cereal production in 2009 amounted to 1 million tons, fruit production 59,133 tons, and vegetable production 113,534 tons.

Togo was predominantly an agricultural country, with about 65 percent of the work force engaged in farming. Most food crops are produced by subsistence farmers using rudimentary tools and inputs on family plots of less than 3 hectares (7 acres). Peanuts and sorghum are grown in the extreme north; sorghum, yams, and cotton in the region around Niamtougou; sorghum, cotton, and corn in the central region; coffee, cocoa, and cotton in the southern plateau; and manioc, corn, and copra near the coast.

Although Togo is nearly self-sufficient in food, certain cereals—notably wheat, which could be grown in Togo—had to be imported.

Leading cash crops were coffee and cocoa, followed by cotton, palm kernels, copra, peanuts, and shea nuts (karité). A state organization, the Togolese Cotton Co., was set up in 1974 to develop the cotton industry. When world prices for coffee and cocoa fell in the mid-1980s, there was a greater emphasis on cotton production, which continued into the early 2010s. Historically, Production of palm kernels has been erratic. Some attempts were being made to encourage the export of pineapples, house plants, vegetables, and palm oil.

23 ANIMAL HUSBANDRY

The UN Food and Agriculture Organization (FAO) reported that Togo dedicated 1 million hectares (2.47 million acres) to permanent pasture or meadow in 2009. During that year, the country tended 18.3 million chickens, 378,050 head of cattle, and 612,250 pigs. The production from these animals amounted to 9,617 tons of beef and veal, 8,877 tons of pork, 24,656 tons of poultry, 5,161 tons of eggs, and 32,435 tons of milk. Togo also produced 1,228 tons of cattle hide.

Alleviation of the tsetse fly in the savanna area north of the Atakora Mountains has permitted the development of small-scale cattle raising. Most of the cattle thus produced, principally the humpless West African shorthorn type, were either consumed locally or, when there were surpluses, driven south for consumption in the main cities and towns. Few cattle were exported. Grazing was communal, in the south on family group lands and in the north on tribal lands. Water supplies were short in certain areas.

Goats and sheep often run free in villages or are herded by young boys. There are slaughterhouses at Lomé, Atakpamé, Sokodé, Lama-Kara, Sansanné-Mango, and Dapaong.

24 FISHING

Togo had 8 decked commercial fishing boats in 2008. The annual capture totaled 20,000 tons according to the UN FAO. The export value of seafood totaled $2.43 million.

Fishing remains relatively unimportant, in part because of the country's limited territorial waters. Almost all fish is sold smoked or dried. A new fishing quay was constructed at Lomé in 2000, and a joint Libyan-Togolese fishing company was established thereafter. Togo imported fish from Europe and its West African neighbors.

25 FORESTRY

Approximately 5% of Togo was covered by forest. The UN FAO estimated the 2009 roundwood production at 166,000 cu m (5.86 million cu ft). The value of all forest products, including roundwood, totaled $28.9 million. Although much of Togo once was forested, the country now has to import wood; much of the local production is for fuel.

26 MINING

As of 2009, Togo was a producer of clinker cement, diamonds, gold, limestone and phosphate rock (14th in the world), the latter of which is found mostly in the coastal region and the production of which accounts for most of the country's industrial activity. Phosphate rock is also a leading export commodity, accounting for around 24% of the country's GDP. Phosphate rock production (by gross weight) in 2009 was 726,000 metric tons, down from 842,000 metric tons in 2008. Togo's output of phosphate rock has been declining since production hit a high of 2.73 million metric tons in 1996. Virtually the entire output was exported, the principal destination being the European Union (EU). However, the phosphate rock currently mined in the coastal region contains a high amount of cadmium (about 150 milligrams per kilogram; mg/kg), and the EU is considering setting a 60mg/kg cadmium limit on imports of phosphate rock within five years, followed by a 20mg/kg limit within 15 years. Although cadmium-free resources have been identified in Togo's northwest, they are not currently being mined. The phosphate industry was nationalized in 1974. In 2009, the government restructured the phosphate sector and laid off 616 employees of the Société Nouvelle des Phosphates du Togo and bought new equipment to replace worn out infrastructure. Two new quarries were expected to open in 2011 and 2012.

Exploitation of marble reserves in the region around Niamtougou was begun in 1970 by the Togolese Marble Co. The state-run Nouvelle Sotoma closed operations in 1991, and the government has been looking for private investors to lease or purchase the operation.

Iron ore reserves east of Bassari were 95 million tons, averaging more than 40% iron. There was some artisanal recovery of diamond and gold. Other mineral deposits include attapulgite, barite, bauxite, bentonite, brick clay, chromite, copper, dolomite, garnet, granite, gypsum, kaolin, kyanite, limestone, manganese, monazite, nickel, peat, rutile, silica sand, and dimension stone. The government considers many of these potential small-scale operations.

27 ENERGY AND POWER

The World Bank reported in 2008 that Togo produced 123 million kWh of electricity and consumed 638 million kWh, or 94 kWh

---

Principal Trading Partners – Togo (2010)

(In millions of US dollars)

Country	Total	Exports	Imports	Balance
World	2,350.0	850.0	1,500.0	-650.0
China	218.6	55.7	162.8	-107.1
France	180.5	5.5	175.0	-169.5
Ghana	98.6	63.7	34.9	28.8
Benin	94.7	88.9	5.8	83.0
Burkina Faso	79.1	77.6	1.6	76.0
Belgium	76.4	2.3	74.2	-71.9
India	68.1	17.9	50.3	-32.4
Côte d'Ivoire	56.3	23.8	32.5	-8.8
Niger	47.6	47.3	0.3	47.0
Nigeria	45.1	34.1	11.0	23.1

(…) data not available or not significant.

(n.s.) not specified.

SOURCE: *2011 Direction of Trade Statistics Yearbook,* New York: United Nations, 2011.

Balance of Payments – Togo (2009)

(In millions of US dollars)

Current Account		**-176.7**
Balance on goods	-412.1	
Imports	-1,315.2	
Exports	903.0	
Balance on services	668.3	
Balance on income	-19.0	
Current transfers	335.7	
Capital Account		**135.2**
Financial Account		**86.5**
Direct investment abroad	-37.4	
Direct investment in Togo	48.5	
Portfolio investment assets	-1.4	
Portfolio investment liabilities	-29.2	
Financial derivatives	0.1	
Other investment assets	-176.8	
Other investment liabilities	282.6	
Net Errors and Omissions		**14.1**
Reserves and Related Items		**-59.0**

(…) data not available or not significant.

SOURCE: *Balance of Payment Statistics Yearbook 2011,* Washington, DC: International Monetary Fund, 2011.

---

per capita. Roughly 14% of energy came from fossil fuels. Per capita oil consumption was 397 kg.

The lack of a sufficient energy infrastructure has been a serious problem for economic development. In January 2009, ContourGlobal Togo signed a $146 million finance agreement with the Overseas Private Investment Corporation (OPIC) for the construction of a 100 MW thermal power plant in Lomé. This event marked the largest electricity investment ever in Togo. When complete, the plant was expected to generate approximately 780 GW hours of electricity each year, doubling capacity.

Togo, as of 1 January 2012, had no proven reserves of crude oil, natural gas, or oil refining capacity; all hydrocarbon needs were met by imports. In 2011 compressed natural gas via the West Africa Gas Pipeline connecting Togo and other West African countries with Nigeria became available. In 2009, Togo imported 15,900 barrels per day. There were no recorded imports or consumption of natural gas in 2009.

28 INDUSTRY

In 2010 industry grew at a rate of 2.5% topped by phosphate mining, agricultural processing, cement, handicrafts, textiles, and beverages. Manufacturing represented a small part of the economy (6–8%). Processing of agricultural products included palm oil extraction, coffee roasting, and cotton ginning and weaving. Other industries included footwear, beverages, confectioneries, salt, and tires. Phosphate mining accounted for 5% of GDP and about one-fourth of exports; as of 2006 Togo was the world's fourth-largest producer of phosphate. Until the mid-1980s, most industries were partly or totally government owned. Sales and leases reduced the parastatal sector by nearly half by 1990, but by 2006 most privatization had stalled. Following the election of Fauré Gnassingbé in 2005, interest in Lomé's free port status increased as the country wished to attract foreign business from Asia and Europe in the industry and service sectors.

Togo is part of the $500 million West Africa Gas Pipeline. Construction of the pipeline began in 2005. The pipeline's estimated capacity is 400 million cubic feet per day. In May 2011 the pipeline company announced that it was ready to begin delivering compressed gas to Togo and Benin. Gas was already being supplied to Ghana.

29 SCIENCE AND TECHNOLOGY

The World Bank reported in 2009 that there were no patent applications in science and technology in Togo. The National Institute of Scientific Research, founded in 1965 at Lomé, was the central scientific coordinating body. Several French research institutes had branches in the capital, and there were pilot farm projects throughout the country. The University of Benin at Lomé maintained faculties of sciences and medicine and schools of engineering and agriculture. Togo also had an agricultural school at Kpalimé and a technical college at Sokodá.

30 DOMESTIC TRADE

The Togolese are among the most active traders on the West African coast, with much of the domestic trade handled by women and by traders of Lebanese origin. The Lomé *Grand Marché* features goods from around the world. The national trade organization Société Nationale de Commerce (SONACOM) has a monopoly on importation and distribution of soaps, cereals, sugar, salt, and industrial products, but there is a flourishing free market both within Togo and with neighboring countries due in part to Lomé's free port without tariffs.

Most wholesalers maintain their headquarters in Lomé, the principal commercial and financial center. In Lomé, some shops specialize in such lines as dry goods, foodstuffs, and hardware. Elsewhere, retailers deal in a wide variety of goods rather than specializing in a few products. In the smaller towns, individual merchants deal in locally grown products and items of the first necessity. Kpalimé, Sokodé, and Tsévié are smaller regional commercial and trade centers. The bulk of trade in everyday necessities is carried out in daily and weekly open-air markets in villages and towns across the country.

Business hours are from 8 a.m. to 5:30 p.m., Monday through Friday, and from 7:30 a.m. to 12:30 p.m. on Saturday. Banks are normally open from 8 a.m. to 4 p.m. on weekdays only.

31 FOREIGN TRADE

Togo imported $1.46 billion worth of goods and services in 2011, while exporting $865 million worth of goods and services. Major import partners in 2010 were China, 48%; France, 8.3%; United States, 6.1%. Its major export partners were India, 12.7%; Germany, 12.2%; Benin, 9.8%; Ghana, 9.7%; Burkina Faso, 9.1%; China, 5.1%; Belgium, 4.9%; Nigeria, 4.3%; and Niger, 4.6%.

Togo's foreign trade is vulnerable to price fluctuations in world markets. Togo's main export commodities are crude fertilizers, cotton, and cement. Other exports include coffee and cocoa. A significant volume of re-export goods such as cigarettes, alcohol, perfume, used cars, and household items move across the border to neighboring countries because of the advantageous cost of goods coming into the Lomé free port.

32 BALANCE OF PAYMENTS

In 2011, the account balance was estimated at -$328 million. Togo had an external debt burden of $1.64 billion in 2009. The country had $828.8 million in reserves of foreign exchange and gold in 2011.

33 BANKING AND SECURITIES

The bank of issue is the Central Bank of the West African States (Banque Centrale des États de l'Afrique de l'Ouest—BCEAO), based in Dakar, which also acts in that capacity for Benin, Côte d'Ivoire, Niger, Senegal, and Burkina Faso. Togo had a 10% share in the BCEAO, the development bank that has its headquarters in Lomé.

The most important commercial and savings banks include the Banque Internationale de L'Afrique (BIA), ECOBANK Togo, the Bank of Credit and Commerce International, the Libyan Arab-Togolese Bank of Foreign Commerce, the Banque Togolaise de Commerce et de L'Industrie (BTCI), and the Union Bank of Togo (the latter two with a state share of 35%).

Development banks include the Togolese Development Bank, founded in 1967, which has a 50% state share; the 36.4% state-owned National Farm Credit Fund; and the state-owned National Investment Co., which is intended to mobilize savings, guarantee loans to small- and medium-sized domestic enterprises, and amortize the public debt. The banking and credit systems are not well developed, and large sections of the population remain outside the monetary economy. The banking system is subject to internal shocks.

There are micro-lending institutions in Togo, but many people are too asset-poor to qualify for their loans. NGO programs such as Kiva were established to assist families who otherwise could not qualify for small loans.

Public Finance – Togo (2009)

(In billions of francs, budgetary central government figures)

Revenue and Grants	318	100.0%
Tax revenue	229.1	72.0%
Social contributions	...	
Grants	64.9	20.4%
Other revenue	24.1	7.6%
Expenditures	326.3	100.0%
General public services	...	...
Defense	...	...
Public order and safety	...	...
Economic affairs	...	...
Environmental protection	...	...
Housing and community amenities	...	...
Health	...	...
Recreational, culture, and religion	...	...
Education	...	...
Social protection	...	...

(...) data not available or not significant.

SOURCE: *Government Finance Statistics Yearbook 2010*, Washington, DC: International Monetary Fund, 2010.

In 2011, the Central Bank discount rate, the rate that the central bank lent to financial institutions in the short term, was 4.25%. There were no securities exchanges in Togo.

34 INSURANCE

In 2011 Togo registered some 25 insurance companies, brokers, and consulting firms operating in the country. The Togolese Insurance Group was 63% state owned.

35 PUBLIC FINANCE

In 2010 the budget of Togo included $602.3 million in public revenue and $692.1 million in public expenditures. Public debt was 12.6% of GDP. The budget deficit amounted to -2.9% of GDP in 2011.

By the late 1970s, public investment expenditures had reached an unsustainable level (exceeding 40% of GDP), touched off by an earlier rise of commodity prices. As a result, large payment arrears on the external debt began to mount. In the mid-1980s, the fiscal deficit was reduced largely through IMF credits and debt reschedulings. The civil unrest of 1991 resulted in decreased revenues and increased expenditures, and led to an overall budget deficit of 7.5% of GDP. In 1992, further civil unrest widened the budget deficit to 8.5% of GDP.

In 1994 Togo entered into new arrangements with the IMF and the World Bank. In 2011 the CIA reported that Togo was on track with its IMF Extended Credit Facility and had reached a HIPC debt relief completion point in 2010 at which 95% of the country's debt was forgiven.

36 TAXATION

Taxes are levied on individual incomes and on corporate profits and capital gains. There is a schedule of taxes that includes a transactions tax, a tax on fuel consumption, social security contributions, registration and stamp taxes, and a tax on income from securities. There was a value-added tax (VAT) of 18%. The combined tax rate as a percentage of profit in 2012 is 49.5%, compared with an average of 57.1% for sub Saharan Africa, and 42.7% for OECD countries. In 2012 Togo ranked 161st out of 183 countries on the tax indicator of the World Bank's Doing Business Index.

37 CUSTOMS AND DUTIES

There are no export controls. Tariffs are based on a nondiscriminatory schedule at 5%, 10%, or 20%, and there is a customs stamp tax and a 3% statistical tax. A common external tariff (CET) for members of the West African Economic and Monetary Union (WAEMU) is set at a maximum of 22% for goods coming from outside the WAEMU. Restricted or prohibited goods include arms, ammunition, narcotics, and explosives. On the World Bank's trading across borders indicator, Togo ranked 98th out of 183 countries in 2011. The cost to export a container of goods was $940; to import a container cost $1,109.

38 FOREIGN INVESTMENT

Foreign direct investment (FDI) in Togo was a net inflow of $50.1 million according to World Bank figures published in 2009. In 2010, gross fixed investment as reported by the CIA was estimated to be 18% of GDP. Over the past 15 years, FDI has fluctuated greatly. The annual inflow of FDI rose from $23 million in 1997 to a high of almost $70 million in 1999. FDI inflow declined to $57.2 million in 2000, but recovered to $67 million in 2001. As a percent of gross fixed capital formation, FDI inflows rose from 11.3% in 1997 to nearly 35% in 1999, averaging about 30% in 2000 and 2001. In 2003, FDI amounted to 1.12% of GDP.

Togo's investment code, enacted in April 1990, relaxed restrictions on FDI and offered foreign investors guaranteed repatriation of capital and profits. The former investment code offered tax exemptions, but these were abused, and were removed in the 1990 revision. The investment code, which applied only to foreign investment of more than $42,000, allowed foreign participation up to 100% ownership in eight sectors (agriculture, fishing, and forestry; manufacturing; mining; low-cost housing; tourist infrastructure; agricultural storage; applied research; and socio-cultural activities), and required that the business employ at least 60% local workers and provide at least 25% of the funding.

The creation of an export processing zone (EPZ) in 1989 gave foreign companies the advantages of duty-free imports of materials for production, a less restrictive labor code, and the ability to hold foreign currency accounts. About 60 firms were operating in the EPZ in 2011, representing investments from France, Italy, Norway, Denmark, the United States, India, and China in light manufacturing, food processing and assembly.

On the World Bank's index of Doing Business in 2012, Togo ranked 162nd out of 183 countries for ease of doing business, and 174th on the "starting a business" indicator. One hindrance to increased levels of FDI was the perception that corruption was widespread in Togo. On Transparency International's Corruption Perception Index (CPI) for 2010, Togo scored a low 2.4 (out of 10 possible points), and ranked 143rd out of 182 countries on the index. Major foreign investors included the United States, France, Germany, and Denmark. Petroleum products distribution, seafood processing, construction, textile milling, and agricultural processing were the main foreign businesses.

39 ECONOMIC DEVELOPMENT

The 1981–85 development plan called for spending roughly equal allocation levels for rural development (26.5%), industry (29.2%), and infrastructure (29.5%). In the 1986–90 development plan, principal allocations were for infrastructure and rural development.

Of the development funds for the 1986–90 plan, 90% were sought from foreign sources. Principal sources of development aid were France, Germany, the United States, China, the EU, the World Bank, and IDA. France ranked first among the bilateral donors, with Germany second. The government was diverted from implementing the plan by international financial considerations and concerns over the process of democratization. In 1998 the EU and World Bank suspended aid because of such considerations and poor economic performance. Accords signed in 1999 brought back some interest in developing the country economically, but the major setback remained inadequate political development. While most bilateral and multilateral aid to Togo remained frozen as of early 2006, the EU initiated a partial resumption of cooperation and development aid to Togo in late 2004, based upon commitments by Togo to expand opportunities for political opposition and liberalize portions of the economy.

In 2009, an IMF team prepared the latest iteration of Togo's Poverty Reduction Strategy Paper (2009–2011). The IMF had begun drafting the PRSP in 2001 with an interim paper adopted in 2008. The 2008 PRSP specified debt relief and financial lending arrangements with partners. As with previous versions, the 2009–11 paper detailed a plan for national reconstruction specifying the roles of various development partners. One of the four pillars of the strategy was to establish a strong foundation for economic growth that included restructuring, improving the business climate, promoting sources of growth, developing infrastructure, creating jobs and redistributing the benefits of growth.

Togo is a member of the Economic Community of West African States (ECOWAS), the development fund of which is located in Lomé. The country is also a member of the West African Economic and Monetary Union (UEMOA). Affiliated with the UEMOA is the West African Development Bank, also based in Lomé.

⁴⁰SOCIAL DEVELOPMENT

Limited social development was a significant contributor to low economic development. On the UN Human Development Index (HDI), Togo ranked 162nd out of 187 countries worldwide in 2010, falling within the "low development" category.

Officially, about 67%of the population lives below the poverty threshold, according to the World Bank. In addition, the IMF judges that with the exception of the HIV/AIDS indicator, Togo likely will not achieve its targets set for the Millennium Development Goals (MDGs) of 2015. Development of human capital was one of the four pillars of the Poverty Reduction Strategy Paper (2009–2011) and emphasized social sector elements such as health, access to clean water and proper sanitation, nutrition, education, and gender equity and social protection.

The government's social welfare program, implemented under a 1973 law and amended in 2001, includes family allowances and maternity benefits; old age, disability, and death benefits; and workers' compensation. Retirement is normally allowed at age 55. The program covers employed persons, students, apprentices and members of cooperatives. Maternity benefits are provided for 14 weeks to working women. The labor code requires employers to provide paid sick leave. In theory, family allowances were available for almost all workers with children, including domestic, casual, and temporary laborers. The program supplements a continued strong sense of social obligation to one's family or clan, even among those in urban centers.

The status of women is improving, but they are still subject to legal and social restrictions. A husband may deny his wife the right to work and has legal control over her earnings. Women face discrimination in employment and access to education. A wife has no financial rights in a divorce and no inheritance rights upon the death of her husband. Polygamy is practiced. Although illegal, female genital mutilation is performed widely on adolescent girls. Domestic abuse and violence are widespread. Child labor also continues to be a problem.

The human rights record of the Togolese government remains poor. Abuses include political repression, excessive force by police (with little accountability), and arbitrary arrest and detention. Prison conditions remain very harsh. Human rights organizations are permitted, although they are subject to intimidation by the government.

In June 2009, the nation's parliament unanimously voted to abolish the death penalty. At the time of the vote, there were six convicts on the nation's death row, but no state executions had been carried out since 1978.

⁴¹HEALTH

According to the CIA, life expectancy in Togo was 63.17 years in 2012. The country spent 5.9% of its GDP on healthcare in 2009, amounting to $29 per person. There was 1 physician, 3 nurses and midwives, and 9 hospital beds per 10,000 inhabitants. The fertility rate was 4.64, while the infant mortality rate was 49.87 per 1,000 live births in 2012. In 2008 the maternal mortality rate, according to the World Bank, was 350 per 100,000 births. It was estimated that 84% of children were vaccinated against measles. The CIA calculated HIV/AIDS prevalence in Togo to be about 3.2% in 2009.

Medical services include permanent treatment centers and a mobile organization for preventive medicine. Special facilities treat leprosy, sleeping sickness, and mental illness. All services are free except at the clinic attached to the hospital in Lomé, where some patients pay a nominal fee. Approximately 60% of the population has access to safe drinking water, but only 12% has adequate sanitation. Poor sanitation was especially acute in rural areas, where only 3% of the population has access to improved facilities.

The Mobile Service for Hygiene and Preventive Medicine performs mass inoculations, carries out pest control campaigns, and provides education in hygiene and basic preventive measures. Its activities have led to significant decreases in mortality caused by smallpox, yellow fever, and sleeping sickness. Yaws, malaria, and leprosy continue to be major medical problems.

⁴²HOUSING

Rural dwellings are generally made from sun-dried mud bricks and mud plaster, with straw roofs. Urban dwellings are typically made of concrete hollow blocks with galvanized iron sheeted roofs. Homes for wealthier home owners are in enclosed compounds surrounded by high concrete walls with broken glass, steel spikes, or razor wire fixed on top of the walls. As of 2008 according to the World Bank, 87% of urban residents had access to an improved water source, while only 41% of rural residents had similar access. In that same year, access to improved sanitation facilities was also divided, with 24% having access in urban areas but only 3% with access in rural areas.

⁴³EDUCATION

In 2009 the World Bank estimated that 94% of age-eligible children in Togo were enrolled in primary school. Tertiary enrollment was estimated at 5%. Overall, the CIA estimated that Togo has a literacy rate of 60.9%, though less than half of females (46.9%) are literate and more than 75% of males are literate. Public expenditure on education represented 4.6% of GDP in 2009.

Six years of primary education (ages 6–12) was compulsory and free of charge. Secondary education lasts for seven years, with students attending either general or technical secondary schools. Mission schools play an important role in education. In 2010 it was estimated that about 63.72% of all students completed their primary education (compared with 12.90% in 1972). The University of Lomé and the University of Kara are the primary sites for higher education. Lomé also has colleges of administration, architecture, and urban planning.

⁴⁴LIBRARIES AND MUSEUMS

The National Library in Lomé has a collection of approximately 18,000 volumes. The University of Lomé Library offers some library services to the public. There is a public library with 26 service points holding a total of 63,000 volumes. The National Museum, founded in Lomé in 1975, has ethnography, history, and art exhibits. There are regional museums in Aného, Kara, Savanes, and Sokode.

⁴⁵MEDIA

In 2010 the CIA reported that there were 213,800 telephone landlines in Togo. In addition to landlines, mobile phone subscriptions averaged 40 per 100 people; there were 2.452 million mobile cell phones in use nationwide. There were 98 radio stations, 9 of which were AM stations, and 4 shortwave radio stations. Internet users numbered 5 per 100 citizens. In 2010, the country had about 860 Internet hosts and in 2009 there were some 356,300 Internet users. Telecommunications links were maintained with major African, European, and American cities. There was an automatic telephone exchange in Lomé.

In 2010, Togo had more than 40 publications including three dailies, one of which was governmental and two that were private. The main governmental newspaper is *Togo-Presse* (circulation 15,000). *The Journal Official de la République du Togo*, which reports official business, publishes daily in Lomé. Many private newspapers publish on a weekly or less frequent basis.

In 2010 there were 12 television stations. Television service, broadcast in French and local languages, began in 1973.

The constitution of Togo provides for freedom of speech and of the press; however, though the government was said to generally respect these rights, it has on at least one occasion intimidated journalists through threats, detention, and other persecution. Opposition media are tolerated, though sometimes censored or prevented access to information. Attacks on journalists are rare, but seldom investigated. The government regulatory authority for media is the Higher Communications and Broadcasting Authority (HAAC). It is known to suspend newspapers for unfavorable views of government.

Quality of media has not kept pace with the proliferation of media in Togo. Reporters often are spokesmen for politicians, and have a general disregard for ethical standards. Part of the problem is poor working conditions—low salaries, enticements, outmoded equipment and lack of training all contribute to weak professionalism. On the Media Sustainability Index (MSI) in 2009, Togo scored 1.54 (out of 4 possible points), which placed it in the "unsustainable, mixed system" range. The MSI measures performance on indicators of freedom of speech, business management, professionalism, plurality of news sources and institutional support.

⁴⁶ORGANIZATIONS

The Chamber of Commerce, Agriculture, and Industry is active in Lomé. The Federation of Non-Government Organizations of Togo helps promote small enterprise development by providing training and lobbying services. The African Organization of Supreme Audit Institutions, a large multinational organization promoting high ethical business and accounting standards, is based in Lomé.

The major women's and youth groups are affiliated with the RPT. There are also a Junior Chamber, the Scout Association of Togo, and YMCA/YWCA programs for youth. Sports associations promote amateur competitions in such pastimes as tae kwon do, baseball and softball, badminton, and track and field and in the national sport, soccer. Cultural organizations, all located in Lomé, include the Alliance Française, American Cultural Center, Goethe-Institute, and Togolese Association for Cultural Exchanges with Foreign Countries.

Social action organizations include Islands of Peace, the Adventist Development and Relief Agency, and the Togo Association of Volunteers for Development. Volunteer service organizations, such as the Lions Clubs International, are also present. There are national chapters of the Red Cross Society, Caritas, UNICEF, and CARE Togo. At the grassroots level, community-based organizations are found throughout the country.

⁴⁷TOURISM, TRAVEL, AND RECREATION

The *Tourism Factbook*, published by the UN World Tourism Organization, reported 150,000 incoming tourists to Togo in 2009; they spent a total of $44 million. Of those incoming tourists, there were 76,000 from Africa and 61,000 from Europe. There were 45,908 hotel beds available in Togo. The estimated daily cost to visit Lomé, the capital, was $250. The cost of visiting other cities averaged $71 per day.

Tourist attractions include the Mandouri hunting reserve in the northeast and the beaches and deep sea fishing of the Gulf of Guinea coast. Even though social and political calm were restored after disturbances in the early 1990s, there continues to be a lack of financial resources for the development of tourism.

According to 2012 estimates of the US Department of State, the average daily cost of staying in Lomé was $271, and Lama Kara and smaller towns averaged $91.

⁴⁸FAMOUS PERSONS

Togo's most prominent statesman was Sylvanus Olympio (1902–63), who led his country's fight for independence and was its first president. Gnassingbé Éyadéma (Étienne Éyadéma, 1937–2005) was president of Togo from 1967 until his death in 2005, when his son Faure Essozimna Gnassingbé (b. 1966) became president. Edem Kodjo (b. 1938) was OAU secretary-general, 1978–84.

⁴⁹DEPENDENCIES

Togo had no territories or colonies.

⁵⁰BIBLIOGRAPHY

Houngnikpo, Mathurin C. *Determinants of Democratization in Africa: A Comparative Study of Benin and Togo.* Lanham, MD: University Press of America, 2001.

Nugent, Paul. *Smugglers, Secessionists & Loyal Citizens on the Ghana-Togo Frontier: The Lie of the Borderlands Since 1914.* Athens: Ohio University Press, 2002.

Seely, Jennifer C. *The Legacies of Transition Governments in Africa: The Cases of Benin and Togo.* New York: Palgrave Macmillan, 2009.

Togo Investment and Business Guide: Strategic and Practical Information. Washington, DC: International Business Publications USA, 2012.

TUNISIA

Republic of Tunisia

Al-Jumhuriyah at-Tunisiyah

CAPITAL: Tunis

FLAG: Centered on a red ground is a white disk bearing a red crescent and a red five-pointed star.

ANTHEM: *Humat Al Hima (Defenders of the Homeland).*

MONETARY UNIT: The Tunisian dinar (TND) is a paper currency of 1,000 millimes. There are coins of 1, 2, 5, 10, 20, 50, and 100 millimes and of ½, 1, and 5 dinars, and notes of 1, 5, 10, and 20, and 30 dinars. TND1 = US$0.6629 (or US$1 = TND1.5085) as of 2012.

WEIGHTS AND MEASURES: The metric system is the legal standard.

HOLIDAYS: New Year's Day, 1 January; Revolution and Youth Day, 14 January; Independence Day, 20 March; Martyrs' Day, 9 April; Labor Day, 1 May; Republic Day, 25 July; Women's Day, 13 August; Evacuation Day, 15 October; Movable religious holidays include Eid al-Fitr, Eid al-Adha, 1st of Muharram (Muslim New Year), and Milad an-Nabi.

TIME: 1 p.m. = noon GMT.

¹LOCATION, SIZE, AND EXTENT

Situated on the northern coast of Africa, Tunisia has an area of 163,610 sq km (63,170 sq mi), extending 792 km (492 mi) N–S and 350 km (217 mi) E–W. Comparatively, the area occupied by Tunisia is slightly larger than the state of Georgia. It is bounded on the N and E by the Mediterranean Sea, on the SE by Libya, and on the W by Algeria, with a total boundary length of 2,572 km (1,598 mi), of which 1,148 km (713 mi) is coastline.

Tunisia's capital city, Tunis, is located on the northern coast.

²TOPOGRAPHY

The Nemencha mountains—eastern extensions of the Atlas chain—divide the country into two distinct regions, the well-watered north and the semiarid south. The latter includes Tunisia's highest point, Jebel Chambi, 1,544 m (5,064 ft), near Kasserine. The northern region is further divided into three subregions: the northwest, with extensive cork forests; the north-central, with its fertile grasslands; and the northeast, from Tunis to Cape el-Tib, noted for its livestock, citrus fruits, and garden produce. The southern region contains a central plateau and a desert area in the extreme south, which merges into the Sahara and is characterized by date palm oases and saline lakes, the largest of which is Chott el Djerid. The Medjerda, the most important river system, rises in Algeria and drains into the Gulf of Tunis.

³CLIMATE

Tunisia consists of two climatic belts, with Mediterranean influences in the north and Saharan in the south. Temperatures are moderate along the coast, with an average annual reading of 18°C (64°F), and hot in the interior south. The summer season in the north, from May through September, is hot and dry; the winter,

which extends from October to April, is mild and characterized by frequent rains. Temperatures at Tunis range from an average minimum of 6°C (43°F) and maximum of 14°C (57°F) in January, to an average minimum of 21°C (70°F) and maximum of 33°C (91°F) in August. Precipitation in the northern region reaches a high of 150 cm (59 in) annually, while rainfall in the extreme south averages less than 20 cm (8 in) a year.

⁴FLORA AND FAUNA

The World Resources Institute estimates that there are 2,196 plant species in Tunisia. Tunisia has a great variety of trees, including cork oak, oak, pines, jujube, and gum. More than one-fourth of the country is covered by esparto grass, which is the characteristic vegetation of the steppe region. Animal species include 78 mammals, 360 birds, 70 reptiles, and 8 amphibians. The calculation reflects the total number of distinct species residing in the country, not the number of endemic species. Jackal, wild boar, and several species of gazelle are numerous. Horned vipers and scorpions are common in the Sahara. The sleeved mouflon, a species of wild sheep, is found in the mountains.

⁵ENVIRONMENT

The World Resources Institute reported that Tunisia had designated 235,200 hectares (581,192 acres) of land for protection as of 2006. Water resources totaled 4.6 cu km (1.1 cu mi) while water usage was 2.64 cu km (0.633 cu mi) per year. Domestic water usage accounted for 14% of total usage, industrial for 4%, and agricultural for 82%. Per capita water usage totaled 261 cu m (9,217 cu ft) per year. The UN reported in 2008 that carbon dioxide emissions in Tunisia totaled 23,849 kilotons.

The loss of agricultural land to erosion, and degradation of range and forest lands because of overgrazing or overcutting of timber for fuel are major concerns for the Tunisian government. Erosion threatens about 76% of the nation's land area. Overcrowding and poor sanitation in urban centers are also major environmental problems. Pollution from industry and farming activities threatens the nation's limited water supply. The nation's cities produce about 0.9 million tons of solid waste annually; inadequate disposal of toxic and hazardous wastes poses health risks.

There are four national parks, including one natural UNESCO World Heritage Site. According to a 2011 report issued by the International Union for Conservation of Nature and Natural Resources (IUCN), the number of threatened species included 13 types of mammals, 6 species of birds, 5 types of reptiles, 35 species of fish, and 6 species of invertebrates. Threatened species in Tunisia include the Barbary hyena, Barbary leopard, two species of gazelle (Cuvier's and slender-horned), the Mediterranean monk seal, and oryx. The Bubal hartebeest has become extinct. A World Wildlife Fund project succeeded in rescuing the Atlas deer from near extinction.

6 POPULATION

The US Central Intelligence Agency (CIA) estimates the population of Tunisia in July 2011 to be approximately 10,673,800, which placed it at number 78 in population among the 196 nations of the world. In 2011, approximately 7.5% of the population was over 65 years of age, with another 23.2% under 15 years of age. The median age in Tunisia was 30 years. There were 1.01 males for every female in the country. The population's annual rate of change was 0.978%. The projected population for the year 2025 was 12,200,000. Population density in Tunisia was calculated at 65 people per sq km (168 people per sq mi).

The UN estimated that 67% of the population lived in urban areas, and that urban populations had an annual rate of change of 1.5%. The largest urban area was Tunis, with a population of 759,000.

7 MIGRATION

Estimates of Tunisia's net migration rate, carried out by the CIA in 2011, amounted to -1.79 migrants per 1,000 citizens. The total number of emigrants living abroad was 651,600, and the total number of immigrants living in Tunisia was 33,600. French and Italian migration to Tunisia dates from the French military occupation of 1881. There were 255,000 Europeans in Tunisia in 1956, but most have since left the country. With the conclusion of the Franco-Algerian war in 1962, 110,000 Algerian refugees returned to their homeland.

Rural unemployment has caused significant population movement to urban centers, where conditions are often harsh. This internal migration constitutes a serious problem especially that a number of these migrants continue their migration across the Mediterranean to illegally enter Italy. Since 1964, the government has sought to decentralize industry and to resettle nomads and seminomads in permanent villages. Many Tunisians seek employment abroad; in the early 1990s there were approximately 350,000 Tunisian workers in foreign countries, mostly Libya and France.

Soon after the fall of the Ben Ali regime on 14 January 2011, a huge influx of over 20,000 Tunisian nationals took advantage of the state of lawlessness and left Tunisia, heading north to the Italian island Lampedusa in small fishing boats with the aim of seeking political asylum in Europe. A number of them left with the goal of joining their families or friends elsewhere in Europe, especially France where most Tunisian migrants reside. In 2011 Tunisia was the largest recipient of migrants fleeing Libya: 195,241.

8 ETHNIC GROUPS

Tunisia has a highly homogeneous population, almost entirely of Arab and Berber descent (98%). The small European population (1%) consists mostly of French and Italians. Tunisian Jews and other groups make up the remaining 1% of the population. The native people of Tunisia are the Berbers who witnessed the arrival of a numerous civilizations and peoples from Phoenicians/Carthaginians, Romans, Vandals, Arabs, Ottoman Turks, and French.

9 LANGUAGES

Arabic is the official language and one language used in commerce. French is taught to all school children and is also commonly used in commerce and administration. Small numbers of people speak Berber.

10 RELIGIONS

Islam is the state religion and nearly all Tunisians are Sunni Muslims. A small number are of the mystical Sufi branch. The Christian community, which contains only about 25,000 people, is made up primarily of Roman Catholics, Russian Orthodox, French Reformists, Anglicans, Greek Orthodox, and a small number of Jehovah's Witnesses and Seventh-Day Adventists. There are approximately 1,600 Jews in the country the majority of whom live in the island Djerba. There is a small number of Baha'is. The constitution only provides for the free exercise of religions that do not disturb the public order. Though members of other established, non-Muslim religions are generally allowed to practice freely, proselytizing is prohibited by law. Muslims who convert to another faith are often denied the right to vote, obtain a passport, and to enlist in the army. According to the International Religious Freedom Report 2008, the majority of Tunisia's population (around 98%) are Muslims, while about 1% follow Christianity and the remaining 1% adhere to Judaism or other religions. Tunisia has a sizable Christian community of around 25,000 adherents, mainly Catholics (22,000) and to a lesser degree Protestants. Judaism is the country's third largest religion with 1,500 members. One-third of the Jewish population lives in and around the capital. The remainder lives on the island of Djerba, with 39 synagogues, and where the Jewish community dates back 2,500 years.

11 TRANSPORTATION

The CIA reported that Tunisia had a total of 19,232 km (11,950 mi) of roads in 2008, of which 12,655 km (7,863 mi) were paved. There are 114 vehicles per 1,000 people in the country. Railroads extend for 1,991 km (1,237 mi). The Tunisian National Railway Co. (Société National des Chemins de Fer Tunisiens) operates standard, narrow, and dual gauge track, located mostly in the northern region and central plateau. The Tunis area is served by a tram network, named Metro Leger, which started in 1985.

Tunisia has excellent shipping facilities at Tunis, the principal port, and at Sfax, Sousse, Bizerte, and Gabes; Sekhira is the port for oil exports. The free port terminal at Zarzis was scheduled for further development at an estimated cost of $20.8 million, in order to expand harbor and storage facilities. Tunisia's modest merchant fleet, established in 1958, operates a freighter service principally to French ports. As of 2008, there were seven ships of 1,000 gross registered tons or more. The Tunisian Navigation Co. is the principal shipping firm.

There were 16 airports with paved runways in 2009. That year, air travel transported 2.28 million passengers according to the World Bank. Tunis-Carthage Airport, about 14 km (9 mi) from the capital, provides direct connections to most of the major cities of Europe and the Middle East. There are five other international airports, at Menzel Bourguiba (Monastir), Zarzis (Jerba), Tozeur, Tabarka, and Sfax. Tunis Air, the national airline, is owned by the Tunisian government (51%), Air France, and Tunisian citizens.

12 HISTORY

The history of early Tunisia and its indigenous inhabitants, the Berbers, is obscure prior to the founding of Carthage by seafaring Phoenicians from Tyre (in present-day Lebanon) in the 9th century BC. A great mercantile state developed at Carthage (near modern-day Tunis), which proceeded to dominate the western Mediterranean world. The great Carthaginian general Hannibal engineered the monumental trans-Alpine assault on Rome in 211 BC and inflicted costly losses on the Roman Empire until choosing suicide rather than capture in 183 BC. Carthage was eventually burned to the ground by the Romans at the culmination of the Punic Wars in 146 BC. The Romans subsequently rebuilt the city, making it one of the great cities of the ancient world. With the decline of the Roman Empire, Tunisia fell successively to Vandal invaders during the 5th century AD, to the Byzantines in the 6th century, and finally to the Arabs in the 7th century. Thenceforth, Tunisia remained an integral part of the Muslim world.

In the 9th century, the governor of Tunisia, Ibrahim ibn Aghlab, founded a local dynasty nominally under the sovereignty of the 'Abbasid caliphs of Baghdād. The Aghlabids conquered Sicily and made Tunisia prosperous. In 909, the Fatimids ended Aghlabid rule, using Tunisia as a base for their subsequent conquest of Egypt. They left Tunisia in control of the subordinate Zirid dynasty until the 11th century, when the Zirids rebelled against Fatimid control. The Fatimids unleashed nomadic Arab tribes, the Banu Hilal and Banu Sulaym, to punish the Zirids, a move resulting in the destruction of the Zirid state and the general economic decline of Tunisia. In the 13th century, the Hafsids, a group subordinate to the Almohad dynasty based in Morocco, restored order to Tunisia. They founded a Tunisian dynasty that, from the 13th century to the 16th, made Tunisia one of the flourishing regions of North Africa. In the beginning of the 16th century, however, Spain's occupation of important coastal locations precipitated the demise of Hafsid rule.

In 1574, the Ottoman Turks occupied Tunisia, ruling it with a dey appointed by the Ottoman ruler. The dey's lieutenants, the beys, gradually became the effective rulers, in fact if not in name. Ultimately, in 1705, the bey Husayn ibn 'Ali established a dynasty. Successive Husaynids ruled Tunisia as vassals of the Ottomans until 1881 and under the French until 1956, the year of Tunisia's independence (the dynasty was abolished in 1957). During the 19th century, the Tunisian dynasts acted virtually as independent rulers, making vigorous efforts to utilize Western knowledge and technology to modernize the state. But these efforts led to fis-

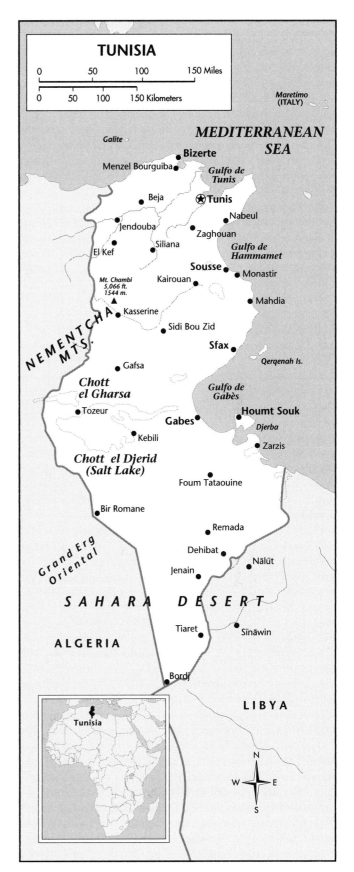

LOCATION: 7°33′ to 11°38′E; 29°54′ to 37°21′ N. BOUNDARY LENGTHS: Mediterranean coastline, 1,028 kilometers (639 miles); Libya, 459 kilometers (285 miles); Algeria, 958 kilometers (595 miles). TERRITORIAL SEA LIMIT: 12 miles.

cal bankruptcy and thus to the establishment of an international commission made up of British, French, and Italian representatives to supervise Tunisian finances. Continued rivalry between French and Italian interests culminated in a French invasion of Tunisia in May 1881. A protectorate was created in that year by the Treaty of Bardo; the Convention of La Marsa (1883) allowed the Tunisian dynasty to continue, although effective direction of affairs passed to the French. French interests invested heavily in Tunisia, and a process of modernization was vigorously pursued; at the same time, direct administration in the name of the dynasty was gradually expanded. The Tunisians, in turn, supported France in World War I.

The beginnings of modern nationalism in Tunisia emerged before the outbreak of the war, with hopes of greater Tunisian participation in government encouraged during the war by pronouncements such as the Fourteen Points (1918) of Woodrow Wilson. When these hopes were not realized, Tunisians formed a moderate nationalist grouping, the Destour ("Constitutional") Party. Dissatisfaction over the group's poor organization led, in 1934, to a split: the more active members, led by Habib Bourguiba, founded the Neo-Destour Party. France responded to demands for internal autonomy with repression, including the deposition and exile of the sovereign Munsif Bey. On 23 August 1945, the two Destour parties proclaimed that the will of the Tunisian people was independence. But the French still held firm. In December 1951, they again rejected a request by the Tunisian government for internal autonomy. The situation worsened when extremists among the French colonists launched a wave of terrorism. Finally, on 31 July 1954, French Premier Pierre Mendès-France promised the bey internal autonomy. After long negotiations accompanied by considerable local disorder, a French-Tunisian convention was signed on 3 June 1955 in Paris. On 20 March 1956, France recognized Tunisian independence.

In April 1956, Habib Bourguiba formed the first government of independent Tunisia, and on 25 July 1957, the National Assembly, having established a republic and transformed itself into a legislative assembly, elected Bourguiba chief of state and deposed the bey. A new constitution came into effect on 1 June 1959. Bourguiba won the first presidential election in 1959 and was reelected in 1964, 1969, and 1974, when the National Assembly amended the constitution to make him president for life.

Economic malaise and political repression during the late 1970s led to student and labor unrest. A general strike called by the General Union of Tunisian Workers (UGTT) on 26 January 1978, in order to protest assaults on union offices and the harassment of labor leaders, brought confrontations with government troops in which at least 50 demonstrators and looters were killed and 200 trade union officials, including UGTT Secretary-General Habib Achour, were arrested. Prime Minister Hedi Nouira was succeeded by Mohamed Mzali in April 1980, marking the advent of a political liberalization. Trade union leaders were released from jails, and Achour ultimately received a full presidential pardon. In July 1981, the formation of opposition political parties was permitted. In elections that November, candidates of Bourguiba's ruling Destourian Socialist Party, aligned in a National Front with the UGTT, garnered all 136 National Assembly seats and 94.6% of the popular vote. An economic slump in 1982–83 brought a renewal of tensions; in January 1984, after five days of rioting in Tunis, the government was forced to rescind the doubling of bread prices that had been ordered as an austerity measure.

After independence, Tunisia pursued a nonaligned course in foreign affairs while maintaining close economic ties with the West. Tunisia's relations with Algeria, strained during the 1970s, improved markedly during the early 1980s, and on 19 March 1983 the two nations signed a 20-year treaty of peace and friendship. Relations with Libya have been stormy since the stillborn Treaty of Jerba (1974), a hastily drafted document that had been intended to merge the two countries into the Islamic Arab Republic; within weeks after signing the accord, Bourguiba, under pressure from Algeria and from members of his own government, retreated to a more gradualist approach toward Arab unity. A further irritant was the territorial dispute between Libya and Tunisia over partition of the oil-rich Gulf of Gabes, resolved by the international Court of Justice in Libya's favor in 1982. Tunisian-Libyan relations reached a low point in January 1980, when some 30 commandos (entering from Algeria but apparently aided by Libya) briefly seized an army barracks and other buildings at Gafsa in an abortive attempt to inspire a popular uprising against Bourguiba. In 1981, Libya vetoed Tunisia's bid to join OAPEC and expelled several thousand Tunisian workers; more Tunisian workers were expelled in 1985.

Following the evacuation of the Palestine Liberation Organization (PLO) from Lebanon in August 1982, Tunisia admitted PLO Chairman Yasir Arafat and nearly 1,000 Palestinian fighters. An October 1985 Israeli bombing raid on the PLO headquarters near Tunis killed about 70 persons. By 1987, the PLO presence was down to about 200, all civilians.

In 1986 and 1987, Bourguiba dealt with labor agitation for wage increases by again jailing UGTT leader Achour and disbanding the confederation. He turned on many of his former political associates, including his wife and son, while blocking two legal opposition parties from taking part in elections. Reasserting his control of Tunisian politics, Bourguiba dismissed Prime Minister Mzali, who fled to Algeria and denounced the regime. A massive roundup of Islamic fundamentalists in 1987 was the president's answer to what he termed a terrorist conspiracy sponsored by Iran, and diplomatic relations with Tehrān were broken. On 27 September 1987, a state security court found 76 defendants guilty of plotting against the government and planting bombs; seven (five in absentia) were sentenced to death.

General Zine el-Abidine Ben Ali, the trusted minister of interior who had conducted the crackdown, was named prime minister in September 1987. Six weeks later, Ben Ali seized power, ousting Bourguiba, whom he said was too ill and senile to govern any longer. He assumed the presidency himself, promising political liberalization. Almost 2,500 political prisoners were released and the special state security courts were abolished. The following year, Tunisia's constitution was revised, ending the presidency for life and permitting the chief executive three five-year terms. Elections were advanced from 1991 to 1989 and Ben Ali ran unopposed. Candidates of the renamed Destour Party, the Constitutional Democratic Rally (RCD), won all of the 141 seats in the Chamber of Deputies, although the Islamist party, an-Nahda, won an average of 18% of the vote where its members contested as independents.

The constitution does not permit political parties based on religion, race, regional, or linguistic affiliation, and thus Islamist parties in Tunisia face an uphill battle in gaining official recognition. After an attack on RCD headquarters in 1990, the government moved decisively against its Islamist opposition. Thousands were arrested and in 1992 military trials, 265 were convicted.

General elections in 1994 elected incumbent Zine El Abidine Ben Ali. The Constitutional Democratic Rally, the party of the president, won 144 of the 163 seats. That year, a new proportional system was established where 144 of the seats were to be contested and were won by the majority party and the remaining 19 were to be distributed to the remaining contesting parties according to their vote draw at the national level. In the parliamentary elections the president's party RCD took all 144 seats with the remaining six parties dividing up the 19 set-aside seats. In the 1995 municipal elections, out of 4,090 seats contested in the 257 constituencies, independent candidates and members of the 5 recognized political parties won only 6 of the seats.

In July 1998 Ben Ali announced his plans to contest the presidential elections scheduled for October 1999. Two other candidates, Mohamed Belhaj Amor of the PUP and Abderrahmane Tlili of the UDU also announced their candidacy. The parliament had again been enlarged to 182 members, with 34 seats guaranteed to the opposition. In the 1999 elections Ben Ali received 99.4% of the votes, with Amor receiving 0.3% and Tlili 0.2%. The RCD was awarded with 148 seats and the 5 other official parties splitting the remaining 34 seats.

In the 1990s Tunisia continued to follow a moderate, nonaligned course in foreign relations, complicated by sporadic difficulties with its immediate neighbors. Relations with Libya remained tense after ties were resumed in 1987. However, Ben Ali pursued normalized relations, which dramatically improved over the next few years. Thousands of Tunisians found work in Libya as the border was reopened. In 1992 the UN Security Council imposed sanctions against Libya due to its decision not to hand over for trial suspects in the Pan Am bombing affair. Tunisia did not wholeheartedly support all of the UN Security Council sanctions due to the real economic ties that the two countries have. Due to these ties Libya's difficulties impacted on the ability of Tunisia and the Union of the Arab Maghreb (UAM) to establish closer relations with the European Union. From 1995 forward, Tunisia lobbied at the international level for the cessation of the sanctions due to the suffering that was caused to the Libyan people as well as to the regional tensions that the sanctions were creating. By 1997 Tunisia had quietly resumed joint economic projects and bilateral visitation with Libya. Following Libya's 1998/99 decision to hand over the Pan Am bombing suspects for trial in the Netherlands for the 1988 Pam Am explosion over Lockerbie, Scotland, Tunisia moved to normalize relations with Libya, including resumption of TunisAir flights to Tripoli in June 2000.

Ben Ali also appeared committed to the promotion of the UAM, an organization that became formalized in 1989 with Mauritania, Morocco, Algeria, Tunisia, and Libya. Ben Ali became president of the organization for 1993, though at this point the active work toward unification of the five countries was put on hold due in large part to the political and economic difficulties that Algeria and Libya faced internally and internationally. In 1999 the leaders of Morocco and Tunisia again called for a resuscitation of the organization and pledged to work toward that end in the following year.

Tunisia's relations with Algeria in the 1990s were controlled by the Islamist issue. The leadership of Tunisia's not-officially-recognized Ennahdha party continued to be closely watched by both countries. With the decision of the Algerian military to annul their January 1992 elections in order to prevent the Islamists from gaining control of the government, relations improved between the two countries. Algeria signed a border agreement in 1993 with Tunisia, ratified during a state visit of the Algerian leader. Reciprocal visits between the leadership of the two countries reinforced their commitment to controlling their joint border and fighting "extremism."

In 1988 'Abu Jihad, the military commander of the PLO, was assassinated near Tunis by Israeli commandos, provoking a Tunisian protest to the UN Security Council and a following resolution of condemnation of the Israeli aggression by the Council. However, relations with Israel then improved, and in 1993, Tunisia welcomed an official Israeli delegation as part of the peace process. Joint naval exercises between the two countries took place in March 1994. The PLO offices in Tunis were closed in 1994 as the new Palestinian Authority (PA) took up residence in Gaza. In 1996, following PA elections, Tunisia moved to establish low-level diplomatic relations with Israel as it also announced its decision to recognize PA passports. However, with the slowing of the peace process and the election of the Netanyahu government in Israel, improving relations between Israel and Tunisia cooled and remained on hold.

Ben Ali also moved to normalize relations with Egypt and visited Cairo in 1990 to that end, the first such trip by a Tunisian president since 1965. In 1997 several agreements regarding economic and cultural cooperation were signed between the two countries.

Although the United States has provided economic and military aid, Tunisia opposed American support for Kuwait following Iraq's invasion in 1990. The support of Iraq in this crisis caused a rift in relations with Kuwait that were finally healed, through Ben Ali's efforts, with the visit of Kuwait's crown prince to Tunis in 1996 and a loan from the Kuwait-based Arab Fund for Economic and Social Development being granted to Tunisia. At the same time, Tunisia continued good relations with Iraq and continued to call for a cessation of UN sanctions against Baghdad.

The consistent stance of Ben Ali's government toward Islamist parties has brought him friends in the West, though his own poor human rights record has provoked consternation from Western governments and vocal criticism from Western media and human rights organizations. Complaints against his regime have included torture under interrogation, deaths in custody, secret or unfair trials and long prison sentences for opposition leaders, inhumane prison conditions, and restrictions on free speech and the press, including controls on the use of satellite dishes. Ironically, the UN Committee against Torture (along with numerous other human rights groups and including the Arab Commission of Human Rights) denounced the police and security forces in Tunisia, while Tunisia was unanimously elected to the UN Human Rights Commission in 1997. This caused international controversy, and by 2006, a Human Rights Council replaced the UN Human Rights Commission. The Human Rights Council was meant to be a standing body that would meet year-round to promote and protect human rights with a membership that excluded the worst human rights violators.

In July 1995, Tunisia signed an association agreement with the European Union that in 2007 would make the country part of a free-trade area around the Mediterranean known as the European Economic Area, the first southern Mediterranean country to be brought into the planned association. The United States has continued to offer praise to Tunisia and encouragement of US investment, but has held off on requested military aid. Relations with Italy, Tunisia's second-largest trading partner after France, have been complicated by the issues of illegal immigration from Tunisia and of fishing rights.

On 11 April 2002, a truck exploded at a synagogue on the Tunisian resort island of Djerba, killing 21 people, including 14 German tourists. German intelligence officials reported the bombing was a terrorist attack, and cited links to the al-Qaeda organization. In November, Ben Ali called for an international conference on terrorism to establish an international code of ethics to which all parties would be committed. In December, the United States praised Tunisia for its efforts in combating terrorism, and for its record of moderation and tolerance in the region.

In a referendum held on 26 May 2002, voters overwhelmingly approved a series of constitutional amendments that would make a marked change in the country's political structure. They included: additional guarantees regarding the pretrial and preventive custody of defendants; the creation of a second legislative body; the elimination of presidential term limits, along with the setting of a maximum age ceiling of 75 years for a presidential candidate; and the consecration of the importance of human rights, solidarity, mutual help, and tolerance as values enshrined in the constitution.

In November 2002, Ben Ali announced a series of electoral reform measures. In addition to the creation of a second legislative body (Chamber of Advisors approved by the May referendum), these included provisions to further guarantee the fairness of voter registration and election processes, and provisions to reduce the minimum requirement for campaign financing and reimbursement by the state. He also called on radio and television operators to provide wider coverage of opposition parties and nongovernmental organizations, and introduced a bill that would guarantee citizens' privacy and protection of personal data.

Presidential and legislative elections were held on 24 October 2004. Ben Ali was reelected for a fourth term with 94.5% of the vote. The legislative election for the Chamber of Deputies was dominated by the RCD, as was the election for the new Chamber of Advisors held on 3 July 2005. That dominance continued in the 2009 elections, as Ben Ali won a fifth-term as president with 90% of the vote. While international observers agreed that the election was free and fair, opposition leaders and human rights groups claimed that free elections had not existed in years, since the oppression of political opponents at the hand of the ruling party left very little choice in elections. The Constitutional Democratic Rally maintained its majority in the Chamber of Deputies with 161 seats of 214 available.

In January 2011, there was an outburst of violent protests starting in the western parts of Tunisia. Civilians marched through the streets, angry about the lack of jobs, corruption, and poverty. For the first time, Ben Ali was criticized by protesters, who demanded

his immediate resignation. Despite his decision not to run for reelection in 2014, protesters continued to fill the streets, stating that the government had lost all legitimacy. A number of violent confrontations took place between police and civilians, leaving many dead or wounded. On 14 January 2011, Ben Ali stepped down and fled the country to Saudi Arabia. The parliamentary speaker Fouad Mebazaa was sworn in as interim president, declaring that the provisional government would remain in effect until the election of a council of representatives with a mandate to rewrite the constitution.

On 3 March 2011, the acting president announced that elections to a constituent assembly would be held on 23 October 2011, which meant that general elections would be further adjourned. The constituent assembly elections took place as scheduled, with international and internal observers declaring it transparent, free, and fair. The Ennahda Movement, formerly banned under the Ben Ali regime, won a plurality of 90 seats out of a total of 217. On 12 December 2011, former dissident and veteran human rights activist Moncef Marzouki was elected president of Tunisia. He was sworn in on 13 December 2011.

13 GOVERNMENT

According to the constitution of 1959, Tunisia is an Islamic republic, although since independence it has been a thoroughly secular state. The president, who is chief of state, must be a Muslim and a Tunisian citizen, born of a Tunisian father and grandfather, and at least 40 years old. The elected president serves a five-year term. He enjoys extensive powers, initiating and directing state policy and appointing judges, provincial governors, the mayor of Tunis, and other high officials. The cabinet, headed by a prime minister, varies in size and is under presidential domination.

The unicameral National Assembly or Chamber of Deputies (Majlis al-Ummah) was expanded in 1993 to 163 members and again in 1997 to 182 members, elected by general, free, direct, and secret ballot. Since 1994 the opposition has been guaranteed a number of seats in the assembly, with the changes introduced in 1997 guaranteeing them 20% of the assembly seats. All citizens 20 years of age or older may vote; candidates must be at least 25 years old and born of a Tunisian father or Tunisian mother. The assembly sits twice a year for five years, but may be extended in the event that a national emergency prevents new elections. Presidential ratification is required before a bill passed by the legislature can become law, but the assembly may override the president's veto by a two-thirds majority. The president may enact decrees in an emergency or when the assembly is in recess.

A series of constitutional amendments were overwhelmingly approved by voters in a 26 May 2002 referendum. Civil liberties were expanded, and human rights were guaranteed. Provisions for a second legislative body, a Chamber of Advisors, were made. Presidential term limits were abolished, and the age limit for a presidential candidate was raised from 70 to 75, thereby making Ben Ali, then age 65, eligible for reelection in 2004 and 2009.

A 2011 revolution deposed Ben Ali and created a multiparty democracy.

14 POLITICAL PARTIES

The Constitutional Democratic Rally (RCD) dominated the country's political life. Its leader from its founding as the Neo-Destour

Party in 1934 to 1987 was Habib Bourguiba. In the first national elections in 1956, all 98 seats in the National Assembly were won by the National Union, a united front of the Neo-Destour Party with the UGTT, the National Union of Tunisian Farmers, and the Tunisian Union of Craftsmen and Merchants. In the November 1959 elections for the National Assembly, the Communist Party (Parti Communiste Tunisien) presented a list of 13 candidates in Tunis and Gafsa; elsewhere, the Neo-Destour Party was unopposed, and the ruling party won all 90 seats at stake. From 1959 to 1994, the RCD (acting in 1981 as part of a National Front with the UGTT) held a monopoly of Assembly seats.

Banned in 1963, the Communist Party was the first opposition group to be fully legalized under the political liberalization of 1981. Two other parties, the Movement of Social Democrats (Mouvement des Démocrates Socialistes—MDS) and the Party of Popular Unity (Parti de l'Unité Populaire—PUP), failed to retain their provisional authorization when each fell short of receiving a 5% share of the total vote in the November 1981 election but nevertheless were formally legalized in 1983. The principal Islamist party, an-Nahda, has been outlawed. In 1992, it was hit hard by the jailing of many of its senior leaders.

Due to a change in the 1994 electoral code to guarantee the opposition would win seats, opposition parties such as the Movement of Social Democrats (MDS) entered the Chamber of Deputies. As of 2006, there were seven officially recognized opposition parties: MDS, PUP, the Union of Democratic Unionists (UDU), Ettajdid (also called the Renewal Movement), the Social Democratic Liberal Party (PSDL), plus the Democratic Progressive Party (PDP) and the Democratic Forum for Labor and Liberties (FDTL), the only two not represented in the Chamber of Deputies as of the October 2004 elections. The RCD held 152 of the 182 seats as of 2006. The Islamist an-Nahda remained an outlawed party.

Soon after Ben Ali fled to Saudi Arabia, a state of emergency was declared all over the Tunisian territory. The Constitutional Court declared Fouad Mebazaa as acting president under Article 57 of the Constitution. A coalition government was also created, including members of Ben Ali's party, the Constitutional Democratic Rally (RCD), in key ministries, while including other opposition figures in other ministries, with the goal of running elections within a couple months. The situation in Tunisia was not calm as daily street protests in Tunis and other towns around Tunisia continued, demanding the resignation of the RCD members of the interim government as well as the total dismantling of this infamous party. On 27 January Prime Minister Mohamed Ghannouchi rearranged the interim government, eliminating all former RCD members. The RCD party was dissolved, as protesters had demanded, on 9 March 2011.

Following the revolution, legally recognized parties included the Tunisian Ba'ath Party (PBT), Congress for the Republic (CPR), Homeland Party, Maghrebi Liberal Party, Ennahda Movement, also Renaissance Party, Patriotic and Democratic Labor Party, Tunisian Workers' Communist Party (PCOT). The Ennahda Movement, formerly banned under the Ben Ali regime, won a plurality of 90 out of a total of 217 seats in constituent assembly elections held in October 2011. Moncef Marzouki was elected president in December of that year.

15 LOCAL GOVERNMENT

Tunisia is divided into 24 provinces (wilayets, or governorates). Each province is headed by a governor appointed by the president through the secretary of interior. The governor is assisted by elected municipal councils and a governmental council, members of which are appointed for a three-year term by the central government on the governor's nomination. Each province is in turn divided into delegations (mutamadiyat), the number of which varies with the size and social and economic importance of the province. In local elections boycotted by the opposition in 1990, RCD candidates won control of all but one of the councils. In 1990 proportional representation for municipal elections was introduced, where the winning party would receive 50% of the council seats with the remaining seats to be proportionally divided between the other political parties according to their electoral draw.

16 JUDICIAL SYSTEM

The constitution provides for an independent judiciary. The judiciary is susceptible to being influenced by the executive branch in practice. Magistrates are appointed by the president upon recommendation of the Supreme Council of the Magistracy; its members are drawn from the Department of Justice and the courts of appeal and cassation. In 2006, there were 51 cantonal courts, 23 courts of first instance, and 3 courts of appeal, located in Tunis, Sousse, and Sfax. A court of cassation in Tunis has three civil sections and one criminal section; it acts as the ultimate court of appeal. In addition, a high court is constituted for the sole purpose of prosecuting a member of the government accused of high treason. The council of state is an administrative tribunal empowered to resolve conflicts between citizens and the state and public authorities; as an accounting department, it is empowered to audit and examine government records.

Civil and criminal law generally follows French-influenced practices that evolved during the period of the protectorate. Since 1956 there has been a steady reform of existing Islamic legislation, including the abolition of polygamy. Shari'ah courts were abolished in 1956.

A military tribunal consisting of a presiding civilian judge from the court of cassation and four military judges hears cases involving military personnel as well as cases concerning civilians when national security is deemed to be at stake. Decisions of the military tribunal may be appealed to the court of cassation.

17 ARMED FORCES

The International Institute for Strategic Studies reports that armed forces in Tunisia totaled 35,800 members in 2011. The force is comprised of 27,000 from the army, 4,800 from the navy, and 4,000 members of the air force. Armed forces represented 1.2% of the labor force in Tunisia. Defense spending totaled $1.4 billion and accounted for 1.4% of GDP. Tunisia participated in peacekeeping efforts in the DROC, Burundi, Côte d'Ivoire and Ethiopia/Eritrea.

18 INTERNATIONAL COOPERATION

Admitted to the UN on 12 November 1956, Tunisia belongs to ECA and several nonregional specialized agencies, such as the World Bank, the FAO, UNESCO, UNHCR, UNIDO, IAEA, and the WHO. The nation also participates in the African Development Bank, the Arab Bank for Economic Development in Africa, the Arab Fund for Economic and Social Development, the Islamic Development Bank, the Arab League, OAPEC, the Organization of the Islamic Conference (OIC), the New Partnership for Africa's Development (NEPAD), the Community of Sahel and Saharan States (CENSAD), G-77, the Arab Maghreb Union, and African Union. The nation has observer status in the OAS and Black Sea Economic Cooperation Zone. Tunisia was the site of the Palestine Liberation Organization (PLO) headquarters from 1982–93. Tunisia is part of the Nonaligned Movement.

In environmental cooperation, Tunisia is part of the Basel Convention, the Convention on Biological Diversity, Ramsar, CITES, the London Convention, the Kyoto Protocol, the Montréal Protocol, MARPOL, the Nuclear Test Ban Treaty, and the UN Conventions on the Law of the Sea, Climate Change, and Desertification.

19 ECONOMY

Tunisia's dynamic economy is based mainly on agriculture, although minerals (crude oil and phosphates in particular), textiles, and tourism also contribute to the country's foreign trade market. Increased privatization of companies and progressive social policies have resulted in significant economic growth and higher standards of living. The food industry has shown steady growth into the 21st century with an increase of 40% from 2004 to 2009. The European Union is the primary destination for agricultural exports, receiving 42% of the nation's products. Olive oil, the Deglet Ennour brand of dates, and Maltese oranges are the primary products.

After a period of socialist economic policies, Tunisia began a structural reform program with the IMF designed to encourage a market-based economy. Tunisia was a founding member of the WTO. Privatization of state-owned enterprises began in 1987 with 67 of the government's 189 companies privatized through 1995. The privatization program, however, focused on smaller companies so as not to disrupt employment. Privatization of the energy, construction materials, and transport sectors, all of which contain unprofitable and overstaffed entities, has yet to occur. The reforms also decontrolled domestic prices and liberalized foreign trade.

With a high level of dependence on European markets for Tunisian exports, the nation faced the threat of major economic decline as a result of the 2008–09 global financial crisis. However, real GDP growth for 2009 was recorded above 3%, which was lower than previous years but higher than expected. The GDP rate of change in 2010 was 3.7%. Inflation stood at 4.5%, and unemployment was reported at 14%. Political instability weakened the economy in 2011. The economic decline led the Central Bank of Tunisia to warn of potential recession in 2012.

20 INCOME

The CIA estimated that in 2010 the GDP of Tunisia was $100 billion. The CIA defines GDP as the value of all final goods and services produced within a nation in a given year and computed on the basis of purchasing power parity (PPP) rather than value as measured on the basis of the rate of the exchange based on current dollars. The per capita GDP was estimated at $9,400. The annual growth rate of GDP was 3.7%. The average inflation rate was 4.5%.

It was estimated that agriculture accounted for 10.6% of GDP, industry 34.6%, and services 54.8%.

According to the World Bank, remittances from citizens living abroad totaled $2 billion or about $185 per capita and accounted for approximately 2% of GDP.

The World Bank reports that in 2009, household consumption in Tunisia totaled $24.9 billion or about $2,338 per capita, measured in current US dollars rather than PPP. Household consumption includes expenditures of individuals, households, and nongovernmental organizations on goods and services, excluding the purchases of dwellings. It was estimated that household consumption was growing at an average annual rate of 9.3%.

As of 2011 the most recent study by the World Bank reported that actual individual consumption in Tunisia was 70.1% of GDP and accounted for 0.12% of world consumption. By comparison, the United States accounted for 25.44% of world individual consumption. The World Bank also estimated that 21.4% of Tunisia's GDP was spent on food and beverages, 15.2% on housing and household furnishings, 6.5% on clothes, 4.5% on health, 6.8% on transportation, 0.7% on communications, 1.8% on recreation, 9.6% on restaurants and hotels, and -1% on miscellaneous goods and services and purchases from abroad.

21 LABOR

As of 2010, Tunisia had a total labor force of 3.829 million people. Within that labor force, CIA estimates in 2009 noted that 18.3% were employed in agriculture, 31.9% in industry, and 49.8% in the service sector.

Since 1958, regional workshops to combat underemployment have provided jobs in land development, reforestation, terracing, and drainage. Full employment has been a goal of successive development plans; however, rates of unemployment and underemployment have remained high.

In one effort to curb the problem, the government approved an early retirement law for public servants in 2009, allowing workers to voluntarily retire at age 57 instead of the general retirement age of 60. Some companies in the commercial and industrial sectors had already initiated similar early retirement plans.

The only trade federation is the General Union of Tunisian Workers (Union Générale des Travailleurs Tunisiens—UGTT). Unions have the right to strike after a mandatory notice period of ten days. Regional labor councils seek to foster cooperation between management and labor. Collective bargaining contracts cover 80% of the private workforce.

The labor code sets the regular workweek at 48 hours with one 24-hour rest period for most sectors. If the workday exceeds 10 hours, overtime rates must be paid. All workers are entitled to annual paid leave of up to 18 working days. All nonagricultural employers with over 40 workers are required to have a medical facility available. In 2010, the minimum wage was between $173 and $188 per month.

The minimum age for agricultural work is 13 years and the minimum age for manufacturing is 16. Children must attend school until 16 and have restricted working hours until the age of 18. The laws are somewhat effectively enforced but children can still be seen performing agricultural work in rural areas and working as vendors in urban areas.

22 AGRICULTURE

Roughly 30% of the total land is farmed, and the country's major crops include olives, olive oil, grain, tomatoes, citrus fruit, sugar beets, dates, and almonds. Cereal production in 2009 amounted to 2.6 million tons, fruit production 1.2 million tons, and vegetable production 2.6 million tons. Fertile land is generally limited to the north. In the southern desert and plateau, desert farming is precarious, but barley is produced in quantity.

Harvests have traditionally yielded sizable surpluses for export, chiefly to France. Tunisia's early growing season allows the nation to profit from exporting fresh produce to Europe before European crops ripen. Crops fluctuate greatly in size, however, depending upon the weather. In very poor years, wheat and barley must be imported to satisfy local food requirements.

The government has undertaken irrigation and soil conservation projects to improve agricultural production and raise the living standard of rural areas. The 1962–71 plan aimed at constructing 40 dams, mostly in the Medjerda River system, plus opening over 1,000 new wells, particularly in the southern regions. In the period 1962–64, the government initiated a program to help the new cooperative farm system; remaining European-owned farms were nationalized as part of the program. In 1969, however, the development of cooperatives was halted, and appropriated land was redistributed to individual Tunisian owners. Irrigation and flood-control projects, many undertaken with foreign aid, were under way in Bizerte, the Medjerda River basin, and other locales in the early 1980s. To increase and direct the flow of capital to this sector, the government has established the Agricultural Investment Promotion Agency and the National Agricultural Development Bank.

23 ANIMAL HUSBANDRY

The UN Food and Agriculture Organization (FAO) reported that Tunisia dedicated 4.8 million hectares (12 million acres) to permanent pasture or meadow in 2009. During that year, the country tended 70 million chickens, 679,080 head of cattle, and 6,000 pigs. The production from these animals amounted to 60,745 tons of beef and veal and 1.08 million tons of milk. Tunisia also produced 4,600 tons of cattle hide and 10,345 tons of raw wool.

24 FISHING

Tunisia had 774 decked commercial fishing boats in 2008. The annual capture totaled 100,241 tons according to the UN FAO. The export value of seafood totaled $156.2 million. Commercial fishing takes place along the Mediterranean coast and in the Lake of Tunis and Lake Achkel. Small quantities of tuna, sardines, shrimp, and lobsters are exported. Except for some trawler and sponge fishing, most activity is on a limited scale. The National Fisheries Office owns part of the trawler fleet.

In 2009 the government announced a joint project with the Italian Cooperation for the Development of Emerging Countries program to boost the Tunisian fishing industry. The project focused on improvements to mullet and eel farms in the northeastern region of the country.

25 FORESTRY

Approximately 7% of Tunisia is covered by forest. The UN FAO estimated the 2009 roundwood production at 218,000 cu m (7.7 million cu ft). The value of all forest products, including roundwood, totaled $44.9 million. The oak and pine forests of the northern highlands provide cork for export and firewood for local use.

26 MINING

In 2009 Tunisia's mineral production included barite, clay, gypsum, iron ore, lead, phosphate rock, silver, zinc and salt. Washed phosphate rock production in 2009 totaled 7,298 metric tons (gross weight) and was entirely controlled by the government-owned Compagnie des Phophates de Gafsa (CPG), founded in 1896. CPG was the largest company in Tunisia, both in terms of employees and capital investment, directly employing 9,000 people and indirectly employing over 200,000. The Kef Eschfair Mine accounted for 28% of total ore volume; the Kef Eddour Mine, 21%; and the Jallabia Mine, 12%. The underground M'rata Mine was closed in 2000. Known reserves of crude phosphate, in the south, amounted to 100 million tons (5% of world reserves). High-grade iron ore was found in the north, while lead and zinc, mined intermittently since Roman times, were widely dispersed. International interest in developing Tunisia's lead-zinc deposits continued to grow. High-quality marine salt was exploited along the coast. Uranium was discovered in 1965. In 2009, iron ore (metal content), 151,000 metric tons, down from 211,000 metric tons in 2008; cement (hydraulic and white), 7.5 million metric tons; marine salt, 1,395,000 metric tons; and gypsum, 360,000 metric tons (estimated). Barite, clays, fertilizers (triple-superphosphate, phosphoric acid, diammonium-phosphate, and ammonium nitrate), gravel, lime, sand, and stone were also produced. No lead, silver, or zinc production has occurred since 2005.

27 ENERGY AND POWER

The World Bank reported in 2008 that Tunisia produced 15.3 billion kWh of electricity and consumed 13.4 billion kWh, or 1,261 kWh per capita. Roughly 86% of energy came from fossil fuels. Per capita oil consumption was 889 kg. Oil production totaled 80,140 barrels of oil a day. Energy conservation and the search for renewable energy resources are priorities for the Tunisian government and have become a key source of foreign investment. In 2008 and 2009, two wind farm projects—sponsored separately by the Spanish government and a private Italian company—were expected to generate increased electrical capacity. Also in 2009 the Abu Dhabi (United Arab Emirates) National Energy Company announced plans to begin construction of a combined cycle gas power plant in Bizerte designed to generate 500 MW of electricity.

28 INDUSTRY

Tunisia has a relatively diversified economy, with agricultural, mining, energy, and manufacturing production. Manufacturing industries, particularly those producing for export, have fueled Tunisia's growth for many years. They contribute one-fifth of total GDP, three-quarters of export earnings, and employ more than one-fifth of the labor force. The manufacturing industry is dominated by textile and leathers operations, followed by the electrical and mechanical industries, chemical exports (mainly phosphate by-products), and agribusiness. Agribusiness includes flour milling; fish, fruit, and vegetable canning; olive oil processing; and sugar refining. As one of the world's largest sources of phosphates, the country's mineral-processing industries are dominated by the manufacture of phosphate fertilizers. Handicrafts industries produce clothing, rugs, pottery, and copper and leather goods for both local and export markets. An oil refinery at Bizerte has a production capacity of 34,000 barrels per day.

The skills of the Tunisian work force and their relatively low wages have led an increasing number of European clothing firms to subcontract their work to Tunisian factories, thereby causing a sharp increase in Tunisia's exports of clothing. Textiles are the primary source of foreign currency revenue, with more than 90% of production being exported. The electrical power industry in Tunisia increased dramatically in the 2000s, with the state supporting major renovations in existing plants, and the construction of new power plants.

Despite political uncertainty, the Tunisian Ministry of Industry and Trade reported an increase of 10.2% in industrial investment for 2011.

29 SCIENCE AND TECHNOLOGY

The World Bank reported in 2009 that there were no patent applications in science and technology in Tunisia. The Pasteur Institute, founded in 1893, conducts medical research in Tunis. That city is also home to institutes for the study of veterinary science (1897) and geology (1962). There are research centers for agronomy (founded in 1914) and forestry (1967) in Ariana. Science and engineering students account for about one-third of college and university enrollments. The University of Sciences, Technologies, and Medicine of Tunis (Tunis II, founded 1988) maintains a comprehensive science program, including faculties of medicine and mathematics, physics, and natural sciences and schools of veterinary medicine, health sciences and technology, engineering, computer science, and agriculture. The University of Sfax (founded in 1988) has faculties of medicine and science.

30 DOMESTIC TRADE

Rades/Tunis is the principal commercial, industrial, and distribution center; most of the import and export houses, banks, and mining firms have their central offices in the city. Other commercial and distribution centers are Sfax, noted for olive oil and phosphate shipments, and Bizerte, known for grain and olive oil. Fairs are held at various times of the year in Sfax, Sousse, Tunis, and other towns. Most businesses are family-owned and operated. The government has posed some resistance to the establishment of foreign firms, particularly foreign franchises. An extensive system of price controls was for the most part eliminated in 1998. The chief advertising media are daily newspapers, outdoor displays, and motion picture theaters. The first private radio station started broadcasting in November 2003, and a private satellite television channel started broadcasting in February 2005. Arabic is the language of sales promotion, French the language of commercial correspondence.

Normal business hours in winter are from 8:30 a.m. to 1 p.m. and 3 to 5:45 p.m., Monday–Friday. Summer business hours are from 8:30 a.m. to 1 p.m. Monday–Saturday.

31 FOREIGN TRADE

Tunisia imported $20.02 billion worth of goods and services in 2008, while exporting $16.11 billion worth of goods and services. Major import partners in 2009 were France, 23.3%; Italy, 19.1%; Germany, 9.2%; and Spain, 4.9% . Its major export partners were France, 27.6%; Italy, 18.7%; Germany, 10.4%; Libya, 6.9%; and Belgium, 4.5%. Tunisia's foreign trade is based upon the export of mineral and agricultural products, textiles, and chemicals in exchange for consumer goods, raw and processed materials, and agricultural and industrial equipment. Apparel, textiles, and leather are now the major exports.

Garments make up a large portion of Tunisia's export commodities. Other exports include crude petroleum, chemicals, manufactured fertilizers, and vegetable oils. The EU is the focus of Tunisia's foreign trade. France is by far Tunisia's largest trading partner.

Tunisia is a world-leader in bulk olive oil exports. Most of the exports go to Italy and Spain, where the oil is blended with local product for the internal market, freeing up local oils for export.

32 BALANCE OF PAYMENTS

In 2010 Tunisia had a foreign trade deficit of $1.2 billion, amounting to 1.7% of GDP. Since 1960, Tunisia has experienced perennial trade deficits. These have been partly covered by tourist income, by remittances from Tunisian workers abroad, and by foreign investment and assistance.

33 BANKING AND SECURITIES

The Central Bank of Tunisia (Banque Centrale de Tunisie—BCT), established in September 1958, is the sole bank of issue. The Tunisian Banking Co. (Société Tunisienne de Banque—STB) was established in 1957; it is the leading commercial and investment bank; the state holds 52% of the STB's capital.

The banking system is a mixture of state-owned and private institutions which offer a variety of financial instruments and services. Commercial banks include Citibank, Amen Bank, Banque International Arabe de Tunisie (BIAT), Banque Nationale Agricole (BNA); and one merchant bank is International Maghreb.

In 2010 the discount rate, the rate at which the central bank lends to banks in the short term, was 5.75%.

A stock exchange began operations in Tunis in May 1970. While its activities have been expanding steadily, they remain limited to transactions in securities issued by the state and the stocks of a few private or government-owned firms. The exchange has completed a shift to fully electronic trading, but remains under the government eye.

34 INSURANCE

Although Tunisians have traditionally resisted taking out insurance, the insurance market has begun to grow rapidly. Vehicle insurance is the biggest category. Both foreign and domestic insurance companies operate in Tunisia. The insurance business is shared roughly equally between state-owned and private companies.

35 PUBLIC FINANCE

In 2010 the budget of Tunisia included $9.806 billion in public revenue and $11.76 billion in public expenditures. The budget def-

Principal Trading Partners – Tunisia (2010)

(In millions of US dollars)

Country	Total	Exports	Imports	Balance
World	38,644.3	16,426.6	22,217.7	-5,791.1
France	9,047.2	4,114.1	4,933.2	-819.1
Italy	7,592.6	2,708.6	4,884.0	-2,175.4
Germany	3,692.2	1,489.3	2,203.0	-713.7
Spain	1,900.7	643.9	1,256.8	-613.0
Libya	1,686.8	954.9	732.0	222.9
China	1,207.3	113.5	1,093.8	-980.3
United Kingdom	1,143.8	862.9	280.9	582.0
Turkey	1,040.2	255.2	785.0	-529.8
Belgium	1,019.1	467.6	551.5	-83.9
United States	1,008.3	379.9	628.4	-248.5

(…) data not available or not significant.

(n.s.) not specified.

SOURCE: *2011 Direction of Trade Statistics Yearbook,* New York: United Nations, 2011.

icit amounted to 4.3% of GDP. Public debt was 49.5% of GDP, with $21.45 billion of the debt held by foreign entities.

36 TAXATION

The statutory corporate tax rate was 30% in 2011. A development of industrial competitiveness tax was levied at 1%. Work accident insurance taxes, paid jointly by employee and employer, were 3.8%. Personal taxes include a progressive income tax and a benefits tax levied on gross salaries and paid quarterly by the employer to the National Social Security Fund. The main indirect tax is Tunisia's value-added tax (VAT), with a standard rate of 18%.

37 CUSTOMS AND DUTIES

Tariffs on textiles and apparel ranged from 0 to 36%. A customs formality fee of 3% of total duties paid also applied. A consumption tax ranged from 10% to as high as 700%. In 1995 Tunisia signed a free trade accord with the renamed European Union that removed tariff and other trade barriers on most nonagricultural goods, services, and capital by 2008. Tunisia is also a member of the World Trade Organization.

38 FOREIGN INVESTMENT

Foreign direct investment (FDI) in Tunisia was a net inflow of $1.6 billion according to World Bank figures published in 2009. FDI represented 4.03% of GDP. As much as 75% of FDI in Tunisia has been in the petroleum sector. Other important sectors are textiles, and mechanical and electrical industries. The telecommunications industry is ready for substantial growth.

In 1972 an investment law provided special benefits to companies manufacturing commodities for export, a regulation that stimulated some foreign involvement, particularly in the textile industry. Incentives consisted of partial or total tax exemption for periods of 10–20 years, as well as exemption from customs and import duties on raw materials and equipment. A similar law that encouraged investment in industries producing for local markets was enacted in 1974 and amended in 1981; the statute required that such firms exhibit partial (in many cases majority) Tunisian ownership. A 1981 law offered incentives for investment in less-

developed regions. Kuwait, Saudi Arabia, Qatar, the United Arab Emirates, and Algeria participated with Tunisia in development banks to channel Arab investment funds.

Tunisia's severe balance of payments crisis forced the government to reverse many of its protectionist and socialist policies under structural adjustment programs supervised by the IMF and World Bank. A new investment code was passed in 1989 offering further tax and customs concessions to local as well as foreign investors, particularly in export-oriented enterprises. Tunisian law still prohibits ownership of land by non-Tunisians, although a special 40-year land lease system permits agricultural development by foreign companies. In January 1994 the government adopted an investment incentives law that, in conjunction with added provisions, offers tax reductions on reinvested profits and revenues, and optional depreciation schedules for production equipment. For companies that export at least 80% of their output, the incentives include a 10-year profits tax holiday, with a 50% reduction thereafter; full tax and duty exemptions on materials and services used in production; full tax exemption on reinvested profits and revenue; and duty-free import of capital goods that have no local equivalent. Large investments with high job creation may qualify to use state land virtually rent-free.

Foreign property is still at risk of expropriation by the Tunisian government and in 1995 an American company had property taken without compensation. The government also reserves the right to take property by eminent domain, in which case just compensation is offered. There remain many restrictions on foreign investment as the government pursues a gradualist approach, caught between pressure to liberalize from the IMF and the WTO, and a fear of igniting a popular uprising. Under the terms of its accession to the WTO (29 March 1995), Tunisia was obligated to relax restrictions on foreign participation in its information, telecommunications, and financial services industries in 2003.

Balance of Payments – Tunisia (2010)

(In millions of US dollars)

Current Account		**-2,104.0**
Balance on goods	-4,575.0	
Imports	-21,005.0	
Exports	16,431.0	
Balance on services	2,460.0	
Balance on income	-1,925.0	
Current transfers	1,935.0	
Capital Account		**82.0**
Financial Account		**1,745.0**
Direct investment abroad	-66.0	
Direct investment in Tunisia	1,401.0	
Portfolio investment assets	…	
Portfolio investment liabilities	-26.0	
Financial derivatives	…	
Other investment assets	-275.0	
Other investment liabilities	711.0	
Net Errors and Omissions		**55.0**
Reserves and Related Items		**222.0**

(…) data not available or not significant.

SOURCE: *Balance of Payment Statistics Yearbook 2011,* Washington, DC: International Monetary Fund, 2011.

39 ECONOMIC DEVELOPMENT

The plan for 1973–76 proposed increasing investments by 75% over the previous ten-year plan. An annual growth rate of 6.6% was targeted for the period. Fully 75% of the plan's investments were to be financed with international aid. Manufacturing industries received the largest single allocation of total investment under the 1977–81 plan. Once again, the burden of financing the program fell on external sources, with Arab funds accounting for 30% of the anticipated foreign capital. Actual growth came close to the target of 7.5% a year in real terms. The development plan for 1982–86 set forth three main goals: employment growth, regional development, and balance of payments equilibrium. Some 33% of the total expenditure was to be invested in labor-intensive industries. Performance fell far short of the goal of 6% a year in real growth.

The inauguration of the 1987–94 development plan followed the foreign exchange crisis of 1986, and the adoption of an International Monetary Fund (IMF) sponsored economic rehabilitation scheme. Services were to receive 39%, agriculture 19%, and manufacturing 16%. This plan was successfully completed, winning the country accolades from investment institutions. The 1994–96 development plan was based on strong expansion in the manufacturing industry (8.7%) and tourism (22%). The plan called for further cuts in consumer subsidies and the privatization of many state assets. The economic development plan of 1997–2001 called for investment in telecommunications infrastructure, continued privatization of industry, and lowering of trade barriers.

The 10th economic development plan of 2002–06 aimed at improving the competitiveness of the economy; increasing the private sector's share in investment; setting up a knowledge economy; and securing sustainable economic and social development and a creation of new jobs while maintaining global balances. Targets set for economic development included: an average economic growth of 5.7% a year; an increase in private sector investment

to 60% (the total investment rate would be brought to 26.6% by 2006); and the consolidation of the national savings rate to reach 26% of GNP by 2006, allowing for the financing of 91% of projected investment.

A surge in demand for new housing and luxury units and a series of plans to expand transportation infrastructure and develop Tunis's growth corridors improved conditions for both the construction industry and foreign investors in 2006. Nonetheless, high unemployment, the existence of the "gray" economy, the continued dominance of the public sector, and masses of bureaucratic red tape persisted throughout the 2000s.

Following the popular uprising in 2011, tourist revenues fell by more than 50 percent. FDI also fell by 20%. Some 80 foreign companies left Tunisia. Additionally, worker layoffs increased, and many Tunisians living in Libya returned to Tunisia following that country's political instability in 2011, worsening the unemployment problem. Tunisia's dependence on Europe as an export market also threatened to drag down the economy, as Europe's banking crisis in 2011 slowed economic growth and, in many countries, fostered a recession. The interim government promised to implement market friendly business polices.

40 SOCIAL DEVELOPMENT

A social insurance system provides benefits including maternity payments, family allowances, disability and life insurance, and old age insurance. The system covers private-sector employees and some categories of fishermen. There are special systems for government workers, agricultural workers, the self-employed, fishermen, artists and intellectuals. Pensions normally are provided at age 60, and benefits are equal to 40% of average earnings, plus 0.5% for each 3 months of contributions above 120. Work injury insurance is compulsory for employers and covers all salaried workers including domestic servants. Unemployment benefits are provided for all salaried nonagricultural workers and payable for six months.

Tunisian women enjoy full civil and political rights under the law. Educational and employment opportunities are growing steadily. The law specifically requires equal pay for equal work and this is generally respected. Inheritance laws, based on Muslim tenets, discriminate against women. Domestic violence occurs but the police and courts regard the issue as a family matter. The rights of children are protected.

41 HEALTH

According to the CIA, life expectancy in Tunisia was 74 years in 2011. The country spent 10.4% of its GDP on healthcare, amounting to $240 per person. There were 12 physicians, 33 nurses and midwives, and 21 hospital beds per 10,000 inhabitants. The fertility rate was 2.1, while the infant mortality rate was 18 per 1,000 live births. In 2008 the maternal mortality rate, according to the World Bank, was 60 per 100,000 births. It was estimated that 98% of children were vaccinated against measles. The CIA calculated HIV/AIDS prevalence in Tunisia to be about less than 0.1% in 2009.

42 HOUSING

The government has spent well over TND1 billion ($663 million) on workers' housing. Since the mid-1960s, trade unions have provided new housing for members. Financial assistance to needy

---

Public Finance – Tunisia (2009)

(In millions of dinars, central government figures)

Revenue and Grants	**16,941**	**100.0%**
Tax revenue	11,685	69.0%
Social contributions	3,237	19.1%
Grants	178	1.1%
Other revenue	1,842	10.9%
Expenditures	**17,860**	**100.0%**
General public services	2,339	13.1%
Defense	763	4.3%
Public order and safety	1,197	6.7%
Economic affairs	3,449	19.3%
Environmental protection	225	1.3%
Housing and community amenities	820	4.6%
Health	826	4.6%
Recreational, culture, and religion	440	2.5%
Education	3,429	19.2%
Social protection	4,373	24.5%

(…) data not available or not significant.

SOURCE: *Government Finance Statistics Yearbook 2010*, Washington, DC: International Monetary Fund, 2010.

homeowners is provided by a national housing fund. About 45% of all housing was considered to be of modern construction, including detached apartment complexes and villas. About 54% of all housing was of traditional construction, such as an Arabic-style home. Squatter communities, called *gourbvilles*, are still prevalent in urban regions.

43 EDUCATION

In 2008 the World Bank estimated that 98% of age-eligible children in Tunisia were enrolled in primary school. Secondary enrollment for age-eligible children stood at 71%. Tertiary enrollment was estimated at 34%. Of those enrolled in tertiary education, there were 100 male students for every 149 female students. Overall, the CIA estimated that Tunisia had a literacy rate of 74.3%. Public expenditure on education represented 7.1% of GDP.

On becoming independent in 1956, Tunisia inherited a small but efficient educational system based on French and, to a lesser extent, Islamic influence. In 1958 the government nationalized most of the existing facilities; remaining private institutions were subject to government regulation. In the same year the government began a comprehensive plan for educational development to achieve universal, free, compulsory primary education and a significant expansion of the secondary school system.

Primary school covers nine years of study in two cycles of six plus three years. Secondary school covers an additional four years, with two years of general education plus two years of specialized education in arts, mathematics, experimental sciences, technology, or economy and management. Vocational studies are also available at the secondary level. The academic year runs from September to June.

The University of Tunis was founded on 31 March 1960. There are over 150 institutions of higher education, including 13 universities.

44 LIBRARIES AND MUSEUMS

The National Library (est. 1885) in Tunis contains a special collection of rare Arabic and Oriental manuscripts. The University of Tunis library has 220,000 volumes. The Arab League Documentation and Information Center, with 25,000 volumes, has been housed at Tunis since 1980. The collections of Tunisia's approximately 380 public libraries hold over 2.7 million volumes. There are also 23 regional libraries throughout the country.

The Bardo National Museum, founded in Tunis in 1888, has the largest collection of Roman mosaics in the world. Another fine collection is located at the museum in Sousse, which contains archaeological remains dating from the 6th century BC to the 6th century AD. The Raqqada Museum, housed in a former presidential palace near Kairouan, has the country's largest collection of Islamic art, including manuscripts of the Koran (Koran) from the Great Mosque of Kairouan. Other museums are in Monastir, Sfax, Qairouan, Maktar, Sbeitla, Sousse, and Carthage. The National Institute of Archaeology is located in Tunis, as is the Center of Living Arts and the Museum of Traditional and Popular Art.

45 MEDIA

In 2009 the CIA reported that there were 1.3 million telephone landlines in Tunisia. In addition to landlines, mobile phone subscriptions averaged 93 per 100 people. There were 7 FM radio stations, 38 AM radio stations, and 2 shortwave radio stations. Internet users numbered 34 per 100 citizens. In 2010 the country had 490 Internet hosts. Prominent newspapers in 2010, with circulation numbers listed parenthetically, included *As-Sabah* (50,000), *As-Sahafa*, and *La Presse de Tunisie* (40,000).

Tunisia's well-developed postal, telephone, and telegraph system is government-operated and links all the important cities. A marine cable connects Tunisia with France, and a land cable links it with Algeria and Morocco. The government-owned Tunisian Radio-Television Broadcasting (ERTT) broadcasts in Arabic, French, and Italian over one national station, one international station, and five regional stations. Relay stations bring in programs from Italian television.

The constitution provides for freedom of speech and of the press. Prior to the 2011 revolution, the government was said to limit these freedoms significantly through economic control, confiscations, imprisonment, and detention. Government control of media was cited as a major factor in Ben Ali's ability to maintain control over Tunisia; following his resignation, previously banned publications reappeared.

46 ORGANIZATIONS

There are chambers of commerce in Tunis, Sfax, Sousse, and Bizerte; the Tunisian Union of Industry, Commerce, and Crafts, a national association of trade federations and business interests, is in Tunis. The National Union of Tunisian Farmers is very active. There are professional associations for several different fields, particularly those involving medicine and healthcare.

The National Union of Tunisian Women promotes greater participation by women in economic, political, and cultural affairs. National youth organizations include the Tunisian General Union of Students, the Young Constitutional Democrats, the League of Arab States Youth and Sports Division, Junior Chamber, and Scouts of Tunisia. Kiwanis and Lions Clubs have active programs. There are several sports associations, including the multinational African Boxing Confederation, African Rugby Football Union, and the African Table Tennis Federation.

The multinational Arab League Educational, Cultural and Scientific Organization encourages cultural unity among Arab countries.

The Arab Institute for Human Rights and the Arab Medical Union, both based in Tunis, are multinational, social action organizations. Other international organizations with national chapters include Greenpeace, Amnesty International, Caritas, UNICEF, and the Red Crescent Society.

47 TOURISM, TRAVEL, AND RECREATION

The *Tourism Factbook*, published by the UN World Tourism Organization, reported 6.9 million incoming tourists to Tunisia in 2009; they spent a total of $3.53 billion. Of those incoming tourists, there were 3.7 million from Europe, 2 million from the Middle East, and 1 million from Africa. There were 239,890 hotel beds available in Tunisia, which had an occupancy rate of 52%. The estimated daily cost to visit Tunis, the capital, was $231. The cost of visiting other cities averaged $156.

Tunisia's cosmopolitan capital city, Tunis, the ruins of Carthage, the ancient Muslim and Jewish quarters of Jerba, and the modern coastal resorts in the vicinity of Monastir and Sousse are among the main tourist attractions. Recreations include hunting, hiking, golf, tennis, and other water sports.

Tourism receipts in 2011 declined sharply (an estimated 50%) due to the political instability associated with the resignation of Ben Ali.

48 FAMOUS PERSONS

Ancient Carthage was located near the site of modern Tunis. Its most famous leader was Hannibal (247–183 BC), the general who campaigned in Italy for several years (218–211 BC) but who was defeated by the Romans under Scipio Africanus at Zama in 202 BC. The dominant figure of modern Tunisia was Habib Bourguiba (Habib bin 'Ali ar-Rugaybah, 1903–2000); he led Tunisia to independence, formed its first government, and was president from 1957 to 1987. Mongi Slim (1908–69) served as president of the 16th session of the UN General Assembly (1961–62). Mohamed Mzali (b. 1925) has served in numerous government posts, including prime minister in 1980–86. Gen. Zine el 'Abidine Ben 'Ali (b. 1936) assumed the presidency in 1987; popular protests forced him from office in 2011.

Tunisia's noteworthy literary figures include Albert Memmi (b. 1920), the author of *The Statue of Salt* (1957), who writes in French; and Mahmoud Messadi (1911–2004), who wrote in Arabic. Prominent Tunisian painters are Ammar Farhat (1911–86) and Jallah bin 'Abdallah (b. 1921).

49 DEPENDENCIES

Tunisia has no territories or colonies.

50 BIBLIOGRAPHY

Borowiec, Andrew. *Taming the Sahara: Tunisia Shows a Way While Others Falter*. Westport, CT: Praeger, 2003.

McDougall, James, ed. *Nation, Society and Culture in North Africa*. London: Frank Cass Publishers, 2003.

Perkins, Kenneth J. *Historical Dictionary of Tunisia*. 2nd ed. Lanham, MD: Scarecrow Press, 1997.

Perkins, Kenneth J. *A History of Modern Tunisia*. New York: Cambridge University Press, 2008.

Tunisia Investment and Business Guide: Strategic and Practical Information. Washington, DC: International Business Publications USA, 2012.

Zeilig, Leo, and David Seddon. *A Political and Economic Dictionary of Africa*. Philadelphia: Routledge/Taylor and Francis, 2005.

UGANDA

Republic of Uganda

CAPITAL: Kampala

FLAG: The national flag consists of six equal horizontal stripes of black, yellow, red, black, yellow, and red (from top to bottom); at the center, within a white circle, is a crested crane, the national bird of Uganda.

ANTHEM: *O Uganda, Land of Beauty!*

MONETARY UNIT: The Uganda shilling (UGX) was introduced in May 1987. There are notes of : 50000, 20000, 10000, 5000, 2000 and 1000. There are coins of 1, 2, 5, 10, 50, 100, 200 and 500 shillings, and notes of 1000, 2000, 5000, 10000, 20000, and 50000 shillings. UGX1 = US$0.00038954 (or US$1 = UGX2,567.1) as of 2011.

WEIGHTS AND MEASURES: The metric system is now in use.

HOLIDAYS: New Year's Day, 1 January; Labor Day, 1 May; Martyrs' Day, 3 June; Independence Day, 9 October; Christmas Day, 25 December; Boxing Day, 26 December. Movable holidays include Good Friday, Easter Monday, Eid al-Fitr, and Eid al-Adha.

TIME: 3 p.m. = noon GMT.

¹LOCATION, SIZE, AND EXTENT

A landlocked country in east-central Africa, situated north and northwest of Lake Victoria, Uganda has a total area of 236,040 sq km (91,136 sq mi), of which 36,330 sq km (14,027 mi) is inland water. Comparatively, the area occupied by Uganda is slightly smaller than the state of Oregon. It extends 787 km (489 mi) NNE–SSW and 486 km (302 mi) ESE–WNW. Bounded on the N by South Sudan, on the E by Kenya, on the S by Tanzania and Rwanda, and on the W by the Democratic Republic of the Congo (DROC). Uganda has a total boundary length of 2,698 km (1,676 mi).

²TOPOGRAPHY

The greater part of Uganda consists of a plateau 800 to 2,000 m (2,600–6,600 ft) in height. Along the western border, in the Ruwenzori Mountains, Margherita Peak reaches a height of 5,109 m (16,762 ft), while on the eastern frontier Mount Elgon rises to 4,321 m (14,178 ft). By contrast, the Western Rift Valley, which runs from north to south through the western half of the country, is below 910 m (3,000 ft) on the surface of Lake Edward and Lake George and 621 m (2,036 ft) on the surface of Lake Albert (L. Mobutu Sese Seko). The White Nile has its source in Lake Victoria; as the Victoria Nile, it runs northward through Lake Kyoga and then westward to Lake Albert, from which it emerges as the Albert Nile to resume its northward course to South Sudan. With 69 lakes, Uganda has the highest number of lakes in Africa.

³CLIMATE

Although Uganda is on the equator, its climate is warm rather than hot, and temperatures vary little throughout the year. Most of the territory receives an annual rainfall of at least 100 cm (40 in). At Entebbe, mean annual rainfall is 162 cm (64 in); in the

northeast, it is only 69 cm (27 in). Temperature generally varies by altitude; on Lake Albert, the mean annual maximum is 29°C (84°F) and the mean annual minimum 22°C (72°F). At Kabale in the southwest, 1,250 m (4,100 ft) higher, the mean annual maximum is 23°C (73°F), and the mean annual minimum 10°C (50°F). At Kampala, these extremes are 27°C (81°F) and 17°C (63°F).

⁴FLORA AND FAUNA

The World Resources Institute estimates that there are 4,900 plant species in Uganda. In the southern half of Uganda, the natural vegetation has been largely replaced by cultivated plots, in which plantain is the most prominent. There are, however, scattered patches of thick forest or of elephant grass and mvuli trees, providing excellent timber. The cooler western highlands contain a higher proportion of long grass and forest. In the extreme southwest, however, cultivation is intensive even on the high mountain slopes. In the drier northern region, short grasses appear, and there are areas of open woodland; thorn trees and borassus palms also grow.

Animal species include 360 mammals, 1,015 birds, 165 reptiles, and 52 amphibians. The calculation reflects the total number of distinct species residing in the country, not the number of endemic species. Elephant, hippopotamus, buffalo, cob, topi, and a variety of monkeys are all plentiful, while lion, giraffe, and rhinoceros also are seen. At least six mammal species are found only in Uganda. The birds of Uganda include the crowned crane (the national emblem), bulbul, weaver, crow, shrike, heron, egret, ibis, guinea fowl, mouse bird, lourie, hornbill, pigeon, dove, bee-eater, hoopoe, darter, lily-trotter, marabou stork, kingfisher, fish eagle, and kite.

There are relatively few varieties of fish, but the lakes and rivers contain plentiful stocks of tilapia, Nile perch, catfish, lungfish, elephant snout fish, and other species. Crocodiles, too, are found in many areas and are particularly evident along the Nile between the Kabalega (Murchison) Falls and Lake Albert. There is a wide variety of snakes, but the more dangerous varieties are rarely observed.

According to a 2011 report issued by the International Union for Conservation of Nature and Natural Resources (IUCN), the number of threatened species included 22 types of mammals, 21 species of birds, 7 species of amphibians, 61 species of fish, 9 types of mollusks, 6 species of other invertebrates, and 39 species of plants. Threatened species include the mountain gorilla, northern white rhinoceros, black rhinoceros, and Nile crocodile. Poaching of protected animals is widespread.

5 ENVIRONMENT

The World Resources Institute reported that Uganda had designated 6.29 million hectares (15.54 million acres) of land for protection as of 2006. Water resources totaled 66 cu km (15.83 cu mi) while water usage was 0.3 cu km (0.072 cu mi) per year. Domestic water usage accounted for 43% of total usage, industrial for 17%, and agricultural for 40%. Per capita water usage totaled 10 cu m (353 cu ft) per year.

Major environmental problems in Uganda include overgrazing, deforestation, and inadequate agricultural methods, all of which lead to soil erosion. Attempts at controlling the propagation of tsetse flies have involved the use of hazardous chemicals. The nation's water supply is threatened by toxic industrial pollutants; mercury from mining activity is also found in the water supply. Deforestation is a serious concern for the nation. Between 1990 and 2010 Uganda lost more than 37.1% of its forest cover. At such a rate of deforestation, all of the nation's remaining forests could be transformed into desert-like regions by 2029. Deforestation in mountain regions often leads to deadly floods and landslides. The country's wetlands are also in danger, as more and more of these ecological systems are being developed for other uses.

In 2009 Uganda implemented a major program known as the Nile Basin Reforestation Project in Uganda. In doing so, it became one of the first countries in Africa to implement a reforestation project with the intention of reducing global warming emissions under the Kyoto Protocol. A pine and mixed native species plantation will be established in the Rwoho Central Forest reserve, an area that has been diminished to grasslands due to deforestation and erosion. Through this project, Uganda will qualify for funds paid out for carbon credits through the World Bank BioCarbon Fund. A portion of the new plantation will be used to support a sustainable timber industry, as the nation has a growing need for wood resources. The UN reported in 2008 that carbon dioxide emissions in Uganda totaled 3,202 kilotons. According to the nongovernmental group Oxfam International, about 70% of the natural disasters in Uganda (including both flooding and drought) have been caused by climate change. This leads to hundreds of thousands of acres of crops lost each year in a nation where many work as subsistence farmers.

6 POPULATION

The US Central Intelligence Agency (CIA) estimates the population of Uganda in 2011 to be approximately 34,612,250, which placed it at number 36 in population among the 196 nations of the world. In 2011, approximately 2% of the population was over 65 years of age, with another 49.9% under 15 years of age. The median age in Uganda was 15.1 years. There were 1.01 males for every female in the country. The population's annual rate of change was 3.576%. The projected population for the year 2025 was 53,400,000. Population density in Uganda was calculated at 144 people per sq km (373 people per sq mi). The UN estimated that 13% of the population lived in urban areas, and that urban populations had an annual rate of change of 4.8%. The largest urban area was Kampala, with a population of 1.5 million.

7 MIGRATION

Estimates of Uganda's net migration rate, carried out by the CIA in 2011, amounted to -0.02 migrants per 1,000 citizens. The total number of emigrants living abroad was 757,500, and the total number of immigrants living in Uganda was 646,500. Uganda accepted 19,382 refugees from Sudan, 81,804 from the Democratic Republic of Congo, 12,590 from Rwanda, 4,950 from Burundi, 3,490 from Eritrea, 2,379 from Kenya, and 11,151 from Somalia. After the fall of the Amin regime, as many as 240,000 people from Amin's West Nile district may have fled to the DROC and Sudan. Many of them returned to Uganda in 1983; government campaigns against guerrillas, however, displaced thousands more.

8 ETHNIC GROUPS

Uganda's ethnic groups are most broadly distinguished by language. In southern Uganda, most of the population speak Bantu languages. Sudanic speakers inhabit the northwest; Nilotic speakers, principally the Acholi and Langi, live in the north; and the Iteso and Karamajong in the northeast. The Baganda, who populate the northern shore of Lake Victoria, constitute the largest single ethnic group in Uganda, making up about 16.9% of the total population. The Banyakole account for about 9.5%, followed by the Basoga at 8.4%, Bakiga at 6.9%, Iteso at 6.4%, Langi at 6.1%, Acholi at 4.7%, Bagisu at 4.6%, Lugbara at 4.2%, and Bunyoro at 2.7%. Perhaps 6% of the population (not counting refugees) is of Rwandan descent, either Tutsi or Hutu. Most of them live in the south. The Karamajong account for 2%. The Bakonjo, Jopodhola, and Rundi groups each account for 2% of the population as well. About 1% is comprised of non-Africans, including Europeans, Asians, and Arabs.

9 LANGUAGES

English is the official national language. It is taught in grade schools, used in courts of law, and by most newspapers and some radio broadcasts. Bantu languages, particularly Luganda (the language of the Baganda), are widespread in the southern, western, and central areas. Luganda is the preferred language for native-language publications and may be taught in school. Nilotic languages are common in the north and northeast. Kiswahili (Swahili) and Arabic are also widely spoken.

10 RELIGIONS

Christianity is the majority religion, practiced by about 85% of the population, with about 42% of all Christians being Roman Catholic and 36% Anglican. Other Christian denominations include Seventh-Day Adventist, Church of Jesus Christ of Latter-Day Saints, Jehovah's Witness, Baptist, Orthodox, and Pentecostal. Muslims account for about 12% of the population; most are of the Sunni sect. Others practice traditional African religions, which are more common in the north and west of Uganda. There are also small numbers of Hindus, Baha'is, and Jews. Traditional beliefs and customs are often practiced in conjunction with other established faiths. Freedom of religion is provided for in the constitution. All religious organizations must register with the government to obtain legal status, which can be done either under the Trustees Incorporation Act or through the Ministry of Internal Affairs Nongovernmental Organizations Board. Good Friday, Easter Monday, Eid al-Fitr, Eid al-Adha, and Christmas are observed as national holidays.

¹¹TRANSPORTATION

The CIA reported that Uganda had a total of 70,746 km (43,960 mi) of roads in 2003 (most recent information available as of March 2012), of which 16,272 km (10,111 mi) were paved. Many roads are not in service due to damage, shortages of fuel and spare parts, and closing of repair and maintenance facilities. There are seven vehicles per 1,000 people in the country. There are 5 airports with paved runaways and 41 with unpaved runaways. According to the World Bank, in 2009 these airports transported 64,234 passengers.

A landlocked country, Uganda depends on links with Tanzania and Kenya for access to the sea. The main rail line runs from Tororo in the east through Jinja and Kampala to the Kilembe copper mines near Kasese. The northwest line runs from Tororo to Pakwach. Eastward from Tororo, the line crosses into Kenya and runs to the port of Mombasa. According to the CIA, as of 2010 Uganda had 1,244 km (773 mi) of railways.

Steamships formerly carried cargo and passengers along the country's major lakes and navigable rivers, but there is no regular service on the Nile. Three Ugandan train ferries ply Lake Victoria, connecting at Kisumu, Kenya, and Mwanza, Tanzania. Important ports and harbors include Entebbe, Jinja, and Port Bell.

¹²HISTORY

San-like peoples were among the Uganda region's earliest inhabitants. Over the centuries, however, they were overcome by waves of migrants, beginning with the Cushitic speakers, who probably penetrated the area around 1000 BC. In the first millennium AD, Bantu-speaking peoples moved into the highland areas of East Africa, where they cultivated the banana as a food crop. After AD 1000, two other migrations filtered through the area: Nilotic-speaking Sudanic people and Luo speakers.

In the region south and west of the Nile, a number of polities formed, most of them strongly centralized. North and east of the Nile, political organization tended to be decentralized. In the south, the kingdom of Bunyoro was the most powerful and extensive, but in the 18th century the neighboring kingdom of Buganda began to challenge its supremacy. The two states were engaged in a critical power struggle when the British explorers John Hanning Speke and J. A. Grant reached Buganda in 1862. They had been preceded some years earlier by Arab ivory and slave traders. Other foreigners soon followed. Sir Samuel Baker entered Uganda from the north shortly after Speke's departure. Baker described a body of water, which he named Lake Albert. Baker returned to Uganda in 1872–73 as a representative of the Egyptian government, which

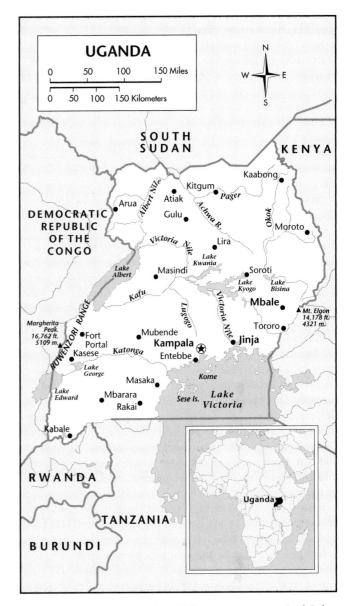

LOCATION: 4°7′ N to 1°30′ S; 29°33′ to 35°20′E. BOUNDARY LENGTHS: South Sudan, 435 kilometers (271 miles); Kenya, 933 kilometers (578 miles); Tanzania, 396 kilometers (247 miles); Rwanda, 169 kilometers (105 miles); Democratic Republic of the Congo (DROC), 765 kilometers (475 miles).

was pursuing a policy of expansion up the Nile. The first Christian missionaries, members of the Church Missionary Society of Great Britain, came to Buganda in 1877. They were followed in 1879 by the Roman Catholic White Fathers. The missionaries were welcomed by the *kabaka* (ruler) of Buganda, Mutesa I, who hoped to gain their support or the support of their countrymen against the Egyptian threat from the north. When the missionaries displayed no interest in military matters and the Egyptian danger was removed by the Mahdist rising in the Sudan in the early 1880s, Mutesa became less amenable. His son, Mwanga, who succeeded Mutesa on the latter's death in 1884, was even more hostile, fearing the influence exerted over his subjects by both the missionaries and the Arab traders. The kabaka, therefore, began to persecute the Bagandan adherents of Christianity and Islam. Both sets of converts joined forces to drive the kabaka from his country in

1888. A few weeks later, the Christians were expelled by the Muslims. Mwanga then appealed to the Christians for help, and they finally succeeded in restoring him to power early in 1890.

In 1888, the Imperial British East African Co. was granted a charter and authorized to administer the British sphere of East Africa. The Anglo-German agreement of 1890 officially outlined imperial spheres of influence in East Africa. By that agreement, what is now Uganda and Kenya were to be considered British spheres and Tanganyika a German sphere. In 1890, Capt. F. D. Lugard was sent to Buganda to establish the company's influence there. Lugard obtained Mwanga's agreement to a treaty that placed Buganda under the company's protection. Shortly afterward, however, lack of funds compelled the company to withdraw its representatives from Buganda.

In 1894, the kingdom of Buganda became a British protectorate, which was extended in 1896 to cover Bunyoro and most of what is now Uganda. In 1897, Mwanga led a revolt against British encroachments; he was quickly defeated and deposed. His infant son, Daudi Chwa, succeeded him, and a regency was established to govern Buganda under British supervision. Under the Uganda Agreement of 1900, Buganda was ruled indirectly by the British, who in turn used the Baganda leadership as agents to extend British control indirectly throughout Uganda. The agreement confirmed the privileged position of Buganda in Uganda and of the traditional chiefs in Buganda. Subsequent treaties for indirect rule were concluded with the remaining kingdoms over a period of years. Buganda's rebuff of British policies following World War II marked the beginning of a conflict over the place of Buganda within the future evolution of the territory. Kabaka Mutesa II was deposed in 1953 when he refused to force his chiefs to cooperate with the British. He was restored to power in 1955 under a compromise agreement.

It was only at the constitutional conference convened in London in October 1961 that a place was agreed for Buganda in a federal relationship to central government. It was also decided at this conference that Uganda should obtain independence on 9 October 1962. At a second constitutional conference in June 1962, Buganda agreed to scale down its demands over financial matters and ended its threats of secession from the central government. In August, a federal relationship with the kingdom of Ankole was agreed upon, and the agreement used as a model for dealing with the remaining two kingdoms, Bunyoro and Toro.

On 9 October 1963, an amendment to the constitution abolished the post of governor-general and replaced it with that of president. Sir Edward Mutesa (Kabaka Mutesa II of Buganda) became Uganda's first president. In February 1966, the 1962 constitution was suspended and the prime minister, Milton Obote, assumed all powers of government. Parliament formally abrogated the 1962 constitution on 15 April 1966 and adopted a new constitution, which created the post of president and commander-in-chief; Obote was elected to fill this position on the same day. Obote declared a state of emergency in Buganda following a clash between the police and dissident Baganda protesting the new constitution. On 24 May, Ugandan troops took control of the kabaka's palace, and the kabaka fled the country.

Further revisions to the constitution enacted in June 1967 abolished the federal relationship of Buganda and the other kingdoms, making Uganda a unitary state. Uganda became a republic with an executive president, who would be concurrently head of state and government. Following a failed assassination attempt on Obote in December 1969, parliament declared a state of emergency on 22 December. Ten opposition leaders were arrested and all opposition parties were banned.

Amin Seizes Power

On 25 January 1971, while Obote was out of the country, Maj. Gen. Idi Amin led a successful military coup. Obote was received by Tanzania as a political exile. The Second Republic of Uganda was proclaimed on 17 March 1971, with Amin as president. In September 1972, Ugandans who had followed Obote into exile in Tanzania staged an abortive invasion. They were immediately overpowered, but tensions between Uganda and Tanzania remained high.

Under Amin, Uganda suffered a reign of terror that had claimed 50,000–300,000 lives by 1977, according to Amnesty International. Idi Amin expelled Asian noncitizens from Uganda in August 1972 causing international tension, especially with the United Kingdom. Expulsion of numerous British nationals in 1973 and the nationalization of UK-owned enterprises beginning in December 1972, further aggravated relations with the United Kingdom. An Israeli commando raid on Entebbe Airport on 3–4 July 1976, which freed 91 Israeli passengers and 12 crew members held captive by pro-Palestinian radicals in a hijacked aircraft, was a severe blow to the prestige of Amin, who was suspected of collusion with the hijackers (20 Ugandan troops were killed during the raid). The expulsion of the Asians took a heavy toll on trade and the economy. Agricultural and industrial production also fell, and educational and health facilities suffered from the loss of skilled personnel. The collapse in 1977, essentially because of political differences, of the 10-year-old East African Community (members-Kenya, Tanzania, and Uganda) also dealt a blow to Uganda's economy.

In late October 1978, Ugandan forces invaded Tanzanian territory, but Tanzanian forces, supported by anti-Amin rebels, struck back and by January 1979 had entered Ugandan territory. Kampala was taken on 11 April 1979, and all of Uganda was cleared of Amin's forces by the end of May; Amin fled first to Libya and later to Saudi Arabia. Yusuf K. Lule, an educator, formed a provisional government but was ousted on 20 June in favor of Godfrey Binaisa. On 13 May 1980, a military takeover ousted Binaisa and installed Paulo Muwanga. parliamentary elections administered by Muwanga and other supporters of Obote, who returned from exile in Tanzania, were held on 10 December 1980. The election results, which opponents claimed were fraudulent, gave Obote's Uganda People's Congress (UPC) a clear majority, and he was sworn in as president on 15 December 1980. A period of reconstruction followed, and Tanzanian troops left in mid-1981. Security remained precarious, however. An undisciplined soldiery committed many outrages, and antigovernment guerrilla groups, especially the National Resistance Army (NRA), which was supported from abroad by Lule and Binaisa, remained active.

Obote's second term in office was marked by continued fighting between the army and guerrilla factions. As many as 100,000 people may have died as a result of massacres, starvation, and hindrance of relief operations. International groups denounced the regime for human rights abuses. On 27 July 1985, Obote was overthrown in a military coup and Lt. Gen. Tito Okello, commander of the armed forces, was installed as president.

The NRA continued fighting, however, and on 26 January 1986 it occupied Kampala. Three days later, NRA leader Yoweri Museveni assumed the presidency. By April the National Resistance Movement (NRM) government was in control of most of the country, but armed supporters of the Obote, Amin, and Okello regimes remained active in northern and northeastern Uganda, as well as opposition from Karamojong separatists and prophetic religious movements, most notably the Holy Spirit rebels of Alice Lakwena in 1987. After 1990, except for tiny groups of bandits, rebel military action was almost eliminated. However, Museveni resisted introducing a multiparty constitution advocating "no-party government" instead. In late August 1992, parliament formalized the ban on party politics which officials of the UPC and Democratic Party, DP (both abolished by Museveni in 1986) rejected at a press conference. Nonetheless, parties became more active, despite the ban and police action.

Although lauded by western countries as a new breed of African leader, and Uganda as a role model for African development, there was growing criticism of Museveni for his lack of democratic credentials. In July 1993, parliament enacted Constituent Assembly Statute No. 6, the basis for nonparty elections to choose a constituent assembly, which would consider the draft constitution released in December 1992 by an appointed commission. In a secret ballot election on 28 March 1994, Ugandans elected 214 delegates to the 288-member assembly. Also included were 10 delegates appointed by the president, 56 representing interest groups, and 8 representing 4 parties that had contested the 1980 election. In addition, the government introduced constitutional changes allowing the Baganda to restore their monarchy purely for ceremonial purposes. Ronald Mutebi, son of the former king, was installed as Kabaka on 31 July 1993. The monarchies had been abolished in the 1967 constitution. A second king was restored and a third was rejected by government.

In October of 1995, the new constitution was finally enacted. It replaced the interim National Resistance Council with a permanent parliament, and made minor changes in executive power, but its most noticed element was the prohibition of political party activity for five years. The first popular elections for president since independence were held on 9 May 1996. Museveni won with 74% of the vote, Paul Ssemogerere got 24%, and Muhammad Mayanja 2%. Nonparty parliamentary elections for the 276-member (214 elected, 62 nominated by special groups) house followed on 27 June 1999. The elections were peaceful and orderly, but election conditions, including restrictions on political party activities, resulted in flaws. Elections were held again in March 2001 with Museveni claiming victory with 69% of the vote to 28% for Kizza Besigye. The results were upheld despite objections by the opposition.

By June 2003, there was growing concern over the government's inability to build political consensus in the country and to maintain peace and security. In the north, the Lord's Resistance Army (LRA), a cult-like Christian rebel group operated from bases in southern Sudan, and in western Uganda, the Allied Democratic Forces (ADF) stepped up rebel attacks from the DRC. Other rebel groups included Rwanda Hutu rebels, Uganda National Rescue Front-II, and the Uganda National Front/Army. Members of these rebel groups murdered, raped, kidnapped, tortured, and abducted children using them as combatants, sex, and labor slaves. UNICEF estimated that the LRA and ADF abducted over 4,900 men, women and children since 1987, most of whom remained missing.

Museveni has tried both diplomatic and military means to end the fighting. He reluctantly accepted an Amnesty Bill in January 2000, which provided for pardon to any rebels who surrendered their arms within six months. Three months later, no rebels had complied. A highly publicized all-out offensive in 2002 also failed to achieve its goals, and independent observers accused government troops of killing innocent civilians including women and children. In 2004, three opposition groups-Reform Agenda, the Parliamentary Advocacy Reform (PAFO), and the National Democratic Forum (NDF)-merged to form the FDC, which became the main challenger to Museveni's NRM party. In 2005, the parliament approved two constitutional amendments that restored a multiparty system and removed the two-term limit for the president. The elimination of the two-term limit, which opposition groups and donors stridently opposed, was significant in that it allowed Museveni to run for another term. Uganda had operated under a no-party system since 1980. Subsequently, some 50 parties formed and began to campaign in the run-up to the 2006 elections. In August, the parliament also approved additional changes to the constitution that increased the power of the executive vis-à-vis the legislature.

The February 2006 polls marked the first multiparty presidential and parliamentary elections in 26 years. In the run-up, three people were killed as a result of violent clashes between security personnel and opposition supporters. Voting day itself was mostly peaceful though many irregularities such as unsealed ballot boxes, under-age voting, and military patrols in the vicinity of polling stations were reported. Thousands of domestic and international observers from the EU, AU, United States and Commonwealth nations observed the polling. Some 80–90% of polling stations were monitored. As the results were announced the following day, the FDC alleged voter-list tampering. International observer missions, though not uniform in their assessments, generally rated the exercise as short of free and fair. The main complaint by observers was that the playing field had been made extremely unlevel mostly because of the rape and treason charges leveled at Dr. Kizza Besigye, Museveni's opponent, by government agencies. In March 2006 the rape charges were dropped. However, the treason trial was due to begin on 15 March 2006. Ironically, Mr. Besigye, who had fled Uganda after losing the 2001 poll, had formerly been Museveni's personal doctor, and the two were allies in the guerrilla war. The official results gave Museveni the victory by a margin of 59.28% of the vote to Dr. Besigye's 37.36%. The FDC immediately challenged the results, but police surrounded FDC headquarters to prevent a mass protest. Voter turnout was 68.6%.

In the 2006 parliamentary contest, the NRM ruling party took the majority of the seats with 202 to 40 for the FDC and 49 seats to other smaller opposition groups. This result assured the president's party of a two-thirds majority. In a hotly contested race in a district in southwest Uganda, the first lady, Janet Museveni, became a member of parliament by beating an FDC incumbent of ten years. Evidence that she used state resources during her campaign did not reverse the outcome. Although the FDC accused the NRM of having stolen the election, it vowed to pursue change through legal and constitutional means. A separate FDC tally showed Museveni winning 51% of the vote with enough votes to exceed a run-off by only 600,000-which the FDC claimed it could prove was rigged.

Internationally, a cease-fire with President Joseph Kabila of DROC signed in 2003 was threatened by alleged evidence of rebel ADF bases in neighboring Ituri province. Additionally, though most Ugandan troops were withdrawn from Congolese territory in early 2003, the Ugandan government was likely to send troops back in if Rwanda were to do the same. Relations with Sudan continued to be unsettled because of unanswered questions following the crash of John Garang's helicopter in July 2005. Garang, former leader of the SPLA, had been a long-time friend of Museveni, but speculation that Uganda was connected to the crash chilled relations with the South Sudan government. For Uganda, this meant that insecurity in the north would likely continue, especially with the rebel group, the Lord's Resistance Army (LRA) able to operate from Sudanese territory.

In July 2006, peace talks between the government and the LRA began in southern Sudan. On 26 August, the two sides signed a truce aimed at ending the conflict. A cease-fire came into force on 29 August. Subsequent peace talks were marred when participants walked out of negotiations. In November 2006, Uganda rejected a UN report accusing the army of using indiscriminate and excessive force in its campaign to disarm tribal warriors in the northeastern region of Karamoja. In March 2007, the UN World Food Program announced it would have to cut food rations in half to more than 1 million people displaced by war in the north. In March 2007, Ugandan peacekeepers were sent to Somalia as part of an African Union (AU) mission to help stabilize the country.

On 11 July 2010, two large bombs exploded in Uganda's capital, Kampala, killing seventy-four people and injuring dozens more. Al-Shabab, a Somalia-based Islamist group, claimed responsibility for the attacks, saying that the bombings were designed to send a message to the governments of Uganda and Burundi. Uganda and Burundi, along with several other African nations, have drawn the ire of al-Shabab for contributing troops to the AU mission in Somalia—a coalition of African nations attempting to bolster the fragile Somali government.

Instability in South Sudan throughout 2011 posed a risk to the Ugandan economy, which counts Sudan as its primary export partner. Further unrest risked increasing the number of South Sudanese refugees in Uganda.

13 GOVERNMENT

Following Gen. Amin's coup of 25 January 1971, provisions of the 1967 constitution dealing with the executive and legislature were suspended, and Amin ruled by decree. As commander-in-chief of the armed forces and president of the military government, he exercised virtually all power. Following Amin's defeat, the Uganda High Court in 1980 declared a modified version of the 1967 constitution to be the law of the land. The constitution was amended in May 1985, but it was suspended with the fall of the Obote government in July, when the National Assembly was dissolved. A 270-person National Resistance Council was established in 1986 to act as the nation's legislative body pending the holding of elections. Nonpartisan elections for the NRC were held in February

1989. There were 382 members, 216 elected and 166 appointed by the president. An appointed cabinet (including members of the banned opposition parties) advised the president. He also sought advice from and consensus with key interest groups and institutions on important policy issues, especially from the National Resistance Army.

The new constitution was enacted in October 1995, replacing the NRC with an elected parliament while leaving the power and structure of the executive largely unchanged. It provided for a 276-member body, with ensured representation for special interest groups (including 39 seats for women, 10 for the Army, 5 for the disabled, 5 for youth, and 3 for trade unions). By 2003 the number and proportion of appointed seats had been altered. In 2005, parliament voted two significant changes to the constitution that restored multipartyism and revoked the two-term limit for presidents.

Parliamentary elections were first held on 27 June 1996 and again on 26 June 2001. The parliamentary term is five years. The 2011 legislative body numbered 375 members—238 members by popular vote, 112 women directly elected, and 25 nominated by legally established special interest groups.

14 POLITICAL PARTIES

The Uganda People's Congress (UPC), founded in 1959, was the leading political party of the pre-Amin era. At the time of independence it formed a ruling coalition with the Kabaka Yekka (The King Only), which drew its support from the Baganda. The opposition party was the Democratic Party (DP), founded in 1953. The marriage of convenience between the UPC and the Kabaka Yekka deteriorated, and in February 1966, Prime Minister Milton Obote, who had been the head of the UPC, suspended the constitution, deposed the president and vice president, and began a move to power, which culminated in the proclamation of the Republic of Uganda under a new constitution adopted in September 1967. The political situation under Obote continued to deteriorate, and after an attempt on his life, Obote's government banned the opposition parties and arrested 10 of their leaders. Uganda was subsequently declared a one-party state in 1969, the UPC remaining as the only legal party. After the military overthrow of the Obote government on 25 January 1971, Maj. Gen. Amin outlawed all political parties.

After the overthrow of Amin, four political parties took part in the parliamentary elections held in December 1980. The UPC was declared to have won 74 seats in the National Assembly; the DP, 51; the Uganda Patriotic Movement, 1; and the Conservative Party, 0. These parties, as well as Yoweri Museveni's National Resistance Movement and the Uganda Freedom Movement, were represented in the cabinet appointed in 1986. The government ordered all parties to suspend active operations, however, and mandated that elections would not be held before 1989.

By 1991, however, party activity, although banned, began to increase. Top officials of the DP and UPC were arrested in January 1992. Museveni insisted that no party activity could precede the new constitution. In August, the DP and UPC held a joint press conference to denounce parliament's formalization of the ban. President Museveni declared that parties were not allowed to participate in either the presidential election or the parliamentary elections held in May and June of 1996, respectively. Nonetheless, 156 of the 276 members of the parliament elected in 1996 were considered to be supporters of General Museveni. The UPC, DP, and CP remained the most important opposition parties.

In June 2000, the no-party system was subjected to a national referendum. Despite accusations of vote rigging and manipulation by the opposition, Ugandans approved it. They also reelected Museveni to a second five-year term in March 2001. In the 303-member National Assembly, 214 seats were directly elected by popular vote, and 81 were nominated by legally established special interest groups including women (56), army (10), disabled (5), youth (5), labor (5), and ex officio members (8). Campaigning by party was not allowed.

In May 2003, the National Executive Committee recommended that subject to another national referendum in 2004, parties be free to operate. Nonetheless, the United States was particularly concerned about the lack of political space and freedom of speech that Museveni's Movement has allowed other political forces. The United States also expressed its disapproval of any attempt by Museveni or his Movement to tamper with the constitution to legalize a run for a third term. Nevertheless, the February 2006 elections showed the grassroots strength of the reconstituted National Resistance Movement (NRM), which despite opposition (FDC) complaints, was confirmed in its victory by parallel vote tabulation. One deciding factor in the outcome, however, was a highly unlevel playing field characterized by the use of state resources, intimidation, and a smear campaign on FDC candidate Dr. Besigye that was launched by the ruling NRM party.

In the February 2011 presidential election, Museveni was reelected to a new term with 68% of the vote. Kizza Besigye from the Forum for Democratic Change gained 26% of the vote. Besigye called the election a sham, accusing the government of ballot stuffing and intimidation at the polls. Observers from the African Union agreed that the vote was neither free nor fair. The parliamentary elections held at the same time resulted in a major victory for the NRM with 279 seats out of 372. The FDC won 34 seats, followed by the Democratic Party with 11 seats, the Ugandan People's Congress with 9 seats, the Conservative Party with 1 seat, and the Justice Forum with 1 seat. Thirty-seven seats were won by independent candidates.

The next elections were scheduled for 2016.

15 LOCAL GOVERNMENT

Until the adoption of the 1967 constitution, local government in Buganda was conducted on behalf of the kabaka by six ministers, advised by the *lukiko* (Buganda council) and by a hierarchy of chiefs. With the abolition of the federal system of government in 1967, Buganda was divided into four districts, and the kabaka's government was dissolved. The federal status of the kingdoms of Ankole, Bunyoro, and Toro was also abolished. Under that constitution, Uganda was divided into 18 districts.

In 1973, President Amin instituted a new system of provincial government establishing 10 provinces subdivided into 26 districts. Later Kampala became Central Province. In 1980 the number of districts increased to 33, and in March 2000, to 39. By 2002, there were 45 districts and by 2006, the number rose to 56. In 2011 there were 112 districts.

Since 1986, National Resistance Movement committees have played leading roles in local and district affairs. In early March 1992, local council elections were held nationwide. Political par-

ties were not allowed to campaign, although many candidates could be identified as members of particular parties. There was disappointment on the part of donors with logistical delays, irregularities in distribution of electoral material and voting, confusion over electoral laws, and electoral violence during the 2002 local elections.

16 JUDICIAL SYSTEM

In 1995, the government restored the legal system to one based on English common law and customary law. At the lowest level are three classes of courts presided over by magistrates. Above these is the chief magistrate's court, which hears appeals from magistrates. The High Court hears appeals and has full criminal and civil jurisdiction. It consists of a chief justice and a number of puisne justices. The three-member Court of Appeal hears appeals from the High Court. A military court system handles offenses involving military personnel. Village resistance councils (RCs) mediate disputes involving land ownership and creditor claims. These councils have at times overstepped their authority in order to hear criminal cases including murder and rape. RC decisions are appealable to magistrate's courts, but ignorance of the right to appeal and the time and cost involved make such appeals rare. In practice, a large backlog of cases delays access to a speedy trial. Although the president retains some control of appointments to the judiciary, the courts appear to engage in independent decision-making and the government normally complies with court decisions. Uganda accepts the jurisdiction of the International Court of Justice with reservations.

17 ARMED FORCES

After Amin's regime was overthrown, a Commonwealth training force was sent to reorganize the Ugandan Army, which proved difficult. In 1987, the National Resistance Army (NRA) was established as the national army in the wake of another civil war. Thousands of defeated guerillas were given amnesty and integrated into the NRA, swelling its ranks to as many as 70,000–100,000 men, armed with outdated US, UK, and Russian weapons. The International Institute for Strategic Studies reports that armed forces in Uganda totaled 45,000 members in 2011, all of which are members of the Ugandan People's Defense Force. Armed forces represented 0.3% of the labor force in Uganda. Defense spending totaled $929.8 million and accounted for 2.2% of GDP.

18 INTERNATIONAL COOPERATION

On 25 October 1962, Uganda became the 110th member of the UN; it is a member of ECA and several nonregional specialized agencies, such as the World Bank, IAEA, FAO, ILO, UNESCO, UNHCR, UNIDO, and WHO. Uganda participated in the establishment of the African Development Bank. It is a member of the Commonwealth of Nations, the ACP Group, the WTO, the East African Development Bank, the Islamic Development Bank, the Organization of the Islamic Conference (OIC), COMESA, the New Partnership for Africa's Development (NEPAD), and G-77. Kampala was the headquarters of the African Union (formerly the Organization of African Unity) for the 1975 summit meeting, and then president Idi Amin was the OAU president for 1975–76.

Uganda generally supports peace efforts in neighboring countries. Relations with Rwanda, Congo and Sudan are sometimes tense, primarily due to unrest in those nations. Uganda fully supports the international war on terrorism. The country is part of the Nonaligned Movement. In environmental cooperation, Uganda is part of the Basel Convention, the Convention on Biological Diversity, Ramsar, CITES, the Kyoto Protocol, the Montréal Protocol, the Nuclear Test Ban Treaty, and the UN Conventions on the Law of the Sea, Climate Change, and Desertification.

¹⁹ECONOMY

Uganda's economy is agriculture based, with agriculture employing over 80% of the population and generating 90% of export earnings. Coffee is the main export crop, with tea and cotton other agricultural products. Uganda also has mineral deposits of copper and cobalt, which contributed 30% of export earnings during the 1960s, although the mining sector is now only a minor contributor to the economy.

The upheavals of the 1970s and the troubles of the 1980s left the economy in disarray. However, economic reforms begun in 1986 have resulted in important progress. The government made significant strides in liberalizing markets and releasing government influence during the 1990s, although some administrative controls remain. Monopolies were abolished in the coffee, cotton, power generation, and telecommunications sectors and restrictions on foreign exchange were removed. The reforms were targeted at taming inflation and boosting export earnings. The reforms succeeded in improving the economy and gained the confidence of international lending agencies. In 2000, donors rewarded Uganda with a debt relief package worth about $2 billion.

The economy has posted growth rates in the GDP averaging 6.9% from 1988 to 1998, 6% from 2000 to 2007, and 6.3% from 2009 to 2011. Still, Uganda is one of the poorest countries in the world, heavily dependent on foreign aid. High growth rates are necessary to balance strong population growth.

With help from foreign countries and international agencies, Uganda has been able to stabilize and strengthen its economy. To continue that trend, in 2010 the World Bank offered $1.97 billion in loans over a five-year period to cover the costs of the nation's new National Development Plan, which was launched in April 2010. Development projects were expected to include the expansion of public infrastructure, the establishment of workforce training programs, and the implementation of measures to improve good governance.

Uganda is a member of the East African Community (EAC), a regional intergovernmental organization established by Kenya, Uganda, and Tanzania in 2000, and expanded to include Rwanda and Burundi in 2007. The EAC Common Market Protocol went into effect on 1 July 2010, under which the members have agreed to implement legislation that will remove barriers to the transport of goods, services, and workers across borders. The development of the common market is one step in the EAC's plan to increase trade to, from, and within the region and to establish a strong political federation by 2015. EAC members hope to launch a new, single, shared currency by 2012.

²⁰INCOME

The CIA estimated that in 2010 the GDP of Uganda was $42.15 billion. The CIA defines GDP as the value of all final goods and services produced within a nation in a given year and computed on the basis of purchasing power parity (PPP) rather than value as measured on the basis of the rate of the exchange based on current dollars. The per capita GDP was estimated at $1,300. The annual growth rate of GDP was 6.4% in 2011. The average inflation rate was 9.4%. It was estimated that agriculture accounted for 23.6% of GDP, industry 24.5%, and services 51.9%. According to the World Bank, remittances from citizens living abroad totaled $749.7 million or about $22 per capita and accounted for approximately 1.8% of GDP. The World Bank reports that in 2009, household consumption in Uganda totaled $11.9 billion or about $343 per capita, measured in current US dollars rather than PPP. Household consumption includes expenditures of individuals, households, and nongovernmental organizations on goods and services, excluding the purchases of dwellings. It was estimated that household consumption was growing at an average annual rate of 12.1%.

As of 2011 a study by the World Bank reported that actual individual consumption in Uganda was 82.2% of GDP and accounted for 0.06% of world consumption. By comparison, the United States accounted for 25.44% of world individual consumption. The World Bank also estimated that 33.8% of Uganda's GDP was spent on food and beverages, 19.6% on housing and household furnishings, 2.5% on clothes, 4.5% on health, 5.1% on transportation, 1.6% on communications, 2.0% on recreation, 2.5% on restaurants and hotels, and 1.5% on miscellaneous goods and services and purchases from abroad.

²¹LABOR

As of 2010, Uganda had a total labor force of 15.51 million people. Within that labor force, CIA estimates in 1999 (most recent available information as of February 2012) noted that 82% were employed in agriculture, 5% in industry, and 13% in the service sector. The minimum working age is 18 but many children work out of economic necessity and because school fees are so high. A large percentage of children do not attend school. Most children work in the informal sector. Wage earners are an extremely small percentage of the workforce. In this sector, the work week is set at 40 hours. Most workers supplement their income with second jobs and family farming. Occupational safety regulations have existed since 1954 but the government lacks the resources to implement them.

²²AGRICULTURE

Roughly 30% of the total land is dedicated to agriculture, and the country's major crops include coffee, tea, cotton, tobacco, cassava (tapioca), potatoes, corn, millet, pulses, and cut flowers. Cereal production in 2009 amounted to 2.8 million tons, fruit production 10.2 million tons, and vegetable production 960,412 tons. Bananas are a leading non-cereal crop and serve as a staple food for more than 70% of the population. However, the banana harvest is susceptible to banana xanthomonas wilt, a bacterial disease that has led to a loss of more than $200 million in export revenues from 2001 through 2010. In July 2010, a group of Ugandan researchers announced the development of genetically modified bananas that show promising resistance to the deadly wilt. The modified bananas, containing genes from sweet peppers, have shown promise in laboratory testing, but have not yet been submitted for larger field trials. Even if such trials prove successful, the government will need to establish legislation pertaining to genetically modified agricultural products before the new bananas can be introduced for large scale planting, harvest, and export. Coffee is still an important export earner for Uganda. Production of robusta, which was cultivated by the Baganda before the arrival of the Arabs and British, and some arabica varieties of coffee provides the most important single source of income for more than one million Ugandan farmers and is the principal earner of foreign exchange.

23 ANIMAL HUSBANDRY

The UN Food and Agriculture Organization (FAO) reported that Uganda dedicated 5.1 million hectares (12.6 million acres) to permanent pasture or meadow in 2009. During that year, the country tended 28.3 million chickens, 7.6 million head of cattle, and 2.3 million pigs. The production from these animals amounted to 105,975 tons of beef and veal, 105,328 tons of pork, 37,696 tons of poultry, 16,001 tons of eggs, and 706,160 tons of milk. Uganda also produced 14,847 tons of cattle hide. The tsetse fly, which infests about 30% of Uganda, limits livestock production . Additionally, cattle rustling remains a problem. The livestock sector has been disrupted by armed rebels, but the UN, EU, Denmark, and several international development banks are contributing to its revitalization.

24 FISHING

Many persons find employment in fishing and the marketing of fish, and many fishermen sell their catch to the main distribution centers. Most fish are caught from dugouts or hand-propelled canoes. Lake Victoria and Lake Kyoga are the major commercial fishing areas; Nile perch and Nile tilapia are the most abundant species. The fishing industry has benefited from a large ice-making plant at Soroti. In 2009, the total annual capture was 400,000 tons and aquaculture production was 76,654 tons.

25 FORESTRY

Approximately 15% of Uganda is covered by forest. About half of the forested area is savanna woodland. The UN FAO estimated the 2009 roundwood production at 3.49 million cu m (123.2 million cu ft). Most wood is burned for fuel. The value of all forest products, including roundwood, totaled $6.27 million.

26 MINING

Mining and quarrying exports amounted to $55 million in 2009. By mid-2009, the government had issued 498 mining licenses, generating $2.4 million in government revenue. In recent years, Uganda has been known to produce cobalt (95% of which was exported), limonite and other iron ore, niobium, steel, tantalum, tin, tungsten, apatite, gypsum, kaolin, brick clays and other clays, hydrated lime, quicklime, limestone, pozzolanic materials (used for pozzolanic cement), and salt (by evaporation of lakes and brine wells).

Gold production began in 1992. Mine gold output (metal content) in 2009 was estimated at 25 kg. In May 2010, Uganda opened its first gold refinery with hopes of tapping into the market by processing raw gold from the Democratic Republic of Congo and other countries in the region. Located in Kampala, the refinery is operated by the Russian-owned Victoria Gold Star and has a capacity to handle 1.2 tons of raw gold per month, producing about

10 kilograms of refined gold per day. The plant also serves as a hopeful investment in the nation's own gold market, as new gold deposits were discovered in the western region in 2009.

Limestone output in 2009 was estimated at 450,000 metric tons. Limestone resources at the largest deposits—Hima, Tororo Hill, and Bukiribo—totaled 46.1 million tons. Output of hydraulic cement in 2009 was estimated at 620,000 tons, down slightly from 650,000 metric tons in 2008; and columbite-tantalite ore and concentrate (gross weight) was estimated at 275 kg. In addition, Uganda presumably produced copper content of slag, corundum, garnet, gemstones, gravel, marble, ruby, sand, and vermiculite. No wolfram, tin, or tungsten was produced in 2009. Extraction of copper was halted in 1980.

The Namekhela high-quality vermiculite deposit had resources of 5 million tons. Pyrochlore resources amounted to 6 million tons. Iron ore resources in Sukulu were 45.7 million tons at an average grade of 62% iron; the Muko deposit, worked by artisanal miners, contained 30 million tons at a grade 61–67% iron; and there were additional resources at Kyanyamuzinda, Metuli, Mugabuzi, and Wambogwe. Inferred resources of wolframite were 20 million tons; gypsum deposits totaled 5.5 million tons; marble resources, 10 million tons; the Sukulu phosphate deposit had resources of 230 million tons; and there were occurrences of silica sand deposits. The abandoned Kilembe copper mine had proven reserves of 5 million tons, and its tailings contained 5.5 million tons. A pilot study in 1991 attempted to process the tailings for cobalt and copper, using a natural strain of bacteria to separate the cobalt metal.

The UN Security Council accused Ugandan government officials, military officers, and businessmen of illegally exploiting columbium, diamonds, gold, and tantalum from Democratic Republic of the Congo; the Ugandan government denied the accusations.

27 ENERGY AND POWER

The CIA reported in 2008 that Uganda produced 2.18 billion kWh of electricity and consumed 1.95 billion kWh, and exported 82.04 million kWh. Considerable oil reserves were discovered in the Lake Albert rift basin along the border with the Democratic Republic of Congo in 2006, with reserves estimated at 2.5 billion barrels. In 2010 the government announced plans to build a major oil refinery, expected to be operational by 2016. When completed, the refinery could meet a local demand of between 20,000 and 25,000 barrels per day. The refinery could eventually produce up to 200,000 barrels per day, providing large quantities for export.

28 INDUSTRY

Production of most industrial products declined in 1973, largely because of the expulsion of skilled Asian personnel. A precipitous decline followed, with output in 1985 little more than a third of the post-independence peak levels of 1970–72. Industrial production returned to growth during the 1990s and 2000s. The industrial growth rate was 8.9% in 2010. The agricultural industry produces cotton, coffee, tea, sugar, tobacco, edible oils, and dairy products. Ugandan industrial production also includes grain milling, brewing, vehicle assembly, textiles, steel, metal products, cement, soap, shoes, animal feed, fertilizers, paint, and matches.

The textile industry suffers from a lack of skilled labor but is being encouraged by funds from the EU and the Arab Development Bank. General Motors is assembling vehicles in Uganda, and Lonrho has returned to manage its previously owned brewery, to build an oil pipeline, and to join in agricultural marketing efforts. Coca-Cola, Pepsi, and Schweppes are producing soft drinks. A tannery will make Uganda self-sufficient in leather products. Batteries, canned foods, pharmaceuticals, and salt are among the other products being produced in Uganda's industrial sector.

29 SCIENCE AND TECHNOLOGY

According to the World Bank, there were no patent applications in science and technology as of 2009. Public financing of science was 0.39% of GDP. Uganda has a medical association, a child malnutrition unit, an agriculture research institute, a forestry research center, and a cotton research station in Kampala. An animal health research center and the Geological Survey and Mines Department are in Entebbe. Makerere University (founded originally in 1922 as a technical school at Kampala) has faculties of science, agriculture and forestry, technology, medicine, and veterinary science.

In 2011 Makerere University developed an environmentally friendly car (Kiira EV) using locally available material. The electric car, made by the Makerere University Vehicle Design Project, was finished and taken for its first test-drive in November 2011.

30 DOMESTIC TRADE

Most retail trade is accomplished through small shops supplied by small distributors. Consumer products are priced based on what the market will bear. Kampala is Uganda's main commercial center, but many concerns have their headquarters or regional offices in Nairobi, Kenya. Bootlegging of cassettes and videos is common. The market for smuggled goods, including fuel, clothing, electronics and other consumer goods, is rather large. English is the business language, although Swahili is often spoken as well. Products are marketed through radio and television advertising. Business hours are from 8 or 8:15 a.m. to 12:30 p.m. and from 2 to 5 p.m. Shops close on Sundays. Banking hours are 8:30 a.m. to 12:30 p.m., Monday-Friday.

31 FOREIGN TRADE

Uganda imported $4.264 billion worth of goods and services in 2010, while exporting $2.164 billion worth of goods and services as of 2010. Major import partners in 2010 were Kenya 17.1%, UAE 14.1%, China 8.5%, India 8.2%, South Africa 6.2%, Japan 5.9%, and Germany 4.3%. Its major export partners were Sudan 15.3%, Kenya 10.2%, Rwanda 8.5%, Democratic Republic of the Congo 7.8%, UAE 7.7%, Netherlands 6.4%, Germany 5.4% and Belgium 4.1%. Principal imports in 2010 included machinery equipment, iron, steel, vehicles and accessories, chemical and related products, medical supplies, petroleum and related products, vegetable products, animal fats and oil. Traditionally, coffee accounts for

Principal Trading Partners – Uganda (2010)				
(In millions of US dollars)				
Country	**Total**	**Exports**	**Imports**	**Balance**
World	7,804.1	3,106.7	4,697.4	-1,590.7
Kenya	750.4	182.2	568.1	-385.9
United Arab Emirates	608.4	138.1	470.4	-332.3
China	307.8	24.1	283.7	-259.6
India	283.4	10.1	273.3	-263.1
Sudan	273.5	273.2	0.3	272.9
Germany	239.4	97.1	142.3	-45.2
South Africa	239.1	31.7	207.4	-175.7
Japan	201.0	4.5	196.5	-192.0
Netherlands	173.8	114.7	59.1	55.6
United States	158.8	55.0	103.8	-48.8

(…) data not available or not significant.

(n.s.) not specified.

SOURCE: *2011 Direction of Trade Statistics Yearbook,* New York: United Nations, 2011.

nearly a third (31%) of Uganda's export commodities. Other exports include gold and tobacco.

32 BALANCE OF PAYMENTS

Uganda had a favorable balance of payments in the 1930s and throughout the postwar years—an unusual feature in an underdeveloped country. The favorable balance with the rest of the world, however, was diminished by deficits in trade with Kenya and Tanzania following independence. Uganda's payments position declined during the 1960s, and during the 1970s, years of deficit outnumbered those of surplus; moreover, the deficits were larger than the surpluses. Poor trade performances and mounting debt service led to a loss of reserves in the 1980s. From 1986 to 1990, merchandise exports fell by 56% (due largely to plummeting coffee prices), while merchandise imports increased by 30%, so that the

Balance of Payments – Uganda (2010)		
(In millions of US dollars)		
Current Account		**-1,739.9**
Balance on goods	-2,100.4	
Imports	-4,264.4	
Exports	2,164.0	
Balance on services	-525.0	
Balance on income	-304.9	
Current transfers	1,190.5	
Capital Account		**…**
Financial Account		**1,148.4**
Direct investment abroad	…	
Direct investment in Uganda	817.2	
Portfolio investment assets	…	
Portfolio investment liabilities	-110.5	
Financial derivatives	-1.4	
Other investment assets	-148.3	
Other investment liabilities	591.5	
Net Errors and Omissions		**295.1**
Reserves and Related Items		**296.4**

(…) data not available or not significant.

SOURCE: *Balance of Payment Statistics Yearbook 2011,* Washington, DC: International Monetary Fund, 2011.

trade deficit widened rapidly from $69 million to $440 million in just a few years. Trade deficits continued through the 1990s. Low levels of foreign investment, coupled with weak coffee exports, led to a decline in foreign exchange reserves and a deteriorating balance of payments position in the early 2000s. In 2010 Uganda had a foreign trade deficit of $1.3 billion, amounting to 0.9% of GDP. That year, the current account balance was -$1.456 billion.

33 BANKING AND SECURITIES

The Bank of Uganda was established on 16 May 1966 as the bank of issue, undertaking the function previously served by the East African Currency Board in Nairobi. The government-owned Uganda Commercial Bank (UCB) provided a full commercial banking service, complementary to and in competition with other commercial banks in the country. Uganda was rocked by a banking scandal in 1989. Lack of public confidence in the system was compounded by a prolonged period of high inflation, which caused rapid erosion in the value of money, and by the liquidity and insolvency problems of some banks.

The Uganda Development Bank is a government bank that channels long-term loans from foreign sources to Ugandan businesses. The East African Development Bank, the last remnant of the defunct East African Community, obtains funds from abroad for Kenya, Tanzania, and Uganda.

In 2010 the discount rate, the rate at which the central bank lends to financial institutions in the short term, was 14%. The commercial bank prime lending rate, the rate at which banks lend to customers, was 20.17%.

The government supported the establishment of a stock exchange in Kampala, and it inaugurated the Capital Markets Authority in 1995/96. The initial stage of capital market development concentrated on the interbank market and the sale of treasury bills, which the Bank of Uganda started selling in 1992 at weekly auctions. The exchange was officially opened in 1997 and became active in 2001.

34 INSURANCE

As of 2012, Uganda has 26 insurance companies. They provide an array of services including health, auto, life, travel, property and other insurance policies.

35 PUBLIC FINANCE

In 2010 the budget of Uganda included $2.457 billion in public revenue and $2.938 billion in public expenditures. The budget deficit amounted to 2.8% of GDP. Public debt was 20.4% of GDP, with $2.854 billion of the debt held by foreign entities. The fiscal year runs from 1 July to 30 June. The main sources of government revenue are export duties on coffee and cotton, import duties, income and profit taxes, excise taxes, and sales taxes. Deficits are chronic. Over half of public monies come from foreign aid.

36 TAXATION

Individual income is taxed progressively. In 2011 corporate income was taxed at 30%. Social security contributions were levied at a rate of 10%. Fuel taxes were included in the base price for fuel. Interest was taxed at 15%, property between 7 and 10%, and trad-

Public Finance – Uganda (2009)		
(In billions of shillings, budgetary central government figures)		
Revenue and Grants	**4,671.4**	**100.0%**
Tax revenue	3,662.3	78.4%
Social contributions	...	...
Grants	884.8	18.9%
Other revenue	124.3	2.7%
Expenditures	**4,949**	**100.0%**
General public services	1,303.2	26.3%
Defense	579.2	11.7%
Public order and safety	296.1	6.0%
Economic affairs	1,209.6	24.4%
Environmental protection	10.8	0.2%
Housing and community amenities	121	2.4%
Health	467.6	9.4%
Recreational, culture, and religion	4.2	0.1%
Education	806.2	16.3%
Social protection	151	3.1%

(…) data not available or not significant.

SOURCE: *Government Finance Statistics Yearbook 2010*, Washington, DC: International Monetary Fund, 2010.

ing licenses and stamp duties at varying rates. The value-added tax (VAT) was 18%.

37 CUSTOMS AND DUTIES

All imports and exports require licenses. As a party to the Lomé Convention, Uganda benefits from EU tariff preferences for its goods. Items that cannot be exported without permission from Uganda include scrap iron, wood charcoal, timber, coffee husks, fresh fish, and game trophies. Other restrictions exist when importing medications, firearms, live animals, endangered species, secondhand clothing, explosives, and plants; and when exporting minerals, fruit, and hides and skins. Prohibited imports include pornographic materials and used tires.

38 FOREIGN INVESTMENT

As a result of political and economic stability, Uganda registered an increase in foreign investment during the late 2000s. After a large number of Asian Ugandan companies were expropriated in 1972, a 1982 law provided for restoration of expropriated property to Asians who returned and for compensation to those who did not. A number of large Asian-owned enterprises resumed operations in 1986 as joint ventures, in which the government held 51% ownership. The United Kingdom group Mitchell Cotts also regained its nationalized property by participating in a similar joint venture. Further measures were taken in 1991 to recompense Asian Ugandans, and a new investment code designed to protect foreigners was issued in 1990. Ugandan law still allows for expropriation for public purposes, but investors are guaranteed compensation within 12 months. The Ugandan government has made attracting foreign investment a central part of its policy. Investors are deterred by pervasive corruption. Corruption infected the privatization process, which had greatly slowed due to a lack of transparency, rampant asset stripping, and the failures of a number of negotiations.

From 1998 to 2001, the average annual inflow of foreign direct investment (FDI) held rather steady at approximately $229 million a year, peaking in 2000 at $275 million. From 2000–2004 FDI averaged $231 million with the year 2004 registering $237 million. Foreign investors include those from the United Kingdom, India, Kenya and South Africa. In 2010 the Uganda Investment Authority reported that total investment in Ugandan projects reached $1.57 billion in 2009. Roughly $655 million of the total investment was licensed by local companies, while the remainder, over $914 million, came as foreign direct investment (FDI). The United Kingdom was the single largest source of FDI, followed by China.

³⁹ECONOMIC DEVELOPMENT

Following decades of political instability, Uganda outlined an economic development policy for the early 1990s. State investment was lowered by 42% from the previous plan, and the export sector was to be revived, particularly the nontraditional export sector. The investment budget was divided equally among the transport and communications sector, social infrastructure, agriculture, and the industry and tourism sector. Inflation, which ran at 240% in 1987 and 42% in mid-1992, was under 5% for 1998. This was further reduced to -0.3% in 2002 but was estimated to have risen to 9.7% in 2005. In 2009 inflation was 13.4%, and in 2010 it fell to 4 %. During the early 2000s, Uganda qualified for debt relief as part of the IMF and World Bank's Heavily Indebted Poor Countries (HIPC) initiative. The government began a Poverty Eradication Action Plan (PEAP) in 1997, with the goal of reducing the incidence of poverty to less than 10% of the population by 2017. PEAP was revised in 2000 and 2004. In 2010 the plan was extended to include development strategies for "structural transformation for growth and increased living standards."

⁴⁰SOCIAL DEVELOPMENT

A social security system was introduced in 1967 and amended in 1985. This program provides old-age and disability pensions for employees of firms with five or more workers. Voluntary coverage is available. Retirement benefits amount to total employee and employer contributions plus interest, payable in a lump sum. Work injury benefits are provided for all workers and are funded by the employer.

Women are accorded equal rights by law, but tradition limits their exercise of them. Under customary law, women may not own or inherit property and are not entitled to custody of their children after divorce. The children of Ugandan women married to foreigners are not entitled to Ugandan citizenship. This stipulation does not apply to Ugandan men married to foreigners. Domestic abuse and violence against women is common. The human rights situation in Uganda has improved in a few areas, but serious violations persist, including excessive force by security forces, incommunicado detention, and prolonged pretrial detention. Prison conditions are very poor.

⁴¹HEALTH

According to the CIA, life expectancy in Uganda was 53 years in 2011. The country spent 8.4% of its GDP on healthcare, amounting to $43 per person. There was 1 physician, 13 nurses and midwives, and 4 hospital beds per 10,000 inhabitants. The fertility rate was 6.3, while the infant mortality rate was 79 per 1,000 live births. In 2008 the maternal mortality rate, according to the World Bank, was 430 per 100,000 births. It was estimated that 68% of children were vaccinated against measles. The CIA calculated HIV/AIDS prevalence in Uganda to be about 6.5% in 2009.

Uganda's health indicators remained poor, even in comparison with those of other African countries. Containment of serious diseases, such as cholera, dysentery, tuberculosis, malaria, schistosomiasis, sleeping sickness, typhus, and leprosy, has been made difficult by poor sanitation and unclean water. Other barriers to health care access for the rural poor were distance from providers, cost of services, and inadequate quality of health care. Less than half the population lives within 5 km (3 mi) of a health care facility. The most serious obstacle to health has arisen from nutritional deficiencies, particularly among children. Malaria remained the country's most serious health threat, even more so than HIV/AIDS. Venereal disease continued to be a problem in adults.

⁴²HOUSING

Most of the inhabitants live in thatched huts with mud and wattle walls, but styles of building vary from group to group. Even in rural areas, however, corrugated iron is used extensively as a roofing material. In urban centers, sun-baked mud bricks, concrete blocks, and even fired bricks were encouraged by the government, which was responsible for a number of housing schemes prior to the Amin era. In that period, housing was neglected and there was considerable damage to the nation's housing stock during the 1978–79 war.

The National Housing and Construction Corp., a government agency founded in 1964, builds residential housing and has sponsored a number of developments in recent years. One of its newest projects is called the Growing House. The Growing House is a basic, one-bedroom detached house that is ready for immediate occupancy but is designed for easy expansion by the owner, as their own financial situation allows.

⁴³EDUCATION

In 2009 the World Bank estimated that 92% of age-eligible children in Uganda were enrolled in primary school. Secondary enrollment for age-eligible children stood at 22%. Tertiary enrollment was estimated at 4%. Of those enrolled in tertiary education, there were 100 male students for every 80 female students. Overall, the CIA estimated that Uganda had a literacy rate of 66.8%. Public expenditure on education represented 3.2% of GDP.

The school system generally comprises a seven-year primary course, a four-year junior secondary course, and a two-year senior secondary course for those who qualify. Those who do not choose to attend general secondary schools may attend technical schools for three years. Agricultural studies are compulsory in all secondary programs. Many of the senior schools are boarding establishments, and bursaries are available from local authorities and various groups for qualified candidates unable to pay the fees. Primary schools are financed from central government grants, local government funds, and fees from pupils. In 1997, the government eliminated fees for education and introduced universal primary education made possible by IMF debt relief. All senior secondary schools, technical schools, and training colleges receive direct grants-in-aid. The academic year runs from October to July.

44 LIBRARIES AND MUSEUMS

Makerere University has the largest and most comprehensive library in East Africa. It consists of a central library with over 566,000 volumes, which functions as the National Reference Library, and the Albert Cook Library of Medicine with over 55,000 volumes, which functions as the National Library of Medicine. The university also has specialized libraries in the fields of technology, education, social sciences, and farm management. The Public Libraries Board, founded in 1964, administers the Uganda Library Service, with 20 branches and 160,000 volumes.

The Uganda Museum, founded in 1908 on the outskirts of Kampala, contains an excellent anthropological collection. The museum conducts a regular education service in collaboration with the Uganda Society. It has a fine collection of East African musical instruments and a growing collection of archaeological specimens. The Zoological Museum at Makerere University has a collection of rock fossils, birds, and mammals indigenous to Uganda, and the university's geology department has natural history collections. Entebbe has botanical gardens, a zoo, an aquarium, and a game and fisheries museum. There are also two fine arts museums in Kampala, regional folk museums at Kabale, Mbarara, and Soroti, a variety of agricultural and forestry collections, and three national park museums.

45 MEDIA

Radio Uganda, founded in 1954, controls the only national radio broadcasting station in the country, broadcasting daily in 22 languages, including English, French, Swahili, and local languages. In 2004, there were about 60 local and regional radio stations that were privately owned. Uganda television sponsors a public broadcasting station with programming in English, Swahili, and Luganda. Prominent newspapers in 2010, with circulation numbers listed parenthetically, included the *Monitor* (34,000) and *New Vision*. In 2010, the country had 19,927 Internet hosts. In 2009, there were some 3.2 million Internet users in Uganda. In 2010 the CIA reported that there were 327,100 telephone landlines in Uganda and 12,828 million mobile phones. The constitution provides for free speech and a free press; however, the government is said at times to restrict these rights in practice. The occasional use of sedition laws and imprisonment of some members of the media lead to the general practice of self-censorship.

46 ORGANIZATIONS

There are various civil society and professional organizations such as the National Chamber of Commerce and Industry and an employers' federation. The cooperative movement is extensive. The Uganda Manufacturers Association sponsors an annual international trade fair in Kampala held in early October. The Uganda Society is the oldest and most prominent cultural organization. The Uganda National Council for Science and Technology was established in 1990 to promote interest, education, and research in various branches of science. There are several professional organizations that also promote education and research in special-ized fields of science and technology, such as the Uganda Medical Association.

There are a number of women's rights groups, including the Committee for the Advancement of Women of the Baha'is of Uganda, the National Association of Women Organizations of Uganda, the Uganda Association of University Women, and the multinational African Women's Leadership Institute. National youth organizations include Boy's Brigade of Uganda, the Uganda Scouts Association, Uganda Girl Guides, Junior Chamber, and YMCA/YWCA. The Mukono Multi-Purpose Youth Organization promotes programs for the health and well-being of youth, particularly those in rural areas. The National Council of Sports is active in promoting amateur athletics programs.

The African Medical and Research Foundation is dedicated to public health issues. The Minsaki Katende Foundation, founded in 2003, serves as a national HIV/AIDS support organization and provides programs for orphans and the disabled. There are national chapters of the Red Cross Society, UNICEF, Habitat for Humanity, and Caritas.

47 TOURISM, TRAVEL, AND RECREATION

The *Tourism Factbook*, published by the UN World Tourism Organization, reported 817,000 incoming tourists to Uganda in 2009; they spent a total of $683 million. Of those incoming tourists, there were 641,000 from Africa. Wildlife, the major tourist attraction, includes the endangered mountain gorilla as well as many other animal species. There are 10 national parks that spread across Uganda and both sides of the equator, all rich in biodiversity. Tourism facilities are adequate in Kampala but limited in other areas. Hiking in the Virunga Mountains is popular along with white-water rafting, and mountain biking.

48 FAMOUS PERSONS

Kabaka Mutesa I (r. 1856–84) contributed to Uganda's modern development. Sir Apollo Kagwa, chief minister (1890–1926) to Kabaka Mwanga and his successor, Kabaka Daudi Chwa, was one of the dominant figures in Uganda's history. Mukama Kabarega of Bunyoro (r. 1896–99) led his people against British and Buganda forces until captured and exiled in 1899; he died in exile in 1923. Apollo Milton Obote (1924–2005), founder of the UPC and prime minister from 1962 to 1966, overthrew the first president, Sir Edward Frederick Mutesa (Kabaka Mutesa II of Buganda, 1924–69), and was himself president of Uganda from 1966 to 1971 and from 1980 to 1985. Maj. Gen. Idi Amin Dada (1925–2003) overthrew Obote in 1971 and led a military government until he was ousted in 1979 by Tanzanian forces and Ugandan rebels. Yoweri Museveni (b. 1944), leader of the National Resistance Movement, became president in 1986 with the help of about 2,000 guerrillas recruited among Tutsi refugee families who had fled Rwanda.

49 DEPENDENCIES

Uganda has no territories or colonies.

50 BIBLIOGRAPHY

Chrétien, Jean-Pierre. *The Great Lakes of Africa: Two Thousand Years of History*. New York: Zone Books, 2003.

Guest, Emma. *Children of AIDS: Africa's Orphan Crisis.* Sterling, VA: Pluto Press, 2001.

McElrath, Karen, ed. *HIV and AIDS: A Global View.* Westport, CT: Greenwood Press, 2002.

Otiso, Kefa M. *Culture and Customs of Uganda.* Westport, CT: Greenwood Press, 2006.

Pirouet, Louise. *Historical Dictionary of Uganda.* Metuchen, NJ: Scarecrow, 1995.

Uganda Investment and Business Guide: Strategic and Practical Information. Washington, DC: International Business Publications USA, 2012.

UNITED KINGDOM
AFRICAN DEPENDENCIES

BRITISH INDIAN OCEAN TERRITORY

In November 1965, the United Kingdom formed the British Indian Ocean Territory. The area contained the island groups of Aldabra, Farquhar, and Des Roches, as well as the Chagos Archipelago, which was formerly a dependency of Mauritius. Aldabra, Farquhar, and Des Roches became part of independent Seychelles in 1976.

The chief island of the Chagos Archipelago is Diego Garcia, on which the United States maintains a naval base under an agreement with the British. In the late 1970s and early 1980s, proposed US expansions of its naval base there—in order to strengthen the US military presence in the Indian Ocean and thereby secure the oil routes from the Persian Gulf—were a sensitive international issue.

The Chagos Archipelago is located at 6° S and 72° E and covers a total land and water area of 54,400 sq km (21,000 sq mi). The land area alone is only 60 sq km (23 sq mi). Diego Garcia is the largest island (44 sq km/17 sq mi). It is located 1,770 km (1,100 mi) E of Mahé, the main island of the Seychelles. It is also the only populated island in the territory. The military installation there has military personnel and civilian contract employees from the United Kingdom, Mauritius, the Philippines, and the United States; they numbered approximately 4,000 as of 2004 (most recent available information as of March 2012). The average temperature on Diego Garcia is 27°C (81°F); annual rainfall ranges from 230 to 255 centimeters (90 to 100 inches).

France took possession of the Chagos Archipelago during the 18th century but ceded it to the United Kingdom in 1814. It was administered as a dependency of Mauritius until 1965. Initially the archipelago was exploited for copra by slave laborers from Mauritius. After emancipation in the 19th century, the slaves became contract employees. Some of them, now known as Ilois, stayed on and became permanent residents. The United Kingdom bought the copra plantations from the private owners in 1967 and decided to close them down. As a result, some 1,200 Ilois were removed to Mauritius during 1967–73. In 1982, after prolonged negotiation, the United Kingdom granted £4 million (about US$7.8 million) to the Ilois on Mauritius, whose government agreed to provide land worth £1 million (US$1.9 million) for their permanent resettlement. The Ilois pursued additional compensation beginning in 1998, but a final ruling by the British House of Lords in 2008 found in favor of the British government.

In 1980, the government of Mauritius demanded that Diego Garcia be returned to its own control, arguing that the United Kingdom had violated a 1967 agreement not to use the island as a military base. The UK government denied making any such agreement. In 2000, a British high court upheld the military status of Diego Garcia. This ruling was bolstered by additional legal opinions in 2006 and 2007.

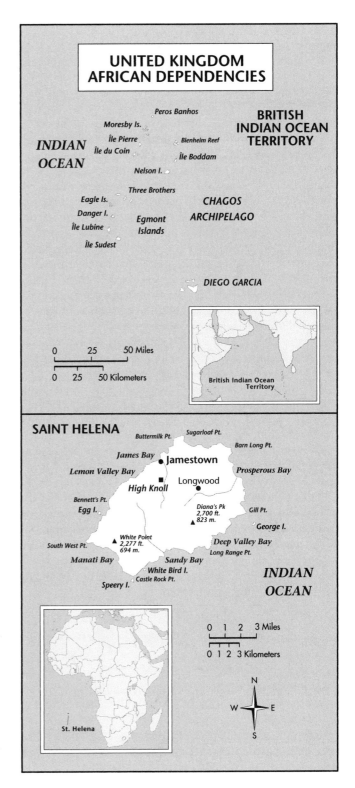

ST. HELENA

The British colony of St. Helena is a mountainous island in the South Atlantic Ocean at approximately 16° S and 5°45′ W, about 1,930 km (1,200 mi) from the west coast of Africa. It has an area of 122 sq km (47 sq mi). The maximum elevation, at Diana's Peak, is 828 meters (2,717 feet). Southeast trade winds give the island a pleasant climate, despite its tropical location. The temperature at Jamestown, the capital, ranges from 18° to 29°C (65 to 85°F). Inland, as the elevation rises, temperatures are somewhat cooler. The annual maximum rainfall is about 100 cm (40 in).

Dependencies of St. Helena are Tristan da Cunha, and Ascension, which are inhabited, and Gough Island, the three Nightingale Islands, and Inaccessible Island, which are not inhabited. Tristan da Cunha is located at 37°15′ S and 12°30′ W, approximately 2,400 km (1,500 mi) SW of St. Helena. It is a partly wooded volcanic island with an area of 98 sq km (38 sq mi), reaching a maximum elevation of 2,060 m (6,760 ft). Annual rainfall averages 168 cm (66 in) on the coast. Ascension, at 7°56′ S and 14°25′ W, about 1,131 km (703 mi) NW of St. Helena, is a bleak volcanic island with an area of 88 sq km (34 sq mi). The island's highest peak, Green Mountain, is 859 m (2,817 ft) above sea level. Ascension became a dependency of St. Helena in 1922 and is an important telecommunications station. Sea turtles come to Ascension between December and May to lay their eggs. Ascension is the breeding ground of the sooty tern, the "wide-awake bird."

The population of St. Helena, Tristan da Cunha, and Ascension was estimated at 7,728 in mid-2012. Those of African origin account for 50% of the population, while those of European or Chinese origin each account for 25%. Approximately 1,000 people lived in Jamestown as of 2009. The principal language is English, and a majority of the people are Anglican Christians.

Jamestown is the only port facility on St. Helena. The island has 138 km (86 mi) of roads, 118 km (73 mi) of which have been paved. A proposed airport, initially approved by the British government in 2008, was under construction in 2012, with an anticipated completion date of year-end 2015. Construction had been delayed due to financing restraints following the 2008–09 global financial crisis.

The island was uninhabited when it was first sighted by the Portuguese navigator João da Nova Castella in 1502. It was claimed by the Dutch in 1633, occupied by the British East India Company in 1659, captured again by the Dutch in 1673, and retaken that same year by the English. It became famous as the place of Napoleon's exile from 1815 until his death in 1821. In 1834, the island officially became a British crown colony.

In October 1961, a volcanic eruption on Tristan da Cunha forced inhabitants to evacuate the island. They were resettled near Southampton, England, in January 1962. Since the island population had been fairly isolated, the islanders discovered that they were particularly vulnerable to respiratory diseases and many of them became ill because of the English climate. In March 1963, a group returned to Tristan da Cunha to repair some of the damaged property and to plant potatoes, the staple subsistence crop. The remaining islanders returned to the island by the end of the year.

St. Helena is administered by a governor, with the aid of a legislative council that includes, in addition to the governor, the speaker, 3 ex officio members, and 12 elected members. Council committees, a majority of whose members belong to the legislative council, are appointed by the governor and charged with executive powers and general supervision of government departments. The Supreme Court of St. Helena, headed by a chief justice, has full criminal and civil jurisdiction. Other judicial institutions include a magistrate's court, a small claims court, and a juvenile court.

The economy depends largely on support from the British government, whose assistance totaled $27 million in fiscal year 2006/07. The construction of an airport was anticipated to create jobs and service the estimated 2,000 tourists that visit the island annually. St. Helena has its own currency, the Saint Helenian pound, which has the same value as its UK equivalent.

Main crops include coffee, corn, potatoes, and vegetables. St. Helenians also are employed on Ascension and the Falkland Islands. Fish, especially skipjack and tuna, are among St. Helena's primary exports. There are no exploitable minerals, and virtually all timber is imported. St. Helena also imports all of its consumer and capital goods. In 2004 (the most recent available information as of March 2012) imports were valued at US$45 million and exports at US$19 million.

There is an unemployment relief system and workers' compensation is paid for death or disablement. Health facilities include a hospital of 58 beds as well as facilities for the elderly and the physically and mentally disabled. Life expectancy was 78.91 years in 2012. The infant mortality rate was 15.8 deaths per 1,000 live births, and the fertility rate was 1.57 children born per woman.

The literacy rate is estimated at nearly 100%. Education is free and compulsory between the ages of 5 and 15. A free public library is located in Jamestown, and there are branch libraries in several rural districts. Longwood House, Napoleon's home in exile, is now French property and a museum. There were 3,000 main telephone lines in use in 2010. There were 900 Internet users in 2009; Internet hosts numbered 6,724 in 2011.

ZAMBIA

Republic of Zambia

CAPITAL: Lusaka

FLAG: The flag is green, with a tricolor of dark red, black, and orange vertical stripes at the lower corner, topped by a golden flying eagle.

ANTHEM: *Lumbanyeni Zambia (Stand and Sing of Zambia, Proud and Free).*

MONETARY UNIT: The kwacha (ZMK) of 100 ngwee replaced the Zambian pound on 15 January 1968. There are coins of 25 ngwee, 50 ngwee, ZMK1, ZMK5, and ZMK10; and notes of 20, 50, 100, 500, 1000, 5000, 10000, 20000, and 100000 kwacha. ZMK1 = US$0.0002 (or US$1 = ZMK5,026.67) as of 2011.

WEIGHTS AND MEASURES: The metric system is used.

HOLIDAYS: New Year's Day, 1 January; Youth Day, 11 March; Labor Day, 1 May; African Freedom Day, 24 May; Heroes' Day, 1st Monday after 1st weekend in July; Unity Day, Tuesday after Heroes' Day; Farmers' Day, 5 August; Independence Day, 24 October; Christmas, 25 December. Movable religious holidays include Good Friday and Easter Monday.

TIME: 2 p.m. = noon GMT.

¹LOCATION, SIZE, AND EXTENT

A landlocked country in south central Africa, Zambia has an area of 752,614 sq km (290,586 sq mi), with a maximum length of 1,206 km (749 mi) E–W and a maximum width of 815 km (506 mi) N–S. Comparatively, the area occupied by Zambia is slightly larger than the state of Texas. Bounded on the NE by Tanzania, on the E by Malawi, on the SE by Mozambique and Zimbabwe, on the S by Zimbabwe, Botswana, and Namibia (South West Africa), on the W by Angola, and on the W and N by the Democratic Republic of the Congo (DROC), Zambia has a total boundary length of 5,664 km (3,519 mi).

Zambia's capital city, Lusaka, is located in the south central part of the country.

²TOPOGRAPHY

Most of the landmass in Zambia is a high plateau lying between 910 and 1,370 m (3,000 and 4,500 ft) above sea level. In the northeast, the Muchinga Mountains exceed 1,800 m (5,900 ft) in height. Elevations below 610 m (2,000 ft) are encountered in the valleys of the major river systems. Plateau land in the northeastern and eastern parts of the country is broken by the low-lying Luangwa River, and in the western half by the Kafue River. Both rivers are tributaries of the upper Zambezi, the major waterway of the area. The frequent occurrence of rapids and falls prevents through navigation of the Zambezi.

There are three large natural lakes—Bangweulu, Mweru, and Tanganyika—all in the northern area. Lake Tanganykia is the largest with an area of about 12,770 sq km (32,893 sq mi). Lake Bangweulu and the swamps at its southern end cover about 9,840 sq km (3,799 sq mi) and are drained by the Luapula River. Kariba, one of the world's largest manmade lakes, is on the southern bor-

der; it was formed by the impoundment of the Zambezi by the construction of the Kariba Dam.

³CLIMATE

Although Zambia lies within the tropics, much of it has a pleasant climate because of the altitude. Temperatures are highest in the valleys of the Zambezi, Luangwa, and Kafue and by the shores of Lakes Tanganyika, Mweru, and Bangweulu.

There are wide seasonal variations in temperature and rainfall. October is the hottest month. The main rainy season starts in mid-November, with heavy tropical storms lasting well into April. The northern and northwestern provinces have an annual rainfall of about 125 cm (50 in), while areas in the far south have as little as 75 cm (30 in). May to mid-August is the cool season, after which temperatures rise rapidly. September is very dry.

Daytime temperatures may range from 23° to 31° C (73–88°F), dropping at night to as low as 5°C (41°F) in June and July. Lusaka, at 1,250 m (4,100 ft), has an average minimum of 9°C (48°F) and an average maximum of 23°C (73°F) in July, with averages of 17°C (63°F) and 26°C (79°F), respectively, in January; normal annual rainfall is 81 cm (32 in).

⁴FLORA AND FAUNA

Most of the territory is plateau and the prevailing type of vegetation is open woodland or savanna. Acacia and baobab trees, thorn trees and bushes, and tall perennial grasses are widespread, becoming coarser and sparser in the drier areas to the south. To the north and east grows a thin forest. The southwest has forests of Zambian teak (Baikiaea plurijuga). The World Resources Institute estimates that there are 4,747 plant species in Zambia. In addition, Zambia is home to 255 mammal, 770 bird, 143 reptile, and 66 amphibian species. The calculation reflects the total number of distinct species residing in the country, not the number of endemic species.

The national parks and game reserves, such as the Kafue National Park, conserve the wildlife threatened by settlement. The Cookson's wildebeest, Senga Kob, Thornicroft giraffe, and red lechwe are unique to Zambia. The many varieties of buck include kudu, impala, duiker, and sten. In Luangwa Valley can be found giraffe, zebra, rhinoceros, elephant, baboon, monkey, hyena, wolf, and lion. Among the nocturnal animals are serval and civet cat, genet, and jackal. Other mammals include the honey badger, ant bear, rock rabbit, wart hog, and bush pig.

Zambia has a wealth of bird life, including the eagle, gull, tern, kingfisher, swift, redwing, lark, babbler, sunbird, weaver, red-billed quelea (in Luangwa Valley), stork, goose, plover, skimmer, bee-eater, wagtail, sparrow, swallow, thrush, shrike, nightingale, dove, nightjar, and an occasional ostrich. White pelican, flamingo, heron, ibis, and the crowned crane are found in the game reserves.

Reptile species include crocodile, tortoise, turtle, terrapin, gecko, agama, nonvenomous python, mamba, viper, and adder. The range of species of fish is also wide and includes bream, snoutfish, butterfish, tigerfish, bottlenose, gorgefish, mudfish, catfish, barbel, "vundu," squeaker, whitebait, perch, carp, bass, and "utaka" (of the sardine type). Insect types number in the thousands, and many are peculiar to the area. The Copperbelt region and the swamps of Lake Bangweulu are especially rich in insect life.

5ENVIRONMENT

Both traditional and modern farming methods in Zambia involve clearing large areas of forest. Zambia has lost large tracts of forestland, mainly to slash-and-burn agriculture but also to firewood gathering and charcoal production. Consequent erosion results in the loss of up to three million tons of topsoil annually. The World Resources Institute reported that Zambia had designated 30.05 million hectares (74.27 million acres) of land for protection as of 2006. The exclusive cultivation of a single crop on agricultural land and the use of fertilizers threaten the soil and contribute to acidification. The Copperbelt region, Zambia's mineral-extraction and refining center, has been polluted by contaminants including acid rain. The buildup of toxins in the soil near many smelters poses a threat to food crops.

Air pollution is caused by vehicle emissions and coal-powered industrial plants. The UN reported in 2008 that carbon dioxide emissions in Zambia totaled 2,689 kilotons. Lack of adequate water-treatment facilities contributes to the prevalence of bilharziasis and other parasitic infections. Water pollution arises from contamination by sewage and toxic industrial chemicals. Water resources totaled 105.2 cu km (25.24 cu mi) while water usage was 1.74 cu km (.417 cu mi) per year.

Wildlife is endangered in some areas by hunting and poaching, although the National Parks and Wildlife Act (1982) mandates automatic imprisonment for trading illicitly in elephant tusks and rhinoceros horns. According to a 2011 report issued by the International Union for Conservation of Nature and Natural Resources (IUCN), the number of threatened species included 9 types of mammals, 14 species of birds, 1 species of amphibian, 20 species of fish, 13 types of mollusks, 1 species of other invertebrate, and 10 species of plants. Threatened species include the African wild dog,

the black rhinoceros, the Madagascar pond heron, and white-winged crake.

6POPULATION

The US Central Intelligence Agency (CIA) estimates the population of Zambia in 2011 to be approximately 13,881,336, which placed it at number 68 in population among the 196 nations of the world. In 2011, approximately 2.5% of the population was more than 65 years of age, with another 46.7% less than 15 years of age. The median age in Zambia was 16.5 years. There were 1.00 males for every female in the country. The population's annual rate of change was 3.062%. The projected population for the year 2025 was 20,400,000. Population density in Zambia was calculated at 18 people per sq km (47 people per sq mi).

The UN estimated that 36% of the population lived in urban areas, and that urban populations was expected to grow at an annual rate of 3.2% between 2010 and 2015. The largest urban area was Lusaka, with a population of 1.4 million.

The prevalence of HIV/AIDS has had a significant impact on the population of Zambia. The AIDS epidemic causes higher death and infant mortality rates, and lowers life expectancy. Approximately 14.3% of Zambians are infected by HIV. More than 800,000 Zambian children have lost one or both of their parents due to HIV/AIDS.

7MIGRATION

Estimates of Zambia's net migration rate, carried out by the CIA in 2011, amounted to -0.84 migrants per 1,000 citizens. The total number of emigrants living abroad was 185,800, and the total number of immigrants living in Zambia was 233,100. Zambia also accepted 42,565 refugees from Angola, 60,874 from the Democratic Republic of the Congo, and 4,100 from Rwanda. Before independence, the size of the European population waxed and waned with the fortunes of the mining industry. During the political upheavals of the mid-1960s, many Europeans in the mining industries left Zambia. In 1999 Zambia was host to nearly 200,000 refugees from the war-torn neighboring countries of Angola, the Democratic Republic of Congo, Rwanda, and Burundi.

8ETHNIC GROUPS

The African community, close to 99.5% of Zambia's total population, is composed of various Bantu groups. (The term "Bantu" refers roughly to all peoples in whose language the root ntu means "man.") The Bemba group—37% of the African population—inhabits the Northern and Copperbelt provinces. Other African societies include the Tonga (19%), Lunda (12%), Nyanja (11%), Mambwe (8%), and Lozi or Barotse (7%). In all, there are at least 73 different African societal classifications. The Europeans, accounting for about 1% of the population, are mainly of British stock, either immigrants or their descendants from the United Kingdom or South Africa. Other European groups include those of Dutch, Italian, and Greek descent. Counting Asians, mainly migrants from the Indian subcontinent, and people of mixed race, other non-Africans constitute only about 0.2% of the population.

9LANGUAGES

Some 80 different languages have been identified, most of them of the Bantu family. Eight main languages are recognized as official

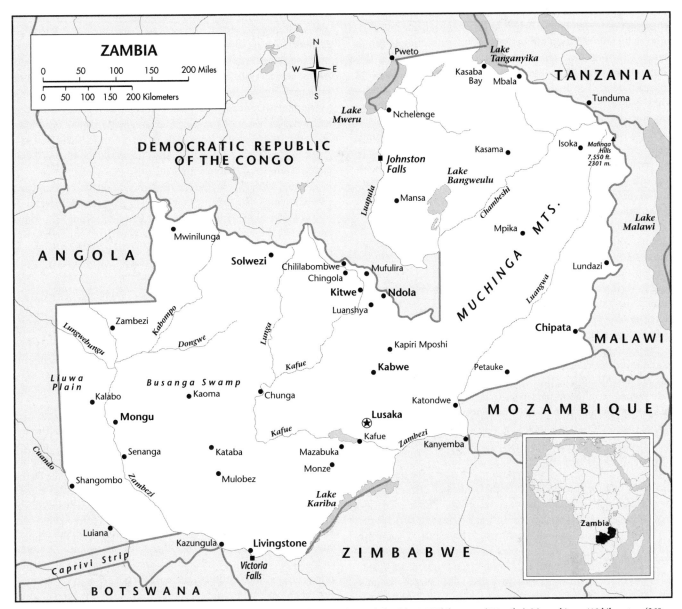

ZAMBIA

0   50   100   150   200 Miles

0   50 100 150 200 Kilometers

LOCATION: 9° to 18° S; 23° to 34°E. BOUNDARY LENGTHS: Tanzania, 338 kilometers (210 miles); Malawi, 837 kilometers (523 miles); Mozambique, 419 kilometers (260 miles); Zimbabwe, 797 kilometers (498 miles); Namibia (Caprivi Strip), 233 kilometers (145 miles); Angola, 1,110 kilometers (690 miles); Democratic Republic of the Congo (DROC), 1,930 kilometers (1,193 miles).

languages: Bemba, Lozi, Lunda, Kaonda, Luvale, Tonga, Nyanja, and English. Bemba, with its various dialects, is widely spoken in northern Zambia and is the lingua franca in the Copperbelt. The Ila and Tonga tongues predominate in the Southern Province. Chewa, Nsenga, and Tumuka are also spoken.

10 RELIGIONS

An estimated 87% of the population professes some form of Christianity. Another 1% are either Muslim or Hindu. Traditionally the majority of Christians were either Roman Catholics or Protestants, but Pentecostalism has been gaining momentum. There has also been a surge in new Pentecostal churches, which have attracted many young followers. Muslims tend to be concentrated in parts of the country where Asians have settled—along the railroad line from Lusaka to Livingstone and in the eastern prov-

ince. A 1996 amendment to the constitution declared the country a Christian nation while providing for freedom of religion in practice. Religious groups must register with the government in order to operate legally; however, most applications for registration are reportedly approved without discrimination. Various ecumenical groups have formed to promote interfaith dialogue and to discuss national political concerns. These include the Zambia Episcopal Conference, the Christian Council of Zambia, and the Evangelical Fellowship of Zambia. Good Friday, Holy Saturday, Easter Monday, and Christmas are observed as national holidays.

11 TRANSPORTATION

Almost all of Zambia's industries, commercial agriculture, and major cities are located along the rail lines, which are often paralleled by highways. The Zambia Railways system consists of all narrow gauge rail. The link with the Atlantic via the Katanga and Benguela railways to Lobito Bay in Angola has been affected periodically by political instability in Angola. Construction began in October 1970 on the Tazara railway, a 1,860-km (1,156-mi) line linking Dar es Salaam in Tanzania with Kapiri Mposhi, north of Lusaka; intended to lessen Zambian dependence on the former white-minority regimes of South Africa and the former Rhodesia (presently Zimbabwe), the line (890 km/553 mi of which is in Zambia) was completed and commissioned in July 1976. Equipment and operational problems have kept the railway from reaching its full potential, however, and rail cargo links with South Africa and Mozambique ports, passing through Zimbabwe, remain important for Zambian commerce.

The principal routes were: the Great North Road (809 km/503 mi), running from Kapiri Mposhi through Tanzania to Dar es Salaam, with a connecting road in Zambia from Kapiri Mposhi south to Livingstone (Maramba); the Great East Road (586 km/364 mi), from Lusaka to Chipata and thence to the Malawi border, with a connecting road (583 km/362 mi) from Mongu to Lusaka; the Zaire Border Road, from Kapiri Mposhi on the Great North Road through the Copperbelt region to Katanga, DROC; and the Kafue-Harare (Zimbabwe) road. Road services continue to play an important role in transporting copper and general cargo to and from Dar es Salaam. Transport services on the main routes also are provided by the National Transport Corp. of Zambia, the state-owned freight and passenger transport service. The United Bus Co. of Zambia is the largest passenger carrier. The CIA reported that Zambia had a total of 91,440 km (56,818 mi) of roads in 2001 (most recent figures available as of 2011), of which 20,117 km (12,500 mi) are paved.

In 2009 Zambia had 94 airports, of which only nine had paved runways. Lusaka International is the principal airport. State-owned Zambia Airways is the national airline. Zambia Airways provides international service from Lusaka to several African and European countries, as well as domestic service to 17 Zambian centers.

Zambia has approximately 2,250 km (1,398 mi) of navigable waterways. The main waterways included Lake Tanganyika, and the Zambezi and Luapula rivers. Mpulungu on Lake Tanganyika is Zambia's only port and receives goods supplied through Tanzania. There are several fishing harbors on Kariba Lake.

12 HISTORY

The history of Zambia before the 19th century can be studied only through archaeology and oral traditions. Iron working and agriculture were practiced in some parts of Zambia by about AD 100. By AD 900, mining and trading were evident in southern Zambia. Between the 15th century (or possibly earlier) and the 18th century, various groups of Bantu migrants from the southern Congo settled in Zambia. By the beginning of the 19th century, three large-scale political units existed in Zambia, in three different types of geographic environment. On the northeast plateau between the valleys of the Luapula and Luangwa, the Bemba had established a system of chieftainships; the Lunda kingdom of Kazembe was in the Luapula Valley; and the kingdom of the Lozi was in the far west, in the floodplain of the upper Zambezi.

Zambia was affected by two "invasions" in the mid-19th century. Shaka's Zulu empire in South Africa set in motion a series of migrations, commonly referred to as the Mfecane; groups of peoples, including the Ngoni, were forced to migrate north across the Zambezi in order to avoid the Zulu raids and conquests. The other invasion came in the form of traders from the north—Nyamwezi, Arabs, and Swahili—drawing Zambia into long-distance trading systems.

The first significant European contact was through Christian missionaries. David Livingstone explored the region near Lake Bangweulu extensively from 1851 to his death in 1873. In 1884, François Coillard, a French Protestant missionary, settled in Barotseland (now the Western Province).

In the 1890s, Cecil Rhodes' British South Africa Company (BSAC), which had already established itself to the south, extended its charter to the lands north of the Zambezi. From 1891 to the end of 1923, the territory—known as Northern Rhodesia—was ruled by this private company. Efforts to stimulate European settlement were disappointing, since anticipated discoveries of mineral wealth failed to materialize.

In the 1920s, new methods of exploiting the extensive mineral deposits in the Copperbelt region transformed the economic life of the territory. Development of these ore bodies, although hampered by the Great Depression, reversed the roles of the two Rhodesias. Northern Rhodesia, formerly viewed as an economic liability in any projected merger with Southern Rhodesia, now was seen as a source of wealth. European settlements rose rapidly, spurred directly by the requirements of the mining industry and indirectly by the subsequent expansion of the economy.

Before the formation of the Federation of Northern and Southern Rhodesia and Nyasaland in 1953, the political development of the territory focused on two relationships: that of the European settlers with the colonial authorities on the one hand, and that between the settlers and the Africans on the other. The European settler community pressed for a greater voice in the colony's affairs. The major political issue involving the relations between Europeans and Africans concerned the allocation of land. Commissions on land policy designated the areas adjacent to the railway line as crown land. Although there was no legal bar to the acquisition of crown land by Africans, the effect of the arrangement was to exclude them from the commercially most attractive acreage.

In 1953, Northern Rhodesia became a member of the Federation of Rhodesia and Nyasaland. Even though the overwhelming majority of Africans in the territory was opposed to the federal arrangement, the British government decided that Northern Rhodesia would participate in the Federation. In 1960, a royal commission reported that, despite clear economic benefits, the majority of Africans in both Northern Rhodesia and Nyasaland was opposed to the continuance of federation in its present form. In early 1962, Nyasaland's desire to secede from the Federation was acknowledged by the British government.

Following its initiation into the Federation, the government of Northern Rhodesia underwent constitutional changes, with a growing emphasis on African representation. Africans had not been represented on the Legislative Council until 1948, when two were named to that body. An enlarged Legislative Council, convened in 1954 just after the formation of the Federation, included four Africans selected by the African Representative Council. A new constitution, introduced in January 1959, aimed at replacing the council with a political system based on a greater degree of co-operation between the races.

Discussions on a revision of this constitution began in December 1960 but were brought to an early close by disagreement between the European-dominated United Federal Party and the United National Independence Party (UNIP). But agreement was finally reached, and a new constitution came into effect in September 1962. Elections later that year produced an African majority in the Legislative Council, which then called for secession from the federation, full internal self-government under a new constitution, and a new National Assembly based on a broader, more democratic franchise.

The Republic of Zambia Is Born

On 31 December 1963, the Federation of Rhodesia and Nyasaland was formally dissolved. On 24 October 1964, Northern Rhodesia became an independent republic, and its name was changed to Zambia. Kenneth Kaunda, the leader of the ruling UNIP, became the nation's first president. Kaunda was reelected in 1969, 1973, 1978, and 1983, surviving a series of coup attempts during 1980–81.

During the 1970s, Zambia played a key role in the movement toward black majority rule in Rhodesia. Zambia's border with Rhodesia was closed from 1973 to 1978 by Kaunda in retaliation for Rhodesian raids into Zambia; the raids were intended to impede the infiltration of Patriotic Front guerrillas into Rhodesia from their Zambian bases. The emergence of independent, black-ruled Zimbabwe eased the political pressure, but a drastic decline of world copper prices in the early 1980s, coupled with a severe drought, left Zambia in a perilous economic position. The continuing civil war in Angola also had repercussions in Zambia, bringing disruption of Zambian trade routes and casualties among Zambians along the border.

A South African air raid near Lusaka on 19 May 1986 was aimed at curbing Zambia's support for black nationalist groups in exile there. Later in the year, Kaunda supported Commonwealth sanctions against South Africa but did not take action himself, since Zambia was heavily dependent on imports from South Africa.

Riots, the worst since independence, broke out on 9 December 1986 in protest against the removal of subsidies for cornmeal, which had caused the price to rise by 120%; 15 people were killed, hundreds were injured, and hundreds of shops were looted. Peace returned two days later when Kaunda restored the subsidy and nationalized the grain-milling industry. He also ruled thenceforth with state of emergency powers. Reduction in government spending in order to reduce the deficit had been demanded by the International Monetary Fund, along with the devaluation of the currency, as a condition for extending new loans to enable Zambia to pay for essential imports. On 1 May 1987, Kaunda rejected the IMF conditions for a new financing package of about $300 million. He limited payments on the foreign debt to well under 10% of export earnings and established a new fixed currency rate of eight kwacha to the dollar. This did little to improve the economy or the popularity of Kaunda and UNIP.

By early 1989, Zambia, in consultation with the IMF and the World Bank, developed a new economic reform plan. In early 1991, Zambia qualified for World Bank assistance for the first time since 1987, although this was later suspended. By 1990, a grow-

ing opposition to UNIP's monopoly of power had coalesced in the Movement for Multiparty Democracy (MMD). A number of UNIP defectors and major labor leaders came together to pressure Kaunda to hold multiparty elections. In December 1990, after a tumultuous year that included riots in Lusaka and a coup attempt, Kaunda signed legislation ending UNIP's legal monopoly of power.

After difficult negotiations between the government and opposition groups, Zambia enacted a new constitution in August 1991. It enlarged the National Assembly, established an electoral commission, and allowed for more than one presidential candidate. Candidates no longer were required to be UNIP members. In September, Kaunda announced the date for Zambia's first multiparty parliamentary and presidential elections in 19 years. On 31 October and 1 November 1991, the 27-year-long state of emergency was terminated. Frederick J. T. Chiluba (MMD) defeated Kaunda, 81% to 15%. The MMD won more than 125 of the 150 elected seats in the Assembly. UNIP won 25 seats, although UNIP swept the Eastern Province, winning 19 seats there.

Despite the change of government, the economy still sputtered. Chiluba's austerity measures may have been popular with Zambia's creditors, but not with its people. Likewise, his privatization plans alarmed the unions, his original base of support. Chiluba's MMD in power became autocratic and corrupt. Kaunda, his family, and UNIP officials were harassed. The press began to criticize Chiluba's government and Chiluba lashed back. An Anticorruption Commission investigated three senior cabinet ministers suspected of abuse of office.

UNIP remained the principal target of Chiluba's wrath. In February 1993, a document known as "Operation Zero Option" was leaked to the press. Allegedly written by Kaunda loyalists, it called for a campaign of strikes, riots and crime to destabilize the government. On 4 March 1993, government declared a three-month state of emergency and detained 26 UNIP members, including three of Kaunda's sons. Chiluba lifted the state of emergency on May 25 and released all but eight of the detainees, whom he charged with offenses from treason to possession of seditious documents.

Throughout the 1990s, Zambia continued to face troubles in its attempts to modernize its economy and to reform its political system. Despite liquidation of the government's huge stake in the nation's industrial sector, and implementing a drastic austerity program to reduce its budget deficit, the country saw only marginal growth. Further, despite the promise of fresh beginnings in 1991, the country momentarily reverted to one-party rule under Chiluba as the MMD fraudulently won huge victories in the November 1996 elections, prompting foreign donors to suspend aid payments briefly in early 1997. Subsequently, a campaign mounted by Chiluba and his party to amend the constitution to allow a third term was defeated. In the election of 27 December 2001, Chiluba's handpicked candidate Levy Mwanawasa was elected president with 29% of the vote; the MMD picked up 68 of 150 seats in the National Assembly. The vote was ruled flawed by international and local poll monitors—mainly on grounds of misuse of state funds and vote buying. An opposition petition to the Supreme Court alleged that the elections were rigged.

In an overture for national unity, or perhaps a bid to save his presidency, Mwanawasa named nine opposition members of parliament to his cabinet in February 2003. The move provoked a constitutional crisis when Mwanawasa refused to back down against a High Court ruling that the appointments were unconstitutional. Opposition parties expelled the members of parliament from the National Assembly. Later that month the Supreme Court declined a petition by former president Chiluba seeking immunity from prosecution under the government's anticorruption drive. Chiluba was accused of abuse of office and 60 counts of theft during his ten-years in office. In May 2003, under pressure from church, women's, and other civil society groups, Mwanawasa conceded to the formation of a constituent assembly to review the constitution. Civic groups contended that the current document grants the executive far-reaching powers, which groups say is at odds with their vision for a people-driven constitution. Activist opponents of the president's vision for the constitutional review process took to wearing green ribbons and honking their horns on Fridays.

Mwanawasa attempted to root out corruption in Zambia unlike the increasingly apparent corruption of the later years of Chiluba's time in office. Chiluba was arrested by Mwanawasa's government and charged with several counts of embezzlement and corruption, firmly quashing initial fears that President Mwanawasa would turn a blind eye to the allegations of his predecessor's corrupt practices. However, his early zeal to root out corruption waned, with key witnesses in the Chiluba trial leaving the country. The Constitutional Review Commission set up by Mwanawasa also hit some turbulence, with arguments as to where its findings should be submitted leading to suspicions that he has been trying to manipulate the outcome. Nevertheless, Zambian people view Mwanawasa's rule as a great improvement on Chiluba's corrupt regime. In May 2007, the High Court in the United Kingdom ruled that Chiluba and four of his associates had conspired to rob Zambia of some $46 million.

In the 2000s the government considered participation in a future free trade area as part of the Southern Africa Development Community (SADC) arrangement. Food security and care for AIDS orphans and vulnerable children were also on the policy agenda. An estimated 1.2 million Zambians were HIV positive, with 21.5% of adults aged between 15 and 49 years infected with the virus. Around 86% of Zambians were classified as poor, which impacted nutritional status. The country's rate of economic growth cannot support rapid population growth or the strain that HIV/AIDS-related issues (i.e., rising medical costs, decline in worker productivity) place on government resources. Unemployment and underemployment are serious problems.

In October 2006, Mwanawasa announced the discovery of oil in the west. In February 2007, Chinese President Hu Jintao inaugurated an enormous mining investment zone at the end of a two-day visit. His itinerary was cut short due to planned protests against the alleged exploitation of local workers by Chinese firms. Although high commodity prices aided the Zambian economy in 2010—which had suffered during the 2008–09 global financial crisis—Zambia remained dependent on strong commodity prices to post consistent economic growth.

In April 2006, Mwanawasa suffered a minor stroke. He resumed light duties after a few weeks and later declared himself fit to run for reelection. In September 2006 presidential elections were held, and Mwanawasa won a second term. However, he died on 19 August 2008 before serving out his term, after suffering another stroke. He was succeeded by his vice president, Rupiah Banda, who won a special election in 2008 but later lost the 2011 presidential election to Michael Sata.

13 GOVERNMENT

From 1953 to 1963, Northern Rhodesia was a protectorate under the jurisdiction of the British crown, within the Federation of Rhodesia and Nyasaland. On 24 October 1964, it became an independent republic. The constitution of January 1964 was amended in 1968 and in 1972, when it was officially announced that Zambia would become a one-party "participatory democracy," with the sole party the ruling United National Independence Party. A new constitution was drafted and received presidential assent in August 1973.

Under the 1973 constitution, the president of the Republic of Zambia was head of state, commander-in-chief of the armed forces, and president of the UNIP. Once chosen by the ruling party, the president had to be confirmed by a majority of the electorate, but there was no limitation on the length of the president's tenure in office. The prime minister was the leader of government business and an ex officio member of the UNIP Central Committee. As provided in the constitution, the Central Committee consisted of not more than 25 members, 20 to be elected at the party's general conference held every 5 years, and 3 to be nominated by the president, who was also a member. Cabinet decisions were subordinate to those of the UNIP Central Committee. The parliament consisted of the president and a National Assembly of 125 elected members, but all Assembly members had to be UNIP members, and their candidacy had to be approved by the party's Central Committee. The constitution also provided for a House of Chiefs of 27 members. A Bill of Rights guaranteed the fundamental freedom and rights of the individual, but if at any time the president felt the security of the state threatened, he had the power to proclaim a state of emergency. Indeed, Zambians lived under a state of emergency for 27 years.

In August 1991, a new constitution was promulgated. The president is now elected directly by universal suffrage and may serve a maximum of two five-year terms. The National Assembly has 150 directly elected members with up to 8 appointed by the president, also for five-year terms.

14 POLITICAL PARTIES

African nationalism began to rise in Northern Rhodesia after World War II. African welfare associations, founded before the war, developed rapidly into political organizations. In 1946, representatives from 14 welfare societies formed the Federation of Welfare Societies. In 1948, the federation was reconstituted as the Northern Rhodesia Congress. It became the North Rhodesian African National Congress (ANC) in 1951 under the leadership of Harry Nkumbula. In 1958, dissatisfaction with Nkumbula's leadership gave rise to a breakaway movement led by the party's secretary-general, Kenneth Kaunda. Kaunda formed the Zambia African National Congress, which was declared illegal the following year. In 1960, the United National Independence Party (UNIP) was formed under Kaunda's leadership. UNIP received a majority of the popular votes in the 1962 elections and formed the first government after independence. The ANC became the chief opposition party.

In 1967, the United Party (UP) was formed by Nalumino Mundia, a Lozi who had been dismissed from the cabinet in 1966. Its support came mainly from Barotseland in the southwest, where the UP promised to restore the power of the chiefs. After violence erupted in the Copperbelt, Kaunda banned the UP as a "threat to public security and peace," and Mundia and his principal officers were arrested. In August 1968, the UP was declared illegal. Mundia was released in 1969, joined the UNIP in 1974, and was named prime minister in 1981.

In the general elections of December 1969, the UNIP won 81 seats in the National Assembly, the ANC 23, and independents 1. Kaunda was reelected president. The elections were followed by violence and political unrest. At the opening of the new Assembly, the speaker refused to recognize the ANC as the official opposition. With the proclamation of a one-party state in December 1972, UNIP became the only legal party in Zambia. The ANC was assimilated into UNIP; the United Progressive Party, formed in August 1971, was summarily disbanded by the government, and its founder, Simon Kapwepwe, briefly arrested.

On 5 December 1973, the first presidential elections held under the new constitution brought the reelection of Kaunda to a third term with 85% of the vote. Voters also filled the 125 elective seats in the National Assembly. In 1975, the UNIP declared its ranks open to former followers of banned parties, but in 1978 candidacy was restricted to those with five years' continuous UNIP membership. National Assembly and presidential elections were held in December 1978, with Kaunda, again unopposed, receiving 80.5% of the vote. In the elections of October 1983, Kaunda's share of the total rose to 93%. A total of 766 candidates ran for the 125 Assembly seats.

After considerable social unrest in 1986 and again in 1990, the Kaunda government came under domestic and international pressure to end UNIP's monopoly in legitimate partisan activity. A Movement for Multiparty Democracy (MMD) was formed and led by trade unionists and defectors from UNIP. Finally, in December 1990, Kaunda signed into law a bill legalizing opposition political parties. In the new constitution adopted in August 1991, candidates are no longer required to belong to UNIP.

These changes paved the way to multiparty presidential and parliamentary elections on 31 October and 1 November 1991, the first in 19 years. The MMD's leader, Frederick Chiluba, easily won the presidency, 81% to 15% for Kaunda. The MMD got 125 seats to 15 for UNIP in the National Assembly. Kaunda and his family were harassed by the MMD, which forced Kaunda to step down as UNIP leader in August 1992. However, he returned a few years later to reclaim UNIP leadership. He briefly considered running on the UNIP ticket in the national presidential elections in 2001.

Since the legalization of multiparty competition, more than 30 parties have operated in the country. Parties include Agenda for Zambia (AZ), Forum for Democracy and Development (FDD), Heritage Party (HP), Progressive Front (PF), Movement for Multiparty Democracy (MMD), National Citizens Coalition (NCC), National Leadership for Development (NLD), National Party (NP), Patriotic Front (PF), Zambian Republican Party (ZRP), Social Democratic Party (SDP), United National Independence Party (UNIP), United Party for National Development (UPND), and

the National Democratic Alliance (NADA). The United Democratic Party and the United Democratic Congress Party are headed by former top UNIP leaders. The National Party (also with prominent ex-MMD figures) was created in August 1993 and won four seats in the Assembly in 1993–94 by-elections. Within the MMD there is a breakaway group, the Caucus for National Unity, to root out corruption in government.

In elections held on 20 November 1996, President Frederick Chiluba and the MMD won more than 85% of the available seats in the National Assembly. However, independent observers condemned the election as being rigged by the MMD.

In the election of 27 December 2001, Levy Mwanawasa was elected president with 29% of the vote to 27% for Anderson Mazoka, 13% for Christon Tembo, 10% for Tilyenji Kaunda, 8% for Godfrey Miyanda, 5% for Benjamin Mwila, and 3% for Michael Sata. In the legislative contest held the same date, eight parties won seats in the National Assembly. The MMD claimed 45.9% of the vote winning 68 seats, followed by the UPND with 32.4% and 48 seats, the UNIP with 8.8% and 13 seats, the FDD with 8.1% and 12 seats, the HP with 2.7% and 4 seats, the PF with 0.7% and one seat, the ZRP with 0.7% and one seat, and independents with 0.7% and one seat. Two seats were not determined.

In the 28 September 2006 presidential election, Mwanawasa won reelection with 43% of the vote. His challengers were Michael Sata of the PF with 29.4%, Hakainde Hichilema of the United Democratic Alliance (UDA) with 25.3% of the vote, Godfrey Miyanda of the HP with 1.6% of the vote, and Winwright Ngondo of the All People's Congress Party (APC) with 0.8% of the vote. In the parliamentary elections held the same day, the MMD secured 73 seats, the Patriotic Front (PF) returned with 43 seats, and the UDA won 26 seats. There were three independents elected, and 2 candidates from the United Liberal Party (ULP), and 1 from the National Democratic Focus (NDF).

Following President Mwanawasa's death, Zambia held elections on 30 October 2008. Acting president Rupiah Banda was declared the winner after narrowly defeating Michael Sata of the opposition PF by only 30,000 votes. Although international observers were satisfied overall with the conduct of the election by the Electoral Commission of Zambia, Sata sued to have the election results nullified. He withdrew his petition in March 2009 after losing preliminary decisions. Banda was sworn in on 2 November 2008.

As the October 2011 elections approached, the PF filed a suit alleging that President Banda was not legally qualified to serve as president (or run for reelection) based on the nature of his citizenship. According to the constitution, both parents of a presidential candidate must be Zambian citizens by birth or descent. The opposition claimed to have learned that Banda's father was born in Nyasaland (modern day Malawi) and not in Chipata of eastern Zambia, as Banda claimed when filing his original candidacy applications. The court dismissed the case, which the ruling party disregarded as malicious. President Banda entered the election with a slightly weakened party after the defection of several party leaders to the political opposition. Presidential and legislative elections were held on 20 September 2011. PF candidate Michael Sata won the presidency and was sworn in on 23 September 2011. In the legislative elections, the PF took 60 seats, the MMD 55, and the United Party for National Development (UPND) 28. No other party won more than one seat.

¹⁵LOCAL GOVERNMENT

Zambia is divided into nine provinces (including the special province of Lusaka), administered by officials appointed by the central government. Each province is further divided into districts, presided over by district secretaries. Zambia has one of the highest urbanization rates in Africa. Lusaka has a city council, and the other large towns have councils or town management boards; most townships, however, are directly administered by government officers. Local elections in urban areas are organized on a ward system with universal adult suffrage. Local urban authorities can levy taxes, borrow money, and own and manage housing projects. They control roads, water, power, town planning, health facilities, and other public services within their areas.

Administrative districts lying outside municipal and township areas are governed by rural councils, consisting of members elected by universal adult suffrage and a minority of nominated members, mainly chiefs, appointed by the under minister of the interior. Councils have evolved from the former native authorities, which were constituted on a tribal basis. The rural councils have frequently cut across African societal boundaries in order to establish larger and more viable units. The functions and powers of rural councils are similar to those of the urban local authorities.

¹⁶JUDICIAL SYSTEM

The judicial system is based on English common law and customary law. Common law is administered by several High Courts, which have authority to hear criminal and civil cases and appeals from lower courts. Resident magistrate's courts are also established at various centers. Local courts mainly administer customary law, especially cases relating to marriage, property, and inheritance.

Under the constitution of 1991, the Supreme Court is the highest court in Zambia and serves as the final court of appeal. The chief justice and other eight judges are appointed by the president. In consultation with the prime minister, the president also appoints the director of public prosecution and the attorney general, the latter being the principal legal adviser to the government. The independence of the judiciary has been respected by the government. Trials in magistrate courts are public.

¹⁷ARMED FORCES

The International Institute for Strategic Studies reports that armed forces in Zambia totaled 15,100 members in 2011. The force is comprised of 13,500 from the army and 1,600 from the air force. Armed forces represented 0.3% of the labor force in Zambia. Defense spending totaled $361.7 million and accounted for 1.8% of GDP.

¹⁸INTERNATIONAL COOPERATION

Zambia joined the UN on 1 December 1964 and participates in ECA and several nonregional specialized agencies, such as the FAO, UNESCO, UNHCR, UNIDO, the FAO, the World Bank, IAEA, and the WHO. It belongs to the African Development Bank, the ACP Group, the Commonwealth of Nations, G-77, the WTO, COMESA, and the African Union. Located in Zambia are the headquarters of the International Red Locust Control Organi-

zation for Central and Southern Africa, as well as COMESA headquarters, an office of the UN High Commissioner of Refugees, and a regional office of the UN Institute for Namibia, established to provide training for future administrators of an independent Namibian state. Zambia belongs to the Southern African Development Community (SADC) and the Preferential Trade Area for Eastern and Southern Africa. Zambia has played an important role in peace negotiation efforts for neighboring states, particularly the Democratic Republic of Congo. The country has also supported UN operations and missions in Kosovo (est. 1999), Ethiopia and Eritrea (est. 2000), Liberia (est. 2003), Sierra Leone (est. 1999), Burundi (est. 2004), and Côte d'Ivoire (est. 2004). Zambia is part of the Nonaligned Movement.

In environmental cooperation, Zambia is part of the Basel Convention, the Convention on Biological Diversity, Ramsar, CITES, the Montréal Protocol, the Nuclear Test Ban Treaty, and the UN Conventions on the Law of the Sea, Climate Change, and Desertification.

¹⁹ECONOMY

Zambia is one of the poorest countries in the world. Copper is the country's economic mainstay. After years of depressed copper prices and mining activities in the 1980s a worldwide increase in commodity prices at the turn of the twenty-first century retuned the copper industry to profitability and encouraged foreign investment. China is the major investor in the Zambian copper mining industry. The government worked to reduce its reliance on the copper industry by encouraging private sector growth in agriculture, tourism, gemstone mining, and hydro power. Zambia's Vision 2030 envisages the country attaining prosperous middle income status by the year 2030. For this to happen, the economy needs to grow at an annual average rate of about 6–7%, slightly higher than rates obtained during the 2000s. However, in 2010 the country attained a growth rate of 7.6 %.

After qualifying for $6 billion of debt relief under the IMF/World Bank Heavily Indebted Poor Countries (HIPC) initiative in 2006, Zambia turned around its image from a country performing considerably below its potential, to a country with good economic management and several years of strong economic growth. Strong macro-economic performance, coupled with fast pace growth in mining, construction, telecommunications and tourism, helped spur GDP growth in 2001–2010. A number of policy reforms such as acceleration of the budget preparation process, increase of electricity tariffs and privatization of remnant parastatals were put in place to enhance economic growth.

In December 2009, the International Monetary Fund (IMF) approved the disbursement of $81.2 million to Zambia as part of its agreement under the Poverty Reduction and Growth Facility (PRGF) program. Since June 2008, Zambia has received $262.5 million in aid through the PRGF. The December disbursement was received after a favorable review of the nation's economy by the IMF, which reported that the 2010 Zambian government budget was well balanced, and that economic reforms have been satisfactorily initiated and maintained.

Despite strong growth through 2011, officials are somewhat concerned about the rise in national debt. The government deficit was estimated at 4% in 2011, an increase over previous years. Between 2011 and 2014, Zambia was slated to borrow about $2 billion to fund additional infrastructure projects.

Foreign investment was generally strong, but 2010 showed a significant increase in foreign direct investment (FDI), which was reported at $4.3 billion from January to November 2010. This was a marked increase from the $959 million in FDI that was reported for all of 2009. The increase was attributed to growth and interest in the manufacturing and mining sectors.

20 INCOME

The CIA estimated that in 2010 the GDP of Zambia was $20.04 billion. The CIA defines GDP as the value of all final goods and services produced within a nation in a given year and computed on the basis of purchasing power parity (PPP) rather than value as measured on the basis of the rate of the exchange based on current dollars. The per capita GDP was estimated at $1,500. The annual growth rate of GDP was 7.6%. The average inflation rate was 8.5%. It was estimated that agriculture accounted for 19.7% of GDP, industry 33.7%, and services 46.6%. Remittances from citizens living abroad totaled $41.3 million or about $3 per capita and accounted for approximately 0.2% of GDP.

As of 2011 the World Bank reported that actual individual consumption in Zambia was 73.9% of GDP and accounted for 0.03% of world consumption. By comparison, the United States accounted for 25.44% of world individual consumption. The World Bank also estimated that 8.4% of Zambia's GDP was spent on food and beverages, 25.4% on housing and household furnishings, 3.9% on clothes, 8.7% on health, 9.6% on transportation, 0.3% on communications, 8.3% on recreation, 0.0% on restaurants and hotels, and 3.7% on miscellaneous goods and services and purchases from abroad.

21 LABOR

The Ministry of Labor and Social Security's Labor Department is responsible for employment exchange services and for enforcing protective labor legislation. There were about 19 large national labor unions, all but one of them affiliated with the Zambia Congress of Trade Unions (ZCTU). With the exception of essential services, all workers have the right to strike. As of 2010, Zambia had a total labor force of 5.524 million people. Within that labor force, CIA estimates in 2004 noted that 85% were employed in agriculture, 6% in industry, and 9% in the service sector.

The minimum wage was ZMK419, 000 per month (US$82) per month in 2011. The maximum regular workweek is 48 hours, but most wage earners work 40-hour weeks. The minimum working age is 16 years. This is enforced in the industrial sector but not in subsistence agriculture, domestic services, or the informal economy where children are more likely to work. The law also regulates minimum health and safety standards in industry but staffing problems at the Ministry of Labor and Social Welfare chronically limit enforcement effectiveness.

22 AGRICULTURE

The development of commercial farming followed the construction of the railroad in the early 20th century, but the main stimulus did not come until World War II (1939–45), when it was necessary to ensure a maximum output of copper and to minimize the shipping space required for food imports. Food production con-

tinued to expand as the copper industry helped raise living standards. Additional European immigration in the 1950s, as well as programs to diversify the economy, gave rise to the production for export of tobacco, cotton, and peanuts. However, partly because of the rapidly rising population, agricultural output never reached the point of meeting domestic food requirements.

Roughly 7% of the total land is farmed, and the country's major crops include corn, sorghum, rice, peanuts, sunflower seed, vegetables, flowers, tobacco, cotton, sugarcane, cassava (tapioca), and coffee. Cereal production in 2009 amounted to 2.2 million tons, fruit production 111,339 tons, and vegetable production 431,711 tons. Throughout the 2000s, the agricultural sector benefitted from of a series of grants from the United States African Development Foundation (USADF), which offered more than $500,000 in funds for grassroots farming organizations. The groups primarily focus on rice production, but include some maize, cassava, and groundnut farmers as well. Grant funds provide jobs, increase incomes for workers, and finance projects to improve crop production.

23 ANIMAL HUSBANDRY

The UN Food and Agriculture Organization (FAO) reported that Zambia dedicated 20 million hectares (49.4 million acres) to permanent pasture or meadow in 2009. During that year, the country tended 30 million chickens, 2.9 million head of cattle, and 340,000 pigs. The production from these animals amounted to 58,523 tons of beef and veal, 11,067 tons of pork, 36,507 tons of poultry, 41,573 tons of eggs, and 90,496 tons of milk. Zambia also produced 7,665 tons of cattle hide. Cattle production in certain regions is limited by sleeping sickness, carried by the tsetse fly.

24 FISHING

Because Zambia's inland waters are a valuable source of food and employment, the fishing industry plays an important part in the rural economy. Large quantities of fish, most of which are transported by rail to processing centers, are frozen or dried. Major quantities are obtained from Bangweulu, Tanganyika, and Mweru lakes, and from the Kafue and Luapula rivers. Zambia had 235 decked commercial fishing boats in 2008. The annual capture totaled 79,403 tons according to the UN FAO. The export value of seafood totaled $3.52 million.

25 FORESTRY

Approximately 67% of Zambia is covered by forest. The UN FAO estimated the 2009 roundwood production at 1.33 million cu m (46.8 million cu ft). The value of all forest products, including roundwood, totaled $9.66 million. Commercial exploitation is concentrated in the southwest and in the Copperbelt. Some 90% of redwood production is for fuel needs.

26 MINING

Zambia's mining sector in 2009 was dominated by the production of copper and cobalt, for which the country ranks 11th and second in the world, respectively. The country was also a leading producer of gem quality emeralds. However, mining and quarrying as a whole, accounted for only 8.9% of Zambia's GDP in 2009. Exports of cobalt and copper were valued at $3.3 billion in 2009 and accounted for 74% of exports. Gemstones, mined mostly by small-scale and artisanal miners, also recorded significant earnings; earnings from this segment may amount to as much as $250 million per year, since much of the output bypassed official counts. Construction was another leading industry, along with the production of chemicals and fertilizers. By 2000, privatization of most of the major mines, including copper, had been completed, and efforts were ongoing to privatize the gemstone and other small mines sectors, and to attract foreign investors to develop other known metallic and industrial mineral resources. Among the difficulties faced by landlocked Zambia were high transportation costs, the threat posed by HIV/AIDS to the labor force, cyclical world commodity prices, and the impact of civil wars in Angola and Democratic Republic of the Congo on foreign investment.

In 2009 total copper mine output (by concentration, cementation, and leaching; metal content) was 697,000 metric tons, up from 546,000 metric tons in 2008. The output of cobalt (metal content), as a by-product of copper mining and processing, was 1,500 metric tons, down from 3,991 metric tons in 2008. The mining industry has been effected by slow global economic growth, labor unrest, transportation difficulties, including port and rail congestion, and shortages of spare parts, raw materials, and fuel. Investment reversals in 2002 involved the Konkola Mines and the Baluba-Luanshya Mines. As a result, the government was forced to reopen privatization bids.

Among the largest copper mines were the Nkana (5.5 million tons ore per year capacity), the Nchanga and Chingola open-pits (4.5 million tons ore per year), the Nchanga underground (2.8 million tons), the Mufalira (2.8 million tons), the Konkola underground (2.2 million tons), the Luanshya underground (1.7 million tons), and the Baluba underground (1.4 million tons). The country's total mineral resources exceeded 2,580 million tons, with ore reserves of 728 million tons. Equinox Resources Ltd.'s Lumwana project, with two large copper-cobalt-gold-uranium deposits (Chimiwunga and Malundwe), had resources of 1 billion tons that contained 0.67% copper, and 481 million tons of ore (1% copper). The Kalimba Group's Nama and Ngosa areas had a resource of 950 million tons.

In April 2010, the government celebrated the official launch of two new copper mines: the Konkola Deep Mining Project (KDMP) in Chililabombwe, north of the capital of Lusaka, and the Nchanga Smelter in nearby Chingola. The launch came only a few days after the announcement that China Nonferrous Metal Mining (CNMC) planned to invest $600 million in Zambian copper mines for 2010–11. CNMC operates the Luanshya and Mulayashi mines. CNMC is one of the largest investors in Zambia's copper sector, having invested more than $1 billion dollars since 1998. Zambia is the second largest copper producer in the world. In 2009, copper mining accounted for about 80% of Zambia's foreign earnings and nearly 16% of its GDP.

The copper industry showed marked potential into mid-2010 as copper prices rose due to increased demand, particularly in the need for construction related products such as pipes and wiring. At least $5 billion was invested in the Zambian copper industry from 2002 through 2010. Although foreign investment is strong, trouble from within might dim the otherwise bright prospects for the industry. In July 2010, the nation's largest mine workers union announced its intention to block the development of a $400 million Brazilian-sponsored mine due to concerns over the company's record of labor relations. The government has urged the unions to overlook some concerns in favor of the socioeconomic benefits to the nation as a whole.

Zambia also produced gold, refined selenium, silver, cement, clays (including brick, china, and ball), gemstones (amethyst, beryl, emerald, red garnet, and tourmaline), calcined lime, limestone, sand and gravel, and sulfur. No iron ore, tin, aquamarine, citrine, feldspar, magnetite, or nitrogen has been produced for several years. Exploration was being carried out for zinc, and for diamonds in western Zambia.

27 ENERGY AND POWER

The World Bank reported in 2008 that Zambia produced 9.7 billion kWh of electricity, of which nearly 100% was from hydropower. It consumed 7.6 billion kWh, or 548 kWh per capita. Roughly 8% of total energy came from fossil fuels, while 11% came from alternative fuels. Per capita oil consumption was 583 kg. Zambia exports almost 30% of its production to Zimbabwe.

In 2010 the government signed loan agreements with China's Sino-Hydro Company and the China Africa Development Fund for major funds to build a 600-MW, $1.5 billion power plant in southern Zambia. Construction on the new Kafue Gorge Lower power plant began in 2011. Frequent power outages in this region of the country, and a lack of capital to improve the situation, have forced the nation to import power from the Democratic Republic of Congo in order to keep the copper mines of the region operational. The Chinese groups have offered loans of $1 billion to set the project in motion. These two groups, combined with the Zambian government power utility ZESCO, formed a joint venture company for the operation of the project. The project was expected to be completed by the end of 2016, creating 2,000 short-term jobs.

28 INDUSTRY

Industry accounted for 33.7% of GDP in 2010. The industrial production growth rate was 9.1% in 2011. Apart from copper refining, the most important industries are those connected with the manufacture of sulfuric acid, fertilizer, compressor lubricants, electrical appliances and parts, glass, batteries, cigarettes, textiles, yarn, glycerine, vehicle and tractor assembling, sawmilling, wood and joinery manufacture, tire retreading, processing of food and drink, and the manufacture of cement and cement products. Nitrogen Chemicals of Zambia, which produces fertilizer, is the largest nonmining enterprise. Since tariff barriers for imports have been lifted, many manufacturing facilities have closed, especially in the clothing industry.

29 SCIENCE AND TECHNOLOGY

The World Bank reported in 2009 that there were no patent applications in science and technology in Zambia. The National Council for Scientific Research, founded in 1967 at Lusaka, advises the government on scientific matters and coordinates and disseminates the results of the Zambian research effort. Scientific learned societies include the Engineering Institution of Zambia, founded in 1955 at Lusaka. Research institutes specialize in fisheries, veterinary science, geology, agriculture, forestry and forest products, tropical diseases, pneumoconiosis, and red locust control. The University of Zambia, founded in 1965 at Lusaka, has de-

Principal Trading Partners – Zambia (2010)

(In millions of US dollars)

Country	Total	Exports	Imports	Balance
World	12,521.1	7,200.3	5,320.8	1,879.5
Switzerland	3,694.1	3,673.5	20.6	3,652.9
South Africa	2,485.3	657.9	1,827.4	-1,169.6
China	1,745.1	1,455.4	289.6	1,165.8
Congo	1,550.6	322.7	1,227.9	-905.2
Kuwait	476.2	13.2	463.0	-449.8
United Arab Emirates	292.9	176.3	116.7	59.6
United Kingdom	240.6	134.8	105.8	29.0
Zimbabwe	189.6	117.8	71.9	45.9
India	163.5	19.0	144.4	-125.4
Malawi	116.1	102.7	13.4	89.2

(…) data not available or not significant.

(n.s.) not specified.

SOURCE: *2011 Direction of Trade Statistics Yearbook*, New York: United Nations, 2011.

partments of natural sciences, engineering, medicine, agricultural sciences, veterinary sciences, and mines. Copperbelt University, founded in 1979 at Kitwe, has schools of environmental studies and technology. Three other colleges offer courses in agriculture and engineering. In 1987–97, science and engineering students accounted for 16% of college and university enrollments. In 1999 (the latest year for which data is available), there were 55 researchers and 17 technicians engaged in research and development per million people. In 2002, high technology exports totaled $2 million, or 2% of the country's manufactured exports.

³⁰DOMESTIC TRADE

Since independence, trading activity has increased in both rural and urban areas, especially in Lusaka. Centers of trading activity are the main towns along the rail line. Wholesale outlets are prevalent in larger towns and cities, while individually owned vendors and smaller retail shops are common in smaller communities and remote areas. Normal business hours are from 8 a.m. to 5 p.m., Monday–Friday, and 8 a.m. to 12:30 p.m. on Saturday. Banks are open from 8:15 a.m. to 12:45 p.m. on most weekdays, but close at noon on Thursdays and 11 a.m. on Saturdays.

³¹FOREIGN TRADE

Zambia imported $4.949 billion worth of goods and services in 2008, while exporting $6.463 billion worth of goods and services. Major import partners in 2009 were South Africa, 40.2%; Democratic Republic of the Congo, 12.9%; Kuwait, 10.6%; and China, 4.7% . Its major export partners were Switzerland, 47.1%; China, 11.2%; South Africa, 9.2%; and Democratic Republic of the Congo, 7%. Mineral commodities account for about 90% of exports, led by copper and cobalt. Other export commodities include zinc, lead, and tobacco. Leading imports are machinery, transportation equipment, foodstuffs, fuels, petroleum products, electricity, and fertilizer.

³²BALANCE OF PAYMENTS

In the early 2000s, the trade deficit worsened due to mining-related imports needed to reform the privatized copper industry. None-

theless, an improvement in official and commercial inflows, supported by a resumption of concessional donor support, prompted a recovery. In 2010 Zambia had a foreign trade surplus of $441 million, amounting to 0.8% of GDP. However, a heavy debt burden frequently gives the country a current account deficit (-$42.7 million in 2011), and hard currency is often in short supply.

³³BANKING AND SECURITIES

In November 1970, the Zambian government announced that it would take a majority interest in all banks operating in Zambia; however, the banking proposals were later modified so that the government became majority shareholder through the State Finance and Development Corporation of the already state-owned Zambia National Commercial Bank Ltd. (ZNCB) and the Commercial Bank of Zambia. The state-owned Bank of Zambia (BOZ), the central bank founded in 1964, sets and controls all currency and banking activities in the country.

There is a Development Bank of Zambia and the Lima Bank financed by the government. Other state-owned financial institutions include the Zambia National Building Society. In 1985 the first locally and privately owned bank was formed, the African Commercial Bank. Its success led to the establishment of several more, including Cavmont Merchant Bank, making Zambia one of Africa's most "overcrowded" countries in terms of banking, with 28 registered commercial banks at the end of December 1994. According to the Bank of Zambia, this number had dropped to 19 in 2011.

In 2009 the discount rate, the interest rate the central bank lends to other financial institutions in the short term, was 8.39%. The commercial bank prime lending rate, the rate at which banks lend to customers, was 20.92%.

Balance of Payments – Zambia (2010)

(In millions of US dollars)

Current Account		**386.1**
Balance on goods		2,703.7
Imports	-4,709.9	
Exports	7,413.6	
Balance on services		-628.1
Balance on income		-1,892.7
Current transfers		203.2
Capital Account		**149.7**
Financial Account		**-574.9**
Direct investment abroad		-288.7
Direct investment in Zambia		1,041.4
Portfolio investment assets		…
Portfolio investment liabilities		73.6
Financial derivatives		…
Other investment assets		-1,693.3
Other investment liabilities		292.1
Net Errors and Omissions		**-107.7**
Reserves and Related Items		**146.7**

(…) data not available or not significant.

SOURCE: *Balance of Payment Statistics Yearbook 2011*, Washington, DC: International Monetary Fund, 2011.

³⁴INSURANCE

On 1 January 1972, the Zambia State Insurance Corp. (ZSIC) took over all insurance transactions in Zambia. The operations of ZSIC cover fire, marine, aviation, accident, motor vehicle, and life insurance. All imports must be insured with this agency.

³⁵PUBLIC FINANCE

With its heavy dependency on copper, Zambia is able to show comfortable surpluses in its public accounts only when the mining industry is prosperous. From 1985 to 1987, Zambia attempted to implement a structural reform program, sponsored by the World Bank and IMF. In 1987, however, the government stopped the program and reverted to deficit spending and monetary creation. By 1992, a new government was committed to curtailing public expenditures through privatization and decreasing the civil service. By 1998, more than 85% of parastatals were privatized. In early 2000, the giant parastatal mining company, Zambian Consolidated Copper Mines (ZCCM) was completely privatized; that transaction helped Zambia satisfy the conditions for balance of payment support. In 2005 Zambia's central government took in revenues of approximately $1.6 billion and had expenditures of $1.8 billion. Revenues minus expenditures totaled approximately -$178 million. Public debt in 2005 amounted to 104.2% of GDP. Total external debt was $5.866 billion. In 2010 the budget of Zambia included $3.2 billion in public revenue and $3.743 billion in public expenditures. The budget deficit amounted to 3.3% of GDP. Public debt was 24.1% of GDP, with $3.456 billion of the debt held by foreign entities.

³⁶TAXATION

As of 2011, Zambia's income and corporate taxes were 35% and sales tax or VAT rate was 16%. Generally, dividends, interest, royalties and management fees are each subject to a 15% withholding tax. There is also a mineral royalty tax and a property transfer tax.

Income taxes include a 1% charge by local Councils on the gross salaries of employees after a deduction of ZMK300,000 (about $66.55) and a 1.015% property tax. In 2011 individual income was taxed according to a progressive schedule with four bands: 0% on the first ZMK9.6 million ($1,920) of annual income; 25% on the next ZMK9.6 million to ZMK16.02 million ($3,204); 30% on the next ZMK16.02 million to ZMK49.2 million ($9,840), and 35% on all incomes above ZMK49.2 million.

A value-added tax (VAT) with a standard rate of 20% replaced the sales tax in 1995. The standard rate was subsequently reduced to 17.5% by 2005 and 16% by 2011. Items exempted from VAT include insurance transactions, mosquito nets and insecticides, and exports.

³⁷CUSTOMS AND DUTIES

Tariff schedules give preferential treatment to imports from the United Kingdom and other Commonwealth countries. Zambia belongs to the Common Market of Eastern and Southern Africa (COMESA) and the Southern African Development Community (SADC), both committed to free trade. Rebates are allowed on certain capital goods and on most materials used in local manufacturing industries. Tariff protection also is accorded to selected new industries. Most imports require licenses. Import duties ranged from 5% for raw materials and capital equipment, 15% for intermediate goods, and 25% on final products. Selected items, such as soaps and vegetable cooking oils, carry special protective tariffs. There are no free trade zones.

³⁸FOREIGN INVESTMENT

In the past, the heaviest concentrations of foreign private capital in Zambia were in the mining enterprises of the Copperbelt. Anglo-American holds only a 27% interest in the national mining company ZCCM, a company that was privatized in 2000. Most investment is from the United Kingdom or South Africa. Although tax holidays have been offered as incentives, Zambia's highly socialized economy has not been conducive to private foreign investment, and exchange controls have made the repatriation of profits and dividends difficult.

Laws concerning retention of foreign exchange have been consistent, achieving full liberalization only recently. In 1983, exporters of nontraditional items could keep 50% of earned foreign exchange to finance imported inputs. This resulted in a fivefold increase in nonmetal exports. This provision was revoked in 1987. The Investment Act of 1991 provided for a 70% foreign exchange retention during the first three years of a license, 60% in the next two years, and 50% for the rest of the license's term. This act was subsequently revised to allow for full retention of foreign exchange earnings.

Annual FDI flow into Zambia reached $207 million in 1997, after which it steadily declined, from $198 million in 1998 to $72 million in 2001. Zambia's success in attracting FDI declined from 1990 to 2000. The FDI flow increased steadily from $82 million in 2002 to $334 million in 2004. For the period 1988 to 1999, Zambia's share of world FDI inflows was more than four times its share in world GDP. For the period 1998 to 2000, its share of world inward FDI was less than twice its share of world GDP. According to the World Bank Zambia`s net FDI inflow was $699.2 in 2009. This FDI represented 5.46% of GDP.

³⁹ECONOMIC DEVELOPMENT

Controlling inflation is a development priority, followed by faster implementation of social sector programs, legal and civil service reform, and privatization. New investment has been slow to form as investors await anticipated lower inflation rates. The lack of administrative capacity lies at the heart of the delays. Various debt cancellations and loans have been prescribed by the World Bank, Paris Club, and the United States.

In 2000 Zambia became eligible for $3.9 billion in debt service relief under the IMF/World Bank Heavily Indebted Poor Countries (HIPC) initiative. In July 2005, the world's eight leading industrialized nations (G8) agreed to provide further debt relief for poor countries including Zambia. The additional relief cut around $2.8 billion of debt, which was combined with the $3.9 billion debt write-off package agreed to under the HIPC initiative. By mid-2006, Zambia's debt burden declined to just $300 million. Debt relief came as a direct result of the government's fiscal austerity measures.

The agricultural sector is viewed as a perennial underachiever, with inconsistent government policy, lack of access to funding, and a weak infrastructure the primary culprits of the sector's stunted growth. Nonetheless, manufacturing and mining continued to sustain strong economic growth, with a 6.7% growth in total GDP projected for 2012. Maintaining single-digit inflation, which the government achieved during 2009–11, was a critical component of future growth. Political stability provided the opportunity for sound fiscal policy that could attract additional foreign investment.

40 SOCIAL DEVELOPMENT

A social insurance system provides benefits to most employed persons. Coverage includes old age pensions, permanent disability benefits, and survivorship payments. Medical care is available to all citizens in government facilities. Workers' compensation is funded totally by the employer. A funeral grant is also provided.

A national provident fund requires employers and employees to make contributions toward a worker's retirement at ages 50–55. This program covers employed persons, including domestic servants in urban areas, and agricultural workers. The lump sum payment is equivalent to contributions plus interest. Maternity leave of 90 days plus a maternity grant for each birth are provided to working women. Medical benefits are available to all citizens in government-run facilities and rural health clinics. Employers are required to fund work injury insurance for all employees.

Domestic violence against women is a widespread problem. Police are hesitant to interfere, although in 2004 the government formed a sex crimes unit to address the issue. Women have full legal rights under law, but customs discriminate against women in areas of inheritance, property ownership, and marriage. Sex-based discrimination in education and employment is pervasive. Women are underrepresented in senior management positions in the private sector and in high-level government positions. However, a growing number of women can be found in local government. Child welfare is a serious concern; there are hundreds of thousands of orphans under the age of 15, mostly attributable to the deaths of parents from HIV/AIDS.

Human rights abuses, including beatings and even the killing of persons in police custody, continue to be reported. A government-created commission is investigating past human rights abuses and some offenders have been punished. Human rights organizations operate freely in Zambia.

41 HEALTH

In 1964 responsibility for public health was transferred from the federation to Zambian authorities. Since then, the government has developed a health plan centered on specialist hospitals, with general and regional hospitals dealing with less complicated cases. At a lower level, district hospitals treat common medical and surgical cases. Rural health centers and clinics with outpatient facilities have been established throughout the country. Services to Zambian nationals are free at the rural health centers and clinics and at hospitals at the large urban centers. Due to government spending restrictions, the public health care sector has suffered from a severe shortage of doctors, medicine, and medical equipment and supplies.

The government records indicated nine hospitals and a few small outpatient clinics. Zambia produced approximately 25% of the pharmaceuticals it consumed. In 2011 there was 1 physician, 7 nurses and midwives, and 19 hospital beds per 10,000 inhabitants. The fertility rate was 5.7, while the infant mortality rate was 86 per

1,000 live births. .Zambia had an estimated 20 hospital beds for every 10,000 people. The country spent 5.9% of its GDP on healthcare, amounting to $47 per person.

Malaria and tuberculosis were major health problems, and hookworm and schistosomiasis afflicted a large proportion of the population. Cholera remained prevalent. In addition, the HIV/AIDS epidemic has increased the incidence of tuberculosis. Other commonly reported diseases in Zambia were diarrheal diseases, leprosy, and measles.

Zambia had one of the highest rates of HIV infection, even in hard-hit sub-Saharan Africa. The HIV/AIDS adult prevalence was 13.5% in 2009. It has been estimated that 500,000–1,000,000 Zambian children have lost both parents to AIDS. Although many international organizations have offered funds for HIV/AIDS education and care, government corruption has hindered many such efforts. In June 2010, the Global Fund to Fight Aids, Tuberculosis, and Malaria announced that it would suspend more than $300 million in general health funding as a result of concerns of corruption within the Zambian health ministry. However, the organization continued to sponsor life-saving treatments for individuals with these diseases.

Life expectancy in 2011 was 52.36 years.

42 HOUSING

Widespread instances of overcrowding and slum growth have for many years focused government attention on urban housing problems. Local authorities have statutory responsibility for housing and housing management. The Zambia National Building Society makes loans to local agencies for the financing of approved schemes and the National Housing Authority established a special fund to support self-help projects for low-income earners. One program gives land ownership to certain residents in recognized informal settlements, thus giving them legal status to build more permanent structures. Mining companies have constructed townships for the families of African workers in the Copperbelt.

The 2000 census counted 1,768,287 housing units nationwide. A 2002/2003 housing survey stated that 66% of all dwellings were defined as traditional structures; these use mud bricks, thatch, straw, and grass as primary building materials. Traditional dwellings accounted for 91% of the housing stock in rural areas and 16% in urban areas. About 34% of the population lived in modern or conventional housing structures. Conventional structures accounted for 86% of the housing stock in Lusaka province and 72% of housing in Copperbelt. About 78% of all dwellings were owner occupied. About 54% of all households lived in units of only one bedroom. Only 50% of all households had access to a source of clean drinking water, 18% had electricity for lighting, and over 50% of all households used pit latrines. The average household size was about five members.

43 EDUCATION

In 2009 the World Bank estimated that 91% of age-eligible children in Zambia were enrolled in primary school. Secondary enrollment for age-eligible children stood at 46%. It is estimated that about 78% of all students complete their primary education. Overall, the CIA estimated that Zambia had a literacy rate of

80.6% in 2004 (most recent information available as of February 2012). Public expenditure on education represented 1.3% of GDP.

Most of the nation's schools are operated by local authorities or by missions and are aided by the central government. A small number of schools are directly administered by the government. Primary education lasts for seven years and is compulsory. Secondary education lasts for five years: two years of junior and three years of senior school. Students must pass an entrance exam to enter senior secondary school.

Higher education opportunities were very limited in Zambia. In 2011 Zambia had six universities: The University of Zambia, Copperbelt University, Zambia Open University, Cavendish University, Zambia Adventist University, and Northrise University. Other institutions of higher learning included technical colleges and a two-year colleges of agriculture. In 2009 it was estimated that about 2% of the tertiary age population were enrolled in tertiary education programs.

44 LIBRARIES AND MUSEUMS

The Zambia Library Service maintains 900 library centers, six regional libraries, six branch libraries, and a central library with 500,000 volumes. The Lusaka Urban District Libraries has 145,000 volumes, and the Zambesi District Library has 120,000. The National Archives of Zambia maintains a library of about 70,000 volumes. The University of Zambia has holdings of more than 2.5 million books.

Zambia's museums include the National Museum, located in Livingstone. It has displays on natural history, archaeology, ethnography, recent history, African art, metallurgy, and memorabilia relating to David Livingstone. The Eastern Cataract Field Museum near Victoria Falls concentrates on archaeology and geology, including illustrations of the formation of the falls and the Stone Age sequence in the area. Lusaka has the Art Center and the Military and Police Museum of Zambia. The Moto Moto Museum in Mbala (founded in 1974) exhibits ethnography and history materials. The Copperbelt Museum at Ndola exhibits geological and historical items as well as ethnic art.

45 MEDIA

In 2009 the CIA reported that there were 90,300 telephone landlines in Zambia. In addition to landlines, mobile phone subscriptions averaged 34 per 100 people. There were 19 FM radio stations, 5 AM radio stations, and 4 shortwave radio stations. Internet users numbered 6 per 100 citizens. In 2010 the country had 14,771 Internet hosts. As of 2009, there were some 816,200 Internet users in Zambia.

There are a number of privately owned newspapers in the country. However, the publications with the largest circulations tend to be politically affiliated. There are three major daily newspapers: the UNIP-owned *Times of Zambia*, founded in Ndola in 1943 and with an estimated 2009 daily circulation of 32,093; the government-owned *Zambia Daily Mail*, published in Lusaka, with a circulation of 40,000; and *The Post*, an independent English-language paper founded in 1991, with a circulation of 40,000.

The constitution provides for free expression, including a free press; however the penal code lists several exceptions and justifies government restrictions and censorship.

46 ORGANIZATIONS

Professional and learned societies include the Wildlife Conservation Society of Zambia, the Zambia Library Association, and the Zambia Medical Association, all in Lusaka. Business groups include chambers of commerce in the major towns. The Zambia Association of Chambers of Commerce and Industry is located in Lusaka. The Consumer Protective Association of Zambia is also active.

National youth organizations include the Catholic Agricultural and Rural Youth Movement, Girl Guides Association of Zambia, YMCA/YWCA, United National Independence Party Youth League, Zambian Youth League, Girl Guides, and the Zambia Scouts Association. There are sports associations promoting amateur competition for athletes of all ages in a wide variety of pastimes, including softball, baseball, squash, lawn tennis, badminton, and weightlifting.

National women's organizations include the National Women's Lobby Group, the Society For Women and AIDS in Zambia, Women for Change, and the Women in Development Department. Among service organizations are the Lions, Rotary, Junior Chamber of Commerce (Jaycees), Professional Women's Club, and Women's Institute. There are national chapters of the Red Cross Society, Habitat for Humanity, the Society of St. Vincent de Paul, UNICEF, and Amnesty International.

47 TOURISM, TRAVEL, AND RECREATION

One of the most impressive tourist attractions in Zambia is Mosi-oa-Tunya ("the smoke that thunders")—Victoria Falls. In 1972, a national park system created 17 parks covering 8% of the entire country. The Kafue National Park, one of the largest in Africa, with 22,500 sq km (8,700 sq mi) of bush, forest, and plain, is well-served with tourist facilities. South Luangwa National Park is another outstanding wildlife area. Tourism in Zambia has maintained a steady increase since the mid-1970s. A valid passport is required to enter Zambia. Most travelers need a visa. Proof of vaccination against yellow fever is required if traveling from an infected country.

The *Tourism Factbook*, published by the UN World Tourism Organization, reported 710,000 incoming tourists to Zambia in 2009; they spent a total of $98 million. Of those incoming tourists, there were 467,000 from Africa. There were 9,894 hotel beds available in Zambia. The estimated daily cost to visit Lusaka, the capital, was $285. The cost of visiting other cities averaged $175.

48 FAMOUS PERSONS

Kenneth David Kaunda (b. 1924) was Zambia's president from independence in 1964 until 1991. Frederick J.T. Chiluba (1943–2011) ousted Kaunda in 1991 in Zambia's first free elections and was reelected in 1996; he served until 2002. Levy Patrick Mwanawasa (1948–2008) was the third president of Zambia from 2002 until his death in office in August 2008.

Harry Nkumbula (1916–83) was the leading and pioneer nationalist leader of Zambia`s liberation movement between the late 1940s and early 1960s. Nalumino Mundia (1927–88), long prominent in Zambian political affairs, was prime minister 1981–85, when he became ambassador to the United States.

49 DEPENDENCIES

Zambia has no territories or colonies.

50 BIBLIOGRAPHY

Guest, Emma. *Children of AIDS: Africa's Orphan Crisis.* Sterling, VA: Pluto Press, 2001.

Kaunda, Kenneth. *Letter to My Children.* London: Longman, 1963.

McElrath, Karen, ed. *HIV and AIDS: A Global View.* Westport, CT: Greenwood Press, 2002.

Mutale, Emmanuel. *The Management of Urban Development in Zambia.* Burlington, VT: Ashgate, 2004.

Phiri, B. J. *A Political History of Zambia: From Colonial Rule to the Third Republic, 1890–2001.* Trenton, NJ: Africa World Press, 2006.

Posner, Daniel N. *Institutions and Ethnic Politics in Africa.* New York: Cambridge University Press, 2005.

Rotberg, Robert I. *Ending Autocracy, Enabling Democracy: The Tribulations of Southern Africa, 1960–2000.* Cambridge, MA: World Peace Foundation, 2002.

Simon, David J, et al. *Historical Dictionary of Zambia.* Lanham, MD: Scarecrow Press, 2008.

Taylor, Scott D. *Culture and Customs of Zambia.* Westport, CT: Greenwood Press, 2006.

Zambian Women Entrepreneurs: Going for Growth. Lusaka, Zambia: ILO Office: Gender in Development Division (GIDD), International Labour Office, 2003.

Zeilig, Leo, and David Seddon. *A Political and Economic Dictionary of Africa.* Philadelphia: Routledge/Taylor and Francis, 2005.

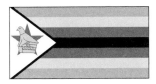

ZIMBABWE

Republic of Zimbabwe

CAPITAL: Harare

FLAG: The flag has seven equal horizontal stripes of green, yellow, red, black, red, yellow, and green. At the hoist is a white triangle, which contains a representation in yellow of the bird of Zimbabwe superimposed on a red star.

ANTHEM: *God Bless Africa.*

MONETARY UNIT: Zimbabwe does not use its own currency (ZWD). It uses multiple foreign currencies such as the South Africa Rand (ZAR), Botswana pula (BWP), British pound (£) and the US dollar (US$). The country effectively abandoned the use of the Zimbabwean dollar as an official currency on 12 April 2009. This was a result of the Reserve Bank of Zimbabwe legalizing the use of foreign currencies for transactions in January 2009. The government of Zimbabwe has insisted that any attempts to reintroduce Zimbabwean currency should be considered only if industrial output improves.

WEIGHTS AND MEASURES: The metric system is used.

HOLIDAYS: New Year's Day, 1 January; Independence Day, 18 April; Workers' Day, 1 May; Africa Day, 25 May;; Unity Day, 22 December; Christmas Day, 25 December; Boxing Day, 26 December. Movable holidays are Good Friday, Holy Saturday, Easter Monday, Heroes Day (2nd Monday in August) and Armed Forces Day (2nd Tuesday in August).

TIME: 2 p.m. = noon GMT.

¹LOCATION, SIZE, AND EXTENT

A landlocked country of south central Africa, Zimbabwe (formerly Rhodesia) lies between the Zambezi River on the N and the Limpopo River on the S. It has an area of 390,580 sq km (150,804 sq mi), with a length of 852 km (529 mi) WNW–ESE and a width of 710 km (441 mi) NNE–SSW. Comparatively, the area occupied by Zimbabwe is slightly larger than the state of Montana. Bounded on the N and E by Mozambique, on the S by the Republic of South Africa, on the SW by Botswana, and on the NW and N by Zambia, Zimbabwe has a total boundary length of 3,066 km (1,905 mi). Zimbabwe's capital city, Harare, is located in the northeast part of the country.

²TOPOGRAPHY

Most of Zimbabwe is rolling plateau, with over 75% of it lying between 600 and 1,500 m (2,000–5,000 ft) above sea level, and almost all of it over 300 m (1,000 ft). The area of high plateau, known as the highveld, is some 650 km (400 mi) long by 80 km (50 mi) wide, and stretches northeast to southwest at 1,200–1,675 m (4,000–5,500 ft). This culminates in the northeast in the Inyanga mountains, reaching the country's highest point at Mt. Inyangani, 2,592 m (8,504 ft). On either side of the highveld is the middleveld, a plateau ranging from about 600–1,200 m (2,000–4,000 ft) in height. Below 610 m (2,000 ft) are areas making up the lowveld, wide and grassy plains in the basins of the Zambezi and the Limpopo.

The highveld is a central ridge forming the country's watershed, with streams flowing southeast to the Limpopo and Sabi rivers and northwest into the Zambezi. Only the largest of the many rivers have an all-year-round flow of water.

³CLIMATE

Altitude and relief greatly affect both temperature and rainfall in Zimbabwe. The higher areas in the east and the highveld receive more rainfall and are cooler than the lower areas. Temperatures on the highveld vary from 12–13°C (54–55°F) in winter to 24°C (75°F) in summer. On the lowveld the temperatures are usually 6°C (11°F) higher, and summer temperatures in the Zambezi and Limpopo valleys average between 32–38°C (90–100°F). Rainfall decreases from east to west. The eastern mountains receive more than 100 cm (40 in) annually, while Harare has 81 cm (32 in) and Bulawayo 61 cm (24 in). The south and southwest receive little rainfall. Seasonal shortages of water are common.

The summer rainy season lasts from November to March. It is followed by a transitional season, during which both rainfall and temperatures decrease. The cool, dry season follows, lasting from mid-May to mid-August. Finally, there is the warm, dry season, which lasts until the onset of the rains.

⁴FLORA AND FAUNA

The World Resources Institute estimates that there are 4,440 plant species in Zimbabwe. The moist and mountainous east supports tropical evergreen and hardwood forests. Trees include teak and mahogany, knobthorn, msasa, and baobab. Among the numerous flowers and shrubs are hibiscus, spider lily, leonotus, cassia, tree wisteria, and dombeya.

Animal species include 222 mammals, 661 birds, 180 reptiles, and 40 amphibians. The calculation reflects the total number of distinct species residing in the country, not the number of endemic species. Mammals include elephant, lion, buffalo, hippopotamus, rhinoceros, gorilla, chimpanzee, baboon, okapi, giraffe, kudu, duiker, eland, sable, gemsbok, waterbuck, zebra, warthog, lynx, aardvark, porcupine, fox, badger, otter, hare, bat, shrew, and scaly anteater.

The largest lizard, the water monitor, is found in many rivers, as are several species of crocodile. Birds include the ant-thrush, barbet, bee-eater, bishop bird, bulbul, bush-warbler, drongo, emerald cuckoo, grouse, gray lourie, and pheasant.

5 ENVIRONMENT

The World Resources Institute reported that Zimbabwe had designated 5.72 million hectares (14.14 million acres) of land for protection as of 2006. Water resources totaled 20 cu km (4.8 cu mi) while water usage was 4.21 cu km (1.01 cu mi) per year. Domestic water usage accounted for 14% of total usage, industrial for 7%, and agricultural for 79%. Per capita water usage totaled 324 cu m (11,442 cu ft) per year. Water pollution results from mining and the use of fertilizers. Zimbabwe's cities produce 0.5 million tons of solid waste per year. The nation has been estimated to have the highest DDT concentrations in the world in its agricultural produce. Zimbabwe's air is polluted by vehicle and industrial emissions. The United Nations (UN) reported in 2008 that carbon dioxide emissions in Zimbabwe totaled 9,629 kilotons.

Among the most serious of Zimbabwe's environmental problems is erosion of its agricultural lands and deforestation. The confinement of large segments of the population to relatively unproductive lands before independence put severe pressure on these lands, a substantial portion of which may have been irreversibly damaged.

According to a 2011 report issued by the International Union for Conservation of Nature and Natural Resources (IUCN), the number of threatened species included 9 types of mammals, 14 species of birds, 6 species of amphibians, 3 species of fish, 5 species of invertebrates, and 16 species of plants. Zimbabwe has about half of the world's population of black rhinoceroses, an endangered species. Rare or threatened species include the cape vulture, the white rhino, black-cheeked lovebird, and brown hyena. For protection, the government has adopted a policy of shooting poachers on sight.

6 POPULATION

The US Central Intelligence Agency (CIA) estimates the population of Zimbabwe in 2011 to be approximately 12,084,304, which placed it at number 72 in population among the 196 nations of the world. In 2011, approximately 3.8% of the population was over 65 years of age, with another 41.9% under 15 years of age. The median age in Zimbabwe was 18.3 years. There were 0.91 males for every female in the country. The population's annual rate of change was 4.31%. The projected population for the year 2025 was

16,800,000. Population density in Zimbabwe was calculated at 31 people per sq km (80 people per sq mi).

The UN estimated that 38% of the population lived in urban areas, and that urban populations had an annual rate of change of 3.4%. The largest urban area was Harare, with a population of 1.6 million.

The prevalence of HIV/AIDS has had a significant impact on the population of Zimbabwe. The AIDS epidemic causes higher death and infant mortality rates, and lowers life expectancy.

7 MIGRATION

By early 1987, about 110,000 whites were estimated to have remained in Zimbabwe, about half the number since independence in 1980. There were also about 25,000 Coloured (of mixed race) and 10,000 Asians. Some 1.5 million people who had left for neighboring states during the civil war returned after independence, putting considerable strain on the new nation. In addition, by the end of 1992, famine and civil war in Mozambique had driven an estimated 136,600 Mozambicans into Zimbabwe. Between 1992 and 1996, 241,000 Mozambican refugees repatriated from Zimbabwe. In the early 1990s, there were about 25,000 Zimbabwe-born whites and 14,000 Zimbabwe-born blacks living in South Africa. As of 1999, there was still a small but steady flow of Zimbabweans into South Africa and Botswana in search of better paid employment. In the context of the country's long-running political and economic crisis of 2000 to 2008 almost 1.5 million Zimbabweans flocked to neighboring countries, especially South Africa. Estimates of Zimbabwe's net migration rate, carried out by the CIA in 2011, amounted to 24.83 migrants per 1,000 citizens. The total number of emigrants living abroad was 1.25 million, and the total number of immigrants living in Zimbabwe was 372,300. Zimbabwe also accepted 2,500 refugees.

8 ETHNIC GROUPS

Africans make up 98% of the total population in Zimbabwe and are mainly related to the two major Bantu-speaking groups, the Shona (about 82% of the population) and the Ndebele (about 14%). Of the former group, the Korekore predominate in the north; the Zezuru are in the center around Harare; the Karanga are in the south; and the Ndau and Manyika in the east. The various clans of the Ndebele, more recent immigrants from the south, occupy the area around Bulawayo and Gwanda. Other groups account for 11% of the African populace and include the Kalanga in the western part of the country near Botswana, the Nambya and the Dombe around Hwange in north-western part of the country, the Tonga near Kariba Lake, and the Sotho, Venda, and Hlengwe along the southern border. Whites make up 1% of the non-African population. Europeans are almost entirely either immigrants from the United Kingdom or South Africa or their descendants; those from South Africa include a substantial number of South African Dutch (Afrikaner) descent. There are small groups of Portuguese, Italians, and other Europeans. Asians and peoples of mixed ancestry make up the remaining 1%.

9 LANGUAGES

The Shona speak dialects of the same Bantu language, Shona. There are four major dialects: Karanga, Zezuru, Korekore, and Manyika.. The Ndebele speak modified versions of Ndebele (or

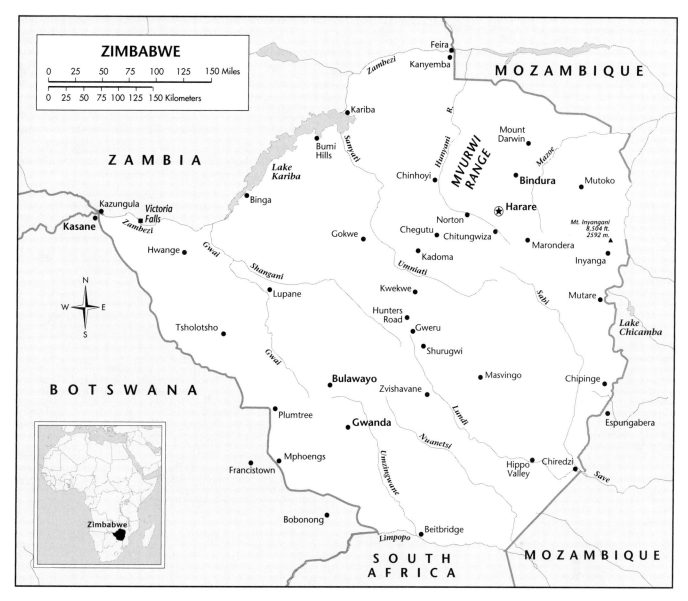

ZIMBABWE

0   25   50   75   100   125   150 Miles

0   25   50   75   100   125   150 Kilometers

ZAMBIA

MOZAMBIQUE

Feira

Kanyemba

Zambezi

Kariba

Lake
Kariba

Bumi
Hills

Binga

Mount
Darwin

MVURWI RANGE

Chinhoyi

Bindura

Mutoko

Harare

Kazungula   Victoria
Falls

Zambezi

Kasane

Hwange

Gwai

Gokwe

Chegutu   Chitungwiza

Norton

Kadoma

Marondera

Mt. Inyangani
8,504 ft.
2592 m.

Inyanga

Shangani

Umniati

Kwekwe

Mutare

Lupane

Hunters
Road

Sabi

Lake
Chicamba

Tsholotsho

Gwai

Gweru

Shurugwi

Masvingo

Chipinge

BOTSWANA

Bulawayo

Zvishavane

Lundi

Plumtree

Gwanda

Nuanetsi

Espungabera

Mphoengs

Umzingwane

Hippo
Valley

Chiredzi

Save

Francistown

Bobonong

Beitbridge

Limpopo

SOUTH
AFRICA

MOZAMBIQUE

Zimbabwe

N
W   E
S

LOCATION: 15°37′ to 22°25′S; 25°14′ to 33°4′ E. BOUNDARY LENGTHS: Mozambique, 1,231 kilometers (762 miles); South Africa, 225 kilometers (140 miles); Botswana, 813 kilometers (505 miles); Zambia, 797 kilometers (498 miles).

Sindebele), which belongs to the Nguni group of southeast Bantu languages. Minority languages include Tonga, Venda and Kalanga. English, the official language, is spoken by Europeans and by most Africans.

¹⁰RELIGION

Historically, Christianity, brought into the region by Portuguese traders and Jesuit priests in the late 1500s, has been the dominant religion of the nation. About 60–70% of the total population belong to various Christian denominations, with the largest being Roman Catholic (between 17–27% of the population). Certain regions of the country have traditional links to specific denominations, based on "areas of interest," which were created by missionaries from groups such as the Catholics, Methodists, Anglicans, Dutch Reformed, and the Salvation Army. As a result, individuals will often claim adherence to their local denomination. At the

turn of the 21st century, Pentecostal and Evangelical Churches began to make serious inroads in the Zimbabwean religious realm such as the Zimbabwe Assembly of God, a branch of the Assemblies of God Church, which adheres strictly to Christian tenets and opposes incorporation of traditional practices and beliefs..

There is a small Muslim community, estimated at less than 1% of the population. They are primarily immigrants from South Asia, the Middle East, and North Africa. There are also small numbers of Greek Orthodox, Jews, Hindus, Buddhists, and atheists.

A good number of African Initiated Churches (AICs) have developed from the mainstream Christian churches. These groups include the Zion Christian Church (ZCC); Johane Masowe; and Johanne Marange Apostolic Church. Some of these churches provide a mixture of traditional religious practices with Christianity. An organization known as Fambidzano formed in the mid-1970s to serve as a support coalition of indigenous churches. One of the goals of the organization is to provide continuing theological and biblical education for church leaders.

Belief in and practice of traditional religions is thought to be quite widespread, as it is sometimes practiced in conjunction with other established belief systems. The belief in and respect for traditional healers resulted in the organization of the Zimbabwe National African Traditional Healers' Association (ZINATHA), which provides licensing and regulation of healers.

In response to widespread belief in and fear of witchcraft, the colonial government passed the Witchcraft Suppression Act (WSA), which prohibits the practice of witchcraft, but also calls for prosecution of those falsely accusing others of the practice or engaging in witch hunts. The African led post-colonial government maintained the act. The act has helped protect those, particularly women, who have been falsely accused of witchcraft. However, members of ZINATHA are seeking an amendment to the law that would redefine certain terms. The Act defines witchcraft as "the use of charms and any other means or devices adopted in the practice of sorcery." The proposed amendment would refocus the law to prohibit any practices that are intended to cause harm.

Though relations between religious groups are generally amicable, some tensions exist between Christians and practitioners of traditional religions. In particular, Christian churches oppose traditional practices that allow polygamy and refuse the use of modern medicine. Some tension exists between the government and indigenous religions which refuse to participate in public health and vaccination programs because of religious beliefs in healing through prayer alone. The Zimbabwe Council of Churches, the Heads of Denominations, and the Evangelical Fellowship of Zimbabwe are ecumenical groups that promote interfaith dialogue and cooperation, while offering forums for discussion of social and political issues.

¹¹TRANSPORTATION

The CIA reports that Zimbabwe has a total of 97,267 km (60,439 mi) of roads in 2002, of which 18,481 km (11,484 mi) are paved. The National Railways of Zimbabwe operates the country's rail lines (all of it narrow gauge), of which 313 km (194 mi) were electrified. Rail links exist with Zambia, Mozambique, Botswana, and the Republic of South Africa. Electrification of the railroads was begun following independence.

The Mazoe and Zambezi rivers are used for transporting chrome ore from Harare to Mozambique. Important ports and harbors are at Binga and Kariba. Zimbabwe operates domestic, regional, and European flights. There are 94 airports in 2010 (only 8 with paved runways), which transported 261,480 passengers in 2009 according to the World Bank. Harare and Bulawayo are the principal airports.

¹²HISTORY

Evidence of Stone Age cultures dating back 100,000 years has been found, and it is thought that the San people, now living mostly in the Kalahari Desert, are the descendants of Zimbabwe's original inhabitants. The remains of ironworking cultures that date back to AD 300 have been discovered. Little is known of the early ironworkers, but it is believed that they were farmers, herdsmen, and hunters who lived in small groups. They put pressure on the San by gradually taking over the land. With the arrival of the Bantu-

speaking Shona from the north between the 10th and 11th centuries AD, the San were driven out or killed, and the early ironworkers were incorporated into the invading groups. The Shona gradually developed gold and ivory trade with the coast, and by the mid-15th century had established a strong empire, with its capital at the ancient city of Great Zimbabwe. With the collapse of Great Zimbabwe around the 16th Century the seat of power shifted to the Munhumutapa empire based in northeastern Zimbabwe. The Munhumutapa was later succeeded by the Rozvi Empire, which flourished for two centuries until its destruction by the Nguni groups such as the Ndebele.

By the time the British began arriving in the mid-19th century, the Shona people had long been subjected to slave raids. The once-powerful Urozwi Empire had been destroyed in the 1830s by the Ndebele, who, under Mzilikaze, had fled from the Zulus in South Africa. David Livingstone, a Scottish missionary and explorer, was chiefly responsible for opening the whole region to European penetration. His explorations in the 1850s focused public attention on Central Africa, and his reports on the slave trade stimulated missionary activity. In 1858, after visiting Mzilikaze, Robert Moffat, Livingstone's father-in-law, established Inyati Mission, the first permanent European settlement in what is now Zimbabwe.

To forestall Portuguese and Boer expansion, both the British government and Cecil Rhodes actively sought to acquire territory. Rhodes, whose fortune had been made through diamond mining in South Africa, became especially active in gaining mineral rights and in sending settlers into Matabeleland (the area occupied by the Ndebele people) and Mashonaland (the area occupied by the Shona people). In 1888, Lobengula, king of the Ndebele, accepted a treaty with Great Britain and granted to Charles Rudd, one of Rhodes's agents, exclusive mineral rights to the lands he controlled. Gold was already known to exist in Mashonaland, so, with the grant of rights, Rhodes was able to obtain a royal charter for his British South Africa Company (BSAC) in 1889. The BSAC sent a group of settlers with a force of European police into Mashonaland, where they founded the town of Salisbury (now Harare). Rhodes gained the right to dispose of land to settlers (a right he was already exercising de facto). With the defeat of the Ndebele and the Shona between 1893 and 1897, Europeans were guaranteed unimpeded settlement. The name Rhodesia was in common usage by 1895.

Under BSAC administration, British settlement continued, but conflicts arose between the settlers and the company. In 1923, Southern Rhodesia was annexed to the crown; its African inhabitants thereby became British subjects, and the colony received its basic constitution. Ten years later, the BSAC ceded its mineral rights to the territory's government for £2 million.

After the onset of self-government, the major issue in Southern Rhodesia was the relationship between the European settlers and the African population. The British government, besides controlling the colony's foreign affairs, retained certain powers to safeguard the rights of Africans. In 1930, however, Southern Rhodesia adopted a land apportionment act that was accepted by the British government. Under this measure, about half the total land area, including all the mining and industrial regions and all the areas served by railroads or roads, was reserved for Europeans. Most of the rest was designated as Tribal Trust Land, native purchase land, or unassigned land. Later acts firmly entrenched the policy of dividing land on a racial basis.

In 1953, the Central African Federation was formed, consisting of the three British territories of Northern Rhodesia (now Zambia), Nyasaland (now Malawi), and Southern Rhodesia (now Zimbabwe), with each territory retaining its original constitutional status. In 1962, in spite of the opposition of the federal prime minister, Sir Roy Welensky, Nyasaland and Northern Rhodesia withdrew from the federation with British approval. The federation disbanded in 1963. Southern Rhodesia, although legally still a colony, sought an independent course under the name of Rhodesia.

Political agitation in Rhodesia increased after the United Kingdom's granting of independence to Malawi and Zambia in the early 1960s. The white-settler government demanded formalization of independence, which it claimed had been in effect since 1923. The African nationalists also demanded independence, but under conditions of universal franchise and African majority rule. The British government refused to yield to settler demands without amendments to the colony's constitution, including a graduated extension of the franchise leading to eventual African rule. Negotiations repeatedly broke down, and on 5 November 1965, Rhodesian Prime Minister Ian Smith declared a state of emergency. On 11 November, the Smith government issued a unilateral declaration of independence (since known as UDI). The British government viewed UDI as illegal and imposed limited economic sanctions, but these measures did not bring about the desired results. In December, the UN Security Council passed a resolution calling for selective mandatory sanctions against Rhodesia. Further attempts at a negotiated settlement ended in failure. In a referendum held on 20 June 1969, the Rhodesian electorate-92% white-approved the establishment of a republic.

The British governor-general, Sir Humphrey Gibbs, resigned on 24 June 1969. The Legislative Council passed the constitution bill in November, and Rhodesia declared itself a republic on 2 March 1970. The United Kingdom called the declaration illegal, and 11 countries closed their consulates in Rhodesia. The UN Security Council called on member states not to recognize any acts by the illegal regime and condemned Portugal and South Africa for maintaining relations with Rhodesia.

Problems in Rhodesia deepened after UDI, largely as a result of regional and international political pressure, African nationalist demands, and African guerrilla activities. Members of the African National Congress(ANC), an African nationalist group, were increasingly subjected to persecution and arrest. Nevertheless, guerrilla activity continued. The principal African nationalist groups, besides the ANC, were the Zimbabwe African People's Union (ZAPU), and the Zimbabwe African National Union (ZANU).

A meeting took place in Geneva in October 1976 between the British and Smith governments and four African nationalist groups. Prominent at the meeting were Joshua Nkomo, the leader of ZAPU; Robert Mugabe, leader of ZANU; Bishop Abel Muzorewa of the ANC; and the Reverend Ndabaningi Sithole, former leader of ZANU. Nkomo and Mugabe had previously formed an alliance, the Patriotic Front. The conference was unable to find the basis for a national settlement; but on 3 March 1978, the Smith regime signed an internal agreement with Muzorewa, Sithole, and other leaders, providing for qualified majority rule and universal suffrage. Although Bishop Muzorewa, whose party won a ma-

jority in the elections of April 1979, became the first black prime minister of the country (now renamed Zimbabwe-Rhodesia), the Patriotic Front disregarded this new arrangement and continued fighting.

Meanwhile, the British government had begun new consultations on the conflict, and at the Commonwealth of Nations Conference in Lusaka, Zambia, in August 1979, committed itself to seeking a settlement. Negotiations that began at Lancaster House, in England, on 10 September resulted in an agreement, by 21 December, on a new, democratic constitution, democratic elections, and independence. On 10 December, the Zimbabwe-Rhodesian parliament had dissolved itself, and the country reverted to formal colonial status during the transition period before independence. That month, sanctions were lifted and a cease-fire declared. Following elections held in February, Robert Mugabe became the first prime minister and formed a coalition government that included Joshua Nkomo. The independent nation of Zimbabwe was proclaimed on 18 April 1980, and the new parliament opened on 14 May 1980.

Independence and Factionalism

Following independence, Zimbabwe initially made significant economic and social progress, but internal dissent became increasingly evident. The long-simmering rivalry erupted between Mugabe's dominant ZANU-Patriotic Front (PF) Party , which represented the majority Shona ethnic groups, and Nkomo's ZAPU, which had the support of the minority Ndebele. A major point of contention was Mugabe's intention to make Zimbabwe a one-party state. Mugabe expelled Nkomo and his (PF) ZAPU allies from the cabinet in February 1982 after the discovery of arms caches that were alleged to be part of a ZAPU-led coup attempt. On 8 March 1983, Nkomo went into exile, but returned to Parliament in August.

Meanwhile, internal security worsened, especially in Matabeleland, where Nkomo supporters allegedly resorted to banditry. The government responded by jailing suspected dissidents, using emergency powers dating from the period of white rule, and by military campaigns against the bandits . The government's Fifth Brigade or Gukurahundi, trained by the Democratic People's Republic of Korea and loyal to Mugabe, was accused of numerous atrocities against civilians in Matabeleland during 1983. By early 1984, it was reported that many residents in Matabeleland and Midlands provinces were starving as a result of the military's interruption of food supplies to the area.

Armed dissidents continued to operate in Matabeleland until 1987, and food supplies in the area continued to be inadequate. A round of particularly brutal killings-men, women, and children-occurred late in the year. The violence abated after the two largest political parties, ZANU and ZAPU, agreed to merge in December 1987. Civic and human rights organizations claim that nearly 20,000 civilians perished in the Matabeleland and Midlands as a result of the government's military campaigns.

A growing problem, however, was the political instability of Zimbabwe's neighbors to the south and east. In 1986, South African forces raided the premises of the South African black-liberation African National Congress in Harare, and 10,000 Zimbabwean troops were deployed in Mozambique, seeking to keep antigovernment forces in that country from severing Zimbabwe's rail, road, and oil-pipeline links with the port of Beira in Mozambique. Although Beira is the closest port to landlocked Zimbabwe, because of the guerrilla war in Mozambique about 85% of Zimbabwe's foreign trade was passing through South Africa instead.

Despite its reputed commitment to socialism, the Mugabe government was slow to dismantle the socioeconomic structures of the old Rhodesia. Until 1990, the government's hands were tied by the Lancaster House accords. Private property, most particularly large white-owned estates, could not be confiscated without fair market compensation. Nevertheless, economic progress was solid and Zimbabwe seemed to have come to terms with its settler minority. There was only modest resettlement of the landless (52,000 out of the target of 162,000 landless families from 1980 to 1990) and when white farmers were bought out, black politicians often benefited. Some 4,000 white farmers owned more than one-third of the best land.

In March 1992, a controversial Land Acquisition Act was passed calling for the government to purchase half of the mostly white-owned commercial farming land at below-market prices, without the right of appeal, in order to redistribute land to black peasants. However, the government continued to move slowly and not until April 1993 was it announced that 70 farms, totaling 470,000 acres, would be purchased. Unease among whites grew, as did fear of unemployment, already at around 40%. Economic conditions also threatened to derail the Economic Structural Adjustment Program (ESAP) designed by the IMF and the World Bank. ESAP pressed for a market-driven economy, reduction of the civil service, and an end to price controls and commodity subsidies.

Meanwhile, in the March 1990 elections, Mugabe was reelected with 78.3% of the vote. The Zimbabwe Unity Movement (ZUM) candidate, Tekere, received about 21.7% of the vote. For parliament, ZANU-PF got 117 seats; ZUM, 2 seats; and ZANU-Ndonga, 1 seat. There was a sharp drop in voter participation, and the election was marred by restrictions on opposition activity and open intimidation of opposition voters. At first, Mugabe insisted that the results were a mandate to establish a one-party state. In 1991, however, growing opposition abroad and domestically, even within ZANU-PF, forced him to postpone his plans. Sensing an erosion of political support, Mugabe restricted human and political rights, weakened the Bill of Rights, placed checks on the judiciary, and tampered with voters' rolls and opposition party financing. The government also suspended the investigation into the 1982–87 Matabeleland Crisis, a decision that prompted a November 1993 reprimand by the Organization of African Unity (OAU)'s Human Rights Commission.

As the economy sputtered, political opposition grew. In January 1992, Sithole returned from seven years of self-imposed exile in the United States. In July, Ian Smith chaired a meeting of Rhodesian-era parties seeking to form a coalition in opposition to Mugabe. Sithole and his ZANU-Ndonga Party, the United African National Congress, the largely white Conservative Alliance, and Edgar Tekere's ZUM were included. Students, church leaders, trade unionists, and the media began to speak out. In May 1992 a new pressure group, the Forum for Democratic Reform, was launched in preparation for the 1995 elections. Parliamentary and presidential elections in 1995 and 1996 though officially won by ZANU-PF, were discredited by opposition boycotts and low voter turnout. Then in 1997, a homegrown pro-democracy coalition

was launched from the constituency for constitutional reform-the National Constitutional Assembly (NCA). The birth of the NCA dovetailed with the growing radicalization of the Zimbabwe Confederation of Trade Unions (ZCTU) and its transformation from a collective bargaining agent for organized urban industrial labor into a broad-based political opposition movement representing a wide spectrum of civil society, the Movement for Democratic Change (MDC). The official launch of the MDC at Rufaro Stadium on 11 September 1999 was followed by the first Congress at which Morgan Tsvangirai was elected president, and Gibson Sibanda his deputy. NCA supporters embraced the MDC as a vehicle for implementing the new constitution should the government be amenable to it.

The MDC's first test came in February 2000 at a national referendum for constitutional changes strongly pro-regime. On 12–13 February, voters soundly rejected the proposals much to the chagrin of the ruling party. The results signaled that ZANU-PF was not invincible, and they catapulted Morgan Tsvangirai and the MDC into a leading position heading into the 24–25 June parliamentary elections. Again threatened, Mugabe cracked down on the opposition. In the run-up to and aftermath of the elections, 34 people were killed, including Tsvangirai's driver and a poll worker who were killed in a gasoline-bomb attack. Officially, but without the sanction of international observers, ZANU-PF claimed 62 of 120 elective seats in the House of Assembly, with the MDC taking 57 seats with a turnout of 60% of eligible voters.

The credibility the regime was further damaged in the 9–11 March 2002 presidential polls, the conduct of which was declared fraudulent by the opposition and-with the exception of the African Union (AU) and Southern African Development Community (SADC)-by the international community. Officially, Mugabe garnered 53.8% of the vote to 40.2% for Tsvangirai while others claimed 6.0%. The government prevented as many voters as possible in urban districts favorable to the MDC from registering, reduced the number of urban polling stations by 50% over the 2000 elections, added 664 rural polling stations, conducted a hostile campaign against the political opposition in the monopolistic and state controlled print and electronic media, and intimidated the opposition. By some reports, 31 people were killed in January and February and 366 tortured. The opposition mounted a legal challenge to the results while the Commonwealth suspended Zimbabwe for one year.

By 2003, the country faced multiple crises. Owing to negative impacts of land grabbing, squatting, and repossessions of large white farms under the government's fast-track land reform program, some 400,000 jobs had been lost in commercial agriculture. Combined with a 90% loss in productivity in large-scale farming since the 1990s, some 5.5 million people in a population of 11.6 million were in need of food aid. Inflation had reached 228% and a fuel crisis threatened the nation. Strikes crippled production, prompting ever more severe repression by the government. More than 30% of the adult population was infected with the AIDS virus.

Given the devastating social impact of these issues, internal and diplomatic pressures were mounting for Mugabe to abandon his survival strategy in favor of a quick and clean exit strategy. One such move afoot was to offer the MDC a form of transitional government in exchange for cooperation in amending the constitution to allow a managed presidential succession and immunity from prosecution for the president and his followers in their retirement. However, there was a reluctance on the part of Tsvangirai's supporters to offer amnesty to a regime that had committed in excess of 550,000 cases of human rights violations ranging from murder, abduction, and rape to arson.

Tsvangirai was arrested and charged with treason in June 2003; he already had an outstanding treason charge from 2002 for attempting to assassinate Mugabe. In October 2004, Tsvangirai was acquitted of the 2002 treason charge. In August 2005, prosecutors dropped the remaining treason charges against Tsvangirai.

In a parliamentary election held in March 2005, the ZANU-PF party won two-thirds of the vote. The opposition claimed the election was rigged, but the MDC won almost all urban seats in the second election in a row. From May to July of that year, tens of thousands of shanty dwellings and illegal street stalls were destroyed as part of a government clean-up program ("Operation Murambatsvina"—"Drive Out Rubbish"). In some cases the police forced people to knock down their own homes. In other cases, trucks and bulldozers moved in. The UN estimated the program left approximately 700,000 people homeless. The government's policy of moving city dwellers to rural areas only worsened the already dire consequences of food shortages. The main opposition to Mugabe's rule came from urban areas.

By May 2006, Zimbabwe's economic crisis had exacerbated: year-on-year inflation exceeded 1,000%. New banknotes, with three zeroes deleted from their values, were introduced in August. In September, riot police disrupted a planned demonstration against the government's mishandling of the economic crisis. Union leaders were taken into custody and later hospitalized, allegedly after being tortured. In December, ZANU-PF attempted to move presidential elections from 2008 to 2010, effectively extending Mugabe's rule by two years. In March 2007, Tsvangirai was hospitalized with a head wound after his arrest at a demonstration. One man was shot dead as riot police moved to disperse the gathering.

By September 2007, the economic crisis had only worsened. The government put a six-month freeze on wages, rents, and service fees to try to sustain the economy. The government said the annual inflation rate exceeded 7,600%, but private economists said the rate was twice that. The freeze followed a decree issued in June 2007 that forced merchants and wholesalers to reduce all prices by at least 50%. People thronged to the stores, buying up clothes, groceries, furniture, and other basic goods. Producers failed to ship new stock because goods were selling for less than it cost to make them. Most commodities as of late 2007 were available only on the black market, where prices are sky high.

However, by September 2007 some hope had returned to Zimbabwe. Legislators from the ruling ZANU-PF party and the opposition MDC met in parliament to unanimously approve constitutional changes that cleared the way for Zimbabwe to hold presidential and parliamentary elections simultaneously in 2008. Mugabe made an important concession in deciding to surrender his power to appoint 10 legislators to the dominant lower house of parliament, the House of Assembly. The brief glimmer of hope arose from talks mediated by South Africa's president, Thabo Mbeki. When the elections were held in June 2008, Mugabe's party suffered heavy losses. His opponent, Morgan Tsvangirai, with-drew from the run-off elections, citing violent attacks on his supporters. When Tsvangirai's Movement for Democratic Change party won 109 seats to the 97 for Mugabe's party, Mugabe agreed in July 2008 to discuss forming a government together. A power-sharing agreement was reached in 2009: Mugabe would serve as president, while Tsvangirai was named prime minister. However, by October 2010, Mugabe stated that he would be reluctant to re-negotiate a unity government plan for 2011, claiming frustration over the inability of the coalition to come to agreements and arguing that the agreement had run its course. Prime Minister Tsvangirai has voiced his own frustrations and dissatisfaction with Mugabe. Tsvangirai accused the president of violating the power-sharing agreement by appointing ambassadors, provincial governors, the Governor of the Reserve Bank of Zimbabwe and the Attorney General without his approval. That year, Mugabe called for elections in 2012—one year earlier than the regularly scheduled elections.

¹³GOVERNMENT

Under the constitution of 18 April 1980, independent Zimbabwe had a bicameral parliament consisting of a house of assembly with 100 members, 20 of whom were elected by white voters, and 80 by persons on the common voters' roll, which included all voters except whites. The upper house, or senate, had 40 members, 14 of whom were chosen by the 80 assembly members elected from the common roll, 10 by the 20 white assembly members, 10 by the council of chiefs, and 6 nominated by the president on the advice of the prime minister. The racial basis of parliament could not be amended until 1987 unless by unanimous vote of parliament; amendment afterward needed only a 70% vote of the assembly. During the first 10 years of independence, the declaration of rights in the constitution could be amended only by a unanimous vote of the assembly; amendment of other clauses required a 70% majority. In August 1987, as soon as the constitution allowed, the separate representation for whites in parliament was abolished and the 20 seats were temporarily filled by representatives selected by the other 80 members.

After the 1990 elections, the two houses of parliament were merged into a single chamber of 150 members-120 elected by popular vote serving for five years, 10 traditional chiefs, 8 provincial governors, and 12 members appointed by the president. A constitutional change created an executive presidency and abolished the office of prime minister. The office of prime minister was restored following a power-sharing agreement in 2009. ZANU leader Robert Mugabe assumed the presidency on 1 December 1987. Amidst controversy, he was reelected in March 1990, March 1996, March 2002 and June 2008.

There is universal suffrage from age 18.

¹⁴POLITICAL PARTIES

The Rhodesian Front Party, which dominated politics from its formation in March 1962 until the establishment of majority rule in 1979, advocated racial separation, division of land on a racial basis, and the protection of the Rhodesian whites. The party won all 20 Assembly seats reserved for whites in both the 1979 and 1980 elections, and in 1981, it changed its name to the Republican Front Party (RFP). Ian Smith, who served (1964–79) as prime minister, remained as party leader until his suspension from parliament in 1987. He was succeeded by Mark Partridge. The name of the party had previously been changed again to the Conservative Alliance Zimbabwe (CAZ). The CAZ won 15 of the 20 seats allotted to whites in the 1985 elections.

The principal black parties in Zimbabwean politics originated in the struggle for independence. The Zimbabwe African People's Union (ZAPU) was formed in December 1961 and led by Joshua Nkomo. It was split in July 1963 by the creation of the Zimbabwe African National Union (ZANU), led by the Reverend Ndabaningi Sithole, and later by Robert Mugabe. ZAPU's constituency was eventually reduced to the Ndebele minority, while ZANU gained wide support among the Shona ethnic group. Both ZAPU and ZANU took up arms against the government and in 1976 allied themselves in the Patriotic Front (PF).

After Bishop Abel Muzorewa accepted the Smith government's proposal for an internal constitutional settlement in 1978, his followers, now known as the United African National Council (UANC), emerged as the major party. In elections on 17–21 April 1979, the UANC captured a majority of 51 seats in the new Assembly, and Muzorewa became the nation's first black prime minister. The elections, however, were boycotted by the PF, which continued its armed opposition to the government.

Under British auspices, a new constitutional settlement obtained ZAPU and ZANU approval in 1979, and the elections of 27–29 February 1980 were contested by nine parties, including ZANU-Patriotic Front, led by Robert Mugabe, and ZAPU (which registered under the name Popular Front). Of the 80 Assembly seats elected from the common rolls, ZANU-Patriotic Front took 57, Popular Front (or ZAPU) 20, and UNAC 3. In the July 1985 elections, ZANU-PF won 63 seats, PF-ZAPU, 15. After much enmity and bitterness during most of the 1980s, ZAPU and ZANU finally agreed to merge in late 1987 under the name of ZANU-PF and the merger was consummated in December 1989.

President Mugabe declared his intention to make Zimbabwe a one-party state by 1990. He regarded his party's victory in the 1990 elections as a mandate to proceed with his plans to establish ZANU-PF as the only legal party. He was soon turned away from that scheme by strong pressure from creditor governments abroad and a chorus of opposition domestically, including from within ZANU-PF. Zimbabwe got caught up in the general press throughout tropical Africa for greater decentralization of power and competitive party politics.

New parties began to emerge in the late 1980s and early 1990s in preparation for the expected elections in 1995. Tekere's Zimbabwe Unity Movement (ZUM) contested the 1990 elections with some success. The UANC merged with ZUM in January 1994. In January, longtime Mugabe rival Sithole returned from exile and to lead his own party, also using the ZANU rubric of ZANU-Ndonga or sometimes ZANU-Sithole.

In March 1993, former Chief Justice Enoch Dumbutshena launched the Forum Party, an outgrowth of the pressure group, Forum for Democratic Reform. The Democratic Party emerged from a split within ZUM.

In 1996 elections for Executive President, Robert Mugabe, the longtime ruler of Zimbabwe, won 93% of the vote, while his party, the Zimbabwe African National Union-Patriotic Front, won 98% of the available seats in elections held a year earlier. However, in both elections it was widely accepted that the result had been pre-

determined. The Zimbabwe government made little pretense of conducting a free and fair election.

Parliamentary elections were scheduled for April 2000, but were postponed until June. Two new strong political parties were formed to challenge Mugabe's ZANU-PF. The United Democratic Front (UDF) party was launched by Lupi Mushayakarara, former Rhodesian leader Ian Smith, Abel Muzorewa, and Ndabaningi Sithole, a pack of leaders that Mugabe dismissed as "ghosts of the past." A more formidable opponent emerged in the form of the Movement for Democratic Change (MDC) led by Morgan Tsvangirai. The MDC successfully campaigned against a government-sponsored draft constitution in the national referendum held in February 2000 with the government securing 45% of the national referendum votes against 55% for the opposition. The opposition argued that the draft constitution further entrenched executive rule allowing Mugabe to dissolve cabinet and parliament, and to rule by decree. Led by the MDC, opposition parties won nearly half of the seats in the House of Assembly in the June 2000 elections.

Parliamentary elections were held on 31 March 2005. ZANU-PF won 78 of 150 seats, or 59.6% of the vote. The MDC won 41 seats, or 39.5% of the vote. One seat was secured by an independent candidate. The elections were not marked by violence as in the past, but the opposition claimed the elections were fraudulent. Human rights groups said that hundreds of thousands of "ghost voters" appeared on the electoral role. Other parties functioning in Zimbabwe were the National Alliance for Good Government (NAGG), the International Socialist Organization, the Shalom Reform Zimbabwe Party, and the Zimbabwe Labour Party.

On 28 March 2008, parliamentary elections were held. ZANU-PF won 97 out of 210 seats, with MDC holding 109. After a highly contested presidential election between Mugabe and Tsvangirai—in which the initial vote was inconclusive and the subsequent run-off boycotted by Tsvangirai—the two candidates agreed to a power-sharing arrangement, with Mugabe as president and Tsvangirai as prime minister. The next elections were scheduled for 2013, although in 2011 Mugabe called for early elections in 2012.

15 LOCAL GOVERNMENT

Each of the eight provinces of Zimbabwe is administered by a provincial governor appointed by the central government. Local services are provided by city, town, and rural councils. The Ministry of Local Government, Rural and Urban Planning is charged with ensuring the establishment of local authorities where necessary and local adherence to legislation. In addition to the eight provinces, two cities have provincial status: Harare and Bulawayo.

16 JUDICIAL SYSTEM

The legal system is based on Roman-Dutch law and has been influenced by the system of South Africa. A four-member Supreme Court, headed by the chief justice, has original jurisdiction over alleged violations of fundamental rights guaranteed in the constitution and appellate jurisdiction over other matters. There is a High Court consisting of general and appellate divisions. Below the High Court are regional magistrate's courts with civil jurisdiction and magistrate's courts with both civil and criminal jurisdiction. Before independence, separate African courts had jurisdiction over cases involving traditional law and custom. Beginning in 1981, these courts were integrated into the national system.

The chief justice of the High Court is appointed by the president upon recommendation of the Judicial Service Commission. The Commission also advises the president on the appointment of the other judges.

In 1990 the Customary Law and Local Courts Act established a unitary court system made up of headmen's courts, chiefs' courts, magisterial courts, the High Court, and the Supreme Court. Under this system, customary law cases can be appealed through all levels to the Supreme Court.

The constitution provides for the right to a fair trial and the judiciary rigorously enforces this right. However, under Mugabe, the judiciary's reputation for independence from the executive branch has been compromised as the executive has refashioned the courts to conform with its dictates. Nevertheless, the High Court has ruled in favor in several of the MDC's elections petitions alleging violence and intimidation that obstructed the election process.

17 ARMED FORCES

The International Institute for Strategic Studies reports that armed forces in Zimbabwe totaled 29,000 members in 2011. The force is comprised of 25,000 from the army and 4,000 from the air force. Armed forces represent 1% of the labor force in Zimbabwe. Defense spending totaled $207.7 million and accounted for 3.8% of gross domestic product (GDP).

18 INTERNATIONAL COOPERATION

Zimbabwe became a UN member on 25 August 1980 and belongs to ECA and several nonregional specialized agencies, such as the World Bank, the FAO, IAEA, UNESCO, UNIDO, and the WHO. It is also a member of the African Development Bank, the Commonwealth of Nations, the ACP Group, G-15, G-77, the African Union, the WTO, COMESA, the Southern African Development Community (SADC), and the Preferential Trade Association (PTA) for eastern and southern Africa. Zimbabwe is part of the Nonaligned Movement.

In environmental cooperation, Zimbabwe is part of the Convention on Biological Diversity, CITES, the Montréal Protocol, and the UN Conventions on the Law of the Sea, Climate Change, and Desertification.

19 ECONOMY

Prior to events in the 21st century, Zimbabwe had one of the most diverse economies in Africa. It had abundant agricultural and mineral resources and a well-developed industrial sector and infrastructure. Traditionally, corn was the largest food crop and tobacco the largest export crop, followed by cotton. But by 2007 store shelves were empty and the economy was in ruins. Average annual growth during the first post independence decade was 2.9%, but has declined by as much as 10% between 2000 and 2006. In 2007 the decline was just over 6%. Deficit spending by the government and the central bank's propensity to print money resulted in an inflation rate that hit a staggering 10,453% by CIA estimates in 2007. That same year the unemployment rate hovered at 80%

with nearly 70% of Zimbabwe's population living below the poverty line on less than $1 a day.

A small white elite continues to dominate economic resources, but repatriation of white farms caused the flight of white capital in 2000. By 2003, the land reform program had created chaos and violence. White farmers left the country taking economic resources and expertise with them. As a result, over 400,000 people lost their jobs in the agricultural sector, as large-scale commercial farming was effectively destroyed. The agricultural sector, once a source of export earnings, could no longer feed the nation, forcing the country to import its food. Inflation seriously threatened the gold mining and tobacco industries and the nation's once enviable infrastructure began to fall into disrepair for lack of maintenance. Roads, railways, power plants, water systems, and telephone service have all deteriorated. Even so, Zimbabwe's infrastructure remains stronger than that of most African countries.

As the economy worsened, the government refused to enact reforms that would return donors and foreign investment. Elections were marred by violence and vote tampering and the government by mismanagement. The IMF suspended support due to arrears on past loans while the country's poor international reputation keeps tourists and foreign investors at bay.

Zimbabwe's debt heavy coffers prompted Tsvangirai to embark on a global tour in 2009 to seek loan guarantees from foreign governments. Many Western governments remained tight-pursed with Zimbabwe's prime minister as he courted their investments, reflecting Western skepticism of Zimbabwe's president, Robert Mugabe. Mugabe, who shares power with Tsvangirai, has a long history of human rights abuse. Because of their distrust for Mugabe, many Western governments chose to issue aid indirectly to Zimbabwe, through international organizations like the UN. China proved more willing to accommodate Tsvangirai's overtures, however, pledging a $950 million loan package directly to the government in 2009.

The once booming tobacco industry saw a major drop in production in the early 2000s as much of the land used by commercial farms owned by whites was seized by the government for the resettlement of blacks. However, this industry appears to be making a comeback. In 2007/08, total production of tobacco was about 48 million kg (105 million pounds). In 2009/10, the total jumped to 119 million kg (262 million pounds). Nearly 70 percent of the tobacco is now produced by some 40,000 small-scale black farmers. Approximately one third of the tobacco crop is exported to China, with Western firms accounting for the majority of sales.

For 2010, higher gold and platinum prices added a much needed boost to exports and favorable weather conditions resulted in better agricultural production. Zimbabwe's finance minister estimated growth of 8.1% for 2010 and 10% for 2011.

20 INCOME

The CIA estimated that in 2010 the GDP of Zimbabwe was $5.457 billion. The CIA defines GDP as the value of all final goods and services produced within a nation in a given year and computed on the basis of purchasing power parity (PPP) rather than value as measured on the basis of the rate of the exchange based on current dollars. The per capita GDP was estimated at $500. The annual growth rate of GDP was 9%. The average inflation rate was

5%. It was estimated that agriculture accounted for 19.5% of GDP, industry 24%, and services 56.5%.

The World Bank reports that in 2009, household consumption in Zimbabwe totaled $6.4 billion or about $526 per capita, measured in current US dollars rather than PPP.

The World Bank estimates that Zimbabwe, with 0.19% of the world's population, accounted for 0.01% of the world's GDP. By comparison, the United States, with 4.85% of the world's population, accounted for 22.51% of world GDP.

The per capita GDP was estimated at $200. The annual growth rate of GDP was estimated at -6.1%. It was estimated that agriculture accounted for 18% of GDP, industry 23%, and services 59%. The average inflation rate in 2007 was 10,453%.

As of 2011 the most recent study by the World Bank reported that actual individual consumption in Zimbabwe was 89.9% of GDP and accounted for 0.01% of world consumption. By comparison, the United States accounted for 25.44% of world individual consumption. The World Bank also estimated that 43.3% of Zimbabwe's GDP was spent on food and beverages, 20.7% on housing and household furnishings, 13.0% on clothes, 1.3% on health, 3.9% on transportation, 0.4% on communications, 2.2% on recreation, 0.3% on restaurants and hotels, and 1.3% on miscellaneous goods and services and purchases from abroad.

21 LABOR

As of 2010, Zimbabwe had a total labor force of 3.848 million people. Within that labor force, CIA estimates in 1996 noted that 66% were employed in agriculture, 10% in industry, and 24% in the service sector. Growing unemployment remains a serious problem as new jobs fail to keep pace with the number of new job seekers.

In 1981, the Zimbabwe Congress of Trade Unions (ZCTU) was formed as an umbrella organization for all trade unions and to promote the formation of a single trade union for each industry. As of 2010, about 350,000 people belonged to the 36 unions that formed the ZCTU. Spontaneous strikes and lockouts are banned. A 2005 Labor Amendment Bill effectively eliminated unionization by public-sector workers, but this provision was not enforced as of 2010.

Since independence, a priority of the government's wage policy has been reduction of the huge variation in earnings among workers, partly by increasing minimum wages and by controlling increases in higher wage brackets. As of 2010 there was no national minimum wage except for agricultural and domestic workers. Although children under the age of 15 are legally banned from employment, child labor is widespread in all aspects of the economy. Workplace safety and health continue to be problems. There are no general standards for the safety of the work environment. The government sets standards and enforces them on an inconsistent basis.

22 AGRICULTURE

Roughly 9% of the total land is farmed, and the country's major crops include corn, cotton, tobacco, wheat, coffee, sugarcane, and peanuts. Cereal production in 2009 amounted to 919,218 tons, fruit production 252,329 tons, and vegetable production 185,261 tons. Most of what is now central Zimbabwe was sparsely populated when Europeans first settled into the region, gradually transforming the bush into fertile farmland.

Since 2000, government policy changes have led to the seizure of 4,000 farms owned by whites, and many who lost land have emigrated elsewhere in Africa or overseas. In April 2000, some 35,000 guerilla veterans of Mugabe's Bush War revolution began expropriating hundreds of white-owned farms, frequently assaulting and occasionally murdering farmers. The farmland occupation cost millions of dollars in crop damage. Zimbabwe's High Court ordered police to evict the squatters from white farms, but the order was not enforced. Mugabe gave an implied approval of the confiscation by publicly declaring all white Zimbabweans as enemies of the state. The mainly white Commercial Farmers Union of Zimbabwe had been willing to negotiate redistribution of much of the farmland owned by whites, but Mugabe and the ruling ZANU-PF party were reluctant to settle.

23 ANIMAL HUSBANDRY

The UN Food and Agriculture Organization (FAO) reported that Zimbabwe dedicated 12.1 million hectares (29.9 million acres) to permanent pasture or meadow in 2009. During that year, the country tended 32.5 million chickens, 5 million head of cattle, and 630,000 pigs. The production from these animals amounted to 103,991 tons of beef and veal, 27,533 tons of pork, 56,683 tons of poultry, 21,025 tons of eggs, and 356,140 tons of milk. Zimbabwe also produced 9,255 tons of cattle hide and 1,981 tons of raw wool. Livestock raising is an important industry, which has been helped by increased diversification initiated after 1965.

24 FISHING

There is some commercial fishing on Kariba Lake. Rural Zimbabweans fish the smaller lakes and rivers. In 2008, the annual capture totaled 10,500 tons according to the UN FAO.

25 FORESTRY

Approximately 40% of Zimbabwe is covered by forest. This classification included scattered tree savanna and considerable areas of grassland likely to be reforested in the foreseeable future. Forestry is gaining importance in Zimbabwe. There are hardwood forests in the western part of the country and in the Victoria Falls area. About 100,000 tons of teak, mahogany, and mukwa (kiaat) are cut annually. The UN FAO estimated the 2009 roundwood production at 770,900 cu m (27.2 million cu ft). The value of all forest products, including roundwood, totaled $13.6 million. Softwood afforestation projects have been undertaken in the eastern districts to supply local needs heretofore met by imports; however, the loss of woodlands may be as high as 1.5% per year.

26 MINING

Zimbabwe's chief minerals were coal, gold, copper, nickel and clays. Zimbabwe was a world leader in the production of lithium minerals, chrysotile asbestos, and ferrochromium, with more than half of the world's known chromium reserves. Zimbabwe was self-sufficient in most minerals, producing 30 commodities mainly from small-scale mines. Minerals accounted for 38% of exports in 2009.

Gold production peaked in 1999 at 27,666 kg, but government policies caused a more than 50% drop to 12,564 kg in 2003. As a result, gold exports also fell, from $236.1 million in 1998 to $137.4 million in 2003. Gold historically had been a major export. Gold production was 4,965 kg in 2009 and the government authorized exports by entities holding gold export permits.

Mineral production in the 2000s generally declined. Among the reasons for the decline were: general domestic economic conditions compounded by the state-sanctioned expropriation of commercial farmlands which threatened to spill over to the mining sector, and the high incidence of HIV/AIDS-25% of the 15–49-year-old population was infected-added substantially to the mining sector's labor costs, through absenteeism, lost productivity, medical treatment, and skill replacement.

Output of other major minerals in 2009 included chromite (gross weight), 193,673 metric tons, down from 442,584 metric tons in 2008; asbestos, 4,971 tons, down from 11,489 in 2008; mine copper concentrate (metal content), 3,572 metric tons, down from 2,827 metric tons in 2008; mined nickel, 4,858 metric tons (estimated), down from 6,354 metric tons; lithium minerals (gross weight), 50,000 metric tons; black granite, 500 metric tons; and marketable phosphate rock concentrate, 20,000 metric tons, down from 21,051 metric tons in 2008. The Madziwa nickel mine was closed down in 2000, the Mhangura Copper Mines were near depletion, and Munyati Copper Mines Ltd. suspended operations in 2000, following its abandoned sale. In the late 1960s and early 1970s, copper replaced gold and asbestos as the most valuable mineral, but its production has not kept pace with other minerals. Zimbabwe in 2009 also produced palladium, platinum, rhodium, selenium, silver, barite, hydraulic cement, clays (including montmorillonite bentonite and fire clay), emerald, feldspar, graphite, kyanite, limestone, magnesite, mica, nitrogen, rough quartz, sulfur, talc, and vermiculite. National PGM metal production grew in 2009 to an estimated 14,600 kg, up from 11,700 kg in 2008. No antimony, lead, zinc, or iron oxide pigments were produced in 2009.

Gold panning is legal, but, by the Gold Trade Act, the Reserve Bank of Zimbabwe had a monopoly on purchasing and exporting of all gold and silver produced in the country. The revised code also permitted unlimited foreign exchange to companies that exported more than 75% of their production, and mining companies were allowed to keep 5% of their export earnings, to buy imported raw materials. Coal deposits in the Hwange area were substantial.

In 2009, investigators from the UN-endorsed group known as the Kimberley Process found credible evidence that the military had organized diamond smuggling syndicates with the permission of the government. The report also presented evidence that members of the military and other security forces used extreme violence against illegal miners in the Marange fields. However, the Kimberley group did not find that the government was producing "conflict diamonds," the term used for those sold to provide financial support of armed conflicts. In November 2009, the Kimberley Process sent investigators to the eastern Marange fields to monitor production and management practices of the mines, giving the government a second chance to work toward compliance with international standards under Kimberley's supervision. Human rights groups criticized the Kimberley response, favoring sanctions against the nation's diamond industry as a means to stop the related abuse of human rights. Diamond production, according to Kimberley Process data, totaled $8.4 million carats in 2010, valued at $339.7 million.

In April 2011, an indigenization policy came into effect, giving locals 51 percent control of Zimbabwe's mining industry. Indigenization is a practice used to force foreign companies to hand over a controlling share of their operations to locals. The new law stipulates that by September 2011, all companies must have at least partial Zimbabwean control.

27 ENERGY AND POWER

Electrical production at the Kariba Hydro-Electric Power Plant is shared with Zambia. Zimbabwe also relies on thermal power generated at Hwange. In 2008, Zimbabwe produced 7.723 billion kWh of electricity. Consumption of electricity in 2008 was 12.47 billion kWh. The country imported 5.268 billion kWh from countries such as South Africa, Zambia and Mozambique. Roughly 26% of energy came from fossil fuels, while 4% came from alternative fuels.

With no proven oil reserves or refining capacity, the country's demand for refined oil is met by imports. In 2010, imports of refined petroleum products averaged 12,651 barrels per day. Demand for refined products averaged 17,000 barrels per day in 2010. A pipeline from the Mozambique port of Beira to Mutare provides the majority of Zimbabwe's refined petroleum and diesel oil; the rest comes from South Africa.

Coal reserves in Zimbabwe were estimated at about 553 million short tons as of 2008. Production in 2010 totaled 3.3 million short tons, with much of that amount going to the coal-fired Hwange plant for electricity production. Imports of coal totaled 12,000 short tons that year.

28 INDUSTRY

Zimbabwe has a substantial and diverse manufacturing base, which is partly a legacy of the international sanctions imposed over the five years prior to independence. Industry accounted for only 24% of GDP in 2010, however. Food and beverages, minerals processing, chemical and petroleum products, and textiles account for the majority of the value added by manufacturing. Lower levels of consumer demand because of high prices have affected producers of many household goods, clothing, footwear, drink, and tobacco products. According to the World Bank economic output declined every single year during the period 1999 to 2008, for a cumulative decline of more than 45%. Levels of productions have not yet recovered to 2000 levels. Growth in manufacturing continues to be sluggish. The sector is heavily undercapitalized, with an important need to refurbish equipment and restore depleted working capital, and is constrained by insufficient and unreliable electricity supply, high labor costs and rigidities, the overall tax and regulatory burden.

The Zimbabwe Iron and Steel Corporation (ZISCO) was operating at 30% in 1996, and supplied 60% of local need. The Zimchem chemical refinery processes a range of chemical products. Cement is produced in large quantities. Zimbabwe also has a substantial cotton and textile industry. The textiles industry has lost some 17,000 jobs in recent years to foreign competition from South Africa, which used subsidies, export incentives, and tariff protection to support its textiles industry. The gold mining industry faced collapse and closure in 2000 because of a lack of foreign exchange. Gold output dropped by half in that year, and 46,000 jobs were in peril. The tobacco industry was also in danger of foreclosure due to farm repatriation. As of 2005, the dire condition of the economy (a severely problematic balance of payments situation, devaluation of the currency, desperate foreign currency shortage, high inflation, very high interest rates, a fall in exports, and fuel shortages) was damaging the operations and viability of the manufacturing, construction, and mining sectors, in addition to agriculture. In 2010 the agriculture and mining sectors were at the front of recovery, with manufacturing and services also registering some growth. Agricultural output grew by 34% in 2010 and was estimated to grow by 19% in 2011, led by recovery in the production of small-holders, principally in the tobacco and cotton sector. In mining, output (value) grew by 8.5% in 2009 and 47% in 2010. Production surged in platinum by 64% between 2008 and 2010 and gold by 125%.

29 SCIENCE AND TECHNOLOGY

The World Bank reported in 2009 that there were no patent applications in science and technology in Zimbabwe. Much of Zimbabwe's research effort is directed at improvements in agriculture. The government's budget for agricultural research is administered by the Agricultural Research Council which is headquartered in Harare and operates seven research institutes, eight research and experiment stations, and the National Herbarium and Botanic Garden. In Harare, at the Blair Research Laboratory, simple, innovative technologies are being developed to improve Zimbabwe's water supply and sewage disposal. Other research organizations, all in Harare, include the Geological Survey of Zimbabwe, the Institute of Mining and Metallurgy, and the Public Health Laboratory. The National University of Science and Technology, founded in 1990 at Bulawayo, has faculties of industrial technology and applied sciences. The University of Zimbabwe, founded in 1955 at Harare, has faculties of agriculture, engineering, medicine, science, and veterinary science. Degrees in agriculture and polytechnic studies are offered by seven colleges.

30 DOMESTIC TRADE

Harare and Bulawayo are the country's principal distribution centers. They are linked by rail and road to smaller towns that serve as centers for their immediate rural areas. Head offices of most of the large companies are in one or the other of the two cities. There are supermarkets and department stores in Harare as well as few newer shopping centers offering a wider variety of goods. Many products are locally produced. Kwe Kwe serves as a processing and distribution center for livestock, tobacco, steel, and chrome. Mutare is a regional trading center. A chaotic, controversial land reform program and uncontrolled inflation have hindered the domestic trade and economy.

Business hours are generally from 8 a.m. to 5 p.m. Monday through Saturday. Banks are open from 8:30 a.m. to 2 p.m. Monday through Friday, except on Wednesday, when they close at noon. Saturday banking hours are from 8:30 to 11 a.m.

31 FOREIGN TRADE

Zimbabwe imported $4.043 billion worth of goods and services in 2008, while exporting $2.54 billion worth of goods and services. Major import partners in 2009 were South Africa, 61%; and China, 5.7% . Its major export partners were Democratic Republic of the Congo, 15.3%; South Africa, 13.9%; Botswana, 13.7%; China,

Principal Trading Partners – Zimbabwe (2010)

(In millions of US dollars)

Country	Total	Exports	Imports	Balance
World	5,462.6	1,757.8	3,704.8	-1,947.0
South Africa	2,314.1	236.1	2,078.0	-1,841.8
China	536.6	223.8	312.9	-89.1
Botswana	360.6	232.9	127.7	105.3
Congo	307.7	261.0	46.7	214.4
Zambia	183.1	65.3	117.8	-52.4
Netherlands	136.5	104.5	32.0	72.4
United States	122.0	54.6	67.4	-12.8
Malawi	103.0	21.2	81.8	-60.6
Italy	102.1	80.7	21.4	59.3
United Kingdom	78.5	40.2	38.3	1.8

(…) data not available or not significant.

(n.s.) not specified.

SOURCE: *2011 Direction of Trade Statistics Yearbook,* New York: United Nations, 2011.

9.5%; Netherlands, 5.6%; and UK, 5.1%. Exports in 2010 were valued at $2.317 billion; imports were valued at $3.673 billion. After nearly a decade of decline, agricultural and mining exports grew substantially in 2010 and 2011. Tobacco and cotton exports drove agricultural growth, while platinum and gold propelled export earnings for mining.

32 BALANCE OF PAYMENTS

Zimbabwe's imports grew by an average of 11% between 1988 and 1998, reflecting a relaxation of import controls and the inflow of capital goods needed for investment, but declined rapidly after 1998. The rapid rise of the current account deficit since 1989 was caused primarily by the surge in imports from the creation of the Open General Import License (OGIL) list of items possible for importation without first obtaining a foreign exchange allocation from the government. Due to the government's disastrous land reform programs, the commercial sector, as the traditional source of exports and foreign exchange, suffered considerably during the early 2000s. However, economic recovery began in the late 2000s. Exports grew by 150% between the setting up of the Government of National Unity in February 2009 and 2011. Despite a growth in export earnings, the current account balance remained negative: -$767.3 in 2010 and -$675.6 in 2011.

33 BANKING AND SECURITIES

Zimbabwe had a relatively well-developed financial sector, second only to that of South Africa. However, the collapse of the economy and subsequent runaway inflation in the mid-2000s, nearly wrecked the nation's banking system. The Reserve Bank of Zimbabwe (RBZ) administers all monetary and exchange controls and is the sole bank of issue. The Zimbabwe Development Bank was established in 1983 as a development finance institution.

Nineteen commercial banks and three merchant banks operated in Zimbabwe as of 2011. Commercial banks include Barclays, Standard Chartered, Stanbic, the ZB Bank Limited, and the CBZ Bank Limited. Merchant banks include the Genesis Investment Bank Limited, the Renaissance Merchant Bank, and the Tetrad Merchant Bank.. High inflation rates in the late 1990s prompted the government to print $250 million worth of Zimbabwean dollars in order to keep the state running, instead of depreciating the currency itself.

In 2010 the discount rate, the rate at which the central bank lends money to banks in the short term, was 7.17%. The commercial bank prime lending rate, the rate at which banks lend to customers, was 36% in 2011.

The Zimbabwe Stock Exchange (ZSE), with floors in Harare, deals in government securities and the securities of many privately owned companies. The stock exchange opened in 1946. Until 1993, it was insignificant as a source of new capital, but the government allowed foreign investment through the ZSE, and by September 1995 the net foreign inflow exceeded US$125 million. In 1997, the value of shares traded more than doubled, but in 1998, there was an 88% decline in the value of shares traded because of social unrest and high interest rates. The year 2001 proved to be a banner year, however, with market capitalization at a soaring all-time high of just under $8 billion, and trading valued at $1.5 billion. The ZSE Industrial Index was up 158% for the year, at 46,351.9, despite the severe economic slowdown caused by President Robert Mugabe's policies. As of 2004, a total of 79 companies were listed on the ZSE, which had a market capitalization of $1.941 billion. In that same year, the ZSE Industrial index rose 173.3% from the previous year to 1,097,492.5. Trading value in 2004 totaled $136 million. As of March 2009, trade was very thin, with very few foreign investors willing to risk trading on the market. Most stocks trade in the US-cent range, with at least 26 different stocks not trading at all. Only six companies were trading at valuations above $1 in February 2012.

34 INSURANCE

Insurance companies must be registered with and licensed by the Registrar of Insurance, make security deposits with the treasury, file annual financial reports, and observe other government regulations. Principal types of insurance written are life, fire, automobile, employers' liability, and accident. Automobile third-party liability is compulsory. About four commercial insurance companies were operating in Zimbabwe as of 2012.

35 PUBLIC FINANCE

Budgets for the 1970s and the 1980s were generally in deficit. Escalating fiscal deficits in the 1980s led to the implementation early in 1991 of an extensive reform program, which focused on fiscal deficit reduction and monetary reforms. A severe drought in 1992, however, set back the program; the deficit rose to more than 10% of GDP in 1993, and 15% of GDP in 2000. In 1999, an estimated one-third of the total budget was spent on troops sent to the Congo. Pay raises from 60% up to 90% were given to the civil service and the army.

The CIA estimated that in 2005 Zimbabwe's central government took in revenues of approximately US$1.4 billion and had expenditures of US$1.9 billion. Revenues minus expenditures totaled approximately - $496 million. Public debt in 2005 amounted to 30.1% of GDP. Total external debt was US$5.17 billion. In 2010 the budget of Zimbabwe included $2.25 billion in public revenue and $2.25 billion in public expenditures. Public debt was 149% of GDP, with $6.027 billion of the debt held by foreign entities. Zimbabwe derives its principal revenues from income taxes, sales tax, customs and excise duties, and interest, dividends, and profits. Principal categories of expenditure are education, defense, debt service, and agriculture. The 2012 budget, originally estimated at $3.4 billion, was increased to $4 billion in November 2011 following permission from the Kimberley Process to reinitiate diamond sales from the Marange fields.

36 TAXATION

The statutory corporate tax rate as of 2011 was 25%, down from the 2005 rate of 30%. Property taxes are applied at various rates. Social security contributions are levied at 3%; there is also an AIDS levy of 3%. The capital gains tax is 20%, and the tax on interest 15%.

The primary tax on individuals is an income tax, which is based on a graduated scale of rates: 0%, 20%, 25%, 30%, 35%, and 40%. The government raised the tax-free threshold for individual taxpayers from $175.00 to $225 in 2011.

As of 2011, Zimbabwe had a value-added tax (VAT) with a standard rate of 15%, which was applied to most goods and services. Exempt from the VAT were rail or road passenger transport, financial, medical, educational and training services, long-term residential leases, tobacco, and fuel. Exports are zero-rated, as are prescribed drugs and tourist services. Tobacco sold on the auction floor is subject to a 1.5% levy. There are excise duties on alcoholic beverages, cigarettes, and tobacco. Other taxes include a betting tax, and stamp, transfer, and estate duties.

37 CUSTOMS AND DUTIES

Zimbabwe uses the GATT system of tariff codes. Imports are subject to duty, import tax, and surtax. Capital goods are exempt from all three. Duties mostly range between 15% and 20% but can go as high as 60%. The surtax is 10% and sales tax is charged to the importer as the end-user. The customs duty for textiles is 5% and the duty for clothes is 15%.

Zimbabwe is a member of the 14-nation Southern African Development Community (SADC), which was formed to promote "regional integration," and the 22-nation Preferential Trade Area (PTA) of the Common Market for Eastern and Southern Africa (COMESA), which provides reduced duties on trade between member countries.

38 FOREIGN INVESTMENT

From independence in 1980 until 1991, the government was very defensive toward foreign investment, subjecting each proposal to careful scrutiny and requiring foreign investors to get permission from the Foreign Investment Center for the development of any new enterprise in Zimbabwe. Enterprises could be 100% foreign owned, especially in priority areas, but there was (and is) in effect a strong preference for joint ventures with at least 30% local participation. In 1991 there was some revision of the regulations but the emphasis on indigenization remained at least as strong as the emphasis on the need to attract foreign investment. In 1992, as part of a structural reform program under the IMF's Enhanced Structural Adjustment Facility (ESAF), the Zimbabwe Investment Centre (ZIC) was established as a one-stop shop for investment approval. In 1995, disbursements under the ESAF program were suspended for failure to meet IMF targets, and in 1996, the government substituted a second plan, the Zimbabwe Program for

Economic and Social Transformation (ZIMPREST), whose operations investors have found much less satisfactory. By the late 1990s, political turbulence and the government's defiance of the IMF had greatly increased investor risk, and brought foreign direct investment flows to a standstill.

In 1998, foreign direct investment (FDI) in Zimbabwe totaled over $444 million; by 2001, FDI in-flow had fallen to $5.4 million. In 2003–05 FDI all but dried up, as the government's focus on political objectives at substantial cost to the economy continued. FDI in Zimbabwe was a net inflow of $60 million according to World Bank figures published in 2009. FDI represented 1.07% of GDP.

39 ECONOMIC DEVELOPMENT

A three-year transitional development plan was adopted for 1982–85. It called for investments in the public sector and assumed an average net growth rate of 8% per year. Manufacturing was to receive 23% of total investment, transport 14%, and agriculture 13%. Total investment fell 30% short of this goal. The Five-Year Development Plan for 1986–90 called for an annual growth rate of 5.1%, some 60% from public-sector investment and 40% from foreign sources. Education, defense, and debt service were the largest categories of government spending. During the 1990s, the International Monetary Fund (IMF) supported Zimbabwe's balance of payments, but in 1999 President Robert Mugabe declared that he would sever ties with the development fund. The president was not willing to "save" the economy under a structural adjustment plan because it would have effectively bankrupted the government. In 2000, economic development slid backwards as inflation spiraled, industries died, and agricultural production fell; but in terms of leveling the distribution of wealth between blacks and whites, it was a red-letter year.

Mugabe's radical land reform program, poor management of the economy, and interference with the judiciary have combined to prevent further investment and development. Shortages of food, fuel, and foreign exchange marked the early 2000s. The IMF adopted a declaration of noncooperation for Zimbabwe in 2002 and suspended its technical assistance to the country, due to the nonpayment of arrears. In 2003, the IMF suspended Zimbabwe's voting and related rights. That year, inflation stood at 385%, and economic and social conditions had deteriorated, including a rise in unemployment and poverty, and a worsening of the HIV/AIDS pandemic in the country. In February 2003, the government launched a National Economic Revival Program (NERP) designed to stabilize the economy.

Beginning in February 2009, Zimbabwe's economy started to recover. Between 1999 to 2008, the economy had shrunk by a cumulative 45%. Agriculture and mining earnings propelled growth in 2009–11. A lack of basic infrastructure, especially electricity, and the government's uneven record on foreign investment were limitations to growth. Although the 2009 power-sharing arrangement between Mugabe and Tsvangirai coincided with economic growth, Mugabe's insistence on early elections in 2012 and Tsvangirai's own dissatisfaction with the power-sharing arrangement kept political stability in the forefront of economic recovery efforts.

40 SOCIAL DEVELOPMENT

The social insurance system, instituted in 1993, has been updated repeatedly—six times between 2001 and 2010 alone. All employed persons between the ages of 16 and 64 who are citizens or residents of Zimbabwe are covered. Old age pensions, disability, and survivorship benefits are provided under the program. Workers' compensation is available to all private-sector employees except domestic workers; government employees are covered under a state plan.

In 1993, a social security system was introduced providing old age, disability, and survivor's pensions. The program covers all employees between the ages of 16 and 65. Retirement is normally allowed at age 60. Free health care is provided for low-income families (about 75% of the population). Maternity benefits provide 70% of regular earnings for 90 days. Workers compensation insurance is provided for private sector employees. The State Disability Act provides coverage to public sector employees.

Domestic violence and abuse is common, and is on the rise due to economic stress and high unemployment. Despite some legislative advances in promoting gender equality, women are bound by traditional customs which are discriminatory in areas of property ownership and inheritance. Sexual harassment in the workplace is prevalent. Rape, including politically motivated assaults, remain a huge and underreported problem. There are hundreds of thousands of orphans due to the large number of deaths from HIV/AIDS. Education is not compulsory, and schooling is not free. The government introduced the Basic Education Assistance Module (BEAM) to assist orphans and other vulnerable children.

There are numerous reports of human rights violations. Abuses included police killings, beatings, and torture, violation of privacy rights, and persecution of journalists. The government has generally failed to take action against those responsible for human rights abuses.

41 HEALTH

All health services are the responsibility of the Ministry of Health. The government has declared its intention to provide free medical services for all. Prior to independence, facilities for Africans were free, but these were greatly inferior to those available to Europeans. Zimbabwe has been focusing on building and/or upgrading rural health care centers and district hospitals and expanding rural health programs, such as immunization, control of diarrheal diseases, training of health care workers, and improving the supply and affordability of essential drugs. The local pharmaceutical industry is well developed. The Ministry of National Supplies operates the Government Medical Stores, which procures goods on behalf of the Ministry of Health. UNICEF provided additional health care support to women and children, including providing vitamin A.

According to the CIA, life expectancy in Zimbabwe was 45 years in 2011. There were 2 physicians, 7 nurses and midwives, and 30 hospital beds per 10,000 inhabitants. The fertility rate was 3.4, while the infant mortality rate was 56 per 1,000 live births. In 2008 the maternal mortality rate, according to the World Bank, was 790 per 100,000 births. It was estimated that 76% of children were vaccinated against measles. The total fertility rate in 2011 was estimated at 3.63 children born per woman.

Guinea worm incidence remained prevalent, although it has been on the decrease. Commonly reported diseases were malaria and measles. Zimbabwe has seen increased resistance of malaria parasites to drugs. Tuberculosis continued to be a major health problem. Local campaigns are under way to control schistosomiasis, which affects a large percentage of the African population.

The AIDS epidemic is among the worst in the world. The HIV/AIDS adult prevalence rate was 14.3% in 2009, the fifth highest in the world.

From August 2008 through May 2009, there were nearly 100,000 reported cases of cholera with over 4,280 deaths reported. The Red Cross launched a cholera relief program in December 2008 resulting in improved access to clean water for nearly 500,000 people. Lack of funding forced the organization to scale-back on some emergency aid measures by May 2009.

42 HOUSING

In rural areas, Africans live in villages and on farms in housing that is mainly of brick or mud and stick construction with thatch or metal roofs. The villages are usually small (except for the massive protected villages), with fewer than 100 inhabitants. Urban housing is generally of brick. In 2011, the country`s housing deficit was estimated at over one million units. The capital city, Harare had a housing backlog of 500,000 units.

The Zimbabwe National Association of Housing Cooperatives (ZINAHCO) is an umbrella organization of over 1,000 national housing cooperatives. The organization was established as a means of providing advice to member groups on dealing with local and national authorities and to offer training in building techniques. ZINAHCO has worked to change urban building standards which dictate that hook-ups to public services must be in place before an owner may begin to build a home. The Cooperatives argue that for many of the urban poor living in slum shacks, it is more appropriate to first allow for the construction of permanent structures with communal utility services. Residents can then install utilities at a later date, as they can afford to do so.

43 EDUCATION

In 2006 the World Bank estimated that 90% of age-eligible children in Zimbabwe were enrolled in primary school. Secondary enrollment for age-eligible children stood at 38%. Tertiary enrollment was estimated at 3%. Overall, the CIA estimated that Zimbabwe had a literacy rate of 92% (2009). A unitary system of education under the Ministry of Education has replaced the dual system of separate educational facilities for Africans and non-Africans formerly maintained by the Rhodesian government. Education is free and compulsory for seven years between the ages of 6 and 13. Secondary education lasts for six years (four years lower and two years upper). The government has developed a strong vocational school and apprenticeship system.

The University of Zimbabwe provides higher education on a multiracial basis. Other universities include the National University of Science and Technology, the Midlands State University, Chinhoyi University of Science and Technology, Masvingo State University, Seventh Day Adventist run Solusi University, and the Africa University, which is sponsored by the United Methodist church.

44 LIBRARIES AND MUSEUMS

The National Free Library of Zimbabwe was founded in 1943 in Bulawayo as a national lending library and center for interlibrary loans. It has over 100,000 volumes. The Bulawayo Public Library holds about 100,000 volumes and operates a mobile library service. Other libraries include the Harare City Library, with 200,000 volumes and the Turner Memorial Library in Mutare. The National Archives of Zimbabwe, located in Harare, receives a copy of every book published in Zimbabwe, as does the Bulawayo Public Library. The library at the University of Zimbabwe is the largest in the country, with 500,000 volumes in the main library and branches. The Parliament of Zimbabwe holds a collection of 115,000 volumes.

The Zimbabwe Museum of Natural History (1901) at Bulawayo has geologic, ethnographic, historical, and zoological collections. A Railway Museum is also located in Bulawayo. Located in Harare are the Zimbabwe Museum of Human Sciences, with archaeological, historical, zoological, and other collections, the National Gallery of Zimbabwe, which displays works of national, regional, and European art, and the Queen Victoria Museum. There is a military museum in Gweru and a children's museum in Marondera.

45 MEDIA

In 2009 the CIA reported that there were 385,100 telephone landlines in Zimbabwe. In addition to landlines, mobile phone subscriptions averaged 24 per 100 people. In 2010, the country had 29,866 Internet hosts. As of 2009, there were some 1.4 million Internet users in Zimbabwe. Internet users numbered 11 per 100 citizens. The Ministry of Information, Posts, and Telecommunications provides telephone, telegraph, and postal services. The state-owned Zimbabwe Broadcasting Corporation controls all domestic broadcasting of television and radio. In 2011 the government owned all local radio stations and the sole television station; foreign shortwave broadcasts and satellite television were available to those who could afford antennas and receivers; in rural areas, access to television broadcasts was extremely limited.

There are a number of independent and government-owned newspapers in the country. Prominent newspapers in 2010, with circulation numbers listed parenthetically, included the state controlled dailies *Chronicle* (74,032) and the *Herald* (122,166). *The Daily News*, an independent publication, was banned in 2003 for criticism of President Robert Mugabe, but was reissued in March 2011. At the time that the paper was banned, it was reported to have the largest circulation in the country. Major independent weeklies include *The Financial Gazette*, *The Independent*, and *The Standard*.

The constitution provides for free expression, but allows for legal limitations in the name of defense, public safety, public order, state economic interest, public morality, and public health. There is said to be a high degree of self-censorship employed by the media, though an increasingly independent press is sometimes critical of the government.

46 ORGANIZATIONS

The government encourages the development of agricultural and other cooperatives, which are seen as a means of improving the subsistence economy. The Zimbabwe National Chamber of Commerce has many branches. The Consumer Council of Zimbabwe is located in Harare. The Africa regional office of Consumers International is in Harare.

The National Arts Council of Zimbabwe is based in Harare. The Zimbabwe Medical Association and the Zimbabwe Scientific Association serve as both professional associations and educational/research organizations. The Wildlife Society of Zimbabwe is an educational and activist group for conservation and environmental issues.

National youth organizations include Youth for Christ, Junior Chamber, the Zimbabwe National Students Union, Zimbabwe Student Christian Movement, the Boy Scouts Association of Zimbabwe, The Girl Guides Association of Zimbabwe, and YMCA/YWCA. There are sports associations promoting amateur competition for athletes of all ages in a wide variety of pastimes, including softball, baseball, badminton, and track and field.

The Zimbabwe Association for Human Rights was established in 1994. Active groups for women's rights and social development include the Kunzwana Women Association, the Musasa Project, the Zimbabwe Association of University Women, Women`s Action Group, and the Zimbabwe Women's Bureau. Amnesty International, Habitat for Humanity, the Society of St. Vincent de Paul, UNICEF, and the Red Cross have national chapters.

47 TOURISM, TRAVEL, AND RECREATION

Tourist attractions include Victoria Falls and the Kariba Dam on the Zambezi River, numerous wildlife sanctuaries and game reserves, including Hwange National Park, the eastern highlands, the Matobo Hills, and the Zimbabwe ruins near Masvingo. There are safari areas in the Zambezi Valley below the Kariba Dam and at Tuli. Resort, camping, and fishing facilities are also available. South African visitors still account for the largest share of the tourist trade.

The *Tourism Factbook*, published by the UN World Tourism Organization, reported 2.02 million incoming tourists to Zimbabwe in 2009; they spent a total of $314 million. Of those incoming tourists, there were 1.7 million from Africa. There were 11,855 hotel beds available in Zimbabwe, which had an occupancy rate of 35%. The estimated daily cost to visit Harare, the capital, was $334. The cost of visiting other cities averaged $175.

48 FAMOUS PERSONS

The country's former name, Rhodesia, was derived from Cecil John Rhodes (1853–1902), whose company administered the area during the late 19th and early 20th centuries. Lobengula (1833–94), king of the Ndebele, whose grant of the minerals concession in his territory to Rhodes in 1888 led to European settlement, headed an unsuccessful rebellion of his people against the settlers in 1893. Prominent African nationalist leaders are Joshua Nkomo (1917–99), leader of ZAPU; Bishop Abel Muzorewa (1925–2010) of the United Methodist Church, who became the nation's first black prime minister in 1979; and ZANU leader Robert Gabriel Mugabe (b. 1924), who became prime minister after independence and later first executive president; he has been head of state since 1980. Ian Smith (1919–2007) was prime minister from 1964 to 1979. Many of the early works of the British novelist Doris Lessing (b. 1919) are set in the Rhodesia where she grew up.

49 DEPENDENCIES

Zimbabwe has no territories or colonies.

50 BIBLIOGRAPHY

Charumbira, Ruramisai. *The History of Zimbabwe*. Westport, CT: Greenwood Press, 2012

Chigara, Ben. *Southern African Development Community Land Issues*. New York: Routledge, 2012.

Harmon, Daniel E. *Southeast Africa: 1880 to the Present: Reclaiming a Region of Natural Wealth*. Philadelphia, PA: Chelsea House Publishers, 2002.

Meldrum, Andrew. *Where We Have Hope: A Memoir of Zimbabwe*. London, Eng.: John Murray, 2004.

Msindo, Enocent. *Ethnicity and Changing Identities in Matabeleland, Zimbabwe*. Rochester, NY: University of Rochester Press, 2012.

Owomoyela, Oyekan. *Culture and Customs of Zimbabwe*. Westport, CT: Greenwood Press, 2002.

Rotberg, Robert I. *Ending Autocracy, Enabling Democracy: The Tribulations of Southern Africa, 1960–2000*. Cambridge, MA: World Peace Foundation, 2002.

Rubert, Steven C. and R. Kent Rasmussen. *Historical Dictionary of Zimbabwe*. Lanham, MD: Scarecrow, 2001.

Sheehan, Sean. *Zimbabwe*. 2nd ed. Tarrytown, NY: Benchmark Books/Marshall Cavendish, 2004.

Zeilig, Leo, and David Seddon. *A Political and Economic Dictionary of Africa*. Philadelphia: Routledge/Taylor and Francis, 2005.

Zimbabwe Investment and Business Guide: Strategic and Practical Information. Washington, DC: International Business Publications USA, 2012.

INDEX TO COUNTRIES AND TERRITORIES

This alphabetical list includes countries and dependencies (colonies, protectorates, and other territories) described in the encyclopedia. Countries and territories described in their own articles are followed by the continental volume (printed in *italics*) in which each appears. Country articles are arranged alphabetically in each volume. For example, Argentina, which appears in *Americas*, is listed this way: Argentina—*Americas*. Dependencies are listed here with the title of the volume in which they are treated, followed by the name of the article in which they are dealt with. In a few cases, an alternative name for the same place is given in parentheses at the end of the entry. The name of the volume *Asia and Oceania* is abbreviated in this list to *Asia*.

Adélie Land—*Asia:* French Pacific Dependencies: French Southern and Antarctic Territories
Afars and the Issas, Territory of the—*Africa:* Djibouti
Afghanistan—*Asia*
Albania—*Europe*
Algeria—*Africa*
American Samoa—*Asia:* US Pacific Dependencies
Andaman Islands—*Asia:* India
Andorra—*Europe*
Angola—*Africa*
Anguilla—*Americas:* UK American Dependencies: Leeward Islands
Antarctica—*United Nations:* Polar Regions
Antigua and Barbuda—*Americas*
Arctic—*United Nations:* Polar Regions
Argentina—*Americas*
Armenia—*Europe*
Aruba—*Americas:* Netherlands American Dependencies: Aruba
Ashmore and Cartier Islands—*Asia:* Australia
Australia—*Asia*
Austria—*Europe*
Azerbaijan—*Asia*
Azores—*Europe:* Portugal

Bahamas—*Americas*
Bahrain—*Asia*
Bangladesh—*Asia*
Barbados—*Americas*
Basutoland—*Africa:* Lesotho
Bechuanaland—*Africa:* Botswana
Belarus—*Europe*
Belau—*Asia:* Palau
Belgium—*Europe*
Belize—*Americas*
Benin—*Africa*
Bermuda—*Americas:* UK American Dependencies
Bhutan—*Asia*
Bolivia—*Americas*
Bonin Islands—*Asia:* Japan (Ogasawara Islands)
Borneo, North—*Asia:* Malaysia
Bosnia and Herzegovina—*Europe*
Botswana—*Africa*

Bouvet Island—*Europe:* Norway
Brazil—*Americas*
British Antarctic Territory—*Americas:* UK American Dependencies
British Guiana—*Americas:* Guyana
British Honduras—*Americas:* Belize
British Indian Ocean Territory—*Africa:* UK African Dependencies
British Virgin Islands—*Americas:* UK American Dependencies
Brunei Darussalam—*Asia*
Bulgaria—*Europe*
Burkina Faso—*Africa*
Burma—*Asia:* Myanmar
Burundi—*Africa*

Caicos Islands—*Americas:* UK American Dependencies
Cambodia—*Asia*
Cameroon—*Africa*
Canada—*Americas*
Canary Islands—*Europe:* Spain
Cape Verde—*Africa*
Caroline Islands—*Asia:* Federated States of Micronesia; Palau
Carriacou—*Americas:* Grenada
Cayman Islands—*Americas:* UK American Dependencies
Central African Republic—*Africa*
Ceuta—*Europe:* Spain
Ceylon—*Asia:* Sri Lanka
Chad—*Africa*
Chile—*Americas*
Chilean Antarctic Territory—*Americas:* Chile
China—*Asia*
Christmas Island (Indian Ocean)—*Asia:* Australia
Christmas Island (Pacific Ocean)—*Asia:* Kiribati
Cocos Islands—*Americas:* Costa Rica
Cocos (Keeling) Islands—*Asia:* Australia
Colombia—*Americas*
Columbus, Archipelago of—*Americas:* Ecuador (Galapagos Islands)
Comoros—*Africa*
Congo—*Africa*
Congo, Democratic Republic of the—*Africa*
Cook Islands—*Asia:* New Zealand

ISBN-13: 978-1-4144-3392-9
ISBN-10: 1-4144-3392-1

90000

9 781414 433929

Algeria

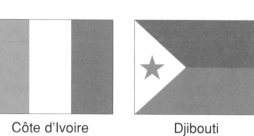

Angola

Benin

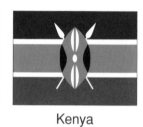

Botswana

Burkina Faso

Comoros

Congo, Democratic
Republic of the

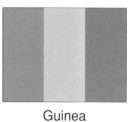

Congo, Republic
of the

Côte d'Ivoire

Djibouti

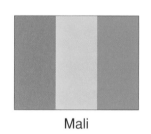

Gambia, The

Ghana

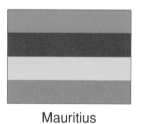

Guinea

Guinea-Bissau

Kenya

Mali

Mauritania

Mauritius

Morocco

Mozambique

Senegal

Seychelles

Sierra Leone

Somalia

South Africa

Tunisia

Uganda

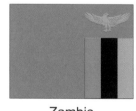

Zambia

Zimbabwe